Masters of British Literature

VOLUME B

David Damrosch
COLUMBIA UNIVERSITY

Kevin J. H. Dettmar
SOUTHERN ILLINOIS UNIVERSITY

Christopher Baswell
UNIVERSITY OF CALIFORNIA, LOS ANGELES

Clare Carroll
QUEENS COLLEGE, CITY UNIVERSITY OF NEW YORK

Heather Henderson

Constance Jordan
CLAREMONT GRADUATE UNIVERSITY

Peter J. Manning
STATE UNIVERSITY OF NEW YORK, STONY BROOK

Anne Howland Schotter
WAGNER COLLEGE

William Chapman Sharpe
BARNARD COLLEGE

Stuart Sherman
FORDHAM UNIVERSITY

Susan J. Wolfson
PRINCETON UNIVERSITY

Masters of British Literature

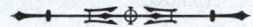

David Damrosch and Kevin J. H. Dettmar
General Editors

VOLUME B

THE ROMANTICS AND THEIR CONTEMPORARIES
Susan Wolfson *and* Peter Manning

THE VICTORIAN AGE
Heather Henderson *and* William Sharpe

THE TWENTIETH CENTURY
Kevin J. H. Dettmar

PEARSON
Longman

New York   San Francisco   Boston
London   Toronto   Sydney   Tokyo   Singapore   Madrid
Mexico City   Munich   Paris   Cape Town   Hong Kong   Montreal

Editor-in-Chief: *Joseph Terry*
Senior Development Editor: *Mikola De Roo*
Director of Development: *Mary Ellen Curley*
Executive Marketing Manager: *Ann Stypuloski*
Senior Supplements Editor: *Donna Campion*
Media Supplements Editor: *Jenna Egan*
Production Manager: *Denise Phillip*
Project Coordination, Text Design, and Page Makeup: *GGS Book Services*
Cover Designer/Cover Design Manager: *Nancy Danahy*
On the Cover: Thomas Phillips, *Lord Byron, 1814.* Courtesy National Portrait Gallery, London.
Photo Researcher: *Julie Tesser*
Manufacturing Buyer: *Lucy Hebard*
Printer and Binder: *Quebecor World/Taunton*
Cover Printer: *The Lehigh Press, Inc.*

For permission to use copyrighted material, grateful acknowledgment is made to the copyright holders on pages 1515–1517, which are hereby made part of this copyright page.

Library of Congress Cataloging-in-Publication Data

Masters of British literature.
    p. cm.
    Vol. A general editors David Damrosch and Kevin J. H. Dettmar.
    Includes index.
    ISBN-13: 978-0-321-33399-5 (v. A)
    ISBN-10: 0-321-33399-3 (v. A)
    ISBN-13: 978-0-321-33400-8 (v. B)
    ISBN-10: 0-321-33400-0 (v. B)
  1. English literature. 2. Great Britain—Literary collections. 3. English literature—History and criticism. I. Damrosch, David. II. Dettmar, Kevin J. H., 1958-
    PR1109.M373 2007
    820.8—dc22

2006102396

Visit us at www.ablongman.com

ISBN-13: 978-0-321-33400-8
ISBN-10:   0-321-33400-0

1 2 3 4 5 6 7 8 9 0—QWT—10 09 08 07

CONTENTS

List of Illustrations   *xxii*

Preface   *xxvi*

Acknowledgments   *xxxi*

The Romantics and Their Contemporaries   3

❧ ANNA LETITIA BARBAULD   28
The Mouse's Petition to Dr. Priestley   29
On a Lady's Writing   30
Inscription for an Ice-House   30
To a Little Invisible Being Who Is Expected Soon to Become Visible   31
Eighteen Hundred and Eleven   32

❧ CHARLOTTE SMITH   40
FROM ELEGIAC SONNETS AND OTHER POEMS   41
To the Moon   41
"Sighing I see you little troop at play"   43
To melancholy. Written on the banks of the Arun October, 1785   43
The sea view   43
The Dead Beggar   44

from Beachy Head   45

❧ WILLIAM BLAKE   48
All Religions Are One   50

SONGS OF INNOCENCE AND OF EXPERIENCE   53
from Songs of Innocence   53
    Introduction   53
    The Shepherd   54
    The Ecchoing Green   54
    The Lamb   55
    The Little Black Boy   56

The Blossom   56
The Chimney Sweeper   57
The Little Boy lost   57
The Little Boy found   58
The Divine Image   58
HOLY THURSDAY   59
Nurses Song   60
Infant Joy   60
A Dream   61
On Anothers Sorrow   61

from Songs of Experience   62
Introduction   62
EARTH'S Answer   63
The CLOD & the PEBBLE   63
HOLY THURSDAY   64
The Little Girl Lost   64
The Little Girl Found   66
The Chimney Sweeper   67
NURSES Song   67
The SICK ROSE   69
THE FLY   70
The Angel   70
The Tyger   70
My Pretty ROSE TREE   71
AH! SUN-FLOWER   71
The GARDEN of LOVE   72
LONDON   72
The Human Abstract   73
INFANT SORROW   73
The Little BOY Lost   74
The Little GIRL Lost   75
The School-Boy   76
A DIVINE IMAGE   77

⇒ PERSPECTIVES ⇐
The Abolition of Slavery and the Slave Trade   78

OLAUDAH EQUIANO   79
from The Interesting Narrative of the Life of Olaudah Equiano   80
MARY PRINCE   88
from The History of Mary Prince, a West Indian Slave   89
THOMAS BELLAMY   93
The Benevolent Planters   93
JOHN NEWTON   99
Amazing Grace!   100

ANN CROMARTIE YEARSLEY   100
   from A Poem on the Inhumanity of the Slave-Trade   101
WILLIAM COWPER   105
   Sweet Meat Has Sour Sauce   106
   The Negro's Complaint   107
HANNAH MORE and EAGLESFIELD SMITH   108
   The Sorrows of Yamba   109
ROBERT SOUTHEY   185
   from Poems Concerning the Slave-Trade   114
DOROTHY WORDSWORTH   119
   from The Grasmere Journals   119
THOMAS CLARKSON   119
   from The History of the Rise, Progress, & Accomplishment
      of the Abolition of the African Slave-Trade by
      the British Parliament   120
WILLIAM WORDSWORTH   128
   To Toussaint L'Ouverture   128
   To Thomas Clarkson   129
   from The Prelude   129
   from Humanity   130
   Letter to Mary Ann Rawson (C. May 1833)   131
THE EDINBURGH REVIEW   131
   from Abstract of the Information laid on the Table of the House of Commons,
      on the Subject of the Slave Trade   132
   GEORGE GORDON, LORD BYRON   134
      from Detached Thoughts   134

MARY ROBINSON   135
   Ode to Beauty   136
   January, 1795   137
   from Sappho and Phaon, in a Series of Legitimate Sonnets   138
      III. The Bower of Pleasure   139
      IV. Sappho discovers her Passion   139
      VII. Invokes Reason   139
      XI. Rejects the influence of Reason   140
      XII. Previous to her Interview with Phaon   140
      XVIII. To Phaon   140
      XXX. Bids farewell to Lesbos   141
      XXXVII. Foresees her Death   141
   The Old Beggar   142

MARY WOLLSTONECRAFT   144
   A Vindication of the Rights of Woman   146
      from To M. Talleyrand-Périgord, Late Bishop of Autun   146
      Introduction   148

from Chapter 1. The Rights and Involved Duties
of Mankind Considered   151
from Chapter 2. The Prevailing Opinion of a Sexual
Character Discussed   153

❧ JOANNA BAILLIE   162
London   162
A Mother to Her Waking Infant   164
A Child to His Sick Grandfather   165
Thunder   166
Song: Woo'd and Married and A'   168

LITERARY BALLADS   169

❧ RELIQUES OF ANCIENT ENGLISH POETRY   170
Sir Patrick Spence   171

❧ ROBERT BURNS   172
To a Mouse   173
To a Louse   174
Flow gently, sweet Afton   175
Ae fond kiss   176
Comin' Thro' the Rye (1)   176
Comin' Thro' the Rye (2)   177
A Red, Red Rose   178
Auld Lang Syne   178
The Fornicator. A New Song   179

❧ SIR WALTER SCOTT   180
Lord Randal   181

❧ THOMAS MOORE   181
The harp that once through Tara's halls   182
Believe me, if all those endearing young charms   182
The time I've lost in wooing   182

❧ WILLIAM WORDSWORTH   183
LYRICAL BALLADS   186
Simon Lee   186
Anecdote for Fathers   188
We are seven   190
Expostulation and Reply   192
Lines written a few miles above Tintern Abbey   193

LYRICAL BALLADS (1800, 1802)   196
from Preface   196
   [The Principal Object of the Poems. Humble and Rustic Life]   198
   ["The Spontaneous Overflow of Powerful Feelings"]   198
   [The Language of Poetry]   200
   [What is a Poet?]   202
   ["Emotion Recollected in Tranquillity"]   206
"Strange fits of passion have I known"   208
Song ("She dwelt among th' untrodden ways")   209
"A slumber did my spirit seal"   209
Lucy Gray   209
Poor Susan   211
Nutting   212
Michael   214

      RESPONSES
      Francis Jeffrey: ["the new poetry"]   225
      Charles Lamb: *from* a letter to William Wordsworth   228
      Charles Lamb: *from* a letter to Thomas Manning   229

SONNETS, 1802–1807   230
Prefatory Sonnet ("Nuns fret not at their Convent's narrow room")   230
Composed upon Westminster Bridge, Sept. 3, 1802   231
"The world is too much with us"   231
"It is a beauteous Evening"   232
London, 1802   232

from THE PRELUDE, OR GROWTH OF A POET'S MIND   234
Book First. Introduction, Childhood, and School time   234
from Book Second. School time continued   249
   [Two Consciousnesses]   249
   [Blessed Infant Babe]   249
from Book Sixth. Cambridge, and the Alps   251
   [Arrival in France]   251
   [Travelling in the Alps. Simplon Pass]   253
from Book Ninth. Residence in France   257
   [Revolution, Royalists, and Patriots]   257
from Book Tenth. Residence in France and French Revolution   259
   [The Reign of Terror. Confusion. Return to England]   259
from Book Eleventh. Imagination, How Impaired and Restored   262
   [Imagination Restored by Nature]   262
   ["Spots of Time." Two Memories from Childhood and Later Reflections]   263
"I travell'd among unknown Men"   267
Resolution and Independence   267
"I wandered lonely as a cloud"   271
"My heart leaps up"   272
Ode: Intimations of Immortality from Recollections of Early Childhood   273
Surprized by joy   278
Scorn not the Sonnet   278

❧ DOROTHY WORDSWORTH   279

Grasmere—A Fragment   280
Thoughts on My Sick-bed   282
When Shall I Tread Your Garden Path?   284
Lines Written (Rather Say *Begun*) on the Morning
   of Sunday April 6th   284
from The Grasmere Journals   286
   [Home Alone]   286
   [A Leech Gatherer]   287
   [A Woman Beggar]   287
   [An Old Soldier]   287
   [The Grasmere Mailman]   288
   [A Vision of the Moon]   289
   [A Field of Daffodils]   289
   [A Beggar Woman from Cockermouth]   290
   [The Circumstances of "Composed upon
     Westminster Bridge"]   291

❧ SAMUEL TAYLOR COLERIDGE   291

Sonnet to the River Otter   292
The Eolian Harp   293
This Lime-Tree Bower My Prison   294
Frost at Midnight   296
The Rime of the Ancient Mariner (1817)   298
Christabel   314
Kubla Khan   330
The Pains of Sleep   332
Dejection: An Ode   334

Biographia Literaria   338
   Chapter 4   338
     [Wordsworth's Earlier Poetry]   338
   Chapter 11   339
     [The Profession of Literature]   339
   Chapter 13   341
     [Imagination and Fancy]   341
   Chapter 14   343
     [Occasion of the *Lyrical Ballads*—Preface to the Second Edition—
       The Ensuing Controversy]   343
     [Philosophic Definitions of a Poem and Poetry]   345
from Lectures on Shakespeare   346
[Mechanic vs. Organic Form]   346

❧ GEORGE GORDON, LORD BYRON   347

She walks in beauty   349
So, we'll go no more a-roving   350
Manfred   351

❦ "MANFRED" AND ITS TIME
The Byronic Hero   386

Byron's Earlier Heroes from *The Giaour* 387 • from *The Corsair* 387 •
from *Lara* 388 • Prometheus 389 • *from* Childe Harold's
Pilgrimage, Canto the Third [Napoleon Buonoparte] 390
Samuel Taylor Coleridge from *The Statesman's Manual* ["Satanic
Pride and Rebellious Self-Idolatry"] 392
Caroline Lamb from *Glenarvon* 393
Mary Wollstonecraft Shelley from *Frankenstein; or The Modern
Prometheus* 395
Felicia Hemans from *The Widow of Crescentius* 397
Percy Bysshe Shelley from *Preface to Prometheus Unbound* •
from *Prometheus Unbound Act 1* 398
Robert Southey from *Preface to A Vision of Judgement* 400
George Gordon, Lord Byron from *The Vision of Judgment* 401

CHILDE HAROLD'S PILGRIMAGE   402
from Canto the Third   402
[Thunderstorm in the Alps]   402
[Byron's Strained Idealism. Apostrophe to His Daughter]   403
from Canto the Fourth   406
[Rome. Political Hopes]   406
[Apostrophe to the Ocean. Conclusion]   407

DON JUAN   411
Dedication   411
Canto 1   415
from Canto 7 [Critique of Military "Glory"]   462
from Canto 11 [Juan in England]   463

Stanzas ("When a man hath no freedom to fight for at home")   466
On This Day I Complete My Thirty-Sixth Year   466

❧ PERCY BYSSHE SHELLEY   467
To Wordsworth   469
Mont Blanc   470
Hymn to Intellectual Beauty   474
Ozymandias   476
Sonnet: Lift not the painted veil   476
Sonnet: England in 1819   477
Ode to the West Wind   477
To a Sky-Lark   480
To—("Music, when soft voices die")   482
Adonais   483
The Cloud   498
from Hellas   501
Chorus ("Worlds on worlds are rolling ever")   501

Chorus ("The world's great age begins anew")   503
from A Defence of Poetry   504

❧ FELICIA HEMANS   514

from TALES, AND HISTORIC SCENES, IN VERSE   516
Evening Prayer, at a Girls' School   516
Casabianca   518

from RECORDS OF WOMAN   519
Indian Woman's Death-Song   519
Joan of Arc, in Rheims   520
The Homes of England   523
The Graves of a Household   524
Corinne at the Capitol   525
Woman and Fame   526

❧ JOHN CLARE   527

Written in November (manuscript)   529
Written in November   529
Songs Eternity   529
[The Mouse's Nest]   531

❧ JOHN KEATS   531

ON FIRST LOOKING INTO CHAPMAN'S HOMER   534
Young Poets   534
On First Looking into Chapman's Homer.   534
"To one who has been long in city pent"   536
On Seeing the Elgin Marbles   536
On sitting down to read King Lear once again   537
Sonnet: When I have fears   537
The Eve of St. Agnes   538
La Belle Dame sans Mercy   548

THE ODES OF 1819   550
Ode to Psyche   551
Ode to a Nightingale   553
Ode on a Grecian Urn   555
Ode on Indolence   557
Ode on Melancholy   558
To Autumn   559
This living hand   560
Bright Star   561

LETTERS   561
To George and Thomas Keats ["intensity" and "Negative Capability"]   561

To Richard Woodhouse [The "Camelion Poet" vs. the "Egotistical
    Sublime"]   562
To Charles Brown [Keats's Last Letter]   564

The Victorian Age   567

❧ THOMAS CARLYLE   591

from Gospel of Mammonism [The Irish Widow]   593
from Labour [Know Thy Work]   594
from Democracy [Liberty to Die by Starvation]   595
Captains of Industry   597

❧ JOHN STUART MILL   601

On Liberty   602
   from Chapter 2. Of the Liberty of Thought and Discussion   602
   from Chapter 3. Of Individuality, as One of the Elements of
      Well-Being   605

❧ ELIZABETH BARRETT BROWNING   613

To George Sand: A Desire   615
To George Sand: A Recognition   616
A Year's Spinning   616
Sonnets from the Portuguese   617
   1 ("I thought once how Theocritus had sung")   617
   13 ("And wilt thou have me fashion into speech")   618
   14 ("If thou must love me, let it be for nought")   618
   21 ("Say over again, and yet once over again")   618
   22 ("When our two souls stand up erect and strong")   619
   43 ("How do I love thee? Let me count the ways")   619
Aurora Leigh   619
Book 1   619
   [Self-Portrait]   619
   [Her Mother's Portrait]   622
   [Aurora's Education]   623
   [Discovery of Poetry]   627
Book 2   628
   [Woman and Artist]   628
   [No Female Christ]   631
Book 5   632
   [Epic Art and Modern Life]   632

❧ ALFRED, LORD TENNYSON   635

The Kraken   638
Mariana   638

The Lady of Shalott   640
The Lotos-Eaters   645
Ulysses   649
Tithonus   651
Break, Break, Break   653
The Epic [Morte d'Arthur]   653

THE PRINCESS   655
Sweet and Low   655
Come Down, O Maid   656
[The Woman's Cause Is Man's]   657

from In Memoriam A. H. H.   659
The Charge of the Light Brigade   689
Idylls of the King   691
    The Coming of Arthur   691
The Higher Pantheism   701
Flower in the Crannied Wall   701
Crossing the Bar   701

CHARLES DARWIN   702
On the Origin of Species by Means of Natural Selection   704
    from Chapter 3. Struggle for Existence   704

PERSPECTIVES
Religion and Science   710

THOMAS BABINGTON MACAULAY   711
    from Lord Bacon   711
CHARLES DICKENS   712
    from Sunday Under Three Heads   712
DAVID FRIEDRICH STRAUSS   715
    from The Life of Jesus Critically Examined   715
CHARLOTTE BRONTË   718
    from Jane Eyre   718
ARTHUR HUGH CLOUGH   720
    Epi-strauss-ium   720
    The Latest Decalogue   721
    from Dipsychus   721
JOHN WILLIAM COLENSO   722
    from The Pentateuch and Book of Joshua Critically Examined   723
JOHN HENRY CARDINAL NEWMAN   724
    from Apologia Pro Vita Sua   725
THOMAS HENRY HUXLEY   732
    from Evolution and Ethics   732

SIR EDMUND GOSSE   737
  from Father and Son   738

ROBERT BROWNING   742

Porphyria's Lover   745
Soliloquy of the Spanish Cloister   747
My Last Duchess   749
The Bishop Orders His Tomb at Saint Praxed's Church   750
Meeting at Night   753
Parting at Morning   754
A Toccata of Galuppi's   754
Memorabilia   756
Love Among the Ruins   756
"Childe Roland to the Dark Tower Came"   758
Fra Lippo Lippi   764
The Last Ride Together   773
Andrea del Sarto   775

CHARLES DICKENS   782

A Christmas Carol   784

SIR ARTHUR CONAN DOYLE   833

A Scandal in Bohemia   834

JOHN RUSKIN   849

Modern Painters   851
  from Definition of Greatness in Art   851
  from Of Water, As Painted by Turner   852
The Storm-Cloud of the Nineteenth Century   853

MATTHEW ARNOLD   858

Isolation. To Marguerite   861
To Marguerite—Continued   862
Dover Beach   863

  RESPONSE
    Anthony Hecht: The Dover Bitch   864

Lines Written in Kensington Gardens   865
The Buried Life   866
The Scholar-Gipsy   868
Culture and Anarchy   874
  from Sweetness and Light   874
  from Doing as One Likes   876

from Hebraism and Hellenism   880
from Conclusion   881

DANTE GABRIEL ROSSETTI   882

The Blessed Damozel   884
The Woodspurge   887
The House of Life   887
    The Sonnet   887
    4. Lovesight   888
    6. The Kiss   888
    Nuptial Sleep   889

CHRISTINA ROSSETTI   889

Song ("She sat and sang alway")   891
Song ("When I am dead, my dearest")   891
Remember   891
After Death   892
A Pause   892
Echo   892
Dead Before Death   893
An Apple-Gathering   893
Up-Hill   894
Goblin Market   894
Promises Like Pie-Crust   907

ALGERNON CHARLES SWINBURNE   908

The Triumph of Time   909
    I Will Go Back to the Great Sweet Mother   909
Hymn to Proserpine   910
A Forsaken Garden   913

WALTER PATER   915

from The Renaissance   916
    Preface   916
    from Leonardo da Vinci   919
    Conclusion   920

GERARD MANLEY HOPKINS   923

God's Grandeur   924
The Windhover   925
Pied Beauty   925
Binsey Poplars   926
Felix Randal   926
As Kingfishers Catch Fire   927
[Carrion Comfort]   927

No Worst, There Is None   928
I Wake and Feel the Fell of Dark, Not Day   928
That Nature Is a Heraclitean Fire and of the Comfort of the Resurrection   929
Thou Art Indeed Just, Lord   929

RUDYARD KIPLING   930
Without Benefit of Clergy   931
from JUST SO STORIES   945
How the Leopard Got His Spots   945

Gunga Din   950
The Widow at Windsor   952
Recessional   953
If—   954

OSCAR WILDE   955
Impression du Matin   958
RESPONSE
Lord Alfred Douglas: Impression de Nuit   958

The Harlot's House   959
Symphony in Yellow   960
Preface to *The Picture of Dorian Gray*   960
The Importance of Being Earnest   961
Aphorisms   1002
from De Profundis   1004

COMPANION READING
H. Montgomery Hyde: *from* The Trials of Oscar Wilde   1011

The Twentieth Century   1019

JOSEPH CONRAD   1043
Preface to *The Nigger of the "Narcissus"*   1046
Heart of Darkness   1048
"HEART OF DARKNESS" AND ITS TIME
Joseph Conrad: from Congo Diary   1104
*Sir Henry Morton Stanley: from Address to the Manchester Chamber
of Commerce*   1106

RESPONSES
Chinua Achebe: An Image of Africa   1110
Gang of Four: We Live As We Dream, Alone   1119

THOMAS HARDY   1120
Hap   1122
Neutral Tones   1122

Wessex Heights   1123
The Darkling Thrush   1124
On the Departure Platform   1124
The Convergence of the Twain   1125
Channel Firing   1126
In Time of "The Breaking of Nations"   1127
I Looked Up from My Writing   1128
"And There Was a Great Calm"   1128
Epitaph   1130

⇒✛ PERSPECTIVES ✛⇐
The Great War: Confronting the Modern   1131

BLAST   1131
    Vorticist Manifesto   1133
REBECCA WEST   1147
    Indissoluble Matrimony   1148
RUPERT BROOKE   1163
    The Great Lover   1164
    The Soldier   1166
SIEGFRIED SASSOON   1166
    Glory of Women   1166
    "They"   1167
    The Rear-Guard   1167
    Everyone Sang   1168
WILFRED OWEN   1168
    Anthem for Doomed Youth   1169
    Strange Meeting   1169
    Disabled   1170
    Dulce Et Decorum Est   1171
ISAAC ROSENBERG   1172
    Break of Day in the Trenches   1172
    Dead Man's Dump   1173
THE WOMEN POETS OF WORLD WAR I   1175
CICELY HAMILTON   1176
    Non-Combatant   1176
MAY WEDDERBURN CANNAN   1176
    Lamplight   1176
    Rouen   1177
PAULINE BARRINGTON   1178
    "Education"   1178
HELEN DIRCKS   1179
    After Bourlon Wood   1179
ALYS FANE TROTTER   1180
    The Hospital Visitor   1180
TERESA HOOLEY   1181
    A War Film   1181

❧ WILLIAM BUTLER YEATS   **1182**

The Lake Isle of Innisfree   1186
Who Goes with Fergus?   1186
No Second Troy   1186
The Fascination of What's Difficult   1187
September 1913   1187
The Wild Swans at Coole   1188
An Irish Airman Foresees His Death   1189
Easter 1916   1189
The Second Coming   1191
A Prayer for My Daughter   1192
Sailing to Byzantium   1194
Leda and the Swan   1194
Among School Children   1195
Byzantium   1197
Crazy Jane Talks with the Bishop   1198
Lapis Lazuli   1198
The Circus Animals' Desertion   1200
Under Ben Bulben   1201

❧ JAMES JOYCE   **1204**

DUBLINERS   1207
Araby   1207
Eveline   1211
Clay   1214
The Dead   1218

❧ T. S. ELIOT   **1245**

The Love Song of J. Alfred Prufrock   1248
Gerontion   1252
The Waste Land   1254

    ❧ RESPONSES
      Fadwa Tuqan: In the Aging City   1267
      Martin Rowson: *from* The Waste Land   1269 ❧

Journey of the Magi   1275
Four Quartets   1276
    Burnt Norton   1276
Tradition and the Individual Talent   1280

❧ VIRGINIA WOOLF   **1285**

The Lady in the Looking-Glass: A Reflection   1288
from A Room of One's Own   1291

❧ KATHERINE MANSFIELD   1317
The Daughters of the Late Colonel   1317

❧ D. H. LAWRENCE   1330
Piano   1333
Song of a Man Who Has Come Through   1333
Tortoise Shout   1333
Snake   1336
Bavarian Gentians   1338
Cypresses   1338
Odour of Chrysanthemums   1340

❧ DYLAN THOMAS   1353
The Force That Through the Green Fuse Drives the Flower   1354
Fern Hill   1355
Poem in October   1356
Do Not Go Gentle into That Good Night   1357

❧ SAMUEL BECKETT   1358
Endgame   1360

POSTWAR POETS: ENGLISH VOICES   1395

❧ W. H. AUDEN   1395
Musée des Beaux Arts   1396
In Memory of W. B. Yeats   1397
Spain 1937   1399
Lullaby   1401
September 1, 1939   1402
In Praise of Limestone   1405

❧ PHILIP LARKIN   1407
Church Going   1408
High Windows   1409
Talking in Bed   1410
MCMXIV   1410

❧ TED HUGHES   1411
Wind   1412
Relic   1412
Theology   1413
Dust As We Are   1413
Leaf Mould   1414
Telegraph Wires   1415

❧ SALMAN RUSHDIE   1416
   The Courter   1416

┌──┐
          ⇒✢ PERSPECTIVES ✢⇐
             Whose Language?   1431

   LOUISE BENNETT   1432
      Back to Africa   1432
      Colonization in Reverse   1433
      Independance   1434
   from NGŨGĨ WA THIONG'O   1435
      Decolonizing the Mind   1436
         Native African Languages   1436
   NADINE GORDIMER   1439
      What Were You Dreaming?   1440
   DEREK WALCOTT   1446
      A Far Cry from Africa   1447
      Wales   1448
      The Fortunate Traveller   1449
   SEAMUS HEANEY   1454
      Punishment   1455
      The Skunk   1456
      The Toome Road   1457
      The Singer's House   1457
      In Memoriam Francis Ledwidge   1458
      Postscript   1460
      A Call   1460
      The Errand   1460
   JAMES KELMAN   1461
      Home for a Couple of Days   1461
   EAVAN BOLAND   1470
      Anorexic   1471
      Mise Eire   1473
      The Pomegranate   1474
      A Woman Painted on a Leaf   1475
   LORNA GOODISON   1476
      The Mulatta as Penelope   1476
      On Becoming a Mermaid   1477
      Annie Pengelly   1477
   AGHA SHAHID ALI   1481
      Beyond English   1481
      In Arabic   1482
      Tonight   1483
   PAUL MULDOON   1484
      Cuba   1484

Aisling   1485
Meeting the British   1485
Sleeve Notes   1486
NUALA NÍ DHOMHNAILL   1492
Feeding a Child   1493
Parthenogenesis   1494
Labasheedy (The Silken Bed)   1496
As for the Quince   1497
Why I Choose to Write in Irish, The Corpse That Sits Up and Talks Back   1498
GWYNETH LEWIS   1506
Therapy   1506
Mother Tongue   1507
ROBERT CRAWFORD   1508
The Saltcoats Structuralists   1508
Alba Einstein   1509
W. N. HERBERT   1510
Cabaret McGonagall   1510
Smirr   1513

Credits   *1515*
Index   *1519*

LIST OF ILLUSTRATIONS

The Romantics and Their Contemporaries

Color Plates   *following page 32*

1. John Martin, *The Bard*

2. Thomas Gainsborough, *Mary Robinson*

3. Thomas Phillips, *Lord Byron*

4. Anonymous, *Portrait of Olaudah Equiano*

5. J. M. W. Turner, *Slavers Throwing the Dead and Dying Overboard, Typhoon Coming On*

6. William Blake, *The Little Black Boy* (second plate only)

7. William Blake, *The Little Black Boy* (another version of #6)

8. William Blake, *The Tyger*

9. William Blake, *The Sick Rose*

10. Joseph Wright, *An Iron Forge Viewed from Without*

Black-and-White Images

Thomas Girtin, *Tintern Abbey*	*page 2*
Thomas Rowlandson, after a drawing by Lord George Murray, *The Contrast, 1729*	12
Thomas Lawrence, *Coronation Portrait of the Prince Regent* (later, *George IV*), 1820	16
Charlotte Smith, engraving for Sonnet IV, "To the Moon"	42
William Blake, frontispiece for *Songs of Innocence*	52
William Blake, *The Lamb*	55
William Blake, *The Little Boy lost*	58
William Blake, *The Little Boy found*	59
William Blake, *THE Chimney Sweeper*	68
William Blake, *THE FLY*	69
William Blake, *A POISON TREE*	74
Packing methods on a slave ship	126
Portrait of Mary Wollstonecraft	144
Ford Madox Brown, *Manfred on the Jungfrau*, 1840	358
Edward Smith, after a painting by Edward Robinson, *Portrait of Felicia Hemans*, 1831	515
Charles Brown, *Portrait of John Keats*, 1819	533

The Victorian Age

Color Plates *following page 576*

11. Sir John Everett Millais, *Mariana*

12. William Holman Hunt, *The Awakening Conscience*

13. Ford Madox Brown, *Work*

14. Augustus Egg, *Past and Present No. 1*

15. Augustus Egg, *Past and Present No. 3*

16. William Morriss, *Guenevere, or La Belle Iseult*

17. Dante Gabriel Rossetti, *The Blessed Damozel*

18. James M. Whistler, *Nocturne in Black and Gold: The Falling Rocket*

19. John Williams Waterhouse, *The Lady of Shalott*

20. Sir Edward Burne-Jones, *Love Among the Ruins*

Black-and-White Images

Gustave Doré, *Ludgate Hill*   page 566

Sunlight Soap advertisement commemorating the 1897 Jubilee
   of Victoria's reign   568

Robert Howlett, *Portrait of Isambard Kingdom Brunel and Launching
   Chains of the Great Eastern, 1857*   571

The Crystal Palace   576

"The Formula of British Conquest," Pears' Soap advertisement   582

Cartoon from *Punch* magazine, 1867   585

Julia Margaret Cameron, *Thomas Carlyle, 1867*   592

Elizabeth Barrett Browning, frontispiece of the revised,
   fourth edition of *Aurora Leigh*   620

Max Beerbohm, *Tennyson Reading "In Memoriam" to his Sovereign, 1904*   637

William Holman Hunt, *The Lady of Shalott*   641

Linley Sambourne, *Man is But a Worm*   703

Julia Margaret Cameron, *Robert Browning, 1866*   742

Hablot K. Browne, *Mr. Scrooge Extinguishing the Spirit*   807

Sidney Paget, *"Good-night, Mr. Sherlock Holmes"*   847

Matthew Arnold and his wife Frances Wightman Arnold   858

Dante Gabriel Rossetti, frontispiece to *Goblin Market*   895

Rudyard Kipling, *How the Leopard Got His Spots*   946

Oscar Wilde and Lord Alfred Douglas, 1893   956

The Twentieth Century

Color Plates   *following page 1024*

21. Paul Nash, *We Are Making a New World*

22. Charles Ginner, *Piccadilly Circus*

23. Vanessa Bell, *The Tub*

24. Vera Willoughby, *General Joy*

25. L. D. Luard, *The Spirit of 1943*

26. Stanley Spencer, *Shipbuilding on the Clyde: Furnaces*

27. Francis Bacon, *Study after Velasquez*

28. Gilbert and George, *Death Hope Life Fear*

29. David Hockney, *Great Pyramid at Giza with Broken Head from Thebes*

30. Chris Ofili, *No Woman, No Cry*

Black-and-White Images

Richard Nevinson, *The Arrival*, 1913–1914	page 1018
Soldiers of the 9th Cameronians division near Arras, France, 24 March 1917	1025
Archibald Hatrick, *A Lift Girl*, 1916	1028
Christopher Richard Wynne Nevinson, *Poster for the Wembley Exhibition*, 1925	1033
London during the Blitz	1034
The Beatles preparing for a television broadcast, c. 1963	1039
Joseph Conrad, London, 11 March 1916	1043
Wyndham Lewis, *The Creditors*, 1912–1913	1132
William Butler Yeats, c. 1933	1182
Man Ray, *Portrait of James Joyce*, 1922	1204
Photo of Sackville Street (now O'Connell Street), with view of Nelson's Pillar	1206
Publicity photo from Barry Hyams, *T. S. Eliot*, 1954	1245
Virginia Woolf	1285
T. S. Eliot and Virginia Woolf	1287
Samuel Beckett, 1971	1358
Salman Rushdie, c. 1999–2000	1416

PREFACE

Literature has a double life. Born in one time and place and read in another, literary works are at once products of their age and independent creations, able to live on long after their original world has disappeared. The goal of this anthology is to present a wealth of poetry, prose, and drama from the literary masters of Great Britain and its empire, and to do so in ways that will bring out these classic works' original cultural contexts and their lasting aesthetic power. These aspects are, in fact, closely related: Form and content, verbal music and social meanings, go hand in hand. This double life makes literature, as Aristotle said, "the most philosophical" of all the arts, intimately connected to ideas and to realities that the writer transforms into moving patterns of words. The challenge is to show these core works in the contexts in which, and for which, they were written, while at the same time not trapping them within those contexts. The warm response this anthology has received from instructors who have reviewed it reflects the growing consensus that we do not have to accept an "either/or" choice between the literature's aesthetic and cultural dimensions. This preface can serve as a road map to this text and the ways in which it reveals the masters of the British literary tradition in a whole new light.

A GENEROUS REPRESENTATION OF MAJOR CLASSIC TEXTS

Major works in all three genres are included in their entirety—among them *Beowulf*, Shakespeare's *The Tempest*, Dickens' *A Christmas Carol*, Wilde's *The Importance of Being Earnest*, Conrad's *Heart of Darkness*, and Beckett's *Endgame*. The book also offers a wealth of significant poetry selections, from Chaucer, Spenser, and Milton to Blake, Keats, and Yeats—and beyond. In addition, enduring works that are taught most frequently have been included:

- J. R. R. Tolkien's translation of *Sir Gawain and the Green Knight*

- the modern translation of Chaucer's General Prologue from *The Canterbury Tales* (appearing on facing pages from the Middle English)

- a generous selection of poems from Sidney's *Astrophil and Stella*

- poems by Lady Mary Wroth

- an extensive excerpt of Milton's *Paradise Lost*, including Books 1 and 9 in their entirety

- chapters from the third voyage and the complete fourth voyage from Swift's *Gulliver's Travels*

- a broad selection of poems from Blake's *Songs of Innocence and of Experience*

- numerous poems by Wordsworth and Keats

- a plethora of World War I poems, including an expansive selection of women poets

- a wide range of works touching on issues of post-colonialism by such authors as Chinua Achebe, Salman Rushdie, Lorna Goodison, Derek Walcott, and Agha Shahid Ali.

LITERATURE IN ITS TIME—AND IN OURS

When we engage with a rich literary history that extends back over a thousand years, we often encounter writers who assume their readers know all sorts of things that are little known today: historical facts, social issues, literary and cultural references. Beyond specific information, these works will have come out of a very different literary culture than our own. Even the contemporary British Isles present a cultural situation—or a mix of cultures—very different from what North American readers encounter at home, and these differences only increase as we go further back in time. A major emphasis of this anthology is to bring the works' original cultural moment to life: not because the works simply or naively reflect that moment of origin, but because they do refract it in fascinating ways. British literature is both a major heritage for modern North America and, in many ways, a very distinct culture; reading British literature will regularly give an experience both of connection and of difference. Great writers create imaginative worlds that have their own compelling internal logic, and a prime purpose of this anthology is to help readers to understand the formal means—whether of genre, rhetoric, or style—with which these writers have created works of haunting beauty. At the same time, as Virginia Woolf says in *A Room of One's Own*, the gossamer threads of the artist's web are joined to reality "with bands of steel." This anthology pursues a range of strategies to bring out both the beauty of these webs of words and their points of contact with reality.

Masters of British Literature brings related authors and works together in several ways:

☞ PERSPECTIVES: **Broad groupings that illuminate underlying issues in a variety of the major works of a period.**

☞ AND ITS TIME: **A focused cluster that illuminates a specific cultural moment or a debate to which an author is responding.**

☞ RESPONSES: **One or more texts in which later authors in the tradition respond creatively to the challenging texts of their forebears.**

For example, Tracts on Women and Gender in the Early Modern section presents Erasmus on marriage, Rachel Speght's defense of womanhood, and a pair of humorous texts on gender and style of dress.

These groupings provide a range of means of access to the literary culture of each period. The Perspectives sections do much more than record what major writers thought about an issue: they give a variety of views in a range of voices, to illustrate the wider culture within which the literature was being written. These and many other vivid readings give rhetorical as well as social contexts for the poems, plays, and stories around them. Perspectives sections typically relate to several major authors of the period, as with a section on The Abolition of Slavery and the Slave-Trade that relates broadly to the work of William Wordsworth and Lord Byron. Many of the writers included in Perspectives sections are important figures of the period who might be neglected if they were listed on their own with just a few pages each; grouping them together has proven to be useful pedagogically as well as intellectually. Perspectives sections may also include work by a major author whose primary listing appears elsewhere in the period, so as to give a rounded presentation of the issue in ways that can inform the reading of those authors in their individual sections.

When we present a major work "And Its Time," we give a cluster of related materials to suggest the context within which the work was written. Thus Jonathan Swift's "A Modest Proposal" is accompanied by a reading showing the tensions that were raging at the time between England and Ireland. Some of the writers in these groupings and in our Perspectives sections have not traditionally been seen as literary figures, but all have produced lively and intriguing works, from medieval writers of King Arthur, to a polemical seventeenth-century tract giving *The Arraignment of Lewd, Idle, Froward, and Unconstant Women*, to the Gang of Four's punk rock anthem derived from Conrad's *Heart of Darkness*.

Also, we include "Responses" to significant texts in the British literary tradition, demonstrating the sometimes far-reaching influence these works have had over the decades and centuries, and sometimes across oceans and continents. *Beowulf* and John Gardiner's *Grendel*, for example, are separated by the Atlantic ocean, perhaps eleven- or twelve hundred years—and, most notably, their attitude toward the poem's monster.

CULTURAL EDITIONS

The publication of *Masters of British Literature* finds eighteen volumes of the Longman Cultural Editions now in print, which carry further the anthology's emphases by presenting major texts along with a generous selection of contextual material. Included in those volumes are frequently taught texts ranging from *Beowulf* and *Hamlet* to *Frankenstein* and *Northanger Abbey*; nearly three dozen new titles are currently being developed, bringing the list of available titles up to the early twentieth century. In some instances, dedicating a full, separate volume to major texts (like *Othello/Miriam* and *Frankenstein*)—available at no additional charge, for course use, with the anthology itself—has helped to free up space for our many additions in this new edition. Taken together, our new edition and the Longman Cultural Editions offer an unparalleled set of materials for the enjoyment and study of British literary culture from its earliest beginnings to the present.

ILLUSTRATING VISUAL CULTURE

Another important context for literary production has been a different kind of culture: the visual. This edition includes a suite of color plates in each volume, along with one hundred black-and-white illustrations throughout the anthology, chosen to show artistic and cultural images that figured importantly for literary creation. Sometimes, a poem refers to a specific painting, or more generally emulates qualities of a school of visual art. At other times, more popular materials like advertisements may underlie scenes in Victorian or Modernist writing. In some cases, visual and literary creation have merged, as in Blake's illustrated engravings of his *Songs of Innocence and of Experience*, several of whose plates are reproduced in color in Volume B. A thumbnail portrait of major authors in each period marks the beginning of author introductions.

AIDS TO UNDERSTANDING

We have attempted to contextualize our selections in suggestive rather than exhaustive ways, trying to enhance rather than overwhelm the experience of reading the texts themselves. Thus, when difficult or archaic words need defining in poems, we use glosses in the margins, so as to disrupt the reader's eye as little as possible; footnotes are intended to be concise and informative, rather than massive or interpretive. Important literary and social terms are defined when they are used; for convenience of reference, there is also an extensive glossary of literary and cultural terms at the end of each volume, together with useful summaries of British political and religious organization, and of money, weights, and measures. For further reading, carefully selected, up-to-date bibliographies for each period and for each author can be found in each volume.

LOOKING—AND LISTENING—FURTHER

Beyond the boundaries of the anthology itself, we have incorporated a pair of CDs, one for each volume, giving a wide range of readings of texts in the anthology and of selections of music from each period. It is only in the past century or two that people usually began to read literature silently; most literature has been written in the expectation that it would be read aloud, or even sung in the case of lyric poetry ("lyric" itself means a work meant to be sung to the accompaniment of a lyre or other instruments). The aural power and beauty of these works is a crucial dimension of their experience. For further explorations, we have also expanded our Web site, available to all users at www.ablongman.com/damroschbritlit3e; this site gives a wealth of information, annotated links to related sites, and an archive of texts for further reading. Links to relevant pages are appended to anthology selections. For instructors, we have revised and expanded our popular companion volume, *Teaching British Literature*, written directly by the anthology editors, 600 pages in length, available free to everyone who adopts the anthology.

WHAT IS BRITISH LITERATURE?

Turning now to the book itself, let us begin by defining our basic terms: What is "British" literature? What is literature itself? And just what should an anthology of this material look like at the present time? The term "British" can mean many things, some of them contradictory, some of them even offensive to people on whom the name has been imposed. If the term "British" has no ultimate essence, it does have a history. The first British were Celtic people who inhabited the British Isles and the northern coast of France (still called Brittany) before various Germanic tribes of Angles and Saxons moved onto the islands in the fifth and sixth centuries. Gradually the Angles and Saxons amalgamated into the Anglo-Saxon culture that became dominant in the southern and eastern regions of Britain and then spread outward; the old British people were pushed west, toward what became known as Cornwall, Wales, and Ireland, which remained independent kingdoms for centuries, as did Celtic Scotland to the north. By an ironic twist of linguistic fate, the Anglo-Saxons began to appropriate the term British from the Britons they had displaced, and they took as a national hero the early, semi-mythic Welsh King Arthur. By the seventeenth century, English monarchs had extended their sway over Wales, Ireland, and Scotland, and they began to refer to their holdings as "Great Britain." Today, Great Britain includes England, Wales, Scotland, and Northern Ireland, but does not include the Republic of Ireland, which has been independent from England since 1922.

This anthology uses "British" in a broad sense, as a geographical term encompassing the whole of the British Isles. For all its fraught history, it seems a more satisfactory term than to speak simply of "English" literature, for two reasons. First: most speakers of English live in countries that are not the focus of this anthology; second, while the English language and its literature have long been dominant in the British Isles, other cultures in the region have always used other languages and have produced great literature in these languages. Important works by Irish, Welsh, and Scots writers appear regularly in the body of this anthology, some of them written directly in their languages and presented here in translation, and others written in an English inflected by the rhythms, habits of thought, and modes of expression characteristic of these other languages and the people who use them.

We use the term "literature" in a similarly capacious sense, to refer to a range of artistically shaped works written in a charged language, appealing to the imagination at least as much as to discursive reasoning. It is only relatively recently that creative writers have been able to make a living composing poems, plays, and novels, and only in the past hundred years or so has creating "belles lettres" or high literary art been thought of as a sharply separate sphere of activity from other sorts of writing that the same authors would regularly produce. Sometimes, Romantic poets wrote sonnets to explore the deepest mysteries of individual perception and memory; at other times, they wrote sonnets the way a person might now write an Op-Ed piece, and such a sonnet would be published and read along with parliamentary debates and letters to the editor on the most pressing contemporary issues.

WOMEN'S WRITING, AND MEN'S

Literary culture has always involved an interplay between central and marginal regions, groupings, and individuals. A major emphasis in literary study in recent years has been the recovery of writing by women writers, some of them little read until recently, others major figures in their time. This anthology emphasizes the presence of women writers with selections by writers like Lady Mary Wroth and Eliza Haywood, as well as by including new voices like the contemporary Welsh poet Gwyneth Lewis and a cluster of women poets writing out of their response to World War I. Attending to these voices gives us a new variety of compelling works, and helps us rethink the entire periods in which they wrote. The first third of the nineteenth century, for example, can be defined more broadly than as a "Romantic Age" dominated by six male poets; looking closely at women's writing as well as at men's, we can deepen our understanding of the period as a whole, including the specific achievements of Blake, William Wordsworth, Coleridge, Keats, Percy Shelley, and Byron, all of whom continue to have a major presence in these pages as most of them did during the nineteenth century.

VARIETIES OF LITERARY EXPERIENCE

Above all, we have striven to give as full a presentation as possible to the varieties of great literature produced over the centuries in the British Isles, by women as well as by men, in outlying regions as well as in the metropolitan center of London, and in prose, drama, and verse alike. We have taken particular care to do justice to prose fiction: we include entire novels or novellas by Charles Dickens and Joseph Conrad, as well as a wealth of short fiction from the eighteenth century to the present. For the earlier periods, we give major space to narrative poetry by Chaucer and Spenser, and to Milton's *Paradise Lost* and Swift's *Gulliver's Travels*, among others. Drama appears throughout the anthology, from the medieval *Second Play of the Shepherds* to William Wycherley's *The Country Wife* to Samuel Beckett's *Endgame*. Finally, lyric poetry appears in profusion throughout the anthology, from early lyrics by anonymous Middle English poets to the powerful contemporary voices of Seamus Heaney, Eavan Boland, and Derek Walcott—himself a product of colonial British education, heir of Shakespeare and James Joyce.

As topical as these contemporary writers are, we hope that this anthology will show that the great works of earlier centuries can also speak to us compellingly today, their value only increased by the resistance they offer to our views of ourselves and our world. To read and reread the full sweep of this literature is to be struck anew by the degree to which the most radically new works are rooted in centuries of prior innovation. Even this preface can close in no better way than by quoting the words written eighteen hundred years ago by Apuleius of Madaura—both a consummate artist and a kind of anthologist of extraordinary tales—when he concluded the prologue to his masterpiece *The Golden Ass*: Attend, reader, and pleasure is yours.

Acknowledgments

In planning and preparing this anthology, the editors have been fortunate to have the support, advice, and assistance of many people. Our editor, Joe Terry, has been unwavering in his enthusiasm for the book and his commitment to it; he and his associates Roth Wilkofsky, Mary Ellen Curley, and Ann Stypuloski have supported us in every possible way throughout the process, ably assisted by Alison Main, Christine Halsey, and Abby Lindquist. Our developmental editor Mika De Roo guided us and our manuscript from start to finish with unfailing acuity and Wildean wit. Our copyeditor marvelously integrated the work of a dozen editors. Jenna Egan, Mika De Roo, Teresa Ward, and Heidi Jacobs have devoted enormous energy and creativity to our Web site and audio CD. Natalie Giboney cleared our many permissions, and Julie Tesser cleared our illustrations. Finally, Valerie Zaborski and Denise Phillips oversaw the production with sunny good humor and kept the book successfully on track on a very challenging schedule, working closely with GGS Book Services.

We are also grateful for the guidance of the reviewers who advised us on the creation of this book. Robert Barrett, University of Illinois-Urbana-Champaign; Bryan P. Davis, Georgia Southwestern State University; Maria Doyle, University of West Georgia; Alison L. Ganze, Valparaiso University; Kevin Gustafson, University of Texas-Arlington; Ruth Jenkins, California State University-Fresno; Tamara Ketabgian, Beloit College; Mary Kramer, University of Massachusetts-Lowell; Jim McKeown, McLennan Community

College; Rebecca M. Mills, Hillsborough Community College; Emily H. Moorer, Hinds Community College; Patricia G. Morgan, Louisiana State University; Barry R. Nowlin, University of South Alabama; and Jackie Walsh, McNeese State University.

Other colleagues brought our developing book into the classroom, teaching from portions of the work-in-progress. Our thanks go to Lisa Abney (Northwestern State University), Charles Lynn Batten (University of California, Los Angeles), Brenda Riffe Brown (College of the Mainland, Texas), John Brugaletta (California State University, Fullerton), Dan Butcher (Southeastern Louisiana University), Lynn Byrd (Southern University at New Orleans), David Cowles (Brigham Young University), Sheila Drain (John Carroll University), Lawrence Frank (University of Oklahoma), Leigh Garrison (Virginia Polytechnic Institute), David Griffin (New York University), Rita Harkness (Virginia Commonwealth University), Linda Kissler (Westmoreland County Community College, Pennsylvania), Brenda Lewis (Motlow State Community College, Tennessee), Paul Lizotte (River College), Wayne Luckman (Green River Community College, Washington), Arnold Markely (Pennsylvania State University, Delaware County), James McKusick (University of Maryland, Baltimore), Eva McManus (Ohio Northern University), Manuel Moyrao (Old Dominion University), Kate Palguta (Shawnee State University, Ohio), Paul Puccio (University of Central Florida), Sarah Polito (Cape Cod Community College), Meredith Poole (Virginia Western Community College), Tracy Seeley (University of San Francisco), Clare Simmons (Ohio State University), and Paul Yoder (University of Arkansas, Little Rock).

As if all this help weren't enough, the editors also drew directly on friends and colleagues in many ways, for advice, for information, sometimes for outright contributions to headnotes and footnotes, even (in a pinch) for aid in proofreading. In particular, we wish to thank David Ackiss, Marshall Brown, James Cain, Cathy Corder, Jeffrey Cox, Michael Coyle, Pat Denison, Tom Farrell, Andrew Fleck, Jane Freilich, Laurie Glover, Lisa Gordis, Joy Hayton, Ryan Hibbet, V. Lauryl Hicks, Nelson Hilton, Jean Howard, David Kastan, Stanislas Kemper, Andrew Krull, Ron Levao, Carol Levin, David Lipscomb, Denise MacNeil, Jackie Maslowski, Richard Matlak, Anne Mellor, James McKusick, Melanie Micir, Michael North, David Paroissien, Stephen M. Parrish, Peter Platt, Cary Plotkin, Desma Polydorou, Gina Renee, Alan Richardson, Esther Schor, Catherine Siemann, Glenn Simshaw, David Tresilian, Shasta Turner, Nicholas Watson, Michael Winckleman, Gillen Wood, and Sarah Zimmerman for all their guidance and assistance.

The pages on the Restoration and the eighteenth century are the work of many collaborators, diligent and generous. Michael F. Suarez, S. J. (Campion Hall, Oxford) edited the Swift and Pope sections; Michael Caldwell (University of Chicago) edited the portions of "Reading Papers" on *The Craftsman* and the South Sea Bubble. Steven N. Zwicker (Washington University) co-wrote the period introduction, and the headnotes for the Dryden section. Bruce Redford (Boston University) crafted the footnotes for Dryden, Gay, Johnson, and Boswell. Susan Brown, Janice Cable, Christine Coch, Marnie Cox, Tara Czechowski, Susan Greenfield, Mary Nassef, Paige Reynolds, and Andrew Tumminia helped with texts, footnotes, and other matters throughout; William Pritchard gathered texts and wrote notes. To all, abiding thanks.

It has been a pleasure to work with all of these colleagues in the ongoing collaborative process that has produced this book and brought it to this new stage of its life and use. This book exists for its readers, whose reactions and suggestions we warmly welcome, as these will in turn reshape this book for later users in the years to come.

David Damrosch & Kevin Dettmar

Masters of
British Literature

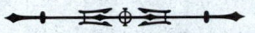

VOLUME B

Thomas Girtin, *Tintern Abbey*, c. 1793. A famously "picturesque" ruin, a favorite of tourists, sketchers, painters, and poets.

The Romantics and Their Contemporaries

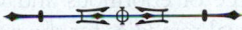

LITERATURE AND THE AGE: "NOUGHT WAS LASTING"

Reviewing Mary Shelley's *Frankenstein* in 1818, the *Edinburgh Magazine* remarked that "never was a wilder story imagined." Even so (the reviewer went on) "like most of the fictions of this age, it has an air of reality attached to it, by being connected with the favourite projects and passions of the times. The real events of the world have, in our day, too, been of so wondrous and gigantic a kind,—the shiftings of the scenes in our stupendous drama have been so rapid and various, that Shakespeare himself, in his wildest flights, has been completely distanced by the eccentricities of actual existence." The turbulent world and whirl of real events shaped the years of the "Romantic" period. It was marked on the one end by the revolutions in America and France, and on the other by the reform of Parliament to extend the vote and re-configure representation, by the emergence of the modern industrial state, and by the abolition of slavery in British colonies. In the early 1820s, Lord Byron protested:

> Talk not of seventy years as age; in seven
>   I have seen more changes, down from monarchs to
> The humblest individual under heaven,
>   Than might suffice a moderate century through.
> I knew that nought was lasting, but now even
>   Change grows too changeable without being new:
> Nought's permanent among the human race . . . (*Don Juan* 11.81)

As the nod toward monarchs indicates, the French Revolution of the 1790s cast a long shadow across British consciousness. Its events had announced a radical break in historical continuity—a sudden, cataclysmic overthrow of a monarchy surrounded by high culture, and the eruption of new social order that no one knew how to "read." New, challenging, and often contradictory energies reverberated across Britain and Europe. Enthusiasts heralded the fall of an oppressive aristocracy and the birth of de-mocratic and egalitarian ideals, a new era, shaped by "the rights of man" rather than the entailments of wealth and privilege, while skeptics and reactionaries rued the end of chivalry, lamented the erosion of order, and foresaw the decline of civilization.

Yet whatever side one took, the upheaval bore a stark realization: politically, so-cially, economically, and philosophically, an irrevocable tide of new ideas had risen against seemingly entrenched structures. "It was now known," as historian E. J. Hobsbawm puts it, "that revolution in a single country could be a European phenom-enon, that its doctrines could spread across the frontiers. . . . It was now known that social revolution was possible, that nations existed as something independent of states, peoples as something independent of their rulers, and even that the poor ex-isted as something independent of the ruling classes." Other challenges appeared,

3

framed in the rhetoric of the Revolution debate and animated by appeals to moral law and natural principle. There were arguments for and against the rights of women (not for the vote, but for better principles of education and improved social attitudes); debates over the abolition of Britain's slave trade and of slavery in its colonies (a moral blight but also a source of enormous and widespread commercial profit); movements for social and political remedies for the poor (versus the traditional spiritual consolations); and a newly emergent class consciousness among discontented workers in Britain's fields, mines, factories, and mills.

Polemical essays and pamphlets helped shape the controversies, and so did various forms of literary writing: sonnets and songs, ballads and poetic epistles, tales and plays, the sensationally turned narrative and the didactic novel. Even literature not forged in the social and political turbulence was caught by a sense of revolution. The first generation of writers (those who made their marks in the 1790s and the first decade of the new century) included William Blake, William Wordsworth, Samuel Taylor Coleridge, and Walter Scott, as well as several remarkable women: Anna Barbauld, Charlotte Smith, Hannah More, Mary Wollstonecraft, Ann Radcliffe, Joanna Baillie, and Mary Robinson. The second generation (emerging before 1820) adds the younger voices and visions of Percy Shelley, Mary Shelley, John Keats, Lord Byron, John Clare. It also witnesses the emergence of international literary celebrity, first and foremost in the charismatic figure of Lord Byron, then extending in the 1820s to the adored Felicia Hemans and at last to venerable Wordsworth, who would become a beloved Poet Laureate in 1843. All these writers were invigorated by a sense of participating in the modern world, of defining its values, and of claiming a place for writers as its instructors, prophets, critics, and inspirers. In 1792 Wollstonecraft urged "a REVOLUTION in female manners," and at the end of the decade, Wordsworth's Preface to the second edition of *Lyrical Ballads* announced his break with "known habits of association" in the genre of poetry—a program, as his collaborator Coleridge later said, of "awakening the mind's attention from the lethargy of custom" (*Biographia Literaria*, 1817). The post-Revolutionary poet "strips the veil of familiarity from the world," declared Shelley in *A Defence of Poetry*, a document he concluded by designating poets the "unacknowledged legislators of the world." This enthusiasm inspired innovations in content and literary form. Lyric, epic, and autobiography became radically subjective, spiraling inward to psychological dramas of mind and memory, or projecting outward into prophecies and visions of new worlds formed by new values. Other hybrid forms, such as political ballads and polemical narrative, emerged to address pressing issues of the day, while novelists were producing new kinds of female heroines and new narrative structures to represent family and social life. Still other writers developed forms such as the personal essay, the travelogue, or the journal, to join the personal and the political, the social and the domestic, the world of feeling to the world of thought, and both to the world of action.

ROMANCE, ROMANTICISM, AND THE POWERS OF THE IMAGINATION

In this vibrant culture of new imaginative possibilities, "Imagination" itself became a subject of reflection, and often debate. Eighteenth-century philosophy and science had argued for objective, verifiable truth and the common basis of our experience in a world of concrete, measurable physical realities. Over the century, however, there emerged a competing interest in individual variations, subjective filterings, and the mind's independence of physical realities, or even creative transformation of them: not just a recorder or mirror, the mind was an active, synthetic, dynamic, even visionary power—of particular importance to poets. Poets tended to define "Imagination" against what it was not, even categorically the opposite of: thus, imagination vs. reality; imagination vs. reason; vs. science; vs. the understanding (especially its "fixities" and "certainties"); vs. mere "fancy"; even vs. religious truth. Blake declared its priority: "What is now proved was once, only imagin'd" (*The Marriage of Heaven and Hell*); it is imagination that can "see a World in a Grain of Sand / And a Heaven in a Wild Flower" (*Auguries of Innocence*). Deeming Wordsworth too wedded to observation and description, he scribbled in the margin of Wordsworth's 1815 *Poems*, "One Power alone makes a Poet.—Imagination The Divine Vision." Yet Wordsworth had moods in which he shared Blake's sense of imagination as most potent when severed from ordinary senses and experiences: "Imagination—here the Power so called / Through sad incompetence of human speech— / That awful Power rose from the Mind's abyss / Like an unfathered vapour" (1850 *Prelude* Book 6, 593–96), he writes at a pivotal moment in a work that is the story of imagination, celebrated in his conclusion as the ultimate synthesizing power: "Imagination . . . in truth, / Is but another name for absolute strength / And clearest insight, and amplitude of mind, / And reason in her most exalted mood" (1805 *Prelude* 13.167–70).

Coleridge defined "Primary Imagination" as "the living Power and prime Agent of all human Perception," analogous to but a lesser power than divine creation. Poetry is written by the "secondary Imagination," an "echo" of the Primary "coexisting with conscious will": it dissolves and diffuses the materials of perception "in order to recreate," and thus shows itself "in the balance or reconciliation of opposite or discordant qualities," among these, the general and the individual, the new and the familiar, emotion and order, judgment and enthusiasm, rationality and passion, the artificial and the natural (*Biographia Literaria* chs. 13, 14). Percy Shelley, who also liked binaries, contrasted "Imagination" to "Reason" in the first paragraph of his *Defence of Poetry*, and following Coleridge, coordinated their powers: "Reason is to imagination as the instrument to the agent, as the body to the spirit, as the shadow to the substance." Byron, when he wasn't dramatizing the torments of imagination, was inclined to look wryly: "Imagination droops her pinion, / And the sad truth which hovers o'er my desk / Turns what was once romantic to burlesque" (*Don Juan* 4.3); "And as for other love, / the illusion's o'er; / And money, that most pure imagination, / Gleams only through the dawn of its creation" (12.2). Keats proposed the imagination as a link to the ideal world at the dawn of creation: "The Imagination may be compared to Adam's dream—he awoke and found it truth," he suggested, referring to the dream of Eve. But he was ultimately more interested in the way imagination operates on real perception: "probably every mental pursuit takes its reality and worth from the ardour of the pursuer—being in itself a nothing." And like his contemporaries, he was drawn by the involvement of imagination with disease, deviance, delusion, egotism, escapism.

As Keats's analogy of Adam's dream suggests, male imagination often projects an eroticized female or feminized object. How did women writers address the imagination? They were prone to a skeptical bias, accenting dangers, a corruption of rational capacity and moral judgment, an alliance with destructive (rather than creative) passion. This view was not just resistance to male schemes of gender; it was also fueled by a discourse of rational education and intellectual dissent that included both men and women. "The imagination should not be allowed to debauch the understanding before it has gained strength, or vanity will become the forerunner of vice," cautioned Wollstonecraft in *A Vindication of the Rights of Woman*; the best books are those "which exercise the understanding and regulate the imagination." When Jane Austen describes Emma's vain, egotistical illusions, she pointedly terms her an "imaginist . . . on fire with speculation and foresight!—especially with such a groundwork of anticipation as her mind had already made" (*Emma* vol. 3, ch. 3).

In her widely read *Plays on the Passions* Joanna Baillie summons the word to name trouble and torment: "strange imaginations," "dark imaginations . . . frightful . . . / The haunt of damned spirits," "the worst imagination" of a "madden'd brain," "a wild imagination / Which has o'erreach'd . . . judgment." Mary Robinson recognized how, Hamlet-wise, "pall'd imagination, sick'ning, spurns / The sanity of reason!" (*The Sicilian Lover* 15.23–24). When Mary Shelley recalls, "My imagination, unbidden, possessed and guided me, gifting the successive images that arose in my mind with a vividness far beyond the usual bounds of reverie," the gift was *Frankenstein*. Men often wrote about these dangers, but usually in a pattern of alternation with enthusiastic, idealizing, visionary projections. And women were not always or only cautionary. Like Byron, Robinson could wax satiric, especially when her object is a self-styled male poet, his garret "the airy throne / Of bold Imagination, rapture-fraught / Above the herds of mortals" (*The Poet's Garret*). Yet of the women poets, she is probably the most enthusiastic: enchanted by Coleridge's opium-inspired *Kubla Khan*, she addresses him as "Spirit Divine!" and offers to "trace / Imagination's boundless space" with him (*To the Poet Coleridge*); writing a poem for his infant son, she celebrates his fortune in being born among "Romantic mountains! from whose brows sublime / Imagination might to frenzy turn."

Imagination was a heady romance—an inspiring force, a dangerous seduction. Not coincidentally, the issues often took shape in the language of romance. The rapid changes, new demands, and confusions of the age often pressed writers into imagining worlds elsewhere, the impulse of the mode from which the "Romantic" era gets its name: the "Romance." In 1755 Samuel Johnson's great *Dictionary* defined it thus: "A military fable of the middle ages; a tale of wild adventures in war and love." Under this appeal, the subtitle "A Romance" graced a host of titles in the Romantic era. Radcliffe perfected the gothic romance novel; Scott elaborated the poetic romance and virtually defined the historical romance, while Byron made his name and fame in exotic quest romance: his first success, *Childe Harold's Pilgrimage* (1812), was subtitled "A Romaunt" (an old "romance" spelling), confirming the aura of the main title. In a variety of genres—ballad, narrative poem, novel—Romance turned to other places and times, or shaped timeless, ahistorical tales of quest and desire, love and adventure. A medieval idiom, which flourished into a "gothic" vogue, supplied vivid language for Radcliffe's novels, Coleridge's *Christabel* and *The Rime of the Ancyent Marinere* (in the patently antiqued version of 1798), Scott's *Lay of the Last Minstrel* (1805), Byron's *Childe Harold*, Keats's *La Belle Dame* and *The Eve of St. Agnes* (1820), and Hemans's many poems of the age of the Crusades. Romance could inhabit the even more distant pasts of Anglo-Saxon legend or classical mythology. Percy Shelley and Keats turned to the landscapes and myths of ancient Greece as resources of imagination before the age of Christian "truth." As the settings of many of these works indicate, Romance is also fascinated with foreign worlds. *Childe Harold*, Coleridge's *Kubla Khan*, and Hemans's *Tales, and Historic Scenes* testify to the vogue of Eastern materials. Byron intrigued readers with a lexicon of "jelicks" and "baracans," "giaours" and "viziers" (*Don Juan*). "Queen of far-away!" Keats hailed "Romance" itself.

In various forms, Romances shared a feature that Victorians would take as exemplary of the literary (if not the polemical) imagination of the age: a turn, even an escape, from the tumultuous and confusing here-and-now. The appeal lay not only in exotic settings and remote ages but also in the freedom these licensed to explore superstitions and customs that had been dismissed by the Enlightenment faith in "Reason," progress, and universal truths. These historically distant worlds were often sites for prophecy of renewed worlds and alternative values. Defined against "neoclassical" values of proportion, rational order, balanced harmony, and a reverence for the traditions that conveyed these values, "romantic" had long stood for a recurrent impulse in the history of the arts: a passion for the wild, the unfamiliar, the irregular, the irrational, even anti-rational. Johnson's *Dictionary* offered a suggestive cluster for "romantick": "1) resembling the tales of romances; wild. 2) Improbable; false. 3) Fanciful; full of wild scenery." All these senses infuse one powerful model for the male Romantic poet: the enraptured, entranced "bard" (see Color Plate 1). Descended from the Old Testament prophet, Englished by Milton and elaborated in the eighteenth-century ode, the bard emerged in the Romantic era as an electrically visionary poet and prophet for the age. Poets as various and as different from one another as Blake, Wordsworth, Coleridge, Shelley, and Keats assume a bardic stance to credit their dreams, hopes, and visions, even as socially oriented reformists, such as Wollstonecraft advocating "the rights of woman" or Wilberforce arguing for the abolition of slavery, adopt bardic tones to project a better, more moral world.

There was another landscape in the Romantic age that overlapped with these exotic worlds: the psychic terrain of imagination. Here a second definition Johnson supplies for "romance"—"A lie; a fiction"—casts its shadow. Romance is the genre not only of enchanted dreams and inspired visions, but also of superstitions and spells, delusions and nightmares. Coleridge said that his work for *Lyrical Ballads* was devoted to "persons and characters supernatural, or at least romantic"; hence the nightmare worlds and sensations of demonic possession in *The Rime of the Ancyent Marinere* and *Christabel*. Infused with sensations of supernatural power, or fed by opiated fantasies, the magical mystery tours of supernatural romance may hold the keys to paradise or the passage to hell, or both by turns—as they do in Thomas De Quincey's bizarrely romantic autobiography, *Confessions of an English Opium Eater*. The genre of romance fairly bristles with complexities. Acutely aware of the chaos of their historical moment, writers often make attraction to another world a critical theme: "magic casements," said Keats, "opening on the foam / Of perilous seas, in faery lands forlorn" (*Ode to a Nightingale*). The dubiously magic casements, moreover, may turn into mirrors: Romances often reflect, and reflect on, the world seemingly escaped or effaced from consciousness. The most celebrated romancers were hardly uncritical practitioners. Byron casts *Childe Harold* as a quest romance, but its path turns repeatedly to modern life, in particular the Napoleonic wars ravaging Europe.

At the same time, the prestige of "romance" and "romanticism" posed problems for women writers. Keats suggests one of these when he casts "Romance" as a dangerous seductress (a "Queen of far-away," a "Fair plumed Syren") and opposes her allure to the demands of epic and tragedy (by which male poets claimed their fame). The sexist critique of "Romance" is ironic, since many women writers were inclined to criticize the genre. If Clara Reeve, Wollstonecraft, Barbauld, and Hannah More divided, often sharply, on a variety of political and social issues, they found common ground on the dangers of "Romance." Especially in the popular form of the novel, it encouraged too much "sensibility"—the cultivation of emotional refinement over rational intellect—and fed an appetite for fantasy over sound judgment. "Romances" deal in "the wild and extravagant," worried Reeve in *The Progress of Romance* (1785); they are "dangerous" for young readers: "they create and encourage the wildest excursions of imagination." "Novels . . . tend to make women the creatures of sensation," warned Wollstonecraft's *Rights of Woman* (1792); "their character is thus formed in the mould of folly." Enfeebled reason courted illusions about "romantic love," with perilous social consequences. By 1810, Barbauld was willing to argue that good novels could teach good values, but she was still cautious about the power of "romances . . . to impress false ideas on the mind." Urging women to cultivate the Enlightenment values of "Reason" and mental strength, these female critics also challenged romance stereotypes proffered as universal truth: the ideals of "feminine" silence, self-sacrifice, passivity, and unquestioning obedience; the ideology of female life contained in the domestic sphere.

There were still more ways that Romance exoticism intersected with the socially immediate world. Encounters with outcasts of all kinds—refugees, the poor, abandoned and fallen women, discharged soldiers, sailors, vagrants, peasants, north-country shepherds and smallholders, abject slaves—supplied the unusual and unexpected, and at the same time provoked social self-reflection. Foreign cultures might be close to home, as in the ballads enthusiastically collected by Scott in *Minstrelsy of the Scottish Border* (1802–1803) and his subsequent use of Highland materials in the series of novels begun with *Waverley*. Scots poet Robert Burns packaged himself as a primitive bard: the son of a tenant-farmer and tenant-farmer himself, a heavy-drinking, illegitimate-child-siring, native genius whose dialect verse and egalitarian sentiments seemed to make him the very voice of the people. William Wordsworth produced incidents from rural life in *Lyrical Ballads*, and his sister Dorothy Wordsworth captured the dialects in her journal. John Clare wrote of rural life in a rural idiom and himself embodied the figure of the peasant poet. Meanwhile, the "wild scenery" of Johnson's definition was caught in new travel books and records of "tours," while "tourists"—a word that emerged around 1800—began to delight in locales ignored by previous generations, or thought unpleasantly rough. Once-isolated Wales became so flooded by tourists that by 1833 a Welsh grammar carried an appendix of useful phrases: "I long to see the monastery"; "Is there a waterfall in this neighbourhood?"

This romance of novelty interplays with a powerful sense of a past that might be renewed. Writers created hybrid forms, building on models anywhere from the middle ages through the eighteenth century. Byron remained loyal to neoclassic poets such as Pope and Dryden, even as he gave their forms new vibrancy and reveled in contemporary political satire. Literary tradition was a cherished, if daunting, national heritage. Many admired Chaucer's tale-telling and descriptive detail; others worked variations on Spenser's allegorical epic, *The Faerie Queene*. Hazlitt honored Spenser as "the poet of our waking dreams," and the Spenserian stanza that conveyed these dreams shaped more than a few new "romances"—among them, Byron's *Childe*

Harold, Hemans's *Forest Sanctuary*, Keats's *Eve of St. Agnes*, Shelley's *Revolt of Islam* and his homage to Keats, *Adonais*. Shakespeare and Milton were the great progenitors. Shakespeare was admired for the intensity of his imagery, his spectacular versatility, his unparalleled characterizations, as well as his mastery of "organic" (as opposed to "mechanical") aesthetic form, a concept elaborated in the criticism of Coleridge. He was an early inspiration for Coleridge's lectures and poetry; Wordsworth, Byron, and Hemans could hardly write without alluding to him; Keats named him his "Presider," and De Quincey wrote vivid essays about him. For this generation of writers, Milton's revolutionary politics provided an example of anti-monarchal courage, and *Paradise Lost* was indisputably the most important poem in English literature. Milton's Eve focuses the feminist grievances of Wollstonecraft's *Rights of Woman*, while for poets, as Byron declares in *Don Juan*, "the word 'Miltonic' mean[s] 'sublime,'" stimulating epic ambitions in works as diverse as Blake's *Milton* and *Jerusalem*, Charlotte Smith's *Emigrants*, Wordsworth's *Prelude*, Percy Shelley's *Prometheus Unbound*, Keats's *Hyperion*, and Byron's *Don Juan*. Milton's Satan, an epitome of the "sublime," is echoed and doubled everywhere, and along with Milton's God and Adam, casts his shadow across the fable of masculine ambition and heroic alienation that Wollstonecraft's daughter Mary Shelley creates for *Frankenstein*.

At the same time, Romantic creativity also defined itself—often defiantly—against tradition, experimenting with new forms and genres. Blake writes visionary epics; Wordsworth spends half a century on his poetic autobiography, "a thing unprecedented in Literary history," he said. Mary Shelley fuses several myths into a complex, interlocking structure of tales and tellers to form *Frankenstein*. Byron interplays stand-up patter with a tale of adventure to shape his burlesque *Don Juan*, "a poem totally of its own species . . . at once the stamp of originality and a defiance of imitation," Percy Shelley exclaimed to him. Individual experience, simultaneously the most exotic and most common region of all, led to excavations of the depths of the single self—which is to say, the unfolding of a self conceived as having depths and mysterious recesses. Reading Wordsworth's *Tintern Abbey*, Keats found "Genius" in its "dark Passages." In the Prospectus to *The Recluse* (1814), Wordsworth himself proclaimed

> Not Chaos, not
> The darkest pit of lowest Erebus,
> Nor aught of blinder vacancy—scooped out
> By help of dreams, can breed such fear and awe
> As fall upon us often when we look
> Into our Minds, into the Mind of Man,
> My haunt, and the main region of my Song.

Byron jibed that Keats's *Sleep and Poetry* was "an ominous title," but when Wordsworth named "the Mind" as his subject, Keats understood completely, and even women poets participated. This post-Enlightenment, bourgeois Protestant individualism moved beyond the rhetorical first-person of eighteenth-century poetry to produce the "I" as an individual authority, for whom the mind, in all its creative powers and passionate testimony of deeply registered sensations, became a compelling focus. The "I" could sponsor extravagant self-display (Robinson and Byron), prophetic self-elevation (Blake and Shelley), poignant song (Hemans), internal debate (Keats), or what Keats, thinking of Wordsworth, called the "egotistical sublime." Many of its forms defined a radical or alienated subjectivity. Wollstonecraft wrote as a nonconformist, Cowper and Hemans were famous for the melancholy autobiography that haunts their poetry, while poets such as Byron, Coleridge, and Shelley cultivated the "I" as antihero: the exile, the damned visionary, the alienated idealist, the outcast, whose affiliates were Cain, Satan, even the paradoxical figure of Napoleon—all joined by the passion of mind and the torments of imagination.

Whether cast as experiment and innovation or allied with liberty and revolution, these new expressive forms were sharpened by a sense of modernity, the writers often viewing old forms and traditions as tyranny or, at the very least, as the strictures of custom and habit. Revoking the neoclassical argument of Dryden (in the seventeenth century) that the poet is responsible for "putting bounds to a wilde over-flowing Fancy," Wordsworth asserted in the Preface to *Lyrical Ballads* (1800) that poetry is a "spontaneous overflow of powerful feelings," in which (he explained in a later version) "the feeling . . . gives importance to the action and situation, and not the action and situation to the feeling." Framing "incidents of common life," he gave importance to the feeling of such socially disenfranchised figures as children, bereft mothers, impoverished shepherds, beggars, and old veterans. In a lecture "On the Living Poets" (1818), William Hazlitt satirized this "mixed rabble of . . . convicts, female vagrants, gipsies, . . . ideot boys and mad mothers . . . peasants, pedlars," but Wordsworth's revolution was to treat them all as vehicles of worthy imagination and passion. Hazlitt had no trouble linking this program to "the sentiments and opinions which produced the French revolution" as well as its "principles and events":

> The change in the belles-lettres was as complete, and . . . as startling, as the change in politics, with which it went hand in hand. . . . According to the prevailing notions, all was to be natural and new. Nothing that was established was to be tolerated. . . . Kings and queens were dethroned from their rank and station in legitimate tragedy or epic poetry, as they were decapitated elsewhere; rhyme was looked upon as a relic of the feudal system, and regular metre was abolished along with regular government.

THE FRENCH REVOLUTION AND ITS REVERBERATIONS

In the 1780s, the American Revolution was a recent memory for the British, at once an inspiration to political progressives, an embarrassment for the prestige of the Empire, and a worry to a conservative ruling class concerned about the arrival of democratic ideas on British shores. When the next Revolution exploded in France only twelve miles across the Channel, rather than a hemisphere away, the press of radical, violent, and inevitable change seemed imminent. With the fall of the Bastille prison, a symbol of royal tyranny, on 14 July 1789, and the *Declaration of the Rights of Man* that soon followed, British consciousness was dominated by French events. Conservatives were alarmed, while liberals welcomed the early phase as a repetition of England's "Glorious Revolution" of 1688, an overdue end to feudal abuse and the inauguration of constitutional government. Radicals hoped for a more thorough-going renovation: "Bliss was it in that dawn to be alive, / But to be young was very heaven!" Wordsworth said in retrospect, in a passage from his poetic autobiography that he published in 1809, and again in 1815 under the title *French Revolution as it Appeared to Enthusiasts at its Commencement*. Everything was infused with "the attraction of a country in Romance!" He was not the only one in rapture. Southey recalled how "a visionary world seemed to open. . . . Old things seemed passing away, and nothing was dreamt of but the regeneration of the human race." Burns was certain that "man to man the world o'er / Shall brithers be for a' that." In their own idioms, Wollstonecraft, Blake, and Charles Lamb joined the chorus, and in subsequent generations, Byron and Percy Shelley continued to hope that what was started in France could be continued elsewhere with better consequences.

Better consequences, because millenarian dreams were soon undermined by harsh developments: the overthrow of the monarchy in August 1792 and in the next month, the massacre of more than a thousand prisoners by a Paris mob. When extremist Jacobins prevailed over moderate Girondins, the Revolution fragmented into the Reign of Terror. Louis XVI was guillotined in January 1793, Queen Marie Antoinette in October. In February, France declared war on Britain and Britain reciprocated, throwing the political ideals of Wordsworth and his generation into sharp conflict with their love of country. Except for the brief interlude of the deceptive Peace of Amiens (1802–1803: "Peace in a week, war in a month," a British diplomat commented), Britain was at war with France until the final defeat of Napoleon at Waterloo in 1815. The shock of these events lasted for decades and lent retroactive credit to the conservative polemic of Edmund Burke's *Reflections on the Revolution in France*, published in 1790, after the arrest and imprisonment of the royal family. In 1790 Burke seemed a sentimental hysteric to political opponents and was quickly subject to sarcastic challenge in Wollstonecraft's *Vindication of the Rights of Men* (1790) and Tom Paine's *Rights of Man* (1791). In 1793 radical philosopher William Godwin's *Political Justice*, though not directly about the Revolution, offered a vision of a society governed by individual reason, without the oppression of social institutions or private property. But the course of the Revolution confirmed Burke's alarm.

Under the systematic Terror of Robespierre (1793–1794), thousands of aristocrats, their employees, the clergy, and ostensible opponents of the Revolution were guillotined, the violence swallowing up Robespierre himself in 1794. British unease increased when France offered to support all revolutions abroad, and then invaded the Netherlands and the German states in 1794, Italy in 1796, and republican Switzerland in 1798. Now "Oppressors in their turn," Wordsworth wrote, "Frenchmen had changed a war of self-defense / For one of conquest, losing sight of all / Which they had struggled for" (1805 *Prelude* 10.791–94). In 1799 Napoleon, a general who consolidated his power in the Italian and Swiss campaigns, staged a *coup d'état* and was named First Consul for life. The Revolution had evolved into a military dictatorship, its despotism confirmed when Napoleon crowned himself Emperor in 1804. A complex personality—a challenger of entrenched monarchies; a charismatic military genius; a ruthless, egotistical imperialist—he generated nearly two decades of war that ravaged the Continent. Although war barely reached Britain, it was a constant threat, cost thousands of British lives and sent its economy into turmoil.

When Napoleon invaded the Iberian Peninsula in 1807, British support for the spontaneous resistance of the Portuguese and Spanish peoples enabled former radicals to return to the patriotic fold, to see their country as the champion of liberty against French imperialism. Napoleon's actions, claimed Coleridge, produced a "national unanimity unexampled in our history since the reign of Elizabeth . . . and

Thomas Rowlandson, after a drawing by Lord George Murray, *The Contrast, 1792*. British propaganda against the revolution in France.

made us all once more Englishmen." English self-definition was energized, the contest with France drawing on historical antagonisms that went back for centuries. Unlike the English, the French rejected their monarchy; if France could thus claim to be the first modern nation in the old world, Britain could feel superior to a country defined by the Terror and then Napoleon. National self-definition had strong literary manifestations. Hemans began her career with patriotic anthems celebrating Britain's support for the "noble" (and highly "romantic") Spanish resistance, and across these decades she published *Welsh Melodies, Greek Songs, Songs of Spain, National Lyrics*, and even the canonical American anthem, "The Landing of the Pilgrim Fathers" (our "Thanksgiving" hymn). Thomas Moore wrote *Irish Melodies* (1807–1834) and championed the grievances of Ireland. Byron wrote *Hebrew Melodies* (1815), got involved with Italian liberation movements, and in his last real-life romance, died in Greece where he had gone to aid the revolution against the Ottoman Empire.

Yet even as class differences blended into a general culture of songs for the salon, and made nationalism a vivid "romance," continuing disturbances pointed to those excluded from Coleridge's ideal of "us all . . . Englishmen." With ever fresh fears of invasion, the government clamped down on any form of political expression that hinted at French ideas. Efforts to reform Parliament begun in the 1780s were stifled, as was the movement to abolish the slave trade, and even moderates were silenced by accusations of "Jacobinism" (sympathy with Revolutionary extremists). In 1791 authorities in Birmingham connived at three days of riots by a loyal "Church and

King" mob against Dissenters who had held a dinner to commemorate the Fall of the Bastille. When his house and laboratory were sacked, the eminent chemist and nonconformist Joseph Priestley fled to London and then emigrated to America. In 1792 Paine fled to France; he was tried and convicted in absentia of sedition for *The Rights of Man*, and his publishers and booksellers were regularly prosecuted. In 1794, twelve London radicals were arrested, including a novelist and playwright, Thomas Holcroft, and Horne Tooke, a philologist whose publications seemed a dangerous attempt to democratize language. Charged with high treason, they were defended by Godwin and acquitted, but the trial was a harbinger.

In 1794 the government suspended the long-established right of habeas corpus, which required the state to show cause for imprisonment and to conduct trials in a timely fashion; now anyone suspected of a crime could be jailed indefinitely. The Gagging Acts of 1795 targeted radical lecturers and societies, defining any criticism of the monarchy as treason and squelching political organization by limiting the size of meetings called to discuss reform. The Combination Act of 1799 forbade workmen, under penalty of conspiracy charges, to unionize or even to associate for purposes of collective bargaining. All these laws were enforced by government spies. Coleridge and Wordsworth, walking and conversing on the coastal hills of the Bristol Channel and plotting nothing more revolutionary than poems for *Lyrical Ballads*, looked suspicious enough to warrant tailing by a government informer. Coleridge was amused that their talk of the philosopher Spinoza was reported as references to "Spy Nozy," but actual radicals suffered severer consequences, for the government was also deploying *agents provocateurs* to incite them into capital offences. These infiltrators played a major role in plotting the Pentridge Rising of 1817 and the Cato Street Conspiracy of 1820, a scheme to murder cabinet ministers (a prime minister had been assassinated in 1812) and stage a coup d'état. "Cato Street" was "exposed" and its radical conspirators hanged or sent to prison in Australia, but the ultimate conspirator had been the government. Policy was still more severe outside England: in Edinburgh, delegates to the first British Convention of reformers were arrested for sedition and doomed to sentences in Australia; in Ireland, where Britain had more troops than on the Continent, a peasants' rebellion was crushed in a bloodbath (1798). Rather than international "fraternity," it was repression at home and wars abroad that defined the legacy of the French Revolution. When Napoleon was finally defeated in 1815 and the Bourbons were restored to the throne of France, the result was to reinforce reactionary measures and despotic monarchies all over Europe.

In the England of 1815, a further affliction was visited on the poor, among whom were many veterans, by Parliament's passage of the Corn Laws. Because importing grain had been impossible during the war years, prices for native grain soared; the Corn Laws now restricted imports in order to sustain the artificially high prices, a boon for landlords and a disaster for the poor, for whom bread was a chief article of diet. Bad harvests further raised costs. For the first time, in the estimate of the *Morning Chronicle*, protests and petitions erupted from "a majority of the adult male population of England," igniting food riots across the country. Under the unreformed electoral system, petitions to Parliament were the only recourse for those without representatives. In 1800 only males, and only five percent of them, were allowed to vote; only Anglicans, members of the state Church, could serve in the House of Lords. Workers did not have a vote, or even a representative in Parliament. The worker-populated cities of Leeds, Manchester, Birmingham, and Sheffield did not have a vote, whereas depopulated "rotten boroughs," consisting of one or two houses owned by a single landlord, enjoyed one or even two representatives in Parliament. As the Prince Regent returned from the opening of Parliament in January 1817, he found his carriage surrounded by a hostile crowd and stoned.

Workers were also being displaced by new machinery; they sometimes retaliated with attacks on the machines themselves, actions punishable by death. (Byron's first speech in the House of Lords was against such a measure, the Frame-breaking Bill provoked by weavers' riots.) Throughout the 1820s, farmworkers, angry at their degraded conditions, erupted into sporadic violence, culminating in a great uprising in 1830, in which barns burned across the countryside, and laborers again attacked machinery. The unemployed starved to death. Men scrambled for employment, while women and children, because they were deemed tractable and obedient, found it at pitiful wages. Prevailing attitudes and institutions were inadequate to ameliorate the misery and consequent disruptions. Since Elizabethan times, England had relied on a network of parishes and justices of the peace: local notables, serving in a largely volunteer capacity that enhanced their status, who kept records, assisted the needy, and administered everyday justice. Indigent newcomers to the cities could not easily be returned to their home parishes for support; they were needed as workers. And the parish system left out many: Irish Catholic immigrants, members of dissenting sects, and those lapsed from an Anglicanism that had failed to build churches for the new populations and at worst seemed remote from their concerns. When Lord John Manners declared that "the only means of Christianizing Manchester" was to revive the monasteries, he made clear the inadequacy of the current state Church to supply moral authority, social structure, and needed assistance.

No wonder that it was in Manchester that the modern vocabulary of class struggle emerged. The eighteenth-century ideal of stable social "orders" and "ranks" was challenged by a growing antagonism between successful capitalist entrepreneurs and their workers. In August 1819, nearly a hundred thousand mill-workers and their families gathered at nearby St. Peter's Field for a peaceful demonstration with banners and parades, capped by an address by the radical "Orator" Hunt calling for parliamentary reform. Alarmed by the spectacle, the local ruling class sent their drunken, sabre-wielding militia to charge the rally and arrest Hunt. Hunt offered no resistance, but the militia struck out at the jeering though unarmed crowd and, backed by mounted Hussars, in ten minutes left an official toll of eleven dead, including one trampled child, and more than four hundred injured, many from sabre wounds. Unreported injuries and later deaths from injury undoubtedly added to the official toll. This pivotal event in nineteenth-century economic and political strife was immediately dubbed "Peterloo" by the left press—a sardonic echo of the celebrated British triumph over Napoleon at Waterloo, four years before. Parliament did not reform, but instead consolidated the repressive measures of previous decades into the notorious Six Acts at the end of 1819. These Acts outlawed demonstrations, empowered magistrates to enter private houses in search of arms, prohibited meetings of more than fifty unless all participants were residents of the parish in which the meeting was held, increased the prosecution of blasphemous or seditious libel (defined as language "tending to bring into hatred or contempt" the monarchy or government), and raised the newspaper tax, thus constricting the circulation of William Cobbett's radical *Political Register* by tripling its price.

The Monarchy

Outraged by the situation summed by "Peterloo," Percy Shelley mordantly surveyed *England in 1819,* the title of a sonnet whose language rendered it unpublishable, even in a radical newspaper such as his friend Leigh Hunt's *Examiner.* It began:

> An old, mad, blind, despised, and dying King,
> Princes, the dregs of their dull race, who flow
> Through public scorn,—mud from a muddy spring,—
> Rulers who neither see, nor feel, nor know . . .

The Lear-like king who inspired this contempt was George III, Washington's antagonist in the American Revolution. He had had an episode of mental instability in 1765 and another in 1788: he talked incessantly and rarely slept, and once his eldest son tried to throttle him. The episode at once epitomized their antagonism and reflected the political conflicts of the late Georgian era. The King lived a domestic life and his successive administrations were firmly Tory—that is, socially and politically "conservative," committed to the constitutional power of the monarchy and the Church, and opposed to concessions of greater religious and political liberties. The Prince lived extravagantly at taxpayers' expense, with a devout Roman Catholic mistress whom he secretly and unconstitutionally married. In 1787 he obtained an extra £10,000 from the King, a relief from Parliament of £100,000 to pay his debts, and an additional £60,000 to build his residence, Carlton House—a total equivalent to almost seven million dollars today. But because his comparative political flexibility held out the hope of some reforms, he was backed by the opposition party, the liberal Whigs. He expected the crown in 1788, but the King unexpectedly recovered, hanging on until November 1810, when he relapsed and became permanently mad. In January 1811 the Prince was appointed "Regent."

In this new position of power, he focused all the contradictions and tensions of the time. In 1812, the *Morning Post* addressed him in the loyalist hyperbole that earned it the nickname of the "Fawning Post": "You are the glory of the People . . . You breathe eloquence, you inspire the Graces—You are an Adonis in loveliness." Leigh and John Hunt replied in *The Examiner,* denouncing "this Adonis in Loveliness" as "a corpulent gentleman of fifty . . . a man who had just closed half a century without one single claim on the gratitude of his country or the respect of posterity." Their scathing rejoinder earned them two-year sentences for libel and fines of £500 each, but Leigh Hunt continued to edit *The Examiner* from his prison cell, which he transformed into a gentleman's parlor, where he was visited as a hero by Byron, Moore, Keats, and Lamb.

Meanwhile, the Prince Regent was transforming the face of London. He and his architects recreated Regent's Park in the north and St. James Park in the south, linking them by extending Regent Street, built Trafalgar Square, elevated Buckingham House into Buckingham Palace, and erected the Hyde Park arch. The "metropolitan improvements" bespoke impressive city planning, but also demarcated the boundaries between rich and poor. The Gothic/Chinese/Indian fantasy of his beloved retreat, the Brighton Pavilion, spoke even more loudly of his distance from the everyday life of his subjects. By 1815, when £150 a year provided a

Thomas Lawrence, *Coronation Portrait of the Prince Regent* (*George IV*), 1820. Thomas Lawrence (1769–1830) succeeded Sir Joshua Reynolds as painter-in-ordinary to George III when still in his twenties, and he remained attached to the monarchy ever afterward. He had painted portraits for the Regent of Frederick William of Prussia and Tsar Alexander and their generals when they visited London after the overthrow of Napoleon in 1814, was knighted in 1815, and was dispatched in 1818 to Europe to complete the Regent's collection of portraits of the restored sovereigns. This image of the Prince Regent in his Coronation robes (1821) was developed from an earlier portrait in Garter robes that had become the Prince's favorite representation of himself.

comfortable living for many, he was £339,000 in debt, an extravagance that brought contempt on the monarchy. The pity many still felt for George III did not extend to the son. On his accession to power, he abandoned his Whig friends, separated his estranged Queen Caroline from their daughter Charlotte, and was absent from Charlotte when she died in childbirth in 1817. In 1820, when George III died and he at last became King, he attempted to divorce Caroline by initiating a sordid investigation of her escapades abroad. The scandal rebounded on a man excoriated, in the Hunts' words, as "a libertine over head and heels in debt and disgrace, a despiser of domestic ties," and provided yet another handle for attacks upon him. The personal elegance that had made him "the first gentleman of Europe" had dissipated; already in 1813, Beau Brummell, an aristocratic "dandy" whose impeccable style and social assurance made him a paragon of the era, responded to a slight by the Regent by loudly inquiring of a fellow dandy, "who's your fat friend?" The Prince was too fat to mount his horse by 1816; by 1818 it was reported that "Prinny has let loose his belly which now reaches his knees." Of his official Coronation portrait, Moore acidly noted that it was "disgraceful both to the King & the painter—a lie upon canvas." It was inevitable that satiric sketches would compete for fame.

INDUSTRIAL ENGLAND AND "NEVER-RESTING LABOUR"

In the decades of this royal extravagance, the general population was rapidly expanding, accompanied by grim social misery. By 1750, the population of England and Wales was around five-and-a-half million; at the turn of the century, when the first census was taken, it was about eight million, with most of the increase in the last two decades. Scotland registered another million and a half, Ireland more than five million. Traditionally viewed as an index to a nation's wealth, population now loomed as a danger, inspiring the dire prophecy of Thomas Malthus's *On the Principle of Population As It Affects the Future Improvement of Society* (1798): "population, when unchecked, increases in a geometrical ratio. Subsistence increases only in an arithmetical ratio. A slight acquaintance with numbers will show the immensity of the first power in comparison of the second." The increase continued: by 1831 the population of Great Britain neared fourteen million.

The numbers tell only part of the story. Ever since the end of the eighteenth century and then with postwar acceleration, the economic base had begun to shift from agriculture, controlled by wealthy aristocrats (the landlords), to manufacture, controlled by new-money industrialists. The war against France fueled a surge: "A race of merchants and manufacturers and bankers and loan jobbers and contractors" was born, remarked Cobbett in 1802. Factories and mills invaded the countryside, pumped small towns into burgeoning cities, and cities into teeming metropolises. In 1800 only London—with about ten percent of the population of England and Wales—had more than a hundred thousand people. By 1837, when Victoria was crowned, there were five such cities, and London was growing by as much as twenty percent a decade. Even more staggering was the growth of the new industrial cities of the north. Manchester's population increased fivefold in fifty years, to 142,000 in 1831. Cobbett denounced these developments as "infernal," and many of his contemporaries, alarmed by the new populations and their demands for wages, food, and housing, feared a repetition at home of the mob violence of France.

This unprecedented concentration was the result of several converging factors. Poor harvests afflicted the countryside in the 1790s, and again in 1815. Scarcities were aggravated by the Corn Laws and ever more "Enclosure acts"—the consolidation and privatization of old common fields into larger, more efficient farms. The modernizing did improve agricultural yield and animal husbandry, offsetting in some measure Malthus's prediction of an inadequate food supply, but it also produced widespread dislocation and misery. The pattern of country landholding changed. Smallholders, from independent, modest farmers to proprietors of estates up to a thousand acres, fell away, while the great estates prospered in size and number: "the big bull frog grasps all," Cobbett pungently remarked. Meanwhile, the farmers and herdsmen rendered landless by enclosure had to settle for meager subsistence wages in the country or migrate to the cities. The census of 1811 revealed that for the first time a majority of families had nonagricultural employment. The yeomen who had represented the mythic heart of sturdy English freedom became day laborers, while others sank into poverty, and centuries-old social structures eroded. Sending the Whig leader in Parliament a copy of *Lyrical Ballads* that he hoped might stir sympathy for the rural poor, Wordsworth lamented that without a "little tract of land" as "a kind of permanent rallying point" in their hardships, "the bonds of domestic feeling . . . have been weakened, and in innumerable instances entirely destroyed."

Uprooted families were pulled by hopes of employment to the new factory towns. Cotton made modern Manchester. By 1802 there were more than fifty spinning mills, and the once-provincial city had become one of the commercial capitals of Europe. Textiles produced in vast quantities by power looms eliminated skilled hand-weavers, and extinguished the traditional supplement to the income of the cottager. The city did not incorporate until 1838, and no regulations controlled manufacture, sanitation, or housing; the unchecked boom enriched the few master manufacturers and immiserated the workers. The factories required a workforce disciplined to the constant output of the machines they tended; families accustomed to the ebb and flow of agricultural rhythms found themselves plunged into a world of industrial clock-time. Twelve- to fifteen-hour shifts, strict discipline, capricious firings, dangerous and unsanitary conditions, injuries, and ruined health were the rule of the day. Children were the preferred staff for the mills, and youngsters of five worked in the mines, their little bodies ideal for hauling coal in the narrow shafts. Workers were often further victimized by debts to their employers for housing and food. There was no philosophy of government restraint and regulation of these practices; all was "laissez-faire," the doctrine associated with Adam Smith's enormously influential *Wealth of Nations* (1777) that national wealth would flourish if businesses were left to operate with unfettered self-interest. By the 1780s there was a measurable gulf between rich and poor, ever more apparent in Manchester in the contrast between the homes of the wealthy in the suburbs and the slums by the polluted city river. "The town is abominably filthy," declared a visitor in 1808, "the Steam Engine is pestiferous, the Dyehouses noisome and offensive, and the water of the river as black as ink or the Stygian lake."

The twin agricultural and industrial revolutions recast both the town and the country and altered the relationship between them. To obtain waterpower, early mills and factories were set by rivers, thereby converting peaceful valleys into sites of production. Gas lighting, first used in such buildings, made possible twenty-four-hour operation, and the resulting spectacle affected contemporaries as a weird and ominous splendor. In regions that were once the "assured domain of calm simplicity / And pensive quiet," wrote Wordsworth in *The Excursion* (1814):

> an unnatural light,
> Prepared for never-resting Labour's eyes,
> Breaks from a many-windowed Fabric huge;
> And at the appointed hour a Bell is heard—
> Of harsher import than the Curfew-knoll
> That spake the Norman Conqueror's stern behest,
> A local summons to unceasing toil!
> Disgorged are now the Ministers of day;
> And, as they issue from the illumined Pile,
> A fresh Band meets them, at the crowded door,—
> And in the Courts—and where the rumbling Stream,
> That turns the multitude of dizzy wheels,
> Glares, like a troubled Spirit, in its bed

> Among the rocks below. Men, Maidens, Youths,
> Mother and little Children, Boys and Girls,
> Enter, and each the wonted task resumes
> Within this Temple—where is offered up
> To Gain—the Master Idol of the Realm,
> Perpetual sacrifice. (8.169–87)

Industry invaded the most picturesque quarters of the British Isles. A center of tourism, Wales was also home to oppressive slate mines. Richard Pennant of North Wales epitomized the fortunes made in the trade in slaves and new-world commodities. Using the profits from his family's Jamaican sugar plantations, Pennant developed and mechanized the slate quarries on his estates. Elected to Parliament from Liverpool in 1783, he led the planters' defense of the slave trade while boosting the market for slate at home. Slate was an ideal roofing material, and the spread of education created a need for slate blackboards; at Port Penrhyn, the town Pennant established to ship slate, a hundred thousand writing slates were manufactured each year. In the eighteenth century, the quarries employed six hundred and the manufactory thirty more; by 1820 the workforce was a thousand, and it expanded rapidly over the next two decades. The concurrent discovery on the estate of minerals useful to the manufacture of Herculaneum pottery in Liverpool generated still more income. The profits underwrote Penryhn Castle, a lush Norman fantasy constructed (from 1821) by Pennant's heir.

The rhetoric of an 1832 history of Wales obscures the dislocations entailed by the progress it lauds: "About forty years ago, this part of the country bore a most wild, barren, and uncultivated appearance, but it is now covered with handsome villas, well built farm houses, neat cottages, rich meadows, well-cultivated fields, and flourishing plantations; bridges have been built, new roads made, bogs and swampy grounds drained and cultivated, neat fences raised, and barren rocks covered with woods." At Portmadoc, about twelve miles south of the sublime scenery of Mount Snowdon in Wales, William Madocks was performing one of the celebrated technological feats of the day, building a massive embankment (1808–1811), draining the tidal estuary behind it, enlarging the harbor, and founding a model village named after himself, Tremadoc—a project on which Percy Shelley enthusiastically collaborated, until he and his household fled from Wales in 1813 in the wake of a murderous attack. Popular biography ascribed the incident to Shelley's propensity to hallucination, but underlying it were genuine conflicts between idealist radicalism, paternalistic planning, local privilege, and labor unrest.

If Romantic poetry is famous for celebrating "Nature," this affection coincides with the peril to actual nature by modern industry. "Our feeling for nature," wrote Friedrich Schiller in the 1790s, "is like the feeling of an invalid for health." Industry scarred previously rural communities. Visiting Scotland in 1803 with her brother, Dorothy Wordsworth noted of one village: "a pretty place it once has been, but a manufactory is established there; and a townish bustle and ugly stone houses are fast taking the place of the brown-roofed thatched cottages." Of the famous Carron Ironworks, "seen at a distance," she noted, "the sky above them was red with a fiery light." Industry ringed even their beloved Lake District, and on its coast the shafts of the coal mines owned by the employer of Wordsworth's father, Sir James Lowther, ran ever deeper and longer, until they extended under the sea and even caused the collapse of houses in Whitehaven, the planned port city from which the coal was shipped.

The need to bring coal and iron into conjunction spurred improvements in transport. In 1759 the Duke of Bridgewater cut an eleven-mile canal between his colliery at Worsley and Manchester; two years later an extension linked Manchester to the sea. Soon canals transected the country; between 1790 and 1794 alone, eighty-one acts for the construction of canals were passed. The cost of carriage was drastically cut, and the interior of England opened for commerce. By 1811 there were steamboats on the rivers; by 1812 locomotives were hauling coal. Large-scale road-building followed, including arteries between Shrewsbury and Holyhead (the port of departure for Ireland) and another between Carlisle and Glasgow in Scotland. During these years, a Scotsman, John Macadam, developed the road surface that bears his name. Across the country, distant regions were joined by a web of new roads and the Royal Mail coaches that ran along them on regular schedules. Decades later, remembering coach travel as it was in 1812, De Quincey recalled the new sensation of speed: "we saw it, we felt it as a thrilling; and this speed was not the product of blind insensate agencies, that had no sympathy to give, but was incarnated in the fiery eyeballs of an animal, in his dilated nostril, spasmodic muscles, and echoing hoofs" (*The English Mail-Coach, or the Glory of Motion*, 1849).

In this age of acceleration, the British Empire was expanding, too. Economically and politically, it had become the preeminent world power. The American colonies had been lost, but Canada and the West Indies remained, and Australia, New Zealand, and India marked a global reach. British forces subjugated natives, defeated rival French ambitions, and held the Turks and Russians in check, while the East India Company, originally a trading organization, gradually assumed administrative control of the subcontinent, even to the point of collecting taxes to protect British interests. The Company penetrated every aspect of British life: Warren Hastings, the first governor-general of India, was tried for cruelty and corruption, having amassed a fortune of over £400,000 in India. His trial, lasting from 1788 to 1795, was a *cause célèbre*, establishing the fame of the prosecutors even though he was acquitted. While his profits were exceptional, they marked a trend of great numbers of younger sons seeking fortunes in India. In a pattern common to north-country boys with the right connections, Wordsworth's family destined his younger brother John for service with the East India Company. "I will work for you," he said to William, "and you shall attempt to do something for the world." Although John lost his life in 1805 in the wreck of a tradeship, so widespread was the phenomenon of English fortunes based on Indian gain that "nabob," Hindi for "vicegerent" or "governor," entered the vernacular as a synonym for a wealthy man.

CONSUMERS AND COMMODITIES

Even more remarkable was the role of the East India Company as the prototype for later colonial rule. At a time when Oxford and Cambridge graduates were preparing for clerical orders, the Company college at Haileybury trained its students for their foreign service. Malthus taught there; both James Mill and son John Stuart Mill worked for the Company; Lamb was a clerk in the home office in London. And thousands more indirectly derived livelihoods or pleasures from the Company's activities. Napoleon sneered at Britain as "a nation of shopkeepers," taking this phrase from Smith's *Wealth of Nations:* "To found a great empire for the sole purpose of raising up a people of customers, may at first sight appear a project fit only for a nation of shopkeepers." But Smith's mercantile empire was a perspicacious forecast, confirmed in

1823 by Byron when he named England's pride as its "haughty shopkeepers, who sternly dealt / Their goods and edicts out from pole to pole, / And made the very billows pay them toll" (*Don Juan* 10.65).

Cotton and tea were major goods. So was opium, and behind the dreams of Coleridge's *Kubla Khan*, Keats's *Ode to a Nightingale* (whose poet compares his state of sensation to intoxication by "some dull opiate"), and De Quincey's *Confessions of an English Opium Eater* were grim realities. Laudanum, opium dissolved in alcohol, was widely prescribed for a variety of complaints; it was the chief ingredient in a host of sedatives for children, especially of the poor, whose families had to leave them at home while they worked. It was also a cheap intoxicant. When Marx said that "religion was the opium of the masses," he was not using a random metaphor. Opium virtually defined foreign profiteering. De Quincey's uncle was a colonel in Bengal, in the military service of the East India Company, which reaped enormous profits from producing opium and smuggling it into China against the prohibition of the Chinese government. A Member of Parliament remarked: "If the Chinese are to be poisoned by opium, I would rather they were poisoned for the benefit of our Indian subjects than for the benefit of any other Exchequer." But the profits accrued less to Indian subjects than to the ruling British, even as the Opium Wars served the larger purpose of opening China to Lancashire cotton, as India had been opened earlier: the Wars concluded with the annexation of Hong Kong, and the opening of five treaty ports to British commerce. Meanwhile, the persistence of slave labor in British colonial plantations (not abolished until 1833) continued to raise ethical questions about the traffic in their commodities. International affairs inescapably cast their shadow on national life: "By foreign wealth are British morals chang'd," charged Barbauld in 1791, "And Afric's sons, and India's, smile aveng'd."

As morals adjusted in relation to economic opportunities, the empire also fed a growing appetite for the exotic among those shut up in urban squalor, or merely in an increasingly routinized commercial life. For those who had the wherewithal, the era proffered a new world of objects, which had begun to proliferate in the late eighteenth century. An exemplary instance of the success of marketing joined to new technological advance is Josiah Wedgwood (1730–1795), whose cream-colored earthenware became known as "Queen's ware" because of Queen Charlotte's patronage in 1765, and, aided by that éclat, soon enjoyed a worldwide sale. In the 1770s he discovered how quickly high art could be transformed into status commodity, and began to produce imitation Greek vases, in vogue because of recent excavations at Herculaneum and Pompeii. The Wedgwood fortune enabled Josiah's sons to offer Coleridge an annuity of £150 so that he could devote himself to literature.

Alfred Bird, inventor of "Bird's Custard," pinned up in his Birmingham shop a telling motto mixing morality and the new imperatives of trade: "Early to bed. Early to rise / Stick to your work . . . And Advertise." From the late eighteenth century on, fashion magazines with colored plates advertised to provincial residents the latest styles of the capital. Even as she denounced the enslavement of women by "the perpetual fluctuation of fashion," Mary Hays conceded that "this constant variation of mode is serviceable to commerce, and promotes a brisk circulation of money" (*Letters and Essays*, 1793). This stimulus reached its acme with the arrival of *Forget Me Not, a Christmas and New Year's Present for 1823*. More than sixty annuals emerged to capitalize on this pioneering venture, bearing such titles as *The Book of Beauty*. Partly because they targeted female readers, they were hospitable to female authors, including Shelley and Hemans. And because they paid so well, they also attracted male writers: Wordsworth, Coleridge, Southey, Lamb, and Scott published in them, even though literary contributions were subordinated to the engravings that were their most compelling feature. The elegantly produced annuals were best-sellers (*The Literary Souvenir* attained a circulation of fifteen thousand); copies were shipped across the empire months in advance.

Not only women and city-dwellers were seduced by the lure of shop windows, magazines, and circulating catalogues. Cobbett hurled jeremiads at the prosperous farmers who aspired to a gentility that set them apart from the workers they had once fed as part of the family:

> Everything about this farm-house was formerly the scene of *plain manners* and *plentiful living*. . . . But all appeared to be in a state of decay and nearly of disuse. There appeared to have been hardly any *family* in that house, where formerly there were, in all probability, from ten to fifteen men, boys, and maids: and, which was the worst of all, there was a *parlour*. Aye, and a *carpet* and a *bell-pull* too! . . . And, there were the decanters, the glasses, the "dinner-set" of crockery-ware, and all just in the true stock-jobber style. And I dare say it has been *'Squire* Charington and the *Miss* Charingtons; and not plain Master Charington, and his son Hodge, and his daughter Betty Charington, all of whom this accursed system has, in all likelihood, transmuted into a species of mock gentlefolks, while it has ground the labourers down into real slaves. (*Rural Rides*, 20 October 1825)

This revolution in manners and family structure reduced "family" to its biological nucleus, replacing the economic unit that enfolded laborers, servants, and dependents. This was but one manifestation of the "acceleration" and "agitation" that, in De Quincey's words, characterized the period well before the French Revolution.

AUTHORSHIP, AUTHORITY, AND "ROMANTICISM"

In this fast-moving world, the fortunes of writers, too, began to rise and fall with new speed. Writing in the *Edinburgh Review* in 1829, the critic Francis Jeffrey meditated on "the perishable nature of modern literary fame":

> Since the beginning of our critical career, we have seen a vast deal of beautiful poetry pass into oblivion, in spite of our feeble efforts to recall or retain it in remembrance. The tuneful quartos of Southey are already little better than lumber:—And the rich melodies of Keats and Shelley,—and the fantastical emphasis of Wordsworth,—and the plebeian pathos of Crabbe, are melting fast from the fields of our vision. The novels of Scott have put out his poetry. Even the splendid strains of Moore are fading into distance and dimness, except where they have been married to immortal music; and the blazing star of Byron himself is receding from its place of pride. . . . The two who have the longest withstood this rapid withering of the laurel, and with the least marks of decay on their branches, are Rogers and Campbell; neither of them, it may be remarked, voluminous writers, and both distinguished rather for the fine taste and consummate elegance of their writings, than for the fiery passion, and disdainful vehemence, which seemed for a time to be so much more in favour with the public. . . . If taste and elegance, however, be titles to enduring fame, we might venture securely to promise that rich boon to the author before us.

The author before Jeffrey as he wrote was Felicia Hemans, a poet widely admired on both sides of the Atlantic but by the end of the century forgotten, except for a few anthology favorites. Meanwhile, with nearly three decades of reviewing experience, Jeffrey was unable to predict the durable fame of some of the writers who by the century's end would be deemed quintessential "romantics": Byron, Wordsworth, Keats, and Shelley. And he misguessed about Rogers and Campbell, though it is clear he would have attributed their demise to degraded public taste rather than intrinsic faults. What Jeffrey helps us see is that naming a literary canon is a matter of selection from a wide field, motivated by personal values. Other than Hemans, for instance, he thinks of English literary tradition as defined by men—even though Jane Austen and Mary Shelley proved to have as much durability as anyone in his census (Austen's novels and Shelley's *Frankenstein* have never been out of print). He also prefers literature of "fine taste" and "elegance" to the fiery passion and disdainful vehemence that other readers would admire in Byron and Shelley.

It was the conservative Jeffrey who first attempted to assess the "new poets," in the inaugural issue of the *Edinburgh Review* (1802). Here he castigates Southey as a member of a heretical "sect of poets, that has established itself in this country within these ten or twelve years, and is looked upon, we believe, as one of its chief champions and apostles." His polemical intent was to brand with all the excesses of the French Revolution a group he called "the Lakers" (from their residence in the Lake District): Southey, Wordsworth, and Coleridge. Well before Hazlitt, Jeffrey was blaming "the revolution in our literature" on "the agitations of the French revolution, and the discussion as well as the hopes and terrors to which it gave occasion." "A splenetic and idle discontent with the existing institutions of society, seems to be at the bottom of all their serious and peculiar sentiments"; "the ambition of Mr. Southey and some of his associates" is not "of that regulated and manageable sort which usually grows up in old established commonwealths," but "of a more undisciplined and revolutionary character which looks, we think with a jealous and contemptuous eye on the old aristocracy of the literary world."

By the Regency, the revolutionary "Lake School" was joined by the upstart "Cockney School," a term of insult fixed on Londoners Hazlitt, Hunt, and Keats, by the Scotsman John Gibson Lockhart, writing in *Blackwood's* in 1817, partly in response to Hunt's celebration of a vigorous school of "Young Poets" in essays he was writing for *The Examiner*. Hunt was a radical; Lockhart despised his politics. In 1821 ex-Laker and now Poet Laureate Southey identified still a third school. His youthful radicalism well behind him, he denounced the men "of diseased hearts and depraved imaginations" who formed "the Satanic School, . . . characterized by a Satanic spirit of pride and audacious impiety." Provoked by the allusion to himself and Percy Shelley, Byron responded with satiric attacks against both Southey personally and the establishment politics he had come to espouse. All these classifications were politically motivated—in most cases sneers at innovators and nonconformists or class-inflected put-downs. The designation of a "Romantic School" was not a product of the age itself, but was applied much later in the century—by literary historians with their own Victorian motivations and nostalgia.

With no sense of a monolithic movement that could be called "Romanticism," the polemical terms of the age itself mark a field animated by differences of location, class, gender, politics, and audience. The boundaries that appear rigid at one moment re-form when the perspective shifts: to Lockhart, Lakers (whom he respected) and Cockneys were distinct; to Byron, a champion of Pope, Keats was both "a tadpole of the Lakes" and a Cockney brat who "abused Pope and Swift." And except for Hunt and Scott, most of these men bonded across class and political lines in their contempt of "Blue Stockings" (intellectual women) and female writers, even as these women were defining themselves for and against the stigmatized precedent of Wollstonecraft. Liberals, conservatives, and radicals; Byron and Shelley, self-exiled aristocrats in Italy; Wordsworth, Coleridge, and Southey praising domesticity in the Lakes; Keats, Hazlitt, and Hunt, an apprentice surgeon and working journalists, all precariously middle-class Londoners; women novelists, poets, and essayists, Blue Stockings and Wollstonecraftians, moralizers and rebels: the array is diverse and engaged in a contest for attention too keen to call debate or conversation.

The difficulty of specifying the term "Romantic" arises in part because it hovers between chronological and conceptual references. Its literature emerges in the social and literary ferment of the 1780s, a benchmark being the publication of Blake's *Songs of Innocence* in the climactic year of 1789. The period's close is usually seen in the 1830s—the decade in which George IV died, as did several writers who defined the age: Scott, Lamb, Coleridge, Hemans. By this time, too, Keats, Byron, and Percy Shelley, Austen, and most of the first generation were dead. In the same decade, Alfred Lord Tennyson's poetic career began, and Victoria was crowned Queen. Yet the temporal boundaries are fluid: "Romantic" Keats and "Victorian" Thomas Carlyle were born the same year, 1795, and Wordsworth's major poem, *The Prelude*, though he worked on it for a half century beginning in 1797 or so, was not published until the year of his death, 1850, the same year that Tennyson's quintessentially Victorian *In Memoriam* appeared. Much of Keats's poetry appeared for the first time after 1848, reviving interest in him among a new generation of readers.

Yet even with these ambiguous boundaries, the "Romantic" movement, from its first description in the nineteenth century until the mid-1980s, was characterized by men's writing. In the age itself, the powers of literary production—publishers, booksellers, reviews, and the press—were men's domains and not always open to female authors, and the culture as a whole was not receptive to female authority. Wollstonecraft's *Rights of Woman* (1792) was one of the first analyses to define "women" as an oppressed class that cut across national distinctions and historical differences—oppressed by lack of education, by lack of legal rights and access to gainful employment, as well as by a "prevailing opinion" about their character: that women were made to feel and be felt, rather than to think; their duty was to bear children and be domestic drudges, to obey their fathers and their husbands without complaint.

Women writers faced more than a few challenges. One was the pervasive cultural attitude that a woman who presumed to authority, published her views, and even aspired to make a living as an author was grossly immodest, decidedly "unfeminine," and probably a truant from her domestic calling. Many women published anonymously, under male pseudonyms, with the proper title "Mrs." or, as in Austen's case, under an anonymous and socially modest signature, "by a Lady" (not one of Austen's novels bore her name). They also maintained propriety by hewing to subjects and genres deemed "feminine"—not political polemic, epic poetry, science or philosophy but children's books, conduct literature, travel writing (if it was clear they had proper escorts), household hints, cookbooks, novels of manners, and poems of sentiment and home, of patriotism and religious piety. Women who transgressed provoked harsh discipline. When Barbauld ventured an anti-imperialist poem, *Eighteen Hundred and Eleven*, the Tory *Quarterly Review* exercised reproof precisely in terms of the gender-genre transgression:

Mrs. Barbauld turned satirist! . . . We had hoped, indeed, that the empire might have been saved without the intervention of a lady-author. . . . Her former works have been of some utility; her "Lessons for Children," her "Hymns in Prose," her "Selections from the Spectator," . . . but we must take the liberty of warning her to desist from satire . . . writing any more pamphlets in verse. (June 1812)

Barbauld took this advice to heart, and desisted from satire. About fifteen years earlier, Anglican arbiter Richard Polwhele viciously listed a whole set of contemporary female writers in his poem *The Unsex'd Females*, with virulent animosity to Wollstonecraft. They are "unsex'd" by their public stance, parading what "ne'er our fathers saw."

The Tory *British Critic*, on the occasion of praising Hemans's excellence "in painting the strength and the weaknesses of her own lovely sex" and the "womanly nature throughout all her thoughts and her aspirations," kept up the surveillance, taking the opportunity to despise anything that advertised the intellectual and critical authority of women. It opened its review of Hemans (1823) not with a discussion of the work at hand but with an assault on the world that was changing before its eyes, against which it invokes every counterauthority, from divine creation, to modern science, to Shakespeare, to the language of ridicule and disgust:

> We heartily abjure Blue Stockings. We make no compromise with any variation of the colour, from sky-blue to Prussian blue, blue stockings are an outrage upon the eternal fitness of things. It is a principle with us to regard an Academicienne of this Society, with the same charity that a cat regards a vagabond mouse. We are inexorable to special justifications. We would fain make a fire in Charing-Cross, of all the bas bleus in the kingdom, and albums, and commonplace books, as accessaries [sic] before or after the fact, should perish in the conflagration.
>
> Our forefathers never heard of such a thing as a Blue Stocking, except upon their sons' legs; the writers of Natural History make no mention of the name. . . . Shakspeare, who painted all sorts and degrees of persons and things, who compounded or created thousands, which, perhaps, never existed, except in his own prolific mind, even he, in the wildest excursion of his fancy never dreamed of such an extraordinary combination as a Blue Stocking! No!

The extraordinary combination, however, was there to stay, and even with all these constraints, women writers thrived. More, Barbauld, Robinson, Charlotte Smith, and Maria Edgeworth stand out among those who earned both reputation and a living through poetry, novels, and tracts on education and politics, freely crossing the borders between public and private spheres, male and female realms.

POPULAR PROSE

When the *Edinburgh Review* was founded in 1802 as an organ of liberal political opinion, it raised the status of periodical writing. "To be an Edinburgh Reviewer," opined Hazlitt, who freelanced in the journal, "is, I suspect, the highest rank in modern literary society." By the end of the decade, the rival Tory *Quarterly Review* arrived on the scene. The quarterlies favored an authoritative, anonymous voice, while new monthly magazines revived the lighter manner of the eighteenth-century "familiar essay." *Blackwood's* (founded 1817) printed raffish conversations set in a nearby tavern, and the *London* (founded 1820) hosted Lamb's essays and De Quincey's *Confessions of an English Opium Eater*. Whether the topic was imaginative literature, social observation, science, or political commentary, the personality of the essayist and the literary performance—by turns meditative, autobiographical, analytical, whimsical, terse and expansive—were what commanded attention. "All the great geniuses of the day are Periodical," declared John Wilson, writing in *Blackwood's* in 1829—a self-interested judgment, but true insofar as it acknowledges the new importance of the periodical essay. Meanwhile, beneath the realm of the respectable journals, though not out of their anxious sight, thrived Cobbett, who published a weekly newspaper, the *Political Register* (founded 1802), its price low enough to evade the stamp tax (thus becoming known as "The Two-Penny Trash"). It reached a circulation of forty or fifty thousand and helped make him the most widely read writer of his era, and surely the most prolific, with an output estimated at more than twenty million words.

If later decades tended to represent "Romanticism" largely as an age of poetry, in the age itself, poetry, traditionally the genre of prestige, had to compete with prose, and not just the engaging new essay form, but also, and quite emphatically, the once-disreputable novel. The novel had begun to command new attention after the success of Godwin's political romance from the 1790s, *Caleb Williams*, and new respect after the critical and popular success of Scott's *Waverley* (1814). With dozens of works of narrative fiction over the next two decades, Scott perfected the genre of historical "romance"—"the interest of which turns upon marvelous and uncommon incidents," he said in a review of Austen. As the occasion indicates, the novel was also a genre in which women achieved considerable success—perhaps why, in addition to its status as a "low" form, Sir Walter kept his authorship of the *Waverley* novels anonymous. In *Waverley*, Scott spoofed the gothic devices that animated Ann Radcliffe's sensational "gothic" novels. But Radcliffe was remarkably popular; the genre that she perfected in the 1790s caught everyone's attention, including publishers'. She received the unheard of sum of £500 for *The Mysteries of Udolpho* (1794), topped by £600 for *The Italian* (1797), and achieved unprecedented fame for a novelist of any sex. Edgeworth's regional-historical novels, their career launched in 1800 with *Castle Rackrent* and extending over a quarter century, also caught the attention of Scott, who dubbed her "the great Maria" both out of admiration for a genre that shaped his own ventures and in recognition of her considerable financial success. Hannah More's only novel, *Coelebs in Search of a Wife* (1808), ran through twelve editions in its first year, and before her death in 1833 had sold thirty thousand copies in America alone. Shelley produced a durable masterpiece with *Frankenstein* (1818 and 1831), while Austen's novels caught public interest with their sharp social observation and stories of heroines coming of age in a world of finely calibrated social codes and financial pressures. With Scott, she would be deemed one of the major figures in the genre.

Throughout the years, social turmoil and technological change fostered a proliferation of writing. In the Preface to *Lyrical Ballads* (1800) Wordsworth deplored the "multitude of causes unknown to former times . . . now acting with a combined force to blunt the discriminating powers of the mind," and diagnosed the most virulent as "the great national events which are daily taking place, and the increasing accumulation of men in cities, where the uniformity of their occupations produces a craving for extraordinary incident which the rapid communication of intelligence hourly gratifies." Newspapers, daily and Sunday, multiplied to meet this craving. In

1814 the London *Times* converted to a steam press, and doubled circulation. Newspaper sales reached thirty million, with yet more readers in the coffee-houses and subscription reading-rooms that took papers that taxes rendered too expensive for individual purchase. Parliamentary commissions and boards of review collected information and compiled statistics and summaries as never before on every aspect of the nation's economy and policies, and the press disseminated them. Cobbett ceaselessly lambasted the fundholders who profited from the debts incurred by the war, even as those who had fought suffered from the postwar depression; John Wade investigated sinecures, aristocratic incomes, pluralism in the Church, corruption in Parliament, and the expenditures of the civil list, and published his findings in the sensational *Black Book* (1820), available in sixpenny installments that sold ten thousand copies each.

The explosion of readers at once liberated authors from patronage and exposed them to the turbulent and precarious world of the literary marketplace. In 1812 Jeffrey reckoned that among "the higher classes" there were twenty thousand readers, but at least "two hundred thousand who read for amusement and instruction, among the middling classes of society," defining "middling" as those "who do not aim at distinction or notoriety beyond the circle of their equals in fortune or station." Faced with an audience fissured along class lines, he thought that it was "easy to see" which group an author should please. But others looked to the growing number of literate poor who lacked traditional education, vast numbers whose allegiance was fought over by radicals like Cobbett and Paine and conservatives such as More, whose *Cheap Repository Tracts* (1795–1799) were circulated by the millions.

Such journalism diffused and intensified troubled perceptions of the functioning of society and one's place in it. "The beginning of Inquiry is Disease," intoned Carlyle; he inveighed against "the diseased self-conscious state of Literature" but this self-consciousness was its character. Uncertain of the audience(s) by whom they would be read, writers resorted to an ironic wavering that sought to forestall being pinned down to a position and dismissed, or devised various strategies to seduce assent: the development of the authorial "I" whom readers might come to trust as an authentic percipient, personae that insiders would be able to penetrate, and codings that would deepen a sense of solidarity among a constituency. Wordsworth had made his name with the highly personal, but culturally resonant, lyric outpouring of "Lines, written a few miles above Tintern Abbey, On Revisiting the Banks of the Wye during a Tour, July 13, 1798" (*Lyrical Ballads*, 1798); he celebrated his return from France in 1802 with a sonnet "Composed in the Valley, near Dover, On the Day of Landing," rejoicing in familiar sights of rivers and boys at play: "All, all are English." In a neighboring sonnet in the same collection, though, he complained, "The world is too much with us," running our lives with "getting and spending" and alienating our hearts from "Nature."

Wordsworth remained ambivalent about developing a voice and a literature that would gain popular reception, and continued to resent those, such as Scott, who were more successful in these terms. But the new world and the new literatures were finding remarkable sympathy in many quarters. Scott's first romance, *The Lay of the Last Minstrel* (1805), sold well over 2,000 copies within a year of publication, and nearly 10,000 more by 1807. His publisher offered him 1,000 guineas, sight unseen, for his next poetic romance, *Marmion* (1808). Scott said the sum "made men's hair stand on end," but the bargain was a good one on both sides: by 1811 it had sold 28,000 copies. These figures were topped by Byron, who, Scott good-naturedly conceded, drove him from the field of poetry, while his own *Waverley* novels proved still more popular. Over his lifetime, Scott made about £80,000 from his writing. That Byron's *Corsair* (1814) could sell 10,000 copies on the day of publication testifies to the mechanisms of production, publicity, and sales the book trade commanded. Byron was not embarrassed to seek £2600 for *Childe Harold IV* (1818). It must have galled Wordsworth that his publisher gave Thomas Moore 3,000 guineas for *Lalla Rookh*, more than had ever been offered for a single poem. Yet along with these stunning successes, other careers were more modestly compensated, and poets, at least, did not often enjoy the degree of prosperity that the novelists did.

The volatility of the market and of public taste points to salient qualities of the period: a heightened awareness of differences and boundaries, and of the energies generated along their unstable edges, and even more, a heightened awareness of time and history, public and cultural as well as personal. "Romanticism" denotes less a unified concept, or even a congeries of ideas, than an era and a literature of clashing systems, each plausibly claiming allegiance, in a world of rapid change.

Anna Letitia Barbauld
1743–1825

Anna Barbauld's long career exemplifies that of the professional woman of letters: a respected poet (and not only on conventionally feminine themes), a writer on radical causes throughout the 1790s, an early welcomer of Coleridge (who presented her with a prepublication copy of *Lyrical Ballads*), and a friend of Priestley, Hannah More, and Joanna Baillie. The daughter of John Aikin, master of Warrington Academy, a celebrated institution of English Dissenting culture where she lived between the ages of fifteen and thirty, Anna Laetitia Aikin is said to have learned to read English by age three, Italian and French not long after, and Greek and Latin while still a child. Her first volume, *Poems* (1773), went through five editions in four years; in the same year, she published *Miscellaneous Pieces in Prose* with her brother John, later editor of the *Monthly Magazine*, an influential radical journal. In 1774 she married Rochemont Barbauld, a Dissenting clergyman, with whom she ran a school. Samuel Johnson derided the activity as the waste of a fine education, but it led to her often reprinted *Lessons for Children* (1778) and *Hymns in Prose for Children* (1781). When her husband's increasing mental instability forced them to close their school, she undertook ambitious editorial projects. In 1794 she produced an edition of Akenside, one of Collins in 1797, and in 1804 a six-volume *Correspondence of Samuel Richardson*, followed by a fifty-volume set of *The British Novelists* (1810), with biographical introductions and a sophisticated preface arguing for the instructive value of a genre depreciated as mere entertainment, as well as a popular anthology for young women, *The Female Speaker* (1811). Like Wollstonecraft, she believed young women should be educated to become wives and mothers. The stark vision of *Eighteen Hundred and Eleven* marks the cultural pessimism that, after decades of war, had succeeded the Enlightenment optimism of her youth; though she continued writing until the 1820s, the harsh review its stern anti-imperialism provoked from John Wilson Croker in the conservative *Quarterly Review* nearly brought her career of publication to an end. His alarm over a woman daring to write about politics and his dismissal, as feminine illogic, of the bold transitions and startling prospects of the poem witness the force of Barbauld's achievement.

The Mouse's Petition to Dr. Priestley[1]

O hear a pensive prisoner's prayer,
    For liberty that sighs;
And never let thine heart be shut
    Against the wretch's cries!

5   For here forlorn and sad I sit,
    Within the wiry grate;
And tremble at the approaching morn,
    Which brings impending fate.

If e'er thy breast with freedom glowed,
10   And spurned a tyrant's chain,
Let not thy strong oppressive force
    A free-born mouse detain!

O do not stain with guiltless blood
    Thy hospitable hearth;
15   Nor triumph that thy wiles betrayed
    A prize so little worth.

The scattered gleanings of a feast
    My frugal meals supply;
But if thine unrelenting heart
20   That slender boon deny,—

The cheerful light, the vital air,
    Are blessings widely given;
Let nature's commoners enjoy
    The common gifts of heaven.

25   The well-taught philosophic mind
    To all compassion gives:
Casts round the world an equal eye,
    And feels for all that lives.

If mind,—as ancient sages taught,—
30   A never-dying flame,
Still shifts through matter's varying forms,
    In every form the same;

Beware, lest in the worm you crush
    A brother's soul you find;
35   And tremble lest thy luckless hand
    Dislodge a kindred mind.

---

1. The title in early editions is *The Mouse's Petition, Found in the trap where he had been confined all night*, accompanied by a motto from Virgil's *Aeneid* (6.853): "Parcere subjectis & debellare superbos" [To spare the conquered, and subdue the proud]. Joseph Priestley (1733–1804), political radical and eminent chemist who discovered oxygen, had been testing the properties of gases on captured household mice. Tradition has it that Barbauld's petition succeeded, and this mouse was released.

Or, if this transient gleam of day
　　Be *all* of life we share,
Let pity plead within thy breast
40　　That little *all* to spare.

So may thy hospitable board
　　With wealth and peace be crowned;
And every charm of heartfelt ease
　　Beneath thy roof be found.

45　So when destruction lurks unseen,
　　Which men, like mice, may share,
May some kind angel clear thy path,
　　And break the hidden snare.

1771   1773

On a Lady's Writing

Her even lines her steady temper show,
Neat as her dress, and polished as her brow;
Strong as her judgment, easy as her air;
Correct though free, and regular though fair:
And the same graces o'er her pen preside,
That form her manners and her footsteps guide.

1773

Inscription for an Ice-House[1]

Stranger, approach! within this iron door
Thrice locked and bolted, this rude arch beneath
That vaults with ponderous stone the cell; confined
By man, the great magician, who controuls
5　Fire, earth and air, and genii of the storm,
And bends the most remote and opposite things
To do him service and perform his will,—
A giant sits; stern Winter; here he piles,
While summer glows around, and southern gales
10　Dissolve the fainting world, his treasured snows°   *sherberts*
Within the rugged cave.—Stranger, approach!
He will not cramp thy limbs with sudden age,
Nor wither with his touch the coyest flower
That decks thy scented hair. Indignant here,
15　Like fettered Sampson[2] when his might was spent
In puny feats to glad the festive halls
Of Gaza's wealthy sons; or he who sat
Midst laughing girls submiss, and patient twirled

1. The ice-house, where blocks of ice were kept cold in the warmer months, was the commonest form of refrigeration before the twentieth century.
2. Judges 16 relates the imprisonment of the blinded Samson in Gaza, forced to make "sport" for the Philistines; the story forms the subject of Milton's tragedy, *Samson Agonistes* (1671).

The slender spindle in his sinewy grasp;[3]
20   The rugged power, fair Pleasure's minister,
Exerts his art to deck the genial board;
Congeals the melting peach, the nectarine smooth,
Burnished and glowing from the sunny wall:
Darts sudden frost into the crimson veins
25   Of the moist berry; moulds the sugared hail:
Cools with his icy breath our flowing cups;
Or gives to the fresh dairy's nectared bowls
A quicker zest. Sullen he plies his task,
And on his shaking fingers counts the weeks
30   Of lingering Summer, mindful of his hour
To rush in whirlwinds forth, and rule the year.

c. 1793   1825

To a Little Invisible Being
Who Is Expected Soon to Become Visible

Germ of new life, whose powers expanding slow
For many a moon their full perfection wait,—
Haste, precious pledge of happy love, to go
Auspicious borne through life's mysterious gate.

5   What powers lie folded in thy curious frame,—
Senses from objects locked, and mind from thought!
How little canst thou guess thy lofty claim
To grasp at all the worlds the Almighty wrought!

And see, the genial season's warmth to share,
10   Fresh younglings shoot, and opening roses glow!
Swarms of new life exulting fill the air,—
Haste, infant bud of being, haste to blow!°   *bloom*

For thee the nurse prepares her lulling songs,
The eager matrons count the lingering day;
15   But far the most thy anxious parent longs
On thy soft cheek a mother's kiss to lay.

She only asks to lay her burden down,
That her glad arms that burden may resume;
And nature's sharpest pangs her wishes crown,
20   That free thee living from thy living tomb.

She longs to fold to her maternal breast
Part of herself, yet to herself unknown;
To see and to salute the stranger guest,
Fed with her life through many a tedious moon.

---

3. In his term as slave to Queen Omphale, Hercules performed women's tasks.

25   Come, reap thy rich inheritance of love!
    Bask in the fondness of a Mother's eye!
    Nor wit nor eloquence her heart shall move
    Like the first accents of thy feeble cry.

    Haste, little captive, burst thy prison doors!
30   Launch on the living world, and spring to light!
    Nature for thee displays her various stores,
    Opens her thousand inlets of delight.

    If charmed verse of muttered prayers had power,
    With favouring spells to speed thee on thy way,
35   Anxious I'd bid my beads° each passing hour,   *tell my rosary*
    Till thy wished smile thy mother's pangs o'erpay.

c. 1795   1825

Eighteen Hundred and Eleven[1]

    Still the loud death-drum, thundering from afar,
    O'er the vext nations pours the storm of war:
    To the stern call still Britain bends her ear,
    Feeds the fierce strife, the alternate hope and fear;
5   Bravely, though vainly, dares to strive with Fate,
    And seeks by turns to prop each sinking state.
    Colossal power with overwhelming force
    Bears down each foot of Freedom in its course;
    Prostrate she lies beneath the despot's° sway,   *Napoleon's*
10   While the hushed nations curse him—and obey.

    Bounteous in vain, with frantic man at strife,
    Glad Nature pours the means—the joys of life;
    In vain with orange-blossoms scents the gale,
    The hills with olives clothes, with corn the vale;
15   Man calls to Famine, nor invokes in vain,
    Disease and Rapine follow in her train;
    The tramp of marching hosts disturbs the plough,
    The sword, not sickle, reaps the harvest now,
    And where the soldier gleans the scant supply,
20   The helpless peasant but retires to die;
    No laws his hut from licensed outrage shield,
    And war's least horror is the ensanguined field.

    Fruitful in vain, the matron counts with pride
    The blooming youths that grace her honored side;
25   No son returns to press her widowed hand,
    Her fallen blossoms strew a foreign strand.

---

1. This dark satire was published as a quarto pamphlet. Its somber tone reflects the times: Britain had been at war with France almost continuously since 1793. At home, the economy had sunk, and distress was widespread; Napoleon controlled the Continent and blockaded British trade; George III had lapsed into madness; conditions with America were strained and verging on war, which broke out the following year.

Color Plate 1   John Martin, *The Bard*, 1817. "Ruin seize thee, ruthless King!" According to the legend retold in Thomas Gray's 1757 ode *The Bard*, in the thirteenth century Edward I attempted to stamp out Welsh resistance to English power by ordering the court poets, bards, put to death. John Martin's large canvas captures the sublime moment at which the last bard denounced the invading monarch before leaping into the River Conway below. *(Tyne and Wear Museums.)*

Color Plate 2 Thomas Gainsborough (1727–1788), *Mrs. Mary Robinson ("Perdita")*. Gainsborough was one of the most fashionable portraitists of his day, surpassed only by his rival Sir Joshua Reynolds. His elegant depiction of the actress and poet Mary Robinson is witness to her social triumph. The locket in Robinson's hand reveals a portrait of the Prince of Wales, whose infatuation with her was the cause of her first celebrity. *(By kind permission of the trustees of the Wallace Collection.)*

Color Plate 3   Thomas Phillips (1770–1845), *George Gordon Byron, 6th Baron Byron,* (c. 1835,
replicated by Thomas Phillips from an 1813 original). Byron himself was the premier model for the
"Byronic hero." He wrote to his mother in 1809, full of admiration for Albanian dress: "the most
magnificent in the world, consisting of a long white kilt, old worked cloak, crimson velvet gold
laced jacket & waistcoat, silver mounted pistols & daggars." He purchased some outfits for himself:
"the only expensive articles in this country they cost 50 guineas each & have so much gold they
would cost in England two hundred." *(By courtesy of The National Portrait Gallery, London.)*

Color Plate 4 *Portrait of Olaudah Equiano,* late-18th century. This handsome portrait vividly attests Equiano's rise from kidnapped slave to British respectability. *(Royal Albert Memorial Museum, Exeter, Devon, UK/Bridgeman Art Library.)*

Color Plate 5 Joseph Mallord William Turner (British 1775–1851), *Slave Ship (Slavers Throwing Overboard the Dead and Dying, Typhoon Coming On)*, 1840. Turner depicts a notorious incident that galvanized the abolition movement. In 1781 the captain of the slave ship *Zong* ordered 133 weak and diseased slaves ejected into shark-infested waters, planning to collect on a policy that held the insurer liable for cargo jettisoned in order to salvage the remainder. In 1783 Olaudah Equiano brought the incident to the attention of the abolition movement; the resulting trial (which debated not the captain's criminal liability but the insurer's financial liability), presided over by Lord Mansfield, sided with the captain. (*Oil on canvas, 90.8 x 122.6 cm [35 3/4 x 48 1/4 in.]. Henry Lillie Pierce Fund. Courtesy, Museum of Fine Arts, Boston.*)

Color Plates 6 and 7 William Blake, two versions of the second plate of *The Little Black Boy*, from *Songs of Innocence*. As can be seen here, Blake sometimes tints the black boy's skin as light as the English boy's (near left); in others, he colors them differently (far left). While the heavenly scene portrays both boys sheltered by the tree and welcomed by Christ, it also puts the black boy outside the inner circle formed by the curve of Christ's body and the praying English boy. The black boy is not part of this configuration of prayer, but rather a witness to it, stroking the hair of the English boy, who has no regard for him. (*Fitzwilliam Museum, University of Cambridge, UK/Bridgeman Art Library.*)

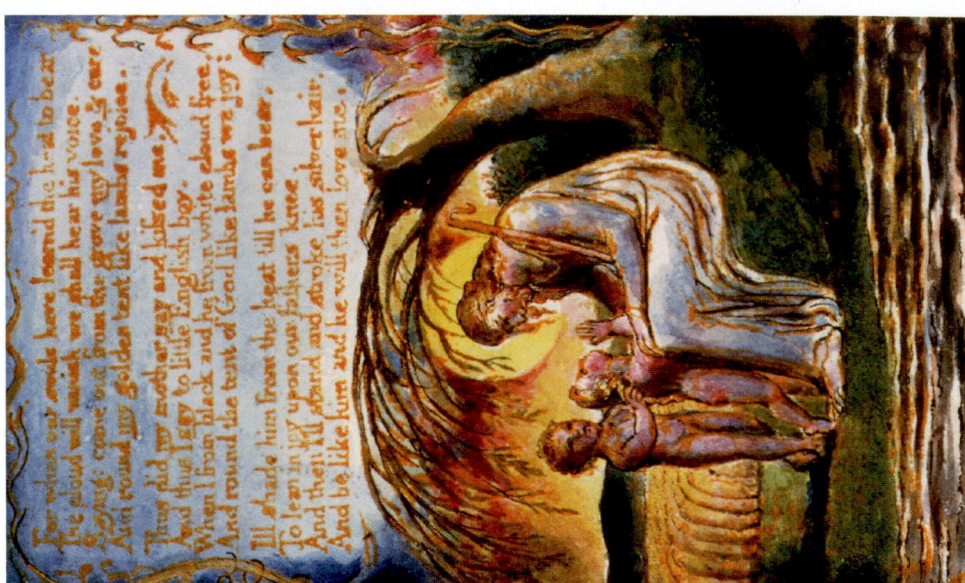

Color Plate 8 (far left) William Blake, *The Tyger,* from *Songs of Experience.* In some copies, Blake colors the tyger in lurid tones; in others, the tyger is colored in pastels. Strangely, the unmenacing, sideways image of the tyger not only fails to display the "fearful symmetry" that alarms the poem's speaker, but also seems no cause for the horrified tone of address. *(Fitzwilliam Museum, University of Cambridge, UK/Bridgeman Art Library.)*

Color Plate 9 (near left) William Blake, *The Sick Rose,* from *Songs of Experience.* The sickness of the rosebush is conveyed not only by its trailing on the ground but also by several particulars: the encircling thorns; the quite visible worm wrapped around the naked body emerging (in joy? in pain?) from the rose; the caterpillars devouring the leaves; a second naked body constricted by a snakelike worm. *(Fitzwilliam Museum, University of Cambridge, UK/Bridgeman Art Library.)*

Color Plate 10 Joseph Wright, *An Iron Forge Viewed from Without*, 1773. Derby was a center of the Industrial Revolution, and Wright (1734–1797), a native, gained fame for his treatment of scientific and industrial subjects. He was particularly renowned for his handling of artificial light, and the dramatic contrast of fire and dark in this painting illustrates the romantic effects that could be drawn from technology. The contrast between the lurid forge and the picturesque background also suggests the contemporary spread of manufacture into peaceful landscapes. *(Hermitage, St. Petersburg, Russia/Bridgeman Art Library.)*

—Fruitful in vain, she boasts her virgin race,
Whom cultured arts adorn and gentlest grace;
Defrauded of its homage, Beauty mourns
30   And the rose withers on its virgin thorns.
Frequent, some stream obscure, some uncouth name,
By deeds of blood is lifted into fame;
Oft o'er the daily page some soft one bends
To learn the fate of husband, brothers, friends,
35   Or the spread map with anxious eye explores,
Its dotted boundaries and pencilled shores,
Asks where the spot that wrecked her bliss is found,
And learns its name but to detest the sound.

And think'st thou, Britain, still to sit at ease,
40   An island queen amidst thy subject seas,
While the vext billows, in their distant roar,
But soothe thy slumbers, and but kiss thy shore?
To sport in wars, while danger keeps aloof,
Thy grassy turf unbruised by hostile hoof?
45   So sing thy flatterers;—but, Britain, know,
Thou who hast shared the guilt must share the woe.
Nor distant is the hour; low murmurs spread,
And whispered fears, creating what they dread;
Ruin, as with an earthquake shock, is here,
50   There, the heart-witherings of unuttered fear,
And that sad death, whence most affection bleeds,
Which sickness, only of the soul, precedes.
Thy baseless wealth dissolves in air away,
Like mists that melt before the morning ray:[2]
55   No more on crowded mart or busy street
Friends, meeting friends, with cheerful hurry greet;
Sad, on the ground thy princely merchants bend
Their altered looks, and evil days portend,
And fold their arms, and watch with anxious breast
60   The tempest blackening in the distant West.°   the United States

Yes, thou must droop; thy Midas dream is o'er;
The golden tide of Commerce leaves thy shore,
Leaves thee to prove the alternate ills that haunt
Enfeebling Luxury and ghastly Want;
65   Leaves thee, perhaps, to visit distant lands,
And deal the gifts of Heaven with equal hands.
Yet, O my Country, name beloved, revered,
By every tie that binds the soul endeared,
Whose image to my infant senses came
70   Mixt with Religion's light and Freedom's holy flame!
If prayers may not avert, if 't is thy fate

2. Echoing Shakespeare's Prospero, on the vanishing of the illusions he has wrought; *The Tempest* 4.1.150–56.

To rank amongst the names that once were great,
Not like the dim, cold Crescent[3] shalt thou fade,
Thy debt to Science and the Muse unpaid;
75   Thine are the laws surrounding states revere,
Thine the full harvest of the mental year,
Thine the bright stars in Glory's sky that shine,
And arts that make it life to live are thine.
If westward streams the light that leaves thy shores,
80   Still from thy lamp the streaming radiance pours.
Wide spreads thy race from Ganges° to the pole,   *river in India*
O'er half the Western world thy accents roll:
Nations beyond the Apalachian hills[4]
Thy hand has planted and thy spirit fills:
85   Soon as their gradual progress shall impart
The finer sense of morals and of art,
Thy stores of knowledge the new states shall know,
And think thy thoughts, and with thy fancy glow;
Thy Lockes, thy Paleys,[5] shall instruct their youth,
90   Thy leading star direct their search for truth;
Beneath the spreading platane's° tent-like shade,   *Asian plane-tree*
Or by Missouri's rushing waters laid,
"Old Father Thames" shall be the poet's theme,
Of Hagley's woods[6] the enamored virgin dream,
95   And Milton's tones the raptured ear enthrall,
Mixt with the roaring of Niagara's fall;
In Thomson's glass the ingenuous youth shall learn
A fairer face of Nature to discern;
Nor of the bards that swept the British lyre
100   Shall fade one laurel, or one note expire.
Then, loved Joanna,[7] to admiring eyes
Thy storied groups in scenic pomp shall rise;
Their high-souled strains and Shakespeare's noble rage
Shall with alternate passion shake the stage.
105   Some youthful Basil from thy moral lay
With stricter hand his fond desires shall sway;
Some Ethwald, as the fleeting shadows pass,
Start at his likeness in the mystic glass;
The tragic Muse resume her just control,
110   With pity and with terror purge the soul,
While wide o'er transatlantic realms thy name
Shall live in light and gather all its fame.

3. Symbol of the Muslim empire.
4. The United States had begun to expand westward with
the Louisiana Purchase of 1803.
5. John Locke, author of *An Essay Concerning Human
Understanding* (1690) and *Two Treatises on Civil Government* (1690); William Paley, author of *The Principles
of Moral and Political Philosophy* (1785), *Evidences of*

Christianity (1794), and *Natural Theology* (1802).
6. The estate of Lord Lyttelton, celebrated in *The Seasons*
(1726–1730), a poem by James Thomson ("Thomson's
glass," i.e., mirror, line 97).
7. Joanna Baillie, whose *Plays on the Passions* include
Count Basil (1798) and *Ethwald* (1802).

Where wanders Fancy down the lapse of years,
Shedding o'er imaged woes untimely tears?
115   Fond, moody power! as hopes—as fears prevail,
She longs, or dreads, to lift the awful veil,
On visions of delight now loves to dwell,
Now hears the shriek of woe or Freedom's knell:
Perhaps, she says, long ages past away,
120   And set in western wave our closing day,
Night, Gothic night, again may shade the plains
Where Power is seated, and where Science reigns;
England, the seat of arts, be only known
By the gray ruin and the mouldering stone;
125   That Time may tear the garland from her brow,
And Europe sit in dust, as Asia now.

Yet then the ingenuous youth whom Fancy fires
With pictured glories of illustrious sires,
With duteous zeal their pilgrimage shall take
130   From the Blue Mountains,° or Ontario's lake,   *in Pennsylvania*
With fond, adoring steps to press the sod
By statesmen, sages, poets, heroes, trod;
On Isis'° banks to draw inspiring air,   *river in Oxford*
From Runnymede[8] to send the patriot's prayer;
135   In pensive thought, where Cam's° slow waters wind,   *Cambridge river*
To meet those shades that ruled the realms of mind;
In silent halls to sculptured marbles bow,
And hang fresh wreaths round Newton's awful brow.[9]
Oft shall they seek some peasant's homely shed,
140   Who toils, unconscious of the mighty dead,
To ask where Avon's winding waters[1] stray,
And thence a knot of wild flowers bear away;
Anxious inquire where Clarkson,[2] friend of man,
Or all-accomplished Jones[3] his race began;
145   If of the modest mansion aught remains
Where Heaven and Nature prompted Cowper's strains;[4]
Where Roscoe, to whose patriot breast belong
The Roman virtue and the Tuscan song,
Led Ceres to the black and barren moor
150   Where Ceres never gained a wreath before:[5]
With curious search their pilgrim steps shall rove
By many a ruined tower and proud alcove,
Shall listen for those strains that soothed of yore

8. The meadow on the banks of the Thames where King John signed the Magna Carta in 1215.
9. Sir Isaac Newton (1642–1727), philosopher, physicist, and mathematician, was professor at Cambridge University.
1. In Stratford, home of Shakespeare.
2. Abolitionist Thomas Clarkson.
3. Sir William Jones (1746–1794), distinguished scholar of Indian language and law.
4. The poet William Cowper, here cited as author of *Olney Hymns* (1779).
5. William Roscoe (1753–1831), noted agricultural improver, a scholar, and opponent of the war. The claim that he led Ceres, Roman goddess of agriculture, where she had never succeeded before, alludes to his achievement of growing high-quality crops on moorland.

Thy rock, stern Skiddaw, and thy fall, Lodore;[6]
155   Feast with Dun Edin's° classic brow their sight,   *Edinburgh's*
And "visit Melross by the pale moonlight."[7]

But who their mingled feelings shall pursue
When London's faded glories rise to view?
The mighty city, which by every road,
160   In floods of people poured itself abroad
Ungirt by walls, irregularly great,
No jealous drawbridge, and no closing gate;
Whose merchants (such the state which commerce brings)
Sent forth their mandates to dependent kings;
165   Streets, where the turbaned Moslem, bearded Jew,
And woolly Afric, met the brown Hindu;
Where through each vein spontaneous plenty flowed,
Where Wealth enjoyed, and Charity bestowed.
Pensive and thoughtful shall the wanderers greet
170   Each splendid square, and still, untrodden street;
Or of some crumbling turret, mined by time,
The broken stairs with perilous step shall climb,
Thence stretch their view the wide horizon round,
By scattered hamlets trace its ancient bound,
175   And, choked no more with fleets, fair Thames survey
Through reeds and sedge pursue his idle way.

With throbbing bosoms shall the wanderers tread
The hallowed mansions of the silent dead.
Shall enter the long aisle and vaulted dome°   *St. Paul's Cathedral*
180   Where Genius and where Valor find a home;
Awe-struck 'midst chill sepulchral marbles breathe,
Where all above is still, as all beneath;
Bend at each antique shrine, and frequent turn
To clasp with fond delight some sculptured urn,
185   The ponderous mass of Johnson's form to greet,
Or breathe the prayer at Howard's sainted feet.[8]

Perhaps some Briton, in whose musing mind
Those ages live which Time has cast behind,
To every spot shall lead his wondering guests
190   On whose known site the beam of glory rests;
Here Chatham's[9] eloquence in thunder broke,
Here Fox persuaded, or here Garrick[1] spoke;
Shall boast how Nelson,[2] fame and death in view,

6. Skiddaw, a mountain, and Lodore, the site of a water-fall, are two tourist spots in the Lake District.
7. Sir Walter Scott, *The Lay of the Last Minstrel* 2.1. The ruined abbey was famously picturesque.
8. Statues of critic and lexicographer Samuel Johnson (1709–1784) and prison reformer John Howard (1726–1790) stand in the nave of St. Paul's Cathedral.
9. William Pitt, first Earl of Chatham (1708–1778), a famous orator and the dominant political figure of his time.

1. Charles James Fox (1749–1806), leader of the Whig opposition; David Garrick (1717–1779), celebrated Shakespearean actor.
2. "Every reader will recollect the sublime telegraphic dispatch, 'England expects every man to do his duty'" [Barbauld's note], sent by Admiral Horatio Nelson (1758–1805), to his fleet, just before he was killed in the victory of the Battle of Trafalgar.

To wonted victory led his ardent crew,
195   In England's name enforced, with loftiest tone,
Their duty,—and too well fulfilled his own:
How gallant Moore,[3] as ebbing life dissolved,
But hoped his country had his fame absolved.
Or call up sages whose capacious mind
200   Left in its course a track of light behind;
Point where mute crowds on Davy's[4] lips reposed,
And Nature's coyest secrets were disclosed;
Join with their Franklin, Priestley's injured name,[5]
Whom, then, each continent shall proudly claim.

205   Oft shall the strangers turn their eager feet
The rich remains of ancient art to greet,
The pictured walls with critic eye explore,
And Reynolds be what Raphael was before.[6]
On spoils from every clime their eyes shall gaze,
210   Egyptian granites and the Etruscan vase;
And when 'midst fallen London they survey
The stone where Alexander's ashes lay,[7]
Shall own with humbled pride the lesson just
By Time's slow finger written in the dust.

215   There walks a Spirit o'er the peopled earth,
Secret his progress is, unknown his birth;
Moody and viewless° as the changing wind,   *invisible*
No force arrests his foot, no chains can bind;
Where'er he turns, the human brute awakes,
220   And, roused to better life, his sordid hut forsakes:
He thinks, he reasons, glows with purer fires,
Feels finer wants, and burns with new desires:
Obedient Nature follows where he leads;
The steaming marsh is changed to fruitful meads;
225   The beasts retire from man's asserted reign,
And prove his kingdom was not given in vain.
Then from its bed is drawn the ponderous ore,
Then Commerce pours her gifts on every shore,
Then Babel's towers and terraced gardens rise,
230   And pointed obelisks invade the skies;
The prince commands, in Tyrian purple drest,
And Egypt's virgins weave the linen vest.
Then spans the graceful arch the roaring tide,

3. "I hope England will be satisfied," were the last words of General Moore [Barbauld's note]. Sir John Moore died while commanding the British retreat at the Battle of Coruña (1809).
4. Sir Humphry Davy (1778–1829), inventor of the miner's safety lamp, gave public lectures on chemistry at the Royal Institution.
5. Benjamin Franklin (1706–1790) and Joseph Priestley corresponded about their work on electricity.

6. Sir Joshua Reynolds (1723–1792), leading British portrait painter and first president of the Royal Academy; Raffaelo Sanzio (1483–1520), great Italian Renaissance artist.
7. A sarcophagus brought for display at the recently opened British Museum in 1802 was thought to be that of Alexander the Great; among the "Egyptian granites" was the Rosetta stone.

And stricter bounds the cultured fields divide.
235   Then kindles Fancy, then expands the heart,
      Then blow° the flowers of Genius and of Art;   *bloom*
      Saints, heroes, sages, who the land adorn,
      Seem rather to descend than to be born;
      While History, 'midst the rolls consigned to fame,
240   With pen of adamant inscribes their name.

      The Genius now forsakes the favored shore,[8]
      And hates, capricious, what he loved before;
      Then empires fall to dust, then arts decay,
      And wasted realms enfeebled despots sway°;   *rule*
245   Even Nature's changed; without his fostering smile
      Ophir° no gold, no plenty yields the Nile;   *region famed for gold*
      The thirsty sand absorbs the useless rill,
      And spotted plagues from putrid fens distil.
      In desert solitudes then Tadmor sleeps,
250   Stern Marius then o'er fallen Carthage weeps;[9]
      Then with enthusiast love the pilgrim roves
      To seek his footsteps in forsaken groves,
      Explores the fractured arch, the ruined tower,
      Those limbs disjointed of gigantic power;
255   Still at each step he dreads the adder's sting,
      The Arab's javelin, or the tiger's spring;
      With doubtful caution treads the echoing ground,
      And asks where Troy or Babylon is found.
      And now the vagrant Power no more detains
260   The vale of Tempe or Ausonian plains;[1]
      Northward he throws the animating ray,
      O'er Celtic nations bursts the mental day;
      And, as some playful child the mirror turns,
      Now here, now there, the moving lustre burns;
265   Now o'er his changeful fancy more prevail
      Batavia's dykes than Arno's purple vale;[2]
      And stinted suns, and rivers bound with frost,
      Than Enna's plains or Baia's viny coast;
      Venice the Adriatic weds in vain,
270   And Death sits brooding o'er Campania's plain;[3]
      O'er Baltic shores and through Hercynian groves,°   *the Black Forest*
      Stirring the soul, the mighty impulse moves;
      Art plies his tools, and Commerce spreads her sail,
      And wealth is wafted in each shifting gale.

8. See Milton's elegy, *Lycidas*, 183.
9. Tadmor is the biblical name for Palmyra, an ancient Syrian city. Roman consul Gaius Marius (157–86 B.C.), vanquished by Sulla, fled to Africa, where he was denied entry. Plutarch records his lament to the governor: "Tell him, then, that thou hast seen Marius a fugitive, seated amid the ruins of Carthage" (a city destroyed by the Romans in 146 B.C.).

1. Tempe is in Greece; Ausonia is Virgil's name for Italy: hence, the realms of classical literature.
2. Batavia is the Netherlands; the Arno flows through Florence.
3. Enna is a valley in Sicily; Baia is a Roman resort on the Bay of Naples. In a grand annual ceremony, Venice symbolically wed the Adriatic. The infamous swamps of Campania enclose Capua and Naples.

275 The sons of Odin° tread on Persian looms,   *Norsemen*
    And Odin's daughters breathe distilled perfumes;
    Loud minstrel bards, in Gothic halls, rehearse
    The Runic rhyme, and "build the lofty verse."[4]
    The Muse, whose liquid notes were wont to swell
280 To the soft breathings of the Æolian shell,
    Submits, reluctant, to the harsher tone,
    And scarce believes the altered voice her own.
    And now, where Cæsar saw with proud disdain
    The wattled hut and skin of azure stain,[5]
285 Corinthian columns rear their graceful forms,
    And light verandas brave the wintry storms,
    While British tongues the fading fame prolong
    Of Tully's eloquence and Maro's song.[6]
    Where once Bonduca[7] whirled the scythed car,
290 And the fierce matrons raised the shriek of war,
    Light forms beneath transparent muslins float,
    And tutored voices swell the artful note.
    Light-leaved acacias and the shady plane
    And spreading cedar grace the woodland reign;
295 While crystal walls the tenderer plants confine,
    The fragrant orange and the nectared pine;
    The Syrian grape there hangs her rich festoons,
    Nor asks for purer air or brighter noons:
    Science and Art urge on the useful toil,
300 New mould a climate and create the soil,
    Subdue the rigor of the Northern Bear,
    O'er polar climes shed aromatic air,
    On yielding Nature urge their new demands,
    And ask not gifts, but tribute, at her hands.

305 London exults:—on London Art bestows
    Her summer ices and her winter rose;
    Gems of the East her mural crown adorn,
    And Plenty at her feet pours forth her horn.°   *cornucopia*
    While even the exiles her just laws disclaim,
310 People a continent, and build a name:
    August she sits, and with extended hands
    Holds forth the book of life to distant lands.

    But fairest flowers expand but to decay;
    The worm is in thy core, thy glories pass away;
315 Arts, arms, and wealth destroy the fruits they bring;
    Commerce, like beauty, knows no second spring.

4. Milton, *Lycidas* (1637): "Who would not sing for Lycidas? he knew / Himself to sing, and build the lofty rhyme"
(10–11). Runic: mysteriously lettered.
5. In *Gallic Wars*, Julius Caesar noted that the ancient
Scots wore blue warpaint.

6. Marcus Tullius Cicero (106–43 B.C.) won renown for
his denunciations of the traitor Catiline; "Maro" is the
surname of Virgil (70–19 B.C.), author of the *Aeneid*.
7. Celtic queen who revolted against the Romans, and
took her own life when she was finally defeated (A.D. 61).

Crime walks thy streets, Fraud earns her unblest bread,
O'er want and woe thy gorgeous robe is spread,
And angel charities in vain oppose:
320   With grandeur's growth the mass of misery grows.
For, see,—to other climes the Genius soars,
He turns from Europe's desolated shores;
And lo! even now, 'midst mountains wrapt in storm,
On Andes' heights he shrouds his awful form;
325   On Chimborazo's summits treads sublime,
Measuring in lofty thought the march of Time;
Sudden he calls: "'Tis now the hour!" he cries,
Spreads his broad hand, and bids the nations rise.
La Plata hears amidst her torrents' roar;
330   Potosi hears it, as she digs the ore:[8]
Ardent, the Genius fans the noble strife,
And pours through feeble souls a higher life,
Shouts to the mingled tribes from sea to sea,
And swears—Thy world, Columbus, shall be free.[9]

1811   1812

—◄═◊═►—

Charlotte Smith
1749–1806

Charlotte Smith was already famous for her *Elegiac Sonnets* when Cambridge student William Wordsworth sought her out in Brighton on his way to France in 1791. In addition to Wordsworth (who would read her sonnets in 1802 to encourage his own exercise in the form) her admirers included Samuel Taylor Coleridge, who credited her and W. L. Bowles for the sonnet-revival in his generation. Bowles's influence flowed from Smith's success. Wordsworth was impressed by her "true feeling for rural nature," so he reflected in the 1830s. In the 1790s, Coleridge cited her sonnets as an "exquisite" example of how "moral Sentiments, Affections, or Feelings" could be "deduced from, and associated with, the scenery of Nature." Smith's poetry involves literary associations, too, full of echoes of, quotations of, and allusions to a host of English poets, as well as Petrarch and Goethe.

Their emotional tone was proved on the pulses of her mostly miserable life. Charlotte Turner was born into a world of comfortable elegance, and although her mother died in childbirth three years later, her youth passed pleasantly enough between her father's London townhouse and Sussex estate. She read avidly and was tutored in landscape painting, dancing, and acting—all evident in her poetic art. This girlhood life came to a sharp conclusion just before her sixteenth birthday, with an arranged marriage to twenty-one-year-old Benjamin Smith, spendthrift heir to a West Indian business and prone to womanizing and temper tantrums. Knowing his son's failings, Benjamin's father wrote a complicated will of inheritance, but the result was decades of litigation, not sorted

---

8. The first of a series of references to the spreading resistance to colonialism in South America: the Andes are mountains in Peru; Chimborazo is a mountain in Equador; La Plata, a city in Argentina; Potosi, a city in

Bolivia, celebrated for its silver.
9. Landing in the Caribbean islands in 1492, Columbus claimed Central and South America for Spain.

out until long after the deaths of Benjamin and Charlotte in 1806. By late 1783, Benjamin had landed in debtors' prison, where Charlotte, leaving their children with her brother, joined him for seven months. On his release in 1784, they fled to France. Pregnant with her twelfth child (she had fourteen in all, three dying in early childhood), Charlotte then moved the entire family to France. By 1785, she had had enough, and legally separated from her husband and returned to England to earn a living as a writer (the deadbeat continued to press legal claims to her income for years afterward). Much earlier than this, Smith realized she would have to support herself and her children, and she found immediate success with her first publication, its title marked by her misery, her lost life of luxury, and her determination to make a name for herself: *Elegiac Sonnets, and Other Essays by Charlotte Smith of Bignor Park, in Sussex.* Its popularity led to eight more, ever-expanding editions over the next sixteen years (we use the ninth [1800], the last she supervised). She also proved a prodigious novelist. Of the ten, *The Old Manor House* (1793) was popular through the nineteenth century, and *Desmond* (1792), a romance set against the background of the French Revolution, has attracted fresh attention today. She also published two long, remarkable poems in blank verse. *The Emigrants* (1793), a complex meditation on Britain's relationship to France in the wake of the Revolution (1793) saw the Terror and Britain's entry into war against France), ultimately evolves into a passionate, maternal indictment of warfare. Her ideals of social justice, which she esteemed in poet Robert Burns, endured.

Smith's long-twinned interests in pedagogy and in nature—not transcendent "visionary nature" or material transformed by the sublime self, but a realm of phenomena to be studied and classified—shape her *Conversations, Introducing Poetry; chiefly on subjects of natural history, for the use of children and young persons* (1804). In these exchanges a mother enlists poetry to educate her children's response to, and understanding of, the natural world. Smith's final work, *Beachy Head* (published posthumously in 1807 by radical bookseller Joseph Johnson) is also a generic mixture: in blank verse punctuated by rhymed lyrics, she produces autobiographical reminiscence, topographical description, geological speculation, reflections on history and natural science (botany and zoology), small narratives, and a final tale of pathos. The Advertisement to *Beachy Head and Other Poems* remarks that the title poem was "not completed according to the original design" because of "the increasing debility of its author."

from ELEGIAC SONNETS AND OTHER POEMS

Sonnet IV: To The Moon

QUEEN of the silver bow![1]—by the pale beam,
   Alone and pensive, I delight to stray,
And watch thy shadow trembling in the stream,
   Or mark the floating clouds that cross thy way.
5   And while I gaze, thy mild and placid light
   Sheds a soft calm upon my troubled breast;
And oft I think—fair planet of the night,
   That in thy orb, the wretched may have rest:
The sufferers of the earth perhaps may go,
10   Releas'd by death—to thy benignant sphere,
And the sad children of despair and woe
   Forget in thee, their cup of sorrow here.
Oh! that I soon may reach thy world serene,
Poor wearied pilgrim—in this toiling scene!

1. Diana, the goddess of the moon, is an archer.

Plate 1.   *Sonnet 4.*

Arbauld del.   *Milton sculp.*

Publish'd Jan.ᵗ 1 1789 by T. Cadell, Strand.

Queen of the Silver Bow, &c.

Engraving for Sonnet IV: "To the Moon" frontispiece to volume 1 of *Elegiac Sonnets and Other Poems*, 8th ed. (1797). Courtesy of Princeton University Library.

Sonnet XXVII

SIGHING I see yon little troop at play;
　　By sorrow yet untouch'd; unhurt by care;
While free and sportive they enjoy to-day,
　　"Content and careless of to-morrow's fare!"[1]
5　Oh happy age! when Hope's unclouded ray
　　Lights their green path, and prompts their simple mirth,
Ere yet they feel the thorns that lurking lay
　　To wound the wretched pilgrims of the earth,
　　Making them rue the hour that gave them birth,
10　　And threw them on a world so full of pain,
Where prosperous folly treads on patient worth,
　　And to deaf pride, misfortune pleads in vain!
Ah! for their future fate how many fears
Oppress my heart—and fill mine eyes with tears![2]

To melancholy. Written on the banks of the Arun October, 1785

When latest Autumn spreads her evening veil,
　　And the grey mists from these dim waves arise,
　　I love to listen to the hollow sighs,
Thro' the half-leafless wood that breathes the gale:
5　For at such hours the shadowy phantom pale,
　　Oft seems to fleet before the poet's eyes;
　　Strange sounds are heard, and mournful melodies,
As of night-wanderers, who their woes bewail!
Here, by his native stream, at such an hour,
10　　Pity's own Otway I methinks could meet,[1]
　　　And hear his deep sighs swell the sadden'd wind!
O Melancholy!—such thy magic power,
　　That to the soul these dreams are often sweet,
　　　And soothe the pensive visionary mind!

1800

The sea view[1]

The upland Shepherd, as reclined he lies
　　On the soft turf that clothes the mountain brow,
Marks the bright Sea-line mingling with the skies;
　　Or from his course celestial, sinking slow,

---

1. Thomson [Smith's note]. In James Thomson's *Autumn* (1730), "lovely young Lavinia," favored by "Fortune" then betrayed to poverty, withdraws with her "widow'd mother, feeble, old" (181) into a secluded vale, to avoid the scorn of the world, and "Almost on Nature's common bounty fed; / Like the gay birds that sung them to repose, / Content, and careless of to-morrow's fare" (189–91).
2. A knowing reprise of Thomas Gray's famous *Ode on a Distant Prospect of Eton College* (1747), which sighs even of privileged Eton schoolboys, "Alas, regardless of their

doom, / The little victims play! / No sense have they of ills to come, / Nor care beyond today" (51–54).
1. Thomas Otway (1652–1685), a dramatist known for pathos.
1. Suggested by the recollection of having seen, some years since, on a beautiful evening of Summer, an engagement between two armed ships, from the high down called the Beacon Hill, near Brighthelmstone [Smith's note, referring to modern Brighton].

5 The Summer-Sun in purple radiance low,
  Blaze on the western waters; the wide scene
   Magnificent, and tranquil, seems to spread
  Even o'er the Rustic's breast a joy serene,
   When, like dark plague-spots by the Demons shed,
10 Charged deep with death, upon the waves, far seen,
   Move the war-freighted ships; and fierce and red,
   Flash their destructive fires—The mangled dead
  And dying victims then pollute the flood.
  Ah! thus man spoils Heaven's glorious works with blood!

1797   1800

The Dead Beggar

*An Elegy, Addressed to a Lady, who was affected at seeing the Funeral
of a nameless Pauper, buried at the Expence of the Parish, in the
Church-Yard at Brighthelmstone, in November 1792.*[1]

  Swells then thy feeling heart, and streams thine eye
   O'er the deserted being, poor and old,
  Whom cold, reluctant, Parish Charity[2]
   Consigns to mingle with his kindred mold?

5 Mourn'st thou, that *here* the time-worn sufferer ends
   Those evil days still threatening woes to come;
  Here, where the friendless feel no want of friends,
   Where even the houseless wanderer finds an home!

  What tho' no kindred croud in sable° forth,   *mourning clothes*
10   And sigh, or seem to sigh, around his bier;
  Tho' o'er his coffin with the humid earth
   No children drop the unavailing tear?

  Rather rejoice that *here* his sorrows cease,
   Whom sickness, age, and poverty oppress'd;
15 Where Death, the Leveller,[3] restores to peace
   The wretch who living knew not where to rest.

1. I have been told that I have incurred blame for having used in this short composition, terms that have become obnoxious to certain persons. Such remarks are hardly worth notice; and it is very little my ambition to obtain the suffrage of those who suffer party prejudice to influence their taste; or of those who desire that because they have themselves done it, every one else should be willing to sell their best birth-rights, the liberty of thought, and of expressing thought, for the *promise* of a mess of pottage.

 It is surely not too much to say, that in a country like ours, where such immense sums are annually raised for the poor, there ought to be some regulation which should prevent any miserable deserted being from perishing through want, as too often happens to such objects as that on whose interment these stanzas were written.

It is somewhat remarkable that a circumstance exactly similar is the subject of a short poem called the Pauper's Funeral, in a volume lately published by Mr. Southey [Smith's note]. The "obnoxious" terms refer to "rights of Man" (20), Smith's endorsement of the principles of the French Revolution. In Genesis (25.27–34), Esau sells his birthright, his inheritance as eldest son, to Jacob, his younger brother for a meal. Robert Southey's *Poems* (1797) contained *The Pauper's Funeral*.

2. Each parish (that is, district Church of England) was responsible for its indigent residents, and some resorted to quite stringent economies.

3. Death-the-Leveller is an old image, referring not just to the leveling of human life, but also to the "democracy" where all are equal.

Rejoice, that tho' an outcast spurn'd by Fate,
 Thro' penury's rugged path his race he ran;
In earth's cold bosom, equall'd with the great,
20 Death vindicates the insulted rights of Man.

Rejoice, that tho' severe his earthly doom,
 And rude, and sown with thorns the way he trod,
Now, (where unfeeling Fortune cannot come)
 He rests upon the mercies of his GOD.

1797

from **Beachy Head**[1]

346 An early worshipper at Nature's shrine;[2]
I loved her rudest scenes—warrens, and heaths,
And yellow commons, and birch-shaded hollows,
And hedge rows, bordering unfrequented lanes
350 Bowered with wild roses, and the clasping woodbine
Where purple tassels of the tangling vetch[3]
With bittersweet, and bryony inweave,[4]
And the dew fills the silver bindweed's[5] cups—
I loved to trace the brooks whose humid banks
355 Nourish the harebell, and the freckled pagil;[6]
And stroll among o'ershadowing woods of beech,
Lending in Summer, from the heats of noon
A whispering shade; while haply there reclines
Some pensive lover of uncultur'd flowers,
360 Who, from the tumps° with bright green mosses clad, *hillock (local usage)*
Plucks the wood sorrel,[7] with its light thin leaves,
Heart-shaped, and triply folded; and its root
Creeping like beaded coral; or who there
Gathers, the copse's pride, anémones,[8]
365 With rays like golden studs on ivory laid
Most delicate: but touch'd with purple clouds,
Fit crown for April's fair but changeful brow.
Ah! hills so early loved! in fancy still
I breathe your pure keen air; and still behold

1. In crossing the Channel from the east coast of France, Beachy Head is the first land made [Smith's note]. This massive headland is the southernmost point of Sussex, directly across the English Channel from the French port of Dieppe.
2. Compare Wordsworth's *Tintern Abbey*. "I, so long / A worshipper of nature, hither came, / Unwearied in that service" (152–54).
3. Vetch. *Vicia sylvatica* [Smith's note].
4. Bittersweet. *Solanum dulcamara*. Bryony, *Bryonia alba* [Smith's note].

5. Bindweed. *Convolvulus sepium* [Smith's note].
6. Harebell. *Hyacinthus non scriptus*. pagil. *Primula veris* [Smith's note].
7. Sorrel. *Oxalis acetosella* [Smith's note].
8. Anémones. *Anemóne nemorosa*. It appears to be settled on late and excellent authorities, that this word should not be accented on the second syllable, but on the penultima. I have however ventured the more known accentuation, as more generally used, and suiting better the nature of my verse. [Smith's note]

370   Those widely spreading views, mocking alike
    The Poet and the Painter's utmost art
    And still, observing objects more minute,
    Wondering remark the strange and foreign forms
    Of sea-shells; with the pale calcareous[9] soil
375   Mingled, and seeming of resembling substance.[1]
    Tho' surely the blue Ocean (from the heights
    Where the downs westward trend, but dimly seen)
    Here never roll'd its surge. Does Nature then
    Mimic, in wanton mood, fantastic shapes
380   Of bivalves, and inwreathed volutes,° that cling   *spiral shells*
    To the dark sea-rock of the wat'ry world?
    Or did this range of chalky mountains, once[2]
    Form a vast bason,° where the Ocean waves   *basin*
    Swell'd fathomless? What time these fossil shells,
385   Buoy'd on their native element, were thrown
    Among the imbedding calx:° when the huge hill   *lime*
    Its giant bulk heaved, and in strange ferment
    Grew up a guardian barrier, 'twixt the sea
    And the green level of the sylvan weald.
390   Ah! very vain is Science' proudest boast,
    And but a little light its flame yet lends
    To its most ardent votaries; since from whence
    These fossil forms are seen, is but conjecture,
    Food for vague theories, or vain dispute,
395   While to his daily task the peasant goes,
    Unheeding such inquiry; with no care
    But that the kindly change of sun and shower,
    Fit for his toil the earth he cultivates.
    As little recks the herdsman of the hill,
400   Who on some turfy knoll, idly reclined,
    Watches his wether flock; that deep beneath[3]
    Rest the remains of men, of whom is left[4]

9. Containing calcium carbonate or carbonate of lime; limestone.

1. Among the crumbling chalk I have often found shells, some quite in fossil state and hardly distinguishable from chalk. Others appeared more recent; cockles, muscles [mussels], and periwinkles, I well remember, were among the number; and some whose names I do not know. A great number were like those of small land snails. It is now many years since I made these observations. The appearance of sea-shells so far from the sea excited my surprise, though I then knew nothing of natural history. I have never read any of the late theories of the earth, nor was I ever satisfied with the attempts to explain many of the phenomena which call forth conjecture in those books I happened to have had access to on this subject [Smith's note].

2. The theory here slightly hinted at, is taken from an idea started by Mr. White [Smith's note]. Gilbert White (1720–1793) published *The Natural History of Selborne* in 1789.

3. Male sheep, kept on high ground.

4. These Downs are not only marked with traces of encampments, which from their forms are called Roman or Danish; but there are numerous tumuli [burial mounds] among them. Some of which having been opened a few years ago, were supposed by a learned antiquary to contain the remains of the original natives of the country [Smith's note].

No traces in the records of mankind,
Save what these half obliterated mounds
405 And half fill'd trenches doubtfully impart
To some lone antiquary; who on times remote,
Since which two thousand years have roll'd away,
Loves to contemplate. He perhaps may trace,
Or fancy he can trace, the oblong square
410 Where the mail'd legions, under Claudius,[5] tear'd,
The rampire,° or excavated fossé° delved;   *rampart / trench or moat*
What time the huge unwieldy Elephant[6]
Auxiliary reluctant, hither led,
From Afric's forest glooms and tawny sands,
415 First felt the Northern blast, and his vast frame
Sunk useless; whence in after ages found,
The wondering hinds, on those enormous bones
Gaz'd;[7] and in giants[8] dwelling on the hills
Believed and marvell'd—

1806   1807

5. That the legions of Claudius were in this part of Britain appears certain. Since this emperor received the submission of Cantii, Atrebates, Irenobates, and Regni, in which later denomination were included the people of Sussex [Smith's note]. Roman emperor Claudius [10 B.C.–54 A.D.] invaded Britain in 43 and made it a province.

6. In the year 1740, some workmen digging in the park at Burton in Sussex, discovered, nine feet below the surface, the teeth and bones of an elephant; two of the former were seven feet eight inches in length. There were besides these, tusks, one of which broke in removing it, a grinder not at all decayed, and a part of the jaw-bone, with bones of the knee and thigh, and several others. Some of them remained very lately at Burton House, the seat of John Biddulph, Esq. Others were in possession of the Rev. Dr. Langrish, minister of Petworth at that period, who was present, when some of these bones were taken up, and gave it as his opinion, that they had remained there since the universal deluge [the time of Noah's Ark]. The Romans under the Emperor Claudius probably brought elephants into Britain. Milton, in the Second Book of his History, in speaking of the expedition, says that "He [. . .] like a great eastern king, with armed elephants, marched through Gallia" [John Milton published *The History of Britain* in 1670]. This is given on the authority of Dion Cassius, in his Life of the Emperor Claudius [Dio Cassius., c. 150–235, wrote an 80-book history of Rome]. It has therefore been conjectured, that the bones found at Burton might have been those of one of these elephants, who perished there soon after its landing; or dying on the high downs, one of which, called Duneton Hill, rises immediately above Burton Park, the bones might have been washed down by the torrents of rain, and buried deep in the soil. They were not found together, but scattered at some distance from each other. The two tusks were twenty feet apart. I had often heard of the elephant's bones at Burton, but never saw them; and I have no books to refer to. I think I saw, in what is now called the National Museum at Paris, the very large bones of an elephant, which were found in North America: though it is certain that this enormous animal is never seen in its natural state, but in the countries under the torrid zone of the old world. I have, since making this note, been told that the bones of the rhinoceros and hippopotamus have been found in America [Smith's note].

7. Compare the famous lines from Virgil's *Georgics*. "Surely a time will come when in those regions / The farmer heaving the soil with his curved plough / Will come on spears all eaten up with rust / Or strike with his heavy hoe on hollow helmets / And gape at the huge bones in the upturned graves" (1.490; trans. by L. P. Wilkinson).

8. The peasants believe that the large bones sometimes found belonged to giants, who formerly lived on the hills. The devil also has a great deal to do with the remarkable forms of hill and vale: the Devil's Punch Bowl, the Devil's Leaps, and the Devil's Dyke, are names given to deep hollows, or high and abrupt ridges, in this and the neighbouring county [Smith's note].

William Blake

1757–1827

It was from William Blake's *Marriage of Heaven and Hell* that a sensationally transgressive rock band of the 1960s, The Doors, took their name:

> If the doors of perception were cleansed
> every thing would appear to man as it is: In-
> > finite.

But unlike The Doors, Blake needed no pharmaceutical assistance in cleansing his vision. His eccentricity and imaginative intensity, which seemed like madness to more than a few contemporaries, emerged from a childhood punctuated by such events as beholding God's face pressed against his window, seeing angels among the haystacks, and being visited by the Old Testament prophet Ezekiel. When his favorite brother died in 1787, Blake claimed that he saw his "released spirit ascend heavenwards, clapping its hand for joy." Soon after, he reports, this spirit visited him with a critical revelation of the method of "Illuminated Printing" that he would use in his major poetical works.

Rebellious, unconventional, fiercely idealistic, Blake became a celebrity in modern counterculture—Allen Ginsberg and many of the Beat poets of the 1950s and 1960s cited him as a major influence. But for a good part of the nineteenth century, he was known only to a coterie. He did not support himself as a poet but got by on patronage and commissions for engraving and painting. His projects included the Book of Job and other scenes from the Bible; Chaucer's Canterbury Pilgrims; characters in Spenser's *Faerie Queene*; Milton's *L'Allegro, Il Penseroso, Paradise Lost,* and *Paradise Regained*; Gray's *The Bard*; Young's *Night Thoughts*; and Blair's *The Grave*. His obscurity as a poet was due in part to the difficulty of his work after the mid-1790s but chiefly to the very limited issue of his books, a consequence of the painstaking and time-consuming process of "Illuminated Printing." He hoped to reach a wider audience with a private exhibition of his illustrations in 1809, but his adventurous originality, coupled with his cantankerous and combative personality, left him ignored, except for one vicious review in *The Examiner,* which called him a lunatic. He died impoverished and almost entirely unknown except to a small group of younger painters. Only in 1863 did interest begin to grow, thanks to Alexander Gilchrist's biography, *The Life of William Blake: Pictor Ignotus,* its second volume a selection of poems edited by Dante Gabriel Rossetti. The revival was fanned by the enthusiasm of the Pre-Raphaelite circle and subsequent essays by Algernon Charles Swinburne, William Michael Rossetti (Dante Gabriel's brother), and William Butler Yeats.

Although Blake had no formal education, he was an avid reader, immersing himself in English poetry, the Bible, and works of mysticism and philosophy, as well as a study of Greek, Latin, and Hebrew. With precocious talent as a sketcher, he hoped to become a painter, but his father could not afford the tuition, and so apprenticed him at age fourteen as an engraver. During this seven-year term, Blake found time to write the poems gathered into his first publication, *Poetical Sketches* (1783), his only unilluminated volume. The later illuminated books were not products of the letter-press, but of a process of hand-etching designs onto copper plates, using these plates to ink-print pages that were then individually hand-colored and hand-bound into volumes. So labor-intensive a method was not adaptable to any production of quantity: there are, for instance, only twenty-seven known copies of *Songs of Innocence and of Experience* and only nine of *The Marriage of Heaven and Hell.* Yet Blake's commitment to involving his verbal text with pictures and pictorial embellishments created books of extraordinary beauty and an innovative "composite art" of word and image. In this art, the script conveys meaning—flowing versus starkly blocked letters, for instance—and the pictorial elements are significant, sometimes illustrating, sometimes adding another perspective or an ironic comment on the verbal text, sometimes even presenting contradictory information. Our selection of plates shows these dynamics, and our transcriptions of the poetry in all cases follow the linear arrangement on the plates.

Blake's popularity is based chiefly on his earlier and most accessible works from the 1790s. *Songs of Innocence and of Experience* (1789–1794) was much admired in his own day by Samuel Taylor Coleridge, Charles Lamb, and William Wordsworth (even though Blake deemed him too enamored of "Natural Piety"—faith in the natural world as spiritual and poetic resource: "I see in Wordsworth the Natural man rising up against the Spiritual Man Continually, & then he is No Poet but a heathen Philosopher at Enmity against all true Poetry or Inspiration"). *Songs* is compelling not only for a concern with the different ways children and adults see and understand their world (a theme that would occupy Wordsworth, too) but also for its acid critiques of social evils, political injustice, and their agents, the triumvirate of "God & his Priest & King" (in the voice of a too-experienced chimney sweeper). Reflecting Blake's familiarity with the range of freethinking contemporary biblical commentary that became the "Higher Criticism," *The Marriage of Heaven and Hell* (1790) brings visionary energy and poetic extravagance to a trenchant argument for imaginative freedom over psychological inhibition, conventional morality, and institutionalized authority. It is also one of the first Romantic-era rethinkings of Milton's *Paradise Lost*, the archetypal story of right and wrong, sin and punishment. Blake takes as an important effect a common reaction (including even Alexander Pope): that Satan and the scenes in Hell provide far more exciting and imaginatively powerful reading than the Angels and God's court in Heaven. "The reason Milton wrote in fetters when / he wrote of Angels & God, and at liberty when of / Devils & Hell," proposes Blake's "Voice of the Devil," is "because he was a true Poet and / of the Devils party without knowing it." Unfettering himself from Milton's moral machinery with this outrageously subversive commentary, Blake presents devils who are a lot more fun than his angels. The *Proverbs of Hell* offer their wisdom with a kind of transgressive glee, sarcastic levity, and diabolical wit that anticipates the sly aphorisms of Oscar Wilde and the exuberance of American Beat poetry.

Visions of the Daughters of Albion (1793), a potent commentary on the tyranny of rape and sexual possession, reflects Blake's admiration for Mary Wollstonecraft, whose *Vindication of the Rights of Woman* had been published to controversial reception the year before. These works and others of the 1790s emerge from Blake's involvement with the London circle of bookseller Joseph Johnson, including Wollstonecraft, William Godwin, Tom Paine, and Dr. Joseph Priestley—a group of artists and religious dissenters joined by progressive politics and support of the French Revolution. Like many of this group, Blake regarded the revolutions in America and France as heralds of a new millennium, and thus inspired, he produced a sequence of (sometimes abstruse) visionary works celebrating the overthrow of tyranny: *The French Revolution* (1791), *America: A Prophecy* (1793), *Europe: A Prophecy* (1794), and *The Book of Urizen* (1794). His later "prophetic" works—*Milton* (1804) and *Jerusalem* (1804–1820)—develop some of these themes with an increasingly esoteric vocabulary and elaborate personal mythology, and are notoriously difficult to read, although they contain passages of impressive energy and imagination.

An emblematic episode from 1803 suggests the real-life consequences of Blake's uncompromising visions. When a drunken dragoon trespassed onto his cottage garden and refused to leave, Blake vigorously ejected him, and was arrested for seditious threats against the crown. With England at war with France, this was a capital offense for which the penalty could have been death. Blake's trial ended in an acquittal loudly applauded by the spectators, but the ordeal exacerbated his memory of having been arrested in 1780 under the suspicion of being a spy for France while on a riverboat sketching excursion, and it crystallized his anger at state authority. Energizing all Blake's works is his commitment to imagination and the potency of visionary idealism, sharpened by resistance to psychological, ideological, institutional, and political tyrannies.

[Plate 1]   The voice of one crying in the
                                    Wilderness[1]

[Plate 2]   **All Religions Are One[2]**

[Plate 3]   The Argument
                            As the true meth-
                            -od of knowledge
                            is experiment,
                            the true faculty
                            of knowing must
                            be the faculty which
                            experiences. This
                            faculty I treat of.

[Plate 4]   PRINCIPLE 1ST

                            That the Poetic Genius is
                            the true Man, and that
                            the body or outward form
                            of Man is derived from the
                            Poetic Genius. Likewise
                            that the forms of all things
                            are derived from their
                            Genius, which by the
                            Ancients was calld an
                            Angel & Spirit & Demon.

[Plate 5]   PRINCIPLE 2D

                            As all men are alike in
                            outward form, So (and
                            with the same infinite
                            variety) all are alike in
                            the Poetic Genius

[Plate 6]   PRINCIPLE 3D

                            No man can think
                            write or speak from his

1. The prophecy of Isaiah 40.3, which Matthew 3.3 takes to refer to John the Baptist.
2. Blake did not sign his name to this potentially heretical declaration, but presents its argument and principles in the voice of a biblical prophet speaking to the modern age.

heart, but he must intend
truth. Thus all sects of
Philosophy are from the
Poetic Genius, adapted
to the weaknesses of
every individual.

[Plate 7]

PRINCIPLE 4TH

As none by trave
ling over known
lands can find out
the unknown, So,
from already ac
quired knowledge,
Man could not ac
quire more; there
fore an universal
Poetic Genius exists.

[Plate 8]

PRINCIPLE 5TH

The Religions of all Nat-
-ions are derived from each
Nations different reception
of the Poetic Genius which
is every where call'd the Spi
rit of Prophecy

[Plate 9]

PRINCIPLE 6TH

The Jewish & Chris-
tian Testaments are
An original derivati-
-on from the Poetic Ge-
nius: this is necessary
from the confined natu
re of bodily sensation

[Plate 10]

PRINCIPLE 7TH

As all men are alike
(tho' infinitely vari
ous) So all Religions:
& as all similars have
one source,
The true Man is the
source, he being the
Poetic Genius

William Blake, Frontispiece
for *Songs of Innocence*.

SONGS OF INNOCENCE AND OF EXPERIENCE   Blake's most popular work appeared in two phases. In 1789 he published *Songs of Innocence*; five years later he bound these poems with a set of new poems in a volume titled *Songs of Innocence and of Experience Shewing the two contrary States of the Human Soul*. "Innocence" and "Experience" are definitions of consciousness that rethink Milton's existential-mythic states of "Paradise" and the "Fall." Blake's categories are modes of perception that tend to coordinate with a chronological story that would become standard in Romanticism: childhood is a time and a state of protected "innocence," but it is a qualified innocence, not immune to the fallen world and its institutions. This world sometimes impinges on childhood itself, and in any event becomes known through "experience," a state of being marked by the loss of childhood vitality, by fear and inhibition, by social and political corruption, and by the manifold oppression of Church, State, and the ruling classes. The volume's "Contrary States" are sometimes signaled by patently repeated or contrasted titles: in *Innocence*, *Infant Joy*, in *Experience*, *Infant Sorrow*; in *Innocence*, *The Lamb*, in *Experience*, *The Fly* and *The Tyger*.

These contraries are not simple oppositions, however. Unlike Milton's narrative of the Fall from Paradise, Blake shows either state of soul possible at any moment. Some children, even infants, have already lost their innocence through a soiling contact with the world; some adults, particularly joyously visionary poets, seem able to retain vitality even in experience. Moreover, the values of "Innocence" and "Experience" are themselves complex. At times, an innocent state of soul reflects a primary, untainted vitality of imagination; at other times, Blake, like Mary Wollstonecraft, implicates innocence with dangerous ignorance and vulnerability to oppression. In rhetorical structure, the songs may present an innocent singer against dark ironies that a more experienced reader, alert to social and political evil, will grasp. But just as trickily, experience can also trap a soul in its own "mind-forg'd manacles." Blake's point is not that children are pure and adults fallen, or that children are naive and adults perspicacious. Contrary possibilities coexist, with different plays and shades of emphasis in different poems. These values are often further complicated by the illustrations that accompany and often frame the song-texts. Sometimes these sustain the singer's tone and point of view (e.g., *The Lamb*), and sometimes (e.g., *The Little Black Boy*) they offer an ironic counter-commentary.

SONGS of INNOCENCE and of EXPERIENCE
Shewing the Two Contrary States of the Human Soul

from SONGS of INNOCENCE

Introduction

Piping down the valleys wild
Piping songs of pleasant glee
On a cloud I saw a child
And he laughing said to me.

5 Pipe a song about a Lamb:
So I piped with merry chear,
Piper, pipe that song again—
So I piped, he wept to hear.

Drop thy pipe thy happy pipe
10 Sing thy songs of happy chear,
So I sang the same again
While he wept with joy to hear

Piper sit thee down and write
In a book that all may read—
15 So he vanish'd from my sight
And I pluck'd a hollow reed

And I made a rural pen,
And I stain'd the water clear,
And I wrote my happy songs,
20 Every child may joy to hear

The Shepherd.

How sweet is the Shepherds sweet lot,
From the morn to the evening he strays:
He shall follow his sheep all the day
And his tongue shall be filled with praise.

5   For he hears the lambs innocent call.
And he hears the ewes tender reply,
He is watchful while they are in peace,
For they know when their Shepherd is nigh.

The Ecchoing Green

The Sun does arise,
And make happy the skies.
The merry bells ring
To welcome the Spring.
5   The sky-lark and thrush,
The birds of the bush,
Sing louder around,
To the bells chearful sound
While our sports shall be seen
10   On the Ecchoing Green.

Old John with white hair
Does laugh away care,
Sitting under the oak,
Among the old folk,
15   They laugh at our play,
And soon they all say,
Such such were the joys
When we all girls & boys,
In our youth time were seen,
20   On the Ecchoing Green.

Till the little ones weary
No more can be merry
The sun does descend,
And our sports have an end:
25   Round the laps of their mothers
Many sisters and brothers,
Like birds in their nest,
Are ready for rest:
And sport no more seen,
30   On the darkening Green.

William Blake, *The Lamb*, from *Songs of Innocence*. Blake pictures the boy in a natural state of nakedness among the lambs, all embraced by twining branches.

The Lamb

Little Lamb who made thee
Dost thou know who made thee
Gave thee life & bid thee feed,
By the stream & o'er the mead;
5 Gave thee clothing of delight,
Softest clothing wooly bright;
Gave thee such a tender voice,
Making all the vales rejoice:
Little Lamb who made thee
10 Dost thou know who made thee

Little Lamb, I'll tell thee.
Little Lamb, I'll tell thee;
He is called by thy name
For he calls himself a Lamb:
15 He is meek & he is mild,
He became a little child:
I a child & thou a lamb,

We are called by his name.
    Little Lamb God bless thee
20   Little Lamb God bless thee

The Little Black Boy[1]

My mother bore me in the southern wild,
And I am black, but O! my soul is white
White as an angel is the English child:
But I am black as if bereav'd of light.

5   My mother taught me underneath a tree
And sitting down before the heat of day,
She took me on her lap and kissed me,
And, pointing to the east, began to say.

Look on the rising sun: there God does live
10   And gives his light and gives his heat away.
And flowers and trees and beasts and men recieve
Comfort in morning joy in the noon day.

And we are put on earth a little space
That we may learn to bear the beams of love.
15   And these black bodies and this sun-burnt face
Is but a cloud, and like a shady grove.

For when our souls have learn'd the heat to bear
The cloud will vanish we shall hear his voice
Saying: come out from the grove, my love & care,
20   And round my golden tent like lambs rejoice.

Thus did my mother say, and kissed me.
And thus I say to little English boy.
When I from black and he from white cloud free,
And round the tent of God like lambs we joy:

25   Ill shade him from the heat till he can bear,
To lean in joy upon our fathers knee
And then Ill stand and stroke his silver hair,
And be like him and he will then love me.

The Blossom.

Merry Merry Sparrow
Under leaves so green
A happy Blossom
Sees you swift as arrow
5   Seek your cradle narrow
Near my Bosom.

1. See Color Plates 6 and 7. In "Copy B" the black boy's skin is as light as the English boy's; other versions use contrasting hues. The second plate shows both boys sheltered by the tree and welcomed by Christ, but also puts the black boy outside the inner cirle formed by the curve of Christ's body and the praying English boy. He is not part of this configuration, but rather a satellite of the English boy.

Pretty Pretty Robin
Under leaves so green
A happy Blossom
10   Hears you sobbing sobbing
Pretty Pretty Robin
Near my Bosom.

The Chimney Sweeper[1]

When my mother died I was very young
And my father sold me while yet my tongue
Could scarcely cry weep weep weep weep.[2]
So your chimneys I sweep & in soot I sleep.

5   Theres little Tom Dacre, who cried when his head
That curl'd like a lambs back, was shav'd, so I said:
Hush Tom never mind it, for when your head's bare
You know that the soot cannot spoil your white hair

And so he was quiet, & that very night,
10   As Tom was a sleeping he had such a sight,
That thousands of sweepers Dick, Joe, Ned & Jack
Were all of them lock'd up in coffins of black,

And by came an Angel who had a bright key,
And he open'd the coffins & set them all free.
15   Then down a green plain leaping laughing they run
And wash in a river and shine in the Sun.

Then naked & white, all their bags left behind,
They rise upon clouds, and sport in the wind
And the Angel told Tom if he'd be a good boy,
20   He'd have God for his father & never want joy

And so Tom awoke and we rose in the dark
And got with our bags & our brushes to work.
Tho' the morning was cold, Tom was happy & warm
So if all do their duty they need not fear harm.[3]

The Little Boy lost

Father, father, where are you going
O do not walk so fast.
Speak father, speak to your little boy
Or else I shall be lost,

1. Chimney-cleaning was done by young boys, whose impoverished parents sold them into the business, or who were orphans, outcasts, or illegitimate children with no other means of living. It was filthy, health-ruining labor, aggravated by overwork and inadequate clothing, food, and shelter. Among the hazards were burns, permanently blackened skin, deformed legs, black lung disease, and cancer of the scrotum. Protective legislation passed in 1788 was never enforced. Blake's outrage also sounds in "London."

Charles Lamb sent this poem to James Montgomery (a topical poet and radical-press editor) for inclusion in *The Chimney-Sweeper's Friend, and Climbing Boy's Album* (1824), which he was assembling for the Society for Ameliorating the Condition of Infant Chimney-Sweepers.
2. The lisping street cry of advertisement ("sweep! sweep!").
3. A typical conduct homily.

William Blake, *The Little Boy lost*, from *Songs of Innocence*.

5   The night was dark no father was there
    The child was wet with dew.
    The mire was deep, & the child did weep
    And away the vapour flew.

The Little Boy found

    The little boy lost in the lonely fen,°   *swamp*
    Led by the wand'ring light,[1]
    Began to cry, but God ever nigh,
    Appeard like his father in white.

5   He kissed the child & by the hand led
    And to his mother brought,
    Who in sorrow pale thro' the lonely dale
    Her little boy weeping sought.

The Divine Image.

    To Mercy Pity Peace and Love,
    All pray in their distress:
    And to these virtues of delight
    Return their thankfulness.

5   For Mercy Pity Peace and Love
    Is God our father dear:

1. Phosphorescent marsh.

The little boy lost in the lonely fen,
Led by the wandring light,
Began to cry, but God ever nigh,
Appeard like his father in white.

He kissed the child & by the hand led
And to his mother brought,
Who in sorrow pale, thro' the lonely dale
Her little boy weeping sought.

William Blake, *The Little Boy found*, from *Songs of Innocence*.

And Mercy Pity Peace and Love,
Is Man his child and care.

For Mercy has a human heart
10   Pity, a human face:
And Love, the human form divine,
And Peace, the human dress.

Then every man, of every clime
That prays in his distress,
15   Prays to the human form divine
Love Mercy Pity Peace.

And all must love the human form,
In heathen, turk or jew.
Where Mercy, Love & Pity dwell,
20   There God is dwelling too.

HOLY THURSDAY[1]

Twas on a Holy Thursday their innocent faces clean
The children walking two & two in red & blue & green[2]
Grey headed beadles[3] walkd before with wands as white as snow
Till into the high dome of Pauls they like Thames waters flow

1. One of the poems with a companion in *Experience* (see page 64). Holy Thursday celebrated the Ascension; it was customary to conduct the children in London's charity schools, many of them orphans, to services at

St. Paul's, the chief Anglican cathedral.
2. The colors of school uniforms.
3. Minor officials for ushering and preserving order.

5   O what a multitude they seemd these flowers of London town
Seated in companies they sit with radiance all their own
The hum of multitudes was there but multitudes of lambs
Thousands of little boys & girls raising their innocent hands

Now like a mighty wind they raise to heaven the voice of song
10   Or like harmonious thunderings the seats of heaven among
Beneath them sit the aged men wise guardians of the poor
Then cherish pity lest you drive an angel from your door[4]

Nurses Song

When the voices of children are heard on the green
And laughing is heard on the hill,
My heart is at rest within my breast
And everything else is still

5   Then come home my children the sun is gone down
And the dews of night arise
Come come leave off play, and let us away
Till the morning appears in the skies

No no let us play, for it is yet day
10   And we cannot go to sleep
Besides in the sky the little birds fly
And the hills are all coverd with sheep

Well well go & play till the light fades away
And then go home to bed
15   The little ones leaped & shouted & laugh'd
And all the hills ecchoed

Infant Joy

I have no name.
I am but two days old—
What shall I call thee?
I happy am
5   Joy is my name—
Sweet joy befall thee!

Pretty joy!
Sweet joy but two days old.
Sweet joy I call thee:
10   Thou dost smile,
I sing the while,
Sweet joy befall thee

4. See Hebrews 13.1–2: "Let brotherly love continue. Be not forgetful to entertain strangers: for thereby some have entertained angels unawares."

A Dream

Once a dream did weave a shade,
O'er my Angel-guarded bed,
That an Emmet° lost it's way   ant
Where on grass methought I lay.

5 Troubled wilderd and folorn
Dark benighted travel-worn,
Over many a tangled spray
All heart-broke I heard her say.

O my children! do they cry
10 Do they hear their father sigh.
Now they look abroad to see,
Now return and weep for me.

Pitying I drop'd a tear;
But I saw a glow-worm near:
15 Who replied. What wailing wight°   creature
Calls the watchman of the night.

I am set to light the ground,
While the beetle goes his round:
Follow now the beetles hum,
20 Little wanderer hie thee home.

On Anothers Sorrow

Can I see anothers woe.
And not be in sorrow too.
Can I see anothers grief,
And not seek for kind relief.

5 Can I see a falling tear,
And not feel my sorrows share,
Can a father see his child,
Weep, nor be with sorrow fill'd.

Can a mother sit and hear,
10 An infant groan an infant fear—
No no never can it be.
Never never can it be.

And can he who smiles on all
Hear the wren with sorrows small,
15 Hear the small birds grief & care
Hear the woes that infants bear—

And not sit beside the nest
Pouring pity in their breast.
And not sit the cradle near
20 Weeping tear on infants tear.

And not sit both night & day.
Wiping all our tears away.
O! no never can it be.
Never never can it be.

25   He doth give his joy to all.
He becomes an infant small.
He becomes a man of woe
He doth feel the sorrow too.

Think not, thou canst sigh a sigh,
30   And thy maker is not by,
Think not, thou canst weep a tear,
And thy maker is not near.

O! he gives to us his joy,
That our grief he may destroy
35   Till our grief is fled & gone
He doth sit by us and moan

from SONGS *of* EXPERIENCE
Introduction.

Hear the voice of the Bard!
Who Present, Past, & Future sees
Whose ears have heard,
The Holy Word,
5   *That walk'd among the ancient trees.*[1]
Calling the lapsed Soul
And weeping in the evening dew:
That might controll
The starry pole:[2]
10   *And fallen fallen light renew!*

O Earth O Earth return![3]
Arise from out the dewy grass:
Night is worn.
And the morn
15   *Rises from the slumberous mass.*

Turn away no more
Why wilt thou turn away
The starry floor
The watry shore
20   *Is givn thee till the break of day.*

1. Adam and Eve (the first lapsed souls), "heard the voice of the Lord God walking in the garden in the cool of the day" and "hid themselves from the presence of the Lord God amongst the trees of the garden" (Genesis 3.8).
2. The star above the North Pole (the North Star), its fixed position a symbol of steadfastness and a focus for navigation; the pivot of celestial order.
3. God exhorts his erring people: "O Earth, earth, earth, hear the word of the Lord" (Jeremiah 22.29). The placement of "return" at the turn of the verse line is a poet's pun (*versus* in Latin means *turn*) replayed in *turn* in lines 16 and 17.

EARTH'S *Answer*[1]

Earth rais'd up her head.
From the darkness dread & drear.
Her light fled:
Stony dread!
5   *And her locks cover'd with grey despair.*

Prison'd on watry shore
Starry Jealousy does keep my den
Cold and hoar
Weeping o'er
10 *I hear the Father of the ancient men.*[2]

Selfish father of men
Cruel jealous selfish fear
Can delight
Chain'd in night
15 *The virgins of youth and morning bear*

Does spring hide its joy
When buds and blossoms grow?
Does the sower?
Sow by night?
20 *Or the plowman in darkness plow?*

Break this heavy chain.
That does freeze my bones around
Selfish! vain!
Eternal bane!
25 *That free Love with bondage bound*

The CLOD & the PEBBLE

Love seeketh not Itself to please,
Nor for itself hath any care;
But for another gives its ease,
And builds a Heaven in Hells despair.[1]

5   *So sung a little Clod of Clay*
       Trodden with the cattles feet:
       But a Pebble of the brook,
       Warbled out these metres meet.

Love seeketh only Self to please
10 *To bind another to Its delight:*

---

1. Blake's plate design surrounds and penetrates the text with sinewy plant stems, which along the bottom turn into a prone serpent, its head slightly raised, with an open mouth and flickering tongue. One effect is to suggest that "Earth's answer" comes from this tongue.

2. On some plates "Father" is "father."
1. I Corinthians 13.4: "Charity suffereth long, and is kind; charity envieth not; charity vaunteth not itself, is not puffed up."

Joys in anothers loss of ease,
And builds a Hell in Heavens despite.[2]

HOLY THURSDAY[1]

Is this a holy thing to see,
In a rich and fruitful land
Babes reducd to misery
Fed with cold and usurous hand?

5   *Is that trembling cry a song?*
Can it be a song of joy?
And so many children poor?
It is a land of poverty!

And their sun does never shine,
10   *And their fields are bleak & bare,*
And their ways are fill'd with thorns
It is eternal winter there.

For where-e'er the sun does shine,
And where-e'er the rain does fall:
15   *Babe can never hunger there,*
Nor poverty the mind appall.

The Little Girl Lost[1]

In futurity
I prophetic see.
That the earth from sleep.
(Grave the sentence deep)

5   Shall arise and seek
For her maker meek:
And the desart wild
Become a garden mild.[2]

In the southern clime,
10   Where the summers prime.
Never fades away;
Lovely Lyca[3] lay.

---

2. In Hell Satan declares, "The mind is its own place, and in itself / Can make a Heaven of Hell, a Hell of Heaven" (*Paradise Lost* 1.254–55).

1. See *Holy Thursday* in *Songs of Innocence* (page 59).

1. This and *The Little Girl Found* were in *Songs of Innocence* in 1789. In *Innocence*, they followed *A Dream* and were followed by *The Little Boy Lost*. In *Experience*, *Holy Thursday* comes before and *The Chimney Sweeper* after. The first plate of *Lost* shows a young naked man and flimsily veiled young woman kissing and embracing under willow branches, as she points to a soaring dove. On the opposite margin are climbing vines, which curl across the plate, entwined with an open-mouthed snake, between the first two and next eight stanzas.

2. The prophecy of Isaiah: "The desert shall rejoice and blossom as the rose" (35.1).

3. A name suggesting affinity with *lykos*, the Greek word for "wolf."

Seven summers old
Lovely Lyca told°,   *tallied*
15   She had wanderd long.
Hearing wild birds song.

Sweet sleep come to me
Underneath this tree;
Do father, mother weep.—
20   Where can Lyca sleep.

Lost in desart wild
Is your little child.
How can Lyca sleep,
If her mother weep.

25   If her heart does ake,
Then let Lyca wake;
If my mother sleep,
Lyca shall not weep.

Frowning frowning night,
30   O'er this desart bright,
Let thy moon arise,
While I close my eyes.

Sleeping Lyca lay:
While the beasts of prey,
35   Come from caverns deep,
View'd the maid asleep

The kingly lion stood
And the virgin view'd,
Then he gambold round
40   O'er the hallowd ground;

Leopards, tygers play,
Round her as she lay;
While the lion old,
Bow'd his mane of gold.

45   And her bosom lick,
And upon her neck,
From his eyes of flame,
Ruby tears there came;

While the lioness,
50   Loos'd her slender dress,
And naked they convey'd
To caves the sleeping maid.[4]

4. On the next plate, depicted beneath the last three stanzas is a woman clad, seated alone under a leafless tree in the woods, looking up.

The Little Girl Found

All the night in woe,
Lyca's parents go:
Over vallies deep
While the desarts weep.

5 Tired and woe-begone,
Hoarse with making moan:
Arm in arm seven days.
They trac'd the desart ways.

Seven nights they sleep,
10 Among shadows deep:
And dream they see their child
Starv'd in desart wild.

Pale thro' pathless ways
The fancied image strays.[1]

15 Famish'd, weeping, weak
With hollow piteous shriek

Rising from unrest,
The trembling woman prest,
With feet of weary woe;
20 She could no further go.

In his arms he bore,
Her arm'd with sorrow sore:
Till before their way,
A couching lion lay.

25 Turning back was vain,
Soon his heavy mane.
Bore them to the ground;
Then he stalk'd around,

Smelling to his prey.
30 But their fears allay,
When he licks their hands:
And silent by them stands.

They look upon his eyes
Fill'd with deep surprise:
35 And wondering behold.
A spirit arm'd in gold.

On his head a crown
On his shoulders down,

---

1. The title and lines 1–14 are on the bottom half of the plate on which *The Little Girl Lost* ends, as if a two-part song. Next to this verse is a lioness under a tree, with her nose in the air (scenting prey?).

40 Flow'd his golden hair.
   Gone was all their care.

   Follow me he said,
   Weep not for the maid;
   In my palace deep,
   Lyca lies asleep.

45 Then they followed,
   Where the vision led:
   And saw their sleeping child,
   Among tygers wild.[2]

   To this day they dwell
50 In a lonely dell
   Nor fear the wolvish howl,
   Nor the lions growl.

THE Chimney Sweeper

   A little black thing among the snow:
   Crying weep, weep, in notes of woe!
   Where are thy father & mother? say?
   They are both gone up to the church to pray.

5 Because I was happy upon the heath
   And smil'd among the winters snow:
   They clothed me in the clothes of death,
   And taught me to sing the notes of woe.

   And because I am happy & dance & sing,
10 They think they have done me no injury:
   And are gone to praise God & his Priest & King
   Who make up a heaven of our misery.[1]

NURSES Song

   When the voices of children, are heard on the green
   And whisprings are in the dale:
   The days of my youth rise fresh in my mind,
   My face turns green and pale.

5 Then come home my children, the sun is gone down
   And the dews of night arise
   Your spring & your day, are wasted in play
   And your winter and night in disguise.

2. The plate with the rest of the song shows intertwined elm trunks, and at their base a small child nestling with a resting lion, two young children playing on the back of a reposing lioness, next to whom a naked woman sleeps, face down.

1. Construct their happiness from the elements of our misery; create an illusion of heavenly will in our misery.

William Blake, *THE Chimney Sweeper*, from *Songs of Experience*. The contrasting colors of soot-burdened sweep and snowstorm also involve a moral recognition: in the adverse winter world where effective home heating requires clean chimneys, the warm homes are closed to the sweep.

William Blake, *THE FLY*, from *Songs of Experience*. How should we read? The activities depicted seem "innocent": a girl bats a shuttlecock; a nurse guides a boy's early steps. But the poem-text provokes a view of the girl as a potential fly-swatter, and, in another frame of reference, of both little ones as analogues to the "little fly." Blake's plate makes the order of the stanzas ambiguous: should we read down or across?

The SICK ROSE[1]

O Rose thou art sick.
The invisible worm,
That flies in the night
In the howling storm:

5   Has found out thy bed
Of crimson joy:
And his dark secret love
Does thy life destroy.[2]

---

1. See Color Plate 9.
2. There are two manuscript versions of 7-8: "O dark secret love / Does life destroy"; "And her dark secret love/ Does thy life destroy."

THE FLY

Little Fly
Thy summer's play,
My thoughtless hand
Has brush'd away.[1]

Am not I
A fly like thee?
Or art not thou
A man like me?

For I dance
And drink & sing:
Till some blind hand
Shall brush my wing.

If thought is life
And strength & breath:[2]
And the want
Of thought is death;

Then am I
A happy fly,
If I live,
Or if I die.

The Angel

I Dreamt a Dream! what can it mean?
And that I was a maiden Queen:
Guarded by an Angel mild:
Witless woe, was ne'er beguil'd!

5   And I wept both night and day
And he wip'd my tears away
And I wept both day and night
And hid from him my hearts delight

So he took his wings and fled:
10   Then the morn blush'd rosy red:
I dried my tears & armd my fears,
With ten thousand shields and spears.

Soon my Angel came again;
I was arm'd, he came in vain:
15   For the time of youth was fled
And grey hairs were on my head

The Tyger[1]

Tyger Tyger, burning bright,
In the forests of the night;[2]
What immortal hand or eye,
Could frame thy fearful symmetry?

---

1. Cf. the blinded Gloucester's bitterly rueful comment in
King Lear: "As flies to wanton boys, are we to th' gods, /
They kill us for their sport" (4.1.36–37).
2. Descartes famously said, "I think, therefore I am."

1. See Color Plate 8.
2. A time of day and a metaphysical location, characterized
by forest mazes—the terrain that conducts to Hell in
Dante's *Inferno.* Cf. "midnight streets" in *London,* line 13.

5　In what distant deeps or skies,
　Burnt the fire of thine eyes?
　On what wings dare he aspire?[3]
　What the hand dare sieze the fire?

　And what shoulder & what art,
10　Could twist the sinews of thy heart?
　And when thy heart began to beat,
　What dread hand? & what dread feet?[4]

　What the hammer? what the chain,
　In what furnace was thy brain?
15　What the anvil? what dread grasp,
　Dare its deadly terrors clasp!

　When the stars threw down their spears
　And water'd heaven with their tears:[5]
　Did he smile his work to see?[6]
20　Did he who made the Lamb make thee?[7]

　Tyger Tyger burning bright,
　In the forests of the night:
　What immortal hand or eye,
　Dare frame thy fearful symmetry?

My Pretty ROSE TREE[1]

A flower was offerd to me;
Such a flower as May never bore.
But I said I've a Pretty Rose-tree:
And I passed the sweet flower o'er.

5　Then I went to my Pretty Rose-tree;
To tend her by day and by night.
But my Rose turnd away with jealousy:
And her thorns were my only delight.

AH! SUN-FLOWER[1]

Ah Sun-flower! weary of time,
Who countest the steps of the Sun:
Seeking after that sweet golden clime
Where the travellers journey is done

3. Icarus, with his father Dedalus, fashioned wings of feathers and wax to escape from prison. Icarus, ignoring his father's cautions, soared too close to the sun; the wax melted and he fell to his death in the sea.
4. One engraving has, "What dread hand Formd thy dread feet?"
5. In the war in Heaven, *Paradise Lost* (bk. 6), Satan is defeated and driven down to Hell. Blake's verb leaves it undecidable whether the stars "threw down their spears" in desperate surrender or in defiance.

6. In a notebook draft, Blake wrote "did he laugh his work to see."
7. An allusion to Jesus, "The Lamb of God" (John 1.29 and 1.36) and, indirectly, to the poem in *Songs of Innocence*, with Blake as the maker.
1. This song and *Ah! Sun-Flower* are on the same plate.
1. In Ovid's *Metamorphoses* (4.192), a nymph spurned by Apollo, the sun god, so pined for him that she turned into a sunflower, a heliotrope (turning its face to follow the sun).

5   Where the Youth pined away with desire,
    And the pale Virgin shrouded in snow:
    Arise from their graves and aspire
    Where my Sun-flower wishes to go.

The GARDEN of LOVE

I went to the Garden of Love.
And saw what I never had seen:
A Chapel was built in the midst,
Where I used to play on the green.

5   *And the gates of this Chapel were shut,*
    And Thou shalt not, writ over the door;[1]
    So I turnd to the Garden of Love,
    That so many sweet flowers bore.

    And I saw it was filled with graves,
10 *And tomb-stones where flowers should be:*
    And Priests in black gowns, were walking their rounds,
    And binding with briars, my joys & desires.[2]

LONDON

    I wander thro' each charter'd street,[1]
    Near where the charter'd Thames does flow
    And mark in every face I meet
    Marks of weakness, marks of woe.

5   In every cry of every Man,
    In every Infants cry of fear,
    In every voice; in every ban,[2]
    The mind-forg'd manacles I hear[3]

    How the Chimney-sweepers cry
10 Every blackning Church appalls.[4]
    And the hapless Soldiers sigh
    Runs in blood down Palace walls

1. A parody of the syntax of the Ten Commandments.
2. A crown of thorns tortured Jesus.
1. A charter is a grant of liberty or privilege, as in Magna Carta (1215). Exclusive: granted to some, it forbids others. Whether rights were chartered or natural was contested in the 1790s.
2. Several meanings: political prohibition, public condemnation, curse, announcement of marriage.
3. The forgers are the authorities of Church and State (Blake first wrote "german forged," referring to the German-born King George III) and the individuals who fetter themselves in fear or compliance. Between this "hear" and its rhyming repetition at the end of line 13, is an acrostic of the first letters of the third stanza H E A R. 4. The capital C makes it clear that this is the institutional Church of England; "blackning" involves soot with the imagery of moral evil; "appalls" continues the indictment, by drawing into the sense of "dismay" (to which the Church is immune) the literal meaning, "make pale"—that is, clean the soot out of; this color-moral extends into the next stanza's "blasts" and "blights."

But most thro' midnight streets I hear
How the youthful Harlots curse[5]
15 Blasts the new-born Infants tear
And blights with plagues the Marriage hearse[6]

The Human Abstract.

Pity would be no more,
If we did not make somebody Poor:
And Mercy no more could be,
If all were as happy as we:

5 And mutual fear brings peace:
Till the selfish loves increase.
Then Cruelty knits a snare,
And spreads his baits with care.

He sits down with holy fears,
10 And waters the ground with tears:
Then Humility takes its root
Underneath his foot.

Soon spreads the dismal shade
Of Mystery over his head;
15 And the Catterpiller and Fly,
Feed on the Mystery.

And it bears the fruit of Deceit,
Ruddy and sweet to eat:
And the Raven his nest has made
20 In its thickest shade.

The Gods of the earth and sea,
Sought thro' Nature to find this Tree
But their search was all in vain:
There grows one in the Human Brain

INFANT SORROW

My mother groand! my father wept.
Into the dangerous world I leapt:
Helpless naked piping loud:
Like a fiend hid in a cloud.

5 Struggling in my fathers hands:
Striving against my swadling bands
Bound and weary I thought best
To sulk upon my mothers breast.

5. Many prostitutes were desperately poor girls barely out of childhood, abandoned or disowned by their families.

6. Prenatal blindness caused by sexually transmitted diseases.

A POISON TREE. The poem was originally titled "Christian Forbearance." We present this Song only in the image of this plate. How does this invite you to read? The tail of the "y" in "My" at the beginning of the last line becomes a clockwise frame of the whole, as a branch of the poison tree. The outstretched body is in the posture of a crucifixion.

A Little BOY Lost

Nought loves another as itself
Nor venerates another so.
Nor is it possible to Thought
A greater than itself to know:

5   And Father, how can I love you,
Or any of my brothers more?
I love you like the little bird
That picks up crumbs around the door.

The Priest sat by and heard the child.
10   In trembling zeal he siez'd his hair:
He led him by his little coat:
And all admir'd the Priestly care.

And standing on the altar high,
Lo what a fiend is here! said he:
15 One who sets reason up for judge
Of our most holy Mystery.°   religion

The weeping child could not be heard.
The weeping parents wept in vain:
They strip'd him to his little shirt.
20 And bound him in an iron chain.

And burn'd him in a holy place,
Where many had been burn'd before:
The weeping parents wept in vain.
Are such things done on Albions° shore.   England's

A Little GIRL Lost

Children of the future Age,
Reading this indignant page;
Know that in a former time.
Love! sweet Love! was thought a crime.

In the Age of Gold,
Free from winters cold:[1]
Youth and maiden bright,
To the holy light,
5 Naked in the sunny beams delight.[2]

Once a youthful pair
Fill'd with softest care:
Met in garden bright.
Where the holy light.
10 Had just removd the curtains of the night.

There in rising day.
On the grass they play:
Parents were afar:
Strangers came not near:
15 And the maiden soon forgot her fear.

Tired with kisses sweet
They agree to meet,
When the silent sleep
Waves o'er heavens deep;
20 And the weary tired wanderers weep.

To her father white
Came the maiden bright:
But his loving look,

---

1. In classical myth, the first idyllic era of existence (always spring), analogous to Adam and Eve in unfallen Eden; here imagined in a visionary present by force of "delight" as verb.
2. Ambiguous or double grammar (noun/verb): "beam's delight" / "Youth and maiden . . . delight."

Like the holy book,
25   *All her tender limbs with terror shook.*

Ona! pale and weak!
To thy father speak:
O the trembling fear!
O the dismal care!   hair[3]
30   *That shakes the blossoms of my hoary.*

The School-Boy[1]

I love to rise in a summer morn,
When the birds sing on every tree;
The distant huntsman winds° his horn,   blows
And the sky-lark sings with me.
5   O! what sweet company.

But to go to school in a summer morn
O! it drives all joy away;
Under a cruel eye outworn
The little ones spend the day,
10   In sighing and dismay.

Ah! then at times I drooping sit,
And spend many an anxious hour.
Nor in my book can I take delight,
Nor sit in learnings bower
15   Worn thro' with the dreary shower.

How can the bird that is born for joy,
Sit in a cage and sing,
How can a child when fears annoy,
But droop his tender wing.
20   And forget his youthful spring.

O father & mother, if buds are nip'd,
And blossoms blown away,
And if the tender plants are strip'd
Of their joy in the springing day,
25   By sorrow and cares dismay.

How shall the summer arise in joy.
Or the summer fruits appear   (troy[2]
Or how shall we gather what griefs des
Or bless the mellowing year
30   When the blasts of winter appear.

3. On the right side of Blake's plate, the curve of a tree-trunk design compels him to etch "hair" above the end of line 30.
1. This song was originally placed in *Songs of Innocence*, then transferred to *Songs of Experience*.
2. On Blake's plate, the word *destroy* is broken into its two syllables, with the second one placed on the line above, its connection to the first indicated by a left parenthesis. While this is a printer's device when page space does not allow the whole line to be printed straight out, Blake's plate shows that he might have had plenty of space after "des" had the syllable not met the tree-trunk of his pictorial design; he displays a destruction of the very word.

A DIVINE IMAGE

Cruelty has a Human Heart
And Jealousy a Human Face
Terror, the Human Form Divine
And Secrecy, the Human Dress

5   The Human Dress, is forged in Iron
The Human Form, a fiery Forge.
The Human Face, a Furnace seal'd
The Human Heart, its hungry Gorge.

⚌ PERSPECTIVES ⚌

The Abolition of Slavery
and the Slave Trade

Slavery and the slave trade provoked sharp controversy in the age of Romanticism, and literary writing played a major role in shaping public opinion. From 1783 to 1793 more than 300,000 slaves were sold in the British colonies, at a value of over £15,000,000. A "triangular trade" flourished, whereby British investors financed expeditions to the African Gold Coast to buy or kidnap human cargo, to be shipped (the "Middle Passage") under brutal conditions to New-World markets. About thirteen percent of this cargo died, while the survivors suffered heat, cramped filthy quarters, fettering, physical abuse, and disease. With the profits, which usually exceeded a hundred percent of the initial investment, the ships were filled with exotic colonial goods—tobacco, sugar, molasses, rum, spices, cotton—to be sold in Europe, also at tremendous profits. Moral opposition to this trade, spearheaded by the Quakers and Evangelical Christian sects, was invigorated by Lord Mansfield's ruling in 1772 declaring the absence of any legal basis for slavery in England. Over the 1770s, several abolitionist tracts appeared, and by the end of the decade, bills were introduced in Parliament to regulate the trade. National attention was galvanized by the scandal of the slave ship *Zong* (1781) whose captain ordered 133 weak and diseased slaves ejected into shark-infested waters in order to collect on a policy that held the insurer liable for cargo jettisoned in order to salvage the remainder. Color Plate 5 shows J. M. W. Turner's famous painting of this event.

In the 1780s the Quakers continued to petition Parliament and distribute pamphlets, while other abolitionists wrote tracts challenging the scriptural as well as economic justifications for slavery, and reformed slave-traders published memoirs detailing the horrors of the trade. By the end of the decade, William Wilberforce was heading a Parliamentary investigation and the former slave Olaudah Equiano's *Interesting Narrative* quickly became a best-seller. But the advent of the French Revolution in 1789 increased fear of slave revolts, and Wilberforce's first bill for abolition was defeated in 1791.

Even so, the abolition movement persisted. In 1792 Edmund Burke's *Sketch of a Negro Code* gave a plan for orderly abolition and emancipation, and in 1793 Wilberforce's second bill for abolition at least won in the House of Commons. By the decade's end, the British treasury was reeling under the cost of regulating the trade and defending the plantation owners. The abolition movement achieved its first major success in 1807, when Parliament abolished British slave-trading. Wilberforce's stirring *Letter on the Abolition of the Slave Trade* (1807), praising the moral importance of the event, helped sustain the movement for abolishing slavery itself (still legal in the colonies)—as did Thomas Clarkson's gripping *History of the Abolition of the African Slave-Trade by the British Parliament* (1808), which detailed the horrors of the trade both for the slaves and the seamen. By the 1820s, the movement was benefiting from the increasing involvement of women, who were horrified by the often violent and sexually abusive treatment of female slaves. In 1823 Clarkson and Wilberforce founded the influential *Anti-Slavery Monthly Reporter,* which relentlessly publicized all the horrors, and Parliament seriously addressed the issue, with Foreign Secretary George Canning declaring that "the spirit of the Christian religion is hostile to slavery." The year 1831 was a critical one, marked not only by a massive slave rebellion in Jamaica, with severe reprisals against slaves and sympathetic missionaries, but also by the publication of former slave Mary Prince's autobiography, with searing reports of atrocities, especially to female slaves. The Reform Parliament of 1832 proved hospitable to emancipation, and in 1833 it passed the Emancipation Bill, liberating 800,000 slaves in British colonies and compensating the owners with more than £20,000,000.

It was the plantation-owners and investors in Bristol and Liverpool, enjoying immense profits, who opposed abolition. Supported by their Standing Committee in Parliament, they justified slavery by arguing that Africans had already enslaved each other; that they were mental and moral primitives, animals and heathens, to whom plantation life brought a work ethic, civilized behavior, and the grace of Christian religion; and finally, that British abolition would not end the trade, only leave the profits to other nations. Their literary propaganda tended toward the genre of "romance," pastoral stories with happy endings in which slaves are grateful and masters benevolent. The appeal to social stability was amplified by alarm at the French Revolution, and in 1791 a massive slave revolt in Santo Domingo made it possible to link abolitionism to Jacobinism and to embarrass at least the Evangelical abolitionists, who tended to be critical of the Revolution.

Abolitionists came from differing, often opposed political groups: Tory, Evangelical, Quaker, Unitarian, Dissenter, Nonconformist, radical. Some, such as Anna Barbauld, Mary Wollstonecraft, and Tom Paine, energized abolitionism with commitments to social reform and the new philosophies of "the rights of man" and "the rights of woman." Wordsworth's excoriation of slavery in *The Prelude* Book 10 powerfully sounds this note. But others, including the Parliamentarians Burke and Wilberforce and most Evangelical Christians, were politically conservative, often wealthy; wanting to avoid political arguments, the Evangelicals condemned slavery as a moral blight on a Christian nation and advocated Parliamentary reform. They refuted the planters' claims of kind treatment on slave-ships and plantations, and vividly purveyed what amounts to a pornography of atrocities, even as the moral stress was on common humanity and Christian values. With their own version of African primitivism, their fables evoked sympathy for the slaves' childlike simplicity and the pathos of their destroyed families, their physical tortures and suffering. In these narratives, redemption for the slaves appears not through rebellion, but through the salvational processes of Christian conversion, forbearance, and an appeal to enlightened authority.

Many well-known writers entered the debate, rallying support by using vivid stories to exemplify the broad social and ethical issues involved. The texts that follow show the range of literary resources, and the range of viewpoints, employed by writers who composed poems, essays, and stories as part of the protracted struggle over abolition.

⊷ ⊱⬥⊰ ⊶

Olaudah Equiano
1745–1797

In the parliamentary inquiry into the condition of the slave trade between 1788 and 1789, evidence came almost exclusively from the traders. A very different perspective is seen in *The Interesting Narrative of the Life of Olaudah Equiano, or Gustavus Vassa. The African. Written by Himself*, published in London in 1789. The force of the account drew in part from this claim of authoritative witness to the harrowing experiences of slavery. Equiano presented himself as born to a high-ranking, prosperous, slave-owning family of the Ebo tribe, in the region of modern Nigeria. At age ten, he says, he was stolen from his village by freelance slavers, and served masters in Africa before being shipped first to Barbados and then to North America.

The disorienting effects are reflected in the series of names given by successive owners: on the slave-ship he was "Michael," then renamed "Jacob" by a Virginia plantation owner, and then dubbed "Gustavus Vassa" after the Swedish hero of a recent play when he was purchased by Lieutenant Michael Pascal of the British navy. Pascal took him to England in 1757, and then to Canada where he fought in the Seven Years' War. He was baptized in London in 1759, and worked for the British navy in the Mediterranean as a servant and gunner's mate, eventually rising to the rank of able seaman. In 1762 Pascal broke his promise to free Equiano and sold him to Captain James Doran. In the West Indies he was sold, again, to an American Quaker merchant, Robert King, on whose trading ships he worked. With profits from private trade conducted by his own initiative and entrepreneurial skill, he earned enough from the system he abhorred to purchase his freedom, for £70, in 1766. Subsequent adventures took him to the Caribbean and even to the Arctic (seeking a polar route to India), where a shipmate was young Horatio Nelson, later the hero of the Battle of Trafalgar. At various times, Equiano managed a plantation in Central America, earned a living as a hairdresser in London, and worked for the Sierra Leone project (a planned colony for freed slaves in Africa), until he protested against financial mismanagement and was dismissed.

Once settled in England, he rediscovered Christianity and worked with the Evangelicals, campaigned tirelessly for abolition, and met the founder of the radical working-class London Corresponding Society. His celebrity stemmed from his *Interesting Narrative,* which movingly renders the cruelty of the Middle Passage, the violence of slavery, and the uncertain status of even the free black; at the same time it is a vivid picaresque adventure, a religious conversion narrative, and a testimony to surprising social mobility. In his own time critics in the slave-holder camp challenged the truthfulness of Equiano's claim to an African origin, and recently historian Vincent Carretta has brought forward documents suggesting that Equiano was born in Carolina. Though Carretta's research confirms the accuracy of Equiano's story of his adult life, doubts of historical fact redouble the literary fascination of the *Interesting Narrative.*

"Olaudah Equiano" may be not the narrator's original name but the persona of the writer, crafted under the influence of Evangelicals and radicals to appeal to their audience and promote abolition. His seemingly artless document raises questions of the artifice of autobiography, the intricacies of identity, and the status of the "author" as a fiction cooperatively produced by writer, publisher, and readers. The *Interesting Narrative,* of which Mary Wollstonecraft published the first review, was an immediate sensation, selling five thousand copies the first year, and going through thirty-six editions over the next half century, including numerous editions in the United States and others as far afield as Germany and Russia. Equiano remained a speaker devoted to abolition, and an emblem of the rise from humble beginnings to middle-class success. In 1792 he married an Englishwoman with whom he had two daughters, and he was well enough off at his death, in 1797, to leave his surviving daughter £950 to inherit on her twenty-first birthday in 1816. A story of triumph as well as of oppression, the *Interesting Narrative* has a complexity the more compelling for its apparent transparency. His portrait (Color Plate 4) suggests the complexities of his African-American-British identity.

From **The Interesting Narrative of the Life of Olaudah Equiano**
or *Gustavus Vassa, the African*
[THE SLAVE SHIP AND ITS CARGO]

The first object that saluted my eyes when I arrived on the coast was the sea, and a slave ship, which was then riding at anchor, and waiting for its cargo.[1] These filled me with astonishment, that was soon converted into terror, which I am yet at a loss to describe, and much more the then feelings of my mind when I was carried on board. I was immediately handled and tossed up to see if I was sound, by some of the crew; and I was now persuaded that I had got into a world of bad spirits, and that they were going to kill me. Their complexions too, differing so much from ours, their long hair, and the language they spoke, which was very different from any I had ever heard, united to confirm me in this belief. Indeed such were the horrors of my views and fears at the moment, that if ten thousand worlds had been my own, I would have freely parted with them all to have exchanged my condition with the meanest slave in my own country.

1. Captured by slavers along with his sister, Equiano was soon separated from her and sold to different masters over a period of several months before reaching the African coast for shipment to Barbados.

When I looked round the ship too, and saw a large furnace or copper boiling and a multitude of black people, of every description, chained together, every one of their countenances expressing dejection and sorrow, I no longer doubted of my fate; and, quite overpowered with horror and anguish, I fell motionless on the deck, and fainted. When I recovered a little, I found some black people about me, who I believed were some of those who brought me on board, and had been receiving their pay: they talked to me in order to cheer me, but all in vain. I asked them if we were not to be eaten by those white men with horrible looks, red faces, and long hair. They told me I was not: and one of the crew brought me a small portion of spirituous liquor in a wine glass; but, being afraid of him, I would not take it out of his hand. One of the blacks therefore took it from him and gave it to me, and I took a little down my palate, which, instead of reviving me, as they thought it would, threw me into the greatest consternation at the strange feeling it produced, having never tasted any such liquor before.

Soon after this the blacks who brought me on board went off, and left me abandoned to despair. I now saw myself deprived of all chance of returning to my native country, or even the least glimpse of gaining the shore, which I now considered as friendly; and I even wished for my former slavery, in preference to my present situation, which was filled with horrors of every kind, still heightened by my ignorance of what I was to undergo. I was not long suffered to indulge my grief. I was soon put down under the decks, and there I received such a salutation in my nostrils as I had never experienced in my life: so that, with the loathsomeness of the stench, and with my crying together, I became so sick and low that I was not able to eat, nor had I the least desire to taste any thing. I now wished for the last friend, death, to relieve me; but soon, to my grief, two of the white men offered me eatables; and, on my refusing to eat, one of them held me fast by the hands, and laid me across, I think, the windlass, and tied my feet, while the other flogged me severely. I had never experienced any thing of this kind before, and although, not being used to the water, I naturally feared that element the first time I saw it, yet nevertheless, could I have got over the nettings, I would have jumped over the side, but I could not; and besides the crew used to watch us very closely, who were not chained down to the decks, lest we should leap into the water. I have seen some of these poor African prisoners most severely cut for attempting to do so, and hourly whipped for not eating. This indeed was often the case with myself. In a little time after, amongst the poor chained men, I found some of my own nation, which in a small degree gave ease to my mind. I inquired of these what was to be done with us. They gave me to understand we were to be carried to these white people's country to work for them. I was then a little revived, and thought if it were no worse than working, my situation was not so desperate. But still I feared I should be put to death, the white people looked and acted, as I thought, in so savage a manner; for I had never seen among any people such instances of brutal cruelty: and this is not only shewn towards us blacks, but also to some of the whites themselves. One white man in particular I saw, when we were permitted to be on deck, flogged so unmercifully with a large rope near the foremast, that he died in consequence of it; and they tossed him over the side as they would have done a brute. This made me fear these people the more; and I expected nothing less than to be treated in the same manner. I could not help expressing my fearful apprehensions to some of my countrymen; I asked them if these people had no country, but lived in this hollow place, the ship. They told me they did not, but came from a distant one. "Then," said I, "how comes it, that in all our country we never heard of them?" They told me, because they lived so very far off. I then asked, where their women were: had they any like themselves. I was told they had. "And why," said I, "do we not see them?" They answered, because they were left behind. I asked how the vessel could go. They told me they could not tell; but that there was cloth put upon the masts by the help of the ropes I saw, and then the vessel went on; and the white men had some spell or magic they put in the water, when they liked, in order to stop the vessel. I was exceedingly amazed at this account, and really thought they were spirits. I therefore wished much to be from amongst them, for I expected they would sacrifice me; but my wishes were in vain, for we were so quartered that it was impossible for any of us to make our escape.

[EQUIANO, AGE 12, REACHES ENGLAND]

One morning, when I got upon deck, I perceived it covered over with the snow that fell overnight. As I had never seen any thing of the kind before, I thought it was salt; so I immediately ran down to the mate and desired him, as well as I could, to come and see how somebody in the night had thrown salt all over the deck. He, knowing what it was, desired me to bring some of it down to him; accordingly I took up a handful of it, which I found very cold indeed; and when I brought it to him he desired me to taste it. I did so, and was surprised above measure. I then asked him what it was; he told me it was snow; but I could not by any means understand him. He asked me if we had no such thing in our country; and I told him "No." I then asked him the use of it, and who made it; he told me a great man in the heavens, called God: but here again I was to all intents and purposes at a loss to understand him; and the more so, when a little after I saw the air filled with it, in a heavy shower, which fell down on the same day.

After this I went to church; and having never been at such a place before, I was again amazed at seeing and hearing the service. I asked all I could about it; and they gave me to understand it was "worshiping God, who made us and all things." I was still at a loss, and soon got into an endless field of inquiries, as well as I was able to speak and ask about things. However, my dear little friend Dick[2] used to be my best interpreter; for I could make free with him and he always instructed me with pleasure. And from what I could understand by him of this God, and in seeing that these white people did not sell one another as we did, I was much pleased: and in this I thought they were much happier than we Africans. I was astonished at the wisdom of the white people in all things which I beheld; but I was greatly amazed at their not sacrificing, not making any offerings, and at their eating with unwashen hands, and touching of the dead. I also could not help remarking the particular slenderness of their women, which I did not at first like, and I thought them not so modest and shamefaced as the African women.

I had often seen my master Dick employed in reading; and I had a great curiosity to talk to the books, as I thought they did; and so to learn how all things had a beginning. For that purpose I have often taken up a book and talked to it, and then put my ears to it, when alone, in hopes it would answer me; and I have been very much concerned when I found it remaining silent.

[READING THE BIBLE; FINDING A "FATHER"; SOLD AGAIN INTO SLAVERY]

There was also one Daniel Queen, about forty years of age, a man very well educated, who messed with me on board this ship,[3] and he likewise dressed and attended the captain. Fortunately this man soon became very much attached to me, and took great

---

2. Richard Baker, an American boy four or five years older than Equiano.

3. The *Etna*, of which Pascal had been given command in 1759; messed: ate.

pains to instruct me in many things. He taught me to shave, and dress hair a little, and also to read in the Bible, explaining many passages to me, which I did not comprehend. I was wonderfully surprised to see the laws and rules of my own country written almost exactly here; a circumstance which, I believe, tended to impress our manners and customs more deeply on my memory. I used to tell him of this resemblance, and many a time we have sat up the whole night together at this employment. In short, he was like a father to me; and some used even to call me after his name: they also styled me "the black Christian." Indeed I almost loved him with the affection of a son. Many things I have denied myself, that he might have them; and when I used to play at marbles or any other game, and won a few halfpence, or got some money for shaving any one, I used to buy him a little sugar or tobacco, as far as my stock of money would go. He used to say that he and I never should part, and that when our ship was paid off, as I was free as himself or any other man on board, he would instruct me in his business, by which I might gain a good livelihood. This gave me new life and spirits; and my heart burned within me, while I thought the time long till I obtained my freedom. For though my master had not promised it to me, yet, besides the assurances I had often received that he had no right to detain me,[4] he always treated me with the greatest kindness, and reposed in me an unbounded confidence. He even paid attention to my morals, and would never suffer me to deceive him, or tell lies, of which he used to tell me the consequences; and that if I did so, God would not love me. So that from all this tenderness I had never once supposed, in all my dreams of freedom, that he would think of detaining me any longer than I wished.

In pursuance of our orders we sailed from Portsmouth for the Thames, and arrived at Deptford the 10th of December, where we cast anchor just as it was high water. The ship was up about half an hour, when my master ordered the barge to be manned; and, all in an instant, without having before given me the least reason to suspect any thing of the matter, he forced me into the barge, saying, I was going to leave him, but he would take care that I did not. I was so struck with the unexpectedness of this proceeding, that for some time I did not make a reply, only I made an offer to go for my books and chest of clothes, but he swore I should not move out of his sight; and if I did, he would cut my throat, at the same time taking out his hanger.[5] I told him that I was free, and he could not by law serve me so. But this only enraged him the more; and he continued to swear, and said he would soon let me know whether he would or not, and at that instant sprung himself into the barge, from the ship, to the astonishment and sorrow of all on board.

The tide, rather unluckily for me, had just turned downward, so that we quickly fell down the river along with it, till we came among some outwardbound West Indiamen; for he was resolved to put me on board the first vessel he could get to receive me. The boat's crew, who pulled against their will, became quite faint at different times, and would have gone ashore, but he would not let them. Some of them strove then to cheer me, and told me he could not sell me, and that they would stand by me, which revived me a little, and I still entertained hopes; for as they pulled me along he asked some vessels to receive me, and they refused.

But, just as we had got a little below Gravesend, we came alongside of a ship going away the next tide for the West-Indies; her name was the Charming Sally, Captain James Doran. My master went on board and agreed with him for me; and in little

---

4. Even before the Mansfield Decision of 1772, contemporary opinion held that Royal Navy ships were British territory, on which slavery was inappropriate.
5. Short sword.

time I was sent for into the cabin. When I came there Captain Doran asked me if I knew him; I answered I did not: "Then," said he, "you are now my slave." I told him my master could not sell me to him nor to any one else. "Why," said he, "did not your master buy you?" I confessed he did. "But I have served him," said I, "many years, and he has taken all my wages and prize-money,[6] for I only got one sixpence during the war. Besides this I have been baptized; and, by the laws of the land, no man has a right to sell me." And I added, that I had heard a lawyer, and others, at different times tell my master so. They both then said, that those people who told me so, were not my friends: but I replied—it was very extraordinary that other people did not know the law as well as they. Upon this, Captain Doran said I talked too much English, and if I did not behave myself well and be quiet, he had a method on board to make me. I was too well convinced of his power over me to doubt what he said; and my former sufferings in the slave-ship presenting themselves to my mind, the recollection of them made me shudder. However, before I retired I told them, that as I could not get any right among men here, I hoped I should hereafter in Heaven, and I immediately left the cabin, filled with resentment and sorrow.

The only coat I had with me my master took away with him, and said, "if your prize-money had been £10,000, I had a right to it all, and would have taken it." I had about nine guineas, which, during my long sea-faring life, I had scraped together from trifling perquisites and little ventures; and I hid it that instant, lest my master should take that from me likewise, still hoping that, by some means or other, I should make my escape to the shore. Indeed some of my old shipmates told me not to despair, for they would get me back again; and that, as soon as they could get their pay, they would immediately come to Portsmouth to me, where this ship was going. But, alas, all my hopes were baffled, and the hour of my deliverance was, as yet, far off. My master, having soon concluded his bargain with the captain, came out of the cabin, and he and his people got into the boat and put off. I followed them with aching eyes as long as I could, and when they were out of sight I threw myself on the deck, with a heart ready to burst with sorrow and anguish.

[EMPLOYMENT IN THE WEST INDIES]

I had the good fortune to please my master[7] in every department in which he employed me; and there was scarcely any part of his business, or household affairs, in which I was not occasionally engaged. I often supplied the place of a clerk, in receiving and delivering cargoes to the ships, in tending stores, and delivering goods; and, besides this, I used to shave and dress my master, when convenient, and take care of his horse; and when it was necessary, which was very often, I worked likewise on board of his different vessels. By these means I became very useful to my master, and saved him, as he used to acknowledge, above a hundred pounds a year. Nor did he scruple to say I was of more advantage to him than any of his clerks; tho' their usual wages in the West-Indies are from sixty to a hundred pounds current a year.

I have sometimes heard it asserted that a negro cannot earn his master the first cost; but nothing can be further from the truth. I suppose nine tenths of the mechanics throughout the West-Indies are negro slaves; and I well know the coopers[8] among them earn two dollars a-day; the carpenters the same, and oftentimes more; also the

6. Profits from an enemy ship and its cargo seized during war, traditionally shared among the victorious crew.
7. In 1763 Equiano was sold to Robert King, a Quaker merchant, and thereafter served in the West Indies in one of his ships under Captain Thomas Farmer.
8. Barrel-makers.

masons, smiths, and fishermen, &c. and I have known many slaves whose masters would not take a thousand pounds current for them. But surely this assertion refutes itself: for, if it be true, why do the planters and merchants pay such a price for slaves? And, above all, why do those, who make this assertion, exclaim the most loudly against the abolition of the slave trade? So much are men blinded, and to such inconsistent arguments are they driven by mistaken interest! I grant, indeed, that slaves are sometimes, by half-feeding, half-clothing, over-working, and stripes,[9] reduced so low, that they are turned out as unfit for service, and left to perish in the woods, or to expire on a dunghill.

My master was several times offered by different gentlemen one hundred guineas[1] for me; but he always told them he would not sell me, to my great joy: and I used to double my diligence and care for fear of getting into the hands of these men, who did not allow a valuable slave the common support of life. Many of them used to find fault with my master for feeding his slaves so well as he did; although I often went hungry, and an Englishman might think my fare very indifferent: but he used to tell them he always would do it, because the slaves thereby looked better and did more work.

While I was thus employed by my master, I was often a witness to cruelties of every kind, which were exercised on my unhappy fellowslaves. I used frequently to have different cargoes of new negroes in my care for sale; and it was almost a constant practice with our clerks, and other whites, to commit violent depredations on the chastity of the female slaves; and to these atrocities I was, though with reluctance, obliged to submit at all times, being unable to help them. When we have had some of these slaves on board my master's vessels to carry them to other islands, or to America, I have known our mates commit these acts most shamefully, to the disgrace not of christians only, but of men. I have even known them gratify their brutal passion with females not ten years old; and these abominations some of them practised to such a scandalous excess, that one of our captains discharged the mate and others on that account. And yet in Montserrat[2] I have seen a negro-man staked to the ground, and cut most shockingly, and then his ears cut off, bit by bit, because he had been connected with a white woman, who was a common prostitute! As if it were no crime in the whites to rob an innocent African girl of her virtue; but most heinous in a black man only to gratify a passion of nature, where the temptation was offered by one of a different colour, though the most abandoned woman of her species.

[The Perils of Being a Freeman]

I have since often seen in Jamaica and other islands, free men, whom I have known in America, thus villainously trepanned[3] and kept in bondage. I have heard of two similar practices even in Philadelphia: and were it not for the benevolence of the Quakers in that city, many of the sable race, who now breathe the air of liberty, would, I believe, be groaning under some planter's chains. These things opened my mind to a new scene of horror, to which I had been before a stranger. Hitherto I had thought only slavery dreadful; but the state of a free negro appeared to me now equally so at least, and in some respects even worse; for they live in constant alarm

---

9. Lashings and the welts they leave.
1. The guinea coin, first struck in 1663 by a company of merchants chartered by the British crown to obtain slaves from the Guinea coast of Africa (hence the name), was worth 21 shillings; made of gold, it often traded for more than its face value and connoted a certain prestige.
2. Island in the British West Indies.
3. Betrayed.

for their liberty, which is but nominal; and they are universally insulted and plundered without the possibility of redress; such being the equity of the West-Indian laws, that no free negro's evidence will be admitted in their courts of justice. * * *

I determined to make every exertion to obtain my freedom, and to return to Old England. For this purpose I thought a knowledge of Navigation might be of use to me; for, though I did not intend to run away unless I should be ill used, yet, in such a case, if I understood navigation, I might attempt my escape in our sloop, which was one of the swiftest sailing vessels in the West-Indies, and I could be at no loss for hands to join me. Had I made this attempt, I had intended to go in her to England; but this, as I said, was only to be in the event of my meeting with any ill usage. I therefore employed the mate of our vessel to teach me Navigation, for which I agreed to give him twenty-four dollars, and actually paid him part of the money down; though when the captain, some time after, came to know that the mate was to have such a sum for teaching me, he rebuked him, and said it was a shame for him to take any money from me. However, my progress in this useful art was much retarded by the constancy of our work.

Had I wished to run away I did not want opportunities, which frequently presented themselves; and particularly at one time, soon after this. When we were at the island of Guadaloupe there was a large fleet of merchantmen bound for Old France; and seamen then being very scarce, they gave from fifteen to twenty pounds a man for the run. Our mate and all the white sailors left our vessel on this account, and went aboard of the French ships. They would have had me also to go with them, for they regarded me, and swore to protect me, if I would go: and, as the fleet was to sail the next day, I really believe I could have got safe to Europe at that time. However, as my master was kind, I would not attempt to leave him; still remembering the old maxim, that *honesty is the best policy*, I suffered them to go without me. Indeed my captain was much afraid of my leaving him and the vessel at that time, as I had so fair an opportunity: but, I thank God, this fidelity of mine turned out much to my advantage hereafter, when I did not in the least think of it; and made me so much in favour with the captain, that he used now and then to teach me some parts of Navigation himself. But some of our passengers, and others, seeing this, found much fault with him for it, saying it was a very dangerous thing to let a negro know Navigation; and thus I was hindered again in my pursuits.

[MANUMISSION]

When we had unladen the vessel, and I had sold my venture,[4] finding myself master of about forty-seven pounds, I consulted my true friend, the Captain, how I should proceed in offering my master the money for my freedom. He told me to come on a certain morning, when he and my master would be at breakfast together. Accordingly, on that morning I went, and met the Captain there, as he had appointed. When I went in I made my obeisance to my master, and with my money in my hand, and many fears in my heart, I prayed him to be as good as his offer to me, when he was pleased to promise me my freedom as soon as I could purchase it. This speech seemed to confound him; he began to recoil; and my heart that instant sunk within me. "What," said he, "give you your freedom? Why, where did you get the money? Have you got forty pounds sterling?" "Yes, sir," I answered. "How did you get it?" replied he. I told him, "very honestly." The Captain then said he knew I got the

---

4. The stock he was permitted to trade for himself.

money very honestly and with much industry, and that I was particularly careful. On which my master replied, I got money much faster than he did; and said he would not have made me the promise which he did, had he thought I should have got the money so soon. "Come, come," said my worthy Captain, clapping my master on the back, "Come, Robert, (which was his name[5]) I think you must let him have his freedom. You have laid your money out very well; you have received good interest for it all this time, and here is now the principal at last. I know GUSTAVUS has earned you more than a hundred a year, and he will still save you money, as he will not leave you. Come, Robert, take the money." My master then said, he would not be worse than his promise; and, taking the money, told me to go to the Secretary at the Register Office, and get my manumission[6] drawn up.

These words of my master were like a voice from heaven to me: in an instant all my trepidation was turned into unutterable bliss, and I most reverently bowed myself with gratitude, unable to express my feelings, but by the overflowing of my eyes, and a heart replete with thanks to God; while my true and worthy friend, the Captain, congratulated us both with a peculiar degree of heartfelt pleasure. As soon as the first transports of my joy were over, and that I had expressed my thanks to these my worthy friends in the best manner I was able, I rose with a heart full of affection and reverence, and left the room, in order to obey my master's joyful mandate of going to the Register Office. As I was leaving the house I called to mind the words of the Psalmist, in the 126th Psalm, and like him, "I glorified God in my heart, in whom I trusted."[7] These words had been impressed on my mind from the very day I was forced from Deptford[8] to the present hour, and I now saw them, as I thought, fulfilled and verified.

My imagination was all rapture as I flew to the Register Office; and in this respect, like the apostle Peter (whose deliverance from prison was so sudden and extraordinary, that he thought he was in a vision)[9] I could scarcely believe I was awake. Heavens! who could do justice to my feelings at this moment? Not conquering heroes themselves, in the midst of a triumph—Not the tender mother who has just regained her long-lost infant, and presses it to her heart—Not the weary, hungry mariner, at the sight of the desired friendly port—Not the lover, when he once more embraces his beloved mistress, after she has been ravished from his arms!—All within my breast was tumult, wildness, and delirium! My feet scarcely touched the ground; for they were winged with joy, and, like Elijah, as he rose to Heaven, they "were with lightning sped as I went on."[1] Every one I met I told of my happiness, and blazed about the virtue of my amiable master and Captain. * * *

In short, the fair as well as black people immediately styled me by a new appellation,—to me the most desirable in the world,—which was "Freeman," and, at the dances I gave, my Georgia superfine blue clothes made no indifferent appearance, as I thought. Some of the sable females, who formerly stood aloof, now began to relax and appear less coy; but my heart was still fixed on London, where I hoped to be ere long. So that my worthy Captain, and his owner, my late master, finding that the bent of my mind was towards London, said to me, "We hope you won't leave us, but

5. Robert King; see n. 7, page 84.
6. The formal liberation of a slave.
7. Psalm 126 celebrates release from captivity; the phrase Equiano quotes does not appear there, though it echoes several other psalms (28, 33, 86, 125).

8. See excerpt on pp. 100–101.
9. Acts 12.9 [Equiano's note].
1. In 2 Kings (2.11), Elijah has a vision of a chariot of fire and is carried to Heaven in a whirlwind.

that you will still be with the vessels." Here gratitude bowed me down; and none but the generous mind can judge of my feelings, struggling between inclination and duty. However, notwithstanding my wish to be in London, I obediently answered my benefactors that I would go in the vessel, and not leave them; and from that day I was entered on board as an able-bodied seaman, at thirty-six shillings per month, besides what perquisites I could make.[2] My intention was to make a voyage or two, entirely to please these my honoured patrons; but I determined that the year following, if it pleased God, I would see Old England once more, and surprise my old master, Captain Pascal, who was hourly in my mind: for I still loved him, notwithstanding his usage to me, and I pleased myself with thinking of what he would say when he saw what the Lord had done for me in so short a time, instead of being, as he might perhaps suppose, under the cruel yoke of some planter.

Mary Prince
c. 1788–after 1833

The History of Mary Prince, a West Indian Slave, Related by Herself is the earliest known slave narrative by a woman. Sponsored by the Anti-Slavery Society to galvanize support for abolition, especially from Britain's women, its saga of overwork, abuse, and sexual violence was chronicled in unprecedented depth and detail. Mary Prince's *History* was a sensation, reaching a third edition the year it was published, 1831.

Prince was born a slave on a farm in Bermuda, a British colony whose major industries were shipbuilding and salting, and whose population was half slave. In her childhood, she was treated with relative kindness, but at age twelve, she was sold to sadistic, sexually abusive new owners. After several years of brutality, she was sold to an even more ghastly situation in the "cruel, horrible" salt ponds of Turks Island, about 200 miles northeast of Bermuda, where her labor left her legs covered with boils and eventually crippled her with rheumatism. Perpetually beaten, and sexually assaulted by an "indecent master," she requested to be sold to a merchant from Antigua, who was impressed by her reputation as a good worker. Overworked and exhausted, she began to rebel, and suffered imprisonment and repeated beatings and floggings. With the help of abolitionists, she escaped from her owners, when they took her to London in 1827. Thomas Pringle, a Methodist and secretary of the Anti-Slavery Society, employed her as a domestic servant. He also edited her *History* as publicity for the movement; it sparked a national controversy when attacked in *Blackwood's Edinburgh Magazine* and *The Glasgow Courier* as fraudulent propaganda by a loose-moraled liar. Libel suits erupted, Prince's owner suing Pringle, and Pringle suing *Blackwood's. Blackwood's* declined to cross-examine her, letting her statement stand, but Pringle lost the other case because he couldn't produce witnesses from the West Indies to substantiate the allegations of *The History.* Even so, *The History* commanded wide readership, influencing the cause not only in its representation of general atrocities, but also in its image of Prince's individual resilience and determination. "All slaves want to be free," she declared in the final paragraph; "to be free is very sweet. . . . I can tell by myself what other slaves feel, and by what they have told me. The man that says slaves be quite happy in slavery—that they don't want to be free—that man is either ignorant or a lying person. I never heard a slave say so."

---

2. Equiano has the right to trade for himself and to receive tips.

from The History of Mary Prince, a West Indian Slave
Related by Herself

It was night when I reached my new home. The house was large, and built at the bottom of a very high hill; but I could not see much of it that night. I saw too much of it afterwards. The stones and the timber were the best things in it; they were not so hard as the hearts of the owners.[1]

Before I entered the house, two slave women, hired from another owner, who were at work in the yard, spoke to me, and asked who I belonged to? I replied, "I am come to live here." "Poor child, poor child!" they both said; "you must keep a good heart, if you are to live here."—When I went in, I stood up crying in a corner. Mrs. I——came and took off my hat, a little black silk hat Miss Pruden[2] made for me, and said in a rough voice, "You are not come here to stand up in corners and cry, you are come here to work." She then put a child into my arms, and, tired as I was, I was forced instantly to take up my old occupation of a nurse.—I could not bear to look at my mistress, her countenance was so stern. She was a stout tall woman with a very dark complexion, and her brows were always drawn together into a frown. I thought of the words of the two slave women when I saw Mrs. I——, and heard the harsh sound of her voice.

The person I took the most notice of that night was a French Black called Hetty, whom my master took in privateering[3] from another vessel, and made his slave. She was the most active woman I ever saw, and she was tasked to her utmost. A few minutes after my arrival she came in from milking the cows, and put the sweet-potatoes on for supper. She then fetched home the sheep, and penned them in the fold; drove home the cattle, and staked them about the pond side;[4] fed and rubbed down my master's horse, and gave the hog and the fed cow[5] their suppers; prepared the beds, and undressed the children, and laid them to sleep. I liked to look at her and watch all her doings, for hers was the only friendly face I had as yet seen, and I felt glad that she was there. She gave me my supper of potatoes and milk, and a blanket to sleep upon, which she spread for me in the passage before the door of Mrs. I——'s chamber.

I got a sad fright, that night. I was just going to sleep, when I heard a noise in my mistress's room; and she presently called out to inquire if some work was finished that she had ordered Hetty to do. "No, Ma'am, not yet," was Hetty's answer from below. On hearing this, my master started up from his bed, and just as he was, in his shirt, ran down stairs with a long cow-skin in his hand.[6] I heard immediately after, the cracking of the thong, and the house rang to the shrieks of poor Hetty, who kept crying out, "Oh, Massa! Massa! me dead. Massa! have mercy upon me—don't kill me outright."—This was a sad beginning for me. I sat up upon my blanket, trembling with terror, like a frightened hound, and thinking that my turn would come next. At length the house became still, and I forgot for a little while all my sorrows by falling fast asleep.

The next morning my mistress set about instructing me in my tasks. She taught me to do all sorts of household work; to wash and bake, pick cotton and wool, and wash floors, and cook. And she taught me (how can I ever forget it!) more things

---

1. These strong expressions, and all of a similar character in this little narrative, are given verbatim as uttered by Mary Prince [Thomas Pringle's note].
2. Prince's first owner, Mrs. Williams, had fallen on hard times and hired her out at age 12 to Mrs. Pruden; with Mrs. Williams's death, she was sold to "Captain I—."
3. Sanctioned raiding of enemy ships by armed private vessels.
4. The cattle on a small plantation in Bermuda are, it seems, often thus staked or tethered, both night and day, in situations where grass abounds [Pringle's note].
5. A cow fed for slaughter [Pringle's note].
6. A thong of hard twisted hide, known by this name in the West Indies [Pringle's note].

than these; she caused me to know the exact difference between the smart of the rope, the cart-whip, and the cow-skin, when applied to my naked body by her own cruel hand. And there was scarcely any punishment more dreadful than the blows I received on my face and head from her hard heavy fist. She was a fearful woman, and a savage mistress to her slaves.

There were two little slave boys in the house, on whom she vented her bad temper in a special manner. One of these children was a mulatto,[7] called Cyrus, who had been bought while an infant in his mother's arms; the other, Jack, was an African from the coast of Guinea, whom a sailor had given or sold to my master. Seldom a day passed without these boys receiving the most severe treatment, and often for no fault at all. Both my master and mistress seemed to think that they had a right to ill-use them at their pleasure; and very often accompanied their commands with blows, whether the children were behaving well or ill. I have seen their flesh ragged and raw with licks.— Lick—lick—they were never secure one moment from a blow, and their lives were passed in continual fear. My mistress was not contented with using the whip, but often pinched their cheeks and arms in the most cruel manner. My pity for these poor boys was soon transferred to myself; for I was licked, and flogged, and pinched by her pitiless fingers in the neck and arms, exactly as they were. To strip me naked—to hang me up by the wrists and lay my flesh open with the cow-skin, was an ordinary punishment for even a slight offence. My mistress often robbed me too of the hours that belong to sleep. She used to sit up very late, frequently even until morning; and I had then to stand at a bench and wash during the greater part of the night, or pick wool and cotton; and often I have dropped down overcome by sleep and fatigue, till roused from a state of stupor by the whip, and forced to start up to my tasks.

Poor Hetty, my fellow slave, was very kind to me, and I used to call her my Aunt; but she led a most miserable life, and her death was hastened (at least the slaves all believed and said so), by the dreadful chastisement she received from my master during her pregnancy. It happened as follows. One of the cows had dragged the rope away from the stake to which Hetty had fastened it, and got loose. My master flew into a terrible passion, and ordered the poor creature to be stripped quite naked, notwithstanding her pregnancy, and to be tied up to a tree in the yard. He then flogged her as hard as he could lick, both with the whip and cow-skin, till she was all over streaming with blood. He rested, and then beat her again and again. Her shrieks were terrible. The consequence was that poor Hetty was brought to bed before her time, and was delivered after severe labour of a dead child. She appeared to recover after her confinement, so far she was repeatedly flogged by both master and mistress afterwards; but her former strength never returned to her. Ere long her body and limbs swelled to a great size; and she lay on a mat in the kitchen, till the water burst out of her body and she died. All the slaves said that death was a good thing for poor Hetty; but I cried very much for her death. The manner of it filled me with horror. I could not bear to think about it; yet it was always present to my mind for many a day.

After Hetty died all her labours fell upon me, in addition to my own. I had now to milk eleven cows every morning before sunrise, sitting among the damp weeds; to take care of the cattle as well as the children; and to do the work of the house. There was no end to my toils—no end to my blows. I lay down at night and rose up in the morning in

---

7. A person of mixed African and Caucasian descent, frequently the issue of rape.

fear and sorrow; and often wished that like poor Hetty I could escape from this cruel bondage and be at rest in the grave. But the hand of God whom then I knew not, was stretched over me; and I was mercifully preserved for better things. It was then, however, my heavy lot to weep, weep, weep, and that for years; to pass from one misery to another, and from one cruel master to a worse. But I must go on with the thread of my story.

One day a heavy squall of wind and rain came on suddenly, and my mistress sent me round the corner of the house to empty a large earthen jar. The jar was already cracked with an old deep crack that divided it in the middle, and in turning it upside down to empty it, it parted in my hand. I could not help the accident, but I was dreadfully frightened, looking forward to a severe punishment. I ran crying to my mistress, "O mistress, the jar has come in two." "You have broken it, have you?" she replied; "come directly here to me." I came trembling; she stripped and flogged me long and severely with the cow-skin; as long as she had strength to use the lash, for she did not give over till she was quite tired.—When my master came home at night, she told him of my fault; and oh, frightful! how he fell a swearing. After abusing me with every ill name he could think of, (too, too bad to speak in England,) and giving me several heavy blows with his hand, he said, "I shall come home to-morrow morning at twelve, on purpose to give you a round hundred." He kept his word—Oh sad for me! I cannot easily forget it. He tied me up upon a ladder, and gave me a hundred lashes with his own hand, and master Benjy[8] stood by to count them for him. When he had licked me for some time he sat down to take breath; then after resting, he beat me again and again, until he was quite wearied, and so hot (for the weather was very sultry), that he sank back in his chair, almost like to faint. While my mistress went to bring him drink, there was a dreadful earthquake.[9] Part of the roof fell down, and every thing in the house went—clatter, clatter, clatter. Oh I thought the end of all things near at hand; and I was so sore with the flogging, that I scarcely cared whether I lived or died. The earth was groaning and shaking; every thing tumbling about; and my mistress and the slaves were shrieking and crying out, "The earthquake! the earthquake!" It was an awful day for us all. * * *

Some little time after this, one of the cows got loose from the stake, and eat one of the sweet-potatoe slips.[1] I was milking when my master found it out. He came to me, and without any more ado, stooped down, and taking off his heavy boot, he struck me such a severe blow in the small of my back, that I shrieked with agony, and thought I was killed; and I feel a weakness in that part to this day. The cow was frightened at his violence, and kicked down the pail and spilt the milk all about. My master knew that this accident was his own fault, but he was so enraged that he seemed glad of an excuse to go on with his ill usage. I cannot remember how many licks he gave me then, but he beat me till I was unable to stand, and till he himself was weary.

After this I ran away and went to my mother, who was living with Mr. Richard Darrel.[2] My poor mother was both grieved and glad to see me; grieved because I had been so ill used, and glad because she had not seen me for a long, long while. She dared not receive me into the house, but she hid me up in a hole in the rocks near, and brought me food at night, after every body was asleep. My father, who lived at Crow-Lane, over the salt-water channel, at last heard of my being hid up in the

8. Captain I——'s son, about Prince's age.
9. An earthquake shook Bermuda on 19 February 1801.
1. A cutting, rooted and planted.

2. Captain Darrell had purchased Prince and her mother, and then gave Prince to his daughter-in-law, Mrs. Williams.

cavern, and he came and took me back to my master. Oh I was loth, loth to go back; but as there was no remedy, I was obliged to submit.

When we got home, my poor father said to Cap. I——, "Sir, I am sorry that my child should be forced to run away from her owner; but the treatment she has received is enough to break her heart. The sight of her wounds has nearly broke mine.—I entreat you, for the love of God, to forgive her for running away, and that you will be a kind master to her in future." Capt. I——said I was used as well as I deserved, and that I ought to be punished for running away. I then took courage and said that I could stand the floggings no longer; that I was weary of my life, and therefore I had run away to my mother; but mothers could only weep and mourn over their children, they could not save them from cruel masters—from the whip, the rope, and the cow-skin. He told me to hold my tongue and go about my work, or he would find a way to settle me. He did not, however, flog me that day. * * *

For five years after this I remained in his house, and almost daily received the same harsh treatment. At length he put me on a sloop, and to my great joy sent me away to Turk's Island. I was not permitted to see my mother or father, or poor sisters and brothers, to say good bye, though going away to a strange land, and might never see them again. Oh the Buckra [white] people who keep slaves think that black people are like cattle, without natural affection. But my heart tells me it is far otherwise. * * *

My new master was one of the owners or holders of the salt ponds, and he received a certain sum for every slave that worked upon his premises, whether they were young or old. This sum was allowed him out of the profits arising from the salt works. I was immediately sent to work in the salt water with the rest of the slaves. The work was perfectly new to me. I was given a half barrel and a shovel, and had to stand up to my knees in the water from four o'clock in the morning till nine, when we were given some Indian corn boiled in water, which we were obliged to swallow as fast as we could for fear the rain should come on and melt the salt. We were then called again to our tasks, and worked through the heat of the day; the sun flaming upon our heads like fire, and raising salt blisters in those parts which were not completely covered. Our feet and legs, from standing in the salt water for so many hours, soon became full of dreadful boils, which eat down in some cases to the very bone, afflicting the sufferers with great torment. We came home at twelve; ate our corn soup, called *blawly*, as fast as we could, and went back to our employment till dark at night. We then shovelled up the salt in large heaps, and went down to the sea, where we washed the pickle from our limbs, and cleaned the barrows and shovels from the salt. When we returned to the house, our master gave us each our allowance of raw Indian corn, which we pounded in a mortar and boiled in water for our suppers.

We slept in a long shed, divided into narrow slips, like the stalls used for cattle. Boards fixed upon stakes driven into the ground, without mat or covering, were our only beds. On Sundays, after we had washed the salt bags, and done other work required of us, we went into the bush and cut the long soft grass, of which we made trusses for our legs and feet to rest upon, for they were so full of the salt boils that we could get no rest lying upon the bare boards.

Though we worked from morning till night, there was no satisfying Mr. D——. I hoped, when I left Capt. I——, that I should have been better off, but I found it was but going from one butcher to another. There was this difference between them: my former master used to beat me while raging and foaming with passion; Mr. D——was usually quite calm. He would stand by and give orders for a slave to be cruelly whipped, and assist in the punishment, without moving a muscle of his face, walking about and taking snuff with the greatest composure. Nothing could touch his hard heart—neither sighs, nor tears, nor prayers, nor streaming blood: he was deaf to our cries, and careless of our sufferings.—Mr. D——has often stripped me naked, hung me up by the wrists, and beat me with the cow-skin with his own hand, till my body was raw with gashes. Yet there was nothing very remarkable in this; for it might serve as a sample of the common usage of slaves on that horrible island.

Thomas Bellamy
1745–1800

Thomas Bellamy had various careers, as a hosier, a bookseller's clerk, a magazine publisher, a writer, and a proprietor of a circulating library. In 1789 he wrote *The Benevolent Planters* in support of the anti-emancipation West Indian lobby. Staged at the Theatre Royal, Haymarket, with some of the leading actors of the day, his playlet presents a world of kindly paternal masters whose slaves proclaim their happiness and gratitude.

The Benevolent Planters
A Dramatic Piece

Scene, Jamaica

Characters

Planters: GOODWIN, STEADY, HEARTFREE
Slaves: ORAN, SELIMA
Archers, &c. &c.

Prologue (By a Friend)[1]

AN AFRICAN SAILOR:
      To Afric's torrid clime, where every day
      The sun oppresses with his scorching ray,
      My birth I owe; and here for many a year,
      I tasted pleasure free from every care.
5   There 'twas my happy fortune long to prove
      The fond endearments of parental love.
      'Twas there my Adela, my favourite maid,
      Return'd my passion, love with love repaid.
      Oft on the banks where golden rivers flow,
10   And aromatic woods enchanting grow,
      With my lov'd Adela I pass'd the day,

1. Spoken by Stephen George Kemble, a leading tragic actor, as "An African Sailor." In the play Kemble performed Oran, whose beloved, Selima, was performed by his wife. The anti–slave trade, pro-liberty prologue is not disputed by the playlet, which instead presents a humane, anti-emancipation image of plantation life.

While suns on suns roll'd unperceiv'd away.
But ah! this happiness was not to last,
Clouds now the brightness of my fate o'ercast;
15   For the white savage fierce upon me sprung,
Wrath in his eye, and fury on his tongue,
And dragg'd me to a loathsome vessel near,
Dragg'd me from every thing I held most dear,
And plung'd me in the horrors of despair.
20   Insensible to all that pass'd around,
Till, in a foreign clime, myself I found,
And sold to slavery!—There with constant toil,
Condemn'd in burning suns to turn the soil.
Oh! if I told you what I suffer'd there,
25   From cruel masters, and the lash severe,
Eyes most unus'd to melt, would drop the tear.
But fortune soon a kinder master gave,
Who made me soon forget I was a slave,
And brought me to this land, this generous land,°   *Jamaica*
30   Where, they inform me, that an hallow'd band,
Impelled by soft humanity's kind laws,
Take up with fervent zeal the Negroe's cause,
And at this very moment, anxious try,
To stop the widespread woes of slavery.
35   But of this hallow'd band a part appears,
Exult my heart, and flow my grateful tears.
Oh sons of mercy! whose extensive mind
Takes in at once the whole of human kind,
Who know the various nations of the earth,
40   To whatsoever clime they owe their birth,
Or of whatever colour they appear,
All children of one gracious Parent are.
And thus united by paternal love,
To all mankind, of all the friend you prove.
45   With fervent zeal pursue your godlike plan,
And man deliver from the tyrant man!
What tho' at first you miss the wish'd-for end,
Success at last your labours will attend.
Then shall your worth, extoll'd in grateful strains,
50   Resound through Gambia's and Angola's plains.[2]
Nations unborn your righteous zeal shall bless,
To them the source of peace and happiness.
Oh mighty Kannoah, thou most holy power,
Whom humbly we thy sable race adore!
55   Prosper the great design—thy children free
From the oppressor's hand, and give them liberty!

---

2. Gambia: northwest African country, with a strong British colonial presence; Angola: Portuguese colony on the south-west coast.

Scene 1

A Room in Goodwin's House; Enter Goodwin, meeting Steady and Heartfree.

GOODWIN: Good morrow, neighbours, friend Steady,[3] is your jetty tribe ready for the diversions?

STEADY: My tribe is prepared and ready to meet thine, and my heart exults on beholding so many happy countenances. But an added joy is come home to my bosom. This English friend, who, some time since, came to settle among us, in order that he might exhibit to his brother Planters, the happy effects of humanity, in the treatment of those who, in the course of human chance, are destined to the bonds of slavery, has honoured my dwelling with his presence, and gladdened my heart with his friendship.

HEARTFREE: A cause like the present, makes brothers of us all, and may heaven increase the brothers of humanity—Friend Steady informs me, that we are to preside as directors of the different diversions.

GOODWIN: It is our wish to prevent a repetition of disorders, that last year disturbed the general happiness. They were occasioned by the admission of one of those games, which, but too often, begin in sport, and end in passion. The offenders, however, were soon made sensible of the folly of attacking each other without provocation, and with no other view than to shew their superior skill, in an art, which white men have introduced among them.[4]

HEARTFREE: If that art was only made use of as a defence against the attacks of an unprincipled and vulgar violence, no man could with propriety form a wish of checking its progress. But while it opens another field where the gambler fills his pocket at the expence of the credulous and unsuspecting, whose families too often mourn in poverty and distress the effects of their folly; every member of society will hold up his hand against it, if his heart feels as it ought. I am sorry likewise to add, that too many recent instances of its fatal effects among my own countrymen, have convinced me of the guilt and folly of venturing *a life* to display *a skill*.

GOODWIN: We are happy to find our union strengthened by corresponding sentiments.

HEARTFREE: The sports, I find, are to continue six days; repeat your design, respecting the successful archers.

STEADY: The archers, friend, to the number of twelve, consist of selected slaves, whose honest industry and attachment have rendered them deserving of reward. They are to advance in pairs, and the youth who speeds the arrow surest, is to be proclaimed victor.

HEARTFREE: And what is his reward?

STEADY: A portion of land for himself, and his posterity—freedom for his life, and the maiden of his heart.

HEARTFREE: Generous men! humanity confers dignity upon authority. The grateful Africans have hearts as large as ours, and shame on the degrading lash, when it can be spared—Reasonable obedience is what we expect, and let those who look for more, feel and severely feel the sting of disappointment.

STEADY: Will your poor fellow attend the festival?

HEARTFREE: He will. I respect your feelings for the sorrows of the worthy Oran.

---

3. "Friend" evokes the Quaker term of address; Bellamy may be suggesting that not all Quakers were adamant abolitionists.

4. Perhaps boxing or dueling.

GOODWIN: Oran, did you say? What know you of him; pardon my abruptness, but relate his story, it may prove a task of pleasure.

HEARTFREE: By the fate of war,[5] Oran had been torn from his beloved Selima. The conquerors were on the point of setting fire to the consuming pile to which he was bound, while the partner of his heart, who was devoted[6] to the arms of the chief of the adverse party, was rending the air with her cries; at this instant a troop of Europeans broke in upon them, and bore away a considerable party to their ships; among the rest was the rescued Oran, who was happily brought to our mart, where I had the good fortune to become his master—he has since served me well and affectionately. But sorrow for his Selima is so deeply rooted in his feeling bosom, that I fear I shall soon lose an excellent domestic and as valuable a friend, whose only consolation springs from a sense of dying in the possession of Christian principles, from whence he acknowledges to have drawn comforts inexpressible.

GOODWIN: And comfort he shall still draw from a worldly as well as a heavenly source. For know, I can produce the Selima he mourns. She has told me her story, which is indeed a tale of woe. Inward grief has preyed upon her mind, and like her faithful Oran, she is bending to her grave. But happiness, love, and liberty shall again restore them.

HEARTFREE: When the mind has made itself up to misery—discoveries admitting of more than hope, ought ever to be made with caution. But you have a heart to feel for the distress of another, and conduct to guide you in giving relief to sorrow; leave me to my poor fellow, and do you prepare his disconsolate partner.

GOODWIN: I'll see her immediately, and when we take our seats on the plain of sports, we will communicate to each other the result of our considerations.

STEADY: Till then, my worthy associates, farewell. [*Exeunt*]

Scene II

Another Apartment in Goodwin's house. Enter Goodwin and Selima.

GOODWIN: Come, my poor disconsolate, be composed, and prepare to meet your friends on those plains, where you never shall experience sorrow; but on the contrary, enjoy every happiness within the power of thy grateful master to bestow; you once told me, Selima, that my participation of your griefs abated their force; will you then indulge me with that pleasing tho' mournful Song you have made, on the loss of him, who, perhaps, may one day be restored?

SELIMA: Good and generous Master! ever consoling me with hope, can I deny you who have given me mind, taught me your language, comforted me with the knowledge of books, and made me every thing I am? Prepared too, my soul for joys, which you say are to succeed the patient bearing of human misery. Oh, Sir, with what inward satisfaction do I answer a request in every way grateful to my feelings!

SONG. SET TO MUSIC BY MR. REEVE[7]

How vain to me the hours of ease,
    When every daily toil is o'er;

---

5. Tribal warfare in Africa.
6. Destined.

7. William Reeve (1757–1815), actor and composer.

In my sad heart no hope I find,
    For Oran is, alas! no more.

Not sunny Africa could please,
    Nor friends upon my native shore,
To me the dreary world's a cave,
    For Oran is, alas! no more.

In bowers of bliss beyond the moon,
    The white man says, his sorrow's o'er,
And comforts me with soothing hope,
    Tho' Oran is, alas, no more.

O come then, messenger of death,
    Convey me to yon starry shore,
Where I may meet with my true love,
    And never part with Oran more.

GOODWIN: There's my kind Selima! and now attend to a discovery, on which depends your future happiness; not only liberty, but love awaits you.

SELIMA: The first I want not—the last can never be! for where shall I find another Oran?

GOODWIN: O my good girl, your song of sorrow shall be changed into that of gladness. For know—the hours of anguish are gone by, your Oran lives, and lives but to bless his faithful Selima.

SELIMA [after a pause]: To that invisible Being who has sustained my suffering heart, I kneel, overwhelmed with an awful[8] sense of his protecting power. But how?

GOODWIN: As we walk on, I will explain every thing. You soon will embrace your faithful Oran, and his beloved Selima shall mourn no more. [Exeunt.]

Scene III

An open Plain.

[On one side a range of men-slaves; on the other a range of women-slaves—at some distance, seated on decorated chairs, Heartfree, Goodwin, and Steady—twelve archers close the line on the men-side, meeting the audience with Oran at their head, distinguished from the rest by a rich dress—Oran, advancing to the front of the stage, stands in a dejected posture.]

HEARTFREE: Now let the air echo to the sound of the enlivening instruments, and beat the ground to their tuneful melody; while myself and my two worthy friends, who since our last festival have reaped the benefit of your honest labours, in full goblets drink to your happiness.

[Flourish of music, and a dance.]

HEARTFREE: Now let the archers advance in pairs, and again, in replenished cups, health and domestic peace to those who surest speed the arrow.

[Flourish. Here the archers advance in pairs to the middle of the Stage, and discharge their arrows through the side wings—the victor is saluted by two female slaves, who

8. Awe-filled.

present to him the maiden of his choice—then a flourish of music, and the parties fall back to the side. After the ceremony has been repeated five times to as many pair of archers, and Oran and Almaboe only remain to advance as the sixth pair, Oran appears absorbed in grief, which is observed with evident concern by Heartfree.]

HEARTFREE: Why Oran, with looks divided between earth and heaven, dost thou appear an alien among those who are encompassed with joy and gladness? Though your beloved Selima is torn from your widowed arms, yet it is a duty you owe yourself, as a man, an obligation due to me, as your friend, to take to your bosom one whom I have provided for you. A contest with Almaboe is needless; he has fixed on his partner, to whom, according to your request, he is now presented. [*A flourish of music—two female slaves advance with a third, who is presented to Almaboe—the parties embrace.*] It remains, therefore, for you to comply with the wishes of those who honour your virtues, and have respected your sorrows.

ORAN: Kind and benevolent masters; I indeed came hither unwillingly, to draw the bow, with a heart already pierced with the arrow of hopeless anguish. You have done generously by my friend, to whom I meant to have relinquished the victor's right, had the chance been mine. For alas, Sirs! Selima was my first and only love; and when I lost her, joy fled from a bosom it will never again revisit. The short date of my existence is therefore devoted alone to that Power whom you have taught me to revere. Sacred to gratitude, and sacred to her whose beckoning spirit seems at this moment to call on me from yonder sky—

GOODWIN: What say you, Oran, if I should produce a maiden whose virtues will bring you comfort, and whose affection you will find as strong as hers, whose loss you so feelingly deplore?

ORAN: O Sirs! had you but known my Selima, you would not attempt to produce her equal! Poor lost excellence! Yes, thy spirit, released from all its sufferings, is now looking down upon its Oran! But let not imagination too far transport me: perhaps she yet lives, a prey to brutal lust. [*Turns to Almaboe.*] Brother of my choice, and friend of my adverse hour, long may your Coanzi be happy in the endearments of her faithful Almaboe. And O my friend! when thy poor Oran is no more, if [it] chance that Selima yet lives, if blessed Providence *should* lead her to these happy shores, if she should escape the cruel enemy, and be brought hither with honour unsullied;[9] tell her how much she owes to these generous men; comfort her afflicted spirit, and teach her to adore the God of truth and mercy.

ALMABOE: Oran must himself endeavour to live for that day, and not by encouraging despair, sink self-devoted to the grave.[1] The same Providence, my friend, which has turned the terrors of slavery into willing bondage, may yet restore thy Selima.

ORAN: The words of Almaboe come charged with the force of truth, and erring Oran bends to offended Heaven! Yet erring Oran must still feel his loss, and erring Oran must for ever lament it.

GOODWIN: It is true, Oran, our arguments to urge thee to be happy, have hitherto proved fruitless. But know, thou man of sorrow, we are possessed of the means which will restore thee to thyself and to thy friends. Hear, then, the important secret, and know, that thy Selima yet lives!

___

9. As a virgin.   1. By suicide; "devoted" means "doomed."

ORAN [*after a pause*]: Yet lives! Selima yet lives! what my Selima! my own dear angel! O speak again, your words have visited my heart, and it is lost in rapture.
HEARTFREE: Nay, Oran, but be calm.
ORAN: I am calm—Heaven will permit me to support my joy, but do you relieve me
from suspence.
GOODWIN: Let the instruments breathe forth the most pleasing strains—Advance,
my happy virgins, with your charge, and restore to Oran his long-lost Selima. You
receive her pure as when you parted, with a mind released from the errors of darkness, and refined by its afflictions.
    [*Soft music—Selima comes down the stage, attended by six virgins in fancied dresses,
    who present her to Oran—the lovers embrace—flourish of music, and a shout.*]
ORAN: Lost in admiration, gratitude, and love, Oran has no words, but can only in
silence own the hand of Heaven; while to his beating heart he clasps his restored
treasure. And O my masters! for such, though free, suffer me still to call you; let
my restored partner and myself bend to such exalted worth; while for ourselves,
and for our surrounding brethren, we declare, that you have proved yourselves *The
Benevolent Planters*, and that under subjection like yours,

SLAVERY IS BUT A NAME

SONG. TO THE TUNE OF *RULE BRITANNIA*.[2]

> In honour of this happy day,
>   Let Afric's sable sons rejoice;
> To mercy we devote the lay,
>   To heaven-born mercy raise the voice.
> Long may she reign, and call each heart her own,
> And nations guard her sacred throne.
>
> Fair child of heaven, our rites approve,
>   With smiles attend the votive song,
> Inspire with universal love,
>   For joy and peace to thee belong.
> Long may'st thou reign, and call each heart thy own,
> While nations guard thy sacred throne.

━━━◄◊►━━━

John Newton
1725–1807

In 1748, John Newton, a former sailor and then captain in the slave trade, converted to
evangelical Christianity, and became a rector. In *An Authentic Narrative of Some Remarkable
and Interesting Particulars in the Life of John Newton* (1764) he related his adventures in a narrative of divine salvation, and so reinforced the spiritual argument for the abolition of the
slave trade. His memoirs, *Thoughts Upon the African Slave Trade* (1788), more starkly

---

2. A famous song, written by James Thomson in 1740, with music by Thomas Arne. Its last stanza: "Blest Isle! with
matchless beauty crowned / And manly hearts to guard the fair. / Rule Britannia, rule the waves, / Britons never will be
slaves!"

detailed the "business at which my heart... (oman of letters), she secured a printer, de-
and the Middle Passage. (Newton guesse... editor, proofreader, and publicist for Years-
the slave cargo was lost.) As a charismati... She also tried to control the proceeds—
mous hymn of personal salvation, now k... ual allowance and establishing a trust fund
Review and Expectation, and was keyed (a... e money herself and when More refused,
17.16–17.   ... tation," Yearsley broke with her and lam-
... graphical Narrative" to the fourth edition
... jects (1787). Although such "ingratitude"
Ama... raise for "genius," and an "unusually sound
... al injustice infuses *Poem on the Inhumanity*
AMAZING grace! how sweet t... *Poem* (1788). Strategically addressing the
   That saved a wretch like... the rending apart of African families, the
I once was lost, but now am... laves, and the affront to Christian con-
   Was blind, but now I see. Evangelical narratives by presenting a re-

5 'Twas grace that taught my h...
   And grace my fears reliev...
How precious did that grace **ty of the Slave-Trade**
   The hour I first believed! ... and strong;
Through many dangers, toil... w'r of song:
10 I have already come; ... stic lyre
'Tis grace has brought me sa... ts *they inspire.*
   And grace will lead me h...
... rl of Bristol, Bishop of Derry, &c. &c.
The Lord has promised good...
   His Word my hope secur...
15 He will my shield and porti... nd Humanity are not confined to *one*
   As long as life endures. ... the Indian Coast.[1] My Intention is
Yes, when this flesh and hea... h powerless Compassion ever gives;
   And mortal life shall cea... your Lordship feels as I do.
I shall possess, within the ve... With the highest Reverence, I am,
20 A life of joy and peace. My Lord
    Your Lordship's much obliged,
The earth shall soon dissolv... And obedient Servant,
   The sun forbear to shine: ANN YEARSLEY.
But God, who call'd me her... glory.—Slaves,
   Will be for ever mine. chains, and gaz'd
... Hence
... give,

---

*Ann Cr*on
... stretch
Freedom.

One of the most bitterly ironic voices of... nd to
and milkseller whose career was launched... n woe,
dairywoman, Ann Cromartie lacked for... ou son,
brother and developed a passion for poetr...
in six years, and suffered near starvation...
Learning of her plight, More read her poe... slave traders, financed by local merchants, de-   gland
she described as "industrious in no comm... to procure Africans.

With the assistance of Elizabeth Montagu (another woman of letters), she secured a printer, developed an impressive subscription list, and served as editor, proofreader, and publicist for Yearsley's first volume, *Poems on Several Occasions* (1785). She also tried to control the proceeds—eventually £600—by placing Yearsley on a small annual allowance and establishing a trust fund for her children. Yearsley insisted on controlling the money herself and when More refused, concerned that she might set her sights "out of her station," Yearsley broke with her and lambasted her treatment of her in a prefatory "Autobiographical Narrative" to the fourth edition (1786), which she reprinted in *Poems on Various Subjects* (1787). Although such "ingratitude" appalled More's friends, Yearsley continued to earn praise for "genius," and an "unusually sound masculine understanding." A passionate sense of social injustice infuses *Poem on the Inhumanity of the Slave-Trade* (1788), a rival to More's *Slavery: A Poem* (1788). Strategically addressing the citizens of Bristol, a hub of the trade, Yearsley details the rending apart of African families, the physical degradation, suffering, and torture of the slaves, and the affront to Christian conscience, but she departs from the salvational model of Evangelical narratives by presenting a rebellious protagonist who is martyred for his resistance.

from A Poem on the Inhumanity of the Slave-Trade

> Go seek the soul refin'd and strong;
> Such aids my wildest pow'r of song:
> For those I strike the rustic lyre
> Who *share* the transports *they inspire*.

To the Right Hon. and Right Rev. Frederick, Earl of Bristol, Bishop of Derry, &c. &c.

My Lord,

Being convinced that your Ideas of Justice and Humanity are not confined to *one* Race of Men, I have endeavoured to lead you to the Indian Coast.[1] My Intention is not to cause that Anguish in your Bosom which powerless Compassion ever gives; yet, my Vanity is flattered, when I but *fancy* that your Lordship feels as I do.

> With the highest Reverence, I am,
> My Lord
> Your Lordship's much obliged,
> And obedient Servant,
> ANN YEARSLEY.

> BRISTOL,[2] thine heart hath throbb'd to glory.—Slaves,
> E'en Christian slaves, have shook their chains, and gaz'd
> With wonder and amazement on thee. Hence
> Ye grov'ling souls, who think the term I give,
> 5   Of Christian slave, a paradox! to *you*
> I do not turn, but leave you to conception
> Narrow; with that be blest, nor dare to stretch
> Your shackled souls along the course of *Freedom*.
>
>   * * *
>
> But come, ye souls who feel for human woe,
> Tho' drest in savage guise! Approach, thou son,

1. West Indies.
2. With Liverpool, one of the chief ports in England from which slave traders, financed by local merchants, departed to procure Africans.

Whose heart would shudder at a father's chains,
And melt o'er thy lov'd brother as he lies
35   Gasping in torment undeserv'd. Oh, sight
Horrid and insupportable! far worse
Than an immediate, an heroic death;
Yet to this sight I summon thee. Approach,
Thou slave of avarice!

                 * * *

      Luco[3] is gone; his little brothers weep,
115   While his fond mother climbs the hoary rock
Whose point o'er-hangs the main. No Luco there,
No sound, save the hoarse billows. On she roves,
With love, fear, hope, holding alternate rage
In her too anxious bosom. Dreary main!
120   Thy murmurs now are riot, while she stands
List'ning to ev'ry breeze, waiting the step
Of gentle Luco. Ah, return! return!
Too hapless mother, thy indulgent arms
Shall never clasp thy fetter'd Luco more.
125   See Incilanda! artless maid, my soul
Keeps pace with thee, and mourns.

                 * * *

                 A father comes,
But not to seek his son, who from the deck
Had breath'd a last adieu: no, he shuts out
The soft, fallacious gleam of hope, and turns
170   Within upon the mind: horrid and dark
Are his wild, unenlighten'd pow'rs: no ray
Of *forc'd* philosophy to calm his soul,
But all the anarchy of wounded nature.

                 * * *

Where now shall Incilanda seek him? Hence,
195   Defenceless mourner, ere the dreary night
Wrap thee in added horror. Oh, Despair,
How eagerly thou rend'st the heart! She pines
In anguish deep, and sullen: Luco's form
Pursues her, lives in restless thought, and chides
200   Soft consolation. Banished from his arms,
She seeks the cold embrace of death; her soul
Escapes in one sad sigh. Too hapless maid!

                 * * *

      Luco is borne around the neighb'ring isles,
Losing the knowledge of his native shore
215   Amid the pathless wave; destin'd to plant
The sweet luxuriant cane.[4] He strives to please,
Nor once complains, but greatly smothers grief.

---

3. A boy kidnapped into slavery; Incilanda is his beloved.
4. Sugarcane, a chief West Indian crop, was processed into rum, molasses, and refined sugar, for sale in England and Europe.

His hands are blister'd, and his feet are worn,
Till ev'ry stroke dealt by his mattock° gives   hoe
220   Keen agony to life; while from his breast
The sigh arises, burthen'd with the name
Of Incilanda. Time inures the youth,
His limbs grow nervous, strain'd by willing toil;
And resignation, or a calm despair,
225   (Most useful either) lulls him to repose.

A Christian renegade, that from his soul
Abjures the tenets of our schools, nor dreads
A future punishment, nor hopes for mercy,
Had fled from England, to avoid those laws
230   Which must have made his life a retribution
To violated justice, and had gain'd,
By fawning guile, the confidence (ill placed)
Of Luco's master. O'er the slave he stands
With knotted whip, lest fainting nature shun
235   The task too arduous, while his cruel soul,
Unnat'ral, ever feeds, with gross delight,
Upon his suff'rings. Many slaves there were,
But none who could suppress the sigh, and bend,
So quietly as Luco: long he bore
240   The stripes,° that from his manly bosom drew   lashes
The sanguine° stream (too little priz'd); at length   bloody
Hope fled his soul, giving her struggles o'er,
And he resolv'd to die. The sun had reach'd
His zenith—pausing faintly, Luco stood,
245   Leaning upon his hoe, while mem'ry brought,
In piteous imag'ry, his aged father,
His poor fond mother, and his faithful maid:
The mental group in wildest motion set
Fruitless imagination; fury, grief,
250   Alternate shame, the sense of insult, all
Conspire to aid the inward storm; yet words
Were no relief, he stood in silent woe.

Gorgon,[5] remorseless Christian, saw the slave
Stand musing, 'mid the ranks, and, stealing soft
255   Behind the studious Luco, struck his cheek
With a too-heavy whip, that reach'd his eye,
Making it dark for ever. Luco turn'd,
In strongest agony, and with his hoe
Struck the rude Christian on the forehead. Pride,
260   With hateful malice, seize[d] on Gorgon's soul,
By nature fierce; while Luco sought the beach,
And plung'd beneath the wave; but near him lay

5. The Gorgons of Greek mythology were monstrous snake-haired sisters whose gaze turned men to stone.

A planter's barge, whose seamen grasp'd his hair,
Dragging to life a wretch who wish'd to die.

265   Rumour now spreads the tale, while Gorgon's breath
Envenom'd, aids her blast: imputed crimes
Oppose the plea of Luco, till he scorns
Even a just defence, and stands prepared.
The planters, conscious that to fear alone
270   They owe their cruel pow'r, resolve to blend
New torment with the pangs of death, and hold
Their victims high in dreadful view, to fright
The wretched number left. Luco is chain'd
To a huge tree, his fellow-slaves are ranged
275   To share the horrid sight; fuel is plac'd
In an increasing train, some paces back,
To kindle slowly, and approach the youth,
With more than native terror. See, it burns!
He gazes on the growing flame, and calls
280   For "water, water!" The small boon's deny'd.
E'en Christians throng each other, to behold
The different alterations of his face,
As the hot death approaches. (Oh, shame, shame
Upon the followers of Jesus! shame
285   On him that dares avow a God!) He writhes,
While down his breast glide the unpity'd tears,
And in their sockets strain their scorched balls.
"Burn, burn me quick! I cannot die!" he cries:
"Bring fire more close!" The planters heed him not,
290   But still prolonging Luco's torture, threat
Their trembling slaves around. His lips are dry,
His senses seem to quiver, e'er they quit
His frame for ever, rallying strong, then driv'n
From the tremendous conflict. Sight no more
295   Is Luco's, his parch'd tongue is ever mute.

* * *

Must our wants
365   Find their supply in murder? Shall the sons
Of Commerce shiv'ring stand, if not employ'd
Worse than the midnight robber? Curses fall
On the destructive system that shall need
Such base supports! Doth England need them? No;
370   Her laws, with prudence, hang the meagre thief
That from his neighbour steals a slender sum,
Tho' famine drove him on. O'er *him* the priest,
Beneath the fatal tree, laments the crime,
Approves the law, and bids him calmly die.
375   Say, doth this law, that dooms the thief, protect
The wretch who makes another's life his prey,
By hellish force to take it at his will?

Is this an English law, whose guidance fails
When crimes are swell'd to magnitude so vast,
380 That *Justice* dare not scan them? Or does *Law*
Bid *Justice* an eternal distance keep
From England's great tribunal, when the slave
Calls loud on *Justice only?* Speak, ye few
Who fill Britannia's senate, and are deem'd
385 The fathers of your country! Boast your laws,
Defend the *honour* of a land so fall'n,
That Fame from ev'ry battlement is flown,
And Heathens start, e'en at a Christian's name.

* * *

Oh, social love,
415 Thou universal good, thou that canst fill
The vacuum of immensity, and live
In endless void! thou that in motion first
Set'st the long lazy atoms, by thy force
Quickly assimilating, and restrain'd
420 By strong attraction; touch the soul of man;
Subdue him; make a fellow-creature's woe
His own by heart-felt sympathy, whilst wealth
Is made subservient to his soft disease.

And when thou hast to high perfection wrought
425 This mighty work, say, *"such is Bristol's soul."*

William Cowper
1731–1800

The son of a rector and a mother who traced her descent to Henry III and John Donne, William Cowper was beset through his life with manic, sometimes suicidal, depressions, aggravated by his attraction to sects emphasizing man's original sin. He studied law but found poetry more congenial, and with the Evangelical minister and abolitionist John Newton published a volume of hymns in 1779, including Newton's great hymn *Amazing Grace*. He followed with a series of moral satires in the early 1780s, and his most famous poem, *The Task* (1785), whose second book opens with a strong critique of slavery. Feeling deeply the moral blight of slavery as an institution sustained only by greed, Cowper responded to Wilberforce's call for popular abolitionist literature with four ballads in 1788 that were widely reprinted. The poet of *The Morning Dream* envisions the goddess Britannia sailing west to a "slave-cultured island" to confront the cruel "Demon" of slave-ownership, who sickens and dies at her sight; the balladeer of *Pity for Poor Africans*, insisting that he is "shock'd at the purchase of slaves," justifies his participation by arguing that foreigners will not give up the trade: "He shar'd in the plunder, but he pitied the man." *Sweet Meat Has Sour Sauce: or, The Slave-Trader in the Dumps* is the ditty of a trader lamenting the inevitable abolition of his business and trying to unload his gear. *The Negro's Complaint*, the most popular of the group in part because of its stark wood-cut illustrations, doubly refutes the view of slaves as subhuman: its slave-speaker not only expresses his own profound humanity but also exposes the inhumanity of the "iron-hearted" masters, whom he calls "slaves of gold." Cowper grew so depressed with his involvement in the slavery issue that eventually he had to stop writing about it. His last poem, written shortly before his death, is the beautifully melancholy *The Castaway*.

Sweet Meat Has Sour Sauce
or, The Slave-Trader in the Dumps

A trader I am to the African shore,
But since that my trading is like to be o'er,
I'll sing you a song that you ne'er heard before,
    Which nobody can deny, deny,
5   Which nobody can deny.

When I first heard the news it gave me a shock,
Much like what they call an electrical knock,
And now I am going to sell off my stock,
    Which nobody can deny.

10 'Tis a curious assortment of dainty regales,°   *choice pieces*
To tickle the Negroes with when the ship sails—
Fine chains for the neck, and a cat with nine tails,[1]
    Which nobody can deny.

Here's supple-jack plenty, and store of rat-tan,[2]
15 That will wind itself round the sides of a man,
As close as a hoop round a bucket or can,
    Which nobody can deny.

Here's padlocks and bolts, and screws for the thumbs,
That squeeze them so lovingly till the blood comes;
20 They sweeten the temper like comfits or plums,
    Which nobody can deny.

When a Negro his head from his victuals withdraws,
And clenches his teeth and thrusts out his paws,
Here's a notable engine to open his jaws,[3]
25   Which nobody can deny.

Thus going to market, we kindly prepare
A pretty black cargo of African ware,
For what they must meet with when they get there,
    Which nobody can deny.

30 'Twould do your heart good to see 'em below
Lie flat on their backs all the way as we go,[4]
Like sprats on a gridiron, scores in a row,[5]
    Which nobody can deny.

---

1. Cat-o'-nine-tails, a whip of nine knotted lashes.
2. Both supple-jack (a woody vine) and rattan (a climbing palm) were used to make whips, canes, and ropes.
3. Force-feeding of a slave meaning to starve to death.
4. A reference to the torturous tight-packing of slave cargo; see illustration, page 126.
5. Sprats are herrings (metaphorically, insignificant people); a gridiron is a griddle—an image of slaves cooking in hot cargo-holds.

35 But ah! if in vain I have studied an art
    So gainful to me, all boasting apart,
    I think it will break my compassionate heart,
            Which nobody can deny.

    For oh! how it enters my soul like an awl!
    This pity, which some people self-pity call,
40 Is sure the most heart-piercing pity of all,
            Which nobody can deny.

    So this is my song, as I told you before;
    Come, buy off my stock, for I must no more
    Carry Caesars and Pompeys to Sugar-cane shore,[6]
45   Which nobody can deny, deny,
            Which nobody can deny.

The Negro's Complaint

    FORCED from home and all its pleasures,
        Afric's coast I left forlorn,
    To increase the stranger's treasures,
        O'er the raging billows borne.
5   Men from England bought and sold me,
        Paid my price in paltry gold;
    But, though slave they have enroll'd me,
        Minds are never to be sold.

    Still in thought as free as ever,
10   What are England's rights, I ask,
    Me from my delights to sever,
        Me to torture, me to task?
    Fleecy locks and black complexion
        Cannot forfeit Nature's claim;
15 Skins may differ, but affection
        Dwells in white and black the same.

    Why did all creating Nature
        Make the plant for which we toil?
    Sighs must fan it, tears must water,
20   Sweat of ours must dress the soil.
    Think, ye masters, iron-hearted,
        Lolling at your jovial boards,
    Think how many backs have smarted
        For the sweets your cane° affords.   *sugarcane*

25 Is there, as ye sometimes tell us,
        Is there One who reigns on high?
    Has He bid you buy and sell us,
        Speaking from his throne, the sky?

---

6. Caesar and Pompey were famous ancient Romans (many slaves were royalty in their African cultures); "Sugar-cane shore" is the West Indies.

Ask Him, if your knotted scourges,°   *whips*
30   Matches, blood-extorting screws,°   *thumbscrews*
Are the means that duty urges
        Agents of his will to use?

Hark! He answers!—Wild tornadoes
        Strewing yonder sea with wrecks,
35 Wasting towns, plantations, meadows,
        Are the voice with which he speaks.
He, foreseeing what vexations
        Afric's sons should undergo,
Fix'd their tyrants' habitations
40   Where his whirlwinds answer—No.¹

By our blood in Afric wasted,
        Ere our necks received the chain;
By the miseries that we tasted,
        Crossing in your barks° the main;°   *ships / sea*
45 By our sufferings, since ye brought us
        To the man-degrading mart,
All sustain'd by patience, taught us
        Only by a broken heart!

Deem our nation brutes no longer,
50   Till some reason ye shall find
Worthier of regard and stronger
        Than the colour of our kind.
Slaves of gold, whose sordid dealings
        Tarnish all your boasted powers,
55 Prove that you have human feelings
        Ere you proudly question ours!

1778

⊷ ⊱✦⊰ ⊶

Hannah More and Eaglesfield Smith

Poet and essayist Hannah More published 114 *Cheap Repository Tracts* between 1795 and 1798. With simple language cast into stories, ballads, poems, dialogues, sermons, prayers, parables, and moral tales, she strove, with an Evangelical view, "to improve the habits, and raise the principles of the common people . . . not only to counteract vice and profligacy on the one hand, but error, discontent, and false religion on the other." Among her concerns were quelling political discontent and class antagonisms and shaping public opinion in favor of abolition. Priced at a halfpenny, and marketed not only in shops but also at fairs and on street corners, the *Tracts* sold quickly and widely, over two million in the first year alone. They were purchased in bulk by preachers for their congregations, landlords for their tenants and laborers,

---

1. Tornados and other natural catastrophes were taken to be signs of divine anger and retribution.

and missionaries for their work in Africa and India, and disseminated in hospitals, prisons, the armed forces, and the workhouses. More had first treated the issue in *Slavery: A Poem* (1788), a 356-line polemical oration aimed at creating support for Wilberforce in Parliament. Eager to involve a popular audience, she devoted four of her Tracts to slavery. The most popular were *The Black Prince* (perhaps co-authored with More's mentor John Newton) and *The Sorrows of Yamba*, which critic Alan Richardson reports was co-authored with Eaglesfield Smith. We also thank him for helping us establish this text.

The Sorrows of Yamba
or, The Negro Woman's Lamentation

"IN St. Lucie's distant isle,[1]
　　Still with Afric's love I burn;
Parted many a thousand mile,
　　Never, never to return.

5　Come, kind death! and give me rest;
　　Yamba has no friend but thee;
Thou can'st ease my throbbing breast,
　　Thou can'st set the Prisoner free.

Down my cheeks the tears are dripping,
10　　Broken is my heart with grief;
Mangled my poor flesh with whipping,
　　Come, kind death! and bring relief.

Born on Afric's Golden Coast,[2]
　　Once I was as blest as you;
15　Parents tender I could boast,
　　Husband dear, and children too.

Whity man he came from far,
　　Sailing o'er the briny flood,
Who with help of British Tar,°　　　　　　　　　　　*seaman*
20　　Buys up human flesh and blood.

With the baby at my breast
　　(Other too were sleeping by)
In my Hut I sat at rest
　　With no thought of danger nigh.

25　From the Bush at even tide,
　　Rushed the fierce man-stealing crew;
Seiz'd the Children by my side,
　　Seiz'd the wretched Yamba too.

Then for love of filthy Gold,
30　　Strait they bore me to the Sea,

---

1. Santa Lucia, in the British West Indies.
2. An evocation of an idyllic world and ironically, the

"Gold Coast," a British West African colony (now Ghana) trading chiefly in gold and slaves.

Cramm'd me down a Slave Ship's hold,
    Where were Hundreds stow'd like me.

Naked on the Platform lying,
    Now we cross the tumbling wave;
35   Shrieking, sickening, fainting, dying;
    Deed of shame for Britons brave.

At the savage Captain's beck,
    Now like Brutes they make us prance:
Smack the Cat° about the Deck,   *whip*
40   And in scorn they make us dance.

Nauseous horse-beans they bring nigh,
    Sick and sad we cannot eat;
Cat must cure the Sulks, they cry,
    Down their throats we'll force the meat.[3]

45   I, in groaning passed the night,
    And did roll my aching head;
At the break of morning light,
    My poor Child was cold and dead.

Happy, happy, there she lies,
50   Thou shalt feel the lash no more.
Thus full many a Negro dies
    Ere we reach the destin'd shore.

Thee, sweet infant, none shall sell,
    Thou hast gained a wat'ry Grave;
55   Clean escap'd the Tyrants fell,°   *fierce*
    While thy mother lives a Slave.

Driven like Cattle to a fair,
    See they sell us, young and old;
Child from Mother too they tear,
60   All for love of filthy Gold.

I was sold to Massa° hard,   *Master*
    Some have Massas kind and good:
And again my back was scarr'd,
    Bad and stinted was my food.

65   Poor and wounded, faint and sick,
    All exposed to burning sky,
Massa bids me grass to pick,
    And I now am near to die.

What and if to death he send me,
70   Savage murder tho' it be,
British Law shall not befriend me,
    They protect not Slaves like me."

3. Forced feeding; horse-beans are food for horses.

Mourning thus my wretched state,
    (Ne'er may I forget the day)
75   Once in dusk of evening late
       Far from home I dar'd to stray;

Dared, alas! with impious haste
    Towards the roaring Sea to fly;
Death itself I longed to taste,
80   Long'd to cast me in and Die.

There I met upon the Strand°   *shore*
    English Missionary Good;
He had Bible book in hand,
    Which poor me no understood.

85   Led by pity from afar,
    He had left his native ground;
Thus, if some inflict a scar,
    Others fly to cure the wound.

Strait he pull'd me from the shore,
90   Bid me no self-murder do;
Talk'd of state when life is o'er,
    All from Bible good and true.

Then he led me to his Cot,°   *cottage*
    Soothed and pitied all my woe;
95   Told me 'twas the Christian's lot
    Much to suffer here below.

Told me then of God's dear Son,
    (Strange and wondrous is the story;)
What sad wrong to him was done,
100   Tho' he was the Lord of Glory.

Told me too, like one who knew him,
    (Can such love as this be true?)
How he died for them that slew him,
    Died for wretched Yamba too.

105   Freely he his mercy proffered,
    And to Sinners he was sent;
E'en to Massa pardons offered;
    O if Massa would repent!

Wicked deed full many a time
110   Sinful Yamba too hath done;
But she wails to God her crime,
    But she trusts his only Son.

O ye slaves whom Massas beat,
    Ye are stained with guilt within;
115   As ye hope for Mercy sweet,
    So forgive your Massas' sin.

And with grief when sinking low,
    Mark the Road that Yamba trod;
Think how all her pain and woe
120   Brought the Captive home to God.

Now let Yamba too adore
    Gracious Heaven's mysterious Plan;
Now I'll count thy mercies o'er,
    Flowing thro' the guilt of man.

125 Now I'll bless my cruel capture,
    (Hence I've known a Saviour's name)
Till my Grief is turn'd to Rapture,
    And I half forget the blame.

But tho' here a convert rare
130   Thanks her God for Grace divine,
Let not man the glory share,
    Sinner, still the guilt is thine.

Here an injured Slave forgives,
    There a Host for vengeance cry;
135 Here a single Yamba lives,
    There a thousand droop and die.

Duly now baptiz'd am I,
    By good Missionary Man:
Lord my nature purify
140   As no outward water can!

All my former thoughts abhorr'd
    Teach me now to pray and praise;
Joy and Glory in my Lord,
    Trust and serve him all my days.

145 Worn indeed with Grief and Pain,
    Death I now will welcome in:
O the Heavenly Prize to gain!
    O to 'scape the power of Sin!

True of heart, and meek and lowly,
150   Pure and blameless let me grow!
Holy may I be, for Holy,
    Is the place to which I go.

But tho' death this hour may find me,
    Still with Afric's love I burn;
155 (There I've left a spouse behind me)
    Still to native land I turn.

And when Yamba sinks in death,
    This my latest° prayer shall be,
While I yield my parting breath,
160   *O that Afric might be free.*

          last

Cease, ye British Sons of murder!
  Cease from forging Afric's chain:
Mock your Saviour's name no further,
  Cease your savage lust of gain.

165 Ye that boast *"Ye rule the waves,"*
  Bid no Slave Ship soil the sea;
Ye, that *"never will be slaves,"*
  Bid poor Afric's land be free.[4]

Where ye gave to war it's birth,
170 Where your traders fix'd their den,
There go publish *"Peace on Earth,"*
  Go, proclaim *"good-will to men."*[5]

Where ye once have carried slaughter,
  Vice, and Slavery, and Sin;
175 Seiz'd on Husband, Wife, and Daughter,
  Let the Gospel enter in.

Thus, where Yamba's native home,
  Humble Hut of Rushes stood,
Oh if there should chance to roam
180 Some dear Missionary good;

Thou in Afric's distant land,
  Still shalt see the man I love;
Join him to the Christian band,
  Guide his Soul to the Realms above.

185 There no Fiend again shall sever
  Those whom God hath join'd and bless'd;
There they dwell with Him for ever,
  There *"the weary are at rest."*[6]

                                        1795

Robert Southey
1774–1843

Author of the children's story *The Three Bears*, Robert Southey was savaged, as Poet Laureate, for his Tory politics by Byron in *Don Juan* and *The Vision of Judgment* (1822). In younger days he had been a political radical with friends William Wordsworth and Samuel Taylor Coleridge, fellow "Lake Poets." In 1794 he and Coleridge planned a utopian community, Pantisocracy, on the banks of the Susquehanna in Pennsylvania. The poets agreed to abolish private property, but the plan fell apart on a disagreement over whether to have servants. Throughout the 1790s and into the next

---

4. Quoting James Thomson's imperialist hymn, *Rule Britannia*. See also page 99.
5. The angels' heralding of the birth of Jesus (Luke 2.14).

6. Job, tormented by Satan on a mission from God as a test of his faith, longs for death, where "the wicked cease from troubling; and . . . the weary be at rest" (3.17).

decade, Southey wrote several political works, including *Wat Tyler* (1794), a drama about the leader
of the English Peasants' Revolt of 1381, and *Joan of Arc* (1796), an epic about the French heroine as
martyred champion of liberty. His abolitionist *Poems Concerning the Slave-Trade*, six sonnets and a
ballad, written in 1798 and published in 1799, emphasize the moral and physical effects of the trade
on the slave-ship crews, themselves often kidnapped like slaves and pressed into service.

from Poems Concerning the Slave-Trade

Sonnet III

Oh he is worn with toil! the big drops run
   Down his dark cheek; hold—hold thy merciless hand,
   Pale tyrant! for, beneath thy hard command
O'er wearied Nature sinks. The scorching Sun,
5 As pityless as proud Prosperity,
   Darts on him his full beams; gasping he lies
   Arraigning with his looks the patient skies,
While that inhuman trader lifts on high
   The mangling scourge. O ye who at your ease
10   Sip the blood-sweetened beverage![1] thoughts like these
Haply ye scorn: I thank thee Gracious God,
   That I do feel upon my cheek the glow
Of indignation, when beneath the rod
   A sable brother writhes in silent woe.

Sonnet IV

'Tis night: the mercenary tyrants sleep
   As undisturb'd as Justice! but no more
   The wretched Slave, as on his native shore,
Rests on his reedy couch: he wakes to weep!
5 Tho' thro' the toil and anguish of the day
   No tear escap'd him, not one suffering groan
   Beneath the twisted thong, he weeps alone
In bitterness; thinking that far away
   Tho' the gay negroes join the midnight song,
10   Tho' merriment resounds on Niger's shore,
She whom he loves far from the chearful throng
   Stands sad and gazes from her lowly door
With dim grown eye, silent and woe-begone,
   And weeps for him who will return no more.

Sonnet V

Did then the Slave rear at last the Sword
   Of Vengeance? drench'd he deep its thirsty blade
   In the cold bosom of his tyrant lord?
   Oh! who shall blame him?[2] thro' the midnight shade

---

1. Tea, with plantation sugar.   2. Vengeance is a mortal sin.

5 Still o'er his tortured memory rush'd the thought
  Of every past delight; his native grove,
  Friendship's best joys, and Liberty and Love,
All lost for ever! Then remembrance wrought
His soul to madness; round his restless bed
10 Freedom's pale spectre stalk'd, with a stern smile
  Pointing the wounds of slavery, the while
She shook her chains and hung her sullen head:
No more on Heaven he calls with fruitless breath,
But sweetens with revenge, the draught of death.

Sonnet VI

High in the air expos'd the Slave is hung,
  To all the birds of Heaven, their living food!
He groans not, tho' awaked by that fierce Sun
  New torturers live to drink their parent blood!
5 He groans not, tho' the gorging Vulture tear
  The quivering fibre! hither gaze O ye
  Who tore this Man from Peace and Liberty!
Gaze hither ye who weigh with scrupulous care
The right and prudent; for beyond the grave
10 There is another world! and call to mind,
  Ere your decrees proclaim to all mankind
Murder is legalized, that there the Slave,
Before the Eternal "thunder-tongued shall plead
Against the deep damnation of your deed."[3]

1794

The Sailor Who had Served in the Slave-Trade

In September, 1798, a dissenting minister of Bristol[1] discovered a sailor, in the neighborhood of that city, groaning and praying in a cow-house. The circumstance which occasioned his agony of mind is detailed in the annexed ballad, without the slightest addition or alteration. By presenting it as a poem, the story is made more public; and such stories ought to be made as public as possible.

It was a Christian minister,[2]
  Who, in the month of flowers,
Walked forth at eve amid the fields
  Near Bristol's ancient towers,—

---

3. The murder of the king in Shakespeare's *Macbeth* (1.7.19–20).
1. In this hub of the slave trade, dissenting sects (refusing the authority of the Church of England) were active in the abolition movement.

2. Southey wrote this ballad of a haunted sailor after reading Coleridge's balladlike *Rime of the Ancyent Marinere* (1798), echoed in the opening line. Though dated "1798" at the close, the text here is the version first published in 1815.

5   When, from a lonely out-house° breathed,   cowshed
           He heard a voice of woe,
       And groans which less might seem from pain
           Than wretchedness to flow.

       Heart-rending groans they were, with words
10   Of bitterest despair,
       Yet with the holy name of Christ
           Pronounced in broken prayer.

       The Christian minister went in:
           A Sailor there he sees,
15   Whose hands were lifted up to heaven;
           And he was on his knees.

       Nor did the Sailor, so intent,
           His entering footsteps heed;
       But now "Our Father"° said, and now   the Lord's Prayer
20   His half-forgotten creed,—

       And often on our Saviour called
           With many a bitter groan,
       But in such anguish as may spring
           From deepest guilt alone.

25   The miserable man was asked
           Why he was kneeling there,
       And what had been the crime that caused
           The anguish of his prayer.

       "I have done a cursed thing!" he cried:
30   "It haunts me night and day;
       And I have sought this lonely place
           Here undisturbed to pray.

       Aboard I have no place for prayer;
           So I came here alone,
35   That I might freely kneel and pray,
           And call on Christ, and groan.

       If to the mainmast-head I go,
           The Wicked One is there;
       From place to place, from rope to rope,
40   He follows everywhere.

       I shut my eyes,—it matters not;
           Still, still the same I see;
       And, when I lie me down at night,
           'Tis always day with me.

45   He follows, follows everywhere;
           And every place is hell:[3]

3. The curse of Milton's Satan: "Me miserable! which way shall I fly / Infinite wrath, and infinite despair? / Which way I fly is Hell; myself am Hell" (*Paradise Lost* 4.73–75).

O God! and I must go with him
    In endless fire to dwell!

He follows, follows everywhere;
50   He's still above, below:
Oh, tell me where to fly from him!
    Oh, tell me where to go!"

"But tell thou," quoth the stranger then,
    "What this thy crime hath been;
55 So haply I may comfort give
    To one who grieves for sin."

"Oh, cursed, cursed is the deed!"
    The wretched man replies;
"And night and day, and everywhere,
60   'Tis still before my eyes.

I sailed on board a Guinea-man,[4]
    And to the slave-coast went:
Would that the sea had swallowed me
    When I was innocent!

65 And we took in our cargo there,—
    Three hundred negro slaves;
And we sailed homeward merrily
    Over the ocean-waves.

But some were sulky of the slaves,
70   And would not touch their meat;
So therefore we were forced by threats
    And blows to make them eat.

One woman, sulkier than the rest,
    Would still refuse her food:
75 O Jesus God! I hear her cries!
    I see her in her blood!

The captain made me tie her up,
    And flog while he stood by;
And then he cursed me if I stayed
80   My hand to hear her cry.

She shrieked, she groaned: I could not spare;
    For the captain he stood by:
Dear God! that I might rest one night
    From that poor creature's cry!

85 What woman's child a sight like that
    Could bear to look upon?

---

4. An armed vessel used for slave-trading, named for Guinea, an old term for the west coast of Africa, and the main source of slave cargo.

And still the captain would not spare,
    But made me still flog on.

90   She could not be more glad than I
        When she was taken down:
    A blessed minute! 'twas the last
        That I have ever known.

    I did not close my eyes all night,
        Thinking what I had done:
95   I heard her groans, and they grew faint
        Towards the rising sun.

    She groaned and moaned, but her voice grew
        Fainter at morning tide;
    Fainter and fainter still it came,
100   Until, at noon, she died.

    They flung her overboard: poor wretch!
        She rested from her pain;
    But when, O Christ! O blessed God!
        Shall I have rest again?

105   I saw the sea close over her:
        Yet she is still in sight;
    I see her twisting everywhere;
        I see her day and night.

    Go where I will, do what I can,
110   The Wicked One I see:
    Dear Christ, have mercy on my soul!
        O God, deliver me!

    Oh, give me comfort, if you can!
        Oh, tell me where to fly!
115   Oh, tell me if there can be hope
        For one so lost as I!"

    What said the minister of Christ?
        He bade him trust in Heaven,
    And call on Him for whose dear sake
120   All sins shall be forgiven.

    He told him of that precious blood°   *Christ's martyrdom*
        Which should his guilt efface
    Told him that none are lost but they
        Who turn from proffered grace.

125   He bade him pray, and knelt with him,
        And joined him in his prayers;
    And some who read the dreadful tale
        Perhaps will aid with theirs.

1798

Dorothy Wordsworth
1771–1855

Dorothy Wordsworth was an ardent advocate of abolition, and closely followed parliamentary events, writing to a friend in May 1792, "I hope you were an *immediate* abolitionist and are angry with the House of Commons for continuing the traffic in human flesh so long as till 96 but you will also rejoice that so much has been done. I hate Mr. Dundas" (the member of Parliament who created the plan to delay abolition until 1796). Her Grasmere journal records the story of a slave-ship sailor, whom she views as a collateral victim of the trade; her brother William touches obliquely on this issue in Book 4 of *The Prelude*, in his recollection of his encounter with a gaunt veteran of service in "the Tropic isles."

For more on Dorothy Wordsworth, see her principal listing, page 279.

from The Grasmere Journals

Monday Morning [March 15, 1802]. . . . a sailor who was travelling from Liverpool[1] to Whitehaven called he was faint & pale when he knocked at the door, a young Man very well dressed. We sate by the kitchen fire talking with him for 2 hours—he told us most interesting stories of his life. His name was Isaac Chapel—he had been at sea since he was 15 years old. He was by trade a sail-maker. His last voyage was to the Coast of Guinea.[2] He had been on board a slave ship the Captain's name Maxwell where one man had been killed a Boy put to lodge with the pigs & was half eaten, one Boy set to watch in the hot sun till he dropped down dead. He had been cast away in North America & had travelled 30 days among the Indians where he had been well treated—He had twice swum from a King's ship in the Night & escaped, he said he would rather be in hell than be pressed.[3] He was now going to wait in England to appear against Captain Maxwell. "O he's a Rascal, Sir, he ought to be put in the papers!" The poor man had not been in bed since Friday Night—he left Liverpool at 2 o'clock on Saturday morning, he had called at a farm house to beg victuals & had been refused. The woman said she would give him nothing. "Won't you? Then I can't help it." He was excessively like my Brother John.[4]

Thomas Clarkson
1760–1846

"The grand mover of the main efforts for the abolition of the Slave Trade," in Dorothy Wordsworth's phrase, Thomas Clarkson was the hero of the movement. In 1785, while a student at Cambridge University, he wrote a prize-winning essay, *On the Slavery and Commerce of the Human Species*, its moral arguments supported with a litany of atrocities documented in the West Indies. When it was published in 1786, one slave owner protested, "I declare to God, I do not believe that a series of more abominable falsehoods ever blotted a page in the wide history

---

1. Another hub of the slave trade.
2. West coast of Africa.
3. Kidnapped and forced into service, a kind of white male slavery.
4. John Wordsworth was captain of a merchant vessel; he would drown in a shipwreck in 1805.

of human depravity!" The next year, Clarkson joined with the English Quakers' Anti-Slavery Society, and at its behest began an arduous investigation of atrocities, centering his research in Bristol and Liverpool, where investors were financing and thriving on the trade. Often at great personal risk, Clarkson gathered detailed information, from the devastating effects on the seamen impressed into the brutal service, to the abuse of the slaves and the conditions aboard ship, to the conduct of the slave-markets. His labor supplied William Wilberforce with material for his parliamentary campaign. In the 1790s, Clarkson traveled to France to urge the Revolutionary government to abolish its slave trade and colonial slavery, agitated in England for a boycott of West Indian sugar and tea, and continued to document the atrocities that the planters' lobby continued to deny and excoriate as falsehoods, working himself into physical collapse in 1794. His most famous work, the *History of . . . the Abolition of the African Slave-Trade* (1808), helped fuel the movement for the abolition of slavery itself, a cause in which Clarkson remained active.

from The History of the Rise, Progress, & Accomplishment of the Abolition of the African Slave-Trade by the British Parliament

["THE NATURE OF THE EVIL"]

To see it as it has been shown to arise in the first case, let us suppose ourselves on the Continent [Africa]. Well then: We are landed; we are already upon our travels; we have just passed through one forest; we are now come to a more open place, which indicates an approach to habitations. And what object is that, which first obtrudes itself upon our sight? Who is that wretched woman, whom we discover under that noble tree, wringing her hands, and beating her breast, as if in the agonies of despair? Three days has she been there at intervals to look and to watch, and this is the fourth morning, and no tidings of her children yet. Beneath its spreading boughs they were accustomed to play: But alas! the savage man-stealer interrupted their playful mirth, and has taken them for ever from her sight.

But let us leave the cries of this unfortunate woman, and hasten into another district: And what do we first see here? Who is he that just now started across the narrow pathway, as if afraid of a human face? What is that sudden rustling among the leaves? Why are those persons flying from our approach, and hiding themselves in yon darkest thicket? Behold, as we get into the plain, a deserted village! The rice-field has been just trodden down around it. An aged man, venerable by his silver beard, lies wounded and dying near the threshold of his hut. War, suddenly instigated by avarice, has just visited the dwellings which we see. The old have been butchered, because unfit for slavery, and the young have been carried off, except such as have fallen in the conflict, or have escaped among the woods behind us. * * *

Let us examine the state of the unhappy Africans, reduced to slavery in this manner, while on board the vessels, which are to convey them across the ocean to other lands. And here I must observe at once, that, as far as this part of the evil is concerned, I am at a loss to describe it. Where shall I find words to express properly their sorrow, as arising from the reflection of being parted for ever from their friends, their relatives, and their country? Where shall I find language to paint in appropriate colours the horror of mind brought on by thoughts of their future unknown destination, of which they can augur nothing but misery from all that they have yet seen? How shall I make known their situation, while labouring under painful disease, or while struggling in the suffocating holds of their prisons, like animals inclosed in an exhausted receiver?[1] How shall I describe their feelings as exposed to all the personal indignities, which lawless appetite or brutal passion may suggest? How shall I exhibit their sufferings as determining to refuse sustenance and die, or as resolving to break their chains and, disdaining to live as slaves, to punish their oppressors? How shall I give an idea of their agony, when under various punishments and tortures for their reputed crimes? Indeed every part of this subject defies my powers, and I must therefore satisfy myself and the reader with a general representation, or in the words of a celebrated member of Parliament [Wilberforce], that "Never was so much human suffering condensed in so small a space."

I come now to the evil, * * * the situation of the unhappy victims of the trade, when their painful voyages are over, or after they have been landed upon their destined shores. And here we are to view them first under the degrading light of cattle.[2] We are to see them examined, handled, selected, separated, and sold. Alas! relatives are separated from relatives, as if, like cattle, they had no rational intellect, no power of feeling the nearness of relationship, nor sense of the duties belonging to the ties of life! We are next to see them labouring, and this for the benefit of those, to whom they are under no obligation, by any law either natural or divine, to obey. We are to see them, if refusing the commands of their purchasers, however weary, or feeble, or indisposed, subject to corporal punishments, and, if forcibly resisting them, to death. We are to see them in a state of general degradation and misery. The knowledge, which their oppressors have of their own crime in having violated the rights of nature, and of the disposition of the injured to seek all opportunities of revenge, produces a fear which dictates to them the necessity of a system of treatment by which they shall keep up a wide distinction between the two, and by which the noble feelings of the latter shall be kept down, and their spirits broken. We are to see them again subject to individual persecution, as anger, or malice, or any bad passion may suggest. Hence the whip; the chain; the iron-collar. Hence the various modes of private torture, of which so many accounts have been truly given. Nor can such horrible cruelties be discovered so as to be made punishable, while the testimony of any number of the oppressed is invalid against the oppressors, however they may be offences against the laws. And; lastly, we are to see their innocent offspring, against whose personal liberty the shadow of an argument cannot be advanced, inheriting all the miseries of their parents' lot.

* * * While the miseries endured by the unfortunate Africans excite our pity on the one hand, the vices, which are connected with them, provoke our indignation and abhorrence on the other. The Slave-trade, in this point of view, must strike us as an immense mass of evil on account of the criminality attached to it. * * * Is not that man made morally worse, who is induced to become a tyger to his species, or who, instigated by avarice, lies in wait in the thicket to get possession of his fellow-man? Is no injustice manifest in the land, where the prince, unfaithful to his duty, seizes his innocent subjects, and sells them for slaves? Are no moral evils produced among those communities, which make war upon other communities for the sake of plunder, and without any previous provocation or offence?

* * * The counterpart of the evil is to be seen in the conduct of those, who purchase the miserable natives in their own country, and convey them to distant lands. And here questions, similar to the former, may be asked. Do they experience no

---

1. Emptied tank.
2. Clarkson's analogy to cattle evokes "chattel," a synonym for "slave" that shares an etymology with "cattle" and "capital."

corruption of their nature, or become chargeable with no violation of right, who, when they go with their ships to this continent, know the enormities which their visits there will occasion, who buy their fellow-creature man, and this, knowing the way in which he comes into their hands, and who chain, and imprison, and scourge him? Do the moral feelings of those persons escape without injury, whose hearts are hardened? And can the hearts of those be otherwise than hardened, who are familiar with the tears and groans of innocent strangers forcibly torn away from every thing that is dear to them in life, who are accustomed to see them on board their vessels in a state of suffocation and in the agonies of despair, and who are themselves in the habits of the cruel use of arbitrary power?

The counterpart of the evil in its third branch is to be seen in the conduct of those, who, when these miserable people have been landed, purchase and carry them to their respective homes. And let us see whether a mass of wickedness is not generated also in the present case. Can those have nothing to answer for, who separate the faithful ties which nature and religion have created? Can their feelings be otherwise than corrupted, who consider their fellow-creatures as brutes, or treat those as cattle, who may become the temples of the Holy Spirit, and in whom the Divinity disdains not himself to dwell? Is there no injustice in forcing men to labour without wages? Is there no breach of duty, when we are commanded to clothe the naked, and feed the hungry, and visit the sick and in prison, in exposing them to want, in torturing them by cruel punishment, and in grinding them down by hard labour, so as to shorten their days? Is there no crime in adopting a system, which keeps down all the noble faculties of their souls, and which positively debases and corrupts their nature? Is there no crime in perpetuating these evils among their innocent offspring? And finally, besides all these crimes, is there not naturally in the familiar sight of the exercise, but more especially in the exercise itself, of uncontrolled power, that which vitiates the internal man? In seeing misery stalk daily over the land, do not all become insensibly hardened? By giving birth to that misery themselves, do they not become abandoned? In what state of society are the corrupt appetites so easily, so quickly, and so frequently indulged, and where else, by means of frequent indulgence, do these experience such a monstrous growth? Where else is the temper subject to such frequent irritation, or passion to such little controul? Yes; if the unhappy slave is in an unfortunate situation, so is the tyrant who holds him. * * *

If we were to take the vast extent of space occupied by these crimes and sufferings from the heart of Africa to its shores, and that which they filled on the continent of America and the islands adjacent, and were to join the crimes and sufferings in one to those in the other by the crimes and sufferings which took place in the track of the vessels successively crossing the Atlantic, we should behold a vast belt as it were of physical and moral evil, reaching through land and ocean to the length of nearly half the circle of the globe.

[THE RECRUITMENT OF SEAMEN FOR THE SLAVE-SHIPS]

The young mariner if a stranger to the port [Bristol] and unacquainted with the nature of the Slave-trade, was sure to be picked up. The novelty of the voyages, the superiority of the wages in this over any other trades, and the privileges of various kinds, were set before him. Gulled in this manner he was frequently enticed to the boat, which was waiting to carry him away. If these prospects did not attract him, he was plied with liquor till he became intoxicated, when a bargain was made over him between the landlord and the mate. After this his senses were kept in such a constant state of stupe-faction by the liquor, that in time the former might do with him what he pleased. Sea-men also were boarded in these houses, who, when the slave-ships were going out, but at no other time, were encouraged to spend more than they had money to pay for; and to these, when they had thus exceeded, but one alternative was given, namely, a slave-vessel, or a jail. These distressing scenes I found myself obliged frequently to witness, for I was no less than nineteen times occupied in making these hateful rounds. And I can say from my own experience, and all the information I could collect from Thomp-son and others, that no such practices were in use to obtain seamen for other trades.

The treatment of the seamen employed in the Slave-trade had so deeply inter-ested me, and now the manner of procuring them, that I was determined to make my-self acquainted with their whole history; for I found by report, that they were not only personally ill-treated, * * * but that they were robbed by artifice of those wages, which had been held up to them as so superior in this service. * * * On whatever branch of the system I turned my eyes, I found it equally barbarous. The trade was, in short, one mass of iniquity from the beginning to the end. * * *

In pursuing another object, which was that of going on board the slave-ships, and learning their construction and dimensions, I was greatly struck, and indeed af-fected, by the appearance of two little sloops, which were fitting out for Africa, the one of only twenty-five tons, which was said to be destined to carry seventy; and the other of only eleven, which was said to be destined to carry thirty slaves. I was told also that which was more affecting, namely, that these were not to act as tenders on the coast, by going up and down the rivers, and receiving three or four slaves at a time, and then carrying them to a large ship, which was to take them to the West In-dies, but that it was actually intended, that they should transport their own slaves themselves. * * * In the vessel of twenty-five tons, the length of the upper part of the hold, or roof, of the room, where the seventy slaves were to be stowed, was but little better than ten yards, or thirty-one feet. The greatest breadth of the bottom, or floor, was ten feet four inches, and the least five. Hence, a grown person must sit down all the voyage, and contract his limbs within the narrow limits of three square feet. In the vessel of eleven tons, the length of the room for the thirty slaves was twenty-two feet. The greatest breadth of the floor was eight, and the least four. The whole height from the keel to the beam was but five feet eight inches, three feet of which were oc-cupied by ballast, cargo, and provisions, so that two feet eight inches remained only as the height between the decks. Hence, each slave would have only four square feet to sit in, and, when in this posture, his head, if he were a full-grown person, would touch the ceiling, or upper deck.

[CLARKSON'S NIGHTMARES]

At Bristol my feelings had been harassed by the cruel treatment of the seamen, which had come to my knowledge there: but now I was doomed to see this treat-ment over again in many other melancholy instances; and additionally to take in the various sufferings of the unhappy slaves. These accounts I could seldom get time to read till late in the evening, and sometimes not till midnight, when the letters containing them were to be answered. The effect of these accounts was in some in-stances to overwhelm me for a time in tears, and in others to produce a vivid indig-nation, which affected my whole frame. Recovering from these, I walked up and down the room. I felt fresh vigour, and made new determinations of perpetual warfare against this impious trade. I implored strength that I might proceed. I then sat down, and continued my work as long as my wearied eyes would permit me to see. Having been agitated in this manner, I went to bed: but my rest was frequently broken by the visions which floated before me. When I awoke, these renewed themselves to me, and they flitted about with me for the remainder of the day. Thus I was kept continually harassed: my mind was confined to one gloomy and heart-breaking subject for months. It had no respite, and my health began now materially to suffer.

[THE DEFENSE OF THE TRADE IN PARLIAMENT]

The public papers began to be filled with such statements as were thought most likely to influence the members of the house of commons, previously to the discussion of the question [the bill for abolition].

The first impression attempted to be made upon them was with respect to the slaves themselves. It was contended, and attempted to be shown by the revival of the old argument of human sacrifices in Africa, that these were better off in the islands than in their own country. It was contended also, that they were people of very inferior capacities, and but little removed from the brute creation; whence an inference was drawn, that their treatment, against which so much clamour had arisen, was adapted to their intellect and feelings.

The next attempt was to degrade the abolitionists in the opinion of the house, by showing the wildness and absurdity of their schemes. It was again insisted upon that emancipation was the real object of the former; so that thousands of slaves would be let loose in the islands to rob or perish, and who could never be brought back again into habits of useful industry.

An attempt was then made to excite their pity in behalf of the planters. The abolition, it was said, would produce insurrections among the slaves. But insurrections would produce the massacre of their masters; and, if any of these should happily escape from butchery, they would be reserved only for ruin.

An appeal was then made to them on the ground of their own interest and of that of the people, whom they represented. It was stated that the ruin of the islands would be the ruin of themselves and of the country. Its revenue would be half annihilated. Its naval strength would decay. Merchants, manufacturers and others would come to beggary. But in this deplorable situation they would expect to be indemnified for their losses. Compensation indeed must follow. It could not be withheld. But what would be the amount of it? The country would have no less than from eighty to a hundred millions to pay the sufferers; and it would be driven to such distress in paying this sum as it had never before experienced.

The last attempt was to show them that a regulation of the trade was all that was now wanted. While this would remedy the evils complained of, it would prevent the mischief which would assuredly follow the abolition. The planters had already done their part. The assemblies of the different islands had most of them made wholesome laws upon the subject. The very bills passed for this purpose in Jamaica and Grenada had arrived in England, and might be seen by the public: the great grievances had been redressed: no slave could now be mutilated or wantonly killed by his owner; one man could not now maltreat, or bruise, or wound the slave of another; the aged could not now be turned off to perish by hunger. There were laws also relative to the better feeding and clothing of the slaves. It remained only that the trade to Africa should be put under as wise and humane regulations as the slavery in the islands had undergone.

[COUNTER-TESTIMONY FROM A SLAVE-SHIP INVESTIGATOR]

Having said thus much on the subject of procuring slaves in Africa, he would now go to that of the transportation of them. * * * This was the most wretched part of the whole subject. He was incapable of impressing the house with what he felt upon it. A description of their conveyance was impossible. So much misery condensed in so little room was more than the human imagination had ever before conceived. Think only of six hundred persons linked together, trying to get rid of each other, crammed in a close vessel with every object that was nauseous and disgusting, diseased, and struggling with all the varieties of wretchedness. It seemed impossible to add any thing more to human misery. Yet shocking as this description must be felt to be by every man, the transportation had been described by several witnesses from Liverpool to be a comfortable conveyance. Mr. Norris had painted the accommodations on board a slaveship in the most glowing colours. He had represented them in a manner which would have exceeded his attempts at praise of the most luxurious scenes. Their apartments, he said, were fitted up as advantageously for them as circumstances could possibly admit: they had several meals a day; some, of their own country provisions, with the best sauces of African cookery; and, by way of variety, another meal of pulse, according to the European taste. After breakfast they had water to wash themselves, while their apartments were perfumed with frankincense and lime-juice. Before dinner they were amused after the manner of their country: instruments of music were introduced: the song and the dance were promoted: games of chance were furnished them: the men played and sang, while the women and girls made fanciful ornaments from beads, with which they were plentifully supplied. They were indulged in all their little fancies, and kept in sprightly humour. Another of them had said, when the sailors were flogged, it was out of the hearing of the Africans, lest it should depress their spirits. He by no means wished to say that such descriptions were wilful misrepresentations. If they were not, it proved that interest or prejudice was capable of spreading a film over the eyes thick enough to occasion total blindness.

Others, however, and these men of the greatest veracity, had given a different account. What would the house think, when by the concurring testimony of these the true history was laid open? The slaves who had been described as rejoicing in their captivity, were so wrung with misery at leaving their country, that it was the constant practice to set sail in the night, lest they should know the moment of their departure. With respect to their accommodation, the right ancle of one was fastened to the left ancle of another by an iron fetter; and if they were turbulent, by another on the wrists. Instead of the apartments described, they were placed in niches, and along the decks, in such a manner, that it was impossible for any one to pass among them, however careful he might be, without treading upon them. Sir George Yonge had testified, that in a slave-ship, on board of which he went, and which had not completed her cargo by two hundred and fifty, instead of the scent of frankincense being perceptible to the nostrils, the stench was intolerable. The allowance of water was so deficient, that the slaves were frequently found gasping for life, and almost suffocated. The pulse with which they had been said to be favoured, were absolutely English horse-beans. The legislature of Jamaica had stated the scantiness both of water and provisions, as a subject which called for the interference of parliament. As Mr. Norris had said, the song and the dance were promoted, he could not pass over these expressions without telling the house what they meant. It would have been much more fair if he himself had explained the word *promoted*. The truth was, that,

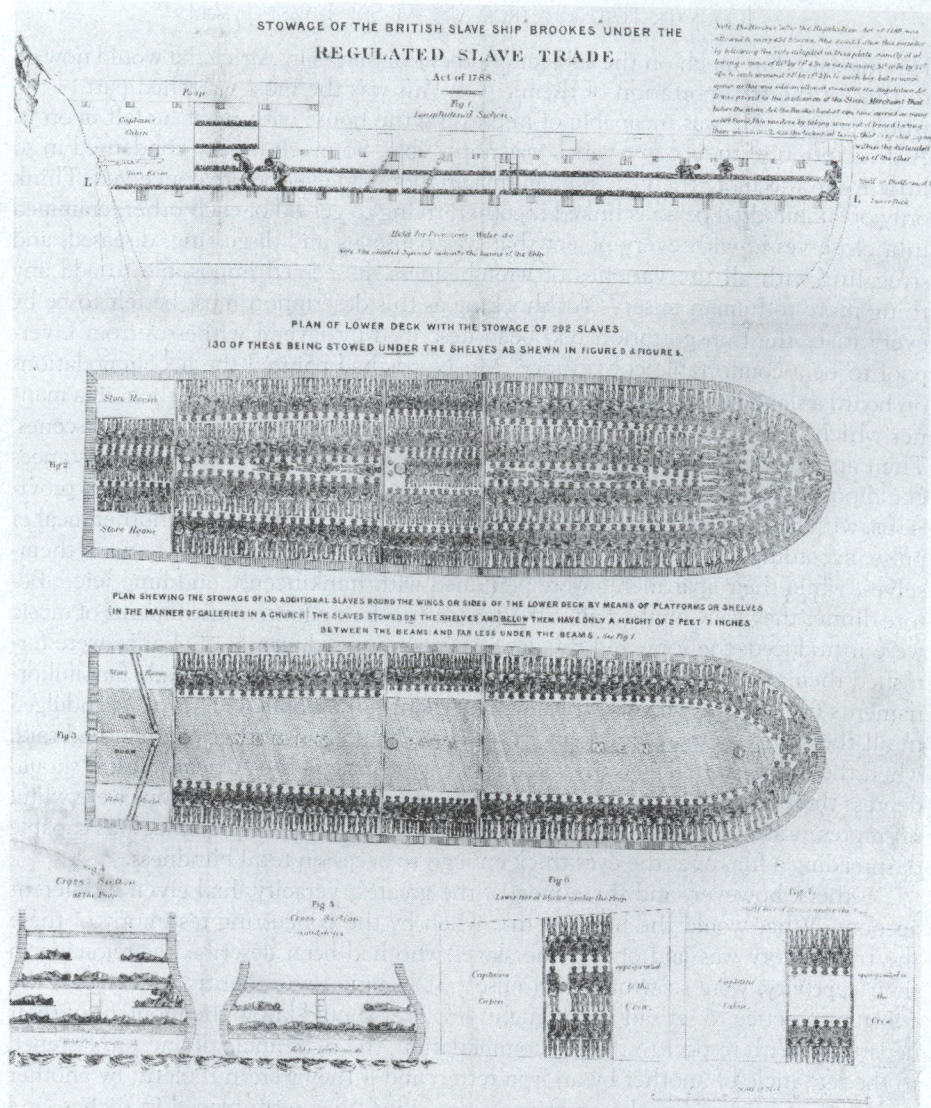

Packing methods on a slave ship. Illustration to *The History of the Rise, Progress, & Accomplishment of the Abolition of the African Slave-Trade by the British Parliament*, by Thomas Clarkson, 1808. The top image is "tight-packing"; the lower, a more "humane" arrangement.

for the sake of exercise, these miserable wretches, loaded with chains and oppressed with disease, were forced to dance by the terror of the lash, and sometimes by the actual use of it. "I," said one of the evidences, "was employed to dance the men, while another person danced the women." Such then was the meaning of the word *promoted;* and it might also be observed with respect to food, that instruments were sometimes carried out, in order to force them to eat; which was the same sort of proof, how much they enjoyed themselves in this instance also. With respect to their singing, it consisted of songs of lamentation for the loss of their country. While they sung they were in tears: so that one of the captains, more humane probably than the rest, threatened a woman with a flogging because the mournfulness of her song was too painful for his feelings. Perhaps he could not give a better proof of the sufferings of these injured people during their passage, than by stating the mortality which accompanied it. This was a species of evidence which was infallible on this occasion. Death was a witness which could not deceive them; and the proportion of deaths would not only confirm, but, if possible, even aggravate our suspicion of the misery of the transit. It would be found, upon an average of all the ships, upon which evidence had been given, that, exclusively of such as perished before they sailed from Africa, not less than twelve and a half per cent. died on their passage: besides these, the Jamaica report stated that four and a half per cent. died while in the harbours, or on shore before the day of sale, which was only about the space of twelve or fourteen days after their arrival there; and one third more died in the seasoning:[3] and this in a climate exactly similar to their own, and where, as some of the witnesses pretended, they were healthy and happy. Thus, out of every lot of one hundred, shipped from Africa, seventeen died in about nine weeks, and not more than fifty lived to become effective labourers in our islands.

["Reflections on This Great Event"]

With respect to the end obtained by this contest, or the great measure of the abolition of the Slave-trade as it has now passed, I know not how to appreciate its importance. To our own country, indeed, it is invaluable. We have lived, in consequence of it, to see the day, when it has been recorded as a principle in our legislation, that commerce itself shall have its moral boundaries. We have lived to see the day, when we are likely to be delivered from the contagion of the most barbarous opinions. * * * though nature shrinks from pain, and compassion is engendered in us when we see it become the portion of others, yet what is physical suffering compared with moral guilt? The misery of the oppressed is, in the first place, not contagious like the crime of the oppressor. Nor is the mischief, which it generates, either so frightful or so pernicious. The body, though under affliction, may retain its shape; and, if it even perish, what is the loss of it but of worthless dust? But when the moral springs of the mind are poisoned, we lose the most excellent part of the constitution of our nature, and the divine image is no longer perceptible in us. Nor are the two evils of similar duration. By a decree of Providence, for which we cannot be too thankful, we are made mortal. Hence the torments of the oppressor are but temporary; whereas the immortal part of us, when once corrupted, may carry its pollutions with it into another world.

But independently of the quantity of physical suffering and the innumerable avenues to vice in more than a quarter of the globe, which this great measure will cut off, there are yet blessings, which we have reason to consider as likely to flow from it. Among these we cannot overlook the great probability, that Africa, now freed from the vicious and barbarous effects of this traffic, may be in a better state to comprehend and receive the sublime truths of the Christian religion. Nor can we overlook the probability, that, a new system of treatment necessarily springing up in our islands, the same

---

3. Breaking-in.

bright sun of consolation may visit her children there. But here a new hope rises to our view. Who knows but that emancipation, like a beautiful plant, may, in its due season, rise out of the ashes of the abolition of the Slave-trade, and that, when its own intrinsic value shall be known, the seed of it may be planted in other lands? And looking at the subject in this point of view, we cannot but be struck with the wonderful concurrence of events as previously necessary for this purpose, namely, that two nations, England and America, the mother and the child, should, in the same month of the same year, have abolished this impious traffic; nations, which at this moment have more than a million of subjects within their jurisdiction to partake of the blessing; and one of which, on account of her local situation and increasing power, is likely in time to give, if not law, at least a tone to the manners and customs of the great continent, on which she is situated.

Reader! Thou art now acquainted with the history of this contest! Rejoice in the manner of its termination! And, if thou feelest grateful for the event, retire within thy closet,[4] and pour out thy thanksgivings to the Almighty for this his unspeakable act of mercy to thy oppressed fellow-creatures.

—⟞⟦◆⟧⟝—

William Wordsworth
1770–1850

When they were all living in the Lake District of England, the Wordsworths and Coleridge became close friends with Thomas Clarkson and his wife, and were inspired by Clarkson's intense commitment to abolition. William Wordsworth's sonnet *To Thomas Clarkson*, published in 1807, honors his heroic persistence in behalf of the Abolition Bill. *To Toussaint L'Ouverture* honors François Dominique Toussaint (1743?–1803), a self-educated slave freed shortly before the 1791 revolt in San Domingo, to become a leader of the revolutionaries (dubbed "L'Ouverture" for his skill in "opening" gaps in enemy ranks, he adopted this as a surname). In 1801, he conquered San Domingo and became governor of the whole island. When, in 1802, he resisted Napoleon's attempt to re-establish French rule and slavery, he was arrested and dungeoned in the French Alps, where he died in April 1803, after ten months of cold and hunger. Wordsworth published his sonnet in *The Morning Post*, 2 February 1803, and then in *Poems* of 1807 under "Sonnets Dedicated to Liberty." *Humanity*—written decades later, in 1829, before colonial emancipation, and published soon after, in 1835—demonstrates his unwavering moral revulsion at slavery and contempt for the economic justifications. But in a letter of 1833, he joined the now Tory Poet Laureate Southey in declining to contribute to a volume of antislavery poetry, arguing that the planters have been too one-sidedly villainized.

For more about Wordsworth, see the principal listing on page 183.

To Toussaint L'Ouverture

> Toussaint, the most unhappy man of men!
> Whether the rural Milk-maid by her Cow
> Sing in thy hearing, or thou liest now
> Alone in some deep dungeon's earless den,
> O miserable Chieftain! where and when
> Wilt thou find patience? Yet die not; be thou

5

---

4. Private sitting room. This is the closing paragraph of the *History*.

Life to thyself in death; with chearful brow:
Live, loving death, nor let one thought in ten
Be painful to thee. Thou hast left behind
10 Powers that will work for thee; air, earth, and skies;
There's not a breathing of the common wind
That will forget thee; thou hast great allies;
Thy friends are exultations, agonies,
And love, and Man's unconquerable mind.

1802   2 February 1803
                                                        W.L.D.[1]

To Thomas Clarkson
On the final passing of the Bill for the Abolition of the Slave Trade,
March, 1807

Clarkson! it was an obstinate Hill to climb;
How toilsome, nay how dire it was, by Thee
Is known,—by none, perhaps, so feelingly;
But Thou, who, starting in thy fervent prime,
5 Didst first lead forth this pilgrimage sublime,
Hast heard the constant Voice its charge repeat,
Which, out of thy young heart's oracular seat,
First roused thee.—O true yoke-fellow of Time
With unabating effort, see, the palm
10 Is won, and by all Nations shall be worn!
The bloody Writing is for ever torn,
And Thou henceforth shalt have a good Man's calm,
A great Man's happiness; thy zeal shall find
Repose at length, firm Friend of human kind!

1807   1807

from The Prelude[1]

When to my native Land,
(After a whole year's absence) I return'd
I found the air yet busy with the stir
Of a contention which had been rais'd up
205 Against the Traffickers in Negro blood,
An effort, which though baffled, nevertheless
Had call'd back old forgotten principles
Dismiss'd from service, had diffus'd some truths
And more of virtuous feeling through the heart

1. According to the poet's brother-in-law, the initials
stand for "Wordsworthius Libertari Dedicavit" (dedicated
to liberty); he signed 7 sonnets this way in 1803.
1. From Book 10, written c. 1805; a revised text appears
in the version of *The Prelude* published in 1850, a moment when it could address the abolition movement in
the United States, where *The Prelude* was also published.

210   Of the English People.[2] And no few of those
          So numerous (little less in verity
          Than a whole Nation crying with one voice)
          Who had been cross'd in this their just intent
          And righteous hope, thereby were well prepared
215   To let that journey sleep a while and join
          Whatever other Caravan appear'd
          To travel forward towards Liberty
          With more success. For me that strife had ne'er
          Fasten'd on my affections, nor did now
220   Its unsuccessful issue much excite
          My sorrow, having laid this faith to heart,
          That if France prosper'd good Men would not long
          Pay fruitless worship to humanity,
          And this most rotten branch of human shame,
225   Object, as seem'd, of a superfluous pains,
          Would fall together with its parent tree.

1805   1926

from Humanity

          Though cold as winter, gloomy as the grave,
          Stone-walls a prisoner make, but not a slave.[1]
          Shall man assume a property in man?[2]
80   Lay on the moral will a withering ban?
          Shame that our laws at distance still protect
          Enormities, which they at home reject!
          "Slaves cannot breathe in England"[3]—yet that boast
          Is but a mockery! when from coast to coast,
85   Though *fettered* slave be none, her floors and soil
          Groan underneath a weight of slavish toil,
          For the poor Many, measured out by rules
          Fetched with cupidity from heartless schools,
          That to an Idol, falsely called "the Wealth
90   Of Nations,"[4] sacrifice a People's health,
          Body and mind and soul; a thirst so keen
          Is ever urging on the vast machine
          Of sleepless Labor, 'mid whose dizzy wheels
          The Power least prized is that which thinks and feels.

1829   1835

2. Wordsworth returned from revolutionary France late in 1792; the "effort" is Wilberforce's unsuccessful 1793 bill for abolition.
1. Revising Lovelace's famous declaration in *To Althea, from Prison* (1649): "Stone walls do not a prison make, / Nor iron bars a cage; // . . . I have freedom in my love, / And in my soul am free" (25ff).
2. A reference to Paine's statement in *The Rights of Man* that "Man has no property in man."

3. The Mansfield Decision of 1772 rejected the claims that "neither the air of England is too pure for a slave to breathe in, nor the laws of England have rejected servitude."
4. An influential argument for laissez-faire capitalism (self-interest, unrestricted by law, best serves the public welfare) put forth in Adam Smith's *Inquiry into the Nature and Causes of the Wealth of Nations* (1776).

Letter to Mary Ann Rawson[1]

[c. May 1833]

Dear Madam,

Your letter which I lose no time in replying to, has placed me under some embarrassment, as I happen to possess some Mss verses of my own[2] upon the subject to which you solicit my attention. But I frankly own to you, that neither with respect to this subject nor to the kindred one, the Slavery of the children in the Factories,[3] which is adverted to in the same Poem, am I prepared to add to the excitement already existing in the public mind upon these, and so many other points of legislation and government. Poetry, if good for any thing, must appeal forcibly to the Imagination and the feelings; but what at this period we want above every thing, is patient examination and sober judgement. It can scarcely be necessary to add that my mind revolts as strongly as any one's can, from the law that permits one human being to sell another. It is in principle monstrous, but it is not the worst thing in human nature. Let precipitate advocates for its destruction bear this in mind. But I will not enter farther into the question than to say, that there are three parties—the Slave—the Slave owner—and the imperial Parliament, or rather the people of the British Islands, acting through that Organ. Surely the course at present pursued is hasty, intemperate, and likely to lead to gross injustice. Who in fact are most to blame? the people—who, by their legislation, have sanctioned not to say encouraged, slavery. But now we are turning round at once upon the planters, and heaping upon them indignation without measure, as if we wished that the Slaves should believe that their Masters alone were culpable—and they alone fit objects of complaint and resentment.

Excuse haste and believe me Dear Madam
respectfully yours,
Wm Wordsworth

The Edinburgh Review

One of the most influential quarterlies of the day, the *Edinburgh Review* was edited by its co-founder Francis Jeffrey (1773–1850) from its inception in 1802 until 1829. Although Jeffrey tended to conservative literary judgment (famously attacking the Lake School for presenting peasants sympathetically), the *Edinburgh* was liberal in political opinion and supported the Whigs in their parliamentary campaign for reform. Among its other cofounders, Henry Brougham (1778–1868) was a leader in the abolitionist movement, and Sydney Smith (1771–1845) excoriated the slave trade as an "enormous wickedness." Although England had

1. An original member of the Sheffield Female Anti-Slavery Society (founded in 1825), Rawson began in 1826 to collect pieces for an anthology of antislavery prose and poetry, *The Bow in the Cloud*, which she published in 1834, after colonial Emancipation, in a small edition of 500.
2. *Humanity*, above.
3. A parliamentary commission issued a shocking report in 1832 about child labor in factories that led to the "Act of 1833," preventing those under nine from such labor and limited those under 13 to 48 hours a week, with no more than nine hours in any one day; it also required these children to receive at least two hours of schooling a day. It failed in its goal to secure a ten-hour day for teenagers.

abolished the trade in 1807, other countries, including France and the United States, had not, and slavery was still legal in England's colonies. Reports such as the one below (October 1821) kept public attention focused on the atrocities.

from Abstract of the Information laid on the Table of the House of Commons, on the Subject of the Slave Trade

The French ship Le Rodeur, of two hundred tons burden, sailed from the port of Havre for the river Calabar on the coast of Africa, where she arrived after a prosperous voyage, and anchored at Bonny on the fourteenth of March. Her crew, of twenty-two men, had enjoyed perfect health; and this continued during her stay of three weeks, while she received on board one hundred and sixty negroes, with whom she set sail for Guadaloupe[1] on the sixth of April. No traces of any epidemy had been perceived among the natives; the cargo (as it is called), no more than the crew, exhibited any symptoms of disease; and the first fortnight of the voyage to the West Indies promised a continuance of all the success which had seemed to attend the earlier stages of the expedition. The vessel had now approached the line,[2] when a frightful malady broke out. At first the symptoms were slight, little more than a redness of the eyes; and this being confined to the negroes, was ascribed to the want of air in the hold, and the narrow space between the decks, into which so large a number of those unhappy beings were crowded; something, too, was imagined to arise from the scarcity of water, which had thus early begun to be felt, and pressed chiefly upon the slaves; for they were allowed only eight ounces, which was soon reduced to half a wine glass per day. By the surgeon's advice, therefore, they were suffered, for the first time, to breathe the purer air upon the deck, where they were brought in succession; but many of these poor creatures being affected with that mighty desire of returning to their native country, which is so strong as to form a disease, termed *Nostalgia* by the physicians, no sooner found they were at liberty, than they threw themselves into the sea, locked in each other's arms, in the vain hope, known to prevail among them, of thus being swiftly transported again to their homes. With the view of counteracting this propensity, the Captain ordered several who were stopt in the attempt, to be shot or hanged in the sight of their companions; but this terrible example was unavailing to deter them; and it became necessary, once more, to confine them entirely to the hold.

The disease proved to be a virulent ophthalmia, and it now spread with irresistible rapidity among the Africans, all of whom were seized; but it soon attacked the crew; and its ravages were attended, perhaps its violence exasperated, by a dysentery, which the use of rain-water was found to have produced. A sailor who slept near the hatch communicating with the hold, was the first who caught it; next day a landsman was taken ill; and in three days more, the Captain and almost all the rest of the crew were infected. The resources of medicine were tried in vain; the sufferings of the people, and the number of the blind, were daily increasing; and they were in constant expectation that the negroes, taking advantage of their numbers, would rise and destroy them. From this danger they were only saved by the mutual hatred of the tribes

1. In the Caribbean.   2. Equator.

to which these unfortunate beings belonged, and which was so fierce and inextinguishable, that, even under the load of chains and sickness, they were ready every instant, in their fury, to tear one another in pieces. * * *

The consternation now became general and horrid; but it did not preclude calculation; for, thirty-six of the negroes having become quite blind, were *thrown into the sea and drowned,* in order to save the expense of supporting slaves rendered unsaleable, and to obtain grounds for a claim against the under-writers.[3] * * *

The reader may think that we have been going back to the times when the slave-trade flourished under the protection of the law in England and France; and that we have been citing from the writings of some political author, some advocate for the abolition. Not so. All these horrors darken the history of the year 1819; and the tale is almost all told incidentally by the scientific compilers of a Medical Journal. Yes—in 1819 * * * twelve years after England had forbidden the traffic—eight years after she had declared it a crime—and four years after France, first by law, and then by solemn treaty, had become a party to its positive, unqualified, immediate abolition.

Dreadful as are the scenes disclosed in the case of the Rodeur, there are even worse horrors in the Parliamentary Papers of which the abstract lies before us. In March 1820, the Tartar, commanded by Sir George Collier, boarded a French vessel, called La Jeune Estelle of Martinique, after a long chase. The captain admitted that he had been engaged in the slave-trade, but denied that he had any slaves on board, declaring that he had been plundered of his cargo. The English officers, however, observed that all the French seamen appeared agitated and alarmed; and this led to an examination of the hold. Nothing, however, was found; and they would have departed with the belief that the captain's story was a true one, had not a sailor happened to strike a cask, and hear, or fancy he heard, a faint voice issue from within. The cask was opened, and two negro girls were found crammed into it, and in the last stage of suffocation. Being brought upon the deck of the Tartar, they were recognised by a person who had before seen them in the possession of an American who had died on the coast. An investigation now took place; and it was ascertained that they formed part of a cargo of fourteen slaves, whom the French captain had carried off by an attack which he and his crew made on the American's property after his decease. This led to a new search of the slave-ship for the other twelve, whom he was thus proved to have obtained by the robbery; when a platform was discovered, on which the negroes must have been laid in a space twenty-three inches in height, and beneath it a negro was found, not, however, one of the twelve, jammed into the crevice between two water casks. Still there were no traces of those twelve slaves; and the French captain persisted in his story, that he had been plundered by a Spanish pirate. But suddenly a most horrible idea darted across the minds of the English officers and men; they recollected that, when the chase began, they had seen several casks floating past them, which, at the time, they could not account for; but now, after the examination of the one which remained on board the Jeune Estelle, little doubt could

---

3. The notorious precedent was the case of the slave ship *Zong* (1781), whose captain ordered 133 weak and diseased slaves ejected into shark-infested waters in order to collect on a policy that held the insurer liable for cargo jettisoned in order to salvage the remainder. The insurance trial (not about the captain's criminal liability but the underwriter's financial liability) was presided over by Mansfield, who ruled in favor of the captain. See Color Plate 5.

be entertained that those casks contained the wretched slaves, whom the infernal monster had thus thrown overboard, to prevent the detection that would have ensued, either upon their being found in his ship, or by their bodies floating exposed on the sea. * * *

May we not then appeal to the body of our most enlightened European neighbours, and call upon them to stimulate their rulers not only to follow the example set by England and America in classing the slave-trade among heinous crimes, but to join them in that measure which, if those three great maritime powers adopt it, must speedily become the law of all nations? That the French people at large are prepared for such a step, there can be little reason to doubt. All their ablest statesmen have the most sound views upon this important question; and the remains of prejudice with respect to the means, when so generous an anxiety is entertained for the attainment of the object, must soon give way to the enlightened genius of the age; and certainly, what has passed in America, is calculated to assist in dispelling those prejudices beyond any thing we can conceive.

Our attention has, in this article, been confined to the portion of the Parliamentary Papers which treats of the French slave-trade, as out of all comparison the most important in every point of view. Much to lament and to amend is, however, contained in the correspondence with Spain, Portugal, and the Netherlands; and it is to be hoped that our Government, acting under the control of the almost unanimous opinion upon this subject entertained both by Parliament and the country, will be enabled, before long, to obtain some more satisfactory arrangements with those three powers. The late Revolutions, and the establishment of a popular constitution in Portugal and Spain, afford additional grounds for such expectations.

⊷ ⊨⟡⊨ ⊶

George Gordon, Lord Byron
1788–1824

from Detached Thoughts[1]

But there is <u>no</u> freedom—even for <u>Masters</u>—in the midst of slaves——it makes my blood boil to see the thing.—I sometimes wish that I was the Owner of Africa—to do at once—what Wilberforce will do in time—viz—sweep Slavery from her desarts— and look on upon the first dance of their Freedom.——As to <u>political</u> slavery—so general—it is men's own fault—if they <u>will</u> be slaves let them!——yet it is but "a word and a blow"—see how England formerly—France—Spain—Portugal— America—Switzerland—freed themselves!——there is no one instance of a <u>long</u> contest in which <u>men</u> did not triumph over Systems.—If Tyranny misses her <u>first</u> spring she is cowardly as the tiger and retires to be hunted.——

⊷ END OF PERSPECTIVES: THE ABOLITION OF SLAVERY AND THE SLAVE TRADE⊷

---

1. Byron recorded these reflections in his journal in late 1821. He quotes *Romeo and Juliet* 3.1.41.

Mary Robinson
1758–1800

As a child, Mary Darby attended a school run by Hannah More's sisters in Bristol. In her teens she married Thomas Robinson, a clerk who landed them and their daughter in debtor's prison. Her beauty and talent rescued her: under the patronage of Richard Brinsley Sheridan and David Garrick, she made her debut in 1776 as Juliet at Drury Lane Theatre, where she appeared with great success for four seasons. Her performance in Shakespeare's *The Winter's Tale* captivated the young Prince of Wales (afterward George IV), who in his letters assumed the role of Florizel to her Perdita, the name by which she was ever afterward known. She became his mistress, but the liaison ended within a year, and the Prince reneged on a promised financial settlement of £20,000. With the aid of the prominent Whig Charles James Fox, also a lover, she obtained an annuity of £500. A series of affairs with such fashionable figures as Colonel Banastre Tarleton, who had fought under Cornwallis in America and later became a Member of Parliament, kept her in the public eye even after her retirement from the stage. Witness this paragraph, under the head "Ship News," from the *Morning Post:*

> Yesterday, a messenger arrived in town, with the very interesting and pleasing intelligence of the Tarleton, armed ship, having, after a chace of some months, captured the Perdita frigate, and brought her safe into Egham port. The Perdita is a prodigious fine clean bottomed vessel, and had taken many prizes during her cruize, particularly the Florizel, a most valuable ship belonging to the Crown, but which was immediately released, after taking out the cargo. The Perdita was captured some time ago by the Fox, but was, afterwards, retaken by the Malden, and had a sumptuous suit of new rigging, when she fell in with the Tarleton. Her manoeuvering to escape was admirable; but the Tarleton, fully determined to take her, or perish, would not give up the chace; and at length, coming alongside the Perdita, fully determined to board her, sword in hand, she instantly surrendered at discretion.

At the height of her fame, Robinson was painted by Cosway, Reynolds, Gainsborough, and Romney. (See the Gainsborough portrait, Color Plate 2.) A miscarriage in 1783 paralyzed her legs, but the affair with Tarleton did not end until he married an heiress in 1798. Though Robinson's literary career was inseparable from her notoriety, it both predated and outlasted her life on the stage. Her first volume of poems appeared in 1775, and the two-volume *Poems* of 1791–1793 attracted 600 subscribers. Working in a variety of genres from the sentimental verse with which she began through ballads, tales, light occasional verse, and odes, producing plays and seven successful novels, Robinson confirmed her twofold status as celebrity and writer, and supported herself, her mother, and her daughter. *Sappho and Phaon* (1796) brought her the title of "the English Sappho" that to some degree overlaid her identity as "Perdita"; arguing in the preface for the "legitimate" Petrarchan sonnet, Robinson combined a poetry of passion (for which Sappho was an honorific female precursor) with formal control, and made a notable contribution to the revival of the sonnet upon which Wordsworth was to capitalize. Succeeding Southey as poetry editor of the *Morning Post*, she became an established figure on the London literary scene. Coleridge thought her "a woman of undoubted Genius . . . she overloads everything; but I never knew a human being with so full a mind—bad, good, and indifferent, I grant you—but full and overflowing." Her collection *Lyrical Tales* (1800), published in the last year of her life, acknowledges *Lyrical Ballads;* Coleridge thought the meter of *The Haunted Beach* "fascinating," and sent her *Kubla Khan* in manuscript, inspiring one of her last works, *To the Poet Coleridge*, a record of response to the poem sixteen years before it was printed. Her career exemplifies the opportunities for self-fashioning the burgeoning literary marketplace offered a resourceful woman.

Ode to Beauty

EXULTING BEAUTY:—phantom of an hour,
    Whose magic spells enchain the heart,
Ah! what avails thy fascinating pow'r,
    Thy thrilling smile, thy witching art?
5   Thy lip, where balmy nectar glows;
        Thy cheek, where round the damask rose
    A thousand nameless Graces move,[1]
        Thy mildly speaking azure eyes,
    Thy golden hair, where cunning Love
10   In many a mazy ringlet lies?
Soon as thy radiant form is seen,
    Thy native blush, thy timid mien,°   *appearance*
Thy hour is past! thy charms are vain!
ILL-NATURE haunts thee with her sallow train,
15   Mean JEALOUSY deceives thy list'ning ear,
And SLANDER stains thy cheek with many a bitter tear.

In calm retirement form'd to dwell,
    NATURE, thy handmaid fair and kind,
    For thee a beauteous garland twin'd;
20   The vale-nurs'd Lily's downcast bell
        Thy modest mien display'd,
    The snow-drop, April's meekest child,
    With myrtle blossoms undefil'd.
        Thy mild and spotless mind pourtray'd;
25   Dear blushing maid, of cottage birth,
     'Twas thine, o'er dewy meads to stray,
While sparkling health, and frolic mirth,
    Led on thy laughing Day.

Lur'd by the babbling tongue of FAME,
30   Too soon, insidious FLATT'RY came;
    Flush'd VANITY her footsteps led,
    To charm thee from thy blest repose,
    While Fashion twin'd about thy head
        A wreath of wounding woes;
35   See Dissipation smoothly glide,
    Cold Apathy, and puny Pride,
    Capricious Fortune, dull, and blind,
        O'er splendid Folly throws her veil,

---

1. A paraphrase of Adam's enchantment with Eve, *Paradise Lost* 8.600–604.

      While Envy's meagre tribe assail
40   Thy gentle form, and spotless mind.

      Their spells prevail! no more those eyes
        Shoot undulating fires;
      On thy wan cheek, the young rose dies,
        Thy lip's deep tint expires;
45   Dark Melancholy chills thy mind;
        Thy silent tear reveals thy woe;
    TIME strews with thorns thy mazy way;
    Where'er thy giddy footsteps stray,
      Thy thoughtless heart is doom'd to find
50   An unrelenting foe.

    'Tis thus, the infant Forest flow'r,
      Bespangled o'er with glitt'ring dew,
  At breezy morn's refreshing hour,
      Glows with pure tints of varying hue,
55 Beneath an aged oak's wide spreading shade,
  Where no rude winds, or beating storms invade.
      Transplanted from its lonely bed,
        No more it scatters perfumes round,
      No more it rears its gentle head,
60   Or brightly paints the mossy ground;
    For ah! the beauteous bud, too soon,
      Scorch'd by the burning eye of day,
    Shrinks from the sultry glare of noon,
  Droops its enamell'd brow, and blushing, dies away.

                                   1791

January, 1795

Pavement slippery, people sneezing
Lords in ermine, beggars freezing;
Titled gluttons dainties carving,
Genius in a garret starving.

5   Lofty mansions, warm and spacious;
Courtiers cringing and voracious;
Misers scarce the wretched heeding;
Gallant soldiers fighting, bleeding.

Wives who laugh at passive spouses;
10 Theatres, and meeting houses;
Balls, where simpering misses languish;
Hospitals, and groans of anguish.

Arts and sciences bewailing;
Commerce drooping, credit failing;
15 Placemen° mocking subjects loyal;   *political appointees*
Separations, weddings royal.

Authors who can't earn a dinner;
Many a subtle rogue a winner;
Fugitives for shelter seeking;
20   Misers hoarding, tradesmen breaking.°   *going bankrupt*

Taste and talents quite deserted;
All the laws of truth perverted;
Arrogance o'er merit soaring;
Merit silently deploring.

25   Ladies gambling night and morning;
Fools the works of genius scorning;
Ancient dames for girls mistaken;
Youthful damsels quite forsaken.

Some in luxury delighting;
30   More in talking than in fighting;
Lovers old, and beaux decrepid;
Lordlings empty and insipid.

Poets, painters, and musicians;
Lawyers, doctors, politicians;
35   Pamphlets, newspapers, and odes,
Seeking fame by different roads.

Gallant souls with empty purses;
Generals only fit for nurses;
School-boys, smit with martial spirit,
40   Taking places of veteran merit.

Honest men who can't get places,
Knaves who show unblushing faces;
Ruin hastened, peace retarded;
Candour spurn'd, and art° rewarded.   *hypocrisy*

1795   1795

from Sappho and Phaon, in a Series of Legitimate Sonnets[1]

Flendus amor meus est; elegeia flebile carmen;
Non facit ad lacrymas barbitos ulla meas.   OVID

Love taught my tears in sadder notes to flow,
And tuned my heart to elegies of woe.   POPE

1. Greek lyric poet Sappho of Lesbos (c. 600 B.C.) was famous for love poems addressed to other women. Little is known of her. According to legend, she was banished from Lesbos, went to Sicily and fell in love with Phaon, a Lesbian boatman granted youth and beauty by Aphrodite. When her love was not returned, she threw herself from the Leucadian rock into the sea. Robinson narrates these events in a series of 44 sonnets, taking her epigraph from Epistle XV of the *Heroides*, by Ovid (43 B.C.–A.D. 18), which popularized the story; the translation is from *Sappho to Phaon* (1712), a free rendering by Alexander Pope (1688–1744) (7–8).

III. The Bower of Pleasure

TURN to yon vale beneath, whose tangled shade
    Excludes the blazing torch of noon-day light,
    Where sportive Fawns, and dimpled Loves invite,[2]
The bow'r of Pleasure opens to the glade:
5   Lull'd by soft flutes, on leaves of violets laid,
    There witching beauty greets the ravish'd sight,
    More gentle than the arbitress of night
In all her silv'ry panoply° array'd![3]   *armor*
    The birds breathe bliss! light zephyrs kiss the ground,
10 Stealing the hyacinth's divine perfume;
    While from the pellucid fountains glitt'ring round,
Small tinkling rills° bid rival flow'rets bloom!   *streamlets*
    HERE, laughing Cupids bathe the bosom's wound;
THERE, tyrant passion finds a glorious tomb!

IV. Sappho discovers her Passion

Why, when I gaze on Phaon's beauteous eyes,
    Why does each thought in wild disorder stray?
    Why does each fainting faculty decay,
And my chill'd breast in throbbing tumults rise?
5   Mute on the ground my lyre neglected lies,
    The Muse forgot, and lost the melting lay;
    My down-cast looks, my faltering lips betray,
That stung by hopeless passion;—Sappho dies!
    Now on a bank of cypress° let me rest;   *emblem of death*
10 Come, tuneful maids, ye pupils of my care,
    Come, with your dulcet° numbers soothe my breast; *sweet, melodious*
And, as the soft vibrations float on air,
    Let pity waft my spirit to the blest,
To mock the barbarous triumphs of despair!

VII. Invokes Reason

Come. Reason, come! each nerve rebellious bind,[4]
    Lull the fierce tempest of my fev'rish soul;
    Come, with the magic of thy meek controul,
And check the wayward wand'rings of my mind:
5   Estrang'd from thee, no solace can I find;
    O'er my rapt brain, where pensive visions stole,
    Now passion reigns and stormy tumults roll—
So the smooth Sea obeys the furious wind!
    In vain Philosophy unfolds his[5] store,
10 O'erwhelm'd is every source of pure delight;

---

2. Fawns: young deer, or mythological figures (fauns), half
men half goats; Loves: cupids.
3. Moon goddess Diana, traditionally a virgin.

4. Compare to Wollstonecraft's *Rights of Woman*, which
urges rational control of erotic passion.
5. Later revised to "her."

Dim is the golden page of wisdom's lore;
All nature fades before my sick'ning sight;
   For what bright scene can fancy's eye explore,
'Midst dreary labyrinths of mental night?

XI. Rejects the Influence of Reason

O Reason! vaunted Sov'reign of the mind!
   Thou pompous vision with a sounding name!
   Can'st thou the soul's rebellious passions tame?
Can'st thou in spells the vagrant fancy bind?
5 Ah, no! capricious as the wav'ring wind
   Are sighs of Love that dim thy boasted flame,
   While Folly's torch consumes the wreath of fame,
And Pleasure's hands the sheaves of Truth unbind.
   Press'd by the storms of fate, hope shrinks and dies,
10 Frenzy darts forth in mightiest ills array'd;
   Around thy throne destructive tumults rise,
   And hell-fraught jealousies, thy rights invade!
   Then, what art thou? O Idol of the wise!
A visionary theme!—a gorgeous shade!°   *shadow; ghost*

XII. Previous to her Interview with Phaon

Now, o'er the tesselated° pavement strew   *mosaic*
   Fresh saffron, steep'd in essence of the rose,
   While down yon agate column gently flows
A glittering streamlet of ambrosial[6] dew!
5 My Phaon smiles! the rich carnation's hue,
   On his flush'd cheek in conscious lustre glows,
   While o'er his breast enamour'd Venus throws
Her starry mantle of celestial blue!
   Breathe soft, ye dulcet flutes, among the trees
10 Where clustering boughs with golden citron° twine;   *citrus fruit*
   While slow vibrations, dying on the breeze
Shall soothe his soul with harmony divine!
   Then let my form his yielding fancy seize,
And all his fondest wishes blend with mine.

XVIII. To Phaon

Why art thou changed? O Phaon! tell me why?
   Love flies reproach, when passion feels decay;
   Or, I would paint the raptures of that day,
When, in sweet converse, mingling sigh with sigh,
5 I mark'd the graceful languor of thine eye

6. In Greek mythology, ambrosia is the nectar of the gods; hence, divinely sweet.

As on a shady bank entranced we lay:
    O! eyes! whose beamy radiance stole away,
    As stars fade trembling from the burning sky!
    Why art thou changed, dear source of all my woes?
10 Though dark my bosom's tint, through every vein
    A ruby tide of purest lustre flows,
Warm'd by thy love, or chill'd by thy disdain;
    And yet no bliss this sensate being knows;
Ah! why is rapture so allied to pain?

XXX. Bids farewell to Lesbos

O'er the tall cliff that bounds the billowy main,
    Shadowing the surge that sweeps the lonely strand,
    While the thin vapours break along the sand,
Day's harbinger unfolds the liquid plain.
5 The rude sea murmurs, mournful as the strain
    That love-lorn minstrels strike with trembling hand,
    While from their green beds rise the Syren band[7]
With tongues aerial to repeat my pain!
    The vessel rocks beside the pebbly shore,
10 The foamy curls its gaudy trappings lave;
    Oh! bark propitious! bear me gently o'er;
Breathe soft, ye winds! rise slow, O swelling wave!
    Lesbos, these eyes shall meet thy sands no more:
I fly, to seek my lover, or my grave!

XXXVII. Foresees her Death

When, in the gloomy mansion of the dead,
    This withering heart, this faded form shall sleep:
    When these fond eyes at length shall cease to weep,
And earth's cold lap receive this feverish head;
5 Envy shall turn away, a tear to shed,
    And time's obliterating pinions sweep
    The spot, where poets shall their vigils keep,
To mourn and wander near my freezing bed!
    Then, my pale ghost, upon th' Elysian shore,
10 Shall smile, released from every mortal care;
    While, doom'd love's victim to repine no more,
My breast shall bathe in endless rapture there!
    Ah! no! my restless shade would still deplore,
Nor taste that bliss, which Phaon did not share.

1796

7. Mythical sea nymphs who, by their singing, lured men to destruction.

The Old Beggar

Do you see the OLD BEGGAR who sits at yon gate,
    With his beard silver'd over like snow?
Tho' he smiles as he meets the keen arrows of fate,
    Still his bosom is wearied with woe.

5   Many years has he sat at the foot of the hill,
    Many days seen the summer sun rise;
And at evening the traveller passes him still,
    While the shadows steal over the skies.

In the bleak blast of winter he hobbles along
10   O'er the heath, at the dawning of day;
And the *dew-drops* that freeze the rude thistles among,
    Are the *stars* that illumine his way.

How mild is his aspect, how modest his eye,
    How meekly his soul bears each wrong!
15 How much does he speak by his eloquent sigh,
    Tho' no accent is heard from his tongue.

Time was, when this beggar, in martial trim dight,°   *dressed*
    Was as bold as the chief of his throng;
When he march'd thro' the storms of the day or the night,
20   And still smil'd as he journey'd along.

Then his form was athletic, his eyes' vivid glance
    Spoke the lustre of youth's glowing day!
And the village all mark'd, in the combat and dance,
    The brave younker° still valiant as gay.   *youth*

25 When the prize was propos'd, how his footsteps wou'd bound,
    While the MAID *of his heart* led the throng,
While the ribands that circled the May-pole around,
    Wav'd the trophies of garlands among!

But love o'er his bosom triumphantly reign'd,
30   Love taught him in secret to pine;
Love wasted his youth, yet he never complain'd,
    For the silence of love—is divine!

The dulcet° ton'd word, and the plaint°of despair,   *sweet / lament*
    Are no signs of the soul-wasting smart;
35 'Tis the pride of affection to cherish its care,
    And to count the quick throbs of the heart.

Amidst the loud din of the battle he stood,
    Like a lion, undaunted and strong;
But the tear of compassion was mingled with blood,
40   When his sword was the first in the throng.

When the bullet whizz'd by, and his arm bore away,
    Still he shrunk not, with anguish oppress'd;
And when victory shouted the fate of the day,
    Not a groan check'd the joy of his breast.

45   To his dear native shore the poor wand'rer hied;
    But he came to complete his despair:
For the maid of his soul was that morning *a bride*!
    And a gay *lordly rival* was there!

From that hour, o'er the world he has wander'd forlorn;
50   But still LOVE his companion would go;
And tho' deeply fond memory planted its thorn,
    Still he silently cherish'd his woe.

See him now, while with age and with sorrow oppress'd,
    He the gate opens slowly, and sighs!
55   See him drop the big tears on his woe-wither'd breast,
    The big tears that fall fast from his eyes!

See his habit all tatter'd, his shrivell'd cheek pale;
    See his locks, waving thin in the air;
See his lip is half froze with the sharp cutting gale,
60   And his head, o'er the temples, all bare!

His eye-beam no longer in lustre displays
    The warm sunshine that visits his breast;
For deep sunk is its orbit, and darken'd its rays,
    And he sighs for the grave's silent rest.

65   And his voice is grown feeble, his accent is slow,
    And he sees not the distant hill's side;
And he hears not the breezes of morn as they blow,
    Nor the streams that soft murmuring glide.

To him all is silent, and mournful, and dim,
70   E'en the seasons pass dreary and slow;
For affliction has plac'd its cold fetters on him,
    And his soul is enamour'd of woe.

See the TEAR, which, imploring, is fearful to roll,
    Tho' in silence he bows as you stray;
75   'Tis the eloquent silence which speaks to the soul,
    'Tis the *star* of his *slow-setting day*!

Perchance, ere the *May-blossoms* cheerfully wave,
    Ere the *zephyrs* of SUMMER soft sigh;
The sun-beams shall dance on the grass o'er his GRAVE,
80   And his *journey* be mark'd—TO THE SKY.

1799   1806

Mary Wollstonecraft
1759–1797

John Opie's famous portrait of Mary Wollstonecraft, probably painted in 1797 when she was pregnant with her and William Godwin's daughter Mary, was etched for this frontispiece of Godwin's posthumous *Memoirs of the Author of a Vindication of the Rights of Woman* (1798). The iconic image of an unadorned, wistful woman could not deflect the barrage of abuse provoked by the memoir's scandalous revelations.

It is hard to imagine how anyone advocating the education of young women, the virtues of sense over sensibility, chastity for men as well as women, school uniforms, and regular physical exercise could be reviled as a radical revolutionary, an atheist, a slut, and a pathologically castrating threat to masculine authority. But Mary Wollstonecraft was thus abused. One provocation was her frequently caustic refutation in *A Vindication of the Rights of Men* of Edmund Burke's *Reflections on the Revolution in France*. She went further in her *Vindication of the Rights of Woman*, a trenchant critique of the ideologies of gender in such culturally revered works as Milton's *Paradise Lost* and the admired "conduct" literature of the day—advice to young women on how to be attractive to men and cultivate the Christian virtues of submission, obedience, and service. It was not only the publications; it was also her private life, taken to be the basis of her ideas. The indictments included helping a sister run away from an abusive husband (an assault on the social institution and religious sacrament of marriage); her financial independence and career as a professional writer (very unfeminine); her enamored pursuit of Swiss artist Henry Fuseli in the early 1790s (most immodest) and her affair with American adventurer Gilbert Imlay a few years later; her out-of-wedlock daughter by Imlay; the two attempts at suicide provoked by Imlay's infidelities; her affair with William Godwin and a premarital pregnancy. When she died from complications in childbirth, her detractors intuited divine judgment, and said so in print.

A brilliant thinker and conversationalist, a prolific polemical writer, a commanding social presence, Wollstonecraft led a life of passionate commitments, and was one of the most impressive figures of the radical circle in England in the 1790s. Born in 1759, she spent a childhood suffering the consequences of her father's failures at various enterprises, as he squandered a large inheritance and sought refuge in drink; more than once she defended her mother from his drunken rages. To escape, she became a lady's companion in Bath but returned after two years to nurse her mother. After her mother's death, she left home for good, supporting herself with eye-straining work as a seamstress and then as a schoolmistress in North London with a friend and another sister. When the school failed, Wollstonecraft wrote to pay off her debts, publishing *Thoughts on the Education of Daughters* in 1786; she worked for a year as a governess in an aristocratic Irish family, during which time she wrote her first novel, *Mary, A Fiction*.

Determined to make a living as a writer, she returned to London where she met Joseph Johnson, a radical bookseller who, in 1788, published *Mary* and her book for children, *Original Stories from Real Life*, and in 1789, her anthology, *The Female Reader* (under a male pen name). He also hired her to work for and write articles for *The Analytical Review* and to produce translations of German and French moral philosophers. In London Wollstonecraft became part of Johnson's lively circle of artists, writers, liberal political thinkers, progressive philosophers, and religious Dissenters—among them, Anna Laetitia Barbauld, Tom Paine, William Blake, Joel Barlow, Joseph Priestley, Fuseli, and Godwin. Blake and Robert Southey were completely enamored of her, though Godwin was at first put off by her forwardness in conversation. In 1790 Johnson published A *Vindication of the Rights of Men*, a rapid response to Edmund Burke's *Reflections on the Revolution in France;* it was anonymous, and when Wollstonecraft signed her name to the second edition, her fame was established.

She began *Rights of Woman* in 1791 and early in 1792 spent time with Talleyrand, the French minister of education, on his visit to London; she dedicated *Rights of Woman* to him when its second edition was published later that year. Her reasonable, modest proposals for the improved education and social development of young women were etched with acid comparisons of the state of women to that of plantation and harem slaves, equally oppressed, tyrannized, and brutalized by morally illegitimate masters. Wollstonecraft called for a "revolution in female manners," arguing that no agenda for "the rights of man" could claim moral authority if it entailed the unchanged degradation of women. At the end of 1792, she left on her own for Paris, partly to wean herself from her crush on Fuseli and partly to witness Revolutionary France. Here she met Helen Maria Williams, and within a few months, Imlay, dashing veteran of the American Revolution. Paris in 1793 was a dangerous world, still reeling from the September massacres of 1792 and the arrest and trial of Louis XVI, who was beheaded in January 1793. Over the course of this year, the Reign of Terror claimed thousands more, including Wollstonecraft's friend Madame Roland and Queen Marie Antoinette in October. Wollstonecraft left Paris to seek safety in the suburbs, but returned to register as Imlay's wife at the American embassy in order to gain protection as an American citizen, France being at war with England. Early in 1794, she and Imlay went to Le Havre, where their daughter Fanny was born. They all returned to Paris; then Imlay went to London, leaving wife and daughter behind.

Wollstonecraft's *Historical and Moral View of the Origin and Progress of the French Revolution* was published later that year. On returning to London, she was devastated to discover Imlay living with an actress. He prevented her attempted suicide, and to distance himself from her, sent her (with Fanny and a French nurse) on a business trip to Scandinavia during the summer of 1795. She returned in October to find him living with yet another actress and again attempted suicide, jumping off a bridge into the Thames. Imlay left for Paris with his new amour in November, and Wollstonecraft, ever resourceful, published her letters to him recording her experiences in Scandinavia. When *Letters Written during a Short Residence in Sweden, Norway, and Denmark* appeared the following year, Godwin exclaimed, "If ever there was a book calculated to make a man in love with its author, this appears to me to be the book." They renewed their friendship in January 1796 and by the summer, "friendship melting into love," they became lovers. When she became pregnant at the end of the year, they set aside principle and decided to marry. They wed in March, but insisted on keeping separate residences. Mary Wollstonecraft Godwin (later, Mary Shelley) was born in August; in ten days, her mother, having suffered agonizing pain from poisoning by an incompletely expelled placenta, was dead, at age thirty-seven.

When Godwin published his *Memoirs* and her unfinished novel, *The Wrongs of Woman, or Maria* in 1798, both works fed anti-Jacobin attacks on her ideas and moral character. His grief clouded his judgment about what he could recount without offending propriety, and the *Memoir* proved a scandal, embarrassing even those who had welcomed *Rights of Woman*. An anonymous *Defence of the Character and Conduct of the Late Mary Wollstonecraft Godwin* (often credited to Mary Hays, her friend and fellow feminist), appeared in 1803, but the defense could hardly rest. Hays did not feel safe including her in her *Female Biography, or Memoirs of Illustrious and Celebrated Women of all Ages and Countries* (also 1803), even though she found space for the Lesbian Sappho and Marat's assassin Charlotte Corday. Decades later, in 1869, John Stuart Mill forgot to mention *Rights of Woman* in his

Subjection of Women. Attacks on Wollstonecraft's character and conduct persisted well into the 1970s, not only stigmatizing the arguments of her writing but providing antifeminists with fuel to impugn any advocacy of women's rights. Yet there always persisted a community of admiration for her courage and intelligence, including (for better or worse) Percy Shelley, and over ensuing decades, such women of intellect as George Eliot, Emma Goldman, and Virginia Woolf.

A VINDICATION OF THE RIGHTS OF WOMAN   The French Revolutionary Assembly's Declaration of the Rights of Man granted participatory citizenship only to men. The vibrant declarations of the "Rights of Man" meant a *fraternity* of "liberty, fraternity, equality." Bluntly comparing marriage to slavery and tyrannical oppression, Wollstonecraft's "second" *Vindication* boldly challenges the thinking that sustains and frequently idealizes this subjection: the view of women's subordination as a universal fact of nature, human history, rational philosophy, and divine ordination. Identifying this view as a sociocultural text, a "prevailing opinion," she subjects it to a sharp critical reading. This critique is energized by the actual literary criticism that fills her pages, incisive and often sarcastic examinations of long-standing misogynist myths (Pandora) and their prestigious literary vehicles: John Milton's *Paradise Lost* (and its informing biblical stories); Alexander Pope's second *Moral Essay*, "Of the Characters of Women" (1735); Samuel Richardson's *Clarissa* (1747–1748); Jean-Jacques Rousseau's education novel *Émile* (1762) and his romance *Julie, ou la Nouvelle Héloïse* (1791); Dr. John Gregory's *A Father's Legacy to His Daughters* (1774); Dr. James Fordyce's *Sermons to Young Women* (1765). She turns an unforgiving focus on a set of interlocked key terms used to flatter women into subjection—*innocent, delicate, feminine, beautiful*—embellished with praise for their "fair defects" of character (an oxymoron she despises) and reverence for them as "angels" or "girls," rather than rationally capable, intelligent, mature adults.

Wollstonecraft's argument for gender-neutral "reason" undoes Milton's assignment of this capacity to men only. To Wollstonecraft, this is no divine arrangement but a social formation. She counters that God would not have created women without this capacity, the source of both virtuous conduct and spiritual salvation—a religious argument that invests her social polemic with unimpeachable moral foundation. Alongside this moral argument, *Vindication* wields the discourse of tyranny and revolution that already had currency with Wollstonecraft's male colleagues, allowing her to point out the reactionary attitudes about women that may be tolerated, even supported, by progressive political thinkers.

from A Vindication of the Rights of Woman
from To M. Talleyrand-Périgord, Late Bishop of Autun[1]

Contending for the rights of woman, my main argument is built on this simple principle, that if she be not prepared by education to become the companion of man, she will stop the progress of knowledge and virtue; for truth must be common to all, or it will be inefficacious with respect to its influence on general practice. * * *

In this work I have produced many arguments, which to me were conclusive, to prove that the prevailing notion respecting a sexual character was subversive of

1. Talleyrand (1754–1838) was Bishop of Autun (1788–1791) when he resigned to serve in the Constituent Assembly of the French Revolutionary government, where he recommended raising revenue by confiscating church properties. In 1791 he rendered a Report on Public Instruction, urging free education for both sexes but following the view of Rousseau's *Émile* (1762) that girls be trained for subservience to men. In the first sentence of her dedicatory letter, Wollstonecraft says she means "to induce [him] to reconsider the subject."

morality, and I have contended, that to render the human body and mind more perfect, chastity[2] must more universally prevail, and that chastity will never be respected in the male world till the person of a woman is not, as it were, idolized, when little virtue or sense embellish it with the grand traces of mental beauty, or the interesting simplicity of affection.

Consider, Sir, dispassionately, these observations—for a glimpse of this truth seemed to open before you when you observed, "that to see one half of the human race excluded by the other from all participation of government, was a political phænomenon that, according to abstract principles, it was impossible to explain."[3] If so, on what does your constitution rest? If the abstract rights of man will bear discussion and explanation, those of woman, by a parity of reasoning, will not shrink from the same test: though a different opinion prevails in this country, built on the very arguments which you use to justify the oppression of woman—prescription.

Consider, I address you as a legislator, whether, when men contend for their freedom, and to be allowed to judge for themselves respecting their own happiness, it be not inconsistent and unjust to subjugate women, even though you firmly believe that you are acting in the manner best calculated to promote their happiness? Who made man the exclusive judge, if woman partake with him the gift of reason?

In this style, argue tyrants of every denomination, from the weak king to the weak father of a family; they are all eager to crush reason; yet always assert that they usurp its throne only to be useful. Do you not act a similar part, when you *force* all women, by denying them civil and political rights, to remain immured in their families groping in the dark? for surely, Sir, you will not assert, that a duty can be binding which is not founded on reason? If indeed this be their destination, arguments may be drawn from reason: and thus augustly supported, the more understanding women acquire, the more they will be attached to their duty—comprehending it—for unless they comprehend it, unless their morals be fixed on the same immutable principle as those of man, no authority can make them discharge it in a virtuous manner. They may be convenient slaves, but slavery will have its constant effect, degrading the master and the abject dependent.

But, if women are to be excluded, without having a voice, from a participation of the natural rights of mankind, prove first, to ward off the charge of injustice and inconsistency, that they want reason—else this flaw in your NEW CONSTITUTION will ever shew that man must, in some shape, act like a tyrant, and tyranny, in whatever part of society it rears its brazen front, will ever undermine morality.

I have repeatedly asserted, and produced what appeared to me irrefragable arguments drawn from matters of fact, to prove my assertion, that women cannot, by force, be confined to domestic concerns; for they will, however ignorant, intermeddle with more weighty affairs, neglecting private duties only to disturb, by cunning tricks, the orderly plans of reason which rise above their comprehension.

Besides, whilst they are only made to acquire personal accomplishments,[4] men will seek for pleasure in variety, and faithless husbands will make faithless wives; such ignorant beings, indeed, will be very excusable when, not taught to respect public good, nor allowed any civil rights, they attempt to do themselves justice by retaliation.

2. Sexual self-control, including abstinence and fidelity to marriage.
3. Quoting Talleyrand's *Report*; the French Constitution of 1791 restricted citizenship to men over age 25; women did not gain the vote until 1944.

4. The 18th-century female curriculum for the leisure-class: basic literacy, embroidery, singing; playing a piano or harpsichord; dancing; sketching; conversational French or Italian.

The box of mischief thus opened in society,[5] what is to preserve private virtue, the only security of public freedom and universal happiness?

Let there be then no coercion *established* in society, and the common law of gravity prevailing, the sexes will fall into their proper places. And, now that more equitable laws are forming your citizens, marriage may become more sacred: your young men may choose wives from motives of affection, and your maidens allow love to root out vanity.

The father of a family will not then weaken his constitution and debase his sentiments, by visiting the harlot, nor forget, in obeying the call of appetite, the purpose for which it was implanted. And, the mother will not neglect her children to practise the arts of coquetry, when sense and modesty secure her the friendship of her husband.

But, till men become attentive to the duty of a father, it is vain to expect women to spend that time in their nursery which they, "wise in their generation,"[6] choose to spend at their glass;[7] for this exertion of cunning is only an instinct of nature to enable them to obtain indirectly a little of that power of which they are unjustly denied a share: for, if women are not permitted to enjoy legitimate rights, they will render both men and themselves vicious, to obtain illicit privileges.

I wish, Sir, to set some investigations of this kind afloat in France; and should they lead to a confirmation of my principles, when your constitution is revised the Rights of Woman may be respected, if it be fully proved that reason calls for this respect, and loudly demands Justice for one half of the human race.

I am, SIR,
Your's respectfully,
M. W.

Introduction

After considering the historic page, and viewing the living world with anxious solicitude, the most melancholy emotions of sorrowful indignation have depressed my spirits, and I have sighed when obliged to confess, that either nature has made a great difference between man and man, or that the civilization which has hitherto taken place in the world has been very partial. I have turned over various books written on the subject of education, and patiently observed the conduct of parents and the management of schools; but what has been the result?—a profound conviction that the neglected education of my fellow-creatures is the grand source of the misery I deplore; and that women, in particular, are rendered weak and wretched by a variety of concurring causes, originating from one hasty conclusion. The conduct and manners of women, in fact, evidently prove that their minds are not in a healthy state; for, like the flowers which are planted in too rich a soil, strength and usefulness are sacrificed to beauty; and the flaunting leaves, after having pleased a fastidious eye, fade, disregarded on the stalk, long before the season when they ought to have arrived at maturity.— One cause of this barren blooming I attribute to a false system of education, gathered

---

5. In the Greek fable, Pandora, overcome by curiosity, opens a forbidden box, letting loose a host of evils on mankind but closing it before "hope" could escape. Wollstonecraft refuses the sexism of the myth by casting male politicians as the box-openers.

6. A sarcastic reference to Jesus's parable about rewarding a shrewd but dishonest steward (Luke 16.8).

7. Mirror.

from the books written on this subject by men who, considering females rather as women than human creatures, have been more anxious to make them alluring mistresses than affectionate wives and rational mothers; and the understanding of the sex has been so bubbled[1] by this specious homage, that the civilized women of the present century, with a few exceptions, are only anxious to inspire love, when they ought to cherish a nobler ambition, and by their abilities and virtues exact respect.

In a treatise, therefore, on female rights and manners, the works which have been particularly written for their improvement must not be overlooked; especially when it is asserted, in direct terms, that the minds of women are enfeebled by false refinement; that the books of instruction, written by men of genius, have had the same tendency as more frivolous productions; and that, in the true style of Mahometanism, they are treated as a kind of subordinate beings, and not as a part of the human species,[2] when improveable reason is allowed to be the dignified distinction which raises men above the brute creation, and puts a natural sceptre in a feeble hand.

Yet, because I am a woman, I would not lead my readers to suppose that I mean violently to agitate the contested question respecting the equality or inferiority of the sex; but as the subject lies in my way, and I cannot pass it over without subjecting the main tendency of my reasoning to misconstruction, I shall stop a moment to deliver, in a few words, my opinion.—In the government of the physical world it is observable that the female in point of strength is, in general, inferior to the male. This is the law of nature; and it does not appear to be suspended or abrogated in favour of woman. A degree of physical superiority cannot, therefore, be denied—and it is a noble prerogative! But not content with this natural pre-eminence, men endeavour to sink us still lower, merely to render us alluring objects for a moment; and women, intoxicated by the adoration which men, under the influence of their senses, pay them, do not seek to obtain a durable interest in their hearts, or to become the friends of the fellow creatures who find amusement in their society.

I am aware of an obvious inference:—from every quarter have I heard exclamations against masculine women; but where are they to be found? If by this appellation men mean to inveigh against their ardour in hunting, shooting, and gaming, I shall most cordially join in the cry; but if it be against the imitation of manly virtues, or, more properly speaking, the attainment of those talents and virtues, the exercise of which ennobles the human character, and which raise females in the scale of animal being, when they are comprehensively termed mankind;—all those who view them with a philosophic eye must, I should think, wish with me, that they may every day grow more and more masculine.

This discussion naturally divides the subject. I shall first consider women in the grand light of human creatures, who, in common with men, are placed on this earth to unfold their faculties; and afterwards I shall more particularly point out their peculiar designation.

I wish also to steer clear of an error which many respectable writers have fallen into; for the instruction which has hitherto been addressed to women, has rather been applicable to *ladies*, if the little indirect advice, that is scattered through Sandford and Merton, be excepted;[3] but, addressing my sex in a firmer tone, I pay particular attention to those in the middle class, because they appear to be in the

---

1. Gas-filled; deluded.
2. A misconception that the sacred texts of Islam stated that women lack souls and therefore have no afterlife in Heaven.

3. The tutor in Thomas Day's popular children's story, *The History of Sandford and Merton* (1786–1789), tells several moral tales.

most natural state.[4] Perhaps the seeds of false-refinement, immorality, and vanity, have ever been shed by the great. Weak, artificial beings, raised above the common wants and affections of their race, in a premature unnatural manner, undermine the very foundation of virtue, and spread corruption through the whole mass of society! As a class of mankind they have the strongest claim to pity; the education of the rich tends to render them vain and helpless, and the unfolding mind is not strengthened by the practice of those duties which dignify the human character.—They only live to amuse themselves, and by the same law which in nature invariably produces certain effects, they soon only afford barren amusement.

But as I purpose taking a separate view of the different ranks of society, and of the moral character of women, in each, this hint is, for the present, sufficient; and I have only alluded to the subject, because it appears to me to be the very essence of an introduction to give a cursory account of the contents of the work it introduces.

My own sex, I hope, will excuse me, if I treat them like rational creatures, instead of flattering their *fascinating* graces, and viewing them as if they were in a state of perpetual childhood, unable to stand alone. I earnestly wish to point out in what true dignity and human happiness consists—I wish to persuade women to endeavour to acquire strength, both of mind and body, and to convince them that the soft phrases, susceptibility of heart, delicacy of sentiment, and refinement of taste, are almost synonymous with epithets of weakness, and that those beings who are only the objects of pity and that kind of love, which has been termed its sister, will soon become objects of contempt.

Dismissing then those pretty feminine phrases, which the men condescendingly use to soften our slavish dependence, and despising that weak elegancy of mind, exquisite sensibility, and sweet docility of manners, supposed to be the sexual characteristics of the weaker vessel, I wish to shew that elegance is inferior to virtue, that the first object of laudable ambition is to obtain a character as a human being, regardless of the distinction of sex; and that secondary views should be brought to this simple touchstone.

This is a rough sketch of my plan; and should I express my conviction with the energetic emotions that I feel whenever I think of the subject, the dictates of experience and reflection will be felt by some of my readers. Animated by this important object, I shall disdain to cull my phrases or polish my style;—I aim at being useful, and sincerity will render me unaffected; for, wishing rather to persuade by the force of my arguments, than dazzle by the elegance of my language, I shall not waste my time in rounding periods,[5] or in fabricating the turgid bombast of artificial feelings, which, coming from the head, never reach the heart.—I shall be employed about things, not words!—and, anxious to render my sex more respectable members of society, I shall try to avoid that flowery diction which has slided from essays into novels, and from novels into familiar letters and conversation.

These pretty superlatives, dropping glibly from the tongue, vitiate the taste, and create a kind of sickly delicacy that turns away from simple unadorned truth; and a deluge of false sentiments and over-stretched feelings, stifling the natural emotions of the heart, render the domestic pleasures insipid, that ought to sweeten the exercise of those severe duties, which educate a rational and immortal being for a nobler field of action.

---

4. "Ladies" are upper-class. The middle class is the most "natural" state because it has not been corrupted by extremes of wealth or poverty.

5. Crafting elaborate sentences—the oratorical style for which Burke was famous.

The education of women has, of late, been more attended to than formerly; yet they are still reckoned a frivolous sex, and ridiculed or pitied by the writers who endeavour by satire or instruction to improve them. It is acknowledged that they spend many of the first years of their lives in acquiring a smattering of accomplishments; meanwhile strength of body and mind are sacrificed to libertine notions of beauty, to the desire of establishing themselves,—the only way women can rise in the world,—by marriage. And this desire making mere animals of them, when they marry they act as such children may be expected to act:—they dress; they paint, and nickname God's creatures.[6]—Surely these weak beings are only fit for a seraglio![7]—Can they be expected to govern a family with judgment, or take care of the poor babes whom they bring into the world?

If then it can be fairly deduced from the present conduct of the sex, from the prevalent fondness for pleasure which takes place of ambition and those nobler passions that open and enlarge the soul; that the instruction which women have hitherto received has only tended, with the constitution of civil society, to render them insignificant objects of desire—mere propagators of fools!—if it can be proved that in aiming to accomplish them, without cultivating their understandings, they are taken out of their sphere of duties, and made ridiculous and useless when the short-lived bloom of beauty is over,[8] I presume that *rational* men will excuse me for endeavouring to persuade them to become more masculine and respectable.

Indeed the word masculine is only a bugbear: there is little reason to fear that women will acquire too much courage or fortitude; for their apparent inferiority with respect to bodily strength, must render them, in some degree, dependent on men in the various relations of life; but why should it be increased by prejudices that give a sex to virtue,[9] and confound simple truths with sensual reveries?

Women are, in fact, so much degraded by mistaken notions of female excellence, that I do not mean to add a paradox when I assert, that this artificial weakness produces a propensity to tyrannize, and gives birth to cunning, the natural opponent of strength, which leads them to play off those contemptible infantine airs that undermine esteem even whilst they excite desire. Let men become more chaste and modest, and if women do not grow wiser in the same ratio, it will be clear that they have weaker understandings. It seems scarcely necessary to say, that I now speak of the sex in general. Many individuals have more sense than their male relatives; and, as nothing preponderates where there is a constant struggle for an equilibrium, without it has naturally more gravity, some women govern their husbands without degrading themselves, because intellect will always govern.

from *Chapter 1. The Rights and Involved Duties of Mankind Considered*

In the present state of society it appears necessary to go back to first principles in search of the most simple truths, and to dispute with some prevailing prejudice every inch of ground. To clear my way, I must be allowed to ask some plain questions, and the answers will probably appear as unequivocal as the axioms on which reasoning is

6. Suspecting Ophelia of treachery, Hamlet rants about all women, "God hath given you one face, and you make yourselves another. You jig and amble, and you lisp; you nickname God's creatures and make your wantonness [seem] your ignorance" (3.1.145–48).

7. Harem.
8. A lively writer . . . asks what business women turned of forty have to do in the world? [Wollstonecraft's note.]
9. The prevailing opinion that only men have the rational and hence moral capacity for virtuous behavior.

built; though, when entangled with various motives of action, they are formally contradicted, either by the words or conduct of men.

In what does man's pre-eminence over the brute creation consist? The answer is as clear as that a half is less than the whole; in Reason.

What acquirement exalts one being above another? Virtue; we spontaneously reply.

For what purpose were the passions implanted? That man by struggling with them might attain a degree of knowledge denied to the brutes; whispers Experience.

Consequently the perfection of our nature and capability of happiness, must be estimated by the degree of reason, virtue, and knowledge, that distinguish the individual, and direct the laws which bind society: and that from the exercise of reason, knowledge and virtue naturally flow, is equally undeniable, if mankind be viewed collectively.

The rights and duties of man thus simplified, it seems almost impertinent to attempt to illustrate truths that appear so incontrovertible; yet such deeply rooted prejudices have clouded reason, and such spurious qualities have assumed the name of virtues, that it is necessary to pursue the course of reason as it has been perplexed and involved in error, by various adventitious circumstances, comparing the simple axiom with casual deviations.

* * * All power inebriates weak man; and its abuse proves that the more equality there is established among men, the more virtue and happiness will reign in society. But this and any similar maxim deduced from simple reason, raises an outcry—the church or the state is in danger, if faith in the wisdom of antiquity is not implicit; and they who, roused by the sight of human calamity, dare to attack human authority, are reviled as despisers of God, and enemies of man. These are bitter calumnies, yet they reached one of the best of men,[1] whose ashes still preach peace, and whose memory demands a respectful pause, when subjects are discussed that lay so near his heart.—

After attacking the sacred majesty of Kings, I shall scarcely excite surprise by adding my firm persuasion that every profession, in which great subordination of rank constitutes its power, is highly injurious to morality.

A standing army, for instance, is incompatible with freedom; because subordination and rigour are the very sinews of military discipline; and despotism is necessary to give vigour to enterprizes that one will directs. A spirit inspired by romantic notions of honour, a kind of morality founded on the fashion of the age, can only be felt by a few officers, whilst the main body must be moved by command, like the waves of the sea; for the strong wind of authority pushes the crowd of subalterns forward, they scarcely know or care why, with headlong fury.

Besides, nothing can be so prejudicial to the morals of the inhabitants of country towns as the occasional residence of a set of idle superficial young men, whose only occupation is gallantry, and whose polished manners render vice more dangerous, by concealing its deformity under gay ornamental drapery. An air of fashion, which is but a badge of slavery, and proves that the soul has not a strong individual character, awes simple country people into an imitation of the vices, when they cannot catch the slippery graces, of politeness. Every corps is a chain of despots, who, submitting and tyrannizing without exercising their reason, become dead weights of vice and folly on the community. A man of rank or fortune, sure of rising

---

1. Dr. Price [Wollstonecraft's note]. "Calumnies" are maliciously false charges. Wollstonecraft's friend, dissenting minister Richard Price, championed the American and French Revolutions. His lecture to the Revolution Society in 1789, *A Discourse on the Love of our Country*, provoked sharp criticism in Burke's *Reflections on the Revolution in France* and a spirited defense in Wollstonecraft's *Vindication of the Rights of Men*.

by interest, has nothing to do but to pursue some extravagant freak; whilst the needy *gentleman*, who is to rise, as the phrase turns, by his merit, becomes a servile parasite or vile pander.

Sailors, the naval gentlemen, come under the same description, only their vices assume a different and a grosser cast. They are more positively indolent, when not discharging the ceremonials of their station; whilst the insignificant fluttering of soldiers may be termed active idleness. More confined to the society of men, the former acquire a fondness for humour and mischievous tricks; whilst the latter, mixing frequently with well-bred women, catch a sentimental cant.—But mind is equally out of the question, whether they indulge the horse-laugh, or polite simper.

May I be allowed to extend the comparison to a profession where more mind is certainly to be found; for the clergy have superior opportunities of improvement, though subordination almost equally cramps their faculties? The blind submission imposed at college to forms of belief serves as a novitiate to the curate, who must obsequiously respect the opinion of his rector or patron, if he mean to rise in his profession. Perhaps there cannot be a more forcible contrast than between the servile dependent gait of a poor curate and the courtly mien of a bishop. And the respect and contempt they inspire render the discharge of their separate functions equally useless.

It is of great importance to observe that the character of every man is, in some degree, formed by his profession. A man of sense may only have a cast of countenance that wears off as you trace his individuality, whilst the weak, common man has scarcely ever any character, but what belongs to the body; at least, all his opinions have been so steeped in the vat consecrated by authority, that the faint spirit which the grape of his own vine yields cannot be distinguished.

Society, therefore, as it becomes more enlightened, should be very careful not to establish bodies of men who must necessarily be made foolish or vicious by the very constitution of their profession.

from *Chapter 2. The Prevailing Opinion of a Sexual Character Discussed*

To account for, and excuse the tyranny of man, many ingenious arguments have been brought forward to prove, that the two sexes, in the acquirement of virtue, ought to aim at attaining a very different character: or, to speak explicitly, women are not allowed to have sufficient strength of mind to acquire what really deserves the name of virtue. Yet it should seem, allowing them to have souls, that there is but one way appointed by Providence to lead *mankind* to either virtue or happiness.

If then women are not a swarm of ephemeron[1] triflers, why should they be kept in ignorance under the specious name of innocence? Men complain, and with reason, of the follies and caprices of our sex, when they do not keenly satirize our headstrong passions and groveling vices.—Behold, I should answer, the natural effect of ignorance! The mind will ever be unstable that has only prejudices to rest on, and the current will run with destructive fury when there are no barriers to break its force. Women are told from their infancy, and taught by the example of their mothers, that a little knowledge of human weakness, justly termed cunning, softness of temper, *outward* obedience, and a scrupulous attention to a puerile kind of propriety, will obtain for them the protection of man; and should they be beautiful, every thing else is needless, for, at least, twenty years of their lives.

---

1. Winged insect that lives for only a day.

Thus Milton describes our first frail mother; though when he tells us that women are formed for softness and sweet attractive grace,[2] I cannot comprehend his meaning, unless, in the true Mahometan strain, he meant to deprive us of souls, and insinuate that we were beings only designed by sweet attractive grace, and docile blind obedience, to gratify the senses of man when he can no longer soar on the wing of contemplation.

How grossly do they insult us who thus advise us only to render ourselves gentle, domestic brutes! For instance, the winning softness so warmly, and frequently, recommended, that governs by obeying. What childish expressions, and how insignificant is the being—can it be an immortal one? who will condescend to govern by such sinister methods! "Certainly," says Lord Bacon, "man is of kin to the beasts by his body; and if he be not of kin to God by his spirit, he is a base and ignoble creature!"[3] Men, indeed, appear to me to act in a very unphilosophical manner when they try to secure the good conduct of women by attempting to keep them always in a state of childhood. Rousseau was more consistent when he wished to stop the progress of reason in both sexes, for if men eat of the tree of knowledge, women will come in for a taste; but, from the imperfect cultivation which their understandings now receive, they only attain a knowledge of evil.[4]

Children, I grant, should be innocent; but when the epithet is applied to men, or women, it is but a civil term for weakness. For if it be allowed that women were destined by Providence to acquire human virtues, and by the exercise of their understandings, that stability of character which is the firmest ground to rest our future hopes upon, they must be permitted to turn to the fountain of light, and not forced to shape their course by the twinkling of a mere satellite. Milton, I grant, was of a very different opinion; for he only bends to the indefeasible right of beauty, though it would be difficult to render two passages which I now mean to contrast, consistent. But into similar inconsistencies are great men often led by their senses.

> To whom thus Eve with *perfect beauty* adorn'd.
> "My Author and Disposer, what thou bidst
> *Unargued* I obey; So God ordains;
> God is *thy law, thou mine:* to know no more
> Is Woman's *happiest* knowledge and her *praise.*"[5]

These are exactly the arguments that I have used to children; but I have added, your reason is now gaining strength, and, till it arrives at some degree of maturity, you must look up to me for advice—then you ought to *think,* and only rely on God.

Yet in the following lines Milton seems to coincide with me; when he makes Adam thus expostulate with his Maker.

> Hast thou not made me here thy substitute,
> And these inferior far beneath me set?
> Among *unequals* what society
> Can sort, what harmony or true delight?
> Which must be mutual, in proportion due
> Giv'n and receiv'd; but in *disparity*
> The one intense, the other still remiss

---

2. Satan's first view of Adam and Eve in *Paradise Lost:* "Not equal, as thir sex not equal seem'd; / For contemplation hee and valor form'd, / For softness shee and sweet attractive Grace, / He for God only, shee for God in him" (4.296–99). Fordyce quotes these lines in *Sermons to* *Young Women,* ch. 13.

3. Francis Bacon, *Essay 16,* "Of Atheism" (1606).

4. See Rousseau's *Émile* (1.1): "Only reason teaches us good from evil."

5. *Paradise Lost* 4.634–38; Wollstonecraft's emphases.

> Cannot well suit with either, but soon prove
> Tedious alike: of *fellowship* I speak
> Such as I seek, fit to participate
> All rational delight[6]—

In treating, therefore, of the manners of women, let us, disregarding sensual arguments, trace what we should endeavour to make them in order to co-operate, if the expression be not too bold, with the supreme Being.

By individual education, I mean, for the sense of the word is not precisely defined, such an attention to a child as will slowly sharpen the senses, form the temper, regulate the passions as they begin to ferment, and set the understanding to work before the body arrives at maturity; so that the man may only have to proceed, not to begin, the important task of learning to think and reason. * * *

In fact, it is a farce to call any being virtuous whose virtues do not result from the exercise of its own reason. This was Rousseau's opinion respecting men: I extend it to women, and confidently assert that they have been drawn out of their sphere by false refinement, and not by an endeavour to acquire masculine qualities. Still the regal homage which they receive is so intoxicating, that till the manners of the times are changed, and formed on more reasonable principles, it may be impossible to convince them that the illegitimate power, which they obtain, by degrading themselves, is a curse, and that they must return to nature and equality, if they wish to secure the placid satisfaction that unsophisticated affections impart. * * *

In the education of women, the cultivation of the understanding is always subordinate to the acquirement of some corporeal accomplishment;[7] even while enervated by confinement and false notions of modesty, the body is prevented from attaining that grace and beauty which relaxed half-formed limbs never exhibit. Besides, in youth their faculties are not brought forward by emulation; and having no serious scientific study, if they have natural sagacity it is turned too soon on life and manners. They dwell on effects, and modifications, without tracing them back to causes; and complicated rules to adjust behaviour are a weak substitute for simple principles.

As a proof that education gives this appearance of weakness to females, we may instance the example of military men, who are, like them, sent into the world before their minds have been stored with knowledge or fortified by principles. The consequences are similar; soldiers acquire a little superficial knowledge, snatched from the muddy current of conversation, and, from continually mixing with society, they gain, what is termed a knowledge of the world; and this acquaintance with manners and customs has frequently been confounded with a knowledge of the human heart. But can the crude fruit of casual observation, never brought to the test of judgment, formed by comparing speculation and experience, deserve such a distinction? Soldiers, as well as women, practice the minor virtues with punctilious politeness. Where is then the sexual difference, when the education has been the same? All the difference that I can discern, arises from the superior advantage of liberty, which enables the former to see more of life.

* * *

Standing armies can never consist of resolute, robust men; they may be well disciplined machines, but they will seldom contain men under the influence of strong passions, or with very vigorous faculties. And as for any depth of understanding, I will

---

6. *Paradise Lost* 8.381–91; Wollstonecraft's emphases.   7. E.g., cosmetic adornment, dancing, singing.

venture to affirm, that it is as rarely to be found in the army as amongst women; and the cause, I maintain, is the same. It may be further observed, that officers are also particularly attentive to their persons, fond of dancing, crowded rooms, adventures, and ridicule.[8] Like the *fair* sex, the business of their lives is gallantry.—They were taught to please, and they only live to please. Yet they do not lose their rank in the distinction of sexes, for they are still reckoned superior to women, though in what their superiority consists, beyond what I have just mentioned, it is difficult to discover.

The great misfortune is this, that they both acquire manners before morals, and a knowledge of life before they have, from reflection, any acquaintance with the grand ideal outline of human nature. The consequence is natural; satisfied with common nature, they become a prey to prejudices, and taking all their opinions on credit, they blindly submit to authority. So that, if they have any sense, it is a kind of instinctive glance, that catches proportions, and decides with respect to manners; but fails when arguments are to be pursued below the surface, or opinions analyzed.

May not the same remark be applied to women? Nay, the argument may be carried still further, for they are both thrown out of a useful station by the unnatural distinctions established in civilized life. Riches and hereditary honours have made cyphers of women to give consequence to the numerical figure; and idleness has produced a mixture of gallantry and despotism into society, which leads the very men who are the slaves of their mistresses to tyrannize over their sisters, wives, and daughters. This is only keeping them in rank and file, it is true. Strengthen the female mind by enlarging it, and there will be an end to blind obedience; but, as blind obedience is ever sought for by power, tyrants and sensualists are in the right when they endeavour to keep women in the dark, because the former only want slaves, and the latter a play-thing. The sensualist, indeed, has been the most dangerous of tyrants, and women have been duped by their lovers, as princes by their ministers, whilst dreaming that they reigned over them. * * *

Probably the prevailing opinion, that woman was created for man, may have taken its rise from Moses's poetical story;[9] yet, as very few, it is presumed, who have bestowed any serious thought on the subject, ever supposed that Eve was, literally speaking, one of Adam's ribs, the deduction must be allowed to fall to the ground; or, only be so far admitted as it proves that man, from the remotest antiquity, found it convenient to exert his strength to subjugate his companion, and his invention to shew that she ought to have her neck bent under the yoke, because the whole creation was only created for his convenience or pleasure.

Let it not be concluded that I wish to invert the order of things; I have already granted, that, from the constitution of their bodies, men seem to be designed by Providence to attain a greater degree of virtue. I speak collectively of the whole sex; but I see not the shadow of a reason to conclude that their virtues should differ in respect to their nature. In fact, how can they, if virtue has only one eternal standard? I must therefore, if I reason consequentially, as strenuously maintain that they have the same simple direction, as that there is a God.

It follows then that cunning should not be opposed to wisdom, little cares to great exertions, or insipid softness, varnished over with the name of gentleness, to that fortitude which grand views alone can inspire.

---

8. Why should women be censured with petulant acrimony, because they seem to have a passion for a scarlet coat? Has not education placed them more on a level with soldiers than any other class of men? [Wollstonecraft's note].

9. The first five books of the Old Testament are traditionally attributed to Moses; in Genesis 2.21–23, followed by Milton, God creates Eve out of Adam's rib.

I shall be told that woman would then lose many of her peculiar graces, and the opinion of a well known poet might be quoted to refute my unqualified assertion. For Pope has said, in the name of the whole male sex,

> Yet ne'er so sure our passion to create,
> As when she touch'd the brink of all we hate.

In what light this sally[1] places men and women, I shall leave to the judicious to determine; meanwhile I shall content myself with observing, that I cannot discover why, unless they are mortal, females should always be degraded by being made subservient to love or lust.

To speak disrespectfully of love is, I know, high treason against sentiment and fine feelings; but I wish to speak the simple language of truth, and rather to address the head than the heart. To endeavour to reason love out of the world, would be to out Quixote Cervantes, and equally offend against common sense;[2] but an endeavour to restrain this tumultuous passion, and to prove that it should not be allowed to dethrone superior powers, or to usurp the sceptre which the understanding should ever coolly wield, appears less wild.

Youth is the season for love in both sexes; but in those days of thoughtless enjoyment provision should be made for the more important years of life, when reflection takes place of sensation. But Rousseau, and most of the male writers who have followed his steps, have warmly inculcated that the whole tendency of female education ought to be directed to one point:—to render them pleasing.[3]

Let me reason with the supporters of this opinion who have any knowledge of human nature, do they imagine that marriage can eradicate the habitude of life? The woman who has only been taught to please will soon find that her charms are oblique sunbeams, and that they cannot have much effect on her husband's heart when they are seen every day, when the summer is passed and gone. Will she then have sufficient native energy to look into herself for comfort, and cultivate her dormant faculties? or, is it not more rational to expect that she will try to please other men; and, in the emotions raised by the expectation of new conquests, endeavour to forget the mortification her love or pride has received? When the husband ceases to be a lover—and the time will inevitably come, her desire of pleasing will then grow languid, or become a spring of bitterness; and love, perhaps, the most evanescent of all passions, gives place to jealousy or vanity.

I now speak of women who are restrained by principle or prejudice; such women, though they would shrink from an intrigue with real abhorrence, yet, nevertheless, wish to be convinced by the homage of gallantry that they are cruelly neglected by their husbands; or, days and weeks are spent in dreaming of the happiness enjoyed by congenial souls till their health is undermined and their spirits broken by discontent. How then can the great art of pleasing be such a necessary study? it is only useful to a mistress; the chaste wife, and serious mother, should only consider her power to please as the polish of her virtues, and the affection of her husband as one of the comforts that render her task less difficult and her life happier.—But, whether she be loved or neglected, her first wish should be to make herself respectable, and not to rely for all her happiness on a being subject to like infirmities with herself.

---

1. The "sally" (an attack by besieged troops; an outburst of wit) is from Pope's *Epistle II, to a Lady*, "Of the Characters of Women" (1735), 51–52.

2. To outdo Cervantes' comic hero Don Quixote in ineffectual idealism, including the ideals of courtly love.
3. *Émile*, ch. 5.

The worthy Dr. Gregory fell into a similar error. I respect his heart; but entirely disapprove of his celebrated Legacy to his Daughters.[4]

He advises them to cultivate a fondness for dress, because a fondness for dress, he asserts, is natural to them. I am unable to comprehend what either he or Rousseau mean, when they frequently use this indefinite term. If they told us that in a pre-existent state the soul was fond of dress, and brought this inclination with it into a new body, I should listen to them with a half smile, as I often do when I hear a rant about innate elegance.—But if he only meant to say that the exercise of the faculties will produce this fondness—I deny it.—It is not natural; but arises, like false ambition in men, from a love of power.

Dr. Gregory goes much further; he actually recommends dissimulation, and ad-vises an innocent girl to give the lie to her feelings, and not dance with spirit, when gaiety of heart would make her feel eloquent without making her gestures immodest. In the name of truth and common sense, why should not one woman acknowledge that she can take more exercise than another? or, in other words, that she has a sound constitution; and why, to damp innocent vivacity, is she darkly to be told that men will draw conclusions which she little thinks of?—Let the libertine draw what inference he pleases; but, I hope, that no sensible mother will restrain the natural frankness of youth by instilling such indecent cautions. * * *

Surely she has not an immortal soul who can loiter life away merely employed to adorn her person, that she may amuse the languid hours, and soften the cares of a fel-low-creature who is willing to be enlivened by her smiles and tricks, when the serious business of life is over.

Besides, the woman who strengthens her body and exercises her mind will, by man-aging her family and practising various virtues, become the friend, and not the humble dependent of her husband; and if she, by possessing such substantial qualities, merit his regard, she will not find it necessary to conceal her affection, nor to pretend to an un-natural coldness of constitution to excite her husband's passions. In fact, if we revert to history, we shall find that the women who have distinguished themselves have neither been the most beautiful nor the most gentle of their sex. * * *

Love, the common passion, in which chance and sensation take place of choice and reason, is, in some degree, felt by the mass of mankind; for it is not necessary to speak, at present, of the emotions that rise above or sink below love. This passion, naturally increased by suspense and difficulties, draws the mind out of its accustomed state, and exalts the affections; but the security of marriage, allowing the fever of love to subside, a healthy temperature is thought insipid, only by those who have not suf-ficient intellect to substitute the calm tenderness of friendship, the confidence of re-spect, instead of blind admiration, and the sensual emotions of fondness.

This is, must be, the course of nature.—Friendship or indifference inevitably succeeds love.—And this constitution seems perfectly to harmonize with the system of government which prevails in the normal world. Passions are spurs to action, and open the mind; but they sink into mere appetites, become a personal and momentary gratification, when the object is gained, and the satisfied mind rests in enjoyment. The man who had some virtue whilst he was struggling for a crown, often becomes a voluptuous tyrant when it graces his brow; and, when the lover is not lost in the hus-band, the dotard, a prey of childish caprices, and fond jealousies, neglects the serious

4. Dr. John Gregory's influential conduct manual, *A Father's Legacy to His Daughters* (1774).

duties of life, and the caresses which should excite confidence in his children are lavished on the overgrown child, his wife.

In order to fulfil the duties of life, and to be able to pursue with vigour the various employments which form the moral character, a master and mistress of a family ought not to continue to love each other with passion. I mean to say, that they ought not to indulge those emotions which disturb the order of society, and engross the thoughts that should be otherwise employed. The mind that has never been engrossed by one object wants vigour—if it can long be so, it is weak.

A mistaken education, a narrow, uncultivated mind, and many sexual prejudices, tend to make women more constant than men; but, for the present, I shall not touch on this branch of the subject. I will go still further, and advance, without dreaming of a paradox, that an unhappy marriage is often very advantageous to a family, and that the neglected wife is, in general, the best mother. * * *

I own it frequently happens that women who have fostered a romantic unnatural delicacy of feeling,[5] waste their lives in *imagining* how happy they should have been with a husband who could love them with a fervid increasing affection every day, and all day. But they might as well pine married as single—and would not be a jot more unhappy with a bad husband than longing for a good one. That a proper education; or, to speak with more precision, a well stored mind, would enable a woman to support a single life with dignity, I grant; but that she should avoid cultivating her taste, lest her husband should occasionally shock it, is quitting a substance for a shadow. To say the truth, I do not know of what use is an improved taste, if the individual be not rendered more independent of the casualties of life; if new sources of enjoyment, only dependent on the solitary operations of the mind, are not opened. People of taste, married or single, without distinction, will ever be disgusted by various things that touch not less observing minds. On this conclusion the argument must not be allowed to hinge; but in the whole sum of enjoyment is taste to be denominated a blessing?

The question is, whether it procures most pain or pleasure? The answer will decide the propriety of Dr. Gregory's advice, and shew how absurd and tyrannic it is thus to lay down a system of slavery; or to attempt to educate moral beings by any other rules than those deduced from pure reason, which apply to the whole species.

Gentleness of manners, forbearance and long-suffering, are such amiable God-like qualities, that in sublime poetic strains the Deity has been invested with them; and, perhaps, no representation of his goodness so strongly fastens on the human affections as those that represent him abundant in mercy and willing to pardon.[6] Gentleness, considered in this point of view, bears on its front all the characteristics of grandeur, combined with the winning graces of condescension; but what a different aspect it assumes when it is the submissive demeanour of dependence, the support of weakness that loves, because it wants protection; and is forbearing, because it must silently endure injuries; smiling under the lash at which it dare not snarl. Abject as this picture appears, it is the portrait of an accomplished woman, according to the received opinion of female excellence, separated by specious reasoners from human

5. For example, the herd of novelists [Wollstonecraft's note, attacking popular sentimental fiction].
6. A repentant sinner will find that God "will have mercy upon him; and to our God, for he will abundantly pardon" (Isaiah 55.7).

excellence. Or, they[7] kindly restore the rib, and make one moral being of a man and woman; not forgetting to give her all the "submissive charms."[8]

How women are to exist in that state where there is to be neither marrying nor giving in marriage, we are not told.[9] For though moralists have agreed that the tenor of life seems to prove that *man* is prepared by various circumstances for a future state, they constantly concur in advising *woman* only to provide for the present. Gentleness, docility, and a spaniel-like affection are, on this ground, consistently recommended as the cardinal virtues of the sex; and, disregarding the arbitrary economy of nature, one writer has declared that it is masculine for a woman to be melancholy. She was created to be the toy of man, his rattle, and it must jingle in his ears whenever, dismissing reason, he chooses to be amused. * * *

As a philosopher, I read with indignation the plausible epithets which men use to soften their insults; and, as a moralist, I ask what is meant by such heterogeneous associations, as fair defects, amiable weaknesses, &c.?[1] If there be but one criterion of morals, but one archetype for man, women appear to be suspended by destiny, according to the vulgar tale of Mahomet's coffin;[2] they have neither the unerring instinct of brutes, nor are allowed to fix the eye of reason on a perfect model. They were made to be loved, and must not aim at respect, lest they should be hunted out of society as masculine.

But to view the subject in another point of view. Do passive indolent women make the best wives? Confining our discussion to the present moment of existence, let us see how such weak creatures perform their part? Do the women who, by the attainment of a few superficial accomplishments, have strengthened the prevailing prejudice, merely contribute to the happiness of their husbands? Do they display their charms merely to amuse them? And have women, who have early imbibed notions of passive obedience, sufficient character to manage a family or educate children? So far from it, that, after surveying the history of woman, I cannot help, agreeing with the severest satirist, considering the sex as the weakest as well as the most oppressed half of the species. What does history disclose but marks of inferiority, and how few women have emancipated themselves from the galling yoke of sovereign man?—So few, that the exceptions remind me of an ingenious conjecture respecting Newton: that he was probably a being of a superior order, accidentally caged in a human body.[3] Following the same train of thinking, I have been led to imagine that the few extraordinary women who have rushed in eccentrical directions out of the orbit prescribed to their sex, were *male* spirits, confined by mistake in female frames. But if it be not philosophical to think of sex when the soul is mentioned, the inferiority

---

7. Vide [see] Rousseau and Swedenborg [Wollstonecraft's note]. In *Émile*, ch. 5, Rousseau argued that because man and wife were one ("one flesh"; Genesis 2.24), the wife could have no independent moral judgment. Emanuel Swedenborg (1688–1772), Swedish scientist, theologian, and mystic, argued that marriage persisted in the afterlife of heaven in the united form of a single angel.

8. In *Paradise Lost*, Adam smiles on Eve "with superior Love," delighted by her "Beauty and submissive Charms" (4.497–99).

9. Asked about the heavenly life of a woman who has married more than once ("whose wife shall she be?"), Jesus answers, "in the resurrection they neither marry, nor are given in marriage, but are as the angels of God in heaven" (Matthew 22.30). Wollstonecraft's *Mary, A Fiction* (1788)

closes with its ever frustrated, dying heroine cheered by the thought of "hastening to that world *where there is neither marrying,* nor giving in marriage"—where women are no longer controlled by fathers and husbands.

1. In *Paradise Lost*, after the Fall, Adam reviles Eve as a "fair defect/Of nature" (10.891–92) prone to Satanic temptation and tempting Adam from his better knowledge. Pope's "Of the Characters of Women" declares that "Ladies, like variegated tulips, show; . . . / Fine by defect, and delicately weak . . ." (41–43); the coloring of tulips is caused by a virus that renders them both beautiful and weak.

2. Muhammad's coffin was reputed to hang magically in the center of his tomb.

3. Isaac Newton (1642–1727), brilliant physicist and mathematician.

must depend on the organs; or the heavenly fire, which is to ferment the clay, is not given in equal portions.[4] * * *

Surely there can be but one rule of right, if morality has an eternal foundation, and whoever sacrifices virtue, strictly so called, to present convenience, or whose *duty* it is to act in such a manner, lives only for the passing day, and cannot be an accountable creature.

The poet then should have dropped his sneer when he says,

> If weak women go astray,
> The stars are more in fault than they.[5]

For that they are bound by the adamantine chain of destiny is most certain, if it be proved that they are never to exercise their own reason, never to be independent, never to rise above opinion, or to feel the dignity of a rational will that only bows to God, and often forgets that the universe contains any being but itself and the model of perfection to which its ardent gaze is turned, to adore attributes that, softened into virtues, may be imitated in kind, though the degree overwhelms the enraptured mind.

If, I say, for I would not impress by declamation when Reason offers her sober light,[6] if they be really capable of acting like rational creatures, let them not be treated like slaves; or, like the brutes who are dependent on the reason of man, when they associate with him; but cultivate their minds, give them the salutary, sublime curb of principle, and let them attain conscious dignity by feeling themselves only dependent on God. Teach them, in common with man, to submit to necessity, instead of giving, to render them more pleasing, a sex to morals.

Further, should experience prove that they cannot attain the same degree of strength of mind, perseverance, and fortitude, let their virtues be the same in kind, though they may vainly struggle for the same degree; and the superiority of man will be equally clear, if not clearer; and truth, as it is a simple principle, which admits of no modification, would be common to both. Nay, the order of society as it is at present regulated would not be inverted, for woman would then only have the rank that reason assigned her, and arts could not be practised to bring the balance even, much less to turn it.

These may be termed Utopian dreams.[7]—Thanks to that Being who impressed them on my soul, and gave me sufficient strength of mind to dare to exert my own reason, till, becoming dependent only on him for the support of my virtue, I view, with indignation, the mistaken notions that enslave my sex.

I love man as my fellow; but his scepter, real, or usurped, extends not to me, unless the reason of an individual demands my homage; and even then the submission is to reason, and not to man. In fact, the conduct of an accountable being must be regulated by the operations of its own reason; or on what foundation rests the throne of God? * * *

---

4. In the 18th century, the question whether the soul had a sex, like the body, was widely debated. "Clay" is a familiar term for the body.

5. "Hans Carvel" (11–12), a satire by Matthew Prior (1664–1721). These lines invert Cassius's remark in *Julius Caesar*: "The fault, dear Brutus, lies not in the stars/ But in ourselves, that we are underlings" (1.2.140–41).

6. This feminine gendering of "Reason" resists Milton's male assignment of Reason and evokes the deity of the French Revolution, "La Raison"—a feminine noun in French.

7. Impossible social ideals, derived from Sir Thomas More's 16th-century treatise, *Utopia*.

‐‐•‐ ⧱ ‐•‐‐

Joanna Baillie

1762–1851

In 1824, *Blackwood's Edinburgh Magazine* noted the influence of Baillie's plays on Lord Byron: "the dark shadows of his Lordship's imagination have received a deeper gloom from his early acquaintance with those wild and midnight forests, in which the passion of De Monfort [*De Monfort*, 1798] consummated its dreadful purpose, and the dim aisles in which it met its retribution." The influence was a nervous admiration. In 1813, Byron insisted that Baillie could not have "a more enthusiastic admirer than myself," and he was eager to meet her; in 1817, in the throes of rewriting his gothic closet drama *Manfred*, he mulled over Voltaire's reply to a question about "why no woman has ever written even a tolerable tragedy": "Ah (said the Patriarch) the composition of a tragedy requires *testicles*." "If this be true," Byron jested to his publisher, "Lord knows what Joanna Baillie does—I suppose she borrows them." Byron's regard for Baillie's potency was shared (without a regendering) by many of her contemporaries, including William Wordsworth, who called her "the bold enchantress," Anna Letitia Barbauld, Maria Edgeworth, Robert Southey, Samuel Taylor Coleridge, Felicia Hemans (who dedicated *Records of Woman* to her), and Sir Walter Scott, who deemed her the finest English dramatist since Shakespeare.

Born in 1762 in Scotland, Baillie traced her ancestry to the famously brave-hearted patriot William Wallace. She never married and lived her adult life with her unmarried sister. Her first literary efforts were issued, unsigned, in 1790 as *Poems: Wherein it is Attempted to Describe Certain Views of Nature and Rustic Manners*. This was unsuccessful, and she turned to drama. *A Series of Plays in Which it is Attempted to Delineate the Stronger Passions of the Mind* appeared in three installments from 1798 to 1812. The first was anonymous, and a curious public speculated about the author, probably male. The "Introductory Discourse" could have been written only by a man, insisted Samuel Rogers in the *Monthly Review*, and he ascribed it to Baillie's brother. Baillie's project of "unveiling the human mind under the dominion of . . . strong and fixed passions" was matched two years later by Wordsworth in Preface to *Lyrical Ballads* (1800), presenting a poetry of "the essential passions of the heart" in states of excitement. *De Monfort* attracted the leading actors of the day, including Sarah Siddons, John Philip Kemble, and Edmund Kean, but the psychological emphases and philosophical introspectiveness of the plays were ill-suited to popular theater, however much other poets were impressed. Even without stage acclaim, Baillie continued to write and publish plays over the next three decades, conceiving them as dramas for "the mental theatre of the reader," in Byron's words, taking a cue from Charles Lamb's essay on the unsuitability of Shakespeare's tragedies for stage representation (1811). In 1821, she published *Metrical Legends of Exalted Characters*, including "chronicles" of her ancestors William Wallace and Lady Griselda Baillie, and she put out an expanded edition of her poems in 1840 titled *Fugitive Verses*. Some pieces show her skill at the poetry in Scots dialect that Robert Burns popularized, while others follow the program of her dramas, voicing passion, sometimes in stormy moods, but often in quieter and more domestic scenes.

London

It is a goodly sight through the clear air,
From Hampstead's heathy height[1] to see at once

---

1. Hampstead heath, to the north, offers a view of London.

England's vast capital in fair expanse,
Towers, belfries,° lengthen'd streets, and structures fair.   *bell-towers*
5   St. Paul's high dome[2] amidst the vassal bands
Of neighb'ring spires, a regal chieftain stands,
And over fields of ridgy roofs appear,
With distance softly tinted, side by side,
In kindred grace, like twain of sisters dear,
10   The Towers of Westminster, her Abbey's pride;[3]
While, far beyond, the hills of Surrey shine[4]
Through thin soft haze, and show their wavy line.
View'd thus, a goodly sight! but when survey'd
Through denser air when moisten'd winds prevail,
15   In her grand panoply° of smoke array'd,   *armor*
While clouds aloft in heavy volumes sail,
She is sublime.—She seems a curtain'd gloom
Connecting heaven and earth,—a threat'ning sign of doom.
With more than natural height, rear'd in the sky
20   'Tis then St. Paul's arrests the wondering eye;
The lower parts in swathing mist conceal'd,
The higher through some half spent shower reveal'd,
So far from earth removed, that well, I trow,°   *believe*
Did not its form man's artful structure show,
25   It might some lofty alpine peak be deem'd,
The eagle's haunt, with cave and crevice seam'd.
Stretch'd wide on either hand, a rugged screen,
In lurid dimness, nearer streets are seen
Like shoreward billows of a troubled main,°   *open sea*
30   Arrested in their rage. Through drizzly rain,
Cataracts of tawny sheen pour from the skies,
Of furnace smoke black curling columns rise,
And many tinted vapours, slowly pass
O'er the wide draping of that pictured mass.

35   So shows by day this grand imperial town,
And, when o'er all the night's black stole is thrown,
The distant traveller doth with wonder mark
Her luminous canopy athwart the dark,
Cast up, from myriads of lamps that shine
40   Along her streets in many a starry line:—
He wondering looks from his yet distant road,
And thinks the northern streamers° are abroad.   *northern lights*
"What hollow sound is that?" approaching near,
The roar of many wheels breaks on his ear.
45   It is the flood of human life in motion!
It is the voice of a tempestuous ocean!

---

2. London's chief Anglican cathedral.
3. Westminster, a city within London, is the seat of government, the location of Westminster Palace (Parliament), Buckingham Palace (the royal family home), and Westminster Abbey (an imposing gothic church).
4. County southwest of London.

With sad but pleasing awe his soul is fill'd,
Scarce heaves his breast, and all within is still'd,
As many thoughts and feelings cross his mind,—
50 Thoughts, mingled, melancholy, undefined,
Of restless, reckless man, and years gone by,
And Time fast wending to Eternity.

1790, 1840

A Mother to Her Waking Infant

Now in thy dazzling half-oped eye,
Thy curled nose, and lip awry,
Thy up-hoist arms, and noddling head,
And little chin with crystal spread,
5 Poor helpless thing! what do I see,
    That I should sing of thee?

From thy poor tongue no accents come,
Which can but rub thy toothless gum:
Small understanding boasts thy face,
10 Thy shapeless limbs nor step, nor grace:
A few short words thy feats may tell,
    And yet I love thee well.

When sudden wakes the bitter shriek,
And redder swells thy little cheek;
15 When rattled keys thy woes beguile,
And thro' the wet eye gleams the smile,
Still for thy weakly self is spent
    Thy little silly plaint.°   lament

But when thy friends are in distress,
20 Thou'lt laugh and chuckle ne'er the less;
Nor e'en with sympathy be smitten,
Tho' all are sad but thee and kitten;
Yet puny varlet that thou art,
    Thou twitchest at the heart.

25 Thy rosy round cheek so soft and warm;
Thy pinky hand, and dimpled arm;
Thy silken locks that scantly peep,
With gold-tip'd ends, where circle deep
Around thy neck in harmless grace
30 So soft and sleekly hold their place,
Might harder hearts with kindness fill,
    And gain our right good will.

Each passing clown bestows his blessing,
Thy mouth is worn with old wives' kissing;
35 E'en lighter looks the gloomy eye
Of surly sense, when thou art by;

And yet I think whoe'er they be,
    They love thee not like me.

40   Perhaps when time shall add a few
Short years to thee, thou'lt love me too.
Then wilt thou, thro' life's weary way
Become my sure and cheering stay:
Wilt care for me, and be my hold,
    When I am weak and old.

45   Thou'lt listen to my lengthen'd tale,
And pity me when I am frail—
But see, the sweepy spinning fly
Upon the window takes thine eye.
Go to thy little senseless play—
50   Thou dost not heed my lay.°   *lullaby*
                                           1790

A Child to His Sick Grandfather

Grand-dad, they say you're old and frail,
Your stocked legs begin to fail:
Your knobbed stick (that was my horse)
Can scarce support your bended corse
5   While back to wall, you lean so sad,
    I'm vex'd to see you, dad.

You us'd to smile, and stroke my head,
And tell me how good children did;
But now I wot° not how it be,   *know*
10   You take me seldom on your knee;
Yet ne'ertheless I am right glad
    To sit beside you, dad.

How lank and thin your beard hangs down!
Scant are the white hairs on your crown:
15   How wan and hollow are your cheeks!
Your brow is rough with crossing streaks
But yet, for all his strength be fled,
    I love my own old dad.

The housewives round their potions brew,
20   And gossips° come to ask for you;   *friends*
And for your weal° each neighbour cares,   *well-being*
And good men kneel, and say their prayers:
And ev'ry body looks so sad,
    When you are ailing, dad.

25   You will not die, and leave us, then?
Rouse up and be our dad again.
When you are quiet and laid in bed,
We'll doff° our shoes and softly tread;   *remove*

And when you wake we'll aye° be near,   *always*
30   To fill old dad his cheer.

When thro' the house you shift your stand,
I'll lead you kindly by the hand:
When dinner's set, I'll with you bide,
And aye be serving by your side:
35   And when the weary fire burns blue,
I'll sit and talk with you.

I have a tale both long and good,
About a partlet° and her brood;   *hen*
And cunning greedy fox, that stole,
40   By dead of midnight thro' a hole,
Which slily to the hen-roost led,—
You love a story, dad?

And then I have a wondrous tale
Of men all clad in coats of mail,
45   With glitt'ring swords—you nod,—I think?
Your fixed eyes begin to wink:
Down on your bosom sinks your head:
You do not hear me, dad.

1790

Thunder

Spirit of strength! to whom in wrath 'tis given,
To mar the earth and shake its vasty dome,
Behold the sombre robes whose gathering folds,
Thy secret majesty conceal. Their skirts
5   Spread on mid air move slow and silently,
O'er noon-day's beam thy sultry shroud is cast,
Advancing clouds from every point of heaven,
Like hosts° of gathering foes in pitchy volumes,   *armies*
Grandly dilated, clothe the fields of air,
10   And brood° aloft o'er the empurpled earth.   *hover*
Spirit of strength! it is thy awful hour;
The wind of every hill is laid to rest,
And far o'er sea and land deep silence reigns.

Wild creatures of the forest homeward hie,
15   And in their dens with fear unwonted° cower;   *unaccustomed*
Pride in the lordly palace is put down,
While in his humble cot° the poor man sits   *cottage*
With all his family round him hush'd and still,
In awful expectation. On his way
20   The traveller stands aghast and looks to heaven.
On the horizon's verge thy lightning gleams,
And the first utterance of thy deep voice
Is heard in reverence and holy fear.

From nearer clouds bright burst more vivid gleams,
25   As instantly in closing darkness lost;
Pale sheeted flashes cross the wide expanse
While over boggy moor or swampy plain,
A streaming cataract of flame appears,
To meet a nether fire from earth cast up,
30   Commingling terribly; appalling gloom
Succeeds, and lo! the rifted° centre pours   *fissured*
A general blaze, and from the war of clouds,
Red, writhing falls the embodied bolt of heaven.
Then swells the rolling peal, full, deep'ning, grand,
35   And in its strength lifts the tremendous roar,
With mingled discord, rattling, hissing, growling;
Crashing like rocky fragments downward hurl'd,
Like the upbreaking of a ruined world,
In awful majesty the explosion bursts
40   Wide and astounding o'er the trembling land.
Mountain, and cliff, repeat the dread turmoil,
And all, to man's distinctive senses known,
Is lost in the immensity of sound.
Peal after peal succeeds with waning strength,
45   And hush'd and deep each solemn pause between.

Upon the lofty mountain's side
The kindled forest blazes wide;
Huge fragments of the rugged steep
Are tumbled to the lashing deep;
50   Firm rooted in his cloven rock,
Crashing falls the stubborn oak.
The lightning keen in wasteful ire
Darts fiercely on the pointed spire,
Rending in twain the iron-knit stone,
55   And stately towers to earth are thrown.
No human strength may brave the storm,
Nor shelter screen the shrinking form,
Nor castle wall its fury stay,
Nor massy gate impede its way:
60   It visits those of low estate,°   *the poor*
It shakes the dwellings of the great,
It looks athwart the vaulted tomb,
And glares upon the prison's gloom.
Then dungeons black in unknown light,
65   Flash hideous on the wretches' sight,
And strangely groans the downward cell,
Where silence deep is wont to dwell.

Now eyes, to heaven up-cast, adore,
Knees bend that never bent before,
70   The stoutest hearts begin to fail,
And many a manly face is pale;

Benumbing fear awhile up-binds,
The palsied action of their minds,
Till waked to dreadful sense they lift their eyes,
75   And round the stricken corse° shrill shrieks of horror rise.   *corpse*

    Now rattling hailstones, bounding as they fall
To earth, spread motley winter o'er the plain;
Receding peals sound fainter on the ear,
And roll their distant grumbling far away:
80   The lightning doth in paler flashes gleam,
And through the rent cloud, silvered with his rays,
The sun on all this wild affray° looks down,   *tumult, quarrel*
As, high enthroned above all mortal ken,°   *understanding*
A higher Power beholds the strife of men.

1790; rev. 1840

Song: Woo'd and Married and A'
(Version taken from an old song of that name)

The bride she is winsome and bonny,
    Her hair it is snooded° sae° sleek,   *tied up / so*
And faithfu' and kind is her Johnny,
    Yet fast fa' the tears on her cheek.
5   New pearlins° are cause of her sorrow,   *fancy lacework*
    New pearlins and plenishing° too,   *furnishings*
The bride that has a' to borrow,
    Has e'en right mickle° ado,   *much*
      Woo'd and married and a'!°   *all*
10   Woo'd and married and a'!
    Is na' she very weel aff
      To be woo'd and married at a'?

Her mither then hastily spak,
    "The lassie is glaikit° wi' pride;   *foolish*
15   In my pouch I had never a plack°   *4-cent coin*
    On the day when I was a bride.
E'en tak' to your wheel° and be clever,   *spinning wheel*
    And draw out your thread in the sun;
The gear° that is gifted° it never   *goods / given*
20   Will last like the gear that is won.°   *earned*
      Woo'd and married and a'!
      Wi' havins° and tocher° sae sma'!   *belongings / dowry*
    I think ye are very weel aff,
      To be woo'd and married at a'!"

25   "Toot, toot!" quo' her grey-headed faither,
    "She's less o' a bride than a bairn,°   *child*
She's ta'en like a cout° frae the heather,   *colt*
    Wi' sense and discretion to learn.
Half husband, I trow,° and half daddy,   *suppose*

30   As humour inconstantly leans,
  The chiel maun° be patient and steady,   *fellow must*
   That yokes wi' a mate in her teens.
    A kerchief sae douce° and sae neat,   *proper*
    O'er her locks that the winds used to blaw!
35   I'm baith like to laugh and to greet,°   *weep*
    When I think o' her married at a'!"

   Then out spak' the wily bridegroom,
    Weel waled° were his wordies, I ween,° *well chosen / suppose*
   "I'm rich, though my coffer be toom,°   *empty*
40   Wi' the blinks o' your bonny blue een.°   *eyes*
   I'm prouder o' thee by my side,
    Though thy ruffles or ribbons be few,
   Than if Kate o' the Croft were my bride,
    Wi' purfles° and pearlins enow.   *embroidery*
45   Dear and dearest of ony!°   *any*
    Ye're woo'd and buikit° and a'!"   *registered*
   And do ye think scorn o' your Johnny,
    And grieve to be married at a'?"

   She turn'd, and she blush'd, and she smiled,
50   And she looket sae bashfully down;
   The pride o' her heart was beguiled,
    And she played wi' the sleeves o' her gown;
   She twirled the tag o' her lace,
    And she nippet her boddice sae blue,
55   Syne° blinket sae sweet in his face,   *then*
    And aff like a maukin° she flew.   *cat, slut*
    Woo'd and married and a'!
    Wi' Johnny to roose° her and a'!   *praise*
   She thinks hersel very weel aff,
60   To be woo'd and married at a'!

                1822, 1840

LITERARY BALLADS

"I never heard the old song of Percy and Douglas," wrote Sir Philip Sidney in *Apology for Poetry* (1595), "that I found not my heart moved more than with a trumpet: and yet it is sung but by some blind crouder [fiddler], with no rougher voice than rude style: which being so evil apparelled in the dust and cobwebs of that uncivil age, what would it work trimmed in the gorgeous elegance of Pindar?" Sidney set the terms in which popular ballads were appreciated for the next three centuries: readers prized their directness, but could scarcely refrain from wishing to sophisticate them. In the eighteenth century, the numerous popular ballads composed between roughly 1200 and 1700 became a cherished alternative to prevailing norms of elegance and decorum. In *Spectator* No. 70 (1711), Joseph Addison devoted to the ballad *Chevy Chase* the kind of criticism previously limited to the classics, preferring its "essential and inherent perfection of simplicity of thought" to the "artificial taste" cultivated by "little fanciful authors and writers of epigram." Like the exalted epics of Homer, Virgil, or Milton, ballads appealed to readers of "plain common sense" across all classes and times. Yet no small part of their appeal was their evocation of a hazily indefinite Middle Ages. Thought to be the work of bards or minstrels in the employ of a chieftain, or anonymous folk songs, ballads signified a living oral tradition imperiled by the growing, standardizing print culture on which the eighteenth century prided itself. They harked back to an immediate contact between singer and audience lost in a culture of private reading and glamorized authors.

The basis of the ballads in music shaped their form—usually quatrains of four-beat lines—and permitted a number of haunting effects: repetitions, unexpected syncopations, and narrative compression. Even dilations, such as refrains or formulaic dialogue, made the expected end seem more inevitable. Often haunted by the supernatural that an age of reason dismissed as primitive, sometimes based on historical incidents, usually tragic, the ballads share an intense spareness that springs the reader's imagination.

Richard Hurd's *Letters on Chivalry and Romance* (1762) voiced the spirit of the ballad revival: the age of realism, reason, and "good sense" had sacrificed "a world of fine fabling." This revival even generated fresh production. Thomas Chatterton (1752–1770) counterfeited a *mélange* of Elizabethan and medieval ballads that he attributed to a fifteenth-century monk, "Thomas Rowley." It was from Chatterton that Wordsworth derived the unusual stanza form of his *Resolution and Independence* (1807), celebrating him there as "the marvellous boy, / The sleepless Soul who perished in his pride," and pairing him with Burns: "Him who walked in glory and in joy / Following his plough." The Scot James Macpherson took Europe by storm with *Fingal* (1762) and other supposed versions of oral epics by the ancient Celtic bard Ossian, and though his fabrications were exposed, admiration remained. Bishop Lowth's Latin *Lectures on the Sacred Poetry of the Hebrews* (1753; translated into English 1793) defended the psalms against neoclassic norms by articulating a standard of impassioned sublimity, embodied in lyric. Concurrently, scholars were suggesting that the Bible was not a unitary text but a composite, and German philologists were similarly dissolving the *Iliad* and *Odyssey* into the stitched-together fragments of oral tradition. By the end of the century, divine scripture, epic, and ballad, high artistic monument and folk culture had come together in a provocative upheaval of the long-established hierarchy of genres.

Reliques of Ancient English Poetry

Thomas Percy (1729–1811), a grocer's son who took a degree at Oxford in 1750, enjoyed a career in the Anglican church that culminated in his appointments as a chaplain to George III (1769), Dean of Carlisle (1778), and Bishop of Dromore, Ireland (1782). His celebrity derives from his three-volume *Reliques of Ancient Poetry* (1765), developed from a manuscript collection he had found at a friend's house "lying dirty on the floor under a Bureau in ye Parlour: being used by the Maids to light the fires." Fewer than fifty of the 175 poems in the first edition can be traced to this trove, however; for the rest Percy scoured manuscript archives and published collections. Traditional ballads were his object, but the *Reliques* mix them with sixteenth- and seventeenth-century poetry (by Shakespeare, Jonson, Carew, Crashaw, and others), works by contemporaries and himself, and substantial essays on "ancient English minstrels" and on the unrhymed alliterative verse of *Piers Plowman* and the Norse poets. A serious churchman, Percy apologized for bestowing "attention on a parcel of OLD BALLADS": his presentation dignified them, however, diminishing the strangeness of the medieval world, not least because (in a tactic excoriated by later scholars) he did not hesitate to "improve" his originals. Subsequent editions appeared across the century, exerting a wide influence on the Romantic period, visible, for example, in the meter of Coleridge's *Christabel* (page 314) and Scott's *The Lay of the Last Minstrel*. Wordsworth declared that British poetry had been "absolutely redeemed" by the *Reliques*, and continued: "I do not think that there is an able writer of verse of the present day who would not be proud to acknowledge his obligations to the Reliques; I know that it is so for my friends; and for myself, I am happy . . . to make a public avowal of my own." Volume I of the *Reliques* printed such famous ballads as *Chevy Chase* and *Edward, Edward*, as well as *Sir Patrick Spence*, which provided Coleridge with the epigraph for his *Dejection: An Ode* (page 334).

Sir Patrick Spence[1]

where

The king sits in Dumferling[2] toune,
   Drinking the blude-reid wine:
O quhar° will I get guid sailòr,   *where*
   To sail this schip of mine?

5 Up and spak an eldern knicht,
   Sat at the kings richt kne:
Sir Patrick Spence is the best sailòr,
   That sails upon the se.

The king has written a braid° letter,   *open*
10   And signd it wi' his hand;
And sent it to Sir Patrick Spence,
   Was walking on the sand.

The first line that Sir Patrick red,
   Loud lauch° lauched he: *laugh*
15 The next line that Sir Patrick red,
   The teir blinded his ee.°   *eye*

O quha° is this has don this deid,   *who*
   This ill deid don to me;
To send me out this time o' the zeir,°   *year*
20   To sail upon the se?[3]

Mak hast, mak haste, my mirry men all,
   Our guid schip sails the morne,°   *on the morrow*
O say na sae, my master deir,
   For I feir a deadlie storme.

25 Late late yestreen I saw the new moone
   Wi' the auld moone in hir arme;
And I feir, I feir, my deir mastèr,
   That we will com to harme.

O our Scots nobles wer richt laith°   *loath*
30   To weet their cork-heild schoone;°   *shoes*
Bot lang owre° a' the play wer playd,   *long ere*
   Thair hats they swam aboone.°   *above (water)*

---

1. Percy confesses ignorance of the historical particulars of the events; Sir Walter Scott's version includes a stanza explaining that the Scots were bound for Norway to deliver their king's daughter for marriage to King Eric. The return voyage ended in shipwreck in 1281.

2. Dunfermline, site of Scottish royal palace.
3. "In the infancy of navigation, such [sailors] as used the northern seas were very liable to shipwreck in the wintry months: hence a law was enacted in the reign of James III," restricting winter ship travel [Percy's comment].

O lang, lang, may thair ladies sit
    Wi' thair fans into their hand,
35   Or eir they se Sir Patrick Spence
    Cum sailing to the land.

O lang, lang, may the ladies stand
    Wi' thair gold kems° in their hair,   *combs*
Waiting for thair ain deir lords,
40   For they'll se thame na mair.

Have owre°, have owre to Aberdour,[4]   *half over*
    It's fiftie fadom deip:
And thair lies guid Sir Patrick Spence,
    Wi' the Scots lords at his feit.

                                            1765

Robert Burns
1759–1796

A "striking example of native genius bursting through the obscurity of poverty and the ob-structions of laborious life" exclaimed the *Edinburgh Magazine* when Burns's *Poems, Chiefly in the Scottish Dialect* appeared from provincial Kilmarnock in 1786. Yet the reality of the "heaven-taught plow-man" was more complex. A tenant farmer like his father, Burns planned to accept a position on a Jamaican plantation until the success of his poetry provided an alternative. Though poor, Burns was well read; his poems, if "chiefly" in dialect, were never exclusively so: the accents and forms of folk culture play against a range of polite English genres. Fame brought Burns to Edinburgh, where he enlarged and reprinted his book. On the profits, he returned to farming and married Jean Armour, who had borne him children in 1786 and 1788.

    The farm failed, as had its three predecessors, and Burns moved his family to Dumfries, where he obtained the post of exciseman, or tax-inspector. Government employment might seem anomalous for one who championed the American and French Revolutions, who believed in the goodness of man against the tenets of the Scots church, which he re-peatedly satirized, and flamboyantly defied in his many erotic escapades, but Burns fulfilled his duties responsibly. An invitation in 1787 to contribute to *The Scots Musical Museum* in-tensified his sense of his Scots identity: for the next six years he became "absolutely crazed," as he put it, with collecting and editing traditional songs for the successive vol-umes, and wrote more than two hundred himself, new or adapted. When the fourth volume was finished in 1792, Burns agreed to participate in a *Select Collection of Scottish Airs*, a far more genteelly refining version of Scottish poetry. The more earthy energies of Burns's po-etry appear in the posthumously published *Merry Muses of Caledonia* (1799–1800), a collec-tion printed at least partly from Burns's papers following his early death from heart disease at the age of thirty-seven. The second version of *Comin' Thro' the Rye* and *The Fornicator* appeared in this work.

4. A harbor in Fife, Scotland.

To a Mouse

On Turning Her Up in Her Nest with the Plough, November, 1785

Wee, sleekit,° cowrin, tim'rous beastie,	*sleek*
O, what a panic's in thy breastie!	
Thou need na start awa sac° hasty	*so*
Wi' bickering brattle!°	*scurry*
5 I wad be laith° to rin an' chase thee,	*loath*
Wi' murdering pattle!°	*plough-scraper*

I'm truly sorry man's dominion
Has broken Nature's social union,
An' justifies that ill opinion
10   Which makes thee startle
At me, thy poor, earth-born companion
    An' fellow mortal!

I doubt na, whyles,° but thou may thieve;	*sometimes*
What then? poor beastie, thou maun° live!	*must*
15 A daimen icker in a thrave°	*odd ear in 24 sheaves*
'S a sma' request;	
I'll get a blessin wi' the lave,°	*rest*
An' never miss 't!	

Thy wee-bit housie, too, in ruin!	
20 Its silly wa's° the win's are strewin!	*feeble walls*
An' naething, now, to big° a new ane,	*build*
O' foggage° green!	*coarse grass*
An' bleak December's win's ensuin,	
Baith snell° an' keen!	*bitter*

25 Thou saw the fields laid bare an' waste,	
An' weary winter comin fast,	
An' cozie here, beneath the blast,	
Thou thought to dwell,	
Till crash! the cruel coulter° past	*plow-blade*
30 Out thro' thy cell.	

That wee bit heap o' leaves an' stibble,°	*stubble*
Has cost thee monie a weary nibble!	
Now thou's turned out, for a' thy trouble,	
But° house or hald,°	*without / goods*
35 To thole° the winter's sleety dribble,	*endure*
An' cranreuch° cauld!	*hoarfrost*

But Mousie, thou art no thy lane,°	*not alone*
In proving foresight may be vain:	
The best-laid schemes o' mice an' men	
40 Gang aft agley,°	*go oft awry*
An' lea'e us nought but grief an' pain,	
For promis'd joy!	

Still thou art blest, compared wi' me!
The present only toucheth thee:
45 But och! I backward cast my e'e,
  On prospects drear!
An' forward, tho' I canna see,
  I guess an' fear!

1785   1786

To a Louse,
On Seeing one on a Lady's Bonnet at Church

Ha! Whare ye gaun,° ye crowlan ferlie!°   *going / creeping wonder*
Your impudence protects you sairly:°   *surely*
I canna say but ye strunt° rarely,   *strut*
  Owre *gawze* and *lace;*
5 Tho' faith, I fear ye dine but sparely,
  On sic a place.

Ye ugly, creepan, blastet° wonner,   *blasted, cursed*
Detested, shunn'd, by saunt an' sinner,
How daur ye set your fit upon her,
10   Sae fine a *Lady!*
Gae somewhere else and seek your dinner,
  On some poor body.

Swith,° in some beggar's haffet° squattle,° *Away! / lock of hair / squat*
There ye may creep, and sprawl,° and sprattle,° *struggle / scramble*
15 Wi'ither kindred, jumping cattle,°   *beasts*
  In shoals and nations;
Whare *horn* nor *bane*[1] ne'er daur unsettle,
  Your thick plantations.

Now haud° you there, ye're out o' sight,   *stay*
20 Below the fatt'rels,° snug and tight,   *ribbon ends*
Na faith ye° yet! Ye'll no be right,   *confound you*
  Till ye've got on it,
The vera tapmost, towrin height
  O' *Miss's bonnet.*

25 My sooth! Right bauld ye set your nose,
As plump an' gray as onie grozet°   *gooseberry*
O for some rank, mercurial rozet,° *rosin soap (used as insecticide)*
  Or fell,° red smeddum,°   *deadly / powder*
I'd gie you sic a hearty dose o't,
30   Wad dress your droddum!°   *beat your backside*

I wad na been surpriz'd to spy
You on an auld wife's *flainen toy;*°   *flannel cap with flaps*

---

1. Combs were made of horn or bone.

Or aiblins° some bit duddie° boy,   *perhaps / ragged*
    On's *wylecoat;*°   *flannel vest*
35 But Miss's fine *Lunardi,*[2] fye!
    How daur ye do't?

O *Jenny* dinna toss your head,
An' set your beauties a' abroad!
Ye little ken what cursed speed
40   The blastie's° makin!   *shrivelled dwarf*
Thae *winks* and *finger-ends,* I dread,
    Are notice takin!

O wad some Pow'r the giftie gie us
To see oursels as others see us!
45 It wad frae monie a blunder free us
    An' foolish notion:
What airs in dress an' gait wad lea'e us,
    And ev'n Devotion!

1785   1786

Flow gently, sweet Afton[1]

Flow gently, sweet Afton, among thy green braes!°   *banks*
Flow gently, I'll sing thee a song in thy praise!
My Mary's asleep by thy murmuring stream—
Flow gently, sweet Afton, disturb not her dream!

5 Thou stock-dove whose echo resounds thro' the glen,
Ye wild whistling blackbirds in yon thorny den,
Thou green-crested lapwing, thy screaming forbear—
I charge you, disturb not my slumbering fair!

How lofty, sweet Afton, thy neighbouring hills,
10 Far mark'd with the courses of clear, winding rills!°   *brooks*
There daily I wander, as noon rises high,
My flocks and my Mary's sweet cot° in my eye.   *cottage*

How pleasant thy banks and green vallies below,
Where wild in the woodlands the primroses blow;
15 There oft, as mild Ev'ning weeps over the lea,°   *meadow*
The sweet-scented birk° shades my Mary and me.   *birch*

Thy crystal stream, Afton, how lovely it glides,
And winds by the cot where my Mary resides!
How wanton thy waters her snowy feet lave,°   *wash*
20 As, gathering sweet flowerets, she stems thy clear wave.

2. Vincenzo Lunardi (1759–1806) was an early balloonist who made several ascents in Scotland in 1785. His celebrity brought a bonnet shaped like a balloon into fashion.

1. "There is a small river, Afton, that falls into [the river] Nith, New Cumnock [in southwest Scotland]; which has some charming wild, romantic scenery on its banks. . . ." [Burns's comment].

Flow gently, sweet Afton, among thy green braes!
Flow gently, sweet river, the theme of my lays!
My Mary's asleep by thy murmuring stream—
Flow gently, sweet Afton, disturb not her dream!

1789   1792

Ae fond kiss[1]

Ae° fond kiss, and then we sever!   *one*
Ae farewell, and then forever!
Deep in heart-wrung tears I'll pledge thee,
Warring sighs and groans I'll wage° thee.   *pledge*
5   Who shall say that Fortune grieves him
While the star of hope she° leaves him   *Fortune*
Me, nae cheerfu' twinkle lights me,
Dark despair around benights me.

I'll ne'er blame my partial fancy:
10   Naething could resist my Nancy!
But to see her was to love her,
Love but her, and love for ever.
Had we never lov'd sae kindly,
Had we never lov'd sae blindly,
15   Never met—or never parted—
We had ne'er been broken-hearted.

Fare-the-weel, thou first and fairest!
Fare-the-weel, thou best and dearest!
Thine be ilka° joy and treasure,   *every*
20   Peace, Enjoyment, Love and Pleasure!
Ae fond kiss, and then we sever!
Ae farewell, alas, for ever!
Deep in heart-wrung tears I'll pledge thee,
Warring sighs and groans I'll wage thee.

1791   1792

Comin' Thro' the Rye (1)[1]

CHORUS
O, Jenny's a' weet, poor body,
Jenny's seldom dry:
She draigl't° a' her petticoatie,   *bedraggled*
Comin thro' the rye!

5   Comin thro' the rye, poor body,
Comin thro' the rye,

---

1. Addressed to Agnes "Nancy" McLehose, leaving Edinburgh in 1792 to rejoin her husband in the West Indies.
1. A revision and expansion of an old song, also popular in various bawdy versions, as in the second version which follows, with obscenities tactfully hyphenated by the 1800 publisher.

She draigl't a' her petticoatie,
   Comin thro' the rye!

Gin° a body meet a body   *if*
10   Comin thro' the rye,
Gin a body kiss a body,
   Need a body cry?

Gin a body meet a body
   Comin thro' the glen,
15 Gin a body kiss a body,
   Need the warld ken?°   *know*

CHORUS

                      1796

Comin' Thro' the Rye (2)

CHORUS

O gin a body meet a body,
   Comin throu the rye;
Gin a body f—k a body,
Need a body cry.

5 Comin' thro' the rye, my jo,°   *sweetheart*
   An' comin' thro' the rye;
She fand a staun° o' staunin' graith,°   *stand / tools*
   Comin' thro' the rye.

Gin a body meet a body,
10   Comin' thro' the glen;
Gin a body f—k a body,
   Need the warld ken.

Gin a body meet a body,
   Comin' thro' the grain;
15 Gin a body f—k a body,
   C—t's a body's ain.°   *own*

Gin a body meet a body,
   By a body's sel,
What na body f—s a body,
20   Wad a body tell.

Mony a body meets a body,
   They dare na weel avow;
Mony a body f—s a body,
   Ye wadna think it true.

                   1799–1800

A Red, Red Rose[1]

O, my luve is like a red, red rose,
    That's newly sprung in June.
O, my luve is like the melodie,
    That's sweetly play'd in tune.

5   As fair art thou, my bonie lass,
      So deep in luve am I,
And I will luve thee still, my dear,
    Till a' the seas gang° dry.   *go*

Till a' the seas gang dry, my dear,
10   And the rocks melt wi' the sun!
And I will luve thee still, my dear,
    While the sands o' life shall run.

And fare thee weel, my only luve,
    And fare thee weel a while!
15   And I will come again, my luve,
    Tho' it were ten thousand mile!

1794   1796

Auld Lang Syne

Should auld acquaintance be forgot,
    And never brought to mind?
Should auld acquaintance be forgot,
    And auld lang syne!°   *long ago times*

CHORUS
5   For auld lang syne, my dear,
        For auld lang syne,
    We'll tak a cup o' kindness yet
        For auld lang syne!

And surely ye'll be° your pint-stowp,°   *buy / pint-cup*
10   And surely I'll be mine,
And we'll tak a cup o' kindness yet
    For auld lang syne!

CHORUS

We twa hae run about the braes,°   *slopes*
    And pou'd° the gowans° fine,   *pulled / daisies*
15   But we've wander'd monie a weary fit°   *foot*
    Sin'° auld lang syne.   *since*

1. This poem incorporates elements of several old ballads and folk songs, a common practice of amalgamation at which Burns had great success.

CHORUS

We twa hae paidl'd in the burn[1]
   Frae morning sun till dine,°   *dinner (noon)*
But seas between us braid° hae roar'd   *broad*
20   Sin' auld lang syne.

CHORUS

And there's a hand, my trusty fiere,°   *friend*
   And gie's a hand o' thine,
And we'll tak a right guid-willie waught°   *good-will swig*
   For auld lang syne!

CHORUS

25   For auld lang syne, my dear,
       For auld lang syne,
       We'll tak a cup o' kindness yet
       For auld lang syne!

1788   1796

The Fornicator. A New Song
Tune, Clout the Caldron

Ye jovial boys who love the joys
   The blissful joys of lovers;
Yet dare avow with dauntless brow,
   When the bony lass discovers:[1]
5   I pray draw near and lend an ear,
      And welcome in a Frater,°   *brother*
For I've lately been on quarantine,
   A proven Fornicator.

Before the Congregation wide
10   I pass'd the muster fairly,[2]
My handsome Betsey by my side,[3]
   We gat° our ditty° rarely;   *received / reproof*
But my downcast eye by chance did spy
   What made my lips to water,
15   Those limbs so clean where I, between
   Commenc'd a Fornicator.

With rueful face and signs of grace
   I pay'd the buttock-hire,[4]
The night was dark and thro the park

---

1. Stream; waters used for brewing. "Burns" would especially appreciate the double sense.
1. Reveals her pregnancy.
2. In the Scottish Church those found guilty of fornication were required to sit, clothed in black, for three successive Sundays on a raised "stool of repentance."
3. Usually taken as Elizabeth Paton, with whom Burns had an illegitimate child.
4. There was a six-pound fine for fornication.

20   I could not but convoy her;
          A parting kiss, what could I less,
               My vows began to scatter,
          My Betsey fell—lal de dal lal lal,
               I am a Fornicator.

25   But for her sake this vow I make,
               And solemnly I swear it,
          That while I own a single crown,
               She's welcome for to share it;
         And my roguish boy his Mother's joy,
30   And the darling of his Pater,°   *father*
         For him I boast my pains and cost,
               Although a Fornicator.

         Ye wenching blades whose hireling jades[5]
               Have tipt you off blue-boram,[6]
35   I tell you plain, I do disdain
               To rank you in the Quorum;
         But a bony lass upon the grass
               To teache her esse Mater,°   *to be a mother*
         And no reward but for regard,
40   O that's a Fornicator.

         Your warlike kings and heroes bold,
               Great Captains and Commanders;
         Your mighty Cèsars fam'd of old,
               And Conquering Alexanders;
45   In fields they fought and laurels bought
               And bulwarks strong did batter,
         But still they grac'd our noble list
               And ranked Fornicator!!!

1784–1785   1799

⊶⊷

Sir Walter Scott
1771–1832

"An eager student" of ballads in his youth, Scott even remembered the tree under which he had first read Percy's "enchanting" *Reliques*. In 1795 Anna Barbauld visited Edinburgh and "electrified" audiences by reading a translation of the German Gottfried Bürger's *Lenore*; the following year, Scott's translations of two of Bürger's ballads (including *Lenore*) made up his first publication. In 1799 Scott set out with a team of assistants to collect the local "raiding" ballads recording the strife along the Scots-English border. The project grew, issuing in the two-volume *Minstrelsy of the Scottish Border* of 1802, so popular that a third volume was added in 1803. By 1812 the

5. Worn-out horses, a contemptuous term for women.   from the notorious Blue Boar Tavern in London.
6. Infected you with syphilis. The term probably derives

Minstrelsy had reached a larger fifth edition, signed "Walter Scott, Esq., Advocate," by then famous in his own right for his verse-romances, the best-selling *The Lay of the Last Minstrel* (1805), *Marmion* (1808), and their successors. *Lord Randal* (1803) is one of Scott's own literary ballads.

Lord Randal

"O where hae ye been, Lord Randal, my son?
O where hae ye been, my handsome young man?"
"I hae been to the wild wood; mother, make my bed soon,
For I'm weary wi' hunting, and fain would lie down."

5   "Where gat ye your dinner, Lord Randal, my son?
Where gat ye your dinner, my handsome young man?"
"I din'd wi' my true-love; mother, make my bed soon,
For I'm weary wi' hunting, and fain would lie down."

"What gat ye to your dinner, Lord Randal, my son?"
10 What gat ye to your dinner, my handsome young man?"
"I gat eels boiled in broo;° mother, make my bed soon,   *broth*
For I'm weary wi' hunting, and fain would lie down."

"What became of your bloodhounds, Lord Randal, my son!
What became of your bloodhounds, my handsome young man?"
15 "O they swelld and they died; mother, make my bed soon,
For I'm weary wi' hunting, and fain would lie down."

"O I fear ye are poisond, Lord Randal, my son!
O I fear ye are poisond, my handsome young man!"
"O yes! I am poisond; mother, make my bed soon.
20 For I'm sick at the heart and I fain would lie down."

* ❧ *

Thomas Moore
1779–1852

"Tommy loves a lord," Byron said of his friend and biographer. Thomas Moore was the Irish Catholic son of a grocer; he attended Trinity College, Dublin, and went to London in 1798 to study law. A translation of Anacreon, dedicated to the Prince of Wales, opened the doors of Whig society and fixed his career. His poetic success—lyrics and songs, seven volumes of satires, political lampoons in the newspapers—was inseparable from his genial presence as a wit and an accomplished singer. Appointed Admiralty Registrar at Bermuda in 1803, Moore soon transferred the work to a deputy and returned to the circles he loved; when the deputy embezzled and decamped in 1818, Moore was responsible for the debt and had to quit England for four years. His fame was by then secure, partly for *Lalla Rookh* (1817), an oriental romance for which his publisher paid £3,000, at the time the highest sum ever paid for a single work, and still more for his *Irish Melodies*, which began to appear in 1807. Set to traditional airs or to his own compositions, Moore's lyrics became a staple of nineteenth-century musical evenings and were enthusiastically recommended by James Joyce to his singer son. If Hazlitt thought Moore converted "the wild harp of Erin into a musical snuffbox," the Tory press was alert to the "rebel words" of a work such as *The harp that once through Tara's halls* and denounced the charm of the *Melodies* as "a vehicle of dangerous politics."

The harp that once through Tara's halls[1]

The harp that once through Tara's halls
    The soul of music shed,
Now hangs as mute on Tara's walls,
    As if that soul were fled.—
5   So sleeps the pride of former days,
        So glory's thrill is o'er,
And hearts, that once beat high for praise,
        Now feel that pulse no more.

No more to chiefs and ladies bright
10   The harp of Tara swells;
The chord alone, that breaks at night,
    Its tale of ruin tells.
Thus Freedom now so seldom wakes,
    The only throb she gives,
15   Is when some heart indignant breaks,
    To show that still she lives.

1834

Believe me, if all those endearing young charms

Believe me, if all those endearing young charms,
    Which I gaze on so fondly to-day,
Were to change by to-morrow, and fleet in my arms,
    Like fairy-gifts fading away,
5   Thou wouldst still be adored, as this moment thou art,
    Let thy loveliness fade as it will,
And around the dear ruin each wish of my heart
    Would entwine itself verdantly still.

It is not while beauty and youth are thine own,
10   And thy cheeks unprofaned by a tear
That the fervor and faith of a soul can be known,
    To which time will but make thee more dear;
No, the heart that has truly loved never forgets,
    But as truly loves on to the close,
15   As the sun-flower turns on her god, when he sets,
    The same look which she turn'd when he rose.[1]

1822

The time I've lost in wooing

The time I've lost in wooing,
In watching and pursuing

---

1. Tara was the ancient seat of the high kings of Ireland, northwest of Dublin.   1. The sunflower is a heliotrope.

The light, that lies
   In woman's eyes,
5   Has been my heart's undoing.
Though Wisdom oft has sought me,
I scorn'd the lore she brought me,
   My only books
   Were woman's looks,
10   And folly's all they've taught me.

Her smile when Beauty granted,
I hung with gaze enchanted,
   Like him the sprite,
   Whom maids by night
15   Oft meet in glen that's haunted.
Like him, too, Beauty won me,[1]
But while her eyes were on me,
   If once their ray
   Was turn'd away,
20   O! winds could not outrun me.

And are those follies going?
And is my proud heart growing
   Too cold or wise
   For brilliant eyes
25   Again to set it glowing?
No, vain, alas! th' endeavor
From bonds so sweet to sever;
   Poor Wisdom's chance
   Against a glance
30   Is now as weak as ever.

                                    1834

━━◆※◆━━

William Wordsworth
1770–1850

Meeting Wordsworth in 1815, Byron told his wife that he had "but one feeling . . . reverence!"
The exemplar of "plain living and high thinking," Wordsworth provided an image of poetry
and "the Poet" as at once humble and exalted, domestic and severely moral. By the end of his
life he had become a cultural institution, respected even by those who opposed his politics.
Admirers made pilgrimages to his home at Rydal Mount in the Lake District. His beginnings
were less auspicious. Born in the beautiful, isolated Lake District, Wordsworth was the son of
the steward of Lord Lonsdale (James Lowther), the dominant landowner. The death of
Wordsworth's mother when he was eight years old broke a stable middle-class family life;
William and his three brothers were sent to Hawkshead to school, and his sister Dorothy sent
to live with various distant relatives. His father died five years later, and Lord Lonsdale resisted

1. According to legend, the Irish sprite (fairy) could be mastered by the fixed gaze of a mortal.

paying monies owed; the children did not receive their due until 1802, when a new Lord Lons-dale, who became Wordsworth's patron, succeeded to the title. "The props of my affection were removed,/And yet the building stood," Wordsworth exclaimed in a passage of *The Prelude* that seems to refer to these early losses and separations; "taught to feel, perhaps too much,/ The self-sufficing power of Solitude," Wordsworth developed a potent myth of himself as a "favoured being" shaped by the severe but mysteriously benevolent ministry of Nature.

In 1787 Wordsworth entered St. John's College, Cambridge, taking his degree in 1791 with-out distinction. As his autobiographical poem *The Prelude* testifies, his travels left deeper impres-sions than his studies: a summer walking tour in 1790 that brought him to France a year after the fall of the Bastille, a trip through North Wales in 1791, and a year-long stay in France (1791–1792). There he became an active partisan in the heady early phase of the Revolution. "Bliss was it in that dawn to be alive, / But to be young was very Heaven!" he wrote in *The Prelude*. The millenarian hopes of a new era were suffused with personal attachments: he had a love affair with Annette Vallon, who bore their daughter in December 1792. By then, lack of funds had forced him back to England, and the English declaration of war against France precluded his return until 1802. In him as in many of his generation, the war produced a crisis of loyalties, aggravated by the increasing violence of revolutionary France. "Sick, wearied out with contrarieties," Wordsworth re-covered "a saving intercourse with [his] true self" only through the struggles that his poetry records.

A turning point came in 1795, when a small legacy of £900 from a friend enabled Wordsworth to devote himself to poetry. He reunited with Dorothy, and met Coleridge; in 1797 brother and sister moved to Alfoxden, to be near Coleridge at Nether Stowey. "[B]uoyant spirits/. . . were our daily portion when we first/Together wantoned in wild poesy," Wordsworth later wrote; comfortably housed, free to wander the countryside, Wordsworth and Coleridge collaborated on the poems that became *Lyrical Ballads*, published anonymously in 1798 to mixed reviews. The strangeness of *The Rime of the Ancyent Marinere* disconcerted some readers, and the audacious simplicity of Wordsworth's subjects and style offended more. But others felt the "power and pathos" of the poetry, even (in Hazlitt's words) "the sense of a new style and a new spirit." In 1800 Wordsworth published a second edition under his own name, adding a volume containing *Michael* and the "Lucy" poems and others written during the cold and lonely winter that he and Dorothy had passed in Germany between 1798 and 1799. A new Preface, defending his princi-ples and repudiating the expectations of his readers, set the terms of his reception and continued to govern the charges against him by critics such as Francis Jeffrey for decades afterward.

In late 1799 William and Dorothy returned to the Lakes and settled in the beautiful Gras-mere valley, where they remained together for the rest of their lives: first at Dove Cottage, then, after 1813, at the more spacious Rydal Mount. In 1802 their household had expanded when Wordsworth married a childhood friend, and the tenor of their life was steady thereafter, though the years were marred by grave losses—his brother John drowned in 1805, when the ship he cap-tained went down in a storm, two of his five children died in 1812, and a rift with Coleridge was not patched up until the 1820s. Harsh reviews of *Poems, in Two Volumes* (1807) and *The Excur-sion* (1814) paradoxically attested to Wordsworth's emerging centrality, and the publication of his revised and reordered *Poems* in 1815 asserted his claim to enter the canon of English poetry. Wordsworth continued to write and publish almost to the end of his long life. Though his increas-ingly conservative politics led some of the next generation to regard him as having betrayed his republican youth, and put him in opposition to the democratic and commercializing spirit of post-Reform Bill England, his reputation grew steadily, and in 1843 he was appointed Poet Laureate.

The Prelude, the poem that has most compelled modern readers, was published posthu-mously. Wordsworth had held back the work ("Title not yet fixed upon") that he had referred to variously as "the poem to Coleridge," "the poem on the growth of my own mind," and "the poem on my own poetical education," in part because he thought it "unprecedented" that an author should talk so much about himself, in part so as to bequeath its copyright as a legacy to his family. Reserving his most intimate and ambitious poem while revising it across four decades must have affected his often touchy attitude to his critics; by the time *The Prelude* appeared in 1850, the same year as Tennyson's *In Memoriam*, not even the "jacobinical" strain that Thomas Macaulay detected could much alter the image of him. For the Victorians, Wordsworth was the poet of nature, whose writings made the Lake District a tourist spot (much to his disgruntlement) and provided a moral philosophy of life, of childhood and "joy in widest commonalty spread," and above all, of memory and consolation. It was chiefly Wordsworth's "healing power" that led Matthew Arnold to declare in 1879 that Wordsworth stood third only to Milton and Shakespeare in English poetry since the Renaissance. Twentieth-century readers have been captivated by the visionary power of his language, those transient moments when "forms and substances . . . through the turnings intricate of verse, / Present themselves as objects recognized, / In flashes, and with a glory scarce their own." In Wordsworth's sustained effort in *The Prelude* to trace the growth of his mind while attending to experiences lying beyond and beneath the rational mind's grasp—"Points have we all of us within our souls / Where all stand single; this I feel, and make / Breathings for incommunicable powers"—some critics have discerned the beginnings of modern subjectivity. For Geoffrey Hartman, Wordsworth is "the most isolated figure among the great English poets." Other readers, though, have found in the tensions and ambivalences of Wordsworth's project a particularly rich embodiment of the strains of the pivotal decades in which he wrote, and he remains a crucial focus for understanding the vivid and contradictory currents of his age.

Other writing by Wordsworth appears in Perspectives: The Abolition of Slavery and the Slave Trade, page 128.

LYRICAL BALLADS In spring 1798 the young Wordsworth and Coleridge had been near neighbors in Somerset for almost a year. In the fall of 1797, they had decided to pay for a brief walking tour by collaborating on a poem to be sold to the *Monthly Magazine*. Uncompleted at the time, *The Rime of the Ancyent Marinere* became the opening poem of a more substantial enterprise: *Lyrical Ballads, with a few other poems*, the joint collection they published anonymously in October 1798. The exchange that nourished the project had been so close that Coleridge said that the two poets regarded the volume as "one work, in kind, though not in degree, as an ode is one work; and that our different poems are stanzas, good, relatively rather than absolutely," though of the twenty-three poems he wrote only four. A friend, Bristol bookseller Joseph Cottle, agreed to pay the poets £30 for the copyright; before the book appeared they had departed for Germany, Coleridge to study philosophy at Göttingen and Wordsworth to learn German at Goslar, in hopes of later earning money as a translator. Priced at five shillings, the volume sold steadily and earned favorable reviews, but the simplicity of style, the focus on rural life and language, and the obscurity of the *Ancyent Marinere* provoked memorably sharp criticism. The volume had been prefixed by an Advertisement describing the majority of the poems as "experiments" to "ascertain how far the language of conversation in the middle and lower classes of society is adapted to the purposes of poetic pleasure." Attacking "the gaudiness and inane phraseology of many modern writers," and anticipating that "readers of superior judgment" would find that many of the poems would not "suit their taste," the Advertisement deliberately positioned the volume as an affront to "pre-established codes of decision," and thereby claimed for its authors the status of innovators.

Returning from Germany in 1800 to live in the Lake District, Wordsworth planned a second edition, which he sold to Longman, an established London publisher. He now dominated the project: the collection was published under his name alone, and the Advertisement was replaced by a long Preface vindicating his principles. A new second volume was made up entirely of his poems; the *Ancyent Marinere* was retitled *The Ancient Mariner: A Poet's Reverie*, and moved from the head of the first volume to the twenty-third position, with a condescending note ("The Poem of my Friend has indeed great defects"). The collection sold quickly, and a revised edition appeared in 1802 with a significant addition to the Preface, "What is a poet?" The harsh critique by Francis Jeffrey in the newly founded *Edinburgh Review* (page 225) might have been welcome notoriety; it surely helped propel the final edition of *Lyrical Ballads* in 1805, after which the contents were dispersed among the author's separate publications. Years later, in 1843, Wordsworth dictated notes on the circumstances of the poems' composition to Isabella Fenwick, indicated here by "[I.F.]."

from Lyrical Ballads (1798)

Simon Lee[1]
The Old Huntsman, with an incident in which he was concerned.

In the sweet shire of Cardigan,
Not far from pleasant Ivor-hall,
An old man dwells, a little man,
I've heard he once was tall.
5   Of years he has upon his back,
No doubt, a burthen weighty;
He says he is three score and ten,°   *seventy years old*
But others say he's eighty.

A long blue livery-coat° has he,   *servant's uniform*
10   That's fair behind, and fair before;
Yet, meet him where you will, you see
At once that he is poor.
Full five and twenty years he lived
A running huntsman merry;
15   And, though he has but one eye left,
His cheek is like a cherry.

No man like him the horn could sound,
And no man was so full of glee;
To say the least, four counties round
20   Had heard of Simon Lee;
His master's dead, and no one now
Dwells in the hall of Ivor;
Men, dogs, and horses, all are dead;
He is the sole survivor.

25   His hunting feats have him bereft
Of his right eye, as you may see:
And then, what limbs those feats have left
To poor old Simon Lee!
He has no son, he has no child,
30   His wife, an aged woman,
Lives with him, near the waterfall,
Upon the village common.[2]

1. "This old man had been huntsman to the squires of Alfoxden. . . . The old man's cottage stood upon the common, a little way from the entrance to Alfoxden Park. . . . I have, after an interval of 45 years, the image of the old man as fresh before my eyes as if I had seen him yesterday" [I.F.]. Wordsworth relocated the site from Somersetshire, where he and his sister Dorothy lived from 1797 to 1798, to Cardiganshire, a former county of southwest Wales. A huntsman manages the hunt and has charge of the hounds. In the Preface, Wordsworth said that he wrote the poem to place the reader "in the way of receiving from ordinary moral sensations another and more salutary impression than we are accustomed to receive from them."
2. Common lands were progressively being enclosed as private property. Wordsworth successfully fought the enclosure of Grasmere's commons.

And he is lean and he is sick,
His little body's half awry
35   His ancles they are swoln and thick;
His legs are thin and dry.
When he was young he little knew
Of husbandry or tillage;
And now he's forced to work, though weak,
40   —The weakest in the village.

He all the country could outrun,
Could leave both man and horse behind;
And often, ere the race was done,
He reeled and was stone-blind.
45   And still there's something in the world
At which his heart rejoices;
For when the chiming hounds are out,
He dearly loves their voices![3]

Old Ruth works out of doors with him,
50   And does what Simon cannot do;
For she, not over stout° of limb,   *hardy*
Is stouter of the two.
And though you with your utmost skill
From labour could not wean them,
55   Alas! 'tis very little, all
Which they can do between them.

Beside their moss-grown hut of clay,
Not twenty paces from the door,
A scrap of land they have, but they
60   Are poorest of the poor.
This scrap of land he from the heath
Enclosed when he was stronger;
But what avails the land to them,
Which they can till no longer?

65   Few months of life has he in store,
As he to you will tell,
For still, the more he works, the more
His poor old ancles swell.
My gentle reader, I perceive
70   How patiently you've waited,
And I'm afraid that you expect
Some tale will be related.

O reader! had you in your mind
Such stores as silent thought can bring,
75   O gentle° reader! you would find   *kind, well-born*
A tale in every thing.

3. "The expression when the hounds were out, 'I dearly love their voices,' was word for word from his own lips" [I.F.].

What more I have to say is short,
I hope you'll kindly take it;
It is no tale; but should you think,
80   Perhaps a tale you'll make it.

One summer-day I chanced to see
This old man doing all he could
About the root of an old tree,
A stump of rotten wood.
85   The mattock° totter'd in his hand;   *pick-ax*
So vain was his endeavour
That at the root of the old tree
He might have worked for ever.

"You're overtasked, good Simon Lee,
90   Give me your tool" to him I said;
And at the word right gladly he
Received my proffer'd aid.
I struck, and with a single blow
The tangled root I sever'd,
95   At which the poor old man so long
And vainly had endeavour'd.

The tears into his eyes were brought,
And thanks and praises seemed to run
So fast out of his heart, I thought
100   They never would have done.
—I've heard of hearts unkind, kind deeds
With coldness still returning.
Alas! the gratitude of men
Has oftner left me mourning.
1798   1798

Anecdote for Fathers,
shewing how the art of lying may be taught

I have a boy of five years old,
His face is fair and fresh to see;
His limbs are cast in beauty's mould,
And dearly he loves me.

5   One morn we stroll'd on our dry walk,
Our quiet house all full in view,
And held such intermitted talk
As we are wont to do.

My thoughts on former pleasures ran;
10   I thought of Kilve's delightful shore,
My pleasant home, when spring began,
A long, long year before.

A day it was when I could bear
To think, and think, and think again;
15 With so much happiness to spare,
I could not feel a pain.

My boy was by my side, so slim
And graceful in his rustic dress!
And oftentimes I talked to him,
20 In very idleness.

The young lambs ran a pretty race;
The morning sun shone bright and warm;
"Kilve," said I, "was a pleasant place,
And so is Liswyn farm."

25 "My little boy, which like you more,"
I said and took him by the arm—
"Our home by Kilve's delightful shore,
Or here at Liswyn farm?"

"And tell me, had you rather be,"
30 I said and held him by the arm,
"At Kilve's smooth shore by the green sea,
Or here at Liswyn farm?"

In careless mood he looked at me,
While still I held him by the arm,
35 And said, "At Kilve I'd rather be
Than here at Liswyn farm."

"Now, little Edward, say why so;
My little Edward, tell me why";
"I cannot tell, I do not know."
40 "Why this is strange," said I.

"For, here are woods and green-hills warm;
There surely must some reason be
Why you would change sweet Liswyn farm
For Kilve by the green sea."

45 At this, my boy, so fair and slim,
Hung down his head, nor made reply;
And five times did I say to him,
"Why? Edward, tell me why?"

His head he raised—there was in sight,
50 It caught his eye, he saw it plain—
Upon the house-top, glittering bright,
A broad and gilded vane.

Then did the boy his tongue unlock,
And thus to me he made reply;
55 "At Kilve there was no weather-cock,
And that's the reason why."

Oh dearest, dearest boy! my heart
For better lore would seldom yearn,
Could I but teach the hundredth part
60   Of what from thee I learn.

We are seven[1]

A simple child, dear brother Jim,
That lightly draws its breath,
And feels its life in every limb,
What should it know of death?

5   I met a little cottage girl,
She was eight years old, she said;
Her hair was thick with many a curl
That cluster'd round her head.

She had a rustic, woodland air,
10   And she was wildly clad;
Her eyes were fair, and very fair,
—Her beauty made me glad.

"Sisters and brothers, little maid,
How many may you be?"
15   "How many? seven in all," she said,
And wondering looked at me.

"And where are they, I pray you tell?"
She answered, "Seven are we,
And two of us at Conway° dwell,   *Welsh seaport*
20   And two are gone to sea.

"Two of us in the church-yard lie,
My sister and my brother,
And in the church-yard cottage, I
Dwell near them with my mother."

25   "You say that two at Conway dwell,
And two are gone to sea,
Yet you are seven; I pray you tell
Sweet Maid, how this may be?"

Then did the little Maid reply,
30   "Seven boys and girls are we;

1. "The little girl who is the heroine I met within the area of Goodrich Castle in the year 1793. . . . I composed it while walking in the grove at Alfoxden. My friends will not deem it too trifling to relate that while walking to and fro I composed the last stanza first having begun with the last line" [I.F.]. In the Preface Wordsworth pointed to this poem as "shewing . . . the perplexity and obscurity which in childhood attend our notion of death, or rather our utter inability to admit that notion." Wordsworth's mother died when he was turning eight, the age of the girl in the poem. Coleridge wrote the first stanza.

Two of us in the church-yard lie,
Beneath the church-yard tree."

"You run about, my little Maid,
Your limbs they are alive;
35   If two are in the church-yard laid,
Then ye are only five."

"Their graves are green, they may be seen,"
The little Maid replied,
"Twelve steps or more from my mother's door,
40   And they are side by side.

"My stockings there I often knit,
My 'kerchief there I hem;
And there upon the ground I sit—
I sit and sing to them.

45   "And often after sunset, Sir,
When it is light and fair,
I take my little porringer,°   *porridge-bowl*
And eat my supper there.

"The first that died was little Jane;
50   In bed she moaning lay,
Till God released her of her pain,
And then she went away.

"So in the church-yard was she laid;
And all the summer dry,
55   Together round her grave we played,
My brother John and I.

"And when the ground was white with snow,
And I could run and slide,
My brother John was forced to go,
60   And he lies by her side."

"How many are you then," said I,
"If they two are in Heaven?"
The little Maiden did reply,
"O Master! we are seven."

65   "But they are dead; those two are dead!
Their spirits are in heaven!"
'Twas throwing words away; for still
The little Maid would have her will,
And said, "Nay, we are seven!"

1798   1798

Expostulation and Reply[1]

"Why William, on that old grey stone,
Thus for the length of half a day,
Why William, sit you thus alone,
And dream your time away?

5 "Where are your books? that light bequeath'd
To beings else forlorn and blind!
Up! Up! and drink the spirit breath'd
From dead men to their kind.

You look round on your mother earth,
10 As if she for no purpose bore you;
As if you were her first-born birth,
And none had lived before you!"

One morning thus, by Esthwaite lake,[2]
When life was sweet I knew not why,
15 To me my good friend Matthew spake,
And thus I made reply.

"The eye it cannot chuse but see,
We cannot bid the ear be still;
Our bodies feel, where'er they be,
20 Against, or with our will.

"Nor less I deem that there are powers,
Which of themselves our minds impress,
That we can feed this mind of ours,
In a wise passiveness.

25 "Think you, mid all this mighty sum
Of things for ever speaking,
That nothing of itself will come,
But we must still be seeking?

"—Then ask not wherefore, here, alone,
30 Conversing as I may,
I sit upon this old grey stone,
And dream my time away."

1798   1798

---

1. This and the poem that followed opened the 1800 *Lyrical Ballads*. The companion pieces, Wordsworth said, "arose out of a conversation with a friend who was somewhat unreasonably attached to modern books of Moral Philosophy" ("Advertisement," 1798)—probably William Hazlitt, who visited in 1798 and argued about metaphysics. Wordsworth later noted this poem's popularity with Quakers, whose worship is informal and spontaneous.
2. At Hawkshead, where Wordsworth went to school.

Lines
written a few miles above Tintern Abbey,
On Revisiting the Banks of the Wye
during a Tour,
July 13, 1798

Five years have passed; five summers, with the length
Of five long winters! and again I hear
These waters, rolling from their mountain-springs
With a sweet inland murmur.[1]—Once again
5   Do I behold these steep and lofty cliffs,
Which on a wild secluded scene impress
Thoughts of more deep seclusion; and connect
The landscape with the quiet of the sky.
The day is come when I again repose
10   Here, under this dark sycamore, and view
These plots of cottage-ground, these orchard-tufts,
Which, at this season, with their unripe fruits,
Among the woods and copses lose themselves,
Nor, with their green and simple hue, disturb
15   The wild green landscape. Once again I see
These hedge-rows, hardly hedge-rows, little lines
Of sportive wood run wild; these pastoral farms
Green to the very door; and wreathes of smoke
Sent up, in silence, from among the trees,
20   With some uncertain notice, as might seem,
Of vagrant dwellers in the houseless woods,
Or of some hermit's cave, where by his fire
The hermit° sits alone.   *religious recluse*

                   Though absent long,
These forms of beauty have not been to me,
25   As is a landscape to a blind man's eye:
But oft, in lonely rooms, and mid the din
Of towns and cities, I have owed to them,
In hours of weariness, sensations sweet,
Felt in the blood, and felt along the heart,
30   And passing even into my purer mind
With tranquil restoration:—feelings too
Of unremembered pleasure; such, perhaps,
As may have had no trivial influence
On that best portion of a good man's life;
35   His little, nameless, unremembered acts
Of kindness and of love. Nor less, I trust,
To them I may have owed another gift,
Of aspect more sublime; that blessed mood,

---

1. The river is not affected by the tides a few miles above Tintern [Wordsworth's note, 1798].

In which the burthen° of the mystery,[2]   *burden*
40   In which the heavy and the weary weight
Of all this unintelligible world
Is lighten'd:—that serene and blessed mood,
In which the affections gently lead us on,
Until, the breath of this corporeal frame,
45   And even the motion of our human blood
Almost suspended, we are laid asleep
In body, and become a living soul:
While with an eye made quiet by the power
Of harmony, and the deep power of joy,
50   We see into the life of things.

                     If this
Be but a vain belief, yet, oh! how oft,
In darkness, and amid the many shapes
Of joyless day-light; when the fretful stir
Unprofitable, and the fever of the world,
55   Have hung upon the beatings of my heart,[3]
How oft, in spirit, have I turned to thee
O sylvan Wye! Thou wanderer through the wood
How often has my spirit turned to thee!

And now, with gleams of half-extinguish'd thought,
60   With many recognitions dim and faint,
And somewhat of a sad perplexity,
The picture of the mind revives again:
While here I stand, not only with the sense
Of present pleasure, but with pleasing thoughts
65   That in this moment there is life and food
For future years. And so I dare to hope
Though changed, no doubt, from what I was, when first
I came among these hills; when like a roe
I bounded o'er the mountains, by the sides
70   Of the deep rivers, and the lonely streams,
Wherever nature led; more like a man
Flying from something that he dreads, than one
Who sought the thing he loved. For nature then
(The coarser pleasures of my boyish days,
75   And their glad animal movements all gone by,)
To me was all in all.—I cannot paint
What then I was. The sounding cataract
Haunted me like a passion: the tall rock,
The mountain, and the deep and gloomy wood,
80   Their colours and their forms, were then to me
An appetite: a feeling and a love,

---

2. Keats thought this phrase the core of Wordsworth's "genius."
3. Echoing Macbeth's sense of life's fitful fever (*Macbeth*

3.2.23) and Hamlet's view of life as "weary, stale, flat, and unprofitable" (*Hamlet* 1.2.133).

That had no need of a remoter charm,
By thought supplied, or any interest
Unborrowed from the eye.—That time is past,
85 And all its aching joys are now no more,
And all its dizzy raptures. Not for this
Faint° I, nor mourn nor murmur: other gifts   *lose heart*
Have followed, for such loss, I would believe,
Abundant recompence. For I have learned
90 To look on nature, not as in the hour
Of thoughtless youth, but hearing oftentimes
The still, sad music of humanity,
Not harsh nor grating, though of ample power
To chasten and subdue. And I have felt
95 A presence that disturbs me with the joy
Of elevated thoughts; a sense sublime
Of something far more deeply interfused,
Whose dwelling is the light of setting suns,
And the round ocean, and the living air,
100 And the blue sky, and in the mind of man,
A motion and a spirit, that impels
All thinking things, all objects of all thought,
And rolls through all things. Therefore am I still
A lover of the meadows and the woods,
105 And mountains; and of all that we behold
From this green earth; of all the mighty world
Of eye and ear, both what they half-create,[4]
And what perceive; well pleased to recognize
In nature and the language of the sense,
110 The anchor of my purest thoughts, the nurse,
The guide, the guardian of my heart, and soul
Of all my moral being.

                    Nor, perchance,
If I were not thus taught, should I the more
Suffer my genial° spirits to decay: *creative*
115 For thou art with me, here, upon the banks
Of this fair river; thou, my dearest Friend,[5]
My dear, dear Friend, and in thy voice I catch°   *sense, arrest*
The language of my former heart, and read
My former pleasures in the shooting lights
120 Of thy wild eyes. Oh! yet a little while
May I behold in thee what I was once,
My dear, dear Sister! And this prayer I make,
Knowing that Nature never did betray
The heart that loved her; 'tis her privilege,

---

4. This line has a close resemblance to an admirable line of Young, the exact expression of which I cannot recollect [Wordsworth's note]. He is thinking of Edward Young's "half create the wondrous world they see" (*The Complaint or Night Thoughts* [1744], 6.427).

5. His sister Dorothy. The language echoes Psalm 23: "Yea, through I walk through the valley of the shadow of death, I will fear no evil: for thou art with me."

125 Through all the years of this our life, to lead
     From joy to joy: for she can so inform
     The mind that is within us, so impress
     With quietness and beauty, and so feed
     With lofty thoughts, that neither evil tongues,[6]
130 Rash judgments, nor the sneers of selfish men,
     Nor greetings where no kindness is, nor all
     The dreary intercourse of daily life,
     Shall e'er prevail against us, or disturb
     Our chearful faith that all which we behold
135 Is full of blessings. Therefore let the moon
     Shine on thee in thy solitary walk;
     And let the misty mountain winds be free
     To blow against thee: and in after years,
     When these wild ecstasies shall be matured
140 Into a sober pleasure, when thy mind
     Shall be a mansion for all lovely forms,
     Thy memory be as a dwelling-place
     For all sweet sounds and harmonies; Oh! then,
     If solitude, or fear, or pain, or grief,
145 Should be thy portion,° with what healing thoughts   dowry, bequest
     Of tender joy wilt thou remember me,
     And these my exhortations! Nor, perchance,
     If I should be, where I no more can hear
     Thy voice, nor catch from thy wild eyes these gleams
150 Of past existence, wilt thou then forget
     That on the banks of this delightful stream
     We stood together; and that I, so long
     A worshipper of Nature, hither came,
     Unwearied in that service: rather say
155 With warmer love, oh! with far deeper zeal
     Of holier love. Nor wilt thou then forget,
     That after many wanderings, many years
     Of absence, these steep woods and lofty cliffs,
     And this green pastoral landscape, were to me
160 More dear, both for themselves, and for thy sake.
1798   1798

from Lyrical Ballads (1800, 1802)

from Preface[1]

The first Volume of these Poems has already been submitted to general perusal. It was published, as an experiment, which, I hoped, might be of some use to ascertain, how far, by fitting to metrical arrangement a selection of the real language of men in

---

6. An echo of Milton's claim to "Sing with mortal voice, unchang'd / To hoarse or mute, though fall'n on evil days, / . . . and evil tongues" (*Paradise Lost* 7.24–26).
1. In 1800 Wordsworth replaced the 1798 Advertisement with a substantial Preface, which he expanded for the 1802 edition (our text). The 1800 publication was two volumes, the first comprised of poems published in the 1798 *Ballads*.

a state of vivid sensation, that sort of pleasure and that quantity of pleasure may be imparted, which a Poet may rationally endeavour to impart.

I had formed no very inaccurate estimate of the probable effect of those Poems: I flattered myself that they who should be pleased with them would read them with more than common pleasure: and, on the other hand, I was well aware, that by those who should dislike them they would be read with more than common dislike. The result has differed from my expectation in this only, that I have pleased a greater number, than I ventured to hope I should please. * * *

Several of my Friends are anxious for the success of these Poems from a belief, that, if the views with which they were composed were indeed realized, a class of Poetry would be produced, well adapted to interest mankind permanently, and not unimportant in the multiplicity, and in the quality of its moral relations: and on this account they have advised me to prefix a systematic defence of the theory, upon which the poems were written. But I was unwilling to undertake the task, because I knew that on this occasion the Reader would look coldly upon my arguments, since I might be suspected of having been principally influenced by the selfish and foolish hope of reasoning him into an approbation of these particular Poems: and I was still more unwilling to undertake the task, because, adequately to display my opinions, and fully to enforce my arguments, would require a space wholly disproportionate to the nature of a preface. For to treat the subject with the clearness and coherence, of which I believe it susceptible, it would be necessary to give a full account of the present state of the public taste in this country, and to determine how far this taste is healthy or depraved; which, again, could not be determined, without pointing out, in what manner language and the human mind act and re-act on each other, and without retracing the revolutions, not of literature alone, but likewise of society itself. I have therefore altogether declined to enter regularly upon this defence; yet I am sensible, that there would be some impropriety in abruptly obtruding upon the Public, without a few words of introduction, Poems so materially different from those, upon which general approbation is at present bestowed.

It is supposed, that by the act of writing in verse an Author makes a formal engagement that he will gratify certain known habits of association; that he not only thus apprizes the Reader that certain classes of ideas and expressions will be found in his book, but that others will be carefully excluded. This exponent or symbol held forth by metrical language must in different eras of literature have excited very different expectations: for example, in the age of Catullus, Terence, and Lucretius and that of Statius or Claudian; and in our own country, in the age of Shakespeare and Beaumont and Fletcher, and that of Donne and Cowley, or Dryden, or Pope.[2] I will not take upon me to determine the exact import of the promise which by the act of writing in verse an Author, in the present day, makes to his Reader; but I am certain, it will appear to many persons that I have not fulfilled the terms of an engagement thus voluntarily contracted. They who have been accustomed to the gaudiness and inane phraseology of many modern writers, if they persist in reading this book to its conclusion, will, no doubt, frequently have to struggle with feelings of strangeness and aukwardness: they will look round for poetry, and will be induced to inquire by what species of courtesy

---

2. Wordsworth contrasts the Silver Age Latin rhetoric of Statius (A.D. 45–96) and the still more elaborate verse of Claudian (c. 370–404) to the earlier less artificial styles of Catullus (84–54 B.C.), Terence (c. 195–159 B.C.), and Lucretius (c. 94–54 B.C.).

these attempts can be permitted to assume that title. I hope therefore the Reader will not censure me, if I attempt to state what I have proposed to myself to perform; and also, (as far as the limits of a preface will permit) to explain some of the chief reasons which have determined me in the choice of my purpose: that at least he may be spared any unpleasant feeling of disappointment, and that I myself may be protected from the most dishonorable accusation which can be brought against an Author, namely, that of an indolence which prevents him from endeavouring to ascertain what is his duty, or, when his duty is ascertained, prevents him from performing it.

[THE PRINCIPAL OBJECT OF THE POEMS. HUMBLE AND RUSTIC LIFE]

The principal object, then, which I proposed to myself in these Poems was to chuse incidents and situations from common life, and to relate or describe them, throughout, as far as was possible, in a selection of language really used by men; and, at the same time, to throw over them a certain colouring of imagination, whereby ordinary things should be presented to the mind in an unusual way; and, further, and above all, to make these incidents and situations interesting by tracing in them, truly though not ostentatiously, the primary laws of our nature: chiefly, as far as regards the manner in which we associate ideas in a state of excitement. Low and rustic life was generally chosen, because in that condition, the essential passions of the heart find a better soil in which they can attain their maturity, are less under restraint, and speak a plainer and more emphatic language; because in that condition of life our elementary feelings co-exist in a state of greater simplicity, and, consequently, may be more accurately contemplated, and more forcibly communicated; because the manners of rural life germinate from those elementary feelings; and, from the necessary character of rural occupations, are more easily comprehended; and are more durable; and lastly, because in that condition the passions of men are incorporated with the beautiful and permanent forms of nature.[3] The language, too, of these men is adopted (purified indeed from what appear to be its real defects, from all lasting and rational causes of dislike or disgust) because such men hourly communicate with the best objects from which the best part of language is originally derived; and because, from their rank in society and the sameness and narrow circle of their intercourse, being less under the influence of social vanity they convey their feelings and notions in simple and unelaborated expressions. Accordingly, such a language, arising out of repeated experience and regular feelings, is a more permanent, and a far more philosophical language, than that which is frequently substituted for it by Poets, who think that they are conferring honour upon themselves and their art, in proportion as they separate themselves from the sympathies of men, and indulge in arbitrary and capricious habits of expression, in order to furnish food for fickle tastes, and fickle appetites, of their own creation.[4]

["THE SPONTANEOUS OVERFLOW OF POWERFUL FEELINGS"]

I cannot, however, be insensible of the present outcry against the triviality and meanness both of thought and language, which some of my contemporaries have occasionally introduced into their metrical compositions; and I acknowledge, that this de-

3. Compare Coleridge's account of the genesis of *Lyrical Ballads* in *Biographia Literaria*, ch. 14 (page 343).
4. It is worth while here to observe that the affecting parts of Chaucer are almost always expressed in language pure and universally intelligible even to this day [Wordsworth's note].

fect, where it exists, is more dishonorable to the Writer's own character than false refinement or arbitrary innovation, though I should contend at the same time that it is
far less pernicious in the sum of its consequences. From such verses the Poems in these
volumes will be found distinguished at least by one mark of difference, that each of
them has a worthy *purpose*. Not that I mean to say, that I always began to write with a
distinct purpose formally conceived; but I believe that my habits of meditation have so
formed my feelings, as that my descriptions of such objects as strongly excite those feelings, will be found to carry along with them a purpose. If in this opinion I am mistaken,
I can have little right to the name of a Poet. For all good poetry is the spontaneous
overflow of powerful feelings: but though this be true, Poems to which any value can be
attached, were never produced on any variety of subjects but by a man, who being possessed of more than usual organic sensibility, had also thought long and deeply. For our
continued influxes of feeling are modified and directed by our thoughts, which are indeed the representatives of all our past feelings; and, as by contemplating the relation of
these general representatives to each other we discover what is really important to
men, so, by the repetition and continuance of this act, our feelings will be connected
with important subjects, till at length, if we be originally possessed of much sensibility,
such habits of mind will be produced, that, by obeying blindly and mechanically the
impulses of those habits, we shall describe objects, and utter sentiments, of such a nature and in such connection with each other, that the understanding of the being to
whom we address ourselves, if he be in a healthful state of association, must necessarily
be in some degree enlightened, and his affections ameliorated.

I have said that each of these poems has a purpose. I have also informed my
Reader what this purpose will be found principally to be: namely to illustrate the manner in which our feelings and ideas are associated in a state of excitement. But, speaking in language somewhat more appropriate, it is to follow the fluxes and refluxes of
the mind when agitated by the great and simple affections of our nature. * * * I should
mention one other circumstance which distinguishes these Poems from the popular
Poetry of the day; it is this, that the feeling therein developed gives importance to the
action and situation, and not the action and situation to the feeling. * * *

I will not suffer a sense of false modesty to prevent me from asserting, that I point
my Reader's attention to this mark of distinction, far less for the sake of these particular Poems than from the general importance of the subject. The subject is indeed
important! For the human mind is capable of being excited without the application
of gross and violent stimulants; and he must have a very faint perception of its beauty
and dignity who does not know this, and who does not further know, that one being
is elevated above another, in proportion as he possesses this capability. It has therefore appeared to me, that to endeavour to produce or enlarge this capability is one of
the best services in which, at any period, a Writer can be engaged; but this service,
excellent at all times, is especially so at the present day. For a multitude of causes, unknown to former times, are now acting with a combined force to blunt the discriminating powers of the mind, and unfitting it for all voluntary exertion to reduce it to a
state of almost savage torpor. The most effective of these causes are the great national events which are daily taking place, and the increasing accumulation of men
in cities, where the uniformity of their occupations produces a craving for extraordinary incident, which the rapid communication of intelligence hourly gratifies.[5] To

---

5. That is, the rapid increase in daily newspaper production at this time. The "events" include the war with France, the
Irish rebellion, and the sedition trials at home.

this tendency of life and manners the literature and theatrical exhibitions of the country have conformed themselves. The invaluable works of our elder writers, I had almost said the works of Shakespear and Milton, are driven into neglect by frantic novels, sickly and stupid German Tragedies, and deluges of idle and extravagant stories in verse.[6]—When I think upon this degrading thirst after outrageous stimulation, I am almost ashamed to have spoken of the feeble effort with which I have endeavoured to counteract it; and, reflecting upon the magnitude of the general evil, I should be oppressed with no dishonorable melancholy, had I not a deep impression of certain inherent and indestructible qualities of the human mind, and likewise of certain powers in the great and permanent objects that act upon it which are equally inherent and indestructible; and did I not further add to this impression a belief, that the time is approaching when the evil will be systematically opposed, by men of greater powers, and with far more distinguished success.

[THE LANGUAGE OF POETRY]

Having dwelt thus long on the subjects and aim of these Poems, I shall request the Reader's permission to apprize him of a few circumstances relating to their style, in order, among other reasons, that I may not be censured for not having performed what I never attempted. The Reader will find that personifications of abstract ideas rarely occur in these volumes; and, I hope, are utterly rejected as an ordinary device to elevate the style, and raise it above prose. I have proposed to myself to imitate, and, as far as is possible, to adopt the very language of men; and assuredly such personifications do not make any natural or regular part of that language. They are, indeed, a figure of speech occasionally prompted by passion, and I have made use of them as such; but I have endeavoured utterly to reject them as a mechanical device of style, or as a family language which Writers in metre seem to lay claim to by prescription. I have wished to keep my Reader in the company of flesh and blood, persuaded that by so doing I shall interest him. I am, however, well aware that others who pursue a different track may interest him likewise; I do not interfere with their claim, I only wish to prefer a different claim of my own. There will also be found in these volumes little of what is usually called poetic diction; I have taken as much pains to avoid it as others ordinarily take to produce it; this I have done for the reason already alleged, to bring my language near to the language of men, and further, because the pleasure which I have proposed to myself to impart is of a kind very different from that which is supposed by many persons to be the proper object of poetry. I do not know how without being culpably particular I can give my Reader a more exact notion of the style in which I wished these poems to be written than by informing him that I have at all times endeavoured to look steadily at my subject, consequently, I hope that there is in these Poems little falsehood of description, and that my ideas are expressed in language fitted to their respective importance. Something I must have gained by this practice, as it is friendly to one property of all good poetry, namely, good sense; but it has necessarily cut me off from a large portion of phrases and figures of speech which from father to son have long been regarded as the common inheritance of Poets. I have also thought it expedient to restrict myself still further, having abstained from the use of many expressions, in themselves proper and

---

6. For example, sentimental melodramas, the popular Gothic novels of Ann Radcliffe and "Monk" Lewis, and the poetry of sensibility.

beautiful, but which have been foolishly repeated by bad Poets, till such feelings of disgust are connected with them as it is scarcely possible by any art of association to overpower.

If in a Poem there should be found a series of lines, or even a single line, in which the language, though naturally arranged and according to the strict laws of metre, does not differ from that of prose, there is a numerous class of critics, who, when they stumble upon these prosaisms as they call them, imagine that they have made a notable discovery, and exult over the Poet as over a man ignorant of his own profession. Now these men would establish a canon of criticism which the Reader will conclude he must utterly reject, if he wishes to be pleased with these volumes. And it would be a most easy task to prove to him, that not only the language of a large portion of every good poem, even of the most elevated character, must necessarily, except with reference to the metre, in no respect differ from that of good prose, but likewise that some of the most interesting parts of the best poems will be found to be strictly the language of prose, when prose is well written. The truth of this assertion might be demonstrated by innumerable passages from almost all the poetical writings, even of Milton himself. * * * [T]o illustrate the subject in a general manner, I will here adduce a short composition of Gray,[7] who was at the head of those who by their reasonings have attempted to widen the space of separation betwixt Prose and Metrical composition, and was more than any other man curiously elaborate in the structure of his own poetic diction.

> In vain to me the smiling mornings shine,
> And reddening Phœbus° lifts his golden fire: [sun god]
> The birds in vain their amorous descant° join,   [song]
> Or chearful fields resume their green attire:
> These ears alas! for other notes repine;°   [languish]
> *A different object do these eyes require;*
> *My lonely anguish melts no heart but mine;*
> *And in my breast the imperfect joys expire;*
> Yet Morning smiles the busy race to cheer,
> And new-born pleasure brings to happier men;
> The fields to all their wonted tribute bear;
> To warm their little loves the birds complain.
> *I fruitless mourn to him that cannot hear*
> *And weep the more because I weep in vain.*

It will easily be perceived that the only part of this Sonnet which is of any value is the lines printed in Italics: it is equally obvious, that, except in the rhyme, and in the use of the single word "fruitless" for fruitlessly, which is so far a defect, the language of these lines does in no respect differ from that of prose.

By the foregoing quotation I have shewn that the language of Prose may yet be well adapted to Poetry; and I have previously asserted that a large portion of the language of every good poem can in no respect differ from that of good Prose. I will go further. I do not doubt that it may be safely affirmed, that there neither is, nor can be, any essential difference between the language of prose and metrical composition. We are fond of tracing the resemblance between Poetry and Painting, and,

---

7. Thomas Gray (1716–1771) is best known for *Elegy Written in a Country Churchyard* (1751). The inset poem, with Wordsworth's italics, is *Sonnet on the Death of Richard West* (1775). Gray had said to West that "the language of the age is never the language of poetry."

accordingly, we call them Sisters: but where shall we find bonds of connection sufficiently strict to typify the affinity betwixt metrical and prose composition? They
both speak by and to the same organs; the bodies in which both of them are clothed
may be said to be of the same substance, their affections are kindred and almost
identical, not necessarily differing even in degree; Poetry[8] sheds no tears "such as
Angels weep," but natural and human tears; she can boast of no celestial Ichor that
distinguishes her vital juices from those of prose; the same human blood circulates
through the veins of them both.

If it be affirmed that rhyme and metrical arrangement of themselves constitute a
distinction which overturns what I have been saying on the strict affinity of metrical
language with that of prose, and paves the way for other artificial distinctions which
the mind voluntarily admits, I answer that the language of such Poetry as I am recommending is, as far as is possible, a selection of the language really spoken by men;
that this selection, wherever it is made with true taste and feeling, will of itself form a
distinction far greater than would at first be imagined, and will entirely separate the
composition from the vulgarity and meanness of ordinary life; and, if metre be super-
added thereto, I believe that a dissimilitude will be produced altogether sufficient for
the gratification of a rational mind. What other distinction would we have? Whence
is it to come? And where is it to exist? Not, surely, where the Poet speaks through the
mouths of his characters: it cannot be necessary here, either for elevation of style, or
any of its supposed ornaments: for, if the Poet's subject be judiciously chosen, it will
naturally, and upon fit occasion, lead him to passions the language of which, if selected truly and judiciously, must necessarily be dignified and variegated, and alive
with metaphors and figures. * * *

[WHAT IS A POET?]

Taking up the subject, then, upon general grounds, I ask what is meant by the
word Poet? What is a Poet? To whom does he address himself? And what language is to
be expected from him? He is a man speaking to men: a man, it is true, endued with
more lively sensibility, more enthusiasm and tenderness, who has a greater knowledge
of human nature, and a more comprehensive soul, than are supposed to be common
among mankind; a man pleased with his own passions and volitions, and who rejoices
more than other men in the spirit of life that is in him; delighting to contemplate similar volitions and passions as manifested in the goings-on of the Universe, and habitually impelled to create them where he does not find them. To these qualities he has
added a disposition to be affected more than other men by absent things as if they were
present; an ability of conjuring up in himself passions, which are indeed far from being
the same as those produced by real events, yet (especially in those parts of the general
sympathy which are pleasing and delightful) do more nearly resemble the passions produced by real events, than any thing which, from the motions of their own minds
merely, other men are accustomed to feel in themselves; whence, and from practice, he
has acquired a greater readiness and power in expressing what he thinks and feels, and

---

8. I here use the word "Poetry" (though against my own judgment) as opposed to the word Prose, and synonomous with
metrical composition. But much confusion has been introduced into criticism by this contradistinction of Poetry and
Prose, instead of the more philosophical one of Poetry and Matter of fact, or Science. The only strict antithesis to Prose is
Metre; nor is this, in truth, a strict antithesis; because lines and passages of metre so naturally occur in writing prose, that
it would be scarcely possible to avoid them, even were it desirable [Wordsworth's note]. The ensuing quotation is from
Paradise Lost, 1.620 (Satan's tears, as he attempts to address his fallen comrades, now in Hell).

especially those thoughts and feelings which, by his own choice, or from the structure of his own mind, arise in him without immediate external excitement.

But, whatever portion of this faculty we may suppose even the greatest Poet to possess, there cannot be a doubt but that the language which it will suggest to him, must, in liveliness and truth, fall far short of that which is uttered by men in real life, under the actual pressure of those passions, certain shadows of which the Poet thus produces, or feels to be produced, in himself. However exalted a notion we would wish to cherish of the character of a Poet, it is obvious, that, while he describes and imitates passions, his situation is altogether slavish and mechanical, compared with the freedom and power of real and substantial action and suffering. So that it will be the wish of the Poet to bring his feelings near to those of the persons whose feelings he describes, nay, for short spaces of time perhaps, to let himself slip into an entire delusion, and even confound and identify his own feelings with theirs; modifying only the language which is thus suggested to him, by a consideration that he describes for a particular purpose, that of giving pleasure. Here, then, he will apply the principle on which I have so much insisted, namely, that of selection * * *

But it may be said by those who do not object to the general spirit of these remarks, that, as it is impossible for the Poet to produce upon all occasions language as exquisitely fitted for the passion as that which the real passion itself suggests, it is proper that he should consider himself as in the situation of a translator, who deems himself justified when he substitutes excellences of another kind for those which are unattainable by him; and endeavours occasionally to surpass his original, in order to make some amends for the general inferiority to which he feels that he must submit. But this would be to encourage idleness and unmanly despair. Further, it is the language of men who speak of what they do not understand; who talk of poetry as a matter of amusement and idle pleasure; who will converse with us as gravely about a taste for Poetry, as they express it, as if it were a thing as indifferent as a taste for Rope-dancing, or Frontiniac[9] or Sherry. Aristotle, I have been told, hath said, that Poetry is the most philosophic of all writing:[1] it is so: its object is truth, not individual and local, but general, and operative; not standing upon external testimony, but carried alive into the heart by passion; truth which is its own testimony, which gives strength and divinity to the tribunal to which it appeals, and receives them from the same tribunal. Poetry is the image of man and nature. The obstacles which stand in the way of the fidelity of the Biographer and Historian, and of their consequent utility, are incalculably greater than those which are to be encountered by the Poet who has an adequate notion of the dignity of his art. The Poet writes under one restriction only, namely, that of the necessity of giving immediate pleasure to a human Being possessed of that information which may be expected from him, not as a lawyer, a physician, a mariner, an astronomer or a natural philosopher, but as a Man. Except this one restriction, there is no object standing between the Poet and the image of things; between this, and the Biographer and Historian there are a thousand.

Nor let this necessity of producing immediate pleasure be considered as a degradation of the Poet's art. It is far otherwise. It is an acknowledgment of the beauty of the universe, an acknowledgment the more sincere because it is not formal, but indirect; it is a task light and easy to him who looks at the world in the spirit of love:

9. A much-prized sweet French wine.
1. "[T]he historian speaks of what has happened, the poet of the kind of thing that *can* happen. Hence poetry is a more philosophical and serious business than history; for poetry speaks more of universals, history of particulars" (Aristotle, *Poetics*, 1451b, Else translation).

further, it is a homage paid to the native and naked dignity of man, to the grand elementary principle of pleasure, by which he knows, and feels, and lives, and moves.[2] We have no sympathy but what is propagated by pleasure: I would not be misunderstood; but wherever we sympathize with pain it will be found that the sympathy is produced and carried on by subtle combinations with pleasure. We have no knowledge, that is, no general principles drawn from the contemplation of particular facts, but what has been built up by pleasure, and exists in us by pleasure alone. The Man of Science, the Chemist and Mathematician, whatever difficulties and disgusts they may have had to struggle with, know and feel this. However painful may be the objects with which the Anatomist's knowledge is connected, he feels that his knowledge is pleasure; and where he has no pleasure he has no knowledge. What then does the Poet? He considers man and the objects that surround him as acting and reacting upon each other, so as to produce an infinite complexity of pain and pleasure; he considers man in his own nature and in his ordinary life as contemplating this with a certain quantity of immediate knowledge, with certain convictions, intuitions, and deductions which by habit become of the nature of intuitions; he considers him as looking upon this complex scene of ideas and sensations, and finding every where objects that immediately excite in him sympathies which, from the necessities of his nature, are accompanied by an overbalance of enjoyment.

To this knowledge which all men carry about with them, and to these sympathies in which without any other discipline than that of our daily life we are fitted to take delight, the Poet principally directs his attention. He considers man and nature as essentially adapted to each other, and the mind of man as naturally the mirror of the fairest and most interesting qualities of nature. And thus the Poet, prompted by this feeling of pleasure which accompanies him through the whole course of his studies, converses with general nature with affections akin to those, which, through labour and length of time, the Man of Science has raised up in himself, by conversing with those particular parts of nature which are the objects of his studies. The knowledge both of the Poet and the Man of Science is pleasure; but the knowledge of the one cleaves to us as a necessary part of our existence, our natural and unalienable inheritance; the other is a personal and individual acquisition, slow to come to us, and by no habitual and direct sympathy connecting us with our fellow-beings. The Man of Science seeks truth as a remote and unknown benefactor; he cherishes and loves it in his solitude: the Poet, singing a song in which all human beings join with him, rejoices in the presence of truth as our visible friend and hourly companion. Poetry is the breath and finer spirit of all knowledge; it is the impassioned expression which is in the countenance of all Science. Emphatically may it be said of the Poet, as Shakespeare hath said of man, "that he looks before and after."[3] He is the rock of defence of human nature; an upholder and preserver, carrying every where with him relationship and love. In spite of difference of soil and climate, of language and manners, of laws and customs, in spite of things silently gone out of mind and things violently destroyed, the Poet binds together by passion and knowledge the vast empire of human society, as it is spread over the whole earth, and over all time. The objects of the Poet's thoughts are every where; though the eyes and senses of man are, it is true, his favorite guides, yet he will follow wheresoever he can find an atmosphere of

2. Echoing St. Paul's declaration that in God "we live, and move, and have our being" (Acts 17.28).
3. From Hamlet's last soliloquy, contemplating the mental activity that distinguishes humans from animals (Hamlet 4.4.37).

sensation in which to move his wings. Poetry is the first and last of all knowledge—it is as immortal as the heart of man. If the labours of men of Science should ever create any material revolution, direct or indirect, in our condition, and in the impressions which we habitually receive, the Poet will sleep then no more than at present, but he will be ready to follow the steps of the man of Science, not only in those general indirect effects, but he will be at his side, carrying sensation into the midst of the objects of the Science itself. The remotest discoveries of the Chemist, the Botanist, or Mineralogist, will be as proper objects of the Poet's art as any upon which it can be employed, if the time should ever come when these things shall be familiar to us, and the relations under which they are contemplated by the followers of these respective Sciences shall be manifestly and palpably material to us as enjoying and suffering beings. If the time should ever come when what is now called Science, thus familiarized to men, shall be ready to put on, as it were, a form of flesh and blood, the Poet will lend his divine spirit to aid the transfiguration, and will welcome the Being thus produced, as a dear and genuine inmate of the household of man. ✳ ✳ ✳

What I have thus far said applies to Poetry in general; but especially to those parts of composition where the Poet speaks through the mouths of his characters; and upon this point it appears to have such weight that I will conclude, there are few persons, of good sense, who would not allow that the dramatic parts of composition are defective, in proportion as they deviate from the real language of nature, and are coloured by a diction of the Poet's own, either peculiar to him as an individual Poet, or belonging simply to Poets in general, to a body of men who, from the circumstance of their compositions being in metre, it is expected will employ a particular language.

It is not, then, in the dramatic parts of composition that we look for this distinction of language; but still it may be proper and necessary where the Poet speaks to us in his own person and character. To this I answer by referring my Reader to the description which I have before given of a Poet. Among the qualities which I have enumerated as principally conducting to form a Poet, is implied nothing differing in kind from other men, but only in degree. The sum of what I have there said is, that the Poet is chiefly distinguished from other men by a greater promptness to think and feel without immediate external excitement, and a greater power in expressing such thoughts and feelings as are produced in him in that manner. But these passions and thoughts and feelings are the general passions and thoughts and feelings of men. And with what are they connected? Undoubtedly with our moral sentiments and animal sensations, and with the causes which excite these; with the operations of the elements and the appearances of the visible universe; with storm and sunshine, with the revolutions of the seasons, with cold and heat, with loss of friends and kindred, with injuries and resentments, gratitude and hope, with fear and sorrow. These, and the like, are the sensations and objects which the Poet describes, as they are the sensations of other men, and the objects which interest them. The Poet thinks and feels in the spirit of the passions of men. How, then, can his language differ in any material degree from that of all other men who feel vividly and see clearly? It might be proved that it is impossible. But supposing that this were not the case, the Poet might then be allowed to use a peculiar language, when expressing his feelings for his own gratification, or that of men like himself. But Poets do not write for Poets alone, but for men. Unless therefore we are advocates for that admiration which depends upon ignorance, and that pleasure which arises from hearing what we do not understand, the Poet must descend from this supposed height, and, in order to excite rational sympathy, he must express himself as other men express themselves. ✳ ✳ ✳

["Emotion Recollected in Tranquillity"]

I have said that Poetry is the spontaneous overflow of powerful feelings: it takes its origin from emotion recollected in tranquillity: the emotion is contemplated till by a species of reaction the tranquillity gradually disappears, and an emotion, kindred to that which was before the subject of contemplation, is gradually produced, and does itself actually exist in the mind. In this mood successful composition generally begins, and in a mood similar to this it is carried on; but the emotion, of whatever kind and in whatever degree, from various causes is qualified by various pleasures, so that in describing any passions whatsoever, which are voluntarily described, the mind will upon the whole be in a state of enjoyment. Now, if Nature be thus cautious in preserving in a state of enjoyment a being thus employed, the Poet ought to profit by the lesson thus held forth to him, and ought especially to take care, that whatever passions he communicates to his Reader, those passions, if his Reader's mind be sound and vigorous, should always be accompanied with an overbalance of pleasure. Now the music of harmonious metrical language, the sense of difficulty overcome, and the blind association of pleasure which has been previously received from works of rhyme or metre of the same or similar construction, an indistinct perception perpetually renewed of language closely resembling that of real life, and yet, in the circumstance of metre, differing from it so widely, all these imperceptibly make up a complex feeling of delight, which is of the most important use in tempering the painful feeling which will always be found intermingled with powerful descriptions of the deeper passions. This effect is always produced in pathetic and impassioned poetry; while, in lighter compositions, the ease and gracefulness with which the Poet manages his numbers are themselves confessedly a principal source of the gratification of the Reader. I might perhaps include all which it is necessary to say upon this subject by affirming, what few persons will deny, that, of two descriptions, either of passions, manners, or characters, each of them equally well executed, the one in prose and the other in verse, the verse will be read a hundred times where the prose is read once. * * *

Having thus explained a few of the reasons why I have written in verse, and why I have chosen subjects from common life, and endeavoured to bring my language near to the real language of men, if I have been too minute in pleading my own cause, I have at the same time been treating a subject of general interest; and it is for this reason that I request the Reader's permission to add a few words with reference solely to these particular poems, and to some defects which will probably be found in them. I am sensible that my associations must have sometimes been particular instead of general, and that, consequently, giving to things a false importance, sometimes from diseased impulses I may have written upon unworthy subjects; but I am less apprehensive on this account, than that my language may frequently have suffered from those arbitrary connections of feelings and ideas with particular words and phrases, from which no man can altogether protect himself. Hence I have no doubt, that, in some instances, feelings even of the ludicrous may be given to my Readers by expressions which appeared to me tender and pathetic. Such faulty expressions, were I convinced they were faulty at present, and that they must necessarily continue to be so, I would willingly take all reasonable pains to correct. But it is dangerous to make these alterations on the simple authority of a few individuals, or even of certain classes of men; for where the understanding of an Author is not convinced, or his feelings altered, this cannot be done without great injury to himself: for his own feelings are his stay and support, and, if he sets them aside in one instance, he may be induced to repeat this act till his mind loses all confidence in itself, and becomes utterly debilitated. To this it may be added, that the Reader ought never to forget that he is himself exposed to the same errors as the Poet, and perhaps in a much greater degree: for there can be no presumption in saying, that it is not probable he will be so well acquainted with the various stages of meaning through which words have passed, or with the fickleness or stability of the relations of particular ideas to each other; and above all, since he is so much less interested in the subject, he may decide lightly and carelessly. * * *

I have one request to make of my Reader, which is, that in judging these Poems he would decide by his own feelings genuinely, and not by reflection upon what will probably be the judgment of others. * * *

If an Author by any single composition has impressed us with respect for his talents, it is useful to consider this as affording a presumption, that, on other occasions where we have been displeased, he nevertheless may not have written ill or absurdly; and, further, to give him so much credit for this one composition as may induce us to review what has displeased us with more care than we should otherwise have bestowed upon it. This is not only an act of justice, but in our decisions upon poetry especially, may conduce in a high degree to the improvement of our own taste: for an accurate taste in poetry, and in all the other arts, as Sir Joshua Reynolds has observed, is an acquired talent, which can only be produced by thought and a long continued intercourse with the best models of composition.[5] This is mentioned, not with so ridiculous a purpose as to prevent the most inexperienced Reader from judging for himself, (I have already said that I wish him to judge for himself;) but merely to temper the rashness of decision, and to suggest, that, if Poetry be a subject on which much time has not been bestowed, the judgment may be erroneous; and that in many cases it necessarily will be so.

I know that nothing would have so effectually contributed to further the end which I have in view as to have shown of what kind the pleasure is, and how the pleasure is produced, which is confessedly produced by metrical composition essentially different from that which I have here endeavoured to recommend: for the Reader will say that he has been pleased by such composition; and what can I do more for him? The power of any art is limited; and he will suspect, that, if I propose to furnish him with new friends, it is only upon condition of his abandoning his old friends. Besides, as I have said, the Reader is himself conscious of the pleasure which he has received from such composition, composition to which he has peculiarly attached the endearing name of Poetry; and all men feel an habitual gratitude, and something of an honorable bigotry for the objects which have long continued to please them: we not only wish to be pleased, but to be pleased in that particular way in which we have been accustomed to be pleased. There is a host of arguments in these feelings; and I should be the less able to combat them successfully, as I am willing to allow, that, in order entirely to enjoy the Poetry which I am recommending, it would be necessary to give up much of what is ordinarily enjoyed. But, would my limits have permitted me to point out how this pleasure is produced, I might have removed many obstacles, and assisted my Reader in perceiving that the powers of language are not so limited as he may

---

5. See Sir Joshua Reynolds, "The reality of a standard of Taste," (Discourse 7, delivered 1776): "He therefore who is acquainted with the works which have pleased different ages and different countries, and has formed his opinion on them, has more materials, and more means of knowing what is analogous to the mind of man, than he who is conversant only with the works of his own age or country. What has pleased, and continues to please, is likely to please again: hence are derived the rules of art, and on this immovable foundation they must ever stand." (*Discourses*, collected 1707; rpt. 1798.)

suppose; and that it is possible that poetry may give other enjoyments, of a purer, more lasting, and more exquisite nature. This part of my subject I have not altogether neglected; but it has been less my present aim to prove, that the interest excited by some other kinds of poetry is less vivid, and less worthy of the nobler powers of the mind, than to offer reasons for presuming, that, if the object which I have proposed to myself were adequately attained, a species of poetry would be produced, which is genuine poetry; in its nature well adapted to interest mankind permanently, and likewise important in the multiplicity and quality of its moral relations.

From what has been said, and from a perusal of the Poems, the Reader will be able clearly to perceive the object which I have proposed to myself: he will determine how far I have attained this object; and, what is a much more important question, whether it be worth attaining; and upon the decision of these two questions will rest my claim to the approbation of the public.

"Strange fits of passion have I known"[1]

Strange fits of passion have I known,
And I will dare to tell,
But in the lover's ear alone,
What once to me befel.

5   When she I lov'd, was strong and gay
And like a rose in June,
I to her cottage bent my way,
Beneath the evening moon.

Upon the moon I fix'd my eye,
10   All over the wide lea;
My horse trudg'd on, and we drew nigh
Those paths so dear to me.

And now we reach'd the orchard plot,
And, as we climb'd the hill,
15   Towards the roof of Lucy's cot°   *cottage*
The moon descended still.

In one of those sweet dreams I slept,
Kind Nature's gentlest boon!
And, all the while, my eyes I kept
20   On the descending moon.

My horse mov'd on; hoof after hoof
He rais'd, and never stopp'd:
When down behind the cottage roof
At once the planet dropp'd.

25   What fond and wayward thoughts will slide
Into a Lover's head—

---

1. This and the two following lyrics written during a lonely winter that William and Dorothy spent in Germany comprise three of six lyrics traditionally called the "Lucy Poems." *Three years she grew* appears later in the volume. *I travell'd among unknown Men* was published in 1807 (see page 267). "Lucy" has not been identified. The name comes from the Latin "lux" (light); "Lucina" is an old name for the goddess of the moon.

"O mercy!" to myself I cried,
"If Lucy should be dead!"[2]

1798–1799   1800

Song ("She dwelt among th' untrodden ways")

She dwelt among th' untrodden ways
    Beside the springs of Dove,[1]
A Maid whom there were none to praise
    And very few to love:

5   A Violet by a mossy stone
        Half-hidden from the Eye![2]
    —Fair, as a star when only one
        Is shining in the sky!

She *liv'd* unknown, and few could know
10   When Lucy ceas'd to be;
But she is in her Grave, and Oh!
    The difference to me!

1798   1800

"A slumber did my spirit seal"[1]

A slumber did my spirit seal,
    I had no human fears:
She seem'd a thing that could not feel
    The touch of earthly years.

5   No motion has she now, no force
    She neither hears nor sees
Roll'd round in earth's diurnal° course   *daily*
    With rocks, and stones, and trees!

1798–1799   1800

Lucy Gray[1]

Oft I had heard of Lucy Gray,
And when I cross'd the Wild,
I chanc'd to see at break of day
The solitary Child.

---

2. A manuscript from 1799 shows a final stanza: "I told her this: her laughter light / Is ringing in my ears: / And when I think upon that night / My eyes are dim with tears."
1. A river in England.
2. See Gray's *Elegy Written in a Country Churchyard*: "Full many a flower is born to blush unseen" (55).
1. Wordsworth published this poem without a title. Coleridge thought that this "most sublime Epitaph" exposed Wordsworth's fear that "his Sister might die."
1. "Founded on a circumstance told me by my Sister, of a little girl who, not far from Halifax in Yorkshire, was bewildered in a snow-storm. . . . Her footsteps were traced by her parents to the middle of the lock of a canal, and no other vestige of her, backward or forward, could be traced. The body, however, was found in the canal. The way in which the incident was treated & the spiritualizing of the character might furnish hints for contrasting the imaginative influences which I have endeavoured to throw over common life with Crabbe's matter of fact style of treating subjects of the same kind." [I.F., referring to poet George Crabbe.] In 1815, Wordsworth changed the title to *Lucy Gray, or Solitude*.

5   No Mate, no comrade Lucy knew;
She dwelt on a wild Moor,
The sweetest Thing that ever grew
Beside a human door!

You yet may spy the Fawn at play,
10   The Hare upon the Green;
But the sweet face of Lucy Gray
Will never more be seen.

"To-night will be a stormy night,
You to the Town must go,
15   And take a lantern, Child, to light
Your Mother thro' the snow."

"That, Father! will I gladly do;
'Tis scarcely afternoon—
The Minster°-clock has struck two,   *church*
20   And yonder is the Moon."[2]

At this the Father rais'd his hook
And snapp'd a faggot-band;°   *bundle of firewood*
He plied his work; and Lucy took
The lantern in her hand.

25   Not blither is the mountain roe,
With many a wanton° stroke   *frolicsome*
Her feet disperse the powd'ry snow
That rises up like smoke.

The storm came on before its time,
30   She wander'd up and down,
And many a hill did Lucy climb
But never reach'd the Town.

The wretched Parents all that night
Went shouting far and wide;
35   But there was neither sound nor sight
To serve them for a guide.

At day-break on a hill they stood
That overlook'd the Moor;
And thence they saw the Bridge of Wood,
40   A furlong° from their door.   *one-eighth of a mile*

And now they homeward turn'd, and cry'd
"In Heaven we all shall meet!"
When in the snow the Mother spied
The print of Lucy's feet.

45   Then downward from the steep hill's edge
They track'd the footmarks small;

2. Wordsworth remarked that "the day-moon" is something "no town or village girl would ever notice" (1816).

And through the broken hawthorn-hedge,
And by the long stone-wall;

50   And then an open field they cross'd,
The marks were still the same;
They track'd them on, nor ever lost,
And to the Bridge they came.

They follow'd from the snowy bank
Those footmarks, one by one,
55   Into the middle of the plank,
And further there were none.

Yet some maintain that to this day
She is a living Child,
That you may see sweet Lucy Gray
60   Upon the lonesome Wild.

O'er rough and smooth she trips along,
And never looks behind;
And sings a solitary song
That whistles in the wind.

1798–1799   1800

Poor Susan[1]

At the corner of Wood-Street, when day-light appears,
There's a Thrush that sings loud, it has sung for three years:
Poor Susan has pass'd by the spot, and has heard
In the silence of morning the song of the bird.

5   'Tis a note of enchantment; what ails her? She sees
A mountain ascending, a vision of trees;
Bright volumes of vapour through Lothbury glide,
And a river flows on through the vale of Cheapside.

Green pastures she views in the midst of the dale,
10   Down which she so often has tripp'd with her pail,
And a single small cottage, a nest like a dove's,
The one only dwelling on earth that she loves.

She looks, and her heart is in Heaven, but they fade,
The mist and the river, the hill and the shade;
15   The stream will not flow, and the hill will not rise,
And the colours have all pass'd away from her eyes.

Poor Outcast! return—to receive thee once more
The house of thy Father will open its door,

1. The title was changed to *The Reverie of Poor Susan* in 1815. The poem is set in London's mercantile district. In the Preface Wordsworth instances *Poor Susan* as exemplifying poetry in which "the feeling therein developed gives importance to the action and situation, and not the action and situation to the feeling."

1800

And thou once again, in thy plain russet gown,
20   May'st hear the thrush sing from a tree of its own.[2]
1798

Nutting[1]

It seems a day,
(I speak of one from many singled out)
One of those heavenly days which cannot die,
When forth I sallied from our cottage-door,[2]
5   And with a wallet o'er my shoulder slung,
A nutting crook in hand, and turn'd my steps
Towards the distant wood, a Figure quaint,
Trick'd out in proud disguise of Beggar's weeds°   *clothing*
Put on for the occasion, by advice
10   And exhortation of my frugal Dame.
Motley accoutrement! of power to smile
At thorns, and brakes, and brambles, and, in truth,
More ragged than need was. Among the woods,
And o'er the pathless rocks, I forc'd my way
15   Until, at length, I came to one dear nook
Unvisited, where not a broken bough
Droop'd with its wither'd leaves, ungracious sign
Of devastation, but the hazels rose
Tall and erect, with milk-white clusters hung,
20   A virgin scene![3]—A little while I stood,
Breathing with such suppression of the heart
As joy delights in; and with wise restraint
Voluptuous, fearless of a rival, eyed
The banquet; or beneath the trees I sate
25   Among the flowers, and with the flowers I play'd;
A temper known to those, who, after long
And weary expectation, have been bless'd
With sudden happiness beyond all hope.—
—Perhaps it was a bower beneath whose leaves
30   The violets of five seasons re-appear
And fade, unseen by any human eye,
Where fairy water-breaks[4] do murmur on
For ever, and I saw the sparkling foam,
And with my cheek on one of those green stones
35   That, fleec'd with moss, beneath the shady trees,

---

2. Charles Lamb felt this last stanza "threw a kind of dubiety upon Susan's moral conduct"; it was dropped after 1800.
1. "Intended as part of a poem on my own life, but struck out as not being wanted there. Like most of my schoolfellows I was an impassioned nutter. For this pleasure, the vale of Esthwaite, abounding in coppice-wood, furnished a very wide range. The verses arose out of the remembrance of feelings I had when a boy" [I.F.].

2. The house at which I boarded during the time I was at School [Wordsworth's note]; it was supervised by Ann Tyson, the Dame of line 10.
3. The moral terrain evokes Spenser's "Bower of Blisse" in *The Faerie Queene*, a dangerously seductive pleasure garden, and the Garden of Eden in Milton's *Paradise Lost*, which Satan invades to ravage Eve.
4. Wordsworth's coinage: "little rapids."

Lay round me, scatter'd like a flock of sheep,
I heard the murmur and the murmuring sound,
In that sweet mood when pleasure loves to pay
Tribute to ease, and, of its joy secure

40 The heart luxuriates with indifferent things,
Wasting its kindliness on stocks° and stones,   *tree stumps*
And on the vacant air. Then up I rose,
And dragg'd to earth both branch and bough, with crash
And merciless ravage; and the shady nook

45 Of hazels, and the green and mossy bower
Deform'd and sullied, patiently gave up
Their quiet being: and unless I now
Confound my present feelings with the past,
Even then, when from[5] the bower I turn'd away,

50 Exulting, rich beyond the wealth of kings
I felt a sense of pain when I beheld
The silent trees, and saw the intruding sky.—
Then, dearest Maiden![6] move along these shades°   *shadows, spirits*
In gentleness of heart with gentle hand

55 Touch,—for there is a Spirit in the woods.

1798–1799   1800

MICHAEL   Sending the 1800 *Lyrical Ballads* to Charles James Fox, leader of the Whig opposition in Parliament, Wordsworth drew attention to *Michael*: "I have attempted to draw a picture of the domestic affections . . . amongst a class of men who are now almost confined to the North of England. They are small independent *proprietors* of land here called statesmen, men of respectable education who daily labour on their own little properties. The domestic affections will always be strong amongst men who live in a country not crowded with population, if these men are placed above poverty. But if they are proprietors of small estates, which have descended to them from their ancestors, the power which these affections will acquire . . . is inconceivable by those who have only had an opportunity of observing hired labourers, farmers, and the manufacturing Poor. Their little tract of land serves as a kind of permanent rallying point for their domestic feelings, as a tablet upon which they are written which makes them objects of memory in a thousand instances when they would otherwise be forgotten"; *Michael* shows "that men who do not wear fine cloaths can feel deeply." Later that year Wordsworth wrote to a friend, "I have attempted to give a picture of a man, of strong mind and lively sensibility, agitated by two of the most powerful affections of the human heart; the parental affection, and the love of property, *landed* property, including the feelings of inheritance, home, and personal and family independence." Wordsworth drew on two local tales, one of "the son of an old couple having become dissolute and run away from his parents" (who once owned Dove Cottage, Wordsworth's home at the time); and one of "an old shepherd having been seven years in building up a sheepfold in a solitary valley." The austere biblical aura of the "covenant" between Michael and his son evokes Old Testament prototypes, and Luke is the Gospel that contains the parable of the Prodigal Son (15.11–32). In focusing on contemporary

5. Later revised to "ere from," making the "sense of pain" precede rather than coincide with "exulting."
6. In a much longer manuscript draft, Wordsworth preceded this poem with the story of a "Lucy" who had been ravaging a bower—her ungentle, unmaidenly action provoking her companion to recount this episode from his past, seemingly to admonish her with his remorse.

conditions and refusing to provide any relief except in Michael's "comfort in the strength of love," Wordsworth significantly revises the genre of pastoral.

Michael
A Pastoral Poem

If from the public way you turn your steps
Up the tumultuous brook of Green-head Gill,[1]
You will suppose that with an upright path
Your feet must struggle; in such bold ascent
5   The pastoral Mountains front you, face to face.
But, courage! for around that boisterous Brook
The mountains have all open'd out themselves,
And made a hidden valley of their own.
No habitation can be seen; but such
10   As journey thither find themselves alone
With a few sheep, with rocks and stones, and kites°   hawks
That overhead are sailing in the sky.
It is in truth an utter solitude;
Nor should I have made mention of this Dell
15   But for one object which you might pass by,
Might see and notice not. Beside the brook
There is a straggling heap of unhewn stones!
And to that place a story appertains,
Which, though it be ungarnish'd with events,
20   Is not unfit, I deem, for the fire-side,
Or for the summer shade. It was the first,
The earliest of those tales that spake to me
Of Shepherds, dwellers in the valleys, men
Whom I already lov'd; not verily
25   For their own sakes, but for the fields and hills
Where was their occupation and abode.
And hence this Tale, while I was yet a boy
Careless of books, yet having felt the power
Of Nature, by the gentle agency
30   Of natural objects, led me on to feel
For passions that were not my own, and think
At random and imperfectly indeed
On man; the heart of man, and human life.
Therefore, although it be a history
35   Homely and rude, I will relate the same
For the delight of a few natural hearts,
And with yet fonder feeling, for the sake
Of youthful Poets, who among these Hills
Will be my second self when I am gone.

---

1. Green-head Gill (valley) and the poem's other settings are near Wordsworth's cottage at Grasmere.

40   Upon the Forest-side in Grasmere Vale
      There dwelt a Shepherd, Michael was his name,
      An old man, stout of heart, and strong of limb.
      His bodily frame had been from youth to age
      Of an unusual strength; his mind was keen
45   Intense and frugal, apt for all affairs,
      And in his Shepherd's calling he was prompt
      And watchful more than ordinary men.
      Hence had he learn'd the meaning of all winds,
      Of blasts of every tone, and often-times,
50   When others heeded not, He heard the South°   *south wind*
      Make subterraneous music, like the noise
      Of Bagpipers on distant Highland hills;
      The Shepherd, at such warning, of his flock
      Bethought him, and he to himself would say
55   The winds are now devising work for me!
      And truly at all times the storm, that drives
      The Traveller to a shelter, summon'd him
      Up to the mountains: he had been alone
      Amid the heart of many thousand mists
60   That came to him, and left him, on the heights.
      So liv'd he till his eightieth year was pass'd.

      And grossly that man errs, who should suppose
      That the green Valleys, and the Streams and Rocks
      Were things indifferent to the Shepherd's thoughts.
65   Fields, where with chearful spirits he had breath'd
      The common air; the hills, which he so oft
      Had climb'd, with vigorous steps; which had impress'd
      So many incidents upon his mind
      Of hardship, skill or courage, joy or fear;
70   Which, like a book, preserv'd the memory
      Of the dumb animals, whom he had sav'd,
      Had fed or shelter'd, linking to such acts,
      So grateful in themselves, the certainty
      Of honourable gains; these fields, these hills
75   Which were his living Being, even more
      Than his own Blood—what could they less? had laid
      Strong hold on his affections, were to him
      A pleasurable feeling of blind love,
      The pleasure which there is in life itself.

80   He had not passed his days in singleness.
      He had a Wife, a comely Matron, old
      Though younger than himself full twenty years.
      She was a woman of a stirring life
      Whose heart was in her house: two wheels she had
85   Of antique form; this large, for spinning wool,
      That small for flax; and if one wheel had rest,
      It was because the other was at work.

The Pair had but one Inmate° in their house, *resident*
An only Child, who had been born to them
When Michael telling° o'er his years began *counting*
To deem that he was old, in Shepherd's phrase,
With one foot in the grave. This only son,
With two brave sheep dogs tried° in many a storm, *tested*
The one of an inestimable worth,
Made all their Household. I may truly say,
That they were as a proverb in the vale
For endless industry. When day was gone,
And from their occupations out of doors
The Son and Father were come home, even then
Their labour did not cease, unless when all
Turn'd to the cleanly supper-board, and there
Each with a mess of pottage° and skimm'd milk, *stew*
Sate round the basket pil'd with oaten cakes,
And their plain home-made cheese. Yet when their meal
Was ended, LUKE (for so the Son was nam'd)
And his old Father, both betook themselves
To such convenient work as might employ
Their hands by the fire-side; perhaps to card° *comb out*
Wool for the House-wife's spindle, or repair
Some injury done to sickle, flail, or scythe,
Or other implement of house or field.

Down from the ceiling, by the chimney's edge,
That in our ancient uncouth country style
Did with a huge projection overbrow
Large space beneath, as duly as the light
Of day grew dim, the House-wife hung a lamp;
An aged utensil, which had perform'd
Service beyond all others of its kind.
Early at evening did it burn and late,
Surviving Comrade of uncounted Hours
Which going by from year to year had found
And left the Couple neither gay perhaps
Nor chearful, yet with objects and with hopes
Living a life of eager industry.
And now, when LUKE was in his eighteenth year,
There by the light of this old lamp they sate,
Father and Son, while late into the night
The House-wife plied her own peculiar work,
Making the cottage thro' the silent hours
Murmur as with the sound of summer flies.
Not with a waste of words, but for the sake
Of pleasure, which I know that I shall give
To many living now, I of this Lamp
Speak thus minutely: for there are no few
Whose memories will bear witness to my tale.
This Light was famous in its neighbourhood,

And was a public Symbol of the life,
That thrifty Pair had liv'd. For, as it chanc'd,
Their Cottage on a plot of rising ground
140   Stood single, with large prospect North and South,
High into Easedale, up to Dunmal-Raise,
And Westward to the village near the Lake;
And from this constant light so regular
And so far seen, the House itself by all
145   Who dwelt within the limits of the vale,
Both old and young, was nam'd The Evening Star.

Thus living on through such a length of years,
The Shepherd, if he lov'd himself, must needs
Have lov'd his Help-mate; but to Michael's heart
150   This Son of his old age was yet more dear—
Effect which might perhaps have been produc'd
By that instinctive tenderness, the same
Blind Spirit, which is in the blood of all,
Or that a child, more than all other gifts,
155   Brings hope with it, and forward-looking thoughts,
And stirrings of inquietude, when they
By tendency of nature needs must fail.
From such, and other causes, to the thoughts
Of the old Man his only Son was now
160   The dearest object that he knew on earth.
Exceeding was the love he bare to him,
His Heart and his Heart's joy! For oftentimes
Old Michael, while he was a babe in arms,
Had done him female service, not alone
165   For dalliance and delight, as is the use
Of Fathers, but with patient mind enforc'd
To acts of tenderness; and he had rock'd
His cradle, as with a woman's gentle hand.

And in a later time, ere yet the Boy
170   Had put on Boy's attire, did Michael love,
Albeit of a stern unbending mind,
To have the young one in his sight, when he
Had work by his own door, or when he sate
With sheep before him on his Shepherd's stool,
175   Beneath that large old Oak, which near their door
Stood, and from its enormous breadth of shade
Chosen for the Shearer's covert from the sun,
Thence in our rustic dialect was call'd
The CLIPPING TREE,[2] a name which yet it bears.
180   There, while they two were sitting in the shade,
With others round them, earnest all and blithe,

2. Clipping is the word used in the North of England for shearing [Wordsworth's note].

Would Michael exercise his heart with looks
Of fond correction and reproof bestow'd
Upon the child, if he disturb'd the sheep
185   By catching at their legs, or with his shouts
Scar'd them, while they lay still beneath the shears.

And when by Heaven's good grace the Boy grew up
A healthy Lad, and carried in his cheek
Two steady roses that were five years old,
190   Then Michael from a winter coppice° cut   *grove of small trees*
With his own hand a sapling, which he hoop'd
With iron, making it throughout in all
Due requisites a perfect Shepherd's Staff,
And gave it to the Boy; wherewith equipp'd
195   He as a Watchman oftentimes was plac'd
At gate or gap, to stem or turn the flock,
And to his office prematurely call'd
There stood the urchin, as you will divine,
Something between a hindrance and a help,
200   And for this cause not always, I believe,
Receiving from his Father hire of praise.
Though nought was left undone which staff or voice,
Or looks, or threatening gestures, could perform.
But soon as Luke, full ten years old, could stand
205   Against the mountain blasts, and to the heights,
Not fearing toil, nor length of weary ways,
He with his Father daily went, and they
Were as companions, why should I relate
That objects which the Shepherd loved before
210   Were dearer now? that from the Boy there came
Feelings and emanations, things which were
Light to the sun and music to the wind;
And that the Old Man's heart seemed born again.
Thus in his Father's sight the Boy grew up:
215   And now, when he had reached his eighteenth year,
He was his comfort and his daily hope.

While this good household thus were living on
From day to day, to Michael's ear there came
Distressful tidings. Long before the time
220   Of which I speak, the Shepherd had been bound
In surety° for his Brother's Son, a man   *guaranteed a loan*
Of an industrious life, and ample means;
But unforeseen misfortunes suddenly
Had press'd upon him, and old Michael now
225   Was summon'd to discharge the forfeiture,°   *collateral*
A grievous penalty, but little less
Than half his substance. This un-look'd for claim,
At the first hearing, for a moment took
More hope out of his life than he supposed

230 That any old man ever could have lost.
     As soon as he had gather'd so much strength
     That he could look his trouble in the face,
     It seem'd that his sole refuge was to sell
     A portion of his patrimonial fields.
235 Such was his first resolve; he thought again,
     And his heart fail'd him. "Isabel," said he,
     Two evenings after he had heard the news,
     "I have been toiling more than seventy years,
     And in the open sun-shine of God's love
240 Have we all liv'd; yet if these fields of ours
     Should pass into a Stranger's hand, I think
     That I could not lie quiet in my grave.
     Our lot is a hard lot; the Sun itself
     Has scarcely been more diligent than I,
245 And I have liv'd to be a fool at last
     To my own family. An evil Man
     That was, and made an evil choice, if he
     Were false to us; and if he were not false,
     There are ten thousand to whom loss like this
250 Had been no sorrow. I forgive him—but
     'Twere better to be dumb than to talk thus.
     When I began, my purpose was to speak
     Of remedies and of a chearful hope.
     Our Luke shall leave us, Isabel; the land
255 Shall not go from us, and it shall be free;°   *not mortgaged*
     He° shall possess it, free as is the wind   *(Luke)*
     That passes over it. We have, thou knowest,
     Another Kinsman, he will be our friend
     In this distress. He is a prosperous man,
260 Thriving in trade, and Luke to him shall go,
     And with his Kinsman's help and his own thrift,
     He quickly will repair this loss, and then
     May come again to us. If here he stay,
     What can be done? Where every one is poor
265 What can be gained?" At this the old Man paus'd,
     And Isabel sate silent, for her mind
     Was busy, looking back into past times.
     There's Richard Bateman, thought she to herself,[3]
     He was a parish-boy° at the church-door   *on welfare*
270 They made a gathering for him, shillings, pence,
     And halfpennies, wherewith the Neighbours bought
     A Basket, which they fill'd with Pedlar's wares,
     And with this Basket on his arm, the Lad
     Went up to London, found a Master° there,   *employer*
275 Who out of many chose the trusty Boy
     To go and overlook his merchandise

3. The story alluded to here is well known in the country [Wordsworth's note, 1802].

Beyond the seas, where he grew wond'rous rich,
And left estates and monies to the poor,
And at his birth-place, built a Chapel, floor'd
280   With Marble, which he sent from foreign lands.
These thoughts, and many others of like sort,
Pass'd quickly thro' the mind of Isabel,
And her face brighten'd. The old Man was glad,
And thus resum'd. "Well! Isabel, this scheme
285   These two days, has been meat and drink to me.
Far more than we have lost is left us yet.
—We have enough—I wish indeed that I
Were younger, but this hope is a good hope.
—Make ready Luke's best garments, of the best
290   Buy for him more, and let us send him forth
To-morrow, or the next day, or to-night:
—If he could go, the Boy should go to-night."

Here Michael ceas'd, and to the fields went forth
With a light heart. The House-wife for five days
295   Was restless° morn and night, and all day long   *without rest*
Wrought on with her best fingers to prepare
Things needful for the journey of her Son.
But Isabel was glad when Sunday came
To stop her in her work; for, when she lay
300   By Michael's side, she through the last two nights
Heard him, how he was troubled in his sleep:
And when they rose at morning she could see
That all his hopes were gone. That day at noon
She said to Luke, while they two by themselves
305   Were sitting at the door, "Thou must not go,
We have no other Child but thee to lose,
None to remember—do not go away,
For if thou leave thy Father he will die."[4]
The Lad made answer with a jocund voice,
310   And Isabel, when she had told her fears,
Recover'd heart. That evening her best fare
Did she bring forth, and all together sate
Like happy people round a Christmas fire.

Next morning Isabel resum'd her work,
315   And all the ensuing week the house appear'd
As chearful as a grove in Spring: at length
The expected letter from their Kinsman came,
With kind assurances that he would do
His utmost for the welfare of the Boy,

4. Echoing the story of Joseph in Genesis 44.22: "The lad cannot leave his father: for if he should leave his father, his father would die."

320 To which requests were added, that forthwith
He might be sent to him. Ten times or more
The letter was read over; Isabel
Went forth to shew it to the neighbours round:
Nor was there at that time on English Land
325 A prouder heart than Luke's. When Isabel
Had to her house return'd, the Old Man said,
"He shall depart to-morrow." To this word
The House-wife answered, talking much of things
Which, if at such short notice he should go,
330 Would surely be forgotten. But at length
She gave consent, and Michael was at ease.

Near the tumultuous brook of Green-head Gill,
In that deep Valley, Michael had design'd
To build a Sheep-fold;[5] and, before he heard
335 The tidings of his melancholy loss,
For this same purpose he had gathered up
A heap of stones, which close to the brook side
Lay thrown together, ready for the work.
With Luke that evening thitherward he walk'd;
340 And soon as they had reach'd the place he stopp'd,
And thus the Old Man spake to him. "My Son,
To-morrow thou wilt leave me; with full heart
I look upon thee, for thou art the same
That wert a promise to me ere thy birth,
345 And all thy life hast been my daily joy.
I will relate to thee some little part
Of our two histories; 'twill do thee good
When thou art from me, even if I should speak
On things thou canst not know of.—After thou
350 First cam'st into the world—as oft befalls
To new-born infants, thou didst sleep away
Two days, and blessings from thy Father's tongue
Then fell upon thee. Day by day pass'd on,
And still I lov'd thee with encreasing love.
355 Never to living ear came sweeter sounds
Than when I heard thee by our own fire-side
First uttering without words a natural tune,
While thou, a feeding babe, didst in thy joy
Sing at thy Mother's breast. Month followed month,
360 And in the open fields my life was pass'd
And on the mountains, else I think that thou
Hadst been brought up upon thy father's knees.

5. A sheepfold in these mountains is an unroofed building of stone walls, with different divisions. It is generally placed by the side of a brook [Wordsworth's note, 1802]. "The Sheepfold . . . remains, or rather ruins of it," Wordsworth remarked in 1843.

—But we were playmates, Luke; among these hills,
As well thou know'st, in us the old and young
365   Have play'd together, nor with me didst thou
Lack any pleasure which a boy can know."

Luke had a manly heart; but at these words
He sobb'd aloud. The Old Man grasp'd his hand,
And said, "Nay do not take it so—I see
370   That these are things of which I need not speak.
—Even to the utmost I have been to thee
A kind and a good Father: and herein
I but repay a gift which I myself
Receiv'd at others' hands, for, though now old
375   Beyond the common life of man, I still
Remember them who lov'd me in my youth.
Both of them sleep together: here they liv'd,
As all their Forefathers had done, and when
At length their time was come, they were not loth
380   To give their bodies to the family mold.
I wish'd that thou should'st live the life they liv'd.
But 'tis a long time to look back, my Son,
And see so little gain from sixty years.
These fields were burthen'd° when they came to me;   *mortgaged*
385   'Till I was forty years of age, not more
Than half of my inheritance was mine.
I toil'd and toil'd; God bless'd me in my work,
And 'till these three weeks past the land was free.
—It looks as if it never could endure
390   Another Master. Heaven forgive me, Luke,
If I judge ill for thee, but it seems good
That thou should'st go." At this the Old Man paus'd;
Then, pointing to the Stones near which they stood,
Thus, after a short silence, he resum'd:
395   "This was a work for us, and now, my Son,
It is a work for me. But, lay one Stone—
Here, lay it for me, Luke, with thine own hands.
I for the purpose brought thee to this place.
Nay, Boy, be of good hope:—we both may live
400   To see a better day. At eighty-four
I still am strong and stout;°—do thou thy part;   *hardy*
I will do mine[6]—I will begin again
With many tasks that were resign'd to thee;
Up to the heights, and in among the storms,

---

6. "Nature . . . hath done her part; / Do thou but thine," Raphael instructs Adam about his responsibility for Eve (*Paradise Lost* 8.561–62); "God toward thee hath done his part, do thine," Adam cautions Eve, before she goes off alone in Eden, the prelude to her Fall (9.375).

405 Will I without thee go again, and do
    All works which I was wont to do alone,
    Before I knew thy face.—Heaven bless thee, Boy!
    Thy heart these two weeks has been beating fast
    With many hopes—it should be so—yes—yes—
410 I knew that thou could'st never have a wish
    To leave me, Luke, thou hast been bound to me
    Only by links of love, when thou art gone
    What will be left to us!—But, I forget
    My purposes. Lay now the corner-stone,
415 As I requested, and hereafter, Luke,
    When thou art gone away, should evil men
    Be thy companions, let this sheep-fold be
    Thy anchor and thy shield; amid all fear
    And all temptation, let it be to thee
420 An emblem of the life thy Fathers liv'd,
    Who, being innocent, did for that cause
    Bestir them in good deeds. Now, fare thee well—
    When thou return'st, thou in this place wilt see
    A work which is not here, a covenant
425 'Twill be between us—but, whatever fate
    Befall thee, I shall love thee to the last,
    And bear thy memory with me to the grave."

    The Shepherd ended here; and Luke stoop'd down,
    And as his Father had requested, laid
430 The first stone of the Sheep-fold; at the sight
    The Old Man's grief broke from him, to his heart
    He press'd his Son, he kissed him and wept;
    And to the House together they return'd.

    Next morning, as had been resolv'd, the Boy
435 Began his journey, and when he had reach'd
    The public Way, he put on a bold face;
    And all the Neighbours, as he pass'd their doors
    Came forth with wishes and with farewell pray'rs,
    That follow'd him 'till he was out of sight.

440 A good report did from their Kinsman come,
    Of Luke and his well-doing; and the Boy
    Wrote loving letters, full of wond'rous news,
    Which, as the House-wife phrased it, were throughout
    The prettiest letters that were ever seen.
445 Both parents read them with rejoicing hearts.
    So, many months pass'd on: and once again
    The Shepherd went about his daily work
    With confident and chearful thoughts; and now
    Sometimes when he could find a leisure hour
450 He to that valley took his way, and there

Wrought at the Sheep-fold. Meantime Luke began
To slacken in his duty; and, at length
He in the dissolute city gave himself
To evil courses: ignominy and shame
455   Fell on him, so that he was driven at last
To seek a hiding-place beyond the seas.

There is a comfort in the strength of love;
'Twill make a thing endurable, which else
Would break the heart:—Old Michael found it so.
460   I have convers'd with more than one who well
Remember the Old Man, and what he was
Years after he had heard this heavy news.
His bodily frame had been from youth to age
Of an unusual strength. Among the rocks
465   He went, and still look'd up upon the sun,
And listen'd to the wind; and as before
Perform'd all kinds of labour for his Sheep,
And for the land, his small inheritance.
And to that hollow Dell from time to time
470   Did he repair, to build the Fold of which
His flock had need. 'Tis not forgotten yet
The pity which was then in every heart
For the Old Man—and 'tis believed by all
That many and many a day he thither went,
475   And never lifted up a single stone.

There, by the Sheep-fold, sometimes was he seen
Sitting alone, with that his faithful Dog,
Then old, beside him, lying at his feet.
The length of full seven years from time to time
480   He at the building of this Sheep-fold wrought,
And left the work unfinished when he died.

Three years, or little more, did Isabel,
Survive her Husband: at her death the estate
Was sold, and went into a Stranger's hand.
485   The Cottage which was nam'd The Evening Star
Is gone, the ploughshare has been through the ground
On which it stood;[7] great changes have been wrought
In all the neighbourhood, yet the Oak is left
That grew beside their Door; and the remains
490   Of the unfinished Sheep-fold may be seen
Beside the boisterous brook of Green-head Gill.

1800   1800

---

7. The grazing fields have been enclosed for agriculture; also evoking the strife between the shepherd Abel and his farming brother Cain.

RESPONSES

Francis Jeffrey: ["the new poetry"][1]

Poetry has this much, at least, in common with religion, that its standards were fixed long ago, by certain inspired writers, whose authority it is no longer lawful to call in question; and that many profess to be entirely devoted to it, who have no *good works* to produce in support of their pretensions. * * * The author who is now before us, belongs to a *sect* of poets, that has established itself in this country within these ten or twelve years, and is looked upon, we believe, as one of its chief champions and apostles. The peculiar doctrines of this sect, it would not, perhaps, be very easy to explain; but, that they are *dissenters* from the established systems in poetry and criticism, is admitted, and proved indeed, by the whole tenor of their compositions. Though they lay claim, we believe, to a creed and a revelation of their own, there can be little doubt, that their doctrines are of *German* origin, and have been derived from some of the great modern reformers in that country. Some of their leading principles, indeed, are probably of an earlier date, and seem to have been borrowed from the great apostle of Geneva.[2] * * *

The disciples of this school boast much of its originality, and seem to value themselves very highly, for having broken loose from the bondage of ancient authority, and re-asserted the independence of genius. Originality, however, we are persuaded, is rarer than mere alteration; and a man may change a good master for a bad one, without finding himself at all nearer to independence. * * * The productions of this school, we conceive, are so far from being entitled to the praise of originality, that they cannot be better characterised, than by an enumeration of the sources from which their materials have been derived. The greater part of them, we apprehend, will be found to be composed of the following elements: 1. The antisocial principles, and distempered sensibility of Rousseau—his discontent with the present constitution of society—his paradoxical morality, and his perpetual hankerings after some unattainable state of voluptuous virtue and perfection. 2. The simplicity and energy (*horresco referens* [I dread to say it]) of Kotzebue and Schiller. 3. The homeliness and harshness of some of Cowper's language and versification, interchanged occasionally with the *innocence* of Ambrose Philips, or the quaintness of Quarles and Dr Donne.[3] * * *

The authors, of whom we are now speaking [Southey, Wordsworth, and Coleridge], have, among them, unquestionably, a very considerable portion of poetical talent, and have, consequently, been enabled to seduce many into an admiration of the false taste (as it appears to us) in which most of their productions are composed. They constitute, at present, the most formidable conspiracy that has lately been

1. By 1802, when this essay appeared in the *Edinburgh Review* (its occasion was Robert Southey's exotic verse romance, *Thalaba, the Destroyer*), the second edition of *Lyrical Ballads*, with the Preface, had appeared. Southey, like fellow "Lake Poet" Wordsworth, advocated political reform in the 1790s (see his abolition poetry, pages 114–18). Francis Jeffrey (1773–1850) was the editor and chief literary critic for the *Edinburgh*, soon to be one of the most influential reviews of the age. His tastes were more neoclassical than modern, and his attacks on Wordsworth's poetic principles persisted for decades.

2. Referring chiefly to Goethe and to German poets of sensational verse narrative. The apostle of Geneva is Rousseau.
3. August von Kotzebue was famed for his sentimental plays. Ambrose Phillips (1675–1749) was admired and ridiculed for his sweet verses; Francic Quarles was best known for *Emblems* (1635), a book of devotional poems with quaint illustrations. John Donne (1572–1631) wrote boldly experimental poetry famed for its passion, its rough meters, and extravagant wit.

formed against sound judgment in matters poetical; and are entitled to a larger share of our censorial notice, than could be spared for an individual delinquent. * * *

Their most distinguishing symbol, is undoubtedly an affection of great simplicity and familiarity of language. They disdain to make use of the common poetical phraseology, or to ennoble their diction by a selection of fine or dignified expressions. There would be too much *art* in this, for that great love of nature with which they are all of them inspired; and their sentiments, they are determined shall be indebted, for their effect, to nothing but their intrinsic tenderness or elevation. There is something very noble and conscientious, we will confess, in this plan of composition; but the misfortune is, that there are passages in all poems, that can neither be pathetic nor sublime; and that, on these occasions, a neglect of the embellishments of language is very apt to produce absolute meanness and insipidity. * * * It is in such passages, accordingly, that we are most frequently offended with low and inelegant expressions; and that the language, which was intended to be simple and natural, is found oftenest to degenerate into mere slovenliness and vulgarity. * * *

One of their own authors, indeed, has very ingeniously set forth, (in a kind of manifesto that preceded one of their most flagrant acts of hostility), that it was their capital object "to adapt to the uses of poetry, the ordinary language of conversation among the middling and lower orders of the people." What advantages are to be gained by the success of this project, we confess ourselves unable to conjecture. The language of the higher and more cultivated orders may fairly be presumed to be better than that of their inferiors: at any rate, it has all those associations in its favour, by means of which, a style can ever appear beautiful or exalted, and is adapted to the purposes of poetry, by having been long consecrated to its use. The language of the vulgar, on the other hand, has all the opposite associations to contend with; and must seem unfit for poetry, (if there were no other reason), merely because it has scarcely ever been employed in it. A great genius may indeed overcome these disadvantages; but we can scarcely conceive that he should court them. We may excuse a certain homeliness of language in the productions of a ploughman or a milkwoman;[4] but we cannot bring ourselves to admire it in an author, who has had occasion to indite odes to his college bell, and inscribe hymns to the Penates.[5]

But the mischief of this new system is not confined to the depravation of language only; it extends to the sentiments and emotions, and leads to the debasement of all those feelings which poetry is designed to communicate. It is absurd to suppose, that an author should make use of the language of the vulgar, to express the sentiments of the refined. His professed object, in employing that language, is to bring his compositions nearer to the true standard of nature; and his intention to copy the sentiments of the lower orders, is implied in his resolution to make use of their style. Now, the different classes of society have each of them a distinct character, as well as a separate idiom; and the names of the various passions to which they are subject respectively, have a signification that varies essentially, according to the condition of the persons to whom they are applied. The love, or grief, or indignation of an enlightened and refined character, is not only expressed in a different language, but is in itself a different emotion from the love, or grief, or anger, of

4. Robert Burns (Scots farmer poet) and Ann Yearsley, "the poetical milkwoman." See pages 100 and 172.
5. A sarcastic reference to Southey's mock ode *The*

Chapel-Bell (1793) and his long *Hymn to the Penates* (1796); penates were Roman household deities.

a clown,[6] a tradesman, or a market-wench. The things themselves are radically and obviously distinct; and the representation of them is calculated to convey a very different train of sympathies and sensations to the mind. The question, therefore, comes simply to be—which of them is the most proper object for poetical imitation? It is needless for us to answer a question, which the practice of all the world has long ago decided irrevocably. The poor and vulgar may interest us, in poetry, by their *situation*; but never, we apprehend, by any sentiments that are peculiar to their condition, and still less by any language that is characteristic of it. The truth is, that is impossible to copy their diction or their sentiments correctly, in a serious composition; and this, not merely because poverty makes men ridiculous, but because just taste and refined sentiment are rarely to be met with among the uncultivated part of mankind; and a language, fitted for their expression, can still more rarely form any part of their "ordinary conversation."

* * * It has been argued, indeed, (for men will argue in support of what they do not venture to practice), that as the middling and lower orders of society constitute by far the greater part of mankind, so, their feelings and expressions should interest more extensively, and may be taken, more fairly than any other, for the standards of what is natural and true. To this, it seems obvious to answer, that the arts that aim at exciting admiration and delight, do not take their models from what is ordinary, but from what is excellent; and that our interest in the representation of any event, does not depend upon our familiarity with the original, but on its intrinsic importance, and the celebrity of the parties it concerns. The sculptor employs his art in delineating the graces of Antinous or Apollo, and not in the representation of those ordinary forms that belong to the crowd of his admirers. When a chieftain perishes in battle, his followers mourn more for him, than for thousands of their equals that may have fallen around him. * * *

The qualities of style and imagery, however, form but a small part of the characteristics by which a literary faction is to be distinguished. The subject and object of their compositions, and the principles and opinions they are calculated to support, constitute a far more important criterion, and one to which it is usually altogether easy to refer. Some poets are sufficiently described as the flatterers of greatness and power, and others as the champions of independence. One set of writers is known by its antipathy to decency and religion; another, by its methodistical cant and intolerance. Our new school of poetry has a moral character also; though it may not be possible, perhaps, to delineate it quite so concisely.

A splenetic and idle discontent with the existing institutions of society, seems to be at the bottom of all their serious and peculiar sentiments. Instead of contemplating the wonders and the pleasures which civilization has created for mankind, they are perpetually brooding over the disorders by which its progress has been attended. They are filled with horror and compassion at the sight of poor men spending their blood in the quarrels of princes, and brutifying their sublime capabilities in the drudgery of unremitting labour. For all sorts of vice and profligacy in the lower orders of society, they have the same virtuous horror, and the same tender compassion. While the existence of these offences overpowers them with grief and confusion, they never permit themselves to feel the smallest indignation or dislike towards the offenders. The present vicious constitution of society alone is responsible for all these enormities: the poor sinners are but the helpless

6. A peasant.

victims or instruments of its disorders, and could not possibly have avoided the errors into which they have been betrayed. Though they can bear with crimes, therefore, they cannot reconcile themselves to punishments; and have an unconquerable antipathy to prisons, gibbets, and houses of correction, as engines of oppression, and instruments of atrocious injustice. While the plea of moral necessity is thus artfully brought forward to convert all the excesses of the poor into innocent misfortunes, no sort of indulgence is shown to the offences of the powerful and rich. Their oppressions, and seductions, and debaucheries, are the theme of many an angry verse; and the indignation and abhorrence of the reader is relentlessly conjured up against those perturbators of society, and scourges of mankind.

It is not easy to say, whether the fundamental absurdity of this doctrine, or the partiality of its application, be entitled to the severest reprehension.

1802

Charles Lamb: from *a letter to William Wordsworth*[1]

[Jan. 30, 1801]

Thanks for your Letter and Present. I had already borrowed your second volume.[2] What most please me are, the Song of Lucy.[3] . . . I will mention one more: the delicate and curious feeling in the wish for the Cumberland Beggar, that he may have about him the melody of Birds, altho' he hear them not. Here the mind knowingly passes a fiction upon herself, first substituting her own feelings for the Beggar's, and, in the same breath detecting the fallacy, will not part with the wish.— * * * I will just add that it appears to me a fault in the Beggar, that the instructions conveyed in it are too direct and like a lecture:[4] they don't slide into the mind of the reader, while he is imagining no such matter. An intelligent reader finds a sort of insult in being told, I will teach you how to think upon this subject. * * * There is implied an unwritten compact between Author and reader; I will tell you a story, and I suppose you will understand it. * * *—I am sorry that Coleridge has christened his Ancient Marinere "a poet's Reverie"—it is as bad as Bottom the Weaver's declaration that he is not a Lion but only the scenical representation of a Lion.[5] What new idea is gained by this Title, but one subversive of all credit, which the tale should force upon us, of its truth? For me, I was never so affected with any human Tale. After first reading it, I was totally possessed with it for many days.—I dislike all the miraculous part of it, but the feelings of the man under the operation of such scenery dragged me along like Tom Piper's magic whistle. I totally differ from your idea that the Marinere should have had a character and profession. This is a Beauty in Gulliver's Travels, where the mind is kept in a placid state of little wonderments; but the Ancient Marinere undergoes such Trials, as overwhelm and bury all individuality or memory of what he was, like the state of a man in a Bad dream, one terrible peculiarity of which is: that all consciousness of personality is gone. Your other observation is I think as well a little

1. At the time of these letters, Lamb was an old friend of Coleridge and a newer acquaintance of the Wordsworths; he had published a novel and some verses, but his major career as an essayist was still to come.
2. Wordsworth had sent *Lyrical Ballads* (1800) to Lamb, who knew the poems in the first volume from the 1798 edition. The poems he discusses are newly published in volume 2.
3. Song (*She dwelt among th'untrodden ways*)
4. See lines 177–78.
5. In 1800, the subtitle was "A Poet's Reverie." In Shakespeare's *Midsummer Night's Dream* (5.1), Snug the Joiner says this, to allay Bottom's fear that the ladies in the audience will take him for a real lion (5.1.220 ff; cf. Bottom, 3.1.35–45).

unfounded: the Marinere from being conversant in supernatural events *has* acquired a supernatural and strange cast of *phrase,* eye, appearance, &c. which frighten the wedding guest. You will excuse my remarks, because I am hurt and vexed that you should think it necessary, with a prose apology,[6] to open the eyes of dead men that cannot see. To sum up a general opinion of the second vol.—I do not feel any one poem in it so forcibly as the Ancient Marinere, the Mad Mother, and the Lines at Tintern Abbey in the first.—I could, too, have wished the Critical preface had appeared in a separate treatise. All its dogmas are true and just, and most of them new, *as* criticism. But they associate a *diminishing* idea with the Poems which follow, as having been written for *Experiment* on the public taste, more than having sprung (as they must have done) from living and daily circumstances.—I am prolix, because I am gratifyed in the opportunity of writing to you, and I don't well know when to leave off. I ought before this to have reply'd to your very kind invitation into Cumberland.[7] With you and your Sister I could gang any where. But I am afraid whether I shall ever be able to afford so desperate a Journey. Separate from the pleasure of your company, I don't much care if I never see a mountain in my life. I have passed all my days in London, until I have formed as many and intense local attachments, as any of you mountaineers can have done with dead nature. The Lighted shops of the Strand and Fleet Street, the innumerable trades, tradesmen and customers, coaches, waggons, playhouses, all the bustle and wickedness round about Covent Garden, the very women of the Town, the Watchmen, drunken scenes, rattles,[8]—life awake, if you awake, at all hours of the night, the impossibility of being dull in Fleet Street, the crowds, the very dirt & mud, the Sun shining upon houses and pavements, the print shops, the old book stalls, parsons cheap'ning books, coffee houses, steams of soups from kitchens, the pantomimes, London itself a pantomime and a masquerade,—all these things work themselves into my mind and feed me, without a power of satiating me. The wonder of these sights impells me into night-walks about her crowded streets, and I often shed tears in the motley Strand from fulness of joy at so much Life.—All these emotions must be strange to you. So are your rural emotions to me. But consider, what must I have been doing all my life, not to have lent great portions of my heart with usury to such scenes?—

Charles Lamb: from *a letter to Thomas Manning*[1]

[Feb. 15, 1801]

I had need be cautious henceforward what opinion I give of the "Lyrical Ballads." All the North of England are in a turmoil. Cumberland and Westmoreland have already declared a state of war.[2] I lately received from Wordsworth a copy of the second volume, accompanied by an acknowledgement of having received from me many months since a copy of a certain Tragedy,[3] with excuses for not having made any acknowledgement sooner, it being owing to an "almost insurmountable aversion from Letter-writing." This letter I answered in due form and time, and enumerated several of the passages which had most affected me, adding, unfortunately, that no single piece had moved me so forcibly as the "Ancient Mariner," "The Mad

---

6. The Preface of 1800.
7. In the Lake District.
8. Watchmen's alarms.
1. One of Lamb's closest friends, Manning (1772–1840), mathematician and traveler, was considered the first scholar of Chinese literature in Europe; he was the first

and, for many years, only Englishman to enter the holy city of Lhasa, Tibet.
2. Coleridge was living in Cumberland county, the Wordsworths in Westmoreland.
3. By Lamb.

Mother," or the "Lines at Tintern Abbey." The Post did not sleep a moment. I received almost instantaneously a long letter of four sweating pages from my Reluctant Letter-Writer, the purport of which was, that he was sorry his 2d vol. had not given me more pleasure (Devil a hint did I give that it had *not pleased me*), and "was compelled to wish that my range of sensibility was more extended, being obliged to believe that I should receive large influxes of happiness and happy Thoughts" (I suppose from the L. B.)—With a deal of stuff about a certain Union of Tenderness and Imagination, which in the sense he used Imagination was not the characteristic of Shakspeare, but which Milton possessed in a degree far exceeding other Poets: which Union, as the highest species of Poetry, and chiefly deserving that name,[4] "He was most proud to aspire to;" then illustrating the said Union by two quotations from his own 2d vol. (which I had been so unfortunate as to miss) [quotes *Michael* 349–53]. These lines [352–53] were thus undermarked, and then followed "This Passage, as combining in an extraordinary degree that Union of Imagination and Tenderness which I am speaking of, I consider as one of the Best I ever wrote!" * * * good Poetry: but after one has been reading Shakspeare twenty of the best years of one's life, to have a fellow start up, and prate about some unknown quality, which Shakspeare possessed in a degree inferior to Milton and *somebody else!!* This was not to be *all* my castigation. Coleridge, who had not written to me some months before, starts up from his bed of sickness to reprove me for my hardy presumption: four long pages, equally sweaty and more tedious, came from him; assuring me that, when the works of a man of true genius such as W. undoubtedly was, do not please me at first sight, I should suspect the fault to lie "in me and not in them," etc. etc. etc. etc. etc. What am I to do with such people? I certainly shall write them a very merry Letter. Writing to *you*, I may say that the 2d vol. has no such pieces. * * * It is full of original thinking and an observing mind, but it does not often make you laugh or cry.—It too artfully aims at simplicity of expression. And you sometimes doubt if Simplicity be not a cover for Poverty. The best Piece in it I will send you, being *short*. I have grievously offended my friends in the North by declaring my undue preference; but I need not fear you:—[quotes *Song (She dwelt among th'untrodden ways)*]. This is choice and genuine, and so are many, many more. But one does not like to have 'em rammed down one's throat. "Pray, take it—it's very good—let me help you—eat faster."

⊱ ⋈⬧⋈ ⊰

SONNETS, 1802–1807[1]
Prefatory Sonnet

Nuns fret not at their Convent's narrow room;[2]
And Hermits are contented with their Cells;

---

4. See page 202.

1. Wordsworth's first publication was his sonnet *On seeing Miss Helen Maria Williams Weep at a Tale of Distress* (1787), and he was encouraged by the revival of sonnet-writing at the end of the 18th century as well as by Milton's political sonnets. He wrote a number of sonnets in 1802, when he briefly visited France during the Peace of Amiens to settle affairs with Annette Vallon, prior to his marriage. For other sonnets from this period see pages 128–29.

2. In 1802 Wordsworth praised Milton's sonnets for the "energetic and varied flow of sound crowding into narrow room more of the combined effect of rhyme and blank verse than can be done by any other kind of verse that I know of." He particularly liked Milton's stanzaic and linear enjambments (see his own wit about this device in line 10 where *bound* is unbound). For another sonnet on sonnet writing, see his *Scorn not the sonnet*, page 278.

And Students with their pensive Citadels;
Maids at the Wheel, the Weaver at his Loom,
5 Sit blithe and happy; Bees that soar for bloom,
High as the highest Peak of Furness fells,°   mountains
Will murmur by the hour in Foxglove bells:
In truth, the prison, into which we doom
Ourselves, no prison is: and hence for me,
10 In sundry moods, 'twas pastime to be bound
Within the Sonnet's scanty plot of ground:
Pleas'd if some Souls (for such there needs must be)
Who have felt the weight of too much liberty,
Should find brief solace there, as I have found.

1802   1807

Composed upon
Westminster Bridge,
Sept. 3, 1802[1]

Earth has not any thing to shew more fair:
Dull would he be of soul who could pass by
A sight so touching in it's majesty:
This City now doth like a garment wear
5 The beauty of the morning; silent, bare,
Ships, towers, domes, theatres, and temples lie
Open unto the fields, and to the sky;
All bright and glittering in the smokeless air.
Never did sun more beautifully steep
10 In his first splendor, valley, rock, or hill;
Ne'er saw I, never felt, a calm so deep!
The river glideth at his own sweet will:
Dear God! the very houses seem asleep;
And all that mighty heart is lying still!

1802   1807

"The world is too much with us"

The world is too much with us; late and soon,
Getting and spending, we lay waste our powers:
Little we see in nature that is ours;
We have given our hearts away, a sordid boon!
5 The Sea that bares her bosom to the moon;
The Winds that will be howling at all hours
And are up-gathered now like sleeping flowers;
For this, for every thing, we are out of tune;
It moves us not. Great God! I'd rather be

1. "Composed on the roof of a coach, on my way to France" [I.F., 1843]. For the circumstances, see Dorothy Wordsworth's *Grasmere Journals*, July 1802, page 291. Wordsworth perhaps finished it in September (on his return), and he did give the year as 1803 (corrected to 1802 in 1838). His confusion may have had to do with his anxiety about his reunion with—and final departure from—Annette Vallon and daughter Caroline.

10   A Pagan° suckled in a creed outworn;   *pre-Christian*
      So might I, standing on this pleasant lea,
      Have glimpses that would make me less forlorn;
      Have sight of Proteus rising from the sea;
      Or hear old Triton blow his wreathed horn.[1]

1802–1804   1807

"It is a beauteous Evening"[1]

      It is a beauteous Evening, calm and free;
      The holy time is quiet as a Nun
      Breathless with adoration; the broad sun
      Is sinking down in its tranquillity;
5   The gentleness of heaven is on[2] the Sea:
      Listen! the mighty Being is awake
      And doth with his eternal motion make
      A sound like thunder—everlastingly.
      Dear Child! dear Girl! that walkest with me here,[3]
10   If thou appear'st untouch'd by solemn thought,
      Thy nature is not therefore less divine:
      Thou liest in Abraham's bosom[4] all the year;
      And worshipp'st at the Temple's inner shrine,
      God being with thee when we know it not.

1802   1807

London,
1802[1]

      Milton! thou should'st be living at this hour:
      England hath need of thee: she is a fen
      Of stagnant waters: altar, sword, and pen,
      Fireside, the heroic wealth of hall and bower,
5   Have forfeited their ancient English dower
      Of inward happiness. We are selfish men;
      Oh! raise us up, return to us again;
      And give us manners, virtue, freedom, power.
      Thy soul was like a Star and dwelt apart:
10   Thou hadst a voice whose sound was like the sea;
      Pure as the naked heavens, majestic, free,
      So didst thou travel on life's common way,

1. Proteus is the shape-changing herdsman of the sea;
Triton, usually depicted blowing a conch shell, is a sea
deity. Cf. the personified "Sea" in line 5.
1. This was composed on the beach near Calais, in the
autumn of 1802 [Wordsworth's note, 1843]. Actually,
late August.
2. [1836] broods o'er.
3. Daughter Caroline.
4. Christ's description of the resting place for heaven-
bound souls (Luke 16.22).

1. Written immediately after my return from France to
London, when I could not but be struck . . . with the vanity and parade of our own country, especially in great
towns and cities as contrasted with the quiet, and I may
say desolation, that the revolution had produced in
France. This must be borne in mind, or else the reader
may think . . . I have exaggerated the mischief engendered and fostered among us by undisturbed wealth
[Wordsworth's note, 1843].

In chearful godliness; and yet thy heart
The lowliest duties on itself did lay.

1802   1807

THE PRELUDE   Now regarded as Wordsworth's major work, *The Prelude* was unknown in his lifetime except to a small circle of family and friends. Though the poem was largely complete by 1805, Wordsworth continued to rework and polish it for the remaining forty-five years of his life, in an ongoing and intense self-inquiry into his childhood and youth. Published posthumously in 1850, *The Prelude* incorporates passages first written in the late 1790s. On a first reading, *The Prelude* appears to be a paean to the recovery of the past; on closer acquaintance it emerges as a great, self-conscious testimony to the construction of the past out of the urgent needs of the present. To compose the poem was also to compose the poet, to create Wordsworth as The Poet, a meditative and resolute figure who had struggled through years of family disruption and revolutionary turmoil to a position of authority.

The Prelude evolved in three principal versions. Isolated in Germany in the coldest winter of the century, 1798–1799, Wordsworth wrote several passages drawing on his childhood experiences in nature, sketches for *The Recluse*, a philosophic poem that Coleridge had urged him to write. By the time he and his sister Dorothy had settled in Grasmere in 1799, he had completed a two-part poem of almost a thousand lines of blank verse, narrating his life from boyhood through the age of seventeen. In 1801 he began to revise, though it was not until 1804 that he set to work in earnest. An initial plan for five books quickly became thirteen books, involving experiences in France and the crisis that followed the failure of his hopes for the French Revolution. The full version finished in 1805 combines earlier and later material, not always in chronological order, suggesting that the sequence of Wordsworth's life is less important than the imperatives shaping its argument. Further revised over the years, the poem was published by Wordsworth's widow in 1850. This was the only known text until 1926, when Ernest de Selincourt published that of 1805, the version we use.

Part confession, a crisis-autobiography descended from Saint Augustine's exemplary *Confessions*, *The Prelude* is also consciously English. Exceptionally personal, it is also a representative story of youthful radicalism and a return to native heritage to become a national poet. To this degree, *The Prelude* stands as a rejoinder to Rousseau's notorious *Confessions*, but its chief, self-conscious parallel is Milton's *Paradise Lost*. *The Prelude* turns epic inward, claiming the growth of the poet's mind as an exalted subject. But it is not everywhere epic and prophetic: it is also an epistle to Coleridge, intimate and domestic, a record of friendship. The result is a shifting interplay between high genre and familiar conversation, between the adult poet looking back and trying to explain and the boy from whose sense of the mysterious the poem derives its originating power. Writing his story, Wordsworth sometimes felt possessed by "Two consciousnesses, conscious of myself / And of some other Being" (2.32–33). As he tries to close the gap in the act of writing, the ungraspable, elusive vacancies generate a structure that circles back in its large patterns, animated throughout by countermovements that uncannily create the effect of authenticity:

As oftentimes a River, it might seem,
Yielding in part to old remembrances,
Part sway'd by fear to tread an onward road
That leads direct to the devouring sea,
Turns and will measure back his course, far back
Towards the very regions which he cross'd
In his first outset; so have we long time
Made motions retrograde, in like pursuit
Detain'd.   (9.1–9)

The simile, in suggesting the "fear" of concluding as well as the pull of "old remembrances," lays open to view the conflicting dynamics of Wordsworth's autobiographical enterprise.

from The Prelude, or Growth of a Poet's Mind

Book First. Introduction, Childhood, and School time

Oh there is blessing in this gentle breeze[1]
That blows from the green fields and from the clouds
And from the sky: it beats against my cheek
And seems half conscious of the joy it gives.
5　O welcome Messenger! O welcome Friend!
A Captive greets thee, coming from a house
Of bondage,[2] from yon City's walls set free,
A prison where he hath been long immured.
Now I am free, enfranchis'd and at large,
10　May fix my habitation where I will.
What dwelling shall receive me? In what Vale
Shall be my harbour? Underneath what grove
Shall I take up my home, and what sweet stream
Shall with its murmurs lull me to my rest?
15　The earth is all before me:[3] with a heart
Joyous, nor scar'd at its own liberty
I look about, and should the guide I chuse
Be nothing better than a wandering cloud
I cannot miss my way. I breathe again;
20　Trances of thought and mountings of the mind
Come fast upon me: it is shaken off,
As by miraculous gift 'tis shaken off,
That burthen of my own unnatural self,
The heavy weight of many a weary day
25　Not mine, and such as were not made for me.
Long months of peace (if such bold word accord
With any promises of human life)
Long months of ease and undisturb'd delight
Are mine in prospect: whither shall I turn
30　By road or pathway or through open field,
Or shall a twig or any floating thing
Upon the river, point me out my course?
　　Enough that I am free; for months to come
May dedicate myself to chosen tasks;
35　May quit the tiresome sea, and dwell on shore,
If not a settler on the soil, at least
To drink wild water, and to pluck green herbs,
And gather fruits fresh from their native bough.

---

1. Lines 1–54, which Wordsworth later called his "glad preamble" (7.4), were composed in late 1799 or 1800. Nature is his inspiring Muse or spirit ("spiritus" in Latin means both "spirit" and "breeze").

2. Evoking Exodus 13.14: "the Lord brought us out from Egypt, from the house of bondage."

3. At the end of *Paradise Lost*, Adam and Eve leave Eden: "the world was all before them" (12.646ff.).

Nay more, if I may trust myself, this hour
40   Hath brought a gift that consecrates my joy;
For I, methought, while the sweet breath of Heaven
Was blowing on my body, felt within
A corresponding mild creative breeze,
A vital breeze which travell'd gently on
45   O'er things which it had made, and is become
A tempest, a redundant° energy   *abounding*
Vexing its own creation. 'Tis a power
That does not come unrecognis'd, a storm,
Which, breaking up a long continued frost
50   Brings with it vernal° promises, the hope   *springtime*
Of active days, of dignity and thought,
Of prowess in an honorable field,
Pure passions, virtue, knowledge, and delight,
The holy life of music and of verse.
55   Thus far, O Friend! did I, not used to make
A present joy the matter of my Song,[4]
Pour out, that day, my soul in measur'd strains,
Even in the very words which I have here
Recorded: to the open fields I told
60   A prophecy: poetic numbers° came   *verses*
Spontaneously, and cloth'd in priestly robe
My spirit, thus singled out, as it might seem,
For holy services: great hopes were mine;
My own voice chear'd me, and, far more, the mind's
65   Internal echo of the imperfect sound:
To both I listen'd, drawing from them both
A chearful confidence in things to come.
      Whereat, being not unwilling now to give
A respite to this passion, I paced on
70   Gently, with careless steps, and came erelong
To a green shady place where down I sate
Beneath a tree, slackening my thoughts by choice
And settling into gentler happiness.
'Twas Autumn, and a calm and placid day,
75   With warmth as much as needed from a sun
Two hours declin'd towards the west, a day
With silver clouds, and sunshine on the grass
And, in the shelter'd grove where I was couch'd,
A perfect stillness. On the ground I lay
80   Passing through many thoughts, yet mainly such
As to myself pertain'd. I made a choice
Of one sweet Vale° whither my steps should turn   *Grasmere*
And saw, methought, the very house and fields
Present before my eyes: nor did I fail

---

4. Coleridge is this Friend. In Preface to *Lyrical Ballads*, Wordsworth calls poetry "emotion recollected in tranquillity."

85   To add, meanwhile, assurance of some work
     Of glory, there forthwith to be begun,[5]
     Perhaps, too, there perform'd. Thus, long I lay
     Chear'd by the genial pillow of the earth
     Beneath my head, sooth'd by a sense of touch
90   From the warm ground, that balanced me, though lost
     Entirely, seeing nought, nought hearing, save
     When here and there, about the grove of Oaks
     Where was my bed, an acorn from the trees
     Fell audibly, and with a startling sound.
95   Thus occupied in mind, I linger'd here
     Contented, nor rose up until the sun
     Had almost touch'd the horizon; bidding then
     A farewell to the City left behind,
     Even on the strong temptation of that hour
100 And with its chance equipment, I resolved
     To journey towards the Vale which I had chosen.
     It was a splendid evening: and my soul
     Did once again make trial of her strength
     Restored to her afresh; nor did she want
105 Eolian visitations;[6] but the harp
     Was soon defrauded, and the banded host
     Of harmony dispers'd in straggling sounds
     And, lastly, utter silence. "Be it so,
     It is an injury," said I, "to this day
110 To think of any thing but present joy."
     So like a Peasant I pursued my road
     Beneath the evening sun; nor had one wish
     Again to bend the sabbath of that time
     To a servile yoke. What need of many words?
115 A pleasant loitering journey, through two days
     Continued, brought me to my hermitage.°   *secluded dwelling*
         I spare to speak, my Friend, of what ensued,
     The admiration and the love, the life
     In common things; the endless store of things
120 Rare, or at least so seeming, every day
     Found all about me in one neighbourhood,
     The self-congratulation,° the complete   *rejoicing*
     Composure, and the happiness entire.
     But speedily a longing in me rose
125 To brace myself to some determin'd aim,
     Reading or thinking, either to lay up
     New stores, or rescue from decay the old
     By timely interference, I had hopes
     Still higher, that with a frame of outward life,

---

5. *The Recluse* (never finished).
6. The Aeolian harp, named for Aeolus, mythic god of   the winds, resounds at the wind's touch.

130 I might endue,° might fix in a visible home   *endow*
     Some portion of those phantoms of conceit°   *mental images*
     That had been floating loose about so long,
     And to such Beings temperately deal forth
     The many feelings that oppress'd my heart.
135 But I have been discouraged: gleams of light
     Flash often from the East, then disappear
     And mock me with a sky that ripens not
     Into a steady morning: if my mind,
     Remembering the sweet promise of the past,
140 Would gladly grapple with some noble theme,
     Vain is her wish; where'er she turns she finds
     Impediments from day to day renew'd.
         And now it would content me to yield up
     Those lofty hopes a while for present gifts
145 Of humbler industry. But, O dear Friend!
     The Poet, gentle creature as he is,
     Hath, like the Lover, his unruly times;
     His fits when he is neither sick nor well,
     Though no distress be near him but his own
150 Unmanageable thoughts. The mind itself,
     The meditative mind, best pleased, perhaps,
     While she, as duteous as the Mother Dove,
     Sits brooding,[7] lives not always to that end
     But hath less quiet instincts, goadings-on
155 That drive her, as in trouble, through the groves.
     With me is now such passion, which I blame
     No otherwise than as it lasts too long.
         When, as becomes a man who would prepare
     For such a glorious work, I through myself
160 Make rigorous inquisition, the report
     Is often chearing; for I neither seem
     To lack, that first great gift! the vital soul,
     Nor general truths which are themselves a sort
     Of Elements and Agents, Under-Powers,
165 Subordinate helpers of the living mind.
     Nor am I naked in external things,
     Forms, images; nor numerous other aids
     Of less regard, though won perhaps with toil,
     And needful to build up a Poet's praise.
170 Time, place, and manners;° these I seek, and these   *customs*
     I find in plenteous store; but nowhere such
     As may be singled out with steady choice;
     No little Band of yet remember'd names
     Whom I, in perfect confidence, might hope
175 To summon back from lonesome banishment
     And make them inmates in the hearts of men

7. Nurturing eggs; but with a pun on mental work.

Now living, or to live in times to come.
Sometimes, mistaking vainly, as I fear,
Proud spring-tide swellings for a regular sea
180 I settle on some British theme, some old
Romantic tale, by Milton left unsung:[8]
More often, resting at some gentle place
Within the groves of Chivalry, I pipe
Among the Shepherds, with reposing Knights
185 Sit by a Fountain-side, and hear their tales.
Sometimes, more sternly mov'd, I would relate
How vanquish'd Mithridates northward pass'd,
And, hidden in the cloud of years, became
That Odin, Father of a Race by whom
190 Perish'd the Roman Empire:[9] how the Friends
And Followers of Sertorius, out of Spain
Flying, found shelter in the Fortunate Isles;[1]
And left their usages, their arts, and laws
To disappear by a slow gradual death;
195 To dwindle and to perish one by one
Starved in those narrow bounds: but not the Soul
Of Liberty, which fifteen hundred years
Surviv'd, and when the European° came   (*Spanish conquerors*)
With skill and power that could not be withstood,
200 Did like a pestilence maintain its hold,
And wasted down by glorious death that Race
Of natural Heroes: or I would record
How in tyrannic times some unknown Man,
Unheard of in the Chronicles of Kings,
205 Suffer'd in silence for the love of truth:
How that one Frenchman,[2] through continued force
Of meditation on the inhuman deeds
Of the first Conquerors of the Indian Isles,
Went single in his ministry across
210 The Ocean, not to comfort the Oppress'd,
But, like a thirsty wind, to roam about,
Withering the Oppressor: how Gustavus found
Help at his need in Dalecarlia's Mines;[3]
How Wallace fought for Scotland,[4] left the name
215 Of Wallace to be found like a wild flower,
All over his dear Country, left the deeds

---

8. Milton considered writing tales of "Heroic Martyrdom" or a "Romantic" epic about Arthurian knights before settling on his biblical theme.
9. In *Decline and Fall of the Roman Empire* (1776–1788), Edward Gibbon had proposed that the Norse god Odin was originally a tribal chieftain who had attacked Rome, perhaps historical King Mithridates of Asia Minor, defeated by the Romans in the 1st century B.C.
1. Canary Islands. Roman general Sertorius, ally of

Mithridates, was assassinated in 72 B.C.
2. In 1568 Dominique de Gourges "went to Florida to avenge the massacre of the French by the Spaniards there" [Wordsworth's note, 1850].
3. Where, in hiding, Gustavus I of Sweden (1496–1530) planned his country's revolt from Danish rule.
4. William Wallace fought for the liberty of Scotland; he was executed by the British in 1305.

Of Wallace, like a Family of Ghosts,
To people the steep rocks and river banks,
Her natural sanctuaries, with a local soul
220   Of independence and stern liberty.
Sometimes it suits me better to shape out
Some Tale from my own heart, more near akin
To my own passions and habitual thoughts,
Some variegated story, in the main
225   Lofty, with interchange of gentler things;
But deadening admonitions will succeed,
And the whole beauteous Fabric seems to lack
Foundation, and, withal, appears throughout
Shadowy and unsubstantial. Then, last wish,
230   My last and favorite aspiration! then
I yearn towards some philosophic Song
Of Truth that cherishes° our daily life;   *holds dear*
With meditations passionate from deep
Recesses in man's heart, immortal verse
235   Thoughtfully fitted to the Orphean lyre;[5]
But from this awful° burthen I full soon   *solemn*
Take refuge, and beguile myself with trust
That mellower years will bring a riper mind
And clearer insight. Thus from day to day
240   I live, a mockery of the brotherhood
Of vice and virtue, with no skill to part
Vague longing that is bred by want of power
From paramount impulse not to be withstood,
A timorous capacity from prudence;
245   From circumspection infinite delay.
Humility and modest awe themselves
Betray me, serving often for a cloak
To a more subtle selfishness, that now
Doth lock my functions up in blank reserve,°   *inertia*
250   Now dupes me by an over anxious eye
That with a false activity beats off
Simplicity and self-presented truth.
—Ah! better far than this, to stray about
Voluptuously° through fields and rural walks,   *luxuriantly*
255   And ask no record of the hours, given up
To vacant musing, unreprov'd neglect
Of all things, and deliberate holiday:
Far better never to have heard the name
Of zeal and just ambition, than to live
260   Thus baffled by a mind that every hour
Turns recreant to her task, takes heart again

5. In Greek myth, musician Orpheus could enthrall all creation. Coleridge praised *The Prelude* as "an Orphic Tale indeed."

Then feels immediately some hollow thought
Hang like an interdict° upon her hopes.   *prohibition*
This is my lot; for either still I find
265   Some imperfection in the chosen theme;
Or see of absolute accomplishment
Much wanting, so much wanting in myself,
That I recoil and droop, and seek repose
In indolence from vain perplexity,
270   Unprofitably travelling towards the grave,
Like a false Steward who hath much receiv'd
And renders nothing back.[6]—Was it for this
That one, the fairest of all Rivers,[7] lov'd
To blend his murmurs with my Nurse's song
275   And from his alder shades and rocky falls,
And from his fords and shallows sent a voice
That flow'd along my dreams? For this didst Thou,
O Derwent! travelling over the green Plains
Near my sweet birth-place,[8] didst thou, beauteous Stream,
280   Make ceaseless music through the night and day
Which with its steady cadence tempering
Our human waywardness, composed my thoughts
To more than infant softness, giving me,
Among the fretful dwellings of mankind,
285   A knowledge, a dim earnest of the calm
Which Nature breathes among the hills and groves.
      When, having left his Mountains, to the Towers
Of Cockermouth that beauteous River came,
Behind my Father's House he pass'd, close by,
290   Along the margin of our Terrace Walk.
He was a Playmate whom we dearly lov'd.
Oh! many a time have I, a five years' Child,
A naked Boy, in one delightful Rill,
A little Mill-race sever'd from his stream,
295   Made one long bathing of a summer's day,
Bask'd in the sun, and plunged, and bask'd again,
Alternate all a summer's day, or cours'd
Over the sandy fields, leaping through groves
Of yellow grunsel,° or when crag and hill,   *ragweed*
300   The woods, and distant Skiddaw's[9] lofty height,
Were bronz'd with a deep radiance, stood alone
Beneath the sky, as if I had been born
On Indian Plains,° and from my Mother's hut   *in America*

6. Jesus's parable of the steward who fails to use his talents (literally a coin; metaphorically, God's gifts), in Matthew 25.14–30, also the referent of Milton's famous sonnet, *On His Blindness.*
7. The Derwent flows behind Wordsworth's childhood home in Cockermouth, Cumberland.
8. Quoting Coleridge's *Frost at Midnight* (line 28).
9. At 3,053 feet, one of the highest peaks of the Lake District, nine miles east of Cockermouth.

Had run abroad in wantonness, to sport,
305 A naked Savage, in the thunder shower.
      Fair seed-time had my soul, and I grew up
Foster'd alike by beauty and by fear;
Much favor'd in my birth-place, and no less
In that beloved Vale[1] to which, erelong,
310 I was transplanted. Well I call to mind,
('Twas at an early age, ere I had seen
Nine summers) when upon the mountain slope
The frost, and breath of frosty wind had snapp'd
The last autumnal crocus, 'twas my joy
315 To wander half the night among the Cliffs
And the smooth Hollows, where the woodcocks ran
Along the open turf. In thought and wish,
That time, my shoulder all with springes° hung,   *bird-traps*
I was a fell destroyer. On the heights
320 Scudding away from snare to snare, I plied
My anxious visitation, hurrying on,
Still hurrying, hurrying onward: moon and stars
Were shining o'er my head; I was alone
And seem'd to be a trouble to the peace
325 That was among them. Sometimes it befel
In these night-wanderings, that a strong desire
O'erpower'd my better reason, and the bird
Which was the captive of another's toils°   *labors, snares*
Became my prey; and, when the deed was done,
330 I heard among the solitary hills
Low breathings coming after me, and sounds
Of undistinguishable motion, steps
Almost as silent as the turf they trod.
      Nor less in spring-time when on southern banks
335 The shining sun had from her knot of leaves
Decoy'd the primrose flower, and when the Vales
And woods were warm, was I a plunderer then
In the high places, on the lonesome peaks
Where'er, among the mountains and the winds,
340 The Mother Bird had built her lodge. Though mean
My object, and inglorious, yet the end
Was not ignoble. Oh! when I have hung
Above the raven's nest, by knots of grass,
And half-inch fissures in the slippery rock
345 But ill sustain'd, and almost, as it seem'd,
Suspended by the blast which blew amain,
Shouldering the naked crag; Oh! at that time,
While on the perilous ridge I hung alone,
With what strange utterance did the loud dry wind
350 Blow through my ears! the sky seem'd not a sky

---

1. Esthwaite, where Wordsworth went to school, 35 miles from Cockermouth.

Of earth, and with what motion mov'd the clouds!
   The mind of man is framed even like the breath
And harmony of music. There is a dark
Invisible workmanship that reconciles
355   Discordant elements, and makes them move
In one society. Ah me! that all
The terrors, all the early miseries,
Regrets, vexations, lassitudes, that all
The thoughts and feelings which have been infus'd
360   Into my mind should ever have made up
The calm existence that is mine when I
Am worthy of myself. Praise to the end!
Thanks likewise for the means! But I believe
That Nature, oftentimes, when she would frame
365   A favor'd Being, from his earliest dawn
Of infancy doth open out the clouds,
As at the touch of lightning, seeking him
With gentlest visitation: not the less,
Though haply° aiming at the self-same end,   *perhaps*
370   Does it delight her sometimes to employ
Severer interventions, ministry
More palpable, and so she dealt with me.
   One evening (surely I was led by her)
I went alone into a Shepherd's Boat,
375   A Skiff that to a Willow tree was tied
Within a rocky Cave, its usual home.
'Twas by the Shores of Patterdale, a Vale
Wherein I was a Stranger, thither come,
A School-boy Traveller, at the Holidays.
380   Forth rambled from the Village Inn alone
No sooner had I sight of this small Skiff,
Discover'd thus by unexpected chance,
Than I unloos'd her tether and embark'd.
The moon was up, the Lake was shining clear
385   Among the hoary mountains: from the Shore
I push'd, and struck the oars and struck again
In cadence, and my little Boat mov'd on
Even like a Man who walks with stately step
Though bent on speed. It was an act of stealth
390   And troubled pleasure: nor without the voice
Of mountain echoes did my Boat move on,
Leaving behind her still on either side
Small circles glittering idly in the moon
Until they melted all into one track
395   Of sparkling light. A rocky steep uprose
Above the Cavern of the Willow tree
And now, as suited one who proudly row'd
With his best skill, I fix'd a steady view

Upon the top of that same craggy ridge,[2]
400 The bound of the horizon, for behind
Was nothing but the stars and the grey sky.
She was an elfin Pinnace;° lustily   *small boat*
I dipp'd my oars into the silent Lake,
And, as I rose upon the stroke, my Boat
405 Went heaving through the water, like a Swan,
When from behind that craggy Steep, till then
The bound of the horizon, a huge Cliff,
As if with voluntary power instinct,°   *endowed*
Uprear'd its head: I struck, and struck again,
410 And, growing still in stature, the huge Cliff
Rose up between me and the stars, and still,
With measur'd motion, like a living thing,
Strode after me. With trembling hands I turn'd,
And through the silent water stole my way
415 Back to the Cavern of the Willow tree.
There, in her mooring-place, I left my Bark
And, through the meadows homeward went with grave
And serious thoughts: and after I had seen
That spectacle, for many days my brain
420 Work'd with a dim and undetermin'd sense
Of unknown modes of being: in my thoughts
There was a darkness, call it solitude,
Or blank desertion, no familiar shapes
Of hourly objects, images of trees,
425 Of sea, or sky, no colours of green fields;
But huge and mighty Forms that do not live
Like living men mov'd slowly through my mind
By day and were the trouble of my dreams.
    Wisdom and Spirit of the Universe![3]
430 Thou Soul that art the Eternity of Thought!
And giv'st to forms and images a breath
And everlasting motion! not in vain,
By day or starlight thus from my first dawn
Of Childhood didst Thou intertwine for me
435 The passions that build up our human Soul,
Not with the mean and vulgar° works of Man,   *lowly and ordinary*
But with high objects, with enduring things,
With life and nature, purifying thus
The elements of feeling and of thought,
440 And sanctifying by such discipline
Both pain and fear until we recognise

---

2. The rower faces the stern and fixes his sight on a shore-point, in order to move the boat in a straight line.
3. Coleridge published 429–90 in *The Friend* (28 December 1809), under the title "Growth of Genius from the Influence of Natural Objects, on the Imagination in Boyhood, and Early Youth."

A grandeur in the beatings of the heart.
    Nor was this fellowship vouchsaf'd to me
With stinted kindness. In November days

445 When vapours, rolling down the valleys, made
A lonely scene more lonesome; among woods
At noon, and 'mid the calm of summer nights,
When by the margin of the trembling Lake
Beneath the gloomy hills I homeward went

450 In solitude, such intercourse was mine;
'Twas mine among the fields both day and night,
And by the waters all the summer long.
—And in the frosty season, when the sun
Was set, and, visible for many a mile,

455 The cottage windows through the twilight blaz'd,
I heeded not the summons:—happy time
It was indeed for all of us; to me
It was a time of rapture: clear and loud
The village clock toll'd six; I wheel'd about,

460 Proud and exulting, like an untired horse,
That cares not for its home.—All shod with steel
We hiss'd along the polish'd ice, in games
Confederate, imitative of the chace,
And woodland pleasures, the resounding horn,

465 The Pack, loud bellowing, and the hunted hare.
So through the darkness and the cold we flew,
And not a voice was idle: with the din,
Meanwhile, the precipices rang aloud,
The leafless trees, and every icy crag

470 Tinkled like iron, while the distant hills
Into the tumult sent an alien sound
Of melancholy, not unnoticed, while the stars,
Eastward, were sparkling clear, and in the west,
The orange sky of evening died away.

475   Not seldom from the uproar I retired
Into a silent bay, or sportively
Glanced sideway, leaving the tumultuous throng,
To cut across the image of a star
That gleam'd upon the ice: and oftentimes,

480 When we had given our bodies to the wind,
And all the shadowy banks, on either side,
Came sweeping through the darkness, spinning still
The rapid line of motion; then at once
Have I, reclining back upon my heels,

485 Stopp'd short, yet still the solitary Cliffs
Wheel'd by me, even as if the earth had roll'd
With visible motion her diurnal° round;   *daily*
Behind me did they stretch in solemn train
Feebler and feebler, and I stood and watch'd

490   Till all was tranquil as [   ]⁴
          Ye Presences of Nature, in the sky
      Or on the earth! Ye Visions of the hills!
      And Souls of lonely places! can I think
      A vulgar hope was yours when Ye employ'd
495   Such ministry, when Ye through many a year
      Haunting me thus among my boyish sports,
      On caves and trees, upon the woods and hills,
      Impress'd upon all forms the characters°   *marks, signs*
      Of danger or desire, and thus did make
500   The surface of the universal earth
      With triumph, and delight, and hope, and fear
      Work° like a sea.   *seethe*
              Not uselessly employ'd,
      I might pursue this theme through every change
      Of exercise and play, to which the year
505   Did summon us in its delightful round.
      —We were a noisy crew; the sun in heaven
      Beheld not vales more beautiful than ours
      Nor saw a race, in happiness and joy
      More worthy of the fields where they were sown.
510   I would record with no reluctant voice
      The woods of autumn and their hazel bowers⁵
      With milk-white clusters hung; the rod and line,
      True symbol of the foolishness of hope,
      Which with its strong enchantment led us on
515   By rocks and pools, shut out from every star
      All the green summer, to forlorn cascades
      Among the windings of the mountain-brooks.
      —Unfading recollections! at this hour
      The heart is almost mine with which I felt
520   From some hill-top, on sunny afternoons,
      The Kite high up among the fleecy clouds
      Pull at its rein, like an impatient Courser,°   *racehorse*
      Or, from the meadows sent on gusty days
      Beheld her breast the wind, then suddenly
525   Dash'd headlong; and rejected by the storm.
          Ye lowly Cottages in which we dwelt,
      A ministration of your own was yours,
      A sanctity, a safeguard, and a love!
      Can I forget you, being as ye were
530   So beautiful among the pleasant fields
      In which ye stood? Or can I here forget
      The plain and seemly countenance with which

---

4. Wordsworth left the end of this line blank in 1805. In   5. *Nutting* (page 212) was originally part of this poem.
1809, it was completed as "a dreamless sleep."

Ye dealt out your plain comforts? Yet had ye
Delights and exultations of your own.
535 Eager and never weary we pursued
Our home amusements by the warm peat fire
At evening; when with pencil and with slate,
In square divisions parcell'd out, and all
With crosses and with cyphers scribbled o'er,°   *tic-tac-toe*
540 We schemed and puzzled, head opposed to head,
In strife too humble to be named in Verse;
Or round the naked Table, snow-white deal,°   *pine*
Cherry, or maple, sate in close array,
And to the combat, Lu or Whist,° led on   *(card games)*
545 A thick-ribb'd Army, not as in the world
Neglected and ungratefully thrown by
Even for the very service they had wrought,
But husbanded through many a long campaign.
Uncouth assemblage was it, where no few
550 Had changed their functions, some, plebean cards,
Which Fate beyond the promise of their birth
Had glorified, and call'd to represent
The persons of departed Potentates.
Oh! with what echoes on the Board they fell!
555 Ironic Diamonds; Clubs, Hearts, Diamonds, Spades,
A congregation piteously akin;
Cheap matter did they give to boyish wit,
Those sooty Knaves, precipitated down
With scoffs and taunts, like Vulcan out of Heaven,
560 The paramount Ace, a moon in her eclipse,
Queens, gleaming through their splendour's last decay,
And Monarchs, surly at the wrongs sustain'd
By royal visages. Meanwhile, abroad
The heavy rain was falling, or the frost
565 Raged bitterly, with keen and silent tooth,
And, interrupting the impassion'd game,
From Esthwaite's neighbouring Lake the splitting ice,
While it sank down towards the water, sent,
Among the meadows and the hills, its long
570 And dismal yellings, like the noise of wolves
When they are howling round the Bothnic Main.°   *Baltic Sea*
        Nor, sedulous[6] as I have been to trace
How Nature by extrinsic passion first
Peopled my mind with beauteous forms or grand,
575 And made me love them, may I well forget
How other pleasures have been mine, and joys
Of subtler origin; how I have felt
Not seldom, even in that tempestuous time,
Those hallow'd and pure motions of the sense

6. Diligent; revising Milton's claim that he is "Not sedulous by Nature" to treat epic themes (*Paradise Lost* 9.27).

580 Which seem, in their simplicity, to own
An intellectual charm, that calm delight
Which, if I err not, surely must belong
To those first-born affinities that fit
Our new existence to existing things
585 And, in our dawn of being, constitute
The bond of union betwixt life and joy.
    Yes, I remember, when the changeful earth,
And twice five seasons on my mind had stamp'd
The faces of the moving year, even then,
590 A Child, I held unconscious intercourse
With the eternal Beauty, drinking in
A pure organic pleasure from the lines
Of curling mist, or from the level plain
Of waters colour'd by the steady clouds.
595 The Sands of Westmoreland, the Creeks and Bays
Of Cumbria's rocky limits, they can tell
How when the Sea threw off his evening shade
And to the Shepherd's hut beneath the crags
Did send sweet notice of the rising moon,
600 How I have stood to fancies such as these,
Engrafted in the tenderness of thought,
A stranger, linking with the spectacle
No conscious memory of a kindred sight,
And bringing with me no peculiar sense
605 Of quietness or peace, yet have I stood,
Even while mine eye has mov'd o'er three long leagues°   *about nine miles*
Of shining water, gathering, as it seem'd,
Through every hair-breadth of that field of light,
New pleasure, like a bee among the flowers.
610 Thus, often in those fits of vulgar° joy   *ordinary*
Which through all seasons, on a child's pursuits
Are prompt attendants, 'mid that giddy bliss
Which, like a tempest, works along the blood
And is forgotten; even then I felt
615 Gleams like the flashing of a shield: the earth
And common face of Nature spake to me
Rememberable things: sometimes, 'tis true,
By chance collisions, and quaint accidents
Like those ill-sorted unions, work suppos'd
620 Of evil-minded fairies, yet not vain,
Nor profitless, if haply they impress'd
Collateral° objects and appearances,   *secondary*
Albeit lifeless then, and doom'd to sleep
Until maturer seasons call'd them forth
625 To impregnate and to elevate the mind.
And if the vulgar joy by its own weight
Wearied itself out of the memory
The scenes which were a witness of that joy

630 Remained, in their substantial lineaments
Depicted on the brain, and to the eye
Were visible, a daily sight: and thus,
By the impressive discipline of fear,
By pleasure, and repeated happiness,
So frequently repeated, and by force
635 Of obscure feelings representative
Of joys that were forgotten, these same scenes,
So beauteous and majestic in themselves,
Though yet the day was distant, did at length
Become habitually dear; and all
640 Their hues and forms were by invisible links
Allied to the affections.
                              I began
My Story early, feeling as I fear,
The weakness of a human love, for days
Disown'd by memory, ere the birth of spring
645 Planting my snow-drops among winter snows.
Nor will it seem to thee, my Friend! so prompt
In sympathy, that I have lengthen'd out,
With fond and feeble tongue, a tedious tale.
Meanwhile, my hope has been that I might fetch
650 Invigorating thoughts from former years,
Might fix the wavering balance of my mind,
And haply meet reproaches, too, whose power
May spur me on, in manhood now mature,
To honorable toil. Yet should these hopes
655 Be vain, and thus should neither I be taught
To understand myself, nor thou to know
With better knowledge how the heart was fram'd
Of him thou lovest, need I dread from thee
Harsh judgments, if I am so loth to quit
660 Those recollected hours that have the charm
Of visionary things, and lovely forms,
And sweet sensations that throw back our life
And almost make our Infancy itself
A visible scene on which the sun is shining.
665   One end hereby, at least, hath been attain'd—
My mind hath been reviv'd, and if this mood
Desert me not, I will forthwith bring down,
Through later years, the story of my life.
The road lies plain before me; 'tis a theme
670 Single, and of determin'd bounds; and hence
I chuse it rather, at this time, than work
Of ampler or more varied argument.[7]

---

7. Wordsworth wrote this last paragraph in 1804, addressing Coleridge's desire for a major philosophical epic.

from **Book Second. School time continued**

[TWO CONSCIOUSNESSES]

Thus far, O Friend! have we, though leaving much
Unvisited, endeavour'd to retrace
My life through its first years, and measur'd back[1]
The way I travell'd when I first began
5   To love the woods and fields: the passion yet
Was in its birth, sustain'd, as might befal,
By nourishment that came unsought; for still,
From week to week, from month to month we liv'd
A round of tumult: duly were our games
10   Prolong'd in summer till the daylight fail'd;
No chair remain'd before the doors, the bench
And threshold steps were empty; fast asleep
The Labourer, and the Old Man who had sate,
A later lingerer, yet the revelry
15   Continued, and the loud uproar: at last,
When all the ground was dark, and the huge clouds
Were edged with twinkling stars, to bed we went
With weary joints, and with a beating mind.
Ah! is there one who ever has been young,
20   And needs a monitory voice to tame
The pride of virtue, and of intellect?
And is there one, the wisest and the best
Of all mankind, who does not sometimes wish
For things which cannot be, who would not give,
25   If so he might, to duty and to truth
The eagerness of infantine desire?
A tranquillizing spirit presses now
On my corporeal frame: so wide appears
The vacancy between me and those days,
30   Which yet have such self-presence in my mind
That, sometimes, when I think of them, I seem
Two consciousnesses, conscious of myself
And of some other Being.

[BLESSED INFANT BABE]

Bless'd the infant Babe,[2]
(For with my best conjectures I would trace
The progress of our being) blest the Babe,
240 Nurs'd in his Mother's arms, the Babe who sleeps
Upon his Mother's breast, who, when his soul
Claims manifest kindred with an earthly soul,

1. A pun on poetic measures (meters).
2. Wordsworth has been discussing how hard it is "to analyse a soul" when no clear origin can be found for one's habits and desires, or even for any "obvious and particular thought." Then follows this general speculation in psychobiography.

Doth gather passion from his Mother's eye!
Such feelings pass into his torpid life
245 Like an awakening breeze, and hence his mind
Even [in the first trial of its powers,][3]
Is prompt and watchful, eager to combine
In one appearance, all the elements
And parts of the same object, else detach'd
250 And loth to coalesce. Thus, day by day,
Subjected to the discipline of love,
His organs and recipient faculties
Are quicken'd, are more vigorous, his mind spreads,
Tenacious of the forms which it receives.
255 In one beloved presence, nay and more,
In that most apprehensive habitude°   *capacity to assimilate*
And those sensations which have been deriv'd
From this beloved Presence, there exists
A virtue which irradiates and exalts
260 All objects through all intercourse of sense.
No outcast he, bewilder'd and depress'd:
Along his infant veins are interfus'd
The gravitation and the filial bond
Of nature, that connect him with the world.
265 Emphatically such a Being lives,
An inmate of this *active* universe;
From nature largely he receives; nor so
Is satisfied, but largely gives again,
For feeling has to him imparted strength,
270 And powerful in all sentiments of grief,
Of exultation, fear, and joy, his mind,
Even as an agent of the one great mind,
Creates, creator and receiver both,
Working but in alliance with the works
275 Which it beholds.—Such, verily, is the first
Poetic spirit of our human life;
By uniform controul of after years
In most abated and suppress'd, in some,
Through every change of growth or of decay,
280 Pre-eminent till death.
                              From early days,
Beginning not long after that first time
In which, a Babe, by intercourse of touch,
I held mute dialogues with my Mother's heart,
I have endeavour'd to display the means
285 Whereby the infant sensibility,
Great birth-right of our Being, was in me
Augmented and sustain'd. Yet is a path

___
3. This line was completed decades later.

More difficult before me, and I fear
That in its broken windings we shall need
290   The chamois'° sinews, and the eagle's wing: *mountain antelope*
For now a trouble came into my mind
From unknown causes. I was left alone,
Seeking the visible world, nor knowing why.
The props of my affections were remov'd,
295   And yet the building stood, as if sustain'd
By its own spirit![4] All that I beheld
Was dear to me, and from this cause it came,
That now to Nature's finer influxes°   *influences, impressions*
My mind lay open, to that more exact
300   And intimate communion which our hearts
Maintain with the minuter properties
Of objects which already are belov'd,
And of those only.

from Book Sixth. Cambridge, and the Alps
[ARRIVAL IN FRANCE][1]

A Fellow Student and myself, he, too,
340   A Mountaineer, together sallied forth
And, Staff in hand, on foot pursu'd our way
Towards the distant Alps. An open slight
Of College cares and study was the scheme,
Nor entertain'd without concern for those
345   To whom my worldly interests were dear:[2]
But Nature then was sovereign in my heart,
And mighty forms seizing a youthful Fancy
Had given a charter to irregular hopes.
In any age, without an impulse sent
350   From work of Nations, and their goings-on,
I should have been possess'd by like desire:
But 'twas a time when Europe was rejoiced,
France standing on the top of golden hours,[3]
And human nature seeming born again.
355   Bound, as I said, to the Alps, it was our lot
To land at Calais on the very Eve
Of that great federal Day;[4] and there we saw
In a mean City, and among a few,
How bright a face is worn when joy of one

4. Perhaps an oblique reference to the death of his mother when he was almost eight years old.

1. In summer 1790, a year after the French Revolution, Wordsworth and a friend toured France, the Swiss Alps, and Italy. France was still in the "golden hours" (353) of Revolutionary optimism.

2. Undergraduates usually spent the third summer studying for impending final examinations, which would determine their rank on graduation and shape their future prospects.

3. Shakespeare, Sonnet 16: "Now stand you on the top of happy hours," he says to a young man.

4. On the Festival of the Federation, 14 July 1790, the first anniversary of the fall of the Bastille, Louis XVI swore fidelity to the new constitution. Calais is a seaport in northern France.

360   Is joy of tens of millions. Southward thence
        We took our way direct, through Hamlets, Towns,
        Gaudy with reliques of that Festival,
        Flowers left to wither on triumphal Arcs,
        And window-garlands. On the public roads,
365   And once, three days successively, through paths
        By which our toilsome journey was abridg'd,
        Among sequester'd villages we walked,
        And found benevolence and blessedness
        Spread like a fragrance every where, like Spring
370   That leaves no corner of the Land untouch'd.
        Where Elms, for many and many a league, in files,
        With their thin umbrage,° on the stately roads   *foliage*
        Of that great Kingdom rustled o'er our heads,
        For ever near us as we paced along,
375   'Twas sweet, at such a time, with such delights
        On every side, in prime of youthful strength,
        To feed a Poet's tender melancholy
        And fond conceit of sadness to the noise
        And gentle undulation which they made.
380   Unhous'd, beneath the Evening Star we saw
        Dances of Liberty, and in late hours
        Of darkness, dances in the open air.
        Among the vine-clad Hills of Burgundy,
        Upon the bosom of the gentle Soane
385   We glided forward with the flowing stream:
        Swift Rhone, thou wert the wings on which we cut
        Between thy lofty rocks! Enchanting show
        Those woods, and farms, and orchards did present,
        And single Cottages, and lurking Towns,
390   Reach after reach, procession without end
        Of deep and stately Vales. A lonely Pair
        Of Englishmen we were, and sail'd along
        Cluster'd together with a merry crowd
        Of those emancipated, with a host
395   Of Travellers, chiefly Delegates, returning
        From the great Spousals newly solemniz'd
        At their chief City in the sight of Heaven.[5]
        Like bees they swarm'd, gaudy and gay as bees;
        Some vapour'd° in the unruliness of joy   *blustered*
400   And flourish'd with their swords, as if to fight
        The saucy air. In this blithe Company
        We landed, took with them our evening meal,
        Guests welcome almost as the Angels were
        To Abraham of old.[6] The Supper done,

5. Louis XVI's oath of fidelity was described as a marriage between monarch and nation.

6. Abraham lavishes hospitality on three disguised angels, who inform him his aged wife will bear a son (Genesis 18).

405	With flowing cups elate, and happy thoughts,
	We rose at signal given, and form'd a ring
	And, hand in hand, danced round and round the Board:
	All hearts were open, every tongue was loud
	With amity and glee: we bore a name
410	Honour'd in France, the name of Englishmen,
	And hospitably did they give us Hail
	As their forerunners in a glorious course,[7]
	And round and round the Board they danced again.
	With this same Throng our voyage we pursued
415	At early dawn; the Monastery Bells
	Made a sweet jingling in our youthful ears;
	The rapid River, flowing without noise,
	And every Spire we saw among the rocks
	Spake with a sense of peace, at intervals
420	Touching the heart amid the boisterous Crew
	With which we were environ'd.

[TRAVELLING IN THE ALPS. SIMPLON PASS]

Yet still in me, mingling with these delights°   *of travel*
Was something of stern mood, an under thirst
490 Of vigour, never utterly asleep.
Far different dejection once was mine,
A deep and genuine sadness then I felt:
The circumstances I will here relate
Even as they were. Upturning with a Band
495 Of Travellers, from the Valais we had clomb
Along the road that leads to Italy;°   *Simplon Pass*
A length of hours, making of these our guides
Did we advance, and having reach'd an Inn
Among the mountains, we together ate
500 Our noon's repast, from which the Travellers rose,
Leaving us at the Board. Erelong we follow'd,
Descending by the beaten road that led
Right to a rivulet's edge, and there broke off.
The only track now visible was one
505 Upon the further side, right opposite,
And up a lofty Mountain. This we took
After a little scruple,° and short pause,   *hesitation*
And climb'd with eagerness, though not, at length,
Without surprize and some anxiety
510 On finding that we did not overtake
Our Comrades gone before. By fortunate chance,
While every moment now encreas'd our doubts,
A Peasant met us and from him we learn'd
That to the place which had perplex'd us first

7. Referring to England's "Glorious Revolution" of 1688, which deposed the autocratic James II.

515 We must descend, and there should find the road
Which in the stony channel of the Stream
Lay a few steps, and then along its Banks,
And, further, that thenceforward all our course
Was downwards, with the current of that Stream.
520 Hard of belief we questioned him again,
And all the answers which the Man return'd
To our inquiries, in their sense and substance,
Translated by the feelings which we had,
Ended in this, that we had cross'd the Alps.
525   Imagination! lifting up itself
Before the eye and progress of my Song°   *this poem*
Like an unfather'd vapour; here that Power,
In all the might of its endowments, came
Athwart me; I was lost as in a cloud,
530 Halted without a struggle to break through,
And now[1] recovering to my Soul I say
I recognize thy glory; in such strength
Of usurpation, in such visitings
Of awful° promise, when the light of sense   *awe-filled*
535 Goes out in flashes that have shewn to us
The invisible world, doth Greatness make abode,
There harbours whether we be young or old.
Our destiny, our nature, and our home
Is with infinitude, and only there;
540 With hope it is, hope that can never die,
Effort, and expectation, and desire,
And something evermore about to be.
The mind beneath such banners militant
Thinks not of spoils, trophies nor of aught
545 That may attest its prowess, blest in thoughts
That are their own perfection and reward,
Strong in itself, and in the access of joy
Which hides it like the overflowing Nile.
     The dull and heavy slackening which ensu'd
550 Upon those tidings by the Peasant given
Was soon dislodg'd; downwards we hurried fast,
And enter'd with the road which we had miss'd
Into a narrow chasm: the brook and road[2]
Were fellow-travellers in this gloomy Pass,
555 And with them did we journey several hours
At a slow step. The immeasurable height
Of woods decaying, never to be decay'd,
The stationary blasts of waterfalls,
And every where along the hollow rent
560 Winds thwarting winds, bewilder'd and forlorn,[3]

---

1. This apostrophe was written in 1804, 14 years after the disappointment of the missed climax.
2. Lines 553 (from "the") through 572 were published as

The Simplon Pass in Wordsworth's 1845 *Poems*, under "Poems of the Imagination."
3. A contrasting echo of 2.261.

The torrents shooting from the clear blue sky,
The rocks that mutter'd close upon our ears,
Black drizzling crags that spake by the way-side
As if a voice were in them, the sick sight
565   And giddy prospect of the raving stream,
The unfetter'd clouds, and region of the heavens,
Tumult and peace, the darkness and the light
Were all like workings of one mind, the features
Of the same face, blossoms upon one tree,
570   Characters° of the great Apocalyps,   *signs, letters*
The types and symbols of Eternity,
Of first and last, and midst, and without end.[4]
    That night our lodging was an Alpine House,
An Inn or Hospital, as they are named,
575   Standing in that same valley by itself
And close upon the confluence of two streams,
A dreary Mansion, large beyond all need,
With high and spacious rooms, deafen'd and stunn'd
By noise of waters, making innocent Sleep
580   Lie melancholy among weary bones.[5]
    Uprisen betimes, our journey we renew'd
Led by the Stream, ere noon-day magnified
Into a lordly River, broad and deep,
Dimpling along in silent majesty,
585   With mountains for its neighbours, and in view
Of distant mountains and their snowy tops,
And thus proceeding to Locarno's Lake,
Fit resting-place for such a Visitant.
—Locarno, spreading out in width like Heaven,
590   And Como, thou a treasure by the earth
Kept to itself, a darling bosom'd up
In Abyssinian[6] privacy, I spake
Of thee, thy chesnut woods, and garden plots
Of Indian corn tended by dark-eyed Maids,
595   Thy lofty steeps, and path-ways roof'd with vines
Winding from house to house, from town to town,
Sole link that binds them to each other, walks
League after league, and cloistral avenues
Where silence is, if music be not there:
600   While yet a Youth, undisciplined in Verse,
Through fond ambition of my heart, I told
Your praises; nor can I approach you now,
Ungreeted by a more melodious Song,
Where tones of learned Art and Nature mix'd

---

4. Milton's terms for God (*Paradise Lost* 5.165), echoing God's self-description in Revelation (the Apocalypse) as "Alpha and Omega, the beginning and the ending"—the first and last letters of the Greek alphabet. "Types" are foreshadowings and prefigurations of God's plans.
5. King-killer Macbeth laments the loss of "innocent sleep" (*Macbeth* 2.2.35).
6. Abyssinia was a legendary location of Paradise.

605   May frame enduring language. Like a breeze
           Or sunbeam over your domain I pass'd
           In motion without pause; but Ye have left
           Your beauty with me, an impassion'd sight
           Of colours and of forms, whose power is sweet
610   And gracious, almost might I dare to say,
           As virtue is, or goodness, sweet as love
           Or the remembrance of a noble deed,
           Or gentlest visitations of pure thought
           When God, the Giver of all joy, is thank'd
615   Religiously, in silent blessedness,
           Sweet as this last itself, for such it is.
               Through those delightful pathways we advanced
           Two days, and still in presence of the Lake,
           Which, winding up among the Alps, now changed
620   Slowly its lovely countenance, and put on
           A sterner character. The second night,
           In eagerness, and by report misled
           Of those Italian Clocks that speak the time
           In fashion different from ours, we rose
625   By moonshine, doubting not that day was near,
           And that, meanwhile, coasting the Water's edge,
           As hitherto, and with as plain a track
           To be our guide, we might behold the scene
           In its most deep repose.—We left the Town
630   Of Gravedona with this hope; but soon
           Were lost, bewilder'd among woods immense,
           Where, having wander'd for a while, we stopp'd
           And on a rock sate down, to wait for day.
           An open place it was, and overlook'd
635   From high the sullen water underneath,
           On which a dull red image of the moon
           Lay bedded, changing oftentimes its form
           Like an uneasy snake: long time we sate,
           For scarcely more than one hour of the night,
640   Such was our error, had been gone, when we
           Renew'd our journey. On the rock we lay,
           And wish'd to sleep but could not for the stings
           Of insects, which with noise like that of noon
           Fill'd all the woods: the cry of unknown birds,
645   The mountains, more by darkness visible[7]
           And their own size than any outward light,
           The breathless wilderness of clouds, the clock
           That told with unintelligible voice
           The widely-parted hours, the noise of streams
650   And sometimes rustling motions nigh at hand
           Which did not leave us free from personal fear,

---

7. Milton's description of Hell (*Paradise Lost* 1.61ff.) resonates throughout this passage.

And lastly the withdrawing Moon, that set
Before us while she yet was high in heaven,
These were our food; and such a summer night
655 Did to that pair of golden days succeed,
With now and then a doze and snatch of sleep,
On Como's Banks, the same delicious Lake.

from Book Ninth. Residence in France[1]
[REVOLUTION, ROYALISTS, AND PATRIOTS]

        day by day the roads,
(While I consorted with these Royalists)
Were crowded with the bravest Youth of France
270 And all the promptest of her Spirits, link'd
In gallant Soldiership, and posting on
To meet the War, upon her Frontier Bounds.[2]
Yet at this very moment do tears start
Into mine eyes; I do not say I weep,
275 I wept not then, but tears have dimm'd my sight
In memory of the farewells of that time,
Domestic severings, female fortitude
At dearest separation, patriot love[3]
And self-devotion,° and terrestrial hope   *self-devoting, self-dooming*
280 Encouraged with a martyr's confidence;
Even files of Strangers merely, seen but once,
And for a moment, men from far with sound
Of music, martial tunes, and banners spread
Entering the City, here and there a face
285 Or person singled out among the rest,
Yet still a stranger and beloved as such,
Even by these passing spectacles my heart
Was oftentimes uplifted, and they seem'd
Like arguments from Heaven that 'twas a cause
290 Good, and which no one could stand up against
Who was not lost, abandon'd, selfish, proud,
Mean, miserable, wilfully depraved,
Hater perverse of equity and truth.
    Among that Band of Officers was one
295 Already hinted at,[4] of other mold,
A Patriot, thence rejected by the rest
And with an oriental loathing spurn'd,
As of a different Cast.° A meeker Man   *caste*
Than this lived never, or a more benign,

---

1. After four months in London in 1791, Wordsworth returned to France. He had an affair with Annette Vallon,
whom he left pregnant when he returned to England in
December 1792, sensing the peril for an Englishman as
the Reign of Terror spread.
2. France declared war on Austria in April 1792.

3. Royalists as well as Republicans regarded themselves
as patriots.
4. Michel Beaupuy (1755–1796), born into the nobility
but devoted to the ideals of the new Republic, was a powerful influence on young Wordsworth.

300   Meek though enthusiastic to the height
        Of highest expectation. Injuries
        Made him more gracious, and his nature then
        Did breathe its sweetness out most sensibly°   *perceptibly*
        As aromatic flowers on Alpine turf
305   When foot hath crush'd them. He thro' the events
        Of that great change wander'd in perfect faith,
        As through a Book, an old Romance or Tale
        Of Fairy, or some dream of actions wrought
        Behind the summer clouds. By birth he rank'd
310   With the most noble, but unto the poor
        Among mankind he was in service bound
        As by some tie invisible, oaths profess'd
        To a religious Order. Man he lov'd
        As man; and to the mean° and the obscure   *humble*
315   And all the homely in their homely works
        Transferr'd a courtesy which had no air
        Of condescension; but did rather seem
        A passion and a gallantry, like that
        Which he, a Soldier, in his idler day
320   Had payed to Woman; somewhat vain he was,
        Or seem'd so, yet it was not vanity
        But fondness, and a kind of radiant joy
        That cover'd him about when he was bent
        On works of love or freedom, or revolved
325   Complacently° the progress of a cause   *with pleasure*
        Whereof he was a part; yet this was meek
        And placid, and took nothing from the Man
        That was delightful: oft in solitude
        With him did I discourse about the end°   *aims*
330   Of civil government, and its wisest forms,
        Of ancient prejudice, and charter'd rights,
        Allegiance, faith, and laws by time matured;
        Custom and habit, novelty and change,
        Of self-respect and virtue in the Few
335   For patrimonial honour set apart,
        And ignorance in the labouring Multitude.

                * * * And when we chanced[5]
        One day to meet a hunger-bitten Girl
        Who crept along, fitting her languid self
        Unto a Heifer's motion, by a cord
515   Tied to her arm, and picking thus from the lane
        Its sustenance, while the Girl with her two hands
        Was busy knitting, in a heartless° mood   *disheartened*
        Of solitude, and at the sight my Friend
        In agitation said, "'Tis against that

5. By this time, Beaupuy had become an officer in the army of the Republic. He died in battle in 1796.

520 Which we are fighting," I with him believed
Devoutly that a spirit was abroad
Which could not be withstood, that poverty,
At least like this, would in a little time
Be found no more, that we should see the earth
525 Unthwarted in her wish to recompense
The industrious and the lowly Child of Toil,
All institutes for ever blotted out
That legalized exclusion, empty pomp
Abolish'd, sensual state and cruel power
530 Whether by edict of the one or few,
And finally, as sum and crown of all,
Should see the People having a strong hand
In making their own Laws, whence better days
To all mankind. * * *

from Book Tenth. Residence in France and French Revolution

[THE REIGN OF TERROR. CONFUSION. RETURN TO ENGLAND]

It was a beautiful and silent day
That overspread the countenance of earth,
Then fading, with unusual quietness
When from the Loire I parted, and through scenes
5 Of vineyard, orchard, meadow-ground and tilth,°   *tilled land*
Calm waters, gleams of sun, and breathless trees
Towards the fierce Metropolis turn'd my steps
Their homeward way to England. From his Throne
The King had fallen;[1] the congregated Host,
10 Dire cloud upon the front of which was written
The tender mercies of the dismal wind
That bore it, on the Plains of Liberty
Had burst innocuously:—say more, the swarm
That came elate and jocund, like a Band
15 Of Eastern Hunters, to enfold in ring
Narrowing itself by moments and reduce
To the last punctual spot of their despair
A race of victims, so they deem'd, themselves
Had shrunk from sight of their own task, and fled
20 In terror; desolation and dismay
Remain'd for them whose fancies had grown rank
With evil expectations, confidence
And perfect triumph to the better cause.
The State, as if to stamp the final seal
25 On her security, and to the world
Shew what she was, a high and fearless soul,
Or rather in a spirit of thanks to those

---

1. Louis XVI was imprisoned in August 1792, and the invading armies of Austria and Prussia were defeated by the French at Valmy on 20 September 1792, a month before Wordsworth returned from Orleans to Paris.

Who had stirr'd up her slackening faculties
To new transition, had assumed with joy
30   The body and the venerable name
Of a Republic:[2] lamentable crimes
'Tis true had gone before this hour, the work
Of massacre in which the senseless sword
Was pray'd to as a judge; but these were past,
35   Earth free from them for ever, as was thought,
Ephemeral monsters, to be seen but once,
Things that could only shew themselves and die.
      This was the time in which enflam'd with hope,
To Paris I return'd. Again I rang'd,
40   More eagerly than I had done before,
Through the wide City and in progress pass'd
The Prison where the unhappy Monarch lay
Associate with his Children and his Wife
In bondage; and the Palace lately storm'd
45   With roar of canon, and a numerous Host.
I cross'd, (a blank and empty area then)
The Square of the Carousel, few weeks back
Heap'd up with dead and dying,[3] upon these
And other sights looking as doth a man
50   Upon a volume whose contents he knows
Are memorable, but from him lock'd up,
Being written in a tongue he cannot read;
So that he questions the mute leaves with pain
And half upbraids their silence. But that night
55   When on my bed I lay I was most mov'd
And felt most deeply in what world I was;
My room was high and lonely, near the roof
Of a large Mansion° or Hotel, a spot   *townhouse*
That would have pleas'd me in more quiet times
60   Nor was it wholly without pleasure then.
With unextinguish'd taper I kept watch,
Reading at intervals; the fear gone by
Press'd on me almost like a fear to come;
I thought of those September Massacres,
65   Divided from me by a little month,[4]
And felt and touch'd them, a substantial dread;
The rest was conjured up from tragic fictions
And mournful Calendars° of true history,   *records*
Remembrances and dim admonishments.
70   "The horse is taught his manage° and the wind   *paces*

2. On 22 September 1792.
3. The royal palace had been stormed by a mob in August, with over a thousand lives lost; their bodies were cremated in the square in front of the palace.

4. Between September 2 and 7, Robespierre's newly powerful radical faction organized the massacres of 3,000 prisoners. Wordsworth echoes Hamlet's anger at his mother's betrayal of his recently deceased father (*Hamlet* 1.2.147).

Of heaven wheels round and treads in his own steps,[5]
Year follows year, the tide returns again,
Day follows day, all things have second birth;
The earthquake is not satisfied at once."
75 And in such way I wrought upon myself
Until I seem'd to hear a voice that cried
To the whole City, "Sleep no more."[6] To this
Add comments of a calmer mind, from which
I could not gather full security,
80 But at the best it seemed a place of fear,
Unfit for the repose of night,
Defenceless as a wood where tigers roam.
    Betimes next morning to the Palace Walk
Of Orleans I repair'd and entering there
85 Was greeted, among divers° other notes,   *various*
By voices of the Hawkers in the crowd
Bawling, *Denunciation of the crimes*
Of Maximilian Robespierre: the speech
Which in their hands they carried was the same
90 Which had been recently pronounced the day
When Robespierre, well-knowing for what mark
Some words of indirect reproof had been
Intended, rose in hardihood and dared
The Man who had an ill surmise of him
95 To bring his charge in openness: whereat
When a dead pause ensued and no one stirr'd,
In silence of all present, from his seat
Louvet walked singly through the avenue
And took his station in the Tribune,° saying   *rostrum*
100 "I, Robespierre, accuse thee"! 'Tis well known
What was the issue of that charge, and how
Louvet was left alone without support
Of his irresolute Friends:[7] but these are things
Of which I speak only as they were storm
105 Or sunshine to my individual mind,
No further. * * *

    Well might my wishes be intense, my thoughts
Strong and perturb'd, not doubting at that time,
Creed which ten shameful years[8] have not annull'd,
But that the virtue of one paramount mind
180 Would have abash'd those impious crests, have quell'd

---

5. The National Convention of France now met at a former riding school near the Tuileries. The quotation is from Shakespeare's *As You Like it* (1.1.11-12).
6. Macbeth's guilty fantasy after he has murdered his king: "Methought I heard a voice cry 'Sleep no more!'" (*Macbeth* 2.2.35).

7. In the National Convention, on 29 October 1792, moderate Girondist J. B. Louvet de Couvray accused Robespierre of tyranny. The phrase "walked singly" in line 98 evokes the solitary resistance of archangel Abdiel to Satan's revolt against God (*Paradise Lost* 5.877ff.).
8. Since 1793.

Outrage and bloody power, and in despite
Of what the People were through ignorance
And immaturity, and, in the teeth
Of desperate opposition from without,
185   Have clear'd a passage for just government,
And left a solid birth-right to the State,
Redeem'd according to example given
By ancient Lawgivers.
              In this frame of mind
Reluctantly to England I return'd,[9]
190   Compell'd by nothing less than absolute want
Of funds for my support, else, well assured
That I both was and must be of small worth,
No better than an alien in the Land,
I doubtless should have made a common cause
195   With some who perish'd, haply° perish'd too,[1]   *perhaps*
A poor mistaken and bewilder'd offering,
Should to the breast of Nature have gone back
With all my resolutions, all my hopes,
A Poet only to myself, to Men
200   Useless, and even, beloved Friend, a soul
To thee unknown.[2]

from Book Eleventh. Imagination, How Impaired and Restored

[IMAGINATION RESTORED BY NATURE]

Long time hath Man's unhappiness and guilt
Detain'd us; with what dismal sights beset
For the outward view, and inwardly oppress'd
With sorrow, disappointment, vexing thoughts,
5   Confusion of the judgement, zeal decay'd
And lastly, utter loss of hope itself,
And things to hope for. Not with these began
Our Song; and not with these our Song must end:
Ye motions of delight that through the fields
10   Stir gently, breezes and soft airs that breathe
The breath of paradise, and find your way
To the recesses of the soul! Ye Brooks
Muttering along the stones, a busy noise
By day, a quiet one in silent night,
15   And you, Ye Groves, whose ministry it is
To interpose the covert of your shades,
Even as a sleep, betwixt the heart of man
And the uneasy world, 'twixt man himself,
Not seldom, and his own unquiet heart,

9. Late in 1792.
1. Wordsworth's sympathies were with the moderate Girondins, almost all of whom were executed or committed suicide following Robespierre's rise to power.
2. Wordsworth met Coleridge in 1795. See page 129 for the next 25 lines.

20   Oh! that I had a music and a voice,
       Harmonious as your own, that I might tell
       What ye have done for me. The morning shines,
       Nor heedeth Man's perverseness; Spring returns,
       I saw the Spring return when I was dead
25   To deeper hope, yet had I joy for her,
       And welcomed her benevolence, rejoiced
       In common with the Children of her Love,
       Plants, insects, beast in field, and bird in bower.
       So neither were complacency° nor peace   *satisfaction*
30   Nor tender yearnings wanting° for my good   *lacking*
       Through those distracted times; in Nature still
       Glorying, I found a counterpoise in her,
       Which, when the spirit of evil was at height
       Maintain'd for me a secret happiness;
35   Her I resorted to, and lov'd so much
       I seem'd to love as much as heretofore;
       And yet this passion, fervent as it was,
       Had suffer'd change; how could there fail to be
       Some change, if merely hence, that years of life
40   Were going on, and with them loss or gain
       Inevitable, sure alternative.
           This History, my Friend, hath chiefly told
       Of intellectual° power, from stage to stage   *mental and spiritual*
       Advancing, hand in hand with love and joy,
45   And of imagination teaching truth
       Until that natural graciousness of mind
       Gave way to over-pressure of the times
       And their disastrous issues. * * *

       ["SPOTS OF TIME." TWO MEMORIES FROM CHILDHOOD AND LATER REFLECTIONS][1]

       In truth, this degradation, howsoe'er
       Induced, effect in whatsoe'er degree
245   Of custom, that prepares such wantonness
       As makes the greatest things give way to least,
       Of any other cause which hath been named,
       Or, lastly, aggravated by the times,
       Which with their passionate sounds might often make
250   The milder minstrelsies of rural scenes
       Inaudible, was transient; I had felt
       Too forcibly, too early in my life
       Visitings of imaginative power,
       For this to last: I shook the habit off

---

1. This passage, which concludes Book 11, was drafted in 1799. Originally set early in part 1 of the *Two-Part Prelude* with other boyhood memories (boat-stealing, ice-skating, the drowned man), it argues that memory can restore power to the imagination. Transferring early memories to this late point in his autobiography, Wordsworth empowers them to enact what they describe—poetic power revivified through recollection.

255　　Entirely and for ever, and again
　　　In Nature's presence stood, as I stand now,
　　　A sensitive and a creative Soul.
　　　　　There are in our existence spots of time,
　　　Which with distinct preeminence retain
260　　A renovating Virtue,° whence, depress'd   *power*
　　　By false opinion and contentious thought,
　　　Or aught of heavier or more deadly weight
　　　In trivial occupations, and the round
　　　Of ordinary intercourse, our minds
265　　Are nourish'd, and invisibly repair'd,
　　　A virtue by which pleasure is enhanced
　　　That penetrates, enables us to mount
　　　When high, more high, and lifts us up when fallen.
　　　This efficacious spirit chiefly lurks
270　　Among those passages of life in which
　　　We have had deepest feeling that the mind
　　　Is lord and master, and that outward sense
　　　Is but the obedient servant of her will.
　　　Such moments, worthy of all gratitude,
275　　Are scatter'd every where, taking their date
　　　From our first childhood; in our childhood even
　　　Perhaps are most conspicuous. Life with me
　　　As far as memory can look back, is full
　　　Of this beneficent influence. At a time
280　　When scarcely (I was then not six years old)
　　　My hand could hold a bridle, with proud hopes
　　　I mounted, and we rode towards the hills:
　　　We were a pair of Horsemen; honest James[2]
　　　Was with me, my encourager and guide.
285　　We had not travell'd long ere some mischance
　　　Disjoin'd me from my Comrade, and through fear
　　　Dismounting, down the rough and stony Moor
　　　I led my Horse, and, stumbling on, at length
　　　Came to a bottom,° where in former times   *dell*
290　　A Murderer had been hung in iron chains.
　　　The Gibbet mast was moulder'd down, the bones
　　　And iron case were gone; but on the turf
　　　Hard by, soon after that fell deed was wrought
　　　Some unknown hand had carved the Murderer's name.
295　　The monumental writing was engraven
　　　In times long past, and still, from year to year,
　　　By superstition of the neighbourhood
　　　The grass is clear'd away; and to this hour
　　　The letters are all fresh and visible.
300　　Faltering, and ignorant where I was, at length
　　　I chanced to espy those characters inscribed

2. 1850] "an ancient servant of my father's house."

On the green sod: forthwith I left the spot
And, reascending the bare Common,° saw   *field*
A naked Pool that lay beneath the hills,
305   The Beacon on the summit, and more near
A Girl who bore a Pitcher on her head
And seem'd with difficult steps to force her way
Against the blowing wind. It was, in truth,
An ordinary sight; but I should need
310   Colours and words that are unknown to man
To paint the visionary dreariness
Which, while I look'd all round for my lost Guide,
Did at that time invest the naked Pool,
The Beacon on the lonely Eminence,
315   The Woman, and her garments vex'd and toss'd
By the strong wind. When in a blessed season[3]
With those two dear Ones,[4] to my heart so dear,
When in the blessed time of early love,
Long afterwards, I roam'd about
320   In daily presence of this very scene;
Upon the naked pool and dreary crags,
And on the melancholy Beacon, fell
The spirit of pleasure, and youth's golden gleam;
And think ye not with radiance more divine
325   From these remembrances, and from the power
They left behind? So feeling comes in aid
Of feeling, and diversity of strength
Attends us, if but once we have been strong.
Oh! mystery of Man, from what a depth
330   Proceed thy honours! I am lost, but see
In simple childhood something of the base
On which thy greatness stands, but this I feel,
That from thyself it is that thou must give,
Else never canst receive. The days gone by
335   Come back upon me from the dawn almost
Of life: the hiding-places of my power
Seem open; I approach, and then they close;[5]
I see by glimpses now; when age comes on
May scarcely see at all, and I would give,
340   While yet we may, as far as words can give,
A substance and a life to what I feel:
I would enshrine the spirit of the past
For future restoration. Yet another
Of these to me affecting incidents
With which we will conclude.

3. Before he left for France in 1802. The verse from here to the end of the paragraph was drafted in 1804, just after he completed the "Intimations" Ode.

4. His sister and his fiancée Mary Hutchinson.

5. 1850] "I would approach them, but they close" (12.280).

345   One Christmas-time,
      The day before the Holidays began,
      Feverish, and tired, and restless, I went forth
      Into the fields, impatient for the sight
      Of those two Horses which should bear us home,
350   My Brothers and myself.[6] There was a Crag,
      An Eminence, which from the meeting point
      Of two high-ways ascending, overlook'd
      At least a long half-mile of those two roads,
      By each of which the expected Steeds might come,
355   The choice uncertain. Thither I repair'd,
      Up to the highest summit: 'twas a day
      Stormy, and rough and wild, and on the grass
      I sate, half shelter'd by a naked wall:
      Upon my right hand was a single sheep,
360   A whistling hawthorn on my left, and there
      With those Companions at my side, I watch'd,
      Straining my eyes intensely, as the mist
      Gave intermitting prospect of the wood
      And plain beneath. Ere I to School return'd
365   That dreary time, ere I had been ten days
      A Dweller in my Father's House, he died
      And I and my two Brothers, Orphans then,
      Followed his Body to the Grave.[7] The event
      With all the sorrow which it brought appear'd
370   A chastisement; and when I call'd to mind
      That day so lately pass'd, when from the crag
      I look'd in such anxiety of hope,
      With trite reflections of morality,
      Yet in the deepest passion, I bow'd low
375   To God, who thus corrected my desires;
      And afterwards, the wind and sleety rain
      And all the business of the elements,
      The single sheep, and the one blasted tree,
      And the bleak music of that old stone wall,
380   The noise of wood and water, and the mist
      Which on the line of each of those two Roads
      Advanced in such indisputable shapes,[8]
      All these were spectacles and sounds to which
      I often would repair, and thence would drink
385   As at a fountain: and I do not doubt
      That in this later time, when storm and rain
      Beat on my roof at midnight, or by day
      When I am in the woods, unknown to me

---

6. December 1783; they were away from home at Hawkshead Grammar School.
7. Wordsworth's father died on 30 December 1783; his
mother had died five years earlier.

8. Hamlet cries to his father's ghost: "Thou com'st in such
a questionable shape / That I will speak to thee" (*Hamlet*
1.4.43–44).

The workings of my spirit thence are brought.
390   Thou wilt not languish here, O Friend! for whom
I travel in these dim uncertain ways;
Thou wilt assist me as a pilgrim gone
In quest of highest truth. Behold me then
Once more in Nature's presence, thus restored
395   Or otherwise, and strengthen'd once again
(With memory left of what had been escaped)
To habits of devoutest sympathy.

"I travell'd among unknown Men"[1]

I travell'd among unknown Men,
    In Lands beyond the Sea;
Nor England! did I know till then
    What love I bore to thee.

5   'Tis past, that melancholy dream!
    Nor will I quit thy shore
A second time; for still I seem
    To love thee more and more.

Among thy mountains did I feel
10   The joy of my desire;
And She I cherish'd turn'd her wheel°   *spinning wheel*
    Beside an English fire.

Thy mornings shew'd—thy nights conceal'd
    The bowers where Lucy play'd;
15   And thine is, too, the last green field
    Which Lucy's eyes survey'd!

1801   1807

Resolution and Independence[1]

There was a roaring in the wind all night;
The rain came heavily and fell in floods;
But now the sun is rising calm and bright;
The birds are singing in the distant woods;
5   Over his own sweet voice the Stock-dove broods;[2]
The Jay makes answers as the Magpie chatters;
And all the air is fill'd with pleasant noise of waters.

---

1. A kin of the "Lucy" poems of *Lyrical Ballads* (1800), this was intended for the 1802 edition.
1. The working title was *The Leech-gatherer*. Leeches were used for blood-letting, the sucking out of supposedly bad blood. In 1843 Wordsworth recalled, "This old Man I met a few hundred yards from my cottage [in Grasmere]; and the account of him is taken from his own mouth. I was in the state of feeling described in the beginning of the poem" [I.F.]. See Dorothy Wordsworth's journal, 3 October 1800 (page 287).

2. The stock-dove is said to *coo*, a sound well imitating the note of the bird; but by the intervention of the metaphor *broods*, the affections are called in by the imagination to assist in marking the manner in which the bird reiterates and prolongs her soft note, as if herself delighting to listen to it, and participating of a still and quiet satisfaction, like that which may be supposed inseparable from the continuous process of incubation [Wordsworth, Preface to 1815 *Poems*].

All things that love the sun are out of doors;
The sky rejoices in the morning's birth;
10   The grass is bright with rain-drops; on the moors
The Hare is running races in her mirth;
And with her feet she from the plashy earth
Raises a mist, which, glittering in the sun,
Runs with her all the way, wherever she doth run.

15   I was a Traveller then upon the moor;
I saw the Hare that rac'd about with joy;
I heard the woods, and distant waters roar;
Or heard them not, as happy as a Boy:
The pleasant season did my heart employ:
20   My old remembrances went from me wholly;
And all the ways of men, so vain and melancholy.

But, as it sometimes chanceth, from the might
Of joy in minds that can no farther go,
As high as we have mounted in delight
25   In our dejection do we sink as low;
To me that morning did it happen so;
And fears, and fancies, thick upon me came;
Dim sadness, and blind thoughts I knew not nor could name.

I heard the Sky-lark singing in the sky;
30   And I bethought me of the playful Hare:
Even such a happy Child of earth am I;
Even as these blissful Creatures do I fare;
Far from the world I walk, and from all care;
But there may come another day to me,
35   Solitude, pain of heart, distress, and poverty.

My whole life I have liv'd in pleasant thought,
As if life's business were a summer mood;
As if all needful things would come unsought
To genial faith, still rich in genial good;
40   But how can He expect that others should
Build for him, sow for him, and at his call
Love him, who for himself will take no heed at all?

I thought of Chatterton, the marvellous Boy,
The sleepless Soul that perish'd in his pride;
45   Of Him who walk'd in glory and in joy
Behind his plough, along the mountain-side:[3]
By our own spirits are we deified:
We Poets in our youth begin in gladness;
But thereof comes in the end despondency and madness.

---

3. In 1770, the year Wordsworth was born, Thomas Chatterton (famed for pseudo-archaic poetry he attributed to a 15th-century monk) committed suicide by arsenic, amid dire poverty in a London garret; dead at 17, he became an icon of youthful suffering and neglected genius (see Shelley's *Adonais*, 379; Keats dedicated his longest poem, *Endymion*, to him). Robert Burns, the "plowman" poet, also died young, poor, and under-appreciated.

50   Now, whether it were by peculiar grace,
        A leading from above, a something given,
        Yet it befel, that, in this lonely place,
        When up and down my fancy thus was driven,
        And I with these untoward thoughts had striven,[4]
55   I saw a Man before me unawares:
        The oldest man he seem'd that ever wore grey hairs.

        My course I stopped as soon as I espied
        The Old Man in that naked wilderness:
        Close by a Pond, upon the further side,
60   He stood alone: a minute's space I guess
        I watch'd him, he continuing motionless:
        To the Pool's further margin then I drew;
        He being all the while me full in view.[5]

        As a huge stone is sometimes seen to lie
65   Couch'd on the bald top of an eminence;
        Wonder to all who do the same espy,
        By what means it could thither come, and whence;
        So that it seems a thing endued with sense:
        Like a Sea-beast crawl'd forth, which on a shelf
70   Of rock or sand reposeth, there to sun itself;[6]

        Such seem'd this Man, not all alive nor dead,
        Nor all asleep; in his extreme old age:
        His body was bent double, feet and head
        Coming together in their pilgrimage;
75   As if some dire constraint of pain, or rage
        Of sickness felt by him in times long past,
        A more than human weight upon his frame had cast.

        Himself he propp'd, limbs, body, and pale face,
        Upon a long grey Staff of shaven wood:
80   And, still as I drew near with gentle pace,
        Beside the little pond or moorish flood
        Motionless as a Cloud the Old Man stood,
        That heareth not the loud winds when they call;
        And moveth altogether, if it move at all.

85   At length, himself unsettling, he the Pond
        Stirred with his Staff, and fixedly did look
        Upon the muddy water, which he conn'd,°   *studied*
        As if he had been reading in a book:
        And now such freedom as I could I took;
90   And, drawing to his side, to him did say,
        "This morning gives us promise of a glorious day."

---

4. 1820] line 53 is deleted; new line 54: "Beside a Pool
bare to the eye of Heaven."
5. This stanza was omitted after 1820.
6. In these images, the conferring, the abstracting, and
the modifying powers of the Imagination, immediately
and mediately acting, are all brought into conjunction
[Wordsworth, 1815 Preface].

A gentle answer did the old Man make,
In courteous speech which forth he slowly drew:
And him with further words I thus bespake,
95   "What kind of work is that which you pursue?
This is a lonesome place for one like you."
He answer'd me with pleasure and surprize;
And there was, while he spake, a fire about his eyes.[7]

His words came feebly, from a feeble chest,
100   But each in solemn order follow'd each,
With something of a lofty utterance drest;
Choice word, and measured phrase; above the reach
Of ordinary men; a stately speech!
Such as grave Livers do in Scotland use,
105   Religious men, who give to God and man their dues.

He told me that he to this Pond had come
To gather Leeches, being old and poor:
Employment hazardous and wearisome![8]
And he had many hardships to endure:
110   From Pond to Pond he roam'd, from moor to moor;
Housing, with God's good help, by choice or chance:
And in this way he gain'd an honest maintenance.

The Old Man still stood talking by my side;
But now his voice to me was like a stream
115   Scarce heard; nor word from word could I divide;
And the whole Body of the man did seem
Like one whom I had met with in a dream;
Or like a Man from some far region sent,
To give me human strength, and strong admonishment.

120   My former thoughts return'd: the fear that kills;
And hope that is unwilling to be fed;
Cold, pain, and labour, and all fleshly ills;
And mighty Poets in their misery dead.
And now, not knowing what the Old Man had said,[9]
125   My question eagerly did I renew,
"How is it that you live, and what is it you do?"

He with a smile did then his words repeat;
And said, that, gathering Leeches, far and wide
He travelled; stirring thus above his feet
130   The waters of the Ponds where they abide.
"Once I could meet with them on every side;
But they have dwindled long by slow decay;
Yet still I persevere, and find them where I may."

---

7. 1820] "He answered, while a flash of mild surprise /
Broke from the sable orbs of his yet-vivid eyes."
8. Leech-gathering required wading bare-legged into
shallow water, stirring the surface to attract them, and
then plucking them off one's legs.
9. 1815] ——Perplexed, and longing to be comforted.

While he was talking thus, the lonely place,
135 The Old Man's shape, and speech, all troubled me:
In my mind's eye I seem'd to see him pace[1]
About the weary moors continually,
Wandering about alone and silently.
While I these thoughts within myself pursued,
140 He, having made a pause, the same discourse renewed.

And soon with this he other matter blended,
Chearfully uttered, with demeanour kind,
But stately in the main; and when he ended,
I could have laugh'd myself to scorn, to find
145 In that decrepit Man so firm a mind.
"God," said I, "be my help and stay secure;
I'll think of the Leech-gatherer on the lonely moor!"[2]

1802   1807

"I wandered lonely as a Cloud"[1]

I wandered lonely as a Cloud
That floats on high o'er Vales and Hills,
When all at once I saw a crowd,
A host, of dancing[2] Daffodils;
5 Along the Lake, beneath the trees,
Ten thousand dancing in the breeze.[3]

Continuous as the stars that shine
And twinkle on the milky way,
They stretched in never-ending line
10 Along the margin of a bay:
Ten thousand saw I at a glance,
Tossing their heads in sprightly dance.

The waves beside them danced; but they
Outdid the sparkling waves in glee:—
15 A Poet could not but be gay,
In such a laughing company:
I gaz'd—and gaz'd—but little thought
What wealth the show to me had brought:

For oft when on my couch I lie
20 In vacant or in pensive mood,

---

1. Hamlet sees his recently deceased father "in my mind's eye" (*Hamlet* 1.2.184–85).
2. Writing to a friend who was "displeased" by this "tedious" poem, Wordsworth exclaims, "I can *confidently* affirm, that, though I believe God has given me a strong imagination, I cannot conceive a figure more impressive than that of an old Man like this . . . travelling alone among the mountains and all lonely places, carrying with him his own fortitude, and the necessities which an unjust state of society has entailed upon him. . . . Everything is tedious when one does not read with the feelings of the Author. . . . It is in the character of the old man to tell his story in a manner in which an *impatient* reader must necessarily feel as tedious" (14 June 1802).
1. See Dorothy Wordsworth's *Grasmere Journal*, 15 April 1802, page 289.
2. Revised to "golden" in 1815.
3. In 1815, Wordsworth changed "Ten thousand" to "Fluttering" and added the next stanza. He also changed "laughing" (16) to "jocund."

They flash upon that inward eye
Which is the bliss of solitude;[4]
And then my heart with pleasure fills,
And dances with the Daffodils.

1804/1815   1807/1815

"My heart leaps up"

My heart leaps up when I behold
    A Rainbow in the sky:
So was it when my life began;
So is it now I am a Man;
5   So be it when I shall grow old,
    Or let me die!
The Child is Father of the Man;
And I could wish my days to be
Bound each to each by natural piety.

1802   1807

ODE: INTIMATIONS OF IMMORTALITY FROM RECOLLECTIONS OF EARLY CHILDHOOD

In a letter from 1814, Wordsworth remarks, "The poem rests entirely on two recollections of childhood, one that of a splendour in the objects of sense which is passed away, and the other an indisposition to bend to the law of death as applying to our particular case. A Reader who has not a vivid recollection of these feelings having existed in his mind cannot understand that Poem." In 1843 he recalled, "Two years at least passed between the writing of the four first stanzas and the remaining part. To the attentive and competent reader the whole sufficiently explains itself; but there may be no harm in adverting here to particular feelings or *experiences* of my own mind on which the structure of the poem partly rests. Nothing was more difficult for me in childhood than to admit the notion of death as a state applicable to my own being. I have said elsewhere—

                A simple child,
        That lightly draws its breath,
        And feels its life in every limb,
        What should it know of death?— [*We Are Seven*, 1–4]

But it was not so much from feelings of animal vivacity that my difficulty came as from a sense of the indomitableness of the Spirit within me. I used to brood over the stories of Enoch and Elijah, and almost to persuade myself that, whatever might become of others, I should be translated, in something of the same way, to heaven.[1] With a feeling congenial to this, I was often unable to think of external things as having external existence, and I communed with all that I saw as something not apart from, but inherent in, my own immaterial nature. Many times while going to school have I grasped at a wall or tree to recall myself from this abyss of idealism to the reality. At that time I was afraid of such processes. In later periods of life I have deplored, as we have all reason to do, a subjugation of an opposite character, and have rejoiced over the remembrances, as is expressed in the lines—

                Obstinate questionings
        Of sense and outward things,
        Fallings from us, vanishings; etc. [141–43]

---

4. Lines 21–22 were composed by Wordsworth's wife. He thought them the "two best lines," though Coleridge called them "mental bombast" (*Biographia Literaria*, ch. 22).

1. Old Testament prophets: Enoch did not die, but was taken directly to heaven (Genesis 5.24) and Elijah was carried to heaven in a chariot of fire (2 Kings 2.11).

To that dream-like vividness and splendour which invest objects of sight in childhood, every one, I believe, if he would look back, could bear testimony, and I need not dwell upon it here: but having in the poem regarded it as presumptive evidence of a prior state of existence, I think it right to protest against a conclusion, which has given pain to some good and pious persons, that I meant to inculcate such a belief. It is far too shadowy a notion to be recommended to faith, as more than an element in our instincts of immortality. But let us bear in mind that, though the idea is not advanced in revelation, there is nothing there to contradict it, and the fall of Man presents an analogy in its favour. Accordingly, a pre-existent state has entered into the popular creeds of many nations; and, among all persons acquainted with classic literature, is known as an ingredient in Platonic philosophy. Archimedes said that he could move the world if he had a point whereon to rest his machine. Who has not felt the same aspirations as regards the world of his own mind? Having to wield some of its elements when I was impelled to write this poem on the 'Immortality of the Soul,' I took hold of the notion of pre-existence as having sufficient foundation in humanity for authorising me to make for my purpose the best use of it I could as a Poet." [I. F.]

Ode
Intimations of Immortality from Recollections of Early Childhood[2]

The Child is Father of the Man;
And I could wish my days to be
Bound each to each by natural piety.

1

There was a time when meadow, grove, and stream,
The earth, and every common sight,
    To me did seem
    Apparelled in celestial light,
5   The glory and the freshness of a dream.
It is not now as it hath been of yore;—
    Turn wheresoe'er I may,
      By night or day,
The things which I have seen I now can see no more.

2

10   The Rainbow comes and goes,
    And lovely is the Rose,
    The Moon doth with delight
Look round her when the heavens are bare,
    Waters on a starry night
15   Are beautiful and fair;
    The sunshine is a glorious birth;
    But yet I know, where'er I go,
That there hath past away a glory from the earth.

3

Now, while the birds thus sing a joyous song,
20   And while the young lambs bound
    As to the tabor's° sound,   *small drum*

2. The ode published in 1807 was titled simply *Ode*, with an epigraph from Virgil's *Fourth* (Messianic) *Eclogue: Paulò majora canamus* (Let us sing of somewhat higher things). The long title and epigraph from *My heart leaps up* were added in 1815, and the Latin motto was dropped.

To me alone there came a thought of grief:
A timely utterance gave that thought relief,
    And I again am strong:
25 The cataracts blow their trumpets from the steep;
No more shall grief of mine the season wrong;
I hear the Echoes through the mountains throng,
The Winds come to me from the fields of sleep,
    And all the earth is gay;
30   Land and sea
    Give themselves up to jollity,
      And with the heart of May
Doth every Beast keep holiday;—
      Thou Child of Joy,
35 Shout round me, let me hear thy shouts, thou happy Shepherd-boy!

          4

Ye blessèd Creatures, I have heard the call
    Ye to each other make; I see
The heavens laugh with you in your jubilee;
    My heart is at your festival,
40   My head hath its coronal,°   *flower wreath*
The fulness of your bliss, I feel—I feel it all.
    Oh evil day! if I were sullen
    While Earth herself is adorning,
      This sweet May-morning,
45   And the Children are culling
      On every side,
In a thousand valleys far and wide,
Fresh flowers; while the sun shines warm,
And the Babe leaps up on his Mother's arm:—
50   I hear, I hear, with joy I hear!
    —But there's a Tree, of many, one,
A single Field which I have looked upon,
Both of them speak of something that is gone:
    The Pansy[3] at my feet
55   Doth the same tale repeat:
Whither is fled the visionary gleam?
Where is it now, the glory and the dream?[4]

          5

Our birth is but a sleep and a forgetting:
The Soul that rises with us, our life's Star,°   *the sun*
60   Hath had elsewhere its setting,
      And cometh from afar:
    Not in entire forgetfulness,
    And not in utter nakedness,

3. From the French *pensée*, "thought," this flower is its emblem.
4. The "Ubi sunt" trope of elegiac literary tradition. In 1802, Wordsworth stopped writing the ode at this point and did not resume for two years.

But trailing clouds of glory do we come[5]
65   From God, who is our home:
Heaven lies about us in our infancy!
Shades of the prison-house begin to close
        Upon the growing Boy,
But He beholds the light, and whence it flows,
70   He sees it in his joy;
The Youth, who daily farther from the east
        Must travel, still is Nature's Priest,
        And by the vision splendid
        Is on his way attended;
75   At length the Man perceives it die away,
And fade into the light of common day.

6

Earth fills her lap with pleasures of her own;
Yearnings she hath in her own natural kind,
And, even with something of a Mother's mind,
80   And no unworthy aim,
        The homely° Nurse doth all she can   *simple*
To make her Foster-child, her Inmate° Man,   *resident*
        Forget the glories he hath known,
And that imperial palace whence he came.

7

85   Behold the Child among his new-born blisses,
A six years' Darling of a pigmy size!
See, where 'mid work of his own hand he lies,
Fretted by sallies of his mother's kisses,
With light upon him from his father's eyes!
90   See, at his feet, some little plan or chart,
Some fragment from his dream of human life,
Shaped by himself with newly-learned art;
        A wedding or a festival,
        A mourning or a funeral;
95   And this hath now his heart,
        And unto this he frames his song:
        Then will he fit his tongue
To dialogues of business, love, or strife;
        But it will not be long
100   Ere this be thrown aside,
        And with new joy and pride
The little Actor cons another part;
Filling from time to time his "humorous stage"[6]
With all the Persons, down to palsied Age,

---

5. Revising a famous line in Thomas Gray's *Elegy Written in a Country Churchyard* (1751): "The paths of glory lead but to the grave."
6. A phrase from the dedicatory sonnet for Samuel Daniel's *Musophilus* (1599), referring to the different character types of Renaissance drama, defined by their "humors" (natural temperaments).

105   That Life brings with her in her equipage;
  As if his whole vocation
  Were endless imitation.

8

Thou, whose exterior semblance doth belie
  Thy Soul's immensity;
110   Thou best Philosopher, who yet dost keep
Thy heritage, thou Eye among the blind,
That, deaf and silent, read'st the eternal deep,
Haunted for ever by the eternal mind,—
  Mighty Prophet! Seer blest!
115   On whom those truths do rest,
Which we are toiling all our lives to find,
In darkness lost, the darkness of the grave;
Thou, over whom thy Immortality
Broods like the Day, a Master o'er a Slave,
120   A Presence which is not to be put by;
Thou little Child, yet glorious in the might
Of heaven-born freedom on thy being's height,
Why with such earnest pains dost thou provoke
The years to bring the inevitable yoke,
125   Thus blindly with thy blessedness at strife?
Full soon thy Soul shall have her earthly freight,
And custom lie upon thee with a weight,
Heavy as frost, and deep almost as life!

9

  O joy! that in our embers
130   Is something that doth live,
  That nature yet remembers
  What was so fugitive!
The thought of our past years in me doth breed
Perpetual benediction: not indeed
135   For that which is most worthy to be blest;
Delight and liberty, the simple creed
Of Childhood, whether busy or at rest,
With new-fledged hope still fluttering in his breast:—
  Not for these I raise
140   The song of thanks and praise;
  But for those obstinate questionings
  Of sense and outward things,
  Fallings from us, vanishings;
  Blank misgivings of a Creature
145   Moving about in worlds not realised,°   *seeming unreal*
High instincts before which our mortal Nature
Did tremble like a guilty Thing surprised:[7]

7. At dawn, the ghost of Hamlet's father "started, like a guilty thing / Upon a fearful summons" and vanished (*Hamlet* 1.1.148–49).

But for those first affections,
Those shadowy recollections,
150 Which, be they what they may,
Are yet the fountain light of all our day,
Are yet a master light of all our seeing;
Uphold us, cherish, and have power to make
Our noisy years seem moments in the being
155 Of the eternal Silence: truths that wake,
To perish never;
Which neither listlessness, nor mad endeavour,
Nor Man nor Boy,
Nor all that is at enmity with joy,
160 Can utterly abolish or destroy!
Hence in a season of calm weather
Though inland far we be,
Our Souls have sight of that immortal sea
Which brought us hither,
165 Can in a moment travel thither,
And see the Children sport upon the shore,
And hear the mighty waters rolling evermore.

10

Then sing, ye Birds, sing, sing a joyous song!
And let the young Lambs bound
170 As to the tabor's sound!
We in thought will join your throng,
Ye that pipe and ye that play,
Ye that through your hearts to-day
Feel the gladness of the May!
175 What though the radiance which was once so bright
Be now for ever taken from my sight,
Though nothing can bring back the hour
Of splendour in the grass, of glory in the flower;
We will grieve not, rather find
180 Strength in what remains behind;
In the primal sympathy
Which having been must ever be;
In the soothing thoughts that spring
Out of human suffering;
185 In the faith that looks through death,
In years that bring the philosophic mind.

11

And O, ye Fountains, Meadows, Hills, and Groves,
Forebode not any severing of our loves!
Yet in my heart of hearts I feel your might;
190 I only have relinquished one delight
To live beneath your more habitual sway.
I love the Brooks which down their channels fret,

Even more than when I tripped lightly as they;
The innocent brightness of a new-born Day

195   Is lovely yet;
The Clouds that gather round the setting sun
Do take a sober colouring from an eye
That hath kept watch o'er man's mortality;
Another race hath been, and other palms° are won.   *prizes*

200 Thanks to the human heart by which we live,
Thanks to its tenderness, its joys, and fears,
To me the meanest° flower that blows can give   *humblest*
Thoughts that do often lie too deep for tears.

1802–1804/1815   1807/1815

Surprized by joy

Surprized by joy—impatient as the Wind
I turned to share the transport—Oh! with whom
But thee, long buried in the silent Tomb,
That spot which no vicissitude can find?[1]

5 Love, faithful love, recalled thee to my mind—
But how could I forget thee? Through what power,
Even for the least division of an hour,
Have I been so beguiled as to be blind
To my most grievous loss!—That thought's return

10 Was the worst pang that sorrow ever bore,
Save one, one only, when I stood forlorn,
Knowing my heart's best treasure was no more;
That neither present time, nor years unborn
Could to my sight that heavenly face restore.

1812–1815   1815

Scorn not the Sonnet[1]

Scorn not the Sonnet; Critic, you have frowned,
Mindless of its just honors; with this key
Shakspeare unlocked his heart; the melody
Of this small lute gave ease to Petrarch's wound;

5 A thousand times this pipe did Tasso sound;
With it Camoëns soothed an exile's grief;
The Sonnet glittered a gay myrtle leaf
Amid the cypress with which Dante crowned
His visionary brow: a glow-worm lamp,

10 It cheered mild Spenser, called from Faëryland
To struggle through dark ways; and, when a damp

---

1. Daughter Catherine died in 1812 at age 3.
1. In this record of devotion to the form and its tradition, Wordsworth combats the regard of sonnet-writing as less mature than epic poetry or tragic drama. Because many women poets were writing sonnets, sonnet-writing could seem "feminine," as opposed to "masculine" epic. The sonnet cites a range of major Renaissance sonnet-writers.

Fell round the path of Milton, in his hand
The Thing became a trumpet; when he blew
Soul-animating strains—alas, too few!

1827   1827

+→ ⩢⧫⩥ →+

Dorothy Wordsworth
1771–1855

Dorothy Wordsworth would probably be surprised to see herself in our pages, for unlike just about everyone else here, she did not think of herself primarily as a writer, and she did not aspire to publication. Her brother William did put a few of her poems in his volumes (including *Address to a Child* and *Floating Island*), identified as "By my Sister"—an apt credit, for this was Dorothy's own chief self-identification. When friends urged her to publish her remarkable account of her community's response to a local tragedy (*George and Sarah Green*, 1808), she protested that she had written it only at her brother's urging and only as a local record; "I should detest the idea of setting myself as an Author," she said. Similar encouragement for her journals of her tours of Scotland and Europe was similarly rebuffed, Dorothy insisting that she had written only for family and friends. When she began her Grasmere journal, she told herself that she was writing to give William "pleasure."

Born in the Lake District of England in 1771, Dorothy Wordsworth lived happily there with her four brothers until 1778, when their mother died. Their father, who was often absent on business, felt unable to sustain the household and sent the boys away to school and Dorothy to live with a series of distant relatives, in situations ranging from happy to bleak. She saw her brothers rarely and especially missed William, with whom she was closest, less than two years his junior. Reunited in 1787, they longed to have a home together, and in 1795, with the advantage of William's legacy from a college friend, they were able to realize this dream. They first lived in southwest England, in Dorset, as a quasi-family with a friend's young son as their ward. Moving to Alfoxden in 1797 to be near Samuel Taylor Coleridge, they became acquainted with Charles and Mary Lamb and Robert Southey. During their summer tour of the Wye valley in 1798, William wrote *Tintern Abbey* with its homage to Dorothy's companionship and her continuing inspiration to him. They spent the next winter miserably in Goslar, Germany (following Coleridge there on a scheme to learn the language), and settled at the end of 1799 in Grasmere, in their beloved native Lake District, where they remained together for the rest of their lives.

Dorothy began her Grasmere journal in May 1800, just as William was beginning to court their childhood friend, Mary Hutchinson, and she left off at the beginning of 1803, a few months after Mary and William returned from their honeymoon. There was never any question about her remaining in the household: Mary married *them*. A beloved aunt to their children, Dorothy was really more a third parent. She not only shared the domestic labors but functioned for William as companion, encourager, sounding-board, secretary, and (along with Mary) perpetual transcriber of his drafts into fair-copy. In 1829 she was stricken by the first in a series of devastating illnesses, with relapses and new afflictions occurring over the next six years, each event wracking her with pain and leaving her further debilitated. By 1835 her temperament and mental acuity were also afflicted in a pre-senile dementia akin to Alzheimer's disease. Cared for with affection by her family, she lived a kind of invalid half-life, with lucid intervals, for the next twenty years, surviving her brother by five.

This demise is especially poignant, given the intelligence, sensitivity, and physical vitality with which she had impressed everyone. It was not until the end of the nineteenth century that her poems and journals were collected and published, and for a long time the journals were read chiefly for information about Coleridge, William, and the circumstances of the poems he wrote between 1798 and 1802. Placed alongside these poems, however, some of Dorothy's passages suggest that William may have been inspired as much by her language as by events and appearances in the external world; and recently Dorothy Wordsworth has been taken seriously as a writer in her own right. Her Grasmere journal is a fascinating chronicle of early nineteenth-century life in the Lake District—full of brilliantly detailed descriptions of nature (admired by Virginia Woolf), accounts of domestic life and household labors, precise observations of the people, the social textures and economic distresses of rural England. In the cast of characters that cross her pages—children, neighbors, local laborers, tinkers and itinerants, beggars and vagrants, abandoned wives and mothers, a leech-gatherer, discharged and often injured soldiers, sailors, and veterans—Dorothy Wordsworth captures, as much as her brother hoped his poetry would, the "language really used by men" (and women). In addition to journals, records of tours, numerous letters, and ceaseless secretarial work and manuscript transcription for William, Dorothy wrote about thirty poems. Composed sporadically from 1805 to 1840, these often allude to or converse with her brother's poetry, sometimes marking different investments of imagination, alternative views of the world they share, or a different sensibility—one less solitary and more social in orientation, less visionary than domestic in idiom, and more self-effacing and self-discrediting in character, especially about the vocation and practice of writing poetry.

A selection from Dorothy Wordsworth's journal appears in Perspectives: The Abolition of Slavery and the Slave Trade, page 119.

Grasmere—A Fragment

Peaceful our valley, fair and green,
And beautiful her cottages,
Each in its nook, its sheltered hold,
Or underneath its tuft of trees

5   Many and beautiful they are;
But there is *one* that I love best,
A lowly shed, in truth, it is,
A brother of the rest.

Yet when I sit on rock or hill,
10   Down looking on the valley fair,
That Cottage with its clustering trees
Summons my heart; it settles there.

Others there are whose small domain
Of fertile fields and hedgerows green
15   Might more seduce a wanderer's mind
To wish that *there* his home had been.

Such wish be his! I blame him not,
My fancies they perchance are wild
—I love that house because it is
20   The very Mountains' child.

Fields hath it of its own, green fields,
But they are rocky steep and bare;
Their fence is of the mountain stone,
And moss and lichen flourish there.

25   And when the storm comes from the North
It lingers near that pastoral spot,
And, piping through the mossy walls,
It seems delighted with its lot.

And let it take its own delight;
30   And let it range the pastures bare;
Until it reach that group of trees,
—It may not enter there!

A green unfading grove it is,
Skirted with many a lesser tree,
35   Hazel & holly, beech and oak,
A bright and flourishing company.

Precious the shelter of those trees;
They screen the cottage that I love;
The sunshine pierces to the roof,
40   And the tall pine-trees tower above.

When first I saw that dear abode,
It was a lovely winter's day:[1]
After a night of perilous storm
The west wind ruled with gentle sway;

45   A day so mild, it might have been
The first day of the gladsome spring;
The robins warbled, and I heard
One solitary throstle sing.

A Stranger, Grasmere, in thy Vale,
50   All faces then to me unknown,
I left my sole companion-friend
To wander out alone.

Lured by a little winding path,
I quitted soon the public road,
55   A smooth and tempting path it was,
By sheep and shepherds trod.[2]

Eastward, towards the lofty hills,
This pathway led me on
Until I reached a stately Rock,
60   With velvet moss o'ergrown.

1. Dorothy and William, her "sole companion-friend"   2. Compare the opening of William's *Michael*, page 214.
(51), moved to Grasmere just before Christmas 1799.

With russet oak and tufts of fern
Its top was richly garlanded;
Its sides adorned with eglantine
Bedropp'd with hips of glossy red.

65 There, too, in many a sheltered chink
The foxglove's broad leaves flourished fair,
And silver birch whose purple twigs
Bend to the softest breathing air.

Beneath that Rock my course I stayed,
70 And, looking to its summit high,
"Thou wear'st," said I, "a splendid garb,
Here winter keeps his revelry."

"Full long a dweller on the Plains,
I griev'd when summer days were gone;
75 No more I'll grieve; for Winter here
Hath pleasure gardens of his own.

What need of flowers? The splendid moss
Is gayer than an April mead;
More rich its hues of various green,
80 Orange, and gold, & glittering red."

—Beside that gay and lovely Rock
There came with merry voice
A foaming streamlet glancing by;
It seemed to say "Rejoice!"

85 My youthful wishes all fulfill'd,
Wishes matured by thoughtful choice,
I stood an Inmate° of this vale   *dweller*
How *could* I but rejoice?

Late 1805

Thoughts on My Sick-bed[1]

And has the remnant of my life
Been pilfered of this sunny Spring?
And have its own prelusive sounds
Touched in my heart no echoing string?

5   Ah! say not so—the hidden life
Couchant° within this feeble frame   *lying down*
Hath been enriched by kindred gifts,
That, undesired, unsought-for, came

With joyful heart in youthful days
10 When fresh each season in its Round

1. Written in spring 1832, by which time Dorothy was stricken with a series of debilitating illnesses.

I welcomed the earliest Celandine[2]
Glittering upon the mossy ground;

With busy eyes I pierced the lane
In quest of known and *unknown* things,
15   —The primrose a lamp on its fortress rock,
The silent butterfly spreading its wings,

The violet betrayed by its noiseless breath,
The daffodil dancing in the breeze,
The carolling thrush, on his naked perch,
20   Towering above the budding trees.[3]

Our cottage-hearth no longer our home,
Companions of Nature were we,
The Stirring, the Still, the Loquacious, the Mute—
To all we gave our sympathy.

25   Yet never in those careless days
When spring-time in rock, field, or bower
Was but a fountain of earthly hope
A promise of fruits & the *splendid* flower.[4]

No! then I never felt a bliss
30   That might with *that* compare
Which, piercing to my couch of rest,
Came on the vernal air.

When loving Friends an offering brought,
The first flowers of the year,
35   Culled from the precincts of our home,
From nooks to Memory dear.[5]

With some sad thoughts the work was done,[6]
Unprompted and unbidden,
But joy it brought to my *hidden* life,
40   To consciousness no longer hidden.

I felt a Power unfelt before,
Controlling weakness, languor, pain;
It bore me to the Terrace walk
I trod the Hills again;—

---

2. A resilient flower, treated by William in *The Small Celandine* (1804; 1807) as an emblem of inevitable old age.
3. A bouquet of references to William's poems: *The Primrose of the Rock* (c. 1831, a flower on the Grasmere-Rydal road); *To a Butterfly* ("Stay near me") and *To a Butterfly* ("I've watched you") (both 1802; 1807); *Song* ("She dwelt among th'untrodden ways") ("a violet by a mossy stone, half hidden from the eye"); *I wandered lonely as a cloud* ("golden daffodils . . . dancing in the breeze").
4. W. Wordsworth's "Intimations" Ode: "Though nothing can bring back the hour / Of splendour in the grass, of glory in the flower; / We will grieve not, rather find /

Strength in what remains behind" (177–80).
5. "Intimations" Ode: "The fulness of your bliss, I feel— I feel it all. / O evil day! if I were sullen / While Earth herself is adorning, / This sweet May-morning, / And the Children are culling / On every side, / In a thousand valleys far and wide, / Fresh flowers" (41–48).
6. W. Wordsworth's *Lines Written in Early Spring* ("I sate reclined, / In that sweet mood when pleasant thoughts / Bring sad thoughts to the mind") and *Three Years She Grew* ("Thus nature spake—The work was done—/ How soon my Lucy's race was run! / She died").

45   No prisoner in this lonely room,
       I *saw* the green Banks of the Wye,
       Recalling thy prophetic words,
       Bard, Brother, Friend from infancy![7]

       No need of motion, or of strength,[8]
50   Or even the breathing air:
       —I thought of Nature's loveliest scenes;
       And with Memory I was there.
1832

When Shall I Tread Your Garden Path?[1]

When shall I tread your garden path?
Or climb your sheltering hill?
When shall I wander, free as air,
And track the foaming rill?

5   A prisoner on my pillowed couch
       Five years in feebleness I've lain,
       Oh! shall I e'er with vigorous step
       Travel the hills again?

                              To Mr Carter DW
                              Novr 11—1835

Lines Written (Rather Say *Begun*) on the Morning of Sunday April 6th
The Third Approach of Spring-Time Since My Illness Began.
It Was a Morning of Surpassing Beauty.

The worship of this sabbath morn,
How sweetly it begins!
With the full choral hymn of birds
Mingles no sad lament for sins.

5   The air is clear, the sunshine bright.
       The dew-drops glitter on the trees;
       My eye beholds a perfect Rest,
       I hardly hear a stirring breeze.

       A robe of quiet overspreads
10   The living lake and verdant field;
       The very earth seems sanctified,
       Protected by a holy shield.

       The steed, now vagrant on the hill,
       Rejoices in this sacred day,

---

7. See *Tintern Abbey*, especially 111ff.
8. W. Wordsworth's *A slumber did my spirit seal* ("No motion has she now, no force").

1. Addressed to John Carter, William's assistant in the stamp office and their handyman for more than 40 years.

15 Forgetful of the plough—the goad—
    And, though subdued, is happy as the gay.

    A chastened call of bleating lambs
    Drops steadily from that lofty Steep;
    —I could believe this sabbath peace
20 Was felt even by the mother sheep.[1]

    Conscious that they are safe from man
    On this glad day of punctual rest,
    By God himself—his work being done—
    Pronounced the holiest and the best

25 'Tis but a fancy, a fond thought,
    To which a waking dream gave birth,
    Yet heavenly, in this brilliant Calm,
    —Yea *heavenly* is the spirit of earth—

    Nature attunes the pious heart
30 To gratitude and fervent love
    By visible stillne[ss] the chearful voice
    Of living things in budding trees & in the air above.

    Fit prelude are these lingering hours
    To man's appointed, holy task
35 Of prayer and social gratitude:
    They prompt our hearts in faith to ask,

    Ask humbly for the precious boon
    Of pious hope and fixed content
    And pardon, sought through trust in Him
40 Who died to save the Penitent.

    And now the chapel bell invites
    The Old, the Middle-aged, and Young
    To meet beneath those sacred walls,
    And give to pious thought a tongue

45 That simple bell of jingling tone
    To careless ears unmusical,
    Speaks to the Serious in a strain
    That might their wisest hours recal.

    Alas! my feet no more may join
50 The chearful sabbath train;
    But if I inwardly lament
    Soon may a will subdued all grief restrain.[2]

---

1. In another copy, Dorothy ends the poem here, adding this last stanza: "Thus have ye passed one gladsome hour / But [earnest?] youth exhausts its power / The weary limbs, the panting breast / The throbbing head / Plead piteously for rest."

2. In yet another copy, Dorothy writes *resigned* instead of *subdued*.

No prisoner am I on this couch
My mind is free to roam,
55   And leisure, peace, and loving Friends
Are the best treasures of an earthly home.

Such gifts are mine: then why deplore
The body's gentle slow decay,
A warning mercifully sent
60   To fix my hopes upon a surer stay?

from The Grasmere Journals

[HOME ALONE]

May 14 1800 [*Wednesday*]. Wm and John set off into Yorkshire[1] after dinner at 1/2
past 2 o'clock—cold pork in their pockets. I left them at the turning of the Low-
wood bay under the trees. My heart was so full that I could hardly speak to W when I
gave him a farewell kiss. I sate a long time upon a stone at the margin of the lake, &
after a flood of tears my heart was easier. The lake looked to me I knew not why dull
and melancholy, the weltering on the shores seemed a heavy sound. I walked as long
as I could amongst the stones of the shore. The wood rich in flowers. A beautiful yellow, palish yellow flower, that looked thick round & double, and smelt very sweet—
I supposed it was a ranunculus—Crowfoot, the grassy-leaved Rabbit-toothed white
flower, strawberries, Geranium—scentless violet, anemones two kinds, orchises,
primroses. The heckberry very beautiful. * * * Met a blind man, driving a very large
beautiful Bull & a cow—he walked with two sticks. Came home by Clappersgate.
The valley very green, many sweet views up to Rydale head when I could juggle away
the fine houses, but they disturbed me even more than when I have been happier—
one beautiful view of the Bridge, without Sir Michaels.[2] Sate down very often, tho' it
was cold. I resolved to write a journal of the time till W & J return, and I set about
keeping my resolve because I will not quarrel with myself, & because I shall give Wm
Pleasure by it when he comes home again. At Rydale a woman of the village, stout &
well dressed, begged a halfpenny—she had never she said done it before, but these
hard times—Arrived at home with a bad head-ach, set some slips of privett. The
evening cold had a fire—my face now flame-coloured. It is nine o'clock. I shall soon
go to bed. A young woman begged at the door—she had come from Manchester on
Sunday morn with two shillings & a slip of paper which she supposed a Bank note—
it was a cheat. She had buried her husband & three children within a year & a half—
all in one grave—burying very dear—paupers all put in one place—20 shillings paid
for as much ground as will bury a man—a stone to be put over it or the right will be
lost—11/6 each time the ground is opened.[3] Oh! that I had a letter from William!

Sunday [*18th.*] Went to church, slight showers, a cold air. The mountains from this
window look much greener & I think the valley is more green than ever. The corn begins to shew itself. The ashes are still bare. * * * A little girl from Coniston came to
beg. She had lain out all night—her step-mother had turned her out of doors.

1. William and younger brother John, who lived with
them at Dove Cottage in 1800; the trip through
Yorkshire was to visit childhood friend Mary Hutchinson, whom William would marry in October 1802.
2. Rydal Hall, the home of Sir Michael le Fleming; in
1813, the Wordsworth household would move to Rydal

Mount, the substantial residence next door, where they
lived the rest of their lives.
3. Eleven shillings, 6 pence; dear: expensive. William and
Dorothy lived modestly but comfortably on £130–140
a year.

[A Leech Gatherer]

3 October 1800. * * * Wm and I * * * met an old man almost double, he had on a coat thrown over his shoulders above his waistcoat & coat. Under this he carried a bundle and had an apron on and a night cap. His face was interesting. He had dark eyes & a long nose. John who afterwards met him at Wythburn took him for a Jew. He was of Scotch parents but had been born in the army. He had had a wife "& a good woman & it pleased God to bless us with ten children"—all these were dead but one of whom he had not heard for many years, a sailor—his trade was to gather leeches,[4] but now leeches are scarce & he had not strength for it—he lived by begging and was making his way to Carlisle where he should buy a few godly books to sell. He said leeches were very scarce partly owing to this dry season, but many years they have been scarce—he supposed it owing to their being much sought after, that they did not breed fast, & were of slow growth. Leeches were formerly 2/6 [per] 100; they are now 30/.[5] He had been hurt in driving a cart, his leg broke his body driven over his skull fractured—he felt no pain till he recovered from his first insensibility. It was then "late in the evening—when the light was just going away."

[A Woman Beggar]

Friday 27th [November 1801] Snow upon the ground thinly scattered. It snowed after we got up & then the sun shone & it was very warm though frosty—now the sun shines sweetly. A woman came who was travelling with her husband—he had been wounded & was going with her to live at Whitehaven. She had been at Ambleside[6] the night before, offered 4d[7] at the Cock for a bed—they sent her to one Harrison's where she and her husband had slept upon the hearth & bought a penny-worth of chips for a fire. Her husband was gone before very lame—"Aye" says she "I was once an officers wife I, as you see me now. My first husband married me at Appleby. I had 18£ a year for teaching a school & because I had no fortune his father turned him out of doors. I have been in the West Indies[8]—I lost the use of this Finger just before he died he came to me and said he must bid farewell to his dear children and me. I had a muslin gown on like yours—I seized hold of his coat as he went from me & slipped the joint of my finger. He was shot directly.[9] I came to London & married this man. He was clerk to Judge Chambray, *that man*, that man that's going on the Road now. If he, Judge Chambray, had been at Kendal he would [have] given us a guinea or two & made nought of it, for he is very generous."[1]

[An Old Soldier]

Tuesday 22nd [December 1801] * * * Wm & I went to Rydale for letters, the road was covered with dirty snow, rough & rather slippery. * * * As we came up the White

---

4. Cf. the poem William wrote 18 months later, first titled *The Leech Gatherer*, then published as *Resolution and Independence* in 1807. Leeches were used medicinally, to suck out supposedly "bad blood."

5. Two shillings, 6 pence per 100 leeches; their value had now risen twelvefold to 30 shillings.

6. A village three miles from Grasmere; the Cock is a small inn.

7. Four pence.

8. Where the plantation economy involves slave labor; her husband may have been assigned with the army there to keep order after numerous slave uprisings and revolts.

9. Perhaps for desertion.

1. At the time, Judge Chambré resided at his home, Abbot Hall, in Kendal, a city about 20 miles away. A guinea is £1, 1 shilling.

Moss[2] we met an old man, who I saw was a beggar by his two bags hanging over his shoulder, but from a half laziness, half indifference & a wanting to try him if he would speak I let him pass. He said nothing, & my heart smote me. I turned back and said You are begging? "Ay," says he—I gave him a halfpenny. William, judging from his appearance joined in, "I suppose you were a sailor?" "Ay," he replied, "I have been 57 years at sea, 12 of them on board a man-of-war under Sir Hugh Palmer." "Why have you not a pension?" "I have no pension, but I could have got into Greenwich hospital[3] but all my officers are dead." He was 75 years of age, had a freshish colour in his cheeks, grey hair, a decent hat with a binding round the edge, the hat worn brown & glossy, his shoes were small thin shoes low in the quarters, pretty good—they had belonged to a gentleman. His coat was blue, frock shaped coming over his thighs, it had been joined up at the seams behind with paler blue to let it out, & there were three Bell-shaped patches of darker blue behind where the Buttons had been. His breeches were either of fustian[4] or grey cloth, with strings hanging down, whole & tight; he had a checked shirt on, & a small coloured hand-kerchief tyed round his neck. His bags were hung over each shoulder & lay on each side of him, below his breast. One was brownish & of coarse stuff, the other was white with meal on the outside, & his blue waistcoat was whitened with meal.[5] In the coarse bag I guessed he put his scraps of meat &c. He walked with a slender stick decently stout, but his legs bowed outwards. We overtook old Fleming at Rydale,[6] leading his little Dutchman-like grandchild along the slippery road. The same pace seemed to be natural to them both, the old man & the little child, and they went hand in hand, the grandfather cautious, yet looking proud of his charge. He had two patches of new cloth at the shoulder blades of his faded claret coloured coat, like eyes at each shoulder, not worn elsewhere. * * * We stopped to look at the Stone seat at the top of the Hill. There was a white cushion upon it round at the edge like a cushion & the Rock behind looked soft as velvet, of a vivid green & so tempting! The snow too looked as soft as a down cushion. A young Foxglove, like a Star in the Centre. There were a few green lichens about it & a few withered Brackens of Fern here & there & upon the ground near. All else was a thick snow—no foot mark to it, not the foot of a sheep.—

[The Grasmere Mailman]

Monday Morning 8th February 1802. It was very windy & rained very hard all the morn-ing. William worked at his poem & I read a little in Lessing and the Grammar.[7] A chaise came past to fetch Ellis the Carrier who had hurt his head. After dinner (i.e. we set off at about 1/2 past 4) we went towards Rydale[8] for letters. It was a cold "*Cauld Clash*"—the Rain had been so cold that it hardly melted the snow. We stopped at Park's to get some straw in William's shoes. The young mother was sitting by a bright wood fire with her youngest child upon her lap & the other two sate on each side of the chimney. The light of the fire made them a beautiful sight, with their innocent counte-nances, their rosy cheeks & glossy curling hair. We sate & talked about poor Ellis, and

2. White Moss Common, a field near Grasmere Lake.
3. For seamen.
4. Sturdy cotton or linen.
5. Flour, part of his provisions.
6. Sir Michael le Fleming of Rydal Hall.
7. William's poem is *The Pedlar*, abandoned as an

independent piece and later incorporated into the first part of Book 1 of his long poem, *The Excursion* (1814). Lessing (1729–1781) is a German dramatist, art theorist, and critic; "the Grammar" is most likely a German gram-mar (Dorothy had learned German in Germany).
8. About a mile away.

our journey over the Hawes. It had been reported that we came over in the night. Willy told us of 3 men who were once lost in crossing that way in the night, they had carried a lantern with them—the lantern went out at the Tarn[9] & they all perished. Willy had seen their cloaks drying at the public house in Patterdale[1] the day before their funeral. We walked on very wet through the clashy cold roads in bad spirits at the idea of having to go as far as Rydale, but before we had come again to the shore of the Lake, we met our patient, bow-bent Friend with his little wooden box at his Back. "Where are you going?" said he. "To Rydale for letters.—I have two for you in my Box." We lifted up the lid & there they lay. Poor Fellow, he straddled & pushed on with all his might but we soon out-stripped him far away when we had turned back with our letters. We were very thankful that we had not to go on, for we should have been sadly tired. In thinking of this I could not help comparing lots with him! He goes at that slow pace every morning, & after having wrought a hard days work returns at night, however weary he may be, takes it all quietly, & though perhaps he neither feels thankfulness, nor pleasure when he eats his supper, & has no luxury to look forward to but falling asleep in bed, yet I daresay he neither murmurs nor thinks it hard. He seems mechanized to labour.

[A Vision of the Moon]

[18 March 1802] * * * As we came along Ambleside vale in the twilight—it was a grave evening—there was something in the air that compelled me to serious thought—the hills were large, closed in by the sky. It was nearly dark * * * night was come on & the moon was overcast. But as I climbed Moss the moon came out from behind a Mountain Mass of Black clouds—O the unutterable darkness of the sky & the Earth below the Moon! & the glorious brightness of the moon itself! There was a vivid sparkling streak of light at this end of Rydale water but the rest was very dark & Loughrigg fell and Silver How were white & bright as if they were covered with hoar frost.[2] The moon retired again & appeared & disappeared several times before I reached home. Once there was no moonlight to be seen but upon the Island house & the promontory of the Island where it stands, "That needs must be a holy place" &c—&c.[3] I had many many exquisite feelings and when I saw this lowly Building in the waters among the dark & lofty hills, with that bright soft light upon it—it made me more than half a poet. I was tired when I reached home. I could not sit down to reading & tried to write verses but alas! I gave up expecting William & went soon to bed. Fletcher's carts came home late.[4]

[A Field of Daffodils]

Thursday 15th. [April 1802] * * * When we were in the woods beyond Gowbarrow[5] park we saw a few daffodils close to the water side, we fancied that the lake had floated the seeds ashore & that the little colony had so sprung up—But as we went along there were more & yet more & at last under the boughs of the trees, we saw

9. Mountain lake.
1. An inn in the village several miles away, reached by a treacherous pass over the high mountains.
2. White Moss Common, Rydale water (a lake nearby Grasmere Lake and the Common), and two peaks to the south of these lakes, Loughrigg and Silver How.

3. Perhaps recalling an early draft of Coleridge's Kubla Khan, line 14, or William's feeling in Home at Grasmere that "dwellers in this holy place / Must need themselves be hallow'd" (366–67).
4. William's ride, via the mail carrier.
5. Several miles away near Patterdale on Ullswater.

that there was a long belt of them along the shore, about the breadth of a country turnpike road.[6] I never saw daffodils so beautiful they grew among the mossy stones about & about them, some rested their heads upon these stones as on a pillow for weariness & the rest tossed & reeled & danced & seemed as if they verily laughed with the wind that blew upon them over the Lake, they looked so gay ever glancing ever changing. This wind blew directly over the lake to them. There was here & there a little knot & a few stragglers a few yards higher up but they were so few as not to disturb the simplicity & unity & life of that one busy highway. We rested again & again. The Bays were stormy, & we heard the waves at different distances and in the middle of the water like the Sea.

[A BEGGAR WOMAN FROM COCKERMOUTH[7]]

Tuesday 4th May [1802]. William had slept pretty well & though he went to bed nervous & jaded in the extreme he rose refreshed. I wrote the Leech Gatherer[8] for him which he had begun the night before & of which he wrote several stanzas in bed this Monday morning. It was very hot, we called at Mr Simpson's door as we passed but did not go in. We rested several times by the way, read & repeated the Leech Gatherer. We were almost melted before we were at the top of the hill. * * * William & I ate a Luncheon, then went on towards the Waterfall. It is a glorious wild solitude under that lofty purple crag. It stood upright by itself. Its own self and its shadow below, one mass—all else was sunshine. We went on further. A Bird at the top of the crags was flying round & round & looked in thinness & transparency, shape & motion, like a moth. We climbed the hill but looked in vain for a shade except at the foot of the great waterfall, & there we did not like to stay on account of the loose stones above our heads. We came down & rested upon a moss covered Rock, rising out of the bed of the River. There we lay ate our dinner & stayed there till about 4 o clock or later. Wm & C[9] repeated & read verses. I drank a little Brandy & water & was in Heaven. The Stags horn is very beautiful & fresh springing upon the fells. Mountain ashes, green. * * * On the Rays we met a woman with 2 little girls one in her arms the other about 4 years old walking by her side, a pretty little thing, but half starved. She had on a pair of slippers that had belonged to some gentlemans child, down at the heels it was not easy to keep them on but, poor thing! young as she was, she walked carefully with them. Alas too young for such cares & such travels. The Mother when we accosted her told us that her husband had left her & gone off with another woman & how she "pursued" them. Then her fury kindled & her eyes rolled about. She changed again to tears. She was a Cockermouth woman 30 years of age— a child at Cockermouth when I was. I was moved & gave her a shilling—I believe 6[d] more than I ought to have given.[1] We had the crescent moon with the "auld moon in her arms."[2] We rested often—always upon the Bridges. Reached home at about 10 o clock.

---

6. Dorothy erased the next words, "the end we did not see." Cf. W. Wordsworth's poem, *I wandered lonely as a cloud*: "They stretched in never-ending line."
7. The small town where Dorothy and her brothers were born and lived until the break-up of the household.
8. The early title for *Resolution and Independence*.

9. Coleridge, whom they met up with on their excursion.
1. Six pence; Dorothy inserted "30 years of age—a child at Cockermouth when I was" to explain the generosity.
2. A line from *Sir Patrick Spence* (see page 171), also quoted by Coleridge in his epigraph for *Dejection: An Ode*.

[THE CIRCUMSTANCES OF "COMPOSED UPON WESTMINISTER BRIDGE"[3]]

[*27 July 1802*] ⁎ ⁎ ⁎ After various troubles & disasters we left London on Saturday morning at 1/2 past 5 or 6. ⁎ ⁎ ⁎ we mounted the Dover Coach at Charing Cross. It was a beautiful morning. The City, St Pauls, with the River & a multitude of little Boats, made a most beautiful sight as we crossed Westminster Bridge. The houses were not overhung by their cloud of smoke & they were spread out endlessly, yet the sun shone so brightly with such a pure light that there was even something like the purity of one of nature's own grand Spectacles.

⁘

Samuel Taylor Coleridge
1772–1834

"Come back into memory, like as thou wert in the dayspring of thy fancies, with hope like a fiery column before thee—the dark pillar not yet turned—Samuel Taylor Coleridge— Logician, Metaphysician, Bard!—How have I seen the casual passer through the cloisters stand still, entranced with admiration . . . while the walls of the old Grey Friars re-echoed to the accents of the *inspired charity-boy!*" When Charles Lamb thus memorialized his former schoolfellow, Coleridge had more than a decade yet to live, but he had already made himself into the mythic Romantic figure of promise and failure whom Lamb salutes.

Born in 1772, the last child of the vicar of Ottery St. Mary's in Devon, Coleridge developed a reputation for precocity even before the death of his father led to his enrollment at Christ's Hospital, a London boarding school for the sons of distressed families, where Lamb met him. A brilliant career at Jesus College, Cambridge, ended in an unhappy attempt to enlist in the army under an assumed name, and he left without a degree in 1794. With Robert Southey, a fellow Oxford enthusiast for poetry and radical politics, he planned an ideal democratic community on the banks of the Susquehanna in Pennsylvania, to be named "Pantisocracy," or equal rule by all. The project collapsed over a dispute whether they would have servants, but not before Coleridge had cemented the social bonds by becoming engaged to Sara Fricker, the sister of Southey's fiancee; the marriage proved unhappy. Coleridge later minimized his youthful "squeaking baby-trumpet of sedition," but he founded a short-lived antigovernment periodical, *The Watchman* (1796); to earn a living, he was pointing in the unorthodox direction of the Unitarian ministry until he was relieved by a moderate annuity of £150 from the Wedgwoods, of the famous pottery firm. In 1796 he published *Poems on Various Subjects*, containing the poem later titled *The Eolian Harp*, and in 1797 he began the collaboration with Wordsworth that produced *Lyrical Ballads* (1798), headed by *The Rime of the Ancyent Marinere*, as the poem was called in its archaizing first version. Before the volume was published, Coleridge and the Wordsworths departed for Germany, where Coleridge studied philosophy at Göttingen. Charges of plagiarism have swirled ever since around the readings of Kant, Schiller, Schelling, and Fichte that animated his lifelong effort to combat what he regarded as the spiritless mechanical world of eighteenth-century British empiricism.

In 1800 Coleridge followed the Wordsworths to the Lake District, where his love for Sara Hutchinson, sister of Wordsworth's future wife, sharpened his estrangement from his own wife. He became addicted to laudanum (opium dissolved in alcohol), a standard medical remedy for the rheumatic pains he suffered, but the stomach disorders it produced increased his dependency. The physiology of addiction was not understood in his day, and what was a widespread

3. See page 231; they are on their way to Calais, France, sailing from Dover, to settle affairs with Annette Vallon and her daughter by William, Caroline, prior to William's marriage to May Hutchinson in October. The City is Westminster, a district of London where Parliament, Westminster Abbey, and Buckingham Palace are located; St. Paul's is the chief Anglican church. Westminster Bridge crosses the Thames river.

social phenomenon Coleridge regarded as a personal moral flaw. His inability to break the habit produced a spiral of depression: guilt, a paralytic doubt of his strength of will, the fear that he was unworthy of love. By 1802, in *Dejection: An Ode*, he declared the failure of his "genial spirits" and "shaping spirit of Imagination," but he carried on an active public career. An important political commentator in the newspapers, he also undertook another periodical, *The Friend* (1809–1810), saw his play *Remorse* succeed at Drury Lane (1813), and gave a series of brilliant lectures on Shakespeare, Milton, poetry, drama, and philosophy (1808–1818). That these enterprises often fell short of the triumphant fullness he forecast for them fixed the myth of promise unfulfilled, even as his accomplishments won increasing influence. From 1816 on, he lived in a London suburb under the care of a young doctor, James Gillman, and he flourished in this stable environment. The fabled talk of the "Sage of Highgate," as Carlyle called him, "had a charm much more than literary, a charm almost religious and prophetic." If the "practical intellects of the world did not much heed him," Carlyle continued, "to the rising spirits of the young generation he had this dusky sublime character; and sat there as a kind of *Magus*." Coleridge became, in the judgment of John Stuart Mill, one of the two seminal minds of the nineteenth century, the idealist, Christian, philosopher of organic unity around whose work the opposition to Benthamite utilitarianism crystalized.

In his final decades, Coleridge joined new work and old into a substantial body of publication. *Christabel*, long known by reputation, appeared with Byron's enthusiastic sponsorship, in 1816, together with *Kubla Khan*. 1817 brought *Sibylline Leaves* (Coleridge's collected poems, including the marginal-gloss version of the lyrical ballad now titled *The Rime of the Ancient Mariner*) and *Biographia Literaria*, the account of his "literary life and opinions" that has provided the starting-point for much twentieth-century literary criticism. In a series of works, Coleridge explicated conservative principles continuous with but far evolved from the Jacobin associations that had led him to urge anonymous publication of the *Lyrical Ballads* because "Wordsworth's name is nothing, and mine stinks": two *Lay Sermons* (1816–1817), articulating his views in the debate over reform; *The Friend*, expanded in 1818 into a three-volume collection of essays on "politics, morals, and religion"; *Aids to Reflection* (1825), emphasizing Christianity as "personal revelation"; and *On the Constitution of Church and State* (1830), outlining conceptions of national culture (and the "clerisy" responsible for preserving it) that resonate throughout the Victorian period. *Table Talk* (1836) posthumously captured the echoes of his voice, and Coleridge has enjoyed a resurrection in our own day. As new scholarly editions bring more writings to light, they deepen the fascination of a man who was the author of some of the most suggestive poems in the language and an erudite philosopher, a poet who in the *Biographia Literaria* transformed the role of the critic, a theorist of the unifying imagination whose works and life are marked by fragments and discontinuities, a believer in the unity of all whose own method has been aptly described as marginal glosses on the works of others, and an idealist engaged with the daily politics of a turbulent era.

SONNET TO THE RIVER OTTER[1]

Dear native Brook! wild Streamlet of the West!
   How many various-fated years have past,
     What happy, and what mournful hours, since last
I skimm'd the smooth thin stone along thy breast,
Numbering its light leaps! yet so deep impresst
Sink the sweet scenes of childhood, that mine eyes
     I never shut amid the sunny ray,

1. In Devon, where Coleridge grew up. His father was the vicar of nearby Ottery St. Mary's.

But strait with all their tints their waters rise,
   Thy crossing plank, thy marge with willows grey,
10   And bedded sand that vein'd with various dyes
Gleam'd through thy bright transparence! On my way,
   Visions of childhood! oft have ye beguiled
Lone manhood's cares, yet waking fondest sighs.
   Ah! that I were once more a careless child!

c. 1796   1797/1817

The Eolian Harp[1]

Composed at Clevedon, Somersetshire

My pensive Sara![2] thy soft cheek reclined
Thus on mine arm, most soothing sweet it is
To sit beside our cot,° our cot o'ergrown   *cottage*
With white-flower'd Jasmin, and the broad-leave'd Myrtle,
5   (Meet° emblems they of Innocence and Love!)   *fit*
And watch the clouds, that late were rich with light,
Slow sad'ning round, and mark the star of eve°   *Venus*
Serenely brilliant (such should wisdom be)
Shine opposite! How exquisite the scents
10   Snatch'd from yon bean-field! and the world so hush'd!
The stilly murmur of the distant Sea
Tells us of Silence.
                    And that simplest Lute,
Placed length-ways in the clasping casement, hark!
How by the desultory breeze caress'd,
15   Like some coy maid half yielding to her lover,
It pours such sweet upbraidings,° as must needs   *reproaches*
Tempt to repeat the wrong! And now, its strings
Boldlier swept, the long sequacious notes
Over delicious surges sink and rise,
20   Such a soft floating witchery of sound
As twilight Elfins make, when they at eve
Voyage on gentle gales from Fairy-Land,
Where Melodies round honey-dropping flowers,
Footless and wild, like birds of Paradise,[3]
25   Nor pause, nor perch, hovering on untamed wing!
O! the one Life, within us and abroad,
Which meets all Motion, and becomes its soul,
A Light in Sound, a sound-like power in Light,
Rhythm in all Thought, and Joyance every where—
30   Methinks, it should have been impossible
Not to love all things in a world so fill'd,

1. Named for Aeolus, god of winds, the harp consisted of a guitarlike box, set in an open window where the breeze would cause its strings to sound. Originally titled *Effusion. xxxv. / Composed August 20th, 1795, at Clevedon, Somersetshire*. This poem was first published in 1796; we print the text of 1817.
2. Formerly Sara Fricker; the poem was composed on the honeymoon.
3. Tropical birds famed for colorful plumage.

Where the breeze warbles and the mute still Air
Is Music slumbering on its instrument.[4]

And thus, my love! as on the midway slope
35 Of yonder hill I stretch my limbs at noon,
Whilst thro' my half-closed eye-lids I behold
The sunbeams dance, like diamonds, on the main,
And tranquil muse upon tranquillity;
Full many a thought uncall'd and undetain'd,
40 And many idle flitting phantasies,
Traverse my indolent and passive brain,
As wild and various as the random gales
That swell and flutter on this subject lute!

And what if all of animated nature
45 Be but organic harps diversely fram'd,
That tremble into thought, as o'er them sweeps
Plastic° and vast, one intellectual breeze,   *creatively shaping*
At once the Soul of each, and God of All?

But thy more serious eye a mild reproof
50 Darts, O beloved woman! nor such thoughts
Dim and unhallow'd dost thou not reject,
And biddest me walk humbly with my God.
Meek daughter in the family of Christ!
Well hast thou said and holily disprais'd
55 These shapings of the unregenerate° mind,   *sinful*
Bubbles that glitter as they rise and break
On vain Philosophy's aye°-babbling spring.   *ever*
For never guiltless may I speak of him,
Th' Incomprehensible! save when with awe
60 I praise him, and with Faith that inly feels;
Who with his saving mercies healed me,
A sinful and most miserable Man,
Wilder'd and dark, and gave me to possess
Peace, and this Cot, and Thee, heart-honor'd Maid!

1795–1817   1817

THIS LIME-TREE BOWER MY PRISON

ADVERTISEMENT

In the June of 1797, some long-expected Friends[1] paid a visit
to the Author's Cottage; and on the morning of their arrival, he
met with an accident, which disabled him from walking during the

---

4. Lines 26–34 were added in 1817, on a corrections page
at the front of the volume, marked for insertion here;
"Its" (33) was later revised to "her."
1. The title of the first publication (1800) added

"A Poem Addressed to Charles Lamb, of the India-House,
London." Lamb was a clerk in the East India Company's
London office.

whole time of their stay. One Evening, when they had left him for a few hours, he composed the following lines in the Garden-Bower.

Well, they are gone, and here must I remain,
This Lime-Tree Bower my Prison! I have lost
Such beauties and such feelings, as had been
Most sweet to my remembrance even when age
5   Had dimmed mine eyes to blindness! They, meanwhile,
My Friends, whom I may never meet again,
On springy heath, along the hill-top edge,
Wander in gladness, and wind down, perchance,
To that still roaring dell, of which I told;
10   The roaring dell, o'erwooded, narrow, deep,
And only speckled by the mid-day Sun;
Where its slim trunk the Ash from rock to rock
Flings arching like a Bridge;—that branchless Ash,
Unsunn'd and damp, whose few poor yellow leaves
15   Ne'er tremble in the gale, yet tremble still,
Fann'd by the water-fall! and there my friends
Behold the dark green file of long lank Weeds,
That all at once (a most fantastic sight!)
Still nod and drip beneath the dripping edge
20   Of the blue clay-stone.

             Now, my Friends emerge
Beneath the wide wide Heaven—and view again
The many-steepled track magnificent
Of hilly fields and meadows, and the sea,
With some fair bark,° perhaps, whose Sails light up   *small boat*
25   The slip of smooth clear blue betwixt two Isles
Of purple shadow! Yes! they wander on
In gladness all; but thou, methinks, most glad,
My gentle-hearted Charles! for thou hast pined
And hunger'd after Nature, many a year,
30   In the great City pent, winning thy way
With sad yet patient soul, through evil and pain
And strange calamity![2] Ah! slowly sink
Behind the western ridge, thou glorious Sun!
Shine in the slant beams of the sinking orb
35   Ye purple heath-flowers! richlier burn, ye clouds!
Live in the yellow light, ye distant groves!
And kindle, thou blue Ocean! So my Friend
Struck with deep joy may stand, as I have stood,
Silent with swimming sense; yea, gazing round
40   On the wide landscape, gaze till all doth seem
Less gross than bodily;° and of such hues   *less than bodied*

2. The fit of insanity in which Mary Lamb, Charles's sister, killed their mother the year before.

As cloath[3] the Almighty Spirit, when yet he makes
Spirits perceive his presence.

A delight

Comes sudden on my heart, and I am glad
45 As I myself were there! Nor in this bower,
This little lime-tree bower, have I not mark'd
Much that has sooth'd me. Pale beneath the blaze
Hung the transparent foliage; and I watch'd
Some broad and sunny leaf, and lov'd to see
50 The shadow of the leaf and stem above
Dappling its sunshine! And that Walnut-tree
Was richly ting'd, and a deep radiance lay
Full on the ancient Ivy, which usurps
Those fronting elms, and now, with blackest mass
55 Makes their dark branches gleam a lighter hue
Through the late twilight: and though now the Bat
Wheels silent by, and not a Swallow twitters,
Yet still the solitary humble Bee
Sings in the bean-flower! Henceforth I shall know
60 That Nature ne'er deserts the wise and pure,
No Plot so narrow, be but Nature there,
No waste so vacant, but may well employ
Each faculty of sense, and keep the heart
Awake to Love and Beauty! and sometimes
65 'Tis well to be bereft of promised good,
That we may lift the Soul, and contemplate
With lively joy the joys we can not share.
My gentle-hearted Charles! when the last Rook
Beat its straight path along the dusky air
70 Homewards, I blest it! deeming, its black wing
(Now a dim speck, now vanishing in light)
Had cross'd the mighty Orb's dilated glory,
While thou stood'st gazing; or when all was still,
Flew creeking o'er thy head, and had a charm
75 For thee, my gentle-hearted Charles, to whom
No Sound is dissonant which tells of Life.

1797/1800   1800/1817

Frost at Midnight

The frost performs its secret ministry,
Unhelped by any wind. The owlet's cry
Came loud—and hark, again! loud as before.
The inmates of my cottage, all at rest,
5 Have left me to that solitude, which suits

---

3. Later, "veil."

Abstruser musings: save that at my side
My cradled infant° slumbers peacefully.   *son Hartley*
'Tis calm indeed! so calm, that it disturbs
And vexes meditation with its strange
10   And extreme silentness. Sea, hill, and wood
This populous village!° Sea, and hill, and wood,   *Nether Stowey*
With all the numberless goings on of life,
Inaudible as dreams! the thin blue flame
Lies on my low burnt fire, and quivers not;
15   Only that film,[1] which fluttered on the grate,
Still flutters there, the sole unquiet thing.
Methinks, its motion in this hush of nature
Gives it dim sympathies with me who live,
Making it a companionable form,
20   Whose puny flaps and freaks the idling Spirit
By its own moods interprets, everywhere
Echo or mirror seeking of itself,
And makes a toy of Thought.

                                                    But O! how oft,
How oft, at school, with most believing mind,
25   Presageful, have I gazed upon the bars,
To watch that fluttering stranger! and as oft
With unclosed lids, already had I dreamt
Of my sweet birth-place, and the old church-tower,
Whose bells, the poor man's only music, rang
30   From morn to evening, all the hot Fair-day,
So sweetly, that they stirred and haunted me
With a wild pleasure, falling on mine ear
Most like articulate sounds of things to come!
So gazed I, till the soothing things I dreamt
35   Lulled me to sleep, and sleep prolonged my dreams!
And so I brooded all the following morn,
Awed by the stern preceptor's° face, mine eye   *teacher's*
Fixed with mock study on my swimming book:
Save if the door half opened, and I snatched
40   A hasty glance, and still my heart leaped up,
For still I hoped to see the stranger's face,
Townsman, or aunt, or sister more beloved,
My play-mate when we both were clothed alike![2]

          Dear Babe, that sleepest cradled by my side,
45   Whose gentle breathings, heard in this deep calm,
Fill up the interspersed vacancies
And momentary pauses of the thought!
My babe so beautiful! it thrills my heart

---

1. A piece of soot. "In all parts of the kingdom these films are called *strangers* and supposed to portend the arrival of some absent friend" (Coleridge's note, 1798).
2. Boys and girls were dressed alike until age 5.

With tender gladness, thus to look at thee,
50   And think that thou shalt learn far other lore
And in far other scenes! For I was reared
In the great city, pent 'mid cloisters dim,
And saw naught lovely but the sky and stars.
But *thou*, my babe! shalt wander like a breeze
55   By lakes and sandy shores, beneath the crags
Of ancient mountain, and beneath the clouds,
Which image in their bulk both lakes and shores
And mountain crags: so shalt thou see and hear
The lovely shapes and sounds intelligible
60   Of that eternal language, which thy God
Utters, who from eternity doth teach
Himself in all, and all things in himself.
Great universal Teacher! he shall mould
Thy spirit, and by giving make it ask.

65   Therefore all seasons shall be sweet to thee,
Whether the summer clothe the general earth
With greenness, or the redbreast sit and sing
Betwixt the tufts of snow on the bare branch
Of mossy apple-tree, while the nigh thatch
70   Smokes in the sun-thaw; whether the eave-drops fall
Heard only in the trances of the blast,
Or if the secret ministry of frost
Shall hang them up in silent icicles,
Quietly shining to the quiet Moon.

[February] 1798   1798–1834[3]

The Rime of the Ancient Mariner[1]

In Seven Parts

Facile credo, plures esse Naturas invisibiles quam visibiles in rerum universitate. Sed horum omnium familiam quis nobis enarrabit? et gradus et cognationes et discrimina et singulorum munera? Quid agunt? quæ loca habitant? Harum rerum notitiam semper ambivit ingenium humanum, nunquam attigit. Juvat, interea, non diffiteor, quandoque in animo, tanquam in Tabulâ, majoris et melioris mundi imaginem contemplari: ne mens assuefacta hodiernæ vitæ minutiis se contrahat nimis, & tota subsidat in pusillas cogitationes. Sed

3. Published in several various forms across these years; the text here is 1834.
1. A somewhat revised *Rime* appeared in the 1800 *Lyrical Ballads*, and each publication thereafter reflected further revisions. It was the first poem proper in *Sibylline Leaves* "By S. T. Coleridge, Esq." (1817), in which the Latin epigraph replaced the "Argument" and the marginal commentary first appeared.

veritati interea invigilandum est, modusque servandus, ut
certa ab incertis, diem a nocte, distinguamus.[2]

T. BURNET. *Archaeol. Phil.* p. 68.

IT is an ancient Mariner,
And he stoppeth one of three.
"By thy long grey beard and glittering eye,
Now wherefore stopp'st thou me?

5   "The Bridegroom's doors are open'd wide,
And I am next of kin;
The guests are met, the feast is set:
May'st hear the merry din."

He holds him with his skinny hand,
10   "There was a ship," quoth he.
"Hold off! unhand me, grey-beard loon!"
immediately   Eftsoons° his hand dropt he.

He holds him with his glittering eye—
The wedding-guest stood still,
15   And listens like a three years child:
The Mariner hath his will.

The wedding-guest sat on a stone:
He can not chuse but hear;
And thus spake on that ancient man,
20   The bright-eyed mariner.

The ship was cheer'd, the harbour clear'd,
Merrily did we drop
Below the kirk,° below the hill,
Below the light-house top.

25   The Sun came up upon the left,
Out of the sea came he;
And he shone bright, and on the right
Went down into the sea.

Higher and higher every day,
30   Till over the mast at noon—
The Wedding-Guest here beat his breast,
For he heard the loud bassoon.

The bride hath paced into the hall,
Red as a rose is she;
35   Nodding their heads before her goes
The merry minstrelsy.

Side glosses:

An ancient Mariner
meeteth three Gallants
bidden to a wedding-
feast, and detaineth one.

The wedding-guest is
spellbound by the eye of
the old sea-faring man,
and constrained to hear
his tale.

The Mariner tells how
the ship sailed southward
with a good wind and
fair weather, till it
reached the line.

The wedding-guest
heareth the bridal music;
but the mariner
continueth his tale.

2. From English theologian Thomas Burnet's *Archaeologiae Philosophicae* (1692): "I can easily believe that there are more invisible creatures in the universe than visible ones. But who will tell us to what family each belongs, their ranks and relationships, and what their distinguishing characteristics may be? What do they do? Where do they live? The human mind has always circled around these matters without finding satisfaction. But I do not doubt that it is beneficial sometimes to contemplate in the mind, as in a picture, the image of a grander and better world; for if the mind becomes used to the trivial things of everyday life, it may limit itself too much and decline completely into worthless thinking. Meanwhile, however, we must be on the lookout for the truth, keeping a sense of proportion so that we can distinguish what is sure from what is uncertain, and day from night."

The Wedding-Guest he beat his breast,
Yet he can not chuse but hear;
And thus spake on that ancient man,
The bright-eyed Mariner.   40

The ship drawn by a storm toward the south pole.
And now the STORM-BLAST came, and he
Was tyrannous and strong:
He struck with his o'ertaking wings,
And chased us south along.

With sloping masts and dipping prow,   45
As who pursued with yell and blow
Still treads the shadow of his foe
And forward bends his head,
The ship drove fast, loud roar'd the blast,
And southward aye° we fled.   50 *even*

And now there came both mist and snow,
And it grew wondrous cold:
And ice, mast-high, came floating by,
As green as emerald.

The land of ice, and of fearful sounds, where no living thing was to be seen.
And through the drifts the snowy clift   55
Did send a dismal sheen:
Nor shapes of men nor beast we ken°—   *knew*
The ice was all between.

The ice was here, the ice was there,
The ice was all around: 60
It cracked and growled, and roar'd and howl'd,
Like noises in a swound!

Till a great sea-bird, called the Albatross, came through the snow-fog, and was received with great joy and hospitality.
At length did cross an Albatross:
Thorough the fog it came;
As if it had been a Christian soul,   65
We hailed it in God's name.

It ate the food it ne'er had eat,
And round and round it flew.
The ice did split with a thunder-fit;
The helmsman steer'd us through!   70

And lo! the Albatross proveth a bird of good omen, and followeth the ship as it returned northward, through fog and floating ice.
And a good south wind sprung up behind;
The Albatross did follow,
And every day, for food or play,
Came to the Mariner's hollo!

In mist or cloud, on mast or shroud,   75
It perch'd for vespers° nine;   *evening prayers*
Whiles all the night, through fog-smoke white,
Glimmered the white Moon-shine.

"God save thee, ancient Mariner!
From the fiends, that plague thee thus!—
Why look'st thou so?"—With my cross-bow
I shot the ALBATROSS!.

80

The ancient Mariner inhospitably killeth the pious bird of good omen.

PART THE SECOND

THE Sun now rose upon the right:
Out of the sea came he,
Still hid in mist, and on the left
Went down into the sea.

And the good south wind still blew behind,
But no sweet bird did follow,
Nor any day for food or play
Came to the mariners' hollo!

And I had done a hellish thing,
And it would work 'em woe:
For all averred, I had killed the bird
That made the breeze to blow.
Ah wretch! said they, the bird to slay,
That made the breeze to blow!

His shipmates cry out against the ancient Mariner, for killing the bird of good luck.

Nor dim nor red, like God's own head,
The glorious Sun uprist:
Then all averred, I had killed the bird
That brought the fog and mist.
'Twas right, said they, such birds to slay,
That bring the fog and mist.

But when the fog cleared off, they justify the same—and thus make themselves accomplices in the crime.

The fair breeze blew, the white foam flew,
The furrow followed free;[3]
We were the first that ever burst
Into that silent sea.

The fair breeze continues; the ship enters the Pacific Ocean, and sails northward, even till it reaches the Line.

Down dropt the breeze, the sails dropt down,
'Twas sad as sad could be;
And we did speak only to break
The silence of the sea!

The ship hath been suddenly becalmed.

All in a hot and copper sky,
The bloody Sun, at noon,
Right up above the mast did stand,
No bigger than the Moon.

Day after day, day after day,
We stuck, nor breath nor motion;
As idle as a painted ship
Upon a painted ocean.

3. In the former edition the line was, "The furrow follow'd free"; but I had not been long on board a ship, before I perceived that this was the image as seen by a spectator from the shore, or from another vessel. From the ship itself the *Wake* appears like a brook flowing off from the stern [Coleridge's note, 1817].

And the Albatross
begins to be avenged.

Water, water, every where,
And all the boards did shrink;   120
Water, water, every where,
Nor any drop to drink.

The very deep did rot: O Christ!
That ever this should be!
Yea, slimy things did crawl with legs   125
Upon the slimy sea.

About, about, in reel and rout
The death-fires danced at night;
The water, like a witch's oils,
Burnt green, and blue and white.   130

A spirit had followed
them; one of the
invisible inhabitants of
this planet, neither
departed souls nor
angels; concerning
whom the learned Jew,
Josephus, and the
Platonic
Constantinopolitan,
Michael Psellus, may

And some in dreams assured were
Of the spirit that plagued us so:
Nine fathom deep he had followed us
From the land of mist and snow.

And every tongue, through utter drought,   135
Was wither'd at the root;
We could not speak, no more than if
We had been choak'd with soot.

be consulted. They are very numerous, and there is no climate or element without one or more.

The shipmates, in their
sore distress, would fain
throw the whole guilt on
the ancient Mariner: in
sign whereof they hang
the dead sea-bird round his neck.

Ah! well a-day! what evil looks
Had I from old and young!   140
Instead of the cross, the Albatross
About my neck was hung.

PART THE THIRD

THERE passed a weary time. Each throat
Was parched, and glazed each eye.
A weary time! a weary time!   145
How glazed each weary eye!

The ancient Mariner
beholdeth a sign in the
element afar off.

When looking westward, I beheld
A something in the sky.

At first it seem'd a little speck,
And then it seem'd a mist!   150
It moved and moved, and took at last
A certain shape, I wist.°   *knew*

A speck, a mist, a shape, I wist!
And still it near'd and near'd:
And as if it dodged a water-sprite,   155
It plunged and tack'd and veer'd.

With throat unslack'd, with black lips baked,
We could nor laugh nor wail;
Through utter drought all dumb we stood!
160 I bit my arm, I sucked the blood,
And cried, A sail! a sail!

At its nearer approach, it seemeth him to be a ship; and at a dear ransom he freeth his speech from the bonds of thirst.

With throat unslacked,[4] with black lips baked,
Agape they heard me call:
Gramercy! they for joy did grin,
165 And all at once their breath drew in,
As they were drinking all.

A flash of joy.

See! see! (I cried) she tacks no more!
benefit Hither to work us weal°
Without a breeze, without a tide,
170 She steddies with upright keel!

And horror follows. For can it be a ship that comes onward without wind or tide?

The western wave was all a-flame.
The day was well nigh done!
Almost upon the western wave
Rested the broad bright Sun;
175 When that strange shape drove suddenly
Betwixt us and the Sun.

And straight the Sun was flecked with bars,
(Heaven's Mother send us grace!)
As if through a dungeon-grate he peer'd
180 With broad and burning face.

It seemeth him but the skeleton of a ship.

Alas! (thought I, and my heart beat loud)
How fast she nears and nears!
Are those *her* sails that glance in the Sun,
cobwebs Like restless gossameres?°

185 Are those *her* ribs through which the Sun
Did peer, as through a grate?
And is that Woman all her crew?
Is that a DEATH? and are there two?
Is DEATH that woman's mate?

And its ribs are seen as bars on the face of the setting Sun. The spectre-woman and her death-mate, and no other on board the skeleton-ship.

190 *Her* lips were red, *her* looks were free,
Her locks were yellow as gold:
Her skin was as white as leprosy,
The Night-Mair LIFE-IN-DEATH was she,
Who thicks man's blood with cold.

Like vessel, like crew!

195 The naked hulk alongside came,
And the twain were casting dice;
"The game is done! I've, I've won!"
Quoth she, and whistles thrice.[5]

DEATH, and LIFE-IN-DEATH have diced for the ship's crew, and she (the latter) winneth the ancient Mariner.

---

4. 1834] throats unslaked.
5. In 1817 only, this stanza followed: "A gust of wind sterte up behind / And whistled through the bones; / Through the holes of his eyes and the hole of his mouth, / Half whistles and half groans." Coleridge had wanted to "erase" this stanza.

No twilight within the
courts of the Sun.

The Sun's rim dips; the stars rush out:
At one stride comes the dark;   200
With far-heard whisper, o'er the sea,
Off shot the spectre-bark.

We listen'd and look'd sideways up!
Fear at my heart, as at a cup,
My life-blood seem'd to sip!   205
The stars were dim, and thick the night,
The steersman's face by his lamp gleam'd white;

At the rising of the
Moon,

From the sails the dew did drip—
Till clombe above the eastern bar
The horned Moon, with one bright star   210
Within the nether tip.

One after another,

One after one, by the star-dogg'd Moon,
Too quick for groan or sigh,
Each turn'd his face with a ghastly pang,
And curs'd me with his eye.   215

His ship-mates drop
down dead;

Four times fifty living men,
(And I heard nor sigh nor groan)
With heavy thump, a lifeless lump,
They dropped down one by one.

But LIFE-IN-DEATH
begins her work on the
ancient Mariner.

The souls did from their bodies fly,—   220
They fled to bliss or woe!
And every soul, it passed me by,
Like the whizz of my CROSS-BOW!

PART THE FOURTH

The wedding-guest
feareth that a spirit is
talking to him;

"I FEAR thee, ancient Mariner!
I fear thy skinny hand!   225
And thou art long, and lank, and brown,
As is the ribbed sea-sand.[6]

I fear thee and thy glittering eye,
And thy skinny hand, so brown."—

But the ancient Mariner
assureth him of his
bodily life, and
proceedeth to relate his
horrible penance.

Fear not, fear not, thou Wedding-Guest!   230
This body dropt not down.

Alone, alone, all, all alone,
Alone on a wide wide sea!
And never a saint took pity on
My soul in agony   235

He despiseth the
creatures of the calm,

The many men, so beautiful!
And they all dead did lie:

6. For the last two lines of this stanza, I am indebted to Mr. Wordsworth. It was on a delightful walk from Nether Stowey to
Dulverton, with him and his sister, in the Autumn of 1797, that this poem was planned, and in part composed [Coleridge's
note].

And a thousand thousand slimy things
Liv'd on; and so did I.

240   I looked upon the rotting sea,
And drew my eyes away;
I looked upon the rotting deck,
And there the dead men lay.

And envieth that they should live, and so many lie dead

I looked to Heaven, and tried to pray;
245   But or ever a prayer had gusht,
A wicked whisper came, and made
My heart as dry as dust.

I closed my lids, and kept them close,
And the balls like pulses beat;
250   For the sky and the sea, and the sea and the sky
Lay, like a load, on my weary eye,
And the dead were at my feet.

The cold sweat melted from their limbs,
Not rot nor reek did they:
255   The look with which they looked on me
Had never passed away.

But the curse liveth for him in the eye of the dead men.

An orphan's curse would drag to Hell
A spirit from on high;
But oh! more horrible than that
260   Is the curse in a dead man's eye!
Seven days, seven nights, I saw that curse,
And yet I could not die.

The moving Moon went up the sky,
And nowhere did abide:
265   Softly she was going up,
And a star or two beside—

In his loneliness and fixedness he yearneth towards the journeying Moon, and the stars that still sojourn, yet still move onward; and every where the blue sky belongs to them, and is their appointed rest, and their native country, and their own natural homes, which they enter unannounced, as lords

Her beams bemock'd the sultry main,
Like April hoar-frost spread;
But where the ship's huge shadow lay,
270   The charmed water burnt alway
A still and awful red.

that are certainly expected, and yet there is a silent joy at their arrival.

Beyond the shadow of the ship,
I watch'd the water-snakes:
They moved in tracks of shining white,
275   And when they reared, the elfish light
Fell off in hoary flakes.

By the light of the Moon he beholdeth God's creatures of the great calm.

Within the shadow of the ship
I watched their rich attire:
Blue, glossy green, and velvet black,

They coiled and swam; and every track   280
Was a flash of golden fire.

Their beauty and their happiness. O happy living things! no tongue
Their beauty might declare:
A spring of love gusht from my heart,
He blesseth them in his heart. And I blessed them unaware!   285
Sure my kind saint took pity on me,
And I blessed them unaware.

The spell begins to break. The self same moment I could pray;
And from my neck so free
The Albatross fell off, and sank   290
Like lead into the sea.

PART THE FIFTH

Oh SLEEP! it is a gentle thing,
Belov'd from pole to pole!
To Mary Queen the praise be given!
She sent the gentle sleep from Heaven,   295
That slid into my soul.

By grace of the holy Mother, the ancient Mariner is refreshed with rain. The silly° buckets on the deck,   *helpless*
That had so long remained,
I dreamt that they were filled with dew;
And when I awoke, it rained.   300

My lips were wet, my throat was cold,
My garments all were dank;
Sure I had drunken in my dreams,
And still my body drank.

I moved, and could not feel my limbs: 305
I was so light—almost
I thought that I had died in sleep,
And was a blessed ghost.

He heareth sounds, and seeth strange sights and commotions in the sky and the element. And soon I heard a roaring wind:
It did not come anear;   310
But with its sound it shook the sails,
That were so thin and sere.

The upper air burst into life!
And a hundred fire-flags° sheen,   *meteors*
To and fro they were hurried about;   315
And to and fro, and in and out,
The wan stars danced between.

And the coming wind did roar more loud,
And the sails did sigh like sedge;°   *marsh grass*
And the rain pour'd down from one black cloud;   320
The Moon was at its edge.

The thick black cloud was cleft, and still
The Moon was at its side:
Like waters shot from some high crag,
325   The lightning fell with never a jag,
A river steep and wide.

The loud wind never reached the ship,
Yet now the ship moved on!
Beneath the lightning and the Moon
330   The dead men gave a groan.

> The bodies of the
> ship's crew are
> inspirited, and the ship
> moves on;

They groan'd, they stirr'd, they all uprose,
Nor spake, nor moved their eyes;
It had been strange, even in a dream,
To have seen those dead men rise.

335   The helmsman steered, the ship moved on;
Yet never a breeze up blew;
The mariners all 'gan work the ropes,
Where they were wont to do:
They raised their limbs like lifeless tools—
340   We were a ghastly crew.

The body of my brother's son
Stood by me, knee to knee:
The body and I pulled at one rope,
But he said nought to me.

345   "I fear thee, ancient Mariner!"
Be calm, thou Wedding-Guest!
'Twas not those souls that fled in pain,
corpses   Which to their corses° came again,
But a troop of spirits blest:

> But not by the souls of
> the men, nor by dæmons
> of earth or middle air,
> but by a blessed troop of
> angelic spirits, sent down
> by the invocation of the
> guardian saint.

350   For when it dawned—they dropped their arms,
And clustered round the mast;
Sweet sounds rose slowly through their mouths,
And from their bodies passed.

Around, around, flew each sweet sound,
355   Then darted to the Sun;
Slowly the sounds came back again,
Now mixed, now one by one.

Sometimes a-dropping from the sky
I heard the sky-lark sing;
360   Sometimes all little birds that are,
How they seem'd to fill the sea and air
warbling   With their sweet jargoning!°

And now 'twas like all instruments,
Now like a lonely flute;
365   And now it is an angel's song,
That makes the Heavens be mute.

It ceased; yet still the sails made on
A pleasant noise till noon,
A noise like of a hidden brook
In the leafy mouth of June,
That to the sleeping woods all night   370
Singeth a quiet tune.

Till noon we quietly sailed on,
Yet never a breeze did breathe:
Slowly and smoothly went the ship,   375
Moved onward from beneath.

The lonesome spirit from the south-pole carries on the ship as far as the line, in obedience to the angelic troop, but still requireth vengeance.

Under the keel nine fathom deep,
From the land of mist and snow,
The spirit slid: and it was he
That made the ship to go.   380
The sails at noon left off their tune,
And the ship stood still also.

The Sun, right up above the mast,
Had fixt her to the ocean;
But in a minute she 'gan stir,   385
With a short uneasy motion—
Backwards and forwards half her length,
With a short uneasy motion.

Then like a pawing horse let go,
She made a sudden bound: 390
It flung the blood into my head,
And I fell down in a swound.

The Polar Spirit's fellow-dæmons, the invisible inhabitants of the element, take part in his wrong; and two of them relate, one to the other, that penance long and heavy for the ancient Mariner hath been accorded to the Polar Spirit, who returneth southward.

How long in that same fit I lay,
I have not to declare;
But ere my living life returned,
I heard and in my soul discerned   395
Two VOICES in the air.

"Is it he?" quoth one, "Is this the man?
By him who died on cross,
With his cruel bow he laid full low,   400
The harmless Albatross.

The spirit who bideth by himself
In the land of mist and snow,
He loved the bird that loved the man
Who shot him with his bow."   405

The other was a softer voice,
As soft as honey-dew.
Quoth he, "The man hath penance done,
And penance more will do."

PART THE SIXTH

FIRST VOICE.

410 But tell me, tell me! speak again,
Thy soft response renewing—
What makes that ship drive on so fast?
What is the OCEAN doing?

SECOND VOICE.

Still as a slave before his lord,
415 The OCEAN hath no blast;
His great bright eye most silently
Up to the Moon is cast—

If he may know which way to go;
For she guides him smooth or grim.
See, brother, see! how graciously
420 She looketh down on him.

FIRST VOICE.

But why drives on that ship so fast,   The Mariner hath been
Without or wave or wind?   cast into a trance; for the
                                                 angelic power causeth
                                                 the vessel to drive
SECOND VOICE.   northward, faster than
                                                 human life could endure.
The air is cut away before,
425 And closes from behind.

Fly, brother, fly! more high, more high!
Or we shall be belated:
For slow and slow that ship will go,
When the Mariner's trance is abated."

430 I woke, and we were sailing on   The supernatural motion
As in a gentle weather: is retarded; the Mariner
'Twas night, calm night, the Moon was high;   awakes, and his penance
The dead men stood together.   begins anew.

All stood together on the deck,
435 *tomb*   For a charnel-dungeon° fitter:
All fixed on me their stony eyes,
That in the Moon did glitter.

The pang, the curse, with which they died,
Had never passed away:
440 I could not draw my eyes from theirs,
Nor turn them up to pray.

And now this spell was snapt: once more   The curse is finally
I viewed the ocean green,   expiated.
And looked far forth, yet little saw
445 Of what had else been seen—

Like one, that on a lonesome road
Doth walk in fear and dread,
And having once turn'd round, walks on,
And turns no more his head;
Because he knows, a frightful fiend   450
Doth close behind him tread.

But soon there breathed a wind on me,
Nor sound nor motion made:
Its path was not upon the sea,
In ripple or in shade.   455

It raised my hair, it fanned my cheek
Like a meadow-gale of spring—
It mingled strangely with my fears,
Yet it felt like a welcoming.

Swiftly, swiftly flew the ship,   460
Yet she sailed softly too:
Sweetly, sweetly blew the breeze—
On me alone it blew.

And the ancient
Mariner beholdeth his
native country.

Oh! dream of joy! is this indeed
The light-house top I see?   465
Is this the hill? is this the kirk?
Is this mine own countree?

We drifted o'er the harbour-bar,
And I with sobs did pray—
O let me be awake, my God!   470
Or let me sleep alway.

The harbour-bay was clear as glass,
So smoothly it was strewn!
And on the bay the moonlight lay,
And the shadow of the moon.   475

The rock shone bright, the kirk no less,
That stands above the rock:
The moonlight steeped in silentness
The steady weathercock.

The angelic spirits
leave the dead bodies,

And the bay was white with silent light,   480
Till rising from the same,
Full many shapes, that shadows were,
In crimson colours came.

And appear in their
own forms of light.

A little distance from the prow
Those crimson shadows were: 485
I turned my eyes upon the deck—
Oh, Christ! what saw I there!

Each corse lay flat, lifeless and flat,
And, by the holy rood!°   *cross*

490   A man all light, a seraph-man,
         On every corse there stood.

         This seraph-band, each waved his hand:
         It was a heavenly sight!
         They stood as signals to the land,
495   Each one a lovely light:

         This seraph-band, each waved his hand,
         No voice did they impart—
         No voice; but oh! the silence sank
         Like music on my heart.

500   But soon I heard the dash of oars,
         I heard the Pilot's cheer;
         My head was turn'd perforce away,
         And I saw a boat appear.

         The Pilot, and the Pilot's boy,
505   I heard them coming fast:
         Dear Lord in Heaven! it was a joy
         The dead men could not blast.

         I saw a third—I heard his voice:
         It is the Hermit good!
510   He singeth loud his godly hymns
         That he makes in the wood.

absolve   He'll shrieve° my soul, he'll wash away
         The Albatross's blood.

PART THE SEVENTH

         This Hermit good lives in that wood   The Hermit of the
515   Which slopes down to the sea.   Wood,
         How loudly his sweet voice he rears!
         He loves to talk with marineres
         That come from a far countree.

         He kneels at morn, and noon, and eve—
520   He hath a cushion plump:
         It is the moss that wholly hides
         The rotted old oak-stump.

         The Skiff-boat near'd: I heard them talk,
         "Why, this is strange, I trow!
525   Where are those lights so many and fair,
         That signal made but now?"

         "Strange, by my faith!" the Hermit said—   Approacheth the ship
         "And they answered not our cheer!   with wonder.
         The planks looked warped! and see those sails,
530   How thin they are and sere!

I never saw aught like to them,
Unless perchance it were

Brown skeletons of leaves that lag
My forest-brook along;
When the ivy-tod° is heavy with snow,   535 *clump*
And the owlet whoops to the wolf below,
That eats the she-wolf's young."

Dear Lord! it hath a fiendish look—
(The Pilot made reply)
I am a-feared—Push on, push on!   540
Said the Hermit cheerily.

The boat came closer to the ship,
But I nor spake nor stirred;
The boat came close beneath the ship,
And straight a sound was heard.   545

The ship suddenly
sinketh.

Under the water it rumbled on,
Still louder and more dread:
It reach'd the ship, it split the bay;
The ship went down like lead.

The ancient Mariner is
saved in the Pilot's
boat.

Stunned by that loud and dreadful sound,   550
Which sky and ocean smote,
Like one that hath been seven days drown'd,
My body lay afloat;
But swift as dreams, myself I found
Within the Pilot's boat.   555

Upon the whirl, where sank the ship,
The boat spun round and round;
And all was still, save that the hill
Was telling of the sound.

I moved my lips—the Pilot shrieked   560
And fell down in a fit;
The holy Hermit raised his eyes,
And prayed where he did sit.

I took the oars: the Pilot's boy,
Who now doth crazy go,   565
Laughed loud and long, and all the while
His eyes went to and fro.
"Ha! ha!" quoth he, "full plain I see,
The Devil knows how to row."

And now, all in my own countree,   570
I stood on the firm land!
The Hermit stepped forth from the boat,
And scarcely he could stand.

"O shrieve me, shrieve me, holy man!"
The Hermit cross'd his brow.
"Say quick," quoth he, "I bid thee say—
What manner of man art thou?"

Forthwith this frame of mine was wrench'd
With a woeful agony,
Which forced me to begin my tale;
And then it left me free.

Since then, at an uncertain hour,
That agony returns;
And till my ghastly tale is told,
This heart within me burns.

I pass, like night, from land to land;
I have strange power of speech;
That moment that his face I see,
I know the man that must hear me:
To him my tale I teach.

What loud uproar bursts from that door!
The wedding-guests are there;
But in the garden-bower the bride
And bride-maids singing are;
And hark the little vesper bell,
Which biddeth me to prayer!

O Wedding-Guest! this soul hath been
Alone on a wide wide sea:
So lonely 'twas, that God himself
Scarce seemed there to be.

O sweeter than the marriage-feast,
'Tis sweeter far to me,
To walk together to the kirk
With a goodly company!—

To walk together to the kirk,
And all together pray,
While each to his great Father bends,
Old men, and babes, and loving friends,
And youths and maidens gay!

Farewell, farewell! but this I tell
To thee, thou Wedding-Guest!
He prayeth well, who loveth well
Both man and bird and beast.

He prayeth best, who loveth best
All things both great and small;
For the dear God who loveth us,
He made and loveth all."

575
580
585
590
595
600
605
610
615

The ancient Mariner
earnestly entreateth
the Hermit to shrieve
him; and the penance
of life falls on him.

And ever and anon
throughout his future
life an agony
constraineth him to
travel from land to land,

And to teach by his own
example, love and
reverence to all things
that God made and
loveth.

620

The Mariner, whose eye is bright,
Whose beard with age is hoar,
Is gone: and now the Wedding-Guest
Turned from the bridegroom's door.

He went like one that hath been stunned,
And is of sense forlorn:
A sadder and a wiser man,

625

He rose the morrow morn.

1817   1798–1817

Christabel[1]
Preface

The first part of the following poem was written in the year one thousand seven hundred and ninety seven,[2] at Stowey, in the county of Somerset. The second part, after my return from Germany, in the year one thousand eight hundred, at Keswick, Cumberland. Since the latter date, my poetic powers have been, till very lately, in a state of suspended animation. But as, in my very first conception of the tale, I had the whole present to my mind, with the wholeness, no less than with the liveliness of a vision; I trust that I shall be able to embody in verse the three parts yet to come, in the course of the present year.

It is probable, that if the poem had been finished at either of the former periods, or if even the first and second part had been published in the year 1800, the impression of its originality would have been much greater than I dare at present expect. But for this, I have only my own indolence to blame. The dates are mentioned for the exclusive purpose of precluding charges of plagiarism or servile imitation from myself. For there is among us a set of critics, who seem to hold, that every possible thought and image is traditional; who have no notion that there are such things as fountains in the world, small as well as great; and who would therefore charitably derive every rill they behold flowing, from a perforation made in some other man's tank. I am confident, however, that as far as the present poem is concerned, the celebrated poets whose writings I might be suspected of having imitated,[3] either in particular passages, or in the tone and the spirit of the whole, would be among the first to vindicate me from the charge, and who, on any striking coincidence, would permit me to address them in this doggerel version of two monkish Latin hexameters:

'Tis mine and it is likewise yours,
But an if this will not do;
Let it be mine, good friend! for I
Am the poorer of the two.

---

1. *Christabel* circulated in manuscript and recitation long before it was published in 1816, along with *Kubla Khan* and *The Pains of Sleep*, by Byron's publisher John Murray, and advertised with Byron's praise: "That wild and singularly original and beautiful Poem." But it proved controversial, some reviewers finding the heroine's encounter with Geraldine confusing, or worse: "disgusting" said one; "obscene" said another. Even so, the volume was popular enough to see two more editions in 1816. Perhaps to answer the reviews, in 1824 Coleridge added nine marginal notes (which we include with a caution: as with the 1817 gloss to *The Ancient Mariner*, these might satirize rather than satisfy desire for clarification). There is no other record of further work on the poem.

2. Actually, spring 1798; it was to be the closing poem of *Lyrical Ballads* 1800 (see Coleridge's account of the project, page 343), but Wordsworth thought it unsuitable and replaced it with *Michael*.

3. He is thinking of Scott's metrical tales, Byron's Eastern tales, and even Wordsworth's *White Doe of Rylstone*.

I have only to add, that the metre of the Christabel is not, properly speaking, irregular, though it may seem so from its being founded on a new principle: namely, that of counting in each line the accents, not the syllables. Though the latter may vary from seven to twelve, yet in each line the accents will be found to be only four. Nevertheless this occasional variation in number of syllables is not introduced wantonly, or for the mere ends of convenience, but in correspondence with some transition, in the nature of the imagery or passion.

PART I

'Tis the middle of night by the castle clock,
And the owls have awakened the crowing cock;
Tu—whit!——Tu—whoo!
And hark, again! the crowing cock,
5   How drowsily it crew.

Sir Leoline, the Baron rich,
Hath a toothless mastiff bitch;
From her kennel beneath the rock
She maketh answer to the clock,
10   Four for the quarters, and twelve for the hour;
Ever and aye,° by shine or shower,   *always*
Sixteen short howls, not over loud;
Some say, she sees my lady's shroud.

Is the night chilly and dark?
15   The night is chilly, but not dark.
The thin gray cloud is spread on high,
It covers but not hides the sky.
The moon is behind, and at the full;
And yet she looks both small and dull.
20   The night is chill, the cloud is gray:
'Tis a month before the month of May,
And the Spring comes slowly up this way.

The lovely lady, Christabel,
Whom her father loves so well,
25   What makes her in the wood so late,
A furlong° from the castle gate?   *220 yards*
She had dreams all yesternight
Of her own betrothed knight;
Dreams that made her moan and leap,
30   As on her bed she lay in sleep;[4]
And she in the midnight wood will pray
For the weal° of her lover that's far away.   *well-being*

She stole along, she nothing spoke,
The sighs she heaved were still also;
35   And nought was green upon the oak,

4. Deleted in 1824.

But moss and rarest mistletoe:[5]
She kneels beneath the huge oak tree,
And in silence prayeth she.

40 The lady leaps up suddenly,
The lovely lady, Christabel!
It moan'd as near, as near can be,
But what it is, she can not tell,—
On the other side it seems to be,
Of the huge, broad-breasted, old oak tree.

45 The night is chill; the forest bare;
Is it the wind that moaneth bleak?
There is not wind enough in the air
To move away the ringlet curl
From the lovely lady's cheek—
50 There is not wind enough to twirl
The one red leaf, the last of its clan,
That dances as often as dance it can,
Hanging so light, and hanging so high,
On the topmost twig that looks up at the sky.
55 Hush! beating heart of Christabel!
Jesu, Maria, shield her well!

She folded her arms beneath her cloak,
And stole to the other side of the oak.
    What sees she there?

60 There she sees a damsel bright,
Drest in a silken robe of white;
Her neck, her feet, her arms were bare;
And the jewels disorder'd in her hair.[6]
I guess, 'twas frightful there to see
65 A lady so richly clad as she—
Beautiful exceedingly!

Mary mother, save me now!
(Said Christabel,) And who art thou?

The lady strange made answer meet,
70 And her voice was faint and sweet:—
Have pity on my sore distress,
I scarce can speak for weariness.
Stretch forth thy hand, and have no fear!
Said Christabel, How cam'st thou here?
75 And the lady, whose voice was faint and sweet,
Did thus pursue her answer meet:—

---

5. Ancient Druids held such a sight in veneration, because the parasite mistletoe is rare on oak.
6. 62–63, revised 1824] That shadowy in the moonlight
shone: / The Neck, that made her white robe wan, / Her
stately Neck, and Arms were bare; / Her blue-vein'd Feet
unsandal'd were; / And wildly glitter'd here and there /
The Gems entangled in her hair!

My sire is of a noble line,
And my name is Geraldine.
Five warriors seiz'd me yestermorn,
80   Me, even me, a maid forlorn:
They chok'd my cries with force and fright,
And tied me on a palfrey° white.   *horse*
The palfrey was as fleet as wind,
And they rode furiously behind.
85   They spurrd amain,° their steeds were white;   *with full force*
And once we cross'd the shade of night.
As sure as Heaven shall rescue me,
I have no thought what men they be;
Nor do I know how long it is
90   (For I have lain in fits I wis°)   *believe*
Since one, the tallest of the five,
Took me from the palfrey's back,
A weary woman, scarce alive.
Some mutter'd words his comrades spoke:
95   He plac'd me underneath this oak,
He swore they would return with haste;
Whither they went I cannot tell—
I thought I heard, some minutes past,
Sounds as of a castle bell.
100   Stretch forth thy hand (thus ended she),
And help a wretched maid to flee.

Then Christabel stretch'd forth her hand
And comforted fair Geraldine,
Saying, that she should command
105   The service of Sir Leoline;
And straight be convoy'd, free from thrall,
Back to her noble father's hall.

So up she rose, and forth they pass'd
With hurrying steps, yet nothing fast.
110   Her lucky stars the lady blest,
And Christabel she sweetly said—
All our household are at rest,
Each one sleeping in his bed;
Sir Leoline is weak in health,
115   And may not well awaken'd be;
So to my room we'll creep in stealth,
And you tonight must sleep with me.[7]

They cross'd the moat, and Christabel
Took the key that fitted well;
120   A little door she opened straight,

---

7. marginal note, 1824] The Strange Lady cannot rise, without the touch of Christabel's Hand: and now she blesses her Stars. She will not praise the Creator of the Heavens, or name the saints.

All in the middle of the gate;
The gate that was iron'd within and without,
Where an army in battle array had march'd out.

The lady sank, belike thro' pain,
125 And Christabel with might and main
Lifted her up, a weary weight,
Over the threshold of the gate:
Then the lady rose again,
And mov'd, as she were not in pain.[8]

130 So free from danger, free from fear,
They cross'd the court: right glad they were.
And Christabel devoutly cried,
To the lady by her side,
Praise we the Virgin all divine
135 Who hath rescued thee from thy distress!
Alas, alas! said Geraldine,
I can not speak for weariness.[9]
So free from danger, free from fear,
They cross'd the court: right glad they were.

140 Outside her kennel, the mastiff old
Lay fast asleep, in moonshine cold.
The mastiff old did not awake,
Yet she an angry moan did make!
And what can ail the mastiff bitch?
145 Never till now she utter'd yell
Beneath the eye of Christabel.
Perhaps it is the owlet's scritch:
For what can ail the mastiff bitch?

They pass'd the hall, that echoes still,
150 Pass as lightly as you will!
The brands° were flat, the brands were dying,   *fireplace logs*
Amid their own white ashes lying;
But when the lady pass'd, there came
A tongue of light, a fit of flame;
155 And Christabel saw the lady's eye,
And nothing else saw she thereby,
Save the boss of the shield of Sir Leoline tall,
Which hung in a murky old nitch in the wall.
O softly tread, said Christabel,
160 My father seldom sleepeth well.

Sweet Christabel her feet she bares,
And they are creeping up the stairs;
Now in glimmer, and now in gloom,

8. marginal note, 1824] The strange lady may not pass the threshold without Christabel's help and will.

9. marginal note, 1824] The strange Lady makes an excuse, not to praise the Holy Virgin.

And now they pass the Baron's room,
165 As still as death with stifled breath!
And now have reach'd her chamber door;
And now doth Geraldine press down
The rushes of the chamber floor.

The moon shines dim in the open air,
170 And not a moonbeam enters here:
But they without its light can see
The chamber carv'd so curiously,
Carv'd with figures strange and sweet,
All made out of the carver's brain,
175 For a lady's chamber meet:
The lamp with twofold silver chain
Is fasten'd to an angel's feet.

The silver lamp burns dead and dim;
But Christabel the lamp will trim.
180 She trimm'd the lamp, and made it bright,
And left it swinging to and fro,
While Geraldine, in wretched plight,
Sank down upon the floor below.

O weary lady, Geraldine,
185 I pray you, drink this cordial wine!
It is a wine of virtuous powers;
My mother made it of wild flowers.

And will your mother pity me,
Who am a maiden most forlorn?

190 Christabel answer'd—Woe is me!
She died the hour that I was born.
I have heard the gray-hair'd friar tell,
How on her death-bed she did say,
That she should hear the castle-bell
195 Strike twelve upon my wedding-day.
O mother dear! that thou wert here!
I would, said Geraldine, she were!

But soon with alter'd voice, said she—
"Off, wandering mother![1] Peak and pine!
200 I have power to bid thee flee."
Alas! what ails poor Geraldine?
Why stares she with unsettled eye?
Can she the bodiless dead espy?[2]
And why with hollow voice cries she,

1. Literally, "hysteria," one symptom being an altered voice.
2. marginal note, 1824] The Mother of Christabel, who is now her Guardian Spirit, appears to Geraldine, as in answer to her wish. Geraldine fears the Spirit, but yet has power over it for a time.

205   "Off, woman, off! this hour is mine—
    Though thou her guardian spirit be,
    Off, woman, off! 'tis given to me."

    Then Christabel knelt by the lady's side,
    And raised to heaven her eyes so blue—
210   Alas! said she, this ghastly ride—
    Dear lady! it hath wilder'd you!
    The lady wip'd her moist cold brow,
    And faintly said, "'Tis over now!"

    Again the wild-flower wine she drank:
215   Her fair large eyes 'gan glitter bright,
    And from the floor whereon she sank,
    The lofty lady stood upright:
    She was most beautiful to see,
    Like a lady of a far countrée.

220   And thus the lofty lady spake—
    All they, who live in the upper sky,
    Do love you, holy Christabel!
    And you love them, and for their sake
    And for the good which me befel,
225   Even I in my degree will try,
    Fair maiden, to requite you well.
    But now unrobe yourself; for I
    Must pray, ere yet in bed I lie.

    Quoth Christabel, so let it be!
230   And as the lady bade, did she.
    Her gentle limbs did she undress,
    And lay down in her loveliness.

    But thro' her brain of weal and woe
    So many thoughts mov'd to and fro,
235   That vain it were her lids to close;
    So half-way from the bed she rose,
    And on her elbow did recline
    To look at the lady Geraldine.

    Beneath the lamp the lady bow'd,
240   And slowly roll'd her eyes around;
    Then drawing in her breath aloud,
    Like one that shudder'd, she unbound
    The cincture° from beneath her breast: *belt*
    Her silken robe, and inner vest,
245   Dropt to her feet, and full in view,
    Behold! her bosom and half her side—
    A sight to dream of, not to tell!
    And she is to sleep by Christabel!

She took two Paces, and a Stride,[3]
250   And lay down by the maiden's side!:[4]
And in her arms the maid she took,
    Ah wel-a-day!
And with low voice and doleful look
These words did say:
255   In the touch of this bosom there worketh a spell,
Which is lord of thy utterance, Christabel!
Thou knowest to-night, and wilt know to-morrow
This mark of my shame, this seal of my sorrow;
    But vainly thou warrest,
260   For this is alone in
    Thy power to declare,
        That in the dim forest
        Thou heard'st a low moaning,
And found'st a bright lady, surpassingly fair:
265   And didst bring her home with thee in love and in charity,
To shield her and shelter her from the damp air.

The Conclusion to Part the First

It was a lovely sight to see
The lady Christabel, when she
Was praying at the old oak tree.
270   Amid the jagged shadows
        Of mossy leafless boughs,
        Kneeling in the moonlight,
        To make her gentle vows;
Her slender palms together prest,
275   Heaving sometimes on her breast;
Her face resigned to bliss or bale°—   *woe, evil*
Her face, oh call it fair not pale;
And both blue eyes more bright than clear,
Each about to have a tear.

280   With open eyes (ah woe is me!)
Asleep, and dreaming fearfully,
Fearfully dreaming, yet I wis,°   *believe*
Dreaming that alone, which is—
O sorrow and shame! Can this be she,
285   The lady, who knelt at the old oak tree?
And lo! the worker of these harms,
That holds the maiden in her arms,
Seems to slumber still and mild,
As a mother with her child.

---

3. 248–49 revised 1817–1824] O shield her! shield sweet
Christabel / But Geraldine nor moves nor stirs; / Ah!
what a stricken Look was her's! / Deep from within she
seems half-way / To lift some weight, with Faint assay, /
And eyes the Maid, and seeks delay: / Then suddenly as
one defied / Collects herself in scorn and pride . . .
4. marginal note, 1824] As soon as the wicked Bosom,
with the mysterious sign of Evil stamped thereby, touches
Christabel, she is deprived of the power of disclosing
what has occurred.

290   A star hath set, a star hath risen,
        O Geraldine! since arms of thine
        Have been the lovely lady's prison.
        O Geraldine! one hour was thine—
        Thou'st had thy will! By tairn° and rill,   *mountain pool*
295   The night-birds all that hour were still.
        But now they are jubilant anew,
        From cliff and tower, tu—whoo! tu—whoo!
        Tu—whoo! tu—whoo! from wood and fell!°   *highland*

        And see! the lady Christabel
300   Gathers herself from out her trance;
        Her limbs relax, her countenance
        Grows sad and soft; the smooth thin lids
        Close o'er her eyes; and tears she sheds—
        Large tears that leave the lashes bright!
305   And oft the while she seems to smile
        As infants at a sudden light!

        Yea, she doth smile, and she doth weep,
        Like a youthful hermitess,
        Beauteous in a wilderness,
310   Who, praying always, prays in sleep.
        And, if she move unquietly,
        Perchance, 'tis but the blood so free,
        Comes back and tingles in her feet.
        No doubt, she hath a vision sweet.
315   What if her guardian spirit 'twere?
        What if she knew her mother near?
        But this she knows, in joys and woes,
        That saints will aid if men will call:
        For the blue sky bends over all!

                    PART II
320   Each matin bell, the Baron saith,
        Knells us back to a world of death.
        These words Sir Leoline first said,
        When he rose and found his lady dead:
        These words Sir Leoline will say,
325   Many a morn to his dying day.

        And hence the custom and law began,
        That still at dawn the sacristan,°   *sexton*
        Who duly pulls the heavy bell,
        Five and forty beads must tell°   *count*
330   Between each stroke—a warning knell,
        Which not a soul can choose but hear
        From Bratha Head to Wyn'dermere.[5]

5. These and the following names refer to places in the Lake District.

Saith Bracy the bard, So let it knell!
And let the drowsy sacristan
335   Still count as slowly as he can!
There is no lack of such, I ween,°   *believe*
As well fill up the space between.
In Langdale Pike and Witch's Lair,
And Dungeon-ghyll° so foully rent,   *ravine*
340   With ropes of rock and bells of air
Three sinful sextons' ghosts are pent,
Who all give back, one after t'other,
The death-note to their living brother;
And oft too, by the knell offended,
345   Just as their one! two! three! is ended,
The devil mocks the doleful tale
With a merry peal from Borrowdale.

The air is still! thro' mist and cloud
That merry peal comes ringing loud;
350   And Geraldine shakes off her dread,
And rises lightly from the bed;
Puts on her silken vestments white,
And tricks her hair in lovely plight,°   *plait*
And nothing doubting of her spell
355   Awakens the lady Christabel.
"Sleep you, sweet lady Christabel?
I trust that you have rested well."

And Christabel awoke and spied
The same who lay down by her side—
360   O rather say, the same whom she
Rais'd up beneath the old oak-tree!
Nay, fairer yet! and yet more fair!
For she belike hath drunken deep
Of all the blessedness of sleep!
365   And while she spake, her looks, her air
Such gentle thankfulness declare,
That (so it seem'd) her girded vests
Grew tight beneath her heaving breasts.
"Sure I have sinn'd!" said Christabel,
370   "Now heaven be prais'd if all be well!"
And in low faltering tones, yet sweet,[6]
Did she the lofty lady greet
With such perplexity of mind
As dreams too lively leave behind.

375   So quickly she rose, and quickly array'd
Her maiden limbs, and having pray'd
That He, who on the cross did groan,

6. marginal note, 1824] Christabel is made to believe, that the fearful Sight had taken place only in a dream.

Might wash away her sins unknown,
She forthwith led fair Geraldine
380   To meet her sire, Sir Leoline.

The lovely maid and the lady tall
Are pacing both into the hall,
And pacing on thro' page and groom
Enter the Baron's presence-room.

385   The Baron rose, and while he prest
His gentle daughter to his breast,
With cheerful wonder in his eyes
The lady Geraldine espies,
And gave such welcome to the same,
390   As might beseem so bright a dame!

But when he heard the lady's tale,
And when she told her father's name,
Why wax'd Sir Leoline so pale,
Murmuring o'er the name again,
395   Lord Roland de Vaux of Tryermaine?

Alas! they had been friends in youth;
But whispering tongues can poison truth;
And constancy lives in realms above;
And life is thorny; and youth is vain;
400   And to be wroth with one we love,
Doth work like madness in the brain.
And thus it chanc'd, as I divine,
With Roland and Sir Leoline.
Each spake words of high disdain
405   And insult to his heart's best brother:
They parted—ne'er to meet again!
But never either found another
To free the hollow heart from paining—
They stood aloof, the scars remaining,
410   Like cliffs which had been rent asunder;
A dreary sea now flows between,
But neither heat, nor frost, nor thunder,
Shall wholly do away, I ween,
The marks of that which once hath been.[7]

415   Sir Leoline, a moment's space,
Stood gazing on the damsel's face;
And the youthful Lord of Tryermaine
Came back upon his heart again.

O then the Baron forgot his age,
420   His noble heart swell'd high with rage;
He swore by the wounds in Jesu's side,
He would proclaim it far and wide

7. Lord Byron and Victorian essayist Walter Pater admired this passage on male friendship.

With trump and solemn heraldry,
That they, who thus had wronged the dame,
425   Were base as spotted infamy!
"And if they dare deny the same,
  My herald shall appoint a week,
  And let the recreant traitors seek
  My tourney court°—that there and then   *jousting arena*
430   I may dislodge their reptile souls
  From the bodies and forms of men!"
He spake: his eye in lightning rolls!
For the lady was ruthlessly seiz'd; and he kenn'd
In the beautiful lady the child of his friend!

435   And now the tears were on his face,
And fondly in his arms he took
Fair Geraldine, who met th' embrace,
Prolonging it with joyous look.
Which when she view'd, a vision fell
440   Upon the soul of Christabel,
The vision of fear, the touch and pain!
She shrunk and shudder'd, and saw again
(Ah, woe is me! Was it for thee,
Thou gentle maid! such sights to see?)[8]
445   Again she saw that bosom old,
Again she felt that bosom cold,
And drew in her breath with a hissing sound:
Whereat the Knight turned wildly round,
And nothing saw, but his own sweet maid
450   With eyes upraised, as one that pray'd.

The touch, the sight, had pass'd away,[9]
And in its stead that vision blest,
Which comforted her after-rest,
While in the lady's arms she lay,
455   Had put a rapture in her breast,
And on her lips and o'er her eyes
Spread smiles like light!
                   With new surprise,
"What ails then my beloved child?"
The Baron said—His daughter mild
460   Made answer, "All will yet be well!"
I ween, she had no power to tell
Aught else: so mighty was the spell.
Yet he, who saw this Geraldine,
Had deem'd her sure a thing divine,
465   Such sorrow with such grace she blended,
As if she fear'd, she had offended

8. marginal note, 1824] Christabel then recollects the whole, and knows that it was not a Dream: but yet cannot disclose the fact, that the strange Lady is a supernatural Being with the stamp of the Evil Ones on her.

9. marginal note, 1824] Christabel for a moment sees her Mother's Spirit.

Sweet Christabel, that gentle maid!
And with such lowly tones she prayed,
She might be sent without delay
470   Home to her father's mansion.
                                                "Nay!
Nay, by my soul!" said Leoline.
"Ho! Bracy, the bard, the charge be thine!
    Go thou, with music sweet and loud,
    And take two steeds with trappings proud,
475   And take the youth whom thou lov'st best
    To bear thy harp, and learn thy song,
    And clothe you both in solemn vest,
    And over the mountains haste along,
    Lest wand'ring folk, that are abroad,
480   Detain you on the valley road.

    And when he has cross'd the Irthing flood,
    My merry bard! he hastes, he hastes
    Up Knorren Moor, thro' Halegarth Wood,
    And reaches soon that castle good
485   Which stands and threatens Scotland's wastes.

    Bard Bracy! bard Bracy! your horses are fleet,[1]
    Ye must ride up the hall, your music so sweet,
    More loud than your horses' echoing feet!
    And loud and loud to Lord Roland call,
490   Thy daughter is safe in Langdale hall!
    Thy beautiful daughter is safe and free—
    Sir Leoline greets thee thus thro' me.
    He bids thee come without delay
    With all thy numerous array;
495   And take thy lovely daughter home,
    And he will meet thee on the way
    With all his numerous array
    White with their panting palfreys' foam:
    And by mine honour! I will say,
500   That I repent me of the day
    When I spake words of fierce disdain
    To Roland de Vaux of Tryermaine!—
    —For since that evil hour hath flown,
    Many a summer's sun have shone;
505   Yet ne'er found I a friend again
    Like Roland de Vaux of Tryermaine."

The lady fell, and clasped his knees,
Her face uprais'd, her eyes o'erflowing;
And Bracy replied, with faltering voice,
510   His gracious hail on all bestowing:—

---

1. marginal note, 1824] How gladly Sir Leoline repeats the names and shows, how familiarly he had once been acquainted with all the spots & paths in the neighborhood of his former Friend's Castle & Residence.

Thy words, thou sire of Christabel,
Are sweeter than my harp can tell;
Yet might I gain a boon° of thee,   favor
This day my journey should not be,
515   So strange a dream hath come to me:
That I had vow'd with music loud
To clear yon wood from thing unblest,
Warn'd by a vision in my rest!
For in my sleep I saw that dove,
520   That gentle bird, whom thou dost love,
And call'st by thy own daughter's name—
Sir Leoline! I saw the same,
Fluttering, and uttering fearful moan,
Among the green herbs in the forest alone.
525   Which when I saw and when I heard,
I wonder'd what might ail the bird:
For nothing near it could I see,
Save the grass and green herbs underneath the old tree.

And in my dream, methought, I went
530   To search out what might there be found;
And what the sweet bird's trouble meant,
That thus lay fluttering on the ground.
I went and peer'd, and could descry
No cause for her distressful cry;
535   But yet for her dear lady's sake
I stoop'd, methought the dove to take,
When lo! I saw a bright green snake
Coil'd around its wings and neck
Green as the herbs on which it couch'd,
540   Close by the dove's its head it crouch'd;
And with the dove it heaves and stirs,
Swelling its neck as she swell'd hers!
I woke; it was the midnight hour,
The clock was echoing in the tower;
545   But tho' my slumber was gone by,
This dream it would not pass away—
It seems to live upon my eye!
And thence I vow'd this self-same day,
With music strong and saintly song
550   To wander through the forest bare,
Lest aught unholy loiter there.

Thus Bracy said: the Baron, the while,
Half-listening heard him with a smile;
Then turn'd to Lady Geraldine,
555   His eyes made up of wonder and love;
And said in courtly accents fine,
Sweet maid, Lord Roland's beauteous dove,
With arms more strong than harp or song,

Thy sire and I will crush the snake!
560   He kiss'd her forehead as he spake,
And Geraldine in maiden wise
Casting down her large bright eyes,
With blushing cheek and courtesy fine
She turn'd her from Sir Leoline;
565   Softly gathering up her train,
That o'er her right arm fell again;
And folded her arms across her chest,
And couch'd her head upon her breast,
And look'd askance at Christabel——
570   Jesu Maria, shield her well!

A snake's small eye blinks dull and shy,
And the lady's eyes they shrunk in her head,
Each shrunk up to a serpent's eye,
And with somewhat of malice, and more of dread,
575   At Christabel she look'd askance!——
One moment—and the sight was fled!
But Christabel in dizzy trance,
Stumbling on the unsteady ground——
Shudder'd aloud, with a hissing sound;
580   And Geraldine again turn'd round,
And like a thing, that sought relief,
Full of wonder and full of grief,
She roll'd her large bright eyes divine
Wildly on Sir Leoline.

585   The maid, alas! her thoughts are gone,
She nothing sees—no sight but one!
The maid, devoid of guile and sin,
I know not how, in fearful wise
So deeply had she drunken in
590   That look, those shrunken serpent eyes,
That all her features were resign'd
To this sole image in her mind:
And passively did imitate
That look of dull and treacherous hate.
595   And thus she stood, in dizzy trance,
Still picturing that look askance
With forc'd unconscious sympathy
Full before her father's view——
As far as such a look could be,
600   In eyes so innocent and blue!

But when the trance was o'er, the maid
Paus'd awhile, and inly pray'd:
Then falling at her father's feet,
"By my mother's soul do I entreat
605   That thou this woman send away!"

She said: and more she could not say,
For what she knew she could not tell,
O'er-master'd by the mighty spell.

Why is thy cheek so wan and wild,
610 Sir Leoline? Thy only child
Lies at thy feet, thy joy, thy pride,
So fair, so innocent, so mild;
The same, for whom thy lady died!
O by the pangs of her dear mother
615 Think thou no evil of thy child!
For her, and thee, and for no other,
She pray'd the moment, ere she died:
Pray'd that the babe for whom she died,
Might prove her dear lord's joy and pride!
620   That prayer her deadly pangs beguil'd,
        Sir Leoline!
    And wouldst thou wrong thy only child,
        Her child and thine?
Within the Baron's heart and brain
625 If thoughts, like these, had any share,
They only swell'd his rage and pain,
And did but work confusion there.
His heart was cleft with pain and rage,
His cheeks they quiver'd, his eyes were wild.
630 Dishonour'd thus in his old age;
Dishonour'd by his only child,
And all his hospitality
To th'insulted daughter of his friend
By more than woman's jealousy,
635 Brought thus to a disgraceful end—
He roll'd his eye with stern regard
Upon the gentle minstrel bard,
And said in tones abrupt, austere—
Why, Bracy! dost thou loiter here?
640 I bade thee hence! The bard obey'd;
And turning from his own sweet maid,
The aged knight, Sir Leoline,
Led forth the lady Geraldine!

THE CONCLUSION TO PART THE SECOND[2]

A little child, a limber elf,
645 Singing, dancing to itself,
A fairy thing with red round cheeks
That always finds, and never seeks,
Makes such a vision to the sight
As fills a father's eyes with light;

2. This conclusion, not in any known manuscript of this poem, was drafted in a letter to Robert Southey, May 1801.

650   And pleasures flow in so thick and fast
       Upon his heart, that he at last
       Must needs express his love's excess
       With words of unmeant bitterness.
       Perhaps 'tis pretty to force together
655   Thoughts so all unlike each other;
       To mutter and mock a broken charm,
       To dally with wrong that does no harm.
       Perhaps 'tis tender too and pretty
       At each wild word to feel within,
660   A sweet recoil of love and pity.
       And what, if in a world of sin
       (O sorrow and shame should this be true!)
       Such giddiness of heart and brain
       Comes seldom save from rage and pain,
665   So talks as it's most used to do.

1797–1801   1816

Kubla Khan:
or
A Vision in a Dream[1]

Of the Fragment of Kubla Kahn

The following fragment is here published at the request of a poet of great and deserved celebrity,[2] and, as far as the Author's own opinions are concerned, rather as a psychological curiosity, than on the ground of any supposed *poetic* merits.

In the summer of the year 1797, the Author, then in ill health, had retired to a lonely farm house between Porlock and Linton, on the Exmoor confines of Somerset and Devonshire. In consequence of a slight indisposition, an anodyne[3] had been prescribed, from the effects of which he fell asleep in his chair at the moment that he was reading the following sentence, or words of the same substance, in "Purchas's Pilgrimage":[4] "Here the Khan Kubla commanded a palace to be built, and a stately garden thereunto: and thus ten miles of fertile ground were inclosed with a wall." The Author continued for about three hours in a profound sleep, at least of the external senses, during which time he has the most vivid confidence, that he could not have composed less than from two to three hundred lines; if that indeed can be called composition in which all the images rose up before him as *things,* with a parallel production of the correspondent expressions, without any sensation or consciousness of effort. On awaking he appeared to himself to have a distinct recollection of the whole, and taking his pen, ink, and paper, instantly and eagerly wrote down the lines that are here preserved. At this moment he was unfortunately called out by a person on business from Porlock, and detained by him above an hour, and on his return to

---

1. Grandson of Genghis Khan and Emperor of China in the 13th century.
2. Byron convinced his own publisher to issue the poem, together with *Christabel* and *The Pains of Sleep.*

3. A painkiller, probably laudanum (tincture of opium).
4. A collection of often fantastical accounts of foreign lands compiled by Samuel Purchas (1613). As a boy, Coleridge was an avid reader of such literature.

his room, found, to his no small surprise and mortification, that though he still retained some vague and dim recollection of the general purpose of the vision, yet, with the exception of some eight or ten scattered lines and images, all the rest had passed away like the images on the surface of a stream into which a stone has been cast, but, alas! without the after restoration of the latter:

> Then all the charm
> Is broken—all that phantom-world so fair
> Vanishes, and a thousand circlets spread,
> And each mis-shape the other. Stay awhile,
> Poor youth! who scarcely dar'st lift up thine eyes—
> The stream will soon renew its smoothness, soon
> The visions will return! And lo, he stays,
> And soon the fragments dim of lovely forms
> Come trembling back, unite, and now once more
> The pool becomes a mirror.[5]

Yet from the still surviving recollections in his mind, the Author has frequently purposed to finish for himself what had been originally, as it were, given to him. Σαμερον αδιον ασω:[6] but the to-morrow is yet to come.

As a contrast to this vision, I have annexed a fragment of a very different character, describing with equal fidelity the dream of pain and disease.[7]

(1816)

In Xanadu did KUBLA KHAN
A stately pleasure-dome decree
Where ALPH, the sacred river, ran
Through caverns measureless to man
5   Down to a sunless sea.
So twice five miles of fertile ground
With walls and towers were girdled round;
And here were gardens bright with sinuous rills
Where blossomed many an incense-bearing tree;
10   And here were forests ancient as the hills,
Enfolding[8] sunny spots of greenery.

But oh that deep romantic chasm which slanted
Down the green hill athwart a cedarn cover!
A savage place! as holy and inchanted
15   As e'er beneath a waning moon was haunted
By woman wailing for her demon-lover!
And from this chasm, with ceaseless turmoil seething,
As if this earth in fast thick pants were breathing,
A mighty fountain momently was forced:
20   Amid whose swift half-intermitted Burst
Huge fragments vaulted like rebounding hail,
Or chaffy grain beneath the thresher's flail:
And mid these dancing rocks at once and ever

---

5. Coleridge, *The Picture* (91–100).
6. From Theocritus, *Idyls*, 1.145: "I'll sing a sweeter song tomorrow."

7. *The Pains of Sleep.*
8. Revised from a likely printer's error, this was "And folding" in 1816.

It flung up momently the sacred river.
25   Five miles meandering with a mazy motion
Through wood and dale the sacred river ran,
Then reached the caverns measureless to man,
And sank in tumult to a lifeless ocean:
And 'mid this tumult Kubla heard from far
30   Ancestral voices prophesying war!

  The shadow of the dome of pleasure
  Floated midway on the waves;
  Where was heard the mingled measure
  From the fountain and the caves.
35   It was a miracle of rare device,
A sunny pleasure-dome with caves of ice!

  A damsel with a dulcimer
  In a vision once I saw:
  It was an Abyssinian maid
40   And on her dulcimer she played,
  Singing of Mount Abora.[9]
  Could I revive within me
  Her symphony and song,
  To such a deep delight 'twould win me
45   That with music loud and long,
I would build that dome in air,
That sunny dome! those caves of ice!
And all who heard should see them there,
And all should cry, Beware! Beware!
50   His flashing eyes, his floating hair!
Weave a circle round him thrice,
And close your eyes with holy dread:
For he on honey-dew hath fed,
And drank[1] the milk of Paradise.

1797   1816

The Pains of Sleep

In September 1803, on his return, alone, from a walking tour of Scotland begun with the Wordsworths, Coleridge sent this poem to brother-in-law Robert Southey, in a letter about his struggle to break a dependency on opium: "I have walked 263 miles in eight Days—so I must have strength somewhere but my spirits are dreadful, owing entirely to the Horrors of every night—I truly dread to sleep it is no shadow with me, but substantial Misery foot-thick, that makes me sit by my bedside of a morning, & <u>cry</u>—. I have abandoned all opiates except Ether be one; & that only in <u>fits</u>—& that is a blessed medicine!—& when you see me drink a glass of Spirit & Water, except by prescription of a physician, you shall despise me—but still I can not get quiet rest. . . . I do not know how I came to scribble down these verses to you—my heart

9. A fabled Paradise in equatorial Abyssinia, thought to be the head of the Nile River, mentioned by Purchas, and by Milton in *Paradise Lost* (4. 280–85).
1. Changed to "drunk" in 1832.

was aching, my head all confused—but they are, doggrels as they may be, a true portrait of my nights.—What to do, I am at a loss, for it hard thus to be withered, having the faculty & attainments, which I have." In 1806, Coleridge drafted *A Child's Evening Prayer*, which begins, "Ere on my bed my limbs I lay, / God grant me grace my prayers to say."

> Ere on my bed my limbs I lay,
> It hath not been my use to pray
> With moving lips or bended knees;
> But silently, by slow degrees,
> 5   My spirit I to Love compose,
> In humble trust mine eye-lids close,
> With reverential resignation,
> No wish conceived, no thought exprest,
> Only a *sense* of supplication;
> 10   A sense o'er all my soul imprest
> That I am weak, yet not unblest,
> Since in me, round me, every where
> Eternal Strength and Wisdom are.
>
> But yester-night I prayed aloud
> 15   In anguish and in agony,
> Up-starting from the fiendish crowd
> Of shapes and thoughts that tortured me:
> A lurid light, a trampling throng,
> Sense of intolerable wrong,
> 20   And whom I scorned, those only strong!
> Thirst of revenge, the powerless will
> Still baffled, and yet burning still!
> Desire with loathing strangely mixed
> On wild or hateful objects fixed.
> 25   Fantastic passions! maddening brawl!
> And shame and terror over all!
> Deeds to be hid which were not hid,
> Which all confused I could not know
> Whether I suffered, or I did:
> 30   For all seemed guilt, remorse or woe,
> My own or others still the same
> Life-stifling fear, soul-stifling shame.
>
> So two nights passed: the night's dismay
> Saddened and stunned the coming day.
> 35   Sleep, the wide blessing, seemed to me
> Distemper's worst calamity.
> The third night, when my own loud scream
> Had waked me from the fiendish dream,
> O'ercome with sufferings strange and wild,
> 40   I wept as I had been a child;
> And having thus by tears subdued
> My anguish to a milder mood,
> Such punishments, I said, were due

To natures deepliest stained with sin,—
45 For aye entempesting anew
The unfathomable hell within,[1]
The horror of their deeds to view,
To know and loathe, yet wish and do!
Such griefs with such men well agree,
50 But wherefore, wherefore fall on me?
To be beloved is all I need,
And whom I love, I love indeed.

1803   1816

DEJECTION:
An Ode[1]

Late, late yestreen I saw the new Moon,
With the old Moon in her arms;
And I fear, I fear, my Master dear!
We shall have a deadly storm.

Ballad of Sir PATRICK SPENCE[2]

I

WELL! If the Bard was weather-wise, who made
The grand old ballad of Sir Patrick Spence,
This night, so tranquil now, will not go hence
Unrous'd by winds, that ply a busier trade
5 Than those which mould yon cloud in lazy flakes,
Or the dull sobbing draft, that moans and rakes
Upon the strings of this Æolian lute,[3]
Which better far were mute.
For lo! the New-moon winter-bright!
10 And overspread with phantom-light,
(With swimming phantom light o'erspread
But rimm'd and circled by a silver thread)
I see the old Moon in her lap, foretelling
The coming on of rain and squally blast.
15 And oh! that even now the gust were swelling,
And the slant night-shower driving loud and fast!
Those sounds which oft have raised me, whilst they awed,
And sent my soul abroad,
Might now perhaps their wonted impulse give,
20 Might startle this dull pain, and make it move and live!

1. A painful affiliation with Milton's Satan: "the hot Hell that always in him burns" *in Paradise Lost* (9.467).
1. Originally a long verse-letter addressed to Sarah Hutchinson (beloved sister of William Wordsworth's wife) in April 1802, after hearing the first four stanzas of Wordsworth's "Intimations" Ode. When Coleridge put it in the *Morning Post* on 4 October 1802, Wordsworth's wedding day and the seventh anniversary of his own unhappy marriage, he cut it by half and made the addressee a generic "Edmund." Our text is from *Sibylline Leaves* (1817).
2. See page 171.
3. See *The Eolian Harp.*

II

A grief without a pang, void, dark, and drear,
    A stifled, drowsy, unimpassion'd grief,
    Which finds no natural outlet, no relief,
        In word, or sigh, or tear—

25 O Lady! in this wan and heartless mood,
To other thoughts by yonder throstle° woo'd,   *thrush*
    All this long eve, so balmy and serene,
Have I been gazing on the western sky,
    And it's peculiar tint of yellow green:

30 And still I gaze—and with how blank an eye!
And those thin clouds above, in flakes and bars,
That give away their motion to the stars;
Those stars, that glide behind them or between,
Now sparkling, now bedimm'd, but always seen;

35 Yon crescent Moon, as fix'd as if it grew
In its own cloudless, starless lake of blue;
I see them all so excellently fair,
I see, not feel how beautiful they are![4]

III

    My genial° spirits fail;[5]   *creative*
40   And what can these avail,
To lift the smothering weight from off my breast?
    It were a vain endeavor,
    Though I should gaze for ever
On that green light that lingers in the west:

45 I may not hope from outward forms to win
The passion and the life, whose fountains are within.

IV

O Lady! we receive but what we give,
And in our life alone does nature live:
Ours is her wedding-garment, ours her shroud!

50   And would we aught behold, of higher worth,
Than that inanimate° cold world allow'd   *soulless*
To the poor loveless ever-anxious crowd,
    Ah! from the soul itself must issue forth,
A light, a glory, a fair luminous cloud

55   Enveloping the Earth—
And from the soul itself must there be sent
    A sweet and potent voice, of its own birth,
Of all sweet sounds the life and element!

---

4. Compare Wordsworth's *Ode*, 36–50.   5. Compare *Tintern Abbey*, lines 114ff.

V

O pure of heart! thou need'st not ask of me
60   What this strong music in the soul may be!
What, and wherein it doth exist,
This light, this glory, this fair luminous mist,
This beautiful and beauty-making power.
    Joy, virtuous Lady! Joy that ne'er was given,
65   Save to the pure, and in their purest hour,
Life, and life's effluence, cloud at once and shower.
Joy, Lady! is the spirit and the power,
Which wedding Nature to us gives in dow'r,
    A new Earth and new Heaven,[6]
70   Undreamt of by the sensual and the proud—
Joy is the sweet voice, Joy the luminous cloud—
        We in ourselves rejoice!
And thence flows all that charms or ear or sight,
    All melodies the echoes of that voice,
75   All colours a suffusion from that light.

VI

There was a time when, though my path was rough,
    This joy within me dallied with distress,
And all misfortunes were but as the stuff
    Whence Fancy made me dreams of happiness:[7]
80   For hope grew round me, like the twining vine,
And fruits, and foliage, not my own, seem'd mine.
But now afflictions bow me down to earth:
Nor care I that they rob me of my mirth,
        But oh! each visitation
85   Suspends what nature gave me at my birth,
    My shaping spirit of Imagination.
For not to think of what I needs must feel,
    But to be still and patient, all I can;
And haply° by abstruse research to steal   perhaps
90   From my own nature all the natural Man—
    This was my sole resource, my only plan:
Till that which suits a part infects the whole,
And now is almost grown the habit of my Soul.

VII

Hence, viper thoughts, that coil around my mind,
95   Reality's dark dream!
I turn from you, and listen to the wind,
    Which long has rav'd unnotic'd. What a scream
Of agony by torture lengthen'd out
That lute sent forth! Thou Wind, that rav'st without,

6. "And I saw a new heaven and a new earth: for the   (Revelation 21.1).
first heaven and the first earth were passed away"   7. Compare the opening of Wordsworth's Ode.

100   Bare craig, or mountain-tairn,[8] or blasted tree,
Or pine-grove whither woodman never clomb,
Or lonely house, long held the witches' home,
    Methinks were fitter instruments for thee,
Mad Lutanist! who in this month of show'rs,
105 Of dark brown gardens, and of peeping flow'rs,
Mak'st Devils' yule,° with worse than wint'ry song,   *Christmas*
The blossoms, buds, and tim'rous leaves among.
    Thou Actor, perfect in all tragic sounds!
Thou mighty Poet, e'en to Frenzy bold!
110   What tell'st thou now about?
    'Tis of the Rushing of an Host in rout,
With groans of trampled men, with smarting wounds—
At once they groan with pain, and shudder with the cold!
But hush! there is a pause of deepest silence![9]
115   And all that noise, as of a rushing crowd,
With groans, and tremulous shudderings—all is over—
    It tells another tale, with sounds less deep and loud!
        A tale of less affright,
        And temper'd with delight,
120 As Otway's self had fram'd the tender lay[1]—
        'Tis of a little child,
        Upon a lonesome wild,
Not far from home, but she hath lost her way:
And now moans low in bitter grief and fear,
125 And now screams loud, and hopes to make her mother hear.

                VIII

'Tis midnight, but small thoughts have I of sleep;
Full seldom may my friend such vigils keep!
Visit her, gentle Sleep! with wings of healing,
    And may this storm be but a mountain-birth,°   *short-lived*
130 May all the stars hang bright above her dwelling,
    Silent as though they watch'd the sleeping Earth!
        With light heart may she rise,
        Gay fancy, cheerful eyes,
Joy lift her spirit, joy attune her voice:
135 To her may all things live, from Pole to Pole,
Their life the eddying of her living soul!
    O simple spirit, guided from above,
Dear Lady! friend devoutest of my choice,
Thus may'st thou ever, evermore rejoice.[2]

1802–1817   1817

8. This address to the wind will not appear extravagant to those who have heard it at night, and in a mountainous country [Coleridge's note]. A tairn is a small mountain lake.
9. Echoing Wordsworth's *There was a Boy*, 17ff.
1. Thomas Otway, author of *The Orphan* (1680) and other tragedies noted for pathos. In earlier versions the poet is "William," alluding to Wordsworth's *Lucy Gray* and its keynote rhymes. (See page 209.)
2. The *Morning Post* version is signed ΕΣΤΗΣΕ, Greek phonics for STC.

BIOGRAPHIA LITERARIA   In 1803 Coleridge contemplated writing "my metaphysical works *as my life, & in* my life—intermixed with all the other events of history of the mind and fortunes of S.T. Coleridge." Nothing came of this Romantic interfusion of personal experience and philosophical generalization until 1815, when Coleridge decided to prefix *Sibylline Leaves* with "a general preface . . . on the principles" of criticism. Wordsworth's *Poems* (1815), with an extensive prefatory essay, further prompted Coleridge to clarify his theoretical divergences from his former collaborator. The resulting *Biographia Literaria*, grown from preface to two independent volumes, is an extraordinary work: a revisionary autobiography, minimizing the youthful radicalism; a philosophical argument to establish the freedom of the will, yet so enmeshed in the material exigencies of book production that publication was delayed for two years; a meditation on original genius heavily indebted to recent German thought; and, in Chapter 13, a comic masquerade that has proved a seminal passage for literary studies. In his sustained, probing commentary on Wordsworth, unprecedented in discussions of modern literature, Coleridge confirmed Wordsworth's stature and, at the same time, by claiming to understand Wordsworth better than he did himself, institutionalized the role of the critic as the reader who completes the poet's task. *Lyrical Ballads* (1798) had been a joint project of Wordsworth and Coleridge; Coleridge said in 1800 that the new Preface "contains our joint opinions on Poetry," but by 1802 he had begun "to suspect, that there is, somewhere or other, a *radical* difference in our opinions."

Biographia Literaria or, Biographical Sketches of My Literary Life and Opinions

from *Chapter 4*
[WORDSWORTH'S EARLIER POETRY]

I was in my twenty-fourth year, when I had the happiness of knowing Mr. Wordsworth personally, and while memory lasts, I shall hardly forget the sudden effect produced on my mind, by his recitation of a manuscript poem, which still remains unpublished.[1] * * * There was here, no mark of strained thought, or forced diction, no crowd or turbulence of imagery, and, as the poet hath himself well described in his lines "on revisiting the Wye," manly reflection, and human associations had given both variety, and an additional interest to natural objects, which in the passion and appetite of the first love they had seemed to him neither to need or permit. The occasional obscurities, which had risen from an imperfect controul over the resources of his native language, had almost wholly disappeared, together with that worse defect of arbitary and illogical phrases, at once hackneyed, and fantastic, which hold so distinguished a place in the *technique* of ordinary poetry, and will, more or less, alloy the earlier poems of the truest genius, unless the attention has been specifically directed to their worthlessness and incongruity.[2] * * * It was not however the freedom from false taste, whether as to common defects, or to those more properly his own, which made so unusual an impression on my feelings immediately, and subsequently on my judgement. It was the union of deep feeling with profound thought; the fine balance of truth in observing with the imaginative faculty in modifying the objects observed; and above all the original gift of spreading the tone, the *atmosphere*, and with it the depth and height of the ideal world around forms, incidents, and situations, of which, for the common view, custom had

---

1. *Guilt and Sorrow; or, Incidents upon Salisbury Plain,* written in 1793–1794, not published until 1842.

2. Coleridge described Wordsworth's *Descriptive Sketches* (1793) as work of "genius" but "knotty and contorted."

bedimmed all the lustre, had dried up the sparkle and the dew drops. To find no contradiction in the union of old and new; to contemplate the ANCIENT of days and all his works with feelings as fresh, as if all had then sprang forth at the first creative fiat;[3] characterizes the mind that feels the riddle of the world, and may help to unravel it. To carry on the feelings of childhood into the powers of manhood; to combine the child's sense of wonder and novelty with the appearances, which every day for perhaps forty years had rendered familiar;

> With sun and moon and stars throughout the year,
> And man and woman;[4]

this is the character and privilege of genius, and one of the marks which distinguish genius from talents. And therefore is it the prime merit of genius and its most unequivocal mode of manifestation, so to represent familiar objects as to awaken in the minds of others a kindred feeling concerning them and that freshness of sensation which is the constant accompaniment of mental, no less than of bodily, convalescence. Who has not a thousand times seen snow fall on water? Who has not watched it with a new feeling, from the time that he has read Burns' comparison of sensual pleasure

> To snow that falls upon a river
> A moment white—then gone for ever![5]

from *Chapter 11*
[THE PROFESSION OF LITERATURE]

With no other privilege than that of sympathy and sincere good wishes, I would address an affectionate exhortation to the youthful literati, grounded on my own experience. It will be but short; for the beginning, middle, and end converge to one charge: NEVER PURSUE LITERATURE AS A TRADE. With the exception of one extraordinary man, I have never known an individual, least of all an individual of genius, healthy or happy without a *profession,* i.e. some *regular* employment, which does not depend on the will of the moment, and which can be carried on so far *mechanically* that an average quantum only of health, spirits, and intellectual exertion are requisite to its faithful discharge. Three hours of leisure, unannoyed by any alien anxiety, and looked forward to with delight as a change and recreation, will suffice to realize in literature a larger product of what is truly *genial,* than weeks of compulsion. Money, and immediate reputation form only an arbitrary and accidental end of literary labor. The *hope* of increasing them by any given exertion will often prove a stimulant to industry; but the *necessity* of acquiring them will in all works of genius convert the stimulant into a *narcotic.* Motives by excess reverse their very nature, and instead of exciting, stun and stupify the mind. For it is one contradistinction of genius from talent, that its predominant end is always comprized in the means; and this is one of the many points, which establish an analogy between genius and virtue. Now though talents may exist without genius, yet as genius cannot exist, certainly not manifest itself, without talents, I would advise every scholar, who feels the genial power working within him, so far to make a division between the two, as that he should devote his *talents* to the acquirement of competence in some known trade or

---

3. Divine command.
4. What Milton can no longer see (*To Mr. Cyriack Skinner*

upon his Blindness, 5–6).
5. Robert Burns, *Tam O'Shanter* (61–62).

profession, and his genius to objects of his tranquil and unbiassed choice; while the consciousness of being actuated in both alike by the sincere desire to perform his duty, will alike ennoble both. My dear young friend (I would say) suppose yourself established in any honourable occupation. From the manufactory or counting-house, from the law-court, or from having visited your last patient, you return at evening,

> Dear tranquil time, when the sweet sense of home
> Is sweetest———[1]

to your family, prepared for its social enjoyments, with the very countenances of your wife and children brightened, and their voice of welcome made doubly welcome, by the knowledge that, as far as they are concerned, you have satisfied the demands of the day by the labor of the day. Then, when you retire into your study, in the books on your shelves you revisit so many venerable friends with whom you can converse. Your own spirit scarcely less free from personal anxieties than the great minds, that in those books are still living for you! Even your writing desk with its blank paper and all its other implements will appear as a chain of flowers, capable of linking your feelings as well as thoughts to events and characters past or to come; not a chain of iron which binds you down to think of the future and the remote by recalling the claims and feelings of the peremptory present. But why should I say *retire*? The habits of active life and daily intercourse with the stir of the world will tend to give you such self-command, that the presence of your family will be no interruption. Nay, the social silence, or undisturbing voices of a wife or sister will be like a restorative atmosphere, or soft music which moulds a dream without becoming its object. If facts are required to prove the possibility of combining weighty performances in literature with full and independent employment, the works of Cicero and Xenophon among the ancients; of Sir Thomas Moore, Bacon, Baxter, or to refer at once to later and contemporary instances, DARWIN and ROSCOE,[2] are at once decisive of the question.

* * * It would be a sort of irreligion, and scarcely less than a libel on human nature to believe, that there is any established and reputable profession or employment, in which a man may not continue to act with honesty and honor; and doubtless there is likewise none, which may not at times present temptations to the contrary. But woefully will that man find himself mistaken, who imagines that the profession of literature, or (to speak more plainly) the *trade* of authorship, besets its members with fewer or with less insidious temptations, than the church, the law, or the different branches of commerce. But I have treated sufficiently on this unpleasant subject in an early chapter of this volume. I will conclude the present therefore with a short extract from HERDER,[3] whose name I might have added to the illustrious list of those, who have combined the successful pursuit of the muses, not only with the faithful discharge, but with the highest honors and honorable emoluments, of an established profession. [Coleridge prints the German passage and translates] "With the greatest possible solicitude avoid authorship. Too early or immoderately employed, it makes the head *waste* and the heart empty; even were there no other worse consequences. A person, who reads only to print, in all probability reads amiss; and he, who sends away through the pen and the press every thought, the moment it occurs to him, will

---

1. Coleridge's *To A Gentleman* (92–93).
2. Cicero and Xenophon were illustrious statesmen. More (1478–1535) and Bacon (1561–1626) both served as Lord Chancellor in their public careers. Erasmus Darwin, a physician and a poet, and William Roscoe, a lawyer and aboli-

tionist, were contemporaries and friends of Coleridge.
3. J. G. Herder (1744–1803), German poet, critic, and philosopher of history, was superintendent of religious and educational affairs at Weimar. Coleridge quotes from his *Letters on the Study of Theology*.

in a short time have sent all away, and will become a mere journeyman of the printing-office, a *compositor*."

To which I may add from myself, that what medical physiologists affirm of certain secretions, applies equally to our thoughts; they too must be taken up again into the circulation, and be again and again re-secreted in order to ensure a healthful vigor, both to the mind and to its intellectual offspring.

from **Chapter 13**
[IMAGINATION AND FANCY]

Thus far had the work been transcribed for the press, when I received the following letter from a friend,[1] whose practical judgement I have had ample reason to estimate and revere, and whose taste and sensibility preclude all the excuses which my self-love might possibly have prompted me to set up in plea against the decision of advisers of equal good sense, but with less tact and feeling.

Dear C.

You ask my opinion concerning your Chapter on the Imagination, both as to the impressions it made on myself, and as to those which I think it will make on the PUBLIC, *i.e. that part of the public, who from the title of the work and from its forming a sort of introduction to a volume of poems, are likely to constitute the great majority of your readers.*

As to myself, and stating in the first place the effect on my understanding, your opinions and method of argument were not only so new to me, but so directly the reverse of all I had ever been accustomed to consider as truth, that even if I had comprehended your premises sufficiently to have admitted them, and had seen the necessity of your conclusions, I should still have been in that state of mind, which in your note, p. 75, 76, you have so ingeniously evolved, as the antithesis to that in which a man is, when he makes a bull.[2] In your own words, I should have felt as if I had been standing on my head.

The effect on my feelings, on the other hand, I cannot better represent, than by supposing myself to have known only our light airy modern chapels of ease, and then for the first time to have been placed, and left alone, in one of our largest Gothic cathedrals in a gusty moonlight night of autumn. "Now in glimmer, and now in gloom;"[3] often in palpable darkness not without a chilly sensation of terror; then suddenly emerging into broad yet visionary lights with coloured shadows, of fantastic shapes yet all decked with holy insignia and mystic symbols; and ever and anon coming out full upon pictures and stone-work images of great men, with whose names I was familiar, but which looked upon me with countenances and an expression, the most dissimilar to all I had been in the habit of connecting with those names. Those whom I had been taught to venerate as almost super-human in magnitude of intellect, I found perched in little fret-work niches, as grotesque dwarfs; while the grotesques, in my hitherto belief, stood guarding the high altar with all the characters of Apotheosis.[4] In short, what I had supposed substances were thinned away into shadows, while every where shadows were deepened into substances:

> If substance may be call'd what shadow seem'd,
> For each seem'd either!   Milton[5]

---

1. Coleridge wrote the letter himself.
2. Contradicts himself, inviting ridicule.
3. *Christabel*, line 163.

4. Divinity.
5. A famous description of Death; *Paradise Lost*, 2.669–70.

Yet after all, I could not but repeat the lines which you had quoted from a MS. poem of your own in the FRIEND[6] *and applied to a work of Mr. Wordsworth's though with a few of the words altered:*

> _____An orphic tale indeed,
> A tale obscure of high and passionate thoughts
> To a strange music chaunted![7]

Be assured, however, that I look forward anxiously to your great book on the CONSTRUCTIVE PHILOSOPHY,[8] *which you have promised and announced: and that I will do my best to understand it. Only I will not promise to descend into the dark cave of Trophonius[9] with you, there to rub my own eyes, in order to make the sparks and figured flashes, which I am required to see.*

So much for myself. But as for the PUBLIC, *I do not hesitate a moment in advising and urging you to withdraw the Chapter from the present work, and to reserve it for your announced treatises on the Logos or communicative intellect in Man and Deity.[1] First, because imperfectly as I understand the present Chapter, I see clearly that you have done too much, and yet not enough. You have been obliged to omit so many links, from the necessity of compression, that what remains, looks (if I may recur to my former illustration) like the fragments of the winding steps of an old ruined tower. Secondly, a still stronger argument (at least one that I am sure will be more forcible with you) is, that your readers will have both right and reason to complain of you. This Chapter, which cannot, when it is printed, amount to so little as an hundred pages, will of necessity greatly increase the expense of the work; and every reader who, like myself, is neither prepared or perhaps calculated for the study of so abstruse a subject so abstrusely treated, will, as I have before hinted, be almost entitled to accuse you of a sort of imposition on him. For who, he might truly observe, could from your title-page, viz. "𝕸𝖞 𝕷𝖎𝖙𝖊𝖗𝖆𝖗𝖞 𝕷𝖎𝖋𝖊 𝖆𝖓𝖉 𝕺𝖕𝖎𝖓𝖎𝖔𝖓𝖘," published too as introductory to a volume of miscellaneous poems, have anticipated, or even conjectured, a long treatise on ideal Realism, which holds the same relation in abstruseness to Plotinus, as Plotinus does to Plato.[2] It will be well, if already you have not too much of metaphysical disquisition in your work, though as the larger part of the disquisition is historical, it will doubtless be both interesting and instructive to many to whose unprepared minds your speculations on the esemplastic[3] power would be utterly unintelligible. Be assured, if you do publish this Chapter in the present work, you will be reminded of Bishop Berkley's Siris,[4] announced as an Essay on Tar-water, which beginning with Tar ends with the Trinity, the omne scibile [everything knowable] forming the interspace. I say in the present work. In that greater work to which you have devoted so many years, and study so intense and various, it will be in its proper place. Your prospectus will have described and announced both its contents and their nature; and if any persons purchase it, who feel no interest in the subjects of which it treats, they will have themselves only to blame.*

---

6. The journal produced by Coleridge in 1809–1810.
7. *To A Gentleman*, 45–47 (variant).
8. Perhaps the *Logic* or *Opus Maximum*, or Coleridge's Kantian model of philosophy.
9. Legendary architect of the temple of Apollo at Delphi. After his death an oracle was consecrated to him; visitors were dragged into a cave filled with strange sounds and glaring lights, where they received the oracle's messages.
1. The Word of God, incarnated in Jesus Christ. Coleridge announced a study of the Gospel of John as part of a work that never appeared, the *Logosophia*.

2. An "ideal realist," Coleridge rejected the Platonic distinction between the essence and appearance of things for an idea of the world and the mind infused by one spirit, a position derived from Plato's inheritor Plotinus.
3. An invented word, meaning unifying or synthesizing.
4. George Berkeley (1685–1753), Irish bishop and philosopher. *Siris* (1744) begins with a chemical description of the medicinal advantages of tar and proceeds to reflections on theology. Coleridge admired philosophy tied to the empirical truths of the natural sciences.

I could add to these arguments one derived from pecuniary[5] motives, and particularly from the probable effects on the sale of your present publication; but they would weigh little with you compared with the preceding. Besides, I have long observed, that arguments drawn from your own personal interests more often act on you as narcotics than as stimulants, and that in money concerns you have some small portion of pig nature in your moral idiosyncracy, and like these amiable creatures, must occasionally be pulled backward from the boat in order to make you enter it. All success attend you, for if hard thinking and hard reading are merits, you have deserved it.

Your affectionate, & c.

In consequence of this very judicious letter, which produced complete conviction on my mind, I shall content myself for the present with stating the main result of the Chapter, which I have reserved for that future publication, a detailed prospectus of which the reader will find at the close of the second volume.

The IMAGINATION then I consider either as primary, or secondary. The primary IMAGINATION I hold to be the living Power and prime Agent of all human Perception, and as a repetition in the finite mind of the eternal act of creation in the infinite I AM. The secondary I consider as an echo of the former, co-existing with the conscious will, yet still as identical with the primary in the *kind* of its agency, and differing only in *degree*, and in the *mode* of its operation. It dissolves, diffuses, dissipates, in order to re-create; or where this process is rendered impossible, yet still at all events it struggles to idealize and to unify. It is essentially *vital*, even as all objects (as objects) are essentially fixed and dead.

FANCY, on the contrary, has no other counters to play with, but fixities and definites. The Fancy is indeed no other than a mode of Memory emancipated from the order of time and space; and blended with, and modified by that empirical phenomenon of the will, which we express by the word CHOICE. But equally with the ordinary memory it must receive all its materials ready made from the law of association.

Whatever more than this, I shall think it fit to declare concerning the powers and privileges of the imagination in the present work, will be found in the critical essay on the uses of the Supernatural in poetry and the principles that regulate its introduction: which the reader will find prefixed to the poem of 𝔗𝔥𝔢 𝔄𝔫𝔠𝔦𝔢𝔫𝔱 𝔐𝔞𝔯𝔦𝔫𝔢𝔯.[6]

from *Chapter 14*

[OCCASION OF THE *LYRICAL BALLADS*—PREFACE TO THE SECOND EDITION— THE ENSUING CONTROVERSY]

During the first year that Mr. Wordsworth and I were neighbours, our conversations turned frequently on the two cardinal points of poetry, the power of exciting the sympathy of the reader by a faithful adherence to the truth of nature, and the power of giving the interest of novelty by the modifying colours of imagination. The sudden charm, which accidents of light and shade, which moon-light or sun-set diffused over a known and familiar landscape, appeared to represent the practicability of combining both. These are the poetry of nature. The thought suggested itself (to which of us I do not recollect) that a series of poems might be composed of two sorts. In the one, the incidents and agents were to be, in part at least, supernatural; and the excellence

---

5. Financial.   6. The essay did not appear.

aimed at was to consist in the interesting of the affections by the dramatic truth of such emotions, as would naturally accompany such situations, supposing them real. And real in *this* sense they have been to every human being who, from whatever source of delusion, has at any time believed himself under supernatural agency. For the second class, subjects were to be chosen from ordinary life; the characters and incidents were to be such, as will be found in every village and its vicinity, where there is a meditative and feeling mind to seek after them, or to notice them, when they present themselves.

In this idea originated the plan of the *Lyrical Ballads*; in which it was agreed, that my endeavours should be directed to persons and characters supernatural, or at least romantic; yet so as to transfer from our inward nature a human interest and a semblance of truth sufficient to procure for these shadows of imagination that willing suspension of disbelief for the moment, which constitutes poetic faith. Mr. Wordsworth, on the other hand, was to propose to himself as his object, to give the charm of novelty to things of every day, and to excite a feeling analogous to the supernatural, by awakening the mind's attention from the lethargy of custom, and directing it to the loveliness and the wonders of the world before us; an inexhaustible treasure, but for which in consequence of the film of familiarity and selfish solicitude we have eyes, yet see not, ears that hear not, and hearts that neither feel nor understand.[1]

With this view I wrote the "Ancient Mariner," and was preparing among other poems, the "Dark Ladie," and the "Christabel," in which I should have more nearly realized my ideal, than I had done in my first attempt. But Mr. Wordsworth's industry had proved so much more successful, and the number of his poems so much greater, that my compositions, instead of forming a balance, appeared rather an interpolation of heterogeneous matter. Mr. Wordsworth added two or three poems written in his own character, in the impassioned, lofty, and sustained diction, which is characteristic of his genius. In this form the *Lyrical Ballads* were published; and were presented by him, as an *experiment*,[2] whether subjects, which from their nature rejected the usual ornaments and extra-colloquial style of poems in general, might not be so managed in the language of ordinary life as to produce the pleasurable interest, which it is the peculiar business of poetry to impart. To the second edition he added a preface of considerable length; in which notwithstanding some passages of apparently a contrary import, he was understood to contend for the extension of this style to poetry of all kinds, and to reject as vicious and indefensible all phrases and forms of style that were not included in what he (unfortunately, I think, adopting an equivocal expression) called the language of *real life*. From this preface, prefixed to poems in which it was impossible to deny the presence of original genius, however mistaken its direction might be deemed, arose the whole long continued controversy. For from the conjunction of perceived power with supposed heresy I explain the inveteracy[3] and in some instances, I grieve to say, the acrimonious passions, with which the controversy has been conducted by the assailants.

Had Mr. Wordsworth's poems been the silly, the childish things, which they were for a long time described as being; had they been really distinguished from the compositions of other poets merely by meanness of language and inanity of thought; had they indeed contained nothing more than what is found in the parodies and

---

1. Echoing Jeremiah 5.21 and Isaiah 6.10.
2. "Experiments" is Wordsworth's term in the Advertisement to the 1798 *Lyrical Ballads*.
3. Deep-seated prejudice.

pretended imitations of them; they must have sunk at once, a dead weight, into the slough of oblivion, and have dragged the preface along with them. But year after year increased the number of Mr. Wordsworth's admirers. They were found too not in the lower classes of the reading public, but chiefly among young men of strong sensibility and meditative minds; and their admiration (inflamed perhaps in some degree by opposition) was distinguished by its intensity, I might almost say, by its *religious* fervour. These facts, and the intellectual energy of the author, which was more or less consciously felt, where it was outwardly and even boisterously denied, meeting with sentiments of aversion to his opinions, and of alarm at their consequences, produced an eddy of criticism, which would of itself have borne up the poems by the violence, with which it whirled them round and round. With many parts of this preface in the sense attributed to them and which the words undoubtedly seem to authorise, I never concurred; but on the contrary objected to them as erroneous in principle, and as contradictory (in appearance at least) both to other parts of the same preface, and to the author's own practice in the greater number of the poems themselves. Mr. Wordsworth in his recent collection[4] has, I find, degraded this prefatory disquisition to the end of his second volume, to be read or not at the reader's choice. But he has not, as far as I can discover, announced any change in his poetic creed. [At] all events, considering it as the source of a controversy, in which I have been honored more, than I deserve, by the frequent conjunction of my name with his, I think it expedient to declare once for all, in what points I coincide with his opinions, and in what points I altogether differ. But in order to render myself intelligible I must previously, in as few words as possible, explain my ideas, first, of a POEM; and secondly, of POETRY itself, in *kind*, and in *essence*.

[PHILOSOPHIC DEFINITIONS OF A POEM AND POETRY]

A poem is that species of composition, which is opposed to works of science, by proposing for its *immediate* object pleasure, not truth; and from all other species (having *this* object in common with it) it is discriminated by proposing to itself such delight from the *whole*, as is compatible with a distinct gratification from each component *part*. * * *

But if this should be admitted as a satisfactory character of a poem, we have still to seek for a definition of poetry. The writings of PLATO, and Bishop TAYLOR, and the *Theoria Sacra* of BURNET,[5] furnish undeniable proofs that poetry of the highest kind may exist without metre, and even without the contra-distinguishing objects of a poem. The first chapter of Isaiah (indeed a very large proportion of the whole book) is poetry in the most emphatic sense; yet it would be not less irrational than strange to assert, that pleasure, and not truth, was the immediate object of the prophet. In short, whatever *specific* import we attach to the word, poetry, there will be found involved in it, as a necessary consequence, that a poem of any length neither can be, or ought to be, all poetry. * * *

What is poetry? is so nearly the same question with, what is a poet? that the answer to the one is involved in the solution of the other. For it is a distinction resulting from the poetic genius itself, which sustains and modifies the images, thoughts, and emotions of the poet's own mind. The poet, described in ideal

---

4. *Poems* (1815).
5. Jeremy Taylor, author of *Holy Living* and *Holy Dying* (1650–1651); and 17th-century theologian Thomas

Burnet (who supplies the epigraph for the 1817 *Ancient Mariner*).

perfection, brings the whole soul of man into activity, with the subordination of its faculties to each other, according to their relative worth and dignity. He diffuses a tone, and spirit of unity, that blends, and (as it were) *fuses*, each into each, by that synthetic and magical power, to which we have exclusively appropriated the name of imagination. This power, first put in action by the will and understanding, and retained under their irremissive, though gentle and unnoticed, controul (*laxis effertur habenis* [guided by loose reins]) reveals itself in the balance or reconciliation of opposite or discordant qualities: of sameness, with difference; of the general, with the concrete; the idea, with the image; the individual, with the representative; the sense of novelty and freshness, with old and familiar objects; a more than usual state of emotion, with more than usual order; judgement ever awake and steady self-possession, with enthusiasm and feeling profound or vehement; and while it blends and harmonizes the natural and the artificial, still subordinates art to nature; the manner to the matter; and our admiration of the poet to our sympathy with the poetry. * * *

Finally, GOOD SENSE is the BODY of poetic genius, FANCY its DRAPERY, MOTION its LIFE, and IMAGINATION the SOUL that is every where, and in each; and forms all into one graceful and intelligent whole.

from Lectures on Shakespeare[1]

[MECHANIC VS. ORGANIC FORM]

—Imagine not that I am about to oppose genius to rules. No! the comparative value of these rules is the very cause to be tried. The spirit of poetry, like all other living powers, must of necessity circumscribe itself by rules, were it only to unite power with beauty. It must embody in order to reveal itself; but a living body is of necessity an organized one; and what is organization but the connection of parts in and for a whole, so that each part is at once end and means?—This is no discovery of criticism;—it is a necessity of the human mind; and all nations have felt and obeyed it, in the invention of metre, and measured sounds, as the vehicle and *involucrum* [covering] of poetry—itself a fellow-growth from the same life—even as the bark is to the tree!

No work of true genius dares want its appropriate form, neither indeed is there any danger of this. As it must not, so genius can not, be lawless; for it is even this that constitutes it genius—the power of acting creatively under laws of its own origination. How then comes it that not only single *Zoili*,[2] but whole nations have combined in unhesitating condemnation of our great dramatist, as a sort of African nature, rich in beautiful monsters—as a wild heath where islands of fertility look the greener from the surrounding waste, where the loveliest plants now shine out among unsightly weeds, and now are choked by their parasitic growth, so intertwined that we can not disentangle the weed without snapping the flower? * * * The true ground of the mistake lies in the confounding mechanical regularity with organic form. The form is mechanic, when on any given material we impress a pre-determined form, not necessarily arising out of the properties of the material;—as when to a mass of wet clay we give whatever shape we wish it to retain when hardened. The organic form,

---

1. Coleridge gave these lectures in 1811–1812, speaking from notes. The texts were assembled from notes by attendees, which scholars later developed.

2. Malicious or pedantic critics. Greek grammarian Zoilus (4th century B.C.) was known for unforgiving criticism of Homer.

on the other hand, is innate; it shapes, as it develops itself from within, and the fulness of its development is one and the same with the perfection of its outward form. Such as the life is, such is the form. Nature, the prime genial artist, inexhaustible in diverse powers, is equally inexhaustible in forms;—each exterior is the physiognomy of the being within—its true image reflected and thrown out from the concave mirror;—and even such is the appropriate excellence of her chosen poet, of our own Shakespeare—himself a nature humanized, a genial understanding directing self-consciously a power and an implicit wisdom deeper even than our consciousness.

✦ ❧ ✦

George Gordon, Lord Byron
1788–1824

"Mad, bad, and dangerous to know," pronounced Lady Caroline Lamb, before becoming his lover; a "splendid and imperishable excellence of sincerity and strength," declared Matthew Arnold: the fascination that made Byron the archetypal Romantic, in Europe even more than in Britain, grew from both judgments. He was born in London in 1788, the son of Captain John "Mad Jack" Byron and his second wife, Catherine Gordon, a Scots heiress. The Captain quickly ran through her fortune and departed; Byron and his mother withdrew to Aberdeen in 1789. He passed the next ten years in straitened circumstances, sensitive to the clubfoot with which he had been born, left with a mother who displaced resentment against her absconded husband onto him, and tended by a Calvinist nurse whom he later said had early awakened his sexuality. In 1798 his great-uncle the fifth Baron Byron, "the wicked Lord," died childless, and just after his tenth birthday Byron unexpectedly inherited his title. He asked his mother "whether she perceived any difference in him since he had been made a lord, as he perceived none himself," but the difference shaped the poet.

Byron and his mother returned to England and moved into Newstead Abbey, near Nottingham, the now debt-ridden estate presented to the Byrons by Henry VIII; to the lonely boy, the Gothic hall embodied his tempestuous family heritage. In 1801 Byron was sent to school at Harrow; in the same year he probably met his half-sister Augusta. He entered Trinity College, Cambridge, in 1805, living extravagantly and entangling himself with moneylenders, but also making enduring friendships. His first published volume, *Hours of Idleness*, appeared in 1807, when he was nineteen; the lofty pose he struck as "Lord Byron: A Minor" provoked a savage notice from the *Edinburgh Review*, to which he retaliated in 1809 with a satire in Popean couplets, *English Bards and Scotch Reviewers*. "Written when I was very young and very angry," Byron later confessed to Coleridge, the poem "has been a thorn in my side ever since; more particularly as almost all the Persons animadverted upon became subsequently my acquaintances, and some of them my friends." He suppressed the fifth edition, but so memorable were its attacks on Coleridge, Southey, Wordsworth, Scott, and others that pirated editions continued to appear. Byron took his seat in the House of Lords the same year, then departed on a grand tour shaped by the Napoleonic wars, which barred much of Europe. He sailed to Lisbon, crossed Spain, and proceeded to Greece and Albania, through country little known to Western Europeans. There he began *Childe Harold's Pilgrimage*. In March 1810 he sailed for Constantinople, visited the site of Troy and swam the Hellespont in imitation of mythical Greek lover, Leander. In the East, Byron not only found a world in which the love of an older aristocrat for a beautiful boy was accepted, but also developed a political identity as the Western hero who would liberate Greece from the Turks.

Byron returned to London in July 1811, but too late to see his mother before she died. In February 1812 he made his first speech in the House of Lords, denouncing the death penalty proposed for weavers who had smashed the machines they blamed for their loss of work. Byron's parliamentary activity was superseded the next month when the first two cantos of *Childe Harold's Pilgrimage* appeared and he "woke to find himself famous." The poem joined the immediacy of a travelogue to the disillusionment of a speaker who voiced the melancholy of a generation wearied by prolonged war. Despite Byron's claim that Harold was a fiction designed merely to connect a picaresque narrative, readers heard his author speaking passionately of his own concerns. The magnetism of this personality offset the cynicism the poem displayed: the handsome, aristocratic poet, returned from exotic travels, himself became a figure of force. Byron followed this success with a series of "Eastern" tales that added to his aura: one, *The Corsair* (1814), written in ten days, sold ten thousand copies on the day of publication. *Hebrew Melodies* (1815) contains some of Byron's most famous lyrics (*She walks in beauty*) and accorded with the vogue for nationalist themes. Byron was both a sensational commercial success and a noble who gave away his copyrights because aristocrats do not write for money. Like all myths, "Byron" embodied contradictions more than he resolved them.

This literary celebrity was enhanced by Byron's lionizing in Whig society. Liaisons with Lady Caroline Lamb and the "autumnal" Lady Oxford magnified his notoriety, but it was his relationship with his half-sister Augusta, now married, that most gave rise to scandal; her daughter Medora, born in 1814 and given the name of the heroine of *The Corsair*, was widely thought to be Byron's, and probably was. Seeking to escape these agitating affairs, and also to repair his debts, Byron proposed to wealthy heiress Annabella Milbanke. They married in January 1815; their daughter Augusta Ada was born at the end of the year, but a few weeks later Annabella left Byron to live with her parents, amid rumors of insanity, incest, and sodomy. Pirated editions of Byron's poems on the separation made marital discord into public scandal.

In April 1816 Byron quit England, bearing the pageant of his bleeding heart, in Matthew Arnold's famous phrase, across Europe. He settled in Geneva, near Percy Bysshe Shelley and Mary Godwin, who had eloped two years before. They were joined by Mary's stepsister, Claire Clairmont, with whom Byron resumed an affair he had begun in England. Poetry was as much in the air as romance: Byron reported that Shelley "dosed him with Wordsworth physic even to nausea"; the influence and resistance the phrase shows are both evident in the third canto of *Childe Harold* (1816). He wrote *The Prisoner of Chillon* at this time and began the closet-drama *Manfred* (1817). At the end of the summer the Shelley party left for England, where Claire gave birth to daughter Allegra; in October Byron departed for Venice, where he rented a palazzo on the Grand Canal.

Byron described his Venetian life in brilliant letters, some of which were meant for circulation in the circle of his publisher John Murray. To a ceaseless round of sexual activity, he joined substantial literary productivity. He studied Armenian, completed *Manfred,* and visited Rome, gathering materials for a fourth canto of *Childe Harold* (1818). The canto was his longest and most sublime, and its invocation of Freedom's torn banner streaming "*against* the wind" fixed his revolutionary reputation. Yet Byron began to feel trapped by the modes that had won him popularity; determining to "repel charges of monotony and mannerism," he wrote *Beppo*, a comic verse tale of a Venetian *ménage-à-trois* (1818). In its colloquial, digressive ease, Byron was testing the form of his greatest poem, *Don Juan,* at once fictional autobiography, picaresque narrative, literary burlesque, and exposure of social, sexual, and religious hypocrisies. The first two cantos were published in 1819 in an expensive edition meant to forestall charges of blasphemy and bearing neither the author's nor the publisher's name. The authorship was nonetheless known: *Blackwood's Magazine* criticized Byron for "a filthy and impious" attack on his wife (the model for Juan's mother), and the second canto, which turns to shipwreck and cannibalism, redoubled charges of nihilism. Shocking the proprieties of one audience, Byron moved toward another; the poem sold well in increasingly cheap editions.

In April 1819 Byron met his "last attachment," Countess Teresa Gamba Guiccioli, nineteen years old and married to a man nearly three times her age. Through her family, Byron was initiated into the Carbonari, a clandestine revolutionary organization devoted to Italian independence from Austria. While continuing *Don Juan*, he wrote *Marino Faliero*, *Sardanapalus*, and *The Two Foscari* (all 1821), historical dramas exploring the relationship between the powerful individual and the post-revolutionary state. To the same year belongs *Cain*, a "mystery" drama refused copyright for its unorthodoxy and immediately pirated by radicals. When Teresa's father and brother were exiled for their part in an abortive uprising, she followed them, and Byron reluctantly went with her to Pisa. There he reunited with Percy Shelley, with whom he planned a radical journal, *The Liberal*. The first number contained *The Vision of Judgment*, a devastating rebuttal to a eulogy of George III by Robert Southey, in the preface to which the Poet Laureate had alluded to Byron as the head of a "Satanic School."

Restive in domestic life with Teresa, Byron agreed to act as agent of a London committee aiding the Greek struggle for independence. In July 1823 he left for Cephalonia, an island in western Greece. Clear of debt and now attentive to his literary income, Byron devoted his fortune to the cause. Philhellenic idealism was soon confronted by motley reality, but Byron founded, paid, and trained a brigade of soldiers. A serious illness in February 1824, followed by the usual remedy of bleeding, weakened him; in April he contracted a fever, treated by further bleeding, from which he died on April 19 at age thirty-six. Deeply mourned, he became a Greek national hero, and throughout Europe his name became synonymous with Romanticism. In England, the stunned reaction of young Tennyson spoke for many: hearing the news, he sadly wrote on a rock "Byron is dead." As Arnold later recalled, in placing Byron with Wordsworth as the great English poets of the century, he had "subjugated" his readers, and his influence was immense and lasting.

Additional writing by Byron appears on page 134.

She walks in beauty[1]

1

She walks in beauty, like the night
   Of cloudless climes and starry skies;
And all that's best of dark and bright
   Meet in her aspect and her eyes:
5   Thus mellow'd to that tender light
   Which heaven to gaudy day denies.

2

One shade the more, one ray the less,
   Had half impair'd the nameless grace
Which waves in every raven tress,
10   Or softly lightens o'er her face;
   Where thoughts serenely sweet express
   How pure, how dear their dwelling-place.

3

And on that cheek, and o'er that brow,
   So soft, so calm, yet eloquent,
15   The smiles that win, the tints that glow,

1. The first poem in *Hebrew Melodies*, a collection initiated by Jewish composer Isaac Nathan, with his music. The subject is Anne Wilmot, the wife of Byron's cousin, whom he had seen at a party wearing "mourning, with dark spangles on her dress."

But tell of days in goodness spent,
A mind at peace with all below,
A heart whose love is innocent!

1814   1815

So, we'll go no more a-roving

1

So, we'll go no more a-roving[1]
  So late into the night,
Though the heart be still as loving,
  And the moon be still as bright.

2

5 For the sword outwears its sheath,
  And the soul wears out the breast.
And the heart must pause to breathe,
  And love itself have rest.

3

Though the night was made for loving,
10 And the day returns too soon,
Yet we'll go no more a-roving
  By the light of the moon.

1817   1830

MANFRED, A DRAMATIC POEM   In summer 1816 English tourists in Switzerland had grist for gossip: Byron and Shelley had settled in neighboring houses near Geneva. With Shelley were Mary Wollstonecraft Godwin, with whom he had eloped, their infant son William, and Mary's stepsister, Claire Clairmont, who had introduced the poets and was pregnant with Byron's daughter (Allegra, born 1817). Rumors swirled about "a league of Incest," which Byron indignantly denied. Into this hothouse in August came a visiting M. G. Lewis, author of the sensational Gothic novel *The Monk* (1796) and the hugely successful Drury Lane melodrama *Castle Spectre* (1797). Lewis translated most of Goethe's *Faust* (Part 1, 1808) *viva voce* to Byron. "I was naturally much struck with it," Byron told John Murray, "but it was the *Staubach* & the *Jungfrau*—and something else—much more than Faustus that made me write Manfred." The effect of the surrounding mountains is corroborated by the many echoes in the play of the journal Byron kept for Augusta of his Alpine tour in September. And before this encounter with *Faust* were the Gothic melodramas that Byron met on the Drury Lane Committee of Management in 1815, the success in 1813 of Coleridge's drama *Remorse* (a title which might serve for an entire heritage), and Byron's general knowledge of the Gothic: William Beckford's Oriental tale *Vathek* (1786) supplied the details of Manfred's underworld journey, and Horace Walpole's seminal *Castle of Otranto* (1764) is the probable source of his name. Subtitling the play "a dramatic poem," Byron signaled that it wasn't for performance—he insisted that he had rendered it *"quite impossible* for the stage"—but he was probably tempted: despite the disavowals, *Manfred* was the first of several of his plays to enjoy theatrical success in the nineteenth century.

---

1. The poem first appeared in a letter Byron wrote from Venice to Thomas Moore: "The Carnival—that is, the latter part of it—and sitting up late o'nights, had knocked me up a little. But it is over—and it is now Lent . . . though I did not dissipate much upon the whole, yet I find 'the sword wearing out the scabbard,' though I have but just turned the corner of twenty-nine." Carnival, literally "farewell to flesh," is the period of festival before Lent.

The momentous "something else" Byron hinted to Murray was his bitterness over the separation from Annabella, from which Augusta was inextricable. By naming Manfred's beloved Astarte (an incestuous pagan goddess) Byron refueled the scandal, and in interrupting the dialogue between Manuel and Herman just as the former is about to name "The lady Astarte, his—" (3.3.47), Byron tantalized prurient or literal-minded readers looking for autobiographical confession. Byron's deepest confrontation was with his own image. Manfred is the epitome of the titanic, gloomy Byronic Hero who dominates *Childe Harold's Pilgrimage* and the popular "Eastern" tales, a figure whose notoriety Byron exploited but by which he was beginning to feel constrained. *Manfred* was "too much in my old style," he told Murray; "I certainly am a devil of a mannerist—and must leave off—but what could I do? without exertion of some kind—I should have sunk under my imagination and reality." The autonomy that Manfred claims—"The mind which is immortal makes itself / Requital for its good or evil thoughts— / Is its own origin of ill and end— / And its own place and time" (3.4.129-32)—is the sign of an independence of all authority that Nietzsche recognized as a precursor of his own Superman, but which in its extremism tips into the self-parody Byron acknowledged to Murray. The rhythm of repeated rejections that constitutes the dramatic action produces an intensifying isolation that tends only toward death.

Manfred
A Dramatic Poem

"There are more things in heaven and earth, Horatio,
Than are dreamt of in your philosophy."[1]

Dramatis Personæ

MANFRED	WITCH OF THE ALPS
CHAMOIS HUNTER	ARIMANES
ABBOT OF ST MAURICE	NEMESIS
MANUEL	THE DESTINIES
HERMAN	SPIRITS, & c.

The Scene of the Drama is amongst the Higher Alps—partly in the Castle of Manfred, and partly in the Mountains.

ACT 1

Scene 1

Manfred alone.—Scene, a Gothic Gallery.—Time, Midnight.

MANFRED: The lamp must be replenish'd, but even then
It will not burn so long as I must watch:
My slumbers—if I slumber—are not sleep,
But a continuance of enduring thought,
5   Which then I can resist not: in my heart
There is a vigil, and these eyes but close
To look within; and yet I live, and bear
The aspect and the form of breathing men.
(But grief should be the instructor of the wise;)

---

1. Hamlet's reminder to his friend after having seen his father's ghost (*Hamlet* 1.5.66–67).

10   Sorrow is knowledge: they who know the most
       Must mourn the deepest o'er the fatal truth,
       The Tree of Knowledge is not that of Life.[2]
       Philosophy and science, and the springs
       Of wonder, and the wisdom of the world,
15   I have essay'd, and in my mind there is
       A power to make these subject to itself—
       But they avail not: I have done men good,
       And I have met with good even among men—
       But this avail'd not: I have had my foes,
20   And none have baffled, many fallen before me—
       But this avail'd not:—Good, or evil, life,
       Powers, passions, all I see in other beings,
       Have been to me as rain unto the sands,
       Since that all-nameless hour. I have no dread,
25   And feel the curse to have no natural fear,
       Nor fluttering throb, that beats with hopes or wishes,
       Or lurking love of something on the earth.—
       Now to my task.—
                         Mysterious Agency!
       Ye spirits of the unbounded Universe!
30   Whom I have sought in darkness and in light—
       Ye, who do compass earth about, and dwell
       In subtler essence—ye, to whom the tops
       Of mountains inaccessible are haunts,
       And earth's and ocean's caves familiar things—
35   I call upon ye by the written charm
       Which gives me power upon you—Rise! appear!
   [A pause.]
       They come not yet.—Now by the voice of him
       Who is the first among you—by this sign,
       Which makes you tremble—by the claims of him
40   Who is undying,—Rise! appear!—Appear!
   [A pause.]
       If it be so.—Spirits of earth and air,
       Ye shall not thus elude me: by a power,
       Deeper than all yet urged, a tyrant-spell,
       Which had its birthplace in a star condemn'd,
45   The burning wreck of a demolish'd world,
       A wandering hell in the eternal space;
       By the strong curse which is upon my soul,
       The thought which is within me and around me,
       I do compel ye to my will.—Appear!
   [A star is seen at the darker end of the gallery: it is stationary; and a voice is heard singing.]

2. See Genesis chs. 2–3; Milton, Paradise Lost, 4.194–222.

FIRST SPIRIT

50 Mortal! to thy bidding bow'd,
From my mansion in the cloud,
Which the breath of twilight builds,
And the summer's sunset gilds
With the azure and vermilion,
55 Which is mix'd for my pavilion;
Though thy quest may be forbidden,
On a star-beam I have ridden;
To thine adjuration bow'd,
Mortal—be thy wish avow'd!

Voice of the SECOND SPIRIT

60 Mont Blanc is the monarch of mountains;[3]
They crown'd him long ago
On a throne of rocks, in a robe of clouds,
With a diadem of snow.
Around his waist are forests braced,
65 The Avalanche in his hand;
But ere it fall, that thundering ball
Must pause for my command.
The Glacier's cold and restless mass
Moves onward day by day;
70 But I am he who bids it pass,
Or with its ice delay.
I am the spirit of the place,
Could make the mountain bow
And quiver to his cavern'd base—
75 And what with me wouldst *Thou*?

Voice of the THIRD SPIRIT

In the blue depth of the waters,
Where the wave hath no strife,
Where the wind is a stranger,
And the sea-snake hath life,
80 Where the Mermaid is decking
Her green hair with shells;
Like the storm on the surface
Came the sound of thy spells;
O'er my calm Hall of Coral
85 The deep echo roll'd—
To the Spirit of Ocean
Thy wishes unfold!

FOURTH SPIRIT

Where the slumbering earthquake
Lies pillow'd on fire,

3. See P. B. Shelley's *Mont Blanc*, page 470.

<pre>
90   And the lakes of bitumen[4]
             Rise boilingly higher;
          Where the roots of the Andes
             Strike deep in the earth,
          As their summits to heaven
95   Shoot soaringly forth;
          I have quitted my birthplace,
             Thy bidding to bide—
          Thy spell hath subdued me,
             Thy will be my guide!
</pre>

FIFTH SPIRIT

<pre>
100   I am the Rider of the wind,
             The Stirrer of the storm;
          The hurricane I left behind
             Is yet with lightning warm;
          To speed to thee, o'er shore and sea
105   I swept upon the blast:
          The fleet I met sail'd well, and yet
             'Twill sink ere night be past.
</pre>

SIXTH SPIRIT

<pre>
          My dwelling is the shadow of the night,
          Why doth thy magic torture me with light?
</pre>

SEVENTH SPIRIT

<pre>
110   The star which rules thy destiny
             Was ruled, ere earth began, by me:
          It was a world as fresh and fair
             As e'er revolved round sun in air;
          Its course was free and regular,
115   Space bosom'd not a lovelier star.
          The hour arrived—and it became
             A wandering mass of shapeless flame,
          A pathless comet, and a curse,
             The menace of the universe;
120   Still rolling on with innate force,
             Without a sphere, without a course,
          A bright deformity on high,
             The monster of the upper sky!
          And thou! beneath its influence born—
125   Thou worm! whom I obey and scorn—
          Forced by a power (which is not thine,
             And lent thee but to make thee mine)
          For this brief moment to descend,
             Where these weak spirits round thee bend
</pre>

4. Cf. the "bituminous lake where Sodom flared" to which Milton compares Hell (*Paradise Lost* 10.562). Bitumen: mineral pitch.

130 　　　　　　And parley with a thing like thee—
　　　　　　　　What wouldst thou, Child of Clay! with me?

THE SEVEN SPIRITS

　　　　　　　　Earth, ocean, air, night, mountains, winds, thy star,
　　　　　　　　Are at thy beck and bidding, Child of Clay!
　　　　　　　　Before thee at thy quest their spirits are—
135 　　　　　　　What wouldst thou with us, son of mortals—say?

MANFRED: Forgetfulness—
FIRST SPIRIT: 　　　　Of what—of whom—and why?
MANFRED: Of that which is within me; read it there—
　　　　Ye know it, and I cannot utter it.
SPIRIT: We can but give thee that which we possess:
140 　　Ask of us subjects, sovereignty, the power
　　　O'er earth, the whole, or portion, or a sign
　　　Which shall control the elements, whereof
　　　We are the dominators, each and all,
　　　These shall be thine.
MANFRED: 　　　　　　　Oblivion, self-oblivion—
145 　　Can ye not wring from out the hidden realms
　　　Ye offer so profusely what I ask?
SPIRIT: It is not in our essence, in our skill;
　　　But—thou mayst die.
MANFRED: 　　　　　　　Will death bestow it on me?
SPIRIT: We are immortal, and do not forget;
150 　　We are eternal; and to us the past
　　　Is, as the future, present. Art thou answer'd?
MANFRED: Ye mock me—but the power which brought ye here
　　　Hath made you mine. Slaves, scoff not at my will!
　　　The mind, the spirit, the Promethean spark,[5]
155 　　The lightning of my being, is as bright,
　　　Pervading, and far darting as your own,
　　　And shall not yield to yours, though coop'd in clay!
　　　Answer, or I will teach you what I am.
SPIRIT: We answer as we answer'd; our reply
160 　　Is even in thine own words.
MANFRED: 　　　　　　　Why say ye so?
SPIRIT: If, as thou say'st, thine essence be as ours,
　　　We have replied in telling thee, the thing
　　　Mortals call death hath nought to do with us.
MANFRED: I then have call'd ye from your realms in vain;
165 　　Ye cannot, or ye will not, aid me.
SPIRIT: 　　　　　　　　　Say;
　　　What we possess we offer; it is thine:

---

5. Greek myths relate that Prometheus stole fire from the gods to give to humankind. "Of the Prometheus of Aeschylus [*Prometheus Bound*] I was passionately fond as a boy," Byron recalled; "[it] has always been so much in my head—that I can easily conceive its influence over all or anything that I have written." Mary Shelley subtitled *Frankenstein* "The Modern Prometheus."

Bethink ere thou dismiss us, ask again—
Kingdom, and sway, and strength, and length of days—
MANFRED: Accursed! what have I to do with days?
170   They are too long already.—Hence—begone!
SPIRIT: Yet pause: being here, our will would do thee service;
Bethink thee, is there then no other gift
Which we can make not worthless in thine eyes?
MANFRED: No, none: yet stay—one moment, ere we part—
175   I would behold ye face to face. I hear
Your voices, sweet and melancholy sounds,
As music on the waters; and I see
The steady aspect of a clear large star;
But nothing more. Approach me as ye are,
180   Or one, or all, in your accustom'd forms.
SPIRIT: We have no forms, beyond the elements
Of which we are the mind and principle:
But choose a form—in that we will appear.
MANFRED: I have no choice; there is no form on earth
185   Hideous or beautiful to me. Let him,
Who is most powerful of ye, take such aspect
As unto him may seem most fitting—Come!
SEVENTH SPIRIT [Appearing in the shape of a beautiful female figure]:[6]
Behold!
MANFRED: Oh God! if it be thus, and thou
Art not a madness and a mockery,
190   I yet might be most happy. I will clasp thee,
And we again will be— [The figure vanishes.]
                    My heart is crush'd! [Manfred falls senseless.]
[A Voice is heard in the Incantation which follows.][7]

When the moon is on the wave,
    And the glow-worm in the grass,
And the meteor on the grave,
195   And the wisp on the morass;
When the falling stars are shooting,
    And the answer'd owls are hooting,
And the silent leaves are still
    In the shadow of the hill,
200   Shall my soul be upon thine,
        With a power and with a sign.

Though thy slumber may be deep,
    Yet thy spirit shall not sleep;
There are shades which will not vanish,

6. Probably an image of Astarte.
7. The "Incantation" was published some months before Manfred, with The Prisoner of Chillon, where it is headed by a note: "The following poem was a Chorus in an unfinished Witch drama, which was begun some years ago." The time aligns the Incantation with Byron's first encounter with excerpts of Goethe's Faust in a "sorry French translation" in de Staël's Corinne and with the success of Coleridge's Remorse. Stanzas 5 and 6, inserted later, were recognized as pointing toward Lady Byron, from whom Byron had separated early in 1816.

205 There are thoughts thou canst not banish;
By a power to thee unknown,
  Thou canst never be alone;
Thou art wrapt as with a shroud,
  Thou art gather'd in a cloud;
210 And for ever shalt thou dwell
  In the spirit of this spell.

Though thou seest me not pass by,
  Thou shalt feel me with thine eye
As a thing that, though unseen,
215   Must be near thee, and hath been;
And when in that secret dread
  Thou hast turn'd around thy head,
Thou shalt marvel I am not
  As thy shadow on the spot,
220 And the power which thou dost feel
  Shall be what thou must conceal.

And a magic voice and verse
  Hath baptized thee with a curse;
And a spirit of the air
225   Hath begirt thee with a snare;
In the wind there is a voice
  Shall forbid thee to rejoice;
And to thee shall Night deny
  All the quiet of her sky;
230 And the day shall have a sun,
  Which shall make thee wish it done.

From thy false tears I did distil
  An essence which hath strength to kill;
From thy own heart I then did wring
235   The black blood in its blackest spring;
From thy own smile I snatch'd the snake,
  For there it coil'd as in a brake;
From thy own lip I drew the charm
  Which gave all these their chiefest harm;
240 In proving every poison known,
  I found the strongest was thine own.

By thy cold breast and serpent smile,
  By thy unfathom'd gulfs of guile,
By that most seeming virtuous eye,
245   By thy shut soul's hypocrisy;
By the perfection of thine art
  Which pass'd for human thine own heart;
By thy delight in others' pain,
  And by thy brotherhood of Cain,[8]

---

8. Kinship with the brother-murderer (Genesis ch. 4).

Ford Madox Brown, *Manfred on the Jungfrau*, 1840. Byron's flamboyant protagonist inspired many later works. Robert Schumann set the play to music (1848–49) and Peter Ilyich Tchaikovsky composed a Manfred symphony (1885). Famous representations include two watercolors by John Martin (1837) and this painting by Ford Madox Brown, imagining the moment in Act I, Scene 2, when Manfred, about to indulge a suicidal leap, is interrupted by a chamois hunter. Standing on the brink of a precipice crowned with thick snow, Manfred clutches his hands to his head in a gesture of despair; his dress is intended to be in the style of the tenth or eleventh century.

250   I call upon thee! and compel
    Thyself to be thy proper Hell![9]

And on thy head I pour the vial
    Which doth devote thee to this trial;
Nor to slumber, nor to die,
255   Shall be in thy destiny;
Though thy death shall still seem near
    To thy wish, but as a fear;
Lo! the spell now works around thee,
    And the clankless chain hath bound thee;
260   O'er thy heart and brain together
    Hath the word been pass'd—now wither!

Scene 2

The Mountain of the Jungfrau.[1]—*Time, Morning.—Manfred alone upon the Cliffs.*

MANFRED: The spirits I have raised abandon me—
    The spells which I have studied baffle me—
    The remedy I reck'd of tortured me;
    I lean no more on super-human aid,
5   It hath no power upon the past, and for
    The future, till the past be gulf'd in darkness,
    It is not of my search.—My mother Earth!

9. "Myself am Hell," says Milton's Satan (*Paradise Lost* 4.75). 1. A peak in the Swiss Alps.

And thou fresh breaking Day, and you, ye Mountains,
Why are ye beautiful? I cannot love ye.
10   And thou, the bright eye of the universe,
That openest over all, and unto all
Art a delight—thou shin'st not on my heart.
And you, ye crags, upon whose extreme edge
I stand, and on the torrent's brink beneath
15   Behold the tall pines dwindled as to shrubs
In dizziness of distance; when a leap,
A stir, a motion, even a breath, would bring
My breast upon its rocky bosom's bed
To rest for ever—wherefore do I pause?
20   I feel the impulse—yet I do not plunge;
I see the peril—yet do not recede;
And my brain reels—and yet my foot is firm:
There is a power upon me which withholds,
And makes it my fatality to live;
25   If it be life to wear within myself
This barrenness of spirit, and to be
My own soul's sepulchre, for I have ceased
To justify my deeds unto myself—
The last infirmity of evil.[2] Ay,
30   Thou winged and cloud-cleaving minister,
   [An eagle passes.]
Whose happy flight is highest into heaven,
Well may'st thou swoop so near me—I should be
Thy prey, and gorge thine eaglets; thou art gone
Where the eye cannot follow thee; but thine
35   Yet pierces downward, onward, or above,
With a pervading vision.—Beautiful!
How beautiful is all this visible world!
How glorious in its action and itself!
But we, who name ourselves its sovereigns, we,
40   Half dust, half deity, alike unfit
To sink or soar, with our mix'd essence make
A conflict of its elements, and breathe
The breath of degradation and of pride,
Contending with low wants and lofty will,
45   Till our mortality predominates,
And men are—what they name not to themselves,
And trust not to each other.[3] Hark! the note,
   [The Shepherd's pipe in the distance is heard.]
The natural music of the mountain reed—
For here the patriarchal days[4] are not

2. An echo of Milton's *Lycidas* (line 71), on fame.
3. Echoing Hamlet's confession of his lost responsiveness to "this goodly frame, the earth" and the despair that to him renders "man, how noble in reason, how infinite in

faculties . . . in action how like an angel" the "quintessence of dust" (*Hamlet* 2.2.301–19).
4. The days of the Old Testament elders, the shepherds Abraham, Isaac, and Jacob.

50   A pastoral fable—pipes in the liberal air,
        Mix'd with the sweet bells of the sauntering herd;
        My soul would drink those echoes.—Oh, that I were
        The viewless° spirit of a lovely sound,   *invisible*
        A living voice, a breathing harmony,
55   A bodiless enjoyment—born and dying
        With the blest tone which made me!
    [*Enter from below a Chamois° Hunter.*]   *native antelope*

CHAMOIS HUNTER: Even so
        This way the chamois leapt: her nimble feet
        Have baffled me; my gains to-day will scarce
        Repay my break-neck travail.—What is here?
60   Who seems not of my trade, and yet hath reach'd
        A height which none even of our mountaineers,
        Save our best hunters, may attain: his garb
        Is goodly, his mien manly, and his air
        Proud as a free-born peasant's, at this distance—
65   I will approach him nearer.

MANFRED [*not perceiving the other*]: To be thus—
        Grey-hair'd with anguish, like these blasted pines,
        Wrecks of a single winter, barkless, branchless,
        A blighted trunk upon a cursed root,
        Which but supplies a feeling to decay—
70   And to be thus, eternally but thus,
        Having been otherwise! Now furrow'd o'er
        With wrinkles, plough'd by moments, not by years
        And hours—all tortured into ages—hours
        Which I outlive!—Ye toppling crags of ice!
75   Ye avalanches, whom a breath draws down
        In mountainous o'erwhelming, come and crush me!
        I hear ye momently above, beneath,
        Crash with a frequent conflict; but ye pass,
        And only fall on things that still would live;
80   On the young flourishing forest, or the hut
        And hamlet of the harmless villager.

CHAMOIS HUNTER: The mists begin to rise from up the valley;
        I'll warn him to descend, or he may chance
        To lose at once his way and life together.

MANFRED: The mists boil up around the glaciers; clouds
86   Rise curling fast beneath me, white and sulphury,
        Like foam from the roused ocean of deep Hell,
        Whose every wave breaks on a living shore,
        Heap'd with the damn'd like pebbles.—I am giddy.

CHAMOIS HUNTER: I must approach him cautiously; if near,
91   A sudden step will startle him, and he
        Seems tottering already.

MANFRED: Mountains have fallen,
        Leaving a gap in the clouds, and with the shock
        Rocking their Alpine brethren; filling up

95   The ripe green valleys with destruction's splinters;
        Damming the rivers with a sudden dash,
        Which crush'd the waters into mist, and made
        Their fountains find another channel—thus,
        Thus, in its old age, did Mount Rosenberg[5]—
100   Why stood I not beneath it?
CHAMOIS HUNTER: Friend! have a care,
        Your next step may be fatal!—for the love
        Of him who made you, stand not on that brink!
MANFRED [*not hearing him*]: Such would have been for me a fitting tomb;
        My bones had then been quiet in their depth;
105   They had not then been strewn upon the rocks
        For the wind's pastime—as thus—thus they shall be—
        In this one plunge.—Farewell, ye opening heavens!
        Look not upon me thus reproachfully—
        Ye were not meant for me—Earth! take these atoms!
     [*As Manfred is in act to spring from the cliff, the Chamois Hunter seizes and retains
     him with a sudden grasp.*]
CHAMOIS HUNTER: Hold, madman!—though aweary of thy life,
111   Stain not our pure vales with thy guilty blood—
        Away with me—I will not quit my hold.
MANFRED: I am most sick at heart—nay, grasp me not—
        I am all feebleness—the mountains whirl
115   Spinning around me—I grow blind—What art thou?
CHAMOIS HUNTER: I'll answer that anon.—Away with me—
        The clouds grow thicker—there—now lean on me—
        Place your foot here—here, take this staff, and cling
        A moment to that shrub—now give me your hand,
120   And hold fast by my girdle—softly—well—
        The Chalet will be gain'd within an hour—
        Come on, we'll quickly find a surer footing,
        And something like a pathway, which the torrent
        Hath wash'd since winter.—Come, 'tis bravely done—
125   You should have been a hunter.—Follow me.
     [*As they descend the rocks with difficulty, the scene closes.*]

                          ACT 2
                         Scene 1

A Cottage amongst the Bernese Alps. [Manfred and the Chamois Hunter.]

CHAMOIS HUNTER: No, no—yet pause—thou must not yet go forth:
        Thy mind and body are alike unfit
        To trust each other; for some hours, at least;
        When thou art better, I will be thy guide—
5   But whither?
MANFRED: It imports not: I do know
        My route full well, and need no further guidance.

---

5. In 1806 an avalanche on Mt. Rossberg had crushed several villages.

CHAMOIS HUNTER: Thy garb and gait bespeak thee of high lineage—
  One of the many chiefs, whose castled crags
  Look o'er the lower valleys—which of these
10 May call thee lord? I only know their portals;
  My way of life leads me but rarely down
  To bask by the huge hearths of those old halls,
  Carousing with the vassals; but the paths,
  Which step from out our mountains to their doors,
15 I know from childhood—which of these is thine?
MANFRED: No matter.
CHAMOIS HUNTER: Well, sir, pardon me the question,
  And be of better cheer. Come, taste my wine;
  'Tis of an ancient vintage; many a day
  'T has thawed my veins among our glaciers, now
20 Let it do thus for thine—Come, pledge me fairly.
MANFRED: Away, away! there's blood upon the brim!
  Will it then never—never sink in the earth?
CHAMOIS HUNTER: What dost thou mean? thy senses wander from thee.
MANFRED: I say 'tis blood—my blood! the pure warm stream
25 Which ran in the veins of my fathers, and in ours
  When we were in our youth, and had one heart,
  And loved each other as we should not love,
  And this was shed: but still it rises up,
  Colouring the clouds, that shut me out from heaven,
30 Where thou art not—and I shall never be.
CHAMOIS HUNTER: Man of strange words, and some half-maddening sin,
  Which makes thee people vacancy, whate'er
  Thy dread and sufferance be, there's comfort yet—
  The aid of holy men, and heavenly patience—
MANFRED: Patience and patience! Hence—that word was made
  For brutes of burthen, not for birds of prey;
  Preach it to mortals of a dust like thine,—
  I am not of thine order.
CHAMOIS HUNTER: Thanks to heaven!
  I would not be of thine for the free fame
40 Of William Tell;[1] but whatsoe'er thine ill,
  It must be borne, and these wild starts are useless.
MANFRED: Do I not bear it?—Look on me—I live.
CHAMOIS HUNTER: This is convulsion, and no healthful life.
MANFRED: I tell thee, man! I have lived many years,
45 Many long years, but they are nothing now
  To those which I must number: ages—ages—
  Space and eternity—and consciousness,
  With the fierce thirst of death—and still unslaked!
CHAMOIS HUNTER: Why, on thy brow the seal of middle age
50 Hath scarce been set; I am thine elder far.

---

1. The legendary 14th-century liberator of Switzerland from Austrian domination.

MANFRED: Think'st thou existence doth depend on time?
        It doth; but actions are our epochs: mine
        Have made my days and nights imperishable,
        Endless, and all alike, as sands on the shore,
55   Innumerable atoms; and one desert,
        Barren and cold, on which the wild waves break,
        But nothing rests, save carcasses and wrecks,
        Rocks, and the salt-surf weeds of bitterness.
CHAMOIS HUNTER: Alas! he's mad—but yet I must not leave him.
MANFRED: I would I were—for then the things I see
        Would be but a distemper'd dream.
CHAMOIS HUNTER: What is it
        That thou dost see, or think thou look'st upon?
MANFRED: Myself, and thee—a peasant of the Alps—
        Thy humble virtues, hospitable home,
65   And spirit patient, pious, proud, and free;
        Thy self-respect, grafted on innocent thoughts;
        Thy days of health, and nights of sleep; thy toils,
        By danger dignified, yet guiltless; hopes
        Of cheerful old age and a quiet grave,
70   With cross and garland over its green turf,
        And thy grandchildren's love for epitaph;
        This do I see—and then I look within—
        It matters not—my soul was scorch'd already!
CHAMOIS HUNTER: And would'st thou then exchange thy lot for mine?
MANFRED: No, friend! I would not wrong thee, nor exchange
        My lot with living being: I can bear—
        However wretchedly, 'tis still to bear—
        In life what others could not brook to dream,
        But perish in their slumber.
CHAMOIS HUNTER: And with this—
80   This cautious feeling for another's pain,
        Canst thou be black with evil?—say not so.
        Can one of gentle thoughts have wreak'd revenge
        Upon his enemies?
MANFRED: Oh! no, no, no!
        My injuries came down on those who loved me—
85   On those whom I best loved: I never quell'd
        An enemy, save in my just defence—
        My wrongs were all on those I should have cherished
        But my embrace was fatal.
CHAMOIS HUNTER: Heaven give thee rest!
        And penitence restore thee to thyself;
90   My prayers shall be for thee.
MANFRED: I need them not,
        But can endure thy pity. I depart—
        'Tis time—farewell!—Here's gold, and thanks for thee—
        No words—it is thy due.—Follow me not—
        I know my path—the mountain peril's past:

95   And once again, I charge thee, follow not!
       [*Exit Manfred.*]

                              Scene 2

A lower Valley in the Alps.—A Cataract. [Enter Manfred.]

MANFRED: It is not noon—the sunbow's rays[2] still arch
       The torrent with the many hues of heaven,
       And roll the sheeted silver's waving column
       O'er the crag's headlong perpendicular,
5   And fling its lines of foaming light along,
       And to and fro, like the pale courser's tail,
       The Giant steed, to be bestrode by Death,
       As told in the Apocalypse.[3] No eyes
       But mine now drink this sight of loveliness;
10   I should be sole in this sweet solitude,
       And with the Spirit of the place divide
       The homage of these waters.—I will call her.
[*Manfred takes some of the water into the palm of his hand, and flings it into the air,
muttering the adjuration. After a pause, the Witch of the Alps rises beneath the arch of
the sunbow of the torrent.*]
       Beautiful Spirit! with thy hair of light,
       And dazzling eyes of glory, in whose form
15   The charms of earth's least mortal daughters grow
       To an unearthly stature, in an essence
       Of purer elements; while the hues of youth,—
       Carnation'd like a sleeping infant's cheek,
       Rock'd by the beating of her mother's heart,
20   Or the rose tints, which summer's twilight leaves
       Upon the lofty glacier's virgin snow,
       The blush of earth embracing with her heaven,—
       Tinge thy celestial aspect, and make tame
       The beauties of the sunbow which bends o'er thee.
25   Beautiful Spirit! in thy calm clear brow,
       Wherein is glass'd serenity of soul,
       Which of itself shows immortality,
       I read that thou wilt pardon to a Son
       Of Earth, whom the abstruser powers permit
30   At times to commune with them—if that he
       Avail him of his spells—to call thee thus,
       And gaze on thee a moment.
WITCH: Son of Earth!
       I know thee, and the powers which give thee power;
       I know thee for a man of many thoughts,

---

2. This iris is formed by the rays of the sun over the lower part of the Alpine torrents: it is exactly like a rainbow come to pay a visit, and so close that you may walk into it: this effect lasts until noon. [Byron's note]

3. Revelation 6.8: "And I looked, and behold a pale horse: and his name that sat on him was Death, and Hell followed with him."

35 And deeds of good and ill, extreme in both,
 Fatal and fated in thy sufferings.
 I have expected this—what would'st thou with me?
MANFRED: To look upon thy beauty—nothing further.
 The face of the earth hath madden'd me, and I
40 Take refuge in her mysteries, and pierce
 To the abodes of those who govern her—
 But they can nothing aid me. I have sought
 From them what they could not bestow, and now
 I search no further.
WITCH: What could be the quest
45 Which is not in the power of the most powerful,
 The rulers of the invisible?
MANFRED: A boon;
 But why should I repeat it? 'twere in vain.
WITCH: I know not that; let thy lips utter it.
MANFRED: Well, though it torture me, 'tis but the same;
50 My pang shall find a voice. From my youth upwards
 My spirit walk'd not with the souls of men,
 Nor look'd upon the earth with human eyes;
 The thirst of their ambition was not mine,
 The aim of their existence was not mine;
55 My joys, my griefs, my passions, and my powers,
 Made me a stranger; though I wore the form,
 I had no sympathy with breathing flesh,
 Nor midst the creatures of clay that girded me
 Was there but one who—but of her anon.
60 I said with men, and with the thoughts of men,
 I held but slight communion; but instead,
 My joy was in the Wilderness, to breathe
 The difficult air of the iced mountain's top,
 Where the birds dare not build, nor insect's wing
65 Flit o'er the herbless granite; or to plunge
 Into the torrent, and to roll along
 On the swift whirl of the new breaking wave
 Of river-stream, or ocean, in their flow.
 In these my early strength exulted; or
70 To follow through the night the moving moon,
 The stars and their development; or catch
 The dazzling lightnings till my eyes grew dim;
 Or to look, list'ning, on the scatter'd leaves,
 While Autumn winds were at their evening song.
75 These were my pastimes, and to be alone;
 For if the beings, of whom I was one,—
 Hating to be so,—cross'd me in my path,
 I felt myself degraded back to them,
 And was all clay again. And then I dived,
80 In my lone wanderings, to the caves of death,
 Searching its cause in its effect; and drew

From wither'd bones, and skulls, and heap'd up dust,
Conclusions most forbidden. Then I pass'd
The nights of years in sciences untaught,
85   Save in the old time; and with time and toil,
And terrible ordeal, and such penance
As in itself hath power upon the air,
And spirits that do compass air and earth,
Space, and the peopled infinite, I made
90   Mine eyes familiar with Eternity,
Such as, before me, did the Magi, and
He who from out their fountain dwellings raised
Eros and Anteros, at Gadara,[4]
As I do thee;—and with my knowledge grew
95   The thirst of knowledge, and the power and joy
Of this most bright intelligence, until—
WITCH: Proceed.
MANFRED: Oh! I but thus prolong'd my words,
Boasting these idle attributes, because
As I approach the core of my heart's grief—
100   But to my task. I have not named to thee
Father or mother, mistress, friend, or being,
With whom I wore the chain of human ties;
If I had such, they seem'd not such to me—
Yet there was one—
WITCH: Spare not thyself—proceed.
MANFRED: She was like me in lineaments—her eyes,
Her hair, her features, all, to the very tone
Even of her voice, they said were like to mine;
But soften'd all, and temper'd into beauty;
She had the same lone thoughts and wanderings,
110   The quest of hidden knowledge, and a mind
To comprehend the universe: nor these
Alone, but with them gentler powers than mine,
Pity, and smiles, and tears—which I had not;
And tenderness—but that I had for her;
115   Humility—and that I never had.
Her faults were mine—her virtues were her own—
I loved her, and destroy'd her!
WITCH: With thy hand?
MANFRED: Not with my hand, but heart—which broke her heart—
It gazed on mine, and wither'd. I have shed
120   Blood, but not hers—and yet her blood was shed—
I saw—and could not stanch it.
WITCH: And for this—
A being of the race thou dost despise,

4. The philosopher Jamblicus. The story of the raising of Eros and Anteros may be found in his life by Eunapius. It is well told [Byron's note]. Jamblicus, a 4th-century Neo-Platonist, called up Eros, the god of love, and Anteros, the god of unrequited love, from the springs named after them in Syria.

The order which thine own would rise above,
Mingling with us and ours, thou dost forego
125   The gifts of our great knowledge, and shrink'st back
To recreant mortality—Away!
MANFRED: Daughter of Air! I tell thee, since that hour—
But words are breath—look on me in my sleep,
Or watch my watchings—Come and sit by me!
130   My solitude is solitude no more,
But peopled with the Furies;[5]—I have gnash'd
My teeth in darkness till returning morn,
Then cursed myself till sunset;—I have pray'd
For madness as a blessing— 'tis denied me.
135   I have affronted death—but in the war
Of elements the waters shrunk from me,
And fatal things pass'd harmless—the cold hand
Of an all-pitiless demon held me back,
Back by a single hair, which would not break.
140   In fantasy, imagination, all
The affluence of my soul—which one day was
A Crœsus[6] in creation—I plunged deep,
But, like an ebbing wave, it dash'd me back
Into the gulf of my unfathom'd thought.
145   I plunged amidst mankind—Forgetfulness
I sought in all, save where 'tis to be found,
And that I have to learn—my sciences,
My long pursued and super-human art,
149   Is mortal here—I dwell in my despair—
And live—and live for ever.[7]
WITCH: It may be
That I can aid thee.
MANFRED: To do this thy power
Must wake the dead, or lay me low with them.
Do so—in any shape—in any hour—
154   With any torture—so it be the last.
WITCH: That is not in my province; but if thou
Wilt swear obedience to my will, and do
My bidding, it may help thee to thy wishes.
MANFRED: I will not swear—Obey! and whom? the spirits
159   Whose presence I command, and be the slave
Of those who served me—Never!
WITCH: Is this all?
Hast thou no gentler answer?—Yet bethink thee,
And pause ere thou rejectest.

5. Greek goddesses of revenge.
6. The legendary wealthy monarch.
7. Byron evokes the legend of the Wandering Jew, who is punished for his cruelty to Jesus by the eternal refusal of the death for which he yearns.

MANFRED: I have said it.
WITCH: Enough!—I may retire then—say!
MANFRED: Retire!
    [*The Witch disappears.*]
MANFRED [*alone*]: We are the fools of time and terror: Days
165   Steal on us and steal from us; yet we live,
     Loathing our life, and dreading still to die.
     In all the days of this detested yoke—
     This heaving burthen, this accursed breath—
     This vital weight upon the struggling heart,
170   Which sinks with sorrow, or beats quick with pain,
     Or joy that ends in agony or faintness—
     In all the days of past and future, for
     In life there is no present, we can number
     How few—how less than few—wherein the soul
175   Forbears to pant for death, and yet draws back
     As from a stream in winter, though the chill
     Be but a moment's. I have one resource
     Still in my science—I can call the dead,
     And ask them what it is we dread to be:
180   The sternest answer can but be the Grave,
     And that is nothing—if they answer not—
     The buried Prophet answered to the Hag
     Of Endor; and the Spartan Monarch drew
     From the Byzantine maid's unsleeping spirit
185   An answer and his destiny—he slew
     That which he loved, unknowing what he slew,
     And died unpardon'd—though he call'd in aid
     The Phyxian Jove, and in Phigalia roused
     The Arcadian Evocators to compel
190   The indignant shadow to depose her wrath,
     Or fix her term of vengeance—she replied
     In words of dubious import, but fulfill'd.[8]
     If I had never lived, that which I love
     Had still been living; had I never loved,
195   That which I love would still be beautiful—
     Happy and giving happiness. What is she?
     What is she now?—a sufferer for my sins—
     A thing I dare not think upon—or nothing.
     Within few hours I shall not call in vain—
200   Yet in this hour I dread the thing I dare:
     Until this hour I never shrunk to gaze
     On spirit, good or evil—now I tremble,

---

8. A pair of grim prophecies, biblical and classical: at the request of Saul, the woman of Endor summons the spirit of the prophet Samuel, who foretells that the Philistines will defeat Saul and kill him and his sons (1 Samuel 28.7–19); King Pausanias, according to Plutarch and a later Pausanias, author of the *Description of Greece*, learns from the ghost of the beloved whom he had inadvertently slain that he will die, despite his calling Jupiter Phyxius for aid and his enlistment of the priests at Phygalia to get her to lay aside ("depose") her anger.

And feel a strange cold thaw upon my heart.
But I can act even what I most abhor,
205 And champion human fears.—The night approaches.[9]

[Exit.]

Scene 3

The Summit of the Jungfrau Mountain.

[Enter First Destiny.]
The moon is rising broad, and round, and bright;
And here on snows, where never human foot
Of common mortal trod, we nightly tread,
And leave no traces; o'er the savage sea,
5   The glassy ocean of the mountain ice,
We skim its rugged breakers, which put on
The aspect of a tumbling tempest's foam,
Frozen in a moment—a dead whirlpool's image:
And this most steep fantastic pinnacle,
10   The fretwork of some earthquake—where the clouds
Pause to repose themselves in passing by—
Is sacred to our revels, or our vigils;
Here do I wait my sisters, on our way
To the Hall of Arimanes,[1] for to-night
15   Is our great festival—'tis strange they come not.

A Voice without, singing.

The Captive Usurper,[2]
    Hurl'd down from the throne,
Lay buried in torpor,
    Forgotten and lone;
20   I broke through his slumbers,
    I shiver'd his chain,
I leagued him with numbers—
    He's Tyrant again!

With the blood of a million he'll answer my care,
25   With a nation's destruction—his flight and despair.

Second Voice, without.

The ship sail'd on, the ship sail'd fast,
But I left not a sail, and I left not a mast;
There is not a plank of the hull or the deck,
And there is not a wretch to lament o'er his wreck;
30   Save one, whom I held, as he swam, by the hair,

---

9. Macbeth says, as Scots forces close on his castle: "I have almost forgot the taste of fears" (*Macbeth* 5.5.9).
1. Arimanes is derived from Ahriman, the principle of evil in Zoroastrianism.

2. Napoleon escaped from captivity on Elba in March 1815, returned triumphantly to France; the Hundred Days of his recovered power ended at Waterloo, and exile to St. Helena. See Byron's *Childe Harold* 3 (page 390).

And he was a subject well worthy my care;
A traitor on land, and a pirate at sea—
But I saved him to wreak further havoc for me!

FIRST DESTINY, *answering.*

The city lies sleeping;
35   The morn, to deplore it,
May dawn on it weeping:
Sullenly, slowly,
The black plague flew o'er it—
Thousands lie lowly;
40   Tens of thousands shall perish—
The living shall fly from
The sick they should cherish;
But nothing can vanquish
The touch that they die from.
45   Sorrow and anguish,
And evil and dread,
Envelope a nation—
The blest are the dead,
Who see not the sight
50   Of their own desolation—
This work of a night—

This wreck of a realm—this deed of my doing—
For ages I've done, and shall still be renewing!
     [*Enter the Second and Third Destinies.*]
THE THREE:

Our hands contain the hearts of men,
55   Our footsteps are their graves;
We only give to take again
The spirits of our slaves!

FIRST DESTINY: Welcome!—Where's Nemesis?
SECOND DESTINY: At some great work;
But what I know not, for my hands were full.
THIRD DESTINY: Behold she cometh.
     [*Enter Nemesis.*]
FIRST DESTINY: Say, where hast thou been?
My sisters and thyself are slow to-night.
NEMESIS: I was detain'd repairing shatter'd thrones,
Marrying fools, restoring dynasties,
Avenging men upon their enemies,
65   And making them repent their own revenge;
Goading the wise to madness; from the dull
Shaping out oracles to rule the world
Afresh, for they were waxing out of date,
And mortals dared to ponder for themselves,
70   To weigh kings in the balance, and to speak

Of freedom, the forbidden fruit.—Away!
We have outstay'd the hour—mount we our clouds![3]

[Exeunt.]

Scene 4

The Hall of Arimanes—Arimanes on his Throne, a Globe of Fire, surrounded by the Spirits.

HYMN OF THE SPIRITS

    Hail to our Master!—Prince of Earth and Air!
      Who walks the clouds and waters—in his hand
    The sceptre of the elements, which tear
      Themselves to chaos at his high command!
5   He breatheth—and a tempest shakes the sea;
      He speaketh—and the clouds reply in thunder;
    He gazeth—from his glance the sunbeams flee;
      He moveth—earthquakes rend the world asunder.
    Beneath his footsteps the volcanoes rise;
10   His shadow is the Pestilence; his path
    The comets herald through the crackling skies;
      And planets turn to ashes at his wrath.
    To him War offers daily sacrifice;
      To him Death pays his tribute; Life is his,
15   With all its infinite of agonies—
      And his the spirit of whatever is!
   [Enter the Destinies and Nemesis.]

FIRST DESTINY: Glory to Arimanes! on the earth
    His power increaseth—both my sisters did
    His bidding, nor did I neglect my duty!
SECOND DESTINY: Glory to Arimanes! we who bow
    The necks of men, bow down before his throne!
THIRD DESTINY: Glory to Arimanes! we await His nod!
NEMESIS: Sovereign of Sovereigns! we are thine,
    And all that liveth, more or less, is ours,
25   And most things wholly so; still to increase
    Our power, increasing thine, demands our care,
    And we are vigilant—Thy late commands
    Have been fulfill'd to the utmost.
   [Enter Manfred.]
A SPIRIT: What is here?
    A mortal!—Thou most rash and fatal wretch,
30   Bow down and worship!
SECOND SPIRIT: I do know the man—
    A Magian° of great power, and fearful skill!   *magus*
THIRD SPIRIT: Bow down and worship, slave!—What, know'st thou not
    Thine and our Sovereign?—Tremble, and obey!

3. The scene blends the Three Witches of *Macbeth* with Byron's review of the restored monarchies of post-Napoleonic Europe.

ALL THE SPIRITS: Prostrate thyself, and thy condemned clay,
35   Child of the Earth! or dread the worst.
MANFRED: I know it;
        And yet ye see I kneel not.
FOURTH SPIRIT: 'Twill be taught thee.
MANFRED: 'Tis taught already;—many a night on the earth,
        On the bare ground, have I bow'd down my face,
        And strew'd my head with ashes; I have known
40   The fulness of humiliation, for
        I sunk before my vain despair, and knelt
        To my own desolation.
FIFTH SPIRIT: Dost thou dare
        Refuse to Arimanes on his throne
        What the whole earth accords, beholding not
45   The terror of his Glory?—Crouch! I say.
MANFRED: Bid *him* bow down to that which is above him,
        The overruling Infinite—the Maker
        Who made him not for worship—let him kneel,
        And we will kneel together.
THE SPIRITS: Crush the worm!
50   Tear him in pieces!—
FIRST DESTINY: Hence! Avaunt!—he's mine.
        Prince of the Powers invisible! This man
        Is of no common order, as his port°   bearing
        And presence here denote; his sufferings
        Have been of an immortal nature, like
55   Our own; his knowledge, and his powers and will,
        As far as is compatible with clay,
        Which clogs the ethereal essence, have been such
        As clay hath seldom borne; his aspirations
        Have been beyond the dwellers of the earth,
60   And they have only taught him what we know—
        That knowledge is not happiness, and science
        But an exchange of ignorance for that
        Which is another kind of ignorance.
        This is not all—the passions, attributes
65   Of earth and heaven, from which no power, nor being,
        Nor breath from the worm upwards is exempt,
        Have pierced his heart; and in their consequence
        Made him a thing, which I, who pity not,
        Yet pardon those who pity. He is mine,
70   And thine, it may be—be it so, or not,
        No other Spirit in this region hath
        A soul like his—or power upon his soul.
NEMESIS: What doth he here then?
FIRST DESTINY: Let him answer that.
MANFRED: Ye know what I have known; and without power
75   I could not be amongst ye: but there are
        Powers deeper still beyond—I come in quest

Of such, to answer unto what I seek.

NEMESIS: What would'st thou?

MANFRED: Thou canst not reply to me.
Call up the dead—my question is for them.

NEMESIS: Great Arimanes, doth thy will avouch°   support, confirm
The wishes of this mortal?

ARIMANES: Yea.

NEMESIS: Whom would'st thou
Uncharnel?

MANFRED: One without a tomb—call up
Astarte.[4]

NEMESIS:

               Shadow! or Spirit!
85   Whatever thou art,
               Which still doth inherit
                    The whole or a part
               Of the form of thy birth,
                    Of the mould of thy clay,
90   Which return'd to the earth,
                    Re-appear to the day!
             Bear what thou borest,
                    The heart and the form,
             And the aspect thou worest
95   Redeem from the worm.

Appear!—Appear!—Appear!
Who sent thee there requires thee here!

[*The Phantom of Astarte rises and stands in the midst.*]

MANFRED: Can this be death? there's bloom upon her cheek;
But now I see it is no living hue,
100   But a strange hectic—like the unnatural red
Which Autumn plants upon the perish'd leaf.
It is the same! Oh, God! that I should dread
To look upon the same—Astarte!—No,
I cannot speak to her—but bid her speak—
105   Forgive me or condemn me.

NEMESIS:

             By the power which hath broken
                 The grace which enthrall'd thee,
             Speak to him who hath spoken,
                 Or those who have call'd thee!

MANFRED: She is silent,
And in that silence I am more than answer'd.

NEMESIS: My power extends no further. Prince of air!
It rests with thee alone—command her voice.

ARIMANES: Spirit—obey this sceptre!

---

4 Astarte is a variant of Ashtareth ("*Astoreth*, whom the *Phoenicians* call'd / *Astarte*, Queen of Heav'n," *Paradise Lost*
1.438–39), the Near Eastern equivalent of the Greek Aphrodite, goddess of love and fertility.

NEMESIS: Silent still!

115   She is not of our order, but belongs
      To the other powers. Mortal! thy quest is vain,
      And we are baffled also.

MANFRED: Hear me, hear me—
      Astarte! my beloved! speak to me:
      I have so much endured—so much endure—

120   Look on me! the grave hath not changed thee more
      Than I am changed for thee. Thou lovedst me
      Too much, as I loved thee: we were not made
      To torture thus each other, though it were
      The deadliest sin to love as we have loved.

125   Say that thou loath'st me not—that I do bear
      This punishment for both—that thou wilt be
      One of the blessed—and that I shall die;
      For hitherto all hateful things conspire
      To bind me in existence—in a life

130   Which makes me shrink from immortality—
      A future like the past. I cannot rest.
      I know not what I ask, nor what I seek:
      I feel but what thou art—and what I am;
      And I would hear yet once before I perish

135   The voice which was my music—Speak to me!
      For I have call'd on thee in the still night,
      Startled the slumbering birds from the hush'd boughs,
      And woke the mountain wolves, and made the caves
      Acquainted with thy vainly echoed name,

140   Which answer'd me—many things answer'd me—
      Spirits and men—but thou wert silent all.
      Yet speak to me! I have outwatch'd the stars,
      And gazed o'er heaven in vain in search of thee.
      Speak to me! I have wander'd o'er the earth,

145   And never found thy likeness—Speak to me!
      Look on the fiends around—they feel for me!
      I fear them not, and feel for thee alone—
      Speak to me! though it be in wrath;—but say—
      I reck not what—but let me hear thee once—

150   This once—once more!

PHANTOM OF ASTARTE: Manfred!

MANFRED: Say on, say on—
      I live but in the sound—it is thy voice!

PHANTOM: Manfred! To-morrow ends thine earthly ills. Farewell!

MANFRED: Yet one word more—am I forgiven?

PHANTOM: Farewell!

MANFRED: Say, shall we meet again?

PHANTOM: Farewell!

MANFRED: One word for mercy! Say, thou lovest me.

PHANTOM: Manfred!

      [*The Spirit of Astarte disappears.*]

NEMESIS: She's gone, and will not be recall'd;
     Her words will be fulfill'd. Return to the earth.
A SPIRIT: He is convulsed—This is to be a mortal
159   And seek the things beyond mortality.
ANOTHER SPIRIT: Yet, see, he mastereth himself, and makes
     His torture tributary to his will.
     Had he been one of us, he would have made
     An awful[5] spirit.
NEMESIS: Hast thou further question
164   Of our great sovereign, or his worshippers?
MANFRED: None.
NEMESIS: Then for a time farewell.
MANFRED: We meet then—
     Where? On the earth?
NEMESIS: That will be seen hereafter.
MANFRED: Even as thou wilt: and for the grace accorded
     I now depart a debtor. Fare ye well!   [*Exit Manfred.*]
          [*Scene closes*]

ACT 3[1]

Scene 1

A Hall in the Castle of Manfred.

[*Manfred and Herman.*]
MANFRED: What is the hour?
HERMAN: It wants but one till sunset,
     And promises a lovely twilight.
MANFRED: Say,
     Are all things so disposed of in the tower
     As I directed?
HERMAN: All, my lord, are ready:
5   Here is the key and casket.
MANFRED: It is well:
     Thou may'st retire.
                   [*Exit Herman.*]
     There is a calm upon me—
     Inexplicable stillness! which till now
     Did not belong to what I knew of life.
     If that I did not know philosophy
10   To be of all our vanities the motliest,
     The merest word that ever fool'd the ear
     From out the schoolman's jargon, I should deem
     The golden secret, the sought "Kalon,"[2] found,

5. The sense wavers between "awe-inspiring" and "despicable."

1. In March 1817 Byron sent Murray from Venice a fair copy of his "very wild—metaphysical—and inexplicable play," and commented "I have really & truly no notion whether it is good or bad." When Murray's literary advisor William Gifford criticized the third act, Byron conceded that "it was certainly d———d bad" and agreed to rewrite it. In the original (see vol. 4 of *Complete Poetical Works*,) the Abbot crudely threatens Manfred, and is carried off by a demon; in the revision, the "Abbot is become a good man."

2. The "Supreme Good" (Greek).

And seated in my soul. It will not last,
15   But it is well to have known it, though but once:
It hath enlarged my thoughts with a new sense,
And I within my tablets would note down
That there is such a feeling. Who is there?
  [Re-enter Herman.]
HERMAN: My lord, the abbot of St Maurice craves
20   To greet your presence.
  [Enter the Abbot of St Maurice.]
ABBOT: Peace be with Count Manfred!
MANFRED: Thanks, holy father! welcome to these walls;
Thy presence honours them, and blesseth those
Who dwell within them.
ABBOT: Would it were so, Count!—
But I would fain confer with thee alone.
MANFRED: Herman, retire.—What would my reverend guest?
ABBOT: Thus, without prelude:—Age and zeal, my office,
And good intent, must plead my privilege;
Our near, though not acquainted neighbourhood,
May also be my herald. Rumours strange,
30   And of unholy nature, are abroad,
And busy with thy name; a noble name
For centuries: may he who bears it now
Transmit it unimpair'd!
MANFRED: Proceed,—I listen.
ABBOT: 'Tis said thou holdest converse with the things
35   Which are forbidden to the search of man;
That with the dwellers of the dark abodes,
The many evil and unheavenly spirits
Which walk the valley of the shade of death,
Thou communest. I know that with mankind,
40   Thy fellows in creation, thou dost rarely
Exchange thy thoughts, and that thy solitude
Is as an anchorite's,° were it but holy.   *ascetic, religious hermit*
MANFRED: And what are they who do avouch these things?
ABBOT: My pious brethren—the scared peasantry—
45   Even thy own vassals—who do look on thee
With most unquiet eyes. Thy life's in peril.
MANFRED: Take it.
ABBOT: I come to save, and not destroy—
I would not pry into thy secret soul;
But if these things be sooth, there still is time
50   For penitence and pity: reconcile thee
With the true church, and through the church to heaven.
MANFRED: I hear thee. This is my reply: whate'er
I may have been, or am, doth rest between
Heaven and myself.—I shall not choose a mortal
55   To be my mediator. Have I sinn'd
Against your ordinances? prove and punish!

ABBOT: My son! I did not speak of punishment,
        But penitence and pardon;—with thyself
        The choice of such remains—and for the last,
60   Our institutions and our strong belief
        Have given me power to smooth the path from sin—
        To higher hope and better thoughts; the first
        I leave to heaven,—"Vengeance is mine alone!"
        So saith the Lord,[3] and with all humbleness
65   His servant echoes back the awful word.
MANFRED: Old man! there is no power in holy men,
        Nor charm in prayer—nor purifying form
        Of penitence—nor outward look—nor fast—
        Nor agony—nor, greater than all these,
70   The innate tortures of that deep despair,
        Which is remorse without the fear of hell,
        But all in all sufficient to itself
        Would make a hell of heaven—can exorcise
        From out the unbounded spirit the quick sense
75   Of its own sins, wrongs, sufferance, and revenge
        Upon itself; there is no future pang
        Can deal that justice on the self-condemn'd
        He deals on his own soul.[4]
ABBOT: All this is well;
        For this will pass away, and be succeeded
80   By an auspicious hope, which shall look up
        With calm assurance to that blessed place,
        Which all who seek may win, whatever be
        Their earthly errors, so they be atoned:
        And the commencement of atonement is
85   The sense of its necessity.—Say on—
        And all our church can teach thee shall be taught;
        And all we can absolve thee shall be pardon'd.
MANFRED: When Rome's sixth emperor was near his last,
        The victim of a self-inflicted wound,
90   To shun the torments of a public death
        From senates once his slaves, a certain soldier,
        With show of loyal pity, would have stanch'd
        The gushing throat with his officious robe;
        The dying Roman thrust him back, and said—
95   Some empire still in his expiring glance,
        "It is too late—is this fidelity?"
ABBOT: And what of this?[5]
MANFRED: I answer with the Roman—
        "It is too late!"

3. Romans 12.19: "Dearly beloved, avenge not yourselves, but *rather* give place unto wrath; for it is written, Vengeance *is* mine; I will repay, saith the Lord."
4. Compare the boast of Milton's Satan: "The mind is
its own place, and in itself / Can make a Heav'n of

Hell, a Hell of Heav'n" (*Paradise Lost*, 1.254–55). Cf.
1.1.251.
5. Byron transposes to Otho, the sixth emperor, a
story Suetonius relates of Nero in his *Lives of the
Emperors*.

ABBOT: It never can be so,
         To reconcile thyself with thy own soul,
100   And thy own soul with heaven. Hast thou no hope?
         'Tis strange—even those who do despair above,
         Yet shape themselves some fantasy on earth,
         To which frail twig they cling, like drowning men.
MANFRED: Ay—father! I have had those earthly visions
105   And noble aspirations in my youth,
         To make my own the mind of other men;
         The enlightener of nations; and to rise
         I knew not whither—it might be to fall;
         But fall, even as the mountain-cataract,
110   Which having leapt from its more dazzling height,
         Even in the foaming strength of its abyss,
         (Which casts up misty columns that become
         Clouds raining from the re-ascended skies,)
         Lies low but mighty still.—But this is past,
115   My thoughts mistook themselves.
ABBOT: And wherefore so?
MANFRED: I could not tame my nature down; for he
         Must serve who fain would sway—and soothe—and sue—
         And watch all time—and pry into all place—
         And be a living lie—who would become
120   A mighty thing amongst the mean, and such
         The mass are; I disdain'd to mingle with
         A herd, though to be leader—and of wolves.
         The lion is alone, and so am I.
ABBOT: And why not live and act with other men?
MANFRED: Because my nature was averse from life;
         And yet not cruel; for I would not make,
         But find a desolation:—like the wind,
         The red-hot breath of the most lone Simoom,[6]
         Which dwells but in the desert, and sweeps o'er
130   The barren sands which bear no shrubs to blast,
         And revels o'er their wild and arid waves,
         And seeketh not, so that it is not sought,
         But being met is deadly; such hath been
         The course of my existence; but there came
135   Things in my path which are no more.
ABBOT: Alas!
         I 'gin to fear that thou art past all aid
         From me and from my calling; yet so young,
         I still would—
MANFRED: Look on me! there is an order
         Of mortals on the earth, who do become
140   Old in their youth, and die ere middle age,
         Without the violence of warlike death:

6. The Simoom, or Simoon, is a seasonal hot sandy wind of the African and Arabian deserts.

Some perishing of pleasure—some of study—
Some worn with toil—some of mere weariness—
Some of disease—and some insanity—
145   And some of wither'd, or of broken hearts;
For this last is a malady which slays
More than are number'd in the lists of Fate,
Taking all shapes, and bearing many names.
Look upon me! for even of all these things
150   Have I partaken; and of all these things,
One were enough; then wonder not that I
Am what I am, but that I ever was,
Or having been, that I am still on earth.

ABBOT: Yet, hear me still—
MANFRED: Old man! I do respect
155   Thine order, and revere thine years; I deem
Thy purpose pious, but it is in vain:
Think me not churlish; I would spare thyself,
Far more than me, in shunning at this time
All further colloquy—and so—farewell.   [Exit Manfred.]

ABBOT: This should have been a noble creature: he
Hath all the energy which would have made
A goodly frame of glorious elements,[7]
Had they been wisely mingled; as it is,
It is an awful chaos—light and darkness—
165   And mind and dust—and passions and pure thoughts
Mix'd, and contending without end or order,
All dormant or destructive: he will perish,
And yet he must not; I will try once more,
For such are worth redemption; and my duty
170   Is to dare all things for a righteous end.
I'll follow him—but cautiously, though surely.

                                                [Exit Abbot.]

Scene 2

Another Chamber.
    [*Manfred and Herman.*]
HERMAN: My lord, you bade me wait on you at sunset:
He sinks behind the mountain.
MANFRED: Doth he so?
I will look on him.
    [*Manfred advances to the Window of the Hall.*]
                            Glorious Orb! the idol
Of early nature, and the vigorous race
5   Of undiseased mankind, the giant sons
Of the embrace of angels, with a sex
More beautiful than they, which did draw down

7. See n. 3, page 359.

The erring spirits who can ne'er return.——8
Most glorious orb! that wert a worship, ere
10   The mystery of thy making was reveal'd!
Thou earliest minister of the Almighty,
Which gladden'd, on their mountain tops, the hearts
Of the Chaldean shepherds, till they pour'd
Themselves in orisons! Thou material God!
15   And representative of the Unknown—
Who chose thee for his shadow! Thou chief star!
Centre of many stars! which mak'st our earth
Endurable, and temperest the hues
And hearts of all who walk within thy rays!
20   Sire of the seasons! Monarch of the climes,
And those who dwell in them! for near or far,
Our inborn spirits have a tint of thee
Even as our outward aspects;—thou dost rise,
And shine, and set in glory. Fare thee well!
25   I ne'er shall see thee more. As my first glance
Of love and wonder was for thee, then take
My latest look: thou wilt not beam on one
To whom the gifts of life and warmth have been
Of a more fatal nature. He is gone:
30   I follow.   [Exit Manfred.]

Scene 3

*The Mountains—The Castle of Manfred at some distance—A Terrace before a Tower.—
Time, Twilight.* [*Herman, Manuel, and other Dependants of Manfred.*]

HERMAN: 'Tis strange enough; night after night, for years,
He hath pursued long vigils in this tower,
Without a witness. I have been within it,—
So have we all been oft-times; but from it,
5   Or its contents, it were impossible
To draw conclusions absolute, of aught
His studies tend to. To be sure, there is
One chamber where none enter: I would give
The fee of what I have to come these three years,
10   To pore upon its mysteries.
MANUEL: 'Twere dangerous;
Content thyself with what thou know'st already.
HERMAN: Ah! Manuel! thou art elderly and wise,
And couldst say much; thou hast dwelt within the castle—
How many years is't?
MANUEL: Ere Count Manfred's birth,
15   I served his father, whom he nought resembles.
HERMAN: There be more sons in like predicament.
But wherein do they differ?

---

8. "There were giants in the earth in those days, and also after that, when the sons of God came in unto the daughters of men, and they bare *children* to them, the same *became* mighty men which *were* of old, men of renown" (Genesis 6.4).

MANUEL: I speak not
      Of features or of form, but mind and habits;
      Count Sigismund was proud,—but gay and free,—
20   A warrior and a reveller; he dwelt not
      With books and solitude, nor made the night
      A gloomy vigil, but a festal time,
      Merrier than day; he did not walk the rocks
      And forests like a wolf, nor turn aside
25   From men and their delights.
HERMAN: Beshrew° the hour,   *curse*
      But those were jocund times! I would that such
      Would visit the old walls again; they look
      As if they had forgotten them.
MANUEL: These walls
      Must change their chieftain first. Oh! I have seen
30   Some strange things in them, Herman.
HERMAN: Come, be friendly;
      Relate me some to while away our watch:
      I've heard thee darkly speak of an event
      Which happen'd hereabouts, by this same tower.
MANUEL: That was a night indeed! I do remember
35   'Twas twilight, as it may be now, and such
      Another evening;—yon red cloud, which rests
      On Eigher's pinnacle,[9] so rested then,—
      So like that it might be the same; the wind
      Was faint and gusty, and the mountain snows
40   Began to glitter with the climbing moon;
      Count Manfred was, as now, within his tower,—
      How occupied, we knew not, but with him
      The sole companion of his wanderings
      And watchings—her, whom of all earthly things
45   That lived, the only thing he seem'd to love,—
      As he, indeed, by blood was bound to do,
      The lady Astarte, his—
                       Hush! who comes here?
   [Enter the Abbot.]
ABBOT: Where is your master?
HERMAN: Yonder in the tower.
ABBOT: I must speak with him.
MANUEL: 'Tis impossible;
50   He is most private, and must not be thus
      Intruded on.
ABBOT: Upon myself I take
      The forfeit of my fault, if fault there be—
      But I must see him.
HERMAN: Thou hast seen him once
      This eve already.

9. The Eigher is an Alpine peak north of the Jungfrau.

ABBOT: Herman! I command thee,
55 Knock, and apprize the Count of my approach.
HERMAN: We dare not.
ABBOT: Then it seems I must be herald
 Of my own purpose.
MANUEL: Reverend father, stop—
 I pray you pause.
ABBOT: Why so?
MANUEL: But step this way,
 And I will tell you further.

               [Exeunt.]

Scene 4

Interior of the Tower.
 [Manfred alone.]

  The stars are forth, the moon above the tops
  Of the snow-shining mountains.—Beautiful!
  I linger yet with Nature, for the night
  Hath been to me a more familiar face
5 Than that of man; and in her starry shade
  Of dim and solitary loveliness,
  I learn'd the language of another world.
  I do remember me, that in my youth,
  When I was wandering,—upon such a night
10 I stood within the Coliseum's wall,
  Midst the chief relics of almighty Rome;
  The trees which grew along the broken arches
  Waved dark in the blue midnight, and the stars
  Shone through the rents of ruin; from afar
15 The watchdog bay'd beyond the Tiber; and
  More near from out the Cæsars' palace came
  The owl's long cry, and, interruptedly,
  Of distant sentinels the fitful song
  Begun and died upon the gentle wind.
20 Some cypresses beyond the time-worn breach
  Appear'd to skirt the horizon, yet they stood
  Within a bowshot—Where the Cæsars dwelt,
  And dwell the tuneless birds of night, amidst
  A grove which springs through levell'd battlements,
25 And twines its roots with the imperial hearths,
  Ivy usurps the laurel's place of growth;—
  But the gladiators' bloody Circus stands,
  A noble wreck in ruinous perfection!
  While Cæsar's chambers, and the Augustan halls,
30 Grovel on earth in indistinct decay.—
  And thou didst shine, thou rolling moon, upon
  All this, and cast a wide and tender light,
  Which soften'd down the hoar austerity
  Of rugged desolation, and fill'd up,

35 As 'twere anew, the gaps of centuries;
   Leaving that beautiful which still was so,
   And making that which was not, till the place
   Became religion, and the heart ran o'er
   With silent worship of the great of old!
40 The dead, but sceptred sovereigns, who still rule
   Our spirits from their urns.—
          'Twas such a night!
   'Tis strange that I recall it at this time;
   But I have found our thoughts take wildest flight
   Even at the moment when they should array
45 Themselves in pensive order.
  [*Enter the Abbot.*]
ABBOT: My good lord!
   I crave a second grace for this approach;
   But yet let not my humble zeal offend
   By its abruptness—all it hath of ill
   Recoils on me; its good in the effect
50 May light upon your head—could I say *heart*—
   Could I touch *that*, with words or prayers, I should
   Recall a noble spirit which hath wander'd;
   But is not yet all lost.
MANFRED: Thou know'st me not;
   My days are number'd, and my deeds recorded:
55 Retire, or 'twill be dangerous—Away!
ABBOT: Thou dost not mean to menace me?
MANFRED: Not I;
   I simply tell thee peril is at hand,
   And would preserve thee.
ABBOT: What dost thou mean?
MANFRED: Look there!
   What dost thou see?
ABBOT: Nothing.
MANFRED: Look there, I say,
60 And steadfastly;—now tell me what thou seest?
ABBOT: That which should shake me,—but I fear it not—
   I see a dusk and awful figure rise,
   Like an infernal god, from out the earth;
   His face wrapt in a mantle, and his form
65 Robed as with angry clouds: he stands between
   Thyself and me—but I do fear him not.
MANFRED: Thou hast no cause—he shall not harm thee—but
   His sight may shock thine old limbs into palsy.
   I say to thee—Retire!
ABBOT: And I reply—
70 Never—till I have battled with this fiend:—
   What doth he here?
MANFRED: Why—ay—what doth he here?—
   I did not send for him,—he is unbidden.

ABBOT: Alas! lost mortal! what with guests like these
    Hast thou to do? I tremble for thy sake:
75   Why doth he gaze on thee, and thou on him?
    Ah! he unveils his aspect: on his brow
    The thunder-scars are graven; from his eye
    Glares forth the immortality of hell[1]—
    Avaunt!°—   *Away, be gone*
MANFRED: Pronounce—what is thy mission?
SPIRIT: Come!
ABBOT: What art thou, unknown being? answer!—speak!
SPIRIT: The genius° of this mortal.—Come! 'tis time.   *presiding spirit*
MANFRED: I am prepared for all things, but deny
    The power which summons me. Who sent thee here?
SPIRIT: Thou'lt know anon—Come! come!
MANFRED: I have commanded
85   Things of an essence greater far than thine,
    And striven with thy masters. Get thee hence!
SPIRIT: Mortal! thine hour is come—Away! I say.
MANFRED: I knew, and know my hour is come, but not
    To render up my soul to such as thee:
90   Away! I'll die as I have lived—alone.
SPIRIT: Then I must summon up my brethren.—Rise!
    [*Other Spirits rise up.*]
ABBOT: Avaunt! ye evil ones!—Avaunt! I say,—
    Ye have no power where piety hath power,
    And I do charge ye in the name—
SPIRIT: Old man!
95   We know ourselves, our mission, and thine order;
    Waste not thy holy words on idle uses,
    It were in vain: this man is forfeited.
    Once more I summon him—Away! away!
MANFRED: I do defy ye,—though I feel my soul
100   Is ebbing from me, yet I do defy ye;
    Nor will I hence, while I have earthly breath
    To breathe my scorn upon ye—earthly strength
    To wrestle, though with spirits; what ye take
    Shall be ta'en limb by limb.
SPIRIT: Reluctant mortal!
105   Is this the Magian who would so pervade
    The world invisible, and make himself
    Almost our equal?—Can it be that thou
    Art thus in love with life? the very life
    Which made thee wretched!
MANFRED: Thou false fiend, thou liest!

---

1. See Milton's description of the fallen Satan: "his face / Deep scars of thunder had intrenched" (*Paradise Lost* 1.600–601).

110   My life is in its last hour,—*that* I know,
      Nor would redeem a moment of that hour;
      I do not combat against death, but thee
      And thy surrounding angels; my past power
      Was purchased by no compact with thy crew,
115   But by superior science—penance—daring—
      And length of watching—strength of mind—and skill
      In knowledge of our fathers—when the earth
      Saw men and spirits walking side by side,
      And gave ye no supremacy: I stand
120   Upon my strength—I do defy—deny—
      Spurn back, and scorn ye!—

SPIRIT: But thy many crimes
      Have made thee—

MANFRED: What are they to such as thee?
      Must crimes be punish'd but by other crimes,
      And greater criminals?[2]—Back to thy hell!
125   Thou hast no power upon me, *that* I feel;
      Thou never shalt possess me, *that* I know:
      What I have done is done; I bear within
      A torture which could nothing gain from thine:
      The mind which is immortal makes itself
130   Requital for its good or evil thoughts—
      Is its own origin of ill and end—
      And its own place and time[3]—its innate sense,
      When stripp'd of this mortality, derives
      No colour from the fleeting things without;
135   But is absorb'd in sufferance or in joy,
      Born from the knowledge of its own desert.
      Thou didst not tempt me, and thou couldst not tempt me;
      I have not been thy dupe, nor am thy prey—
      But was my own destroyer, and will be
140   My own hereafter.—Back, ye baffled fiends!
      The hand of death is on me—but not yours!

      [*The Demons disappear.*]

ABBOT: Alas! how pale thou art—thy lips are white—
      And thy breast heaves—and in thy gasping throat
      The accents rattle—Give thy prayers to Heaven—
145   Pray—albeit but in thought,—but die not thus.

MANFRED: 'Tis over—my dull eyes can fix thee not;
      But all things swim around me, and the earth
      Heaves as it were beneath me. Fare thee well—
      Give me thy hand.

ABBOT: Cold—cold—even to the heart—
150   But yet one prayer—Alas! how fares it with thee?

2. Compare *Childe Harold's Pilgrimage*, "Can tyrants but   3. See n. 4, page 377.
by tyrants conquer'd be" (4.96; page 406).

MANFRED: Old man! 'tis not so difficult to die.[4]
   [*Manfred expires.*]
ABBOT: He's gone—his soul hath ta'en its earthless flight—
   Whither? I dread to think—but he is gone.

August 1815–February 1817

❀ "MANFRED" AND ITS TIME ❀
The Byronic Hero

In *Manfred,* Byron trades on and pushes to an unstable extreme an established character type, the Byronic Hero. To some, Manfred seems a tragic figure of modern existential angst, with a taint of mysterious crime, possibly of an incestuous nature. To others, he is a case study in narcissism, psychological disease, and antisocial pride. And to still others, he seems a gothic parody of this character type, Byron's strategic exhaustion of a figure who was to give way within a year to an altogether different type, the boyish hero of *Don Juan,* perpetually resilient, unburdened by memory or remorse. Whatever the view, the focus is the Byronic Hero, "mad, bad, and dangerous to know," so said Byron's onetime lover, Caroline Lamb, of the author himself. The defining traits are a contempt of conventional morality, alienation, burning inward torment, and a heroic defiance of fate. A "strange union of opposite extremes," Thomas Macaulay wrote in the *Edinburgh Review* in 1831; "proud, moody, cynical,—with defiance on his brow, and misery in his heart; a scorner of his kind, implacable in revenge, yet capable of deep and strong affection."

The contours draw on Shakespeare's tormented heroes—Hamlet, Othello, Macbeth, and Coriolanus—and their descendant, Milton's Satan, the antihero of *Paradise Lost,* a figure who in the Romantic era focused interest as a complex psychology, even a potential political hero. In *The Marriage of Heaven and Hell,* William Blake, one of the earliest voices of this "Romantic Satanism," argued that the magnificent poetry Milton wrote for Satan showed Milton to be of "the devil's party," and that Satan was the true hero of *Paradise Lost,* the caustic antagonist of a vengeful oppressor called God. Percy Shelley (in *A Defence of Poetry,* written 1820; published 1840) argued that Satan's "magnificence" called into question the "superiority of moral virtue" in Milton's God, and in so doing confirmed "the supremacy of Milton's own genius." The Byronic Hero frequently evokes the Romantic Satan, emulating his oppositional energy, sharing a torment by unredeemable sin, and bearing an anguished heart. Byron's modern articulation is psychological and dramatic, rather than judgmental and moralistic, the very quality of the Byronic Hero confounding easy determinations. This hero debuted in the sensationally successful *Childe Harold's Pilgrimage* (1812), at once defining the type and implying an authorial investment. Across the next decade, Byron produced a series of dashing, transgressive heroes, and was not above performing the role himself, as seen in his famous portrait in exotic Eastern garb (Color Plate 3).

Byron was not the only producer of the Byronic Hero. Its magnetic popularity guaranteed its attraction to other writers. Caroline Lamb's roman à clef, *Glenarvon,* published in 1816, combined moral evil, devastating seductiveness, and political courage in its Satanic/Byronic Hero. Mary Shelley's *Frankenstein,* begun the same year at Byron's villa on Lake Geneva, links both Frankenstein and his Creature to the Byronic type, and ultimately to Milton's Satan. Felicia Hemans, wondering if women could play the part, presents a cross-dressed Byronic Heroine in *The Widow of Crescentius.* Even as Byron was casting Napoleon as a Byronic Hero, a

---

4. When this line was dropped in the first edition, Byron told Murray, "You have destroyed the whole effect & moral of the poem by omitting the last line of Manfred's speaking."

mixture of antitheses, extreme in all things, Samuel Taylor Coleridge was linking Napoleon to an un-Byronic Satan, all pride and aggression. And conservative monitors, such as Tory Poet Laureate Robert Southey, feeling a danger to the nation in the vogue of Byronism, sounded the alarm, dubbing the whole literary culture "the Satanic School" and holding Byron responsible. Byron replied in *The Vision of Judgment* by bringing Satan himself on stage as the latest version of the Byronic Hero: wry, urbane, not particularly damnable, and with a polite disdain of Southey, another character in this poem. The Byronic Hero outlasted Byron, enduring in cultural imagination, in such figures as Charlotte Brontë's Rochester (*Jane Eyre*), Emily Brontë's Heathcliff (*Wuthering Heights*), Herman Melville's Captain Ahab, Robert Louis Stevenson's Dr. Jekyll, Oscar Wilde's Dorian Gray, and every hard-boiled detective of Hollywood *film noir*.

Byron's Earlier Heroes

from *The Giaour*[1]

The Mind, that broods o'er guilty woes,
　　Is like the Scorpion girt by fire,
In circle narrowing as it glows,
425　The flames around their captive close,
Till inly search'd by thousand throes,
　　And maddening in her ire,
One sad and sole relief she knows,
The sting she nourish'd for her foes,
430　Whose venom never yet was vain,
Gives but one pang, and cures all pain,
And darts into her desperate brain;
So do the dark in soul expire,
Or live like Scorpion girt by fire;[2]
435　So writhes the mind Remorse hath riven,
Unfit for earth, undoom'd for heaven,
Darkness above, despair beneath,
Around it flame, within it death!

1812–1813　　　　　　　　　　　　　　　　　　　1813

from *The Corsair*[1]

II

His soul was changed, before his deeds had driven
Him forth to war with man and forfeit heaven.
Warp'd by the world in Disappointment's school,
In words too wise, in conduct *there* a fool;

1. The tormented hero of this tale is an aristocratic Venetian, a "giaour," or infidel, by Arabic/Muslim lights. This famous passage impressed Percy Shelley and Felicia Hemans.
2. Alluding to the dubious suicide of the scorpion, so placed for experiment by gentle philosophers. Some maintain that the position of the sting, when turned toward the head, is merely a convulsive movement; but others have actually brought in the verdict "Felo de se." The scorpions are surely interested in a speedy decision of the question; as, if once fairly established as insect Catos, they will probably be allowed to live as long as they think proper, without being marryred for the sake of an hypothesis [Byron's note]. Cato the Republican committed suicide ("Felo de se") rather than surrender to Julius Caesar.
1. This immensely popular tale sold 10,000 copies on the day of publication, and burned through several editions over the next few years. Its hero is a pirate, described in this stanza from Canto 1.

255   Too firm to yield, and far too proud to stoop,
       Doom'd by his very virtues for a dupe,
       He cursed those virtues as the cause of ill,
       And not the traitors who betray'd him still;
       Nor deem'd that gifts bestow'd on better men
260   Had left him joy, and means to give again.
       Fear'd—shunn'd—belied—ere youth had lost her force,
       He hated man too much to feel remorse,
       And thought the voice of wrath a sacred call,
       To pay the injuries of some on all.
265   He knew himself a villain—but he deem'd
       The rest no better than the thing he seem'd;
       And scorn'd the best as hypocrites who hid
       Those deeds the bolder spirit plainly did.
       He knew himself detested, but he knew
270   The hearts that loath'd him, crouch'd and dreaded too.
       Lone, wild, and strange, he stood alike exempt
       From all affection and from all contempt:
       His name could sadden, and his acts surprise;
       But they that fear'd him dared not to despise:
275   Man spurns the worm, but pauses ere he wake
       The slumbering venom of the folded snake;
       The first may turn—but not avenge the blow;
       The last expires—but leaves no living foe;
       Fast to the doom'd offender's form it clings,
280   And he may crush—not conquer—still it stings!

1813   1814

from *Lara*[1]

       Whate'er he be, 'twas not what he had been:
       That brow in furrow'd lines had fix'd at last,
       And spake of passions, but of passion past:
       The pride, but not the fire, of early days,
70   Coldness of mien, and carelessness of praise;
       A high demeanour, and a glance that took
       Their thoughts from others by a single look;
       And that sarcastic levity of tongue,
       The stinging of a heart the world hath stung,
75   That darts in seeming playfulness around,
       And makes those feel that will not own the wound;
       All these seem'd his, and something more beneath
       Than glance could well reveal, or accent breathe.
       Ambition, glory, love, the common aim,
80   That some can conquer, and that all would claim,
       Within his breast appear'd no more to strive,

1. Byron followed the success of *The Corsair* with *Lara*, whose hero has a mysterious, possibly criminal past. This passage from Canto 1 became a set piece of the character type.

Yet seem'd as lately they had been alive;
And some deep feeling it were vain to trace
At moments lighten'd o'er his livid face.

1814   1814

Prometheus[1]

Titan! to whose immortal eyes
   The sufferings of mortality,
   Seen in their sad reality,
Were not as things that gods despise;
5   What was thy pity's recompense?
A silent suffering, and intense;
The rock, the vulture, and the chain,
All that the proud can feel of pain,
The agony they do not show,
10   The suffocating sense of woe,
   Which speaks but in its loneliness,
And then is jealous lest the sky
Should have a listener, nor will sigh
   Until its voice is echoless.

15   Titan! to thee the strife was given
   Between the suffering and the will,
   Which torture where they cannot kill;
And the inexorable Heaven,
And the deaf tyranny of Fate,
20   The ruling principle of Hate,
Which for its pleasure doth create
The things it may annihilate,
Refused thee even the boon to die:
The wretched gift eternity
25   Was thine—and thou hast borne it well.
All that the Thunderer[2] wrung from thee
Was but the menace which flung back
On him the torments of thy rack;[3]
The fate thou didst so well foresee,[4]
30   But would not to appease him tell;
And in thy Silence was his Sentence,
And in his Soul a vain repentance,
And evil dread so ill dissembled
That in his hand the lightnings trembled.

---

1. The Greek god punished by Jupiter for stealing fire from heaven and bestowing it, in compassion, on humankind. Jupiter has Prometheus chained to a mountain, where a vulture gnaws eternally at his heart.
2. Jupiter is also the god of thunder; "Thunderer" is aptly Satan's name for God (*Paradise Lost* 1.258).
3. An instrument of bone-breaking torture; heroically defiant, Prometheus was eventually liberated by Hercules.
4. Prometheus, whose name means "foreseeing," prophesied the downfall not only of his fellow Titans but also of their conqueror, Jupiter. Jupiter offered to end Prometheus's torture if he would tell him the secret of averting his downfall—a crisis that shapes Percy Shelley's *Prometheus Unbound* (written 1818–1819).

35   Thy Godlike crime was to be kind,
            To render with thy precepts less
            The sum of human wretchedness,
        And strengthen Man with his own mind;
        But baffled as thou wert from high,
40   Still in thy patient energy,
        In the endurance, and repulse
            Of thine impenetrable Spirit,
        Which Earth and Heaven could not convulse,
            A mighty lesson we inherit:
45   Thou art a symbol and a sign
        To Mortals of their fate and force;
        Like thee, Man is in part divine,
            A troubled stream from a pure source;
        And Man in portions can foresee
50   His own funereal destiny;
        His wretchedness, and his resistance,
        And his sad unallied existence:
        To which his Spirit may oppose
        Itself—and equal to all woes,
55   And a firm will, and a deep sense,
        Which even in torture can descry
            Its own concenter'd recompense,
        Triumphant where it dares defy,
        And making Death a Victory.

Diodati, July 1816   1816

from *Childe Harold's Pilgrimage, Canto the Third*

[NAPOLEON BUONAPARTE][1]

36

        There sunk the greatest, nor the worst of men,
        Whose spirit antithetically mixt
        One moment of the mightiest, and again
        On little objects with like firmness fixt,
320   Extreme in all things! hadst thou been betwixt,
        Thy throne had still been thine, or never been;
        For daring made thy rise as fall: thou seek'st
        Even now to re-assume the imperial mien,
        And shake again the world, the Thunderer[2] of the scene!

37

325   Conqueror and captive of the earth art thou!
        She trembles at thee still, and thy wild name

---

1. Napoleon was defeated at Waterloo in June 1815 by the allied forces of Britain and Prussia, then exiled for the rest of his life to St. Helena, a small island in the Atlantic Ocean. Amid British triumphalism, Byron visited Waterloo in May 1816. He reflected on the fate of this extraordinary figure.

2. "Thunder" is Satan's term for God's surprising potency against his rebel forces (*Paradise Lost* 1.93, 174).

Was ne'er more bruited° in men's minds than now   *reported*
That thou art nothing, save the jest of Fame,
Who woo'd thee once, thy vassal, and became

330   The flatterer of thy fierceness, till thou wert
A god unto thyself; nor less the same
To the astounded kingdoms all inert,
Who deem'd thee for a time whate'er thou didst assert.

38

Oh, more or less than man—in high or low,
335   Battling with nations, flying from the field;
Now making monarchs' necks thy footstool, now
More than thy meanest° soldier taught to yield;   *lowest*
An empire thou couldst crush, command, rebuild,
But govern not thy pettiest passion, nor,
340   However deeply in men's spirits skill'd,
Look through thine own, nor curb the lust of war,
Nor learn that tempted Fate will leave the loftiest star.

39

Yet well thy soul hath brook'd the turning tide
With that untaught innate philosophy,
345   Which, be it wisdom, coldness, or deep pride,
Is gall and wormwood to an enemy.
When the whole host of hatred stood hard by,
To watch and mock thee shrinking, thou hast smiled
With a sedate and all-enduring eye;—
350   When Fortune fled her spoil'd and favourite child,
He stood unbow'd beneath the ills upon him piled.

40

Sager than in thy fortunes; for in them
Ambition steel'd thee on too far to show
That just habitual scorn, which could contemn
355   Men and their thoughts; 'twas wise to feel, not so
To wear it ever on thy lip and brow,
And spurn the instruments thou wert to use
Till they were turn'd unto thine overthrow;
'Tis but a worthless world to win or lose;
360   So hath it proved to thee, and all such lot who choose.

41

If, like a tower upon a headlong rock,
Thou hadst been made to stand or fall alone,
Such scorn of man had help'd to brave the shock;
But men's thoughts were the steps which paved thy throne,
365   *Their* admiration thy best weapon shone;
The part of Philip's son[3] was thine, not then

---

3. Alexander the Great, son of Philip II of Macedon, famed for his conquest of the eastern Mediterranean world in the 4th century B.C. Purple is the color of royalty.

(Unless aside thy purple had been thrown)
Like stern Diogenes to mock at men;
For sceptred cynics earth were far too wide a den.[4]

42

370   But quiet to quick bosoms is a hell,
And *there* hath been thy bane; there is a fire
And motion of the soul which will not dwell
In its own narrow being, but aspire
Beyond the fitting medium of desire;
375   And, but once kindled, quenchless evermore,
Preys upon high adventure, nor can tire
Of aught but rest; a fever at the core,
Fatal to him who bears, to all who ever bore.

1816   1816

Samuel Taylor Coleridge
from *The Statesman's Manual*[1]
["SATANIC PRIDE AND REBELLIOUS SELF-IDOLATRY"]

[I]n its utmost abstraction and consequent state of reprobation, the Will becomes Satanic pride and rebellious self-idolatry in the relations of the spirit to itself, and remorseless despotism relatively to others; the more hopeless as the more obdurate by its subjugation of sensual impulses, by its superiority to toil and pain and pleasure; in short, by the fearful resolve to find in itself alone the one absolute motive of action, under which all other motives from within and from without must be either subordinated or crushed.

This is the character which Milton has so philosophically as well as sublimely embodied in the Satan of his Paradise Lost. Alas! too often has it been embodied in *real* life! Too often has it given a dark and savage grandeur to the historic page! And wherever it has appeared, under whatever circumstances of time and country, the same ingredients have gone to its composition; and it has been identified by the same attributes. Hope in which there is no Chearfulness; Stedfastness within and immovable Resolve, with outward Restlessness and whirling Activity; Violence with Guile; Temerity with Cunning; and, as the result of all, Interminableness of Object with perfect Indifference of Means; these are the qualities that have constituted the Commanding GENIUS! these are the Marks, that have characterized the Masters of Mischief, the Liberticides,[2] and mighty Hunters of Mankind, from NIMROD[3] to NAPOLEON. And from inattention to the possibility of such a character as well as

---

4. The great error of Napoleon, . . . was a continued obtrusion on mankind of his want of all community of feeling for, or with them; perhaps more offensive to human vanity than the active cruelty of more trembling and suspicious tyranny. Such were his speeches to public assemblies as well as individuals; and the single expression which he is said to have used on returning to Paris after the Russian winter had destroyed his army, rubbing his hands over a fire, "This is pleasanter than Moscow," would probably alienate more favour from his cause than the destruction and reverses which led to the remark [Byron's note]. Greek philosopher Diogenes the Cynic

(4th century B.C.) impressed Alexander with his resolute independence.
1. The defeat of Napoleon in 1815 ended nearly 25 years of war, but peacetime brought new crises: unemployment, inflation, food shortages, and agitations for political and social reform. Coleridge joined the debates with a set of pamphlets, of which *The Statesman's Manual*, "Addressed to the higher classes of society," was the first, published in 1816.
2. "Killers of liberty."
3. "The mighty hunter" (Genesis 10.8–9).

from ignorance of its elements, even men of honest intentions too frequently become fascinated. Nay, whole nations have been so far duped by this want of insight and reflection as to regard with palliative admiration, instead of wonder and abhorrence, the Molocks[4] of human nature, who are indebted for the larger portion of their meteoric success, to their total want of principle, and who surpass the generality of their fellow creatures in one act of courage only, that of daring to say with their whole heart, "Evil, be thou my good!"[5]—All *system* so far is power; and a *systematic* criminal, self-consistent and entire in wickedness, who entrenches villainy within villainy and barricadoes crime by crime, has removed a world of obstacles by the mere decision, that he will have no obstacles, but those of force and brute matter.

1816

Caroline Lamb[1]
from *Glenarvon*

Those who have given way to the violence of any uncontrouled passion know that during its influence, all other considerations vanish. It is of little use to upbraid or admonish the victim who pursues his course: the fires that goad him on to his ruin, prevent his return. A kind word, an endearing smile, may excite one contrite tear; but he never pauses to reflect, or turns his eyes from the object of his pursuit. In vain the cold looks of an offended world, the heavy censures, and the pointed, bitter sarcasms of friends and dependants. Misfortunes, poverty, pain, even to the rack, are nothing if he obtain his view. It is a madness that falls upon the brain and heart. All is at stake for that one throw; and he who dares all, is desperate, and cannot fear. It was phrenzy, not love, that raged in Calantha's bosom.

To the prayers of a heart-broken parent, Lady Avondale opposed the agonizing threats of a distempered mind. "I will leave you all, if you take him from me. On earth there is nothing left me but Glenarvon.—Oh name not virtue and religion to me.—What are its hopes, its promises, if I lose him." The fever of her mind was such, that she could not for one hour rest: he saw the dreadful power he had gained, and he lost no opportunity of encreasing it. Ah did he share it? In language the sweetest, and the most persuasive, he worked upon her passions, till he inflamed them beyond endurance.

"This, this is sin," he cried, as he held her to his bosom, and breathed vows of ardent, burning love. "This is what moralists rail at, and account degrading. Now tell them, Calantha, thou who didst affect to be so pure—so chaste, whether the human heart can resist it? Religion bids thee fly me," he cried: "every hope of heaven and hereafter warns thee from my bosom. Glenarvon is the hell thou art to shun:—this is the hour of trial. Christians must resist. Calantha arise, and fly me; leave me alone, as before I found thee. Desert me, and thy father and relations shall bless thee for the sacrifice: and thy God, who redeemed thee, shall mark thee for his own." With bitter taunts he smiled as he thus spoke: then clasping her nearer to his heart, "Tell both priests and parents," he said exultingly, "that one kiss from the lips of those we love, is dearer than every future hope."

4. The idol to whom children were sacrificed in the Old Testament world (Leviticus 18.21), and in *Paradise Lost*, Satan's compatriot in Hell (1.392–96).
5. Satan's oath (*Paradise Lost* 4.110).
1. Caroline Lamb (1785–1828) had a tempestuous affair with Byron across 1812. When an exasperated Byron bluntly ditched her, she collapsed in hysterics, but by 1816, after Byron's marriage to her cousin Annabella Milbanke had collapsed, she avenged herself with a *roman à clef*, whose evil hero, the Earl of Glenarvon, is not only Byronic, but transparently Byron. The heroine, Calantha, Lady Avondale, has fallen under his spell, even though she is married to a good man, has children, and her course is opposed by her family.

All day,—every hour in the day,—every instant of passing time Glenarvon thought but of Calantha. It was not love, it was distraction. When near him, she felt ecstasy; but if separated, though but for one moment, she was sullen and desponding. At night she seldom slept; a burning fever quickened every pulse: the heart beat as if with approaching dissolution,—delirium fell upon her brain. No longer innocent, her fancy painted but visions of love; and to be his alone, was all she now wished for, or desired on earth. He felt, he saw, that the peace of her mind, her life itself were gone for ever, and he rejoiced in the thought.

* * *

[Calantha dies after being jilted by Glenarvon; Glenarvon, in the disguise of "Viviani," has murdered a child and the sister of the duke to whom he is talking in the following passage, describing himself. In another character, Glenarvon is the leader of Irish patriots plotting a rebellion—they are the multitude to whom the passage refers.]

The duke started, and looked full in the face of Glenarvon. "Who is this Viviani?" he said, in a tone of voice loud and terrible. "An idol," replied Glenarvon, "whom the multitude have set up for themselves, and worshipped, forsaking their true faith, to follow after a false light—a man who is in love with crime and baseness—one, of whom it has been said, that he hath an imagination of fire playing around a heart of ice—one whom the never-dying worm feeds on by night and day—a hypocrite," continued Glenarvon, with a smile of bitterness, "who wears a mask to his friends, and defeats his enemies by his unexpected sincerity—a coward, with more of bravery than some who fear nothing; for, even in his utmost terror, he defies that which he fears." "And where is this wretch?" said the duke: "what dungeon is black enough to hold him? What rack has been prepared to punish him for his crimes?" "He is as I have said," replied Glenarvon triumphantly, "the idol of the fair, and the great. Is it virtue that women prize? Is it honour and renown they worship? Throw but the dazzling light of genius upon baseness, and corruption, and every crime will be to them but an additional charm."

* * *

[Glenarvon goes on to ruin several women, fatally wounds Calantha's husband in a duel, and abandons the Irish patriots, whose rebellion is crushed; having confessed all to the duke, he flees Ireland for England. At the novel's end, he has become captain of a ship in the navy. Commanding his ship in an engagement against the French, he fights bravely, but is then seized with a vision of a ghost-ship, which he is determined to pursue.]

Madness to phrenzy came upon him. In vain his friends, and many of the brave companions in his ship, held him struggling in their arms. He seized his opportunity. "Bear on," he cried: "pursue, till death and vengeance—" and throwing himself from the helm, plunged headlong into the waters. They rescued him; but it was too late. In the struggles of ebbing life, even as the spirit of flame rushed from the bands of mortality, visions of punishment and hell pursued him. Down, down, he seemed to sink with horrid precipitance from gulf to gulf, till immured in darkness; and as he closed his eyes in death, a voice, loud and terrible, from beneath, thus seemed to address him:

"Hardened and impenitent sinner! the measure of your iniquity is full: the price of crime has been paid: here shall your spirit dwell for ever, and for ever. You have dreamed away life's joyous hour, nor made atonement for error, nor denied yourself aught that the fair earth presented you. You did not controul the fiend in your bosom, or stifle him in his first growth: he now has mastered you, and brought you here: and you did not bow the knee for mercy whilst time was given you: now mercy shall not be shewn. O, cry upwards from these lower pits, to the friends and companions you have left, to the sinner who hardens himself against his Creator—who basks in the ray of prosperous guilt, nor dreams that his hour like your's is at hand. Tell him how terrible a thing is death; how fearful at such an hour is remembrance of the past. Bid him repent, but he shall not hear you. Bid him amend, but like you he shall delay till it is too late. Then, neither his arts, nor talents, nor his possessions, shall save him, nor friends, though leagued together more than ten thousand strong; for the axe of justice must fall. God is just; and the spirit of evil infatuates before he destroys."

1816   1816

Mary Wollstonecraft Shelley
from *Frankenstein; or The Modern Prometheus* [1]
[VICTOR FRANKENSTEIN IN THE LABORATORY]

No one can conceive the variety of feelings which bore me onwards, like a hurricane, in the first enthusiasm of success. Life and death appeared to me ideal bounds, which I should first break through, and pour a torrent of light into our dark world. A new species would bless me as its creator and source; many happy and excellent natures would owe their being to me. No father could claim the gratitude of his child so completely as I should deserve their's. Pursuing these reflections, I thought, that if I could bestow animation upon lifeless matter, I might in process of time (although I now found it impossible) renew life where death had apparently devoted the body to corruption.

These thoughts supported my spirits, while I pursued my undertaking with unremitting ardour. My cheek had grown pale with study, and my person had become emaciated with confinement. Sometimes, on the very brink of certainty, I failed; yet still I clung to the hope which the next day or the next hour might realize. One secret which I alone possessed was the hope to which I had dedicated myself; and the moon gazed on my midnight labours, while, with unrelaxed and breathless eagerness, I pursued nature to her hiding places. Who shall conceive the horrors of my secret toil, as I dabbled among the unhallowed damps of the grave, or tortured the living animal to animate the lifeless clay? [2] My limbs now tremble, and my eyes swim with the remembrance; but then a resistless, and almost frantic impulse, urged me forward; I seemed to have lost all soul or sensation but for this one pursuit. It was indeed but a passing trance, that only made me feel with renewed acuteness so soon as, the unnatural stimulus ceasing to operate, I had returned to my old habits. I collected bones from charnel houses; and disturbed, with profane fingers, the tremendous secrets of the human frame. In a

1. Shelley began this novel at Byron's villa in 1816 and it was published in 1818. The subtitle, "the Modern Prometheus," may describe both Frankenstein and his Creature, the former as a transgressor against divine law, stealing power from heaven, the latter as a compassionate fire-bringer to suffering humanity, punished for his deed. In this excerpt from vol. 1, ch. 3, Frankenstein recounts his project to create life, a daring idealism betrayed and tormented by horrific consequences: a malformed creature, whom he calls "Monster" and "Demon." In the excerpt from vol. 2, ch. 7, the Creature, having finally caught up

with the creator who abandoned him at birth, tells his story, a narrative in which he is the victim, alienated and tormented by his physical difference from humanity, anguished in his loneliness. Having learned to read, the Creature studies *Paradise Lost* (found by chance in a satchel in the woods) and what amounts to his prenatal biography, Victor's laboratory notes on his science project.

2. In the Greek myth, Prometheus fashions man out of clay, and breathes life into him, later giving him fire to raise him above the level of the beasts. In the story of Genesis (2.7), God creates man out of clay and breathes life into him.

solitary chamber, or rather cell, at the top of the house, and separated from all the other apartments by a gallery and staircase, I kept my workshop of filthy creation; my eyeballs were starting from their sockets in attending to the details of my employment. The dissecting room and the slaughter-house furnished many of my materials; and often did my human nature turn with loathing from my occupation, whilst, still urged on by an eagerness which perpetually increased, I brought my work near to a conclusion.

[THE CREATURE, NOW LITERATE, READS *PARADISE LOST*]

But *Paradise Lost* excited different and far deeper emotions. I read it, as I had read the other volumes which had fallen into my hands, as a true history. It moved every feeling of wonder and awe, that the picture of an omnipotent God warring with his creatures was capable of exciting. I often referred the several situations, as their similarity struck me, to my own. Like Adam, I was created apparently united by no link to any other being in existence; but his state was far different from mine in every other respect. He had come forth from the hands of God a perfect creature, happy and prosperous, guarded by the especial care of his Creator; he was allowed to converse with, and acquire knowledge from beings of a superior nature:[3] but I was wretched, helpless, and alone. Many times I considered Satan as the fitter emblem of my condition; for often, like him, when I viewed the bliss of my protectors, the bitter gall of envy rose within me.[4]

Another circumstance strengthened and confirmed these feelings. Soon after my arrival in the hovel, I discovered some papers in the pocket of the dress[5] which I had taken from your laboratory. At first I had neglected them; but now that I was able to decypher the characters in which they were written, I began to study them with diligence. It was your journal of the four months that preceded my creation. You minutely described in these papers every step you took in the progress of your work; this history was mingled with accounts of domestic occurrences. You, doubtless, recollect these papers. Here they are. Every thing is related in them which bears reference to my accursed origin; the whole detail of that series of disgusting circumstances which produced it is set in view; the minutest description of my odious and loathsome person is given, in language which painted your own horrors, and rendered mine ineffaceable. I sickened as I read. "Hateful day when I received life!" I exclaimed in agony. "Cursed creator! Why did you form a monster so hideous that even you turned from me in disgust? God in pity made man beautiful and alluring, after his own image;[6] but my form is a filthy type of your's, more horrid from its very resemblance. Satan had his companions, fellow-devils, to admire and encourage him; but I am solitary and detested."[7]

1816   1818

---

3. *Paradise Lost* 8.250–559; Adam recounts several conversations with his Creator, and he is tutored in Eden by the "affable" Archangel Raphael.
4. *Paradise Lost* 4.358–69.

5. Lab coat.
6. "God created man in his own image" (Genesis 1.27).
7. *Frankenstein* may be read in full in the Longman Cultural Edition, edited by Susan Wolfson.

Felicia Hemans
from *The Widow of Crescentius* [1]

So wildly sweet, its° notes might seem   *Guido's song*
Th' ethereal music of a dream,
125   A spirit's voice from worlds unknown,
Deep thrilling power in every tone!
Sweet is that lay, and yet its flow
Hath language only given to woe;
And if at times its wakening swell
130   Some tale of glory seems to tell,
Soon the proud notes of triumph die,
Lost in a dirge's harmony:
Oh! many a pang the heart hath proved,
Hath deeply suffer'd, fondly loved,
135   Ere the sad strain could catch from thence
Such deep impassion'd eloquence!—
Yes! gaze on him, that minstrel boy—
He is no child of hope and joy;
Though few his years, yet have they been
140   Such as leave traces on the mien,
And o'er the roses of our prime
Breathe other blights than those of time.

Yet, seems his spirit wild and proud,
By grief unsoften'd and unbow'd.
145   Oh! there are sorrows which impart
A sternness foreign to the heart,
And rushing with an earthquake's power,
That makes a desert in an hour;
Rouse the dread passions in their course,
150   As tempests wake the billows' force!—
'Tis sad, on youthful Guido's face,
The stamp of woes like these to trace.
Oh! where can ruins awe mankind,
Dark as the ruins of the mind?

155   His mien is lofty, but his gaze
Too well a wandering soul betrays:
His full dark eye at times is bright
With strange and momentary light,
Whose quick uncertain flashes throw
160   O'er his pale cheek a hectic glow:
And oft his features and his air
A shade of troubled mystery wear,

1. For Hemans, see page 514. This poem is in *Tales, and Historic Scenes*, published in 1819 by John Murray, also Byron's publisher. Hemans was one of many female poets inspired by Byron's poetry. In this historically based poem, Stephania's husband, a Republican opponent of papal rule in late 10th-century Rome, has been tortured and executed by the Holy Roman Emperor, Otto III of Germany. Stephania takes revenge by disguising herself as the minstrel-boy Guido and insinuating herself into Otto's court, where she eventually poisons him, gloating in her triumph before she is led off to execution. This excerpt from part 2 describes the mysteriously sad "Guido," before "his" true identity is disclosed.

A glance of hurried wildness, fraught
With some unfathomable thought.[2]
165   Whate'er that thought, still, unexpress'd,
Dwells the sad secret in his breast;
The pride his haughty brow reveals,
All other passion well conceals.[3]
He breathes each wounded feeling's tone,
170   In music's eloquence alone;
His soul's deep voice is only pour'd
Through his full song and swelling chord.

Percy Bysshe Shelley
from *Preface to Prometheus Unbound* [1]

The only imaginary being resembling in any degree Prometheus, is Satan; and Prometheus is, in my judgement, a more poetical character than Satan, because, in addition to courage, and majesty, and firm and patient opposition to omnipotent force, he is susceptible of being described as exempt from the taints of ambition, envy, revenge, and a desire for personal aggrandisement, which, in the Hero of Paradise Lost, interfere with the interest. The character of Satan engenders in the mind a pernicious casuistry[2] which leads us to weigh his faults and his wrongs,[3] and to excuse the former because the latter exceed all measure. In the minds of those who consider that magnificent fiction with a religious feeling it engenders something worse. But Prometheus is, as it were, the type of the highest perfection of moral and intellectual nature, impelled by the purest and the truest motives to the best and noblest ends.

from *Prometheus Unbound*, Act 1[4]

Monarch of Gods and Dæmons,[5] and all Spirits
But One,° who throng those bright and rolling worlds   *i.e., himself*
Which Thou and I alone of living things
Behold with sleepless eyes! regard this Earth
5   Made multitudinous with thy slaves, whom thou
Requitest for knee-worship, prayer, and praise,
And toil, and hecatombs[6] of broken hearts,
With fear and self-contempt and barren hope;
Whilst me, who am thy foe, eyeless° in hate,   *blind*
10   Hast thou made reign and triumph, to thy scorn,
O'er mine own misery and thy vain revenge.
Three thousand years of sleep-unsheltered hours,
And moments aye° divided by keen pangs   *forever*
Till they seemed years, torture and solitude,

2. Readers of *The Giaour* and *Lara* would grasp the allusion to a Byronic heroine in page's guise, and recognize the iconography of the Byronic hero.
3. In Byron's portrait of the charismatic, mysterious hero of *The Corsair* (1814) this rhyme is a keynote: "And oft perforce his rising lip reveals / The haughtier thought it curbs, but scarce conceals" (1.205–6).
1. Shelley's epic verse drama, written in 1818–1819 and published in 1820, concerns Prometheus's struggle against and eventual liberation from Jupiter's tyranny, an emblem of modern tyrannies as well.
2. Specious moral reasoning.
3. Oppression and suffering.
4. Prometheus, bound to a precipice in a ravine of icy rocks, invokes Jupiter.
5. Beings between mortals and gods able to communicate with both.
6. Massive sacrifices (heca: 100).

15   Scorn and despair,—these are mine empire:—
     More glorious far than that which thou surveyest
     From thine unenvied throne, O Mighty God!
     Almighty, had I deigned to share the shame
     Of thine ill tyranny, and hung not here
20   Nailed to this wall of eagle-baffling mountain,
     Black, wintry, dead, unmeasured; without herb,
     Insect, or beast, or shape or sound of life.
     Ah me! alas, pain, pain ever, for ever!

     No change, no pause, no hope! Yet I endure.
25   I ask the Earth, have not the mountains felt?
     I ask yon Heaven, the all-beholding Sun,
     Has it not seen? The Sea, in storm or calm
     Heaven's ever-changing Shadow, spread below,
     Have its deaf waves not heard my agony?
30   Ah me! alas, pain, pain ever, for ever!

     The crawling glaciers pierce me with the spears
     Of their moon-freezing crystals; the bright chains
     Eat with their burning cold into my bones.
     Heaven's winged hound, polluting from thy lips
35   His beak in poison not his own, tears up
     My heart;[7] and shapeless sights come wandering by,
     The ghastly people of the realm of dream,
     Mocking me: and the Earthquake-fiends are charged
     To wrench the rivets from my quivering wounds
40   When the rocks split and close again behind;
     While from their loud abysses howling throng
     The genii of the storm, urging the rage
     Of whirlwind, and afflict me with keen hail.
     And yet to me welcome is day and night,
45   Whether one breaks the hoar frost of the morn,
     Or starry, dim, and slow, the other climbs
     The leaden-coloured east; for then they lead
     The wingless, crawling hours, one among whom
     —As some dark Priest hales° the reluctant victim—   hauls
50   Shall drag thee, cruel King, to kiss the blood
     From these pale feet, which then might trample thee
     If they disdained not such a prostrate slave.
     Disdain! Ah no! I pity thee. What ruin
     Will hunt thee undefended through the wide Heaven!
55   How will thy soul, cloven to its depth with terror,
     Gape like a Hell within! I speak in grief,
     Not exultation, for I hate no more,
     As then ere misery made me wise. The curse
     Once breathed on thee I would recall.

1818–1819   1820

7. See page 389, n. 1. Jupiter kisses the vulture on his return.

Robert Southey
from *Preface to A Vision of Judgement* [1]
[THE "SATANIC SCHOOL"]

Would that [the public's "literary intolerance"] were directed against those monstrous combinations of horrors and mockery, lewdness and impiety, with which English poetry has, in our days, first been polluted! For more than half a century English literature had been distinguished by its moral purity, the effect, and in its turn, the cause of an improvement in national manners. A father might, without apprehension of evil, have put into the hands of his children any book which issued from the press, if it did not bear, either in its title-page or frontispiece, manifest signs that it was intended as furniture for the brothel. There was no danger in any work which bore the name of a respectable publisher, or was to be procured at any respectable bookseller's. This was particularly the case with regard to our poetry. It is now no longer so; and woe to those by whom the offence cometh! The greater the talents of the offender, the greater is his guilt, and the more enduring will be his shame. Whether it be that the laws are in themselves unable to abate an evil of this magnitude, or whether it be that they are remissly administered, and with such injustice that the celebrity of an offender serves as a privilege whereby he obtains impunity, individuals are bound to consider that such pernicious works would neither be published nor written, if they were discouraged as they might, and ought to be, by public feeling; every person, therefore, who purchases such books, or admits them into his house, promotes the mischief, and thereby, as far as in him lies, becomes an aider and abettor of the crime.

The publication of a lascivious book is one of the worst offences that can be committed against the well-being of society. It is a sin, to the consequences of which no limits can be assigned, and those consequences no after repentance in the writer can counteract. Whatever remorse of conscience he may feel when his hour comes (and come it must!) will be of no avail. The poignancy of a death-bed repentance cannot cancel one copy of the thousands which are sent abroad; and as long as it continues to be read, so long is he the pandar of posterity, and so long is he heaping up guilt upon his soul in perpetual accumulation.

These remarks are not more severe than the offence deserves, even when applied to those immoral writers who have not been conscious of any evil intention in their writings, who would acknowledge a little levity, a little warmth of colouring, and so forth, in that sort of language with which men gloss over their favourite vices, and deceive themselves. What then should be said of those for whom the thoughtlessness and inebriety of wanton youth can no longer be pleaded, but who have written in sober manhood and with deliberate purpose? . . Men of diseased hearts and depraved imaginations, who, forming a system of opinions to suit their own unhappy course of conduct, have rebelled against the holiest ordinances of human society, and hating that revealed religion which, with all their efforts and bravadoes, they are unable entirely to disbelieve, labour to make others as miserable as themselves, by infecting them with a moral virus that eats into the soul! The school which they have set up may properly be called the Satanic school; for though their productions breathe the

---

1. When Poet Laureate Southey published *A Vision of Judgement* in 1821, on the occasion of the death of George III, he took the opportunity to settle scores with his detractors, chiefly Byron. In *A Vision* Satan arrives at the gates of heaven, where the king's spirit is to be admitted amid beatification, to carry the monarch's political antagonists off to hell. In his preface Southey wished the same for Byron and his compeers, in punishment for polluting the "moral purity" of English literature with the works of a "Satanic school."

spirit of Belial in their lascivious parts, and the spirit of Moloch in those loathsome images of atrocities and horrors which they delight to represent, they are more especially characterised by a Satanic spirit of pride and audacious impiety, which still betrays the wretched feeling of hopelessness wherewith it is allied.

   This evil is political as well as moral for indeed moral and political evils are inseparably connected. * * * Let rulers of the state look to this, in time!

George Gordon, Lord Byron
from *The Vision of Judgment*[1]

24

185   But bringing up the rear of this bright host
           A Spirit of a different aspect waved
       His wings, like thunder-clouds above some coast
           Whose barren beach with frequent wrecks is paved;
       His brow was like the deep when tempest-toss'd;
190   Fierce and unfathomable thoughts engraved
       Eternal wrath on his immortal face,
       And *where* he gazed a gloom pervaded space.

                         * * *

33

       But here they were in neutral space: we know
           From Job, that Satan hath the power to pay
       A heavenly visit thrice a year or so;[2]
260   And that 'the sons of God,' like those of clay,°   *mortals*
       Must keep him company; and we might show
           From the same book, in how polite a way
       The dialogue is held between the Powers
       Of Good and Evil—but 'twould take up hours.

                         * * *

35

       The spirits were in neutral space, before
           The gate of heaven; like eastern thresholds is
275   The place where Death's grand cause is argued o'er,
           And souls despatch'd to that world or to this;
       And therefore Michael and the other wore
           A civil aspect: though they did not kiss,
       Yet still between his Darkness and his Brightness
280   There pass'd a mutual glance of great politeness.

---

1. Outraged by Southey's politics of Heaven, whereby a reactionary king was canonized and his political opponents damned, Byron began a counter-*Vision* immediately, in the spring of 1821, but his longtime publisher John Murray, tied in with the Tories, demurred and delayed its publication. Testing other London publishers, even the radical press, without success, Byron put the poem in the first issue of *The Liberal*, October 1822. Its publisher John Hunt was prosecuted for "calumniating the late king, and wounding the feelings of his present majesty," and was fined £100. In this excerpt, Satan arrives at the gates of heaven to make his claim for the king's soul and is greeted by Archangel Michael.
2. Job 1.2

36

The Archangel bow'd, not like a modern beau,
    But with a graceful oriental bend,
Pressing one radiant arm just where below
    The heart in good men is supposed to tend.
285 He turn'd as to an equal, not too low,
    But kindly; Satan met his ancient friend
With more hauteur, as might an old Castilian[3]
Poor noble meet a mushroom rich civilian.

END OF "MANFRED" AND ITS TIME

❂

from CHILDE HAROLD'S PILGRIMAGE

Canto the Third[1]

[THUNDERSTORM IN THE ALPS][2]

92

860 Thy sky is changed!—and such a change! Oh night,
    And storm, and darkness, ye are wondrous strong,
    Yet lovely in your strength, as is the light
    Of a dark eye in woman! Far along,
    From peak to peak, the rattling crags among
865 Leaps the live thunder! Not from one lone cloud,
    But every mountain now hath found a tongue,
    And Jura answers, through her misty shroud,
Back to the joyous Alps, who call to her aloud![3]

93

And this is in the night:—Most glorious night!
870 Thou wert not sent for slumber! let me be
    A sharer in thy fierce and far delight,—
    A portion of the tempest and of thee!
    How the lit lake shines, a phosphoric sea,
    And the big rain comes dancing to the earth!
875 And now again 'tis black,—and now, the glee
    Of the loud hills shakes with its mountain-mirth,
As if they did rejoice o'er a young earthquake's birth.

---

3. Old nobility, descended from the medieval Spanish kingdom of Castile.

1. The first two cantos appeared in 1812. As the subtitle "A Romaunt" indicated, Byron had adopted the genre of romance for his unnervingly contemporary poem. The Spenserian stanzas and mock-archaisms—a "childe" is a youth of noble birth—played discordantly against the account of his travels in 1809–1811 through Spain and then on into parts of Greece unfrequented by Westerners. The overwhelming success of the poem ensured that Byron would be identified with Childe Harold. Byron protested, but the connection is reinforced by the manuscripts, which disclose that Childe Harold was once Childe Burun, an ancient form of his family name. Although Canto 3 was published independently in 1816,

protagonist and poet had come to figure each other. Byron left England on 25 April 1816, and wrote the opening stanzas while crossing the Channel. For a counterpoint to the poem's melancholy sublimity see Byron's letter of 28 January 1817 to Thomas Moore, page 809.
2. "The thunder-storms to which these lines refer occurred on the thirteenth of June, 1816, at midnight. I have seen among the Acroceraunian mountains of Chimari several more terrible, but none more beautiful" [Byron's note]. Byron moved into Villa Diodati on 10 June, near the Shelley party; a few days after these storms Mary Shelley began *Frankenstein* at Byron's Villa.
3. The Jura Mountains, north and west of Geneva, form the boundary between Switzerland and France; the Alps run to the east and south.

94

Now, where the swift Rhone cleaves his way between
Heights which appear as lovers who have parted
880   In hate, whose mining depths so intervene,
That they can meet no more, though broken-hearted!
Though in their souls, which thus each other thwarted,
Love was the very root of the fond rage
Which blighted their life's bloom, and then departed:——
885   Itself expired, but leaving them an age
Of years all winters,—war within themselves to wage.[4]

95

Now, where the quick Rhone thus hath cleft his way,
The mightiest of the storms hath ta'en his stand:
For here, not one, but many, make their play,
890   And fling their thunder-bolts from hand to hand,
Flashing and cast around: of all the band,
The brightest through these parted hills hath fork'd
His lightnings,—as if he did understand,
That in such gaps as desolation work'd,
895 There the hot shaft should blast whatever therein lurk'd.

96

Sky, mountains, river, winds, lake, lightnings! ye!
With night, and clouds, and thunder, and a soul
To make these felt and feeling, well may be
Things that have made me watchful; the far roll
900   Of your departing voices, is the knoll
Of what in me is sleepless,—if I rest.
But where of ye, oh tempests! is the goal?
Are ye like those within the human breast?
Or do ye find, at length, like eagles, some high nest?

97

905   Could I embody and unbosom now
That which is most within me,—could I wreak
My thoughts upon expression, and thus throw
Soul, heart, mind, passions, feelings, strong or weak,
All that I would have sought, and all I seek,
910   Bear, know, feel, and yet breathe—into *one* word,
And that one word were Lightning, I would speak;
But as it is, I live and die unheard,
With a most voiceless thought, sheathing it as a sword.

[BYRON'S STRAINED IDEALISM. APOSTROPHE TO HIS DAUGHTER]

111

Thus far have I proceeded in a theme
Renew'd with no kind auspices°:—to feel   *hopeful signs*

---

4. The simile, obliquely recalling Byron's separation from his wife, illustrates his tendency to turn nature into sublime self-projection.

We are not what we have been, and to deem
We are not what we should be,—and to steel
1035   The heart against itself; and to conceal,
With a proud caution, love, or hate, or aught,—
Passion or feeling, purpose, grief, or zeal,—
Which is the tyrant spirit of our thought,
Is a stern task of soul:—No matter,—it is taught.

112

1040   And for these words, thus woven into song,
It may be that they are a harmless wile,—
The colouring of the scenes which fleet along,
Which I would seize, in passing, to beguile
My breast, or that of others, for a while.
1045   Fame is the thirst of youth,—but I am not
So young as to regard men's frown or smile,
As loss or guerdon° of a glorious lot;   *prize*
I stood and stand alone,—remember'd or forgot.

113

I have not loved the world, nor the world me;
1050   I have not flatter'd its rank breath,[5] nor bow'd
To it's idolatries a patient knee,—
Nor coin'd my cheek to smiles,—nor cried aloud
In worship of an echo; in the crowd
They could not deem me one of such; I stood
1055   Among them, but not of them; in a shroud
Of thoughts which were not their thoughts, and still could,
Had I not filed° my mind, which thus itself subdued.[6]   *defiled*

114

I have not loved the world, nor the world me,—
But let us part fair foes; I do believe,
1060   Though I have found them not, that there may be
Words which are things,—hopes which will not deceive,
And virtues which are merciful, nor weave
Snares for the failing: I would also deem
O'er others' griefs that some sincerely grieve;[7]
1065   That two, or one, are almost what they seem,—
That goodness is no name, and happiness no dream.

115

My daughter![8] with thy name this song begun—
My daughter! with thy name thus much shall end—
I see thee not,—I hear thee not,—but none
1070   Can be so wrapt in thee; thou art the friend

---

5. Echoing Shakespeare's *Coriolanus*, 3.1.66–67. Byron frequently voices himself through this willful Roman general, who retorts to the plebeians who banish him: "I banish you" (3.3.124).
6. Byron adds a note citing *Macbeth*, 3.1.65.

7. It is said by Rochefoucault that "there is *always* something in the misfortunes of men's best friends not displeasing to them" [Byron's note].
8. Ada, whom Byron never saw again, after leaving England in her infancy. These stanzas close the canto.

To whom the shadows of far years extend:
Albeit my brow thou never should'st behold,
My voice shall with thy future visions blend
And reach into thy heart,—when mine is cold,—
1075   A token and a tone, even from thy father's mould.

116

To aid thy mind's developement,—to watch
Thy dawn of little joys,—to sit and see
Almost thy very growth,—to view thee catch
Knowledge of objects,—wonders yet to thee!
1080   To hold thee lightly on a gentle knee,
And print on thy soft cheek a parent's kiss,—
This, it should seem, was not reserved for me;
Yet this was in my nature:—as it is,
I know not what is there, yet something like to this.

117

1085   Yet, though dull Hate as duty should be taught,
I know that thou wilt love me; though my name
Should be shut from thee, as a spell still fraught
With desolation,—and a broken claim:
Though the grave closed between us,—'twere the same,
1090   I know that thou wilt love me; though to drain
My blood from out thy being were an aim,
And an attainment,—all would be in vain,—
Still thou would'st love me, still that more than life retain.

118

The child of love,—though born in bitterness
1095   And nurtured in convulsion. Of thy sire
These were the elements,—and thine no less.
As yet such are around thee,—but thy fire
Shall be more temper'd, and thy hope far higher.
Sweet be thy cradled slumbers! O'er the sea,
1100   And from the mountains where I now respire,
Fain would I waft such blessing upon thee,
As, with a sigh, I deem thou might'st have been to me!

from Canto the Fourth[1]

[ROME. POLITICAL HOPES]

93

What from this barren being° do we reap?   *Napoleon*
830   Our senses narrow, and our reason frail,
Life short, and truth a gem which loves the deep,

---

1. Begun in June 1817, published April 1818. In the dedication Byron announced that the reader would find "less of the pilgrim" than in preceding cantos: "I had become weary," he declared of the fiction, "of drawing a line which every one seemed determined not to perceive." Canto 4 is spoken in his own person and carries the account of his travels into Italy.

And all things weigh'd in custom's falsest scale;
Opinion an omnipotence,—whose veil
Mantles the earth with darkness, until right
835   And wrong are accidents, and men grow pale
Lest their own judgments should become too bright,
And their free thoughts be crimes, and earth have too much light.

94

And thus they plod in sluggish misery,
Rotting from sire to son, and age to age,
840   Proud of their trampled nature, and so die,
Bequeathing their hereditary rage
To the new race of inborn slaves, who wage
War for their chains, and rather than be free,
Bleed gladiator-like, and still engage
845   Within the same arena where they see
Their fellows fall before, like leaves of the same tree.

95

I speak not of men's creeds—they rest between
Man and his Maker—but of things allowed,
Averr'd,° and known,—and daily, hourly seen—   affirmed
850   The yoke that is upon us doubly bowed,
And the intent of tyranny avowed,
The edict of Earth's rulers, who are grown
The apes of him who humbled once the proud,
And shook them from their slumbers on the throne;
855   Too glorious, were this all his mighty arm had done.[2]

96

Can tyrants but by tyrants conquered be,
And Freedom find no champion and no child
Such as Columbia saw arise when she
Sprung forth a Pallas, armed and undefiled?[3]
860   Or must such minds be nourished in the wild,
Deep in the unpruned forest, 'midst the roar
Of cataracts, where nursing Nature smiled
On infant Washington?[4] Has Earth no more
Such seeds within her breast, or Europe no such shore?

2. At the Congress of Vienna in 1815, the nations that defeated Napoleon implemented a system of alliances to check the power of France. Reactionary regimes were installed throughout Europe; in France, the pre-Revolutionary Bourbon monarchy was restored.
3. The Greek goddess of wisdom and counsel in war, Pallas Athena, sprang fully formed from the head of Zeus, as Columbia, the figure of America, sprang from Britain.

4. Byron's admiration for George Washington was constant. He ended Ode to Napoleon Buonaparte (1814) declaring him "the first—the last—the best / The Cincinnatus of the West, / Whom envy dared not hate, / Bequeath'd the name of Washington, / To make man blush there was but one!" Cincinnatus, a type of Republican virtue, left his plough in 458 B.C. to defend Rome; having succeeded, he resigned his command and returned to his farm.

97

865   But France got drunk with blood to vomit crime,
       And fatal have her Saturnalia⁵ been
       To Freedom's cause, in every age and clime;
       Because the deadly days which we have seen,
       And vile Ambition, that built up between
870   Man and his hopes an adamantine° wall,   impregnable
       And the base pageant last upon the scene,
       Are grown the pretext for the eternal thrall
Which nips life's tree, and dooms man's worst—his second fall.⁶

98

       Yet, Freedom! yet thy banner, torn, but flying,
875   Streams like the thunder-storm *against* the wind;
       Thy trumpet voice, though broken now and dying,
       The loudest still the tempest leaves behind;
       Thy tree hath lost its blossoms, and the rind,°   bark
       Chopp'd by the axe, looks rough and little worth,
880   But the sap lasts, and still the seed we find
       Sown deep, even in the bosom of the North;
So shall a better spring less bitter fruit bring forth.

[APOSTROPHE TO THE OCEAN. CONCLUSION]

178

       There is a pleasure in the pathless woods,
1595   There is a rapture on the lonely shore,
       There is society, where none intrudes,
       By the deep Sea, and music in its roar:
       I love not Man the less, but Nature more,
       From these our interviews, in which I steal
1600   From all I may be, or have been before,
       To mingle with the Universe, and feel
What I can ne'er express, yet can not all conceal.

179

       Roll on, thou deep and dark blue ocean—roll!
       Ten thousand fleets sweep over thee in vain;
1605   Man marks the earth with ruin—his control
       Stops with the shore;—upon the watery plain
       The wrecks are all thy deed, nor doth remain
       A shadow of man's ravage, save his own,
       When, for a moment, like a drop of rain,

5. The Roman festival of the god Saturn was a time of general license.
6. The "base pageant" is the Congress of Vienna; the concept of a second fall, repeating the eating of the apple by Adam and Eve, originates in St. Augustine.

1610   He sinks into thy depths with bubbling groan,
        Without a grave, unknell'd, uncoffin'd, and unknown.

                            180
            His steps are not upon thy paths,—thy fields
            Are not a spoil for him,—thou dost arise
            And shake him from thee; the vile strength he wields
1615   For earth's destruction thou dost all despise,
            Spurning him from thy bosom to the skies,
            And send'st him, shivering in thy playful spray
            And howling, to his Gods, where haply lies
            His petty hope in some near port or bay,
1620   And dashest him again to earth:—there let him lay.[7]

                            181
            The armaments which thunderstrike the walls
            Of rock-built cities, bidding nations quake,
            And monarchs tremble in their capitals,
            The oak leviathans, whose huge ribs make
1625   Their clay creator the vain title take
            Of lord of thee, and arbiter of war;[8]
            These are thy toys, and, as the snowy flake,
            They melt into thy yeast of waves, which mar
        Alike the Armada's pride, or spoils of Trafalgar.[9]

                            182
1630   Thy shores are empires, changed in all save thee—
            Assyria, Greece, Rome, Carthage, what are they?
            Thy waters wasted them while they were free,
            And many a tyrant since; their shores obey
            The stranger, slave, or savage; their decay
1635   Has dried up realms to desarts:—not so thou,
            Unchangeable save to thy wild waves' play—
            Time writes no wrinkle on thine azure brow—
        Such as creation's dawn beheld, thou rollest now.

                            183
            Thou glorious mirror, where the Almighty's form
1640   Glasses itself in tempests; in all time,
            Calm or convuls'd—in breeze, or gale, or storm,
            Icing the pole, or in the torrid clime
            Dark-heaving;—boundless, endless, and sublime—
            The image of Eternity—the throne

---

7. When his publisher's reader queried, "I have a doubt about *lay*" (instead of *lie*, perhaps the most famous solecism in English poetry), Byron replied: "So have I—but the *poet* and *indolence* and *illness!*" He "manages his pen with the careless and negligent ease of a man of quality," Scott wrote of Byron; the nonchalant manner marked his aristocratic status.
8. The imagery is from the Book of Job: bemoaning his condition, Job acknowledges that God has made him "as the clay" (Job 10.9); God, showing his power, asks: "Canst thou draw out leviathan with a hook?" (41.1). The comparison of ships to this sea beast was familiar.
9. Storms severely damaged the Spanish fleet sent against England in 1588; a subsequent storm destroyed many of the ships taken as prizes in Admiral Nelson's victory over the French fleet at Trafalgar (1805).

1645　　　Of the Invisible; even from out thy slime
　　　　　The monsters of the deep are made; each zone
　　　Obeys thee; thou goest forth, dread, fathomless, alone.

184

　　　　　And I have loved thee, Ocean! and my joy
　　　　　Of youthful sports was on thy breast to be
1650　　　Borne, like thy bubbles, onward: from a boy
　　　　　I wantoned with thy breakers—they to me
　　　　　Were a delight; and if the freshening sea
　　　　　Made them a terror—'twas a pleasing fear,
　　　　　For I was as it were a child of thee,
1655　　　And trusted to thy billows far and near,
　　　And laid my hand upon thy mane—as I do here.

185

　　　　　My task is done—my song hath ceased—my theme
　　　　　Has died into an echo; it is fit
　　　　　The spell should break of this protracted dream.
1660　　　The torch shall be extinguish'd which hath lit
　　　　　My midnight lamp—and what is writ, is writ,—
　　　　　Would it were worthier! but I am not now
　　　　　That which I have been—and my visions flit
　　　　　Less palpably before me—and the glow
1665　　Which in my spirit dwelt is fluttering, faint, and low.

186

　　　　　Farewell! a word that must be, and hath been—
　　　　　A sound which makes us linger;—yet—farewell!
　　　　　Ye! who have traced the Pilgrim to the scene
　　　　　Which is his last, if in your memories dwell
1670　　　A thought which once was his, if on ye swell
　　　　　A single recollection, not in vain
　　　　　He wore his sandal-shoon, and scallop-shell;[1]
　　　　　Farewell! with *him* alone may rest the pain,
　　　If such there were—with *you*, the moral of his strain!

Don Juan　"Give me a poem," Byron's publisher John Murray wrote him in January 1817, "a good Venetian tale describing manners formerly from the story itself, and now from your own observations." The response was *Beppo*, which Byron based on an anecdote heard from the husband of his mistress, turning it into a seemingly effortless comparison of Italian and British manners. Its success led Murray to ask in July 1818: "Have you not another lively tale like *Beppo*? Or will you not give me some prose in three volumes?—all the adventures that you have undergone, seen, heard of, or imagined, with your reflections on life and manners." In the same week Byron had begun *Don Juan*; his own inclination consorted with the publisher's sketch of a suitable "work to open [his] campaign" for fall sales.

---

1. The shell of a scallop found on the Mediterranean coast was formerly worn by pilgrims returned from the Holy Land.

For a work of which he remarked "I *have* no plan—I *had* no plan—but I had or have materials," Byron found an ideal model in the seriocomic Italian romances of the fifteenth and sixteenth centuries by Pulci, Berni, and Ariosto. Their episodic, digressive mode, flexible enough to incorporate a wide range of moods and stylistic levels, enabled Byron to stage aspects of himself that had not appeared in the titanism of his Eastern tales and the loftiness of *Childe Harold's Pilgrimage*. He could treat public issues with the conversational fluency of a skeptical intelligence engaged with the ordinary materiality of the world: brand names and ship's pumps, indigestion and thinning hair, literary rivalries and reviewers. The story was a "hinge" on which to mount his reflections, and as the poem proceeds its title character retreats before the ceaseless inventions of the narrator, who both is and is not Byron. "If people contradict themselves," he wrote, "can I / Help contradicting them, and everybody, / Even my veracious self?" Truth's streams, he continued, "cut through such canals of contradiction, / That she must often navigate o'er fiction" (15.88). Such teasing of the borders between fiction and fact intrigued readers, and enhanced the allure of "Byron." *Don Juan* is a seemingly inexhaustible improvisatory monologue—sixteen cantos were published between 1819 and 1824, with a fragmentary seventeenth left uncompleted at Byron's death. Through a range of voices, by allusion and quotation, and in the number of perspectives entertained or denounced, the poem generates a sense of dialogue and exchange. As critic Jerome McGann has argued, the poem superimposes three historical levels: Juan's own late eighteenth-century career; to Byron's years of fame in Regency London (1812–1816); and the post-Napoleonic moment of the actual writing (1818–1823). As it proceeds, *Don Juan* depicts Greek pirates and Turkish harems, Russian armies and Spanish families, British highwaymen and British aristocrats, story and commentary together building a critical portrait of the Europe of Byron's era, torn by revolution and now subsiding into the conservative restoration the poet condemns. Though he might have begun the poem intending only "to giggle and make giggle," Byron's purposes deepened as he advanced, often in opposition to his friends and publisher.

Byron intensifies the sense that he is speaking in *Don Juan*—forms of the first-person pronoun occur almost two thousand times—and he repeatedly reminds the reader of his capricious playing with form. The poem is personal in a more specific way as well. Readers familiar with Byron's life—and his celebrity had assured that many were—could perceive in Juan's mother, Donna Inez, a caricature of Byron's estranged wife Lady Byron. The account of Juan's youth with Inez also draws on Byron's childhood, "an only son left with an only mother" (1.37). Like Wordsworth's *Prelude*, *Don Juan* is autobiography—but in the form of oblique and theatricalized fiction. It is also picaresque adventure, satire, and mock-Homeric epic, whose hero belies the legacy of his name, seduced more often than seducing, kindhearted rather than ruthless and conniving. As Byron's rhymes make clear (*Juan* rhymes with *new one*), this half-Englished modern hero is not the legendary Don Juan. Byron's genre-crossing revision of literary tradition made "something wholly new & relative to the age," as Shelley recognized.

Much of the poem's power arises from Byron's fluent handling of the ottava rima stanza, rhyming *abababcc*. He credited *The Monks and the Giants* (1817) by his friend John Hookham Frere for the inspiration, but Frere's work shows little of Byron's deftness. Byron employed a fantastic wealth of rhymes ("Plato" with "potato," "intellectual" with "henpeck'd you all"), often emphasizing the snap of the concluding couplet for comic surprise; he could also downplay the rhymes and enjamb lines to yield a rhythm like blank verse. "The most readable poem of its length ever written," Virginia Woolf marveled, because its "method is a discovery by itself . . . an elastic shape which will hold whatever you choose to put in it." "Like all free and easy things," she added, "only the skilled and mature really bring them off successfully. But Byron was full of ideas—a quality that gives his verse a toughness." The rare combination of ease and power to which both Shelley and Woolf point keeps *Don Juan* subversively fresh today.

from **DON JUAN**

Dedication[1]

1

Bob Southey! You're a poet, Poet-laureate,[2]
    And representative of all the race,
Although 'tis true that you turn'd out a Tory at
    Last,—yours has lately been a common case,—
5 And now, my Epic Renegade! what are ye at?
    With all the Lakers,[3] in and out of place?
A nest of tuneful persons, to my eye
Like "four and twenty Blackbirds in a pye;[4]

2

"Which pye being open'd they began to sing"
10   (This old song and new simile holds good),
"A dainty dish to set before the King,"
    Or Regent, who admires such kind of food;—
And Coleridge, too, has lately taken wing,
    But like a hawk encumber'd with his hood,—
15 Explaining metaphysics to the nation—
I wish he would explain his Explanation.[5]

3

You, Bob! are rather insolent, you know,
    At being disappointed in your wish
To supersede all warblers here below,
20   And be the only Blackbird in the dish;
And then you overstrain yourself, or so,
    And tumble downward like the flying fish
Gasping on deck, because you soar too high, Bob,
And fall, for lack of moisture quite a-dry, Bob![6]

4

25 And Wordsworth, in a rather long "Excursion"[7]
    (I think the quarto holds five hundred pages),
Has given a sample from the vasty version
    Of his new system to perplex the sages;

---

1. Byron sent the dedication to his publisher in November 1818 with Canto 1. When Cantos 1 and 2 were published together, anonymously, in 1819, Byron removed the dedication because he did not want "to attack the dog [Southey] so fiercely without putting my name." It appeared for the first time in the 1832–1833 edition of Byron's works.

2. Southey became Poet Laureate in 1813, and earned Byron's contempt, not only for abandoning the republican principles of his youth but also for his malicious gossip in 1816 about Byron, Shelley, Claire Clairmont, and Mary Shelley: "The Son of a Bitch . . . said that Shelley and I 'had formed a League of Incest and practiced our precepts with &c'." The phrase "Epic Renegade" (5)

glances both at Southey's political reversal and his series of epic poems such as *Thalaba* (1801) and *The Curse of Kehama* (1810). For Southey's attack on "the Satanic School" see page 400.

3. Applied by the *Edinburgh Review* to Coleridge, Southey, and Wordsworth, from their common residence in the Lake District.

4. Henry James Pye (1745–1813), Poet Laureate before Southey; his first official ode had provoked the nursery-rhyme parody Byron repeats here.

5. *The Statesman's Manual* (1816) and *Biographia Literaria* (1817).

6. A "dry bob" was slang for sex without ejaculation.

7. This nine-book poem appeared in 1814.

'Tis poetry—at least by his assertion,
30   And may appear so when the dog-star rages—
And he who understands it would be able
To add a story to the Tower of Babel.[8]

5

You—Gentlemen! by dint of long seclusion
From better company, have kept your own
35   At Keswick,[9] and, through still continued fusion
Of one another's minds, at last have grown
To deem as a most logical conclusion,
That Poesy has wreaths for you alone:
There is a narrowness in such a notion,
40   Which makes me wish you'd change your lakes for ocean.

6

I would not imitate the petty thought,
Nor coin my self-love to so base a vice,
For all the glory your conversion brought,
Since gold alone should not have been its price.
45   You have your salary; was't for that you wrought?
And Wordsworth has his place in the Excise.[1]
You're shabby fellows—true—but poets still,
And duly seated on the immortal hill.°   *Parnassus*

7

Your bays° may hide the baldness of your brows[2]—   *laurel wreaths*
50   Perhaps some virtuous blushes;—let them go—
To you I envy neither fruit nor boughs—
And for the fame you would engross below,
The field is universal, and allows
Scope to all such as feel the inherent glow:
55   Scott, Rogers, Campbell, Moore, and Crabbe,[3] will try
'Gainst you the question with posterity.

8

For me, who, wandering with pedestrian Muses,
Contend not with you on the winged steed,[4]
I wish your fate may yield ye, when she chooses,
60   The fame you envy, and the skill you need;

---

8. To punish human presumption, God destroys the Tower of Babel and institutes the multiplicity of languages (Genesis 11.1–9); note the pun on "story."
9. Southey's home, where the Coleridges moved in 1800; Wordsworth lived nearby in Grasmere.
1. In March 1813 Wordsworth obtained a sinecure as distributor of tax stamps for Westmoreland through the aid of his patron, the Earl of Lonsdale, to whom he dedicated *The Excursion*.
2. See *Childe Harold* 4.144.
3. In ranking the living poets in an 1813 journal, Byron declared Walter Scott the "Monarch of Parnassus,"

Samuel Rogers (1763–1855) next, Thomas Moore (1779–1852) and Thomas Campbell (1777–1844) third, "Southey-Wordsworth-Coleridge" below these. George Crabbe (1754–1832) he elsewhere praised for being "free" of the "wrong revolutionary poetical system" that he and his contemporaries exemplified: "and if I had to begin again—I would model myself accordingly—Crabbe's the man."
4. The "musa pedestris" of Latin poet Horace (65–8 B.C.) signals a humble, as opposed to exalted or epic, style (*Satires* 2.6.17). The winged horse Pegasus is an old symbol of poetic imagination.

And recollect a poet nothing loses
   In giving to his brethren their full meed°   *reward*
Of merit, and complaint of present days
Is not the certain path to future praise.

9

65 He that reserves his laurels for posterity
   (Who does not often claim the bright reversion)
Has generally no great crop to spare it, he
   Being only injured by his own assertion;
And although here and there some glorious rarity
70   Arise like Titan from the sea's immersion,
The major part of such appellants go
To—God knows where—for no one else can know.

10

If, fallen in evil days on evil tongues,
   Milton appeal'd to the Avenger, Time,[5]
75 If Time, the Avenger, execrates his wrongs,
   And makes the word "Miltonic" mean "*sublime*,"
He deign'd not to belie his soul in songs,
   Nor turn his very talent to a crime;
He did not loathe the Sire to laud the Son,
80 But closed the tyrant-hater he begun.[6]

11

Think'st thou, could he—the blind Old Man—arise
   Like Samuel from the grave, to freeze once more
The blood of monarchs with his prophecies,[7]
   Or be alive again—again all hoar
85 With time and trials, and those helpless eyes,
   And heartless daughters[8]—worn—and pale—and poor;
Would *he* adore a sultan? *he* obey
The intellectual eunuch Castlereagh?[9]

12

Cold-blooded, smooth-faced, placid miscreant!
90   Dabbling its sleek young hands in Erin's° gore,   *Ireland's*
And thus for wider carnage taught to pant,
   Transferr'd to gorge upon a sister shore,
The vulgarest tool that Tyranny could want,
   With just enough of talent, and no more,

---

5. Milton's self-description in Book 7 of *Paradise Lost:* "On evil days though fall'n, and evil tongues" (26).

6. A supporter of the Commonwealth party that overthrew Charles I in 1649, Milton held to principle and did not praise Charles II after the Restoration in 1660.

7. King Saul, attacked by the Philistines, raises the ghost of the prophet Samuel to ask advice, only to learn that he has disobeyed the Lord and will be delivered to the enemy (1 Samuel 28).

8. Milton's two elder daughters are said to have robbed

him of his books, besides cheating and plaguing him in the economy of his house [Byron's note].

9. Irish nobleman Robert Stewart, Viscount Castlereagh, as chief secretary for Ireland (1799–1801), suppressed the Irish rebellion and secured the Act of Union with England that ended the Irish Parliament. As British Foreign Secretary (1812–1822), he was instrumental in arranging the balance of power in post-Napoleonic Europe, for which he was detested by Byron and the liberals.

95 To lengthen fetters by another fix'd,
And offer poison long already mix'd.[1]

13

An orator of such set trash of phrase
Ineffably—legitimately vile,[2]
That even its grossest flatterers dare not praise,
100   Nor foes—all nations—condescend to smile,—
Not even a sprightly blunder's spark can blaze
From that Ixion grindstone's ceaseless toil,[3]
That turns and turns to give the world a notion
Of endless torments and perpetual motion.

14

105 A bungler even in its disgusting trade,
And botching, patching, leaving still behind
Something of which its masters are afraid,
States to be curb'd, and thoughts to be confined,
Conspiracy or Congress to be made—[4]
110   Cobbling at manacles for all mankind—
A tinkering slave-maker, who mends old chains,
With God and man's abhorrence for its gains.

15

If we may judge of matter by the mind,
Emasculated to the marrow *It*
115 Hath but two objects, how to serve, and bind,
Deeming the chain it wears even men may fit,
Eutropius[5] of its many masters,—blind
To worth as freedom, wisdom as to wit,
Fearless—because *no* feeling dwells in ice,
120 Its very courage stagnates to a vice.

16

Where shall I turn me not to *view* its bonds,
For I will never *feel* them;—Italy!
Thy late reviving Roman soul desponds
Beneath the lie this State-thing breathed o'er thee—
125 Thy clanking chain, and Erin's yet green wounds,

---

1. His opponents regarded Castlereagh as the pawn of the Austrian foreign minister, Prince Metternich.
2. Castlereagh's poor speaking was notorious: "It is the first time indeed since the Normans," Byron wrote in the preface to Cantos 6–8, "that England has been insulted by a *Minister* (at least) who could not speak English, and that Parliament permitted itself to be dictated to in the language of Mrs. Malaprop" [the character from R. B. Sheridan's *The Rivals* (1773) who has given her name to verbal slips].
3. In Greek mythology Ixion is punished in Hades by being chained to a perpetually rolling wheel.
4. In 1814 Austria, Russia, Prussia, and England formed the Quadruple Alliance; after the fall of Napoleon,

Castlereagh and Metternich reestablished the "legitimate" governments of Europe at the Congress of Vienna (1815), restoring the Bourbons in France and acknowledging Ferdinand VII in Spain.
5. The career of Eutropius, a eunuch who became a magistrate and general in the Eastern Roman Empire (395–408), is narrated by Gibbon, *Decline and Fall* (ch. 32). Byron's denunciation of Castlereagh as a "eunuch" and an "It" may hint at private knowledge. Castlereagh's suicide in 1822, officially attributed to overwork, was preceded by an attempt to blackmail him on the grounds of homosexuality: sodomy was a capital crime.

Have voices—tongues to cry aloud for me.
Europe has slaves—allies—kings—armies still,
And Southey lives to sing them very ill.

17

Meantime—Sir Laureate—I proceed to dedicate,
130   In honest simple verse, this song to you.
And, if in flattering strains I do not predicate,
'Tis that I still retain my "buff and blue";[6]
My politics as yet are all to educate:
Apostasy's so fashionable, too,
135   To keep *one* creed's a task grown quite Herculean;
Is it not so, my Tory, ultra-Julian?[7]

Canto 1

1

I want a hero: an uncommon want,
When every year and month sends forth a new one,
Till, after cloying the gazettes with cant,
The age discovers he is not the true one;
5   Of such as these I should not care to vaunt,
I'll therefore take our ancient friend Don Juan—
We all have seen him, in the pantomime,
Sent to the devil somewhat ere his time.[1]

2

Vernon, the butcher Cumberland, Wolfe, Hawke,
10   Prince Ferdinand, Granby, Burgoyne, Keppel, Howe,[2]
Evil and good, have had their tithe of talk,
And fill'd their sign-posts then, like Wellesley now;[3]
Each in their turn like Banquo's monarchs stalk,
Followers of fame, "nine farrow" of that sow:[4]
15   France, too, had Buonaparté and Dumourier
Recorded in the Moniteur and Courier.[5]

6. Colors adopted by the Whigs and by the *Edinburgh Review*.
7. Julian was raised as a Christian, but on becoming Roman emperor in 361 he revived the worship of the pagan gods. He was killed in battle in 363. See Gibbon, *Decline and Fall*, ch. 23.
1. Popular melodrama portrayed Don Juan as a seducer who ends in hell; Byron plays against his own reputation as notorious lover by presenting Juan as an innocent boy overwhelmed by women. "Juan" is Anglicized into two syllables, as the rhymes with "true one" and "new one" indicate. "Inez" rhymes with "fine as" and "Jóse" with "nosey."
2. Recent military heroes. The Duke of Cumberland defeated the Stuart army in 1745; he earned the title "Butcher" for his subsequent suppression of Jacobitism in

Scotland.
3. Arthur Wellesley, Duke of Wellington, born in Ireland, the most celebrated British general of his time. Granted a peerage for his victory over the French at Talavera (1808), he led the British forces at Waterloo.
4. In Shakespeare's *Macbeth* (4.1), the witches show Macbeth a vision of future Scots kings descended from the murdered Banquo, establishing the triumph of his line and the frustration of Macbeth's ambitions.
5. Charles Dumouriez was a French general and Girondist (moderate); suspected by the Jacobins in 1793, he fled to the Austrians whom he had defeated the year before. He settled in England in 1804, and advised the British in their war against Buonaparte. The *Moniteur* and *Courier* were French newspapers.

3

Barnave, Brissot, Condorcet, Mirabeau,
　　Petion, Clootz, Danton, Marat, La Fayette,[6]
Were French, and famous people, as we know;
20　　　And there were others, scarce forgotten yet,
Joubert, Hoche, Marceau, Lannes, Desaix, Moreau,
　　With many of the military set,
Exceedingly remarkable at times,
But not at all adapted to my rhymes.

4

25   Nelson was once Britannia's god of war,
　　　And still should be so, but the tide is turn'd;
There's no more to be said of Trafalgar
　　'Tis with our hero quietly inurn'd;[7]
Because the army's grown more popular,
30　　　At which the naval people are concern'd;
Besides, the prince is all for the land-service,
Forgetting Duncan, Nelson, Howe, and Jervis.[8]

5

Brave men were living before Agamemnon[9]
　　And since, exceeding valorous and sage,
35   A good deal like him too, though quite the same none;
　　　But then they shone not on the poet's page,
And so have been forgotten:—I condemn none,
　　But can't find any in the present age
Fit for my poem (that is, for my new one);
40   So, as I said, I'll take my friend Don Juan.

6

Most epic poets plunge "in medias res"
　　(Horace makes this the heroic turnpike road),[1]
And then your hero tells, whene'er you please,
　　What went before—by way of episode,
45   While seated after dinner at his ease,
　　Beside his mistress in some soft abode,
Palace, or garden, paradise, or cavern,
Which serves the happy couple for a tavern.

---

6. All figures of the French Revolution. Jean Baptiste, Baron von Cloots, a zealot, dropped his title and took the pseudonym Anacharsis; elected to the Convention in 1792, he voted for the King's death and was himself executed in 1794. Byron wrote that he meant Juan "to finish as *Anacharsis Cloots*—in the French Revolution."
7. Admiral Horatio Nelson died in the Battle of Trafalgar (1805) at which he defeated the French fleet.
8. Byron plays the four distinguished British admirals against the Regent's support of the army.
9. An adaptation of Horace (*Odes* 4.9.25–28): "Many heroes lived before Agamemnon; but all are overwhelmed in unending night, unwept, unknown, because they lacked a sacred bard" (trans. by C. E. Bennett).
1. In *Ars Poetica* Horace recommends that the epic poet begin dramatically, like Homer, by taking the audience directly "into the midst of things."

7

That is the usual method, but not mine—
50   —My way is to begin with the beginning;
The regularity of my design
        Forbids all wandering as the worst of sinning,[2]
And therefore I shall open with a line
        (Although it cost me half an hour in spinning)
55 Narrating somewhat of Don Juan's father,
And also of his mother, if you'd rather.

8

In Seville was he born, a pleasant city,
        Famous for oranges and women—he
Who has not seen it will be much to pity,
60   So says the proverb—and I quite agree;
Of all the Spanish towns is none more pretty,
        Cadiz perhaps—but that you soon may see:—
Don Juan's parents lived beside the river,
A noble stream, and call'd the Guadalquivir.

9

65 His father's name was Jóse—*Don*, of course,
        A true Hidalgo,° free from every stain   *nobleman*
Of Moor or Hebrew blood, he traced his source
        Through the most Gothic gentlemen of Spain;
A better cavalier ne'er mounted horse,
70   Or, being mounted, e'er got down again,
Than Jóse, who begot our hero, who
Begot—but that's to come———Well, to renew:

10

His mother was a learned lady, famed
        For every branch of every science known—
75 In every Christian language ever named,
        With virtues equall'd by her wit alone,
She made the cleverest people quite ashamed,
        And even the good with inward envy groan,
Finding themselves so very much exceeded
80 In their own way by all the things that she did.

11

Her memory was a mine: she knew by heart
        All Calderon and greater part of Lopé,[3]
So that if any actor miss'd his part
        She could have served him for the prompter's copy;
85 For her Feinagle's were an useless art,[4]

2. That is, digression, literally "off the path." The Latin word for "wandering," *erratus*, also means "sinning."
3. Pedro Calderón de la Barca (1600–1681) and Lopé de
Vega (1562–1635), Spanish dramatists.
4. In 1812 Gregor von Feinagle lectured on mnemonics, under bluestocking patronage.

And he himself obliged to shut up shop—he
Could never make a memory so fine as
That which adorn'd the brain of Donna Inez.

12

Her favourite science was the mathematical,
90   Her noblest virtue was her magnanimity,
Her wit (she sometimes tried at wit) was Attic° all,   *refined*
       Her serious sayings darken'd to sublimity;
In short, in all things she was fairly what I call
       A prodigy—her morning dress was dimity,°   *plain cotton*
95 Her evening silk, or, in the summer, muslin,
And other stuffs, with which I won't stay puzzling.

13

She knew the Latin—that is, "the Lord's prayer,"
       And Greek—the alphabet—I'm nearly sure;
She read some French romances here and there,
100   Although her mode of speaking was not pure;
For native Spanish she had no great care,
       At least her conversation was obscure;
Her thoughts were theorems, her words a problem,
As if she deem'd that mystery would ennoble 'em.

14

105 She liked the English and the Hebrew tongue,
       And said there was analogy between 'em;
She proved it somehow out of sacred song,
       But I must leave the proofs to those who've seen 'em,
But this I heard her say, and can't be wrong,
110   And all may think which way their judgments lean 'em,
"'Tis strange—the Hebrew noun which means 'I am,'[5]
The English always use to govern d—n."

15

Some women use their tongues—she *look'd* a lecture,
       Each eye a sermon, and her brow a homily,
115 An all-in-all-sufficient self-director,
       Like the lamented late Sir Samuel Romilly,
The Law's expounder, and the State's corrector,
       Whose suicide was almost an anomaly—
One sad example more, that "All is vanity,"—
120 (The jury brought their verdict in "Insanity.")[6]

16

In short, she was a walking calculation,
       Miss Edgeworth's novels stepping from their covers,

---

5. "God," *Yahweh* in Hebrew, which God renders to Moses as "I AM THAT I AM" (Exodus 3.14).
6. Romilly (1757–1818), a liberal member of Parliament, accepted a retainer to represent Byron in the separation proceedings but then switched to Lady Byron. Even his suicide did not soften Byron's resentment; Murray refused to print this stanza in the first edition. "All is vanity" (emptiness) is the Preacher's refrain in Ecclesiastes.

Or Mrs. Trimmer's books on education,
    Or "Cœlebs' Wife" set out in quest of lovers,[7]
125 Morality's prim personification,
    In which not Envy's self a flaw discovers;
To others' share let "female errors fall,"[8]
For she had not even one—the worst of all.

17

Oh! she was perfect past all parallel—
130   Of any modern female saint's comparison;
So far above the cunning powers of hell,
    Her guardian angel had given up his garrison;
Even her minutest motions went as well
    As those of the best time-piece made by Harrison:[9]
135 In virtues nothing earthly could surpass her,
Save thine "incomparable oil," Macassar![1]

18

Perfect she was, but as perfection is
    Insipid in this naughty world of ours,
Where our first parents never learn'd to kiss
140   Till they were exiled from their earlier bowers,
Where all was peace, and innocence, and bliss
    (I wonder how they got through the twelve hours)
Don Jóse, like a lineal son of Eve,
Went plucking various fruit without her leave.

19

145 He was a mortal of the careless kind,
    With no great love for learning, or the learn'd,
Who chose to go where'er he had a mind,
    And never dream'd his lady was concern'd;
The world, as usual, wickedly inclined
150   To see a kingdom or a house o'erturn'd,
Whisper'd he had a mistress, some said *two*,
But for domestic quarrels *one* will do.

20

Now Donna Inez had, with all her merit,
    A great opinion of her own good qualities;
155 Neglect, indeed, requires a saint to bear it,
    And such, indeed, she was in her moralities;
But then she had a devil of a spirit,
    And sometimes mix'd up fancies with realities,

---

7. Maria Edgeworth was a popular Irish novelist and educational writer; Sarah Trimmer (1741–1810) was a popular writer on education and of children's books. *Cœlebs in Search of a Wife* (1809)—its title deliberately distorted by Byron—was the only, but quite successful novel of Hannah More.
8. Alexander Pope, *The Rape of the Lock* (1714), 2.17.

9. In 1762 English clockmaker John Harrison claimed the government prize of £20,000 for a chronometer able to determine longitude. Byron called Lady Byron "the Princess of Parellelograms."
1. Byron cites the advertisements of the firm A. Rowland and Son for their widely used hair oil.

And let few opportunities escape
160   Of getting her liege lord into a scrape.

21

This was an easy matter with a man
    Oft in the wrong, and never on his guard;
And even the wisest, do the best they can,
    Have moments, hours, and days, so unprepared,
165   That you might "brain them with their lady's fan";[2]
    And sometimes ladies hit exceeding hard,
And fans turn into falchions° in fair hands,   swords
And why and wherefore no one understands.

22

'Tis pity learned virgins ever wed
170   With persons of no sort of education,
Or gentlemen, who, though well born and bred,
    Grow tired of scientific conversation:
I don't choose to say much upon this head,
    I'm a plain man, and in a single station,
175   But—Oh! ye lords of ladies intellectual,
Inform us truly, have they not hen-peck'd you all?

23

Don Jóse and his lady quarrell'd—why,
    Not any of the many could divine,
Though several thousand people chose to try,
180   'Twas surely no concern of theirs nor mine;
I loathe that low vice—curiosity;
    But if there's any thing in which I shine,
'Tis in arranging all my friends' affairs,
Not having, of my own, domestic cares.

24

185   And so I interfered, and with the best
    Intentions, but their treatment was not kind;
I think the foolish people were possess'd,
    For neither of them could I ever find,
Although their porter afterwards confess'd—
190   But that's no matter, and the worst's behind,
For little Juan o'er me threw, down stairs,
A pail of housemaid's water unawares.

25

A little curly-headed, good-for-nothing,
    And mischief-making monkey from his birth;
195   His parents ne'er agreed except in doting
    Upon the most unquiet imp on earth;

2. Shakespeare, *1 Henry IV*, 2.3.23.

Instead of quarrelling, had they been but both in
　　Their senses, they'd have sent young master forth
To school, or had him soundly whipp'd at home,
200　To teach him manners for the time to come.

26

Don Jóse and the Donna Inez led
　　For some time an unhappy sort of life,
Wishing each other, not divorced, but dead;
　　They lived respectably as man and wife,
205　Their conduct was exceedingly well-bred,
　　And gave no outward signs of inward strife,
Until at length the smother'd fire broke out,
And put the business past all kind of doubt.

27

For Inez call'd some druggists, and physicians,
210　And tried to prove her loving lord was *mad*,[3]
But as he had some lucid intermissions,
　　She next decided he was only *bad*;
Yet when they ask'd her for her depositions,
　　No sort of explanation could be had,
215　Save that her duty both to man and God
Required this conduct—which seem'd very odd.

28

She kept a journal, where his faults were noted,
　　And open'd certain trunks of books and letters,
All which might, if occasion served, be quoted;
220　And then she had all Seville for abettors,
Besides her good old grandmother (who doted);
　　The hearers of her case became repeaters,
Then advocates, inquisitors, and judges,
Some for amusement, others for old grudges.

29

225　And then this best and meekest woman bore
　　With such serenity her husband's woes,
Just as the Spartan ladies did of yore,
　　Who saw their spouses kill'd, and nobly chose
Never to say a word about them more—
230　Calmly she heard each calumny that rose,
And saw *his* agonies with such sublimity,
That all the world exclaim'd, "What magnanimity!"

30

No doubt this patience, when the world is damning us,
　　Is philosophic in our former friends;
235　'Tis also pleasant to be deem'd magnanimous,

3. As Byron believed Lady Byron had tried to do; stanzas 27 and 28 replay details of their separation.

The more so in obtaining our own ends;
And what the lawyers call a *"malus animus"*°   *ill will*
   Conduct like this by no means comprehends:
Revenge in person's certainly no virtue,
240 But then 'tis not *my* fault, if *others* hurt you.

31

And if our quarrels should rip up old stories,
   And help them with a lie or two additional,
I'm not to blame, as you well know—no more is
   Any one else—they were become traditional;
245 Besides, their resurrection aids our glories
   By contrast, which is what we just were wishing all:
And science profits by this resurrection—
Dead scandals form good subjects for dissection.

32

Their friends had tried at reconciliation,
250   Then their relations, who made matters worse.
('Twere hard to tell upon a like occasion
   To whom it may be best to have recourse—
I can't say much for friend or yet relation):
   The lawyers did their utmost for divorce,
255 But scarce a fee was paid on either side
Before, unluckily, Don Jóse died.

33

He died: and most unluckily, because,
   According to all hints I could collect
From counsel learned in those kinds of laws,
260   (Although their talk's obscure and circumspect)
His death contrived to spoil a charming cause;
   A thousand pities also with respect
To public feeling, which on this occasion
Was manifested in a great sensation.

34

265 But ah! he died; and buried with him lay
   The public feeling and the lawyers' fees:
His house was sold, his servants sent away,
   A Jew took one of his two mistresses,
A priest the other—at least so they say:
270   I ask'd the doctors after his disease—
He died of the slow fever call'd the tertian,°   *malaria*
And left his widow to her own aversion.

35

Yet Jóse was an honourable man,[4]
   That I must say, who knew him very well;

---

4. Parodying Marc Antony's ironic praise of assassin Brutus at Caesar's funeral (*Julius Caesar* 3.2.84).

275 Therefore his frailties I'll no further scan,
  Indeed there were not many more to tell:
And if his passions now and then outran
  Discretion, and were not so peaceable
As Numa's (who was also named Pompilius),[5]
280 He had been ill brought up, and was born bilious.

36

Whate'er might be his worthlessness or worth,
  Poor fellow! he had many things to wound him.
Let's own—since it can do no good on earth—
  It was a trying moment that which found him
285 Standing alone beside his desolate hearth,
  Where all his household gods lay shiver'd round him
No choice was left his feelings or his pride,
Save death or Doctors' Commons[6]—so he died.

37

Dying intestate,° Juan was sole heir   *without a will*
290   To a chancery suit, and messuages,° and lands,   *houses*
Which, with a long minority and care,
  Promised to turn out well in proper hands:
Inez became sole guardian, which was fair,
  And answer'd but to nature's just demands;
295 An only son left with an only mother
Is brought up much more wisely than another.

38

Sagest of women, even of widows, she
  Resolved that Juan should be quite a paragon,
And worthy of the noblest pedigree:
300   (His sire was of Castile, his dam from Aragon.)
Then for accomplishments of chivalry,
  In case our lord the king should go to war again,
He learn'd the arts of riding, fencing, gunnery,
And how to scale a fortress—or a nunnery.

39

305 But that which Donna Inez most desired,
  And saw into herself each day before all
The learned tutors whom for him she hired,
  Was, that his breeding should be strictly moral:
Much into all his studies she enquired,
310   And so they were submitted first to her, all,
Arts, sciences, no branch was made a mystery
To Juan's eyes, excepting natural history.

---

5. The second king of Rome, renowned for his piety.   presided over inheritance.
6. The court that presided over divorces; Chancery

40

The languages, especially the dead,
    The sciences, and most of all the abstruse,
315   The arts, at least all such as could be said
        To be the most remote from common use,
In all these he was much and deeply read;
    But not a page of any thing that's loose,
Or hints continuation of the species,
320   Was ever suffer'd, lest he should grow vicious.

41

His classic studies made a little puzzle,
    Because of filthy loves of gods and goddesses,
Who in the earlier ages raised a bustle,
    But never put on pantaloons or bodices;
325   His reverend tutors had at times a tussle,
        And for their Aeneids, Iliads, and Odysseys,
Were forced to make an odd sort of apology,
For Donna Inez dreaded the Mythology.

42

Ovid's a rake, as half his verses show him,
330   Anacreon's morals are a still worse sample,
Catullus scarcely has a decent poem,
    I don't think Sappho's Ode a good example,
Although Longinus tells us there is no hymn
    Where the sublime soars forth on wings more ample;
335   But Virgil's songs are pure, except that horrid one
Beginning with "Formosum Pastor Corydon."[7]

43

Lucretius' irreligion is too strong
    For early stomachs, to prove wholesome food;
I can't help thinking Juvenal was wrong,
340   Although no doubt his real intent was good,
For speaking out so plainly in his song,
    So much indeed as to be downright rude;
And then what proper person can be partial
To all those nauseous epigrams of Martial?[8]

44

345   Juan was taught from out the best edition,
    Expurgated by learned men, who place,
Judiciously, from out the schoolboy's vision,
    The grosser parts; but fearful to deface

7. All erotic poets: the Roman Ovid (43 B.C.–A.D. 18), author of the *Amores* and *The Art of Love*; Anacreon, 6th-century B.C.; Catullus (c. 84–54 B.C.); Sappho, 7th-century B.C. Greek poet; her ode beginning "To me he seems like a god / as he sits facing you" (trans. by Willis Barnstone) was praised by Longinus in his essay *On the Sublime* (1st century B.C.). The second Eclogue of Virgil (70–19 B.C.), is homoerotic: "Corydon the shepherd burned for lovely Alexis, / His master's beloved."

8. *De Rerum Natura* ("On the Nature of Things"), by 1st-century B.C. Roman poet Lucretius, argues a materialistic view of the world; the 16 satires of Juvenal (c. A.D. 60–130) sternly denounce Roman society; the epigrams of Martial (A.D. 40–104) are witty but often blunt.

Too much their modest bard by this omission,
350   And pitying sore his mutilated case,
They only add them all in an appendix,
Which saves, in fact, the trouble of an index;[9]

45

For there we have them all "at one fell swoop,"
      Instead of being scatter'd through the pages;
355 They stand forth marshall'd in a handsome troop,
      To meet the ingenuous youth of future ages,
Till some less rigid editor shall stoop
      To call them back into their separate cages,
Instead of standing staring altogether,
360 Like garden gods—and not so decent either.

46

The Missal too (it was the family Missal)
      Was ornamented in a sort of way
Which ancient mass-books often are, and this all
      Kinds of grotesques illumined; and how they,
365 Who saw those figures on the margin kiss all,
      Could turn their optics to the text and pray,
Is more than I know—but Don Juan's mother
Kept this herself, and gave her son another.

47

Sermons he read, and lectures he endured,
370   And homilies, and lives of all the saints;
To Jerome and to Chrysostom inured,[1]
      He did not take such studies for restraints;
But how faith is acquired, and then ensured,
      So well not one of the aforesaid paints
375 As Saint Augustine in his fine Confessions,
Which make the reader envy his transgressions.[2]

48

This, too, was a seal'd book to little Juan—
      I can't but say that his mamma was right,
If such an education was the true one.
380   She scarcely trusted him from out her sight;
Her maids were old, and if she took a new one,
      You might be sure she was a perfect fright,
She did this during even her husband's life—
I recommend as much to every wife.

---

9. Fact. There is, or was, such an edition, with all the obnoxious epigrams of Martial placed by themselves at the end [Byron's note].
1. St. Jerome (340–420), translator of the Vulgate, and St. John Chrysostom (c. 345–407) were famous ascetics.
2. Augustine's *Confessions* (397–398) describes his life in Carthage, "a hissing cauldron of lust," before his conversion to Christianity.

49

385 Young Juan wax'd in goodliness and grace;
　　　At six a charming child, and at eleven
　　With all the promise of as fine a face
　　　As e'er to man's maturer growth was given:
　　He studied steadily, and grew apace,
390　　And seem'd, at least, in the right road to heaven,
　　For half his days were pass'd at church, the other
　　Between his tutors, confessor, and mother.

50

　　At six, I said, he was a charming child,
　　　At twelve he was a fine, but quiet boy;
395 Although in infancy a little wild,
　　　They tamed him down amongst them: to destroy
　　His natural spirit not in vain they toil'd.
　　　At least it seem'd so; and his mother's joy
　　Was to declare how sage, and still, and steady,
400 Her young philosopher was grown already.

51

　　I had my doubts, perhaps I have them still,
　　　But what I say is neither here nor there:
　　I knew his father well, and have some skill
　　　In character—but it would not be fair
405 From sire to son to augur good or ill:
　　　He and his wife were an ill-sorted pair—
　　But scandal's my aversion—I protest
　　Against all evil speaking, even in jest.

52

　　For my part I say nothing—nothing—but
410 　　*This* I will say—my reasons are my own—
　　That if I had an only son to put
　　　To school (as God be praised that I have none),
　　'Tis not with Donna Inez I would shut
　　　Him up to learn his catechism alone,
415 No—no—I'd send him out betimes to college,
　　For there it was I pick'd up my own knowledge.

53

　　For there one learns—'tis not for me to boast,
　　　Though I acquired—but I pass over *that,*
　　As well as all the Greek I since have lost:
420 　　I say that there's the place—but "*Verbum sat,*"[3]
　　I think I pick'd up too, as well as most,
　　　Knowledge of matters—but no matter *what*—
　　I never married—but, I think, I know
　　That sons should not be educated so.

3. Proverbial: "A word to the wise suffices."

54

425   Young Juan now was sixteen years of age,
      Tall, handsome, slender, but well knit: he seem'd
  Active, though not so sprightly, as a page;
      And every body but his mother deem'd
  Him almost man; but she flew in a rage
430   And bit her lips (for else she might have scream'd)
  If any said so, for to be precocious
  Was in her eyes a thing the most atrocious.

55

  Amongst her numerous acquaintance, all
      Selected for discretion and devotion,
435   There was the Donna Julia, whom to call
      Pretty were but to give a feeble notion
  Of many charms in her as natural
      As sweetness to the flower, or salt to ocean,
  Her zone to Venus,[4] or his bow to Cupid,
440   (But this last simile is trite and stupid.)

56

  The darkness of her Oriental eye
      Accorded with her Moorish origin;
  (Her blood was not all Spanish, by the by;
      In Spain, you know, this is a sort of sin.)
445   When proud Granada fell, and, forced to fly,
      Boabdil[5] wept, of Donna Julia's kin
  Some went to Africa, some stay'd in Spain,
  Her great great grandmamma chose to remain.

57

  She married (I forget the pedigree)
450   With an Hidalgo, who transmitted down
  His blood less noble than such blood should be;
      At such alliances his sires would frown,
  In that point so precise in each degree
      That they bred in and in, as might be shown,
455   Marrying their cousins—nay, their aunts, and nieces,
  Which always spoils the breed, if it increases.

58

  This heathenish cross restored the breed again,
      Ruin'd its blood, but much improved its flesh;
  For from a root the ugliest in Old Spain
460   Sprung up a branch as beautiful as fresh;
  The sons no more were short, the daughters plain:
      But there's a rumour which I fain would hush,

4. The belt ("zone") of Venus was sexy.

5. Mohammed XI, the last Moorish king of Granada, expelled by Ferdinand and Isabella in 1492.

'Tis said that Donna Julia's grandmamma
Produced her Don more heirs at love than law.

59

465   However this might be, the race went on
  Improving still through every generation,
Until it centred in an only son,
  Who left an only daughter; my narration
May have suggested that this single one
470   Could be but Julia (whom on this occasion
I shall have much to speak about), and she
Was married, charming, chaste, and twenty-three.

60

Her eye (I'm very fond of handsome eyes)
  Was large and dark, suppressing half its fire
475   Until she spoke, then through its soft disguise
  Flash'd an expression more of pride than ire,
And love than either; and there would arise
  A something in them which was not desire,
But would have been, perhaps, but for the soul
480   Which struggled through and chasten'd down the whole.

61

Her glossy hair was cluster'd o'er a brow
  Bright with intelligence, and fair, and smooth;
Her eyebrow's shape was like th' aërial bow,
  Her cheek all purple with the beam of youth,
485   Mounting, at times, to a transparent glow,
  As if her veins ran lightning; she, in sooth,
Possess'd an air and grace by no means common:
Her stature tall—I hate a dumpy woman.

62

Wedded she was some years, and to a man
490   Of fifty, and such husbands are in plenty;
And yet, I think, instead of such a ONE
  'Twere better to have TWO of five-and-twenty,
Especially in countries near the sun:
  And now I think on't, "mi vien in mente,"°   *it comes to mind*
495   Ladies even of the most uneasy virtue
Prefer a spouse whose age is short of thirty.

63

'Tis a sad thing, I cannot choose but say,
  And all the fault of that indecent sun,
Who cannot leave alone our helpless clay,
500   But will keep baking, broiling, burning on,
That howsoever people fast and pray,
  The flesh is frail, and so the soul undone:
What men call gallantry, and gods adultery,
Is much more common where the climate's sultry.

64

505 Happy the nations of the moral North!
    Where all is virtue, and the winter season
Sends sin, without a rag on, shivering forth
    ('Twas snow that brought St. Anthony to reason);⁶
Where juries cast up what a wife is worth,
510   By laying whate'er sum, in mulct,° they please on   *penalty*
The lover, who must pay a handsome price,
Because it is a marketable vice.

65

Alfonso was the name of Julia's lord,
    A man well looking for his years, and who
515 Was neither much beloved nor yet abhorr'd:
    They lived together, as most people do,
Suffering each other's foibles by accord,
    And not exactly either *one* or *two*;
Yet he was jealous, though he did not show it,
520 For jealousy dislikes the world to know it.

66

Julia was—yet I never could see why—
    With Donna Inez quite a favourite friend;
Between their tastes there was small sympathy,
    For not a line had Julia ever penn'd:
525 Some people whisper (but, no doubt, they lie,
    For malice still imputes some private end)
That Inez had, ere Don Alfonso's marriage,
Forgot with him her very prudent carriage;

67

And that still keeping up the old connection,
530   Which time had lately render'd much more chaste,
She took his lady also in affection,
    And certainly this course was much the best:
She flatter'd Julia with her sage protection,
    And complimented Don Alfonso's taste;
535 And if she could not (who can?) silence scandal,
At least she left it a more slender handle.

68

I can't tell whether Julia saw the affair
    With other people's eyes, or if her own
Discoveries made, but none could be aware
540   Of this, at least no symptom e'er was shown;
Perhaps she did not know, or did not care,
    Indifferent from the first, or callous grown:
I'm really puzzled what to think or say,
She kept her counsel in so close a way.

6. Byron later realized it was St. Francis of Assisi (1181?–1226) who cast himself on the snow to quell his desires.

69

545 Juan she saw, and, as a pretty child,
    Caress'd him often—such a thing might be
Quite innocently done, and harmless styled,
    When she had twenty years, and thirteen he;
But I am not so sure I should have smiled
550   When he was sixteen, Julia twenty-three;
These few short years make wondrous alterations,
Particularly amongst sun-burnt nations.

70

Whate'er the cause might be, they had become
    Changed; for the dame grew distant, the youth shy,
555 Their looks cast down, their greetings almost dumb,
    And much embarrassment in either eye;
There surely will be little doubt with some
    That Donna Julia knew the reason why,
But as for Juan, he had no more notion
560 Than he who never saw the sea of ocean.

71

Yet Julia's very coldness still was kind,
    And tremulously gentle her small hand
Withdrew itself from his, but left behind
    A little pressure, thrilling, and so bland
565 And slight, so very slight, that to the mind
    'Twas but a doubt; but ne'er magician's wand
Wrought change with all Armida's fairy art[7]
Like what this light touch left on Juan's heart.

72

And if she met him, though she smiled no more,
570   She look'd a sadness sweeter than her smile,
As if her heart had deeper thoughts in store
    She must not own, but cherish'd more the while
For that compression in its burning core;
    Even innocence itself has many a wile,
575 And will not dare to trust itself with truth,
And love is taught hypocrisy from youth.

73

But passion most dissembles, yet betrays
    Even by its darkness; as the blackest sky
Foretells the heaviest tempest, it displays
580   Its workings through the vainly guarded eye,
And in whatever aspect it arrays
    Itself, 'tis still the same hypocrisy;
Coldness or anger, even disdain or hate,
Are masks it often wears, and still too late.

---

7. Armida, sorceress in *Jerusalem Delivered* by Torquato Tasso (1544–1595), causes the crusader hero to forget his vows.

74

585 Then there were sighs, the deeper for suppression,
    And stolen glances, sweeter for the theft,
And burning blushes, though for no transgression,
    Tremblings when met, and restlessness when left;
All these are little preludes to possession,
590   Of which young passion cannot be bereft,
And merely tend to show how greatly love is
Embarrass'd at first starting with a novice.

75

Poor Julia's heart was in an awkward state;
    She felt it going, and resolved to make
595 The noblest efforts for herself and mate,
    For honour's, pride's, religion's, virtue's sake;
Her resolutions were most truly great,
    And almost might have made a Tarquin quake:[8]
She pray'd the Virgin Mary for her grace,
600 As being the best judge of a lady's case.

76

She vow'd she never would see Juan more,
    And next day paid a visit to his mother,
And look'd extremely at the opening door,
    Which, by the Virgin's grace, let in another;
605 Grateful she was, and yet a little sore—
    Again it opens, it can be no other,
'Tis surely Juan now—No! I'm afraid
That night the Virgin was no further pray'd.

77

She now determined that a virtuous woman
610   Should rather face and overcome temptation,
That flight was base and dastardly, and no man
    Should ever give her heart the least sensation;
That is to say, a thought beyond the common
    Preference, that we must feel upon occasion,
615 For people who are pleasanter than others,
But then they only seem so many brothers.

78

And even if by chance—and who can tell?
    The devil's so very sly—she should discover
That all within was not so very well,
620   And, if still free, that such or such a lover
Might please perhaps, a virtuous wife can quell
    Such thoughts, and be the better when they're over;
And if the man should ask, 'tis but denial:
I recommend young ladies to make trial.

8. The Tarquins were noted for arrogance and cruelty; after his son Sextus raped Lucretia, Tarquinius Superbus, the last king of Rome, was exiled in a revolt led by Brutus. See Shakespeare, *The Rape of Lucrece* (1594).

79

625 And then there are such things as love divine,
    Bright and immaculate, unmix'd and pure,
Such as the angels think so very fine,
    And matrons, who would be no less secure,
Platonic, perfect, "just such love as mine":
630   Thus Julia said—and thought so, to be sure;
And so I'd have her think, were I the man
On whom her reveries celestial ran.

80

Such love is innocent, and may exist
    Between young persons without any danger.
635 A hand may first, and then a lip be kist;
    For my part, to such doings I'm a stranger,
But *hear* these freedoms form the utmost list
    Of all o'er which such love may be a ranger:
If people go beyond, 'tis quite a crime,
640 But not my fault—I tell them all in time.

81

Love, then, but love within its proper limits,
    Was Julia's innocent determination
In young Don Juan's favour, and to him its
    Exertion might be useful on occasion;
645 And, lighted at too pure a shrine to dim its
    Ethereal lustre, with what sweet persuasion
He might be taught, by love and her together—
I really don't know what, nor Julia either.

82

Fraught with this fine intention, and well fenced
650   In mail of proof—her purity of soul,
She, for the future of her strength convinced,
    And that her honour was a rock, or mole,°   *breakwater*
Exceeding sagely from that hour dispensed
    With any kind of troublesome control;
655 But whether Julia to the task was equal
Is that which must be mention'd in the sequel.

83

Her plan she deem'd both innocent and feasible,
    And, surely, with a stripling of sixteen
Not scandal's fangs could fix on much that's seizable,
660   Or if they did so, satisfied to mean
Nothing but what was good, her breast was peaceable—
    A quiet conscience makes one so serene!
Christians have burnt each other, quite persuaded
That all the Apostles would have done as they did.

84

665 And if in the mean time her husband died,
　　　　But Heaven forbid that such a thought should cross
　　Her brain, though in a dream! (and then she sigh'd)
　　　　Never could she survive that common loss;
　　But just suppose that moment should betide,
670　　　　I only say suppose it—*inter nos.*°　　　　　　　　*between us (Latin)*
　　(This should be *entre nous*, for Julia thought
　　In French, but then the rhyme would go for nought.)

85

　　I only say suppose this supposition:
　　　　Juan being then grown up to man's estate
675　Would fully suit a widow of condition,
　　　　Even seven years hence it would not be too late
　　And in the interim (to pursue this vision)
　　　　The mischief, after all, could not be great,
　　For he would learn the rudiments of love,
680　I mean the seraph° way of those above.　　　　　　*angelic*

86

　　So much for Julia. Now we'll turn to Juan,
　　　　Poor little fellow! he had no idea
　　Of his own case, and never hit the true one;
　　　　In feelings quick as Ovid's Miss Medea,[9]
685　He puzzled over what he found a new one,
　　　　But not as yet imagined it could be a
　　Thing quite in course, and not at all alarming,
　　Which, with a little patience, might grow charming.

87

　　Silent and pensive, idle, restless, slow,
690　　　　His home deserted for the lonely wood,
　　Tormented with a wound he could not know,
　　　　His, like all deep grief, plunged in solitude:
　　I'm fond myself of solitude or so,
　　　　But then, I beg it may be understood,
695　By solitude I mean a sultan's, not
　　A hermit's, with a haram for a grot.

88

　　"Oh Love! in such a wilderness as this,
　　　　Where transport and security entwine,
　　Here is the empire of thy perfect bliss,
700　　　　And here thou art a god indeed divine."[1]
　　The bard I quote from does not sing amiss,

9. Ovid's *Metamorphoses* 7 tells of how Medea was overcome by passion for Jason; though she struggled, her reason could not defeat her desire.
1. Campbell's *Gertrude of Wyoming*, (I think) the opening
of Canto II; but quote from memory [Byron's note; see
Thomas Campbell's *Gertrude of Wyoming* (1809), Canto
III, 1–4].

With the exception of the second line,
For that same twining "transport and security"
Are twisted to a phrase of some obscurity.

89

705 The poet meant, no doubt, and thus appeals
    To the good sense and senses of mankind,
The very thing which every body feels,
    As all have found on trial, or may find,
That no one likes to be disturb'd at meals
710   Or love.—I won't say more about "entwined"
Or "transport," as we knew all that before,
But beg "Security" will bolt the door.

90

Young Juan wander'd by the glassy brooks
    Thinking unutterable things; he threw
715 Himself at length within the leafy nooks
    Where the wild branch of the cork forest grew:
There poets find materials for their books,
    And every now and then we read them through,
So that their plan and prosody are eligible,
720 Unless, like Wordsworth, they prove unintelligible.

91

He, Juan, (and not Wordsworth) so pursued
    His self-communion with his own high soul,
Until his mighty heart, in its great mood,
    Had mitigated part, though not the whole
725 Of its disease; he did the best he could
    With things not very subject to control,
And turn'd, without perceiving his condition,
Like Coleridge, into a metaphysician.

92

He thought about himself, and the whole earth,
730   Of man the wonderful, and of the stars,
And how the deuce they ever could have birth;
    And then he thought of earthquakes, and of wars,
How many miles the moon might have in girth,
    Of air-balloons, and of the many bars
735 To perfect knowledge of the boundless skies;—
And then he thought of Donna Julia's eyes.

93

In thoughts like these true wisdom may discern
    Longings sublime, and aspirations high,
Which some are born with, but the most part learn
740   To plague themselves withal, they know not why:
'Twas strange that one so young should thus concern
    His brain about the action of the sky;

If *you* think 'twas philosophy that this did,
I can't help thinking puberty assisted.

94

745   He pored upon the leaves, and on the flowers,
          And heard a voice in all the winds; and then
      He thought of wood-nymphs and immortal bowers,
          And how the goddesses came down to men:
      He miss'd the pathway, he forgot the hours,
750   And when he look'd upon his watch again,
      He found how much old Time had been a winner—
      He also found that he had lost his dinner.

95

      Sometimes he turn'd to gaze upon his book,
          Boscan, or Garcilasso;[2]—by the wind
755   Even as the page is rustled while we look,
          So by the poesy of his own mind
      Over the mystic leaf his soul was shook,
          As if 'twere one whereon magicians bind
      Their spells, and give them to the passing gale,
760   According to some good old woman's tale.

96

      Thus would he while his lonely hours away
          Dissatisfied, nor knowing what he wanted;
      Nor glowing reverie, nor poet's lay,
          Could yield his spirit that for which it panted,
765   A bosom whereon he his head might lay,
          And hear the heart beat with the love it granted,
      With——several other things, which I forget,
      Or which, at least, I need not mention yet.

97

      Those lonely walks, and lengthening reveries,
770   Could not escape the gentle Julia's eyes;
      She saw that Juan was not at his ease;
          But that which chiefly may, and must surprise,
      Is, that the Donna Inez did not tease
          Her only son with question or surmise;
775   Whether it was she did not see, or would not,
      Or, like all very clever people, could not.

98

      This may seem strange, but yet 'tis very common;
          For instance—gentlemen, whose ladies take
      Leave to o'erstep the written rights of woman,
780   And break the——Which commandment is't they break?

2. Juan Boscán Almogáver and Garcilaso de la Vega, 16th-century poets who introduced the Petrarchan style in Castilian poetry.

(I have forgot the number, and think no man
    Should rashly quote, for fear of a mistake.)
I say, when these same gentlemen are jealous,
They make some blunder, which their ladies tell us.

99

785 A real husband always is suspicious,
        But still no less suspects in the wrong place,
    Jealous of some one who had no such wishes,
        Or pandering blindly to his own disgrace,
    By harbouring some dear friend extremely vicious;
790   The last indeed's infallibly the case:
    And when the spouse and friend are gone off wholly,
    He wonders at their vice, and not his folly.

100

    Thus parents also are at times short-sighted;
        Though watchful as the lynx, they ne'er discover,
795 The while the wicked world beholds delighted,
        Young Hopeful's mistress, or Miss Fanny's lover,
    Till some confounded escapade has blighted
        The plan of twenty years, and all is over;
    And then the mother cries, the father swears,
800 And wonders why the devil he got heirs.

101

    But Inez was so anxious, and so clear
        Of sight, that I must think, on this occasion,
    She had some other motive much more near
        For leaving Juan to this new temptation;
805 But what that motive was, I sha'n't say here;
        Perhaps to finish Juan's education,
    Perhaps to open Don Alfonso's eyes,
    In case he thought his wife too great a prize.

102

    It was upon a day, a summer's day;—
810   Summer's indeed a very dangerous season,
    And so is spring about the end of May;
        The sun, no doubt, is the prevailing reason;
    But whatsoe'er the cause is, one may say,
        And stand convicted of more truth than treason,
815 That there are months which nature grows more merry in,—
    March has its hares,[3] and May must have its heroine.

103

    'Twas on a summer's day—the sixth of June:—
        I like to be particular in dates,
    Not only of the age, and year, but moon;

---

3. Proverbial: "Mad as a March hare" (the mating season).

820   They are a sort of post-house, where the Fates
      Change horses, making history change its tune,
        Then spur away o'er empires and o'er states,
      Leaving at last not much besides chronology,
      Excepting the post-obits of theology.

104

825   'Twas on the sixth of June, about the hour
        Of half-past six—perhaps still nearer seven—
      When Julia sate within as pretty a bower
        As e'er held houri in that heathenish heaven
      Described by Mahomet, and Anacreon Moore,[4]
830   To whom the lyre and laurels have been given,
      With all the trophies of triumphant song—
      He won them well, and may he wear them long!

105

    She sate, but not alone; I know not well
        How this same interview had taken place,
835   And even if I knew, I should not tell—
        People should hold their tongues in any case;
      No matter how or why the thing befell,
        But there were she and Juan, face to face—
      When two such faces are so, 'twould be wise,
840   But very difficult, to shut their eyes.

106

    How beautiful she look'd! her conscious heart
        Glow'd in her cheek, and yet she felt no wrong.
      Oh Love! how perfect is thy mystic art,
        Strengthening the weak, and trampling on the strong,
845   How self-deceitful is the sagest part
        Of mortals whom thy lure hath led along—
      The precipice she stood on was immense,
      So was her creed in her own innocence.

107

    She thought of her own strength, and Juan's youth,
850   And of the folly of all prudish fears,
      Victorious virtue, and domestic truth,
        And then of Don Alfonso's fifty years:
      I wish these last had not occurr'd, in sooth,
        Because that number rarely much endears,
855   And through all climes, the snowy and the sunny,
      Sounds ill in love, whate'er it may in money.

108

    When people say, "I've told you *fifty* times,"
        They mean to scold, and very often do;

---

4. The houris are the maidens who await heroes in the Muslim paradise; Thomas Moore translated the erotic odes of Anacreon in 1800 and described the "heathenish heaven" in his popular poem *Lalla Rookh* (1817).

When poets say, "I've written *fifty* rhymes,"
860   They make you dread that they'll recite them too;
In gangs of *fifty*, thieves commit their crimes;
      At *fifty* love for love is rare, 'tis true,
But then, no doubt, it equally as true is,
A good deal may be bought for *fifty* Louis.°   *gold coins*

109

865 Julia had honour, virtue, truth, and love,
      For Don Alfonso; and she inly swore,
By all the vows below to powers above,
      She never would disgrace the ring she wore,
Nor leave a wish which wisdom might reprove;
870   And while she ponder'd this, besides much more,
One hand on Juan's carelessly was thrown,
Quite by mistake—she thought it was her own;

110

Unconsciously she lean'd upon the other,
      Which play'd within the tangles of her hair;
875 And to contend with thoughts she could not smother
      She seem'd, by the distraction of her air.
'Twas surely very wrong in Juan's mother
      To leave together this imprudent pair,
She who for many years had watch'd her son so—
880 I'm very certain *mine* would not have done so.

111

The hand which still held Juan's, by degrees
      Gently, but palpably confirm'd its grasp,
As if it said, "Detain me, if you please";
      Yet there's no doubt she only meant to clasp
885 His fingers with a pure Platonic squeeze;
      She would have shrunk as from a toad, or asp,
Had she imagined such a thing could rouse
A feeling dangerous to a prudent spouse.

112

I cannot know what Juan thought of this,
890   But what he did, is much what you would do;
His young lip thank'd it with a grateful kiss,
      And then, abash'd at its own joy, withdrew
In deep despair, lest he had done amiss,
      Love is so very timid when 'tis new:
895 She blush'd, and frown'd not, but she strove to speak,
And held her tongue, her voice was grown so weak.

113

The sun set, and up rose the yellow moon:
      The devil's in the moon for mischief; they
Who call'd her chaste, methinks, began too soon

900
 Their nomenclature; there is not a day,
The longest, not the twenty-first of June,
  Sees half the business in a wicked way
On which three single hours of moonshine smile—
And then she looks so modest all the while.

114

905
There is a dangerous silence in that hour,
  A stillness, which leaves room for the full soul
To open all itself, without the power
  Of calling wholly back its self-control;
The silver light which, hallowing tree and tower,
910
  Sheds beauty and deep softness o'er the whole,
Breathes also to the heart, and o'er it throws
A loving languor, which is not repose.

115

And Julia sate with Juan, half embraced
  And half retiring from the glowing arm,
915
Which trembled like the bosom where 'twas placed;
  Yet still she must have thought there was no harm,
Or else 'twere easy to withdraw her waist;
  But then the situation had its charm,
And then——God knows what next—I can't go on;
920
I'm almost sorry that I e'er begun.

116

Oh Plato! Plato! you have paved the way,
  With your confounded fantasies, to more
Immoral conduct by the fancied sway
  Your system feigns o'er the controulless core
925
Of human hearts, than all the long array
  Of poets and romancers:—You're a bore,
A charlatan, a coxcomb—and have been,
At best, no better than a go-between.

117

And Julia's voice was lost, except in sighs,
930
  Until too late for useful conversation;
The tears were gushing from her gentle eyes,
  I wish, indeed, they had not had occasion,
But who, alas! can love, and then be wise?
  Not that remorse did not oppose temptation,
935
A little still she strove, and much repented,
And whispering "I will ne'er consent"—consented.

118

'Tis said that Xerxes[5] offer'd a reward
  To those who could invent him a new pleasure:

5. An anecdote drawn from Cicero and Montaigne (*Of Experience*).

Methinks, the requisition's rather hard,
940   And must have cost his majesty a treasure:
For my part, I'm a moderate-minded bard,
        Fond of a little love (which I call leisure);
I care not for new pleasures, as the old
Are quite enough for me, so they but hold.

119

945   Oh Pleasure! you are indeed a pleasant thing,
        Although one must be damn'd for you, no doubt:
I make a resolution every spring
        Of reformation, ere the year run out,
But somehow, this my vestal vow takes wing,
950   Yet still, I trust, it may be kept throughout:
I'm very sorry, very much ashamed,
And mean, next winter, to be quite reclaim'd.

120

Here my chaste Muse a liberty must take—
        Start not! still chaster reader—she'll be nice hence-
955   Forward, and there is no great cause to quake;
        This liberty is a poetic licence,
Which some irregularity may make
        In the design, and as I have a high sense
Of Aristotle and the Rules, 'tis fit
960   To beg his pardon when I err a bit.

121

This licence is to hope the reader will
        Suppose from June the sixth (the fatal day,
Without whose epoch my poetic skill
        For want of facts would all be thrown away),
965   But keeping Julia and Don Juan still
        In sight, that several months have pass'd; we'll say
'Twas in November, but I'm not so sure
About the day—the era's more obscure.

122

We'll talk of that anon.—'Tis sweet to hear
970   At midnight on the blue and moonlit deep
The song and oar of Adria's gondolier,[6]
        By distance mellow'd, o'er the waters sweep;
'Tis sweet to see the evening star° appear;   *Venus*
        'Tis sweet to listen as the night-winds creep
975   From leaf to leaf; 'tis sweet to view on high
The rainbow, based on ocean, span the sky.

6. The famous singing of the boatmen of Venice, on the Adriatic Sea.

123

'Tis sweet to hear the watch-dog's honest bark
    Bay deep-mouth'd welcome as we draw near home;
'Tis sweet to know there is an eye will mark
980   Our coming, and look brighter when we come;
'Tis sweet to be awaken'd by the lark,
    Or lull'd by falling waters; sweet the hum
Of bees, the voice of girls, the song of birds,
The lisp of children, and their earliest words.

124

985 Sweet is the vintage, when the showering grapes
    In Bacchanal[7] profusion reel to earth
Purple and gushing: sweet are our escapes
    From civic revelry to rural mirth;
Sweet to the miser are his glittering heaps,
990   Sweet to the father is his first-born's birth,
Sweet is revenge—especially to women,
Pillage to soldiers, prize-money to seamen.

125

Sweet is a legacy, and passing sweet
    The unexpected death of some old lady
995 Or gentleman of seventy years complete,
    Who've made "us youth" wait too—too long already
For an estate, or cash, or country-seat,
    Still breaking, but with stamina so steady,[8]
That all the Israelites are fit to mob its
1000 Next owner for their double-damn'd post-obits.[9]

126

'Tis sweet to win, no matter how, one's laurels,
    By blood or ink; 'tis sweet to put an end
To strife; 'tis sometimes sweet to have our quarrels,
    Particularly with a tiresome friend:
1005 Sweet is old wine in bottles, ale in barrels;
    Dear is the helpless creature we defend
Against the world; and dear the schoolboy spot
We ne'er forget, though there we are forgot.

127

But sweeter still than this, than these, than all,
1010 Is first and passionate love—it stands alone,
Like Adam's recollection of his fall;
    The tree of knowledge has been pluck'd—all's known—

---

7. Bacchus is the Greek god of wine.
8. "Us youth" is a phrase of Falstaff (Shakespeare, *1 Henry IV* 2.2.85); Byron glances at his estranged wife's mother, who did not die until the age of 70 in 1822, when Byron received the inheritance.
9. At college Byron had borrowed from Jewish money-lenders on the prospects of his inheritance; "post-obit," after death.

And life yields nothing further to recall
    Worthy of this ambrosial sin, so shown,
1015   No doubt in fable, as the unforgiven
Fire which Prometheus filch'd for us from heaven.[1]

128

Man's a strange animal, and makes strange use
    Of his own nature, and the various arts,
And likes particularly to produce
1020   Some new experiment to show his parts;
This is the age of oddities let loose,
    Where different talents find their different marts;
You'd best begin with truth, and when you've lost your
Labour, there's a sure market for imposture.

129

1025   What opposite discoveries we have seen!
    (Signs of true genius, and of empty pockets.)
One makes new noses, one a guillotine,
    One breaks your bones, one sets them in their sockets;
But vaccination certainly has been
1030   A kind antithesis to Congreve's rockets,[2]
With which the Doctor paid off an old pox,
By borrowing a new one from an ox.[3]

130

Bread has been made (indifferent) from potatoes;
    And galvanism has set some corpses grinning,[4]
1035   But has not answer'd like the apparatus
    Of the Humane Society's beginning
By which men are unsuffocated gratis:[5]
    What wondrous new machines have late been spinning!
I said the small-pox has gone out of late;
1040   Perhaps it may be follow'd by the great.

131

'Tis said the great came from America;
    Perhaps it may set out on its return,—
The population there so spreads, they say
    'Tis grown high time to thin it in its turn,
1045   With war, or plague, or famine, any way,
    So that civilisation they may learn;
And which in ravage the more loathsome evil is—
Their real lues, or our pseudo-syphilis?

1. See *Prometheus*, page 389.
2. Sir William Congreve invented the rockets used against the French at the Battle of Leipzig in 1813.
3. Edward Jenner first vaccinated against smallpox in 1796 with a serum made from cowpox. In the first edition the references to syphilis (the "great pox" and "lues") caused this couplet and several ensuing lines to be omitted.

4. Theories that electricity might be the vital force of life led to a number of experiments, on both living and dead bodies, with Galvanism, or electricity generated by chemical reaction. Mary Shelley's *Frankenstein* (1818) reflects these experiments.
5. The Humane Society rescued drowned persons and sought means to revive them.

132

1050
This is the patent-age of new inventions
For killing bodies, and for saving souls,
All propagated with the best intentions;
Sir Humphry Davy's lantern, by which coals
Are safely mined for in the mode he mentions,[6]
Timbuctoo travels, voyages to the Poles,
1055
Are ways to benefit mankind, as true,
Perhaps, as shooting them at Waterloo.

133

Man's a phenomenon, one knows not what,
And wonderful beyond all wondrous measure;
'Tis pity though, in this sublime world, that
1060
Pleasure's a sin, and sometimes sin's a pleasure;
Few mortals know what end they would be at,
But whether glory, power, or love, or treasure,
The path is through perplexing ways, and when
The goal is gain'd, we die, you know—and then—

134

1065
What then?—I do not know, no more do you—
And so good night.—Return we to our story:
'Twas in November, when fine days are few,
And the far mountains wax a little hoary,
And clap a white cape on their mantles blue[7]
1070
And the sea dashes round the promontory,
And the loud breaker boils against the rock,
And sober suns must set at five o'clock.

135

'Twas, as the watchmen say, a cloudy night;
No moon, no stars, the wind was low or loud
1075
By gusts, and many a sparkling hearth was bright
With the piled wood, round which the family crowd;
There's something cheerful in that sort of light,
Even as a summer sky's without a cloud:
I'm fond of fire, and crickets, and all that,
1080
A lobster salad, and champagne, and chat.

136

'Twas midnight—Donna Julia was in bed,
Sleeping, most probably,—when at her door
Arose a clatter might awake the dead,
If they had never been awoke before,
1085
And that they have been so we all have read,
And are to be so, at the least, once more;

6. Sir Humphry Davy in 1815 invented the safety lamp that protected miners from explosions of gas.   7. A comic echo of the end of Milton's elegy, *Lycidas*.

The door was fasten'd, but with voice and fist
First knocks were heard, then "Madam—Madam—hist!

137

"For God's sake, Madam—Madam—here's my master,
1090   With more than half the city at his back—
Was ever heard of such a curst disaster!
      'Tis not my fault—I kept good watch—Alack!
Do pray undo the bolt a little faster—
      They're on the stair just now, and in a crack
1095 Will all be here; perhaps he yet may fly—
Surely the window's not so *very* high!"

138

By this time Don Alfonso was arrived,
      With torches, friends, and servants in great number;
The major part of them had long been wived,
1100   And therefore paused not to disturb the slumber
Of any wicked woman, who contrived
      By stealth her husband's temples to encumber:[8]
Examples of this kind are so contagious,
Were *one* not punish'd, *all* would be outrageous.

139

1105 I can't tell how, or why, or what suspicion
      Could enter into Don Alfonso's head;
But for a cavalier of his condition
      It surely was exceedingly ill-bred,
Without a word of previous admonition,
1110   To hold a levee[9] round his lady's bed,
And summon lackeys, arm'd with fire and sword,
To prove himself the thing he most abhorr'd.

140

Poor Donna Julia! starting as from sleep,
      (Mind—that I do not say—she had not slept)
1115 Began at once to scream, and yawn, and weep;
      Her maid Antonia, who was an adept,
Contrived to fling the bed-clothes in a heap,
      As if she had just now from out them crept:
I can't tell why she should take all this trouble
1120 To prove her mistress had been sleeping double.

141

But Julia mistress, and Antonia maid,
      Appear'd like two poor harmless women, who
Of goblins, but still more of men afraid,
      Had thought one man might be deterr'd by two,

---

8. With horns, traditional sign of a cuckold.   9. A formal morning reception.

1125 And therefore side by side were gently laid,
    Until the hours of absence should run through,
And truant husband should return, and say,
"My dear, I was the first who came away."

142

    Now Julia found at length a voice, and cried,
1130   "In heaven's name, Don Alfonso, what d' ye mean?
Has madness seized you? would that I had died
    Ere such a monster's victim I had been!
What may this midnight violence betide,
    A sudden fit of drunkenness or spleen?
1135 Dare you suspect me, whom the thought would kill?
Search, then, the room!"—Alfonso said, "I will."

143

He search'd, *they* search'd, and rummaged every where,
    Closet and clothes' press, chest and window-seat,
And found much linen, lace, and several pair
1140   Of stockings, slippers, brushes, combs, complete,
With other articles of ladies fair,
    To keep them beautiful, or leave them neat:
Arras° they prick'd and curtains with their swords,   *tapestry*
And wounded several shutters, and some boards.

144

1145 Under the bed they search'd, and there they found—
    No matter what—it° was not that they sought;   *a chamber pot*
They open'd windows, gazing if the ground
    Had signs or footmarks, but the earth said nought;
And then they stared each others' faces round:
1150   'Tis odd, not one of all these seekers thought,
And seems to me almost a sort of blunder,
Of looking *in* the bed as well as under.

145

During this inquisition, Julia's tongue
    Was not asleep—"Yes, search and search," she cried,
1155 "Insult on insult heap, and wrong on wrong!
    It was for this that I became a bride!
For this in silence I have suffer'd long
    A husband like Alfonso at my side;
But now I'll bear no more, nor here remain.
1160 If there be law, or lawyers, in all Spain.

146

"Yes, Don Alfonso! husband now no more,
    If ever you indeed deserved the name,
Is't worthy of your years?—you have threescore—
    Fifty, or sixty, it is all the same—
1165 Is't wise or fitting, causeless to explore

For facts against a virtuous woman's fame?
Ungrateful, perjured, barbarous Don Alfonso,
How dare you think your lady would go on so?

147

"Is it for this I have disdain'd to hold
1170   The common privileges of my sex?
That I have chosen a confessor so old
    And deaf, that any other it would vex,
And never once he has had cause to scold,
    But found my very innocence perplex
1175 So much, he always doubted I was married—
How sorry you will be when I've miscarried!

148

"Was it for this that no Cortejo[1] e'er
    I yet have chosen from out the youth of Seville?
Is it for this I scarce went anywhere,
1180   Except to bull-fights, mass, play, rout, and revel?
Is it for this, whate'er my suitors were,
    I favour'd none—nay, was almost uncivil?
Is it for this that General Count O'Reilly,
Who took Algiers, declares I used him vilely?[2]

149

1185 "Did not the Italian Musico° Cazzani   musician
    Sing at my heart six months at least in vain?
Did not his countryman, Count Corniani,
    Call me the only virtuous wife in Spain?[3]
Were there not also Russians, English, many?
1190   The Count Strongstroganoff I put in pain,
And Lord Mount Coffeehouse, the Irish peer,
Who kill'd himself for love (with wine) last year.

150

"Have I not had two bishops at my feet?
    The Duke of Ichar, and Don Fernan Nunez,
1195 And is it thus a faithful wife you treat?
    I wonder in what quarter now the moon is:
I praise your vast forbearance not to beat
    Me also, since the time so opportune is—
Oh, valiant man! with sword drawn and cock'd trigger,
1200 Now, tell me, don't you cut a pretty figure?

151

"Was it for this you took your sudden journey,
    Under pretence of business indispensable

---

1. The socially accepted "escort" (lover) of a married woman.
2. Donna Julia here made a mistake. Count O'Reilly did not take Algiers—but Algiers very nearly took him

[Byron's note]. Irish-born Spanish general O'Reilly led an unsuccessful expedition to Algiers in 1775.

3. "Cazzano" is slang for a penis, by extension a dunce or a rogue; "Cornuto" means horned, that is, cuckolded.

With that sublime of rascals your attorney,
    Whom I see standing there, and looking sensible
1205 Of having play'd the fool? though both I spurn, he
    Deserves the worst, his conduct's less defensible,
Because, no doubt, 'twas for his dirty fee,
And not from any love to you nor me.

           152

"If he comes here to take a deposition,
    By all means let the gentleman proceed;
1210 You've made the apartment in a fit condition:—
    There's pen and ink for you, sir, when you need—
Let every thing be noted with precision,
    I would not you for nothing should be fee'd—
1215 But, as my maid's undrest, pray turn your spies out."
"Oh!" sobb'd Antonia, "I could tear their eyes out."

           153

"There is the closet, there the toilet,° there   *dressing table*
    The antechamber—search them under, over;
There is the sofa, there the great arm-chair,
1220   The chimney—which would really hold a lover.
I wish to sleep, and beg you will take care
    And make no further noise, till you discover
The secret cavern of this lurking treasure—
And when 'tis found, let me, too, have that pleasure.

           154

1225 "And now, Hidalgo! now that you have thrown
    Doubt upon me, confusion over all,
Pray have the courtesy to make it known
    Who is the man you search for? how d'ye call
Him? what's his lineage? let him but be shown—
1230   I hope he's young and handsome—is he tall?
Tell me—and be assured, that since you stain
My honour thus, it shall not be in vain.

           155

"At least, perhaps, he has not sixty years,
    At that age he would be too old for slaughter,
1235 Or for so young a husband's jealous fears—
    (Antonia! let me have a glass of water.)
I am ashamed of having shed these tears,
    They are unworthy of my father's daughter;
My mother dream'd not in my natal hour
1240 That I should fall into a monster's power.

           156

"Perhaps 'tis of Antonia you are jealous,
    You saw that she was sleeping by my side
When you broke in upon us with your fellows:

Look where you please—we've nothing, sir, to hide;
1245   Only another time, I trust, you'll tell us,
        Or for the sake of decency abide
A moment at the door, that we may be
Drest to receive so much good company.

157

"And now, sir, I have done, and say no more;
1250   The little I have said may serve to show
The guileless heart in silence may grieve o'er
        The wrongs to whose exposure it is slow:—
I leave you to your conscience as before,
        'Twill one day ask you *why* you used me so?
1255   God grant you feel not then the bitterest grief!—
Antonia! where's my pocket-handkerchief?"

158

She ceased, and turn'd upon her pillow; pale
        She lay, her dark eyes flashing through their tears,
Like skies that rain and lighten; as a veil,
1260   Waved and o'ershading her wan cheek, appears
Her streaming hair; the black curls strive, but fail,
        To hide the glossy shoulder, which uprears
Its snow through all;—her soft lips lie apart,
And louder than her breathing beats her heart.

159

1265   The Senhor Don Alfonso stood confused;
        Antonia bustled round the ransack'd room,
And, turning up her nose, with looks abused
        Her master, and his myrmidons, of whom
Not one, except the attorney, was amused;
1270   He, like Achates, faithful to the tomb,[4]
So there were quarrels, cared not for the cause,
Knowing they must be settled by the laws.

160

With prying snub-nose, and small eyes, he stood,
        Following Antonia's motions here and there,
1275   With much suspicion in his attitude;
        For reputations he had little care;
So that a suit or action were made good,
        Small pity had he for the young and fair,
And ne'er believed in negatives, till these
1280   Were proved by competent false witnesses.

161

But Don Alfonso stood with downcast looks,
        And, truth to say, he made a foolish figure;

---

4. Aeneas's loyal companion, a synonym for fidelity. The Myrmidons are the private army of Greek hero Achilles.

When, after searching in five hundred nooks,
　　And treating a young wife with so much rigour,
1285　He gain'd no point, except some self-rebukes,
　　Added to those his lady with such vigour
Had pour'd upon him for the last half-hour,
　　Quick, thick, and heavy—as a thunder-shower.

162

At first he tried to hammer an excuse,
1290　　To which the sole reply was tears, and sobs,
And indications of hysterics, whose
　　Prologue is always certain throes, and throbs,
Gasps, and whatever else the owners choose:
　　Alfonso saw his wife, and thought of Job's;[5]
1295　He saw too, in perspective, her relations,
And then he tried to muster all his patience.

163

He stood in act to speak, or rather stammer,
　　But sage Antonia cut him short before
The anvil of his speech received the hammer,
1300　　With "Pray, sir, leave the room, and say no more,
Or madam dies."—Alfonso mutter'd, "D—n her,"
　　But nothing else, the time of words was o'er;
He cast a rueful look or two, and did,
He knew not wherefore, that which he was bid.

164

1305　With him retired his "*posse comitatus,*"[6]
　　The attorney last, who linger'd near the door,
Reluctantly, still tarrying there as late as
　　Antonia let him—not a little sore
At this most strange and unexplain'd "*hiatus*"
1310　　In Don Alfonso's facts, which just now wore
An awkward look; as he revolved the case,
The door was fasten'd in his legal face.

165

No sooner was it bolted, than—Oh shame!
　　Oh sin! Oh sorrow! and Oh womankind!
1315　How can you do such things and keep your fame,
　　Unless this world, and t' other too, be blind?
Nothing so dear as an unfilch'd good name![7]
　　But to proceed—for there is more behind:
With much heartfelt reluctance be it said,
1320　Young Juan slipp'd, half-smother'd, from the bed.

---

5. Job's wife advises him to "curse God, and die" (2.9).
6. The "power of the country," a group deputized to maintain order.

7. Thus Iago says, leading Othello to believe that his new bride has been unfaithful and so a scandal to his good name (*Othello*, 3.3.159).

166

He had been hid—I don't pretend to say
        How, nor can I indeed describe the where—
Young, slender, and pack'd easily, he lay,
        No doubt, in little compass, round or square;
1325   But pity him I neither must nor may
        His suffocation by that pretty pair;
'Twere better, sure, to die so, than be shut
With maudlin Clarence in his Malmsey butt.[8]

167

And, secondly, I pity not, because
1330   He had no business to commit a sin,
Forbid by heavenly, fined by human laws,
        At least 'twas rather early to begin;
But at sixteen the conscience rarely gnaws
        So much as when we call our old debts in
1335   At sixty years, and draw the accompts of evil,
And find a deuced balance with the devil.

168

Of his position I can give no notion:
        'Tis written in the Hebrew Chronicle,
How the physicians, leaving pill and potion,
1340   Prescribed, by way of blister, a young belle,
When old King David's blood grew dull in motion,
        And that the medicine answer'd very well;[9]
Perhaps 'twas in a different way applied,
For David lived, but Juan nearly died.

169

1345   What's to be done? Alfonso will be back
        The moment he has sent his fools away.
Antonia's skill was put upon the rack,
        But no device could be brought into play—
And how to parry the renew'd attack?
1350   Besides, it wanted but few hours of day:
Antonia puzzled; Julia did not speak,
But press'd her bloodless lip to Juan's cheek.

170

He turn'd his lip to hers, and with his hand
        Call'd back the tangles of her wandering hair;
1355   Even then their love they could not all command,
        And half forgot their danger and despair:
Antonia's patience now was at a stand—
        "Come, come, 'tis no time now for fooling there,"

8. In Shakespeare's *Richard III* (1.4), the Duke of Clarence is murdered by being drowned in a cask of sweet wine.

9. When the aged King David was afflicted with chills, a beautiful maiden was found to warm him at night (1 Kings 1).

She whisper'd, in great wrath—"I must deposit
1360   This pretty gentleman within the closet:

171

"Pray, keep your nonsense for some luckier night—
    Who can have put my master in this mood?
What will become on 't—I'm in such a fright,
    The devil's in the urchin, and no good—
1365 Is this a time for giggling? this a plight?
    Why, don't you know that it may end in blood?
You'll lose your life, and I shall lose my place,
My mistress all, for that half-girlish face.

172

"Had it but been for a stout cavalier
1370   Of twenty-five or thirty—(Come, make haste)
But for a child, what piece of work is here!
    I really, madam, wonder at your taste—
(Come, sir, get in)—my master must be near:
    There, for the present, at the least, he's fast,
1375 And if we can but till the morning keep
Our counsel—(Juan, mind, you must not sleep.)"

173

Now, Don Alfonso entering, but alone,
    Closed the oration of the trusty maid:
She loiter'd, and he told her to be gone,
1380   An order somewhat sullenly obey'd;
However, present remedy was none,
    And no great good seem'd answer'd if she staid:
Regarding both with slow and sidelong view,
She snuff'd the candle, curtsied, and withdrew.

174

1385 Alfonso paused a minute—then begun
    Some strange excuses for his late proceeding;
He would not justify what he had done,
    To say the best, it was extreme ill-breeding;
But there were ample reasons for it, none
1390   Of which he specified in this his pleading:
His speech was a fine sample, on the whole,
Of rhetoric, which the learn'd call "*rigmarole.*"

175

Julia said nought; though all the while there rose
    A ready answer, which at once enables
1395 A matron, who her husband's foible knows,
    By a few timely words to turn the tables,
Which, if it does not silence, still must pose,—
    Even if it should comprise a pack of fables;
'Tis to retort with firmness, and when he
1400 Suspects with *one*, do you reproach with *three*.

176

176

Julia, in fact, had tolerable grounds,—
    Alfonso's loves with Inez were well known;
But whether 'twas that one's own guilt confounds—
    But that can't be, as has been often shown,
1405 A lady with apologies° abounds;—   *defenses*
    It might be that her silence sprang alone
From delicacy to Don Juan's ear,
To whom she knew his mother's fame° was dear.   *good reputation*

177

There might be one more motive, which makes two;
1410   Alfonso ne'er to Juan had alluded,—
Mention'd his jealousy, but never who
    Had been the happy lover, he concluded,
Conceal'd amongst his premises; 'tis true,
    His mind the more o'er this its mystery brooded;
1415 To speak of Inez now were, one may say,
Like throwing Juan in Alfonso's way.

178

A hint, in tender cases, is enough;
    Silence is best, besides there is a *tact*—
(That modern phrase appears to me sad stuff,
1420   But it will serve to keep my verse compact)—
Which keeps, when push'd by questions rather rough,
    A lady always distant from the fact:
The charming creatures lie with such a grace,
There's nothing so becoming to the face.

179

1425 They blush, and we believe them; at least I
    Have always done so; 'tis of no great use,
In any case, attempting a reply,
    For then their eloquence grows quite profuse;
And when at length they're out of breath, they sigh,
1430   And cast their languid eyes down, and let loose
A tear or two, and then we make it up;
And then—and then—and then—sit down and sup.

180

Alfonso closed his speech, and begg'd her pardon,
    Which Julia half withheld, and then half granted,
1435 And laid conditions, he thought, very hard on,
    Denying several little things he wanted:
He stood like Adam lingering near his garden,[1]
    With useless penitence perplex'd and haunted,
Beseeching she no further would refuse,
1440 When, lo! he stumbled o'er a pair of shoes.

---

1. After his expulsion from Eden (Milton, *Paradise Lost,* 12.637–39).

181

A pair of shoes!—what then? not much, if they
   Are such as fit with ladies' feet, but these
(No one can tell how much I grieve to say)
   Were masculine; to see them, and to seize,
1445 Was but a moment's act.—Ah! well-a-day!
   My teeth begin to chatter, my veins freeze—
Alfonso first examined well their fashion,
And then flew out into another passion.

182

He left the room for his relinquish'd sword,
1450   And Julia instant to the closet flew.
"Fly, Juan, fly! for heaven's sake—not a word—
   The door is open—you may yet slip through
The passage you so often have explored—
   Here is the garden-key—Fly—fly—Adieu!
1455 Haste—haste! I hear Alfonso's hurrying feet—
Day has not broke—there's no one in the street."

183

None can say that this was not good advice,
   The only mischief was, it came too late;
Of all experience 'tis the usual price,
1460   A sort of income-tax laid on by fate:
Juan had reach'd the room-door in a trice,
   And might have done so by the garden-gate,
But met Alfonso in his dressing-gown,
Who threaten'd death—so Juan knock'd him down.

184

1465 Dire was the scuffle, and out went the light;
   Antonia cried out "Rape!" and Julia "Fire!"
But not a servant stirr'd to aid the fight.
   Alfonso, pommell'd to his heart's desire,
Swore lustily he'd be revenged this night;
1470   And Juan, too, blasphemed an octave higher;
His blood was up: though young, he was a Tartar,°   *fierce warrior*
And not at all disposed to prove a martyr.

185

Alfonso's sword had dropp'd ere he could draw it,
   And they continued battling hand to hand,
1475 For Juan very luckily ne'er saw it;
   His temper not being under great command,
If at that moment he had chanced to claw it,
   Alfonso's days had not been in the land
Much longer.—Think of husbands', lovers' lives!
1480 And how ye may be doubly widows—wives!

186

Alfonso grappled to detain the foe,
   And Juan throttled him to get away,
And blood ('twas from the nose) began to flow;
   At last, as they more faintly wrestling lay,
Juan contrived to give an awkward blow,
   And then his only garment quite gave way;
He fled, like Joseph, leaving it; but there,
I doubt, all likeness ends between the pair.[2]

187

Lights came at length, and men, and maids, who found
   An awkward spectacle their eyes before;
Antonia in hysterics, Julia swoon'd,
   Alfonso leaning, breathless, by the door;
Some half-torn drapery scatter'd on the ground,
   Some blood, and several footsteps, but no more:
Juan the gate gain'd, turn'd the key about,
And liking not the inside, lock'd the out.

188

Here ends this canto.—Need I sing, or say,
   How Juan, naked, favour'd by the night,
Who favours what she should not, found his way,
   And reach'd his home in an unseemly plight?
The pleasant scandal which arose next day,
   The nine days' wonder which was brought to light,
And how Alfonso sued for a divorce,
Were in the English newspapers, of course.

189

If you would like to see the whole proceedings,
   The depositions, and the cause at full,
The names of all the witnesses, the pleadings
   Of counsel to nonsuit, or to annul,
There's more than one edition, and the readings
   Are various, but they none of them are dull;
The best is that in short-hand ta'en by Gurney,
Who to Madrid on purpose made a journey.[3]

190

But Donna Inez, to divert the train
   Of one of the most circulating scandals
That had for centuries been known in Spain,
   At least since the retirement of the Vandals,
First vow'd (and never had she vow'd in vain)
   To Virgin Mary several pounds of candles;

1485

1490

1495

1500

1505

1510

1515

2. The chaste Joseph fled Potiphar's seductive wife, leaving "his garment in her hand" (Genesis 39).

3. William Brodie Gurney (1777–1855) was the official shorthand writer to Parliament and a noted trial reporter.

And then, by the advice of some old ladies,
1520 She sent her son to be shipp'd off from Cadiz.

191

She had resolved that he should travel through
　All European climes, by land or sea,
To mend his former morals, and get new,
　Especially in France and Italy,
1525 (At least this is the thing most people do.)
　　Julia was sent into a convent: she
Grieved, but, perhaps, her feelings may be better
Shown in the following copy of her Letter:—

192

"They tell me 'tis decided; you depart:
1530 　'Tis wise, 'tis well, but not the less a pain;
I have no further claim on your young heart,
　Mine was the victim, and would be again;
To love too much has been the only art
　I used;—I write in haste, and if a stain
1535 Be on this sheet, 'tis not what it appears;
My eyeballs burn and throb, but have no tears.

193

"I loved, I love you, for this love have lost
　State, station, heaven, mankind's, my own esteem,
And yet can not regret what it hath cost,
1540 　So dear is still the memory of that dream;
Yet, if I name my guilt, 'tis not to boast,
　None can deem harshlier of me than I deem:
I trace this scrawl because I cannot rest—
I've nothing to reproach, or to request.

194

1545 "Man's love is of man's life a thing apart,
　'Tis woman's whole existence; man may range
The court, camp, church, the vessel, and the mart,
　Sword, gown, gain, glory, offer in exchange
Pride, fame, ambition, to fill up his heart,
1550 　And few there are whom these can not estrange;
Men have all these resources, we but one,
To love again, and be again undone.

195

"You will proceed in pleasure, and in pride,
　Beloved and loving many; all is o'er
1555 For me on earth, except some years to hide
　My shame and sorrow deep in my heart's core;
These I could bear, but cannot cast aside
　The passion which still rages as before,—
And so farewell—forgive me, love me—No,
1560 That word is idle now—but let it go.

196

"My breast has been all weakness, is so yet;
    But still I think I can collect my mind;
My blood still rushes where my spirit's set,
    As roll the waves before the settled wind;
1565   My heart is feminine, nor can forget—
    To all, except one image, madly blind;
So shakes the needle, and so stands the pole,
As vibrates my fond heart to my fix'd soul.

197

"I have no more to say, but linger still,
1570   And dare not set my seal upon this sheet,
And yet I may as well the task fulfil,
    My misery can scarce be more complete:
I had not lived till now, could sorrow kill;
    Death shuns the wretch who fain the blow would meet,
1575   And I must even survive this last adieu,
And bear with life, to love and pray for you!"

198

This note was written upon gilt-edged paper
    With a neat little crow-quill, slight and new;
Her small white hand could hardly reach the taper,
1580   It trembled as magnetic needles do,
And yet she did not let one tear escape her;
    The seal a sun-flower; "*Elle vous suit partout*,"[4]
The motto, cut upon a white cornelian;
The wax was superfine, its hue vermilion.

199

1585   This was Don Juan's earliest scrape; but whether
    I shall proceed with his adventures is
Dependent on the public altogether;
    We'll see, however, what they say to this,
Their favour in an author's cap's a feather,
1590   And no great mischief's done by their caprice;
And if their approbation we experience,
Perhaps they'll have some more about a year hence.

200

My poem's epic, and is meant to be
    Divided in twelve books; each book containing,
1595   With love, and war, a heavy gale at sea,
    A list of ships, and captains, and kings reigning,
New characters; the episodes are three:
    A panoramic view of hell's in training,
After the style of Virgil and of Homer,
1600   So that my name of Epic's no misnomer.

---

4. "She follows you everywhere," the motto of one of Byron's own seals, also inscribed on a jewel he gave to John Edleston, his beloved at Cambridge.

201

All these things will be specified in time,
    With strict regard to Aristotle's rules,
The *Vade Mecum°* of the true sublime,   *handbook*
    Which makes so many poets, and some fools:
1605   Prose poets like blank-verse, I'm fond of rhyme,
    Good workmen never quarrel with their tools;
I've got new mythological machinery,
And very handsome supernatural scenery.

202

There's only one slight difference between
1610   Me and my epic brethren gone before,
And here the advantage is my own, I ween;
    (Not that I have not several merits more,
But this will more peculiarly be seen);
    They so embellish, that 'tis quite a bore;
1615   Their labyrinth of fables to thread through,
Whereas this story's actually true.

203

If any person doubt it, I appeal
    To history, tradition, and to facts,
To newspapers, whose truth all know and feel,
1620   To plays in five, and operas in three acts;
All these confirm my statement a good deal,
    But that which more completely faith exacts
Is, that myself, and several now in Seville,
Saw Juan's last elopement with the devil.

204

1625   If ever I should condescend to prose,
    I'll write poetical commandments, which
Shall supersede beyond all doubt all those
    That went before; in these I shall enrich
My text with many things that no one knows,
1630   And carry precept to the highest pitch:
I'll call the work "Longinus o'er a Bottle,
Or, Every Poet his *own* Aristotle."[5]

205

Thou shalt believe in Milton, Dryden, Pope;[6]
    Thou shalt not set up Wordsworth, Coleridge, Southey;
1635   Because the first is crazed beyond all hope,
    The second drunk, the third so quaint and mouthy:

5. Two famous ancient literary treatises: the *Poetics* of Aristotle, and Longinus, *On the Sublime.*
6. This parody of the Ten Commandments provoked cries of blasphemy. Byron feared that if Murray put his name on the poem "in these canting days—any lawyer might oppose my Guardian right of my daughter in Chancery—on the plea of it's containing the parody—such are the perils of a foolish jest." Percy Shelley lost custody of children by his first wife on such charges.

With Crabbe it may be difficult to cope,
    And Campbell's Hippocrene[7] is somewhat drouthy:
Thou shalt not steal from Samuel Rogers, nor
1640   Commit—flirtation with the muse of Moore.

206

Thou shalt not covet Mr. Sotheby's Muse,
    His Pegasus, nor any thing that's his;[8]
Thou shalt not bear false witness like "the Blues"—
    (There's one, at least, is very fond of this);[9]
1645 Thou shalt not write, in short, but what I choose:
    This is true criticism, and you may kiss—
Exactly as you please, or not,—the rod;
But if you don't, I'll lay it on, by G—d!

207

If any person should presume to assert
1650   This story is not moral, first, I pray,
That they will not cry out before they're hurt,
    Then that they'll read it o'er again, and say,
(But, doubtless, nobody will be so pert,)
    That this is not a moral tale, though gay;
1655 Besides, in Canto Twelfth, I mean to show
The very place where wicked people go.

208

If, after all, there should be some so blind
    To their own good this warning to despise,
Led by some tortuosity of mind,
1660   Not to believe my verse and their own eyes,
And cry that they "the moral cannot find,"
    I tell him, if a clergyman, he lies;
Should captains the remark, or critics, make,
They also lie too—under a mistake.

209

1665 The public approbation I expect,
    And beg they'll take my word about the moral,
Which I with their amusement will connect
    (So children cutting teeth receive a coral);
Meantime, they'll doubtless please to recollect
1670   My epical pretensions to the laurel:
For fear some prudish readers should grow skittish.
I've bribed my grandmother's review—the British.[1]

---

7. Fountain on Mount Helicon, sacred to the Muses.
8. William Sotheby (1757–1833), minor poet, man of letters, and translator of Wieland's *Oberon,* is satirized in Byron's *Beppo.* Samuel Rogers, a popular poet, published his *Jacqueline* with Byron's *Lara* in 1814.

9. Probably Lady Byron; "Blue Stockings" is a derogatory term for intellectual women.
1. William Roberts, editor of the *British Review,* missed this joke and printed a solemn denial.

210

I sent it in a letter to the Editor,
    Who thank'd me duly by return of post—
1675   I'm for a handsome article his creditor;
    Yet, if my gentle Muse he please to roast,
And break a promise after having made it her,
    Denying the receipt of what it cost,
And smear his page with gall instead of honey,
1680   All I can say is—that he had the money.

211

I think that with this holy new alliance[2]
    I may ensure the public, and defy
All other magazines of art or science,
    Daily, or monthly, or three monthly; I
1685   Have not essay'd to multiply their clients,
    Because they tell me 'twere in vain to try,
And that the Edinburgh Review and Quarterly
Treat a dissenting author very martyrly.

212

"*Non ego hoc ferrem calida juventâ*
1690   *Consule Planco*," Horace said,[3] and so
Say I; by which quotation there is meant a
    Hint that some six or seven good years ago
(Long ere I dreamt of dating from the Brenta)[4]
    I was most ready to return a blow,
1695   And would not brook at all this sort of thing
In my hot youth—when George the Third was King.

213

But now at thirty years my hair is grey—
    (I wonder what it will be like at forty?
I thought of a peruke° the other day—)   *wig*
1700   My heart is not much greener; and, in short, I
Have squander'd my whole summer while 'twas May,
    And feel no more the spirit to retort; I
Have spent my life, both interest and principal,
And deem not, what I deem'd, my soul invincible.

214

1705   No more—no more—Oh! never more on me
    The freshness of the heart can fall like dew,
Which out of all the lovely things we see

---

2. Glancing at the Holy Alliance formed in 1815 between Russia, Austria, and Prussia to join their countries in Christian brotherhood.
3. Horace, *Odes* 3.14.27: "I had not brooked such insult when hot with youth in Plancus's consulship" (trans. by C. E. Bennett). The joke, clinched in the last two lines of the stanza, is that George III was still king.
4. In the summer of 1817 Byron rented a villa on the river Brenta, near Venice.

Extracts emotions beautiful and new,
Hived in our bosoms like the bag o' the bee:
1710   Think'st thou the honey with those objects grew?
Alas! 'twas not in them, but in thy power
To double even the sweetness of a flower.

215

No more—no more—Oh! never more, my heart.
Canst thou be my sole world, my universe!
1715   Once all in all, but now a thing apart,
Thou canst not be my blessing or my curse:
The illusion's gone for ever, and thou art
Insensible, I trust, but none the worse,
And in thy stead I've got a deal of judgment,
1720   Though heaven knows how it ever found a lodgement.

216

My days of love are over; me no more
The charms of maid, wife, and still less of widow,
Can make the fool of which they made before,[5]
In short, I must not lead the life I did do;
1725   The credulous hope of mutual minds is o'er,
The copious use of claret is forbid too,
So for a good old-gentlemanly vice,
I think I must take up with avarice.

217

Ambition was my idol, which was broken
1730   Before the shrines of Sorrow, and of Pleasure;
And the two last have left me many a token
O'er which reflection may be made at leisure:
Now, like Friar Bacon's brazen head, I've spoken,
"Time is, Time was, Time's past:"[6]—a chymic° treasure   alchemic
1735   Is glittering youth, which I have spent betimes—
My heart in passion, and my head on rhymes.

218

What is the end of Fame? 'tis but to fill
A certain portion of uncertain paper:
Some liken it to climbing up a hill,
1740   Whose summit, like all hills, is lost in vapour;
For this men write, speak, preach, and heroes kill,
And bards burn what they call their "midnight taper,"

5. Horace, *Odes* 4.1.29–32: "Neither boy nor woman can please me any more . . . nor drinking bouts and brows with garlands bound."
6. Quoting *Friar Bacon and Friar Bungay* (1594), a comedy based on the legend of Roger Bacon, a 13th-century Oxford philosopher regarded as a necromancer and said to have constructed a brazen head capable of speech.

To have, when the original is dust,
A name, a wretched picture, and worse bust.

219

¹⁷⁴⁵ What are the hopes of man? Old Egypt's King
    Cheops erected the first pyramid
And largest, thinking it was just the thing
    To keep his memory whole, and mummy hid;
But somebody or other rummaging,
¹⁷⁵⁰   Burglariously broke his coffin's lid:
Let not a monument give you or me hopes,
Since not a pinch of dust remains of Cheops.

220

But I being fond of true philosophy,
    Say very often to myself, "Alas!
¹⁷⁵⁵ All things that have been born were born to die,
    And flesh (which Death mows down to hay) is grass;
You've pass'd your youth not so unpleasantly,
    And if you had it o'er again—'twould pass—
So thank your stars that matters are no worse,
¹⁷⁶⁰ And read your Bible, sir, and mind your purse."

221

But for the present, gentle reader! and
    Still gentler purchaser! the bard—that's I—
Must, with permission, shake you by the hand,
    And so your humble servant, and good-b'ye!
¹⁷⁶⁵ We meet again, if we should understand
    Each other; and if not, I shall not try
Your patience further than by this short sample—
'Twere well if others follow'd my example.

222

"Go, little book, from this my solitude!
¹⁷⁷⁰   I cast thee on the waters—go thy ways!
And if, as I believe, thy vein be good,
    The world will find thee after many days."[7]
When Southey's read, and Wordsworth understood,
    I can't help putting in my claim to praise—
¹⁷⁷⁵ The four first rhymes are Southey's every line:
For God's sake, reader! take them not for mine.

7. Byron quotes from the final stanza of Southey's *Carmen Nuptiale: The Lay of the Laureate* (1816).

from **Canto 7**[1]
[CRITIQUE OF MILITARY "GLORY"][2]

78

—The work of glory still went on
    In preparations for a cannonade
As terrible as that of Ilion,[3]
620   If Homer had found mortars ready made;
But now, instead of slaying Priam's son,[4]
    We only can but talk of escalade,°   *scaling walls by ladder*
Bombs, drums, guns, bastions, batteries, bayonets, bullets;
Hard words, which stick in the soft Muses' gullets.

79

625 Oh, thou eternal Homer! who couldst charm
    All ears, though long; all ages, though so short,
By merely wielding with poetic arm
    Arms to which men will never more resort,
Unless gunpowder should be found to harm
630   Much less than is the hope of every court,
Which now is leagued young Freedom to annoy;
But they will not find Liberty a Troy:—

80

Oh, thou eternal Homer! I have now
    To paint a siege, wherein more men were slain,
635 With deadlier engines and a speedier blow,
    Than in thy Greek gazette of that campaign;
And yet, like all men else, I must allow,
    To vie with thee would be about as vain
As for a brook to cope with ocean's flood;
640 But still we moderns equal you in blood;

81

If not in poetry, at least in fact;
    And fact is truth, the grand desideratum!
Of which, howe'er the Muse describes each act,

---

1. Byron composed Cantos 6–8 between January and July 1822. He intended to publish as usual with John Murray, but increasing controversy—his drama *Cain* had caused an outcry in 1821—and the violent critique in the new cantos caused Murray to delay. In a preface, Byron denounced Castlereagh, a recent suicide, as a Minister "the most despotic in intention and weakest in intellect that ever tyrannized over a country," and he attacked "the degraded and hypocritical mass" of "this double-dealing and false-speaking time of selfish Spoilers." See also the Dedication, pages 413–15. Byron moved from his respectable Tory publisher to John Hunt, brother of Leigh Hunt, with whom he was engaged on *The Liberal;* in 1813 both Hunts had been sentenced to two years' imprisonment for libeling the Prince Regent. Hunt published Cantos 6–8 in July 1823, still anonymously, though Byron's authorship had never been doubted. A motto from Shakespeare on the title page marked Byron's repudiation of English censoriousness: "Dost thou think, because thou art virtuous, there shall be no more Cakes and Ale?"—"Yes, by St. Anne; and Ginger shall be hot i' the mouth too!" (*Twelfth Night* 2.3.104–106).

2. The idyll of Haidée and Juan is ended by the unexpected return of her father, who sells him as a slave in Constantinople. Juan is bought by the Sultan's wife, who disguises him as "Juanna" and hides him in her husband's harem. There his adventures with a harem girl arouse the Sultana's wrath. He escapes a death sentence and joins the Russian army, then besieging Ismail, a Turkish town on the north shore of the Danube, during November–December 1790.

3. Troy; the Siege of Ismail corresponds both to the *Iliad* and, in its hellish quality, to the underworld journey of epic.

4. Hector, the Trojan hero.

There should be ne'ertheless a slight substratum.
645 But now the town is going to be attack'd;
　　Great deeds are doing—how shall I relate 'em?
Souls of immortal generals! Phoebus° watches　　　　　　　　　*the sun god*
To colour up his rays from your despatches.
1822　　　　　　　　　　　　　　　　　　　　　　　　　　　　　1823

from Canto 11[1]
[JUAN IN ENGLAND][2]

21

Through Groves, so call'd as being void of trees,
　　(Like *lucus* from *no* light);[3] through prospects named
Mount Pleasant, as containing nought to please,
　　Nor much to climb; through little boxes framed
165 Of bricks, to let the dust in at your ease,
　　With "To be let,"° upon their doors proclaim'd;　　　　　　*rented*
Through "Rows" most modestly call'd "Paradise,"
Which Eve might quit without much sacrifice;—

22

Through coaches, drays, choked turnpikes, and a whirl
170 　　Of wheels, and roar of voices, and confusion;
Here taverns wooing to a pint of "purl,"°　　　　　　　　　*gin and beer*
　　There mails° fast flying off like a delusion;　　　　　　　*mail-coaches*
There barbers' blocks with periwigs in curl
　　In windows; here the lamplighter's infusion
175 Slowly distill'd into the glimmering glass
(For in those days we had not got to gas—);[4]

23

Through this, and much, and more, is the approach
　　Of travellers to mighty Babylon:
Whether they come by horse, or chaise, or coach,
180 　　With slight exceptions, all the ways seem one.
I could say more, but do not choose to encroach
　　Upon the Guide-book's privilege. The sun
Had set some time, and night was on the ridge
Of twilight, as the party cross'd the bridge.

24

185 That's rather fine, the gentle sound of Thamis°—　　　　*River Thames*
　　Who vindicates a moment, too, his stream—

1. Composed October 1822. John Hunt published Cantos 9–11 in August 1823, again anonymously.
2. Having distinguished himself at Ismail, Juan is sent to St. Petersburg, where he becomes the favorite of Empress Catherine the Great, whose sexual appetite was notorious. Amply rewarded but exhausted, Juan is sent on a diplomatic mission to England to restore his declining health. His journey across Europe enabled Byron lightly to revisit the materials of *Childe Harold's Pilgrimage*, and the arrival in England returns *Don Juan*, in a vivid act of memory, to the Regency England in which Byron had shined. Here Juan is approaching London.
3. A famous ancient false etymology derived the Latin word for "grove," *lucus*, from the lack of light (*lux*) under the trees.
4. Gas came into use in London in 1812.

Though hardly heard through multifarious "damme's."
   The lamps of Westminster's more regular gleam,
The breadth of pavement, and yon shrine[5] where fame is
190   A spectral resident—whose pallid beam
In shape of moonshine hovers o'er the pile—
   Make this a sacred part of Albion's isle.

25

The Druids' groves are gone—so much the better:
   Stone-Henge[6] is not—but what the devil is it?—
195   But Bedlam still exists with its sage fetter,
   That madmen may not bite you on a visit;
The Bench too seats or suits full many a debtor;
   The Mansion House too (though some people quiz it)
To me appears a stiff yet grand erection;
200   But then the Abbey's worth the whole collection.[7]

26

The line of lights too up to Charing Cross,
   Pall Mall,[8] and so forth, have a coruscation°   *sparkle*
Like gold as in comparison to dross,
   Match'd with the Continent's illumination,
205 Whose cities Night by no means deigns to gloss.
   The French were not yet a lamp-lighting nation,
And when they grew so—on their new-found lantern,
Instead of wicks, they made a wicked man turn.[9]

27

A row of gentlemen along the streets
210   Suspended, may illuminate mankind,
As also bonfires made of country seats;
   But the old way is best for the purblind:
The other looks like phosphorus on sheets,
   A sort of ignis fatuus° to the mind,   *will-o'-the-wisp*
215 Which, though 'tis certain to perplex and frighten,
Must burn more mildly ere it can enlighten.

28

But London's so well lit, that if Diogenes
   Could recommence to hunt his *honest man*,[1]
And found him not amidst the various progenies
220   Of this enormous city's spreading spawn,
'Twere not for want of lamps to aid his dodging his
   Yet undiscover'd treasure. What *I* can,

---

5. Westminster Abbey, filled with shrines.
6. Interest in the ancient Celtic Druids, to whom the oak was sacred, and Stonehenge, the Druid stone circle on Salisbury Plain, had grown in the 18th century.
7. Bedlam, a corruption of Bethlehem Hospital for the insane; the Bench, the Court of Common Pleas; the Mansion House, the residence of the Lord Mayor.

8. Juan is proceeding to the fashionable West End.
9. A punning capsule history, from the rationalism of the Enlightenment to the hanging of offending persons from lampposts during the French Revolution.
1. Greek philosopher Diogenes the Cynic (c. 423–323 B.C.) took a lantern in broad daylight to search for an honest man.

I've done to find the same throughout life's journey,
But see the world is only one attorney.

* * *

65[2]

His morns he pass'd in business—which dissected,
    Was like all business, a laborious nothing,
515 That leads to lassitude, the most infected
    And Centaur Nessus garb of mortal clothing,[3]
And on our sofas makes us lie dejected,
    And talk in tender horrors of our loathing
All kinds of toil, save for our country's good—.
520 Which grows no better, though 'tis time it should.

66

His afternoons he pass'd in visits, luncheons,
    Lounging, and boxing; and the twilight hour
In riding round those vegetable puncheons
    Call'd "Parks," where there is neither fruit nor flower
525 Enough to gratify a bee's slight munchings;
    But after all it is the only "bower,"
(In Moore's phrase) where the fashionable fair
Can form a slight acquaintance with fresh air.

67

Then dress, then dinner, then awakes the world!
530 Then glare the lamps, then whirl the wheels, then roar
Through street and square fast flashing chariots hurl'd
    Like harness'd meteors; then along the floor
Chalk mimics painting; then festoons are twirl'd;
    Then roll the brazen thunders of the door,
535 Which opens to the thousand happy few
An earthly Paradise of "Or Molu."[4]

* * *

74

585 Our hero, as a hero, young and handsome,
    Noble, rich, celebrated, and a stranger,
Like other slaves of course must pay his ransom
    Before he can escape from so much danger
As will environ a conspicuous man.[5] Some
590   Talk about poetry, and "rack and manger,"°   *rack and ruin*
And ugliness, disease, as toil and trouble;—
I wish they knew the life of a young noble.

---

2. The intervening stanzas record Juan's enthusiastic reception by high society.
3. When her husband Hercules was unfaithful, Deianira sent him the tunic of the Centaur Nessus, whom he had killed. Believing it to be a love charm, Hercules died in agony.

4. Gilded bronze, a popular ornamental material.
5. Echoing Samuel Butler's satiric poem, *Hudibras* (1663–1678), "Ah me! what perils do environ / The man who meddles with cold iron" (pt. 1, ch. 3).

75

They are young, but know not youth—it is anticipated;
    Handsome but wasted, rich without a sou;
595 Their vigour in a thousand arms is dissipated;
    Their cash comes *from*, their wealth goes to a Jew;
Both senates see their nightly votes participated
    Between the tyrant's and the tribunes' crew;[6]
And having voted, dined, drank, gamed, and whored,
600 The family vault receives another lord.

1822   1823

Stanzas[1]

When a man hath no freedom to fight for at home,
    Let him combat for that of his neighbours;
Let him think of the glories of Greece and of Rome,
    And get knock'd on the head for his labours.

5 To do good to mankind is the chivalrous plan,
    And is always as nobly requited;
Then battle for freedom wherever you can,
    And, if not shot or hang'd, you'll get knighted.

1820   1830

On This Day I Complete My Thirty-Sixth Year
Missolonghi, Jan. 22. 1824[1]

'Tis time this heart should be unmoved,
    Since others it hath ceased to move:
Yet, though I cannot be beloved,
    Still let me love!

5 My days are in the yellow leaf;[2]
    The flowers and fruits of love are gone;
The worm, the canker, and the grief
    Are mine alone!

The fire that on my bosom preys
10   Is lone as some volcanic isle;
No torch is kindled at its blaze—
    A funeral pile!

The hope, the fear, the jealous care,
    The exalted portion of the pain

6. The tyrants are the Tories, in power; the tribunes, representatives of the people, are the opposition Whigs and radicals. The Jews are moneylenders.
1. Sent to Thomas Moore in a letter of 5 November 1820, and published posthumously, the poem reflects—with his usual irony—Byron's involvement with the Carbonari, rebels against the Austrian domination of Italy.
1. Two weeks earlier, Byron had arrived in Missolonghi, a

marshy town in western Greece, to support the Greeks in their war against Turkish rule. The poem is the final entry in his Missolonghi journal; he died from a fever and the ignorant medical practice of the day on April 19. The poem reflects Byron's feelings for his 15-year-old page, Loukas Chalandritsanos.
2. Echoing Shakespeare, *Macbeth*, 5.3.22, on old age.

15 And power of love, I cannot share,
        But wear the chain.

But 'tis not *thus*—and 'tis not *here*—
    Such thoughts should shake my soul, nor *now*,
Where glory decks the hero's bier,
20   Or binds his brow.

The sword, the banner, and the field,
    Glory and Greece, around me see!
The Spartan, borne upon his shield,[3]
    Was not more free.

25 Awake! (not Greece—she *is* awake!)
    Awake, my spirit! Think through *whom*
Thy life-blood tracks its parent lake,
    And then strike home!

Tread those reviving passions down,
30   Unworthy manhood!—unto thee
Indifferent should the smile or frown
    Of beauty be.

If thou regret'st thy youth, *why* live?
    The land of honourable death
35 Is here:—up to the field, and give
    Away thy breath!

Seek out—less often sought than found—
    A soldier's grave, for thee the best;
Then look around, and choose thy ground,
40   And take thy rest.

1824   1824

———— ✦ ————

Percy Bysshe Shelley
1792–1822

One of the most radically visionary of the Romantics, Percy Bysshe Shelley has always had countercultural prestige. In the nineteenth century, Karl Marx and Friedrich Engels praised his "prophetic genius," and in the twentieth century, Paul Foot, head of England's Socialist Workers Party, edited an inexpensive volume of his political writing both to answer "the enthusiasm of the members of the SWP for Shelley's revolutionary writings" and to give socialists a means to disseminate their views not "with dogmatic propaganda but with the poetry which carries revolutionary ideas through the centuries."

Shelley's esteem in these countercultures emerges from a selective reading of his work and life, the full range of which complicates and challenges partisan evaluation. Variously

---

3. Spartan warriors were exhorted not to drop their shields and flee battle but to return either with their shields or carried, dead, upon them.

described as a selflessly devoted, often misunderstood idealist and as appallingly selfish, Shelley was always a risk-taker, and could be careless of the consequences. As an Oxford undergraduate, he collaborated with a friend on *The Necessity of Atheism,* a pamphlet that got them promptly expelled after they sent it to every university professor and administrative official, as well as every bishop in the United Kingdom. His first long poem *Queen Mab* included a vitriolic attack on "Priestcraft" and "Kingcraft" that earned him celebrity in the radical press and infamy in the conservative press; well into the nineteenth century, these atheist and revolutionary passages were expurgated. This censorship was part of the refashioning of Shelley in the Victorian period. In a well-orchestrated campaign by his grieving widow and devoted disciples of his poetry, he was made safe for parlors, refurbished from a dangerous thinker into an impossibly delicate visionary given to chanting at skylarks, "Hail to thee, blithe Spirit!"

Shelley's life is marked by idealism, scandal, and passionate but shifting emotional commitments, especially to women. Grandson of a wealthy landowner and son of a member of Parliament, he was born into conservative aristocracy. Expected to continue in this world, he was sent to the best schools. But he began to rebel early. At Eton (1804–1810), he challenged the tyrannical system of "fagging," whereby upperclassmen had the privilege of abusing their juniors. He no sooner enrolled in Oxford, in 1810, than he got himself expelled for that pamphlet on atheism, an event that at once surprised him and enraged his father. He took off for London, where he met Harriet Westbrook and, believing her oppressed by her father, convinced her to elope with him in August 1811 (he was eighteen, she sixteen). The next year, he was in Ireland irritating its Protestant aristocracy by distributing pamphlets urging Catholic emancipation and improved conditions for its large population of the poor. Eager to meet William Godwin, author of *Political Justice,* he returned to London, and began *Queen Mab,* a Godwinian dream vision. In 1813 Harriet bore a daughter, and he published *Mab* at his own expense. At once celebrated (and pirated) by the radical press and denounced by the Tory press, this poem would be linked to Shelley for the rest of his life, its infamy persisting even into his obituaries.

In the heat of his Godwinian enthusiasms and mindful of Godwin's disdain of the institution of marriage, Shelley allowed himself to tire of Harriet and become enamored of Godwin and Wollstonecraft's beautiful, intelligent daughter Mary. In July 1814, he and Mary eloped to France, accompanied by her stepsister Claire Clairmont. After a six-week tour of Europe, marveling at the Alps and dismayed by the ravages of the Napoleonic wars, they returned to England and the scandal of their elopement. In December Harriet bore her second child by Percy but declined his invitation to join their menage as a platonic sister. When Shelley's grandfather died at the beginning of 1815, he gained a modest fortune of £1000 per year, one-fifth of which was paid directly to Harriet and a good portion of which he would always spend on philanthropy and loans to friends. Mary's first child, a daughter, was born prematurely in February, and died within a few weeks, an event that devastated her. During this year, they experimented with an "open" relationship, in which Percy had a romance with Claire and Mary with his college friend T. J. Hogg (collaborator on the pamphlet on atheism). Still at odds with their fathers, Mary and Percy were further strained by debts and a constant shift of residences to avoid creditors and bailiffs. Percy wrote *Alastor,* a somewhat equivocally framed story of a young visionary poet alienated by life in the world who seeks visionary fulfillment, finding this ultimately in death. Their second child, William, was born early in 1816.

They left for Switzerland in May 1816 with Claire, to meet Lord Byron, now Claire's lover. During this summer, Mary wrote *Frankenstein,* and Percy wrote *Hymn to Intellectual Beauty* and *Mont Blanc,* and toured the lakes with Byron. At the summer's end, the Shelley party returned to England and several catastrophes. Mary's half-sister Fanny Imlay committed suicide in October on discovering that Godwin was not her father, and in November, Harriet, pregnant by a new lover and in despair over rejection by him, drowned herself. Percy and Mary were now able to marry, but the scandal of his life and political writings cost him custody of his children by Harriet—an extraordinary ruling in an age when fathers automatically had custody. He was shocked by this judgment, which deepened his self-mythology as an idealist persecuted by social and political injustice and despised by a world unable to appreciate his "beautiful ide-alisms of moral excellence" (as he would phrase it in the Preface to *Prometheus Unbound*).

Over the course of 1817, Shelley consoled himself with new political writing and his friendship with Leigh Hunt, man of letters and editor of the radical newspaper *The Examiner;* through Hunt he met John Keats. Mary was pregnant again, and Clara was born in September. In 1818 they moved to Europe. Eager to spend as much time as possible with Byron, now in Italy, Percy subjected his family to much arduous travel during an oppressively hot summer. Clara did not fare well and died in September. The year 1819 was a productive one for Shelley's writing. He finished *Prometheus Unbound,* an epic "closet-drama" begun the year be-fore about the Titan's war with his oppressor; he wrote *The Cenci,* a gothic political tragedy of incestuous rape, parricide, and persecution; several other political poems, including *The Mask of Anarchy,* in reaction to the infamous "Peterloo Massacre" of a peaceful workers' rally; a long proto-Marxist political pamphlet, *A Philosophical View of Reform;* and a witty satire of Wordsworth (*Peter Bell the Third*), energized by dismay at the middle-aged poet's didacticism and swing to the political right. He also composed one of his most famous poems, *Ode to the West Wind,* an impassioned cry for spiritual transformation rendered in the astonishingly intri-cate, overflowing verse of terza-rima sonnet-stanzas. The death of William in June, at age three and a half, wrenched the Shelleys with a grief only partly allayed by the birth, five months later, of a second son, Percy Florence—the only of their children to survive into adulthood.

Shelley continued to write poetry over the next two years, including *To a Sky-Lark,* and *Adonais,* an elegy for Keats, representing him as a martyr to vicious, politically motivated re-views. Increasingly identifying with this myth himself, and despairing of his bid for poetic fame, in 1821 he began his *Defence of Poetry* (published posthumously by Mary in 1840), in which he set forth his views on the relation of poets both to their immediate social and historical circum-stances and to the "Eternity" that authorized their visions and would vindicate their merits. He was also becoming infatuated with Jane Williams, who with her common-law husband Edward had joined their circle in Pisa, Italy. The Williamses and the Shelleys decided to live together on the Bay of Spezia in the summer of 1822. More and more alienated from Mary, who was under-standably moody (pregnant for the fifth time in six years and still grieving for her first three chil-dren), Percy frequently left her behind to enjoy excursions with the Williamses or Jane alone. He was charmed by their company, jealous of their relationship, and in love with Jane, to whom he addressed a set of beautiful lyrics interwoven with his affection for her, his resentment of Edward, and his withdrawal from Mary. Mary suffered a nearly fatal miscarriage in June. In July, Percy and Edward sailed to Leghorn to greet Leigh Hunt, who was joining Shelley and Byron in Italy to es-tablish *The Liberal,* a journal of opinion and the arts. On the sail back, Percy and Edward were caught in a sudden storm, and both drowned. Byron wrote to his publisher, sponsor of the most influential Tory periodical of the day, *The Quarterly Review* (which had savaged Shelley): "You are all brutally mistaken about Shelley who was without exception—the *best* and least selfish man I ever knew.—I never knew one who was not a beast in comparison." Whether or not one shares this judgment of the man, Shelley's accomplishment as an artist has always compelled ad-miration. Wordsworth, who thought him too fantastic by half and who was famously sparing in praise of other poets, judged Shelley "one of the best *artists* of us all . . . in workmanship of style."

The opening of *Prometheus Unbound* is included in "*Manfred* and Its Time," pages 398–99.

To Wordsworth[1]

Poet of Nature, thou hast wept to know
That things depart which never may return:

---

1. By 1816 Wordsworth had abandoned the radicalism of his youth and was inclined to spiritual rather than political remedies, a view frequently voiced in his long poem, *The Excursion* (1814). Now in a government patronage position, he was supporting conservative (Tory) politics. Deploying a form dear to Wordsworth, Shelley's sonnet interweaves several critical allusions to his early poetry, including his "Intimations" Ode (lines 9, 56–57) and his sonnet *London, 1802.*

Childhood and youth, friendship, and love's first glow,
Have fled like sweet dreams, leaving thee to mourn.
5   These common woes I feel. One loss is mine,
Which thou too feel'st, yet I alone deplore.[2]
Thou wert as a lone star whose light did shine
On some frail bark in winter's midnight roar:
Thou hast like to a rock-built refuge stood
10   Above the blind and battling multitude:
In honoured poverty thy voice did weave
Songs consecrate to truth and liberty.[3]
Deserting these, thou leavest me to grieve,
Thus having been, that thou shouldst cease to be.[4]

1816

Mont Blanc
Lines Written in the Vale of Chamouni[1]

1

The everlasting universe of things
Flows through the mind, and rolls its rapid waves,
Now dark—now glittering—now reflecting gloom—
Now lending splendour, where from secret springs
5   The source of human thought its tribute brings
Of waters,—with a sound but half its own,
Such as a feeble brook will oft assume
In the wild woods, among the mountains lone,
Where waterfalls around it leap for ever,
10   Where woods and winds contend, and a vast river
Over its rocks ceaselessly bursts and raves.[2]

2

Thus thou, Ravine of Arve—dark, deep Ravine—
Thou many-coloured, many-voiced vale,
Over whose pines and crags and caverns sail
15   Fast cloud-shadows and sunbeams: awful° scene,   awesome
Where Power in likeness of the Arve comes down

---

2. Lament, disparage.
3. *Sonnets Dedicated to Liberty* (including *London, 1802*) was a subsection of Wordsworth's *Poems* of 1807.
4. A potentially satiric echo of *Song* ("She dwelt among th'untrodden ways"), "Lucy ceased to be" (10).
1. At nearly 16,000 ft. Mont Blanc, in the French Alps, is the highest peak in Europe, a must-see on everyone's Grand Tour as the epitome of "the sublime"; its summit had been attained only a few times by 1816. In Mary's *History of a Six Weeks' Tour*, Percy said the poem "was composed under the immediate impression of the deep and powerful feelings excited by the objects which it attempts to describe; and, as an undisciplined overflowing of the soul, rests its claim to approbation on an attempt to imitate the untamable wildness and inaccessible solemnity from which those feelings sprang." The "imitation" involves a dizzying play of imagery and language: wildly dilated and

piled-up syntaxes, dazzling verbal transformations and a welter of sublime negatives (*unknown, infinite, unearthly, unfathomable, viewless*). Amid this drama, Shelley poses questions of the mind's ability to perceive and comprehend transcendent power, and ultimately its existence. He portrays the perceiving "mind" with metaphors drawn from the scene before him, as he stands on a bridge over the River Arve, a deep ravine, and the valley below, the mountain and glacier above. Echoing with a difference Wordsworth's love for "all the mighty world / Of eye, and ear,—both what they half create, / And what perceive; / well pleased to recognise / In nature and the language of the sense / The anchor of my purest thoughts" (*Tintern Abbey* 105–109), Shelley alludes to and contests this philosophy of "Nature."
2. Echoing Coleridge's *Kubla Khan* (1816) 17–21; the landscape of this poem also appears at 122.

From the ice gulphs that gird his secret throne,
Bursting thro' these dark mountains like the flame
Of lightning through the tempest;—thou dost lie,—
20 Thy giant brood of pines around thee clinging,
Children of elder° time, in whose devotion   *older and earlier*
The chainless winds still come and ever came
To drink their odours, and their mighty swinging
To hear, an old and solemn harmony;
25 Thine earthly rainbows stretched across the sweep
Of the ethereal waterfall, whose veil
Robes some unsculptured image;[3] the strange sleep
Which, when the voices of the desart fail,
Wraps all in its own deep eternity;—
30 Thy caverns echoing to the Arve's commotion,
A loud, lone sound no other sound can tame;
Thou art pervaded with that ceaseless motion
Thou art the path of that unresting sound—
Dizzy Ravine! and when I gaze on thee
35 I seem as in a trance sublime and strange
To muse on my own separate phantasy,°   *fantasy, delusion*
My own, my human mind, which passively
Now renders and receives fast influencings,
Holding an unremitting interchange
40 With the clear universe of things around;
One legion of wild thoughts, whose wandering wings
Now float above thy darkness, and now rest
Where that° or thou° art no unbidden guest,   *thy darkness / ravine*
In the still cave of the witch Poesy,
45 Seeking among the shadows that pass by,
Ghosts of all things that are, some shade of thee,
Some phantom, some faint image; till the breast
From which they fled recalls them, thou art there![4]

                              3
Some say that gleams of a remoter world
50 Visit the soul in sleep,[5]—that death is slumber,
And that its shapes the busy thoughts outnumber
Of those who wake and live.—I look on high;
Has some unknown omnipotence unfurled
The veil of life and death?[6] or do I lie
55 In dream, and does the mightier world of sleep
Spread far around and inaccessibly
Its circles? For the very spirit fails,

3. Rocks behind the waterfall.
4. Plato's allegory in *Republic* 7 compares the mind to a cave in which our sense of reality consists of the shadows cast by firelight on its walls, ignorant of the light of "Reality" outside. Shelley's difficult syntax blurs the distinction of inner and outer, human mind and Ravine.
5. Revising Wordsworth's philosophy of Platonic amnesia in stanza 5 of the "Intimations" Ode, Shelley offers the idea that this spiritual reality is not forgotten but visits the soul in sleep.
6. The screen of phenomena separating physical from spiritual reality (lifted in sleep, in daydreams and visions); see *Lift not the painted veil*, page 476.

Driven like a homeless cloud from steep to steep
That vanishes among the viewless° gales!   *unseeing, invisible*
60   Far, far above, piercing the infinite sky,
Mont Blanc appears,—still, snowy, and serene—
Its subject mountains their unearthly forms
Pile around it, ice and rock; broad vales between
Of frozen floods, unfathomable deeps,
65   Blue as the overhanging heaven, that spread
And wind among the accumulated steeps;
A desert peopled by the storms alone,
Save° when the eagle brings some hunter's bone,   *except*
And the wolf tracts° her there—how hideously   *tracks, traces*
70   Its shapes are heaped around! rude, bare, and high,
Ghastly, and scarred, and riven.°—Is this the scene   *split*
Where the old Earthquake-dæmon[7] taught her young
Ruin? Were these their toys? or did a sea
Of fire, envelope once this silent snow?
75   None can reply—all seems eternal now.
The wilderness has a mysterious tongue
Which teaches awful doubt,° or faith so mild,   *awe-filled questioning*
So solemn, so serene, that man may be
But for such faith, with nature reconciled.[8]
80   Thou hast a voice, great Mountain, to repeal
Large codes of fraud and woe; not understood
By all, but which the wise and great and good
Interpret, or make felt, or deeply feel.

4

The fields, the lakes, the forests, and the streams,
85   Ocean, and all the living things that dwell
Within the daedal[9] earth, lightning, and rain,
Earthquake, and fiery flood, and hurricane,
The torpor of the year when feeble dreams
Visit the hidden buds, or dreamless sleep
90   Holds every future leaf and flower;—the bound
With which from that detested trance they leap;
The works and ways of man, their death and birth,
And that of him, and all that his may be;
All things that move and breathe with toil and sound
95   Are born and die; revolve, subside, and swell.
Power dwells apart in its tranquillity
Remote, serene, and inaccessible:
And *this*, the naked countenance of earth,

7. In Greek mythology daemons are (often playful) spirits, usually personifications of natural forces.
8. Shelley first wrote "In such wise faith with Nature
reconciled," then revised to "But for such faith" and
lowercased "nature." The sense is ambiguous: "But for"
may indicate "Only by means of" faith in Nature, over
the "Large codes of fraud and woe" promulgated by

institutional religions (81). Or it may mean "Except for":
a bland faith in a nature that is unknowable and perhaps
indifferent to human needs and values is, paradoxically,
no faith.
9. From Daedalus, architect of the famous labyrinth in
Crete, and of wings for flight crafted with feathers and
wax; hence, a wonderfully wrought, inspired creation.

On which I gaze, even these primaeval mountains
100 Teach the adverting mind. The glaciers creep
Like snakes that watch their prey, from their far fountains,
Slow rolling on; there, many a precipice,
Frost and the Sun in scorn of mortal power
Have piled: dome, pyramid, and pinnacle,
105 A city of death, distinct with many a tower
And wall impregnable of beaming ice.
Yet not a city, but a flood of ruin
Is there, that from the boundary of the sky
Rolls its perpetual stream; vast pines are strewing
110 Its destined path, or in the mangled soil
Branchless and shattered stand: the rocks, drawn down
From yon remotest waste, have overthrown
The limits of the dead and living world,
Never to be reclaimed. The dwelling-place
115 Of insects, beasts, and birds, becomes its spoil;
Their food and their retreat for ever gone,
So much of life and joy is lost. The race
Of man, flies far in dread; his work and dwelling
Vanish, like smoke before the tempest's stream,
120 And their place is not known.[1] Below, vast caves
Shine in the rushing torrent's restless gleam,
Which from those secret chasms in tumult welling
Meet in the vale, and one majestic River,
The breath and blood of distant lands, for ever
125 Rolls its loud waters to the ocean waves,
Breathes its swift vapours to the circling air.

5

Mont Blanc yet gleams on high:—the power is there,
The still and solemn power, of many sights,
And many sounds, and much of life and death.
130 In the calm darkness of the moonless nights,
In the lone glare of day, the snows descend
Upon that Mountain; none beholds them there,
Nor when the flakes burn in the sinking sun,
Or the star-beams dart through them:—Winds contend
135 Silently there, and heap the snow with breath
Rapid and strong, but silently! Its home
The voiceless lightning in these solitudes
Keeps innocently, and like vapour broods
Over the snow. The secret strength of things
140 Which governs thought, and to the infinite dome
Of heaven is as a law, inhabits thee!
And what were thou,° and earth, and stars, and sea,   *Mont Blanc*

---

1. Echoing Psalm 103: "As for man, his days are as grass . . . For the wind passeth over it, and it is gone; and the place thereof shall know it no more" (15–16).

If to the human mind's imaginings
Silence and solitude were vacancy?

23 July 1816   1817

Hymn to Intellectual Beauty[1]

1

The awful° shadow of some unseen Power   *awe-inspiring*
    Floats, though unseen, amongst us, visiting
    This various world with as inconstant wing
As summer winds that creep from flower to flower.—
5   Like moonbeams that behind some piny mountain shower,°   *(verb)*
    It visits with inconstant glance
    Each human heart and countenance;
Like hues and harmonies of evening,—
    Like clouds in starlight widely spread,—
10   Like memory of music fled,—
    Like aught that for its grace may be
Dear, and yet dearer for its mystery.

2

Spirit of BEAUTY, that dost consecrate
    With thine own hues all thou dost shine upon
15   Of human thought or form,—where art thou gone?
Why dost thou pass away, and leave our state,
This dim vast vale of tears, vacant and desolate?—
    Ask why the sunlight not for ever
    Weaves rainbows o'er yon mountain river;
20   Why aught should fail and fade that once is shown;
    Why fear and dream and death and birth
    Cast on the daylight of this earth
    Such gloom,—why man has such a scope
For love and hate, despondency and hope?

3

25   No voice from some sublimer world hath ever
    To sage or poet these responses given—
    Therefore the names of God and ghost and Heaven,
Remain the records of their° vain endeavour,   *sages and poets*
Frail spells[2]—whose uttered charm might not avail to sever
30   From all we hear and all we see,
    Doubt, chance, and mutability.
Thy light alone like mist o'er mountains driven,
    Or music by the night wind sent
    Through strings of some still instrument,[3]

---

1. Composed the same summer as *Mont Blanc* (1816), *Hymn* shares its metaphysics. "Intellectual" refers to the ideal Spirit apprehended by the mind, over the faint and fleeting information of the senses; Shelley may have taken this term from Wollstonecraft's lament in *Rights of Woman* over the low cultural esteem of women's "intellectual beauty" (ch. 3). As in *Mont Blanc*, "unseen Power" is evoked by a language of negation, questions, and merely proximate similes.
2. The languages of institutional religion.

35   Or moonlight on a midnight stream,
Gives grace and truth to life's unquiet dream.

4

Love, Hope, and Self-esteem, like clouds depart
     And come, for some uncertain moments lent.
     Man were° immortal, and omnipotent,   *would be*
40   Didst thou,° unknown and awful as thou art,   *if thou didst*
Keep with thy glorious train firm state within his heart.
          Thou messenger of sympathies
          That wax and wane in lovers' eyes—
Thou, that to human thought art nourishment,
45   Like darkness to a dying flame![4]
          Depart not—as thy shadow came:
          Depart not, lest the grave should be,
Like life and fear, a dark reality!

5

While yet a boy, I sought for ghosts, and sped
50   Through many a listening chamber, cave and ruin,
          And starlight wood, with fearful steps pursuing
Hopes of high talk with the departed dead.[5]
I called on poisonous names with which our youth is fed.[6]
          I was not heard—I saw them not—
55   When musing deeply on the lot
Of life at that sweet time when winds are wooing
          All vital things that wake to bring
          News of birds and blossoming,—
          Sudden, thy shadow fell on me;
60   I shrieked, and clasped my hands in exstasy!

6

I vowed that I would dedicate my powers
     To thee and thine—have I not kept the vow?
     With beating heart and streaming eyes, even now
I call the phantoms of a thousand hours
65   Each from his voiceless grave: they have in visioned bowers
          Of studious zeal or love's delight
          Outwatched with me the envious night—
They know that never joy illumed my brow
          Unlinked with hope that thou wouldst free
70   This world from its dark slavery,
          That thou, O awful LOVELINESS,
Wouldst give whate'er these words cannot express.

3. An aeolian or "wind" harp; see Coleridge's *The Eolian Harp*.
4. Darkness offsets its glow, even as the flame ultimately dies into darkness.
5. Evoking Wordsworth's shadowy recollection in the "Intimations" Ode of a boyhood sense of a spiritual reality behind the veil of phenomena; see lines 141–147 (page 276). Shelley is referring to boyhood experiments in conjuration.
6. The vocabulary for divinity in institutional religions.

7

The day becomes more solemn and serene
    When noon is past—there is a harmony
75   In autumn, and a lustre in its sky,
Which through the summer is not heard or seen,
As if it could not be, as if it had not been!
    Thus let thy power, which like the truth
    Of Nature on my passive youth
80 Descended, to my onward life supply
    Its calm—to one who worships thee,
    And every form containing thee,
    Whom, SPIRIT fair, thy spells did bind
To fear° himself, and love all humankind.   *revere, fear for*

1816   1817

Ozymandias[1]

I met a traveller from an antique land
Who said: "Two vast and trunkless° legs of stone   *lacking a torso*
Stand in the desert. . . . Near them on the sand,
Half sunk, a shattered visage° lies, whose frown,   *face*
5 And wrinkled lip, and sneer of cold command,
Tell that its sculptor well those passions read
Which yet survive, stamped on these lifeless things,
The hand that mocked them, and the heart that fed.[2]
And on the pedestal, these words appear:
10 "My name is Ozymandias, King of Kings:
Look on my works, ye Mighty, and despair!"[3]
Nothing beside remains. Round the decay
Of that colossal[4] Wreck, boundless and bare,
The lone and level sands stretch far away."

1817   1818

Sonnet: Lift not the painted veil[1]

Lift not the painted veil which those who live
Call Life: though unreal shapes be pictured there,
And it but mimic all we would believe
With colours idly spread,—behind, lurk Fear
5 And Hope, twin Destinies; who ever weave

1. Ozymandias (the Greek name for Ramses II) reigned 1292–1225 B.C.; he is thought to be the pharaoh of Exodus whom Moses challenged. The story of the statue and its inscription is taken from the Greek historian Diodorus Siculus, 1st century B.C.
2. The sculptor read well those passions that survive his hand and the tyrant's heart; "mocked": "imitated," with a sense of caricature or derision. The passions survive in modern tyrants. Shelley published this sonnet in 1818 in Leigh Hunt's radical paper, *The Examiner*.
3. According to Diodorus, this is the actual boast; by Shelley's time, its language echoes ironically against the subsequent application of this title to Christ.
4. An adjective derived from "colossus," the term in antiquity for any large statue; there were several such of 50 to 60 feet in height in ancient Egypt. Shelley is also recalling the depiction of Julius Caesar by one of the conspirators in his assassination: "he doth bestride the narrow world / Like a Colossus" (*Julius Caesar* 1.2.135–36).
1. The veil is all the visual (and all sensory) phenomena normally called "Life."

Their shadows, o'er the chasm, sightless and drear.
I knew one who had lifted it—he sought,
For his lost heart was tender, things to love,
But found them not, alas! nor was there aught
10   The world contains, the which he could approve.
Through the unheeding many he did move,
A splendour among shadows, a bright blot
Upon this gloomy scene, a Spirit that strove
For truth, and like the Preacher found it not.[2]

1818   1824

Sonnet: England in 1819[1]

An old, mad, blind, despised, and dying King,—
Princes, the dregs of their dull race, who flow
Through public scorn,—mud from a muddy spring,—
Rulers who neither see nor feel nor know,
5   But leechlike to their fainting country cling,
Till they drop, blind in blood, without a blow,—
A people starved and stabbed in the untilled field,[2]—
An army, which liberticide[3] and prey
Make as a two-edged sword to all who wield;—
10   Golden and sanguine laws which tempt and slay;[4]
Religion Christless, Godless, a book sealed;
A Senate,—Time's worst statute unrepealed,[5]—
Are graves from which a glorious Phantom[6] may
Burst, to illumine our tempestuous day.

1819   1839

Ode to the West Wind[1]

1

O wild West Wind, thou breath of Autumn's being,
Thou from whose unseen presence the leaves dead
Are driven like ghosts from an enchanter fleeing,

---

2. The refrain of the Preacher of Ecclesiastes, "all is vanity and vexation of spirit." Shelley's first draft read, "I should be happier had I ne'er known / This mournful man—he was himself alone."

1. Unpublishable in 1819 for its probable libel; first printed in Mary Shelley's edition of 1839 (when George III was long dead). George III, king since 1760, had been declared insane in 1811, when his son became Prince Regent. The first line echoes Lear's self-description on the heath: "a poor, infirm, weak, and despised old man" (3.3.20); *King Lear* was kept out of production by the Examiner of Plays because of its suggestion of George III. George III's sons were notoriously dissolute, given to sexual scandal, gluttony, gambling, outrageous expenditure, and taking bribes for army commissions.

2. The "Peterloo Massacre," 16 August 1819.

3. Liberty-killing; normally a term for a tyrant (*Adonais* 32), this is the first use in this sense noted by OED.

4. Laws procured with gold and enacted with bloodshed; *Mask of Anarchy*, 65, 298.

5. Referring to the exclusion of most citizens, including Catholics, Dissenters, women, and workers, from representation in Parliament.

6. The spirit of revolt and revolution.

1. There is a tradition, as old as the Bible, of wind as metaphor of life and inspiration—particularly the West Wind as harbinger of future seasons, events, and transformations, not only in weather, but by symbolic extension, in emotional, spiritual, and political life. The Latin for "wind," *spiritus*, also means "breath" (1) and soul or spirit (13, 61–62), as well as being the root-word for "inspiration" (a taking-in of energy). The ode is in terza rima sonnet stanzas.

Yellow, and black, and pale, and hectic° red,   *feverish*
5   Pestilence-stricken multitudes!² O Thou
Who chariotest to their dark wintry bed

The winged seeds, where they lie cold and low,
Each like a corpse within its grave, until
Thine azure sister of the Spring° shall blow   *spring wind*

10   Her clarion° o'er the dreaming earth, and fill   *shrill trumpet*
(Driving sweet buds like flocks to feed in air)
With living hues and odours plain and hill:

Wild Spirit, which art moving everywhere;
Destroyer and Preserver;³ hear, O hear!

2

15   Thou on whose stream, mid the steep sky's commotion,
Loose clouds like earth's decaying leaves are shed,
Shook from the tangled boughs of heaven and ocean,

Angels° of rain and lightning! there are spread   *messengers*
On the blue surface of thine airy surge,
20   Like the bright hair uplifted from the head

Of some fierce Maenad, even from the dim verge
Of the horizon to the zenith's height,
The locks of the approaching storm.⁴ Thou dirge°   *funeral chant*

Of the dying year, to which this closing night
25   Will be the dome of a vast sepulchre,
Vaulted with all thy congregated might

Of vapours, from whose solid atmosphere
Black rain, and fire, and hail, will burst: Oh hear!

3

Thou who didst waken from his summer dreams
30   The blue Mediterranean, where he lay,
Lulled by the coil of his crystalline streams,

Beside a pumice° isle in Baiae's bay,   *volcanic*
And saw in sleep old palaces and towers
Quivering within the wave's intenser day,

35   All overgrown with azure moss, and flowers
So sweet, the sense faints picturing them!⁵ Thou
For whose path the Atlantic's level powers

2. A traditional epic simile (Milton, Dante, Virgil) compares the dead to wind-driven fallen leaves.
3. Titles for major Hindu gods, Siva the Destroyer and Vishnu the Preserver.
4. The Greek god of wine Bacchus was attended by Maenads, female votaries who danced in wild worship. Viewing a sculpture of them in Florence, Shelley commented: "The tremendous spirit of superstition aided by drunkenness . . .

seems to have caught them in its whirlwinds, and to bear them over the earth as the rapid volutions of a tempest have the ever-changing trunk of a water-spout. . . . Their hair, loose and floating, seems caught in tempest of their own tumultuous motion." Associated with vegetation, Bacchus was fabled to die in the autumn and be reborn in the spring.
5. Ruins of imperial Roman villas in the Bay of Baiae, west of Naples.

Cleave themselves into chasms, while far below
The sea-blooms and the oozy woods which wear
40   The sapless foliage of the ocean, know

Thy voice, and suddenly grow grey with fear,
And tremble and despoil themselves:[6] O hear!

4

If I were a dead leaf thou mightest bear;
If I were a swift cloud to fly with thee;
45   A wave to pant beneath thy power, and share

The impulse of thy strength, only less free
Than thou, O uncontrollable! if even
I were as in my boyhood, and could be

The comrade of thy wanderings over heaven,
50   As then, when to outstrip thy skiey speed
Scarce seemed a vision,—I would ne'er have striven

As thus with thee in prayer in my sore need.
Oh lift me as a wave, a leaf, a cloud!
I fall upon the thorns of life![7] I bleed!

55   A heavy weight of hours has chained and bowed
One too like thee—tameless, and swift, and proud.

5

Make me thy lyre,[8] even as the forest is:
What if my leaves are falling like its own?
The tumult of thy mighty harmonies

60   Will take from both a deep autumnal tone,
Sweet though in sadness. Be thou, Spirit fierce,
My spirit! Be thou me, impetuous one![9]

Drive my dead thoughts over the universe,
Like withered leaves, to quicken a new birth;
65   And, by the incantation of this verse,

Scatter, as from an unextinguished hearth
Ashes and sparks, my words among mankind!
Be through my lips to unawakened earth

The trumpet of a prophecy! O Wind,
70   If Winter comes, can Spring be far behind?
1819   1820

---

6. In a note, Shelley says he is alluding to the seasonal change (despoiling) of seaweed, a process he imagines as instigated by the autumn wind.
7. A risky self-comparison to Jesus's torture by a crown of thorns; see also *Adonais* 305–306, page 493.

8. A wind-harp, an image used again in *A Defence* (page 505), and in Coleridge's *The Eolian Harp*.
9. Shelley hazards the ungrammatical objective case ("me" instead of "I") not only to chime with "Be" but also to represent himself as an object.

To a Sky-Lark

Hail to thee, blithe Spirit!
   Bird thou never wert—
That from Heaven or near it
   Pourest thy full heart
5 In profuse strains of unpremeditated art.[1]

Higher still and higher
   From the earth thou springest,
Like a cloud of fire;
   The blue deep thou wingest,
10 And singing still dost soar, and soaring ever singest.

In the golden lightning
   Of the sunken sun,
O'er which clouds are bright'ning,
   Thou dost float and run,
15 Like an unbodied joy whose race is just begun.

The pale purple even°   *evening*
   Melts around thy flight;
Like a star of Heaven,
   In the broad daylight
20 Thou art unseen, but yet I hear thy shrill delight—

Keen as are the arrows
   Of that silver sphere°   *morning star*
Whose intense lamp narrows
   In the white dawn clear
25 Until we hardly see—we feel, that it is there.

All the earth and air
   With thy voice is loud,
As, when night is bare,
   From one lonely cloud
30 The moon rains out her beams, and Heaven is overflowed.

What thou art we know not;
   What is most like thee?
From rainbow clouds there flow not
   Drops so bright to see
35 As from thy presence showers a rain of melody:—

Like a Poet hidden
   In the light of thought,
Singing hymns unbidden,
   Till the world is wrought
40 To sympathy with hopes and fears it heeded not:

1. The skylark sings only in flight; Shelley evokes Milton's thanks to his "Celestial patroness," who "inspires / Easy [his] unpremeditated Verse" (*Paradise Lost* 9.21–24).

Like a high-born maiden
   In a palace tower,
Soothing her love-laden
   Soul in secret hour
45 With music sweet as love which overflows her bower:

Like a glow-worm golden
   In a dell of dew,
Scattering unbeholden
   Its aerial hue
50 Among the flowers and grass which screen it from the view:

Like a rose embowered
   In its own green leaves,
By warm winds deflowered,
   Till the scent it gives
55 Makes faint with too much sweet these heavy-winged thieves:

Sound of vernal° showers   *springtime*
   On the twinkling grass,
Rain-awakened flowers,
   All that ever was,
60 Joyous and clear and fresh,—thy music doth surpass.

Teach us, Sprite° or Bird,   *spirit, fairy*
   What sweet thoughts are thine:
I have never heard
   Praise of love or wine
65 That panted forth a flood of rapture so divine.

Chorus Hymeneal°   *wedding song*
   Or triumphal° chaunt,   *military*
Matched with thine, would be all
   But an empty vaunt—
70 A thing wherein we feel there is some hidden want.

What objects are the fountains
   Of thy happy strain?
What fields, or waves, or mountains?
   What shapes of sky or plain?
75 What love of thine own kind? what ignorance of pain?

With thy clear keen joyance
   Languor cannot be:
Shadow of annoyance
   Never came near thee:
80 Thou lovest—but ne'er knew love's sad satiety.°   *(over)fullness*

Waking or asleep,
   Thou of death must deem
Things more true and deep
   Than we mortals dream,
85 Or how could thy notes flow in such a crystal stream?

We look before and after,[2]
   And pine for what is not:
Our sincerest laughter
   With some pain is fraught;
90   Our sweetest songs are those that tell of saddest thought.

Yet if we could scorn
   Hate and pride and fear,
If we were things born
   Not to shed a tear,
95   I know not how thy joy we ever should come near.

Better than all measures
   Of delightful sound,
Better than all treasures
   That in books are found,
100   Thy skill to poet were, thou scorner of the ground!

Teach me half the gladness
   That thy brain must know,
Such harmonious madness[3]
   From my lips would flow
105   The world should listen then—as I am listening now.
1820   1820

To ———

Music, when soft voices die,
Vibrates in the memory;
Odours, when sweet violets sicken,
Live within the sense they quicken;°   *enliven*

5   Rose-leaves, when the rose is dead,
Are heaped for the beloved's bed;
And so thy thoughts, when thou art gone,
Love itself shall slumber on.
1821   1824

ADONAIS Shelley was only casually acquainted with Keats, but was impressed by his poetry and pained by his abuse in the Tory press for his political sentiments. When he and Mary Shelley learned of Keats's failing health, they invited him to Italy as their guest; Keats went first to Rome for treatment, and he died there after a few months, in February 1821. Shelley had heard that his demise was brought on by the vicious reviews of his poetry that began to appear in 1818, capped by ridicule of *Endymion* in the chief Tory periodical, *The Quarterly Review*, which had also cut into Shelley. Shelley's intent in *Adonais* is both to honor its subject (the protocol of elegy) and to wage his own polemic against the reviews. Deploying Spenserian stanzas (Keats's verse form in *The Eve of St. Agnes*) and classical allusions, he fashioned a self-advertising, "highly wrought

---

2. Echoing Hamlet's comment on the human capability of "looking before and after" (*Hamlet* 4.4.36), as well as alluding to Wordsworth's use of this phrase in Preface to *Lyrical Ballads* (see page 204).

3. Echoing Wordsworth's rhyme in *Resolution and Independence*: "We Poets in our youth begin in gladness; / But thereof come in the end despondency and madness" (48–49). See also the last lines of Coleridge's *Kubla Khan*.

piece of art." As in his other angry poems, Shelley took risks, notably with stanza 34, a daring self-portrait in the combined figure of tormented Christ and branded Cain. Though he had expected a drubbing from the Tory press, he was crushed when the poem did not sell well. Enough of the poem was quoted in the first reviews, however, to launch the legend of Keats's death, which proved durable: until the late 1840s, Keats was known more widely by *Adonais* than by his own poetry. Using the standard pattern of "pastoral elegy" (the call to mourning; the grieving accusation in the invocation of the muse; the sympathy of nature with the death; the procession of mourners; the turn from grief to consolation), Shelley develops a master-myth: a "beautiful," "frail," "defenceless" poet fatally savaged, and vindicated in "Eternity"—a judgment Shelley means for himself as well. So disdainful is he of a world where "*We* decay / Like corpses in a charnel," that *Adonais* strains the traditional obligation of elegy to reconcile mourners to death, all but recommending escape to the world beyond: "Die, / If thou wouldst be with that which thou dost seek!" In an elegiac tribute to a friend and former band member (Brian Jones) at a huge concert in Hyde Park, London, Mick Jagger read part of this famous stanza in a tone of celebration.

Shelley's investment in Keats received fresh credit when he drowned in a storm at sea a little over a year after publishing *Adonais*. "Who but will regard as a prophecy the last stanza?" Mary Shelley wrote in a note in her 1839 edition; the poem now seemed "more applicable to Shelley, than to the young and gifted poet whom he mourned. The poetic view he takes of death, and the lofty scorn he displays towards his calumniators, are as a prophecy on his own destiny, when received among immortal names, and the poisonous breath of critics has vanished into emptiness before the fame he inherits." The double applications involve some weirdly textual elements. When Shelley's ravaged corpse washed ashore, a friend identified it by a copy of Keats's 1820 volume in the coat pocket, which he knew Shelley had taken with him. Then, after a cremation in which Shelley's heart, hardened by calcium, did not burn, this same friend snatched it from the embers and presented it to Mary Shelley, who kept it thereafter in her desk, wrapped in a copy of *Adonais*.

Adonais
An Elegy on the Death of John Keats, Author of Endymion, Hyperion, Etc.

Ἀστὴρ πρὶν μὲν ἔλαμπες ἐνὶ ζωοῖσιν Ἐῴος·
νῦν δὲ θανὼν λάμπεις Ἕσπερος ἐν φθιμένοις.

Plato[1]

Preface

Φάρμακον ἦλθε, Βίων, ποτὶ σὸν στόμα, φάρμακον εἶδες.
πως τεν τοῖς χείλεσσι ποτέδραμε, κοὐκ ἐγλυκάνθη;
τίς δὲ βροτὸς τοσσοῦτον ἀνάμερος ἢ κεράσαι τοι,
ἢ δοῦναι λαλέοντι τὸ φάρμακον; ἔκφυγεν ᾠδάν.

Moschus, Epitaph. Bion[2]

1. "Thou wert the morning star among the living, / Ere thy fair light had fled; / Now, having died, thou art as Hesperus, giving / New splendour to the dead"; Shelley's translation of *Epigram on Aster* by Plato; Aster (Star) was a young man whom he loved. Hesperus is the evening star; it and the morning star are really the planet Venus. Shelley's Greek texts for both epigraphs designate an elite audience.
2. From *Lament for Bion*: "Poison came, Bion, to thy mouth; thou didst know poison. To such lips as thine did it come, and was not sweetened? What mortal was so cruel that could mix poison for thee, or give thee venom, who heard thy voice? Surely he had no music in his soul." The next line, which Shelley does not quote, is "Yet justice overtakes all." As this Preface makes clear, Bion is Keats, and his poison, the reviews. Moschus (2nd century B.C.) also wrote a *Lament for Adonis*.

It is my intention to subjoin to the London edition[3] of this poem a criticism upon the claims of its lamented object to be classed among the writers of the highest genius who have adorned our age. My known repugnance to the narrow principles of taste on which several of his earlier compositions were modelled proves at least that I am an impartial judge. I consider the fragment of *Hyperion* as second to nothing that was ever produced by a writer of the same years.[4]

John Keats died at Rome of a consumption, in his twenty-fourth year, on the [23rd] of [February] 1821; and was buried in the romantic and lonely cemetery of the protestants in that city, under the pyramid which is the tomb of Cestius, and the massy walls and towers, now mouldering and desolate, which formed the circuit of ancient Rome. The cemetery is an open space among the ruins, covered in winter with violets and daisies. It might make one in love with death to think that one should be buried in so sweet a place.[5]

The genius of the lamented person to whose memory I have dedicated these unworthy verses was not less delicate and fragile than it was beautiful; and, where canker-worms abound, what wonder if its young flower was blighted in the bud? The savage criticism on his *Endymion* which appeared in the *Quarterly Review* produced the most violent effect on his susceptible mind.[6] The agitation thus originated ended in the rupture of a blood-vessel in the lungs; a rapid consumption ensued; and the succeeding acknowledgements, from more candid critics,[7] of the true greatness of his powers, were ineffectual to heal the wound thus wantonly inflicted.

It may be well said that these wretched men know not what they do.[8] They scatter their insults and their slanders without heed as to whether the poisoned shaft lights on a heart made callous by many blows, or one, like Keats's, composed of more penetrable stuff.[9] One of their associates is, to my knowledge, a most base and unprincipled calumniator. As to *Endymion*, was it a poem, whatever might be its defects, to be treated contemptuously by those who had celebrated with various degrees of complacency and panegyric *Paris*, and *Woman*, and *A Syrian Tale*, and Mrs. Lefanu, and Mr. Barret, and Mr. Howard Payne, and a long list of the illustrious obscure? Are these the men who, in their venal good-nature, presumed to draw a parallel between the Rev. Mr. Milman and Lord Byron?[1] What gnat did they strain at here, after having swallowed all those camels? Against what woman taken in adultery

---

3. *Adonais* was printed in Pisa, Italy, in 1821; although the London reviews quoted it extensively, its first English edition did not appear until 1829.

4. The fragment of *Hyperion* published in Keats's 1820 volume was written in late 1819, around his twenty-fourth birthday. The "narrow principles of taste" were voiced chiefly in *Sleep and Poetry*, the final poem in his harshly reviewed debut volume of 1817.

5. The Shelleys' son William, who died in Rome in 1819 at age three, is buried there, as would be Shelley himself in 1822. Shelley is echoing Keats's *Ode to a Nightingale:* "I have been half in love with easeful Death" (line 52).

6. Shelley believed the reviewer of *Endymion* for *The Quarterly Review* (April 1818) to have been Poet Laureate Robert Southey (now a Tory); it was actually John Wilson Croker (the savager of Barbauld's *Eighteen Hundred and Eleven*). Croker was less unkind than others (e.g., *Blackwood's*), but *The Quarterly's* wide circulation, influence, and establishment credentials made its voice the most damaging—to Shelley and others, as well as to Keats.

7. Francis Jeffrey, for example, gave a favorable review to Keats's 1820 volume in the *Edinburgh Review*.

8. Jesus's exculpation of his crucifiers, "Father, forgive them; for they know not what they do" (Luke 23.34).

9. An allusion both to Hamlet's sneer at his remarried mother—whether her heart is insensitive, or "made of penetrable stuff" (*Hamlet* 3.4.36–40)—and to Byron's use of this phrase in *English Bards and Scotch Reviewers*, when he warns his hostile reviewers that "they too are 'penetrable stuff'"; Shelley refers to this poem in stanza 28.

1. Now forgotten writers: *Paris in 1815* (1817) by Rev. George Croly was favorably reviewed in *The Quarterly* (he would go on to write a nasty review of *Adonais*); *The Quarterly* also reviewed *Woman* (1810) by Eaton Stannard Barrett, a Tory wit, and H. Galley Knight's *Ilderim: A Syrian Tale* (1816), and gave favorable reviews to Rev. Henry Hart Milman's *Saviour, Lord of the Bright City* and *Fall of Jerusalem* but drubbed *Brutus* by American dramatist John Howard Payne (who would court the widowed Mary Shelley). Alicia Lefanu wrote *The Flowers* (1809).

dares the foremost of these literary prostitutes to cast his opprobrious stone? Miserable man: you, one of the meanest, have wantonly defaced one of the noblest, specimens of the workmanship of God. Nor shall it be your excuse that, murderer as you are, you have spoken daggers, but used none.[2]

The circumstances of the closing scene of poor Keats's life were not made known to me until the Elegy was ready for the press. I am given to understand that the wound which his sensitive spirit had received from the criticism of *Endymion* was exasperated by the bitter sense of unrequited benefits; the poor fellow seems to have been hooted from the stage of life, no less by those on whom he had wasted the promise of his genius than those on whom he had lavished his fortune and his care. He was accompanied to Rome, and attended in his last illness, by Mr. Severn, a young artist of the highest promise, who, I have been informed, "almost risked his own life, and sacrificed every prospect to unwearied attendance upon his dying friend." Had I known these circumstances before the completion of my poem, I should have been tempted to add my feeble tribute of applause to the more solid recompense which the virtuous man finds in the recollection of his own motives. Mr. Severn can dispense with a reward from "such stuff as dreams are made of."[3] His conduct is a golden augury of the success of his future career. May the unextinguished spirit of his illustrious friend animate the creations of his pencil, and plead against oblivion for his name!

Adonais

I

I weep for Adonais[4]—he is dead!
Oh weep for Adonais, though our tears
Thaw not the frost which binds so dear a head!
And thou, sad Hour° selected from all years   *goddess of the season*
5   To mourn our loss, rouse thy obscure compeers,
And teach them thine own sorrow! Say: "With me
Died Adonais! Till the Future dares
Forget the Past, his fate and fame shall be
An echo and a light unto eternity!"

II

10   Where wert thou, mighty Mother, when he lay,
When thy Son lay, pierced by the shaft which flies
In darkness? Where was lorn° Urania   *forlorn*
When Adonais died?[5] With veilèd eyes,

2. Shelley's pile of allusions are to Jesus's upbraiding of the "blind guides, which strain at a gnat, and swallow a camel" (Matthew 23.24), his challenge to the would-be executioners of the woman taken in adultery (John 8.3–11), and to Hamlet's barely restrained anger at his mother, his intent to "speak daggers to her, but use none" (*Hamlet* 3.2.404). Opprobrious: punitive, bearing public disgrace.
3. Prospero's elegy for his art: "We are such stuff / As dreams are made on, and our little life / Is rounded with a sleep" (*Tempest* 4.1.156–58). Joseph Severn, a painter and friend of Keats, accompanied him to Rome and nursed him in his final months, holding him in his arms as he died.
4. "Adonais" is derived from Adonis, a beautiful youth in classical mythology fatally gored while hunting a boar.

To settle the contention between Venus and Persephone over who should possess him in the afterlife, Zeus decreed that he would spend half the year in the underworld with Persephone and half the year aboveground with Venus—a perpetual death and rebirth reflecting the seasonal cycles of vegetation. Keats treated Venus's love for Adonis in Book 2 of *Endymion*.
5. Urania, the mighty Mother, is the "Heav'nly Muse" of astronomy whom Milton invokes at the opening of *Paradise Lost* (1.6) and in the first line of Book 7. The name is also an epithet of Aphrodite (Venus, the goddess who loved Adonis), "Aphrodite Urania," the heavenly goddess of pure or spiritual love. The fatal shaft images *The Quarterly*'s supposedly fatal review of Keats; "in darkness" refers to its lack of signature.

Mid listening Echoes,° in her Paradise   *personified echoes*
15   She sate, while one,° with soft enamoured breath,   *an Echo*
Rekindled all the fading melodies°   *Keats's poetry*
With which, like flowers that mock the corse beneath,
He had adorned and hid the coming bulk of Death.

III

Oh weep for Adonais—he is dead!
20   Wake, melancholy Mother, wake and weep!—
Yet wherefore? Quench within their burning bed
Thy fiery tears, and let thy loud heart keep
Like his, a mute and uncomplaining sleep;
For he is gone where all things wise and fair
25   Descend. Oh dream not that the amorous Deep°   *abyss*
Will yet restore him to the vital air;
Death feeds on his mute voice, and laughs at our despair.

IV

Most musical of mourners, weep again!
Lament anew, Urania!—He° died   *Milton*
30   Who was the Sire of an immortal strain,
Blind, old, and lonely, when his country's pride,
The priest, the slave, and the liberticide,°   *liberty-killer*
Trampled and mocked with many a loathèd rite
Of lust and blood; he went unterrified
35   Into the gulf of death; but his clear Sprite°   *spirit*
Yet reigns o'er earth, the third among the sons of light.[6]

V

Most musical of mourners, weep anew!
Not all to that bright station dared to climb:
And happier they their happiness who knew,
40   Whose tapers yet burn through that night of time
In which suns perished. Others more sublime,
Struck by the envious wrath of man or god,
Have sunk, extinct in their refulgent° prime;   *radiant*
And some yet live, treading the thorny road
45   Which leads, through toil and hate, to Fame's serene abode.

VI

But now thy youngest, dearest one has perished,
The nursling of thy widowhood, who grew,
Like a pale flower by some sad maiden cherished,
And fed with true-love tears instead of dew.
50   Most musical of mourners, weep anew!
Thy extreme° hope, the loveliest and the last,   *final, highest*
The bloom whose petals, nipped before they blew,°   *blossomed*

---

6. Milton served Cromwell's parliamentary government, which had executed Charles I. After the monarchy was restored in 1660, Milton was imprisoned, heavily fined, and only narrowly escaped the execution suffered by others of Cromwell's party. The other two are Homer and Dante.

Died on the promise of the fruit, is waste;
The broken lily lies—the storm is overpast.

VII

55 To that high Capital° where kingly Death   *Rome*
Keeps his pale court° in beauty and decay   *the cemetery*
He came; and bought, with price of purest breath,
A grave among the eternal.—Come away!
Haste, while the vault of blue Italian day
60 Is yet his fitting charnel-roof, while still
He lies, as if in dewy sleep he lay.
Awake him not! surely he takes his fill
Of deep and liquid rest, forgetful of all ill.

VIII

He will awake no more, oh never more!
65 Within the twilight chamber spreads apace
The shadow of white Death, and at the door
Invisible Corruption waits to trace
His extreme way to her dim dwelling-place;
The eternal Hunger sits, but pity and awe
70 Soothe her pale rage, nor dares she to deface
So fair a prey, till darkness and the law
Of change shall o'er his sleep the mortal curtain draw.

IX

Oh weep for Adonais!—The quick Dreams,°   *living poetry*
The passion-winged Ministers of thought,
75 Who were his flocks, whom near the living streams
Of his young spirit he fed, and whom he taught
The love which was its music, wander not—
Wander no more from kindling brain to brain,
But droop there whence they sprung; and mourn their lot
80 Round the cold heart where, after their sweet pain,
They ne'er will gather strength or find a home again.

X

And one° with trembling hands clasps his cold head,   *of the Dreams*
And fans him with her moonlight wings, and cries,
"Our love, our hope, our sorrow, is not dead!
85 See, on the silken fringe of his faint eyes,
Like dew upon a sleeping flower, there lies
A tear some Dream has loosened from his brain."
Lost Angel of a ruined Paradise!
She knew not 'twas her own,—as with no stain
90 She faded, like a cloud which had outwept its rain.

XI

One from a lucid urn of starry dew
Washed his light limbs, as if embalming them;
Another clipped her profuse locks, and threw
The wreath upon him, like an anadem°   *head-garland*

95   Which frozen tears instead of pearls begem;
        Another in her wilful grief would break
        Her bow and winged reeds,° as if to stem   *arrows*
        A greater loss with one which was more weak,—
And dull the barbed fire against his frozen cheek.

                        XII
100   Another Splendour on his mouth alit,
        That mouth whence it was wont° to draw the breath   *used*
        Which gave it strength to pierce the guarded wit,°   *mind*
        And pass into the panting heart beneath
        With lightning and with music: the damp death
105   Quenched its caress upon his icy lips;
        And, as a dying meteor stains a wreath
        Of moonlight vapour which the cold night clips,°   *clasps, cuts off*
It flushed through his pale limbs, and passed to its eclipse.

                        XIII
        And others came. Desires and Adorations;
110   Wingèd Persuasions, and veiled Destinies;
        Splendours, and Glooms, and glimmering incarnations
        Of Hopes and Fears, and twilight Phantasies;
        And Sorrow, with her family of Sighs;
        And Pleasure, blind with tears, led by the gleam
115   Of her own dying smile instead of eyes,
        Came in slow pomp;—the moving pomp might seem
Like pageantry of mist on an autumnal stream.

                        XIV
        All he had loved, and moulded into thought
        From shape and hue and odour and sweet sound,
120   Lamented Adonais. Morning sought
        Her eastern watch-tower, and her hair unbound,
        Wet with the tears which should adorn the ground,
        Dimmed the aerial eyes that kindle day;
        Afar the melancholy Thunder moaned,
125   Pale Ocean in unquiet slumber lay,
And the wild Winds flew round, sobbing in their dismay.

                        XV
        Lost Echo sits amid the voiceless mountains,
        And feeds her grief with his remembered lay,°   *song*
        And will no more reply to winds or fountains,
130   Or amorous birds perched on the young green spray,
        Or herdsman's horn, or bell° at closing day;   *church bell*
        Since she can mimic not his lips, more dear
        Than those for whose disdain she pined away
        Into a shadow of all sounds:[7]—a drear
135 Murmur, between their songs, is all the woodmen hear.

7. Narcissus rejected the nymph Echo who, lovelorn, faded into an echo.

XVI

Grief made the young Spring wild, and she threw down
Her kindling buds, as if she Autumn were,
Or they dead leaves; since her delight is flown,
For whom should she have waked the sullen Year?
140   To Phoebus was not Hyacinth so dear,
Nor to himself Narcissus,[8] as to both°   *as dear to both are*
Thou, Adonais; wan they stand and sere°   *withered*
Amid the faint companions of their youth,
With dew all turned to tears,—odour, to sighing ruth.°   *pity*

XVII

145   Thy spirit's sister, the lorn nightingale,
Mourns not her mate with such melodious pain;[9]
Not so the eagle, who like thee could scale
Heaven, and could nourish in the sun's domain
Her mighty youth with morning, doth complain,°   *lament*
150   Soaring and screaming round her empty nest,[1]
As Albion° wails for thee: the curse of Cain[2]   *mythical England*
Light on his° head who pierced thy innocent breast,   *the reviewer's*
And scared the angel soul that was its earthly guest!

XVIII

Ah woe is me! Winter is come and gone,
155   But grief returns with the revolving year.
The airs and streams renew their joyous tone;
The ants, the bees, the swallows, re-appear;
Fresh leaves and flowers deck the dead Seasons' bier;°   *coffin platform*
The amorous birds now pair in every brake,°   *thicket*
160   And build their mossy homes in field and brere;°   *briar*
And the green lizard and the golden snake,
Like unimprisoned flames, out of their trance° awake.   *hibernation*

XIX

Through wood and stream and field and hill and Ocean,
A quickening life from the Earth's heart has burst,
165   As it has ever done, with change and motion,
From the great morning of the world when first
God dawned on Chaos.[3] In its steam immersed,
The lamps° of heaven flash with a softer light;   *lights, stars*
All baser things pant with life's sacred thirst,
170   Diffuse themselves, and spend in love's delight
The beauty and the joy of their renewed might.

8. In punishment for his scorn of love from others, Narcissus was cursed to fall in love with his reflection in a pool of water; he pined away until he turned into a narcissus flower. The beautiful youth Hyacinthus was loved by Phoebus (Apollo, god of poetry); when Hyacinthus rebuffed the advances of Zephyr (Keats's reviewer), Zephyr caused him to be slain, but Apollo engendered the hyacinth flower from his blood.
9. Shelley returns the happy nightingale of Keats's *Ode* to its tradition of sorrowful, lovelorn song.
1. Although the eagle bewails the death of her brood (the empty nest), she may (as legend has it) soar toward the sun, which restores her to youth.
2. For murdering Abel, Cain is "cursed from the earth," (Genesis 4.10–15).
3. Alluding to Genesis 1.3–5 and evoking the myth of Adonis's seasonal rebirth.

XX

The leprous corpse, touched by this spirit tender,
Exhales itself in flowers of gentle breath;
Like incarnations° of the stars, when splendour   *embodiments*
175   Is changed to fragrance, they illumine death,
And mock the merry worm that wakes beneath.
Nought we know dies: shall that alone which knows°   *the mind*
Be as a sword consumed before the sheath
By sightless° lightning? The intense atom glows   *invisible, morally blind*
180   A moment, then is quenched in a most cold repose.

XXI

Alas that all we loved of him should be,
But for our grief, as if it had not been,
And grief itself be mortal! Woe is me!
Whence are we, and why are we? of what scene
185   The actors or spectators? Great and mean
Meet massed in death, who lends what life must borrow.
As long as skies are blue and fields are green,
Evening must usher night, night urge the morrow,
Month follow month with woe, and year wake year to sorrow.

XXII

190   *He* will awake no more, oh never more!
"Wake thou," cried Misery, "childless Mother! Rise
Out of thy sleep, and slake in thy heart's core
A wound more fierce than his, with tears and sighs."
And all the Dreams that watched Urania's eyes,
195   And all the Echoes whom their Sister's° song   *Echo's*
Had held in holy silence, cried "Arise";
Swift as a Thought by the snake Memory stung,
From her ambrosial⁴ rest the fading Splendour° sprung.   *Urania*

XXIII

She rose like an autumnal Night that springs
200   Out of the East, and follows wild and drear
The golden Day, which, on eternal wings,
Even as a ghost abandoning a bier,
Had left the Earth a corpse. Sorrow and fear
So struck, so roused, so rapt, Urania;
205   So saddened round her like an atmosphere
Of stormy mist; so swept her on her way,
Even to the mournful place where Adonais lay.

XXIV

Out of her secret Paradise she sped,
Through camps and cities rough with stone and steel
210   And human hearts, which, to her aery tread

---

4. Delightful; ambrosia (from Greek for "immortal, immune to murder") is the food of the gods in classical myth.

Yielding not, wounded the invisible
Palms of her tender feet where'er they fell.
And barbed tongues, and thoughts more sharp than they,
Rent° the soft form they never could repel,   *tore*
215　　Whose sacred blood, like the young tears of May,
　　Paved with eternal flowers that undeserving way.

XXV

In the death-chamber for a moment Death,
Shamed by the presence of that living Might,
Blushed to annihilation, and the breath
220　　Revisited those° lips, and life's pale light   *Adonais's*
Flashed through those limbs so late° her dear delight.   *recently*
"Leave me not wild and drear and comfortless,
As silent lightning leaves the starless night!
Leave me not!" cried Urania. Her distress
225　　Roused Death: Death rose and smiled, and met her vain caress.

XXVI

"Stay yet awhile! speak to me once again!
Kiss me, so long but as a kiss may live!
And in my heartless° breast and burning brain   *love-lorn*
That word, that kiss, shall all thoughts else survive,
230　　With food of saddest memory kept alive,
Now thou art dead, as if it were a part
Of thee, my Adonais! I would give
All that I am, to be as thou now art!
　　But I am chained to Time, and cannot thence depart.

XXVII

235　　O gentle child, beautiful as thou wert,
Why didst thou leave the trodden paths of men
Too soon, and with weak hands though mighty heart
Dare° the unpastured dragon° in his den?   *provoke / the reviewer*
Defenceless as thou wert, oh where was then
240　　Wisdom the mirrored shield,⁵ or scorn° the spear?—   *(Keats's)*
Or, hadst thou waited the full cycle when
Thy spirit should have filled its crescent sphere,⁶
　　The monsters of life's waste had fled from thee like deer.

XXVIII

The herded wolves bold only to pursue,
245　　The obscene ravens clamorous o'er the dead,
The vultures to the conqueror's banner true,
Who feed where Desolation first has fed,
And whose wings rain contagion,—how they° fled,   *these reviewers*
When, like Apollo from his golden bow,

5. Because the stare of gorgon Medusa turned its beholders to stone, shields often bore her image, including the
shield of warrior Athena, goddess of Wisdom. In the
fable, Perseus manages to decapitate Medusa by viewing
her reflection in his shield.
6. Reached maturity, like the full moon.

250   The Pythian of the age one arrow sped,
         And smiled!—The spoilers tempt no second blow,
    They fawn on the proud feet that spurn them lying low.[7]

                         XXIX
    The sun comes forth, and many reptiles spawn;
         He sets, and each ephemeral° insect then   *living for one day*
255 Is gathered into death without a dawn,
         And the immortal stars awake again.
         So is it in the world of living men:
         A godlike mind soars forth, in its delight
         Making earth bare and veiling heaven; and, when
260 It sinks, the swarms that dimmed or shared its light
    Leave to its kindred lamps° the spirit's awful° night."   *stars / awesome*

                          XXX
    Thus ceased she:° and the mountain shepherds° came,   *Urania / fellow poets*
         Their garlands sere, their magic mantles° rent.   *capes*
         The Pilgrim of Eternity,° whose fame   *Byron*
265 Over his living head like heaven is bent,
         An early but enduring monument,
         Came, veiling all the lightnings of his song
         In sorrow. From her wilds Ierne° sent   *Ireland*
         The sweetest lyrist of her saddest wrong,
270 And love taught grief to fall like music from his tongue.[8]

                         XXXI
    Midst others of less note came one frail Form,°   *(Shelley)*
         A phantom among men, companionless
         As the last cloud of an expiring storm
         Whose thunder is its knell.° He, as I guess,   *funeral bell*
275 Had gazed on Nature's naked loveliness
         Actaeon-like; and now he fled astray
         With feeble steps o'er the world's wilderness,
         And his own thoughts along that rugged way
    Pursued like raging hounds their father and their prey.[9]

                        XXXII
280 A pard-like° Spirit beautiful and swift—   *leopard-like*
         A Love in desolation masked—a Power
         Girt round with weakness; it can scarce uplift
         The weight of the superincumbent hour.[1]
         It is a dying lamp, a falling shower,
285 A breaking billow;—even whilst we speak

---

7. Byron skewered his harsh reviewers in *English Bards and Scotch Reviewers;* by 1821, many had been converted to praise. Apollo earns the title "Pythian" from slaying the dragon Python.
8. Thomas Moore's *Irish Melodies* voiced the "wrongs"

Ireland suffered from Britain.
9. Hunter Actaeon angered the goddess Diana by accidentally beholding her bathing naked; she turned him into a stag, and his own hounds tore him apart.
1. The overhanging hour of Adonais-Keats's death.

Is it not broken? On the withering flower
The killing sun smiles brightly: on a cheek
The life can burn in blood even while the heart may break.

XXXIII

His head was bound with pansies overblown,°   *past blooming*
290   And faded violets, white and pied and blue;
And a light spear topped with a cypress-cone,
Round whose rude shaft dark ivy-tresses grew[2]
Yet dripping with the forest's noonday dew,
Vibrated, as the ever-beating heart
295   Shook the weak hand that grasped it. Of that crew
He came the last, neglected and apart;
A herd-abandoned deer struck by the hunter's dart.

XXXIV

All stood aloof, and at his partial° moan   *compassionate, partisan*
Smiled through their tears. Well knew that gentle band
300   Who in another's fate now wept his own.
As in the accents of an unknown land
He sang new sorrow, sad Urania scanned
The Stranger's mien, and murmured "Who art thou?"
He answered not, but with a sudden hand
305   Made bare his branded and ensanguined° brow,   *bloody*
Which was like Cain's or Christ's—oh that it should be so![3]

XXXV

What softer voice is hushed over the dead?
Athwart what brow is that dark mantle thrown?
What form leans sadly o'er the white death-bed,
310   In mockery° of monumental stone,   *imitation*
The heavy heart heaving without a moan?
If it be He who, gentlest of the wise,
Taught, soothed, loved, honoured, the departed one,[4]
Let me not vex with inharmonious sighs
315   The silence of that heart's accepted sacrifice.

XXXVI

Our Adonais has drunk poison—oh
What deaf and viperous murderer could crown
Life's early cup with such a draught of woe?
The nameless worm° would now itself disown;   *anonymous reviewer*
320   It felt, yet could escape, the magic tone
Whose prelude held all envy, hate, and wrong,
But what was howling in one breast alone,

---

2. Among these emblems of sorrow, death, and mourning, some signify potential rebirth: the spear decorated with evergreen cypress and ivy evokes the thyrsus staff of Dionysius, Greek god of fertility.
3. A stanza deemed blasphemous in the first reviews, not only for the comparison of Shelley's suffering to Christ's torture by the crown of thorns, but also for his refusal to distinguish Christ's agony from Cain's.
4. Leigh Hunt, radical journalist, poet, and close friend of Shelley and Keats; grateful for his encouragement, Keats dedicated his first volume to him.

Silent with expectation of the song
Whose master's hand is cold, whose silver lyre unstrung.[5]

XXXVII

325 Live thou, whose infamy is not thy fame!
Live! fear no heavier chastisement from me,
Thou noteless[6] blot on a remembered name!
But be thyself, and know thyself to be!
And ever at thy season be thou free
330 To spill the venom when thy fangs o'erflow:
Remorse and Self-contempt shall cling to thee,
Hot Shame shall burn upon thy secret brow,
And like a beaten hound tremble thou shalt—as now.

XXXVIII

Nor let us weep that our delight is fled
335 Far from these carrion kites° that scream below.   *corpse-eating hawks*
He wakes or sleeps with the enduring dead;
Thou canst not soar where he is sitting now.[7]
Dust to the dust[8] but the pure spirit shall flow
Back to the burning fountain whence it came,
340 A portion of the Eternal,[9] which must glow
Through time and change, unquenchably the same,
Whilst thy cold embers choke the sordid hearth of shame.

XXXIX

Peace, peace! he is not dead, he doth not sleep!
He hath awakened from the dream of life.
345 'Tis we who, lost in stormy visions, keep
With phantoms an unprofitable strife,
And in mad trance strike with our spirit's knife
Invulnerable nothings. *We* decay
Like corpses in a charnel; fear and grief
350 Convulse us and consume us day by day,
And cold hopes swarm like worms within our living clay.

XL

He has outsoared the shadow of our night.
Envy and calumny° and hate and pain,   *slander*
And that unrest which men miscall delight,
355 Can touch him not and torture not again.
From the contagion of the world's slow stain
He is secure; and now can never mourn

---

5. Keats's tomb bears an image of a Greek lyre with half its strings broken, signifying, in Severn's words, "his Classical Genius cut off by death before its maturity."
6. "Noteless" for several reasons: its anonymity, its insignificance and forgettability against Keats's assured fame, and its own lack of poetic music (notes).
7. A sympathetic echo of Satan's reminder of his former glory to the Angelic Squadron who eject him from Eden

(where he had been corrupting Eve's dreams): "said Satan, fill'd with scorn, / Know ye not mee? ye knew me once no mate / For you, there sitting where ye durst not soar" (*Paradise Lost* 4.827–829); see also *Defence*, page 874.
8. Body to the earth; see the Lord's chastisement of fallen Adam, "dust thou art, and unto dust shalt thou return" (Genesis 3.19).
9. Eternal Spirit and Eternity.

A heart grown cold, a head grown grey, in vain—
Nor, when the spirit's self has ceased to burn,

360 With sparkless ashes load an unlamented urn.°   *burial urn*

XLI

He lives, he wakes—'tis Death is dead, not he;[1]
Mourn not for Adonais.—Thou young Dawn,
Turn all thy dew to splendour, for from thee
The spirit thou lamentest is not gone!

365 Ye caverns and ye forests, cease to moan!
Cease, ye faint flowers and fountains! and, thou Air,
Which like a mourning-veil thy scarf hadst thrown
O'er the abandoned Earth, now leave it bare
Even to the joyous stars which smile on its despair!

XLII

370 He is made one with Nature. There is heard
His voice in all her music, from the moan
Of thunder to the song of night's sweet bird.[2]
He is a presence to be felt and known
In darkness and in light, from herb and stone,—

375 Spreading itself where'er that Power may move
Which has withdrawn his being to its own,
Which wields the world with never-wearied love,
Sustains it from beneath, and kindles it above.

XLIII

He is a portion of the loveliness

380 Which once he made more lovely. He doth bear
His part, while the one Spirit's plastic° stress   *shaping, formative*
Sweeps through the dull dense world; compelling there
All new successions to the forms they wear;
Torturing th'unwilling dross, that checks its flight

385 To its° own likeness, as each mass may bear;   *the Spirit's*
And bursting in its beauty and its might
From trees and beasts and men into the Heaven's light.

XLIV

The splendours of the firmament of time
May be eclipsed, but are extinguished not;

390 Like stars to their appointed height they climb,
And death is a low mist which cannot blot
The brightness it may veil. When lofty thought
Lifts a young heart above its mortal lair,°   *sleeping-place*
And love and life contend in it° for what°   *the heart / whatever*

395 Shall be its earthly doom, the dead live there°   *in lofty thought*
And move like winds of light on dark and stormy air.

---

1. The consolation of Donne's famous sonnet (1633), *Death be not proud.*

2. From the Titans of Keats's *Hyperion* fragment to *Ode to a Nightingale.*

XLV

The inheritors of unfulfilled renown
Rose from their thrones, built beyond mortal thought
Far in the Unapparent. Chatterton
400   Rose pale, his solemn agony had not
Yet faded from him; Sidney, as he fought,
And as he fell, and as he lived and loved,
Sublimely mild, a Spirit without spot,
Arose; and Lucan, by his death approved;°—   *honored*
405   Oblivion as they rose shrank like a thing reproved.[3]

XLVI

And many more, whose names on earth are dark,
But whose transmitted effluence° cannot die   *radiance, influence*
So long as fire outlives the parent spark,
Rose, robed in dazzling immortality.
410   "Thou art become as one of us," they cry;
"It was for thee yon kingless° sphere has long   *awaiting its king*
Swung blind in unascended majesty,
Silent alone amid an Heaven of song.
Assume thy winged throne, thou Vesper° of our throng!"   *evening star*

XLVII

415   Who mourns for Adonais? Oh come forth,
Fond wretch, and know thyself and him aright.
Clasp with thy panting soul the pendulous earth;
As from a centre, dart thy spirit's light
Beyond all worlds, until its spacious might°   *power*
420   Satiate the void circumference: then shrink
Even to a point within our day and night;°   *ordinary time*
And keep thy heart light, lest it make thee sink,
When hope has kindled hope, and lured thee to the brink.

XLVIII

Or go to Rome, which is the sepulchre,
425   Oh not of him, but of our joy. 'Tis nought
That ages, empires, and religions, there
Lie buried in the ravage they have wrought;
For such as he° can lend°—they borrow not   *Keats / bestow (glory)*
Glory from those° who made the world their prey;   *Romans*
430   And he is gathered to the kings of thought
Who waged contention with their time's° decay,   *own life's or age's*
And of the past are all that cannot pass away.

---

3. Poets who, dying young, did not achieve their full potential for fame ("renown"). Thomas Chatterton (1752–1770), in despair of success, killed himself with arsenic at age 17; Keats addressed one of his *Poems* of 1817 to him, and dedicated his longest work, *Endymion* (1818), to his memory. Sir Philip Sidney (1554–1586) died heroically in battle at age 32. Roman poet Lucan (A.D. 39–65), in preference to execution for conspiring against the tyrant Nero, committed suicide at age 26; he recited his poetry to his friends while he bled to death.

XLIX

Go thou to Rome,—at once the Paradise,
The grave, the city, and the wilderness;
435 And where its wrecks° like shattered mountains rise,   ruins
And flowering weeds and fragrant copses° dress   thickets
The bones of Desolation's nakedness,
Pass, till the Spirit of the spot shall lead
Thy footsteps to a slope of green access,
440 Where, like an infant's smile, over the dead
A light of laughing flowers along the grass is spread.[4]

L

And grey walls moulder round, on which dull Time
Feeds, like slow fire upon a hoary brand;°   ash-covered log
And one keen pyramid with wedge sublime,
445 Pavilioning the dust of him who planned
This refuge for his memory, doth stand
Like flame transformed to marble; and beneath
A field is spread, on which a newer band
Have pitched in Heaven's smile their camp of death,[5]
450 Welcoming him we lose with scarce-extinguished breath.

LI

Here pause. These graves are all too young as yet
To have outgrown the sorrow which consigned
Its charge to each; and, if the seal is set
Here on one fountain of a mourning mind,
455 Break it not thou! too surely shalt thou find
Thine own well full, if thou returnest home,
Of tears and gall. From the world's bitter wind[6]
Seek shelter in the shadow of the tomb.
What Adonais is why fear we to become?

LII

460 The One remains, the many change and pass;
Heaven's light for ever shines, earth's shadows fly;
Life, like a dome of many-coloured glass,
Stains the white radiance of eternity,[7]
Until Death tramples it to fragments.—Die,
465 If thou wouldst be with that which thou dost seek!
Follow where all is fled!—Rome's azure sky,
Flowers, ruins, statues, music, words, are weak
The glory they transfuse with fitting truth to speak.

---

4. The Protestant Cemetery in Rome, where Keats is buried; one of its walls incorporates the pyramid-tomb of Caius Cestius, a Roman tribune. The image of "the infant's smile" evokes the grave of the Shelleys' son William (see Preface).

5. Military imagery with a pun on *campo* (field); *camposanto* ("sacred field") is Italian for cemetery.
6. A hint of the malaria ("bad air" or "bitter wind") that was fatal to William Shelley.
7. "Stain" can mean color, refract, discolor, or degrade.

LIII

Why linger, why turn back, why shrink, my Heart?
470 Thy hopes are gone before: from all things here
They have departed;[8] thou shouldst now depart.
A light is past from the revolving year,
And man and woman; and what still is dear
Attracts to crush, repels to make thee wither.
475 The soft sky smiles, the low wind whispers near:
'Tis Adonais calls! Oh hasten thither!
No more let Life divide what Death can join together.

LIV

That Light whose smile kindles the Universe,
That Beauty in which all things work and move,
480 That Benediction which the eclipsing Curse
Of birth can quench not, that sustaining Love
Which through the web of being blindly wove
By man and beast and earth and air and sea,
Burns bright or dim, as° each are mirrors of   *to the extent that*
485 The fire for which all thirst, now beams on me,
Consuming the last clouds of cold mortality.

LV

The breath whose might I have invoked in song[9]
Descends on me; my spirit's bark is driven
Far from the shore, far from the trembling throng
490 Whose sails were never to the tempest given.
The massy earth and sphered skies are riven!
I am borne darkly, fearfully, afar!
Whilst, burning through the inmost veil of Heaven,
The soul of Adonais, like a star,
495 Beacons from the abode where the Eternal are.
1821   1821

The Cloud[1]

1

I bring fresh showers for the thirsting flowers,
      From the seas and streams;
I bear light shade for the leaves when laid
      In their noon-day dreams.
5 From my wings are shaken the dews that waken
      The sweet buds every one,

---

8. Multiple possible allusions to lost hopes: the death of two children and the lost custody of two others, exile from England, estrangement from Mary, tensions with Byron, neglect by his publisher, hostile reviews, failure to find a broad audience and fame, despair over his health, loss of hope for his political ideals.
9. Other poems expressing such ideal thirsting, e.g., *Ode to the West Wind*.
1. This poem is a rare representation, for Shelley, of ceaseless transformation without agony.

When rocked to rest on their mother's breast,
    As she dances about the sun.
I wield the flail of the lashing hail,
10   And whiten the green plains under,
And then again I dissolve it in rain,
    And laugh as I pass in thunder.

2

I sift the snow on the mountains below,
    And their great pines groan aghast;
15 And all the night 'tis my pillow white,
    While I sleep in the arms of the blast.
Sublime on the towers of my skiey bowers,
    Lightning my pilot sits,
In a cavern under is fettered the thunder,
20   It struggles and howls at fits;°   *fitfully*
Over earth and ocean, with gentle motion,
    This pilot is guiding me,
Lured by the love of the genii that move
    In the depths of the purple sea;
25 Over the rills, and the crags, and the hills,
    Over the lakes and the plains,
Wherever he dream, under mountain or stream,
    The Spirit he loves remains;
And I all the while bask in heaven's blue smile,
30   Whilst he is dissolving in rains.

3

The sanguine sunrise, with his meteor eyes,
    And his burning plumes outspread,
Leaps on the back of my sailing rack,[2]
    When the morning star shines dead.
35 As on the jag of a mountain crag,
    Which an earthquake rocks and swings,
An eagle alit one moment may sit
    In the light of its golden wings.
And when sunset may breathe, from the lit sea beneath,
40   Its ardours of rest and of love,
And the crimson pall of eve may fall
    From the depth of heaven above,
With wings folded I rest, on mine aëry nest,
    As still as a brooding dove.[3]

---

2. A mass of wind-blown clouds scattered in the upper air.
3. An echo of Milton's description of his muse at the outset of *Paradise Lost* as an original agent of creation: "Thou

. . . with mighty wings outspread / Dove-like satst brooding on the vast Abyss / And mad'st it pregnant" (1.19–22); brooding: incubating.

4

45   That orbèd maiden, with white fire laden,
         Whom mortals call the moon,
      Glides glimmering o'er my fleece-like floor,
         By the midnight breezes strewn;
      And wherever the beat of her unseen feet,
50   Which only the angels hear,
      May have broken the woof° of my tent's thin roof,   *fabric*
         The stars peep behind her, and peer;
      And I laugh to see them whirl and flee,
         Like a swarm of golden bees,
55   When I widen the rent in my wind-built tent,
         Till the calm rivers, lakes, and seas,
      Like strips of the sky fallen through me on high,
         Are each paved with the moon and these.°   *stars*

5

      I bind the sun's throne with a burning zone,°   *sash*
60   And the moon's with a girdle of pearl;
      The volcanos are dim, and the stars reel and swim,
         When the whirlwinds my banner unfurl.
      From cape to cape, with a bridge-like shape,
         Over a torrent sea,
65   Sunbeam-proof, I hang like a roof,
         The mountains its columns be,
      The triumphal arch through which I march
         With hurricane, fire, and snow,
      When the powers of the air are chained to my chair,
70   Is the million-coloured bow;°   *rainbow*
      The sphere-fire° above its soft colours wove,   *sunlight*
         While the moist earth was laughing below.

6

      I am the daughter of earth and water,
         And the nursling of the sky:
75   I pass through the pores of the ocean and shores;
         I change, but I cannot die.
      For after the rain when with never a stain,
         The pavilion of heaven is bare,
      And the winds and sunbeams with their convex gleams,
80   Build up the blue dome of air,
      I silently laugh at my own cenotaph,[4]
         And out of the caverns of rain,
      Like a child from the womb, like a ghost from the tomb,
         I arise and unbuild it again.

1820   1820/1839

4. A monument honoring someone interred elsewhere.

from **Hellas**[1]

195 MAHMUD: . . . Kings are like stars: they rise and set, they have
The worship of the world, but no repose. [*exeunt severally*]

Chorus[2]

Worlds on worlds are rolling ever
  From creation to decay,
    Like the bubbles on a river,
200   Sparkling, bursting, borne away.
        But *they*[3] are still immortal
          Who, through birth's orient° portal   *eastern, dawning*
And death's dark chasm hurrying to and fro,
      Clothe their unceasing flight
205   In the brief dust and light
Gathered around their chariots as they go:
    New shapes they still may weave,
    New gods, new laws, receive:
Bright or dim are they, as the robes they last
210   On Death's bare ribs had cast.

  A Power from the unknown God,
    A Promethean Conqueror, came;[4]
  Like a triumphal path he trod
    The thorns of death and shame.
215   A mortal shape to him
      Was like the vapour dim
Which the orient planet animates with light.[5]
      Hell, sin, and Slavery, came,

1. Shelley wrote *Hellas* (classical name for Greece) in October 1821, inspired by a Greek revolt against centuries of Turkish domination, initiating the war won in 1832. In his Preface, he says he gives "a series of lyric pictures," its "figures of indistinct and visionary delineation" meant to "suggest the final triumph of the Greek cause as a portion of the cause of civilization and social improvement"; a later sentence, censored by his publisher, went on to declare, "This is the age of the war of the oppressed against the oppressors." His enthusiasm derives from his conviction that "we are all Greeks—our laws, our literature, our religion, our arts have their root in Greece," a widely shared sympathy that has been named "Romantic Hellenism." He modeled *Hellas* on Aeschylus's *Persians* (472 B.C.), which records the defeat of the invading Persians under Xerxes at the naval battle of Salamis eight years before. As in the Greek tragedy, Shelley uses a chorus for communal comment, reflection, hope, and sometimes prophecy. His Chorus is the "Greek Captive Women" in Constantinople, the city in Turkey founded A.D. 330 by the first Christian Emperor of Rome (Constantine the Great), who made it the capital of the Roman Empire; it was conquered by the Ottoman Empire in 1453. In the first excerpt, Sultan Mahmud (Mahmud II, named for the prophet Muhammed, founder of Islam) has woken from a dream of the destruction of his empire so disturbing that

he has asked a mystical Jew to interpret it; he has ordered the silencing of drunken sailors (one by decapitation) who are vexing his "need of rest."
2. The popular notions of christianity are represented in this chorus as true in their relation to the worship they superseded. . . . The first stanza contrasts the immortality of the living and thinking beings which inhabit the planets . . . with the transience of the noblest manifestations of the external world. . . . [T]he concluding verses indicate a progressive state of more or less exalted existence, according to the degree of perfection which every distinct intelligence may have attained . . . the condition of that futurity towards which we are all impelled by an inextinguishable thirst for immortality . . . the strongest and the only presumption that eternity is the inheritance of every thinking being [Shelley's note].
3. "The living and thinking beings" of the previous note.
4. The identity of God was "unknown" in ancient Greece and Rome (Acts 17.23) before Jesus Christ, whom Shelley compares to Prometheus, the god of classical myth who stole fire from heaven and gave it to humanity; tortured for this transgression by Jupiter, he was often compared to Christ, the bearer of God's light into the mortal world. See Byron's *Prometheus*, page 389.
5. Venus appears as the morning star in the eastern, or orient, sky.

Like bloodhounds mild and tame,
220   Nor preyed until their Lord had taken flight.
The moon of Mahomet[6]
Arose, and it shall set:
While blazoned as on heaven's immortal noon,
The cross leads generations on.[7]

225   Swift as the radiant shapes of sleep
From one whose dreams are Paradise
Fly, when the fond wretch wakes to weep,
And Day peers forth with her blank eyes;
So fleet, so faint, so fair,
230   The Powers of Earth and Air

Fled from the folding-star[8] of Bethlehem:
Apollo, Pan, and Love,
And even Olympian Jove,
Grew weak, for killing Truth had glared on them.[9]
235   Our hills and seas and streams,
Dispeopled of their dreams,
Their waters turned to blood, their dew to tears,
Wailed for the golden years.[1]

Enter Mahmud [and associates]

MAHMUD: More gold? Our ancestors bought gold with victory,
And shall I sell it for defeat?
240   DAOD: The Janizars[2]
Clamour for pay.
MAHMUD: Go bid them pay themselves
With Christian blood! Are there no Grecian virgins
Whose shrieks and spasms and tears they may enjoy?
No infidel° children to impale on spears?   *non-Islamic*
245   No hoary priests after that Patriarch
Who bent to curse against his country's heart,
Which clove his own at last?[3] Go bid them kill:
Blood is the seed of gold.

* * *

6. The emblem of Islam; these lines echo 195–96 (see n. 1).

7. Before a battle with rivals for the rule of Rome in 312, Constantine I is said to have beheld a flaming cross in front of the noonday sun, inscribed "In this sign, thou shalt conquer." He converted to Christianity and was victorious; the Roman empire was henceforth safe for Christians. *Hellas* is set in Constantinople.

8. Called thus because it appeared in the sky at evening, when shepherds return their grazing flocks to the fold (pen).

9. Shelley follows Milton's *Ode on the Morning of Christ's Nativity* (165–236) in portraying the classical gods fleeing from and even annihilated by Christian "Truth."

1. Nature is "dispeopled" of classical river- and sea-gods, mountain-nymphs, etc.; blood and tears report their "killing" by Christian "Truth"; "the golden years" are the Golden Age of Saturn's rule, an era of perfect peace and plenty, analogous to the Judaeo-Christian Eden before the Fall.

2. The chief standing army of the Turkish Empire.

3. After the Greek rebels killed Turks in Greece, the Turks massacred the Greeks in Asia Minor; on 22 April 1821, they hanged Gregorios, the Orthodox Patriarch of Constantinople.

Chorus[1]

1060   The world's great age begins anew,
        The golden years° return,   *the Golden Age*
    The earth doth like a snake renew
        Her winter weeds[2] outworn:
    Heaven smiles, and faiths and empires gleam
1065   Like wrecks of a dissolving dream.

    A brighter Hellas rears its mountains
        From waves serener far;
    A new Peneus[3] rolls his fountains°   *waters*
        Against the morning star;°   *eastward*
1070   Where fairer Tempes[4] bloom, there sleep
    Young Cyclads[5] on a sunnier deep.°   *sea*

    A loftier Argo[6] cleaves the main,
        Fraught with a later prize;
    Another Orpheus sings again,
1075   And loves, and weeps, and dies;[7]
    A new Ulysses leaves once more
    Calypso for his native shore.[8]

    Oh write no more the tale of Troy,
        If earth Death's scroll must be—
1080   Nor mix with Laian rage the joy
        Which dawns upon the free,
    Although a subtler Sphinx renew
    Riddles of death Thebes never knew.[9]

1. After the Turks have vanquished the Greek rebels, the Chorus is comforted by the thought that "Greece which was dead is arisen!" (1059), and concludes the play with this song. "The final chorus is indistinct and obscure, as the event of the living drama whose arrival it foretells. Prophecies of wars . . . may safely be made by poet or prophet in any age, but to anticipate however darkly a period of regeneration and happiness is a more hazardous exercise which bards possess or fain. It will remind the reader . . . of Isaiah and Virgil, whose ardent spirits overleaping the actual reign of evil which we endure and bewail, already saw the possible and perhaps approaching state of society in which the *'lion shall lie down with the lamb'* and 'omnis feret omnia tellus [each land will produce all things].' Let these great names be my authority and excuse" [Shelley's note, paraphrasing Isaiah (11.6, 35.9, 65.25) and Virgil's *Eclogue* IV ("The Golden Age Returns")].
2. Dead grass; also mourning clothes to be shed.
3. River in northeast Greece.
4. Tempe is the valley reputed to be a playground of the gods.
5. Cyclades, an island chain in the Aegean.
6. The ship in which Jason and his crew (Argonauts) sailed in quest of the Golden Fleece.
7. In Greek legend, Orpheus played the lyre so beautifully that he charmed even the rocks and stones. When his beloved Eurydice was killed by a snake while fleeing a ravisher, he descended to the underworld to find her, and so moved its ruler, Hades, with his music that he was allowed to reclaim her—provided he did not look back at her until they reached the upper world. He anxiously looked back, and lost her forever. In grief, he refused all women, so enraging the Thracian women that they tore him to pieces at a Bacchanalian revel.
8. Sailing home to Greece from the Trojan War, Ulysses was shipwrecked on the island of the nymph Calypso, where he dallied for seven years before returning to his wife.
9. A reference to the story of the riddle-solver Oedipus, whose father Laius, alarmed by a prophecy that he would be killed by his son, ordered the newborn's death by exposure. Oedipus was rescued, and as a young man got into an argument with Laius (not knowing him), and killed him in rage. He later married Laius's widow, not knowing she was his mother. When his parentage was revealed, she committed suicide and he blinded himself.

Another Athens shall arise,
1085   And to remoter time
Bequeath, like sunset to the skies,
       The splendour of its prime;
And leave, if nought so bright may live,
All earth can take or heaven can give.

1090   Saturn and Love their long repose
       Shall burst, more bright and good
Than all who fell, than one who rose,
       Than many unsubdued:[1]
Not gold, not blood, their altar dowers,°   *gifts, dowries*
1095   But votive tears and symbol flowers.

Oh cease! must hate and death return?
       Cease! must men kill and die?
Cease! drain not to its dregs the urn
       Of bitter prophecy!
1100   The world is weary of the past,—
Oh might it die or rest at last!

A DEFENCE OF POETRY

A DEFENCE OF POETRY   Shelley was called to the *Defence* by an extravagant essay published in 1820 by his friend Thomas Love Peacock. Peacock described a fall from the grandeur of former ages into a modern poetry of triviality, vulgarity, and a studious ignorance "of history, society, and human nature": Wordsworth gives the "phantastical parturition of the moods of his own mind"; "Scott digs up the poachers and cattle-stealers of the ancient border. Lord Byron cruises for thieves and pirates," and Coleridge "superadds the dreams of crazy theologians and the mysticisms of German metaphysics." Replete with "obsolete customs, and exploded superstitions . . . the whine of exaggerated feeling, and the cant of factitious sentiment," such poetry, Peacock argued, lacks relevance to the modern world being shaped by the intellectual power of "mathematicians, astronomers, chemists, moralists, metaphysicians, historians, politicians, and political economists." Even as Shelley recognized the comedy of Peacock's essay, he also knew that such views had currency in contemporary Utilitarian philosophies. He began his *Defence* early the next year, but put it aside in the distraction of other projects and a tumultuous personal life. Left unfinished at his death, the fragment did not appear until Mary Shelley published it in 1840.

"Poets are the unacknowledged legislators of the world," Shelley famously concluded his defense, designating the poet as visionary legislator in his own right. Yet what makes *A Defence* so compelling is not any skillful, coherent legal argumentation toward this verdict, but its welter of impassioned, often conflicting arguments and its evocative, often contradictory images for poetic authority and value. On the one hand, a radical dualism invests all truth in "the eternal, the infinite, and the one"—a transcendent realm to which the poet's imagination has visionary access. This is a theme elaborated throughout Shelley's career, with some of its most succinct expressions in *Adonais* (lines 343–69 and 460–95). Shelley concedes the frustration of any artist who would convey his visions: "the mind in creation is as a fading coal. . . .

---

1. Saturn and Love were among the deities of a real or imaginary state of innocence and happiness. *All those who fell* [are] the Gods of Greece, Asia, and Egypt; the *One who rose* [is] Jesus Christ, at whose appearance the idols of the Pagan World were amerced [deprived] of their worship; and *the many unsubdued* [are] the monstrous objects of the idolatry of China, India, the Antarctic islands, and the native tribes of America. [Shelley's note, which goes on to lament the lack of "temperance and chastity" in otherwise "innocent" Grecian gods, to praise "the sublime human character of Jesus Christ," to honor true Christian martyrs, and to denigrate the "horrors of the Mexican, the Peruvian, and the Indian superstitions."]

when composition begins, inspiration is already on the decline, and the most glorious poetry that has ever been communicated to the world is probably a feeble shadow of the original conception." On the other hand, this inevitability has not thwarted poets, Shelley among them, from laboring to make beautiful poems in order to awaken readers' minds to higher values—a precondition for effective political action. In this other line of defense, poetry is not just weak communication of truths beyond the reach of words but is a force of revelation and vital creation in itself. Many of the *Defence's* sentences, including the celebration of the "electric life" of inspired words and of poets as "unacknowledged legislators," were ones Shelley first drafted for his political pamphlet (also unfinished), *A Philosophical Review of Reform*.

from A Defence of Poetry
or Remarks Suggested by an Essay Entitled "The Four Ages of Poetry"

According to one mode of regarding those two classes of mental action which are called reason and imagination, the former may be considered as mind contemplating the relations borne by one thought to another, however produced; and the latter as mind acting upon those thoughts so as to color them with its own light, and composing from them, as from elements, other thoughts, each containing within itself the principle of its own integrity. The one is the τὸ ποιεῖν,[1] or the principle of synthesis, and has for its object those forms which are common to universal nature and existence itself; the other is the τὸ λογίζειν,[2] or principle of analysis, and its action regards the relations of things simply as relations; considering thoughts not in their integral unity, but as the algebraical representations which conduct to certain general results. Reason is the enumeration of quantities already known; imagination is the perception of the value of those quantities, both separately and as a whole. Reason respects the differences, and imagination the similitudes of things. Reason is to imagination as the instrument to the agent, as the body to the spirit, as the shadow to the substance.

Poetry, in a general sense, may be defined to be "the expression of the imagination"; and poetry is connate with the origin of man. Man is an instrument over which a series of external and internal impressions are driven, like the alternations of an ever-changing wind over an Aeolian lyre,[3] which move it by their motion to ever-changing melody. But there is a principle within the human being (and perhaps within all sentient beings) which acts otherwise than in the lyre, and produces not melody alone, but harmony, by an internal adjustment of the sounds and motions thus excited to the impressions which excite them. It is as if the lyre could accommodate its chords to the motions of that which strikes them, in a determined proportion of sound—even as the musician can accommodate his voice to the sound of the lyre. A child at play by itself will express its delight by its voice and motions, and every inflection of tone and every gesture will bear exact relation to a corresponding antitype in the pleasurable impressions which awakened it. It will be the reflected image of that impression; and as the lyre trembles and sounds after the wind has died away, so the child seeks, by prolonging in its voice and motions the duration of the effect, to prolong also a consciousness of the cause. In relation to the objects which delight a child, these expressions are what poetry is to higher objects.

---

1. "Making something," the derivation of "poet." Sir Philip Sidney refers to the poet as "maker" in his late 16th-century *Defense of Poesie*.

2. The logic or reason.
3. Wind harp.

The savage (for the savage is to ages what the child is to years) expresses the emotions produced in him by surrounding objects in a similar manner; and language and gesture, together with plastic[4] or pictorial imitation, become the image of the combined effect of those objects and his apprehension of them. Man in society, with all his passions and his pleasures, next becomes the object of the passions and pleasures of man; an additional class of emotions produces an augmented treasure of expression; and language, gesture, and the imitative arts become at once the representation and the medium, the pencil and the picture, the chisel and the statue, the chord and the harmony. The social sympathies, or those laws from which, as from its elements, society results, begin to develop themselves from the moment that two human beings coexist; the future is contained within the present as the plant within the seed; and equality, diversity, unity, contrast, mutual dependence, become the principles alone capable of affording the motives according to which the will of a social being is determined to action (inasmuch as he is social), and constitute pleasure in sensation, virtue in sentiment, beauty in art, truth in reasoning, and love in the intercourse of kind. Hence men, even in the infancy of society, observe a certain order in their words and actions distinct from that of the objects and the impressions represented by them, all expression being subject to the laws of that from which it proceeds.

But let us dismiss those more general considerations which might involve an inquiry into the principles of society itself, and restrict our view to the manner in which the imagination is expressed upon its forms.

In the youth of the world, men dance and sing and imitate natural objects, observing[5] in these actions (as in all others) a certain rhythm or order. And, although all men observe a similar, they observe not the same order in the motions of the dance, in the melody of the song, in the combinations of language, in the series of their imitations of natural objects. For there is a certain order or rhythm belonging to each of these classes of mimetic representation, from which the hearer and the spectator receive an intenser and purer pleasure than from any other. The sense of an approximation to this order has been called taste by modern writers. Every man in the infancy of art observes an order which approximates more or less closely to that from which this highest delight results. But the diversity is not sufficiently marked as that its gradations should be sensible, except in those instances where the predominance of this faculty of approximation to the beautiful (for so we may be permitted to name the relation between this highest pleasure and its cause) is very great. Those in whom it exists to excess are poets, in the most universal sense of the word; and the pleasure resulting from the manner in which they express the influence of society or nature upon their own minds, communicates itself to others, and gathers a sort of reduplication from the community. Their language is vitally metaphorical; that is, it marks the before unapprehended relations of things, and perpetuates their apprehension, until words which represent them, become through time signs for portions or classes of thought instead of pictures of integral thoughts; and then, if no new poets should arise to create afresh the associations which have been thus disorganized, language will be dead to all the nobler purposes of human intercourse.

These similitudes or relations are finely said by Lord Bacon to be "the same footsteps of nature impressed upon the various subjects of the world"—and he considers

---

4. Shaping (cf. *Adonais*, line 381, page 495).   5. Seeing and following.

the faculty which perceives them as the storehouse of axioms common to all knowledge.[6] In the infancy of society every author is necessarily a poet, because language itself is poetry; and to be a poet is to apprehend the true and the beautiful, in a word, the good which exists in the relation subsisting, first between existence and perception, and secondly between perception and expression. Every original language near to its source is in itself the chaos of a cyclic poem:[7] the copiousness of lexicography and the distinctions of grammar are the works of a later age, and are merely the catalogue and the form of the creations of poetry.

But Poets, or those who imagine and express this indestructible order, are not only the authors of language and of music, of the dance and architecture and statuary and painting; they are the institutors of laws, and the founders of civil society, and the inventors of the arts of life, and the teachers who draw into a certain propinquity with the beautiful and the true that partial apprehension of the agencies of the invisible world which is called religion. Hence all original religions are allegorical, or susceptible of allegory, and like Janus have a double face of false and true. Poets, according to the circumstances of the age and nation in which they appeared, were called in the earlier epochs of the world, legislators or prophets. A poet essentially comprises and unites both these characters. For he not only beholds intensely the present as it is, and discovers those laws according to which present things ought to be ordered, but he beholds the future in the present, and his thoughts are the germs of the flower and the fruit of latest time. Not that I assert poets to be prophets in the gross sense of the word, or that they can foretell the form as surely as they foreknow the spirit of events; such is the pretence of superstition, which would make poetry an attribute of prophecy, rather than prophecy an attribute of poetry.[8]

A Poet participates in the eternal, the infinite, and the one; as far as relates to his conceptions, time and place and number are not. The grammatical forms which express the moods of time, and the difference of persons and the distinction of place are convertible with respect to the highest poetry without injuring it as poetry and the choruses of Aeschylus, and the Book of Job, and Dante's Paradise would afford, more than any other writings, examples of this fact, if the limits of this essay did not forbid citation.[9] The creations of sculpture, painting, and music, are illustrations still more decisive.

Language, colour, form, and religious and civil habits of action are all the instruments and materials of poetry; they may be called poetry[1] by that figure of speech which considers the effect as a synonym of the cause. But poetry in a more restricted sense expresses those arrangements of language, and especially metrical language, which are created by that imperial faculty whose throne is curtained within the invisible nature of man. And this springs from the nature itself of language, which is a more direct representation of the actions and passions of our internal being, and is susceptible of more various and delicate combinations, than colour, form, or motion, and is more plastic and obedient to the control of that faculty of which it is the creation. For language is arbitrarily produced by the

6. In a note, Shelley cites Francis Bacon's *Of the Advancement of Learning* (1605), bk. 3, ch. 1.
7. An extended set of poems, not necessarily by the same author, with a common subject, event, or character, first applied to a series of Greek epic poems supplementing Homer's *Iliad*; the most famous example of the genre in British literature is "the Arthurian Cycle," dealing with the court of King Arthur.
8. Sidney's *Defence* observes that the Roman word for poet, *vates*, means "prophet" or "oracle."
9. In addition to Job, referring to the Greek tragedian (525–456 B.C.), and *Paradiso*, the third and final part of Dante's epic *Divina Commedia* (completed 1321).
1. Creative imagination and creative arts.

imagination, and has relation to thoughts alone; but all other materials, instruments and conditions of art have relations among each other which limit and interpose between conception and expression. The former is as a mirror which reflects, the latter as a cloud which enfeebles, the light of which both are mediums of communication. Hence the fame of sculptors, painters and musicians (although the intrinsic powers of the great masters of these arts may yield in no degree to that of those who have employed language as the hieroglyphic of their thoughts) has never equalled that of poets in the restricted sense of the term, as two performers of equal skill will produce unequal effects from a guitar and a harp. The fame of legislators and founders of religions (so long as their institutions last) alone seems to exceed that of poets in the restricted sense; but it can scarcely be a question whether, if we deduct the celebrity which their flattery of the gross opinions of the vulgar usually conciliates, together with that which belonged to them in their higher character of poets, any excess will remain. * * *

Poetry is ever accompanied with pleasure: all spirits on which it falls, open themselves to receive the wisdom which is mingled with its delight. * * * it acts in a divine and unapprehended manner, beyond and above consciousness; and it is reserved for future generations to contemplate and measure the mighty cause and effect in all the strength and splendour of their union. * * * no living poet ever arrived at the fulness of his fame; the jury which sits in judgement upon a poet, belonging as he does to all time, must be composed of his peers: it must be impanelled by Time from the selectest of the wise of many generations. A Poet is a nightingale, who sits in darkness and sings to cheer its own solitude with sweet sound; his auditors are as men entranced by the melody of an unseen musician, who feel that they are moved and softened, yet know not whence or why.[2] * * *

The whole objection * * * of the immorality of poetry rests upon a misconception of the manner in which poetry acts to produce the moral improvement of man.[3] Ethical science[4] arranges the elements which poetry has created, and propounds schemes and proposes examples of civil and domestic life. Nor is it for want of admirable doctrines that men hate, and despise, and censure, and deceive, and subjugate one another. But poetry acts in another and diviner manner. It awakens and enlarges the mind itself by rendering it the receptacle of a thousand unapprehended combinations of thought. Poetry lifts the veil from the hidden beauty of the world, and makes familiar objects be as if they were not familiar; it re-produces all that it represents, and the impersonations clothed in its Elysian light[5] stand thenceforward in the minds of those who have once contemplated them as memorials of that gentle and exalted content[6] which extends itself over all thoughts and actions with which it co-exists. The great secret of morals is love, or a going out of our own[7] nature, and an identification of ourselves with the beautiful which exists in thought, action, or person, not our own. A man, to be greatly good,

2. Compare *To a Sky-Lark*, (page 480), especially lines 36–40 and 101–105.
3. In the previous paragraph. Shelley defended poetry from the charge of immorality (leveled famously by Plato in *The Republic*, renewed by the English Puritans of the 17th century and the Evangelicals of Shelley's own age) for depicting characters "remote from moral perfection" and thus offering no "edifying pattern for general imitation" by their readers. Throughout, *A Defence* also counters Plato's other charge, that all art is only representation, and thus a diminishment of Ideal Truth.

4. Moral philosophy.
5. In Greek myth, Elysium is the abode of the blessed after death.
6. Noun: both "content" and "contentment."
7. In the argument of Plato's *Symposium*, a key sentence reads, "Love, therefore, and every thing else that desires anything, desires that which is absent and beyond his reach, that which it has not, that which is not itself, that which it wants" (Shelley's translation); "wants" means both "desires" and "lacks."

must imagine intensely and comprehensively; he must put himself in the place of another and of many others; the pains and pleasures of his species must become his own. The great instrument of moral good is the imagination; and poetry administers to the effect by acting upon the cause.

Poetry enlarges the circumference of the imagination by replenishing it with thoughts of ever new delight, which have the power of attracting and assimilating to their own nature all other thoughts, and which form new intervals and interstices whose void forever craves fresh food. Poetry strengthens the faculty which is the organ of the moral nature of man, in the same manner as exercise strengthens a limb. A poet therefore would do ill to embody his own conceptions of right and wrong (which are usually those of his place and time) in his poetical creations (which participate in neither). By this assumption of the inferior office of interpreting the effect, in which perhaps after all he might acquit himself but imperfectly, he would resign a glory in the participation of the cause. There was little danger that Homer, or any of the eternal poets, should have so far misunderstood themselves as to have abdicated this throne of their widest dominion. Those in whom the poetical faculty, though great, is less intense (as Euripides, Lucan, Tasso, Spenser) have frequently affected a moral aim, and the effect of their poetry is diminished in exact proportion to the degree in which they compel us to advert to this purpose.[8] * * *

We have more moral, political and historical wisdom than we know how to reduce into practice; we have more scientific and economical knowledge than can be accommodated to the just distribution of the produce which it multiplies. The poetry in these systems of thought is concealed by the accumulation of facts and calculating processes. There is no want of knowledge respecting what is wisest and best in morals, government, and political economy, or at least what is wiser and better than what men now practise and endure. But we let "*I dare not* wait upon *I would*, like the poor cat i' the adage."[9] We want the creative faculty to imagine that which we know; we want the generous impulse to act that which we imagine; we want the poetry of life:[1] our calculations have outrun conception; we have eaten more than we can digest. The cultivation of those sciences which have enlarged the limits of the empire of man over the external world, has, for want of the poetical faculty, proportionally circumscribed those of the internal world; and man, having enslaved the elements, remains himself a slave. To what but a cultivation of the mechanical arts in a degree disproportioned to the presence of the creative faculty (which is the basis of all knowledge) is to be attributed the abuse of all invention for abridging and combining labour, to the exasperation of the inequality of mankind? From what other cause has it arisen that these inventions, which should have lightened, have added a weight to the curse imposed on Adam?[2] Poetry, and the principle of Self (of which money is the visible incarnation) are the God and Mammon of the world.[3]

8. Euripides: Greek tragedian, 5th century B.C.; Lucan: Roman epic poet, A.D. 1st century (see *Adonais* 404); Torquato Tasso: Italian epic poet, 16th century; Edmund Spenser: 16th-century English poet, best known for the romance epic, *The Faerie Queene*.
9. *Macbeth* 1.7.44–45. So Lady Macbeth taunts her reluctant husband, referring to the cat that has a taste for fish but won't get its paws wet.
1. In these declarations, "want" means "lack" and "need," shaded by a sense of "desire," "wish for."
2. The Lord says to Adam, in punishment for his sin, "cursed is the ground for thy sake; in sorrow shalt thou eat of it all the days of thy life; thorns also and thistles shall it bring forth. . . . In the sweat of thy face shalt thou eat bread, till thou return unto the ground; . . . dust thou art, and unto dust shalt thou return" (Genesis 3.17–19).
3. Mammon is the false idol of money and worldly goods, against whom Jesus cautions, "Ye cannot serve God and mammon" (Luke 16.13). Keats told Shelley the year before he wrote his *Defence*, "A modern work it is said must have a purpose, which may be the God—*an artist* must serve Mammon—he must have 'self concentration' selfishness perhaps. You I am sure will forgive me for sincerely remarking that you might curb your magnanimity and be more of an artist".

The functions of the poetical faculty are twofold: by one it creates new materials of knowledge and power and pleasure; by the other it engenders in the mind a desire to reproduce and arrange them according to a certain rhythm and order which may be called the beautiful and the good. The cultivation of poetry is never more to be desired than in periods when, from an excess of the selfish and calculating principle, the accumulation of the materials of external life exceed the quantity of the power of assimilating them to the internal laws of human nature. The body has then become too unwieldy for that which animates it.

Poetry is indeed something divine. It is at once the centre and circumference of knowledge;[4] it is that which comprehends all science, and that to which all science must be referred. It is at the same time the root and blossom of all other systems of thought. It is that from which all spring, and that which adorns all; and that which, if blighted, denies the fruit and the seed, and withholds from the barren world the nourishment and the succession of the scions of the tree of life. It is the perfect and consummate surface and bloom of all things; it is as the odour and the colour of the rose to the texture of the elements which compose it, as the form and splendour of unfaded beauty to the secrets of anatomy and corruption. What were [would be] Virtue, Love, Patriotism, Friendship, etc., what were the scenery of this beautiful Universe which we inhabit; what were our consolations on this side of the grave, and what were our aspirations beyond it,—if Poetry did not ascend to bring light and fire from those eternal regions where the owl-winged faculty of calculation dare not ever soar? Poetry is not like reasoning, a power to be exerted according to the determination of the will. A man cannot say, "I will compose poetry." The greatest poet even cannot say it: for the mind in creation is as a fading coal which some invisible influence, like an inconstant wind, awakens to transitory brightness. This power arises from within, like the colour of a flower which fades and changes as it is developed, and the conscious portions of our natures are un-prophetic either of its approach or its departure. Could this influence be durable in its original purity and force, it is impossible to predict the greatness of the results; but when composition begins, inspiration is already on the decline, and the most glorious poetry that has ever been communicated to the world is probably a feeble shadow of the original conceptions of the poet. I appeal to the greatest poets of the present day whether it is not an error to assert that the finest passages of poetry are produced by labour and study. The toil and the delay recommended by critics can be justly interpreted to mean no more than a careful observation of the inspired moments, and an artificial connection of the spaces between their suggestions by the intertexture of conventional expressions—a necessity only imposed by a limit-edness of the poetical faculty itself. For Milton conceived the Paradise Lost as a whole before he executed it in portions. We have his own authority also for the muse having "dictated" to him the "unpremeditated song."[5] And let this be an an-swer to those who would allege the fifty-six various readings of the first line of the Orlando Furioso.[6] Compositions so produced are to poetry what mosaic is to paint-ing. The instinct and intuition of the poetical faculty is still more observable in the

---

4. A description of God often attributed to St. Augustine (4th–5th century), as the circle whose center is every-where and circumference nowhere.

5. In *Paradise Lost*, Milton says that his celestial muse

"dictates to me slumb'ring, or inspires / Easy my un-premeditated verse" (9.23–24); compare *To a Sky-Lark*, 5 (page 480).

6. Epic poem by Italian poet Ariosto (1632).

plastic and pictorial arts: a great statue or picture grows under the power of the artist as a child in the mother's womb, and the very mind which directs the hands in formation is incapable of accounting to itself for the origin, the gradations, or the media of the process.

Poetry is the record of the best and happiest moments of the happiest and best minds. We are aware of evanescent visitations of thought and feeling sometimes associated with place or person, sometimes regarding our own mind alone, and always arising unforeseen and departing unbidden, but elevating and delightful beyond all expression; so that even in the desire and the regret they leave, there cannot but be pleasure, participating as it does in the nature of its object. It is, as it were, the interpenetration of a diviner nature through our own, but its footsteps are like those of a wind over a sea, which the morning calm erases, and whose traces remain only as on the wrinkled sand which paves it. These and corresponding conditions of being are experienced principally by those of the most delicate sensibility and the most enlarged imagination; and the state of mind produced by them is at war with every base desire. The enthusiasm of virtue, love, patriotism, and friendship is essentially linked with emotions; and whilst they last, self appears as what it is, an atom to a Universe. Poets are not only subject to these experiences as spirits of the most refined organization, but they can colour all that they combine with the evanescent hues of this etherial world; a word or a trait in the representation of a scene or a passion will touch the enchanted chord, and reanimate, in those who have ever experienced these emotions, the sleeping, the cold, the buried image of the past. Poetry thus makes immortal all that is best and most beautiful in the world; it arrests the vanishing apparitions which haunt the interlunations[7] of life, and veiling them or [either] in language or in form, sends them forth among mankind, bearing sweet news of kindred joy to those with whom their sisters abide—abide, because there is no portal of expression from the caverns of the spirit which they inhabit into the universe of things.[8] Poetry redeems from decay the visitations of the divinity in man.

Poetry turns all things to loveliness: it exalts the beauty of that which is most beautiful, and it adds beauty to that which is most deformed; it marries exultation and horror, grief and pleasure, eternity and change; it subdues to union under its light yoke all irreconcilable things.[9] It transmutes all that it touches, and every form moving within the radiance of its presence is changed by wondrous sympathy to an incarnation of the spirit which it breathes; its secret alchemy turns to potable gold the poisonous waters which flow from death through life; it strips the veil of familiarity from the world, and lays bare the naked and sleeping beauty which is the spirit of its forms.

All things exist as they are perceived: at least in relation to the percipient. "The mind is its own place, and of itself can make a heaven of hell, a hell of heaven."[1] But poetry defeats the curse which binds us to be subjected to the

7. The dark intervals between the old and new moons.
8. Poetry is valuable because it articulates not only what the poet apprehends—those "vanishing apparitions"—but also their "sisters" in the spiritual selves of ordinary mankind, who would lack connection to what is "best and most beautiful in the world" and "the universe of things," were it not for poetry. In his *Defense*, Sidney calls the inner potential for understanding the "foreconceit," and grants poets similar power.

9. Coleridge's description of imagination, *Biographia Literaria* (1817), the end of ch. 14 (see page 345).
1. A small but significant misquotation of Satan's boast in Hell, *Paradise Lost* 1.254–55; Milton wrote "in itself" (not "of"), in order to set up, along with the second half of the chiasmus that Shelley goes on to deflect, the horribly ironic return of this boast of mind over place when Satan beholds Eve and Eden in the morning (9.467–70).

accident of surrounding impressions. And whether it spreads its own figured curtain or withdraws life's dark veil from before the scene of things,[2] it equally creates for us a being within our being. It makes us the inhabitant of a world to which the familiar world is a chaos. It reproduces the common universe of which we are portions and percipients, and it purges from our inward sight the film of familiarity which obscures from us the wonder of our being. It compels us to feel that which we perceive, and to imagine that which we know. It creates anew the universe after it has been annihilated in our minds by the recurrence of impressions blunted by reiteration. It justifies that bold and true word of Tasso: *Non merita nome di creatore, se non Iddio ed il Poeta*.[3]

A Poet, as he is the author to others of the highest wisdom, pleasure, virtue, and glory, so he ought personally to be the happiest, the best, the wisest, and the most illustrious of men. As to his glory, let time be challenged to declare whether the fame of any other institutor of human life be comparable to that of a poet. That he is the wisest, the happiest, and the best, inasmuch as he is a poet, is equally incontrovertible: the greatest poets have been men of the most spotless virtue, of the most consummate prudence, and (if we would look into the interior of their lives) the most fortunate of men. And the exceptions, as they regard those who possessed the poetic faculty in a high yet inferior degree, will be found on consideration to confirm rather than destroy the rule. Let us for a moment stoop to the arbitration of popular breath, and usurping and uniting in our own persons the incompatible characters of accuser, witness, judge and executioner, let us decide without trial, testimony, or form, that certain motives of those who are "there sitting where we dare not soar,"[4] are reprehensible. Let us assume that Homer was a drunkard, that Virgil was a flatterer, that Horace was a coward, that Tasso was a madman, that Lord Bacon was a peculator, that Raphael was a libertine, that Spenser was a Poet Laureate.[5] It is inconsistent with this division of our subject to cite living poets, but posterity has done ample justice to the great names now referred to. Their errors have been weighed and found to have been dust in the balance; if their sins "were as scarlet, they are now white as snow"; they have been washed in the blood of the mediator and redeemer, Time.[6] Observe in what a ludicrous chaos the imputations of real or fictitious crime have been confused in the contemporary calumnies against poetry and poets; con-

---

2. *Lift not the painted veil* (page 476) and *Mont Blanc* 53–54 (page 471).

3. *None merits the name of creator except God and the Poet*; from Serassi's *Life of Torquato Tasso* (1785). Sidney's *Defense* refers to God as the "Maker of [the] maker" (punning on the Greek word root for "poet").

4. Poets whose reprehensible motives Shelley is willing to concede for the sake of argument. His quotation adapts Satan's sneering reminder to his former peers of his former state in Heaven: "ye knew me once no mate / For you, there sitting where ye durst not soar" (*Paradise Lost* 4.428–29); recall this phrase in *Adonais* 337.

5. All charges made against these poets. Homer: epic poet of ancient Greece; Horace: Roman lyric poet and satirist, 1st century B.C.; Virgil: Roman pastoral and epic poet, 1st century B.C., sometimes accused of being an apologist for Roman imperialism; Bacon: English Renaissance philosopher, essayist, statesman, and scientist, whose public

career was ruined by a conviction for accepting bribes (a peculator is an embezzler); Raphael: 16th-century Italian painter (a libertine is given to immoral sensual indulgence); for Tasso and Spenser, see n. 8, page 509. The first Poet Laureate, a royally bestowed office and honor, was Dryden (1670–1689), but because the position is associated with royal patronage and devotion to the monarchy, other court poets, including Spenser, have been retroactively accorded the title. Shelley uses the charge against Spenser to sneer at one particular "living poet," the current Laureate, Robert Southey (see also Preface to *Adonais* and Byron's Dedication to *Don Juan*).

6. See Isaiah: "Come now, and let us reason together, saith the Lord: though your sins be as scarlet, they shall be as white as snow" (1.18); and Revelation: those in white robes at the throne of God "came out of great tribulation, and have washed their robes, and made them white in the blood of the Lamb" (i.e., Christ; 7.14).

sider how little is as it appears—or appears as it is; look to your own motives, and judge not, lest ye be judged.[7]

Poetry, as has been said, differs in this respect from logic: that it is not subject to the controul of the active power of the mind, and that its birth and recurrence has no necessary connection with the consciousness or will. It is presumptuous to determine that these are the necessary conditions of all mental causation, when mental effects are experienced insusceptible of being referred to them.[8] The frequent recurrence of the poetical power, it is obvious to suppose, may produce in the mind a habit of order and harmony correlative with its own nature and with its effects upon other minds. But in the intervals of inspiration (and they may be frequent without being durable) a poet becomes a man, and is abandoned to the sudden reflux of the influences under which others habitually live. But as he is more delicately organized than other men, and sensible to pain and pleasure (both his own and that of others), in a degree unknown to them,[9] he will avoid the one [pain] and pursue the other [pleasure] with an ardor proportioned to this difference. And he renders himself obnoxious to calumny, when he neglects to observe the circumstances under which these objects of universal pursuit and flight have disguised themselves in one another's garments.

But there is nothing necessarily evil in this error, and thus cruelty, envy, revenge, avarice, and the passions purely evil, have never formed any portion of the popular imputations on the lives of poets.

I have thought it most favourable to the cause of truth to set down these remarks according to the order in which they were suggested to my mind by a consideration of the subject itself, instead of following that of the treatise that excited me to make them public. Thus although devoid of the formality of a polemical reply, if the views which they contain be just, they will be found to involve a refutation of the doctrines of "The Four Ages of Poetry" so far at least as regards the first division of the subject. I can readily conjecture what should have moved the gall of the learned and intelligent author of that paper; I confess myself like him unwilling to be stunned by the *Theseids* of the hoarse Codri of the day. Bavius and Maevius undoubtedly are, as they ever were, insufferable persons. But it belongs to a philosophical critic to distinguish rather than confound.[1]

The first part of these remarks has related to poetry in its elements and principles; and it has been shown, as well as the narrow limits assigned them would permit, that what is called poetry in a restricted sense has a common source with all other forms of order and of beauty according to which the materials of human life are susceptible of being arranged, and which is poetry in a universal sense.

---

7. Christ admonishes: "Judge not, that ye be not judged. For with what judgment ye judge, ye shall be judged" (Matthew 7.1–2); by "contemporary calumnies," slanders and lies intended to ruin reputations, Shelley refers to attacks on himself and others in Tory journals, especially *The Quarterly* (see Preface to *Adonais*). In the Preface of his panegyric on the death of King George III (1820), Poet Laureate Southey described Shelley and Byron as "the Satanic School"; see page 400.
8. "Consciousness and will" in the previous sentence.
9. An echo of Wordsworth's Preface to *Lyrical Ballads*.

1. Theseids are epic poems about Theseus, hero of ancient Greek legend; one of the worst and longest, by Roman poet Codrus (*Codri*, the plural, names poems of this type), was savaged by Juvenal and other satirists. Two other inferior Roman poets, Bavius and Maevius, were satirized by Virgil and Horace; the names became bywords for bad poetry. In the 1790s William Gifford (who would go on to edit *The Anti-Jacobin* and *The Quarterly*) gave the titles *The Baviad* and *The Maeviad* to his devastating mock-heroic satires of the sentimental-aesthetic poetry of the day.

The second part will have for its object an application of these principles to the present state of the cultivation of poetry, and a defense of the attempt to idealize the modern forms of manners and opinions, and compel them into a subordination to the imaginative and creative faculty.[2] For the literature of England, an energetic development of which has ever preceded or accompanied a great and free development of the national will, has arisen, as it were, from a new birth. In spite of the low-thoughted envy which would undervalue contemporary merit, our own will be a memorable age in intellectual achievements, and we live among such philosophers and poets as surpass beyond comparison any who have appeared since the last national struggle for civil and religious liberty.[3] The most unfailing herald, companion, and follower of the awakening of a great people to work a beneficial change in opinion or institution, is poetry. At such periods there is an accumulation of the power of communicating and receiving intense and impassioned conceptions respecting man and nature. The persons in whom this power resides may often (as far as regards many portions of their nature) have little apparent correspondence with that spirit of good of which they are the ministers. But even whilst they deny and abjure, they are yet compelled to serve the power which is seated on the throne of their own soul. It is impossible to read the compositions of the most celebrated writers of the present day[4] without being startled with the electric life which burns within their words. They measure the circumference and sound the depths of human nature with a comprehensive and all-penetrating spirit, and they are themselves perhaps the most sincerely astonished at its manifestations, for it is less their spirit than the spirit of the age. Poets are the hierophants[5] of an unapprehended inspiration, the mirrors of the gigantic shadows which futurity casts upon the present, the words which express what they understand not; the trumpets which sing to battle, and feel not what they inspire; the influence which is moved not, but moves.[6] Poets are the unacknowledged legislators of the world.

<hr />

Felicia Hemans
1793–1835

A best-selling poet in England and America through most of the nineteenth century, Felicia Hemans (née Browne) was prolific. In addition to numerous publications in magazines and gift-books, she produced nineteen volumes of poems and plays between 1808 and 1834. Lord Byron, with whom she shared the publisher John Murray, was sensitive to the competition. In letters to Murray, he tags her "your feminine *He-Man*" or "Mrs. Hewoman's," his punning turning her commercial prowess into a sexual monstrosity. Byron preferred women in their place, not his. "I do not despise Mrs. Heman—but if [she] knit blue stockings instead of wearing them it would be better," he declared to Murray, referring to the "bluestockings," a derisive term for learned women.

<hr />

2. Never drafted.
3. The Civil Wars of the 1640s, concluding in the execution of Charles I, and the Glorious Revolution of the late 1680s, unseating James II. Among "philosophers and poets," Shelley has Byron in mind.

4. Again, himself and Byron.
5. Ancient priests who interpret sacred mysteries; oracles of revelation.
6. Aristotle (Greek philosopher, 4th century B.C.) described God as the "Unmoved Mover" of the universe.

Edward Smith, after a painting by
Edward Robertson, *Portrait of Felicia
Hemans*, 1831. Robertson's portrait
captures the melancholy beauty
that was the poet's hallmark.

Born in Liverpool in 1793, the year of the Terror in France and the execution of its king and queen, Felicia Browne was raised in the distant calms of North Wales. Under the devoted tutelage of her mother, she became a child prodigy, learning Latin, German, French, and Italian, devouring Shakespeare, and quickly developing a talent for writing; when she was fourteen, her parents underwrote the publication of her first volume. Learning of her talents and beauty, Percy Shelley ventured a correspondence, but (fortunately for the young poet) her mother intervened and nothing came of his overture. The romance that did blossom was with Captain Alfred Hemans, a veteran of the Peninsular Campaign in Spain in which her brothers also served. They married in 1812, the year of her nineteenth birthday and third volume, *The Domestic Affections*. By 1818, she had produced three more volumes to favorable reviews, as well as five sons. Just before the birth of the last, the Captain left for Italy; the "story" was ill health. They never saw each other again, the breach mirroring her father's desertion of his wife and children in 1810, for a fresh start in Canada. The collapse of her own and her mother's marriages haunts the idealism of home for which "Mrs. Hemans" was becoming famous, shadowing it with repeated stories of men's unreliability or treachery and the necessity of maternal responsibility.

Determined to support herself and her sons with her writing, Hemans returned to her mother's home in Wales. With no wifely obligations or husband to "obey," and with sisters, mother, and brothers to help care for her boys and run the home, Hemans had considerable time to read, study, write, and publish. Moreover, as a daughter under "the maternal wing" and an "affectionate, tender, and vigilant mother" herself (as prefaces to her works later in the century put it), the professional writer was immunized against the stigma of "unfeminine" independence. The death of her mother in 1827 was a deep and devastating grief, aggravated by the disintegration of her home as sons grew up and brothers and sisters married or moved away. Her health suffered, and after a long decline, she died in Dublin in 1835, a few months before her forty-second birthday. William Wordsworth warmly honored her in the memorial verses of his *Extempore Effusion*, even as he indicated his discomfort with her ignorance of household skills and her affectation of being a "literary lady."

Among Hemans's most successful volumes, both critically and commercially, were *Tales, and Historic Scenes in Verse* (1819), *The Forest Sanctuary* (1825), *Records of Woman* (1828), which she dedicated to Joanna Baillie, and *Songs of the Affections* (1830). She was popular well into the Victorian age, especially among women. By the middle of the twentieth century, she was remembered only by a few favorite poems, including *The Homes of England, The Landing of the Pilgrim Fathers* ("The breaking waves dashed high, / On a stern and rockbound coast") and *Casabianca* ("The boy stood on the burning deck")—this last a parlor-recitation and school-assembly favorite, as well as the subject of multiple parodies. By the 1980s, she was virtually forgotten. In the subsequent recovery of the "lost" women writers of the Romantic era, her work has received fresh attention, especially for its reflection of many key social, psychological, and emotional concerns for women in her day. These involve not only woman's celebrated roles as a patient, devoted, and often long-suffering lover, wife, and mother, but also tensions within these definitions. Some still read her poetry as primers of traditional gender values: women's place at home and upholding "domestic affections," religious faith, and patriotic sentiment. But others find this same poetry haunted by the futility and vulnerability of the ideals it celebrates, invaded by sadness, melancholy, betrayal, suffering, and violence, and repeatedly staging women's heroism in scenes of defeat and death. Hemans was particularly tuned to conflicts besetting women who achieve fame in nontraditional roles, especially as artists, typically at great cost in personal happiness. Poetry by Hemans also appears in "*Manfred* and Its Time," page 397.

from TALES, AND HISTORIC SCENES, IN VERSE

Evening Prayer, at a Girls' School[1]

> Now in thy youth, beseech of Him
>   Who giveth, upbraiding not,
> That his light in thy heart becomes not dim,
>   And his love be unforgot;
> And thy God, in the darkest of days, will be
> Greenness, and beauty, and strength to thee.
>
> —*Bernard Barton*[2]

Hush! 'tis a holy hour—the quiet room
    Seems like a temple, while yon soft lamp sheds
A faint and starry radiance, through the gloom
    And the sweet stillness, down on bright young heads,
5   With all their clustering locks, untouch'd by care,
    And bowed, as flowers are bowed with night, in prayer.

Gaze on—'tis lovely! childhood's lip and cheek,
    Mantling° beneath its earnest brow of thought!   blushing
Gaze, yet what seest thou in those fair and meek
10   And fragile things, as but for sunshine wrought?

---

1. First published in *Forget Me Not*, a gift-book annual, this poem was an anthology favorite in the 19th century.
2. From *The Ivy, Addressed to a Young Friend*. Barton, "the Quaker poet," first sponsored by Quakers, would later secure a pension after he dedicated *Household Verses* (1845) to Queen Victoria.

Thou seest what grief must nurture for the sky,
What Death must fashion for eternity!

O joyous creatures! that will sink to rest,
    Lightly, when those pure orisons° are done,   *prayers*
15 As birds with slumber's honey-dew oppres'd,
    Midst the dim folded leaves, at set of sun—
Lift up your hearts! though yet no sorrow lies
Dark in the summer-heaven of those clear eyes.

Though fresh within your breasts th' untroubled springs
20   Of hope make melody where'er ye tread,
And o'er your sleep bright shadows, from the wings
        Of spirits visiting but youth, be spread—
Yet in those flute-like voices, mingling low,
Is woman's tenderness—how soon her wo!

25 Her lot° is on you!—silent tears to weep,   *fate*
        And patient smiles to wear through suffering's hour,
And sumless riches, from affection's deep,
        To pour on broken reeds—a wasted shower!
And to make idols, and to find them clay,[3]
30 And to bewail that worship—therefore pray!

Her lot is on you!—to be found untir'd,
        Watching the stars out by the bed of pain,
With a pale cheek, and yet a brow inspir'd,
        And a true heart of hope, though hope be vain;
35 Meekly to bear with wrong, to cheer decay,
And, oh! to love through all things—therefore pray!

And take the thought of this calm vesper-time,°   *evening prayer*
        With its low murmuring sounds and silvery light,
On through the dark days fading from their prime,
40   As a sweet dew to keep your souls from blight!
Earth will forsake—Oh! happy to have given
Th'unbroken heart's first fragrance unto Heaven.

1826

CASABIANCA Hemans's most famous (and most scurrilously parodied) poem is based on an episode from the British campaign against Napoleon in Egypt. Ten-year-old Giacomo Jocante Casabianca was a boy-sailor on *L'Orient*, the admiral ship of Napoleon's fleet, commanded by fellow Corsican Louis de Casabianca (Giacomo's father) and destroyed in the Battle of the Nile, August 1798, by the British fleet, commanded by Horatio Nelson. Widely celebrated for this crucial victory, Nelson lost his life in 1805 in the Battle of Trafalgar, his even more celebrated victory over the restored French fleet. The coffin that conveyed him home was crafted from the iron and wrecked mainmast of *L'Orient*, a strange trophy for his future burial presented to him by one of his captains just after the Battle of the Nile. It did not serve this ultimate purpose, but, famously, "was cut in pieces, which were distributed as relics," so Southey writes in *Life of*

3. Stock metaphors: "suffering's hour" is any affliction and particularly childbirth; "broken reeds" are those who die; "idols" of "clay" are those (probably husbands) who prove unworthy of the worship they court.

Horatio, Lord Nelson (1813, much reissued). This *Life* was Hemans's likely source, but one she noticeably alters. Southey reports that "Casa-Bianca, and his son, a brave boy, only ten years old ... were seen floating on a shattered mast when the ship blew up"—"a tremendous explosion ... followed by a silence not less awful"; "the first sound which broke the silence was the dash of her shattered masts and yards, falling into the water from the vast height to which they been exploded. ... no incident in war ... has ever equalled the sublimity of this co-instantaneous pause, and all its circumstances." One of Southey's sources reports that the mast to which the Casabiancas clung was the mainmast used for Nelson's trophy-coffin.

Casabianca[1]

The boy stood on the burning deck
    Whence all but he had fled;
The flame that lit the battle's wreck,
    Shone round him o'er the dead.

5   Yet beautiful and bright he stood,
    As born to rule the storm;
A creature of heroic blood,
    A proud, though child-like form.

The flames rolled on—he would not go,
10   Without his Father's word;
That Father, faint in death below,
    His voice no longer heard.

He called aloud:—"Say, Father, say
    If yet my task is done?"
15   He knew not that the chieftain lay
    Unconscious of his son.

"Speak, Father!" once again he cried,
    "If I may yet be gone!"
And"—but the booming shots replied,
20   And fast the flames rolled on.

Upon his brow he felt their breath,
    And in his waving hair,
And looked from that lone post of death,
    In still, yet brave despair.

25   And shouted but once more aloud,
    "My Father! must I stay?"
While o'er him fast, through sail and shroud,
    The wreathing fires made way.

They wrapt the ship in splendour wild,
30   They caught the flag on high,
And streamed above the gallant child,
    Like banners in the sky.

1. Young Casabianca, a boy about thirteen years old, son to the Admiral of the Orient, remained at his post (in the Battle of the Nile) after the ship had taken fire, and all the guns had been abandoned; and perished in the explosion of the vessel, when the flames had reached the powder. [Hemans's note; Hemans makes the boy older.]

There came a burst of thunder sound—
    The boy—oh! where was he?
35 Ask of the winds that far around
    With fragments strewed the sea!—

With mast, and helm, and pennon° fair,   *pennant*
    That well had borne their part—
But the noblest thing which perished there
40   Was that young faithful heart!
1826   1829

from Records of Woman[1]
Indian Woman's Death-Song

An Indian woman, driven to despair by her husband's desertion of her for another wife, entered a canoe with her children, and rowed it down the Mississippi towards a cataract. Her voice was heard from the shore singing a mournful death-song, until overpowered by the sound of the waters in which she perished. The tale is related in Long's Expedition to the source of St Peter's River.[2]

> Non, je ne puis vivre avec un coeur brisé. Il faut que je retrouve la joie, et que je m'unisse aux esprits libres de l'air.
>
>   *Bride of Messina*, Translated by Madame de Staël[3]

> Let not my child be a girl, for very sad is the life of a woman.
>
>   *The Prairie*[4]

Down a broad river of the western wilds,
Piercing thick forest glooms, a light canoe
Swept with the current: fearful was the speed
Of the frail bark, as by a tempest's wing
5 Borne leaf-like on to where the mist of spray
Rose with the cataract's thunder.—Yet within,
Proudly, and dauntlessly, and all alone,
Save that a babe lay sleeping at her breast,
A woman stood: upon her Indian brow
10 Sat a strange gladness, and her dark hair wav'd
As if triumphantly. She press'd her child,
In its bright slumber, to her beating heart,
And lifted her sweet voice, that rose awhile
Above the sound of waters, high and clear,
15 Wafting a wild proud strain, her song of death.

---

1. Hemans's most popular volume was published in 1828, with a dedication to Joanna Baillie; as in Wollstonecraft, *Woman* identifies a universal category. A subsection of *Miscellaneous Poems* included *The Graves of a Household* and *The Homes of England*.

2. William Hippolytus Keating, *Narrative of an Expedition to the Source of St. Peter's River* (1824), which includes notes from Stephen Long's narrative of his explorations in the American plains states in the 1820s.

3. "No, I cannot live with a broken heart. I must regain joy and join the free spirits of the air"; de Staël's translation of Friedrich Schiller's verse in *De L'Allemagne* (1810).

4. From Chapter 26 of the novel by American James Fenimore Cooper (1827), spoken by the third wife of a Sioux Chief, who has proposed a fourth marriage to a "white" Mexican woman captured by his tribe, promising her status as favorite. The third wife never fully recovers from this betrayal and her sense of inferiority to the white woman.

Roll swiftly to the Spirit's land, thou mighty stream and free!
Father of ancient waters,[5] roll! and bear our lives with thee!
The weary bird that storms have toss'd, would seek the sunshine's calm,
And the deer that hath the arrow's hurt, flies to the woods of balm.

20   Roll on!—my warrior's eye hath look'd upon another's face,
And mine hath faded from his soul, as fades a moonbeam's trace;
My shadow comes not o'er his path, my whisper to his dream,
He flings away the broken reed—roll swifter yet, thou stream!

The voice that spoke of other days is hush'd within *his* breast,
25   But *mine* its lonely music haunts, and will not let me rest;
It sings a low and mournful song of gladness that is gone,
I cannot live without that light—Father of waves! roll on!

Will he not miss the bounding step that met him from the chase?°   *hunt*
The heart of love that made his home an ever sunny place?
30   The hand that spread the hunter's board, and deck'd his couch of yore?—
He will not!—roll, dark foaming stream, on to the better shore!

Some blessed fount amidst the woods of that bright land must flow,
Whose waters from my soul may lave the memory of this wo;
Some gentle wind must whisper there, whose breath may waft away
35   The burden of the heavy night, the sadness of the day.

And thou, my babe! tho' born, like me, for woman's weary lot,
Smile!—to that wasting of the heart, my own! I leave thee not;
Too bright a thing art *thou* to pine in aching love away,
Thy mother bears thee far, young Fawn! from sorrow and decay.

40   She bears thee to the glorious bowers where none are heard to weep,
And where th' unkind one hath no power again to trouble sleep;
And where the soul shall find its youth, as wakening from a dream,—
One moment, and that realm is ours—On, on, dark rolling stream!

Joan of Arc, in Rheims

Jeanne d'Arc avait eu la joie de voir à Chalons quelques amis de son enfance. Une joie
plus ineffable encore l'attendait à Rheims, au sein de son triomphe: Jacques d'Arc, son
père y se trouva, aussitôt que de troupes de Charles VII y furent entrées; et comme les
deux frères de notre Héroïne l'avaient accompagnés, elle se vit, pour un instant au milieu de sa famille, dans les bras d'un père vertueux. *Vie de Jeanne d'Arc.*[1]

---

5. "Father of waters," the Indian name for the Mississippi
[Hemans's note].

1. Joan of Arc had the pleasure of seeing at Chalons some
childhood friends. A still more exquisite pleasure awaited
her at Rheims in the scene of her triumph: Jacques d'Arc,
her father, arrived there just as the troops of Charles VII
made their entry; and as the two brothers of our Heroine
had accompanied him, she found herself for a moment, in
the midst of her family, in the arms of a good father
(*Almanach de Gotha*, 1822). French national heroine,
Jeanne d'Arc (1412–1431), inspired by what she took to
be holy voices, encouraged the Dauphin (prince and

claimant to the throne) to throw off the English claim to
France. She led his troops against the siege of Orleans
and conducted him to the cathedral at Rheims, where he
was crowned Charles VII and she received acclaim. She
continued to lead the war against the English but suffered
defeats and was taken prisoner in 1430; with Charles's
cowardly acquiescence, she was turned over to the
French ecclesiastical court, which tried her for witchcraft, blasphemy, and dressing in male armor; uneasy
about punishing so popular a heroine, however, they
handed her over to the English, who burned her at the
stake in the marketplace at Rouen.

Thou hast a charmed cup, O Fame!
  A draught that mantles° high,   *froths*
And seems to lift this earth-born frame
  Above mortality:
Away! to me—a woman—bring
Sweet waters from affection's spring.[2]

That was a joyous day in Rheims of old,
When peal on peal of mighty music roll'd
Forth from her throng'd cathedral; while around,
A multitude, whose billows made no sound,
5 Chain'd to a hush of wonder, tho' elate
With victory, listen'd at their temple's gate.
And what was done within?—within, the light
  Thro' the rich gloom of pictured windows flowing,
Tinged with soft awfulness a stately sight,
10   The chivalry of France, their proud heads bowing
In martial vassalage!—while midst that ring,
And shadow'd by ancestral tombs, a king
Receiv'd his birthright's crown. For this, the hymn
  Swell'd out like rushing waters, and the day
15 With the sweet censer's misty breath grew dim,
  As thro' long aisles it floated o'er th' array
Of arms and sweeping stoles. But who, alone
And unapproach'd, beside the altar-stone,
With the white banner, forth like sunshine streaming,
20 And the gold helm, thro' clouds of fragrance gleaming,
Silent and radiant stood?—the helm was rais'd,
And the fair face reveal'd, that upward gaz'd,
  Intensely worshipping:—a still, clear face,
Youthful, but brightly solemn!—Woman's cheek
25 And brow were there, in deep devotion meek,
  Yet glorified with inspiration's trace
On its pure paleness; while, enthron'd above,
The pictur'd virgin, with her smile of love,
Seem'd bending o'er her votaress.—That slight form!
30 Was that the leader thro' the battle storm?
Had the soft light in that adoring eye,
Guided the warrior where the swords flash'd high?
'Twas so, even so!—and thou, the shepherd's child,
Joanne,[3] the lowly dreamer of the wild!
35 Never before, and never since that hour,
Hath woman, mantled° with victorious power,   *flushed, covered*
Stood forth as *thou* beside the shrine didst stand,
Holy amidst the knighthood of the land;
And beautiful with joy and with renown,

---

2. The first stanza of Hemans's *Woman and Fame*.   3. A hybrid of French "Jeanne" and English "Joan."

40   Lift thy white banner o'er the olden crown,
       Ransom'd for France by thee!

                              The rites are done.
      Now let the dome with trumpet-notes be shaken,
      And bid the echoes of the tombs awaken,
        And come thou forth, that Heaven's rejoicing sun
45   May give thee welcome from thine own blue skies,
        Daughter of victory!—A triumphant strain,
      A proud rich stream of warlike melodies,
        Gush'd thro' the portals of the antique fane,°   *temple*
      And forth she came.—Then rose a nation's sound—
50   Oh! what a power to bid the quick heart bound,
      The wind bears onward with the stormy cheer
      Man gives to glory on her high career!
      Is there indeed such power?—far deeper dwells
      In one kind household voice, to reach the cells
55   Whence happiness flows forth!—The shouts that fill'd
      The hollow heaven tempestuously, were still'd
      One moment; and in that brief pause, the tone,
      As of a breeze that o'er her home had blown,
      Sank on the bright maid's heart.—"Joanne!"—Who spoke
60   Like those whose childhood with *her* childhood grew
      Under one roof?—"Joanne!"—*that* murmur broke
        With sounds of weeping forth!—She turn'd—she knew
      Beside her, mark'd from all the thousands there,
      In the calm beauty of his silver hair,
65   The stately shepherd; and the youth, whose joy
      From his dark eye flash'd proudly; and the boy,
      The youngest-born, that ever lov'd her best:
      "Father! and ye, my brothers!"—On the breast
      Of that grey sire she sank—and swiftly back,
70   Ev'n in an instant, to their native track
      Her free thoughts flowed.—She saw the pomp no more—
      The plumes, the banners:—to her cabin-door,
      And to the Fairy's fountain in the glade,[4]
      Where her young sisters by her side had play'd,
75   And to her hamlet's chapel, where it rose
      Hallowing the forest unto deep repose,
      Her spirit turn'd.—The very wood-note, sung
        In early spring-time by the bird, which dwelt
      Where o'er her father's roof the beech-leaves hung,
80   Was in her heart; a music heard and felt,
      Winning her back to nature.[5]—She unbound

---

4. A beautiful fountain near Domremi, believed to be haunted by fairies, and a favourite resort of Jeanne d'Arc in her childhood [Hemans's note].

5. The world of nature and also her deepest female "nature" as daughterly maid, before her days of fame.

The helm of many battles from her head,
And, with her bright locks bow'd to sweep the ground,
Lifting her voice up, wept for joy, and said,—
85 "Bless me, my father, bless me! and with thee,
To the still cabin and the beechen-tree,
Let me return!"[6]
                    Oh! never did thine eye
Thro' the green haunts of happy infancy
Wander again, Joanne!—too much of fame
90 Had shed its radiance on thy peasant-name;
And bought alone by gifts beyond all price,[7]
The trusting heart's repose, the paradise
Of home with all its loves, doth fate allow
The crown of glory unto woman's brow.[8]

1826   1828

The Homes of England

"Where's the coward that would not dare
To fight for such a land?"   —*Marmion*[1]

The stately Homes of England,
    How beautiful they stand!
Amidst their tall ancestral trees,
    O'er all the pleasant land.
5 The deer across their greensward bound
    Through shade and sunny gleam,
And the swan glides past them with the sound
    Of some rejoicing stream.

The merry Homes of England!
10   Around their hearths by night,
What gladsome looks of household love
    Meet, in the ruddy light!
There woman's voice flows forth in song,
    Or childhood's tale is told,
15 Or lips move tunefully along
    Some glorious page of old.

The blessed Homes of England!
    How softly on their bowers
Is laid the holy quietness
20   That breathes from Sabbath-hours!
Solemn, yet sweet, the church-bell's chime

---

6. Evoking Jesus's parable of the prodigal son, Luke 15.11–32.
7. Salvation through Christ is a promise "great beyond price" (2 Peter).
8. "Thou never from that hour in Paradise / Found'st either sweet repast, or sound repose," Milton writes of Eve as she leaves Adam's side (*Paradise Lost* 9.406–407).
1. A poetic romance (1808) by Walter Scott.

  Floats through their woods at morn;
   All other sounds, in that still time,
    Of breeze and leaf are born.

25   The Cottage Homes of England!
    By thousands on her plains,
   They are smiling o'er the silvery brooks,
    And round the hamlet-fanes.
   Thro' glowing orchards forth they peep,
30   Each from its nook of leaves,
   And fearless there the lowly° sleep,   *the poor*
    As the bird beneath their eaves.

   The free, fair Homes of England!
    Long, long, in hut and hall,
35   May hearts of native proof be rear'd
    To guard each hallowed wall!
   And green for ever be the groves,
    And bright the flowery sod,
   Where first the child's glad spirit loves
40   Its country and its God!
1827   1828

The Graves of a Household

  They grew in beauty, side by side,
   They filled one home with glee;—
  Their graves are sever'd, far and wide,
   By mount, and stream, and sea.[1]

5 The same fond mother bent at night
   O'er each fair sleeping brow;
  She had each folded flower in sight,—
   Where are those dreamers now?

  One, midst the forest of the west,
10   By a dark stream is laid—
  The Indian knows his place of rest,
   Far in the cedar shade.

  The sea, the blue lone sea, hath one,
   He lies where pearls lie deep;
15 *He* was the lov'd of all, yet none
   O'er his low bed may weep.

  One sleeps where southern vines are drest
   Above the noble slain:
  He wrapt his colours round his breast
20   On a blood-red field of Spain.[2]

1. Hemans's younger brother died in Canada in 1821.
2. Hemans's brothers and husband had served in the war in Spain against Napoleon; her first long poem was *England and Spain, or Valour and Patriotism* (1808).

And one—o'er *her* the myrtle showers
   Its leaves, by soft winds fann'd;
She faded midst Italian flowers,—
   The last of that bright band.

25   And parted thus they rest, who play'd
   Beneath the same green tree;
Whose voices mingled as they pray'd
   Around one parent knee!

They that with smiles lit up the hall,
30   And cheer'd with song the hearth,—
Alas, for love! if *thou* wert all,
   And naught beyond, oh, earth!

1825   1828

Corinne at the Capitol[1]

"Les femmes doivent penser [. . .] qu'il est dans cette car-
rière
   bien peu de sorts qui puissent valoir la plus obscure vie d'une
   femme aimée et d'une mère heureuse."   —*Madame de Staël*[2]

Daughter of th' Italian heaven!
Thou, to whom its fires are given,
Joyously thy car hath roll'd
Where the conqueror's pass'd of old;
5   And the festal sun that shone,
O'er three hundred triumphs gone,[3]
Makes thy day of glory bright,
With a shower of golden light.

Now thou tread'st th' ascending road,
10   Freedom's foot so proudly trode;
While, from tombs of heroes borne,
From the dust of empire shorn,
Flowers upon thy graceful head,
Chaplets° of all hues, are shed,   *head-wreaths*

1. Hemans's title is that of Book 2 of Germaine de Staël's *Corinne, ou l'Italie* (1807). Quickly translated into English, this novel was immensely popular, especially with women, not only Hemans, but also Jane Austen, Mary Godwin (Shelley), Elizabeth Barrett (Browning), George Eliot, and Harriet Beecher (Stowe). It was read as the definitive story of female "genius"—an inspirational and cautionary tale about artistic celebrity at the cost of domestic happiness. De Staël was famous for her intellect, her social charm, her essays, her forthright conversation (including blunt criticism of Napoleon), and her salons, attended by political and literary celebrities. Her heroine, Corinne, half English and half Italian, is a famous performing poet living in Italy, where she meets English Lord Nelvil. With him, we see her for the first time, at the Roman Capitol, celebrated in all her glorious genius. De Staël elaborates her triumph, transcribing "Corinne's Improvisation at the Capitol," and concluding in apotheosis: "No longer a fearful woman, she was an inspired priestess, joyously devoting herself to the cult of genius." Corinne and Nelvil fall in love, but she declines his proposal of marriage, fearing a too-constrained life as an English wife. He returns to England and marries her half sister, a fully proper English maid. When Corinne learns of this, she dies of grief.

2. *De L'influence des Passions* (1796): "Women should consider that in this career there are very few destinies equal in worth to the most obscure life of a beloved wife and a happy mother." *Femme* means both *wife* and *woman*.

3. The trebly hundred triumphs.—Byron [Hemans's note, referring to *Childe Harold's Pilgrimage*, 4.731, a comment on the number of triumphs (victory parades), in ancient Rome.]

15   In a soft and rosy rain,
        Touch'd with many a gemlike stain.

        Thou hast gain'd the summit now!
        Music hails thee from below;—
        Music, whose rich notes might stir
20   Ashes of the sepulchre;
        Shaking with victorious notes
        All the bright air as it floats.
        Well may woman's heart beat high
        Unto that proud harmony!

25   Now afar it rolls—it dies—
        And thy voice is heard to rise
        With a low and lovely tone
        In its thrilling power alone;
        And thy lyre's deep silvery string,
30   Touch'd as by a breeze's wing,
        Murmurs tremblingly at first,
        Ere the tide of rapture burst.

        All the spirit of thy sky
        Now hath lit thy large dark eye,
35   And thy cheek a flush hath caught
        From the joy of kindled thought;
        And the burning words of song
        From thy lip flow fast and strong,
        With a rushing stream's delight
40   In the freedom of its might.

        Radiant daughter of the sun!
        Now thy living wreath is won.
        Crown'd of Rome!—Oh! art thou not
        Happy in that glorious lot?—
45   Happier, happier far than thou,
        With the laurel on thy brow,[4]
        She that makes the humblest hearth
        Lovely but to one on earth!

1827   1830

Woman and Fame[1]

        Happy—happier far than thou,
        With the laurel on thy brow;
        She that makes the humblest hearth,
        Lovely but to one on earth.

---

4. The laurel wreath is a public honor for glorious accomplishment; laurel is the badge of Apollo, classical god of poetry (whence "Poet Laureate").

1. Published in *The Amulet*, an annual. The epigraph is a self-quotation from the end of *Corinne at the Capitol*.

Thou hast a charmed cup, O Fame!
   A draught° that mantles° high,   *drink / blushes*
And seems to lift this earthly frame
   Above mortality.
5   Away! to me—a woman—bring
Sweet waters from affection's spring.[2]

Thou hast green laurel-leaves that twine
   Into so proud a wreath;[3]
For that resplendent gift of thine,
10   Heroes have smiled in death.
Give *me* from some kind hand a flower,
The record of one happy hour!

Thou hast a voice, whose thrilling tone
   Can bid each life-pulse beat,
15 As when a trumpet's note hath blown,
   Calling the brave to meet:
But mine, let mine—a woman's breast,
By words of home-born love be bless'd.

A hollow sound is in thy song,
20   A mockery in thine eye,
To the sick heart that doth but long
   For aid, for sympathy;
For kindly looks to cheer it on,
For tender accents that are gone.

25 Fame, Fame! thou canst not be the stay
    Unto the drooping reed,
The cool fresh fountain, in the day
    Of the soul's feverish need;
Where must the lone one turn or flee?—
30 Not unto thee, oh! not to thee!

1827–1829   1829

⊢ ⊨⊠⊨ ⊣

John Clare
1793–1864

The horizon of John Clare's world was defined by the village of Helpston, Northamptonshire, in which he was born to a barely literate farmhand and an illiterate mother. His formal education was sparse, though his poetry shows his knowledge of Milton and Thomson, and he read Wordsworth, Coleridge, Keats, and Byron (two late long poems are titled *Childe Harold* and *Don Juan*). By the "indefatigable savings of a penny and a half-penny," young Clare purchased fairy tales from hawkers, recalling, "I firmly believed every page I read and considerd I possessd

---

2. The epigraph for *Joan of Arc, in Rheims*.   3. See page 525 n. 4 to *Corinne at the Capitol*.

in these the chief learning and literature of the country." His own writing was produced swiftly and with few revisions in time seized from agricultural labor, then hid "with all secresy possible" in "an old unused cubbard" or hole in the wall.

Clare's condition placed him in the line of those "natural geniuses" eagerly sought by eighteenth-century primitivism: Stephen Duck "The Thresher Poet" (1705–1756), Robert Bloomfield (*The Farmer's Boy*, 1800), Ann Yearsley "The Milkmaid Poet" (1752–1806), and Robert Burns (1759–1796) had all been fit into the stereotype of the peasant poet. In 1817 John Taylor saw Clare's proposal to publish a volume of poetry by subscription; in 1820 his firm brought out *Poems Descriptive of Rural Life and Scenery*, marketing it as the work of a young "Northamptonshire Peasant," a description that fixed Clare's regional and class identity. The book enjoyed critical and popular success, with four editions in a year. The vogue that brought Clare attention quickly came to constrain him: his Evangelical patron disapproved of his social criticism and "vulgar" manner, while Taylor sought to broaden his appeal by standardizing his language and cutting his poems. Clare's pungent dialect usages—which illustrate by contrast how thoroughly Wordsworth "purified" the "language really used by men" in *Lyrical Ballads*—and belief "that what ever is intellig[i]ble to others is grammer and what ever is commonsense is not far from correctness" offended the norms of polite literature. "Grammer in learning," Clare adamantly insisted to Taylor in a phrase that by linking style and politics makes clear the twin offenses he posed to the urban book-buying public, "is like Tyranny in government—confound the bitch Ill never be her slave." Taylor found himself in the awkward position of intermediary between an audience for poetry increasingly represented by genteel women and a prickly lower-class male writer: "*false delicasy* damn it I hate it beyond every thing those primpt up misses brought up in those seminaries of mysterious wickedness (Boarding Schools) what will please 'em? why we well know—but while their heart & soul loves to extravagance (what we dare not mention) false delicasy's seriousness muscles [muzzles] up the mouth & condemns it." If that explosion reminds one of the "rhodomontade" with which Keats defended his sexually more explicit revisions to *The Eve of St. Agnes*, the distance between the literariness of Keats, whom Clare admired, and Clare's plainness is manifest in his objection that Keats "keeps up a constant alusion or illusion to the grecian mythology & there I cannot follow . . . the frequency of such classical accompaniment makes it wearisome to the reader where behind every rose bush he looks for a Venus & under every laurel a thrumming Appollo."

Before long, readers lost interest in Clare's rough independence from their expectations of verse. *The Village Minstrel* (1821) sold badly and *The Shepherd's Calendar* (1827) even worse; *The Rural Muse* (1835) got good reviews but not a readership. By then Clare had left Helpston for Northborough, where he moved to a cottage provided by another patron, hoping to set himself up as a farmer. Though the move measured only a few miles, it broke his firm sense of place. In 1837 Clare was admitted to an asylum for the mentally ill in southeast England, from which he escaped in 1841, walking back the eighty miles to Northborough. He was recommitted to an asylum in Northampton, where he spent the remaining years of his life. Yet Clare never ceased to write. His early poetry depicts with marked individuality a rural existence threatened by enclosure and by widening difference between classes; long and close observation of the landscape, of animals and birds, produced sharply detailed images in "a language that is ever green" (*Pastoral Poesy*) and far removed from the "egotistical sublime" to which Wordsworth's experience of nature gives rise. Clare once proclaimed of *Composed Upon Westminster Bridge* "I think it (& woud say it to the teeth of the critic in spite of his rule & compass) that it owns no equal in the English language," but he mocked Wordsworth's "affectations of simplicity." The delusions and instabilities of Clare's identity in the asylum period led to a poetry of fantasized memory and loss that possesses a strange and often visionary power.

New editions of Clare's writings have freed his texts from the emendations of their first publication and have brought unpublished materials to view, winning him the audience he missed in his own time. As illustration, we print two versions of *Written in November*, the first from the manuscripts edited by Eric Robinson and David Powell, the source of our texts, the second as the poem appeared in *The Village Minstrel* (1821).

Written in November (manuscript)

Autumn I love thy latter end to view
In cold novembers day so bleak & bare
When like lifes dwindled thread worn nearly thro
Wi lingering pottering° pace & head bleached bare   *dawdling, uncertain*
5   Thou like an old man bids the world adieu
I love thee well & often when a child
Have roamd the bare brown heath a flower to find
& in the moss clad vale & wood bank wild
Have cropt the little bell flowers paley blue
10   That trembling peept the sheltering bush behind
When winnowing north winds cold & blealy° blew   *coldly, bleakly*
How have I joyd wi dithering° hands to find   *shivering*
Each fading flower & still how sweet the blast
Would bleak novembers hour Restore the joy thats past

Written in November

Autumn, I love thy parting look to view
    In cold November's day, so bleak and bare,
When, thy life's dwindled thread worn nearly thro',
    With ling'ring pott'ring pace, and head bleach'd bare,
5   Thou, like an old man, bidd'st the world adieu.
    I love thee well: and often, when a child,
Have roam'd the bare brown heath a flower to find;
    And in the moss-clad vale, and wood-bank wild
Have cropt the little bell-flowers, pearly blue,
10   That trembling peep the shelt'ring bush behind.
When winnowing north-winds cold and bleaky blew,
    How have I joy'd, with dithering hands, to find
Each fading flower; and still how sweet the blast,
    Would bleak November's hour restore the joy that's past.

c. 1812   1821

Songs Eternity

What is songs eternity
Come and see
Can it noise and bustle be
Come and see
5   Praises sung or praises said
Can it be

Wait awhile and these are dead
Sigh sigh
Be they high or lowly bred
10   They die

What is songs eternity
Come and see
Melodys of earth and sky
Here they be
15   Songs once sung to adams ears
Can it be
—Ballads of six thousand years
Thrive thrive
Songs awakened with the spheres
20   Alive

Mighty songs that miss decay
What are they
Crowds and citys pass away
Like a day
25   Books are writ and books are read
What are they
Years will lay them with the dead
Sigh sigh
Trifles unto nothing wed
30   They die

Dreamers list the honey be[e]
Mark the tree
Where the blue cap tootle tee
Sings a glee
35   Sung to adam and to eve
Here they be
When floods covered every bough
Noahs ark
Heard that ballad singing now
40   Hark hark

Tootle tootle tootle tee
Can it be
Pride and fame must shadows be
Come and see
45   Every season own her own
Bird and be[e]
Sing creations music on
Natures glee
Is in every mood and tone
50   Eternity

The eternity of song
Liveth here

Natures universal tongue
Singeth here
55 Songs Ive heard and felt and seen
Everywhere
Songs like the grass are evergreen
The giver
Said live and be and they have been
For ever
1812–1831

[The Mouse's Nest]

I found a ball of grass among the hay
And proged° it as I passed and went away   *prodded*
And when I looked I fancied somthing stirred
And turned agen and hoped to catch the bird
5 When out an old mouse bolted in the wheat
With all her young ones hanging at her teats
She looked so odd and so grotesque to me
I ran and wondered what the thing could be
And pushed the knapweed° bunches where I stood   *purple flower*
10 When the mouse hurried from the crawling brood
The young ones squeaked and when I went away
She found her nest again among the hay
The water oer the pebbles scarce could run
And broad old cesspools° glittered in the sun   *pools of standing water*
c. 1835–1837   1935

John Keats
1795–1821

"A thing of beauty is a joy for ever"; "tender is the night"; "Beauty is truth; truth Beauty"—these phrases are so well known that we may forget that they were unheard before John Keats. Keats's brief career ran only from 1814, when he wrote his first poem, to 1820, when he revised his sonnet *Bright Star* on board a ship to Italy. "Oh, for ten years, that I may overwhelm / Myself in poesy," he said in 1816. Not even getting this decade, his active life as a writer stopped around his twenty-fourth birthday. At age twenty-four, Chaucer had yet to write anything, and if Shakespeare had died at twenty-four, he would be known only (if at all) by a few early works. What if Keats had lived until 1881, like that Victorian sage Thomas Carlyle, also born in 1795?

The drama of Keats is not just the poignancy of genius cut off in youth but also his humble origins—a focus of ridicule during and after his lifetime by class-conscious reviewers and aristocratic poets. Son of a livery-stable keeper who had married the owner's daughter and inherited the suburban London business, Keats attended the progressive Enfield School. Here he was tutored and befriended by Charles Cowden Clarke, the headmaster's son, who introduced him to literature, music, the theater. When Keats was nine years old, his father died in a riding accident and his mother remarried immediately; her commitment to her children was as erratic as it was doting, and her presence at home was inconstant. Keats was deeply attached to her and devastated when she disappeared for four years, leaving them all with his grandmother. When she returned sick and consumptive, he nursed her, and she died when he was fourteen; the welter of emotions she left in him is reflected in the series of adored, inconstant women around which so much of his poetry revolves. The children were remanded to the guardianship of a practical businessman whose chief concern was to apprentice the boys to some viable trade. Unimaginative himself and unsympathetic to any passion for learning and poetry, he apprenticed Keats to a London hospital surgeon in the grim days before anesthesia. Keats stayed with this training long enough to be licensed as an apothecary (more a general practitioner than a druggist), but he frequently took time off to read and to write poetry. When he came of age in 1817, he gave up medicine and set out to make a living as a poet.

Keats was already enjoying the society of Clarke and his circle of politically progressive thinkers, artists, poets, journalists, and publishers, many of whom became close friends—among them Leigh Hunt, also a poet as well as a radical journalist. Hunt launched Keats's career, publishing him in his weekly paper, *The Examiner,* and advertising him as one of the rising "Young Poets." It was through Hunt that Keats met some of the chief nonestablishment writers of the day— William Wordsworth, William Hazlitt, Charles Lamb, Percy Shelley—and the controversial painter Benjamin Robert Haydon. His inaugural volume, published in 1817, included twenty sonnets, a favorite form for him, as well as Spenserian stanzas, odes, verse epistles, romance fragments, and meditative long poems on the subject of poetry itself. The writers that mattered most to him were Spenser (his first poem, written in 1814, was a deft "Imitation of Spenser" in Spenserian stanzas), Shakespeare, and ambivalently, Milton, and among his contemporaries, Wordsworth and Byron, though again with intelligent ambivalence. Keats warmly dedicated the 1817 *Poems* to Hunt and in a long concluding piece (*Sleep and Poetry*) voiced sharp criticism of what he saw as the arid formalism of eighteenth-century neoclassical poetry, which still had prestige with conservative or aristocratic writers, including Byron. Byron never forgave Keats for this tirade, and it immediately provoked the Tory journalists, who were only too eager to jab at their political enemy Hunt through his protégé. Published in a year when civil rights were weakened and the radical publisher William Hone brought to trial, *Poems* was viciously ridiculed in reviews marked by social snobbery and political prejudice, and Keats was indelibly tagged "the Cockney Poet"—one of Hunt's suburban radicals. He was stung, but determined to prove himself with his next effort, *Endymion,* initiated as part of a contest with Hunt and Shelley to see who could write a 4,000-line poem by the end of 1817. The only one to complete the challenge, Keats set off with a sense that it would be "a test" or "trial" of his talents. "A thing of beauty is a joy for ever" begins this tale of a shepherd-prince who dreams of a goddess, and on waking is profoundly alienated from ordinary life in the world. Book I narrates this episode; over the course of the next three books, Endymion dreams of her again, loses her, searches high (more dreams) and low (underground to the Bower of Venus and Adonis and several other labyrinthine terrains), and finally gives up, falling for a maid he finds abandoned in the woods. She turns out to be his goddess in disguise, and his dream comes true. This is the last time in Keats's poetry that dreams are so happily realized.

The same reviewers who had hooted at Keats's debut were waiting to savage *Endymion,* which they did with glee in the summer of 1818. But Keats himself had already grown weary of this poem, calling it "slipshod," and coming to feel that the most powerful poets did not write escapist, "golden-tongued Romance" but embraced the "fierce dispute" of life in the world. In 1818 he was attending Hazlitt's London lectures on English poetry, rereading *Paradise Lost, Hamlet, King Lear,* and Henry Cary's recent translation of Dante's *Divine Comedy.* He was also acknowledging that Wordsworth, whose didacticism and egotism he disliked, had a profoundly modern sense of the "dark passages" of life—the misfortunes, miseries, and griefs that could not be dispelled by simple romance or explained away by simplistic moral philosophies. It was in this temper that Keats began a revisionary Miltonic epic, *Hyperion,* whose hero was intended to be Apollo, the god of knowledge, po-

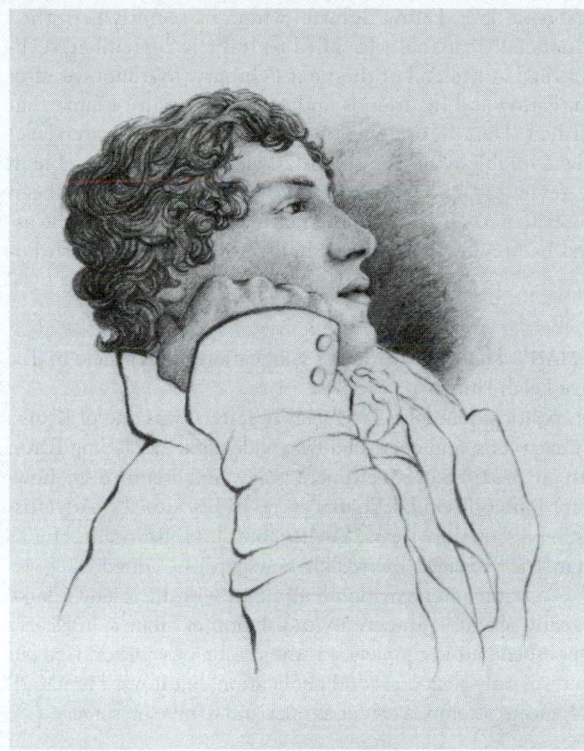

Charles Brown, *Portrait of John Keats*, 1819. Brown, Keats's friend, and traveling companion in the summer of 1818, invited Keats to move in with him after the death of Keats's brother Tom in December. Keats remained at Wentworth Place until the end of summer 1820, when he left for Italy. This charcoal sketch, which was unknown in the 19th century, presents Keats in a stylish Regency mode: handsome, contemplative, rakishly "poetic."

etry, and medicine—a linkage dear to Keats. Its most deeply felt poetry, however—in the two books that Keats completed—involved the sorrows and anxieties of gods suffering their ejection from heaven, and the plight of the sun god Hyperion, not yet fallen but sensing his fate. When Keats turned to Apollo in Book 3, he lost inspiration, in part because he was feeling acutely the very mortal pain of nursing his beloved brother Tom, dying of tuberculosis, the disease that had killed their mother and that would kill Keats himself three years later (already he was suffering from a chronically sore throat).

Tom died at the end of 1818, and Keats sought relief in his poetry. In a burst of inspiration that lasted well into the fall of 1819 (when he revised *Hyperion*), he produced the work that established his fame: *The Eve of St. Agnes* (a part serious, part ironic romance), *La Belle Dame sans Mercy* (a romance with a vengeance), *Lamia* (a wickedly satirical, bitter romance), all the Great Odes, and a clutch of brilliant sonnets, including *Bright Star*. Although (unlike most of his contemporaries) he wrote no prefaces, defenses, self-promoting polemics, or theoretical essays, his letters display a critical intelligence as brilliant as the poetic talent. A number of their off-the-cuff formulations—the "finer tone" of repetition, "negative capability," "the camelion Poet," "the egotistical sublime," truth "proved upon our pulses"—have become standard terms in literary criticism and theory, and his letters from their first publication, after his death, have been admired for their generosity and playfulness, their insight, their candor, and their critical penetration.

His health worsening over the course of 1819, Keats suffered a major lung hemorrhage early in 1820; with the accuracy of his medical training, he read his "death warrant" and was devastated. For despite the shaky reception of *Poems* and *Endymion*, he was hopeful about his forthcoming volume and full of plans for new writing (journalism or plays); he was also deeply in love with the girl next door, Fanny Brawne, whom he secretly betrothed and hoped to marry once he was financially capable. He sailed to Italy in September, seeking health in a warmer climate, but died at the end of the next February, four months after his twenty-fifth birthday—far from Fanny and his friends and in such despair of fame that he asked his tombstone to be inscribed "Here lies one whose name was writ in water." Yet he did live long enough to see some favorable reviews of his 1820 volume. Shelley's fable in *Adonais* of Keats killed by hostile reviewers, though often credited, could not have been more out of tune with Keats's own resilience. "This is a mere matter of the moment," he assured his brother George of the first bad reviews; "I think I shall be among the English Poets after my death."

ON FIRST LOOKING INTO CHAPMAN'S HOMER   (from its publication in an article in *The Examiner*, 1 December 1816, by editor Leigh Hunt).

Leigh Hunt (1784–1859), poet, political journalist, and man of letters, was one of Keats's earliest, warmest and most devoted champions, and cherished by a wide circle, including Byron and Shelley. His radical politics, both on questions of government policy and literary taste, however, made Keats an unlucky target for John Gibson Lockhart's essays in *Blackwood's*. Advertising a rising generation of new poets, represented by Keats, Shelley, and J. H. Reynolds, Hunt's essay appeared on 1 December 1816 in *The Examiner*, the weekly newspaper he edited. This was the first publication of the sonnet Keats wrote after staying up all night with his friend Clarke reading George Chapman's vibrant, early seventeenth-century translation of Homer; in Keats's day, Alexander Pope's rendering in polished heroic couplets was the prestigious version (see our samples from both, below) the sonnet was only Keats's second publication, but it was Hunt's advertisement of him that encouraged Keats to attempt a career as poet and to give up surgery.

YOUNG POETS

In sitting down to this subject, we happen to be restricted by time to a much shorter notice than we could wish: but we mean to take it up again shortly. Many of our readers however have perhaps observed for themselves, that there has been a new school of poetry rising of late, which promises to extinguish the French one that has prevailed among us since the time of Charles the 2d.[1] It began with something excessive, like most revolutions, but this gradually wore away; and an evident aspiration after real nature and original fancy remained, which called to mind the finer times of the English Muse. In fact it is wrong to call it a new school, and still more so to represent it as one of innovation, it's only object being to restore the same love of Nature, and of *thinking* instead of mere *talking*, which formerly rendered us real poets, and not merely versifying wits, and bead-rollers of couplets.

We were delighted to see the departure of the old school acknowledged in the number of the *Edinburgh Review* just published,—a candour more generous and spirited, inasmuch as that work has hitherto been the greatest surviving ornament of the same school in prose and criticism, as it is now destined, we trust, to be still the leader in the new.[2]

---

1. For Keats's rejection of the influence of French neoclassicism on 18th century British poets, see *Sleep and Poetry* 181–206.
2. A long essay in the September 1816 issue on 18th-

century poet and satirist Jonathan Swift's *Works* declared that "the writers who adorned the beginning of the last century have been eclipsed by those of our own time . . . a revolution in our literature."

We also felt the same delight at the third canto of Lord Byron's *Child Harolde* [sic], in which, to our conceptions at least, he has fairly renounced a certain leaven of the French style, and taken his place where we always said he would be found,— among the poets who have a real feeling for numbers, and who go directly to Nature for inspiration. * * *

The object of the present article is merely to notice three young writers, who appear to us to promise a considerable addition of strength to the new school. Of the first who came before us, we have, it is true, yet seen only one or two specimens, and these were no sooner sent us than we unfortunately mislaid them; but we shall procure what he has published, and if the rest answer to what we have seen, we shall have no hesitation in announcing him for a very striking and original thinker. His name is PERCY BYSSHE SHELLEY, and he is the author of a poetical work entitled *Alastor, or the Spirit of Solitude*.[3]

The next with whose name we became acquainted, was JOHN HENRY REYNOLDS, author of a tale called *Safie*, written, we believe in imitation of Lord Byron, and more lately of a small set of poems published by Taylor and Hessey,[4] the principal of which is called the *Naiad*. [quotes lines 1–27] * * * The author's style is too artificial, though he is evidently an admirer of Mr. Wordsworth. Like all young poets too, properly so called, his love of detail is too over-wrought and indiscriminate; but still he is a young poet, and only wants a still closer attention to things as opposed to the seduction of words, to realize all that he promises. His nature seems very true and amiable.

The last of these young aspirants, whom we have met with, and who promises to help the new school to revive Nature and

> "To put a spirit of youth in every thing,"—[5]

is, we believe, the youngest of them all, and just of age. His name is JOHN KEATS. He has not yet published any thing except in a newspaper;[6] but a set of his manuscripts was handed us the other day, and fairly surprised us with the truth of their ambition, and ardent grappling with Nature. In the following Sonnet there is one incorrect rhyme, which might be easily altered, but which shall serve in the mean time as a peace-offering to the rhyming critics. The rest of the composition, with the exception of a little vagueness in calling the regions of poetry "the realms of gold," we do not hesitate to pronounce excellent, especially the first six lines. The word *swims* is complete; and the conclusion is equally powerful and quiet:—

On First Looking into Chapman's Homer.

Much have I travel'd in the realms of Gold,[7]
    And many goodly states and Kingdoms seen;
    Round many western Islands have I been,

3. Published March 1816, this 720-line poem in heroic blank verse is a tale of visionary quest fulfilled in death. Keats's *Endymion* (1818) is an oblique quarrel with its metaphysics.
4. After the publishers of Keats's first volume dropped him, this firm would publish *Endymion* and the 1820 volume. The poet's middle name is actually Hamilton.
5. Shakespeare, Sonnet 98, describing April.

6. The sonnet *To Solitude* in *The Examiner* 5 May 1816 was Keats's first (and thus far, only) publication.
7. In *A Defence of Poesie* (1595), Sir Philip Sidney wrote that poets "deliver a golden" world from the "brazen" one of nature; Keats's metaphor also involves early modern explorations for gold by new-world adventurers such as Cortez, conquistador of Mexico.

Which Bards in fealty to Apollo[8] hold.
But of one wide expanse had I been told
    That deep-brow'd Homer ruled as his demesne;[9]
    Yet could I never judge what men could mean,[1]
Till I heard CHAPMAN speak out loud and bold,
Then felt I like some watcher of the skies,
    When a new planet swims into his ken;[2]
Or like stout CORTEZ, when with eagle eyes
He stared at the Pacific,—and all his men
Looked at each other with a wild surmise,—
Silent, upon a peak in Darien.[3]

Oct. 1816   JOHN KEATS.

"To one who has been long in city pent"

To one who has been long in city pent,[1]
    'Tis very sweet to look into the fair
    And open face of heaven,—to breathe a prayer
Full in the smile of the blue firmament.
5   Who is more happy, when, with hearts content,
    Fatigued he sinks into some pleasant lair
    Of wavy grass, and reads a debonair
And gentle tale of love and languishment?
Returning home at evening, with an ear
10   Catching the notes of Philomel,[2]—an eye
Watching the sailing cloudlet's bright career,
    He mourns that day so soon has glided by:
E'en like the passage of an angel's tear
    That falls through the clear ether° silently.   *upper air*

1816   1817

On Seeing the Elgin Marbles[1]

My spirit is too weak—Mortality
    Weighs heavily on me like unwilling sleep,

---

8. God of poetry.
9. Domain or realm.
1. *Poems* 1817] Yet did I never breathe its pure serene. (serene: expanse of clear sky.)
2. Range of apprehension; Uranus was discovered in 1781.
3. Panama. There is no reason to agree with Tennyson that Cortez is a mistake for Balboa (the first European to see the Pacific Ocean), and a sign of Keats's inferior education.
1. An allusion to *Paradise Lost* 9.445ff, an extended simile for Satan, on his first morning in the Garden of Eden (he is there to seduce Eve): "As one who long in populous city pent, / Where houses thick and sewers annoy the air, / Forth issuing on a summer's morn to breathe / Among the pleasant villages and farms. . . ." Keats's alignment instances a Romantic embrace of Milton's Satan as a psychological ally rather than moral antagonist.

2. Literally, "lover of song." The poetic name for nightingale evokes the Philomel of Ovid's *Metamorphoses*, a maiden raped, tortured, and ultimately turned by the gods into a nightingale, who sings in pain. See n. 8 on page 544.
1. Keats viewed these sculptural fragments from the Athenian Parthenon with Haydon, a champion of Lord Elgin's purchase of them in 1806 from the Turks, then occupying Greece. Elgin (hard g) was motivated both by admiration for their powerful beauty and a desire to preserve them from erosion and the further peril of being turned into mortar or used for target practice by Turkish soldiers. Their aesthetic value was debated (some found them crude and even inauthentic), and their purchase by the government in 1816 for deposit in the British Museum (they are still there) was (and still is) controversial. Keats's sonnet appeared in *The Examiner* in 1817 (our text) and in Haydon's *Annals of the Fine Arts* in 1818.

And each imagined pinnacle and steep
Of godlike hardship, tells me I must die
5   Like a sick Eagle looking at the sky.
      Yet 'tis a gentle luxury to weep
That I have not the cloudy winds to keep,
Fresh for the opening of the morning's eye.
Such dim-conceived glories of the brain
10   Bring round the heart an undescribable feud;
So do these wonders a most dizzy pain,
      That mingles Grecian grandeur with the rude
Wasting of old time—with a billowy main°—   *sea*
    A sun—a shadow of a magnitude.

1817   J.K.   1817

On sitting down to read King Lear once again[1]

O golden-tongued Romance, with serene lute!
Fair plumed Syren![2] Queen of far-away!
Leave melodizing on this wintry day,
Shut up thine olden pages, and be mute:
5   Adieu! for, once again, the fierce dispute,
      Betwixt damnation and impassion'd clay[3]
Must I burn through; once more assay[4]
The bitter sweet of this Shakesperean fruit:
Chief Poet! and ye clouds of Albion,[5]
10   Begetters of our deep eternal theme!
When through the old oak forest I am gone,
      Let me not wander in a barren dream,
But when I am consumed in the Fire,
Give me new Phoenix-wings to fly at my desire.[6]

January 1818   (1838, 1848), 1899

Sonnet: When I have fears

When I have fears that I may cease to be[1]
Before my pen has glean'd my teeming brain,
Before high piled books, in charact'ry,°   *written symbols*

---

1. The emphasis on reading is critical, for Keats would not have been able to see Shakespeare's play. The stage was held by Nahum Tate's "romance" revision (1681): Lear doesn't die but regains the throne, then abdicates to newlyweds Edgar and Cordelia (she doesn't die either), and happily retires with Gloucester (ditto) and Kent.
2. Temptress and seductress; the Sirens of myth seemed women above the waist but were really birds of prey, whose singing lured men to destruction.
3. The body and its mortal limitations; in *Childe Harold III* (1816), Byron described man as "clay" that inevitably "will sink / Its spark immortal" (14). In a letter-draft, Keats wrote "Hell-torment" instead of "Damnation."
4. Analyze the contents of, more specifically, the gold

content of ore.
5. Old Celtic name for England, frequent in Romance; *King Lear* is set in the Celtic era.
6. Phoenix: bird fabled to rejuvenate itself with cyclical self-immolation and rebirth from its ashes.
1. Several allusive echoes: Shakespeare's "When I do count the clock that tells the time"; Wordsworth's "few could know / When Lucy ceased to be" (*She dwelt among th'untrodden ways*; see page 209); Shelley's lament that by 1816 the radical Wordsworth should "cease to be" (*To Wordsworth*; see page 470); Milton's sonnet, "When I consider how my light is spent / Ere half my days, in this dark world and wide . . ."

> Hold like rich garners the full-ripened grain;
5   When I behold, upon the night's starr'd face,
>   Huge cloudy symbols of a high romance,
> And think that I may never live to trace
>   Their shadows, with the magic hand of chance;
> And when I feel, fair creature of an hour!
10   That I shall never look upon thee more,
> Never have relish in the faery power
>   Of unreflecting love!—then on the shore
> Of the wide world I stand alone, and think
> Till Love and Fame to nothingness do sink.

January 1818   1848

THE EVE OF ST. AGNES   Keats began this poem in the winter months of early 1819, setting it on St. Agnes' Eve, when, according to legend, a young virgin who has performed certain rituals may dream of her future husband. The story of this patron saint of virgins is quite violent. A thirteen-year-old Christian martyr in early fourth-century Rome, she was condemned to a night of rape in the brothels before execution. This preliminary torture was prevented by a miraculous storm of thunder and lightning, a climate that Keats writes into the end of his poem. Working in the intricate form of Spenserian stanzas, popularized by Byron's *Childe Harold's Pilgrimage* (1812–1818), Keats spins an ironic romance—at once indulging the traditional pleasures of the genre (love, imagination, gorgeous sensuality with a spiritual aura) and bringing a playful, sometimes satiric, sometimes darkly shaded perspective to its illusions. With *Romeo and Juliet* in mind, Keats portrayed the sexual desire of his hero and heroine, but his publishers, worried about indecency, forced him to revise. Though he complied with angry reluctance, the imagery of stars and flowers in stanza 36 shows his skill in retaining some of the original pulsation. We give some of his original draft in our footnotes.

The Eve of St. Agnes

I

> St. Agnes' Eve—Ah, bitter chill it was!
> The owl, for all his feathers, was a-cold;
> The hare limp'd trembling through the frozen grass,
> And silent was the flock in woolly fold:
5 Numb were the Beadsman's fingers, while he told
> His rosary,[1] and while his frosted breath,
> Like pious incense from a censer old,
> Seem'd taking flight for heaven, without a death,
> Past the sweet Virgin's picture, while his prayer he saith.

II

10 His prayer he saith, this patient, holy man;
> Then takes his lamp, and riseth from his knees,
> And back returneth, meagre, barefoot, wan,
> Along the chapel aisle by slow degrees:

---

1. A pensioner paid to say prayers, this beadsman is saying a rosary in the estate's cold chapel for the salvation of the ancestors.

The sculptur'd dead, on each side, seem to freeze,
15   Emprison'd in black, purgatorial rails:
       Knights, ladies, praying in dumb orat'ries,°   *chapels*
       He passeth by; and his weak spirit fails
To think how they may ache in icy hoods and mails.°   *armor*

                              III

       Northward he turneth through a little door,
20   And scarce three steps, ere Music's golden tongue
       Flatter'd to tears this aged man and poor;
       But no—already had his deathbell rung;
       The joys of all his life were said and sung:
       His was harsh penance on St. Agnes' Eve:
25   Another way he went, and soon among
       Rough ashes sat he for his soul's reprieve,
And all night kept awake, for sinners' sake to grieve.

                              IV

       That ancient Beadsman heard the prelude soft;
       And so it chanc'd, for many a door was wide,
30   From hurry to and fro. Soon, up aloft,
       The silver, snarling trumpets 'gan to chide:
       The level chambers, ready with their pride,
       Were glowing to receive a thousand guests:
       The carved angels, ever eager-eyed,
35   Star'd, where upon their heads the cornice rests,
With hair blown back, and wings put cross-wise on their breasts.

                              V

       At length burst in the argent° revelry,   *silvery*
       With plume, tiara, and all rich array,
       Numerous as shadows haunting fairily
40   The brain, new stuff'd, in youth, with triumphs gay
       Of old romance.[2] These let us wish away,
       And turn, sole-thoughted, to one Lady there,
       Whose heart had brooded, all that wintry day,
       On love, and wing'd St. Agnes' saintly care,
45   As she had heard old dames full many times declare.

                              VI

       They told her how, upon St. Agnes' Eve,
       Young virgins might have visions of delight,
       And soft adorings from their loves receive
       Upon the honey'd middle of the night,
50   If ceremonies due they did aright;
       As, supperless to bed they must retire,
       And couch supine their beauties, lily white;

2. The literary genre; see the sonnet on *Lear* page 537.

Nor look behind, nor sideways, but require°   *beseech*
Of Heaven with upward eyes for all that they desire.[3]

VII

55 Full of this whim was thoughtful Madeline:[4]
The music, yearning like a God in pain,
She scarcely heard: her maiden eyes divine,
Fix'd on the floor, saw many a sweeping train°   *long skirt*
Pass by—she heeded not at all: in vain
60 Came many a tiptoe, amorous cavalier,
And back retir'd; not cool'd by high disdain,
But she saw not: her heart was otherwhere:
She sigh'd for Agnes' dreams, the sweetest of the year.

VIII

She danc'd along with vague, regardless eyes,
65 Anxious her lips, her breathing quick and short:[5]
The hallow'd hour was near at hand: she sighs
Amid the timbrels,° and the throng'd resort   *tambourines*
Of whisperers in anger, or in sport;
'Mid looks of love, defiance, hate, and scorn,
70 Hoodwink'd° with faery fancy; all amort,°   *blinded / dead*
Save to St. Agnes and her lambs unshorn,
And all the bliss to be before to-morrow morn.[6]

IX

So, purposing each moment to retire,
She linger'd still. Meantime, across the moors,
75 Had come young Porphyro,[7] with heart on fire
For Madeline. Beside the portal doors,
Buttress'd from moonlight,[8] stands he, and implores
All saints to give him sight of Madeline,
But for one moment in the tedious hours,
80 That he might gaze and worship all unseen;
Perchance speak, kneel, touch, kiss—in sooth such things have been.

X

He ventures in: let no buzz'd whisper tell:
All eyes be muffled, or a hundred swords

---

3. Keats's publishers forced him to cancel as too explicitly erotic a stanza that followed this one, recounting the fable of a maid's "future lord" appearing in her dreams, bringing "delicious food even to her lips": "Viands, and wine, and fruit, and sugared cream, / To touch her palate with the fine extreme / Of relish; the soft music heard; and then / More pleasures followed in a dizzy stream, / Palpable almost; then to wake again / Warm in the virgin morn, no weeping Magdalen"—i.e., Mary Magdalen, the prostitute befriended by Jesus; in Keats's day hospitals for unwed mothers were called Magdalens.
4. A name derived from Magdalen.
5. Originally: "Her anxious lips mouth full pulp'd with rosy thoughts."
6. It was a custom at St. Agnes' Day mass, during the singing of Agnus Dei (Lamb of God), to bless two white unshorn lambs, whose wool nuns then spun and wove.
7. From porphyra, "purple," a precious dye for garments of the nobility; "purple blood" signifies royalty and nobility; a porphyre is a purple-colored serpent. Moreover, Porphyry (3rd c. A.D.), famous antagonist of Christianity, instituted Neoplatonism throughout the Roman Empire a few decades before the martyrdom of St. Agnes.
8. Hidden in the shadow of a buttress (the external architecture that supports the castle walls).

Will storm his heart,[9] Love's fev'rous citadel:
85 For him, those chambers held barbarian hordes,
Hyena foemen, and hot-blooded lords,
Whose very dogs would execrations howl
Against his lineage: not one breast affords
Him any mercy, in that mansion foul,
90 Save one old beldame,[1] weak in body and in soul.

XI

Ah, happy chance! the aged creature came,
Shuffling along with ivory-headed wand,°   *staff*
To where he stood, hid from the torch's flame,
Behind a broad hall-pillar, far beyond
95 The sound of merriment and chorus bland:°   *soft*
He startled her; but soon she knew his face,
And grasp'd his fingers in her palsied hand,
Saying, "Mercy, Porphyro! hie thee from this place;
They are all here to-night, the whole blood-thirsty race!

XII

100 Get hence! get hence! there's dwarfish Hildebrand;
He had a fever late, and in the fit
He cursed thee and thine, both house and land:
Then there's that old Lord Maurice, not a whit
More tame for his grey hairs—Alas me! flit!
105 Flit like a ghost away."—"Ah, Gossip° dear,   *confidant*
We're safe enough; here in this arm-chair sit,
And tell me how"—"Good Saints! not here, not here;
Follow me, child, or else these stones will be thy bier."°   *coffin-platform*

XIII

He follow'd through a lowly arched way,
110 Brushing the cobwebs with his lofty plume,
And as she mutter'd "Well-a—well-a-day!"
He found him in a little moonlight room,
Pale, lattic'd, chill, and silent as a tomb.
"Now tell me where is Madeline," said he,
115 "O tell me, Angela, by the holy loom
Which none but secret sisterhood may see,
When they St. Agnes' wool are weaving piously."

XIV

"St. Agnes! Ah! it is St. Agnes' Eve—
Yet men will murder upon holy days:
120 Thou must hold water in a witch's sieve,

9. An echo of Burke's famous account of the arrest of Marie
Antoinette: "A band of cruel ruffians and assassins . . .
rushed into the chamber of the queen, and pierced with a
hundred strokes of bayonets and poniards the bed, from
whence this persecuted woman had but just time to fly
almost naked."
1. Grandmother or old nurse; Angela evokes Juliet's
nurse Angelica in *Romeo and Juliet*, also a go-between for
the lovers.

And be liege-lord of all the Elves and Fays,°   *fairies*
To venture so: it fills me with amaze
To see thee, Porphyro!—St. Agnes' Eve!
God's help! my lady fair the conjuror plays
125   This very night: good angels her deceive!
But let me laugh awhile, I've mickle° time to grieve."   *much*

XV

Feebly she laugheth in the languid moon,
While Porphyro upon her face doth look,
Like puzzled urchin on an aged crone
130   Who keepeth clos'd a wond'rous riddle-book,
As spectacled she sits in chimney nook.
But soon his eyes grew brilliant, when she told
His lady's purpose; and he scarce could brook°   *hold back*
Tears, at the thought of those enchantments cold,
135   And Madeline asleep in lap of legends old.

XVI

Sudden a thought came like a full-blown rose,
Flushing his brow, and in his pained heart
Made purple riot:[2] then doth he propose
A stratagem, that makes the beldame start:
140   "A cruel man and impious thou art:
Sweet lady, let her pray, and sleep, and dream
Alone with her good angels, far apart
From wicked men like thee. Go, go!—I deem
Thou canst not surely be the same that thou didst seem."

XVII

145   "I will not harm her, by all saints I swear,"
Quoth Porphyro: "O may I ne'er find grace
When my weak voice shall whisper its last prayer,
If one of her soft ringlets I displace,
Or look with ruffian passion in her face:
150   Good Angela, believe me by these tears;
Or I will, even in a moment's space,
Awake, with horrid shout, my foemen's ears,
And beard° them, though they be more fang'd than wolves and bears."   *defy*

XVIII

"Ah! why wilt thou affright a feeble soul?
155   A poor, weak, palsy-stricken, churchyard thing,
Whose passing-bell° may ere the midnight toll;   *death knell*
Whose prayers for thee, each morn and evening,
Were never miss'd."—Thus plaining,° doth she bring   *lamenting*
A gentler speech from burning Porphyro;
160   So woful, and of such deep sorrowing,

2. Originally: Heated his Brow / Made riot fierce.

That Angela gives promise she will do
Whatever he shall wish, betide her weal or woe.

XIX

Which was, to lead him, in close secrecy,
Even to Madeline's chamber, and there hide
165   Him in a closet,° of such privacy   *private room*
That he might see her beauty unespied,
And win perhaps that night a peerless bride,
While legion'd fairies pac'd the coverlet,
And pale enchantment held her sleepy-eyed.
170   Never on such a night have lovers met,
Since Merlin paid his Demon all the monstrous debt.[3]

XX

"It shall be as thou wishest," said the Dame:
"All cates° and dainties shall be stored there   *delicacies*
Quickly on this feast-night: by the tambour frame[4]
175   Her own lute thou wilt see: no time to spare,
For I am slow and feeble, and scarce dare
On such a catering trust my dizzy head.
Wait here, my child, with patience; kneel in prayer
The while: Ah! thou must needs the lady wed,
180   Or may I never leave my grave among the dead."

XXI

So saying, she hobbled off with busy fear.
The lover's endless minutes slowly pass'd;
The dame return'd, and whisper'd in his ear
To follow her; with aged eyes aghast
185   From fright of dim espial.[5] Safe at last,
Through many a dusky gallery, they gain
The maiden's chamber, silken, hush'd, and chaste;
Where Porphyro took covert,[6] pleas'd amain.°   *fully*
His poor guide hurried back with agues° in her brain.   *trembling*

XXII

190   Her falt'ring hand upon the balustrade,°   *bannister*
Old Angela was feeling for the stair,
When Madeline, St. Agnes' charmed maid,
Rose, like a mission'd spirit,[7] unaware:
With silver taper's° light, and pious care,   *candle's*
195   She turn'd, and down the aged gossip led
To a safe level matting. Now prepare,
Young Porphyro, for gazing on that bed;
She comes, she comes again, like ring-dove fray'd° and fled.   *frightened*

3. In Arthurian legend, magician Merlin had his powers turned against him by enchantress Vivien, who repaid his love by imprisoning him in a cave, where he died.
4. Frame for embroidering, shaped like a tambourine.

5. Being espied, even in dim light.
6. Originally: where he in panting covert.
7. Commissioned, as if an angel-messenger.

XXIII

Out went the taper° as she hurried in;   *candle*
200   Its little smoke, in pallid moonshine, died:
She clos'd the door, she panted, all akin
To spirits of the air, and visions wide:
No uttered syllable, or, woe betide!
But to her heart, her heart was voluble,
205   Paining with eloquence her balmy side;
As though a tongueless nightingale should swell
Her throat in vain, and die, heart-stifled, in her dell.[8]

XXIV

A casement° high and triple-arch'd there was,   *window*
All garlanded with carven imag'ries
210   Of fruits, and flowers, and bunches of knot-grass,
And diamonded with panes of quaint device,
Innumerable of stains and splendid dyes,
As are the tiger-moth's deep-damask'd wings;
And in the midst, 'mong thousand heraldries,°   *genealogical emblems*
215   And twilight saints, and dim emblazonings,
A shielded scutcheon° blush'd with blood of queens and kings.[9]   *coat of arms*

XXV

Full on this casement shone the wintry moon,
And threw warm gules° on Madeline's fair breast,   *red*
As down she knelt for heaven's grace and boon;°   *favor*
220   Rose-bloom fell on her hands, together prest,
And on her silver cross soft amethyst,
And on her hair a glory,° like a saint: *halo*
She seem'd a splendid angel, newly drest,
Save wings, for heaven:—Porphyro grew faint:
225   She knelt, so pure a thing, so free from mortal taint.

XXVI

Anon his heart revives: her vespers done,
Of all its wreathed pearls her hair she frees;
Unclasps her warmed jewels one by one;
Loosens her fragrant bodice;[1] by degrees
230   Her rich attire creeps rustling to her knees:
Half-hidden, like a mermaid in sea-weed,
Pensive awhile she dreams awake, and sees,
In fancy, fair St. Agnes in her bed,
But dares not look behind, or all the charm is fled.[2]

8. In a story in Ovid's *Metamorphoses*, Tereus, after raping his wife's sister Philomela, cut out her tongue to prevent her report; but she wove its imagery, which her sister understood, and was so enraged that she butchered her and Tereus's son and fed him a dinner of the flesh. With Tereus on the verge of violent revenge, all three were turned into birds, Philomela into a nightingale; her name means "lover of honey, sweetness, song."
9. Although "blood" evokes bloodshed, here it refers to Madeline's royal bloodline.

1. Keats's drafts: her bosom jewels / loosens her bursting boddice / her Boddice lace string / her Boddice and her bosom bar[e] / Loosens her fragrant boddice and does bare her.
2. Evoking the myth of Orpheus and Eurydice, with Madeline in the male role of the lover who wins the opportunity to lead his dead beloved back to life from Hades, on the condition that he not look back at her until they reach the upper world. Orpheus violated this injunction and lost Eurydice forever.

XXVII

235 Soon, trembling in her soft and chilly nest,
In sort of wakeful swoon, perplex'd she lay,
Until the poppied° warmth of sleep oppress'd   *fragrant, narcotic*
Her soothed limbs, and soul fatigued away;
Flown, like a thought, until the morrow-day;
240 Blissfully haven'd both from joy and pain;
Clasp'd like a missal where swart Paynims pray;[3]
Blinded alike from sunshine and from rain,
As though a rose should shut, and be a bud again.

XXVIII

Stol'n to this paradise,[4] and so entranced,
245 Porphyro gazed upon her empty dress,
And listen'd to her breathing, if it chanced
To wake into a slumberous tenderness;
Which when he heard, that minute did he bless,
And breath'd himself: then from the closet crept,
250 Noiseless as fear in a wide wilderness,
And over the hush'd carpet, silent, stept,
And 'tween the curtains peep'd, where, lo!—how fast she slept.

XXIX

Then by the bed-side, where the faded moon
Made a dim, silver twilight, soft he set
255 A table, and, half anguish'd, threw thereon
A cloth of woven crimson, gold, and jet:—
O for some drowsy Morphean amulet![5]
The boisterous, midnight, festive clarion,
The kettle-drum, and far-heard clarionet,
260 Affray° his ears, though but in dying tone:—   *frighten*
The hall door shuts again, and all the noise is gone.

XXX

And still she slept an azure-lidded sleep,
In blanched linen, smooth, and lavender'd,
While he from forth the closet brought a heap
265 Of candied apple, quince, and plum, and gourd;°   *melon*
With jellies soother[6] than the creamy curd,
And lucent syrops, tinct° with cinnamon;   *clear syrups, tinged*
Manna° and dates, in argosy° transferr'd   *rare food / merchant fleet*
From Fez; and spiced dainties, every one,
270 From silken Samarcand to cedar'd Lebanon.[7]

---

3. Clasped shut and held like a prayer-book concealed from the sight of hostile, dark-skinned pagans (Muslims); "clasped" also suggests "arrested," with "pray" punning as "prey" (on), or persecute.
4. Alluding to Satan's entry into the Garden of Eden to corrupt Eve (*Paradise Lost*, bk. 9).
5. Charm; Morpheus is the divine agent of sleep.

6. A Keats-coinage: smoother and more soothing.
7. All major places in the British trade in exotic goods, the luxuries of the feudal aristocracy: Fez in northern Morocco was a source of sugar; the ancient Persian city of Samarkand was famous for its silk markets, and Lebanon for its fine cedar timber.

XXXI

These delicates he heap'd with glowing hand
On golden dishes and in baskets bright
Of wreathed silver: sumptuous they stand
In the retired quiet of the night,
275   Filling the chilly room with perfume light.—
"And now, my love, my seraph° fair, awake!   *angel*
Thou art my heaven, and I thine eremite:°   *worshipper*
Open thine eyes, for meek St. Agnes' sake,
Or I shall drowse beside thee, so my soul doth ache."

XXXII

280   Thus whispering, his warm, unnerved arm
Sank in her pillow. Shaded was her dream
By the dusk curtains:—'twas a midnight charm
Impossible to melt as iced stream:
The lustrous salvers° in the moonlight gleam;   *trays*
285   Broad golden fringe upon the carpet lies:
It seem'd he never, never could redeem
From such a stedfast spell his lady's eyes;
So mus'd awhile, entoil'd in woofed° phantasies.   *woven*

XXXIII

Awakening up, he took her hollow lute,—
290   Tumultuous,—and, in chords that tenderest be,
He play'd an ancient ditty, long since mute,
In Provence call'd, "La belle dame sans mercy":[8]
Close to her ear touching the melody;—
Wherewith disturb'd, she utter'd a soft moan:
295   He ceased—she panted quick—and suddenly
Her blue affrayed° eyes wide open shone: *frightened*
Upon his knees he sank, pale as smooth-sculptured stone.

XXXIV

Her eyes were open, but she still beheld,
Now wide awake, the vision of her sleep:
300   There was a painful change, that nigh expell'd
The blisses of her dream so pure and deep
At which fair Madeline began to weep,
And moan forth witless° words with many a sigh;   *uncomprehending*
While still her gaze on Porphyro would keep;
305   Who knelt, with joined hands and piteous eye,
Fearing to move or speak, she look'd so dreamingly.

XXXV

"Ah, Porphyro!" said she, "but even now
Thy voice was at sweet tremble in mine ear,
Made tuneable with every sweetest vow;

---

8. Provence is a region of southern France famed for troubadours; in the poem by Alain Chartier (1424; translated by Chaucer), a lady earns this title for refusing a suitor. In a few months, Keats would write his own ballad of a lady "sans mercy" / "sans merci."

310 And those sad eyes were spiritual and clear:
     How chang'd thou art! how pallid, chill, and drear!
     Give me that voice again, my Porphyro,
     Those looks immortal, those complainings° dear!   laments
     Oh leave me not in this eternal woe,
315 For if thou diest, my Love, I know not where to go."

                          XXXVI
     Beyond a mortal man impassion'd far
     At these voluptuous accents, he arose,
     Ethereal, flush'd, and like a throbbing star
     Seen mid the sapphire heaven's deep repose;
320 Into her dream he melted, as the rose
     Blendeth its odour with the violet,⁹—
     Solution° sweet: meantime the frost-wind blows   fusion
     Like Love's alarum,° pattering the sharp sleet   Cupid's warning
     Against the window-panes; St. Agnes' moon hath set.

                          XXXVII
325 'Tis dark: quick pattereth the flaw-blown° sleet: storm-driven
     "This is no dream, my bride, my Madeline!"
     'Tis dark: the iced gusts still rave and beat:
     "No dream, alas! alas! and woe is mine!
     Porphyro will leave me here to fade and pine.—
330 Cruel! what traitor could thee hither bring?
     I curse not, for my heart is lost in thine,
     Though thou forsakest a deceived thing;—
     A dove forlorn and lost with sick unpruned° wing."   bedraggled

                          XXXVIII
     "My Madeline! sweet dreamer! lovely bride!
335 Say, may I be for aye° thy vassal blest?¹   ever
     Thy beauty's shield, heart-shaped and vermeil° dyed?   vermillion
     Ah, silver shrine, here will I take my rest
     After so many hours of toil and quest,
     A famish'd pilgrim,—saved by miracle.
340 Though I have found, I will not rob thy nest
     Saving of thy sweet self; if thou think'st well
     To trust, fair Madeline, to no rude infidel.°   unbeliever

                          XXXIX
     Hark! 'tis an elfin-storm from faery land,
     Of haggard° seeming, but a boon indeed:
345 Arise—arise! the morning is at hand;—   wild, bewitched
     The bloated wassaillers will never heed:—
     Let us away, my love, with happy speed;

9. Keats's publishers refused his revision of 314–22, in
which Porphyro's "arms encroaching slow . . . zon'd her,
heart to heart" as he spoke into "her burning ear," and
then "with her wild dream . . . mingled as a rose / Mar-
ryeth its odour to a violet."
1. Keats would tell Fanny Brawne (25 July 1819): "the
very first week I knew you I wrote myself your vassal"
(page 1005). Vassal: devoted servant.

There are no ears to hear, or eyes to see,—
Drown'd all in Rhenish and the sleepy mead:°   *sweet wine*
350   Awake! arise! my love, and fearless be,
For o'er the southern moors I have a home for thee."

XL

She hurried at his words, beset with fears,
For there were sleeping dragons all around,
At glaring watch, perhaps, with ready spears—
355   Down the wide stairs a darkling° way they found.—   *dark, in the dark*
In all the house was heard no human sound.
A chain-droop'd lamp was flickering by each door;
The arras,° rich with horseman, hawk, and hound,   *tapestry*
Flutter'd in the besieging wind's uproar;
360   And the long carpets rose along the gusty floor.

XLI

They glide, like phantoms, into the wide hall;
Like phantoms to the iron porch they glide;
Where lay the Porter,° in uneasy sprawl,   *gate-keeper*
With a huge empty flagon by his side:
365   The wakeful bloodhound rose, and shook his hide,
But his sagacious eye an inmate owns:[2]
By one, and one, the bolts full easy slide:—
The chains lie silent on the footworn stones;—
The key turns, and the door upon its hinges groans.

XLII

370   And they are gone: ay, ages long ago
These lovers fled away into the storm.
That night the Baron dreamt of many a woe,
And all his warrior-guests, with shade and form
Of witch, and demon, and large coffin-worm,
375   Were long be-nightmar'd. Angela the old
Died palsy-twitch'd, with meagre face deform;
The Beadsman, after thousand aves told,[3]
For aye unsought for slept among his ashes cold.

1819   1820

La belle dame sans merci / LA BELLE DAME SANS MERCY

The title, French for "The beautiful lady without mercy," names her refusal to satisfy a lover's desire. Derived from the medieval word *merces*, price or wages, both *merci* and *mercy* involve an erotic economy: granting sexual favor for gifts and service. Women who did not honor this tacit contract suffered the charge of "sans merci." Keats's literary ballad joins a long lore of "femmes fatales," women whose allure is fatal to the men they enchant. We annotate the publication of 1819; our text is transcribed from Keats's long journal letter to George and Georgiana Keats, 21 April 1819.

---

2. Recognizes a resident (i.e., Madeline).   3. "Ave Maria" (Hail Mary) prayers, part of the rosary.

La belle dame sans merci—

O what can ail thee Knight at arms
    Alone and palely loitering?
The sedge has wither'd from the Lake
    And no birds sing!

5   O what can ail thee Knight at arms
    So haggard and so woe begone?
The squirrel's granary is full
    And the harvest's done.

           a
I see ~~death's~~ lilly on thy brow
10   With anguish moist and fever dew,
              a
And on thy cheeks ~~death's~~ fading rose
Fast Withereth too-

I met a Lady in the ~~Wilds~~ Meads
    Full beautiful, a faery's child,
15   Her hair was long, her foot was light
    And her eyes were wild-

I made a Garland for her head,
    And bracelets too, and fragrant Zones
She look'd at me as she did love
20   And made sweet moan-

I set her on my pacing steed
    And nothing else saw all day long
For sidelong would she bend, and sing
    A faerys song-
25   She found me roots of relish sweet,
                manna
    And honey wild, and ~~honey~~ dew
And sure in language strange she said
    I love thee true-
She took me to her elfin grot,
             and sigh'd full sore
30   And there she wept ~~and there she sighed fill sore~~
And there I shut her wild wild eyes
    With kisses four.

And there she lulled me asleep,
    And there I dream'd Ah woe betide!
35   The latest dream I ever dreamt
      On the cold hill side

I saw pale Kings and Princes too
    Pale warriors death pale were they all
They cried-La belle dame sans merci
40   Thee hath in thrall-

I saw their starv'd lips in the gloam
~~All tremble~~   gaped
        With horrid warning ^ wide agape
And I awoke and found me here
        On the cold hill's side.

45   And this is why I ~~wither~~ sojourn here,
        Alone and palely loitering,
Though the sedge is wither'd from the lake,
        And no birds sing — ⁻ . . . .

Why four Kisses ⁻ you will say ⁻ why four because I wish to restrain the headlong impetuousity of my Muse ⁻ she would have fain said 'score' without hurting the rhyme—but we must temper the Imagination as the Critics say with Judgment. I was obliged to choose an even number that both eyes might have fair play: and to speak truly I think two a piece quite sufficient—Suppose I had said seven; there would have been three and a half a piece—a very awkward affair-and well got out of on my side–

From *The Indicator* 31 (10 May 1820), pp. 246–248. This is Leigh Hunt's aesthetic (as opposed to political) periodical.

THE ODES OF 1819   In Keats's career of ode-writing (from *Ode to Apollo*, 1814, to *Ode to Fanny*, 1820), the remarkable group composed in a burst of inspiration between April and September 1819 is regarded as his highest achievement. Except for *Ode on Indolence*, first published in 1848, all appeared, though not as a sequence, in Keats's 1820 volume (our text). *Ode to Psyche* was written in April, the others probably in May, and *To Autumn* the last, in September. The odes reflect personal, cultural, and political contexts of 1819, having to do with everything from the Elgin Marbles controversy, to the widespread use of opium as a painkiller, to social misery and political unrest, to Keats's grief over one brother's death and the other's emigration to America, to his nagging sensation that he was doomed to die young. Their language is enriched by literary allusion, as dense as it is casual, ranging through the Bible, Keats's earlier poetry and the hostile reviews of it, and favorite writers: Spenser, Shakespeare, Milton, Thomson, Collins, Chatterton, Coleridge, and Wordsworth. Even so, the odes also have an independent appeal that has made them, like Shakespeare's sonnets, general primers of the pleasure of reading poetry—of how verbal nuance and reverberation, and complex interplays of imagery, shape a dynamic process of thought. Nineteenth-century readers admired the beautiful phrases and sensuous language—the tactile, auditory, visual qualities, even sensations of smell and taste. Later readers have added an enthusiasm for the intellectual complexity and mental drama, variously described as a poetry of "internal debate," a structure of "paradox" and "contradiction," a "rhetoric of irony" or a poetics of "indeterminacy."

Keats once suggested that "a question is the best beacon toward a little speculation," and that knowledge was less a matter of "seeming sure points of Reasoning" than of "question and answer—a little pro and con." The key questions in his odes—"Was it a vision, or a waking dream?"; "What leaf-fringed legend haunts about thy shape . . . ?"; "Where are the songs of spring?"—are met less with answers than with pro and con: a poet's mind as a "rosy sanctuary" and a place of mere "shadowy thought"; a bird-song that evokes "full-throated ease" and "easeful death"; a world of art in which human figures are both "for ever young" and a "cold pastoral"; an intensity of "Beauty" that is always a "Beauty that must die"; a sensuous "indolence" that cannot stay "sheltered from annoy" of busy thoughts; an autumn that is inextricably a season of ripe fruition and of death.

Ode to Psyche[1]

    O GODDESS! hear these tuneless numbers,° wrung   *meters*
        By sweet enforcement and remembrance dear,
    And pardon that thy secrets should be sung
        Even into thine own soft-conchèd° ear: *shell-shaped*
5   Surely I dreamt to-day, or did I see
        The winged Psyche with awaken'd eyes?
    I wander'd in a forest thoughtlessly,
        And, on the sudden, fainting with surprise,
    Saw two fair creatures, couched side by side
10   In deepest grass, beneath the whisp'ring roof
        Of leaves and trembled blossoms, where there ran
        A broklet, scarce espied:[2]

    'Mid hush'd, cool-rooted flowers, fragrant-eyed,
        Blue, silver-white, and budded Tyrian,°   *deep purple*
15   They lay calm-breathing on the bedded grass;
        Their arms embraced, and their pinions° too;   *wings*
        Their lips touch'd not, but had not bade adieu
    As if disjoined by soft-handed slumber,
    And ready still past kisses to outnumber
20   At tender eye-dawn of aurorean° love: *dawning*
        The winged boy° I knew;   *Cupid*
    But who wast thou, O happy, happy dove?
        His Psyche true!

    O latest born and loveliest vision far
25   Of all Olympus' faded hierarchy![3]
    Fairer than Phœbe's sapphire-region'd star,
        Or Vesper, amorous glow-worm of the sky;[4]
    Fairer than these, though temple thou hast none,
        Nor altar heap'd with flowers;
30   Nor virgin-choir to make delicious moan
        Upon the midnight hours;

---

1. "Psyche" means *soul* or *mind* and *butterfly* in Greek; in Greek myth the nymph Psyche personified soul, sometimes in the form of a butterfly. In Apuleius's *The Golden Ass* (2nd century), she is a mortal loved by Cupid, who visited her only at night, to keep his identity secret and prevent discovery by his mother Venus, jealous of Psyche's beauty. "Psyche was not embodied as a goddess before the time of Apul[ei]us the Platonist who lived afte[r] the Augustan age, and consequently the goddess was never worshipped or sacrificed to with any of the ancient fervour—and perhaps never thought of in the old religion—I am more orthodox tha[n] to let a hethan Goddess be so neglected," wrote Keats, who knew Mary Tighe's *Psyche* (1805), a romance in Spenserian stanzas also based on Apuleius, which his ode echoes in several places. Keats was reflecting at this time on the development of the soul through suffering.

2. The scene evokes Satan's view of Adam and Eve in Eden: "the loveliest pair . . . Under a tuft of shade that on a green / Stood whispering soft, by a fresh Fountain side / They sat them down" (*Paradise Lost* 4.321–27); and later, the epic narrator's account of the pair "side by side" in "thir inmost bower" making "connubial Love" (4.742–43), then as "two fair Creatures . . . asleep secure of harm" (4.790–91).

3. The gods who lived on Mount Olympus in classical mythology, now eclipsed by Christianity.

4. Phoebe is the moon-goddess whose "star" is the moon; Vesper: Venus, the evening star, and in the fable of Psyche, Cupid's jealous mother.

No voice, no lute, no pipe, no incense sweet
    From chain-swung censer teeming;
No shrine, no grove, no oracle, no heat
35   Of pale-mouth'd prophet dreaming.[5]

O brightest! though too late for antique vows,
    Too, too late for the fond believing lyre,°   *religious worship*
When holy were the haunted° forest boughs,   *spirit-filled*
    Holy the air, the water, and the fire;
40 Yet even in these days so far retir'd
    From happy pieties, thy lucent fans,°   *wings*
    Fluttering among the faint° Olympians,   *weak, faded*
I see, and sing, by my own eyes inspired.
So let me be thy choir, and make a moan
45   Upon the midnight hours;
Thy voice, thy lute, thy pipe, thy incense sweet
    From swinged censer teeming;
Thy shrine, thy grove, thy oracle, thy heat
    Of pale-mouth'd prophet dreaming.

50 Yes, I will be thy priest, and build a fane°   *temple*
    In some untrodden region of my mind,[6]
Where branched thoughts, new grown with pleasant pain,
    Instead of pines shall murmur in the wind:
Far, far around shall those dark-cluster'd trees
55   Fledge° the wild-ridged mountains steep by steep;   *feather*
And there by zephyrs,° streams, and birds, and bees,   *breezes*
    The moss-lain Dryads° shall be lull'd to sleep;   *wood-nymphs*
And in the midst of this wide quietness
A rosy sanctuary will I dress
60 With the wreath'd trellis of a working brain,
    With buds, and bells, and stars without a name,
With all the gardener Fancy[7] e'er could feign,
    Who breeding flowers, will never breed the same:
And there shall be for thee all soft delight
65   That shadowy thought can win,
A bright torch, and a casement ope at night,
    To let the warm Love in!

---

5. Alluding to the rout by Christianity of the pagan Greek deities in Milton's *On the Morning of Christ's Nativity* (1629): "The Oracles are dumb, / No voice . . . No nightly trance, or breathed spell, / Inspires the pale-ey'd priest from the prophetic cell" (19).

6. Echoing Spenser's *Amoretti* 22: "Her temple fayre is built within my mind, / In which her glorious ymage placèd is, / On which my thoughts doo day and night attend / Like sacred priests" (5–8).

7. Fancy is often represented in literary tradition as a gardener who improves nature. Feign: invent, dissemble, with Shakespearean punning on *fain* and *fane* (50). Keats's language is allusively embedded in a stanza of Spenser's *Hymne in Honour of Love* (1596), about a jealous lover whose fears "to his fayning fansie represent / Sights never seene, and thousand shadowes vaine, / To break his sleepe, and waste his ydle braine" (254–56).

Ode to a Nightingale[1]

1

My heart aches, and a drowsy numbness pains
   My sense, as though of hemlock I had drunk,
Or emptied some dull opiate to the drains
   One minute past, and Lethe-wards had sunk:[2]
5 'Tis not through envy of thy happy lot,
   But being too happy in thine happiness,—
      That thou, light-winged Dryad° of the trees,   *wood-nymph*
      In some melodious plot
Of beechen green, and shadows numberless,
10   Singest of summer in full-throated ease.

2

O, for a draught of vintage!° that hath been   *wine*
   Cool'd a long age in the deep-delved earth,
Tasting of Flora and the country green,
   Dance, and Provençal song, and sunburnt mirth![3]
15 O for a beaker full of the warm South,
   Full of the true, the blushful Hippocrene,[4]
      With beaded bubbles winking at the brim,
      And purple-stained mouth;
That I might drink, and leave the world unseen,[5]
20   And with thee fade away into the forest dim:

3

Fade far away, dissolve, and quite forget
   What thou among the leaves hast never known,
The weariness, the fever, and the fret
   Here, where men sit and hear each other groan;
25 Where palsy shakes a few, sad, last gray hairs,
   Where youth grows pale, and spectre-thin, and dies;[6]
      Where but to think is to be full of sorrow
      And leaden-eyed despairs,
Where Beauty cannot keep her lustrous eyes,
30   Or new Love pine at them beyond to-morrow.

---

1. First published in *Annals of the Fine Arts*, 1819. Keats's stanza incorporates sonnet elements: a Shakespearean quatrain (*abab*) followed by a Petrarchan sestet (*cdecde*), also the form of the odes on "Melancholy" and "Indolence." The nightingale in literary tradition (including Milton, Charlotte Smith, Wordsworth, Coleridge) often evokes Ovid's story of Philomela; see page 544, n. 8. Keats was also inspired by an actual nightingale's song at the house where he was living.
2. In small doses hemlock is a sedative; in large doses, such as Socrates', it is fatal; an opiate is any sense-duller, particularly opium, widely used as a painkiller; Lethe is the mythic river of the underworld whose waters produce forgetfulness of previous life.
3. Magician Merlin dwells "in a deep delve, farre from the view of day, / That of no living wight he mote be found"

(*Faerie Queene* 3.3.7). Flora: Roman goddess of flowers. Provence: region in southern France famed for troubadours.
4. The fountain of the muses on Mount Helicon.
5. "Unseen" can modify both "I" and "world."
6. An echo of Wordsworth's memory in *Tintern Abbey* of himself in "darkness, and amid the many shapes / Of joyless day-light; when the fretful stir / Unprofitable, and the fever of the world, / Have hung upon the beatings of my heart" (52–55); Both poets recall Macbeth's envy of Duncan "in his grave; / After life's fitful fever he sleeps well" (*Macbeth* 3.322–323). Also echoed is Wordsworth's image of an ideal life "from diminution safe and weakening age; / While man grows old, and dwindles, and decays" (*Excursion* 4.759–60).

4

Away! away! for I will fly to thee,

  Not charioted by Bacchus and his pards,[7]

But on the viewless wings of Poesy,

  Though the dull brain perplexes and retards:

35 Already with thee! tender is the night,

    And haply° the Queen-Moon is on her throne,   *happily, perhaps*

      Cluster'd around by all her starry Fays;°   *fairies*

        But here there is no light,

  Save what from heaven is with the breezes blown

40   Through verdurous glooms and winding mossy ways.

5

I cannot see what flowers are at my feet,

  Nor what soft incense hangs upon the boughs,

But, in embalmed darkness, guess each sweet

  Wherewith the seasonable month endows

45 The grass, the thicket, and the fruit-tree wild;

    White hawthorn, and the pastoral eglantine;

      Fast fading violets cover'd up in leaves;

      And mid-May's eldest child,

  The coming musk-rose, full of dewy wine,

50   The murmurous haunt of flies on summer eves.[8]

6

Darkling° I listen; and, for many a time   *in the dark*

  I have been half in love with easeful Death,

Call'd him soft names in many a mused rhyme,

  To take into the air my quiet breath;

55 Now more than ever seems it rich to die,

    To cease upon the midnight with no pain,

      While thou art pouring forth thy soul abroad

      In such an ecstasy!

  Still wouldst thou sing, and I have ears in vain—

60   To thy high requiem° become a sod.   *funeral mass*

7

Thou wast not born for death, immortal Bird!

  No hungry generations tread thee down;

The voice I hear this passing night was heard

  In ancient days by emperor and clown:°   *rustic, peasant*

65 Perhaps the self-same song that found a path

    Through the sad heart of Ruth, when, sick for home,

      She stood in tears amid the alien corn;[9]

      The same that oft-times hath

---

7. Bacchus, god of wine and revelry, whose chariot is drawn by leopards.

8. This guessing of flowers echoes Oberon's description in *A Midsummer Night's Dream* of a verdant bank where one may find a snakeskin whose juices make a sleeper fall in love with whatever is first seen on waking (2.1.249–58).

9. See Ruth 1–2: compelled by famine to leave her home, Ruth eked out a living as a gleaner in faraway fields.

Charm'd magic casements, opening on the foam
70   Of perilous seas, in faery lands forlorn.

8

Forlorn! the very word is like a bell
To toll me back from thee to my sole self!
Adieu! the fancy cannot cheat so well[1]
As she is fam'd to do, deceiving elf.
75   Adieu! adieu! thy plaintive anthem fades
Past the near meadows, over the still stream,
Up the hill-side; and now 'tis buried deep
In the next valley-glades:
Was it a vision, or a waking dream?
80   Fled is that music:—Do I wake or sleep?

Ode on a Grecian Urn[1]

1

THOU still unravish'd bride of quietness,
Thou foster-child of silence and slow time,
Sylvan° historian, who canst thus express   *woodland*
A flowery tale more sweetly than our rhyme:
5   What leaf-fring'd legend haunts about thy shape
Of deities or mortals, or of both,
In Tempe or the dales of Arcady?[2]
What men or gods are these? What maidens loth?
What mad pursuit? What struggle to escape?
10   What pipes and timbrels?° What wild ecstasy?   *tambourines*

2

Heard melodies are sweet, but those unheard
Are sweeter; therefore, ye soft pipes, play on;
Not to the sensual° ear, but, more endear'd,   *physical*
Pipe to the spirit ditties of no tone:
15   Fair youth, beneath the trees, thou canst not leave
Thy song, nor ever can those trees be bare;
Bold Lover, never, never canst thou kiss,

1. The adieu echoes the opening line of Charlotte Smith's On the Departure of the Nightingale (1784), "Sweet poet of the woods!—a long adieu!" The closing question bears several echoes: Psyche 5–6; the opening of Spenser's Amoretti 77: "Was it a dreame, or did I see it playne?"; Hazlitt's remark that "Spenser was the poet of our waking dreams," his "music . . . lulling the senses into a deep oblivion of the jarring noises of the world from which we have no wish ever to be recalled" (On Chaucer and Spenser, 1818); a spellbound lover's confusion in Midsummer Night's Dream: "Are you sure / That we are awake? It seems to me / That yet we sleep, we dream" (4.1.194–96); Wordsworth's lament in the "Intimations" Ode, "Whither is fled the visionary gleam? / Where is it

now, the glory and the dream?" (56–57), and his phrase "waking dream" in Yarrow Visited (pub. 1815).
1. First published in Annals of the Fine Arts. Keats describes three scenes on an imaginary urn. The first is an image of revelry and sexual pursuit; the second (stanzas 2–3) is either a detail of this or another: a piper, and a lover in pursuit of a fair maid; in both, the story of Pan is implied. The third (stanza 4) is a sacrificial ritual, perhaps inspired by one of the Elgin Marble friezes.
2. A design of leaves frames a "legend" or caption on some vases; Tempe and Arcadia are districts of ancient Greece famed for beauty and serenity, where the gods often frolicked.

Though winning near the goal—yet, do not grieve;
  She cannot fade, though thou hast not thy bliss,
20   For ever wilt thou love, and she be fair!

3

Ah, happy, happy° boughs! that cannot shed   *joyous, fortunate*
  Your leaves, nor ever bid the Spring adieu;
And, happy melodist, unwearied,
  For ever piping songs for ever new;
25 More happy love! more happy, happy love!
  For ever warm and still to be enjoy'd,
    For ever panting, and for ever young;
All breathing human passion far above,
  That leaves a heart high-sorrowful and cloy'd,
30   A burning forehead, and a parching tongue.

4

Who are these coming to the sacrifice?
  To what green altar, O mysterious[3] priest,
Lead'st thou that heifer lowing at the skies,
  And all her silken flanks with garlands drest?
35 What little town by river or sea shore,
  Or mountain-built with peaceful citadel,°   *fortress*
    Is emptied of this folk, this pious morn?
And, little town, thy streets for evermore
  Will silent be; and not a soul to tell
40   Why thou art desolate, can e'er return.

5

O Attic shape! Fair attitude°! with brede°   *pose / intricate design*
  Of marble men and maidens overwrought,[4]
With forest branches and the trodden weed;
  Thou, silent form, dost tease us out of thought
45 As doth eternity: Cold Pastoral!
  When old age shall this generation waste,
    Thou shalt remain, in midst of other woe
Than ours, a friend to man, to whom thou say'st,
  "Beauty is truth, truth beauty,"[5]—that is all
50   Ye know on earth, and all ye need to know.

3. Unknown; also denoting religious rites.
4. The urn, made in Attica (where Athens is located), is "overwrought" (overlaid) with its design; Keats may be implying "over-elaborated," with a hint of psychological or emotional anguish in the frozen figures; thus "brede" puns on what cannot happen, "breed."

5. The quotation marks do not appear in any manuscript of the ode. Keats ponders the relation between beauty and truth throughout his career: see his letters of 22 November 1817, 21–27 December 1817, and 19 March 1819.

Ode on Indolence[1]

"They toil not, neither do they spin"[2]

I

One morn before me were three figures seen,
    With bowed necks, and joined hands, side-faced;
And one behind the other stepp'd serene,
    In placid sandals, and in white robes graced;
5   They pass'd, like figures on a marble urn,
    When shifted round to see the other side;
They came again; as when the urn once more
    Is shifted round, the first seen shades return;
    And they were strange to me, as may betide
10 With vases, to one deep in Phidian lore.[3]

II

How is it, Shadows!° that I knew ye not?   *shady figures, phantoms*
    How came ye muffled in so hush a mask?[4]
Was it a silent deep-disguised plot
    To steal away, and leave without a task
15   My idle days? Ripe was the drowsy hour;
    The blissful cloud of summer-indolence
Benumb'd my eyes; my pulse grew less and less;
    Pain had no sting, and pleasure's wreath no flower:
    O, why did ye not melt, and leave my sense
20 Unhaunted quite of all but—nothingness?

III

A third time pass'd they by, and, passing, turn'd
    Each one the face a moment whiles to me;
Then faded, and to follow them I burn'd
    And ached for wings, because I knew the three;
25   The first was a fair Maid, and Love her name;
    The second was Ambition, pale of cheek,
And ever watchful with fatigued eye;
    The last, whom I love more, the more of blame
    Is heap'd upon her, maiden most unmeek,—
30 I knew to be my demon Poesy.[5]

---

1. Indolence is usually seen as a laxity boding moral dissolution; James Thomson's *Castle of Indolence* (1748) begins, however, by detailing its lush pleasures before the
moral is applied. Keats mentions this poem in the journal-
letter of 19 March 1819 in which he recounts the mood
that inspires this ode. Our text is the first publication, in
1848.
2. In the Sermon on the Mount, Jesus advises: "Take no
thought for your life, what ye shall eat, or what ye shall
drink; nor yet for your body, what ye shall put on. Is not
the life more than meat, and the body than raiment . . .
why take ye thought for raiment? Consider the lilies of
the field, how they grow; they toil not, neither do they
spin: And yet I say unto you, That even Solomon in all

his glory was not arrayed like one of these" (Matthew
6.26–29). The spinning of garments obliquely relates to
textuality (and writing) through the tacit pun on *textum*
("woven" in Latin).
3. The famous Athenian sculptor Phidias (5th century
B.C.) created the Elgin Marbles.
4. Another manuscript has "masque," a theatrical ritual;
Keats allows the puns.
5. In Greek myth, a "demon" or "daemon" is a semi-
divine spirit; the word also carries a Christian sense of
"evil spirit." The image hints at the kind of "unmeek"
("vulgar," "sensuous," "immodest") poetry for which
Keats was criticized in the reviews of 1817–1818.

IV

They faded, and, forsooth! I wanted° wings: *lacked and ached for*
  O folly! What is Love? and where is it?
And for that poor Ambition! it springs
  From a man's little heart's short fever-fit;
35   For Poesy!—no,—she has not a joy,—
    At least for me,—so sweet as drowsy noons,
And evenings steep'd in honeyed indolence;
  O, for an age so shelter'd from annoy,°   *annoyance, harm*
    That I may never know how change the moons,
40 Or hear the voice of busy common-sense!

V

And once more came they by;—alas! wherefore?
  My sleep had been embroider'd with dim dreams;
My soul had been a lawn besprinkled o'er
  With flowers, and stirring shades, and baffled beams:
45   The morn was clouded, but no shower fell,
    Tho' in her lids hung the sweet tears of May;
The open casement press'd a new-leaved vine,
  Let in the budding warmth and throstle's lay;6
    O Shadows! 'twas a time to bid farewell!
50 Upon your skirts had fallen no tears of mine.

VI

So, ye three Ghosts, adieu! Ye cannot raise
  My head cool-bedded in the flowery grass;
For I would not be dieted with praise,
  A pet-lamb in a sentimental farce!7
55   Fade softly from my eyes, and be once more
    In masque-like figures on the dreamy urn;
Farewell! I yet have visions for the night,
  And for the day faint visions there is store;
Vanish, ye Phantoms! from my idle spright,8
60   Into the clouds, and never more return!

1848

Ode on Melancholy1

1

No, no, go not to Lethe,° neither twist   *river of forgetfulness*
  Wolf's-bane, tight-rooted, for its poisonous wine;

---

6. Thrush's song, but with a possible pun related to the epigraph, on "throstle" as a frame for spinning.
7. In a letter of June 1819, Keats claimed to be disenchanted with the idea of fame: "I hope I am a little more of a Philosopher than I was, consequently a little less of a versifying Pet-lamb."
8. Old term for spirit or soul but also denoting a diminutive: ghost, elf, fairy.
1. In May 1819, Keats paraphrased a couplet from Wordsworth's "Intimations" Ode: "Nothing can bring back the hour / Of splendour in the grass and glory in the flower" (177–78), commenting, "I once thought this a

Melancholist's dream." "Melancholy" is a traditional term for "the blues," or even "black" moods; Hamlet is famously "The Melancholy Dane." Robert Burton's treatise, *Anatomy of Melancholy* (1621), which Keats studied, offers an elaborate medical analysis as well as an anthology of notable remarks. Taking a stock subject for poets in the 18th century (see Charlotte Smith's sonnet *To Melancholy*), Keats prizes melancholy as a sensibility that accepts, even relishes, evanescence. He originally began the ode with a macabre, mock-heroic stanza about the quest for the goddess Melancholy: "Though you should build a bark of dead men's bones, / And rear a phantom

Nor suffer thy pale forehead to be kiss'd
   By nightshade, ruby grape of Proserpine;[2]

5   Make not your rosary of yew-berries,[3]
     Nor let the beetle, nor the death-moth be
      Your mournful Psyche,[4] nor the downy owl
A partner in your sorrow's mysteries;°   *secret rites*
   For shade to shade will come too drowsily,
10   And drown the wakeful anguish of the soul.

2

But when the melancholy fit shall fall
   Sudden from heaven like a weeping cloud,
That fosters the droop-headed flowers all,
   And hides the green hill in an April shroud;
15   Then glut thy sorrow on a morning rose,
     Or on the rainbow of the salt sand-wave,
      Or on the wealth of globed peonies;
Or if thy mistress some rich anger shows,
   Emprison her soft hand, and let her rave,
20   And feed deep, deep upon her peerless eyes.

3

She[5] dwells with Beauty—Beauty that must die;
   And Joy, whose hand is ever at his lips
Bidding adieu; and aching Pleasure nigh,
   Turning to poison while the bee-mouth sips:
25   Ay, in the very temple of Delight
     Veil'd Melancholy has her sovran shrine,
      Though seen of none save him whose strenuous tongue
Can burst Joy's grape against his palate fine;°   *sensitive, refined*
   His soul shall taste the sadness of her might,
30   And be among her cloudy trophies hung.

To Autumn[1]

1

SEASON of mists and mellow fruitfulness,
   Close bosom-friend of the maturing sun;

---

gibbet for a mast, / Stitch creeds together for a sail, with groans / To fill it out, bloodstained and aghast; / Although your rudder be a Dragon's tail, / Long sever'd, yet still hard with agony, / Your cordage large uprootings from the skull / Of bald Medusa: certes you would fail / To find the Melancholy, whether she / Dreameth in any isle of Lethe dull . . . "
2. Wolfsbane and nightshade are poisons; Proserpine was abducted to the underworld by its ruler, Hades, but an appeal by her mother Ceres (goddess of grain) allowed her to return to the upper world from spring to fall—a seasonal flux relevant to the aesthetic of Melancholy.
3. Yew is an emblem of death; rosary: prayer beads.
4. In Greek, "psyche" means both "soul" and "butterfly" (its emblem); the markings on the death's-head moth resemble a human skull; the beetle may be the scarab, a jewel-bug placed in tombs by the ancient Egyptians as a portent of resurrection.

5. A double reference, to the mistress and to Melancholy.
1. Composed 19–21 September 1819 in Winchester, a tranquil town in southern England, from which Keats wrote to a friend: "How beautiful the season is now— How fine the air. A temperate sharpness about it. . . . I never lik'd stubble fields so much as now—Aye better than the chilly green of the spring. Somehow a stubble plain looks warm—in the same way that some pictures look warm—this struck me so much in my sunday's walk that I composed upon it." The ode evokes two competing but related senses of autumn: the social context of harvest bounty; and the symbolic association with death—the reaper as grim reaper, autumn as the presage of winter (see Shakespeare's Sonnet 73, "That time of year thou may'st in me behold"). Among other poems echoed are Thomson's *Autumn* in *The Seasons* (1740) and the last stanza of Coleridge's *Frost at Midnight*.

Conspiring with him how to load and bless
   With fruit the vines that round the thatch-eaves[2] run;
5 To bend with apples the moss'd cottage-trees,
   And fill all fruit with ripeness to the core;
      To swell the gourd, and plump the hazel shells
With a sweet kernel; to set budding more,
   And still more, later flowers for the bees,
10 Until they think warm days will never cease,
   For Summer has o'er-brimm'd their clammy cells.

2

Who hath not seen thee oft amid thy store?
   Sometimes whoever seeks abroad may find
Thee sitting careless on a granary floor,
15   Thy hair soft-lifted by the winnowing wind;
Or on a half-reap'd furrow sound asleep,
   Drows'd with the fume of poppies, while thy hook°   *scythe*
      Spares the next swath and all its twined flowers:
And sometimes like a gleaner thou dost keep
20   Steady thy laden head across a brook;
Or by a cyder-press, with patient look,
      Thou watchest the last oozings hours by hours.

3

Where are the songs of Spring? Ay, where are they?[3]
   Think not of them, thou hast thy music too,—
25 While barred clouds bloom the soft-dying day,
   And touch the stubble-plains with rosy hue;
Then in a wailful choir the small gnats mourn
   Among the river sallows,[4] borne aloft
      Or sinking as the light wind lives or dies;
30 And full-grown lambs loud bleat from hilly bourn;°   *boundary, region*
   Hedge-crickets sing; and now with treble soft°   *faint high pitch*
   The red-breast whistles from a garden-croft;°   *enclosure*
   And gathering swallows twitter in the skies.

This living hand[1]

This living hand, now warm and capable
Of earnest grasping, would, if it were cold
and in the icy silence of the tomb,
So haunt thy days and chill thy dreaming nights
5 That thou would wish thine own hea[r]t[2] dry of blood

---

2. The eaves of thatched cottage roofs.
3. The "Ubi sunt" trope ("where are they now?") traditionally prefaces a lament for lost worlds, the implied answer being "gone"; cf. Wordsworth's "Intimations" Ode, stanza 4 (page 274).
4. Willows (an emblem of death).
1. A mysterious fragment, context unknown; "hand" is also a term for "handwriting": for the relation of these two senses, see *Fall of Hyperion* 1.16–18.
2. Keats inserted "heat" as superscript between "thine" and "own"; his characteristic dropping of "r" in handwriting makes it possible that he meant "heart," which best fits the context (although "heat" is relevant).

So in my veins red life might stream again,
and thou be conscience-calm'd—see here it is—
I hold it towards you—

c. 1819   1898

Bright Star[1]

Bright star! would I were steadfast as thou art—
   Not in lone splendour hung aloft the night,
And watching, with eternal lids apart,
   Like Nature's patient sleepless Eremite,°   *worshipper*
5   The moving waters at their priestlike task
   Of pure ablution° round earth's human shores,   *ritual washing*
Or gazing on the new soft fallen mask
   Of snow upon the mountains and the moors—
No—yet still steadfast, still unchangeable,
10   Pillow'd upon my fair love's ripening breast,
   To feel for ever its soft fall and swell,[2]
   Awake for ever in a sweet unrest,
Still, still to hear her tender-taken breath,
And so live ever—or else swoon to death.

1820   (1838), 1848

Letters[1]

To George and Thomas Keats[2]
["Intensity" and "Negative Capability"]

My dear Brothers   December 181[7]

[21 Dec.] * * * I saw Kean return to the public in Richard III,[3] & finely he did it.
* * * Hone the publisher's trial, you must find very amusing; & as Englishmen very
encouraging—his <u>Not Guilty</u> is a thing, which not to have been, would have dulled
still more Liberty's Emblazoning – Lord Ellenborough has been paid in his own
coin–Wooler & Hone have done us an essential service[4] * * * I spent Friday evening

1. In summer 1818, Keats remarked that the scenery of the lake country "refine[s] one's sensual vision into a sort of north star which can never cease to be open lidded and stedfast over the wonders of the great Power"; sometime before summer 1819, he drafted this sonnet, then wrote this revised version in early autumn 1820 into the volume of Shakespeare's poems he took to Italy; perhaps the last poetry he wrote, it was titled in 19th-century editions "Keats's last sonnet." The opening recalls the heroic self-description of Julius Caesar: "I could be well moved . . . but I am constant as the Northern Star, / Of whose true-fixed and resting quality / There is no fellow in the firmament" (*Julius Caesar* 3.1.58–62).
2. One draft has: swell and fall.
1. In order to convey the character of Keats's letter-writing, idiosyncrasies of spelling, punctuation, and capitalization are for the most part preserved. Our insertions for clarity appear in square brackets [ ].
2. The brothers had lived together since 1816; George (1797–1841) had taken Tom to Teignmouth,

Devonshire for his health.
3. Edmund Kean (1787–1833), charismatic and scandal-ridden actor who revolutionized the Shakespearean stage with his passionate performances. Richard III was one of his celebrated roles; Keats had just published an article on him in *The Champion*.
4. Two notorious prosecutions. William Hone had just been found not guilty on three counts of blasphemous libel for his parodies of the liturgy, of which nearly 100,000 copies had sold. Lord Chief Justice Ellenborough, who had earlier sentenced John and Leigh Hunt for libel, presided at two of his trials and was humiliated by the loudly applauded verdict. Thomas Wooler, politician, journalist, and editor of the radical weekly *The Black Dwarf*, was acquitted on similar charges the previous June. The trials were well attended and extremely amusing because the "offenses" had to be read into the record, thus gaining audience not only in the courtroom but also in reports in the "legitimate" press.

with Wells & went the next morning to see <u>Death on the Pale horse</u>.[5] It is a wonderful picture, when West's age is considered; But there is nothing to be intense upon; no women one feels mad to kiss; no face swelling into reality. the excellence of every Art is its intensity, capable of making all disagreeables evaporate, from their being in close relationship with Beauty & Truth – Examine King Lear[6] & you will find this examplified throughout; but in this picture we have unpleasantness without any momentous depth of speculation excited, in which to bury its repulsiveness. * * * [?27 Dec.] * * * I had not a dispute but a disquisition[7] with Dilke, on various subjects; several things dovetailed in my mind, & at once it struck me, what quality went to form a Man of Achievement especially in Literature & which Shakespeare posessed so enormously – I mean <u>Negative Capability</u>, that is when man is capable of being in uncertainties, Mysteries, doubts, without any irritable reaching after fact & reason[8]— Coleridge, for instance, would let go by a fine isolated verisimilitude caught from the Penetralium of mystery, from being incapable of remaining content with half knowledge.[9] This pursued through Volumes would perhaps take us no further than this, that with a great poet the sense of Beauty overcomes every other consideration, or rather obliterates all consideration.

Shelley's poem is out & there are words about its being objected too, as much as Queen Mab was. Poor Shelley I think he has his Quota of good qualities, in sooth la!!![1]   Write soon to your most sincere friend & affectionate Brother

John

To Richard Woodhouse[2]
[The "Camelion Poet" vs. The "Egotistical Sublime"]

My dear Woodhouse,   27 October 1818

Your Letter gave me a great satisfaction; more on account of its friendliness, than any relish of that matter in it which is accounted so acceptable in the 'genus irritabile'[3] The best answer I can give you is in a clerklike manner to make some observations on two principle points, which seem to point like indices into the midst of the whole pro and con, about genius, and views and atchievements and ambition and cœtera.[4] 1st As to the poetical Character itself, (I mean that sort of which, if I am any thing, I am a Member; that sort distinguished from the wordsworthian or

---

5. Wells was a schoolmate of Tom; *Death on a Pale Horse*, by American painter Benjamin West, is based on the image in Revelation of the fourth horseman of the apocalypse.
6. West's painting of the storm scene in the play (Keats's rereading of the play the next month would provoke very different terms of description: see his sonnet, page 537).
7. Legalese for formal inquiry. Charles Dilke (1789–1864), government worker and amateur scholar, was a new friend.
8. <u>Negative Capability</u>, Keats's most famous formulation, is a self-conscious oxymoron; compare Keats's antipathy to egotistical assertions of "certain philosophy," "resting places and seeming sure points of Reasoning" (letters to Reynolds, 3 February and 3 May 1818).
9. In 1817, Coleridge published *Biographia Literaria* and *The Rime of the Ancient Mariner* with a marginal gloss. "Penetralium" is Keats's faux-Latin singular of "pene-

tralia," the inmost chamber of a temple.
1. Shelley was forced to withdraw *Laon and Cythna* (1817), an epic featuring the incestuous love of its sibling hero and heroine; the outcry was as heated as that against *Queen Mab* (1813), a visionary political epic attacking "Kingcraft, Priestcraft, and Statecraft." Keats's "sooth la!" ("the truth!") echoes Cleopatra as she tries, ineptly, to help Antony put on his armor after their night of debauchery (*Antony and Cleopatra* 4.4.8).
2. Legal and literary adviser to Keats's second publishers, Woodhouse adored Keats and assiduously preserved or transcribed his letters, manuscripts, and proof-sheets, as well as collected anecdotes. This is one of Keats's most famous letters, written after a summer of negative reviews in highly visible journals.
3. Horace's term for poets, "the irritable tribe" (*Epistles* 2.2.102).
4. The rest.

egotistical sublime;[5] which is a thing per se and stands alone[6]) it is not itself – it has no self – it is every thing and nothing – It has no character – it enjoys light and shade; it lives in gusto, be it foul or fair, high or low, rich or poor, mean or elevated – It has as much delight in conceiving an Iago as an Imogen.[7] What shocks the virtuous philosoper, delights the camelion[8] Poet. It does no harm from its relish of the dark side of things any more than from its taste for the bright one; because they both end in speculation. A Poet is the most unpoetical of any thing in existence; because he has no Identity – he is continually infor–[9] and filling some other Body – The Sun, the Moon, the Sea and Men and Women who are creatures of impulse are poetical and have about them an unchangeable attribute – the poet has none; no identity – he is certainly the most unpoetical of all God's Creatures. If then he has no self, and if I am a Poet, where is the Wonder that I should say I would ~~right~~ write no more? Might I not at that very instant been cogitating on the Characters of Saturn and Ops?[1] It is a wretched thing to confess; but is a very fact that not one word I ever utter can be taken for granted as an opinion growing out of my identical nature – how can it, when I have no nature? When I am in a room with People if I ever am free from speculating on creations of my own brain, then not myself goes home to myself: but the identity of every one in the room begins to press upon me that, I am in a very little time anhilated – not only among Men; it would be the same in a Nursery of children: I know not whether I make myself wholly understood: I hope enough so to let you see that no dependence is to be placed on what I said that day.

In the second place I will speak of my views, and of the life I purpose to myself – I am ambitious of doing the world some good: if I should be spared that may be the work of maturer years – in the interval I will assay to reach to as high a summit in Poetry as the nerve bestowed upon me will suffer. The faint conceptions I have of Poems to come brings the blood frequently into my forehead – All I hope is that I may not lose all interest in human affairs – that the solitary indifference I feel for applause even from the finest Spirits, will not blunt any acuteness of vision I may have. I do not think it will — I feel assured I should write from the mere yearning and fondness I have for the Beautiful even if my night's labours should be burnt every morning and no eye ever shine upon them. But even now I am perhaps not speaking from myself; but from some character in whose soul I now live – I am sure however that this next sentence is from myself. I feel your anxiety, good opinion and friendliness in the highest degree, and am

Your's most sincerely
John Keats

5. "Character" means not only a poet's personality but also the visibility of his identity, biases, philosophy, etc. in his work. In Keats's day, Shakespeare was admired, by Coleridge and others, for the invisibility of this "character"; in an influential lecture of 1818 (attended by Keats), Hazlitt called Shakespeare "the least of an egotist that it was possible to be. He was nothing in himself; but . . . all that others were". Milton and Wordsworth were typical contrasts, as poets of egotism.

6. A foolish soldier in Shakespeare's *Troilus and Cressida* is described as "a very man per se" who "stands alone" (1.2.15–16).

7. Hazlitt's *On Gusto*, begins, "Gusto in art is power or passion defining any object." Iago is the scheming villain

of *Othello*; Imogen is the virtuous heroine of *Cymbeline*.

8. A chameleon can change color according to circumstance.

9. At the bottom of the first letter-page, Keats writes "infor—" as if meaning to hyphenate, and complete the word on the next page. He began page 2 however with no such completion, but rather, "and filling."

1. Keats had remarked to Woodhouse that he felt preempted by the great poets of the past. In Greek mythology, Saturn is the king of the Titan gods and Ops a harvest goddess; cast out of heaven by the revolt of their children, the fallen Titans appear in the poem Keats was working on during these months, *Hyperion*.

To Charles Brown[2]
[KEATS'S LAST LETTER]

My Dear Brown,   Rome. 30th *November*, 1820.

'Tis the most difficult thing in the world to me to write a letter. My stomach continues so bad, that I feel it worse on opening any book,—yet I am much better than I was in quarantine.[3] Then I am afraid to encounter the pro-ing and con-ing of any thing interesting to me in England. I have an habitual feeling of my real life having passed, and that I am leading a posthumous existence. God knows how it would have been—but it appears to me—however, I will not speak of that subject. I must have been at Bedhampton nearly at the time you were writing to me from Chichester—how unfortunate—and to pass on the river too![4] There was my star predominant! I cannot answer any thing in your letter, which followed me from Naples to Rome, because I am afraid to look it over again. I am so weak (in mind) that I cannot bear the sight of any handwriting of a friend I love so much as I do you. Yet I ride the little horse,[5] and, at my worst, even in quarantine, summoned up more puns, in a sort of desperation, in one week than in any year of my life. There is one thought enough to kill me; I have been well, healthy, alert, &c., walking with her,[6] and now—the knowledge of contrast, feeling for light and shade, all that information (primitive sense) necessary for a poem are great enemies to the recovery of the stomach. There, you rogue, I put you to the torture; but you must bring your philosophy to bear, as I do mine, really, or how should I be able to live? Dr Clarke is very attentive to me; he says, there is very little the matter with my lungs,[7] but my stomach, he says, is very bad. I am well disappointed in hearing good news from George, for it runs in my head we shall all die young.[8] I have not written to Reynolds yet, which he must think very neglectful; being anxious to send him a good account of my health, I have delayed it from week to week. If I recover, I will do all in my power to correct the mistakes made during sickness; and if I should not, all my faults will be forgiven. Severn is very well, though he leads so dull a life with me. Remember me to all friends, and tell Haslam I should not have left London without taking leave of him, but from being so low in body and mind. Write to George as soon as you receive this, and tell him how I am, as far as you can guess: and also a note to my sister—who walks about my imagination like a ghost—she is so like Tom. I can scarcely bid you good-bye, even in a letter. I always made an awkward bow.

God bless you!
John Keats.

2. Charles Brown (1787–1842), a man of various literary and amorous pursuits, was a close friend, traveling companion, and housemate. He cared assiduously for Keats after his first major hemorrhage in February 1820, then left for his usual summer vacation in May. Keats earnestly hoped Brown would accompany him to Italy, but he could not be located. Our text of this letter is the one published in 1848.

3. The ship on which Keats sailed was held for quarantine outside Naples, in oppressive summer weather.

4. The towns are near Portsmouth harbor, from which Keats would sail.

5. Recommended by Keats's doctor in Rome as exercise.

6. Fanny Brawne; Brown deleted her name, as well as those of Keats's friends, when he included the letter in a biography of Keats.

7. Actually, Keats's lungs were nearly destroyed.

8. Tom died at 19, George lived to his mid-forties, and the youngest, Fanny, lived into her eighties.

Gustave Doré, *Ludgate Hill,* from *London: A Pilgrimage,* 1872.

The Victorian Age

1832–1901

> Never since the beginning of Time was there, that we hear or read of, so intensely self-conscious a Society. Our whole relations to the Universe and to our fellow-man have become an Inquiry, a Doubt.
>
> —*Thomas Carlyle, 1831*

Nothing characterizes Victorian society so much as its quest for self-definition. The sixty-three years of Victoria's reign were marked by momentous and intimidating social changes, startling inventions, prodigious energies; the rapid succession of events produced wild prosperity and unthinkable poverty, humane reforms and flagrant exploitation, immense ambitions and devastating doubts. Between 1800 and 1850 the population doubled from nine to eighteen million, and Britain became the richest country on earth, the first urban industrial society in history. For some, it was a period of great achievement, deep faith, indisputable progress. For others, it was "an age of destruction," religious collapse, vicious profiteering. To almost everyone it was apparent that, as Sir Henry Holland put it in 1858, "we are living in *an age of transition*."

But what Matthew Arnold called the "multitudinousness" of British culture overwhelmed all efforts to give the era a collective identity or a clear sense of purpose. Dazzled and dazed by their steam-powered printing presses, their railways and telegraphs, journalism and junk mail, Victorians suffered from both future shock and the information explosion. For the first time a nation had become self-consciously modern: people were sure only of their differences from previous generations, certain only that traditional ways of life were fast being transformed into something perilously unstable and astonishingly new. As the novelist William Makepeace Thackeray noted, "We are of the time of chivalry. . . . We are of the age of steam."

VICTORIA AND THE VICTORIANS

In an unpredictable, tumultuous era, the stern, staid figure of Queen Victoria came to represent stability and continuity. The adjective "Victorian" was first used in 1851 to celebrate the nation's mounting pride in its institutions and commercial success. That year, the global predominance of British industry had emerged incontestably at the original "world's fair" in London, the "Great Exhibition of the Works of Industry of All Nations," which Prince Albert helped organize. Arrayed for the world to see in a vast "Crystal Palace" of iron and glass, the marvels of British manufacture achieved a regal stature of their own and cast their allure upon the monarchy in turn. In the

Sunlight Soap advertisement commemorating the 1897 Jubilee of Victoria's reign.

congratulatory rhetoric that surrounded the event, the conservative, retiring queen emerged as the durable symbol of her dynamic, aggressively businesslike realm.

In succeeding decades, the official portraits of Queen Victoria, gradually aging, reflected her country's sense of its own maturation as a society and world power. Etched by conflict with her prime ministers, the birth of nine children, and the early death of her beloved Prince Albert, Victoria's once pretty face became deeply lined and heavily jowled. Represented as a fairy-tale teenaged queen at her coronation in 1837, she radiated a youthful enthusiasm that corresponded to the optimism of the earlier 1830s. It seemed a decade of new beginnings. Settling into the role of fertile matron-monarch, she offered a domestic image to match the booming productivity of the 1850s. Reclusive after Albert died in 1861, she eventually took on the austere role of the black-satined Empress of India, projecting a world-weary glumness that lent gravity to the imperial heyday of the 1870s. Finally, as the aged, venerated Widow of Windsor, she became a universal icon, prompting the nostalgic worldwide spectacles of the Golden and Diamond Jubilees in 1887 and 1897. When Victoria died in 1901, after the longest reign in English history, a newspaper wrote: "Few of us, perhaps, have realized till now how large a part she had in the life of everyone of us; how the thread of her life [bound] the warp of the nation's progress."

During the seven decades of her rule, Victoria's calm profile, stamped on currency and displayed in offices and outposts from London to Bombay, presided over the expansion of Britain into the world's greatest empire. Economically and politically,

Britannia ruled not only the waves but more than a quarter of the globe's landmass. Among its domains were Canada, Australia, New Zealand, South Africa, the Indian subcontinent and Ceylon, Malaya, Hong Kong, Singapore, Burma, Jamaica, Trinidad, British Guiana, Bermuda, the Bahamas, Rhodesia, Kenya, Uganda, and Nigeria. By the 1890s one out of every four people on earth was a "subject" of Queen Victoria.

Victoria stood not only for England and Empire, but also for Duty, Family, and, especially, Propriety. "We have come to regard the Crown as the head of our morality" wrote the historian Walter Bagehot. As a description of behavior, "Victorian" signifies social conduct governed by strict rules, formal manners, and rigidly defined gender roles. Relations between the sexes were hedged about with sexual prudery and an intense concern for maintaining the appearance of propriety in public, whatever the private facts. But although she was presented as the ultimate role model, Victoria herself could not escape the contradictions of her era. The most powerful woman on earth, she denounced "this mad, wicked folly of Women's Rights." Her quiet reserve restored the dignity of the monarchy after the rakish ways of George IV, but she allowed advertisers to trade shamelessly on her image and product endorsements. Her face was universally known, featured on everything from postage stamps to tea trays, yet after Albert's death she lived in seclusion, rarely seeing either her ministers or the public. An icon of motherhood, she detested pregnancy, childbirth, and babies. As an emblem of Britain's greatness, Queen Victoria gave her subjects the public identity and purpose that privately they—and she, in her diaries—recognized as an unfulfilled ideal.

The Victorians have left us a contradictory picture of themselves. On the one hand, they were phenomenally energetic, dedicated to the Gospel of Work and driven by a solemn sense of duty to the Public Good. Popular authors like Dickens and Trollope churned out three-volume novels, engaged in numerous philanthropic projects, devoured twelve-course dinners, took twenty-mile walks, and produced a voluminous correspondence. Explorers and missionaries such as Burton, Speke, Stanley, and Livingston took enormous risks to map uncharted territory or spread Christianity "in darkest Africa." Although an invalid, Florence Nightingale revamped the entire British military medical and supply system from her bedroom office. All this activity was sustained by belief in its implicit moral benefit. In matters of character Victorians prized respectability, earnestness, a sense of duty and public service; most would have regarded an industrious, pious conventionality as the best road not only to material recompense but to heavenly rewards as well.

Yet the fabled self-confidence of this overachieving society often rings hollow. Their literature conveys an uneasy sense that their obsession with work was in part a deliberate distraction, as if Victorians were discharging public responsibilities in order to ease nagging doubts about their religious faith, about changing gender roles, about the moral quandaries of class privilege and imperial rule. Much of the era's social conservatism, such as its resistance to women's rights and to class mobility, may be traced to the fear of change. They struggled to dominate the present moment in order to keep an uncertain future at bay. Few questioned that tremendous advances were taking place in science, public health, transportation, and the general standard of living, but each new idea or discovery seemed to have unexpected, distressing repercussions.

The critic J. A. Froude remarked in 1841 that "the very truths which have come forth have produced doubts . . . this dazzle has too often ended in darkness." Discoveries in geology, biology, and textual scholarship shattered belief in the literal truth of the Bible. The Industrial Revolution shifted power from the landed aristocracy toward an insecure, expanding middle class of businessmen and professionals, impoverishing millions of once rural laborers along the way. Strident, riotous campaigns to extend voting rights to males of the middle and working classes produced fears of armed insurrection. Coupled with the agitations for and against trade unions, women's equality, socialism, and the separation of church and state, the fitful transformation of Britain's political and economic structure often teetered on the brink of open class warfare. In the national clamor for reform, every sector of the population fought for its privileges and feared for its rights. The following pages introduce the Victorian period by looking at several key issues: the era's energy and invention, its doubts about religion and industrialism, its far-reaching social reforms, its conflicted fascination with Empire, the commercialization and expansion of the reading public, and the period's vigorous self-scrutiny in the mirror of literature.

THE AGE OF ENERGY AND INVENTION

The most salient characteristic of life in this latter portion of the 19th century is its SPEED.

—*W. R. Greg,* Life at High Pressure, *1875*

The "newness" of Victorian society—its speed, progress, and triumphant ingenuity—was epitomized by the coming of the railway. Until the 1830s, the fastest ways to travel or transport goods were still the most ancient ones, by sail or horse. But on seeing the first train pass through the Rugby countryside in 1839, Thomas Arnold astutely remarked: "Feudality is gone forever." The earliest passenger railway line opened in 1830 between Liverpool and Manchester; by 1855, eight thousand miles of track had been laid. Speeds of fifty miles per hour were soon routine; the journey from London to Edinburgh that had taken two weeks in 1800 now took less than a day.

Carrying passengers, freight, newspapers, and mail, the railways helped create a national consciousness by linking once remote parts of the country into a single economy and culture. Networks of information, distribution, and services moved news, goods, and people from one end of Britain to the other to the rhythm of the railway timetable. The accelerating pace of life that railways introduced became one of the defining features of the age.

Moreover, the railway irrevocably altered the face of the landscape. Its bridges, tunnels, cuttings, crossings, viaducts, and embankments permanently scarred a rural landscape whose fields, hedgerows, and highways were rooted deep in history. In the cities, engineers and entrepreneurs carved room for vast railyards and stations by demolishing populous districts. Discharging commodities and crowds, the railways transformed town centers everywhere, bolstering local economies and stimulating construction as they arrived, but depriving once thriving coaching inns and former mail routes of traffic and trade. Underground trains restructured the experience of

Robert Howlett, *Portrait of Isambard Kingdom Brunel and Launching Chains of the Great Eastern,* 1857. Howlett's interest in contemporary subjects, ranging from steamships and Crimean War heroes to telescopic views of the moon, exemplified the belief that as a new medium itself, photography was supremely suited to capture "progress" in all its manifestations. In his portrait of Brunel, the audacious engineer who designed the Great Western Railway and the world's largest steamship, *The Great Eastern,* Howlett evoked both industrial might and Victorian self-confidence; the man of genius dominates the chains that dwarf him.

travel within the city as well: the world's first subway line opened in 1863 in London; a complete inner London system was operating by 1884. Finally, railway-sponsored mass tourism eroded the regional distinctiveness and insularity of individual places. The inventor of the organized excursion, Thomas Cook, saw his advertising slogan, "RAILWAYS FOR THE MILLIONS," turned into a simple statement of fact.

Optimistic social prophets envisioned all classes reaping the fruits of the Industrial Revolution. The widespread Victorian belief in Progress was sustained by many factors, including rising incomes, the greater availability of goods, the perception of surplus production, and the leading role of Britain in world affairs. Many people were awed by the sheer size of industrial achievement: the heaviest ships, the longest tunnels, the biggest warehouses, the most massive factory outputs ever known, all contributed to a sublimity of scale that staggered the public's imagination.

Every decade brought impressive innovations that transformed the rhythms of everyday life. The first regular Atlantic steamship crossings began in 1838, flouting the age-old dependence on wind and tide, importing tea from China, cotton from India or Alabama, beef from Australia, and exporting to world markets finished goods ranging from Sheffield cutlery and Manchester textiles to Pear's Soap and the latest Dickens novel.

Equally momentous in its own way was Henry Fox Talbot's discovery between 1839 and 1841 of how to produce and print a photographic negative. The technology of his "sun-pictures" revolutionized the entire visual culture and changed the human relationship to the past. A moment in time could now be "fixed" forever. Thus, more than a century later, we have photographic records of many subsequent innovations: the construction of the London sewer system; the laying of the transatlantic cable in 1865, putting London and New York in almost instantaneous contact via telegraph; the popularity in the 1890s of bicycles, gramophones, electric trams, and the first regular motion picture shows; and in the year of Victoria's death, 1901, Marconi's first transatlantic wireless radio message.

Capturing the public mood, Disraeli wrote in 1862: "It is a privilege to live in this age of rapid and brilliant events. What an error to consider it a utilitarian age. It is one of infinite romance." For the growing middle class there was an Aladdin-like sense of wonderment at the astounding abundance of *things*: an incredible hodge-podge of inventions, gimmicks, and gadgets began to make up the familiar paraphernalia of modern life, including chain stores, washing and sewing machines, postage stamps, canned foods, toothpaste, sidewalk newsstands, illustrated magazines and newspapers, typewriters, breakfast cereal, slide projectors, skin creams, diet pills, shampoo, ready-to-wear clothes, sneakers (called "plimsolls"), and even a cumbersome prototype computer, designed by Charles Babbage.

Victorian architecture, interior design, and clothing embodied the obsession with plenitude, presenting a bewildering variety of prefabricated, highly ornamented styles. A house might feature Gothic revival, neoclassical, Egyptian, Moorish, baronial, or Arts-and-Crafts motifs, every inch of its interior covered with wallpapers, etchings, draperies, carvings, lacework, and knickknacks. Though fashions varied, men and women were usually as well upholstered as their furniture, tightly buttoned from top to toe in sturdy fabrics, their clothes complexly layered on the outside (men's waistcoats, jackets, cravats, and watches) and inside (women's crinolines, petticoats, bustles, corsets, and drawers).

In a Protestant culture that linked industriousness with godliness, both capitalism and consumerism were fueled by prevailing religious attitudes. For Thomas Carlyle, work itself had a divine sanction: "Produce! Produce!" he wrote in *Sartor Resartus*: "Were it but the pitifullest infinitesimal fraction of a Product, produce it in God's name!" His compatriots obliged: by 1848 Britain's output of cotton cloth and iron was more than half of the world total, and the coal output two-thirds of world production. At the Great Exhibition of 1851, when Britain was dubbed "the workshop of the world," the display struck the Reverend Charles Kingsley as triumphant evidence of God's will: "If these forefathers of ours could rise from their graves this day they would be inclined to see in our hospitals, in our railroads, in the achievements of our physical science . . . proofs of the kingdom of God . . . vaster than any of which they had dreamed."

But for Karl Marx, laboring to write *Das Kapital* (1867) at a desk in the British Museum Reading Room, it was not enough to find God in the material world. He saw that through the hoopla of the marketplace, products had acquired a "mystical character" and "theological niceties" of their own. Yet Marx did not regard commodities as proof of God's existence; instead, he argued that they functioned as deities in their own right. An ignored subversive stationed at the heart of the empire, Marx perceived how status-filled objects seemed to take on lives that defined human social relations, even as they degraded the workers that produced them.

Looking around at the wonders of British industry, Marx decided that people had become, finally, less important than things. For him, it was the Age of Commodity Fetishism.

THE AGE OF DOUBT

It was the age of science, new knowledge, searching criticism, followed by multiplied doubts and shaken beliefs.

—*John Morley*

Despite their reverence for material accomplishment and the tenets of organized religion, the Victorians were deeply conflicted in their beliefs and intentions. In retrospect, the forces that shook the foundations of Victorian society might be summed up in two names, Marx and Darwin: though Marx was virtually unknown at the time, his radical critique of unbridled free enterprise brought to the most acute level contemporary analyses of economic injustice and the class system. Darwin's staggering evolutionary theories implied that biblical accounts of creation could not be literally true. But well before either had published a word, British thought was in crisis: "The Old has passed away," wrote Carlyle in 1831, "but, alas, the New appears not in its stead." In his 1851 novel *Yeast*, Charles Kingsley described how deluged the Victorians felt by challenges to their faith and social order: "The various stereotyped systems . . . received by tradition [are] breaking up under them like ice in a thaw," he wrote; "a thousand facts and notions, which they know not how to classify, [are] pouring in on them like a flood."

The Crisis of Faith

In the midst of this tumult, the Victorians were troubled by Time. On the one hand, there was not enough of it: the accelerated pace of change kept people too busy to assimilate the torrent of new ideas and technologies. In the 1880s the essayist F. R. Harrison contended that Victorians were experiencing "a life lived so full . . . that we have no time to reflect where we have been and whither we intend to go." On the other hand, there was too much time: well before Darwin, scientists were showing that vast eons of geological and cosmic development had preceded human history, itself suddenly lengthening due to such discoveries as the Neanderthal skeletons found in 1856.

Their sense of worth diminished by both time clocks and time lines, Victorians felt they had little opportunity for reflection and often took scant comfort in it. Matthew Arnold complained of "this strange disease of modern life with its sick hurry, its divided aims." Yet this climate of anxious uncertainty provoked intense religious fervor, and debates about church doctrine and the proper forms of Christian worship occupied the national consciousness throughout the century. "This is the age of experiment," wrote the historian E. P. Hood in 1850, regarding the constant testing of belief, "but the cheerful fact is, that almost all men are yearning after a faith."

The most influential group were the "Evangelicals," a term which covers not only "dissenting" or "nonconformist" Protestant sects outside the Church of England (such as Methodists, Presbyterians, Congregationalists, and Baptists), but also the Evangelical party or "Low Church" faction within the Church of England. Anti-Catholic,

Bible-oriented, concerned with humanitarian issues, and focused on the salvation of individual souls within a rigid framework of Christian conduct, Evangelicalism dominated the religious and often the social life of working- and middle-class Britons. Evangelicals practiced self-denial and frugality; they rejected most forms of entertainment as sinful or frivolous, and regarded any but the simplest church service as a "popish" throwback to Catholicism, which they abhorred on nationalistic as well as religious grounds. It was Evangelicalism that was largely responsible for the freeing of slaves in the British colonies in 1833, for the strictness of Victorian morality at home, and for British missionary zeal abroad.

At the other end of the spectrum were the Anglo-Catholics of the Tractarian or Oxford Movement, which flourished in the 1830s and 1840s. Through an appeal to early church history, they sought to revitalize the power and spiritual intensity of the Church of England, insisting on the authority of the Church hierarchy, and reaffirming the Church's traditional position as a grace-granting intermediary between Christians and their God. The movement collapsed when its leader, John Henry Newman, converted to Roman Catholicism in 1845. But the antirational, romantic spirit of this small group left a substantial legacy in the renewed ritualism of "High Church" practices. Gothic revival architecture, the burning of altar candles and incense, the resplendent vestments of the clergy—all these were aspects of a religious apprehension of sensuous beauty and mysticism that had not been seen in England since before the Reformation. This "High Church" aestheticism came into direct and ongoing conflict with "Low Church" sobriety.

The crisis of religious doubt occasioned by biblical scholarship and scientific discoveries hit Christian belief hard. But it prompted an array of coping strategies and new ideas about the position of human beings in the universe that remain significant to this day. Most Victorian authors and intellectuals found a way to reassert religious ideas. Thus George Eliot, for instance, maintained that an Evangelical sense of duty and ethics was essential as a social "glue" to prevent the disintegration of society in the absence of religious authority. That it was still an era which *wanted* to believe is evident from the huge success of Tennyson's *In Memoriam* (1850), in which the poet's hard-won religious faith finally triumphs over science-induced despair. Extending evolutionary theory to spiritual advantage, Tennyson hoped man might transcend animality by encouraging his divine soul to "Move upward, working out the beast, / And let the ape and tiger die." Even Darwin's defender Thomas Huxley, who coined the word "agnostic," also celebrated Auguste Comte's positivism and "the Religion of Humanity." Huxley spoke for many who had renounced organized religion but not spiritual impulses when he said that Carlyle's *Sartor Resartus* "led me to know that a deep sense of religion was compatible with the entire absence of theology." Finally, some artists and writers used Christian icons as an avant-garde protest against the secular direction of modern life. "The more materialistic science becomes," said the artist Edward Burne-Jones, "the more angels shall I paint."

The Industrial Catastrophe

In principle, the Victorian crisis of faith should at least have pleased the Utilitarians. The creed of these atheistic, rationalist followers of Jeremy Bentham was strictly practical: measure all human endeavor by its ability to produce "the greatest happiness for the greatest number." Sharing a committed, "can do" philosophy of social reform, Utilitarianism and Evangelicalism were the two dominant ideologies shaping early and mid-Victorian life. But despite the significant changes they effected in government and education during the 1820s and 1830s, even the Utilitarians ran out of self-assurance and moral steam in the morass of mid-Victorian cultural ferment.

A few energetic idealists dreamed of leveling age-old inequalities. "Glory to Man in the highest!" wrote Swinburne in 1869, "for Man is the master of things." But here too a form of evolutionary theory was undercutting the conventional pieties of social discourse. "Love thy neighbor" had no more moral authority for the "Social Darwinist" than it had historical accuracy for the textual scholar. Summed up in the phrase "survival of the fittest"—coined by the philosopher Herbert Spencer in 1852, seven years before *The Origin of Species* appeared—Social Darwinism viewed as dangerous any attempt to regulate the supposedly immutable laws of society. Evolutionary forces decreed that only the fittest should survive in capitalist competition as well as in nature. Applied to nations and races as well as individuals, this theory supported the apparent destiny of England to prosper and rule the world.

Social Darwinism was a brutal offshoot of the influential economic theory of laissez-faire capitalism. Drawing on Adam Smith's *The Wealth of Nations* (1776), businessmen argued that the unfettered pursuit of self-interest, in the form of unrestricted competition in a free market, would be best for society. This was an idea that Utilitarians and many Evangelicals rejected in favor of legislative regulation, since their view of the imperfections of humanity indicated that one person's self-interest was likely to mean another's exploitation. The desperate need to protect the poor and disadvantaged, and the difficulty of doing so, was cause for much soul-searching, particularly among those who had made a religion of social reform.

Concern about the fairness and efficacy of the social structure was exacerbated by the unprecedented rate of urbanization. "Our age is preeminently the age of great cities" declared historian Robert Vaughan in 1843. At the beginning of the nineteenth century only one-fifth of the British population lived in cities; by the end of the century, more than three-quarters did. Such vast numbers of people crowding into the cities created hideous problems of housing, sanitation, and disease. For the poor, living and working conditions were appalling, particularly in the 1830s and 1840s, when neither housing nor factories were regulated. Industrial workers labored six days a week, for as many as fourteen or sixteen hours a day, in stifling, deafening, dangerous workshops, then went home to unheated rooms they often shared with other families, six or seven people to a bed of rags. Drinking water often came from rivers filled with industrial pollution and human waste. Without job security, healthcare, or pensions, the injured, the sick, and the aged fell by the wayside. In manufacturing cities the competition for survival was indeed intense: the life expectancy among working people in Manchester in 1841 was about twenty years.

Foreign visitors in particular were struck with wonder and horror at the conjunction of so much misery and so much wealth. "From this filthy sewer pure gold flows," marveled the French historian Alexis de Tocqueville: "From this foul drain the greatest stream of human industry flows out to fertilize the whole world." Friedrich Engels spent a year in Manchester, producing the most detailed and shocking firsthand account of Victorian industrial life, *The Condition of the Working Class in England in 1844*. Karl Marx, who lived in England for thirty-four years, worked his observations into his famous

The Crystal Palace, site of the Great Exhibition of 1851, after its re-erection at Sydenham, c. 1855.

theory of "surplus labor value." Under the current system, he said, wretched factory hands would never receive adequate payment for the wealth they created by transforming raw materials into precious commodities. Like many people at the time, both liberal and conservative, Marx expected that violent class warfare was imminent.

On average real wages went up and prices went down in Victoria's reign, with per capita income doubling between 1800 and 1860. But the boom-and-bust cycles of free trade made for unsteady wages, seesaw prices, sudden layoffs, and volatile labor relations, as Britain made a lurching transition to an industrial and commercial economy. There were serious depressions or slowdowns almost every decade, but the worst took place during "the Hungry Forties." Scarce food, widespread unemployment, and general despair provoked riots and fears of revolution. The statesman Charles Greville noted in his diary in 1842, "There is an immense and continually increasing population, no adequate demand for labor . . . no confidence, but a universal alarm, disquietude, and discontent." An American observer of the industrial scene named Henry Coleman remarked, "Every day that I live I thank Heaven that I am not a poor man with a family in England." When the economy recovered, many fled. Between the years 1850 and 1880, three million emigrants left Britain, two-thirds for the United States.

THE AGE OF REFORM

The whole meaning of Victorian England is lost if it is thought of as a country of stuffy complacency and black top-hatted moral priggery. Its frowsty crinolines and dingy hansom cabs, its gas-lit houses

Color Plate 11 Sir John Everett Millais, *Mariana*, 1851. Millais based this painting on Tennyson's poem *Mariana* (page 1139). When first exhibited, the painting was accompanied by these lines: "She only said, 'My life is dreary, / He cometh not,' she said; / She said, 'I am aweary, aweary, / I would that I were dead!'" Millais's painting is typically Pre-Raphaelite in its use of bright colors, narrative details, and medieval trappings. The stained glass windows depict the Annunciation, suggesting an ironic contrast between the Virgin's fulfillment and Mariana's frustration. Not everyone was moved by this vision of anguished longing; the art critic John Ruskin snorted derisively that had Millais "depicted Mariana working in a meadowed grange, instead of idle in a moated one, it had been to better purpose." *(Tate Gallery, London/Art Resource, NY.)*

Color Plate 12   William Holman Hunt, *The Awakening Conscience*, 1853. A "kept" woman (she wears no wedding ring) and her lover have been blithely singing at the piano when suddenly she has a spiritual revelation: she sees the light and realizes it is not too late to reform. The painting is full of symbolic details: the cat toying with the bird suggests the true nature of the gentleman's relationship with his mistress; the glove carelessly tossed aside hints at her probable future as a prostitute. Ruskin wrote, "the very hem of the poor girl's dress, at which the painter has laboured so closely, thread by thread, has a story in it, if we think how soon its pure whiteness may be soiled with dust and rain, her outcast feet failing in the street." The sunny garden reflected in the mirror symbolizes the possibility of redemption if she can escape the importuning arms that encircle her. *(Tate Gallery, London/Art Resource, NY.)*

Color Plate 13 Ford Madox Brown, *Work*, 1852–1865. Inspired by the sight of men laying sewers in London, this Dickensian novel of a painting portrays work across the entire social spectrum. Brown called the young British excavator in the center "The outward and visible type of Work"— he is the hero, "the strong fully developed navvy who does his work and loves his beer." On horseback is a very rich gentleman, "probably a Colonel in the army, with a seat in Parliament, and fifteen thousand a year" and his daughter. Standing on the right are two influential intellectuals, Thomas Carlyle and the Reverend F. D. Maurice (who founded the Working Man's College where Brown taught art); they are "the brain workers, who seeming to be idle, work, and are the cause of well-ordained work and happiness, in others." The beer seller, who grew up in the slums of Birmingham, is "humpbacked, dwarfish, and . . . vulgar," yet has prospered through energy and hard work; "in his way he also is a sort of hero." The flower seller is a "ragged wretch who has never been taught to work." The neglected children are motherless, as "the baby's black ribbons and their extreme dilapidation indicate," and "the care of the two little ones is an anxious charge for the elder girl." *(© Manchester Art Gallery.)*

Color Plates 14 and 15   Augustus Egg, *Past and Present, No. 1* (above) and *Past and Present, No. 3* (below), 1858. *Past and Present* tells the story of an adulterous woman's downfall in three scenes. In the first, the distraught husband holds the letter that has just revealed his wife's infidelity; she lies prostrate with grief and shame, while the house of cards their children are building collapses (on the wall one picture depicts the expulsion of Adam and Eve from Eden; the other shows a shipwreck). The third scene takes place five years later; the mother is now a homeless outcast, huddled under a bridge with her illegitimate child (behind her a poster advertises two plays, *Victims* and *The Cure for Love*, while another describes "Pleasure Excursions to Paris"). Meanwhile, in the second scene (not illustrated here) her two orphaned daughters gaze forlornly at the same moon as their mother, from whom they are forever separated. Egg's use of symbolic detail recalls Holman Hunt's *The Awakening Conscience* (Color Plate 12), another version of the theme of the "fallen woman." (*Tate Gallery, London/Art Resource, NY.*)

Color Plate 16   William Morris, *Guenevere*, or *La Belle Iseult*, 1858. Morris published his first book of poems, *The Defence of Guenevere*, in March 1858, and this painting was long believed to depict Guenevere, King Arthur's adulterous queen, standing beside her rumpled bed. Arthurian themes were enormously popular among the Victorians (Tennyson published his first *Idylls of the King* in 1858). But the picture is now thought to portray Queen Iseult grieving over the absence of her exiled lover, Sir Tristram. Either way, the brooding posture of the "fallen woman" is accentuated by the sensuous richness of her dress and surroundings: the illuminated missal, Turkish carpet, and elaborately patterned hangings and tapestries. The model was Jane Burden, whom Morris married the following year. (*Tate Gallery, London/Art Resource, NY.*)

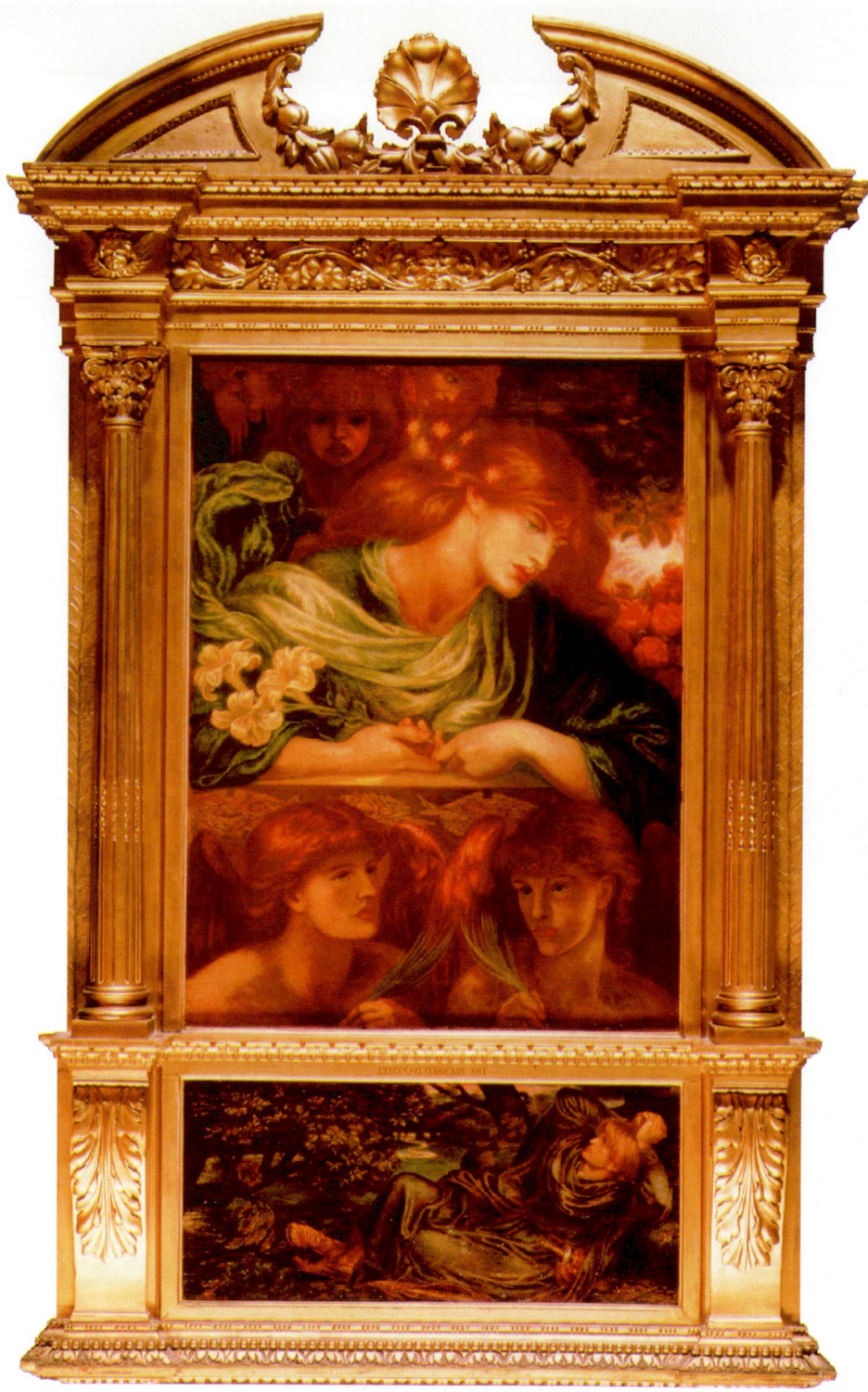

Color Plate 17 Dante Gabriel Rossetti, *The Blessed Damozel*, 1871–1879. Rossetti based this painting on his poem *The Blessed Damozel*, written before he was 20 years old. The Damozel, surrounded by angels, leans over the golden bar of Heaven and gazes wistfully down toward her lover below on earth. The painting is split into two parts—rather like a Renaissance altarpiece—emphasizing the separation of the lovers. *(Courtesy, National Museums Liverpool [The Walker].)*

Color Plate 18   James McNeill Whistler, *Nocturne in Black and Gold: The Falling Rocket*, 1875. Working at the limit of representation, Whistler aggressively opposed the literary, anecdotal qualities of Pre-Raphaelite and mainstream Victorian art. This painting of fireworks exploding at the Cremorne Gardens amusement park so riled the critic John Ruskin that he wrote, "I have seen, and heard, much of Cockney impudence before now; but never expected to hear a coxcomb ask two hundred guineas for flinging a pot of paint in the public's face." Whistler sued Ruskin for libel, and Whistler's brilliant defense of his work at the ensuing trial paved the way for the impressionist and abstract styles of the modern era. *(Gift of Dexter M. Ferry, Jr. Photograph © 1988 The Detroit Institute of Arts.)*

Color Plate 19 John Williams Waterhouse, *The Lady of Shalott*, 1888. Tennyson's poem *The Lady of Shalott* (page 640) inspired many Victorian paintings, including one by Holman Hunt (page 641). Hunt shows the lady imprisoned in her tower; Waterhouse depicts her floating "down the river's dim expanse / Like some bold seer in a trance" toward Camelot. The painting shows her loosening the boat's chain and "singing her last song," as in the poem, but Waterhouse has added the crucifix and candles. *(Tate Gallery, London/Art Resource, NY.)*

Color Plate 20 Sir Edward Burne-Jones, *Love Among the Ruins*, 1894. The painting's title is taken from Robert Browning's poem (page 756), but it is not so much an illustration of the poem as a romantic evocation of its subject. The languid poses and pale faces, sumptuous colors and flowing drapery, show how the Pre-Raphaelite influence continued late in the century. Unlike narrative paintings (such as *Mariana, The Awakening Conscience,* and *Past and Present,* Color Plates 11, 12, 14, and 15), there is no story to be "read" in the details. As Burne-Jones wrote, "I mean by a picture, a beautiful romantic dream of something that never was, never will be—in a better light than any light that ever shone—in a land that no-one can define or remember, only desire—and the forms divinely beautiful." *(Wightwick Manor, The Mander Collection [The National Trust] NTPL. Photo by Derrick E. Witty.)*

and over-ornate draperies, concealed a people engaged in a tremendously exciting adventure—the daring experiment of fitting industrial man into a democratic society.

—*Historian David Thompson, 1950*

Despite crushing problems and the threat of social breakdown, the Victorian period can justly be called an age of reform. Each of the issues that threatened to bring the country into open conflict or destroy the social fabric was in the course of the century addressed peacefully through legislation: voting rights were extended, working conditions improved, and women's rights began to gain ground, without the bloody revolutions or insurrections that struck France in 1838, 1848, and 1870, and Germany in 1848. As fears of revolution receded, the subtler worries of Mill and Arnold, based on their observation of American democracy, seemed more to the point. How could liberty of thought be preserved in a mass culture dedicated to majority rule? How could the best ideas elevate, rather than succumb to, the lowest common denominator?

Politics and Class

The key to the century's relatively peaceful progress was the passage of legislation for political and social reform. The start of the Victorian era is often dated 1832, five years before Victoria's coronation, because in that year the First Reform Bill was enacted. It gave representation to the new industrial towns, such as Manchester, Birmingham, and Leeds, all cities of over 100,000 inhabitants that had lacked a single seat in Parliament. It also enlarged the electorate by about 50 percent, granting the vote to some propertied portions of the middle class. Still, only one in six adult males could vote, and the aristocracy retained parliamentary control. Agitation for reform continued, especially in the Chartist movement of 1838–1848. Taking its name from the People's Charter of 1838, it was a loose alliance of artisans and factory workers that called for sweeping reforms, including universal male suffrage, the secret ballot, equal electoral districts, and annual elections. Chartism was the world's first independent working-class movement, its membership swelling into the millions during the depressions of the 1840s. The Chartists presented giant petitions, signed by one to five million people, to Parliament in 1839, 1842, and 1848. But each time they were rejected, and the movement collapsed after a government show of force effectively defused the demonstrations accompanying the petition of 1848.

The lot of workers was to improve piecemeal, not through the grand political reorganization envisioned by Chartism, as Parliament grudgingly passed acts regulating food, factories, and the right to unionize. An important breakthrough came with the repeal of the Corn Laws in 1846. The laws levied tariffs on the importation of foreign grain; they were sponsored by the landed aristocracy to protect the high price of their home-grown grains (called "corn" in Britain). Therefore, as the poet Thomas Hood wrote in 1842, "bread was dear and flesh and blood were cheap." The new urban business interests fought the protectionist tariffs in the name of "Free Trade." They preferred a stable, better-fed workforce to one that rioted or starved in times of scarcity, but they also wanted cheap bread to keep their workers' wages down. Later, the Public Health acts of 1848 and 1869 improved the availability of tea, sugar, and beer. In the 1870s the importation of wheat from the United States and refrigerated meat and fruit from Australia and New Zealand meant a more varied diet for the working classes, who could by now also afford the new custom of having large bacon-and-egg breakfasts.

Beginning in 1833, a crucial series of Factory Acts slowly curtailed the horrors of industrial labor. The 1833 Act provided for safety inspections of machinery, prohibited the employment of children under nine, and limited the workweek to forty-eight hours for children under twelve. Though the law was poorly enforced, a trend had begun. The Ten Hours Act of 1847 limited the time women and children could work daily in textile factories, and ensuing acts gradually regulated safety and working conditions in other industries. Workers' political power increased when the Second Reform Bill (1867) doubled the electorate, including all male urban householders. During this period employers also felt increasing pressure from extralegal trade union movements, including miners, textile workers, and women garment workers. An uncomprehending middle class (including Dickens and Gaskell) often regarded unionists as anarchists and murderers. But trade unions were finally legalized in 1871, and the first working-class Members of Parliament were unionist miners elected in 1874. By the 1890s there were 1.5 million trade union members, many of them part of the growing Socialist movement, and the foundations of the modern Labour Party had been laid.

Thus the high hopes of Chartism had in a sense succeeded, many of its supposedly dangerous demands eventually met. As Engels noted, these changes also benefited the middle class who resisted them, as people realized the value—social as well as economic—of reduced hostilities and improved cooperation between classes. Everyone also gained from related reforms that reflected weakening class barriers and increasing social mobility. In 1870 the Education Act initiated nationally funded public education in England and Wales. In the 1880s, middle-class investigators and social workers spearheaded the "discovery of poverty" in London's East End, one of a range of efforts that brought better housing, nutrition, and education to the poor. Finally, the nation as a whole benefited from what historian Asa Briggs has called "the one great political invention in Victorian England"—a civil service staffed through open examinations rather than patronage.

By the last decades of the century, Britain had become a more democratic and pluralistic society; it enjoyed greater freedom in matters of religion, political views, and intellectual life than any other country. Overall, the middle class were the chief generators and beneficiaries of social change. Outsiders before 1832, they became key players in the Victorian period. Though they never dominated politics, which remained largely an aristocratic preserve, they set the tone and agenda for the era's socioeconomic evolution.

"The Woman Question"

Still, one group found almost all doors closed against it. Throughout much of Victoria's reign, women had few opportunities for higher education or satisfying employment: from scullery maids to governesses, female workers of all ranks were severely exploited, and prior to the 1870s married women had no legal rights. What contemporaries called "the Woman Question" was hotly debated in every decade, but only at the end of the century were the first women allowed to vote in local elections. Full female suffrage came only after World War I. Despite articulate champions such as Harriet Martineau and John Stuart Mill, and the examples of successful women such as George Eliot, the Brontës, Florence Nightingale, and the Queen herself, proponents of women's rights made slow headway against prevailing norms. Though Victorians acknowledged the undeniable literary achievements of numerous women writers, many regarded this "brain-work" as a serious aberration that unfitted women for motherhood. The medical establishment backed the conventional view that women were physically and intellectually inferior, a "weaker sex" that would buckle under the weight of strong passion, serious thought, or vigorous exercise. Only in their much vaunted "femininity" did women have an edge, as nurturers of children and men's better instincts.

The ideal Victorian woman was supposed to be domestic and pure, selflessly motivated by the desire to serve others rather than fulfill her own needs. In particular, her duty was to soothe the savage beast her husband might become as he fought in the jungle of free trade. Her role prescribed by Coventry Patmore's wildly popular poem, *The Angel in the House* (1854–1862), the model woman would provide her family with an uplifting refuge from the moral squalor of the working world. Only a small portion of the nation's women could afford to remain at home, but the constant celebration of home and hearth by politicians, the press, and respected authors made conspicuous domesticity the expected role for well-born and well-married women. Many upper- and middle-class women spent their days paying social calls or acquiring "female accomplishments" such as needlework, sketching, or flower arranging. Though this leisure played an important part in generating new literary markets targeted at women, it provoked devastating satires of time-wasting females by Elizabeth Barrett Browning, Charles Dickens, and Florence Nightingale, among others. By the 1860s, with the birth of the department store and modern advertising, leisured women were also for the first time wooed as consumers and portrayed as smart shoppers.

Though their contribution was minimized, women were in fact heavily involved in the labor force, making up one-third of all workers, and 90 percent of the nation's largest labor category, household servants. For so-called "redundant" women who could not find husbands or work, the situation was especially grim. Low wages and unemployment drove tens of thousands of girls and women into prostitution, which, due to the growth of the military and repressive Victorian sexual mores, became one more "boom industry" whose workers reaped few rewards.

If a woman's life was economically precarious outside marriage, her existence was legally terminated within that bond. A woman lost the few civil rights she had as she became "one body" with her husband. Married women had, at the start of the era, no legal right to custody of their own children or to own property. The Divorce and Matrimonial Causes Act of 1857 established a civil divorce court in London, and subsequent acts created protection against assault, desertion, and cruelty, but only a wealthy few could afford legal proceedings. The Married Women's Property Acts of 1870 and 1882, however, gave women the right to possess wages they earned after marriage, as well as any property they owned before it.

Gradually, with the aid of male allies, women created educational opportunities for themselves. The first women's college opened in London in 1848, and the first women's colleges opened at Cambridge in 1869 and at Oxford in 1879—though women were not allowed to take Oxbridge degrees. Elizabeth Blackwell, the first woman M.D., became an accredited physician both in Britain and the United States in 1859; by 1895 there were 264 women doctors. In the 1890s, the much parodied image of the liberated "New Woman" began circulating in the press. By then many young women were braving a conservative backlash to take new positions in office work, the civil service, nursing, and teaching. They also enjoyed the social freedom that accompanied their expanding role in the economy. The novelist Walter Besant wrote admiringly in 1897 of the "personal independence that is the keynote of the situation. . . . The girls go off by themselves on their bicycles; they go about as they please. . . . For the first time in man's history it is regarded as a right and proper thing to trust a girl as a boy insists on being trusted."

The uphill battle that feminists faced is conveyed in the cautious motto of a national-market periodical for women. Published from 1890 to 1912, *Woman* magazine declared its mission: "Forward, but not too fast." Antisuffragists of both sexes found willing allies among those who regarded women as weak and unworldly, better equipped for housekeeping than speechmaking. As the nineteenth century waned, many women and most men would still have endorsed Dickens's parodic view of the public woman, Mrs Jellyby in *Bleak House*: she is so focused on missionary work in Africa that she cannot see the lamentable state of her family in the very next room.

THE AGE OF EMPIRE

> I contend that we are the first race in the world, and the more of
> the world we inhabit, the better it is for the human race.
>
> —*Cecil Rhodes*

With the prime meridian conveniently located at Greenwich, just southeast of London, Victorians could measure all the world in relation to a British focal point, culturally as well as geographically. Abroad, as at home, it was an Englishman's duty to rule whatever childlike or womanly peoples he came across, for their own good. For Queen Victoria, the mission of empire was obvious: "to protect the poor natives and advance civilization." The conviction of innate superiority was reinforced by the implacable desire of British business to dominate world markets. The vast size of Britain's naval and commercial fleets and its head start in industrial production helped the cause, and Britain's military and commercial might was unsurpassed. Victorian advertising reveals the global realities and hopes of the emerging merchant empires. Tetley's tea ads depicted their plantations in Ceylon, as well as the ships, trains, and turbanned laborers that secured "the largest sale in the world." Pear's Soap advertising campaigns kept up with British expeditionary forces worldwide, finding potential customers in temporary adversaries such as the "Fuzzy-Wuzzies" of the Sudanese wars or the Boers of South Africa. One advertiser even challenged convention by speaking of "Brightest Africa"—because of the continent's vast market potential.

Yet the empire was hard to assemble and expensive—monetarily and morally—to maintain. Slavery was abolished in British dominions in 1833, but many fortunes still depended on the cheap production of sugar at West Indian plantations, as well as slave-produced cotton from the United States. Thus British implication in the slave trade remained a volatile issue. All Britain took sides in the Governor Eyre scandal of 1865, when the acting governor of Jamaica imposed severe martial law to put down a rebellion by plantation workers. Carlyle, Dickens, and Ruskin supported the executions and floggings, while John Stuart Mill sought to have Eyre tried for murder.

Closer to home, the perennial "Irish Question" resurfaced urgently during the potato famine of 1845–1847. Through the British government's callousness and ineptitude, a million and a half Irish died of starvation and disease and an equal number emigrated. In the wake of this disaster, the Irish engaged in rebellions, uprisings, and massive political efforts to gain parliamentary "Home Rule" for Ireland. But concern about the unity of the Empire, the safety of Protestants in the north of Ireland, and the supposed inability of the Irish to govern themselves led Parliament to defeat all efforts at Irish autonomy during Victoria's reign.

The Asian empire captured the popular imagination for the first time through the so-called "Indian Mutiny" of 1857–1859, a broad-based rebellion against the East India Company, the commercial entity that ruled most of India. The gory details of Indian atrocities, followed by equally bloody and more extensive British reprisals, filled the press and inflamed the public. The crown now took possession, and henceforth British policy was much more guarded, attempting to respect local institutions and practices. Later, as Rudyard Kipling recorded in his novel *Kim* (1901), India became an important setting for the "Great Game" of espionage to prevent foreign destabilization of British interests worldwide.

In the second half of the century, frequent and often bungled conflicts riveted public attention. The Crimean War of 1854–1856, in which Britain fought on the side of Turkey to prevent Russian expansion in the Middle East, cost 21,000 British lives but made little change in the European balance of power. "Some one had blunder'd," as Tennyson wrote in *The Charge of the Light Brigade*. The newspapers' exposure of the gross mismanagement of the war effort, however, led to improved supply systems, medical care, and weapons, and the rebuilding of the armed forces, all of which served Britain in ensuing colonial wars. A veteran of the Crimea, General George Gordon, rose to fame in 1860, capturing Peking and protecting far-flung Britons in the Second Opium War. But in 1884 he and several thousand others were massacred at Khartoum in the Sudan after a year's siege by religiously inspired rebels. Governmental dithering caused the British relief force to arrive two days too late. On another front, the Boer War of 1899–1902 stimulated war mania at home but tarnished Britain's image throughout the world. In pursuit of freer access to South African gold and diamond mines, the world's greatest military power bogged down in a guerilla war that ended only when British forces herded Afrikaner civilians into concentration camps, where 20,000 died.

Many viewed these conflicts as part of "the White Man's burden," as Kipling phrased it: the duty to spread British order and culture throughout the world. Yet imperialism had many opponents. In 1877 the Liberal leader William Gladstone argued that the Empire was a drain on the economy and population, serving only "to compromise British character in the judgment of the impartial world." Even Queen Victoria complained of the "overbearing and offensive behavior" of the Indian Civil Service for "trying to trample on the people and continually reminding them and making them feel that they are a conquered people." Like the growth of Victorian cities, the unplanned agglomeration of British colonies involved such a haphazard mixture of economic expansion, high-minded sentiment, crass exploitation, political

PEARS' SOAP IN THE SOUDAN.
"Even if our invasion of the Soudan has done nothing else it has at any rate left the Arab something to puzzle his fuzzy head over, for the legend
PEARS' SOAP IS THE BEST,
inscribed in huge white characters on the rock which marks the farthest point of our advance towards Berber, will tax all the wits of the Dervishes of the Desert to translate."—Phil Robinson, War Correspondent [in the Soudan] of the Daily Telegraph in London, 1884.

"The Formula of British Conquest," Pears' Soap advertisement from *Illustrated London News,* 27 August 1887.

expediency, and blatant racism that it apparently had no clear rationale. "We seem," said Cambridge historian J. R. Seeley in 1883, "to have conquered and peopled half the world in a fit of absence of mind."

Victorians did not only go to the ends of the earth; they saw the world's abundance come home to them. Britain and especially London became a magnet for all manner of people and things, a world within a world. There were many distinguished foreign sojourners at the center of empire. Among the artists, exiles, and expatriates who visited or stayed were the deposed French emperor Louis Napoleon, the painters Vincent Van Gogh and James McNeill Whistler, and the writers Arthur Rimbaud, Paul Verlaine, and Stephen Crane. Many of the era's great images and cultural moments came from outsiders: London was memorably painted by Claude Monet, anatomized by Henry James, serenaded by Frédéric Chopin and Franz Liszt, and entertained by Buffalo Bill. It received possibly its most searching critique from Karl Marx and Friedrich Engels, who drafted the *Communist Manifesto* there in 1847. Not only the country's prosperity and cultural prestige attracted people, but also its tolerance and democracy. Despite the wage slavery and imperialist ideology that he saw only too clearly, Engels was forced to admit: "England is unquestionably the freest—that is, the least unfree—country in the world, North America not excepted."

THE AGE OF READING

> Even idleness is eager now,—eager for amusement; prone to excursion-trains, art-museums, periodical literature, and exciting novels.
>
> *—George Eliot*

Publishing was a major industry in the Victorian period. Magazines, newspapers, novels, poetry, histories, travel narratives, sporting news, scandal sheets, and penny cyclopedias kept people entertained and informed as never before. A thriving commercial literary culture was built on rising literacy rates, with as many as 97 percent of both sexes able to read by 1900. The expansion of the reading public went hand-in-hand with new print technologies, including steam-powered presses, the introduction of cheaper wood-pulp (instead of rag-based) paper, and, eventually, mechanized typesetting. Illustrations were widely used, notably in serialized fiction, where they helped unpracticed readers to follow the story. After 1875 wood engravings gave way to photogravure, and in the 1880s halftone printing enabled photographs to replace hand-drawn works as the primary means of visual communication. Colored illustrations were handtinted at first, often by poor women and children working at home; later chromolithography made colored reproductions of artwork possible. British publishing gradually transformed itself into a modern industry with worldwide distribution and influence. Copies of *The Times* circulated in uncharted Africa; illustrations torn from magazines adorned bushmen's huts in the Great Karoo.

Readers' tastes varied according to class, income, and education. The well-educated but unintellectual upper class formed only a small portion of the Victorian reading public. As the historian Walter Bagehot noted at the time, "A great part of the 'best' English people keep their minds in a state of decorous dullness." At the other end of the social scale, working-class literacy rates were far below the general standard but increased as working hours diminished, housing improved, and public libraries spread. The appetite for cheap literature steadily grew, feeding on a diet of religious tracts, self-help manuals, reprints of classics, penny newspapers, and the expanding range of sensational entertainment: "penny dreadfuls and shilling shockers," serials, bawdy ballads, and police reports of lurid crimes.

It was the burgeoning middle class, however, that formed the largest audience for new prose and poetry and produced the authors to meet an increasing demand for books that would edify, instruct, and entertain. This was the golden age of the English novel, but poetry and serious nonfiction also did a brisk trade, as did "improving" works on religion, science, philosophy, and economics. But new books, especially fiction, were still a luxury in the earlier Victorian period. Publishers inflated prices so that readers would rent novels and narrative poems—just as people rent movies today—from commercial circulating libraries, which provided a larger and steadier income than individual sales. The collaboration between publishers and libraries required authors to produce "three deckers," long novels packaged in three separate volumes that thereby tripled rental fees and allowed three readers to peruse a single novel at one time. An economical alternative was to buy the successive "numbers" of a book as they appeared in individual, illustrated monthly installments. This form of publication became common with the tremendous success of Dickens's first novel, *Pickwick Papers*, which came out in parts in 1836 and 1837. By the 1860s most novels were serialized in weekly or monthly magazines, giving the reader a wealth of additional material for about the same price.

The serialization of novels had a significant impact on literary form. Most of the major novelists, including Dickens, Thackeray, Collins, Gaskell, Trollope, and Eliot, had to organize their work into enticing, coherent morsels that kept characters and story lines clear from month to month, and left readers eager to buy the next installment. Authors felt pressure to keep ahead of deadlines, often not knowing which turn a story might take. But they also enjoyed the opportunity to stay in the public eye, to weave in references to current events, or to make adjustments based on sales and reviews. For their part, readers experienced literature as an ongoing part of their lives. They had time to absorb and interpret their reading, and even to influence the outcome of literary events: throughout his career, Dickens was badgered by readers who wanted to see more of one character, less of another, or prevent the demise of a third.

The close relationship authors shared with their public had its drawbacks: writers had to censor their content to meet the prim standards of "circulating library morality." In keeping with the Evangelical temper of the times, middle-class Victorian recreation centered on the home, where one of the most sacred institutions was the family reading circle. Usually wives or daughters read aloud to the rest of the household. Any hint of impropriety, anything that might bring "a blush to the cheek of the Young Person"—as Dickens warily satirized the trend—was aggressively ferreted out by publishers and libraries. Even revered poets such as Tennyson and Barrett Browning found themselves edited by squeamish publishers.

A better testimony to the intelligence and perceptiveness of the Victorian reading public is the fact that so many of today's classics were best-sellers then, including the novels of the Brontës, Dickens, and George Eliot; the poetry of Tennyson, Elizabeth and Robert Browning, and Christina Rossetti; and the essays of Carlyle, Ruskin, and Arnold. These works were addressed to readers who had an impressive level of literary and general culture, kept up to snuff by the same magazines and reviews in which the best fiction, poetry, and prose appeared. Educated Victorians had an insatiable appetite for "serious" literature on religious issues, socioeconomic theory, scientific developments, and general information of all sorts. It was an era of outstanding, influential periodicals that combined entertaining writing with intellectual substance: politically oriented quarterlies such as the Whig *Edinburgh Review* and the Benthamite *Westminster Review;* more varied monthlies such as *Fraser's Magazine,* where Carlyle's *Sartor Resartus* first appeared, and *Cornhill,* which published works by Ruskin, Thackeray, Eliot, Trollope, and Hardy; the satirical weekly *Punch,* still published today; and Dickens's low-priced weeklies *Household Words* and *All the Year Round* for a more general readership. As a rule, the public had faith in the press, regarding it as a forum essential to the progress and management of democracy. At the same time, as political and cultural power broadened, the press took seriously its new role as creator, shaper, and transmitter of public opinion.

A NOVEL FACT.

Old-fashioned Party (with old-fashioned prejudices). "AH! VERY CLEVER, I DARE SAY. BUT I SEE IT'S WRITTEN BY A LADY, AND *I WANT A BOOK THAT MY DAUGHTERS MAY READ.* GIVE ME SOMETHING ELSE!"

Cartoon from *Punch* magazine, 1867.

Celebrated authors were hailed as heroes, regarded as public property, and respected as sages; they inspired a passionate adulation. Robert Browning first approached Elizabeth Barrett by writing her a fan letter. The public sought instruction and guidance from authors, who were alternately flattered and dismayed by the responsibilities thrust upon them. The critic Walter Houghton points out that "every writer had his congregation of devoted or would-be devoted disciples who read his work in much the spirit they had once read the Bible." Robert Browning lived to see an international proliferation of Browning Societies, dedicated to expounding his supposed moral teachings. Hero worship was yet another Victorian invention.

THE AGE OF SELF-SCRUTINY

The energy of Victorian literature is its most striking trait, and self-exploration is its favorite theme. Victorians produced a staggeringly large body of literature, renowned for its variety and plenitude. Their writing is distinguished by its particularity, eccentricity, long-windedness, earnestness, ornateness, fantasy, humor, experimentation, and self-consciousness. As befits a scientific age, most authors exhibited a willingness to experiment with new forms of representation, coupled with a penchant for realism, a love of closely observed detail: Tennyson was famous for his myopic descriptions of flowers; Browning transcribed tics of speech like a clinical psychologist; Eliot compared her scenes to Dutch genre paintings; and Dickens indignantly defended the accuracy of his characterization and the plausibility of his plots. Sustained labor was as important as keen observation: "lyric" poems ran to hundreds of lines, novels spanned a thousand pages, essayists constructed lengthy paragraphs with three or four generous sentences. One single book, alternately discredited and revered, underpinned the whole literary enterprise. The King James Version of the Bible shaped the cadences, supplied the imagery, and proposed the structures through which Victorians apprehended the universe; knowledge of it immensely deepens one's appreciation of the time.

Like the photographic close-ups invented by Julia Margaret Cameron, much Victorian literature tries to get at what Matthew Arnold called "the buried life" of individuals struggling for identity in a commercial, technocratic society. In the 1830s Carlyle was already alluding to "these autobiographical times of ours." Autobiography rapidly assumed new importance as a literary form, driven by the apparent necessity of each person working out a personal approach to the universe and a position within the culture. As Matthew Arnold announced in 1853, "the dialogue of the mind with itself has commenced."

Often written under intense emotional pressure, nonfiction prose on social or aesthetic issues turned into an art form as personal as lyric poetry, expressing the writers' interior lives as well as their ideas. Yet the very variety of disguised or semiautobiographical forms (such as the dramatic monologue) suggests that introspection produced its own moral perplexities. In a culture that stressed action, production, civic duty, and family responsibility, such apparently self-indulgent self-scrutiny might well seem unworthy: "I sometimes hold it half a sin / To put in words the grief I feel," said Tennyson about the loss of his best friend. Thus the guilty confessional impulse was forced underground to reemerge almost everywhere: in first-person narratives, devotional poems, travelogues, novels of religious or emotional crisis, intimate essays, dramatic lyrics, fictionalized memoirs, and recollections of famous people and places.

The Major Genres

Victorian literature is remarkable in that there were three great literary genres: nonfiction prose emerged as the artistic equal of poetry and fiction. Topical and influential in their day, the criticism and essays of such writers as Carlyle, Mill, Newman, Ruskin, Darwin, Arnold, Nightingale, Pater, and Wilde achieved classic status by virtue of their distinctive styles and force of intellect. In richly varied rhythms they record the process of original minds seeking to understand the relation of individuals to nature and culture in the new industrial world. Though their works might be categorized as religion, politics, aesthetics, or science, all these authors wrote revealingly of their intellectual development, and all explored the literary resources of the language, from simile and metaphor to fable and fantasy. Oscar Wilde argued for the supreme creativity of the autobiographical critic-as-artist: "That is what the highest criticism really is, the record of one's own soul." His teacher Walter Pater remarked simply that prose is "the special and opportune art of the modern world."

Poets struggled to refute this sentiment. Poetry commanded more respect than prose as a literary genre, but despite the immense success of Tennyson, it gradually lost ground in popularity. Whether this occurred because of, or in spite of, poetry's deliberate cultivation of a mass audience is difficult to say. But whereas Victorians regarded the Romantic poets as visionaries who opened dazzling new vistas onto the self and nature, they encouraged contemporary poets to keep their ideas down to earth, to offer practical advice about managing the vicissitudes of heart and soul in a workaday world. What was viewed, with some suspicion, as the Romantic emphasis on self-expression gave way to more qualified soul-searching with an eye toward moral content that the public could grasp and apply. Carlyle's famous admonition in *Sartor Resartus* set the tone for the period: "Close thy *Byron*; open thy *Goethe*." In other words, forget the tormented introspection and alienation associated with Byronic heroes; strive instead to improve society and practice greater artistic control; know your work and do it.

Whether they felt guilty, inspired, infuriated, or amused over their audience's thirst for instruction, Victorian poets took advantage of it to expand the resources of poetry in English. Though there are obvious lines of influence from the Romantics—Tennyson acknowledged Keats, Shelley was an early influence on Browning, and Arnold steeped himself in Wordsworth—the innovations are perhaps even more striking. Eclectic poets introduced their readers to a bewildering variety of rhythms, stanzas, topics, words, and ideas. Contemporary social concerns vied with—and sometimes merged into—Greek mythology and Arthurian legend as subject matter. Swinburne and Hopkins engaged in verbal pyrotechnics that produced new meters amid an ecstasy of sound; Elizabeth Barrett Browning unleashed stormy feminist lyrics marked by a dazzling intellect; Arnold captured readers with his startling emotional honesty; Christina Rossetti whittled her lines down to a thought-teasing purity; Arthur Symons and William Ernest Henley adapted French *vers libre* to create modern "free verse."

Perhaps the most important development was the rise of the dramatic monologue. Almost every poet found occasion to speak through characters apparently quite foreign in time, place, or social situation. Tennyson's liquid vowel sounds and Browning's clotted consonant clusters are trademarks of very different styles, but both poets use their distinctive music to probe the psychology of the speakers in their dramatic poems. Adapting the sound of their lines to fit the rhythms of their speakers' thoughts, poets acquired a more conversational tone and expanded the psychological range of their craft. While Browning was preoccupied with extreme psychological states, many poets shared his desire to represent a person or event from multiple perspectives, through shifting voices and unreliable narrators. These relativistic approaches also encouraged poets to experiment with new angles of vision suggested by the initially disorienting array of developments in visual culture. Photography, panoramas, stereopticons, impressionist painting, illustrated newspapers, and the mass reproduction of art images all left their mark on poetic practice. The ultimate effect was to engender poems whose ability to please or even communicate depended on the active participation of the reader.

Though nonfiction prose and poetry flourished, the Victorian era is still considered the great age of British fiction. Novelists strove to embody the character and genius of the time. The novel's triumphant adaptation of practically any material into "realistic" narrative and detail fueled an obsession with storytelling that spilled over into anecdotal painting, program music, and fictive or autobiographical frames for essays and histories. The novels themselves generally explored the relation between individuals and their society through the mechanism of a central love plot, around which almost any subject could be investigated, including the quest for self-knowledge, religious crises, industrialism, education, women's roles, crime and punishment, or the definition of gentlemanliness.

Convoluted by later standards, Victorian novels received their most famous assessment from Henry James, who regarded them as "loose baggy monsters." The English novel, he said, is "a treasure house of detail, but an indifferent whole." Shrewd as the observation was, it overlooks the thematic density that unifies Dickens's sprawling three-deckers; the moral consciousness that registers every nuance of thought in George Eliot's rural panoramas; the intricate narrative structures and ardent self-questioning that propel the tormented romances of the Brontës. Their novels work within an established social frame, focusing on the characters' freedom to act within fairly narrow moral codes in an unpredictable universe; they deal with questions of social responsibility and personal choice, the impulses of passion and the dictates of conscience. Yet even as they portrayed familiar details of contemporary social life, novelists challenged the confines of "realist" fiction, experimenting with multiple perspectives, unreliable narrators, stories within stories, direct appeals to the reader, and strange extremes of behavior.

The Role of Art in Society

"The past for poets, the present for pigs." This polemical statement by the painter Samuel Palmer sums up much of the period's literary debate. Because Victorian times seemed so thoroughly to break from the past, "modern" became a common but often prejudicial word. Was there anything of lasting artistic value to be found in ordinary everyday life? Many writers felt there was not; they preferred to indulge instead in what Tennyson called the "passion of the past." Most poetry shunned the details of contemporary urban existence, and even the great novelists like Dickens, Eliot, and Thackeray situated much of their work in the pre-Victorian world of their parents. Some of this writing was escapist, but many authors saw in earlier times a more ethically and aesthetically coherent world that could serve as a model for Victorian social reform. The Pre-Raphaelite painters and their literary allies sought out medieval models, while Matthew Arnold returned to the Greco-Roman classics: "They, at any rate, knew what they wanted in art, and we do not."

But another group vigorously disagreed; they stressed the importance of creating an up-to-date art that would validate or at least grapple with the uniqueness of Victorian life. In *Aurora Leigh* Elizabeth Barrett Browning contended that "this live throbbing age" should take precedence over all other topics: "if there's room for poets in this world," she said, "Their sole work is to represent the age / Their age, not Charlemagne's." In 1850 the critic F. G. Stephens argued that poets should emphasize "the poetry of the things about us; our railways, factories, mines, roaring cities, steam vessels, and the endless novelties and wonders produced every day." As the century wore on, there was a broadening in social scope: the life of the working classes became a serious literary topic, and in the 1870s and 1880s "naturalist" writers probed the structures of everyday life at near-subsistence level. Thomas Hardy wrote searching studies of rural life; George Gissing, whose first wife was a prostitute, documented in harsh detail "the nether world" of backstreet London.

Whether they favored the past or present as a literary landscape, whether they criticized or lauded the times they lived in, most Victorian writers felt at home in their era. Though they had their own interests, they did not act as alienated outcasts but addressed social needs and responded to the public desire for instruction and reassurance. They recognized the force of John Stuart Mill's remark: "Whatever we may think or affect to think of the present age, we cannot get out of it; we must suffer with its sufferings, and enjoy with its enjoyments; we must share in its lot."

Amid all this energetic literary production, a substantial portion of readers demanded to know if literature had any value at all. Utilitarians regarded art as a waste of time and energy, while Evangelicals were suspicious of art's appeal to the senses and emotions rather than the soul and the conscience. "All poetry is misrepresentation," said the founder of Utilitarianism, Jeremy Bentham, who could not see how fanciful words might be of service to humanity. Such was the temper of the time that writers strove mightily to prove that audiences could derive moral and religious benefit from impractical things like circuses or watercolors. Even secular critics sought to legitimize art's role in society by contending that if religion failed, literature would take its place as a guiding light. "Literature is but a branch of Religion," said Carlyle; "in our time, it is the only branch that still shows any greenness." "More and more," said Arnold, "mankind will discover that we have to turn to poetry to interpret life for us, to console us, to sustain us."

The great expectations most Victorians had for their literature inevitably produced reactions against such moral earnestness. In the theater, a huge variety of comedies, melodramas, pantomimes, and music-hall skits amused all classes; 150,000 people a day went to theaters in London during the 1860s. Yet in comparison to other literary forms, little of lasting value remains. Though leading authors such as Browning, Tennyson, and Henry James tried their hand at writing for the stage, it was not until the 1890s, with the sophisticated wit of Oscar Wilde, the subtle social inquiry of Arthur Wing Pinero, and the provocative "problem plays" of Bernard Shaw, that British theater offered more than light entertainment for the masses. The way for serious drama had been prepared by the wonderfully clever musicals of W. S. Gilbert and Arthur Sullivan, which satirized such topics as Aestheticism (*Patience*, 1881), the House of Lords (*Iolanthe*, 1882), and the struggle for sexual equality (*Princess Ida*, 1884). Victorian social drama came into its own late in the era, when it began directly to explore its own relevance, dissecting social and theatrical conventions even as it questioned whether art could—or should—teach anything at all.

Doubts about the mission of art to improve society culminated in the Aesthetic movement of the 1880s and 1890s, whose writers sought to show, in Oscar Wilde's words, that "there is no such thing as a moral or an immoral book. Books are well written or badly written. That is all." In an era of practicality, art declared its freedom by positing its sheer uselessness. Wilde argued that it is "through Art, and through Art only, that we can shield ourselves from the sordid perils of actual existence." Thus many authors at the end of the Victorian period renounced the values that characterize the age as a whole.

And yet the Aesthetes were still quintessentially Victorian in feeling that, as writers, they had to expose their inner being, whether uplifting or shocking, to the public gaze. In their thoughts and deeds, but especially in their words, writers were expected to harness their autobiographical impulses to society's need for guidance and amusement—or even outrage. "I never travel without my diary," one of Wilde's characters remarks: "One should always have something sensational to read in the train."

Every generalization about the Victorians comes with a ready-made contradiction: they were materialist but religious, self-confident but insecure, monstrous exploiters who devoted themselves to humane reforms; they were given to blanket pronouncements about the essential nature of sexes and races, the social order, and the Christian universe, but they relentlessly probed the foundations of their thought; they demanded a moral literature and thrilled to mindless page-turners. Yet in all these matters they were constantly concerned with rules, codes of duty and behavior, their places in a complex and often frustrating social order. Even the alienated rebels of the 1890s cared intensely (a favorite word) what people thought and how shocking their calculated transgressions might make them.

For a few decades after World War I, the Victorians' obsession with the tightly buttoned structures of everyday life seemed their only legacy, offering an easy target for Modernists who sought to declare their own free-thinking independence. "Queen Victoria was like a great paper-weight," wrote H. G. Wells, "that for half a century sat upon men's minds, and when she was removed their ideas began to blow about all over the place haphazardly." But the end of the Victorian period is now more than a century past, and the winds of change have blown many Victorian ideas back into favor. More and more readers delight to discover beneath the stiff manners and elaborate conventions of a bygone era an anxious, humorous, dynamic people very much like ourselves.

Thomas Carlyle
1795–1881

Thomas Carlyle was a difficult and cranky character whose imaginative, eccentric works of history and social criticism had an immense influence on his fellow Victorians. Mill, Tennyson, Browning, Dickens, Ruskin, and many others idolized him. George Eliot believed that even if all Carlyle's books were burnt, "it would be only like cutting down an oak after its acorns have sown a forest. For there is hardly a superior or active mind of this generation that has not been modified by Carlyle's writings; there has hardly been an English book written for the last ten or twelve years that would not have been different if Carlyle had not lived."

Carlyle was born in the small village of Ecclefechan in Scotland, the eldest son of a stonemason and his wife who gave their numerous children a strict Calvinist upbringing. From his devout and self-disciplined parents, Carlyle learned early the value of hard work, and he later preached the Gospel of Work to his generation. His parents recognized his exceptional abilities and sent him to the University of Edinburgh to study for the ministry.

Religious doubts, however, prevented him from seeking ordination; at nineteen he wrote, "I am growing daily and hourly more lukewarm about this preaching business." He tried schoolteaching instead, but hated it, and feared that his youth was "hurrying darkly and uselessly away." Tormented by ill health and his lack of a vocation, Carlyle gradually turned to a literary career. Inspired by German literature and philosophy, he began reviewing and translating.

In 1821 Carlyle met Jane Welsh. Middle-class, well-educated, and with literary aspirations of her own, Jane did not at first take Carlyle seriously as a suitor, but he was determined to marry her. Prophetically, he wrote to a friend that he expected their marriage to be "the most turbulent, incongruous thing on earth—a mixture of honey and wormwood" with "thunder and lightning and furious storms—all mingled together into the same season—and the sunshine always in the *smallest* quantity!" Despite this gloomy forecast, they married in 1826, embarking on one of the century's most famous, and most speculated about, marriages. Jane was sharp-tongued and high-strung, Thomas was perpetually irritable, depressed, and complaining, yet they stayed together for nearly forty years. Samuel Butler rather nastily remarked that "it was very good of God to let Carlyle and Mrs. Carlyle marry one another and so make only two people miserable instead of four, besides being very amusing."

In 1828 they left the social and intellectual pleasures of Edinburgh for six years of self-imposed exile in Craigenputtoch, a bleak, remote sheep farm. Here Carlyle wrote the essays that would begin to make his name, *Signs of the Times, On History*, and *Characteristics*, as well as his first book, *Sartor Resartus* (1833–1834). A symbolic autobiography, *Sartor* records Carlyle's struggle to find meaning in life after his loss of faith. A decade earlier, during a period of despair and spiritual crisis which he terms "The Everlasting No," Carlyle had experienced a kind of epiphany, a profound and lifelong conviction of the existence of a transcendent reality. *Sartor*, however, is a strange book, mixing metaphorical philosophy and narrative hijinks in the reconstruction of the odd life of its comic hero, Diogenes Teufelsdröckh. Carlyle had a long and discouraging struggle to find a publisher for it.

In 1834 the Carlyles moved to London, to a house in Chelsea where they spent the rest of their lives. The bustling city was a great contrast to the lonely farm, providing more access to stimulating books and friendships, but Carlyle continued to struggle with poverty, poor health, and insomnia. He set to work on his chronicle of *The French Revolution* (1837), the most dramatic and apocalyptic event in recent European history. In impassioned and impressionistic prose, he traced the downfall of an aristocracy of corrupt impostors, who had to be swept away to allow for the rebirth of a healthy society. In their destruction he read a warning

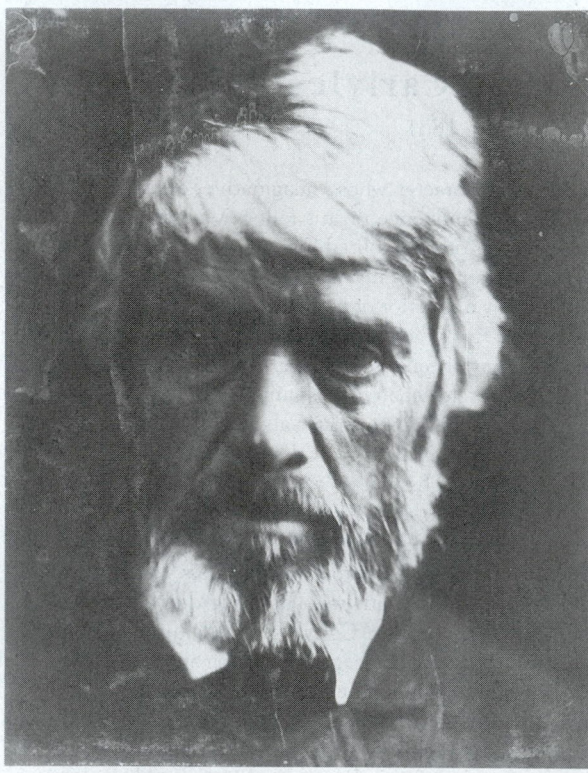

Julia Margaret Cameron, *Thomas Carlyle*, 1867. The greatest of Victorian portrait photographers, Cameron lived near Tennyson on the Isle of Wight, and by virtue of her irrepressible personality managed to get his many distinguished visitors to sit through grueling photo sessions in her drafty greenhouse. Tennyson once brought the American poet Longfellow to her, saying "You will have to do whatever she tells you. I will come back soon and see what is left of you." Cameron's portrait of Carlyle conveys not only his stern prophetic power but also her own sense of photography's ability to discover a transcendent energy in simple human features: "My mortal but yet divine! Art of photography."

for England, whose leaders seemed to be abandoning the country to democracy and laissez-faire capitalism.

After completing the first of three volumes, Carlyle suffered a catastrophic setback: he lent the manuscript to his friend John Stuart Mill, whose housemaid accidentally burned it in the fireplace. Carlyle was devastated, but he forced himself to begin again. Rewriting was torture: Carlyle called *The French Revolution* "a wild savage Book" that "has come out of my own soul; born in blackness, whirl-wind and sorrow."

Yet, to his own surprise, this was the book that finally brought him widespread public recognition and some relief from financial strain. He enjoyed the admiration, and savored his new role as Sage and Prophet—though he complained that nobody listened when he addressed his contemporaries on a variety of social issues. Invited to give a series of lectures, later published as *On Heroes and Hero-Worship* (1841), Carlyle offered historical examples of what he considered true leadership. Then, in *Past and Present* (1843), he contrasted the coherent social and religious fabric of life in the Middle Ages with the chaos of the modern world. Democracy, to Carlyle, meant the breakdown of political order, the "despair of finding any heroes to govern you." He urged the "Captains of Industry" to become modern heroes, as feudal lords had been in an idealized medieval past, and to reestablish a sense of human community in mechanized England.

Carlyle believed that strong leaders were the only hope for social reform. Turning to history once again for examples, he wrote about *Oliver Cromwell* (1845) and *Frederick the Great* (1858–1865). Six volumes long, *Frederick* was hailed as Carlyle's masterpiece, and Carlyle was elected Rector of Edinburgh University. While he was in Scotland delivering his inaugural speech in 1866, Jane Welsh Carlyle died. In his grief, Carlyle wrote a moving memoir of his wife, to which he added others, including portraits of his friend Edward Irving, and Wordsworth; these were published after his death as *Reminiscences* (1881).

Although Carlyle continued to have public honors heaped upon him in old age, a reaction against his authoritarianism had begun as early as 1850, when he published the *Latter-Day Pamphlets*, a jeremiad against democracy, and *Shooting Niagara, and After?* (1867), an attack on the Second Reform Bill. While he remained an important figure, admired and respected, he was frustrated at feeling, as the critic G. B. Tennyson has put it, "everywhere honored and nowhere heeded." Carlyle's lifelong insistence on divine purpose at work in the universe was deeply attractive to a society in the grip of social unrest and religious malaise—but few were willing to accept the tasks that Carlyle claimed God had set for them. Carlyle's reputation rests on his vigorous denunciation of a materialist society and his rousing calls for social reform. Like a biblical prophet, Carlyle exhorts his followers to mend their ways. In powerfully idiosyncratic language, he condemns laziness and greed, alienation and mechanization, and urges the necessity for spiritual rebirth.

from *Gospel of Mammonism*[1]
[THE IRISH WIDOW]

One of Dr. Alison's Scotch facts struck us much. A poor Irish Widow, her husband having died in one of the Lanes of Edinburgh, went forth with her three children, bare of all resource, to solicit help from the Charitable Establishments of that City. At this Charitable Establishment and then at that she was refused; referred from one to the other, helped by none;—till she had exhausted them all; till her strength and heart failed her: she sank down in typhus-fever; died, and infected her Lane with fever, so that "seventeen other persons" died of fever there in consequence. The humane Physician asks thereupon, as with a heart too full for speaking, Would it not have been *economy* to help this poor Widow? She took typhus-fever, and killed seventeen of you!—Very curious. The forlorn Irish Widow applies to her fellow-creatures, as if saying, "Behold I am sinking, bare of help: ye must help me! I am your sister, bone of your bone; one God made us: ye must help me!" They answer, "No, impossible; thou art no sister of ours." But she proves her sisterhood; her typhus-fever kills *them:* they actually were her brothers, though denying it! Had human creature ever to go lower for a proof?

For, as indeed was very natural in such case, all government of the Poor by the Rich has long ago been given over to Supply-and-demand, Laissez-faire and such-like,[2] and universally declared to be "impossible." "You are no sister of ours; what shadow of proof is there? Here are our parchments, our padlocks, proving indisputably our money-safes to be *ours*, and you to have no business with them. Depart! It is impossible!"—Nay, what wouldst thou thyself have us do? cry indignant readers. Nothing, my friends,—till you have got a soul for yourselves again. Till then all things are "impossible." Till then I cannot even bid you buy, as the old Spartans would have done, two-pence worth of powder and lead, and compendiously shoot to death this poor Irish Widow: even that is "impossible" for you. Nothing is left but that she prove her sisterhood by dying, and infecting you with typhus. Seventeen of you lying dead will not deny such proof that she *was* flesh of your flesh; and perhaps some of the living may lay it to heart.

---

1. From Book 3, ch. 2.
2. The free trade philosophy of British industrialists who believed in the market's ability to regulate itself and in the right to do business unhampered by government regulation.

from *Labour*[3]
[KNOW THY WORK]

For there is a perennial nobleness, and even sacredness, in Work. Were he never so benighted, forgetful of his high calling, there is always hope in a man that actually and earnestly works: in Idleness alone is there perpetual despair. Work, never so Mammonish,[4] mean, *is* in communication with Nature; the real desire to get Work done will itself lead one more and more to truth, to Nature's appointments and regulations, which are truth.

The latest Gospel in this world is, Know thy work and do it. "Know thyself": long enough has that poor "self" of thine tormented thee; thou wilt never get to "know" it, I believe! Think it not thy business, this of knowing thyself; thou art an unknowable individual: know what thou canst work at; and work at it, like a Hercules![5] That will be thy better plan.

It has been written, "an endless significance lies in Work"; a man perfects himself by working. Foul jungles are cleared away, fair seedfields rise instead, and stately cities; and withal the man himself first ceases to be a jungle and foul unwholesome desert thereby. Consider how, even in the meanest sorts of Labour, the whole soul of a man is composed into a kind of real harmony, the instant he sets himself to work! Doubt, Desire, Sorrow, Remorse, Indignation, Despair itself, all these like helldogs lie beleaguering the soul of the poor dayworker, as of every man: but he bends himself with free valour against his task, and all these are stilled, all these shrink murmuring far off into their caves. The man is now a man. The blessed glow of Labour in him, is it not as purifying fire, wherein all poison is burnt up, and of sour smoke itself there is made bright blessed flame!

Destiny, on the whole, has no other way of cultivating us. A formless Chaos, once set it *revolving,* grows round and ever rounder; ranges itself, by mere force of gravity, into strata, spherical courses; is no longer a Chaos, but a round compacted World. What would become of the Earth, did she cease to revolve? In the poor old Earth, so long as she revolves, all inequalities, irregularities disperse themselves; all irregularities are incessantly becoming regular. Hast thou looked on the Potter's wheel,—one of the venerablest objects; old as the Prophet Ezechiel and far older? Rude lumps of clay, how they spin themselves up, by mere quick whirling, into beautiful circular dishes. And fancy the most assiduous Potter, but without his wheel; reduced to make dishes, or rather amorphous botches, by mere kneading and baking! Even such a Potter were Destiny, with a human soul that would rest and lie at ease, that would not work and spin! Of an idle unrevolving man the kindest Destiny, like the most assiduous Potter without wheel, can bake and knead nothing other than a botch; let her spend on him what expensive colouring, what gilding and enamelling she will, he is but a botch. Not a dish; no, a bulging, kneaded, crooked, shambling, squint-cornered, amorphous botch,—a mere enamelled vessel of dishonour! Let the idle think of this.

Blessed is he who has found his work; let him ask no other blessedness. He has a work, a life-purpose; he has found it, and will follow it! How, as a free-flowing channel, dug and torn by noble force through the sour mud-swamp of one's existence, like

3. From Book 3, ch. 9.
4. Mammon is the personification of material wealth. "Ye cannot serve God and mammon" (Matthew 7.24).

5. Hercules had to perform twelve labors.

an ever-deepening river there, it runs and flows;—draining-off the sour festering water, gradually from the root of the remotest grass-blade; making, instead of pestilential swamp, a green fruitful meadow with its clear-flowing stream. How blessed for the
meadow itself, let the stream and *its* value be great or small! Labour is Life: from the
inmost heart of the Worker rises his god-given Force, the sacred celestial Life-essence
breathed into him by Almighty God; from his inmost heart awakens him to all
nobleness,—to all knowledge, "self-knowledge" and much else, so soon as Work fitly
begins. Knowledge? The knowledge that will hold good in working, cleave thou to
that; for Nature herself accredits that, says Yea to that. Properly thou hast no other
knowledge but what thou hast got by working: the rest is yet all a hypothesis of
knowledge; a thing to be argued of in schools, a thing floating in the clouds, in endless logic-vortices, till we try it and fix it. "Doubt, of whatever kind, can be ended by
Action alone."

from *Democracy*[6]
[Liberty to Die by Starvation]

Life was never a May-game for men: in all times the lot of the dumb millions born to
toil was defaced with manifold sufferings, injustices, heavy burdens, avoidable and
unavoidable; not play at all, but hard work that made the sinews sore and the heart
sore. As bond-slaves, *villani, bordarii, sochemanni,* nay indeed as dukes, earls and kings,
men were oftentimes made weary of their life; and had to say, in the sweat of their
brow and of their soul, Behold, it is not sport, it is grim earnest, and our back can bear
no more! Who knows not what massacrings and harryings there have been; grinding,
long-continuing, unbearable injustices,—till the heart had to rise in madness, and
some "*Eu Sachsen, nimith euer sachses,* You Saxons, out with your gully-knives, then!"
You Saxons, some "arrestment," partial "arrestment of the Knaves and Dastards" has
become indispensable!—The page of Dryasdust[7] is heavy with such details.

And yet I will venture to believe that in no time, since the beginnings of Society, was the lot of those same dumb millions of toilers so entirely unbearable as it is
even in the days now passing over us. It is not to die, or even to die of hunger, that
makes a man wretched; many men have died; all men must die,—the last exit of us
all is in a Fire-Chariot of Pain.[8] But it is to live miserable we know not why; to work
sore and yet gain nothing; to be heart-worn, weary, yet isolated, unrelated, girt-in
with a cold universal Laissez-faire: it is to die slowly all our life long, imprisoned in a
deaf, dead, Infinite Injustice, as in the accursed iron belly of a Phalaris' Bull![9] This is
and remains forever intolerable to all men whom God has made. Do we wonder at
French Revolutions, Chartisms, Revolts of Three Days? The times, if we will consider them, are really unexampled.

Never before did I hear of an Irish Widow reduced to "prove her sisterhood by
dying of typhus-fever and infecting seventeen persons,"—saying in such undeniable
way, "You *see* I was your sister!" Sisterhood, brotherhood, was often forgotten; but
not till the rise of these ultimate Mammon and Shotbelt Gospels[1] did I ever see it so
expressly denied. If no pious Lord or *Law-ward* would remember it, always some pious
Lady ("*Hlaf-dig,*" Benefactress, "*Loaf-giveress,*" they say she is,—blessings on her

---

6. From Book 3, ch. 13.
7. Sir Walter Scott's name for an imaginary historian
who is a pedantic and dull scholar.
8. 2 Kings 2.11–12.

9. Phalaris was a Sicilian tyrant who killed his enemies by
roasting them in the belly of a brass bull.
1. Carlyle is referring to the landed aristocracy's concern
with maintaining their exclusive rights to shoot game.

beautiful heart!) was there, with mild mother-voice and hand, to remember it; some pious thoughtful *Elder*, what we now call "Prester," *Presbyter* or "Priest," was there to put all men in mind of it, in the name of the God who had made all.

Not even in Black Dahomey[2] was it ever, I think, forgotten to the typhus-fever length. Mungo Park,[3] resourceless, had sunk down to die under the Negro Village-Tree, a horrible White object in the eyes of all. But in the poor Black Woman, and her daughter who stood aghast at him, whose earthly wealth and funded capital consisted of one small calabash of rice, there lived a heart richer than *Laissez-faire*: they, with a royal munificence, boiled their rice for him; they sang all night to him, spinning assiduous on their cotton distaffs, as he lay to sleep: "Let us pity the poor white man; no mother has he to fetch him milk, no sister to grind him corn!" Thou poor black Noble One,—thou *Lady* too: did not a God make thee too; was there not in thee too something of a God!—

Gurth, born thrall of Cedric the Saxon,[4] has been greatly pitied by Dryasdust and others. Gurth, with the brass collar round his neck, tending Cedric's pigs in the glades of the wood, is not what I call an exemplar of human felicity: but Gurth, with the sky above him, with the free air and tinted boscage and umbrage[5] round him, and in him at least the certainty of supper and social lodging when he came home; Gurth to me seems happy, in comparison with many a Lancashire and Buckinghamshire man of these days, not born thrall of anybody! Gurth's brass collar did not gall him: Cedric *deserved* to be his master. The pigs were Cedric's, but Gurth too would get his parings of them. Gurth had the inexpressible satisfaction of feeling himself related indissolubly, though in a rude brass-collar way, to his fellow-mortals in this Earth. He had superiors, inferiors, equals.—Gurth is now "emancipated" long since; has what we call "Liberty." Liberty, I am told, is a divine thing. Liberty when it becomes the "Liberty to die by starvation" is not so divine!

Liberty? The true liberty of a man, you would say, consisted in his finding out, or being forced to find out the right path, and to walk thereon. To learn, or to be taught, what work he actually was able for; and then by permission, persuasion, and even compulsion, to set about doing of the same! That is his true blessedness, honour, "liberty" and maximum of wellbeing: if liberty be not that, I for one have small care about liberty. You do not allow a palpable madman to leap over precipices; you violate his liberty, you that are wise; and keep him, were it in strait-waistcoats, away from the precipices! Every stupid, every cowardly and foolish man is but a less palpable madman: his true liberty were that a wiser man, that any and every wiser man, could, by brass collars, or in whatever milder or sharper way, lay hold of him when he was going wrong, and order and compel him to go a little righter. O, if thou really art my *Senior*, Seigneur, my *Elder*, Presbyter or Priest,—if thou art in very deed my *Wiser*, may a beneficent instinct lead and impel thee to "conquer" me, to command me! If thou do know better than I what is good and right, I conjure thee in the name of God, force me to do it; were it by never such brass collars, whips and handcuffs, leave me not to walk over precipices! That I have been called, by all the Newspapers, a "free man" will avail me little, if my pilgrimage have ended in death and wreck. O that the Newspapers had called me slave, coward, fool, or what it pleased

2. A former French territory in West Africa where cannibalism was rumored to persist.
3. Scottish explorer of Africa, and author of *Travels in the Interior of Africa* (1799), Park was killed by Africans in 1806.

4. In Sir Walter Scott's novel *Ivanhoe* (1819), the swineherd Gurth is a serf belonging to the well-to-do farmer, Cedric.
5. Thickets and shade.

their sweet voices to name me, and I had attained not death, but life!—Liberty requires new definitions.

Captains of Industry[6]

If I believed that Mammonism with its adjuncts was to continue henceforth the one serious principle of our existence, I should reckon it idle to solicit remedial measures from any Government, the disease being insusceptible of remedy. Government can do much, but it can in nowise do all. Government, as the most conspicuous object in Society, is called upon to give signal of what shall be done; and, in many ways, to preside over, further, and command the doing of it. But the Government cannot do, by all its signaling and commanding, what the Society is radically indisposed to do. In the long-run every Government is the exact symbol of its People, with their wisdom and unwisdom; we have to say, Like People like Government.—The main substance of this immense Problem of Organising Labour, and first of all of Managing the Working Classes, will, it is very clear, have to be solved by those who stand practically in the middle of it; by those who themselves work and preside over work. Of all that can be enacted by any Parliament in regard to it, the germs must already lie potentially extant in those two Classes, who are to obey such enactment. A Human Chaos *in* which there is no light, you vainly attempt to irradiate by light shed *on* it: order never can arise there.

But it is my firm conviction that the "Hell of England" will *cease* to be that of "not making money"; that we shall get a nobler Hell and a nobler Heaven! I anticipate light *in* the Human Chaos, glimmering, shining more and more; under manifold true signals from without That light shall shine. Our deity no longer being Mammon,—O Heavens, each man will then say to himself: "Why such deadly haste to make money? I shall not go to Hell, even if I do not make money! There is another Hell, I am told!" Competition, at railway-speed, in all branches of commerce and work will then abate:—good felt-hats for the head, in every sense, instead of seven-feet lath-and-plaster hats on wheels, will then be discoverable! Bubble-periods,[7] with their panics and commercial crises, will again become infrequent; steady modest industry will take the place of gambling speculation. To be a noble Master, among noble Workers, will again be the first ambition with some few; to be a rich Master only the second. How the Inventive Genius of England, with the whirr of its bobbins and billy-rollers[8] shoved somewhat into the backgrounds of the brain, will contrive and devise, not cheaper produce exclusively, but fairer distribution of the produce at its present cheapness! By degrees, we shall again have a Society with something of Heroism in it, something of Heaven's Blessing on it; we shall again have, as my German friend[9] asserts, "instead of Mammon-Feudalism with unsold cotton-shirts and Preservation of the Game, noble just Industrialism and Government by the Wisest!"

It is with the hope of awakening here and there a British man to know himself for a man and divine soul, that a few words of parting admonition, to all persons to whom the Heavenly Powers have lent power of any kind in this land, may now be addressed. And first to those same Master-Workers, Leaders of Industry; who stand nearest and in fact powerfulest, though not most prominent, being as yet in too many senses a Virtuality rather than an Actuality.

---

6. From Book 4, ch. 4.
7. Ups and downs in the stock market.

8. Machines that prepare cotton or wool for spinning.
9. Teufelsdröckh, the central character in *Sartor Resartus*.

The Leaders of Industry, if Industry is ever to be led, are virtually the Captains of the World! if there be no nobleness in them, there will never be an Aristocracy more. But let the Captains of Industry consider: once again, are they born of other clay than the old Captains of Slaughter; doomed forever to be no Chivalry, but a mere gold-plated *Doggery*,—what the French well name *Canaille*, "Doggery" with more or less gold carrion at its disposal? Captains of Industry are the true Fighters, henceforth recognisable as the only true ones: Fighters against Chaos, Necessity and the Devils and Jötuns;[1] and lead on Mankind in that great, and alone true, and universal warfare; the stars in their courses fighting for them, and all Heaven and all Earth saying audibly, Well done! Let the Captains of Industry retire into their own hearts, and ask solemnly, If there is nothing but vulturous hunger, for fine wines, valet reputation and gilt carriages, discoverable there? Of hearts made by the Almighty God I will not believe such a thing. Deep-hidden under wretchedest god-forgetting Cants, Epicurisms, Dead-Sea Apisms;[2] forgotten as under foulest fat Lethe mud and weeds, there is yet, in all hearts born into this God's-World, a spark of the Godlike slumbering. Awake, O nightmare sleepers; awake, arise, or be forever fallen! This is not playhouse poetry; it is sober fact. Our England, our world cannot live as it is. It will connect itself with a God again, or go down with nameless throes and fire-consummation to the Devils. Thou who feelest aught of such a Godlike stirring in thee, any faintest intimation of it as through heavy-laden dreams, follow *it*, I conjure thee. Arise, save thyself, be one of those that save thy country.

Bucaniers, Chactaw Indians, whose supreme aim in fighting is that they may get the scalps, the money, that they may amass scalps and money: out of such came no Chivalry, and never will! Out of such came only gore and wreck, infernal rage and misery; desperation quenched in annihilation. Behold it, I bid thee, behold there, and consider! What is it that thou have a hundred thousand-pound bills laid-up in thy strong-room, a hundred scalps hung-up in thy wigwam? I value not them or thee. Thy scalps and thy thousand-pound bills are as yet nothing, if no nobleness from within irradiate them; if no Chivalry, in action, or in embryo ever struggling towards birth and action, be there.

Love of men cannot be bought by cash-payment; and without love men cannot endure to be together. You cannot lead a Fighting World without having it regimented, chivalried: the thing, in a day, becomes impossible; all men in it, the highest at first, the very lowest at last, discern consciously, or by a noble instinct, this necessity. And can you any more continue to lead a Working World unregimented, anarchic? I answer, and the Heavens and Earth are now answering, No! The thing becomes not "in a day" impossible; but in some two generations it does. Yes, when fathers and mothers, in Stockport hunger-cellars, begin to eat their children, and Irish widows have to prove their relationship by dying of typhus-fever; and amid Governing "Corporations of the Best and Bravest," busy to preserve their game by "bushing," dark millions of God's human creatures start up in mad Chartisms, impracticable Sacred-Months, and Manchester Insurrections;[3]—and there is a virtual Industrial Aristocracy as yet only half-alive, spell-bound amid money-bags and ledgers; and an actual Idle Aristocracy seemingly near dead in somnolent delusions, in trespasses

1. Giants in Norse mythology.
2. An Islamic myth held that a tribe living near the Dead Sea were turned into apes because they refused to heed the prophecies of Moses.
3. Manchester was the site of Chartist agitation in

1838–1839. In 1819, the infamous "Peterloo Massacre" occurred there when charging cavalry killed a dozen people at an outdoor workers' meeting. See Shelley's *The Mask of Anarchy* (1819), written in response to the killing.

and double-barrels; "sliding," as on inclined-planes, which every new year they *soap* with new Hansard's-jargon[4] under God's sky, and so are "sliding," ever faster, towards a "scale" and balance-scale whereon is written *Thou art found Wanting*:—in such days, after a generation or two, I say, it does become, even to the low and simple, very palpably impossible! No Working World, any more than a Fighting World, can be led on without a noble Chivalry of Work, and laws and fixed rules which follow out of that,—far nobler than any Chivalry of Fighting was. As an anarchic multitude on mere Supply-and-demand, it is becoming inevitable that we dwindle in horrid suicidal convulsion and self-abrasion, frightful to the imagination, into *Chactaw* Workers. With wigwams and scalps,—with palaces and thousand-pound bills; with savagery, depopulation, chaotic desolation! Good Heavens, will not one French Revolution and Reign of Terror suffice us, but must there be two? There will be two if needed; there will be twenty if needed; there will be precisely as many as are needed. The Laws of Nature will have themselves fulfilled. That is a thing certain to me.

Your gallant battle-hosts and work-hosts, as the others did, will need to be made loyally yours; they must and will be regulated, methodically secured in their just share of conquest under you;—joined with you in veritable brotherhood, sonhood, by quite other and deeper ties than those of temporary day's wages! How would mere red-coated regiments, to say nothing of chivalries, fight for you, if you could discharge them on the evening of the battle, on payment of the stipulated shillings,—and they discharge you on the morning of it! Chelsea Hospitals,[5] Pensions, promotions, rigorous lasting covenant on the one side and on the other, are indispensable even for a hired fighter. The Feudal Baron, much more,—how could he subsist with mere temporary mercenaries round him, at sixpence a day; ready to go over to the other side, if sevenpence were offered? He could not have subsisted;—and his noble instinct saved him from the necessity of even trying! The Feudal Baron had a Man's Soul in him; to which anarchy, mutiny, and the other fruits of temporary mercenaries, were intolerable: he had never been a Baron otherwise, but had continued a Chactaw and Bucanier. He felt it precious, and at last it became habitual, and his fruitful enlarged existence included it as a necessity, to have men round him who in heart loved him; whose life he watched over with rigour yet with love; who were prepared to give their life for him, if need came. It was beautiful; it was human! Man lives not otherwise, nor can live contented, anywhere or anywhen. Isolation is the sum-total of wretchedness to man. To be cut off, to be left solitary: to have a world alien, not your world; all a hostile camp for you; not a home at all, of hearts and faces who are yours, whose you are! It is the frightfulest enchantment; too truly a work of the Evil One. To have neither superior, nor inferior, nor equal, united manlike to you. Without father, without child, without brother. Man knows no sadder destiny. "How is each of us," exclaims Jean Paul,[6] "so lonely in the wide bosom of the All!" Encased each as in his transparent "ice-palace"; our brother visible in his, making signals and gesticulations to us;—visible, but forever unattainable: on his bosom we shall never rest, nor he on ours. It was not a God that did this; no!

Awake, ye noble Workers, warriors in the one true war: all this must be remedied. It is you who are already half-alive, whom I will welcome into life; whom I will conjure, in God's name, to shake off your enchanted sleep, and live wholly! Cease to count scalps, gold-purses; not in these lies your or our salvation. Even these, if you

---

4. *Hansard* is the official record of parliamentary debate.   6. Jean Paul Richter (1763–1825), German writer.
5. A home and hospital for disabled soldiers.

count only these, will not long be left. Let bucaniering be put far from you; alter, speedily abrogate all laws of the bucaniers, if you would gain any victory that shall endure. Let God's justice, let pity, nobleness and manly valour, with more gold-purses or with fewer, testify themselves in this your brief Life-transit to all the Eternities, the Gods and Silences. It is to you I call; for ye are not dead, ye are already half-alive: there is in you a sleepless dauntless energy, the prime-matter of all nobleness in man. Honour to you in your kind. It is to you I call: ye know at least this, That the mandate of God to His creature man is: Work! The future Epic of the World rests not with those that are near dead, but with those that are alive, and those that are coming into life.

Look around you. Your world-hosts are all in mutiny, in confusion, destitution; on the eve of fiery wreck and madness! They will not march farther for you, on the sixpence a day and supply-and-demand principle: they will not; nor ought they, nor can they. Ye shall reduce them to order, begin reducing them. To order, to just subordination; noble loyalty in return for noble guidance. Their souls are driven nigh mad; let yours be sane and ever saner. Not as a bewildered bewildering mob; but as a firm regimented mass, with real captains over them, will these men march any more. All human interests, combined human endeavours, and social growths in this world, have, at a certain stage of their development, required organising: and Work, the grandest of human interests, does now require it.

God knows, the task will be hard: but no noble task was ever easy. This task will wear away your lives, and the lives of your sons and grandsons: but for what purpose, if not for tasks like this, were lives given to men? Ye shall cease to count your thousand-pound scalps, the noble of you shall cease! Nay the very scalps, as I say, will not long be left if you count only these. Ye shall cease wholly to be barbarous vulturous Chactaws, and become noble European Nineteenth-Century Men. Ye shall know that Mammon, in never such gigs[7] and flunky "respectabilities," is not the alone God; that of himself he is but a Devil, and even a Brute-god.

Difficult? Yes, it will be difficult. The short-fibre cotton; that too was difficult. The waste cotton-shrub, long useless, disobedient, as the thistle by the wayside,—have ye not conquered it: made it into beautiful bandana webs; white woven shirts for men; bright-tinted air-garments wherein flit goddesses? Ye have shivered mountains asunder, made the hard iron pliant to you as soft putty: the Forest-giants, Marsh-jötuns bear sheaves of golden-grain; Aegir the Sea-demon himself stretches his back for a sleek highway to you, and on Firehorses and Windhorses ye career. Ye are most strong. Thor red-bearded, with his blue sun-eyes, with his cheery heart and strong thunder-hammer, he and you have prevailed. Ye are most strong, ye Sons of the icy North, of the far East,—far marching from your rugged Eastern Wildernesses, hitherward from the gray Dawn of Time! Ye are Sons of the *Jötun*-land; the land of Difficulties Conquered. Difficult? You must try this thing. Once try it with the understanding that it will and shall have to be done. Try it as ye try the paltrier thing, making of money! I will bet on you once more, against all Jötuns, Tailor-gods, Double-barrelled Law-wards, and Denizens of Chaos whatsoever!

1843   1843

---

7. A two-wheeled, one-horse carriage.

John Stuart Mill
1806–1873

The name John Stuart Mill has become synonymous with genius. But for the Victorians it was also associated with outrageously radical views: Mill advocated sexual equality, the right to divorce, universal suffrage, free speech, and proportional representation. He first gained public attention as a social reformer, promoting the rationalist ideas of his godfather, Jeremy Bentham, founder of Utilitarianism. Mill went on to become the era's leading philosopher and political theorist, an outspoken member of Parliament, and Britain's most prestigious proponent of women's rights.

Mill's education is legendary: the Victorians were fond of social experiments, but few were stranger or more disturbing than James Mill's efforts to prove that a child could learn so much so early in life. He began teaching his son Greek at the age of three, making him memorize long lists of Greek words and their English translations. He also "home-schooled" his son in history, languages, calculus, logic, political economy, geography, psychology, and rhetoric. The boy's responsibilities included tutoring his younger siblings—eventually, eight of them— in these subjects. All this went on while his father, busy writing his multivolume *History of British India*, surveyed his children from the other end of the dining-room table.

As Mill's *Autobiography* shows, the human cost of the experiment was high. In an early draft he wrote that "I . . . grew up in the absence of love & in the presence of fear." His stern father denied Mill both pleasures and playmates, and so dominated the boy's mother that he interpreted her submissiveness as indifference to his existence. At fourteen, when his father declared his education finished, Mill had, by his own account, the knowledge of a man of forty—but he still could not brush his own hair.

Undaunted by such trivia, Mill decided he wanted to be "a reformer of the world." When he was seventeen, he founded the Utilitarian Society, which vigorously debated how to achieve the Utilitarian goal of bringing the greatest happiness to the greatest number of people. But at twenty he was plunged into depression when he realized that achieving all his goals would not satisfy him: "I seemed to have nothing left to live for." Overwork and the utter neglect of human emotion in his otherwise comprehensive education led Mill to a nervous breakdown in 1826.

Discovering that "the habit of analysis has a tendency to wear away the feelings," Mill gradually recovered by reading poetry, especially that of Wordsworth. The poet aroused his interest in "the common feelings and common destiny of human beings." Despite his assessment of himself as an "unpoetical nature," Mill became one of the most astute critics of his generation, recognizing before anyone else the unusual strengths and psychological motivations of both Tennyson and Browning. His essay *What is Poetry?* (1833) argues that true poetry expresses the passionate, solitary meditations of the author; it is not so much heard as "overheard."

In 1823 Mill followed in his father's footsteps by taking a clerkship in the Examiner's Office of the East India Company, the commercial enterprise that, in effect, governed British India. He eventually headed the department, as his father had before him. The center of his professional life, however, was his own writing and political activism. His position allowed him time to become an energetic propagandist for radical causes and legal reform—he was even arrested at age seventeen, a few weeks after the job began, for distributing information on birth control. He also edited the *London and Westminster Review* (1836–1840), while writing important essays on Coleridge and Jeremy Bentham. His *System of Logic* (1843) and *Principles of Political Economy* (1848) immediately became standard works in the field; he followed these with influential books on philosophy, politics, and economics, including *Thoughts on Parliamentary Reform* (1859), *Utilitarianism* (1861), *Representative Government* (1861), and *Auguste Comte and Positivism* (1865).

The most significant event of Mill's adult life was meeting the brilliant and beautiful Harriet Taylor in 1830. She shared his radical views on women's rights, and they soon formed an intimate friendship. But she was married and the mother of three children, a fact which lent piquancy to their efforts to establish the legal right of divorce. They finally married in 1851, after the death of her husband. Mill claimed that she deserved equal credit for his works, calling them "joint productions" of their intellectual life together. "When two persons have their thoughts and speculations completely in common," he wrote in his *Autobiography*, "it is of little consequence ... which of them holds the pen." After Harriet Taylor died in 1858, her daughter Helen became Mill's companion; she carried on their work in woman's rights into the twentieth century.

Mill retired from the East India Company in 1858 when the British government took over the company's affairs. Although he refused to seek votes or curry favor with any constituency, Mill was elected Member of Parliament for Westminster from 1865 to 1868, making memorable speeches on behalf of political reform, Irish freedom, and women's voting rights. A century ahead of mainstream Anglo-American lawmakers, he demanded nonsexist language for legislation, including a proposal that the Second Reform Bill (1867) be rewritten to replace the word "man" with the word "person." After his defeat in the election of 1868, Mill spent most of his remaining years in Avignon, France, where he died in 1873.

In the twentieth century, Mill's reputation has been sustained by the continuing relevance of his work. *On Liberty* (1859) has become the classic defense of the individual's right, in a modern society dominated by bureaucracy and mass culture, to resist the constraints of both government and public opinion. *The Subjection of Women* (1869) insists that men should grant "perfect equality" to women, demonstrating that "what is now called the nature of women is an eminently artificial thing—the result of forced repression in some directions, unnatural stimulation in others." Finally, the *Autobiography* (1873) poignantly applies these insights to the construction of the author's own identity, revealing how Mill's life was shaped by the forced repressions and stimulations of his unusual family environment.

These three works also embody Mill's distinctive qualities as a writer and thinker: he advances his arguments with exceptional clarity, anticipating objections and providing interesting examples to prove his points; he makes his appeals to the reader on the basis of reason, no matter how emotionally charged the topic may be; and he displays an underlying concern for what is good for the public at large. Never content merely to assert human rights or display moral outrage, Mill dedicated himself to convincing others that freedom of thought and action—for women as well as for men—is not simply right but beneficial to society as a whole.

from On Liberty
from Chapter 2. Of the Liberty of Thought and Discussion

The time, it is to be hoped, is gone by, when any defence would be necessary of the "liberty of the press" as one of the securities against corrupt or tyrannical government. * * * If all mankind minus one, were of one opinion, and only one person were of the contrary opinion, mankind would be no more justified in silencing that one person, than he, if he had the power, would be justified in silencing mankind. Were an opinion a personal possession of no value except to the owner; if to be obstructed in the enjoyment of it were simply a private injury, it would make some difference whether the injury was inflicted only on a few persons or on many. But the peculiar evil of silencing the expression of an opinion is, that it is robbing the human race; posterity as well as the existing generation; those who dissent from the opinion, still more than those who hold it. If the opinion is right, they are deprived of the opportunity of exchanging error for truth: if wrong, they lose, what is almost as great a benefit, the clearer perception and livelier impression of truth, produced by its collision with error.

   * * * The majority of the eminent men of every past generation held many opinions now known to be erroneous, and did or approved numerous things which no one will now justify. Why is it, then, that there is on the whole a preponderance among mankind of rational opinions and rational conduct? If there really is this preponderance—which there must be unless human affairs are, and have always been, in an almost desperate state—it is owing to a quality of the human mind, the source of everything respectable in man either as an intellectual or as a moral being, namely, that his errors are corrigible. He is capable of rectifying his mistakes, by discussion and experience. Not by experience alone. There must be discussion, to show how experience is to be interpreted. Wrong opinions and practices gradually yield to fact and argument: but facts and arguments, to produce any effect on the mind, must be brought before it. Very few facts are able to tell their own story, without comments to bring out their meaning. The whole strength and value, then, of human judgment, depending on the one property, that it can be set right when it is wrong, reliance can be placed on it only when the means of setting it right are kept constantly at hand. In the case of any person whose judgment is really deserving of confidence, how has it become so? Because he has kept his mind open to criticism of his opinions and conduct. Because it has been his practice to listen to all that could be said against him; to profit by as much of it as was just, and expound to himself, and upon occasion to others, the fallacy of what was fallacious. Because he has felt, that the only way in which a human being can make some approach to knowing the whole of a subject, is by hearing what can be said about it by persons of every variety of opinion, and studying all modes in which it can be looked at by every character of mind. No wise man ever acquired his wisdom in any mode but this. * * *

   In the present age—which has been described as "destitute of faith, but terrified at scepticism"[1]—in which people feel sure, not so much that their opinions are true, as that they should not know what to do without them—the claims of an opinion to be protected from public attack are rested not so much on its truth, as on its importance to society. There are, it is alleged, certain beliefs, so useful, not to say indispensable to well-being, that it is as much the duty of governments to uphold those beliefs, as to protect any other of the interests of society. In a case of such necessity, and so directly in the line of their duty, something less than infallibility may, it is maintained, warrant, and even bind, governments, to act on their own opinion, confirmed by the general opinion of mankind. It is also often argued, and still oftener thought, that none but bad men would desire to weaken these salutary beliefs; and there can be nothing wrong, it is thought, in restraining bad men, and prohibiting what only such men would wish to practise. This mode of thinking makes the justification of restraints on discussion not a question of the truth of doctrines, but of their usefulness; and flatters itself by that means to escape the responsibility of claiming to be an infallible judge of opinions. But those who thus satisfy themselves, do not perceive that the assumption of infallibility is merely shifted from one point to another. The usefulness of an opinion is itself matter of opinion: as disputable, as open to discussion, and requiring discussion as much, as the opinion itself. There is the same need of an infallible judge of opinions to decide an opinion to be noxious,

---

1. By Thomas Carlyle in *Memoirs of the Life of Scott* (1838).

as to decide it to be false, unless the opinion condemned has full opportunity of defending itself. And it will not do to say that the heretic may be allowed to maintain the utility or harmlessness of his opinion, though forbidden to maintain its truth. The truth of an opinion is part of its utility. If we would know whether or not it is desirable that a proposition should be believed, is it possible to exclude the consideration of whether or not it is true? * * *

We have now recognised the necessity to the mental well-being of mankind (on which all their other well-being depends) of freedom of opinion, and freedom of the expression of opinion, on four distinct grounds; which we will now briefly recapitulate.

First, if any opinion is compelled to silence, that opinion may, for aught we can certainly know, be true. To deny this is to assume our own infallibility.

Secondly, though the silenced opinion be an error, it may, and very commonly does, contain a portion of truth; and since the general or prevailing opinion on any subject is rarely or never the whole truth, it is only by the collision of adverse opinions that the remainder of the truth has any chance of being supplied.

Thirdly, even if the received opinion be not only true, but the whole truth; unless it is suffered to be, and actually is, vigorously and earnestly contested, it will, by most of those who receive it, be held in the manner of a prejudice, with little comprehension or feeling of its rational grounds. And not only this, but, fourthly, the meaning of the doctrine itself will be in danger of being lost, or enfeebled, and deprived of its vital effect on the character and conduct: the dogma becoming a mere formal profession, inefficacious for good, but cumbering the ground, and preventing the growth of any real and heartfelt conviction, from reason or personal experience.

Before quitting the subject of freedom of opinion, it is fit to take some notice of those who say, that the free expression of all opinions should be permitted, on condition that the manner be temperate, and do not pass the bounds of fair discussion. Much might be said on the impossibility of fixing where these supposed bounds are to be placed; for if the test be offence to those whose opinion is attacked, I think experience testifies that this offence is given whenever the attack is telling and powerful, and that every opponent who pushes them hard, and whom they find it difficult to answer, appears to them, if he shows any strong feeling on the subject, an intemperate opponent. But this, though an important consideration in a practical point of view, merges in a more fundamental objection. Undoubtedly the manner of asserting an opinion, even though it be a true one, may be very objectionable, and may justly incur severe censure. But the principal offences of the kind are such as it is mostly impossible, unless by accidental self-betrayal, to bring home to conviction. The gravest of them is, to argue sophistically,[2] to suppress facts or arguments, to misstate the elements of the case, or misrepresent the opposite opinion. But all this, even to the most aggravated degree, is so continually done in perfect good faith, by persons who are not considered, and in many other respects may not deserve to be considered, ignorant or incompetent, that it is rarely possible on adequate grounds conscientiously to stamp the misrepresentation as morally culpable; and still less could law presume to interfere with this kind of controversial misconduct. With regard to what is commonly meant by intemperate discussion, namely invective, sarcasm, personality, and the like, the denunciation of these weapons would deserve more sympathy if it were ever proposed to interdict them equally to both sides; but it

2. In a plausible but fallacious manner.

is only desired to restrain the employment of them against the prevailing opinion: against the unprevailing they may not only be used without general disapproval, but will be likely to obtain for him who uses them the praise of honest zeal and righteous indignation. Yet whatever mischief arises from their use, is greatest when they are employed against the comparatively defenceless; and whatever unfair advantage can be derived by any opinion from this mode of asserting it, accrues almost exclusively to received opinions. The worst offence of this kind which can be committed by a polemic, is to stigmatize those who hold the contrary opinion as bad and immoral men. To calumny of this sort, those who hold any unpopular opinion are peculiarly exposed, because they are in general few and uninfluential, and nobody but themselves feels much interested in seeing justice done them; but this weapon is, from the nature of the case, denied to those who attack a prevailing opinion: they can neither use it with safety to themselves, nor, if they could, would it do anything but recoil on their own cause. In general, opinions contrary to those commonly received can only obtain a hearing by studied moderation of language, and the most cautious avoidance of unnecessary offence, from which they hardly every deviate even in a slight degree without losing ground: while unmeasured vituperation employed on the side of the prevailing opinion, really does deter people from professing contrary opinions, and from listening to those who profess them. For the interest, therefore, of truth and justice, it is far more important to restrain this employment of vituperative language than the other; and, for example, if it were necessary to choose, there would be much more need to discourage offensive attacks on infidelity, than on religion. It is, however, obvious that law and authority have no business with restraining either, while opinion ought, in every instance, to determine its verdict by the circumstances of the individual case; condemning every one, on whichever side of the argument he places himself, in whose mode of advocacy either want of candour, or malignity, bigotry, or intolerance of feeling manifest themselves; but not inferring these vices from the side which a person takes, though it be the contrary side of the question to our own: and giving merited honour to every one, whatever opinion he may hold, who has calmness to see and honesty to state what his opponents and their opinions really are, exaggerating nothing to their discredit, keeping nothing back which tells or can be supposed to tell, in their favour. This is the real morality of public discussion: and if often violated, I am happy to think that there are many controversialists who to a great extent observe it, and a still greater number who conscientiously strive towards it.

from *Chapter 3. Of Individuality, as One of the Elements of Well-Being*

Such being the reasons which make it imperative that human beings should be free to form opinions, and to express their opinions without reserve; and such the baneful consequences to the intellectual, and through that to the moral nature of man, unless this liberty is either conceded, or asserted in spite of prohibition; let us next examine whether the same reasons do not require that men should be free to act upon their opinions—to carry these out in their lives, without hindrance, either physical or moral, from their fellow-men, so long as it is at their own risk and peril. This last proviso is of course indispensable. No one pretends that actions should be as free as opinions. On the contrary, even opinions lose their immunity, when the circumstances in which they are expressed are such as to constitute their expression a positive instigation to some mischievous act. An opinion that corn-dealers are starvers of the poor, or that private property is robbery, ought to be unmolested when simply circulated through the press, but may justly incur punishment when delivered orally to an excited mob assembled before the house of a corn-dealer, or when handed about among the same mob in the form of a placard. Acts, of whatever kind, which, without justifiable cause, do harm to others, may be, and in the more important cases absolutely require to be, controlled by the unfavourable sentiments, and, when needful, by the active interference of mankind. The liberty of the individual must be thus far limited; he must not make himself a nuisance to other people. But if he refrains from molesting others in what concerns them, and merely acts according to his own inclination and judgment in things which concern himself, the same reasons which show that opinion should be free, prove also that he should be allowed, without molestation, to carry his opinions into practice at his own cost. * * * As it is useful that while mankind are imperfect there should be different opinions, so is it that there should be different experiments of living; that free scope should be given to varieties of character, short of injury to others; and that the worth of different modes of life should be proved practically, when any one thinks fit to try them. It is desirable, in short, that in things which do not primarily concern others, individuality should assert itself. * * *

* * * The majority, being satisfied with the ways of mankind as they now are (for it is they who make them what they are), cannot comprehend why those ways should not be good enough for everybody; and what is more, spontaneity forms no part of the ideal of the majority of moral and social reformers, but is rather looked on with jealousy, as a troublesome and perhaps rebellious obstruction to the general acceptance of what these reformers, in their own judgment, think would be best for mankind. Few persons, out of Germany, even comprehend the meaning of the doctrine which Wilhelm Von Humboldt, so eminent both as a *savant* and as a politician, made the text of a treatise—that "the end of man, or that which is prescribed by the eternal or immutable dictates of reason, and not suggested by vague and transient desires, is the highest and most harmonious development of his powers to a complete and consistent whole;" that, therefore, the object "towards which every human being must ceaselessly direct his efforts, and on which especially those who design to influence their fellow-men must ever keep their eyes, is the individuality of power and development;" that for this there are two requisites, "freedom, and variety of situations;" and that from the union of these arise "individual vigour and manifold diversity," which combine themselves in "originality."[1]

Little, however, as people are accustomed to a doctrine like that of Von Humboldt, and surprising as it may be to them to find so high a value attached to individuality, the question, one must nevertheless think, can only be one of degree. No one's idea of excellence in conduct is that people should do absolutely nothing but copy one another. No one would assert that people ought not to put into their mode of life, and into the conduct of their concerns, any impress whatever of their own judgment, or of their own individual character. On the other hand, it would be absurd to pretend that people ought to live as if nothing whatever had been known in the world before they came into it; as if experience had as yet done nothing towards showing that one mode of existence, or of conduct, is preferable to another. Nobody denies that people should be so taught and trained in youth, as to know and

---

1. From *The Sphere and Duties of Government* by Baron Wilhelm von Humboldt. Although written in 1791, this treatise was not published until 1852; it was translated into English in 1854.

benefit by the ascertained results of human experience. But it is the privilege and proper condition of a human being, arrived at the maturity of his faculties, to use and interpret experience in his own way. It is for him to find out what part of recorded experience is properly applicable to his own circumstances and character. * * *

He who lets the world, or his own portion of it, choose his plan of life for him, has no need of any other faculty than the ape-like one of imitation. He who chooses his plan for himself, employs all his faculties. He must use observation to see, reasoning and judgment to foresee, activity to gather materials for decision, discrimination to decide, and when he has decided, firmness and self-control to hold to his deliberate decision. And these qualities he requires and exercises exactly in proportion as the part of his conduct which he determines according to his own judgment and feelings is a large one. It is possible that he might be guided in some good path, and kept out of harm's way, without any of these things. But what will be his comparative worth as a human being? It really is of importance, not only what men do, but also what manner of men they are that do it. Among the works of man, which human life is rightly employed in perfecting and beautifying, the first in importance surely is man himself. Supposing it were possible to get houses built, corn grown, battles fought, causes tried, and even churches erected and prayers said, by machinery—by automatons in human form—it would be a considerable loss to exchange for these automatons even the men and women who at present inhabit the more civilized parts of the world, and who assuredly are but starved specimens of what nature can and will produce. Human nature is not a machine to be built after a model, and set to do exactly the work prescribed for it, but a tree, which requires to grow and develop itself on all sides, according to the tendency of the inward forces which make it a living thing.

It will probably be conceded that it is desirable people should exercise their understandings, and that an intelligent following of custom, or even occasionally an intelligent deviation from custom, is better than a blind and simply mechanical adhesion to it. To a certain extent it is admitted, that our understanding should be our own: but there is not the same willingness to admit that our desires and impulses should be our own likewise; or that to possess impulses of our own, and of any strength, is anything but a peril and a snare. Yet desires and impulses are as much a part of a perfect human being, as beliefs and restraints: and strong impulses are only perilous when not properly balanced; when one set of aims and inclinations is developed into strength, while others, which ought to co-exist with them, remain weak and inactive. It is not because men's desires are strong that they act ill; it is because their consciences are weak. There is no natural connexion between strong impulses and a weak conscience. The natural connexion is the other way. * * * A person whose desires and impulses are his own—are the expression of his own nature, as it has been developed and modified by his own culture—is said to have a character. One whose desires and impulses are not his own, has no character, no more than a steam-engine has a character. If, in addition to being his own, his impulses are strong, and are under the government of a strong will, he has an energetic character. Whoever thinks that individuality of desires and impulses should not be encouraged to unfold itself, must maintain that society has no need of strong natures—is not the better for containing many persons who have much character—and that a high general average of energy is not desirable.

In some early states of society, these forces might be, and were, too much ahead of the power which society then possessed of disciplining and controlling them. There has been a time when the element of spontaneity and individuality was in excess, and the social principle had a hard struggle with it. The difficulty then was, to induce men of strong bodies or minds to pay obedience to any rules which required them to control their impulses. To overcome this difficulty, law and discipline, like the Popes struggling against the Emperors, asserted a power over the whole man, claiming to control all his life in order to control his character—which society had not found any other sufficient means of binding. But society has now fairly got the better of individuality; and the danger which threatens human nature is not the excess, but the deficiency, of personal impulses and preferences. Things are vastly changed, since the passions of those who were strong by station or by personal endowment were in a state of habitual rebellion against laws and ordinances, and required to be rigorously chained up to enable the persons within their reach to enjoy any particle of security. In our times, from the highest class of society down to the lowest, every one lives as under the eye of a hostile and dreaded censorship. Not only in what concerns others, but in what concerns only themselves, the individual or the family do not ask themselves—what do I prefer? or, what would suit my character and disposition? or, what would allow the best and highest in me to have fair play, and enable it to grow and thrive? They ask themselves, what is suitable to my position? what is usually done by persons of my station and pecuniary circumstances? or (worse still) what is usually done by persons of a station and circumstances superior to mine? I do not mean that they choose what is customary, in preference to what suits their own inclination. It does not occur to them to have any inclination, except for what is customary. Thus the mind itself is bowed to the yoke: even in what people do for pleasure, conformity is the first thing thought of; they like in crowds; they exercise choice only among things commonly done: peculiarity of taste, eccentricity of conduct, are shunned equally with crimes: until by dint of not following their own nature, they have no nature to follow: their human capacities are withered and starved: they become incapable of any strong wishes or native pleasures, and are generally without either opinions or feelings of home growth, or properly their own. Now is this, or is it not, the desirable condition of human nature?

* * * Many persons, no doubt, sincerely think that human beings thus cramped and dwarfed, are as their Maker designed them to be; just as many have thought that trees are a much finer thing when clipped into pollards,[2] or cut out into figures of animals, than as nature made them. But if it be any part of religion to believe that man was made by a good Being, it is more consistent with that faith to believe, that this Being gave all human faculties that they might be cultivated and unfolded, not rooted out and consumed, and that he takes delight in every nearer approach made by his creatures to the ideal conception embodied in them, every increase in any of their capabilities of comprehension, of action, or of enjoyment. There is a different type of human excellence from the Calvinistic;[3] a conception of humanity as having its nature bestowed on it for other purposes than merely to be abnegated. "Pagan self-assertion" is one of the elements of human worth, as well as "Christian self-denial."[4] There is a Greek ideal of self-development, which the Platonic and Christian ideal of self-government blends with, but does not supersede. It may be better to be a John

2. Trees pruned severely to create a thick growth of branches and foliage overhead.
3. Followers of the French Protestant theologian, John Calvin (1509–1564), believed that human nature was depraved and sinful. Elsewhere in the essay, Mill says that the Calvinist idea is that "the one great offence of man is self-will. All the good of which humanity is capable, is comprised in obedience. . . . Human nature being radically corrupt, there is no redemption for any one until human nature is killed within him."
4. From "Simonides" in John Sterling's *Essays* (1848).

Knox than an Alcibiades, but it is better to be a Pericles than either;[5] nor would a Pericles, if we had one in these days, be without anything good which belonged to John Knox.

It is not by wearing down into uniformity all that is individual in themselves, but by cultivating it and calling it forth, within the limits imposed by the rights and interests of others, that human beings become a noble and beautiful object of contemplation; and as the works partake the character of those who do them, by the same process human life also becomes rich, diversified, and animating, furnishing more abundant aliment[6] to high thoughts and elevating feelings, and strengthening the tie which binds every individual to the race, by making the race infinitely better worth belonging to. In proportion to the development of his individuality, each person becomes more valuable to himself, and is therefore capable of being more valuable to others. There is a greater fulness of life about his own existence, and when there is more life in the units there is more in the mass which is composed of them. As much compression as is necessary to prevent the stronger specimens of human nature from encroaching on the rights of others, cannot be dispensed with; but for this there is ample compensation even in the point of view of human development. The means of development which the individual loses by being prevented from gratifying his inclinations to the injury of others, are chiefly obtained at the expense of the development of other people. And even to himself there is a full equivalent in the better development of the social part of his nature, rendered possible by the restraint put upon the selfish part. To be held to rigid rules of justice for the sake of others, developes the feelings and capacities which have the good of others for their object. But to be restrained in things not affecting their good, by their mere displeasure, developes nothing valuable, except such force of character as may unfold itself in resisting the restraint. If acquiesced in, it dulls and blunts the whole nature. To give any fair play to the nature of each, it is essential that different persons should be allowed to lead different lives. In proportion as this latitude has been exercised in any age, has that age been noteworthy to posterity. Even despotism does not produce its worst effects, so long as individuality exists under it; and whatever crushes individuality is despotism, by whatever name it may be called, and whether it professes to be enforcing the will of God or the injunctions of men.

Having said that Individuality is the same thing with development, and that it is only the cultivation of individuality which produces, or can produce, well-developed human beings, I might here close the argument: for what more or better can be said of any condition of human affairs, than that it brings human beings themselves nearer to the best thing they can be? or what worse can be said of any obstruction to good, than that it prevents this? Doubtless, however, these considerations will not suffice to convince those who most need convincing; and it is necessary further to show, that these developed human beings are of some use to the undeveloped—to point out to those who do not desire liberty, and would not avail themselves of it, that they may be in some intelligible manner rewarded for allowing other people to make use of it without hindrance.

In the first place, then, I would suggest that they might possibly learn something from them. It will not be denied by anybody, that originality is a valuable element in

---

5. John Knox (1505–1572), Scottish Calvinist reformer; Alcibiades (450–404 B.C.), dissolute Athenian general; Pericles (500–429 B.C.), wise and virtuous Athenian statesman.
6. Nourishment.

human affairs. There is always need of persons not only to discover new truths, and point out when what were once truths are true no longer, but also to commence new practices, and set the example of more enlightened conduct, and better taste and sense in human life. * * * Persons of genius, it is true, are, and are always likely to be, a small minority; but in order to have them, it is necessary to preserve the soil in which they grow. Genius can only breathe freely in an *atmosphere* of freedom. Persons of genius are, *ex vi termini* [by definition], *more* individual than any other people—less capable, consequently, of fitting themselves, without hurtful compression, into any of the small number of moulds which society provides in order to save its members the trouble of forming their own character. If from timidity they consent to be forced into one of these moulds, and to let all that part of themselves which cannot expand under the pressure remain unexpanded, society will be little the better for their genius. If they are of a strong character, and break their fetters, they become a mark for the society which has not succeeded in reducing them to commonplace, to point at with solemn warning as "wild," "erratic," and the like; much as if one should complain of the Niagara river for not flowing smoothly between its banks like a Dutch canal.

I insist thus emphatically on the importance of genius, and the necessity of allowing it to unfold itself freely both in thought and in practice, being well aware that no one will deny the position in theory, but knowing also that almost every one, in reality, is totally indifferent to it. People think genius a fine thing if it enables a man to write an exciting poem, or paint a picture. But in its true sense, that of originality in thought and action, though no one says that it is not a thing to be admired, nearly all, at heart, think that they can do very well without it. Unhappily this is too natural to be wondered at. Originality is the one thing which unoriginal minds cannot feel the use of. They cannot see what it is to do for them: how should they? If they could see what it would do for them, it would not be originality. The first service which originality has to render them, is that of opening their eyes: which being once fully done, they would have a chance of being themselves original. Meanwhile, recollecting that nothing was ever yet done which some one was not the first to do, and that all good things which exist are the fruits of originality, let them be modest enough to believe that there is something still left for it to accomplish, and assure themselves that they are more in need of originality, the less they are conscious of the want.

In sober truth, whatever homage may be professed, or even paid, to real or supposed mental superiority, the general tendency of things throughout the world is to render mediocrity the ascendant power among mankind. In ancient history, in the middle ages, and in a diminishing degree through the long transition from feudality to the present time, the individual was a power in himself; and if he had either great talents or a high social position, he was a considerable power. At present individuals are lost in the crowd. In politics it is almost a triviality to say that public opinion now rules the world. The only power deserving the name is that of masses, and of governments while they make themselves the organ of the tendencies and instincts of masses. This is as true in the moral and social relations of private life as in public transactions. Those whose opinions go by the name of public opinion, are not always the same sort of public: in America they are the whole white population; in England, chiefly the middle class. But they are always a mass, that is to say, collective mediocrity. And what is a still greater novelty, the mass do not now take their opinions from dignitaries in Church or State, from ostensible leaders, or from books. Their thinking is done for them by men much like themselves, addressing them or speaking in their name, on the spur of the moment, through the newspapers. I am not complaining of all this. I do not assert that anything better is compatible, as a general rule, with the present low state of the human mind. But that does not hinder the government of mediocrity from being mediocre government. No government by a democracy or a numerous aristocracy, either in its political acts or in the opinions, qualities, and tone of mind which it fosters, ever did or could rise above mediocrity, except in so far as the sovereign Many have let themselves be guided (which in their best times they always have done) by the counsels and influence of a more highly gifted and in-structed One or Few. The initiation of all wise or noble things, comes and must come from individuals; generally at first from some one individual. The honour and glory of the average man is that he is capable of following that initiative; that he can respond internally to wise and noble things, and be led to them with his eyes open. I am not countenancing the sort of "hero-worship" which applauds the strong man of genius for forcibly seizing on the government of the world and making it do his bidding in spite of itself.[7] All he can claim is, freedom to point out the way. The power of com-pelling others into it, is not only inconsistent with the freedom and development of all the rest, but corrupting to the strong man himself. It does seem, however, that when the opinions of masses of merely average men are everywhere become or be-coming the dominant power, the counterpoise and corrective to that tendency would be, the more and more pronounced individuality of those who stand on the higher eminences of thought. It is in these circumstances most especially, that exceptional individuals, instead of being deterred, should be encouraged in acting differently from the mass. In other times there was no advantage in their doing so, unless they acted not only differently, but better. In this age, the mere example of nonconfor-mity, the mere refusal to bend the knee to custom, is itself a service. Precisely because the tyranny of opinion is such as to make eccentricity a reproach, it is desirable, in order to break through that tyranny, that people should be eccentric. Eccentricity has always abounded when and where strength of character has abounded; and the amount of eccentricity in a society has generally been proportional to the amount of genius, mental vigour, and moral courage which it contained. That so few now dare to be eccentric, marks the chief danger of the time. * * *

There is one characteristic of the present direction of public opinion, peculiarly calculated to make it intolerant of any marked demonstration of individuality. The general average of mankind are not only moderate in intellect, but also moderate in inclinations: they have no tastes or wishes strong enough to incline them to do any-thing unusual, and they consequently do not understand those who have, and class all such with the wild and intemperate whom they are accustomed to look down upon. * * * These tendencies of the times cause the public to be more disposed than at most former periods to prescribe general rules of conduct, and endeavour to make every one conform to the approved standard. And that standard, express or tacit, is to desire nothing strongly. Its ideal of character is to be without any marked charac-ter; to maim by compression, like a Chinese lady's foot, every part of human nature which stands out prominently, and tends to make the person markedly dissimilar in outline to commonplace humanity.

As is usually the case with ideals which exclude one-half of what is desirable, the present standard of approbation produces only an inferior imitation of the other half.

---

7. Cf. Thomas Carlyle, *On Heroes and Hero-Worship* (1841).

Instead of great energies guided by vigorous reason, and strong feelings strongly controlled by a conscientious will, its result is weak feelings and weak energies, which therefore can be kept in outward conformity to rule without any strength either of will or of reason. Already energetic characters on any large scale are becoming merely traditional. There is now scarcely any outlet for energy in this country except business. The energy expended in this may still be regarded as considerable. What little is left from that employment, is expended on some hobby; which may be a useful, even a philanthropic hobby, but is always some one thing, and generally a thing of small dimensions. The greatness of England is now all collective: individually small, we only appear capable of anything great by our habit of combining; and with this our moral and religious philanthropists are perfectly contented. But it was men of another stamp than this that made England what it has been; and men of another stamp will be needed to prevent its decline.

The despotism of custom is everywhere the standing hindrance to human advancement, being in unceasing antagonism to that disposition to aim at something better than customary, which is called, according to circumstances, the spirit of liberty, or that of progress or improvement. The spirit of improvement is not always a spirit of liberty, for it may aim at forcing improvements on an unwilling people; and the spirit of liberty, in so far as it resists such attempts, may ally itself locally and temporarily with the opponents of improvement; but the only unfailing and permanent source of improvement is liberty, since by it there are as many possible independent centres of improvement as there are individuals. The progressive principle, however, in either shape, whether as the love of liberty or of improvement, is antagonistic to the sway of Custom, involving at least emancipation from that yoke; and the contest between the two constitutes the chief interest of the history of mankind. The greater part of the world has, properly speaking, no history, because the despotism of Custom is complete. This is the case over the whole East. Custom is there, in all things, the final appeal; justice and right mean conformity to custom; the argument of custom no one, unless some tyrant intoxicated with power, thinks of resisting. And we see the result. Those nations must once have had originality; they did not start out of the ground populous, lettered, and versed in many of the arts of life; they made themselves all this, and were then the greatest and most powerful nations of the world. What are they now? The subjects or dependents of tribes whose forefathers wandered in the forests when theirs had magnificent palaces and gorgeous temples, but over whom custom exercised only a divided rule with liberty and progress. A people, it appears, may be progressive for a certain length of time, and then stop: when does it stop? When it ceases to possess individuality. If a similar change should befall the nations of Europe, it will not be in exactly the same shape: the despotism of custom with which these nations are threatened is not precisely stationariness. It proscribes singularity, but it does not preclude change, provided all change together. We have discarded the fixed costumes of our forefathers; every one must still dress like other people, but the fashion may change once or twice a year. We thus take care that when there is change it shall be for change's sake, and not from any idea of beauty or convenience; for the same idea of beauty or convenience would not strike all the world at the same moment, and be simultaneously thrown aside by all at another moment. But we are progressive as well as changeable: we continually make new inventions in mechanical things, and keep them until they are again superseded by better; we are eager for improvement in politics, in education, even in morals, though in this last our idea of improvement chiefly consists in persuading or forcing other people to be as good as ourselves. It is not progress that we object to; on the contrary, we flatter ourselves that we are the most progressive people who ever lived. It is individuality that we war against: we should think we had done wonders if we had made ourselves all alike; forgetting that the unlikeness of one person to another is generally the first thing which draws the attention of either to the imperfection of his own type, and the superiority of another, or the possibility, by combining the advantages of both, of producing something better than either. We have a warning example in China—a nation of much talent, and, in some respects, even wisdom, owing to the rare good fortune of having been provided at an early period with a particularly good set of customs, the work, in some measure, of men to whom even the most enlightened European must accord, under certain limitations, the title of sages and philosophers. They are remarkable, too, in the excellence of their apparatus for impressing, as far as possible, the best wisdom they possess upon every mind in the community, and securing that those who have appropriated most of it shall occupy the posts of honour and power. Surely the people who did this have discovered the secret of human progressiveness, and must have kept themselves steadily at the head of the movement of the world. On the contrary, they have become stationary—have remained so for thousands of years; and if they are ever to be farther improved, it must be by foreigners. They have succeeded beyond all hope in what English philanthropists are so industriously working at—in making a people all alike, all governing their thoughts and conduct by the same maxims and rules; and these are the fruits. The modern *régime* of public opinion is, in an unorganized form, what the Chinese educational and political systems are in an organized; and unless individuality shall be able successfully to assert itself against this yoke, Europe, notwithstanding its noble antecedents and its professed Christianity, will tend to become another China.

1859

Elizabeth Barrett Browning
1806–1861

Elizabeth Barrett Browning was the most celebrated woman poet of the Victorian era. She was admired by contemporaries as varied as William Wordsworth, Queen Victoria, Edgar Allan Poe (who introduced an American edition of her work), Christina Rossetti, and John Ruskin (who proclaimed *Aurora Leigh* the greatest poem in English). Her popularity was especially remarkable because she interspersed her ardent love lyrics with hard-hitting poems on radical political causes and feminist themes. In the United States, she influenced not only sequestered writers like Emily Dickinson but also political activists like Susan B. Anthony.

The eldest of eleven children, Elizabeth Barrett grew up in a country manor house called Hope End in Hertfordshire. The Barretts were a wealthy family whose fortune derived from a slave plantation in Jamaica. While her submissive mother, Mary Clark, encouraged her to write, it was her protective but authoritarian father, Edward Moulton-Barrett, who dominated her affections and received laudatory poems on his birthdays. From an early age Barrett envisioned herself combining male and female attributes to become "the feminine of Homer." As the critic Dorothy Mermin has pointed out, the ambitious child-poet was already imaginatively inhabiting two gender roles, the imprisoned female muse and the active male quester: "At five I supposed myself a heroine and in my day dreams of bliss I constantly imaged to myself a forlorn damsel in distress rescued by some noble knight."

Barrett took advantage of her family's resources to give herself an exceptional education, unusual for a woman of her day. Her passion for Greek poetry led her to translate Aeschylus's *Prometheus Bound* (1833). Two earlier works also reflected her wide reading: at twelve she wrote a four-book epic, *The Battle of Marathon*, which her father had privately printed, and at twenty she anonymously published a long philosophical poem, *An Essay on Mind, with Other Poems* (1826). But her intellectual development was offset by an illness that broke her health at the age of fifteen. Thereafter, her bold aspirations and mental energy were at odds with her semi-invalid state. Her sense of isolation increased in 1828 when her mother died, and again when declining family fortunes led her father to move the family from the home she loved, first to Sidmouth, Devon, in 1832 and then to London in 1835, where they eventually settled at 50 Wimpole Street.

It was here that Barrett became almost a recluse. Disliking the dirty, foggy city, she hardly left the house, but she corresponded avidly with a circle of literary and public figures. In 1838 chronic lung disease weakened her further; she already had developed what would be a lifelong dependence on morphine as a painkiller. Her doctors insisted that she go to Mediterranean climes, but the farthest her father would allow was Torquay, on the south coast of England. She lived there for three years, returning prostrate with grief after her brother Edward died in a boating accident. For the next several years, her spirits sustained only by her poetry, she worked, slept, and received visitors on a couch in a room sealed against the London air. Often exhausted, she was unable to see the aged Wordsworth when he came to pay his respects.

As she and her small circle of friends were quick to realize, Elizabeth Barrett had become like Tennyson's Lady of Shalott, having no other life but to weave her poetic web in solitude. *The Seraphim and Other Poems* (1838) established her reputation, and the two volumes of *Poems* (1844) consolidated her position as the era's finest "poetess." The latter book included *A Drama of Exile*, a sequel to Milton's *Paradise Lost* in which Eve emerges as a heroine, and also *The Cry of the Children*, condemning child labor in factories. Despite her oppositional politics, the suppleness of her thought and her passionate voice were so highly regarded by critics and public alike that she was mentioned as a candidate for Poet Laureate when Wordsworth died in 1850.

But by then she had utterly transformed her life. In 1845 she began corresponding with Robert Browning—she was nearly forty, and famous; he was thirty-three and his only reputation was for obscurity. Their literary friendship rapidly blossomed into romance, which they had to hide from her father, who had tacitly forbidden his children to marry. After a secret marriage in London in 1846, the couple eloped to Italy, where they settled in Florence at Casa Guidi. There, the fairy tale continued: happily married and living in a warm climate, she recovered much of her health, wrote her best work, gained the love of the Italians with her nationalistic verse, and gave birth to a son, Robert Weidemann Browning ("Pen"), in 1849. She had prophetically written to Browning, in the last letter before their elopement: "I begin to think that none are so bold as the timid, when they are fairly roused."

Her union with Robert Browning was responsible for two works that have since formed the cornerstone of her reputation. The first is their justly famous correspondence. The story of their courtship was widely known, but its intimate details were not revealed until the publication of their letters in 1899. Second, as their relationship developed she wrote a series of love poems to Browning. She finished the last poem two days before their wedding, and the collection was published in 1850, under the deliberately misleading title *Sonnets from the Portuguese*. Among the most significant sonnet sequences since those of Shakespeare and Sidney, these poems revived the form in Victorian England and revised in brilliant new ways what had hitherto been a primarily masculine poetic tradition. Casting the male recipient of her sonnets in the role of sexual object, yet also allowing for his reciprocal passion and poetic drive, Barrett

Browning records the interplay of gifted lovers whose desire is inseparable from their quest for verbal mastery.

In her final years Barrett Browning's career continued to flourish. She and her husband enjoyed a wide circle of friends, including Tennyson, Ruskin, Carlyle, Rossetti, and Margaret Fuller. They traveled a great deal, to Rome, Paris, and several times back to London where they were warmly received by both their families—with the exception of her father, who refused to forgive or even see her again. In 1851 she published *Casa Guidi Windows*, which promoted the cause of Italian independence from Austria. *Poems Before Congress* (1860) stirred controversy in England over its volatile and "unwomanly" political views, particularly its scathing attack on American slavery. But her health was failing, and after recurrent illnesses, she died in Florence in her husband's arms. *Last Poems* appeared posthumously in 1862.

Her greatest achievement, however, lies in her verse novel, *Aurora Leigh* (1856), a daring combination of epic, romance, and *bildungsroman*. The first major poem in English in which the heroine, like the author, is a woman writer, *Aurora Leigh* rewrites Wordsworth's *The Prelude* from a female point of view. With its Miltonic echoes, the blank-verse format claims epic importance not only for the growth of the woman poet, but also for a woman's struggle to achieve artistic and economic independence in modern society. The poem blends these themes, moreover, with a witty, Byronic treatment of Victorian manners and social issues, and an emotionally charged love plot that recalls Charlotte Brontë's *Jane Eyre*. The story of how the aspiring poet Aurora Leigh overcomes the prejudices of both a masculine audience and the man she loves, in order to find fame and happiness in Italy, closely mirrors Barrett Browning's own. The poem was an overwhelming success, even though many contemporary readers were scandalized by its radical revision of Victorian ideals of femininity and its picture of how the two sexes might work together so that each could achieve its fullest human potential. Scorning to measure herself against any but the greatest male authors, Elizabeth Barrett Browning was the first to show English readers the enormous possibilities of a poetic tradition in which women participated on equal terms.

To George Sand[1]
A Desire

Thou large-brained woman and large-hearted man,
Self-called George Sand! whose soul, amid the lions
Of thy tumultuous senses, moans defiance
And answers roar for roar, as spirits can:
5   I would some mild miraculous thunder ran
Above the applauded circus,[2] in appliance
Of thine own nobler nature's strength and science,
Drawing two pinions,° white as wings of swan,   wings
From thy strong shoulders, to amaze the place
10   With holier light! that thou to woman's claim
And man's, mightst join beside the angel's grace
Of a pure genius sanctified from blame,

---

1. George Sand was the pseudonym of Aurore Dudevant (1804–1876), a French Romantic novelist noted for her free and unconventional ways, including the adoption of male dress. Barrett Browning admired Sand's genius, and defended her against those critical of her morality.
2. Roman arena where Christians were thrown to the lions.

Till child and maiden pressed to thine embrace
To kiss upon thy lips a stainless fame.

1844

To George Sand
A Recognition

True genius, but true woman! dost deny
The woman's nature with a manly scorn,
And break away the gauds° and armlets worn   *jewelry*
By weaker women in captivity?
5   Ah, vain denial! that revolted cry
Is sobbed in by a woman's voice forlorn,—
Thy woman's hair, my sister, all unshorn
Floats back dishevelled strength in agony,
Disproving thy man's name: and while before
10 The world thou burnest in a poet-fire,
We see thy woman-heart beat evermore
Through the large flame. Beat purer, heart, and higher,
Till God unsex thee on the heavenly shore
Where unincarnate spirits purely aspire!

1844

A Year's Spinning

1

He listened at the porch that day,
    To hear the wheel go on, and on;
And then it stopped, ran back away,
    While through the door he brought the sun:
5   But now my spinning is all done.

2

He sat beside me, with an oath
    That love ne'er ended, once begun;
I smiled—believing for us both,
    What was the truth for only one:
10   And now my spinning is all done.

3

My mother cursed me that I heard
    A young man's wooing as I spun:
Thanks, cruel mother, for that word,—
    For I have, since, a harder known!
15   And now my spinning is all done.

4

I thought—O God!—my first-born's cry
    Both voices to mine ear would drown:
I listened in mine agony—

It was the *silence* made me groan!
20   And now my spinning is all done.

5

Bury me 'twixt my mother's grave,
          (Who cursed me on her death-bed lone)
And my dead baby's (God it save!)
          Who, not to bless me, would not moan.
25   And now my spinning is all done.

6

A stone upon my heart and head,
          But no name written on the stone!
Sweet neighbours, whisper low instead,
          "This sinner was a loving one—
30   And now her spinning is all done."

7

And let the door ajar remain,
          In case he should pass by anon;
And leave the wheel out very plain,—
          That HE, when passing in the sun,
35   May see the spinning is all done.

1850

from Sonnets from the Portuguese[1]

1

I thought once how Theocritus had sung
Of the sweet years, the dear and wished-for years,
Who each one in a gracious hand appears
To bear a gift for mortals, old or young:[2]
5   And, as I mused it in his antique tongue,[3]
I saw, in gradual vision through my tears,
The sweet, sad years, the melancholy years,
Those of my own life, who by turns had flung
A shadow across me. Straightway I was 'ware,
10   So weeping, how a mystic Shape did move
Behind me, and drew me backward by the hair;
And a voice said in mastery, while I strove,—
"Guess now who holds thee?"—"Death," I said. But, there,
The silver answer rang,—"Not Death, but Love."

1. These very personal poems chronicle Elizabeth Barrett's courtship with Robert Browning. She did not show
them to him until after they were married, when he pronounced them "the finest sonnets written in any language since Shakespeare's." He overcame her reluctance
to publish them by proposing the somewhat cryptic title
implying that they are merely translations.

2. In *Idylls* 15, Theocritus, a Greek pastoral poet of the
3rd century B.C., tells how "the dainty-footed Hours"
brought Adonis to Aphrodite. The song celebrates the
return of spring, the season when Elizabeth Barrett first
met Robert Browning.
3. I.e., Greek.

13

And wilt thou have me fashion into speech
The love I bear thee, finding words enough,
And hold the torch out, while the winds are rough,
Between our faces, to cast light on each?—
5   I drop it at thy feet. I cannot teach
My hand to hold my spirit so far off
From myself—me—that I should bring thee proof
In words, of love hid in me out of reach.
Nay, let the silence of my womanhood
10   Commend my woman-love to thy belief,—
Seeing that I stand unwon, however wooed,
And rend the garment of my life, in brief,
By a most dauntless, voiceless fortitude,
Lest one touch of this heart convey its grief.

14

If thou must love me, let it be for nought
Except for love's sake only. Do not say
"I love her for her smile—her look—her way
Of speaking gently,—for a trick of thought
5   That falls in well with mine, and certes brought
A sense of pleasant ease on such a day"—
For these things in themselves, Belovèd, may
Be changed, or change for thee,—and love, so wrought,
May be unwrought so. Neither love me for
10   Thine own dear pity's wiping my cheeks dry,—
A creature might forget to weep, who bore
Thy comfort long, and lose thy love thereby!
But love me for love's sake, that evermore
Thou mayst love on, through love's eternity.

21

Say over again, and yet once over again,
That thou dost love me. Though the word repeated
Should seem "a cuckoo-song,"[4] as thou dost treat it,
Remember, never to the hill or plain,
5   Valley and wood, without her cuckoo-strain
Comes the fresh Spring in all her green completed.
Belovèd, I, amid the darkness greeted
By a doubtful spirit-voice, in that doubt's pain
Cry, "Speak once more—thou lovest!" Who can fear
10   Too many stars, though each in heaven shall roll,
Too many flowers, though each shall crown the year?
Say thou dost love me, love me, love me—toll

---

4. Repetitious, like the cuckoo's song.

The silver iterance!°—only minding, Dear,   *repetition*
To love me also in silence with thy soul.

22

When our two souls stand up erect and strong,
Face to face, silent, drawing nigh and nigher,
Until the lengthening wings break into fire
At either curvèd point,—what bitter wrong
5   Can the earth do to us, that we should not long
Be here contented? Think. In mounting higher,
The angels would press on us and aspire
To drop some golden orb of perfect song
Into our deep, dear silence. Let us stay
10   Rather on earth, Belovèd,—where the unfit
Contrarious moods of men recoil away
And isolate pure spirits, and permit
A place to stand and love in for a day,
With darkness and the death-hour rounding it.

43

How do I love thee? Let me count the ways.
I love thee to the depth and breadth and height
My soul can reach, when feeling out of sight
For the ends of Being and ideal Grace.
5   I love thee to the level of everyday's
Most quiet need, by sun and candle-light.
I love thee freely, as men strive for Right;
I love thee purely, as they turn from Praise.
I love thee with the passion put to use
10   In my old griefs, and with my childhood's faith.
I love thee with a love I seemed to lose
With my lost saints,—I love with the breath,
Smiles, tears, of all my life!—and, if God choose,
I shall but love thee better after death.

1845–1847   1850

from **Aurora Leigh**[1]
from *Book 1*
[SELF-PORTRAIT]

Of writing many books there is no end;
And I who have written much in prose and verse
For others' uses, will write now for mine,—
Will write my story for my better self,
5   As when you paint your portrait for a friend,

---

1. Barrett Browning called *Aurora Leigh*, a poem in nine books, a "verse novel." It portrays the struggles of a young poet to find her artistic voice and pursue her vocation despite the obstacles confronting a woman writer.

Elizabeth Barrett Browning, from the frontispiece of the fourth edition of *Aurora Leigh* (1859). This etched portrait of Barrett Browning—with the disheveled hair, frank gaze, and bohemian-looking jacket—signals to the reader that the author has a lot in common with her heroine, the feminist poet Aurora Leigh. During this period Barrett Browning was living in Florence and at the height of her fame, passionately involved in denouncing the slave trade in America and demanding independence for her adoptive country, Italy.

Who keeps it in a drawer and looks at it
Long after he has ceased to love you, just
To hold together what he was and is.
I, writing thus, am still what men call young;
10   I have not so far left the coasts of life
To travel inward, that I cannot hear
That murmur of the outer Infinite
Which unweaned babies smile at in their sleep
When wondered at for smiling; not so far,
15   But still I catch my mother at her post
Beside the nursery door, with finger up,
"Hush, hush—here's too much noise!" while her sweet eyes
Leap forward, taking part against her word
In the child's riot. Still I sit and feel
20   My father's slow hand, when she had left us both,
Stroke out my childish curls across his knee,
And hear Assunta's daily jest (she knew
He liked it better than a better jest)
Inquire how many golden scudi[2] went
25   To make such ringlets. O my father's hand,

2. Italian coins; Assunta was Aurora's nurse.

Stroke heavily, heavily the poor hair down,
Draw, press the child's head closer to thy knee!
I'm still too young, too young, to sit alone.
I write. My mother was a Florentine,

30 Whose rare blue eyes were shut from seeing me
When scarcely I was four years old, my life
A poor spark snatched up from a failing lamp
Which went out therefore. She was weak and frail;
She could not bear the joy of giving life,

35 The mother's rapture slew her. If her kiss
Had left a longer weight upon my lips
It might have steadied the uneasy breath,
And reconciled and fraternised my soul
With the new order. As it was, indeed,

40 I felt a mother-want about the world,
And still went seeking, like a bleating lamb
Left out at night in shutting up the fold,—
As restless as a nest-deserted bird
Grown chill through something being away, though what

45 It knows not. I, Aurora Leigh, was born
To make my father sadder, and myself
Not overjoyous, truly. Women know
The way to rear up children (to be just),
They know a simple, merry, tender knack

50 Of tying sashes, fitting baby-shoes,
And stringing pretty words that make no sense,
And kissing full sense into empty words,
Which things are corals to cut life upon,
Although such trifles: children learn by such,

55 Love's holy earnest in a pretty play
And get not over-early solemnised,
But seeing, as in a rose-bush, Love's Divine
Which burns and hurts not,—not a single bloom,—
Become aware and unafraid of Love.

60 Such good do mothers. Fathers love as well
—Mine did, I know,—but still with heavier brains,
And wills more consciously responsible,
And not as wisely, since less foolishly;
So mothers have God's license to be missed.

65 My father was an austere Englishman,
Who, after a dry lifetime spent at home
In college-learning, law, and parish talk,
Was flooded with a passion unaware,
His whole provisioned and complacent past

70 Drowned out from him that moment. As he stood
In Florence, where he had come to spend a month
And note the secret of Da Vinci's drains,[3]

3. Leonardo da Vinci (1452–1519) was an architect and engineer, as well as an artist; he designed the aqueduct that supplied Milan's water.

He musing somewhat absently perhaps
Some English question . . . whether men should pay
75   The unpopular but necessary tax
With left or right hand—in the alien sun
In that great square of the Santissima[4]
There drifted past him (scarcely marked enough
To move his comfortable island scorn)
80   A train of priestly banners, cross and psalm,
The white-veiled rose-crowned maidens holding up
Tall tapers, weighty for such wrists, aslant
To the blue luminous tremor of the air,
And letting drop the white wax as they went
85   To eat the bishop's wafer[5] at the church;
From which long trail of chanting priests and girls,
A face flashed like a cymbal on his face
And shook with silent clangour brain and heart,
Transfiguring him to music. Thus, even thus,
90   He too received his sacramental gift
With eucharistic meanings; for he loved.

[HER MOTHER'S PORTRAIT]

And as I grew
In years, I mixed, confused, unconsciously,
Whatever I last read or heard or dreamed,
Abhorrent, admirable, beautiful,
150   Pathetical, or ghastly, or grotesque,
With still that face . . . which did not therefore change,
But kept the mystic level of all forms,
Hates, fears, and admirations, was by turns
Ghost, fiend, and angel, fairy, witch, and sprite,
155   A dauntless Muse who eyes a dreadful Fate,
A loving Psyche who loses sight of Love,[6]
A still Medusa[7] with mild milky brows
All curdled and all clothed upon with snakes
Whose slime falls fast as sweat will; or anon
160   Our Lady of the Passion, stabbed with swords
Where the Babe sucked; or Lamia[8] in her first
Moonlighted pallor, ere she shrunk and blinked
And shuddering wriggled down to the unclean;
Or my own mother, leaving her last smile
165   In her last kiss upon the baby-mouth
My father pushed down on the bed for that,—

4. The Florentine church of the Santissima Annunziata, or Holy Annunciation.
5. To take Holy Communion.
6. Psyche was beloved of Cupid (or Eros), whom she had never seen because he always came to her after dark; one night she lit her lamp to look at him as he slept, where-

upon he left her.
7. A gorgon, a female monster with serpents for hair, the sight of whom turned people to stone.
8. A monster with the head and upper body of a maiden, and lower body of a serpent.

Or my dead mother, without smile or kiss,
Buried at Florence. All which images,
Concentred on the picture, glassed themselves
170   Before my meditative childhood, as
The incoherencies of change and death
Are represented fully, mixed and merged,
In the smooth fair mystery of perpetual Life.

[Aurora's Education]

Then, land!—then, England! oh, the frosty cliffs[9]
Looked cold upon me. Could I find a home
Among those mean red houses through the fog?
And when I heard my father's language first
255   From alien lips which had no kiss for mine
I wept aloud, then laughed, then wept, then wept,
And some one near me said the child was mad
Through much sea-sickness. The train swept us on:
Was this my father's England? the great isle?
260   The ground seemed cut up from the fellowship
Of verdure, field from field,[1] as man from man;
The skies themselves looked low and positive,
As almost you could touch them with a hand,
And dared to do it they were so far off
265   From God's celestial crystals;[2] all things blurred
And dull and vague. Did Shakespeare and his mates
Absorb the light here?—not a hill or stone
With heart to strike a radiant colour up
Or active outline on the indifferent air.

270   I think I see my father's sister stand
Upon the hall-step of her country-house
To give me welcome. She stood straight and calm,
Her somewhat narrow forehead braided tight
As if for taming accidental thoughts
275   From possible pulses;[3] brown hair pricked with gray
By frigid use of life (she was not old,
Although my father's elder by a year),
A nose drawn sharply, yet in delicate lines;
A close mild mouth, a little soured about
280   The ends, through speaking unrequited loves
Or peradventure niggardly half-truths;
Eyes of no colour,—once they might have smiled,
But never, never have forgot themselves
In smiling; cheeks, in which was yet a rose
285   Of perished summers, like a rose in a book,

9. The white chalk cliffs of Dover.
1. English fields are divided by hedgerows.
2. The stars, or perhaps the crystalline sphere the ancients believed lay beyond them.
3. Pulsations of strong emotion.

Kept more for ruth° than pleasure,—if past bloom,   *remorse*
Past fading also.

           She had lived, we'll say,
A harmless life, she called a virtuous life,
A quiet life, which was not life at all
290   (But that, she had not lived enough to know),
Between the vicar and the country squires,
The lord-lieutenant looking down sometimes
From the empyrean to assure their souls
Against chance vulgarisms, and, in the abyss,
295   The apothecary, looked on once a year
To prove their soundness of humility.
The poor-club exercised her Christian gifts
Of knitting stockings, stitching petticoats,
Because we are of one flesh, after all,
300   And need one flannel° (with a proper sense   *petticoat*
Of difference in the quality)—and still
The book-club, guarded from your modern trick
Of shaking dangerous questions from the crease,[4]
Preserved her intellectual. She had lived
305   A sort of cage-bird life, born in a cage,
Accounting that to leap from perch to perch
Was act and joy enough for any bird.
Dear heaven, how silly are the things that live
In thickets, and eat berries!

               I, alas,
310   A wild bird scarcely fledged, was brought to her cage,
And she was there to meet me. Very kind.
Bring the clean water, give out the fresh seed.

                * * *
              So it was.
385   I broke the copious curls upon my head
In braids, because she liked smooth-ordered hair.
I left off saying my sweet Tuscan words
Which still at any stirring of the heart
Came up to float across the English phrase
390   As lilies (*Bene* or *Che che*[5]), because
She liked my father's child to speak his tongue.
I learnt the collects and the catechism,
The creeds, from Athanasius back to Nice,
The Articles,[6] the Tracts *against* the times[7]

---

4. Books were sold with their pages uncut; one had to cut the folds, or creases, to open the pages and read the book.
5. "Good" and "no, indeed" (Italian).
6. The Thirty-nine Articles are the principles of Angli-can faith; collects are Anglican prayers.
7. An ironic reference to the High Church movement's *Tracts for the Times*, written by Newman, Keble, and Pusey; thus, the aunt is Low Church.

395 (By no means Buonaventure's "Prick of Love"[8]),
And various popular synopses of
Inhuman doctrines never taught by John,[9]
Because she liked instructed piety.
I learnt my complement of classic French
400 (Kept pure of Balzac and neologism[1])
And German also, since she liked a range
Of liberal education,—tongues, not books.
I learnt a little algebra, a little
Of the mathematics,—brushed with extreme flounce
405 The circle of the sciences, because
She misliked women who are frivolous.
I learnt the royal genealogies
Of Oviedo, the internal laws
Of the Burmese empire,—by how many feet
410 Mount Chimborazo outsoars Teneriffe.
What navigable river joins itself
To Lara, and what census of the year five
Was taken at Klagenfurt,—because she liked
A general insight into useful facts.
415 I learnt much music,—such as would have been
As quite impossible in Johnson's day[2]
As still it might be wished—fine sleights of hand
And unimagined fingering, shuffling off
The hearer's soul through hurricanes of notes
420 To a noisy Tophet;° and I drew . . . costumes   *Hell*
From French engravings, nereids neatly draped
(With smirks of simmering godship): I washed in°   *water-colored*
Landscapes from nature (rather say, washed out).
I danced the polka and Cellarius,
425 Spun glass, stuffed birds, and modelled flowers in wax,
Because she liked accomplishments in girls.
I read a score of books on womanhood
To prove, if women do not think at all,
They may teach thinking (to a maiden aunt
430 Or else the author),—books that boldly assert
Their right of comprehending husband's talk
When not too deep, and even of answering
With pretty "may it please you," or "so it is,"—
Their rapid insight and fine aptitude,
435 Particular worth and general missionariness,
As long as they keep quiet by the fire

8. Saint Buonaventure (1221–1274) wrote of ecstatic, mystical Christian experiences; he believed in the power of love over the power of reason.
9. The author of the gospel.
1. Honoré de Balzac (1799–1850), French realist novelist who described things considered unpleasant or immoral, hence unsuitable reading for young ladies. A neologism is a newly coined word.
2. When informed that a piece of music being played by a young lady was extremely difficult, Samuel Johnson responded, "Would that it had been impossible."

And never say "no" when the world says "ay,"
For that is fatal,—their angelic reach
Of virtue, chiefly used to sit and darn,
440 And fatten household sinners,—their, in brief,
Potential faculty in everything
Of abdicating power in it: she owned
She liked a woman to be womanly,
And English women, she thanked God and sighed
445 (Some people always sigh in thanking God)
Were models to the universe. And last
I learnt cross-stitch, because she did not like
To see me wear the night with empty hands
A-doing nothing. So, my shepherdess
450 Was something after all (the pastoral saints
Be praised for't), leaning lovelorn with pink eyes
To match her shoes, when I mistook the silks;
Her head uncrushed by that round weight of hat
So strangely similar to the tortoise-shell
455 Which slew the tragic poet.[3]
                                    By the way,
The works of women are symbolical.
We sew, sew, prick our fingers, dull our sight,
Producing what? A pair of slippers, sir,
To put on when you're weary—or a stool
460 To stumble over and vex you . . . "curse that stool!"
Or else at best, a cushion, where you lean
And sleep, and dream of something we are not
But would be for your sake. Alas, alas!
This hurts most, this—that, after all, we are paid
465 The worth of our work, perhaps.
                                    In looking down
Those years of education (to return)
I wonder if Brinvilliers suffered more
In the water-torture[4] . . . flood succeeding flood
To drench the incapable throat and split the veins . . .
470 Than I did. Certain of your feebler souls
Go out in such a process; many pine
To a sick, inodorous light; my own endured:
I had relations in the Unseen, and drew
The elemental nutriment and heat
475 From nature, as earth feels the sun at nights,
Or as a babe sucks surely in the dark.
I kept the life thrust on me, on the outside
Of the inner life with all its ample room

---

3. The Greek playwright Aeschylus was supposed to have
been killed when an eagle, mistaking his bald head for a
stone, dropped a tortoise on it to break the shell.

4. In 1676 Marie Marguerite, Marquise de Brinvilliers,
was tortured by having water forced down her throat,
then executed.

For heart and lungs, for will and intellect,
480   Inviolable by conventions. God,
I thank thee for that grace of thine!

[DISCOVERY OF POETRY]

815   The cygnet finds the water, but the man
Is born in ignorance of his element
And feels out blind at first, disorganised
By sin i' the blood,—his spirit-insight dulled
And crossed by his sensations. Presently
820   He feels it quicken in the dark sometimes,
When, mark, be reverent, be obedient,
For such dumb motions of imperfect life
Are oracles of vital Deity
Attesting the Hereafter. Let who says
825   "The soul's a clean white paper," rather say,
A palimpsest,[5] a prophet's holograph
Defiled, erased and covered by a monk's,—
The apocalypse, by a Longus![6] poring on
Which obscene text, we may discern perhaps
830   Some fair, fine trace of what was written once,
Some upstroke of an alpha and omega
Expressing the old scripture.
                 Books, books, books!
I had found the secret of a garret-room
Piled high with cases in my father's name,
835   Piled high, packed large,—where, creeping in and out
Among the giant fossils of my past,
Like some small nimble mouse between the ribs
Of a mastodon, I nibbled here and there
At this or that box, pulling through the gap,
840   In heats of terror, haste, victorious joy,
The first book first. And how I felt it beat
Under my pillow, in the morning's dark,
An hour before the sun would let me read!
My books! At last because the time was ripe,
845   I chanced upon the poets.

          As the earth
Plunges in fury, when the internal fires
Have reached and pricked her heart, and, throwing flat
The marts and temples, the triumphal gates
And towers of observation, clears herself
850   To elemental freedom—thus, my soul,
At poetry's divine first finger-touch,

---

5. Parchment where the original writing has been scraped off so it can be reused.
6. I.e., imagine that the words of the apocalyse have been erased and written over by Longus, a Greek writer of romances.

Let go conventions and sprang up surprised,
Convicted of the great eternities
Before two worlds.

                    What's this, Aurora Leigh,
855   You write so of the poets, and not laugh?
Those virtuous liars, dreamers after dark,
Exaggerators of the sun and moon,
And soothsayers in a tea-cup?

                              I write so
Of the only truth-tellers now left to God,
860   The only speakers of essential truth,
Opposed to relative, comparative,
And temporal truths; the only holders by
His sun-skirts, through conventional gray glooms;
The only teachers who instruct mankind
865   From just a shadow on a charnel-wall[7]
To find man's veritable stature out
Erect, sublime,—the measure of a man,
And that's the measure of an angel, says
The apostle. Ay, and while your common men
870   Lay telegraphs, gauge railroads, reign, reap, dine,
And dust the flaunty carpets of the world
For kings to walk on, or our president,
The poet suddenly will catch them up
With his voice like a thunder,—"This is soul,
875   This is life, this word is being said in heaven,
Here's God down on us! what are you about?"
How all those workers start amid their work,
Look round, look up, and feel, a moment's space,
That carpet-dusting, though a pretty trade,
880   Is not the imperative labour after all.

from *Book 2*
[WOMAN AND ARTIST]

Times followed one another. Came a morn
I stood upon the brink of twenty years,
And looked before and after, as I stood
Woman and artist,—either incomplete,
5   Both credulous of completion. There I held
The whole creation in my little cup,
And smiled with thirsty lips before I drank
"Good health to you and me, sweet neighbor mine,
And all these peoples."

7. Wall of a building where bodies or bones are deposited.

I was glad, that day;
10 The June was in me, with its multitudes
Of nightingales all singing in the dark,
And rosebuds reddening where the calyx[1] split.
I felt so young, so strong, so sure of God!
So glad, I could not choose be very wise!
15 And, old at twenty, was inclined to pull
My childhood backward in a childish jest
To see the face of't once more, and farewell!
In which fantastic mood I bounded forth
At early morning,—would not wait so long
20 As even to snatch my bonnet by the strings,
But, brushing a green trail across the lawn
With my gown in the dew, took will and away
Among the acacias of the shrubberies,
To fly my fancies in the open air
25 And keep my birthday, till my aunt awoke
To stop good dreams. Meanwhile I murmured on
As honeyed bees keep humming to themselves,
"The worthiest poets have remained uncrowned
Till death has bleached their foreheads to the bone;
30 And so with me it must be unless I prove
Unworthy of the grand adversity,
And certainly I would not fail so much.
What, therefore, if I crown myself to-day
In sport, not pride, to learn the feel of it,
35 Before my brows be numbed as Dante's own
To all the tender pricking of such leaves?
Such leaves! what leaves?"

            I pulled the branches down
To choose from.

              "Not the bay![2] I choose no bay
(The fates deny us if we are overbold),
40 Nor myrtle—which means chiefly love; and love
Is something awful which one dares not touch
So early o' mornings. This verbena strains
The point of passionate fragrance; and hard by,
This guelder-rose, at far too slight a beck
45 Of the wind, will toss about her flower-apples.
Ah—there's my choice,—that ivy on the wall,
That headlong ivy! not a leaf will grow
But thinking of a wreath. Large leaves, smooth leaves,
Serrated like my vines, and half as green.
50 I like such ivy, bold to leap a height
'Twas strong to climb; as good to grow on graves
As twist about a thyrsus;[3] pretty too

---

1. The green outer leaves which protect a flowerbud.
2. Laurel; Apollo, the god of poetry, wore a wreath of   laurel leaves.
3. Ivy-covered staff carried by the Greek god Dionysus.

(And that's not ill) when twisted round a comb."
Thus speaking to myself, half singing it,
55 Because some thoughts are fashioned like a bell
To ring with once being touched, I drew a wreath
Drenched, blinding me with dew, across my brow,
And fastening it behind so, turning faced
. . . My public!—cousin Romney—with a mouth
60 Twice graver than his eyes.

              I stood there fixed,—
My arms up, like the caryatid,[4] sole
Of some abolished temple, helplessly
Persistent in a gesture which derides
A former purpose. Yet my blush was flame,
65 As if from flax, not stone.

              "Aurora Leigh,
The earliest of Auroras!"[5]

              Hand stretched out
I clasped, as shipwrecked men will clasp a hand,
Indifferent to the sort of palm. The tide
Had caught me at my pastime, writing down
70 My foolish name too near upon the sea
Which drowned me with a blush as foolish. "You,
My cousin!"
              The smile died out in his eyes
And dropped upon his lips, a cold dead weight,
For just a moment, "Here's a book I found!
75 No name writ on it—poems, by the form;
Some Greek upon the margin,—lady's Greek
Without the accents. Read it? Not a word.
I saw at once the thing had witchcraft in't,
Whereof the reading calls up dangerous spirits:
80 I rather bring it to the witch."

              "My book.
You found it" . . .

           "In the hollow by the stream
That beech leans down into—of which you said
The Oread in it has a Naiad's heart
And pines for waters."[6]

           "Thank you."
              "Thanks to *you*

85 My cousin! that I have seen you not too much
Witch, scholar, poet, dreamer, and the rest,
To be a woman also."

---

4. Female figure with upraised arms, used as a supporting architectural column.

5. Aurora, the goddess of the dawn.

6. An Oread is a tree nymph; a Naiad is a water nymph.

With a glance
The smile rose in his eyes again and touched
The ivy on my forehead, light as air.
90   I answered gravely "Poets needs must be
Or men or women—more's the pity."

"Ah,
But men, and still less women, happily,
Scarce need be poets. Keep to the green wreath,
Since even dreaming of the stone and bronze
95   Brings headaches, pretty cousin, and defiles
The clean white morning dresses."

"So you judge!
Because I love the beautiful I must
Love pleasure chiefly, and be overcharged
For ease and whiteness! well, you know the world,
100   And only miss your cousin, 'tis not much.
But learn this; I would rather take my part
With God's Dead, who afford to walk in white
Yet spread His glory, than keep quiet here
And gather up my feet from even a step
105   For fear to soil my gown in so much dust.
I choose to walk at all risks.—Here, if heads
That hold a rhythmic thought, much ache perforce,
For my part I choose headaches,—and to-day's
My birthday."

"Dear Aurora, choose instead
110   To cure them. You have balsams."

"I perceive.
The headache is too noble for my sex.
You think the heartache would sound decenter,
Since that's the woman's special, proper ache,
And altogether tolerable, except
115   To a woman."

[No Female Christ]

"There it is!—
180   You play beside a death-bed like a child,
Yet measure to yourself a prophet's place
To teach the living. None of all these things
Can women understand. You generalise
Oh, nothing,—not even grief! Your quick-breathed hearts,
185   So sympathetic to the personal pang,
Close on each separate knife-stroke, yielding up
A whole life at each wound, incapable
Of deepening, widening a large lap of life
To hold the world-full woe. The human race
190   To you means, such a child, or such a man,
You saw one morning waiting in the cold,

Beside that gate, perhaps. You gather up
A few such cases, and when strong sometimes
Will write of factories and of slaves, as if
195   Your father were a negro, and your son
A spinner in the mills. All's yours and you,
All, coloured with your blood, or otherwise
Just nothing to you. Why, I call you hard
To general suffering. Here's the world half-blind
200   With intellectual light, half-brutalised
With civilisation, having caught the plague
In silks from Tarsus,[7] shrieking east and west
Along a thousand railroads, mad with pain
And sin too! . . . does one woman of you all
205   (You who weep easily) grow pale to see
This tiger shake his cage?—does one of you
Stand still from dancing, stop from stringing pearls,
And pine and die because of the great sum
Of universal anguish?—Show me a tear
210   Wet as Cordelia's,[8] in eyes bright as yours,
Because the world is mad. You cannot count,
That you should weep for this account, not you!
You weep for what you know. A red-haired child
Sick in a fever, if you touch him once,
215   Though but so little as with a finger-tip,
Will set you weeping; but a million sick . . .
You could as soon weep for the rule of three
Or compound fractions. Therefore, this same world,
Uncomprehended by you, must remain
220   Uninfluenced by you.—Women as you are,
Mere women, personal and passionate,
You give us doating mothers, and perfect wives,
Sublime Madonnas, and enduring saints!
We get no Christ from you,—and verily
225   We shall not get a poet, in my mind."

from *Book 5*

[EPIC ART AND MODERN LIFE]

The critics say that epics have died out
140   With Agamemnon and the goat-nursed gods;[1]
I'll not believe it. I could never deem,
As Payne Knight[2] did (the mythic mountaineer

---

7. I.e., with civilized luxuries come evils, just as the trading ships bringing silks from Tarsus—a wealthy center of
trade in the ancient Middle East—might also have
brought rats that spread the plague.
8. Cordelia weeps when she is reunited with her father
(*King Lear*, 4.7.71); her feelings are entirely personal.
Romney mentions Cordelia to bolster his argument that

women cannot play any role in world affairs because they
are incapable of taking a broad view of human suffering.
1. Agamemnon led the Greeks in the Trojan War, as
chronicled in Homer's epic, the *Iliad*; Zeus was nursed by
a goat.
2. Richard Payne Knight (1750–1824), a classical scholar
who speculated about Homer and the Elgin marbles.

Who travelled higher than he was born to live,
And showed sometimes the goitre in his throat[3]
145 Discoursing of an image seen through fog),
That Homer's heroes measured twelve feet high.
They were but men:—his Helen's hair turned grey
Like any plain Miss Smith's who wears a front;[4]
And Hector's infant whimpered at a plume[5]
150 As yours last Friday at a turkey-cock.
All actual heroes are essential men,
And all men possible heroes: every age,
Heroic in proportions, double-faced,
Looks backward and before, expects a morn
155 And claims an epos.°   epic poem

        Ay, but every age
Appears to souls who live in't (ask Carlyle[6])
Most unheroic. Ours, for instance, ours:
The thinkers scout it, and the poets abound
160 Who scorn to touch it with a finger-tip:
A pewter age,[7]—mixed metal, silver-washed;
An age of scum, spooned off the richer past,
An age of patches for old gaberdines,°   overcoats
An age of mere transition,[8] meaning nought
Except that what succeeds must shame it quite
165 If God please. That's wrong thinking, to my mind,
And wrong thoughts make poor poems.

                Every age,
Through being beheld too close, is ill-discerned
By those who have not lived past it. We'll suppose
Mount Athos carved, as Alexander schemed,
170 To some colossal statue of a man.[9]
The peasants, gathering brushwood in his ear,
Had guessed as little as the browsing goats
Of form or feature of humanity
Up there,—in fact, had travelled five miles off
175 Or ere the giant image broke on them,
Full human profile, nose and chin distinct,
Mouth, muttering rhythms of silence up the sky
And fed at evening with the blood of suns;
Grand torso,—hand, that flung perpetually

3. A swelling of the throat (caused by lack of iodine in the water at high altitudes), symbolizing the foolishness of Payne Knight's utterances.
4. Hairpiece worn over the forehead; artificial bangs.
5. When the Trojan warrior Hector tried to embrace his infant son before going into battle, the baby was terrified of his father's plumed helmet.
6. In *On Heroes and Hero-Worship* (1841) Thomas Carlyle urges a renewal of the idea of the heroic.

7. Inferior to the Golden, the Silver, or even the Bronze Age; Hesiod proposed that history is a constant process of decline.
8. In *The Spirit of the Age* (1831) John Stuart Mill says the present era is "an age of transition."
9. Alexander the Great thought of having Mount Athos carved in the form of a gigantic statue of a conqueror, with a basin in one hand to collect water for the pastures below.

180 The largesse of a silver river down
To all the country pastures. 'Tis even thus
With times we live in,—evermore too great
To be apprehended near.

But poets should
Exert a double vision; should have eyes
185 To see near things as comprehensively
As if afar they took their point of sight,
And distant things as intimately deep
As if they touched them. Let us strive for this.
I do distrust the poet who discerns
190 No character or glory in his times,
And trundles back his soul five hundred years,
Past moat and drawbridge, into a castle-court,
To sing—oh, not of lizard or of toad
Alive i' the ditch there,—'twere excusable,
195 But of some black chief, half knight, half sheep-lifter,
Some beauteous dame, half chattel and half queen,
As dead as must be, for the greater part,
The poems made on their chivalric bones;
And that's no wonder: death inherits death.

200 Nay, if there's room for poets in this world
A little overgrown (I think there is),
Their sole work is to represent the age,
Their age, not Charlemagne's,[1]—this live, throbbing age,
That brawls, cheats, maddens, calculates, aspires,
205 And spends more passion, more heroic heat,
Betwixt the mirrors of its drawing-rooms,
Than Roland with his knights at Roncesvalles.[2]
To flinch from modern varnish, coat or flounce,
Cry out for togas and the picturesque,
210 Is fatal,—foolish too. King Arthur's self
Was commonplace to Lady Guenever;
And Camelot to minstrels seemed as flat
As Fleet Street to our poets.[3]

Never flinch,
But still, unscrupulously epic, catch
215 Upon the burning lava of a song
The full-veined, heaving, double-breasted Age:
That, when the next shall come, the men of that
May touch the impress with reverent hand, and say

---

1. Charlemagne was king of the Franks (768–814) and emperor of the West, laying the foundation for the Holy Roman Empire.
2. Legendary hero whose defeat at Roncesvalles (in the Spanish Pyrenees) was disastrous for Charlemagne's forces; his exploits are the subject of a medieval epic

poem, *Le Chanson de Roland*.
3. I.e., to his wife Guenevere, even the glorious King Arthur was ordinary, and his kingdom was no more a subject for the poets of his own time than Fleet Street— location of London publishers and newspaper offices—is for the poets of the 19th century.

"Behold,—behold the paps we all have sucked!
220   This bosom seems to beat still, or at least
            It sets ours beating: this is living art,
            Which thus presents and thus records true life."
1853–1856   1856

—✦✦✦—

Alfred, Lord Tennyson
1809–1892

"There, that is the first money you have ever earned by your poetry, and, take my word for it, it will be the last." These were the words of Tennyson's crusty grandfather, as he doled out ten shillings for the teenager's ode on the death of his grandmother. The pen proved mightier than the prediction, however, as Tennyson went on to become the most celebrated poet of the age. His books sold tens of thousands of copies; the Queen and Parliament named him Poet Laureate, then Lord, and finally Baron Tennyson; his annual income surpassed ten thousand pounds a year; and he was widely regarded as something more than a poet—a prophet, a sage, and an infallible moneymaker. A New York publisher once offered him a thousand pounds for any three-stanza poem he cared to write.

It is often said that Tennyson's greatness lay in eloquently presenting the anxieties and aspirations of his era. In poems such as *Ulysses*, *In Memoriam*, and *Idylls of the King*, he expressed the energy, resolve, faith, and idealism of an industrious society that was nonetheless racked by deep doubts about its materialism, the truth of the Bible, and the possibility of achieving a truly Christian society. But Tennyson was not just a mouthpiece for his age: in the early and mid-Victorian period Tennyson was one of its most progressive voices, espousing views that were all the more daring for a shy and sensitive man struggling to realize his dream of becoming "a *popular* poet." His assertion in *The Princess* (1847) that "the woman's cause is man's" anticipates Mill's *The Subjection of Women* by more than twenty years; in the course of writing *In Memoriam* (1850) he lucidly formulated some of the main principles of evolutionary theory well before Darwin's *Origin of Species* (1859); he called public attention to the industrialized misery and revolutionary anger of the poor during the 1840s while the contemporaneous works of Marx and Engels were virtually unknown; and in *Locksley Hall* (1842) he evoked the technological promise of the future as compellingly as any science fiction writer.

One key to Tennyson's poetic success was his prosaic devotion to the Victorian gospel of hard work. He labored patiently, in poverty and without recognition, to overcome his troubled background. Born in Somersby, Lincolnshire, Tennyson was the third surviving son in a close-knit but emotionally unstable family of eleven children, two of whom suffered lifelong mental illness, while two more were addicted to drugs and alcohol. The poet's father, George, was an awkward, tormented man whose ill temper was aggravated into alcoholism and violence when he was disinherited in favor of his younger brother and then forced to accept a position as village rector. It seems that the entire family was prone to epilepsy. Well into maturity, Alfred was haunted by fear of "the black blood of the Tennysons."

Tennyson's grim childhood was brightened by his mother's warmth and affection, his father's extensive library, and both parents' love of poetry. The rectory was surrounded by large gardens and open countryside, and as a child Tennyson composed nature poetry in the manner of James Thomson's *Seasons*. Early years at a brutally strict grammar school, followed by intensive tutoring from his erudite father, gave Tennyson a solid grounding in Greek, Latin, English, and modern languages by the time he went to Cambridge University in 1827. He had already mastered the styles of poets ranging from Horace and Virgil to Shakespeare, Milton, Scott, and Byron, and earlier that year he published his first book, *Poems by Two Brothers*. It was written with his brother Charles, with whom he used to exchange lines on their country walks, shouting them out across the hedges. The habit of building poems around a series of sonorous individual lines would remain with Tennyson all his life.

At Cambridge the timid country boy began gradually to assume the artistic persona that would be revered throughout the empire. Tall, ruggedly handsome, and with a faraway look in his eyes that was actually due to myopia, Tennyson fit everyone's idea of how a poet should look. He distinguished himself by the quality of his talk, his humorous storytelling, and his acting ability. In 1829 he received the Chancellor's Medal for *Timbuctoo*, the first poem in blank verse ever to win. The same year he and his best friend Arthur Henry Hallam joined "The Apostles," a select group of undergraduates who met to discuss social, philosophical, and literary issues. Members became lifelong friends, and their admiration of his early work helped convince the reticent Tennyson to publish *Poems, Chiefly Lyrical* in 1830. The book received mixed reviews.

In 1831 his father died, and Tennyson had to return home without a degree. Yet Tennyson persevered, issuing in 1832 a new volume, *Poems*. This time, the reviews were actively hostile. Tennyson's morale was sustained only by the visits to Somersby of Hallam, who by now was engaged to Tennyson's sister Emily. Then in 1833 Hallam died suddenly of a cerebral hemorrhage while on a trip to Vienna, and Tennyson's life changed forever.

Within a week of hearing the news, Tennyson began work on his greatest poem, though he did not know then that the brief lyric passages of love, loss, and doubt that he composed to assuage his grief would eventually become *In Memoriam*, an epic meditation on mortality, evolution, and the hard-won consolations of inner faith. He was already proficient, like his early hero Byron, in turning his own private misery into virtuoso evocations of emotionally charged landscapes. As John Stuart Mill wrote in 1835, Tennyson excelled in "the power of *creating* scenery, in keeping with some state of human feeling, so fitted to it as to be the embodied symbol of it, and to summon up the state of feeling itself, with a force not to be surpassed by anything but reality." Quoting *Mariana* as an example, Mill concluded that "words surely never created a more vivid feeling of physical and spiritual dreariness."

Outwardly Tennyson was calm, actively reading, writing, and socializing, but in his poetry he pictured himself as a weeping widower who mourned "a loss forever new." In 1842 he reluctantly published a two-volume edition of *Poems*, improving earlier works and introducing new ones, most notably *Ulysses* and *Morte d'Arthur*. Although his reputation was now rising, the poet was at a low ebb. He was so poor and hampered by responsibilities to his unraveling family that he was forced to postpone indefinitely his marriage to Emily Sellwood, to whom he had become engaged in 1838.

At this point Tennyson lost all his money in a scheme for carving wood by machinery. His friends feared he was on the verge of suicide. Here, as at other dark times in his life, he relied on sheer willpower to follow the advice he once offered to a depressed friend: "Just go grimly on." Eventually travel, hydropathic cures, new acquaintances, and improving finances assuaged his melancholia. Publication of *The Princess* in 1847 finally gave him the popular notice he had long sought.

But it was not until 1850 that Tennyson triumphed in life and art. In May, after seventeen years' brooding, he published *In Memoriam* to great acclaim; on June 13 he married Emily; and by the end of June one reviewer was calling him "the greatest living poet." The sentiment was timely, since Wordsworth had died in April, and by November Tennyson was named Poet Laureate. In 1852 his first son, Hallam, was born, and in 1853 the Tennysons moved to a neo-Gothic country estate called Farringford on the Isle of Wight.

His experimental "monodrama" *Maud* (1855) sold well though it baffled the critics, one of whom remarked that there was one vowel too many, no matter which, in the title. But the combined sales of his works enabled him to buy Farringford, where he could work in peace

Max Beerbohm, *Tennyson Reading "In Memoriam" to his Sovereign,* 1904.

amid wreaths of tobacco smoke, adored by Emily and protected from his fans by a large staff. There he entertained great personages of the day, from Prince Albert and Garibaldi to his neighbor Julia Margaret Cameron, who badgered him into photographic immortality. Henceforth, whenever he visited London, he was sought after in society and mobbed by admirers.

The stability of his new life enabled Tennyson to pursue many longer projects, including the best-selling narrative poem *Enoch Arden* (1864) and several successful plays. Most of his energies were taken up, however, with the great work of his later life, *Idylls of the King.* A trip to Wales helped fuel his interest in Arthurian legends, and he published groups of *Idylls* in 1859 and 1869. As with *In Memoriam* and *Maud,* the poet gradually felt his way, as he composed the parts, toward a larger design for the whole. All the while he held before him the image of "my lost Arthur," until recollections of his actual friend Arthur Hallam blended with the two literary Arthurs of *In Memoriam* and *Idylls of the King.* He rounded out his tale to an epic twelve books, not producing a final version until 1888, just a few years before his death.

In the *Idylls* as in much of his earlier poetry, Tennyson is a poet of deferment. His most memorable characters—Mariana, the Lotos Eaters, Ulysses, Tithonus, and the speakers of *In Memoriam* and *Maud,* among them—long for reunions and releases that are ever yet to come, as distant as the return of King Arthur from Avalon. In old age Tennyson remembered of his youth that even before he could read, "the words 'far, far away' always had a strange charm for me."

After Tennyson's death in 1892 and his burial with great pomp in Westminster Abbey, his reputation suffered a decline that lasted till the end of the Modernist period around 1945. But Tennyson's lyric genius was admired by poets as various as the Pre-Raphaelites and Whitman, Poe, and Hopkins. Auden and Eliot were in rare agreement that he had "the finest ear of any English poet since Milton." Critics continue to dispute whether the sense of Tennyson's poetry is equal to its magnificent sound, but any close reading of his work will reveal Tennyson's deep ambivalence about the world of which he gradually became both oracle and icon. Often beneath his harmonies we hear echoes of his favorite childhood sound, "voices crying in the wind." As Eliot observed, Tennyson was "the most instinctive rebel against the society in which he was the most perfect conformist."

The Kraken[1]

Below the thunders of the upper deep;
Far, far beneath in the abysmal sea,
His ancient, dreamless, uninvaded sleep
The Kraken sleepeth: faintest sunlights flee
5   About his shadowy sides: above him swell
Huge sponges of millennial growth and height;
And far away into the sickly light,
From many a wondrous grot° and secret cell   grotto, cave
Unnumber'd and enormous polypi°   octopuses
10   Winnow with giant arms the slumbering green.
There hath he lain for ages and will lie
Battening upon huge seaworms in his sleep,
Until the latter fire[2] shall heat the deep;
Then once by man and angels to be seen,
15   In roaring he shall rise and on the surface die.

1830

Mariana

"Mariana in the moated grange."[1]

Measure for Measure

With blackest moss the flower-plots
    Were thickly crusted, one and all:
The rusted nails fell from the knots
    That held the pear to the gable-wall.
5   The broken sheds look'd sad and strange:
        Unlifted was the clinking latch;
        Weeded and worn the ancient thatch
Upon the lonely moated grange.
    She only said, "My life is dreary,
10   He cometh not," she said;
        She said, "I am aweary, aweary,
            I would that I were dead!"

Her tears fell with the dews at even;
    Her tears fell ere the dews were dried;
15   She could not look on the sweet heaven,
        Either at morn or eventide.
After the flitting of the bats,
    When thickest dark did trance° the sky,   traverse
    She drew her casement-curtain by,
20   And glanced athwart the glooming flats.

1. Giant mythical sea monster.
2. The fire of Judgment Day, which will consume the world.
1. The *moated grange* was no particular grange, but one which rose to the music of Shakespeare's words: "There,

at the moated grange, resides this dejected Mariana" (*Measure for Measure* Act 3. Sc. 1) [Tennyson's note]. In Shakespeare's play, Angelo refuses to marry Mariana after her brother and her dowry are lost in a shipwreck. See Sir John Everett Millais's painting *Mariana* (Color Plate 11).

She only said, "The night is dreary,
  He cometh not," she said;
She said, "I am aweary, aweary,
  I would that I were dead!"

25 Upon the middle of the night,
      Waking she heard the night-fowl crow:
    The cock sung out an hour ere light:
      From the dark fen the oxen's low
    Came to her: without hope of change,
30   In sleep she seem'd to walk forlorn,
      Till cold winds woke the gray-eyed morn
    About the lonely moated grange.
      She only said, "The day is dreary,
        He cometh not," she said;
35   She said, "I am aweary, aweary,
        I would that I were dead!"

    About a stone-cast from the wall
      A sluice with blacken'd waters slept,
    And o'er it many, round and small,
40   The cluster'd marish-mosses² crept.
    Hard by a poplar shook alway,
      All silver-green with gnarled bark:
      For leagues no other tree did mark
    The level waste, the rounding gray.
45   She only said, "My life is dreary,
        He cometh not," she said;
      She said, "I am aweary, aweary,
        I would that I were dead!"

    And ever when the moon was low,
50   And the shrill winds were up and away,
    In the white curtain, to and fro,
      She saw the gusty shadow sway.
    But when the moon was very low,
      And wild winds bound within their cell,³
55   The shadow of the poplar fell
    Upon her bed, across her brow.
      She only said, "The night is dreary,
        He cometh not," she said;
      She said, "I am aweary, aweary,
60   I would that I were dead!"

    All day within the dreamy house,
      The doors upon their hinges creak'd;
    The blue fly sung in the pane; the mouse

---

2. The little marsh-moss lumps that float on the surface   3. The cave of Aeolus, god of the winds.
of water [Tennyson's note].

Behind the mouldering wainscot shriek'd,
65   Or from the crevice peer'd about.
    Old faces glimmer'd thro' the doors,
    Old footsteps trod the upper floors,
Old voices called her from without.
    She only said, "My life is dreary,
70   He cometh not," she said;
    She said, "I am aweary, aweary,
      I would that I were dead!"

The sparrow's chirrup on the roof,
  The slow clock ticking, and the sound
75 Which to the wooing wind aloof
  The poplar made, did all confound
Her sense; but most she loathed the hour
  When the thick-moted sunbeam lay
  Athwart the chambers, and the day
80 Was sloping toward his western bower.
    Then, said she, "I am very dreary,
      He will not come," she said;
    She wept, "I am aweary, aweary,
      Oh God, that I were dead!"

                                1830

The Lady of Shalott[1]
Part 1

On either side the river lie
Long fields of barley and of rye,
That clothe the wold° and meet the sky;   *rolling uplands*
And thro' the field the road runs by
5   To many-tower'd Camelot;
And up and down the people go,
Gazing where the lilies blow°   *bloom*
Round an island there below,
    The island of Shalott.

10 Willows whiten, aspens quiver,
Little breezes dusk and shiver
Thro' the wave that runs for ever
By the island in the river
    Flowing down to Camelot.
15 Four gray walls, and four gray towers,
Overlook a space of flowers,
And the silent isle imbowers
    The Lady of Shalott.

---

1. The Lady of Shalott is evidently the Elaine of the *Morte d'Arthur*, but I do not think that I had ever heard of the latter when I wrote the former [Tennyson's note]. In Malory, Elaine dies of grief for love of Lancelot, but the curse, the weaving, and the mirror are all Tennyson's inventions.

William Holman Hunt, *The Lady of Shalott*, from the Moxon edition of Tennyson's poems, 1857. This edition was a high point in Victorian book illustration, including drawings by Rossetti and Millais as well as Hunt. Tennyson, however, complained about this illustration because it depicts the lady entangled in the threads of her tapestry, making her unable to leave the loom, as she does in his poem. Hunt responded: "I had only half a page on which to convey the impression of weird fate, whereas you use about fifteen pages to give expression to the complete idea." See also *The Lady of Shalott* by John Williams Waterhouse (Color Plate 19).

	By the margin, willow-veil'd,	
20	Slide the heavy barges trail'd	
	By slow horses; and unhail'd	
	The shallop° flitteth silken-sail'd	*small boat*
	Skimming down to Camelot:	
	But who hath seen her wave her hand?	
25	Or at the casement seen her stand?	
	Or is she known in all the land,	
	The Lady of Shalott?	

Only reapers, reaping early
In among the bearded barley,
30   Hear a song that echoes cheerly
From the river winding clearly,
     Down to tower'd Camelot:
And by the moon the reaper weary,
Piling sheaves in uplands airy,
35   Listening, whispers "'Tis the fairy
     Lady of Shalott.'"

Part 2

There she weaves by night and day
A magic web with colours gay.
She has heard a whisper say,
40   A curse is on her if she stay
     To look down to Camelot.

She knows not what the curse may be,
And so she weaveth steadily,
And little other care hath she,
45   The Lady of Shalott.

And moving thro' a mirror clear[2]
That hangs before her all the year,
Shadows of the world appear.
There she sees the highway near
50   Winding down to Camelot:
There the river eddy whirls,
And there the surly village-churls,°   peasants
And the red cloaks of market girls,
          Pass onward from Shalott.

55   Sometimes a troop of damsels glad,
An abbot on an ambling pad,°   horse
Sometimes a curly shepherd-lad,
Or long-hair'd page in crimson clad,
          Goes by to tower'd Camelot;
60   And sometimes thro' the mirror blue
The knights come riding two and two:
She hath no loyal knight and true,
          The Lady of Shalott.

But in her web she still delights
65   To weave the mirror's magic sights,
For often thro' the silent nights
A funeral, with plumes and lights
          And music, went to Camelot:
Or when the moon was overhead,
70   Came two young lovers lately wed;
"I am half sick of shadows," said
          The Lady of Shalott.

Part 3

A bow-shot from her bower-eaves,
He rode between the barley-sheaves,
75   The sun came dazzling thro' the leaves,
And flamed upon the brazen greaves°   leg armor
          Of bold Sir Lancelot.[3]
A red-cross knight for ever kneel'd
To a lady in his shield,[4]
80   That sparkled on the yellow field,
          Beside remote Shalott.

2. Working from the back of their tapestries, weavers placed mirrors on the other side to see the effect of their work.
3. The greatest of King Arthur's knights, Lancelot was in love with Queen Guinevere.
4. Lancelot's shield depicts the Redcrosse Knight—a character in Spenser's *Faerie Queene* who champions holiness—kneeling in homage to his lady.

The gemmy bridle glitter'd free,
Like to some branch of stars we see
Hung in the golden Galaxy.
85   The bridle bells rang merrily
      As he rode down to Camelot:
And from his blazon'd baldric° slung   *ornamented belt*
A mighty silver bugle hung,
And as he rode his armour rung,
90   Beside remote Shalott.

All in the blue unclouded weather
Thick-jewell'd shone the saddle-leather,
The helmet and the helmet-feather
Burn'd like one burning flame together,
95   As he rode down to Camelot.
As often thro' the purple night,
Below the starry clusters bright,
Some bearded meteor, trailing light,
      Moves over still Shalott.

100   His broad clear brow in sunlight glow'd;
On burnish'd hooves his war-horse trode;
From underneath his helmet flow'd
His coal-black curls as on he rode,
      As he rode down to Camelot.
105   From the bank and from the river
He flash'd into the crystal mirror,
"Tirra lirra," by the river
      Sang Sir Lancelot.

She left the web, she left the loom,
110   She made three paces thro' the room,
She saw the water-lily bloom,
She saw the helmet and the plume,
      She look'd down to Camelot.
Out flew the web and floated wide;
115   The mirror crack'd from side to side;
"The curse is come upon me," cried
      The Lady of Shalott.

Part 4

In the stormy east-wind straining,
The pale yellow woods were waning,
120   The broad stream in his banks complaining,
Heavily the low sky raining
      Over tower'd Camelot;
Down she came and found a boat
Beneath a willow left afloat,
125   And round about the prow she wrote
      The Lady of Shalott.

And down the river's dim expanse
Like some bold seër in a trance,
Seeing all his own mischance—
130   With a glassy countenance
     Did she look to Camelot.
And at the closing of the day
She loosed the chain, and down she lay;
The broad stream bore her far away,
135   The Lady of Shalott.

Lying, robed in snowy white
That loosely flew to left and right—
The leaves upon her falling light—
Thro' the noises of the night
140   She floated down to Camelot:
And as the boat-head wound along
The willowy hills and fields among,
They heard her singing her last song,
     The Lady of Shalott.

145   Heard a carol, mournful, holy,
Chanted loudly, chanted lowly,
Till her blood was frozen slowly,
And her eyes were darken'd wholly,
     Turn'd to tower'd Camelot.
150   For ere she reach'd upon the tide
The first house by the water-side,
Singing in her song she died,
     The Lady of Shalott.

Under tower and balcony,
155   By garden-wall and gallery,
A gleaming shape she floated by,
Dead-pale between the houses high,
     Silent into Camelot.
Out upon the wharfs they came;
160   Knight and burgher, lord and dame,
And round the prow they read her name,
     The Lady of Shalott.

Who is this? and what is here?
And in the lighted palace near
165   Died the sound of royal cheer;
And they cross'd themselves for fear,
     All the knights at Camelot:
But Lancelot mused a little space;
He said, "She has a lovely face;
170   God in his mercy lend her grace,
     The Lady of Shalott."

                                    1832, 1842

Falls, and floats adown the air.
Lo! sweeten'd with the summer light,
The full-juiced apple, waxing over-mellow,
Drops in a silent autumn night.
80   All its allotted length of days,
The flower ripens in its place,
Ripens and fades, and falls, and hath no toil,
Fast-rooted in the fruitful soil.

4

Hateful is the dark-blue sky,
85   Vaulted o'er the dark-blue sea.
Death is the end of life; ah, why
Should life all labour be?
Let us alone. Time driveth onward fast,
And in a little while our lips are dumb.
90   Let us alone. What is it that will last?
All things are taken from us, and become
Portions and parcels of the dreadful Past.
Let us alone. What pleasure can we have
To war with evil? Is there any peace
95   In ever climbing up the climbing wave?
All things have rest, and ripen toward the grave
In silence; ripen, fall and cease:
Give us long rest or death, dark death, or dreamful ease.

5

How sweet it were, hearing the downward stream,
100   With half-shut eyes ever to seem
Falling asleep in a half-dream!
To dream and dream, like yonder amber light,
Which will not leave the myrrh-bush on the height;
To hear each other's whisper'd speech;
105   Eating the Lotos day by day,
To watch the crisping ripples on the beach,
And tender curving lines of creamy spray;
To lend our hearts and spirits wholly
To the influence of mild-minded melancholy;
110   To muse and brood and live again in memory,
With those old faces of our infancy
Heap'd over with a mound of grass,
Two handfuls of white dust, shut in an urn of brass!

6

Dear is the memory of our wedded lives,
115   And dear the last embraces of our wives
And their warm tears: but all hath suffer'd change:
For surely now our household hearths are cold:
Our sons inherit us: our looks are strange:
And we should come like ghosts to trouble joy.

120   Or else the island princes[9] over-bold
      Have eat our substance, and the minstrel sings
      Before them of the ten years' war in Troy,[1]
      And our great deeds, as half-forgotten things.
      Is there confusion in the little isle?
125   Let what is broken so remain.
      The Gods are hard to reconcile:
      'Tis hard to settle order once again.
      There *is* confusion worse than death,
      Trouble on trouble, pain on pain,
130   Long labour unto aged breath,
      Sore task to hearts worn out by many wars
      And eyes grown dim with gazing on the pilot-stars.

7

      But, propt on beds of amaranth and moly,[2]
      How sweet (while warm airs lull us, blowing lowly)
135   With half-dropt eyelid still,
      Beneath a heaven dark and holy,
      To watch the long bright river drawing slowly
      His waters from the purple hill—
      To hear the dewy echoes calling
140   From cave to cave thro' the thick-twined vine—
      To watch the emerald-colour'd water falling
      Thro' many a wov'n acanthus-wreath[3] divine!
      Only to hear and see the far-off sparkling brine,
      Only to hear were sweet, stretch'd out beneath the pine.

8

145   The Lotos blooms below the barren peak:
      The Lotos blows by every winding creek:
      All day the wind breathes low with mellower tone:
      Thro' every hollow cave and alley lone
      Round and round the spicy downs the yellow Lotos-dust is blown.
150   We have had enough of action, and of motion we,
      Roll'd to starboard, roll'd to larboard, when the surge was seething free,
      Where the wallowing monster spouted his foam-fountains in the sea.
      Let us swear an oath, and keep it with an equal mind,
      In the hollow Lotos-land to live and lie reclined
155   On the hills like Gods together, careless of mankind.
      For they lie beside their nectar, and the bolts[4] are hurl'd
      Far below them in the valleys, and the clouds are lightly curl'd
      Round their golden houses, girdled with the gleaming world:

---

9. The suitors of Penelope, Odysseus's wife and presumed widow.

1. The Trojan War, from which Odysseus and his men are returning.

2. *Amaranth*, the immortal flower of legend; *moly*, the sacred herb of mystical power, used as a charm by Odysseus against Circe [Tennyson's note].

3. The plant seen in the capitals of Corinthian pillars [Tennyson's note].

4. Nectar is the food of the gods, and thunderbolts their weapons.

Where they smile in secret, looking over wasted lands,
160 Blight and famine, plague and earthquake, roaring deeps and fiery sands,
Clanging fights, and flaming towns, and sinking ships, and praying hands.
But they smile, they find a music centred in a doleful song
Steaming up, a lamentation and an ancient tale of wrong,
Like a tale of little meaning tho' the words are strong;
165 Chanted from an ill-used race of men that cleave the soil,
Sow the seed, and reap the harvest with enduring toil,
Storing yearly little dues of wheat, and wine and oil;
Till they perish and they suffer—some, 'tis whisper'd—down in hell
Suffer endless anguish, others in Elysian[5] valleys dwell,
170 Resting weary limbs at last on beds of asphodel.[6]
Surely, surely, slumber is more sweet than toil, the shore
Than labour in the deep mid-ocean, wind and wave and oar;
Oh rest ye, brother mariners, we will not wander more.

1832, 1842

Ulysses[1]

It little profits that an idle king,
By this still hearth, among these barren crags,
Match'd with an aged wife, I mete and dole
Unequal laws unto a savage race,
5 That hoard, and sleep, and feed, and know not me.

I cannot rest from travel: I will drink
Life to the lees: all times I have enjoy'd
Greatly, have suffer'd greatly, both with those
That loved me, and alone; on shore, and when
10 Thro' scudding drifts the rainy Hyades[2]
Vext the dim sea: I am become a name;
For always roaming with a hungry heart
Much have I seen and known; cities of men
And manners, climates, councils, governments,
15 Myself not least, but honour'd of them all;
And drunk delight of battle with my peers,
Far on the ringing plains of windy Troy.
I am a part of all that I have met;
Yet all experience is an arch wherethro'
20 Gleams that untravell'd world, whose margin fades

5. Paradisical; Elysium was the part of the underworld where the blessed dwelled after death.
6. Flowering plant of the lily family, said to grow in the Elysian fields.
1. The poem was written soon after Arthur Hallam's death, and it gives the feeling about the need of going further and braving the struggle of life perhaps more simply than anything in *In Memoriam* [Tennyson's note]. In Homer's *Odyssey*, Ulysses returns home to Ithaca, after ten years of wandering following the fall of Troy, and slays the suitors who have been harassing his wife

Penelope. "My father," wrote Tennyson's son, "takes up the story of further wanderings at the end of the *Odyssey*. Ulysses has lived in Ithaca for a long while before the craving for fresh travel seizes him. The comrades he addresses are of the same heroic mould as his old comrades." Dante also has Ulysses set off on another voyage, this time westward through the Strait of Gibraltar (*Inferno* 26).
2. The Hyades were a constellation of seven stars whose rising was believed to bring rain.

For ever and for ever when I move.
How dull it is to pause, to make an end,
To rust unburnish'd, not to shine in use!
As tho' to breathe were life. Life piled on life
25   Were all too little, and of one to me
Little remains: but every hour is saved
From that eternal silence, something more,
A bringer of new things; and vile it were
For some three suns to store and hoard myself,
30   And this gray spirit yearning in desire
To follow knowledge like a sinking star,
Beyond the utmost bound of human thought.

This is my son, mine own Telemachus,
To whom I leave the sceptre and the isle—
35   Well-loved of me, discerning to fulfil
This labour, by slow prudence to make mild
A rugged people, and thro' soft degrees
Subdue them to the useful and the good.
Most blameless is he, centred in the sphere
40   Of common duties, decent not to fail
In offices of tenderness, and pay
Meet adoration to my household gods,
When I am gone. He works his work, I mine.

There lies the port; the vessel puffs her sail:
45   There gloom the dark broad seas. My mariners,
Souls that have toil'd, and wrought, and thought with me—
That ever with a frolic welcome took
The thunder and the sunshine, and opposed
Free hearts, free foreheads—you and I are old;
50   Old age hath yet his honour and his toil;
Death closes all: but something ere the end,
Some work of noble note, may yet be done,
Not unbecoming men that strove with Gods.
The lights begin to twinkle from the rocks:
55   The long day wanes: the slow moon climbs: the deep
Moans round with many voices. Come, my friends,
'Tis not too late to seek a newer world.
Push off, and sitting well in order smite
The sounding furrows; for my purpose holds
60   To sail beyond the sunset, and the baths
Of all the western stars,[3] until I die.
It may be that the gulfs will wash us down:
It may be we shall touch the Happy Isles,[4]

---

3. The Greeks believed that the flat earth was encircled by an ocean into which the stars dipped at times.
4. The Islands of the Blessed were a land of perpetual summer thought to lie in the western ocean beyond the Pillars of Hercules (the Straits of Gibraltar). Great heroes—such as Achilles, the Greek warrior who killed the Trojan prince, Hector—were sent by the gods to live there as immortals.

And see the great Achilles, whom we knew.
65 Tho' much is taken, much abides; and tho'
We are not now that strength which in old days
Moved earth and heaven; that which we are, we are;
One equal temper of heroic hearts,
Made weak by time and fate, but strong in will
70 To strive, to seek, to find, and not to yield.
1833   1842

Tithonus[1]

The woods decay, the woods decay and fall,
The vapours weep their burthen to the ground,
Man comes and tills the field and lies beneath,
And after many a summer dies the swan.[2]
5 Me only cruel immortality
Consumes: I wither slowly in thine arms,[3]
Here at the quiet limit of the world,
A white-hair'd shadow roaming like a dream
The ever-silent spaces of the East,
10 Far-folded mists, and gleaming halls of morn.

   Alas! for this gray shadow, once a man—
So glorious in his beauty and thy choice,
Who madest him thy chosen, that he seem'd
To his great heart none other than a God!
15 I ask'd thee, "Give me immortality."
Then didst thou grant mine asking with a smile,
Like wealthy men who care not how they give.
But thy strong Hours indignant work'd their wills,
And beat me down and marr'd and wasted me,
20 And tho' they could not end me, left me maim'd
To dwell in presence of immortal youth,
Immortal age beside immortal youth,
And all I was, in ashes. Can thy love,
Thy beauty, make amends, tho' even now,
25 Close over us, the silver star,[4] thy guide,
Shines in those tremulous eyes that fill with tears
To hear me? Let me go: take back thy gift:
Why should a man desire in any way
To vary from the kindly race of men,
30 Or pass beyond the goal of ordinance[5]
Where all should pause, as is most meet for all?

1. Beloved by Aurora, who gave him eternal life but not eternal youth. He grew old and infirm, and as he could not die, according to the legend, was turned into a grasshopper [Tennyson's note]. Aurora was the goddess of the dawn.
2. Swans can live as many as 50 years.
3. Tithonus ages in Aurora's arms.
4. Venus, the morning star, is Aurora's guide because it shines just before the dawn.
5. Appointed limit [Tennyson's note]; i.e., to exceed the ordained length of ordinary human life.

A soft air fans the cloud apart; there comes
A glimpse of that dark world where I was born.
Once more the old mysterious glimmer steals
35 From thy pure brows, and from thy shoulders pure,
And bosom beating with a heart renew'd.
Thy cheek begins to redden thro' the gloom,
Thy sweet eyes brighten slowly close to mine,
Ere yet they blind the stars, and the wild team[6]
40 Which love thee, yearning for thy yoke, arise,
And shake the darkness from their loosen'd manes,
And beat the twilight into flakes of fire.

Lo! ever thus thou growest beautiful
In silence, then before thine answer given
45 Departest, and thy tears are on my cheek.

Why wilt thou ever scare me with thy tears,
And make me tremble lest a saying learnt,
In days far-off, on that dark earth, be true?
"The Gods themselves cannot recall their gifts."

50 Ay me! ay me! with what another heart
In days far-off, and with what other eyes
I used to watch—if I be he that watch'd—
The lucid outline forming round thee; saw
The dim curls kindle into sunny rings;
55 Changed with thy mystic change, and felt my blood
Glow with the glow that slowly crimson'd all
Thy presence and thy portals, while I lay,
Mouth, forehead, eyelids, growing dewy-warm
With kisses balmier than half-opening buds
60 Of April, and could hear the lips that kiss'd
Whispering I knew not what of wild and sweet,
Like that strange song I heard Apollo sing,
While Ilion like a mist rose into towers.[7]

Yet hold me not for ever in thine East:
65 How can my nature longer mix with thine?
Coldly thy rosy shadows bathe me, cold
Are all thy lights, and cold my wrinkled feet
Upon thy glimmering thresholds, when the steam
Floats up from those dim fields about the homes
70 Of happy men that have the power to die,
And grassy barrows of the happier dead.
Release me, and restore me to the ground;
Thou seëst all things, thou wilt see my grave:
Thou wilt renew thy beauty morn by morn;

6. The horses of dawn, who pull Aurora's chariot into the sky each morning.

7. Apollo built the walls of Ilion (Troy) with the music of his lyre.

75   I earth in earth forget these empty courts,
      And thee returning on thy silver wheels.
1833, 1859   1860

Break, Break, Break[1]

Break, break, break,
    On thy cold gray stones, O Sea!
And I would that my tongue could utter
    The thoughts that arise in me.

5   O well for the fisherman's boy,
      That he shouts with his sister at play!
    O well for the sailor lad,
      That he sings in his boat on the bay!

And the stately ships go on
10   To their haven under the hill;
But O for the touch of a vanish'd hand,
    And the sound of a voice that is still!

Break, break, break
    At the foot of thy crags, O Sea!
15   But the tender grace of a day that is dead
      Will never come back to me.

1834   1842

The Epic [Morte d'Arthur][1]

At Francis Allen's on the Christmas-eve,—
The game of forfeits[2] done—the girls all kiss'd
Beneath the sacred bush° and past away—   *mistletoe*
The parson Holmes, the poet Everard Hall,
5   The host, and I sat round the wassail-bowl,°   *punch bowl*
Then half-way ebb'd: and there we held a talk,
How all the old honour had from Christmas gone,
Or gone, or dwindled down to some odd games
In some odd nooks like this; till I, tired out
10   With cutting eights that day upon the pond,
Where, three times slipping from the outer edge,
I bump'd the ice into three several stars,
Fell in a doze; and half-awake I heard
The parson taking wide and wider sweeps,
15   Now harping on the church-commissioners,[3]

1. Inspired by the death of the poet's friend, Arthur Hallam. Cf. In Memoriam, page 659.
1. One of Tennyson's lifelong projects was an epic poem about King Arthur, which ultimately became *Idylls of the King*. The last poem in the sequence, describing the death of Arthur, was actually written first: it was begun in 1833, when Arthur Hallam died, and was called *Morte d'Arthur*. Tennyson framed the poem with *The Epic*, a description of contemporary (i.e., 19th century) Christmas Eve festivities, during which the poet—here called Everard Hall—was encouraged to read *Morte d'Arthur* aloud.
2. A party game where players have to forfeit an item, then redeem it by performing a silly task.
3. In 1835 the government set up a system of commissioners to oversee the finances of the Anglican Church.

Now hawking at Geology and schism;[4]
Until I woke, and found him settled down
Upon the general decay of faith
Right thro' the world, "at home was little left,
20 And none abroad: there was no anchor, none,
To hold by." Francis, laughing, clapt his hand
On Everard's shoulder, with "I hold by him."
"And I," quoth Everard, "by the wassail-bowl."
"Why yes," I said, "we knew your gift that way
25 At college: but another which you had,
I mean of verse (for so we held it then),
What came of that?" "You know," said Frank, "he burnt
His epic, his King Arthur, some twelve books"—
And then to me demanding why? "Oh, sir,
30 He thought that nothing new was said, or else
Something so said 'twas nothing—that a truth
Looks freshest in the fashion of the day;
God knows: he has a mint of reasons: ask.
It pleased *me* well enough." "Nay, nay," said Hall,
35 "Why take the style of those heroic times?
For nature brings not back the Mastodon,
Nor we those times; and why should any man
Remodel models? these twelve books of mine
Were faint Homeric echoes,[5] nothing-worth,
40 Mere chaff and draff, much better burnt." "But I,"
Said Francis, "pick'd the eleventh from this hearth
And have it: keep a thing, its use will come.
I hoard it as a sugar-plum for Holmes."
He laugh'd, and I, tho' sleepy, like a horse
45 That hears the corn-bin open, prick'd my ears;
For I remember'd Everard's college fame
When we were Freshmen: then at my request
He brought it; and the poet little urged,
But with some prelude of disparagement,
50 Read, mouthing out his hollow oes and aes,
Deep-chested music, and to this result.[6]

                    * * *

    Here ended Hall, and our last light, that long
325 Had wink'd and threaten'd darkness, flared and fell:
At which the Parson, sent to sleep with sound,
And waked with silence, grunted "Good!" but we

---

4. A reference to current scientific and religious controversies.
5. I.e., Hall claims his poems merely echoed the great epics of Homer. He may have been fishing for a compliment: when the poet Walter Savage Landor read Tennyson's

Morte d'Arthur in manuscript, he declared, "it is more Homeric than any poem of our time, and rivals some of the noblest parts of the Odyssey."
6. At this point Hall reads aloud *Morte d'Arthur.* (See lines 170–440 of *The Passing of Arthur.*)

Sat rapt: it was the tone with which he read—
Perhaps some modern touches here and there
330 Redeem'd it from the charge of nothingness—
Or else we loved the man, and prized his work;
I know not: but we sitting, as I said,
The cock crew loud; as at that time of year
The lusty bird takes every hour for dawn:
335 Then Francis, muttering, like a man ill-used,
"There now—that's nothing!" drew a little back,
And drove his heel into the smoulder'd log,
That sent a blast of sparkles up the flue:
And so to bed; where yet in sleep I seem'd
340 To sail with Arthur under looming shores,
Point after point; till on to dawn, when dreams
Begin to feel the truth and stir of day,
To me, methought, who waited with a crowd,
There came a bark that, blowing forward, bore
345 King Arthur, like a modern gentleman
Of stateliest port;° and all the people cried,   *bearing*
"Arthur is come again: he cannot die."[7]
Then those that stood upon the hills behind
Repeated—"Come again, and thrice as fair;"
350 And, further inland, voices echo'd—"Come
With all good things, and war shall be no more."
At this a hundred bells began to peal,
That with the sound I woke, and heard indeed
The clear church-bells ring in the Christmas-morn.

1833–1838   1842

from THE PRINCESS[1]
Sweet and Low

Sweet and low, sweet and low,
  Wind of the western sea,
Low, low, breathe and blow,
  Wind of the western sea!
5 Over the rolling waters go,
Come from the dying moon, and blow,
  Blow him again to me;
While my little one, while my pretty one, sleeps.

7. There is a legend that King Arthur will return once more to lead his people.
1. *The Princess* (1847) is a long narrative poem, set in a fairy-tale realm, about the effort to found a women's college. (The first British institution for the higher educa-

tion of women, Queen's College, London, opened the next year.) The story is interspersed with brief "songs" or lyrics—some of them added later—whose musicality and depth of emotion soon won them admiration as independent works of art.

Sleep and rest, sleep and rest,
10   Father will come to thee soon;
Rest, rest, on mother's breast,
            Father will come to thee soon;
Father will come to his babe in the nest,
Silver sails all out of the west
15   Under the silver moon:
Sleep, my little one, sleep, my pretty one, sleep.

Come Down, O Maid[1]

Come down, O maid, from yonder mountain height:
What pleasure lives in height (the shepherd sang)
In height and cold, the splendour of the hills?
But cease to move so near the Heavens, and cease
5   To glide a sunbeam by the blasted Pine,
To sit a star upon the sparkling spire;
And come, for Love is of the valley, come,
For Love is of the valley, come thou down
And find him; by the happy threshold, he,
10   Or hand in hand with Plenty in the maize,
Or red with spirted purple of the vats,
Or foxlike in the vine; nor cares to walk
With Death and Morning on the silver horns,[2]
Nor wilt thou snare him in the white ravine,
15   Nor find him dropt upon the firths of ice,°   *glaciers*
That huddling slant in furrow-cloven falls
To roll the torrent out of dusky doors:[3]
But follow; let the torrent dance thee down
To find him in the valley; let the wild
20   Lean-headed Eagles yelp alone, and leave
The monstrous ledges there to slope, and spill
Their thousand wreaths of dangling water-smoke,
That like a broken purpose waste in air:
So waste not thou; but come; for all the vales
25   Await thee; azure pillars of the hearth[4]
Arise to thee; the children call, and I
Thy shepherd pipe, and sweet is every sound,
Sweeter thy voice, but every sound is sweet;
Myriads of rivulets hurrying thro' the lawn,
30   The moan of doves in immemorial elms,
And murmuring of innumerable bees.

1. Written in Switzerland in 1846 after Tennyson had seen the Jungfrau (German for "Maiden"), a mountain peak near the villages of Lauterbrunnen and Grindelwald.
2. Death is the lifelessness on the high snow peaks [Tennyson's note]. The silver horns are mountain peaks;
the Silberhorn is a spur of the Jungfrau.
3. The opening of the gorge is called dusky as a contrast with the snows all about [Tennyson's note].
4. Smoke rising from the chimneys of cottages in the valley.

["THE WOMAN'S CAUSE IS MAN'S"][1]

"Blame not thyself too much," I said, "nor blame
240   Too much the sons of men and barbarous laws;
These were the rough ways of the world till now.
Henceforth thou hast a helper, me, that know
The woman's cause is man's: they rise or sink
Together, dwarf'd or godlike, bond or free:
245   For she that out of Lethe[2] scales with man
The shining steps of Nature, shares with man
His nights, his days, moves with him to one goal,
Stays all the fair young planet in her hands[3]—
If she be small, slight-natured, miserable,
250   How shall men grow? but work no more alone!
Our place is much: as far as in us lies
We two will serve them both in aiding her—
Will clear away the parasitic forms
That seem to keep her up but drag her down—
255   Will leave her space to burgeon out of all
Within her—let her make herself her own
To give or keep, to live and learn and be
All that not harms distinctive womanhood.
For woman is not undevelopt man,
260   But diverse: could we make her as the man,
Sweet Love were slain: his dearest bond is this,
Not like to like, but like in difference.
Yet in the long years liker must they grow;
The man be more of woman, she of man;
265   He gain in sweetness and in moral height,
Nor lose the wrestling thews° that throw the world;   *muscles*
She mental breadth, nor fail in childward care,
Nor lose the childlike in the larger mind;
Till at the last she set herself to man,
270   Like perfect music unto noble words;
And so these twain, upon the skirts of Time,
Sit side by side, full-summ'd in all their powers,
Dispensing harvest, sowing the To-be,
Self-reverent each and reverencing each,

1. Princess Ida, the heroine of *The Princess*, founds a women's college, and swears she will never marry. But through various exploits—including masquerading as a woman to attend her college—Prince Florian convinces her that her feminist experiment is futile. She turns her college into a hospital and agrees to marry him. In this, his concluding speech (from Book 7), Florian envisions a future in which men and women will be more alike, and the relations between them will be improved.
2. The waters of forgetfulness, here implying a new beginning.
3. Hallam Tennyson notes: "Cf. Ross Wallace's lines:

'The hand that rocks the cradle is the hand that rules the world.' My father felt that woman must train herself more earnestly than heretofore to do the large work that lies before her, even though she may not be destined to be wife or mother, cultivating her understanding not her memory only, her imagination in its highest phases, her inborn spirituality and her sympathy with all that is pure, noble and beautiful, rather than mere social accomplishments; and that then and then only will she further the progress of humanity, then and then only men will continue to hold her in reverence."

275   Distinct in individualities,
        But like each other ev'n as those who love.
        Then comes the statelier Eden back to men:
        Then reign the world's great bridals, chaste and calm:
        Then springs the crowning race of humankind.
280   May these things be!"
                        Sighing she spoke "I fear
        They will not."
                        "Dear, but let us type them now
        In our own lives, and this proud watchword rest
        Of equal; seeing either sex alone
        Is half itself, and in true marriage lies
285   Nor equal, nor unequal: each fulfils
        Defect in each, and always thought in thought,
        Purpose in purpose, will in will, they grow,
        The single pure and perfect animal,
        The two-cell'd heart beating, with one full stroke,
290   Life."
                        And again sighing she spoke: "A dream
        That once was mine! what woman taught you this?"

1839–1847   1847

IN MEMORIAM A. H. H.   When Tennyson was twenty-four, his closest friend Arthur Henry Hallam died suddenly in Vienna. Regarded by all who knew him as the most promising intellect of his generation, Hallam had been Tennyson's confidante, best critic, and strongest supporter. It was Hallam who encouraged Tennyson to publish, helped him get his work through the press, and sustained him amidst criticism, self-doubt, and family crises. His perceptive review of the early poems remains among the best essays ever written on Tennyson. The poet learned of Hallam's death on 1 October 1833, and soon began composing short lyrics exploring the dark questions raised by so devastating an event. "I did not write them with any view of weaving them into a whole," Tennyson later said, "or for publication, until I found I had written so many."

The 131 sections of In Memoriam, produced over sixteen years, constitute a new type of elegy, what T. S. Eliot called "the concentrated diary" of a man confessing his love, sorrow, and doubts about the immortality of the soul. Tennyson drew on many sources, ranging from Greek pastoral elegy and Horace's Odes, to the sonnet sequences of Petrarch and Shakespeare. As in traditional elegy, the death of a friend blights joy in all living things, until the poet asserts his omnipresence in nature. But Tennyson expands his personal loss into the potential death of the human species, questioning the direction of evolution, science's challenges to Christian belief, and the ultimate destiny of the human spirit. The result is an intensely private autobiography of grief that nonetheless registers the troubled spiritual condition of Victorian England.

Presented as a broken narrative of the poet's fitful progress from despair to solace, In Memoriam covers a three-year period, from the death of Hallam in the autumn of 1833 to the spring of 1836. Sections 9–15 describe the return of Hallam's body to England by sea; section 19, its burial. The structural heart of the poem is the succession of three Christmases (sections 28–30, 78, 104–106), whose celebration of Christian rebirth gradually rings less hollow, more convincing. The poet's acceptance of his loss also deepens over the three springs that follow (sections 39, 86, and 115); the timeless renewal of nature eventually reawakens the poet to life. Yet for many readers, the bleak evidence of blindly predatory Nature at the poem's emotional nadir (sections 54, 55, and 56) nearly overshadows the brighter hopes of later sections. As Eliot remarked, *In Memoriam* triumphs not "because of the quality of its faith, but because of the quality of its doubt."

The form of the poem is justly famous. At the time he was writing Tennyson mistakenly thought he had created a new stanza—iambic tetrameter quatrains, rhyming *abba*—unaware that Sidney and Jonson had preceded him. But Tennyson's brilliant, sustained use of the quatrains was so well adapted to his material that the form has come to be called "the *In Memoriam* stanza." The first line-ending lingers in the memory while the central couplet pushes other sounds to the fore, then the rhyme is completed across that divide just as the stanza ends. This aural pattern of separation and completion parallels the intellectual and emotional progress of the poem: sound and substance combine in a verbal embrace of Tennyson's loss.

from In Memoriam A. H. H.
Obiit MDCCCXXXIII[1]

> Strong Son of God, immortal Love,
>   Whom we, that have not seen thy face,
>   By faith, and faith alone, embrace,
> Believing where we cannot prove;
>
> 5   Thine are these orbs of light and shade;[2]
>   Thou madest Life in man and brute;
>   Thou madest Death; and lo, thy foot
> Is on the skull which thou hast made.
>
> Thou wilt not leave us in the dust:
> 10   Thou madest man, he knows not why,
>   He thinks he was not made to die;
> And thou hast made him: thou art just.
>
> Thou seemest human and divine,
>   The highest, holiest manhood, thou:
> 15   Our wills are ours, we know not how,
> Our wills are ours, to make them thine.
>
> Our little systems have their day;[3]
>   They have their day and cease to be:
>   They are but broken lights of thee,
> 20   And thou, O Lord, art more than they.
>
> We have but faith: we cannot know;
>   For knowledge is of things we see;
>   And yet we trust it comes from thee,
> A beam in darkness: let it grow.

1. Died 1833. Tennyson wrote the introductory stanzas below, addressed to Christ, in 1849 after he had completed the poem.
2. Sun and moon [Tennyson's note].
3. Current notions of religion and philosophy.

25   Let knowledge grow from more to more,
          But more of reverence in us dwell;
          That mind and soul, according well,
     May make one music as before,[4]

     But vaster. We are fools and slight;
30   We mock thee when we do not fear:
          But help thy foolish ones to bear;
     Help thy vain worlds to bear thy light.

     Forgive what seem'd my sin in me;
          What seem'd my worth since I began;
35   For merit lives from man to man,
     And not from man, O Lord, to thee.

     Forgive my grief for one removed,
          Thy creature, whom I found so fair.
          I trust he lives in thee, and there
40   I find him worthier to be loved.

     Forgive these wild and wandering cries,
          Confusions of a wasted° youth;   *ruined*
          Forgive them where they fail in truth,
     And in thy wisdom make me wise.

1

     I held it truth, with him who sings
          To one clear harp in divers tones,[5]
          That men may rise on stepping-stones
     Of their dead selves to higher things.

5   But who shall so forecast the years
          And find in loss a gain to match?
          Or reach a hand thro' time to catch
     The far-off interest of tears?[6]

     Let Love clasp Grief lest both be drown'd,
10   Let darkness keep her raven gloss:
          Ah, sweeter to be drunk with loss,
     To dance with death, to beat the ground,

     Than that the victor Hours should scorn
          The long result of love, and boast,
15   "Behold the man that loved and lost,
     But all he was is overworn."

2

     Old Yew, which graspest at the stones
          That name the under-lying dead,

---

4. As in the ages of faith [Tennyson's note].
5. Goethe, according to Tennyson.

6. The good that grows for us out of grief [Tennyson's note].

Thy fibres net the dreamless head,
Thy roots are wrapt about the bones.

5 The seasons bring the flower again,
  And bring the firstling to the flock;
  And in the dusk of thee, the clock
Beats out the little lives of men.

O not for thee the glow, the bloom,
10 Who changest not in any gale,
  Nor branding summer suns avail
To touch thy thousand years of gloom:[7]

And gazing on thee, sullen tree,
  Sick° for thy stubborn hardihood,   *envious*
15 I seem to fail from out my blood
And grow incorporate into thee.

3

O Sorrow, cruel fellowship,
  O Priestess in the vaults of Death,
  O sweet and bitter in a breath,
What whispers from thy lying lip?

5 "The stars," she whispers, "blindly run;
  A web is wov'n across the sky;
  From out waste places comes a cry,
And murmurs from the dying sun:

"And all the phantom, Nature, stands—
10 With all the music in her tone,
  A hollow echo of my own,—
A hollow form with empty hands."

And shall I take a thing so blind,[8]
  Embrace her as my natural good;
15 Or crush her, like a vice of blood,
Upon the threshold of the mind?

4

To Sleep I give my powers away;
  My will is bondsman to the dark;
  I sit within a helmless bark,
And with my heart I muse and say:

5 O heart, how fares it with thee now,
  That thou should'st fail from thy desire,
  Who scarcely darest to inquire,
"What is it makes me beat so low?"

---

7. Hallam Tennyson says: "No autumn tints ever change 8. The blind thing is sorrow.
the green gloom of the yew."

Something it is which thou hast lost,
10   Some pleasure from thine early years.
        Break, thou deep vase of chilling tears,
That grief hath shaken into frost![9]

Such clouds of nameless trouble cross
        All night below the darken'd eyes;
15   With morning wakes the will, and cries,
"Thou shalt not be the fool of loss."

5

I sometimes hold it half a sin
        To put in words the grief I feel;
        For words, like Nature, half reveal
And half conceal the Soul within.

5   But, for the unquiet heart and brain,
        A use in measured language lies;
        The sad mechanic exercise,
Like dull narcotics, numbing pain.

In words, like weeds,° I'll wrap me o'er,   *mourning clothes*
10   Like coarsest clothes against the cold:
        But that large grief which these enfold
Is given in outline and no more.

6

One writes, that "Other friends remain,"
        That "Loss is common to the race"—
        And common is the commonplace,
And vacant chaff well meant for grain.

5   That loss is common would not make
        My own less bitter, rather more:
        Too common! Never morning wore
To evening, but some heart did break.

O father, wheresoe'er thou be,
10   Who pledgest° now thy gallant son;   *toasts*
        A shot, ere half thy draught be done,
Hath still'd the life that beat from thee.

O mother, praying God will save
        Thy sailor,—while thy head is bow'd,
15   His heavy-shotted hammock-shroud[1]
Drops in his vast and wandering grave.

Ye know no more than I who wrought
        At that last hour to please him well;[2]

---

9. Water can be brought below freezing-point and not turn into ice—if it be kept still; but if it be moved suddenly it turns into ice and may break the vase [Tennyson's note].

1. For a burial at sea, the shroud must be weighted to make the corpse sink.
2. Hallam Tennyson says: "My father was writing to Arthur Hallam in the hour that he died."

Who mused on all I had to tell,
20   And something written, something thought;

Expecting still his advent home;
      And ever met him on his way
      With wishes, thinking, "here to-day,"
Or "here to-morrow will he come."

25   O somewhere, meek, unconscious dove,
      That sittest ranging[3] golden hair;
      And glad to find thyself so fair,
Poor child, that waitest for thy love!

For now her father's chimney glows
30   In expectation of a guest;
      And thinking "this will please him best,"
She takes a riband or a rose;

For he will see them on to-night;
      And with the thought her colour burns;
35   And, having left the glass, she turns
Once more to set a ringlet right;

And, even when she turn'd, the curse
      Had fallen, and her future Lord
      Was drown'd in passing thro' the ford,
40   Or kill'd in falling from his horse.

O what to her shall be the end?
      And what to me remains of good?
      To her, perpetual maidenhood,
And unto me no second friend.

7

Dark house, by which once more I stand
      Here in the long unlovely street,[4]
      Doors, where my heart was used to beat
So quickly, waiting for a hand,

5   A hand that can be clasp'd no more—
      Behold me, for I cannot sleep,
      And like a guilty thing I creep
At earliest morning to the door.

He is not here;[5] but far away
10   The noise of life begins again,
      And ghastly thro' the drizzling rain
On the bald street breaks the blank day.

---

3. Arranging; the "meek, unconscious dove" was Tennyson's sister Emily, who had been engaged to marry Hallam.

4. Hallam's house at 67 Wimpole Street in London.
5. "He is not here, but is risen," said the angel at Jesus' tomb (Luke 24.6).

8

A happy lover who has come
    To look on her that loves him well,
    Who 'lights and rings the gateway bell,
And learns her gone and far from home;

5   He saddens, all the magic light
    Dies off at once from bower and hall,
    And all the place is dark, and all
The chambers emptied of delight:

So find I every pleasant spot
10   In which we two were wont to meet,
    The field, the chamber and the street,
For all is dark where thou art not.

Yet as that other, wandering there
    In those deserted walks, may find
15   A flower beat with rain and wind,
Which once she foster'd up with care;

So seems it in my deep regret,
    O my forsaken heart, with thee
    And this poor flower of poesy
20   Which little cared for fades not yet.

But since it pleased a vanish'd eye,
    I go to plant it on his tomb,
    That if it can it there may bloom,
Or dying, there at least may die.

9

Fair ship, that from the Italian shore
    Sailest the placid ocean-plains
    With my lost Arthur's loved remains,
Spread thy full wings, and waft him o'er.

5   So draw him home to those that mourn
    In vain; a favourable speed
    Ruffle thy mirror'd mast, and lead
Thro' prosperous floods his holy urn.

All night no ruder air perplex
10   Thy sliding keel, till Phosphor,[6] bright
    As our pure love, thro' early light
Shall glimmer on the dewy decks.

Sphere all your lights around, above;
    Sleep, gentle heavens, before the prow;
15   Sleep, gentle winds, as he sleeps now,
My friend, the brother of my love;

6. The morning star.

My Arthur, whom I shall not see
 Till all my widow'd race be run;
 Dear as the mother to the son,
20 More than my brothers are to me.

10

I hear the noise about thy keel;
 I hear the bell struck in the night:
 I see the cabin-window bright;
I see the sailor at the wheel.

5 Thou bring'st the sailor to his wife,
 And travell'd men from foreign lands;
 And letters unto trembling hands;
And, thy dark freight, a vanish'd life.

So bring him: we have idle dreams:
10 This look of quiet flatters thus
 Our home-bred fancies: O to us,
The fools of habit, sweeter seems

To rest beneath the clover sod,
 That takes the sunshine and the rains,
15 Or where the kneeling hamlet drains
The chalice of the grapes of God;[7]

Than if with thee the roaring wells
 Should gulf him fathom-deep in brine;
 And hands so often clasp'd in mine,
20 Should toss with tangle° and with shells.   *seaweed*

11

Calm is the morn without a sound,
 Calm as to suit a calmer grief,
 And only thro' the faded leaf
The chestnut pattering to the ground:

5 Calm and deep peace on this high wold,[8]
 And on these dews that drench the furze,°   *heath shrubs*
 And all the silvery gossamers
That twinkle into green and gold:

Calm and still light on yon great plain
10 That sweeps with all its autumn bowers,
 And crowded farms and lessening towers,
To mingle with the bounding main:

Calm and deep peace in this wide air,
 These leaves that redden to the fall;
15 And in my heart, if calm at all,
If any calm, a calm despair:

---

7. A burial in England, either inside the church itself, near the area where people take communion, or outdoors, "beneath the clover sod," is preferable to burial at sea.

8. A Lincolnshire wold or upland from which the whole range of marsh to the sea is visible [Tennyson's note].

Calm on the seas, and silver sleep,
    And waves that sway themselves in rest,
    And dead calm in that noble breast
20   Which heaves but with the heaving deep.[9]

12

Lo, as a dove when up she springs
    To bear thro' Heaven a tale of woe,
    Some dolorous message knit below
The wild pulsation of her wings;

5   Like her I go; I cannot stay;
    I leave this mortal ark behind,[1]
    A weight of nerves without a mind,
And leave the cliffs, and haste away

O'er ocean-mirrors rounded large,
10   And reach the glow of southern skies,
    And see the sails at distance rise,
And linger weeping on the marge,

And saying; "Comes he thus, my friend?
    Is this the end of all my care?"
15   And circle moaning in the air:
"Is this the end? Is this the end?"

And forward dart again, and play
    About the prow, and back return
    To where the body sits, and learn
20   That I have been an hour away.

13

Tears of the widower, when he sees
    A late-lost form that sleep reveals,
    And moves his doubtful arms, and feels
Her place is empty, fall like these;

5   Which weep a loss for ever new,
    A void where heart on heart reposed;
    And, where warm hands have prest and closed,
Silence, till I be silent too.

Which weep the comrade of my choice,
10   An awful thought, a life removed,
    The human-hearted man I loved,
A Spirit, not a breathing voice.

Come Time, and teach me,[2] many years,
    I do not suffer in a dream;

9. The poet imagines Hallam's body being transported home by ship in autumn 1833, shortly after he died; the actual voyage took place later that winter.
1. My spirit flies out from my material self [Tennyson's note]. Cf. Genesis 8.8–12, where Noah sends out a dove from the ark to see if the Flood has abated.
2. Hallam Tennyson remarks: "Time will teach him the full reality of his loss, whereas now he scarce believes in it, and is like one who between sleeping and waking can weep and has dream-fancies."

15   For now so strange do these things seem,
        Mine eyes have leisure for their tears;

        My fancies time to rise on wing,
           And glance about the approaching sails,
           As tho' they brought but merchants' bales,
20   And not the burthen that they bring.

14

        If one should bring me this report,
           That thou° hadst touch'd the land to-day,   *the ship*
           And I went down unto the quay,
        And found thee lying in the port;

5   And standing, muffled round with woe,
           Should see thy passengers in rank
           Come stepping lightly down the plank,
        And beckoning unto those they know;

        And if along with these should come
10   The man I held as half-divine;
           Should strike a sudden hand in mine,
        And ask a thousand things of home;

        And I should tell him all my pain,
           And how my life had droop'd of late,
15   And he should sorrow o'er my state
        And marvel what possess'd my brain;

        And I perceived no touch of change,
           No hint of death in all his frame,
           But found him all in all the same,
20   I should not feel it to be strange.

15

        To-night the winds begin to rise
           And roar from yonder dropping day:[3]
           The last red leaf is whirl'd away,
        The rooks are blown about the skies;

5   The forest crack'd, the waters curl'd,
           The cattle huddled on the lea;
           And wildly dash'd on tower and tree
        The sunbeam strikes along the world:

        And but for fancies, which aver
10   That all thy motions gently pass
           Athwart a plane of molten glass,[4]
        I scarce could brook the strain and stir

        That makes the barren branches loud;
           And but for fear it is not so,

---

3. From the west, the direction of sunset.   4. A calm sea [Tennyson's note].

15   The wild unrest that lives in woe
      Would dote and pore on yonder cloud

      That rises upward always higher,
          And onward drags a labouring breast,
          And topples round the dreary west,
20   A looming bastion fringed with fire.

* * *

19

      The Danube to the Severn[5] gave
          The darken'd heart that beat no more;
          They laid him by the pleasant shore,
      And in the hearing of the wave.

5   There twice a day the Severn fills;
          The salt sea-water passes by,
          And hushes half the babbling Wye,[6]
      And makes a silence in the hills.

      The Wye is hush'd nor moved along,
10   And hush'd my deepest grief of all,
          When fill'd with tears that cannot fall,
      I brim with sorrow drowning song.

      The tide flows down, the wave again
          Is vocal in its wooded walls;
15   My deeper anguish also falls,
      And I can speak a little then.

* * *

24

      And was the day of my delight
          As pure and perfect as I say?
          The very source and fount of Day
      Is dash'd with wandering isles of night.[7]

5   If all was good and fair we met,
          This earth had been the Paradise
          It never look'd to human eyes
      Since our first Sun arose and set.

      And is it that the haze of grief
10   Makes former gladness loom so great?
          The lowness of the present state,
      That sets the past in this relief?

      Or that the past will always win
          A glory from its being far;

---

5. Arthur Hallam died in Vienna, which is on the Danube, and was buried at Clevedon, near the Severn River in southwest England.
6. Taken from my own observation—the rapids of the Wye are stilled by the incoming sea [Tennyson's note]. The Wye is a tributary of the Severn, a tidal river.
7. Moving sunspots.

15   And orb into the perfect star
        We saw not, when we moved therein?[8]

* * *

27

        I envy not in any moods
            The captive void of noble rage,
            The linnet° born within the cage,   *finch*
        That never knew the summer woods:

5   I envy not the beast that takes
            His license in the field of time,
            Unfetter'd by the sense of crime,
        To whom a conscience never wakes;

        Nor, what may count itself as blest,
10   The heart that never plighted troth
            But stagnates in the weeds of sloth;
        Nor any want-begotten rest.[9]

        I hold it true, whate'er befall;
            I feel it, when I sorrow most;
15   'Tis better to have loved and lost
        Than never to have loved at all.

28

        The time draws near the birth of Christ:[1]
            The moon is hid; the night is still;
            The Christmas bells from hill to hill
        Answer each other in the mist.

5   Four voices of four hamlets round,
            From far and near, on mead and moor,
            Swell out and fail, as if a door
        Were shut between me and the sound:

        Each voice four changes[2] on the wind,
10   That now dilate, and now decrease,
            Peace and goodwill, goodwill and peace,
        Peace and goodwill, to all mankind.

        This year I slept and woke with pain,
            I almost wish'd no more to wake,
15   And that my hold on life would break
        Before I heard those bells again:

        But they my troubled spirit rule,
            For they controll'd me when a boy;
            They bring me sorrow touch'd with joy,
20   The merry merry bells of Yule.

* * *

8. From a distance the earth would look like a perfect orb.
9. Peace of mind owing to lack or "want" of having made
commitments.

1. The first Christmas after Hallam's death.
2. Arrangements of church bell ringing.

30

With trembling fingers did we weave
    The holly round the Christmas hearth;
    A rainy cloud possess'd the earth,
And sadly fell our Christmas-eve.

5   At our old pastimes in the hall
    We gambol'd, making vain pretence
    Of gladness, with an awful sense
Of one mute Shadow watching all.

We paused: the winds were in the beech:
10   We heard them sweep the winter land;
    And in a circle hand-in-hand
Sat silent, looking each at each.

Then echo-like our voices rang;
    We sung, tho' every eye was dim,
15   A merry song we sang with him
Last year: impetuously we sang:

We ceased: a gentler feeling crept
    Upon us: surely rest is meet:°   *fitting*
    "They rest," we said, "their sleep is sweet,"
20   And silence follow'd, and we wept.

Our voices took a higher range;
    Once more we sang: "They do not die
    Nor lose their mortal sympathy,
Nor change to us, although they change;

25   "Rapt° from the fickle and the frail   *carried away*
    With gather'd power, yet the same,
    Pierces the keen seraphic flame
From orb° to orb, from veil to veil."   *star*

Rise, happy morn, rise, holy morn,
30   Draw forth the cheerful day from night:
    O Father, touch the east, and light
The light that shone when Hope was born.

* * *

34

My own dim life should teach me this,
    That life shall live for evermore,
    Else earth is darkness at the core,
And dust and ashes all that is;

5   This round of green, this orb of flame,[3]
    Fantastic beauty; such as lurks
    In some wild Poet, when he works
Without a conscience or an aim.

3. The earth; the sun.

What then were God to such as I?
  'Twere hardly worth my while to choose
  Of things all mortal, or to use
A little patience ere I die;

'Twere best at once to sink to peace,
  Like birds the charming serpent draws,[4]
  To drop head-foremost in the jaws
Of vacant darkness and to cease.

* * *

39

Old warder[5] of these buried bones,
  And answering now my random stroke
  With fruitful cloud and living smoke,[6]
Dark yew, that graspest at the stones

And dippest toward the dreamless head,
  To thee too comes the golden hour
  When flower is feeling after flower;
But Sorrow—fixt upon the dead,

And darkening the dark graves of men,—
  What whisper'd from her lying lips?
  Thy gloom is kindled at the tips,[7]
And passes into gloom again.

* * *

50

Be near me when my light is low,
  When the blood creeps, and the nerves prick
  And tingle; and the heart is sick,
And all the wheels of Being slow.

Be near me when the sensuous frame
  Is rack'd with pangs that conquer trust;
  And Time, a maniac scattering dust,
And Life, a Fury slinging flame.[8]

Be near me when my faith is dry,
  And men the flies of latter spring,
  That lay their eggs, and sting and sing
And weave their petty cells and die.

Be near me when I fade away,
  To point the term of human strife,
  And on the low dark verge of life
The twilight of eternal day.

* * *

---

4. Some snakes were believed to hypnotize their prey.
5. The yew tree that stands by Hallam's grave; cf. Section 2. This section was written and added in 1868.
6. The yew, when flowering, in a wind or if struck sends up its pollen like smoke [Tennyson's note].
7. The tips of the yew branches are in flower.
8. The Furies—avengers of crime—carry torches.

54

Oh yet we trust that somehow good
    Will be the final goal of ill,
    To pangs of nature, sins of will,
Defects of doubt, and taints of blood;

5   That nothing walks with aimless feet;
    That not one life shall be destroy'd,
    Or cast as rubbish to the void,
When God hath made the pile complete;

That not a worm is cloven in vain;
10   That not a moth with vain desire
    Is shrivell'd in a fruitless fire,
Or but subserves another's gain.

Behold, we know not anything;
    I can but trust that good shall fall
15   At last—far off—at last, to all,
And every winter change to spring.

So runs my dream: but what am I?
    An infant crying in the night:
    An infant crying for the light:
20   And with no language but a cry.

55

The wish, that of the living whole
    No life may fail beyond the grave,
    Derives it not from what we have
The likest God within the soul?[9]

5   Are God and Nature then at strife,
    That Nature lends such evil dreams?
    So careful of the type[1] she seems,
So careless of the single life;

That I, considering everywhere
10   Her secret meaning in her deeds,
    And finding that of fifty seeds
She often brings but one to bear,

I falter where I firmly trod,
    And falling with my weight of cares
15   Upon the great world's altar-stairs
That slope thro' darkness up to God,

I stretch lame hands of faith, and grope,
    And gather dust and chaff, and call

---

9. The inner consciousness—the divine in man [Tennyson's note].

1. Species; i.e., Nature ensures the preservation of the species but is indifferent to the fate of the individual.

To what I feel is Lord of all,
20   And faintly trust the larger hope.[2]

56

"So careful of the type?" but no.
   From scarpèd[3] cliff and quarried stone
   She° cries, "A thousand types are gone: *Nature*
I care for nothing, all shall go."

5   "Thou makest thine appeal to me:
   I bring to life, I bring to death:
   The spirit does but mean the breath:
I know no more." And he, shall he,

Man, her last work, who seem'd so fair,
10   Such splendid purpose in his eyes,
   Who roll'd the psalm to wintry skies,
Who built him fanes° of fruitless prayer,   *temples*

Who trusted God was love indeed
   And love Creation's final law—
15   Tho' Nature, red in tooth and claw
With ravine, shriek'd against his creed—

Who loved, who suffer'd countless ills,
   Who battled for the True, the Just,
   Be blown about the desert dust,
20   Or seal'd° within the iron hills?   *fossilized*

No more? A monster then, a dream,
   A discord. Dragons of the prime,
   That tare° each other in their slime,[4]   *tore*
Were mellow music match'd° with him.   *compared*

25   O life as futile, then, as frail!
   O for thy voice to soothe and bless!
   What hope of answer, or redress?
Behind the veil, behind the veil.

* * *

59

O Sorrow,[5] wilt thou live with me
   No casual mistress, but a wife,
   My bosom-friend and half of life;
As I confess it needs must be;

5   O Sorrow, wilt thou rule my blood,
   Be sometimes lovely like a bride,

---

2. Hallam Tennyson notes: "My father means by 'the larger hope' that the whole human race would through, perhaps, ages of suffering, be at length purified and saved."

3. Steep cut-away cliffs with the strata exposed.
4. The geologic monsters of the early ages [Tennyson's note].
5. Cf. Section 3. Tennyson added this section in 1851.

And put thy harsher moods aside,
If thou wilt have me wise and good.

My centred passion cannot move,
10 Nor will it lessen from to-day;
 But I'll have leave at times to play
As with the creature of my love;

And set thee forth, for thou art mine,
 With so much hope for years to come,
15 That, howsoe'er I know thee, some
Could hardly tell what name were thine.

* * *

67

When on my bed the moonlight falls,
 I know that in thy place of rest
 By that broad water of the west,[6]
There comes a glory on the walls;

5 Thy marble bright in dark appears,
 As slowly steals a silver flame
 Along the letters of thy name,
And o'er the number of thy years.

The mystic glory swims away;
10 From off my bed the moonlight dies;
 And closing eaves of wearied eyes
I sleep till dusk is dipt in gray:

And then I know the mist is drawn
 A lucid veil from coast to coast,
15 And in the dark church like a ghost
Thy tablet glimmers to the dawn.

* * *

72

Risest thou thus, dim dawn, again,[7]
 And howlest, issuing out of night,
 With blasts that blow the poplar white,
And lash with storm the streaming pane?

5 Day, when my crown'd estate° begun   *happiness*
 To pine in that reverse of doom,[8]
 Which sicken'd every living bloom,
And blurr'd the splendour of the sun;

Who usherest in the dolorous hour
10 With thy quick tears that make the rose

---

6. The Severn, near which Hallam was buried at Clevedon.
7. It is 15 September 1834, the first anniversary of Hallam's death.

8. I.e., the disastrous reversal of fortune brought about by doom, in the form of Hallam's death.

Pull sideways, and the daisy close
    Her crimson fringes to the shower;

Who might'st have heaved a windless flame
    Up the deep East, or, whispering, play'd
15   A chequer-work of beam and shade
Along the hills, yet look'd the same.

As wan, as chill, as wild as now;
    Day, mark'd as with some hideous crime,
    When the dark hand struck down thro' time,
20   And cancell'd nature's best: but thou,

Lift as thou may'st thy burthen'd brows
    Thro' clouds that drench the morning star,
    And whirl the ungarner'd sheaf afar,
And sow the sky with flying boughs,

25   And up thy vault with roaring sound
    Climb thy thick noon, disastrous day;
    Touch thy dull goal of joyless gray,[9]
And hide thy shame beneath the ground.

* * *

78

Again at Christmas[1] did we weave
    The holly round the Christmas hearth;
    The silent snow possess'd the earth,
And calmly fell our Christmas-eve:

5   The yule-clog° sparkled keen with frost,   *log*
    No wing of wind the region swept,
    But over all things brooding slept
The quiet sense of something lost.

As in the winters left behind,
10   Again our ancient games had place,
    The mimic picture's breathing grace,[2]
And dance and song and hoodman-blind.°   *blindman's bluff*

Who show'd a token of distress?
    No single tear, no mark of pain:
15   O sorrow, then can sorrow wane?
O grief, can grief be changed to less?

O last regret, regret can die!
    No—mixt with all this mystic frame,
    Her° deep relations are the same,   *sorrow's*
20   But with long use her tears are dry.

* * *

---

9. The dull sunset.
1. The second Christmas after Hallam's death.

2. Tableaux-vivants, an entertainment in which performers reenact a well-known work of art or historical event,

80

If any vague desire should rise,
 That holy Death ere Arthur died
 Had moved me kindly from his side,
And dropt the dust on tearless eyes;

5 Then fancy shapes, as fancy can,
 The grief my loss in him had wrought,
 A grief as deep as life or thought,
But stay'd in peace with God and man.

I make a picture in the brain;
10 I hear the sentence that he speaks;
 He bears the burthen of the weeks
But turns his burthen into gain.

His credit thus shall set me free;
 And, influence rich to soothe and save,
15 Unused example from the grave
Reach out dead hands to comfort me.

* * *

86

Sweet after showers, ambrosial air,
 That rollest from the gorgeous gloom
 Of evening over brake and bloom
And meadow, slowly breathing bare

5 The round of space, and rapt below
 Thro' all the dewy-tassell'd wood,
 And shadowing down the hornèd flood[3]
In ripples, fan my brows and blow

The fever from my cheek, and sigh
10 The full new life that feeds thy breath
 Throughout my frame, till Doubt and Death,
Ill brethren, let the fancy fly

From belt to belt of crimson seas
 On leagues of odour streaming far,
15 To where in yonder orient star
A hundred spirits whisper "Peace."

* * *

89

Witch-elms that counterchange[4] the floor
 Of this flat lawn with dusk and bright;
 And thou, with all thy breadth and height
Of foliage, towering sycamore;

---

3. Between two promontories [Tennyson's note].   4. The shadows cast by the elm tree checkered the lawn.

How often, hither wandering down,
  My Arthur found your shadows fair,
  And shook to all the liberal air
The dust and din and steam of town:

He brought an eye for all he saw;
  He mixt in all our simple sports;
  They pleased him, fresh from brawling courts
And dusty purlieus of the law.[5]

O joy to him in this retreat,
  Immantled in ambrosial dark,
  To drink the cooler air, and mark
The landscape winking thro' the heat:

O sound to rout the brood of cares,
  The sweep of scythe in morning dew,
  The gust that round the garden flew,
And tumbled half the mellowing pears!

O bliss, when all in circle drawn
  About him, heart and ear were fed
  To hear him, as he lay and read
The Tuscan poets[6] on the lawn:

Or in the all-golden afternoon
  A guest, or happy sister, sung,
  Or here she brought the harp and flung
A ballad to the brightening moon:

Nor less it pleased in livelier moods,
  Beyond the bounding hill to stray,
  And break the livelong summer day
With banquet in the distant woods;

Whereat we glanced from theme to theme,
  Discuss'd the books to love or hate,
  Or touch'd the changes of the state,
Or threaded some Socratic dream;

But if I praised the busy town,
  He loved to rail against it still,
  For "ground in yonder social mill
We rub each other's angles down,

"And merge," he said, "in form and gloss
  The picturesque of man and man."
  We talk'd: the stream beneath us ran,
The wine-flask lying couch'd in moss,

5. Hallam had been a law student   6. Petrarch and Dante.

45   Or cool'd within the glooming wave;
            And last, returning from afar,
            Before the crimson-circled star
        Had fall'n into her father's grave,

        And brushing ankle-deep in flowers,
50   We heard behind the woodbine veil
            The milk that bubbled in the pail,
        And buzzings of the honied hours.

                        * * *

                        93
        I shall not see thee. Dare I say
            No spirit ever brake the band
            That stays him from the native land
        Where first he walk'd when claspt in clay?[7]

5   No visual shade of some one lost,
            But he, the Spirit himself, may come
            Where all the nerve of sense is numb;
        Spirit to Spirit, Ghost to Ghost.

        O, therefore from thy sightless° range   *invisible*
10   With gods in unconjectured bliss,
            O, from the distance of the abyss
        Of tenfold-complicated change,

        Descend, and touch, and enter; hear
            The wish too strong for words to name;
15   That in this blindness of the frame
        My Ghost may feel that thine is near.

                        94
        How pure at heart and sound in head,
            With what divine affections bold
            Should be the man whose thought would hold
        An hour's communion with the dead.

5   In vain shalt thou, or any, call
            The spirits from their golden day,
            Except, like them, thou too canst say,
        My spirit is at peace with all.

        They haunt the silence of the breast,
10   Imaginations calm and fair,
            The memory like a cloudless air,
        The conscience as a sea at rest:

        But when the heart is full of din,
            And doubt beside the portal waits,
15   They can but listen at the gates,
        And hear the household jar within.

---

7. Flesh; in other words, when he was alive.

95

By night we linger'd on the lawn,
  For underfoot the herb was dry;
  And genial warmth; and o'er the sky
The silvery haze of summer drawn;

5   And calm that let the tapers burn
  Unwavering: not a cricket chirr'd:
  The brook alone far-off was heard,
And on the board the fluttering urn:[8]

And bats went round in fragrant skies,
10   And wheel'd or lit the filmy shapes°   *moths*
  That haunt the dusk, with ermine capes
And woolly breasts and beaded eyes;

While now we sang old songs that peal'd
  From knoll to knoll, where, couch'd at ease,
15   The white kine° glimmer'd, and the trees   *cows*
Laid their dark arms about the field.

But when those others, one by one,
  Withdrew themselves from me and night,
  And in the house light after light
20   Went out, and I was all alone,

A hunger seized my heart; I read
  Of that glad year which once had been,
  In those fall'n leaves which kept their green,
The noble letters of the dead:

25   And strangely on the silence broke
  The silent-speaking words, and strange
  Was love's dumb cry defying change
To test his worth; and strangely spoke

The faith, the vigour, bold to dwell
30   On doubts that drive the coward back,
  And keen thro' wordy snares to track
Suggestion to her inmost cell.

So word by word, and line by line,
  The dead man touch'd me from the past.
35   And all at once it seem'd at last
The living soul[9] was flash'd on mine,

And mine in this was wound, and whirl'd
  About empyreal heights of thought,
  And came on that which is, and caught
40   The deep pulsations of the world,

---

8. Hot-water urn for making tea or coffee, heated by a fluttering flame.
9. "His living soul" in the first edition; the next line originally read "And mine in his was wound." Tennyson said that the first version "troubled me, as perhaps giving a wrong impression."

Aeonian music[1] measuring out
   The steps of Time—the shocks of Chance—
   The blows of Death. At length my trance
Was cancell'd, stricken thro' with doubt.[2]

45   Vague words! but ah, how hard to frame
   In matter-moulded forms of speech,
   Or ev'n for intellect to reach
Thro' memory that which I became:

Till now the doubtful dusk reveal'd
50   The knolls once more where, couch'd at ease,
   The white kine glimmer'd, and the trees
Laid their dark arms about the field:

And suck'd from out the distant gloom
   A breeze began to tremble o'er
55   The large leaves of the sycamore,
And fluctuate all the still perfume,

And gathering freshlier overhead,
   Rock'd the full-foliaged elms, and swung
   The heavy-folded rose, and flung
60   The lilies to and fro, and said

"The dawn, the dawn," and died away;
   And East and West, without a breath,
   Mixt their dim lights, like life and death,
To broaden into boundless day.

96

You say, but with no touch of scorn,
   Sweet-hearted, you, whose light-blue eyes
   Are tender over drowning flies,
You tell me, doubt is Devil-born.

5   I know not: one[3] indeed I knew
   In many a subtle question versed,
   Who touch'd a jarring lyre at first,
But ever strove to make it true:

Perplext in faith, but pure in deeds,
10   At last he beat his music out.
   There lives more faith in honest doubt,
Believe me, than in half the creeds.

He fought his doubts and gather'd strength,
   He would not make his judgment blind,
15   He faced the spectres of the mind
And laid them: thus he came at length

---

1. The music of the aeons.
2. The trance came to an end in a moment of critical doubt, but the doubt was dispelled by the glory of the

dawn of the "boundless day" [Tennyson's note].
3. Arthur Hallam.

To find a stronger faith his own;
　　And Power was with him in the night,
　　Which makes the darkness and the light,
20 And dwells not in the light alone,

But in the darkness and the cloud,
　　As over Sinai's peaks of old,[4]
　　While Israel made their gods of gold,
Altho' the trumpet blew so loud.

* * *

99

Risest thou thus, dim dawn, again,[5]
　　So loud with voices of the birds,
　　So thick with lowings of the herds,
Day, when I lost the flower of men;

5 Who tremblest thro' thy darkling red
　　On yon swoll'n brook that bubbles fast
　　By meadows breathing of the past,
And woodlands holy to the dead;

Who murmurest in the foliaged eaves
10 　　A song that slights the coming care,[6]
　　And Autumn laying here and there
A fiery finger on the leaves;

Who wakenest with thy balmy breath
　　To myriads on the genial earth,
15 　　Memories of bridal, or of birth,
And unto myriads more, of death.

O wheresoever those[7] may be,
　　Betwixt the slumber of the poles,[8]
　　To-day they count as kindred souls;
20 They know me not, but mourn with me.

* * *

104

The time draws near the birth of Christ;[9]
　　The moon is hid, the night is still;
　　A single church below the hill
Is pealing, folded in the mist.

5 A single peal of bells below,
　　That wakens at this hour of rest
　　A single murmur in the breast,
That these are not the bells I know.

---

4. In Exodus (19.16) God speaks to Moses after sending a dark cloud of smoke to cloak Mount Sinai.
5. It is now 15 September 1835, the second anniversary of Hallam's death.
6. The approach of winter.

7. The "myriads" who have memories of death.
8. The ends of the axis of the earth, which move so slowly that they seem not to move, but slumber [Tennyson's note].
9. It is now the third Christmas since Hallam's death.

Like strangers' voices here they sound,
10   In lands where not a memory strays,
    Nor landmark breathes of other days,
But all is new unhallow'd ground.

105

To-night ungather'd let us leave
    This laurel, let this holly stand:
    We live within the stranger's land,[1]
And strangely falls our Christmas-eve.

5   Our father's dust is left alone
    And silent under other snows:
    There in due time the woodbine blows,
The violet comes, but we are gone.

No more shall wayward grief abuse
10   The genial hour with mask and mime;
    For change of place, like growth of time,
Has broke the bond of dying use.

Let cares that petty shadows cast,
    By which our lives are chiefly proved,
15   A little spare the night I loved,
And hold it solemn to the past.

But let no footstep beat the floor,
    Nor bowl of wassail mantle warm;
    For who would keep an ancient form
20 Thro' which the spirit breathes no more?

Be neither song, nor game, nor feast;
    Nor harp be touch'd, nor flute be blown;
    No dance, no motion, save alone
What lightens in the lucid east

25 Of rising worlds° by yonder wood.   *stars*
    Long sleeps the summer in the seed;
    Run out your measured arcs, and lead
The closing cycle rich in good.

106

Ring out, wild bells, to the wild sky,
    The flying cloud, the frosty light:
    The year is dying in the night;
Ring out, wild bells, and let him die.

5   Ring out the old, ring in the new,
    Ring, happy bells, across the snow:

---

1. The Tennyson family have moved away from their old home in Lincolnshire and can no longer bring themselves to observe their former festive customs, such as gathering holly for Christmas or dancing and drinking hot punch (the "bowl of wassail" in line 18).

The year is going, let him go;
Ring out the false, ring in the true.

Ring out the grief that saps the mind,
10   For those that here we see no more;
      Ring out the feud of rich and poor,
Ring in redress to all mankind.

Ring out a slowly dying cause,
      And ancient forms of party strife;
15   Ring in the nobler modes of life,
With sweeter manners, purer laws.

Ring out the want, the care, the sin,
      The faithless coldness of the times;
      Ring out, ring out my mournful rhymes,
20 But ring the fuller minstrel in.

Ring out false pride in place and blood,
      The civic slander and the spite;
      Ring in the love of truth and right,
Ring in the common love of good.

25 Ring out old shapes of foul disease;
      Ring out the narrowing lust of gold;
      Ring out the thousand wars of old,
Ring in the thousand years of peace.

Ring in the valiant man and free,
30   The larger heart, the kindlier hand;
      Ring out the darkness of the land,
Ring in the Christ that is to be.

107

It is the day when he was born,[2]
      A bitter day that early sank
      Behind a purple-frosty bank
Of vapour, leaving night forlorn.

5 The time admits not flowers or leaves
      To deck the banquet. Fiercely flies
      The blast of North and East, and ice
Makes daggers at the sharpen'd eaves,

And bristles all the brakes and thorns
10   To yon hard crescent, as she hangs
      Above the wood which grides° and clangs   *grinds*
Its leafless ribs and iron horns

2. Hallam's birthday was 1 February 1811.

Together, in the drifts, that pass
    To darken on the rolling brine
15   That breaks the coast. But fetch the wine,
Arrange the board and brim the glass;

Bring in great logs and let them lie,
    To make a solid core of heat;
    Be cheerful-minded, talk and treat
20 Of all things ev'n as he were by;

We keep the day. With festal cheer,
    With books and music, surely we
    Will drink to him, whate'er he be,
And sing the songs he loved to hear.

108

I will not shut me from my kind,
    And, lest I stiffen into stone,
    I will not eat my heart alone,
Nor feed with sighs a passing wind:

5 What profit lies in barren faith,
    And vacant yearning, tho' with might
    To scale the heaven's highest height,
Or dive below the wells of Death?

What find I in the highest place,
10   But mine own phantom chanting hymns?
    And on the depths of death there swims
The reflex of a human face.[3]

I'll rather take what fruit may be
    Of sorrow under human skies:
15   'Tis held that sorrow makes us wise,
Whatever wisdom sleep with thee.

* * *

115

Now fades the last long streak of snow,
    Now burgeons every maze of quick[4]
    About the flowering squares, and thick
By ashen roots the violets blow.

5 Now rings the woodland loud and long,
    The distance takes a lovelier hue,
    And drown'd in yonder living blue
The lark becomes a sightless song.

Now dance the lights on lawn and lea,
10   The flocks are whiter down the vale,

---

3. The reflection of his own face.
4. Hawthorn hedges are budding; the "flowering squares" in the next line are fields.

And milkier every milky sail
On winding stream or distant sea;

Where now the seamew pipes, or dives
In yonder greening gleam, and fly
15   The happy birds, that change their sky
To build and brood; that live their lives

From land to land; and in my breast
Spring wakens too; and my regret
Becomes an April violet,
20   And buds and blossoms like the rest.

* * *

117

O days and hours, your work is this
To hold me from my proper place,
A little while from his embrace,
For fuller gain of after bliss:

5   That out of distance might ensue
Desire of nearness doubly sweet;
And unto meeting when we meet,
Delight a hundredfold accrue,

For every grain of sand that runs,[5]
10   And every span of shade[6] that steals,
And every kiss of toothed wheels,[7]
And all the courses of the suns.

118

Contemplate all this work of Time,
The giant labouring in his youth;
Nor dream of human love and truth,
As dying Nature's earth and lime;

5   But trust that those we call the dead
Are breathers of an ampler day
For ever nobler ends. They° say,   *scientists*
The solid earth whereon we tread

In tracts of fluent heat began,
10   And grew to seeming-random forms,
The seeming prey of cyclic storms,
Till at the last arose the man;

Who throve and branch'd from clime to clime,
The herald of a higher race,
15   And of himself in higher place,
If so he type[8] this work of time

5. Through an hourglass.   7. In the works of a clock.
6. On a sundial.   8. Typifies or prefigures.

Within himself, from more to more;
   Or, crown'd with attributes of woe
   Like glories, move his course, and show
20   That life is not as idle ore,

But iron dug from central gloom,
   And heated hot with burning fears,
   And dipt in baths of hissing tears,
And batter'd with the shocks of doom

25   To shape and use. Arise and fly
   The reeling Faun, the sensual feast;
   Move upward, working out the beast,
And let the ape and tiger die.

119

Doors, where my heart was used to beat
   So quickly, not as one that weeps
   I come once more;[9] the city sleeps;
I smell the meadow in the street;

5   I hear a chirp of birds; I see
   Betwixt the black fronts long-withdrawn
   A light-blue lane of early dawn,
And think of early days and thee,

And bless thee, for thy lips are bland,
10   And bright the friendship of thine eye;
   And in my thoughts with scarce a sigh
I take the pressure of thine hand.

120

I trust I have not wasted breath:
   I think we are not wholly brain,
   Magnetic mockeries;° not in vain,   *automatons*
Like Paul with beasts,[1] I fought with Death;

5   Not only cunning casts in clay:
   Let Science prove we are, and then
   What matters Science unto men,
At least to me? I would not stay.

Let him, the wiser man who springs
10   Hereafter, up from childhood shape
   His action like the greater ape,[2]
But I was *born* to other things.

* * *

9. Tennyson has returned to Hallam's house in London;
see Section 7, page 663.
1. St. Paul said: "If after the manner of men I have fought
with beasts at Ephesus, what advantageth it me, if the
dead rise not" (1 Corinthians 15.32).
2. Spoken ironically against mere materialism, not
against evolution [Tennyson's note].

123

There rolls the deep where grew the tree.
   O earth, what changes hast thou seen!
   There where the long street roars, hath been
The stillness of the central sea.

5   The hills are shadows, and they flow
   From form to form, and nothing stands;
   They melt like mist, the solid lands,
Like clouds they shape themselves and go.

But in my spirit will I dwell,
10   And dream my dream, and hold it true;
   For tho' my lips may breathe adieu,
I cannot think the thing farewell.

124

That which we dare invoke to bless;
   Our dearest faith; our ghastliest doubt;
   He, They, One, All; within, without;
The Power in darkness whom we guess;

5   I found Him not in world or sun,
   Or eagle's wing, or insect's eye;[3]
   Nor thro' the questions men may try,
The petty cobwebs we have spun:

If e'er when faith had fall'n asleep,
10   I heard a voice "believe no more"
   And heard an ever-breaking shore
That tumbled in the Godless deep;

A warmth within the breast would melt
   The freezing reason's colder part,
15   And like a man in wrath the heart
Stood up and answer'd "I have felt."

No, like a child in doubt and fear:
   But that blind clamour made me wise;
   Then was I as a child that cries,
20   But, crying, knows his father near;

And what I am beheld again
   What is, and no man understands;
   And out of darkness came the hands
That reach thro' nature, moulding men.

* * *

---

3. Tennyson rejects the argument that God's existence can be inferred from Nature—i.e., that the design of the universe is so orderly and complex that there must have been a designer.

130

Thy voice is on the rolling air;
    I hear thee where the waters run;
    Thou standest in the rising sun,
And in the setting thou art fair.

5   What art thou then? I cannot guess;
    But tho' I seem in star and flower
    To feel thee some diffusive power,
I do not therefore love thee less:

My love involves the love before;
10   My love is vaster passion now;
    Tho' mix'd with God and Nature thou,
I seem to love thee more and more.

Far off thou art, but ever nigh;
    I have thee still, and I rejoice;
15   I prosper, circled with thy voice;
I shall not lose thee tho' I die.

131

O living will[4] that shalt endure
    When all that seems shall suffer shock,
    Rise in the spiritual rock,[5]
Flow thro' our deeds and make them pure,

5   That we may lift from out of dust
    A voice as unto him that hears,
    A cry above the conquer'd years
To one that with us works, and trust,

With faith that comes of self-control,
10   The truths that never can be proved
    Until we close with all we loved,
And all we flow from, soul in soul.

* * *

from *Epilogue*[6]

And rise, O moon, from yonder down,
110   Till over down and over dale
    All night the shining vapour sail
And pass the silent-lighted town,

---

4. That which we know as Free-will in man [Tennyson's note].
5. "And did all drink the same spiritual drink: for they drank of that spiritual Rock that followed them: and that Rock was Christ" (1 Corinthians 10.4).
6. The *Epilogue* opens with a description of the marriage of Cecilia Tennyson, the poet's sister, to Edmund

Lushington on 10 October 1842. Tennyson said *In Memoriam* "begins with a funeral and ends with a marriage—begins with death and ends in promise of a new life—a sort of Divine Comedy, cheerful at the close." The last nine stanzas take place after the wedding is over, as the poet, leaving the reception, looks out over the darkened countryside.

The white-faced halls, the glancing rills,
  And catch at every mountain head,
115 And o'er the friths° that branch and spread   *estuaries*
Their sleeping silver thro' the hills;

And touch with shade the bridal doors,
  With tender gloom the roof, the wall;
  And breaking let the splendour fall
120 To spangle all the happy shores

By which they rest, and ocean sounds,
  And, star and system rolling past,
  A soul shall draw from out the vast
And strike his being into bounds,[7]

125 And, moved thro' life of lower phase,
  Result in man, be born and think,
  And act and love, a closer link
Betwixt us and the crowning race

Of those that, eye to eye, shall look
130 On knowledge; under whose command
  Is Earth and Earth's, and in their hand
Is Nature like an open book;

No longer half-akin to brute,
  For all we thought and loved and did,
135 And hoped, and suffer'd, is but seed
Of what in them is flower and fruit;

Whereof the man, that with me trod
  This planet, was a noble type
  Appearing ere the times were ripe,
140 That friend of mine who lives in God,

That God, which ever lives and loves,
  One God, one law, one element,
  And one far-off divine event,
To which the whole creation moves.
1833–1850   1850

The Charge of the Light Brigade[1]

1

Half a league, half a league,
Half a league onward,
All in the valley of Death

---

7. The poet anticipates the conception of a child, who will pass through various stages of embryonic development to "result in man" (line 126). His development will correspond to the stages of human evolution, perhaps even looking forward to the emergence of a higher form of life, of which Hallam was a precursor, "a noble type" (line 138).

1. In 1854, during the Crimean War, a misunderstood order caused a brigade of 600 British cavalry to make a foolhardy charge upon the batteries of Russian artillery at Balaclava, near Sebastopol. More than 400 soldiers were killed.

Rode the six hundred.
5   "Forward, the Light Brigade!
Charge for the guns!" he said:
Into the valley of Death
        Rode the six hundred.[2]

                    2

    "Forward, the Light Brigade!"
10 Was there a man dismay'd?
    Not tho' the soldier knew
        Some one had blunder'd:
    Their's not to make reply,
    Their's not to reason why,
15 Their's but to do and die:
    Into the valley of Death
        Rode the six hundred.

                    3

    Cannon to right of them,
    Cannon to left of them,
20 Cannon in front of them
        Volley'd and thunder'd;
    Storm'd at with shot and shell,
    Boldly they rode and well,
    Into the jaws of Death,
25 Into the mouth of Hell
        Rode the six hundred.

                    4

    Flash'd all their sabres bare,
    Flash'd as they turn'd in air
    Sabring the gunners there,
30 Charging an army, while
        All the world wonder'd:
    Plunged in the battery-smoke
    Right thro' the line they broke;
    Cossack and Russian
35 Reel'd from the sabre-stroke
        Shatter'd and sunder'd.
    Then they rode back, but not
        Not the six hundred.

                    5

    Cannon to right of them,
40 Cannon to left of them,
    Cannon behind them
        Volley'd and thunder'd;
    Storm'd at with shot and shell,

2. In his Lincolnshire accent, Tennyson apparently pronounced "hundred" as "hunderd"—thus making it an exact rhyme with "blundered" and "thundered."

	While horse and hero fell,
45	They that had fought so well
	Came thro' the jaws of Death,
	Back from the mouth of Hell,
	All that was left of them,
	Left of six hundred.

6

	When can their glory fade?
50	O the wild charge they made!
	All the world wonder'd.
	Honour the charge they made!
	Honour the Light Brigade,
55	Noble six hundred!

1854   1854

IDYLLS OF THE KING   An "idyll" typically describes picturesque and harmonious scenes of rustic life. Tennyson's idylls, in contrast, are glorious but also bitter and bloody tapestries of love, lust, deceit, and betrayal. He composed the twelve books of *Idylls of the King* over the course of fifty-three years (1833–1885), drawing not only on Thomas Malory's fifteenth-century *Morte D'Arthur*, his major source, but on many other ancient tales, including the Welsh *Mabinogion*. Some contemporaries thought that the effort could have been better spent dealing with current social problems: Carlyle sarcastically called the first four idylls "lollipops." But Tennyson intended an "allegorical or . . . parabolic drift in the poem," and many readers soon perceived the metaphoric parallels between Camelot and Victorian Britain—their virtues, vices, and moral vulnerability.

The poet arranged the tales to create a mythic portrayal of a civilization's aspiration and decline. The story of the Round Table's creation and dissolution follows the seasons of the year, from Arthur and Guinevere's union in the springtime, when they redeem the wasted land, to Arthur's vanishing at the winter solstice. Throughout, Tennyson focuses on the human potential for either moral evolution or regression. Poised "between the man and beast" at the coming of Arthur, his people rise under the influence of the mysterious and almost supernatural king to become fully human and spiritually motivated. But as the knights of the Round Table fail to keep their vows, the "realm / Reels back into the beast." The adulterous love of Guinevere and Lancelot eventually provokes treachery and disillusion, and the fellowship of the Round Table perishes. *Pelleas and Ettarre* is a pivotal tale showing the disastrous encounter of youthful idealism with the poisonous hypocrisy and sexual indulgence that eat away at the heart of Arthur's dream. Finally, *The Passing of Arthur* describes the apocalyptic battle "where all of high and holy dies away" except the faint hope that, Christlike, Arthur may come again.

from **Idylls of the King**
The Coming of Arthur

	Leodogran, the King of Cameliard,[1]
	Had one fair daughter, and none other child;
	And she was fairest of all flesh on earth,
	Guinevere, and in her his one delight.

---

1. Tradition situates the realms of Leodogran and Arthur somewhere in the west of England or southern Wales. Tennyson uses the geographic imprecision of Arthurian legend for imaginative effect: both the wasteland and Camelot could be anywhere, more states of mind than actual places. Tennyson hints at this in the second Idyll, *Gareth and Lynette*, when a character marvels at Camelot's shimmering towers, saying "there is no such city anywhere, but all a vision."

5   For many a petty king ere Arthur came
       Ruled in this isle, and ever waging war
       Each upon other, wasted all the land;
       And still from time to time the heathen host[2]
       Swarm'd overseas, and harried what was left.
10   And so there grew great tracts of wilderness,
       Wherein the beast was ever more and more,
       But man was less and less, till Arthur came.
       For first Aurelius lived and fought and died,
       And after him King Uther[3] fought and died,
15   But either fail'd to make the kingdom one.
       And after these King Arthur for a space,
       And thro' the puissance of his Table Round,
       Drew all their petty princedoms under him,
       Their king and head, and made a realm, and reign'd.

20   And thus the land of Cameliard was waste,
       Thick with wet woods, and many a beast therein,
       And none or few to scare or chase the beast;
       So that wild dog, and wolf and boar and bear
       Came night and day, and rooted in the fields,
25   And wallow'd in the gardens of the King.
       And ever and anon the wolf would steal
       The children and devour, but now and then,
       Her own brood lost or dead, lent her fierce teat
       To human sucklings; and the children, housed
30   In her foul den, there at their meat would growl,
       And mock their foster-mother on four feet,
       Till, straighten'd, they grew up to wolf-like men,
       Worse than the wolves. And King Leodogran
       Groan'd for the Roman legions here again,
35   And Caesar's eagle:[4] then his brother king,
       Urien,[5] assail'd him: last a heathen horde,
       Reddening the sun with smoke and earth with blood,
       And on the spike that split the mother's heart
       Spitting the child, brake on him,[6] till, amazed,
40   He knew not whither he should turn for aid.

           But—for he heard of Arthur newly crown'd,
       Tho' not without an uproar made by those

---

2. Pagan Germanic tribes—Angles, Jutes, and Saxons—invaded the British isles periodically during the 5th century, further weakening what remained of Romanized British civilization. Arthur apparently rose to power as Roman influence declined, but since Malory, writers have set the events of Arthurian legend in an idealized era of medieval chivalry, which creates certain historical anachronisms.

3. Arthur's father, but Arthur was brought up as the foster son of a knight, unaware of his true identity until adulthood. Aurelius was Uther's brother.

4. Caesar's eagle—the regimental standard of the Roman legions—was a symbol of imperial power. The Roman conquest of Britain began with the invasion of Julius Caesar in 55–54 B.C.; by the 5th century, the Roman Empire was disintegrating and could no longer administer such distant possessions. Leodogran longs for the protection and orderly rule of the Romans.

5. King of North Wales.

6. The heathen horde assaulted Leodogran like a breaking wave, with pikes that figuratively pierced mothers' hearts by impaling their children.

Who cried, "He is not Uther's son"—the King
Sent to him, saying, "Arise, and help us thou!
45   For here between the man and beast we die."

    And Arthur yet had done no deed of arms,
But heard the call, and came: and Guinevere
Stood by the castle walls to watch him pass;
But since he neither wore on helm or shield
50   The golden symbol of his kinglihood,
But rode a simple knight among his knights,
And many of these in richer arms than he,
She saw him not, or mark'd not, if she saw,
One among many, tho' his face was bare.
55   But Arthur, looking downward as he past,
Felt the light of her eyes into his life
Smite on the sudden, yet rode on, and pitch'd
His tents beside the forest. Then he drave
The heathen; after, slew the beast, and fell'd
60   The forest, letting in the sun, and made
Broad pathways for the hunter and the knight
And so return'd.

               For while he linger'd there,
A doubt that ever smoulder'd in the hearts
Of those great Lords and Barons of his realm
65   Flash'd forth and into war: for most of these,
Colleaguing with a score of petty kings,
Made head against him, crying, "Who is he
That he should rule us? who hath proven him
King Uther's son? for lo! we look at him,
70   And find nor face nor bearing, limbs nor voice,
Are like to those of Uther whom we knew.
This is the son of Gorloïs,[7] not the King;
This is the son of Anton,[8] not the King."

    And Arthur, passing thence to battle, felt
75   Travail, and throes and agonies of the life,
Desiring to be join'd with Guinevere;
And thinking as he rode, "Her father said
That there between the man and beast they die.
Shall I not lift her from this land of beasts
80   Up to my throne, and side by side with me?
What happiness to reign a lonely king,
Vext—O ye stars that shudder over me,
O earth that soundest hollow under me,
Vext with waste dreams? for saving I be join'd
85   To her that is the fairest under heaven,
I seem as nothing in the mighty world,

---

7. King of Cornwall and husband of Arthur's mother,   8. The knight who brought up Arthur.
Ygerne.

And cannot will my will, nor work my work
Wholly, nor make myself in mine own realm
Victor and lord. But were I join'd with her,
90   Then might we live together as one life,
And reigning with one will in everything
Have power on this dark land to lighten it,
And power on this dead world to make it live."

Thereafter—as he speaks who tells the tale—
95   When Arthur reach'd a field-of-battle bright
With pitch'd pavilions of his foe, the world
Was all so clear about him, that he saw
The smallest rock far on the faintest hill,
And even in high day the morning star.
100 So when the King had set his banner broad,
At once from either side, with trumpet-blast,
And shouts, and clarions shrilling unto blood,
The long-lanced battle let their horses run.
And now the Barons and the kings prevail'd,
105 And now the King, as here and there that war
Went swaying; but the Powers who walk the world
Made lightnings and great thunders over him,
And dazed all eyes, till Arthur by main might,
And mightier of his hands with every blow,
110 And leading all his knighthood threw the kings
Carádos, Urien, Cradlemont of Wales,
Claudias, and Clariance of Northumberland,
The King Brandagoras of Latangor,
With Anguisant of Erin, Morganore,
115 And Lot of Orkney. Then, before a voice
As dreadful as the shout of one who sees
To one who sins, and deems himself alone
And all the world asleep, they swerved and brake
Flying, and Arthur call'd to stay the brands
120 That hack'd among the flyers,[9] "Ho! they yield!"
So like a painted battle the war stood
Silenced, the living quiet as the dead,
And in the heart of Arthur joy was lord.
He laugh'd upon his warrior whom he loved
125 And honour'd most.[1] "Thou dost not doubt me King,
So well thine arm hath wrought for me to-day."
"Sir and my liege," he cried, "the fire of God
Descends upon thee in the battle-field:
I know thee for my King!" Whereat the two,
130 For each had warded either in the fight,
Sware on the field of death a deathless love.
And Arthur said, "Man's word is God in man:
Let chance what will, I trust thee to the death."

9. I.e., Arthur commanded his men to stop hacking their   1. Sir Lancelot.
retreating enemies with their swords (brands).

Then quickly from the foughten field he sent
135   Ulfius, and Brastias, and Bedivere,
His new-made knights, to King Leodogran,
Saying, "If I in aught have served thee well,
Give me thy daughter Guinevere to wife."

Whom when he heard, Leodogran in heart
140   Debating—"How should I that am a king,
However much he holp me at my need,
Give my one daughter saving to a king,
And a king's son?"—lifted his voice, and call'd
A hoary man, his chamberlain, to whom
145   He trusted all things, and of him required
His counsel: "Knowest thou aught of Arthur's birth?"

Then spake the hoary chamberlain and said,
"Sir King, there be but two old men that know:
And each is twice as old as I; and one
150   Is Merlin, the wise man that ever served
King Uther thro' his magic art; and one
Is Merlin's master (so they call him) Bleys,
Who taught him magic; but the scholar ran
Before the master, and so far, that Bleys
155   Laid magic by, and sat him down, and wrote
All things and whatsoever Merlin did
In one great annal-book, where after-years
Will learn the secret of our Arthur's birth."

To whom the King Leodogran replied,
160   "O friend, had I been holpen half as well
By this King Arthur as by thee to-day,
Then beast and man had had their share of me:
But summon here before us yet once more
Ulfius, and Brastias, and Bedivere."

165   Then, when they came before him, the King said,
"I have seen the cuckoo chased by lesser fowl,
And reason in the chase: but wherefore now
Do these your lords stir up the heat of war,
Some calling Arthur born of Gorloïs,
170   Others of Anton? Tell me, ye yourselves,
Hold ye this Arthur for King Uther's son?"

And Ulfius and Brastias answer'd, "Ay."
Then Bedivere, the first of all his knights
Knighted by Arthur at his crowning, spake—
175   For bold in heart and act and word was he,
Whenever slander breathed against the King—

"Sir, there be many rumours on this head:
For there be those who hate him in their hearts,
Call him baseborn, and since his ways are sweet,
180   And theirs are bestial, hold him less than man:

And there be those who deem him more than man,
And dream he dropt from heaven: but my belief
In all this matter—so ye care to learn—
Sir, for ye know that in King Uther's time
185 The prince and warrior Gorloïs, he that held
Tintagil castle by the Cornish sea,
Was wedded with a winsome wife, Ygerne:
And daughters had she borne him,—one whereof,
Lot's wife, the Queen of Orkney, Bellicent,
190 Hath ever like a loyal sister cleaved
To Arthur,—but a son she had not borne.
And Uther cast upon her eyes of love:
But she, a stainless wife to Gorloïs,
So loathed the bright dishonour of his love,
195 That Gorloïs and King Uther went to war:
And overthrown was Gorloïs and slain.
Then Uther in his wrath and heat besieged
Ygerne within Tintagil, where her men,
Seeing the mighty swarm about their walls,
200 Left her and fled, and Uther enter'd in,
And there was none to call to but himself.
So, compass'd by the power of the King,
Enforced she was to wed him in her tears,
And with a shameful swiftness: afterward,
205 Not many moons, King Uther died himself,
Moaning and wailing for an heir to rule
After him, lest the realm should go to wrack.
And that same night, the night of the new year,
By reason of the bitterness and grief
210 That vext his mother, all before his time
Was Arthur born, and all as soon as born
Deliver'd at a secret postern-gate
To Merlin, to be holden far apart
Until his hour should come; because the lords
215 Of that fierce day were as the lords of this,
Wild beasts, and surely would have torn the child
Piecemeal among them, had they known; for each
But sought to rule for his own self and hand,
And many hated Uther for the sake
220 Of Gorloïs. Wherefore Merlin took the child,
And gave him to Sir Anton, an old knight
And ancient friend of Uther; and his wife
Nursed the young prince, and rear'd him with her own;
And no man knew. And ever since the lords
225 Have foughten like wild beasts among themselves,
So that the realm has gone to wrack: but now,
This year, when Merlin (for his hour had come)
Brought Arthur forth, and set him in the hall,
Proclaiming, 'Here is Uther's heir, your king,'

230 A hundred voices cried, 'Away with him!
No king of ours! a son of Gorloïs he,
Or else the child of Anton, and no king,
Or else baseborn.' Yet Merlin thro' his craft,
And while the people clamour'd for a king,
235 Had Arthur crown'd; but after, the great lords
Banded, and so brake out in open war."

Then while the King debated with himself
If Arthur were the child of shamefulness,
Or born the son of Gorloïs, after death,
240 Or Uther's son, and born before his time,
Or whether there were truth in anything
Said by these three, there came to Cameliard,
With Gawain and young Modred, her two sons,
Lot's wife, the Queen of Orkney, Bellicent;[2]
245 Whom as he could, not as he would, the King
Made feast for, saying, as they sat at meat,

"A doubtful throne is ice on summer seas.
Ye come from Arthur's court. Victor his men
Report him! Yea, but ye—think ye this king—
250 So many those that hate him, and so strong,
So few his knights, however brave they be—
Hath body enow to hold his foemen down?"

"O King," she cried, "and I will tell thee: few,
Few, but all brave, all of one mind with him;
255 For I was near him when the savage yells
Of Uther's peerage died, and Arthur sat
Crown'd on the daïs, and his warriors cried,
'Be thou the king, and we will work thy will
Who love thee.' Then the King in low deep tones,
260 And simple words of great authority,
Bound them by so strait° vows to his own self,   strict
That when they rose, knighted from kneeling, some
Were pale as at the passing of a ghost,
Some flush'd, and others dazed, as one who wakes
265 Half-blinded at the coming of a light.

"But when he spake and cheer'd his Table Round
With large, divine, and comfortable words,
Beyond my tongue to tell thee—I beheld
From eye to eye thro' all their Order flash
270 A momentary likeness of the King:
And ere it left their faces, thro' the cross
And those around it and the Crucified,

2. The daughter of Gorloïs and Ygerne, Bellicent is Arthur's older half-sister. Her sons are Arthur's nephews: Gawain becomes one of Arthur's knights, but Modred eventually leads the rebellion against him.

Down from the casement over Arthur, smote
Flame-colour, vert and azure,[3] in three rays,
275   One falling upon each of three fair queens,
Who stood in silence near his throne, the friends
Of Arthur, gazing on him, tall, with bright
Sweet faces, who will help him at his need.

"And there I saw mage Merlin, whose vast wit
280   And hundred winters are but as the hands
Of loyal vassals toiling for their liege.

"And near him stood the Lady of the Lake,[4]
Who knows a subtler magic than his own—
Clothed in white samite,[5] mystic, wonderful.
285   She gave the King his huge cross-hilted sword,
Whereby to drive the heathen out: a mist
Of incense curl'd about her, and her face
Wellnigh was hidden in the minster° gloom;   cathedral
But there was heard among the holy hymns
290   A voice as of the waters, for she dwells
Down in a deep; calm, whatsoever storms
May shake the world, and when the surface rolls,
Hath power to walk the waters like our Lord.

"There likewise I beheld Excalibur[6]
295   Before him at his crowning borne, the sword
That rose from out the bosom of the lake,
And Arthur row'd across and took it—rich
With jewels, elfin Urim,[7] on the hilt,
Bewildering heart and eye—the blade so bright
300   That men are blinded by it—on one side,
Graven in the oldest tongue of all this world,
'Take me,' but turn the blade and ye shall see,
And written in the speech ye speak yourself,
'Cast me away!' And sad was Arthur's face
305   Taking it, but old Merlin counsell'd him,
'Take thou and strike! the time to cast away
Is yet far-off.' So this great brand the king
Took, and by this will beat his foemen down."

Thereat Leodogran rejoiced, but thought
310   To sift his doubtings to the last, and ask'd,

---

3. Red, green and blue; presumably the cross is part of a stained glass window set in the wall above Arthur. In *Morte D'Arthur* Malory said of the three queens: "one was king Arthur's sister Morgan le Fay; the other was the queene of Northgalis; and the third was the queene of the wast lands." In *The Passing of Arthur* they reappear to take Arthur to Avalon. Tennyson also identified them with Faith, Hope, and Charity.

4. The Lady of the Lake in the old Legends is the Church [Tennyson's note].
5. A rich silk stuff inwrought with gold and silver threads [Tennyson's note].
6. Arthur's legendary sword.
7. Cf. Exodus 28.30: "And thou shalt put in the breastplate of judgment the Urim and the Thummim," objects used for casting lots to determine God's will.

Fixing full eyes of question on her face,
"The swallow and the swift are near akin,
But thou art closer to this noble prince,
Being his own dear sister;" and she said,
315 "Daughter of Gorloïs and Ygerne am I;"
"And therefore Arthur's sister?" ask'd the King
She answer'd, "These be secret things," and sign'd
To those two sons to pass, and let them be.
And Gawain went, and breaking into song
320 Sprang out, and follow'd by his flying hair
Ran like a colt, and leapt at all he saw:
But Modred laid his ear beside the doors,
And there half-heard;[8] the same that afterward
Struck for the throne, and striking found his doom.

[Queen Bellicent tells Leodogran that, while she doesn't know if Arthur is her brother, both Bleys and Merlin had confirmed her presentiment that Arthur would become a great king.]

She spake and King Leodogran rejoiced,
425 But musing "Shall I answer yea or nay?"
Doubted, and drowsed, nodded and slept, and saw,
Dreaming, a slope of land that ever grew,
Field after field, up to a height, the peak
Haze-hidden, and thereon a phantom king,
430 Now looming, and now lost; and on the slope
The sword rose, the hind fell, the herd was driven,
Fire glimpsed; and all the land from roof and rick,
In drifts of smoke before a rolling wind,
Stream'd to the peak, and mingled with the haze
435 And made it thicker; while the phantom king
Sent out at times a voice; and here or there
Stood one who pointed toward the voice, the rest
Slew on and burnt, crying, "No king of ours,
No son of Uther, and no king of ours;"
440 Till with a wink his dream was changed, the haze
Descended, and the solid earth became
As nothing, but the King stood out in heaven,
Crown'd. And Leodogran awoke, and sent
Ulfius, and Brastias and Bedivere,
445 Back to the court of Arthur answering yea.

Then Arthur charged his warrior whom he loved
And honour'd most, Sir Lancelot, to ride forth
And bring the Queen;[9]—and watch'd him from the gates:
And Lancelot past away among the flowers,

---

8. Bellicent sends her sons away so they will not hear her discuss the mystery surrounding Arthur's birth, but Modred eavesdrops.
9. Although Arthur told Lancelot, "I trust thee to the death" (line 133 above), subsequent Idylls reveal that Lancelot betrayed this trust by falling in love with Guinevere when he was sent to escort her to her wedding.

450   (For then was latter April) and return'd
          Among the flowers, in May, with Guinevere.
          To whom arrived, by Dubric the high saint,[1]
          Chief of the church in Britain, and before
          The stateliest of her altar-shrines, the King
455   That morn was married, while in stainless white,
          The fair beginners of a nobler time,
          And glorying in their vows and him, his knights
          Stood round him, and rejoicing in his joy.
          Far shone the fields of May thro' open door,
460   The sacred altar blossom'd white with May,
          The Sun of May descended on their King,
          They gazed on all earth's beauty in their Queen,
          Roll'd incense, and there past along the hymns
          A voice as of the waters, while the two
465   Sware at the shrine of Christ a deathless love:
          And Arthur said, "Behold, thy doom is mine.
          Let chance what will, I love thee to the death!"
          To whom the Queen replied with drooping eyes,
          "King and my lord, I love thee to the death!"
470   And holy Dubric spread his hands and spake,
          "Reign ye, and live and love, and make the world
          Other, and may thy Queen be one with thee,
          And all this Order of thy Table Round
          Fulfil the boundless purpose of their King!"

                              * * *

          There at the banquet those great Lords from Rome,[2]
          The slowly-fading mistress of the world,
505   Strode in, and claim'd their tribute as of yore.
          But Arthur spake, "Behold, for these have sworn
          To wage my wars, and worship me their King;
          The old order changeth, yielding place to new;
          And we that fight for our fair father Christ,
510   Seeing that ye be grown too weak and old
          To drive the heathen from your Roman wall,
          No tribute will we pay": so those great lords
          Drew back in wrath, and Arthur strove with Rome.

          And Arthur and his knighthood for a space
515   Were all one will, and thro' that strength the King
          Drew in the petty princedoms under him,
          Fought, and in twelve great battles overcame
          The heathen hordes, and made a realm and reign'd.

1868–1869   1869

---

1. Archbishop of Caerleon.   Arthur asserts his independence and refuses to pay, argu-
2. Emissaries from Rome, which still claimed tribute from   ing that Rome had grown too weak to defend Britain
Britain as part of the Roman Empire. In lines 506–512   from other invaders.

The Higher Pantheism[1]

The sun, the moon, the stars, the seas, the hills and the plains—
Are not these, O Soul, the Vision of Him who reigns?

Is not the Vision He? tho' He be not that which He seems?
Dreams are true while they last, and do we not live in dreams?

5   Earth, these solid stars, this weight of body and limb,
Are they not sign and symbol of thy division from Him?

Dark is the world to thee: thyself art the reason why;
For is He not all but that which has power to feel "I am I"?

Glory about thee, without thee; and thou fulfillest thy doom
10   Making Him broken gleams, and a stifled splendour and gloom.

Speak to Him thou for He hears, and Spirit with Spirit can meet—
Closer is He than breathing, and nearer than hands and feet.

God is law, say the wise; O Soul, and let us rejoice,
For if He thunder by law the thunder is yet His voice.

15   Law is God, say some: no God at all, says the fool;
For all we have power to see is a straight staff bent in a pool;

And the ear of man cannot hear, and the eye of man cannot see;
But if we could see and hear, this Vision—were it not He?

1869

Flower in the Crannied Wall

Flower in the crannied wall,
I pluck you out of the crannies,
I hold you here, root and all, in my hand,
Little flower—but *if* I could understand
What you are, root and all, and all in all,
I should know what God and man is.

1869

Crossing the Bar[1]

Sunset and evening star,
  And one clear call for me!
And may there be no moaning of the bar,[2]
  When I put out to sea,

1. Tennyson's son noted that this was written for the Metaphysical Society in 1869. Pantheism views God as coexistent with nature and its laws; the "higher pantheism" proposed by Tennyson sees nature not as God, but as merely a visible sign of a distinct and all-pervading Spirit that is beyond the power of imperfect human senses to grasp. Tennyson's paradoxes inspired Swinburne to produce a brutal but hilarious parody.

1. Tennyson instructed that this poem should appear at the end of every collection of his work, though it was not in fact the last poem he wrote. The poem, he said, "came in a moment" while he was crossing the Solent to return home to Farringford on the Isle of Wight.
2. The sandbank that forms at the mouth of a harbor. The "moaning" may be the sound of the river and the sea meeting.

5   But such a tide as moving seems asleep,
    Too full for sound and foam,
When that which drew from out the boundless deep
    Turns again home.

    Twilight and evening bell,
10   And after that the dark!
And may there be no sadness of farewell,
    When I embark;

For tho' from out our bourne° of Time and Place   *boundary*
    The flood may bear me far,
15   I hope to see my Pilot face to face[3]
    When I have crost the bar.

1889   1889

＊━━◆≋━━＊

Charles Darwin
1809–1882

Charles Darwin's five-year excursion on the *Beagle* has become the stuff of legend. No voyage since that of Columbus has had such a profound impact on the world. Darwin's ideas concerning evolution and natural selection brought about a revolution in human thought; they radically transformed our sense of our place in the universe. Yet *The Voyage of the Beagle* is a modestly written account of the meticulous observations of a young naturalist, as interested in ordinary beetles and coral formations as in the weirdly monstrous creatures he saw on the Galapagos Islands.

Nothing in Darwin's youth suggested a great man in the making. His father once warned him, "You care for nothing but shooting, dogs, and rat-catching, and you will be a disgrace to yourself and all your family." Darwin's father was a prosperous doctor, and he sent his son to Edinburgh University for two years to study medicine, but Darwin detested the subject and neglected his studies. Casting about for an occupation for this unpromising son, his father proposed the undemanding career of a country clergyman. Darwin agreed and spent the next three years at Cambridge where, according to his autobiography, he did little except collect beetles.

Although he considered his formal education a complete waste, Darwin was busy educating himself in natural history. The turning point in his life was an invitation to become the ship's naturalist on the H.M.S. *Beagle*'s surveying expedition. Knowing the ship would be away for years, Darwin's father initially refused permission to accept. At a time when the word "scientist" did not even exist, he could not see how such an undertaking could lead to any respectable profession. But he left a loophole, telling his son, "If you can find any man of common sense, who advises you to go, I will give my consent." Fortunately, Darwin's uncle supported the idea, and in 1831 the *Beagle* sailed for South America with the twenty-two-year-old Darwin aboard.

Darwin had to put up with cramped quarters, seasickness, and the captain's volatile temper, but he accomplished an extraordinary amount of work. He collected specimens, filled

---

3. The pilot has been on board all the while, but in the dark I have not seen him [Tennyson's note]. Cf. 1 Corinthians 13.12: "For now we see through a glass, darkly; but then face to face: now I know in part; but then shall I know even as also I am known."

MAN·IS·BVT·A·WORM·

Linley Sambourne, *Man is But a Worm*, from *Punch's Almanack for 1882* (published December 1881). In 1881, Darwin, who had studied earthworms for forty years, published *The Formation of Vegetable Mould through the Action of Worms with Observations on their Habits*. Darwin justified his interest in the lowly worm by pointing out that "All the fertile areas of this planet have at least once passed through the bodies of earthworms." But it was his conclusion that sparked public attention, causing many to link worms with Darwin's evolutionary theory: "Worms," wrote Darwin, "although standing low in the scale of organization, possess some degree of intelligence." *Punch's* Linley Sambourne (1844–1910), one of the great Victorian caricaturists, depicted the ape-browed scientist sitting like Michelangelo's Adam as depicted on the Sistine Chapel ceiling. Mixing Creationism and Evolution, the Adamic Darwin retrospectively bestows life and consciousness on his ancestors, an evolving chain of monkeys that have sprung from worms. Emerging from CHAOS at the lower left, the creatures spin around "Time's Meter" until they arrive at the modern Victorian gentleman who doffs his hat to Darwin.

eighteen notebooks with scientific observations, and spent long periods ashore studying plants and animals, fossils, and indigenous cultures. He also kept a diary that eventually became the basis of *The Voyage of the Beagle* (1839, rev. 1845), one of the great classics of travel literature. Out of these investigations, particularly in the volcanic Galapagos Islands off the coast of South America, grew the theory of evolution.

Yet it is a myth that Darwin had a sudden insight concerning the origin of species while examining the strange tortoises, lizards, and finches in the Galapagos. Though he had read with interest the evolutionary speculations of his grandfather, Erasmus Darwin, he had remained a creationist: during the voyage he continued to believe that species were fixed forever at the moment of their creation, as described in the Bible. Only back in England, working through his huge volume of notes, did he become convinced of the mutability of species.

Within a few months of his return home in 1836, Darwin had accepted evolution as the explanation for the natural phenomena he had observed. But he was in no hurry to publish his findings. In fact, twenty years went by before he learned in 1858 that a young naturalist, Alfred Russel Wallace, had arrived independently at the theory of natural selection. A joint paper of their findings was presented to the Linnaean Society, and Darwin at long last rushed to compile and publish *On the Origin of Species by Means of Natural Selection* (1859). Darwin realized that most living organisms produce far more offspring than can survive: not every acorn becomes an oak. Certain genetically favored individuals have a competitive edge in the struggle for life. Nature thus ensures the "survival of the fittest," and eventually their descendants evolve into new and better-adapted species.

The book created an immediate sensation. The original edition sold out the day it was published. Darwin was not the first to propose a theory of evolution, but he was the first to offer a persuasive account of the means by which evolution works. Geologists such as Charles Lyell had already shown that the earth was immensely older than six thousand years, the traditional estimate based on biblical chronology. In further undermining the biblical account of creation, Darwin shook the faith of his contemporaries.

Darwin was not eager to offend people, nor did he enjoy controversy. Thus in *The Origin of Species* he tactfully avoided any discussion of human origins, although he was already confident that evolution applied to human beings as well. In *The Descent of Man* (1871) he finally made his position clear: man is an animal. Darwin's ideas were profoundly unsettling. No longer sure of belonging to an ordered world overseen by a beneficent Creator, many people felt they had been set adrift in an indifferent cosmos. Tennyson's memorable phrase, "Nature, red in tooth and claw," expressed the Victorians' collective horror at Darwin's vision of nature as a cruel and violent battlefield.

Darwin's theories were earthshaking, but his private life was not. When the *Beagle* voyage ended, he debated the pros and cons of marriage, telling himself that a wife would provide an "object to be beloved and played with—better than a dog anyhow." Despite these unromantic musings, his marriage to his cousin Emma Wedgwood was long and happy. They settled down in a country house and had many children. For the rest of his life Darwin suffered from mysterious illnesses; they prevented his going into society, but they did not stop him working and writing. He never traveled again.

from On the Origin of Species by Means of Natural Selection
or
The Preservation of Favoured Races in the Struggle for Life
from *Chapter 3. Struggle for Existence*

Before entering on the subject of this chapter, I must make a few preliminary remarks, to show how the struggle for existence bears on Natural Selection. * * * The mere existence of individual variability and of some few well-marked varieties, though necessary as the foundation for the work, helps us but little in understanding how species arise in nature. How have all those exquisite adaptations of one part of the organisation to another part, and to the conditions of life, and of one distinct organic being to another being, been perfected? We see these beautiful co-adaptations most plainly in the woodpecker and missletoe; and only a little less plainly in the humblest parasite which clings to the hairs of a quadruped or feathers of a bird; in the structure of the beetle which dives through the water; in the plumed seed which is wafted by the gentlest breeze; in short, we see beautiful adaptations everywhere and in every part of the organic world.

Again, it may be asked, how is it that varieties which I have called incipient species, become ultimately converted into good and distinct species, which in most cases obviously differ from each other far more than do the varieties of the same species? How do those groups of species, which constitute what are called distinct genera,[1] and which differ from each other more than do the species of the same genus, arise? All these results, as we shall more fully see in the next chapter, follow inevitably from the struggle for life. Owing to this struggle for life, any variation, however slight and from whatever cause proceeding, if it be in any degree profitable to an individual of any species, in its infinitely complex relations to other organic beings and to external nature, will tend to the preservation of that individual, and will generally be inherited by its offspring. The offspring, also, will thus have a better chance of surviving, for, of the many individuals of any species which are periodically born, but a small number can survive. I have called this principle, by which each slight variation, if useful, is preserved, by the term of Natural Selection, in order to mark its relation to man's power of selection. We have seen that man by selection can certainly produce great results, and can adapt organic beings to his own uses, through the accumulation of slight but useful variations, given to him by the hand of Nature. But Natural Selection, as we shall hereafter see, is a power incessantly ready for action, and is as immeasurably superior to man's feeble efforts, as the works of Nature are to those of Art.

We will now discuss in a little more detail the struggle for existence. * * * Nothing is easier than to admit in words the truth of the universal struggle for life, or more difficult—at least I have found it so—than constantly to bear this conclusion in mind. Yet unless it be thoroughly engrained in the mind, I am convinced that the whole economy of nature, with every fact on distribution, rarity, abundance, extinction, and variation, will be dimly seen or quite misunderstood. We behold the face of nature bright with gladness, we often see superabundance of food; we do not see, or we forget, that the birds which are idly singing round us mostly live on insects or seeds, and are thus constantly destroying life; or we forget how largely these songsters, or their eggs, or their nestlings, are destroyed by birds and beasts of prey; we do not always bear in mind, that though food may be now superabundant, it is not so at all seasons of each recurring year.

I should premise that I use the term Struggle for Existence in a large and metaphorical sense, including dependence of one being on another, and including (which is more important) not only the life of the individual, but success in leaving progeny. Two canine animals in a time of dearth, may be truly said to struggle with each other which shall get food and live. But a plant on the edge of a desert is said to struggle for life against the drought, though more properly it should be said to be dependent on the moisture. A plant which annually produces a thousand seeds, of

1. Plural of genus, a class of species with common characteristics.

which on an average only one comes to maturity, may be more truly said to struggle with the plants of the same and other kinds which already clothe the ground. The missletoe is dependent on the apple and a few other trees, but can only in a far-fetched sense be said to struggle with these trees, for if too many of these parasites grow on the same tree, it will languish and die. But several seedling missletoes, growing close together on the same branch, may more truly be said to struggle with each other. As the missletoe is disseminated by birds, its existence depends on birds; and it may metaphorically be said to struggle with other fruit-bearing plants, in order to tempt birds to devour and thus disseminate its seeds rather than those of other plants. In these several senses, which pass into each other, I use for convenience sake the general term of struggle for existence.

A struggle for existence inevitably follows from the high rate at which all organic beings tend to increase. Every being, which during its natural lifetime produces several eggs or seeds, must suffer destruction during some period of its life, and during some season or occasional year, otherwise, on the principle of geometrical increase, its numbers would quickly become so inordinately great that no country could support the product. Hence, as more individuals are produced than can possibly survive, there must in every case be a struggle for existence, either one individual with another of the same species, or with the individuals of distinct species or with the physical conditions of life. It is the doctrine of Malthus[2] applied with manifold force to the whole animal and vegetable kingdoms; for in this case there can be no artificial increase of food, and no prudential restraint from marriage. Although some species may be now increasing, more or less rapidly, in numbers, all cannot do so, for the world would not hold them.

There is no exception to the rule that every organic being naturally increases at so high a rate, that if not destroyed, the earth would soon be covered by the progeny of a single pair. Even slow-breeding man has doubled in twenty-five years, and at this rate, in a few thousand years, there would literally not be standing room for his progeny. Linnaeus[3] has calculated that if an annual plant produced only two seeds—and there is no plant so unproductive as this—and their seedlings next year produced two, and so on, then in twenty years there would be a million plants. The elephant is reckoned to be the slowest breeder of all known animals, and I have taken some pains to estimate its probable minimum rate of natural increase: it will be under the mark to assume that it breeds when thirty years old, and goes on breeding till ninety years old, bringing forth three pairs of young in this interval; if this be so, at the end of the fifth century there would be alive fifteen million elephants, descended from the first pair.

But we have better evidence on this subject than mere theoretical calculations, namely, the numerous recorded cases of the astonishingly rapid increase of various animals in a state of nature, when circumstances have been favourable to them during two or three following seasons. Still more striking is the evidence from our domestic animals of many kinds which have run wild in several parts of the world: if the statements of the rate of increase of slow-breeding cattle and horses in South America, and latterly in Australia, had not been well authenticated, they would have

---

2. In his *Essay on the Principle of Population* (1803), English economist Thomas Malthus argued that unchecked population growth would threaten the food supply; he proposed "moral restraint" as a partial solution.
3. Carl von Linné (1707–1778), Swedish botanist and founder of scientific classification systems.

been quite incredible. So it is with plants: cases could be given of introduced plants which have become common throughout whole islands in a period of less than ten years. ✳ ✳ ✳

In looking at Nature, it is most necessary to keep the foregoing considerations always in mind—never to forget that every single organic being around us may be said to be striving to the utmost to increase in numbers; that each lives by a struggle at some period of its life; that heavy destruction inevitably falls either on the young or old, during each generation or at recurrent intervals. Lighten any check, mitigate the destruction ever so little, and the number of the species will almost instantaneously increase to any amount. The face of Nature may be compared to a yielding surface, with ten thousand sharp wedges packed close together and driven inwards by incessant blows, sometimes one wedge being struck, and then another with greater force. ✳ ✳ ✳

The amount of food for each species of course gives the extreme limit to which each can increase; but very frequently it is not the obtaining food, but the serving as prey to other animals, which determines the average numbers of a species. Thus, there seems to be little doubt that the stock of partridges, grouse, and hares on any large estate depends chiefly on the destruction of vermin. If not one head of game were shot during the next twenty years in England, and, at the same time, if no vermin were destroyed, there would, in all probability, be less game than at present, although hundreds of thousands of game animals are now annually killed. On the other hand, in some cases, as with the elephant and rhinoceros, none are destroyed by beasts of prey: even the tiger in India most rarely dares to attack a young elephant protected by its dam.

Climate plays an important part in determining the average numbers of a species, and periodical seasons of extreme cold or drought, I believe to be the most effective of all checks. I estimated that the winter of 1854–55 destroyed four-fifths of the birds in my own grounds; and this is a tremendous destruction, when we remember that ten per cent. is an extraordinarily severe mortality from epidemics with man. The action of climate seems at first sight to be quite independent of the struggle for existence; but in so far as climate chiefly acts in reducing food, it brings on the most severe struggle between the individuals, whether of the same or of distinct species, which subsist on the same kind of food. Even when climate, for instance extreme cold, acts directly, it will be the least vigorous, or those which have got least food through the advancing winter, which will suffer most. When we travel from south to north, or from a damp region to a dry, we invariably see some species gradually getting rarer and rarer, and finally disappearing; and the change of climate being conspicuous, we are tempted to attribute the whole effect to its direct action. But this is a very false view: we forget that each species, even where it most abounds, is constantly suffering enormous destruction at some period of its life, from enemies or from competitors for the same place and food; and if these enemies or competitors be in the least degree favoured by any slight change of climate, they will increase in numbers, and, as each area is already fully stocked with inhabitants, the other species will decrease. ✳ ✳ ✳

That climate acts in main part indirectly by favouring other species, we may clearly see in the prodigious number of plants in our gardens which can perfectly well endure our climate, but which never become naturalised, for they cannot compete with our native plants, nor resist destruction by our native animals. ✳ ✳ ✳

Many cases are on record showing how complex and unexpected are the checks and relations between organic beings, which have to struggle together in the same country. I will give only a single instance, which, though a simple one, has interested me. In Staffordshire, on the estate of a relation where I had ample means of investigation, there was a large and extremely barren heath, which had never been touched by the hand of man; but several hundred acres of exactly the same nature had been enclosed twenty-five years previously and planted with Scotch fir. The change in the native vegetation of the planted part of the heath was most remarkable, more than is generally seen in passing from one quite different soil to another: not only the proportional numbers of the heath-plants were wholly changed, but twelve species of plants (not counting grasses and carices) flourished in the plantations, which could not be found on the heath. The effect on the insects must have been still greater, for six insectivorous birds were very common in the plantations, which were not to be seen on the heath; and the heath was frequented by two or three distinct insectivorous birds. Here we see how potent has been the effect of the introduction of a single tree, nothing whatever else having been done, with the exception that the land had been enclosed, so that cattle could not enter. * * *

A corollary of the highest importance may be deduced from the foregoing remarks, namely, that the structure of every organic being is related, in the most essential yet often hidden manner, to that of all other organic beings, with which it comes into competition for food or residence, or from which it has to escape, or on which it preys. This is obvious in the structure of the teeth and talons of the tiger; and in that of the legs and claws of the parasite which clings to the hair on the tiger's body. But in the beautifully plumed seed of the dandelion, and in the flattened and fringed legs of the water-beetle, the relation seems at first confined to the elements of air and water. Yet the advantage of plumed seeds no doubt stands in the closest relation to the land being already thickly clothed by other plants; so that the seeds may be widely distributed and fall on unoccupied ground. In the water-beetle, the structure of its legs, so well adapted for diving, allows it to compete with other aquatic insects, to hunt for its own prey, and to escape serving as prey to other animals.

The store of nutriment laid up within the seeds of many plants seems at first sight to have no sort of relation to other plants. But from the strong growth of young plants produced from such seeds (as peas and beans), when sown in the midst of long grass, I suspect that the chief use of the nutriment in the seed is to favour the growth of the young seedling, whilst struggling with other plants growing vigorously all around.

Look at a plant in the midst of its range, why does it not double or quadruple its numbers? We know that it can perfectly well withstand a little more heat or cold, dampness or dryness, for elsewhere it ranges into slightly hotter or colder, damper or drier districts. In this case we can clearly see that if we wished in imagination to give the plant the power of increasing in number, we should have to give it some advantage over its competitors, or over the animals which preyed on it. On the confines of its geographical range, a change of constitution with respect to climate would clearly be an advantage to our plant; but we have reason to believe that only a few plants or animals range so far, that they are destroyed by the rigour of the climate alone. Not until we reach the extreme confines of life, in the arctic regions or on the borders of an utter desert, will competition cease. The land may be extremely cold or dry, yet there will be competition between some few species, or between the individuals of the same species, for the warmest or dampest spots.

Hence, also, we can see that when a plant or animal is placed in a new country amongst new competitors, though the climate may be exactly the same as in its former home, yet the conditions of its life will generally be changed in an essential manner. If we wished to increase its average numbers in its new home, we should have to modify it in a different way to what we should have done in its native country; for we should have to give it some advantage over a different set of competitors or enemies.

It is good thus to try in our imagination to give any form some advantage over another. Probably in no single instance should we know what to do, so as to succeed. It will convince us of our ignorance on the mutual relations of all organic beings; a conviction as necessary, as it seems to be difficult to acquire. All that we can do, is to keep steadily in mind that each organic being is striving to increase at a geometrical ratio; that each at some period of its life, during some season of the year, during each generation or at intervals, has to struggle for life, and to suffer great destruction. When we reflect on this struggle, we may console ourselves with the full belief, that the war of nature is not incessant, that no fear is felt, that death is generally prompt, and that the vigorous, the healthy, and the happy survive and multiply.

1859

⇒ PERSPECTIVES ⇐

Religion and Science

"If only the Geologists would let me alone, I could do very well, but those dreadful Hammers! I hear the clink of them at the end of every cadence of the Bible verses." John Ruskin's anxious words reflect the widespread fear that science was chipping away at the foundations of faith. The fossil record showed that the earth was vastly older than anyone had thought, thus casting doubt on the biblical account of Creation, conventionally dated around four thousand years before the birth of Christ. Suddenly a scale of millions and even billions of years was being employed. "The riddle of the rocks" having been deciphered, the physicist John Tyndall said in 1874, "the leaves of that stone book . . . carry the mind back into abysses of past time."

Yet, far from being opposed to science, many early Victorian clergymen were amateur geologists and naturalists. The word "scientist" did not even exist until 1840, and science was scarcely imagined as an independent profession: for all his love of natural history, Charles Darwin studied to be a clergyman. In his day, it was common to take a university degree with no scientific education at all. Until the mid-nineteenth century, science and religion had often been seen as being in harmony. In *Natural Theology* (1802) the philosopher and Anglican priest William Paley had proposed a famous analogy: when we see a complex mechanism such as a watch, we infer that the watch must have had a maker; similarly, when we see the order and beauty of the universe, we must infer the existence of a Creator. Paley's "Argument from Design" was enormously influential. As the geologist Hugh Miller put it, "I am confident that there is not half the ingenuity, or half the mathematical knowledge, displayed in the dome of St Paul's at London, that we find exhibited in the construction of this simple shell."

Increasingly, though, scientists began to question the evidence of God's artistry. In *Principles of Geology* (1830–1833), Charles Lyell argued that geological phenomena resulted from the gradual actions of nature over immense stretches of time. And in 1859, Darwin's *The Origin of Species* extended this perspective to the formation of living creatures, including human beings. Years of scientific observations had convinced him that the animate world is not the product of divine creation but of natural selection: "We can no longer argue that, for instance, the beautiful hinge of a bivalve shell must have been made by an intelligent being. . . . There seems to be no more design in the variability of organic beings and in the action of natural selection, than in the course which the wind blows."

Scientific methods, moreover, were being applied to the study of the Bible itself. Even as scientists undermined "natural" theology, a new wave of biblical criticism from Germany undermined the "revealed" theology given in the Bible. These scholars treated Scripture like any other text, probing into questions of dates and sources, authorship and authenticity. They concluded that Moses could not have written the Pentateuch, and that many episodes in the Bible could not be regarded as historically accurate; some even denied that Jesus was the son of God.

The claims of both science and the "Higher Criticism" provoked storms of controversy. They shattered certainties about the nature of truth, the meaning of life, and man's place in the universe. The historian J. A. Froude recalled the 1840s as a period when "All round us, the intellectual lightships had broken from their moorings. . . . The present generation . . . will never know what it was to find the lights all drifting, the compasses all awry, and nothing left to steer by except the stars." This was not only a personal problem; many assumed that a collapse of Christian faith would lead to the disintegration of society as a whole. The critic Walter Houghton points out the connection to the fear of revolution: in the reviews of *The Descent of Man* (1871) Darwin was severely censured for "revealing his zoological conclusions to the general public at a moment when the sky of Paris was red with the incendiary flames of the Commune."

Some—particularly the literal-minded Evangelicals—reacted to these upheavals by denying any validity to the new scientific theories; others struggled to repress their concerns.

The educator Thomas Arnold suggested that doubts "should be kept, I think, to ourselves, and not talked of even to our nearest friends." If we put a searching question to our neighbor, wrote Ruskin, we risk discovering "that he doubts of many things which we ourselves do not believe strongly enough to hear doubted without danger." To some Victorians, on the other hand, the new theories offered an opportunity for a fresh assessment of long-unquestioned beliefs. George Eliot wrote with exhilaration that her soul had been "liberated from the wretched giant's bed of dogmas on which it has been racked and stretched." The philosopher Leslie Stephen welcomed agnosticism: "I did not feel that the solid ground was giving way beneath my feet, but rather that I was being relieved of a cumbrous burden."

Stopping short of agnosticism, the liberal "Broad Church" centrists of the Church of England sought a clarified, "demythologized" faith, finding moral rather than historical truths in the old stories of creation. At times they treated even Jesus' miracles as more on a par with his parables than as crucial historical events. Bishop William Colenso's careful weighing of historical probabilities, excerpted below, struck many of his first readers as scandalous, but over time mainstream Church of England thought came to accept a comparable coexistence of myth and history in the biblical stories. The book of nature and the book of the acts of God alike now required active and engaged readers, in a world less of facts and certainties than of hypotheses and interpretations.

+—+ ≍◆≍ +—+

Thomas Babington Macaulay
1800–1859

Always a staunch believer in material progress, Macaulay extolled scientific achievements as entirely beneficial for society. In 1837 his lavish and unqualified praise of applied science did not jar any sensibilities, for religion and science had not yet clashed as violently as they were to do later in the century. Railroads and steamships, feats of engineering and astronomy, military and industrial technology—it was still possible to admire them all unreservedly. Macaulay's enthusiasm for science was untempered by any sense of the possible dangers of science, or of the threat science would soon pose to the very foundations of religious belief.

from Lord Bacon
[SCIENCE AS PROGRESS]

It has lengthened life; it has mitigated pain; it has extinguished diseases; it has increased the fertility of the soil; it has given new securities to the mariner; it has furnished new arms to the warrior; it has spanned great rivers and estuaries with bridges of form unknown to our fathers; it has guided the thunderbolt innocuously from heaven to earth; it has lighted up the night with the splendour of the day; it has extended the range of the human vision; it has multiplied the power of the human muscles; it has accelerated motion; it has annihilated distance; it has facilitated intercourse, correspondence, all friendly offices, all despatch of business; it has enabled man to descend to the depths of the sea, to soar into the air, to penetrate securely into the noxious recesses of the earth, to traverse the land in cars which whirl along without horses, and the ocean in ships which run ten knots an hour against the wind. These are but a part of its fruits, and of its first fruits. For it is a philosophy which never rests, which has never attained, which is never perfect. Its law is progress. A point which yesterday was invisible is its goal today, and will be its starting-post to-morrow.

1837

Charles Dickens
1812–1870

Victorian morality permeated British life in the mid-nineteenth century—but there was sharp disagreement as to how that morality should be fostered and expressed. In this selection, Dickens argues passionately for a relaxed standard of Sunday observance, against the strict rules that the Evangelicals were attempting to legislate. A broadly based group that included Methodists, Congregationalists, Baptists, and "Low Church" Anglicans, Evangelicals were concerned not only with individual salvation (through rigorous conduct, prayer, and Bible reading) but also with the moral reform of society. In the mid–1830s, Sir Andrew Agnew repeatedly proposed a Sunday Observance Bill in Parliament. As Dickens points out in his scathing attack, the effects of the Bill would have been felt disproportionately by the lower classes, for whom Sunday was the only day of relaxation; he argues that the cause of religion itself, as well as working people's well-being, would be harmed by overly strict observance.

For more about Dickens, see his principal listing on page 782.

from Sunday Under Three Heads

The provisions of the bill introduced into the House of Commons by Sir Andrew Agnew, and thrown out by that House on the motion for the second reading, on the 18th of May in the present year, by a majority of 32, may very fairly be taken as a test of the length to which the fanatics, of which the honourable Baronet is the distinguished leader, are prepared to go. * * *

The proposed enactments of the bill are briefly these:—All work is prohibited on the Lord's day, under heavy penalties, increasing with every repetition of the offence. There are penalties for keeping shops open—penalties for drunkenness—penalties for keeping open houses of entertainment—penalties for being present at any public meeting or assembly—penalties for letting carriages, and penalties for hiring them—penalties for travelling in steam-boats, and penalties for taking passengers—penalties on vessels commencing their voyage on Sundays—penalties on the owners of cattle who suffer them to be driven on the Lord's day—penalties on constables who refuse to act, and penalties for resisting them when they do. In addition to these trifles, the constables are invested with arbitrary, vexatious, and most extensive powers; and all this in a bill which sets out with the hypocritical and canting declaration that "nothing is more acceptable to God than the *true and sincere* worship of Him according to His holy will, and that it is the bounden duty of Parliament to promote the observance of the Lord's day, by protecting every class of society against being required to sacrifice their comfort, health, religious privileges, and conscience, for the convenience, enjoyment, or supposed advantage of any other class on the Lord's day"! The idea of making a man truly moral through the ministry of constables, and sincerely religious under the influence of penalties, is worthy of the mind which could form such a mass of monstrous absurdity as this bill is composed of. * * *

In the first place, it is by no means the worst characteristic of this bill, that it is a bill of blunders: it is, from beginning to end, a piece of deliberate cruelty, and crafty injustice. If the rich composed the whole population of this country, not a single comfort of one single man would be affected by it. It is directed exclusively, and without the exception of a solitary instance, against the amusements and recreations of the poor. * * *

Take the very first clause, the provision that no man shall be allowed to work on Sunday—"That no person, upon the Lord's day, shall do, or hire, or employ any person to do any manner of labour, or any work of his or her ordinary calling." What class of persons does this affect? The rich man? No. Menial servants, both male and female, are specially exempted from the operation of the bill. "Menial servants" are among the poor people. The bill has no regard for them. The Baronet's dinner must be cooked on Sunday, the Bishop's horses must be groomed, and the Peer's carriage must be driven. So the menial servants are put utterly beyond the pale of grace;—unless indeed, they are to go to heaven through the sanctity of their masters, and possibly they might think even that, rather an uncertain passport. * * *

With one exception, there are perhaps no clauses in the whole bill, so strongly illustrative of its partial operation, and the intention of its framer, as those which relate to travelling on Sunday. Penalties of ten, twenty, and thirty pounds, are mercilessly imposed upon coach proprietors who shall run their coaches on the Sabbath; one, two, and ten pounds upon those who hire, or let to hire, horses and carriages upon the Lord's day, but not one syllable about those who have no necessity to hire, because they have carriages and horses of their own; not one word of a penalty on liveried coachmen and footmen. The whole of the saintly venom is directed against the hired cabriolet, the humble fly, or the rumbling hackney coach, which enables a man of the poorer class to escape for a few hours from the smoke and dirt, in the midst of which he has been confined throughout the week: while the escutcheoned[1] carriage and the dashing cab, may whirl their wealthy owners to Sunday feasts and private oratorios, setting constables, informers, and penalties, at defiance. Again, in the description of the places of public resort which it is rendered criminal to attend on Sunday, there are no words comprising a very fashionable promenade. Public discussions, public debates, public lectures and speeches, are cautiously guarded against; for it is by their means that the people become enlightened enough, to deride the last efforts of bigotry and superstition. There is a stringent provision for punishing the poor man who spends an hour in a news-room, but there is nothing to prevent the rich one, from lounging away the day in the Zoological Gardens.

There is, in four words, a mock proviso, which affects to forbid travelling "with any animal" on the Lord's day. This, however, is revoked, as relates to the rich man, by a subsequent provision. We have then a penalty of not less than fifty, nor more than one hundred pounds, upon any person participating in the controul, or having the command of any vessel which shall commence her voyage on the Lord's day, should the wind prove favourable. The next time this bill is brought forward (which will no doubt be at an early period of the next session of Parliament) perhaps it will be better to amend this clause by declaring, that from and after the passing of the act, it shall be deemed unlawful for the wind to blow at all upon the Sabbath. It would remove a great deal of temptation from the owners and captains of vessels. * * *

---

1. Bearing a coat of arms.

Let us suppose such a bill as this, to have actually passed both branches of the legislature; to have received the royal assent; and to have come into operation. Imagine its effect in a great city like London.

Sunday comes, and brings with it a day of general gloom and austerity. The man who has been toiling hard all the week, has been looking towards the Sabbath, not as to a day of rest from labour, and healthy recreation, but as one of grievous tyranny and grinding oppression. The day which his Maker intended as a blessing, man has converted into a curse. Instead of being hailed by him as his period of relaxation, he finds it remarkable only as depriving him of every comfort and enjoyment. He has many children about him, all sent into the world at an early age, to struggle for a livelihood; one is kept in a warehouse all day, with an interval of rest too short to enable him to reach home, another walks four or five miles to his employment at the docks, a third earns a few shillings weekly, as an errand boy, or office messenger; and the employment of the man himself, detains him at some distance from his home from morning till night. Sunday is the only day on which they could all meet together, and enjoy a homely meal in social comfort; and now they sit down to a cold and cheerless dinner: the pious guardians of the man's salvation, having, in their regard for the welfare of his precious soul, shut up the bakers' shops.[2] The fire blazes high in the kitchen chimney of these well-fed hypocrites, and the rich steams of the savoury dinner scent the air. What care they to be told that this class of men have neither a place to cook in—nor means to bear the expense, if they had?

Look into your churches—diminished congregations, and scanty attendance. People have grown sullen and obstinate, and are becoming disgusted with the faith which condemns them to such a day as this, once in every seven. And as you cannot make people religious by Act of Parliament, or force them to church by constables, they display their feeling by staying away.

Turn into the streets, and mark the rigid gloom that reigns over everything around. The roads are empty, the fields are deserted, the houses of entertainment are closed. Groups of filthy and discontented-looking men, are idling about at the street corners, or sleeping in the sun; but there are no decently-dressed people of the poorer class, passing to and fro. Where should they walk to? It would take them an hour, at least, to get into the fields, and when they reached them, they could procure neither bit nor sup, without the informer and the penalty. Now and then, a carriage rolls smoothly on, or a well-mounted horseman followed by a liveried attendant, canters by; but with these exceptions, all is as melancholy and quiet, as if a pestilence had fallen on the city.

Bend your steps through the narrow and thickly-inhabited streets, and observe the sallow faces of the men and women, who are lounging at the doors, or lolling from the windows. Regard well, the closeness of these crowded rooms, and the noisome exhalations that rise from the drains and kennels; and then laud the triumph of religion and morality, which condemns people to drag their lives out in such stews[3] as these, and makes it criminal for them to eat or drink in the fresh air, or under the clear sky. * * *

It may be asked, what motives can actuate a man who has so little regard for the comfort of his fellow-beings, so little respect for their wants and necessities, and so

2. Lacking ovens at home, working people brought their dinners to cook at bakers' shops on Sundays. Dickens returned to the subject in *A Christmas Carol*, where the reformed Scrooge is indignant about Sunday closings, particularly of bakeries; see pages 810–11.
3. Overheated, congested areas.

distorted a notion of the beneficence of his Creator. I reply, an envious, heartless, ill-conditioned dislike, to seeing those whom fortune has placed below him, cheerful and happy—an intolerant confidence in his own high worthiness before God, and a lofty impression of the demerits of others—pride, selfish pride, as inconsistent with the spirit of Christianity itself, as opposed to the example of its Founder upon earth.

1836

David Friedrich Strauss
1808–1874

Evolution and geology were not the only threats to traditional Christian faith: German scholars who applied methods of historical and literary analysis to the Bible demonstrated that it was, as the historian J. A. Froude put it, "a human composition—parts of it of doubtful authenticity." Such scholarship, known as the "higher criticism," undermined the Bible's stature as divine revelation. Biblical criticism made Charles Kingsley, the Anglican clergyman associated with "Muscular Christianity," feel as though he were standing "on a cliff which is crumbling beneath one, and falling piecemeal into the dark sea." But it liberated George Eliot from her evangelical beliefs. In 1846 she helped bring German scholarship to the attention of the British public with her translation, excerpted here, of *Das Leben Jesu*, David Friedrich Strauss's controversial treatment of Jesus as a historical figure, not the son of God.

from The Life of Jesus Critically Examined
Translated by George Eliot

Having shown the possible existence of the mythical and the legendary in the gospels, both on extrinsic and intrinsic grounds, and defined their distinctive characteristics, it remains in conclusion to inquire how their actual presence may be recognized in individual cases?

The mythus[1] presents two phases; in the first place it is not history; in the second it is fiction, the product of the particular mental tendency of a certain community. These two phases afford the one a negative, the other a positive criterion, by which the mythus is to be recognized.

I. *Negative*. That an account is not historical—that the matter related could not have taken place in the manner described is evident.

First. When the narration is irreconcileable with the known and universal laws which govern the course of events. * * *

Secondly. An account which shall be regarded as historically valid must neither be inconsistent with itself, nor in contradiction with other accounts. * * *

It may here be asked: is it to be regarded as a contradiction if one account is wholly silent respecting a circumstance mentioned by another? In itself, apart from all other considerations, the argumentum ex silentio is of no weight; but it is certainly to be accounted of moment when, at the same time, it may be shown that had the author known the circumstance he could not have failed to mention it, and also that he must have known it had it actually occurred.

1. Myth; this was a contentious word to use in connection with Scripture.

II. *Positive*. The positive characters of legend and fiction are to be recognized sometimes in the form, sometimes in the substance of a narrative.

If the form be poetical, if the actors converse in hymns, and in a more diffuse and elevated strain than might be expected from their training and situations, such discourses, at all events, are not to be regarded as historical. The absence of these marks of the unhistorical do not however prove the historical validity of the narration, since the mythus often wears the most simple and apparently historical form: in which case the proof lies in the substance.

If the contents of a narrative strikingly accords with certain ideas existing and prevailing within the circle from which the narrative proceeded, which ideas themselves seem to be the product of preconceived opinions rather than of practical experience, it is more or less probable, according to circumstances, that such a narrative is of mythical origin. The knowledge of the fact, that the Jews were fond of representing their great men as the children of parents who had long been childless, cannot but make us doubtful of the historical truth of the statement that this was the case with John the Baptist;[2] knowing also that the Jews saw predictions every where in the writings of their prophets and poets, and discovered types[3] of the Messiah in all the lives of holy men recorded in their Scriptures; when we find details in the life of Jesus evidently sketched after the pattern of these prophecies and prototypes, we cannot but suspect that they are rather mythical than historical. * * *

Yet each of these tests, on the one hand, and each narrative on the other, considered apart, will rarely prove more than the possible or probable unhistorical character of the record. The concurrence of several such indications, is necessary to bring about a more definite result. The accounts of the visit of the Magi, and of the murder of the innocents at Bethlehem, harmonize remarkably with the Jewish Messianic notion, built upon the prophecy of Balaam, respecting the star which should come out of Jacob; and with the history of the sanguinary command of Pharaoh.[4] Still this would not alone suffice to stamp the narratives as mythical. But we have also the corroborative facts that the described appearance of the star is contrary to the physical, the alleged conduct of Herod to the psychological laws; that Josephus,[5] who gives in other respects so circumstantial an account of Herod, agrees with all other historical authorities in being silent concerning the Bethlehem massacre; and that the visit of the Magi together with the flight into Egypt related in the one Gospel, and the presentation in the temple related in another Gospel, mutually exclude one another.[6] Wherever, as in this instance, the several criteria of the mythical character concur, the result is certain, and certain in proportion to the accumulation of such grounds of evidence. * * *

In these last remarks we are, to a certain extent, anticipating the question which is, in conclusion, to be considered: viz., whether the mythical character is restricted to those features of the narrative, upon which such character is actually stamped; and whether a contradiction between two accounts invalidates one

2. Elizabeth, the mother of John the Baptist, was well past childbearing years when he was born. See Luke 1.5–25.
3. Antecedents who foreshadowed the coming of the Messiah.
4. The Magi were the three kings or wise men who visited the infant Jesus (Matthew 2.1); the "murder of the innocents" refers to King Herod's slaughter of all the male infants in Bethlehem (Matthew 2.16); Balaam's words in Numbers 24.17 have been interpreted as a prophecy

concerning Jesus; the Pharaoh of Egypt, fearing the people of Israel, plotted to kill all the male infants born to them (Exodus 1.8, 22).
5. Flavius Josephus (37–c.100), Jewish historian.
6. Joseph and Mary fled into Egypt with their child, Jesus, after a dream warning of the wrath of Herod (Matthew 2.13–15); when Jesus was 12, his parents took him to the Temple in Jerusalem, where he amazed the rabbis with his wisdom (Luke 2.41–52).

account only, or both? That is to say, what is the precise boundary line between the historical and the unhistorical?—the most difficult question in the whole province of criticism.

In the first place, when two narratives mutually exclude one another, one only is thereby proved to be unhistorical. If one be true the other must be false, but though the one be false the other may be true. Thus, in reference to the original residence of the parents of Jesus, we are justified in adopting the account of Luke which places it at Nazareth, to the exclusion of that of Matthew, which plainly supposes it to have been at Bethlehem; and, generally speaking, when we have to choose between two irreconcileable accounts, in selecting as historical that which is the least opposed to the laws of nature, and has the least correspondence with certain national or party opinions. But upon a more particular consideration it will appear that, since one account is false, it is possible that the other may be so likewise: the existence of a mythus respecting some certain point, shows that the imagination has been active in reference to that particular subject; (we need only refer to the genealogies); and the historical accuracy of either of two such accounts cannot be relied upon, unless substantiated by its agreement with some other well-authenticated testimony.

Concerning the different parts of one and the same narrative: it might be thought for example, that though the appearance of an angel, and his announcement to Mary that she should be the Mother of the Messiah,[7] must certainly be regarded as unhistorical, still, that Mary should have indulged this hope before the birth of the child, is not in itself incredible. But what should have excited this hope in Mary's mind? It is at once apparent that that which is credible in itself is nevertheless unhistorical when it is so intimately connected with what is incredible that, if you discard the latter, you at the same time remove the basis on which the former rests. * * *

The following examples will serve to illustrate the mode of deciding in such cases. According to the narrative, as Mary entered the house and saluted her cousin Elizabeth, who was then pregnant, the babe leaped in her womb, she was filled with the Holy Ghost, and she immediately addressed Mary as the mother of the Messiah. This account bears indubitable marks of an unhistorical character. Yet, it is not, in itself, impossible that Mary should have paid a visit to her cousin, during which every thing went on quite naturally. The fact is, however, that there are psychological difficulties connected with this journey of the betrothed; and that the visit, and even the relationship of the two women, seem to have originated entirely in the wish to exhibit a connexion between the mother of John the Baptist, and the mother of the Messiah. Or when in the history of the transfiguration[8] it is stated, that the men who appeared with Jesus on the Mount were Moses and Elias; and that the brilliancy which illuminated Jesus was supernatural; it might seem here also that, after deducting the marvellous, the presence of two men and a bright morning beam might be retained as the historical facts. But the legend was predisposed, by virtue of the current idea concerning the relation of the Messiah to these two prophets, not merely to make any two men (whose persons, object, and conduct, if they were not what the narrative represents them, remain in the highest degree mysterious) into Moses and Elias, but to create the whole occurrence; and in like manner not merely to conceive of some certain illumination as a supernatural effulgence (which, if a natural one, is much exaggerated and misrepresented), but to create it at once after the pattern of the brightness which illuminated the face of Moses on Mount Sinai.

---

7. See Luke 1.26.
8. Jesus took several disciples up a mountain, "And was transfigured before them: and his face did shine as the sun, and his raiment was white as the light. And, behold, there appeared unto them Moses and Elias talking with him" (Matthew 17.1–3).

Hence is derived the following rule. Where not merely the particular nature and manner of an occurrence is critically suspicious, its external circumstances represented as miraculous and the like; but where likewise the essential substance and groundwork is either inconceivable in itself, or is in striking harmony with some Messianic idea of the Jews of that age, then not the particular alleged course and mode of the transaction only, but the entire occurrence must be regarded as unhistorical. Where on the contrary, the form only, and not the general contents of the narration, exhibits the characteristics of the unhistorical, it is at least possible to suppose a kernel of historical fact; although we can never confidently decide whether this kernel of fact actually exists, or in what it consists; unless, indeed, it be discoverable from other sources. In legendary narratives, or narratives embellished by the writer, it is less difficult,—by divesting them of all that betrays itself as fictitious imagery, exaggeration, &c.—by endeavouring to abstract from them every extraneous adjunct and to fill up every hiatus—to succeed, proximately at least, in separating the historical groundwork.

The boundary line, however, between the historical and the unhistorical, in records, in which as in our Gospels this latter element is incorporated, will ever remain fluctuating and unsusceptible of precise attainment. Least of all can it be expected that the first comprehensive attempt to treat these records from a critical point of view should be successful in drawing a sharply defined line of demarcation. In the obscurity which criticism has produced, by the extinction of all lights hitherto held historical, the eye must accustom itself by degrees to discriminate objects with precision; and at all events the author of this work, wishes especially to guard himself, in those places where he declares he knows not what happened, from the imputation of asserting that he knows that nothing happened.

1835; 1846

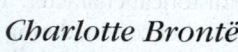

Charlotte Brontë
1816–1855

Charlotte Brontë's savage portrait in her novel *Jane Eyre* of an evangelical clergyman as a sadistic and hypocritical bully is based on a real-life figure, the founder of the school where her two elder sisters died. The Reverend Mr. Brocklehurst, who hectors a small child about death and hell-fire, represents the worst excesses of the Evangelical movement. Convinced of mankind's essentially sinful nature, Evangelicals stressed Bible reading, prayer, and regular examinations of conscience as the means to salvation. Brontë satirizes the self-serving piety which urges humility and self-denial on others—particularly dependents—while complacently exempting itself.

from **Jane Eyre**

I feared to return to the nursery, and feared to go forward to the parlour; ten minutes I stood in agitated hesitation; the vehement ringing of the breakfast-room bell decided me; I *must* enter.

"Who could want me?" I asked inwardly, as with both hands I turned the stiff door-handle which, for a second or two, resisted my efforts. "What should I see besides Aunt Reed in the apartment?—a man or a woman?" The handle turned, the door unclosed, and passing through and curtseying low, I looked up at—a black pillar!—such, at least, appeared to me, at first sight, the straight, narrow, sable-clad shape standing erect on the rug; the grim face at the top was like a carved mask, placed above the shaft by way of capital.

Mrs Reed occupied her usual seat by the fireside; she made a signal to me to approach; I did so, and she introduced me to the stony stranger with the words—

"This is the little girl respecting whom I applied to you."

He—for it was a man—turned his head slowly towards where I stood, and having examined me with the two inquisitive looking gray eyes which twinkled under a pair of bushy brows, said solemnly, and in a bass voice—

"Her size is small; what is her age?"

"Ten years."

"So much?" was the doubtful answer; and he prolonged his scrutiny for some minutes. Presently he addressed me—

"Your name, little girl?"

"Jane Eyre, sir."

In uttering these words I looked up: he seemed to me a tall gentleman, but then I was very little; his features were large, and they and all the lines of his frame were equally harsh and prim.

"Well, Jane Eyre, and are you a good child?"

Impossible to reply to this in the affirmative: my little world held a contrary opinion: I was silent. Mrs Reed answered for me by an expressive shake of the head, adding soon, "Perhaps the less said on that subject the better, Mr Brocklehurst."

"Sorry indeed to hear it! She and I must have some talk"; and bending from the perpendicular, he installed his person in the arm-chair, opposite Mrs Reed's. "Come here," he said.

I stepped across the rug: he placed me square and straight before him. What a face he had, now that it was almost on a level with mine! what a great nose! and what a mouth! and what large, prominent teeth!

"No sight so sad as that of a naughty child," he began, "especially a naughty little girl. Do you know where the wicked go after death?"

"They go to hell," was my ready and orthodox answer.

"And what is hell? Can you tell me that?"

"A pit full of fire."

"And should you like to fall into that pit, and to be burning there for ever?"

"No, sir."

"What must you do to avoid it?"

I deliberated a moment: my answer, when it did come, was objectionable: "I must keep in good health, and not die."

"How can you keep in good health? Children younger than you die daily. I buried a little child of five years old only a day or two since—a good little child, whose soul is now in heaven. It is to be feared the same could not be said of you, were you to be called thence."

Not being in a condition to remove his doubt, I only cast my eyes down on the two large feet planted on the rug, and sighed, wishing myself far enough away.

"I hope that sigh is from the heart, and that you repent of ever having been the occasion of discomfort to your excellent benefactress."

"Benefactress! benefactress!" said I inwardly: "they all call Mrs Reed my benefactress; if so, a benefactress is a disagreeable thing."

"Do you say your prayers night and morning?" continued my interrogator.

"Yes, sir."

"Do you read your Bible?"

"Sometimes."

"With pleasure? Are you fond of it?"

"I like Revelations, and the Book of Daniel, and Genesis, and Samuel, and a little bit of Exodus, and some parts of Kings and Chronicles, and Job and Jonah."

"And the Psalms? I hope you like them?"

"No, sir."

"No? Oh, shocking! I have a little boy, younger than you, who knows six Psalms by heart: and when you ask him which he would rather have, a ginger-bread-nut to eat, or a verse of a Psalm to learn, he says: 'Oh! the verse of a Psalm! angels sing Psalms,' says he; 'I wish to be a little angel here below.' He then gets two nuts in recompense for his infant piety."

"Psalms are not interesting," I remarked.

"That proves you to have a wicked heart; and you must pray to God to change it: to give you a new and clean one: to take away your heart of stone and give you a heart of flesh."

I was about to propound a question, touching the manner in which that operation of changing my heart was to be performed, when Mrs Reed interposed, telling me to sit down; she then proceeded to carry on the conversation herself.

1847

—◆—✠◆✠—◆—

Arthur Hugh Clough
1819–1861

Clever, witty, and ironic, Arthur Hugh Clough satirized religious hypocrisy and bankrupt values. But his humor only thinly veiled his genuine concern at the erosion of Christianity's spiritual authority. Clough took religion seriously enough to resign his Oxford fellowship rather than subscribe to the Thirty-Nine Articles of Anglican doctrine. He used his poetry to probe the ways Victorians had adjusted their religion to suit an increasingly secular age. The title *Epi-strauss-ium* refers to David Friedrich Strauss, whose *Life of Jesus* denied the divinity of Christ: the poem concludes that the Sun/Son of God can still illuminate, despite skepticism about the authenticity of the gospels. *The Latest Decalogue* casts a cynical eye on a materialist version of the Ten Commandments. *"There is no God," the Wicked Saith*, a lyric interlude from his long poem *Dipsychus*, contrasts the self-absorption of doubters to those whose love, innocence, or suffering make them believers.

Epi-strauss-ium[1]

Matthew and Mark and Luke and holy John
Evanished all and gone!
Yea, he° that erst, his dusky curtains quitting,   *the sun*
Through Eastern pictured panes his level beams transmitting,
5   With gorgeous portraits blent,

1. "On-Strauss-ism."

On them his glories intercepted spent,
Southwestering now, through windows plainly glassed,
On the inside face his radiance keen hath cast,
And in the lustre lost, invisible and gone,
10 Are, say you, Matthew, Mark and Luke and holy John?
Lost, is it? lost, to be recovered never?
However,
The place of worship the meantime with light
Is, if less richly, more sincerely bright,
15 And in blue skies the Orb is manifest to sight.
1847   1869

The Latest Decalogue[1]

Thou shalt have one God only; who
Would be at the expense of two?
No graven images may be
Worshipped, except the currency:
5   Swear not at all; for for thy curse
Thine enemy is none the worse:
At church on Sunday to attend
Will serve to keep the world thy friend:
Honour thy parents; that is, all
10 From whom advancement may befall:

Thou shalt not kill; but needst not strive
Officiously to keep alive:
Do not adultery commit;
Advantage rarely comes of it:
15 Thou shalt not steal; an empty feat,
When it's so lucrative to cheat:
Bear not false witness; let the lie
Have time on its own wings to fly:
Thou shalt not covet; but tradition
20 Approves all forms of competition.

The sum of all is, thou shalt love,
If any body, God above:
At any rate shall never labour
More than thyself to love thy neighbour.
                                            1862; 1951

from Dipsychus[1]

"There Is No God," the Wicked Saith

"There is no God," the wicked saith,
   "And truly it's a blessing,

---

1. The Ten Commandments. The last four lines were not
published until 1951; they were added from Clough's
manuscript.

1. Dipsychus ("two-souled" or "of two minds") is the hero
of a long poem by Clough, published in 1865; this excerpt
from scene 5 was published separately in 1862.

For what he might have done with us
    It's better only guessing."

5   "There is no God," a youngster thinks,
    "Or really, if there may be,
He surely didn't mean a man
    Always to be a baby."

     "There is no God, or if there is,"
10   The tradesman thinks, "'twere funny
If he should take it ill in me
    To make a little money."

    "Whether there be," the rich man says,
    "It matters very little,
15   For I and mine, thank somebody,
    Are not in want of victual."

    Some others, also, to themselves
    Who scarce so much as doubt it,
Think there is none, when they are well,
20   And do not think about it.

    But country folks who live beneath
    The shadow of the steeple;
The parson and the parson's wife,
    And mostly married people;

25   Youths green and happy in first love,
    So thankful for illusion;
And men caught out in what the world
    Calls guilt, in first confusion;

    And almost every one when age,
30   Disease, or sorrows strike him,
Inclines to think there is a God,
    Or something very like Him.

1850   1862

John William Colenso
1814–1883

Shortly after *The Origin of Species* appeared in 1859, an even greater furor erupted, this time with the publication of a work of biblical criticism written by an Anglican bishop. A mathematician who had become the Bishop of Natal in South Africa, Colenso was translating the Scriptures into Zulu when he began to have doubts about their historical veracity. His knowledge of geology made him realize that the Flood "could not possibly have taken place." Further research convinced him that Moses had not written the first five books of the Bible. Colenso was angrily attacked for challenging the divine authenticity of the Bible—he was even accused of insanity. He was deposed as bishop and excommunicated, though later reinstated. Colenso argued, however, that a vital religious belief could not ultimately conflict with the findings of historical scholarship, and that modern Christianity would be strengthened by being freed from outdated mythological beliefs.

from The Pentateuch and Book of Joshua Critically Examined

You will, of course, expect that, since I have had the charge of this Diocese, I have been closely occupied in the study of the Zulu tongue, and in translating the Scriptures into it. Through the blessing of God, I have now translated the New Testament completely, and several parts of the Old, among the rest the books of Genesis and Exodus. In this work I have been aided by intelligent natives; and, having also published a Zulu Grammar and Dictionary, I have acquired sufficient knowledge of the language, to be able to have intimate communion with the native mind. * * *

Here, however, as I have said, amidst my work in this land, I have been brought face to face with the very questions which I then put by. While translating the story of the Flood, I have had a simple-minded, but intelligent, native,—one with the docility of a child, but the reasoning powers of mature age,—look up, and ask, "Is all that true? Do you really believe that all this happened thus,—that all the beasts, and birds, and creeping things, upon the earth, large and small, from hot countries and cold, came thus by pairs, and entered into the ark with Noah? And did Noah gather food for them *all*, for the beasts and birds of prey, as well as the rest?" My heart answered in the words of the Prophet, "Shall a man speak lies in the Name of the Lord?" Zech.xiii.3. I dared not do so. My own knowledge of some branches of science, of Geology in particular, had been much increased since I left England; and I now knew for certain, on geological grounds, a fact, of which I had only had misgivings before, viz. that a *Universal* Deluge, such as the Bible manifestly speaks of, could not possibly have taken place in the way described in the Book of Genesis, not to mention other difficulties which the story contains. * * * Of course, I am well aware that some have attempted to show that Noah's Deluge was only a *partial* one. But such attempts have ever seemed to me to be made in the very teeth of the Scripture statements, which are as plain and explicit as words can possibly be. Nor is anything really gained by supposing the Deluge to have been partial. For, as waters must find their own level on the Earth's surface, without a special miracle, of which the Bible says nothing, a Flood, which should begin by covering the top of Ararat,[1] (if that were conceivable), or a much lower mountain, must necessarily become universal, and in due time sweep over the hills of Auvergne.[2] Knowing this, I felt that I dared not, as a servant of the God of Truth, urge my brother man to believe that, which I did not myself believe, which I knew to be untrue, as a matter-of-fact, historical, narrative. I gave him, however, such a reply as satisfied him for the time, without throwing any discredit upon the general veracity of the Bible history.

But I was thus driven,—against my will at first, I may truly say,—to search more deeply into these questions; and I have since done so, to the best of my power, with the means at my disposal in this colony. And now I tremble at the result of my enquiries, rather, I should do so, were it not that I believe firmly in a God of Righteousness and Truth and Love, who both "IS, and is a rewarder of them that diligently seek him." * * *

---

1. A mountain in Turkey on which Noah's ark was supposed to have landed at the end of the Flood (Genesis 8.4).

2. Part of the Massif Central in France.

The first five books of the Bible,—commonly called the Pentateuch (ηπεντατευχος βιβλος, Pentateuchus, sc. liber), or Book of Five Volumes,—are supposed by most English readers of the Bible to have been written by Moses, except the last chapter of Deuteronomy, which records the death of Moses, and which, of course, it is generally allowed, must have been added by another hand, perhaps that of Joshua. It is believed that Moses wrote under such special guidance and teaching of the Holy Spirit, that he was preserved from making any error in recording those matters, which came within his own cognisance, and was instructed also in respect of events, which took place before he was born,—before, indeed, there was a human being on the earth to take note of what was passing. He was in this way, it is supposed, enabled to write a true account of the Creation. And, though the accounts of the Fall and of the Flood, as well as of later events, which happened in the time of Abraham, Isaac, and Jacob, may have been handed down by tradition from one generation to another, and even, some of them, perhaps, written down in words, or represented in hieroglyphics, and Moses may, probably, have derived assistance from these sources also in the composition of his narrative, yet in all his statements, it is believed, he was under such constant control and superintendence of the Spirit of God, that he was kept from making any serious error, and certainly from writing anything altogether untrue. We may rely with undoubting confidence—such is the statement usually made—on the historical veracity, and infallible accuracy, of the Mosaic narrative in all its main particulars. * * *

But, among the many results of that remarkable activity in scientific enquiry of every kind, which, by God's own gift, distinguishes the present age, this also must be reckoned, that attention and labour are now being bestowed, more closely and earnestly than ever before, to search into the real foundations for such a belief as this. * * * The time is come, as I believe, in the Providence of God, when this question can no longer be put by,—when it must be resolutely faced, and the whole matter fully and freely examined, if we would be faithful servants of the God of Truth. * * *

The result of my enquiry is this, that I have arrived at the conviction,—as painful to myself at first, as it may be to my reader, though painful now no longer under the clear shining of the Light of Truth,—that the Pentateuch, as a whole, cannot possibly have been written by Moses, or by any one acquainted personally with the facts which it professes to describe, and, further, that the (so-called) Mosaic narrative, by whomsoever written, and though imparting to us, as I fully believe it does, revelations of the Divine Will and Character, cannot be regarded as *historically true*.

1862

—◄═✦═►—

John Henry Cardinal Newman
1801–1890

Newman's conversion to Catholicism in 1845 sent shock waves throughout England. Newman, an Anglican clergyman and a leading figure in the Oxford Movement, was well known for his efforts to construct a *via media*, or middle way, between Protestantism and Catholicism. But his struggle to locate the authority of the Anglican church in early church history gradually convinced him that Rome was right. Anti-Catholic feeling was strong, and Newman's "going over" was regarded as a terrible betrayal of his friends and colleagues. But when Charles Kingsley incautiously accused him of lying, Newman finally got a chance to explain his conversion to the public; the *Apologia Pro Vita Sua* became a classic of spiritual autobiography. Unlike some of his contemporaries, whose religious beliefs were shaken by scientific discoveries and biblical criticism, Newman's faith never wavered: "Ten thousand difficulties do not make one doubt."

from **Apologia Pro Vita Sua**

from *Chapter 1. History of My Religious Opinions to the Year 1833*

I was brought up from a child to take great delight in reading the Bible; but I had no formed religious convictions till I was fifteen. Of course I had a perfect knowledge of my Catechism.[1]

After I was grown up, I put on paper my recollections of the thoughts and feelings on religious subjects, which I had at the time that I was a child and a boy,—such as had remained on my mind with sufficient prominence to make me then consider them worth recording. Out of these, written in the Long Vacation of 1820, and transcribed with additions in 1823, I select two, which are at once the most definite among them, and also have a bearing on my later convictions.

1. "I used to wish the Arabian Tales were true: my imagination ran on unknown influences, on magical powers, and talismans. . . . I thought life might be a dream, or I an Angel, and all this world a deception, my fellow-angels by a playful device concealing themselves from me, and deceiving me with the semblance of a material world."

Again: "Reading in the Spring of 1816 a sentence from [Dr. Watts's] 'Remnants of Time,'[2] entitled 'the Saints unknown to the world,' to the effect, that 'there is nothing in their figure or countenance to distinguish them,' &c, &c, I supposed he spoke of Angels who lived in the world, as it were disguised."

2. The other remark is this: "I was very superstitious, and for some time previous to my conversion [when I was fifteen] used constantly to cross myself on going into the dark."

Of course I must have got this practice from some external source or other; but I can make no sort of conjecture whence; and certainly no one had ever spoken to me on the subject of the Catholic religion, which I only knew by name. The French master was an *émigré* Priest, but he was simply made a butt, as French masters too commonly were in that day, and spoke English very imperfectly. There was a Catholic family in the village, old maiden ladies we used to think; but I knew nothing about them. I have of late years heard that there were one or two Catholic boys in the school; but either we were carefully kept from knowing this, or the knowledge of it made simply no impression on our minds. My brother[3] will bear witness how free the school was from Catholic ideas. * * *

---

1. A summary of religious doctrine (in Newman's case, the Church of England's) set forth in a series of questions and answers.
2. Isaac Watts (1674–1748), Nonconformist cleric; the full title is *The Improvement of the Mind, with a discourse*

on Education, and the Remnants of Time, employed in prose and verse.
3. Francis William Newman (1805–1897), professor of Latin at University College, London, and a prominent freethinker.

When I was fifteen, (in the autumn of 1816), a great change of thought took place in me. I fell under the influences of a definite Creed, and received into my intellect impressions of dogma, which, through God's mercy, have never been effaced or obscured. * * * [I] believed that the inward conversion of which I was conscious, (and of which I still am more certain than that I have hands and feet,) would last into the next life, and that I was elected to eternal glory. I have no consciousness that this belief had any tendency whatever to lead me to be careless about pleasing God. I retained it till the age of twenty-one, when it gradually faded away; but I believe that it had some influence on my opinions, in the direction of those childish imaginations which I have already mentioned, viz. in isolating me from the objects which surrounded me, in confirming me in my mistrust of the reality of material phenomena, and making me rest in the thought of two and two only absolute and luminously self-evident beings, myself and my Creator;—for while I considered myself predestined to salvation, my mind did not dwell upon others, as fancying them simply passed over, not predestined to eternal death. I only thought of the mercy to myself. * * *

Calvinists[4] make a sharp separation between the elect and the world; there is much in this that is cognate or parallel to the Catholic doctrine; but they go on to say, as I understand them, very differently from Catholicism,—that the converted and the unconverted can be discriminated by man, that the justified are conscious of their state of justification, and that the regenerate cannot fall away. Catholics on the other hand shade and soften the awful antagonism between good and evil, which is one of their dogmas, by holding that there are different degrees of justification, that there is a great difference in point of gravity between sin and sin, that there is the possibility and the danger of falling away, and that there is no certain knowledge given to any one that he is simply in a state of grace, and much less that he is to persevere to the end:—of the Calvinistic tenets the only one which took root in my mind was the fact of heaven and hell, divine favour and divine wrath, of the justified and the unjustified. The notion that the regenerate and the justified were one and the same, and that the regenerate, as such, had the gift of perseverance, remained with me not many years, as I have said already. * * *

I am obliged to mention, though I do it with great reluctance, another deep imagination, which at this time, the autumn of 1816, took possession of me,—there can be no mistake about the fact; viz. that it would be the will of God that I should lead a single life. This anticipation, which has held its ground almost continuously ever since,—with the break of a month now and a month then, up to 1829, and, after that date, without any break at all,—was more or less connected in my mind with the notion, that my calling in life would require such a sacrifice as celibacy involved; as, for instance, missionary work among the heathen, to which I had a great drawing for some years. It also strengthened my feeling of separation from the visible world, of which I have spoken above.

from *Chapter 5. The Position of My Mind Since 1845*

From the time that I became a Catholic, of course I have no further history of my religious opinions to narrate. In saying this, I do not mean to say that my mind has

---

4. Followers of John Calvin (1509–1564), French theologian whose doctrines included predestination, the natural depravity of human beings, and salvation through God's grace.

been idle, or that I have given up thinking on theological subjects; but that I have had no variations to record, and have had no anxiety of heart whatever. I have been in perfect peace and contentment; I never have had one doubt. I was not conscious to myself, on my conversion, of any change, intellectual or moral, wrought in my mind. I was not conscious of firmer faith in the fundamental truths of Revelation, or of more self-command; I had not more fervour; but it was like coming into port after a rough sea; and my happiness on that score remains to this day without interruption.

Nor had I any trouble about receiving those additional articles, which are not found in the Anglican Creed. Some of them I believed already, but not any one of them was a trial to me. I made a profession of them upon my reception with the greatest ease, and I have the same ease in believing them now. I am far of course from denying that every article of the Christian Creed, whether as held by Catholics or by Protestants, is beset with intellectual difficulties; and it is simple fact, that, for myself, I cannot answer those difficulties. Many persons are very sensitive of the difficulties of Religion; I am as sensitive of them as any one; but I have never been able to see a connexion between apprehending those difficulties, however keenly, and multiplying them to any extent, and on the other hand doubting the doctrines to which they are attached. Ten thousand difficulties do not make one doubt, as I understand the subject; difficulty and doubt are incommensurate. There of course may be difficulties in the evidence; but I am speaking of difficulties intrinsic to the doctrines themselves, or to their relations with each other. A man may be annoyed that he cannot work out a mathematical problem, of which the answer is or is not given to him, without doubting that it admits of an answer, or that a certain particular answer is the true one. Of all points of faith, the being of a God is, to my own apprehension, encompassed with most difficulty, and yet borne in upon our minds with most power.

People say that the doctrine of Transubstantiation[1] is difficult to believe; I did not believe the doctrine till I was a Catholic. I had no difficulty in believing it, as soon as I believed that the Catholic Roman Church was the oracle of God, and that she had declared this doctrine to be part of the original revelation. It is difficult, impossible, to imagine, I grant;—but how is it difficult to believe? Yet Macaulay thought it so difficult to believe, that he had need of a believer in it of talents as eminent as Sir Thomas More,[2] before he could bring himself to conceive that the Catholics of an enlightened age could resist "the overwhelming force of the argument against it." "Sir Thomas More," he says, "is one of the choice specimens of wisdom and virtue; and the doctrine of transubstantiation is a kind of proof charge. A faith which stands that test, will stand any test." But for myself, I cannot indeed prove it, I cannot tell *how* it is; but I say, "Why should it not be? What's to hinder it? What do I know of substance or matter? just as much as the greatest philosophers, and that is nothing at all;"—so much is this the case, that there is a rising school of philosophy now, which considers phenomena to constitute the whole of our knowledge in physics. The Catholic doctrine leaves phenomena alone. It does not say that the phenomena go; on the contrary, it says that they remain; nor does it say that the same phenomena are in several places at once. It deals with what no one on earth knows any thing about, the material substances themselves. And, in like manner, of

1. Doctrine that the elements of bread and wine in the rite of Holy Communion are actually converted into the Body and Blood of Christ in all but external appearance.
2. Sir Thomas More (1478–1535) was an English statesman beheaded for his opposition to the church policy of Henry VIII. Macaulay invokes More in his 1840 review of Ranke's *History of the Popes*.

that majestic Article of the Anglican as well as of the Catholic Creed,—the doctrine of the Trinity in Unity.[3] What do I know of the Essence of the Divine Being? I know that my abstract idea of three is simply incompatible with my idea of one; but when I come to the question of concrete fact, I have no means of proving that there is not a sense in which one and three can equally be predicated of the Incommunicable God.

But I am going to take upon myself the responsibility of more than the mere Creed of the Church; as the parties accusing me are determined I shall do. They say, that now, in that I am a Catholic, though I may not have offences of my own against honesty to answer for, yet, at least, I am answerable for the offences of others, of my co-religionists, of my brother priests, of the Church herself. I am quite willing to accept the responsibility; and, as I have been able, as I trust, by means of a few words, to dissipate, in the minds of all those who do not begin with disbelieving me, the suspicion with which so many Protestants start, in forming their judgment of Catholics, viz. that our Creed is actually set up in inevitable superstition and hypocrisy, as the original sin of Catholicism; so now I will proceed, as before, identifying myself with the Church and vindicating it,—not of course denying the enormous mass of sin and error which exists of necessity in that world-wide multiform Communion,—but going to the proof of this one point, that its system is in no sense dishonest, and that therefore the upholders and teachers of that system, as such, have a claim to be acquitted in their own persons of that odious imputation.

Starting then with the being of a God, (which, as I have said, is as certain to me as the certainty of my own existence, though when I try to put the grounds of that certainty into logical shape I find a difficulty in doing so in mood and figure to my satisfaction,) I look out of myself into the world of men, and there I see a sight which fills me with unspeakable distress. The world seems simply to give the lie to that great truth, of which my whole being is so full; and the effect upon me is, in consequence, as a matter of necessity, as confusing as if it denied that I am in existence myself. If I looked into a mirror, and did not see my face, I should have the sort of feeling which actually comes upon me, when I look into this living busy world, and see no reflexion of its Creator. This is, to me, one of those great difficulties of this absolute primary truth, to which I referred just now. Were it not for this voice, speaking so clearly in my conscience and my heart, I should be an atheist, or a pantheist, or a polytheist when I looked into the world. I am speaking for myself only; and I am far from denying the real force of the arguments in proof of a God, drawn from the general facts of human society and the course of history, but these do not warm me or enlighten me; they do not take away the winter of my desolation, or make the buds unfold and the leaves grow within me, and my moral being rejoice. The sight of the world is nothing else than the prophet's scroll, full of "lamentations, and mourning, and woe."[4]

To consider the world in its length and breadth, its various history, the many races of man, their starts, their fortunes, their mutual alienation, their conflicts; and then their ways, habits, governments, forms of worship; their enterprises, their aimless courses, their random achievements and acquirements, the impotent conclusion of long-standing facts, the tokens so faint and broken of a superintending design, the blind evolution of what turn out to be great powers or truths, the progress of things, as if from unreasoning elements, not towards final causes, the greatness and littleness

---

3. The belief that God is three (Father, Son, and Holy Spirit) and yet only one.

4. Ezekiel 2.9–10.

of man, his far-reaching aims, his short duration, the curtain hung over his futurity, the disappointments of life, the defeat of good, the success of evil, physical pain, mental anguish, the prevalence and intensity of sin, the pervading idolatries, the corruptions, the dreary hopeless irreligion, that condition of the whole race, so fearfully yet exactly described in the Apostle's words, "having no hope and without God in the world,"[5]—all this is a vision to dizzy and appal; and inflicts upon the mind the sense of a profound mystery, which is absolutely beyond human solution.

What shall be said to this heart-piercing, reason-bewildering fact? I can only answer, that either there is no Creator, or this living society of men is in a true sense discarded from His presence. Did I see a boy of good make and mind, with the tokens on him of a refined nature, cast upon the world without provision, unable to say whence he came, his birth-place or his family connexions, I should conclude that there was some mystery connected with his history, and that he was one, of whom, from one cause or other, his parents were ashamed. Thus only should I be able to account for the contrast between the promise and the condition of his being. And so I argue about the world;—*if* there be a God, *since* there is a God, the human race is implicated in some terrible aboriginal calamity. It is out of joint with the purposes of its Creator. This is a fact, a fact as true as the fact of its existence; and thus the doctrine of what is theologically called original sin becomes to me almost as certain as that the world exists, and as the existence of God.

And now, supposing it were the blessed and loving will of the Creator to interfere in this anarchical condition of things, what are we to suppose would be the methods which might be necessarily or naturally involved in His purpose of mercy? Since the world is in so abnormal a state, surely it would be no surprise to me, if the interposition were of necessity equally extraordinary—or what is called miraculous. But that subject does not directly come into the scope of my present remarks. Miracles as evidence, involve a process of reason, or an argument; and of course I am thinking of some mode of interference which does not immediately run into argument. I am rather asking what must be the face-to-face antagonist, by which to withstand and baffle the fierce energy of passion and the all-corroding, all-dissolving scepticism of the intellect in religious inquiries? I have no intention at all of denying, that truth is the real object of our reason, and that, if it does not attain to truth, either the premiss or the process is in fault; but I am not speaking here of right reason, but of reason as it acts in fact and concretely in fallen man. I know that even the unaided reason, when correctly exercised, leads to a belief in God, in the immortality of the soul, and in a future retribution; but I am considering the faculty of reason actually and historically; and in this point of view, I do not think I am wrong in saying that its tendency is towards a simple unbelief in matters of religion. No truth, however sacred, can stand against it, in the long run; and hence it is that in the pagan world, when our Lord came, the last traces of the religious knowledge of former times were all but disappearing from those portions of the world in which the intellect had been active and had had a career.

And in these latter days, in like manner, outside the Catholic Church things are tending,—with far greater rapidity than in that old time from the circumstance of the age,—to atheism in one shape or other. What a scene, what a prospect, does the

5. Ephesians 2.12.

whole of Europe present at this day! and not only Europe, but every government and every civilization through the world, which is under the influence of the European mind! Especially, for it most concerns us, how sorrowful, in the view of religion, even taken in its most elementary, most attenuated form, is the spectacle presented to us by the educated intellect of England, France, and Germany! Lovers of their country and of their race, religious men, external to the Catholic Church, have attempted various expedients to arrest fierce wilful human nature in its onward course, and to bring it into subjection. The necessity of some form of religion for the interests of humanity, has been generally acknowledged: but where was the concrete representative of things invisible, which would have the force and the toughness necessary to be a breakwater against the deluge? Three centuries ago the establishment of religion, material, legal, and social, was generally adopted as the best expedient for the purpose, in those countries which separated from the Catholic Church; and for a long time it was successful; but now the crevices of those establishments are admitting the enemy. Thirty years ago, education was relied upon: ten years ago there was a hope that wars would cease for ever, under the influence of commercial enterprise and the reign of the useful and fine arts; but will any one venture to say that there is any thing any where on this earth, which will afford a fulcrum for us, whereby to keep the earth from moving onwards? * * *

Supposing then it to be the Will of the Creator to interfere in human affairs, and to make provisions for retaining in the world a knowledge of Himself, so definite and distinct as to be proof against the energy of human scepticism, in such a case,—I am far from saying that there was no other way,—but there is nothing to surprise the mind, if He should think fit to introduce a power into the world, invested with the prerogative of infallibility in religious matters. Such a provision would be a direct, immediate, active, and prompt means of withstanding the difficulty; it would be an instrument suited to the need; and, when I find that this is the very claim of the Catholic Church, not only do I feel no difficulty in admitting the idea, but there is a fitness in it, which recommends it to my mind. And thus I am brought to speak of the Church's infallibility, as a provision, adapted by the mercy of the Creator, to preserve religion in the world, and to restrain that freedom of thought, which of course in itself is one of the greatest of our natural gifts, and to rescue it from its own suicidal excesses. And let it be observed that, neither here nor in what follows, shall I have occasion to speak directly of Revelation in its subject-matter, but in reference to the sanction which it gives to truths which may be known independently of it,—as it bears upon the defence of natural religion. I say, that a power, possessed of infallibility in religious teaching, is happily adapted to be a working instrument, in the course of human affairs, for smiting hard and throwing back the immense energy of the aggressive, capricious, untrustworthy intellect:—and in saying this, as in the other things that I have to say, it must still be recollected that I am all along bearing in mind my main purpose, which is a defence of myself.

I am defending myself here from a plausible charge brought against Catholics, as will be seen better as I proceed. The charge is this:—that I, as a Catholic, not only make profession to hold doctrines which I cannot possibly believe in my heart, but that I also believe in the existence of a power on earth, which at its own will imposes upon men any new set of *credenda* [beliefs], when it pleases, by a claim to infallibility; in consequence, that my own thoughts are not my own property; that I cannot tell that tomorrow I may not have to give up what I hold to-day, and that the necessary effect of such a condition of mind must be a degrading bondage, or a bitter inward rebellion relieving itself in secret infidelity, or the necessity of ignoring the whole subject of religion in a sort of disgust, and of mechanically saying every thing that the Church says, and leaving to others the defence of it. As then I have above spoken of the relation of my mind towards the Catholic Creed, so now I shall speak of the attitude which it takes up in the view of the Church's infallibility.

And first, the initial doctrine of the infallible teacher must be an emphatic protest against the existing state of mankind. Man had rebelled against his Maker. It was this that caused the divine interposition: and to proclaim it must be the first act of the divinely-accredited messenger. The Church must denounce rebellion as of all possible evils the greatest. She must have no terms with it; if she would be true to her Master, she must ban and anathematize it. This is the meaning of a statement of mine which has furnished matter for one of those special accusations to which I am at present replying: I have, however, no fault at all to confess in regard to it; I have nothing to withdraw, and in consequence I here deliberately repeat it. I said, "The Catholic Church holds it better for the sun and moon to drop from heaven, for the earth to fail, and for all the many millions on it to die of starvation in extremest agony, as far as temporal affliction goes, than that one soul, I will not say, should be lost, but should commit one single venial sin, should tell one wilful untruth, or should steal one poor farthing without excuse." I think the principle here enunciated to be the mere preamble in the formal credentials of the Catholic Church, as an Act of Parliament might begin with a "Whereas." It is because of the intensity of the evil which has possession of mankind, that a suitable antagonist has been provided against it; and the initial act of that divinely-commissioned power is of course to deliver her challenge and to defy the enemy. Such a preamble then gives a meaning to her position in the world, and an interpretation to her whole course of teaching and action. * * *

* * * We live in a wonderful age; the enlargement of the circle of secular knowledge just now is simply a bewilderment, and the more so, because it has the promise of continuing, and that with greater rapidity, and more signal results. Now these discoveries, certain or probable, have in matter of fact an indirect bearing upon religious opinions, and the question arises how are the respective claims of revelation and of natural science to be adjusted. Few minds in earnest can remain at ease without some sort of rational grounds for their religious belief; to reconcile theory and fact is almost an instinct of the mind. When then a flood of facts, ascertained or suspected, comes pouring in upon us, with a multitude of others in prospect, all believers in Revelation, be they Catholic or not, are roused to consider their bearing upon themselves, both for the honour of God, and from tenderness for those many souls who, in consequence of the confident tone of the schools of secular knowledge, are in danger of being led away into a bottomless liberalism of thought.

I am not going to criticize here that vast body of men, in the mass, who at this time would profess to be liberals in religion; and who look towards the discoveries of the age, certain or in progress, as their informants, direct or indirect, as to what they shall think about the unseen and the future. The Liberalism which gives a colour to society now, is very different from that character of thought which bore the name thirty or forty years ago. Now it is scarcely a party; it is the educated lay world.

1864

⊶ ⩫⧫⩤ ⊷

Thomas Henry Huxley
1825–1895

Huxley was known as "Darwin's bulldog" for the vigorous way he defended Darwin in the controversies over *The Origin of Species*. In 1860 he took on Bishop Wilberforce in a famous debate at Oxford: when the bishop asked sarcastically whether "it was through his grandfather or his grandmother that he claimed his descent from a monkey?" Huxley carried the day by replying that "he was not ashamed to have a monkey for his ancestor; but he would be ashamed to be connected with a man who used great gifts to obscure the truth." In *Evolution and Ethics* he built on Darwinian ideas, arguing that although humankind is the natural product of evolutionary forces, we are inescapably at war with nature. Huxley rejected any direct "social Darwinist" view of society as a struggle for the survival of the fittest, and sought instead to envision a humanist ethics free from natural and from supernatural control alike.

from Evolution and Ethics
from Prolegomena
[MAN'S WAR WITH NATURE]

It may be safely assumed that, two thousand years ago, before Caesar set foot in southern Britain,[1] the whole country-side visible from the windows of the room in which I write, was in what is called "the state of nature." Except, it may be, by raising a few sepulchral mounds, such as those which still, here and there, break the flowing contours of the downs, man's hands had made no mark upon it; and the thin veil of vegetation which overspread the broad-backed heights and the shelving sides of the coombs[2] was unaffected by his industry. The native grasses and weeds, the scattered patches of gorse, contended with one another for the possession of the scanty surface soil; they fought against the droughts of summer, the frosts of winter, and the furious gales which swept, with unbroken force, now from the Atlantic, and now from the North Sea, at all times of the year; they filled up, as they best might, the gaps made in their ranks by all sorts of underground and overground animal ravagers. One year with another, an average population, the floating balance of the unceasing struggle for existence among the indigenous plants, maintained itself. It is as little to be doubted, that an essentially similar state of nature prevailed, in this region, for many thousand years before the coming of Caesar; and there is no assignable reason for denying that it might continue to exist through an equally prolonged futurity, except for the intervention of man.

Reckoned by our customary standards of duration, the native vegetation, like the "everlasting hills" which it clothes, seems a type of permanence. The little Amarella Gentians, which abound in some places to-day, are the descendants of those that were trodden underfoot by the prehistoric savages who have left their flint tools about, here and there; and they followed ancestors which, in the climate of the glacial epoch, probably flourished better than they do now. Compared with the long past of this humble plant, all the history of civilized men is but an episode.

---

1. Julius Caesar conquered Britain for the Roman Empire   2. Deep valleys.
in the last century B.C.

Yet nothing is more certain than that, measured by the liberal scale of time-keeping of the universe, this present state of nature, however it may seem to have gone and to go on for ever, is but a fleeting phase of her infinite variety; merely the last of the series of changes which the earth's surface has undergone in the course of the millions of years of its existence. Turn back a square foot of the thin turf, and the solid foundation of the land, exposed in cliffs of chalk five hundred feet high on the adjacent shore, yields full assurance of a time when the sea covered the site of the "everlasting hills"; and when the vegetation of what land lay nearest, was as different from the present Flora of the Sussex downs, as that of Central Africa now is. No less certain is it that between the time during which the chalk was formed and that at which the original turf came into existence, thousands of centuries elapsed, in the course of which, the state of nature of the ages during which the chalk was deposited, passed into that which now is, by changes so slow that, in the coming and going of the generations of men, had such witnessed them, the contemporary conditions would have seemed to be unchanging and unchangeable.

But it is also certain that, before the deposition of the chalk, a vastly longer period had elapsed, throughout which it is easy to follow the traces of the same process of ceaseless modification and of the internecine struggle for existence of living things; and that even when we can get no further back, it is not because there is any reason to think we have reached the beginning, but because the trail of the most ancient life remains hidden, or has become obliterated.

Thus that state of nature of the world of plants, which we began by considering, is far from possessing the attribute of permanence. Rather its very essence is impermanence. It may have lasted twenty or thirty thousand years, it may last for twenty or thirty thousand years more, without obvious change; but, as surely as it has followed upon a very different state, so it will be followed by an equally different condition. That which endures is not one or another association of living forms, but the process of which the cosmos is the product, and of which these are among the transitory expressions. And in the living world, one of the most characteristic features of this cosmic process is the struggle for existence, the competition of each with all, the result of which is the selection, that is to say, the survival of those forms which, on the whole, are best adapted to the conditions which at any period obtain; and which are, therefore, in that respect, and only in that respect, the fittest. The acme reached by the cosmic process in the vegetation of the downs is seen in the turf, with its weeds and gorse. Under the conditions, they have come out of the struggle victorious; and, by surviving, have proved that they are the fittest to survive. * * *

As a natural process, of the same character as the development of a tree from its seed, or of a fowl from its egg, evolution excludes creation and all other kinds of supernatural intervention. As the expression of a fixed order, every stage of which is the effect of causes operating according to definite rules, the conception of evolution no less excludes that of chance. It is very desirable to remember that evolution is not an explanation of the cosmic process, but merely a generalized statement of the method and results of that process. And, further, that, if there is proof that the cosmic process was set going by any agent, then that agent will be the creator of it and of all its products, although supernatural intervention may remain strictly excluded from its further course.

So far as that limited revelation of the nature of things, which we call scientific knowledge, has yet gone, it tends, with constantly increasing emphasis, to the belief that, not merely the world of plants, but that of animals; not merely living things, but the whole fabric of the earth; not merely our planet, but the whole solar system; not merely our star and its satellites, but the millions of similar bodies which bear witness to the order which pervades boundless space, and has endured through boundless time; are all working out their predestined courses of evolution.

* * * Three or four years have elapsed since the state of nature, to which I have referred, was brought to an end, so far as a small patch of the soil is concerned, by the intervention of man. The patch was cut off from the rest by a wall; within the area thus protected, the native vegetation was, as far as possible, extirpated; while a colony of strange plants was imported and set down in its place. In short, it was made into a garden. At the present time, this artificially treated area presents an aspect extraordinarily different from that of so much of the land as remains in the state of nature, outside the wall. Trees, shrubs, and herbs, many of them appertaining to the state of nature of remote parts of the globe, abound and flourish. Moreover, considerable quantities of vegetables, fruits, and flowers are produced, of kinds which neither now exist, nor have ever existed, except under conditions such as obtain in the garden; and which, therefore, are as much works of the art of man as the frames and glass-houses in which some of them are raised. That the "state of Art," thus created in the state of nature by man, is sustained by and dependent on him, would at once become apparent, if the watchful supervision of the gardener were withdrawn, and the antagonistic influences of the general cosmic process were no longer sedulously warded off, or counteracted. The walls and gates would decay; quadrupedal and bipedal intruders would devour and tread down the useful and beautiful plants; birds, insects, blight, and mildew would work their will; the seeds of the native plants, carried by winds or other agencies, would immigrate, and in virtue of their long-earned special adaptation to the local conditions, these despised native weeds would soon choke their choice exotic rivals. A century or two hence, little beyond the foundations of the wall and of the houses and frames would be left, in evidence of the victory of the cosmic powers at work in the state of nature, over the temporary obstacles to their supremacy, set up by the art of the horticulturist.

It will be admitted that the garden is as much a work of art,[3] or artifice, as anything that can be mentioned. The energy localised in certain human bodies, directed by similarly localised intellects, has produced a collocation[4] of other material bodies which could not be brought about in the state of nature. The same proposition is true of all the works of man's hands, from a flint implement to a cathedral or a chronometer; and it is because it is true, that we call these things artificial, term them works of art, or artifice, by way of distinguishing them from the products of the cosmic process, working outside man, which we call natural, or works of nature. The distinction thus drawn between the works of nature and those of man, is universally recognised; and it is, as I conceive, both useful and justifiable. * * *

The process of colonization presents analogies to the formation of a garden which are highly instructive. Suppose a shipload of English colonists sent to form a settlement, in such a country as Tasmania was in the middle of the last century. On landing, they find themselves in the midst of a state of nature, widely different from that left behind them in everything but the most general physical conditions. The common plants, the common birds and quadrupeds, are as totally distinct as the men

---

3. The sense of the term "Art" is becoming narrowed; "work of Art" to most people means a picture, a statue, or a piece of *bijouterie*; by way of compensation "artist" has included in its wide embrace cooks and ballet girls, no less than painters and sculptors [Huxley's note].
4. Bringing together.

from anything to be seen on the side of the globe from which they come. The colonists proceed to put an end to this state of things over as large an area as they desire to occupy. They clear away the native vegetation, extirpate or drive out the animal population, so far as may be necessary, and take measures to defend themselves from the re-immigration of either. In their place, they introduce English grain and fruit trees; English dogs, sheep, cattle, horses; and English men; in fact, they set up a new Flora and Fauna and a new variety of mankind, within the old state of nature. Their farms and pastures represent a garden on a great scale, and themselves the gardeners who have to keep it up, in watchful antagonism to the old *régime*. Considered as a whole, the colony is a composite unit introduced into the old state of nature; and, thenceforward, a competitor in the struggle for existence, to conquer or be vanquished.

Under the conditions supposed, there is no doubt of the result, if the work of the colonists be carried out energetically and with intelligent combination of all their forces. On the other hand, if they are slothful, stupid, and careless; or if they waste their energies in contests with one another, the chances are that the old state of nature will have the best of it. The native savage will destroy the immigrant civilized man; of the English animals and plants some will be extirpated by their indigenous rivals, others will pass into the feral state and themselves become components of the state of nature. In a few decades, all other traces of the settlement will have vanished. * * *

Moralists of all ages and of all faiths, attending only to the relations of men towards one another in an ideal society, have agreed upon the "golden rule," "Do as you would be done by." In other words, let sympathy be your guide; put yourself in the place of the man towards whom your action is directed; and do to him what you would like to have done to yourself under the circumstances. However much one may admire the generosity of such a rule of conduct; however confident one may be that average men may be thoroughly depended upon not to carry it out to its full logical consequences; it is nevertheless desirable to recognise the fact that these consequences are incompatible with the existence of a civil state, under any circumstances of this world which have obtained, or, so far as one can see, are, likely to come to pass.

For I imagine there can be no doubt that the great desire of every wrongdoer is to escape from the painful consequences of his actions. If I put myself in the place of the man who has robbed me, I find that I am possessed by an exceeding desire not to be fined or imprisoned; if in that of the man who has smitten me on one cheek, I contemplate with satisfaction the absence of any worse result than the turning of the other cheek for like treatment. Strictly observed, the "golden rule" involves the negation of law by the refusal to put it in motion against law-breakers; and, as regards the external relations of a polity,[5] it is the refusal to continue the struggle for existence. It can be obeyed, even partially, only under the protection of a society which repudiates it. Without such shelter, the followers of the "golden rule" may indulge in hopes of heaven, but they must reckon with the certainty that other people will be masters of the earth.

What would become of the garden if the gardener treated all the weeds and slugs and birds and trespassers as he would like to be treated, if he were in their place? * * *

That progressive modification of civilization which passes by the name of the "evolution of society," is, in fact, a process of an essentially different character, both

5. Government.

from that which brings about the evolution of species, in the state of nature, and from that which gives rise to the evolution of varieties, in the state of art.

There can be no doubt that vast changes have taken place in English civilization since the reign of the Tudors.[6] But I am not aware of a particle of evidence in favour of the conclusion that this evolutionary process has been accompanied by any modification of the physical, or the mental, characters of the men who have been the subjects of it. I have not met with any grounds for suspecting that the average Englishmen of to-day are sensibly different from those that Shakspere knew and drew. We look into his magic mirror of the Elizabethan age, and behold, nowise darkly, the presentment of ourselves.

During these three centuries, from the reign of Elizabeth to that of Victoria, the struggle for existence between man and man has been so largely restrained among the great mass of the population (except for one or two short intervals of civil war), that it can have had little, or no, selective operation. As to anything comparable to direct selection, it has been practised on so small a scale that it may also be neglected. The criminal law, in so far as by putting to death, or by subjecting to long periods of imprisonment, those who infringe its provisions, it prevents the propagation of hereditary criminal tendencies; and the poor-law, in so far as it separates married couples, whose destitution arises from hereditary defects of character, are doubtless selective agents operating in favour of the non-criminal and the more effective members of society. But the proportion of the population which they influence is very small; and, generally, the hereditary criminal and the hereditary pauper have propagated their kind before the law affects them. In a large proportion of cases, crime and pauperism have nothing to do with heredity; but are the consequence, partly, of circumstances and, partly, of the possession of qualities, which, under different conditions of life, might have excited esteem and even admiration. It was a shrewd man of the world who, in discussing sewage problems, remarked that dirt is riches in the wrong place; and that sound aphorism has moral applications. The benevolence and open-handed generosity which adorn a rich man, may make a pauper of a poor one; the energy and courage to which the successful soldier owes his rise, the cool and daring subtlety to which the great financier owes his fortune, may very easily, under unfavourable conditions, lead their possessors to the gallows, or to the hulks. Moreover, it is fairly probable that the children of a "failure" will receive from their other parent just that little modification of character which makes all the difference. I sometimes wonder whether people, who talk so freely about extirpating the unfit, ever dispassionately consider their own history. Surely, one must be very "fit," indeed, not to know of an occasion, or perhaps two, in one's life, when it would have been only too easy to qualify for a place among the "unfit."

In my belief the innate qualities, physical, intellectual, and moral, of our nation have remained substantially the same for the last four or five centuries. If the struggle for existence has affected us to any serious extent (and I doubt it) it has been, indirectly, through our military and industrial wars with other nations. * * *

To return, once more, to the parallel of horticulture. In the modern world, the gardening of men by themselves is practically restricted to the performance, not of selection, but of that other function of the gardener, the creation of conditions more favourable than those of the state of nature; to the end of facilitating the free expansion

6. Reigned 1485–1603.

of the innate faculties of the citizen, so far as it is consistent with the general good. And the business of the moral and political philosopher appears to me to be the ascertainment, by the same method of observation, experiment, and ratiocination, as is practised in other kinds of scientific work, of the course of conduct which will best conduce to that end.

But, supposing this course of conduct to be scientifically determined and carefully followed out, it cannot put an end to the struggle for existence in the state of nature; and it will not so much as tend, in any way, to the adaptation of man to that state. Even should the whole human race be absorbed in one vast polity, within which "absolute political justice" reigns, the struggle for existence with the state of nature outside it, and the tendency to the return of the struggle within, in consequence of over-multiplication, will remain; and, unless men's inheritance from the ancestors who fought a good fight in the state of nature, their dose of original sin, is rooted out by some method at present unrevealed, at any rate to disbelievers in supernaturalism, every child born into the world will still bring with him the instinct of unlimited self-assertion. He will have to learn the lesson of self-restraint and renunciation. But the practice of self-restraint and renunciation is not happiness, though it may be something much better.

That man, as a "political animal," is susceptible of a vast amount of improvement, by education, by instruction, and by the application of his intelligence to the adaptation of the conditions of life to his higher needs, I entertain not the slightest doubt. But, so long as he remains liable to error, intellectual or moral; so long as he is compelled to be perpetually on guard against the cosmic forces, whose ends are not his ends, without and within himself; so long as he is haunted by inexpugnable memories and hopeless aspirations; so long as the recognition of his intellectual limitations forces him to acknowledge his incapacity to penetrate the mystery of existence; the prospect of attaining untroubled happiness, or of a state which can, even remotely, deserve the title of perfection, appears to me to be as misleading an illusion as ever was dangled before the eyes of poor humanity. And there have been many of them.

That which lies before the human race is a constant struggle to maintain and improve, in opposition to the State of Nature, the State of Art of an organized polity; in which, and by which, man may develop a worthy civilization, capable of maintaining and constantly improving itself, until the evolution of our globe shall have entered so far upon its downward course that the cosmic process resumes its sway; and, once more, the State of Nature prevails over the surface of our planet.

1893

Sir Edmund Gosse
1849–1928

Gosse's autobiography relates his effort to forge an identity in opposition to loving but fanatical parents. His father, Philip Henry Gosse, was a prominent zoologist, and a zealous member of the Plymouth Brethren, a fundamentalist Evangelical sect. They disapproved of art and the imagination: the father was proud of not knowing a word of Shakespeare; the son devoted his life to literature. The turning point of Philip Gosse's career was his publication of *Omphalos* (1857), an absurd attempt to counter Darwin's impending *The Origin of Species* by arguing that the natural world presents a false picture of its own history: "God hid the fossils in the rocks." His argument was ridiculed by scientists and rejected even by churchmen, but it illustrates the desperate lengths to which some were willing to go to refute Darwin's theories.

from Father and Son

[NO FICTION OF ANY KIND]

I found my greatest pleasure in the pages of books. The range of these was limited, for story-books of every description were sternly excluded. No fiction of any kind, religious or secular, was admitted into the house. In this it was to my Mother, not to my Father, that the prohibition was due. She had a remarkable, I confess to me still somewhat unaccountable impression that "to tell a story," that is, to compose fictitious narrative of any kind, was a sin. She carried this conviction to extreme lengths. * * *

My own state, however, was, I should think, almost unique among the children of cultivated parents. In consequence of the stern ordinance which I have described, not a single fiction was read or told to me during my infancy. The rapture of the child who delays the process of going to bed by cajoling "a story" out of his mother or his nurse, as he sits upon her knee, well tucked up, at the corner of the nursery fire,—this was unknown to me. Never, in all my early childhood, did anyone address to me the affecting preamble, "Once upon a time!" I was told about missionaries, but never about pirates, I was familiar with humming-birds, but I had never heard of fairies. Jack the Giant-Killer, Rumpelstiltskin and Robin Hood were not of my acquaintance, and though I understood about wolves, Little Red Ridinghood was a stranger even by name. So far as my "dedication"[1] was concerned, I can but think that my parents were in error thus to exclude the imaginary from my outlook upon facts. They desired to make me truthful; the tendency was to make me positive and sceptical. Had they wrapped me in the soft folds of supernatural fancy, my mind might have been longer content to follow their traditions in an unquestioning spirit.

[A MOTH INTERRUPTS FAMILY PRAYERS]

Another instance of the remarkable way in which the interests of daily life were mingled, in our strange household, with the practice of religion, made an impression upon my memory. We had all three been much excited by a report that a certain dark geometer-moth, generated in underground stables, had been met with in Islington. Its name, I think, is *boletobia fuliginaria,* and I believe that it is excessively rare in England. We were sitting at family prayers, on a summer morning, I think in 1855, when through the open window a brown moth came sailing. My Mother immediately interrupted the reading of the Bible by saying to my Father, "O! Henry, do you think that can be *boletobia?*" My Father rose up from the sacred book, examined the insect, which had now perched, and replied: "No! it is only the common Vapourer, *orgygia antiqua,*" resuming his seat, and the exposition of the Word, without any apology or embarrassment.

---

1. Earlier, Gosse described how when he was two months old, his mother had written a "solemn dedication of me to the Lord, which was repeated in public in my Mother's arms" at church. Similarly, in *Praeterita* Ruskin described how his mother "solemnly 'devoted me to God' before I was born; in imitation of Hannah."

[A Scientific Experiment in Idolatry]

My theological misdeeds culminated, however, in an act so puerile and preposterous that I should not venture to record it if it did not throw some glimmering of light on the subject which I have proposed to myself in writing these pages. My mind continued to dwell on the mysterious question of prayer. It puzzled me greatly to know why, if we were God's children, and if he was watching over us by night and day, we might not supplicate for toys and sweets and smart clothes as well as for the conversion of the heathen. * * *

All these matters drew my thoughts to the subject of idolatry, which was severely censured at the missionary meeting. I cross-examined my Father very closely as to the nature of this sin, and pinned him down to the categorical statement that idolatry consisted in praying to any one or anything but God himself. Wood and stone, in the words of the hymn, were peculiarly liable to be bowed down to by the heathen in their blindness. I pressed my Father further on this subject, and he assured me that God would be very angry, and would signify His anger, if any one, in a Christian country, bowed down to wood and stone. I cannot recall why I was so pertinacious on this subject, but I remember that my Father became a little restive under my cross-examination. I determined, however, to test the matter for myself, and one morning, when both my parents were safely out of the house, I prepared for the great act of heresy. I was in the morning-room on the ground-floor, where, with much labour, I hoisted a small chair on to the table close to the window. My heart was now beating as if it would leap out of my side, but I pursued my experiment. I knelt down on the carpet in front of the table, and looking up I said my daily prayer in a loud voice, only substituting the address "O Chair!" for the habitual one.

Having carried this act of idolatry safely through, I waited to see what would happen. It was a fine day, and I gazed up at the slip of white sky above the houses opposite, and expected something to appear in it. God would certainly exhibit his anger in some terrible form, and would chastise my impious and wilful action. I was very much alarmed, but still more excited; I breathed the high, sharp air of defiance. But nothing happened; there was not a cloud in the sky, not an unusual sound in the street. Presently I was quite sure that nothing would happen. I had committed idolatry, flagrantly and deliberately, and God did not care. The result of this ridiculous act was not to make me question the existence and power of God; those were forces which I did not dream of ignoring. But what it did was to lessen still further my confidence in my Father's knowledge of the Divine mind. My Father had said, positively, that if I worshipped a thing made of wood, God would manifest his anger. I had then worshipped a chair, made (or partly made) of wood, and God had made no sign whatever. My Father, therefore, was not really acquainted with the Divine practice in cases of idolatry. And with that, dismissing the subject, I dived again into the unplumbed depths of the "Penny Cyclopædia."

[Did God Hide the Fossils in the Rocks?]

So, through my Father's brain, in that year of scientific crisis, 1857, there rushed two kinds of thought, each absorbing, each convincing yet totally irreconcilable. There is a peculiar agony in the paradox that truth has two forms, each of them indisputable, yet each antagonistic to the other. It was this discovery, that there were two theories of physical life, each of which was true, but the truth of each incompatible with the truth of the other, which shook the spirit of my Father with perturbation. It was not, really, a paradox, it was a fallacy, if he could only have known it, but he allowed the turbid volume of superstition to drown the delicate stream of reason. He took one step in the service of truth, and then he drew back in an agony, and accepted the servitude of error.

This was the great moment in the history of thought when the theory of the mutability of species was preparing to throw a flood of light upon all departments of human speculation and action. It was becoming necessary to stand emphatically in one army or the other. Lyell[2] was surrounding himself with disciples, who were making strides in the direction of discovery. Darwin had long been collecting facts with regard to the variation of animals and plants. Hooker and Wallace, Asa Gray and even Agassiz,[3] each in his own sphere, were coming closer and closer to a perception of that secret which was first to reveal itself clearly to the patient and humble genius of Darwin. In the year before, in 1856, Darwin, under pressure from Lyell, had begun that modest statement of the new revelation, that "abstract of an essay," which developed so mightily into "The Origin of Species." Wollaston's "Variation of Species" had just appeared,[4] and had been a nine days' wonder in the wilderness.

On the other side, the reactionaries, although never dreaming of the fate which hung over them, had not been idle. In 1857 the astounding question had for the first time been propounded with contumely, "What, then, did we come from an orangoutang?" The famous "Vestiges of Creation"[5] had been supplying a sugar-and-water panacea for those who could not escape from the trend of evidence, and who yet clung to revelation. Owen[6] was encouraging reaction by resisting, with all the strength of his prestige, the theory of the mutability of species.

In this period of intellectual ferment, as when a great political revolution is being planned, many possible adherents were confidentially tested with hints and encouraged to reveal their bias in a whisper. It was the notion of Lyell, himself a great mover of men, that before the doctrine of natural selection was given to a world which would be sure to lift up at it a howl of execration, a certain body-guard of sound and experienced naturalists, expert in the description of species, should be privately made aware of its tenour. Among those who were thus initiated, or approached with a view towards possible illumination, was my Father. He was spoken to by Hooker, and later on by Darwin, after meetings of the Royal Society in the summer of 1857.

My Father's attitude towards the theory of natural selection was critical in his career, and, oddly enough, it exercised an immense influence on my own experience as a child. Let it be admitted at once, mournful as the admission is, that every instinct in his intelligence went out at first to greet the new light. It had hardly done so, when a recollection of the opening chapter of Genesis checked it at the outset. He consulted with Carpenter, a great investigator, but one who was fully as incapable

---

2. Sir Charles Lyell (1797–1875), Victorian Britain's most influential geologist, author of *Principles of Geology* (1830–1833), which argued that geological change had occurred gradually over vast periods of time, not through sudden and violent natural catastrophes. His theory was inconsistent with the Christian reckoning that the earth was only six thousand years old.
3. Sir Joseph Dalton Hooker (1817–1911), English botanist; Alfred Russel Wallace (1823–1913), co-originator, with Darwin, of the theory of evolution; Asa Gray (1810–1888), American botanist and taxonomist; Louis Agassiz (1807–1873), Swiss-American zoologist

and geologist who studied the natural history of North America.
4. *On the Variation of Species* (1856) by Thomas Vernon Wollaston (1822–1878), entomologist and conchologist, and a friend of Darwin's.
5. The controversial *Vestiges of the Natural History of Creation* (1844), by the Scottish scientist Robert Chambers, introduced the British public to the idea of evolution, although in the context of a divine Creator.
6. Sir Richard Owen (1804–1892), naturalist and anatomist who attacked Darwin's theory of natural selection.

as himself of remodelling his ideas with regard to the old, accepted hypotheses. They both determined, on various grounds, to have nothing to do with the terrible theory, but to hold steadily to the law of the fixity of species. It was exactly at this juncture that we left London, and the slight and occasional, but always extremely salutary personal intercourse with men of scientific leading which my Father had enjoyed at the British Museum and at the Royal Society came to an end. His next act was to burn his ships, down to the last beam and log out of which a raft could have been made. By a strange act of wilfulness, he closed the doors upon himself for ever.

My Father had never admired Sir Charles Lyell. I think that the famous "Lord Chancellor manner" of the geologist intimidated him, and we undervalue the intelligence of those whose conversation puts us at a disadvantage. For Darwin and Hooker, on the other hand, he had a profound esteem, and I know not whether this had anything to do with the fact that he chose, for his impetuous experiment in reaction, the field of geology, rather than that of zoölogy or botany. Lyell had been threatening to publish a book on the geological history of Man, which was to be a bomb-shell flung into the camp of the catastrophists. My Father, after long reflection, prepared a theory of his own, which, as he fondly hoped, would take the wind out of Lyell's sails, and justify geology to godly readers of "Genesis." It was, very briefly, that there had been no gradual modification of the surface of the earth, or slow development of organic forms, but that when the catastrophic act of creation took place, the world presented, instantly, the structural appearance of a planet on which life had long existed.

The theory, coarsely enough, and to my Father's great indignation, was defined by a hasty press as being this—that God hid the fossils in the rocks in order to tempt geologists into infidelity. In truth, it was the logical and inevitable conclusion of accepting, literally, the doctrine of a sudden act of creation; it emphasised the fact that any breach in the circular course of nature could be conceived only on the supposition that the object created bore false witness to past processes, which had never taken place. For instance, Adam would certainly possess hair and teeth and bones in a condition which it must have taken many years to accomplish, yet he was created full-grown yesterday. He would certainly—though Sir Thomas Browne[7] denied it— display an *omphalos* [navel], yet no umbilical cord had ever attached him to a mother.

Never was a book cast upon the waters with greater anticipations of success than was this curious, this obstinate, this fanatical volume. My Father lived in a fever of suspense, waiting for the tremendous issue. This "Omphalos" of his, he thought, was to bring all the turmoil of scientific speculation to a close, fling geology into the arms of Scripture, and make the lion eat grass with the lamb. It was not surprising, he admitted, that there had been experienced an ever-increasing discord between the facts which geology brings to light and the direct statements of the early chapters of "Genesis." Nobody was to blame for that. My Father, and my Father alone, possessed the secret of the enigma; he alone held the key which could smoothly open the lock of geological mystery. He offered it, with a glowing gesture, to atheists and Christians alike. This was to be the universal panacea; this the system of intellectual therapeutics which could not but heal all the maladies of the age. But, alas! atheists and Christians alike looked at it and laughed, and threw it away.

7. Sir Thomas Browne (1605 1682), author and physician; his *Religio Medici* attempted to reconcile science and religion.

In the course of that dismal winter, as the post began to bring in private letters, few and chilly, and public reviews, many and scornful, my Father looked in vain for the approval of the churches, and in vain for the acquiescence of the scientific societies, and in vain for the gratitude of those "thousands of thinking persons," which he had rashly assured himself of receiving. As his reconciliation of Scripture statements and geological deductions was welcomed nowhere; as Darwin continued silent, and the youthful Huxley was scornful, and even Charles Kingsley,[8] from whom my Father had expected the most instant appreciation, wrote that he could not "give up the painful and slow conclusion of five and twenty years' study of geology, and believe that God has written on the rocks one enormous and superfluous lie,"—as all this happened or failed to happen, a gloom, cold and dismal, descended upon our morning teacups. It was what the poets mean by an "inspissated" gloom; it thickened day by day, as hope and self-confidence evaporated in thin clouds of disappointment. My Father was not prepared for such a fate. He had been the spoiled darling of the public, the constant favourite of the press, and now, like the dark angels of old,

> so huge a rout
> Encumbered him with ruin.

He could not recover from amazement at having offended everybody by an enterprise which had been undertaken in the cause of universal reconciliation.

1907

⇒ END OF PERSPECTIVES: RELIGION AND SCIENCE ⇐

Robert Browning
1812–1889

Julia Margaret Cameron, *Robert Browning*, 1866.

Throughout his life Robert Browning was something of an enigma, a Byronic dandy sporting lemon-yellow gloves and gorgeous waistcoats, who loved dining out and yet kept both his private life and poetic practice out of the conversation. He longed for public recognition but would not make his work more accessible by stepping from behind his elaborate artistic masks. Unable to reconcile the hearty dinner guest with the experimental poet, Henry James concluded that Browning lived equally on both sides of an inner wall which "contained an invisible door through which, working the lock at will, he could swiftly pass." Although Browning sometimes suggested that he was a mere ventriloquist or puppeteer, the genius with which he impersonated other voices extended the range and complexity of English poetry in bold new directions. More than any other nineteenth-century figure, Browning shaped the poetry of the twentieth, influencing British and American poets from Hardy and Yeats to Eliot, Pound, Frost, Lowell, and Stevens.

---

8. Huxley had been an early defender of Darwin's; Charles Kingsley (1819–1875) was a prominent clergyman.

Browning's early years were quiet, even sheltered. He was born in Camberwell, a rural suburb south of London, and with the exception of a year spent at London University, he lived at home with his parents and sister until the age of thirty-four. His father was an official in the Bank of England, and his mother a pious Nonconformist, both of whom encouraged their son in his passion for poetry, painting, and music. The chief source of his education was extensive, haphazard reading in his father's vast private library. Brought up to be a gentleman, Browning received lessons in dancing, fencing, boxing, drawing, and music, as well as Greek and Latin. His doting parents denied him nothing: when, at fourteen, he expressed an interest in the poetry of Shelley—whose works were unavailable because of his atheism—Browning's devout mother took him to London to find an out-of-print copy.

Uncertain what his genuine calling was, Browning considered and rejected careers in art, music, law, and business. A turning point came in October 1832, when he saw the aging Edmund Kean play Richard III. Stunned by the power of a performance in which the brilliant but weary actor alternately electrified and embarrassed the audience as he struggled to dominate his role, Browning found dramatic confirmation of his evolving theory that all personality was staged and variable. Taking Shakespeare as a model, he envisioned himself as performer, playwright, and stage manager of his own artistic world. That night he conceived a grand plan to "assume I know not how many different characters" in order to write poems, operas, novels, and speeches under different names so that "the world was never to guess" that Robert Browning had been the author.

It is a fascinating literary mystery why Browning should have wanted simultaneously to conceal his own identity and yet dazzle the world by impersonating other people—especially since the authors he most admired (Byron, Keats, and particularly Shelley) seemed to him to speak so personally. In 1833, Browning began his career anonymously with a long romantic poem, *Pauline*, in which he took an indirect approach, speaking through a narrator who confided: "I will tell / My state, as though 'twere none of mine." *Pauline* failed to sell a single copy, but the book found its way to John Stuart Mill, who commented that the poet possessed "a more intense and morbid self-consciousness than I ever knew in any sane being."

In the next decade Browning produced a string of introspective plays and experimental dramatic poems, including *Paracelsus* (1835), *Strafford* (1837), *Sordello* (1840), and *Pippa Passes* (1841). The notorious difficulty of these unpopular works gave Browning a reputation for obscurity that he labored for the rest of his life to overcome. But by the early 1840s he had discovered where his talent lay: applying to lyric poetry his theatrical instincts and his aversion to self-revelation, he found he could produce startling new effects. Henceforth he would present his audience with a cast of aberrant personalities, each starring in his or her own miniplay. In language adapted to their insecurities and obsessions, Browning's characters unwittingly reveal their own, often shocking secrets—but only if readers make the effort to follow the uncanny logic of their contorted confessions.

In the advertisement for his breakthrough book, *Dramatic Lyrics* (1842), Browning offered the disclaimer that, though the poems are "lyric in expression," they are the "utterances of so many imaginary persons, not mine." These imaginary persons range from the Greek goddess Artemis to lovers in a Venetian gondola, from a medieval damsel in distress to a Spanish monk so consumed by hatred that his soliloquy begins with a growl: "Gr-r-r." The sheer physicality of Browning's words, the thick-textured lines, the aggressive consonant clusters that seem to mock Tennyson's liquid vowels, the staccato lines and convoluted syntax that convey the twistings of tongue and mind struggling to express themselves—all are trademarks of Browning's style. As Gerard Manley Hopkins said, Browning talks like "a man bouncing up from table with his mouth full of bread and cheese and saying that he meant to stand no blasted nonsense."

Browning did not invent the poetic form known as the dramatic monologue—it is used in such classics as Marvell's *To His Coy Mistress* and Tennyson's *Ulysses*—but he brought the form to new levels of complexity. He usually situates his speakers in specific historical places and periods. Sometimes they are well-known figures from the past, such as the Italian painters

Andrea del Sarto and Fra Lippo Lippi, or literary characters, such as Caliban and Childe Roland. Browning catches them at a moment of great emotional intensity as they attempt to explain why they think and act as they do. In these passionate outbursts, they reveal their characters as much by idiomatic language, patterns of imagery, speech rhythms, and unintended ironies as by what they actually say.

Browning induces his readers to sympathize—even identify—with speakers of dubious morality and intentions. His gallery of rogues includes a duke who may have murdered his wife, a painter who savors his own cuckoldry, and a dying bishop who recalls with gusto the fleshly delights he has enjoyed. As the critic Robert Langbaum has pointed out, "the utter outrageousness" of such behavior "makes condemnation the least interesting response." Just as Satan becomes the most intriguing figure in *Paradise Lost*, so Browning's narrators elicit a reluctant fascination. Alternating between admiration and revulsion, and compelled by the intricacies of human motivation to suspend judgment, the reader struggles to come to terms with these disclosures.

This theatrical world of passionate utterance spilled over into reality in 1845, when Browning became the coauthor and hero of his own romantic drama. On January 10, he wrote a fan letter to the famous poet Elizabeth Barrett, whom he had never seen. He was thirty-three, she nearly forty, and her poetry was far better known than his. "I love your verses with all my heart," he wrote boldly, "—and I love you too." Her reply was encouraging, and thus began the century's most celebrated literary correspondence. She was an invalid suffering from tuberculosis, and they did not meet until May. But when Browning entered her darkened room, he fell instantly in love with the frail, fiery woman lying on her couch swathed in shawls and blankets. For more than a year and half they kept the nature of their relationship secret, to circumvent the wrath of her tyrannical father, who had permitted none of his children to marry. Finally, Browning decided they must break free: they were married secretly during a morning walk, in September 1846, and eloped to Italy, where they eventually settled in Florence.

Though their marriage was rhapsodic, Browning was frustrated with his art. Preoccupied with his wife, her work, their son "Pen" (born in 1849), and the charms of Florence, the usually prolific Browning wrote only one poem in the first three years of marriage and published just two books in the fifteen years they lived together. Though she acknowledged his genius, Elizabeth joined with her husband's friends in urging him to write "in the most directest and most impressive way, the mask thrown off." Unable or unwilling to do so, Browning gloomily found that he had acquired a further mask that he had not sought: that of "Mrs. Browning's husband."

Hoping finally to make his name with a wider public, Browning channeled his energies into a new project, fifty monologues published in 1855 as *Men and Women*. These animated self-portraits by artists, lovers, questors, skeptics, and impostors form a dazzling picture gallery containing many of Browning's greatest poems, including *Love Among the Ruins, Fra Lippo Lippi,* and *Childe Roland.* The plural title of *Men and Women* insists on the variability of human experience and the centrality of sexual difference to every individual's self-definition. But the book was poorly received at the time, except by the Pre-Raphaelites, and was soon overshadowed by the tumultuous acclaim bestowed on Elizabeth Barrett Browning's *Aurora Leigh* in 1856. Dejected by his readers' failure to make the effort to comprehend his art, Browning complained to his friend John Ruskin: "I cannot begin writing poetry till my imaginary reader has conceded licenses to me. . . . You would have me paint it all plain out, which can't be; but by various artifices I try to make shift with touches and bits of outlines which *succeed* if they bear the conception from me to you. You ought, I think, to keep pace with the thought."

Elizabeth Barrett Browning died suddenly in 1861 in Florence. "My life is fixed and sure now," the devastated widower wrote to his sister, "I shall live out the remainder in her direct influence." Browning returned to England with his son and settled down to a steady rhythm of writing and dining out. But with renewed vigor he resumed his demanding experiments with dramatic lyrics, more determined than ever to pursue the indirect forms of expression that the reading public had resisted.

The result was his second masterpiece, *The Ring and the Book*, a novel in verse published in four monthly installments, between 1868 and 1869. The poem reimagines a sensational seventeenth-century Roman murder trial. In extended monologues the various participants tell their versions of the story. We hear the pleas of the dying young bride Pompilia, her cruel husband Guido, her priest and would-be rescuer Caponsacchi, and then the rationale of the Pope, who decides the case. In this sordid tale of marital abuse and dubious justice, Browning explores the relativity of human understanding, the rights of women, and the role of religious belief in determining earthly action.

"Art remains the one way possible," the poet says, "Of speaking truth. . . ." But then, typically, he hedges his assertion: "—to mouths like mine, at least." In a world of becoming, no single perspective is ever sufficient, but Browning shows how, seen from the inside, each self, no matter how bizarre, finds words to justify its actions. Browning's truth is always contingent, evolving, and dependent on the flawed language we have to express it: "For how else know we save by worth of word?"

The success of *The Ring and the Book*, together with the increasing popularity of his earlier work, meant that in the 1870s and 1880s Browning was finally recognized as sharing with Tennyson the title of the era's leading poet. He was especially amused and gratified by the adulation of the Browning Societies that sprang up in England and around the world during his later years. When asked if he objected to the amateurish enthusiasm of the clubs that met to discuss his philosophy of life, he replied: "Object to it? No, I like it! . . . I have waited forty years for it, and now—I like it!" In the United States, where Browning mania hit hardest, brown clothing, curtains, and tableware became the rage, and his works were excerpted on railroad timetables. Mark Twain even gave a series of readings of which he boasted: "I can read Browning so Browning himself can understand it."

Browning's last book, *Asolando*, was published to wide acclaim the day he died at his son's home in Venice. Shortly before his death, Browning read aloud from the book's *Epilogue* the stanza that described his dogged determination to keep on striving in a world of limitation and imperfection: "One who never turned his back but marched breast forward, / Never doubted clouds would break." Ultimately, this confidence underlies the bold relativity and deep skepticism that animate Browning's work. Like Hopkins, Browning insists that all of nature, even human nature, bespeaks some part of an unknowable absolute. Thus everything becomes material for poetry, the dirty, deformed, and despicable no less than the beautiful, pure, and radiantly good. As Browning says in *Fra Lippo Lippi*, "This world's no blot for us, / Nor blank; it means intensely, and means good: / To find its meaning is my meat and drink."

Porphyria's Lover[1]

> The rain set early in to-night,
>   The sullen wind was soon awake,
> It tore the elm-tops down for spite,
>   And did its worst to vex the lake:
> 5   I listened with heart fit to break.
> When glided in Porphyria; straight
>   She shut the cold out and the storm,
> And kneeled and made the cheerless grate
>   Blaze up, and all the cottage warm;
> 10   Which done, she rose, and from her form

---

1. The poem was originally published with another of Browning's dramatic monologues, *Johannes Agricola in Meditation*, under the general title of *Madhouse Cells*.

Withdrew the dripping cloak and shawl,
   And laid her soiled gloves by, untied
Her hat and let the damp hair fall,
   And, last, she sat down by my side
15   And called me. When no voice replied,
She put my arm about her waist,
   And made her smooth white shoulder bare,
And all her yellow hair displaced,
   And, stooping, made my cheek lie there,
20   And spread, o'er all, her yellow hair,
Murmuring how she loved me—she
   Too weak, for all her heart's endeavour,
To set its struggling passion free
   From pride, and vainer ties dissever,
25   And give herself to me for ever.
But passion sometimes would prevail,
   Nor could to-night's gay feast restrain
A sudden thought of one so pale
   For love of her, and all in vain:
30   So, she was come through wind and rain.
Be sure I looked up at her eyes
   Happy and proud; at last I knew
Porphyria worshipped me; surprise
   Made my heart swell, and still it grew
35   While I debated what to do.
That moment she was mine, mine, fair,
   Perfectly pure and good: I found
A thing to do, and all her hair
   In one long yellow string I wound
40   Three times her little throat around,
And strangled her. No pain felt she;
   I am quite sure she felt no pain.
As a shut bud that holds a bee,
   I warily oped her lids: again
45   Laughed the blue eyes without a stain.
And I untightened next the tress
   About her neck; her cheek once more
Blushed bright beneath my burning kiss:
   I propped her head up as before,
50   Only, this time my shoulder bore
Her head, which droops upon it still:
   The smiling rosy little head,
So glad it has its utmost will,
   That all it scorned at once is fled,
55   And I, its love, am gained instead!
Porphyria's love: she guessed not how
   Her darling one wish would be heard.
And thus we sit together now,

And all night long we have not stirred,
60   And yet God has not said a word!

c. 1835   1836, 1842

Soliloquy of the Spanish Cloister

1

Gr-r-r—there go, my heart's abhorrence!
    Water your damned flower-pots, do!
If hate killed men, Brother Lawrence,
    God's blood, would not mine kill you!
5 What? your myrtle-bush wants trimming?
    Oh, that rose has prior claims—
Needs its leaden vase filled brimming?
    Hell dry you up with its flames!

2

At the meal we sit together:
10   *Salve tibi!°* I must hear   *hail to thee*
Wise talk of the kind of weather,
    Sort of season, time of year:
Not a plenteous cork-crop: scarcely
    Dare we hope oak-galls,[1] *I doubt:*
15 *What's the Latin name for "parsley"?*
    What's the Greek name for Swine's Snout?°   *dandelion*

3

Whew! We'll have our platter burnished,
    Laid with care on our own shelf!
With a fire-new spoon we're furnished,
20   And a goblet for ourself,
Rinsed like something sacrificial
    Ere 'tis fit to touch our chaps°—   *chops, jaws*
Marked with L. for our initial!
    (He-he! There his lily snaps!)

4

25 *Saint,* forsooth! While brown Dolores
    Squats outside the Convent bank
With Sanchicha, telling stories,
    Steeping tresses in the tank,
Blue-black, lustrous, thick like horsehairs,
30   —Can't I see his dead eye glow,
Bright as't were a Barbary corsair's?[2]
    (That is, if he'd let it show!)

---

1. Growths on oaks which produce tannin.   2. A pirate from the Barbary Coast of Africa.

5

When he finishes refection,
   Knife and fork he never lays
35 Cross-wise, to my recollection,
   As do I, in Jesu's praise.
I the Trinity illustrate,
   Drinking watered orange-pulp—
In three sips the Arian[3] frustrate;
40   While he drains his at one gulp.

6

Oh, those melons? If he's able
   We're to have a feast! so nice!
One goes to the Abbot's table,
   All of us get each a slice.
45 How go on your flowers? None double?
   Not one fruit-sort can you spy?
Strange!—And I, too, at such trouble,
   Keep them close-nipped on the sly!

7

There's a great text in Galatians,
50   Once you trip on it, entails
Twenty-nine distinct damnations,
   One sure, if another fails:
If I trip him just a-dying,[4]
   Sure of heaven as sure can be,
55 Spin him round and send him flying
   Off to hell, a Manichee?°   *heretic*

8

Or, my scrofulous° French novel   *degenerate*
   On grey paper with blunt type!
Simply glance at it, you grovel
60   Hand and foot in Belial's gripe:[5]
If I double down its pages
   At the woeful sixteenth print,
When he gathers his greengages,°   *plums*
   Ope a sieve and slip it in't?

9

65 Or, there's Satan!—one might venture
   Pledge one's soul to him, yet leave
Such a flaw in the indenture
   As he'd miss till, past retrieve,
Blasted lay that rose-acacia

---

3. The Arian heresy denied the doctrine of the Trinity.
4. The speaker would like to ensure Brother Lawrence's damnation by tripping him up with St. Paul's difficult Epistle to the Galatians. Focusing on Galatians 5.19–21, which lists 17 mortal sins, the speaker overlooks Galatians

5.14–15: "Thou shalt love thy neighbour as thyself. But if ye hate and devour one another, take heed that ye be not consumed one of another."
5. In the grip of the Devil.

70　　　　We're so proud of! *Hy, Zy, Hine* . . .[6]
　　　　'St, there's Vespers! *Plena gratiâ*
　　　　Ave, Virgo![7] Gr-r-r—you swine!

1839　　　　　　　　　　　　　　　　　　　　　　　　　1842

My Last Duchess[1]
Ferrara

　　　　That's my last Duchess painted on the wall,
　　　　Looking as if she were alive. I call
　　　　That piece a wonder, now: Frà Pandolf's[2] hands
　　　　Worked busily a day, and there she stands.
5　　　　Will't please you sit and look at her? I said
　　　　"Frà Pandolf" by design, for never read
　　　　Strangers like you that pictured countenance,
　　　　The depth and passion of its earnest glance,
　　　　But to myself they turned (since none puts by
10　　　　The curtain I have drawn for you, but I)
　　　　And seemed as they would ask me, if they durst,
　　　　How such a glance came there; so, not the first
　　　　Are you to turn and ask thus. Sir, 'twas not
　　　　Her husband's presence only, called that spot
15　　　　Of joy into the Duchess' cheek: perhaps
　　　　Frà Pandolf chanced to say "Her mantle laps
　　　　Over my lady's wrist too much," or "Paint
　　　　Must never hope to reproduce the faint
　　　　Half-flush that dies along her throat:" such stuff
20　　　　Was courtesy, she thought, and cause enough
　　　　For calling up that spot of joy. She had
　　　　A heart—how shall I say?—too soon made glad,
　　　　Too easily impressed; she liked whate'er
　　　　She looked on, and her looks went everywhere.
25　　　　Sir, 'twas all one! My favour at her breast,
　　　　The dropping of the daylight in the West,
　　　　The bough of cherries some officious fool
　　　　Broke in the orchard for her, the white mule
　　　　She rode with round the terrace—all and each
30　　　　Would draw from her alike the approving speech,
　　　　Or blush, at least. She thanked men,—good! but thanked
　　　　Somehow—I know not how—as if she ranked
　　　　My gift of a nine-hundred-years-old name
　　　　With anybody's gift. Who'd stoop to blame

6. The speaker considers selling his own soul to Satan in return for blasting Lawrence, but he would leave a clever loophole in the bargain and thus escape damnation himself. "Hy, Zy, Hine" may be the beginning of a curse against Lawrence.
7. "Full of Grace, hail, Virgin!"—a garbled form of the Ave Maria, or prayer to Mary. Vespers are evening prayers.

1. The speaker is modeled on Alfonso II, Duke of Ferrara, who married the 14-year-old Lucrezia de Medici in 1558. When she died three years later, poisoning was suspected. In 1565 the Duke married the daughter of Ferdinand I, Count of Tyrol.
2. Brother Pandolf, the imaginary painter of the duchess's portrait.

35   This sort of trifling? Even had you skill
      In speech—(which I have not)—to make your will
      Quite clear to such an one, and say, "Just this
      Or that in you disgusts me; here you miss,
      Or there exceed the mark"—and if she let
40   Herself be lessoned so, nor plainly set
      Her wits to yours, forsooth, and made excuse,
      —E'en then would be some stooping; and I choose
      Never to stoop. Oh sir, she smiled, no doubt,
      Whene'er I passed her, but who passed without
45   Much the same smile? This grew; I gave commands;
      Then all smiles stopped together. There she stands
      As if alive. Will't please you rise? We'll meet
      The company below, then. I repeat,
      The Count your master's known munificence
50   Is ample warrant that no just pretence
      Of mine for dowry will be disallowed;
      Though his fair daughter's self, as I avowed
      At starting, is my object.[3] Nay, we'll go
      Together down, sir. Notice Neptune, though,
55   Taming a sea-horse, thought a rarity,
      Which Claus of Innsbruck cast in bronze for me!

1842   1842

The Bishop Orders His Tomb at Saint Praxed's Church[1]
Rome, 15—

      Vanity, saith the preacher, vanity![2]
      Draw round my bed: is Anselm keeping back?
      Nephews—sons mine[3] . . . ah God, I know not! Well—
      She, men would have to be your mother once,
5   Old Gandolf envied me, so fair she was!
      What's done is done, and she is dead beside,
      Dead long ago, and I am Bishop since,
      And as she died so must we die ourselves,
      And thence ye may perceive the world's a dream.
10   Life, how and what is it? As here I lie
      In this state-chamber, dying by degrees,
      Hours and long hours in the dead night, I ask

3. Only now does the reader learn that the duke is conducting negotiations for his second marriage and has been addressing the envoy of his bride-to-be's father.
1. John Ruskin admired Browning's portrait of a dying bishop's obsession with ordering a sumptuous tomb: "I know of no other piece of modern English, prose or poetry, in which there is so much told, as in these lines, of the Renaissance spirit—its worldliness, inconsistency, pride, hypocrisy, ignorance of itself, love of art, of luxury,

and of good Latin. It is nearly all that I have said of the central Renaissance in thirty pages of the *Stones of Venice*, put into as many lines, Browning's also being the antecedent work" (*Modern Painters*, vol. 4, ch. 20, sec. 34).
2. "Vanity of vanities, saith the Preacher, vanity of vanities; all is vanity" (Ecclesiastes 1.2).
3. The supposedly celibate clergy could not marry but sometimes took mistresses; the Bishop euphemistically calls his illegitimate sons "nephews."

"Do I live, am I dead?" Peace, peace seems all.
Saint Praxed's ever was the church for peace;
15 And so, about this tomb of mine. I fought
With tooth and nail to save my niche, ye know:
—Old Gandolf me cozened,° despite my care;   *cheated*
Shrewd was that snatch from out the corner South
He graced his carrion with, God curse the same!
20 Yet still my niche is not so cramped but thence
One sees the pulpit o' the epistle-side,[4]
And somewhat of the choir, those silent seats,
And up into the aery dome where live
The angels, and a sunbeam's sure to lurk:
25 And I shall fill my slab of basalt there,
And 'neath my tabernacle[5] take my rest,
With those nine columns round me, two and two,
The odd one at my feet where Anselm stands:
Peach-blossom marble all, the rare, the ripe
30 As fresh-poured red wine of a mighty pulse.[6]
—Old Gandolf with his paltry onion-stone,°   *cheap marble*
Put me where I may look at him! True peach,
Rosy and flawless: how I earned the prize!
Draw close: that conflagration of my church
35 —What then? So much was saved if aught were missed!
My sons, ye would not be my death? Go dig
The white-grape vineyard where the oil-press stood,
Drop water gently till the surface sink,
And if ye find . . . Ah God, I know not, I! . . .
40 Bedded in store of rotten fig-leaves soft,
And corded up in a tight olive-frail,°   *basket*
Some lump, ah God, of *lapis lazuli*,[7]
Big as a Jew's head cut off at the nape,
Blue as a vein o'er the Madonna's breast . . .
45 Sons, all have I bequeathed you, villas, all,
That brave Frascati[8] villa with its bath,
So, let the blue lump poise between my knees,
Like God the Father's globe on both his hands
Ye worship in the Jesu Church so gay,
50 For Gandolf shall not choose but see and burst!
Swift as a weaver's shuttle fleet our years:[9]
Man goeth to the grave, and where is he?
Did I say basalt for my slab, sons? Black—
'Twas ever antique-black I meant! How else

---

4. The right side, as one faces the altar, from which the Epistles of the New Testament are read.
5. Stone canopy beneath which the sculpted effigy of the bishop will repose on his tomb.
6. The pulpy mash of grapes from which strong wine could be made.

7. A semiprecious bright blue stone.
8. A resort near Rome.
9. Job 7.6: "My days are swifter than a weaver's shuttle and are spent without hope." The next line alludes to Job 7.9 and 14.10.

55   Shall ye contrast my frieze° to come beneath?   *sculpted band*
       The bas-relief in bronze ye promised me,
       Those Pans and Nymphs ye wot of, and perchance
       Some tripod, thyrsus, with a vase or so,
       The Saviour at his sermon on the mount,
60   Saint Praxed in a glory, and one Pan
       Ready to twitch the Nymph's last garment off,
       And Moses with the tables[1] . . . but I know
       Ye mark me not! What do they whisper thee,
       Child of my bowels, Anselm? Ah, ye hope
65   To revel down my villas while I gasp
       Bricked o'er with beggar's mouldy travertine°   *limestone*
       Which Gandolf from his tomb-top chuckles at!
       Nay, boys, ye love me—all of jasper, then!
       'Tis jasper ye stand pledged to, lest I grieve.
70   My bath must needs be left behind, alas!
       One block, pure green as a pistachio-nut,
       There's plenty jasper somewhere in the world—
       And have I not Saint Praxed's ear to pray
       Horses for ye, and brown Greek manuscripts,
75   And mistresses with great smooth marbly limbs?
       —That's if ye carve my epitaph aright,
       Choice Latin, picked phrase, Tully's every word,
       No gaudy ware like Gandolf's second line—
       Tully, my masters? Ulpian serves his need![2]
80   And then how I shall lie through centuries,
       And hear the blessed mutter of the mass,
       And see God made and eaten all day long,[3]
       And feel the steady candle-flame, and taste
       Good strong thick stupefying incense-smoke!
85   For as I lie here, hours of the dead night,
       Dying in state and by such slow degrees,
       I fold my arms as if they clasped a crook,
       And stretch my feet forth straight as stone can point,
       And let the bedclothes, for a mortcloth, drop
90   Into great laps and folds of sculptor's-work:[4]
       And as yon tapers dwindle, and strange thoughts
       Grow, with a certain humming in my ears,
       About the life before I lived this life,
       And this life too, popes, cardinals and priests,
95   Saint Praxed at his sermon on the mount,[5]
       Your tall pale mother with her talking eyes,

1. The bronze bas-relief sculptures will mingle pagan and Christian scenes, the goatlike lecherous Pan next to Moses receiving the Ten Commandments. In *Contrasts* (1841) A. W. Pugin criticized such juxtapositions, which were typical of the Renaissance.
2. Domitius Ulpianus (A.D. 170–228) was considered inferior to Marcus Tullius Cicero (106–43 B.C.), regarded during the Renaissance as the greatest Latin prose stylist.
3. According to the doctrine of transubstantiation, the bread and wine of Holy Communion become the body and blood of Christ.
4. As he lies in bed, the bishop positions himself like a carved effigy lying on a tomb, holding his ceremonial staff and draping his bedsheets like a "mortcloth" over a corpse.
5. Jesus gave the sermon on the mount, not St. Praxed (who was a woman); the bishop's mind is getting confused.

And new-found agate urns as fresh as day,
And marble's language, Latin pure, discreet,
—Aha, ELUCESCEBAT[6] quoth our friend?
100 No Tully, said I, Ulpian at the best!
Evil and brief hath been my pilgrimage.[7]
All *lapis*, all, sons! Else I give the Pope
My villas! Will ye ever eat my heart?
Ever your eyes were as a lizard's quick,
105 They glitter like your mother's for my soul,
Or ye would heighten my impoverished frieze,
Piece out its starved design, and fill my vase
With grapes, and add a vizor and a Term,[8]
And to the tripod ye would tie a lynx
110 That in his struggle throws the thyrsus down,
To comfort me on my entablature°   *platform*
Whereon I am to lie till I must ask
"Do I live, am I dead?" There, leave me, there!
For ye have stabbed me with ingratitude
115 To death—ye wish it—God, ye wish it! Stone—
Gritstone, a-crumble![9] Clammy squares which sweat
As if the corpse they keep were oozing through—
And no more *lapis* to delight the world!
Well go! I bless ye. Fewer tapers there,
120 But in a row: and, going, turn your backs
—Ay, like departing altar-ministrants,
And leave me in my church, the church for peace,
That I may watch at leisure if he leers—
Old Gandolf, at me, from his onion-stone,
125 As still he envied me, so fair she was!

1844   1845

Meeting at Night

1

The grey sea and the long black land;
And the yellow half-moon large and low;
And the startled little waves that leap
In fiery ringlets from their sleep,
5 As I gain the cove with pushing prow,
And quench its speed i' the slushy sand.

2

Then a mile of warm sea-scented beach;
Three fields to cross till a farm appears;

6. Gandolf's epitaph: "He was illustrious." The bishop disapproves of the verb form; Cicero would have written *elucebat*.
7. Cf. Genesis 47.9, where Jacob says: "The days of the years of my pilgrimage are an hundred and thirty years: few and evil have the days of the years of my life been."
8. The vizor of a helmet is sometimes represented in sculpture; the bishop suggests that his sons might also add a statue of Terminus, the Roman god of boundaries.
9. He fears they might use crumbly sandstone after all.

10 A tap at the pane, the quick sharp scratch
And blue spurt of a lighted match
And a voice less loud, thro' its joys and fears,
Than the two hearts beating each to each!

1845

Parting at Morning

Round the cape of a sudden came the sea,
And the sun looked over the mountain's rim:
And straight was a path of gold for him,°   *the sun*
And the need of a world of men for me.

1845

A Toccata of Galuppi's[1]

1

Oh, Galuppi, Baldassaro, this is very sad to find!
I can hardly misconceive you; it would prove me deaf and blind;
But although I take your meaning, 'tis with such a heavy mind!

2

Here you come with your old music, and here's all the good it brings.
5 What, they lived once thus at Venice where the merchants were the kings,
Where Saint Mark's is, where the Doges used to wed the sea with rings?[2]

3

Ay, because the sea's the street there; and 'tis arched by . . . what you call
. . . Shylock's bridge with houses on it, where they kept the carnival:[3]
I was never out of England—it's as if I saw it all.

4

10 Did young people take their pleasure when the sea was warm in May?
Balls and masks begun at midnight, burning ever to midday,
When they made up fresh adventures for the morrow, do you say?

5

Was a lady such a lady, cheeks so round and lips so red,—
On her neck the small face buoyant, like a bell-flower on its bed,
15 O'er the breast's superb abundance where a man might base his head?

6

Well, and it was graceful of them—they'd break talk off and afford
—She, to bite her mask's black velvet—he, to finger on his sword,
While you sat and played Toccatas, stately at the clavichord?

1. Baldassare Galuppi (1706–1785) was a Venetian composer for harpsichord. (Baldassaro is Browning's spelling of the composer's name.) A toccata is a fast-moving keyboard composition that displays the performer's virtuosity. The speaker is an imaginary Englishman of the 19th century for whom the music of Galuppi evokes scenes of Venice—and thoughts of death.
2. The Doges of Venice performed an annual ceremony of throwing a gold ring into the water near St. Mark's church, celebrating Venice's maritime power through a symbolic marriage to the sea.
3. The Rialto, a bridge over the Grand Canal, was the Venetian Merchants' Exchange where Shylock does business in *The Merchant of Venice*. Venice is famous for its celebrations of Carnival during the weeks preceding Lent.

7

What? Those lesser thirds[4] so plaintive, sixths diminished, sigh on sigh,
20 Told them something? Those suspensions, those solutions—"Must we die?"
Those commiserating sevenths—"Life might last! we can but try!"

8

"Were you happy?"—"Yes."—"And are you still as happy?"—"Yes. And you?"
—"Then, more kisses!"—"Did *I* stop them, when a million seemed so few?"
Hark, the dominant's persistence till it must be answered to!

9

25 So, an octave struck the answer. Oh, they praised you, I dare say!
"Brave Galuppi! that was music! good alike at grave and gay!
I can always leave off talking when I hear a master play!"

10

Then they left you for their pleasure: till in due time, one by one,
Some with lives that came to nothing, some with deeds as well undone,
30 Death stepped tacitly and took them where they never see the sun.

11

But when I sit down to reason, think to take my stand nor swerve,
While I triumph o'er a secret wrung from nature's close reserve,
In you come with your cold music till I creep thro' every nerve.

12

Yes, you, like a ghostly cricket, creaking where a house was burned:[5]
35 "Dust and ashes, dead and done with, Venice spent what Venice earned.
The soul, doubtless, is immortal—where a soul can be discerned.

13

"Yours for instance: you know physics, something of geology,
Mathematics are your pastime; souls shall rise in their degree;
Butterflies may dread extinction,—you'll not die, it cannot be!

14

40 "As for Venice and her people, merely born to bloom and drop,
Here on earth they bore their fruitage, mirth and folly were the crop:
What of soul was left, I wonder, when the kissing had to stop?

15

"Dust and ashes!" So you creak it, and I want° the heart to scold.   lack
Dear dead women, with such hair, too—what's become of all the gold
45 Used to hang and brush their bosoms? I feel chilly and grown old.

1855

---

4. Musical intervals, as are the sixths, sevenths, and octaves in later lines. Browning uses these and harmonic terms such as "suspension" and "dominant" evocatively—to convey the emotional effect of the toccata on the speaker—rather than in strict accordance with musical theory; there is no such interval as a "lesser third," for example.
5. Listening to Galuppi's music, the speaker imagines the lines that follow being spoken to him by the dead composer.

Memorabilia[1]

1

Ah, did you once see Shelley plain,
    And did he stop and speak to you
And did you speak to him again?
    How strange it seems and new!

2

5   But you were living before that,
      And also you are living after;
    And the memory I started at—
      My starting moves your laughter.

3

I crossed a moor, with a name of its own
10   And a certain use in the world no doubt,
Yet a hand's-breadth of it shines alone
    'Mid the blank miles round about:

4

For there I picked up on the heather
    And there I put inside my breast
15   A moulted feather, an eagle-feather!
    Well, I forget the rest.

1851   1855

Love Among the Ruins[1]

1

Where the quiet-coloured end of evening smiles,
    Miles and miles
On the solitary pastures where our sheep
    Half-asleep
5   Tinkle homeward thro' the twilight, stray or stop
    As they crop—
Was the site once of a city great and gay,
    (So they say)
Of our country's very capital, its prince
10   Ages since
Held his court in, gathered councils, wielding far
    Peace or war.

1. Things worthy of remembrance. Browning recalled meeting a man who had known Shelley, the poet he admired beyond all others: "I was one day in the shop of Hodgson, the well-known London bookseller, when a stranger came in, who, in the course of conversation with the bookseller, spoke of something that Shelley had once said to him. Suddenly the stranger paused, and burst into laughter as he observed me staring at him with blanched face; and . . . I still vividly remember how strangely the presence of a man who had seen and spoken with Shelley affected me."

1. The poem's scenery suggests the Roman Campagna but may also allude to archaeological excavations at Babylon, Nineveh, and Egyptian Thebes. Browning invented this stanza form. See Edward Burne-Jones's painting of the same name (Color Plate 20).

2

Now,—the country does not even boast a tree
    As you see,
15   To distinguish slopes of verdure, certain rills
    From the hills
Intersect and give a name to, (else they run
    Into one)
Where the domed and daring palace shot its spires
20   Up like fires
O'er the hundred-gated circuit of a wall
    Bounding all,
Made of marble, men might march on nor be pressed
    Twelve abreast.

3

25   And such plenty and perfection, see, of grass
    Never was!
Such a carpet as, this summer-time, o'erspreads
    And embeds
Every vestige of the city, guessed alone,
30   Stock or stone—
Where a multitude of men breathed joy and woe
    Long ago;
Lust of glory pricked their hearts up, dread of shame
    Struck them tame;
35   And that glory and that shame alike, the gold
    Bought and sold.

4

Now,—the single little turret that remains
    On the plains,
By the caper° overrooted, by the gourd   *shrub*
40   Overscored,
While the patching houseleek's head of blossom winks
    Through the chinks—
Marks the basement whence a tower in ancient time
    Sprang sublime,
45   And a burning ring, all round, the chariots traced
    As they raced,
And the monarch and his minions and his dames
    Viewed the games.

5

And I know, while thus the quiet-coloured eve
50   Smiles to leave
To their folding, all our many-tinkling fleece
    In such peace,
And the slopes and rills in undistinguished grey
    Melt away—
55   That a girl with eager eyes and yellow hair
    Waits me there

In the turret whence the charioteers caught soul
    For the goal,
When the king looked, where she looks now, breathless, dumb
60   Till I come.

6

But he looked upon the city, every side,
    Far and wide,
All the mountains topped with temples, all the glades'
    Colonnades,
65 All the causeys,° bridges, aqueducts,—and then,   *causeways*
    All the men!
When I do come, she will speak not, she will stand,
    Either hand
On my shoulder, give her eyes the first embrace
70   Of my face,
Ere we rush, ere we extinguish sight and speech
    Each on each.

7

In one year they sent a million fighters forth
    South and North,
75 And they built their gods a brazen pillar high
    As the sky,
Yet reserved a thousand chariots in full force—
    Gold, of course.
Oh heart! oh blood that freezes, blood that burns!
80   Earth's returns
For whole centuries of folly, noise and sin!
    Shut them in,
With their triumphs and their glories and the rest!
    Love is best.

c. 1852   1855

"Childe Roland to the Dark Tower Came"[1]
(See Edgar's Song in "Lear")[2]

1

My first thought was, he lied in every word,
    That hoary cripple, with malicious eye
    Askance to watch the working of his lie
On mine, and mouth scarce able to afford
5 Suppression of the glee, that pursed and scored
    Its edge, at one more victim gained thereby.

---

1. Roland was a hero of Charlemagne legends, and a "childe" was a young candidate for knighthood. Although critics have proposed many different interpretations of Roland's strange, nightmarish quest, Browning himself said only that the poem "came upon me as a kind of dream. I had to write it, then and there, and I finished it the same day, I believe. But it was simply that I had to do it. I did not know then what I meant beyond that, and I'm sure I don't know now. But I am very fond of it."
2. In Shakespeare's *King Lear*, Edgar, disguised as the mad beggar Poor Tom, sings: "Child Rowland to the dark tower came; / His word was still, 'Fie, foh and fum, / I smell the blood of a British man'" (3.4.181–83).

2

What else should he be set for, with his staff?
   What, save to waylay with his lies, ensnare
   All travellers who might find him posted there,
And ask the road? I guessed what skull-like laugh
Would break, what crutch 'gin write my epitaph
   For pastime in the dusty thoroughfare,

3

If at his counsel I should turn aside
   Into that ominous tract which, all agree,
   Hides the Dark Tower. Yet acquiescingly
I did turn as he pointed: neither pride
Nor hope rekindling at the end descried,
   So much as gladness that some end might be.

4

For, what with my whole world-wide wandering,
   What with my search drawn out thro' years, my hope
   Dwindled into a ghost not fit to cope
With that obstreperous joy success would bring,—
I hardly tried now to rebuke the spring
   My heart made, finding failure in its scope.

5

As when a sick man very near to death
   Seems dead indeed, and feels begin and end
   The tears and takes the farewell of each friend,
And hears one bid the other go, draw breath
Freelier outside, ("since all is o'er," he saith,
   "And the blow fallen no grieving can amend;")

6

While some discuss if near the other graves
   Be room enough for this, and when a day
   Suits best for carrying the corpse away,
With care about the banners, scarves and staves:
And still the man hears all, and only craves
   He may not shame such tender love and stay.

7

Thus, I had so long suffered in this quest,
   Heard failure prophesied so oft, been writ
   So many times among "The Band"—to wit,
The knights who to the Dark Tower's search addressed
Their steps—that just to fail as they, seemed best,
   And all the doubt was now—should I be fit?

8

So, quiet as despair, I turned from him,
   That hateful cripple, out of his highway
   Into the path he pointed. All the day

10

15

20

25

30

35

40

45

Had been a dreary one at best, and dim
Was settling to its close, yet shot one grim
   Red leer to see the plain catch its estray.°   *stray animal*

9

For mark! no sooner was I fairly found
50   Pledged to the plain, after a pace or two,
      Than, pausing to throw backward a last view
O'er the safe road, 'twas gone; grey plain all round:
Nothing but plain to the horizon's bound.
     I might go on; nought else remained to do.

10

55   So, on I went. I think I never saw
       Such starved ignoble nature; nothing throve:
      For flowers—as well expect a cedar grove!
But cockle, spurge,° according to their law   *weeds*
Might propagate their kind, with none to awe,
60   You'd think; a burr had been a treasure-trove.

11

No! penury, inertness and grimace,
       In some strange sort, were the land's portion. "See
      Or shut your eyes," said Nature peevishly,
"It nothing skills: I cannot help my case:
65   'Tis the Last Judgment's fire must cure this place,
       Calcine° its clods and set my prisoners free."   *burn to ashes*

12

If there pushed any ragged thistle-stalk
       Above its mates, the head was chopped; the bents°   *coarse grasses*
      Were jealous else. What made those holes and rents
70   In the dock's° harsh swarth leaves, bruised as to baulk   *weed*
All hope of greenness? 'tis a brute must walk
       Pashing° their life out, with a brute's intents.   *crushing*

13

As for the grass, it grew as scant as hair
       In leprosy; thin dry blades pricked the mud
75   Which underneath looked kneaded up with blood.
One stiff blind horse, his every bone a-stare,
Stood stupefied, however he came there:
       Thrust out past service from the devil's stud!

14

Alive? he might be dead for aught I know,
80   With that red gaunt and colloped neck a-strain,
      And shut eyes underneath the rusty mane;
Seldom went such grotesqueness with such woe;
I never saw a brute I hated so;
       He must be wicked to deserve such pain.

15

85   I shut my eyes and turned them on my heart.
       As a man calls for wine before he fights,
       I asked one draught of earlier, happier sights,
    Ere fitly I could hope to play my part.
    Think first, fight afterwards—the soldier's art:
90   One taste of the old time sets all to rights.

16

    Not it! I fancied Cuthbert's reddening face
      Beneath its garniture of curly gold,
      Dear fellow, till I almost felt him fold
    An arm in mine to fix me to the place,
95   That way he used. Alas, one night's disgrace!
      Out went my heart's new fire and left it cold.

17

    Giles then, the soul of honour—there he stands
      Frank as ten years ago when knighted first.
      What honest man should dare (he said) he durst.
100   Good—but the scene shifts—faugh! what hangman-hands
    Pin to his breast a parchment? His own bands
      Read it. Poor traitor, spit upon and curst!

18

    Better this present than a past like that;
      Back therefore to my darkening path again!
105   No sound, no sight as far as eye could strain.
    Will the night send a howlet° or a bat?   *owl*
    I asked: when something on the dismal flat
      Came to arrest my thoughts and change their train.

19

    A sudden little river crossed my path
110   As unexpected as a serpent comes.
      No sluggish tide congenial to the glooms;
    This, as it frothed by, might have been a bath
    For the fiend's glowing hoof—to see the wrath
      Of its black eddy bespate with flakes and spumes.

20

115   So petty yet so spiteful! All along,
      Low scrubby alders kneeled down over it;
      Drenched willows flung them headlong in a fit
    Of mute despair, a suicidal throng:
    The river which had done them all the wrong,
120   Whate'er that was, rolled by, deterred no whit.

21

    Which, while I forded,—good saints, how I feared
      To set my foot upon a dead man's cheek,
      Each step, or feel the spear I thrust to seek

For hollows, tangled in his hair or beard!
125 —It may have been a water-rat I speared,
　　But, ugh! it sounded like a baby's shriek.

22

Glad was I when I reached the other bank.
　　Now for a better country. Vain presage!
　　Who were the strugglers, what war did they wage,
130 Whose savage trample thus could pad° the dank　　　　　　　*tread*
Soil to a plash? Toads in a poisoned tank,
　　Or wild cats in a red-hot iron cage—

23

The fight must so have seemed in that fell cirque.°　　　　*terrible arena*
　　What penned them there, with all the plain to choose?
135 　　No foot-print leading to that horrid mews,
None out of it. Mad brewage set to work
Their brains, no doubt, like galley-slaves the Turk
　　Pits for his pastime, Christians against Jews.

24

And more than that—a furlong on—why, there!
140 　　What bad use was that engine for, that wheel,
　　Or brake, not wheel—that harrow fit to reel
Men's bodies out like silk? with all the air
Of Tophet's° tool, on earth left unaware,　　　　　　　　*hell's*
　　Or brought to sharpen its rusty teeth of steel.

25

145 Then came a bit of stubbed ground, once a wood,
　　Next a marsh, it would seem, and now mere earth
　　Desperate and done with; (so a fool finds mirth,
Makes a thing and then mars it, till his mood
Changes and off he goes!) within a rood°—　　　　　　*quarter of an acre*
150 　　Bog, clay and rubble, sand and stark black dearth.

26

Now blotches rankling, coloured gay and grim,
　　Now patches where some leanness of the soil's
　　Broke into moss or substances like boils;
Then came some palsied oak, a cleft in him
155 Like a distorted mouth that splits its rim
　　Gaping at death, and dies while it recoils.

27

And just as far as ever from the end!
　　Nought in the distance but the evening, nought
　　To point my footstep further! At the thought,
160 A great black bird, Apollyon's[3] bosom-friend,

---

3. Devil mentioned in Revelation 9.11 and in Bunyan's *Pilgrim's Progress*.

Sailed past, nor beat his wide wing dragon-penned°   *pinioned*
   That brushed my cap—perchance the guide I sought.

28

For, looking up, aware I somehow grew,
   'Spite of the dusk, the plain had given place
165   All round to mountains—with such name to grace
Mere ugly heights and heaps now stolen in view.
How thus they had surprised me,—solve it, you!
   How to get from them was no clearer case.

29

Yet half I seemed to recognize some trick
170   Of mischief happened to me, God knows when—
   In a bad dream perhaps. Here ended, then,
Progress this way. When, in the very nick
Of giving up, one time more, came a click
   As when a trap shuts—you're inside the den!

30

175 Burningly it came on me all at once,
   This was the place! those two hills on the right,
   Crouched like two bulls locked horn in horn in fight;
While to the left, a tall scalped mountain . . . Dunce,
Dotard, a-dozing at the very nonce,°   *moment*
180   After a life spent training for the sight!

31

What in the midst lay but the Tower itself?
   The round squat turret, blind as the fool's heart,[4]
   Built of brown stone, without a counterpart
In the whole world. The tempest's mocking elf
185 Points to the shipman thus the unseen shelf
   He strikes on, only when the timbers start.

32

Not see? because of night perhaps?—why, day
   Came back again for that! before it left,
   The dying sunset kindled through a cleft:
190 The hills, like giants at a hunting, lay,
Chin upon hand, to see the game at bay,—
   "Now stab and end the creature—to the heft!"°   *hilt*

33

Not hear? when noise was everywhere! it tolled
   Increasing like a bell. Names in my ears
195   Of all the lost adventurers my peers,—
How such a one was strong, and such was bold,
And such was fortunate, yet each of old
   Lost, lost! one moment knelled the woe of years.

---

4. "The fool hath said in his heart, There is no God" (Psalm 14.1).

34

There they stood, ranged along the hill-sides, met
200   To view the last of me, a living frame
            For one more picture! in a sheet of flame
      I saw them and I knew them all. And yet
      Dauntless the slug-horn[5] to my lips I set,
            And blew. "*Childe Roland to the Dark Tower came.*"

c. 1852   1855

Fra Lippo Lippi[1]

      I am poor brother Lippo, by your leave!
      You need not clap your torches to my face.
      Zooks, what's to blame? you think you see a monk!
      What, 'tis past midnight, and you go the rounds,
5   And here you catch me at an alley's end
      Where sportive ladies leave their doors ajar?
      The Carmine's my cloister:[2] hunt it up,
      Do,—harry out, if you must show your zeal,
      Whatever rat, there, haps on his wrong hole,
10   And nip each softling of a wee white mouse,
      Weke, weke, that's crept to keep him company!
      Aha, you know your betters! Then, you'll take
      Your hand away that's fiddling on my throat,
      And please to know me likewise. Who am I?
15   Why, one, sir, who is lodging with a friend
      Three streets off—he's a certain . . . how d'ye call?
      Master—a . . . Cosimo of the Medici,[3]
      I' the house that caps the corner. Boh! you were best!
      Remember and tell me, the day you're hanged,
20   How you affected such a gullet's-gripe![4]
      But you, sir,[5] it concerns you that your knaves
      Pick up a manner nor discredit you:
      Zooks, are we pilchards,° that they sweep the streets   sardines
      And count fair prize what comes into their net?
25   He's Judas to a tittle, that man is![6]
      Just such a face! Why, sir, you make amends:
      Lord, I'm not angry! Bid your hangdogs go
      Drink out this quarter-florin to the health
      Of the munificent House that harbours me
30   (And many more beside, lads! more beside!)
      And all's come square again. I'd like his face—

5. Scottish word for slogan, or battle cry, though Browning seems to mean "trumpet."
1. Filippo Lippi (1406–1469) was an early Renaissance painter and monk whose life is described in Giorgio Vasari's *The Lives of the Painters* (1550, 1568); "Fra" means brother.
2. Santa Maria del Carmine, a Carmelite monastery in Florence.

3. Cosimo de' Medici (1389–1464), a banker and ruler of Florence, was Lippi's patron.
4. How you choked me by the throat.
5. Lippi now addresses the leader of the watchmen.
6. One of the watchmen is the spitting image of Judas.

His, elbowing on his comrade in the door
With the pike and lantern,—for the slave that holds
John Baptist's head a-dangle by the hair
35 With one hand ("Look you, now," as who should say)
And his weapon in the other, yet unwiped!
It's not your chance to have a bit of chalk,
A wood-coal or the like? or you should see!
Yes, I'm the painter, since you style me so.
40 What, brother Lippo's doings, up and down,
You know them and they take you? like enough!
I saw the proper twinkle in your eye—
'Tell you, I liked your looks at very first.
Let's sit and set things straight now, hip to haunch.
45 Here's spring come, and the nights one makes up bands
To roam the town and sing out carnival,[7]
And I've been three weeks shut within my mew,
A-painting for the great man, saints and saints
And saints again. I could not paint all night—
50 Ouf! I leaned out of window for fresh air.
There came a hurry of feet and little feet,
A sweep of lute-strings, laughs, and whifts of song,—
Flower o' the broom,
Take away love, and our earth is a tomb!
55 *Flower o' the quince,*
I let Lisa go, and what good in life since?
Flower o' the thyme[8]—and so on. Round they went.
Scarce had they turned the corner when a titter
Like the skipping of rabbits by moonlight,—three slim shapes,
60 And a face that looked up . . . zooks, sir, flesh and blood,
That's all I'm made of! Into shreds it went,
Curtain and counterpane and coverlet,
All the bed-furniture—a dozen knots,
There was a ladder! Down I let myself,
65 Hands and feet, scrambling somehow, and so dropped,
And after them. I came up with the fun
Hard by Saint Laurence,[9] hail fellow, well met,—
Flower o' the rose,
If I've been merry, what matter who knows?
70 And so as I was stealing back again
To get to bed and have a bit of sleep
Ere I rise up to-morrow and go work
On Jerome[1] knocking at his poor old breast
With his great round stone to subdue the flesh,
75 You snap me of the sudden. Ah, I see!

---

7. A season of festivities before Lent.
8. The "flower songs" Lippi sings are called *stornelli*, three-line Tuscan folk songs.

9. The Church of San Lorenzo.
1. The pleasure-loving Lippi is painting the chaste and ascetic St. Jerome.

Though your eye twinkles still, you shake your head—
Mine's shaved[2]—a monk, you say—the sting's in that!
If Master Cosimo announced himself,
Mum's the word naturally; but a monk!
80   Come, what am I a beast for? tell us, now!
I was a baby when my mother died
And father died and left me in the street.
I starved there, God knows how, a year or two
On fig-skins, melon-parings, rinds and shucks,
85   Refuse and rubbish. One fine frosty day,
My stomach being empty as your hat,
The wind doubled me up and down I went.
Old Aunt Lapaccia trussed me with one hand,
(Its fellow was a stinger as I knew)
90   And so along the wall, over the bridge,
By the straight cut to the convent. Six words there,
While I stood munching my first bread that month:
"So, boy, you're minded," quoth the good fat father
Wiping his own mouth, 'twas refection-time,°—   *mealtime*
95   "To quit this very miserable world?
Will you renounce" . . . . "the mouthful of bread?" thought I;
By no means! Brief, they made a monk of me;
I did renounce the world, its pride and greed,
Palace, farm, villa, shop and banking-house,
100 Trash, such as these poor devils of Medici
Have given their hearts to—all at eight years old.
Well, sir, I found in time, you may be sure,
'Twas not for nothing—the good bellyful,
The warm serge and the rope that goes all round,
105 And day-long blessed idleness beside!
"Let's see what the urchin's fit for"—that came next.
Not overmuch their way, I must confess.
Such a to-do! They tried me with their books:
Lord, they'd have taught me Latin in pure waste!
110 *Flower o' the clove,*
All the Latin I construe is, "amo," I love!
But, mind you, when a boy starves in the streets
Eight years together, as my fortune was,
Watching folk's faces to know who will fling
115 The bit of half-stripped grape-bunch he desires,
And who will curse or kick him for his pains,—
Which gentleman processional and fine,
Holding a candle to the Sacrament,
Will wink and let him lift a plate and catch
120 The droppings of the wax to sell again,
Or holla for the Eight[3] and have him whipped,—

2. The tonsure, or partially shaved head, was the emblem   3. Send for the magistrates of Florence.
of the monk.

How say I?—nay, which dog bites, which lets drop
His bone from the heap of offal in the street,—
Why, soul and sense of him grow sharp alike,
125   He learns the look of things, and none the less
For admonition from the hunger-pinch.
I had a store of such remarks, be sure,
Which, after I found leisure, turned to use.
I drew men's faces on my copy-books,
130   Scrawled them within the antiphonary's marge,[4]
Joined legs and arms to the long music-notes,
Found eyes and nose and chin for A's and B's,
And made a string of pictures of the world
Betwixt the ins and outs of verb and noun,
135   On the wall, the bench, the door. The monks looked black.
"Nay," quoth the Prior, "turn him out, d' ye say?
In no wise. Lose a crow and catch a lark.
What if at last we get our man of parts,
We Carmelites, like those Camaldolese
140   And Preaching Friars, to do our church up fine
And put the front on it that ought to be!"[5]
And hereupon he bade me daub away.
Thank you! my head being crammed, the walls a blank,
Never was such prompt disemburdening.
145   First, every sort of monk, the black and white,
I drew them, fat and lean: then, folk at church,
From good old gossips waiting to confess
Their cribs° of barrel-droppings, candle-ends,—   *small thefts*
To the breathless fellow at the altar-foot,
150   Fresh from his murder,[6] safe and sitting there
With the little children round him in a row
Of admiration, half for his beard and half
For that white anger of his victim's son
Shaking a fist at him with one fierce arm,
155   Signing himself[7] with the other because of Christ
(Whose sad face on the cross sees only this
After the passion° of a thousand years)   *suffering*
Till some poor girl, her apron o'er her head,
(Which the intense eyes looked through) came at eve
160   On tiptoe, said a word, dropped in a loaf,
Her pair of earrings and a bunch of flowers
(The brute took growling), prayed, and so was gone.
I painted all, then cried "'Tis ask and have;
Choose, for more's ready!"—laid the ladder flat,
165   And showed my covered bit of cloister-wall

---

4. The margin of his hymnbook.
5. The Prior, or head of the monastery, wants to outdo rival orders of monks by having Lippi paint the church splendidly.
6. Criminals could take refuge in the church because it was a sanctuary where civil law had no power.
7. Making the sign of the cross.

The monks closed in a circle and praised loud
Till checked, taught what to see and not to see,
Being simple bodies,—"That's the very man!
Look at the boy who stoops to pat the dog!
170   That woman's like the Prior's niece[8] who comes
To care about his asthma: it's the life!"
But there my triumph's straw-fire flared and funked;°   smoked
Their betters took their turn to see and say:
The Prior and the learned pulled a face
175   And stopped all that in no time. "How? what's here?
Quite from the mark of painting, bless us all!
Faces, arms, legs and bodies like the true
As much as pea and pea! it's devil's-game!
Your business is not to catch men with show,
180   With homage to the perishable clay,
But lift them over it, ignore it all,
Make them forget there's such a thing as flesh.
Your business is to paint the souls of men—
Man's soul, and it's a fire, smoke . . . no, it's not . . .
185   It's vapour done up like a new-born babe—
(In that shape when you die it leaves your mouth)
It's . . . well, what matters talking, it's the soul!
Give us no more of body than shows soul!
Here's Giotto,[9] with his Saint a-praising God,
190   That sets us praising,—why not stop with him?
Why put all thoughts of praise out of our head
With wonder at lines, colours, and what not?
Paint the soul, never mind the legs and arms!
Rub all out, try at it a second time.
195   Oh, that white smallish female with the breasts,
She's just my niece . . . Herodias, I would say,—
Who went and danced and got men's heads cut off![1]
Have it all out!" Now, is this sense, I ask?
A fine way to paint soul, by painting body
200   So ill, the eye can't stop there, must go further
And can't fare worse! Thus, yellow does for white
When what you put for yellow's simply black,
And any sort of meaning looks intense
When all beside itself means and looks nought.
205   Why can't a painter lift each foot in turn,
Left foot and right foot, go a double step,
Make his flesh liker and his soul more like,
Both in their order? Take the prettiest face,
The Prior's niece . . . patron-saint—is it so pretty

8. Probably a euphemism for the Prior's mistress.
9. Giotto di Bondone (c. 1266–1337), late-medieval Florentine artist and architect.
1. The gospel of Matthew tells how Herod's niece Salomé danced before him and requested as a reward the head of John the Baptist (14.6–8). According to Vasari, however, it was Salomé's mother, Herodias, who danced.

210 You can't discover if it means hope, fear,
     Sorrow or joy? won't beauty go with these?
     Suppose I've made her eyes all right and blue,
     Can't I take breath and try to add life's flash,
     And then add soul and heighten them threefold?
215 Or say there's beauty with no soul at all—
     (I never saw it—put the case the same—)
     If you get simple beauty and nought else,
     You get about the best thing God invents:
     That's somewhat: and you'll find the soul you have missed,
220 Within yourself, when you return him thanks.
     "Rub all out!" Well, well, there's my life, in short,
     And so the thing has gone on ever since.
     I'm grown a man no doubt, I've broken bounds:
     You should not take a fellow eight years old
225 And make him swear to never kiss the girls.
     I'm my own master, paint now as I please—
     Having a friend, you see, in the Corner-house!°   *Medici palace*
     Lord, it's fast holding by the rings in front—
     Those great rings serve more purposes than just
230 To plant a flag in, or tie up a horse!
     And yet the old schooling sticks, the old grave eyes
     Are peeping o'er my shoulder as I work,
     The heads shake still—"It's art's decline, my son!
     You're not of the true painters, great and old;
235 Brother Angelico's the man, you'll find;
     Brother Lorenzo stands his single peer:[2]
     Fag° on at flesh, you'll never make the third!"   *struggle*
     Flower o' the pine,
     You keep your mistr . . . manners, and I'll stick to mine!
240 I'm not the third, then: bless us, they must know!
     Don't you think they're the likeliest to know,
     They with their Latin? So, I swallow my rage,
     Clench my teeth, suck my lips in tight, and paint
     To please them—sometimes do and sometimes don't;
245 For, doing most, there's pretty sure to come
     A turn, some warm eve finds me at my saints—
     A laugh, a cry, the business of the world—
     (*Flower o' the peach,*
     Death for us all, and his own life for each!)
250 And my whole soul revolves, the cup runs over,
     The world and life's too big to pass for a dream,
     And I do these wild things in sheer despite,
     And play the fooleries you catch me at,
     In pure rage! The old mill-horse, out at grass
255 After hard years, throws up his stiff heels so,

2. Fra Angelico (1387–1455) and Lorenzo Monaco (1370–1425) were important painters in the traditional formalist style.

Although the miller does not preach to him
The only good of grass is to make chaff.°   *straw*
What would men have? Do they like grass or no—
May they or mayn't they? all I want's the thing
260   Settled for ever one way. As it is,
You tell too many lies and hurt yourself:
You don't like what you only like too much,
You do like what, if given you at your word,
You find abundantly detestable.
265   For me, I think I speak as I was taught;
I always see the garden and God there
A-making man's wife: and, my lesson learned,
The value and significance of flesh,
I can't unlearn ten minutes afterwards.

270   You understand me: I'm a beast, I know.
But see, now—why, I see as certainly
As that the morning-star's about to shine,
What will hap some day. We've a youngster here
Comes to our convent, studies what I do,
275   Slouches and stares and lets no atom drop:
His name is Guidi—he'll not mind the monks—
They call him Hulking Tom,[3] he lets them talk—
He picks my practice up—he'll paint apace,
I hope so—though I never live so long,
280   I know what's sure to follow. You be judge!
You speak no Latin more than I, belike,
However, you're my man, you've seen the world
—The beauty and the wonder and the power,
The shapes of things, their colours, lights and shades,
285   Changes, surprises,—and God made it all!
—For what? Do you feel thankful, ay or no,
For this fair town's face, yonder river's line,
The mountain round it and the sky above,
Much more the figures of man, woman, child,
290   These are the frame to? What's it all about?
To be passed over, despised? or dwelt upon,
Wondered at? oh, this last of course!—you say.
But why not do as well as say,—paint these
Just as they are, careless what comes of it?
295   God's works—paint anyone, and count it crime
To let a truth slip. Don't object, "His works
Are here already; nature is complete:
Suppose you reproduce her—(which you can't)
There's no advantage! you must beat her, then."
300   For, don't you mark? we're made so that we love

---

3. Tommaso Guidi (1401–1428), called Masaccio ("Sloppy Tom"), was probably Lippi's teacher, but Browning casts him as his pupil. Both painters revolted against the highly stylized conventions of medieval art in favor of increased realism.

First when we see them painted, things we have passed
Perhaps a hundred times nor cared to see;
And so they are better, painted—better to us,
Which is the same thing. Art was given for that;
305 God uses us to help each other so,
Lending our minds out. Have you noticed, now,
Your cullion's hanging face?[4] A bit of chalk,
And trust me but you should, though! How much more,
If I drew higher things with the same truth!
310 That were to take the Prior's pulpit-place,
Interpret God to all of you! Oh, oh,
It makes me mad to see what men shall do
And we in our graves! This world's no blot for us,
Nor blank; it means intensely, and means good:
315 To find its meaning is my meat and drink.
"Ay, but you don't so instigate to prayer!"
Strikes in the Prior: "when your meaning's plain
It does not say to folk—remember matins,°   *morning prayers*
Or, mind you fast next Friday!" Why, for this
320 What need of art at all? A skull and bones,
Two bits of stick nailed crosswise, or, what's best,
A bell to chime the hour with, does as well.
I painted a Saint Laurence six months since
At Prato, splashed the fresco in fine style:
325 "How looks my painting, now the scaffold's down?"
I ask a brother: "Hugely," he returns—
Already not one phiz° of your three slaves   *face*
Who turn the Deacon off his toasted side,[5]
But's scratched and prodded to our heart's content,
330 The pious people have so eased their own
With coming to say prayers there in a rage:
We get on fast to see the bricks beneath.
Expect another job this time next year,
For pity and religion grow i' the crowd—
335 Your painting serves its purpose!" Hang the fools!

    —That is—you'll not mistake an idle word
Spoke in a huff by a poor monk, God wot,
Tasting the air this spicy night which turns
The unaccustomed head like Chianti wine!
340 Oh, the church knows! don't misreport me, now!
It's natural a poor monk out of bounds
Should have his apt word to excuse himself:
And hearken how I plot to make amends.
I have bethought me: I shall paint a piece
345 . . . There's for you! Give me six months, then go, see

4. That rascal's drooping face (or perhaps "born to be hanged"—cf. line 19).
5. St. Laurence, a deacon who was martyred by being roasted, is reputed to have asked to be turned over, as he was done on one side.

Something in Sant' Ambrogio's![6] Bless the nuns!
They want a cast o' my office. I shall paint
God in the midst, Madonna and her babe,
Ringed by a bowery flowery angel-brood,
350   Lilies and vestments and white faces, sweet
As puff on puff of grated orris-root
When ladies crowd to Church at midsummer.
And then i' the front, of course a saint or two—
Saint John, because he saves the Florentines,
355   Saint Ambrose, who puts down in black and white
The convent's friends and gives them a long day,
And Job, I must have him there past mistake,
The man of Uz (and Us without the z,
Painters who need his patience). Well, all these
360   Secured at their devotion, up shall come
Out of a corner when you least expect,
As one by a dark stair into a great light,
Music and talking, who but Lippo! I!—
Mazed, motionless and moonstruck—I'm the man!
365   Back I shrink—what is this I see and hear?
I, caught up with my monk's-things by mistake,
My old serge gown and rope that goes all round,
I, in this presence, this pure company!
Where's a hole, where's a corner for escape?
370   Then steps a sweet angelic slip of a thing
Forward, puts out a soft palm—"Not so fast!"
—Addresses the celestial presence, "nay—
He made you and devised you, after all,
Though he's none of you! Could Saint John there draw—
375   His camel-hair[7] make up a painting-brush?
We come to brother Lippo for all that,
Iste perfecit opus!"[8] So, all smile—
I shuffle sideways with my blushing face
Under the cover of a hundred wings
380   Thrown like a spread of kirtles° when you're gay   skirts
And play hot cockles,[9] all the doors being shut,
Till, wholly unexpected, in there pops
The hothead husband! Thus I scuttle off
To some safe bench behind, not letting go
385   The palm of her, the little lily thing
That spoke the good word for me in the nick,
Like the Prior's niece . . . Saint Lucy, I would say.[1]

6. Lippi's *Coronation of the Virgin* was painted for the church of Sant' Ambrogio's convent in Florence.
7. "And John was clothed with camel's hair, and with a girdle of a skin about his loins; and he did eat locusts and wild honey" (Mark 1.6). John the Baptist is the patron saint of Florence.
8. "This man made the work." These words appear beside

a figure in the painting, which was assumed to be a self-portrait of Lippi. (It actually depicts the patron who ordered the painting.)
9. A blindfolded game, here a euphemism for sex.
1. Lippi will paint the Prior's "niece" as the virgin martyr Lucy, whom he has imagined interceding on his behalf with "the celestial presence" (lines 370–77).

And so all's saved for me, and for the church
A pretty picture gained. Go, six months hence!
390   Your hand, sir, and good-bye: no lights, no lights!
The street's hushed, and I know my own way back,
Don't fear me! There's the grey beginning. Zooks!

1853   1855

The Last Ride Together

1

I said—Then, dearest, since 'tis so,
Since now at length my fate I know,
Since nothing all my love avails,
Since all, my life seemed meant for, fails,
5   Since this was written and needs must be—
My whole heart rises up to bless
Your name in pride and thankfulness!
Take back the hope you gave,—I claim
Only a memory of the same,
10   —And this beside, if you will not blame,
    Your leave for one more last ride with me.

2

My mistress bent that brow of hers;
Those deep dark eyes where pride demurs
When pity would be softening through,
15   Fixed me a breathing-while or two
    With life or death in the balance: right!
The blood replenished me again;
My last thought was at least not vain:
I and my mistress, side by side
20   Shall be together, breathe and ride,
So, one day more am I deified.
    Who knows but the world may end to-night?

3

Hush! if you saw some western cloud
All billowy-bosomed, over-bowed
25   By many benedictions—sun's
And moon's and evening-star's at once—
    And so, you, looking and loving best,
Conscious grew, your passion drew
Cloud, sunset, moonrise, star-shine too,
30   Down on you, near and yet more near,
Till flesh must fade for heaven was here!—
Thus leant she and lingered—joy and fear!
    Thus lay she a moment on my breast.

4

Then we began to ride. My soul
35   Smoothed itself out, a long-cramped scroll

Freshening and fluttering in the wind.
Past hopes already lay behind.
    What need to strive with a life awry?
Had I said that, had I done this,
40   So might I gain, so might I miss.
Might she have loved me? just as well
She might have hated, who can tell!
Where had I been now if the worst befell?
    And here we are riding, she and I.

5

45   Fail I alone, in words and deeds?
Why, all men strive and who succeeds?
We rode; it seemed my spirit flew,
Saw other regions, cities new,
    As the world rushed by on either side.
50   I thought,—All labour, yet no less
Bear up beneath their unsuccess.
Look at the end of work, contrast
The petty done, the undone vast,
This present of theirs with the hopeful past!
55   I hoped she would love me; here we ride.

6

What hand and brain went ever paired?
What heart alike conceived and dared?
What act proved all its thought had been?
What will but felt the fleshy screen?
60   We ride and I see her bosom heave.
There's many a crown for who can reach.
Ten lines, a statesman's life in each!
The flag stuck on a heap of bones,
A soldier's doing! what atones?
65   They scratch his name on the Abbey-stones.[1]
    My riding is better, by their leave.

7

What does it all mean, poet? Well,
Your brains beat into rhythm, you tell
What we felt only; you expressed
70   You hold things beautiful the best,
    And pace them in rhyme so, side by side.
'Tis something, nay 'tis much: but then,
Have you yourself what's best for men?
Are you—poor, sick, old ere your time—
75   Nearer one whit your own sublime
Than we who never have turned a rhyme?
    Sing, riding's a joy! For me, I ride.

---

1. Glorious human achievement ends in a ten-line biographical summary, a memorial flag, or a tomb in Westminster Abbey.

8

And you, great sculptor—so, you gave
A score of years to Art, her slave,
80 And that's your Venus, whence we turn
To yonder girl that fords the burn!°   *crosses the stream*
You acquiesce, and shall I repine?
What, man of music, you grown grey
With notes and nothing else to say,
85 Is this your sole praise from a friend,
"Greatly his opera's strains intend,
But in music we know how fashions end!"
I gave my youth; but we ride, in fine.

9

Who knows what's fit for us? Had fate
90 Proposed bliss here should sublimate°   *make sublime, exalt*
My being—had I signed the bond—
Still one must lead some life beyond,
Have a bliss to die with, dim-descried.[2]
This foot once planted on the goal,
95 This glory-garland round my soul,
Could I descry such? Try and test!
I sink back shuddering from the quest.
Earth being so good, would heaven seem best?
Now, heaven and she are beyond this ride.

10

100 And yet—she has not spoke so long
What if heaven be that, fair and strong
At life's best, with our eyes upturned
Whither life's flower is first discerned,
We, fixed so, ever should so abide?
105 What if we still ride on, we two
With life for ever old yet new,
Changed not in kind but in degree,
The instant made eternity,—
And heaven just prove that I and she
110 Ride, ride together, for ever ride?

1855

Andrea del Sarto[1]
(called "The Faultless Painter")

But do not let us quarrel any more,
No, my Lucrezia; bear with me for once:

2. At death one looks forward to heavenly bliss (whereas, had his earthly love been successful, he might have had nothing better to hope for in heaven).

1. Browning's depiction of Andrea del Sarto (1486–1531), a technically gifted Florentine Renaissance painter who never quite lived up to his early promise, is based in part on Giorgio Vasari's *The Lives of the Painters*

(1550, 1568). Vasari, who had been Andrea's pupil, considered that "had his spirit been as bold as his judgment was profound, he would doubtless have been unequaled. But a timidity of spirit and a yielding simple nature prevented him from exhibiting a burning ardour and dash that, joined to his other qualities, would have made him divine."

Sit down and all shall happen as you wish.
You turn your face, but does it bring your heart?
5   I'll work then for your friend's friend, never fear,
Treat his own subject after his own way,
Fix his own time, accept too his own price,
And shut the money into this small hand
When next it takes mine. Will it? tenderly?
10 Oh, I'll content him,—but to-morrow, Love!
I often am much wearier than you think,
This evening more than usual, and it seems
As if—forgive now—should you let me sit
Here by the window with your hand in mine
15 And look a half-hour forth on Fiesole,[2]
Both of one mind, as married people use,
Quietly, quietly the evening through,
I might get up to-morrow to my work
Cheerful and fresh as ever. Let us try.
20 To-morrow, how you shall be glad for this!
Your soft hand is a woman of itself,
And mine the man's bared breast she curls inside.
Don't count the time lost, neither; you must serve
For each of the five pictures we require:
25 It saves a model. So! keep looking so—
My serpentining beauty, rounds on rounds!
—How could you ever prick those perfect ears,
Even to put the pearl there! oh, so sweet—
My face, my moon, my everybody's moon,
30 Which everybody looks on and calls his,
And, I suppose, is looked on by in turn,
While she looks—no one's: very dear, no less.
You smile? why, there's my picture ready made,
There's what we painters call our harmony!
35 A common greyness silvers everything,[3]—
All in a twilight, you and I alike
—You, at the point of your first pride in me
(That's gone you know),—but I, at every point;
My youth, my hope, my art, being all toned down
40 To yonder sober pleasant Fiesole.
There's the bell clinking from the chapel-top;
That length of convent-wall across the way
Holds the trees safer, huddled more inside;
The last monk leaves the garden; days decrease,
45 And autumn grows, autumn in everything.
Eh? the whole seems to fall into a shape

2. A suburb of Florence.
3. The grey tones of Andrea del Sarto's paintings were regarded in Browning's day as characteristic of his art (rather than the effect of fading and aging); the unusually muted rhythms of this poem attempt to convey the same qualities of restraint and understatement.

As if I saw alike my work and self
And all that I was born to be and do,
A twilight-piece. Love, we are in God's hand.
50 How strange now, looks the life he makes us lead;
So free we seem, so fettered fast we are!
I feel he laid the fetter: let it lie!
This chamber for example—turn your head—
All that's behind us! You don't understand
55 Nor care to understand about my art,
But you can hear at least when people speak:
And that cartoon,° the second from the door   *drawing*
—It is the thing, Love! so such things should be—
Behold Madonna!—I am bold to say.
60 I can do with my pencil what I know,
What I see, what at bottom of my heart
I wish for, if I ever wish so deep—
Do easily, too—what I say, perfectly,
I do not boast, perhaps: yourself are judge,
65 Who listened to the Legate's[4] talk last week,
And just as much they used to say in France.
At any rate 'tis easy, all of it!
No sketches first, no studies, that's long past:
I do what many dream of, all their lives,
70 —Dream? strive to do, and agonize to do,
And fail in doing. I could count twenty such
On twice your fingers, and not leave this town,
Who strive—you don't know how the others strive
To paint a little thing like that you smeared
75 Carelessly passing with your robes afloat,—
Yet do much less, so much less, Someone[5] says,
(I know his name, no matter)—so much less!
Well, less is more, Lucrezia: I am judged.
There burns a truer light of God in them,
80 In their vexed beating stuffed and stopped-up brain,
Heart, or whate'er else, than goes on to prompt
This low-pulsed forthright craftsman's hand of mine.
Their works drop groundward, but themselves, I know,
Reach many a time a heaven that's shut to me,
85 Enter and take their place there sure enough,
Though they come back and cannot tell the world.
My works are nearer heaven, but I sit here.
The sudden blood of these men! at a word—
Praise them, it boils, or blame them, it boils too.
90 I, painting from myself and to myself,
Know what I do, am unmoved by men's blame
Or their praise either. Somebody remarks

4. A representative of the Pope.   5. Probably Michelangelo.

Morello's[6] outline there is wrongly traced,
His hue mistaken; what of that? or else,
95   Rightly traced and well ordered; what of that?
Speak as they please, what does the mountain care?
Ah, but a man's reach should exceed his grasp,
Or what's a heaven for? All is silver-grey
Placid and perfect with my art: the worse!
100   I know both what I want and what might gain,
And yet how profitless to know, to sigh
"Had I been two, another and myself,
Our head would have o'erlooked the world!" No doubt.
Yonder's a work now, of that famous youth
105   The Urbinate who died five years ago.[7]
('Tis copied, George Vasari sent it me.)
Well, I can fancy how he did it all,
Pouring his soul, with kings and popes to see,
Reaching, that heaven might so replenish him,
110   Above and through his art—for it gives way;
That arm is wrongly put—and there again—
A fault to pardon in the drawing's lines,
Its body, so to speak: its soul is right,
He means right—that, a child may understand.
115   Still, what an arm! and I could alter it:
But all the play, the insight and the stretch—
Out of me, out of me! And wherefore out?
Had you enjoined them on me, given me soul,
We might have risen to Rafael, I and you!
120   Nay, Love, you did give all I asked, I think—
More than I merit, yes, by many times.
But had you—oh, with the same perfect brow,
And perfect eyes, and more than perfect mouth,
And the low voice my soul hears, as a bird
125   The fowler's pipe, and follows to the snare—
Had you, with these the same, but brought a mind!
Some women do so. Had the mouth there urged
"God and the glory! never care for gain.
The present by the future, what is that?
130   Live for fame, side by side with Agnolo![8]
Rafael is waiting: up to God, all three!"
I might have done it for you. So it seems:
Perhaps not. All is as God over-rules.
Beside, incentives come from the soul's self;
135   The rest avail not. Why do I need you?
What wife had Rafael, or has Agnolo?

6. A mountain near Florence.
7. Raphael (1483–1520) was born in Urbino. Thus the poem is set in 1525 (when, far from being in autumnal decline, Andrea was at the height of his powers).
8. Michelangelo (Michel Agnolo Buonarroti), Italian painter (1475–1564).

In this world, who can do a thing, will not;
And who would do it, cannot, I perceive:
Yet the will's somewhat—somewhat, too, the power—
140 And thus we half-men struggle. At the end,
God, I conclude, compensates, punishes.
'Tis safer for me, if the award be strict,
That I am something underrated here,
Poor this long while, despised, to speak the truth.
145 I dared not, do you know, leave home all day,
For fear of chancing on the Paris lords.[9]
The best is when they pass and look aside;
But they speak sometimes; I must bear it all.
Well may they speak! That Francis, that first time,
150 And that long festal year at Fontainebleau!
I surely then could sometimes leave the ground,
Put on the glory, Rafael's daily wear,
In that humane great monarch's golden look,—
One finger in his beard or twisted curl
155 Over his mouth's good mark that made the smile,
One arm about my shoulder, round my neck,
The jingle of his gold chain in my ear,
I painting proudly with his breath on me,
All his court round him, seeing with his eyes,
160 Such frank French eyes, and such a fire of souls
Profuse, my hand kept plying by those hearts,—
And, best of all, this, this, this face beyond,
This in the background, waiting on my work,
To crown the issue with a last reward!
165 A good time, was it not, my kingly days?
And had you not grown restless . . . but I know—
'Tis done and past; 'twas right, my instinct said;
Too live the life grew, golden and not grey,
And I'm the weak-eyed bat no sun should tempt
170 Out of the grange whose four walls make his world.
How could it end in any other way?
You called me, and I came home to your heart.
The triumph was—to reach and stay there; since
I reached it ere the triumph, what is lost?
175 Let my hands frame your face in your hair's gold,
You beautiful Lucrezia that are mine!
"Rafael did this, Andrea painted that;
The Roman's[1] is the better when you pray,
But still the other's Virgin was his wife—"
180 Men will excuse me. I am glad to judge

9. In 1518 Andrea was invited to Fontainebleau by the French king, Francis I, who became his patron. Rumor had it that when he left the court to return to Italy, the king entrusted him with funds, which he spent on a house for Lucrezia. Now he is ashamed to face the scorn of visiting French nobles.
1. Raphael worked in Rome after 1509.

Both pictures in your presence; clearer grows
My better fortune, I resolve to think.
For, do you know, Lucrezia, as God lives,
Said one day Agnolo, his very self,
185   To Rafael . . . I have known it all these years . . .
(When the young man was flaming out his thoughts
Upon a palace-wall for Rome to see,
Too lifted up in heart because of it)
"Friend, there's a certain sorry little scrub[2]
190   Goes up and down our Florence, none cares how,
Who, were he set to plan and execute
As you are, pricked on by your popes and kings,
Would bring the sweat into that brow of yours!"
To Rafael's!—And indeed the arm is wrong.
195   I hardly dare . . . yet, only you to see,
Give the chalk here—quick, thus the line should go!
Ay, but the soul! he's Rafael! rub it out!
Still, all I care for, if he spoke the truth,
(What he? why, who but Michel Agnolo?
200   Do you forget already words like those?)[3]
If really there was such a chance, so lost,—
Is, whether you're—not grateful—but more pleased.
Well, let me think so. And you smile indeed!
This hour has been an hour! Another smile?
205   If you would sit thus by me every night
I should work better, do you comprehend?
I mean that I should earn more, give you more.
See, it is settled dusk now; there's a star;
Morello's gone, the watch-lights show the wall,
210   The cue-owls[4] speak the name we call them by.
Come from the window, love,—come in, at last,
Inside the melancholy little house
We built to be so gay with. God is just.
King Francis may forgive me: oft at nights
215   When I look up from painting, eyes tired out,
The walls become illumined, brick from brick
Distinct, instead of mortar, fierce bright gold,
That gold of his I did cement them with!
Let us but love each other. Must you go?
220   That Cousin here again?[5] he waits outside?
Must see you—you, and not with me? Those loans?
More gaming debts to pay? you smiled for that?
Well, let smiles buy me! have you more to spend?
While hand and eye and something of a heart
225   Are left me, work's my ware, and what's it worth?

---

2. I.e., Andrea, who is boasting to Lucrezia that
Michelangelo once praised his abilities to Raphael.
3. Lucrezia, bored, has lost the thread of Andrea's story.

4. Owls whose cry sounds like the Italian word *ciù*.
5. Lucrezia's lover, whose gambling debts Andrea has
already agreed to pay (lines 5–10).

I'll pay my fancy. Only let me sit
The grey remainder of the evening out,
Idle, you call it, and muse perfectly
How I could paint, were I but back in France,
230   One picture, just one more—the Virgin's face,
Not yours this time! I want you at my side
To hear them—that is, Michel Agnolo—
Judge all I do and tell you of its worth.
Will you? To-morrow, satisfy your friend.
235   I take the subjects for his corridor,
Finish the portrait out of hand—there, there,
And throw him in another thing or two
If he demurs; the whole should prove enough
To pay for this same Cousin's freak. Beside,
240   What's better and what's all I care about,
Get you the thirteen scudi° for the ruff!   *coins*
Love, does that please you? Ah, but what does he,
The Cousin! what does he to please you more?

I am grown peaceful as old age to-night.
245   I regret little, I would change still less.
Since there my past life lies, why alter it?
The very wrong to Francis!—it is true
I took his coin, was tempted and complied,
And built this house and sinned, and all is said.
250   My father and my mother died of want.[6]
Well, had I riches of my own? you see
How one gets rich! Let each one bear his lot.
They were born poor, lived poor, and poor they died:
And I have laboured somewhat in my time
255   And not been paid profusely. Some good son
Paint my two hundred pictures—let him try!
No doubt, there's something strikes a balance. Yes,
You loved me quite enough, it seems to-night.
This must suffice me here. What would one have?
260   In heaven, perhaps, new chances, one more chance—
Four great walls in the New Jerusalem,[7]
Meted° on each side by the angel's reed,   *measured*
For Leonard,[8] Rafael, Agnolo and me
To cover—the three first without a wife,
265   While I have mine! So—still they overcome
Because there's still Lucrezia,—as I choose.

Again the Cousin's whistle! Go, my Love.
c. 1853   1855

6. Vasari claimed that Andrea abandoned his aged parents and spent his money on Lucrezia and her family.
7. Cf. Revelation 21.10–21.

8. Leonardo da Vinci (1452–1519), third in the trio of great Italian Renaissance artists whom del Sarto has failed to equal.

Charles Dickens

1812–1870

Charles Dickens was the most popular novelist of his century. Anthony Trollope observed that Dickens's works could be found "in every house in which books are kept." He published his novels in monthly or weekly parts, and whole families would gather in suspense to hear a newly published episode read aloud. He was equally renowned in America: a ship arriving in New York from England was mobbed by crowds frantic to learn whether one of his characters, Little Nell, had died.

Dickens's own story was like a rags-to-riches fairy tale. His parents were lower-middle class, precariously clinging to gentility as they drifted downward into poverty. As a boy he was sent to school and taken to the theater; he read voraciously and amused himself by impersonating his favorite characters: "I have been Tom Jones . . . for a week together. I have sustained my own idea of Roderick Random for a month at a stretch."

But before Dickens was twelve, family fortunes took a turn for the worse. He was taken out of school and later sent to work for six months beside common laboring boys in a warehouse. For the rest of his life he would wonder bitterly "how I could have been so easily cast away at such an age." Many years later he wrote: "No words can express the secret agony of my soul as I sunk into this companionship; compared these every day associates with those of my happier childhood; and felt my early hopes of growing up to be a learned and distinguished man, crushed in my breast."

As if this were not dreadful enough, his father was arrested for debt and thrown into the Marshalsea debtors' prison, where his wife and younger children soon joined him. The twelve-year-old Charles was left to fend for himself. Even after his father was released, Charles's mother opposed his decision to take the boy away from the factory: "I never afterwards forgot, I never shall forget, I never can forget, that my mother was warm for my being sent back."

Dickens went on to become England's most celebrated novelist, but no achievements could erase the terrible memory of shame: "My whole nature was so penetrated with the grief and humiliation . . . that even now, famous and caressed and happy, I often forget in my dreams that I have a dear wife and children; even that I am a man; and wander desolately back to that time of my life." The traumatic recollections of his family's disgrace and his own abandonment motivated both his intense ambition for success and also his lifelong sympathy with suffering children.

As a young man, Dickens became a parliamentary reporter, then began writing. First *Sketches by Boz* (1836–1837) appeared, then *Pickwick Papers* (1836–1837), using the method of serial publication that he would continue with all his novels. Pickwick-mania suddenly swept the nation as readers of all classes were captivated by Dickens's humor.

In the next five years Dickens—still only in his twenties—produced four more long novels: *Oliver Twist* (1837–1839), *Nicholas Nickleby* (1838–1839), *The Old Curiosity Shop* (1840–1841), and *Barnaby Rudge* (1841). These early novels satirize the cruelties of workhouses and orphanages, bad schools, inhuman factories, and hideous slums. They reflect Dickens's growing compassion for orphans, outcasts, and the afflicted, and his outrage at the hypocrisies of a society that exploited them. Some readers missed the merry fun of Pickwick, but most welcomed his new earnestness. *The Old Curiosity Shop* in particular was a triumph, a runaway bestseller of over a hundred thousand copies.

In 1842 Dickens embarked on a trip to America, where he was given a hero's welcome. Bursting with enthusiasm for the young democracy, he was soon disillusioned, for when he complained about the pirating of his books (foreign authors did not have copyright protection in the United States until 1891), American newspapers attacked him as greedy. They were even more offended by *American Notes* (1842): far from lauding American landscapes and public institutions, Dickens's account of his travels focused obsessively on prisons and lunatic asylums. His moral crusading on behalf of the poor, the insane, and the imprisoned struck readers as a boorish affront to national honor. His next novel, *Martin Chuzzlewit* (1843–1844), set partially in America, did not mend matters; in fact, it was his first experience of failure.

Dickens was alarmed to realize that the public's love affair with his novels was at a low ebb, but he wooed them afresh with *A Christmas Carol* (1843). This parable of redemption and metamorphosis is one of Dickens's most representative works. The story of Scrooge, the cantankerous old miser who repents, dramatizes the fundamental Dickensian theme of rebirth. Scrooge's selfishness and coldness anticipate a host of later characters with frozen hearts. Scrooge's recollections of his unloved boyhood evoke Dickens's own past and illustrate his preoccupation with the insidious effects of a warped childhood.

These concerns pervaded Dickens's subsequent novels: in *Dombey and Son* (1846–1848) Mr. Dombey stonily spurns his daughter's love. The hero of *David Copperfield* (1849–1850) is maltreated by a repressive stepfather, then shipped off to a harsh boarding school. *Bleak House* (1852–1853) is full of unwanted orphans, including the illegitimate Esther and the illiterate Jo. In *Hard Times* (1854) the children are oppressed by a grinding system of education, and in *Little Dorrit* (1855–1857) the protagonist's childhood has been stunted by a narrow system of religion.

Dickens's extraordinary productivity was matched by his prodigious energy. In addition to writing one massive novel after another, he was actively involved in public affairs and charitable projects, including a home for "fallen women." In 1850 he founded *Household Words*, a weekly magazine later incorporated into *All the Year Round*, which he edited until his death. He serialized three of his novels in these periodicals, and contributed frequent essays. His exuberant vitality also found outlet in the theater; he loved performing in amateur theatricals and, later on, giving readings of his own works. An actor at heart, Dickens revelled in the applause and admiration of an audience.

Even amid these successes, Dickens kept returning to the theme of imprisonment: in *Little Dorrit* the Marshalsea debtors' prison in London had been the dominant setting; in *A Tale of Two Cities* (1859) it is the French Bastille. In *Great Expectations* (1860–1861) an escaped convict turns out to be the hidden agent behind the hero's transformation into a gentleman. In Dickens's last completed novel, *Our Mutual Friend* (1864–1865), the Thames becomes a river of the dead where outcasts scrounge a living by pickpocketing drowned bodies: "I can't get away from it," says the daughter of one of these river rats.

As these grim images suggest, there was a darker side to Dickens's art. Despite his flourishing career and convivial nature, Dickens felt a lifelong sense of restlessness and loss, of some "happiness I have missed in life." His unsatisfying marriage gradually came to seem claustrophobic, and Dickens's decision in 1858 to separate from his wife, after ten children and more than two decades together, did considerable harm to his reputation. Flamboyant and charming, Dickens was also emotionally insecure. In his later years he wore himself out with an arduous round of public readings, courting audiences nightly by bringing his famous characters to life on stage. Exhausted from his unceasing activities, Dickens collapsed and died while still at work on his last novel, *The Mystery of Edwin Drood* (1870). He was only fifty-eight. From America Longfellow wrote: "I never knew an author's death to cause such general mourning. It is no exaggeration to say that this whole country is stricken with grief."

Contemporary readers, associating Dickens with jollity, were sometimes alienated by his indignation about the human costs of industrialism and materialism. His attack on the complacent brutality of laissez-faire capitalism in *Hard Times* irritated conservatives, as did his portrayal of Sir Leicester Dedlock, a doddering aristocrat, in *Bleak House*. Meanwhile, the liberal John Stuart Mill—author of *The Subjection of Women*—was annoyed by Mrs. Jellyby, Dickens's satirical portrait of a woman who neglects her home and family to devote herself to philanthropic causes.

But Dickens's comic genius always enabled him to combine serious themes with laughter. His novels are populated with an extraordinary gallery of peculiar characters, whose names—Scrooge, Gradgrind, Uriah Heep, Mr Micawber, Oliver Twist, Fagin—have become part of the language. Dickens delighted in the absurd, but he was also an astute observer of human nature, and he insisted that his memorable eccentrics were true to life: "Mrs Nickleby herself, sitting bodily before me in a solid chair, once asked me whether I believed there ever was such a woman." Keenly aware of how figures of speech pervade everyday language, Dickens gloried in flights of linguistic fancy: literalizing metaphors, personifying inanimate objects, turning people into their possessions, and using verbal ticks to limn a character or construct a scene. This attention to how language creates and reveals personality not only made Dickens a brilliant comic novelist; it also, especially in his later novels, helped him probe the darker sides of human nature with the psychological acuity of one of his fans, Sigmund Freud.

Later generations of readers have sometimes found Dickens's sentimentality hard to take: Oscar Wilde said that "one must have a heart of stone to read the death of Little Nell without laughing." But they have also been fascinated by Dickens's deftly elaborated symbolism. Almost all his works are permeated by a dominant symbol-system (railways in *Dombey and Son*, prisons in *Little Dorrit*, dustheaps in *Our Mutual Friend*) that helped him establish thematic unity among the monthly installments. With an inventiveness of character and density of imagery equaled only by Shakespeare, Dickens worked out in astonishing detail the complex connections binding members of a society to their environment, to their institutions, and to each other. He is the quintessential urban novelist: his mythic vision of Victorian London is so intense, surprising, and phantasmagoric that the fractured, paranoid modernist landscapes of Conrad, T. S. Eliot, Joyce, and Woolf all seem to have originated with Dickens.

Additional work by Dickens is included in Perspectives: Religion and Science, page 710.

A CHRISTMAS CAROL   An instant success when it was first published in December 1843, *A Christmas Carol* is still the best-known work of Victorian short fiction. Thackeray called it "a national benefit" and noted that it provoked such an outpouring of Yuletide conviviality that "had the book appeared a fortnight earlier all the prize cattle would have been gobbled up in pure love and friendship, Epping denuded of sausages, and not a turkey left in Norfolk." Even before Dickens gave his tour-de-force readings of the story, pirated productions filled the stages and bookstalls. Its overwhelming popularity has turned this fable of moral metamorphosis into a cultural icon.

But *A Christmas Carol* is not all holiday cheer. Near its beginning Ebenezer Scrooge brusquely refuses to contribute to charity: "Are there no prisons?" he asks. Dickens is satirizing his society's harsh treatment of the indigent; as the Poor Law of 1834 had established, paupers were little better than criminals, to be incarcerated in workhouses for the crime of poverty. Echoing Thomas Malthus, the grim analyst of overpopulation, Scrooge says that if the poor would rather die than subsist in workhouses, "they had better do it, and decrease the surplus population."

Like Carlyle's *Past and Present*, published earlier in 1843, *A Christmas Carol* is in part a response to the Hungry Forties, a period of high unemployment and suffering among factory workers. Both Dickens and Carlyle expose the brutality of laissez-faire capitalism, where profit is the only goal, and employers and employees are united by nothing except the "cash nexus." Scrooge's gradual awakening to a more generous sense of responsibility toward his dependents and fellow beings illustrates the redemptive power of imaginative sympathy.

A Christmas Carol is a story of catharsis and renewal, of a crabbed old miser who miraculously gets a second chance at life. His change of heart is brought about by ghostly visitors who lead him on a tour of his past: Scrooge pities his own solitary boyhood, delights in recalling Ali Baba and Robinson Crusoe, and grieves for his dead sister and lost love. These dream visions offer insight into the psychological sources of Scrooge's monstrous egotism, and the similarities to Dickens's own childhood suggest an autobiographical identification with his character. By recovering his past, Scrooge recovers his humanity.

A *Christmas Carol* is thus both an allegory of social responsibility and a fable of individual transformation through symbolic rebirth. Beside himself with joy, Scrooge splutters "I'm quite a baby. Never mind. I don't care. I'd rather be a baby." Like Wordsworth and Blake, Dickens explores the nature of memory and childhood, innocence and experience, exalting the power of the imagination to transcend a fallen world. But he situates these archetypal themes in a classically Dickensian fairy-tale universe, where inanimate objects, from bedposts to buildings, come to life and the supernatural permeates the prosaic.

A Christmas Carol
Stave One
MARLEY'S GHOST

Marley was dead: to begin with. There is no doubt whatever about that. The register of his burial was signed by the clergyman, the clerk, the undertaker, and the chief mourner. Scrooge signed it: and Scrooge's name was good upon 'Change, for anything he chose to put his hand to. Old Marley was as dead as a door-nail.

Mind! I don't mean to say that I know, of my own knowledge, what there is particularly dead about a door-nail. I might have been inclined, myself, to regard a coffin-nail as the deadest piece of ironmongery in the trade. But the wisdom of our ancestors is in the simile; and my unhallowed hands shall not disturb it, or the Country's done for. You will therefore permit me to repeat, emphatically, that Marley was as dead as a door-nail.

Scrooge knew he was dead? Of course he did. How could it be otherwise? Scrooge and he were partners for I don't know how many years. Scrooge was his sole executor, his sole administrator, his sole assign, his sole residuary legatee,[1] his sole friend and sole mourner. And even Scrooge was not so dreadfully cut up by the sad event, but that he was an excellent man of business on the very day of the funeral, and solemnised it with an undoubted bargain.

The mention of Marley's funeral brings me back to the point I started from. There is no doubt that Marley was dead. This must be distinctly understood, or nothing wonderful can come of the story I am going to relate. If we were not perfectly convinced that Hamlet's Father died before the play began,[2] there would be nothing more remarkable in his taking a stroll at night, in an easterly wind, upon his own ramparts, than there would be in any other middle-aged gentleman rashly turning out after dark in a breezy spot—say Saint Paul's Churchyard for instance—literally to astonish his son's weak mind.

Scrooge never painted out Old Marley's name. There it stood, years afterwards, above the warehouse door: Scrooge and Marley. The firm was known as Scrooge and Marley. Sometimes people new to the business called Scrooge Scrooge, and sometimes Marley, but he answered to both names: it was all the same to him.

---

1. Legal terms meaning that Scrooge was Marley's only heir.

2. In Shakespeare's *Hamlet*, the appearance of the ghost of Hamlet's murdered father sets the plot in motion.

Oh! but he was a tight-fisted hand at the grindstone, Scrooge! a squeezing, wrenching, grasping, scraping, clutching, covetous old sinner! Hard and sharp as flint, from which no steel had ever struck out generous fire; secret, and self-contained, and solitary as an oyster. The cold within him froze his old features, nipped his pointed nose, shrivelled his cheek, stiffened his gait; made his eyes red, his thin lips blue; and spoke out shrewdly in his grating voice. A frosty rime was on his head, and on his eyebrows, and his wiry chin. He carried his own low temperature always about with him; he iced his office in the dog-days;[3] and didn't thaw it one degree at Christmas.

External heat and cold had little influence on Scrooge. No warmth could warm, nor wintry weather chill him. No wind that blew was bitterer than he, no falling snow was more intent upon its purpose, no pelting rain less open to entreaty. Foul weather didn't know where to have him. The heaviest rain, and snow, and hail, and sleet, could boast of the advantage over him in only one respect. They often "came down"[4] handsomely, and Scrooge never did.

Nobody ever stopped him in the street to say, with gladsome looks, "My dear Scrooge, how are you? when will you come to see me?" No beggars implored him to bestow a trifle, no children asked him what it was o'clock, no man or woman ever once in all his life inquired the way to such and such a place, of Scrooge. Even the blindmen's dogs appeared to know him; and when they saw him coming on, would tug their owners into doorways and up courts; and then would wag their tails as though they said, "no eye at all is better than an evil eye, dark master!"

But what did Scrooge care? It was the very thing he liked. To edge his way along the crowded paths of life, warning all human sympathy to keep its distance, was what the knowing ones call "nuts" to Scrooge.[5]

Once upon a time—of all the good days in the year, on Christmas Eve—old Scrooge sat busy in his counting-house. It was cold, bleak, biting weather: foggy withal: and he could hear the people in the court outside, go wheezing up and down, beating their hands upon their breasts, and stamping their feet upon the pavement-stones to warm them. The city clocks had only just gone three, but it was quite dark already: it had not been light all day: and candles were flaring in the windows of the neighbouring offices, like ruddy smears upon the palpable brown air. The fog came pouring in at every chink and keyhole, and was so dense without, that although the court was of the narrowest, the houses opposite were mere phantoms. To see the dingy cloud come drooping down, obscuring everything, one might have thought that Nature lived hard by, and was brewing on a large scale.

The door of Scrooge's counting-house was open that he might keep his eye upon his clerk, who in a dismal little cell beyond, a sort of tank, was copying letters. Scrooge had a very small fire, but the clerk's fire was so very much smaller that it looked like one coal. But he couldn't replenish it, for Scrooge kept the coal-box in his own room; and so surely as the clerk came in with the shovel, the master predicted that it would be necessary for them to part. Wherefore the clerk put on his white comforter,[6] and tried to warm himself at the candle; in which effort, not being a man of a strong imagination, he failed.

"A merry Christmas, uncle! God save you!" cried a cheerful voice. It was the voice of Scrooge's nephew, who came upon him so quickly that this was the first intimation he had of his approach.

---

3. The hot weather of late summer.
4. A pun, playing on the slang meaning, to give money.

5. A source of pleasure to him (slang).
6. A long scarf.

"Bah!" said Scrooge, "Humbug!"

He had so heated himself with rapid walking in the fog and frost, this nephew of Scrooge's, that he was all in a glow; his face was ruddy and handsome; his eyes sparkled, and his breath smoked again.

"Christmas a humbug, uncle!" said Scrooge's nephew. "You don't mean that, I am sure?"

"I do," said Scrooge. "Merry Christmas! What right have you to be merry? what reason have you to be merry? You're poor enough."

"Come, then," returned the nephew gaily. "What right have you to be dismal? what reason have you to be morose? You're rich enough."

Scrooge having no better answer ready on the spur of the moment, said, "Bah!" again; and followed it up with "Humbug."

"Don't be cross, uncle," said the nephew.

"What else can I be," returned the uncle, "when I live in such a world of fools as this? Merry Christmas! Out upon merry Christmas! What's Christmas time to you but a time for paying bills without money; a time for finding yourself a year older, and not an hour richer; a time for balancing your books and having every item in 'em through a round dozen of months presented dead against you? If I could work my will," said Scrooge, indignantly, "every idiot who goes about with 'Merry Christmas,' on his lips, should be boiled with his own pudding, and buried with a stake of holly through his heart. He should!"

"Uncle!" pleaded the nephew.

"Nephew!" returned the uncle, sternly, "keep Christmas in your own way, and let me keep it in mine."

"Keep it!" repeated Scrooge's nephew. "But you don't keep it."

"Let me leave it alone, then," said Scrooge. "Much good may it do you! Much good it has ever done you!"

"There are many things from which I might have derived good, by which I have not profited, I dare say," returned the nephew: "Christmas among the rest. But I am sure I have always thought of Christmas time, when it has come round—apart from the veneration due to its sacred name and origin, if anything belonging to it can be apart from that—as a good time: a kind, forgiving, charitable, pleasant time: the only time I know of, in the long calendar of the year, when men and women seem by one consent to open their shut-up hearts freely, and to think of people below them as if they really were fellow-passengers to the grave, and not another race of creatures bound on other journeys. And therefore, uncle, though it has never put a scrap of gold or silver in my pocket, I believe that it *has* done me good, and *will* do me good; and I say, God bless it!"

The clerk in the tank involuntarily applauded: becoming immediately sensible of the impropriety, he poked the fire, and extinguished the last frail spark for ever.

"Let me hear another sound from *you*," said Scrooge, "and you'll keep your Christmas by losing your situation. You're quite a powerful speaker, sir," he added, turning to his nephew. "I wonder you don't go into Parliament."

"Don't be angry, uncle. Come! Dine with us to-morrow."

Scrooge said that he would see him—yes, indeed he did. He went the whole length of the expression, and said that he would see him in that extremity first.[7]

---

7. I.e., that he would see his nephew in hell first.

"But why?" cried Scrooge's nephew. "Why?"

"Why did you get married?" said Scrooge.

"Because I fell in love."

"Because you fell in love!" growled Scrooge, as if that were the only one thing in the world more ridiculous than a merry Christmas. "Good afternoon!"

"Nay, uncle, but you never came to see me before that happened. Why give it as a reason for not coming now?"

"Good afternoon," said Scrooge.

"I want nothing from you; I ask nothing of you; why cannot we be friends?"

"Good afternoon," said Scrooge.

"I am sorry, with all my heart, to find you so resolute. We have never had any quarrel, to which I have been a party. But I have made the trial in homage to Christmas, and I'll keep my Christmas humour to the last. So A Merry Christmas, uncle!"

"Good afternoon!" said Scrooge.

"And A Happy New Year!"

"Good afternoon!" said Scrooge.

His nephew left the room without an angry word, notwithstanding. He stopped at the outer door to bestow the greetings of the season on the clerk, who, cold as he was, was warmer than Scrooge; for he returned them cordially.

"There's another fellow," muttered Scrooge; who overheard him: "my clerk, with fifteen shillings a-week, and a wife and family, talking about a merry Christmas. I'll retire to Bedlam."[8]

This lunatic, in letting Scrooge's nephew out, had let two other people in. They were portly gentlemen, pleasant to behold, and now stood, with their hats off, in Scrooge's office. They had books and papers in their hands, and bowed to him.

"Scrooge and Marley's, I believe," said one of the gentlemen, referring to his list. "Have I the pleasure of addressing Mr Scrooge, or Mr Marley?"

"Mr Marley has been dead these seven years," Scrooge replied. "He died seven years ago, this very night."

"We have no doubt his liberality is well represented by his surviving partner," said the gentleman, presenting his credentials.

It certainly was; for they had been two kindred spirits. At the ominous word "liberality," Scrooge frowned, and shook his head, and handed the credentials back.

"At this festive season of the year, Mr Scrooge," said the gentleman, taking up a pen, "it is more than usually desirable that we should make some slight provision for the poor and destitute, who suffer greatly at the present time. Many thousands are in want of common necessaries; hundreds of thousands are in want of common comforts, sir."

"Are there no prisons?" asked Scrooge.

"Plenty of prisons," said the gentleman, laying down the pen again.

"And the Union workhouses?"[9] demanded Scrooge. "Are they still in operation?"

"They are. Still," returned the gentleman, "I wish I could say they were not."

"The Treadmill[1] and the Poor Law are in full vigour, then?" said Scrooge.

"Both very busy, sir."

---

8. An insane asylum.

9. Established under the Poor Law Amendment Act of 1834, the workhouses provided a place of refuge for the poor but offered degrading subsistence conditions, justified by the theory that the inhabitants of workhouses ought to be worse off than the poorest of the gainfully employed.

1. Prisoners were required to perform meaningless hard labor, such as walking on treadmills.

"Oh! I was afraid, from what you said at first, that something had occurred to stop them in their useful course," said Scrooge. "I'm very glad to hear it."

"Under the impression that they scarcely furnish Christian cheer of mind or body to the multitude," returned the gentleman, "a few of us are endeavouring to raise a fund to buy the Poor some meat and drink, and means of warmth. We choose this time because it is a time, of all others, when Want is keenly felt, and Abundance rejoices. What shall I put you down for?"

"Nothing!" Scrooge replied.

"You wish to be anonymous?"

"I wish to be left alone," said Scrooge. "Since you ask me what I wish, gentlemen, that is my answer. I don't make merry myself at Christmas, and I can't afford to make idle people merry. I help to support the establishments I have mentioned: they cost enough: and those who are badly off must go there."

"Many can't go there; and many would rather die."

"If they would rather die," said Scrooge, "they had better do it, and decrease the surplus population.[2] Besides—excuse me—I don't know that."

"But you might know it," observed the gentleman.

"It's not my business," Scrooge returned. "It's enough for a man to understand his own business, and not to interfere with other people's. Mine occupies me constantly. Good afternoon, gentlemen!"

Seeing clearly that it would be useless to pursue their point, the gentlemen withdrew. Scrooge resumed his labours with an improved opinion of himself, and in a more facetious temper than was usual with him.

Meanwhile the fog and darkness thickened so, that people ran about with flaring links,[3] proffering their services to go before horses in carriages, and conduct them on their way. The ancient tower of a church, whose gruff old bell was always peeping slily down at Scrooge out of a gothic window in the wall, became invisible, and struck the hours and quarters in the clouds, with tremulous vibrations afterwards, as if its teeth were chattering in its frozen head up there. The cold became intense. In the main street, at the corner of the court, some labourers were repairing the gas-pipes, and had lighted a great fire in a brazier, round which a party of ragged men and boys were gathered: warming their hands and winking their eyes before the blaze in rapture. The water-plug being left in solitude, its overflowings sullenly congealed, and turned to misanthropic ice. The brightness of the shops where holly sprigs and berries crackled in the lamp-heat of the windows, made pale faces ruddy as they passed. Poulterers' and grocers' trades became a splendid joke: a glorious pageant, with which it was next to impossible to believe that such dull principles as bargain and sale had anything to do. The Lord Mayor, in the stronghold of the mighty Mansion House, gave orders to his fifty cooks and butlers to keep Christmas as a Lord Mayor's household should; and even the little tailor, whom he had fined five shillings on the previous Monday for being drunk and blood-thirsty in the streets, stirred up to-morrow's pudding in his garret, while his lean wife and the baby sallied out to buy the beef.

Foggier yet, and colder! Piercing, searching, biting cold. If the good Saint Dunstan[4] had but nipped the Evil Spirit's nose with a touch of such weather as that, instead of using his familiar weapons, then indeed he would have roared to lusty purpose. The

---

2. In 1803, Thomas Malthus published his *Essay on the Principle of Population,* warning that unchecked population growth would lead to starvation.

3. Torches.

4. St. Dunstan was a smith who once seized the devil by the nose with a pair of red-hot pincers.

owner of one scant young nose, gnawed and mumbled by the hungry cold as bones are gnawed by dogs, stooped down at Scrooge's keyhole to regale him with a Christmas carol: but at the first sound of—

"God bless you merry gentleman!
May nothing you dismay!"

Scrooge seized the ruler with such energy of action, that the singer fled in terror, leaving the keyhole to the fog and even more congenial frost.

At length the hour of shutting up the counting-house arrived. With an ill-will Scrooge dismounted from his stool, and tacitly admitted the fact to the expectant clerk in the Tank, who instantly snuffed his candle out, and put on his hat.

"You'll want all day to-morrow, I suppose?" said Scrooge.

"If quite convenient, sir."

"It's not convenient," said Scrooge, "and it's not fair. If I was to stop half-a-crown for it, you'd think yourself ill used, I'll be bound?"

The clerk smiled faintly.

"And yet," said Scrooge, "you don't think *me* ill used, when I pay a day's wages for no work."

The clerk observed that it was only once a year.

"A poor excuse for picking a man's pocket every twenty-fifth of December!" said Scrooge, buttoning his great-coat to the chin. "But I suppose you must have the whole day. Be here all the earlier next morning!"

The clerk promised that he would; and Scrooge walked out with a growl. The office was closed in a twinkling, and the clerk, with the long ends of his white comforter dangling below his waist (for he boasted no great-coat), went down a slide on Cornhill, at the end of a lane of boys, twenty times, in honour of its being Christmas-eve, and then ran home to Camden Town[5] as hard as he could pelt, to play at blind-man's-buff.

Scrooge took his melancholy dinner in his usual melancholy tavern; and having read all the newspapers, and beguiled the rest of the evening with his banker's-book, went home to bed. He lived in chambers which had once belonged to his deceased partner. They were a gloomy suite of rooms, in a lowering pile of building up a yard, where it had so little business to be, that one could scarcely help fancying it must have run there when it was a young house, playing at hide-and-seek with other houses, and have forgotten the way out again. It was old enough now, and dreary enough, for nobody lived in it but Scrooge, the other rooms being all let out as offices. The yard was so dark that even Scrooge, who knew its every stone, was fain to grope with his hands. The fog and frost so hung about the black old gateway of the house, that it seemed as if the Genius of the Weather sat in mournful meditation on the threshold.

Now, it is a fact, that there was nothing at all particular about the knocker on the door, except that it was very large. It is also a fact, that Scrooge had seen it night and morning during his whole residence in that place; also that Scrooge had as little of what is called fancy about him as any man in the City of London, even including—which is a bold word—the corporation, aldermen, and livery. Let it also be borne in mind that Scrooge had not bestowed one thought on Marley, since his

5. A northern suburb of London; in Dickens's era the home of the working poor.

last mention of his seven-years' dead partner that afternoon. And then let any man explain to me, if he can, how it happened that Scrooge, having his key in the lock of the door, saw in the knocker, without its undergoing any intermediate process of change: not a knocker, but Marley's face.

Marley's face. It was not in impenetrable shadow as the other objects in the yard were, but had a dismal light about it, like a bad lobster in a dark cellar. It was not angry or ferocious, but looked at Scrooge as Marley used to look: with ghostly spectacles turned up upon its ghostly forehead. The hair was curiously stirred, as if by breath or hot-air; and though the eyes were wide open, they were perfectly motionless. That, and its livid colour, made it horrible; but its horror seemed to be, in spite of the face and beyond its control, rather than a part of its own expression.

As Scrooge looked fixedly at this phenomenon, it was a knocker again.

To say that he was not startled, or that his blood was not conscious of a terrible sensation to which it had been a stranger from infancy, would be untrue. But he put his hand upon the key he had relinquished, turned it sturdily, walked in, and lighted his candle.

He *did* pause, with a moment's irresolution, before he shut the door; and he *did* look cautiously behind it first, as if he half-expected to be terrified with the sight of Marley's pigtail sticking out into the hall. But there was nothing on the back of the door, except the screws and nuts that held the knocker on; so he said "Pooh, pooh!" and closed it with a bang.

The sound resounded through the house like thunder. Every room above, and every cask in the wine-merchant's cellars below, appeared to have a separate peal of echoes of its own. Scrooge was not a man to be frightened by echoes. He fastened the door, and walked across the hall, and up the stairs: slowly too: trimming his candle as he went.

You may talk vaguely about driving a coach-and-six up a good old flight of stairs, or through a bad young Act of Parliament; but I mean to say you might have got a hearse up that staircase, and taken it broadwise, with the splinter-bar towards the wall, and the door towards the balustrades: and done it easy. There was plenty of width for that, and room to spare; which is perhaps the reason why Scrooge thought he saw a locomotive hearse going on before him in the gloom. Half a dozen gas-lamps out of the street wouldn't have lighted the entry too well, so you may suppose that it was pretty dark with Scrooge's dip.[6]

Up Scrooge went, not caring a button for that: darkness is cheap, and Scrooge liked it. But before he shut his heavy door, he walked through his rooms to see that all was right. He had just enough recollection of the face to desire to do that.

Sitting room, bed-room, lumber-room. All as they should be. Nobody under the table, nobody under the sofa; a small fire in the grate; spoon and basin ready; and the little saucepan of gruel[7] (Scrooge had a cold in his head) upon the hob.[8] Nobody under the bed; nobody in the closet; nobody in his dressing-gown, which was hanging up in a suspicious attitude against the wall. Lumber-room as usual. Old fire-guard, old shoes, two fish-baskets, washing-stand on three legs, and a poker.

Quite satisfied, he closed his door, and locked himself in; double-locked himself in, which was not his custom. Thus secured against surprise, he took off his cravat;

---

6. Candle.
7. Thin porridge.

8. A shelf in the fireplace where something may be kept warm.

put on his dressing-gown and slippers, and his night-cap; and sat down before the fire to take his gruel.

It was a very low fire indeed; nothing on such a bitter night. He was obliged to sit close to it, and brood over it, before he could extract the least sensation of warmth from such a handful of fuel. The fireplace was an old one, built by some Dutch merchant long ago, and paved all round with quaint Dutch tiles, designed to illustrate the Scriptures. There were Cains and Abels; Pharaoh's daughters, Queens of Sheba, Angelic messengers descending through the air on clouds like feather-beds, Abrahams, Belshazzars, Apostles putting off to sea in butter-boats, hundreds of figures to attract his thoughts; and yet that face of Marley, seven years dead, came like the ancient Prophet's rod,[9] and swallowed up the whole. If each smooth tile had been a blank at first, with power to shape some picture on its surface from the disjointed fragments of his thoughts, there would have been a copy of old Marley's head on every one.

"Humbug!" said Scrooge; and walked across the room.

After several turns, he sat down again. As he threw his head back in the chair, his glance happened to rest upon a bell, a disused bell, that hung in the room, and communicated for some purpose now forgotten with a chamber in the highest story of the building. It was with great astonishment, and with a strange, inexplicable dread, that as he looked, he saw this bell begin to swing. It swung so softly in the outset that it scarcely made a sound; but soon it rang out loudly, and so did every bell in the house.

This might have lasted half a minute, or a minute, but it seemed an hour. The bells ceased as they had begun, together. They were succeeded by a clanking noise, deep down below; as if some person were dragging a heavy chain over the casks in the wine-merchant's cellar. Scrooge then remembered to have heard that ghosts in haunted houses were described as dragging chains.

The cellar-door flew open with a booming sound, and then he heard the noise much louder, on the floors below; then coming up the stairs; then coming straight towards his door.

"It's humbug still!" said Scrooge. "I won't believe it."

His colour changed though, when, without a pause, it came on through the heavy door, and passed into the room before his eyes. Upon its coming in, the dying flame leaped up, as though it cried "I know him! Marley's Ghost!" and fell again.

The same face: the very same. Marley in his pig-tail, usual waistcoat, tights, and boots; the tassels on the latter bristling, like his pigtail, and his coat-skirts, and the hair upon his head. The chain he drew was clasped about his middle. It was long, and wound about him like a tail; and it was made (for Scrooge observed it closely) of cash-boxes, keys, padlocks, ledgers, deeds, and heavy purses wrought in steel. His body was transparent: so that Scrooge, observing him, and looking through his waistcoat, could see the two buttons on his coat behind.

Scrooge had often heard it said that Marley had no bowels, but he had never believed it until now.

No, nor did he believe it even now. Though he looked the phantom through and through, and saw it standing before him; though he felt the chilling influence of its death-cold eyes; and marked the very texture of the folded kerchief bound about

---

9. Aaron, the brother of Moses, transformed his rod into a serpent, which swallowed up those of the magicians of Egypt (Exodus 7.12).

its head and chin, which wrapper he had not observed before: he was still incredulous, and fought against his senses.

"How now!" said Scrooge, caustic and cold as ever. "What do you want with me?"

"Much!"—Marley's voice, no doubt about it.

"Who are you?"

"Ask me who I *was*."

"Who *were* you then?" said Scrooge, raising his voice. "You're particular—for a shade." He was going to say "*to* a shade," but substituted this, as more appropriate.

"In life I was your partner, Jacob Marley."

"Can you—can you sit down?" asked Scrooge, looking doubtfully at him.

"I can."

"Do it then."

Scrooge asked the question, because he didn't know whether a ghost so transparent might find himself in a condition to take a chair; and felt that in the event of its being impossible, it might involve the necessity of an embarrassing explanation. But the ghost sat down on the opposite side of the fireplace, as if he were quite used to it.

"You don't believe in me," observed the Ghost.

"I don't," said Scrooge.

"What evidence would you have of my reality, beyond that of your senses?"

"I don't know," said Scrooge.

"Why do you doubt your senses?"

"Because," said Scrooge, "a little thing affects them. A slight disorder of the stomach makes them cheats. You may be an undigested bit of beef, a blot of mustard, a crumb of cheese, a fragment of an underdone potato. There's more of gravy than of grave about you, whatever you are!"

Scrooge was not much in the habit of cracking jokes, nor did he feel, in his heart, by any means waggish then. The truth is, that he tried to be smart, as a means of distracting his own attention, and keeping down his terror; for the spectre's voice disturbed the very marrow in his bones.

To sit, staring at those fixed, glazed eyes, in silence for a moment, would play, Scrooge felt, the very deuce with him. There was something very awful, too, in the spectre's being provided with an infernal atmosphere of its own. Scrooge could not feel it himself, but this was clearly the case; for though the Ghost sat perfectly motionless, its hair, and skirts, and tassels, were still agitated as by the hot vapour from an oven.

"You see this toothpick?" said Scrooge, returning quickly to the charge, for the reason just assigned; and wishing, though it were only for a second, to divert the vision's stony gaze from himself.

"I do," replied the Ghost.

"You are not looking at it," said Scrooge.

"But I see it," said the Ghost, "notwithstanding."

"Well!" returned Scrooge. "I have but to swallow this, and be for the rest of my days persecuted by a legion of goblins, all of my own creation. Humbug, I tell you—humbug!"

At this, the spirit raised a frightful cry, and shook its chain with such a dismal and appalling noise, that Scrooge held on tight to his chair, to save himself from falling in a swoon. But how much greater was his horror, when the phantom taking off the bandage round its head, as if it were too warm to wear in-doors, its lower jaw dropped down upon its breast!

Scrooge fell upon his knees, and clasped his hands before his face.

"Mercy!" he said. "Dreadful apparition, why do you trouble me?"

"Man of the worldly mind!" replied the Ghost, "do you believe in me or not?"

"I do," said Scrooge. "I must. But why do spirits walk the earth, and why do they come to me?"

"It is required of every man," the Ghost returned, "that the spirit within him should walk abroad among his fellowmen, and travel far and wide; and if that spirit goes not forth in life, it is condemned to do so after death. It is doomed to wander through the world—oh, woe is me!—and witness what it cannot share, but might have shared on earth, and turned to happiness!"

Again the spectre raised a cry, and shook its chain and wrung its shadowy hands.

"You are fettered," said Scrooge, trembling. "Tell me why?"

"I wear the chain I forged in life," replied the Ghost. "I made it link by link, and yard by yard; I girded it on of my own free will, and of my own free will I wore it. Is its pattern strange to *you?*"

Scrooge trembled more and more.

"Or would you know," pursued the Ghost, "the weight and length of the strong coil you bear yourself? It was full as heavy and as long as this, seven Christmas Eves ago. You have laboured on it, since. It is a ponderous chain!"

Scrooge glanced about him on the floor, in the expectation of finding himself surrounded by some fifty or sixty fathoms of iron cable: but he could see nothing.

"Jacob," he said, imploringly. "Old Jacob Marley, tell me more. Speak comfort to me, Jacob."

"I have none to give," the Ghost replied. "It comes from other regions, Ebenezer Scrooge, and is conveyed by other ministers, to other kinds of men. Nor can I tell you what I would. A very little more is all permitted to me. I cannot rest, I cannot stay, I cannot linger anywhere. My spirit never walked beyond our counting-house—mark me!—in life my spirit never roved beyond the narrow limits of our money-changing hole; and weary journeys lie before me!"

It was a habit with Scrooge, whenever he became thoughtful, to put his hands in his breeches pockets. Pondering on what the Ghost had said, he did so now, but without lifting up his eyes, or getting off his knees.

"You must have been very slow about it, Jacob," Scrooge observed, in a business-like manner, though with humility and deference.

"Slow!" the Ghost repeated.

"Seven years dead," mused Scrooge. "And travelling all the time?"

"The whole time," said the Ghost. "No rest, no peace. Incessant torture of remorse."

"You travel fast?" said Scrooge.

"On the wings of the wind," replied the Ghost.

"You might have got over a great quantity of ground in seven years," said Scrooge.

The Ghost, on hearing this, set up another cry, and clanked its chain so hideously in the dead silence of the night, that the Ward[1] would have been justified in indicting it for a nuisance.

"Oh! captive, bound, and double-ironed," cried the phantom, "not to know, that ages of incessant labour by immortal creatures, for this earth must pass into eternity before the good of which it is susceptible is all developed. Not to know that any Christian spirit working kindly in its little sphere, whatever it may be, will find its mortal life too short for its vast means of usefulness. Not to know that no space of regret can make amends for one life's opportunity misused! Yet such was I! Oh! such was I!"

1. A constable who patrolled the streets of London at night.

"But you were always a good man of business, Jacob," faultered Scrooge, who now began to apply this to himself.

"Business!" cried the Ghost, wringing its hands again. "Mankind was my business. The common welfare was my business; charity, mercy, forbearance, and benevolence, were, all, my business. The dealings of my trade were but a drop of water in the comprehensive ocean of my business!"

It held up its chain at arm's length, as if that were the cause of all its unavailing grief, and flung it heavily upon the ground again.

"At this time of the rolling year," the spectre said, "I suffer most. Why did I walk through crowds of fellow-beings with my eyes turned down, and never raise them to that blessed Star which led the Wise Men to a poor abode? Were there no poor homes to which its light would have conducted *me!*"

Scrooge was very much dismayed to hear the spectre going on at this rate, and began to quake exceedingly.

"Hear me!" cried the Ghost. "My time is nearly gone."

"I will," said Scrooge. "But don't be hard upon me! Don't be flowery, Jacob! Pray!"

"How it is that I appear before you in a shape that you can see, I may not tell. I have sat invisible beside you many and many a day."

It was not an agreeable idea. Scrooge shivered, and wiped the perspiration from his brow.

"That is no light part of my penance," pursued the Ghost. "I am here to-night to warn you, that you have yet a chance and hope of escaping my fate. A chance and hope of my procuring, Ebenezer."

"You were always a good friend to me," said Scrooge. "Thank'ee!"

"You will be haunted," resumed the Ghost, "by Three Spirits."

Scrooge's countenance fell almost as low as the Ghost's had done.

"Is that the chance and hope you mentioned, Jacob?" he demanded, in a faultering voice.

"It is."

"I—I think I'd rather not," said Scrooge.

"Without their visits," said the Ghost, "you cannot hope to shun the path I tread. Expect the first to-morrow, when the bell tolls one."

"Couldn't I take 'em all at once, and have it over, Jacob?" hinted Scrooge.

"Expect the second on the next night at the same hour. The third upon the next night when the last stroke of twelve has ceased to vibrate. Look to see me no more; and look that, for your own sake, you remember what has passed between us!"

When it had said these words, the spectre took its wrapper from the table, and bound it round its head, as before. Scrooge knew this, by the smart sound its teeth made, when the jaws were brought together by the bandage. He ventured to raise his eyes again, and found his supernatural visitor confronting him in an erect attitude, with its chain wound over and about its arm.

The apparition walked backward from him; and at every step it took, the window raised itself a little, so that when the spectre reached it, it was wide open. It beckoned Scrooge to approach, which he did. When they were within two paces of each other, Marley's Ghost held up its hand, warning him to come no nearer. Scrooge stopped.

Not so much in obedience, as in surprise and fear: for on the raising of the hand, he became sensible of confused noises in the air; incoherent sounds of lamentation and regret; wailings inexpressibly sorrowful and self-accusatory. The spectre, after listening for a moment, joined in the mournful dirge; and floated out upon the bleak, dark night.

Scrooge followed to the window: desperate in his curiosity. He looked out.

The air filled with phantoms, wandering hither and thither in restless haste, and moaning as they went. Every one of them wore chains like Marley's Ghost; some few (they might be guilty governments) were linked together; none were free. Many had been personally known to Scrooge in their lives. He had been quite familiar with one old ghost, in a white waistcoat, with a monstrous iron safe attached to its ankle, who cried piteously at being unable to assist a wretched woman with an infant, whom it saw below, upon a door-step. The misery with them all was, clearly, that they sought to interfere, for good, in human matters, and had lost the power for ever.

Whether these creatures faded into mist, or mist enshrouded them, he could not tell. But they and their spirit voices faded together; and the night became as it had been when he walked home.

Scrooge closed the window, and examined the door by which the Ghost had entered. It was double-locked, as he had locked it with his own hands, and the bolts were undisturbed. He tried to say "Humbug!" but stopped at the first syllable. And being, from the emotion he had undergone, or the fatigues of the day, or his glimpse of the Invisible World, or the dull conversation of the Ghost, or the lateness of the hour, much in need of repose; went straight to bed, without undressing, and fell asleep upon the instant.

Stave Two
THE FIRST OF THE THREE SPIRITS

When Scrooge awoke, it was so dark, that looking out of bed, he could scarcely distinguish the transparent window from the opaque walls of his chamber. He was endeavouring to pierce the darkness with his ferret eyes, when the chimes of a neighbouring church struck the four quarters. So he listened for the hour.

To his great astonishment the heavy bell went on from six to seven, and from seven to eight, and regularly up to twelve; then stopped. Twelve! It was past two when he went to bed. The clock was wrong. An icicle must have got into the works. Twelve!

He touched the spring of his repeater, to correct this most preposterous clock. Its rapid little pulse beat twelve; and stopped.

"Why, it isn't possible," said Scrooge, "that I can have slept through a whole day and far into another night. It isn't possible that anything has happened to the sun, and this is twelve at noon!"

The idea being an alarming one, he scrambled out of bed, and groped his way to the window. He was obliged to rub the frost off with the sleeve of his dressing-gown before he could see anything; and could see very little then. All he could make out was, that it was still very foggy and extremely cold, and that there was no noise of people running to and fro, and making a great stir, as there unquestionably would have been if night had beaten off bright day, and taken possession of the world. This was a great relief, because "three days after sight of this First of Exchange pay to Mr Ebenezer Scrooge or his order," and so forth, would have become a mere United States' security[2] if there were no days to count by.

Scrooge went to bed again, and thought, and thought, and thought it over and over and over, and could make nothing of it. The more he thought, the more perplexed he was; and the more he endeavoured not to think, the more he thought.

---

2. Individual American states borrowed heavily from foreign capitalists in the 1830s; in 1837 a financial crisis caused many to default.

Marley's Ghost bothered him exceedingly. Every time he resolved within himself, after mature inquiry, that it was all a dream, his mind flew back again, like a strong spring released, to its first position, and presented the same problem to be worked all through, "Was it a dream or not?"

Scrooge lay in this state until the chimes had gone three quarters more, when he remembered, on a sudden, that the Ghost had warned him of a visitation when the bell tolled one. He resolved to lie awake until the hour was passed; and, considering that he could no more go to sleep than go to Heaven, this was perhaps the wisest resolution in his power.

The quarter was so long, that he was more than once convinced he must have sunk into a doze unconsciously, and missed the clock. At length it broke upon his listening ear.

"Ding, dong!"

"A quarter past," said Scrooge, counting.

"Ding, dong!"

"Half past!" said Scrooge.

"Ding, dong!"

"A quarter to it," said Scrooge.

"Ding, dong!"

"The hour itself," said Scrooge, triumphantly, "and nothing else!"

He spoke before the hour bell sounded, which it now did with a deep, dull, hollow, melancholy ONE. Light flashed up in the room upon the instant, and the curtains of his bed were drawn.

The curtains of his bed were drawn aside, I tell you, by a hand. Not the curtains at his feet, nor the curtains at his back, but those to which his face was addressed. The curtains of his bed were drawn aside; and Scrooge, starting up into a half-recumbent attitude, found himself face to face with the unearthly visitor who drew them: as close to it as I am now to you, and I am standing in the spirit at your elbow.

It was a strange figure—like a child: yet not so like a child as like an old man, viewed through some supernatural medium, which gave him the appearance of having receded from the view, and being diminished to a child's proportions. Its hair, which hung about its neck and down its back, was white as if with age; and yet the face had not a wrinkle in it, and the tenderest bloom was on the skin. The arms were very long and muscular; the hands the same, as if its hold were of uncommon strength. Its legs and feet, most delicately formed, were, like those upper members, bare. It wore a tunic of the purest white; and round its waist was bound a lustrous belt, the sheen of which was beautiful. It held a branch of fresh green holly in its hand; and, in singular contradiction of that wintry emblem, had its dress trimmed with summer flowers. But the strangest thing about it was, that from the crown of its head there sprung a bright clear jet of light, by which all this was visible; and which was doubtless the occasion of its using, in its duller moments, a great extinguisher for a cap,[3] which it now held under its arm.

Even this, though, when Scrooge looked at it with increasing steadiness, was *not* its strangest quality. For as its belt sparkled and glittered now in one part and now in another, and what was light one instant, at another time was dark, so the figure itself fluctuated in its distinctness: being now a thing with one arm, now with one leg, now with twenty legs, now a pair of legs without a head, now a head without a body: of

---

3. A candle snuffer.

which dissolving parts, no outline would be visible in the dense gloom wherein they melted away. And in the very wonder of this, it would be itself again; distinct and clear as ever.

"Are you the Spirit, sir, whose coming was foretold to me?" asked Scrooge.

"I am!"

The voice was soft and gentle. Singularly low, as if instead of being so close beside him, it were at a distance.

"Who, and what are you?" Scrooge demanded.

"I am the Ghost of Christmas Past."

"Long Past?" inquired Scrooge: observant of its dwarfish stature.

"No. Your past."

Perhaps, Scrooge could not have told anybody why, if anybody could have asked him; but he had a special desire to see the Spirit in his cap; and begged him to be covered.

"What!" exclaimed the Ghost, "would you so soon put out, with worldly hands, the light I give? Is it not enough that you are one of those whose passions made this cap, and force me through whole trains of years to wear it low upon my brow!"

Scrooge reverently disclaimed all intention to offend, or any knowledge of having wilfully "bonneted" the Spirit at any period of his life. He then made bold to inquire what business brought him there.

"Your welfare!" said the Ghost.

Scrooge expressed himself much obliged, but could not help thinking that a night of unbroken rest would have been more conducive to that end. The Spirit must have heard him thinking for it said immediately:

"Your reclamation, then. Take heed!"

It put out its strong hand as it spoke, and clasped him gently by the arm.

"Rise! and walk with me!"

It would have been in vain for Scrooge to plead that the weather and the hour were not adapted to pedestrian purposes; that bed was warm, and the thermometer a long way below freezing; that he was clad but lightly in his slippers, dressing-gown, and nightcap; and that he had a cold upon him at that time. The grasp, though gentle as a woman's hand, was not to be resisted. He rose: but finding that the Spirit made towards the window, clasped its robe in supplication.

"I am a mortal," Scrooge remonstrated, "and liable to fall."

"Bear but a touch of my hand *there*," said the Spirit, laying it upon his heart, "and you shall be upheld in more than this!"

As the words were spoken, they passed through the wall, and stood upon an open country road, with fields on either hand. The city had entirely vanished. Not a vestige of it was to be seen. The darkness and the mist had vanished with it, for it was a clear, cold, winter day, with snow upon the ground.

"Good Heaven!" said Scrooge, clasping his hands together, as he looked about him. "I was bred in this place. I was a boy here!"

The Spirit gazed upon him mildly. Its gentle touch, though it had been light and instantaneous, appeared still present to the old man's sense of feeling. He was conscious of a thousand odours floating in the air, each one connected with a thousand thoughts, and hopes, and joys, and cares long, long, forgotten!

"Your lip is trembling," said the Ghost. "And what is that upon your cheek?"

Scrooge muttered, with an unusual catching in his voice, that it was a pimple; and begged the Ghost to lead him where he would.

"You recollect the way?" inquired the Spirit.

"Remember it!" cried Scrooge with fervour—"I could walk it blindfold."

"Strange to have forgotten it for so many years!" observed the Ghost. "Let us go on."

They walked along the road; Scrooge recognising every gate, and post, and tree; until a little market-town appeared in the distance, with its bridge, its church, and winding river. Some shaggy ponies now were seen trotting towards them with boys upon their backs, who called to other boys in country gigs and carts, driven by farmers. All these boys were in great spirits, and shouted to each other, until the broad fields were so full of merry music, that the crisp air laughed to hear it.

"These are but shadows of the things that have been," said the Ghost. "They have no consciousness of us."

The jocund travellers came on; and as they came, Scrooge knew and named them every one. Why was he rejoiced beyond all bounds to see them! Why did his cold eye glisten, and his heart leap up as they went past! Why was he filled with gladness when he heard them give each other Merry Christmas, as they parted at crossroads and bye-ways, for their several homes! What was merry Christmas to Scrooge? Out upon merry Christmas! What good had it ever done to him?

"The school is not quite deserted," said the Ghost. "A solitary child, neglected by his friends, is left there still."

Scrooge said he knew it. And he sobbed.

They left the high-road, by a well remembered lane, and soon approached a mansion of dull red brick, with a little weathercock-surmounted cupola on the roof, and a bell hanging in it. It was a large house, but one of broken fortunes; for the spacious offices were little used, their walls were damp and mossy, their windows broken, and their gates decayed. Fowls clucked and strutted in the stables; and the coach-houses and sheds were over-run with grass. Nor was it more retentive of its ancient state, within; for entering the dreary hall, and glancing through the open doors of many rooms, they found them poorly furnished, cold, and vast. There was an earthy savour in the air, a chilly bareness in the place, which associated itself somehow with too much getting up by candle-light, and not too much to eat.

They went, the Ghost and Scrooge, across the hall, to a door at the back of the house. It opened before them, and disclosed a long, bare, melancholy room, made barer still by lines of plain deal forms and desks. At one of these a lonely boy was reading near a feeble fire; and Scrooge sat down upon a form, and wept to see his poor forgotten self as he had used to be.

Not a latent echo in the house, not a squeak and scuffle from the mice behind the panelling, not a drip from the half-thawed water-spout in the dull yard behind, not a sigh among the leafless boughs of one despondent poplar, not the idle swinging of an empty store-house door, no, not a clicking in the fire, but fell upon the heart of Scrooge with a softening influence, and gave a freer passage to his tears.

The Spirit touched him on the arm, and pointed to his younger self, intent upon his reading. Suddenly a man, in foreign garments: wonderfully real and distinct to look at: stood outside the window, with an axe stuck in his belt, and leading an ass laden with wood by the bridle.

"Why, it's Ali Baba!"[4] Scrooge exclaimed in ecstasy. "It's dear old honest Ali Baba! Yes, yes, I know! One Christmas time, when yonder solitary child was left here all alone, he *did* come, for the first time, just like that. Poor boy! And Valentine," said Scrooge,

4. From *The Arabian Nights*.

"and his wild brother, Orson;[5] there they go! And what's his name, who was put down in his drawers, asleep, at the Gate of Damascus; don't you see him! And the Sultan's Groom turned upside-down by the Genii; there he is upon his head! Serve him right. I'm glad of it. What business had *he* to be married to the Princess!"

To hear Scrooge expending all the earnestness of his nature on such subjects, in a most extraordinary voice between laughing and crying; and to see his heightened and excited face; would have been a surprise to his business friends in the city, indeed.

"There's the Parrot!" cried Scrooge. "Green body and yellow tail, with a thing like a lettuce growing out of the top of his head; there he is! Poor Robin Crusoe, he called him, when he came home again after sailing round the island. 'Poor Robin Crusoe, where have you been, Robin Crusoe?' The man thought he was dreaming, but he wasn't. It was the Parrot, you know. There goes Friday, running for his life to the little creek! Halloa! Hoop! Halloo!"[6]

Then, with a rapidity of transition very foreign to his usual character, he said, in pity for his former self, "Poor boy!" and cried again.

"I wish," Scrooge muttered, putting his hand in his pocket, and looking about him, after drying his eyes with his cuff: "but it's too late now."

"What is the matter?" asked the Spirit.

"Nothing," said Scrooge. "Nothing. There was a boy singing a Christmas Carol at my door last night. I should like to have given him something: that's all."

The Ghost smiled thoughtfully, and waved its hand: saying as it did so, "Let us see another Christmas!"

Scrooge's former self grew larger at the words, and the room became a little darker and more dirty. The panels shrunk, the windows cracked; fragments of plaster fell out of the ceiling, and the naked laths were shown instead; but how all this was brought about, Scrooge knew no more than you do. He only knew that it was quite correct; that everything had happened so; that there he was, alone again, when all the other boys had gone home for the jolly holidays.

He was not reading now, but walking up and down despairingly. Scrooge looked at the Ghost, and with a mournful shaking of his head, glanced anxiously towards the door.

It opened; and a little girl, much younger than the boy, came darting in, and putting her arms about his neck, and often kissing him, addressed him as her "Dear, dear brother."

"I have come to bring you home, dear brother!" said the child, clapping her tiny hands, and bending down to laugh. "To bring you home, home, home!"

"Home, little Fan?" returned the boy.

"Yes!" said the child, brimful of glee. "Home, for good and all. Home, for ever and ever. Father is so much kinder than he used to be, that home's like Heaven! He spoke so gently to me one dear night when I was going to bed, that I was not afraid to ask him once more if you might come home; and he said Yes, you should; and sent me in a coach to bring you. And you're to be a man!" said the child, opening her eyes, "and are never to come back here; but first, we're to be together all the Christmas long, and have the merriest time in all the world."

"You are quite a woman, little Fan!" exclaimed the boy.

5. The medieval story of the knight Valentine, and his brother Orson who had been reared as a wild man in the woods, had become a popular folktale by Dickens's time.

6. The incidents in this paragraph allude to Daniel Defoe's *Robinson Crusoe* (1719).

She clapped her hands and laughed, and tried to touch his head; but being too little, laughed again, and stood on tiptoe to embrace him. Then she began to drag him, in her childish eagerness, towards the door; and he, nothing loth to go, accompanied her.

A terrible voice in the hall cried, "Bring down Master Scrooge's box, there!" and in the hall appeared the schoolmaster himself, who glared on Master Scrooge with a ferocious condescension, and threw him into a dreadful state of mind by shaking hands with him. He then conveyed him and his sister into the veriest old well of a shivering best-parlour that ever was seen, where the maps upon the wall, and the celestial and terrestrial globes in the windows were waxy with cold. Here he produced a decanter of curiously light wine, and a block of curiously heavy cake, and administered instalments of those dainties to the young people: at the same time, sending out a meagre servant to offer a glass of "something" to the postboy, who answered that he thanked the gentleman, but if it was the same tap as he had tasted before, he had rather not. Master Scrooge's trunk being by this time tied on to the top of the chaise, the children bade the schoolmaster good-bye right willingly; and getting into it, drove gaily down the garden-sweep: the quick wheels dashing the hoar-frost and snow from off the dark leaves of the evergreens like spray.

"Always a delicate creature, whom a breath might have withered," said the Ghost. "But she had a large heart!"

"So she had," cried Scrooge. "You're right. I'll not gainsay it, Spirit. God forbid!"

"She died a woman," said the Ghost, "and had, as I think, children."

"One child," Scrooge returned.

"True," said the Ghost. "Your nephew!"

Scrooge seemed uneasy in his mind; and answered briefly, "Yes."

Although they had but that moment left the school behind them, they were now in the busy thoroughfares of a city, where shadowy passengers passed and repassed; where shadowy carts and coaches battled for the way, and all the strife and tumult of a real city were. It was made plain enough, by the dressing of the shops, that here too it was Christmas time again; but it was evening, and the streets were lighted up.

The Ghost stopped at a certain warehouse door, and asked Scrooge if he knew it.

"Know it!" said Scrooge. "Was I apprenticed here?"

They went in. At sight of an old gentleman in a Welch wig,[7] sitting behind such a high desk, that if he had been two inches taller he must have knocked his head against the ceiling, Scrooge cried in great excitement:

"Why, it's old Fezziwig! Bless his heart; it's Fezziwig alive again!"

Old Fezziwig laid down his pen, and looked up at the clock, which pointed to the hour of seven. He rubbed his hands; adjusted his capacious waistcoat; laughed all over himself, from his shoes to his organ of benevolence;[8] and called out in a comfortable, oily, rich, fat, jovial voice:

"Yo ho, there! Ebenezer! Dick!"

Scrooge's former self, now grown a young man, came briskly in, accompanied by his fellow-'prentice.

"Dick Wilkins, to be sure!" said Scrooge to the Ghost. "Bless me, yes. There he is. He was very much attached to me, was Dick. Poor Dick! Dear, dear!"

---

7. A knit cap.
8. The top of the forehead. Phrenology, a system for analyzing character based on the shape of the head, was widely credited in Victorian times.

"Yo ho, my boys!" said Fezziwig. "No more work tonight. Christmas Eve, Dick. Christmas, Ebenezer! Let's have the shutters up," cried old Fezziwig, with a sharp clap of his hands, "before a man can say, Jack Robinson!"

You wouldn't believe how those two fellows went at it! They charged into the street with the shutters—one, two, three—had 'em up in their places—four, five, six—barred 'em and pinned 'em—seven, eight, nine—and came back before you could have got to twelve, panting like race-horses.

"Hilli-ho!" cried old Fezziwig, skipping down from the high desk, with wonderful agility. "Clear away, my lads, and let's have lots of room here! Hilli-ho, Dick! Chirrup, Ebenezer!"

Clear away! There was nothing they wouldn't have cleared away, or couldn't have cleared away, with old Fezziwig looking on. It was done in a minute. Every movable was packed off, as if it were dismissed from public life for evermore; the floor was swept and watered, the lamps were trimmed, fuel was heaped upon the fire; and the warehouse was as snug, and warm, and dry, and bright a ball-room, as you would desire to see upon a winter's night.

In came a fiddler with a music-book, and went up to the lofty desk, and made an orchestra of it, and tuned like fifty stomach-aches. In came Mrs Fezziwig, one vast substantial smile. In came the three Miss Fezziwigs, beaming and lovable. In came the six young followers whose hearts they broke. In came all the young men and women employed in the business. In came the housemaid, with her cousin, the baker. In came the cook, with her brother's particular friend, the milkman. In came the boy from over the way, who was suspected of not having board enough from his master; trying to hide himself behind the girl from next door but one, who was proved to have had her ears pulled by her Mistress. In they all came, one after another; some shyly, some boldly, some gracefully, some awkwardly, some pushing, some pulling; in they all came, anyhow and everyhow. Away they all went, twenty couple at once, hands half round and back again the other way; down the middle and up again; round and round in various stages of affectionate grouping; old top couple always turning up in the wrong place; new top couple starting off again, as soon as they got there; all top couples at last, and not a bottom one to help them. When this result was brought about, old Fezziwig, clapping his hands to stop the dance, cried out, "Well done!" and the fiddler plunged his hot face into a pot of porter, especially provided for that purpose. But scorning rest upon his reappearance, he instantly began again, though there were no dancers yet, as if the other fiddler had been carried home, exhausted, on a shutter; and he were a bran-new man resolved to beat him out of sight, or perish.

There were more dances, and there were forfeits, and more dances, and there was cake, and there was negus, and there was a great piece of Cold Roast, and there was a great piece of Cold Boiled, and there were mince-pies, and plenty of beer. But the great effect of the evening came after the Roast and Boiled, when the fiddler (an artful dog, mind! The sort of man who knew his business better than you or I could have told it him!) struck up "Sir Roger de Coverley." Then old Fezziwig stood out to dance with Mrs Fezziwig. Top couple, too; with a good stiff piece of work cut out for them; three or four and twenty pair of partners; people who were not to be trifled with; people who *would* dance, and had no notion of walking.

But if they had been twice as many: ah, four times: old Fezziwig would have been a match for them, and so would Mrs Fezziwig. As to *her*, she was worthy to be his partner in every sense of the term. If that's not high praise, tell me higher, and I'll use it.

A positive light appeared to issue from Fezziwig's calves. They shone in every part of the dance like moons. You couldn't have predicted, at any given time, what would become of 'em next. And when old Fezziwig and Mrs Fezziwig had gone all through the dance; advance and retire, hold hands with your partner; bow and curtsey; corkscrew; thread-the-needle, and back again to your place; Fezziwig "cut"[9]—cut so deftly, that he appeared to wink with his legs, and came upon his feet again without a stagger.

When the clock struck eleven, this domestic ball broke up. Mr and Mrs Fezziwig took their stations, one on either side the door, and shaking hands with every person individually as he or she went out, wished him or her a Merry Christmas. When everybody had retired but the two 'prentices, they did the same to them; and thus the cheerful voices died away, and the lads were left to their beds; which were under a counter in the back-shop.

During the whole of this time, Scrooge had acted like a man out of his wits. His heart and soul were in the scene, and with his former self. He corroborated everything, remembered everything, enjoyed everything, and underwent the strangest agitation. It was not until now, when the bright faces of his former self and Dick were turned from them, that he remembered the Ghost, and became conscious that it was looking full upon him, while the light upon its head burnt very clear.

"A small matter," said the Ghost, "to make these silly folks so full of gratitude."

"Small!" echoed Scrooge.

The Spirit signed to him to listen to the two apprentices, who were pouring out their hearts in praise of Fezziwig: and when he had done so, said,

"Why! Is it not? He has spent but a few pounds of your mortal money: three or four, perhaps. Is that so much that he deserves this praise?"

"It isn't that," said Scrooge, heated by the remark, and speaking unconsciously like his former, not his latter, self. "It isn't that, Spirit. He has the power to render us happy or unhappy; to make our service light or burdensome; a pleasure or a toil. Say that his power lies in words and looks; in things so slight and insignificant that it is impossible to add and count 'em up: what then? The happiness he gives, is quite as great as if it cost a fortune."

He felt the Spirit's glance, and stopped.

"What is the matter?" asked the Ghost.

"Nothing particular," said Scrooge.

"Something, I think?" the Ghost insisted.

"No," said Scrooge, "No. I should like to be able to say a word or two to my clerk just now! That's all."

His former self turned down the lamps as he gave utterance to the wish; and Scrooge and the Ghost again stood side by side in the open air.

"My time grows short," observed the Spirit. "Quick!"

This was not addressed to Scrooge, or to any one whom he could see, but it produced an immediate effect. For again Scrooge saw himself. He was older now; a man in the prime of life. His face had not the harsh and rigid lines of later years; but it had begun to wear the signs of care and avarice. There was an eager, greedy, restless motion in the eye, which showed the passion that had taken root, and where the shadow of the growing tree would fall.

9. A "cut" in dancing meant to leap in the air and wiggle the legs back and forth quickly.

He was not alone, but sat by the side of a fair young girl in a mourning-dress: in whose eyes there were tears, which sparkled in the light that shone out of the Ghost of Christmas Past.

"It matters little," she said, softly. "To you, very little. Another idol has displaced me; and if it can cheer and comfort you in time to come, as I would have tried to do, I have no just cause to grieve."

"What Idol has displaced you?" he rejoined.

"A golden one."

"This is the even-handed dealing of the world!" he said. "There is nothing on which it is so hard as poverty; and there is nothing it professes to condemn with such severity as the pursuit of wealth!"

"You fear the world too much," she answered, gently. "All your other hopes have merged into the hope of being beyond the chance of its sordid reproach. I have seen your nobler aspirations fall off one by one, until the master-passion, Gain, engrosses you. Have I not?"

"What then?" he retorted. "Even if I have grown so much wiser, what then? I am not changed towards you."

She shook her head.

"Am I?"

"Our contract is an old one. It was made when we were both poor and content to be so, until, in good season, we could improve our worldly fortune by our patient industry. You *are* changed. When it was made, you were another man."

"I was a boy," he said impatiently.

"Your own feeling tells you that you were not what you are," she returned. "I am. That which promised happiness when we were one in heart, is fraught with misery now that we are two. How often and how keenly I have thought of this, I will not say. It is enough that I *have* thought of it, and can release you."

"Have I ever sought release?"

"In words. No. Never."

"In what, then?"

"In a changed nature; in an altered spirit; in another atmosphere of life; another Hope as its great end. In everything that made my love of any worth or value in your sight. If this had never been between us," said the girl, looking mildly, but with steadiness, upon him; "tell me, would you seek me out and try to win me now? Ah, no!"

He seemed to yield to the justice of this supposition, in spite of himself. But he said, with a struggle, "You think not."

"I would gladly think otherwise if I could," she answered, "Heaven knows! When I have learned a Truth like this, I know how strong and irresistible it must be. But if you were free to-day, to-morrow, yesterday, can even I believe that you would choose a dowerless girl—you who, in your very confidence with her, weigh everything by Gain: or, choosing her, if for a moment you were false enough to your one guiding principle to do so, do I not know that your repentance and regret would surely follow? I do; and I release you. With a full heart, for the love of him you once were."

He was about to speak; but with her head turned from him, she resumed.

"You may—the memory of what is past half makes me hope you will—have pain in this. A very, very brief time, and you will dismiss the recollection of it, gladly, as an unprofitable dream, from which it happened well that you awoke. May you be happy in the life you have chosen!"

She left him; and they parted.

"Spirit!" said Scrooge, "show me no more! Conduct me home. Why do you delight to torture me?"

"One shadow more!" exclaimed the Ghost.

"No more!" cried Scrooge. "No more. I don't wish to see it. Show me no more!"

But the relentless Ghost pinioned him in both his arms, and forced him to observe what happened next.

They were in another scene and place: a room, not very large or handsome, but full of comfort. Near to the winter fire sat a beautiful young girl, so like the last that Scrooge believed it was the same, until he saw *her,* now a comely matron, sitting opposite her daughter. The noise in this room was perfectly tumultuous, for there were more children there, than Scrooge in his agitated state of mind could count; and, unlike the celebrated herd in the poem,[1] they were not forty children conducting themselves like one, but every child was conducting itself like forty. The consequences were uproarious beyond belief; but no one seemed to care; on the contrary, the mother and daughter laughed heartily, and enjoyed it very much; and the latter, soon beginning to mingle in the sports, got pillaged by the young brigands most ruthlessly. What would I not have given to be one of them! Though I never could have been so rude, no, no! I wouldn't for the wealth of all the world have crushed that braided hair, and torn it down; and for the precious little shoe, I wouldn't have plucked it off, God bless my soul! to save my life. As to measuring her waist in sport, as they did, bold young brood, I couldn't have done it; I should have expected my arm to have grown round it for a punishment, and never come straight again. And yet I should have dearly liked, I own, to have touched her lips; to have questioned her, that she might have opened them; to have looked upon the lashes of her downcast eyes, and never raised a blush; to have let loose waves of hair, an inch of which would be a keepsake beyond price: in short, I should have liked, I do confess, to have had the lightest licence of a child, and yet been man enough to know its value.

But now a knocking at the door was heard, and such a rush immediately ensued that she with laughing face and plundered dress was borne towards it the centre of a flushed and boisterous group, just in time to greet the father, who came home attended by a man laden with Christmas toys and presents. Then the shouting and the struggling, and the onslaught that was made on the defenceless porter! The scaling him with chairs for ladders, to dive into his pockets, despoil him of brown-paper parcels, hold on tight by his cravat, hug him round the neck, pommel his back, and kick his legs in irrepressible affection! The shouts of wonder and delight with which the development of every package was received! The terrible announcement that the baby had been taken in the act of putting a doll's frying-pan into his mouth, and was more than suspected of having swallowed a fictitious turkey, glued on a wooden platter! The immense relief of finding this a false alarm! The joy, and gratitude, and ecstasy! They are all indescribable alike. It is enough that by degrees the children and their emotions got out of the parlour and by one stair at a time, up to the top of the house; where they went to bed, and so subsided.

And now Scrooge looked on more attentively than ever, when the master of the house, having his daughter leaning fondly on him, sat down with her and her mother at his own fireside; and when he thought that such another creature, quite as graceful

1. A reference to Wordsworth's *Written in March:* "The cattle are grazing, / Their heads never raising; / There are forty feeding like one!"

and as full of promise, might have called him father, and been a spring-time in the haggard winter of his life, his sight grew very dim indeed.

"Belle," said the husband, turning to his wife with a smile, "I saw an old friend of yours this afternoon."

"Who was it?"

"Guess!"

"How can I? Tut, don't I know," she added in the same breath, laughing as he laughed. "Mr Scrooge."

"Mr Scrooge it was. I passed his office window; and as it was not shut up, and he had a candle inside, I could scarcely help seeing him. His partner lies upon the point of death, I hear; and there he sat alone. Quite alone in the world, I do believe."

"Spirit!" said Scrooge in a broken voice, "remove me from this place."

"I told you these were shadows of the things that have been," said the Ghost. "That they are what they are, do not blame me!"

"Remove me!" Scrooge exclaimed. "I cannot bear it!"

He turned upon the Ghost, and seeing that it looked upon him with a face, in which in some strange way there were fragments of all the faces it had shown him, wrestled with it.

"Leave me! Take me back. Haunt me no longer!"

In the struggle, if that can be called a struggle in which the Ghost with no visible resistance on its own part was undisturbed by any effort of its adversary, Scrooge observed that its light was burning high and bright; and dimly connecting that with its influence over him, he seized the extinguisher-cap, and by a sudden action pressed it down upon its head.

The Spirit dropped beneath it, so that the extinguisher covered its whole form; but though Scrooge pressed it down with all his force, he could not hide the light: which streamed from under it, in an unbroken flood upon the ground.

He was conscious of being exhausted, and overcome by an irresistible drowsiness; and, further, of being in his own bedroom. He gave the cap a parting squeeze, in which his hand relaxed; and had barely time to reel to bed, before he sank into a heavy sleep.

Stave Three
THE SECOND OF THE THREE SPIRITS

Awaking in the middle of a prodigiously tough snore, and sitting up in bed to get his thoughts together, Scrooge had no occasion to be told that the bell was again upon the stroke of One. He felt that he was restored to consciousness in the right nick of time, for the especial purpose of holding a conference with the second messenger despatched to him through Jacob Marley's intervention. But, finding that he turned uncomfortably cold when he began to wonder which of his curtains this new spectre would draw back, he put them every one aside with his own hands; and lying down again, established a sharp look-out all round the bed. For he wished to challenge the Spirit on the moment of its appearance, and did not wish to be taken by surprise and made nervous.

Gentlemen of the free-and-easy sort, who plume themselves on being acquainted with a move or two, and being usually equal to the time-of-day, express the wide range of their capacity for adventure by observing that they are good for anything from pitch-and-toss to manslaughter; between which opposite extremes, no

Hablot K. Browne ("Phiz"), *Mr. Scrooge Extinguishing the Spirit*. Mr. Scrooge uses a giant extinguisher cap (for snuffing candles or oil lamps) to escape the reproachful haunting of the Ghost of Christmas Past. The illustrator Hablot K. Browne (1815–1882), who called himself "Phiz" to complement Dickens's nickname "Boz," closely collaborated with the author on ten of his novels, thereby indelibly imprinting the faces and forms of Dickens's characters on the Victorian consciousness. Here Browne produces a stark yet comic image of Scrooge's ineffectual struggle to repress his selfish past and his awakening conscience: "but though Scrooge pressed it down with all his force, he could not hide the light: which streamed from under it."

doubt, there lies a tolerably wide and comprehensive range of subjects. Without venturing for Scrooge quite as hardily as this, I don't mind calling on you to believe that he was ready for a good broad field of strange appearances, and that nothing between a baby and a rhinoceros would have astonished him very much.

Now, being prepared for almost anything, he was not by any means prepared for nothing; and, consequently, when the Bell struck One, and no shape appeared, he was taken with a violent fit of trembling. Five minutes, ten minutes, a quarter of an hour went by, yet nothing came. All this time, he lay upon his bed, the very core and centre of a blaze of ruddy light, which streamed upon it when the clock proclaimed the hour; and which being only light, was more alarming than a dozen ghosts, as he was powerless to make out what it meant, or would be at; and was sometimes apprehensive that he might be at that very moment an interesting case of spontaneous combustion,[2] without having the consolation of knowing it. At last, however, he began to think—as you or I would have thought at first; for it is always the person not in the predicament who knows what ought to have been done in it, and would unquestionably have done it too—at last, I say, he began to think that the source and secret of this ghostly light might be in the adjoining room: from whence, on further tracing it, it seemed to shine. This idea taking full possession of his mind, he got up softly and shuffled in his slippers to the door.

The moment Scrooge's hand was on the lock, a strange voice called him by his name, and bade him enter. He obeyed.

It was his own room. There was no doubt about that. But it had undergone a surprising transformation. The walls and ceiling were so hung with living green, that it looked a perfect grove, from every part of which, bright gleaming berries glistened. The crisp leaves of holly, mistletoe, and ivy reflected back the light, as if so many little mirrors had been scattered there; and such a mighty blaze went roaring up the chimney, as that dull petrification of a hearth had never known in Scrooge's time, or Marley's, or for many and many a winter season gone. Heaped up on the floor, to form a kind of throne, were turkeys, geese, game, poultry, brawn, great joints of meat, sucking-pigs, long wreaths of sausages, mince-pies, plum-puddings, barrels of oysters, red-hot chestnuts, cherry-cheeked apples, juicy oranges, luscious pears, immense twelfth-cakes,[3] and seething bowls of punch, that made the chamber dim with their delicious steam. In easy state upon this couch, there sat a jolly Giant, glorious to see; who bore a glowing torch, in shape not unlike Plenty's horn, and held it up, high up, to shed its light on Scrooge, as he came peeping round the door.

"Come in!" exclaimed the Ghost. "Come in! and know me better, man!"

Scrooge entered timidly, and hung his head before this Spirit. He was not the dogged Scrooge he had been; and though the Spirit's eyes were clear and kind, he did not like to meet them.

"I am the Ghost of Christmas Present," said the Spirit. "Look upon me!"

Scrooge reverently did so. It was clothed in one simple deep green robe, or mantle, bordered with white fur. This garment hung so loosely on the figure, that its capacious breast was bare, as if disdaining to be warded or concealed by any artifice. Its feet, observable beneath the ample folds of the garment, were also bare; and on its head it wore no other covering than a holly wreath, set here and there with shining icicles. Its dark brown curls were long and free: free as its genial face, its sparkling eye, its open hand, its cheery voice, its unconstrained demeanour, and its joyful air. Girded round its middle was an antique scabbard; but no sword was in it, and the ancient sheath was eaten up with rust.

"You have never seen the like of me before!" exclaimed the Spirit.

"Never," Scrooge made answer to it.

"Have never walked forth with the younger members of my family; meaning (for I am very young) my elder brothers born in these later years?" pursued the Phantom.

"I don't think I have," said Scrooge. "I am afraid I have not. Have you had many brothers, Spirit?"

"More than eighteen hundred," said the Ghost.

---

2. Dickens was fascinated by the theory that under certain conditions a human body could go up in flames spontaneously; in his novel *Bleak House* the rag-and-bone dealer, Krook, perishes this way.

3. Decorated cakes eaten on Twelfth Night (January 5), the eve of Epiphany; traditionally, the end of Christmas festivities.

"A tremendous family to provide for!" muttered Scrooge.

The Ghost of Christmas Present rose.

"Spirit," said Scrooge submissively, "conduct me where you will. I went forth last night on compulsion, and I learnt a lesson which is working now. To-night, if you have aught to teach me, let me profit by it."

"Touch my robe!"

Scrooge did as he was told, and held it fast.

Holly, mistletoe, red berries, ivy, turkeys, geese, game, poultry, brawn, meat, pigs, sausages, oysters, pies, puddings, fruit, and punch, all vanished instantly. So did the room, the fire, the ruddy glow, the hour of night, and they stood in the city streets on Christmas morning, where (for the weather was severe) the people made a rough, but brisk and not unpleasant kind of music, in scraping the snow from the pavement in front of their dwellings, and from the tops of their houses: whence it was mad delight to the boys to see it come plumping down into the road below, and splitting into artificial little snow-storms.

The house fronts looked black enough, and the windows blacker, contrasting with the smooth white sheet of snow upon the roofs, and with the dirtier snow upon the ground; which last deposit had been ploughed up in deep furrows by the heavy wheels of carts and waggons; furrows that crossed and re-crossed each other hundreds of times where the great streets branched off, and made intricate channels, hard to trace, in the thick yellow mud and icy water. The sky was gloomy, and the shortest streets were choked up with a dingy mist, half thawed, half frozen, whose heavier particles descended in a shower of sooty atoms, as if all the chimneys in Great Britain had, by one consent, caught fire, and were blazing away to their dear hearts' content. There was nothing very cheerful in the climate or the town, and yet was there an air of cheerfulness abroad that the clearest summer air and brightest summer sun might have endeavoured to diffuse in vain.

For the people who were shovelling away on the housetops were jovial and full of glee; calling out to one another from the parapets, and now and then exchanging a facetious snow-ball—better-natured missile far than many a wordy jest—laughing heartily if it went right, and not less heartily if it went wrong. The poulterers' shops were still half open, and the fruiterers' were radiant in their glory. There were great round, pot-bellied baskets of chestnuts, shaped like the waistcoats of jolly old gentlemen, lolling at the doors, and tumbling out into the street in their apoplectic opulence. There were ruddy, brown-faced, broad-girthed Spanish Onions, shining in the fatness of their growth like Spanish Friars; and winking from their shelves in wanton slyness at the girls as they went by, and glanced demurely at the hung-up mistletoe. There were pears and apples, clustered high in blooming pyramids; there were bunches of grapes, made in the shopkeepers' benevolence to dangle from conspicuous hooks, that people's mouths might water gratis as they passed; there were piles of filberts, mossy and brown, recalling, in their fragrance, ancient walks among the woods, and pleasant shufflings ankle deep through withered leaves; there were Norfolk Biffins,[4] squab and swarthy, setting off the yellow of the oranges and lemons, and, in the great compactness of their juicy persons, urgently entreating and beseeching to be carried home in paper bags and eaten after dinner. The very gold and silver fish, set forth among these choice fruits in a bowl, though members of a dull

4. Cooking apples.

and stagnant-blooded race, appeared to know that there was something going on; and, to a fish, went gasping round and round their little world in slow and passionless excitement.

The Grocers'! oh the Grocers'! nearly closed, with perhaps two shutters down, or one; but through those gaps such glimpses! It was not alone that the scales descending on the counter made a merry sound, or that the twine and roller parted company so briskly, or that the canisters were rattled up and down like juggling tricks, or even that the blended scents of tea and coffee were so grateful to the nose, or even that the raisins were so plentiful and rare, the almonds so extremely white, the sticks of cinnamon so long and straight, the other spices so delicious, the candied fruits so caked and spotted with molten sugar as to make the coldest lookers-on feel faint and subsequently bilious. Nor was it that the figs were moist and pulpy, or that the French plums blushed in modest tartness from their highly-decorated boxes, or that everything was good to eat and in its Christmas dress: but the customers were all so hurried and so eager in the hopeful promise of the day, that they tumbled up against each other at the door, clashing their wicker baskets wildly, and left their purchases upon the counter, and came running back to fetch them, and committed hundreds of the like mistakes in the best humour possible; while the Grocer and his people were so frank and fresh that the polished hearts with which they fastened their aprons behind might have been their own, worn outside for general inspection, and for Christmas daws to peck at if they chose.[5]

But soon the steeples called good people all, to church and chapel, and away they came, flocking through the streets in their best clothes, and with their gayest faces. And at the same time there emerged from scores of bye streets, lanes, and nameless turnings, innumerable people, carrying their dinners to the bakers' shops.[6] The sight of these poor revellers appeared to interest the Spirit very much, for he stood with Scrooge beside him in a baker's doorway, and taking off the covers as their bearers passed, sprinkled incense on their dinners from his torch. And it was a very uncommon kind of torch, for once or twice when there were angry words between some dinner-carriers who had jostled each other, he shed a few drops of water on them from it, and their good humour was restored directly. For they said, it was a shame to quarrel upon Christmas Day. And so it was! God love it, so it was!

In time the bells ceased, and the bakers' were shut up; and yet there was a genial shadowing forth of all these dinners and the progress of their cooking, in the thawed blotch of wet above each baker's oven; where the pavement smoked as if its stones were cooking too.

"Is there a peculiar flavour in what you sprinkle from your torch?" asked Scrooge.

"There is. My own."

"Would it apply to any kind of dinner on this day?" asked Scrooge.

"To any kindly given. To a poor one most."

"Why to a poor one most?" asked Scrooge.

"Because it needs it most."

"Spirit," said Scrooge, after a moment's thought, "I wonder you, of all the beings in the many worlds about us, should desire to cramp these people's opportunities of innocent enjoyment."

---

5. Cf. *Othello*, 1.1.65–66: "But I will wear my heart upon my sleeve / For daws to peck at."
6. Bakers were forbidden to bake bread on Sundays and holidays, so working-class families brought their meals to cook in the ovens.

"I!" cried the Spirit.

"You would deprive them of their means of dining every seventh day, often the only day on which they can be said to dine at all," said Scrooge. "Wouldn't you?"

"I!" cried the Spirit.

"You seek to close these places on the Seventh Day?"[7] said Scrooge. "And it comes to the same thing."

"*I* seek!" exclaimed the Spirit.

"Forgive me if I am wrong. It has been done in your name, or at least in that of your family," said Scrooge.

"There are some upon this earth of yours," returned the Spirit, "who lay claim to know us, and who do their deeds of passion, pride, ill-will, hatred, envy, bigotry, and selfishness in our name, who are as strange to us and all our kith and kin, as if they had never lived. Remember that, and charge their doings on themselves, not us."

Scrooge promised that he would; and they went on, invisible, as they had been before, into the suburbs of the town. It was a remarkable quality of the Ghost (which Scrooge had observed at the baker's) that notwithstanding his gigantic size, he could accommodate himself to any place with ease; and that he stood beneath a low roof quite as gracefully and like a supernatural creature, as it was possible he could have done in any lofty hall.

And perhaps it was the pleasure the good Spirit had in showing off this power of his, or else it was his own kind, generous, hearty nature, and his sympathy with all poor men, that led him straight to Scrooge's clerk's; for there he went, and took Scrooge with him, holding to his robe; and on the threshold of the door the Spirit smiled, and stopped to bless Bob Cratchit's dwelling with the sprinkling of his torch. Think of that! Bob had but fifteen "Bob" a-week himself; he pocketed on Saturdays but fifteen copies of his Christian name; and yet the Ghost of Christmas Present blessed his four-roomed house!

Then up rose Mrs Cratchit, Cratchit's wife, dressed out but poorly in a twice-turned gown,[8] but brave in ribbons, which are cheap and make a goodly show for six-pence; and she laid the cloth, assisted by Belinda Cratchit, second of her daughters, also brave in ribbons; while Master Peter Cratchit plunged a fork into the saucepan of potatoes, and getting the corners of his monstrous shirt-collar (Bob's private property, conferred upon his son and heir in honour of the day) into his mouth, rejoiced to find himself so gallantly attired, and yearned to show his linen in the fashionable Parks. And now two smaller Cratchits, boy and girl, came tearing in, screaming that outside the baker's they had smelt the goose, and known it for their own; and basking in luxurious thoughts of sage and onion, these young Cratchits danced about the table, and exalted Master Peter Cratchit to the skies, while he (not proud, although his collars nearly choked him) blew the fire, until the slow potatoes bubbling up, knocked loudly at the saucepan-lid to be let out and peeled.

"What has ever got your precious father then," said Mrs Cratchit. "And your brother, Tiny Tim; and Martha warn't as late last Christmas Day by half-an-hour!"

"Here's Martha, mother!" said a girl, appearing as she spoke.

"Here's Martha, mother!" cried the two young Cratchits. "Hurrah! There's *such* a goose, Martha!"

7. Dickens strongly opposed efforts in the 1830s to pass a Sunday Observance Bill limiting the recreations of working people on their only day off. (See *Sunday Under Three* *Heads* in Perspectives: Religion and Science, page 712.)
8. A worn out and remade dress.

"Why, bless your heart alive, my dear, how late you are!" said Mrs Cratchit, kissing her a dozen times, and taking off her shawl and bonnet for her, with officious zeal.

"We'd a deal of work to finish up last night," replied the girl, "and had to clear away this morning, mother!"

"Well! Never mind so long as you are come," said Mrs Cratchit. "Sit ye down before the fire, my dear, and have a warm, Lord bless ye!"

"No no! There's father coming," cried the two young Cratchits, who were everywhere at once. "Hide Martha, hide!"

So Martha hid herself, and in came little Bob, the father, with at least three feet of comforter exclusive of the fringe, hanging down before him; and his thread-bare clothes darned up and brushed, to look seasonable; and Tiny Tim upon his shoulder. Alas for Tiny Tim, he bore a little crutch, and had his limbs supported by an iron frame!

"Why, where's our Martha?" cried Bob Cratchit looking round.

"Not coming," said Mrs Cratchit.

"Not coming!" said Bob, with a sudden declension in his high spirits; for he had been Tim's blood horse[9] all the way from church, and had come home rampant. "Not coming upon Christmas Day!"

Martha didn't like to see him disappointed, if it were only in joke; so she came out prematurely from behind the closet door, and ran into his arms, while the two young Cratchits hustled Tiny Tim, and bore him off into the wash-house, that he might hear the pudding singing in the copper.

"And how did little Tim behave?" asked Mrs Cratchit, when she had rallied Bob on his credulity and Bob had hugged his daughter to his heart's content.

"As good as gold," said Bob, "and better. Somehow he gets thoughtful sitting by himself so much, and thinks the strangest things you ever heard. He told me, coming home, that he hoped the people saw him in the church, because he was a cripple, and it might be pleasant to them to remember upon Christmas Day, who made lame beggars walk and blind men see."

Bob's voice was tremulous when he told them this, and trembled more when he said that Tiny Tim was growing strong and hearty.

His active little crutch was heard upon the floor, and back came Tiny Tim before another word was spoken, escorted by his brother and sister to his stool before the fire; and while Bob, turning up his cuffs—as if, poor fellow, they were capable of being made more shabby—compounded some hot mixture in a jug with gin and lemons, and stirred it round and round and put it on the hob to simmer; Master Peter, and the two ubiquitous young Cratchits went to fetch the goose, with which they soon returned in high procession.

Such a bustle ensued that you might have thought a goose the rarest of all birds; a feathered phenomenon, to which a black swan was a matter of course; and in truth it was something very like it in that house. Mrs Cratchit made the gravy (ready beforehand in a little saucepan) hissing hot; Master Peter mashed the potatoes with incredible vigour; Miss Belinda sweetened up the apple-sauce; Martha dusted the hot plates; Bob took Tiny Tim beside him in a tiny corner at the table; the two young Cratchits set chairs for everybody, not forgetting themselves, and mounting guard upon their posts, crammed spoons into their mouths, lest they should shriek for goose before their turn came to be helped. At last the dishes were set on, and grace was said. It was succeeded by a breathless pause, as Mrs Cratchit, looking slowly all

9. I.e., Bob was carrying Tim on his shoulders.

along the carving-knife, prepared to plunge it in the breast; but when she did, and when the long expected gush of stuffing issued forth, one murmur of delight arose all round the board, and even Tiny Tim, excited by the two young Cratchits, beat on the table with the handle of his knife, and feebly cried Hurrah!

There never was such a goose. Bob said he didn't believe there ever was such a goose cooked. Its tenderness and flavour, size and cheapness, were the themes of universal admiration. Eked out by the apple-sauce and mashed potatoes, it was a sufficient dinner for the whole family; indeed, as Mrs Cratchit said with great delight (surveying one small atom of a bone upon the dish), they hadn't ate it all at last! Yet every one had had enough, and the youngest Cratchits in particular, were steeped in sage and onion to the eyebrows! But now, the plates being changed by Miss Belinda, Mrs Cratchit left the room alone—too nervous to bear witnesses—to take the pudding up, and bring it in.

Suppose it should not be done enough! Suppose it should break in turning out! Suppose somebody should have got over the wall of the back-yard, and stolen it, while they were merry with the goose: a supposition at which the two young Cratchits became livid! All sorts of horrors were supposed.

Hallo! A great deal of steam! The pudding was out of the copper. A smell like a washing-day! That was the cloth. A smell like an eating-house, and a pastry cook's next door to each other, with a laundress's next door to that! That was the pudding. In half a minute Mrs Cratchit entered: flushed, but smiling proudly: with the pudding, like a speckled cannon-ball, so hard and firm, blazing in half of half-a-quartern of ignited brandy, and bedight with Christmas holly stuck into the top.

Oh, a wonderful pudding! Bob Cratchit said, and calmly too, that he regarded it as the greatest success achieved by Mrs Cratchit since their marriage. Mrs Cratchit said that now the weight was off her mind, she would confess she had had her doubts about the quantity of flour. Everybody had something to say about it, but nobody said or thought it was at all a small pudding for a large family. It would have been flat heresy to do so. Any Cratchit would have blushed to hint at such a thing.

At last the dinner was all done, the cloth was cleared, the hearth swept, and the fire made up. The compound in the jug being tasted, and considered perfect, apples and oranges were put upon the table, and a shovel-full of chestnuts on the fire. Then all the Cratchit family drew round the hearth, in what Bob Cratchit called a circle, meaning half a one; and at Bob Cratchit's elbow stood the family display of glass; two tumblers, and a custard-cup without a handle.

These held the hot stuff from the jug, however, as well as golden goblets would have done; and Bob served it out with beaming looks, while the chestnuts on the fire sputtered and crackled noisily. Then Bob proposed:

"A Merry Christmas to us all, my dears. God bless us!"

Which all the family re-echoed.

"God bless us every one!" said Tiny Tim, the last of all.

He sat very close to his father's side, upon his little stool. Bob held his withered little hand in his, as if he loved the child, and wished to keep him by his side, and dreaded that he might be taken from him.

"Spirit," said Scrooge, with an interest he had never felt before, "tell me if Tiny Tim will live."

"I see a vacant seat," replied the Ghost, "in the poor chimney corner, and a crutch without an owner, carefully preserved. If these shadows remain unaltered by the Future, the child will die."

"No, no," said Scrooge. "Oh no, kind Spirit! say he will be spared."

"If these shadows remain unaltered by the Future, none other of my race," returned the Ghost, "will find him here. What then? If he be like to die, he had better do it, and decrease the surplus population."

Scrooge hung his head to hear his own words quoted by the Spirit, and was overcome with penitence and grief.

"Man," said the Ghost, "if man you be in heart, not adamant, forbear that wicked cant until you have discovered What the surplus is, and Where it is. Will you decide what men shall live, what men shall die? It may be, that in the sight of Heaven, you are more worthless and less fit to live than millions like this poor man's child. Oh God! to hear the Insect on the leaf pronouncing on the too much life among his hungry brothers in the dust!"

Scrooge bent before the Ghost's rebuke, and trembling cast his eyes upon the ground. But he raised them speedily, on hearing his own name.

"Mr Scrooge!" said Bob; "I'll give you Mr Scrooge, the Founder of the Feast!"

"The Founder of the Feast indeed!" cried Mrs Cratchit, reddening. "I wish I had him here. I'd give him a piece of my mind to feast upon, and I hope he'd have a good appetite for it."

"My dear," said Bob, "the children; Christmas Day."

"It should be Christmas Day, I am sure," said she, "on which one drinks the health of such an odious, stingy, hard, unfeeling man as Mr Scrooge. You know he is, Robert! Nobody knows it better than you do, poor fellow!"

"My dear," was Bob's mild answer, "Christmas Day."

"I'll drink his health for your sake and the Day's," said Mrs Cratchit, "not for his. Long life to him! A merry Christmas and a happy new year!—he'll be very merry and very happy, I have no doubt!"

The children drank the toast after her. It was the first of their proceedings which had no heartiness in it. Tiny Tim drank it last of all, but he didn't care twopence for it. Scrooge was the Ogre of the family. The mention of his name cast a dark shadow on the party, which was not dispelled for full five minutes.

After it had passed away, they were ten times merrier than before, from the mere relief of Scrooge the Baleful being done with. Bob Cratchit told them how he had a situation in his eye for Master Peter, which would bring in, if obtained, full five-and-sixpence weekly. The two young Cratchits laughed tremendously at the idea of Peter's being a man of business; and Peter himself looked thoughtfully at the fire from between his collars, as if he were deliberating what particular investments he should favour when he came into the receipt of that bewildering income. Martha, who was a poor apprentice at a milliner's, then told them what kind of work she had to do, and how many hours she worked at a stretch, and how she meant to lie a-bed tomorrow morning for a good long rest; to-morrow being a holiday she passed at home. Also how she had seen a countess and a lord some days before, and how the lord "was much about as tall as Peter"; at which Peter pulled up his collars so high that you couldn't have seen his head if you had been there. All this time the chestnuts and the jug went round and round; and bye and bye they had a song, about a lost child travelling in the snow, from Tiny Tim; who had a plaintive little voice, and sang it very well indeed.

There was nothing of high mark in this. They were not a handsome family; they were not well dressed; their shoes were far from being water-proof; their clothes were scanty; and Peter might have known, and very likely did, the inside of a pawnbroker's. But they were happy, grateful, pleased with one another, and contented with the time; and when they faded, and looked happier yet in the bright sprinklings of the Spirit's torch at parting, Scrooge had his eye upon them, and especially on Tiny Tim, until the last.

By this time it was getting dark, and snowing pretty heavily; and as Scrooge and the Spirit went along the streets, the brightness of the roaring fires in kitchens, parlours, and all sorts of rooms, was wonderful. Here, the flickering of the blaze showed preparations for a cosy dinner, with hot plates baking through and through before the fire, and deep red curtains, ready to be drawn, to shut out cold and darkness. There, all the children of the house were running out into the snow to meet their married sisters, brothers, cousins, uncles, aunts, and be the first to greet them. Here, again, were shadows on the window-blind of guests assembling; and there a group of handsome girls, all hooded and fur-booted, and all chattering at once, tripped lightly off to some near neighbour's house; where, woe upon the single man who saw them enter—artful witches: well they knew it—in a glow!

But if you had judged from the numbers of people on their way to friendly gatherings, you might have thought that no one was at home to give them welcome when they got there, instead of every house expecting company, and piling up its fires half-chimney high. Blessings on it, how the Ghost exulted! How it bared its breadth of breast, and opened its capacious palm, and floated on, outpouring, with a generous hand, its bright and harmless mirth on everything within its reach! The very lamplighter, who ran on before dotting the dusky street with specks of light, and who was dressed to spend the evening somewhere, laughed out loudly as the Spirit passed: though little kenned the lamplighter that he had any company but Christmas!

And now, without a word of warning from the Ghost, they stood upon a bleak and desert moor, where monstrous masses of rude stone were cast about, as though it were the burial-place of giants; and water spread itself wheresoever it listed—or would have done so, but for the frost that held it prisoner; and nothing grew but moss and furze, and coarse, rank grass. Down in the west the setting sun had left a streak of fiery red, which glared upon the desolation for an instant, like a sullen eye, and frowning lower, lower, lower yet, was lost in the thick gloom of darkest night.

"What place is this?" asked Scrooge.

"A place where Miners live, who labour in the bowels of the earth," returned the Spirit. "But they know me. See!"

A light shone from the window of a hut, and swiftly they advanced towards it. Passing through the wall of mud and stone, they found a cheerful company assembled round a glowing fire. An old, old man and woman, with their children and their children's children, and another generation beyond that, all decked out gaily in their holiday attire. The old man, in a voice that seldom rose above the howling of the wind upon the barren waste, was singing them a Christmas song; it had been a very old song when he was a boy; and from time to time they all joined in the chorus. So surely as they raised their voices, the old man got quite blithe and loud; and so surely as they stopped, his vigour sang again.

The Spirit did not tarry here, but bade Scrooge hold his robe, and passing on above the moor, sped whither? Not to sea? To sea. To Scrooge's horror, looking back, he saw the last of the land, a frightful range of rocks, behind them; and his ears were deafened by the thundering of water, as it rolled, and roared, and raged among the dreadful caverns it had worn, and fiercely tried to undermine the earth.

Built upon a dismal reef of sunken rocks, some league or so from shore, on which the waters chafed and dashed, the wild year through, there stood a solitary lighthouse. Great heaps of sea-weed clung to its base, and storm-birds—born of the wind one might suppose, as sea-weed of the water—rose and fell about it, like the waves they skimmed.

But even here, two men who watched the light had made a fire, that through the loophole in the thick stone wall shed out a ray of brightness on the awful sea. Joining their horny hands over the rough table at which they sat, they wished each other Merry Christmas in their can of grog; and one of them: the elder, too, with his face all damaged and scarred with hard weather, as the figure-head of an old ship might be: struck up a sturdy song that was like a Gale in itself.

Again the Ghost sped on, above the black and heaving sea—on, on—until, being far away, as he told Scrooge, from any shore, they lighted on a ship. They stood beside the helmsman at the wheel, the look-out in the bow, the officers who had the watch; dark, ghostly figures in their several stations; but every man among them hummed a Christmas tune, or had a Christmas thought, or spoke below his breath to his companion of some bygone Christmas Day, with homeward hopes belonging to it. And every man on board, waking or sleeping, good or bad, had had a kinder word for another on that day than on any day in the year; and had shared to some extent in its festivities; and had remembered those he cared for at a distance, and had known that they delighted to remember him.

It was a great surprise to Scrooge, while listening to the moaning of the wind, and thinking what a solemn thing it was to move on through the lonely darkness over an unknown abyss, whose depths were secrets as profound as Death: it was a great surprise to Scrooge, while thus engaged, to hear a hearty laugh. It was a much greater surprise to Scrooge to recognise it as his own nephew's, and to find himself in a bright, dry, gleaming room, with the Spirit standing smiling by his side, and looking at that same nephew with approving affability!

"Ha, ha!" laughed Scrooge's nephew. "Ha, ha, ha!"

If you should happen, by any unlikely chance, to know a man more blest in a laugh than Scrooge's nephew, all I can say is, I should like to know him too. Introduce him to me, and I'll cultivate his acquaintance.

It is a fair, even-handed, noble adjustment of things, that while there is infection in disease and sorrow, there is nothing in the world so irresistibly contagious as laughter and good-humour. When Scrooge's nephew laughed in this way: holding his sides, rolling his head, and twisting his face into the most extravagant contortions: Scrooge's niece, by marriage, laughed as heartily as he. And their assembled friends being not a bit behindhand, roared out, lustily.

"Ha, ha! Ha, ha, ha, ha!"

"He said that Christmas was a humbug, as I live!" cried Scrooge's nephew. "He believed it too!"

"More shame for him, Fred!" said Scrooge's niece, indignantly. Bless those women; they never do anything by halves. They are always in earnest.

She was very pretty: exceedingly pretty. With a dimpled, surprised-looking, capital face; a ripe little mouth, that seemed made to be kissed—as no doubt it was; all kinds of good little dots about her chin, that melted into one another when she laughed; and the sunniest pair of eyes you ever saw in any little creature's head. Altogether she was what you would have called provoking, you know; but satisfactory too. Oh, perfectly satisfactory!

"He's a comical old fellow," said Scrooge's nephew, "that's the truth: and not so pleasant as he might be. However, his offences carry their own punishment, and I have nothing to say against him."

"I'm sure he is very rich, Fred," hinted Scrooge's niece. "At least you always tell *me* so."

"What of that, my dear!" said Scrooge's nephew. "His wealth is of no use to him. He don't do any good with it. He don't make himself comfortable with it. He hasn't the satisfaction of thinking—ha, ha, ha!—that he is ever going to benefit Us with it."

"I have no patience with him," observed Scrooge's niece. Scrooge's niece's sisters, and all the other ladies, expressed the same opinion.

"Oh, I have!" said Scrooge's nephew. "I am sorry for him; I couldn't be angry with him if I tried. Who suffers by his ill whims! Himself, always. Here, he takes it into his head to dislike us, and he won't come and dine with us. What's the consequence? He don't lose much of a dinner."

"Indeed, I think he loses a very good dinner," interrupted Scrooge's niece. Everybody else said the same, and they must be allowed to have been competent judges, because they had just had dinner; and, with the dessert upon the table, were clustered round the fire, by lamplight.

"Well! I'm very glad to hear it," said Scrooge's nephew, "because I haven't great faith in these young housekeepers. What do *you* say, Topper?"

Topper had clearly got his eye upon one of Scrooge's niece's sisters, for he answered that a bachelor was a wretched outcast, who had no right to express an opinion on the subject. Whereat Scrooge's niece's sister—the plump one with the lace tucker: not the one with the roses—blushed.

"Do go on, Fred," said Scrooge's niece, clapping her hands. "He never finishes what he begins to say! He is such a ridiculous fellow!"

Scrooge's nephew revelled in another laugh, and as it was impossible to keep the infection off; though the plump sister tried hard to do it with aromatic vinegar; his example was unanimously followed.

"I was going to say," said Scrooge's nephew, "that the consequence of his taking a dislike to us, and not making merry with us, is, as I think, that he loses some pleasant moments, which could do him no harm. I am sure he loses pleasanter companions than he can find in his own thoughts, either in his mouldy old office, or his dusty chambers. I mean to give him the same chance every year, whether he likes it or not, for I pity him. He may rail at Christmas till he dies, but he can't help thinking better of it—I defy him—if he finds me going there, in good temper, year after year, and saying Uncle Scrooge, how are you? If it only puts him in the vein to leave his poor clerk fifty pounds, *that's* something; and I think I shook him, yesterday."

It was their turn to laugh now, at the notion of his shaking Scrooge. But being thoroughly good-natured, and not much caring what they laughed at, so that they laughed at any rate, he encouraged them in their merriment, and passed the bottle, joyously.

After tea, they had some music. For they were a musical family, and knew what they were about, when they sung a Glee or Catch,[1] I can assure you: especially Topper, who could growl away in the bass like a good one, and never swell the large veins in his forehead, or get red in the face over it. Scrooge's niece played well upon the harp; and played among other tunes a simple little air (a mere nothing: you might learn to whistle it in two minutes), which had been familiar to the child who fetched Scrooge from the boarding-school, as he had been reminded by the Ghost of Christmas Past. When this strain of music sounded, all the things that Ghost had shown him, came upon his mind; he softened more and more; and thought that if he could

---

1. A glee is an unaccompanied song for three or more voices; a catch is a round.

have listened to it often, years ago, he might have cultivated the kindnesses of life for his own happiness with his own hands, without resorting to the sexton's spade that buried Jacob Marley.

But they didn't devote the whole evening to music. After a while they played at forfeits;[2] for it is good to be children sometimes, and never better than at Christmas, when its mighty Founder was a child himself. Stop! There was first a game at blind-man's buff. Of course there was. And I no more believe Topper was really blind than I believe he had eyes in his boots. My opinion is, that it was a done thing between him and Scrooge's nephew; and that the Ghost of Christmas Present knew it. The way he went after that plump sister in the lace tucker, was an outrage on the credulity of human nature. Knocking down the fire-irons, tumbling over the chairs, bumping against the piano, smothering himself among the curtains, wherever she went, there went he. He always knew where the plump sister was. He wouldn't catch anybody else. If you had fallen up against him, as some of them did, and stood there; he would have made a feint of endeavouring to seize you, which would have been an affront to your understanding; and would instantly have sidled off in the direction of the plump sister. She often cried out that it wasn't fair; and it really was not. But when at last, he caught her; when, in spite of all her silken rustlings, and her rapid flutterings past him, he got her into a corner whence there was no escape; then his conduct was the most execrable. For his pretending not to know her; his pretending that it was necessary to touch her head-dress, and further to assure himself of her identity by pressing a certain ring upon her finger, and a certain chain about her neck; was vile, monstrous! No doubt she told him her opinion of it, when, another blind-man being in office, they were so very confidential together, behind the curtains.

Scrooge's niece was not one of the blind-man's buff party, but was made comfortable with a large chair and a footstool, in a snug corner, where the Ghost and Scrooge were close behind her. But she joined in the forfeits, and loved her love to admiration with all the letters of the alphabet. Likewise at the game of How, When, and Where, she was very great, and to the secret joy of Scrooge's nephew, beat her sisters hollow: though they were sharp girls too, as Topper could have told you. There might have been twenty people there, young and old, but they all played, and so did Scrooge; for wholly forgetting in the interest he had in what was going on, that his voice made no sound in their ears, he sometimes came out with his guess quite loud, and very often guessed quite right, too; for the sharpest needle, best Whitechapel,[3] warranted not to cut in the eye, was not sharper than Scrooge: blunt as he took it in his head to be.

The Ghost was greatly pleased to find him in this mood, and looked upon him with such favour that he begged like a boy to be allowed to stay until the guests departed. But this the Spirit said could not be done.

"Here's a new game," said Scrooge. "One half hour, Spirit, only one!"

It was a Game called Yes and No, where Scrooge's nephew had to think of something, and the rest must find out what; he only answering to their questions yes or no as the case was. The brisk fire of questioning to which he was exposed, elicited from him that he was thinking of an animal, a live animal, rather a disagreeable animal, a savage animal, an animal that growled and grunted sometimes, and talked sometimes, and lived in London, and walked about the streets, and wasn't made a show of,

---

2. A game in which penalties are exacted when the player makes a mistake.

3. Whitechapel, a district in East London, was known for its manufacturing.

and wasn't led by anybody, and didn't live in a menagerie, and was never killed in a market, and was not a horse, or an ass, or a cow, or a bull, or a tiger, or a dog, or a pig, or a cat, or a bear. At every fresh question that was put to him, this nephew burst into a fresh roar of laughter; and was so inexpressibly tickled, that he was obliged to get up off the sofa and stamp. At last the plump sister, falling into a similar state, cried out:

"I have found it out! I know what it is, Fred! I know what it is!"

"What is it?" cried Fred.

"It's your Uncle Scro-o-o-o-oge!"

Which it certainly was. Admiration was the universal sentiment, though some objected that the reply to "Is it a bear?" ought to have been "Yes;" inasmuch as an answer in the negative was sufficient to have diverted their thoughts from Mr Scrooge, supposing they had ever had any tendency that way.

"He has given us plenty of merriment, I am sure," said Fred, "and it would be ungrateful not to drink his health. Here is a glass of mulled wine ready to our hand at the moment; and I say 'Uncle Scrooge!'"

"Well! Uncle Scrooge!" they cried.

"A Merry Christmas and a Happy New Year to the old man, whatever he is!" said Scrooge's nephew. "He wouldn't take it from me, but may he have it, nevertheless. Uncle Scrooge!"

Uncle Scrooge had imperceptibly become so gay and light of heart, that he would have pledged the unconscious company in return, and thanked them in an inaudible speech, if the Ghost had given him time. But the whole scene passed off in the breath of the last word spoken by his nephew; and he and the Spirit were again upon their travels.

Much they saw, and far they went, and many homes they visited, but always with a happy end. The Spirit stood beside sick beds, and they were cheerful; on foreign lands, and they were close at home; by struggling men, and they were patient in their greater hope; by poverty, and it was rich. In almshouse, hospital, and jail, in misery's every refuge, where vain man in his little brief authority[4] had not made fast the door, and barred the Spirit out, he left his blessing, and taught Scrooge his precepts.

It was a long night, if it were only a night; but Scrooge had his doubts of this, because the Christmas Holidays appeared to be condensed into the space of time they passed together. It was strange, too, that while Scrooge remained unaltered in his outward form, the Ghost grew older, clearly older. Scrooge had observed this change, but never spoke of it, until they left a children's Twelfth Night party, when, looking at the Spirit as they stood together in an open place, he noticed that its hair was gray.

"Are spirits' lives so short?" asked Scrooge.

"My life upon this globe, is very brief," replied the Ghost. "It ends to-night."

"To-night!" cried Scrooge.

"To-night at midnight. Hark! The time is drawing near."

The chimes were ringing the three quarters past eleven at that moment.

"Forgive me if I am not justified in what I ask," said Scrooge, looking intently at the Spirit's robe, "but I see something strange, and not belonging to yourself, protruding from your skirts. Is it a foot or a claw!"

"It might be a claw, for the flesh there is upon it," was the Spirit's sorrowful reply. "Look here."

---

4. *Measure for Measure*, 2.2.121–22: "but man, proud man, / Dress'd in a little brief authority."

From the foldings of its robe, it brought two children; wretched, abject, frightful, hideous, miserable. They knelt down at its feet, and clung upon the outside of its garment.

"Oh, Man! look here. Look, look, down here!" exclaimed the Ghost.

They were a boy and girl. Yellow, meagre, ragged, scowling, wolfish; but prostrate, too, in their humility. Where graceful youth should have filled their features out, and touched them with its freshest tints, a stale and shrivelled hand, like that of age, had pinched, and twisted them, and pulled them into shreds. Where angels might have sat enthroned, devils lurked; and glared out menacing. No change, no degradation, no perversion of humanity, in any grade, through all the mysteries of wonderful creation, has monsters half so horrible and dread.

Scrooge started back, appalled. Having them shown to him in this way, he tried to say they were fine children, but the words choked themselves, rather than be parties to a lie of such enormous magnitude.

"Spirit! are they yours?" Scrooge could say no more.

"They are Man's," said the Spirit, looking down upon them. "And they cling to me, appealing from their fathers. This boy is Ignorance. This girl is Want. Beware them both, and all of their degree, but most of all beware this boy, for on his brow I see that written which is Doom, unless the writing be erased. Deny it!" cried the Spirit, stretching out its hand towards the city. "Slander those who tell it ye! Admit it for your factious purposes, and make it worse. And bide the end!"

"Have they no refuge or resource?" cried Scrooge.

"Are there no prisons?" said the Spirit, turning on him for the last time with his own words. "Are there no workhouses?"

The bell struck twelve.

Scrooge looked about him for the Ghost, and saw it not. As the last stroke ceased to vibrate, he remembered the prediction of old Jacob Marley, and lifting up his eyes, beheld a solemn Phantom, draped and hooded, coming, like a mist along the ground, towards him.

Stave Four
THE LAST OF THE SPIRITS

The Phantom slowly, gravely, silently, approached. When it came near him, Scrooge bent down upon his knee; for in the very air through which this Spirit moved it seemed to scatter gloom and mystery.

It was shrouded in a deep black garment, which concealed its head, its face, its form, and left nothing of it visible save one outstretched hand. But for this it would have been difficult to detach its figure from the night, and separate it from the darkness by which it was surrounded.

He felt that it was tall and stately when it came beside him, and that its mysterious presence filled him with a solemn dread. He knew no more, for the Spirit neither spoke nor moved.

"I am in the presence of the Ghost of Christmas Yet To Come?" said Scrooge.

The Spirit answered not, but pointed onward with its hand.

"You are about to show me shadows of the things that have not happened, but will happen in the time before us," Scrooge pursued. "Is that so, Spirit?"

The upper portion of the garment was contracted for an instant in its folds, as if the Spirit had inclined its head. That was the only answer he received.

Although well used to ghostly company by this time, Scrooge feared the silent shape so much that his legs trembled beneath him, and he found that he could hardly stand when he prepared to follow it. The Spirit paused a moment, as observing his condition, and giving him time to recover.

But Scrooge was all the worse for this. It thrilled him with a vague uncertain horror, to know that behind the dusky shroud, there were ghostly eyes intently fixed upon him, while he, though he stretched his own to the utmost, could see nothing but a spectral hand and one great heap of black.

"Ghost of the Future!" he exclaimed, "I fear you more than any Spectre I have seen. But as I know your purpose is to do me good, and as I hope to live to be another man from what I was, I am prepared to bear you company, and do it with a thankful heart. Will you not speak to me?"

It gave him no reply. The hand was pointed straight before them.

"Lead on!" said Scrooge. "Lead on! The night is waning fast, and it is precious time to me, I know. Lead on, Spirit!"

The Phantom moved away as it had come towards him. Scrooge followed in the shadow of its dress, which bore him up, he thought, and carried him along.

They scarcely seemed to enter the city; for the city rather seemed to spring up about them, and encompass them of its own act. But there they were, in the heart of it; on 'Change, amongst the merchants; who hurried up and down, and chinked the money in their pockets, and conversed in groups, and looked at their watches, and trifled thoughtfully with their great gold seals; and so forth, as Scrooge had seen them often.

The Spirit stopped beside one little knot of business men. Observing that the hand was pointed to them, Scrooge advanced to listen to their talk.

"No," said a great fat man with a monstrous chin, "I don't know much about it, either way. I only know he's dead."

"When did he die?" inquired another.

"Last night, I believe."

"Why, what was the matter with him?" asked a third, taking a vast quantity of snuff out of a very large snuff-box. "I thought he'd never die."

"God knows," said the first, with a yawn.

"What has he done with his money?" asked a red-faced gentleman with a pendulous excrescence on the end of his nose, that shook like the gills of a turkey-cock.

"I haven't heard," said the man with the large chin, yawning again. "Left it to his Company, perhaps. He hasn't left it to *me*. That's all I know."

This pleasantry was received with a general laugh.

"It's likely to be a very cheap funeral," said the same speaker; "for upon my life I don't know of anybody to go to it. Suppose we make up a party and volunteer?"

"I don't mind going if a lunch is provided," observed the gentleman with the excrescence on his nose. "But I must be fed, if I make one."

Another laugh.

"Well, I am the most disinterested among you, after all," said the first speaker, "for I never wear black gloves, and I never eat lunch. But I'll offer to go, if anybody else will. When I come to think of it, I'm not at all sure that I wasn't his most particular friend; for we used to stop and speak whenever we met. Bye, bye!"

Speakers and listeners strolled away, and mixed with other groups. Scrooge knew the men, and looked towards the Spirit for an explanation.

The Phantom glided on into a street. Its finger pointed to two persons meeting. Scrooge listened again, thinking that the explanation might lie here.

He knew these men, also, perfectly. They were men of business: very wealthy, and of great importance. He had made a point always of standing well in their esteem: in a business point of view, that is; strictly in a business point of view.

"How are you?" said one.

"How are you?" returned the other.

"Well!" said the first. "Old Scratch[5] has got his own at last, hey?"

"So I am told," returned the second. "Cold, isn't it?"

"Seasonable for Christmas time. You're not a skaiter, I suppose?"

"No. No. Something else to think of. Good morning!"

Not another word. That was their meeting, their conversation, and their parting.

Scrooge was at first inclined to be surprised that the Spirit should attach importance to conversations apparently so trivial; but feeling assured that they must have some hidden purpose, he set himself to consider what it was likely to be. They could scarcely be supposed to have any bearing on the death of Jacob, his old partner, for that was Past, and this Ghost's province was the Future. Nor could he think of any one immediately connected with himself, to whom he could apply them. But nothing doubting that to whomsoever they applied they had some latent moral for his own improvement, he resolved to treasure up every word he heard, and everything he saw; and especially to observe the shadow of himself when it appeared. For he had an expectation that the conduct of his future self would give him the clue he missed, and would render the solution of these riddles easy.

He looked about in that very place for his own image; but another man stood in his accustomed corner, and though the clock pointed to his usual time of day for being there, he saw no likeness of himself among the multitudes that poured in through the Porch. It gave him little surprise, however; for he had been revolving in his mind a change of life, and thought and hoped he saw his new-born resolutions carried out in this.

Quiet and dark, beside him stood the Phantom, with its outstretched hand. When he roused himself from his thoughtful quest, he fancied from the turn of the hand, and its situation in reference to himself, that the Unseen Eyes were looking at him keenly. It made him shudder, and feel very cold.

They left the busy scene, and went into an obscure part of the town, where Scrooge had never penetrated before although he recognised its situation, and its bad repute. The ways were foul and narrow; the shops and houses wretched; the people half-naked, drunken, slipshod, ugly. Alleys and archways, like so many cesspools, disgorged their offences of smell, and dirt, and life, upon the straggling streets; and the whole quarter reeked with crime, with filth, and misery.

Far in this den of infamous resort, there was a low-browed, beetling shop, below a pent-house roof,[6] where iron, old rags, bottles, bones, and greasy offal, were bought. Upon the floor within, were piled up heaps of rusty keys, nails, chains, hinges, files, scales, weights, and refuse iron of all kinds. Secrets that few would like to scrutinise were bred and hidden in mountains of unseemly rags, masses of corrupted fat, and sepulchres of bones. Sitting in among the wares he dealt in, by a charcoal-stove, made of old bricks, was a gray-haired rascal, nearly seventy years of age; who had screened himself from the cold air without, by a frousy curtaining of miscellaneous tatters, hung upon a line; and smoked his pipe in all the luxury of calm retirement.

5. The devil.   6. A roof sloping out from a building.

Scrooge and the Phantom came into the presence of this man, just as a woman with a heavy bundle slunk into the shop. But she had scarcely entered, when another woman, similarly laden, came in too; and she was closely followed by a man in faded black, who was no less startled by the sight of them, than they had been upon the recognition of each other. After a short period of blank astonishment, in which the old man with the pipe had joined them, they all three burst into a laugh.

"Let the charwoman alone to be the first!" cried she who had entered first. "Let the laundress alone to be the second; and let the undertaker's man alone to be the third. Look here, old Joe, here's a chance! If we haven't all three met here without meaning it."

"You couldn't have met in a better place," said old Joe, removing his pipe from his mouth. "Come into the parlour. You were made free of it long ago, you know; and the other two an't strangers. Stop till I shut the door of the shop. Ah! How it skreeks! There an't such a rusty bit of metal in the place as its own hinges, I believe; and I'm sure there's no such old bones here, as mine. Ha, ha! We're all suitable to our calling, we're well matched. Come into the parlour. Come into the parlour."

The parlour was the space behind the screen of rags. The old man raked the fire together with an old stair-rod, and having trimmed his smoky lamp (for it was night), with the stem of his pipe, put it in his mouth again.

While he did this, the woman who had already spoken threw her bundle on the floor and sat down in a flaunting manner on a stool; crossing her elbows on her knees, and looking with a bold defiance at the other two.

"What odds then! What odds, Mrs Dilber?" said the woman. "Every person has a right to take care of themselves. *He* always did!"

"That's true, indeed!" said the laundress. "No man more so."

"Why then, don't stand staring as if you was afraid, woman; who's the wiser? We're not going to pick holes in each other's coats, I suppose?"

"No, indeed!" said Mrs Dilber and the man together. "We should hope not."

"Very well, then!" cried the woman. "That's enough. Who's the worse for the loss of a few things like these? Not a dead man, I suppose."

"No, indeed," said Mrs Dilber, laughing.

"If he wanted to keep 'em after he was dead, a wicked old screw," pursued the woman, "why wasn't he natural in his lifetime? If he had been, he'd have had somebody to look after him when he was struck with Death, instead of lying gasping out his last there, alone by himself."

"It's the truest word that ever was spoke," said Mrs Dilber. "It's a judgment on him."

"I wish it was a little heavier one," replied the woman; "and it should have been, you may depend upon it, if I could have laid my hands on anything else. Open that bundle, old Joe, and let me know the value of it. Speak out plain. I'm not afraid to be the first, nor afraid for them to see it. We knew pretty well that we were helping ourselves, before we met here, I believe. It's no sin. Open the bundle, Joe."

But the gallantry of her friends would not allow of this; and the man in faded black, mounting the breach first, produced *his* plunder. It was not extensive. A seal or two, a pencil-case, a pair of sleeve-buttons, and a brooch of no great value, were all. They were severally examined and appraised by old Joe, who chalked the sums he was disposed to give for each, upon the wall, and added them up into a total when he found there was nothing more to come.

"That's your account," said Joe, "and I wouldn't give another sixpence, if I was to be boiled for not doing it. Who's next?"

Mrs Dilber was next. Sheets and towels, a little wearing apparel, two old-fashioned silver teaspoons, a pair of sugar-tongs, and a few boots. Her account was stated on the wall in the same manner.

"I always give too much to ladies. It's a weakness of mine, and that's the way I ruin myself," said old Joe. "That's your account. If you asked me for another penny, and made it an open question, I'd repent of being so liberal and knock off half-a-crown."

"And now undo *my* bundle, Joe," said the first woman.

Joe went down on his knees for the greater convenience of opening it, and having unfastened a great many knots, dragged out a large and heavy roll of some dark stuff.

"What do you call this?" said Joe. "Bed-curtains!"

"Ah!" returned the woman, laughing and leaning forward on her crossed arms. "Bed-curtains!"

"You don't mean to say you took 'em down, rings and all, with him lying there?" said Joe.

"Yes I do," replied the woman. "Why not?"

"You were born to make your fortune," said Joe, "and you'll certainly do it."

"I certainly shan't hold my hand, when I get anything in it by reaching it out, for the sake of such a man as He was, I promise you, Joe," returned the woman coolly. "Don't drop that oil upon the blankets, now."

"His blankets?" asked Joe.

"Whose else's do you think?" replied the woman. "He isn't likely to take cold without 'em, I dare say."

"I hope he didn't die of anything catching? Eh?" said old Joe, stopping in his work, and looking up.

"Don't you be afraid of that," returned the woman. "I an't so fond of his company that I'd loiter about him for such things, if he did. Ah! you may look through that shirt till your eyes ache; but you won't find a hole in it, nor a threadbare place. It's the best he had, and a fine one too. They'd have wasted it, if it hadn't been for me."

"What do you call wasting of it?" asked old Joe.

"Putting it on him to be buried in, to be sure," replied the woman with a laugh. "Somebody was fool enough to do it, but I took it off again. If calico an't good enough for such a purpose, it isn't good enough for anything. It's quite as becoming to the body. He can't look uglier than he did in that one."

Scrooge listened to this dialogue in horror. As they sat grouped about their spoil, in the scanty light afforded by the old man's lamp, he viewed them with a detestation and disgust, which could hardly have been greater, though they had been obscene demons, marketing the corpse itself.

"He, ha!" laughed the same woman, when old Joe, producing a flannel bag with money in it, told out their several gains upon the ground. "This is the end of it, you see! He frightened every one away from him when he was alive, to profit us when he was dead! Ha, ha, ha!"

"Spirit!" said Scrooge, shuddering from head to foot. "I see, I see. The case of this unhappy man might be my own. My life tends that way, now. Merciful Heaven, what is this!"

He recoiled in terror, for the scene had changed, and now he almost touched a bed: a bare, uncurtained bed: on which, beneath a ragged sheet, there lay a some-thing covered up, which, though it was dumb, announced itself in awful language.

The room was very dark, too dark to be observed with any accuracy, though Scrooge glanced round it in obedience to a secret impulse, anxious to know what kind of room it was. A pale light, rising in the outer air, fell straight upon the bed; and on it, plundered and bereft, unwatched, unwept, uncared for, was the body of this man.

Scrooge glanced towards the Phantom. Its steady hand was pointed to the head. The cover was so carelessly adjusted that the slightest raising of it, the motion of a finger upon Scrooge's part, would have disclosed the face. He thought of it, felt how easy it would be to do, and longed to do it; but had no more power to withdraw the veil than to dismiss the spectre at his side.

Oh cold, cold, rigid, dreadful Death, set up thine altar here, and dress it with such terrors as thou hast at thy command: for this is thy dominion! But of the loved, revered, and honoured head, thou canst not turn one hair to thy dread purposes, or make one feature odious. It is not that the hand is heavy and will fall down when released; it is not that the heart and pulse are still; but that the hand WAS open, generous, and true; the heart brave, warm, and tender; and the pulse a man's. Strike, Shadow, strike! And see his good deeds springing from the wound, to sow the world with life immortal!

No voice pronounced these words in Scrooge's ears, and yet he heard them when he looked upon the bed. He thought, if this man could be raised up now, what would be his foremost thoughts? Avarice, hard dealing, griping cares? They have brought him to a rich end, truly!

He lay, in the dark empty house, with not a man, a woman, or a child, to say that he was kind to me in this or that, and for the memory of one kind word I will be kind to him. A cat was tearing at the door, and there was a sound of gnawing rats beneath the hearth-stone. What *they* wanted in the room of death, and why they were so restless and disturbed, Scrooge did not dare to think.

"Spirit!" he said, "this is a fearful place. In leaving it, I shall not leave its lesson, trust me. Let us go!"

Still the Ghost pointed with an unmoved finger to the head.

"I understand you," Scrooge returned, "and I would do it, if I could. But I have not the power, Spirit. I have not the power."

Again it seemed to look upon him.

"If there is any person in the town, who feels emotion caused by this man's death," said Scrooge quite agonised, "show that person to me, Spirit, I beseech you!"

The Phantom spread its dark robe before him for a moment, like a wing; and withdrawing it, revealed a room by daylight, where a mother and her children were.

She was expecting some one, and with anxious eagerness; for she walked up and down the room; started at every sound; looked out from the window; glanced at the clock; tried, but in vain, to work with her needle; and could hardly bear the voices of the children in their play.

At length the long-expected knock was heard. She hurried to the door, and met her husband; a man whose face was care-worn and depressed, though he was young. There was a remarkable expression in it now; a kind of serious delight of which he felt ashamed, and which he struggled to repress.

He sat down to the dinner that had been hoarding for him by the fire; and when she asked him faintly what news (which was not until after a long silence), he appeared embarrassed how to answer.

"Is it good," she said, "or bad?"—to help him.

"Bad," he answered.

"We are quite ruined?"

"No. There is hope yet, Caroline."

"If *he* relents," she said, amazed, "there is! Nothing is past hope, if such a miracle has happened."

"He is past relenting," said her husband. "He is dead."

She was a mild and patient creature if her face spoke truth; but she was thankful in her soul to hear it, and she said so, with clasped hands. She prayed forgiveness the next moment, and was sorry; but the first was the emotion of her heart.

"What the half-drunken woman whom I told you of last night, said to me, when I tried to see him and obtain a week's delay; and what I thought was a mere excuse to avoid me; turns out to have been quite true. He was not only very ill, but dying, then."

"To whom will our debt be transferred?"

"I don't know. But before that time we shall be ready with the money; and even though we were not, it would be bad fortune indeed to find so merciless a creditor in his successor. We may sleep to-night with light hearts, Caroline!"

Yes. Soften it as they would, their hearts were lighter. The children's faces, hushed and clustered round to hear what they so little understood, were brighter; and it was a happier house for this man's death! The only emotion that the Ghost could show him, caused by the event, was one of pleasure.

"Let me see some tenderness connected with a death," said Scrooge; "or that dark chamber, Spirit, which we left just now, will be for ever present to me."

The Ghost conducted him through several streets familiar to his feet; and as they went along, Scrooge looked here and there to find himself, but nowhere was he to be seen. They entered poor Bob Cratchit's house; the dwelling he had visited before; and found the mother and the children seated round the fire.

Quiet. Very quiet. The noisy little Cratchits were as still as statues in one corner, and sat looking up at Peter, who had a book before him. The mother and her daughters were engaged in sewing. But surely they were very quiet!

"'And He took a child, and set him in the midst of them.'"[7]

Where had Scrooge heard those words? He had not dreamed them. The boy must have read them out, as he and the Spirit crossed the threshold. Why did he not go on?

The mother laid her work upon the table, and put her hand up to her face.

"The colour hurts my eyes," she said.

The colour? Ah, poor Tiny Tim!

"They're better now again," said Cratchit's wife. "It makes them weak by candle-light; and I wouldn't show weak eyes to your father when he comes home, for the world. It must be near his time."

"Past it rather," Peter answered, shutting up his book. "But I think he's walked a little slower than he used, these few last evenings, mother."

They were very quiet again. At last she said, and in a steady, cheerful voice, that only faultered once:

"I have known him walk with—I have known him walk with Tiny Tim upon his shoulder, very fast indeed."

"And so have I," cried Peter. "Often."

"And so have I!" exclaimed another. So had all.

"But he was very light to carry," she resumed, intent upon her work, "and his father loved him so, that it was no trouble—no trouble. And there is your father at the door!"

7. Matthew 18.2.

She hurried out to meet him; and little Bob in his comforter—he had need of it, poor fellow—came in. His tea was ready for him on the hob, and they all tried who should help him to it most. Then the two young Cratchits got upon his knees and laid, each child a little cheek, against his face, as if they said, "Don't mind it, father. Don't be grieved!"

Bob was very cheerful with them, and spoke pleasantly to all the family. He looked at the work upon the table, and praised the industry and speed of Mrs Cratchit and the girls. They would be done long before Sunday, he said.

"Sunday! You went to-day then, Robert?" said his wife.

"Yes, my dear," returned Bob. "I wish you could have gone. It would have done you good to see how green a place it is. But you'll see it often. I promised him that I would walk there on a Sunday. My little, little child!" cried Bob. "My little child!"

He broke down all at once. He couldn't help it. If he could have helped it, he and his child would have been farther apart perhaps than they were.

He left the room, and went up stairs into the room above, which was lighted cheerfully, and hung with Christmas. There was a chair set close beside the child, and there were signs of some one having been there, lately. Poor Bob sat down in it, and when he had thought a little and composed himself, he kissed the little face. He was reconciled to what had happened, and went down again quite happy.

They drew about the fire, and talked; the girls and mother working still. Bob told them of the extraordinary kindness of Mr Scrooge's nephew, whom he had scarcely seen but once, and who, meeting him in the street that day, and seeing that he looked a little—"just a little down you know" said Bob, inquired what had happened to distress him. "On which," said Bob, "for he is the pleasantest-spoken gentleman you ever heard, I told him. 'I am heartily sorry for it, Mr Cratchit,' he said, 'and heartily sorry for your good wife.' By the bye, how he ever knew *that*, I don't know."

"Knew what, my dear."

"Why, that you were a good wife," replied Bob.

"Everybody knows that!" said Peter.

"Very well observed, my boy!" cried Bob. "I hope they do. 'Heartily sorry,' he said, 'for your good wife. If I can be of any service to you in any way,' he said, giving me his card, 'that's where I live. Pray come to me.' Now, it wasn't," cried Bob, "for the sake of anything he might be able to do for us, so much as for his kind way, that this was quite delightful. It really seemed as if he had known our Tiny Tim, and felt with us."

"I'm sure he's a good soul!" said Mrs Cratchit.

"You would be surer of it, my dear," returned Bob, "if you saw and spoke to him. I shouldn't be at all surprised, mark what I say, if he got Peter a better situation."

"Only hear that, Peter," said Mrs Cratchit.

"And then," cried one of the girls, "Peter will be keeping company with some one, and setting up for himself."

"Get along with you!" retorted Peter, grinning.

"It's just as likely as not," said Bob, "one of these days; though there's plenty of time for that, my dear. But however and whenever we part from one another, I am sure we shall none of us forget poor Tiny Tim—shall we—or this first parting that there was among us?"

"Never, father!" cried they all.

"And I know," said Bob, "I know, my dears, that when we recollect how patient and how mild he was; although he was a little, little child; we shall not quarrel easily among ourselves, and forget poor Tiny Tim in doing it."

"No, never, father!" they all cried again.

"I am very happy," said little Bob, "I am very happy!"

Mrs Cratchit kissed him, his daughters kissed him, the two young Cratchits kissed him, and Peter and himself shook hands. Spirit of Tiny Tim, thy childish essence was from God!

"Spectre," said Scrooge, "something informs me that our parting moment is at hand. I know it, but I know not how. Tell me what man that was whom we saw lying dead?"

The Ghost of Christmas Yet To Come conveyed him, as before—though at a different time, he thought: indeed, there seemed no order in these latter visions, save that they were in the Future—into the resorts of business men, but showed him not himself. Indeed, the Spirit did not stay for anything, but went straight on, as to the end just now desired, until besought by Scrooge to tarry for a moment.

"This court," said Scrooge, "through which we hurry now, is where my place of occupation is, and has been for a length of time. I see the house. Let me behold what I shall be, in days to come."

The Spirit stopped; the hand was pointed elsewhere.

"The house is yonder," Scrooge exclaimed. "Why do you point away?"

The inexorable finger underwent no change.

Scrooge hastened to the window of his office, and looked in. It was an office still, but not his. The furniture was not the same, and the figure in the chair was not himself. The Phantom pointed as before.

He joined it once again, and wondering why and whither he had gone, accompanied it until they reached an iron gate. He paused to look round before entering.

A churchyard. Here, then, the wretched man whose name he had now to learn, lay underneath the ground. It was a worthy place. Walled in by houses; overrun by grass and weeds, the growth of vegetation's death, not life; choked up with too much burying; fat with repleted appetite. A worthy place!

The Spirit stood among the graves, and pointed down to One. He advanced towards it trembling. The Phantom was exactly as it had been, but he dreaded that he saw new meaning in its solemn shape.

"Before I draw nearer to that stone to which you point," said Scrooge, "answer me one question. Are these the shadows of the things that Will be, or are they shadows of things that May be, only?"

Still the Ghost pointed downward to the grave by which it stood.

"Men's courses will foreshadow certain ends, to which, if persevered in, they must lead," said Scrooge. "But if the courses be departed from, the ends will change. Say it is thus with what you show me!"

The Spirit was immovable as ever.

Scrooge crept towards it, trembling as he went; and following the finger, read upon the stone of the neglected grave his own name, EBENEZER SCROOGE.

"Am I that man who lay upon the bed?" he cried, upon his knees.

The finger pointed from the grave to him, and back again.

"No, Spirit! Oh, no, no!"

The finger still was there.

"Spirit!" he cried, tight clutching at its robe, "hear me! I am not the man I was. I will not be the man I must have been but for this intercourse. Why show me this, if I am past all hope?"

For the first time the hand appeared to shake.

"Good Spirit," he pursued, as down upon the ground he fell before it: "Your nature intercedes for me, and pities me. Assure me that I yet may change these shadows you have shown me, by an altered life!"

The kind hand trembled.

"I will honour Christmas in my heart, and try to keep it all the year. I will live in the Past, Present, and the Future. The Spirits of all Three shall strive within me. I will not shut out the lessons that they teach. Oh, tell me I may sponge away the writing on this stone!"

In his agony, he caught the spectral hand. It sought to free itself, but he was strong in his entreaty, and detained it. The Spirit, stronger yet, repulsed him.

Holding up his hands in a last prayer to have his fate reversed, he saw an alteration in the Phantom's hood and dress. It shrunk, collapsed, and dwindled down into a bedpost.

Stave Five
THE END OF IT

Yes! and the bedpost was his own. The bed was his own, the room was his own. Best and happiest of all, the Time before him was his own, to make amends in!

"I will live in the Past, the Present, and the Future!" Scrooge repeated, as he scrambled out of bed. "The Spirits of all Three shall strive within me. Oh Jacob Marley! Heaven, and the Christmas Time be praised for this! I say it on my knees, old Jacob; on my knees!"

He was so fluttered and so glowing with his good intentions, that his broken voice would scarcely answer to his call. He had been sobbing violently in his conflict with the Spirit, and his face was wet with tears.

"They are not torn down," cried Scrooge, folding one of his bed-curtains in his arms, "they are not torn down, rings and all. They are here: I am here: the shadows of the things that would have been, may be dispelled. They will be. I know they will!"

His hands were busy with his garments all this time: turning them inside out, putting them on upside down, tearing them, mislaying them, making them parties to every kind of extravagance.

"I don't know what to do!" cried Scrooge, laughing and crying in the same breath; and making a perfect Laocoön of himself with his stockings.[8] I am as light as a feather, I am as happy as an angel, I am as merry as a school-boy. I am as giddy as a drunken man. A merry Christmas to everybody! A happy New Year to all the world! Hallo here! Whoop! Hallo!"

He had frisked into the sitting-room, and was now standing there: perfectly winded.

"There's the saucepan that the gruel was in!" cried Scrooge, starting off again, and frisking round the fire-place. "There's the door, by which the Ghost of Jacob Marley entered! There's the corner where the Ghost of Christmas Present, sat! There's the window where I saw the wandering Spirits! It's all right, it's all true, it all happened. Ha ha ha!"

Really, for a man who had been out of practice for so many years, it was a splendid laugh, a most illustrious laugh. The father of a long, long line of brilliant laughs!

---

8. Scrooge struggles with his stockings as Laocoön struggles with two sea serpents (see Virgil's *Aeneid*, Book 2).

"I don't know what day of the month it is!" said Scrooge. "I don't know how long I've been among the Spirits. I don't know anything. I'm quite a baby. Never mind. I don't care. I'd rather be a baby. Hallo! Whoop! Hallo here!"

He was checked in his transports by the churches ringing out the lustiest peals he had ever heard. Clash, clang, hammer, ding, dong, bell. Bell, dong, ding, hammer, clang, clash! Oh, glorious, glorious!

Running to the window, he opened it, and put out his head. No fog, no mist; clear, bright, jovial, stirring, cold; cold, piping for the blood to dance to; Golden sunlight; Heavenly sky; sweet fresh air; merry bells. Oh, glorious. Glorious!

"What's to-day?" cried Scrooge, calling downward to a boy in Sunday clothes, who perhaps had loitered in to look about him.

"EH?" returned the boy, with all his might of wonder.

"What's to-day, my fine fellow?" said Scrooge.

"To-day!" replied the boy. "Why, CHRISTMAS DAY."

"It's Christmas Day!" said Scrooge to himself. "I haven't missed it. The Spirits have done it all in one night. They can do anything they like. Of course they can. Of course they can. Hallo, my fine fellow!"

"Hallo!" returned the boy.

"Do you know the Poulterer's, in the next street but one, at the corner?" Scrooge inquired.

"I should hope I did," replied the lad.

"An intelligent boy!" said Scrooge. "A remarkable boy! Do you know whether they've sold the prize Turkey that was hanging up there? Not the little prize Turkey: the big one?"

"What, the one as big as me?" returned the boy.

"What a delightful boy!" said Scrooge. "It's a pleasure to talk to him. Yes, my buck!"

"It's hanging there now," replied the boy.

"Is it?" said Scrooge. "Go and buy it."

"Walk-ER!"[9] exclaimed the boy.

"No, no," said Scrooge, "I am in earnest. Go and buy it, and tell 'em to bring it here, that I may give them the direction where to take it. Come back with the man, and I'll give you a shilling. Come back with him in less than five minutes, and I'll give you half-a-crown!"

The boy was off like a shot. He must have had a steady hand at a trigger who could have got a shot off half so fast.

"I'll send it to Bob Cratchit's!" whispered Scrooge, rubbing his hands, and splitting with a laugh. "He shan't know who sends it. It's twice the size of Tiny Tim. Joe Miller[1] never made such a joke as sending it to Bob's will be!"

The hand in which he wrote the address was not a steady one, but write it he did, somehow, and went down stairs to open the street door, ready for the coming of the poulterer's man. As he stood there, waiting his arrival, the knocker caught his eye.

"I shall love it, as long as I live!" cried Scrooge, patting it with his hand. "I scarcely ever looked at it before. What an honest expression it has in its face! It's a wonderful knocker!—Here's the Turkey. Hallo! Whoop! How are you! Merry Christmas!"

It *was* a Turkey! He never could have stood upon his legs, that bird. He would have snapped 'em short off in a minute, like sticks of sealing-wax.

---

9. Cockney exclamation of incredulity.   1. Eighteenth-century actor and comedian. *Joe Miller's Jests* (1739) was a popular jokebook.

"Why, it's impossible to carry that to Camden Town," said Scrooge. "You must have a cab."

The chuckle with which he said this, and the chuckle with which he paid for the Turkey, and the chuckle with which he paid for the cab, and the chuckle with which he recompensed the boy, were only to be exceeded by the chuckle with which he sat down breathless in his chair again, and chuckled till he cried.

Shaving was not an easy task, for his hand continued to shake very much; and shaving requires attention, even when you don't dance while you are at it. But if he had cut the end of his nose off, he would have put a piece of sticking-plaister over it, and been quite satisfied.

He dressed himself "all in his best," and at last got out into the streets. The people were by this time pouring forth, as he had seen them with the Ghost of Christmas Present; and walking with his hands behind him, Scrooge regarded every one with a delighted smile. He looked so irresistibly pleasant, in a word, that three or four good-humoured fellows said, "Good morning, sir! A merry Christmas to you!" And Scrooge said often afterwards, that of all the blithe sounds he had ever heard, those were the blithest in his ears.

He had not gone far, when coming on towards him he beheld the portly gentleman, who had walked into his counting-house the day before and said, "Scrooge and Marley's, I believe?" It sent a pang across his heart to think how this old gentleman would look upon him when they met; but he knew what path lay straight before him, and he took it.

"My dear sir," said Scrooge, quickening his pace, and taking the old gentleman by both his hands. "How do you do? I hope you succeeded yesterday. It was very kind of you. A merry Christmas to you, sir!"

"Mr Scrooge?"

"Yes," said Scrooge. "That is my name, and I fear it may not be pleasant to you. Allow me to ask your pardon. And will you have the goodness"—here Scrooge whispered in his ear.

"Lord bless me!" cried the gentleman, as if his breath were gone. "My dear Mr Scrooge, are you serious?"

"If you please," said Scrooge. "Not a farthing less. A great many back-payments are included in it, I assure you. Will you do me that favour?"

"My dear sir," said the other, shaking hands with him. "I don't know what to say to such munifi—"

"Don't say anything, please," retorted Scrooge. "Come and see me. Will you come and see me?"

"I will!" cried the old gentleman. And it was clear he meant to do it.

"Thank'ee," said Scrooge. "I am much obliged to you. I thank you fifty times. Bless you!"

He went to church, and walked about the streets, and watched the people hurrying to and fro, and patted children on the head, and questioned beggars, and looked down into the kitchens of houses, and up to the windows; and found that everything could yield him pleasure. He had never dreamed that any walk—that anything—could give him so much happiness. In the afternoon, he turned his steps towards his nephew's house.

He passed the door a dozen times, before he had the courage to go up and knock. But he made a dash, and did it:

"Is your master at home, my dear?" said Scrooge to the girl. Nice girl! Very.

"Yes, sir."

"Where is he, my love?" said Scrooge.

"He's in the dining-room, sir, along with mistress. I'll show you up stairs, if you please."

"Thank'ee. He knows me," said Scrooge, with his hand already on the dining-room lock. "I'll go in here, my dear."

He turned it gently, and sidled his face in, round the door. They were looking at the table (which was spread out in great array); for these young housekeepers are always nervous on such points, and like to see that everything is right.

"Fred!" said Scrooge.

Dear heart alive, how his niece by marriage started! Scrooge had forgotten, for the moment, about her sitting in the corner with the footstool, or he wouldn't have done it, on any account.[2]

"Why bless my soul!" cried Fred, "who's that?"

"It's I. Your uncle Scrooge. I have come to dinner. Will you let me in, Fred?"

Let him in! It is a mercy he didn't shake his arm off. He was at home in five minutes. Nothing could be heartier. His niece looked just the same. So did Topper when *he* came. So did the plump sister, when *she* came. So did every one when *they* came. Wonderful party, wonderful games, wonderful unanimity, won-der-ful happiness!

But he was early at the office next morning. Oh, he was early there. If he could only be there first, and catch Bob Cratchit coming late! That was the thing he had set his heart upon.

And he did it; yes, he did! The clock struck nine. No Bob. A quarter past. No Bob. He was full eighteen minutes and a half behind his time. Scrooge sat with his door wide open, that he might see him come into the Tank.

His hat was off, before he opened the door; his comforter too. He was on his stool in a jiffy; driving away with his pen, as if he were trying to overtake nine o'clock.

"Hallo!" growled Scrooge, in his accustomed voice as near as he could feign it. "What do you mean by coming here at this time of day?"

"I am very sorry, sir," said Bob. "I *am* behind my time."

"You are?" repeated Scrooge. "Yes. I think you are. Step this way, if you please."

"It's only once a year, sir," pleaded Bob, appearing from the Tank. "It shall not be repeated. I was making rather merry yesterday, sir."

"Now, I'll tell you what, my friend," said Scrooge, "I am not going to stand this sort of thing any longer. And therefore," he continued, leaping from his stool, and giving Bob such a dig in the waistcoat that he staggered back into the Tank again: "and therefore I am about to raise your salary!"

Bob trembled, and got a little nearer to the ruler. He had a momentary idea of knocking Scrooge down with it; holding him; and calling to the people in the court for help and a strait-waistcoat.

"A merry Christmas, Bob!" said Scrooge, with an earnestness that could not be mistaken, as he clapped him on the back. "A merrier Christmas, Bob, my good fellow, than I have given you, for many a year! I'll raise your salary, and endeavour to assist your struggling family, and we will discuss your affairs this very afternoon, over a Christmas bowl of smoking bishop,[3] Bob! Make up the fires, and buy another coal-scuttle before you dot another i, Bob Cratchit!"

---

2. Scrooge alludes to the fact that Fred's wife is pregnant.   3. A hot punch made of red wine, oranges, sugar, and spices.

Scrooge was better than his word. He did it all, and infinitely more; and to Tiny Tim, who did NOT die, he was a second father. He became as good a friend, as good a master, and as good a man, as the good old city knew, or any other good old city, town, or borough, in the good old world. Some people laughed to see the alteration in him, but he let them laugh, and little heeded them; for he was wise enough to know that nothing ever happened on this globe, for good, at which some people did not have their fill of laughter in the outset; and knowing that such as these would be blind anyway, he thought it quite as well that they should wrinkle up their eyes in grins, as have the malady in less attractive forms. His own heart laughed: and that was quite enough for him.

He had no further intercourse with Spirits, but lived upon the Total Absti-nence Principle, ever afterwards; and it was always said of him, that he knew how to keep Christmas well, if any man alive possessed the knowledge. May that be truly said of us, and all of us! And so, as Tiny Tim observed, God bless Us, Every One!

The End

1843

✦✦✦

Sir Arthur Conan Doyle
1859–1930

Sherlock Holmes may not have been the first detective in English fiction, but he quickly became *the* detective, a near-mythic character whose cloak and deerstalker cap, pipe and magnifying glass have defined our image of the "private eye" for over a century. Edgar Allan Poe, Charles Dickens, and Wilkie Collins had preceded Doyle in creating detectives of their own, but Doyle's genius was to construct a rational aesthete: Holmes's languid manner and bohemian tastes suggest *fin de siècle* decadence, but his suave imperturbability stems from his extraordinary powers of reasoning and observation. A quintessentially urban figure, Sherlock Holmes penetrates the foggy chaos of London with his mastery of disguise and his uncanny ability to guess occupations through telltale signs. In an urban world of anonymous strangers, Holmes can "place" people instantly, deciphering the clues to identity that elude and perplex the ordinary observer. Like his plodding sidekick Watson, readers trail along in the wake of Holmes's deft ratiocinations, awed and reas-sured by his effortless omniscience. His successful detections keep at bay threats to middle-class values and social harmony; he offers a comforting promise of legibility, order, and justice.

Holmes's adventures appeared monthly in *The Strand Magazine*, and they were the making of Arthur Conan Doyle, a doctor-turned-writer who capitalized on the Victorian fascination with crime. So wildly popular was his brilliant investigator that when Doyle grew bored and decided to slay his hero, the public wore mourning-bands, and Doyle was forced to revive him. Indeed, Sherlock Holmes has always seemed oddly more real than his creator: T. S. Eliot wrote that when we talk of Holmes, "we invariably fall into the fancy of his existence." To this day, thousands of letters are addressed to him at 221B Baker Street.

A Scandal in Bohemia[1]

To Sherlock Holmes she is always *the* woman. I have seldom heard him mention her under any other name. In his eyes she eclipses and predominates the whole of her sex. It was not that he felt any emotion akin to love for Irene Adler. All emotions, and that one particularly, were abhorrent to his cold, precise, but admirably balanced mind. He was, I take it, the most perfect reasoning and observing machine that the world has seen; but, as a lover, he would have placed himself in a false position. He never spoke of the softer passions, save with a gibe and a sneer. They were admirable things for the observer—excellent for drawing the veil from men's motives and actions. But for the trained reasoner to admit such intrusions into his own delicate and finely adjusted temperament was to introduce a distracting factor which might throw a doubt upon all his mental results. Grit in a sensitive instrument, or a crack in one of his own high-power lenses, would not be more disturbing than a strong emotion in a nature such as his. And yet there was but one woman to him, and that woman was the late Irene Adler, of dubious and questionable memory.

I had seen little of Holmes lately. My marriage had drifted us away from each other. My own complete happiness, and the home-centred interests which rise up around the man who first finds himself master of his own establishment, were sufficient to absorb all my attention; while Holmes, who loathed every form of society with his whole Bohemian soul,[2] remained in our lodgings in Baker-street, buried among his old books, and alternating from week to week between cocaine and ambition, the drowsiness of the drug, and the fierce energy of his own keen nature. He was still, as ever, deeply attracted by the study of crime, and occupied his immense faculties and extraordinary powers of observation in following out those clues, and clearing up those mysteries, which had been abandoned as hopeless by the official police. From time to time I heard some vague account of his doings: of his summons to Odessa in the case of the Trepoff murder, of his clearing up of the singular tragedy of the Atkinson brothers at Trincomalee, and finally of the mission which he had accomplished so delicately and successfully for the reigning family of Holland. Beyond these signs of his activity, however, which I merely shared with all the readers of the daily press, I knew little of my former friend and companion.

One night—it was on the 20th of March, 1888—I was returning from a journey to a patient (for I had now returned to civil practice),[3] when my way led me through Baker-street. As I passed the well-remembered door, which must always be associated in my mind with my wooing, and with the dark incidents of the Study in Scarlet,[4] I was seized with a keen desire to see Holmes again, and to know how he was employing his extraordinary powers. His rooms were brilliantly lit, and, even as I looked up, I saw his tall spare figure pass twice in a dark silhouette against the blind. He was pacing the room swiftly, eagerly, with his head sunk upon his chest, and his hands clasped behind him. To me, who knew his every mood and habit, his attitude and manner told their own story. He was at work again. He had arisen out of his drug-created dreams, and was hot upon the scent of some new problem. I rang the bell, and was shown up to the chamber which had formerly been in part my own.

1. First published in *The Strand Magazine* in July 1891.
2. Like the artists in Henri Murger's *Scènes de la vie de Bohème* (1848), Holmes's tastes are aesthetic and eccentric. His bohemianism contrasts with the conventional soul of the King of Bohemia later in the story.

3. Watson, who had been invalided out of the Army medical corps, had resumed private practice upon his marriage.
4. Doyle's first Sherlock Holmes novel (1887).

His manner was not effusive. It seldom was; but he was glad, I think, to see me. With hardly a word spoken, but with a kindly eye, he waved me to an armchair, threw across his case of cigars, and indicated a spirit case and a gasogene in the corner.[5] Then he stood before the fire, and looked me over in his singular introspective fashion.

"Wedlock suits you," he remarked. "I think, Watson, that you have put on seven and a half pounds since I saw you."

"Seven," I answered.

"Indeed, I should have thought a little more. Just a trifle more, I fancy, Watson. And in practice again, I observe. You did not tell me that you intended to go into harness."

"Then, how do you know?"

"I see it, I deduce it. How do I know that you have been getting yourself very wet lately, and that you have a most clumsy and careless servant girl?"

"My dear Holmes," said I, "this is too much. You would certainly have been burned, had you lived a few centuries ago.[6] It is true that I had a country walk on Thursday and came home in a dreadful mess; but, as I have changed my clothes, I can't imagine how you deduce it. As to Mary Jane, she is incorrigible, and my wife has given her notice; but there again I fail to see how you work it out."

He chuckled to himself and rubbed his long nervous hands together.

"It is simplicity itself," said he; "my eyes tell me that on the inside of your left shoe, just where the fire-light strikes it, the leather is scored by six almost parallel cuts. Obviously they have been caused by someone who has very carelessly scraped round the edges of the sole in order to remove crusted mud from it. Hence, you see, my double deduction that you had been out in vile weather, and that you had a particularly malignant boot-slitting specimen of the London slavey.[7] As to your practice, if a gentleman walks into my rooms smelling of iodoform, with a black mark of nitrate of silver upon his right fore-finger, and a bulge on the side of his top-hat to show where he has secreted his stethoscope, I must be dull indeed, if I do not pronounce him to be an active member of the medical profession."

I could not help laughing at the ease with which he explained his process of deduction. "When I hear you give your reasons," I remarked, "the thing always appears to me to be so ridiculously simple that I could easily do it myself, though at each successive instance of your reasoning I am baffled, until you explain your process. And yet I believe that my eyes are as good as yours."

"Quite so," he answered, lighting a cigarette, and throwing himself down into an armchair. "You see, but you do not observe. The distinction is clear. For example, you have frequently seen the steps which lead up from the hall to this room."

"Frequently."

"How often?"

"Well, some hundreds of times."

"Then how many are there?"

"How many! I don't know."

"Quite so! You have not observed. And yet you have seen. That is just my point. Now, I know that there are seventeen steps, because I have both seen and observed.

5. I.e., he invited Watson to make himself a drink (a gasogene makes carbonated water).
6. I.e., his uncanny powers would have led to his being

burned at the stake as a warlock.
7. Maidservant.

By the way, since you are interested in these little problems, and since you are good enough to chronicle one or two of my trifling experiences, you may be interested in this." He threw over a sheet of thick pink-tinted notepaper which had been lying open upon the table. "It came by the last post," said he. "Read it aloud."

The note was undated, and without either signature or address.

"There will call upon you to-night, at a quarter to eight o'clock," it said, "a gentleman who desires to consult you upon a matter of the very deepest moment. Your recent services to one of the Royal Houses of Europe have shown that you are one who may safely be trusted with matters which are of an importance which can hardly be exaggerated. This account of you we have from all quarters received. Be in your chamber then at that hour, and do not take it amiss if your visitor wear a mask."

"This is indeed a mystery," I remarked. "What do you imagine that it means?"

"I have no data yet. It is a capital mistake to theorise before one has data. Insensibly one begins to twist facts to suit theories, instead of theories to suit facts. But the note itself. What do you deduce from it?"

I carefully examined the writing, and the paper upon which it was written.

"The man who wrote it was presumably well to do," I remarked, endeavouring to imitate my companion's processes. "Such paper could not be bought under half a crown a packet. It is peculiarly strong and stiff."

"Peculiar—that is the very word," said Holmes. "It is not an English paper at all. Hold it up to the light."

I did so, and saw a large E with a small g, a P, and a large G with a small t woven into the texture of the paper.

"What do you make of that?" asked Holmes.

"The name of the maker, no doubt; or his monogram, rather."

"Not at all. The G with the small t stands for 'Gesellschaft,' which is the German for 'Company.' It is a customary contraction like our 'Co.' P, of course, stands for 'Papier.' Now for the Eg. Let us glance at our Continental Gazetteer." He took down a heavy brown volume from his shelves. "Eglow, Eglonitz—here we are, Egria. It is in a German-speaking country—in Bohemia,[8] not far from Carlsbad. 'Remarkable as being the scene of the death of Wallenstein, and for its numerous glass factories and paper mills.' Ha, ha, my boy, what do you make of that?" His eyes sparkled, and he sent up a great blue triumphant cloud from his cigarette.

"The paper was made in Bohemia," I said.

"Precisely. And the man who wrote the note is a German. Do you note the peculiar construction of the sentence—'This account of you we have from all quarters received.' A Frenchman or Russian could not have written that. It is the German who is so uncourteous to his verbs. It only remains, therefore, to discover what is wanted by this German who writes upon Bohemian paper, and prefers wearing a mask to showing his face. And here he comes, if I am not mistaken, to resolve all our doubts."

As he spoke there was the sharp sound of horses' hoofs and grating wheels against the curb, followed by a sharp pull at the bell. Holmes whistled.

"A pair, by the sound," said he. "Yes," he continued, glancing out of the window. "A nice little brougham and a pair of beauties.[9] A hundred and fifty guineas apiece. There's money in this case, Watson, if there is nothing else."

8. Country in Eastern Central Europe, then part of the Austrian Empire, now part of the Czech Republic. Prague was the capital.
9. A closed four-wheeled carriage drawn by two horses.

"I think that I had better go, Holmes."

"Not a bit, Doctor. Stay where you are. I am lost without my Boswell.[1] And this promises to be interesting. It would be a pity to miss it."

"But your client—"

"Never mind him. I may want your help, and so may he. Here he comes. Sit down in that armchair, Doctor, and give us your best attention."

A slow and heavy step, which had been heard upon the stairs and in the passage, paused immediately outside the door. Then there was a loud and authoritative tap.

"Come in!" said Holmes.

A man entered who could hardly have been less than six feet six inches in height, with the chest and limbs of a Hercules. His dress was rich with a richness which would, in England, be looked upon as akin to bad taste. Heavy bands of Astrakhan[2] were slashed across the sleeves and fronts of his double-breasted coat, while the deep blue cloak which was thrown over his shoulders was lined with flame-coloured silk, and secured at the neck with a brooch which consisted of a single flaming beryl. Boots which extended half way up his calves, and which were trimmed at the tops with rich brown fur, completed the impression of barbaric opulence which was suggested by his whole appearance. He carried a broad-brimmed hat in his hand, while he wore across the upper part of his face, extending down past the cheekbones, a black vizard mask,[3] which he had apparently adjusted that very moment, for his hand was still raised to it as he entered. From the lower part of the face he appeared to be a man of strong character, with a thick, hanging lip, and a long straight chin, suggestive of resolution pushed to the length of obstinacy.

"You had my note?" he asked, with a deep harsh voice and a strongly marked German accent. "I told you that I would call." He looked from one to the other of us, as if uncertain which to address.

"Pray take a seat," said Holmes. "This is my friend and colleague, Dr Watson, who is occasionally good enough to help me in my cases. Whom have I the honour to address?"

"You may address me as the Count Von Kramm, a Bohemian nobleman. I understand that this gentleman, your friend, is a man of honour and discretion, whom I may trust with a matter of the most extreme importance. If not, I should much prefer to communicate with you alone."

I rose to go, but Holmes caught me by the wrist and pushed me back into my chair. "It is both, or none," said he. "You may say before this gentleman anything which you may say to me."

The Count shrugged his broad shoulders. "Then I must begin," said he, "by binding you both to absolute secrecy for two years, at the end of that time the matter will be of no importance. At present it is not too much to say that it is of such weight that it may have an influence upon European history."

"I promise," said Holmes.

"And I."

"You will excuse this mask," continued our strange visitor. "The august person who employs me wishes his agent to be unknown to you, and I may confess at once that the title by which I have just called myself is not exactly my own."

"I was aware of it," said Holmes dryly.

1. James Boswell (1740–1795), biographer of Samuel Johnson.
2. A luxurious wool, made from lambs that are killed in their mother's womb.
3. A mask that conceals the eyes.

"The circumstances are of great delicacy, and every precaution has to be taken to quench what might grow to be an immense scandal and seriously compromise one of the reigning families of Europe. To speak plainly, the matter implicates the great House of Ormstein, hereditary kings of Bohemia."

"I was also aware of that," murmured Holmes, settling himself down in his arm-chair, and closing his eyes.

Our visitor glanced with some apparent surprise at the languid, lounging figure of the man who had been no doubt depicted to him as the most incisive reasoner, and most energetic agent in Europe. Holmes slowly reopened his eyes, and looked impatiently at his gigantic client.

"If your Majesty would condescend to state your case," he remarked, "I should be better able to advise you."

The man sprang from his chair, and paced up and down the room in uncontrollable agitation. Then, with a gesture of desperation, he tore the mask from his face and hurled it upon the ground. "You are right," he cried, "I am the King. Why should I attempt to conceal it?"

"Why, indeed?" murmured Holmes. "Your Majesty had not spoken before I was aware that I was addressing Wilhelm Gottsreich Sigismond von Ormstein, Grand Duke of Cassel-Felstein, and hereditary King of Bohemia."

"But you can understand," said our strange visitor, sitting down once more and passing his hand over his high, white forehead, "you can understand that I am not accustomed to doing such business in my own person. Yet the matter was so delicate that I could not confide it to an agent without putting myself in his power. I have come *incognito* from Prague for the purpose of consulting you."

"Then, pray consult," said Holmes, shutting his eyes once more.

"The facts are briefly these: Some five years ago, during a lengthy visit to Warsaw, I made the acquaintance of the well-known adventuress Irene Adler. The name is no doubt familiar to you."

"Kindly look her up in my index, Doctor," murmured Holmes, without opening his eyes. For many years he had adopted a system of docketing all paragraphs concerning men and things, so that it was difficult to name a subject or a person on which he could not at once furnish information. In this case I found her biography sandwiched in between that of a Hebrew Rabbi and that of a staff-commander who had written a monograph upon the deep sea fishes.

"Let me see," said Holmes. "Hum! Born in New Jersey in the year 1858. Contralto—hum! La Scala,[4] hum! Prima donna Imperial Opera of Warsaw—Yes! Retired from operatic stage—ha! Living in London—quite so! Your Majesty, as I understand, became entangled with this young person, wrote her some compromising letters, and is now desirous of getting those letters back."

"Precisely so. But how—"

"Was there a secret marriage?"

"None."

"No legal papers or certificates?"

"None."

"Then I fail to follow your Majesty. If this young person should produce her letters for blackmailing or other purposes, how is she to prove their authenticity?"

"There is the writing."

---

4. A famous opera house in Milan.

"Pooh, pooh! Forgery."

"My private notepaper."

"Stolen."

"My own seal."

"Imitated."

"My photograph."

"Bought."

"We were both in the photograph."

"Oh dear! That is very bad! Your Majesty has indeed committed an indiscretion."

"I was mad—insane."

"You have compromised yourself seriously."

"I was only Crown Prince then. I was young. I am but thirty now."

"It must be recovered."

"We have tried and failed."

"Your Majesty must pay. It must be bought."

"She will not sell."

"Stolen, then."

"Five attempts have been made. Twice burglars in my pay ransacked her house. Once we diverted her luggage when she travelled. Twice she has been waylaid. There has been no result."

"No sign of it?"

"Absolutely none."

Holmes laughed. "It is quite a pretty little problem," said he.

"But a very serious one to me," returned the King, reproachfully.

"Very, indeed. And what does she propose to do with the photograph?"

"To ruin me."

"But how?"

"I am about to be married."

"So I have heard."

"To Clotilde Lothman von Saxe-Meningen, second daughter of the King of Scandinavia. You may know the strict principles of her family. She is herself the very soul of delicacy. A shadow of a doubt as to my conduct would bring the matter to an end."

"And Irene Adler?"

"Threatens to send them the photograph. And she will do it. I know that she will do it. You do not know her, but she has a soul of steel. She has the face of the most beautiful of women, and the mind of the most resolute of men. Rather than I should marry another woman, there are no lengths to which she would not go—none."

"You are sure that she has not sent it yet?"

"I am sure."

"And why?"

"Because she has said that she would send it on the day when the betrothal was publicly proclaimed. That will be next Monday."

"Oh, then, we have three days yet," said Holmes, with a yawn. "That is very fortunate, as I have one or two matters of importance to look into just at present. Your Majesty will, of course, stay in London for the present?"

"Certainly. You will find me at the Langham, under the name of the Count Von Kramm."

"Then I shall drop you a line to let you know how we progress."

"Pray do so. I shall be all anxiety."

"Then, as to money?"

"You have *carte blanche*."[5]

"Absolutely?"

"I tell you that I would give one of the provinces of my kingdom to have that photograph."

"And for present expenses?"

The king took a heavy chamois leather bag from under his cloak, and laid it on the table.

"There are three hundred pounds in gold, and seven hundred in notes," he said.

Holmes scribbled a receipt upon a sheet of his note-book, and handed it to him.

"And mademoiselle's address?" he asked.

"Is Briony Lodge, Serpentine-avenue, St. John's Wood."[6]

Holmes took a note of it. "One other question," said he. "Was the photograph a cabinet?"[7]

"It was."

"Then, good night, your Majesty, and I trust that we shall soon have some good news for you. And good night, Watson," he added, as the wheels of the Royal brougham rolled down the street. "If you will be good enough to call tomorrow afternoon, at three o'clock, I should like to chat this little matter over with you."

2

At three o'clock precisely I was at Baker-street, but Holmes had not yet returned. The landlady informed me that he had left the house shortly after eight o'clock in the morning. I sat down beside the fire, however, with the intention of awaiting him, however long he might be. I was already deeply interested in his inquiry, for, though it was surrounded by none of the grim and strange features which were associated with the two crimes which I have already recorded,[8] still, the nature of the case and the exalted station of his client gave it a character of its own. Indeed, apart from the nature of the investigation which my friend had on hand, there was something in his masterly grasp of a situation, and his keen, incisive reasoning, which made it a pleasure to me to study his system of work, and to follow the quick, subtle methods by which he disentangled the most inextricable mysteries. So accustomed was I to his invariable success that the very possibility of his failing had ceased to enter into my head.

It was close upon four before the door opened, and a drunken-looking groom, ill-kempt and side-whiskered, with an inflamed face and disreputable clothes, walked into the room. Accustomed as I was to my friend's amazing powers in the use of disguises, I had to look three times before I was certain that it was indeed he. With a nod he vanished into the bedroom, whence he emerged in five minutes tweed-suited and respectable, as of old. Putting his hands into his pockets, he stretched out his legs in front of the fire, and laughed heartily for some minutes.

"Well, really!" he cried, and then he choked; and laughed again until he was obliged to lie back, limp and helpless, in the chair.

"What is it?"

"It's quite too funny. I am sure you could never guess how I employed my morning, or what I ended by doing."

5. I.e., complete freedom of action and unlimited funds.
6. A London area favored by authors, artists, and well-known courtesans.

7. A cabinet photo was 5½ by 4 inches.
8. In *A Study in Scarlet* (1887) and *The Sign of the Four* (1890).

"I can't imagine. I suppose that you have been watching the habits, and perhaps the house, of Miss Irene Adler."

"Quite so, but the sequel was rather unusual. I will tell you, however. I left the house a little after eight o'clock this morning, in the character of a groom out of work. There is a wonderful sympathy and freemasonry among horsey men. Be one of them, and you will know all that there is to know. I soon found Briony Lodge. It is a *bijou* villa,[9] with a garden at the back, but built out in front right up to the road, two stories. Chubb lock to the door. Large sitting-room on the right side, well furnished, with long windows almost to the floor, and those preposterous English window fasteners which a child could open. Behind there was nothing remarkable, save that the passage window could be reached from the top of the coach-house. I walked round it and examined it closely from every point of view, but without noting anything else of interest.

"I then lounged down the street, and found, as I expected, that there was a mews[1] in a lane which runs down by one wall of the garden. I lent the ostlers a hand in rubbing down their horses, and I received in exchange twopence, a glass of half-and-half, two fills of shag tobacco, and as much information as I could desire about Miss Adler, to say nothing of half a dozen other people in the neighbourhood in whom I was not in the least interested, but whose biographies I was compelled to listen to."

"And what of Irene Adler?" I asked.

"Oh, she has turned all the men's heads down in that part. She is the daintiest thing under a bonnet on this planet. So say the Serpentine-mews, to a man. She lives quietly, sings at concerts, drives out at five every day, and returns at seven sharp for dinner. Seldom goes out at other times, except when she sings. Has only one male visitor, but a good deal of him. He is dark, handsome, and dashing; never calls less than once a day, and often twice. He is a Mr Godfrey Norton, of the Inner Temple.[2] See the advantages of a cabman as a confidant. They had driven him home a dozen times from Serpentine-mews, and knew all about him. When I had listened to all that they had to tell, I began to walk up and down near Briony Lodge once more, and to think over my plan of campaign.

"This Godfrey Norton was evidently an important factor in the matter. He was a lawyer. That sounded ominous. What was the relation between them, and what the object of his repeated visits? Was she his client, his friend, or his mistress? If the former, she had probably transferred the photograph to his keeping. If the latter, it was less likely. On the issue of this question depended whether I should continue my work at Briony Lodge, or turn my attention to the gentleman's chambers in the Temple. It was a delicate point, and it widened the field of my inquiry. I fear that I bore you with these details, but I have to let you see my little difficulties, if you are to understand the situation."

"I am following you closely," I answered.

"I was still balancing the matter in my mind, when a hansom cab drove up to Briony Lodge, and a gentleman sprang out. He was a remarkably handsome man, dark, aquiline, and moustached—evidently the man of whom I had heard. He appeared to be in a great hurry, shouted to the cabman to wait, and brushed past the maid who opened the door with the air of a man who was thoroughly at home.

"He was in the house about half an hour, and I could catch glimpses of him, in the windows of the sitting-room, pacing up and down, talking excitedly and waving

9. A small, charming house.
1. A back lane, used for stables and deliveries.

2. One of the four Inns of Court, where the offices and residences of barristers are located.

his arms. Of her I could see nothing. Presently he emerged, looking even more flurried than before. As he stepped up to the cab, he pulled a gold watch from his pocket and looked at it earnestly. 'Drive like the devil,' he shouted, 'first to Gross & Hankey's in Regent-street, and then to the church of St. Monica in the Edgware-road. Half a guinea if you do it in twenty minutes!'

"Away they went, and I was just wondering whether I should not do well to follow them, when up the lane came a neat little landau, the coachman with his coat only half buttoned, and his tie under his ear, while all the tags of his harness were sticking out of the buckles. It hadn't pulled up before she shot out of the hall door and into it. I only caught a glimpse of her at the moment, but she was a lovely woman, with a face that a man might die for.

"'The Church of St. Monica, John,' she cried, 'and half a sovereign if you reach it in twenty minutes.'

"This was quite too good to lose, Watson. I was just balancing whether I should run for it, or whether I should perch behind her landau, when a cab came through the street. The driver looked twice at such a shabby fare; but I jumped in before he could object. 'The Church of St. Monica,' said I, 'and half a sovereign if you reach it in twenty minutes.' It was twenty-five minutes to twelve, and of course it was clear enough what was in the wind.[3]

"My cabby drove fast. I don't think I ever drove faster, but the others were there before us. The cab and the landau with their steaming horses were in front of the door when I arrived. I paid the man, and hurried into the church. There was not a soul there save the two whom I had followed and a surpliced clergyman, who seemed to be expostulating with them. They were all three standing in a knot in front of the altar. I lounged up the side aisle like any other idler who has dropped into a church. Suddenly, to my surprise, the three at the altar faced round to me, and Godfrey Norton came running as hard as he could towards me.

"'Thank God!' he cried. 'You'll do. Come! Come!'

"'What then?' I asked.

"'Come man, come, only three minutes, or it won't be legal.'

"I was half dragged up to the altar, and, before I knew where I was, I found myself mumbling responses which were whispered in my ear, and vouching for things of which I knew nothing, and generally assisting in the secure tying up of Irene Adler, spinster, to Godfrey Norton, bachelor. It was all done in an instant, and there was the gentleman thanking me on the one side and the lady on the other, while the clergyman beamed on me in front. It was the most preposterous position in which I ever found myself in my life, and it was the thought of it that started me laughing just now. It seems that there had been some informality about their licence, that the clergyman absolutely refused to marry them without a witness of some sort, and that my lucky appearance saved the bridegroom from having to sally out into the streets in search of a best man. The bride gave me a sovereign, and I mean to wear it on my watch chain in memory of the occasion."

"This is a very unexpected turn of affairs," said I; "and what then?"

"Well, I found my plans very seriously menaced. It looked as if the pair might take an immediate departure, and so necessitate very prompt and energetic measures on my part. At the church door, however, they separated, he driving back to the Temple, and she to her own house. 'I shall drive out in the Park at five as usual,' she

3. Until 1886, marriages could be legally performed only before noon.

said as she left him. I heard no more. They drove away in different directions, and I went off to make my own arrangements."

"Which are?"

"Some cold beef and a glass of beer," he answered, ringing the bell. "I have been too busy to think of food, and I am likely to be busier still this evening. By the way, Doctor, I shall want your co-operation."

"I shall be delighted."

"You don't mind breaking the law?"

"Not in the least."

"Nor running a chance of arrest?"

"Not in a good cause."

"Oh, the cause is excellent!"

"Then I am your man."

"I was sure that I might rely on you."

"But what is it you wish?"

"When Mrs Turner has brought in the tray I will make it clear to you. Now," he said, as he turned hungrily on the simple fare that our landlady had provided, "I must discuss it while I eat, for I have not much time. It is nearly five now. In two hours we must be on the scene of action. Miss Irene, or Madame, rather, returns from her drive at seven. We must be at Briony Lodge to meet her."

"And what then?"

"You must leave that to me. I have already arranged what is to occur. There is only one point on which I must insist. You must not interfere, come what may. You understand?"

"I am to be neutral?"

"To do nothing whatever. There will probably be some small unpleasantness. Do not join in it. It will end in my being conveyed into the house. Four or five minutes afterwards the sitting-room window will open. You are to station yourself close to that open window."

"Yes."

"You are to watch me, for I will be visible to you."

"Yes."

"And when I raise my hand—so—you will throw into the room what I give you to throw, and will, at the same time, raise the cry of fire. You quite follow me?"

"Entirely."

"It is nothing very formidable," he said, taking a long cigar-shaped roll from his pocket. "It is an ordinary plumber's smoke rocket,[4] fitted with a cap at either end to make it self-lighting. Your task is confined to that. When you raise your cry of fire, it will be taken up by quite a number of people. You may then walk to the end of the street, and I will rejoin you in ten minutes. I hope that I have made myself clear?"

"I am to remain neutral, to get near the window, to watch you, and, at the signal, to throw in this object, then to raise the cry of fire, and to await you at the corner of the street."

"Precisely."

"Then you may entirely rely on me."

"That is excellent. I think perhaps it is almost time that I prepared for the new rôle I have to play."

4. A device to test pipes for leaks.

He disappeared into his bedroom, and returned in a few minutes in the character of an amiable and simple-minded Nonconformist clergyman. His broad black hat, his baggy trousers, his white tie, his sympathetic smile, and general look of peering and benevolent curiosity were such as Mr John Hare[5] alone could have equalled. It was not merely that Holmes changed his costume. His expression, his manner, his very soul seemed to vary with every fresh part that he assumed. The stage lost a fine actor, even as science lost an acute reasoner, when he became a specialist in crime.

It was a quarter past six when we left Baker-street, and it still wanted ten minutes to the hour when we found ourselves in Serpentine-avenue. It was already dusk, and the lamps were just being lighted as we paced up and down in front of Briony Lodge, waiting for the coming of its occupant. The house was just such as I had pictured it from Sherlock Holmes's succinct description, but the locality appeared to be less private than I expected. On the contrary, for a small street in a quiet neighbourhood, it was remarkably animated. There was a group of shabbily-dressed men smoking and laughing in a corner, a scissors grinder with his wheel,[6] two guardsmen who were flirting with a nurse-girl, and several well-dressed young men who were lounging up and down with cigars in their mouths.

"You see," remarked Holmes, as we paced to and fro in front of the house, "this marriage rather simplifies matters. The photograph becomes a double-edged weapon now. The chances are that she would be as averse to its being seen by Mr Godfrey Norton, as our client is to its coming to the eyes of his Princess. Now the question is—Where are we to find the photograph?"

"Where, indeed?"

"It is most unlikely that she carries it about with her. It is cabinet size. Too large for easy concealment about a woman's dress. She knows that the King is capable of having her waylaid and searched. Two attempts of the sort have already been made. We may take it then that she does not carry it about with her."

"Where, then?"

"Her banker or her lawyer. There is that double possibility. But I am inclined to think neither. Women are naturally secretive, and they like to do their own secreting. Why should she hand it over to anyone else? She could trust her own guardianship, but she could not tell what indirect or political influence might be brought to bear upon a business man. Besides, remember that she had resolved to use it within a few days. It must be where she can lay her hands upon it. It must be in her own house."

"But it has twice been burgled."

"Pshaw! They did not know how to look."

"But how will you look?"

"I will not look."

"What then?"

"I will get her to show me."

"But she will refuse."

"She will not be able to. But I hear the rumble of wheels. It is her carriage. Now carry out my orders to the letter."

As he spoke the gleam of the sidelights of a carriage came round the curve of the avenue. It was a smart little landau which rattled up to the door of Briony Lodge. As it pulled up one of the loafing men at the corner dashed forward to open the door in the hope of earning a copper, but was elbowed away by another loafer who had rushed up

---

5. A popular character actor of the era.   6. A door-to-door knife sharpener.

with the same intention. A fierce quarrel broke out, which was increased by the two guardsmen, who took sides with one of the loungers, and by the scissors grinder, who was equally hot upon the other side. A blow was struck, and in an instant the lady, who had stepped from her carriage, was the centre of a little knot of flushed and struggling men who struck savagely at each other with their fists and sticks. Holmes dashed into the crowd to protect the lady; but, just as he reached her, he gave a cry and dropped to the ground, with the blood running freely down his face. At his fall the guardsmen took to their heels in one direction and the loungers in the other, while a number of better dressed people who had watched the scuffle without taking part in it, crowded in to help the lady and to attend to the injured man. Irene Adler, as I will still call her, had hurried up the steps; but she stood at the top with her superb figure outlined against the lights of the hall, looking back into the street.

"Is the poor gentleman much hurt?" she asked.

"He is dead," cried several voices.

"No, no, there's life in him," shouted another. "But he'll be gone before you can get him to hospital."

"He's a brave fellow," said a woman. "They would have had the lady's purse and watch if it hadn't been for him. They were a gang, and a rough one too. Ah, he's breathing now."

"He can't lie in the street. May we bring him in, marm?"

"Surely. Bring him into the sitting-room. There is a comfortable sofa. This way, please!"

Slowly and solemnly he was borne into Briony Lodge, and laid out in the principal room, while I still observed the proceedings from my post by the window. The lamps had been lit, but the blinds had not been drawn, so that I could see Holmes as he lay upon the couch. I do not know whether he was seized with compunction at that moment for the part he was playing, but I know that I never felt more heartily ashamed of myself in my life than when I saw the beautiful creature against whom I was conspiring, or the grace and kindliness with which she waited upon the injured man. And yet it would be the blackest treachery to Holmes to draw back now from the part which he had entrusted to me. I hardened my heart, and took the smoke-rocket from under my ulster.[7] After all, I thought, we are not injuring her. We are but preventing her from injuring another.

Holmes had sat up upon the couch, and I saw him motion like a man who is in need of air. A maid rushed across and threw open the window. At the same instant I saw him raise his hand, and at the signal I tossed my rocket into the room with a cry of "Fire." The word was no sooner out of my mouth than the whole crowd of spectators, well dressed and ill—gentlemen, ostlers, and servant maids—joined in a general shriek of "Fire." Thick clouds of smoke curled through the room, and out at the open window. I caught a glimpse of rushing figures, and a moment later the voice of Holmes from within, assuring them that it was a false alarm. Slipping through the shouting crowd I made my way to the corner of the street, and in ten minutes was rejoiced to find my friend's arm in mine, and to get away from the scene of uproar. He walked swiftly and in silence for some few minutes, until we had turned down one of the quiet streets which lead towards the Edgware-road.

"You did it very nicely, Doctor," he remarked. "Nothing could have been better. It is all right."

7. A long, loose overcoat.

"You have the photograph!"

"I know where it is."

"And how did you find out?"

"She showed me, as I told you that she would."

"I am still in the dark."

"I do not wish to make a mystery," said he laughing. "The matter was perfectly simple. You, of course, saw that everyone in the street was an accomplice. They were all engaged for the evening."

"I guessed as much."

"Then, when the row broke out, I had a little moist red paint in the palm of my hand. I rushed forward, fell down, clapped my hand to my face, and became a piteous spectacle. It is an old trick."

"That also I could fathom."

"Then they carried me in. She was bound to have me in. What else could she do? And into her sitting-room, which was the very room which I suspected. It lay between that and her bedroom, and I was determined to see which. They laid me on a couch, I motioned for air, they were compelled to open the window, and you had your chance."

"How did that help you?"

"It was all-important. When a woman thinks that her house is on fire, her instinct is at once to rush to the thing which she values most. It is a perfectly overpowering impulse, and I have more than once taken advantage of it. In the case of the Darlington Substitution Scandal it was of use to me, and also in the Arnsworth Castle business. A married woman grabs at her baby—an unmarried one reaches for her jewel box. Now it was clear to me that our lady of to-day had nothing in the house more precious to her than what we are in quest of. She would rush to secure it. The alarm of fire was admirably done. The smoke and shouting were enough to shake nerves of steel. She responded beautifully. The photograph is in a recess behind a sliding panel just above the right bell pull. She was there in an instant, and I caught a glimpse of it as she half drew it out. When I cried out that it was a false alarm, she replaced it, glanced at the rocket, rushed from the room, and I have not seen her since. I rose, and, making my excuses, escaped from the house. I hesitated whether to attempt to secure the photograph at once; but the coachman had come in, and, as he was watching me narrowly, it seemed safer to wait. A little over-precipitance may ruin all."

"And now?" I asked.

"Our quest is practically finished. I shall call with the King to-morrow, and with you, if you care to come with us. We will be shown into the sitting-room to wait for the lady, but it is probable that when she comes she may find neither us nor the photograph. It might be a satisfaction to His Majesty to regain it with his own hands."

"And when will you call?"

"At eight in the morning. She will not be up, so that we shall have a clear field. Besides, we must be prompt, for this marriage may mean a complete change in her life and habits. I must wire to the King without delay."

We had reached Baker-street, and had stopped at the door. He was searching his pockets for the key, when someone passing said:—

"Good-night, Mister Sherlock Holmes."

There were several people on the pavement at the time, but the greeting appeared to come from a slim youth in an ulster who had hurried by.

"I've heard that voice before," said Holmes, staring down the dimly lit street. "Now, I wonder who the deuce that could have been."

Sidney Paget, *Good-night, Mr. Sherlock Holmes*. At the doorway of 221B Baker Street, Watson and Holmes (disguised as a clergyman) are hailed by a mysterious stranger. The artist Sidney Paget (1850–1908), who illustrated the Sherlock Holmes stories as they appeared in *The Strand Magazine* in the early 1890s, was responsible for creating the instantly recognizable image of Holmes as the tall, lean, hook-nosed sleuth who smokes a curved meerschaum pipe and wears a deerstalker cap and cloak when out on the trail of a criminal. But Doyle made his detective as adept at disguise as at deduction. In almost every story, Holmes becomes someone else in order to pass unnoticed at all levels of society. Here Paget explores one of Doyle's main themes, that skill in disguise must be matched by skill in penetrating the disguises of others.

3

I slept at Baker-street that night, and we were engaged upon our toast and coffee in the morning when the King of Bohemia rushed into the room.

"You have really got it!" he cried, grasping Sherlock Holmes by either shoulder, and looking eagerly into his face.

"Not yet."

"But you have hopes?"

"I have hopes."

"Then, come. I am all impatience to be gone."

"We must have a cab."

"No, my brougham is waiting."

"Then that will simplify matters." We descended, and started off once more for Briony Lodge.

"Irene Adler is married," remarked Holmes.

"Married! When?"

"Yesterday."

"But to whom?"

"To an English lawyer named Norton."

"But she could not love him?"

"I am in hopes that she does."

"And why in hopes?"

"Because it would spare your Majesty all fear of future annoyance. If the lady loves her husband, she does not love your Majesty. If she does not love your Majesty, there is no reason why she should interfere with your Majesty's plan."

"It is true. And yet—! Well! I wish she had been of my own station! What a queen she would have made!" He relapsed into a moody silence which was not broken, until we drew up in Serpentine-avenue.

The door of Briony Lodge was open, and an elderly woman stood upon the steps. She watched us with a sardonic eye as we stepped from the brougham.

"Mr Sherlock Holmes, I believe?" said she.

"I am Mr Holmes," answered my companion, looking at her with a questioning and rather startled gaze.

"Indeed! My mistress told me that you were likely to call. She left this morning with her husband, by the 5.15 train from Charing-cross, for the Continent."

"What!" Sherlock Holmes staggered back, white with chagrin and surprise. "Do you mean that she has left England?"

"Never to return."

"And the papers?" asked the King, hoarsely. "All is lost."

"We shall see." He pushed past the servant, and rushed into the drawing-room, followed by the King and myself. The furniture was scattered about in every direction, with dismantled shelves, and open drawers, as if the lady had hurriedly ransacked them before her flight. Holmes rushed at the bell-pull, tore back a small sliding shutter, and, plunging in his hand, pulled out a photograph and a letter. The photograph was of Irene Adler herself in evening dress, the letter was superscribed to "Sherlock Holmes, Esq. To be left till called for." My friend tore it open, and we all three read it together. It was dated at midnight of the preceding night, and ran in this way:—

"MY DEAR MR SHERLOCK HOLMES,—You really did it very well. You took me in completely. Until after the alarm of fire, I had not a suspicion. But then, when I found how I had betrayed myself, I began to think. I had been warned against you months ago. I had been told that, if the King employed an agent, it would certainly be you. And your address had been given me. Yet, with all this, you made me reveal what you wanted to know. Even after I became suspicious, I found it hard to think evil of such a dear, kind old clergyman. But, you know, I have been trained as an actress myself. Male costume is nothing new to me. I often take advantage of the freedom which it gives. I sent John, the coachman, to watch you, ran upstairs, got into my walking clothes, as I call them, and came down just as you departed.

"Well, I followed you to your door, and so made sure that I was really an object of interest to the celebrated Mr Sherlock Holmes. Then I, rather imprudently, wished you good night, and started for the Temple to see my husband.

"We both thought the best resource was flight, when pursued by so formidable an antagonist; so you will find the nest empty when you call to-morrow. As to the photograph, your client may rest in peace. I love and am loved by a better man than he. The King may do what he will without hindrance from one whom he has cruelly wronged. I keep it only to safeguard myself, and to preserve a weapon which will always secure me from any steps which he might take in the future. I leave a photograph which he might care to possess; and I remain, dear Mr Sherlock Holmes, very truly yours,

"IRENE NORTON, née ADLER."

"What a woman—oh, what a woman!" cried the King of Bohemia, when we had all three read this epistle. "Did I not tell you how quick and resolute she was? Would she not have made an admirable queen? Is it not a pity that she was not on my level?"

"From what I have seen of the lady, she seems, indeed, to be on a very different level to your Majesty," said Holmes, coldly. "I am sorry that I have not been able to bring your Majesty's business to a more successful conclusion."

"On the contrary, my dear sir," cried the King. "Nothing could be more successful. I know that her word is inviolate. The photograph is now as safe as if it were in the fire."

"I am glad to hear your Majesty say so."

"I am immensely indebted to you. Pray tell me in what way I can reward you. This ring—." He slipped an emerald snake ring from his finger, and held it out upon the palm of his hand.

"Your Majesty has something which I should value even more highly," said Holmes.

"You have but to name it."

"This photograph!"

The King stared at him in amazement.

"Irene's photograph!" he cried. "Certainly, if you wish it."

"I thank your Majesty. Then there is no more to be done in the matter. I have the honour to wish you a very good morning." He bowed, and, turning away without observing the hand which the King had stretched out to him, he set off in my company for his chambers.

And that was how a great scandal threatened to affect the kingdom of Bohemia, and how the best plans of Mr Sherlock Holmes were beaten by a woman's wit. He used to make merry over the cleverness of women, but I have not heard him do it of late. And when he speaks of Irene Adler, or when he refers to her photograph, it is always under the honourable title of *the* woman.

1891

+—⊨⬥⊨—+

John Ruskin
1819–1900

John Ruskin began his career as the most perceptive English art critic of the nineteenth century. But for Ruskin, art was inextricably linked to the moral temper of the age in which it was produced. Thus he was drawn inevitably from art criticism to social criticism, denouncing ugliness and injustice as aspects of the same spiritual decline. His prodigious output of books on painting, literature, architecture, politics, and society culminated with a beautiful and moving autobiography, *Praeterita*, which means "of things past."

For all the magnificence of his prose and the brilliance of his vision, John Ruskin was a rather peculiar man. He was the only child of middle-class parents who lived in the suburbs near London and whose dearest wish, he wrote, was "to make an evangelical clergyman of me." Forbidden toys, he passed his time studying the patterns in the nursery carpet and garden leaves, delighting already in the visual pleasures that would engross him all his life. His upbringing was strict, secluded, and overprotected: he was educated at home until his mother accompanied him to Oxford, where she remained for the duration of his studies.

Perhaps because he was so sheltered, Ruskin's love life was a series of disastrous ordeals. As a teenager he suffered a hopeless passion for Adèle Domecq, who was rich, French, and Catholic—unsuitable on every count. Later, a miserable six-year marriage to his cousin Effie Gray was annulled on the grounds of nonconsummation (she then married the Pre-Raphaelite painter John Everett Millais, with whom she had many children). The annulment created a scandal, and the whole episode was so painful that Ruskin omitted any reference to his marriage in *Praeterita*. Finally, he became morbidly obsessed with Rose La Touche, thirty years his junior, and only nine years old when he met her. His tragic relationship with her became a secret thread running through his later work.

Ruskin's intensity of vision was already evident in his first book, *Modern Painters*, in which he declared that "to see clearly is poetry, prophecy, and religion—all in one." Ruskin insisted that the impressionistic canvasses of J. M. W. Turner were actually more faithful to nature than the carefully rendered detail of Dutch realists. Reading *Modern Painters*, Charlotte Brontë wrote: "I feel . . . as if I had been walking blindfold—this book seems to give me eyes." Published over seventeen years (1843–1860), the five volumes of *Modern Painters* reflect their author's changing preoccupations: from art and nature in the early volumes to humanism and society in the last one, following an experience of religious "unconversion" in 1858.

From boyhood Ruskin loved to travel on the Continent, and his autobiography relates with deep pleasure the many journeys he took, usually with his parents. Venice aroused him to write what the critic John Rosenberg has called "the most elaborate and eloquent monument to a city in our literature," *The Stones of Venice* (1851–1853). Ruskin's Venice is "a ghost upon the sands of the sea, so weak—so quiet,—so bereft of all but her loveliness." The decline and fall of the Venetian empire serves as a warning to the British, which, "if it forget their example, may be led through prouder eminence to less pitied destruction."

The book's central chapter, *The Nature of Gothic*, became the touchstone for Ruskin's subsequent radical social critique of England. He argues that Gothic workmanship, though rude and imperfect, reflected a culture that respected the individual soul of the workman. Societies which demand machinelike perfection dehumanize the craftsman, turning him into a soulless operative. Ruskin thus mingled his hymn to the beauty of Venice with a scathing indictment of the Industrial Revolution.

In *Modern Manufacture and Design* (1859) and *Unto This Last* (1862), Ruskin turned from architecture to economics, raging like a biblical prophet against the savagery of laissez-faire capitalism and exhorting employers to take responsibility for the well-being of their workers. Contemporary response was hostile, but Ruskin's reforms have had a lasting influence on radical political thinkers from the founders of the British Labour Party to Gandhi, who felt himself transformed by reading *Unto This Last*: "All Ruskin's words captivated me . . . I lay awake all night and there and then I decided to change my whole life."

Ruskin's later writings became increasingly fragmented as he suffered a long, slow decline into madness. "The doctors said I went mad . . . from overwork," he wrote, but "I went mad because nothing came of my work." Yet from 1871 to 1884 he was able to lecture about art at Oxford and to produce an impassioned series of open letters to English workmen, entitled *Fors Clavigera*. Many of the letters describe the Guild of St. George, a utopian society Ruskin had founded. Tormented by the brutality and folly he saw everywhere around him, Ruskin chose in his final work to record only "what it gives me joy to remember." In the serene and radiant *Praeterita* (1885–1889), which was to inspire Proust's *Remembrance of Things Past*, Ruskin transcended his apocalyptic fury to produce one of the most enchanting yet poignant autobiographies ever written in English.

from **Modern Painters**
from Definition of Greatness in Art[1]

Painting, or art generally, as such, with all its technicalities, difficulties, and particular ends, is nothing but a noble and expressive language, invaluable as the vehicle of thought, but by itself nothing. He who has learned what is commonly considered the whole art of painting, that is, the art of representing any natural object faithfully, has as yet only learned the language by which his thoughts are to be expressed. He has done just as much towards being that which we ought to respect as a great painter, as a man who has learnt how to express himself grammatically and melodiously has towards being a great poet. The language is, indeed, more difficult of acquirement in the one case than in the other, and possesses more power of delighting the sense, while it speaks to the intellect; but it is, nevertheless, nothing more than language, and all those excellences which are peculiar to the painter as such, are merely what rhythm, melody, precision, and force are in the words of the orator and the poet, necessary to their greatness, but not the tests of their greatness. It is not by the mode of representing and saying, but by what is represented and said, that the respective greatness either of the painter or the writer is to be finally determined. * * *

If I say that the greatest picture is that which conveys to the mind of the spectator the greatest number of the greatest ideas, I have a definition which will include as subjects of comparison every pleasure which art is capable of conveying. If I were to say, on the contrary, that the best picture was that which most closely imitated nature, I should assume that art could only please by imitating nature; and I should cast out of the pale of criticism those parts of works of art which are not imitative, that is to say, intrinsic beauties of colour and form, and those works of art wholly, which, like the Arabesques of Raffaelle in the Loggias,[2] are not imitative at all. Now, I want a definition of art wide enough to include all its varieties of aim. I do not say, therefore, that the art is greatest which gives most pleasure, because perhaps there is some art whose end is to teach, and not to please. I do not say that the art is greatest which teaches us most, because perhaps there is some art whose end is to please, and not to teach. I do not say that the art is greatest which imitates best, because perhaps there is some art whose end is to create and not to imitate. But I say that the art is greatest which conveys to the mind of the spectator, by any means whatsoever, the greatest number of the greatest ideas; and I call an idea great in proportion as it is received by a higher faculty of the mind, and as it more fully occupies, and in occupying, exercises and exalts, the faculty by which it is received.

If this, then, be the definition of great art, that of a great artist naturally follows. He is the greatest artist who has embodied, in the sum of his works, the greatest number of the greatest ideas.

1843

---

1. From vol. 1, part 1, sec. 1, ch. 2.
2. The Italian Renaissance painter Raphael (1483–1520) decorated the Loggia of the Vatican with arabesques, wall paintings of interwoven foliage, animals, and human figures.

from *Of Water, As Painted by Turner*
["THE SLAVE SHIP"][1]

But, I think, the noblest sea that Turner[2] has ever painted, and, if so, the noblest certainly ever painted by man, is that of the Slave Ship, the chief Academy picture of the Exhibition of 1840.[3] It is a sunset on the Atlantic, after prolonged storm; but the storm is partially lulled, and the torn and streaming rain-clouds are moving in scarlet lines to lose themselves in the hollow of the night. The whole surface of sea included in the picture is divided into two ridges of enormous swell, not high, nor local, but a low broad heaving of the whole ocean, like the lifting of its bosom by deep-drawn breath after the torture of the storm. Between these two ridges the fire of the sunset falls along the trough of the sea, dyeing it with an awful but glorious light, the intense and lurid splendour which burns like gold, and bathes like blood. Along this fiery path and valley, the tossing waves by which the swell of the sea is restlessly divided, lift themselves in dark, indefinite, fantastic forms, each casting a faint and ghastly shadow behind it along the illumined foam. They do not rise everywhere, but three or four together in wild groups, fitfully and furiously, as the under strength of the swell compels or permits them; leaving between them treacherous spaces of level and whirling water, now lighted with green and lamp-like fire, now flashing back the gold of the declining sun, now fearfully dyed from above with the undistinguishable images of the burning clouds, which fall upon them in flakes of crimson and scarlet, and give to the reckless waves the added motion of their own fiery flying. Purple and blue, the lurid shadows of the hollow breakers are cast upon the mist of night, which gathers cold and low, advancing like the shadow of death upon the guilty ship[4] as it labours amidst the lightning of the sea, its thin masts written upon the sky in lines of blood, girded with condemnation in that fearful hue which signs the sky with horror, and mixes its flaming flood with the sunlight, and, cast far along the desolate heave of the sepulchral waves, incarnadines the multitudinous sea.[5]

I believe, if I were reduced to rest Turner's immortality upon any single work, I should choose this. Its daring conception, ideal in the highest sense of the word, is based on the purest truth, and wrought out with the concentrated knowledge of a life; its colour is absolutely perfect, not one false or morbid hue in any part or line, and so modulated that every square inch of canvas is a perfect composition; its drawing as accurate as fearless; the ship buoyant, bending, and full of motion; its tones as true as they are wonderful; and the whole picture dedicated to the most sublime of subjects and impressions (completing thus the perfect system of all truth, which we have shown to be formed by Turner's works)—the power, majesty, and deathfulness of the open, deep, illimitable sea.

1843

---

1. From vol. 1, part 2, sec. 5, ch. 3.
2. J. M. W. Turner (1775–1851), English Romantic landscape painter. See Color Plate 5.
3. In 1844 Ruskin's father gave him this dramatic painting; it now hangs in the Museum of Fine Arts in Boston. The annual exhibition of the Royal Academy of Arts was the primary showcase for new paintings.
4. She is a slaver, throwing her slaves overboard. The near sea is encumbered with corpses [Ruskin's note].
5. "No, this my hand will rather / The multitudinous seas incarnadine, / Making the green one red" (*Macbeth* 2.2.59–61).

The Storm-Cloud of the Nineteenth Century
Lecture I[1]

Let me first assure my audience that I have no *arrière pensée*[2] in the title chosen for this lecture. I might, indeed, have meant, and it would have been only too like me to mean, any number of things by such a title;—but, to-night, I mean simply what I have said, and propose to bring to your notice a series of cloud phenomena, which, so far as I can weigh existing evidence, are peculiar to our own times; yet which have not hitherto received any special notice or description from meteorologists.

So far as the existing evidence, I say, of former literature can be interpreted, the storm-cloud—or more accurately plague-cloud, for it is not always stormy—which I am about to describe to you, never was seen but by now living, or *lately* living eyes. It is not yet twenty years that this—I may well call it, wonderful—cloud has been, in its essence, recognizable. There is no description of it, so far as I have read, by any ancient observer. Neither Homer nor Virgil, neither Aristophanes nor Horace, acknowledge any such clouds among those compelled by Jove. Chaucer has no word of them, nor Dante; Milton none, nor Thomson.[3] In modern times, Scott, Wordsworth, and Byron are alike unconscious of them; and the most-observant and descriptive of scientific men, De Saussure[4] is utterly silent concerning them. Taking up the traditions of air from the year before Scott's death, I am able, by my own constant and close observation, to certify you that in the forty following years (1831 to 1871 approximately—for the phenomena in question came on gradually)—no such clouds as these are, and are now often for months without intermission, were ever seen in the skies of England, France, or Italy.

In those old days, when weather was fine, it was luxuriously fine; when it was bad—it was often abominably bad, but it had its fit of temper and was done with it—it didn't sulk for three months without letting you see the sun,—nor send you one cyclone inside out, every Saturday afternoon, and another outside in, every Monday morning.

In fine weather the sky was either blue or clear in its light; the clouds, either white or golden, adding to, not abating, the lustre of the sky. In wet weather, there were two different species of clouds,—those of beneficent rain, which for distinction's sake I will call the non-electric rain-cloud, and those of storm, usually charged highly with electricity. The beneficent rain-cloud was indeed often extremely dull and grey for days together, but gracious nevertheless, felt to be doing good, and often to be delightful after drought; capable also of the most exquisite colouring, under certain conditions; and continually traversed in clearing by the rainbow:—and, secondly, the storm-cloud, always majestic, often dazzlingly beautiful, and felt also to be

---

1. Given at the London Institution, 4 February 1884, followed by a second and final lecture a week later. The impassioned, almost hypersensitive lectures mix pioneering environmentalism, based on careful observation and record-keeping, with Ruskin's biblically inflected sense of dread; the Storm-Cloud contains a grim moral message for all beneath its shadow. Over the course of his lifetime Ruskin's immensely acute vision registered climactic changes as finely as any scientific instrument, but he could not and would not separate any observation from moral considerations—and human failings. In the second lecture, Ruskin remarked that "had the weather when I was young been such as it is now, no book such as *Modern Painters* ever would... have been written," since that

work was founded on "the beauty and blessing of nature," whereas now "month by month the darkness gains upon the day, and the ashes of the Antipodes glare through the night." The glaring ashes that troubled Ruskin were those of Krakatau, whose eruption in Java in 1883 also produced the horrifying reddish sky recorded in Edvard Munch's painting *The Scream*.
2. Ulterior motive or hidden meaning.
3. James Thomson (1700–1748), whose poem *The Seasons* (1726–1730), contains many descriptions of British weather.
4. The geologist and naturalist Horace Bénédict de Saussure, author of *Voyages in the Alps* (1779–1796), the third man ever to scale Mont Blanc.

beneficent in its own way, affecting the mass of the air with vital agitation, and purging it from the impurity of all morbific elements.

In the entire system of the Firmament, thus seen and understood, there appeared to be, to all the thinkers of those ages, the incontrovertible and unmistakable evidence of a Divine Power in creation, which had fitted, as the air for human breath, so the clouds for human sight and nourishment;—the Father who was in heaven feeding day by day the souls of His children with marvels, and satisfying them with bread, and so filling their hearts with food and gladness. * * *

The first time I recognized the clouds brought by the plague-wind as distinct in character was in walking back from Oxford, after a hard day's work, to Abingdon,[5] in the early spring of 1871: it would take too long to give you any account this evening of the particulars which drew my attention to them; but during the following months I had too frequent opportunities of verifying my first thoughts of them, and on the first of July in that year wrote the description of them which begins the *Fors Clavigera*[6] of August, thus:—

> "It is the first of July, and I sit down to write by the dismallest light that ever yet I wrote by; namely, the light of this midsummer morning, in mid-England (Matlock, Derbyshire),[7] in the year 1871.
>
> "For the sky is covered with grey cloud;—not rain-cloud, but a dry black veil, which no ray of sunshine can pierce; partly diffused in mist, feeble mist, enough to make distant objects unintelligible, yet without any substance, or wreathing, or colour of its own. And everywhere the leaves of the trees are shaking fitfully, as they do before a thunderstorm; only not violently, but enough to show the passing to and fro of a strange, bitter, blighting wind. Dismal enough, had it been the first morning of its kind that summer had sent. But during all this spring, in London, and at Oxford, through meagre March, through changelessly sullen April, through despondent May, and darkened June, morning after morning has come grey-shrouded thus.
>
> "And it is a new thing to me, and a very dreadful one. I am fifty years old, and more; and since I was five, have gleaned the best hours of my life in the sun of spring and summer mornings; and I never saw such as these, till now.
>
> "And the scientific men are busy as ants, examining the sun and the moon, and the seven stars, and can tell me all about *them*, I believe, by this time; and how they move, and what they are made of.
>
> "And I do not care, for my part, two copper spangles how they move, nor what they are made of. I can't move them any other way than they go, nor make them of anything else, better than they are made. But I would care much and give much, if I could be told where this bitter wind comes from, and what *it* is made of.
>
> "For, perhaps, with forethought, and fine laboratory science, one might make it of something else.
>
> "It looks partly as if it were made of poisonous smoke; very possibly it may be: there are at least two hundred furnace chimneys in a square of two miles on every side of me. But mere smoke would not blow to and fro in that wild way. It looks more to me as if it were made of dead men's souls—such of them as are not gone yet where they have to go, and may be flitting hither and thither, doubting, themselves, of the fittest place for them.

---

5. Market town about six miles south of Oxford.
6. Ruskin's series of open letters to British workingmen, published irregularly from 1871 until 1884. The Latin words mean "Fate, the club-bearer," and are taken from Horace's *Odes* 1. 35.

7. A scenic area in north-central England, much developed during the Industrial Revolution due to its abundant water power.

"You know, if there are such things as souls, and if ever any of them haunt places where they have been hurt, there must be many above us, just now, displeased enough!"

The last sentence refers of course to the battles of the Franco-German campaign[8] which was especially horrible to me, in its digging, as the Germans should have known, a moat flooded with waters of death between the two nations for a century to come.

Since that Midsummer day, my attention, however otherwise occupied, has never relaxed in its record of the phenomena characteristic of the plague-wind; and I now define for you, as briefly as possible, the essential signs of it.

(1.) It is a wind of darkness,—all the former conditions of tormenting winds, whether from the north or east, were more or less capable of co-existing with sunlight, and often with steady and bright sunlight; but whenever, and wherever the plague-wind blows, be it but for ten minutes, the sky is darkened instantly.

(2.) It is a malignant *quality* of wind, unconnected with any one quarter of the compass; it blows indifferently from all, attaching its own bitterness and malice to the worst characters of the proper winds of each quarter. It will blow either with drenching rain, or dry rage, from the south,—with ruinous blasts from the west,—with bitterest chills from the north,—and with venomous blight from the east.

Its own favourite quarter, however, is the south-west, so that it is distinguished in its malignity equally from the Bise of Provence, which is a north wind always, and from our own old friend, the east.

(3.) It always blows *tremulously*, making the leaves of the trees shudder as if they were all aspens, but with a peculiar fitfulness which gives them—and I watch them this moment as I write—an expression of anger as well as of fear and distress. You may see the kind of quivering, and hear the ominous whimpering, in the gusts that precede a great thunderstorm; but plague-wind is more panic-struck, and feverish; and its sound is a hiss instead of a wail.

When I was last at Avallon, in South France, I went to see *Faust* played at the little country theatre: it was done with scarcely any means of pictorial effect, except a few old curtains, and a blue light or two. But the night on the Brocken[9] was nevertheless extremely appalling to me,—a strange ghastliness being obtained in some of the witch scenes merely by fine management of gesture and drapery; and in the phantom scenes, by the half-palsied, half-furious, faltering or fluttering past of phantoms stumbling as into graves; as if of not only soulless, but senseless, Dead, moving with the very action, the rage, the decrepitude, and the trembling of the plague-wind.

(4.) Not only tremulous at every moment, it is also *intermittent* with a rapidity quite unexampled in former weather. There are, indeed, days—and weeks, on which it blows without cessation, and is as inevitable as the Gulf Stream; but also there are days when it is contending with healthy weather, and on such days it will remit for half an hour, and the sun will begin to show itself, and then the wind will come back and cover the whole sky with clouds in ten minutes; and so on, every half-hour, through the whole day; so that it is often impossible to go on with any kind of drawing in colour, the light being never for two seconds the same from morning till evening.

(5.) It degrades, while it intensifies, ordinary storm; but before I read you any description of its efforts in this kind, I must correct an impression which has got abroad

---

8. The Franco-Prussian war of 1870–1871, in which nearly 200,000 persons died.

9. In Goethe's drama *Faust* (1808), witches meet at night on the high mountain of Brocken in central Germany.

through the papers, that I speak as if the plague-wind blew now always, and there were no more any natural weather. On the contrary, the winter of 1878–9 was one of the most healthy and lovely I ever saw ice in;–Coniston lake[1] shone under the calm clear frost in one marble field, as strong as the floor of Milan Cathedral, half a mile across and four miles down; and the first entries in my diary which I read you shall be from the 22nd to 26th June, 1876, of perfectly lovely and natural weather: * * *

"*Monday, 26th June*, 1876.

Yesterday an entirely perfect summer light on the Old Man; Lancaster Bay all clear; Ingleborough and the great Pennine fault as on a map.[2] Divine beauty of western colour on thyme and rose,—then twilight of clearest *warm* amber far into night, of *pale* amber all night long; hills dark-clear against it.

"And so it continued, only growing more intense in blue and sunlight, all day. After breakfast, I came in from the well under strawberry bed, to say I had never seen anything like it, so pure or intense, in Italy; and so it went glowing on, cloudless, with soft north wind, all day."

"*16th July*.

"The sunset almost too bright *through the blinds* for me to read Humboldt[3] at tea by, finally, new moon like a lime-light, reflected on breeze-struck water; traces, across dark calm, of reflected hills."

These extracts are, I hope, enough to guard you against the absurdity of supposing that it only means that I am myself soured, or doting, in my old age, and always in an ill humour. Depend upon it, when old men are worth anything, they are better-humoured than young ones; and have learned to see what good there is, and pleasantness, in the world they are likely so soon to have orders to quit.

Now then—take the following sequences of accurate description of thunderstorm, *with* plague-wind. * * *

"*Brantwood, 13th August*, 1879.

"The most terrific and horrible thunderstorm, this morning, I ever remember. It waked me at six, or a little before—then rolling incessantly, like railway luggage trains, quite ghastly in its mockery of them—the air one loathsome mass of sultry and foul fog, like smoke; scarcely raining at all, but increasing to heavier rollings, with flashes quivering vaguely through all the air, and at last terrific double streams of reddish-violent fire, not forked or zigzag, but rippled rivulets—two at the same instant some twenty to thirty degrees apart, and lasting on the eye at least half a second, with grand artillery-peals following; not rattling crashes, or irregular cracklings, but delivered volleys. It lasted an hour, then passed off, clearing a little, without rain to speak of,—not a glimpse of blue,—and now, half-past seven, seems settling down again into Manchester devil's darkness.

"Quarter to eight, morning.—Thunder returned, all the air collapsed into one black fog, the hills invisible, and scarcely visible the opposite shore; heavy rain in short fits, and frequent though less formidable, flashes, and shorter thunder. While I

1. Coniston, in the Lake District, is the site of Ruskin's home, Brantwood.
2. Sites in the Lake District.
3. Alexander von Humboldt (1769–1859), German geol-

ogist and naturalist described by Darwin as "the greatest scientific traveler who ever lived," a founder of modern meteorology.

have written this sentence the cloud has again dissolved itself, like a nasty solution in a bottle, with miraculous and unnatural rapidity, and the hills are in sight again; a double-forked flash—rippled, I mean, like the others—starts into its frightful ladder of light between me and Wetherlam, as I raise my eyes. All black above, a rugged spray cloud on the Eaglet. (The 'Eaglet' is my own name for the bold and elevated crag to the west of the little lake above Coniston mines. It had no name among the country people, and is one of the most conspicuous features of the mountain chain, as seen from Brantwood.)

"Half-past eight.—Three times light and three times dark since last I wrote, and the darkness seeming each time as it settles more loathsome, at last stopping my reading in mere blindness. One lurid gleam of white cumulus in upper lead-blue sky, seen for half a minute through the sulphurous chimney-pot vomit of blackguardly cloud beneath, where its rags were thinnest."

"Thursday, 22nd Feb. 1883.

"Yesterday a fearfully dark mist all afternoon, with steady, south plague-wind of the bitterest, nastiest, poisonous blight, and fretful flutter. I could scarcely stay in the wood for the horror of it. To-day, really rather bright blue, and bright semi-cumuli, with the frantic Old Man[4] blowing sheaves of lancets and chisels across the lake— not in strength enough, or whirl enough, to raise it in spray, but tracing every squall's outline in black on the silver grey waves, and whistling meanly, and as if on a flute made of a file."

"Sunday, 17th August, 1879.

"Raining in foul drizzle, slow and steady; sky pitchdark, and I just get a little light by sitting in the bow-window; diabolic clouds over everything: and looking over my kitchen garden yesterday, I found it one miserable mass of weeds gone to seed, the roses in the higher garden putrefied into brown sponges, feeling like dead snails; and the half-ripe strawberries all rotten at the stalks."

(6.) And now I come to the most important sign of the plague-wind and the plague-cloud: that in bringing on their peculiar darkness, they *blanch* the sun instead of reddening it. And here I must note briefly to you the uselessness of observation by instruments, or machines, instead of eyes. In the first year when I had begun to notice the specialty of the plague-wind, I went of course to the Oxford observatory to consult its registrars. They have their anemometer always on the twirl, and can tell you the force, or at least the pace, of a gale, by day or night. But the anemometer can only record for you how often it has been driven round, not at all whether it went round *steadily*, or went round *trembling*. And on that point depends the entire question whether it is a plague breeze or a healthy one: and what's the use of telling you whether the wind's strong or not, when it can't tell you whether it's a strong medicine, or a strong poison? * * *

Blanched Sun,—blighted grass—blinded man.—If, in conclusion, you ask me for any conceivable cause or meaning of these things—I can tell you none, according to your modern beliefs; but I can tell you what meaning it would have borne to the men of old time. Remember, for the last twenty years, England, and all foreign

4. An 800-meter tall crag overlooking Coniston Water.

nations, either tempting her, or following her, have blasphemed the name of God deliberately and openly; and have done iniquity by proclamation, every man doing as much injustice to his brother as it is in his power to do. Of states in such moral gloom every seer of old predicted the physical gloom, saying, "The light shall be darkened in the heavens thereof, and the stars shall withdraw their shining."[5] All Greek, all Christian, all Jewish prophecy insists on the same truth through a thousand myths; but of all the chief, to former thought, was the fable of the Jewish warrior and prophet, for whom the sun hasted not to go down,[6] with which I leave you to compare at leisure the physical result of your own wars and prophecies, as declared by your own elect journal not fourteen days ago,—that the Empire of England, on which formerly the sun never set, has become one on which he never rises.[7]

What is best to be done, do you ask me? The answer is plain. Whether you can affect the signs of the sky or not, you *can* the signs of the times. Whether you can bring the *sun* back or not, you can assuredly bring back your own cheerfulness, and your own honesty. You may not be able to say to the winds, "Peace; be still," but you can cease from the insolence of your own lips, and the troubling of your own passions. And all *that* it would be extremely well to do, even though the day *were* coming when the sun should be as darkness, and the moon as blood. But, the paths of rectitude and piety once regained, who shall say that the promise of old time would not be found to hold for us also?—"Bring ye all the tithes into my storehouse, and prove me now herewith, saith the Lord God, if I will not open you the windows of heaven, and pour you out a blessing, that there shall not be room enough to receive it."[8]

1884

Matthew Arnold
1822–1888

Matthew Arnold and his wife Frances Wightman Arnold, 1860s, *carte de visite* photographs by Elliot and Fry, London.

"I am glad you like the Gipsy Scholar," Matthew Arnold wrote to a friend in 1853, "—but what does it *do* for you?" No Victorian gave more attention than Arnold to the momentous question of how art should affect an audience, and no writer was ever more tortured by it. For much as he delighted in creating the "pleasing melancholy" of *The Scholar-Gipsy*, one of his greatest poems, Arnold felt that literature must directly address the

---

5. A biblical citation combining Isaiah 5.30 and Joel 3.15.
6. In the Bible the Lord kept the sun from setting so that Joshua could win a battle; see Joshua 10.12–14.

7. The year 1883 ended with a totally sunless week in London, according to the *Pall Mall Gazette* (2 January 1884).
8. See Malachi 3.10.

moral needs of readers, "to *animate* and *ennoble* them." This concern with the practical emotional effects of art, Arnold said simply, is "the basis of my nature—and of my poetics."

But in trying to realize his goal, Arnold became a deeply divided man. Author of the era's most distinctive poems of alienation and doubt, he gave up poetry to work for the public good, passionately defending classic literature as a means of remaking the materialist society he abhorred. As a social critic, he aspired to embody his ideal of a balanced mind, to be a man "who saw life steadily and saw it whole." But as a private individual he viewed himself as a forlorn romantic quester, disenchanted with modernity. Unable to believe in the religion of the past and unwilling to accept the secular values of the present, he described himself as "wandering between two worlds, one dead, / The other powerless to be born." Arnold is unique among the eminent Victorian writers, admired equally for his heartfelt poetry of disillusionment and for his sophisticated prose aimed at pragmatic social reform.

Matthew Arnold was the oldest son of Dr. Thomas Arnold, headmaster of Rugby School, who had become famous for reshaping the curriculum to instill a healthy respect for Christian values, classical languages, and competitive games. Matthew's mother, Mary Penrose Arnold, encouraged her son to be creative, self-conscious, and alert to the comic or dramatic side of daily events. Nicknamed "Crabby" by his father when he wore leg braces for two years, Arnold adopted a sidelong, crab-like approach to his goal of becoming a poet. A lazy, dilettantish, facetious student, Arnold managed through last-minute heroics to win the top prizes: a scholarship in 1840 to Balliol College, Oxford; the renowned Newdigate Prize for poetry in 1843; and in 1845 a Fellowship at Oriel College.

Throughout his life, Arnold seemed most comfortable outdoors and free of the classroom, whether blasting away at game on the English moors (he was a terrible shot) or hiking in the Alps. He spent his early childhood at Laleham, a village on the Thames, perhaps the source of his frequent river imagery. When he should have been studying at Oxford, he roamed the idyllic countryside surrounding it, hunting, fishing, and composing verses. He once pranced naked on a riverbank after swimming, prompting a rebuke from a passing clergyman. Waving his towel, Arnold replied: "Is it possible that you see anything indelicate in the human form divine?"

In 1847 Arnold became private secretary to the liberal politician Lord Lansdowne, spending most of his time in London, working on his poetry, and arguing about poetry and religion with his best friend, the poet Arthur Hugh Clough. They both agreed on the spiritual bankruptcy of modern life: "These are damned times," Arnold wrote to Clough in 1849; "everything is against one . . . the absence of great *natures*, the unavoidable contact with millions of small ones . . . our own selves, and the sickening consciousness of our difficulties."

Arnold dealt with these difficulties by casting them in poetic form. His first book of poems, *The Strayed Reveller, and Other Poems*, by "A," appeared in 1849, followed by *Empedocles on Etna, and Other Poems* (1852) and *Poems* (1853). Many other important poems, including *Dover Beach*, also date from this fertile period, though not published until later, in *Poems, Second Series* (1855) and *New Poems* (1867).

Arnold's finest poetry is imbued with a love of the countryside. He spent family vacations in the Lake District, whose beauty and poetic associations made a deep impression on him. His parents were friendly with Wordsworth, who was to become the chief influence on Arnold's poetry; when Wordsworth died he mourned, "who will teach us how to feel?" Like Wordsworth, Arnold evokes memorable landscapes in many of his key works in order to ponder the relation between hidden emotions and external objects, and to explore the themes of lost childhood, nostalgia for the past, and the quest for identity. But Arnold rarely found in nature a means of contact with other people or with a deeper self: "The disease of the present age," he wrote in his journal, "is divorce from oneself."

Arnold felt a growing dissatisfaction with his society and with his own poetry. In a controversial preface to his *Poems* of 1853, he justified not reprinting his major earlier work, *Empedocles on Etna*, because he felt that it failed to "inspirit and rejoice" readers and teach them how to live. He went on to condemn poetry that merely presents "a continuous state of mental distress . . . unrelieved by incident, hope, or resistance; in which there is everything to be endured, nothing to be done." In these words he accurately summed up—and dismissed—what was most powerful and moving in his own work.

Provoking a heated debate about the poet's relation to contemporary life, Arnold urged that modern poets should turn from their own troubles to build upon timeless, universal "great actions," such as those found in Sophocles and Aeschylus. The Victorian age, he concluded, was an unlikely source of poetic material, because it was "an age wanting in moral grandeur . . . an age of spiritual discomfort."

Too much a man of his time to be able to follow his own advice, Arnold largely abandoned poetry after the mid-1850s. In 1851, two important events occurred that contributed to this abdication: his marriage to Frances Lucy Wightman and his taking a job as a school inspector to support his family. This turned out to be a grueling position assessing the quality of instruction in government-funded schools for the poor. Initially surmising that the job would do well enough "for the next three or four years," Arnold doggedly kept at it for thirty-five years, traveling constantly throughout Britain and later in Europe. He soon realized the importance of expanding and reforming public education, arguing for the schools' crucial role "in civilizing the next generation of the lower classes, who, as things are going, will have most of the political power of the country in their hands."

Thus the anguished poet transformed himself into an energetic public servant, strenuously trying to remedy with his progressive criticism a society that he privately despaired of as hopelessly materialist. In 1857 Arnold was elected Professor of Poetry at Oxford University. He was the first to lecture in English rather than Latin, and for the next ten years he used the occasion of his public lectures to reach the broadest possible audience, promoting his belief that a careful reading of classic literature produces civilizing and morally sustaining effects. He reworked many of his lectures into books and essays, including *On Translating Homer* (1861) and *On the Modern Element in Literature* (1869). The work begun at Oxford eventually helped establish literature as a cornerstone of university programs in the liberal arts.

In 1865 Arnold published *Essays in Criticism*, which began with his famous essay, *The Function of Criticism at the Present Time*. There he argued that criticism is "a free creative activity," one that may well be the most useful and satisfying activity available to an inquiring mind in a modern, unpoetical era. With examples ranging from high art to tabloid journalism, Arnold revealed how British thought is entangled in class relations and political exigencies; his essay anticipates the scope and methods of modern culture studies. In his most important work of social criticism, *Culture and Anarchy* (1869), Arnold called for "disinterested" analysis free of partisan politics. He deplored English pride in "doing as one likes" and found in the self-serving behavior of all classes an anarchic lack of concern for the public good. Only education, he contended, could unite the antagonistic factions of British society, by teaching respect for beauty and intellect—what Arnold termed the virtues of "sweetness and light."

The mocking irony, Olympian assurance, and lucid, cascading style of these works make them exhilarating—or exasperating—reading. Arnold's high-minded attitudes enraged many of his opponents, and his loftiness of tone led even his friends and family to nickname him "the Emperor." For Arnold, education was a lifelong task, and few measured up to the cosmopolitan, European standards he set. He was particularly savage with anyone he considered guilty of self-interest or fuzzy thinking, and he attacked politicians and bishops by name. Leslie Stephen, Virginia Woolf's father, remarked satirically that "I often wished . . . that I too had a little sweetness and light that I might be able to say such nasty things of my enemies."

In the 1870s, Arnold scandalized many people with his attacks on orthodox religion in *St. Paul and Protestantism* (1870), *Literature and Dogma* (1873), and *God and the Bible* (1875). In *The Study of Poetry* (1880), he went so far as to argue that "most of what now passes for religion and philosophy will be replaced by poetry."

In 1883, weary, in debt, and desperate to retire, Arnold tried to raise money by select-ing, with his daughter Nelly, 365 mottoes to create a *Matthew Arnold Birthday Book*. In the same year he went on a money-making lecture tour of the United States, meeting with mixed success. The chief intellectual product of his travel was *Discourses in America* (1885), which contained his essay *Literature and Science*. There, Arnold defended the idea of a liberal arts education founded on ancient and modern literatures against Thomas Huxley's contention in *Science and Culture* (1881) that an education based on the natural sciences would do just as well. Arnold felt that the debate had particular relevance for Americans, whose respect for "the average man" was fraught with "danger to the ideal of a high and rare excellence," best conveyed by a humanistic education. Arnold died suddenly of a heart attack in 1888.

Arnold was not a prophetic critic like Carlyle, nor a visionary poet of social reform like Eliz-abeth Barrett Browning, nor a moral crusader like Dickens. Instead, Arnold offered thoughtful prescriptions for guiding a changing and increasingly democratic society to a fuller understand-ing of its problems, and a more effective realization of its goals. As a school inspector he devel-oped a deeper understanding of ineffective institutions and the ignorance of the British public than any other important Victorian author. While few have agreed fully with his pronounce-ments on literature and society, he has influenced almost every significant English-speaking critic since his time, including T. S. Eliot, F. R. Leavis, Lionel Trilling, and Raymond Williams.

Arnold has remained a literary force to be reckoned with as well. In its honest, introspec-tive, sometimes awkward way, Arnold's poetry speaks unforgettably of the anxieties of his era. Though he saw himself as having "less poetical sentiment than Tennyson, and less intellectual vigor and abundance than Browning," he felt that his more balanced "fusion" of these qualities would continue to assure him an audience. His open approach to his innermost feelings is echoed almost everywhere in modern poetry.

Isolation. To Marguerite[1]

We were apart; yet, day by day,
I bade my heart more constant be.
I bade it keep the world away,
And grow a home for only thee;
5   Nor feared but thy love likewise grew,
Like mine, each day, more tried, more true.

The fault was grave! I might have known,
What far too soon, alas! I learned—
The heart can bind itself alone,
10   And faith may oft be unreturned.
Self-swayed our feelings ebb and swell—
Thou lov'st no more;—Farewell! Farewell!

Farewell!—and thou, thou lonely heart,
Which never yet without remorse
15   Even for a moment didst depart
From thy remote and spheréd course
To haunt the place where passions reign—
Back to thy solitude again!

1. The identity of Marguerite has long been a puzzle. She has been variously identified as an unknown woman whom Arnold met in Switzerland in the 1840s, or as Mary Claude, an Englishwoman whom he knew at about the same time.

Back! with the conscious thrill of shame
20 Which Luna felt, that summer-night,
Flash through her pure immortal frame,
When she forsook the starry height
To hang over Endymion's sleep
Upon the pine-grown Latmian steep.

25 Yet she, chaste queen, had never proved
How vain a thing is mortal love,
Wandering in Heaven, far removed.
But thou hast long had place to prove
This truth—to prove, and make thine own:
30 "Thou hast been, shalt be, art, alone."

Or, if not quite alone, yet they
Which touch thee are unmating things—
Ocean and clouds and night and day;
Lorn autumns and triumphant springs;
35 And life, and others' joy and pain,
And love, if love, of happier men.

Of happier men—for they, at least,
Have *dreamed* two human hearts might blend
In one, and were through faith released
40 From isolation without end
Prolonged; nor knew, although not less
Alone than thou, their loneliness.

1849   1857

To Marguerite—Continued

Yes! in the sea of life enisled,
With echoing straits between us thrown,
Dotting the shoreless watery wild,
We mortal millions live *alone*.
5   The islands feel the enclasping flow,
And then their endless bounds they know.

But when the moon their hollows lights,
And they are swept by balms of spring,
And in their glens, on starry nights,
10 The nightingales divinely sing;
And lovely notes, from shore to shore,
Across the sounds and channels pour—

Oh! then a longing like despair
Is to their farthest caverns sent;
15 For surely once, they feel, we were
Parts of a single continent!
Now round us spreads the watery plain—
Oh might our marges meet again!

Who ordered, that their longing's fire
20   Should be, as soon as kindled, cooled?
Who renders vain their deep desire?—
A God, a God their severance ruled!
And bade betwixt their shores to be
The unplumbed, salt, estranging sea.

1849   1852

Dover Beach

The sea is calm to-night.
The tide is full, the moon lies fair
Upon the straits; on the French coast the light
Gleams and is gone; the cliffs of England stand,
5   Glimmering and vast, out in the tranquil bay.
Come to the window, sweet is the night-air!
Only, from the long line of spray
Where the sea meets the moon-blanched land,
Listen! you hear the grating roar
10   Of pebbles which the waves draw back, and fling,
At their return, up the high strand,
Begin, and cease, and then again begin,
With tremulous cadence slow, and bring
The eternal note of sadness in.

15   Sophocles long ago
Heard it on the Aegean,[1] and it brought
Into his mind the turbid ebb and flow
Of human misery; we
Find also in the sound a thought,
20   Hearing it by this distant northern sea.

The Sea of Faith
Was once, too, at the full, and round earth's shore
Lay like the folds of a bright girdle° furled.   sash
But now I only hear
25   Its melancholy, long, withdrawing roar,
Retreating, to the breath
Of the night-wind, down the vast edges drear
And naked shingles° of the world.   pebble beaches

Ah, love, let us be true
30   To one another! for the world, which seems
To lie before us like a land of dreams,
So various, so beautiful, so new,
Hath really neither joy, nor love, nor light,
Nor certitude, nor peace, nor help for pain;
35   And we are here as on a darkling plain

---

1. Sophocles was a 5th century B.C. Greek dramatist; the Aegean Sea lies between Greece and Turkey.

Swept with confused alarms of struggle and flight,
Where ignorant armies clash by night.

c. 1851   1867

❧

RESPONSE
Anthony Hecht: The Dover Bitch
A Criticism of Life[1]

for Andrews Wanning

So there stood Matthew Arnold and this girl
With the cliffs of England crumbling away behind them,
And he said to her, "Try to be true to me,
And I'll do the same for you, for things are bad
5   All over, etc., etc."
Well now, I knew this girl. It's true she had read
Sophocles in a fairly good translation
And caught that bitter allusion to the sea,
But all the time he was talking she had in mind
10   The notion of what his whiskers would feel like
On the back of her neck. She told me later on
That after a while she got to looking out
At the lights across the channel, and really felt sad,
Thinking of all the wine and enormous beds
15   And blandishments in French and the perfumes.
And then she got really angry. To have been brought
All the way down from London, and then be addressed
As a sort of mournful cosmic last resort
Is really tough on a girl, and she was pretty.
20   Anyway, she watched him pace the room
And finger his watch-chain and seem to sweat a bit,
And then she said one or two unprintable things.
But you mustn't judge her by that. What I mean to say is,
She's really all right. I still see her once in a while
25   And she always treats me right. We have a drink
And I give her a good time, and perhaps it's a year
Before I see her again, but there she is,
Running to fat, but dependable as they come.
And sometimes I bring her a bottle of *Nuit d'Amour*.[2]

1967

❧

1. The Pulitzer Prize–winning American poet Anthony Hecht (1923–2004) was known for a polished, musical verse whose beauty was built on dark undertones. But he had a lighter side, and here he uses his fascination with literary history to imagine how the self-involved "cosmic" concerns of a poet like Arnold (or Hecht) might strike a woman more interested in sex than in Sophocles. With its memorable setting and uneasy mixture of desire and doubt, *Dover Beach* is perhaps the single most popular poem of the Victorian era; it has played host to endless interpretations. Many scholars believe that Arnold wrote the poem to his wife on his honeymoon, so Hecht's outrageous but intriguing suggestion that the poem's auditor is a woman of easy virtue shows just how open the text is to a reader's imagination. But is Hecht's worldly speaker any more open-minded than Arnold's? And in Arnold's poem, can we even be sure a man is speaking? Hecht's subtitle wryly alludes to Arnold's famous definition in *The Study of Poetry* (1880) that poetry is "a criticism of life."
2. Night of Love (French); presumably a perfume.

Lines Written in Kensington Gardens[1]

In this lone, open glade I lie,
Screened by deep boughs on either hand;
And at its end, to stay the eye,
Those black-crowned, red-boled pine-trees stand!

5   Birds here make song, each bird has his,
Across the girdling city's hum.
How green under the boughs it is!
How thick the tremulous sheep-cries come!

Sometimes a child will cross the glade
10   To take his nurse his broken toy;
Sometimes a thrush flit overhead
Deep in her unknown day's employ.

Here at my feet what wonders pass,
What endless, active life is here!
15   What blowing daisies, fragrant grass!
An air-stirred forest, fresh and clear.

Scarce fresher is the mountain-sod
Where the tired angler lies, stretched out,
And, eased of basket and of rod,
20   Counts his day's spoil, the spotted trout.

In the huge world, which roars hard by,
Be others happy if they can!
But in my helpless cradle I
Was breathed on by the rural Pan.

25   I, on men's impious uproar hurled,
Think often, as I hear them rave,
That peace has left the upper world
And now keeps only in the grave.

Yet here is peace for ever new!
30   When I who watch them am away,
Still all things in this glade go through
The changes of their quiet day.

Then to their happy rest they pass!
The flowers upclose, the birds are fed,
35   The night comes down upon the grass,
The child sleeps warmly in his bed.

Calm soul of all things! make it mine
To feel, amid the city's jar,
That there abides a peace of thine,
40   Man did not make, and cannot mar.

1. A park in London.

The will to neither strive nor cry,
The power to feel with others give!
Calm, calm me more! nor let me die
Before I have begun to live.

c. 1852   1852

The Buried Life

Light flows our war of mocking words, and yet,
Behold, with tears mine eyes are wet!
I feel a nameless sadness o'er me roll.
Yes, yes, we know that we can jest,
5   We know, we know that we can smile!
But there's a something in this breast,
To which thy light words bring no rest,
And thy gay smiles no anodyne.
Give me thy hand, and hush awhile,
10   And turn those limpid eyes on mine,
And let me read there, love! thy inmost soul.

Alas! is even love too weak
To unlock the heart, and let it speak?
Are even lovers powerless to reveal
15   To one another what indeed they feel?
I knew the mass of men concealed
Their thoughts, for fear that if revealed
They would by other men be met
With blank indifference, or with blame reproved;
20   I knew they lived and moved
Tricked in disguises, alien to the rest
Of men, and alien to themselves—and yet
The same heart beats in every human breast!

But we, my love!—doth a like spell benumb
25   Our hearts, our voices? must we too be dumb?

Ah! well for us, if even we,
Even for a moment, can get free
Our heart, and have our lips unchained;
For that which seals them hath been deep-ordained!

30   Fate, which foresaw
How frivolous a baby man would be—
By what distractions he would be possessed,
How he would pour himself in every strife,
And well-nigh change his own identity—
35   That it might keep from his capricious play
His genuine self, and force him to obey
Even in his own despite his being's law,
Bade through the deep recesses of our breast
The unregarded river of our life

40   Pursue with indiscernible flow its way;
        And that we should not see
        The buried stream, and seem to be
        Eddying at large in blind uncertainty,
        Though driving on with it eternally.

45   But often, in the world's most crowded streets,
        But often, in the din of strife,
        There rises an unspeakable desire
        After the knowledge of our buried life;
        A thirst to spend our fire and restless force
50   In tracking out our true, original course;
        A longing to inquire
        Into the mystery of this heart which beats
        So wild, so deep in us—to know
        Whence our lives come and where they go.

55   And many a man in his own breast then delves,
        But deep enough, alas! none ever mines.
        And we have been on many thousand lines,
        And we have shown, on each, spirit and power;
        But hardly have we, for one little hour,
60   Been on our own line, have we been ourselves—
        Hardly had skill to utter one of all
        The nameless feelings that course through our breast,
        But they course on for ever unexpressed.
        And long we try in vain to speak and act
65   Our hidden self, and what we say and do
        Is eloquent, is well—but 'tis not true!
        And then we will no more be racked
        With inward striving, and demand
        Of all the thousand nothings of the hour
70   Their stupefying power;
        Ah yes, and they benumb us at our call!
        Yet still, from time to time, vague and forlorn,
        From the soul's subterranean depth upborne
        As from an infinitely distant land,
75   Come airs, and floating echoes, and convey
        A melancholy into all our day.

        Only—but this is rare—
        When a belovéd hand is laid in ours,
        When, jaded with the rush and glare
80   Of the interminable hours,
        Our eyes can in another's eyes read clear,
        When our world-deafened ear
        Is by the tones of a loved voice caressed—
        A bolt is shot back somewhere in our breast,
85   And a lost pulse of feeling stirs again.
        The eye sinks inward, and the heart lies plain,
        And what we mean, we say, and what we would, we know.

A man becomes aware of his life's flow,
And hears its winding murmur; and he sees
90   The meadows where it glides, the sun, the breeze.

And there arrives a lull in the hot race
Wherein he doth for ever chase
That flying and elusive shadow, rest.
An air of coolness plays upon his face,
95   And an unwonted calm pervades his breast.
And then he thinks he knows
The hills where his life rose,
And the sea where it goes.

                                                                1852

THE SCHOLAR-GIPSY   While at Oxford in the mid-1840s, Arnold read the seventeenth-century tale of a young man who left his studies at the university to join a band of gypsies, intending to master their lore. Fascinated by the story, Arnold imagined the scholar still wandering the hills around Oxford, magically untouched by time and change. The poem Arnold eventually wrote, circa 1853, celebrated his own youth at Oxford, "the *freest* and most delightful part, perhaps, of my life," he told his brother Tom, "when with you and Clough . . . I shook off all the bonds and formalities of the place, and enjoyed the spring of life and that unforgotten Oxfordshire and Berkshire country." Arnold accompanied the poem with a note based on his source, Joseph Glanvill's *Vanity of Dogmatizing* (1661):

> There was very lately a lad in the University of Oxford, who was by his poverty forced to leave his studies there; and at last to join himself to a company of vagabond gipsies. Among these extravagant people, by the insinuating subtilty of his carriage, he quickly got so much of their love and esteem as that they discovered to him their mystery. After he had been a pretty while well exercised in the trade, there chanced to ride by a couple of scholars, who had formerly been of his acquaintance. They quickly spied out their old friend among the gipsies; and he gave them an account of the necessity which drove him to that kind of life, and told them that the people he went with were not such impostors as they were taken for, but that they had a traditional kind of learning among them, and could do wonders by the power of imagination, their fancy binding that of others: that himself had learned much of their art, and when he had compassed the whole secret, he intended, he said, to leave their company, and give the world an account of what he had learned.

The Scholar-Gipsy

Go, for they call you, shepherd, from the hill;
        Go, shepherd, and untie the wattled cotes![1]
            No longer leave thy wistful flock unfed,
            Nor let thy bawling fellows rack their throats,
5   Nor the cropped herbage shoot another head.
                But when the fields are still,
            And the tired men and dogs all gone to rest,
                And only the white sheep are sometimes seen

---

1. Fences made of woven sticks, used to pen sheep.

Cross and recross the strips of moon-blanched green,
10   Come, shepherd, and again begin the quest!

Here, where the reaper was at work of late—
   In this high field's dark corner, where he leaves
      His coat, his basket, and his earthen cruse,°   *jug*
   And in the sun all morning binds the sheaves,
15   Then here, at noon, comes back his stores to use—
         Here will I sit and wait,
   While to my ear from uplands far away
      The bleating of the folded° flocks is borne,   *penned up*
      With distant cries of reapers in the corn—
20   All the live murmur of a summer's day.

Screened is this nook o'er the high, half-reaped field,
   And here till sun-down, shepherd! will I be.
      Through the thick corn the scarlet poppies peep,
   And round green roots and yellowing stalks I see
25   Pale pink convolvulus° in tendrils creep;   *morning glory*
         And air-swept lindens yield
   Their scent, and rustle down their perfumed showers
      Of bloom on the bent grass where I am laid,
      And bower me from the August sun with shade;
30   And the eye travels down to Oxford's towers.

And near me on the grass lies Glanvil's book—
   Come, let me read the oft-read tale again!
      The story of the Oxford scholar poor,
   Of pregnant parts° and quick inventive brain,   *bursting with ideas*
35   Who, tired of knocking at preferment's door,
         One summer-morn forsook
   His friends, and went to learn the gipsy-lore,
      And roamed the world with that wild brotherhood,
      And came, as most men deemed, to little good,
40   But came to Oxford and his friends no more.

But once, years after, in the country-lanes,
   Two scholars, whom at college erst he knew,
      Met him, and of his way of life enquired;
   Whereat he answered, that the gipsy-crew,
45   His mates, had arts to rule as they desired
         The workings of men's brains,
   And they can bind them to what thoughts they will.
      "And I," he said, "the secret of their art,
      When fully learned, will to the world impart;
50   But it needs heaven-sent moments for this skill."

This said, he left them, and returned no more.
   But rumours hung about the country-side,
      That the lost Scholar long was seen to stray,
   Seen by rare glimpses, pensive and tongue-tied,

55   In hat of antique shape, and cloak of grey,
            The same the gipsies wore.
        Shepherds had met him on the Hurst[2] in spring;
            At some lone alehouse in the Berkshire moors,
            On the warm ingle-bench, the smock-frocked boors[3]
60   Had found him seated at their entering,

        But, 'mid their drink and clatter, he would fly.
        And I myself seem half to know thy looks,
            And put the shepherds, wanderer! on thy trace;
            And boys who in lone wheatfields scare the rooks
65   I ask if thou hast passed their quiet place;
            Or in my boat I lie
        Moored to the cool bank in the summer-heats,
            'Mid wide grass meadows which the sunshine fills,
            And watch the warm, green-muffled Cumner hills,
70   And wonder if thou haunt'st their shy retreats.

        For most, I know, thou lov'st retiréd ground!
        Thee at the ferry Oxford riders blithe,
            Returning home on summer-nights, have met
        Crossing the stripling Thames at Bab-lock-hithe,
75   Trailing in the cool stream thy fingers wet,
            As the punt's° rope chops round;   *small boat*
        And leaning backward in a pensive dream,
            And fostering in thy lap a heap of flowers
            Plucked in shy fields and distant Wychwood bowers,
80   And thine eyes resting on the moonlit stream.

        And then they land, and thou art seen no more!
        Maidens, who from the distant hamlets come
            To dance around the Fyfield elm in May,
        Oft through the darkening fields have seen thee roam,
85   Or cross a stile into the public way.
            Oft thou hast given them store
        Of flowers—the frail-leafed, white anemone,
            Dark bluebells drenched with dews of summer eves,
            And purple orchises with spotted leaves—
90   But none hath words she can report of thee.

        And, above Godstow Bridge, when hay-time's here
        In June, and many a scythe in sunshine flames,
            Men who through those wide fields of breezy grass
        Where black-winged swallows haunt the glittering Thames,
95   To bathe in the abandoned lasher pass,[4]
            Have often passed thee near
        Sitting upon the river bank o'ergrown;

2. Hill near Oxford; most of the places mentioned are in the countryside around Oxford.

3. Rustic peasants; an ingle-bench is beside the fireplace.

4. Pool where water spilling over a dam collects.

Marked thine outlandish garb, thy figure spare,
  Thy dark vague eyes, and soft abstracted air—
100 But, when they came from bathing, thou wast gone!

At some lone homestead in the Cumner hills,
  Where at her open door the housewife darns,
    Thou hast been seen, or hanging on a gate
To watch the threshers in the mossy barns.
105   Children, who early range these slopes and late
      For cresses from the rills,
  Have known thee eying, all an April-day,
    The springing pastures and the feeding kine;
    And marked thee, when the stars come out and shine,
110 Through the long dewy grass move slow away.

In autumn, on the skirts of Bagley Wood—
  Where most the gipsies by the turf-edged way
    Pitch their smoked tents, and every bush you see
With scarlet patches tagged and shreds of grey,[5]
115   Above the forest-ground called Thessaly—
      The blackbird, picking food,
  Sees thee, nor stops his meal, nor fears at all;
    So often has he known thee past him stray,
    Rapt, twirling in thy hand a withered spray,
120 And waiting for the spark from heaven to fall.

And once, in winter, on the causeway chill
  Where home through flooded fields foot-travellers go,
    Have I not passed thee on the wooden bridge,
Wrapped in thy cloak and battling with the snow,
125   Thy face tow'rd Hinksey and its wintry ridge?
      And thou hast climbed the hill,
  And gained the white brow of the Cumner range;
    Turned once to watch, while thick the snowflakes fall,
    The line of festal light in Christ-Church hall[6]—
130 Then sought thy straw in some sequestered grange.

But what—I dream! Two hundred years are flown
  Since first thy story ran through Oxford halls,
    And the grave Glanvil did the tale inscribe
That thou wert wandered from the studious walls
135   To learn strange arts, and join a gipsy-tribe;
      And thou from earth art gone
  Long since, and in some quiet churchyard laid—
    Some country-nook, where o'er thy unknown grave
    Tall grasses and white flowering nettles wave,
140 Under a dark, red-fruited yew-tree's shade.

---

5. Gypsies spread their clothes on bushes to dry.   6. The dining hall of Christ Church, an Oxford college.

—No, no, thou hast not felt the lapse of hours!
   For what wears out the life of mortal men?
     'Tis that from change to change their being rolls;
   'Tis that repeated shocks, again, again,
145   Exhaust the energy of strongest souls
      And numb the elastic powers.
   Till having used our nerves with bliss and teen,°   *grief*
     And tired upon a thousand schemes our wit,
     To the just-pausing Genius[7] we remit
150   Our worn-out life, and are—what we have been.

Thou hast not lived, why should'st thou perish, so?
   Thou hadst *one* aim, *one* business, *one* desire;
     Else wert thou long since numbered with the dead!
   Else hadst thou spent, like other men, thy fire!
155   The generations of thy peers are fled,
      And we ourselves shall go;
   But thou possessest an immortal lot,
     And we imagine thee exempt from age
     And living as thou liv'st on Glanvil's page,
160   Because thou hadst—what we, alas! have not.

For early didst thou leave the world, with powers
   Fresh, undiverted to the world without,
     Firm to their mark, not spent on other things;
   Free from the sick fatigue, the languid doubt,
165   Which much to have tried, in much been baffled, brings.
      O life unlike to ours!
   Who fluctuate idly without term or scope,
     Of whom each strives, nor knows for what he strives,
     And each half-lives a hundred different lives;
170   Who wait like thee, but not, like thee, in hope.

Thou waitest for the spark from heaven! and we,
   Light half-believers of our casual creeds,
     Who never deeply felt, nor clearly willed,
   Whose insight never has borne fruit in deeds,
175   Whose vague resolves never have been fulfilled;
      For whom each year we see
   Breeds new beginnings, disappointments new;
     Who hesitate and falter life away,
     And lose to-morrow the ground won to-day—
180   Ah! do not we, wanderer! await it too?

Yes, we await it!—but it still delays,
   And then we suffer! and amongst us one,[8]
     Who most has suffered, takes dejectedly

7. The guardian spirit that the ancients believed accompanied a person through life; here it pauses for only a moment to receive back the life it has shepherded.

8. Either Goethe, whom Arnold admired, or Tennyson, whose *In Memoriam* had recently been published.

His seat upon the intellectual throne;
185   And all his store of sad experience he
      Lays bare of wretched days;
Tells us his misery's birth and growth and signs,
    And how the dying spark of hope was fed,
    And how the breast was soothed, and how the head,
190   And all his hourly varied anodynes.

This for our wisest! and we others pine,
    And wish the long unhappy dream would end,
    And waive all claim to bliss, and try to bear;
With close-lipped patience for our only friend,
195   Sad patience, too near neighbour to despair—
      But none has hope like thine!
Thou through the fields and through the woods dost stray,
    Roaming the country-side, a truant boy,
    Nursing thy project in unclouded joy,
200   And every doubt long blown by time away.

O born in days when wits were fresh and clear,
    And life ran gaily as the sparkling Thames;
    Before this strange disease of modern life,
    With its sick hurry, its divided aims,
205   Its heads o'ertaxed, its palsied hearts, was rife—
      Fly hence, our contact fear!
Still fly, plunge deeper in the bowering wood!
    Averse, as Dido did with gesture stern
    From her false friend's approach in Hades turn,[9]
210   Wave us away, and keep thy solitude!

Still nursing the unconquerable hope,
    Still clutching the inviolable shade,
    With a free, onward impulse brushing through,
    By night, the silvered branches of the glade—
215   Far on the forest-skirts, where none pursue,
      On some mild pastoral slope
Emerge, and resting on the moonlit pales
    Freshen thy flowers as in former years
    With dew, or listen with enchanted ears,
220   From the dark dingles,° to the nightingales!   *small wooded valleys*

But fly our paths, our feverish contact fly!
    For strong the infection of our mental strife,
    Which, though it gives no bliss, yet spoils for rest;
    And we should win thee from thy own fair life,
225   Like us distracted, and like us unblest.
      Soon, soon thy cheer would die,

---

9. In Virgil's *Aeneid*, Dido, queen of Carthage, kills herself after her lover, Aeneas, deserts her. When they meet in Hades, she turns away sternly.

Thy hopes grow timorous, and unfixed thy powers,
   And thy clear aims be cross and shifting made;
   And then thy glad perennial youth would fade,
230   Fade, and grow old at last, and die like ours.

Then fly our greetings, fly our speech and smiles!
   —As some grave Tyrian trader,[1] from the sea,
   Descried at sunrise an emerging prow
   Lifting the cool-haired creepers stealthily,
235   The fringes of a southward-facing brow
        Among the Aegean isles;
   And saw the merry Grecian coaster come,
      Freighted with amber grapes, and Chian wine,
      Green, bursting figs, and tunnies steeped in brine—
240   And knew the intruders on his ancient home,

The young light-hearted masters of the waves—
   And snatched his rudder, and shook out more sail;
   And day and night held on indignantly
   O'er the blue Midland waters with the gale,
245   Betwixt the Syrtes[2] and soft Sicily,
        To where the Atlantic raves
   Outside the western straits; and unbent sails
      There, where down cloudy cliffs, through sheets of foam,
      Shy traffickers, the dark Iberians come;
250   And on the beach undid his corded bales.[3]

c. 1853   1853

from Culture and Anarchy[1]
from Sweetness and Light

The disparagers of culture make its motive curiosity; sometimes, indeed, they make its motive mere exclusiveness and vanity. The culture which is supposed to plume itself on a smattering of Greek and Latin is a culture which is begotten by nothing so

1. From Tyre, capital of ancient Phoenicia, in Northern Africa. The poet urges the solitary scholar to shun modern contacts just as he imagines the Tyrian trader once fled from intrusive Greeks.
2. Shoals off North Africa.
3. The last stanza continues the comparison between the scholar and the Tyrian. According to Herodotus's *History* 4.196, the Carthaginians—who came originally from Tyre—would sail out of the Mediterranean to West Africa, place their bales on the beach, and withdraw to their ships. The timid inhabitants would then set gold by the goods and withdraw in turn; thus the two sides could do business and never meet. Arnold's "shy traffickers" are not Africans but "dark Iberians" (Spanish or Portuguese). He implies that in them—people reminiscent of the dark-skinned reclusive gypsies who "trade" in the Oxford countryside—the sensitive Tyrian has found others as wary as he is.
1. Arnold's most important work of social criticism,

Culture and Anarchy (1869) grew out of his final Oxford lecture in 1867. Deploring English pride in "doing as one likes," Arnold connected the self-serving behavior of all classes to the worst effects of laissez-faire capitalism. He felt that Britain was heading toward anarchy; no one seemed to have any concern for the public good. The best of Western culture, Arnold contended, depends on a balance between the Judeo-Christian emphasis on moral conduct (Hebraism) and the Greek ideal of intellectual and artistic cultivation (Hellenism). But in his view a Puritan "strictness of conscience" was now impeding a classical "spontaneity of consciousness." There was only one way to bridge the gap between privileged "Barbarians" (the aristocracy), intolerant "Philistines" (the middle classes), and the uneducated "Populace" (the working classes): by spreading to all parts of society a Hellenistic respect for beauty and intellect—what Arnold termed "sweetness and light."

intellectual as curiosity; it is valued either out of sheer vanity and ignorance or else as an engine of social and class distinction, separating its holder, like a badge or title, from other people who have not got it. No serious man would call this *culture*, or attach any value to it, as culture, at all. To find the real ground for the very different estimate which serious people will set upon culture, we must find some motive for culture in the terms of which may lie a real ambiguity; and such a motive the word *curiosity* gives us.

I have before now pointed out that we English do not, like the foreigners, use this word in a good sense as well as in a bad sense. With us the word is always used in a somewhat disapproving sense. A liberal and intelligent eagerness about the things of the mind may be meant by a foreigner when he speaks of curiosity, but with us the word always conveys a certain notion of frivolous and unedifying activity. In the *Quarterly Review*, some little time ago, was an estimate of the celebrated French critic, M. Sainte-Beuve,[2] and a very inadequate estimate it in my judgment was. And its inadequacy consisted chiefly in this: that in our English way it left out of sight the double sense really involved in the word *curiosity*, thinking enough was said to stamp M. Sainte-Beuve with blame if it was said that he was impelled in his operations as a critic by curiosity, and omitting either to perceive that M. Sainte-Beuve himself, and many other people with him, would consider that this was praiseworthy and not blameworthy, or to point out why it ought really to be accounted worthy of blame and not of praise. For as there is a curiosity about intellectual matters which is futile, and merely a disease, so there is certainly a curiosity,—a desire after the things of the mind simply for their own sakes and for the pleasure of seeing them as they are,—which is, in an intelligent being, natural and laudable. Nay, and the very desire to see things as they are implies a balance and regulation of mind which is not often attained without fruitful effort, and which is the very opposite of the blind and diseased impulse of mind which is what we mean to blame when we blame curiosity. Montesquieu[3] says: "The first motive which ought to impel us to study is the desire to augment the excellence of our nature, and to render an intelligent being yet more intelligent." This is the true ground to assign for the genuine scientific passion, however manifested, and for culture, viewed simply as a fruit of this passion; and it is a worthy ground, even though we let the term *curiosity* stand to describe it.

But there is of culture another view, in which not solely the scientific passion, the sheer desire to see things as they are, natural and proper in an intelligent being, appears as the ground of it. There is a view in which all the love of our neighbour, the impulses towards action, help, and beneficence, the desire for removing human error, clearing human confusion, and diminishing human misery, the noble aspiration to leave the world better and happier than we found it,—motives eminently such as are called social,—come in as part of the grounds of culture, and the main and pre-eminent part. Culture is then properly described not as having its origin in curiosity, but as having its origin in the love of perfection; it is *a study of perfection*. It moves by the force, not merely or primarily of the scientific passion for pure knowledge, but also of the moral and social passion for doing good. As, in the first view of it, we took for its worthy motto Montesquieu's words: "To render an intelligent being yet more intelligent!" so, in the second view of it, there is no better motto which it

2. Charles Augustine Sainte-Beuve (1804–1869), French critic whom Arnold admired.

3. Baron de la Brède et de Montesquieu (1689–1755), French political and legal philosopher.

can have than these words of Bishop Wilson: "To make reason and the will of God prevail!"[4] * * *

The pursuit of perfection, then, is the pursuit of sweetness and light.[5] He who works for sweetness and light, works to make reason and the will of God prevail. He who works for machinery, he who works for hatred, works only for confusion. Culture looks beyond machinery, culture hates hatred; culture has one great passion, the passion for sweetness and light. It has one even yet greater!—the passion for making them *prevail*. It is not satisfied till we *all* come to a perfect man; it knows that the sweetness and light of the few must be imperfect until the raw and unkindled masses of humanity are touched with sweetness and light. If I have not shrunk from saying that we must work for sweetness and light, so neither have I shrunk from saying that we must have a broad basis, must have sweetness and light for as many as possible. Again and again I have insisted how those are the happy moments of humanity, how those are the marking epochs of a people's life, how those are the flowering times for literature and art and all the creative power of genius, when there is a *national* glow of life and thought, when the whole of society is in the fullest measure permeated by thought, sensible to beauty, intelligent and alive. Only it must be *real* thought and *real* beauty; *real* sweetness and *real* light. Plenty of people will try to give the masses, as they call them, an intellectual food prepared and adapted in the way they think proper for the actual condition of the masses. The ordinary popular literature is an example of this way of working on the masses. Plenty of people will try to indoctrinate the masses with the set of ideas and judgments constituting the creed of their own profession or party. Our religious and political organisations give an example of this way of working on the masses. I condemn neither way; but culture works differently. It does not try to teach down to the level of inferior classes; it does not try to win them for this or that sect of its own, with ready-made judgments and watchwords. It seeks to do away with classes; to make the best that has been thought and known in the world current everywhere; to make all men live in an atmosphere of sweetness and light, where they may use ideas, as it uses them itself, freely,—nourished, and not bound by them.

* * *

from *Doing as One Likes*

It is said that a man with my theories of sweetness and light is full of antipathy against the rougher or coarser movements going on around him, that he will not lend a hand to the humble operation of uprooting evil by their means, and that therefore the believers in action grow impatient with him. But what if rough and coarse action, ill-calculated action, action with insufficient light, is, and has for a long time been, our bane? What if our urgent want now is, not to act at any price, but rather to lay in a stock of light for our difficulties? In that case, to refuse to lend a hand to the rougher and coarser movements going on round us, to make the primary need, both for oneself and others, to consist in enlightening ourselves and qualifying ourselves to act less at random, is surely the best and in real truth the most practical line our

---

4. Thomas Wilson (1663–1755), Bishop of Sodor and Man. His *Maxims*, though little known, were a favorite of Arnold's.
5. The phrase comes from a fable in Swift's *The Battle of the Books* (1704): the Bee (representing ancient culture) ventures forth to fill its hive with honey and wax for light-giving candles, but the home-bound Spider (representing modern culture) produces from itself only cobwebs and poison. The Bee thus provides "the two noblest of things, which are sweetness and light."

endeavours can take. So that if I can show what my opponents call rough or coarse action, but what I would rather call random and ill-regulated action,—action with insufficient light, action pursued because we like to be doing something and doing it as we please, and do not like the trouble of thinking and the severe constraint of any kind of rule,—if I can show this to be, at the present moment, a practical mischief and dangerous to us, then I have found a practical use for light in correcting this state of things, and have only to exemplify how, in cases which fall under everybody's observation, it may deal with it.

When I began to speak of culture, I insisted on our bondage to machinery, on our proneness to value machinery as an end in itself, without looking beyond it to the end for which alone, in truth, it is valuable. Freedom, I said, was one of those things which we thus worshipped in itself, without enough regarding the ends for which freedom is to be desired. In our common notions and talk about freedom, we eminently show our idolatry of machinery. Our prevalent notion is,—and I quoted a number of instances to prove it,—that it is a most happy and important thing for a man merely to be able to do as he likes. On what he is to do when he is thus free to do as he likes, we do not lay so much stress. Our familiar praise of the British Constitution under which we live, is that it is a system of checks,—a system which stops and paralyses any power in interfering with the free action of individuals. To this effect Mr Bright,[6] who loves to walk in the old ways of the Constitution, said forcibly in one of his great speeches, what many other people are every day saying less forcibly, that the central idea of English life and politics is *the assertion of personal liberty*. Evidently this is so; but evidently, also, as feudalism, which with its ideas and habits of subordination was for many centuries silently behind the British Constitution, dies out, and we are left with nothing but our system of checks, and our notion of its being the great right and happiness of an Englishman to do as far as possible what he likes, we are in danger of drifting towards anarchy. We have not the notion, so familiar on the Continent and to antiquity, of *the State*,—the nation in its collective and corporate character, entrusted with stringent powers for the general advantage, and controlling individual wills in the name of an interest wider than that of individuals. We say, what is very true, that this notion is often made instrumental to tyranny; we say that a State is in reality made up of the individuals who compose it, and that every individual is the best judge of his own interests. Our leading class is an aristocracy, and no aristocracy likes the notion of a State-authority greater than itself, with a stringent administrative machinery superseding the decorative inutilities of lord-lieutenancy, deputy-lieutenancy, and the *posse comitatus*,[7] which are all in its own hands. Our middle class, the great representative of trade and Dissent, with its maxims of every man for himself in business, every man for himself in religion, dreads a powerful administration which might somehow interfere with it; and besides, it has its own decorative inutilities of vestrymanship and guardianship, which are to this class what lord-lieutenancy and the county magistracy are to the aristocratic class, and a stringent administration might either take these functions out of its hands, or prevent its exercising them in its own comfortable, independent manner, as at present.

---

6. John Bright (1811–1889), Quaker radical who led the left wing of the Liberal Party under Gladstone.
7. Power of the county (Latin); a "posse" was an outdated method of preserving public order by local authority rather than by the government.

Then as to our working class. This class, pressed constantly by the hard daily compulsion of material wants, is naturally the very centre and stronghold of our national idea, that it is man's ideal right and felicity to do as he likes. I think I have somewhere related how M. Michelet said to me of the people of France, that it was "a nation of barbarians civilised by the conscription."[8] He meant that through their military service the idea of public duty and of discipline was brought to the mind of these masses, in other respects so raw and uncultivated. Our masses are quite as raw and uncultivated as the French; and so far from their having the idea of public duty and of discipline, superior to the individual's self-will, brought to their mind by a universal obligation of military service, such as that of the conscription,—so far from their having this, the very idea of a conscription is so at variance with our English notion of the prime right and blessedness of doing as one likes, that I remember the manager of the Clay Cross works in Derbyshire told me during the Crimean war, when our want of soldiers was much felt and some people were talking of a conscription, that sooner than submit to a conscription the population of that district would flee to the mines, and lead a sort of Robin Hood life under ground.

For a long time, as I have said, the strong feudal habits of subordination and deference continued to tell upon the working class. The modern spirit has now almost entirely dissolved those habits, and the anarchical tendency of our worship of freedom in and for itself, of our superstitious faith, as I say, in machinery, is becoming very manifest. More and more, because of this our blind faith in machinery, because of our want of light to enable us to look beyond machinery to the end for which machinery is valuable, this and that man, and this and that body of men, all over the country, are beginning to assert and put in practice an Englishman's right to do what he likes; his right to march where he likes, meet where he likes, enter where he likes, hoot as he likes, threaten as he likes, smash as he likes. All this, I say, tends to anarchy; and though a number of excellent people, and particularly my friends of the Liberal or progressive party, as they call themselves, are kind enough to reassure us by saying that these are trifles, that a few transient outbreaks of rowdyism signify nothing, that our system of liberty is one which itself cures all the evils which it works, that the educated and intelligent classes stand in overwhelming strength and majestic repose, ready, like our military force in riots, to act at a moment's notice,—yet one finds that one's Liberal friends generally say this because they have such faith in themselves and their nostrums,[9] when they shall return, as the public welfare requires, to place and power. But this faith of theirs one cannot exactly share, when one has so long had them and their nostrums at work, and sees that they have not prevented our coming to our present embarrassed condition. And one finds, also, that the outbreaks of rowdyism tend to become less and less of trifles, to become more frequent rather than less frequent; and that meanwhile our educated and intelligent classes remain in their majestic repose, and somehow or other, whatever happens, their overwhelming strength, like our military force in riots, never does act.

How, indeed, *should* their overwhelming strength act, when the man who gives an inflammatory lecture, or breaks down the park railings,[1] or invades a Secretary of State's office, is only following an Englishman's impulse to do as he likes; and our own

8. From Arnold's *The Popular Education of France* (1861); Jules Michelet (1798–1874), French historian.
9. Panaceas, quack medicine.
1. On 23 July 1866 the Reform League organized a mass

meeting in Hyde Park. When they were refused entrance, the demonstrators broke down the park railings and trampled the flowers. The incident was widely viewed as a symptom of impending anarchy.

conscience tells us that we ourselves have always regarded this impulse as something primary and sacred? Mr Murphy lectures at Birmingham,[2] and showers on the Catholic population of that town "words," says the Home Secretary, "only fit to be addressed to thieves or murderers." What then? Mr Murphy has his own reasons of several kinds. He suspects the Roman Catholic Church of designs upon Mrs Murphy; and he says if mayors and magistrates do not care for their wives and daughters, he does. But, above all, he is doing as he likes; or, in worthier language, asserting his personal liberty. "I will carry out my lectures if they walk over my body as a dead corpse; and I say to the Mayor of Birmingham that he is my servant while I am in Birmingham, and as my servant he must do his duty and protect me." Touching and beautiful words, which find a sympathetic chord in every British bosom! The moment it is plainly put before us that a man is asserting his personal liberty, we are half disarmed; because we are believers in freedom, and not in some dream of a right reason to which the assertion of our freedom is to be subordinated. Accordingly, the Secretary of State had to say that although the lecturer's language was "only fit to be addressed to thieves or murderers," yet, "I do not think he is to be deprived, I do not think that anything I have said could justify the inference that he is to be deprived, of the right of protection in a place built by him for the purpose of these lectures; because the language was not language which afforded grounds for a criminal prosecution." No, nor to be silenced by Mayor, or Home Secretary, or any administrative authority on earth, simply on their notion of what is discreet and reasonable! This is in perfect consonance with our public opinion, and with our national love for the assertion of personal liberty. * * *

Now, if culture, which simply means trying to perfect oneself, and one's mind as part of oneself, brings us light, and if light shows us that there is nothing so very blessed in merely doing as one likes, that the worship of the mere freedom to do as one likes is worship of machinery, that the really blessed thing is to like what right reason ordains, and to follow her authority, then we have got a practical benefit out of culture. We have got a much wanted principle, a principle of authority, to counteract the tendency to anarchy which seems to be threatening us. * * *

Well, then, what if we tried to rise above the idea of class to the idea of the whole community, *the State*, and to find our centre of light and authority there? Every one of us has the idea of country, as a sentiment; hardly any one of us has the idea of *the State*, as a working power. And why? Because we habitually live in our ordinary selves, which do not carry us beyond the ideas and wishes of the class to which we happen to belong. And we are all afraid of giving to the State too much power, because we only conceive of the State as something equivalent to the class in occupation of the executive government, and are afraid of that class abusing power to its own purposes. If we strengthen the State with the aristocratic class in occupation of the executive government, we imagine we are delivering ourselves up captive to the ideas and wishes of our fierce aristocratical baronet; if with the middle class in occupation of the executive government, to those of our truculent middle-class Dissenting minister;[3] if with the working class, to those of its notorious tribune, Mr Bradlaugh.[4] And with much justice; owing to the exaggerated notion which we English, as I have said, entertain of the right and blessedness of the mere doing as one likes, of

2. In 1867 William Murphy, an anti-Catholic agitator, delivered a series of lectures in Birmingham that led to riots.
3. Rev. William Cattle, chairman at William Murphy's

anti-Catholic lectures (see n. 2).
4. Charles Bradlaugh, radical agitator, eventually the first atheist Member of Parliament.

the affirming oneself, and oneself just as it is. People of the aristocratic class want to affirm their ordinary selves, their likings and dislikings; people of the middle class the same, people of the working class the same. By our everyday selves, however, we are separate, personal, at war; we are only safe from one another's tyranny when no one has any power; and this safety, in its turn, cannot save us from anarchy. And when, therefore, anarchy presents itself as a danger to us, we know not where to turn.

But by our *best self* we are united, impersonal, at harmony. We are in no peril from giving authority to this, because it is the truest friend we all of us can have; and when anarchy is a danger to us, to this authority we may turn with sure trust. Well, and this is the very self which culture, or the study of perfection, seeks to develop in us; at the expense of our old untransformed self, taking pleasure only in doing what it likes or is used to do, and exposing us to the risk of clashing with every one else who is doing the same! So that our poor culture, which is flouted as so unpractical, leads us to the very ideas capable of meeting the great want of our present embarrassed times! We want an authority, and we find nothing but jealous classes, checks, and a dead-lock; culture suggests the idea of *the State.* We find no basis for a firm State-power in our ordinary selves; culture suggests one to us in our *best self.*[5] * * *

from *Hebraism and Hellenism*

This fundamental ground is our preference of doing to thinking. Now this preference is a main element in our nature, and as we study it we find ourselves opening up a number of large questions on every side.

Let me go back for a moment to Bishop Wilson, who says: "First, never go against the best light you have; secondly, take care that your light be not darkness."[6] We show, as a nation, laudable energy and persistence in walking according to the best light we have, but are not quite careful enough, perhaps, to see that our light be not darkness. This is only another version of the old story that energy is our strong point and favourable characteristic, rather than intelligence. But we may give to this idea a more general form still, in which it will have a yet larger range of application. We may regard this energy driving at practice, this paramount sense of the obligation of duty, self-control, and work, this earnestness in going manfully with the best light we have, as one force. And we may regard the intelligence driving at those ideas which are, after all, the basis of right practice, the ardent sense for all the new and changing combinations of them which man's development brings with it, the indomitable impulse to know and adjust them perfectly, as another force. And these two forces we may regard as in some sense rivals,—rivals not by the necessity of their own nature, but as exhibited in man and his history,—and rivals dividing the empire of the world between them. And to give these forces names from the two races of men who have supplied the most signal and splendid manifestations of them, we may call them respectively the forces of Hebraism and Hellenism.[7] Hebraism and Hellenism,— between these two points of influence moves our world. At one time it feels

---

5. Chapter 3, omitted here, explores the class-bound "ordinary selves" that Arnold wishes to transcend: the "Barbarian" aristocracy who value individualism, courage, and athleticism over intellect and sensitivity; the middle-class Philistines who stubbornly resist new ideas; and the dangerously "raw and half-developed" working class he calls simply "the Populace."

6. Quoting Thomas Wilson, *Maxims* (see page 876, n. 4).

7. In Arnold's view Hebraism (the Judeo-Christian tradition) emphasizes duty, industriousness, and a sense of sin. In contrast, Hellenism (the Greek tradition) values rationality, "clearness of mind," and the quest for perfection. While Arnold emphasizes the importance of both traditions, it is Hellenism that he associates with sweetness and light.

more powerfully the attraction of one of them, at another time of the other; and it ought to be, though it never is, evenly and happily balanced between them.

The final aim of both Hellenism and Hebraism, as of all great spiritual disciplines, is no doubt the same: man's perfection or salvation. The very language which they both of them use in schooling us to reach this aim is often identical. * * *

Still, they pursue this aim by very different courses. The uppermost idea with Hellenism is to see things as they really are; the uppermost idea with Hebraism is conduct and obedience. Nothing can do away with this ineffaceable difference. The Greek quarrel with the body and its desires is, that they hinder right thinking; the Hebrew quarrel with them is, that they hinder right acting. * * *

* * * Eighteen hundred years ago it was altogether the hour of Hebraism. Primitive Christianity was legitimately and truly the ascendant force in the world at that time, and the way of mankind's progress lay through its full development. Another hour in man's development began in the fifteenth century, and the main road of his progress then lay for a time through Hellenism. Puritanism was no longer the central current of the world's progress, it was a side stream crossing the central current and checking it. The cross and the check may have been necessary and salutary, but that does not do away with the essential difference between the main stream of man's advance and a cross or side stream. For more than two hundred years the main stream of man's advance has moved towards knowing himself and the world, seeing things as they are, spontaneity of consciousness; the main impulse of a great part, and that the strongest part, of our nation has been towards strictness of conscience. They have made the secondary the principal at the wrong moment, and the principal they have at the wrong moment treated as secondary. This contravention of the natural order has produced, as such contravention always must produce, a certain confusion and false movement, of which we are now beginning to feel, in almost every direction, the inconvenience. In all directions our habitual courses of action seem to be losing efficaciousness, credit, and control, both with others and even with ourselves. Everywhere we see the beginnings of confusion, and we want a clue to some sound order and authority. This we can only get by going back upon the actual instincts and forces which rule our life, seeing them as they really are, connecting them with other instincts and forces, and enlarging our whole view and rule of life.

from *Conclusion*

And so we bring to an end what we had to say in praise of culture, and in evidence of its special utility for the circumstances in which we find ourselves, and the confusion which environs us. Through culture seems to lie our way, not only to perfection, but even to safety. Resolutely refusing to lend a hand to the imperfect operations of our Liberal friends, disregarding their impatience, taunts, and reproaches, firmly bent on trying to find in the intelligible laws of things a firmer and sounder basis for future practice than any which we have at present, and believing this search and discovery to be, for our generation and circumstances, of yet more vital and pressing importance than practice itself, we nevertheless may do more, perhaps, we poor disparaged followers of culture, to make the actual present, and the frame of society in which we live, solid and seaworthy, than all which our bustling politicians can do.

For we have seen how much of our disorders and perplexities is due to the disbelief, among the classes and combinations of men, Barbarian or Philistine, which have hitherto governed our society, in right reason, in a paramount best self; to the inevitable decay and break-up of the organisations by which, asserting and expressing in these organisations their ordinary self only, they have so long ruled us; and to their irresolution, when the society, which their conscience tells them they have made and still manage not with right reason but with their ordinary self, is rudely shaken, in offering resistance to its subverters. But for us,—who believe in right reason, in the duty and possibility of extricating and elevating our best self, in the progress of humanity towards perfection,—for us the framework of society, that theatre on which this august drama has to unroll itself, is sacred; and whoever administers it, and however we may seek to remove them from their tenure of administration, yet, while they administer, we steadily and with undivided heart support them in repressing anarchy and disorder; because without order there can be no society, and without society there can be no human perfection.

And this opinion of the intolerableness of anarchy we can never forsake, however our Liberal friends may think a little rioting, and what they call popular demonstrations, useful sometimes to their own interests and to the interests of the valuable practical operations they have in hand, and however they may preach the right of an Englishman to be left to do as far as possible what he likes, and the duty of his government to indulge him and connive as much as possible and abstain from all harshness of repression. And even when they artfully show us operations which are undoubtedly precious, such as the abolition of the slave-trade, and ask us if, for their sake, foolish and obstinate governments may not wholesomely be frightened by a little disturbance, the good design in view and the difficulty of overcoming opposition to it being considered,—still we say no, and that monster-processions in the streets and forcible irruptions into the parks, even in professed support of this good design, ought to be unflinchingly forbidden and repressed; and that far more is lost than is gained by permitting them. Because a State in which law is authoritative and sovereign, a firm and settled course of public order, is requisite if man is to bring to maturity anything precious and lasting now, or to found anything precious and lasting for the future. * * *

1867–1868; 1869

+•+ ⊰◈⊱ +•+

Dante Gabriel Rossetti
1828–1882

"If any man has any poetry in him he should paint it," Dante Gabriel Rossetti once said. Like Blake, whose work he rediscovered for a Victorian audience, Rossetti was gifted as both a poet and painter. So many of Rossetti's poems became subjects of his own paintings—and vice versa—that his friend James McNeill Whistler once suggested combining the two: "Why not frame the sonnet?"

Christened Gabriele Charles Dante, Rossetti rearranged his name to signal his determination to devote himself to what was most spiritual in love, poetry, and art. He grew up in London in a poor but exceptionally cultivated milieu: his father was an ardent Italian poet, patriot, and Dante scholar in exile; his mother was a devout, half-Italian but very English governess.

His sister Christina composed poetry before she was old enough to write it down. Dante himself showed such early signs of genius that he was spared work and sent to art school despite his family's poverty. In 1848 Dante joined with two other young students at the Royal Academy, William Holman Hunt and John Everett Millais, to found the Pre-Raphaelite Brotherhood.

Rossetti published his early poems, including *The Blessed Damozel,* in the Pre-Raphaelite journal, *The Germ,* in 1850. His paintings of the time exhibit many traits of the short-lived group: a flattened picture plane, luminous detail, careful observation of nature, purity of line and color, and an earnest treatment of religious subjects that sought to capture the intensity of feeling of art before Raphael—i.e., before the High Renaissance.

Members of the group soon went their separate ways, and Rossetti's own art and writing became increasingly preoccupied with two subjects that often overlapped: a "medievalism" that lost itself in densely designed interpretations of scenes from Dante and Malory, and a luscious, almost claustrophobic exploration of love in its most spiritual and sensuous manifestations. Rossetti's distinctive style included elements that shaped the meaning of "Pre-Raphaelitism" as a literary and artistic term: vivid color, formal harmony, and symbolic detail used to create distant (and decidedly un-Victorian) settings for the expression of amorous passion.

Bohemian, gregarious, brilliant, and worldly, Rossetti moved in a circle of artists and writers that included Ruskin, William Morris, Swinburne, Edward Burne-Jones, Whistler, George Meredith, and Ford Madox Brown. The wittiness of *The Burden of Nineveh,* about the eventual decline of the British Empire, and the jaded sophistication of *Jenny,* about a poet's night with a prostitute, convey a different side of Rossetti: the urbane and self-assured Londoner who was the center of attention at any gathering, who taught art at the Working Men's College, and who for a while shared his house with a menagerie that included kangaroos, peacocks, and a wombat.

But Rossetti's personal life was erratic, eccentric, and often miserable. As one critic put it: "He married a woman he did not love, loved a woman he could not marry, and lived with a woman he neither loved nor married." The woman he married, in 1860, was the poet, artist, and model Elizabeth Siddall. She committed suicide in 1862, a devastating event that Rossetti commemorated by portraying her as a transfigured Beatrice (Dante's love lost early to death) in his painting *Beata Beatrix* (c. 1863). In a fit of remorse Rossetti thrust the manuscript of his poems into her coffin at the funeral—only to exhume them years later in order to publish his first collection, *Poems* (1870). By then he had fallen hopelessly in love with William Morris's wife, Jane, who posed for many of his later portrait-fantasies, among them *Astarte Syrica* (1877) and *Proserpine* (1873–1877). The woman he finally lived with was Fanny Cornforth, who also modeled for Rossetti's languid, steamy fantasies of long-necked, thick-haired beauties.

In 1871 the poet Robert Buchanan published a scathing attack on Rossetti, *The Fleshly School of Poetry.* Rossetti counterattacked in 1872 with *The Stealthy School of Criticism,* but the experience wounded him deeply, contributing to declining health and mental depression, aggravated by large doses of narcotics and whiskey. Spiritual and sensuous at the same time, Rossetti could not seem to find happiness in a world scandalized by his efforts to unite these qualities in art and life. He had approached his ideal most fully, perhaps, in *The Blessed Damozel,* where he transformed the Dantesque vision of a heavenly beloved by giving her a very Rossettian physical body: he could not separate the purity of his passion from the warmth of her bosom. It was this combination of eroticism and idealism, together with his commingling of the visual and the poetic, that made Rossetti's work a decisive force in the shaping of English aestheticism, the Arts and Crafts movement, and art nouveau. And it was Rossetti's powerful influence on the symbolist poets of the *fin de siècle* that made Yeats declare of his own youthful aspirations that he was "in all things Pre-Raphaelite."

The Blessed Damozel[1]

The blessed damozel leaned out
    From the gold bar of Heaven;
Her eyes were deeper than the depth
    Of waters stilled at even;
5   She had three lilies in her hand,
    And the stars in her hair were seven.

Her robe, ungirt from clasp to hem,
    No wrought flowers did adorn,
But a white rose of Mary's gift,
10   For service meetly worn;
Her hair that lay along her back
    Was yellow like ripe corn.

Herseemed° she scarce had been a day   *it seemed to her*
    One of God's choristers;
15   The wonder was not yet quite gone
    From that still look of hers;
Albeit, to them she left, her day
    Had counted as ten years.

(To one, it is ten years of years.
20   . . . Yet now, and in this place,
Surely she leaned o'er me—her hair
    Fell all about my face . . .
Nothing: the autumn-fall of leaves.
    The whole year sets apace.)

25   It was the rampart of God's house
    That she was standing on;
By God built over the sheer depth
    The which is Space begun;
So high, that looking downward thence
30   She scarce could see the sun.

It lies in Heaven, across the flood
    Of ether, as a bridge.
Beneath, the tides of day and night
    With flame and darkness ridge
35   The void, as low as where this earth
    Spins like a fretful midge.

Around her, lovers, newly met
    'Mid deathless love's acclaims,
Spoke evermore among themselves

---

1. Damsel, young woman. Rossetti explained the connection between this poem and Edgar Allan Poe's *The Raven* (1844): "I saw that Poe had done the utmost it was possible to do with the grief of the lover on earth, and so I determined to reverse the conditions, and give utterance to the yearning of the loved one in heaven" (quoted in T. Hall Caine's *Recollections of Dante Gabriel Rossetti*, 1882). See Rossetti's painting *The Blessed Damozel*, Color Plate 17.

40 Their heart-remembered names;
   And the souls mounting up to God
     Went by her like thin flames.

And still she bowed herself and stooped
     Out of the circling charm;
45 Until her bosom must have made
     The bar she leaned on warm,
And the lilies lay as if asleep
     Along her bended arm.

From the fixed place of Heaven she saw
50   Time like a pulse shake fierce
Through all the worlds. Her gaze still strove
     Within the gulf to pierce
Its path; and now she spoke as when
     The stars sang in their spheres.

55 The sun was gone now; the curled moon
     Was like a little feather
Fluttering far down the gulf; and now
     She spoke through the still weather.
Her voice was like the voice the stars
60   Had when they sang together.

(Ah sweet! Even now, in that bird's song,
     Strove not her accents there,
Fain to be hearkened? When those bells
     Possessed the mid-day air,
65 Strove not her steps to reach my side
     Down all the echoing stair?)

"I wish that he were come to me,
     For he will come," she said.
"Have I not prayed in Heaven?—on earth,
70   Lord, Lord, has he not pray'd?
Are not two prayers a perfect strength?
     And shall I feel afraid?

"When round his head the aureole° clings,   *halo*
     And he is clothed in white,
75 I'll take his hand and go with him
     To the deep wells of light;
As unto a stream we will step down,
     And bathe there in God's sight.

"We two will stand beside that shrine,
80   Occult,° withheld, untrod,   *hidden*
Whose lamps are stirred continually
     With prayer sent up to God;
And see our old prayers, granted, melt
     Each like a little cloud.

85 "We two will lie i' the shadow of
  That living mystic tree[2]
Within whose secret growth the Dove
  Is sometimes felt to be,
While every leaf that His plumes touch
90 Saith His Name audibly.

"And I myself will teach to him,
  I myself, lying so,
The songs I sing here; which his voice
  Shall pause in, hushed and slow,
95 And find some knowledge at each pause,
  Or some new thing to know."

(Alas! we two, we two, thou say'st!
  Yea, one wast thou with me
That once of old. But shall God lift
100 To endless unity
The soul whose likeness with thy soul
  Was but its love for thee?)

"We two," she said, "will seek the groves
  Where the lady Mary is,
105 With her five handmaidens, whose names
  Are five sweet symphonies,
Cecily, Gertrude, Magdalen,
  Margaret and Rosalys.

"Circlewise sit they, with bound locks
110 And foreheads garlanded;
Into the fine cloth white like flame
  Weaving the golden thread,
To fashion the birth-robes for them
  Who are just born, being dead.

115 "He shall fear, haply, and be dumb:
  Then will I lay my cheek
To his, and tell about our love,
  Not once abashed or weak:
And the dear Mother will approve
120 My pride, and let me speak.

"Herself shall bring us, hand in hand,
  To Him round whom all souls
Kneel, the clear-ranged unnumbered heads
  Bowed with their aureoles:
125 And angels meeting us shall sing
  To their citherns and citoles.[3]

---

2. The tree of life; cf. Revelation 22.2.

3. Stringed instruments from the Middle Ages and Renaissance.

"There will I ask of Christ the Lord
    Thus much for him and me:—
Only to live as once on earth
130   With Love,—only to be,
As then awhile, for ever now
    Together, I and he."

She gazed and listened and then said,
    Less sad of speech than mild,—
135 "All this is when he comes." She ceased.
    The light thrilled towards her, fill'd
With angels in strong level flight.
    Her eyes prayed, and she smil'd.

(I saw her smile.) But soon their path
140   Was vague in distant spheres:
And then she cast her arms along
    The golden barriers,
And laid her face between her hands,
    And wept. (I heard her tears.)

1847   1850

The Woodspurge[1]

The wind flapped loose, the wind was still,
Shaken out dead from tree and hill:
I had walked on at the wind's will,—
I sat now, for the wind was still.

5   Between my knees my forehead was,—
My lips, drawn in, said not Alas!
My hair was over in the grass,
My naked ears heard the day pass.

My eyes, wide open, had the run
10 Of some ten weeds to fix upon;
Among those few, out of the sun,
The woodspurge flowered, three cups in one.

From perfect grief there need not be
Wisdom or even memory:
15 One thing then learnt remains to me,—
The woodspurge has a cup of three.

1856   1870

from The House of Life
The Sonnet

A Sonnet is a moment's monument,—
  Memorial from the Soul's eternity

---

1. A flowering weed that exudes a milky fluid.

To one dead deathless hour. Look that it be,
Whether for lustral° rite or dire portent,   *purification*
5   Of its own arduous fulness reverent:
    Carve it in ivory or in ebony,
    As Day or Night may rule; and let Time see
Its flowering crest impearled and orient.

A Sonnet is a coin: its face reveals
10   The soul,—its converse, to what Power 'tis due:[1]—
Whether for tribute to the august appeals
    Of Life, or dower in Love's high retinue,
It serve; or, 'mid the dark wharf's cavernous breath,
In Charon's[2] palm it pay the toll to Death.

1880   1881

4. Lovesight

When do I see thee most, belovèd one?
    When in the light the spirits of mine eyes
    Before thy face, their altar, solemnize
The worship of that Love through thee made known?
5   Or when in the dusk hours, (we two alone,)
    Close-kissed and eloquent of still replies
    Thy twilight-hidden glimmering visage lies,
And my soul only sees thy soul its own?

O love, my love! if I no more should see
10 Thyself, nor on the earth the shadow of thee,
    Nor image of thine eyes in any spring,—
How then should sound upon Life's darkening slope
The ground-whirl of the perished leaves of Hope,
    The wind of Death's imperishable wing?

1869   1870

6. The Kiss

What smouldering senses in death's sick delay
    Or seizure of malign vicissitude
    Can rob this body of honour, or denude
This soul of wedding-raiment worn to-day?
5   For lo! even now my lady's lips did play
    With these my lips such consonant interlude
    As laurelled Orpheus[1] longed for when he wooed
The half-drawn hungering face with that last lay.

I was a child beneath her touch,—a man
10   When breast to breast we clung, even I and she,—

1. Cf. Luke 20.21–26.
2. The ferryman whom the dead would pay to row them across the River Styx of Hades.
1. Orpheus tried to rescue his wife Eurydice from the underworld by the power of his music. She was permitted to leave provided he did not look back at her, but he disobeyed and she had to return to Hades. In his grief he wandered the earth for years.

A spirit when her spirit looked through me,—
A god when all our life-breath met to fan
Our life-blood, till love's emulous ardours ran,
  Fire within fire, desire in deity.

1869   1870

Nuptial Sleep[1]

At length their long kiss severed, with sweet smart:
  And as the last slow sudden drops are shed
  From sparkling eaves when all the storm has fled,
So singly flagged the pulses of each heart.
5 Their bosoms sundered, with the opening start
  Of married flowers to either side outspread
  From the knit stem; yet still their mouths, burnt red,
Fawned on each other where they lay apart.

Sleep sank them lower than the tide of dreams,
10 And their dreams watched them sink, and slid away.
Slowly their souls swam up again, through gleams
  Of watered light and dull drowned waifs of day;
Till from some wonder of new woods and streams
  He woke, and wondered more: for there she lay.

1869   1870

•—⊫◈⊐—•

Christina Rossetti
1830–1894

"Here is a great discovery," Christina Rossetti wrote to her brother Dante Gabriel in 1870, as he tried to advise her about her poetic career: "'Women are not Men,' and you must not expect me to possess a tithe of your capacities, though I humbly—or proudly—lay claim to family-likeness." The remark hints at many sides of Rossetti's complex nature: her modest yet firm manner; the touch of irony in her deference; and the "family-likeness" not only of poetic genius but personal temperament—their parents called them the "two storms" in childhood because they were both difficult, irritable, volatile, and creative. Her declaration signals Rossetti's recognition that as a woman and artist she had had to take a very different path from her more famous brother. She renounced from an early age any pleasures or relationships that did not conform to her strict Anglo-Catholic principles—even to the point of giving up chess because it made her too eager to win. Instead she found poetic fulfillment in haunting lyrics about goblin men and love beyond the grave.

    Rossetti was born in London in 1830, the youngest of four precocious children of Gabriele Rossetti, an Italian poet-in-exile, and his English-Italian wife, Frances Polidori, whose brother John was Byron's physician and traveling companion. Amid a stream of foreign visitors the

---

1. In a review titled *The Fleshly School of Poetry* (1871), the poet and critic Robert Buchanan viciously attacked Rossetti for having "so sickening a desire to reproduce the sensual mood." Buchanan singled out *Nuptial Sleep*: "we merely shudder at the shameless nakedness." Rossetti omitted this poem from the 1881 edition of his work.

bilingual Rossetti children listened to animated discussions of art, music, and revolutionary politics. This atmosphere "made us . . . not a little different from British children," her brother William recalled, "and, when Dante and Christina Rossetti proved, as poetic writers, somewhat devious from the British tradition and the insular mind, we may say, if not 'so much the better,' at any rate, 'no wonder.'"

Like many Victorian women of letters, Christina Rossetti suffered from mysterious maladies that served to protect her time and talent. "I am rejoiced to feel that my health does really unfit me for miscellaneous governessing *en permanence*," she confided to William in 1855. Freed from "the necessity of teaching the small daughters of the neighbouring hairdresser or the neighbouring pork-butcher their p's and q's," she was "anxious to secure any literary pickings which might offer."

Shy, devout, and self-sacrificing, Rossetti nevertheless found time for a literary and social life that included as acquaintances Browning, Ruskin, Swinburne, Lewis Carroll, Edmund Gosse, and the Pre-Raphaelites. She modeled as the Virgin Mary in two of Dante Gabriel's finest paintings, *The Girlhood of Mary Virgin* (1848–1849) and *Ecce Ancilla Domini* (1849–1850). Because of her sex, Christina was denied membership in the Pre-Raphaelite Brotherhood, but she did publish her first poems in their journal, *The Germ*, in 1850. With the appearance of *Goblin Market and Other Poems* in 1862, she acquired a growing critical and popular following. Hailed by Gosse as the "High Priestess of Pre-Raphaelitism" because of her superb technique and keenness of observation, she won even wider fame as an author of religious poetry, inspiring, among others, Gerard Manley Hopkins.

Admirers of Rossetti's passionate, frustrated love poetry have long puzzled over the scanty details of her romantic life. She rejected two suitors because she found their faith wanting. Early biographers assumed that these broken relationships blighted Rossetti's life, but recently critics have regarded her choice of a single life as an act of artistic self-preservation. For Christina not only witnessed Dante's tormented affairs but also had the opportunity to view passion's consequences in a clinical light during the decade she worked as a volunteer at the Highgate House of Charity for "fallen women."

Though brightened by many touches of humor, Rossetti's writing focuses mostly on religious topics or some combination of themes arising from troubled love, grave illness, and anticipations of death—themes she must have pondered during the extended periods she spent taking care of dying family members at home, beginning with her father and continuing with her sister, her brother Dante, her mother (who was always her closest companion), and two maiden aunts. Despite severe illness in later life, she maintained a strict professionalism toward her career, publishing new work during the 1870s and 1880s, then issuing revised editions until her death in 1894.

A spontaneous writer whose lucidity of phrasing has sometimes caused readers to overlook her emotional and symbolic depths, Rossetti mastered a variety of forms, ranging from hymns and a sonnet-sequence to nursery rhymes and a well-known Christmas carol, *In the Bleak Mid-Winter*. Like Emily Dickinson, whose poems she admired when the first selection was published in 1890, Rossetti displays a quirky independence of vision, mingling the morbid, the whimsical, the cooly ironic. What is today her most famous poem, *Goblin Market*, features the enticements of sensual knowledge. Regarded chiefly as a children's tale in the nineteenth century, the poem has subsequently attracted much critical attention, including analyses of it as a struggle between self and soul, a comment on sex as a capitalist commodity, a parable of feminist solidarity, a lesson about poetry's subversive power, and a lesbian love story. This fable about the danger of desire provides insight into the dualistic world of Victorian fantasy. Magical events permitted writers and readers to enter forbidden realms of violence, temptation, and transformation, yet moralized endings sought to tame even the wildest tales for social and ethical instruction. Something similar may be said of Christina Rossetti's life and art: a stormy nature finds release in the tight formal control of the polished artist.

Song

She sat and sang alway
    By the green margin of a stream,
Watching the fishes leap and play
    Beneath the glad sunbeam.

5   I sat and wept away
    Beneath the moon's most shadowy beam,
Watching the blossoms of the May
    Weep leaves into the stream.

I wept for memory;
10   She sang for hope that is so fair:
My tears were swallowed by the sea;
    Her songs died on the air.

1848   1862

Song

When I am dead, my dearest,
    Sing no sad songs for me;
Plant thou no roses at my head,
    Nor shady cypress tree:
5   Be the green grass above me
    With showers and dewdrops wet;
And if thou wilt, remember,
    And if thou wilt, forget.

I shall not see the shadows,
10   I shall not feel the rain;
I shall not hear the nightingale
    Sing on, as if in pain:
And dreaming through the twilight
    That doth not rise nor set,
15   Haply° I may remember,   *perhaps*
    And haply may forget.

1848   1862

Remember

Remember me when I am gone away,
    Gone far away into the silent land;
    When you can no more hold me by the hand,
Nor I half turn to go yet turning stay.
5   Remember me when no more day by day
    You tell me of our future that you planned:
    Only remember me; you understand
It will be late to counsel then or pray.
Yet if you should forget me for a while

10   And afterwards remember, do not grieve:
      For if the darkness and corruption leave
      A vestige of the thoughts that once I had,
Better by far you should forget and smile
      Than that you should remember and be sad.

1849   1862

After Death

The curtains were half drawn, the floor was swept
      And strewn with rushes, rosemary and may[1]
      Lay thick upon the bed on which I lay,
Where thro' the lattice ivy-shadows crept.
5   He leaned above me, thinking that I slept
      And could not hear him; but I heard him say:
      "Poor child, poor child:" and as he turned away
Came a deep silence, and I knew he wept.
He did not touch the shroud, or raise the fold
10   That hid my face, or take my hand in his,
         Or ruffle the smooth pillows for my head:
      He did not love me living; but once dead
      He pitied me; and very sweet it is
To know he still is warm tho' I am cold.

1849   1862

A Pause

They made the chamber sweet with flowers and leaves,
      And the bed sweet with flowers on which I lay;
      While my soul, love-bound, loitered on its way.
I did not hear the birds about the eaves,
5   Nor hear the reapers talk among the sheaves:
      Only my soul kept watch from day to day,
      My thirsty soul kept watch for one away:—
Perhaps he loves, I thought, remembers, grieves.
At length there came the step upon the stair,
10   Upon the lock the old familiar hand:
Then first my spirit seemed to scent the air
      Of Paradise; then first the tardy sand
Of time ran golden; and I felt my hair
      Put on a glory, and my soul expand.

1853   1896

Echo

Come to me in the silence of the night;
      Come in the speaking silence of a dream;

1. Flowers traditionally associated with death.

Come with soft rounded cheeks and eyes as bright
   As sunlight on a stream;
5   Come back in tears,
O memory, hope, love of finished years.

Oh dream how sweet, too sweet, too bitter sweet,
   Whose wakening should have been in Paradise,
Where souls brimfull of love abide and meet;
10   Where thirsting longing eyes
      Watch the slow door
That opening, letting in, lets out no more.

Yet come to me in dreams, that I may live
   My very life again tho' cold in death:
15 Come back to me in dreams, that I may give
   Pulse for pulse, breath for breath:
     Speak low, lean low,
As long ago, my love, how long ago.

1854   1862

Dead Before Death

Ah! changed and cold, how changed and very cold!
   With stiffened smiling lips and cold calm eyes:
   Changed, yet the same; much knowing, little wise;
This was the promise of the days of old!
5   Grown hard and stubborn in the ancient mould,
   Grown rigid in the sham of lifelong lies:
We hoped for better things as years would rise,
But it is over as a tale once told.
All fallen the blossom that no fruitage bore,
10   All lost the present and the future time,
All lost, all lost, the lapse that went before:
So lost till death shut-to the opened door,
   So lost from chime to everlasting chime,
So cold and lost for ever evermore.

1854   1862

An Apple-Gathering

I plucked pink blossoms from mine apple tree
   And wore them all that evening in my hair:
Then in due season when I went to see
   I found no apples there.

5 With dangling basket all along the grass
   As I had come I went the selfsame track:
My neighbours mocked me while they saw me pass
   So empty-handed back.

Lilian and Lilias smiled in trudging by,
10   Their heaped-up basket teazed me like a jeer;
Sweet-voiced they sang beneath the sunset sky,
      Their mother's home was near.

Plump Gertrude passed me with her basket full,
      A stronger hand than hers helped it along;
15 A voice talked with her thro' the shadows cool
      More sweet to me than song.

Ah Willie, Willie, was my love less worth
      Than apples with their green leaves piled above?
I counted rosiest apples on the earth
20   Of far less worth than love.

So once it was with me you stooped to talk
      Laughing and listening in this very lane:
To think that by this way we used to walk
      We shall not walk again!

25 I let my neighbours pass me, ones and twos
      And groups; the latest said the night grew chill,
And hastened: but I loitered, while the dews
      Fell fast I loitered still.

1857   1862

Up-Hill

Does the road wind up-hill all the way?
      Yes, to the very end.
Will the day's journey take the whole long day?
      From morn to night, my friend.

5   But is there for the night a resting-place?
      A roof for when the slow dark hours begin.
May not the darkness hide it from my face?
      You cannot miss that inn.

Shall I meet other wayfarers at night?
10   Those who have gone before.
Then must I knock, or call when just in sight?
      They will not keep you standing at that door.

Shall I find comfort, travel-sore and weak?
      Of labour you shall find the sum.
15 Will there be beds for me and all who seek?
      Yea, beds for all who come.

1858   1862

Goblin Market

Morning and evening
Maids heard the goblins cry:

Dante Gabriel Rossetti,
frontispiece to the first edition of Christina Rossetti's
Goblin Market, 1862.

"Come buy our orchard fruits,
Come buy, come buy:
5   Apples and quinces,
Lemons and oranges,
Plump unpecked cherries,
Melons and raspberries,
Bloom-down-cheeked peaches,
10   Swart°-headed mulberries,   dark
Wild free-born cranberries,
Crab-apples, dewberries,
Pine-apples, blackberries,
Apricots, strawberries;—
15   All ripe together
In summer weather,—
Morns that pass by,
Fair eves that fly;
Come buy, come buy:
20   Our grapes fresh from the vine,
Pomegranates full and fine,
Dates and sharp bullaces,

Rare pears and greengages,
Damsons[1] and bilberries,
25   Taste them and try:
Currants and gooseberries,
Bright-fire-like barberries,
Figs to fill your mouth,
Citrons from the South,
30   Sweet to tongue and sound to eye;
Come buy, come buy."

Evening by evening
Among the brookside rushes,
Laura bowed her head to hear,
35   Lizzie veiled her blushes:
Crouching close together
In the cooling weather,
With clasping arms and cautioning lips,
With tingling cheeks and finger tips.
40   "Lie close," Laura said,
Pricking up her golden head:
"We must not look at goblin men,
We must not buy their fruits:
Who knows upon what soil they fed
45   Their hungry thirsty roots?"
"Come buy," call the goblins
Hobbling down the glen.
"Oh," cried Lizzie, "Laura, Laura,
You should not peep at goblin men."
50   Lizzie covered up her eyes,
Covered close lest they should look;
Laura reared her glossy head,
And whispered like the restless brook:
"Look, Lizzie, look, Lizzie,
55   Down the glen tramp little men.
One hauls a basket,
One bears a plate,
One lugs a golden dish
Of many pounds weight.
60   How fair the vine must grow
Whose grapes are so luscious;
How warm the wind must blow
Thro' those fruit bushes."
"No," said Lizzie: "No, no, no;
65   Their offers should not charm us,
Their evil gifts would harm us."
She thrust a dimpled finger
In each ear, shut eyes and ran:

1. Bullaces, greengages, and damsons are types of plums.

Curious Laura chose to linger
70   Wondering at each merchant man.
One had a cat's face,
One whisked a tail,
One tramped at a rat's pace,
One crawled like a snail,
75   One like a wombat prowled obtuse and furry,
One like a ratel[2] tumbled hurry skurry.
She heard a voice like voice of doves
Cooing all together:
They sounded kind and full of loves
80   In the pleasant weather.

Laura stretched her gleaming neck
Like a rush-imbedded swan,
Like a lily from the beck,°   *brook*
Like a moonlit poplar branch,
85   Like a vessel at the launch
When its last restraint is gone.

Backwards up the mossy glen
Turned and trooped the goblin men,
With their shrill repeated cry,
90   "Come buy, come buy."
When they reached where Laura was
They stood stock still upon the moss,
Leering at each other,
Brother with queer brother;
95   Signalling each other,
Brother with sly brother.
One set his basket down,
One reared his plate;
One began to weave a crown
100   Of tendrils, leaves and rough nuts brown
(Men sell not such in any town);
One heaved the golden weight
Of dish and fruit to offer her:
"Come buy, come buy," was still their cry.
105   Laura stared but did not stir,
Longed but had no money:
The whisk-tailed merchant bade her taste
In tones as smooth as honey,
The cat-faced purr'd,
110   The rat-paced spoke a word
Of welcome, and the snail-paced even was heard;
One parrot-voiced and jolly
Cried "Pretty Goblin" still for "Pretty Polly;"—
One whistled like a bird.

---

2. A tropical badger-like nocturnal animal (pronounced "ray-tell").

115   But sweet-tooth Laura spoke in haste:
     "Good folk, I have no coin;
     To take were to purloin:
     I have no copper in my purse,
     I have no silver either,
120   And all my gold is on the furze[3]
     That shakes in windy weather
     Above the rusty heather."
     "You have much gold upon your head,"
     They answered all together:
125   "Buy from us with a golden curl."
     She clipped a precious golden lock,
     She dropped a tear more rare than pearl,
     Then sucked their fruit globes fair or red:
     Sweeter than honey from the rock.
130   Stronger than man-rejoicing wine,
     Clearer than water flowed that juice;
     She never tasted such before,
     How should it cloy with length of use?
     She sucked and sucked and sucked the more
135   Fruits which that unknown orchard bore;
     She sucked until her lips were sore;
     Then flung the emptied rinds away
     But gathered up one kernel-stone,
     And knew not was it night or day
140   As she turned home alone.

     Lizzie met her at the gate
     Full of wise upbraidings:
     "Dear, you should not stay so late,
     Twilight is not good for maidens;
145   Should not loiter in the glen
     In the haunts of goblin men.
     Do you not remember Jeanie,
     How she met them in the moonlight,
     Took their gifts both choice and many,
150   Ate their fruits and wore their flowers
     Plucked from bowers
     Where summer ripens at all hours?
     But ever in the noonlight
     She pined and pined away;
155   Sought them by night and day,
     Found them no more but dwindled and grew grey;
     Then fell with the first snow,
     While to this day no grass will grow
     Where she lies low:
160   I planted daisies there a year ago

---

3. An evergreen shrub that grows on the heath.

That never blow.
You should not loiter so."
"Nay, hush," said Laura:
"Nay, hush, my sister:
165   I ate and ate my fill,
Yet my mouth waters still;
Tomorrow night I will
Buy more:" and kissed her:
"Have done with sorrow;
170   I'll bring you plums tomorrow
Fresh on their mother twigs,
Cherries worth getting;
You cannot think what figs
My teeth have met in,
175   What melons icy-cold
Piled on a dish of gold
Too huge for me to hold,
What peaches with a velvet nap,
Pellucid° grapes without one seed: *translucent*
180   Odorous indeed must be the mead
Whereon they grow, and pure the wave they drink
With lilies at the brink,
And sugar-sweet their sap."

Golden head by golden head,
185   Like two pigeons in one nest
Folded in each other's wings,
They lay down in their curtained bed:
Like two blossoms on one stem,
Like two flakes of new-fall'n snow,
190   Like two wands of ivory
Tipped with gold for awful° kings.   *awe-inspiring*
Moon and stars gazed in at them,
Wind sang to them lullaby,
Lumbering owls forbore to fly,
195   Not a bat flapped to and fro
Round their rest:
Cheek to cheek and breast to breast
Locked together in one nest.

Early in the morning
200   When the first cock crowed his warning,
Neat like bees, as sweet and busy,
Laura rose with Lizzie:
Fetched in honey, milked the cows,
Aired and set to rights the house,
205   Kneaded cakes of whitest wheat,
Cakes for dainty mouths to eat,
Next churned butter, whipped up cream,
Fed their poultry, sat and sewed;

Talked as modest maidens should:
210   Lizzie with an open heart,
Laura in an absent dream,
One content, one sick in part;
One warbling for the mere bright day's delight,
One longing for the night.

215   At length slow evening came:
They went with pitchers to the reedy brook;
Lizzie most placid in her look,
Laura most like a leaping flame.
They drew the gurgling water from its deep;
220   Lizzie plucked purple and rich golden flags,
Then turning homewards said: "The sunset flushes
Those furthest loftiest crags;
Come, Laura, not another maiden lags,
No wilful squirrel wags,
225   The beasts and birds are fast asleep."
But Laura loitered still among the rushes
And said the bank was steep.

And said the hour was early still,
The dew not fall'n, the wind not chill:
230   Listening ever, but not catching
The customary cry,
"Come buy, come buy,"
With its iterated jingle
Of sugar-baited words:
235   Not for all her watching
Once discerning even one goblin
Racing, whisking, tumbling, hobbling;
Let alone the herds
That used to tramp along the glen,
240   In groups or single,
Of brisk fruit-merchant men.
Till Lizzie urged, "O Laura, come;
I hear the fruit-call but I dare not look:
You should not loiter longer at this brook:
245   Come with me home.
The stars rise, the moon bends her arc,
Each glowworm winks her spark,
Let us get home before the night grows dark:
For clouds may gather
250   Tho' this is summer weather,
Put out the lights and drench us thro';
Then if we lost our way what should we do?"

Laura turned cold as stone
To find her sister heard that cry alone,
255   That goblin cry,

"Come buy our fruits, come buy."
Must she then buy no more such dainty fruit?
Must she no more such succous° pasture find,   *juicy*
Gone deaf and blind?
260   Her tree of life drooped from the root:
She said not one word in her heart's sore ache;
But peering thro' the dimness, nought discerning,
Trudged home, her pitcher dripping all the way;
So crept to bed, and lay
265   Silent till Lizzie slept;
Then sat up in a passionate yearning,
And gnashed her teeth for baulked desire, and wept
As if her heart would break.

Day after day, night after night,
270   Laura kept watch in vain
In sullen silence of exceeding pain.
She never caught again the goblin cry:
"Come buy, come buy;"—
She never spied the goblin men
275   Hawking their fruits along the glen:
But when the noon waxed bright
Her hair grew thin and gray;
She dwindled, as the fair full moon doth turn
To swift decay and burn
280   Her fire away.

One day remembering her kernel-stone
She set it by a wall that faced the south;
Dewed it with tears, hoped for a root,
Watched for a waxing shoot,
285   But there came none;
It never saw the sun,
It never felt the trickling moisture run:
While with sunk eyes and faded mouth
She dreamed of melons, as a traveller sees
290   False waves in desert drouth
With shade of leaf-crowned trees,
And burns the thirstier in the sandful breeze.

She no more swept the house,
Tended the fowls or cows,
295   Fetched honey, kneaded cakes of wheat,
Brought water from the brook:
But sat down listless in the chimney-nook
And would not eat.

Tender Lizzie could not bear
300   To watch her sister's cankerous° care   *festering*
Yet not to share.
She night and morning

Caught the goblins' cry:
"Come buy our orchard fruits,
305 Come buy, come buy:"—
Beside the brook, along the glen,
She heard the tramp of goblin men,
The voice and stir
Poor Laura could not hear;
310 Longed to buy fruit to comfort her,
But feared to pay too dear.
She thought of Jeanie in her grave,
Who should have been a bride;
But who for joys brides hope to have
315 Fell sick and died
In her gay prime,
In earliest Winter time,
With the first glazing rime,
With the first snow-fall of crisp Winter time.

320 Till Laura dwindling
Seemed knocking at Death's door:
Then Lizzie weighed no more
Better and worse;
But put a silver penny in her purse,
325 Kissed Laura, crossed the heath with clumps of furze
At twilight, halted by the brook:
And for the first time in her life
Began to listen and look.

Laughed every goblin
330 When they spied her peeping:
Came towards her hobbling,
Flying, running, leaping,
Puffing and blowing,
Chuckling, clapping, crowing,
335 Clucking and gobbling,
Mopping and mowing,
Full of airs and graces,
Pulling wry faces,
Demure grimaces,
340 Cat-like and rat-like,
Ratel- and wombat-like,
Snail-paced in a hurry,
Parrot-voiced and whistler,
Helter skelter, hurry skurry,
345 Chattering like magpies,
Fluttering like pigeons,
Gliding like fishes,—
Hugged her and kissed her,
Squeezed and caressed her:
350 Stretched up their dishes,

Panniers, and plates:
"Look at our apples
Russet and dun,
Bob at our cherries,
355 Bite at our peaches,
Citrons and dates,
Grapes for the asking,
Pears red with basking
Out in the sun,
360 Plums on their twigs;
Pluck them and suck them,
Pomegranates, figs."—

"Good folk," said Lizzie,
Mindful of Jeanie:
365 "Give me much and many:"—
Held out her apron,
Tossed them her penny.
"Nay, take a seat with us,
Honour and eat with us,"
370 They answered grinning:
"Our feast is but beginning.
Night yet is early,
Warm and dew-pearly,
Wakeful and starry:
375 Such fruits as these
No man can carry;
Half their bloom would fly,
Half their dew would dry,
Half their flavour would pass by.
380 Sit down and feast with us,
Be welcome guest with us,
Cheer you and rest with us."—
"Thank you," said Lizzie: "But one waits
At home alone for me:
385 So without further parleying,
If you will not sell me any
Of your fruits tho' much and many,
Give me back my silver penny
I tossed you for a fee."—
390 They began to scratch their pates,
No longer wagging, purring,
But visibly demurring,
Grunting and snarling.
One called her proud,
395 Cross-grained, uncivil;
Their tones waxed loud,
Their looks were evil.
Lashing their tails

They trod and hustled her,
400 Elbowed and jostled her,
Clawed with their nails,
Barking, mewing, hissing, mocking,
Tore her gown and soiled her stocking,
Twitched her hair out by the roots,
405 Stamped upon her tender feet,
Held her hands and squeezed their fruits
Against her mouth to make her eat.
White and golden Lizzie stood,
Like a lily in a flood,—
410 Like a rock of blue-veined stone
Lashed by tides obstreperously,—
Like a beacon left alone
In a hoary roaring sea,
Sending up a golden fire,—
415 Like a fruit-crowned orange-tree
White with blossoms honey-sweet
Sore beset by wasp and bee,—
Like a royal virgin town
Topped with gilded dome and spire
420 Close beleaguered by a fleet
Mad to tug her standard down.

One may lead a horse to water,
Twenty cannot make him drink.
Tho' the goblins cuffed and caught her,
425 Coaxed and fought her,
Bullied and besought her,
Scratched her, pinched her black as ink,
Kicked and knocked her,
Mauled and mocked her,
430 Lizzie uttered not a word;
Would not open lip from lip
Lest they should cram a mouthful in:
But laughed in heart to feel the drip
Of juice that syrupped all her face,
435 And lodged in dimples of her chin,
And streaked her neck which quaked like curd.
At last the evil people
Worn out by her resistance
Flung back her penny, kicked their fruit
440 Along whichever road they took,
Not leaving root or stone or shoot;
Some writhed into the ground,
Some dived into the brook
With ring and ripple,
445 Some scudded on the gale without a sound,
Some vanished in the distance.

In a smart, ache, tingle,
Lizzie went her way;
Knew not was it night or day;
450 Sprang up the bank, tore thro' the furze,
Threaded copse and dingle,
And heard her penny jingle
Bouncing in her purse,
Its bounce was music to her ear.
455 She ran and ran
As if she feared some goblin man
Dogged her with gibe or curse
Or something worse:
But not one goblin skurried after,
460 Nor was she pricked by fear;
The kind heart made her windy-paced
That urged her home quite out of breath with haste
And inward laughter.

She cried "Laura," up the garden,
465 "Did you miss me?
Come and kiss me.
Never mind my bruises,
Hug me, kiss me, suck my juices
Squeezed from goblin fruits for you,
470 Goblin pulp and goblin dew.
Eat me, drink me, love me;
Laura, make much of me:
For your sake I have braved the glen
And had to do with goblin merchant men."

475 Laura started from her chair,
Flung her arms up in the air,
Clutched her hair:
"Lizzie, Lizzie, have you tasted
For my sake the fruit forbidden?
480 Must your light like mine be hidden,
Your young life like mine be wasted,
Undone in mine undoing
And ruined in my ruin,
Thirsty, cankered, goblin-ridden?"—
485 She clung about her sister,
Kissed and kissed and kissed her:
Tears once again
Refreshed her shrunken eyes,
Dropping like rain
490 After long sultry drouth;
Shaking with aguish fear, and pain,
She kissed and kissed her with a hungry mouth.

Her lips began to scorch,
That juice was wormwood to her tongue,
495   She loathed the feast:
Writhing as one possessed she leaped and sung,
Rent all her robe, and wrung
Her hands in lamentable haste,
And beat her breast.
500   Her locks streamed like the torch
Borne by a racer at full speed,
Or like the mane of horses in their flight,
Or like an eagle when she stems° the light   *makes headway against*
Straight toward the sun,
505   Or like a caged thing freed,
Or like a flying flag when armies run.

Swift fire spread thro' her veins, knocked at her heart,
Met the fire smouldering there
And overbore its lesser flame;
510   She gorged on bitterness without a name:
Ah! fool, to choose such part
Of soul-consuming care!
Sense failed in the mortal strife:
Like the watch-tower of a town
515   Which an earthquake shatters down,
Like a lightning-stricken mast,
Like a wind-uprooted tree
Spun about,
Like a foam-topped waterspout
520   Cast down headlong in the sea,
She fell at last;
Pleasure past and anguish past,
Is it death or is it life?

Life out of death.
525   That night long Lizzie watched by her,
Counted her pulse's flagging stir,
Felt for her breath,
Held water to her lips, and cooled her face
With tears and fanning leaves:
530   But when the first birds chirped about their eaves,
And early reapers plodded to the place
Of golden sheaves,
And dew-wet grass
Bowed in the morning winds so brisk to pass,
535   And new buds with new day
Opened of cup-like lilies on the stream,
Laura awoke as from a dream,
Laughed in the innocent old way,
Hugged Lizzie but not twice or thrice;
540   Her gleaming locks showed not one thread of grey,

Her breath was sweet as May
And light danced in her eyes.

Days, weeks, months, years
Afterwards, when both were wives
545   With children of their own;
Their mother-hearts beset with fears,
Their lives bound up in tender lives;
Laura would call the little ones
And tell them of her early prime,
550   Those pleasant days long gone
Of not-returning time:
Would talk about the haunted glen,
The wicked, quaint fruit-merchant men,
Their fruits like honey to the throat
555   But poison in the blood;
(Men sell not such in any town:)
Would tell them how her sister stood
In deadly peril to do her good,
And win the fiery antidote:
560   Then joining hands to little hands
Would bid them cling together,
"For there is no friend like a sister
In calm or stormy weather;
To cheer one on the tedious way,
565   To fetch one if one goes astray,
To lift one if one totters down,
To strengthen whilst one stands."

1859   1862

Promises Like Pie-Crust[1]

Promise me no promises,
    So will I not promise you;
Keep we both our liberties,
    Never false and never true:
5   Let us hold the die uncast,
    Free to come as free to go;
For I cannot know your past,
    And of mine what can you know?

You, so warm, may once have been
10   Warmer towards another one;
I, so cold, may once have seen
    Sunlight, once have felt the sun:
Who shall show us if it was
    Thus indeed in time of old?
15   Fades the image from the glass
    And the fortune is not told.

1. English proverb: "Promises are like pie-crust, made to be broken."

If you promised, you might grieve
    For lost liberty again;
If I promised, I believe
20   I should fret to break the chain:
Let us be the friends we were,
    Nothing more but nothing less;
Many thrive on frugal fare
    Who would perish of excess.

1861   1896

Algernon Charles Swinburne
1837–1909

Algernon Charles Swinburne is the most notorious bad boy in English poetry. His verse contains everything calculated to affront a "respectable" audience—incest, sadomasochism, necrophilia, atheism, cannibalism, aestheticism, revolutionary politics—all conveyed in virtuoso rhythms that intensify his lurid, seductive appeal. Drunk or sober, sliding naked down banisters or rhapsodizing over the Marquis de Sade, Swinburne managed to offend people wherever he went. Yet despite the uproar, his extraordinary talent won him many admirers. Ruskin regarded him as a force of nature: "I should as soon think of finding fault with you as with a thundercloud or a nightshade blossom." Tennyson declared: "Swinburne is a reed through which all things blow into music."

Raised on the Isle of Wight, the son of an admiral and an earl's daughter, Swinburne was obsessed with the sea. His family nicknamed him "Seagull," and his earliest memory was "being held up naked in my father's arms . . . then shot like a stone from a sling through the air, shouting and laughing with delight, head foremost into the coming wave." The surging rhythms of his lines give proof of what he called "my endless passionate returns to the sea in all my verse."

Educated at Eton and Oxford, he became friends with Dante Gabriel Rossetti and William Morris in the late 1850s and embarked on a wild, bohemian life in London, where he dazzled people with impromptu recitations of his own erotic verse. But he was devastated when his beloved cousin Mary Gordon married in 1865. Her "loss" was the major event in his adult emotional life, inspiring many poems that dwell on the curiously pleasurable pain of unrequited love. Swinburne spent another fourteen self-destructive yet amazingly productive years in London, punctuated by visits to flagellation brothels, drunken sprees, seizures, breakdowns, and recuperations. In 1879 he was taken into "protective custody" by his friend Theodore Watts-Dunton, and spent his last three decades living quietly in the rural suburb of Putney.

Swinburne burst upon public notice with two key works: *Atalanta in Calydon* (1865), an effort to recreate in English the measures and feeling of Greek tragedy, and *Poems and Ballads* (1866), sixty-two lyrics of metric genius and scandalous subject matter. These revealed his particular flair for decadent dramatic monologues and poems. His speakers include a necrophiliac lover in *The Leper*, a connoisseur of erotic cruelty in *Dolores*, an incestuous mother in *Phaedra*, and a wary admirer of a nymphomaniac Roman empress in *Faustine*. Public outrage was nearly unanimous: even a friend who conceded Swinburne's "audacious courage" and musical "swing of words" accused the author of "grovelling down among the nameless shameless abominations which inspire him with such frenzied delight." *Punch* suggested simply that the poet should change his name to "Swineborn."

When he wasn't writing flagellation pornography for the amusement of his friends, Swinburne wrote more poems, two novels, and influential critical essays. His lush prose and fervent worship of beauty for its own sake made him an important influence on the Aesthetes, especially Walter Pater. Swinburne's outrageous acts and radical sympathies made him *the* symbol of social, political, and religious revolt in Victorian Britain. His friend and biographer Edmund Gosse recalled: "He was not merely a poet, but a flag, and not merely a flag but the Red Flag incarnate."

Swinburne is most admired for his startling style. Like his hero Shelley, he tried "to render the effect of the thing rather than the thing itself." Desiring to convey sensations acutely, Swinburne glorified all the senses except sight. This approach is so rare in English poetry that he is often accused of caring more for sound effects than ideas or images. Poets like Browning or Hopkins challenge the reader because of their intense particularity; Swinburne challenges because he is so diffuse—his deluge of words threatens to overwhelm the reader with hypnotic cadences and intricate, echoing patterns of association.

Yet, as T. S. Eliot declared, "his diffuseness is one of his glories." Like J. M. W. Turner, the English painter who said "indistinctness is my forte," Swinburne thrives on elemental forces of nature clashing and combining. He constructs his stanzas by piling up parallels and contrasts. Passionate about love's impossibility, he weaves his rich textures mostly from monosyllables, discovering in the process what the critic John D. Rosenberg calls "the bleak beauty of little words." As Ezra Pound remarked, summing up the effect of his verse, "no one else has made such music in English . . . the passion, not merely for political, but also for personal, liberty is the bedrock of Swinburne's writing."

from The Triumph of Time[1]
I Will Go Back to the Great Sweet Mother

I will go back to the great sweet mother,
    Mother and lover of men, the sea.
I will go down to her, I and none other,
260   Close with her, kiss her and mix her with me;
Cling to her, strive with her, hold her fast:
O fair white mother, in days long past
Born without sister, born without brother,
    Set free my soul as thy soul is free.

265   O fair green-girdled mother of mine,
    Sea, that art clothed with the sun and the rain,
Thy sweet hard kisses are strong like wine,
    Thy large embraces are keen like pain.
Save me and hide me with all thy waves,
270 Find me one grave of thy thousand graves,
Those pure cold populous graves of thine
    Wrought without hand in a world without stain.

I shall sleep, and move with the moving ships,
    Change as the winds change, veer in the tide;
275 My lips will feast on the foam of thy lips,
    I shall rise with thy rising, with thee subside;

---

1. *The Triumph of Time* is a long monologue in which the speaker laments that his love has forsaken him; he wishes that they had died together. In this excerpt the speaker envisions finding comfort by drowning his sorrows—or himself—in the sea.

Sleep, and not know if she[2] be, if she were,
    Filled full with life to the eyes and hair,
    As a rose is fulfilled to the roseleaf tips
280   With splendid summer and perfume and pride.

This woven raiment of nights and days,
    Were it once cast off and unwound from me,
    Naked and glad would I walk in thy ways,
        Alive and aware of thy ways and thee;
285   Clear of the whole world, hidden at home,
    Clothed with the green and crowned with the foam,
    A pulse of the life of thy straits and bays,
        A vein in the heart of the streams of the sea.

Fair mother, fed with the lives of men,
290   Thou art subtle and cruel of heart, men say.
    Thou hast taken, and shalt not render again;
        Thou art full of thy dead, and cold as they.
    But death is the worst that comes of thee;
    Thou art fed with our dead, O mother, O sea,
295   But when hast thou fed on our hearts? or when,
        Having given us love, hast thou taken away?

O tender-hearted, O perfect lover,
        Thy lips are bitter, and sweet thine heart.
    The hopes that hurt and the dreams that hover,
300   Shall they not vanish away and apart?
    But thou, thou art sure, thou art older than earth;
    Thou art strong for death and fruitful of birth;
    Thy depths conceal and thy gulfs discover;
        From the first thou wert; in the end thou art.

        1866

Hymn to Proserpine[1]
(After the Proclamation in Rome of the Christian Faith)
VICISTI, GALILAEE[2]

I have lived long enough, having seen one thing, that love hath an end;
Goddess and maiden and queen, be near me now and befriend.
Thou art more than the day or the morrow, the seasons that laugh or that weep;
For these give joy and sorrow; but thou, Proserpina, sleep.
5   Sweet is the treading of wine, and sweet the feet of the dove;
But a goodlier gift is thine than foam of the grapes or love.

---

2. The woman he has lost.
1. Proserpine (Persephone) was the queen of the underworld. The daughter of Demeter (Ceres), the goddess of planting and harvest, she was abducted by Hades and forced to live as his consort in the underworld for six months of each year.
2. "Thou hast conquered, O Galilean." Legend has it that these words were spoken by the Roman Emperor Julian the Apostate (331–363) on his deathbed. The Galilean is Jesus, and the proclamation in the subtitle is Constantine's Edict of Milan in 313, which extended religious tolerance to Christians. Julian had tried to discourage the spread of Christianity and promote a return to paganism. The speaker of the poem, a Roman poet, shares Julian's admiration for the traditional gods.

Yea, is not even Apollo, with hair and harpstring of gold,
A bitter God to follow, a beautiful God to behold?
I am sick of singing: the bays[3] burn deep and chafe: I am fain
10   To rest a little from praise and grievous pleasure and pain.
For the Gods we know not of, who give us our daily breath,
We know they are cruel as love or life, and lovely as death.
O Gods dethroned and deceased, cast forth, wiped out in a day!
From your wrath is the world released, redeemed from your chains, men say.
15   New Gods are crowned in the city; their flowers have broken your rods;
They are merciful, clothed with pity, the young compassionate Gods.
But for me their new device is barren, the days are bare;
Things long past over suffice, and men forgotten that were.
Time and the Gods are at strife; ye dwell in the midst thereof,
20   Draining a little life from the barren breasts of love.
I say to you, cease, take rest; yea, I say to you all, be at peace,
Till the bitter milk of her breast and the barren bosom shall cease.
Wilt thou yet take all, Galilean? but these thou shalt not take,
The laurel, the palms and the paean, the breasts of the nymphs in the brake;
25   Breasts more soft than a dove's, that tremble with tenderer breath;
And all the wings of the Loves, and all the joy before death;
All the feet of the hours that sound as a single lyre,
Dropped and deep in the flowers, with strings that flicker like fire.
More than these wilt thou give, things fairer than all these things?
30   Nay, for a little we live, and life hath mutable wings.
A little while and we die; shall life not thrive as it may?
For no man under the sky lives twice, outliving his day.
And grief is a grievous thing, and a man hath enough of his tears:
Why should he labour, and bring fresh grief to blacken his years?
35   Thou hast conquered, O pale Galilean; the world has grown grey from thy breath;
We have drunken of things Lethean,[4] and fed on the fullness of death.
Laurel is green for a season, and love is sweet for a day;
But love grows bitter with treason, and laurel outlives not May.
Sleep, shall we sleep after all? for the world is not sweet in the end;
40   For the old faiths loosen and fall, the new years ruin and rend.
Fate is a sea without shore, and the soul is a rock that abides;
But her ears are vexed with the roar and her face with the foam of the tides.
O lips that the live blood faints in, the leavings of racks and rods!
O ghastly glories of saints, dead limbs of gibbeted Gods![5]
45   Though all men abase them before you in spirit, and all knees bend,
I kneel not neither adore you, but standing, look to the end.
All delicate days and pleasant, all spirits and sorrows are cast
Far out with the foam of the present that sweeps to the surf of the past:
Where beyond the extreme sea-wall, and between the remote sea-gates,
50   Waste water washes, and tall ships founder, and deep death waits:
Where, mighty with deepening sides, clad about with the seas as with wings,

3. Leaves from the poet's laurel wreath.
4. The River Lethe in the underworld; the dead who
drank of its waters forgot their past.

5. A reference to the Crucifixion.

And impelled of invisible tides, and fulfilled of unspeakable things,
White-eyed and poisonous-finned, shark-toothed and serpentine-curled,
Rolls, under the whitening wind of the future, the wave of the world.
55 The depths stand naked in sunder behind it, the storms flee away;
In the hollow before it the thunder is taken and snared as a prey;
In its sides is the north-wind bound; and its salt is of all men's tears;
With light of ruin, and sound of changes, and pulse of years;
With travail of day after day, and with trouble of hour upon hour;
60 And bitter as blood is the spray; and the crests are as fangs that devour:
And its vapour and storm of its steam as the sighing of spirits to be;
And its noise as the noise in a dream; and its depth as the roots of the sea:
And the height of its heads as the height of the utmost stars of the air:
And the ends of the earth at the might thereof tremble, and time is made bare.
65 Will ye bridle the deep sea with reins, will ye chasten the high sea with rods?
Will ye take her to chain her with chains, who is older than all ye Gods?
All ye as a wind shall go by, as a fire shall ye pass and be past;
Ye are Gods, and behold, ye shall die, and the waves be upon you at last.
In the darkness of time, in the deeps of the years, in the changes of things,
70 Ye shall sleep as a slain man sleeps, and the world shall forget you for kings.
Though the feet of thine high priests tread where thy lords and our forefathers trod,
Though these that were Gods are dead, and thou being dead art a God,
Though before thee the throned Cytherean[6] be fallen, and hidden her head,
Yet thy kingdom shall pass, Galilean, thy dead shall go down to thee dead.
75 Of the maiden thy mother men sing as a goddess with grace clad around;
Thou art throned where another was king; where another was queen she is crowned.
Yea, once we had sight of another: but now she is queen, say these.
Not as thine, not as thine was our mother, a blossom of flowering seas,
Clothed round with the world's desire as with raiment, and fair as the foam,
80 And fleeter than kindled fire, and a goddess, and mother of Rome.[7]
For thine came pale and a maiden, and sister to sorrow; but ours,
Her deep hair heavily laden with odour and colour of flowers,
White rose of the rose-white water, a silver splendour, a flame,
Bent down unto us that besought her, and earth grew sweet with her name.
85 For thine came weeping, a slave among slaves, and rejected; but she
Came flushed from the full-flushed wave, and imperial, her foot on the sea.
And the wonderful waters knew her, the winds and the viewless ways,
And the roses grew rosier, and bluer the sea-blue stream of the bays.
Ye are fallen, our lords, by what token? we wist that ye should not fall.
90 Ye were all so fair that are broken; and one more fair than ye all.
But I turn to her[8] still, having seen she shall surely abide in the end;
Goddess and maiden and queen, be near me now and befriend.
O daughter of earth, of my mother, her crown and blossom of birth,
I am also, I also, thy brother; I go as I came unto earth.
95 In the night where thine eyes are as moons are in heaven, the night where thou art,
Where the silence is more than all tunes, where sleep overflows from the heart,

---

6. Aphrodite (Venus) was born near the island of Cythera.   Rome.
7. Aphrodite was the mother of Aeneas, the founder of   8. Proserpine.

Where the poppies are sweet as the rose in our world, and the red rose is white,
And the wind falls faint as it blows with the fume of the flowers of the night,
And the murmur of spirits that sleep in the shadow of Gods from afar
100 Grows dim in thine ears and deep as the deep dim soul of a star,
In the sweet low light of thy face, under heavens untrod by the sun,
Let my soul with their souls find place, and forget what is done and undone.
Thou art more than the Gods who number the days of our temporal breath;
For these give labour and slumber; but thou, Proserpina, death.
105 Therefore now at thy feet I abide for a season in silence. I know
I shall die as my fathers died, and sleep as they sleep; even so.
For the glass of the years is brittle wherein we gaze for a span;
A little soul for a little bears up this corpse which is man.
So long I endure, no longer; and laugh not again, neither weep.
110 For there is no God found stronger than death; and death is a sleep.

                                                                    1866

A Forsaken Garden[1]

In a coign[2] of the cliff between lowland and highland,
     At the sea-down's edge between windward and lee,
Walled round with rocks as an inland island,
     The ghost of a garden fronts the sea.
5   A girdle of brushwood and thorn encloses
     The steep square slope of the blossomless bed
Where the weeds that grew green from the graves of its roses
          Now lie dead.

The fields fall southward, abrupt and broken,
10   To the low last edge of the long lone land.
If a step should sound or a word be spoken,
     Would a ghost not rise at the strange guest's hand?
So long have the grey bare walks lain guestless,
     Through branches and briars if a man make way,
15   He shall find no life but the sea-wind's, restless
          Night and day.

The dense hard passage is blind and stifled
     That crawls by a track none turn to climb
To the strait waste place that the years have rifled
20   Of all but the thorns that are touched not of time.
The thorns he spares when the rose is taken;
     The rocks are left when he wastes the plain.
The wind that wanders, the weeds wind-shaken,
          These remain.

25   Not a flower to be pressed of the foot that falls not;
     As the heart of a dead man the seed-plots are dry;

---

1. The poem is set at East Dene on the Isle of Wight,   2. Corner.
where Swinburne grew up.

From the thicket of thorns whence the nightingale calls not,
    Could she call, there were never a rose to reply.
Over the meadows that blossom and wither
30   Rings but the note of a sea-bird's song;
Only the sun and the rain come hither
      All year long.

The sun burns sere and the rain dishevels
One gaunt bleak blossom of scentless breath.
35 Only the wind here hovers and revels
    In a round where life seems barren as death.
Here there was laughing of old, there was weeping,
    Haply, of lovers none ever will know,
Whose eyes went seaward a hundred sleeping
40   Years ago.

Heart handfast in heart as they stood, "Look thither,"
    Did he whisper? "look forth from the flowers to the sea;
For the foam-flowers endure when the rose-blossoms wither,
    And men that love lightly may die—but we?"
45 And the same wind sang and the same waves whitened,
    And or ever the garden's last petals were shed,
In the lips that had whispered, the eyes that had lightened,
    Love was dead.

Or they loved their life through, and then went whither?
50   And were one to the end—but what end who knows?
Love deep as the sea as a rose must wither,
    As the rose-red seaweed that mocks the rose.
Shall the dead take thought for the dead to love them?
    What love was ever as deep as a grave?
55 They are loveless now as the grass above them
    Or the wave.

All are at one now, roses and lovers,
    Not known of the cliffs and the fields and the sea.
Not a breath of the time that has been hovers
60   In the air now soft with a summer to be.
Not a breath shall there sweeten the seasons hereafter
    Of the flowers or the lovers that laugh now or weep,
When as they that are free now of weeping and laughter
    We shall sleep.

65 Here death may deal not again for ever;
    Here change may come not till all change end.
From the graves they have made they shall rise up never,
    Who have left nought living to ravage and rend.
Earth, stones, and thorns of the wild ground growing,
70   While the sun and the rain live, these shall be;
Till a last wind's breath upon all these blowing
    Roll the sea.

Till the slow sea rise and the sheer cliff crumble,
  Till terrace and meadow the deep gulfs drink,
75 Till the strength of the waves of the high tides humble
  The fields that lessen, the rocks that shrink,
Here now in his triumph where all things falter,
  Stretched out on the spoils that his own hand spread,
As a god self-slain on his own strange altar,
80   Death lies dead.

1876

━━ ⊰◈⊱ ━━

Walter Pater
1839–1894

"It doesn't matter what is said as long as it is said beautifully." The young Walter Pater's casual, deliberately shocking remark forecast a career that would undermine Victorian confidence in the morality of art and spark a transition to the Aesthetic creed of "art for art's sake." But if Pater was, as Oscar Wilde said, "the most perfect master of English prose now creating amongst us," *what* he said also mattered immensely. He was an elegant pioneer of subjective, impressionistic criticism, intent on subverting moral and religious absolutes.

Pater's first publication, on Coleridge (1866), announced his main theme: "To the modern spirit nothing is or can be rightly known except relatively." Pater dismissed the notion of critical objectivity, preferring to explore art's effect on himself. In preface to *The Renaissance*, he startled his readers by asking: "What is this song or picture, this engaging personality presented in life or in a book, to *me*?"

As a boy, Pater loved to play at being a priest; his schoolmates called him "Parson Pater." Even though he lost his faith at Oxford, scandalizing friends with his irreverent talk, he was so attracted to the beauty of church ritual that he considered ordination anyway. Instead, in 1864 he became a Fellow of Brasenose College, Oxford. Regarded by friends as a "queer, strange creature," Pater developed a reputation for wittily trivializing serious topics. After his first tutorial with Pater, Gerard Manley Hopkins noted in his diary: "Pater talking two hours against Xtianity." From 1869 onward, Pater lived with his two sisters, first at Oxford, then in London. Their house was an Aesthetic oasis, decorated with Morris wallpaper, blue china pots, delicate embroidery, engravings from Botticelli, and a few artfully arranged flowers. The teas they gave for students subtly challenged decorum, as Pater's favored guests were young athletes who approached a Greek ideal of male beauty.

The publication of *Studies in the History of the Renaissance* (1873) brought Pater both recognition and notoriety. His appointment as university proctor appears to have been blocked because the amoral tone of his writing drew attention to his private behavior—a romantic friendship with an undergraduate. His reputation also suffered from his well-known influence on Oscar Wilde. Pater's efforts to defend himself were characteristically prim: "I wish they would not call me a hedonist. It gives such a wrong impression to those who do not know Greek."

Yet *The Renaissance* became the key book of the Aesthetic movement. It marked the end of High Victorianism by displacing reverence for the organicism and spirituality of medieval society—as imagined by Carlyle, Ruskin, and Morris—in favor of the sensuous, pagan self-consciousness and materiality of Renaissance artists like Botticelli and Leonardo. Pater denied that morality had anything to do with art, or that organized religion had any claim on the individual. Arguing that life was sheer flux—"that strange perpetual weaving and unweaving of ourselves"—Pater insisted that the intense appreciation of passionate, beautiful, transitory moments mattered more than anything else. Life's aim, he concluded, is "not the fruit of experience, but experience itself." Wilde called *The Renaissance* "the holy writ of beauty."

In 1878 Pater transformed his earliest memories into *The Child in the House*, a haunting exploration of how identity is born. Later, he obliquely elaborated his own moral sensibility in the dreamy novel *Marius the Epicurean* (1885), in which his pagan protagonist dies alongside a Christian martyr who befriends him. The works of Pater's last decade include the quasi-autobiographical musings in *Imaginary Portraits* (1887); his finest book of literary criticism, *Appreciations, with an Essay on Style* (1889); *Plato and Platonism* (1893), and a posthumous unfinished novel, *Gaston de Latour* (1896).

Elevating criticism to an expressive art, Pater opened new possibilities both for critics and for English prose. Though Arnold had claimed that criticism should "see the object as in itself it really is," Pater asserted that first one had to "know one's own impression as it really is" and make that elusive feeling, as Wilde put it, the "starting point for a new creation." As Wilde saw, Pater's famous description of the Mona Lisa achieves independent stature as a work of art. Yeats admired the passage so much he pronounced it the first modern poem, and reprinted it—in free verse form—at the start of his *Oxford Book of Modern Verse* (1936). Pater's emphasis on flux, sensation, perception, and the mysteries of identity—all that betokened the "quickened, multiplied consciousness" of modern life—carried his influence far beyond Aestheticism. Joyce imitated him in *A Portrait of the Artist* and *Ulysses*, and Wilde, Hopkins, Symons, Yeats, Eliot, Pound, and Woolf all acknowledged their debt to him. As he announced in his famous essay on style: "imaginative prose" is "the special art of the modern world."

from The Renaissance
Preface

Many attempts have been made by writers on art and poetry to define beauty in the abstract, to express it in the most general terms, to find some universal formula for it. The value of these attempts has most often been in the suggestive and penetrating things said by the way. Such discussions help us very little to enjoy what has been well done in art or poetry, to discriminate between what is more and what is less excellent in them, or to use words like beauty, excellence, art, poetry, with a more precise meaning than they would otherwise have. Beauty, like all other qualities presented to human experience, is relative; and the definition of it becomes unmeaning and useless in proportion to its abstractness. To define beauty, not in the most abstract but in the most concrete terms possible, to find not its universal formula, but the formula which expresses most adequately this or that special manifestation of it, is the aim of the true student of aesthetics.

"To see the object as in itself it really is,"[1] has been justly said to be the aim of all true criticism whatever; and in aesthetic criticism the first step towards seeing one's object as it really is, is to know one's own impression as it really is, to discriminate it, to realise it distinctly. The objects with which aesthetic criticism deals—music, poetry, artistic and accomplished forms of human life—are indeed receptacles of so many powers or forces: they possess, like the products of nature, so many virtues or qualities. What is this song or picture, this engaging personality presented in life or in a book, to *me*? What effect does it really produce on me? Does it give me pleasure? and if so, what sort or degree of pleasure? How is my nature modified by its presence, and under its influence? The answers to these questions are the original facts with

---

1. Quoting Matthew Arnold, *The Function of Criticism at the Present Time.*

which the aesthetic critic has to do; and, as in the study of light, of morals, of number, one must realise such primary data for one's self, or not at all. And he who experiences these impressions strongly, and drives directly at the discrimination and analysis of them, has no need to trouble himself with the abstract question what beauty is in itself, or what its exact relation to truth or experience—metaphysical questions, as unprofitable as metaphysical questions elsewhere. He may pass them all by as being, answerable or not, of no interest to him.

The aesthetic critic, then, regards all the objects with which he has to do, all works of art, and the fairer forms of nature and human life, as powers or forces producing pleasurable sensations, each of a more or less peculiar or unique kind. This influence he feels, and wishes to explain, by analysing and reducing it to its elements. To him, the picture, the landscape, the engaging personality in life or in a book, *La Gioconda*, the hills of Carrara, Pico of Mirandola,[2] are valuable for their virtues, as we say, in speaking of a herb, a wine, a gem; for the property each has of affecting one with a special, a unique, impression of pleasure. Our education becomes complete in proportion as our susceptibility to these impressions increases in depth and variety. And the function of the aesthetic critic is to distinguish, to analyse, and separate from its adjuncts, the virtue by which a picture, a landscape, a fair personality in life or in a book, produces this special impression of beauty or pleasure, to indicate what the source of that impression is, and under what conditions it is experienced. His end is reached when he has disengaged that virtue, and noted it, as a chemist notes some natural element, for himself and others; and the rule for those who would reach this end is stated with great exactness in the words of a recent critic of Sainte-Beuve:— *De se borner à connaître de près les belles choses, et à s'en nourrir en exquis amateurs, en humanistes accomplis*.[3]

What is important, then, is not that the critic should possess a correct abstract definition of beauty for the intellect, but a certain kind of temperament, the power of being deeply moved by the presence of beautiful objects. He will remember always that beauty exists in many forms. To him all periods, types, schools of taste, are in themselves equal. In all ages there have been some excellent workmen, and some excellent work done. The question he asks is always:—In whom did the stir, the genius, the sentiment of the period find itself? where was the receptacle of its refinement, its elevation, its taste? "The ages are all equal," says William Blake, "but genius is always above its age."[4]

Often it will require great nicety to disengage this virtue from the commoner elements with which it may be found in combination. Few artists, not Goethe or Byron even, work quite cleanly, casting off all *débris*, and leaving us only what the heat of their imagination has wholly fused and transformed. Take, for instance, the writings of Wordsworth. The heat of his genius, entering into the substance of his work, has crystallised a part, but only a part, of it; and in that great mass of verse there is much which might well be forgotten. But scattered up and down it, sometimes fusing and transforming entire compositions, like the Stanzas on *Resolution and Independence*, or the *Ode on the Recollections of Childhood*,[5] sometimes,

---

2. *La Gioconda* is another title for the *Mona Lisa* by Leonardo da Vinci (1452–1519); the hills of Carrara contain marble quarries; Pico della Mirandola (1463–1494) was an Italian philosopher and classical scholar about whom Pater wrote an essay in *The Renaissance*.
3. To limit oneself to knowing beautiful things well, and to be nourished by them, as might an exquisite amateur

or an accomplished humanist (French). In fact, this was written by Charles Sainte-Beuve (1804–1869).
4. From Blake's annotations to *The Works of Sir Joshua Reynolds*.
5. The actual title of Wordsworth's poem is *Ode: Intimations of Immortality from Recollections of Early Childhood*.

as if at random, depositing a fine crystal here or there, in a matter it does not wholly search through and transmute, we trace the action of his unique, incommunicable faculty, that strange, mystical sense of a life in natural things, and of man's life as a part of nature, drawing strength and colour and character from local influences, from the hills and streams, and from natural sights and sounds. Well! that is the *virtue*, the active principle in Wordsworth's poetry; and then the function of the critic of Wordsworth is to follow up that active principle, to disengage it, to mark the degree in which it penetrates his verse.

The subjects of the following studies are taken from the history of the *Renaissance*, and touch what I think the chief points in that complex, many-sided movement. I have explained in the first of them what I understand by the word, giving it a much wider scope than was intended by those who originally used it to denote that revival of classical antiquity in the fifteenth century which was only one of many results of a general excitement and enlightening of the human mind, but of which the great aim and achievements of what, as Christian art, is often falsely opposed to the Renaissance, were another result. This outbreak of the human spirit may be traced far into the middle age itself, with its motives already clearly pronounced, the care for physical beauty, the worship of the body, the breaking down of those limits which the religious system of the middle age imposed on the heart and the imagination. I have taken as an example of this movement, this earlier Renaissance within the middle age itself, and as an expression of its qualities, two little compositions in early French; not because they constitute the best possible expression of them, but because they help the unity of my series, inasmuch as the Renaissance ends also in France, in French poetry, in a phase of which the writings of Joachim du Bellay[6] are in many ways the most perfect illustration. The Renaissance, in truth, put forth in France an aftermath, a wonderful later growth, the products of which have to the full that subtle and delicate sweetness which belongs to a refined and comely decadence, just as its earliest phases have the freshness which belongs to all periods of growth in art, the charm of *ascêsis* [self-denial], of the austere and serious girding of the loins in youth.

But it is in Italy, in the fifteenth century, that the interest of the Renaissance mainly lies,—in that solemn fifteenth century which can hardly be studied too much, not merely for its positive results in the things of the intellect and the imagination, its concrete works of art, its special and prominent personalities, with their profound aesthetic charm, but for its general spirit and character, for the ethical qualities of which it is a consummate type.

The various forms of intellectual activity which together make up the culture of an age, move for the most part from different starting-points, and by unconnected roads. As products of the same generation they partake indeed of a common character, and unconsciously illustrate each other; but of the producers themselves, each group is solitary, gaining what advantage or disadvantage there may be in intellectual isolation. Art and poetry, philosophy and the religious life, and that other life of refined pleasure and action in the conspicuous places of the world, are each of them confined to its own circle of ideas, and those who prosecute either of them are generally little curious of the thoughts of others. There come, however, from time to time, eras of more favourable conditions, in which the thoughts of men draw nearer together than is their wont, and the many interests of the intellectual world combine

6. French poet and critic, (1524–1560), about whom Pater wrote an essay in *The Renaissance*.

in one complete type of general culture. The fifteenth century in Italy is one of these happier eras, and what is sometimes said of the age of Pericles is true of that of Lorenzo:[7]—it is an age productive in personalities, many-sided, centralised, complete. Here, artists and philosophers and those whom the action of the world has elevated and made keen, do not live in isolation, but breathe a common air, and catch light and heat from each other's thoughts. There is a spirit of general elevation and enlightenment in which all alike communicate. The unity of this spirit gives unity to all the various products of the Renaissance; and it is to this intimate alliance with mind, this participation in the best thoughts which that age produced, that the art of Italy in the fifteenth century owes much of its grave dignity and influence.

I have added an essay on Winckelmann,[8] as not incongruous with the studies which precede it, because Winckelmann, coming in the eighteenth century, really belongs in spirit to an earlier age. By his enthusiasm for the things of the intellect and the imagination for their own sake, by his Hellenism, his life-long struggle to attain to the Greek spirit, he is in sympathy with the humanists of a previous century. He is the last fruit of the Renaissance, and explains in a striking way its motive and tendencies.

1873

from *Leonardo da Vinci*
[LA GIOCONDA][1]

La Gioconda is, in the truest sense, Leonardo's masterpiece, the revealing instance of his mode of thought and work. In suggestiveness, only the *Melancholia* of Dürer[2] is comparable to it; and no crude symbolism disturbs the effect of its subdued and graceful mystery. We all know the face and hands of the figure, set in its marble chair, in that circle of fantastic rocks, as in some faint light under sea. Perhaps of all ancient pictures time has chilled it least. As often happens with works in which invention seems to reach its limit, there is an element in it given to, not invented by, the master. In that inestimable folio of drawings, once in the possession of Vasari, were certain designs by Verrocchio,[3] faces of such impressive beauty that Leonardo in his boyhood copied them many times. It is hard not to connect with these designs of the elder, by-past master, as with its germinal principle, the unfathomable smile, always with a touch of something sinister in it, which plays over all Leonardo's work. Besides, the picture is a portrait. From childhood we see this image defining itself on the fabric of his dreams; and but for express historical testimony, we might fancy that this was but his ideal lady, embodied and beheld at last. What was the relationship of a living Florentine to this creature of his thought? By what strange affinities had the dream and the person grown up thus apart, and yet so closely together? Present from the first incorporeally in Leonardo's brain, dimly traced in the designs of Verrocchio, she is found present at last in *Il Giocondo's* house. That there is much of mere portraiture in

---

7. Pericles, Athenian statesman during the 5th century B.C.; Lorenzo de Medici (1449–1492), Florentine ruler and patron of the arts.
8. Johann Joachim Winckelmann (1717–1768), German classicist and art historian.
1. Better known as the *Mona Lisa*, this painting by Italian Renaissance artist and inventor Leonardo da Vinci (1452–1519) hangs in the Louvre Museum in Paris. The model was probably the wife of Francesco del Giocondo; hence, "La Gioconda."
2. Engraving of the spirit of Melancholy, represented as a seated female figure, by the German artist Albrecht Dürer (1471–1528).
3. Andrea del Verrocchio (1435–1488), Florentine painter and sculptor; Giorgio Vasari (1511–1574), was the author of *Lives of the Most Excellent Italian Painters*.

the picture is attested by the legend that by artificial means, the presence of mimes and flute-players, that subtle expression was protracted on the face. Again, was it in four years and by renewed labour never really completed, or in four months and as by stroke of magic, that the image was projected?

The presence that rose thus so strangely beside the waters, is expressive of what in the ways of a thousand years men had come to desire. Hers is the head upon which all "the ends of the world are come,"[4] and the eyelids are a little weary. It is a beauty wrought out from within upon the flesh, the deposit, little cell by cell, of strange thoughts and fantastic reveries and exquisite passions. Set it for a moment beside one of those white Greek goddesses or beautiful women of antiquity, and how would they be troubled by this beauty, into which the soul with all its maladies has passed! All the thoughts and experience of the world have etched and moulded there, in that which they have of power to refine and make expressive the outward form, the animalism of Greece, the lust of Rome, the mysticism of the middle age with its spiritual ambition and imaginative loves, the return of the Pagan world, the sins of the Borgias.[5] She is older than the rocks among which she sits; like the vampire, she has been dead many times, and learned the secrets of the grave; and has been a diver in deep seas, and keeps their fallen day about her; and trafficked for strange webs with Eastern merchants and, as Leda, was the mother of Helen of Troy, and, as Saint Anne, the mother of Mary;[6] and all this has been to her but as the sound of lyres and flutes, and lives only in the delicacy with which it has moulded the changing lineaments, and tinged the eyelids and the hands. The fancy of a perpetual life, sweeping together ten thousand experiences, is an old one; and modern philosophy has conceived the idea of humanity as wrought upon by, and summing up in itself, all modes of thought and life. Certainly Lady Lisa might stand as the embodiment of the old fancy, the symbol of the modern idea.

1871

Conclusion[1]

Λέγει που Ἡράκλειτος ὅτι πάντα χωρεῖ καὶ οὐδὲν μένι[2]

To regard all things and principles of things as inconstant modes or fashions has more and more become the tendency of modern thought. Let us begin with that which is without—our physical life. Fix upon it in one of its more exquisite intervals, the moment, for instance, of delicious recoil from the flood of water in summer heat. What is the whole physical life in that moment but a combination of natural elements to which science gives their names? But those elements, phosphorus and lime and delicate fibres, are present not in the human body alone: we detect them in places most remote from it. Our physical life is a perpetual motion of them—the passage of the blood, the waste and repairing of the lenses of the eye, the modification of the tissues

---

4. "Now all these things happened unto them for examples: and they are written for our admonition, upon whom the ends of the world are come" (1 Corinthians 10.11).
5. An Italian Renaissance family notorious for their ruthlessness in the pursuit of power.
6. A bold juxtaposition of St. Anne, mother of the Virgin Mary, with the mythic Leda, who gave birth to Helen of Troy after being raped by Zeus.
1. This brief "Conclusion" was omitted in the second edi-

tion of this book, as I conceived it might possibly mislead some of those young men into whose hands it might fall. On the whole, I have thought it best to reprint it here, with some slight changes which bring it closer to my original meaning. I have dealt more fully in *Marius the Epicurean* with the thoughts suggested by it [Pater's note to the third edition, 1888].
2. Heraclitus says, All things give way; nothing remaineth [Pater's translation, from Plato's *Cratylus*].

of the brain under every ray of light and sound—processes which science reduces to simpler and more elementary forces. Like the elements of which we are composed, the action of these forces extends beyond us: it rusts iron and ripens corn. Far out on every side of us those elements are broadcast, driven in many currents; and birth and gesture and death and the springing of violets from the grave[3] are but a few out of ten thousand resultant combinations. That clear, perpetual outline of face and limb is but an image of ours, under which we group them—a design in a web, the actual threads of which pass out beyond it. This at least of flamelike our life has, that it is but the concurrence, renewed from moment to moment, of forces parting sooner or later on their ways.

Or if we begin with the inward world of thought and feeling, the whirlpool is still more rapid, the flame more eager and devouring. There it is no longer the gradual darkening of the eye, the gradual fading of colour from the wall—movements of the shore-side, where the water flows down indeed, though in apparent rest—but the race of the mid-stream, a drift of momentary acts of sight and passion and thought. At first sight experience seems to bury us under a flood of external objects, pressing upon us with a sharp and importunate reality, calling us out of ourselves in a thousand forms of action. But when reflexion begins to play upon those objects they are dissipated under its influence; the cohesive force seems suspended like some trick of magic; each object is loosed into a group of impressions—colour, odour, texture—in the mind of the observer. And if we continue to dwell in thought on this world, not of objects in the solidity with which language invests them, but of impressions, unstable, flickering, inconsistent, which burn and are extinguished with our consciousness of them, it contracts still further: the whole scope of observation is dwarfed into the narrow chamber of the individual mind. Experience, already reduced to a group of impressions, is ringed round for each one of us by that thick wall of personality through which no real voice has ever pierced on its way to us, or from us to that which we can only conjecture to be without. Every one of those impressions is the impression of the individual in his isolation, each mind keeping as a solitary prisoner its own dream of a world. Analysis goes a step farther still, and assures us that those impressions of the individual mind to which, for each one of us, experience dwindles down, are in perpetual flight; that each of them is limited by time, and that as time is infinitely divisible, each of them is infinitely divisible also; all that is actual in it being a single moment, gone while we try to apprehend it, of which it may ever be more truly said that it has ceased to be than that it is. To such a tremulous wisp constantly re-forming itself on the stream, to a single sharp impression, with a sense in it, a relic more or less fleeting, of such moments gone by, what is real in our life fines itself down. It is with this movement, with the passage and dissolution of impressions, images, sensations, that analysis leaves off— that continual vanishing away, that strange, perpetual weaving and unweaving of ourselves.

Philosophiren, says Novalis, *ist dephlegmatisiren vivificiren*.[4] The service of philosophy, of speculative culture, towards the human spirit, is to rouse, to startle it to a life of constant and eager observation. Every moment some form grows perfect in hand or face; some tone on the hills or the sea is choicer than the rest; some mood of passion

---

3. When Ophelia is being buried, her brother says: "Lay her i' th' earth; / And from her fair and unpolluted flesh / May violets spring!" (*Hamlet* 5.1.238–40).

4. "To philosophize is to become unsluggish, to come alive." Novalis is the pseudonym of Friedrich von Hardenberg (1772–1801), a German Romantic writer.

or insight or intellectual excitement is irresistibly real and attractive to us,—for that moment only. Not the fruit of experience, but experience itself, is the end. A counted number of pulses only is given to us of a variegated, dramatic life. How may we see in them all that is to be seen in them by the finest senses? How shall we pass most swiftly from point to point, and be present always at the focus where the greatest number of vital forces unite in their purest energy?

To burn always with this hard, gemlike flame, to maintain this ecstasy, is success in life. In a sense it might even be said that our failure is to form habits: for, after all, habit is relative to a stereotyped world, and meantime it is only the roughness of the eye that makes any two persons, things, situations, seem alike. While all melts under our feet, we may well grasp at any exquisite passion, or any contribution to knowledge that seems by a lifted horizon to set the spirit free for a moment, or any stirring of the senses, strange dyes, strange colours, and curious odours, or work of the artist's hands, or the face of one's friend. Not to discriminate every moment some passionate attitude in those about us, and in the very brilliancy of their gifts some tragic dividing of forces on their ways, is, on this short day of frost and sun, to sleep before evening. With this sense of the splendour of our experience and of its awful brevity, gathering all we are into one desperate effort to see and touch, we shall hardly have time to make theories about the things we see and touch. What we have to do is to be for ever curiously testing new opinions and courting new impressions, never acquiescing in a facile orthodoxy of Comte, or of Hegel,[5] or of our own. Philosophical theories or ideas, as points of view, instruments of criticism, may help us to gather up what might otherwise pass unregarded by us. "Philosophy is the microscope of thought."[6] The theory or idea or system which requires of us the sacrifice of any part of this experience, in consideration of some interest into which we cannot enter, or some abstract theory we have not identified with ourselves, or of what is only conventional, has no real claim upon us.

One of the most beautiful passages of Rousseau is that in the sixth book of the *Confessions*,[7] where he describes the awakening in him of the literary sense. An undefinable taint of death had clung always about him, and now in early manhood he believed himself smitten by mortal disease. He asked himself how he might make as much as possible of the interval that remained; and he was not biassed by anything in his previous life when he decided that it must be by intellectual excitement, which he found just then in the clear, fresh writings of Voltaire.[8] Well! we are all *condamnés*, as Victor Hugo[9] says: we are all under sentence of death but with a sort of indefinite reprieve—*les hommes sont tous condamnés à mort avec des sursis indéfinis*: we have an interval, and then our place knows us no more. Some spend this interval in listlessness, some in high passions, the wisest, at least among "the children of this world,"[1] in art and song. For our one chance lies in expanding that interval, in getting as many pulsations as possible into the given time. Great passions may give us this quickened sense of life, ecstasy and sorrow of love, the various forms of enthusiastic activity, disinterested or otherwise, which come naturally to many of us. Only be sure

5. Auguste Comte (1798–1857), French philosopher, was the founder of positivism; George W. F. Hegel (1770–1831), was a major German philosopher of history and of art.
6. Victor Hugo, *Les Misérables* (1862) pt. 5, bk. 2, ch. 2.
7. The *Confessions* is an autobiographical work by Jean-Jacques Rousseau (1712–1778), French writer and philosopher.
8. The critic Donald Hill notes that Rousseau never

mentions reading Voltaire (1694–1778), French writer and skeptic.
9. Condemned. Victor Hugo, French novelist; the passage Pater quotes is from *Le dernier jour d'un condamné* (1832).
1. "And the Lord commended the unjust steward, because he had done wisely; for the children of this world are in their generation wiser than the children of light" (Luke 16.8).

it is passion—that it does yield you this fruit of a quickened, multiplied conscious-ness. Of such wisdom, the poetic passion, the desire of beauty, the love of art for its own sake, has most. For art comes to you proposing frankly to give nothing but the highest quality to your moments as they pass, and simply for those moments' sake.

1868   1868, 1873

Gerard Manley Hopkins
1844–1889

Gerard Manley Hopkins is the most modern of Victorian poets, and the most Victorian of modern poets. His stunningly original poems were, with a few exceptions, not published until 1918, placing him at first glance in the company of Eliot and Pound. But his struggle to main-tain religious faith, his respect for conventional verse forms, and his quest to find proof of God's work in nature all mark him as quintessentially Victorian. Hopkins combines a micro-scopic keenness of vision with a Joycean genius for compound words, new coinages, unex-pected rhymes, and startling distortions of syntax. The result is a poetry of modernist intensity and compression, fraught with bold ellipses and daring line breaks, but nonetheless dedicated to describing a world "charged with the grandeur of God." Orthodox and self-denying in mat-ters of religion, Hopkins was also the era's most radical literary rebel.

Hopkins was born into a prosperous, pious Anglican family. After attending school in London, he went in 1863 to study classics at Balliol College, Oxford, where the agnostic aes-thete Walter Pater was one of his tutors. At the same time, Hopkins came under the influence of the "Oxford Movement." He read John Henry Newman's account of his gravitation toward Roman Catholicism in *Apologia Pro Vita Sua*; subsequent talks with Newman led to Hopkins's own agonizing conversion to Catholicism in 1866. In 1868 he entered the novitiate of the So-ciety of Jesus and burned almost all his early, Keatsian poems. He called his action the "slaugh-ter of the innocents," and resolved "to write no more, as not belonging to my profession, unless it were by the wish of my superiors."

Seven years of poetic silence ensued, as Hopkins studied for the priesthood. But he was also meditating on his idiosyncratic theories of poetic composition. When five nuns were drowned in a shipwreck in 1875, he was suddenly moved to compose the first poem in his new style, *The Wreck of the Deutschland*. But there was no audience prepared to fathom his highly wrought style. Hopkins offered the work to a Jesuit magazine but, he said, "they dared not print it." He never again tried to publish.

Hopkins was ordained a Jesuit priest in 1877. Joyous, he produced a series of radiant sonnets celebrating the presence of God in nature. But his remaining years tested his faith sorely. Often in ill-health, he labored as a parish priest and teacher throughout Britain, including missionary work in the slums of Liverpool. He suffered physically and spiritually from the "vice and horrors" he found in his dreary urban duties: "It made even life a burden to me," he confessed. Then in 1884 he was appointed Professor of Greek and Latin at the Catholic, newly formed University College in Dublin. Already estranged from his family and the English church, he felt separated from his country, too. "I am in Ireland now," he wrote in a sonnet, "now I am at a third / Remove." Yet even as he despaired of accomplishing work of lasting value, he produced many of his best poems, including the famed "terrible sonnets" that describe his sense of spiritual and poetic sterility. Ex-hausted by his strenuous duties, Hopkins died in Dublin of typhoid at the age of forty-five.

Although Hopkins read the important nineteenth-century poets with care, he deliber-ately carved his own way. "The effect of studying masterpieces," he said, "is to make me admire and do otherwise." In his journals Hopkins often sounds like an English Thoreau, finely attuned to every nuance of the natural world. His entries are always searching to grasp the essential particularity of a thing, its inner landscape—what he called "inscape." Elaborating his theory in a letter to Robert Bridges, an Oxford friend who later became Poet Laureate, Hopkins admitted that "no doubt my poetry errs on the side of oddness. . . . it is the vice of distinctiveness to become queer." But he asserted the absolute importance of such "distinctiveness"—this "design, pattern or what I am in the habit of calling *inscape* is what I above all aim at in poetry." Hopkins needed another term to express the dynamic energy that not only makes the inscape cohere but also projects it outward toward the observer. This force that both unifies an object and arouses the senses of its beholder Hopkins called "instress." Taken together, the terms "inscape" and "instress" convey the organic beauty that for Hopkins speaks of God's presence in nature.

To apply these concepts poetically, Hopkins developed a new verse line based on "sprung rhythm." As in Old English poetry or nursery rhymes, each line in sprung rhythm has a fixed number of stresses, but the number and placement of unstressed syllables can vary widely. Many poets had employed individual lines of this type, but Hopkins took the idea of flexible metrics to new heights. He loaded his lines with internal rhyme, alliteration, assonance, and strong Anglo-Saxon words, and drove them forward with crashing consonants and wrenching enjambments. Responding to Bridges's confusion, he explained: "Why do I employ sprung rhythm at all? Because it is the nearest to the rhythm of prose, that is the native and natural rhythm of speech, the least forced, the most rhetorical and emphatic of all possible rhythms." Since Hopkins connected the sight and sound of individual words to the religious intensity with which he viewed objects in nature, the effect is akin to impassioned prayer. "My verse is less to be read than heard," he concluded; "it is oratorical."

In his later poetry a tangle of religious and sexual imagery expresses his sense of thwarted love and meager poetic production. He portrays himself as a sapless tree, or as barren sand: "I am soft sift / In an hourglass." In 1885 he wrote to Bridges in frustration, "if I could but produce work I should not mind its being buried, silenced, and going no further; but it kills me to be time's eunuch and never to beget." Such passages, with their images of sexual impotency, poetic infertility, and self-abnegation, suggest what Bridges called "the naked encounter of sensualism and asceticism" in Hopkins's work.

Despite his disclaimers, Hopkins was preoccupied with his lack of an audience. He once informed Bridges: "You are my public and I hope to convert you." Missionary-like, Hopkins's poetry seeks to "convert" the reader with its ecstatic particularity, its intensity of perception. But he speaks of his efforts as a one-way correspondence to God and his public; his poems are "cries like dead letters sent / To dearest him that lives alas! away." Hopkins could not have known that Bridges, despite his difficulty grasping these "dead letters," would finally publish the poems to great acclaim at the close of World War I. Then, like the works of Emily Dickinson and Vincent Van Gogh, they would suddenly seize a central artistic place in a past that had been unaware of their existence. And yet, Hopkins did recognize that his mingling of sensuality and spirituality allied him with another great proto-modernist. "I always knew in my heart Walt Whitman's mind to be more like my own than any other man's living," he told Bridges. "As he is a great scoundrel this is not a pleasant confession."

God's Grandeur

The world is charged with the grandeur of God.
It will flame out, like shining from shook foil;[1]

---

1. I mean foil in its sense of leaf or tinsel . . . . Shaken goldfoil gives off broad glares like sheet lightning and also, and this is true of nothing else, owing to its zigzag dints and creasings and network of small many cornered facets, a sort of fork lightning too [Hopkins's note].

It gathers to a greatness, like the ooze of oil
Crushed.[2] Why do men then now not reck° his rod?   heed
5 Generations have trod, have trod, have trod;
     And all is seared with trade; bleared, smeared with toil;
     And wears man's smudge and shares man's smell: the soil
Is bare now, nor can foot feel, being shod.

And for° all this, nature is never spent;   despite
10   There lives the dearest freshness deep down things;
And though the last lights off the black West went
     Oh, morning, at the brown brink eastward, springs—
Because the Holy Ghost over the bent
     World broods with warm breast and with ah! bright wings.
1877   1895

The Windhover:[1]
To Christ Our Lord

I caught this morning morning's minion,[2] king-
     dom of daylight's dauphin,[3] dapple-dawn-drawn Falcon, in his riding
     Of the rolling level underneath him steady air, and striding
High there, how he rung upon the rein[4] of a wimpling wing
5 In his ecstasy! then off, off forth on swing,
     As a skate's heel sweeps smooth on a bow-bend: the hurl and gliding
     Rebuffed the big wind. My heart in hiding
Stirred for a bird,—the achieve of, the mastery of the thing!

Brute beauty and valour and act, oh, air, pride, plume, here
10   Buckle! AND the fire that breaks from thee then, a billion
Times told lovelier, more dangerous, O my chevalier!

     No wonder of it: shéer plód makes plough down sillion[5]
Shine, and blue-bleak embers, ah my dear,
     Fall, gall[6] themselves, and gash gold-vermilion.
1877   1918

Pied[1] Beauty

Glory be to God for dappled things—
     For skies of couple-colour as a brinded[2] cow;
          For rose-moles all in stipple[3] upon trout that swim;
Fresh-firecoal chestnut-falls;[4] finches' wings;

2. Oil made by crushing seeds or olives.
1. Kestrel falcon—a small hawk—that appears to hover in the air.
2. Darling, from the French *mignon*.
3. The dauphin was the heir to the French throne.
4. In falconry, a bird rings when it rises in spirals (like a horse circling at the end of a tether or rein). Wimpling means rippling.
5. The furrows of a plowed field.
6. Break their surfaces.
1. Blotched with different colors.
2. Brindled, having dark patches on a tawny ground.
3. Stippled, painted or drawn with dots instead of lines.
4. Chestnuts as bright as coals [Hopkins's journal].

5   Landscape plotted and pieced—fold, fallow, and plough;[5]
              And áll trádes, their gear and tackle and trim.°   *equipment*

        All things counter,[6] original, spare, strange;
           Whatever is fickle, freckled (who knows how?)
           With swift, slow; sweet, sour; adazzle, dim;
10   He fathers-forth whose beauty is past change:
                Praise him.

1877   1918

Binsey Poplars
felled 1879

     My aspens dear, whose airy cages quelled,
     Quelled or quenched in leaves the leaping sun,
     All felled, felled, are all felled;
        Of a fresh and following folded rank
5   Not spared, not one
              That dandled a sandalled
          Shadow that swam or sank
On meadow and river and wind-wandering weed-winding bank.

      O if we but knew what we do
10   When we delve or hew—
       Hack and rack the growing green!
          Since country is so tender
     To touch, her being só slender,
     That, like this sleek and seeing ball°   *eye*
15   But a prick will make no eye at all,
     Where we, even where we mean
         To mend her we end her,
       When we hew or delve:
After-comers cannot guess the beauty been.
20   Ten or twelve, only ten or twelve
        Strokes of havoc únselve
       The sweet especial scene,
      Rural scene, a rural scene,
      Sweet especial rural scene.

1879   1918

Felix Randal

Felix Randal the farrier,[1] O he is dead then? my duty all ended,
Who have watched his mould of man, big-boned and hardy-handsome
Pining, pining, till time when reason rambled in it and some
Fatal four disorders, fleshed there, all contended?

---

5. Landscape of differently colored fields, some used as pasture ("fold"), some lying fallow, some plowed.

6. Contrary; "spare" means rare.
1. Blacksmith.

5 Sickness broke him. Impatient he cursed at first, but mended
Being anointed[2] and all; though a heavenlier heart began some
Months earlier, since I had our sweet reprieve and ransom[3]
Tendered to him. Ah well, God rest him all road ever he offended!

This seeing the sick endears them to us, us too it endears.
10 My tongue had taught thee comfort, touch had quenched thy tears,
Thy tears that touched my heart, child, Felix, poor Felix Randal;

How far from then forethought of, all thy more boisterous years,
When thou at the random[4] grim forge, powerful amidst peers,
Didst fettle° for the great grey drayhorse his bright and battering sandal!   *prepare*

1880   1918

As Kingfishers Catch Fire

As kingfishers catch fire, dragonflies dráw fláme;
As tumbled over rim in roundy wells
Stones ring; like each tucked° string tells, each hung bell's   *plucked*
Bow swung finds tongue to fling out broad its name;
5 Each mortal thing does one thing and the same:
Deals out that being indoors each one dwells;
Selves—goes itself; *myself* it speaks and spells;
Crying *Whát I dó is me: for that I came.*

Í say móre: the just man justices;
10 Kéeps gráce; thát keeps all his goings graces;
Acts in God's eye what in God's eye he is—
Christ—for Christ plays in ten thousand places,
Lovely in limbs, and lovely in eyes not his
To the Father through the features of men's faces.

1881–1882?   1918

[Carrion Comfort][1]

Not, I'll not, carrion comfort, Despair, not feast on thee;
Not untwist—slack they may be—these last strands of man
In me ór, most weary, cry *I can no more*. I can;
Can something, hope, wish day come, not choose not to be.
5 But ah, but O thou terrible, why wouldst thou rude on me
Thy wring-world right foot rock? lay a lionlimb against me? scan
With darksome devouring eyes my bruisèd bones? and fan,
O in turns of tempest, me heaped there; me frantic to avoid thee and flee?

Why? That my chaff might fly; my grain lie, sheer and clear.
10 Nay in all that toil, that coil,[2] since (seems) I kissed the rod,

2. Having received Extreme Unction, the sacrament for the dying.
3. Confession, absolution, and Holy Communion.
4. Built of rough irregular stones.

1. The title was added by Robert Bridges. This poem is one of the "terrible sonnets" of 1885, as are the next two.
2. Turmoil.

Hand rather,[3] my heart lo! lapped strength, stole joy, would laugh, chéer.
Cheer whom though? the hero whose heaven-handling flung me, fóot tród
Me? or me that fought him? O which one? is it each one? That night, that year
Of now done darkness I wretch lay wrestling with (my God!) my God.

1885   1918

No Worst, There Is None

No worst, there is none. Pitched past pitch of grief,
More pangs will, schooled at forepangs, wilder wring.
Comforter, where, where is your comforting?
Mary, mother of us, where is your relief?
5   My cries heave, herds-long;[1] huddle in a main, a chief
Woe, world-sorrow; on an age-old anvil wince and sing—
Then lull, then leave off. Fury had shrieked "No ling-
ering! Let me be fell°: force° I must be brief."   *fierce/perforce*

    O the mind, mind has mountains; cliffs of fall
10   Frightful, sheer, no-man-fathomed. Hold them cheap
May who ne'er hung there. Nor does long our small
Durance° deal with that steep or deep. Here! creep,   *endurance*
Wretch, under a comfort serves in a whirlwind: all
Life death does end and each day dies with sleep.

1885   1918

I Wake and Feel the Fell of Dark, Not Day

I wake and feel the fell[1] of dark, not day.
What hours, O what black hoürs we have spent
This night! what sights you, heart, saw; ways you went!
And more must, in yet longer light's delay.
5   With witness I speak this. But where I say
Hours I mean years, mean life. And my lament
Is cries countless, cries like dead letters sent
To dearest him that lives alas! away.

    I am gall, I am heartburn. God's most deep decree
10   Bitter would have me taste: my taste was me;
Bones built in me, flesh filled, blood brimmed the curse.
    Selfyeast of spirit a dull dough sours. I see
The lost° are like this, and their scourge to be   *souls in Hell*
As I am mine, their sweating selves; but worse.

1885   1918

---

3. I.e., the hand that holds the rod the speaker has kissed.
1. Like a cry of sheep or cattle repeated successively the length of the herd.

1. Gall, bitterness; but also a hide or covering; a wasteland; as an adjective, "fell" means fierce or cruel.

That Nature Is a Heraclitean Fire[1]
and of the Comfort of the Resurrection

Cloud-puffball, torn tufts, tossed pillows | flaunt forth, then
    chevy° on an air-   *race*
built thoroughfare: heaven-roysterers, in gay-gangs | they throng; they
    glitter in marches.
Down roughcast, down dazzling whitewash, | wherever an elm arches,
Shivelights[2] and shadowtackle in long | lashes lace, lance, and pair.
5 Delightfully the bright wind boisterous | ropes, wrestles, beats earth bare
Of yestertempest's creases; | in pool and rut peel parches
Squandering ooze to squeezed | dough, crust, dust; stanches,[3] starches
Squadroned masks and manmarks | treadmire toil there
Footfretted in it. Million-fuelèd, | nature's bonfire burns on.
10 But quench her bonniest, dearest | to her, her clearest-selvèd spark
Man, how fast his firedint, | his mark on mind, is gone!
Both are in an unfathomable, all is in an enormous dark
Drowned. O pity and indig | nation! Manshape, that shone
Sheer off, disseveral,[4] a star, | death blots black out; nor mark
15   Is any of him at all so stark
But vastness blurs and time | beats level. Enough! the Resurrection,
A heart's-clarion! Away grief's gasping, | joyless days, dejection.
                  Across my foundering deck shone
A beacon, an eternal beam. | Flesh fade, and mortal trash
20 Fall to the residuary worm; | world's wildfire, leave but ash:
                  In a flash, at a trumpet crash,
I am all at once what Christ is, | since he was what I am, and
This Jack, joke, poor potsherd,[5] | patch,[6] matchwood, immortal diamond,
                  Is immortal diamond.

1888   1918

Thou Art Indeed Just, Lord

*Justus quidem tu es, Domine, si disputem tecum: verumtamen
justa loquar ad te: Quare via impiorum prosperatur? & c.[1]*

Thou art indeed just, Lord, if I contend
With thee; but, sir, so what I plead is just.
Why do sinners' ways prosper? and why must
Disappointment all I endeavour end?
5   Wert thou my enemy, O thou my friend,
How wouldst thou worse, I wonder, than thou dost
Defeat, thwart me? Oh, the sots and thralls of lust

---

1. The Greek philosopher Heraclitus (c. 535 B.C.–475 B.C.) taught that the basic element of the universe was fire, and that all things were constantly in flux as mere transient manifestations of that fire. Hopkins sets this idea against his belief in the resurrection of an immortal, unchanging Christ.
2. Slivers of light.

3. Makes staunch or firm.
4. Neologism combining "dissever" and "several."
5. A broken piece of pottery.
6. Fool.
1. The first lines of the poem translate these words from Jeremiah 12.1.

Do in spare hours more thrive than I that spend,
Sir, life upon thy cause. See, banks and brakes°   *thickets*
10 Now, leavèd how thick! lacèd they are again
With fretty chervil,° look, and fresh wind shakes   *cow-parsley*
Them; birds build—but not I build; no, but strain,
Time's eunuch, and not breed one work that wakes.
Mine, O thou lord of life, send my roots rain.

1889   1893

⊷ ⊱⊰ ⊶

Rudyard Kipling
1865–1936

"The infant monster," Henry James called him. In his early twenties the "shockingly precocious" Rudyard Kipling was already a literary celebrity, acclaimed for his vivid stories of life
in India. Like Dickens, to whom he was inevitably compared, Kipling was both popular and
prolific. In addition to hundreds of short stories, he wrote poetry, essays, and children's
books, including the *Jungle Books* (1894, 1895) and *Just So Stories* (1902). He also wrote several novels, of which the best-known are *The Light That Failed* (1890), *Captains Courageous*
(1896–1897), and *Kim* (1901). In 1907 he became the first English writer to win the Nobel
Prize for literature.

Rudyard Kipling was born in Bombay, and his idyllic early years gave him a lifelong attachment to India. He and his younger sister were cared for by indulgent servants with whom
they spoke Hindustani; English was almost a second language, "haltingly translated out of the
vernacular idiom that one thought and dreamed in." But when he was five years old Kipling's
parents sent the children "home" to England, where they were badly treated by the English
family who were paid to look after them. They did not see their parents for five years. After
this period of bitter unhappiness, boarding school came as a relief; Kipling later recorded his
experiences of schoolboy life in the stories of *Stalky & Co.* (1899).

In 1882, not yet seventeen, Kipling returned to India to work as a journalist. Once again
the people and landscape got under his skin: "I would wander till dawn in all manner of odd
places—liquor-shops, gambling- and opium-dens . . . wayside entertainments such as puppet-
shows, native dances; or in and about the narrow gullies under the Mosque of Wazir Khan for
the sheer sake of looking." After seven years in India, he returned to England with a growing
literary reputation, for his first collection of stories, *Plain Tales from the Hills* (1888), had
caught the public's imagination. His exotic settings and vigorous prose struck readers as fresh
and original—particularly in contrast to the writing of his jaded *fin-de-siècle* contemporaries.
Somerset Maugham described the magic of Kipling's Indian stories: "They give you the tang of
the East, the smell of the bazaars, the torpor of the rains, the heat of the sun-scorched earth,
the rough life of the barracks."

Kipling married an American and lived in Vermont for several years, but eventually the
couple settled in Sussex. Kipling wrote: "I am slowly discovering England which is the most
wonderful foreign land I have ever been in." Although he was always something of an outsider
in England, his love for the English countryside is reflected in much of his later writing, including the haunting story, *They*, and the children's book *Puck of Pook's Hill* (1906).

Many critics consider Kipling the greatest short story writer in English. Describing his
own economy of style, Kipling wrote that tightening up his stories had taught him "that a
tale from which pieces have been raked out is like a fire that has been poked." His intense

and enigmatic stories reveal a meticulous attention to detail. In addition, Kipling captured the cadences of everyday speech in many dialects and accents—Indian, Cockney, Yorkshire, Irish, Sussex—and he was adept with an astonishing range of narrative voices. He particularly excelled at reproducing the slang and shoptalk of the rough-and-ready men doing the work of empire: soldiers, sailors, engineers. Kipling's genius for capturing the "language of common men,"—to use Wordsworth's phrase from his preface to *Lyrical Ballads* (1800)—is even more pronounced in his poetry than in his prose. *Barrack-Room Ballads* (1892), for instance, pursues the Wordsworthian fascination with the imaginative side of ordinary life, but life as it is lived at the ends of a far-flung Empire, to the tempo of a military band. His first book of poems, *Departmental Ditties* (1886), revealed that he had learned his swinging rhythms and ballad meters from Swinburne and Scott, while he also admired the American dialect styles of Bret Harte, Mark Twain, and Joel Chandler Harris's Uncle Remus stories.

Fusing these varied influences with subject matter that was completely new to English verse, he deliberately rejected the introspective poetry of private life that the Aesthetes were making fashionable. Instead Kipling produced a public-oriented poetry that dealt with the wider world of Empire, using poetry as a vehicle to express the social and political views of his down-to-earth narrators. Though his exceptional skill with rhyme and meter has been widely praised, people often quote Kipling without realizing it, when they use such phrases as "a good cigar is a Smoke," "the female of the species," "but that is another story," or "the White Man's burden."

At times Kipling has been better known for his political views than for his literary works. But attention to the more reactionary moments of his later life (his opposition to Home Rule in India, for instance) has obscured the complexity of his attitudes. His opinions of imperialism, the colonies, and people of other cultures can be extremely hard to pin down. Like Robert Browning or Joseph Conrad, he adopts a range of narrative devices and speaking voices, presenting himself in a variety of roles, from the common British soldier to the Islamic sage. Though he is often accused of supporting British imperialism, Kipling persistently probes the human toll that empire building takes on those who bear the brunt of it: British soldiers and administrators on the one hand and native soldiers and servants on the other.

A reading of Kipling's work on its own terms reveals a complicated art in which human qualities such as love, fidelity, and devotion to duty can bridge national and racial boundaries. What comes through strongly in Kipling's writing is his respect for hard work and his admiration for courage in the face of death. He satirizes and condemns vanity and bullying among all peoples. Above all else, perhaps, he is fascinated with both subtle and crude manifestations of English power: its uses, abuses, and—especially—its painful responsibilities. Kipling's sympathy for both colonized and colonizer, as well as his evident pleasure in the myriad inflections and accents of speech, makes his work, as the critic Craig Raine has said, "the expression of a profoundly democratic artistry."

Without Benefit of Clergy[1]

"But if it be a girl?"

"Lord of my life, it cannot be. I have prayed for so many nights, and sent gifts to Sheikh Badl's shrine so often, that I know God will give us a son—a man-child that shall grow into a man. Think of this and be glad. My mother shall be his mother till I can take him again, and the mullah[2] of the Pattan mosque shall cast his nativity—God send he be born in an auspicious hour!—and then, and then thou wilt never weary of me, thy slave."

---

1. First published in *Macmillan's Magazine* (1890). "Benefit of clergy" means the traditional right of clergymen to be tried by a church court; Kipling, however, means that the union of the two protagonists has not been blessed by the clergy—i.e., they are unmarried.
2. Muslim religious leader.

"Since when hast thou been a slave, my queen?"

"Since the beginning—till this mercy[3] came to me. How could I be sure of thy love when I knew that I had been bought with silver?"

"Nay, that was the dowry. I paid it to thy mother."

"And she has buried it, and sits upon it all day long like a hen. What talk is yours of dower! I was bought as though I had been a Lucknow dancing-girl[4] instead of a child."

"Art thou sorry for the sale?"

"I have sorrowed; but to-day I am glad. Thou wilt never cease to love me now?—answer, my king."

"Never—never. No."

"Not even though the *mem-log*—the white women of thy own blood—love thee? And remember, I have watched them driving in the evening; they are very fair."

"I have seen fire-balloons[5] by the hundred. I have seen the moon, and—then I saw no more fire-balloons."

Ameera clapped her hands and laughed. "Very good talk," she said. Then with an assumption of great stateliness: "It is enough. Thou hast my permission to depart,—if thou wilt."

The man did not move. He was sitting on a low red-lacquered couch in a room furnished only with a blue and white floor-cloth, some rugs, and a very complete collection of native cushions. At his feet sat a woman of sixteen, and she was all but all the world in his eyes. By every rule and law she should have been otherwise, for he was an Englishman, and she a Mussulman's daughter bought two years before from her mother, who, being left without money, would have sold Ameera shrieking to the Prince of Darkness if the price had been sufficient.

It was a contract entered into with a light heart; but even before the girl had reached her bloom she came to fill the greater portion of John Holden's life. For her, and the withered hag her mother, he had taken a little house overlooking the great red-walled city, and found,—when the marigolds had sprung up by the well in the courtyard, and Ameera had established herself according to her own ideas of comfort, and her mother had ceased grumbling at the inadequacy of the cooking-places, the distance from the daily market, and at matters of house-keeping in general,—that the house was to him his home. Any one could enter his bachelor's bungalow by day or night, and the life that he led there was an unlovely one. In the house in the city his feet only could pass beyond the outer courtyard to the women's rooms; and when the big wooden gate was bolted behind him he was king in his own territory, with Ameera for queen. And there was going to be added to this kingdom a third person whose arrival Holden felt inclined to resent. It interfered with his perfect happiness. It disarranged the orderly peace of the house that was his own. But Ameera was wild with delight at the thought of it, and her mother not less so. The love of a man, and particularly a white man, was at the best an inconstant affair, but it might, both women argued, be held fast by a baby's hands. "And then," Ameera would always say, "then he will never care for the white *mem-log*. I hate them all—I hate them all."

"He will go back to his own people in time," said the mother; "but by the blessing of God that time is yet afar off."

Holden sat silent on the couch thinking of the future, and his thoughts were not pleasant. The drawbacks of a double life are manifold. The Government, with singular care, had ordered him out of the station for a fortnight on special duty in the place of a man who was watching by the bedside of a sick wife. The verbal notification of the transfer had been edged by a cheerful remark that Holden ought to think himself lucky in being a bachelor and a free man. He came to break the news to Ameera.

"It is not good," she said slowly, "but it is not all bad. There is my mother here, and no harm will come to me—unless indeed I die of pure joy. Go thou to thy work and think no troublesome thoughts. When the days are done I believe . . . nay, I am sure. And—and then I shall lay *him* in thy arms, and thou wilt love me for ever. The train goes tonight, at midnight is it not? Go now, and do not let thy heart be heavy by cause of me. But thou wilt not delay in returning? Thou wilt not stay on the road to talk to the bold white *mem-log*. Come back to me swiftly, my life."

As he left the courtyard to reach his horse that was tethered to the gatepost, Holden spoke to the white-haired old watchman who guarded the house, and bade him under certain contingencies despatch the filled-up telegraph-form that Holden gave him. It was all that could be done, and with the sensations of a man who has attended his own funeral Holden went away by the night-mail to his exile. Every hour of the day he dreaded the arrival of the telegram, and every hour of the night he pictured to himself the death of Ameera. In consequence his work for the State was not of first-rate quality, nor was his temper towards his colleagues of the most amiable. The fortnight ended without a sign from his home, and, torn to pieces by his anxieties, Holden returned to be swallowed up for two precious hours by a dinner at the club, wherein he heard, as a man hears in a swoon, voices telling him how execrably he had performed the other man's duties, and how he had endeared himself to all his associates. Then he fled on horseback through the night with his heart in his mouth. There was no answer at first to his blows on the gate, and he had just wheeled his horse round to kick it in when Pir Khan appeared with a lantern and held his stirrup.

"Has aught occurred?" said Holden.

"The news does not come from my mouth, Protector of the Poor, but—" He held out his shaking hand as befitted the bearer of good news who is entitled to a reward.

Holden hurried through the courtyard. A light burned in the upper room. His horse neighed in the gateway and he heard a shrill little wail that sent all the blood into the apple of his throat. It was a new voice, but it did not prove that Ameera was alive.

"Who is there?" he called up the narrow brick staircase.

There was a cry of delight from Ameera, and then the voice of the mother, tremulous with old age and pride—"We be two women and—the—man—thy—son."

On the threshold of the room Holden stepped on a naked dagger, that was laid there to avert ill-luck, and it broke at the hilt under his impatient heel.

"God is great!" cooed Ameera in the half-light. "Thou hast taken his misfortunes on thy head."

"Ay, but how is it with thee, life of my life? Old woman, how is it with her?"

"She has forgotten her sufferings for joy that the child is born. There is no harm; but speak softly," said the mother.

"It only needed thy presence to make me all well," said Ameera. "My king, thou hast been very long away. What gifts hast thou for me? Ah, ah! It is I that bring gifts this time. Look, my life, look. Was there ever such a babe? Nay, I am too weak even to clear my arm from him."

"Rest then, and do not talk. I am here, *bachari* (little woman)."

"Well said, for there is a bond and a heel-rope (*peecharee*) between us now that nothing can break. Look—canst thou see in this light? He is without spot or blemish. Never was such a man-child. *Ya illah!* [My God] he shall be a pundit[6]—no, a trooper of the Queen. And, my life, dost thou love me as well as ever, though I am faint and sick and worn? Answer truly."

"Yea. I love as I have loved, with all my soul. Lie still, pearl, and rest."

"Then do not go. Sit by my side here—so. Mother, the lord of this house needs a cushion. Bring it." There was an almost imperceptible movement on the part of the new life that lay in the hollow of Ameera's arm. "Aho!" she said, her voice breaking with love. "The babe is a champion from his birth. He is kicking me in the side with mighty kicks. Was there ever such a babe! And he is ours to us—thine and mine. Put thy hand on his head, but carefully, for he is very young, and men are unskilled in such matters."

Very cautiously Holden touched with the tips of his fingers the downy head.

"He is of the Faith," said Ameera; "for lying here in the night-watches I whispered the call to prayer and the profession of faith into his ears. And it is most marvellous that he was born upon a Friday,[7] as I was born. Be careful of him, my life; but he can almost grip with his hands."

Holden found one helpless little hand that closed feebly on his finger. And the clutch ran through his limbs till it settled about his heart. Till then his sole thought had been for Ameera. He began to realize that there was some one else in the world, but he could not feel that it was a veritable son with a soul. He sat down to think, and Ameera dozed lightly.

"Get hence, *sahib*,"[8] said her mother under her breath. "It is not good that she should find you here on waking. She must be still."

"I go," said Holden submissively. "Here be rupees. See that my *baba* gets fat and finds all that he needs."

The chink of the silver roused Ameera. "I am his mother, and no hireling," she said weakly. "Shall I look to him more or less for the sake of money? Mother, give it back. I have born my lord a son."

The deep sleep of weakness came upon her almost before the sentence was completed. Holden went down to the courtyard very softly with his heart at ease. Pir Khan, the old watchman, was chuckling with delight. "This house is now complete," he said, and without further comment thrust into Holden's hands the hilt of a sabre worn many years ago when he, Pir Khan, served the Queen in the police. The bleat of a tethered goat came from the well-kerb.

"There be two," said Pir Khan, "two goats of the best. I bought them, and they cost much money; and since there is no birth-party assembled their flesh will be all mine. Strike craftily, *sahib*! 'Tis an ill-balanced sabre at the best. Wait till they raise their heads from cropping the marigolds."

"And why?" said Holden, bewildered.

6. Teacher.
7. The Islamic holy day.

8. A deferential term meaning lord or master.

"For the birth-sacrifice. What else? Otherwise the child being unguarded from fate may die. The Protector of the Poor knows the fitting words to be said."

Holden had learned them once with little thought that he would ever speak them in earnest. The touch of the cold sabre-hilt in his palm turned suddenly to the clinging grip of the child up stairs—the child that was his own son—and a dread of loss filled him.

"Strike!" said Pir Khan. "Never life came into the world but life was paid for it. See, the goats have raised their heads. Now! With a drawing cut!"

Hardly knowing what he did Holden cut twice as he muttered the Mohammedan prayer that runs:—"Almighty! In place of this my son I offer life for life, blood for blood, head for head, bone for bone, hair for hair, skin for skin." The waiting horse snorted and bounded in his pickets at the smell of the raw blood that spirted over Holden's riding-boots.

"Well smitten!" said Pir Khan wiping the sabre. "A swordsman was lost in thee. Go with a light heart, Heaven-born. I am thy servant, and the servant of thy son. May the Presence live a thousand years and. . . . the flesh of the goats is all mine?" Pir Khan drew back richer by a month's pay. Holden swung himself into the saddle and rode off through the low-hanging wood-smoke of the evening. He was full of riotous exultation, alternating with a vast vague tenderness directed towards no particular object, that made him choke as he bent over the neck of his uneasy horse. "I never felt like this in my life," he thought. "I'll go to the club and pull myself together."

A game of pool was beginning, and the room was full of men. Holden entered, eager to get to the light and the company of his fellows, singing at the top of his voice:

> In Baltimore a-walking, a lady I did meet!

"Did you?" said the club-secretary from his corner. "Did she happen to tell you that your boots were wringing wet? Great goodness, man, it's blood!"

"Bosh!" said Holden, picking his cue from the rack. "May I cut in? It's dew. I've been riding through high crops. My faith! my boots are in a mess though!

> And if it be a girl she shall wear a wedding ring,
> And if it be a boy he shall fight for his king,
> With his dirk, and his cap, and his little jacket blue,
> He shall walk the quarter-deck—

"Yellow on blue—green next player," said the marker monotonously.

"He *shall walk the quarter-deck*,—am I green, marker? He *shall walk the quarter-deck*,—eh! that's a bad shot,—*as his daddy used to do!*"

"I don't see that you have anything to crow about," said a zealous junior civilian acidly. "The Government is not exactly pleased with your work when you relieved Sanders."

"Does that mean a wigging[9] from head-quarters?" said Holden with an abstracted smile. "I think I can stand it."

The talk beat up round the ever-fresh subject of each man's work, and steadied Holden till it was time to go to his dark empty bungalow, where his butler received him as one who knew all his affairs. Holden remained awake for the greater part of the night, and his dreams were pleasant ones.

9. Reprimand.

2

"How old is he now?"

"*Ya illah!* What a man's question! He is all but six weeks old; and on this night I go up to the house-top with thee, my life, to count the stars. For that is auspicious. And he was born on a Friday under the sign of the sun, and it has been told to me that he will outlive us both and get wealth. Can we wish for aught better, beloved?"

"There is nothing better. Let us go up to the roof, and thou shalt count the stars—but a few only, for the sky is heavy with cloud."

"The winter rains are late, and maybe they come out of season. Come, before all the stars are hid. I have put on my richest jewels."

"Thou hast forgotten the best of all."

"*Ai!* Ours. He comes also. He has never yet seen the skies."

Ameera climbed the narrow staircase that led to the flat roof. The child, placid and unwinking, lay in the hollow of her right arm, gorgeous in silver-fringed muslin with a small skull-cap on his head. Ameera wore all that she valued most. The diamond nose-stud that takes the place of the Western patch[1] in drawing attention to the curve of the nostril, the gold ornament in the centre of the forehead studded with tallow-drop emeralds and flawed rubies, the heavy circlet of beaten gold that was fastened round her neck by the softness of the pure metal, and the chinking curb-patterned silver anklets hanging low over the rosy ankle-bone. She was dressed in jade-green muslin as befitted a daughter of the Faith, and from shoulder to elbow and elbow to wrist ran bracelets of silver tied with floss silk, frail glass bangles slipped over the wrist in proof of the slenderness of the hand, and certain heavy gold bracelets that had no part in her country's ornaments but, since they were Holden's gift and fastened with a cunning European snap, delighted her immensely.

They sat down by the low white parapet of the roof, overlooking the city and its lights.

"They are happy down there," said Ameera. "But I do not think that they are as happy as we. Nor do I think the white *mem-log* are as happy. And thou?"

"I know they are not."

"How dost thou know?"

"They give their children over to the nurses."

"I have never seen that," said Ameera with a sigh, "nor do I wish to see. *Ahi!*"— she dropped her head on Holden's shoulder,—"I have counted forty stars, and I am tired. Look at the child, love of my life, he is counting too."

The baby was staring with round eyes at the dark of the heavens. Ameera placed him in Holden's arms, and he lay there without a cry.

"What shall we call him among ourselves?" she said. "Look! Art thou ever tired of looking? He carries thy very eyes. But the mouth—"

"Is thine, most dear. Who should know better than I?"

"'Tis such a feeble mouth. Oh, so small! And yet it holds my heart between its lips. Give him to me now. He has been too long away."

"Nay, let him lie; he has not yet begun to cry."

"When he cries thou wilt give him back—eh! What a man of mankind thou art! If he cried he were only the dearer to me. But, my life, what little name shall we give him?"

---

1. Reference to the "beauty patches" popular in England in the 18th century.

The small body lay close to Holden's heart. It was utterly helpless and very soft. He scarcely dared to breathe for fear of crushing it. The caged green parrot that is regarded as a sort of guardian spirit in most native households moved on its perch and fluttered a drowsy wing.

"There is the answer," said Holden. "Mian Mittu has spoken. He shall be the parrot. When he is ready he will talk mightily and run about. Mian Mittu is the parrot in thy—in the Mussulman tongue, is it not?"

"Why put me so far off?" said Ameera fretfully. "Let it be like unto some English name—but not wholly. For he is mine."

"Then call him Tota, for that is likest English."

"Ay, Tota, and that is still the parrot. Forgive me, my lord, for a minute ago, but in truth he is too little to wear all the weight of Mian Mittu for name. He shall be Tota—our Tota to us. Hearest thou, oh, small one? Littlest, thou art Tota." She touched the child's cheek, and he waking wailed, and it was necessary to return him to his mother, who soothed him with the wonderful rhyme of *Aré koko, Ja ré koko!* which says:

> Oh, crow! Go crow! Baby's sleeping sound,
> And the wild plums grow in the jungle, only a penny a pound.
> Only a penny a pound, *baba,* only a penny a pound.

Reassured many times as to the price of those plums, Tota cuddled himself down to sleep. The two sleek, white well-bullocks in the courtyard were steadily chewing the cud of their evening meal; old Pir Khan squatted at the head of Holden's horse, his police sabre across his knees, pulling drowsily at a big water-pipe that croaked like a bull-frog in a pond. Ameera's mother sat spinning in the lower verandah, and the wooden gate was shut and barred. The music of a marriage procession came to the roof above the gentle hum of the city, and a string of flying-foxes crossed the face of the low moon.

"I have prayed," said Ameera after a long pause, "I have prayed for two things. First, that I may die in thy stead if thy death is demanded, and in the second that I may die in the place of the child. I have prayed to the Prophet and to Beebee Miriam [the Virgin Mary]. Thinkest thou either will hear?"

"From thy lips who would not hear the lightest word?"

"I asked for straight talk, and thou hast given me sweet talk. Will my prayers be heard?"

"How can I say? God is very good."

"Of that I am not sure. Listen now. When I die, or the child dies, what is thy fate? Living, thou wilt return to the bold white *mem-log,* for kind calls to kind."

"Not always."

"With a woman, no; with a man it is otherwise. Thou wilt in this life, later on, go back to thine own folk. That I could almost endure, for I should be dead. But in thy very death thou wilt be taken away to a strange place and a paradise that I do not know."

"Will it be paradise?"

"Surely, for who would harm thee? But we two—I and the child—shall be elsewhere, and we cannot come to thee, nor canst thou come to us. In the old days, before the child was born, I did not think of these things; but now I think of them always. It is very hard talk."

"It will fall as it will fall. Tomorrow we do not know, but to-day and love we know well. Surely we are happy now."

"So happy that it were well to make our happiness assured. And thy Beebee Miriam should listen to me; for she is also a woman. But then she would envy me! It is not seemly for men to worship a woman."

Holden laughed aloud at Ameera's little spasm of jealousy.

"Is it not seemly? Why didst thou not turn me from worship of thee, then?"

"Thou a worshipper! And of me! My king, for all thy sweet words, well I know that I am thy servant and thy slave, and the dust under thy feet. And I would not have it otherwise. See!"

Before Holden could prevent her she stooped forward and touched his feet; recovering herself with a little laugh she hugged Tota closer to her bosom. Then, almost savagely—

"Is it true that the bold white *mem-log* live for three times the length of my life? Is it true that they make their marriages not before they are old women?"

"They marry as do others—when they are women."

"That I know, but they wed when they are twenty-five. Is that true?"

"That is true."

"*Ya illah!* At twenty-five! Who would of his own will take a wife even of eighteen? She is a woman—ageing every hour. Twenty-five! I shall be an old woman at that age, and—Those *mem-log* remain young for ever. How I hate them!"

"What have they to do with us?"

"I cannot tell. I know only that there may now be alive on this earth a woman ten years older than I who may come to thee and take thy love ten years after I am an old woman, grey headed, and the nurse of Tota's son. That is unjust and evil. They should die too."

"Now, for all thy years thou art a child, and shalt be picked up and carried down the staircase."

"Tota! Have a care for Tota, my lord! Thou at least art as foolish as any babe!" Ameera tucked Tota out of harm's way in the hollow of her neck, and was carried down stairs laughing in Holden's arms, while Tota opened his eyes and smiled after the manner of the lesser angels.

He was a silent infant, and, almost before Holden could realize that he was in the world, developed into a small gold-coloured little god and unquestioned despot of the house overlooking the city. Those were months of absolute happiness to Holden and Ameera—happiness withdrawn from the world, shut in behind the wooden gate that Pir Khan guarded. By day Holden did his work with an immense pity for such as were not so fortunate as himself, and a sympathy for small children that amazed and amused many mothers at the little station-gatherings. At nightfall he returned to Ameera,—Ameera full of the wondrous doings of Tota, how he had been seen to clap his hands together and move his fingers with intention and purpose—which was manifestly a miracle—how later, he had of his own initiative crawled out of his low bedstead on to the floor and swayed on both feet for the space of three breaths.

"And they were long breaths, for my heart stood still with delight," said Ameera.

Then he took the beasts into his councils—the well-bullocks, the little grey squirrels, the mongoose that lived in a hole near the well, and especially Mian Mittu, the parrot, whose tail he grievously pulled, and Mian Mittu screamed till Ameera and Holden arrived.

"Oh, villain! Child of strength! This to thy brother on the house-top! *Tobah, tobah!* Fie! Fie! But I know a charm to make him wise as Suleiman and Aflatoun

[Solomon and Plato]. Now look," said Ameera. She drew from an embroidered bag a handful of almonds. "See! we count seven. In the name of God!"

She placed Mian Mittu, very angry and rumpled, on the top of his cage, and seating herself between the babe and the bird she cracked and peeled an almond less white than her teeth. "This is a true charm, my life, and do not laugh. See! I give the parrot one half and Tota the other." Mian Mittu with careful beak took his share from between Ameera's lips, and she kissed the other half into the mouth of the child, who ate it slowly with wondering eyes. "This I will do each day of seven, and without doubt he who is ours will be a bold speaker and wise. Eh, Tota, what wilt thou be when thou art a man and I am grey-headed?" Tota tucked his fat legs into adorable creases. He could crawl, but he was not going to waste the spring of his youth in idle speech. He wanted Mian Mittu's tail to tweak.

When he was advanced to the dignity of a silver belt—which, with a magic-square engraved on silver and hung round his neck, made up the greater part of his clothing—he staggered on a perilous journey down the garden to Pir Khan and proffered him all his jewels in exchange for one little ride on Holden's horse, having seen his mother's mother chaffering with pedlars in the verandah. Pir Khan wept and set the untried feet on his own grey head in sign of fealty, and brought the bold adventurer to his mother's arms, vowing that Tota would be a leader of men ere his beard was grown.

One hot evening while he sat on the roof between his father and mother watching the never-ending warfare of the kites, that the city boys flew, he demanded a kite of his own with Pir Khan to fly it, because he had a fear of dealing with anything larger than himself, and when Holden called him a "spark," he rose to his feet and answered slowly in defence of his newfound individuality: "*Hum 'park nahin hai. Hom admi hai.* (I am no spark, but a man.)"

The protest made Holden choke and devote himself very seriously to a consideration of Tota's future. He need hardly have taken the trouble. The delight of that life was too perfect to endure. Therefore it was taken away as many things are taken away in India—suddenly and without warning. The little lord of the house, as Pir Khan called him, grew sorrowful and complained of pains who had never known the meaning of pain. Ameera, wild with terror, watched him through the night, and in the dawning of the second day the life was shaken out of him by fever—the seasonal autumn fever. It seemed altogether impossible that he could die, and neither Ameera nor Holden at first believed the evidence of the little body on the bedstead. Then Ameera beat her head against the wall and would have flung herself down the well in the garden had Holden not restrained her by main force.

One mercy only was granted to Holden. He rode to his office in broad daylight and found waiting him an unusually heavy mail that demanded concentrated attention and hard work. He was not, however, alive to this kindness of the gods.

3

The first shock of a bullet is no more than a brisk pinch. The wrecked body does not send in its protest to the soul till ten or fifteen seconds later. Holden realized his pain slowly, exactly as he had realized his happiness, and with the same imperious necessity for hiding all trace of it. In the beginning he only felt that there had been a loss, and that Ameera needed comforting, where she sat with her head on her knees shivering as Mian Mittu from the house-top called, *Tota! Tota! Tota!* Later all his world and the daily life of it rose up to hurt him. It was an outrage that any one of the children at the band-stand in the evening should be alive and clamorous, when his own child lay dead. It was more than mere pain when one of them touched him, and stories told by over-fond fathers of their children's latest performances cut him to the quick. He could not declare his pain. He had neither help, comfort, nor sympathy; and Ameera at the end of each weary day would lead him through the hell of self-questioning reproach which is reserved for those who have lost a child, and believe that with a little—just a little more care—it might have been saved.

"Perhaps," Ameera would say, "I did not take sufficient heed. Did I, or did I not? The sun on the roof that day when he played so long alone and I was—*ahi!* braiding my hair—it may be that the sun then bred the fever. If I had warned him from the sun he might have lived. But, oh my life, say that I am guiltless! Thou knowest that I loved him as I love thee. Say that there is no blame on me, or I shall die—I shall die!"

"There is no blame,—before God, none. It was written and how could we do aught to save? What has been, has been. Let it go, beloved."

"He was all my heart to me. How can I let the thought go when my arm tells me every night that he is not here? *Ahi! Ahi!* Oh Tota come back to me—come back again, and let us be all together as it was before!"

"Peace, peace! For thine own sake, and for mine also, if thou lovest me—rest."

"By this I know thou dost not care; and how shouldst thou? The white men have hearts of stone and souls of iron. Oh that I had married a man of mine own people—though he beat me, and had never eaten the bread of an alien!"

"Am I an alien—mother of my son?"

"What else—*sahib?* . . . Oh forgive me—forgive! The death has driven me mad. Thou art the life of my heart, and the light of my eyes, and the breath of my life, and—and I have put thee from me though it was but for a moment. If thou goest away to whom shall I look for help? Do not be angry. Indeed, it was the pain that spoke and not thy slave."

"I know, I know. We be two who were three. The greater need therefore that we should be one."

They were sitting on the roof as of custom. The night was a warm one in early spring, and sheet-lightning was dancing on the horizon to a broken tune played by far-off thunder. Ameera settled herself in Holden's arms.

"The dry earth is lowing like a cow for the rain, and I—I am afraid. It was not like this when we counted the stars. But thou lovest me as much as before, though a bond is taken away? Answer!"

"I love more because a new bond has come out of the sorrow that we have eaten together, and that thou knowest."

"Yea, I knew," said Ameera in a very small whisper. "But it is good to hear thee say so, my life, who art so strong to help. I will be a child no more, but a woman and an aid to thee. Listen! Give me my *sitar*[2] and I will sing bravely."

She took the light silver-studded *sitar* and began a song of the great hero Rajah Rasalu. The hand failed on the strings, the tune halted, checked, and at a low note turned off to the poor little nursery-rhyme about the wicked crow:

> And the wild plums grow in the jungle, only a penny a pound.
> Only a penny a pound, *baba*—only . . .

2. Indian stringed instrument.

Then came the tears, and the piteous rebellion against fate till she slept, moaning a little in her sleep, with the right arm thrown clear of the body as though it protected something that was not there. It was after this night that life became a little easier for Holden. The ever-present pain of loss drove him into his work, and the work repaid him by filling up his mind for eight or nine hours a day. Ameera sat alone in the house and brooded, but grew happier when she understood that Holden was more at ease, according to the custom of women. They touched happiness again, but this time with caution.

"It was because we loved Tota that he died. The jealousy of God was upon us," said Ameera. "I have hung up a large black jar before our window to turn the evil eye from us, and we must make no protestations of delight but go softly underneath the stars, lest God find us out. Is that not good talk, worthless one?"

She had shifted the accent on the word that means "beloved," in proof of the sincerity of her purpose. But the kiss that followed the new christening was a thing that any deity might have envied. They went about henceforward saying, "It is naught, it is naught;" and hoping that all the Powers heard.

The Powers were busy on other things. They had allowed thirty million people four years of plenty wherein men fed well and the crops were certain and the birth-rate rose year by year: the districts reported a purely agricultural population varying from nine hundred to two thousand to the square mile of the overburdened earth; and the Member for Lower Tooting,[3] wandering about India in top-hat and frock-coat talked largely of the benefits of British rule, and suggested as the one thing needful the establishment of a duly qualified electoral system and a general bestowal of the franchise. His long-suffering hosts smiled and made him welcome, and when he paused to admire, with pretty picked words, the blossom of the blood-red *dhak* tree that had flowered untimely for a sign of what was coming, they smiled more than ever.

It was the Deputy Commissioner of Kot-Kumharsen, staying at the club for a day, who lightly told a tale that made Holden's blood run cold as he overheard the end.

"He won't bother any one any more. Never saw a man so astonished in my life. By Jove, I thought he meant to ask a question in the House about it. Fellow-passenger in his ship—dined next him—bowled over by cholera and died in eighteen hours. You needn't laugh, you fellows. The Member for Lower Tooting is awfully angry about it; but he's more scared. I think he's going to take his enlightened self out of India."

"I'd give a good deal if he were knocked over. It might keep a few vestrymen[4] of his kidney to their own parish. But what's this about cholera? It's full early for anything of that kind," said a warden of an unprofitable salt-lick.

"Don't know," said the Deputy Commissioner reflectively. "We've got locusts with us. There's sporadic cholera all along the north—at least we're calling it sporadic for decency's sake. The spring crops are short in five districts, and nobody seems to know where the rains are. It's nearly March now. I don't want to scare anybody, but it seems to me that Nature's going to audit her accounts with a big red pencil this summer."

"Just when I wanted to take leave, too!" said a voice across the room.

---

3. A Member of Parliament who has come to India to give advice on matters about which, Kipling suggests, he knows nothing.

4. Members of a Church of England parish council; Kipling uses the term satirically to refer to Members of Parliament.

"There won't be much leave this year, but there ought to be a great deal of promotion. I've come in to persuade the Government to put my pet canal on the list of famine relief-works. It's an ill-wind that blows no good. I shall get that canal finished at last."

"Is it the old programme then," said Holden; "famine, fever, and cholera?"

"Oh no. Only local scarcity and an unusual prevalence of seasonal sickness. You'll find it all in the reports if you live till next year. You're a lucky chap. You haven't got a wife to put out of harm's way. The hill-stations ought to be full of women this year."

"I think you're inclined to exaggerate the talk in the *bazars*," said a young civilian in the Secretariat. "Now I have observed——"

"I dare say you have," said the Deputy Commissioner, "but you've a great deal more to observe, my son. In the meantime, I wish to observe to you—" and he drew him aside to discuss the construction of the canal that was so dear to his heart. Holden went to his bungalow and began to understand that he was not alone in the world, and also that he was afraid for the sake of another,—which is the most soul-satisfying fear known to man.

Two months later, as the Deputy had foretold, Nature began to audit her accounts with a red pencil. On the heels of the spring-reapings came a cry for bread, and the Government, which had decreed that no man should die of want, sent wheat. Then came the cholera from all four quarters of the compass. It struck a pilgrim-gathering of half a million at a sacred shrine. Many died at the feet of their god; the others broke and ran over the face of the land carrying the pestilence with them. It smote a walled city and killed two hundred a day. The people crowded the trains, hanging on to the foot-boards and squatting on the roofs of the carriages, and the cholera followed them, for at each station they dragged out the dead and the dying. They died by the roadside, and the horses of the Englishmen shied at the corpses in the grass. The rains did not come, and the earth turned to iron lest man should escape death by hiding in her. The English sent their wives away to the hills and went about their work, coming forward as they were bidden to fill the gaps in the fighting-line. Holden, sick with fear of losing his chiefest treasure on earth, had done his best to persuade Ameera to go away with her mother to the Himalayas.

"Why should I go?" said she one evening on the roof.

"There is sickness, and people are dying, and all the white *mem-log* have gone."

"All of them?"

"All—unless perhaps there remain some old scald-head who vexes her husband's heart by running risk of death."

"Nay; who stays is my sister, and thou must not abuse her, for I will be a scald-head too. I am glad all the bold *mem-log* are gone."

"Do I speak to a woman or a babe? Go to the hills and I will see to it that thou goest like a queen's daughter. Think, child. In a red-lacquered bullock cart, veiled and curtained, with brass peacocks upon the pole and red cloth hangings. I will send two orderlies for guard and—"

"Peace! Thou art the babe in speaking thus. What use are those toys to me? *He* would have patted the bullocks and played with the housings. For his sake, perhaps,—thou hast made me very English—I might have gone. Now, I will not. Let the *mem-log* run."

"Their husbands are sending them, beloved."

"Very good talk. Since when hast thou been my husband to tell me what to do? I have but born thee a son. Thou art only all the desire of my soul to me. How shall I depart when I know that if evil befall thee by the breadth of so much as my littlest fingernail—is that not small?—I should be aware of it though I were in paradise. And here, this summer thou mayst die—*ai, janee*, die! and in dying they might call to tend thee a white woman, and she would rob me in the last of thy love!"

"But love is not born in a moment or on a death-bed!"

"What dost thou know of love, stone-heart? She would take thy thanks at least and, by God and the Prophet and Beebee Miriam the mother of thy Prophet, that I will never endure. My lord and my love, let there be no more foolish talk of going away. Where thou art, I am. It is enough." She put an arm round his neck and a hand on his mouth.

There are not many happinesses so complete as those that are snatched under the shadow of the sword. They sat together and laughed, calling each other openly by every pet name that could move the wrath of the gods. The city below them was locked up in its own torments. Sulphur fires blazed in the streets; the conches in the Hindu temples screamed and bellowed, for the gods were inattentive in those days. There was a service in the great Mahomedan shrine, and the call to prayer from the minarets was almost unceasing. They heard the wailing in the houses of the dead, and once the shriek of a mother who had lost a child and was calling for its return. In the grey dawn they saw the dead borne out through the city gates, each litter with its own little knot of mourners. Wherefore they kissed each other and shivered.

It was a red and heavy audit, for the land was very sick and needed a little breathing-space ere the torrent of cheap life should flood it anew. The children of immature fathers and undeveloped mothers made no resistance. They were cowed and sat still, waiting till the sword should be sheathed in November if it were so willed. There were gaps among the English, but the gaps were filled. The work of superintending famine-relief, cholera-sheds, medicine-distribution, and what little sanitation was possible, went forward because it was so ordered.

Holden had been told to keep himself in readiness to move to replace the next man who should fall. There were twelve hours in each day when he could not see Ameera, and she might die in three. He was considering what his pain would be if he could not see her for three months, or if she died out of his sight. He was absolutely certain that her death would be demanded—so certain that when he looked up from the telegram and saw Pir Khan breathless in the doorway, he laughed aloud, "And?" said he,——

"When there is a cry in the night and the spirit flutters into the throat, who has a charm that will restore? Come swiftly, Heaven-born! It is the black cholera."

Holden galloped to his home. The sky was heavy with clouds, for the long deferred rains were near and the heat was stifling. Ameera's mother met him in the courtyard, whimpering, "She is dying. She is nursing herself into death. She is all but dead. What shall I do, *sahib?*"

Ameera was lying in the room in which Tota had been born. She made no sign when Holden entered because the human soul is a very lonely thing and, when it is getting ready to go away, hides itself in a misty borderland where the living may not follow. The black cholera does its work quietly and without explanation. Ameera was being thrust out of life as though the Angel of Death had himself put his hand upon her. The quick breathing seemed to show that she was neither afraid nor in pain, but neither eyes nor mouth gave any answer to Holden's kisses. There was nothing to be said or done. Holden could only wait and suffer. The first drops of the rain began to fall on the roof and he could hear shouts of joy in the parched city.

The soul came back a little and the lips moved. Holden bent down to listen. "Keep nothing of mine," said Ameera. "Take no hair from my head. *She* would make thee burn it later on. That flame I should feel. Lower! Stoop lower! Remember only that I was thine and bore thee a son. Though thou wed a white woman to-morrow, the pleasure of receiving in thy arms thy first son is taken from thee for ever. Remember me when thy son is born—the one that shall carry thy name before all men. His misfortunes be on my head. I bear witness—I bear witness"—the lips were forming the words on his ear—"that there is no God but—thee, beloved!"

Then she died. Holden sat still, and all thought was taken from him,—till he heard Ameera's mother lift the curtain.

"Is she dead, *sahib?*"

"She is dead."

"Then I will mourn, and afterwards take an inventory of the furniture in this house. For that will be mine. The *sahib* does not mean to resume it? It is so little, so very little, *sahib*, and I am an old woman. I would like to lie softly."

"For the mercy of God be silent, a while. Go out and mourn where I cannot hear."

"*Sahib*, she will be buried in four hours."

"I know the custom. I shall go ere she is taken away. That matter is in thy hands. Look to it, that the bed on which—on which she lies—"

"Aha! That beautiful red-lacquered bed. I have long desired——"

"That the bed is left here untouched for my disposal. All else in the house is thine. Hire a cart, take everything, go hence, and before sunrise let there be nothing in this house but that which I have ordered thee to respect."

"I am an old woman. I would stay at least for the days of mourning, and the rains have just broken. Whither shall I go?"

"What is that to me? My order is that there is a going. The house-gear is worth a thousand rupees and my orderly shall bring thee a hundred rupees to-night."

"That is very little. Think of the cart-hire."

"It shall be nothing unless thou goest, and with speed. O woman, get hence and leave me to my dead!"

The mother shuffled down the staircase, and in her anxiety to take stock of the house-fittings forgot to mourn. Holden stayed by Ameera's side and the rain roared on the roof. He could not think connectedly by reason of the noise, though he made many attempts to do so. Then four sheeted ghosts glided dripping into the room and stared at him through their veils. They were the washers of the dead. Holden left the room and went out to his horse. He had come in a dead, stifling calm through ankle-deep dust. He found the court-yard a rain-lashed pond alive with frogs; a torrent of yellow water ran under the gate, and a roaring wind drove the bolts of the rain like buck-shot against the mud walls. Pir Khan was shivering in his little hut by the gate, and the horse was stamping uneasily in the water.

"I have been told the *sahib*'s order," said Pir Khan. "It is well. This house is now desolate. I go also, for my monkey-face would be a reminder of that which has been. Concerning the bed, I will bring that to thy house yonder in the morning; but remember, *sahib*, it will be to thee a knife turned in a green wound. I go upon a pilgrimage, and I will take no money. I have grown fat in the protection of the Presence whose sorrow is my sorrow. For the last time I hold his stirrup."

He touched Holden's foot with both hands and the horse sprang out into the road, where the creaking bamboos were whipping the sky and all the frogs were chuckling. Holden could not see for the rain in his face. He put his hands before his eyes and muttered,

"Oh you brute! You utter brute!"

The news of his trouble was already in his bungalow. He read the knowledge in his butler's eyes when Ahmed Khan brought in food, and for the first and last time in his life laid a hand upon his master's shoulder, saying: "Eat, *sahib*, eat. Meat is good against sorrow. I also have known. Moreover the shadows come and go, *sahib*; the shadows come and go. These be curried eggs."

Holden could neither eat nor sleep. The heavens sent down eight inches of rain in that night and washed the earth clean. The waters tore down walls, broke roads, and scoured open the shallow graves on the Mahomedan burying-ground. All next day it rained, and Holden sat still in his house considering his sorrow. On the morning of the third day he received a telegram which said only: "Rickells, Myndonie. Dying. Holden relieve. Immediate." Then he thought that before he departed he would look at the house wherein he had been master and lord. There was a break in the weather, and the rank earth steamed with vapour.

He found that the rains had torn down the mud pillars of the gateway, and the heavy wooden gate that had guarded his life hung lazily from one hinge. There was grass three inches high in the courtyard; Pir Khan's lodge was empty, and the sodden thatch sagged between the beams. A gray squirrel was in possession of the verandah, as if the house had been untenanted for thirty years instead of three days. Ameera's mother had removed everything except some mildewed matting. The *tick-tick* of the little scorpions as they hurried across the floor was the only sound in the house. Ameera's room and the other one where Tota had lived were heavy with mildew; and the narrow staircase leading to the roof was streaked and stained with rain-borne mud. Holden saw all these things, and came out again to meet in the road Durga Dass, his landlord,—portly, affable, clothed in white muslin, and driving a C-spring buggy. He was overlooking his property to see how the roofs stood the stress of the first rains.

"I have heard," said he, "you will not take this place any more, *sahib?*"

"What are you going to do with it?"

"Perhaps I shall let it again."

"Then I will keep it on while I am away."

Durga Dass was silent for some time. "You shall not take it on, *sahib*," he said. "When I was a young man I also——, but to-day I am a member of the Municipality. Ho! Ho! No. When the birds have gone what need to keep the nest? I will have it pulled down—the timber will sell for something always. It shall be pulled down, and the Municipality shall make a road across, as they desire, from the burning-*ghaut*[5] to the city wall, so that no man may say where this house stood."

1890

from JUST SO STORIES[1]

How the Leopard Got His Spots

In the days when everybody started fair, Best Beloved, the Leopard lived in a place called the High Veldt.[2] 'Member it wasn't the Low Veldt, or the Bush Veldt, or the

---

5. Place where bodies are cremated.
1. *Just So Stories for Little Children* (1902) contains 12 stories and 12 poems, most of which were first published in various magazines between 1897 and 1902. They show the influence of the time Kipling spent in South Africa. G. K. Chesterton said of them "The peculiar splendour . . .

of these new Kipling stories is the fact that they do not read like fairy tales told to children by the modern fireside, so much as like fairy tales told to men in the morning of the world.
2. Open grassy plain.

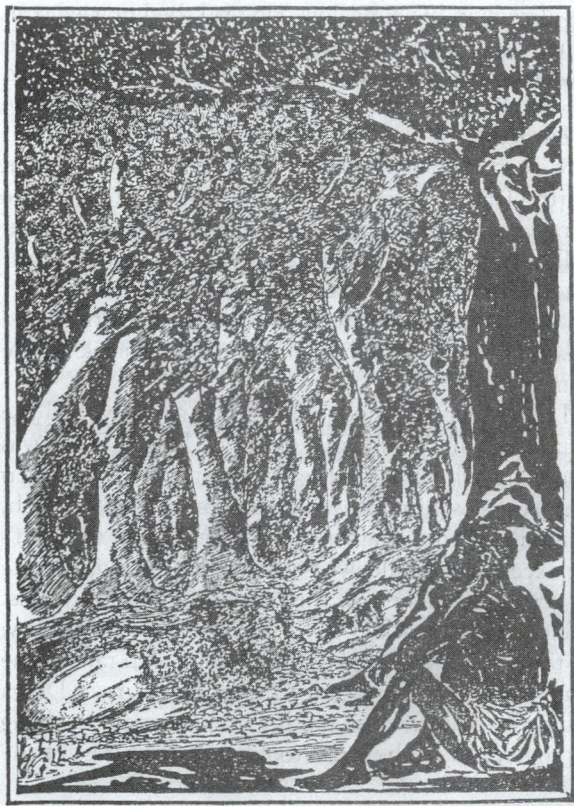

Kipling himself illustrated the *Just So Stories,* showing here how the man and the leopard (in the lower foreground) learned to blend in with their surroundings to hunt their prey, the giraffe (above the man near the crook of the tree) and the zebra (in the woods above the leopard). While today it is unusual for authors to be also skilled artists, learning to draw was part of the Victorian gentleman or lady's education. William Makepeace Thackeray illustrated his novels, John Ruskin's watercolors rivaled those of the artists he critiqued, Lewis Carroll did the first depictions of Alice's adventures, the poet Gerard Manley Hopkins sketched plants and self-portraits in his journals, and Beatrix Potter's pictures of Peter Rabbit and his fellow animals are still world famous.

Sour Veldt, but the 'sclusively bare, hot, shiny High Veldt, where there was sand and sandy-coloured rock and 'sclusively tufts of sandy-yellowish grass. The Giraffe and the Zebra and the Eland and the Koodoo and the Hartebeest[3] lived there; and they were 'sclusively sandy-yellow-brownish all over; but the Leopard, he was the 'sclusivest sandiest-yellowish-brownest of them all—a greyish-yellowish catty-shaped kind of beast, and he matched the 'sclusively yellowish-greyish-brownish colour of the High Veldt to one hair. This was very bad for the Giraffe and the Zebra and the rest of them; for he would lie down by a 'sclusively yellowish-greyish-brownish stone or clump of grass, and when the Giraffe or the Zebra or the Eland or the Koodoo or the Bush-Buck or the Bonte-Buck came by he would surprise them out of their

3. Varieties of African antelope, as are Bush-Buck and Bonte-Buck, mentioned below.

jumpsome lives. He would indeed! And, also, there was an Ethiopian with bows and arrows (a 'sclusively greyish-brownish-yellowish man he was then), who lived on the High Veldt with the Leopard; and the two used to hunt together—the Ethiopian with his bows and arrows, and the Leopard 'sclusively with his teeth and claws—till the Giraffe and the Eland and the Koodoo and the Quagga[4] and all the rest of them didn't know which way to jump, Best Beloved. They didn't indeed!

After a long time—things lived for ever so long in those days—they learned to avoid anything that looked like a Leopard or an Ethiopian; and bit by bit—the Giraffe began it, because his legs were the longest—they went away from the High Veldt. They scuttled for days and days and days till they came to a great forest, 'sclusively full of trees and bushes and stripy, speckly, patchy-blatchy shadows, and there they hid: and after another long time, what with standing half in the shade and half out of it, and what with the slippery-slidy shadows of the trees falling on them, the Giraffe grew blotchy, and the Zebra grew stripy, and the Eland and the Koodoo grew darker, with little wavy grey lines on their backs like bark on a tree trunk; and so, though you could hear them and smell them, you could very seldom see them, and then only when you knew precisely where to look. They had a beautiful time in the 'sclusively speckly-spickly shadows of the forest, while the Leopard and the Ethiopian ran about over the 'sclusively greyish-yellowish-reddish High Veldt outside, wondering where all their breakfasts and their dinners and their teas had gone. At last they were so hungry that they ate rats and beetles and rock-rabbits, the Leopard and the Ethiopian, and then they had the Big Tummy-ache, both together; and then they met Baviaan—the dog-headed, barking Baboon, who is Quite the Wisest Animal in All South Africa.

Said Leopard to Baviaan (and it was a very hot day), "Where has all the game gone?"

And Baviaan winked. *He* knew.

Said the Ethiopian to Baviaan, "Can you tell me the present habitat of the aboriginal Fauna?" (That meant just the same thing, but the Ethiopian always used long words. He was a grown-up.)

And Baviaan winked. *He* knew.

Then said Baviaan, "The game has gone into other spots; and my advice to you, Leopard, is to go into other spots as soon as you can."

And the Ethiopian said, "That is all very fine, but I wish to know whither the aboriginal Fauna has migrated."

Then said Baviaan, "The aboriginal Fauna has joined the aboriginal Flora because it was high time for a change; and my advice to you, Ethiopian, is to change as soon as you can."

That puzzled the Leopard and the Ethiopian, but they set off to look for the aboriginal Flora, and presently, after ever so many days, they saw a great, high, tall forest full of tree trunks all 'sclusively speckled and sprottled and spottled, dotted and splashed and slashed and hatched and cross-hatched with shadows. (Say that quickly aloud, and you will see how *very* shadowy the forest must have been.)

"What is this," said the Leopard, "that is so 'sclusively dark, and yet so full of little pieces of light?"

"I don't know," said the Ethiopian, "but it ought to be the aboriginal Flora. I can smell Giraffe, and I can hear Giraffe, but I can't see Giraffe."

4. Zebra-like animal, extinct since the 19th century.

"That's curious," said the Leopard. "I suppose it is because we have just come in out of the sunshine. I can smell Zebra, and I can hear Zebra, but I can't see Zebra."

"Wait a bit," said the Ethiopian. "It's a long time since we've hunted 'em. Perhaps we've forgotten what they were like."

"Fiddle!" said the Leopard. "I remember them perfectly on the High Veldt, especially their marrow-bones. Giraffe is about seventeen feet high, of a 'sclusively fulvous golden-yellow from head to heel; and Zebra is about four and a half feet high, of a 'sclusively grey-fawn colour from head to heel."

"Umm," said the Ethiopian, looking into the speckly-spickly shadows of the aboriginal Flora-forest. "Then they ought to show up in this dark place like ripe bananas in a smokehouse."

But they didn't. The Leopard and the Ethiopian hunted all day; and though they could smell them and hear them, they never saw one of them.

"For goodness' sake," said the Leopard at tea-time, "let us wait till it gets dark. This daylight hunting is a perfect scandal."

So they waited till dark, and then the Leopard heard something breathing sniffily in the starlight that fell all stripy through the branches, and he jumped at the noise, and it smelt like Zebra, and it felt like Zebra, and when he knocked it down it kicked like Zebra, but he couldn't see it. So he said, "Be quiet, O you person without any form. I am going to sit on your head till morning, because there is something about you that I don't understand."

Presently he heard a grunt and a crash and a scramble, and the Ethiopian called out, "I've caught a thing that I can't see. It smells like Giraffe, and it kicks like Giraffe, but it hasn't any form."

"Don't you trust it," said the Leopard. "Sit on its head till the morning—same as me. They haven't any form—any of 'em."

So they sat down on them hard till bright morning-time, and then Leopard said, "What have you at your end of the table, Brother?"

The Ethiopian scratched his head and said, "It ought to be 'sclusively a rich fulvous orange-tawny from head to heel, and it ought to be Giraffe; but it is covered all over with chestnut blotches. What have you at *your* end of the table, Brother?"

And the Leopard scratched his head and said, "It ought to be 'sclusively a delicate greyish-fawn, and it ought to be Zebra; but it is covered all over with black and purple stripes. What in the world have you been doing to yourself, Zebra? Don't you know that if you were on the High Veldt I could see you ten miles off? You haven't any form."

"Yes," said the Zebra, "but this isn't the High Veldt. Can't you see?"

"I can now," said the Leopard. "But I couldn't all yesterday. How is it done?"

"Let us up," said the Zebra, "and we will show you."

They let the Zebra and the Giraffe get up; and Zebra moved away to some little thornbushes where the sunlight fell all stripy, and Giraffe moved off to some tallish trees where the shadows fell all blotchy.

"Now watch," said the Zebra and the Giraffe. "This is the way it's done. One—two—three! And where's your breakfast?"

Leopard stared, and Ethiopian stared, but all they could see were stripy shadows and blotched shadows in the forest, but never a sign of Zebra and Giraffe. They had just walked off and hidden themselves in the shadowy forest.

"Hi! Hi!" said the Ethiopian. "That's a trick worth learning. Take a lesson by it, Leopard. You show up in this dark place like a bar of soap in a coal-scuttle."

"Ho! Ho!" said the Leopard. "Would it surprise you very much to know that you show up in this dark place like a mustard-plaster on a sack of coals?"

"Well, calling names won't catch dinner," said the Ethiopian. "The long and the little of it is that we don't match our backgrounds. I'm going to take Baviaan's advice. He told me I ought to change; and as I've nothing to change except my skin I'm going to change that."

"What to?" said the Leopard, tremendously excited.

"To a nice working blackish-brownish colour, with a little purple in it, and touches of slaty-blue. It will be the very thing for hiding in hollows and behind trees."

So he changed his skin then and there, and the Leopard was more excited than ever; he had never seen a man change his skin before.

"But what about me?" he said, when the Ethiopian had worked his last little finger into his fine new black skin.

"You take Baviaan's advice too. He told you to go into spots."

"So I did," said the Leopard. "I went into other spots as fast as I could. I went into this spot with you, and a lot of good it has done me."

"Oh," said the Ethiopian, "Baviaan didn't mean spots in South Africa. He meant spots on your skin."

"What's the use of that?" said the Leopard.

"Think of Giraffe," said the Ethiopian. "Or if you prefer stripes, think of Zebra. They find their spots and stripes give them per-fect satisfaction."

"Umm," said the Leopard. "I wouldn't look like Zebra—not for ever so."

"Well, make up your mind," said the Ethiopian, "because I'd hate to go hunting without you, but I must if you insist on looking like a sun-flower against a tarred fence."

"I'll take spots, then," said the Leopard; "but don't make 'em too vulgar-big. I wouldn't look like Giraffe—not for ever so."

"I'll make 'em with the tips of my fingers," said the Ethiopian. "There's plenty of black left on my skin still. Stand over!"

Then the Ethiopian put his five fingers close together (there was plenty of black left on his new skin still) and pressed them all over the Leopard, and wherever the five fingers touched they left five little black marks, all close together. You can see them on any Leopard's skin you like, Best Beloved. Sometimes the fingers slipped and the marks got a little blurred; but if you look closely at any Leopard now you will see that there are always five spots—off five fat black finger-tips.

"Now you *are* a beauty!" said the Ethiopian. "You can lie out on the bare ground and look like a heap of pebbles. You can lie out on the naked rocks and look like a piece of pudding-stone. You can lie out on a leafy branch and look like sunshine sifting through the leaves; and you can lie right across the centre of a path and look like nothing in particular. Think of that and purr!"

"But if I'm all this," said the Leopard, "why didn't you go spotty too?"

"Oh, plain black's best for a nigger," said the Ethiopian. "Now come along and we'll see if we can't get even with Mr. One-Two-Three-Where's-your-Breakfast!"

So they went away and lived happily ever afterward, Best Beloved. That is all.

Oh, now and then you will hear grown-ups say, "Can the Ethiopian change his skin or the Leopard his spots?" I don't think even grown-ups would keep on saying such a silly thing if the Leopard and the Ethiopian hadn't done it once—do you? But they will never do it again, Best Beloved. They are quite contented as they are.

I AM the Most Wise Baviaan, saying in most wise tones,
"Let us melt into the landscape—just us two by our lones."
People have come—in a carriage—calling. But Mummy is there. . . .
Yes, I can go if you take me—Nurse says she don't care.
Let's go up to the pig-sties and sit on the farmyard rails!
Let's say things to the bunnies, and watch 'em skitter their tails!
Let's—oh, anything, daddy, so long as it's you and me,
And going truly exploring, and not being in till tea!
Here's your boots (I've brought 'em), and here's your cap and stick,
And here's your pipe and tobacco. Oh, come along out of it—quick.

1902

Gunga Din

You may talk o' gin and beer
When you're quartered safe out 'ere,
An' you're sent to penny-fights an' Aldershot[1] it;
But when it comes to slaughter
5   You will do your work on water,
An' you'll lick the bloomin' boots of 'im that's got it.
Now in Injia's sunny clime,
Where I used to spend my time
A-servin' of 'Er Majesty the Queen,
10   Of all them blackfaced crew
The finest man I knew
Was our regimental bhisti,° Gunga Din.   water carrier
          He was "Din! Din! Din!
      "You limpin' lump o' brick-dust, Gunga Din!
15   "Hi! Slippy hitherao!°   come here
          "Water, get it! Panee lao,°   bring water quickly
      "You squidgy-nosed old idol, Gunga Din."

The uniform 'e wore
Was nothin' much before,
20   An' rather less than 'arf o' that be'ind,
For a piece o' twisty rag
An' a goatskin water-bag
Was all the field-equipment 'e could find.
When the sweatin' troop-train lay
25   In a sidin' through the day,
Where the 'eat would make your bloomin' eyebrows crawl,
We shouted "Harry By!"[2]
Till our throats were bricky-dry,
Then we wopped 'im 'cause 'e couldn't serve us all.
30   It was "Din! Din! Din!
      "You 'eathen, where the mischief 'ave you been?

---

1. The speaker is back from India, addressing recruits who will be training at Aldershot, a military camp in Hampshire.
2. *Hari bhai*, Hindustani for "Hey, brother!"

> "You put some *juldee*° in it   speed
> "Or I'll *marrow*° you this minute   hit
> "If you don't fill up my helmet, Gunga Din!"

35   'E would dot an' carry one
Till the longest day was done;
An' 'e didn't seem to know the use o' fear.
If we charged or broke or cut,
You could bet your bloomin' nut,
40   'E'd be waitin' fifty paces right flank rear.
With 'is mussick° on 'is back,   water-bag
'E would skip with our attack,
An' watch us till the bugles made "Retire,"
An' for all 'is dirty 'ide
45   'E was white, clear white, inside
When 'e went to tend the wounded under fire!
    It was "Din! Din! Din!"
  With the bullets kickin' dust-spots on the green.
    When the cartridges ran out,
50   You could hear the front-ranks shout,
  "Hi! ammunition-mules an' Gunga Din!"

I shan't forgit the night
When I dropped be'ind the fight
With a bullet where my belt-plate should 'a' been.
55   I was chokin' mad with thirst,
An' the man that spied me first
Was our good old grinnin', gruntin' Gunga Din.
'E lifted up my 'ead,
An' he plugged me where I bled,
60   An' 'e guv me 'arf-a-pint o' water green.
It was crawlin' and it stunk,
But of all the drinks I've drunk,
I'm gratefullest to one from Gunga Din.
    It was "Din! Din! Din!
65   "'Ere's a beggar with a bullet through 'is spleen;
    "'E's chawin' up the ground,
    "An' 'e's kickin' all around:
  "For Gawd's sake git the water, Gunga Din!"

'E carried me away
70   To where a dooli° lay,   stretcher
An' a bullet come an' drilled the beggar clean.
'E put me safe inside,
An' just before 'e died,
"I 'ope you liked your drink," sez Gunga Din.
75   So I'll meet 'im later on
At the place where 'e is gone—
Where it's always double drill and no canteen.
'E'll be squattin' on the coals

Givin' drink to poor damned souls,
80   An' I'll get a swig in hell from Gunga Din!
                Yes, Din! Din! Din!
        You Lazarushian-leather[3] Gunga Din!
                Though I've belted you and flayed you,
                By the livin' Gawd that made you,
85   You're a better man than I am, Gunga Din!

1890

The Widow at Windsor[1]

        'Ave you 'eard o' the Widow at Windsor
                With a hairy gold crown on 'er 'ead?
        She 'as ships on the foam—she 'as millions at 'ome,
                An' she pays us poor beggars in red.[2]
5   (Ow, poor beggars in red!)
        There's 'er nick on the cavalry 'orses,[3]
                There's 'er mark on the medical stores—
        An' 'er troopers[4] you'll find with a fair wind be'ind
                That takes us to various wars.
10   (Poor beggars!—barbarious wars!)
                Then 'ere's to the Widow at Windsor,
                        An' 'ere's to the stores an' the guns,
                The men an' the 'orses what makes up the forces
                        O' Missis Victorier's sons.
15   (Poor beggars! Victorier's sons!)

        Walk wide o' the Widow at Windsor,
                For 'alf o' Creation she owns:
        We 'ave bought 'er the same with the sword an' the flame,
                An' we've salted it down with our bones.
20   (Poor beggars!—it's blue with our bones!)
        Hands off o' the sons o' the Widow,
                Hands off o' the goods in 'er shop,
        For the Kings must come down an' the Emperors frown
                When the Widow at Windsor says "Stop!"
25   (Poor beggars!—we're sent to say "Stop!")
                Then 'ere's to the Lodge o' the Widow,
                        From the Pole to the Tropics it runs[5]—
                To the Lodge that we tile with the rank an' the file,
                        An' open in form with the guns.
30   (Poor beggars!—it's always they guns!)

---

3. Kipling has coined a phrase, a cross between Russian leather (like Gunga Din's skin) and Lazarus, the beggar in Luke 16 who goes to heaven while the rich man who spurned him burns in hell begging for a drink of water.
1. Queen Victoria, who entered into lifelong mourning after the death of her husband, Prince Albert, in 1861.
2. British soldiers wore red coats.

3. Army horses had a nick on their hooves identifying them as property of the queen.
4. Troopships.
5. The Lodge is being used as a synonym for the British Empire, with a probable allusion to Freemasonry, a secret society whose members group themselves into "lodges" or local chapters. Kipling was a Freemason.

We 'ave 'eard o' the Widow at Windsor,
   It's safest to leave 'er alone:
For 'er sentries we stand by the sea an' the land
   Wherever the bugles are blown.
35   (Poor beggars!—an' don't we get blown!)
Take 'old o' the Wings o' the Mornin',[6]
   An' flop round the earth till you're dead;
But you won't get away from the tune that they play[7]
   To the bloomin' old rag over'ead.
40   (Poor beggars!—it's 'ot over'ead!)
      Then 'ere's to the Sons o' the Widow,
       Wherever, 'owever they roam.
   'Ere's all they desire, an' if they require
    A speedy return to their 'ome.
45   (Poor beggars!—they'll never see 'ome!)

                                      1890

Recessional[1]
1897

God of our fathers, known of old,
   Lord of our far-flung battle-line,
Beneath whose awful Hand we hold
   Dominion over palm and pine—
5   Lord God of Hosts, be with us yet,
   Lest we forget—lest we forget![2]

The tumult and the shouting dies;
   The Captains and the Kings depart:
Still stands Thine ancient sacrifice,
10   An humble and a contrite heart.[3]
Lord God of Hosts, be with us yet,
   Lest we forget—lest we forget!

Far-called, our navies melt away;
   On dune and headland sinks the fire:[4]
15 Lo, all our pomp of yesterday
   Is one with Nineveh and Tyre![5]
Judge of the Nations, spare us yet,
   Lest we forget—lest we forget!

If, drunk with sight of power, we loose
20   Wild tongues that have not Thee in awe,
Such boastings as the Gentiles use,

---

6. "If I take the wings of the morning / A dwell in the uttermost parts of the sea" (Psalm 139.9).
7. *God Save the Queen*, the British national anthem.
1. Hymn sung at the end of a church service. Kipling wrote this cautionary hymn for Queen Victoria's Diamond Jubilee.

2. "Then beware lest thou forget the Lord, which brought thee forth out of the land of Egypt" (Deuteronomy 6.21).
3. Paraphrasing Psalm 51.17.
4. Celebratory bonfires were lit all over Britain in honor of the Jubilee.
5. The ruined capitals of once-great empires.

Or lesser breeds without the Law[6]—
Lord God of Hosts, be with us yet,
Lest we forget—lest we forget!

25 For heathen heart that puts her trust
In reeking tube and iron shard,
All valiant dust that builds on dust,
And guarding, calls not Thee to guard,
For frantic boast and foolish word—
30 Thy mercy on Thy People, Lord!

If—[1]

If you can keep your head when all about you
Are losing theirs and blaming it on you,
If you can trust yourself when all men doubt you,
But make allowance for their doubting too;
5 If you can wait and not be tired by waiting,
Or being lied about, don't deal in lies,
Or being hated, don't give way to hating,
And yet don't look too good, nor talk too wise:

If you can dream—and not make dreams your master;
10 If you can think—and not make thoughts your aim;
If you can meet with Triumph and Disaster
And treat those two impostors just the same;
If you can bear to hear the truth you've spoken
Twisted by knaves to make a trap for fools,
15 Or watch the things you gave your life to, broken,
And stoop and build 'em up with worn-out tools:

If you can make one heap of all your winnings
And risk it on one turn of pitch-and-toss,[2]
And lose, and start again at your beginnings
20 And never breathe a word about your loss;
If you can force your heart and nerve and sinew
To serve your turn long after they are gone,
And so hold on when there is nothing in you
Except the Will which says to them: "Hold on!"

25 If you can talk with crowds and keep your virtue,
Or walk with Kings—nor lose the common touch,
If neither foes nor loving friends can hurt you,
If all men count with you, but none too much;
If you can fill the unforgiving minute

---

6. "For when the Gentiles, which have not the law, do by nature the things contained in the law, these having not the law, are a law unto themselves" (Romans 2.14). Kipling associates the English with the Chosen People, and the rest of the world with the Gentiles.
1. First published in the *American Magazine* in October

1910, *If* soon became one of the best-known poems of the day. It was reprinted widely; Kipling included it in his children's book *Rewards and Fairies* (1910). Its theme and meter recall Browning's *Epilogue* to *Asolando*.
2. Game in which players pitch coins.

30   With sixty seconds' worth of distance run,
             Yours is the Earth and everything that's in it,
               And—which is more—you'll be a Man, my son!

1910

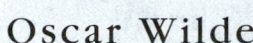

Oscar Wilde
1854–1900

"He hasn't a single redeeming vice." Oscar Wilde's witticism hardly applied to himself: his character was a quixotic mixture of brilliance and folly. Flamboyant, extravagant, outrageous, the most splendid playwright of the century lived his own life on center stage. Though his flagrant self-promotion irritated many, he was generous and good-natured, unable to imagine that the Victorian morality he satirized would finally bring about his own fall.

Wilde was born in Dublin, and although he spent much of his adult life in England, he never lost the sense of himself as a foreigner. His parents—Irish Protestants, ardent nationalists, and prolific writers—were notable figures in their own right: Sir William Robert Wilde was a famous surgeon, fathered three illegitimate children, and was sued by a former patient who claimed he had drugged and raped her. Lady Wilde, who changed her name from Jane Frances to Speranza Francesca, was a self-dramatizing and unconventional woman whom her son adored.

Wilde was educated in Ireland until 1874 when he won a scholarship to Oxford. Here he began to establish a reputation as an Aesthete and an admirer of Pre-Raphaelite poets such as Swinburne, Rossetti, and William Morris. He was also attracted to the contradictory artistic creeds of both John Ruskin and Walter Pater, Ruskin proclaiming that all good art is moral art, Pater preferring "poetic passion, the desire of beauty, the love of art for art's sake." Wilde dressed ostentatiously, wore his hair long, and decorated his rooms with lilies, a favorite symbol of the Aesthetes. His literary abilities won him both the Newdigate Prize for poetry and a double first (highest honors). But along with these academic awards he was celebrated for a remark which seemed to epitomize aestheticism: "I find it harder and harder every day to live up to my blue china."

Following his triumphs at Oxford, Wilde cast about for a career. His father had died leaving only a small inheritance, and Wilde's attempts to win a university fellowship failed. In London he set about making himself conspicuous, and soon he was the center of the social scene. Few could help being dazzled by his witty conversation. Yet some were skeptical, including an actress who said: "What has he done, this young man, that one meets him everywhere? Oh yes he talks well, but what has he done? He has written nothing, he does not sing or paint or act—he does nothing but talk."

Wilde's talk, however, was glorious and eventually would find lasting expression in his plays. Meanwhile, he played the dandy, and was satirized by Gilbert and Sullivan in *Patience* (1881) as the most illustrious Aesthete of the day, who had walked "down Piccadilly with a poppy or a lily in his medieval hand." Wilde reacted with good humor, observing that "To have done it was nothing, but to make people think one had done it was a triumph."

In the early 1880s Wilde began to refute the charge that he did nothing but talk. He wrote his first play, called *Vera; or, The Nihilists* (1880), about Russian czars and revolutionaries; the play's portrayal of an assassination attempt made it politically unacceptable, and the

Oscar Wilde and Lord Alfred
Douglas, 1893.

production was canceled. He privately published a book of poems in 1881, opening with the
sonnet *Hélas!* They were praised by Matthew Arnold and by Swinburne, but elsewhere denounced as immoral.

Wilde's finances received an unexpected boost when the New York production of
Patience led to an invitation to lecture in the United States. His arrival in New York in 1882
was a media event: he was mobbed by reporters, and his every utterance was quoted or mis-
quoted in both the American and British press. He was reported to have been disappointed in
the Atlantic—"It is not so majestic as I expected"—and to have told the customs officers, "I
have nothing to declare except my genius." He stayed a full year, earned quite a lot of money,
and returned home internationally famous.

Wilde followed up his conquest of America with a few months in Paris, where he met
many leading painters and writers. Back in London, and short of money once again, his
thoughts turned to marriage, and in 1884 he wed Constance Lloyd. She was well educated and
well-off, and at first Wilde enjoyed the new roles of husband and then father to two sons, Cyril
and Vyvyan. But he soon found married life a bore. Even during his honeymoon in Paris his
thoughts were elsewhere: he became enamored of a book known as the Bible of decadence,
A Rebours (1884) by Joris-Karl Huysmans. As his biographer Richard Ellmann has put it, this
book "summoned him towards an underground life."

Wilde was a celebrity. He spent several years lecturing and reviewing, then entered
the most inventive period of his life. Although he would later remark, "I have put only my
talent into my works. I have put my genius into my life," the creative work of the early
1890s belies him. He articulated his theories on Art and Nature in two dialogues full of

provocative paradoxes, *The Decay of Lying* (1888) and *The Critic as Artist* (1890). Then in his essay *The Soul of Man Under Socialism* (1891) he argued that the final goal of social evolution was joyous individualism. He continued his exploration of the relation of art to life in his only novel, *The Picture of Dorian Gray* (1890), which tells of a promising golden boy fascinated by the seductively amoral ideas of a jaded cynic. Dorian makes a Faustian bargain: his corrupted soul will be mirrored, not in his own face—he remains eternally youthful—but in his portrait. Much influenced by *A Rebours*, *Dorian Gray* achieved instantaneous notoriety, not so much for its aestheticism as for its thinly veiled suggestions of homosexuality.

Lady Windermere's Fan (1891) met with the opposite reception: this sparkling comedy depicting a mother's secret sacrifice for her daughter was an immediate success. Inspired in part by the French symbolist poet, Stéphane Mallarmé, Wilde was also writing—in French—a very different play, *Salomé*, about the fatal perversity of love and desire. To Wilde's indignation, *Salomé* was banned in England. However, in 1894 he published an English translation, with dramatic and daring illustrations by Aubrey Beardsley.

Wilde wrote two more comedies, *A Woman of No Importance* and *An Ideal Husband*, followed by his masterpiece, *The Importance of Being Earnest* (1895). Its philosophy, Wilde said, is "That we should treat all trivial things very seriously, and all the serious things of life with sincere and studied triviality." The triumphant opening night of this delightfully sophisticated farce marked the culmination of Wilde's career.

Then, at the very crest of success, Wilde was brought down by catastrophe. Although homosexuality was a criminal offense in Britain, Wilde had made little effort to conceal his relations with younger men, particularly Lord Alfred Douglas. But if society turned a blind eye, Douglas's father, the Marquess of Queensberry, did not. He hounded his son's lover relentlessly, finally sending Wilde a ludicrously misspelled note calling him a "Somdomite." Egged on by Douglas, Wilde sued for libel. It was a fatal mistake. His private affairs were mercilessly exposed in court, and he lost the case. Wilde himself was then prosecuted for committing indecent acts, convicted, and sentenced to two years at hard labor.

His obsession with the young aristocrat—beautiful, vicious, and volatile—had been ruinous in every sense. Wilde was disgraced and bankrupted. So great was the collective repugnance for him that both of his currently running plays, *An Ideal Husband* and *The Importance of Being Earnest*, were obliged to close. But the nightmare was only beginning: following the public humiliation of the trials was the horror of prison. Confined in a small cell with a bare plank bed, revolting food, and no latrine, he suffered constantly from diarrhea. He was allowed only one twenty-minute visit every three months. No talking was permitted. Dreading that he might lose his sanity, Wilde pleaded in vain for early release.

He gave vent to his sufferings in a long letter to Douglas entitled *De Profundis*. It is a terrible indictment of Douglas's selfish behavior, but more than that it is an autobiography, the anguished confession of a soul coming face to face with itself. Painfully he reviews the events that led to his downfall, finding at last his own salvation in forgiveness: "I don't write this letter to put bitterness into your heart, but to pluck it out of mine. For my own sake I must forgive you." Wilde was allowed to take the letter with him when he left prison, but chose not to have it published until after his death.

Wilde emerged from the degradation of prison a broken and penniless man. He spent the remainder of his life in exile outside Britain. He was never again allowed to see his young sons, and their surname was changed to protect them from scandal. All but a few loyal friends shunned him. The man who had lavished champagne on his friends was reduced to scrounging drinks from strangers who pitied him. He was unable to resume his writing, except for *The Ballad of Reading Gaol* (1898), a long poem based upon his prison experience. He converted to Catholicism on his deathbed, in a Paris hotel, but continued bravely inventing witticisms to the end: "I am dying beyond my means."

Impression du Matin[1]

The Thames nocturne of blue and gold
   Changed to a harmony in gray:[2]
   A barge with ochre-coloured hay
Dropt° from the wharf: and chill and cold   *went downstream*

5   The yellow fog came creeping down
   The bridges, till the houses' walls
   Seemed changed to shadows and St. Paul's
Loomed like a bubble o'er the town.

Then suddenly arose the clang
10   Of waking life; the streets were stirred
   With country wagons: and a bird
Flew to the glistening roofs and sang.

But one pale woman all alone,
   The daylight kissing her wan hair,
15   Loitered beneath the gas lamps' flare,
With lips of flame and heart of stone.

1877   1881

RESPONSE
Lord Alfred Douglas: Impression de Nuit[1]
London

See what a mass of gems the city wears
Upon her broad live bosom! row on row
Rubies and emeralds and amethysts glow.
See! that huge circle like a necklace, stares
5   With thousands of bold eyes to heaven, and dares
The golden stars to dim the lamps below,
And in the mirror of the mire I know
The moon has left her image unawares.

That's the great town at night: I see her breasts,
10   Pricked out with lamps they stand like huge black towers.
I think they move! I hear her panting breath.
And that's her head where the tiara rests.

1. Impression of the morning (French). The title evokes the paintings of the French Impressionists and their attempts to show how light transforms the landscape. The group received its name in 1874 when a critic singled out Monet's *Impression: Sunrise* as representative.
2. The American James McNeill Whistler painted a series of Thames night scenes, called "nocturnes" (see Color Plate 18). He entitled some of his daytime scenes "harmonies." His close friendship with Wilde turned into a bitter rivalry by the mid-1880s; Whistler accused Wilde of plagiarizing his ideas.
1. Lord Alfred Douglas received not only Wilde's amorous attentions but also his literary encouragement.

The sonnet *Impression de Nuit* ("impression of the night") complements Wilde's *Impression du Matin* (itself a reaction to Whistler's painting *Nocturne in Blue and Gold*) by enlarging and transforming Wilde's conventional final image of a prostitute beneath a streetlamp. In Douglas's poem, the city becomes a gigantic, panting woman, the streetlights her jewelry. Wilde builds his poem on a seemingly objective series of visual images that balances the natural and the artificial; Douglas elaborates a personal vision of urban life that invokes both the decadent fascination with the *femme fatale* and a gay man's quest for nocturnal sexual adventure.

And in her brain, through lanes as dark as death,
Men creep like thoughts . . . The lamps are like pale flowers.

1894

The Harlot's House

We caught the tread of dancing feet,
We loitered down the moonlit street,
And stopped beneath the harlot's house.

Inside, above the din and fray,
5   We heard the loud musicians play
The "Treues Liebes Herz" of Strauss.[1]

Like strange mechanical grotesques,
Making fantastic arabesques,[2]
The shadows raced across the blind.

10   We watched the ghostly dancers spin
To sound of horn and violin,
Like black leaves wheeling in the wind.

Like wire-pulled automatons,
Slim silhouetted skeletons
15   Went sidling through the slow quadrille.[3]

They took each other by the hand,
And danced a stately saraband;
Their laughter echoed thin and shrill.

Sometimes a clockwork puppet pressed
20   A phantom lover to her breast,
Sometimes they seemed to try to sing.

Sometimes a horrible marionette
Came out, and smoked its cigarette
Upon the steps like a live thing.

25   Then, turning to my love, I said,
"The dead are dancing with the dead,
The dust is whirling with the dust."

But she—she heard the violin,
And left my side, and entered in:
30   Love passed into the house of Lust.

Then suddenly the tune went false,
The dancers wearied of the waltz,
The shadows ceased to wheel and whirl.

---

1. "The Heart of True Love," a waltz by Viennese composer Johann Strauss (1825–1899).
2. "Arabesque" is a term both for a ballet posture and, in art, for patterns of interlaced lines.
3. Square dance for four couples. The saraband (line 17) is an old Spanish dance.

35 And down the long and silent street,
The dawn, with silver-sandalled feet,
Crept like a frightened girl.

1885, 1908

Symphony in Yellow[1]

An omnibus across the bridge
    Crawls like a yellow butterfly,
    And, here and there, a passer-by
Shows like a little restless midge.

5 Big barges full of yellow hay
    Are moored against the shadowy wharf,
    And, like a yellow silken scarf,
The thick fog hangs along the quay.

The yellow leaves begin to fade
10   And flutter from the Temple elms,[2]
    And at my feet the pale green Thames
Lies like a rod of rippled jade.

1889

Preface to *The Picture of Dorian Gray*[1]

The artist is the creator of beautiful things.
    To reveal art and conceal the artist is art's aim.
The critic is he who can translate into another manner or a new material
his impression of beautiful things.
    The highest as the lowest form of criticism is a mode of autobiography.
Those who find ugly meanings in beautiful things are corrupt without being
charming. This is a fault.
        Those who find beautiful meanings in beautiful things are the
        cultivated. For these there is hope.
They are the elect to whom beautiful things mean only Beauty.
    There is no such thing as a moral or an immoral book.
    Books are well written, or badly written. That is all.
The nineteenth century dislike of Realism is the rage of Caliban[2] seeing his
own face in a glass.

1. The title suggests Whistler's series of paintings that he called "symphonies" in various colors. The Aesthetic vogue for titles that mingle the arts originated with the French poet Théophile Gautier, who in 1852 named a poem *Symphony in White Major*. In the 1880s yellow—the color of sunflowers and paperback French novels—became associated with the Aesthetic movement.
2. The Middle Temple and Inner Temple form part of the Inns of Court; their garden runs down to the River Thames.
1. When Wilde's novel *Dorian Gray* first appeared in *Lippincott's Monthly Magazine* in July 1890, it scandalized readers with its portrayal of a cruelly hedonistic young man who remains unblemished by his crimes while his

portrait ages hideously. Responding to his critics' charges that the novel fostered immoral ideas, Wilde published the preface separately in *The Fortnightly Review* in March 1891. He then added it to the revised novel when it came out in book form a month later. In its defiant tone and "art for art's sake" insistence that literature has no moral content, Wilde's preface echoes Théophile Gautier's preface to *Mademoiselle de Maupin* (1835), a founding text of the Aesthetic movement.
2. In Shakespeare's *The Tempest*, the "monster" Caliban is the offspring of the witch Sycorax and is a native of Prospero's island.

The nineteenth century dislike of Romanticism is the rage of Caliban not seeing his own face in a glass.

The moral life of man forms part of the subject-matter of the artist, but the morality of art consists in the perfect use of an imperfect medium.

No artist desires to prove anything. Even things that are true can be proved.

No artist has ethical sympathies. An ethical sympathy in an artist is an unpardonable mannerism of style.

No artist is ever morbid. The artist can express everything.

Thought and language are to the artist instruments of an art.

Vice and virtue are to the artist materials for an art.

From the point of view of form, the type of all the arts is the art of the musician. From the point of view of feeling, the actor's craft is the type.

All art is at once surface and symbol.

Those who go beneath the surface do so at their peril.

Those who read the symbol do so at their peril.

It is the spectator, and not life, that art really mirrors.

Diversity of opinion about a work of art shows that the work is new, complex, and vital.

When critics disagree the artist is in accord with himself.

We can forgive a man for making a useful thing as long as he does not admire it. The only excuse for making a useless thing is that one admires it intensely.

All art is quite useless.

OSCAR WILDE

THE IMPORTANCE OF BEING EARNEST   Wilde's last play, *The Importance of Being Earnest,* is one of the great comedies in the English language. Fast-paced and sparkling, the play opened on 14 February 1895, to widespread acclaim. But it was forced to close less than three months later, amidst the scandal surrounding Wilde's trials for sodomy in April 1895. Eventually, however, the play's reputation was firmly established, and Wilde's witty master-piece took its place in an Anglo-Irish tradition of classic comedies that includes Goldsmith's *She Stoops to Conquer,* Sheridan's *The Rivals,* and Synge's *Playboy of the Western World.* The ti-tle alludes to the Victorian obsession with earnestness as both character trait and moral ideal. The play's philosophy, Wilde claimed, was that "We should treat all the trivial things of life seriously, and all the serious things of life with sincere and studied triviality." In the dandified world of this drama, paying scrupulous attention to surfaces is an act of the deepest sincerity.

Wilde drafted the play in four acts, then at the request of the producer revised it to a tauter three-act version that has become the standard text for performance and reading. For-mally, *The Importance of Being Earnest* shows the clever construction and neat resolution popu-lar in nineteenth-century British and French drama. But it also fulfills the classical definition of comedy as beginning in error and confusion, and ending in knowledge, recognition, and self-discovery. Questioning social hierarchies based on birth, the plot turns on the mysteries of social and personal identity: "Would you kindly inform me who I am?" asks Jack Worthing at the play's climactic moment.

To explore the fictions of personality, Wilde meticulously sketches the trivialities that constitute social ritual and class distinction. From cucumber sandwiches at the start of the play to champagne and muffins in Act 3, the way Wilde's well-bred sophisticates consume food and drink becomes evidence of their character, emotional state, and social status. While the rigid conventions of this world apparently force young men like Jack and Algy to live double lives, they freely exploit their fictive selves as events dictate. Yet they are easily stage-managed by the women they love. Gwendolen and Cecily, who are more preoccupied with writing in their diaries than with the events they record in them, deploy their self-conscious sexual innocence to make life and love conform to the conventions of literature. *The Importance of Being Earnest* presents life as an aesthetic spectacle, in which the careful observation of outward form is the truest path toward an ironic authenticity and self-fulfillment.

"If I were asked of myself as a dramatist," Wilde mused, "I would say that my unique position was that I had taken the Drama, the most objective form known to art, and made it as personal a mode of expression as the Lyric or the Sonnet, while enlarging the characterization of the stage." Wilde refashioned the late-Victorian theater in his own image through the self-conscious brilliance of his language and the outrageousness of his comic invention. He delighted in artifice and exaggeration for their own sake. As he argued in *The Decay of Lying*, art is not an imitation of life but a more aesthetically satisfying restructuring of it. With droll wordplay, paradox, and ridiculous coincidence casting existential dilemmas into comic relief, *The Importance of Being Earnest* anticipates the modern Theater of the Absurd; it heralds the profound slapstick of Pirandello, Ionesco, Beckett, and Stoppard.

The Importance of Being Earnest
A Trivial Comedy for Serious People

FIRST ACT

SCENE: *Morning-room in Algernon's flat in Half Moon Street.*[1] *The room is luxuriously and artistically furnished. The sound of a piano is heard in the adjoining room.*

[*Lane is arranging afternoon tea on the table, and after the music has ceased, Algernon enters.*]

ALGERNON: Did you hear what I was playing, Lane?

LANE: I didn't think it polite to listen, sir.

ALGERNON: I'm sorry for that, for your sake. I don't play accurately—anyone can play accurately—but I play with wonderful expression. As far as the piano is concerned, sentiment is my forte. I keep science for Life.

LANE: Yes, sir.

ALGERNON: And, speaking of the science of Life, have you got the cucumber sandwiches cut for Lady Bracknell?

LANE: Yes, sir. [*Hands them on a salver.*]

ALGERNON [*inspects them, takes two, and sits down on the sofa*]: Oh! . . . by the way, Lane, I see from your book that on Thursday night, when Lord Shoreham and Mr Worthing were dining with me, eight bottles of champagne are entered as having been consumed.

LANE: Yes, sir; eight bottles and a pint.

ALGERNON: Why is it that at a bachelor's establishment the servants invariably drink the champagne? I ask merely for information.

LANE: I attribute it to the superior quality of the wine, sir. I have often observed that in married households the champagne is rarely of a first-rate brand.

ALGERNON: Good Heavens! Is marriage so demoralizing as that?

LANE: I believe it *is* a very pleasant state, sir. I have had very little experience of it myself up to the present. I have only been married once. That was in consequence of a misunderstanding between myself and a young person.

---

1. A fashionable address in the West End of London.

ALGERNON [*languidly*]: I don't know that I am much interested in your family life, Lane.

LANE: No, sir; it is not a very interesting subject. I never think of it myself.

ALGERNON: Very natural, I am sure. That will do, Lane, thank you.

LANE: Thank you, sir. [*Lane goes out.*]

ALGERNON: Lane's views on marriage seem somewhat lax. Really, if the lower orders don't set us a good example, what on earth is the use of them? They seem, as a class, to have absolutely no sense of moral responsibility.

    [*Enter Lane.*]

LANE: Mr Ernest Worthing.

    [*Enter Jack. Lane goes out.*]

ALGERNON: How are you, my dear Ernest? What brings you up to town?

JACK: Oh, pleasure, pleasure! What else should bring one anywhere? Eating as usual, I see, Algy!

ALGERNON [*stiffly*]: I believe it is customary in good society to take some slight refreshment at five o'clock. Where have you been since last Thursday?

JACK [*sitting down on the sofa*]: In the country.

ALGERNON: What on earth do you do there?

JACK [*pulling off his gloves*]: When one is in town one amuses oneself. When one is in the country one amuses other people. It is excessively boring.

ALGERNON: And who are the people you amuse?

JACK [*airily*]: Oh, neighbours, neighbours.

ALGERNON: Got nice neighbours in your part of Shropshire?[2]

JACK: Perfectly horrid! Never speak to one of them.

ALGERNON: How immensely you must amuse them! [*Goes over and takes sandwich.*] By the way, Shropshire is your county, is it not?

JACK: Eh? Shropshire? Yes, of course. Hallo! Why all these cups? Why cucumber sandwiches? Why such reckless extravagance in one so young? Who is coming to tea?

ALGERNON: Oh! merely Aunt Augusta and Gwendolen.

JACK: How perfectly delightful!

ALGERNON: Yes, that is all very well; but I am afraid Aunt Augusta won't quite approve of your being here.

JACK: May I ask why?

ALGERNON: My dear fellow, the way you flirt with Gwendolen is perfectly disgraceful. It is almost as bad as the way Gwendolen flirts with you.

JACK: I am in love with Gwendolen. I have come up to town expressly to propose to her.

ALGERNON: I thought you had come up for pleasure? . . . I call that business.

JACK: How utterly unromantic you are!

ALGERNON: I really don't see anything romantic in proposing. It is very romantic to be in love. But there is nothing romantic about a definite proposal. Why, one may be accepted. One usually is, I believe. Then the excitement is all over. The very essence of romance is uncertainty. If I ever get married, I'll certainly try to forget the fact.

JACK: I have no doubt about that, dear Algy. The Divorce Court was specially invented for people whose memories are so curiously constituted.

2. Worthing's estate is actually in Hertfordshire, which is a long way from Shropshire.

ALGERNON: Oh! there is no use speculating on that subject. Divorces are made in Heaven—[*Jack puts out his hand to take a sandwich. Algernon at once interferes.*] Please don't touch the cucumber sandwiches. They are ordered specially for Aunt Augusta. [*Takes one and eats it.*]

JACK: Well, you have been eating them all the time.

ALGERNON: That is quite a different matter. She is my aunt. [*Takes plate from below.*] Have some bread and butter. The bread and butter is for Gwendolen. Gwendolen is devoted to bread and butter.

JACK [*advancing to table and helping himself*]: And very good bread and butter it is too.

ALGERNON: Well, my dear fellow, you need not eat as if you were going to eat it all. You behave as if you were married to her already. You are not married to her already, and I don't think you ever will be.

JACK: Why on earth do you say that?

ALGERNON: Well, in the first place girls never marry the men they flirt with. Girls don't think it right.

JACK: Oh, that is nonsense!

ALGERNON: It isn't. It is a great truth. It accounts for the extraordinary number of bachelors that one sees all over the place. In the second place, I don't give my consent.

JACK: Your consent!

ALGERNON: My dear fellow, Gwendolen is my first cousin. And before I allow you to marry her, you will have to clear up the whole question of Cecily. [*Rings bell.*]

JACK: Cecily! What on earth do you mean? What do you mean, Algy, by Cecily? I don't know anyone of the name of Cecily.
  [*Enter Lane.*]

ALGERNON: Bring me that cigarette case Mr Worthing left in the smoking-room the last time he dined here.

LANE: Yes, sir. [*Lane goes out.*]

JACK: Do you mean to say you have had my cigarette case all this time? I wish to goodness you had let me know. I have been writing frantic letters to Scotland Yard[3] about it. I was very nearly offering a large reward.

ALGERNON: Well, I wish you would offer one. I happen to be more than usually hard up.

JACK: There is no good offering a large reward now that the thing is found.
  [*Enter Lane with the cigarette case on a salver. Algernon takes it at once. Lane goes out.*]

ALGERNON: I think that is rather mean of you, Ernest, I must say. [*Opens case and examines it.*] However, it makes no matter, for, now that I look at the inscription inside, I find that the thing isn't yours after all.

JACK: Of course it's mine. [*Moving to him.*] You have seen me with it a hundred times, and you have no right whatsoever to read what is written inside. It is a very ungentlemanly thing to read a private cigarette case.

ALGERNON: Oh! it is absurd to have a hard-and-fast rule about what one should read and what one shouldn't. More than half of modern culture depends on what one shouldn't read.

3. London police headquarters.

JACK: I am quite aware of the fact, and I don't propose to discuss modern culture. It isn't the sort of thing one should talk of in private. I simply want my cigarette case back.

ALGERNON: Yes; but this isn't your cigarette case. This cigarette case is a present from someone of the name of Cecily, and you said you didn't know anyone of that name.

JACK: Well, if you want to know, Cecily happens to be my aunt.

ALGERNON: Your aunt!

JACK: Yes. Charming old lady she is, too. Lives at Tunbridge Wells.⁴ Just give it back to me, Algy.

ALGERNON [*retreating to back of sofa*]: But why does she call herself little Cecily if she is your aunt and lives at Tunbridge Wells? [*Reading.*] "From little Cecily with her fondest love."

JACK [*moving to sofa and kneeling upon it*]: My dear fellow, what on earth is there in that? Some aunts are tall, some aunts are not tall. That is a matter that surely an aunt may be allowed to decide for herself. You seem to think that every aunt should be exactly like your aunt! That is absurd! For Heaven's sake give me back my cigarette case. [*Follows Algernon round the room.*]

ALGERNON: Yes. But why does your aunt call you her uncle? "From little Cecily, with her fondest love to her dear Uncle Jack." There is no objection, I admit, to an aunt being a small aunt, but why an aunt, no matter what her size may be, should call her own nephew her uncle, I can't quite make out. Besides, your name isn't Jack at all; it is Ernest.

JACK: It isn't Ernest; it's Jack.

ALGERNON: You have always told me it was Ernest. I have introduced you to everyone as Ernest. You answer to the name of Ernest. You look as if your name was Ernest. You are the most earnest looking person I ever saw in my life. It is perfectly absurd your saying that your name isn't Ernest. It's on your cards. Here is one of them. [*Taking it from case.*] "Mr Ernest Worthing, B. 4, The Albany." I'll keep this as a proof that your name is Ernest if ever you attempt to deny it to me, or to Gwendolen, or to anyone else. [*Puts the card in his pocket.*]

JACK: Well, my name is Ernest in town and Jack in the country, and the cigarette case was given to me in the country.

ALGERNON: Yes, but that does not account for the fact that your small Aunt Cecily, who lives at Tunbridge Wells, calls you her dear uncle. Come, old boy, you had much better have the thing out at once.

JACK: My dear Algy, you talk exactly as if you were a dentist. It is very vulgar to talk like a dentist when one isn't a dentist. It produces a false impression.

ALGERNON: Well, that is exactly what dentists always do. Now, go on! Tell me the whole thing. I may mention that I have always suspected you of being a confirmed and secret Bunburyist, and I am quite sure of it now.

JACK: Bunburyist? What on earth do you mean by a Bunburyist?

ALGERNON: I'll reveal to you the meaning of that incomparable expression as soon as you are kind enough to inform me why you are Ernest in town and Jack in the country.

JACK: Well, produce my cigarette case first.

ALGERNON: Here it is. [*Hands cigarette case.*] Now produce your explanation, and pray make it improbable. [*Sits on sofa.*]

4. A fashionable resort.

JACK: My dear fellow, there is nothing improbable about my explanation at all. In fact it's perfectly ordinary. Old Mr Thomas Cardew, who adopted me when I was a little boy, made me in his will guardian to his granddaughter, Miss Cecily Cardew. Cecily who addresses me as her uncle from motives of respect that you could not possibly appreciate, lives at my place in the country under the charge of her admirable governess, Miss Prism.

ALGERNON: Where is that place in the country, by the way?

JACK: That is nothing to you, dear boy. You are not going to be invited. . . . I may tell you candidly that the place is not in Shropshire.

ALGERNON: I suspected that, my dear fellow! I have Bunburyed all over Shropshire on two separate occasions. Now, go on. Why are you Ernest in town and Jack in the country?

JACK: My dear Algy, I don't know whether you will be able to understand my real motives. You are hardly serious enough. When one is placed in the position of guardian, one has to adopt a very high moral tone on all subjects. It's one's duty to do so. And as a high moral tone can hardly be said to conduce very much to either one's health or one's happiness, in order to get up to town I have always pretended to have a younger brother of the name of Ernest, who lives in the Albany, and gets into the most dreadful scrapes. That, my dear Algy, is the whole truth pure and simple.

ALGERNON: The truth is rarely pure and never simple. Modern life would be very tedious if it were either, and modern literature a complete impossibility!

JACK: That wouldn't be at all a bad thing.

ALGERNON: Literary criticism is not your forte, my dear fellow. Don't try it. You should leave that to people who haven't been at a University. They do it so well in the daily papers. What you really are is a Bunburyist. I was quite right in saying you were a Bunburyist. You are one of the most advanced Bunburyists I know.

JACK: What on earth do you mean?

ALGERNON: You have invented a very useful younger brother called Ernest, in order that you may be able to come up to town as often as you like. I have invented an invaluable permanent invalid called Bunbury, in order that I may be able to go down into the country whenever I choose. Bunbury is perfectly invaluable. If it wasn't for Bunbury's extraordinary bad health, for instance, I wouldn't be able to dine with you at Willis's[5] tonight, for I have been really engaged[6] to Aunt Augusta for more than a week.

JACK: I haven't asked you to dine with me anywhere tonight.

ALGERNON: I know. You are absurdly careless about sending out invitations. It is very foolish of you. Nothing annoys people so much as not receiving invitations.

JACK: You had much better dine with your Aunt Augusta.

ALGERNON: I haven't the smallest intention of doing anything of the kind. To begin with, I dined there on Monday, and once a week is quite enough to dine with one's own relations. In the second place, whenever I do dine there I am always treated as a member of the family, and sent down[7] with either no woman at all, or two. In the third place, I know perfectly well whom she will place me next to, tonight. She will place me next Mary Farquhar, who always flirts with her own husband across the dinner-table. That is not very pleasant. Indeed, it is not even

---

5. An expensive London restaurant.
6. I.e., pledged to attend her dinner party.

7. Sent in to the dining room as someone's escort.

decent . . . and that sort of thing is enormously on the increase. The amount of women in London who flirt with their own husbands is perfectly scandalous. It looks so bad. It is simply washing one's clean linen in public. Besides, now that I know you to be a confirmed Bunburyist I naturally want to talk to you about Bunburying. I want to tell you the rules.

JACK: I'm not a Bunburyist at all. If Gwendolen accepts me, I am going to kill my brother, indeed I think I'll kill him in any case. Cecily is a little too much interested in him. It is rather a bore. So I am going to get rid of Ernest. And I strongly advise you to do the same with Mr . . . with your invalid friend who has the absurd name.

ALGERNON: Nothing will induce me to part with Bunbury, and if you ever get married, which seems to me extremely problematic, you will be very glad to know Bunbury. A man who marries without knowing Bunbury has a very tedious time of it.

JACK: That is nonsense. If I marry a charming girl like Gwendolen, and she is the only girl I ever saw in my life that I would marry, I certainly won't want to know Bunbury.

ALGERNON: Then your wife will. You don't seem to realize, that in married life three is company and two is none.

JACK [*sententiously*]: That, my dear young friend, is the theory that the corrupt French Drama[8] has been propounding for the last fifty years.

ALGERNON: Yes; and that the happy English home has proved in half the time.

JACK: For heaven's sake, don't try to be cynical. It's perfectly easy to be cynical.

ALGERNON: My dear fellow, it isn't easy to be anything nowadays. There's such a lot of beastly competition about. [*The sound of an electric bell is heard.*] Ah! that must be Aunt Augusta. Only relatives, or creditors, ever ring in that Wagnerian manner.[9] Now, if I get her out of the way for ten minutes, so that you can have an opportunity for proposing to Gwendolen, may I dine with you tonight at Willis's?

JACK: I suppose so, if you want to.

ALGERNON: Yes, but you must be serious about it. I hate people who are not serious about meals. It is so shallow of them.

   [*Enter Lane.*]

LANE: Lady Bracknell and Miss Fairfax.

   [*Algernon goes forward to meet them. Enter Lady Bracknell and Gwendolen.*]

LADY BRACKNELL: Good afternoon, dear Algernon, I hope you are behaving very well.

ALGERNON: I'm feeling very well, Aunt Augusta.

LADY BRACKNELL: That's not quite the same thing. In fact the two things rarely go together. [*Sees Jack and bows to him with icy coldness.*]

ALGERNON [*to Gwendolen*]: Dear me, you are smart![1]

GWENDOLEN: I am always smart! Aren't I, Mr Worthing?

JACK: You're quite perfect, Miss Fairfax.

GWENDOLEN: Oh! I hope I am not that. It would leave no room for developments, and I intend to develop in many directions. [*Gwendolen and Jack sit down together in the corner.*]

---

8. Late 19th-century French plays frequently focused on marital infidelity.

9. I.e., loud and dramatic, like the grand operas of Richard Wagner (1813–1883).

1. Chic.

LADY BRACKNELL: I'm sorry if we are a little late, Algernon, but I was obliged to call on dear Lady Harbury. I hadn't been there since her poor husband's death. I never saw a woman so altered; she looks quite twenty years younger. And now I'll have a cup of tea, and one of those nice cucumber sandwiches you promised me.

ALGERNON: Certainly, Aunt Augusta. [Goes over to tea-table.]

LADY BRACKNELL: Won't you come and sit here, Gwendolen?

GWENDOLEN: Thanks, mamma, I'm quite comfortable where I am.

ALGERNON [picking up empty plate in horror]: Good heavens! Lane! Why are there no cucumber sandwiches? I ordered them specially.

LANE [gravely]: There were no cucumbers in the market this morning, sir. I went down twice.

ALGERNON: No cucumbers!

LANE: No, sir. Not even for ready money.

ALGERNON: That will do, Lane, thank you.

LANE: Thank you, sir. [Goes out.]

ALGERNON: I am greatly distressed, Aunt Augusta, about there being no cucumbers, not even for ready money.

LADY BRACKNELL: It really makes no matter, Algernon. I had some crumpets with Lady Harbury, who seems to me to be living entirely for pleasure now.

ALGERNON: I hear her hair has turned quite gold from grief.

LADY BRACKNELL: It certainly has changed its colour. From what cause I, of course, cannot say. [Algernon crosses and hands tea.] Thank you. I've quite a treat for you tonight, Algernon. I am going to send you down with Mary Farquhar. She is such a nice woman, and so attentive to her husband. It's delightful to watch them.

ALGERNON: I am afraid, Aunt Augusta, I shall have to give up the pleasure of dining with you tonight after all.

LADY BRACKNELL [frowning]: I hope not, Algernon. It would put my table completely out. Your uncle would have to dine upstairs. Fortunately he is accustomed to that.

ALGERNON: It is a great bore, and, I need hardly say, a terrible disappointment to me, but the fact is I have just had a telegram to say that my poor friend Bunbury is very ill again. [Exchanges glances with Jack.] They seem to think I should be with him.

LADY BRACKNELL: It is very strange. This Mr Bunbury seems to suffer from curiously bad health.

ALGERNON: Yes; poor Bunbury is a dreadful invalid.

LADY BRACKNELL: Well, I must say, Algernon, that I think it is high time that Mr Bunbury made up his mind whether he was going to live or to die. This shilly-shallying with the question is absurd. Nor do I in any way approve of the modern sympathy with invalids. I consider it morbid. Illness of any kind is hardly a thing to be encouraged in others. Health is the primary duty of life. I am always telling that to your poor uncle, but he never seems to take much notice . . . as far as any improvement in his ailments goes. I should be much obliged if you would ask Mr Bunbury, from me, to be kind enough not to have a relapse on Saturday, for I rely on you to arrange my music for me. It is my last reception, and one wants something that will encourage conversation, particularly at the end of the season[2] when everyone has practically said whatever they had to say, which, in most cases, was probably not much.

---

2. Fashionable people left their country estates to spend the social season in London; it began in late spring and lasted through July.

ALGERNON: I'll speak to Bunbury, Aunt Augusta, if he is still conscious, and I think I can promise you he'll be all right by Saturday. Of course the music is a great difficulty. You see, if one plays good music, people don't listen, and if one plays bad music people don't talk. But I'll run over the programme I've drawn out, if you will kindly come into the next room for a moment.

LADY BRACKNELL: Thank you, Algernon. It is very thoughtful of you. [*Rising, and following Algernon.*] I'm sure the programme will be delightful, after a few expurgations. French songs I cannot possibly allow. People always seem to think that they are improper, and either look shocked, which is vulgar, or laugh, which is worse. But German sounds a thoroughly respectable language, and indeed, I believe is so. Gwendolen, you will accompany me.

GWENDOLEN: Certainly, mamma.

[*Lady Bracknell and Algernon go into the music-room, Gwendolen remains behind.*]

JACK: Charming day it has been, Miss Fairfax.

GWENDOLEN: Pray don't talk to me about the weather, Mr Worthing. Whenever people talk to me about the weather, I always feel quite certain that they mean something else. And that makes me so nervous.

JACK: I do mean something else.

GWENDOLEN: I thought so. In fact, I am never wrong.

JACK: And I would like to be allowed to take advantage of Lady Bracknell's temporary absence . . .

GWENDOLEN: I would certainly advise you to do so. Mamma has a way of coming back suddenly into a room that I have often had to speak to her about.

JACK [*nervously*]: Miss Fairfax, ever since I met you I have admired you more than any girl . . . I have ever met since . . . I met you.

GWENDOLEN: Yes, I am quite aware of the fact. And I often wish that in public, at any rate, you had been more demonstrative. For me you have always had an irresistible fascination. Even before I met you I was far from indifferent to you. [*Jack looks at her in amazement.*] We live, as I hope you know, Mr Worthing, in an age of ideals. The fact is constantly mentioned in the more expensive monthly magazines, and has reached the provincial pulpits I am told: and my ideal has always been to love some one of the name of Ernest. There is something in that name that inspires absolute confidence. The moment Algernon first mentioned to me that he had a friend called Ernest, I knew I was destined to love you.

JACK: You really love me, Gwendolen?

GWENDOLEN: Passionately!

JACK: Darling! You don't know how happy you've made me.

GWENDOLEN: My own Ernest!

JACK: But you don't really mean to say that you couldn't love me if my name wasn't Ernest?

GWENDOLEN: But your name is Ernest.

JACK: Yes, I know it is. But supposing it was something else? Do you mean to say you couldn't love me then?

GWENDOLEN [*glibly*]: Ah! that is clearly a metaphysical speculation, and like most metaphysical speculations has very little reference at all to the actual facts of real life, as we know them.

JACK: Personally, darling, to speak quite candidly, I don't much care about the name of Ernest . . . I don't think the name suits me at all.

GWENDOLEN: It suits you perfectly. It is a divine name. It has a music of its own. It produces vibrations.

JACK: Well, really, Gwendolen, I must say that I think there are lots of other much nicer names. I think Jack, for instance, a charming name.

GWENDOLEN: Jack?...No, there is very little music in the name Jack, if any at all, indeed. It does not thrill. It produces absolutely no vibrations...I have known several Jacks, and they all, without exception, were more than usually plain. Besides, Jack is a notorious domesticity for John! And I pity any woman who is married to a man called John. She would probably never be allowed to know the entrancing pleasure of a single moment's solitude. The only really safe name is Ernest.

JACK: Gwendolen, I must get christened at once—I mean we must get married at once. There is no time to be lost.

GWENDOLEN: Married, Mr Worthing?[3]

JACK [astounded]: Well...surely. You know that I love you, and you led me to believe, Miss Fairfax, that you were not absolutely indifferent to me.

GWENDOLEN: I adore you. But you haven't proposed to me yet. Nothing has been said at all about marriage. The subject has not even been touched on.

JACK: Well...may I propose to you now?

GWENDOLEN: I think it would be an admirable opportunity. And to spare you any possible disappointment, Mr Worthing, I think it only fair to tell you quite frankly beforehand that I am fully determined to accept you.

JACK: Gwendolen!

GWENDOLEN: Yes, Mr Worthing, what have you got to say to me?

JACK: You know what I have got to say to you.

GWENDOLEN: Yes, but you don't say it.

JACK: Gwendolen, will you marry me? [Goes on his knees.]

GWENDOLEN: Of course I will, darling. How long you have been about it! I am afraid you have had very little experience in how to propose.

JACK: My own one, I have never loved anyone in the world but you.

GWENDOLEN: Yes, but men often propose for practice. I know my brother Gerald does. All my girl-friends tell me so. What wonderfully blue eyes you have, Ernest! They are quite, quite, blue. I hope you will always look at me just like that, especially when there are other people present.

[Enter Lady Bracknell.]

LADY BRACKNELL: Mr Worthing! Rise, sir, from this semi-recumbent posture. It is most indecorous.

GWENDOLEN: Mamma! [He tries to rise; she restrains him.] I must beg you to retire. This is no place for you. Besides, Mr Worthing has not quite finished yet.

LADY BRACKNELL: Finished what, may I ask?

GWENDOLEN: I am engaged to Mr Worthing, mamma. [They rise together.]

LADY BRACKNELL: Pardon me, you are not engaged to anyone. When you do become engaged to some one, I, or your father, should his health permit him, will inform you of the fact. An engagement should come on a young girl as a surprise, pleasant or unpleasant, as the case may be. It is hardly a matter that she could be allowed to arrange for herself....And now I have a few questions to put to you,

---

3. Gwendolen reverts to using Jack's last name when she is reminded that he has not yet formally proposed.

Mr Worthing. While I am making these inquiries, you, Gwendolen, will wait for
me below in the carriage.

GWENDOLEN [*reproachfully*]: Mamma!

LADY BRACKNELL: In the carriage, Gwendolen! [*Gwendolen goes to the door. She
and Jack blow kisses to each other behind Lady Bracknell's back. Lady Bracknell looks
vaguely about as if she could not understand what the noise was. Finally turns round.*]
Gwendolen, the carriage!

GWENDOLEN: Yes, mamma. [*Goes out, looking back at Jack.*]

LADY BRACKNELL [*sitting down*]: You can take a seat, Mr Worthing.
     [*Looking in her pocket for note-book and pencil.*]

JACK: Thank you, Lady Bracknell, I prefer standing.

LADY BRACKNELL [*pencil and note-book in hand*]: I feel bound to tell you that you
are not down on my list of eligible young men, although I have the same list as the
dear Duchess of Bolton has. We work together, in fact. However, I am quite ready
to enter your name, should your answers be what a really affectionate mother requires. Do you smoke?

JACK: Well, yes, I must admit I smoke.

LADY BRACKNELL: I am glad to hear it. A man should always have an occupation
of some kind. There are far too many idle men in London as it is. How old are you?

JACK: Twenty-nine.

LADY BRACKNELL: A very good age to be married at. I have always been of opinion that a man who desires to get married should know either everything or nothing. Which do you know?

JACK [*after some hesitation*]: I know nothing, Lady Bracknell.

LADY BRACKNELL: I am pleased to hear it. I do not approve of anything that
tampers with natural ignorance. Ignorance is like a delicate exotic fruit; touch it
and the bloom is gone. The whole theory of modern education is radically unsound. Fortunately in England, at any rate, education produces no effect whatsoever. If it did, it would prove a serious danger to the upper classes, and probably
lead to acts of violence in Grosvenor Square.[4] What is your income?

JACK: Between seven and eight thousand a year.

LADY BRACKNELL [*makes a note in her book*]: In land, or in investments?

JACK: In investments, chiefly.

LADY BRACKNELL: That is satisfactory. What between the duties expected of
one during one's lifetime, and the duties exacted from one after one's death,[5] land
has ceased to be either a profit or a pleasure. It gives one position, and prevents
one from keeping it up. That's all that can be said about land.

JACK: I have a country house with some land, of course, attached to it, about fifteen
hundred acres, I believe; but I don't depend on that for my real income. In fact, as
far as I can make out, the poachers are the only people who make anything out of it.

LADY BRACKNELL: A country house! How many bedrooms? Well, that point can
be cleared up afterwards. You have a town house, I hope? A girl with a simple, unspoiled nature, like Gwendolen, could hardly be expected to reside in the country.

JACK: Well, I own a house in Belgrave Square,[6] but it is let by the year to Lady
Bloxham. Of course, I can get it back whenever I like, at six months' notice.

---

4. A fashionable area in the West End of London.   6. A fashionable West End address in Belgravia.
5. "Death duties" are inheritance taxes.

LADY BRACKNELL: Lady Bloxham? I don't know her.

JACK: Oh, she goes about very little. She is a lady considerably advanced in years.

LADY BRACKNELL: Ah, nowadays that is no guarantee of respectability of character. What number in Belgrave Square?

JACK: 149.

LADY BRACKNELL [*shaking her head*]: The unfashionable side. I thought there was something. However, that could easily be altered.

JACK: Do you mean the fashion, or the side?

LADY BRACKNELL [*sternly*]: Both, if necessary, I presume. What are your politics?

JACK: Well, I am afraid I really have none. I am a Liberal Unionist.[7]

LADY BRACKNELL: Oh, they count as Tories. They dine with us. Or come in the evening, at any rate. Now to minor matters. Are your parents living?

JACK: I have lost both my parents.

LADY BRACKNELL: Both? To lose one parent may be regarded as a misfortune— to lose *both* seems like carelessness. Who was your father? He was evidently a man of some wealth. Was he born in what the Radical papers call the purple of commerce, or did he rise from the ranks of the aristocracy?

JACK: I am afraid I really don't know. The fact is, Lady Bracknell, I said I had lost my parents. It would be nearer the truth to say that my parents seem to have lost me . . . I don't actually know who I am by birth. I was . . . well, I was found.

LADY BRACKNELL: Found!

JACK: The late Mr Thomas Cardew, an old gentleman of a very charitable and kindly disposition, found me, and gave me the name of Worthing, because he happened to have a first-class ticket for Worthing in his pocket at the time. Worthing is a place in Sussex. It is a seaside resort.

LADY BRACKNELL: Where did the charitable gentleman who had a first-class ticket for this seaside resort find you?

JACK [*gravely*]: In a hand-bag.

LADY BRACKNELL: A hand-bag?

JACK [*very seriously*]: Yes, Lady Bracknell. I was in a hand-bag—a somewhat large, black leather hand-bag, with handles to it—an ordinary hand-bag in fact.

LADY BRACKNELL: In what locality did this Mr James, or Thomas, Cardew come across this ordinary hand-bag?

JACK: In the cloak-room at Victoria Station. It was given to him in mistake for his own.

LADY BRACKNELL: The cloak-room at Victoria Station?

JACK: Yes. The Brighton line.

LADY BRACKNELL: The line is immaterial. Mr Worthing, I confess I feel somewhat bewildered by what you have just told me. To be born, or at any rate bred, in a hand-bag, whether it had handles or not, seems to me to display a contempt for the ordinary decencies of family life that reminds one of the worst excesses of the French Revolution. And I presume you know what that unfortunate movement led to? As for the particular locality in which the hand-bag was found, a cloak-room at a railway station might serve to conceal a social indiscretion—has probably, indeed, been used for that purpose before now—but it could hardly be regarded as an assured basis for a recognized position in good society.

---

7. In 1886 Liberal Unionists joined the Conservatives (the "Tories") in voting against the Liberal Prime Minister Gladstone's bill supporting Home Rule for Ireland.

JACK: May I ask you then what you would advise me to do? I need hardly say I would do anything in the world to ensure Gwendolen's happiness.

LADY BRACKNELL: I would strongly advise you, Mr Worthing, to try and acquire some relations as soon as possible, and to make a definite effort to produce at any rate one parent, of either sex, before the season is quite over.

JACK: Well, I don't see how I could possibly manage to do that. I can produce the hand-bag at any moment. It is in my dressing-room at home. I really think that should satisfy you, Lady Bracknell.

LADY BRACKNELL: Me, sir! What has it to do with me? You can hardly imagine that I and Lord Bracknell would dream of allowing our only daughter—a girl brought up with the utmost care—to marry into a cloak-room, and form an alliance with a parcel? Good morning, Mr Worthing!

[*Lady Bracknell sweeps out in majestic indignation.*]

JACK: Good morning! [*Algernon, from the other room, strikes up the Wedding March. Jack looks perfectly furious, and goes to the door.*] For goodness' sake don't play that ghastly tune, Algy! How idiotic you are!

[*The music stops, and Algernon enters cheerily.*]

ALGERNON: Didn't it go off all right, old boy? You don't mean to say Gwendolen refused you? I know it is a way she has. She is always refusing people. I think it is most ill-natured of her.

JACK: Oh, Gwendolen is as right as a trivet.[8] As far as she is concerned, we are engaged. Her mother is perfectly unbearable. Never met such a Gorgon[9] . . . I don't really know what a Gorgon is like, but I am quite sure Lady Bracknell is one. In any case, she is a monster, without being a myth, which is rather unfair . . . I beg your pardon, Algy, I suppose I shouldn't talk about your own aunt in that way before you.

ALGERNON: My dear boy, I love hearing my relations abused. It is the only thing that makes me put up with them at all. Relations are simply a tedious pack of people, who haven't got the remotest knowledge of how to live, nor the smallest instinct about when to die.

JACK: Oh, that is nonsense!

ALGERNON: It isn't!

JACK: Well, I won't argue about the matter. You always want to argue about things.

ALGERNON: That is exactly what things were originally made for.

JACK: Upon my word, if I thought that, I'd shoot myself . . . [*A pause.*] You don't think there is any chance of Gwendolen becoming like her mother in about a hundred and fifty years, do you Algy?

ALGERNON: All women become like their mothers. That is their tragedy. No man does. That's his.

JACK: Is that clever?

ALGERNON: It is perfectly phrased! and quite as true as any observation in civilized life should be.

JACK: I am sick to death of cleverness. Everybody is clever nowadays. You can't go anywhere without meeting clever people. The thing has become an absolute public nuisance. I wish to goodness we had a few fools left.

ALGERNON: We have.

8. Reliable and steady, like a stand used to hold a pot over the fire.   9. A mythical female monster with snakes for hair.

JACK: I should extremely like to meet them. What do they talk about?

ALGERNON: The fools? Oh! about the clever people, of course.

JACK: What fools!

ALGERNON: By the way, did you tell Gwendolen the truth about your being Ernest in town, and Jack in the country?

JACK [in a very patronizing manner]: My dear fellow, the truth isn't quite the sort of thing one tells to a nice sweet refined girl. What extraordinary ideas you have about the way to behave to a woman!

ALGERNON: The only way to behave to a woman is to make love to her,[1] if she is pretty, and to someone else if she is plain.

JACK: Oh, that is nonsense.

ALGERNON: What about your brother? What about the profligate Ernest?

JACK: Oh, before the end of the week I shall have got rid of him. I'll say he died in Paris of apoplexy. Lots of people die of apoplexy, quite suddenly, don't they?

ALGERNON: Yes, but it's hereditary, my dear fellow. It's a sort of thing that runs in families. You had much better say a severe chill.

JACK: You are sure a severe chill isn't hereditary, or anything of that kind?

ALGERNON: Of course it isn't!

JACK: Very well, then. My poor brother Ernest is carried off suddenly in Paris, by a severe chill. That gets rid of him.

ALGERNON: But I thought you said that . . . Miss Cardew was a little too much interested in your poor brother Ernest? Won't she feel his loss a good deal?

JACK: Oh, that is all right. Cecily is not a silly romantic girl, I am glad to say. She has got a capital appetite, goes long walks, and pays no attention at all to her lessons.

ALGERNON: I would rather like to see Cecily.

JACK: I will take very good care you never do. She is excessively pretty, and she is only just eighteen.

ALGERNON: Have you told Gwendolen yet that you have an excessively pretty ward who is only just eighteen?

JACK: Oh! one doesn't blurt these things out to people. Cecily and Gwendolen are perfectly certain to be extremely great friends. I'll bet you anything you like that half an hour after they have met, they will be calling each other sister.

ALGERNON: Women only do that when they have called each other a lot of other things first. Now, my dear boy, if we want to get a good table at Willis's, we really must go and dress. Do you know it is nearly seven?

JACK [irritably]: Oh! it always is nearly seven.

ALGERNON: Well, I'm hungry.

JACK: I never knew you when you weren't. . . .

ALGERNON: What shall we do after dinner? Go to a theatre?

JACK: Oh no! I loathe listening.

ALGERNON: Well, let us go to the Club?

JACK: Oh, no! I hate talking.

ALGERNON: Well, we might trot round to the Empire[2] at ten?

JACK: Oh, no! I can't bear looking at things. It is so silly.

ALGERNON: Well, what shall we do?

---

1. I.e., to flirt with or court her.   2. A popular music hall.

JACK: Nothing!

ALGERNON: It is awfully hard work doing nothing. However, I don't mind hard work where there is no definite object of any kind.

[*Enter Lane.*]

LANE: Miss Fairfax.

[*Enter Gwendolen. Lane goes out.*]

ALGERNON: Gwendolen, upon my word!

GWENDOLEN: Algy, kindly turn your back. I have something very particular to say to Mr Worthing.

ALGERNON: Really, Gwendolen, I don't think I can allow this at all.

GWENDOLEN: Algy, you always adopt a strictly immoral attitude towards life. You are not quite old enough to do that.

[*Algernon retires to the fireplace.*]

JACK: My own darling!

GWENDOLEN: Ernest, we may never be married. From the expression on mamma's face I fear we never shall. Few parents nowadays pay any regard to what their children say to them. The old-fashioned respect for the young is fast dying out. Whatever influence I ever had over mamma, I lost at the age of three. But although she may prevent us from becoming man and wife, and I may marry someone else, and marry often, nothing that she can possibly do can alter my eternal devotion to you.

JACK: Dear Gwendolen!

GWENDOLEN: The story of your romantic origin, as related to me by mamma, with unpleasing comments, has naturally stirred the deeper fibres of my nature. Your Christian name has an irresistible fascination. The simplicity of your character makes you exquisitely incomprehensible to me. Your town address at the Albany I have. What is your address in the country?

JACK: The Manor House, Woolton, Hertfordshire.

[*Algernon, who has been carefully listening, smiles to himself, and writes the address on his shirt-cuff. Then picks up the Railway Guide.*]

GWENDOLEN: There is a good postal service, I suppose? It may be necessary to do something desperate. That of course will require serious consideration. I will communicate with you daily.

JACK: My own one!

GWENDOLEN: How long do you remain in town?

JACK: Till Monday.

GWENDOLEN: Good! Algy, you may turn round now.

ALGERNON: Thanks, I've turned round already.

GWENDOLEN: You may also ring the bell.

JACK: You will let me see you to your carriage, my own darling?

GWENDOLEN: Certainly.

JACK [*to Lane, who now enters*]: I will see Miss Fairfax out.

LANE: Yes, sir. [*Jack and Gwendolen go off.*]

[*Lane presents several letters on a salver to Algernon. It is to be surmised that they are bills, as Algernon, after looking at the envelopes, tears them up.*]

ALGERNON: A glass of sherry, Lane.

LANE: Yes, sir.

ALGERNON: Tomorrow, Lane, I'm going Bunburying.

LANE: Yes, sir.

ALGERNON: I shall probably not be back till Monday. You can put up my dress clothes, my smoking jacket, and all the Bunbury suits . . .

LANE: Yes, sir. [*Handing sherry.*]

ALGERNON: I hope tomorrow will be a fine day, Lane.

LANE: It never is, sir.

ALGERNON: Lane, you're a perfect pessimist.

LANE: I do my best to give satisfaction, sir.

   [*Enter Jack. Lane goes off.*]

JACK: There's a sensible, intellectual girl! the only girl I ever cared for in my life. [*Algernon is laughing immoderately.*] What on earth are you so amused at?

ALGERNON: Oh, I'm a little anxious about poor Bunbury, that is all.

JACK: If you don't take care, your friend Bunbury will get you into a serious scrape some day.

ALGERNON: I love scrapes. They are the only things that are never serious.

JACK: Oh, that's nonsense, Algy. You never talk anything but nonsense.

ALGERNON: Nobody ever does.

   [*Jack looks indignantly at him, and leaves the room. Algernon lights a cigarette, reads his shirt-cuff, and smiles.*]

                                                                        ACT DROP

SECOND ACT

SCENE: *Garden at the Manor House. A flight of gray stone steps leads up to the house. The garden, an old-fashioned one, full of roses. Time of year, July. Basket chairs, and a table covered with books, are set under a large yew tree.*

   [*Miss Prism discovered seated at the table. Cecily is at the back watering flowers.*]

MISS PRISM [*calling*]: Cecily, Cecily! Surely such a utilitarian occupation as the watering of flowers is rather Moulton's duty than yours? Especially at a moment when intellectual pleasures await you. Your German grammar is on the table. Pray open it at page fifteen. We will repeat yesterday's lesson.

CECILY [*coming over very slowly*]: But I don't like German. It isn't at all a becoming language. I know perfectly well that I look quite plain after my German lesson.

MISS PRISM: Child, you know how anxious your guardian is that you should improve yourself in every way. He laid particular stress on your German, as he was leaving for town yesterday. Indeed, he always lays stress on your German when he is leaving for town.

CECILY: Dear Uncle Jack is so very serious! Sometimes he is so serious that I think he cannot be quite well.

MISS PRISM [*drawing herself up*]: Your guardian enjoys the best of health, and his gravity of demeanour is especially to be commended in one so comparatively young as he is. I know no one who has a higher sense of duty and responsibility.

CECILY: I suppose that is why he often looks a little bored when we three are together.

MISS PRISM: Cecily! I am surprised at you. Mr Worthing has many troubles in his life. Idle merriment and triviality would be out of place in his conversation. You must remember his constant anxiety about that unfortunate young man his brother.

CECILY: I wish Uncle Jack would allow that unfortunate young man, his brother, to come down here sometimes. We might have a good influence over him, Miss Prism. I am sure you certainly would. You know German, and geology, and things of that kind influence a man very much. [*Cecily begins to write in her diary.*]

MISS PRISM [*shaking her head*]: I do not think that even I could produce any effect on a character that according to his own brother's admission is irretrievably weak and vacillating. Indeed I am not sure that I would desire to reclaim him. I am not in favour of this modern mania for turning bad people into good people at a moment's notice. As a man sows so let him reap.[3] You must put away your diary, Cecily. I really don't see why you should keep a diary at all.

CECILY: I keep a diary in order to enter the wonderful secrets of my life. If I didn't write them down I should probably forget all about them.

MISS PRISM: Memory, my dear Cecily, is the diary that we all carry about with us.

CECILY: Yes, but it usually chronicles the things that have never happened, and couldn't possibly have happened. I believe that Memory is responsible for nearly all the three-volume novels that Mudie sends us.[4]

MISS PRISM: Do not speak slightly of the three-volume novel, Cecily. I wrote one myself in earlier days.

CECILY: Did you really, Miss Prism? How wonderfully clever you are! I hope it did not end happily? I don't like novels that end happily. They depress me so much.

MISS PRISM: The good ended happily, and the bad unhappily. That is what Fiction means.

CECILY: I suppose so. But it seems very unfair. And was your novel ever published?

MISS PRISM: Alas! no. The manuscript unfortunately was abandoned. I use the word in the sense of lost or mislaid. To your work, child, these speculations are profitless.

CECILY [*smiling*]: But I see dear Dr Chasuble coming up through the garden.

MISS PRISM [*rising and advancing*]: Dr Chasuble! This is indeed a pleasure.
    [*Enter Canon Chasuble.*][5]

CHASUBLE: And how are we this morning? Miss Prism, you are, I trust, well?

CECILY: Miss Prism has just been complaining of a slight headache. I think it would do her so much good to have a short stroll with you in the Park, Dr Chasuble.

MISS PRISM: Cecily, I have not mentioned anything about a headache.

CECILY: No, dear Miss Prism, I know that, but I felt instinctively that you had a headache. Indeed I was thinking about that, and not about my German lesson, when the Rector came in.

CHASUBLE: I hope Cecily, you are not inattentive.

CECILY: Oh, I am afraid I am.

CHASUBLE: That is strange. Were I fortunate enough to be Miss Prism's pupil, I would hang upon her lips. [*Miss Prism glares.*] I spoke metaphorically.—My metaphor was drawn from bees. Ahem! Mr Worthing I suppose, has not returned from town yet?

MISS PRISM: We do not expect him till Monday afternoon.

CHASUBLE: Ah yes, he usually likes to spend his Sunday in London. He is not one of those whose sole aim is enjoyment, as, by all accounts, that unfortunate young man his brother seems to be. But I must not disturb Egeria[6] and her pupil any longer.

---

3. "Be not deceived; God is not mocked: for whatsoever a man soweth, that shall he also reap" (Galatians 6.7).

4. Mudie's Select Library lent novels to subscribers for a fee; at the time of this play, both Mudie's and the three-volume novel were becoming outmoded.

5. A canon is a cathedral clergyman; a chasuble is a vestment.

6. Roman goddess of fountains; her name was used for a woman who instructed other women.

MISS PRISM: Egeria? My name is Laetitia, Doctor.

CHASUBLE [*bowing*]: A classical allusion merely, drawn from the Pagan authors. I shall see you both no doubt at Evensong?[7]

MISS PRISM: I think, dear Doctor, I will have a stroll with you. I find I have a headache after all, and a walk might do it good.

CHASUBLE: With pleasure, Miss Prism, with pleasure. We might go as far as the schools and back.

MISS PRISM: That would be delightful. Cecily, you will read your Political Economy in my absence. The chapter on the Fall of the Rupee you may omit.[8] It is somewhat too sensational. Even these metallic problems have their melodramatic side. [*Goes down the garden with Dr Chasuble.*]

CECILY [*picks up books and throws them back on table*]: Horrid Political Economy! Horrid Geography! Horrid, horrid German!

[*Enter Merriman with a card on a salver.*]

MERRIMAN: Mr Ernest Worthing has just driven over from the station. He has brought his luggage with him.

CECILY [*takes the card and reads it*]: "Mr Ernest Worthing, B.4 The Albany, W." Uncle Jack's brother! Did you tell him Mr Worthing was in town?

MERRIMAN: Yes, Miss. He seemed very much disappointed. I mentioned that you and Miss Prism were in the garden. He said he was anxious to speak to you privately for a moment.

CECILY: Ask Mr Ernest Worthing to come here. I suppose you had better talk to the housekeeper about a room for him.

MERRIMAN: Yes, Miss. [*Merriman goes off.*]

CECILY: I have never met any really wicked person before. I feel rather frightened. I am so afraid he will look just like everyone else.

[*Enter Algernon, very gay and debonair.*]

He does!

ALGERNON [*raising his hat*]: You are my little cousin Cecily, I'm sure.

CECILY: You are under some strange mistake. I am not little. In fact, I believe I am more than usually tall for my age. [*Algernon is rather taken aback.*] But I am your cousin Cecily. You, I see from your card, are Uncle Jack's brother, my cousin Ernest, my wicked cousin Ernest.

ALGERNON: Oh! I am not really wicked at all, cousin Cecily. You mustn't think that I am wicked.

CECILY: If you are not, then you have certainly been deceiving us all in a very inexcusable manner. I hope you have not been leading a double life, pretending to be wicked and being really good all the time. That would be hypocrisy.

ALGERNON [*looks at her in amazement*]: Oh! Of course I have been rather reckless.

CECILY: I am glad to hear it.

ALGERNON: In fact, now you mention the subject, I have been very bad in my own small way.

CECILY: I don't think you should be so proud of that, although I am sure it must have been very pleasant.

ALGERNON: It is much pleasanter being here with you.

---

7. Evening church services.
8. The declining value of the Indian rupee would hurt   British civil servants in India, who were paid in rupees.

CECILY: I can't understand how you are here at all. Uncle Jack won't be back till Monday afternoon.

ALGERNON: That is a great disappointment. I am obliged to go up by the first train on Monday morning. I have a business appointment that I am anxious . . . to miss.

CECILY: Couldn't you miss it anywhere but in London?

ALGERNON: No: the appointment is in London.

CECILY: Well, I know, of course, how important it is not to keep a business engagement, if one wants to retain any sense of the beauty of life, but still I think you had better wait till Uncle Jack arrives. I know he wants to speak to you about your emigrating.

ALGERNON: About my what?

CECILY: Your emigrating. He has gone up to buy your outfit.

ALGERNON: I certainly wouldn't let Jack buy my outfit. He has no taste in neckties at all.

CECILY: I don't think you will require neckties. Uncle Jack is sending you to Australia.[9]

ALGERNON: Australia! I'd sooner die.

CECILY: Well, he said at dinner on Wednesday night, that you would have to choose between this world, the next world, and Australia.

ALGERNON: Oh, well! The accounts I have received of Australia and the next world are not particularly encouraging. This world is good enough for me, cousin Cecily.

CECILY: Yes, but are you good enough for it?

ALGERNON: I'm afraid I'm not that. That is why I want you to reform me. You might make that your mission, if you don't mind, cousin Cecily.

CECILY: I'm afraid I've no time, this afternoon.

ALGERNON: Well, would you mind my reforming myself this afternoon?

CECILY: It is rather Quixotic[1] of you. But I think you should try.

ALGERNON: I will. I feel better already.

CECILY: You are looking a little worse.

ALGERNON: That is because I am hungry.

CECILY: How thoughtless of me. I should have remembered that when one is going to lead an entirely new life, one requires regular and wholesome meals. Won't you come in?

ALGERNON: Thank you. Might I have a buttonhole[2] first? I never have any appetite unless I have a buttonhole first.

CECILY: A Maréchal Niel?[3] [Picks up scissors.]

ALGERNON: No, I'd sooner have a pink rose.

CECILY: Why? [Cuts a flower.]

ALGERNON: Because you are like a pink rose, Cousin Cecily.

CECILY: I don't think it can be right for you to talk to me like that. Miss Prism never says such things to me.

ALGERNON: Then Miss Prism is a short-sighted old lady. [Cecily puts the rose in his buttonhole.] You are the prettiest girl I ever saw.

CECILY: Miss Prism says that all good looks are a snare.

---

9. Australia was no longer a penal colony, but it was still a place where families sent their ne'er-do-well sons.
1. Hopelessly idealistic, like Don Quixote.

2. A flower to wear in his lapel.
3. A yellow rose.

ALGERNON: They are a snare that every sensible man would like to be caught in.

CECILY: Oh! I don't think I would care to catch a sensible man. I shouldn't know what to talk to him about.

[*They pass into the house. Miss Prism and Dr Chasuble return.*]

MISS PRISM: You are too much alone, dear Dr Chasuble. You should get married. A misanthrope I can understand—a womanthrope, never!

CHASUBLE [*with a scholar's shudder*][4]: Believe me, I do not deserve so neologistic a phrase. The precept as well as the practice of the Primitive Church was distinctly against matrimony.[5]

MISS PRISM [*sententiously*]: That is obviously the reason why the Primitive Church has not lasted up to the present day. And you do not seem to realize, dear Doctor, that by persistently remaining single, a man converts himself into a permanent public temptation. Men should be more careful; this very celibacy leads weaker vessels astray.

CHASUBLE: But is a man not equally attractive when married?

MISS PRISM: No married man is ever attractive except to his wife.

CHASUBLE: And often, I've been told, not even to her.

MISS PRISM: That depends on the intellectual sympathies of the woman. Maturity can always be depended on. Ripeness can be trusted. Young women are green. [*Dr Chasuble starts.*] I spoke horticulturally. My metaphor was drawn from fruits. But where is Cecily?

CHASUBLE: Perhaps she followed us to the schools.

[*Enter Jack slowly from the back of the garden. He is dressed in the deepest mourning, with crape hat-band and black gloves.*]

MISS PRISM: Mr Worthing!

CHASUBLE: Mr Worthing?

MISS PRISM: This is indeed a surprise. We did not look for you till Monday afternoon.

JACK [*shakes Miss Prism's hand in a tragic manner*]: I have returned sooner than I expected. Dr Chasuble, I hope you are well?

CHASUBLE: Dear Mr Worthing, I trust this garb of woe does not betoken some terrible calamity?

JACK: My brother.

MISS PRISM: More shameful debts and extravagance?

CHASUBLE: Still leading his life of pleasure?

JACK [*shaking his head*]: Dead!

CHASUBLE: Your brother Ernest dead?

JACK: Quite dead.

MISS PRISM: What a lesson for him! I trust he will profit by it.

CHASUBLE: Mr Worthing, I offer you my sincere condolence. You have at least the consolation of knowing that you were always the most generous and forgiving of brothers.

JACK: Poor Ernest! He had many faults, but it is a sad, sad blow.

CHASUBLE: Very sad indeed. Were you with him at the end?

---

4. He shudders because Miss Prism has mangled the language by coining a word, "womanthrope," to describe someone who dislikes women, instead of using the correct term, "misogynist." A neologism is a newly invented word.

5. Protestant clergy are allowed to marry, but as a High Church Anglican, Chasuble is interested in preserving the rituals and practices of the early Catholic church.

JACK: No. He died abroad; in Paris, in fact. I had a telegram last night from the manager of the Grand Hotel.

CHASUBLE: Was the cause of death mentioned?

JACK: A severe chill, it seems.

MISS PRISM: As a man sows, so shall he reap.

CHASUBLE [*raising his hand*]: Charity, dear Miss Prism, charity! None of us are perfect. I myself am peculiarly susceptible to draughts. Will the interment take place here?

JACK: No. He seemed to have expressed a desire to be buried in Paris.

CHASUBLE: In Paris! [*Shakes his head.*] I fear that hardly points to any very serious state of mind at the last. You would no doubt wish me to make some slight allusion to this tragic domestic affliction next Sunday. [*Jack presses his hand convulsively.*] My sermon on the meaning of the manna in the wilderness[6] can be adapted to almost any occasion, joyful, or, as in the present case, distressing. [*All sigh.*] I have preached it at harvest celebrations, christenings, confirmations, on days of humiliation and festal days. The last time I delivered it was in the Cathedral, as a charity sermon on behalf of the Society for the Prevention of Discontent among the Upper Orders. The Bishop, who was present, was much struck by some of the analogies I drew.

JACK: Ah! that reminds me, you mentioned christenings I think, Dr Chasuble? I suppose you know how to christen all right? [*Dr Chasuble looks astounded.*] I mean, of course, you are continually christening, aren't you?

MISS PRISM: It is, I regret to say, one of the Rector's most constant duties in this parish. I have often spoken to the poorer classes on the subject. But they don't seem to know what thrift is.

CHASUBLE: But is there any particular infant in whom you are interested, Mr Worthing? Your brother was, I believe, unmarried, was he not?

JACK: Oh, yes.

MISS PRISM [*bitterly*]: People who live entirely for pleasure usually are.

JACK: But it is not for any child, dear Doctor. I am very fond of children. No! the fact is, I would like to be christened myself, this afternoon, if you have nothing better to do.

CHASUBLE: But surely, Mr Worthing, you have been christened already?

JACK: I don't remember anything about it.

CHASUBLE: But have you any grave doubts on the subject?

JACK: I certainly intend to have. Of course I don't know if the thing would bother you in any way, or if you think I am a little too old now.

CHASUBLE: Not at all. The sprinkling, and, indeed, the immersion of adults is a perfectly canonical practice.

JACK: Immersion!

CHASUBLE: You need have no apprehensions. Sprinkling is all that is necessary, or indeed I think advisable. Our weather is so changeable. At what hour would you wish the ceremony performed?

JACK: Oh, I might trot round about five if that would suit you.

CHASUBLE: Perfectly, perfectly! In fact I have two similar ceremonies to perform at that time. A case of twins that occurred recently in one of the outlying cottages on your own estate. Poor Jenkins the carter, a most hard-working man.

JACK: Oh! I don't see much fun in being christened along with other babies. It would be childish. Would half-past five do?

6. Cf. Exodus 16.

CHASUBLE: Admirably! Admirably! [*Takes out watch.*] And now, dear Mr Worthing, I will not intrude any longer into a house of sorrow. I would merely beg you not to be too much bowed down by grief. What seem to us bitter trials are often blessings in disguise.

MISS PRISM: This seems to me a blessing of an extremely obvious kind.

[*Enter Cecily from the house.*]

CECILY: Uncle Jack! Oh, I am pleased to see you back. But what horrid clothes you have got on! Do go and change them.

MISS PRISM: Cecily!

CHASUBLE: My child! my child!

[*Cecily goes towards Jack; he kisses her brow in a melancholy manner.*]

CECILY: What is the matter, Uncle Jack? Do look happy! You look as if you had toothache, and I have got such a surprise for you. Who do you think is in the dining-room? Your brother!

JACK: Who?

CECILY: Your brother Ernest. He arrived about half an hour ago.

JACK: What nonsense! I haven't got a brother.

CECILY: Oh, don't say that. However badly he may have behaved to you in the past he is still your brother. You couldn't be so heartless as to disown him. I'll tell him to come out. And you will shake hands with him, won't you, Uncle Jack? [*Runs back into the house.*]

CHASUBLE: These are very joyful tidings.

MISS PRISM: After we had all been resigned to his loss, his sudden return seems to me peculiarly distressing.

JACK: My brother is in the dining-room? I don't know what it all means. I think it is perfectly absurd.

[*Enter Algernon and Cecily hand in hand. They come slowly up to Jack.*]

JACK: Good heavens! [*Motions Algernon away.*]

ALGERNON: Brother John, I have come down from town to tell you that I am very sorry for all the trouble I have given you, and that I intend to lead a better life in the future.

[*Jack glares at him and does not take his hand.*]

CECILY: Uncle Jack, you are not going to refuse your own brother's hand?

JACK: Nothing will induce me to take his hand. I think his coming down here disgraceful. He knows perfectly well why.

CECILY: Uncle Jack, do be nice. There is some good in everyone. Ernest has just been telling me about his poor invalid friend Mr Bunbury whom he goes to visit so often. And surely there must be much good in one who is kind to an invalid, and leaves the pleasures of London to sit by a bed of pain.

JACK: Oh! he has been talking about Bunbury has he?

CECILY: Yes, he has told me all about poor Mr Bunbury, and his terrible state of health.

JACK: Bunbury! Well, I won't have him talk to you about Bunbury or about anything else. It is enough to drive one perfectly frantic.

ALGERNON: Of course I admit that the faults were all on my side. But I must say that I think that Brother John's coldness to me is peculiarly painful. I expected a more enthusiastic welcome, especially considering it is the first time I have come here.

CECILY: Uncle Jack, if you don't shake hands with Ernest I will never forgive you.

JACK: Never forgive me?

CECILY: Never, never, never!

JACK: Well, this is the last time I shall ever do it. [*Shakes hands with Algernon and glares.*]

CHASUBLE: It's pleasant, is it not, to see so perfect a reconciliation? I think we might leave the two brothers together.

MISS PRISM: Cecily, you will come with us.

CECILY: Certainly, Miss Prism. My little task of reconciliation is over.

CHASUBLE: You have done a beautiful action today, dear child.

MISS PRISM: We must not be premature in our judgements.

CECILY: I feel very happy. [*They all go off.*]

JACK: You young scoundrel, Algy, you must get out of this place as soon as possible. I don't allow any Bunburying here.

[*Enter Merriman.*]

MERRIMAN: I have put Mr Ernest's things in the room next to yours, sir. I suppose that is all right?

JACK: What?

MERRIMAN: Mr Ernest's luggage, sir. I have unpacked it and put it in the room next to your own.

JACK: His luggage?

MERRIMAN: Yes, sir. Three portmanteaus, a dressing-case, two hat-boxes, and a large luncheon-basket.

ALGERNON: I am afraid I can't stay more than a week this time.

JACK: Merriman, order the dog-cart[7] at once. Mr Ernest has been suddenly called back to town.

MERRIMAN: Yes, sir. [*Goes back into the house.*]

ALGERNON: What a fearful liar you are, Jack. I have not been called back to town at all.

JACK: Yes, you have.

ALGERNON: I haven't heard anyone call me.

JACK: Your duty as a gentleman calls you back.

ALGERNON: My duty as a gentleman has never interfered with my pleasures in the smallest degree.

JACK: I can quite understand that.

ALGERNON: Well, Cecily is a darling.

JACK: You are not to talk of Miss Cardew like that. I don't like it.

ALGERNON: Well, I don't like your clothes. You look perfectly ridiculous in them. Why on earth don't you go up and change? It is perfectly childish to be in deep mourning for a man who is actually staying for a whole week with you in your house as a guest. I call it grotesque.

JACK: You are certainly not staying with me for a whole week as a guest or anything else. You have got to leave . . . by the four-five train.

ALGERNON: I certainly won't leave you so long as you are in mourning. It would be most unfriendly. If I were in mourning you would stay with me, I suppose. I should think it very unkind if you didn't.

JACK: Well, will you go if I change my clothes?

ALGERNON: Yes, if you are not too long. I never saw anybody take so long to dress, and with such little result.

JACK: Well, at any rate, that is better than being always over-dressed as you are.

---

7. A horse-drawn cart with seats, and a box for hunting dogs.

ALGERNON: If I am occasionally a little over-dressed, I make up for it by being always immensely over-educated.

JACK: Your vanity is ridiculous, your conduct an outrage, and your presence in my garden utterly absurd. However, you have got to catch the four-five, and I hope you will have a pleasant journey back to town. This Bunburying, as you call it, has not been a great success for you. [*Goes into the house.*]

ALGERNON: I think it has been a great success. I'm in love with Cecily, and that is everything.

[*Enter Cecily at the back of the garden. She picks up the can and begins to water the flowers.*]

But I must see her before I go, and make arrangements for another Bunbury. Ah, there she is.

CECILY: Oh, I merely came back to water the roses. I thought you were with Uncle Jack.

ALGERNON: He's gone to order the dog-cart for me.

CECILY: Oh, is he going to take you for a nice drive?

ALGERNON: He's going to send me away.

CECILY: Then have we got to part?

ALGERNON: I am afraid so. It's a painful parting.

CECILY: It is always painful to part from people whom one has known for a very brief space of time. The absence of old friends one can endure with equanimity. But even a momentary separation from anyone to whom one has just been introduced is almost unbearable.

ALGERNON: Thank you.

[*Enter Merriman.*]

MERRIMAN: The dog-cart is at the door, sir.

[*Algernon looks appealingly at Cecily.*]

CECILY: It can wait, Merriman . . . for . . . five minutes.

MERRIMAN: Yes, Miss. [*Exit Merriman.*]

ALGERNON: I hope, Cecily, I shall not offend you if I state quite frankly and openly that you seem to me to be in every way the visible personification of absolute perfection.

CECILY: I think your frankness does you great credit, Ernest. If you will allow me I will copy your remarks into my diary. [*Goes over to table and begins writing in diary.*]

ALGERNON: Do you really keep a diary? I'd give anything to look at it. May I?

CECILY: Oh no. [*Puts her hand over it.*] You see, it is simply a very young girl's record of her own thoughts and impressions, and consequently meant for publication. When it appears in volume form I hope you will order a copy. But pray, Ernest, don't stop. I delight in taking down from dictation. I have reached "absolute perfection." You can go on. I am quite ready for more.

ALGERNON [*somewhat taken aback*]: Ahem! Ahem!

CECILY: Oh, don't cough, Ernest. When one is dictating one should speak fluently and not cough. Besides, I don't know how to spell a cough. [*Writes as Algernon speaks.*]

ALGERNON [*speaking very rapidly*]: Cecily, ever since I first looked upon your wonderful and incomparable beauty, I have dared to love you wildly, passionately, devotedly, hopelessly.

CECILY: I don't think that you should tell me that you love me wildly, passionately, devotedly, hopelessly. Hopelessly doesn't seem to make much sense, does it?

ALGERNON: Cecily!

[Enter Merriman.]

MERRIMAN: The dog-cart is waiting, sir.

ALGERNON: Tell it to come round next week, at the same hour.

MERRIMAN [looks at Cecily, who makes no sign]: Yes, sir. [Merriman retires.]

CECILY: Uncle Jack would be very much annoyed if he knew you were staying on till next week, at the same hour.

ALGERNON: Oh, I don't care about Jack. I don't care for anybody in the whole world but you. I love you, Cecily. You will marry me, won't you?

CECILY: You silly boy! Of course. Why, we have been engaged for the last three months.

ALGERNON: For the last three months?

CECILY: Yes, it will be exactly three months on Thursday.

ALGERNON: But how did we become engaged?

CECILY: Well, ever since dear Uncle Jack first confessed to us that he had a younger brother who was very wicked and bad, you of course have formed the chief topic of conversation between myself and Miss Prism. And of course a man who is much talked about is always very attractive. One feels there must be something in him after all. I daresay it was foolish of me, but I fell in love with you, Ernest.

ALGERNON: Darling! And when was the engagement actually settled?

CECILY: On the 14th of February last. Worn out by your entire ignorance of my existence, I determined to end the matter one way or the other, and after a long struggle with myself I accepted you under this dear old tree here. The next day I bought this little ring in your name, and this is the little bangle with the true lovers' knot I promised you always to wear.

ALGERNON: Did I give you this? It's very pretty, isn't it?

CECILY: Yes, you've wonderfully good taste, Ernest. It's the excuse I've always given for your leading such a bad life. And this is the box in which I keep all your dear letters. [Kneels at table, opens box, and produces letters tied up with blue ribbon.]

ALGERNON: My letters! But my own sweet Cecily, I have never written you any letters.

CECILY: You need hardly remind me of that, Ernest. I remember only too well that I was forced to write your letters for you. I wrote always three times a week, and sometimes oftener.

ALGERNON: Oh, do let me read them, Cecily?

CECILY: Oh, I couldn't possibly. They would make you far too conceited. [Replaces box.] The three you wrote me after I had broken off the engagement are so beautiful, and so badly spelled, that even now I can hardly read them without crying a little.

ALGERNON: But was our engagement ever broken off?

CECILY: Of course it was. On the 22nd of last March. You can see the entry if you like. [Shows diary.] "Today I broke off my engagement with Ernest. I feel it is better to do so. The weather still continues charming."

ALGERNON: But why on earth did you break it off? What had I done? I had done nothing at all. Cecily, I am very much hurt indeed to hear you broke it off. Particularly when the weather was so charming.

CECILY: It would hardly have been a really serious engagement if it hadn't been broken off at least once. But I forgave you before the week was out.

ALGERNON [*crossing to her, and kneeling*]: What a perfect angel you are, Cecily.

CECILY: You dear romantic boy. [*He kisses her, she puts her fingers through his hair.*] I hope your hair curls naturally, does it?

ALGERNON: Yes, darling, with a little help from others.

CECILY: I am so glad.

ALGERNON: You'll never break off our engagement again, Cecily?

CECILY: I don't think I could break it off now that I have actually met you. Besides, of course, there is the question of your name.

ALGERNON: Yes, of course. [*Nervously.*]

CECILY: You must not laugh at me, darling, but it had always been a girlish dream of mine to love some one whose name was Ernest. [*Algernon rises, Cecily also.*] There is something in that name that seems to inspire absolute confidence. I pity any poor married woman whose husband is not called Ernest.

ALGERNON: But, my dear child, do you mean to say you could not love me if I had some other name?

CECILY: But what name?

ALGERNON: Oh, any name you like—Algernon—for instance . . .

CECILY: But I don't like the name of Algernon.

ALGERNON: Well, my own dear, sweet, loving little darling, I really can't see why you should object to the name of Algernon. It is not at all a bad name. In fact, it is rather an aristocratic name. Half of the chaps who get into the Bankruptcy Court are called Algernon. But seriously, Cecily . . . [*moving to her*] . . . if my name was Algy, couldn't you love me?

CECILY [*rising*]: I might respect you, Ernest, I might admire your character, but I fear that I should not be able to give you my undivided attention.

ALGERNON: Ahem! Cecily! [*Picking up hat.*] Your Rector here is, I suppose, thoroughly experienced in the practice of all the rites and ceremonials of the Church?

CECILY: Oh yes. Dr Chasuble is a most learned man. He has never written a single book, so you can imagine how much he knows.

ALGERNON: I must see him at once on a most important christening—I mean on most important business.

CECILY: Oh!

ALGERNON: I shan't be away more than half an hour.

CECILY: Considering that we have been engaged since February the 14th, and that I only met you today for the first time, I think it is rather hard that you should leave me for so long a period as half an hour. Couldn't you make it twenty minutes?

ALGERNON: I'll be back in no time. [*Kisses her and rushes down the garden.*]

CECILY: What an impetuous boy he is! I like his hair so much. I must enter his proposal in my diary.

[*Enter Merriman.*]

MERRIMAN: A Miss Fairfax has just called to see Mr Worthing. On very important business Miss Fairfax states.

CECILY: Isn't Mr Worthing in his library?

MERRIMAN: Mr Worthing went over in the direction of the Rectory some time ago.

CECILY: Pray ask the lady to come out here; Mr Worthing is sure to be back soon. And you can bring tea.

MERRIMAN: Yes, Miss. [*Goes out.*]

CECILY: Miss Fairfax! I suppose one of the many good elderly women who are associated with Uncle Jack in some of his philanthropic work in London. I don't quite like women who are interested in philanthropic work. I think it is so forward of them. [*Enter Merriman.*]

MERRIMAN: Miss Fairfax.
  [*Enter Gwendolen. Exit Merriman.*]

CECILY [*advancing to meet her*]: Pray let me introduce myself to you. My name is Cecily Cardew.

GWENDOLEN: Cecily Cardew? [*Moving to her and shaking hands.*] What a very sweet name! Something tells me that we are going to be great friends. I like you already more than I can say. My first impressions of people are never wrong.

CECILY: How nice of you to like me so much after we have known each other such a comparatively short time. Pray sit down.

GWENDOLEN [*still standing up*]: I may call you Cecily, may I not?

CECILY: With pleasure!

GWENDOLEN: And you will always call me Gwendolen, won't you.

CECILY: If you wish.

GWENDOLEN: Then that is all quite settled, is it not?

CECILY: I hope so.
  [*A pause. They both sit down together.*]

GWENDOLEN: Perhaps this might be a favourable opportunity for my mentioning who I am. My father is Lord Bracknell. You have never heard of papa, I suppose?

CECILY: I don't think so.

GWENDOLEN: Outside the family circle, papa, I am glad to say, is entirely unknown. I think that is quite as it should be. The home seems to me to be the proper sphere for the man. And certainly once a man begins to neglect his domestic duties he becomes painfully effeminate, does he not? And I don't like that. It makes men so very attractive. Cecily, mamma, whose views on education are remarkably strict, has brought me up to be extremely short-sighted; it is part of her system; so do you mind my looking at you through my glasses?

CECILY: Oh! not at all, Gwendolen. I am very fond of being looked at.

GWENDOLEN: [*after examining Cecily carefully through a lorgnette*]: You are here on a short visit I suppose.

CECILY: Oh no! I live here.

GWENDOLEN [*severely*]: Really? Your mother, no doubt, or some female relative of advanced years, resides here also?

CECILY: Oh no! I have no mother, nor, in fact, any relations.

GWENDOLEN: Indeed?

CECILY: My dear guardian, with the assistance of Miss Prism, has the arduous task of looking after me.

GWENDOLEN: Your guardian?

CECILY: Yes, I am Mr Worthing's ward.

GWENDOLEN: Oh! It is strange he never mentioned to me that he had a ward. How secretive of him! He grows more interesting hourly. I am not sure, however, that the news inspires me with feelings of unmixed delight. [*Rising and going to her.*] I am very fond of you, Cecily; I have liked you ever since I met you! But I am bound to state that now that I know that you are Mr Worthing's ward, I cannot help expressing a wish you were—well just a little older than you seem to be—and not quite so very alluring in appearance. In fact, if I may speak candidly—

CECILY: Pray do! I think that whenever one has anything unpleasant to say, one should always be quite candid.

GWENDOLEN: Well, to speak with perfect candour, Cecily, I wish that you were fully forty-two, and more than usually plain for your age. Ernest has a strong upright nature. He is the very soul of truth and honour. Disloyalty would be as impossible to him as deception. But even men of the noblest possible moral character are extremely susceptible to the influence of the physical charms of others. Modern, no less than Ancient History, supplies us with many most painful examples of what I refer to. If it were not so, indeed, History would be quite unreadable.

CECILY: I beg your pardon, Gwendolen, did you say Ernest?

GWENDOLEN: Yes.

CECILY: Oh, but it is not Mr Ernest Worthing who is my guardian. It is his brother—his elder brother.

GWENDOLEN [sitting down again]: Ernest never mentioned to me that he had a brother.

CECILY: I am sorry to say they have not been on good terms for a long time.

GWENDOLEN: Ah! that accounts for it. And now that I think of it I have never heard any man mention his brother. The subject seems distasteful to most men. Cecily, you have lifted a load from my mind. I was growing almost anxious. It would have been terrible if any cloud had come across a friendship like ours, would it not? Of course you are quite, quite sure that it is not Mr Ernest Worthing who is your guardian?

CECILY: Quite sure. [A pause.] In fact, I am going to be his.

GWENDOLEN [enquiringly]: I beg your pardon?

CECILY [rather shy and confidingly]: Dearest Gwendolen, there is no reason why I should make a secret of it to you. Our little county newspaper is sure to chronicle the fact next week. Mr Ernest Worthing and I are engaged to be married.

GWENDOLEN [quite politely, rising]: My darling Cecily, I think there must be some slight error. Mr Ernest Worthing is engaged to me. The announcement will appear in the "Morning Post" on Saturday at the latest.

CECILY [very politely, rising]: I am afraid you must be under some misconception. Ernest proposed to me exactly ten minutes ago. [Shows diary.]

GWENDOLEN [examines diary through her lorgnette carefully]: It is certainly very curious, for he asked me to be his wife yesterday afternoon at 5.30. If you would care to verify the incident, pray do so. [Produces diary of her own.] I never travel without my diary. One should always have something sensational to read in the train. I am so sorry, dear Cecily, if it is any disappointment to you, but I am afraid I have the prior claim.

CECILY: It would distress me more than I can tell you, dear Gwendolen, if it caused you any mental or physical anguish, but I feel bound to point out that since Ernest proposed to you he clearly has changed his mind.

GWENDOLEN [meditatively]: If the poor fellow has been entrapped into any foolish promise I shall consider it my duty to rescue him at once, and with a firm hand.

CECILY [thoughtfully and sadly]: Whatever unfortunate entanglement my dear boy may have got into, I will never reproach him with it after we are married.

GWENDOLEN: Do you allude to me, Miss Cardew, as an entanglement? You are presumptuous. On an occasion of this kind it becomes more than a moral duty to speak one's mind. It becomes a pleasure.

CECILY: Do you suggest, Miss Fairfax, that I entrapped Ernest into an engagement? How dare you? This is no time for wearing the shallow mask of manners. When I see a spade I call it a spade.

GWENDOLEN [*satirically*]: I am glad to say that I have never seen a spade. It is obvious that our social spheres have been widely different.

[*Enter Merriman, followed by the footman. He carries a salver, table cloth, and plate stand. Cecily is about to retort. The presence of the servants exercises a restraining influence, under which both girls chafe.*]

MERRIMAN: Shall I lay tea here as usual, Miss?

CECILY [*sternly, in a calm voice*]: Yes, as usual.

[*Merriman begins to clear table and lay cloth. A long pause. Cecily and Gwendolen glare at each other.*]

GWENDOLEN: Are there many interesting walks in the vicinity, Miss Cardew?

CECILY: Oh! yes! a great many. From the top of one of the hills quite close one can see five counties.

GWENDOLEN: Five counties! I don't think I should like that. I hate crowds.

CECILY [*sweetly*]: I suppose that is why you live in town?

[*Gwendolen bites her lip, and beats her foot nervously with her parasol.*]

GWENDOLEN [*looking round*]: Quite a well-kept garden this is, Miss Cardew.

CECILY: So glad you like it, Miss Fairfax.

GWENDOLEN: I had no idea there were any flowers in the country.

CECILY: Oh, flowers are as common here, Miss Fairfax, as people are in London.

GWENDOLEN: Personally, I cannot understand how anybody manages to exist in the country, if anybody who is anybody does. The country always bores me to death.

CECILY: Ah! This is what the newspapers call agricultural depression,[8] is it not? I believe the aristocracy are suffering very much from it just at present. It is almost an epidemic amongst them, I have been told. May I offer you some tea, Miss Fairfax?

GWENDOLEN [*with elaborate politeness*]: Thank you. [*Aside.*] Detestable girl! But I require tea!

CECILY [*sweetly*]: Sugar?

GWENDOLEN [*superciliously*]: No, thank you. Sugar is not fashionable any more.

[*Cecily looks angrily at her, takes up the tongs and puts four lumps of sugar into the cup.*]

CECILY [*severely*]: Cake or bread and butter?

GWENDOLEN [*in a bored manner*]: Bread and butter, please. Cake is rarely seen at the best houses nowadays.

CECILY [*cuts a very large slice of cake, and puts it on the tray*]: Hand that to Miss Fairfax.

[*Merriman does so, and goes out with footman. Gwendolen drinks the tea and makes a grimace. Puts down cup at once, reaches out her hand to the bread and butter, looks at it, and finds it is cake. Rises in indignation.*]

GWENDOLEN: You have filled my tea with lumps of sugar, and though I asked most distinctly for bread and butter, you have given me cake. I am known for the

---

8. A pun on the word "depression"; beginning in the 1870s, British agriculture had been in a slump, causing losses and hardship among landowners.

gentleness of my disposition, and the extraordinary sweetness of my nature, but I warn you, Miss Cardew, you may go too far.

CECILY [*rising*]: To save my poor, innocent, trusting boy from the machinations of any other girl there are no lengths to which I would not go.

GWENDOLEN: From the moment I saw you I distrusted you. I felt that you were false and deceitful. I am never deceived in such matters. My first impressions of people are invariably right.

CECILY: It seems to me, Miss Fairfax, that I am trespassing on your valuable time. No doubt you have many other calls of a similar character to make in the neighbourhood.
     [*Enter Jack.*]

GWENDOLEN [*catching sight of him*]: Ernest! My own Ernest!

JACK: Gwendolen! Darling! [*Offers to kiss her.*]

GWENDOLEN [*drawing back*]: A moment! May I ask if you are engaged to be married to this young lady? [*Points to Cecily.*]

JACK [*laughing*]: To dear little Cecily! Of course not! What could have put such an idea into your pretty little head?

GWENDOLEN: Thank you. You may! [*Offers her cheek.*]

CECILY [*very sweetly*]: I knew there must be some misunderstanding, Miss Fairfax. The gentleman whose arm is at present round your waist is my dear guardian, Mr John Worthing.

GWENDOLEN: I beg your pardon?

CECILY: This is Uncle Jack.

GWENDOLEN [*receding*]: Jack! Oh!
     [*Enter Algernon.*]

CECILY: Here is Ernest.

ALGERNON [*goes straight over to Cecily without noticing anyone else*]: My own love!
     [*Offers to kiss her.*]

CECILY [*drawing back*]: A moment, Ernest! May I ask you—are you engaged to be married to this young lady?

ALGERNON [*looking round*]: To what young lady? Good heavens! Gwendolen!

CECILY: Yes, to good heavens, Gwendolen, I mean to Gwendolen.

ALGERNON [*laughing*]: Of course not! What could have put such an idea into your pretty little head?

CECILY: Thank you. [*Presenting her cheek to be kissed.*] You may.
     [*Algernon kisses her.*]

GWENDOLEN: I felt there was some slight error, Miss Cardew. The gentleman who is now embracing you is my cousin, Mr Algernon Moncrieff.

CECILY [*breaking away from Algernon*]: Algernon Moncrieff! Oh!
     [*The two girls move towards each other and put their arms round each other's waists as if for protection.*]

CECILY: Are you called Algernon?

ALGERNON: I cannot deny it.

CECILY: Oh!

GWENDOLEN: Is your name really John?

JACK [*standing rather proudly*]: I could deny it if I liked. I could deny anything if I liked. But my name certainly is John. It has been John for years.

CECILY [*to Gwendolen*]: A gross deception has been practised on both of us.

GWENDOLEN: My poor wounded Cecily!

CECILY: My sweet wronged Gwendolen!

GWENDOLEN [*slowly and seriously*]: You will call me sister, will you not?
  [*They embrace. Jack and Algernon groan and walk up and down.*]
CECILY [*rather brightly*]: There is just one question I would like to be allowed to
  ask my guardian.
GWENDOLEN: An admirable idea! Mr Worthing, there is just one question I
  would like to be permitted to put to you. Where is your brother Ernest? We are
  both engaged to be married to your brother Ernest, so it is a matter of some importance to us to know where your brother Ernest is at present.
JACK [*slowly and hesitatingly*]: Gwendolen—Cecily—It is very painful for me to be
  forced to speak the truth. It is the first time in my life that I have ever been reduced to such a painful position, and I am really quite inexperienced in doing anything of the kind. However I will tell you quite frankly that I have no brother
  Ernest. I have no brother at all. I never had a brother in my life, and I certainly
  have not the smallest intention of ever having one in the future.
CECILY [*surprised*]: No brother at all?
JACK [*cheerily*]: None!
GWENDOLEN [*severely*]: Had you never a brother of any kind?
JACK [*pleasantly*]: Never. Not even of any kind.
GWENDOLEN: I am afraid it is quite clear, Cecily, that neither of us is engaged to
  be married to anyone.
CECILY: It is not a very pleasant position for a young girl suddenly to find herself
  in. Is it?
GWENDOLEN: Let us go into the house. They will hardly venture to come after us
  there.
CECILY: No, men are so cowardly, aren't they?
  [*They retire into the house with scornful looks.*]
JACK: This ghastly state of things is what you call Bunburying, I suppose?
ALGERNON: Yes, and a perfectly wonderful Bunbury it is. The most wonderful
  Bunbury I have ever had in my life.
JACK: Well, you've no right whatsoever to Bunbury here.
ALGERNON: That is absurd. One has a right to Bunbury anywhere one chooses.
  Every serious Bunburyist knows that.
JACK: Serious Bunburyist! Good heavens!
ALGERNON: Well, one must be serious about something, if one wants to have any
  amusement in life. I happen to be serious about Bunburying. What on earth you
  are serious about I haven't got the remotest idea. About everything, I should
  fancy. You have such an absolutely trivial nature.
JACK: Well, the only small satisfaction I have in the whole of this wretched business
  is that your friend Bunbury is quite exploded. You won't be able to run down to the
  country quite so often as you used to do, dear Algy. And a very good thing too.
ALGERNON: Your brother is a little off colour, isn't he, dear Jack? You won't be
  able to disappear to London quite so frequently as your wicked custom was. And
  not a bad thing either.
JACK: As for your conduct towards Miss Cardew, I must say that your taking in a
  sweet, simple, innocent girl like that is quite inexcusable. To say nothing of the
  fact that she is my ward.
ALGERNON: I can see no possible defence at all for your deceiving a brilliant,
  clever, thoroughly experienced young lady like Miss Fairfax. To say nothing of the
  fact that she is my cousin.

JACK: I wanted to be engaged to Gwendolen, that is all. I love her.

ALGERNON: Well, I simply wanted to be engaged to Cecily. I adore her.

JACK: There is certainly no chance of your marrying Miss Cardew.

ALGERNON: I don't think there is much likelihood, Jack, of you and Miss Fairfax being united.

JACK: Well, that is no business of yours.

ALGERNON: If it was my business, I wouldn't talk about it. [*Begins to eat muffins.*] It is very vulgar to talk about one's business. Only people like stockbrokers do that, and then merely at dinner parties.

JACK: How you can sit there, calmly eating muffins when we are in this horrible trouble, I can't make out. You seem to me to be perfectly heartless.

ALGERNON: Well, I can't eat muffins in an agitated manner. The butter would probably get on my cuffs. One should always eat muffins quite calmly. It is the only way to eat them.

JACK: I say it's perfectly heartless your eating muffins at all, under the circumstances.

ALGERNON: When I am in trouble, eating is the only thing that consoles me. Indeed, when I am in really great trouble, as anyone who knows me intimately will tell you, I refuse everything except food and drink. At the present moment I am eating muffins because I am unhappy. Besides, I am particularly fond of muffins. [*Rising.*]

JACK [*rising*]: Well, that is no reason why you should eat them all in that greedy way.
  [*Takes muffins from Algernon.*]

ALGERNON [*offering tea-cake*]: I wish you would have tea-cake instead. I don't like tea-cake.

JACK: Good heavens! I suppose a man may eat his own muffins in his own garden.

ALGERNON: But you have just said it was perfectly heartless to eat muffins.

JACK: I said it was perfectly heartless of you, under the circumstances. That is a very different thing.

ALGERNON: That may be. But the muffins are the same. [*He seizes the muffin-dish from Jack.*]

JACK: Algy, I wish to goodness you would go.

ALGERNON: You can't possibly ask me to go without having some dinner. It's absurd. I never go without my dinner. No one ever does, except vegetarians and people like that. Besides I have just made arrangements with Dr Chasuble to be christened at a quarter to six under the name of Ernest.

JACK: My dear fellow, the sooner you give up that nonsense the better. I made arrangements this morning with Dr Chasuble to be christened myself at 5.30, and I naturally will take the name of Ernest. Gwendolen would wish it. We can't both be christened Ernest. It's absurd. Besides, I have a perfect right to be christened if I like. There is no evidence at all that I ever have been christened by anybody. I should think it extremely probable I never was, and so does Dr Chasuble. It is entirely different in your case. You have been christened already.

ALGERNON: Yes, but I have not been christened for years.

JACK: Yes, but you have been christened. That is the important thing.

ALGERNON: Quite so. So I know my constitution can stand it. If you are not quite sure about your ever having been christened, I must say I think it rather dangerous your venturing on it now. It might make you very unwell. You can hardly have forgotten that someone very closely connected with you was very nearly carried off this week in Paris by a severe chill.

JACK: Yes, but you said yourself that a severe chill was not hereditary.

ALGERNON: It usen't to be, I know—but I daresay it is now. Science is always making wonderful improvements in things.

JACK [*picking up the muffin-dish*]: Oh, that is nonsense; you are always talking nonsense.

ALGERNON: Jack, you are at the muffins again! I wish you wouldn't. There are only two left. [*Takes them.*] I told you I was particularly fond of muffins.

JACK: But I hate tea-cake.

ALGERNON: Why on earth then do you allow tea-cake to be served up for your guests? What ideas you have of hospitality!

JACK: Algernon! I have already told you to go. I don't want you here. Why don't you go!

ALGERNON: I haven't quite finished my tea yet! and there is still one muffin left.
[*Jack groans, and sinks into a chair. Algernon still continues eating.*]   ACT DROP

THIRD ACT

SCENE: *Morning-room*[9] *at the Manor House.*

[*Gwendolen and Cecily are at the window, looking out into the garden.*]

GWENDOLEN: The fact that they did not follow us at once into the house, as anyone else would have done, seems to me to show that they have some sense of shame left.

CECILY: They have been eating muffins. That looks like repentance.

GWENDOLEN [*after a pause*]: They don't seem to notice us at all. Couldn't you cough?

CECILY: But I haven't got a cough.

GWENDOLEN: They're looking at us. What effrontery!

CECILY: They're approaching. That's very forward of them.

GWENDOLEN: Let us preserve a dignified silence.

CECILY: Certainly. It's the only thing to do now.
[*Enter Jack followed by Algernon. They whistle some dreadful popular air from a British Opera.*][1]

GWENDOLEN: This dignified silence seems to produce an unpleasant effect.

CECILY: A most distasteful one.

GWENDOLEN: But we will not be the first to speak.

CECILY: Certainly not.

GWENDOLEN: Mr Worthing, I have something very particular to ask you. Much depends on your reply.

CECILY: Gwendolen, your common sense is invaluable. Mr Moncrieff, kindly answer me the following question. Why did you pretend to be my guardian's brother?

ALGERNON: In order that I might have an opportunity of meeting you.

CECILY [*to Gwendolen*]: That certainly seems a satisfactory explanation, does it not?

---

9. An informal room for receiving morning calls from friends (afternoon visitors were received in the formal drawing room).

1. Probably a reference to Gilbert and Sullivan, who had made fun of Wilde and the Aesthetic movement in *Patience* (1881).

GWENDOLEN: Yes, dear, if you can believe him.

CECILY: I don't. But that does not affect the wonderful beauty of his answer.

GWENDOLEN: True. In matters of grave importance, style, not sincerity is the vital thing. Mr Worthing, what explanation can you offer to me for pretending to have a brother? Was it in order that you might have an opportunity of coming up to town to see me as often as possible?

JACK: Can you doubt it, Miss Fairfax?

GWENDOLEN: I have the gravest doubts upon the subject. But I intend to crush them. This is not the moment for German scepticism.[2] [*Moving to Cecily.*] Their explanations appear to be quite satisfactory, especially Mr Worthing's. That seems to me to have the stamp of truth upon it.

CECILY: I am more than content with what Mr Moncrieff said. His voice alone inspires one with absolute credulity.

GWENDOLEN: Then you think we should forgive them?

CECILY: Yes. I mean no.

GWENDOLEN: True! I had forgotten. There are principles at stake that one cannot surrender. Which of us should tell them? The task is not a pleasant one.

CECILY: Could we not both speak at the same time?

GWENDOLEN: An excellent idea! I nearly always speak at the same time as other people. Will you take the time from me?

CECILY: Certainly.

[*Gwendolen beats time with uplifted finger.*]

GWENDOLEN AND CECILY [*speaking together*]: Your Christian names are still an insuperable barrier. That is all!

JACK AND ALGERNON [*speaking together*]: Our Christian names! Is that all? But we are going to be christened this afternoon.

GWENDOLEN [*to Jack*]: For my sake you are prepared to do this terrible thing?

JACK: I am.

CECILY [*to Algernon*]: To please me you are ready to face this fearful ordeal?

ALGERNON: I am!

GWENDOLEN: How absurd to talk of the equality of the sexes! Where questions of self-sacrifice are concerned, men are infinitely beyond us.

JACK: We are. [*Clasps hands with Algernon.*]

CECILY: They have moments of physical courage of which we women know absolutely nothing.

GWENDOLEN [*to Jack*]: Darling!

ALGERNON [*to Cecily*]: Darling! [*They fall into each other's arms.*]

[*Enter Merriman. When he enters he coughs loudly, seeing the situation.*]

MERRIMAN: Ahem! Ahem! Lady Bracknell!

JACK: Good heavens!

[*Enter Lady Bracknell. The couples separate in alarm.*] [*Exit Merriman.*]

LADY BRACKNELL: Gwendolen! What does this mean?

GWENDOLEN: Merely that I am engaged to be married to Mr Worthing, mamma.

LADY BRACKNELL: Come here. Sit down. Sit down immediately. Hesitation of any kind is a sign of mental decay in the young, of physical weakness in the old. [*Turns to Jack.*] Apprised, sir, of my daughter's sudden flight by her trusty maid, whose confidence I purchased by means of a small coin, I followed her at once by

---

2. Many 19th-century German scholars were skeptical in their treatment of religious texts.

a luggage train. Her unhappy father is, I am glad to say, under the impression that she is attending a more than usually lengthy lecture by the University Extension Scheme on the Influence of a permanent income on Thought. I do not propose to undeceive him. Indeed I have never undeceived him on any question. I would consider it wrong. But of course, you will clearly understand that all communication between yourself and my daughter must cease immediately from this moment. On this point, as indeed on all points, I am firm.

JACK: I am engaged to be married to Gwendolen, Lady Bracknell!

LADY BRACKNELL: You are nothing of the kind, sir. And now, as regards Algernon! . . . Algernon!

ALGERNON: Yes, Aunt Augusta.

LADY BRACKNELL: May I ask if it is in this house that your invalid friend Mr Bunbury resides?

ALGERNON [*stammering*]: Oh! No! Bunbury doesn't live here. Bunbury is somewhere else at present. In fact, Bunbury is dead.

LADY BRACKNELL: Dead! When did Mr Bunbury die? His death must have been extremely sudden.

ALGERNON [*airily*]: Oh! I killed Bunbury this afternoon. I mean poor Bunbury died this afternoon.

LADY BRACKNELL: What did he die of?

ALGERNON: Bunbury? Oh, he was quite exploded.

LADY BRACKNELL: Exploded! Was he the victim of a revolutionary outrage?[3] I was not aware that Mr Bunbury was interested in social legislation. If so, he is well punished for his morbidity.

ALGERNON: My dear Aunt Augusta, I mean he was found out! The doctors found out that Bunbury could not live, that is what I mean—so Bunbury died.

LADY BRACKNELL: He seems to have had great confidence in the opinion of his physicians. I am glad, however, that he made up his mind at the last to some definite course of action, and acted under proper medical advice. And now that we have finally got rid of this Mr Bunbury, may I ask, Mr Worthing, who is that young person whose hand my nephew Algernon is now holding in what seems to me a peculiarly unnecessary manner?

JACK: That lady is Miss Cecily Cardew, my ward.

[*Lady Bracknell bows coldly to Cecily.*]

ALGERNON: I am engaged to be married to Cecily, Aunt Augusta.

LADY BRACKNELL: I beg your pardon?

CECILY: Mr Moncrieff and I are engaged to be married, Lady Bracknell.

LADY BRACKNELL [*with a shiver, crossing to the sofa and sitting down*]: I do not know whether there is anything peculiarly exciting in the air of this particular part of Hertfordshire, but the number of engagements that go on seems to me considerably above the proper average that statistics have laid down for our guidance. I think some preliminary enquiry on my part would not be out of place. Mr Worthing, is Miss Cardew at all connected with any of the larger railway stations in London? I merely desire information. Until yesterday I had no idea that there were any families or persons whose origins was a Terminus.[4]

[*Jack looks perfectly furious, but restrains himself.*]

---

3. Anarchy and political assassination were much in the news; Wilde's earliest drama, *Vera, or the Nihilists* (1881),   dealt with the subject.
4. A railway station at the end of the line.

JACK [*in a clear, cold voice*]: Miss Cardew is the granddaughter of the late Mr Thomas Cardew of 149, Belgrave Square, S.W.; Gervase Park, Dorking, Surrey; and the Sporran, Fifeshire, N.B.[5]

LADY BRACKNELL: That sounds not unsatisfactory. Three addresses always inspire confidence, even in tradesmen. But what proof have I of their authenticity?

JACK: I have carefully preserved the Court Guides[6] of the period. They are open to your inspection, Lady Bracknell.

LADY BRACKNELL [*grimly*]: I have known strange errors in that publication.

JACK: Miss Cardew's family solicitors are Messrs Markby, Markby, and Markby.

LADY BRACKNELL: Markby, Markby, and Markby? A firm of the very highest position in their profession. Indeed I am told that one of the Mr Markbys is occasionally to be seen at dinner parties. So far I am satisfied.

JACK [*very irritably*]: How extremely kind of you, Lady Bracknell! I have also in my possession, you will be pleased to hear, certificates of Miss Cardew's birth, baptism, whooping cough, registration, vaccination, confirmation, and the measles; both the German and the English variety.

LADY BRACKNELL: Ah! A life crowded with incident, I see; though perhaps somewhat too exciting for a young girl. I am not myself in favour of premature experiences. [*Rises, looks at her watch.*] Gwendolen! the time approaches for our departure. We have not a moment to lose. As a matter of form, Mr Worthing, I had better ask you if Miss Cardew has any little fortune?

JACK: Oh! about a hundred and thirty thousand pounds in the Funds.[7] That is all. Goodbye, Lady Bracknell. So pleased to have seen you.

LADY BRACKNELL [*sitting down again*]: A moment, Mr Worthing. A hundred and thirty thousand pounds! And in the Funds! Miss Cardew seems to me a most attractive young lady, now that I look at her. Few girls of the present day have any really solid qualities, any of the qualities that last, and improve with time. We live, I regret to say, in an age of surfaces. [*To Cecily.*] Come over here, dear. [*Cecily goes across.*] Pretty child! your dress is sadly simple, and your hair seems almost as Nature might have left it. But we can soon alter all that. A thoroughly experienced French maid produces a really marvellous result in a very brief space of time. I remember recommending one to young Lady Lancing, and after three months her own husband did not know her.

JACK [*aside*]: And after six months nobody knew her.

LADY BRACKNELL [*glares at Jack for a few moments. Then bends, with a practised smile, to Cecily.*]: Kindly turn round, sweet child. [*Cecily turns completely round.*] No, the side view is what I want. [*Cecily presents her profile.*] Yes, quite as I expected. There are distinct social possibilities in your profile. The two weak points in our age are its want of principle and its want of profile. The chin a little higher, dear. Style largely depends on the way the chin is worn. They are worn very high, just at present. Algernon!

ALGERNON: Yes, Aunt Augusta!

LADY BRACKNELL: There are distinct social possibilities in Miss Cardew's profile.

ALGERNON: Cecily is the sweetest, dearest, prettiest girl in the whole world. And I don't care twopence about social possibilities.

---

5. North Britain, i.e., Scotland.
6. Annual publications listing the names and London addresses of the upper classes.

7. The Consolidated Funds, reliable interest-bearing government bonds.

LADY BRACKNELL: Never speak disrespectfully of Society, Algernon. Only people who can't get into it do that. [*To Cecily.*] Dear child, of course you know that Algernon has nothing but his debts to depend upon. But I do not approve of mercenary marriages. When I married Lord Bracknell I had no fortune of any kind. But I never dreamed for a moment of allowing that to stand in my way. Well, I suppose I must give my consent.

ALGERNON: Thank you, Aunt Augusta.

LADY BRACKNELL: Cecily, you may kiss me!

CECILY [*kisses her*]: Thank you, Lady Bracknell.

LADY BRACKNELL: You may also address me as Aunt Augusta for the future.

CECILY: Thank you, Aunt Augusta.

LADY BRACKNELL: The marriage, I think, had better take place quite soon.

ALGERNON: Thank you, Aunt Augusta.

CECILY: Thank you, Aunt Augusta.

LADY BRACKNELL: To speak frankly, I am not in favour of long engagements. They give people the opportunity of finding out each other's character before marriage, which I think is never advisable.

JACK: I beg your pardon for interrupting you, Lady Bracknell, but this engagement is quite out of the question. I am Miss Cardew's guardian, and she cannot marry without my consent until she comes of age. That consent I absolutely decline to give.

LADY BRACKNELL: Upon what grounds may I ask? Algernon is an extremely, I may almost say an ostentatiously, eligible young man. He has nothing, but he looks everything. What more can one desire?

JACK: It pains me very much to have to speak frankly to you, Lady Bracknell, about your nephew, but the fact is that I do not approve at all of his moral character. I suspect him of being untruthful.

[*Algernon and Cecily look at him in indignant amazement.*]

LADY BRACKNELL: Untruthful! My nephew Algernon? Impossible! He is an Oxonian.[8]

JACK: I fear there can be no possible doubt about the matter. This afternoon, during my temporary absence in London on an important question of romance, he obtained admission to my house by means of the false pretence of being my brother. Under an assumed name he drank, I've just been informed by my butler, an entire pint bottle of my Perrier-Jouet, Brut, '89; a wine I was specially reserving for myself. Continuing his disgraceful deception, he succeeded in the course of the afternoon in alienating the affections of my only ward. He subsequently stayed to tea, and devoured every single muffin. And what makes his conduct all the more heartless is, that he was perfectly well aware from the first that I have no brother, that I never had a brother, and that I don't intend to have a brother, not even of any kind. I distinctly told him so myself yesterday afternoon.

LADY BRACKNELL: Ahem! Mr Worthing, after careful consideration I have decided entirely to overlook my nephew's conduct to you.

JACK: That is very generous of you, Lady Bracknell. My own decision, however, is unalterable. I decline to give my consent.

LADY BRACKNELL [*to Cecily*]: Come here, sweet child. [*Cecily goes over.*] How old are you, dear?

8. I.e., he attended Oxford University.

CECILY: Well, I am really only eighteen, but I always admit to twenty when I go to evening parties.

LADY BRACKNELL: You are perfectly right in making some slight alteration. Indeed, no woman should ever be quite accurate about her age. It looks so calculating. . . . [*In a meditative manner.*] Eighteen, but admitting to twenty at evening parties. Well, it will not be very long before you are of age and free from the restraints of tutelage. So I don't think your guardian's consent is, after all, a matter of any importance.

JACK: Pray excuse me, Lady Bracknell, for interrupting you again, but it is only fair to tell you that according to the terms of her grandfather's will Miss Cardew does not come legally of age till she is thirty-five.

LADY BRACKNELL: That does not seem to me to be a grave objection. Thirty-five is a very attractive age. London society is full of women of the very highest birth who have, of their own free choice, remained thirty-five for years. Lady Dumbleton is an instance in point. To my own knowledge she has been thirty-five ever since she arrived at the age of forty, which was many years ago now. I see no reason why our dear Cecily should not be even still more attractive at the age you mention than she is at present. There will be a large accumulation of property.

CECILY: Algy, could you wait for me till I was thirty-five?

ALGERNON: Of course I could, Cecily. You know I could.

CECILY: Yes, I felt it instinctively, but I couldn't wait all that time. I hate waiting even five minutes for anybody. It always makes me rather cross. I am not punctual myself, I know, but I do like punctuality in others, and waiting, even to be married, is quite out of the question.

ALGERNON: Then what is to be done, Cecily?

CECILY: I don't know, Mr Moncrieff.

LADY BRACKNELL: My dear Mr Worthing, as Miss Cardew states positively that she cannot wait till she is thirty-five—a remark which I am bound to say seems to me to show a somewhat impatient nature—I would beg of you to reconsider your decision.

JACK: But my dear Lady Bracknell, the matter is entirely in your own hands. The moment you consent to my marriage with Gwendolen, I will most gladly allow your nephew to form an alliance with my ward.

LADY BRACKNELL [*rising and drawing herself up*]: You must be quite aware that what you propose is out of the question.

JACK: Then a passionate celibacy is all that any of us can look forward to.

LADY BRACKNELL: That is not the destiny I propose for Gwendolen. Algernon, of course, can choose for himself. [*Pulls out her watch.*] Come, dear; [*Gwendolen rises.*] we have already missed five, if not six, trains. To miss any more might expose us to comment on the platform.

    [*Enter Dr Chasuble.*]

CHASUBLE: Everything is quite ready for the christenings.

LADY BRACKNELL: The christenings, sir! Is not that somewhat premature?

CHASUBLE [*looking rather puzzled, and pointing to Jack and Algernon*]: Both these gentlemen have expressed a desire for immediate baptism.

LADY BRACKNELL: At their age? The idea is grotesque and irreligious! Algernon, I forbid you to be baptized. I will not hear of such excesses. Lord Bracknell would be highly displeased if he learned that that was the way in which you wasted your time and money.

CHASUBLE: Am I to understand then that there are to be no christenings at all this afternoon?

JACK: I don't think that, as things are now, it would be of much practical value to either of us, Dr Chasuble.

CHASUBLE: I am grieved to hear such sentiments from you, Mr Worthing. They savour of the heretical views of the Anabaptists,[9] views that I have completely refuted in four of my unpublished sermons. However, as your present mood seems to be one peculiarly secular, I will return to the church at once. Indeed, I have just been informed by the pew-opener[1] that for the last hour and a half Miss Prism has been waiting for me in the vestry.

LADY BRACKNELL [starting]: Miss Prism! Did I hear you mention a Miss Prism?

CHASUBLE: Yes, Lady Bracknell. I am on my way to join her.

LADY BRACKNELL: Pray allow me to detain you for a moment. This matter may prove to be one of vital importance to Lord Bracknell and myself. Is this Miss Prism a female of repellent aspect, remotely connected with education?

CHASUBLE [somewhat indignantly]: She is the most cultivated of ladies, and the very picture of respectability.

LADY BRACKNELL: It is obviously the same person. May I ask what position she holds in your household?

CHASUBLE [severely]: I am a celibate, madam.

JACK [interposing]: Miss Prism, Lady Bracknell, has been for the last three years Miss Cardew's esteemed governess and valued companion.

LADY BRACKNELL: In spite of what I hear of her, I must see her at once. Let her be sent for.

CHASUBLE [looking off]: She approaches; she is nigh.

[Enter Miss Prism hurriedly.]

MISS PRISM: I was told you expected me in the vestry, dear Canon. I have been waiting for you there for an hour and three quarters. [Catches sight of Lady Bracknell who has fixed her with a stony glare. Miss Prism grows pale and quails. She looks anxiously round as if desirous to escape.]

LADY BRACKNELL [in a severe, judicial voice]: Prism! [Miss Prism bows her head in shame.] Come here, Prism! [Miss Prism approaches in a humble manner.] Prism! Where is that baby? [General consternation. The Canon starts back in horror. Algernon and Jack pretend to be anxious to shield Cecily and Gwendolen from hearing the details of a terrible public scandal.] Twenty-eight years ago, Prism, you left Lord Bracknell's house, Number 104, Upper Grosvenor Street, in charge of a perambulator that contained a baby, of the male sex. You never returned. A few weeks later, through the elaborate investigations of the Metropolitan police, the perambulator was discovered at midnight, standing by itself in a remote corner of Bayswater.[2] It contained the manuscript of a three-volume novel of more than usually revolting sentimentality. [Miss Prism starts in involuntary indignation.] But the baby was not there! [Everyone looks at Miss Prism.] Prism! Where is that baby? [A pause.]

MISS PRISM: Lady Bracknell, I admit with shame that I do not know. I only wish I did. The plain facts of the case are these. On the morning of the day you mention, a day that is for ever branded on my memory, I prepared as usual to take the baby

---

9. A 16th-century Protestant sect that believed in adult baptism.
1. Usher.

2. An area in the West End of London, near Kensington Gardens.

out in its perambulator. I had also with me a somewhat old, but capacious hand-bag in which I had intended to place the manuscript of a work of fiction that I had written during my few unoccupied hours. In a moment of mental abstraction, for which I never can forgive myself, I deposited the manuscript in the bassinette, and placed the baby in the hand-bag.

JACK [who has been listening attentively]: But where did you deposit the hand-bag?

MISS PRISM: Do not ask me, Mr Worthing.

JACK: Miss Prism, this is a matter of no small importance to me. I insist on knowing where you deposited the hand-bag that contained that infant.

MISS PRISM: I left it in the cloak-room of one of the larger railway stations in London.

JACK: What railway station?

MISS PRISM [quite crushed]: Victoria. The Brighton line. [Sinks into a chair.]

JACK: I must retire to my room for a moment. Gwendolen, wait here for me.

GWENDOLEN: If you are not too long, I will wait here for you all my life.

[Exit Jack in great excitement.]

CHASUBLE: What do you think this means, Lady Bracknell?

LADY BRACKNELL: I dare not even suspect, Dr Chasuble. I need hardly tell you that in families of high position strange coincidences are not supposed to occur. They are hardly considered the thing.

[Noises heard overhead as if someone was throwing trunks about. Everyone looks up.]

CECILY: Uncle Jack seems strangely agitated.

CHASUBLE: Your guardian has a very emotional nature.

LADY BRACKNELL: This noise is extremely unpleasant. It sounds as if he was having an argument. I dislike arguments of any kind. They are always vulgar, and often convincing.

CHASUBLE [looking up]: It has stopped now. [The noise is redoubled.]

LADY BRACKNELL: I wish he would arrive at some conclusion.

GWENDOLEN: This suspense is terrible. I hope it will last.

[Enter Jack with a hand-bag of black leather in his hand.]

JACK [rushing over to Miss Prism]: Is this the hand-bag, Miss Prism? Examine it carefully before you speak. The happiness of more than one life depends on your answer.

MISS PRISM [calmly]: It seems to be mine. Yes, here is the injury it received through the upsetting of a Gower Street omnibus in younger and happier days. Here is the stain on the lining caused by the explosion of a temperance beverage, an incident that occurred at Leamington. And here, on the lock, are my initials. I had forgotten that in an extravagant mood I had had them placed there. The bag is undoubtedly mine. I am delighted to have it so unexpectedly restored to me. It has been a great inconvenience being without it all these years.

JACK [in a pathetic voice]: Miss Prism, more is restored to you than this hand-bag. I was the baby you placed in it.

MISS PRISM [amazed]: You?

JACK [embracing her]: Yes . . . mother!

MISS PRISM [recoiling in indignant astonishment]: Mr Worthing! I am unmarried!

JACK: Unmarried! I do not deny that is a serious blow. But after all, who has the right to cast a stone against one who has suffered?[3] Cannot repentance wipe out an act of folly? Why should there be one law for men, and another for women? Mother, I forgive you. [Tries to embrace her again.]

---

3. Jesus saves a woman who is about to be stoned for committing adultery, saying, "He that is without sin among you, let him first cast a stone at her" (John 8.7).

MISS PRISM [*still more indignant*]: Mr Worthing, there is some error. [*Pointing to Lady Bracknell.*] There is the lady who can tell you who you really are.

JACK [*after a pause*]: Lady Bracknell, I hate to seem inquisitive, but would you kindly inform me who I am?

LADY BRACKNELL: I am afraid that the news I have to give you will not altogether please you. You are the son of my poor sister, Mrs Moncrieff, and consequently Algernon's elder brother.

JACK: Algy's elder brother! Then I have a brother after all. I knew I had a brother! I always said I had a brother! Cecily—how could you have ever doubted that I had a brother. [*Seizes hold of Algernon.*] Dr Chasuble, my unfortunate brother. Miss Prism, my unfortunate brother. Gwendolen, my unfortunate brother. Algy, you young scoundrel, you will have to treat me with more respect in the future. You have never behaved to me like a brother in all your life.

ALGERNON: Well, not till today, old boy, I admit. I did my best, however, though I was out of practice. [*Shakes hands.*]

GWENDOLEN [*to Jack*]: My own! But what own are you? What is your Christian name, now that you have become someone else?

JACK: Good heavens! . . . I had quite forgotten that point. Your decision on the subject of my name is irrevocable, I suppose?

GWENDOLEN: I never change, except in my affections.

CECILY: What a noble nature you have, Gwendolen!

JACK: Then the question had better be cleared up at once. Aunt Augusta, a moment. At the time when Miss Prism left me in the hand-bag, had I been christened already?

LADY BRACKNELL: Every luxury that money could buy, including christening, had been lavished on you by your fond and doting parents.

JACK: Then I was christened! That is settled. Now, what name was I given? Let me know the worst.

LADY BRACKNELL: Being the eldest son you were naturally christened after your father.

JACK [*irritably*]: Yes, but what was my father's Christian name?

LADY BRACKNELL [*meditatively*]: I cannot at the present moment recall what the General's Christian name was. But I have no doubt he had one. He was eccentric, I admit. But only in later years. And that was the result of the Indian climate, and marriage, and indigestion, and other things of that kind.

JACK: Algy! Can't you recollect what our father's Christian name was?

ALGERNON: My dear boy, we were never even on speaking terms. He died before I was a year old.

JACK: His name would appear in the Army Lists of the period, I suppose, Aunt Augusta?

LADY BRACKNELL: The General was essentially a man of peace, except in his domestic life. But I have no doubt his name would appear in any military directory.

JACK: The Army Lists of the last forty years are here. These delightful records should have been my constant study. [*Rushes to bookcase and tears the books out.*] M. Generals . . . Mallam, Maxbohm,[4] Magley, what ghastly names they have— Markby, Migsby, Mobbs, Moncrieff! Lieutenant 1840, Captain, Lieutenant-Colonel, Colonel, General 1869, Christian names, Ernest John. [*Puts book very quietly down and speaks quite calmly.*] I always told you, Gwendolen, my name was Ernest, didn't I? Well, it is Ernest after all. I mean it naturally is Ernest.

---

4. A pun on the name of Wilde's friend Max Beerbohm.

LADY BRACKNELL: Yes, I remember now that the General was called Ernest. I knew I had some particular reason for disliking the name.

GWENDOLEN: Ernest! My own Ernest! I felt from the first that you could have no other name!

JACK: Gwendolen, it is a terrible thing for a man to find out suddenly that all his life he has been speaking nothing but the truth. Can you forgive me?

GWENDOLEN: I can. For I feel that you are sure to change.

JACK: My own one!

CHASUBLE [to Miss Prism]: Laetitia! [Embraces her.]

MISS PRISM [enthusiastically]: Frederick! At last!

ALGERNON: Cecily! [Embraces her.] At last!

JACK: Gwendolen! [Embraces her.] At last!

LADY BRACKNELL: My nephew, you seem to be displaying signs of triviality.

JACK: On the contrary, Aunt Augusta, I've now realized for the first time in my life the vital Importance of Being Earnest.

TABLEAU

1894, performed 1895

CURTAIN
1899

Aphorisms[1]

[On arriving in America] I have nothing to declare except my genius.

F. Harris, Oscar Wilde

We have really everything in common with America nowadays, except, of course, language.

The Canterville Ghost

A poet can survive everything but a misprint.

The Children of the Poets

Meredith is a prose Browning, and so is Browning. He used poetry as a medium for writing in prose.

The Critic as Artist

Anybody can make history. Only a great man can write it.

Ibid.

The one duty we owe to history is to rewrite it.

Ibid.

A little sincerity is a dangerous thing, and a great deal of it is absolutely fatal.

Ibid.

---

1. Wilde's aphorisms often cleverly invert a cliché in order to produce a seeming paradox; they are perhaps his most characteristic form of expression in his conversation and writing alike. Wilde kept track of his favorite maxims, sometimes revising them in later works. In addition to the epigrammatic preface to *Dorian Gray*, he published two selections: *A Few Maxims for the Instruction of the Over-Educated* appeared anonymously in the *Saturday Review* in November 1894; *Phrases and Philosophies for the Use of the Young* was published in *The Chameleon* in December 1894.

There is only one thing in the world worse than being talked about, and that is not being talked about.

The Picture of Dorian Gray

Being natural is simply a pose, and the most irritating pose I know.

Ibid.

A man cannot be too careful in the choice of his enemies.

Ibid.

American girls are as clever at concealing their parents, as English women are at concealing their past.

Ibid.

Perhaps, after all, America never has been discovered. I myself would say that it had merely been detected.

Ibid.

Women give to men the very gold of their lives. But they invariably want it back in such very small change.

Ibid.

I hate vulgar realism in literature. The man who could call a spade a spade should be compelled to use one. It is the only thing he is fit for.

Ibid.

It is better to be beautiful than to be good. But . . . it is better to be good than to be ugly.

Ibid.

I can resist everything except temptation.

Lady Windermere's Fan

It's most dangerous nowadays for a husband to pay any attention to his wife in public. It always makes people think that he beats her when they're alone.

Ibid.

We are all in the gutter, but some of us are looking at the stars.

Ibid.

In this world there are only two tragedies. One is not getting what one wants, and the other is getting it.

Ibid.

What is a cynic? A man who knows the price of everything and the value of nothing.

Ibid.

Experience is the name everyone gives to their mistakes.

Ibid.

Repentance is quite out of date. And besides, if a woman really repents, she has to go to a bad dressmaker, otherwise no one believes in her.

Ibid.

It is perfectly monstrous the way people go about, nowadays, saying things against one behind one's back that are absolutely and entirely true.

A Woman of No Importance

The youth of America is their oldest tradition. It has been going on now for three hundred years.

Ibid.

The English country gentleman galloping after a fox—the unspeakable in full pursuit of the uneatable.

Ibid.

Twenty years of romance make a woman look like a ruin; but twenty years of marriage make her look like a public building.

Ibid.

One should never trust a woman who tells one her real age. A woman who would tell one that, would tell one anything.

Ibid.

The first duty in life is to be as artificial as possible. What the second duty is no one has as yet discovered.

Phrases and Philosophies for the Use of the Young

To love oneself is the beginning of a lifelong romance.

Ibid.

My wallpaper and I are fighting a duel to the death. One or the other of us has to go.

Richard Ellmann, *Oscar Wilde*

from **De Profundis**[1]

[January–March 1897]

H.M. Prison, Reading

Dear Bosie, After long and fruitless waiting I have determined to write to you myself, as much for your sake as for mine, as I would not like to think that I had

---

1. "Out of the depths" [have I cried unto thee, O Lord] (Latin), the first words of Psalm 130. While imprisoned in Reading Gaol, Wilde was allowed pen and paper only to write letters. He thus composed a meditation on his life in the form of a long letter to Lord Alfred Douglas (nicknamed Bosie), written from January to March 1897. Wilde referred to the text as "Epistola: In Carcere et Vinculis" (Letter: In Prison and in Chains). When he was released, he gave the manuscript to his friend, Robert Ross ("Robbie"), who entitled it *De Profundis* and published an abridged version—omitting all mention of Douglas—in 1905, after Wilde's death. In 1949, when Douglas had died, Wilde's son Vyvyan published a fuller text, based on an unreliable typescript supplied by Ross. Only in 1962, when scholars were allowed to consult the original manuscript—given by Ross to the British Museum—did a complete version finally appear.

passed through two long years of imprisonment without ever having received a single line from you, or any news or message even, except such as gave me pain.

Our ill-fated and most lamentable friendship has ended in ruin and public infamy for me, yet the memory of our ancient affection is often with me, and the thought that loathing, bitterness and contempt should for ever take that place in my heart once held by love is very sad to me: and you yourself will, I think, feel in your heart that to write to me as I lie in the loneliness of prison-life is better than to publish my letters without my permission or to dedicate poems to me unasked, though the world will know nothing of whatever words of grief or passion, of remorse or indifference you may choose to send as your answer or your appeal.

I have no doubt that in this letter in which I have to write of your life and of mine, of the past and of the future, of sweet things changed to bitterness and of bitter things that may be turned into joy, there will be much that will wound your vanity to the quick. If it prove so, read the letter over and over again till it kills your vanity. If you find in it something of which you feel that you are unjustly accused, remember that one should be thankful that there is any fault of which one can be unjustly accused. If there be in it one single passage that brings tears to your eyes, weep as we weep in prison where the day no less than the night is set apart for tears. It is the only thing that can save you. If you go complaining to your mother, as you did with reference to the scorn of you I displayed in my letter to Robbie, so that she may flatter and soothe you back into self-complacency or conceit, you will be completely lost. If you find one false excuse for yourself, you will soon find a hundred, and be just what you were before. Do you still say, as you said to Robbie in your answer, that I "*attribute unworthy motives*" to you? Ah! you had no motives in life. You had appetites merely. A motive is an intellectual aim. That you were "*very young*" when our friendship began? Your defect was not that you knew so little about life, but that you knew so much. The morning dawn of boyhood with its delicate bloom, its clear pure light, its joy of innocence and expectation you had left far behind. With very swift and running feet you had passed from Romance to Realism. The gutter and the things that live in it had begun to fascinate you. That was the origin of the trouble in which you sought my aid, and I, so unwisely according to the wisdom of this world, out of pity and kindness gave it to you. You must read this letter right through, though each word may become to you as the fire or knife of the surgeon that makes the delicate flesh burn or bleed. Remember that the fool in the eyes of the gods and the fool in the eyes of man are very different. One who is entirely ignorant of the modes of Art in its revolution or the moods of thought in its progress, of the pomp of the Latin line or the richer music of the vowelled Greek, of Tuscan sculpture or Elizabethan song may yet be full of the very sweetest wisdom. The real fool, such as the gods mock or mar, is he who does not know himself. I was such a one too long. You have been such a one too long. Be so no more. Do not be afraid. The supreme vice is shallowness. Everything that is realised is right. Remember also that whatever is misery to you to read, is still greater misery to me to set down. To you the Unseen Powers have been very good. They have permitted you to see the strange and tragic shapes of Life as one sees shadows in a crystal. The head of Medusa that turns living men to stone,[2] you have been allowed to look at in a mirror merely. You yourself have walked free among the flowers. From me the beautiful world of colour and motion has been taken away.

---

2. Medusa was a snake-haired monster, so horrifying that anyone who looked at her turned to stone.

I will begin by telling you that I blame myself terribly. As I sit here in this dark cell in convict clothes, a disgraced and ruined man, I blame myself. In the perturbed and fitful nights of anguish, in the long monotonous days of pain, it is myself I blame. I blame myself for allowing an unintellectual friendship, a friendship whose primary aim was not the creation and contemplation of beautiful things, to entirely dominate my life. From the very first there was too wide a gap between us. You had been idle at your school, worse than idle at your university. You did not realise that an artist, and especially such an artist as I am, one, that is to say, the quality of whose work depends on the intensification of personality, requires for the development of his art the companionship of ideas, and intellectual atmosphere, quiet, peace, and solitude. You admired my work when it was finished: you enjoyed the brilliant successes of my first nights, and the brilliant banquets that followed them: you were proud, and quite naturally so, of being the intimate friend of an artist so distinguished: but you could not understand the conditions requisite for the production of artistic work. I am not speaking in phrases of rhetorical exaggeration but in terms of absolute truth to actual fact when I remind you that during the whole time we were together I never wrote one single line. Whether at Torquay, Goring, London, Florence or elsewhere, my life, as long as you were by my side, was entirely sterile and uncreative. And with but few intervals you were, I regret to say, by my side always. * * *

You send me a very nice poem, of the undergraduate school of verse, for my approval: I reply by a letter of fantastic literary conceits:[3] I compare you to Hylas, or Hyacinth, Jonquil or Narcisse,[4] or someone whom the great god of Poetry favoured, and honoured with his love. The letter is like a passage from one of Shakespeare's sonnets, transposed to a minor key. It can only be understood by those who have read the *Symposium* of Plato, or caught the spirit of a certain grave mood made beautiful for us in Greek marbles. It was, let me say frankly, the sort of letter I would, in a happy if wilful moment, have written to any graceful young man of either University who had sent me a poem of his own making, certain that he would have sufficient wit or culture to interpret rightly its fantastic phrases. Look at the history of that letter! It passes from you into the hands of a loathsome companion: from him to a gang of blackmailers: copies of it are sent about London to my friends, and to the manager of the theatre where my work is being performed: every construction but the right one is put on it: Society is thrilled with the absurd rumours that I have had to pay a huge sum of money for having written an infamous letter to you: this forms the basis of your father's worst attack: I produce the original letter myself in Court to show what it really is: it is denounced by your father's Counsel as a revolting and insidious attempt to corrupt Innocence: ultimately it forms part of a criminal charge: the Crown takes it up: the Judge sums up on it with little learning and much morality: I go to prison for it at last. That is the result of writing you a charming letter. * * *

---

3. Douglas's poem is *In Praise of Shame*. Wilde's letter, written in January 1893, was eventually read aloud at his trial:

My own Boy,

Your sonnet is quite lovely, and it is a marvel that those red rose-leaf lips of yours should have been made no less for the music of song than for madness of kisses. Your slim gilt soul walks between passion and poetry. I know Hyacinthus, whom Apollo loved so madly, was you in Greek days.

Why are you alone in London, and when do you go to Salisbury? Do go there to cool your hands in the grey twilight of Gothic things, and come here whenever you like. It is a lovely place—it only lacks you; but go to Salisbury first.

Always, with undying love,

Yours, Oscar

4. Beautiful young men whom Apollo loved.

Other miserable men, when they are thrown into prison, if they are robbed of the beauty of the world, are at least safe, in some measure, from the world's most deadly slings, most awful arrows. They can hide in the darkness of their cells, and of their very disgrace make a mode of sanctuary. The world, having had its will, goes its way, and they are left to suffer undisturbed. With me it has been different. Sorrow after sorrow has come beating at the prison doors in search of me. They have opened the gates wide and let them in. Hardly, if at all, have my friends been suffered to see me. But my enemies have had full access to me always. Twice in my public appearances at the Bankruptcy Court, twice again in my public transferences from one prison to another, have I been shown under conditions of unspeakable humiliation to the gaze and mockery of men. The messenger of Death has brought me his tidings and gone his way,[5] and in entire solitude, and isolated from all that could give me comfort, or suggest relief, I have had to bear the intolerable burden of misery and remorse that the memory of my mother placed upon me, and places on me still. Hardly has that wound been dulled, not healed, by time, when violent and bitter and harsh letters come to me from my wife through her solicitor. I am, at once, taunted and threatened with poverty. That I can bear. I can school myself to worse than that. But my two children are taken from me by legal procedure.[6] That is and always will remain to me a source of infinite distress, of infinite pain, of grief without end or limit. That the law should decide, and take upon itself to decide, that I am one unfit to be with my own children is something quite horrible to me. The disgrace of prison is as nothing compared to it. I envy the other men who tread the yard along with me. I am sure that their children wait for them, look for their coming, will be sweet to them.

The poor are wiser, more charitable, more kind, more sensitive than we are. In their eyes prison is a tragedy in a man's life, a misfortune, a casualty, something that calls for sympathy in others. They speak of one who is in prison as of one who is "in trouble" simply. It is the phrase they always use, and the expression has the perfect wisdom of Love in it. With people of our rank it is different. With us prison makes a man a pariah. I, and such as I am, have hardly any right to air and sun. Our presence taints the pleasures of others. We are unwelcome when we reappear. To revisit the glimpses of the moon is not for us.[7] Our very children are taken away. Those lovely links with humanity are broken. We are doomed to be solitary, while our sons still live. We are denied the one thing that might heal us and help us, that might bring balm to the bruised heart, and peace to the soul in pain.

And to all this has been added the hard, small fact that by your actions and by your silence, by what you have done and by what you have left undone,[8] you have made every day of my long imprisonment still more difficult for me to live through. The very bread and water of prison fare you have by your conduct changed. You have rendered the one bitter and the other brackish to me. The sorrow you should have shared you have doubled, the pain you should have sought to lighten you have quickened to anguish. I have no doubt that you did not mean to do so. I know that you did not mean to do so. It was simply that "one really fatal defect of your character, your entire lack of imagination."

5. Wilde's mother died while he was in prison.

6. In February 1897 Constance Wilde petitioned for custody of their children, Cyril and Vyvyan, whom Wilde never saw again. Their surname was changed to Holland.

7. Cf. Hamlet 1.4.51–53.

8. The Anglican rite of confession asks forgiveness "for what we have done and for what we have left undone."

And the end of it all is that I have got to forgive you. I must do so. I don't write this letter to put bitterness into your heart, but to pluck it out of mine. For my own sake I must forgive you. One cannot always keep an adder in one's breast to feed on one, nor rise up every night to sow thorns in the garden of one's soul. It will not be difficult at all for me to do so, if you help me a little. Whatever you did to me in old days I always readily forgave. It did you no good then. Only one whose life is without stain of any kind can forgive sins. But now when I sit in humiliation and disgrace it is different. My forgiveness should mean a great deal to you now. Some day you will realise it. Whether you do so early or late, soon or not at all, my way is clear before me. I cannot allow you to go through life bearing in your heart the burden of having ruined a man like me. The thought might make you callously indifferent, or morbidly sad. I must take the burden from you and put it on my own shoulders.

I must say to myself that neither you nor your father, multiplied a thousand times over, could possibly have ruined a man like me: that I ruined myself: and that nobody, great or small, can be ruined except by his own hand. I am quite ready to do so. I am trying to do so, though you may not think it at the present moment. If I have brought this pitiless indictment against you, think what an indictment I bring without pity against myself. Terrible as what you did to me was, what I did to myself was far more terrible still.

I was a man who stood in symbolic relations to the art and culture of my age. I had realised this for myself at the very dawn of my manhood, and had forced my age to realise it afterwards. Few men hold such a position in their own lifetime and have it so acknowledged. It is usually discerned, if discerned at all, by the historian, or the critic, long after both the man and his age have passed away. With me it was different. I felt it myself, and made others feel it. Byron was a symbolic figure, but his relations were to the passion of his age and its weariness of passion. Mine were to something more noble, more permanent, of more vital issue, of larger scope.

The gods had given me almost everything. I had genius, a distinguished name, high social position, brilliancy, intellectual daring: I made art a philosophy, and philosophy an art: I altered the minds of men and the colours of things: there was nothing I said or did that did not make people wonder: I took the drama, the most objective form known to art, and made it as personal a mode of expression as the lyric or the sonnet, at the same time that I widened its range and enriched its characterisation: drama, novel, poem in rhyme, poem in prose, subtle or fantastic dialogue, whatever I touched I made beautiful in a new mode of beauty: to truth itself I gave what is false no less than what is true as its rightful province, and showed that the false and the true are merely forms of intellectual existence. I treated Art as the supreme reality, and life as a mere mode of fiction: I awoke the imagination of my century so that it created myth and legend around me: I summed up all systems in a phrase, and all existence in an epigram.

Along with these things, I had things that were different. I let myself be lured into long spells of senseless and sensual ease. I amused myself with being a *flâneur* [idle stroller], a dandy, a man of fashion. I surrounded myself with the smaller natures and the meaner minds. I became the spendthrift of my own genius, and to waste an eternal youth gave me a curious joy. Tired of being on the heights I deliberately went to the depths in the search for new sensations. What the paradox was to me in the sphere of thought, perversity became to me in the sphere of passion. Desire, at the end, was a malady, or a madness, or both. I grew careless of the lives of others. I took pleasure where it pleased me and passed on. I forgot that every little action of the common day makes or unmakes character, and that therefore what one has done in the secret chamber one has some day to cry aloud on the housetops. I ceased to be Lord over myself. I was no longer the Captain of my Soul, and did not know it. I allowed you to dominate me, and your father to frighten me. I ended in horrible disgrace. There is only one thing for me now, absolute Humility: just as there is only one thing for you, absolute Humility also. You had better come down into the dust and learn it beside me.

I have lain in prison for nearly two years. Out of my nature has come wild despair; an abandonment to grief that was piteous even to look at: terrible and impotent rage: bitterness and scorn: anguish that wept aloud: misery that could find no voice: sorrow that was dumb. I have passed through every possible mood of suffering. Better than Wordsworth himself I know what Wordsworth meant when he said:

> Suffering is permanent, obscure, and dark
> And has the nature of Infinity.[9]

But while there were times when I rejoiced in the idea that my sufferings were to be endless, I could not bear them to be without meaning. Now I find hidden away in my nature something that tells me that nothing in the whole world is meaningless, and suffering least of all. That something hidden away in my nature, like a treasure in a field, is Humility.

It is the last thing left in me, and the best: the ultimate discovery at which I have arrived: the starting-point for a fresh development. It has come to me right out of myself, so I know that it has come at the proper time. It could not have come before, nor later. Had anyone told me of it, I would have rejected it. Had it been brought to me, I would have refused it. As I found it, I want to keep it. I must do so. It is the one thing that has in it the elements of life, of a new life, a *Vita Nuova*[1] for me. Of all things it is the strangest. One cannot give it away, and another may not give it to one. One cannot acquire it, except by surrendering everything that one has. It is only when one has lost all things, that one knows that one possesses it.

Now that I realise that it is in me, I see quite clearly what I have got to do, what, in fact, I must do. And when I use such a phrase as that, I need not tell you that I am not alluding to any external sanction or command. I admit none. I am far more of an individualist than I ever was. Nothing seems to me of the smallest value except what one gets out of oneself. My nature is seeking a fresh mode of self-realisation. That is all I am concerned with. And the first thing that I have got to do is to free myself from any possible bitterness of feeling against you.

I am completely penniless, and absolutely homeless. Yet there are worse things in the world than that. I am quite candid when I tell you that rather than go out from this prison with bitterness in my heart against you or against the world I would gladly and readily beg my bread from door to door. If I got nothing at the house of the rich, I would get something at the house of the poor. Those who have much are often greedy. Those who have little always share. I would not a bit mind sleeping in the cool grass in summer, and when winter came on sheltering myself by the warm close-thatched rick, or under the penthouse of a great barn, provided I had love in my heart. The external things of life seem to me now of no importance at all. You can

9. From *The Borderers* (act 3).
1. New life (Italian); Dante's book of this name was one of the few books Wilde was able to have sent to him in prison.

see to what intensity of individualism I have arrived, or am arriving rather, for the journey is long, and "where I walk there are thorns."[2]

Of course I know that to ask for alms on the highway is not to be my lot, and that if ever I lie in the cool grass at night-time it will be to write sonnets to the Moon. When I go out of prison, Robbie will be waiting for me on the other side of the big iron-studded gate, and he is the symbol not merely of his own affection, but of the affection of many others besides. I believe I am to have enough to live on for about eighteen months at any rate, so that, if I may not write beautiful books, I may at least read beautiful books, and what joy can be greater? After that, I hope to be able to recreate my creative faculty. But were things different: had I not a friend left in the world: were there not a single house open to me even in pity: had I to accept the wallet and ragged cloak of sheer penury: still as long as I remained free from all resentment, hardness, and scorn, I would be able to face life with much more calm and confidence than I would were my body in purple and fine linen, and the soul within it sick with hate. And I shall really have no difficulty in forgiving you. But to make it a pleasure for me you must feel that you want it. When you really want it you will find it waiting for you.

I need not say that my task does not end there. It would be comparatively easy if it did. There is much more before me. I have hills far steeper to climb, valleys much darker to pass through. And I have to get it all out of myself. Neither Religion, Morality, nor Reason can help me at all.

Morality does not help me. I am a born antinomian.[3] I am one of those who are made for exceptions, not for laws. But while I see that there is nothing wrong in what one does, I see that there is something wrong in what one becomes. It is well to have learned that.

Religion does not help me. The faith that others give to what is unseen, I give to what one can touch, and look at. My Gods dwell in temples made with hands, and within the circle of actual experience is my creed made perfect and complete: too complete it may be, for like many or all of those who have placed their Heaven in this earth, I have found in it not merely the beauty of Heaven, but the horror of Hell also. When I think about Religion at all, I feel as if I would like to found an order for those who cannot believe: the Confraternity of the Fatherless one might call it, where on an altar, on which no taper burned, a priest, in whose heart peace had no dwelling, might celebrate with unblessed bread and a chalice empty of wine. Everything to be true must become a religion. And agnosticism should have its ritual no less than faith. It has sown its martyrs, it should reap its saints, and praise God daily for having hidden Himself from man. But whether it be faith or agnosticism, it must be nothing external to me. Its symbols must be of my own creating. Only that is spiritual which makes its own form. If I may not find its secret within myself, I shall never find it. If I have not got it already, it will never come to me.

Reason does not help me. It tells me that the laws under which I am convicted are wrong and unjust laws, and the system under which I have suffered a wrong and unjust system. But, somehow, I have got to make both of these things just and right to me. And exactly as in Art one is only concerned with what a particular thing is at a particular moment to oneself, so it is also in the ethical evolution of one's character. I have got to make everything that has happened to me good for me. The

---

2. From Wilde's play, *A Woman of No Importance* (act 4).   3. A person who rejects conventional morality.

plank-bed, the loathsome food, the hard ropes shredded into oakum[4] till one's fingertips grow dull with pain, the menial offices with which each day begins and finishes, the harsh orders that routine seems to necessitate, the dreadful dress that makes sorrow grotesque to look at, the silence, the solitude, the shame—each and all of these things I have to transform into a spiritual experience. There is not a single degradation of the body which I must not try and make into a spiritualising of the soul.

I want to get to the point when I shall be able to say, quite simply and without affectation, that the two great turning-points of my life were when my father sent me to Oxford, and when society sent me to prison. I will not say that it is the best thing that could have happened to me, for that phrase would savour of too great bitterness towards myself. I would sooner say, or hear it said of me, that I was so typical a child of my age that in my perversity, and for that perversity's sake, I turned the good things of my life to evil, and the evil things of my life to good. What is said, however, by myself or by others matters little. The important thing, the thing that lies before me, the thing that I have to do, or be for the brief remainder of my days one maimed, marred, and incomplete, is to absorb into my nature all that has been done to me, to make it part of me, to accept it without complaint, fear, or reluctance. The supreme vice is shallowness. Whatever is realised is right.

When first I was put into prison some people advised me to try and forget who I was. It was ruinous advice. It is only by realising what I am that I have found comfort of any kind. Now I am advised by others to try on my release to forget that I have ever been in a prison at all. I know that would be equally fatal. It would mean that I would be always haunted by an intolerable sense of disgrace, and that those things that are meant as much for me as for anyone else—the beauty of the sun and the moon, the pageant of the seasons, the music of daybreak and the silence of great nights, the rain falling through the leaves, or the dew creeping over the grass and making it silver— would all be tainted for me, and lose their healing power and their power of communicating joy. To reject one's own experiences is to arrest one's own development. To deny one's own experiences is to put a lie into the lips of one's own life. It is no less than a denial of the Soul.

✦

COMPANION READING
H. Montgomery Hyde: from *The Trials of Oscar Wilde*[1]

[THE FIRST TRIAL]

Queensberry's leading counsel[2] rose from his place in the front row of barristers' seats in the Old Bailey courtroom to begin his cross-examination of the prosecutor. As he

---

4. Prisoners were often forced to pick oakum—i.e., to shred used ropes into fibers.

1. After Lord Alfred Douglas's father, the Marquess of Queensberry, accused Wilde of sodomy, Wilde brought suit for libel. Wilde lost his case, and was in turn prosecuted, in two subsequent criminal trials, for committing indecent acts. He was found guilty and sentenced to two years in prison with hard labor. The three trials took place in 1895, in the Old Bailey in London, and were the focus of immense public curiosity; the sensational story

was followed daily in almost every London newspaper. The following excerpts are from H. Montgomery Hyde's *The Trials of Oscar Wilde* (1948); it should be noted that since no authoritative transcripts of the court proceedings exist, his book is a reconstruction of events based on contemporary press reports and personal reminiscences.
2. Edward Carson, a renowned barrister, had been a classmate of Wilde's at Trinity College, Dublin. He successfully defended Queensberry against Wilde's charge of libel in the first trial.

faced his old college classmate in the witness box, the two figures on whom every eye in court was now fixed presented a striking contrast. There was Wilde, dressed in the height of fashion, a flower in the buttonhole of his frock coat, and exuding an air of easy confidence; opposite him stood Carson, tall, saturnine, and with the most determined expression on his lantern-jawed countenance. * * *

The opening question immediately revealed the cross-examiner's skill. * * *

"You stated that your age was thirty-nine. I think you are over forty. You were born on the 16th of October 1854?" Carson emphasized the point by holding up a copy of the witness's birth certificate.

Wilde appeared momentarily disconcerted, but he quickly recovered his composure. "I have no wish to pose as being young," he replied sweetly. "You have my certificate and that settles the matter."

"But," Carson persisted, "being born in 1854 makes you more than forty?"

"Ah! Very well," Wilde agreed with a sigh, as if to congratulate his opponent on a remarkable feat of mathematics.

It was a small point that Carson had scored in this duel of wits, but not without considerable importance. At the very outset Wilde had been detected in a stupid lie, the effect of which was not lost upon the jury, particularly when Carson followed it up by contrasting Wilde's true age with that of Lord Alfred Douglas,[3] with whom Wilde admitted to having stayed at many places, including hotels, both in England and on the Continent. Furthermore, it appeared that Douglas had also contributed to *The Chameleon*,[4] namely two poems. Wilde was asked about these poems, which he admitted that he had seen. "I thought them exceedingly beautiful poems," he added. "One was 'In Praise of Shame' and the other 'Two Loves.'"

"These loves," Carson asked, with a note of distaste in his voice. "They were two boys?"

"Yes."

"One boy calls his love 'true love,' and the other boy calls his love 'shame'?"

"Yes."

"Did you think they made any improper suggestion?"

"No, none whatever."

Carson passed on to "The Priest and the Acolyte," which Wilde admitted that he had read.

"You have no doubt whatever that that was an improper story?"

"From the literary point of view it was highly improper. It is impossible for a man of literature to judge it otherwise; by literature, meaning treatment, selection of subject, and the like. I thought the treatment rotten and the subject rotten."

"You are of opinion, I believe, that there is no such thing as an immoral book?"

"Yes."

"May I take it that you think 'The Priest and the Acolyte' was not immoral?"

"It was worse. It was badly written."[5]

"Was not the story that of a priest who fell in love with a boy who served him at the altar, and was discovered by the rector in the priest's room, and a scandal arose?"

---

3. Douglas was 24 years old; Wilde was 40.

4. Edited by Jack Bloxam, an Oxford undergraduate, *The Chameleon* was a literary magazine with a homoerotic tone; it appeared only once, in 1894. Bloxam was the author of *The Priest and the Acolyte*. At Douglas's request, Wilde had submitted some of his aphorisms to the

magazine, and his legal opponents sought to make Wilde appear guilty by association with the allegedly immoral contributions of Douglas and Bloxam.

5. Wilde is paraphrasing his preface to *The Picture of Dorian Gray* (see page 960).

"I have read it only once, last November, and nothing will induce me to read it again. I don't care for it. It doesn't interest me."

"Do you think the story blasphemous?"

"I think it violated every artistic canon of beauty."

"That is not an answer."

"It is the only one I can give."

"I want to see the position you pose in."

"I do not think you should say that."

"I have said nothing out of the way. I wish to know whether you thought the story blasphemous."

"The story filled me with disgust. The end was wrong."

"Answer the question, sir," Carson rapped out sharply. "Did you or did you not consider the story blasphemous?"

"I thought it disgusting."

Professing himself satisfied with this reply, Carson turned to a particular incident in the story. "You know that when the priest in the story administers poison to the boy, he uses the words of the sacrament of the Church of England?"

"That I entirely forgot."

"Do you consider that blasphemous?"

"I think it is horrible. 'Blasphemous' is not a word of mine." When Carson put the passage in question to him and asked whether he approved of the words used by the author, Wilde repeated his previous opinion: "I think them disgusting, perfect twaddle."

"I think you will admit that anyone who would approve of such a story would pose as guilty of improper practices?"

"I do not think so in the person of another contributor to the magazine. It would show very bad literary taste. Anyhow I strongly objected to the whole story. * * * Of course, I am aware that *The Chameleon* may have circulated among the undergraduates of Oxford. But I do not believe that any book or work of art ever had any effect whatever on morality."

"Am I right in saying that you do not consider the effect in creating morality or immorality?"

"Certainly, I do not."

"So far as your works are concerned, you pose as not being concerned about morality or immorality?"

"I do not know whether you use the word 'pose' in any particular sense."

"Is it a favourite word of your own?"

"Is it? I have no pose in this matter. In writing a play or a book, I am concerned entirely with literature—that is, with art. I aim not at doing good or evil, but in trying to make a thing that will have some quality of beauty." * * *

Carson now turned to *The Picture of Dorian Gray*[6] * * *

"'There is no such thing as a moral or an immoral book. Books are well written or badly written.' That expresses your view?"

"My view on art, yes."

"Then I take it, no matter how immoral a book may be, if it is well written, it is, in your opinion, a good book?"

---

6. Wilde's novel describes the passion felt by an artist, Basil Hallward, for a beautiful young man, Dorian Gray, whose portrait he paints.

"Yes, if it were well written so as to produce a sense of beauty, which is the highest sense of which a human being can be capable. If it were badly written, it would produce a sense of disgust."

"Then a well-written book putting forward perverted moral views may be a good book?"

"No work of art ever puts forward views. Views belong to people who are not artists."

"A perverted novel might be a good book?" Carson persisted.

"I don't know what you mean by a 'perverted' novel," Wilde answered crisply.

This gave Carson the opening he sought. "Then I will suggest *Dorian Gray* is open to the interpretation of being such a novel?"

Wilde brushed aside the suggestion with contempt. "That could only be to brutes and illiterates," he said. "The views of Philistines on art are unaccountable."

"An illiterate person reading *Dorian Gray* might consider it such a novel?"

"The views of illiterates on art are unaccountable. I am concerned only with my own view of art. I don't care twopence what other people think of it."

"The majority of persons come under your definition of Philistines and illiterates?"

"I have found wonderful exceptions."

"Do you think that the majority of people live up to the position you are giving us?"

"I am afraid they are not cultivated enough."

"Not cultivated enough to draw the distinction between a good book and a bad book?" The note of sarcasm in Carson's voice was unmistakable.

"Certainly not," Wilde replied blandly.

"The affection and love of the artist of *Dorian Gray* might lead an ordinary individual to believe that it might have a certain tendency?"

"I have no knowledge of the views of ordinary individuals."

"You did not prevent the ordinary individual from buying your book?"

"I have never discouraged him!" * * *

Having covered Wilde's published writings, Carson passed on to the allegedly compromising letters Wilde had written to Lord Alfred Douglas. * * *

"Why should a man of your age address a boy nearly twenty years younger as 'My own Boy'?"[7]

"I was fond of him. I have always been fond of him."

"Do you adore him?"

"No, but I have always liked him." Wilde then went on to elaborate upon the letter. "I think it is a beautiful letter. It is a poem. I was not writing an ordinary letter. You might as well cross-examine me as to whether *King Lear* or a sonnet of Shakespeare was proper."

"Apart from art, Mr Wilde?"

"I cannot answer apart from art."

"Suppose a man who was not an artist had written this letter, would you say it was a proper letter?"

"A man who was not an artist could not have written that letter."

"Why?"

"Because nobody but an artist could write it. He certainly could not write the language unless he were a man of letters."

7. For the text of this letter, a response to Douglas's poem *In Praise of Shame*, see page 1006, n. 3.

"I can suggest, for the sake of your reputation, that there is nothing very wonderful in this 'red rose-leaf lips of yours'?"

"A great deal depends on the way it is read."

"'Your slim gilt soul walks between passion and poetry,'" Carson continued. "Is that a beautiful phrase?"

"Not as you read it, Mr Carson. You read it very badly."

It was now Carson's turn to be nettled. "I do not profess to be an artist," he exclaimed, "and when I hear you give evidence, I am glad I am not."

These words immediately brought Sir Edward Clarke[8] to his feet. "I don't think my learned friend should talk like that," he observed. Then, turning towards his client in the witness box, he added: "Pray do not criticize my learned friend's reading again."

This clash caused a buzz of excitement in the courtroom. When it had died down, Carson went on with his cross-examination, indicating the document he was holding in his hand. "Is not that an exceptional letter?"

"It is unique, I should say." Wilde's answer produced loud laughter in court, which was still largely on the side of the witness.

"Was that the ordinary way in which you carried on your correspondence?"

"No. But I have often written to Lord Alfred Douglas, though I never wrote to another young man in the same way."

"Have you often written letters in the same style as this?"

"I don't repeat myself in style."

Carson held out another sheet of paper. "Here is another letter which I believe you also wrote to Lord Alfred Douglas. Will you read it?"

Wilde refused this invitation. "I don't see why I should," he said.

"Then I will," retorted Carson.

Savoy Hotel
Victoria Embankment
London

Dearest of all Boys,

> Your letter was delightful, red and yellow wine to me; but I am sad and out of sorts. Bosie, you must not make scenes with me. They kill me, they wreck the loveliness of life. I cannot see you, so Greek and gracious, distorted with passion. I cannot listen to your curved lips saying hideous things to me. I would sooner—than have you bitter unjust, hating. . . .

> I must see you soon. You are the divine thing I want, the thing of grace and beauty; but I don't know how to do it. Shall I come to Salisbury? My bill here is £49 for a week. I have also got a new sitting-room. . . .

> Why are you not here, my dear, my wonderful boy? I fear I must leave—no money, no credit, and a heart of lead.

Your own
OSCAR

"Is that an ordinary letter?" Carson asked, when he had finished reading it.

"Everything I wrote is extraordinary," Wilde answered with a show of impatience. "I do not pose as being ordinary, great heavens! Ask me any question you like about it."

---

8. Clarke was Wilde's attorney in all three trials.

Carson had only one question to ask about this letter, but its effect was deadly. "Is it the kind of letter a man writes to another?"

[THE SECOND TRIAL]

"During 1893 and 1894 you were a great deal in the company of Lord Alfred Douglas?"

"Oh, yes."

"Did he read that poem to you?"[1]

"Yes."

"You can perhaps understand that such verses as these would not be acceptable to the reader with an ordinary balanced mind?"

"I am not prepared to say," Wilde answered. "It appears to me to be a question of taste, temperament, and individuality. I should say that one man's poetry is another man's poison!"

"I daresay!" commented Gill[2] dryly, when the laughter had subsided. "The next poem is one described as 'Two Loves.' * * * Was that poem explained to you?"

"I think that is clear."

"There is no question as to what it means?"

"Most certainly not."

"Is it not clear that the love described relates to natural love and unnatural love?"

"No."

"What is the 'Love that dare not speak its name'?"[3] Gill now asked.

"'The love that dare not speak its name' in this century is such a great affection of an elder for a younger man as there was between David and Jonathan, such as Plato made the very basis of his philosophy, and such as you find in the sonnets of Michelangelo and Shakespeare.[4] It is that deep, spiritual affection that is as pure as it is perfect. It dictates and pervades great works of art like those of Shakespeare and Michelangelo, and those two letters of mine, such as they are. It is in this century misunderstood, so much misunderstood that it may be described as the 'Love that dare not speak its name,' and on account of it I am placed where I am now. It is beautiful, it is fine, it is the noblest form of affection. There is nothing unnatural about it. It is intellectual, and it repeatedly exists between an elder and a younger man, when the elder has intellect, and the younger man has all the joy, hope, and glamour of life before him. That it should be so, the world does not understand. The world mocks at it and sometimes puts one in the pillory for it."

Wilde's words produced a spontaneous outburst of applause from the public gallery, mingled with some hisses, which moved the judge to say he would have the Court cleared if there were any further manifestation of feeling.

❧

---

1. Douglas's sonnet *In Praise of Shame*.
2. Charles Gill was counsel for the prosecution during the second and third trial.
3. Cf. *Two Loves*, line 74.
4. King David of Israel, and Jonathan, the son of King Saul, were inseparable friends. On Jonathan's death, David declared that "your love to me was wonderful, passing the love of women" (2 Samuel 1.26). Plato argued that the passion of an older man for a younger one could be translated into a contemplation of the ideal and the universal. Both Shakespeare and Michelangelo wrote sonnets that can be read as describing platonic and/or erotic love between men.

Richard Nevinson, *The Arrival*, 1913–1914.

The Twentieth Century

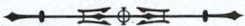

BEYOND THE PALE

Modern British literature has consistently been distinguished by its movement "beyond the pale." The Pale was originally the fenced-in territory established around Dublin by the invading English in the medieval period, a border between English civilization and Celtic foreignness. In later usage, the phrase "beyond the pale" came to have a purely metaphoric meaning: to stand outside the conventional boundaries of law, behavior, or social class. To snobbish members of the British elite, a poor flower-seller like Eliza Doolittle in Shaw's *Pygmalion* would be beyond the pale in a social sense; at its most serious, the phrase can designate actions violating universal standards of human decency, such as the colonists' appalling treatment of Africans that Conrad chillingly describes in *Heart of Darkness*. Throughout the twentieth century, writers active in the British Isles increasingly probed actions and locations beyond the pale of proper middle-class Englishness. Many of the century's greatest writers, such as the Pole Joseph Conrad, the Irishmen William Butler Yeats and James Joyce, and the Americans Ezra Pound and T. S. Eliot, themselves came from beyond the boundaries of England; others came from social strata within England less often visible before: provincial working-class writers like D. H. Lawrence and the Scots writer James Kelman; women like Rebecca West and Katherine Mansfield; men and women whose sexuality transcended conventional boundaries, such as E. M. Forster, Virginia Woolf, and W. H. Auden.

As the century went on, more and more writers active in the British Isles and its former colonies have been "beyond the pale" in a very literal sense, as people of color: Salman Rushdie, who grew up in India and Pakistan before establishing himself as a writer in England; V. S. Naipaul, a Caribbean of Indian ancestry; Ngugi wa-Thiongo, educated by British missionaries in Kenya; Derek Walcott, whose poetry moves between the Caribbean, England, North America, and Africa. With the ending of England's role as a colonial power, a new and dynamic relation of former colonies and colonizers has arisen, a pervasive interfusion of people and of roles, aptly symbolized by dizzying role changes in Caryl Churchill's comic masterpiece *Cloud 9*. British literature has become a world literature, overflowing what were once its borders.

Earlier centuries had periodically seen the eruption of writers, and of issues, from beyond the pale of accepted norms and educated social groups, but these writers had often faced severe struggles against dominant values of upper-middle-class propriety and the strictures of established literary conventions. The fate of Oscar Wilde was a case in point: his arrest on sodomy charges in 1895 at the peak of his career as a playwright, his sentencing to hard labor and then his exile and death in France in 1900, all pointed up the ways in which late Victorian society could retaliate against the challenges posed by a brilliant, flamboyant, homosexual Irishman. A new generation of writers at the turn of the century set themselves to change this situation, seeking variously to infiltrate the Pale of established British literary expression, to expand its dimensions, or to abolish it altogether. For many of these young writers, a prime strategy for achieving these goals was to attack their predecessors, and they set about this task with gusto.

BURYING VICTORIA

Writing in 1928, Virginia Woolf described the cultural atmosphere of the Victorian era in the following way:

> Damp now began to make its way into every house. . . . The damp struck within. Men felt the chill in their hearts; the damp in their minds. . . . The life of the average woman was a succession of childbirths. She married at nineteen and had fifteen or eighteen children by the time she was thirty; for twins abounded. Thus the British Empire came into existence; and thus—for there is no stopping damp; it gets into inkpots as it gets into the wood-work—sentences swelled, adjectives multiplied, lyrics became epics, and little trifles that had been essays a column long were now encyclopedias in ten or twenty volumes.

Woolf of course exaggerates here for her own effect; yet this passage does capture nicely the stereotypical view of the Victorians that flourished during the modern period—and helped make it possible. Ezra Pound, for instance, called the later nineteenth century "a rather blurry, messy sort of period, a rather sentimentalistic, mannerish sort of period." Polemical descriptions like these served the rhetorical purposes of writers at the start of the new century as they attempted to stake out their terrain and to forge a literature and a perspective of their own.

The opening decade of the new century was a time of transition. Woolf later suggested, her tongue perhaps in her cheek, that as a result of a Post-Impressionist exhibition of paintings in London, "on or about December, 1910, human character changed." Almost no one, however, seems to have maintained that anything changed very decisively on the morning of 1 January 1900. Queen Victoria, at that time on the throne for nearly sixty-five years and in mourning for her husband Prince Albert for almost forty, lived and ruled on into the following year; the subsequent reign of Edward VII (1901–1910) differed only slightly from that of his mother in many respects, the entire nation mourning the loss of their queen as she had the loss of her husband. But Woolf, in a 1924 essay, saw a gulf between herself and the Edwardians: Edwardian novelists, she writes, "established conventions which do their business; and that business is not our business." Edward VII himself, in fact, was clearly not a Victorian. He had a reputation as a playboy and implicitly rebelled against the conventions that his mother had upheld. During his reign, the mannered decadence of the 1890s modulated into a revived social realism seen in ambitious novels like Joseph Conrad's *Nostromo* and H. G. Wells's darkly comic masterpiece *Tono-Bungay*, while poets like Yeats and Hardy produced major poems probing the relations of self, society, and history. Writers in general considered themselves to be voices of a nation taking stock of its place in the world in a new century. They saw their times as marked by accelerating social and technological change and by the burden of a worldwide empire, which achieved its greatest extent in the years between 1900 and 1914—encompassing as much as a quarter of the world's population and dominating world trade through a global network of ports.

This period of consolidation and reflection abruptly came to an end four years into the reign of George V, with the start of World War I in August 1914; the relatively tranquil prewar years of George's early reign were quickly memorialized, and nostalgized, in the wake of the war's disruption to the traditionally English way of life. This first Georgian period was abruptly elevated into a cultural "golden age" by the British public and British publishers, a process that was typified by the pastoral poetry gathered by Edward Marsh in his hugely popular series of five anthologies called *Georgian Poetry*, the first of which was published in 1912. As a consequence of Marsh's skill as a tastemaker, this brief period before the war is frequently known as the Georgian period in British literature, though George V himself remained on the throne until 1936, when the distant rumble of World War II was to be heard by those with ears to hear.

The quarter century from 1914 until the start of the war in 1939 is now conventionally known as the modernist period. To be modern was, in one respect, to rebel openly and loudly against one's philosophical and artistic inheritance, in much the same way that the Romantic writers of the late eighteenth and early nineteenth centuries had sought to distinguish themselves from their Augustan forebears. This gesture—the way in which a new artistic movement seeks to define itself through caricature of the movement(s) that gave it birth—is a recurrent feature in literary history, but it took on a particular urgency and energy among the modernists, who advanced the view summarized in Pound's bold slogan, "Make It New." A great modernist monument to this anti-Victorian sentiment was Lytton Strachey's elegantly ironic *Eminent Victorians* (1918), whose probing biographical portraits punctured a series of Victorian pieties. Much of Bernard Shaw's writing (including *Pygmalion*) is animated by anti-Victorian animus as well, taking the theatrical wit of Oscar Wilde and turning it against specific targets. Exaggerated though it was, the ritualized slaughter performed by modernists like Woolf, Strachey, and Shaw seems to have achieved a clearing of the literary and artistic terrain that formed a necessary prelude to further innovation. The modernists' "Victorians" were oversimplified, sometimes straw figures, but the battle that was waged against them was real indeed, and the principles of modernism were forged and refined in the process.

THE FOUNDATIONS OF MODERN SKEPTICISM

The best Victorian writers had not been afraid to ask difficult, unsettling questions. Tennyson's restless skepticism in *In Memoriam*, for example, exemplifies the spirit of Victorian inquiry. But the conclusion of that poem foresees an ongoing progress toward future perfection, guided by "One God, one law, one element, / And one far-off divine event, / To which the whole creation moves." Tennyson himself doubted that such unities could be embodied in the present; twentieth-century writers found increasing fragmentation around them and became more and more suspicious of narratives of historical progress and of social unity.

Modern explorations are undertaken with absolutely no confidence as to the results that will be discovered, still less that a public exists who could understand the writers' discoveries. For that reason Thomas Hardy's ruthless skepticism now seems quintessentially modern. This new attitude is quite clear in Ford Madox Ford's *The Good Soldier* (1915), the first installment of which was published in the inaugural issue of Wyndham Lewis's violently modern magazine *Blast*. John Dowell, the narrator/protagonist of Ford's novel, worries for 250 pages about his sense that the "givens" of civil society seem to have been knocked out from under him, and that he has been left to create values and meaning on his own. Struggling to extract the moral of the story he tells us—the story of his wife's long-standing affair with his best friend, and their consequent deaths—Dowell can only conclude:

> I don't know. And there is nothing to guide us. And if everything is so nebulous about a matter so elementary as the morals of sex, what is there to guide us in the more subtle morality of all other personal contacts, associations, and activities? Or are we meant to act on impulse alone? It is all a darkness.

In Conrad's *Heart of Darkness*, the narrator Charlie Marlow suffers from a similar moral vertigo. When, at the novella's close, he resolves to perform an action he finds deeply repugnant—to tell a lie—he worries that his willful violation of the moral order will provoke an immediate act of divine retribution. None, however, is forthcoming: "It seemed to me that the house would collapse before I could escape, that the heavens would fall upon my head. But nothing happened. The heavens do not fall for such a trifle." In works like these, a voyage is undertaken into a vast, unknown, dark expanse. Those few who come out alive have seen too much ever to be the same.

Similar perceptions underlie modern humor. The Theater of the Absurd that flourished in the 1950s and 1960s, in the work of playwrights like Samuel Beckett and Harold Pinter, had roots in Wilde and Shaw and their comic explorations of the arbitrary conventionality of long-held social values. Throughout the twentieth century, writers devoted themselves to unfolding many varieties of irony—from the severe ironies of Conrad and Yeats to the more tender ironies of Woolf and Auden, to the farcical absurdities of Tom Stoppard and Joe Orton. Joyce described his mixture of high and low comedy as "jocoserious"; asked the meaning of his dense book *Finnegans Wake*, he replied, "It's meant to make you laugh."

Whether seen in comic or tragic light, the sense of a loss of moorings was pervasive. Following the rapid social and intellectual changes of the previous century, the early twentieth century suffered its share of further concussions tending to heighten modern uncertainty. It was even becoming harder to understand the grounds of uncertainty itself. The critiques of Marx and Darwin had derived new messages from bodies of evidence available in principle to all literate citizens; the most important paradigm shifts of the early twentieth century, on the other hand, occurred in the fields of philosophy, psychology, and physics, and often rested on evidence invisible to the average citizen. The German philosopher Friedrich Nietzsche (1844–1900) was, as his dates suggest, wholly a nineteenth-century man, yet his ideas had their most profound impact in the twentieth century. Nietzsche described his lifelong philosophical project as "the revaluation of all values"; in his 1882 treatise *The Joyful Science*, he went so far as to assert that "God is dead." This deliberately provocative statement came as the culmination of a long and complicated argument, and did not mean simply that Nietzsche was an atheist (though he was). Nietzsche was suggesting that traditional religion had been discredited by advances in the natural and physical sciences, and as transcendent standards of truth disappeared, so logically must all moral and ethical systems depending on some faith for their force. It was from this base that Nietzsche created the idea of the *Übermensch*, the "superman" who because of his intellectual and moral superiority to others must not be bound by social conventions. Conrad's tragic figure Kurtz and Shaw's comic Professor Henry Higgins represent two very different takes on this idea, building on Nietzsche's interest in showing how all values are "constructed" rather than given—at some level arbitrary, all truths being merely opinions, all social identities merely roles.

The new psychology, whose earliest stirrings are to be found in the last decades of the nineteenth century, came of age at the turn of the twentieth. Sigmund Freud's

The Interpretation of Dreams (1900) and *Psychopathology of Everyday Life* (1901) together illustrate in an especially vivid way his evolving theories about the influence of the unconscious mind, and past (especially childhood) experience, on our daily lives. The whole of Freud's work was translated into English by James Strachey (Lytton's brother), and was published in conjunction with the Hogarth Press, owned and run by Leonard and Virginia Woolf; for this reason, among others, the Freudian revolution was felt early, and strongly, among the London intelligentsia. The new psychology was frequently distorted and misunderstood by the larger public; among the artistic community Freud provoked a wide range of response, from the enthusiastic adoption of his theories by some to nervous rejection by writers like Joyce. This response is complicated, in part, by the fact that Freud himself took an interest in artistic and creative processes, and presumed to explain to writers the psychopathology at the heart of their own genius; as the Freudian literary critic Lionel Trilling succinctly put it, "the poet is a poet by reason of his sickness as well as by reason of his power." As Freud's supporter W. H. Auden wrote in his elegy, *In Memory of Sigmund Freud* (1939):

> If often he was wrong and at times absurd,
> To us he is no more a person
> Now but a whole climate of opinion
> Under whom we conduct our different lives.

A further intellectual shock wave was the revolution in physics that was spearheaded by Albert Einstein's *Special Theory of Relativity* (1905). In both this theory (dealing with motion) and later in the general theory of relativity (dealing with gravity), Einstein shook the traditional understanding of the universe and our relationship to it; the certainty and predictability of the Newtonian description of the universe had been undone. The "uncertainty" of Einstein's universe was seemingly reinforced by developments in quantum physics, such as the work of Niels Bohr (who won the Nobel Prize in physics in 1922) and Werner Heisenberg, author of the famous "Uncertainty Principle" and the principle of complementarity, which together assert that the movement of subatomic particles can be predicted only by probability and not measured, as the very act of measurement alters their behavior. Ironically enough, the true import of these ideas is not, as the truism has it, that "everything is relative"—in fact, Einstein says almost the exact opposite. In Einstein's vision of the world, *nothing* is relative: everything is absolute, and absolutely fixed—except for us, fallible and limited observers, who have no secure standpoint from which "to see the thing as in itself it really is," to quote Matthew Arnold's 1867 formulation of the critic's goal. The only way to experience the truth, it would seem, would be to find what T. S. Eliot called "the still point of the turning world," an "unmoved mover" outside the flux and change of our day-to-day world. Einstein himself never really rejected the idea of transcendent truth; he once said to an interviewer that to him, the idea of our universe without a Creator was inconceivable. In this case, however, the popular fiction has been more influential than the facts, and the work of Einstein, Heisenberg, and Bohr has been used to support the widespread sense that, as Irish playwright Sean O'Casey's character Captain Jack Boyle puts it in *Juno and the Paycock* (1924), "the whole worl's in a state o' chassis!"

The philosophical and moral upheavals of these years were given added force by the profound shock of World War I—"The Great War," as it came to be known. The

British entered the conflict against Germany partly in order to preserve their influence in Europe and their dominance around the globe, and partly out of altruistic notions of gallantry and fair play—to aid their weaker allies against German aggression. The conflict was supposed to take a few weeks; it lasted four grueling years and cost hundreds of thousands of British lives. Notions of British invincibility, of honor, even of the viability of civilization all weakened over the years of vicious trench warfare in France. The progress of technology, which had raised Victorian standards of living, now led to a mechanization of warfare that produced horrific numbers of deaths—as many as a million soldiers died in the single protracted battle of the Somme in 1916. As poets discovered as they served in the trenches, and as the people back home came to learn, modernity had arrived with a vengeance.

REVOLUTIONS OF STYLE

The end of the war was accompanied by a sense of physical and moral exhaustion. To be modern has been defined as a persistent sense of having arrived on the stage of history after history has finished. The critic Perry Meisel, for instance, describes modernism as "a structure of compensation, a way of adjusting to the paradox of belatedness." Behind Ezra Pound's struggle to reinvent poetry lay a nagging suspicion that there was nothing new left to make or say, and Pound claimed that the very slogan "Make It New" was taken off the bathtub of an ancient Chinese emperor. As T. S. Eliot explains in his essay *Tradition and the Practice of Poetry*, "The perpetual task of poetry is to *make all things new*. Not necessarily to make new things. . . . It is always partly a revolution, or a reaction, from the work of the previous generation."

That revolution was carried out both on the level of subject matter and often on the level of style. Some important early twentieth-century fiction writers, like John Galsworthy and H. G. Wells, felt no real need to depart from inherited narrative models, and hewed more or less to a realist or naturalist line, carrying on from the French naturalists like Emile Zola and the Norwegian dramatist Henrik Ibsen. But for those writers we now call modernist, these conventions came to seem too limiting and lifeless. The modern writer was faced with an enormous, Nietzschean task: to create new and appropriate values for modern culture, and a style appropriate to those values. As a consequence, there is often a probing, nervous quality in the modernist explorations of ultimate questions. This quality can be seen at the very start of the century in Conrad's *Heart of Darkness*, a novel about psychological depth and social disintegration that simultaneously implicates its readers in the moral ambiguities of its events. These ambiguities, moreover, are reflected in the very presentation of the narrative itself. In the modern novel, we are no longer allowed to watch from a safe distance while our protagonists mature and change through their trials; instead, we are made to undergo those trials ourselves, through the machinations of the narrative. This technique had already been employed in the nineteenth century, as for instance in the dramatic monologues of Robert Browning; but this narrative of process becomes pervasive in modernist texts, where the uncertainties of the form, the waverings and unpredictability of the narrative, mirror similar qualities in the mind of the narrator or protagonist. Often the reader is drawn into the story's crisis by a heightened use of the technique of plunging the narrative suddenly *in medias res*:

Color Plate 21   Paul Nash, *We Are Making a New World*, 1918. An Irish painter especially noted for his extraordinary depictions of World War I, Nash is perhaps best known for this stark land-scape of the no-man's-land nightmare of trench warfare, a scene empty of human beings, an apocalyptic vision of the horrors created by the modern technology of war, the nightmare "new world" of his painting's ironic title. *(The Imperial War Museum, London.)*

Color Plate 22 Charles Ginner, *Piccadilly Circus*, 1912. A depiction of London shortly before World War I, the scene features a seemingly quaint flower seller in the midst of urban change. Like Eliza Doolittle in *Pygmalion*, she is surrounded by evidence of the energies and transformations of the modern city: automobiles, advertising, and even a woman boldly strolling alone down the sidewalk. The word "new" on the poster sums up the social scene. (*© Charles Ginner. Tate Gallery, London/Art Resource, NY.*)

Color Plate 23   Vanessa Bell, *The Tub*, 1917. Bell was Virginia Woolf's sister and, like her, a member of the Bloomsbury Group—a casual association of friends, family, and lovers who were at the forefront of Britain's literary, artistic, and cultural scene for three decades. Bell was a gifted painter with an astonishing color sense; her innovative abstract and figural paintings make her England's strongest female artist of the period. She was known as well for decorative and crafts work such as the furniture, painting and china she created for Omega Workshops, led by Roger Fry. Together with Duncan Grant and Clive Bell, she decorated Charleston, the legendary Bloomsbury country house now on England's register of cultural landmarks. (*© Vanessa Bell. Tate Gallery, London/Art Resource, NY.*)

Color Plate 24 Vera Willoughby, *General Joy*, 1928. As the 20th century opened, public transportation systems in and around London—including the city's impressive subway system, known as the Underground or the Tube—were consolidated under the direction of a single company, soon known as the Underground Group. A committment to innovative and effective maps, signs, and advertising quickly earned the Underground Group a place in the forefront of graphic design, and together with its successor organizations it remained a strong patron of the arts for much of the century. Posters commissioned by the Authority from new and established artists often advertised underground or ground transportation in novel and artistic ways. *General Joy* reflects the exuberance of London in the 1920s, but just as often the posters offered public art, political messages, and cultural rallying points. Clarissa Dalloway's daughter Elizabeth rides just such an open-air bus through a sparkling London day in June in Virginia Woolf's *Mrs Dalloway*. (*London's Transport Museum.*)

Color Plate 25 L. D. Luard, *The Spirit of 1943*, 1943. By the 1940s the Underground Group had been absorbed into the still larger London Transport company, but the emphasis on strong graphic design and the tradition of commissioning posters from artists continued. This striking graphic image conveys Britain's determination in the midst of World War II. It was meant to bolster the fighting spirit of a country still two years and hundreds of thousands of deaths away from victory over the Axis forces. (*London's Transport Museum.*)

The Spirit of 1943

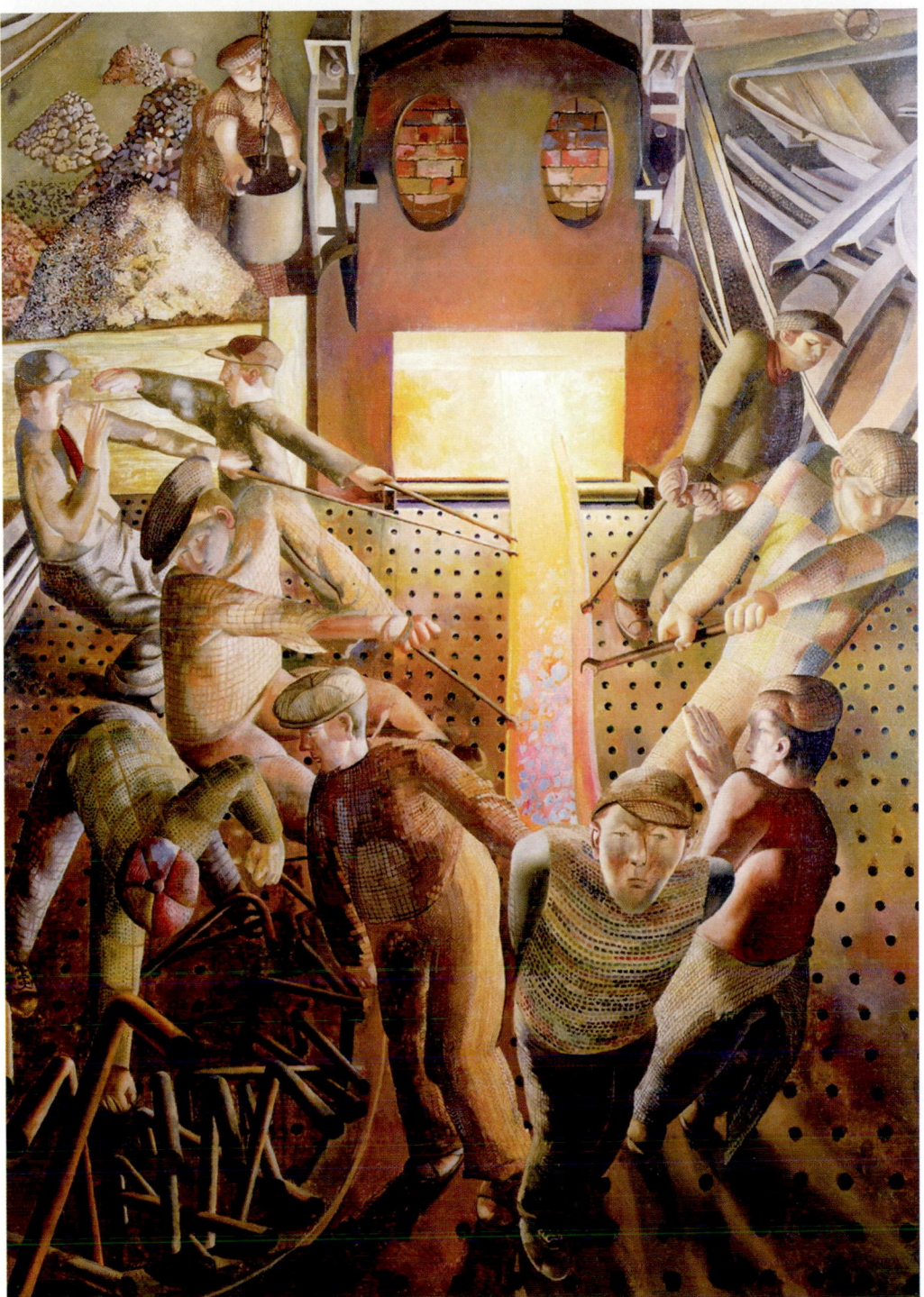

Color Plate 26 Stanley Spencer, *Shipbuilding on the Clyde. Furnaces*, 1946. Twentieth-century British painting is unusual in modern art, for the best of it is not abstract but rather portrays the human figure. Spencer's work was resolutely figural, yet it manages to be modern nonetheless because of the almost transcendent, mystical effects his human figures create. Spencer spent most of his eccentric life in a small English village, whose citizens he depicted swept up in great religious mysteries, such as the Annunciation or the Resurrection. Even his portraits of everyday activities such as shipbuilding or baking are gilded with radiant transfiguration. *(Imperial War Museum, London.)*

Color Plate 27   Francis Bacon, *Study After Velasquez*, 1950. Irish painter Francis Bacon lived for most of his life in London, where his squalid studio, now reconstructed at the Hugh Lane Gallery in Dublin, was famous as a hub of creativity. Bacon was surely one of the great artists of the modern period; his innovations in portraiture are unforgettable icons of modernity. Perhaps his most iconic works are the series of screaming popes. Based on classical portraits of a pope by Velasquez, Bacon's nameless pope has a face haunted with knowledge of the holocausts of the twentieth century. He seems to scream at us from behind a wasteland of totalitarian bars. Bacon was a highly literary painter, and he was inspired to create some of his most tragic and innovative painting by the poetry of Eliot and Yeats. (*© 2004 The Estate of Francis Bacon/ARS, New York/ DACS, London.*)

Color Plate 28 Gilbert and George (b. 1943, b. 1942), *Death Hope Life Fear*, 1984. Performance artists and photographers, the gay couple Gilbert and George have offered provocative art for decades, beginning with their first performance piece, for which they gilded themselves with metallic paint and stood motionless for a long, long time. Other pieces have included simply declaring their everyday life to be performance art. Since the 1980s they have also produced huge photographic canvases with religious, political, and homoerotic imagery. Cultural agents-provocateurs, Gilbert and George try to create witty yet highly charged confrontations between spectators and their own cultural beliefs, wishes, and secrets. *(© Gilbert and George. Tate Gallery, London/Art Resource, NY.)*

Color Plate 29 David Hockney, *Great Pyramid at Giza with Broken Head from Thebes*, 1963. Hockney has become a premier artist of our time by reinventing portraiture. Unlike Francis Bacon, who basically deconstructed the human body in his work, Hockney's paintings are filled with sunlight and color. Long stints in Los Angeles have made Hockney the visual poet of the California swimming pool, its aqua waters set shimmering by the beautiful young men Hockney places there. Branching out into many media, Hockney's recent work includes photographic collages and theater stage design. The Egyptian scene depicted here is less typical, but it shows his fascination both with other cultures and countries and with the "deadpan vistas of postmodern and postimperial tourism." *(Earl of Pembroke, Wilton House, Wilton, Salisbury, UK.)*

Color Plate 30 Chris Ofili, *No Woman, No Cry*, 1998. In the 1990s London took the crown from New York as the world's hottest art scene. Young British visual artists have caused a veritable Sensation—the name of one of their group shows—and even prompted the Tate Gallery to build an entirely new wing to house contemporary work. Chris Ofili is one of the most exciting painters in the group. Nigerian by birth, Ofili represents the multicultural Britain that is remaking British art, literature, and popular culture. Ofili integrates African cultural symbols into a painting style drawn from American pop art and British figural painting. Titled after a Bob Marley song, the painting here makes a vivid icon of a black British woman, her clothes a landscape of hot color studded with dried elephant dung, a sacred substance in African rites. "Mr. Ofili generously supports the six London Zoo elephants whose dung is dried for his paintings." *(Acrylic, oil, and mixed media on canvas. © Chris Ofili. Courtesy, Victoria Miro Gallery, London. Photo: Tate Gallery, London/Art Resource, NY.)*

Soldiers of the 9th Cameronians division prepare to go "over the top" during a daylight raid near Arras, France, 24 March 1917. During such an offensive, troops would make their way quickly across the contested territory between the opposing armies' trenches—the area known as No Man's Land—and attempt to take control of an enemy trench in order to conduct bombing raids and gain whatever intelligence might be found in the abandoned foxholes. The pace of this warfare—where a week's progress might be measured in yards, rather than miles—was, according to troops on both sides, the most salient feature of trench warfare. The human costs included diseases caused by standing water (like infamous "trench foot") and emotional disorders caused by the stress of waiting and constant shelling ("shell shock").

"There was no hope for him this time: it was the third stroke" (Joyce, *The Sisters*); "A sudden blow:" (Yeats, *Leda and the Swan*); "'Yes, of course, if it's fine tomorrow,' said Mrs. Ramsay" (Woolf, *To the Lighthouse*). The customary preliminary information—the sort of dossier about the characters that we expect—isn't given; the reader is put in the position of a detective who has to sort all this information out unaided. This narrative decontextualization reaches its culmination in the theater of Beckett and Pinter, who typically withhold any and all background information about characters. "Confusion," Samuel Beckett told an interviewer in 1956, "is all around us and our only chance now is to let it in. The only chance of renovation is to open our eyes and see the mess. It is not a mess you can make sense of."

Early in the century, a number of poets began to dispense with the frames of reference provided by conventional poetic forms. The first important Anglo-American poetic movement of the century was Imagism, a reaction against the expansive wordiness of Victorian poetry like Tennyson's *Idylls of the King* or Browning's *The Ring and the Book*. Imagists like Pound and H. D. wrote short, spare poems embodying a revelatory image or moment. The most memorable Imagist poems have the concentrated impact of a haiku. But the form leaves little scope for narrative development; that path seems to have been opened by a rediscovery of the seventeenth-century metaphysical poets, notably by T. S. Eliot. The techniques of metaphysical poets like John Donne suggested to Eliot a means for expanding the repertory of Imagist poetry, which he used to good effect in poems like *The Love Song of J. Alfred Prufrock*, which opens with a thoroughly modernized metaphysical conceit:

> Let us go then, you and I,
> when the evening is spread out against the sky
> Like a patient etherized upon a table.

One strategy for making literature new was to make it difficult; this notion was, in part, a response to the proliferation of popular entertainments during the early twentieth century, a development that both disturbed and intrigued many artists, writers, and cultural critics. In such a context, "difficult" literature (such as the densely allusive poetry of Eliot, or the multilayered prose of Joyce) was seen to be of greater artistic merit than the products of an easily consumable mass culture—even as both Eliot and Joyce drew on popular culture and diction as they reshaped the norms of their literary art. Thus, while one of the primary targets of modernist renovation was Victorian literary manners, another was the complacent taste and sensibility of a large, and growing, middle class. Artists had been declaring the need to shock the bourgeoisie since time immemorial; Matthew Arnold worried publicly, and at length, about the dilution of a natural aristocracy of taste by the pseudoculture of newly educated British philistines, at the same time that he campaigned for greatly expanded public education. The Education Act of 1870 resulted in the explosive growth of elementary education, which meant that the reading class grew exponentially. Within the art world, the most obvious result of this anxiety was the "art for art's sake" movement associated with Walter Pater that began in the 1870s. Art was becoming its own material—as, for instance, in French artist Marcel Duchamp's mustache on the Mona Lisa.

In some ways modernist art and literature turned inward, becoming cannibalistic and self-referential. This is demonstrated well in Joyce's novel *A Portrait of the Artist as a Young Man*, whose protagonist is autobiographical in genesis yet critical in intent; the way Joyce accomplishes this is by moving Stephen Dedalus, his artist-protagonist, through various prose poses—writing now like Gustave Flaubert, now like Cardinal Newman, now like Pater. Stephen can only mimic—not create—a style; such is the situation of the modern writer, Joyce suggests, and his novel *Ulysses* dramatizes this by adopting a kaleidoscopic array of styles in its eighteen chapters. It thus becomes increasingly difficult to think of "style" as the achievement of an individual, and more and more it becomes the culmination of a cultural, national, or ethnic project or history. As the French critic Roland Barthes has written, the text in the modern period becomes a "multidimensional space in which a variety of writings, none of them original, blend and clash," "a tissue of quotations drawn from innumerable centres of culture"—an apt and dramatic description of modernist texts like Eliot's *The Waste Land*, Joyce's *Ulysses*, and Pound's *Cantos*. To be textual is, during this period, to be intertextual and interdisciplinary as well.

The stylistic experimentation of modernist writers was fueled by the era's technological advances. From the mid-nineteenth century on, Britain had prided itself on its industrial strength and leadership; with the electrification of Britain at the turn of the century, however, the Industrial Revolution was gradually overtaken by a technological revolution. If the sinking of the *Titanic* on her maiden voyage in 1912 stands as a symbol of the vulnerability of progress—a sort of watery funeral for traditional British industry—the first transatlantic flight in 1919 pointed toward the future. Advances in photographic technology made documentary photographs a part of daily life and brought a heightened visual dimension to political campaigns and to advertising; the advent of quick and inexpensive newspaper photographs put vivid images of the carnage of World War I on Britain's breakfast tables. The texture and pace of daily life changed in the early years of the century to such a degree that average men and women were comfortable referring to themselves by that hopelessly awkward designation, "modern" (from the Latin *modo*, "just now"). And clearly, the London inhabited by the denizens of Eliot's *Waste Land* is a profoundly different place from the London of Dickens. Eliot portrays a woman who works in an office, composes letters on a typewriter, talks to clients on the telephone, plays records on the phonograph at her flat after having casual sex with a co-worker, and eats her evening meal from tins.

The advent of technology had far-reaching effects on the writing of the period. Beckett, famously, imagined a tape recorder before he had ever seen one in order to make possible the memory play of his *Krapp's Last Tape* (1959); more generally, the technology of the transistor radio, and government sponsorship of radio and television by the British Broadcasting Corporation, made possible wholly new literary genres. Beckett and Dylan Thomas were among the first to take advantage of the new media, writing plays for radio and then for television. A generation earlier, Joyce made use of early art film strategies in his "Circe" episode of *Ulysses*. In the most advanced writing of the modernist period we find an increasing sense that the technologies of print affect the text itself. Pound's *Cantos* were composed, not just transcribed, on a typewriter, and cannot be imagined in their current form composed with pen and ink; Joyce plays with the typographic conventions of newspaper headlines in the "Aeolus" chapter of *Ulysses* to create an ironic running commentary on the action. A crucial scene in Joyce's *Finnegans Wake* features a television broadcast (which was not available commercially when the novel was published), blending with a nuclear explosion (also several years before the fact). The scene culminates in "the abnihilisation of the etym"—both a destruction of atom/Adam/etym and its recovery *from* ("ab") nothingness.

MODERNISM AND THE MODERN CITY

Paralleling the new social and artistic opportunities of the twentieth century was a kind of anomie or alienation created by the rush toward industrialization. Vast numbers of human figures remained undifferentiated and the mass-manufactured hats and clothing worn by British industrial workers served only to heighten the monotony of their daily routines. Newspapers eagerly published photographs of thousands of sooty-faced miners. The members of the workforce, which Marx had called "alienated labor," were seen to be estranged not just from their work but from one another as well, as they themselves became mass products. This situation is dramatized especially vividly in the silent films of the period—from the dystopian vision of Fritz

Archibald Hatrick, *A Lift Girl*, 1916. The Scottish artist A. S. Hatrick (1864–1950) was part of the vibrant art movement in Glasgow, which he joined after studying art in France, where he had met the painters Van Gogh and Gauguin; as a wartime artist, he became especially interested in recording women's efforts. *A Lift Girl* is a multidimensional portrait of these efforts, as it depicts a young woman whose service to her country in the war comes about as an elevator operator carrying civilians and military personnel down to the underground refuges meant to protect families and soldiers alike from the constant aerial bombardment of German airplanes.

Lang's *Metropolis* (1926) to the more comic vision presented by the British-American Charlie Chaplin in *Modern Times* (1936). The sense of major cities being overrun by crowds of nameless human locusts recurs in the poetry of the period:

> A crowd flowed over London Bridge, so many,
> I had not thought death had undone so many.
> Sighs, short and infrequent, were exhaled,
> And each man fixed his eyes before his feet.

(Eliot, *The Waste Land*)

> I have met them at close of day
> Coming with vivid faces
> From counter or desk among grey
> Eighteenth-century houses.

(Yeats, *Easter 1916*)

The Victorian concern over huge numbers of urban poor was seconded by a fear of large numbers of restive urban lower-middle-class workers and their families.

The city also appeared in far more positive guises, as the modernists were urban sophisticates above all else. Joyce famously remarked that if Dublin were one day destroyed, it could be recreated whole from the pages of his *Ulysses*. Virginia Woolf's great novel *Mrs Dalloway* is among other things a glowing tribute to

London as the center of incongruous juxtapositions and unexpected connections, the quintessence of life itself: "Heaven only knows why one loves it so," Clarissa Dalloway thinks,

> how one sees it so, making it up, building it round one, tumbling it, creating it every moment afresh. . . . In people's eyes, in the swing, tramp, and trudge; in the bellow and the uproar; the carriages, motor cars, omnibuses, vans, sandwich men shuffling and swinging; brass bands; barrel organs; in the triumph and the jingle and the strange high singing of some aeroplane overhead was what she loved; life; London; this moment of June.

London had a magnetic attraction for many American writers as well, as a transatlantic literary culture blossomed. Henry James based novels like *The American* and *Portrait of a Lady* on the adventures of Americans living abroad; James himself was an American who lived most of the last thirty-five years of his life in London, and was naturalized as a British citizen three months before his death. T. S. Eliot moved to London in 1915 and lived there until his death in 1965, becoming a British subject, a communicant of the Church of England, and being knighted along the way. The great comic writer P. G. Wodehouse commuted back and forth across the Atlantic in the 1920s and 1930s as his plays and musical comedies were staged in New York and London. In many ways, New York and London had never been so close. This artistic diaspora resulted in a richer, more complex and urbane literature.

PLOTTING THE SELF

The Freudian revolution grew from and reinforced an intense interest in the workings of the individual psyche, and modernists like Woolf and Joyce devoted themselves to capturing the mind's modulations. Both Woolf and Joyce employed versions of what came to be known as the "stream-of-consciousness" technique, in which fragmentary thoughts gradually build up a portrayal of characters' perceptions and of their unstated concerns. Consider this passage from the "interior monologue" of Joyce's protagonist Leopold Bloom, as he prepares a saucer of milk for his cat:

> They call them stupid. They understand what we say better than we understand them. She understands all she wants to. Vindictive too. Wonder what I look like to her. Height of a tower? No, she can jump me. . . . Cruel. Her nature. Curious mice never squeal. Seem to like it.

On the surface, Bloom's staccato thoughts reflect on the cat; at the same time, he identifies the cat with his unfaithful wife Molly, and—without admitting it to himself—he reflects on the cat's foreign psyche as a way of coming to terms with Molly's needs and desires. The development of stream-of-consciousness narrative grows out of a sense that the self is not "natural" or "given" but a construction—specifically a social construction—and that, consequently, traditional methods for depicting character no longer suffice. We are all the products of our own past and we are also, powerfully, products of larger social forces that shape the stories we tell about ourselves, and which others tell about us.

In the Victorian novel, plot crises were typically resolved in some definitive way, such as by a marriage or a change in the financial status of the protagonist. In the modern novel, lasting resolutions growing out of a common vision are few and far between. Walter Pater had counseled his readers, at the conclusion of *The Renaissance*, that "to burn always with a hard, gemlike flame, to maintain this ecstasy" was "success in life"; in the modern period, everyone wants that ecstasy, but no one is sure quite what it looks like amid the ruthless individualism of modern life. "We live as we dream, alone," Conrad's narrator Marlow mutters despondently; "Only connect," the epigraph to E. M. Forster's *Howards End* (1910) implores. On the eve of the London Blitz, however, the characters in Woolf's *Between the Acts* (still the most powerful British novel of World War II) are united only as they sing the refrain, "Dispersed are we." The texts of the modern period, bookended as they are by two world wars, represent a real, agonized meditation on how modern individuals can become united as community again. Woolf herself was skeptical of the possibility and her last novel remains unfinished—or finished only by her husband Leonard—because she took her own life before she could complete it. In the novels of Woolf and Joyce, and in the poetry of Yeats and Auden, community is the glimpsed prospect, the promised land: seen as a possibility but never realized, or embodied precariously in a gesture, a moment, a metaphor, and above all in art itself.

After the modernist high-water mark of the 1920s, the atmosphere darkened amid the international financial depression of the 1930s triggered by the U.S. stock market crash of 1929. The decade saw the growth of British Marxism and widespread labor agitation. The decade also witnessed the international growth of fascism and totalitarianism; writers like Shaw, Wyndham Lewis, Eliot, Yeats, Pound, and Lawrence for a time saw the order and stability promised by authoritarian governments as the only antidote to the "mere anarchy" Yeats decries in his poem *The Second Coming*. In the late thirties, however, intellectual sentiment turned increasingly against the fascist movements being led in Germany by Hitler, in Italy by Mussolini and in Spain by Franco. During Spain's brutal civil war (1936–1939), many writers supported the democratic Republicans against the ultimately victorious fascist General Franco. Meanwhile a series of weak British governments did little to oppose Hitler's increasing belligerence and extremism; the failure to stand up for democratic principles, coupled with worldwide economic depression, led many young intellectuals and artists to become Leftists.

Compared to the stylistic experiments of the previous two decades, British writing of the 1930s sometimes looks rather flat, neutral. This can be attributed in part to the disillusionment that followed World War I, and the very real sense throughout the thirties that things were building up to another war, that art had become something of an irrelevancy. The German cultural critic Theodor Adorno was to write after the war, "no poetry after Auschwitz"; writers of the thirties seem to have had this sense well in advance of Auschwitz. Yeats admired the character in Auguste de Villiers de L'Isle-Adam's drama *Axël* who said, "As for living, we let the servants do that for us"; the young writers of the thirties, however, were concerned that (in Auden's phrase) "poetry makes nothing happen," and were committed to the idea that it must. "Late modernism," as the critic Tyrus Miller has described this writing, was newly engaged with popular culture and political events alike.

THE RETURN OF THE REPRESSED

Modern British literature is characterized by the increasing presence of women's voices, working-class voices, and voices expressing varied ethnic, religious, and sexual perspectives which, whether methodically or inadvertently, had often been excluded from the British literary tradition. The writings of an author like Woolf made England think hard about who she really was, as did, in another sense, the writings of the former colonial administrator George Orwell. In the modern period, Britain begins to deal in a fully conscious way with its human rights problems—most significantly, its treatment of women and the diverse ethnic groups of its colonial possessions.

The gradual enfranchisement and political and economic liberation of British women in the early years of the twentieth century comprised a fundamental social change; the novelist D. H. Lawrence, a rather equivocal friend of the women's movement, called it "perhaps the greatest revolution of modern times." The Women's Property Act—passed in 1882, the year of Woolf's birth—for the first time allowed married women to own property. Decades of sometimes violent suffragist agitation led finally to full voting rights for women in 1928 and to the gradual opening up of opportunities in higher education and the professions.

The quick pace of these changes naturally made many men uneasy. In their monumental three-volume study *No Man's Land: The Place of the Woman Writer in the Twentieth Century*, critics Sandra Gilbert and Susan Gubar suggest that this "war between the sexes" was one of the primary driving forces behind the modernist literary movement. Having emphasized the revolutionary force of the women's movement, Lawrence goes on to warn that the movement, "is even going beyond, and becoming a tyranny of woman, of the individual woman in the house, and of the feminine ideas and ideals in the world." In a half-serious essay titled *Cocksure Women and Hensure Men*, Lawrence complained of women

> more cocky, in their assurance, than the cock himself. . . . It is really out of scheme, it is not in relation to the rest of things. . . . They find, so often, that instead of having laid an egg, they have laid a vote, or an empty ink-bottle, or some other absolutely unhatchable object, which means nothing to them.

On the level of literary principles, a masculinist emphasis can be seen in Ezra Pound's insistence that modern poetry should "move against poppy-cock," "be harder and saner . . . 'nearer the bone' . . . as much like granite as it can be."

Other writers, male and female, supported women's rights; almost all writers sought to rebel against Victorian sexual norms and gender roles. Joyce battled with censors beginning in 1906, and his *Ulysses* was put on trial in New York on obscenity charges in 1933 (and cleared of those charges in the same week that the United States repealed Prohibition). Defending his sexual and scatological scenes, Joyce put the modernists' case for frankness this way:

> The modern writer has other problems facing him, problems which are more intimate and unusual. We prefer to search in the corners for what has been hidden, and moods, atmospheres and intimate relationships are the modern writers' theme. . . . The modern theme is the subterranean forces, those hidden tides which govern everything and run humanity counter to the apparent flood: those poisonous subtleties which envelop the soul, the ascending fumes of sex.

In defense of his "dirty" book *Lady Chatterley's Lover* (1928), whose full text was banned as obscene until 1960, Lawrence wrote: "In spite of all antagonism, I put forth this novel as an honest, healthy book, necessary for us today. . . . We are today, as human beings, evolved and cultured far beyond the taboos which are inherent in

our culture. . . . The mind has an old groveling fear of the body and the body's poten-
cies. It is the mind we have to liberate, to civilize on these points." In a rich irony,
Joyce and Lawrence hated one another's writing: Joyce insisted on calling Lawrence's
best-known novel "Lady Chatterbox's Lover." He dismissed the novel as "a piece of
propaganda in favour of something which, outside of D. H. L.'s country at any rate,
makes all the propaganda for itself." Lawrence, for his part, thought the last chapter
of *Ulysses* (Molly Bloom's famous soliloquy) "the dirtiest, most indecent, obscene
thing ever written."

Sexuality of all stripes was on trial. The lesbian writer Radclyffe Hall was tried for
obscenity in 1928 for her novel *The Well of Loneliness*—whose most obscene sentence
is, "That night they were not divided." The trial became a public spectacle, and was a
rallying point for writers like Woolf and E. M. Forster, who spoke valiantly in favor of
Hall's right to explore her subject, which was primarily the loneliness, rather than the
fleshly joys, of same-sex love. Forster's overtly homosexual writings, including his
novel *Maurice*, were not published until after his death in 1970. Woolf was somewhat
more open in her novel *Orlando* (1928), whose protagonist changes sex from male to
female. In Joyce's *Ulysses*, Leopold Bloom fantasizes about becoming a "new womanly
man" and dreams of being chastised by a dominatrix who appears first as Bella and
then as Bello Cohen. It was not only sexual taboos that were challenged in the writing of the period; in practice there began to be a loosening of the strict gender and
sexual roles, which had been reinforced by the homophobia resulting from Oscar
Wilde's trial. Gay, lesbian, and bisexual writers like Forster, Woolf, Hall, Stein, Natalie Barney, Djuna Barnes, H. D., Ronald Firbank, and Carl Van Vechten pushed the
comfort level of the British reading public; even the "healthy" version of sexuality celebrated by D. H. Lawrence in his greatest novel *Women in Love* begins to suggest that
heterosexuality and homosexuality are shifting boundaries, not immutable categories.

The growing independence of the individual subject began to be matched by
drives for independence among imperial subjects as well. In "John Bull's other island," as Bernard Shaw called Ireland in his play of that title, agitations for independence grew widespread from the late nineteenth century onward, culminating in the
Easter Rising of 1916 and the 1922 partitioning of Ireland, when the Irish Republic
became an independent nation while Northern Ireland remained part of Great
Britain. No match for England militarily, the Irish used words as their chief weapon
in the struggle for independence.

The liberation of Britain's overseas colonial holdings began in the early decades of
the century and gathered momentum thereafter. The history of Great Britain in the
twentieth century is, in some ways, the story of the centrifugal forces that have largely
stripped Britain of its colonial possessions. Britain suffered humiliating losses in the
Boer War (1899–1902), fought by the British to take possession of the Boer Republic
of South Africa. Half a million British troops were unable to win outright victory over
eighty thousand Boers; finally the British adopted a scorched-earth policy that entailed massive arrests and the deaths of thousands of captives in unsanitary camps.
This debilitating and unsavory conquest marked the low point of British imperialism,
and public disgust led to a reaction against empire itself. Independence movements
sprang up in colonies around the world, most notably in India, Britain's largest colony,
"the jewel in the crown" of Queen Victoria, where Mohandas Gandhi's Congress Party
struggled through nonviolent resistance to force Britain to grant its independence.

Christopher Richard Wynne Nevinson, *Poster for the Wembley Exhibition,* 1925. Advertising the Wembley Empire Exhibition, this bus poster conveys its quite effective attempt to turn empire into spectacular entertainment, and imperial colonies into a multicultural festival for the British masses. Labor strikes and unemployment within England had made the working public aware of the huge costs of maintaining empire at their expense; the ruling class responded by trying to force the working class and the poor to emigrate to the colonies. The latter coercive approach appears in *Mrs Dalloway,* where Lady Bruton, whose last name conveys the brutality of this attempt to get rid of what she calls a "superfluous" population, is joined by Clarissa Dalloway's husband, a prominent member of the government, at a posh luncheon meeting to launch what was called in real life, although not in Woolf's novel, the "Get Out!" movement.

WORLD WAR II AND ITS AFTERMATH

The year 1939 and the start of World War II closed the modernist era. It was the year that saw the publication of Joyce's *Finnegans Wake,* which the critic Ihab Hassan calls a "monstrous prophecy" of postmodernity. The seminal modernist careers of Joyce, Woolf, Yeats, Ford, and Freud all came to an end—as did the social and political order of the previous decades. Throughout the late thirties, the government had engaged in futile efforts at diplomacy as Hitler expanded German control in central Europe. Prime Minister Neville Chamberlain finally denounced Hitler when the Germans invaded Czechoslovakia early in 1939; on September 1, Germany invaded Poland, and within days Britain declared war. In contrast to the "Great War," this conflict began with few illusions—but with the knowledge that Britain was facing an implacable and better-armed enemy. Unlike the Great War, fought on foreign soil, the new war hit home directly; during "the Blitz" from July 1940 through 1941, the German Luftwaffe carried out massive bombing raids on London and many other targets around Britain.

During these years, Winston Churchill emerged as a pivotal figure both strategically and morally. First as commander in chief of the navy, and starting in May 1940 as prime minister, he directed British military operations while rallying popular support through stirring speeches and radio addresses. The war had profound effects

London during the Blitz, seen from the north transept of Saint Paul's Cathedral.

throughout British society, as almost every man—and many women—between the ages of 14 and 64 came to be involved in the war effort, in conditions that weakened old divisions of region and class and that provided the impetus for new levels of government involvement in social planning. At the war's end in September of 1945, Britain emerged victorious, in concert with its allies. In contrast with the United States, though, Britain had suffered enormous civilian casualties and crushing economic losses, both within Great Britain and throughout its far-flung colonies. As much as a quarter of Britain's national wealth had been consumed by the war. The great city of London had undergone horrific bombing during the the Blitz, whose attacks left the face of this world capital as scarred as had the Great Fire three centuries before. Although morally and socially triumphant in its defeat of Nazism and fascism, Britain was left shattered economically and exhausted spiritually. Its people had come through the war gallantly, only to face grim conditions at home and political unrest throughout the empire.

The global effort of that war, whose battles were fought not only in Europe but in Africa, Asia, Latin America, the Middle East, and the Pacific, had forced Britain to draw massively on its colonies for raw materials, money, and soldiers. Since the resistance to the British empire had begun long before World War II, the drafting of millions of already restive colonial subjects into the armed forces intensified the tensions and the conflicts running beneath the surface of the empire. One of the most important political phenomena of the twentieth century was about to hit a depleted

Britain with a vengeance: the decolonization of most of the conquered globe in the great wave of independence movements that swept the world after 1945. One by one, with greater and lesser degrees of violence and agony, colonies slipped out of Britain's imperial net. From the independence of India (1947) to the independence struggles of Kenya, Nigeria, Zaire, Palestine, Egypt, and many others, Britain experienced the accelerated loss of the largest empire in Western history. Retaining only a handful of Caribbean, Latin American, and Pacific Rim possessions, the empire had radically shrunk. India, Pakistan, Canada, Australia, and a few other countries adopted commonwealth status, remaining commercially linked but becoming essentially independent politically. The empire on which the sun never set was fast becoming largely confined to England, Scotland, Wales, and Northern Ireland—the latter, especially, an ongoing area of tension and conflict to the present day.

The dizzying pace of decolonization after the war put Britain in a paradoxically modern position ahead of many other Western countries: the unquestioned ability, and the rarely questioned right, of Western societies to dominate the globe had finally encountered decisive opposition. Within fifty years Britain found itself transformed from the dominant global power into a relatively small and, for a time, impoverished island nation, no longer a dictator of the world's history, but merely part of it. This dislocation was profoundly registered in British culture, and British writers strove to assess these losses—and to define the new possibilities for a freer and more open society that might emerge from the wreckage of empire.

One of the exciting aspects of British literature after World War II, then, is its very incoherence. New players not only joined the game, but in some instances began to call the shots, as the struggles for independence from British colonial control provided vivid and critical literary subjects—"subjects" in the sense of topics as well as those newly empowered writers whose subjectivity emerged on the page. At the same time, the shrinking of empire was turning Great Britain back into a small nation. Vita Sackville-West's story *Seducers in Ecuador* serves as a beautiful pre-war parable of Britain's precarious global significance; its main character travels around the Mediterranean by yacht with a group of fellow English citizens, with many if not most of their exotic ports of call under British imperial control. When the man buys a pair of blue spectacles in Egypt, he finds that he cannot bear to take them off: the story subtly suggests that they are imperial sunglasses, affording him a way of looking at the world—a gaze of control and domination—that ironically destroys his life when he tries to wear them back in England. The British literature that comes after the loss of Suez, of Egypt and Palestine and Arabia, reverses Sackville-West's prescient parable. The inhabitants of colonized zones don spectacles themselves, and use them to look unsparingly at their colonizers.

A new generation of writers also took on the task of evaluating English culture from inside. John of Gaunt's beautiful paean to "this sceptered isle, this England," in Shakespeare's *Richard II* had to be rewritten now: what was "this England" to be? In the absence of its colonial possessions, and in the general misery of shortages and rationing after the war, there was suddenly a sharp new scrutiny of British society. Its class-bound hierarchies appeared in an even harsher light, and its failures at home became the source of profound self-examination. Rage and anger accompanied this process of self-awareness, and a generation of literary artists dubbed the "angry young men" arose to meet the failures head-on, often in realist drama so faithful to its shabby subjects it was called "kitchen sink" drama, after the cold-water flat settings where the characters played out their rage. Playwrights such as John Osborne (as in the aptly titled *Look Back in Anger*) and novelists such as Anthony Burgess (*A Clockwork Orange*) angrily or satirically probed the discrepancy between England's glorious past and its seemingly squalid present.

A sense of diminishment in the world's eyes led to a passionate critique of British institutions, particularly its class structure, even where the literature produced was conservative in its looking backward. The extraordinary poet Philip Larkin might be seen as a key figure in this generation of writers. Larkin was a librarian in a rural town for most of his adult life. His poetry takes on the sardonic voice of the disenfranchised and the dispossessed—speaking not for the poor or the downtrodden but instead articulating the sense of loss and fury of middle and upper-class England, bereft of its historical prestige, impoverished by modern culture. He sings of nature, home, and country in a voice that is lacerating and self-mocking, using jazzy and colloquial poetic diction and Anglo-Saxon expletives. As one of his poems memorably declares:

> They fuck you up, your mum and dad.
>   They may not mean to, but they do.
> They fill you with the faults they had
>   And add some extra, just for you.

Larkin also wrote several notable novels at this time, among them *A Girl in Winter*, which explores from a surprisingly feminine and even feminist point of view the struggles of an emigré to Britain who must conceal the traumas her family experienced during the war, in order to "fit in" with a blithe and cavalier aristocratic British family. Larkin's artistry joins that of a host of other postwar writers, mostly male, who write from the center of an England now put off-kilter by the wrenching changes after the war.

Profound historical changes were to continue after the war with the commencement of the Cold War, in which the new world superpowers, the United States and the former Soviet Union, became locked in an intense battle for ideological, political, and economic dominance. Human beings now possessed the technological means to destroy the planet and its inhabitants, and these weapons of destruction were amassed by two societies with sharply conflicting goals. Britain along with Western Europe unequivocally aligned itself on the side of the United States, joining in the long fight against communism and Soviet socialism. While not itself a superpower, Britain had to shape its own social goals in light of the Cold War raging around it. A supremely eloquent voice in the articulation of what was at stake was that of the British writer George Orwell, known for his lucid essays on politics and language, including *Politics and the English Language*, to cite one of his classic works. Immediately after the war Orwell crafted *1984*, an enduring parable of Cold War culture. This book envisions a future society in the year 1984 when the infamous "Big Brother" is watching everyone. That tale of a society of totalitarian surveillance was a thinly veiled allegory of the possibilities inherent not only in a Soviet takeover but even in Western societies and their implicit tendencies toward control and bureaucracy. It may be that Orwell was able to be prophetic about the cultural touchstones of the next several decades because as a British writer he wrote from an oblique angle: the colonial relationship of Britain to the United States had become reversed, with Britain almost becoming an outpost of the United States in terms of its Cold War dominance, reminiscent of Britain's dominance of the fate of the American colonies in the centuries leading up to the American Revolution. It is sometimes possible to see more clearly from a position outside the exact center—and Britain was, in this sense, no longer the center of English-speaking Western civilization. Strangely enough, that ex-centricity granted its literary writers a certain kind of insight.

The British novel after World War II made a retreat from modernist experimentalism. One explanation for a return to the realism that Woolf had so passionately argued against comes, paradoxically, from feminism of the very sort Woolf espouses in *A Room of One's Own* and *Three Guineas*. For as women began to write in large numbers, the novel with characters and a plot became a kind of room these writers needed to make their own. A host of important women writers emerged who revived the novel—which had been declared dead by the French, at least, around 1950—by using its traditions to incorporate their experiences as women, "making it new" not by formal experiments, but by opening that familiar, even a little shabby, room to new voices and new stories. Among the practitioners of this "feminist realism"—although some of them would vehemently deny the label "feminist"—are Jean Rhys, Doris Lessing, Margaret Drabble, A. S. Byatt, Muriel Spark, Iris Murdoch, Nadine Gordimer, and Buchi Emecheta. In every case these are writers who ring changes on ostensibly traditional forms.

A particularly vibrant arena of British literary innovation after the postwar period was British drama; the dramatic form seemed to lend itself to the staging of new social and aesthetic experiments which, with the exception of women's writing as noted above, largely bypassed the British novel of this period. The most innovative of all British dramatists of the twentieth century after World War I was indubitably the Irishman Samuel Beckett. Living in a form of self-imposed exile in France, and a further self-imposed exile within the French language, Beckett moved from being the writer of mordant novels (*Molloy; Malone Dies*) to becoming an extraordinary dramatist. He often wrote his plays first in French, later translating them into English, so that English was their "secondary" language, leading to multiple puns in both English and French. Beckett's contribution to dramatic form, for which he received the Nobel Prize, is nonetheless a creation within British literature. Beckett sculpted his plays out of silence, paring down lines of dialogue until their short sentences and sometimes single words reverberate with the unspoken. More than any other dramatist in English, Samuel Beckett found the pockets of silence in English speech, and made those silences speak. His characters do not inhabit a real place, like England, but instead occupy an abstract space of human existence, where the human predicaments of longing and desire for redemption, the failures of understanding, and the bafflement of death are experienced in their purest form.

Within England a host of dramatic luminaries gave vital energy to the British stage after 1945. While John Osborne created realist dramas of rage and dispossession, Harold Pinter emphasized the careful chiseling of language, bringing out the full ambiguity hidden in seemingly innocuous social conversation. Tom Stoppard joins Harold Pinter in his postwar longevity as a master of the British drama, despite or perhaps because of being an immigrant—"a bounced Czech," as he has called himself. Stoppard employs a brilliant rhetorical surface in his plays, which are often modernist puzzle boxes in their annihilation of the rules of time and space. In his meteoric but short dramatic career the playwright Joe Orton took a reverse tack to that of Beckettian silence and economy, or Pinterian ordinary language, and returned to the example of Oscar Wilde. Using a wildly baroque vocabulary and an epigrammatic wit, Orton brought an explicit gay drama and gay sensibility to the postwar theater, in works like *Loot,* which revolves around a seductive lower-class character who wreaks sexual havoc with all the inhabitants of a country estate, male and female, young and old. In *What the Butler Saw,* Orton imagines a monumental statue, bearing the national "phallus," which is hilariously blown to bits.

The impoverishment of the fifties abated in the sixties, at least for the middle class, as British banking and finance reinvigorated the economy. "Swinging London" became a household phrase, as British urban culture set the pace in music, fashion, and style. The Carnaby Street mode of dress and fashion mavens like Mary Quant, Jean Muir, and Zandra Rhodes were copied all over the world, worn by Jean Shrimpton and Twiggy, who were among the first supermodels. British film came out of a postwar slump and movies like *Morgan* and *Georgy Girl* had huge audiences at home and in the United States. A delirious excitement invested British popular culture, and London became a hub of the new once more. The critique of British society mounted by Joe Orton's work found its double in the youth culture of "Mods" and "Rockers." Asked which he was, the Beatles' drummer Ringo Starr claimed to synthesize both: "I'm a mocker."

Amid the cultural ferment of the sixties and seventies, successive British governments struggled with intractable problems of inflation and unemployment, punctuated by frequent strikes by Britain's powerful unions, and rising violence in Northern Ireland. The generally pro-union government of Harold Wilson (1964–1970) was followed by the Conservative government of Edward Heath, who put new stress on private enterprise. A major shift away from the "welfare state," however, came only at the end of the decade, when Heath was succeeded by the formidable Margaret Thatcher, the prime minister of Britain for a record twelve years. The daughter of a lower middle-class family, Thatcher vaulted into politics when that was an exceptionally rare opportunity not only for a woman, but for a person whose father was a shopkeeper. Trained as a chemist, Thatcher worked long and hard for the Conservative (Tory) Party, even as Britain was ruled by a succession of Labour and Socialist governments. When her chance came to lead England as its Tory prime minister, Thatcher and her political and ideological colleagues began a governmental revolution by adopting free-market policies similar to those identified with the Ronald Reagan school of U.S. Republicanism. Thatcher set about dismantling as much of the welfare state of postwar modern Britain as she could—and that was a considerable amount.

Margaret Thatcher had an enormous impact on British identity, as well as on British society. Among the very small number of women worldwide who have ever wielded such substantial political power—Golda Meir and Indira Gandhi come to mind as others—Thatcher's polished good looks, her extreme toughness, and her uncompromising political dictates combined to produce a caricature of her as the domineering English governess, laying down the rules of what would be good for Britain's unruly citizens. Thatcher's economic policies emphasized productivity as never before; under her rule, an entrepreneurial culture began to flourish at the expense of once-sacred British social entitlements in education, health care, and civic subsidy of the arts and culture. Margaret Thatcher's most breathtaking

The Beatles preparing for a television broadcast, c. 1963.

quotation, and the one summing up her philosophy of government, was uttered in response to complaints about what was happening to the fabric of British society and, especially, to its poor, elderly, immigrants, and the mass numbers of the unemployed. "There is no such thing as society," she declared. What she meant was that government had no role to play in creating a unitary, egalitarian society. The forces of the unleashed free market, and the will of private individuals, would replace any notion of a social contract or social compact between and among British citizens. There was irony, of course, in Thatcher's seeming to turn her back on members of her own class and those below it, and despite the power and immense reputation she acquired worldwide, there was always scathing and vocal opposition to her within Britain, as she privatized the universities and abolished tenure, made inroads on the National Health Service, dissolved city councils and established poll taxes. Prime Minister Thatcher declared and fought Britain's last imperial war of modern times, against Argentina over the control of the Falkland Islands, and she was fierce opponent of nationalist sentiment among the Scottish and the Welsh, a firm upholder of Britain's right to control Northern Ireland in perpetuity, and strongly against the move toward joining the European Community. Thatcher became an icon in Britain, as well as its longest-governing prime minister: an icon for her certainty, her confidence, and her personification of the huge changes she brought about. Though she provoked sharp opposition, her brilliance and energy were never in question, nor was her international influence.

By and large, the literary response to Thatcher's vision of Britain was electrifying in its opposition to everything she stood for. The jolt of anti-Thatcherism galvanized fiction, poetry, drama, visual art, and film. Among the many superb artists honed in the crucible of anti-Thatcherism is the playwright Caryl Churchill. While Churchill was plying her craft well before Maggie's reign began, she is an apt symbol of the passionate creativity unleashed from the later 1970s into the mid–1990s, especially given the gender she shares with Thatcher. Without question Caryl Churchill is among the foremost playwrights in the world today; such singularity means for her that gender—in addition to class, race, age, sexuality, nationality, ethnicity and the like—is foregrounded in her plays. Churchill's provocative theater is designed in part to open that Pandora's box which Thatcher herself ignored. Her play *Top Girls*, for example, sets Thatcher's political rise into collision with a contemporary feminism that questions whether female power is simply identical to masculine power—i.e., just a matter of who's on top, and who's at the top. By those lights, Thatcher's success made her a top girl par excellence, yet the play sets up a dinner party to debate this, a conversation between and among powerful women throughout the centuries from around the world, some of them historical figures, others images and icons, legends or myths, all eager to investigate whether or not women's liberation inheres in a simple exchange of dominance.

Major changes occurred in the last several years of the twentieth century, changes sweeping enough to have diminished Margaret Thatcher's iconic stature, and to have partially reversed the social revolution she began. At the turn of the century, the Labour Party reclaimed control of the country, changing course economically and emphasizing the very social contract Thatcher had set aside. Despite its refusal to adopt the European common currency, the Euro, Britain is an increasingly pivotal member of the European Community alliance, and its own internal divisions have come productively to the fore. Surprisingly, the twentieth century ended in much the same way as did the nineteenth century for Britain, with a nationwide debate on home rule. In 1886 and again in 1893 the eminent British prime minister William Gladstone fought for the establishment of a separate Irish parliament—thus the term "home rule"—to allow the Irish colony, with its differing religion of Roman Catholicism and its unique Gaelic culture, to have control over its own internal affairs. Gladstone and his Liberal Party formed an alliance with the Irish National Party's members of Parliament, who were led by the great Charles Stewart Parnell, a Protestant Irishman known as "the uncrowned king of Ireland." Parnell's political fall due to an extramarital scandal removed a key player in Gladstone's strategy, and his final attempt in 1893 at voting in home rule failed. This failure led to the Irish revolution, the Irish Civil War, and the continuing violence within Northern Ireland, the six counties still belonging to Britain and occupied by their army.

Britain's new prime minister, Tony Blair, was elected in 1997 from the Labour Party, breaking the Conservative Party's eighteen-year hold on the position under Thatcher and her chosen successor, the rather low-key John Major. One of Blair's main campaign promises was bringing home rule to both Scotland and Wales, regions of Britain with their own language and dialect, their own cultural mores, and a long history of armed conflict with England. The referendum on the Scottish parliament, with the power to raise and lower income taxes within Scotland, and a considerable budget to operate as Scotland chooses, for its schools, health, housing and transport, overwhelmingly passed the popular vote; Wales has voted as well for the creation of a Welsh assembly with many of the same powers and responsibilities. While the Republic of Ireland is now a nation in its own right, Tony Blair's commitment to the peace talks in Northern Ireland, and to the inclusion of Sinn Fein in those talks, has also provided the first stirrings of political momentum in resolving the century-old conflict between Northern Irish Protestants who largely wish to remain attached to Britain, and the Northern Irish Catholics who have fought for the autonomy of this part of Ireland.

LANGUAGE AND IDENTITY

Complicated questions of language and identity have increasingly come to dominate the most recent phase of British literature. A great paradox of the British postwar period, in its time of imperial shrinkage, involves the fate of the English language. Britain may have been "kicked out" of many of its former colonies as a governing presence, but English was rarely shown the door at the same time. For economic and cultural reasons English as a global language became even more widely dispersed and dominant after World War II. Of course, the spread of U.S. interests has played a role in the hegemony of English. However, the old contours of the British empire continue to shape much of the production of English literature today. In this way, the former British empire has become part of the fabric of British literature. V. S. Naipaul, for example, has long resided in England, but he was born to Indian parents in Trinidad, where the British had deployed Indian labor. His writing is as much in dialogue with the British literary tradition, and an extension of it, as that of any native-born British author. Naipaul's winning of the 2001 Nobel Prize for literature both confirms his international standing and highlights the altered literary geography of England itself.

Salman Rushdie, who is of Pakistani parentage, is another intriguing example of this process of crossing the increasingly porous boundaries of Britishness, as well as a cautionary tale of how powerful literature can be. Rushdie's novels are part of British literature at its modernist best, drawing on the entire English literary tradition, yet informed by a cosmopolitan and a non-Western literary tradition as well. Eight years after he achieved great acclaim for his novel *Midnight's Children* (1980), a book that adapted the "magic realism" of Latin American fiction to the history of Indian independence, Rushdie published *The Satanic Verses*. This novel recounts a magical mystery tour of sorts, the arrival of two South Asian refugees to modern London: one a film star from Bombay, the other a kind of trickster figure. Embedded in this complex tale of migration and identity is a brief dream sequence satirizing the prophet Mohammed. In response to this dream-within-a-dream passage, the Iranian theocratic government delivered a *fatwa*—an edict sentencing Rushdie to death for treachery to the religion of Islam. Rushdie did not write the book in Arabic, nor did he write it for a Muslim audience, but that was irrelevant to the clerics who pronounced sentence on him before millions of devout adherents. From that time until the late 1990s, Rushdie was forced to live in a form of self-imposed house arrest, guarded by the British government. In an ironic twist, British literature itself had become his prison house of language, his internal exile. It is this tradition that "protects" him as a great writer, and, because of its porous literary borders, is responsible for his predicament.

In recent years British literature has been infused with new life both from foreign-born writers and from new voices bubbling up from within the British Isles, in the shape of Welsh, Scottish, and Irish literary prose and poetry. The Nobel Prize-winning Irish poet Seamus Heaney is a kind of internal outsider, since, as he has written, he does not consider himself to be part of "British" literature as ordinarily defined, while he nonetheless writes English poetry deeply influenced by English poets from Milton to Wordsworth to Eliot. Some writers have deliberately taken themselves out of British literature for political and literary reasons, using the strongest means possible: they have decided to write in a language other than English. For example, the Kenyan writer Ngugi wa Thiong'o, educated by British missionaries and then at a British university, whose first memorized poem was Wordsworth's *Daffodils*, now writes in the Kikuyu language, and translates his work into English. The Irish poet Nuala Ní Dhomhnaill has made a similar decision: she writes and publishes her poetry first in Irish, and only later translates it into English as a "second" language.

In recent years British writing has been invigorated from "below," as well as from "outside": there has been a profusion of working-class or lower-middle-class novelists, poets, and screenwriters, many of whom adopt the dialect or argot of lower-class Welsh, Scottish, and Irish English. The Scottish writer Irvine Welsh is one example of this cross-fertilization today; his novel *Trainspotting* received ample literary accolades and was made into a widely seen film that, like the book, circulated throughout Europe, the Americas, and much of the globe. Its picaresque tale of down-and-out yet lively and smart urban twenty-somethings trying to find fulfillment in drugs, travel, and petty crime made Glaswegian knockabouts and their dialect emblematic of the modern condition. When James Kelman won the Booker Prize for the best novel published in England in 1994, there was widespread outrage: the working-class, expletive-laced speech of his Scottish protagonist was deemed unliterary by many, or at least unreadable and not in conformity with what was revered as the Queen's English. Poetry too has become a vehicle for a range of literary experiments, linking music and film to rhymed and unrhymed, and often performed, verse, connecting the popular and the literary. This upsurge of vivacious and often provocative writing is primarily the work of younger writers, and in many instances the novels are almost immediately being turned into films with international audiences.

In the past hundred years British literature has seen upheavals of aesthetic form, of geographic location, and of linguistic content. What is no longer in question, oddly enough, despite the current age of cyberspace and interactive media, is whether literature itself will survive. As Mark Twain once commented dryly after reading his own obituary in the newspaper: "The reports of my death are greatly exaggerated." The reports of literature's inevitable eclipse at the hands of media and mass culture have, it seems, been greatly exaggerated too. At this moment, British literary creativity is fed from many streams, welling up unpredictably, located in unexpected places. British literature has not merely survived; it remains a vital index of contemporary social and cultural life, and a crucial indication of the shape of things to come.

Joseph Conrad

1857–1924

Joseph Conrad, London, 11 March 1916.

One of the ironies of twentieth-century British literature is that many of its greatest writers were not conventionally "British." In the case of Joseph Conrad, arguably the first modern British writer, the irony is even more extreme, because Conrad was born a Pole, and learned English only when he was in his twenties. The transformation of Josef Konrad Nalecz Korzeniowski into "Joseph Conrad" is as fascinating and mysterious a story as the transforming journeys at the heart of his fiction.

Joseph Conrad was a lifelong exile from a country that no longer existed on the map of Europe as a separate country. At the time of Conrad's birth in 1857, Poland was divided between Russia and the Austro-Hungarian empire. His parents, Apollo and Eva, were Polish patriots, and after an uprising against Russia in 1863, the family was exiled to a village in the far north of Russia. Eva died when Josef was seven years old; Apollo when he was twelve. Apollo had been both a political activist and a man of letters, a poet and a translator of French and English literature into Polish. In a sense, by becoming a British novelist writing in English, Conrad was carrying on a project of translation begun by his father, a translation across cultures and literatures as well as languages. Hidden within Conrad's poetic and impressionistic literary language is a secret language—Polish—and a secret history of exile from his homeland.

After Conrad's parents died, he was raised by a cosmopolitan uncle, Tadeusz Bobrowski, who was also imbued with patriotic political leanings and a deep love of literature. Josef was sent to school in Cracow, Poland, where he was bored and restless. His uncle then sent him to Switzerland with a private tutor; they argued constantly for a year, and the tutor resigned. Not quite seventeen years old, Conrad proceeded to Marseilles and joined the French merchant navy. He spent twenty years as a sailor and as a ship's captain, spending four years sailing under the French flag, and then sixteen years with British trading ships. In 1894 Josef Korzeniowski completed his transformation into the writer Joseph Conrad by changing his name and settling in England to become a full-time writer.

By the end of the nineteenth century, the nationalistic wars that had led to a divided Poland had been followed by another historical phenomenon: the dividing-up of the globe by the nations of Europe as these powers consolidated empires. The oceans were crucial pathways in these struggles, not simply vast, watery landscapes outside of history. The seafaring Conrad, who had wanted to leave the frustrations of school behind him and see the world, became intimately involved in the everyday business of the making of empires, playing a minor role behind the scenes of the major political forces of the age. Merchant ships of the kind he served on traced the routes of trade and commerce, which now had become the routes of colonization and political conquest as well. As he came to realize he was an eyewitness to modern history in the making, Joseph Conrad discovered his abiding subject as a writer.

Conrad's voyages during this twenty-year odyssey took him East and West, to Indonesia and the Philippines, to Venezuela, the West Indies, and Africa. Working all the while, he watched as bit by bit the patchwork quilt of empire was put together. Wishing to avoid conscription in the French navy when he came of age, in 1878 Conrad joined the British merchant navy. The British empire had become the most extensive and mighty of any imperial power, and in his capacity as seaman Conrad worked in the main ports of call of the empire upon which the sun supposedly never set. He adopted British citizenship in 1886; after his uncle Tadeusz's death in 1894, Conrad made the final decision to become a writer, and to write in English rather than in French. At the age of thirty-seven, Joseph Conrad was newly born.

As a British writer, Conrad was a sort of ventriloquist. On the surface, he was as English as any other writer in his circle: he married an Englishwoman, Jessie George, and became a recognized part of British literary life, forming friendships with other major writers like Henry James and Ford Madox Ford, and achieving great popularity with the British reading public. A stranger from an exotically foreign place, by British standards, a newcomer to the English language, he nonetheless spoke through an English "voice" he created. From his distanced perspective, he was able to make English do things it had not done in the past for native writers of English. Language in Conrad's writing is always a bit off kilter, reading as if it had been translated instead of being, as it was, originally written in English. His prose has a hallucinatory effect, and a poetic intensity linked to his approaching the words of the English language afresh. The most famous of Conrad's narrators is the character Marlow, who appears in several of his major works as an elusive commentator on the action. His Englishness is as real as it can be, for an imitation. Marlow is perhaps even more British than the British, lapsing often into British slang like "By Jove!" as if to authenticate the reality of Conrad's vision of the British world. Through narrative voices like that of Marlow, Conrad can tell stories that may appear to be familiar and ordinary but are in fact anything but that. If modernist writers succeed in making us doubt that we can truly be at home in the world, Conrad can be said to have been the first writer to convey this homelessness in English.

There is another paradox at the heart of Joseph Conrad's work. His writing straddles the nineteenth and the twentieth centuries, with the five major works he wrote in the years before 1900—*Almayer's Folly*, *The Nigger of the "Narcissus,"* *Heart of Darkness*, *Lord Jim*, and *Typhoon*—thought of by many critics as more modernist and experimental than later novels he wrote in the twentieth century—*Nostromo*, *The Secret Agent*, *Under Western Eyes*, *Chance*, and *Victory*. The critic Ian Watt claims that the "intense experimentation which began in 1896 and ended in 1900" resulted from Conrad's concentration in those five earlier works on his own personal experience, a personal experience of travel, exile, and solitude that was a radical premonition of the conditions of modernity. Works like *Heart of Darkness*, written during Queen Victoria's reign, for Watt present "the obdurate incompatibility of the self and the world in which it exists." In book after book, he sets a lone individual into confrontation with the complexities of the modern world, whether the world be that of European imperialism, or political anarchism, or the secret world of spies, or the world of political revolution. His heroes and (much less often) heroines have to find their bearings as society crumbles around them, and Conrad usually depicts them at a moment of choice, when they have to act on their lonely knowledge without any guarantee that they have chosen rightly.

A reliance on personal experience might seem to be a recipe for a straightforward, realist style, but Conrad's prose throughout his work is complex and symbolic, relying on images that are spun into complicated and ambiguous webs of symbolism. What stands out prominently in Conrad's style is its visual nature, the emphasis on making the reader "see." Critics of Conrad's writing early on seized on the strikingly visual aspect of his effects, and his friend and fellow modernist writer Ford Madox Ford wrote an essay in 1913, *On Impressionism*, which put Conrad in a newly invented camp of impressionist writers. Conrad never fully agreed with this description of his style, nor did he have any special fondness for impressionist painting or the works of its greatest practitioners, Monet and Cézanne. Nonetheless, his own preface to *The Nigger of the "Narcissus"* describes all successful art as based on "an impression conveyed through the senses," and in each of his first five books narrators recount what they have *seen*. The narrator goes back over an experience in retelling it to an audience, an experience whose significance is not necessarily clear even to the narrator but whose meaning is revealed through the accumulation of imagistic details. The powers of sight are directly related to the powers of insight, or self-knowledge. A famous passage from *Heart of Darkness* explains the storytelling technique of the narrator Marlow, but also explains a philosophical conviction at the core of Conrad's writing: "The yarns of seamen have a direct simplicity, the whole meaning of which lies within the shell of a cracked nut. But Marlow was not typical (if his propensity to spin yarns be excepted), and to him the meaning of an episode was not inside like a kernel but outside, enveloping the tale which brought it out only as a glow brings out a haze, in the likeness of one of these misty halos that are sometimes made visible by the spectral illumination of moonshine." Events cast a visual glow and haze where meaning can be found only in the most subtle shades and ambiguous highlights of language. The reader must participate in the gradual, and partial, process of accumulating meaning.

Heart of Darkness is a work at the heart of modern British literature. First published serially in *Blackwood's Magazine* in 1899, it was reprinted as a complete work along with a companion novella, *Youth*, in 1902, and writers have returned to it again and again, in the form of quotations and allusions and imitations of its style; its story has been rewritten by each successive generation, in novels, films like *Apocalypse Now*, and even rock lyrics. Almost mythic in resonance, *Heart of Darkness* itself is structured around a mythical core—that is, the hero's quest. The journey or quest motif pervades world literature and English literature alike, from the *Odyssey* and the *Epic of Gilgamesh* to Dante's *Divine Comedy*, Bunyan's *Pilgrim's Progress*, and Byron's *Childe Harold*. *Heart of Darkness* condenses in its pages an epic range of theme and experience, both the social themes of empire and cultural clash, and the personal theme of the hero's quest for self-discovery.

As with all his early work, Conrad based *Heart of Darkness* on his own experience, in this case a trip he took up the Congo River in 1890 in order to become captain of a small steamship. The trip was an unusual one even by Conrad's standards, as he had been sailing the major oceans of the world on large ships. Conrad had reasons for choosing the assignment, however; he had been fascinated by maps since boyhood, and the blank space on the continent of Africa represented by the then-unexplored interior impelled him on. He was curious to see for himself the scandalous imperial practices of the Belgian King Leopold II in the Congo, who possessed what he called the Congo Free State (now Zaire) as his own private property, draining it of raw materials like ivory, while claiming to be suppressing savagery and spreading European civilization. After traveling two hundred miles upriver to Kinshasa to join his ship, however, he found it was undergoing repairs. He traveled as a passenger on a trip to Stanley Falls, to bring back an ailing company agent, Georges Klein, who died on the return trip to Kinshasa. These events provided the germ of Conrad's novella, which transformed Klein ("Little," in German) into the uncanny figure of Kurtz.

A diary Conrad kept during his journey (excerpted beginning on p. 1104) records his dawning awareness that King Leopold's policy in the Congo was nothing other than slave labor, ultimately causing the deaths of more than a million Africans. Initially an observer, Conrad became a passionately informed partisan, and made known his findings in the form of journalism and essays in the attempt to halt the King's genocidal policies. *Heart of Darkness* records these evils, and the ravages of Belgian colonialism on the African tribal societies it encountered and uprooted. Scholars of African history have shown how accurate his descriptions are, from the bit of white thread worn around the neck of a certain tribal group, to the construction of the railroad to Kinshasa and its devastating human impact. Conrad never names the Congo, nor the places and landmarks his character Marlow visits, yet he himself later called the book a "Kodak," or a snapshot, of the Congo.

The location is left unnamed in part because Conrad wishes to show that the heart of this darkness can shift on its axis. Marlow is telling the tale to several anonymous Englishmen as they sail the Thames on their yacht. Under the Roman empire, Britain had itself been thought of as a savage wilderness, a dark continent. The journey upriver, as Marlow points out, has been a reverse journey as well, a journey back from Africa to the darkness that lies at the heart of an England that claims to be civilizing those whom it is merely conquering. The seemingly clear-cut boundaries of light and dark, black and white, have blurred and even reversed themselves, and the nested narrative of the story itself challenges our understanding and even our sense of self. In this narrative, as in Conrad's other works, we are confronted with the tragic irony that human knowledge always comes too late.

Preface to *The Nigger of the "Narcissus"*[1]

A work that aspires, however humbly, to the condition of art should carry its justification in every line. And art itself may be defined as a single-minded attempt to render the highest kind of justice to the visible universe, by bringing to light the truth, manifold and one, underlying its every aspect. It is an attempt to find in its forms, in its colours, in its light, in its shadows, in the aspects of matter, and in the facts of life what of each is fundamental, what is enduring and essential—their one illuminating and convincing quality—the very truth of their existence. The artist, then, like the thinker or the scientist, seeks the truth and makes his appeal. Impressed by the aspect of the world the thinker plunges into ideas, the scientist into facts—whence, presently, emerging they make their appeal to those qualities of our being that fit us best for the hazardous enterprise of living. They speak authoritatively to our common sense, to our intelligence, to our desire of peace, or to our desire of unrest; not seldom to our prejudices, sometimes to our fears, often to our egoism—but always to our credulity. And their words are heard with reverence, for their concern is with weighty matters: with the cultivation of our minds and the proper care of our bodies, with the attainment of our ambitions, with the perfection of the means and the glorification of our precious aims.

It is otherwise with the artist.

Confronted by the same enigmatical spectacle the artist descends within himself, and in that lonely region of stress and strife, if he be deserving and fortunate, he finds the terms of his appeal. His appeal is made to our less obvious capacities: to that part of our nature which, because of the warlike conditions of existence, is necessarily kept out of sight within the more resisting and hard qualities—like the vulnerable body within a steel armour. His appeal is less loud, more profound, less distinct, more stirring—and sooner forgotten. Yet its effect endures for ever. The changing wisdom of successive generations discards ideas, questions facts, demolishes theories. But the artist appeals to that part of our being which is not dependent on wisdom; to that in us which is a gift and not an acquisition—and, therefore, more permanently enduring. He speaks to our capacity for delight and wonder, to the sense of mystery surrounding our lives; to our sense of pity, and beauty, and pain; to the latent feeling of fellowship with all creation—and to the subtle but invincible conviction of solidarity that knits together the loneliness of innumerable hearts, to the solidarity in dreams, in joy, in sorrow, in aspirations, in illusions, in hope, in fear, which binds men to each other, which binds together all humanity—the dead to the living and the living to the unborn.

It is only some such train of thought, or rather of feeling, that can in a measure explain the aim of the attempt, made in the tale which follows, to present an unrestful episode in the obscure lives of a few individuals out of all the disregarded multitude of

---

1. Conrad's novella *The Nigger of the "Narcissus"* deals with the tragic death of a black seaman aboard a merchant ship named the *Narcissus;* Conrad had served as first mate on a ship of that name in the Indian Ocean in 1883. He published the novella in *The New Review* in 1897, then added this preface when it came out in book form in 1898.

the bewildered, the simple, and the voiceless. For, if any part of truth dwells in the belief confessed above, it becomes evident that there is not a place of splendour or a dark corner of the earth that does not deserve, if only a passing glance of wonder and pity. The motive, then, may be held to justify the matter of the work; but this preface, which is simply an avowal of endeavour, cannot end here—for the avowal is not yet complete.

Fiction—if it at all aspires to be art—appeals to temperament. And in truth it must be, like painting, like music, like all art, the appeal of one temperament to all the other innumerable temperaments whose subtle and resistless power endows passing events with their true meaning, and creates the moral, the emotional atmosphere of the place and time. Such an appeal to be effective must be an impression conveyed through the senses; and, in fact, it cannot be made in any other way, because temperament, whether individual or collective, is not amenable to persuasion. All art, therefore, appeals primarily to the senses, and the artistic aim when expressing itself in written words must also make its appeal through the senses, if its high desire is to reach the secret spring of responsive emotions. It must strenuously aspire to the plasticity of sculpture, to the colour of painting, and to the magic suggestiveness of music—which is the art of arts. And it is only through complete, unswerving devotion to the perfect blending of form and substance; it is only through an unremitting never-discouraged care for the shape and ring of sentences that an approach can be made to plasticity, to colour, and that the light of magic suggestiveness may be brought to play for an evanescent instant over the commonplace surface of words: of the old, old words, worn thin, defaced by ages of careless usage.

The sincere endeavour to accomplish that creative task, to go as far on that road as his strength will carry him, to go undeterred by faltering, weariness, or reproach, is the only valid justification for the worker in prose. And if his conscience is clear, his answer to those who, in the fullness of a wisdom which looks for immediate profit, demand specifically to be edified, consoled, amused; who demand to be promptly improved, or encouraged, or frightened, or shocked, or charmed, must run thus: My task which I am trying to achieve is, by the power of the written word to make you hear, to make you feel—it is, before all, to make you see. That—and no more, and it is everything. If I succeed, you shall find there according to your deserts: encouragement, consolation, fear, charm—all you demand—and, perhaps, also that glimpse of truth for which you have forgotten to ask.

To snatch in a moment of courage, from the remorseless rush of time, a passing phase of life, is only the beginning of the task. The task approached in tenderness and faith is to hold up unquestioningly, without choice and without fear, the rescued fragment before all eyes in the light of a sincere mood. It is to show its vibration, its colour, its form; and through its movement, its form, and its colour, reveal the substance of its truth—disclose its inspiring secret: the stress and passion within the core of each convincing moment. In a single-minded attempt of that kind, if one be deserving and fortunate, one may perchance attain to such clearness of sincerity that at last the presented vision of regret or pity, of terror or mirth, shall awaken in the hearts of the beholders that feeling of unavoidable solidarity; of the solidarity in mysterious origin, in toil, in joy, in hope, in uncertain fate, which binds men to each other and all mankind to the visible world.

It is evident that he who, rightly or wrongly, holds by the convictions expressed above cannot be faithful to any one of the temporary formulas of his craft. The enduring part of them—the truth which each only imperfectly veils—should abide with him as the most precious of his possessions, but they all: Realism, Romanticism, Naturalism, even the unofficial sentimentalism (which, like the poor, is exceedingly difficult to get rid of), all these gods must, after a short period of fellowship, abandon him—even on the very threshold of the temple—to the stammerings of his conscience and to the outspoken consciousness of the difficulties of his work. In that uneasy solitude the supreme cry of Art for Art itself, loses the exciting ring of its apparent immorality. It sounds far off. It has ceased to be a cry, and is heard only as a whisper, often incomprehensible, but at times and faintly encouraging.

Sometimes, stretched at ease in the shade of a roadside tree, we watch the motions of a labourer in a distant field, and after a time, begin to wonder languidly as to what the fellow may be at. We watch the movements of his body, the waving of his arms, we see him bend down, stand up, hesitate, begin again. It may add to the charm of an idle hour to be told the purpose of his exertions. If we know he is trying to lift a stone, to dig a ditch, to uproot a stump, we look with a more real interest at his efforts; we are disposed to condone the jar of his agitation upon the restfulness of the landscape; and even, if in a brotherly frame of mind, we may bring ourselves to forgive his failure. We understood his object, and, after all, the fellow has tried, and perhaps he had not the strength—and perhaps he had not the knowledge. We forgive, go on our way—and forget.

And so it is with the workman of art. Art is long and life is short, and success is very far off. And thus, doubtful of strength to travel so far, we talk a little about the aim—the aim of art, which, like life itself, is inspiring, difficult—obscured by mists. It is not in the clear logic of a triumphant conclusion; it is not in the unveiling of one of those heartless secrets which are called the Laws of Nature. It is not less great, but only more difficult.

To arrest, for the space of a breath, the hands busy about the work of the earth, and compel men entranced by the sight of distant goals to glance for a moment at the surrounding vision of form and colour, of sunshine and shadows; to make them pause for a look, for a sigh, for a smile—such is the aim, difficult and evanescent, and reserved only for a very few to achieve. But sometimes, by the deserving and the fortunate, even that task is accomplished. And when it is accomplished—behold!—all the truth of life is there: a moment of vision, a sigh, a smile—and the return to an eternal rest.

Heart of Darkness
1

The *Nellie*, a cruising yawl,[1] swung to her anchor without a flutter of the sails, and was at rest. The flood had made, the wind was nearly calm, and being bound down the river, the only thing for it was to come to and wait for the turn of the tide.

The sea-reach of the Thames stretched before us like the beginning of an interminable waterway. In the offing the sea and the sky were welded together without a joint, and in the luminous space the tanned sails of the barges drifting up with the tide seemed to stand still in red clusters of canvas sharply peaked, with gleams of varnished sprits. A haze rested on the low shores that ran out to sea in vanishing flatness. The air was dark above Gravesend, and farther back still seemed condensed

---

1. A two-masted ship.

into a mournful gloom, brooding motionless over the biggest, and the greatest, town on earth.[2]

The Director of Companies was our captain and our host. We four affectionately watched his back as he stood in the bows looking to seaward. On the whole river there was nothing that looked half so nautical. He resembled a pilot, which to a seaman is trustworthiness personified. It was difficult to realise his work was not out there in the luminous estuary, but behind him, within the brooding gloom.

Between us there was, as I have already said somewhere, the bond of the sea. Besides holding our hearts together through long periods of separation, it had the effect of making us tolerant of each other's yarns—and even convictions. The Lawyer—the best of old fellows—had, because of his many years and many virtues, the only cushion on deck, and was lying on the only rug. The Accountant had brought out already a box of dominoes, and was toying architecturally with the bones. Marlow sat cross-legged right aft, leaning against the mizzen-mast.[3] He had sunken cheeks, a yellow complexion, a straight back, an ascetic aspect, and, with his arms dropped, the palms of hands outwards, resembled an idol. The Director, satisfied the anchor had good hold, made his way aft and sat down amongst us. We exchanged a few words lazily. Afterwards there was silence on board the yacht. For some reason or other we did not begin that game of dominoes. We felt meditative, and fit for nothing but placid staring. The day was ending in a serenity of still and exquisite brilliance. The water shone pacifically; the sky, without a speck, was a benign immensity of unstained light; the very mist on the Essex marshes was like a gauzy and radiant fabric, hung from the wooded rises inland, and draping the low shores in diaphanous folds. Only the gloom to the west, brooding over the upper reaches, became more sombre every minute, as if angered by the approach of the sun.

And at last, in its curved and imperceptible fall, the sun sank low, and from glowing white changed to a dull red without rays and without heat, as if about to go out suddenly, stricken to death by the touch of that gloom brooding over a crowd of men.

Forthwith a change came over the waters, and the serenity became less brilliant but more profound. The old river in its broad reach rested unruffled at the decline of day, after ages of good service done to the race that peopled its banks, spread out in the tranquil dignity of a waterway leading to the uttermost ends of the earth. We looked at the venerable stream not in the vivid flush of a short day that comes and departs for ever, but in the august light of abiding memories. And indeed nothing is easier for a man who has, as the phrase goes, "followed the sea" with reverence and affection, than to evoke the great spirit of the past upon the lower reaches of the Thames. The tidal current runs to and fro in its unceasing service, crowded with memories of men and ships it has borne to the rest of home or to the battles of the sea. It had known and served all the men of whom the nation is proud, from Sir Francis Drake to Sir John Franklin, knights all, titled and untitled—the great knights-errant of the sea.[4] It had borne all the ships whose names are like jewels flashing in the night of time, from the *Golden Hind* returning with her round flanks full of treasure, to be visited by the Queen's Highness and

---

2. London. Gravesend is the last major town on the Thames estuary, from which the river joins the North Sea.
3. A secondary mast at the stern of the ship.
4. Sir Francis Drake (1540–1596) was captain of *The Golden Hind* in the service of Queen Elizabeth I; his

reputation came from the successful raids he mounted against Spanish ships returning laden with gold from the New World (South America). In 1845 Sir John Franklin led an expedition in the *Erebus* and *Terror* in search of the Northwest Passage (to the Pacific); all perished.

thus pass out of the gigantic tale, to the *Erebus* and *Terror*, bound on other conquests—and that never returned. It had known the ships and the men. They had sailed from Deptford, from Greenwich, from Erith—the adventurers and the settlers; kings' ships and the ships of men on 'Change; captains, admirals, the dark "interlopers" of the Eastern trade, and the commissioned "generals" of East India fleets.[5] Hunters for gold or pursuers of fame, they all had gone out on that stream, bearing the sword, and often the torch, messengers of the might within the land, bearers of a spark from the sacred fire. What greatness had not floated on the ebb of that river into the mystery of an unknown earth! . . . The dreams of men, the seed of commonwealths, the germs of empires.

The sun set; the dusk fell on the stream, and lights began to appear along the shore. The Chapman lighthouse, a three-legged thing erect on a mudflat, shone strongly. Lights of ships moved in the fairway—a great stir of lights going up and going down. And farther west on the upper reaches the place of the monstrous town was still marked ominously on the sky, a brooding gloom in sunshine, a lurid glare under the stars.

"And this also," said Marlow suddenly, "has been one of the dark places of the earth."

He was the only man of us who still "followed the sea." The worst that could be said of him was that he did not represent his class. He was a seaman, but he was a wanderer too, while most seamen lead, if one may so express it, a sedentary life. Their minds are of the stay-at-home order, and their home is always with them—the ship; and so is their country—the sea. One ship is very much like another, and the sea is always the same. In the immutability of their surroundings the foreign shores, the foreign faces, the changing immensity of life, glide past, veiled not by a sense of mystery but by a slightly disdainful ignorance; for there is nothing mysterious to a seaman unless it be the sea itself, which is the mistress of his existence and as inscrutable as Destiny. For the rest, after his hours of work, a casual stroll or a casual spree on shore suffices to unfold for him the secret of a whole continent, and generally he finds the secret not worth knowing. The yarns of seamen have a direct simplicity, the whole meaning of which lies within the shell of a cracked nut. But Marlow was not typical (if his propensity to spin yarns be excepted), and to him the meaning of an episode was not inside like a kernel but outside, enveloping the tale which brought it out only as a glow brings out a haze, in the likeness of one of these misty halos that sometimes are made visible by the spectral illumination of moonshine.

His remark did not seem at all surprising. It was just like Marlow. It was accepted in silence. No one took the trouble to grunt even; and presently he said, very slow,—

"I was thinking of very old times, when the Romans first came here, nineteen hundred years ago[6]—the other day. . . . Light came out of this river since—you say Knights? Yes; but it is like a running blaze on a plain, like a flash of lightning in the clouds. We live in the flicker—may it last as long as the old earth keeps rolling! But darkness was here yesterday. Imagine the feelings of a commander of a fine—what d'ye call 'em?—trireme in the Mediterranean, ordered suddenly to the north; run overland across the Gauls in a hurry;[7] put in charge of one of these craft the legionaries,—a wonderful lot of handy men they must have been too—used to build, apparently by the hundred, in a month or two, if we may believe what we read. Imagine him here—the very end of the world, a sea the colour of lead, a sky the colour of smoke, a kind of ship about as rigid as a concertina—and going up this river with stores, or orders, or what you like. Sandbanks, marshes, forests, savages,—precious little to eat fit for a civilised man, nothing but Thames water to drink. No Falernian wine here, no going ashore. Here and there a military camp lost in a wilderness, like a needle in a bundle of hay—cold, fog, tempests, disease, exile, and death,—death skulking in the air, in the water, in the bush. They must have been dying like flies here. Oh yes—he did it. Did it very well, too, no doubt, and without thinking much about it either, except afterwards to brag of what he had gone through in his time, perhaps. They were men enough to face the darkness. And perhaps he was cheered by keeping his eye on a chance of promotion to the fleet at Ravenna by-and-by, if he had good friends in Rome and survived the awful climate. Or think of a decent young citizen in a toga—perhaps too much dice, you know—coming out here in the train of some prefect, or tax-gatherer, or trader even, to mend his fortunes. Land in a swamp, march through the woods, and in some inland post feel the savagery, the utter savagery, had closed round him,—all that mysterious life of the wilderness that stirs in the forest, in the jungles, in the hearts of wild men. There's no initiation either into such mysteries. He has to live in the midst of the incomprehensible, which is also detestable. And it has a fascination, too, that goes to work upon him. The fascination of the abomination—you know. Imagine the growing regrets, the longing to escape, the powerless disgust, the surrender, the hate."

He paused.

"Mind," he began again, lifting one arm from the elbow, the palm of the hand outwards, so that, with his legs folded before him, he had the pose of a Buddha preaching in European clothes and without a lotus-flower—"Mind, none of us would feel exactly like this. What saves us is efficiency—the devotion to efficiency. But these chaps were not much account, really. They were no colonists; their administration was merely a squeeze, and nothing more, I suspect. They were conquerors, and for that you want only brute force—nothing to boast of, when you have it, since your strength is just an accident arising from the weakness of others. They grabbed what they could get for the sake of what was to be got. It was just robbery with violence, aggravated murder on a great scale, and men going at it blind—as is very proper for those who tackle a darkness. The conquest of the earth, which mostly means the taking it away from those who have a different complexion or slightly flatter noses than ourselves, is not a pretty thing when you look into it too much. What redeems it is the idea only. An idea at the back of it; not a sentimental pretence but an idea; and an unselfish belief in the idea—something you can set up, and bow down before, and offer a sacrifice to. . . ."

He broke off. Flames glided in the river, small green flames, red flames, white flames, pursuing, overtaking, joining, crossing each other—then separating slowly or hastily. The traffic of the great city went on in the deepening night upon the sleepless river. We looked on, waiting patiently—there was nothing else to do till the end

---

7. A *trireme* is an ancient warship, propelled by oarsmen; the Gauls were the pre-Roman tribes who occupied present-day France; they were subdued by Julius Caesar between 58–50 B.C.

of the flood; but it was only after a long silence, when he said, in a hesitating voice, "I suppose you fellows remember I did once turn fresh-water sailor for a bit," that we knew we were fated, before the ebb began to run, to hear about one of Marlow's inconclusive experiences.

"I don't want to bother you much with what happened to me personally," he began, showing in this remark the weakness of many tellers of tales who seem so often unaware of what their audience would best like to hear; "yet to understand the effect of it on me you ought to know how I got out there, what I saw, how I went up that river to the place where I first met the poor chap. It was the farthest point of navigation and the culminating point of my experience. It seemed somehow to throw a kind of light on everything about me—and into my thoughts. It was sombre enough too—and pitiful—not extraordinary in any way—not very clear either. No, not very clear. And yet it seemed to throw a kind of light.

"I had then, as you remember, just returned to London after a lot of Indian Ocean, Pacific, China Seas—a regular dose of the East—six years or so, and I was loafing about, hindering you fellows in your work and invading your homes, just as though I had got a heavenly mission to civilise you. It was very fine for a time, but after a bit I did get tired of resting. Then I began to look for a ship—I should think the hardest work on earth. But the ships wouldn't even look at me. And I got tired of that game too.

"Now when I was a little chap I had a passion for maps. I would look for hours at South America, or Africa, or Australia, and lose myself in all the glories of exploration. At that time there were many blank spaces on the earth, and when I saw one that looked particularly inviting on a map (but they all look that) I would put my finger on it and say, When I grow up I will go there. The North Pole was one of these places, I remember. Well, I haven't been there yet, and shall not try now. The glamour's off. Other places were scattered about the Equator, and in every sort of latitude all over the two hemispheres. I have been in some of them, and. . . well, we won't talk about that. But there was one yet—the biggest, the most blank, so to speak—that I had a hankering after.

"True, by this time it was not a blank space any more. It had got filled since my boyhood with rivers and lakes and names. It had ceased to be a blank space of delightful mystery—a white patch for a boy to dream gloriously over. It had become a place of darkness. But there was in it one river especially, a mighty big river, that you could see on the map, resembling an immense snake uncoiled, with its head in the sea, its body at rest curving afar over a vast country, and its tail lost in the depths of the land. And as I looked at the map of it in a shop-window, it fascinated me as a snake would a bird—a silly little bird. Then I remembered there was a big concern, a Company for trade on that river. Dash it all! I thought to myself, they can't trade without using some kind of craft on that lot of fresh water—steamboats! Why shouldn't I try to get charge of one. I went on along Fleet Street, but could not shake off the idea. The snake had charmed me.

"You understand it was a Continental concern, that Trading Society; but I have a lot of relations living on the Continent, because it's cheap and not so nasty as it looks, they say.

"I am sorry to own I began to worry them. This was already a fresh departure for me. I was not used to get things that way, you know. I always went my own road and on my own legs where I had a mind to go. I wouldn't have believed it of myself; but, then—you see—I felt somehow I must get there by hook or by crook.

So I worried them. The men said 'My dear fellow,' and did nothing. Then—would you believe it?—I tried the women. I, Charlie Marlow, set the women to work—to get a job. Heavens! Well, you see, the notion drove me. I had an aunt, a dear enthusiastic soul. She wrote: 'It will be delightful. I am ready to do anything, anything for you. It is a glorious idea. I know the wife of a very high personage in the Administration, and also a man who has lots of influence with,' &c., &c. She was determined to make no end of fuss to get me appointed skipper of a river steamboat, if such was my fancy.

"I got my appointment—of course; and I got it very quick. It appears the Company had received news that one of their captains had been killed in a scuffle with the natives. This was my chance, and it made me the more anxious to go. It was only months and months afterwards, when I made the attempt to recover what was left of the body, that I heard the original quarrel arose from a misunderstanding about some hens. Yes, two black hens. Fresleven—that was the fellow's name, a Dane—thought himself wronged somehow in the bargain, so he went ashore and started to hammer the chief of the village with a stick. Oh, it didn't surprise me in the least to hear this, and at the same time to be told that Fresleven was the gentlest, quietest creature that ever walked on two legs. No doubt he was; but he had been a couple of years already out there engaged in the noble cause, you know, and he probably felt the need at last of asserting his self-respect in some way. Therefore he whacked the old nigger mercilessly, while a big crowd of his people watched him, thunderstruck, till some man,—I was told the chief's son,—in desperation at hearing the old chap yell, made a tentative jab with a spear at the white man—and of course it went quite easy between the shoulder-blades. Then the whole population cleared into the forest, expecting all kinds of calamities to happen, while, on the other hand, the steamer Fresleven commanded left also in a bad panic, in charge of the engineer, I believe. Afterwards nobody seemed to trouble much about Fresleven's remains, till I got out and stepped into his shoes. I couldn't let it rest, though; but when an opportunity offered at last to meet my predecessor, the grass growing through his ribs was tall enough to hide his bones. They were all there. The supernatural being had not been touched after he fell. And the village was deserted, the huts gaped black, rotting, all askew within the fallen enclosures. A calamity had come to it, sure enough. The people had vanished. Mad terror had scattered them, men, women, and children, through the bush, and they had never returned. What became of the hens I don't know either. I should think the cause of progress got them, anyhow. However, through this glorious affair I got my appointment, before I had fairly begun to hope for it.

"I flew around like mad to get ready, and before forty-eight hours I was crossing the Channel to show myself to my employers, and sign the contract. In a very few hours I arrived in a city that always makes me think of a whited sepulchre.[8] Prejudice no doubt. I had no difficulty in finding the Company's offices. It was the biggest thing in the town, and everybody I met was full of it. They were going to run an oversea empire, and make no end of coin by trade.

"A narrow and deserted street in deep shadow, high houses, innumerable windows with venetian blinds, a dead silence, grass sprouting between the stones, imposing

---

8. Brussels was the headquarters of the Société Anonyme Belge pour le Commerce du Haut-Congo (Belgian Corporation for Trade in the Upper Congo), with which Conrad obtained his post through the influence of his aunt, Marguerite Poradowska.

carriage archways right and left, immense double doors standing ponderously ajar. I slipped through one of these cracks, went up a swept and ungarnished staircase, as arid as a desert, and opened the first door I came to. Two women, one fat and the other slim, sat on straw-bottomed chairs, knitting black wool. The slim one got up and walked straight at me—still knitting with downcast eyes—and only just as I began to think of getting out of her way, as you would for a somnambulist, stood still, and looked up. Her dress was as plain as an umbrella-cover, and she turned round without a word and preceded me into a waiting-room. I gave my name, and looked about. Deal table in the middle, plain chairs all round the walls, on one end a large shining map, marked with all the colours of a rainbow. There was a vast amount of red—good to see at any time, because one knows that some real work is done in there, a deuce of a lot of blue, a little green, smears of orange, and, on the East Coast, a purple patch, to show where the jolly pioneers of progress drink the jolly lager-beer.[9] However, I wasn't going into any of these. I was going into the yellow. Dead in the centre. And the river was there—fascinating—deadly—like a snake. Ough! A door opened, a white-haired secretarial head, but wearing a compassionate expression, appeared, and a skinny forefinger beckoned me into the sanctuary. Its light was dim, and a heavy writing-desk squatted in the middle. From behind that structure came out an impression of pale plumpness in a frock-coat. The great man himself. He was five feet six, I should judge, and had his grip on the handle-end of ever so many millions. He shook hands, I fancy, murmured vaguely, was satisfied with my French. *Bon voyage.*

"In about forty-five seconds I found myself again in the waiting-room with the compassionate secretary, who, full of desolation and sympathy, made me sign some document. I believe I undertook amongst other things not to disclose any trade secrets. Well, I am not going to.

"I began to feel slightly uneasy. You know I am not used to such ceremonies, and there was something ominous in the atmosphere. It was just as though I had been let into some conspiracy—I don't know—something not quite right; and I was glad to get out. In the outer room the two women knitted black wool feverishly. People were arriving, and the younger one was walking back and forth introducing them. The old one sat on her chair. Her flat cloth slippers were propped up on a foot-warmer, and a cat reposed on her lap. She wore a starched white affair on her head, had a wart on one cheek, and silver-rimmed spectacles hung on the tip of her nose. She glanced at me above the glasses. The swift and indifferent placidity of that look troubled me. Two youths with foolish and cheery countenances were being piloted over, and she threw at them the same quick glance of unconcerned wisdom. She seemed to know all about them and about me too. An eerie feeling came over me. She seemed uncanny and fateful. Often far away there I thought of these two, guarding the door of Darkness, knitting black wool as for a warm pall, one introducing, introducing continuously to the unknown, the other scrutinising the cheery and foolish faces with unconcerned old eyes. *Ave!* Old knitter of black wool. *Morituri te salutant.*[1] Not many of those she looked at ever saw her again—not half, by a long way.

"There was yet a visit to the doctor. 'A simple formality,' assured me the secretary, with an air of taking an immense part in all my sorrows. Accordingly a young

9. British territories were traditionally marked in red on colonial maps; lager was originally a continental beer, not much drunk in England.

1. Hail!. . . Those who are about to die salute you!— traditional cry of Roman gladiators.

chap wearing his hat over the left eyebrow, some clerk I suppose,—there must have been clerks in the business, though the house was as still as a house in a city of the dead,—came from somewhere upstairs, and led me forth. He was shabby and careless, with ink-stains on the sleeves of his jacket, and his cravat was large and billowy, under a chin shaped like the toe of an old boot. It was a little too early for the doctor, so I proposed a drink, and thereupon he developed a vein of joviality. As we sat over our vermouths he glorified the Company's business, and by-and-by I expressed casually my surprise at him not going out there. He became very cool and collected all at once. 'I am not such a fool as I look, quoth Plato to his disciples,' he said sententiously, emptied his glass with great resolution, and we rose.

"The old doctor felt my pulse, evidently thinking of something else the while. 'Good, good for there,' he mumbled, and then with a certain eagerness asked me whether I would let him measure my head. Rather surprised, I said Yes, when he produced a thing like calipers and got the dimensions back and front and every way, taking notes carefully. He was an unshaven little man in a threadbare coat like a gaberdine, with his feet in slippers, and I thought him a harmless fool. 'I always ask leave, in the interests of science, to measure the crania of those going out there,' he said. 'And when they come back too?' I asked. 'Oh, I never see them,' he remarked; 'and moreover, the changes take place inside, you know.' He smiled, as if at some quiet joke. 'So you are going out there. Famous. Interesting too.' He gave me a searching glance, and made another note. 'Ever any madness in your family?' he asked, in a matter-of-fact tone. I felt very annoyed. 'Is that question in the interests of science too?' 'It would be,' he said, without taking notice of my irritation, 'interesting for science to watch the mental changes of individuals, on the spot, but. . .' 'Are you an alienist?'[2] I interrupted. 'Every doctor should be—a little,' answered that original, imperturbably. 'I have a little theory which you Messieurs who go out there must help me to prove. This is my share in the advantages my country shall reap from the possession of such a magnificent dependency. The mere wealth I leave to others. Pardon my questions, but you are the first Englishman coming under my observation . . .' I hastened to assure him I was not in the least typical. 'If I were,' said I, 'I wouldn't be talking like this with you.' 'What you say is rather profound, and probably erroneous,' he said, with a laugh. 'Avoid irritation more than exposure to the sun. Adieu. How do you English say, eh? Good-bye. Ah! Good-bye. Adieu. In the tropics one must before everything keep calm.' . . . He lifted a warning forefinger. . . . 'Du calme, du calme. Adieu.'

"One thing more remained to do—say good-bye to my excellent aunt. I found her triumphant. I had a cup of tea—the last decent cup of tea for many days—and in a room that most soothingly looked just as you would expect a lady's drawing-room to look, we had a long quiet chat by the fireside. In the course of these confidences it became quite plain to me I had been represented to the wife of the high dignitary, and goodness knows to how many more people besides, as an exceptional and gifted creature—a piece of good fortune for the Company—a man you don't get hold of every day. Good heavens! and I was going to take charge of a twopenny-half-penny river-steamboat with a penny whistle attached! It appeared, however, I was also one of the Workers, with a capital—you know. Something like an emissary of light, something like a lower sort of apostle. There had been a lot of such rot let loose in print and talk just about that time, and the excellent woman, living right in the rush

2. A psychologist.

of all that humbug, got carried off her feet. She talked about 'weaning those ignorant millions from their horrid ways,' till, upon my word, she made me quite uncomfortable. I ventured to hint that the Company was run for profit.

"'You forget, dear Charlie, that the labourer is worthy of his hire,' she said, brightly.[3] It's queer how out of touch with truth women are. They live in a world of their own, and there had never been anything like it, and never can be. It is too beautiful altogether, and if they were to set it up it would go to pieces before the first sunset. Some confounded fact we men have been living contentedly with ever since the day of creation would start up and knock the whole thing over.

"After this I got embraced, told to wear flannel, be sure to write often, and so on—and I left. In the street—I don't know why—a queer feeling came to me that I was an impostor. Odd thing that I, who used to clear out for any part of the world at twenty-four hours' notice, with less thought than most men give to the crossing of a street, had a moment—I won't say of hesitation, but of startled pause, before this commonplace affair. The best way I can explain it to you is by saying that, for a second or two, I felt as though, instead of going to the centre of a continent, I were about to set off for the centre of the earth.

"I left in a French steamer, and she called in every blamed port they have out there, for, as far as I could see, the sole purpose of landing soldiers and custom-house officers. I watched the coast. Watching a coast as it slips by the ship is like thinking about an enigma. There it is before you—smiling, frowning, inviting, grand, mean, insipid, or savage, and always mute with an air of whispering, Come and find out. This one was almost featureless, as if still in the making, with an aspect of monotonous grimness. The edge of a colossal jungle, so dark-green as to be almost black, fringed with white surf, ran straight, like a ruled line, far, far away along a blue sea whose glitter was blurred by a creeping mist. The sun was fierce, the land seemed to glisten and drip with steam. Here and there greyish-whitish specks showed up, clustered inside the white surf, with a flag flying above them perhaps—settlements some centuries old, and still no bigger than pin-heads on the untouched expanse of their background. We pounded along, stopped, landed soldiers; went on, landed custom-house clerks to levy toll in what looked like a Godforsaken wilderness, with a tin shed and a flag-pole lost in it; landed more soldiers—to take care of the custom-house clerks, presumably. Some, I heard, got drowned in the surf; but whether they did or not, nobody seemed particularly to care. They were just flung out there, and on we went. Every day the coast looked the same, as though we had not moved; but we passed various places—trading places—with names like Gran' Bassam, Little Popo,[4] names that seemed to belong to some sordid farce acted in front of a sinister backcloth. The idleness of a passenger, my isolation amongst all these men with whom I had no point of contact, the oily and languid sea, the uniform sombreness of the coast, seemed to keep me away from the truth of things, within the toil of a mournful and senseless delusion. The voice of the surf heard now and then was a positive pleasure, like the speech of a brother. It was something natural, that had its reason, that had a meaning. Now and then a boat from the shore gave one a momentary contact with reality. It was paddled by black fellows. You could see from afar the white of their eyeballs

---

3. 1 Timothy 5.18.

4. Grand Bassam and Grand Popo are the names of ports where Conrad's ship called on its way to the Congo.

glistening. They shouted, sang; their bodies streamed with perspiration; they had faces like grotesque masks—these chaps; but they had bone, muscle, a wild vitality, an intense energy of movement, that was as natural and true as the surf along their coast. They wanted no excuse for being there. They were a great comfort to look at. For a time I would feel I belonged still to a world of straightforward facts; but the feeling would not last long. Something would turn up to scare it away. Once, I remember, we came upon a man-of-war anchored off the coast. There wasn't even a shed there, and she was shelling the bush. It appears the French had one of their wars going on thereabouts. Her ensign dropped limp like a rag; the muzzles of the long eight-inch guns stuck out all over the low hull; the greasy, slimy swell swung her up lazily and let her down, swaying her thin masts. In the empty immensity of earth, sky, and water, there she was, incomprehensible, firing into a continent. Pop, would go one of the eight-inch guns; a small flame would dart and vanish, a little white smoke would disappear, a tiny projectile would give a feeble screech—and nothing happened. Nothing could happen. There was a touch of insanity in the proceeding, a sense of lugubrious drollery in the sight; and it was not dissipated by somebody on board assuring me earnestly there was a camp of natives—he called them enemies!—hidden out of sight somewhere.

"We gave her letters (I heard the men in that lonely ship were dying of fever at the rate of three a day) and went on. We called at some more places with farcical names, where the merry dance of death and trade goes on in a still and earthy atmosphere as of an overheated catacomb;[5] all along the formless coast bordered by dangerous surf, as if Nature herself had tried to ward off intruders; in and out of rivers, streams of death in life, whose banks were rotting into mud, whose waters, thickened into slime, invaded the contorted mangroves, that seemed to writhe at us in the extremity of an impotent despair. Nowhere did we stop long enough to get a particularised impression, but the general sense of vague and oppressive wonder grew upon me. It was like a weary pilgrimage amongst hints for nightmares.

"It was upward of thirty days before I saw the mouth of the big river. We anchored off the seat of the government. But my work would not begin till some two hundred miles farther on. So as soon as I could I made a start for a place thirty miles higher up.

"I had my passage on a little sea-going steamer. Her captain was a Swede, and knowing me for a seaman, invited me on the bridge. He was a young man, lean, fair, and morose, with lanky hair and a shuffling gait. As we left the miserable little wharf, he tossed his head contemptuously at the shore. 'Been living there?' he asked. I said, 'Yes.' 'Fine lot these government chaps—are they not?' he went on, speaking English with great precision and considerable bitterness. 'It is funny what some people will do for a few francs a month. I wonder what becomes of that kind when it goes up country?' I said to him I expected to see that soon. 'So-o-o!' he exclaimed. He shuffled athwart, keeping one eye ahead vigilantly. 'Don't be too sure,' he continued. 'The other day I took up a man who hanged himself on the road. He was a Swede, too.' 'Hanged himself! Why, in God's name?' I cried. He kept on looking out watchfully. 'Who knows? The sun too much for him, or the country perhaps.'

5. In a letter in May 1890 Conrad wrote: "What makes me rather uneasy is the information that 60 per cent. of our Company's employés return to Europe before they have completed even six months' service. Fever and dysentery! There are others who are sent home in a hurry at the end of a year, so that they shouldn't die in the Congo." According to a 1907 report, 150 out of every 2,000 native Congolese laborers died each month while in company employ; "All along the [railroad] track one would see corpses."

"At last we opened a reach. A rocky cliff appeared, mounds of turned-up earth by the shore, houses on a hill, others, with iron roofs, amongst a waste of excavations, or hanging to the declivity. A continuous noise of the rapids above hovered over this scene of inhabited devastation. A lot of people, mostly black and naked, moved about like ants. A jetty projected into the river. A blinding sunlight drowned all this at times in a sudden recrudescence of glare. 'There's your Company's station,' said the Swede, pointing to three wooden barrack-like structures on the rocky slope. 'I will send your things up. Four boxes did you say? So. Farewell.'

"I came upon a boiler wallowing in the grass, then found a path leading up the hill. It turned aside for the boulders, and also for an undersized railway-truck lying there on its back with its wheels in the air. One was off. The thing looked as dead as the carcass of some animal. I came upon more pieces of decaying machinery, a stack of rusty rails. To the left a clump of trees made a shady spot, where dark things seemed to stir feebly. I blinked, the path was steep. A horn tooted to the right, and I saw the black people run. A heavy and dull detonation shook the ground, a puff of smoke came out of the cliff, and that was all. No change appeared on the face of the rock. They were building a railway. The cliff was not in the way or anything; but this objectless blasting was all the work going on.

"A slight clinking behind me made me turn my head. Six black men advanced in a file, toiling up the path. They walked erect and slow, balancing small baskets full of earth on their heads, and the clink kept time with their footsteps. Black rags were wound round their loins, and the short ends behind wagged to and fro like tails. I could see every rib, the joints of their limbs were like knots in a rope; each had an iron collar on his neck, and all were connected together with a chain whose bights swung between them, rhythmically clinking. Another report from the cliff made me think suddenly of that ship of war I had seen firing into a continent. It was the same kind of ominous voice; but these men could by no stretch of imagination be called enemies. They were called criminals, and the outraged law, like the bursting shells, had come to them, an insoluble mystery from over the sea. All their meagre breasts panted together, the violently dilated nostrils quivered, the eyes stared stonily up-hill. They passed me within six inches, without a glance, with that complete, deathlike indifference of unhappy savages. Behind this raw matter one of the reclaimed, the product of the new forces at work, strolled despondently, carrying a rifle by its middle. He had a uniform jacket with one button off, and seeing a white man on the path, hoisted his weapon to his shoulder with alacrity. This was simple prudence, white men being so much alike at a distance that he could not tell who I might be. He was speedily reassured, and with a large, white, rascally grin, and a glance at his charge, seemed to take me into partnership in his exalted trust. After all, I also was a part of the great cause of these high and just proceedings.

"Instead of going up, I turned and descended to the left. My idea was to let that chain-gang get out of sight before I climbed the hill. You know I am not particularly tender; I've had to strike and to fend off. I've had to resist and to attack sometimes—that's only one way of resisting—without counting the exact cost, according to the demands of such sort of life as I had blundered into. I've seen the devil of violence, and the devil of greed, and the devil of hot desire; but, by all the stars! these were strong, lusty, red-eyed devils, that swayed and drove men—men, I tell you. But as I stood on this hillside, I foresaw that in the blinding sunshine of that land I would become acquainted with a flabby, pretending, weak-eyed devil of a rapacious and pitiless folly. How insidious he could be, too, I was only to find out several months later and a thousand miles farther. For a moment I stood appalled, as though by a warning. Finally I descended the hill, obliquely, towards the trees I had seen.

"I avoided a vast artificial hole somebody had been digging on the slope, the purpose of which I found it impossible to divine. It wasn't a quarry or a sandpit, anyhow. It was just a hole. It might have been connected with the philanthropic desire of giving the criminals something to do. I don't know. Then I nearly fell into a very narrow ravine, almost no more than a scar in the hillside. I discovered that a lot of imported drainage-pipes for the settlement had been tumbled in there. There wasn't one that was not broken. It was a wanton smash-up. At last I got under the trees. My purpose was to stroll into the shade for a moment; but no sooner within than it seemed to me I had stepped into the gloomy circle of some Inferno. The rapids were near, and an uninterrupted, uniform, headlong, rushing noise filled the mournful stillness of the grove, where not a breath stirred, not a leaf moved, with a mysterious sound—as though the tearing pace of the launched earth had suddenly become audible.

"Black shapes crouched, lay, sat between the trees, leaning against the trunks, clinging to the earth, half coming out, half effaced within the dim light, in all the attitudes of pain, abandonment, and despair. Another mine on the cliff went off, followed by a slight shudder of the soil under my feet. The work was going on. The work! And this was the place where some of the helpers had withdrawn to die.

"They were dying slowly—it was very clear. They were not enemies, they were not criminals, they were nothing earthly now,—nothing but black shadows of disease and starvation, lying confusedly in the greenish gloom. Brought from all the recesses of the coast in all the legality of time contracts, lost in uncongenial surroundings, fed on unfamiliar food, they sickened, became inefficient, and were then allowed to crawl away and rest. These moribund shapes were free as air—and nearly as thin. I began to distinguish the gleam of eyes under the trees. Then, glancing down, I saw a face near my hand. The black bones reclined at full length with one shoulder against the tree, and slowly the eyelids rose and the sunken eyes looked up at me, enormous and vacant, a kind of blind, white flicker in the depths of the orbs, which died out slowly. The man seemed young—almost a boy—but you know with them it's hard to tell. I found nothing else to do but to offer him one of my good Swede's ship's biscuits I had in my pocket. The fingers closed slowly on it and held—there was no other movement and no other glance. He had tied a bit of white worsted round his neck—Why? Where did he get it? Was it a badge—an ornament—a charm—a propitiatory act? Was there any idea at all connected with it? It looked startling round his black neck, this bit of white thread from beyond the seas.

"Near the same tree two more bundles of acute angles sat with their legs drawn up. One, with his chin propped on his knees, stared at nothing, in an intolerable and appalling manner: his brother phantom rested its forehead, as if overcome with a great weariness; and all about others were scattered in every pose of contorted collapse, as in some picture of a massacre or a pestilence. While I stood horror-struck, one of these creatures rose to his hands and knees, and went off on all-fours towards the river to drink. He lapped out of his hand, then sat up in the sunlight, crossing his shins in front of him, and after a time let his woolly head fall on his breastbone.

"I didn't want any more loitering in the shade, and I made haste towards the station. When near the buildings I met a white man, in such an unexpected elegance of get-up that in the first moment I took him for a sort of vision. I saw a high starched collar, white cuffs, a light alpaca jacket, snowy trousers, a clear silk necktie, and varnished boots. No hat. Hair parted, brushed, oiled, under a green-lined parasol held in a big white hand. He was amazing, and had a penholder behind his ear.

"I shook hands with this miracle, and I learned he was the Company's chief accountant, and that all the book-keeping was done at this station. He had come out for a moment, he said, 'to get a breath of fresh air.' The expression sounded wonderfully odd, with its suggestion of sedentary desk-life. I wouldn't have mentioned the fellow to you at all, only it was from his lips that I first heard the name of the man who is so indissolubly connected with the memories of that time. Moreover, I respected the fellow. Yes; I respected his collars, his vast cuffs, his brushed hair. His appearance was certainly that of a hairdresser's dummy; but in the great demoralisation of the land he kept up his appearance. That's backbone. His starched collars and got-up shirt-fronts were achievements of character. He had been out nearly three years; and, later on, I could not help asking him how he managed to sport such linen. He had just the faintest blush, and said modestly, 'I've been teaching one of the native women about the station. It was difficult. She had a distaste for the work.' Thus this man had verily accomplished something. And he was devoted to his books, which were in apple-pie order.

"Everything else in the station was in a muddle,—heads, things, buildings. Strings of dusty niggers with splay feet arrived and departed; a stream of manufactured goods, rubbishy cottons, beads, and brass-wire set into the depths of darkness, and in return came a precious trickle of ivory.

"I had to wait in the station for ten days—an eternity. I lived in a hut in the yard, but to be out of the chaos I would sometimes get into the accountant's office. It was built of horizontal planks, and so badly put together that, as he bent over his high desk, he was barred from neck to heels with narrow strips of sunlight. There was no need to open the big shutter to see. It was hot there too; big flies buzzed fiendishly, and did not sting, but stabbed. I sat generally on the floor, while, of faultless appearance (and even slightly scented), perching on a high stool, he wrote, he wrote. Sometimes he stood up for exercise. When a truckle-bed with a sick man (some invalided agent from up-country) was put in there, he exhibited a gentle annoyance. 'The groans of this sick person,' he said, 'distract my attention. And without that it is extremely difficult to guard against clerical errors in this climate.'

"One day he remarked, without lifting his head, 'In the interior you will no doubt meet Mr Kurtz.' On my asking who Mr Kurtz was, he said he was a first-class agent; and seeing my disappointment at this information, he added slowly, laying down his pen, 'He is a very remarkable person.' Further questions elicited from him that Mr Kurtz was at present in charge of a trading-post, a very important one, in the true ivory-country, at 'the very bottom of there. Sends in as much ivory as all the others put together . . .' He began to write again. The sick man was too ill to groan. The flies buzzed in a great peace.

"Suddenly there was a growing murmur of voices and a great tramping of feet. A caravan had come in. A violent babble of uncouth sounds burst out on the other side of the planks. All the carriers were speaking together, and in the midst of the uproar the lamentable voice of the chief agent was heard 'giving it up' tearfully for the twentieth time that day. . . . He rose slowly. 'What a frightful row,' he said. He crossed the room gently to look at the sick man, and returning, said to me, 'He does not hear.' 'What! Dead?' I asked, startled. 'No, not yet,' he answered, with great composure. Then, alluding with a toss of the head to the tumult in the station-yard, 'When one has got to make correct entries, one comes to hate those savages—hate them to the death.' He remained thoughtful for a moment. 'When you see Mr Kurtz,' he went on, 'tell him from me that everything here'—he glanced at the desk—'is very satisfactory. I don't like to write to him—with those messengers of ours you never know who may get hold of your letter—at that Central Station.' He stared at me for a moment with his mild, bulging eyes. 'Oh, he will go far, very far,' he began again. 'He will be a somebody in the Administration before long. They, above—the Council in Europe, you know—mean him to be.'

"He turned to his work. The noise outside had ceased, and presently in going out I stopped at the door. In the steady buzz of flies the homeward-bound agent was lying flushed and insensible; the other, bent over his books, was making correct entries of perfectly correct transactions; and fifty feet below the doorstep I could see the still tree-tops of the grove of death.

"Next day I left that station at last, with a caravan of sixty men, for a two-hundred-mile tramp.

"No use telling you much about that. Paths, paths, everywhere; a stamped-in network of paths spreading over the empty land, through long grass, through burnt grass, through thickets, down and up chilly ravines, up and down stony hills ablaze with heat; and a solitude, a solitude, nobody, not a hut. The population had cleared out a long time ago. Well, if a lot of mysterious niggers armed with all kinds of fearful weapons suddenly took to travelling on the road between Deal[6] and Gravesend, catching the yokels right and left to carry heavy loads for them, I fancy every farm and cottage thereabouts would get empty very soon. Only here the dwellings were gone too. Still, I passed through several abandoned villages. There's something pathetically childish in the ruins of grass walls. Day after day, with the stamp and shuffle of sixty pair of bare feet behind me, each pair under a 60-lb. load. Camp, cook, sleep, strike camp, march. Now and then a carrier dead in harness, at rest in the long grass near the path, with an empty water-gourd and his long staff lying by his side. A great silence around and above. Perhaps on some quiet night the tremor of far-off drums, sinking, swelling, a tremor vast, faint; a sound weird, appealing, suggestive, and wild—and perhaps with as profound a meaning as the sound of bells in a Christian country. Once a white man in an un-buttoned uniform, camping on the path with an armed escort of lank Zanzibaris,[7] very hospitable and festive—not to say drunk. Was looking after the upkeep of the road, he declared. Can't say I saw any road or any upkeep, unless the body of a middle-aged negro, with a bullet-hole in the forehead, upon which I absolutely stumbled three miles farther on, may be considered as a permanent improvement. I had a white companion too, not a bad chap, but rather too fleshy and with the exasperating habit of fainting on the hot hillsides, miles away from the least bit of shade and water. Annoying, you know, to hold your own coat like a parasol over a man's head while he is coming-to. I couldn't help asking him once what he meant by coming there at all. 'To make money, of course. What do you think?' he said, scornfully. Then he got fever, and had to be carried in a hammock slung under a

---

6. An English port.

7. Africans from Zanzibar, in East Africa; they were widely used as mercenaries.

pole. As he weighed sixteen stone I had no end of rows with the carriers. They jibbed, ran away, sneaked off with their loads in the night—quite a mutiny. So, one evening, I made a speech in English with gestures, not one of which was lost to the sixty pairs of eyes before me, and the next morning I started the hammock off in front all right. An hour afterwards I came upon the whole concern wrecked in a bush—man, hammock, groans, blankets, horrors. The heavy pole had skinned his poor nose. He was very anxious for me to kill somebody, but there wasn't the shadow of a carrier near. I remembered the old doctor,—'It would be interesting for science to watch the mental changes of individuals, on the spot.' I felt I was becoming scientifically interesting. However, all that is to no purpose. On the fifteenth day I came in sight of the big river again, and hobbled into the Central Station. It was on a back water surrounded by scrub and forest, with a pretty border of smelly mud on one side, and on the three others enclosed by a crazy fence of rushes. A neglected gap was all the gate it had, and the first glance at the place was enough to let you see the flabby devil was running that show. White men with long staves in their hands appeared languidly from amongst the buildings, strolling up to take a look at me, and then retired out of sight somewhere. One of them, a stout, excitable chap with black moustaches, informed me with great volubility and many digressions, as soon as I told him who I was, that my steamer was at the bottom of the river. I was thunderstruck. What, how, why? Oh, it was 'all right.' The 'manager himself' was there. All quite correct. 'Everybody had behaved splendidly! splendidly!'—'You must,' he said in agitation, 'go and see the general manager at once. He is waiting!'

"I did not see the real significance of that wreck at once. I fancy I see it now, but I am not sure—not at all. Certainly the affair was too stupid—when I think of it—to be altogether natural. Still. . . . But at the moment it presented itself simply as a confounded nuisance. The steamer was sunk. They had started two days before in a sudden hurry up the river with the manager on board, in charge of some volunteer skipper, and before they had been out three hours they tore the bottom out of her on stones, and she sank near the south bank. I asked myself what I was to do there, now my boat was lost. As a matter of fact, I had plenty to do in fishing my command out of the river. I had to set about it the very next day. That, and the repairs when I brought the pieces to the station, took some months.

"My first interview with the manager was curious. He did not ask me to sit down after my twenty-mile walk that morning. He was commonplace in complexion, in feature, in manners, and in voice. He was of middle size and of ordinary build. His eyes, of the usual blue, were perhaps remarkably cold, and he certainly could make his glance fall on one as trenchant and heavy as an axe. But even at these times the rest of his person seemed to disclaim the intention. Otherwise there was only an indefinable, faint expression of his lips, something stealthy—a smile—not a smile—I remember it, but I can't explain. It was unconscious, this smile was, though just after he had said something it got intensified for an instant. It came at the end of his speeches like a seal applied on the words to make the meaning of the commonest phrase appear absolutely inscrutable. He was a common trader, from his youth up employed in these parts—nothing more. He was obeyed, yet he inspired neither love nor fear, nor even respect. He inspired uneasiness. That was it! Uneasiness. Not a definite mistrust—just uneasiness—nothing more. You have no idea how effective such a . . . a . . . faculty can be. He had no genius for organising, for initiative, or for order even. That was evident in such things as the deplorable state of the station. He had no learning, and no intelligence. His position had come to him—why? Perhaps because he was never ill . . . He had served three terms of three years out there . . . Because triumphant health in the general rout of constitutions is a kind of power in itself. When he went home on leave he rioted on a large scale—pompously. Jack ashore—with a difference—in externals only. This one could gather from his casual talk. He originated nothing, he could keep the routine going—that's all. But he was great. He was great by this little thing that it was impossible to tell what could control such a man. He never gave that secret away. Perhaps there was nothing within him. Such a suspicion made one pause—for out there there were no external checks. Once when various tropical diseases had laid low almost every 'agent' in the station, he was heard to say, 'Men who come out here should have no entrails.' He sealed the utterance with that smile of his, as though it had been a door opening into a darkness he had in his keeping. You fancied you had seen things—but the seal was on. When annoyed at meal-times by the constant quarrels of the white men about precedence, he ordered an immense round table to be made, for which a special house had to be built. This was the station's mess-room. Where he sat was the first place—the rest were nowhere. One felt this to be his unalterable conviction. He was neither civil nor uncivil. He was quiet. He allowed his 'boy'—an overfed young negro from the coast—to treat the white men, under his very eyes, with provoking insolence.

"He began to speak as soon as he saw me. I had been very long on the road. He could not wait. Had to start without me. The up-river stations had to be relieved. There had been so many delays already that he did not know who was dead and who was alive, and how they got on—and so on, and so on. He paid no attention to my explanations, and, playing with a stick of sealing-wax, repeated several times that the situation was 'very grave, very grave.' There were rumours that a very important station was in jeopardy, and its chief, Mr Kurtz, was ill. Hoped it was not true. Mr Kurtz was . . . I felt weary and irritable. Hang Kurtz, I thought. I interrupted him by saying I had heard of Mr Kurtz on the coast. 'Ah! So they talk of him down there,' he murmured to himself. Then he began again, assuring me Mr Kurtz was the best agent he had, an exceptional man, of the greatest importance to the Company; therefore I could understand his anxiety. He was, he said, 'very, very uneasy.' Certainly he fidgeted on his chair a good deal, exclaimed, 'Ah, Mr Kurtz!' broke the stick of sealing-wax and seemed dumbfounded by the accident. Next thing he wanted to know 'how long it would take to' . . . I interrupted him again. Being hungry, you know, and kept on my feet too, I was getting savage. 'How can I tell?' I said. 'I haven't even seen the wreck yet—some months, no doubt.' All this talk seemed to me so futile. 'Some months,' he said. 'Well, let us say three months before we can make a start. Yes. That ought to do the affair.' I flung out of his hut (he lived all alone in a clay hut with a sort of verandah) muttering to myself my opinion of him. He was a chattering idiot. Afterwards I took it back when it was borne in upon me startlingly with what extreme nicety he had estimated the time requisite for the 'affair.'

"I went to work the next day, turning, so to speak, my back on that station. In that way only it seemed to me I could keep my hold on the redeeming facts of life. Still, one must look about sometimes; and then I saw this station, these men strolling aimlessly about in the sunshine of the yard. I asked myself sometimes what it all meant. They wandered here and there with their absurd long staves in their hands, like a lot of faithless pilgrims bewitched inside a rotten fence. The word 'ivory' rang in the air, was whispered, was sighed. You would think they were praying to it. A taint of imbecile rapacity blew through it all, like a whiff from some corpse. By Jove! I've never seen anything so unreal in my life. And outside, the silent wilderness surrounding this cleared speck on the earth struck me as something great and invincible, like evil or truth, waiting patiently for the passing away of this fantastic invasion.

"Oh, those months! Well, never mind. Various things happened. One evening a grass shed full of calico, cotton prints, beads, and I don't know what else, burst into a blaze so suddenly that you would have thought the earth had opened to let an avenging fire consume all that trash. I was smoking my pipe quietly by my dismantled steamer, and saw them all cutting capers in the light, with their arms lifted high, when the stout man with moustaches came tearing down to the river, a tin pail in his hand, assured me that everybody was 'behaving splendidly, splendidly,' dipped about a quart of water and tore back again. I noticed there was a hole in the bottom of his pail.

"I strolled up. There was no hurry. You see the thing had gone off like a box of matches. It had been hopeless from the very first. The flame had leaped high, driven everybody back, lighted up everything—and collapsed. The shed was already a heap of embers glowing fiercely. A nigger was being beaten near by. They said he had caused the fire in some way; be that as it may, he was screeching most horribly. I saw him, later on, for several days, sitting in a bit of shade looking very sick and trying to recover himself: afterwards he arose and went out—and the wilderness without a sound took him into its bosom again. As I approached the glow from the dark I found myself at the back of two men, talking. I heard the name of Kurtz pronounced, then the words, 'take advantage of this unfortunate accident.' One of the men was the manager. I wished him a good evening. 'Did you ever see anything like it—eh? it is incredible,' he said, and walked off. The other man remained. He was a first-class agent, young, gentlemanly, a bit reserved, with a forked little beard and a hooked nose. He was stand-offish with the other agents, and they on their side said he was the manager's spy upon them. As to me, I had hardly ever spoken to him before. We got into talk, and by-and-by we strolled away from the hissing ruins. Then he asked me to his room, which was in the main building of the station. He struck a match, and I perceived that this young aristocrat had not only a silver-mounted dressing-case but also a whole candle all to himself. Just at that time the manager was the only man supposed to have any right to candles. Native mats covered the clay walls; a collection of spears, assegais,[8] shields, knives was hung up in trophies. The business intrusted to this fellow was the making of bricks—so I had been informed; but there wasn't a fragment of a brick anywhere in the station, and he had been there more than a year—waiting. It seems he could not make bricks without something, I don't know what—straw maybe. Anyway, it could not be found there, and as it was not likely to be sent from Europe, it did not appear clear to me what he was waiting for. An act of special creation perhaps. However, they were all waiting—all the sixteen or twenty pilgrims of them—for something; and upon my word it did not seem an uncongenial occupation, from the way they took it, though the only

8. Slender African spears.

thing that ever came to them was disease—as far as I could see. They beguiled the time by backbiting and intriguing against each other in a foolish kind of way. There was an air of plotting about that station, but nothing came of it, of course. It was as unreal as everything else—as the philanthropic pretence of the whole concern, as their talk, as their government, as their show of work. The only real feeling was a desire to get appointed to a trading-post where ivory was to be had, so that they could earn percentages. They intrigued and slandered and hated each other only on that account,—but as to effectually lifting a little finger—oh, no. By heavens! there is something after all in the world allowing one man to steal a horse while another must not look at a halter. Steal a horse straight out. Very well. He has done it. Perhaps he can ride. But there is a way of looking at a halter that would provoke the most charitable of saints into a kick.

"I had no idea why he wanted to be sociable, but as we chatted in there it suddenly occurred to me the fellow was trying to get at something—in fact, pumping me. He alluded constantly to Europe, to the people I was supposed to know there—putting leading questions as to my acquaintances in the sepulchral city, and so on. His little eyes glittered like mica discs—with curiosity,—though he tried to keep up a bit of superciliousness. At first I was astonished, but very soon I became awfully curious to see what he would find out from me. I couldn't possibly imagine what I had in me to make it worth his while. It was very pretty to see how he baffled himself, for in truth my body was full of chills, and my head had nothing in it but that wretched steamboat business. It was evident he took me for a perfectly shameless prevaricator. At last he got angry, and, to conceal a movement of furious annoyance, he yawned. I rose. Then I noticed a small sketch in oils, on a panel, representing a woman, draped and blind-folded, carrying a lighted torch. The background was sombre—almost black. The movement of the woman was stately, and the effect of the torchlight on the face was sinister.

"It arrested me, and he stood by civilly, holding a half-pint champagne bottle (medical comforts) with the candle stuck in it. To my question he said Mr Kurtz had painted this—in this very station more than a year ago—while waiting for means to go to his trading-post. 'Tell me, pray,' said I, 'who is this Mr Kurtz?'

"'The chief of the Inner Station,' he answered in a short tone, looking away. 'Much obliged,' I said, laughing. 'And you are the brickmaker of the Central Station. Every one knows that.' He was silent for a while. 'He is a prodigy,' he said at last. 'He is an emissary of pity, and science, and progress, and devil knows what else. We want,' he began to declaim suddenly, 'for the guidance of the cause intrusted to us by Europe, so to speak, higher intelligence, wide sympathies, a singleness of purpose.' 'Who says that?' I asked. 'Lots of them,' he replied. 'Some even write that; and so *he* comes here, a special being, as you ought to know.' 'Why ought I to know?' I interrupted, really surprised. He paid no attention. 'Yes. To-day he is chief of the best station, next year he will be assistant-manager, two years more and . . . but I daresay you know what he will be in two years' time. You are of the new gang—the gang of virtue. The same people who sent him specially also recommended you. Oh, don't say no. I've my own eyes to trust.' Light dawned upon me. My dear aunt's influential acquaintances were producing an unexpected effect upon that young man. I nearly burst into a laugh. 'Do you read the Company's confidential correspondence?' I asked. He hadn't a word to say. It was great fun. 'When Mr Kurtz,' I continued severely, 'is General Manager, you won't have the opportunity.'

"He blew the candle out suddenly, and we went outside. The moon had risen. Black figures strolled about listlessly, pouring water on the glow, whence proceeded a sound of hissing; steam ascended in the moonlight; the beaten nigger groaned somewhere. 'What a row the brute makes!' said the indefatigable man with the moustaches, appearing near us. 'Serve him right. Transgression—punishment—bang! Pitiless, pitiless. That's the only way. This will prevent all conflagrations for the future. I was just telling the manager . . .' He noticed my companion, and became crestfallen all at once. 'Not in bed yet,' he said, with a kind of servile heartiness; 'it's so natural. Ha! Danger—agitation.' He vanished. I went on to the river-side, and the other followed me. I heard a scathing murmur at my ear, 'Heap of muffs—go to.' The pilgrims could be seen in knots gesticulating, discussing. Several had still their staves in their hands. I verily believe they took these sticks to bed with them. Beyond the fence the forest stood up spectrally in the moonlight, and through the dim stir, through the faint sounds of that lamentable courtyard, the silence of the land went home to one's very heart,—its mystery, its greatness, the amazing reality of its concealed life. The hurt nigger moaned feebly somewhere near by, and then fetched a deep sigh that made me mend my pace away from there. I felt a hand introducing itself under my arm. 'My dear sir,' said the fellow, 'I don't want to be misunderstood, and especially by you, who will see Mr Kurtz long before I can have that pleasure. I wouldn't like him to get a false idea of my disposition . . . .'

"I let him run on, this papier-mâché Mephistopheles,[9] and it seemed to me that if I tried I could poke my forefinger through him, and would find nothing inside but a little loose dirt, maybe. He, don't you see, had been planning to be assistant-manager by-and-by under the present man, and I could see that the coming of that Kurtz had upset them both not a little. He talked precipitately, and I did not try to stop him. I had my shoulders against the wreck of my steamer, hauled up on the slope like a carcass of some big river animal. The smell of mud, of primeval mud, by Jove! was in my nostrils, the high stillness of primeval forest was before my eyes; there were shiny patches on the black creek. The moon had spread over everything a thin layer of silver—over the rank grass, over the mud, upon the wall of matted vegetation standing higher than the wall of a temple, over the great river I could see through a sombre gap glittering, glittering, as it flowed broadly by without a murmur. All this was great, expectant, mute, while the man jabbered about himself. I wondered whether the stillness on the face of the immensity looking at us two were meant as an appeal or as a menace. What were we who had strayed in here? Could we handle that dumb thing, or would it handle us? I felt how big, how confoundedly big, was that thing that couldn't talk, and perhaps was deaf as well. What was in there? I could see a little ivory coming out from there, and I had heard Mr Kurtz was in there. I had heard enough about it too—God knows! Yet somehow it didn't bring any image with it—no more than if I had been told an angel or a fiend was in there. I believed it in the same way one of you might believe there are inhabitants in the planet Mars. I knew once a Scotch sail-maker who was certain, dead sure, there were people in Mars. If you asked him for some idea how they looked and behaved, he would get shy and mutter something about 'walking on all-fours.' If you as much as smiled, he would—though a man of sixty—offer to fight you. I would not have gone so far as to fight for Kurtz, but I went

9. One of the devils who tempts Faust.

for him near enough to a lie. You know I hate, detest, and can't bear a lie, not because I am straighter than the rest of us, but simply because it appals me. There is a taint of death, a flavour of mortality in lies,—which is exactly what I hate and detest in the world—what I want to forget. It makes me miserable and sick, like biting something rotten would do. Temperament, I suppose. Well, I went near enough to it by letting the young fool there believe anything he liked to imagine as to my influence in Europe. I became in an instant as much of a pretence as the rest of the bewitched pilgrims. This simply because I had a notion it somehow would be of help to that Kurtz whom at the time I did not see—you understand. He was just a word for me. I did not see the man in the name any more than you do. Do you see him? Do you see the story? Do you see anything? It seems to me I am trying to tell you a dream—making a vain attempt, because no relation of a dream can convey the dream-sensation, that commingling of absurdity, surprise, and bewilderment in a tremor of struggling revolt, that notion of being captured by the incredible which is of the very essence of dreams . . . ."

He was silent for a while.

". . . No, it is impossible; it is impossible to convey the life-sensation of any given epoch of one's existence,—that which makes its truth, its meaning—its subtle and penetrating essence. It is impossible. We live, as we dream—alone . . . ."

He paused again as if reflecting, then added—

"Of course in this you fellows see more than I could then. You see me, whom you know . . . ."

It had become so pitch dark that we listeners could hardly see one another. For a long time already he, sitting apart, had been no more to us than a voice. There was not a word from anybody. The others might have been asleep, but I was awake. I listened, I listened on the watch for the sentence, for the word, that would give me the clue to the faint uneasiness inspired by this narrative that seemed to shape itself without human lips in the heavy night-air of the river.

". . . Yes—I let him run on," Marlow began again, "and think what he pleased about the powers that were behind me. I did! And there was nothing behind me! There was nothing but that wretched, old, mangled steamboat I was leaning against, while he talked fluently about 'the necessity for every man to get on.' 'And when one comes out here, you conceive, it is not to gaze at the moon.' Mr Kurtz was a 'universal genius,' but even a genius would find it easier to work with 'adequate tools—intelligent men.' He did not make bricks—why, there was a physical impossibility in the way—as I was well aware; and if he did secretarial work for the manager, it was because 'no sensible man rejects wantonly the confidence of his superiors.' Did I see it? I saw it. What more did I want? What I really wanted was rivets, by heaven! Rivets. To get on with the work—to stop the hole. Rivets I wanted. There were cases of them down at the coast—cases—piled up—burst—split! You kicked a loose rivet at every second step in that station yard on the hillside. Rivets had rolled into the grove of death. You could fill your pockets with rivets for the trouble of stooping down—and there wasn't one rivet to be found where it was wanted. We had plates that would do, but nothing to fasten them with. And every week the messenger, a lone negro, letter-bag on shoulder and staff in hand, left our station for the coast. And several times a week a coast caravan came in with trade goods,—ghastly glazed calico that made you shudder only to look at it, glass beads value about a penny a quart, confounded spotted cotton handkerchiefs. And no rivets. Three carriers could have brought all that was wanted to set that steamboat afloat.

"He was becoming confidential now, but I fancy my unresponsive attitude must have exasperated him at last, for he judged it necessary to inform me he feared neither God nor devil, let alone any mere man. I said I could see that very well, but what I wanted was a certain quantity of rivets—and rivets were what really Mr Kurtz wanted, if he had only known it. Now letters went to the coast every week. . . . 'My dear sir,' he cried, 'I write from dictation.' I demanded rivets. There was a way—for an intelligent man. He changed his manner; became very cold, and suddenly began to talk about a hippopotamus; wondered whether sleeping on board the steamer (I stuck to my salvage night and day) I wasn't disturbed. There was an old hippo that had the bad habit of getting out on the bank and roaming at night over the station grounds. The pilgrims used to turn out in a body and empty every rifle they could lay hands on at him. Some even had sat up o' nights for him. All this energy was wasted, though. 'That animal has a charmed life,' he said; 'but you can say this only of brutes in this country. No man—you apprehend me?—no man here bears a charmed life.' He stood there for a moment in the moonlight with his delicate hooked nose set a little askew, and his mica eyes glittering without a wink, then, with a curt Good night, he strode off. I could see he was disturbed and considerably puzzled, which made me feel more hopeful than I had been for days. It was a great comfort to turn from that chap to my influential friend, the battered, twisted, ruined, tin-pot steamboat. I clambered on board. She rang under my feet like an empty Huntley & Palmer[1] biscuit-tin kicked along a gutter; she was nothing so solid in make, and rather less pretty in shape, but I had expended enough hard work on her to make me love her. No influential friend would have served me better. She had given me a chance to come out a bit—to find out what I could do. No, I don't like work. I had rather laze about and think of all the fine things that can be done. I don't like work—no man does—but I like what is in the work,—the chance to find yourself. Your own reality—for yourself, not for others—what no other man can ever know. They can only see the mere show, and never can tell what it really means.

"I was not surprised to see somebody sitting aft, on the deck, with his legs dangling over the mud. You see I rather chummed with the few mechanics there were in that station, whom the other pilgrims naturally despised—on account of their imperfect manners, I suppose. This was the foreman—a boiler-maker by trade—a good worker. He was a lank, bony, yellow-faced man, with big intense eyes. His aspect was worried, and his head was as bald as the palm of my hand; but his hair in falling seemed to have stuck to his chin, and had prospered in the new locality, for his beard hung down to his waist. He was a widower with six young children (he had left them in charge of a sister of his to come out there), and the passion of his life was pigeon-flying. He was an enthusiast and a connoisseur. He would rave about pigeons. After work hours he used sometimes to come over from his hut for a talk about his children and his pigeons; at work, when he had to crawl in the mud under the bottom of the steamboat, he would tie up that beard of his in a kind of white serviette[2] he brought for the purpose. It had loops to go over his ears. In the evening he could be seen squatted on the bank rinsing that wrapper in the creek with great care, then spreading it solemnly on a bush to dry.

---

1. A brand of English cookies.   2. Napkin.

"I slapped him on the back and shouted 'We shall have rivets!' He scrambled to his feet exclaiming 'No! Rivets!' as though he couldn't believe his ears. Then in a low voice, 'You . . . eh?' I don't know why we behaved like lunatics. I put my finger to the side of my nose and nodded mysteriously. 'Good for you!' he cried, snapped his fingers above his head, lifting one foot. I tried a jig. We capered on the iron deck. A frightful clatter came out of that hulk, and the virgin forest on the other bank of the creek sent it back in a thundering roll upon the sleeping station. It must have made some of the pilgrims sit up in their hovels. A dark figure obscured the lighted doorway of the manager's hut, vanished, then, a second or so after, the doorway itself vanished too. We stopped, and the silence driven away by the stamping of our feet flowed back again from the recesses of the land. The great wall of vegetation, an exuberant and entangled mass of trunks, branches, leaves, boughs, festoons, motionless in the moonlight, was like a rioting invasion of soundless life, a rolling wave of plants, piled up, crested, ready to topple over the creek, to sweep every little man of us out of his little existence. And it moved not. A deadened burst of mighty splashes and snorts reached us from afar, as though an ichthyosaurus had been taking a bath of glitter in the great river. 'After all,' said the boiler-maker in a reasonable tone, 'why shouldn't we get the rivets?' Why not, indeed! I did not know of any reason why we shouldn't. 'They'll come in three weeks,' I said, confidently.

"But they didn't. Instead of rivets there came an invasion, an infliction, a visitation. It came in sections during the next three weeks, each section headed by a donkey carrying a white man in new clothes and tan shoes, bowing from that elevation right and left to the impressed pilgrims. A quarrelsome band of footsore sulky niggers trod on the heels of the donkey; a lot of tents, camp-stools, tin boxes, white cases, brown bales would be shot down in the courtyard, and the air of mystery would deepen a little over the muddle of the station. Five such instalments came, with their absurd air of disorderly flight with the loot of innumerable outfit shops and provision stores, that, one would think, they were lugging, after a raid, into the wilderness for equitable division. It was an inextricable mess of things decent in themselves but that human folly made look like the spoils of thieving.

"This devoted band called itself the Eldorado Exploring Expedition,[3] and I believe they were sworn to secrecy. Their talk, however, was the talk of sordid buccaneers: it was reckless without hardihood, greedy without audacity, and cruel without courage; there was not an atom of foresight or of serious intention in the whole batch of them, and they did not seem aware these things are wanted for the work of the world. To tear treasure out of the bowels of the land was their desire, with no more moral purpose at the back of it than there is in burglars breaking into a safe. Who paid the expenses of the noble enterprise I don't know; but the uncle of our manager was leader of that lot.

"In exterior he resembled a butcher in a poor neighbourhood, and his eyes had a look of sleepy cunning. He carried his fat paunch with ostentation on his short legs, and during the time his gang infested the station spoke to no one but his nephew. You could see these two roaming about all day long with their heads close together in an everlasting confab.

3. Eldorado, legendary land of gold in South America and the object of many fruitless 16th-century Spanish expeditions.

"I had given up worrying myself about the rivets. One's capacity for that kind of folly is more limited than you would suppose. I said Hang!—and let things slide. I had plenty of time for meditation, and now and then I would give some thought to Kurtz. I wasn't very interested in him. No. Still, I was curious to see whether this man, who had come out equipped with moral ideas of some sort, would climb to the top after all, and how he would set about his work when there."

2

"One evening as I was lying flat on the deck of my steamboat, I heard voices approaching—and there were the nephew and the uncle strolling along the bank. I laid my head on my arm again, and had nearly lost myself in a doze, when somebody said in my ear, as it were: 'I am as harmless as a little child, but I don't like to be dictated to. Am I the manager—or am I not? I was ordered to send him there. It's incredible.'. . . I became aware that the two were standing on the shore alongside the forepart of the steamboat, just below my head. I did not move; it did not occur to me to move: I was sleepy. 'It is unpleasant,' grunted the uncle. 'He has asked the Administration to be sent there,' said the other, 'with the idea of showing what he could do; and I was instructed accordingly. Look at the influence that man must have. Is it not frightful?' They both agreed it was frightful, then made several bizarre remarks: 'Make rain and fine weather—one man—the Council—by the nose'—bits of absurd sentences that got the better of my drowsiness, so that I had pretty near the whole of my wits about me when the uncle said, 'The climate may do away with this difficulty for you. Is he alone there?' 'Yes,' answered the manager; 'he sent his assistant down the river with a note to me in these terms: "Clear this poor devil out of the country, and don't bother sending more of that sort. I had rather be alone than have the kind of men you can dispose of with me." It was more than a year ago. Can you imagine such impudence?' 'Anything since then?' asked the other, hoarsely. 'Ivory,' jerked the nephew; 'lots of it—prime sort—lots—most annoying, from him.' 'And with that?' questioned the heavy rumble. 'Invoice,' was the reply fired out, so to speak. Then silence. They had been talking about Kurtz.

"I was broad awake by this time, but, lying perfectly at ease, remained still, having no inducement to change my position. 'How did that ivory come all this way?' growled the elder man, who seemed very vexed. The other explained that it had come with a fleet of canoes in charge of an English half-caste clerk Kurtz had with him; that Kurtz had apparently intended to return himself, the station being by that time bare of goods and stores, but after coming three hundred miles, had suddenly decided to go back, which he started to do alone in a small dug-out with four paddlers, leaving the half-caste to continue down the river with the ivory. The two fellows there seemed astounded at anybody attempting such a thing. They were at a loss for an adequate motive. As to me, I seemed to see Kurtz for the first time. It was a distinct glimpse: the dug-out, four paddling savages, and the lone white man turning his back suddenly on the headquarters, on relief, on thoughts of home—perhaps; setting his face towards the depths of the wilderness, towards his empty and desolate station. I did not know the motive. Perhaps he was just simply a fine fellow who stuck to his work for its own sake. His name, you understand, had not been pronounced once. He was 'that man.' The half-caste, who, as far as I could see, had conducted a difficult trip with great prudence and pluck, was invariably alluded to as 'that scoundrel.' The 'scoundrel' had reported that the 'man' had been very ill—had recovered imperfectly. . . . The two below me moved away then a few paces, and strolled back and forth at some little distance. I heard: 'Military post—doctor—two hundred miles—quite alone now—unavoidable delays—nine months—no news—strange rumours.' They approached again, just as the manager was saying, 'No one, as far as I know, unless a species of wandering trader—a pestilential fellow, snapping ivory from the natives.' Who was it they were talking about now? I gathered in snatches that this was some man supposed to be in Kurtz's district, and of whom the manager did not approve. 'We will not be free from unfair competition till one of these fellows is hanged for an example,' he said. 'Certainly,' grunted the other; 'get him hanged! Why not? Anything—anything can be done in this country. That's what I say; nobody here, you understand, *here,* can endanger your position. And why? You stand the climate—you outlast them all. The danger is in Europe; but there before I left I took care to—' They moved off and whispered, then their voices rose again. 'The extraordinary series of delays is not my fault. I did my possible.' The fat man sighed, 'Very sad.' 'And the pestiferous absurdity of his talk,' continued the other; 'he bothered me enough when he was here. "Each station should be like a beacon on the road towards better things, a centre for trade of course, but also for humanising, improving, instructing." Conceive you—that ass! And he wants to be manager! No, it's—' Here he got choked by excessive indignation, and I lifted my head the least bit. I was surprised to see how near they were—right under me. I could have spat upon their hats. They were looking on the ground, absorbed in thought. The manager was switching his leg with a slender twig: his sagacious relative lifted his head. 'You have been well since you came out this time?' he asked. The other gave a start. 'Who? I? Oh! Like a charm—like a charm. But the rest—oh, my goodness! All sick. They die so quick, too, that I haven't the time to send them out of the country—it's incredible!' 'H'm. Just so,' grunted the uncle. 'Ah! my boy, trust to this—I say, trust to this.' I saw him extend his short flipper of an arm for a gesture that took in the forest, the creek, the mud, the river,—seemed to beckon with a dishonouring flourish before the sunlit face of the land a treacherous appeal to the lurking death, to the hidden evil, to the profound darkness of its heart. It was so startling that I leaped to my feet and looked back at the edge of the forest, as though I had expected an answer of some sort to that black display of confidence. You know the foolish notions that come to one sometimes. The high stillness confronted these two figures with its ominous patience, waiting for the passing away of a fantastic invasion.

"They swore aloud together—out of sheer fright, I believe—then, pretending not to know anything of my existence, turned back to the station. The sun was low; and leaning forward side by side, they seemed to be tugging painfully uphill their two ridiculous shadows of unequal length, that trailed behind them slowly over the tall grass without bending a single blade.

"In a few days the Eldorado Expedition went into the patient wilderness, that closed upon it as the sea closes over a diver. Long afterwards the news came that all the donkeys were dead. I know nothing as to the fate of the less valuable animals. They, no doubt, like the rest of us, found what they deserved. I did not inquire. I was then rather excited at the prospect of meeting Kurtz very soon. When I say very soon I mean it comparatively. It was just two months from the day we left the creek when we came to the bank below Kurtz's station.

"Going up that river was like travelling back to the earliest beginnings of the world, when vegetation rioted on the earth and the big trees were kings. An empty stream, a great silence, an impenetrable forest. The air was warm, thick, heavy, sluggish. There was no joy in the brilliance of sunshine. The long stretches of the waterway ran on, deserted, into the gloom of overshadowed distances. On silvery sandbanks hippos and alligators sunned themselves side by side. The broadening waters flowed through a mob of wooded islands; you lost your way on that river as you would in a desert, and butted all day long against shoals, trying to find the channel, till you thought yourself bewitched and cut off for ever from everything you had known once—somewhere—far away—in another existence perhaps. There were moments when one's past came back to one, as it will sometimes when you have not a moment to spare to yourself; but it came in the shape of an unrestful and noisy dream, remembered with wonder amongst the overwhelming realities of this strange world of plants, and water, and silence. And this stillness of life did not in the least resemble a peace. It was the stillness of an implacable force brooding over an inscrutable intention. It looked at you with a vengeful aspect. I got used to it afterwards; I did not see it any more; I had no time. I had to keep guessing at the channel; I had to discern, mostly by inspiration, the signs of hidden banks; I watched for sunken stones; I was learning to clap my teeth smartly before my heart flew out, when I shaved by a fluke some infernal sly old snag that would have ripped the life out of the tin-pot steamboat and drowned all the pilgrims; I had to keep a look-out for the signs of dead wood we could cut up in the night for next day's steaming. When you have to attend to things of that sort, to the mere incidents of the surface, the reality—the reality, I tell you—fades. The inner truth is hidden—luckily, luckily. But I felt it all the same; I felt often its mysterious stillness watching me at my monkey tricks, just as it watches you fellows performing on your respective tight-ropes for—what is it? half-a-crown a tumble—"

"Try to be civil, Marlow," growled a voice, and I knew there was at least one listener awake besides myself.

"I beg your pardon. I forgot the heartache which makes up the rest of the price. And indeed what does the price matter, if the trick be well done? You do your tricks very well. And I didn't do badly either, since I managed not to sink that steamboat on my first trip. It's a wonder to me yet. Imagine a blindfolded man set to drive a van over a bad road. I sweated and shivered over that business considerably, I can tell you. After all, for a seaman, to scrape the bottom of the thing that's supposed to float all the time under his care is the unpardonable sin. No one may know of it, but you never forget the thump—eh? A blow on the very heart. You remember it, you dream of it, you wake up at night and think of it—years after—and go hot and cold all over. I don't pretend to say that steamboat floated all the time. More than once she had to wade for a bit, with twenty cannibals splashing around and pushing. We had enlisted some of these chaps on the way for a crew. Fine fellows—cannibals—in their place. They were men one could work with, and I am grateful to them. And, after all, they did not eat each other before my face: they had brought along a provision of hippo-meat which went rotten, and made the mystery of the wilderness stink in my nostrils. Phoo! I can sniff it now. I had the manager on board and three or four pilgrims with their staves—all complete. Sometimes we came upon a station close by the bank, clinging to the skirts of the unknown, and the white men rushing out of a tumble-down hovel, with great gestures of joy and surprise and welcome, seemed very strange,—had the appearance of being held there captive by a spell. The word 'ivory' would ring in the air for a while—and on we went again into the silence, along empty reaches, round the still bends, between the high walls of our winding way, reverberating in hollow claps the ponderous beat of the stern-wheel. Trees, trees, millions of trees, massive, immense, running up high; and at their foot, hugging the bank against the stream, crept the little begrimed steamboat, like a sluggish beetle crawling on the floor of a lofty portico. It made you feel very small, very lost, and yet it was not altogether depressing that feeling. After all, if you were small, the grimy beetle crawled on—which was just what you wanted it to do. Where the pilgrims imagined it crawled to I don't know. To some place where they expected to get something, I bet! For me it crawled towards Kurtz—exclusively; but when the steam-pipes started leaking we crawled very slow. The reaches opened before us and closed behind, as if the forest had stepped leisurely across the water to bar the way for our return. We penetrated deeper and deeper into the heart of darkness. It was very quiet there. At night sometimes the roll of drums behind the curtain of trees would run up the river and remain sustained faintly, as if hovering in the air high over our heads, till the first break of day. Whether it meant war, peace, or prayer we could not tell. The dawns were heralded by the descent of a chill stillness; the woodcutters slept, their fires burned low; the snapping of a twig would make you start. We were wanderers on a prehistoric earth, on an earth that wore the aspect of an unknown planet. We could have fancied ourselves the first of men taking possession of an accursed inheritance, to be subdued at the cost of profound anguish and of excessive toil. But suddenly, as we struggled round a bend, there would be a glimpse of rush walls, of peaked grass-roofs, a burst of yells, a whirl of black limbs, a mass of hands clapping, of feet stamping, of bodies swaying, of eyes rolling, under the droop of heavy and motionless foliage. The steamer toiled along slowly on the edge of a black and incomprehensible frenzy. The prehistoric man was cursing us, praying to us, welcoming us—who could tell? We were cut off from the comprehension of our surroundings; we glided past like phantoms, wondering and secretly appalled, as sane men would be before an enthusiastic outbreak in a madhouse. We could not understand, because we were too far and could not remember, because we were travelling in the night of first ages, of those ages that are gone, leaving hardly a sign—and no memories.

"The earth seemed unearthly. We are accustomed to look upon the shackled form of a conquered monster, but there—there you could look at a thing monstrous and free. It was unearthly, and the men were—No, they were not inhuman. Well, you know, that was the worst of it—this suspicion of their not being inhuman. It would come slowly to one. They howled, and leaped, and spun, and made horrid faces; but what thrilled you was just the thought of their humanity—like yours—the thought of your remote kinship with this wild and passionate uproar. Ugly. Yes, it was ugly enough; but if you were man enough you would admit to yourself that there was in you just the faintest trace of a response to the terrible frankness of that noise, a dim suspicion of there being a meaning in it which you—you so remote from the night of first ages—could comprehend. And why not? The mind of man is capable of anything—because everything is in it, all the past as well as all the future. What was there after all? Joy, fear, sorrow, devotion, valour, rage—who can tell?—but truth—truth stripped of its cloak of time. Let the fool gape and shudder—the man knows, and can look on without a wink. But he must at least be as much of a man as these on the shore. He must meet that truth with his own true stuff—with his own inborn strength. Principles? Principles won't do. Acquisitions, clothes, pretty rags—rags that would fly off at the first good shake. No; you want a deliberate belief. An appeal to me in this fiendish row—is there? Very well; I hear; I admit, but I have a voice too, and for good or evil mine is the speech that cannot be silenced. Of course, a fool, what with sheer fright and fine sentiments, is always safe. Who's that grunting? You wonder I didn't go ashore for a howl and a dance? Well, no—I didn't. Fine sentiments, you say? Fine sentiments be hanged! I had no time. I had to mess about with white-lead and strips of woollen blanket helping to put bandages on those leaky steam-pipes—I tell you. I had to watch the steering, and circumvent those snags, and get the tin-pot along by hook or by crook. There was surface-truth enough in these things to save a wiser man. And between whiles I had to look after the savage who was fireman. He was an improved specimen; he could fire up a vertical boiler. He was there below me, and, upon my word, to look at him was as edifying as seeing a dog in a parody of breeches and a feather hat, walking on his hind-legs. A few months of training had done for that really fine chap. He squinted at the steam-gauge and at the water-gauge with an evident effort of intrepidity—and he had filed teeth too, the poor devil, and the wool of his pate shaved into queer patterns, and three ornamental scars on each of his cheeks. He ought to have been clapping his hands and stamping his feet on the bank, instead of which he was hard at work, a thrall to strange witchcraft, full of improving knowledge. He was useful because he had been instructed; and what he knew was this—that should the water in that transparent thing disappear, the evil spirit inside the boiler would get angry through the greatness of his thirst, and take a terrible vengeance. So he sweated and fired up and watched the glass fearfully (with an impromptu charm, made of rags, tied to his arm, and a piece of polished bone, as big as a watch, stuck flatways through his lower lip), while the wooded banks slipped past us slowly, the short noise was left behind, the interminable miles of silence—and we crept on, towards Kurtz. But the snags were thick, the water was treacherous and shallow, the boiler seemed indeed to have a sulky devil in it, and thus neither that fireman nor I had any time to peer into our creepy thoughts.

"Some fifty miles below the Inner Station we came upon a hut of reeds, an inclined and melancholy pole, with the unrecognisable tatters of what had been a flag of some sort flying from it, and a neatly stacked wood-pile. This was unexpected. We came to the bank, and on the stack of firewood found a flat piece of board with some faded pencil-writing on it. When deciphered it said: 'Wood for you. Hurry up. Approach cautiously.' There was a signature, but it was illegible—not Kurtz—a much longer word. Hurry up. Where? Up the river? 'Approach cautiously.' We had not done so. But the warning could not have been meant for the place where it could be only found after approach. Something was wrong above. But what—and how much? That was the question. We commented adversely upon the imbecility of that telegraphic style. The bush around said nothing, and would not let us look very far, either. A torn curtain of red twill hung in the doorway of the hut, and flapped sadly in our faces. The dwelling was dismantled; but we could see a white man had lived there not very long ago. There remained a rude table—a plank on two posts; a heap of rubbish reposed in a dark corner, and by the door I picked up a book. It had lost its covers, and the pages had been thumbed into a state of extremely dirty softness; but the back had been lovingly stitched afresh with white cotton thread, which looked clean yet. It was an extraordinary find. Its title was, 'An Inquiry into some Points of Seamanship,' by a man Tower, Towson—some such name—Master in his Majesty's Navy. The matter looked dreary reading enough, with illustrative diagrams and repulsive tables of figures, and the copy was sixty years old. I handled this amazing antiquity with the greatest possible tenderness, lest it should dissolve in my hands. Within, Towson or Towser was inquiring earnestly into the breaking strain of ships' chains and tackle, and other such matters. Not a very enthralling book; but at the first glance you could see there a singleness of intention, an honest concern for the right way of going to work, which made these humble pages, thought out so many years ago, luminous with another than a professional light. The simple old sailor, with his talk of chains and purchases, made me forget the jungle and the pilgrims in a delicious sensation of having come upon something unmistakably real. Such a book being there was wonderful enough; but still more astounding were the notes pencilled in the margin, and plainly referring to the text. I couldn't believe my eyes! They were in cipher! Yes, it looked like cipher. Fancy a man lugging with him a book of that description into this nowhere and studying it—and making notes—in cipher at that! It was an extravagant mystery.

"I had been dimly aware for some time of a worrying noise, and when I lifted my eyes I saw the wood-pile was gone, and the manager, aided by all the pilgrims, was shouting at me from the river-side. I slipped the book into my pocket. I assure you to leave off reading was like tearing myself away from the shelter of an old and solid friendship.

"I started the lame engine ahead. 'It must be this miserable trader—this intruder,' exclaimed the manager, looking back malevolently at the place we had left. 'He must be English,' I said. 'It will not save him from getting into trouble if he is not careful,' muttered the manager darkly. I observed with assumed innocence that no man was safe from trouble in this world.

"The current was more rapid now, the steamer seemed at her last gasp, the stern-wheel flopped languidly, and I caught myself listening on tiptoe for the next beat of the float, for in sober truth I expected the wretched thing to give up every moment. It was like watching the last flickers of a life. But still we crawled. Sometimes I would pick out a tree a little way ahead to measure our progress towards Kurtz by, but I lost it invariably before we got abreast. To keep the eyes so long on one thing was too much for human patience. The manager displayed a beautiful resignation. I fretted and fumed and took to arguing with myself whether or no I would talk openly with Kurtz; but before I could come to any conclusion it occurred to me that my speech or my silence, indeed any action of mine, would be a mere futility. What did it matter what any one knew or ignored? What did it matter who was manager? One gets sometimes such a flash of insight. The essentials of this affair lay deep under the surface, beyond my reach, and beyond my power of meddling.

"Towards the evening of the second day we judged ourselves about eight miles from Kurtz's station. I wanted to push on; but the manager looked grave, and told me the navigation up there was so dangerous that it would be advisable, the sun being very low already, to wait where we were till next morning. Moreover, he pointed out that if the warning to approach cautiously were to be followed, we must approach in daylight—not at dusk, or in the dark. This was sensible enough. Eight miles meant nearly three hours' steaming for us, and I could also see suspicious ripples at the upper end of the reach. Nevertheless, I was annoyed beyond expression at the delay, and most unreasonably too, since one night more could not matter much after so many months. As we had plenty of wood, and caution was the word, I brought up in the middle of the stream. The reach was narrow, straight, with high sides like a railway cutting. The dusk came gliding into it long before the sun had set. The current ran smooth and swift, but a dumb immobility sat on the banks. The living trees, lashed together by the creepers and every living bush of the undergrowth, might have been changed into stone, even to the slenderest twig, to the lightest leaf. It was not sleep—it seemed unnatural, like a state of trance. Not the faintest sound of any kind could be heard. You looked on amazed, and began to suspect yourself of being deaf—then the night came suddenly, and struck you blind as well. About three in the morning some large fish leaped, and the loud splash made me jump as though a gun had been fired. When the sun rose there was a white fog, very warm and clammy, and more blinding than the night. It did not shift or drive; it was just there, standing all round you like something solid. At eight or nine, perhaps, it lifted as a shutter lifts. We had a glimpse of the towering multitude of trees, of the immense matted jungle, with the blazing little ball of the sun hanging over it—all perfectly still—and then the white shutter came down again, smoothly, as if sliding in greased grooves. I ordered the chain, which we had begun to heave in, to be paid out again. Before it stopped running with a muffled rattle, a cry, a very loud cry, as of infinite desolation, soared slowly in the opaque air. It ceased. A complaining clamour, modulated in savage discords, filled our ears. The sheer unexpectedness of it made my hair stir under my cap. I don't know how it struck the others: to me it seemed as though the mist itself had screamed, so suddenly, and apparently from all sides at once, did this tumultuous and mournful uproar arise. It culminated in a hurried outbreak of almost intolerably excessive shrieking, which stopped short, leaving us stiffened in a variety of silly attitudes, and obstinately listening to the nearly as appalling and excessive silence. 'Good God! What is the meaning—?' stammered at my elbow one of the pilgrims,—a little fat man, with sandy hair and red whiskers, who wore side-spring boots, and pink pyjamas tucked into his socks. Two others remained open-mouthed a whole minute, then dashed into the little cabin, to rush out incontinently and stand darting scared glances, with Winchesters at 'ready' in their hands. What we could see was just the steamer we were on, her outlines blurred as though she had been on the point of dissolving, and a misty strip of water, perhaps two feet broad, around her—and that was all. The rest of the world was nowhere, as far as our eyes and ears were concerned. Just nowhere. Gone, disappeared; swept off without leaving a whisper or a shadow behind.

"I went forward, and ordered the chain to be hauled in short, so as to be ready to trip the anchor and move the steamboat at once if necessary. 'Will they attack?' whispered an awed voice. 'We will all be butchered in this fog,' murmured another. The faces twitched with the strain, the hands trembled slightly, the eyes forgot to wink. It was very curious to see the contrast of expressions of the white men and of the black fellows of our crew, who were as much strangers to that part of the river as we, though their homes were only eight hundred miles away. The whites, of course greatly discomposed, had besides a curious look of being painfully shocked by such an outrageous row. The others had an alert, naturally interested expression; but their faces were essentially quiet, even those of the one or two who grinned as they hauled at the chain. Several exchanged short, grunting phrases, which seemed to settle the matter to their satisfaction. Their headman, a young, broad-chested black, severely draped in dark-blue fringed cloths, with fierce nostrils and his hair all done up artfully in oily ringlets, stood near me. 'Aha!' I said, just for good fellowship's sake. 'Catch 'im,' he snapped, with a bloodshot widening of his eyes and a flash of sharp teeth—'catch 'im. Give 'im to us.' 'To you, eh?' I asked; 'what would you do with them?' 'Eat 'im!' he said, curtly, and, leaning his elbow on the rail, looked out into the fog in a dignified and profoundly pensive attitude. I would no doubt have been properly horrified, had it not occurred to me that he and his chaps must be very hungry: that they must have been growing increasingly hungry for at least this month past. They had been engaged for six months (I don't think a single one of them had any clear idea of time, as we at the end of countless ages have. They still belonged to the beginnings of time—had no inherited experience to teach them, as it were), and of course, as long as there was a piece of paper written over in accordance with some farcical law or other made down the river, it didn't enter anybody's head to trouble how they would live. Certainly they had brought with them some rotten hippo-meat, which couldn't have lasted very long, anyway, even if the pilgrims hadn't, in the midst of a shocking hullabaloo, thrown a considerable quantity of it overboard. It looked like a high-handed proceeding; but it was really a case of legitimate self-defence. You can't breathe dead hippo waking, sleeping, and eating, and at the same time keep your precarious grip on existence. Besides that, they had given them every week three pieces of brass wire, each about nine inches long; and the theory was they were to buy their provisions with that currency in river-side villages. You can see how *that* worked. There were either no villages, or the people were hostile, or the director, who like the rest of us fed out of tins, with an occasional old he-goat thrown in, didn't want to stop the steamer for some more or less recondite reason. So, unless they swallowed the wire itself, or made loops of it to snare the fishes with, I don't see what good their extravagant salary could be to them. I must say it was paid with a regularity worthy of a large and honourable trading company. For the rest, the only thing to eat—though it didn't look eatable in the least—I saw in their possession was a few lumps of some stuff like half-cooked dough, of a dirty lavender colour, they kept wrapped in leaves, and now and then swallowed a piece of, but so small that it seemed done more for the looks of the thing than for any serious purpose of sustenance. Why in the name of all the gnawing devils of hunger they didn't go for us—they were thirty to five—and have a good tuck-in for once, amazes me now when I think of it. They were big powerful men, with not much capacity to weigh the consequences, with courage, with strength, even yet, though their skins were no longer glossy and their muscles no longer hard. And I saw that something restraining, one of those human secrets that baffle probability, had come into play there. I looked at them with a swift quickening of interest—not because it occurred to me I might be eaten by them before very long, though I own to you that just then I perceived—in a new light, as it were—how unwholesome the pilgrims looked, and I hoped, yes, I positively hoped, that my aspect was not so—what shall I say?—so—unappetising: a touch of fantastic vanity which fitted well with the dream-sensation that pervaded all my days at that time. Perhaps I had a little fever too. One can't live with one's finger everlastingly on one's pulse. I had often 'a little fever,' or a little touch of other things—the playful pawstrokes of the wilderness, the preliminary trifling before the more serious onslaught which came in due course. Yes; I looked at them as you would on any human being, with a curiosity of their impulses, motives, capacities, weaknesses, when brought to the test of an inexorable physical necessity. Restraint! What possible restraint? Was it superstition, disgust, patience, fear—or some kind of primitive honour? No fear can stand up to hunger, no patience can wear it out, disgust simply does not exist where hunger is; and as to superstition, beliefs, and what you may call principles, they are less than chaff in a breeze. Don't you know the dev-ilry of lingering starvation, its exasperating torment, its black thoughts, its sombre and brooding ferocity? Well, I do. It takes a man all his inborn strength to fight hunger properly. It's really easier to face bereavement, dishonour, and the perdi-tion of one's soul—than this kind of prolonged hunger. Sad, but true. And these chaps too had no earthly reason for any kind of scruple. Restraint! I would just as soon have expected restraint from a hyena prowling amongst the corpses of a bat-tlefield. But there was the fact facing me—the fact dazzling, to be seen, like the foam on the depths of the sea, like a ripple on an unfathomable enigma, a mystery greater—when I thought of it—than the curious, inexplicable note of desperate grief in this savage clamour that had swept by us on the river-bank, behind the blind whiteness of the fog.

"Two pilgrims were quarrelling in hurried whispers as to which bank. 'Left.' 'No, no; how can you? Right, right, of course.' 'It is very serious,' said the manager's voice behind me; 'I would be desolated if anything should happen to Mr Kurtz be-fore we came up.' I looked at him, and had not the slightest doubt he was sincere. He was just the kind of man who would wish to preserve appearances. That was his restraint. But when he muttered something about going on at once, I did not even take the trouble to answer him. I knew, and he knew, that it was impossible. Were we to let go our hold of the bottom, we would be absolutely in the air—in space. We wouldn't be able to tell where we were going to—whether up or down stream, or across—till we fetched against one bank or the other,—and then we wouldn't know at first which it was. Of course I made no move. I had no mind for a smash-up. You couldn't imagine a more deadly place for a shipwreck. Whether drowned at once or not, we were sure to perish speedily in one way or another. 'I authorise you to take all the risks,' he said, after a short silence. 'I refuse to take any,' I said shortly; which was just the answer he expected, though its tone might have surprised him. 'Well, I must defer to your judgment. You are captain,' he said, with marked civility. I turned my shoulder to him in sign of my appreciation, and looked into the fog. How long would it last? It was the most hopeless look-out. The approach to this Kurtz grubbing for ivory in the wretched bush was beset by as many dangers as though he had been an enchanted princess sleeping in a fabulous castle. 'Will they attack, do you think?' asked the manager, in a confidential tone.

"I did not think they would attack, for several obvious reasons. The thick fog was one. If they left the bank in their canoes they would get lost in it, as we would be if we attempted to move. Still, I had also judged the jungle of both banks quite impenetrable—and yet eyes were in it, eyes that had seen us. The river-side bushes were certainly very thick; but the undergrowth behind was evidently penetrable. However, during the short lift I had seen no canoes anywhere in the reach—cer-tainly not abreast of the steamer. But what made the idea of attack inconceivable to me was the nature of the noise—of the cries we had heard. They had not the fierce character boding of immediate hostile intention. Unexpected, wild, and violent as they had been, they had given me an irresistible impression of sorrow. The glimpse of the steamboat had for some reason filled those savages with unrestrained grief. The danger, if any, I expounded, was from our proximity to a great human passion let loose. Even extreme grief may ultimately vent itself in violence—but more generally takes the form of apathy. . . .

"You should have seen the pilgrims stare! They had no heart to grin, or even to revile me; but I believe they thought me gone mad—with fright, maybe. I delivered a regular lecture. My dear boys, it was no good bothering. Keep a look-out? Well, you may guess I watched the fog for the signs of lifting as a cat watches a mouse; but for anything else our eyes were of no more use to us than if we had been buried miles deep in a heap of cotton-wool. It felt like it too—choking, warm, stifling. Besides, all I said, though it sounded extravagant, was absolutely true to fact. What we afterwards alluded to as an attack was really an attempt at repulse. The action was very far from being aggressive—it was not even defensive, in the usual sense: it was undertaken under the stress of desperation, and in its essence was purely protective.

"It developed itself, I should say, two hours after the fog lifted, and its commencement was at a spot, roughly speaking, about a mile and a half below Kurtz's station. We had just floundered and flopped round a bend, when I saw an islet, a mere grassy hummock of bright green, in the middle of the stream. It was the only thing of the kind; but as we opened the reach more, I perceived it was the head of a long sandbank, or rather of a chain of shallow patches stretching down the middle of the river. They were discoloured, just awash, and the whole lot was seen just under the water, exactly as a man's backbone is seen running down the middle of his back under the skin. Now, as far as I did see, I could go to the right or to the left of this. I didn't know either channel, of course. The banks looked pretty well alike, the depth appeared the same; but as I had been informed the station was on the west side, I naturally headed for the western passage.

"No sooner had we fairly entered it than I became aware it was much narrower than I had supposed. To the left of us there was the long uninterrupted shoal, and to the right a high, steep bank heavily overgrown with bushes. Above the bush the trees stood in serried ranks. The twigs overhung the current thickly, and from distance to distance a large limb of some tree projected rigidly over the stream. It was then well on in the afternoon, the face of the forest was gloomy, and a broad strip of shadow had already fallen on the water. In this shadow we steamed up—very slowly, as you may imagine. I sheered her well inshore—the water being deepest near the bank, as the sounding-pole informed me.

"One of my hungry and forbearing friends was sounding in the bows just below me. This steamboat was exactly like a decked scow.[4] On the deck there were two little teak-wood houses, with doors and windows. The boiler was in the fore-end, and the machinery right astern. Over the whole there was a light roof, supported on stanchions. The funnel projected through that roof, and in front of the funnel a small cabin built of light planks served for a pilot-house. It contained a couch, two camp-stools, a loaded Martini-Henry[5] leaning in one corner, a tiny table, and the steering-wheel. It had a wide door in front and a broad shutter at each side. All these were always thrown open, of course. I spent my days perched up there on the extreme fore-end of that roof, before the door. At night I slept, or tried to, on the couch. An athletic black belonging to some coast tribe, and educated by my poor predecessor, was the helmsman. He sported a pair of brass ear-rings, wore a blue cloth wrapper from the waist to the ankles, and thought all the

---

4. A flat-bottomed boat.   5. A rifle.

world of himself. He was the most unstable kind of fool I had ever seen. He steered with no end of a swagger while you were by; but if he lost sight of you, he became instantly the prey of an abject funk, and would let that cripple of a steamboat get the upper hand of him in a minute.

"I was looking down at the sounding-pole, and feeling much annoyed to see at each try a little more of it stick out of that river, when I saw my poleman give up the business suddenly, and stretch himself flat on the deck, without even taking the trouble to haul his pole in. He kept hold on it though, and it trailed in the water. At the same time the fireman, whom I could also see below me, sat down abruptly before his furnace and ducked his head. I was amazed. Then I had to look at the river mighty quick, because there was a snag in the fairway. Sticks, little sticks, were flying about—thick: they were whizzing before my nose, dropping below me, striking behind me against my pilot-house. All this time the river, the shore, the woods, were very quiet—perfectly quiet. I could only hear the heavy splashing thump of the stern-wheel and the patter of these things. We cleared the snag clumsily. Arrows, by Jove! We were being shot at! I stepped in quickly to close the shutter on the landside. That fool-helmsman, his hands on the spokes, was lifting his knees high, stamping his feet, champing his mouth, like a reined-in horse. Confound him! And we were staggering within ten feet of the bank. I had to lean right out to swing the heavy shutter, and I saw a face amongst the leaves on the level with my own, looking at me very fierce and steady; and then suddenly, as though a veil had been removed from my eyes, I made out, deep in the tangled gloom, naked breasts, arms, legs, glaring eyes,—the bush was swarming with human limbs in movement, glistening, of bronze colour. The twigs shook, swayed, and rustled, the arrows flew out of them, and then the shutter came to. 'Steer her straight,' I said to the helmsman. He held his head rigid, face forward; but his eyes rolled, he kept on lifting and setting down his feet gently, his mouth foamed a little. 'Keep quiet!' I said in a fury. I might just as well have ordered a tree not to sway in the wind. I darted out. Below me there was a great scuffle of feet on the iron deck; confused exclamations; a voice screamed, 'Can you turn back?' I caught sight of a V-shaped ripple on the water ahead. What? Another snag! A fusillade burst out under my feet. The pilgrims had opened with their Winchesters, and were simply squirting lead into that bush. A deuce of a lot of smoke came up and drove slowly forward. I swore at it. Now I couldn't see the ripple or the snag either. I stood in the doorway, peering, and the arrows came in swarms. They might have been poisoned, but they looked as though they wouldn't kill a cat. The bush began to howl. Our wood-cutters raised a warlike whoop; the report of a rifle just at my back deafened me. I glanced over my shoulder, and the pilot-house was yet full of noise and smoke when I made a dash at the wheel. The fool-nigger had dropped everything, to throw the shutter open and let off that Martini-Henry. He stood before the wide opening, glaring, and I yelled at him to come back, while I straightened the sudden twist out of that steamboat. There was no room to turn even if I had wanted to, the snag was somewhere very near ahead in that confounded smoke, there was no time to lose, so I just crowded her into the bank—right into the bank, where I knew the water was deep.

"We tore slowly along the overhanging bushes in a whirl of broken twigs and flying leaves. The fusillade below stopped short, as I had foreseen it would when the squirts got empty. I threw my head back to a glinting whizz that traversed the pilot-house, in at one shutter-hole and out at the other. Looking past that mad helmsman, who was shaking the empty rifle and yelling at the shore, I saw vague forms of men running bent double, leaping, gliding, distinct, incomplete, evanescent. Something big appeared in the air before the shutter, the rifle went overboard, and the man stepped back swiftly, looked at me over his shoulder in an extraordinary, profound, familiar manner, and fell upon my feet. The side of his head hit the wheel twice, and the end of what appeared a long cane clattered round and knocked over a little camp-stool. It looked as though after wrenching that thing from somebody ashore he had lost his balance in the effort. The thin smoke had blown away, we were clear of the snag, and looking ahead I could see that in another hundred yards or so I would be free to sheer off, away from the bank; but my feet felt so very warm and wet that I had to look down. The man had rolled on his back and stared straight up at me; both his hands clutched that cane. It was the shaft of a spear that, either thrown or lunged through the opening, had caught him in the side just below the ribs; the blade had gone in out of sight, after making a frightful gash; my shoes were full; a pool of blood lay very still, gleaming dark-red under the wheel; his eyes shone with an amazing lustre. The fusillade burst out again. He looked at me anxiously, gripping the spear like something precious, with an air of being afraid I would try to take it away from him. I had to make an effort to free my eyes from his gaze and attend to the steering. With one hand I felt above my head for the line of the steam-whistle, and jerked out screech after screech hurriedly. The tumult of angry and warlike yells was checked instantly, and then from the depths of the woods went out such a tremulous and prolonged wail of mournful fear and utter despair as may be imagined to follow the flight of the last hope from the earth. There was a great commotion in the bush; the shower of arrows stopped, a few dropping shots rang out sharply—then silence, in which the languid beat of the stern-wheel came plainly to my ears. I put the helm hard astarboard at the moment when the pilgrim in pink pyjamas, very hot and agitated, appeared in the doorway. 'The manager sends me—' he began in an official tone, and stopped short. 'Good God!' he said, glaring at the wounded man.

"We two whites stood over him, and his lustrous and inquiring glance enveloped us both. I declare it looked as though he would presently put to us some question in an understandable language; but he died without uttering a sound, without moving a limb, without twitching a muscle. Only in the very last moment, as though in response to some sign we could not see, to some whisper we could not hear, he frowned heavily, and that frown gave to his black death-mask an inconceivably sombre, brooding, and menacing expression. The lustre of inquiring glance faded swiftly into vacant glassiness. 'Can you steer?' I asked the agent eagerly. He looked very dubious; but I made a grab at his arm, and he understood at once I meant him to steer whether or no. To tell you the truth, I was morbidly anxious to change my shoes and socks. 'He is dead,' murmured the fellow, immensely impressed. 'No doubt about it,' said I, tugging like mad at the shoelaces. 'And, by the way, I suppose Mr Kurtz is dead as well by this time.'

"For the moment that was the dominant thought. There was a sense of extreme disappointment, as though I had found out I had been striving after something altogether without a substance. I couldn't have been more disgusted if I had travelled all this way for the sole purpose of talking with Mr Kurtz. Talking with . . . I flung one shoe overboard, and became aware that that was exactly what I had been looking forward to—a talk with Kurtz. I made the strange discovery that I had never imagined him as doing, you know, but as discoursing. I didn't say to myself, 'Now I will never see him,' or 'Now I will never shake him by the hand,' but, 'Now I will never hear him.' The man presented himself as a voice. Not of course that I did not connect him with some sort of action. Hadn't I been told in all the tones of jealousy and admiration that he had collected, bartered, swindled, or stolen more ivory than all the other agents together. That was not the point. The point was in his being a gifted creature, and that of all his gifts the one that stood out pre-eminently, that carried with it a sense of real presence, was his ability to talk, his words—the gift of expression, the bewildering, the illuminating, the most exalted and the most contemptible, the pulsating stream of light, or the deceitful flow from the heart of an impenetrable darkness.

"The other shoe went flying unto the devil-god of that river. I thought, By Jove! it's all over. We are too late; he has vanished—the gift has vanished, by means of some spear, arrow, or club. I will never hear that chap speak after all,—and my sorrow had a startling extravagance of emotion, even such as I had noticed in the howling sorrow of these savages in the bush. I couldn't have felt more of lonely desolation somehow, had I been robbed of a belief or had missed my destiny in life. . . . Why do you sigh in this beastly way, somebody? Absurd? Well, absurd. Good Lord! mustn't a man ever—Here, give me some tobacco.". . .

There was a pause of profound stillness, then a match flared, and Marlow's lean face appeared, worn, hollow, with downward folds and dropped eyelids, with an aspect of concentrated attention; and as he took vigorous draws at his pipe, it seemed to retreat and advance out of the night in the regular flicker of the tiny flame. The match went out.

"Absurd!" he cried. "This is the worst of trying to tell . . . Here you all are, each moored with two good addresses, like a hulk with two anchors, a butcher round one corner, a policeman round another, excellent appetites, and temperature normal—you hear—normal from year's end to year's end. And you say, Absurd! Absurd be—exploded! Absurd! My dear boys, what can you expect from a man who out of sheer nervousness had just flung overboard a pair of new shoes? Now I think of it, it is amazing I did not shed tears. I am, upon the whole, proud of my fortitude. I was cut to the quick at the idea of having lost the inestimable privilege of listening to the gifted Kurtz. Of course I was wrong. The privilege was waiting for me. Oh yes, I heard more than enough. And I was right, too. A voice. He was very little more than a voice. And I heard—him—it—this voice—other voices—all of them were so little more than voices—and the memory of that time itself lingers around me, impalpable, like a dying vibration of one immense jabber, silly, atrocious, sordid, savage, or simply mean, without any kind of sense. Voices, voices—even the girl herself—now—"

He was silent for a long time.

"I laid the ghost of his gifts at last with a lie," he began suddenly. "Girl! What? Did I mention a girl? Oh, she is out of it—completely. They—the women I mean—are out of it—should be out of it. We must help them to stay in that beautiful world of their own, lest ours gets worse. Oh, she had to be out of it. You should have heard the disinterred body of Mr Kurtz saying, "My Intended." You would have perceived directly then how completely she was out of it. And the lofty frontal bone of Mr Kurtz! They say the hair goes on growing sometimes, but this—ah—specimen was impressively bald. The wilderness had patted him on the head, and, behold, it was like a ball—an ivory ball; it had caressed him, and—lo!—he had withered; it had taken him, loved him, embraced him, got into his veins, consumed his flesh, and sealed his soul to its own by the inconceivable ceremonies of some devilish initiation. He was its spoiled and pampered favourite. Ivory? I should think so. Heaps of it, stacks of it. The old mud shanty was bursting with it. You would think there was not a single tusk left either above or below the ground in the whole country. 'Mostly fossil,' the manager had remarked disparagingly. It was no more fossil than I am; but they call it fossil when it is dug up. It appears these niggers do bury the tusks sometimes—but evidently they couldn't bury this parcel deep enough to save the gifted Mr Kurtz from his fate. We filled the steamboat with it, and had to pile a lot on the deck. Thus he could see and enjoy as long as he could see, because the appreciation of this favour had remained with him to the last. You should have heard him say, 'My ivory.' Oh yes, I heard him. 'My Intended, my ivory, my station, my river, my—' everything belonged to him. It made me hold my breath in expectation of hearing the wilderness burst into a prodigious peal of laughter that would shake the fixed stars in their places. Everything belonged to him—but that was a trifle. The thing was to know what he belonged to, how many powers of darkness claimed him for their own. That was the reflection that made you creepy all over. It was impossible—it was not good for one either—trying to imagine. He had taken a high seat amongst the devils of the land—I mean literally. You can't understand. How could you?—with solid pavement under your feet, surrounded by kind neighbours ready to cheer you or to fall on you, stepping delicately between the butcher and the policeman, in the holy terror of scandal and gallows and lunatic asylums—how can you imagine what particular region of the first ages a man's untrammelled feet may take him into by the way of solitude—utter solitude without a policeman—by the way of silence—utter silence, where no warning voice of a kind neighbour can be heard whispering of public opinion? These little things make all the great difference. When they are gone you must fall back upon your own innate strength, upon your own capacity for faithfulness. Of course you may be too much of a fool to go wrong—too dull even to know you are being assaulted by the powers of darkness. I take it, no fool ever made a bargain for his soul with the devil: the fool is too much of a fool, or the devil too much of a devil—I don't know which. Or you may be such a thunderingly exalted creature as to be altogether deaf and blind to anything but heavenly sights and sounds. Then the earth for you is only a standing place—and whether to be like this is your loss or your gain I won't pretend to say. But most of us are neither one nor the other. The earth for us is a place to live in, where we must put up with sights, with sounds, with smells too, by Jove!—breathe dead hippo, so to speak, and not be contaminated. And there, don't you see? your strength comes in, the faith in your ability for the digging of unostentatious holes to bury the stuff in—your power of devotion, not to yourself, but to an obscure, back-breaking business. And that's difficult enough. Mind, I am not trying to excuse or even explain—I am trying to account to myself for—for— Mr Kurtz—for the shade of Mr Kurtz. This initiated wraith from the back of Nowhere honoured me with its amazing confidence before it vanished altogether. This was because it could speak English to me. The original Kurtz had been educated partly in England, and—as he was good enough to say himself—his sympathies were in the right place. His mother was half-English, his father was half-French. All Europe contributed to the making of Kurtz; and by-and-by I learned that, most appropriately, the International Society for the Suppression of Savage Customs had intrusted him with the making of a report, for its future guidance. And he had written it too. I've seen it. I've read it. It was eloquent, vibrating with eloquence, but too high-strung, I think.

Seventeen pages of close writing he had found time for! But this must have been before his—let us say—nerves went wrong, and caused him to preside at certain midnight dances ending with unspeakable rites, which—as far as I reluctantly gathered from what I heard at various times—were offered up to him—do you understand?— to Mr Kurtz himself. But it was a beautiful piece of writing. The opening paragraph, however, in the light of later information, strikes me now as ominous. He began with the argument that we whites, from the point of development we had arrived at, 'must necessarily appear to them [savages] in the nature of supernatural beings—we approach them with the might as of a deity,' and so on, and so on. 'By the simple exercise of our will we can exert a power for good practically unbounded,' &c., &c. From that point he soared and took me with him. The peroration was magnificent, though difficult to remember, you know. It gave me the notion of an exotic Immensity ruled by an august Benevolence. It made me tingle with enthusiasm. This was the unbounded power of eloquence—of words—of burning noble words. There were no practical hints to interrupt the magic current of phrases, unless a kind of note at the foot of the last page, scrawled evidently much later, in an unsteady hand, may be regarded as the exposition of a method. It was very simple, and at the end of that moving appeal to every altruistic sentiment it blazed at you, luminous and terrifying, like a flash of lightning in a serene sky: 'Exterminate all the brutes!' The curious part was that he had apparently forgotten all about that valuable postscriptum, because, later on, when he in a sense came to himself, he repeatedly entreated me to take good care of 'my pamphlet' (he called it), as it was sure to have in the future a good influence upon his career. I had full information about all these things, and, besides, as it turned out, I was to have the care of his memory. I've done enough for it to give me the indisputable right to lay it, if I choose, for an everlasting rest in the dust-bin of progress, amongst all the sweepings and, figuratively speaking, all the dead cats of civilisation. But then, you see, I can't choose. He won't be forgotten. Whatever he was, he was not common. He had the power to charm or frighten rudimentary souls into an aggravated witch-dance in his honour; he could also fill the small souls of the pilgrims with bitter misgivings: he had one devoted friend at least, and he had conquered one soul in the world that was neither rudimentary nor tainted with self-seeking. No; I can't forget him, though I am not prepared to affirm the fellow was exactly worth the life we lost in getting to him. I missed my late helmsman awfully,—I missed him even while his body was still lying in the pilot-house. Perhaps you will think it passing strange this regret for a savage who was no more account than a grain of sand in a black Sahara. Well, don't you see, he had done something, he had steered; for months I had him at my back—a help—an instrument. It was a kind of partnership. He steered for me—I had to look after him, I worried about his deficiencies, and thus a subtle bond had been created, of which I only became aware when it was suddenly broken. And the intimate profundity of that look he gave me when he received his hurt remains to this day in my memory—like a claim of distant kinship affirmed in a supreme moment.

"Poor fool! If he had only left that shutter alone. He had no restraint, no restraint—just like Kurtz—a tree swayed by the wind. As soon as I had put on a dry pair of slippers, I dragged him out, after first jerking the spear out of his side, which operation I confess I performed with my eyes shut tight. His heels leaped together over the little doorstep; his shoulders were pressed to my breast; I hugged him from behind desperately. Oh! he was heavy, heavy; heavier than any man on earth, I should imagine. Then without more ado I tipped him overboard. The current snatched him as though he had been a wisp of grass, and I saw the body roll over twice before I lost sight of it for ever. All the pilgrims and the manager were then congregated on the awning-deck about the pilot-house, chattering at each other like a flock of excited magpies, and there was a scandalised murmur at my heartless promptitude. What they wanted to keep that body hanging about for I can't guess. Embalm it, maybe. But I had also heard another, and a very ominous, murmur on the deck below. My friends the woodcutters were likewise scandalised, and with a better show of reason—though I admit that the reason itself was quite inadmissible. Oh, quite! I had made up my mind that if my late helmsman was to be eaten, the fishes alone should have him. He had been a very second-rate helmsman while alive, but now he was dead he might have become a first-class temptation, and possibly cause some startling trouble. Besides, I was anxious to take the wheel, the man in pink pyjamas showing himself a hopeless duffer at the business.

"This I did directly the simple funeral was over. We were going half-speed, keeping right in the middle of the stream, and I listened to the talk about me. They had given up Kurtz, they had given up the station; Kurtz was dead, and the station had been burnt—and so on—and so on. The red-haired pilgrim was beside himself with the thought that at least this poor Kurtz had been properly revenged. 'Say! We must have made a glorious slaughter of them in the bush. Eh? What do you think? Say?' He positively danced, the bloodthirsty little gingery beggar. And he had nearly fainted when he saw the wounded man! I could not help saying, 'You made a glorious lot of smoke, anyhow.' I had seen, from the way the tops of the bushes rustled and flew, that almost all the shots had gone too high. You can't hit anything unless you take aim and fire from the shoulder; but these chaps fired from the hip with their eyes shut. The retreat, I maintained—and I was right—was caused by the screeching of the steam-whistle. Upon this they forgot Kurtz, and began to howl at me with indignant protests.

"The manager stood by the wheel murmuring confidentially about the necessity of getting well away down the river before dark at all events, when I saw in the distance a clearing on the river-side and the outlines of some sort of building. 'What's this?' I asked. He clapped his hands in wonder. 'The station!' he cried. I edged in at once, still going half-speed.

"Through my glasses I saw the slope of a hill interspersed with rare trees and perfectly free from undergrowth. A long decaying building on the summit was half buried in the high grass; the large holes in the peaked roof gaped black from afar; the jungle and the woods made a background. There was no enclosure or fence of any kind; but there had been one apparently, for near the house half-a-dozen slim posts remained in a row, roughly trimmed, and with their upper ends ornamented with round carved balls. The rails, or whatever there had been between, had disappeared. Of course the forest surrounded all that. The river-bank was clear, and on the water-side I saw a white man under a hat like a cart-wheel beckoning persistently with his whole arm. Examining the edge of the forest above and below, I was almost certain I could see movements—human forms gliding here and there. I steamed past prudently, then stopped the engines and let her drift down. The man on the shore began to shout, urging us to land. 'We have been attacked,' screamed the manager. 'I know—I know. It's all right,' yelled back the other, as cheerful as you please. 'Come along. It's all right. I am glad.'

"His aspect reminded me of something I had seen—something funny I had seen somewhere. As I manoeuvred to get alongside, I was asking myself, 'What does this fellow look like?' Suddenly I got it. He looked like a harlequin. His clothes had been made of some stuff that was brown holland[6] probably, but it was covered with patches all over, with bright patches, blue, red, and yellow,—patches on the back, patches on front, patches on elbows, on knees; coloured binding round his jacket, scarlet edging at the bottom of his trousers; and the sunshine made him look extremely gay and wonderfully neat withal, because you could see how beautifully all this patching had been done. A beardless, boyish face, very fair, no features to speak of, nose peeling, little blue eyes, smiles and frowns chasing each other over that open countenance like sunshine and shadow on a wind-swept plain. 'Look out, captain!' he cried; 'there's a snag lodged in here last night.' What! Another snag? I confess I swore shamefully. I had nearly holed my cripple, to finish off that charming trip. The harlequin on the bank turned his little pug nose up to me. 'You English?' he asked, all smiles. 'Are you?' I shouted from the wheel. The smiles vanished, and he shook his head as if sorry for my disappointment. Then he brightened up. 'Never mind!' he cried encouragingly. 'Are we in time?' I asked. 'He is up there,' he replied, with a toss of the head up the hill, and becoming gloomy all of a sudden. His face was like the autumn sky, overcast one moment and bright the next.

"When the manager, escorted by the pilgrims, all of them armed to the teeth, had gone to the house, this chap came on board. 'I say, I don't like this. These natives are in the bush,' I said. He assured me earnestly it was all right. 'They are simple people,' he added; 'well, I am glad you came. It took me all my time to keep them off.' 'But you said it was all right,' I cried. 'Oh, they meant no harm,' he said; and as I stared he corrected himself, 'Not exactly.' Then vivaciously, 'My faith, your pilot-house wants a clean-up!' In the next breath he advised me to keep enough steam on the boiler to blow the whistle in case of any trouble. 'One good screech will do more for you than all your rifles. They are simple people,' he repeated. He rattled away at such a rate he quite overwhelmed me. He seemed to be trying to make up for lots of silence, and actually hinted, laughing, that such was the case. 'Don't you talk with Mr Kurtz?' I said. 'You don't talk with that man—you listen to him,' he exclaimed with severe exaltation. 'But now—' He waved his arm, and in the twinkling of an eye was in the uttermost depths of despondency. In a moment he came up again with a jump, possessed himself of both my hands, shook them continuously, while he gabbled: 'Brother sailor . . . honour . . . pleasure . . . delight . . . introduce myself . . . Russian . . . son of an arch-priest . . . Government of Tambov[7] . . . What? Tobacco! English tobacco; the excellent English tobacco! Now, that's brotherly. Smoke? Where's a sailor that does not smoke?'

"The pipe soothed him, and gradually I made out he had run away from school, had gone to sea in a Russian ship; ran away again; served some time in English ships; was now reconciled with the arch-priest. He made a point of that. 'But when one is young one must see things, gather experience, ideas; enlarge the mind.' 'Here!' I interrupted. 'You can never tell! Here I have met Mr Kurtz,' he said, youthfully solemn and reproachful. I held my tongue after that. It appears he had persuaded a Dutch trading-house on the coast to fit him out with stores and goods, and had started for the interior with a light heart, and no more idea of what would happen to him than a baby. He had been wandering about that river for nearly two

---

6. A smooth linen fabric.   7. A province of Western Russia.

years alone, cut off from everybody and everything. 'I am not so young as I look. I am twenty-five,' he said. 'At first old Van Shuyten would tell me to go to the devil,' he narrated with keen enjoyment; 'but I stuck to him, and talked and talked, till at last he got afraid I would talk the hind-leg off his favorite dog, so he gave me some cheap things and a few guns, and told me he hoped he would never see my face again. Good old Dutchman, Van Shuyten. I sent him one small lot of ivory a year ago, so that he can't call me a little thief when I get back. I hope he got it. And for the rest, I don't care. I had some wood stacked for you. That was my old house. Did you see?'

"I gave him Towson's book. He made as though he would kiss me, but restrained himself. 'The only book I had left, and I thought I had lost it,' he said, looking at it ecstatically. 'So many accidents happen to a man going about alone, you know. Canoes get upset sometimes—and sometimes you've got to clear out so quick when the people get angry.' He thumbed the pages. 'You made notes in Russian?' I asked. He nodded. 'I thought they were written in cipher,' I said. He laughed, then became serious. 'I had lots of trouble to keep these people off,' he said. 'Did they want to kill you?' I asked. 'Oh no!' he cried, and checked himself. 'Why did they attack us?' I pursued. He hesitated, then said shamefacedly, 'They don't want him to go.' 'Don't they?' I said, curiously. He nodded a nod full of mystery and wisdom. 'I tell you,' he cried, 'this man has enlarged my mind.' He opened his arms wide, staring at me with his little blue eyes that were perfectly round."

3

"I looked at him, lost in astonishment. There he was before me, in motley, as though he had absconded from a troupe of mimes, enthusiastic, fabulous. His very existence was improbable, inexplicable, and altogether bewildering. He was an insoluble problem. It was inconceivable how he had existed, how he had succeeded in getting so far, how he had managed to remain—why he did not instantly disappear. 'I went a little farther,' he said, 'then still a little farther—till I had gone so far that I don't know how I'll ever get back. Never mind. Plenty time. I can manage. You take Kurtz away quick—quick—I tell you.' The glamour of youth enveloped his particoloured rags, his destitution, his loneliness, the essential desolation of his futile wanderings. For months—for years—his life hadn't been worth a day's purchase; and there he was gallantly, thoughtlessly alive, to all appearance indestructible solely by the virtue of his few years and of his unreflecting audacity. I was seduced into something like admiration—like envy. Glamour urged him on, glamour kept him unscathed. He surely wanted nothing from the wilderness but space to breathe in and to push on through. His need was to exist, and to move onwards at the greatest possible risk, and with a maximum of privation. If the absolutely pure, uncalculating, unpractical spirit of adventure had ever ruled a human being, it ruled this be-patched youth. I almost envied him the possession of this modest and clear flame. It seemed to have consumed all thought of self so completely, that, even while he was talking to you, you forgot that it was he—the man before your eyes—who had gone through these things. I did not envy him his devotion to Kurtz, though. He had not meditated over it. It came to him, and he accepted it with a sort of eager fatalism. I must say that to me it appeared about the most dangerous thing in every way he had come upon so far.

"They had come together unavoidably, like two ships becalmed near each other, and lay rubbing sides at last. I suppose Kurtz wanted an audience, because on a certain occasion, when encamped in the forest, they had talked all night, or more probably Kurtz had talked. 'We talked of everything,' he said, quite transported at the recollection. 'I forgot there was such a thing as sleep. The night did not seem to last an hour. Everything! Everything! . . . Of love too.' 'Ah, he talked to you of love!' I said, much amused. 'It isn't what you think,' he cried, almost passionately. 'It was in general. He made me see things—things.'

"He threw his arms up. We were on deck at the time, and the headman of my wood-cutters, lounging near by, turned upon him his heavy and glittering eyes. I looked around, and I don't know why, but I assure you that never, never before, did this land, this river, this jungle, the very arch of this blazing sky, appear to me so hopeless and so dark, so impenetrable to human thought, so pitiless to human weakness. 'And, ever since, you have been with him, of course?' I said.

"On the contrary. It appears their intercourse had been very much broken by various causes. He had, as he informed me proudly, managed to nurse Kurtz through two illnesses (he alluded to it as you would to some risky feat), but as a rule Kurtz wandered alone, far in the depths of the forest. 'Very often coming to this station, I had to wait days and days before he would turn up,' he said. 'Ah, it was worth waiting for!—sometimes.' 'What was he doing? exploring or what?' I asked. 'Oh yes, of course'; he had discovered lots of villages, a lake too—he did not know exactly in what direction; it was dangerous to inquire too much—but mostly his expeditions had been for ivory. 'But he had no goods to trade with by that time,' I objected. 'There's a good lot of cartridges left even yet,' he answered, looking away. 'To speak plainly, he raided the country,' I said. He nodded. 'Not alone, surely!' He muttered something about the villages round that lake. 'Kurtz got the tribe to follow him, did he?' I suggested. He fidgeted a little. 'They adored him,' he said. The tone of these words was so extraordinary that I looked at him searchingly. It was curious to see his mingled eagerness and reluctance to speak of Kurtz. The man filled his life, occupied his thoughts, swayed his emotions. 'What can you expect?' he burst out; 'he came to them with thunder and lightning, you know—and they had never seen anything like it—and very terrible. He could be very terrible. You can't judge Mr Kurtz as you would an ordinary man. No, no, no! Now—just to give you an idea—I don't mind telling you, he wanted to shoot me too one day—but I don't judge him.' 'Shoot you!' I cried. 'What for?' 'Well, I had a small lot of ivory the chief of that village near my house gave me. You see I used to shoot game for them. Well, he wanted it, and wouldn't hear reason. He declared he would shoot me unless I gave him the ivory and then cleared out of the country, because he could do so, and had a fancy for it, and there was nothing on earth to prevent him killing whom he jolly well pleased. And it was true too. I gave him the ivory. What did I care! But I didn't clear out. No, no. I couldn't leave him. I had to be careful, of course, till we got friendly again for a time. He had his second illness then. Afterwards I had to keep out of the way; but I didn't mind. He was living for the most part in those villages on the lake. When he came down to the river, sometimes he would take to me, and sometimes it was better for me to be careful. This man suffered too much. He hated all this, and somehow he couldn't get away. When I had a chance I begged him to try and leave while there was time; I offered to go back with him. And he would say yes, and then he would remain; go off on another ivory hunt; disappear for weeks; forget himself amongst these people—forget himself—you know.' 'Why! he's mad,' I said. He protested indignantly. Mr Kurtz couldn't be mad. If I had heard him talk, only two days ago, I wouldn't dare hint at such a thing. . . . I had taken up my binoculars while we talked, and was looking at the shore, sweeping the limit of the forest at each side and at the back of the house. The consciousness of there being people in that bush, so silent, so quiet—as silent and quiet as the ruined house on the hill—made me uneasy. There was no sign on the face of nature of this amazing tale that was not so much told as suggested to me in desolate exclamations, completed by shrugs, in interrupted phrases, in hints ending in deep sighs. The woods were unmoved, like a mask— heavy, like the closed door of a prison—they looked with their air of hidden knowl- edge, of patient expectation, of unapproachable silence. The Russian was explaining to me that it was only lately that Mr Kurtz had come down to the river, bringing along with him all the fighting men of that lake tribe. He had been absent for several months—getting himself adored, I suppose—and had come down unexpectedly, with the intention to all appearance of making a raid either across the river or down stream. Evidently the appetite for more ivory had got the better of the—what shall I say?—less material aspirations. However, he had got much worse suddenly. 'I heard he was lying helpless, and so I came up—took my chance,' said the Russian. 'Oh, he is bad, very bad.' I directed my glass to the house. There were no signs of life, but there was the ruined roof, the long mud wall peeping above the grass, with three lit- tle square window-holes, no two of the same size; all this brought within reach of my hand, as it were. And then I made a brusque movement, and one of the remaining posts of that vanished fence leaped up in the field of my glass. You remember I told you I had been struck at the distance by certain attempts at ornamentation, rather re- markable in the ruinous aspect of the place. Now I had suddenly a nearer view, and its first result was to make me throw my head back as if before a blow. Then I went carefully from post to post with my glass, and I saw my mistake. These round knobs were not ornamental but symbolic; they were expressive and puzzling, striking and disturbing—food for thought and also for the vultures if there had been any looking down from the sky; but at all events for such ants as were industrious enough to as- cend the pole. They would have been even more impressive, those heads on the stakes, if their faces had not been turned to the house. Only one, the first I had made out, was facing my way. I was not so shocked as you may think. The start back I had given was really nothing but a movement of surprise. I had expected to see a knob of wood there, you know. I returned deliberately to the first I had seen—and there it was, black, dried, sunken, with closed eyelids,—a head that seemed to sleep at the top of that pole, and, with the shrunken dry lips showing a narrow white line of the teeth, was smiling too, smiling continuously at some endless and jocose dream of that eternal slumber.

"I am not disclosing any trade secrets. In fact the manager said afterwards that Mr Kurtz's methods had ruined the district. I have no opinion on that point, but I want you clearly to understand that there was nothing exactly profitable in these heads being there. They only showed that Mr Kurtz lacked restraint in the gratifica- tion of his various lusts, that there was something wanting in him—some small mat- ter which, when the pressing need arose, could not be found under his magnificent eloquence. Whether he knew of this deficiency himself I can't say. I think the knowl- edge came to him at last—only at the very last. But the wilderness had found him out early, and had taken on him a terrible vengeance for the fantastic invasion. I think it had whispered to him things about himself which he did not know, things of which he had no conception till he took counsel with this great solitude—and the whisper had proved irresistibly fascinating. It echoed loudly within him because he was hollow at the core. . . . I put down the glass, and the head that had appeared near enough to be spoken to seemed at once to have leaped away from me into inaccessible distance.

"The admirer of Mr Kurtz was a bit crestfallen. In a hurried, indistinct voice he began to assure me he had not dared to take these—say, symbols—down. He was not afraid of the natives; they would not stir till Mr Kurtz gave the word. His ascendancy was extraordinary. The camps of these people surrounded the place, and the chiefs came every day to see him. They would crawl . . . 'I don't want to know anything of the ceremonies used when approaching Mr Kurtz,' I shouted. Curious, this feeling that came over me that such details would be more intolerable than those heads drying on the stakes under Mr Kurtz's windows. After all, that was only a savage sight, while I seemed at one bound to have been transported into some lightless region of subtle horrors, where pure, uncomplicated savagery was a positive relief, being something that had a right to exist—obviously—in the sunshine. The young man looked at me with surprise. I suppose it did not occur to him Mr Kurtz was no idol of mine. He forgot I hadn't heard any of these splendid monologues on, what was it? on love, justice, conduct of life—or what not. If it had come to crawling before Mr Kurtz, he crawled as much as the veriest savage of them all. I had no idea of the conditions, he said: these heads were the heads of rebels. I shocked him excessively by laughing. Rebels! What would be the next definition I was to hear? There had been enemies, criminals, workers—and these were rebels. Those rebellious heads looked very subdued to me on their sticks. 'You don't know how such a life tries a man like Kurtz,' cried Kurtz's last disciple. 'Well, and you?' I said. 'I! I! I am a simple man. I have no great thoughts. I want nothing from anybody. How can you compare me to . . . ?' His feelings were too much for speech, and suddenly he broke down. 'I don't understand,' he groaned. 'I've been doing my best to keep him alive, and that's enough. I had no hand in all this. I have no abilities. There hasn't been a drop of medicine or a mouthful of invalid food for months here. He was shamefully abandoned. A man like this, with such ideas. Shamefully! Shamefully! I—I—haven't slept for the last ten nights. . . .'

"His voice lost itself in the calm of the evening. The long shadows of the forest had slipped down-hill while we talked, had gone far beyond the ruined hovel, beyond the symbolic row of stakes. All this was in the gloom, while we down there were yet in the sunshine, and the stretch of the river abreast of the clearing glittered in a still and dazzling splendour, with a murky and overshadowed bend above and below. Not a living soul was seen on the shore. The bushes did not rustle.

"Suddenly round the corner of the house a group of men appeared, as though they had come up from the ground. They waded waist-deep in the grass, in a compact body, bearing an improvised stretcher in their midst. Instantly, in the emptiness of the landscape, a cry arose whose shrillness pierced the still air like a sharp arrow flying straight to the very heart of the land; and, as if by enchantment, streams of human beings—of naked human beings—with spears in their hands, with bows, with shields, with wild glances and savage movements, were poured into the clearing by the dark-faced and pensive forest. The bushes shook, the grass swayed for a time, and then everything stood still in attentive immobility.

"'Now, if he does not say the right thing to them we are all done for,' said the Russian at my elbow. The knot of men with the stretcher had stopped too, half-way to the steamer, as if petrified. I saw the man on the stretcher sit up, lank and with an uplifted arm, above the shoulders of the bearers. 'Let us hope that the man who can talk so well of love in general will find some particular reason to spare us this time,' I said. I resented bitterly the absurd danger of our situation, as if to be at the mercy of that atrocious phantom had been a dishonouring necessity. I could not hear a sound, but through my glasses I saw the thin arm extended commandingly, the lower jaw moving, the eyes of that apparition shining darkly far in its bony head that nodded with grotesque jerks. Kurtz—Kurtz—that means 'short' in German—don't it? Well, the name was as true as everything else in his life—and death. He looked at least seven feet long. His covering had fallen off, and his body emerged from it pitiful and appalling as from a winding-sheet. I could see the cage of his ribs all astir, the bones of his arm waving. It was as though an animated image of death carved out of old ivory had been shaking its hand with menaces at a motionless crowd of men made of dark and glittering bronze. I saw him open his mouth wide—it gave him a weirdly voracious aspect, as though he had wanted to swallow all the air, all the earth, all the men before him. A deep voice reached me faintly. He must have been shouting. He fell back suddenly. The stretcher shook as the bearers staggered forward again, and almost at the same time I noticed that the crowd of savages was vanishing without any perceptible movement of retreat, as if the forest that had ejected these beings so suddenly had drawn them in again as the breath is drawn in a long aspiration.

"Some of the pilgrims behind the stretcher carried his arms—two shot-guns, a heavy rifle, and a light revolver-carbine—the thunderbolts of that pitiful Jupiter. The manager bent over him murmuring as he walked beside his head. They laid him down in one of the little cabins—just a room for a bed-place and a camp-stool or two, you know. We had brought his belated correspondence, and a lot of torn envelopes and open letters littered his bed. His hand roamed feebly amongst these papers. I was struck by the fire of his eyes and the composed languor of his expression. It was not so much the exhaustion of disease. He did not seem in pain. This shadow looked satiated and calm, as though for the moment it had its fill of all the emotions.

"He rustled one of the letters, and looking straight in my face said, 'I am glad.' Somebody had been writing to him about me. These special recommendations were turning up again. The volume of tone he emitted without effort, almost without the trouble of moving his lips, amazed me. A voice! a voice! It was grave, profound, vibrating, while the man did not seem capable of a whisper. However, he had enough strength in him—factitious no doubt—to very nearly make an end of us, as you shall hear directly.

"The manager appeared silently in the doorway; I stepped out at once and he drew the curtain after me. The Russian, eyed curiously by the pilgrims, was staring at the shore. I followed the direction of his glance.

"Dark human shapes could be made out in the distance, flitting indistinctly against the gloomy border of the forest, and near the river two bronze figures, leaning on tall spears, stood in the sunlight under fantastic head-dresses of spotted skins, warlike and still in statuesque repose. And from right to left along the lighted shore moved a wild and gorgeous apparition of a woman.

"She walked with measured steps, draped in striped and fringed cloths, treading the earth proudly, with a slight jingle and flash of barbarous ornaments. She carried her head high; her hair was done in the shape of a helmet; she had brass leggings to the knee, brass wire gauntlets to the elbow, a crimson spot on her tawny cheek, innumerable necklaces of glass beads on her neck; bizarre things, charms, gifts of witchmen, that hung about her, glittered and trembled at every step. She must have had the value of several elephant tusks upon her. She was savage and superb, wild-eyed and magnificent; there was something ominous and stately in her deliberate progress. And in the hush that had fallen suddenly upon the whole sorrowful land, the immense wilderness, the colossal body of the fecund and mysterious life seemed to look at her, pensive, as though it had been looking at the image of its own tenebrous and passionate soul.

"She came abreast of the steamer, stood still, and faced us. Her long shadow fell to the water's edge. Her face had a tragic and fierce aspect of wild sorrow and of dumb pain mingled with the fear of some struggling, half-shaped resolve. She stood looking at us without a stir, and like the wilderness itself, with an air of brooding over an inscrutable purpose. A whole minute passed, and then she made a step forward. There was a low jingle, a glint of yellow metal, a sway of fringed draperies, and she stopped as if her heart had failed her. The young fellow by my side growled. The pilgrims murmured at my back. She looked at us all as if her life had depended upon the unswerving steadiness of her glance. Suddenly she opened her bared arms and threw them up rigid above her head, as though in an uncontrollable desire to touch the sky, and at the same time the swift shadows darted out on the earth, swept around on the river, gathering the steamer in a shadowy embrace. A formidable silence hung over the scene.

"She turned away slowly, walked on, following the bank, and passed into the bushes to the left. Once only her eyes gleamed back at us in the dusk of the thickets before she disappeared.

"'If she had offered to come aboard I really think I would have tried to shoot her,' said the man of patches, nervously. 'I had been risking my life every day for the last fortnight to keep her out of the house. She got in one day and kicked up a row about those miserable rags I picked up in the storeroom to mend my clothes with. I wasn't decent. At least it must have been that, for she talked like a fury to Kurtz for an hour, pointing at me now and then. I don't understand the dialect of this tribe. Luckily for me, I fancy Kurtz felt too ill that day to care, or there would have been mischief. I don't understand. . . . No—it's too much for me. Ah, well, it's all over now.'

"At this moment I heard Kurtz's deep voice behind the curtain, 'Save me!—save the ivory, you mean. Don't tell me. Save *me*! Why, I've had to save you. You are interrupting my plans now. Sick! Sick! Not so sick as you would like to believe. Never mind. I'll carry my ideas out yet—I will return. I'll show you what can be done. You with your little peddling notions—you are interfering with me. I will return. I. . .'

"The manager came out. He did me the honour to take me under the arm and lead me aside. 'He is very low, very low,' he said. He considered it necessary to sigh, but neglected to be consistently sorrowful. 'We have done all we could for him—haven't we? But there is no disguising the fact, Mr Kurtz has done more harm than good to the Company. He did not see the time was not ripe for vigorous action. Cautiously, cautiously—that's my principle. We must be cautious yet. The district is closed to us for a time. Deplorable! Upon the whole, the trade will suffer. I don't deny there is a remarkable quantity of ivory—mostly fossil. We must save it, at all events—but look how precarious the position is—and why? Because the method is unsound.' 'Do you,' said I, looking at the shore, 'call it "unsound method"?' 'Without doubt,' he exclaimed, hotly. 'Don't you?'. . . 'No method at all,' I murmured after a while. 'Exactly,' he exulted. 'I anticipated this. Shows a complete want of judgment. It is my duty to point it out in the proper quarter.' 'Oh,' said I, 'that fellow—what's his name?—the brickmaker, will make a readable report for you.' He appeared confounded for a moment. It seemed to me I had never breathed an atmosphere so vile, and I turned mentally to Kurtz for relief—positively for relief. 'Nevertheless, I think Mr Kurtz is a remarkable man,' I said with emphasis. He started, dropped on me a cold heavy glance, said very quietly, 'He was,' and turned his back on me. My hour of favour was over; I found myself lumped along with Kurtz as a partisan of methods for which the time was not ripe: I was unsound! Ah! but it was something to have at least a choice of nightmares.

"I had turned to the wilderness really, not to Mr Kurtz, who, I was ready to admit, was as good as buried. And for a moment it seemed to me as if I also were buried in a vast grave full of unspeakable secrets. I felt an intolerable weight oppressing my breast, the smell of the damp earth, the unseen presence of victorious corruption, the darkness of an impenetrable night. . . . The Russian tapped me on the shoulder. I heard him mumbling and stammering something about 'brother seaman—couldn't conceal—knowledge of matters that would affect Mr Kurtz's reputation.' I waited. For him evidently Mr Kurtz was not in his grave; I suspect that for him Mr Kurtz was one of the immortals. 'Well!' said I at last, 'speak out. As it happens, I am Mr Kurtz's friend—in a way.'

"He stated with a good deal of formality that had we not been 'of the same profession,' he would have kept the matter to himself without regard to consequences. He suspected 'there was an active ill-will towards him on the part of these white men that—' 'You are right,' I said, remembering a certain conversation I had overheard. 'The manager thinks you ought to be hanged.' He showed a concern at this intelligence which amused me at first. 'I had better get out of the way quietly,' he said, earnestly. 'I can do no more for Kurtz now, and they would soon find some excuse. What's to stop them? There's a military post three hundred miles from here.' 'Well, upon my word,' said I, 'perhaps you had better go if you have any friends amongst the savages near by.' 'Plenty,' he said. 'They are simple people—and I want nothing, you know.' He stood biting his lip, then: 'I don't want any harm to happen to these whites here, but of course I was thinking of Mr Kurtz's reputation—but you are a brother seaman and—' 'All right,' said I, after a time. 'Mr Kurtz's reputation is safe with me.' I did not know how truly I spoke.

"He informed me, lowering his voice, that it was Kurtz who had ordered the attack to be made on the steamer. 'He hated sometimes the idea of being taken away—and then again . . . But I don't understand these matters. I am a simple man. He thought it would scare you away—that you would give it up, thinking him dead. I could not stop him. Oh, I had an awful time of it this last month.' 'Very well,' I said. 'He is all right now.' 'Ye-e-es,' he muttered, not very convinced apparently. 'Thanks,' said I; 'I shall keep my eyes open.' 'But quiet—eh?' he urged, anxiously. 'It would be awful for his reputation if anybody here—' I promised a complete discretion with great gravity. 'I have a canoe and three black fellows waiting not very far. I am off. Could you give me a few Martini-Henry cartridges?' I could, and did, with proper secrecy. He helped himself, with a wink at me, to a handful of my tobacco. 'Between sailors—you know—good English tobacco.' At the door of the pilot-house he turned round—'I say, haven't you a pair of shoes you could spare?' He raised one leg. 'Look.' The soles were tied with knotted strings sandal-wise under his bare feet. I rooted out an old pair, at which he looked with admiration before tucking it under his left arm. One of his pockets (bright red) was bulging with cartridges, from the other (dark blue) peeped 'Towson's Inquiry,' &c., &c. He seemed to think himself excellently well equipped for a renewed encounter with the wilderness. 'Ah! I'll never, never meet such a man again. You ought to have heard him recite poetry—his own too it was, he told me. Poetry!' He rolled his eyes at the recollection of these delights. 'Oh, he enlarged my mind!' 'Good-bye,' said I. He shook hands and vanished in the night. Sometimes I ask myself whether I had ever really seen him—whether it was possible to meet such a phenomenon!. . .

"When I woke up shortly after midnight his warning came to my mind with its hint of danger that seemed, in the starred darkness, real enough to make me get up for the purpose of having a look round. On the hill a big fire burned, illuminating fitfully a crooked corner of the station-house. One of the agents with a picket of a few of our blacks, armed for the purpose, was keeping guard over the ivory; but deep within the forest, red gleams that wavered, that seemed to sink and rise from the ground amongst confused columnar shapes of intense blackness, showed the exact position of the camp where Mr Kurtz's adorers were keeping their uneasy vigil. The monotonous beating of a big drum filled the air with muffled shocks and a lingering vibration. A steady droning sound of many men chanting each to himself some weird incantation came out from the black, flat wall of the woods as the humming of bees comes out of a hive, and had a strange narcotic effect upon my half-awake senses. I believe I dozed off leaning over the rail, till an abrupt burst of yells, an overwhelming outbreak of a pent-up and mysterious frenzy, woke me up in a bewildered wonder. It was cut short all at once, and the low droning went on with an effect of audible and soothing silence. I glanced casually into the little cabin. A light was burning within, but Mr Kurtz was not there.

"I think I would have raised an outcry if I had believed my eyes. But I didn't believe them at first—the thing seemed so impossible. The fact is, I was completely unnerved by a sheer blank fright, pure abstract terror, unconnected with any distinct shape of physical danger. What made this emotion so overpowering was—how shall I define it?—the moral shock I received, as if something altogether monstrous, intolerable to thought and odious to the soul, had been thrust upon me unexpectedly. This lasted of course the merest fraction of a second, and then the usual sense of commonplace, deadly danger, the possibility of a sudden onslaught and massacre, or something of the kind, which I saw impending, was positively welcome and composing. It pacified me, in fact, so much, that I did not raise an alarm.

"There was an agent buttoned up inside an ulster[8] and sleeping on a chair on deck within three feet of me. The yells had not awakened him; he snored very slightly; I left him to his slumbers and leaped ashore. I did not betray Mr Kurtz—it was ordered I should never betray him—it was written I should be loyal to the nightmare of my choice. I was anxious to deal with this shadow by myself alone,—and to this day I don't know why I was so jealous of sharing with any one the peculiar blackness of that experience.

"As soon as I got on the bank I saw a trail—a broad trail through the grass. I remember the exultation with which I said to myself, 'He can't walk—he is crawling on all-fours—I've got him.' The grass was wet with dew. I strode rapidly with clenched fists. I fancy I had some vague notion of falling upon him and giving him a drubbing. I don't know. I had some imbecile thoughts. The knitting old woman with the cat obtruded herself upon my memory as a most improper person to be sitting at the other end of such an affair. I saw a row of pilgrims squirting lead in the air out of

8. Long overcoat.

Winchesters held to the hip. I thought I would never get back to the steamer, and imagined myself living alone and unarmed in the woods to an advanced age. Such silly things—you know. And I remember I confounded the beat of the drum with the beating of my heart, and was pleased at its calm regularity.

"I kept to the track though—then stopped to listen. The night was very clear: a dark blue space, sparkling with dew and starlight, in which black things stood very still. I thought I could see a kind of motion ahead of me. I was strangely cocksure of everything that night. I actually left the track and ran in a wide semicircle (I verily believe chuckling to myself) so as to get in front of that stir, of that motion I had seen—if indeed I had seen anything. I was circumventing Kurtz as though it had been a boyish game.

"I came upon him, and, if he had not heard me coming, I would have fallen over him too, but he got up in time. He rose, unsteady, long, pale, indistinct, like a vapour exhaled by the earth, and swayed slightly, misty and silent before me; while at my back the fires loomed between the trees, and the murmur of many voices issued from the forest. I had cut him off cleverly; but when actually confronting him I seemed to come to my senses, I saw the danger in its right proportion. It was by no means over yet. Suppose he began to shout? Though he could hardly stand, there was still plenty of vigour in his voice. 'Go away—hide yourself,' he said, in that profound tone. It was very awful. I glanced back. We were within thirty yards from the nearest fire. A black figure stood up, strode on long black legs, waving long black arms, across the glow. It had horns—antelope horns, I think—on its head. Some sorcerer, some witch-man, no doubt: it looked fiend-like enough. 'Do you know what you are doing?' I whispered. 'Perfectly,' he answered, raising his voice for that single word: it sounded to me far off and yet loud, like a hail through a speaking-trumpet. If he makes a row we are lost, I thought to myself. This clearly was not a case for fisticuffs, even apart from the very natural aversion I had to beat that Shadow—this wandering and tormented thing. 'You will be lost,' I said—'utterly lost.' One gets sometimes such a flash of inspiration, you know. I did say the right thing, though indeed he could not have been more irretrievably lost than he was at this very moment, when the foundations of our intimacy were being laid—to endure—to endure—even to the end—even beyond.

" 'I had immense plans,' he muttered irresolutely. 'Yes,' said I; 'but if you try to shout I'll smash your head with—' there was not a stick or a stone near. 'I will throttle you for good,' I corrected myself. 'I was on the threshold of great things,' he pleaded, in a voice of longing, with a wistfulness of tone that made my blood run cold. 'And now for this stupid scoundrel—' 'Your success in Europe is assured in any case,' I affirmed, steadily. I did not want to have the throttling of him, you understand—and indeed it would have been very little use for any practical purpose. I tried to break the spell—the heavy, mute spell of the wilderness—that seemed to draw him to its pitiless breast by the awakening of forgotten and brutal instincts, by the memory of gratified and monstrous passions. This alone, I was convinced, had driven him out to the edge of the forest, to the bush, towards the gleam of fires, the throb of drums, the drone of weird incantations; this alone had beguiled his unlawful soul beyond the bounds of permitted aspirations. And, don't you see, the terror of the position was not in being knocked on the head—though I had a very lively sense of that danger too—but in this, that I had to deal with a being to whom I could not appeal in the name of anything high or low. I had, even like the niggers, to invoke him—himself—his own exalted and incredible degradation. There was nothing either above or below him, and I knew it. He had kicked himself loose of the earth. Confound the man! he had kicked the very earth to pieces. He was alone, and I before him did not know whether I stood on the ground or floated in the air. I've been telling you what we said—repeating the phrases we pronounced,—but what's the good? They were common everyday words,—the familiar, vague sounds exchanged on every waking day of life. But what of that? They had behind them, to my mind, the terrific suggestiveness of words heard in dreams, of phrases spoken in nightmares. Soul! If anybody had ever struggled with a soul, I am the man. And I wasn't arguing with a lunatic either. Believe me or not, his intelligence was perfectly clear—concentrated, it is true, upon himself with horrible intensity, yet clear; and therein was my only chance—barring, of course, the killing him there and then, which wasn't so good, on account of unavoidable noise. But his soul was mad. Being alone in the wilderness, it had looked within itself, and, by heavens! I tell you, it had gone mad. I had—for my sins, I suppose—to go through the ordeal of looking into it myself. No eloquence could have been so withering to one's belief in mankind as his final burst of sincerity. He struggled with himself, too. I saw it,—I heard it. I saw the inconceivable mystery of a soul that knew no restraint, no faith, and no fear, yet struggling blindly with itself. I kept my head pretty well; but when I had him at last stretched on the couch, I wiped my forehead, while my legs shook under me as though I had carried half a ton on my back down that hill. And yet I had only supported him, his bony arm clasped round my neck—and he was not much heavier than a child.

"When next day we left at noon, the crowd, of whose presence behind the curtain of trees I had been acutely conscious all the time, flowed out of the woods again, filled the clearing, covered the slope with a mass of naked, breathing, quivering, bronze bodies. I steamed up a bit, then swung down-stream, and two thousand eyes followed the evolutions of the splashing, thumping, fierce river-demon beating the water with its terrible tail and breathing black smoke into the air. In front of the first rank, along the river, three men, plastered with bright red earth from head to foot, strutted to and fro restlessly. When we came abreast again, they faced the river, stamped their feet, nodded their horned heads, swayed their scarlet bodies; they shook towards the fierce river-demon a bunch of black feathers, a mangy skin with a pendent tail—something that looked like a dried gourd; they shouted periodically together strings of amazing words that resembled no sounds of human language; and the deep murmurs of the crowd, interrupted suddenly, were like the responses of some satanic litany.

"We had carried Kurtz into the pilot-house: there was more air there. Lying on the couch, he stared through the open shutter. There was an eddy in the mass of human bodies, and the woman with helmeted head and tawny cheeks rushed out to the very brink of the stream. She put out her hands, shouted something, and all that wild mob took up the shout in a roaring chorus of articulated, rapid, breathless utterance.

" 'Do you understand this?' I asked.

"He kept on looking out past me with fiery, longing eyes, with a mingled expression of wistfulness and hate. He made no answer, but I saw a smile, a smile of indefinable meaning, appear on his colourless lips that a moment after twitched convulsively. 'Do I not?' he said slowly, gasping, as if the words had been torn out of him by a supernatural power.

"I pulled the string of the whistle, and I did this because I saw the pilgrims on deck getting out their rifles with an air of anticipating a jolly lark. At the sudden screech there was a movement of abject terror through that wedged mass of bodies. 'Don't! don't! you frighten them away,' cried some one on deck disconsolately. I pulled the string time after time. They broke and ran, they leaped, they crouched, they swerved, they dodged the flying terror of the sound. The three red chaps had fallen flat, face down on the shore, as though they had been shot dead. Only the barbarous and superb woman did not so much as flinch, and stretched tragically her bare arms after us over the sombre and glittering river.

"And then that imbecile crowd down on the deck started their little fun, and I could see nothing more for smoke.

"The brown current ran swiftly out of the heart of darkness, bearing us down towards the sea with twice the speed of our upward progress; and Kurtz's life was running swiftly too, ebbing, ebbing out of his heart into the sea of inexorable time. The manager was very placid, he had no vital anxieties now, he took us both in with a comprehensive and satisfied glance: the 'affair' had come off as well as could be wished. I saw the time approaching when I would be left alone of the party of 'unsound method.' The pilgrims looked upon me with disfavour. I was, so to speak, numbered with the dead. It is strange how I accepted this unforeseen partnership, this choice of nightmares forced upon me in the tenebrous land invaded by these mean and greedy phantoms.

"Kurtz discoursed. A voice! a voice! It rang deep to the very last. It survived his strength to hide in the magnificent folds of eloquence the barren darkness of his heart. Oh, he struggled! he struggled! The wastes of his weary brain were haunted by shadowy images now—images of wealth and fame revolving obsequiously round his unextinguishable gift of noble and lofty expression. My Intended, my station, my career, my ideas—these were the subjects for the occasional utterances of elevated sentiments. The shade of the original Kurtz frequented the bedside of the hollow sham, whose fate it was to be buried presently in the mould of primeval earth. But both the diabolic love and the unearthly hate of the mysteries it had penetrated fought for the possession of that soul satiated with primitive emotions, avid of lying fame, of sham distinction, of all the appearances of success and power.

"Sometimes he was contemptibly childish. He desired to have kings meet him at railway-stations on his return from some ghastly Nowhere, where he intended to accomplish great things. 'You show them you have in you something that is really profitable, and then there will be no limits to the recognition of your ability,' he would say. 'Of course you must take care of the motives—right motives—always.' The long reaches that were like one and the same reach, monotonous bends that were exactly alike, slipped past the steamer with their multitude of secular[9] trees looking patiently after this grimy fragment of another world, the forerunner of change, of conquest, of trade, of massacres, of blessings. I looked ahead—piloting. 'Close the shutter,' said Kurtz suddenly one day; 'I can't bear to look at this.' I did so. There was a silence. 'Oh, but I will wring your heart yet!' he cried at the invisible wilderness.

"We broke down—as I had expected—and had to lie up for repairs at the head of an island. This delay was the first thing that shook Kurtz's confidence. One morning he gave me a packet of papers and a photograph,—the lot tied together with a shoestring. 'Keep this for me,' he said. 'This noxious fool' (meaning the manager) 'is capable of prying into my boxes when I am not looking.' In the afternoon I saw him. He was lying on his back with closed eyes, and I withdrew quietly, but I heard him mutter, 'Live rightly, die, die . . . ' I listened. There was nothing more. Was he rehearsing

9. Ancient.

some speech in his sleep, or was it a fragment of a phrase from some newspaper article? He had been writing for the papers and meant to do so again, 'for the furthering of my ideas. It's a duty.'

"His was an impenetrable darkness. I looked at him as you peer down at a man who is lying at the bottom of a precipice where the sun never shines. But I had not much time to give him, because I was helping the engine-driver to take to pieces the leaky cylinders, to straighten a bent connecting-rod, and in other such matters. I lived in an infernal mess of rust, filings, nuts, bolts, spanners, hammers, ratchet-drills—things I abominate, because I don't get on with them. I tended the little forge we fortunately had aboard; I toiled wearily in a wretched scrap-heap—unless I had the shakes too bad to stand.

"One evening coming in with a candle I was startled to hear him say a little tremulously, 'I am lying here in the dark waiting for death.' The light was within a foot of his eyes. I forced myself to murmur, 'Oh, nonsense!' and stood over him as if transfixed.

"Anything approaching the change that came over his features I have never seen before, and hope never to see again. Oh, I wasn't touched. I was fascinated. It was as though a veil had been rent. I saw on that ivory face the expression of sombre pride, of ruthless power, of craven terror—of an intense and hopeless despair. Did he live his life again in every detail of desire, temptation, and surrender during that supreme moment of complete knowledge? He cried in a whisper at some image, at some vision,—he cried out twice, a cry that was no more than a breath—

" 'The horror! The horror!'

"I blew the candle out and left the cabin. The pilgrims were dining in the mess-room, and I took my place opposite the manager, who lifted his eyes to give me a questioning glance, which I successfully ignored. He leaned back, serene, with that peculiar smile of his sealing the unexpressed depths of his meanness. A continuous shower of small flies streamed upon the lamp, upon the cloth, upon our hands and faces. Suddenly the manager's boy put his insolent black head in the doorway, and said in a tone of scathing contempt—

" 'Mistah Kurtz—he dead.'

"All the pilgrims rushed out to see. I remained, and went on with my dinner. I believe I was considered brutally callous. However, I did not eat much. There was a lamp in there—light, don't you know—and outside it was so beastly, beastly dark. I went no more near the remarkable man who had pronounced a judgment upon the adventures of his soul on this earth. The voice was gone. What else had been there? But I am of course aware that next day the pilgrims buried something in a muddy hole.

"And then they very nearly buried me.

"However, as you see, I did not go to join Kurtz there and then. I did not. I remained to dream the nightmare out to the end, and to show my loyalty to Kurtz once more. Destiny. My destiny! Droll thing life is—that mysterious arrangement of merciless logic for a futile purpose. The most you can hope from it is some knowledge of yourself—that comes too late—a crop of unextinguishable regrets. I have wrestled with death. It is the most unexciting contest you can imagine. It takes place in an impalpable greyness, with nothing underfoot, with nothing around, without spectators, without clamour, without glory, without the great desire of victory, without the great fear of defeat, in a sickly atmosphere of tepid scepticism, without much belief in your own right, and still less in that of your adversary. If such is the form of ultimate wisdom, then life is a greater riddle than some of us think it to be. I was within a hair's-breadth of the last opportunity for pronouncement, and I found with humiliation that probably

I would have nothing to say. This is the reason why I affirm that Kurtz was a remarkable man. He had something to say. He said it. Since I had peeped over the edge myself, I understand better the meaning of his stare, that could not see the flame of the candle, but was wide enough to embrace the whole universe, piercing enough to penetrate all the hearts that beat in the darkness. He had summed up—he had judged. 'The horror!' He was a remarkable man. After all, this was the expression of some sort of belief; it had candour, it had conviction, it had a vibrating note of revolt in its whisper, it had the appalling face of a glimpsed truth—the strange commingling of desire and hate. And it is not my own extremity I remember best—a vision of greyness without form filled with physical pain, and a careless contempt for the evanescence of all things—even of this pain itself. No! It is his extremity that I seem to have lived through. True, he had made that last stride, he had stepped over the edge, while I had been permitted to draw back my hesitating foot. And perhaps in this is the whole difference; perhaps all the wisdom, and all truth, and all sincerity, are just compressed into that inappreciable moment of time in which we step over the threshold of the invisible. Perhaps! I like to think my summing-up would not have been a word of careless contempt. Better his cry—much better. It was an affirmation, a moral victory paid for by innumerable defeats, by abominable terrors, by abominable satisfactions. But it was a victory! That is why I have remained loyal to Kurtz to the last, and even beyond, when a long time after I heard once more, not his own voice, but the echo of his magnificent eloquence thrown to me from a soul as translucently pure as a cliff of crystal.

"No, they did not bury me, though there is a period of time which I remember mistily, with a shuddering wonder, like a passage through some inconceivable world that had no hope in it and no desire. I found myself back in the sepulchral city resenting the sight of people hurrying through the streets to filch a little money from each other, to devour their infamous cookery, to gulp their unwholesome beer, to dream their insignificant and silly dreams. They trespassed upon my thoughts. They were intruders whose knowledge of life was to me an irritating pretence, because I felt so sure they could not possibly know the things I knew. Their bearing, which was simply the bearing of commonplace individuals going about their business in the assurance of perfect safety, was offensive to me like the outrageous flauntings of folly in the face of a danger it is unable to comprehend. I had no particular desire to enlighten them, but I had some difficulty in restraining myself from laughing in their faces, so full of stupid importance. I daresay I was not very well at that time. I tottered about the streets—there were various affairs to settle—grinning bitterly at perfectly respectable persons. I admit my behaviour was inexcusable, but then my temperature was seldom normal in these days. My dear aunt's endeavours to 'nurse up my strength' seemed altogether beside the mark. It was not my strength that wanted nursing, it was my imagination that wanted soothing. I kept the bundle of papers given me by Kurtz, not knowing exactly what to do with it. His mother had died lately, watched over, as I was told, by his Intended. A clean-shaved man, with an official manner and wearing gold-rimmed spectacles, called on me one day and made inquiries, at first circuitous, afterwards suavely pressing, about what he was pleased to denominate certain 'documents.' I was not surprised, because I had had two rows with the manager on the subject out there. I had refused to give up the smallest scrap out of that package, and I took the same attitude with the spectacled man. He became darkly menacing at last, and with much heat argued that the Company had the right to every bit of information about its 'territories.' And, said he, 'Mr Kurtz's knowledge of unexplored regions must have been necessarily extensive and peculiar—owing to his great abilities and to the deplorable circumstances in which he had been placed: therefore—' I assured him Mr Kurtz's knowledge, however extensive, did not bear upon the problems of commerce or administration. He invoked then the name of science. 'It would be an incalculable loss if,' &c., &c. I offered him the report on the 'Suppression of Savage Customs,' with the postscriptum torn off. He took it up eagerly, but ended by sniffing at it with an air of contempt. 'This is not what we had a right to expect,' he remarked. 'Expect nothing else,' I said. 'There are only private letters.' He withdrew upon some threat of legal proceedings, and I saw him no more; but another fellow, calling himself Kurtz's cousin, appeared two days later, and was anxious to hear all the details about his dear relative's last moments. Incidentally he gave me to understand that Kurtz had been essentially a great musician. 'There was the making of an immense success,' said the man, who was an organist, I believe, with lank grey hair flowing over a greasy coat-collar. I had no reason to doubt his statement; and to this day I am unable to say what was Kurtz's profession, whether he ever had any—which was the greatest of his talents. I had taken him for a painter who wrote for the papers, or else for a journalist who could paint—but even the cousin (who took snuff during the interview) could not tell me what he had been—exactly. He was a universal genius—on that point I agreed with the old chap, who thereupon blew his nose noisily into a large cotton handkerchief and withdrew in senile agitation, bearing off some family letters and memoranda without importance. Ultimately a journalist anxious to know something of the fate of his 'dear colleague' turned up. This visitor informed me Kurtz's proper sphere ought to have been politics 'on the popular side.' He had furry straight eyebrows, bristly hair cropped short, an eye-glass on a broad ribbon, and, becoming expansive, confessed his opinion that Kurtz really couldn't write a bit—'but heavens! how that man could talk! He electrified large meetings. He had faith—don't you see?—he had the faith. He could get himself to believe anything—anything. He would have been a splendid leader of an extreme party.' 'What party?' I asked. 'Any party,' answered the other. 'He was an—an—extremist.' Did I not think so? I assented. Did I know, he asked, with a sudden flash of curiosity, 'what it was that had induced him to go out there?' 'Yes,' said I, and forthwith handed him the famous Report for publication, if he thought fit. He glanced through it hurriedly, mumbling all the time, judged 'it would do,' and took himself off with this plunder.

"Thus I was left at last with a slim packet of letters and the girl's portrait. She struck me as beautiful—I mean she had a beautiful expression. I know that the sunlight can be made to lie too, yet one felt that no manipulation of light and pose could have conveyed the delicate shade of truthfulness upon those features. She seemed ready to listen without mental reservation, without suspicion, without a thought for herself. I concluded I would go and give her back her portrait and those letters myself. Curiosity? Yes; and also some other feeling perhaps. All that had been Kurtz's had passed out of my hands: his soul, his body, his station, his plans, his ivory, his career. There remained only his memory and his Intended—and I wanted to give that up too to the past, in a way,—to surrender personally all that remained of him with me to that oblivion which is the last word of our common fate. I don't defend myself. I had no clear perception of what it was I really wanted. Perhaps it was an impulse of unconscious loyalty, or the fulfilment of one of those ironic necessities that lurk in the facts of human existence. I don't know. I can't tell. But I went.

"I thought his memory was like the other memories of the dead that accumulate in every man's life,—a vague impress on the brain of shadows that had fallen on it in their swift and final passage; but before the high and ponderous door, between the tall houses of a street as still and decorous as a well-kept alley in a cemetery, I had a vision of him on the stretcher, opening his mouth voraciously, as if to devour all the earth with all its mankind. He lived then before me; he lived as much as he had ever lived—a shadow insatiable of splendid appearances, of frightful realities; a shadow darker than the shadow of the night, and draped nobly in the folds of a gorgeous eloquence. The vision seemed to enter the house with me—the stretcher, the phantom-bearers, the wild crowd of obedient worshippers, the gloom of the forests, the glitter of the reach between the murky bends, the beat of the drum, regular and muffled like the beating of a heart—the heart of a conquering darkness. It was a moment of triumph for the wilderness, an invading and vengeful rush which, it seemed to me, I would have to keep back alone for the salvation of another soul. And the memory of what I had heard him say afar there, with the horned shapes stirring at my back, in the glow of fires, within the patient woods, those broken phrases came back to me, were heard again in their ominous and terrifying simplicity. I remembered his abject pleading, his abject threats, the colossal scale of his vile desires, the meanness, the torment, the tempestuous anguish of his soul. And later on I seemed to see his collected languid manner, when he said one day, 'This lot of ivory now is really mine. The Company did not pay for it. I collected it myself at a very great personal risk. I am afraid they will try to claim it as theirs though. H'm. It is a difficult case. What do you think I ought to do—resist? Eh? I want no more than justice.' . . . He wanted no more than justice—no more than justice. I rang the bell before a mahogany door on the first floor, and while I waited he seemed to stare at me out of the glassy panel—stare with that wide and immense stare embracing, condemning, loathing all the universe. I seemed to hear the whispered cry, 'The horror! The horror!'

"The dusk was falling. I had to wait in a lofty drawing-room with three long windows from floor to ceiling that were like three luminous and bedraped columns. The bent gilt legs and backs of the furniture shone in indistinct curves. The tall marble fireplace had a cold and monumental whiteness. A grand piano stood massively in a corner, with dark gleams on the flat surfaces like a sombre and polished sarcophagus. A high door opened—closed. I rose.

"She came forward, all in black, with a pale head, floating towards me in the dusk. She was in mourning. It was more than a year since his death, more than a year since the news came; she seemed as though she would remember and mourn for ever. She took both my hands in hers and murmured, 'I had heard you were coming.' I noticed she was not very young—I mean not girlish. She had a mature capacity for fidelity, for belief, for suffering. The room seemed to have grown darker, as if all the sad light of the cloudy evening had taken refuge on her forehead. This fair hair, this pale visage, this pure brow, seemed surrounded by an ashy halo from which the dark eyes looked out at me. Their glance was guileless, profound, confident, and trustful. She carried her sorrowful head as though she were proud of that sorrow, as though she would say, I—I alone know how to mourn for him as he deserves. But while we were still shaking hands, such a look of awful desolation came upon her face that I perceived she was one of those creatures that are not the playthings of Time. For her he had died only yesterday. And, by Jove! the impression was so powerful that for me too he seemed to have died only yesterday—nay, this very minute. I saw her and him in the same instant of time—his death and her sorrow—I saw her sorrow in the very moment of his death. Do you understand? I saw them together—I heard them together. She had said, with a deep catch of the breath, 'I have survived'; while my strained ears seemed to hear distinctly, mingled with her tone of despairing regret, the summing-up whisper of his eternal condemnation. I asked myself what I was doing there, with a sensation of panic in my heart as though I had blundered into a place of cruel and absurd mysteries not fit for a human being to behold. She motioned me to a chair. We sat down. I laid the packet gently on the little table, and she put her hand over it. . . . 'You knew him well,' she murmured, after a moment of mourning silence.

" 'Intimacy grows quickly out there,' I said. 'I knew him as well as it is possible for one man to know another.'

" 'And you admired him,' she said. 'It was impossible to know him and not to admire him. Was it?'

" 'He was a remarkable man,' I said, unsteadily. Then before the appealing fixity of her gaze, that seemed to watch for more words on my lips, I went on, 'It was impossible not to—'

" 'Love him,' she finished eagerly, silencing me into an appalled dumbness. 'How true! how true! But when you think that no one knew him so well as I! I had all his noble confidence. I knew him best.'

" 'You knew him best,' I repeated. And perhaps she did. But with every word spoken the room was growing darker, and only her forehead, smooth and white, remained illumined by the unextinguishable light of belief and love.

" 'You were his friend,' she went on. 'His friend,' she repeated, a little louder. 'You must have been, if he had given you this, and sent you to me. I feel I can speak to you—and oh! I must speak. I want you—you who have heard his last words—to know I have been worthy of him. . . . It is not pride. . . . Yes! I am proud to know I understood him better than any one on earth—he told me so himself. And since his mother died I have had no one—no one—to—to—'

"I listened. The darkness deepened. I was not even sure whether he had given me the right bundle. I rather suspect he wanted me to take care of another batch of his papers which, after his death, I saw the manager examining under the lamp. And the girl talked, easing her pain in the certitude of my sympathy; she talked as thirsty men drink. I had heard that her engagement with Kurtz had been disapproved by her people. He wasn't rich enough or something. And indeed I don't know whether he had not been a pauper all his life. He had given me some reason to infer that it was his impatience of comparative poverty that drove him out there.

" '. . . Who was not his friend who had heard him speak once?' she was saying. 'He drew men towards him by what was best in them.' She looked at me with intensity. 'It is the gift of the great,' she went on, and the sound of her low voice seemed to have the accompaniment of all the other sounds, full of mystery, desolation, and sorrow, I had ever heard—the ripple of the river, the soughing of the trees swayed by the wind, the murmurs of wild crowds, the faint ring of incomprehensible words cried from afar, the whisper of a voice speaking from beyond the threshold of an eternal darkness. 'But you have heard him! You know!' she cried.

" 'Yes, I know,' I said with something like despair in my heart, but bowing my head before the faith that was in her, before that great and saving illusion that shone with an unearthly glow in the darkness, in the triumphant darkness from which I could not have defended her—from which I could not even defend myself.

" 'What a loss to me—to us!'—she corrected herself with beautiful generosity; then added in a murmur, 'To the world.' By the last gleams of twilight I could see the glitter of her eyes, full of tears—of tears that would not fall.

" 'I have been very happy—very fortunate—very proud,' she went on. 'Too fortunate. Too happy for a little while. And now I am unhappy for—for life.'

"She stood up; her fair hair seemed to catch all the remaining light in a glimmer of gold. I rose too.

" 'And of all this,' she went on, mournfully, 'of all his promise, and of all his greatness, of his generous mind, of his noble heart, nothing remains—nothing but a memory. You and I—'

" 'We shall always remember him,' I said, hastily.

" 'No!' she cried. 'It is impossible that all this should be lost—that such a life should be sacrificed to leave nothing—but sorrow. You know what vast plans he had. I knew of them too—I could not perhaps understand,—but others knew of them. Something must remain. His words, at least, have not died.'

" 'His words will remain,' I said.

" 'And his example,' she whispered to herself. 'Men looked up to him,—his goodness shone in every act. His example—'

" 'True,' I said; 'his example too. Yes, his example. I forgot that.'

" 'But I do not. I cannot—I cannot believe—not yet. I cannot believe that I shall never see him again, that nobody will see him again, never, never, never.'

"She put out her arms as if after a retreating figure, stretching them black and with clasped pale hands across the fading and narrow sheen of the window. Never see him! I saw him clearly enough then. I shall see this eloquent phantom as long as I live, and I shall see her too, a tragic and familiar Shade, resembling in this gesture another one, tragic also, and bedecked with powerless charms, stretching bare brown arms over the glitter of the infernal stream, the stream of darkness. She said suddenly very low, 'He died as he lived.'

" 'His end,' said I, with dull anger stirring in me, 'was in every way worthy of his life.'

" 'And I was not with him,' she murmured. My anger subsided before a feeling of infinite pity.

" 'Everything that could be done—' I mumbled.

" 'Ah, but I believed in him more than any one on earth—more than his own mother, more than—himself. He needed me! Me! I would have treasured every sigh, every word, every sign, every glance.'

"I felt like a chill grip on my chest. 'Don't,' I said, in a muffled voice.

" 'Forgive me. I—I—have mourned so long in silence—in silence. . . . You were with him—to the last? I think of his loneliness. Nobody near to understand him as I would have understood. Perhaps no one to hear . . . .'

" 'To the very end,' I said, shakily. 'I heard his very last words . . . .' I stopped in a fright.

" 'Repeat them,' she said in a heart-broken tone. 'I want—I want—something—something—to—to live with.'

"I was on the point of crying at her, 'Don't you hear them?' The dusk was repeating them in a persistent whisper all around us, in a whisper that seemed to swell menacingly like the first whisper of a rising wind. 'The horror! the horror!'

" 'His last word—to live with,' she murmured. 'Don't you understand I loved him—I loved him—I loved him!'

"I pulled myself together and spoke slowly.

" 'The last word he pronounced was—your name.'

"I heard a light sigh, and then my heart stood still, stopped dead short by an exulting and terrible cry, by the cry of inconceivable triumph and of unspeakable pain. 'I knew it—I was sure!' . . . She knew. She was sure. I heard her weeping; she had hidden her face in her hands. It seemed to me that the house would collapse before I could escape, that the heavens would fall upon my head. But nothing happened. The heavens do not fall for such a trifle. Would they have fallen, I wonder, if I had rendered Kurtz that justice which was his due? Hadn't he said he wanted only justice? But I couldn't. I could not tell her. It would have been too dark—too dark altogether . . . ."

Marlow ceased, and sat apart, indistinct and silent, in the pose of a meditating Buddha. Nobody moved for a time. "We have lost the first of the ebb," said the Director, suddenly. I raised my head. The offing was barred by a black bank of clouds, and the tranquil waterway leading to the uttermost ends of the earth flowed sombre under an overcast sky—seemed to lead into the heart of an immense darkness.

❈ "HEART OF DARKNESS" AND ITS TIME ❈

Joseph Conrad
from *Congo Diary*[1]

Arrived at Matadi[2] on the 13th of June, 1890.

Mr Gosse, chief of the station (O.K.) retaining us for some reason of his own.

Made the acquaintance of Mr Roger Casement,[3] which I should consider as a great pleasure under any circumstances and now it becomes a positive piece of luck.

Thinks, speaks well, most intelligent and very sympathetic.

Feel considerably in doubt about the future. Think just now that my life amongst the people (white) around here cannot be very comfortable. Intend avoid acquaintances as much as possible. * * *

24th. Gosse and R.C. gone with a large lot of ivory down to Boma. On G.['s] return to start to up the river. Have been myself busy packing ivory in casks. Idiotic employment. Health good up to now. * * *

Prominent characteristic of the social life here: people speaking ill of each other.

* * *

Friday, 4th July.

Left camp at 6h a.m. after a very unpleasant night. Marching across a chain of hills and then in a maze of hills. At 8:15 opened out into an undulating plain. Took bearings of a break in the chain of mountains on the other side. * * *

Saw another dead body lying by the path in an attitude of meditative repose.

In the evening three women of whom one albino passed our camp. Horrid chalky white with pink blotches. Red eyes. Red hair. Features very Negroid and ugly. Mosquitos. At night when the moon rose heard shouts and drumming in distant villages. Passed a bad night.

* * *

1. The following excerpts are taken from the diary Conrad kept when he was employed to go to the Congo in 1889; he kept the diary only from his landing at Matadi on June 13, 1890, until his arrival at Kinchassa on August 1.
2. Colonial station near the mouth of the Congo River. Conrad arrived there on his way to take up his command of a steamship upriver at Kinshasa.

3. Casement (1864–1916) and Conrad were employed at the time by the same company. Casement later served as British consul in various parts of Africa, and was the author of a report on the Congo (1904) that did much to make public the terrible conditions there. He was knighted in 1912. In 1916 he was executed by the British for his part in the Easter Rising in Ireland.

Saturday, 5th July. go.

Left at 6:15. Morning cool, even cold and very damp. Sky densely overcast. Gentle breeze from NE. Road through a narrow plain up to R. Kwilu. Swift-flowing and deep, 50 yds. wide. Passed in canoes. After[war]ds up and down very steep hills intersected by deep ravines. Main chain of heights running mostly NW-SE or W and E at times. Stopped at Manyamba. Camp[in]g place bad—in hollow—water very indifferent. Tent set at 10:15.

Section of today's road. NNE Distance 12 m. [a drawing]

Today fell into a muddy puddle. Beastly. The fault of the man that carried me. After camp[in]g went to a small stream, bathed and washed clothes. Getting jolly well sick of this fun.

Tomorrow expect a long march to get to Nsona, 2 days from Manyanga. No sunshine today.

* * *

Saturday, 26th.

Left very early. Road ascending all the time. Passed villages. Country seems thickly inhabited. At 11h arrived at large market place. Left at noon and camped at 1h p.m.

[section of the day's march with notes]

a camp—a white man died here—market—govt. post—mount—crocodile pond—Mafiesa. * * *

Sunday, 27th.

Left at 8h am. Sent luggage carriers straight on to Luasi and went ourselves round by the Mission of Sutili.

Hospitable reception by Mrs Comber. All the missio[naries] absent.

The looks of the whole establishment eminently civilized and very refreshing to see after the lots of tumble-down hovels in which the State and Company agents are content to live—fine buildings. Position on a hill. Rather breezy.

Left at 3h pm. At the first heavy ascent met Mr Davis, miss[ionary] returning from a preaching trip. Rev. Bentley away in the South with his wife. * * *

Tuesday, 29th.

Left camp at 7h after a good night's rest. Continuous ascent; rather easy at first. Crossed wooded ravines and the river Lunzadi by a very decent bridge.

At 9h met Mr Louette escorting a sick agent of the Comp[an]y back to Matadi. Looking very well. Bad news from up the river. All the steamers disabled. One wrecked. Country wooded. At 10:30 camped at Inkissi. * * *

Today did not set the tent but put up in Gov[ernmen]t shimbek.[4] Zanzibari in charge—very obliging. Met ripe pineapple for the first time. On the road today passed a skeleton tied up to a post. Also white man's grave—no name. Heap of stones in the form of a cross.

Health good now.

Wednesday, 30th.

Left at 6 a.m. intending to camp at Kinfumu. Two hours' sharp walk brought me to Nsona na Nsefe. Market. $\frac{1}{2}$ hour after, Harou arrived very ill with billious [sic] attack and fever. Laid him down in Gov[ernmen]t shimbek. Dose of Ipeca.[5]

---

4. A group of huts.   5. A medicine.

Vomiting bile in enormous quantities. At 11h gave him 1 gramme of quinine and lots of hot tea. Hot fit ending in heavy perspiration. At 2 p.m. put him in hammock and started for Kinfumu. Row with carriers all the way. Harou suffering much through the jerks of the hammock. Camped at a small stream.

At 4h Harou better. Fever gone. * * *

Up till noon, sky clouded and strong NW wind very chilling. From 1h pm to 4h pm sky clear and very hot day. Expect lots of bother with carriers tomorrow. Had them all called and made a speech which they did not understand. They promise good behaviour. * * *

Friday, 1st of August 1890.

* * * Row between the carriers and a man stating himself in Gov[ernmen]t employ, about a mat. Blows with sticks raining hard. Stopped it. Chief came with a youth about 13 suffering from gunshot wound in the head. Bullet entered about an inch above the right eyebrow and came out a little inside. The roots of the hair, fairly in the middle of the brow in a line with the bridge of the nose. Bone not damaged apparently. Gave him a little glycerine to put on the wound made by the bullet on coming out. Harou not very well. Mosquitos. Frogs. Beastly. Glad to see the end of this stupid tramp. Feel rather seedy. Sun rose red. Very hot day. Wind S[ou]th.

Sir Henry Morton Stanley
from *Address to the Manchester Chamber of Commerce*[1]

There is not one manufacturer here present who could not tell me if he had the opportunity how much he personally suffered through the slackness of trade; and I dare say that you have all some vague idea that if things remain as they are the future of the cotton manufacture is not very brilliant. New inventions are continually cropping up, so that your power of producing, if stimulated, is almost incalculable; but new markets for the sale of your products are not of rapid growth, and as other nations, by prohibitive tariffs, are bent upon fostering native manufacturers to the exclusion of your own, such markets as are now open to you are likely to be taken away from you in course of time. Well, then, I come to you with at least one market where there are at present, perhaps, 6,250,000 yards of cheap cottons sold every year on the Congo banks and in the Congo markets.[2]

I was interested the other day in making a curious calculation, which was, supposing that all the inhabitants of the Congo basin were simply to have one Sunday dress each, how many yards of Manchester cloth would be required; and the amazing number was 320,000,000 yards, just for one Sunday dress! (Cheers.) Proceeding still further with these figures I found that two Sunday dresses and four everyday dresses would in one year amount to 3,840,000,000 yards, which at 2d. [two

1. The journalist and adventurer Henry Morton Stanley wrote best-selling accounts of his exploits in Africa. He delivered this address to the textile manufacturers of Manchester in 1886, seeking their support for the commercial exploitation of the Congo. This speech gives a striking example of the outlook—and rhetoric—of the people who created the conditions Conrad encountered when he went to the Congo in 1890.
2. The Congo Free State (later Zaire), a vast area of central Africa around the Congo River, was formally brought under the ownership of Leopold II of Belgium and other investors in the International Association of the Congo by the Berlin West Africa Conference of 1884–1885. Stanley's expeditions there (from 1876) had been financed by Leopold, and from 1879 Stanley had set up trading stations along the river to facilitate the exploitation of the area's natural resources.

pence] per yard would be of the value of £16,000,000. The more I pondered upon these things I discovered that I could not limit these stores of cotton cloth to day dresses. I would have to provide for night dresses also—(laughter)—and these would consume 160,000,000 yards. (Cheers.) Then the grave cloths came into mind, and, as a poor lunatic, who burned Bolobo Station,[3] destroyed 30,000 yards of cloth in order that he should not be cheated out of a respectable burial, I really feared for a time that the millions would get beyond measurable calculation. However, putting such accidents aside, I estimate that, if my figures of population are approximately correct, 2,000,000 die every year, and to bury these decently, and according to the custom of those who possess cloth, 16,000,000 yards will be required, while the 40,000 chiefs will require an average of 100 yards each, or 4,000,000 yards. I regarded these figures with great satisfaction, and I was about to close my remarks upon the millions of yards of cloth that Manchester would perhaps be required to produce when I discovered that I had neglected to provide for the family wardrobe or currency chest, for you must know that in the Lower Congo there is scarcely a family that has not a cloth fund of about a dozen pieces of about 24 yards each. This is a very important institution, otherwise how are the family necessities to be provided for? How are the fathers and mothers of families to go to market to buy greens, bread, oil, ground nuts, chickens, fish, and goats, and how is the petty trade to be conducted? How is ivory to be purchased, the gums, rubber, dye powders, gunpowder, copper slugs, guns, trinkets, knives, and swords to be bought without a supply of cloth? Now, 8,000,000 families at 300 yards each will require 2,400,000,000. (Cheers.) You all know how perishable such currency must be; but if you sum up these several millions of yards, and value all of them at the average price of 2d. per yard, you will find that it will be possible for Manchester to create a trade—in the course of time—in cottons in the Congo basin amounting in value to about £26,000,000 annually. (Loud cheers.) I have said nothing about Rochdale savelist, or your own superior prints, your gorgeous handkerchiefs, with their variegated patterns, your checks and striped cloths, your ticking and twills.[4] I must satisfy myself with suggesting them; your own imaginations will no doubt carry you to the limbo of immeasurable and incalculable millions. (Laughter and cheers.)

Now, if your sympathy for yourselves and the fate of Manchester has been excited sufficiently, your next natural question would be as follows: We acknowledge, sir, that you have contrived by an artful array of imposing millions to excite our attention, at least, to this field; but we beg to ask you what Manchester is to do in order that we may begin realising this sale of untold millions of yards of cotton cloth? I answer that the first thing to do is for you to ask the British Government to send a cruiser to the mouth of the Congo to keep watch and ward over that river until the European nations have agreed among themselves as to what shall be done with the river, lest one of these days you will hear that it is too late. (Hear, hear.) Secondly, to study whether, seeing that it will never do to permit Portugal to assume sovereignty over that river[5]—and England publicly disclaims any wish to possess that river for herself—it would not be as well to allow the International Association to act as

---

3. The London *Times* carried frequent reports of disturbances in the Congo at this time; in March 1884, for example, Congolese attacks on foreign trading establishments at Nokki in the Lower Congo had caused the Europeans to "declare war against the natives."

4. Savelist is cheap fabric; ticking is a strong cotton or linen fabric; twill is a kind of textile weave.
5. The mouth of the Congo River had been discovered by the Portuguese in 1482.

guardians of international right to free trade and free entrance and exit into and out of the river. (Hear, hear.) The main point, remember, always is a guarantee that the lower river shall be free, that, however the Upper Congo may be developed, no Power, inspired by cupidity, shall seize upon the mouth of the river and build custom houses. (Hear, hear.) The Lower Congo in the future will only be valuable because down its waters will have to be floated the produce of the rich basin above to the ocean steamships. It will always have a fair trade of its own, but it bears no proportion to the almost limitless trade that the Upper Congo could furnish. If the Association could be assured that the road from Europe to Vivi[6] was for ever free, the first steps to realise the sale of those countless millions of yards of cotton cloth would be taken. Over six millions of yards are now used annually; but we have no means of absorbing more, owing to the difficulties of transport. Every man capable and willing to carry a load is employed. When human power was discovered to be not further available we tested animal power and discovered it to be feebler and more costly than the other; and we have come to the conclusion that steam power must now assist us or we remain *in statu quo* [as things now stand]. But before having recourse to this steam power, and building the iron road along which your bales of cotton fabrics may roll on to the absorbing markets of the Upper Congo unceasingly, the Association pauses to ask you, and the peoples of other English cities, such as London, Liverpool, Glasgow, Birmingham, Leeds, Preston, Sheffield, who profess to understand the importance of the work we have been doing, and the absorbing power of those markets we have reached, what help you will render us, for your own sakes, to make those markets accessible? (Hear, hear.) The Association will not build that railway to the Upper Congo, nor invest one piece of sterling gold in it, unless they are assured they will not be robbed of it, and the Lower Congo will be placed under some flag that shall be a guarantee to all the world that its waters and banks are absolutely free. (Cheers.)

You will agree with me, I am sure, that trade ought to expand and commerce grow, and if we can coax it into mature growth in this Congo basin that it would be a praiseworthy achievement, honoured by men and gods; for out of this trade, this intercourse caused by peaceful barter, proceed all those blessings which you and I enjoy. The more trade thrives, the more benefits to mankind are multipled, and nearer to gods do men become. (Hear, hear.) The builders of railroads through wildernesses generally require large concessions of lands; but the proposed builders of this railway to connect the Lower with the Upper Congo do not ask for any landed concessions; but they ask for a concession of authority over the Lower Congo in order that the beneficent policy which directs the civilising work on the Upper Congo may be extended to the Lower River, and that the mode of government and action may be uniform throughout. The beneficent policy referred to is explained in the treaty made and concluded with the United States Government.[7] That treaty says: "That with the object of enabling civilisation and commerce to penetrate into Equatorial Africa the Free States of the Congo have resolved to levy no customs duties whatever. The Free States also guarantee to all men who establish themselves in their territories the right of purchasing, selling, or leasing any land and buildings, of creating factories and of trade on the sole condition that they conform to the law. The International Association of the Congo is prepared

---

6. A town on the Upper Congo river; from 1882 Stanley had been arguing that a railway should be built between the Lower and Upper Congo to facilitate the exploitation of the interior. It was completed in 1898.

7. The United States was the first country to recognize the right of the International Association to govern the Congo territories in April 1884.

to enter into engagements with other nations who desire to secure the free admission of their products on the same terms as those agreed upon with the United States."

Here you have in brief the whole policy. I might end here, satisfied with having reminded you of these facts, which probably you had forgotten. Obedience to the laws—that is, laws drawn for protection of all—is the common law of all civilised communities, without which men would soon become demoralised. Can anybody object to that condition? Probably many of you here recollect reading those interesting letters from the Congo which were written by an English clerk in charge of an English factory. They ended with the cry of "Let us alone." In few words he meant to say, "We are doing very well as we are, we do not wish to be protected, and least of all taxed—therefore, let us alone. Our customers, the natives, are satisfied with us. The native chiefs are friendly and in accord with us; the disturbances, if any occur, are local; they are not general, and they right themselves quickly enough, for the trader cannot exist here if he is not just and kind in his dealings. The obstreperous and violent white is left to himself and ruin. Therefore, let us alone." Most heartily do I echo this cry; but unfortunately the European nations will not heed this cry; they think that some mode of government is necessary to curb those inclined to be refractory, and if there is at present a necessity to exhibit judicial power and to restrict evil-minded and ill-conditioned whites, as the Congo basin becomes more and more populated this necessity will be still more apparent. At the same time, if power appears on the Congo with an arbitrary and unfeeling front—with a disposition to tax and levy burdensome tariffs just as trade begins to be established—the outlook for enterprise becomes dismal and dark indeed.[8] (Hear, hear.) * * *

No part of Africa, look where I might, appeared so promising to me as this neglected tenth part of the continent. I have often fancied myself—when I had nothing to do better than dream—gazing from some lofty height, and looking down upon this square compact patch of 800,000,000 acres, with its 80,000 native towns, its population of 40,000,000 souls, its 17,000 miles of river waters, and its 30,000 square miles of lakes, all lying torpid, lifeless, inert, soaked in brutishness and bestiality, and I have never yet descended from that airy perch in the empyrean and touched earth but I have felt a purpose glow in me to strive to do something to awaken it into life and movement, and I have sometimes half fancied that the face of aged Livingstone,[9] vague and indistinct as it were, shone through the warm, hazy atmosphere, with a benignant smile encouraging me in my purpose. * * *

Yet, though examined from every point of view, a study of the Upper Congo and its capabilities produces these exciting arrays of figures and possibilities, I would not pay a two-shilling piece for it all so long as it remains as it is. It will absorb easily the revenue of the wealthiest nation in Europe without any return. I would personally one hundred times over prefer a snug little freehold in a suburb of Manchester to being the owner of the 1,300,000 English square miles of the Congo basin if it is to remain as inaccessible as it is to-day, or if it is to be blocked by that fearful tariff-loving nation, the Portuguese. (Hear, hear.) But if I were assured that the Lower Congo would remain free, and the flag of the Association guaranteed its freedom, I would if I were able

---

8. The right of the International Association to govern the Congo was eventually ended in 1908, following widespread protests against the regime's brutality.
9. David Livingstone (1813–1873), Scottish explorer and missionary. His expeditions into central Africa, in search of the source of the Nile River, were heavily publicized; when Livingstone "disappeared" in the course of what proved to be his last expedition, Stanley, then a correspondent for the *New York Herald*, was sent to find him. The two men met on the banks of Lake Tanganyika in East Africa in 1871; Stanley published an account of their meeting in *How I Found Livingstone* (1872).

build that railway myself—build it solid and strong—and connect the Lower Congo with the Upper Congo, perfectly satisfied that I should be followed by the traders and colonists of all nations. * * * The Portuguese have had nearly 400 years given them to demonstrate to the world what they could do with the river whose mouth they discovered, and they have been proved to be incapable to do any good with it, and now civilisation is inclined to say to them, "Stand off from this broad highway into the regions beyond—(cheers); let others who are not paralytic strive to do what they can with it to bring it within the number of accessible markets. There are 40,000,000 of naked people beyond that gateway, and the cotton spinners of Manchester are waiting to clothe them. Rochdale and Preston women are waiting for the word to weave them warm blue and crimson savelist. Birmingham foundries are glowing with the red metal that shall presently be made into ironwork in every fashion and shape for them, and the trinkets that shall adorn those dusky bosoms; and the ministers of Christ are zealous to bring them, the poor benighted heathen, into the Christian fold." (Cheers.)

Mr JACOB BRIGHT, M.P., who was received with loud cheers, said: I have listened with extreme interest to one of the ablest, one of the most eloquent addresses which have ever been delivered in this city—(cheers); and I have heard with uncommon pleasure the views of a man whose ability, whose splendid force of character, whose remarkable heroism, have given him a world-wide reputation. (Cheers.) * * *

Mr GRAFTON, M.P., moved:—

> That the best thanks of this meeting be and are hereby given to Mr H. M. Stanley for his address to the members of the Chamber, and for the interesting information conveyed by him respecting the Congo and prospects of international trade on the West Coast and interior of Africa.

He remarked that Mr Stanley's name was already enrolled in the pages of history, and would be handed down to posterity with the names of the greatest benefactors of our species, such as Columbus, who had opened out the pathways of the world. Long might Mr Stanley be spared to witness the benefit of his arduous and beneficent labours. (Cheers.)

 END OF HEART AND DARKNESS AND ITS TIME

❈

❦

RESPONSES
Chinua Achebe: An Image of Africa[1]

It was a fine autumn morning at the beginning of this academic year such as encouraged friendliness to passing strangers. Brisk youngsters were hurrying in all directions, many of them obviously freshmen in their first flush of enthusiasm. An older man, going the same way as I, turned and remarked to me how very young they came these

---

1. More than any other author, Chinua Achebe (1930–) is responsible for creating a consciousness of modern African writing in the West. In 1958, Achebe published *Things Fall Apart*, a novel that has since become the single most widely read text by an African author. Achebe's demand for Western recognition of African historicity in this work is often read as a direct response to Conrad's *Heart of Darkness*, the tale of a journey into Africa, toward savagery, away from both civilization and civilized behavior; Achebe offers a critique of Conrad's novella directly in his essay, *An Image of Africa*. In later novels such as *No Longer at Ease* (1960) and *A Man of the People* (1966), Achebe concerns himself less with Africa's colonial past than with the first years of its independence.

days. I agreed. Then he asked me if I was a student too. I said no, I was a teacher. What did I teach? African literature. Now that was funny, he said, because he never had thought of Africa as having that kind of stuff, you know. By this time I was walking much faster. "Oh well," I heard him say finally, behind me, "I guess I have to take your course to find out."

A few weeks later I received two very touching letters from high school children in Yonkers, New York, who—bless their teacher—had just read *Things Fall Apart*. One of them was particularly happy to learn about the customs and superstitions of an African tribe.

I propose to draw from these rather trivial encounters rather heavy conclusions which at first sight might seem somewhat out of proportion to them: But only at first sight.

The young fellow from Yonkers, perhaps partly on account of his age but I believe also for much deeper and more serious reasons, is obviously unaware that the life of his own tribesmen in Yonkers, New York, is full of odd customs and superstitions and, like everybody else in his culture, imagines that he needs a trip to Africa to encounter those things.

The other person being fully my own age could not be excused on the grounds of his years. Ignorance might be a more likely reason; but here again I believe that something more willful than a mere lack of information was at work. For did not that erudite British historian and Regius Professor at Oxford, Hugh Trevor Roper, pronounce a few years ago that African history did not exist?

If there is something in these utterances more than youthful experience, more than a lack of factual knowledge, what is it? Quite simply it is the desire—one might indeed say the need—in Western psychology to set Africa up as a foil in Europe, a place of negations at once remote and vaguely familiar in comparison with which Europe's own state of spiritual grace will be manifest.

This need is not new: which should relieve us of considerable responsibility and perhaps make us even willing to look at this phenomenon dispassionately. I have neither the desire nor, indeed, the competence to do so with the tools of the social and biological sciences. But, I can respond, as a novelist, to one famous book of European fiction, Joseph Conrad's *Heart of Darkness*, which better than any other work I know displays that Western desire and need which I have just spoken about. Of course, there are whole libraries of books devoted to the same purpose, but most of them are so obvious and so crude that few people worry about them today. Conrad, on the other hand, is undoubtedly one of the great stylists of modern fiction and a good storyteller into the bargain. His contribution therefore falls automatically into a different class—permanent literature—read and taught and constantly evaluated by serious academics. *Heart of Darkness* is indeed so secure today that a leading Conrad scholar has numbered it "among the half-dozen greatest short novels in the English language."[2] I will return to this critical option in due course because it may seriously modify my earlier suppositions about who may or may not be guilty in the things of which I will now speak.

Heart of Darkness projects the image of Africa as "the other world," the antithesis of Europe and therefore of civilization, a place where a man's vaunted intelligence and refinement are finally mocked by triumphant bestiality. The book opens on the River Thames, tranquil, resting peacefully "at the decline of day after ages of good service done to the race that peopled its banks." But the actual story takes place on the River

2. Albert J. Guerard, Introduction to *Heart of Darkness* (New York: New American Library, 1950), p. 9 [Achebe's note].

Congo, the very antithesis of the Thames. The River Congo is quite decidedly not a River Emeritus. It has rendered no service and enjoys no old-age pension. We are told that "going up that river was like travelling back to the earliest beginning of the world."

Is Conrad saying then that these two rivers are very different, one good, the other bad? Yes, but that is not the real point. What actually worries Conrad is the lurking hint of kinship, of common ancestry. For the Thames, too, "has been one of the dark places of the earth." It conquered its darkness, of course, and is now at peace. But if it were to visit its primordial relative, the Congo, it would run the terrible risk of hearing grotesque, suggestive echoes of its own forgotten darkness, and of falling victim to an avenging recrudescence of the mindless frenzy of the first beginnings.

I am not going to waste your time with examples of Conrad's famed evocation of the African atmosphere. In the final consideration it amounts to no more than a steady, ponderous, fake-ritualistic repetition of two sentences, one about silence and the other about frenzy. An example of the former is "It was the stillness of an implacable force brooding over an inscrutable intention" and of the latter, "The steamer toiled along slowly on the edge of a black and incomprehensible frenzy." Of course, there is a judicious change of adjective from time to time so that instead of "inscrutable," for example, you might have "unspeakable," etc., etc.

The eagle-eyed English critic, F. R. Leavis, drew attention nearly thirty years ago to Conrad's "adjectival insistence upon inexpressible and incomprehensible mystery." That insistence must not be dismissed lightly, as many Conrad critics have tended to do, as a mere stylistic flaw. For it raises serious questions of artistic good faith. When a writer, while pretending to record scenes, incidents and their impact, is in reality engaged in inducing hypnotic stupor in his readers through a bombardment of emotive words and other forms of trickery much more has to be at stake than stylistic felicity. Generally, normal readers are well armed to detect and resist such underhand activity. But Conrad chose his subject well—one which was guaranteed not to put him in conflict with the psychological predisposition of his readers or raise the need for him to contend with their resistance. He chose the role of purveyor of comforting myths.

The most interesting and revealing passages in *Heart of Darkness* are, however, about people. I must quote a long passage from the middle of the story in which representatives of Europe in a steamer going down the Congo encounter the denizens of Africa:

> We were wanderers on a prehistoric earth, on an earth that wore the aspect of an unknown planet. We could have fancied ourselves the first of men taking possession of an accursed inheritance, to be subdued at the cost of profound anguish and of excessive toil. But suddenly, as we struggled round a bend, there would be a glimpse of rush walls, of peaked grass-roofs, a burst of yells, a whirl of black limbs, a mass of hands clapping, of feet stamping, of bodies swaying, of eyes rolling, under the droop of heavy and motionless foliage. The steamer toiled along slowly on the edge of a black and incomprehensible frenzy. The prehistoric man was cursing us, praying to us, welcoming us—who could tell? We were cut off from the comprehension of our surroundings; we glided past like phantoms, wondering and secretly appalled, as sane men would be before an enthusiastic outbreak in a madhouse. We could not remember because we were travelling in the night of first ages, of those ages that are gone, leaving hardly a sign—and no memories.
>
> The earth seemed unearthly. We are accustomed to look upon the shackled form of a conquered monster, but there—there you could look at a thing monstrous and free. It was unearthly, and the men were—No, they were not inhuman. Well, you know, that was the worst of it—this suspicion of their not being inhuman. It would come slowly to one. They

howled and leaped, and spun, and made horrid faces; but what thrilled you was just the thought of your remote kinship with this wild and passionate uproar. Ugly. Yes, it was ugly enough; but if you were man enough you would admit to yourself that there was in you just the faintest trace of a response to the terrible frankness of that noise, a dim suspicion of there being a meaning in it which you—you so remote from the night of first ages—could comprehend.

Herein lies the meaning of *Heart of Darkness* and the fascination it holds over the Western mind: "What thrilled you was just the thought of their humanity—like yours. . . . Ugly."

Having shown us Africa in the mass, Conrad then zeros in on a specific example, giving us one of his rare descriptions of an African who is not just limbs or rolling eyes:

And between whiles I had to look after the savage who was fireman. He was an improved specimen; he could fire up a vertical boiler. He was there below me, and, upon my word, to look at him was as edifying as seeing a dog in a parody of breeches and a feather hat, walking on his hind legs. A few months of training had done for that really fine chap. He squinted at the steam gauge and at the water gauge with an evident effort of intrepidity—and he had filed his teeth, too, the poor devil, and the wool of his pate shaved into queer patterns, and three ornamental scars on each of his cheeks. He ought to have been clapping his hands and stamping his feet on the bank, instead of which he was hard at work, a thrall to strange witchcraft, full of improving knowledge.

As everybody knows, Conrad is a romantic on the side. He might not exactly admire savages clapping their hands and stamping their feet but they have at least the merit of being in their place, unlike this dog in a parody of breeches. For Conrad, things (and persons) being in their place is of the utmost importance.

Towards the end of the story, Conrad lavishes great attention quite unexpectedly on an African woman who has obviously been some kind of mistress to Mr. Kurtz and now presides (if I may be permitted a little imitation of Conrad) like a formidable mystery over the inexorable imminence of his departure:

She was savage and superb, wild-eyed and magnificent . . . She stood looking at us without a stir and like the wilderness itself, with an air of brooding over an inscrutable purpose.

This Amazon is drawn in considerable detail, albeit of a predictable nature, for two reasons. First, she is in her place and so can win Conrad's special brand of approval; and second, she fulfills a structural requirement of the story; she is a savage counterpart to the refined, European woman with whom the story will end:

She came forward, all in black with a pale head, floating towards me in the dusk. She was in mourning. . . . She took both my hands in hers and murmured, "I had heard you were coming" . . . She had a mature capacity for fidelity, for belief, for suffering.

The difference in the attitude of the novelist to these two women is conveyed in too many direct and subtle ways to need elaboration. But perhaps the most significant difference is the one implied in the author's bestowal of human expression to the one and the withholding of it from the other. It is clearly not part of Conrad's purpose to confer language on the "rudimentary souls" of Africa. They only "exchanged short grunting phrases" even among themselves but mostly they were too busy with their frenzy. There are two occasions in the book, however, when Conrad departs somewhat from his practice and confers speech, even English speech, on the savages. The first occurs when cannibalism gets the better of them:

"Catch 'im," he snapped, with a bloodshot widening of his eyes and a flash of sharp white teeth—"catch 'im. Give 'im to us." "To you, eh?" I asked; "what would you do with them?" "Eat 'im!" he said curtly . . .

The other occasion is the famous announcement:

Mistah Kurtz—he dead.

At first sight, these instances might be mistaken for unexpected acts of generosity from Conrad. In reality, they constitute some of his best assaults. In the case of the cannibals, the incomprehensible grunts that had thus far served them for speech suddenly proved inadequate for Conrad's purpose of letting the European glimpse the unspeakable craving in their hearts. Weighing the necessity for consistency in the portrayal of the dumb brutes against the sensational advantages of securing their conviction by clear, unambiguous evidence issuing out of their own mouth, Conrad chose the latter. As for the announcement of Mr. Kurtz's death by the "insolent black head of the doorway," what better or more appropriate *finis* could be written to the horror story of that wayward child of civilization who willfully had given his soul to the powers of darkness and "taken a high seat amongst the devils of the land" than the proclamation of his physical death by the forces he had joined?

It might be contended, of course, that the attitude to the African in *Heart of Darkness* is not Conrad's but that of his fictional narrator, Marlow, and that far from endorsing it Conrad might indeed be holding it up to irony and criticism. Certainly, Conrad appears to go to considerable pains to set up layers of insulation between himself and the moral universe of his story. He has, for example, a narrator behind a narrator. The primary narrator is Marlow but his account is given to us through the filter of a second, shadowy person. But if Conrad's intention is to draw a *cordon sanitaire* between himself and the moral and psychological malaise of his narrator, his care seems to me totally wasted because he neglects to hint however subtly or tentatively at an alternative frame of reference by which we may judge the actions and opinions of his characters. It would not have been beyond Conrad's power to make that provision if he had thought it necessary. Marlow seems to me to enjoy Conrad's complete confidence—a feeling reinforced by the close similarities between their careers.

Marlow comes through to us not only as a witness of truth, but one holding those advanced and humane views appropriate to the English liberal tradition which required all Englishmen of decency to be deeply shocked by atrocities in Bulgaria or the Congo of King Leopold of the Belgians or wherever. Thus Marlow is able to toss out such bleeding-heart sentiments as these:

They were all dying slowly—it was very clear. They were not enemies, they were not criminals, they were nothing earthly now—nothing but black shadows of disease and starvation, lying confusedly in the greenish gloom. Brought from all the recesses of the coast in all the legality of time contracts, lost in uncongenial surroundings, fed on unfamiliar food, they sickened, became inefficient, and were then allowed to crawl away and rest.

The kind of liberalism espoused here by Marlow/Conrad touched all the best minds of the age in England, Europe, and America. It took different forms in the minds of different people but almost always managed to sidestep the ultimate question of equality between white people and black people. That extraordinary missionary, Albert Schweitzer, who sacrificed brilliant careers in music and theology in Europe for a life of service to Africans in much the same area as Conrad writes about, epitomizes the ambivalence. In a comment which I have often quoted but must quote one last time Schweitzer says: "The African is indeed my brother but my junior brother." And so he proceeded to build a hospital appropriate to the needs of junior brothers with standards of hygiene reminiscent of medical practice in the days before the germ theory of disease came into being. Naturally, he became a sensation in Europe and America. Pilgrims flocked, and I believe still flock even after he has passed on, to witness the prodigious miracle in Lamberene, on the edge of the primeval forest.

Conrad's liberalism would not take him quite as far as Schweitzer's, though. He would not use the word "brother" however qualified; the farthest he would go was "kinship." When Marlow's African helmsman falls down with a spear in his heart he gives his white master one final disquieting look.

> And the intimate profundity of that look he gave me when he received his hurt remains to this day in my memory—like a claim of distant kinship affirmed in a supreme moment.

It is important to note that Conrad, careful as ever with his words, is not talking so much about *distant kinship* as about someone *laying a claim* on it. The black man lays a claim on the white man which is well-nigh intolerable. It is the laying of this claim which frightens and at the same time fascinates Conrad, ". . . the thought of their humanity—like yours . . . Ugly."

The point of my observations should be quite clear by now, namely, that *Conrad was a bloody racist*. That this simple truth is glossed over in criticism of his work is due to the fact that white racism against Africa is such a normal way of thinking that its manifestations go completely undetected. Students of *Heart of Darkness* will often tell you that Conrad is concerned not so much with Africa as with the deterioration of one European mind caused by solitude and sickness. They will point out to you that Conrad is, if anything, less charitable to the Europeans in the story than he is to the natives. A Conrad student told me in Scotland last year that Africa is merely a setting for the disintegration of the mind of Mr. Kurtz.

Which is partly the point: Africa as setting and backdrop which eliminates the African as human factor. Africa as a metaphysical battlefield devoid of all recognizable humanity, into which the wandering European enters at his peril. Of course, there is a preposterous and perverse kind of arrogance in thus reducing Africa to the role of props for the breakup of one petty European mind. But that is not even the point. The real question is the dehumanization of Africa and Africans which this age-long attitude has fostered and continues to foster in the world. And the question is whether a novel which celebrates this dehumanization, which depersonalizes a portion of the human race, can be called a great work of art. My answer is: No, it cannot. I would not call that man an artist, for example, who composes an eloquent instigation to one people to fall upon another and destroy them. No matter how striking his imagery or how beautiful his cadences fall such a man is no more a great artist than another may be called a priest who reads the mass backwards or a physician who poisons his patients. All those men in Nazi Germany who lent their talent to the service of virulent racism whether in science, philosophy or the arts have generally and rightly been condemned for their perversions. The time is long overdue for taking a hard look at the work of creative artists who apply their talents, alas often considerable as in the case of Conrad, to set people against people. This, I take it, is what Yevtushenko is after when he tells us that a poet cannot be a slave trader at the same time, and gives the striking example of Arthur Rimbaud who was fortunately honest enough to give up any pretenses to poetry when he opted for slave trading. For poetry surely can only be on the side of man's deliverance and not his enslavement; for the brotherhood and unity of all mankind and against the doctrines of Hitler's master races or Conrad's "rudimentary souls."

Last year was the 50th anniversary of Conrad's death. He was born in 1857, the very year in which the first Anglican missionaries were arriving among my own people in Nigeria. It was certainly not his fault that he lived his life at a time when the reputation of the black man was at a particularly low level. But even after due allowances have been made for all the influences of contemporary prejudice on his sensibility, there remains still in Conrad's attitude a residue of antipathy to black people which his peculiar psychology alone can explain. His own account of his first encounter with a black man is very revealing:

> A certain enormous buck nigger encountered in Haiti fixed my conception of blind, furious, unreasoning rage, as manifested in the human animal to the end of my days. Of the nigger I used to dream for years afterwards.

Certainly, Conrad had a problem with niggers. His inordinate love of that word itself should be of interest to psychoanalysts. Sometimes his fixation on blackness is equally interesting as when he gives us this brief description:

> A black figure stood up, strode on long black legs, waving long black arms.[3]

as though we might expect a black figure striding along on black legs to have *white* arms! But so unrelenting is Conrad's obsession.

As a matter of interest Conrad gives us in *A Personal Record* what amounts to a companion piece to the buck nigger of Haiti. At the age of sixteen Conrad encountered his first Englishman in Europe. He calls him "my unforgettable Englishman" and describes him in the following manner:

> [his] calves exposed to the public gaze . . . dazzled the beholder by the splendor of their marble-like condition and their rich tone of young ivory . . . The light of a headlong, exalted satisfaction with the world of men . . . illumined his face . . . and triumphant eyes. In passing he cast a glance of kindly curiosity and a friendly gleam of big, sound, shiny teeth . . . his white calves twinkled sturdily.[4]

Irrational love and irrational hate jostling together in the heart of that tormented man. But whereas irrational love may at worst engender foolish acts of indiscretion, irrational hate can endanger the life of the community. Naturally, Conrad is a dream for psychoanalytic critics. Perhaps the most detailed study of him in this direction is by Bernard C. Meyer, M.D. In this lengthy book, Dr. Meyer follows every conceivable lead (and sometimes inconceivable ones) to explain Conrad. As an example, he gives us long disquisitions on the significance of hair and hair-cutting in Conrad. And yet not even one word is spared for his attitude to black people. Not even the discussion of Conrad's antisemitism was enough to spark off in Dr. Meyer's mind those other dark and explosive thoughts. Which only leads one to surmise that Western psychoanalysts must regard the kind of racism displayed by Conrad as absolutely normal despite the profoundly important work done by Frantz Fanon in the psychiatric hospitals of French Algeria.

Whatever Conrad's problems were, you might say he is now safely dead. Quite true. Unfortunately, his heart of darkness plagues us still. Which is why an offensive and totally deplorable book can be described by a serious scholar as "among the half dozen greatest short novels in the English language," and why it is today perhaps the

---

3. Jonah Raskin, *The Mythology of Imperialism* (New York: Random House, 1971), p. 143 [Achebe's note].
4. Bernard C. Meyer, M.D., *Joseph Conrad: A Psychoanalytic*

Biography (Princeton, N.J.: Princeton University Press, 1967), p. 30 [Achebe's note].

most commonly prescribed novel in the twentieth-century literature courses in our own English Department here. Indeed the time is long overdue for a hard look at things.

There are two probable grounds on which what I have said so far may be contested. The first is that it is no concern of fiction to please people about whom it is written. I will go along with that. But I am not talking about pleasing people. I am talking about a book which parades in the most vulgar fashion prejudices and insults from which a section of mankind has suffered untold agonies and atrocities in the past and continues to do so in many ways and many places today. I am talking about a story in which the very humanity of black people is called in question. It seems to me totally inconceivable that great art or even good art could possibly reside in such unwholesome surroundings.

Secondly, I may be challenged on the grounds of actuality. Conrad, after all, sailed down the Congo in 1890 when my own father was still a babe in arms, and recorded what he saw. How could I stand up in 1975, fifty years after his death and purport to contradict him? My answer is that as a sensible man I will not accept just any traveller's tales solely on the grounds that I have not made the journey myself: I will not trust the evidence even of a man's very eyes when I suspect them to be as jaundiced as Conrad's. And we also happen to know that Conrad was, in the words of his biographer, Bernard C. Meyer, "notoriously inaccurate in the rendering of his own history."[5]

But more important by far is the abundant testimony about Conrad's savages which we could gather if we were so inclined from other sources and which might lead us to think that these people must have had other occupations besides merging into the evil forest or materializing out of it simply to plague Marlow and his dispirited band. For as it happened, soon after Conrad had written his book an event of far greater consequence was taking place in the art world of Europe. This is how Frank Willett, a British art historian, describes it:

> Gaugin had gone to Tahiti, the most extravagant individual act of turning to a non-European culture in the decades immediately before and after 1900, when European artists were avid for new artistic experiences, but it was only about 1904–5 that African art began to make its distinctive impact. One piece is still identifiable; it is a mask that had been given to Maurice Vlaminck in 1905. He records that Derain was "speechless" and "stunned" when he saw it, bought it from Vlaminck and in turn showed it to Picasso and Matisse, who were also greatly affected by it. Ambroise Vollard then borrowed it and had it cast in bronze . . . The revolution of twentieth century art was under way![6]

The mask in question was made by other savages living just north of Conrad's River Congo. They have a name, the Fang people, and are without a doubt among the world's greatest masters of the sculptured form. As you might have guessed, the event to which Frank Willett refers marked the beginning of cubism and the infusion of new life into European art that had run completely out of strength.

The point of all this is to suggest that Conrad's picture of the people of the Congo seems grossly inadequate even at the height of their subjection to the ravages of King Leopold's International Association for the Civilization of Central Africa. Travellers with closed minds can tell us little except about themselves. But even those not blinkered, like Conrad, with xenophobia, can be astonishingly blind.

5. Ibid., p. 30 [Achebe's note].

6. Frank Willett, African Art (New York: Praeger, 1971), pp. 35–36 [Achebe's note].

Let me digress a little here. One of the greatest and most intrepid travellers of all time, Marco Polo, journeyed to the Far East from the Mediterranean in the thirteenth century and spent twenty years in the court of Kublai Khan in China. On his return to Venice he set down in his book entitled *Description of the World* his impressions of the peoples and places and customs he had seen. There are at least two extraordinary omissions in his account. He says nothing about the art of printing unknown as yet in Europe but in full flower in China. He either did not notice it at all or if he did, failed to see what use Europe could possibly have for it. Whatever reason, Europe had to wait another hundred years for Gutenberg. But even more spectacular was Marco Polo's omission of any reference to the Great Wall of China nearly 4000 miles long and already more than 1000 years old at the time of his visit. Again, he may not have seen it; but the Great Wall of China is the only structure built by man which is visible from the moon![7] Indeed, travellers can be blind.

As I said earlier, Conrad did not originate the image of Africa which we find in his book. It was and is the dominant image of Africa in the Western imagination and Conrad merely brought the peculiar gifts of his own mind to bear on it. For reasons which can certainly use close psychological inquiry, the West seems to suffer deep anxieties about the precariousness of its civilization and to have a need for constant reassurance by comparing it with Africa. If Europe, advancing in civilization, could cast a backward glance periodically at Africa trapped in primordial barbarity, it could say with faith and feeling: There go I but for the grace of God. Africa is to Europe as the picture is to Dorian Gray—a carrier onto whom the master unloads his physical and moral deformities so that he may go forward, erect and immaculate. Consequently, Africa is something to be avoided just as the picture has to be hidden away to safeguard the man's jeopardous integrity. Keep away from Africa, or else! Mr. Kurtz of *Heart of Darkness* should have heeded that warning and the prowling horror in his heart would have kept its place, chained to its lair. But he foolishly exposed himself to the wild irresistible allure of the jungle and lo! the darkness found him out.

In my original conception of this talk I had thought to conclude it nicely on an appropriately positive note in which I would suggest from my privileged position in African and Western culture some advantages the West might derive from Africa once it rid its mind of old prejudices and began to look at Africa not through a haze of distortions and cheap mystification but quite simply as a continent of people—not angels, but not rudimentary souls either—just people, often highly gifted people and often strikingly successful in their enterprise with life and society. But as I thought more about the stereotype image, about its grip and pervasiveness, about the willful tenacity with which the West holds it to its heart; when I thought of your television and the cinema and newspapers, about books read in schools and out of school, of churches preaching to empty pews about the need to send help to the heathen in Africa, I realized that no easy optimism was possible. And there is something totally wrong in offering bribes to the West in return for its good opinion of Africa. Ultimately, the abandonment of unwholesome thoughts must be its own and only reward. Although I have used the word *willful* a few times in this talk to characterize the West's view of Africa it may well be that what is happening at this stage is more akin to reflex action than calculated malice. Which does not make the situation more, but less, hopeful. Let me give you one last and really minor example of what I mean.

---

7. About the omission of the Great Wall of China I am indebted to *The Journey of Marco Polo* as recreated by artist Michael Foreman, published by *Pegasus* Magazine, 1974 [Achebe's note].

Last November the *Christian Science Monitor* carried an interesting article written by its Education Editor on the serious psychological and learning problems faced by little children who speak one language at home and then go to school where something else is spoken. It was a wide-ranging article taking in Spanish-speaking children in this country, the children of migrant Italian workers in Germany, the quadrilingual phenomenon in Malaysia and so on. And all this while the article speaks unequivocally about *language*. But then out of the blue sky comes this:

> In London there is an enormous immigration of children who speak Indian or Nigerian dialects, or some other native language.[8]

I believe that the introduction of *dialects*, which is technically erroneous in the context, is almost a reflex action caused by an instinctive desire of the writer to downgrade the discussion to the level of Africa and India. And this is quite comparable to Conrad's withholding of language from his rudimentary souls. Language is too grand for these chaps; let's give them dialects. In all this business a lot of violence is inevitably done to words and their meaning. Look at the phrase "native language" in the above excerpt. Surely the only native language possible in London is Cockney English. But our writer obviously means something else—something Indians and Africans speak.

Perhaps a change will come. Perhaps this is the time when it can begin, when the high optimism engendered by the breathtaking achievements of Western science and industry is giving way to doubt and even confusion. There is just the possibility that Western man may begin to look seriously at the achievements of other people. I read in the papers the other day a suggestion that what America needs at this time is somehow to bring back the extended family. And I saw in my mind's eye future African Peace Corps Volunteers coming to help you set up the system.

Seriously, although the work which needs to be done may appear too daunting, I believe that it is not one day too soon to begin. And where better than at a University?

Gang of Four: We Live As We Dream, Alone[1]

Everybody is in too many pieces
No man's land surrounds our desires
To crack the shell we mix with others
Some lie in the arms of lovers

5   The city is the place to be
With no money you go crazy
I need an occupation
You have to pay for satisfaction

We live as we dream, alone
10   To crack this shell we mix with others

8. *Christian Science Monitor*, Nov. 25, 1974, p. 11 [Achebe's note].
1. In 1976 the Sex Pistols set off the British punk revolution with their first single, *Anarchy in the U.K.* The Gang of Four is one of many bands that arose during the early years of punk, when a wide range of musical possibilities seemed open to anyone with a guitar. The Gang of Four's music combines the assaultive sound of punk bands with an infectious dance sensibility—lacing this unlikely hybrid with neo-Marxist lyrics about consumerism and labor. *We Live As We Dream, Alone*, from their 1982 album *Songs of the Free*, takes a famous line from *Heart of Darkness* and makes it the cry of alienated labor, thereby reframing Conrad's message for a nation dominated by the conservative policies of Thatcherism.

Some flirt with fascism
Some lie in the arms of lovers

We live as we dream, alone
(repeat)

Everybody is in too many pieces
15   No man's land surrounds me
Without money we'll all go crazy

Man and woman need to work
It helps to define ourselves
We were not born in isolation
20   But sometimes it seems that way

We live as we dream, alone
(repeat)

We live as we dream, alone
The space between our work and its product
Some fall into fatalism
25   As if it started out this way

We live as we dream, alone
(repeat)

We live as we dream, alone
We were not born in isolation
But sometimes it seems that way
30   The space between our work and its product
As if it must always be this way

With our money we'll. . . .

Thomas Hardy
1840–1928

Thomas Hardy led a double life: one of the great Victorian novelists, he abandoned fiction in 1896 and reinvented himself as a poet. In a series of volumes published from 1898 through the early decades of the twentieth century, Hardy emerged as one of the most compelling voices in modern poetry. How should this strangely bifurcated literary career be read? There are continuities as well as divergences between Hardy's fiction and his poetry, and the shifts in his work provide a telling instance of the interwoven links and discontinuities between the Victorian era and the new modernism of the twentieth century.

   Hardy was born and reared in the village of Higher Bockhampton, Stinsford, in the rural county of Dorset in southern England. He left home in his early twenties and worked as a church architect in London for five years, then returned to the family home in 1867; he continued to accept architectural commissions while trying his hand at fiction and poetry. In early poems such as *Hap* and *Neutral Tones* Hardy revealed his abiding sense of a universe ruled by a blind or hostile fate, a world whose landscapes are etched with traces of the fleeting stories of their inhabitants. He was not able to find a publisher for such works, and he largely stopped writing poetry, but his first novel, *Desperate Remedies*, was published in 1871. By 1874 he was earning a steady income from his writing and was able to marry Emma Lavinia Gifford, the sister-in-law of a rector whose church he had been restoring. He produced twenty novels within a twenty-five year period, achieving fame, popularity, and no little controversy for the provocative and dark worlds he created. In *Far from the Madding Crowd*, *The Return of the Native*, *Tess of the d'Urbervilles*, and *Jude the Obscure*, Hardy transformed the realist novel of manners into tragic accounts of the industrialization of rural Britain, the bankruptcy of religious faith, and irreconcilable tensions between social classes and between men and women. Though he had become a master of characterization and plot, in his later novels Hardy grew increasingly preoccupied with fundamentally lyrical questions of interiority, subjective perception, and personal voice. After the sexual frankness of *Jude the Obscure* provoked shocked reviews—the Bishop of Wakefield went so far as to burn the book—Hardy decided to abandon his prose writing altogether and to mine his chosen territory with the tools of a poet.

He began by recreating in poetry the landscape of his fiction. Hardy's first poetry collection, published when he was fifty-eight, was *Wessex Poems* (1898), its title referring to the imaginary countryside that he had created in his novels, loosely based on regions in the south of England but named for a long-vanished medieval kingdom. Hardy's "Wessex" was a place whose towns and roads and forests and fields were breathed into life by the novelist. The Wessex novels were published with maps of the territory, and the landmarks were to remain constant throughout the disparate books. The region took such a hold on readers' imaginations that a Wessex tourist industry emerged, one which is still in place today. Hardy was as painstaking in giving the precise (although imaginary) coordinates of a village pathway as he was in tracing the path of a character's destiny.

Many of Hardy's poems take root in this same creative landscape, now viewed by an intensely self-aware speaker who retraces his personal history, himself "tracked by phantoms having weird detective ways," as he says in *Wessex Heights*. Burning logs, a photograph, a diminishing figure on a train platform, a deer at a window all provide "moments of vision" (the title of one of his collections) that foreshadow the modernist "epiphanies" of Joyce and Woolf. Like the major modernists, Hardy explored the workings of memory, of perception, and of individual vision. In other poems, he focused on contemporary events, most notably in a series of poems written during World War I, unsparing in their presentation both of the necessity of waging the conflict and of its horrifying waste.

In his poetry as in his prose, Hardy's modern themes are typically set in a rural landscape with ancient roots. A constant feature of the Wessex novels involves characters setting off on one of the myriad footpaths connecting obscure villages and solitary cottages with one another. Hardy invented his own geography for Wessex, but the footpaths really existed and were the most important trails carved into the landscape by travelers over many years. Called "ley lines" in folk culture, such footpaths are thought to gather their energy over time, as hundreds of people gradually wear down a shared path and leave traces of themselves in the form of memory and tradition. Hardy's poems move between personal, historical, and natural levels of experience, but it is the landscape above all that conveys the power of these events.

Hardy embodied his moments of vision in poems that recall old oral and religious forms of verse, especially those of ballads and hymns. Like Wordsworth, Burns, and Kipling, Hardy was fascinated by the power of popular verse forms to convey deep truths in seemingly simple meters and diction; like his predecessors, Hardy brought his traditional forms to life by subtle modulations of their elements. The lines of Hardy's poetry are measured with extreme care and precision—not in any way approaching "free verse." As W. H. Auden wrote of Hardy's poetry: "No English poet, not even Donne or Browning, employed so many and so complicated stanza forms.

Anyone who imitates his style will learn at least one thing, how to make words fit into a complicated structure." With architectural care, Hardy built up his words into complicated structures, lines, and stanzas following well-used poetic paths. With its compelling mixture of tradition and modernity, stoic calm and deep emotional intensity, Hardy's poetry has become a touchstone for modern poets writing in English, from Ezra Pound, who said he "needed no other poet," to Philip Larkin, Seamus Heaney, and Derek Walcott. "Auden worshiped his honesty, Eliot disliked his heresy," the critic Irving Howe has commented; "but Hardy prepared the ground for both."

Hardy mined his native landscape, and his own memory, until his death, composing many of his best poems in his seventies and eighties. He had built a house on the outskirts of Dorchester in 1885, and he lived there for the rest of his life, with his wife Emma until her death in 1912, and subsequently with his secretary, Florence Dugdale, whom he married in 1914. When he died, his body was buried in Westminster Abbey; but his heart, as he had directed, was buried in the grave of his wife Emma, next to his father's grave, in the Stinsford churchyard.

Hap°

             chance

If but some vengeful god would call to me
From up the sky, and laugh: "Thou suffering thing,
Know that thy sorrow is my ecstasy,
That thy love's loss is my hate's profiting!"

5   Then would I bear it, clench myself, and die,
Steeled by the sense of ire unmerited;
Half-eased in that a Powerfuller than I
Had willed and meted° me the tears I shed.   *given*

But not so. How arrives it joy lies slain,
10 And why unblooms the best hope ever sown?
—Crass Casualty obstructs the sun and rain,
And dicing° Time for gladness casts a moan. . . .   *gambling*
These purblind° Doomsters had as readily strown   *half-blind*
Blisses about my pilgrimage as pain.

1866   11898

Neutral Tones

We stood by a pond that winter day,
And the sun was white, as though chidden° of God,   *rebuked*
And a few leaves lay on the starving sod;
—They had fallen from an ash, and were gray.

5   Your eyes on me were as eyes that rove
Over tedious riddles of years ago;
And some words played between us to and fro
    On which lost the more by our love.

The smile on your mouth was the deadest thing
10 Alive enough to have strength to die;
And a grin of bitterness swept thereby
    Like an ominous bird a-wing. . . .

Since then, keen lessons that love deceives,
And wrings with wrong, have shaped to me
15   Your face, and the God-curst sun, and a tree,
And a pond edged with grayish leaves.

1867

1898

Wessex Heights

There are some heights in Wessex,[1] shaped as if by a kindly hand
For thinking, dreaming, dying on, and at crises when I stand,
Say, on Ingpen Beacon eastward, or on Wylls-Neck westwardly,
I seem where I was before my birth, and after death may be.

5   In the lowlands I have no comrade, not even the lone man's friend—
Her who suffereth long and is kind;[2] accepts what he is too weak to mend:
Down there they are dubious and askance; there nobody thinks as I,
But mind-chains do not clank where one's next neighbour is the sky.

In the towns I am tracked by phantoms having weird detective ways—
10   Shadows of beings who fellowed with myself of earlier days:
They hang about at places, and they say harsh heavy things—
Men with a wintry sneer, and women with tart disparagings.

Down there I seem to be false to myself, my simple self that was,
And is not now, and I see him watching, wondering what crass cause
15   Can have merged him into such a strange continuator as this,
Who yet has something in common with himself, my chrysalis.

I cannot go to the great grey Plain; there's a figure against the moon,
Nobody sees it but I, and it makes my breast beat out of tune;
I cannot go to the tall-spired town, being barred by the forms now passed
20   For everybody but me, in whose long vision they stand there fast.
There's a ghost at Yell'ham Bottom chiding loud at the fall of the night,
There's a ghost in Froom-side Vale, thin-lipped and vague, in a shroud
of white,
There is one in the railway train whenever I do not want it near,
I see its profile against the pane, saying what I would not hear.

25   As for one rare fair woman, I am now but a thought of hers,
I enter her mind and another thought succeeds me that she prefers,
Yet my love for her in its fulness she herself even did not know;
Well, time cures hearts of tenderness, and now I can let her go.

So I am found on Ingpen Beacon, or on Wylls-Neck to the west,
30   Or else on homely Bulbarrow, or little Pilsdon Crest,
Where men have never cared to haunt, nor women have walked with me,
And ghosts then keep their distance; and I know some liberty.

1898

---

1. An imaginary county in southwest England that forms the setting for Hardy's writings; the place names that follow are in "Wessex."

2. Cf. Corinthians 13.4: "Charity suffereth long, and is kind."

The Darkling Thrush[1]

I leant upon a coppice° gate   *wood*
  When Frost was spectre-gray,
And Winter's dregs made desolate
  The weakening eye of day.
5 The tangled bine-stems° scored the sky   *stems of bushes*
  Like strings of broken lyres,
And all mankind that haunted nigh
  Had sought their household fires.

The land's sharp features seemed to be
10 The Century's corpse outleant,[2]
His crypt the cloudy canopy,
  The wind his death-lament.
The ancient pulse of germ° and birth   *seed*
  Was shrunken hard and dry,
15 And every spirit upon earth
  Seemed fervourless as I.

At once a voice arose among
  The bleak twigs overhead
In a full-hearted evensong
20 Of joy illimited;
An aged thrush, frail, gaunt, and small,
  In blast-beruffled plume,
Had chosen thus to fling his soul
  Upon the growing gloom.

25 So little cause for carolings
  Of such ecstatic sound
Was written on terrestrial things
  Afar or nigh around,
That I could think there trembled through
30 His happy good-night air
Some blessed Hope, whereof he knew
  And I was unaware.

On the Departure Platform

We kissed at the barrier; and passing through
She left me, and moment by moment got
Smaller and smaller, until to my view
  She was but a spot;

5 A wee white spot of muslin fluff
That down the diminishing platform bore

---

1. The poem was published on 31 December 1900. 2. As if leaning out from a coffin.

Through hustling crowds of gentle and rough
    To the carriage door.

Under the lamplight's fitful glowers,
Behind dark groups from far and near,
Whose interests were apart from ours,
    She would disappear,

Then show again, till I ceased to see
That flexible form, that nebulous white;
And she who was more than my life to me
    Had vanished quite. . . .

We have penned new plans since that fair fond day,
And in season she will appear again—
Perhaps in the same soft white array—
    But never as then!

—"And why, young man, must eternally fly
A joy you'll repeat, if you love her well?"
—O friend, nought happens twice thus; why,
    I cannot tell!

1909

The Convergence of the Twain
(Lines on the loss of the "Titanic")[1]

1

In a solitude of the sea
Deep from human vanity,
And the Pride of Life that planned her, stilly couches she.

2

Steel chambers, late the pyres
Of her salamandrine° fires,   *white-hot*
Cold currents thrid,° and turn to rhythmic tidal lyres.   *thread*

3

Over the mirrors meant
To glass the opulent
The sea-worm crawls—grotesque, slimed, dumb, indifferent.

4

Jewels in joy designed
To ravish the sensuous mind
Lie lightless, all their sparkles bleared and black and blind.

---

1. The largest ocean-liner of its day, the supposedly unsinkable *Titanic* sank on 15 April 1912 on its maiden voyage after colliding with an iceberg; two-thirds of its 2,200 passengers died.

5

Dim moon-eyed fishes near
Gaze at the gilded gear
And query: "What does this vaingloriousness down here?". . .

6

Well: while was fashioning
This creature of cleaving wing,
The Immanent Will that stirs and urges everything

7

Prepared a sinister mate
For her—so gaily great—
A Shape of Ice, for the time far and dissociate.[2]

8

And as the smart ship grew
In stature, grace, and hue,
In shadowy silent distance grew the Iceberg too.

9

Alien they seemed to be:
No mortal eye could see
The intimate welding of their later history,

10

Or sign that they were bent
By paths coincident
On being anon twin halves of one august event,

11

Till the Spinner of the Years
Said "Now!" And each one hears,
And consummation comes, and jars two hemispheres.

1912   1912

Channel Firing[1]

That night your great guns, unawares,
Shook all our coffins as we lay,
And broke the chancel window-squares,
We thought it was the Judgment-day

5

And sat upright. While drearisome
Arose the howl of wakened hounds:
The mouse let fall the altar-crumb,

---

2. According to Hardy, the Immanent Will is that which
secretly guides events.

1. The poem refer to military in the English channel prior
to World War I.

The worms drew back into the mounds,
The glebe° cow drooled. Till God called, "No;   field
10   It's gunnery practice out at sea
Just as before you went below;
The world is as it used to be:
"All nations striving strong to make
Red war yet redder. Mad as hatters
15   They do no more for Christés sake
Than you who are helpless in such matters.

"That this is not the judgment-hour
For some of them's a blessed thing,
For if it were they'd have to scour
20   Hell's floor for so much threatening. . . .

"Ha, ha. It will be warmer when
I blow the trumpet (if indeed
I ever do; for you are men,
And rest eternal sorely need)."

25   So down we lay again. "I wonder,
Will the world ever saner be,"
Said one, "than when He sent us under
In our indifferent century!"

And many a skeleton shook his head.
30   "Instead of preaching forty year,"
My neighbour Parson Thirdly said,
"I wish I had stuck to pipes and beer."

Again the guns disturbed the hour,
Roaring their readiness to avenge,
35   As far inland as Stourton Tower,
And Camelot, and starlit Stonehenge.[2]

April 1914   1914

In Time of "The Breaking of Nations"[1]

1

Only a man harrowing clods
    In a slow silent walk
With an old horse that stumbles and nods
    Half asleep as they stalk.

2

5   Only thin smoke without flame
    From the heaps of couch-grass;

---

2. The town of Stour Head, which Hardy calls Stourton, is in the county of Dorset. According to legend, Camelot was the site of King Arthur's court; Stonehenge is a prehistoric site in southwest England.

1. Cf. Jeremiah 51.20: "Thou art my battle axe and weapons of war: for with thee will I break in pieces the nations, and with thee will I destroy kingdoms."

Yet this will go onward the same
　　　Though Dynasties pass.

3

Yonder a maid and her wight°　　　　　　　　　　　　man
10　　　Come whispering by:
War's annals will cloud into night
　　　Ere their story die.

1915　　　　　　　　　　　　　　　　　　　　　　　　1916

I Looked Up from My Writing

I looked up from my writing,
　　　And gave a start to see,
As if rapt in my inditing,
　　　The moon's full gaze on me.

5　Her meditative misty head
　　　Was spectral in its air,
And I involuntarily said,
　　　"What are you doing there?"

"Oh, I've been scanning pond and hole
10　　　And waterway hereabout
For the body of one with a sunken soul
　　　Who has put his life-light out.

"Did you hear his frenzied tattle?
　　　It was sorrow for his son
15　Who is slain in brutish battle,
　　　Though he has injured none.

"And now I am curious to look
　　　Into the blinkered mind
Of one who wants to write a book
20　　　In a world of such a kind."

Her temper overwrought me,
　　　And I edged to shun her view,
For I felt assured she thought me
　　　One who should drown him too.

1917

"And There Was a Great Calm"[1]
(On the Signing of the Armistice, 11 Nov. 1918)[2]

1

There had been years of Passion—scorching, cold,
And much Despair, and Anger heaving high,
Care whitely watching, Sorrows manifold,

---

1. A phrase from Mark 4.39, after Jesus has calmed a storm at sea.

2. The armistice ending World War I was signed by Germany and the Allies on this date.

Among the young, among the weak and old,
5   And the pensive Spirit of Pity whispered, "Why?"

2

Men had not paused to answer. Foes distraught
Pierced the thinned peoples in a brute-like blindness,
Philosophies that sages long had taught,
And Selflessness, were as an unknown thought,
10   And "Hell!" and "Shell!" were yapped at Lovingkindness.

3

The feeble folk at home had grown full-used
To "dug-outs," "snipers," "'Huns,"[3] from the war-adept
In the mornings heard, and at evetides perused;
To day-dreamt men in millions, when they mused—
15   To nightmare-men in millions when they slept.

4

Waking to wish existence timeless, null,
Sirius[4] they watched above where armies fell;
He seemed to check his flapping when, in the lull
Of night a boom came thencewise, like the dull
20   Plunge of a stone dropped into some deep well.

5

So, when old hopes that earth was bettering slowly
Were dead and damned, there sounded "War is done!"
One morrow. Said the bereft, and meek, and lowly,
"Will men some day be given to grace? yea, wholly,
25   And in good sooth,° as our dreams used to run?"   *truth*

6

Breathless they paused. Out there men raised their glance
To where had stood those poplars lank and lopped,
As they had raised it through the four years' dance
Of Death in the now familiar flats of France;
30   And murmured, "Strange, this! How? All firing stopped?"

7

Aye; all was hushed. The about-to-fire fired not,
The aimed-at moved away in trance-lipped song.
One checkless regiment slung a clinching shot
And turned. The Spirit of Irony smirked out, "What?
35   Spoil peradventures° woven of Rage and Wrong?"   *perhaps*

8

Thenceforth no flying fires inflamed the gray,
No hurtlings shook the dewdrop from the thorn,
No moan perplexed the mute bird on the spray;
Worn horses mused: "We are not whipped to-day;"

---

3. Slang for "Germans" during the war.   4. The brightest star in the night sky.

40   No weft-winged engines° blurred the moon's thin horn.   *early airplanes*

9

Calm fell. From Heaven distilled a clemency;
There was peace on earth, and silence in the sky;
Some could, some could not, shake off misery:
The Sinister Spirit sneered: "It had to be!"

45   And again the Spirit of Pity whispered, "Why?"

1918   1919, 1922

Epitaph

I never cared for Life: Life cared for me,
And hence I owed it some fidelity.
It now says, "Cease; at length thou hast learnt to grind
Sufficient toll for an unwilling mind,
And I dismiss thee—not without regard
That thou didst ask no ill-advised reward,
Nor sought in me much more than thou couldst find."

1922

≈PERSPECTIVES≈

The Great War: Confronting the Modern

The multiplying technological, artistic, and social changes at the turn of the twentieth century impressed that generation's artists as a rupture with the past. And no event so graphically suggested that human history had "changed, changed utterly," as World War I—"the Great War."

Great Britain, like its enemy Germany, entered the war with idealistic aims. Prime Minister H. H. Asquith put the justice of the British case this way in a speech to the House of Commons on 7 August 1914: "I do not think any nation ever entered into a great conflict—and this is one of the greatest that history will ever know—with a clearer conscience or stronger conviction that it is fighting not for aggression, not for the maintenance of its own selfish ends, but in defence of principles the maintenance of which is vital to the civilization of the world." But cynicism set in quickly—first among ground troops on the Western Front, dug into trenches and watching "progress" that could be measured in yards per day. Soon the British public became disillusioned with the war effort, partly as a result of technological advances in the news media. Daily papers in England carried photographs from the front, and while editorial policy generally supported the British government and printed heroic images of the fighting, this sanitized version of the war was largely offset by the long published lists of casualties; during the four years and three months that Britain was involved in the war, more than a million British troops—an average of fifteen hundred per day—were killed in action.

The war's lasting legacy was a sense of bitterly rebuffed idealism, bringing with it a suspicion of progress, technology, government, bureaucracy, nationalism, and conventional morality—themes probed in new ways by the period's writers. Just as the war had involved radically new strategies and new technologies, writers intensified their search for new forms and modes of expression as they and their compatriots found themselves in the midst of a conflict unlike anything previously known in the annals of history.

Blast

Wyndham Lewis (1884–1957), founder of the provocative arts magazine *Blast,* was often at odds with his sometime co-conspirator Ezra Pound: indeed both men were usually at odds with most of their friends. But they did agree on one thing: that the writers of Edwardian and Georgian England had failed to throw off the deadening literary mannerisms of the previous century. "As for the nineteenth century," Pound wrote, "with all respects to its achievements, I think we shall look back upon it as a rather blurry, messy sort of a period, a rather sentimentalistic, mannerish sort of a period."

Some violent corrective was needed. The name of Lewis's magazine was intended to suggest an explosive charge that would blow away tired literary and social conventions. It was a calculated assault on good taste, both in its contents and, more immediately, in its form: an oversized, bright pink cover with the single word *BLAST* splashed diagonally across it. Lewis carefully oversaw the details of typography; visually and rhetorically, *Blast* is indebted to the polemical style of the Italian artist F. T. Marinetti (1876–1944), the founder of Italian futurism. Marinetti's vivid manifestos for futurism celebrated a modern aesthetic of speed, technology, and power. Lewis in turn founded a movement he called Vorticism, and *Blast* bore the subtitle *The Review of the Great English Vortex.*

The definition of *vorticism* was left intentionally hazy; as canny an observer as the Vorticist painter William Roberts, one of the signatories of the manifesto, claimed that Vorticism

Wyndham Lewis, *The Creditors* (design for *Timon of Athens*), 1912–1913.

was first and foremost "a slogan." In 1915 Lewis defined it this way: "By Vorticism we mean (a) ACTIVITY as opposed to the tasteful PASSIVITY of Picasso; (b) SIGNIFICANCE as opposed to the dull or anecdotal character to which the Naturalist is condemned; (c) ESSENTIAL MOVEMENT and ACTIVITY (such as the energy of a mind) as opposed to the imitative cinematography, the fuss and hysterics of the Futurists."

In its disorienting layout of typography, the *Vorticist Manifesto* is as much a visual as a literary statement, reflecting the multiple and always skewed interest of its primary author, Lewis. Born on a yacht off the coast of Nova Scotia, he had moved to London with his mother when his parents separated in 1893. A precocious painter, he won a scholarship to the progressive Slade School of Art at age sixteen, but moved to Paris before completing his studies. He returned to London in 1909 and began a career as a painter and writer. During the War, he served both as an artillery officer and as a commissioned war artist. He also wrote an experimental novel, *Tarr* (1918), and went on to produce a range of works in the dozen years thereafter, including pro-fascist political theory in *The Art of Being Ruled* (1926) and more general cultural criticism in *Time and Western Man* (1927), in which he attacked the modern cult of subjectivity. During the thirties, he became increasingly unpopular in London, first as a result of a satirical novel, *The Apes of God*, which lampooned figures in the literary and art world and their patrons; following two libel actions against him, publishers became wary of taking on his works. Lewis and his wife spent the years of World War II living in poverty in America and Canada; after the war, he returned to England, where he became an art critic for the British Broadcasting Corporation. He continued to draw, paint, and write memoirs, satirical stories, and an allegorical fantasy in several volumes.

Along with the *Vorticist Manifesto*, the first issue of *Blast* included poetry by Pound, fiction by Ford Madox Ford and Rebecca West, a play by Lewis, and illustrations by Lewis and others. The timing of the first issue couldn't have been worse: after delays caused by typesetting difficulties, *Blast* went on sale in London on 20 June 1914; World War 1 began just a few weeks later. While Lewis and his confederates had declared war on conventional artistic and literary taste with their "puce monster"—an advertisement for the first issue announced the "END OF THE CHRISTIAN ERA"—they were usurped by a much more pressing conflict. As Lewis later wrote, "In 1914 I produced a huge review called *Blast,* which for the most part I wrote myself. That was my first public appearance. Immediately the War broke out and put an end to all that." Lewis brought out a second issue in July 1915, attempting to fend off charges of irrelevancy with a special "War Number" that included T. S. Eliot's *Preludes* and *Rhapsody on a Windy Night* and a manifesto from the sculptor Henri Gaudier-Brzeska, "written from the trenches," which concludes poignantly with an obituary for Gaudier, "Mort pour la Patrie" (died for the fatherland). But by this time, *Blast* itself was for all intents and purposes dead; its second issue was its last. Short-lived though it was, however, *Blast* was remarkably important in clearing the way for the new art of modernism.

VORTICIST MANIFESTO
LONG LIVE THE VORTEX!

Long live the great art vortex sprung up in the centre of this town!

We stand for the Reality of the Present—not for the sentimental Future, or the sacripant[1] Past.

We want to leave Nature and Men alone.

We do not want to make people wear Futurist Patches, or fuss men to take to pink and sky-blue trousers.

We are not their wives or tailors.

The only way Humanity can help artists is to remain independent and work unconsciously.

WE NEED THE UNCONSCIOUSNESS OF HUMANITY—their stupidity, animalism and dreams.

We believe in no perfectibility except our own.

Intrinsic beauty is in the Interpreter and Seer, not in the object or content.[2]

We do not want to change the appearance of the world, because we are not Naturalists, Impressionists or Futurists (the latest form of Impressionism), and do not depend on the appearance of the world for our art.

WE ONLY WANT THE WORLD TO LIVE, and to feel its crude energy flowing through us.

It may be said that great artists in England are always revolutionary, just as in France any really fine artist had a strong traditional vein.

Blast sets out to be an avenue for all those vivid and violent ideas that could reach the Public in no other way.

Blast will be popular, essentially. It will not appeal to any particular class, but to the fundamental and popular instincts in every class and description of people, **TO THE INDIVIDUAL.** The moment a man feels or realizes himself as an artist, he ceases to belong to any milieu or time. Blast is created for this timeless, fundamental Artist that exists in everybody.

---

1. Boasting of valor.
2. Although the Vorticists go on to differentiate themselves from the impressionists, this statement is very close

to the impressionism articulated by Walter Pater in *The Renaissance* (1873); see page 915.

The Man in the Street and the Gentleman are equally ignored.

Popular art does not mean the art of the poor people, as it is usually supposed to. It means the art of the individuals.

Education (art education and general education) tends to destroy the creative instinct. Therefore it is in times when education has been non-existent that art chiefly flourished.

But it is nothing to do with "the People."

It is a mere accident that that is the most favourable time for the individual to appear.

To make the rich of the community shed their education skin, to destroy politeness, standardization and academic, that is civilized, vision, is the task we have set ourselves.

We want to make in England not a popular art, not a revival of lost folk art, or a romantic fostering of such unactual conditions, but to make individuals, wherever found.

We will convert the King if possible.

A VORTICIST KING! WHY NOT?

DO YOU THINK LLOYD GEORGE[3] HAS THE VORTEX IN HIM?

MAY WE HOPE FOR ART FROM LADY MOND?[4]

We are against the glorification of "the People," as we are against snobbery. It is not necessary to be an outcast bohemian, to be unkempt or poor, any more than it is necessary to be rich or handsome, to be an artist. Art is nothing to do with the coat you wear. A top-hat can well hold the Sixtine.[5] A cheap cap could hide the image of Kephren.

AUTOMOBILISM (Marinetteism) bores us. We don't want to go about making a hullo-bulloo about motor cars, anymore than about knives and forks, elephants or gas-pipes.

Elephants are **VERY BIG.** Motor cars go quickly.

Wilde gushed twenty years ago about the beauty of machinery. Gissing,[6] in his romantic delight with modern lodging houses was futurist in this sense.

The futurist is a sensational and sentimental mixture of the aesthete of 1890 and the realist of 1870.

The "Poor" are detestable animals! They are only picturesque and amusing for the sentimentalist or the romantic! The "Rich" are bores without a single exception, *en tant que riches* [so far as they are rich]!

We want those simple and great people found everywhere.

Blast presents an art of Individuals.

MANIFESTO.

1

BLAST First (from politeness) ENGLAND

CURSE ITS CLIMATE FOR ITS SINS AND INFECTIONS

DISMAL SYMBOL, SET round our bodies,
of effeminate lout within.

---

3. David Lloyd George, British statesman, and Prime Minister 1916–1922.
4. A leader of fashionable London society.

5. The Sistine Chapel in the Vatican.
6. George Gissing (1857–1903), naturalist novelist.

VICTORIAN VAMPIRE, the LONDON cloud sucks
the TOWN'S heart.

A 1000 MILE LONG, 2 KILOMETER Deep

BODY OF WATER even, is pushed against us
from the Floridas, TO MAKE US MILD.
OFFICIOUS MOUNTAINS keep back DRASTIC WINDS

SO MUCH VAST MACHINERY TO PRODUCE

THE CURATE of "Eltham"
BRITANNIC AESTHETE
WILD NATURE CRANK
DOMESTICATED POLICEMAN
LONDON COLISEUM
SOCIALIST-PLAYWRIGHT
DALY'S MUSICAL COMEDY
GAIETY CHORUS GIRL
TONKS[7]

CURSE

the flabby sky that can manufacture no snow, but can only drop the sea on us in a
drizzle like a poem by Mr. Robert Bridges.[8]

CURSE

the lazy air that cannot stiffen the back of the **SERPENTINE**, or put
Aquatic steel half way down the **MANCHESTER CANAL.**

But ten years ago we saw distinctly both snow and ice
here.
May some vulgarly inventive, but useful person, arise,
and restore to us the necessary **BLIZZARDS.**

LET US ONCE MORE WEAR THE ERMINE
OF THE NORTH.

WE BELIEVE IN THE EXISTENCE OF THIS USEFUL LITTLE CHEMIST IN OUR MIDST!

7. Henry Tonks, a teacher at the Slade School of Art (where Lewis and other Vorticists studied) who resisted as "contamination" such modern innovations as post-impressionism and cubism.

8. Poet Laureate from 1913 until his death in 1930, noted for his technical skill and high moral tone.

2
OH BLAST FRANCE

pig plagiarism
BELLY
SLIPPERS
POODLE TEMPER
BAD MUSIC

SENTIMENTAL GALLIC GUSH
SENSATIONALISM
FUSSINESS.

PARISIAN PAROCHIALISM.

Complacent young man, so much
respect for Papa and his son!—Oh!—
Papa is wonderful: but all papas are!

BLAST

APERITIFS (Pernots, Amers picon)
Bad change
Naively seductive Houri salon-
    picture Cocottes
Slouching blue porters (can carry
    a pantechnicon)
Stupidly rapacious people at
    every step
Economy maniacs
Bouillon Kub (for being a bad pun)

PARIS.

Clap-trap Heaven of amative
    German professor.
Ubiquitous lines of silly little trees.
Arcs de Triomphe.
Imperturbable, endless prettiness.
Large empty cliques, higher up.
Bad air for the individual.

BLAST
MECCA OF THE AMERICAN

because it is not other side of Suez Canal, instead of an
afternoon's ride from London.

3
CURSE
WITH EXPLETIVE OF WHIRLWIND
THE BRITANNIC AESTHETE

CREAM OF THE SNOBBISH EARTH
ROSE OF SHARON OF GOD-PRIG
   OF SIMIAN VANITY
SNEAK AND SWOT OF THE SCHOOL-ROOM
IMBERB (or Berbed when in Belsize)-PEDANT

PRACTICAL JOKER
DANDY
CURATE

BLAST all products of phlegmatic cold
Life of **LOOKER-ON.**
CURSE

SNOBBERY
(disease of feminity)
FEAR OF RIDICULE
(arch vice of inactive, sleepy)
PLAY
STYLISM
SINS AND PLAGUES
of this **LYMPHATIC** finished
(we admit in every sense
finished)
VEGETABLE HUMANITY.

4
BLAST

THE SPECIALIST
"PROFESSIONAL"
"GOOD WORKMAN"
"GROVE-MAN"
ONE ORGAN MAN

BLAST THE

AMATEUR
SCIOLAST
ART-PIMP
JOURNALIST
SELF MAN
NO-ORGAN MAN

5
BLAST HUMOUR

Quack ENGLISH drug for stupidity and sleepiness.
Arch enemy of REAL, conventionalizing like

gunshot, freezing supple
REAL in ferocious chemistry
of laughter.

BLAST SPORT
HUMOUR'S FIRST COUSIN AND ACCOMPLICE.

Impossibility for Englishman to be grave and
keep his end up, psychologically.
Impossible for him to use Humour as well
and be <u>persistently</u> grave.
Alas! necessity for big doll's show in front of
mouth.
Visitation of Heaven on
English Miss
gums, canines of **FIXED GRIN**
Death's head symbol of Anti-Life.

CURSE those who will hang over this
Manifesto with SILLY CANINES exposed.

6
BLAST

years 1837 to 1900

Curse abysmal inexcusable middle-class (also Aristocracy and
Proletariat).

BLAST

pasty shadow cast by gigantic BOEHM[9]
(Imagined at introduction of BOURGEOIS VICTORIAN
VISTAS).
WRING THE NECK OF all sick inventions born in that
progressive white wake.

9. Joseph Edgar Boehm (1834–1890), sculptor for Queen Victoria.

BLAST their weeping whiskers—hirsute
RHETORIC of EUNUCH and STYLIST—
SENTIMENTAL HYGIENICS
ROUSSEAUISMS (wild Nature cranks)
FRATERNIZING WITH MONKEYS
DIABOLICS—raptures and roses
     of the erotic bookshelves
     culminating in
     PURGATORY OF PUTNEY.[1]

CHAOS OF ENOCH ARDENS[2]
     laughing Jennys[3]
     Ladies with Pains
     good-for-nothing Guineveres.

SNOBBISH BORROVIAN running after
    GIPSY KINGS and **ESPADAS**[4]
     bowing the knee to
     wild Mother Nature,
     her feminine contours,
     Unimaginative insult to
     MAN.

DAMN

all those to-day who have taken on that Rotten Menagerie, and still crack their whips and tumble in Piccadilly Circus, as though London were a provincial town.

WE WHISPER IN YOUR EAR A GREAT SECRET.

LONDON IS <u>NOT</u> A PROVINCIAL TOWN.

We will allow Wonder Zoos. But we do not want the
GLOOMY VICTORIAN CIRCUS in
Piccadilly Circus.

IT IS PICCADILLY'S CIRCUS!

NOT MEANT FOR MENAGERIES trundling

     out of Sixties DICKENSIAN CLOWNS,
     CORELLI[5] LADY RIDERS, TROUPS
     OF PERFORMING GIPSIES (who
     complain besides that 1/6 a night
     does not pay fare back to Clapham).

1. A middle-class suburb of London.
2. *Enoch Arden* (1864), a sentimental narrative poem by Tennyson.
3. From Dante Gabriel Rossetti's popular poem *Jenny* (1870), again disliked for its sentimentality.

4. Refers to the contemporary popularity of the gypsy romances of George Borrow, such as *The Zincali* (1841).
5. Marie Corelli, pseud. of Mary Mackay (1855–1924), author of best-selling religious novels and romances.

BLAST[6]

The Post Office   Frank Brangwyn   Robertson Nicol
Rev. Pennyfeather   Galloway Kyle
(Bells)   (Cluster of Grapes)
Bishop of London and all his posterity
Galsworthy   Dean Inge   Croce Matthews
Rev Meyer   Seymour Hicks
Lionel Cust   C. B. Fry   Bergson Abdul Bahai
Hawtrey   Edward Elgar   Sardlea
Filson Young   Marie Corelli   Geddes
Codliver Oil   St. Loe Strachey   Lyceum Club
Rhabindraneth Tagore   Lord Glenconner of Glen
Weiniger   Norman Angel   Ad. Mahon
Mr. and Mrs. Dearmer   Beecham   Ella
A. C. Benson   (Pills, Opera, Thomas)   Sydney Webb
British Academy   Messrs. Chapell
Countess of Warwick   George Edwards
Willie Ferraro   Captain Cook   R. J. Campbell
Clan Thesiger   Martin Harvey   William Archer
George Grossmith   R. H. Benson
Annie Besant   Chenil   Clan Meynell
Father Vaughan   Joseph Holbrooke   Clan Strachey

1

BLESS ENGLAND!

BLESS ENGLAND

FOR ITS SHIPS

which switchback on Blue, Green and
Red **SEAS** all around the **PINK**
EARTH-BALL,

BIG BETS ON EACH.

BLESS ALL SEAFARERS.

THEY exchange not one LAND for another, but one ELEMENT for
ANOTHER. The MORE against the LESS ABSTRACT.

---

6. The list of those blasted by the Vorticists falls, according to the critic William Wees, into seven categories: (1) members of the (literary and cultural) Establishment (e.g., William Archer, drama critic of the *Nation*); (2) people who represented popular or snobbish fads (e.g., Sir Abdul Baha Bahai, leader of the Bahai faith); (3) high-minded popular writers, (e.g., Marie Corelli); (4) mediocre but popular figures (e.g., the poet Ella Wheeler Wilcox); (5) fuzzy-minded reformers and idealists (e.g., Sidney Webb, a leader of the Fabian Socialist organization); (6) "popular figures whom the Vorticists just didn't like" (e.g., C. B. Fry, a cricket player); and (7) "blasting just for the fun of it . . . or blasting that grew from special circumstances and private reasons known only to insiders" (e.g., the Post Office and Cod Liver Oil). See William C. Wees, *Vorticism and the English Avant-Garde* (1972), pp. 217–27.

BLESS the vast planetary abstraction of the **OCEAN.**

BLESS THE ARABS OF THE **ATLANTIC.**
THIS ISLAND MUST BE CONTRASTED WITH THE BLEAK WAVES.

BLESS ALL PORTS.

PORTS, RESTLESS MACHINES of

scooped out basins
heavy insect dredgers
monotonous cranes
stations
lighthouses, blazing
   through the frosty
   starlight, cutting the
   storm like a cake
beaks of infant boats,
   side by side,
heavy chaos of
   wharves,
steep walls of
   factories
womanly town

BLESS these **MACHINES** that work the little boats across
clean liquid space, in beelines.

BLESS the great **PORTS**

HULL
LIVERPOOL
LONDON
NEWCASTLE-ON-TYNE
BRISTOL
GLASGOW

BLESS ENGLAND,

Industrial Island machine, pyramidal workshop,
its apex at Shetland, discharging itself on the sea.

BLESS

cold
magnanimous
delicate
gauche
fanciful
stupid

ENGLISHMEN.

2
BLESS the HAIRDRESSER.

He attacks Mother Nature for a small fee.
Hourly he ploughs heads for sixpence,
Scours chins and lips for threepence.
He makes systematic mercenary war on this
WILDNESS.
He trims aimless and retrograde growths into
CLEAN ARCHED SHAPES and
ANGULAR PLOTS.

BLESS this HESSIAN (or SILESIAN) **EXPERT**[7]
correcting the grotesque anachronisms
of our physique.

3
BLESS ENGLISH HUMOUR

It is the great barbarous weapon of
the genius among races.
The wild MOUNTAIN RAILWAY from IDEA
to IDEA, in the ancient Fair of LIFE.

BLESS **SWIFT**   for his solemn bleak
wisdom of laughter.

SHAKESPEARE   for his bitter Northern
Rhetoric of humour.

BLESS ALL ENGLISH EYES
that grow crows-feet with their
FANCY and ENERGY.

BLESS this hysterical WALL built round
the EGO.

BLESS the solitude of LAUGHTER.

BLESS the separating, ungregarious

BRITISH GRIN.

4
BLESS FRANCE

for its **BUSHELS** of **VITALITY**
to the square inch.

---

7. From German industrial regions.

HOME OF MANNERS (the Best, the WORST and interesting mixtures).
MASTERLY PORNOGRAPHY (great enemy of progress).
COMBATIVENESS
GREAT HUMAN SCEPTICS
DEPTHS OF ELEGANCE
FEMALE QUALITIES
FEMALES
BALLADS of its PREHISTORIC APACHE
Superb hardness and hardiesse of its
Voyou° type, rebellious adolescent.   *disreputable*
Modesty and humanity of many there.
GREAT FLOOD OF LIFE pouring out
of wound of 1797.[8]
Also bitterer stream from 1870.[9]
STAYING POWER, like a cat.

BLESS[1]

Bridget   Berrwolf   Bearline   Cranmer Byng
Frieder Graham   The Pope   Maria de Tomaso
Captain Kemp   Munroe   Gaby   Jenkins
R. B. Cuningham Grahame   Barker
(not his brother)   (John and Granville)
Mrs. Wil Finnimore   Madame Strindberg   Carson
Salvation Army   Lord Howard de Walden
Capt. Craig   Charlotte Corday   Cromwell
Mrs. Duval   Mary Robertson   Lillie Lenton
Frank Rutter   Castor Oil   James Joyce
Leveridge   Lydia Yavorska   Preb. Carlyle   Jenny
Mon. le compte de Gabulis   Smithers   Dick Burge
33 Church Street   Sievier   Gertie Millar
Norman Wallis   Miss Fowler   Sir Joseph Lyons
Martin Wolff   Watt   Mrs. Hepburn
Alfree   Tommy   Captain Kendell   Young Ahearn
Wilfred Walter   Kate Lechmere   Henry Newbolt
Lady Aberconway   Frank Harris   Hamel
Gilbert Canaan   Sir James Mathew Barry
Mrs. Belloc Lowdnes   W. L. George   Rayner
George Robey   George Mozart   Harry Weldon

8. The rise of Napoleon Bonaparte.
9. Beginning of Franco-Prussian War and end of the Second Empire, led by Napoleon Bonaparte's nephew Napoleon III.
1. This list of the blessed falls, according to William Wees, into four categories: (1) "some of the blessings, like most of the blasts, seemed designed to affront respectable public opinion" (e.g., the Pope and the Salvation Army); (2) "working class entertainments such as boxing and music halls"; (3) "a few selected representatives of the fine arts" (e.g., James Joyce); and (4) "friends of the Vorticists or of the avant-garde in general" (e.g., Frank Rutter and P. J. Konody, two sympathetic art critics).

Chaliapine George Hirst Graham White
Hucks Salmet Shirley Kellogg Bandsman Rice
Petty Officer Curran Applegarth Konody
Colin Bell Lewis Hind LEFRANC
Hubert Commercial Process Co.

MANIFESTO.

I.

1 Beyond Action and Reaction we would establish ourselves.
2 We start from opposite statements of a chosen world. Set up violent structure of adolescent clearness between two extremes.
3 We discharge ourselves on both sides.
4 We fight first on one side, then on the other, but always for the SAME cause, which is neither side or both sides and ours.
5 Mercenaries were always the best troops.
6 We are Primitive Mercenaries in the Modern World.
7 Our <u>Cause</u> is NO-MAN'S.
8 We set Humour at Humour's throat.
Stir up Civil War among peaceful apes.
9 We only want Humour if it has fought like Tragedy.
10 We only want Tragedy if it can clench its side-muscles like hands on its belly, and bring to the surface a laugh like a bomb.

II.

1 We hear from America and the Continent all sorts of disagreeable things about England: "the unmusical, anti-artistic, unphilosophic country."
2 We quite agree.
3 Luxury, sport, the famous English "Humour," the thrilling ascendancy and idée fixe of Class, producing the most intense snobbery in the World; heavy stagnant pools of Saxon blood, incapable of anything but the song of a frog, in home-counties:— these phenomena give England a peculiar distinction in the wrong sense, among the nations.
4 This is why England produces such good artists from time to time.
5 This is also the reason why a movement towards art and imagination could burst up here, from this lump of compressed life, with more force than any-where else.
6 To believe that it is necessary for or conducive to art, to "improve" life, for instance—make architecture, dress, ornament, in "better taste," is absurd.
7 The Art-instinct is permanently primitive.
8 In a chaos of imperfection, discord, etc., it finds the same stimulus as in Nature.
9 The artist of the modern movement is a savage (in no sense an "advanced," perfected, democratic, Futurist individual of Mr. Marinetti's limited imagina-tion): this enormous, jangling, journalistic, fairy desert of modern life serves him as Nature did more technically primitive man.

[10] As the steppes and the rigours of the Russian winter, when the peasant has to lie for weeks in his hut, produces that extraordinary acuity of feeling and intelligence we associate with the Slav; so England is just now the most favourable country for the appearance of a great art.

III.

[1] We have made it quite clear that there is nothing Chauvinistic or picturesquely patriotic about our contentions.

[2] But there is violent boredom with that feeble Europeanism, abasement of the miserable "intellectual" before anything coming from Paris, Cosmopolitan sentimentality, which prevails in so many quarters.

[3] Just as we believe that an Art must be organic with its Time,
So we insist that what is actual and vital for the South, is ineffectual and unactual in the North.

[4] Fairies have disappeared from Ireland (despite foolish attempts to revive them)[2] and the bull-ring languishes in Spain.

[5] But mysticism on the one hand, gladiatorial instincts, blood and asceticism on the other, will be always actual, and springs of Creation for these two peoples.

[6] The English Character is based on the Sea.

[7] The particular qualities and characteristics that the sea always engenders in men are those that are, among the many diagnostics of our race, the most fundamently English.

[8] That unexpected universality as well, found in the completest English artists, is due to this.

IV.

[1] We assert that the art for these climates, then, must be a northern flower.

[2] And we have implied what we believe should be the specific nature of the art destined to grow up in this country, and models of whose flue decorate the pages of this magazine.

[3] It is not a question of the characterless material climate around us.
Were that so the complication of the Jungle, dramatic Tropic growth, the vastness of American trees, would not be for us.

[4] But our industries, and the Will that determined, face to face with its needs, the direction of the modern world, has reared up steel trees where the green ones were lacking; has exploded in useful growths, and found wilder intricacies than those of Nature.

V.

[1] We bring clearly forward the following points, before further defining the character of this necessary native art.

2. The Celtic Revival was a nostalgic movement in Irish arts and letters.

2 At the freest and most vigorous period of ENGLAND'S history, her literature, then chief Art, was in many ways identical with that of France.

3 Chaucer was very much cousin of Villon[3] as an artist.

4 Shakespeare and Montaigne[4] formed one literature.

5 But Shakespeare reflected in his imagination a mysticism, madness and delicacy peculiar to the North, and brought equal quantities of Comic and Tragic together.

6 Humour is a phenomenon caused by sudden pouring of culture into Barbary.[5]

7 It is intelligence electrified by flood of Naivety.

8 It is Chaos invading Concept and bursting it like nitrogen.

9 It is the Individual masquerading as Humanity like a child in clothes too big for him.

10 Tragic Humour is the birthright of the North.

11 Any great Northern Art will partake of this insidious and volcanic chaos.

12 No great ENGLISH Art need be ashamed to share some glory with France, tomorrow it may be with Germany, where the Elizabethans did before it.

13 But it will never be French, any more than Shakespeare was, the most catholic and subtle Englishman.

VI.

1 The Modern World is due almost entirely to Anglo-Saxon genius,—its appearance and its spirit.

2 Machinery, trains, steam-ships, all that distinguishes externally our time, came far more from here than anywhere else.

3 In dress, manners, mechanical inventions, LIFE, that is, ENGLAND, has influenced Europe in the same way that France has in Art.

4 But busy with this LIFE-EFFORT, she has been the last to become conscious of the Art that is an organism of this new Order and Will of Man.

5 Machinery is the greatest Earth-medium: incidentally it sweeps away the doctrines of a narrow and pedantic Realism at one stroke.

6 By mechanical inventiveness, too, just as Englishmen have spread themselves all over the Earth, they have brought all the hemispheres about them in their original island.

7 It cannot be said that the complication of the Jungle, dramatic tropic growths, the vastness of American trees, is not for us.

8 For, in the forms of machinery, Factories, new and vaster buildings, bridges and works, we have all that, naturally, around us.

VII.

1 Once this consciousness towards the new possibilities of expression in present life has come, however, it will be more the legitimate property of Englishmen than of any other people in Europe.

---

3. François Villon (1431–1463?), French poet.
4. Michel de Montaigne (1533–1592), French essayist.

5. An old name for the western part of North Africa; possibly used here to mean "barbarity."

2 It should also, as it is by origin theirs, inspire them more forcibly and directly.

3 They are the inventors of this bareness and hardness, and should be the great enemies of Romance.

4 The Romance peoples will always be, at bottom, its defenders.

5 The Latins are at present, for instance, in their "discovery" of sport, their Futuristic gush over machines, aeroplanes, etc., the most romantic and sentimental "moderns" to be found.

6 It is only the second-rate people in France or Italy who are thorough revolutionaries.

7 In England, on the other hand, there Is no vulgarity in revolt.

8 Or, rather, there is no revolt, it is the normal state.

9 So often rebels of the North and the South are diametrically opposed species.

10 The nearest thing in England to a great traditional French artist, is a great revolutionary English one.

Signatures for Manifesto[6]

R. Aldington

Arbuthnot

L. Atkinson

Gaudier Brzeska

J. Dismorr

C. Hamilton

E. Pound

W. Roberts

H. Sanders

E. Wadsworth

Wyndham Lewis

Rebecca West
1892–1983

Rebecca West is increasingly appreciated as a writer of fiction, literary criticism, political commentary, and biography, as well as one of the most important journalists of the century. Born Cicely Fairfield in Ireland, she was educated in Edinburgh after her father died when she was ten years old. She became an actress in London, taking the stage name "Rebecca West" from a heroine she had played in Ibsen's drama *Rosmersholm*. By the time she was twenty, she was becoming active in left-wing journalism and in agitation for women's rights. In 1914, when she wrote *Indissoluble Matrimony*, she was involved in a love affair with the free-thinking but married novelist H. G. Wells, with whom she had a son; at the same time, she was working on a critical biography of Henry James. She went on to write searching and sometimes critical essays on male modernists like Joyce, Eliot, and Lawrence, and perceptive essays on Virginia

6. The signatories to the manifesto are Richard Aldington, English writer and man of letters; Malcolm Arbuthnot, professional photographer; Lawrence Atkinson, Vorticist artist; Henri Gaudier-Brzeska, Vorticist sculptor and contributor to *Blast* who was killed in the trenches in World War I and whose obituary was included in *Blast II*; Jessica Dismorr, artist whose illustrations were included in *Blast*; Cuthbert Hamilton, avant-garde artist; Ezra Pound; William Roberts, painter; Helen Saunders, Vorticist designer; Edward Wadsworth, Vorticist painter; and Wyndham Lewis.

Woolf and Katherine Mansfield. Throughout her life, she wrote both novels and political jour-nalism, notably a major study of Balkan politics and culture, *Black Lamb and Grey Falcon* (1942), and a series of brilliant reports on the Nuremberg trials of Nazi war criminals at the end of World War II, collected as *A Train of Powder* (1955). She was made Dame Commander of the British Empire in 1959. Like her political writing, her fiction is notable for its irreverent probing of modernity's fault lines. Though never an orthodox feminist, West demonstrated a keen insight into the psychology of women and men, and portrayed the straitened thinking that made feminism's ultimate victory anything but a foregone conclusion.

Indissoluble Matrimony

When George Silverton opened the front door he found that the house was not empty for all its darkness. The spitting noise of the striking of damp matches and mild, growling exclamations of annoyance told him that his wife was trying to light the dining-room gas. He went in and with some short, hostile sound of greeting lit a match and brought brightness into the little room. Then, irritated by his own folly in bringing private papers into his wife's presence, he stuffed the letters he had brought from the office deep into the pockets of his overcoat. He looked at her suspiciously, but she had not seen them, being busy in unwinding her orange motor-veil. His eyes remained on her face to brood a little sourly on her moving loveliness, which he had not been sure of finding: for she was one of those women who create an illusion alter-nately of extreme beauty and extreme ugliness. Under her curious dress, designed in some pitifully cheap and worthless stuff by a successful mood of her indiscreet taste—she had black blood in her—her long body seemed pulsing with some exaltation. The blood was coursing violently under her luminous yellow skin, and her lids, dusky with fatigue, drooped contentedly over her great humid black eyes. Perpetually she raised her hand to the mass of black hair that was coiled on her thick golden neck, and stroked it with secretive enjoyment, as a cat licks its fur. And her large mouth smiled frankly, but abstractedly, at some digested pleasure.

There was a time when George would have looked on this riot of excited loveli-ness with suspicion. But now he knew it was almost certainly caused by some trifle—a long walk through stinging weather, the report of a Socialist victory at a by-election, or the intoxication of a waltz refrain floating from the municipal band-stand across the flats of the local recreation ground. And even if it had been caused by some amorous interlude he would not have greatly cared. In the ten years since their mar-riage he had lost the quality which would have made him resentful. He now believed that quality to be purely physical. Unless one was in good condition and responsive to the messages sent out by the flesh Evadne could hardly concern one. He turned the bitter thought over in his heart and stung himself by deliberately gazing unmoved upon her beautiful joyful body.

"Let's have supper now!" she said rather greedily.

He looked at the table and saw she had set it before she went out. As usual she had been in an improvident hurry: it was carelessly done. Besides, what an absurd supper to set before a hungry solicitor's clerk! In the centre, obviously intended as the principal dish, was a bowl of plums, softly red, soaked with the sun, glowing like jewels in the downward stream of the incandescent light. Besides them was a great yellow melon, its sleek sides fluted with rich growth, and a honey-comb glistening on a willow-pattern dish. The only sensible food to be seen was a plate of tongue laid at his place.

"I can't sit down to supper without washing my hands!"

While he splashed in the bathroom upstairs he heard her pull in a chair to the table and sit down to her supper. It annoyed him. There was no ritual about it. While he was eating the tongue she would be crushing honey on new bread, or stripping a plum of its purple skin and holding the golden globe up to the gas to see the light filter through. The meal would pass in silence. She would innocently take his dumbness for a sign of abstraction and forbear to babble. He would find the words choked on his lips by the weight of dullness that always oppressed him in her presence. Then, just about the time when he was beginning to feel able to formulate his obscure grievances against her, she would rise from the table without a word and run upstairs to her work, humming in that uncanny, negro way of hers.

And so it was. She ate with an appalling catholicity of taste, with a nice child's love of sweet foods, and occasionally she broke into that hoarse beautiful croon. Every now and then she looked at him with too obvious speculations as to whether his silence was due to weariness or uncertain temper. Timidly she cut him an enormous slice of the melon, which he did not want. Then she rose abruptly and flung herself into the rocking chair on the hearth. She clasped her hands behind her head and strained backwards so that the muslin stretched over her strong breasts. She sang softly to the ceiling.

There was something about the fantastic figure that made him feel as though they were not properly married.

"Evadne?"

"S?"

"What have you been up to this evening?"

"I was at Milly Stafordale's."

He was silent again. That name brought up the memory of his courting days. It was under the benign eyes of blonde, plebeian Milly that he had wooed the distracting creature in the rocking chair.

Ten years before, when he was twenty-five, his firm had been reduced to hysteria over the estates of an extraordinarily stupid old woman, named Mrs. Mary Ellerker. Her stupidity, grappling with the complexity of the sources of the vast income which rushed in spate from the properties of four deceased husbands, demanded oceans of explanations even over her weekly rents. Silverton alone in the office, by reason of a certain natural incapacity for excitement, could deal calmly with this marvel of imbecility. He alone could endure to sit with patience in the black-panelled drawing-room amidst the jungle of shiny mahogany furniture and talk to a mass of darkness, who rested heavily in the window-seat and now and then made an idiotic remark in a bright, hearty voice. But it shook even him. Mrs. Mary Ellerker was obscene. Yet she was perfectly sane and, although of that remarkable plainness noticeable in most oft-married women, in good enough physical condition. She merely presented the loathsome spectacle of an ignorant mind, contorted by the artificial idiocy of coquetry, lack of responsibility, and hatred of discipline, stripped naked by old age. That was the real horror of her. One feared to think how many women were really like Mrs. Ellerker under their armour of physical perfection or social grace. For this reason he turned eyes of hate on Mrs. Ellerker's pretty little companion, Milly Stafordale, who smiled at him over her embroidery with wintry northern brightness. When she was old she too would be obscene.

This horror obsessed him. Never before had he feared anything. He had never lived more than half-an-hour from a police station, and, as he had by some chance missed the melancholy clairvoyance of adolescence, he had never conceived of any horror with which the police could not deal. This disgust of women revealed to him that the world is a place of subtle perils. He began to fear marriage as he feared death. The thought of intimacy with some lovely, desirable and necessary wife turned him sick as he sat at his lunch. The secret obscenity of women! He talked darkly of it to his friends. He wondered why the Church did not provide a service for the absolution of men after marriage. Wife desertion seemed to him a beautiful return of the tainted body to cleanliness.

On his fifth visit to Mrs. Ellerker he could not begin his business at once. One of Milly Stafordale's friends had come in to sing to the old lady. She stood by the piano against the light, so that he saw her washed with darkness. Amazed, of tropical fruit. And before he had time to apprehend the sleepy wonder of her beauty, she had begun to sing. Now he knew that her voice was a purely physical attribute, built in her as she lay in her mother's womb, and no index of her spiritual values. But then, as it welled up from the thick golden throat and clung to her lips, it seemed a sublime achievement of the soul. It was smouldering contralto such as only those of black blood can possess. As she sang her great black eyes lay on him with the innocent shamelessness of a young animal, and he remembered hopefully that he was good looking. Suddenly she stood in silence, playing with her heavy black plait. Mrs. Ellerker broke into silly thanks. The girl's mother, who had been playing the accompaniment, rose and stood rolling up her music. Silverton, sick with excitement, was introduced to them. He noticed that the mother was a little darker than the conventions permit. Their name was Hannan—Mrs. Arthur Hannan and Evadne. They moved lithely and quietly out of the room, the girl's eyes still lingering on his face.

The thought of her splendour and the rolling echoes of her voice disturbed him all night. Next day, going to his office, he travelled with her on the horse-car that bound his suburb to Petrick. One of the horses fell lame, and she had time to tell him that she was studying at a commercial college. He quivered with distress. All the time he had a dizzy illusion that she was nestling up against him. They parted shyly. During the next few days they met constantly. He began to go and see them in the evening at their home—a mean flat crowded with cheap glories of bead curtains and Oriental hangings that set off the women's alien beauty. Mrs. Hannan was a widow and they lived alone, in a wonderful silence. He talked more than he had ever done in his whole life before. He took a dislike to the widow, she was consumed with fiery subterranean passions, no fit guardian for the tender girl.

Now he could imagine with what silent rapture Evadne had watched his agitation. Almost from the first she had meant to marry him. He was physically attractive, though not strong. His intellect was gently stimulating like a mild white wine. And it was time she married. She was ripe for adult things. This was the real wound in his soul. He had tasted of a divine thing created in his time for dreams out of her rich beauty, her loneliness, her romantic poverty, her immaculate youth. He had known love. And Evadne had never known anything more than a magnificent physical adventure which she had secured at the right time as she would have engaged a cab to take her to the station in time for the cheapest excursion train. It was a quick way to light-hearted living. With loathing he remembered how in the days of their engagement she used to gaze purely into his blinking eyes and with her unashamed kisses incite him to extravagant embraces. Now he cursed her for having obtained his spiritual revolution on false pretences. Only for a little time had he had his illusion, for their marriage was hastened by Mrs. Hannan's sudden death. After three months of savage mourning Evadne flung herself into marriage, and her excited candour had enlightened him very soon.

That marriage had lasted ten years. And to Evadne their relationship was just the same as ever. Her vitality needed him as it needed the fruit on the table before him. He shook with wrath and a sense of outraged decency.

"O George!" She was yawning widely.

"What's the matter?" he said without interest.

"It's so beastly dull."

"I can't help that, can I?"

"No." She smiled placidly at him. "We're a couple of dull dogs, aren't we? I wish we had children."

After a minute she suggested, apparently as an alternative amusement, "Perhaps the post hasn't passed."

As she spoke there was a rat-tat and the slither of a letter under the door. Evadne picked herself up and ran out into the lobby. After a second or two, during which she made irritating inarticulate exclamations, she came in reading the letter and stroking her bust with a gesture of satisfaction.

"They want me to speak at Longton's meeting on the nineteenth," she purred.

"Longton? What's he up to?"

Stephen Longton was the owner of the biggest iron works in Petrick, a man whose refusal to adopt the livery of busy oafishness thought proper to commercial men aroused the gravest suspicions.

"He's standing as Socialist candidate for the town council."

". . . Socialist!" he muttered.

He set his jaw. That was a side of Evadne he considered as little as possible. He had never been able to assimilate the fact that Evadne had, two years after their marriage, passed through his own orthodox Radicalism[1] to a passionate Socialism, and that after reading enormously of economics she had begun to write for the Socialist press and to speak successfully at meetings. In the jaundiced recesses of his mind he took it for granted that her work would have the lax fibre of her character: that it would be infected with her Oriental crudities. Although once or twice he had been congratulated on her brilliance, he mistrusted this phase of her activity as a caper of the sensualist. His eyes blazed on her and found the depraved, over-sexed creature, looking milder than a gazelle, holding out a hand-bill to him.

"They've taken it for granted!"

He saw her name—his name—

MRS. EVADNE SILVERTON.[2]

It was at first the blaze of stout scarlet letters on the dazzling white ground that made him blink. Then he was convulsed with rage.

"Georgie dear!"

She stepped forward and caught his weak body to her bosom. He wrenched himself away. Spiritual nausea made him determined to be a better man than her.

"A pair of you! You and Longton—!" he snarled scornfully. Then, seeing her startled face, he controlled himself.

"I thought it would please you," said Evadne, a little waspishly.

"You mustn't have anything to do with Longton," he stormed.

A change passed over her. She became ugly. Her face was heavy with intellect, her lips coarse with power. He was at arms with a Socialist lead. Much he would have preferred the bland sensualist again.

---

1. An extreme form of Liberalism, still comfortably within the continuum of British democratic politics; Socialism, which Evadne has embraced, advocates the abolition of the current system and is thus too extreme for George's bourgeois attitudes.

2. Evadne would have been addressed in polite society as "Mrs. George Silverton"; George reads this breach of decorum as one more sign that his wife is out of control. Leopold Bloom, the protagonist of James Joyce's *Ulysses*, makes a similar observation when his wife Molly receives a letter from her lover addressed to "Mrs. Marion Bloom."

"Why?"

"Because—his lips stuck together like blotting-paper—he's not the sort of man my wife should—should—"

With movements which terrified him by their rough energy, she folded up the bills and put them back in the envelope.

"George. I suppose you mean that he's a bad man." He nodded.

"I know quite well that the girl who used to be his typist is his mistress." She spoke it sweetly, as if reasoning with an old fool. "But she's got consumption. She'll be dead in six months. In fact, I think it's rather nice of him. To look after her and all that."

"My God!" He leapt to his feet, extending a shaking forefinger. As she turned to him, the smile dying on her lips, his excited weakness wrapped him in a paramnesic illusion:[3] it seemed to him that he had been through all this before—a long, long time ago. "My God, you talk like a woman off the streets!"

Evadne's lips lifted over her strong teeth. With clever cruelty she fixed his eyes with hers, well knowing that he longed to fall forward and bury his head on the table in a transport of hysterical sobs. After a moment of this torture she turned away, herself distressed by a desire to cry.

"How can you say such dreadful, dreadful things!" she protested, chokingly.

He sat down again. His eyes looked little and red, but they blazed on her. "I wonder if you are," he said softly.

"Are what?" she asked petulantly, a tear rolling down her nose.

"You know," he answered, nodding.

"George, George, George!" she cried.

"You've always been keen on kissing and making love, haven't you, my precious? At first you startled me, you did! I didn't know women were like that." From that morass he suddenly stepped on to a high peak of terror. Amazed to find himself sincere, he cried—"I don't believe good women are!"

"Georgie, how can you be so silly!" exclaimed Evadne shrilly. "You know quite well I've been as true to you as any woman could be." She sought his eyes with a liquid glance of reproach. He averted his gaze, sickened at having put himself in the wrong. For even while he degraded his tongue his pure soul fainted with loathing of her fleshliness.

"I—I'm sorry."

Too wily to forgive him at once, she showed him a lowering profile with downcast lids. Of course, he knew it was a fraud: an imputation against her chastity was no more poignant than a reflection on the cleanliness of her nails—rude and spiteful, but that was all. But for a time they kept up the deception, while she cleared the table in a steely silence.

"Evadne, I'm sorry. I'm tired." His throat was dry. He could not bear the discord of a row added to the horror of their companionship. "Evadne, do forgive me—I don't know what I meant by—"

"That's all right, silly!" she said suddenly and bent over the table to kiss him. Her brow was smooth. It was evident from her splendid expression that she was pre-occupied. Then she finished clearing up the dishes and took them into the kitchen. While she was out of the room he rose from his seat and sat down in the armchair by the fire, setting his bull-dog pipe alight. For a very short time he was free of her voluptuous presence. But she ran back soon, having put the kettle on and changed her blouse for a loose dressing-jacket, and sat down on the arm of his

---

3. A condition in which fact and fiction become confused.

chair. Once or twice she bent and kissed his brow, but for the most part she lay back with his head drawn to her bosom, rocking herself rhythmically. Silverton, a little disgusted by their contact, sat quite motionless and passed into a doze. He revolved in his mind the incidents of his day's routine and remembered a snub from a superior. So he opened his eyes and tried to think of something else. It was then that he became conscious that the rhythm of Evadne's movement was not regular. It was broken as though she rocked in time to music. Music? His sense of hearing crept up to hear if there was any sound of music in the breaths she was emitting rather heavily every now and then. At first he could hear nothing. Then it struck him that each breath was a muttered phrase. He stiffened, and hatred flamed through his veins. The words came clearly through her lips. . . . "The present system of wage-slavery. . . . "

"Evadne!" He sprang to his feet. "You're preparing your speech!"

She did not move. "I am," she said.

"Damn it, you shan't speak!"

"Damn it, I will!"

"Evadne, you shan't speak! If you do I swear to God above I'll turn you out into the streets—." She rose and came towards him. She looked black and dangerous. She trod softly like a cat with her head down. In spite of himself, his tongue licked his lips in fear and he cowered a moment before he picked up a knife from the table. For a space she looked down on him and the sharp blade.

"You idiot, can't you hear the kettle's boiling over?"

He shrank back, letting the knife fall on the floor. For three minutes he stood there controlling his breath and trying to still his heart. Then he followed her into the kitchen. She was making a noise with a basinful of dishes.

"Stop that row."

She turned round with a dripping dish-cloth in her hand and pondered whether to throw it at him. But she was tired and wanted peace: so that she could finish the rough draft of her speech. So she stood waiting.

"Did you understand what I said then? If you don't promise me here and now—"

She flung her arms upwards with a cry and dashed past him. He made to run after her upstairs, but stumbled on the threshold of the lobby and sat with his ankle twisted under him, shaking with rage. In a second she ran downstairs again, clothed in a big cloak with black bundle clutched to her breast. For the first time in their married life she was seized with a convulsion of sobs. She dashed out of the front door and banged it with such passion that a glass pane shivered to fragments behind her.

"What's this? What's this?" he cried stupidly, standing up. He perceived with an insane certainty that she was going out to meet some unknown lover. "I'll come and tell him what a slut you are!" he shouted after her and stumbled to the door. It was jammed now and he had to drag at it.

The night was flooded with the yellow moonshine of midsummer: it seemed to drip from the lacquered leaves of the shrubs in the front garden. In its soft clarity he could see her plainly, although she was now two hundred yards away. She was hastening to the north end of Sumatra Crescent, an end that curled up the hill like a silly kitten's tail and stopped abruptly in green fields. So he knew that she was going to the young man who had just bought the Georgian Manor, whose elm-trees crowned the hill. Oh, how he hated her! Yet he must follow her, or else she would cover up her adulteries so that he could not take his legal revenge. So he began to run—silently, for he wore his carpet slippers. He was only a hundred yards behind her when she slipped through a gap in the hedge to tread a field-path. She still walked with pride, for though she was town-bred, night in the open seemed not at all fearful to her. As he shuffled in pursuit his carpet slippers were engulfed in a shining pool of mud: he raised one with a squelch, the other was left. This seemed the last humiliation. He kicked the other one off his feet and padded on in his socks, snuffling in anticipation of a cold. Then physical pain sent him back to the puddle to pluck out the slippers; it was a dirty job. His heart battered his breast as he saw that Evadne had gained the furthest hedge and was crossing the stile into the lane that ran up to the Manor gates.

"Go on, you beast!" he muttered, "Go on, go on!" After a scamper he climbed the stile and thrust his lean neck beyond a mass of wilted hawthorn bloom that crumbled into vagrant petals at his touch.

The lane mounted yellow as cheese to where the moon lay on his iron tracery of the Manor gates. Evadne was not there. Hardly believing his eyes he hobbled over into the lane and looked in the other direction. There he saw her disappearing round the bend of the road. Gathering himself up to a run, he tried to think out his bearings. He had seldom passed this way, and like most people without strong primitive instincts he had no sense of orientation. With difficulty he remembered that after a mile's mazy wanderings between high hedges this lane sloped suddenly to the bowl of heather overhung by the moorlands, in which lay the Petrick reservoirs, two untamed lakes.

"Eh! she's going to meet him by the water!" he cursed to himself. He remembered the withered ash tree, seared by lightning to its root, that stood by the road at the bare frontier of the moor. "May God strike her like that," he prayed," "as she fouls the other man's lips with her kisses. O God! let me strangle her. Or bury a knife deep in her breast." Suddenly he broke into a lolloping run. "O my Lord, I'll be able to divorce her. I'll be free. Free to live alone. To do my day's work and sleep my night's sleep without her. I'll get a job somewhere else and forget her. I'll bring her to the dogs. No clean man or woman in Petrick will look at her now. They won't have her to speak at that meeting now!" His throat swelled with joy, he leapt high in the air.

"I'll lie about her. If I can prove that she's wrong with this man they'll believe me if I say she's a bad woman and drinks. I'll make her name a joke. And then—"

He flung wide his arms in ecstasy: the left struck against stone. More pain than he had thought his body could hold convulsed him, so that he sank on the ground hugging his aching arm. He looked backwards as he writhed and saw that the hedge had stopped; above him was the great stone wall of the county asylum. The question broke on him—was there any lunatic in its confines so slavered with madness as he himself? Nothing but madness could have accounted for the torrent of ugly words, the sea of uglier thoughts that was now a part of him. "O God, me to turn like this!" he cried, rolling over full-length on the grassy bank by the roadside. That the infidelity of his wife, a thing that should have brought out the stern manliness of his true nature, should have discovered him as lecherous-lipped as any pot-house[4] lounger, was the most infamous accident of his married life. The sense of sin descended on him so that his tears flowed hot and bitterly. "Have I gone to the Unitarian chapel every Sunday morning and to the Ethical Society every evening for nothing?" his spirit asked itself in its travail. "All those Browning lectures for nothing. . . ."[5] He said the Lord's Prayer several times and lay for a minute quietly crying. The relaxation of his muscles brought him a sense of rest which seemed forgiveness falling from

---

4. Tavern.
5. George's activities—Unitarian church, Ethical Society, Browning Society—suggest that he participated in

public exercises of a high moral nature without giving himself over to traditional religious faith, which he would have seen as "irrational" and "unmanly."

God. The tears dried on his cheeks. His calmer consciousness heard the sound of rushing waters mingled with the beating of blood in his ears. He got up and scrambled round the turn of the road that brought him to the withered ash-tree.

He walked forward on the parched heatherland to the mound whose scarred sides, heaped with boulders, tufted with mountain grasses, shone before him in the moonlight. He scrambled up to it hurriedly and hoisted himself from ledge to ledge till he fell on his knees with a squeal of pain. His ankle was caught in a crevice of the rock. Gulping down his agony at this final physical humiliation he heaved himself upright and raced on to the summit, and found himself before the Devil's Cauldron, filled to the brim with yellow moonshine and the fiery play of summer lightning. The rugged crags opposite him were a low barricade against the stars to which the mound where he stood shot forward like a bridge. To the left of this the long Lisbech pond lay like a trailing serpent; its silver scales glittered as the wind swept down from the vaster moorlands to the east. To the right under a steep drop of twenty feet was the Whimsey pond, more sinister, shaped in an unnatural oval, sheltered from the wind by the high ridge so that the undisturbed moonlight lay across it like a sharp-edged sword.

He looked about for some sign of Evadne. She could not be on the land by the margin of the lakes, for the light blazed so strongly that each reed could be clearly seen like a black dagger stabbing the silver. He looked down Lisbech and saw far east a knot of red and green and orange lights. Perhaps for some devilish purpose Evadne had sought Lisbech railway station. But his volcanic mind had preserved one grain of sense that assured him that, subtle as Evadne's villainy might be, it would not lead her to walk five miles out of her way to a terminus which she could have reached in fifteen minutes by taking a train from the station down the road. She must be under cover somewhere here. He went down the gentle slope that fell from the top of the ridge to Lisbech pond in a disorder of rough heather, unhappy patches of cultivated grass, and coppices of silver birch, fringed with flaming broom that seemed faintly tarnished in the moonlight. At the bottom was a roughly hewn path which he followed in hot aimless hurry. In a little he approached a riot of falling waters. There was a slice ten feet broad carved out of the ridge, and to this narrow channel of black shining rock the floods of Lisbech leapt some feet and raced through to Whimsey. The noise beat him back. The gap was spanned by a gaunt thing of paint-blistered iron, on which he stood dizzily and noticed how the wide step that ran on each side of the channel through to the other pond was smeared with sinister green slime. Now his physical distress reminded him of Evadne, whom he had almost forgotten in contemplation of these lonely waters. The idea of her had been present but obscured, as sometimes toothache may cease active torture. His blood lust set him on and he staggered forward with covered ears. Even as he went something caught his eye in a thicket high up on the slope near the crags. Against the slender pride of some silver birches stood a gnarled hawthorn tree, its branches flattened under the stern moorland winds so that it grew squat like an opened umbrella. In its dark shadows, faintly illumined by a few boughs of withered blossom, there moved a strange bluish light. Even while he did not know what it was it made his flesh stir.

The light emerged. It was the moonlight reflected from Evadne's body. She was clad in a black bathing dress, and her arms and legs and the broad streak of flesh laid bare by a rent down the back shone brilliantly white, so that she seemed like a grotesquely patterned wild animal as she ran down to the lake. Whirling her arms above her head she trampled down into the water and struck out strongly. Her movements were full of brisk delight and she swam quickly. The moonlight made her the centre of a little feathery blur of black and silver, with a comet's tail trailing in her wake.

Nothing in all his married life had ever staggered Silverton so much as this. He had imagined his wife's adultery so strongly that it had come to be. It was now as real as their marriage; more real than their courtship. So this seemed to be the last crime of the adulteress. She had dragged him over those squelching fields and these rough moors and changed him from a man of irritations, but no passions, into a cold designer of murderous treacheries, so that he might witness a swimming exhibition! For a minute he was stunned. Then he sprang down to the rushy edge and ran along in the direction of her course, crying—"Evadne! Evadne!" She did not hear him. At last he achieved a chest note and shouted—"Evadne! come here!" The black and silver feather shivered in mid-water. She turned immediately and swam back to shore. He suspected sullenness in her slowness, but was glad of it, for after the shock of this extraordinary incident he wanted to go to sleep. Drowsiness lay on him like lead. He shook himself like a dog and wrenched off his linen collar, winking at the bright moon to keep himself awake. As she came quite near he was exasperated by the happy, snorting breaths she drew, and strolled a pace or two up the bank. To his enragement the face she lifted as she waded to dry land was placid, and she scrambled gaily up the bank to his side.

"O George, why did you come!" she exclaimed quite affectionately, laying a damp hand on his shoulder.

"O damn it, what does this mean!" he cried, committing a horrid tenor squeak. "What are you doing?"

"Why, George," she said," "I came here for a bathe."

He stared into her face and could make nothing of it. It was only sweet surfaces of flesh, soft radiances of eye and lip, a lovely lie of comeliness. He forgot this present grievance in a cold search for the source of her peculiar hatefulness. Under this sick gaze she pouted and turned away with a peevish gesture. He made no sign and stood silent, watching her saunter to that gaunt iron bridge. The roar of the little waterfall did not disturb her splendid nerves and she drooped sensuously over the hand-rail, sniffing up the sweet night smell; too evidently trying to abase him to another apology.

A mosquito whirred into his face. He killed it viciously and strode off towards his wife, who showed by a common little toss of the head that she was conscious of his coming.

"Look here, Evadne!" he panted. "What did you come here for? Tell me the truth and I promise I'll not—I'll not—"

"Not WHAT, George?"

"O please, please tell me the truth, do Evadne!" he cried pitifully.

"But, dear, what is there to carry on about so? You went on so queerly about my meeting that my head felt fit to split, and I thought the long walk and the dip would do me good." She broke off, amazed at the wave of horror that passed over his face.

His heart sank. From the loose-lipped hurry in the telling of her story, from the bigness of her eyes and the lack of subtlety in her voice, he knew that this was the truth. Here was no adulteress whom he could accuse in the law courts and condemn into the street, no resourceful sinner whose merry crimes he could discover. Here was merely his good wife, the faithful attendant of his hearth, relentless wrecker of his soul.

She came towards him as a cat approaches a displeased master, and hovered about him on the stone coping of the noisy sluice.

"Indeed!" he found himself saying sarcastically. "Indeed!"

"Yes, George Silverton, indeed!" she burst out, a little frightened. "And why shouldn't I? I used to come here often enough on summer nights with poor Mamma—"

"Yes!" he shouted. It was exactly the sort of thing that would appeal to that weird half-black woman from the back of beyond. "Mamma!" he cried tauntingly, "Mamma!"

There was a flash of silence between them before Evadne, clutching her breast and balancing herself dangerously on her heels on the stone coping, broke into gentle shrieks. "You dare talk of my Mamma, my poor Mamma, and she cold in her grave! I haven't been happy since she died and I married you, you silly little misery, you!" Then the rage was suddenly wiped off her brain by the perception of a crisis.

The trickle of silence overflowed into a lake, over which their spirits flew, looking at each other's reflection in the calm waters: in the hurry of their flight they had never before seen each other. They stood facing one another with dropped heads, quietly thinking.

The strong passion which filled them threatened to disintegrate their souls as a magnetic current decomposes the electrolyte, so they fought to organise their sensations. They tried to arrange themselves and their lives for comprehension, but beyond sudden lyric visions of old incidents of hatefulness—such as a smarting quarrel of six years ago as to whether Evadne had or had not cheated the railway company out of one and eightpence on an excursion ticket—the past was intangible. It trailed behind this intense event as the pale hair trails behind the burning comet. They were pre-occupied with the moment. Quite often George had found a mean pleasure in the thought that by never giving Evadne a child he had cheated her out of one form of experience, and now he paid the price for this unnatural pride of sterility. For now the spiritual offspring of their intercourse came to birth. A sublime loathing was between them. For a little time it was a huge perilous horror, but afterwards, like men aboard a ship whose masts seek the sky through steep waves, they found a drunken pride in the adventure. This was the very absolute of hatred. It cheapened the memory of the fantasias of irritation and ill-will they had performed in the less boring moments of their marriage, and they felt dazed, as amateurs who had found themselves creating a masterpiece. For the first time they were possessed by a supreme emotion and they felt a glad desire to strip away restraint and express it nakedly. It was ecstasy; they felt tall and full of blood.

Like people who, bewitched by Christ, see the whole earth as the breathing body of God, so they saw the universe as the substance and the symbol of their hatred. The stars trembled overhead with wrath. A wind from behind the angry crags set the moonlight on Lisbech quivering with rage, and the squat hawthorn-tree creaked slowly like the irritation of a dull little man. The dry moors, parched with harsh anger, waited thirstily and, sending out the murmur of rustling mountain grass and the cry of wakening fowl, seemed to huddle closer to the lake. But this sense of the earth's sympathy slipped away from them and they loathed all matter as the dull wrapping of their flame-like passion. At their wishing matter fell away and they saw sarcastic visions. He saw her as a toad squatting on the clean earth, obscuring the stars and pressing down its hot moist body on the cheerful fields. She felt his long boneless body coiled round the roots of the lovely tree of life. They shivered fastidiously. With an uplifting sense of responsibility they realised that they must kill each other.

A bird rose over their heads with a leaping flight that made it seem as though its black body was bouncing against the bright sky. The foolish noise and motion precipitated their thoughts. They were broken into a new conception of life. They perceived that God is war and his creatures are meant to fight. When dogs walk through the world cats must climb trees. The virgin must snare the wanton, the fine lover must put the prude to the sword. The gross man of action walks, spurred on the bloodless bodies of the men of thought, who lie quiet and cunningly do not tell him where his grossness leads him. The flesh must smother the spirit, the spirit must set the flesh on fire and watch it burn. And those who were gentle by nature and shrank from the ordained brutality were betrayers of their kind, surrendering the earth to the seed of their enemies.

In this war there is no discharge. If they succumbed to peace now, the rest of their lives would be dishonourable, like the exile of a rebel who has begged his life as the reward of cowardice. It was their first experience of religious passion, and they abandoned themselves to it so that their immediate personal qualities fell away from them. Neither his weakness nor her prudence stood in the way of the event.

They measured each other with the eye. To her he was a spidery thing against the velvet blackness and hard silver surfaces of the pond. The light soaked her bathing dress so that she seemed, against the jagged shadows of the rock cutting, as though she were clad in a garment of dark polished mail. Her knees were bent so clearly, her toes gripped the coping so strongly. He understood very clearly that if he did not kill her instantly she would drop him easily into the deep riot of waters. Yet for a space he could not move, but stood expecting a degrading death. Indeed, he gave her time to kill him. But she was without power too, and struggled weakly with a hallucination. The quarrel in Sumatra Crescent with its suggestion of vast and unmentionable antagonisms; her swift race through the moon-drenched countryside, all crepitant with night noises: the swimming in the wine-like lake: their isolation on the moor, which was expressedly hostile to them, as nature always is to lonely man: and this stark contest face to face, with their resentments heaped between them like a pile of naked swords—these things were so strange that her civilised self shrank back appalled. There entered into her the primitive woman who is the curse of all women: a creature of the most utter femaleness, useless, save for childbirth, with no strong brain to make her physical weakness a light accident, abjectly and corruptingly afraid of man. A squaw, she dared not strike her lord.

The illusion passed like a moment of faintness and left her enraged at having forgotten her superiority even for an instant. In the material world she had a thousand times been defeated into making prudent reservations and practising unnatural docilities. But in the world of thought she had maintained unfalteringly her masterfulness in spite of the strong yearning of her temperament towards voluptuous surrenders. That was her virtue. Its violation whipped her to action and she would have killed him at once, had not his moment come a second before hers. Sweating horribly, he had dropped his head forward on his chest: his eyes fell on her feet and marked the plebeian moulding of her ankle, which rose thickly over a crease of flesh from the heel to the calf. The woman was coarse in grain and pattern.

He had no instinct for honourable attack, so he found himself striking her in the stomach. She reeled from pain, not because his strength overcame hers. For the first time her eyes looked into his candidly open, unveiled by languor or lust: their hard brightness told him how she despised him for that unwarlike blow. He cried out as he realised that this was another of her despicable victories and that the whole burden of the crime now lay on him, for he had begun it. But the rage was stopped on his lips as her arms, flung wildly out as she fell backwards, caught him about the waist with abominable justness of eye and evil intention. So they fell body to body into the quarrelling waters.

The feathery confusion had looked so soft, yet it seemed the solid rock they struck. The breath shot out of him and suffocation warmly stuffed his ears and nose. Then the rock cleft and he was swallowed by a brawling blackness in which whirled a vortex that flung him again and again on a sharp thing that burned his shoulder. All about him fought the waters, and they cut his flesh like knives. His pain was past belief. Though God might be war, he desired peace in his time, and he yearned for another God—a child's God, an immense arm coming down from the hills and lifting him to a kindly bosom. Soon his body would burst for breath, his agony would smash in his breast bone. So great was his pain that his consciousness was strained to apprehend it, as a too tightly stretched canvas splits and rips.

Suddenly the air was sweet on his mouth. The starlight seemed as hearty as a cheer. The world was still there, the world in which he had lived, so he must be safe. His own weakness and loveableness induced enjoyable tears, and there was a delicious moment of abandonment to comfortable whining before he realised that the water would not kindly buoy him up for long, and that even now a hostile current clasped his waist. He braced his flaccid body against the sucking blackness and flung his head back so that the water should not bubble so hungrily against the cords of his throat. Above him the slime of the rock was sticky with moonbeams, and the leprous light brought to his mind a newspaper paragraph, read years ago, which told him that the dawn had discovered floating in some oily Mersey dock, under walls as infected with wet growth as this, a corpse whose blood-encrusted finger-tips were deeply cleft. On the instant his own finger-tips seemed hot with blood and deeply cleft from clawing at the impregnable rock. He screamed gaspingly and beat his hands through the strangling flood. Action, which he had always loathed and dreaded, had broken the hard mould of his self-possession, and the dry dust of his character was blown hither and thither by fear. But one sharp fragment of intelligence which survived this detrition of his personality perceived that a certain gleam on the rock about a foot above the water was not the cold putrescence of the slime, but certainly the hard and merry light of a moon-ray striking on solid metal. His left hand clutched upwards at it, and he swung from a rounded projection. It was, his touch told him, a leaden ring hanging obliquely from the rock, to which his memory could visualise precisely in some past drier time when Lisbech sent no flood to Whimsey, a waterman mooring a boat strewn with pale-bellied perch. And behind the stooping waterman he remembered a flight of narrow steps that led up a buttress to a stone shelf that ran through the cutting. Unquestionably he was safe. He swung in a happy rhythm from the ring, his limp body trailing like a caterpillar through the stream to the foot of the steps, while he gasped in strength. A part of him was in agony, for his arm was nearly dragged out of its socket and a part of him was embarrassed because his hysteria shook him with a deep rumbling chuckle that sounded as though he meditated on some unseemly joke; the whole was pervaded by a twilight atmosphere of unenthusiastic gratitude for his rescue, like the quietly cheerful tone of a Sunday evening sacred concert. After a minute's deep breathing he hauled himself up by the other hand and prepared to swing himself on to the steps.

But first, to shake off the wet worsted rags, once his socks, that now stuck uncomfortably between his toes, he splashed his feet outwards to midstream. A certain porpoise-like surface met his left foot. Fear dappled his face with goose flesh. Without turning his head he knew what it was. It was Evadne's fat flesh rising on each side of her deep-furrowed spine through the rent in her bathing dress.

Once more hatred marched through his soul like a king: compelling service by his godhead and, like all gods, a little hated for his harsh lieu[6] on his worshipper. He saw his wife as the curtain of flesh between him and celibacy, and solitude and all those delicate abstentions from life which his soul desired. He saw her as the invisible worm destroying the rose of the world with her dark secret love.[7] Now he knelt on the lowest stone step watching her wet seal-smooth head bobbing nearer on the waters. As her strong arms, covered with little dark points where her thick hairs were clotted with moisture, stretched out towards safety he bent forward and laid his hands on her head. He held her face under water. Scornfully he noticed the bubbles that rose to the surface from her

---

6. Discipline.
7. A reference to William Blake's poem *The Sick Rose*, in which a worm has entered a rose's "bed/of crimson joy;/ And his dark secret love/Does thy life destroy."

protesting mouth and nostrils, and the foam raised by her arms and her thick ankles. To the end the creature persisted in turmoil, in movement, in action. . . .

She dropped like a stone. His hands, with nothing to resist them, slapped the water foolishly and he nearly overbalanced forward into the stream. He rose to his feet very stiffly. "I must be a very strong man," he said, as he slowly climbed the steps. "I must be a very strong man," he repeated, a little louder, as with a hot and painful rigidity of the joints he stretched himself out at full length along the stone shelf. Weakness closed him in like a lead coffin. For a little time the wetness of his clothes persisted in being felt: then the sensation oozed out of him and his body fell out of knowledge. There was neither pain nor joy nor any other reckless ploughing of the brain by nerves. He knew unconsciousness, or rather the fullest consciousness he had ever known. For the world became nothingness, and nothingness which is free from the yeasty nuisance of matter and the ugliness of generation was the law of his being. He was absorbed into vacuity, the untamed substance of the universe, round which he conceived passion and thought to circle as straws caught up by the wind. He saw God and lived.

In Heaven a thousand years are a day. And this little corner of time in which he found happiness shrank to a nut-shell as he opened his eyes again. This peace was hardly printed on his heart, yet the brightness of the night was blurred by the dawn. With the grunting carefulness of a man drunk with fatigue, he crawled along the stone shelf to the iron bridge, where he stood with his back to the roaring sluice and rested. All things seemed different now and happier. Like most timid people he disliked the night, and the commonplace hand which the dawn laid on the scene seemed to him a sanctification. The dimmed moon sank to her setting behind the crags. The jewel lights of Lisbech railway station were weak, cheerful twinklings. A steaming bluish milk of morning mist had been spilt on the hard silver surface of the lake, and the reeds no longer stabbed it like little daggers, but seemed a feathery fringe, like the pampas grass in the front garden in Sumatra Crescent. The black crags became brownish, and the mist disguised the sternness of the moor. This weakening of effects was exactly what he had always thought the extinction of Evadne would bring the world. He smiled happily at the moon.

Yet he was moved to sudden angry speech. "If I had my time over again," he said, "I wouldn't touch her with the tongs." For the cold he had known all along he would catch had settled in his head, and his handkerchief was wet through.

He leaned over the bridge and looked along Lisbech and thought of Evadne. For the first time for many years he saw her image without spirits, and wondered without indignation why she had so often looked like the cat about to steal the cream. What was the cream? And did she ever steal it? Now he would never know. He thought of her very generously and sighed over the perversity of fate in letting so much comeliness.

"If she had married a butcher or a veterinary surgeon she might have been happy," he said, and shook his head at the glassy black water that slid under the bridge to that boiling sluice.

A gust of ague[8] reminded him that wet clothes clung to his fevered body and that he ought to change as quickly as possible, or expect to be laid up for weeks. He turned along the path that led back across the moor to the withered ash tree, and was learning the torture of bare feet on gravel when he cried out to himself: "I shall be hanged for killing my wife." It did not come as a trumpet-call, for he was one of those people who never quite hear what is said to them, and this deafishness extended in him to emotional things. It stole on him calmly, like a fog closing on a city. When he first felt hemmed in by this certainty he looked over his shoulder to the crags, remembering

8. Fever.

tales of how Jacobite fugitives had hidden on the moors for many weeks. There lay at least another day of freedom. But he was the kind of man who always goes home. He stumbled on, not very unhappy, except for his feet. Like many people of weak temperament he did not fear death. Indeed, it had a peculiar appeal to him; for while it was important, exciting, it did not, like most important and exciting things try to create action. He allowed his imagination the vanity of painting pictures. He saw himself standing in their bedroom, plotting this last event, with the white sheet and the high lights of the mahogany wardrobe shining ghostly at him through the darkness. He saw himself raising a thin hand to the gas bracket and turning on the tap. He saw himself staggering to their bed while death crept in at his nostrils. He saw his corpse lying in full daylight, and for the first time knew himself certainly, unquestionably dignified.

He threw back his chest in pride: but at that moment the path stopped and he found himself staggering down the mound of heatherland and boulders with bleeding feet. Always he had suffered from sore feet, which had not exactly disgusted but, worse still, disappointed Evadne. A certain wistfulness she had always evinced when she found herself the superior animal had enraged and humiliated him many times. He felt that sting him now, and flung himself down the mound cursing. When he stumbled up to the withered ash tree he hated her so much that it seemed as though she were alive again, and a sharp wind blowing down from the moor terrified him like her touch.

He rested there. Leaning against the stripped grey trunk, he smiled up at the sky, which was now so touched to ineffectiveness by the dawn that it looked like a tent of faded silk. There was the peace of weakness in him, which he took to be spiritual, because it had no apparent physical justification: but he lost it as his dripping clothes chilled his tired flesh. His discomfort reminded him that the phantasmic night was passing from him. Daylight threatened him: the daylight in which for so many years he had worked in the solicitor's office and been snubbed and ignored. "'The garish day,'" he murmured disgustedly, quoting the blasphemy of some hymn writer. He wanted his death to happen in this phantasmic night.

So he limped his way along the road. The birds had not yet begun to sing, but the rustling noises of the night had ceased. The silent highway was consecrated to his proud progress. He staggered happily like a tired child returning from a lovely birthday walk: his death in the little bedroom, which for the first time he would have to himself, was a culminating treat to be gloated over like the promise of a favourite pudding for supper. As he walked he brooded dozingly on large and swelling thoughts. Like all people of weak passions and enterprise he loved to think of Napoleon, and in the shadow of the great asylum wall he strutted a few steps of his advance from murder to suicide, with arms crossed on his breast and thin legs trying to strut massively. He was so happy. He wished that a military band went before him, and pretended that the high hedges were solemn lines of men, stricken in awe to silence as their king rode out to some nobly self-chosen doom. Vast he seemed to himself, and magnificent like music, and solemn like the Sphinx. He had saved the earth from corruption by killing Evadne, for whom he now felt the unremorseful pity a conqueror might bestow on a devastated empire. He might have grieved that his victory brought him death, but with immense pride he found that the occasion was exactly described by a text. "He saved others, Himself He could not save."[9] He had missed the stile in the field above Sumatra Crescent and had to go back and hunt for it in the hedge. So quickly had his satisfaction borne him home.

9. These are the words of the priests and elders mocking Jesus at his crucifixion; Matthew 27.42.

The field had the fantastic air that jerry-builders[1] give to land poised on the knife-edge of town and country, so that he walked in romance to his very door. The unmarred grass sloped to a stone-hedge of towers of loose brick, trenches and mounds of shining clay, and the fine intentful spires of the scaffolding round the last unfinished house. And he looked down on Petrick. Though to the actual eye it was but a confusion of dark distances through the twilight, a breaking of velvety perspectives, he saw more intensely than ever before its squalid walls and squalid homes where mean men and mean women enlaced their unwholesome lives. Yet he did not shrink from entering for his great experience: as Christ did not shrink from being born in a stable. He swaggered with humility over the trodden mud of the field and the new white flags of Sumatra Crescent. Down the road before him there passed a dim figure, who paused at each lamp post and raised a long wand to behead the yellow gas-flowers that were now wilting before the dawn: a ghostly herald preparing the world to be his deathbed. The Crescent curved in quiet darkness, save for one house, where blazed a gas-lit room with undrawn blinds. The brightness had the startling quality of a scream. He looked in almost anxiously as he passed, and met the blank eyes of a man in evening clothes who stood by the window shaking a medicine. His face was like a wax mask softened by heat: the features were blurred with the suffering which comes from the spectacle of suffering. His eyes lay unshiftingly on George's face as he went by and he went on shaking the bottle. It seemed as though he would never stop.

In the hour of his grandeur George was not forgetful of the griefs of the little human people, but interceded with God for the sake of this stranger. Everything was beautiful, beautiful, beautiful.

His own little house looked solemn as a temple. He leaned against the lamppost at the gate and stared at its empty windows and neat bricks. The disorder of the shattered pane of glass could be overlooked by considering a sign that this house was a holy place: like the Passover blood on the lintel. The propriety of the evenly drawn blind pleased him enormously. He had always known that this was how the great tragic things of the world had accomplished themselves: quietly. Evadne's raging activity belonged to trivial or annoying things like spring-cleaning or thunderstorms. Well, the house belonged to him now. He opened the gate and went up the asphalt path, sourly noticing that Evadne had as usual left out the lawn-mower, though it might very easily have rained, with the wind coming up as it was. A stray cat that had been sleeping in the tuft of pampas grass in the middle of the lawn was roused by his coming, and fled insolently close to his legs. He hated all wild homeless things, and bent for a stone to throw at it. But instead his fingers touched a slug, which reminded him of the feeling of Evadne's flesh through the slit in her bathing dress. And suddenly the garden was possessed by her presence: she seemed to amble there as she had so often done, sowing seeds unwisely and tormenting the last days of an ailing geranium by insane transplantation, exclaiming absurdly over such mere weeds as morning glory. He caught the very clucking of her voice. . . . The front door opened at his touch.

The little lobby with its closed doors seemed stuffed with expectant silence. He realised that he had come to the theatre of his great adventure. Then panic seized him. Because this was the home where he and she had lived together so horribly he doubted whether he could do this splendid momentous thing, for here he had always been a poor thing with the habit of failure. His heart beat in him more quickly than his raw feet could pad up the oil-clothed stairs. Behind the deal door at the end of the

---

1. Low-wage, slipshod workers.

passage was death. Nothingness! It would escape him, even the idea of it would escape him if he did not go to it at once. When he burst at last into its presence he felt so victorious that he sank back against the door waiting for death to come to him without turning on the gas. He was so happy. His death was coming true.

But Evadne lay on his deathbed. She slept there soundly, with her head flung back on the pillows so that her eyes and brow seemed small in shadow, and her mouth and jaw huge above her thick throat in the light. Her wet hair straggled across the pillow on to a broken cane chair covered with her tumbled clothes. Her breast, silvered with sweat, shone in the ray of the street lamp that had always disturbed their nights. The counterpane rose enormously over her hips in rolls of glazed linen. Out of mere innocent sleep her sensuality was distilling a most drunken pleasure.

Not for one moment did he think this a phantasmic appearance. Evadne was not the sort of woman to have a ghost.

Still leaning against the door, he tried to think it all out: but his thoughts came brokenly, because the dawnlight flowing in at the window confused him by its pale glare and that lax figure on the bed held his attention. It must have been that when he laid his murderous hands on her head she had simply dropped below the surface and swum a few strokes under water as any expert swimmer can. Probably he had never even put her into danger, for she was a great lusty creature and the weir was a little place. He had imagined the wonder and peril of the battle as he had imagined his victory. He sneezed exhaustingly, and from his physical distress realised how absurd it was ever to have thought that he had killed her. Bodies like his do not kill bodies like hers.

Now his soul was naked and lonely as though the walls of his body had fallen in at death, and the grossness of Evadne's sleep made him suffer more unlovely a destitution than any old beggarwoman squatting by the roadside in the rain. He had thought he had had what every man most desires: one night of power over a woman for the business of murder or love. But it had been a lie. Nothing beautiful had ever happened to him. He would have wept, but the hatred he had learnt on the moors obstructed all tears in his throat. At least this night had given him passion enough to put an end to it all.

Quietly he went to the window and drew down the sash. There was no fireplace, so that sealed the room. Then he crept over to the gas bracket and raised his thin hand, as he had imagined in his hour of vain glory by the lake.

He had forgotten Evadne's thrifty habit of turning off the gas at the main to prevent leakage when she went to bed.

He was beaten. He undressed and got into bed: as he had done every night for ten years, and as he would do every night until he died. Still sleeping, Evadne caressed him with warm arms.

Rupert Brooke
1887–1915

Rupert Brooke was the first of Britain's "war poets," and the last poem he completed during his short lifetime—*The Soldier*—is alone enough to guarantee his lasting place in modern poetry.

Brooke rose with extraordinary speed to the center of the British literary establishment. While an undergraduate, he worked with the *Cambridge Review* and came into contact with such influential writers as Henry James, W. B. Yeats, Virginia Woolf, and Lytton Strachey, and the editor and publisher Edward Marsh. In 1912, after the publication of his first volume of poetry, Brooke suffered a nervous breakdown; after a short recovery period, he spent most of the next three years traveling. World War I began shortly after he returned to England in the spring of 1914; Brooke enlisted immediately and was commissioned on a ship that sailed to Antwerp, Belgium, where Brooke saw no action through early 1915. During this lull, Brooke wrote the war sonnets for which he is best remembered today. While his ship was sailing to Gallipoli, Brooke died of blood poisoning, before seeing combat duty.

It is nearly impossible, even at this late date, to separate Brooke the myth from Brooke the poet; he was something of a national hero even before his death, thanks to the popular reception of his volume of war sonnets, *Nineteen Fourteen*. In Brooke's writings about the war, the irony of early poems like *Heaven* ("And in that Heaven of all their wish, / There shall be no more land, say fish") falls away. These patriotic poems—and most especially *The Soldier*, in which Brooke seemed to have foreseen his own death—meshed perfectly with the temperament of the British people as the nation entered into war. When *The Soldier* was read aloud at Saint Paul's Cathedral in London on Easter Sunday, 1915, Brooke the man—whom Yeats called "the handsomest man in England"—was permanently immortalized as the symbol of English pride.

The Great Lover

    I have been so great a lover: filled my days
    So proudly with the splendour of Love's praise,
    The pain, the calm, and the astonishment,
    Desire illimitable, and still content,
5   And all dear names men use, to cheat despair,
    For the perplexed and viewless streams that bear
    Our hearts at random down the dark of life.
    Now, ere the unthinking silence on that strife
    Steals down, I would cheat drowsy Death so far,
10   My night shall be remembered for a star
    That outshone all the suns of all men's days.
    Shall I not crown them with immortal praise
    Whom I have loved, who have given me, dared with me
    High secrets, and in darkness knelt to see
15   The inenarrable° godhead of delight?   *indescribable*
    Love is a flame;—we have beaconed the world's night.
    A city:—and we have built it, these and I.
    An emperor:—we have taught the world to die.
    So, for their sakes I loved, ere I go hence,
20   And the high cause of Love's magnificence,
    And to keep loyalties young, I'll write those names
    Golden for ever, eagles, crying flames,
    And set them as a banner, that men may know,
    To dare the generations, burn, and blow
25   Out on the wind of Time, shining and streaming. . . .

    These I have loved:
                 White plates and cups, clean-gleaming,
    Ringed with blue lines; and feathery, faëry dust;
    Wet roofs, beneath the lamp-light; the strong crust
    Of friendly bread; and many-tasting food;

30   Rainbows; and the blue bitter smoke of wood;
    And radiant raindrops couching in cool flowers;
    And flowers themselves, that sway through sunny hours,
    Dreaming of moths that drink them under the moon;
    Then, the cool kindliness of sheets, that soon
35   Smooth away trouble; and the rough male kiss
    Of blankets; grainy wood; live hair that is
    Shining and free; blue-massing clouds; the keen
    Unpassioned beauty of a great machine;
    The benison° of hot water; furs to touch;   *benediction*
40   The good smell of old clothes; and other such—
    The comfortable smell of friendly fingers,
    Hair's fragrance, and the musty reek that lingers
    About dead leaves and last year's ferns. . . .
                             Dear names,
    And thousand other throng to me! Royal flames;
45   Sweet water's dimpling laugh from tap or spring;
    Holes in the ground; and voices that do sing;
    Voices in laughter, too; and body's pain,
    Soon turned to peace; and the deep-panting train;
    Firm sands; the little dulling edge of foam
50   That browns and dwindles as the wave goes home;
    And washen stones, gay for an hour; the cold
    Graveness of iron; moist black earthen mould;
    Sleep; and high places; footprints in the dew;
    And oaks; and brown horse-chestnuts, glossy-new;
55   And new-peeled sticks; and shining pools on grass;—
    All these have been my loves. And these shall pass,
    Whatever passes not, in the great hour,
    Nor all my passion, all my prayers, have power
    To hold them with me through the gate of Death.
60   They'll play deserter, turn with the traitor breath,
    Break the high bond we made, and sell Love's trust
    And sacramented covenant to the dust.
    —Oh, never a doubt but, somewhere, I shall wake,
    And give what's left of love again, and make
    New friends, now strangers. . . .
65   But the best I've known,
    Stays here, and changes, breaks, grows old, is blown
    About the winds of the world, and fades from brains
    Of living men, and dies.
    Nothing remains.

          O dear my loves, O faithless, once again
70   This one last gift I give: that after men
    Shall know, and later lovers, far-removed,
    Praise you, "All these were lovely"; say, "He loved."

MATAIEA, 1914

The Soldier

If I should die, think only this of me:
    That there's some corner of a foreign field
That is forever England. There shall be
    In that rich earth a richer dust concealed;
5   A dust whom England bore, shaped, made aware,
    Gave, once, her flowers to love, her ways to roam,
A body of England's, breathing English air,
    Washed by the rivers, blest by suns of home.

And think, this heart, all evil shed away,
10   A pulse in the Eternal mind, no less
        Gives somewhere back the thoughts by England given;
Her sights and sounds; dreams happy as her day;
    And laughter, learnt of friends; and gentleness,
        In hearts at peace, under an English heaven.

Siegfried Sassoon
1886–1967

It is tempting to describe a poet like Siegfried Sassoon by emphasizing his differences from the hugely popular Rupert Brooke. Sassoon was born to a wealthy Jewish family, who made their fortune in India; he lived a life of ease before the war, writing slight Georgian poetry and hunting foxes. World War I suddenly and unequivocally changed all that. Sassoon served with the Royal Welch Fusiliers, and before the end of 1915 saw action in France; he helped a wounded soldier to safety during heavy fire, for which he was awarded a Military Cross. After being wounded himself, Sassoon refused to return to battle; from his hospital bed, he wrote an open letter to the war department suggesting that the war was being unnecessarily prolonged, and as a result, he narrowly avoided a court-martial. Owing to the intervention of his fellow soldier the poet Robert Graves, he was instead committed to a hospital and treated for "shell shock." He returned to the front in 1919, and was wounded a second time.

    Where the war poetry of Brooke is patriotic to the point of sentimentality, Sassoon's verse is characterized by an unrelentingly realistic portrayal of the horrors of modern warfare. And where Brooke's poetry was eagerly welcomed by an anxious public, Sassoon's was largely rejected as either unpatriotic or unnecessarily grotesque. After the war, he lived in seclusion in the country, writing memoirs and poetry—though rarely with the shock value of his early war poems.

Glory of Women

You love us when we're heroes, home on leave,
Or wounded in a mentionable place.
You worship decorations; you believe
That chivalry redeems the war's disgrace.
5   You make us shells. You listen with delight,
By tales of dirt and danger fondly thrilled.
You crown our distant ardours while we fight,

And mourn our laurelled memories when we're killed.
You can't believe that British troops "retire"
10   When hell's last horror breaks them, and they run,
Trampling the terrible corpses—blind with blood.
    O German mother dreaming by the fire,
While you are knitting socks to send your son
His face is trodden deeper in the mud.

Craiglockhart,[1] 1917

"They"

The Bishop tells us: "When the boys come back
"They will not be the same; for they'll have fought
"In a just cause: they lead the last attack
"On Anti-Christ;[1] their comrades' blood has bought
5   "New right to breed an honourable race,
"They have challenged Death and dared him face to face."

"We're none of us the same!" the boys reply.
"For George lost both his legs; and Bill's stone blind;
"Poor Jim's shot through the lungs and like to die;
10   "And Bert's gone syphilitic:[2] you'll not find
"A chap who's served that hasn't found *some* change."
And the Bishop said: "The ways of God are strange!"

The Rear-Guard
(Hindenburg Line, April 1917)

Groping along the tunnel, step by step,
He winked his prying torch° with patching glare   *lantern or flashlight*
From side to side, and sniffed the unwholesome air.

Tins, boxes, bottles, shapes too vague to know;
5   A mirror smashed, the mattress from a bed;
And he, exploring fifty feet below
The rosy gloom of battle overhead.

Tripping, he grabbed the wall; saw some one lie
Humped at his feet, half-hidden by a rug,
10   And stooped to give the sleeper's arm a tug.
"I'm looking for headquarters." No reply.
"God blast your neck!" (For days he'd had no sleep,)
"Get up and guide me through this stinking place."
Savage, he kicked a soft, unanswering heap,
15   And flashed his beam across the livid face
Terribly glaring up, whose eyes yet wore
Agony dying hard ten days before;
And fists of fingers clutched a blackening wound.

1. A hospital near Edinburgh, Scotland, where Sassoon
(along with Wilfred Owen) was treated for shell shock.
1. In Christian tradition, the archenemy of Christ whose

appearance will signal the beginning of the "end times."
2. Infected with syphilis.

Alone he staggered on until he found
20   Dawn's ghost that filtered down a shafted stair
To the dazed, muttering creatures underground
Who hear the boom of shells in muffled sound.
At last, with sweat of horror in his hair,
He climbed through darkness to the twilight air,
25   Unloading hell behind him step by step.

Everyone Sang

Everyone suddenly burst out singing;
And I was filled with such delight
As prisoned birds must find in freedom,
Winging wildly across the white
5   Orchards and dark-green fields; on—on—and out of sight.
Everyone's voice was suddenly lifted;
And beauty came like the setting sun:
My heart was shaken with tears; and horror
Drifted away . . . O, but Everyone
10   Was a bird; and the song was wordless; the singing will never be done.
April 1919

⊷ ⛤ ⊷

Wilfred Owen
1893–1918

The poet C. Day Lewis wrote that Wilfred Owen's poems were "certainly the finest written by any English poet of the First War." In his small body of poems Owen manages to combine his friend Siegfried Sassoon's outrage at the horror of the war with a formal and technical skill reminiscent of his idols Keats and Shelley. Sassoon himself characterized their differences as poets this way: "My trench-sketches were like rockets, sent up to illuminate the darkness. . . . It was Owen who revealed how, out of realistic horror and scorn, poetry might be made."

Owen grew up on the Welsh border in Shropshire, the landscape A. E. Housman was to celebrate in his poetry. After finishing technical school, Owen spent two years in training with an evangelical Church of England vicar, trying to decide whether to pursue formal training as a clergyman. As a result of his experiences, Owen became dissatisfied with the institutional church's response to the poverty and suffering of England's least privileged citizens. In October 1915 he enlisted with the Artists' Rifles, and on 29 December 1916, he left for France as a lieutenant with the Lancashire Fusiliers.

Owen quickly became disillusioned with the war; as a result of almost unimaginable privations, which included being blown into the air while he slept in a foxhole, Owen suffered a breakdown, and was sent to the Craiglockhart War Hospital in Edinburgh. Owen composed nearly all of his poetry in the fourteen months of his rehabilitation, between August 1917 and September 1918; though hard to imagine, it is quite possible that if he had not been sent back to Great Britain to recover from his "shell shock," we might now know nothing of his poetry. While at Craiglockhart he met Sassoon and found his true voice and mode; he published his first poems on war themes anonymously in the hospital's magazine, which he edited. In September 1918 Owen returned to the battlefields of France; he was killed in action at Sambre Canal on November 4, 1918, one week before the Armistice. Dylan Thomas called Owen "one of the four most profound influences upon the poets who came after him"—the others being Hopkins, Yeats, and Eliot.

Anthem for Doomed Youth

What passing-bells for these who die as cattle?
   Only the monstrous anger of the guns.
   Only the stuttering rifles' rapid rattle
Can patter out their hasty orisons.°   *prayers*
5   No mockeries now for them; no prayers nor bells,
   Nor any voice of mourning save the choirs,—
The shrill, demented choirs of wailing shells;
   And bugles calling for them from sad shires.

What candles may be held to speed them all?
10   Not in the hands of boys, but in their eyes
Shall shine the holy glimmers of good-byes.
   The pallor of girls' brows shall be their pall;[1]
Their flowers the tenderness of patient minds,
And each slow dusk a drawing-down of blinds.

Strange Meeting

It seemed that out of battle I escaped
Down some profound dull tunnel, long since scooped
Through granites which titanic wars had groined.°   *joined together*
Yet also there encumbered sleepers groaned,
5   Too fast in thought or death to be bestirred.
Then, as I probed them, one sprang up, and stared
With piteous recognition in fixed eyes,
Lifting distressful hands as if to bless.
And by his smile, I knew that sullen hall,
10   By his dead smile I knew we stood in Hell.
With a thousand pains that vision's face was grained;
Yet no blood reached there from the upper ground,
And no guns thumped, or down the flues made moan.
"Strange friend," I said, "here is no cause to mourn."
15   "None," said that other, "save the undone years,
The hopelessness. Whatever hope is yours,
Was my life also; I went hunting wild
After the wildest beauty in the world,
Which lies not calm in eyes, or braided hair,
20   But mocks the steady running of the hour,
And if it grieves, grieves richlier than here.
For of my glee might many men have laughed,
And of my weeping something had been left,
Which must die now. I mean the truth untold,
25   The pity of war, the pity war distilled.
Now men will go content with what we spoiled,
Or, discontent, boil bloody, and be spilled.
They will be swift with swiftness of the tigress.

1. The cloth draped over a coffin.

None will break ranks, though nations trek from progress.
30 Courage was mine, and I had mystery,
Wisdom was mine, and I had mastery:
To miss the march of this retreating world
Into vain citadels that are not walled.
Then, when much blood had clogged their chariot-wheels,
35 I would go up and wash them from sweet wells,
Even with truths that lie too deep for taint.
I would have poured my spirit without stint
But not through wounds; not on the cess of war.
Foreheads of men have bled where no wounds were.
40 I am the enemy you killed, my friend.
I knew you in this dark: for so you frowned
Yesterday through me as you jabbed and killed.
I parried; but my hands were loath and cold.
Let us sleep now. . . . "

Disabled

He sat in a wheeled chair, waiting for dark,
And shivered in his ghastly suit of grey,
Legless, sewn short at elbow. Through the park
Voices of boys rang saddening like a hymn,
5 Voices of play and pleasure after day,
Till gathering sleep had mothered them from him.

About this time Town used to swing so gay
When glow-lamps budded in the light blue trees,
And girls glanced lovelier as the air grew dim,—
10 In the old times, before he threw away his knees.
Now he will never feel again how slim
Girls' waists are, or how warm their subtle hands.
All of them touch him like some queer disease.

There was an artist silly for his face,
15 For it was younger than his youth, last year.
Now, he is old; his back will never brace;
He's lost his colour very far from here,
Poured it down shell-holes till the veins ran dry,
And half his lifetime lapsed in the hot race
20 And leap of purple spurted from his thigh.

One time he liked a blood-smear down his leg,
After the matches, carried shoulder-high.
It was after football, when he'd drunk a peg,[1]
He thought he'd better join.—He wonders why.
25 Someone had said he'd look a god in kilts,
That's why; and maybe, too, to please his Meg,
Aye, that was it, to please the giddy jilts°   *girls or women*

---

1. Alcoholic drink, such as brandy and soda.

He asked to join. He didn't have to beg;
Smiling they wrote his lie: aged nineteen years.

30   Germans he scarcely thought of; all their guilt,
And Austria's, did not move him. And no fears
Of Fear came yet. He thought of jewelled hilts
For daggers in plaid socks; of smart salutes;
And care of arms; and leave; and pay arrears;
35   Esprit de corps;² and hints for young recruits.
And soon, he was drafted out with drums and cheers.
Some cheered him home, but not as crowds cheer Goal.
Only a solemn man who brought him fruits
Thanked him; and then enquired about his soul.

40   Now, he will spend a few sick years in institutes,
And do what things the rules consider wise,
And take whatever pity they may dole.
Tonight he noticed how the women's eyes
Passed from him to the strong men that were whole.
45   How cold and late it is! Why don't they come
And put him into bed? Why don't they come?

Dulce Et Decorum Est¹

Bent double, like old beggars under sacks,
Knock-kneed, coughing like hags, we cursed through sludge,
Till on the haunting flares we turned our backs
And towards our distant rest began to trudge.
5   Men marched asleep. Many had lost their boots
But limped on, blood-shod. All went lame; all blind;
Drunk with fatigue; deaf even to the hoots
Of tired, outstripped Five-Nines² that dropped behind.

Gas! Gas! Quick, boys!—An ecstasy of fumbling,
10   Fitting the clumsy helmets just in time;
But someone still was yelling out and stumbling
And flound'ring like a man in fire or lime³ . . .
Dim, through the misty panes and thick green light,
As under a green sea, I saw him drowning.

15   In all my dreams, before my helpless sight,
He plunges at me, guttering, choking, drowning.

If in some smothering dreams you too could pace
Behind the wagon that we flung him in,
And watch the white eyes writhing in his face,
20   His hanging face, like a devil's sick of sin;
If you could hear, at every jolt, the blood
Come gargling from the froth-corrupted lungs,

---

2. Spirit of the group (French); camaraderie.
1. From the *Odes* of the Roman satirist Horace (65–8
B.C.): Dulce et decorum est pro patria mori [sweet and fitting it is to die for your fatherland].

2. Artillery shells used by the Germans.
3. Calcium oxide, a powerfully caustic alkali used, among
other purposes, for cleaning the flesh off the bones of
corpses.

Obscene as cancer, bitter as the cud
Of vile, incurable sores on innocent tongues,—
25   My friend, you would not tell with such high zest
To children ardent for some desperate glory,
The old Lie: Dulce et decorum est
Pro patria mori.

━ ⇒✦⇒ ━

Isaac Rosenberg
1890–1918

World War I was the spur that goaded some poets, like Wilfred Owen, into the writing of poetry; for Isaac Rosenberg the war was simply the catalyst for a more vivid and powerful verse. Rosenberg began writing poetry on Jewish themes when he was just fifteen; he had published two volumes of poems and a verse play, *Moses*, by the time he joined the army in 1916. Rosenberg's experience of the war was, in important ways, different from the other poets represented here. To begin with, he was the son of Lithuanian Jewish immigrants who had settled in the East End, London's Jewish ghetto. As a child, Rosenberg lived with severe poverty; he was forced to leave school at fourteen to help support his family. He went to war not as an officer, but as a private; as the critic Irving Howe writes, "No glamorous fatality hangs over Rosenberg's head: he was just a clumsy, stuttering Jewish doughboy." He was killed while on patrol outside the trenches—a private's dangerous assignment.

His experiences on the Western Front seem to have provided him with the perfect canvas for his essentially religious art. Siegfried Sassoon, alluding to Rosenberg's training as an artist at the Slade School, later described his poems as "scriptural and sculptural": "His experiments were a strenuous effort for impassioned expression; his imagination had a sinewy and muscular aliveness; often he saw things in terms of sculpture, but he did not carve or chisel; he *modeled* words with fierce energy and aspiration." His less-than-genteel background also made Rosenberg impatient with the patriotic sentiments of a poet like Rupert Brooke, for whose "begloried sonnets" he had nothing but contempt. In the poetry of Rosenberg, by contrast—according to Sassoon—"words and images obey him, instead of leading him into over-elaboration." Interest in Rosenberg's poetry has recently been revived by critics interested in his use of Jewish themes; the critic Harold Bloom, for instance, calls Rosenberg "an English poet with a Jewish difference," and suggests that he is "the best Jewish poet writing in English that our century has given us."

Break of Day in the Trenches

The darkness crumbles away—
It is the same old druid[1] Time as ever.
Only a live thing leaps my hand—
A queer sardonic rat—
5   As I pull the parapet's poppy
To stick behind my ear.

---

1. Member of an ancient Celtic religion.

Droll rat, they would shoot you if they knew
Your cosmopolitan sympathies.
Now you have touched this English hand
10   You will do the same to a German—
Soon, no doubt, if it be your pleasure
To cross the sleeping green between.
It seems you inwardly grin as you pass
Strong eyes, fine limbs, haughty athletes
15   Less chanced than you for life,
Bonds to the whims of murder,
Sprawled in the bowels of the earth,
The torn fields of France.
What do you see in our eyes
20   At the shrieking iron and flame
Hurled through still heavens?
What quaver—what heart aghast?
Poppies whose roots are in man's veins
Drop, and are ever dropping;
25   But mine in my ear is safe,
Just a little white with the dust.

1916   1922

Dead Man's Dump

The plunging limbers over the shattered track
Racketed with their rusty freight,
Stuck out like many crowns of thorns,
And the rusty stakes like sceptres old
5   To stay the flood of brutish men
Upon our brothers dear.

The wheels lurched over sprawled dead
But pained them not, though their bones crunched,
Their shut mouths made no moan.
10   They lie there huddled, friend and foeman,
Man born of man, and born of woman,
And shells go crying over them
From night till night and now.

Earth has waited for them,
15   All the time of their growth
Fretting for their decay:
Now she has them at last!
In the strength of their strength
Suspended—stopped and held.

20   What fierce imaginings their dark souls lit?
Earth! have they gone into you!
Somewhere they must have gone,
And flung on your hard back
Is their soul's sack

25   Emptied of God-ancestralled essences.
      Who hurled them out? Who hurled?

      None saw their spirits' shadow shake the grass,
      Or stood aside for the half used life to pass
      Out of those doomed nostrils and the doomed mouth,
30   When the swift iron burning bee
      Drained the wild honey of their youth.

      What of us who, flung on the shrieking pyre,°   *funeral bonfire*
      Walk, our usual thoughts untouched,
      Our lucky limbs as on ichor[1] fed,
35   Immortal seeming ever?
      Perhaps when the flames beat loud on us,
      A fear may choke in our veins
      And the startled blood may stop.

      The air is loud with death,
40   The dark air spurts with fire,
      The explosions ceaseless are.
      Timelessly now, some minutes past,
      These dead strode time with vigorous life,
      Till the shrapnel called 'An end!'
45   But not to all. In bleeding pangs
      Some borne on stretchers dreamed of home,
      Dear things, war-blotted from their hearts.

      Maniac Earth! howling and flying, your bowel
      Seared by the jagged fire, the iron love,
50   The impetuous storm of savage love.
      Dark Earth! dark Heavens! swinging in chemic smoke,
      What dead are born when you kiss each soundless soul
      With lightning and thunder from your mined heart,
      Which man's self dug, and his blind fingers loosed?

55   A man's brains splattered on
      A stretcher-bearer's face;
      His shook shoulders slipped their load,
      But when they bent to look again
      The drowning soul was sunk too deep
60   For human tenderness.

      They left this dead with the older dead,
      Stretched at the cross roads.

      Burnt black by strange decay
      Their sinister faces lie,

---

1. The vital fluid flowing in the veins of the Gods in classical mythology.

65   The lid over each eye,
    The grass and coloured clay
    More motion have than they,
    Joined to the great sunk silences.

    Here is one not long dead;
70   His dark hearing caught our far wheels,
    And the choked soul stretched weak hands
    To reach the living word the far wheels said,
    The blood-dazed intelligence beating for light,
    Crying through the suspense of the far torturing wheels
75   Swift for the end to break
    Or the wheels to break,
    Cried as the tide of the world broke over his sight.

    Will they come? Will they ever come?
    Even as the mixed hoofs of the mules,
80   The quivering-bellied mules,
    And the rushing wheels all mixed
    With his tortured upturned sight.
    So we crashed round the bend,
    We heard his weak scream,
85   We heard his very last sound,
    And our wheels grazed his dead face.

The Women Poets of World War I

Although men made up the bulk of combatants in the Great War, and comprised as well the vast majority of the war's casualties, it would be wrong to assume that the war had little or no effect on women. Some women saw action, primarily in military hospitals; others were engaged with the war from the home front—following vicariously the news of brothers, husbands, and lovers, or more generally affected by the large-scale changes the war brought on Great Britain. Cicely Hamilton was active on the home front in the women's suffrage movement and served in a British military hospital in France during the war. May Wedderburn Cannan served in the Intelligence Service during the war and was a widely published poet and novelist. Pauline Barrington wrote poetry that was very controversial during her time, expressing as it did real doubts about the justice of Britain's war effort. Helen Dircks published two volumes of poetry in the years following the war, *Finding* (1918) and *Passengers* (1920), the latter including the biting social satire *After Bourbon Wood*. Alys Fane Trotter moved to South Africa with her husband in the 1890s, writing about Cape Dutch houses; when she returned to England she wrote poetry, contributing to such popular magazines as *Punch* and *Cornhill Magazine*. Teresa Hooley, born in Derbyshire, brought the new technology of film to bear on the modern horrors of war in her poem, *A War Film*. Siegfried Sassoon complained of women noncombatants in his poem *The Glory of Women*: "You make us shells." Taken together, however, the voices of the women poets of World War I suggest that the men often made shells of the women, too, and that their reactions were often much more sympathetic, intelligent, and complex than the men gave them credit for.

Cicely Hamilton[1]

Non-Combatant

Before one drop of angry blood was shed
    I was sore hurt and beaten to my knee;
Before one fighting man reeled back and died
    The War-Lords struck at me.

5   They struck me down—an idle, useless mouth,
    As cumbrous—may, more cumbrous—than the dead,
With life and heart afire to give and give
    I take a dole instead.

With life and heart afire to give and give
10   I take and eat the bread of charity.
In all the length of all this eager land,
    No man has need of me.

That is my hurt—my burning, beating wound;
    That is the spear-thrust driven through my pride!
15   With aimless hands, and mouth that must be fed,
    I wait and stand aside.

Let me endure it, then, with stiffened lip:
    I, even I, have suffered in the strife!
Let me endure it then—I give my pride
20   Where others give a life.

1916

May Wedderburn Cannan[1]

Lamplight

We planned to shake the world together, you and I
Being young, and very wise;
Now in the light of the green shaded lamp
Almost I see your eyes
5 Light with the old gay laughter; you and I
Dreamed greatly of an Empire in those days,
Setting our feet upon laborious ways,
And all you asked of fame
Was crossed swords in the Army List,

1. (1872–1952), playwright, social activist, feminist;
founder of the Women Writers' Suffrage League.

1. (1893–1973), poet, involved in espionage for the
British government during the war.

10   My Dear, against your name.

        We planned a great Empire together, you and I,
        Bound only by the sea;
        Now in the quiet of a chill Winter's night
        Your voice comes hushed to me
15   Full of forgotten memories: you and I
        Dreamed great dreams of our future in those days,
        Setting our feet on undiscovered ways,
        And all I asked of fame
        A scarlet cross on my breast, my Dear,
20   For the swords by your name.

        We shall never shake the world together, you and I,
        For you gave your life away;
        And I think my heart was broken by the war,
        Since on a summer day
25   You took the road we never spoke of: you and I
        Dreamed greatly of an Empire in those days;
        You set your feet upon the Western ways
        And have no need of fame—
        There's a scarlet cross on my breast, my Dear,
30   And a torn cross with your name.

                                        December 1916

Rouen
26 April – 25 May 1915

        Early morning over Rouen, hopeful, high, courageous morning,
        And the laughter of adventure and the steepness of the stair,
        And the dawn across the river, and the wind across the bridges,
        And the empty littered station and the tired people there.

5   Can you recall those mornings and the hurry of awakening,
        And the long-forgotten wonder if we should miss the way,
        And the unfamiliar faces, and the coming of provisions,
        And the freshness and the glory of the labour of the day?

        Hot noontide over Rouen, and the sun upon the city,
10   Sun and dust unceasing, and the glare of cloudless skies,
        And the voices of the Indians and the endless stream of soldiers,
        And the clicking of the tatties, and the buzzing of the flies.

        Can you recall those noontides and the reek of steam and coffee,
        Heavy-laden noontides with the evening's peace to win,
15   And the little piles of Woodbines, and the sticky soda bottles,
        And the crushes in the "Parlour," and the letters coming in?

        Quiet night-time over Rouen, and the station full of soldiers,
        All the youth and pride of England from the ends of all the earth;
        And the rifles piled together, and the creaking of the sword-belts,
20   And the faces bent above them, and the gay, heart-breaking mirth.

Can I forget the passage from the cool white-bedded Aid Post
Past the long sun-blistered coaches of the khaki Red Cross train
To the truck train full of wounded, and the weariness and laughter,
And "Good-bye, and thank you, Sister," and the empty yards again?

25 Can you recall the parcels that we made them for the railroad,
Crammed and bulging parcels held together by their string,
And the voices of the sergeants who called the Drafts together,
And the agony and splendour when they stood to save the King?

Can you forget their passing, the cheering and the waving,
30 The little group of people at the doorway of the shed,
The sudden awful silence when the last train swung to darkness,
And the lonely desolation, and the mocking stars o'erhead?

Can you recall the midnights, and the footsteps of night watchers,
Men who came from darkness and went back to dark again,
35 And the shadows on the rail-lines and the all-inglorious labour,
And the promise of the daylight firing blue the window-pane?

Can you recall the passing through the kitchen door to morning,
Morning very still and solemn breaking slowly on the town,
And the early coastways engines that had met the ships at daybreak,
40 And the Drafts just out from England, and the day shift coming down?

Can you forget returning slowly, stumbling on the cobbles,
And the white-decked Red Cross barges dropping seawards for the tide,
And the search for English papers, and the blessed cool of water,
And the peace of half-closed shutters that shut out the world outside?

45 Can I forget the evenings and the sunsets on the island,
And the tall black ships at anchor far below our balcony,
And the distant call of bugles, and the white wine in the glasses,
And the long line of the street lamps, stretching Eastwards to the sea?

. . . When the world slips slow to darkness, when the office fire burns lower,
50 My heart goes out to Rouen, Rouen all the world away;
When other men remember I remember our Adventure
And the trains that go from Rouen at the ending of the day.

                                                        1916

—⬥≡⬥—

Pauline Barrington[1]

"Education"

The rain is slipping, dripping down the street;
The day is grey as ashes on the hearth.

---

1. Though details of her life are sketchy, Pauline Barrington's poetry was included in the important anthology *Poems Written During the Great War 1914–1918*, edited by Bertram Lloyd.

The children play with soldiers made of tin,
    While you sew
5   Row after row.

The tears are slipping, dripping one by one;
Your son has shot and wounded his small brother.
The mimic battle's ended with a sob,
    While you dream
10   Over your seam.

The blood is slipping, dripping drop by drop;
The men are dying in the trenches' mud.
The bullets search the quick among the dead.
    While you drift,
15   The Gods sift.

The ink is slipping, dripping from the pens,
On papers, White and Orange, Red and Grey,—
History for the children of tomorrow,—
    While you prate
20   About Fate.

War is slipping, dripping death on earth.
If the child is father of the man,
Is the toy gun father of the Krupps?
    For Christ's sake think!
25   While you sew
    Row after row.

1918

Helen Dircks[1]

After Bourlon Wood

In one of London's most exclusive haunts,
Amid the shining lights and table ware,
We sat, where meagre Mistress Ration flaunts
Herself in syncopated music there.

5   He was a Major twenty-six years old,
Back from the latest party of the Hun,
He said: "The beastly blighters had me bowled
Almost before the picnic had begun.

"By Jove! I was particularly cross,
10 I had looked forward to a little fling!

---

1. Helen Dircks's poems were published in her lifetime in the volumes *Finding* (1918) and *Passenger* (1920), from which "After Bourlon Wood" is taken.

(These censored wine lists have me at a loss.)
But what have you been doing, dear old thing?"

"I go to bed," I said, "at half-past ten,
And lead the life of any simple Waac—
15 Alas! a meatless, sweetless one—and then
I have a little joy when you come back.

"But mostly life is dull upon this isle,
And is inclined to be a trifle limp."
"I hate," he said, "the Hun to cramp my style,
20 We'll try and give it just a little crimp."

"On Saturday," I cried, "we stop at one:
To help you with the crimping would be grand!"
"Sorry," he said, "it simply can't be done,
I've got a most unpleasant job on hand."

25 "Unpleasant job!" I asked. "What do you mean?"
"I would," he said, "avoid it if I could,
But Georgius Rex, it seems, is awfully keen
To give me the M.C.[2] for being good."

1920

———— ✠ ————

Alys Fane Trotter[1]

The Hospital Visitor

When yesterday I went to see my friends—
    (Watching their patient faces in a row
I want to give each boy a D.S.O.)
When yesterday I went to see my friends
5 With cigarettes, and foolish odds and ends,
    (Knowing they understand how well I know
That nothing I can do may make amends,
    But that I must not grieve, or tell them so),
A pale-faced Iniskilling, just eighteen,
10   Who'd fought two years; with eyes a little dim
Smiled up and showed me, there behind the screen
    On the humped bandage that replaced a limb,
How someone left him, where the leg had been
    A tiny green glass pig to comfort him.

15 These are the men who've learned to laugh at pain.
    And if their lips have quivered when they spoke,

---

2. Military cross.

1. (1863–1961), writer, graphic artist, author of a history of South Africa.

They've said brave words, or tried to make a joke.
Said it's not worse than trenches in the rain,
Or pools of water on a chalky plain,
20   Or bitter cold from which you stiffly woke,
Or deep wet mud that left you hardly sane,
      Or the tense wait for "Fritz's master stroke."
You seldom hear them talk of their "bad luck,"
      And suffering has not spoiled their ready wit.
25   And oh! you'd hardly doubt their fighting pluck
      When each new operation shows their grit,
Who never brag of blows for England struck,
      But only yearn to "get about a bit."

1924

Teresa Hooley[1]

A War Film

I saw,
With a catch of the breath and the heart's uplifting,
Sorrow and pride,
    The "week's great draw"—
5   The Mons Retreat;
The "Old Contemptibles" who fought, and died,
The horror and the anguish and the glory.

As in a dream,
Still hearing machine-guns rattle and shells scream,
10   I came out into the street.

When the day was done,
My little son
Wondered at bath-time why I kissed him so,
Naked upon my knee.
15   How could he know
The sudden terror that assaulted me? . . .
The body I had borne
Nine moons beneath my heart,
A part of me . . .
20   If, someday,
It should be taken away
To War. Tortured. Torn.
Slain.
Rotting in No Man's Land, out in the rain—

---

1. (1888–1973), pseud. Mrs. F. H. Butler, Derbyshire writer.

25   My little son . . .
      Yet all those men had mothers, every one.

      How should he know
      Why I kissed and kissed and kissed him, crooning his name?
      He thought that I was daft.
30   He thought it was a game,
      And laughed, and laughed.

1927

━━┿ END OF PERSPECTIVES: THE GREAT WAR: CONFRONTING THE MODERN ┿━━

William Butler Yeats
1865–1939

William Butler Yeats, c. 1933.

Beginning his career as a poet during the languid 1880s and 1890s, William Butler Yeats fought, as Ezra Pound said of T. S. Eliot, to modernize himself on his own. At a time when Irish poetry seemed to be in danger of ossifying into a sentimental, self-indulgent luxury, Yeats instead forged a verse that would serve as an exacting instrument of introspection and national inquiry. As a consequence, all modern Irish writing—most clearly poetry, but prose, drama, and literary nonfiction as well—is directly in his debt.

Yeats was born in the Dublin suburb of Sandymount, but his spiritual home, the land of his mother Susan Pollexfen and her people, was the countryside of County Sligo. His father, John Butler Yeats, was an amateur philosopher, an insolvent painter, and a refugee from the legal profession; his grandfather and great-grandfather were both clergymen of the Church of Ireland. Through his mother's family, Yeats traced a close connection with the countryside of Ireland, and the myths and legends of the Irish people. Both parents belonged to the Anglo-Irish Protestant ascendancy, a heritage Yeats remained fiercely proud of all his life; but the success of his poetry, in part, lay in his ability to reconcile the British literary tradition with the native materials of the Irish Catholic tradition.

As he tells it in his autobiography, Yeats's childhood was not a happy one; in 1915 he wrote: "I remember little of childhood but its pain." His father, though a talented painter, lacked the ability to turn his gifts to profit; he would linger over a single portrait for months and sometimes years, revising ceaselessly. When Yeats was three, his father moved his family to London in order to put himself to school as a painter; their existence, though intellectually and artistically rich and stimulating, was quite straitened financially. The young Yeats found London sterile and joyless; fortunately for his imagination, and his future poetry, portions of each year were spent in the Sligo countryside, where Yeats spent time gathering the local folklore and taking long, wide-ranging walks and pony rides. The family remained in London until 1875, and had four more children (though one brother died in childhood). All his surviving siblings were to remain important to Yeats in his artistic life: his brother Jack B. Yeats became an important Irish painter, and his sisters Lily and Lolly together founded the Dun Emer Press, later called the Cuala Press, which published limited-edition volumes of some of Yeats's poetry.

In 1880 the family returned permanently to Ireland, settling first in Howth, in Dublin Bay; the city of Dublin, with its largely unsung history and tradition, fueled Yeats's imagination in a way that London never had. When the time for college came, Yeats was judged unlikely to pass Trinity College's entrance exams, and he was sent instead to the Metropolitan School of Art, apparently in preparation to follow in his father's footsteps. His true gift, it soon appeared, was not for drawing and painting but for poetry. He steeped himself in the Romantic poets, especially Shelley and Keats, as well as the English poet of Irish residence Edmund Spenser. His first poems were published in the *Dublin University Review* in March 1885.

Yeats's early work is self-evidently apprentice work; it draws heavily on the late-Romantic, Pre-Raphaelite ambience so important in the painting of his father and his father's colleagues. He also began to take an active interest in the various mystical movements that were then finding a foothold in Dublin and London, and with friends formed a Hermetic Society in Dublin as an antidote to the humanist rationalism to which his father was so passionately attached. At the same time—almost as a self-administered antidote to the teachings of mystics like the Brahmin teacher Mohini Chatterji—Yeats began to attend the meetings of several Dublin political and debating societies, and became increasingly interested in the nationalist artistic revival that would become known as the Irish Renaissance or Celtic Revival. Unlike most of his debating society comrades, Yeats imagined this political and cultural renaissance as resulting from a marriage of Blakean opposites: "I had noticed that Irish Catholics among whom had been born so many political martyrs had not the good taste, the household courtesy and decency of the Protestant Ireland I had known, yet Protestant Ireland seemed to think of nothing but getting on in the world. I thought we might bring the halves together if we had a national literature that made Ireland beautiful in the memory, and yet had been freed from provincialism by an exacting criticism, a European pose."

The Yeats family moved back to London in 1887; finances were difficult as ever, and Yeats contributed to the family's upkeep by editing two anthologies, *Poems and Ballads of Young Ireland* (1888) and *Fairy and Folk Tales of the Irish Peasantry* (1888). His own first collection of poems, *The Wanderings of Oisin and Other Poems*, was published in the following year; the poems are resolutely romantic, Yeats himself describing his manner at the time as "in all things Pre-Raphaelite." The poems were well received, but the praise of one reader in particular caught Yeats's attention. The statuesque beauty Maud Gonne appeared at Yeats's door with an introduction from the Irish revolutionary John O'Leary, and declared that the title poem had brought her to tears. It was a fateful meeting; throughout five decades Yeats continued to write to Gonne, for Gonne—the critic M. L. Rosenthal has suggested that "virtually every poem celebrating a woman's beauty or addressing a beloved woman has to do with her." Rosenthal might have added, every poem decrying the sacrifice of life to politics, including *No Second Troy, Easter 1916, A Prayer for My Daughter*, and others, all of which lament Gonne's increasing political fanaticism. This fanaticism, which Gonne considered simply patriotism, made impossible the spiritual and emotional consummation that Yeats so fervently desired. He proposed marriage, but she declined, marrying instead an Irish soldier who would later be executed for his role in the Easter Rising of 1916. Yeats is, among his other distinctions, a great poet of unrequited love.

The 1890s in London were heady times for a young poet. Yeats became even more active in his studies of the occult, studying with the charismatic Theosophist Madame Blavatsky and attending meetings of the Order of the Golden Dawn, a Christian cabalist society. The practical upshot of these activities for his later poetry was a confirmed belief in a storehouse of all human experience and knowledge, which he called variously the *Spiritus Mundi* and *Anima Mundi*, invoked in later poems like *The Second Coming* (1920). In 1891 Yeats, together with Ernest Rhys, founded the Rhymers' Club, which brought him into almost nightly contact with such important literary figures as Lionel Johnson, Ernest Dowson, Arthur Symons, and Oscar Wilde; during this same period, he established the Irish Literary Society in London, and the National Literary Society in Dublin. Clearly, something of a program for modern Irish poetry was beginning to emerge, even if Yeats himself wasn't yet quite ready to write it. Yeats also spent the years from 1887 to 1891 studying the writings of that most mystic of English poets,

William Blake; working with his father's friend Edwin Ellis, he produced an edition of and extended commentary on Blake's prophetic writings. Summing up the lesson of Blake's writings, Yeats wrote: "I had learned from Blake to hate all abstractions."

Romantic abstraction was easier to abjure in principle than in practice; Yeats's poetry of the 1890s still hankers after what one of his dramatis personae would later call "the loveliness that has long faded from the world." As one critic has written, "Early Yeats was the best poetry in English in late Victorian times; but they were bad times." Yeats began the process of throwing off the false manners of his Pre-Raphaelite upbringing with his play *The Countess Cathleen*, first performed by the Abbey Theatre, funded by subscriptions collected by his good friend Lady Augusta Gregory. Yeats's play, like Synge's *Playboy of the Western World* years later on that same stage, offended Irish sensibilities; in it, Cathleen sells her soul in order to protect Irish peasants from starvation. Yeats's volume *The Wind Among the Reeds* (1899) closes out the 1890s quite conveniently; it is ethereal, beautiful, and mannered. With this volume, Yeats's early phase comes to a close.

The early years of the twentieth century found Yeats concentrating his energies on the writing of poetic dramas, including, *The Pot of Broth* (1902) and *On Baile's Strand* (1904), for his fledgling Irish National Theatre. In 1903, the small Dun Emer Press published his volume of poems *In the Seven Woods*. These poems, including *Adam's Curse*, show Yeats working in a more spare idiom, the cadences and rhythms closer to those of actual speech—a consequence, some have argued, of his years writing for the stage. New poems published in *The Green Helmet and Other Poems* (1910) display Yeats as an increasingly mature and confident poet; his treatment of Maud Gonne in *No Second Troy*, for instance, shows a tragic acceptance of the fact that he will never have her, nor master her indomitable spirit. In *A Coat*, the poem that closes the 1914 collection *Responsibilities*, Yeats writes of the embroidered cloak he had fashioned for himself in his early poems, whose vanity is now brought home to him by the gaudiness of his imitators. He resolves, in the volume's closing lines, to set his cloak aside, "For there's more enterprise / In walking naked." This sense was strengthened by his close work, during the winter of 1912–1913, with Ezra Pound, in a cottage in rural Sussex. Both studied the stripped-down Japanese Noh drama and the Orientalist Ernest Fennollosa's work on the Chinese ideogram, and both men no doubt reinforced one another's increasing desire for a poetry that would be, in Pound's phrase, "closer to the bone."

The Easter Rising of 1916 took Yeats by surprise; he was in England at the time and complained of not having been informed in advance. A number of the rebel leaders were personal friends; he writes their names into Irish literature in *Easter 1916*, an excruciatingly honest, and ambivalent, exploration of the nature of heroism and nationalism. Yeats's mixed feelings about the revolution derived in part from a concern that some of his early writings, like the nationalist *Cathleen ní Houlihan*, might have contributed to the slaughter that followed in the wake of Easter 1916; as he wrote many years later, he couldn't help but wonder, "Did that play of mine send out / Certain men the English shot?"

The intricacies of Yeats's emotional and romantic life would require an essay of their own. His first marriage proposal to Maud Gonne in 1891, politely refused, set a pattern that was to remain in place for many years; though a number of poems try to reason through the affair, Yeats remained tragically attracted to this woman who did not return his affection, and multiple proposals were turned down as routinely as the first. He would have done as well, he was to write years later, to profess his love "to a statue in a museum." In the summer of 1917 things reached such a pass that Yeats proposed to Maud Gonne's adopted daughter Iseult; here, again, he was refused. Then, hastily, in October 1917 he married a longtime friend Georgiana ("George") Hyde-Lees. For all the tragicomedy leading up to the marriage, Yeats could not have chosen better; George was intelligent and sympathetic, and she brought the additional gift of an interest in mysticism and a facility in automatic writing that Yeats was soon to take full advantage of. Since early childhood, Yeats had heard voices speaking to him, and when he was twenty-one a voice commanded him "Hammer your thoughts into unity"; this charge had weighed on his mind for years, and his various experiments in mysticism and esoteric religions were intended to discover the system wherein his thoughts might be made to cohere.

With George, Yeats finally created that system on his own; its fullest exposition is found in *A Vision* (1928), though elements of it turn up in his poems beginning as early as *No Second Troy*. The system is complicated enough to fill out over 300 pages in the revised (1937) edition; at the heart of the system, though, is a simple diagram of two interpenetrating cones, oriented horizontally, such that the tip of each cone establishes the center of the base of the opposite cone. These two cones describe the paths of two turning gyres, or spirals, representing two alternating antithetical ages which make up human history. Yeats saw history as composed of cycles of approximately 2,000 years; his apocalyptic poem *The Second Coming*, for instance, describes the anxiety caused by the recognition that the 2,000 years of Christian (in Yeats's terms, "primary") values were about to be succeeded by an antithetical age—the "rough beast" of a time characterized by values and beliefs in every way hostile to those of the Christian era. For Yeats, however, as for William Blake, this vacillation and tension between contraries was not to be regretted; Blake taught that "without Contraries is no progression," and Yeats, that "all the gains of man come from conflict with the opposite of his true being."

Yeats's greatest phase begins with the poems of *Michael Robartes and the Dancer* (1921). His mytho-historical system informs a number of the poems written in the 1920s and after; it explains, for instance, why Yeats saw the brutal rape of Leda by Zeus in the form of a swan as a precursor of the traditional Christian iconography of the Virgin Mary "visited" by God the Father in the form of a dove. A logical corollary of Yeats's belief in historical recurrence was the philosophy, articulated best in his late poem *Lapis Lazuli*, of tragic joy: "All things fall and are built again, / And those that build them again are gay." In a letter inspired by the gift of lapis lazuli that the poem celebrates, Yeats wrote to a friend: "To me the supreme aim is an act of faith or reason to make one rejoice in the midst of tragedy." The influence of the writing of Nietzsche, whom Yeats had been reading, is apparent in these formulations.

While continuing to push at the boundaries of modern literature and modern poetry, Yeats also enjoyed the role of statesman. In the fall of 1922, Yeats was made a senator of the new Irish Free State; in 1923 he was awarded the Nobel Prize for literature, the first Irish writer ever to receive the award. The 1930s also saw Yeats flirt briefly with fascism, as did other writers like Pound and Wyndham Lewis. Yeats's belief in the importance of an aristocracy, and his disappointment over the excesses of revolutionary zeal demonstrated in the Irish civil war, for a time during the 1930s made the fascist program of the Irish Blueshirt movement look attractive. He composed *Three Songs to the Same Tune* as rallying songs for the Blueshirts, but the poems were too recherché for any such use. He soon became disillusioned with the party.

Yeats continued to write major poetry almost until his death; his growing ill health seems only to have made his poetry stronger and more defiant, as evidenced in such sinuous and clearsighted poems as *Lapis Lazuli* and the bawdy Crazy Jane poems. In the work published as *Last Poems* (1939), Yeats most satisfactorily put into practice what he had much earlier discovered in theory: that he must, as he wrote in *The Circus Animals' Desertion*, return for his poetry to "the foul rag-and-bone shop of the heart." After a long period of heart trouble, Yeats died on 28 January 1939; he was buried in Roquebrune, France, where he and George had been spending the winter. In 1948 he was reinterred, as he had wished, in Drumcliff churchyard near Sligo, where his grandfather and great-grandfather had served as rectors. Again according to his wishes, his epitaph is that which he wrote for himself in *Under Ben Bulben*:

> *Cast a cold eye*
> *On life, on death.*
> *Horseman, pass by!*

The Lake Isle of Innisfree[1]

I will arise and go now, and go to Innisfree,
And a small cabin build there, of clay and wattles° made: *woven twigs*
Nine bean-rows will I have there, a hive for the honey-bee,
And live alone in the bee-loud glade.

5   And I shall have some peace there, for peace comes dropping slow,
Dropping from the veils of the morning to where the cricket sings;
There midnight's all a glimmer, and noon a purple glow,
And evening full of the linnet's° wings.   *song bird*

I will arise and go now, for always night and day
10   I hear lake water lapping with low sounds by the shore;
While I stand on the roadway, or on the pavements grey,
I hear it in the deep heart's core.

1890   1890

Who Goes with Fergus?[1]

Who will go drive with Fergus now,
And pierce the deep wood's woven shade,
And dance upon the level shore?
Young man, lift up your russet brow,
5   And lift your tender eyelids, maid,
And brood on hopes and fear no more.

And no more turn aside and brood
Upon love's bitter mystery;
For Fergus rules the brazen° cars,   *brass*
10   And rules the shadows of the wood,
And the white breast of the dim sea
And all dishevelled wandering stars.

1893

No Second Troy[1]

Why should I blame her that she filled my days
With misery, or that she would of late
Have taught to ignorant men most violent ways,
Or hurled the little streets upon the great,
5   Had they but courage equal to desire?
What could have made her peaceful with a mind
That nobleness made simple as a fire,
With beauty like a tightened bow, a kind
That is not natural in an age like this,
10   Being high and solitary and most stern?

---

1. A small island in Lough Gill outside the town of Sligo, near the border with Northern Ireland.
1. The poem is a lyric from the second scene of Yeats's play *The Countess Cathleen*. Fergus was an ancient Irish

king who gave up his throne to feast, fight, and hunt.
1. Yeats here compares Maud Gonne to Helen of Troy; the Trojan War began from two kings' rivalry over Helen.

Why, what could she have done, being what she is?
Was there another Troy for her to burn?

1908   1910

The Fascination of What's Difficult

The fascination of what's difficult
Has dried the sap out of my veins, and rent
Spontaneous joy and natural content
Out of my heart. There's something ails our colt[1]
5   That must, as if it had not holy blood
Nor on Olympus leaped from cloud to cloud,
Shiver under the lash, strain, sweat and jolt
As though it dragged road metal. My curse on plays
That have to be set up in fifty ways,
10   On the day's war with every knave and dolt,
Theatre business, management of men.
I swear before the dawn comes round again
I'll find the stable and pull out the bolt.

1910   1910

September 1913[1]

What need you, being come to sense,
But fumble in a greasy till
And add the halfpence to the pence
And prayer to shivering prayer, until
5   You have dried the marrow from the bone;
For men were born to pray and save:
Romantic Ireland's dead and gone,
It's with O'Leary[2] in the grave.

Yet they were of a different kind,
10   The names that stilled your childish play,
They have gone about the world like wind,
But little time had they to pray
For whom the hangman's rope was spun,
And what, God help us, could they save?
15   Romantic Ireland's dead and gone,
It's with O'Leary in the grave.
Was it for this the wild geese[3] spread
The grey wing upon every tide;

1. Pegasus, winged horse of Greek mythology.
1. Yeats wrote the poem on 7 September 1913, and it was
published the following day in the *Irish Times*.
2. John O'Leary (1830–1907) was involved first in the
nationalist Young Ireland movement, and later went on
to cofound its successor, the Fenian movement. After
serving nine years of penal servitude for his republican
activities, he was exiled in Paris for 15 years, before being
allowed to return to Dublin in 1885. O'Leary was a friend
of Yeats's father, John Butler Yeats.
3. The "wild geese" were those Irishmen who fled Ireland
in the wake of the Penal Laws of 1691; many of them
fought as soldiers in the French, Spanish, and Austrian
armies. About 120,000 "wild geese" are thought to have
left Ireland between 1691 and 1730.

20 For this that all the blood was shed,
For this Edward Fitzgerald[4] died,
And Robert Emmet[5] and Wolfe Tone,[6]
All that delirium of the brave?
Romantic Ireland's dead and gone,
It's with O'Leary in the grave.

25 Yet could we turn the years again,
And call those exiles as they were
In all their loneliness and pain,
You'd cry, 'Some woman's yellow hair
Has maddened every mother's son':
30 They weighed so lightly what they gave.
But let them be, they're dead and gone,
They're with O'Leary in the grave.

The Wild Swans at Coole[1]

The trees are in their autumn beauty,
The woodland paths are dry,
Under the October twilight the water
Mirrors a still sky;
5 Upon the brimming water among the stones
Are nine-and-fifty swans.

The nineteenth autumn has come upon me
Since I first made my count;
I saw, before I had well finished,
10 All suddenly mount
And scatter wheeling in great broken rings
Upon their clamorous wings.

I have looked upon those brilliant creatures,
And now my heart is sore.
15 All's changed since I, hearing at twilight,
The first time on this shore,
The bell-beat of their wings above my head,
Trod with a lighter tread.

Unwearied still, lover by lover,
20 They paddle in the cold
Companionable streams or climb the air;
Their hearts have not grown old;
Passion or conquest, wander where they will,
Attend upon them still.

4. Lord Edward Fitzgerald (1763–1798) was a leader of the nationalist United Irishmen and died of wounds he received while being taken into custody by authorities.
5. Robert Emmet (1778–1803) led an unsuccessful revolt against the British government in 1803 and was hanged.
6. Theobald Wolfe Tone (1763–1798) led a friendly French force to Ireland to help oust the British in the ill-fated "year of the French" uprising in 1798. He was arrested and committed suicide while in prison awaiting execution.
1. Coole Park was the name of the estate of Yeats's patron Lady Gregory in Galway.

25   But now they drift on the still water,
Mysterious, beautiful;
Among what rushes will they build,
By what lake's edge or pool
Delight men's eyes when I awake some day
30   To find they have flown away?

1916   1917

An Irish Airman Foresees His Death[1]

I know that I shall meet my fate
Somewhere among the clouds above;
Those that I fight I do not hate,
Those that I guard I do not love;
5   My country is Kiltartan Cross,[2]
My countrymen Kiltartan's poor,
No likely end could bring them loss
Or leave them happier than before.
Nor law, nor duty bade me fight,
10   Nor public men, nor cheering crowds,
A lonely impulse of delight
Drove to this tumult in the clouds;
I balanced all, brought all to mind,
The years to come seemed waste of breath,
15   A waste of breath the years behind
In balance with this life, this death.

1918   1919

Easter 1916[1]

I have met them at close of day
Coming with vivid faces
From counter or desk among grey
Eighteenth-century houses.
5   I have passed with a nod of the head
Or polite meaningless words,
Or have lingered awhile and said
Polite meaningless words,
And thought before I had done
10   Of a mocking tale or a gibe°   *taunt*
To please a companion
Around the fire at the club,
Being certain that they and I
But lived where motley° is worn: *jester's outfit*
15   All changed, changed utterly:

1. The particular airman Yeats had in mind was Major Robert Gregory (1881–1918), only child of his dear friend Lady Augusta Gregory, who was killed in action in Italy during World War I.

2. The crossroads in Kiltartan, near the Gregory estate at Coole Park.
1. The Irish Republic was declared on Easter Monday, 24 April 1916.

A terrible beauty is born.
That woman's days were spent
In ignorant good-will,
Her nights in argument
20   Until her voice grew shrill.[2]
What voice more sweet than hers
When, young and beautiful,
She rode to harriers?°   *hunting dogs*
This man[3] had kept a school
25   And rode our wingèd horse;
This other[4] his helper and friend
Was coming into his force;
He might have won fame in the end,
So sensitive his nature seemed,
30   So daring and sweet his thought.
This other man[5] I had dreamed
A drunken, vainglorious lout.
He had done most bitter wrong
To some who are near my heart,
35   Yet I number him in the song;
He, too, has resigned his part
In the casual comedy;
He, too, has been changed in his turn,
Transformed utterly:
40   A terrible beauty is born.

Hearts with one purpose alone
Through summer and winter seem
Enchanted to a stone
To trouble the living stream.
45   The horse that comes from the road,
The rider, the birds that range
From cloud to tumbling cloud,
Minute by minute they change;
A shadow of cloud on the stream
50   Changes minute by minute;
A horse-hoof slides on the brim,
And a horse plashes within it;
The long-legged moor-hens dive,
And hens to moor-cocks call;
55   Minute by minute they live:
The stone's in the midst of all.

Too long a sacrifice
Can make a stone of the heart.

---

2. Countess Markiewicz, née Constance Gore-Booth, played a prominent part in the Easter Rising and was sentenced to be executed; her sentence was later reduced to imprisonment.
3. Padraic Pearse.

4. Thomas MacDonagh, poet executed for his role in the rebellion.
5. Major John MacBride, briefly married to Maud Gonne, was also executed.

60	O when may it suffice?
	That is Heaven's part, our part
	To murmur name upon name,
	As a mother names her child
	When sleep at last has come
	On limbs that had run wild.
65	What is it but nightfall?
	No, no, not night but death;
	Was it needless death after all?
	For England may keep faith
	For all that is done and said.
70	We know their dream; enough
	To know they dreamed and are dead;
	And what if excess of love
	Bewildered them till they died?
	I write it out in a verse—
75	MacDonagh and MacBride
	And Connolly[6] and Pearse
	Now and in time to be,
	Wherever green is worn,
	Are changed, changed utterly:
80	A terrible beauty is born.

1916   1916

The Second Coming[1]

Turning and turning in the widening gyre°   *circle or spiral*
The falcon cannot hear the falconer;
Things fall apart; the centre cannot hold;
Mere anarchy is loosed upon the world,
5   The blood-dimmed tide is loosed, and everywhere
The ceremony of innocence is drowned;
The best lack all conviction, while the worst
Are full of passionate intensity.

Surely some revelation is at hand;
10 Surely the Second Coming is at hand.
The Second Coming! Hardly are those words out
When a vast image out of *Spiritus Mundi*[2]
Troubles my sight: somewhere in sands of the desert
A shape with lion body and the head of a man,
15 A gaze blank and pitiless as the sun,
Is moving its slow thighs, while all about it
Reel shadows of the indignant desert birds.

6. James Connolly, Marxist commander-in-chief of the Easter rebels; also executed.
1. Traditionally, the return of Christ to earth on Judgment Day.

2. A storehouse of images and symbols common to all humankind; similar to Carl Jung's notion of the collective unconscious.

The darkness drops again; but now I know
That twenty centuries° of stony sleep   *the Christian era*
20   Were vexed to nightmare by a rocking cradle,
And what rough beast, its hour come round at last,
Slouches towards Bethlehem to be born?

1919   1921

A Prayer for My Daughter[1]

Once more the storm is howling, and half hid
Under this cradle-hood and coverlid
My child sleeps on. There is no obstacle
But Gregory's wood and one bare hill
5   Whereby the haystack- and roof-levelling wind,
Bred on the Atlantic, can be stayed;
And for an hour I have walked and prayed
Because of the great gloom that is in my mind.

I have walked and prayed for this young child an hour
10   And heard the sea-wind scream upon the tower,
And under the arches of the bridge, and scream
In the elms above the flooded stream;
Imagining in excited reverie
That the future years had come,
15   Dancing to a frenzied drum,
Out of the murderous innocence of the sea.

May she be granted beauty and yet not
Beauty to make a stranger's eye distraught,
Or hers before a looking-glass, for such,
20   Being made beautiful overmuch,
Consider beauty a sufficient end,
Lose natural kindness and maybe
The heart-revealing intimacy
That chooses right, and never find a friend.

25   Helen[2] being chosen found life flat and dull
And later had much trouble from a fool,
While that great Queen,[3] that rose out of the spray,
Being fatherless could have her way
Yet chose a bandy-leggèd smith[4] for man.
30   It's certain that fine women eat
A crazy salad with their meat
Whereby the Horn of Plenty is undone.
In courtesy I'd have her chiefly learned;
Hearts are not had as a gift but hearts are earned
35   By those that are not entirely beautiful;

1. Anne Butler Yeats was born 26 February 1919.
2. Helen of Troy, who left her husband Menelaus for Paris.
3. Aphrodite, Greek goddess of love, born from the sea.

4. Aphrodite's husband Hephaestus, the god of fire, was lame.

Yet many, that have played the fool
For beauty's very self, has charm made wise,
And many a poor man that has roved,
Loved and thought himself beloved,
40   From a glad kindness cannot take his eyes.

May she become a flourishing hidden tree
That all her thoughts may like the linnet° be,   *song bird*
And have no business but dispensing round
Their magnanimities of sound,
45   Nor but in merriment begin a chase,
Nor but in merriment a quarrel.
O may she live like some green laurel
Rooted in one dear perpetual place.

My mind, because the minds that I have loved,
50   The sort of beauty that I have approved,
Prosper but little, has dried up of late,
Yet knows that to be choked with hate
May well be of all evil chances chief.
If there's no hatred in a mind
55   Assault and battery of the wind
Can never tear the linnet from the leaf.

An intellectual hatred is the worst,
So let her think opinions are accursed.
Have I not seen the loveliest woman born
60   Out of the mouth of Plenty's horn,
Because of her opinionated mind
Barter that horn and every good
By quiet natures understood
For an old bellows full of angry wind?

65   Considering that, all hatred driven hence,
The soul recovers radical innocence
And learns at last that it is self-delighting,
Self-appeasing, self-affrighting,
And that its own sweet will is Heaven's will;
70   She can, though every face should scowl
And every windy quarter howl
Or every bellows burst, be happy still.

And may her bridegroom bring her to a house
Where all's accustomed, ceremonious;
75   For arrogance and hatred are the wares
Peddled in the thoroughfares.
How but in custom and in ceremony
Are innocence and beauty born?
Ceremony's a name for the rich horn,
80   And custom for the spreading laurel tree.

June 1919   1919

Sailing to Byzantium[1]

1

That is no country for old men. The young
In one another's arms, birds in the trees,
—Those dying generations—at their song,
The salmon-falls, the mackerel-crowded seas,
5   Fish, flesh, or fowl, commend all summer long
Whatever is begotten, born, and dies.
Caught in that sensual music all neglect
Monuments of unageing intellect.

2

An aged man is but a paltry thing,
10   A tattered coat upon a stick, unless
Soul clap its hands and sing, and louder sing
For every tatter in its mortal dress,
Nor is there singing school but studying
Monuments of its own magnificence;
15   And therefore I have sailed the seas and come
To the holy city of Byzantium.

3

O sages standing in God's holy fire
As in the gold mosaic of a wall,
Come from the holy fire, perne° in a gyre,   *spin*
20   And be the singing-masters of my soul.
Consume my heart away; sick with desire
And fastened to a dying animal
It knows not what it is; and gather me
Into the artifice of eternity.

4

25   Once out of nature I shall never take
My bodily form from any natural thing,
But such a form as Grecian goldsmiths make
Of hammered gold and gold enamelling
To keep a drowsy Emperor awake;—
30   Or set upon a golden bough to sing
To lords and ladies of Byzantium
Of what is past, or passing, or to come.

1926   1927

Leda and the Swan[1]

A sudden blow: the great wings beating still
Above the staggering girl, her thighs caressed

---

1. Constantinople, now called Istanbul, capital of the Byzantine Empire and the holy city of Eastern Christianity.
1. In Greek mythology, Zeus came to Leda in the form of a swan and raped her; Helen of Troy and Clytemnestra were their offspring.

By the dark webs, her nape caught in his bill,
He holds her helpless breast upon his breast.

5   How can those terrified vague fingers push
The feathered glory from her loosening thighs?
And how can body, laid in that white rush,
But feel the strange heart beating where it lies?

A shudder in the loins engenders there
10   The broken wall, the burning roof and tower
And Agamemnon[2] dead.
                              Being so caught up,
So mastered by the brute blood of the air,
Did she put on his knowledge with his power
Before the indifferent beak could let her drop?

1923   1924

Among School Children

1

I walk through the long schoolroom questioning;[1]
A kind old nun in a white hood replies;
The children learn to cipher and to sing,
To study reading-books and history,
5   To cut and sew, be neat in everything
In the best modern way—the children's eyes
In momentary wonder stare upon
A sixty-year-old smiling public man.

2

I dream of a Ledaean[2] body, bent
10   Above a sinking fire, a tale that she
Told of a harsh reproof, or trivial event
That changed some childish day to tragedy—
Told, and it seemed that our two natures blent
Into a sphere from youthful sympathy,
15   Or else, to alter Plato's parable,
Into the yolk and white of the one shell.[3]

3

And thinking of that fit of grief or rage
I look upon one child or t'other there
And wonder if she stood so at that age—

2. Brother of Menelaus, husband of Helen. When she was abducted by Paris, Agamemnon fought to rescue her. He was murdered by his wife Clytemnestra on his return home.
1. While an Irish senator, Yeats visited St. Otteran's School in Waterford.

2. Of Leda, the mother of Helen of Troy (or Helen herself).
3. According to Plato's parable in the *Symposium*, male and female were once the two halves of a single body; it was subsequently cut in half like a hard-boiled egg.

20   For even daughters of the swan can share
        Something of every paddler's heritage—
        And had that colour upon cheek or hair,
        And thereupon my heart is driven wild:
        She stands before me as a living child.

                            4

25   Her present image floats into the mind—
        Did Quattrocento[4] finger fashion it
        Hollow of cheek as though it drank the wind
        And took a mess of shadows for its meat?
        And I though never of Ledaean kind
30   Had pretty plumage once—enough of that,
        Better to smile on all that smile, and show
        There is a comfortable kind of old scarecrow.

                            5

        What youthful mother, a shape upon her lap
        Honey of generation had betrayed,
35   And that must sleep, shriek, struggle to escape
        As recollection or the drug decide,
        Would think her son, did she but see that shape
        With sixty or more winters on its head,
        A compensation for the pang of his birth,
40   Or the uncertainty of his setting forth?

                            6

        Plato thought nature but a spume° that plays   froth
        Upon a ghostly paradigm of things;
        Solider Aristotle played the taws[5]
        Upon the bottom of a king of kings;
45   World-famous golden-thighed Pythagoras[6]
        Fingered upon a fiddle-stick or strings
        What a star sang and careless Muses heard:
        Old clothes upon old sticks to scare a bird.

                            7

        Both nuns and mothers worship images,
50   But those the candles light are not as those
        That animate a mother's reveries,
        But keep a marble or a bronze repose.
        And yet they too break hearts—O Presences
        That passion, piety or affection knows,
55   And that all heavenly glory symbolise—
        O self-born mockers of man's enterprise;

---

4. Fifteenth-century artists of Italy's Renaissance.
5. A leather strap, used to spin a top.

6. A 6th-century B.C. Greek philosopher who developed a mathematical basis for the universe and music.

8

Labour is blossoming or dancing where
The body is not bruised to pleasure soul,
Nor beauty born out of its own despair,
60   Nor blear-eyed wisdom out of midnight oil.
O chestnut tree, great rooted blossomer,
Are you the leaf, the blossom or the bole?
O body swayed to music, O brightening glance,
How can we know the dancer from the dance?

1926   1927

Byzantium

The unpurged images of day recede;
The Emperor's drunken soldiery are abed;
Night resonance recedes, night-walkers' song
After great cathedral gong;
5   A starlit or a moonlit dome disdains
All that man is,
All mere complexities,
The fury and the mire of human veins.
Before me floats an image, man or shade,
10   Shade more than man, more image than a shade;
For Hades' bobbin° bound in mummy-cloth   *spool*
May unwind the winding path;
A mouth that has no moisture and no breath
Breathless mouths may summon;
15   I hail the superhuman;
I call it death-in-life and life-in-death.

Miracle, bird or golden handiwork,
More miracle than bird or handiwork,
Planted on the starlit golden bough,
20   Can like the cocks of Hades crow,
Or, by the moon embittered, scorn aloud
In glory of changeless metal
Common bird or petal
And all complexities of mire or blood.

25   At midnight on the Emperor's pavement flit
Flames that no faggot° feeds, nor steel has lit,   *bundle of sticks*
Nor storm disturbs, flames begotten of flame,
Where blood-begotten spirits come
And all complexities of fury leave,
30   Dying into a dance,
An agony of trance,
An agony of flame that cannot singe a sleeve.

Astraddle on the dolphin's mire and blood,
Spirit after spirit! The smithies break the flood,

35   The golden smithies of the Emperor!
Marbles of the dancing floor
Break bitter furies of complexity,
Those images that yet
Fresh images beget,
40   That dolphin-torn, that gong-tormented sea.

1930

1932

Crazy Jane Talks with the Bishop

I met the Bishop on the road
And much said he and I.
"Those breasts are flat and fallen now
Those veins must soon be dry;
5   Live in a heavenly mansion,
Not in some foul sty."

"Fair and foul are near of kin,
And fair needs foul," I cried.
"My friends are gone, but that's a truth
10   Nor grave nor bed denied,
Learned in bodily lowliness
And in the heart's pride.

"A woman can be proud and stiff
When on love intent;
15   But Love has pitched his mansion in
The place of excrement;
For nothing can be sole or whole
That has not been rent."

1931

1932

Lapis Lazuli[1]
(For Harry Clifton[2])

I have heard that hysterical women say
They are sick of the palette and fiddle-bow,
Of poets that are always gay,
For everybody knows or else should know
5   That if nothing drastic is done
Aeroplane and Zeppelin will come out,
Pitch like King Billy bomb-balls[3] in
Until the town lie beaten flat.

1. A rich blue mineral producing the pigment ultramarine; used by the ancients for decoration.
2. A friend who gave Yeats a carving in lapis lazuli on his birthday.
3. German bombs; "King Billy" is a nickname for Kaiser

Wilhelm II. Yeats may also mean to invoke King William I of England, "William of Orange," whose defeat of King James II at the Battle of the Boyne in 1690 resulted in the Protestant ascendancy in Ireland.

All perform their tragic play,
10   There struts Hamlet, there is Lear,
That's Ophelia, that Cordelia;[4]
Yet they, should the last scene be there,
The great stage curtain about to drop,
If worthy their prominent part in the play,
15   Do not break up their lines to weep.
They know that Hamlet and Lear are gay;
Gaiety transfiguring all that dread.
All men have aimed at, found and lost;
Black out; Heaven blazing into the head:
20   Tragedy wrought to its uttermost.
Though Hamlet rambles and Lear rages,
And all the drop scenes drop at once
Upon a hundred thousand stages,
It cannot grow by an inch or an ounce.

25   On their own feet they came, or on shipboard,
Camel-back, horse-back, ass-back, mule-back,
Old civilisations put to the sword.
Then they and their wisdom went to rack:
No handiwork of Callimachus[5]
30   Who handled marble as if it were bronze,
Made draperies that seemed to rise
When sea-wind swept the corner, stands;
His long lamp chimney shaped like the stem
Of a slender palm, stood but a day;
35   All things fall and are built again
And those that build them again are gay.

Two Chinamen, behind them a third,
Are carved in Lapis Lazuli,
Over them flies a long-legged bird
40   A symbol of longevity;
The third, doubtless a serving-man,
Carries a musical instrument.

Every discolouration of the stone,
Every accidental crack or dent
45   Seems a water-course or an avalanche,
Or lofty slope where it still snows
Though doubtless plum or cherry-branch
Sweetens the little half-way house
Those Chinamen climb towards, and I

---

4. Characters from *Hamlet* and *King Lear*.   5. Greek poet, grammarian, critic, and sculptor (c. 310–c. 240 B.C.).

50   Delight to imagine them seated there;
      There, on the mountain and the sky,
      On all the tragic scene they stare.
      One asks for mournful melodies;
      Accomplished fingers begin to play.
55   Their eyes mid many wrinkles, their eyes,
      Their ancient, glittering eyes, are gay.

1936   1938

The Circus Animals' Desertion

1

I sought a theme and sought for it in vain,
I sought it daily for six weeks or so.
Maybe at last being but a broken man
I must be satisfied with my heart, although
5   Winter and summer till old age began
My circus animals were all on show,
Those stilted boys, that burnished chariot,
Lion and woman and the Lord knows what.

2

What can I but enumerate old themes,
10   First that sea-rider Oisin[1] led by the nose
Through three enchanted islands, allegorical dreams,
Vain gaiety, vain battle, vain repose,
Themes of the embittered heart, or so it seems,
That might adorn old songs or courtly shows;
15   But what cared I that set him on to ride,
I, starved for the bosom of his fairy bride.

And then a counter-truth filled out its play,
"The Countess Cathleen"[2] was the name I gave it,
She, pity-crazed, had given her soul away
20   But masterful Heaven had intervened to save it.
I thought my dear must her own soul destroy
So did fanaticism and hate enslave it,
And this brought forth a dream and soon enough
This dream itself had all my thought and love.

25   And when the Fool and Blind Man stole the bread
Cuchulain[3] fought the ungovernable sea;
Heart mysteries there, and yet when all is said

---

1. Mythical Irish poet-warrior, son of the great Finn, who crossed the sea on an enchanted horse; hero of Yeats's early narrative poem *The Wanderings of Oisin*.
2. Yeats's play *Cathleen ní Houlihan* (1902) tells the traditional story of its title character, allegorical symbol of Ireland.
3. Hero of the medieval Irish epic *The Tain*, who single-handedly defended Ulster.

It was the dream itself enchanted me:
Character isolated by a deed
30 To engross the present and dominate memory.
Players and painted stage took all my love
And not those things that they were emblems of.

3

Those masterful images because complete
Grew in pure mind but out of what began?
35 A mound of refuse or the sweepings of a street,
Old kettles, old bottles, and a broken can,
Old iron, old bones, old rags, that raving slut
Who keeps the till. Now that my ladder's gone
I must lie down where all the ladders start
40 In the foul rag and bone shop of the heart.

1939

Under Ben Bulben[1]

1

Swear by what the Sages spoke
Round the Mareotic Lake[2]
That the Witch of Atlas[3] knew,
Spoke and set the cocks a-crow.

5   Swear by those horsemen, by those women
Complexion and form prove superhuman,
That pale, long-visaged company
That airs an immortality
Completeness of their passions won;
10 Now they ride the wintry dawn
Where Ben Bulben sets the scene.

Here's the gist of what they mean.

2

Many times man lives and dies
Between his two eternities,
15 That of race and that of soul,
And ancient Ireland knew it all.
Whether man dies in his bed
Or the rifle knocks him dead,
A brief parting from those dear
20 Is the worst man has to fear.

1. A mountain in County Sligo.
2. An ancient region south of Alexandria, Egypt, known
as a center of Neoplatonism.
3. *The Witch of Atlas* is the title of a poem by Percy Shelley.

Though grave-diggers' toil is long,
Sharp their spades, their muscle strong,
They but thrust their buried men
Back in the human mind again.

3

25   You that Mitchel's prayer have heard,
"Send war in our time, O Lord!"[4]
Know that when all words are said
And a man is fighting mad,
Something drops from eyes long blind,
30   He completes his partial mind,
For an instant stands at ease,
Laughs aloud, his heart at peace.
Even the wisest man grows tense
With some sort of violence
35   Before he can accomplish fate,
Know his work or choose his mate.

4

Poet and sculptor do the work,
Nor let the modish painter shirk
What his great forefathers did,
40   Bring the soul of man to God,
Make him fill the cradles right.

Measurement began our might:
Forms a stark Egyptian[5] thought,
Forms that gentler Phidias wrought.
45   Michael Angelo left a proof
On the Sistine Chapel roof,
Where but half-awakened Adam
Can disturb globe-trotting Madam
Till her bowels are in heat,
50   Proof that there's a purpose set
Before the secret working mind:
Profane perfection of mankind.

Quattrocento[6] put in paint
On backgrounds for a God or Saint
55   Gardens where a soul's at ease;
Where everything that meets the eye,
Flowers and grass and cloudless sky
Resemble forms that are, or seem

4. John Mitchel, revolutionary patriot, wrote "Give us war in our time, O Lord!" while in prison.
5. Plotinus, 3rd-century A.D. Egyptian-born philosopher, founder of Neoplatonism.
6. Fifteenth-century artists of Italy's Renaissance.

When sleepers wake and yet still dream,
60 And when it's vanished still declare,
With only bed and bedstead there,
That Heavens had opened.

Gyres run on;
When that greater dream had gone
Calvert and Wilson, Blake and Claude,[7]
65 Prepared a rest for the people of God,
Palmer's phrase,[8] but after that
Confusion fell upon our thought.

5

Irish poets learn your trade,
Sing whatever is well made,
70 Scorn the sort now growing up
All out of shape from toe to top,
Their unremembering hearts and heads
Base-born products of base beds.
Sing the peasantry, and then
75 Hard-riding country gentlemen,
The holiness of monks, and after
Porter-drinkers' randy° laughter;   *lusty*
Sing the lords and ladies gay
That were beaten into the clay
80 Through seven heroic centuries;[9]
Cast your mind on other days
That we in coming days may be
Still the indomitable Irishry.

6

Under bare Ben Bulben's head
85 In Drumcliff[1] churchyard Yeats is laid.
An ancestor was rector there
Long years ago; a church stands near,
By the road an ancient cross.
No marble, no conventional phrase,
90 On limestone quarried near the spot
By his command these words are cut:

> *Cast a cold eye*
> *On life, on death.*
> *Horseman, pass by!*

1938   1939

---

7. Edward Calvert (1799–1883), English painter and engraver, disciple of William Blake; Richard Wilson (1714–1782), British landscape painter; Claude Lorrain (1600–1682), French landscape painter.
8. Samuel Palmer (1805–1881), English painter of vision-ary landscapes and admirer of Blake.
9. I.e., the seven centuries since the conquest of Ireland by Henry II.
1. A village lying on the slopes of Ben Bulben, where Yeats was buried.

James Joyce
1882–1941

Man Ray (1890–1976), *Portrait of James Joyce*, 1922.

James Joyce was one of the great innovators who brought the novel into the modern era. As T. S. Eliot put it, Joyce made "the modern world possible for art." The poet Edith Sitwell wrote that by the turn of the century, "language had become, not so much an abused medium, as a dead and outworn thing, in which there was no living muscular system. Then came the rebirth of the medium, and this was effected, as far as actual vocabularies were concerned, very largely by such prose writers as Mr. James Joyce and Miss Gertrude Stein." Joyce objected to this flaccidity, citing examples in the work of George Moore, the most important Irish novelist of the first decade of the twentieth century; Moore's novel *The Untilled Field*, Joyce complained to his brother Stanislaus, was "damned stupid," "dull and flat," and "ill written." In a comment that would have pleased Joyce, one critic writing in 1929 declared that Joyce had by that date "conclusively reduced all the pretensions of the realistic novel to absurdity."

James Augustus Aloysius Joyce was born in Rathgar, a middle-class suburb of Dublin; though he was to leave Ireland more or less permanently at age twenty-two, Ireland generally, and "Dear Dirty Dublin" specifically, were never far from his mind and writing. He was the eldest surviving son in a large family consisting, according to his father, of "sixteen or seventeen children." His father, John Stanislaus Joyce, born and raised in Cork, was a tax collector and sometime Parnellite political employee; his mother was Mary Jane Joyce, née Murray. There is no better imaginative guide to the twists and turns of Joyce's family fortunes, and their effect on the young writer, than his first novel, *A Portrait of the Artist as a Young Man*; the life of Joyce's autobiographical hero Stephen Dedalus closely follows Joyce's own. The novel brings young Stephen from his earliest memories, through his Catholic schooling at Clongowes Wood College and Belvedere College, up to his graduation from University College, Dublin, and departure for Paris. Like Stephen, Joyce in these years first considered entering the priesthood, then began regarding Catholicism with increasing skepticism and irony, coming to view religion, family, and nation as three kinds of net or trap. One of the most important events of the early part of Joyce's life was the betrayal and subsequent death of "the uncrowned king of Ireland," Charles Stewart Parnell, the political leader who was working hard to make Home Rule for Ireland a reality; his demise, after his adulterous affair with Kitty O'Shea was discovered, was remembered by Joyce in his first poem, *Et Tu, Healy*—which he wrote at the age of eight—and in a haunting story, *Ivy Day in the Committee Room*. Joyce moved to Paris after graduation in 1902 and began medical studies, but he soon had to return to Dublin, as his mother was dying. Joyce gave up the idea of a medical career, which his father could not afford to finance in any event; he briefly tried teaching school and sought to define himself as a writer.

Like Dedalus, the young Joyce first concentrated on writing poetry. The majority of his early poems were collected in the volume *Chamber Music* (1907); both the strength and weakness of the poems is suggested by the praise of Arthur Symons, who in his review in the *Nation* described the lyrics as "tiny, evanescent things." Poetry was ultimately to prove a dead end for Joyce; though he brought out one more volume of thirteen poems during his lifetime (*Pomes Penyeach*, 1927), and wrote one forgettable play (*Exiles*, 1918), prose fiction is the primary area in which Joyce's influence continues to be felt.

The year 1904 proved to be an absolute watershed in Joyce's development as a writer. In January 1904—indeed, perhaps in the single day 7 January 1904—Joyce wrote an impressionistic prose sketch which would ultimately serve as the manifesto for his first novel. From this beginning, Joyce shaped his novel, which was to have been called *Stephen Hero;* and though he worked on it steadily for more than three years, and the manuscript grew to almost a thousand pages, the novel was not coming together in quite the way Joyce had hoped. Hence in the fall of 1907, he began cutting and radically reshaping the material into what would become *A Portrait of the Artist as a Young Man,* one of the finest examples of the *Künstlerroman* (novel of artistic growth) in English; H. G. Wells called it "by far the most living and convincing picture that exists of an Irish Catholic upbringing."

June 16, 1904, in particular is a crucial day in the Joycean calendar, for it is "Bloomsday"— the day on which the events narrated in *Ulysses* take place—and according to legend, it is the day that Nora Barnacle first agreed to go out walking with Joyce. Joyce's father thought Nora's maiden name a good omen, suggesting that she would "stick to him," and indeed she did; without the benefit of marriage, she agreed to accompany him four months later on his artistic exile to the Continent, and though they were not legally married until 1931, she proved a faithful and devoted partner, a small spot of stability amidst the chaos of Joyce's life. They settled for several years in Trieste, Italy, where Joyce taught English at a Berlitz school and where their two children, Giorgio and Lucia, were born. Joyce returned briefly to Ireland in 1909, seeking unsuccessfully to get work published and to start a movie theater; after another brief visit in 1912, he never returned. He spent most of World War I in Zurich, then moved to Paris, where he eked out an existence with the help of several benefactors as his reputation began to grow.

He had begun his first book in June or July 1904, invited by the Irish man of letters "A.E." (George Russell) to submit a short story to his paper *The Irish Homestead.* Joyce began writing the series of fifteen stories that would be published in 1914 as *Dubliners.* In letters to London publisher Grant Richards about his conception for the short stories, Joyce wrote that he planned the volume to be a chapter of Ireland's "moral history" and that in writing it he had "taken the first step towards the spiritual liberation of my country." Richards, however, objected to the stark realism—or sordidness—of several scenes, and pressed Joyce to eliminate vulgarisms; Joyce refused. Finally, desperate to have the book published, Joyce wrote to Richards: "I seriously believe that you will retard the course of civilisation in Ireland by preventing the Irish people from having one good look at themselves in my nicely polished looking-glass."

During this period, Joyce also experimented with a form of short prose sketch that he called the "epiphany." An epiphany, as it is defined in *Stephen Hero,* is "a sudden spiritual manifestation, whether in the vulgarity of speech or of gesture or in a memorable phase of the mind itself." It consequently falls to the artist to "record these epiphanies with extreme care, seeing that they themselves are the most delicate and evanescent of moments." One benefit of Joyce's experimentation with prose epiphanies is that the searching realism and psychological richness of the stories in *Dubliners* are conveyed with a lucid economy of phrasing—what Joyce called "a style of scrupulous meanness"—and by a similar penchant for understatement on the level of plot. The stories often seem to "stop," rather than end; time and again, Joyce withholds the tidy conclusion that conventional fiction had trained readers to expect. In story after story, characters betray what Joyce termed their "paralysis"—a paralysis of the will that prevents them from breaking out of deadening habit. The final story of the collection, *The Dead*—written after the volume had ostensibly been completed, and comprising a broader scope and larger cast of characters than the other stories—is Joyce's finest work of short fiction, and justly praised as one of the great stories of our time; it was filmed, quite sensitively and beautifully, by director John Huston, the last film project before his death.

A second decisive year for Joyce was 1914. Having completed *Dubliners,* Joyce seems never to have thought seriously about writing short fiction again; and throughout the period he was writing his stories, he continued to work on *A Portrait.* As was the case with *Dubliners,* negotiations for the publication of *A Portrait* were extremely difficult; despite its dazzling

Photo of Sackville Street (now O'Connell Street), Dublin, with view of Nelson's Pillar.

language, few editors could get beyond the opening pages, with their references to bedwetting and their use of crude slang. Even though the novel had been published serially in *The Egoist* beginning in 1914, and was praised by influential writers like W. B. Yeats, H. G. Wells, and Ezra Pound, the book was rejected by every publisher in London to whom Joyce offered it, before finally being accepted by B. W. Huebsch in New York, and published in December 1916.

With both his stories and his first novel between hard covers, Joyce was finally able to concentrate his energies on the one novel for which, more than any other, he will be remembered—*Ulysses;* that work, too, had begun in 1914. The novel is structured, loosely, on eighteen episodes from Homer's *Odyssey;* Leopold Bloom, advertising salesman, is a modern-day Ulysses, the streets of Dublin his Aegean Sea, and Molly Bloom his (unfaithful) Penelope. Stephen Dedalus, stuck teaching school and estranged from his real father, is an unwitting Telemachus (Ulysses' son) in search of a father. Critics have disagreed over the years as to how seriously readers should take these Homeric parallels; Eliot understood them to be of the utmost importance—"a way of controlling, of ordering, of giving a shape and a significance to the immense panorama of futility and anarchy which is contemporary history"—while the equally supportive Pound suggested that the parallel structure was merely "the remains of a medieval allegorical culture; it matters little, it is a question of cooking, which does not restrict the action, nor inconvenience it, nor harm the realism, nor the contemporaneity of the action."

Concomitant with the Homeric structure, Joyce sought to give each of his eighteen chapters its own style. Chapter 12, focusing on Bloom's encounter with Dublin's Cyclops, called "the Citizen," is written in a style of "gigantism"—full of mock-epic epithets and catalogues, playfully suggestive of the style of ancient Celtic myth and legend. Chapter 13, which parallels Odysseus's encounter with Nausicaa, is written in the exaggerated style of Victorian women's magazines and sentimental fiction, a style which Joyce characterized as "a namby-pamby jammy marmalady drawersy (alto-là!) style with effects of incense, mariolatry, masturbation, stewed cockles, painter's palette, chitchat, circumlocutions, etc etc." While realist writers sought constantly to flush artifice from their writing, to arrive finally at a style which would be value-neutral, Joyce takes the English language on a voyage in the opposite direction; each chapter, as he wrote to his patron Harriet Shaw Weaver, left behind it "a burnt-up field." It would be difficult to overestimate the influence that *Ulysses* has had on modern writing; Eliot's candid response to the novel, reported in a letter to Joyce, was "I have nothing but admiration; in fact, I wish, for my own sake, that I had not read it."

Other people wanted to make sure that no one else would read it. *Ulysses* was promptly banned as obscene, in Ireland, England, and many other countries. Copies were smuggled into the United States, where a pirated edition was published, paying Joyce no royalties. Finally in 1933, in a landmark decision, a federal judge found that the book's frank language and sexual discussions were fully justified artistically—though he allowed that "*Ulysses* is a rather strong draught to ask some sensitive, though normal, persons to take."

In 1923, with *Ulysses* completed, Joyce suddenly reinvented himself and his writing once again, and turned his attention to the writing of the novel that would occupy him almost until his death—*Finnegans Wake*. If *Ulysses* attacks the novel form at the level of style, *Finnegans Wake* targets the very structures of the English language. The story, in its broad outlines, is adapted from a vaudeville music-hall number, "Finnegan's Wake"; the novel's "protagonist," called by myriad names most of which bear the initials H.C.E. (Humphrey Chimpden Earwicker, Here Comes Everybody), has fallen in a drunken stupor, and the content of his dream is, apparently, the novel we read. But since the book is a night book, so Joyce felt that the language must be a night language, a meeting-place of dream and desire, rather than the straightforward language of the day. The novel's language is a neologismic amalgam of more than a dozen modern and ancient languages—a hybrid that devotees call "Wakese"; when questioned as to the wisdom of such a strategy, Joyce replied that *Ulysses* had proved English to be inadequate. "I'd like a language," he told his friend Stefan Zweig, "which is above all languages, a language to which all will do service. I cannot express myself in English without enclosing myself in a tradition." Though *Finnegans Wake* is of a complexity to frustrate even some of Joyce's most ardent admirers, interest in the novel has, if anything, increased in the wake of poststructuralist criticism, and shows no signs of letting up soon.

On 13 January 1941, Joyce died of a perforated ulcer; his illness and death almost certainly owed something to an adult life of rather heavy drinking and surely to the pain of his self-exile. Though his oeuvre consists largely of one volume of short stories and three novels, his importance for students of modern literature is extraordinary. As Richard Ellmann writes at the opening of his magisterial biography, "We are still learning to be James Joyce's contemporaries, to understand our interpreter."

from DUBLINERS

Araby

North Richmond Street, being blind,[1] was a quiet street except at the hour when the Christian Brothers' School set the boys free. An uninhabited house of two storeys stood at the blind end, detached from its neighbours in a square ground. The other houses of the street, conscious of decent lives within them, gazed at one another with brown imperturbable faces.

The former tenant of our house, a priest, had died in the back drawing-room. Air, musty from having been long enclosed, hung in all the rooms, and the waste room behind the kitchen was littered with old useless papers. Among these I found a few paper-covered books, the pages of which were curled and damp: *The Abbot*, by

1. A dead end.

Walter Scott,[2] *The Devout Communicant*[3] and *The Memoirs of Vidocq.*[4] I liked the last best because its leaves were yellow. The wild garden behind the house contained a central apple-tree and a few straggling bushes under one of which I found the late tenant's rusty bicycle-pump. He had been a very charitable priest; in his will he had left all his money to institutions and the furniture of his house to his sister.

When the short days of winter came dusk fell before we had well eaten our dinners. When we met in the street the houses had grown sombre. The space of sky above us was the colour of ever-changing violet and towards it the lamps of the street lifted their feeble lanterns. The cold air stung us and we played till our bodies glowed. Our shouts echoed in the silent street. The career of our play brought us through the dark muddy lanes behind the houses where we ran the gantlet[5] of the rough tribes from the cottages, to the back doors of the dark dripping gardens where odours arose from the ashpits, to the dark odorous stables where a coachman smoothed and combed the horse or shook music from the buckled harness. When we returned to the street light from the kitchen windows had filled the areas. If my uncle was seen turning the corner we hid in the shadow until we had seen him safely housed. Or if Mangan's sister came out on the doorstep to call her brother in to his tea we watched her from our shadow peer up and down the street. We waited to see whether she would remain or go in and, if she remained, we left our shadow and walked up to Mangan's steps resignedly. She was waiting for us, her figure defined by the light from the half-opened door. Her brother always teased her before he obeyed and I stood by the railings looking at her. Her dress swung as she moved her body and the soft rope of her hair tossed from side to side.

Every morning I lay on the floor in the front parlour watching her door. The blind was pulled down to within an inch of the sash so that I could not be seen. When she came out on the doorstep my heart leaped. I ran to the hall, seized my books and followed her. I kept her brown figure always in my eye and, when we came near the point at which our ways diverged, I quickened my pace and passed her. This happened morning after morning. I had never spoken to her, except for a few casual words, and yet her name was like a summons to all my foolish blood.

Her image accompanied me even in places the most hostile to romance. On Saturday evenings when my aunt went marketing I had to go to carry some of the parcels. We walked through the flaring streets, jostled by drunken men and bargaining women, amid the curses of labourers, the shrill litanies of shop-boys who stood on guard by the barrels of pigs' cheeks, the nasal chanting of street-singers, who sang a *come-all-you*[6] about O'Donovan Rossa,[7] or a ballad about the troubles in our native land. These noises converged in a single sensation of life for me: I imagined that I bore my chalice safely through a throng of foes. Her name sprang to my lips at moments in strange prayers and praises which I myself did not understand. My eyes were often full of tears (I could not tell why) and at times a flood from my heart seemed to pour itself out into my bosom. I thought little of the future. I did not know whether I would ever speak to her or not or, if I spoke to her, how I could tell her of my confused adoration. But my body was like a harp and her words and gestures were like fingers running upon the wires.

2. A romantic novel concerning Mary Queen of Scots, published in 1820.
3. A religious tract written by a Franciscan friar.
4. François Vidocq was chief of detectives with the Paris police in the early 19th century, before being dismissed from the force for falsifying records. He probably did not write the *Memoirs*.
5. Risk; challenge (variation of "gauntlet").
6. A popular type of ballad beginning with the formula, "Come all you Irishmen. . . ."
7. Jeremiah O'Donovan, an Irish nationalist exiled to the United States.

One evening I went into the back drawing-room in which the priest had died. It was a dark rainy evening and there was no sound in the house. Through one of the broken panes I heard the rain impinge upon the earth, the fine incessant needles of water playing in the sodden beds. Some distant lamp or lighted window gleamed below me. I was thankful that I could see so little. All my senses seemed to desire to veil themselves and, feeling that I was about to slip from them, I pressed the palms of my hands together until they trembled, murmuring: *O love! O love!* many times.

At last she spoke to me. When she addressed the first words to me I was so confused that I did not know what to answer. She asked me was I going to *Araby*. I forget whether I answered yes or no. It would be a splendid bazaar, she said; she would love to go.

—And why can't you? I asked.

While she spoke she turned a silver bracelet round and round her wrist. She could not go, she said, because there would be a retreat[8] that week in her convent. Her brother and two other boys were fighting for their caps and I was alone at the railings. She held one of the spikes, bowing her head towards me. The light from the lamp opposite our door caught the white curve of her neck, lit up her hair that rested there and, falling, lit up the hand upon the railing. It fell over one side of her dress and caught the white border of a petticoat, just visible as she stood at ease.

—It's well for you, she said.

—If I go, I said, I will bring you something.

What innumerable follies laid waste my waking and sleeping thoughts after that evening! I wished to annihilate the tedious intervening days. I chafed against the work of school. At night in my bedroom and by day in the classroom her image came between me and the page I strove to read. The syllables of the word *Araby* were called to me through the silence in which my soul luxuriated and cast an Eastern enchantment over me. I asked for leave to go to the bazaar on Saturday night. My aunt was surprised and hoped it was not some Freemason affair.[9] I answered few questions in class. I watched my master's face pass from amiability to sternness; he hoped I was not beginning to idle. I could not call my wandering thoughts together. I had hardly any patience with the serious work of life which, now that it stood between me and my desire, seemed to me child's play, ugly monotonous child's play.

On Saturday morning I reminded my uncle that I wished to go to the bazaar in the evening. He was fussing at the hallstand, looking for the hat-brush, and answered me curtly:

—Yes, boy, I know.

As he was in the hall I could not go into the front parlour and lie at the window. I left the house in bad humour and walked slowly towards the school. The air was pitilessly raw and already my heart misgave me.

When I came home to dinner my uncle had not yet been home. Still it was early. I sat staring at the clock for some time and, when its ticking began to irritate me, I left the room. I mounted the staircase and gained the upper part of the house. The high cold empty gloomy rooms liberated me and I went from room to room singing. From the front window I saw my companions playing below in the street. Their cries reached me weakened and indistinct and, leaning my forehead against the cool glass, I looked over at the dark house where she lived. I may have stood there for an hour, seeing nothing but the

---

8. A period of withdrawal for prayer, meditation, and religious study.

9. The Masonic Order was a guild thought to be an enemy of the Catholic Church.

brown-clad figure cast by my imagination, touched discreetly by the lamplight at the curved neck, at the hand upon the railings and at the border below the dress.

When I came downstairs again I found Mrs Mercer sitting at the fire. She was an old garrulous woman, a pawnbroker's widow, who collected used stamps for some pious purpose. I had to endure the gossip of the tea-table. The meal was prolonged beyond an hour and still my uncle did not come. Mrs Mercer stood up to go: she was sorry she couldn't wait any longer, but it was after eight o'clock and she did not like to be out late, as the night air was bad for her. When she had gone I began to walk up and down the room, clenching my fists. My aunt said:

—I'm afraid you may put off your bazaar for this night of Our Lord.

At nine o'clock I heard my uncle's latchkey in the halldoor. I heard him talking to himself and heard the hallstand rocking when it had received the weight of his overcoat. I could interpret these signs. When he was midway through his dinner I asked him to give me the money to go to the bazaar. He had forgotten.

—The people are in bed and after their first sleep now, he said.

I did not smile. My aunt said to him energetically:

—Can't you give him the money and let him go? You've kept him late enough as it is.

My uncle said he was very sorry he had forgotten. He said he believed in the old saying: *All work and no play makes Jack a dull boy*. He asked me where I was going and, when I had told him a second time he asked me did I know *The Arab's Farewell to his Steed*.[1] When I left the kitchen he was about to recite the opening lines of the piece to my aunt.

I held a florin[2] tightly in my hand as I strode down Buckingham Street towards the station. The sight of the streets thronged with buyers and glaring with gas recalled to me the purpose of my journey. I took my seat in a third-class carriage of a deserted train. After an intolerable delay the train moved out of the station slowly. It crept onward among ruinous houses and over the twinkling river. At Westland Row Station a crowd of people pressed to the carriage doors; but the porters moved them back, saying that it was a special train for the bazaar. I remained alone in the bare carriage. In a few minutes the train drew up beside an improvised wooden platform. I passed out on to the road and saw by the lighted dial of a clock that it was ten minutes to ten. In front of me was a large building which displayed the magical name.

I could not find any sixpenny entrance and, fearing that the bazaar would be closed, I passed in quickly through a turnstile, handing a shilling to a weary-looking man. I found myself in a big hall girdled at half its height by a gallery. Nearly all the stalls were closed and the greater part of the hall was in darkness. I recognised a silence like that which pervades a church after a service. I walked into the centre of the bazaar timidly. A few people were gathered about the stalls which were still open. Before a curtain, over which the words *Café Chantant*[3] were written in coloured lamps, two men were counting money on a salver.[4] I listened to the fall of the coins.

Remembering with difficulty why I had come I went over to one of the stalls and examined porcelain vases and flowered tea-sets. At the door of the stall a young lady was talking and laughing with two young gentlemen. I remarked their English accents and listened vaguely to their conversation.

---

1. A sentimental poem by Caroline Norton, in which the speaker imagines his despair upon selling his favorite horse.

2. A coin worth two shillings.
3. A café with musical entertainment.
4. A tray for food and drinks.

—O, I never said such a thing!

—O, but you did!

—O, but I didn't!

—Didn't she say that?

—Yes. I heard her.

—O, there's a. . . fib!

Observing me the young lady came over and asked me did I wish to buy anything. The tone of her voice was not encouraging; she seemed to have spoken to me out of a sense of duty. I looked humbly at the great jars that stood like eastern guards at either side of the dark entrance to the stall and murmured:

—No, thank you.

The young lady changed the position of one of the vases and went back to the two young men. They began to talk of the same subject. Once or twice the young lady glanced at me over her shoulder.

I lingered before her stall, though I knew my stay was useless, to make my interest in her wares seem the more real. Then I turned away slowly and walked down the middle of the bazaar. I allowed the two pennies to fall against the sixpence in my pocket. I heard a voice call from one end of the gallery that the light was out. The upper part of the hall was now completely dark.

Gazing up into the darkness I saw myself as a creature driven and derided by vanity; and my eyes burned with anguish and anger.

Eveline

She sat at the window watching the evening invade the avenue. Her head was leaned against the window curtains and in her nostrils was the odour of dusty cretonne.[1] She was tired.

Few people passed. The man out of the last house passed on his way home; she heard his footsteps clacking along the concrete pavement and afterwards crunching on the cinder path before the new red houses. One time there used to be a field there in which they used to play every evening with other people's children. Then a man from Belfast bought the field and built houses in it—not like their little brown houses but bright brick houses with shining roofs. The children of the avenue used to play together in that field—the Devines, the Waters, the Dunns, little Keogh the cripple, she and her brothers and sisters. Ernest, however, never played: he was too grown up. Her father used often to hunt them in out of the field with his blackthorn stick; but usually little Keogh used to keep nix[2] and call out when he saw her father coming. Still they seemed to have been rather happy then. Her father was not so bad then; and besides, her mother was alive. That was a long time ago; she and her brothers and sisters were all grown up; her mother was dead. Tizzie Dunn was dead, too, and the Waters had gone back to England. Everything changes. Now she was going to go away like the others, to leave her home.

Home! She looked round the room, reviewing all its familiar objects which she had dusted once a week for so many years, wondering where on earth all the dust came from. Perhaps she would never see again those familiar objects from which she had never dreamed of being divided. And yet during all those years she had never found out the name of the priest whose yellowing photograph hung on the wall

---

1. Heavy cotton fabric.   2. To serve as a lookout.

above the broken harmonium[3] beside the coloured print of the promises made to
Blessed Margaret Mary Alacoque.[4] He had been a school friend of her father. Whenever he showed the photograph to a visitor her father used to pass it with a casual
word:

—He is in Melbourne now.

She had consented to go away, to leave her home. Was that wise? She tried to
weigh each side of the question. In her home anyway she had shelter and food; she
had those whom she had known all her life about her. Of course she had to work hard
both in the house and at business. What would they say of her in the Stores when
they found out that she had run away with a fellow? Say she was a fool, perhaps; and
her place would be filled up by advertisement. Miss Gavan would be glad. She had always had an edge on her, especially whenever there were people listening.

—Miss Hill, don't you see these ladies are waiting?

—Look lively, Miss Hill, please.

She would not cry many tears at leaving the Stores.

But in her new home, in a distant unknown country, it would not be like that.
Then she would be married—she, Eveline. People would treat her with respect then.
She would not be treated as her mother had been. Even now, though she was over
nineteen, she sometimes felt herself in danger of her father's violence. She knew it
was that that had given her the palpitations. When they were growing up he had
never gone for her, like he used to go for Harry and Ernest, because she was a girl; but
latterly he had begun to threaten her and say what he would do to her only for her
dead mother's sake. And now she had nobody to protect her. Ernest was dead and
Harry, who was in the church decorating business, was nearly always down somewhere in the country. Besides, the invariable squabble for money on Saturday nights
had begun to weary her unspeakably. She always gave her entire wages—seven
shillings—and Harry always sent up what he could but the trouble was to get any
money from her father. He said she used to squander the money, that she had no
head, that he wasn't going to give her his hard-earned money to throw about the
streets, and much more, for he was usually fairly bad of a Saturday night. In the end
he would give her the money and ask her had she any intention of buying Sunday's
dinner. Then she had to rush out as quickly as she could and do her marketing, holding her black leather purse tightly in her hand as she elbowed her way through the
crowds and returning home late under her load of provisions. She had hard work to
keep the house together and to see that the two young children who had been left to
her charge went to school regularly and got their meals regularly. It was hard work—
a hard life—but now that she was about to leave it she did not find it a wholly unde-
sirable life.

She was about to explore another life with Frank. Frank was very kind, manly,
open-hearted. She was to go away with him by the night-boat to be his wife and to
live with him in Buenos Ayres where he had a home waiting for her. How well she
remembered the first time she had seen him; he was lodging in a house on the main
road where she used to visit. It seemed a few weeks ago. He was standing at the gate,
his peaked cap pushed back on his head and his hair tumbled forward over a face of
bronze. Then they had come to know each other. He used to meet her outside the

3. A small reed organ.
4. Catholic saint who took a vow of chastity at age four
and carved the name "Jesus" into her chest with a knife as
an adolescent. In 1673 she experienced a series of revelations; these resulted in the founding of the Devotion to
the Sacred Heart of Jesus.

Stores every evening and see her home. He took her to see *The Bohemian Girl*[5] and she felt elated as she sat in an unaccustomed part of the theatre with him. He was awfully fond of music and sang a little. People knew that they were courting and, when he sang about the lass that loves a sailor, she always felt pleasantly confused. He used to call her Poppens out of fun. First of all it had been an excitement for her to have a fellow and then she had begun to like him. He had tales of distant countries. He had started as a deck boy at a pound a month on a ship of the Allan Line going out to Canada. He told her the names of the ships he had been on and the names of the different services. He had sailed through the Straits of Magellan and he told her stories of the terrible Patagonians.[6] He had fallen on his feet in Buenos Ayres, he said, and had come over to the old country just for a holiday. Of course, her father had found out the affair and had forbidden her to have anything to say to him.

—I know these sailor chaps, he said.

One day he had quarrelled with Frank and after that she had to meet her lover secretly.

The evening deepened in the avenue. The white of two letters in her lap grew indistinct. One was to Harry; the other was to her father. Ernest had been her favorite but she liked Harry too. Her father was becoming old lately, she noticed; he would miss her. Sometimes he could be very nice. Not long before, when she had been laid up for a day, he had read her out a ghost story and made toast for her at the fire. Another day, when their mother was alive, they had all gone for a picnic to the Hill of Howth.[7] She remembered her father putting on her mother's bonnet to make the children laugh.

Her time was running out but she continued to sit by the window, leaning her head against the window curtain, inhaling the odour of dusty cretonne. Down far in the avenue she could hear a street organ playing. She knew the air.[8] Strange that it should come that very night to remind her of the promise to her mother, her promise to keep the home together as long as she could. She remembered the last night of her mother's illness; she was again in the close dark room at the other side of the hall and outside she heard a melancholy air of Italy. The organ-player had been ordered to go away and given sixpence. She remembered her father strutting back into the sickroom saying:

—Damned Italians! coming over here!

As she mused the pitiful vision of her mother's life laid its spell on the very quick of her being—that life of commonplace sacrifices closing in final craziness. She trembled as she heard again her mother's voice saying constantly with foolish insistence:

—Derevaun Seraun! Derevaun Seraun![9]

She stood up in a sudden impulse of terror. Escape! She must escape! Frank would save her. He would give her life, perhaps love, too. But she wanted to live. Why should she be unhappy? She had a right to happiness. Frank would take her in his arms, fold her in his arms. He would save her.

She stood among the swaying crowd in the station at the North Wall.[1] He held her hand and she knew that he was speaking to her, saying something about the passage

---

5. An opera (1843) by Irish composer Michael William Balfe, based on a tale by Cervantes about a rich girl kidnapped by gypsies and an exiled nobleman.
6. Native peoples of Southern Argentina.
7. Northeast of Dublin, the hill dominates Dublin Bay.
8. Tune.

9. Though some commentators have suggested the phrase is Irish, it seems more likely to be incoherent nonsense.
1. A point of embarkation in Dublin for passenger ships—but those, as critic Hugh Kenner points out, heading for Liverpool, not Buenos Aires.

over and over again. The station was full of soldiers with brown baggages. Through the wide doors of the sheds she caught a glimpse of the black mass of the boat, lying in beside the quay wall, with illumined portholes. She answered nothing. She felt her cheek pale and cold and, out of a maze of distress, she prayed to God to direct her, to show her what was her duty. The boat blew a long mournful whistle into the mist. If she went, tomorrow she would be on the sea with Frank, steaming toward Buenos Ayres. Their passage had been booked. Could she still draw back after all he had done for her? Her distress awoke a nausea in her body and she kept moving her lips in silent fervent prayer.

A bell clanged upon her heart. She felt him seize her hand:

—Come!

All the seas of the world tumbled about her heart. He was drawing her into them: he would drown her. She gripped with both hands at the iron railing.

—Come!

No! No! No! It was impossible. Her hands clutched the iron in frenzy. Amid the seas she sent a cry of anguish!

—Eveline! Evvy!

He rushed beyond the barrier and called to her to follow. He was shouted at to go on but he still called to her. She set her white face to him, passive, like a helpless animal. Her eyes gave him no sign of love or farewell or recognition.

Clay

The matron had given her leave to go out as soon as the women's tea was over and Maria looked forward to her evening out. The kitchen was spick and span: the cook said you could see yourself in the big copper boilers. The fire was nice and bright and on one of the side-tables were four very big barmbracks.[1] These barmbracks seemed uncut; but if you went closer you would see that they had been cut into long thick even slices and were ready to be handed round at tea. Maria had cut them herself.

Maria was a very, very small person indeed but she had a very long nose and a very long chin. She talked a little through her nose, always soothingly: *Yes, my dear,* and *No, my dear.* She was always sent for when the women quarrelled over their tubs and always succeeded in making peace. One day the matron had said to her:

—Maria, you are a veritable peace-maker!

And the sub-matron and two of the Board ladies[2] had heard the compliment. And Ginger Mooney was always saying what she wouldn't do to the dummy[3] who had charge of the irons if it wasn't for Maria. Everyone was so fond of Maria.

The women would have their tea at six o'clock and she would be able to get away before seven. From Ballsbridge to the Pillar, twenty minutes; from the Pillar to Drumcondra, twenty minutes; and twenty minutes to buy the things. She would be there before eight. She took out her purse with the silver clasps and read again the words *A Present from Belfast.* She was very fond of that purse because Joe had brought it to her five years before when he and Alphy had gone to Belfast on a Whit-Monday[4] trip. In the purse were two half-crowns and some coppers. She would have five shillings clear after paying tram fare. What a nice evening they would have, all the children singing! Only she hoped that Joe wouldn't come in drunk. He was so different when he took any drink.

---

1. Speckled cakes or currant buns.
2. Members of the governing board of the Dublin by Lamplight Laundry.
3. Slang for a mute person.
4. Holiday following Whitsunday, the seventh Sunday after Easter.

Often he had wanted her to go and live with them; but she would have felt herself in the way (though Joe's wife was ever so nice with her) and she had become accustomed to the life of the laundry. Joe was a good fellow. She had nursed him and Alphy too; and Joe used often say:

—Mamma is mamma but Maria is my proper mother.

After the break-up at home the boys had got her that position in the *Dublin by Lamplight* laundry,[5] and she liked it. She used to have such a bad opinion of Protestants but now she thought they were very nice people, a little quiet and serious, but still very nice people to live with. Then she had her plants in the conservatory and she liked looking after them. She had lovely ferns and wax-plants and, whenever anyone came to visit her, she always gave the visitor one or two slips from her conservatory. There was one thing she didn't like and that was the tracts[6] on the walls; but the matron was such a nice person to deal with, so genteel.

When the cook told her everything was ready she went into the women's room and began to pull the big bell. In a few minutes the women began to come in by twos and threes, wiping their steaming hands in their petticoats and pulling down the sleeves of their blouses over their red steaming arms. They settled down before their huge mugs which the cook and the dummy filled up with hot tea, already mixed with milk and sugar in huge tin cans. Maria superintended the distribution of the barmbrack and saw that every woman got her four slices. There was a great deal of laughing and joking during the meal. Lizzie Fleming said Maria was sure to get the ring and, though Fleming had said that for so many Hallow Eves, Maria had to laugh and say she didn't want any ring or man either; and when she laughed her grey-green eyes sparkled with disappointed shyness and the tip of her nose nearly met the tip of her chin. Then Ginger Mooney lifted up her mug of tea and proposed Maria's health while all the other women clattered with their mugs on the table, and said she was sorry she hadn't a sup of porter[7] to drink it in. And Maria laughed again till the tip of her nose nearly met the tip of her chin and till her minute body nearly shook itself asunder because she knew that Mooney meant well though, of course, she had the notions of a common woman.

But wasn't Maria glad when the women had finished their tea and the cook and the dummy had begun to clear away the tea-things! She went into her little bedroom and, remembering that the next morning was a mass morning, changed the hand of the alarm from seven to six. Then she took off her working skirt and her house-boots and laid her best skirt out on the bed and her tiny dress-boots beside the foot of the bed. She changed her blouse too and, as she stood before the mirror, she thought of how she used to dress for mass on Sunday morning when she was a young girl; and she looked with quaint affection at the diminutive body which she had so often adorned. In spite of its years she found it a nice tidy little body.

When she got outside the streets were shining with rain and she was glad of her old brown raincloak. The tram was full and she had to sit on the little stool at the end of the car, facing all the people, with her toes barely touching the floor. She arranged in her mind all she was going to do and thought how much better it was to be independent and to have your own money in your pocket. She hoped they would

5. Joyce's invented benevolent society, run by Protestant women, "saves" Dublin's prostitutes from a life on the streets by giving them honest work in a laundry. Maria works for the laundry but appears not to be a reformed prostitute herself.
6. Evangelical religious texts.
7. A heavy, dark brown ale.

have a nice evening. She was sure they would but she could not help thinking what a pity it was Alphy and Joe were not speaking. They were always falling out now but when they were boys together they used to be the best of friends: but such was life.

She got out of her tram at the Pillar and ferreted her way quickly among the crowds. She went into Downes's cakeshop but the shop was so full of people that it was a long time before she could get herself attended to. She bought a dozen of mixed penny cakes, and at last came out of the shop laden with a big bag. Then she thought what else would she buy: she wanted to buy something really nice. They would be sure to have plenty of apples and nuts. It was hard to know what to buy and all she could think of was cake. She decided to buy some plumcake but Downes's plumcake had not enough almond icing on top of it so she went over to a shop in Henry Street. Here she was a long time in suiting herself and the stylish young lady behind the counter, who was evidently a little annoyed by her, asked her was it wedding-cake she wanted to buy. That made Maria blush and smile at the young lady; but the young lady took it all very seriously and finally cut a thick slice of plumcake, parcelled it up and said:

—Two-and-four, please.

She thought she would have to stand in the Drumcondra tram because none of the young men seemed to notice her but an elderly gentleman made room for her. He was a stout gentleman and he wore a brown hard hat; he had a square red face and a greyish moustache. Maria thought he was a colonel-looking gentleman and she reflected how much more polite he was than the young men who simply stared straight before them. The gentleman began to chat with her about Hallow Eve and the rainy weather. He supposed the bag was full of good things for the little ones and said it was only right that the youngsters should enjoy themselves while they were young. Maria agreed with him and favoured him with demure nods and hems. He was very nice with her, and when she was getting out at the Canal Bridge she thanked him and bowed, and he bowed to her and raised his hat and smiled agreeably; and while she was going up along the terrace, bending her tiny head under the rain, she thought how easy it was to know a gentleman even when he has a drop taken.

Everybody said: O, here's Maria! when she came to Joe's house. Joe was there, having come home from business, and all the children had their Sunday dresses on. There were two big girls in from next door and games were going on. Maria gave the bag of cakes to the eldest boy, Alphy, to divide and Mrs Donnelly said it was too good of her to bring such a big bag of cakes and made all the children say:

—Thanks, Maria.

But Maria said she had brought something special for papa and mamma, something they would be sure to like, and she began to look for her plumcake. She tried in Downes's bag and then in the pockets of her raincloak and then on the hallstand but nowhere could she find it. Then she asked all the children had any of them eaten it—by mistake, of course—but the children all said no and looked as if they did not like to eat cakes if they were to be accused of stealing. Everybody had a solution for the mystery and Mrs Donnelly said it was plain that Maria had left it behind her in the tram. Maria, remembering how confused the gentleman with the greyish moustache had made her, coloured with shame and vexation and disappointment. At the thought of the failure of her little surprise and of the two and fourpence she had thrown away for nothing she nearly cried outright.

But Joe said it didn't matter and made her sit down by the fire. He was very nice with her. He told her all that went on in his office, repeating for her a smart answer which he had made to the manager. Maria did not understand why Joe laughed so much over the answer he had made but she said that the manager must have been a very overbearing person to deal with. Joe said he wasn't so bad when you knew how to take him, that he was a decent sort so long as you didn't rub him the wrong way. Mrs Donnelly played the piano for the children and they danced and sang. Then the two next-door girls handed round the nuts. Nobody could find the nutcrackers and Joe was nearly getting cross over it and asked how did they expect Maria to crack nuts without a nutcracker. But Maria said she didn't like nuts and that they weren't to bother about her. Then Joe asked would she take a bottle of stout[8] and Mrs Donnelly said there was port wine too in the house if she would prefer that. Maria said she would rather they didn't ask her to take anything: but Joe insisted.

So Maria let him have his way and they sat by the fire talking over old times and Maria thought she would put in a good word for Alphy. But Joe cried that God might strike him stone dead if ever he spoke a word to his brother again and Maria said she was sorry she had mentioned the matter. Mrs Donnelly told her husband it was a great shame for him to speak that way of his own flesh and blood but Joe said that Alphy was no brother of his and there was nearly being a row[9] on the head of it. But Joe said he would not lose his temper on account of the night it was and asked his wife to open some more stout. The two next-door girls had arranged some Hallow Eve games[1] and soon everything was merry again. Maria was delighted to see the children so merry and Joe and his wife in such good spirits. The next-door girls put some saucers on the table and then led the children up to the table, blindfold. One got the prayer-book and the other three got the water; and when one of the next-door girls got the ring Mrs Donnelly shook her finger at the blushing girl as much as to say: O, *I know all about it!* They insisted then on blindfolding Maria and leading her up to the table to see what she would get; and, while they were putting on the bandage, Maria laughed and laughed again till the tip of her nose nearly met the tip of her chin.

They led her up to the table amid laughing and joking and she put her hand out in the air as she was told to do. She moved her hand about here and there in the air and descended on one of the saucers. She felt a soft wet substance with her fingers and was surprised that nobody spoke or took off her bandage. There was a pause for a few seconds; and then a great deal of scuffling and whispering. Somebody said something about the garden, and at last Mrs Donnelly said something very cross to one of the next-door girls and told her to throw it out at once: that was no play. Maria understood that it was wrong that time and so she had to do it over again: and this time she got the prayer-book.

After that Mrs Donnelly played Miss McCloud's Reel for the children and Joe made Maria take a glass of wine. Soon they were all quite merry again and Mrs Donnelly said Maria would enter a convent before the year was out because she had got the prayer-book. Maria had never seen Joe so nice to her as he was that night, so full of pleasant talk and reminiscences. She said they were all very good to her.

At last the children grew tired and sleepy and Joe asked Maria would she not sing some little song before she went, one of the old songs. Mrs Donnelly said *Do, please,*

---

8. A dark, full-bodied beer.
9. Argument.
1. The primary game that Maria and the girls play is a traditional Irish Halloween game. In its original version, a blindfolded girl would be led to three plates, and would choose one. Choosing the plate with a ring meant that she would soon marry; water meant she would emigrate (probably to America); and soil, or clay, meant she would soon die. In modern times, a prayer book was substituted for this unsavory third option, suggesting that the girl would enter a convent.

Maria! and so Maria had to get up and stand beside the piano. Mrs Donnelly bade the children be quiet and listen to Maria's song. Then she played the prelude and said *Now, Maria!* and Maria, blushing very much, began to sing in a tiny quavering voice. She sang *I Dreamt that I Dwelt*,[2] and when she came to the second verse she sang again:

> *I dreamt that I dwelt in marble halls*
> > *With vassals and serfs at my side*
> *And of all who assembled within those walls*
> > *That I was the hope and the pride.*
> *I had riches too great to count, could boast*
> > *Of a high ancestral name,*
> *But I also dreamt, which pleased me most,*
> > *That you loved me still the same.*

But no one tried to show her her mistake;[3] and when she had ended her song Joe was very much moved. He said that there was no time like the long ago and no music for him like poor old Balfe, whatever other people might say; and his eyes filled up so much with tears that he could not find what he was looking for and in the end he had to ask his wife to tell him where the corkscrew was.

The Dead

Lily, the caretaker's daughter, was literally run off her feet. Hardly had she brought one gentleman into the little pantry behind the office on the ground floor and helped him off with his overcoat than the wheezy hall-door bell clanged again and she had to scamper along the bare hallway to let in another guest. It was well for her she had not to attend to the ladies also. But Miss Kate and Miss Julia had thought of that and had converted the bathroom upstairs into a ladies' dressing-room. Miss Kate and Miss Julia were there, gossiping and laughing and fussing, walking after each other to the head of the stairs, peering down over the banisters and calling down to Lily to ask her who had come.

It was always a great affair, the Misses Morkan's annual dance. Everybody who knew them came to it, members of the family, old friends of the family, the members of Julia's choir, any of Kate's pupils that were grown up enough and even some of Mary Jane's pupils too. Never once had it fallen flat. For years and years it had gone off in splendid style as long as anyone could remember; ever since Kate and Julia, after the death of their brother Pat, had left the house in Stoney Batter[1] and taken Mary Jane, their only niece, to live with them in the dark gaunt house on Usher's Island,[2] the upper part of which they had rented from Mr Fulham, the cornfactor on the ground floor. That was a good thirty years ago if it was a day. Mary Jane, who was then a little girl in short clothes, was now the main prop of the household for she had the organ in Haddington Road.[3] She had been through the Academy[4] and gave a pupils' concert every year in the upper room of the Antient Concert Rooms. Many of her pupils belonged to better-class families on the Kingstown and Dalkey line.[5] Old as they were, her aunts also did their share. Julia, though she was quite grey, was still

---

2. Aria from Act 2 of *The Bohemian Girl*.
3. Maria repeats the first verse rather than singing the second.
1. A district in northwest Dublin.
2. Two adjoining quays on the south side of the River

Liffey.
3. Played the organ in a church on the Haddington Road.
4. Royal Academy of Music.
5. The train line connecting Dublin to the affluent suburbs south of the city.

the leading soprano in Adam and Eve's,[6] and Kate, being too feeble to go about much, gave music lessons to beginners on the old square piano in the back room. Lily, the caretaker's daughter, did housemaid's work for them. Though their life was modest they believed in eating well; the best of everything: diamond-bone sirloins, three-shilling tea and the best bottled stout.[7] But Lily seldom made a mistake in the orders so that she got on well with her three mistresses. They were fussy, that was all. But the only thing they would not stand was back answers.

Of course they had good reason to be fussy on such a night. And then it was long after ten o'clock and yet there was no sign of Gabriel and his wife. Besides they were dreadfully afraid that Freddy Malins might turn up screwed.[8] They would not wish for worlds that any of Mary Jane's pupils should see him under the influence; and when he was like that it was sometimes very hard to manage him. Freddy Malins always came late but they wondered what could be keeping Gabriel: and that was what brought them every two minutes to the banisters to ask Lily had Gabriel or Freddy come.

—O, Mr Conroy, said Lily to Gabriel when she opened the door for him, Miss Kate and Miss Julia thought you were never coming. Good-night, Mrs Conroy.

—I'll engage[9] they did, said Gabriel, but they forget that my wife here takes three mortal hours to dress herself.

He stood on the mat, scraping the snow from his goloshes, while Lily led his wife to the foot of the stairs and called out:

—Miss Kate, here's Mrs Conroy.

Kate and Julia came toddling down the dark stairs at once. Both of them kissed Gabriel's wife, said she must be perished alive and asked was Gabriel with her.

—Here I am as right as the mail, Aunt Kate! Go on up. I'll follow, called out Gabriel from the dark.

He continued scraping his feet vigorously while the three women went upstairs, laughing, to the ladies' dressing-room. A light fringe of snow lay like a cape on the shoulders of his overcoat and like toecaps on the toes of his goloshes; and, as the buttons of his overcoat slipped with a squeaking noise through the snow-stiffened frieze, a cold fragrant air from out-of-doors escaped from crevices and folds.

—Is it snowing again, Mr Conroy? asked Lily.

She had preceded him into the pantry to help him off with his overcoat. Gabriel smiled at the three syllables she had given his surname and glanced at her. She was a slim, growing girl, pale in complexion and with hay-coloured hair. The gas in the pantry made her look still paler. Gabriel had known her when she was a child and used to sit on the lowest step nursing a rag doll.

—Yes, Lily, he answered, and I think we're in for a night of it.

He looked up at the pantry ceiling, which was shaking with the stamping and shuffling of feet on the floor above, listened for a moment to the piano and then glanced at the girl, who was folding his overcoat carefully at the end of a shelf.

—Tell me, Lily, he said in a friendly tone, do you still go to school?

—O no, sir, she answered. I'm done schooling this year and more.

—O, then, said Gabriel gaily, I suppose we'll be going to your wedding one of these fine days with your young man, eh?

The girl glanced back at him over her shoulder and said with great bitterness:

6. A Dublin church.
7. An extra-strength ale.

8. Drunk.
9. Wager.

—The men that is now is only all palaver[1] and what they can get out of you.

Gabriel coloured as if he felt he had made a mistake and, without looking at her, kicked off his goloshes and flicked actively with his muffler at his patent-leather shoes.

He was a stout tallish young man. The high colour of his cheeks pushed upwards even to his forehead where it scattered itself in a few formless patches of pale red; and on his hairless face there scintillated restlessly the polished lenses and the bright gilt rims of the glasses which screened his delicate and restless eyes. His glossy black hair was parted in the middle and brushed in a long curve behind his ears where it curled slightly beneath the groove left by his hat.

When he had flicked lustre into his shoes he stood up and pulled his waistcoat down more tightly on his plump body. Then he took a coin rapidly from his pocket.

—O Lily, he said, thrusting it into her hands, it's Christmas-time, isn't it? Just. . . here's a little. . . .

He walked rapidly towards the door.

—O no, sir! cried the girl, following him. Really, sir, I wouldn't take it.

—Christmas-time! Christmas-time! said Gabriel, almost trotting to the stairs and waving his hand to her in deprecation.

The girl, seeing that he had gained the stairs, called out after him:

—Well, thank you, sir.

He waited outside the drawing-room door until the waltz should finish, listening to the skirts that swept against it and to the shuffling of feet. He was still discomposed by the girl's bitter and sudden retort. It had cast a gloom over him which he tried to dispel by arranging his cuffs and the bows of his tie. Then he took from his waistcoat pocket a little paper and glanced at the headings he had made for his speech. He was undecided about the lines from Robert Browning for he feared they would be above the heads of his hearers. Some quotation that they could recognise from Shakespeare or from the Melodies[2] would be better. The indelicate clacking of the men's heels and the shuffling of their soles reminded him that their grade of culture differed from his. He would only make himself ridiculous by quoting poetry to them which they could not understand. They would think that he was airing his superior education. He would fail with them just as he had failed with the girl in the pantry. He had taken up a wrong tone. His whole speech was a mistake from first to last, an utter failure.

Just then his aunts and his wife came out of the ladies' dressing-room. His aunts were two small plainly dressed old women. Aunt Julia was an inch or so taller. Her hair, drawn low over the tops of her ears, was grey; and grey also, with darker shadows, was her large flaccid face. Though she was stout in build and stood erect her slow eyes and parted lips gave her the appearance of a woman who did not know where she was or where she was going. Aunt Kate was more vivacious. Her face, healthier than her sister's, was all puckers and creases, like a shrivelled red apple, and her hair, braided in the same old-fashioned way, had not lost its ripe nut colour.

They both kissed Gabriel frankly. He was their favourite nephew, the son of their dead elder sister, Ellen, who had married T.J. Conroy of the Port and Docks.

—Gretta tells me you're not going to take a cab back to Monkstown[3] to-night, Gabriel, said Aunt Kate.

---

1. Empty talk.
2. Thomas Moore's *Irish Melodies*, a perennial favorite
volume of poetry.
3. An elegant suburb south of Dublin.

—No, said Gabriel, turning to his wife, we had quite enough of that last year, hadn't we. Don't you remember, Aunt Kate, what a cold Gretta got out of it? Cab windows rattling all the way, and the east wind blowing in after we passed Merrion. Very jolly it was. Gretta caught a dreadful cold.

Aunt Kate frowned severely and nodded her head at every word.

—Quite right, Gabriel, quite right, she said. You can't be too careful.

—But as for Gretta there, said Gabriel, she'd walk home in the snow if she were let.

Mrs Conroy laughed.

—Don't mind him, Aunt Kate, she said. He's really an awful bother, what with green shades for Tom's eyes at night and making him do the dumb-bells, and forcing Eva to eat the stirabout.[4] The poor child! And she simply hates the sight of it! . . . O, but you'll never guess what he makes me wear now!

She broke out into a peal of laughter and glanced at her husband, whose admiring and happy eyes had been wandering from her dress to her face and hair. The two aunts laughed heartily too, for Gabriel's solicitude was a standing joke with them.

—Goloshes! said Mrs Conroy. That's the latest. Whenever it's wet underfoot I must put on my goloshes. Tonight even he wanted me to put them on, but I wouldn't. The next thing he'll buy me will be a diving suit.

Gabriel laughed nervously and patted his tie reassuringly while Aunt Kate nearly doubled herself, so heartily did she enjoy the joke. The smile soon faded from Aunt Julia's face and her mirthless eyes were directed towards her nephew's face. After a pause she asked:

—And what are goloshes, Gabriel?

—Goloshes, Julia! exclaimed her sister. Goodness me, don't you know what goloshes are? You wear them over your . . . over your boots, Gretta, isn't it?

—Yes, said Mrs Conroy. Guttapercha[5] things. We both have a pair now. Gabriel says everyone wears them on the continent.

—O, on the continent, murmured Aunt Julia, nodding her head slowly.

Gabriel knitted his brows and said, as if he were slightly angered:

—It's nothing very wonderful but Gretta thinks it very funny because she says the word reminds her of Christy Minstrels.[6]

—But tell me, Gabriel, said Aunt Kate, with brisk tact. Of course, you've seen about the room. Gretta was saying . . .

—O, the room is all right, replied Gabriel. I've taken one in the Gresham.[7]

—To be sure, said Aunt Kate, by far the best thing to do. And the children, Gretta, you're not anxious about them?

—O, for one night, said Mrs Conroy. Besides, Bessie will look after them.

—To be sure, said Aunt Kate again. What a comfort it is to have a girl like that, one you can depend on! There's that Lily, I'm sure I don't know what has come over her lately. She's not the girl she was at all.

Gabriel was about to ask his aunt some questions on this point but she broke off suddenly to gaze after her sister who had wandered down the stairs and was craning her neck over the banisters.

—Now, I ask you, she said, almost testily, where is Julia going? Julia! Julia! Where are you going?

---

4. Porridge.
5. Rubberized fabric.

6. A 19th-century minstrel show.
7. The most elegant hotel in Dublin.

Julia, who had gone halfway down one flight, came back and announced blandly:

—Here's Freddy.

At the same moment a clapping of hands and a final flourish of the pianist told that the waltz had ended. The drawing-room door was opened from within and some couples came out. Aunt Kate drew Gabriel aside hurriedly and whispered into his ear:

—Slip down, Gabriel, like a good fellow and see if he's all right, and don't let him up if he's screwed. I'm sure he's screwed. I'm sure he is.

Gabriel went to the stairs and listened over the banisters. He could hear two persons talking in the pantry. Then he recognised Freddy Malins' laugh. He went down the stairs noisily.

—It's such a relief, said Aunt Kate to Mrs Conroy, that Gabriel is here. I always feel easier in my mind when he's here. . . . Julia, there's Miss Daly and Miss Power will take some refreshment. Thanks for your beautiful waltz, Miss Daly. It made lovely time.

A tall wizen-faced man, with a stiff grizzled moustache and swarthy skin, who was passing out with his partner said:

—And may we have some refreshment, too, Miss Morkan?

—Julia, said Aunt Kate summarily, and here's Mr Browne and Miss Furlong. Take them in, Julia, with Miss Daly and Miss Power.

—I'm the man for the ladies, said Mr Browne, pursing his lips until his moustache bristled and smiling in all his wrinkles. You know, Miss Morkan, the reason they are so fond of me is—

He did not finish his sentence, but, seeing that Aunt Kate was out of earshot, at once led the three young ladies into the back room. The middle of the room was occupied by two square tables placed end to end, and on these Aunt Julia and the caretaker were straightening and smoothing a large cloth. On the sideboard were arrayed dishes and plates, and glasses and bundles of knives and forks and spoons. The top of the closed square piano served also as a sideboard for viands[8] and sweets. At a smaller sideboard in one corner two young men were standing, drinking hop-bitters.[9]

Mr Browne led his charges thither and invited them all, in jest, to some ladies' punch, hot, strong and sweet. As they said they never took anything strong he opened three bottles of lemonade for them. Then he asked one of the young men to move aside, and, taking hold of the decanter, filled out for himself a goodly measure of whisky. The young men eyed him respectfully while he took a trial sip.

—God help me, he said, smiling, it's the doctor's orders.

His wizened face broke into a broader smile, and the three young ladies laughed in musical echo to his pleasantry, swaying their bodies to and fro, with nervous jerks of their shoulders. The boldest said:

—O, now, Mr Browne, I'm sure the doctor never ordered anything of the kind.

Mr Browne took another sip of his whisky and said, with sidling mimicry:

—Well, you see, I'm like the famous Mrs Cassidy, who is reported to have said: *Now, Mary Grimes, if I don't take it, make me take it, for I feel I want it.*

His hot face had leaned forward a little too confidentially and he had assumed a very low Dublin accent so that the young ladies, with one instinct, received his speech in silence. Miss Furlong, who was one of Mary Jane's pupils, asked Miss Daly what was the name of the pretty waltz she had played; and Mr Browne, seeing that he was ignored, turned promptly to the two young men who were more appreciative.

8. Meats.   9. Dry ale.

A red-faced young woman, dressed in pansy, came into the room, excitedly clapping her hands and crying:

—Quadrilles![1] Quadrilles!

Close on her heels came Aunt Kate, crying:

—Two gentlemen and three ladies, Mary Jane!

—O, here's Mr Bergin and Mr Kerrigan, said Mary Jane. Mr Kerrigan, will you take Miss Power? Miss Furlong, may I get you a partner, Mr Bergin. O, that'll just do now.

—Three ladies, Mary Jane, said Aunt Kate.

The two young gentlemen asked the ladies if they might have the pleasure, and Mary Jane turned to Miss Daly.

—O, Miss Daly, you're really awfully good, after playing for the last two dances, but really we're so short of ladies to-night.

—I don't mind in the least, Miss Morkan.

—But I've a nice partner for you, Mr Bartell D'Arcy, the tenor. I'll get him to sing later on. All Dublin is raving about him.

—Lovely voice, lovely voice! said Aunt Kate.

As the piano had twice begun the prelude to the first figure Mary Jane led her recruits quickly from the room. They had hardly gone when Aunt Julia wandered slowly into the room, looking behind her at something.

—What is the matter, Julia? asked Aunt Kate anxiously. Who is it?

Julia, who was carrying in a column of table-napkins, turned to her sister and said, simply, as if the question had surprised her:

—It's only Freddy, Kate, and Gabriel with him.

In fact right behind her Gabriel could be seen piloting Freddy Malins across the landing. The latter, a young man of about forty, was of Gabriel's size and build, with very round shoulders. His face was fleshy and pallid, touched with colour only at the thick hanging lobes of his ears and at the wide wings of his nose. He had coarse features, a blunt nose, a convex and receding brow, tumid and protruded lips. His heavy-lidded eyes and the disorder of his scanty hair made him look sleepy. He was laughing heartily in a high key at a story which he had been telling Gabriel on the stairs and at the same time rubbing the knuckles of his left fist backwards and forwards into his left eye.

—Good-evening, Freddy, said Aunt Julia.

Freddy Malins bade the Misses Morkan good-evening in what seemed an offhand fashion by reason of the habitual catch in his voice and then, seeing that Mr Browne was grinning at him from the sideboard, crossed the room on rather shaky legs and began to repeat in an undertone the story he had just told to Gabriel.

—He's not so bad, is he? said Aunt Kate to Gabriel.

Gabriel's brows were dark but he raised them quickly and answered:

—O no, hardly noticeable.

—Now, isn't he a terrible fellow! she said. And his poor mother made him take the pledge on New Year's Eve. But come on, Gabriel, into the drawing-room.

Before leaving the room with Gabriel she signalled to Mr Browne by frowning and shaking her forefinger in warning to and fro. Mr Browne nodded in answer and, when she had gone, said to Freddy Malins:

—Now, then, Teddy, I'm going to fill you out a good glass of lemonade just to buck you up.

---

1. A French square dance.

Freddy Malins, who was nearing the climax of his story, waved the offer aside impatiently but Mr Browne, having first called Freddy Malins' attention to a disarray in his dress, filled out and handed him a full glass of lemonade. Freddy Malins' left hand accepted the glass mechanically, his right hand being engaged in the mechanical readjustment of his dress. Mr Browne, whose face was once more wrinkling with mirth, poured out for himself a glass of whisky while Freddy Malins exploded, before he had well reached the climax of his story, in a kink of high-pitched bronchitic laughter and, setting down his untasted and overflowing glass, began to rub the knuckles of his left fist backwards and forwards into his left eye, repeating words of his last phrase as well as his fit of laughter would allow him.

Gabriel could not listen while Mary Jane was playing her Academy piece, full of runs and difficult passages, to the hushed drawing-room. He liked music but the piece she was playing had no melody for him and he doubted whether it had any melody for the other listeners, though they had begged Mary Jane to play something. Four young men, who had come from the refreshment-room to stand in the door-way at the sound of the piano, had gone away quietly in couples after a few minutes. The only persons who seemed to follow the music were Mary Jane herself, her hands racing along the key-board or lifted from it at the pauses like those of a priestess in momentary imprecation, and Aunt Kate standing at her elbow to turn the page.

Gabriel's eyes, irritated by the floor, which glittered with beeswax under the heavy chandelier, wandered to the wall above the piano. A picture of the balcony scene in *Romeo and Juliet* hung there and beside it was a picture of the two murdered princes[2] in the Tower which Aunt Julia had worked in red, blue and brown wools when she was a girl. Probably in the school they had gone to as girls that kind of work had been taught, for one year his mother had worked for him as a birthday present a waistcoat of purple tabinet,[3] with little foxes' heads upon it, lined with brown satin and having round mulberry buttons. It was strange that his mother had had no musical talent though Aunt Kate used to call her the brains carrier of the Morkan family. Both she and Julia had always seemed a little proud of their serious and matronly sister. Her photograph stood before the pierglass.[4] She held an open book on her knees and was pointing out something in it to Constantine who, dressed in a man-o'-war suit, lay at her feet. It was she who had chosen the names for her sons for she was very sensible of the dignity of family life. Thanks to her, Constantine was now senior curate in Balbriggan[5] and, thanks to her, Gabriel himself had taken his degree in the Royal University.[6] A shadow passed over his face as he remembered her sullen opposition to his marriage. Some slighting phrases she had used still rankled in his memory; she had once spoken of Gretta as being country cute and that was not true of Gretta at all. It was Gretta who had nursed her during all her last long illness in their house at Monkstown.

He knew that Mary Jane must be near the end of her piece for she was playing again the opening melody with runs of scales after every bar and while he waited for the end the resentment died down in his heart. The piece ended with a trill of octaves in the treble and a final deep octave in the bass. Great applause greeted Mary Jane as, blushing and rolling up her music nervously, she escaped from the room. The most vigorous clapping came from the four young men in the doorway who had gone

---

2. The young sons of Edward IV, murdered in the Tower of London by order of their uncle, Edward III.
3. Silk and wool fabric.

4. A large high mirror.
5. Seaport 19 miles southeast of Dublin.
6. The Royal University of Ireland, established in 1882.

away to the refreshment-room at the beginning of the piece but had come back when the piano had stopped.

Lancers[7] were arranged. Gabriel found himself partnered with Miss Ivors. She was a frank-mannered talkative young lady, with a freckled face and prominent brown eyes. She did not wear a low-cut bodice and the large brooch which was fixed in the front of her collar bore on it an Irish device.

When they had taken their places she said abruptly:

—I have a crow to pluck with you.

—With me? said Gabriel.

She nodded her head gravely.

—What is it? asked Gabriel, smiling at her solemn manner.

—Who is G. C.? answered Miss Ivors, turning her eyes upon him.

Gabriel coloured and was about to knit his brows, as if he did not understand, when she said bluntly:

—O, innocent Amy! I have found out that you write for *The Daily Express*.[8] Now, aren't you ashamed of yourself?

—Why should I be ashamed of myself? asked Gabriel, blinking his eyes and trying to smile.

—Well, I'm ashamed of you, said Miss Ivors frankly. To say you'd write for a rag like that. I didn't think you were a West Briton.[9]

A look of perplexity appeared on Gabriel's face. It was true that he wrote a literary column every Wednesday in *The Daily Express*, for which he was paid fifteen shillings. But that did not make him a West Briton surely. The books he received for review were almost more welcome than the paltry cheque. He loved to feel the covers and turn over the pages of newly printed books. Nearly every day when his teaching in the college was ended he used to wander down the quays to the second-hand booksellers, to Hickey's on Bachelor's Walk, to Webb's or Massey's on Aston's Quay, or to O'Clohissey's in the by-street. He did not know how to meet her charge. He wanted to say that literature was above politics. But they were friends of many years' standing and their careers had been parallel, first at the University and then as teachers: he could not risk a grandiose phrase with her. He continued blinking his eyes and trying to smile and murmured lamely that he saw nothing political in writing reviews of books.

When their turn to cross had come he was still perplexed and inattentive. Miss Ivors promptly took his hand in a warm grasp and said in a soft friendly tone:

—Of course, I was only joking. Come, we cross now.

When they were together again she spoke of the University question[1] and Gabriel felt more at ease. A friend of hers had shown her his review of Browning's poems. That was how she had found out the secret: but she liked the review immensely. Then she said suddenly:

—O, Mr Conroy, will you come for an excursion to the Aran Isles[2] this summer? We're going to stay there a whole month. It will be splendid out in the Atlantic. You

---

7. A type of quadrille for 8 or 16 people.
8. A conservative paper opposed to the struggle for Irish independence.
9. Disparaging term for people wishing to identify Ireland as British.
1. Ireland's oldest and most prestigious university, Trinity College, was open only to Protestants; the "University question" involved, in part, the provision of quality university education to Catholics.
2. Islands off the west coast of Ireland where the people still retained their traditional culture and spoke Irish.

ought to come. Mr Clancy is coming, and Mr Kilkelly and Kathleen Kearney. It would be splendid for Gretta too if she'd come. She's from Connacht,[3] isn't she?

—Her people are, said Gabriel shortly.

—But you will come, won't you? said Miss Ivors, laying her warm hand eagerly on his arm.

—The fact is, said Gabriel, I have already arranged to go—

—Go where? asked Miss Ivors.

—Well, you know, every year I go for a cycling tour with some fellows and so—

—But where? asked Miss Ivors.

—Well, we usually go to France or Belgium or perhaps Germany, said Gabriel awkwardly.

—And why do you go to France and Belgium, said Miss Ivors, instead of visiting your own land?

—Well, said Gabriel, it's partly to keep in touch with the languages and partly for a change.

—And haven't you your own language to keep in touch with—Irish? asked Miss Ivors.

—Well, said Gabriel, if it comes to that, you know, Irish is not my language.

Their neighbours had turned to listen to the cross-examination. Gabriel glanced right and left nervously and tried to keep his good humour under the ordeal which was making a blush invade his forehead.

—And haven't you your own land to visit, continued Miss Ivors, that you know nothing of, your own people, and your own country?

—O, to tell you the truth, retorted Gabriel suddenly, I'm sick of my own country, sick of it!

—Why? asked Miss Ivors.

Gabriel did not answer for his retort had heated him.

—Why? repeated Miss Ivors.

They had to go visiting together and, as he had not answered her, Miss Ivors said warmly:

—Of course, you've no answer.

Gabriel tried to cover his agitation by taking part in the dance with great energy. He avoided her eyes for he had seen a sour expression on her face. But when they met in the long chain he was surprised to feel his hand firmly pressed. She looked at him from under her brows for a moment quizzically until he smiled. Then, just as the chain was about to start again, she stood on tiptoe and whispered into his ear:

—West Briton!

When the lancers were over Gabriel went away to a remote corner of the room where Freddy Malins' mother was sitting. She was a stout feeble old woman with white hair. Her voice had a catch in it like her son's and she stuttered slightly. She had been told that Freddy had come and that he was nearly all right. Gabriel asked her whether she had had a good crossing. She lived with her married daughter in Glasgow and came to Dublin on a visit once a year. She answered placidly that she had had a beautiful crossing and that the captain had been most attentive to her. She spoke also of the beautiful house her daughter kept in Glasgow, and of all the nice friends they had there. While her tongue rambled on Gabriel tried to banish from his

3. A province on the west coast of Ireland.

mind all memory of the unpleasant incident with Miss Ivors. Of course the girl or woman, or whatever she was, was an enthusiast but there was a time for all things. Perhaps he ought not to have answered her like that. But she had no right to call him a West Briton before people, even in joke. She had tried to make him ridiculous before people, heckling him and staring at him with her rabbit's eyes.

He saw his wife making her way towards him through the waltzing couples. When she reached him she said into his ear:

—Gabriel, Aunt Kate wants to know won't you carve the goose as usual. Miss Daly will carve the ham and I'll do the pudding.

—All right, said Gabriel.

—She's sending in the younger ones first as soon as this waltz is over so that we'll have the table to ourselves.

—Were you dancing? asked Gabriel.

—Of course I was. Didn't you see me? What words had you with Molly Ivors?

—No words. Why? Did she say so?

—Something like that. I'm trying to get that Mr D'Arcy to sing. He's full of conceit, I think.

—There were no words, said Gabriel moodily, only she wanted me to go for a trip to the west of Ireland and I said I wouldn't.

His wife clasped her hands excitedly and gave a little jump.

—O, do go, Gabriel, she cried. I'd love to see Galway again.

—You can go if you like, said Gabriel coldly.

She looked at him for a moment, then turned to Mrs Malins and said:

—There's a nice husband for you, Mrs Malins.

While she was threading her way back across the room Mrs Malins, without adverting to the interruption, went on to tell Gabriel what beautiful places there were in Scotland and beautiful scenery. Her son-in-law brought them every year to the lakes and they used to go fishing. Her son-in-law was a splendid fisher. One day he caught a fish, a beautiful big big fish, and the man in the hotel boiled it for their dinner.

Gabriel hardly heard what she said. Now that supper was coming near he began to think again about his speech and about the quotation. When he saw Freddy Malins coming across the room to visit his mother Gabriel left the chair free for him and retired into the embrasure of the window. The room had already cleared and from the back room came the clatter of plates and knives. Those who still remained in the drawing-room seemed tired of dancing and were conversing quietly in little groups. Gabriel's warm trembling fingers tapped the cold pane of the window. How cool it must be outside! How pleasant it would be to walk out alone, first along by the river and then through the park! The snow would be lying on the branches of the trees and forming a bright cap on the top of the Wellington Monument.[4] How much more pleasant it would be there than at the supper-table!

He ran over the headings of his speech: Irish hospitality, sad memories, the Three Graces, Paris, the quotation from Browning. He repeated to himself a phrase he had written in his review: *One feels that one is listening to a thought-tormented music.* Miss Ivors had praised the review. Was she sincere? Had she really any life of her own behind all her propagandism? There had never been any ill-feeling between them until

---

4. A monument to the Duke of Wellington, an Irish-born English military hero, located in Phoenix Park, Dublin's major public park.

that night. It unnerved him to think that she would be at the supper-table, looking up at him while he spoke with her critical quizzing eyes. Perhaps she would not be sorry to see him fail in his speech. An idea came into his mind and gave him courage. He would say, alluding to Aunt Kate and Aunt Julia: *Ladies and Gentlemen, the generation which is now on the wane among us may have had its faults but for my part I think it had certain qualities of hospitality, of humour, of humanity, which the new and very serious and hypereducated generation that is growing up around us seems to me to lack.* Very good: that was one for Miss Ivors. What did he care that his aunts were only two ignorant old women?

A murmur in the room attracted his attention. Mr Browne was advancing from the door, gallantly escorting Aunt Julia, who leaned upon his arm, smiling and hanging her head. An irregular musketry of applause escorted her also as far as the piano and then, as Mary Jane seated herself on the stool, and Aunt Julia, no longer smiling, half turned so as to pitch her voice fairly into the room, gradually ceased. Gabriel recognised the prelude. It was that of an old song of Aunt Julia's—*Arrayed for the Bridal*.[5] Her voice, strong and clear in tone, attacked with great spirit the runs which embellish the air and though she sang very rapidly she did not miss even the smallest of the grace notes. To follow the voice, without looking at the singer's face, was to feel and share the excitement of swift and secure flight. Gabriel applauded loudly with all the others at the close of the song and loud applause was borne in from the invisible supper-table. It sounded so genuine that a little colour struggled into Aunt Julia's face as she bent to replace in the music-stand the old leather-bound song-book that had her initials on the cover. Freddy Malins, who had listened with his head perched sideways to hear her better, was still applauding when everyone else had ceased and talking animatedly to his mother who nodded her head gravely and slowly in acquiescence. At last, when he could clap no more, he stood up suddenly and hurried across the room to Aunt Julia whose hand he seized and held in both his hands, shaking it when words failed him or the catch in his voice proved too much for him.

—I was just telling my mother, he said, I never heard you sing so well, never. No, I never heard your voice so good as it is to-night. Now! Would you believe that now? That's the truth. Upon my word and honour that's the truth. I never heard your voice sound so fresh and so . . . so clear and fresh, never.

Aunt Julia smiled broadly and murmured something about compliments as she released her hand from his grasp. Mr Browne extended his open hand towards her and said to those who were near him in the manner of a showman introducing a prodigy to an audience:

—Miss Julia Morkan, my latest discovery!

He was laughing very heartily at this himself when Freddy Malins turned to him and said:

—Well, Browne, if you're serious you might make a worse discovery. All I can say is I never heard her sing half so well as long as I am coming here. And that's the honest truth.

—Neither did I, said Mr. Browne. I think her voice has greatly improved.

Aunt Julia shrugged her shoulders and said with meek pride:

—Thirty years ago I hadn't a bad voice as voices go.

—I often told Julia, said Aunt Kate emphatically, that she was simply thrown away in that choir. But she never would be said by me.

---

5. A popular but challenging song set to music from Bellini's opera *I Puritani* (1835).

She turned as if to appeal to the good sense of the others against a refractory child while Aunt Julia gazed in front of her, a vague smile of reminiscence playing on her face.

—No, continued Aunt Kate, she wouldn't be said or led by anyone, slaving there in that choir night and day, night and day. Six o'clock on Christmas morning! And all for what?

—Well, isn't it for the honour of God, Aunt Kate? asked Mary Jane, twisting round on the piano-stool and smiling.

Aunt Kate turned fiercely on her niece and said:

—I know all about the honour of God, Mary Jane, but I think it's not at all honourable for the pope to turn out the women out of the choirs that have slaved there all their lives and put little whipper-snappers of boys over their heads. I suppose it is for the good of the Church if the pope does it. But it's not just, Mary Jane, and it's not right.

She had worked herself into a passion and would have continued in defence of her sister for it was a sore subject with her but Mary Jane, seeing that all the dancers had come back, intervened pacifically:

—Now, Aunt Kate, you're giving scandal to Mr Browne who is of the other persuasion.

Aunt Kate turned to Mr Browne, who was grinning at this allusion to his religion, and said hastily:

—O, I don't question the pope's being right. I'm only a stupid old woman and I wouldn't presume to do such a thing. But there's such a thing as common everyday politeness and gratitude. And if I were in Julia's place I'd tell that Father Healy straight up to his face . . .

—And besides, Aunt Kate, said Mary Jane, we really are all hungry and when we are hungry we are all very quarrelsome.

—And when we are thirsty we are also quarrelsome, added Mr Browne.

—So that we had better go to supper, said Mary Jane, and finish the discussion afterwards.

On the landing outside the drawing-room Gabriel found his wife and Mary Jane trying to persuade Miss Ivors to stay for supper. But Miss Ivors, who had put on her hat and was buttoning her cloak, would not stay. She did not feel in the least hungry and she had already overstayed her time.

—But only for ten minutes, Molly, said Mrs Conroy. That won't delay you.

—To take a pick itself, said Mary Jane, after all your dancing.

—I really couldn't, said Miss Ivors.

—I am afraid you didn't enjoy yourself at all, said Mary Jane hopelessly.

—Ever so much, I assure you, said Miss Ivors, but you really must let me run off now.

—But how can you get home? asked Mrs Conroy.

—O, it's only two steps up the quay.

Gabriel hesitated a moment and said:

—If you will allow me, Miss Ivors, I'll see you home if you really are obliged to go.

But Miss Ivors broke away from them.

—I won't hear of it, she cried. For goodness sake go in to your suppers and don't mind me. I'm quite well able to take care of myself.

—Well, you're the comical girl, Molly, said Mrs Conroy frankly.

—*Beannacht libh,*[6] cried Miss Ivors, with a laugh, as she ran down the staircase.

Mary Jane gazed after her, a moody puzzled expression on her face, while Mrs Conroy leaned over the banisters to listen for the hall-door. Gabriel asked himself was he the cause of her abrupt departure. But she did not seem to be in ill humour: she had gone away laughing. He stared blankly down the staircase.

At that moment Aunt Kate came toddling out of the supper-room, almost wringing her hands in despair.

—Where is Gabriel? she cried. Where on earth is Gabriel? There's everyone waiting in there, stage to let, and nobody to carve the goose!

—Here I am, Aunt Kate! cried Gabriel, with sudden animation, ready to carve a flock of geese, if necessary.

A fat brown goose lay at one end of the table and at the other end, on a bed of creased paper strewn with sprigs of parsley, lay a great ham, stripped of its outer skin and peppered over with crust crumbs, a neat paper frill round its shin and beside this was a round of spiced beef. Between these rival ends ran parallel lines of side-dishes: two little minsters of jelly, red and yellow; a shallow dish full of blocks of blanc-mange and red jam, a large green leaf-shaped dish with a stalk-shaped handle, on which lay bunches of purple raisins and peeled almonds, a companion dish on which lay a solid rectangle of Smyrna figs, a dish of custard topped with grated nut-meg, a small bowl full of chocolates and sweets wrapped in gold and silver papers and a glass vase in which stood some tall celery stalks. In the centre of the table there stood, as sentries to a fruit-stand which upheld a pyramid of oranges and American apples, two squat old-fashioned decanters of cut glass, one containing port and the other dark sherry. On the closed square piano a pudding in a huge yellow dish lay in waiting and behind it were three squads of bottles of stout and ale and minerals, drawn up according to the colours of their uniforms, the first two black, with brown and red labels, the third and smallest squad white, with transverse green sashes.

Gabriel took his seat boldly at the head of the table and, having looked to the edge of the carver, plunged his fork firmly into the goose. He felt quite at ease now for he was an expert carver and liked nothing better than to find himself at the head of a well-laden table.

—Miss Furlong, what shall I send you? he asked. A wing or a slice of the breast?

—Just a small slice of the breast.

—Miss Higgins, what for you?

—O, anything at all, Mr Conroy.

While Gabriel and Miss Daly exchanged plates of goose and plates of ham and spiced beef Lily went from guest to guest with a dish of hot floury potatoes wrapped in a white napkin. This was Mary Jane's idea and she had also suggested apple sauce for the goose but Aunt Kate had said that plain roast goose without apple sauce had always been good enough for her and she hoped she might never eat worse. Mary Jane waited on her pupils and saw that they got the best slices and Aunt Kate and Aunt Julia opened and carried across from the piano bottles of stout and ale for the gentlemen and bottles of minerals for the ladies. There was a great deal of confusion and laughter and noise, the noise of orders and counter-orders, of knives and forks, of

6. Farewell (Irish).

corks and glass-stoppers. Gabriel began to carve second helpings as soon as he had finished the first round without serving himself. Everyone protested loudly so that he compromised by taking a long draught of stout for he had found the carving hot work. Mary Jane settled down quietly to her supper but Aunt Kate and Aunt Julia were still toddling round the table, walking on each other's heels, getting in each other's way and giving each other unheeded orders. Mr Browne begged of them to sit down and eat their suppers and so did Gabriel but they said there was time enough so that, at last, Freddy Malins stood up and, capturing Aunt Kate, plumped her down on her chair amid general laughter.

When everyone had been well served Gabriel said, smiling:

—Now, if anyone wants a little more of what vulgar people call stuffing let him or her speak.

A chorus of voices invited him to begin his own supper and Lily came forward with three potatoes which she had reserved for him.

—Very well, said Gabriel amiably, as he took another preparatory draught, kindly forget my existence, ladies and gentlemen, for a few minutes.

He set to his supper and took no part in the conversation with which the table covered Lily's removal of the plates. The subject of talk was the opera company which was then at the Theatre Royal. Mr Bartell D'Arcy, the tenor, a dark-complexioned young man with a smart moustache, praised very highly the leading contralto of the company but Miss Furlong thought she had a rather vulgar style of production. Freddy Malins said there was a negro chieftain singing in the second part of the Gaiety pantomime who had one of the finest tenor voices he had ever heard.

—Have you heard him? he asked Mr Bartell D'Arcy across the table.

—No, answered Mr Bartell D'Arcy carelessly.

—Because, Freddy Malins explained, now I'd be curious to hear your opinion of him. I think he has a grand voice.

—It takes Teddy to find out the really good things, said Mr Browne familiarly to the table.

—And why couldn't he have a voice too? asked Freddy Malins sharply. Is it because he's only a black?

Nobody answered this question and Mary Jane led the table back to the legitimate opera. One of her pupils had given her a pass for *Mignon*. Of course it was very fine, she said, but it made her think of poor Georgina Burns. Mr Browne could go back farther still, to the old Italian companies that used to come to Dublin—Tietjens, Ilma de Murzka, Campanini, the great Trebelli, Giuglini, Ravelli, Aramburo.[7] Those were the days, he said, when there was something like singing to be heard in Dublin. He told too of how the top gallery of the old Royal used to be packed night after night, of how one night an Italian tenor had sung five encores to *Let Me Like a Soldier Fall*, introducing a high C every time, and of how the gallery boys would sometimes in their enthusiasm unyoke the horses from the carriage of some great *prima donna* and pull her themselves through the streets to her hotel. Why did they never play the grand old operas now, he asked, *Dinorah, Lucrezia Borgia*? Because they could not get the voices to sing them: that was why.

—O, well, said Mr Bartell D'Arcy, I presume there are as good singers to-day as there were then.

---

7. Famous 19th-century operatic singers.

—Where are they? asked Mr Browne defiantly.

—In London, Paris, Milan, said Mr Bartell D'Arcy warmly. I suppose Caruso,[8] for example, is quite as good, if not better than any of the men you have mentioned.

—Maybe so, said Mr Browne. But I may tell you I doubt it strongly.

—O, I'd give anything to hear Caruso sing, said Mary Jane.

—For me, said Aunt Kate, who had been picking a bone, there was only one tenor. To please me, I mean. But I suppose none of you ever heard of him.

—Who was he, Miss Morkan? asked Mr Bartell D'Arcy politely.

—His name, said Aunt Kate, was Parkinson. I heard him when he was in his prime and I think he had then the purest tenor voice that was ever put into a man's throat.

—Strange, said Mr Bartell D'Arcy. I never even heard of him.

—Yes, yes, Miss Morkan is right, said Mr Browne. I remember hearing of old Parkinson but he's too far back for me.

—A beautiful pure sweet mellow English tenor, said Aunt Kate with enthusiasm.

Gabriel having finished, the huge pudding was transferred to the table. The clatter of forks and spoons began again. Gabriel's wife served out spoonfuls of the pudding and passed the plates down the table. Midway down they were held up by Mary Jane, who replenished them with raspberry or orange jelly or with blancmange and jam. The pudding was of Aunt Julia's making and she received praises for it from all quarters. She herself said that it was not quite brown enough.

—Well, I hope, Miss Morkan, said Mr Browne, that I'm brown enough for you because, you know, I'm all brown.

All the gentlemen, except Gabriel, ate some of the pudding out of compliment to Aunt Julia. As Gabriel never ate sweets the celery had been left for him. Freddy Malins also took a stalk of celery and ate it with his pudding. He had been told that celery was a capital thing for the blood and he was just then under doctor's care. Mrs Malins, who had been silent all through the supper, said that her son was going down to Mount Melleray[9] in a week or so. The table then spoke to Mount Melleray, how bracing the air was down there, how hospitable the monks were and how they never asked for a penny-piece from their guests.

—And do you mean to say, asked Mr Browne incredulously, that a chap can go down there and put up there as if it were a hotel and live on the fat of the land and then come away without paying a farthing?

—O, most people give some donation to the monastery when they leave, said Mary Jane.

—I wish we had an institution like that in our Church, said Mr Browne candidly.

He was astonished to hear that the monks never spoke, got up at two in the morning and slept in their coffins. He asked what they did it for.

—That's the rule of the order, said Aunt Kate firmly.

—Yes, but why? asked Mr Browne.

Aunt Kate repeated that it was the rule, that was all. Mr Browne still seemed not to understand. Freddy Malins explained to him, as best he could, that the monks were trying to make up for the sins committed by all the sinners in the outside world. The explanation was not very clear for Mr Browne grinned and said:

8. Enrico Caruso (1874–1921), a famous tenor.   9. Site of a Trappist monastery in the south of Ireland.

—I like that idea very much but wouldn't a comfortable spring bed do them as well as a coffin?

—The coffin, said Mary Jane, is to remind them of their last end.

As the subject had grown lugubrious it was buried in a silence of the table during which Mrs Malins could be heard saying to her neighbour in an indistinct undertone:

—They are very good men, the monks, very pious men.

The raisins and almonds and figs and apples and oranges and chocolates and sweets were now passed about the table and Aunt Julia invited all the guests to have either port or sherry. At first Mr Bartell D'Arcy refused to take either but one of his neighbours nudged him and whispered something to him upon which he allowed his glass to be filled. Gradually as the last glasses were being filled the conversation ceased. A pause followed, broken only by the noise of the wine and by unsettlings of chairs. The Misses Morkan, all three, looked down at the tablecloth. Someone coughed once or twice and then a few gentlemen patted the table gently as a signal for silence. The silence came and Gabriel pushed back his chair and stood up.

The patting at once grew louder in encouragement and then ceased altogether. Gabriel leaned his ten trembling fingers on the tablecloth and smiled nervously at the company. Meeting a row of upturned faces he raised his eyes to the chandelier. The piano was playing a waltz tune and he could hear the skirts sweeping against the drawing-room door. People, perhaps, were standing in the snow on the quay outside, gazing up at the lighted windows and listening to the waltz music. The air was pure there. In the distance lay the park where the trees were weighted with snow. The Wellington Monument wore a gleaming cap of snow that flashed westward over the white field of Fifteen Acres.[1]

He began:

—Ladies and Gentlemen.

—It has fallen to my lot this evening, as in years past, to perform a very pleasing task but a task for which I am afraid my poor powers as a speaker are all too inadequate.

—No, no! said Mr Browne.

—But, however that may be, I can only ask you tonight to take the will for the deed and to lend me your attention for a few moments while I endeavour to express to you in words what my feelings are on this occasion.

—Ladies and Gentlemen. It is not the first time that we have gathered together under this hospitable roof, around this hospitable board. It is not the first time that we have been the recipients—or perhaps, I had better say, the victims—of the hospitality of certain good ladies.

He made a circle in the air with his arm and paused. Everyone laughed or smiled at Aunt Kate and Aunt Julia and Mary Jane who all turned crimson with pleasure. Gabriel went on more boldly:

—I feel more strongly with every recurring year that our country has no tradition which does it so much honour and which it should guard so jealously as that of its hospitality. It is a tradition that is unique as far as my experience goes (and I have visited not a few places abroad) among the modern nations. Some would say, perhaps, that with us it is rather a failing than anything to be boasted of. But granted even that, it is, to my mind, a princely failing, and one that I trust will long be cultivated among us. Of one thing, at least, I am sure. As long as this one roof shelters the good ladies aforesaid—and I wish from my heart it may do so for many and many a

1. A section of Phoenix Park.

long year to come—the tradition of genuine warm-hearted courteous Irish hospital-ity, which our forefathers have handed down to us and which we in turn must hand down to our descendants, is still alive among us.

A hearty murmur of assent ran round the table. It shot through Gabriel's mind that Miss Ivors was not there and that she had gone away discourteously: and he said with confidence in himself:

—Ladies and Gentlemen.

—A new generation is growing up in our midst, a generation actuated by new ideas and new principles. It is serious and enthusiastic for these new ideas and its en-thusiasm, even when it is misdirected, is, I believe, in the main sincere. But we are living in a sceptical and, if I may use the phrase, a thought-tormented age: and some-times I fear that this new generation, educated or hypereducated as it is, will lack those qualities of humanity, of hospitality, of kindly humour which belonged to an older day. Listening to-night to the names of all those great singers of the past it seemed to me, I must confess, that we were living in a less spacious age. Those days might, without exaggeration, be called spacious days: and if they are gone beyond re-call let us hope, at least, that in gatherings such as this we shall still speak of them with pride and affection, still cherish in our hearts the memory of those dead and gone great ones whose fame the world will not willingly let die.

—Hear, hear! said Mr Browne loudly.

—But yet, continued Gabriel, his voice falling into a softer inflection, there are always in gatherings such as this sadder thoughts that will recur to our minds: thoughts of the past, of youth, of changes, of absent faces that we miss here to-night. Our path through life is strewn with many such sad memories: and were we to brood upon them always we could not find the heart to go on bravely with our work among the living. We have all of us living duties and living affections which claim, and rightly claim, our strenuous endeavours.

—Therefore, I will not linger on the past. I will not let any gloomy moralising in-trude upon us here to-night. Here we are gathered together for a brief moment from the bustle and rush of our everyday routine. We are met here as friends, in the spirit of good-fellowship, as colleagues, also to a certain extent, in the true spirit of *camaraderie*, and as the guests of—what shall I call them?—the Three Graces[2] of the Dublin musical world.

The table burst into applause and laughter at this sally. Aunt Julia vainly asked each of her neighbors in turn to tell her what Gabriel had said.

—He says we are the Three Graces, Aunt Julia, said Mary Jane.

Aunt Julia did not understand but she looked up, smiling, at Gabriel, who con-tinued in the same vein:

—Ladies and Gentlemen.

—I will not attempt to play to-night the part that Paris[3] played on another occa-sion. I will not attempt to choose between them. The task would be an invidious one and one beyond my poor powers. For when I view them in turn, whether it be our chief hostess herself, whose good heart, whose too good heart, has become a byword with all who know her, or her sister, who seems to be gifted with perennial youth and whose singing must have been a surprise and a revelation to us all to-night, or, last but not least, when I consider our youngest hostess, talented, cheerful, hard-working and the best of nieces, I confess, Ladies and Gentlemen, that I do not know to which of them I should award the prize.

2. Companions to the Muses in Greek mythology.
3. Paris was the judge of a divine beauty contest in which

Hera, Athena, and Aphrodite competed; his selection of Aphrodite was, indirectly, the cause of the Trojan War.

Gabriel glanced down at his aunts and, seeing the large smile on Aunt Julia's face and the tears which had risen to Aunt Kate's eyes, hastened to his close. He raised his glass of port gallantly, while every member of the company fingered a glass expectantly, and said loudly:

—Let us toast them all three together. Let us drink to their health, wealth, long life, happiness and prosperity and may they long continue to hold the proud and self-won position which they hold in their profession and the position of honour and affection which they hold in our hearts.

All the guests stood up, glass in hand, and, turning towards the three seated ladies, sang in unison, with Mr Browne as leader:

> *For they are jolly gay fellows,*
> *For they are jolly gay fellows,*
> *For they are jolly gay fellows,*
> *Which nobody can deny.*

Aunt Kate was making frank use of her handkerchief and even Aunt Julia seemed moved. Freddy Malins beat time with his pudding-fork and the singers turned towards one another, as if in melodious conference, while they sang, with emphasis:

> *Unless he tells a lie,*
> *Unless he tells a lie.*

Then, turning once more towards their hostesses, they sang:

> *For they are jolly gay fellows,*
> *For they are jolly gay fellows,*
> *For they are jolly gay fellows,*
> *Which nobody can deny.*

The acclamation which followed was taken up beyond the door of the supper-room by many of the other guests and renewed time after time, Freddy Malins acting as officer with his fork on high.

The piercing morning air came into the hall where they were standing so that Aunt Kate said:

—Close the door, somebody. Mrs Malins will get her death of cold.

—Browne is out there, Aunt Kate, said Mary Jane.

—Browne is everywhere, said Aunt Kate, lowering her voice.

Mary Jane laughed at her tone.

—Really, she said archly, he is very attentive.

—He has been laid on here like the gas, said Aunt Kate in the same tone, all during the Christmas.

She laughed herself this time good-humouredly and then added quickly:

—But tell him to come in, Mary Jane, and close the door. I hope to goodness he didn't hear me.

At that moment the hall-door was opened and Mr Browne came in from the doorstep, laughing as if his heart would break. He was dressed in a long green overcoat with mock astrakhan cuffs and collar and wore on his head an oval fur cap. He pointed down the snow-covered quay from where the sound of shrill prolonged whistling was borne in.

—Teddy will have all the cabs in Dublin out, he said.

Gabriel advanced from the little pantry behind the office, struggling into his overcoat and looking round the hall, said:

—Gretta not down yet?

—She's getting on her things, Gabriel, said Aunt Kate.

—Who's playing up there? asked Gabriel.

—Nobody. They're all gone.

—O no, Aunt Kate, said Mary Jane. Bartell D'Arcy and Miss O'Callaghan aren't gone yet.

—Someone is strumming at the piano, anyhow, said Gabriel.

Mary Jane glanced at Gabriel and Mr Browne and said with a shiver:

—It makes me feel cold to look at you two gentlemen muffled up like that. I wouldn't like to face your journey home at this hour.

—I'd like nothing better this minute, said Mr Browne stoutly, than a rattling fine walk in the country or a fast drive with a good spanking goer between the shafts.

—We used to have a very good horse and trap at home, said Aunt Julia sadly.

—The never-to-be-forgotten Johnny, said Mary Jane, laughing.

Aunt Kate and Gabriel laughed too.

—Why, what was wonderful about Johnny? asked Mr Browne.

—The late lamented Patrick Morkan, our grandfather, that is, explained Gabriel, commonly known in his later years as the old gentleman, was a glue-boiler.

—O, now, Gabriel, said Aunt Kate, laughing, he had a starch mill.

—Well, glue or starch, said Gabriel, the old gentleman had a horse by the name of Johnny. And Johnny used to work in the old gentleman's mill, walking round and round in order to drive the mill. That was all very well; but now comes the tragic part about Johnny. One fine day the old gentleman thought he'd like to drive out with the quality to a military review in the park.

—The Lord have mercy on his soul, said Aunt Kate compassionately.

—Amen, said Gabriel. So the old gentleman, as I said, harnessed Johnny and put on his very best tall hat and his very best stock collar and drove out in grand style from his ancestral mansion somewhere near Back Lane, I think.

Everyone laughed, even Mrs Malins, at Gabriel's manner and Aunt Kate said:

—O now, Gabriel, he didn't live in Back Lane, really. Only the mill was there.

—Out from the mansion of his forefathers, continued Gabriel, he drove with Johnny. And everything went on beautifully until Johnny came in sight of King Billy's statue:[4] and whether he fell in love with the horse King Billy sits on or whether he thought he was back again in the mill, anyhow he began to walk round the statue.

Gabriel paced in a circle round the hall in his goloshes amid the laughter of the others.

—Round and round he went, said Gabriel, and the old gentleman, who was a very pompous old gentleman, was highly indignant. *Go on, sir! What do you mean, sir? Johnny! Johnny! Most extraordinary conduct! Can't understand the horse!*

The peals of laughter which followed Gabriel's imitation of the incident were interrupted by a resounding knock at the hall-door. Mary Jane ran to open it and let in Freddy Malins. Freddy Malins, with his hat well back on his head and his shoulders humped with cold, was puffing and steaming after his exertions.

—I could only get one cab, he said.

---

4. Statue of William of Orange, who defeated the Irish Catholic forces in the Battle of the Boyne in 1690, which stood in College Green in front of Trinity College in the heart of Dublin. It was seen as a symbol of British imperial oppression.

—O, we'll find another along the quay, said Gabriel.

—Yes, said Aunt Kate. Better not keep Mrs Malins standing in the draught.

Mrs Malins was helped down the front steps by her son and Mr Browne and, after many manoeuvres, hoisted into the cab. Freddy Malins clambered in after her and spent a long time settling her on the seat, Mr Browne helping him with advice. At last she was settled comfortably and Freddy Malins invited Mr Browne into the cab. There was a good deal of confused talk, and then Mr Browne got into the cab. The cabman settled his rug over his knees, and bent down for the address. The confusion grew greater and the cabman was directed differently by Freddy Malins and Mr Browne, each of whom had his head out through a window of the cab. The difficulty was to know where to drop Mr Browne along the route and Aunt Kate, Aunt Julia and Mary Jane helped the discussion from the doorstep with cross-directions and contradictions and abundance of laughter. As for Freddy Malins he was speechless with laughter. He popped his head in and out of the window every moment, to the great danger of his hat, and told his mother how the discussion was progressing till at last Mr Browne shouted to the bewildered cabman above the din of everybody's laughter:

—Do you know Trinity College?

—Yes, sir, said the cabman.

—Well, drive bang up against Trinity College gates, said Mr Browne, and then we'll tell you where to go. You understand now?

—Yes, sir, said the cabman.

—Make like a bird for Trinity College.

—Right, sir, cried the cabman.

The horse was whipped up and the cab rattled off along the quay amid a chorus of laughter and adieus.

Gabriel had not gone to the door with the others. He was in a dark part of the hall gazing up the staircase, a woman was standing near the top of the first flight, in the shadow also. He could not see her face but he could see the terracotta and salmonpink panels of her skirt which the shadow made appear black and white. It was his wife. She was leaning on the banisters, listening to something. Gabriel was surprised at her stillness and strained his ear to listen also. But he could hear little save the noise of laughter and dispute on the front steps, a few chords struck on the piano and a few notes of a man's voice singing.

He stood still in the gloom of the hall, trying to catch the air that the voice was singing and gazing up at his wife. There was grace and mystery in her attitude as if she were a symbol of something. He asked himself what is a woman standing on the stairs in the shadow, listening to distant music, a symbol of. If he were a painter he would paint her in that attitude. Her blue felt hat would show off the bronze of her hair against the darkness and the dark panels of her skirt would show off the light ones. *Distant Music* he would call the picture if he were a painter.

The hall-door was closed; and Aunt Kate, Aunt Julia and Mary Jane came down the hall, still laughing.

—Well, isn't Freddy terrible? said Mary Jane. He's really terrible.

Gabriel said nothing but pointed up the stairs towards where his wife was standing. Now that the hall-door was closed the voice and the piano could be heard more clearly. Gabriel held up his hand for them to be silent. The song seemed to be in the old Irish tonality and the singer seemed uncertain both of his words and of his voice. The voice, made plaintive by distance and by the singer's hoarseness, faintly illuminated the cadence of the air with words expressing grief:

> *O, the rain falls on my heavy locks*
> *And the dew wets my skin,*
> *My babe lies cold . . .*

—O, exclaimed Mary Jane. It's Bartell D'Arcy singing and he wouldn't sing all the night. O, I'll get him to sing a song before he goes.

—O do, Mary Jane, said Aunt Kate.

Mary Jane brushed past the others and ran to the staircase but before she reached it the singing stopped and the piano was closed abruptly.

—O, what a pity! she cried. Is he coming down, Gretta?

Gabriel heard his wife answer yes and saw her come down towards them. A few steps behind her were Mr Bartell D'Arcy and Miss O'Callaghan.

—O, Mr D'Arcy, cried Mary Jane, it's downright mean of you to break off like that when we were all in raptures listening to you.

—I have been at him all the evening, said Miss O'Callaghan, and Mrs Conroy too and he told us he had a dreadful cold and couldn't sing.

—O, Mr D'Arcy, said Aunt Kate, now that was a great fib to tell.

—Can't you see that I'm as hoarse as a crow? said Mr D'Arcy roughly.

He went into the pantry hastily and put on his overcoat. The others, taken aback by his rude speech, could find nothing to say. Aunt Kate wrinkled her brows and made signs to the others to drop the subject. Mr D'Arcy stood swathing his neck carefully and frowning.

—It's the weather, said Aunt Julia, after a pause.

—Yes, everybody has colds, said Aunt Kate readily, everybody.

—They say, said Mary Jane, we haven't had snow like it for thirty years; and I read this morning in the newspapers that the snow is general all over Ireland.

—I love the look of snow, said Aunt Julia sadly.

—So do I, said Miss O'Callaghan. I think Christmas is never really Christmas unless we have the snow on the ground.

—But poor Mr D'Arcy doesn't like the snow, said Aunt Kate, smiling.

Mr D'Arcy came from the pantry, full swathed and buttoned, and in a repentant tone told them the history of his cold. Everyone gave him advice and said it was a great pity and urged him to be very careful of his throat in the night air. Gabriel watched his wife who did not join in the conversation. She was standing right under the dusty fanlight and the flame of the gas lit up the rich bronze of her hair which he had seen her drying at the fire a few days before. She was in the same attitude and seemed unaware of the talk about her. At last she turned towards them and Gabriel saw that there was colour on her cheeks and that her eyes were shining. A sudden tide of joy went leaping out of his heart.

—Mr D'Arcy, she said, what is the name of that song you were singing?

—It's called *The Lass of Aughrim*, said Mr D'Arcy, but I couldn't remember it properly. Why? Do you know it?

—*The Lass of Aughrim*, she repeated. I couldn't think of the name.

—It's a very nice air, said Mary Jane. I'm sorry you were not in voice to-night.

—Now, Mary Jane, said Aunt Kate, don't annoy Mr D'Arcy. I won't have him annoyed.

Seeing that all were ready to start she shepherded them to the door where good-night was said:

—Well, good-night, Aunt Kate, and thanks for the pleasant evening.

—Good-night, Gabriel. Good-night, Gretta!

—Good-night, Aunt Kate, and thanks ever so much. Good-night, Aunt Julia.

—O, good-night, Gretta, I didn't see you.

—Good-night, Mr D'Arcy. Good-night, Miss O'Callaghan.

—Good-night, Miss Morkan.

—Good-night, again.

—Good-night, all. Safe home.

—Good-night. Good-night.

The morning was still dark. A dull yellow light brooded over the houses and the river; and the sky seemed to be descending. It was slushy underfoot; and only streaks and patches of snow lay on the roofs, on the parapets of the quay and on the area railings. The lamps were still burning redly in the murky air and, across the river, the palace of the Four Courts[5] stood out menacingly against the heavy sky.

She was walking on before him with Mr Bartell D'Arcy, her shoes in a brown parcel tucked under one arm and her hands holding her skirt up from the slush. She had no longer any grace of attitude but Gabriel's eyes were still bright with happiness. The blood went bounding along his veins; and the thoughts went rioting through his brain, proud, joyful, tender, valorous.

She was walking on before him so lightly and so erect that he longed to run after her noiselessly, catch her by the shoulders and say something foolish and affectionate into her ear. She seemed to him so frail that he longed to defend her against something and then to be alone with her. Moments of their secret life together burst like stars upon his memory. A heliotrope envelope was lying beside his breakfast-cup and he was caressing it with his hand. Birds were twittering in the ivy and the sunny web of the curtain was shimmering along the floor: he could not eat for happiness. They were standing on the crowded platform and he was placing a ticket inside the warm palm of her glove. He was standing with her in the cold, looking in through a grated window at a man making bottles in a roaring furnace. It was very cold. Her face, fragrant in the cold air, was quite close to his; and suddenly she called out to the man at the furnace:

—Is the fire hot, sir?

But the man could not hear her with the noise of the furnace. It was just as well. He might have answered rudely.

A wave of yet more tender joy escaped from his heart and went coursing in warm flood along his arteries. Like the tender fires of stars moments of their life together, that no one knew of or would ever know of, broke upon and illumined his memory. He longed to recall to her those moments, to make her forget the years of their dull existence together and remember only their moments of ecstasy. For the years, he felt, had not quenched his soul or hers. Their children, his writing, her household cares had not quenched all their souls' tender fire. In one letter that he had written to her then he had said: *Why is it that words like these seem to me so dull and cold? Is it because there is no word tender enough to be your name?*

Like distant music these words that he had written years before were borne towards him from the past. He longed to be alone with her. When the others had gone away, when he and she were in their room in the hotel, then they would be alone together. He would call her softly:

—Gretta!

5. The Irish law courts.

Perhaps she would not hear at once: she would be undressing. Then something in his voice would strike her. She would turn and look at him. . . .

At the corner of Winetavern Street they met a cab. He was glad of its rattling noise as it saved him from conversation. She was looking out of the window and seemed tired. The others spoke only a few words, pointing out some building or street. The horse galloped along wearily under the murky morning sky, dragging his old rattling box after his heels, and Gabriel was again in a cab with her, galloping to catch the boat, galloping to their honeymoon.

As the cab drove across O'Connell Bridge Miss O'Callaghan said:

—They say you never cross O'Connell Bridge without seeing a white horse.

—I see a white man this time, said Gabriel.

—Where? asked Mr Bartell D'Arcy.

Gabriel pointed to the statue, on which lay patches of snow. Then he nodded familiarly to it and waved his hand.

—Good-night, Dan,[6] he said gaily.

When the cab drew up before the hotel Gabriel jumped out and, in spite of Mr Bartell D'Arcy's protest, paid the driver. He gave the man a shilling over his fare. The man saluted and said:

—A prosperous New Year to you, sir.

—The same to you, said Gabriel cordially.

She leaned for a moment on his arm in getting out of the cab and while standing at the curbstone, bidding the others good-night. She leaned lightly on his arm, as lightly as when she had danced with him a few hours before. He had felt proud and happy then, happy that she was his, proud of her grace and wifely carriage. But now, after the kindling again of so many memories, the first touch of her body, musical and strange and perfumed, sent through him a keen pang of lust. Under cover of her silence he pressed her arm closely to his side; and, as they stood at the hotel door, he felt that they had escaped from their lives and duties, escaped from home and friends and run away together with wild and radiant hearts to a new adventure.

An old man was dozing in a great hooded chair in the hall. He lit a candle in the office and went before them to the stairs. They followed him in silence, their feet falling in soft thuds on the thickly carpeted stairs. She mounted the stairs behind the porter, her head bowed in the ascent, her frail shoulders curved as with a burden, her skirt girt tightly about her. He could have flung his arms about her hips and held her still for his arms were trembling with desire to seize her and only the stress of his nails against the palms of his hands held the wild impulse of his body in check. The porter halted on the stairs to settle his guttering candle. They halted too on the steps below him. In the silence Gabriel could hear the falling of the molten wax into the tray and the thumping of his own heart against his ribs.

The porter led them along a corridor and opened a door. Then he set his unstable candle down on a toilet-table and asked at what hour they were to be called in the morning.

—Eight, said Gabriel.

The porter pointed to the tap of the electric-light and began a muttered apology but Gabriel cut him short.

6. A statue of Daniel O'Connell, 19th-century nationalist leader, stands at the south end of Sackville Street (now called O'Connell Street).

—We don't want any light. We have light enough from the street. And I say, he added, pointing to the candle, you might remove that handsome article, like a good man.

The porter took up his candle again, but slowly for he was surprised by such a novel idea. Then he mumbled good-night and went out. Gabriel shot the lock to.

A ghostly light from the street lamp lay in a long shaft from one window to the door. Gabriel threw his overcoat and hat on a couch and crossed the room towards the window. He looked down into the street in order that his emotion might calm a little. Then he turned and leaned against a chest of drawers with his back to the light. She had taken off her hat and cloak and was standing before a large swinging mirror, unhooking her waist. Gabriel paused for a few moments, watching her, and then said:

—Gretta!

She turned away from the mirror slowly and walked along the shaft of light towards him. Her face looked so serious and weary that the words would not pass Gabriel's lips. No, it was not the moment yet.

—You looked tired, he said.

—I am a little, she answered.

—You don't feel ill or weak?

—No, tired: that's all.

She went on to the window and stood there, looking out. Gabriel waited again and then, fearing that diffidence was about to conquer him, he said abruptly:

—By the way, Gretta!

—What is it?

—You know that poor fellow Malins? he said quickly.

—Yes. What about him?

—Well, poor fellow, he's a decent sort of chap after all, continued Gabriel in a false voice. He gave me back that sovereign I lent him and I didn't expect it really. It's a pity he wouldn't keep away from that Browne, because he's not a bad fellow at heart.

He was trembling now with annoyance. Why did she seem so abstracted? He did not know how he could begin. Was she annoyed, too, about something? If she would only turn to him or come to him of her own accord! To take her as she was would be brutal. No, he must see some ardour in her eyes first. He longed to be master of her strange mood.

—When did you lend him the pound? she asked, after a pause.

Gabriel strove to restrain himself from breaking out into brutal language about the sottish Malins and his pound. He longed to cry to her from his soul, to crush her body against his, to overmaster her. But he said:

—O, at Christmas, when he opened that little Christmas-card shop in Henry Street.

He was in such a fever of rage and desire that he did not hear her come from the window. She stood before him for an instant, looking at him strangely. Then, suddenly raising herself on tiptoe and resting her hands lightly on his shoulders, she kissed him.

—You are a very generous person, Gabriel, she said.

Gabriel, trembling with delight at her sudden kiss and at the quaintness of her phrase, put his hands on her hair and began smoothing it back, scarcely touching it with his fingers. The washing had made it fine and brilliant. His heart was brimming over with happiness. Just when he was wishing for it she had come to him of her own accord. Perhaps her thoughts had been running with his. Perhaps she had felt the impetuous desire that was in him and then the yielding mood had come upon her. Now that she had fallen to him so easily he wondered why he had been so diffident.

He stood, holding her head between his hands. Then, slipping one arm swiftly about her body and drawing her towards him, he said softly:

—Gretta dear, what are you thinking about?

She did not answer nor yield wholly to his arm. He said again, softly:

—Tell me what it is, Gretta. I think I know what is the matter. Do I know?

She did not answer at once. Then she said in an outburst of tears:

—O, I am thinking about that song, *The Lass of Aughrim.*

She broke loose from him and ran to the bed and, throwing her arms across the bed-rail, hid her face. Gabriel stood stock-still for a moment in astonishment and then followed her. As he passed in the way of the cheval-glass he caught sight of himself in full length, his broad, well-filled shirt-front, the face whose expression always puzzled him when he saw it in a mirror and his glimmering gilt-rimmed eye-glasses. He halted a few paces from her and said:

—What about the song? Why does that make you cry?

She raised her head from her arms and dried her eyes with the back of her hand like a child. A kinder note than he had intended went into his voice.

—Why, Gretta? he asked.

—I am thinking about a person long ago who used to sing that song.

—And who was the person long ago? asked Gabriel, smiling.

—It was a person I used to know in Galway when I was living with my grandmother, she said.

The smile passed away from Gabriel's face. A dull anger began to gather again at the back of his mind and the dull fires of his lust began to glow angrily in his veins.

—Someone you were in love with? he asked ironically.

—It was a young boy I used to know, she answered, named Michael Furey. He used to sing that song, *The Lass of Aughrim.* He was very delicate.

Gabriel was silent. He did not wish her to think that he was interested in this delicate boy.

—I can see him so plainly, she said after a moment. Such eyes as he had: big dark eyes! And such an expression in them—an expression!

—O then, you were in love with him? said Gabriel.

—I used to go out walking with him, she said, when I was in Galway.

A thought flew across Gabriel's mind.

—Perhaps that was why you wanted to go to Galway with that Ivors girl? he said coldly.

She looked at him and asked in surprise:

—What for?

Her eyes made Gabriel feel awkward. He shrugged his shoulders and said:

—How do I know? To see him perhaps.

She looked away from him along the shaft of light towards the window in silence.

—He is dead, she said at length. He died when he was only seventeen. Isn't it a terrible thing to die so young as that?

—What was he? asked Gabriel, still ironically.

—He was in the gasworks, she said.

Gabriel felt humiliated by the failure of his irony and by the evocation of this figure from the dead, a boy in the gasworks. While he had been full of memories of their secret life together, full of tenderness and joy and desire, she had been comparing him in her mind with another. A shameful consciousness of his own person assailed him. He saw himself as a ludicrous figure, acting as a pennyboy[7] for his aunts, a nervous well-meaning sentimentalist, orating to vulgarians and idealising his own clownish lusts, the pitiable fatuous fellow he had caught a glimpse of in the mirror. Instinctively he turned his back more to the light lest she might see the shame that burned upon his forehead.

He tried to keep up his tone of cold interrogation but his voice when he spoke was humble and indifferent.

—I suppose you were in love with this Michael Furey, Gretta, he said.

—I was great with him at that time, she said.

Her voice was veiled and sad. Gabriel, feeling now how vain it would be to try to lead her whither he had purposed, caressed one of her hands and said, also sadly:

—And what did he die of so young, Gretta? Consumption, was it?

—I think he died for me, she answered.[8]

A vague terror seized Gabriel at this answer as if, at that hour when he had hoped to triumph, some impalpable and vindictive being was coming against him, gathering forces against him in its vague world. But he shook himself free of it with an effort of reason and continued to caress her hand. He did not question her again for he felt that she would tell him of herself. Her hand was warm and moist: it did not respond to his touch but he continued to caress it just as he had caressed her first letter to him that spring morning.

—It was in the winter, she said, about the beginning of the winter when I was going to leave my grandmother's and come up here to the convent. And he was ill at the time in his lodgings in Galway and wouldn't be let out and his people in Oughterard[9] were written to. He was in decline, they said, or something like that. I never knew rightly.

She paused for a moment and sighed.

—Poor fellow, she said. He was very fond of me and he was such a gentle boy. We used to go out together, walking, you know, Gabriel, like the way they do in the country. He was going to study singing only for his health. He had a very good voice, poor Michael Furey.

—Well; and then? asked Gabriel.

—And then when it came to the time for me to leave Galway and come up to the convent he was much worse and I wouldn't be let see him so I wrote a letter saying I was going up to Dublin and would be back in the summer and hoping he would be better then.

She paused for a moment to get her voice under control and then went on:

—Then the night before I left I was in my grandmother's house in Nuns' Island, packing up, and I heard gravel thrown up against the window. The window was so wet I couldn't see so I ran downstairs as I was and slipped out the back into the garden and there was the poor fellow at the end of the garden, shivering.

7. Errand boy.
8. Gretta here echoes the words of Yeats's Cathleen ní Houlihan: "Singing I am about a man I knew one time, yellow-haired Donough that was hanged in Galway. . . . He died for love of me: many a man has died for love of me." The play was first performed in Dublin on 2 April 1902.
9. A small village in Western Ireland.

—And did you not tell him to go back? asked Gabriel.

—I implored him to go home at once and told him he would get his death in the rain. But he said he did not want to live. I can see his eyes as well as well! He was standing at the end of the wall where there was a tree.

—And did he go home? asked Gabriel.

—Yes, he went home. And when I was only a week in the convent he died and he was buried in Oughterard where his people came from. O, the day I heard that, that he was dead!

She stopped, choking with sobs, and, overcome by emotion, flung herself face downward on the bed, sobbing in the quilt. Gabriel held her hand for a moment longer, irresolutely, and then, shy of intruding on her grief, let it fall gently and walked quietly to the window.

She was fast asleep.

Gabriel, leaning on his elbow, looked for a few moments unresentfully on her tangled hair and half-open mouth, listening to her deep-drawn breath. So she had had that romance in her life: a man had died for her sake. It hardly pained him now to think how poor a part he, her husband, had played in her life. He watched her while she slept as though he and she had never lived together as man and wife. His curious eyes rested long upon her face and on her hair: and, as he thought of what she must have been then, in that time of her first girlish beauty, a strange friendly pity for her entered his soul. He did not like to say even to himself that her face was no longer beautiful but he knew that it was no longer the face for which Michael Furey had braved death.

Perhaps she had not told him all the story. His eyes moved to the chair over which she had thrown some of her clothes. A petticoat string dangled to the floor. One boot stood upright, its limp upper fallen down: the fellow of it lay upon its side. He wondered at his riot of emotions of an hour before. From what had it proceeded? From his aunt's supper, from his own foolish speech, from the wine and dancing, the merry-making when saying good-night in the hall, the pleasure of the walk along the river in the snow. Poor Aunt Julia! She, too, would soon be a shade with the shade of Patrick Morkan and his horse. He had caught that haggard look upon her face for a moment when she was singing *Arrayed for the Bridal*. Soon, perhaps, he would be sitting in that same drawing-room, dressed in black, his silk hat on his knees. The blinds would be drawn down and Aunt Kate would be sitting beside him, crying and blowing her nose and telling him how Julia had died. He would cast about in his mind for some words that might console her, and would find only lame and useless ones. Yes, yes: that would happen very soon.

The air of the room chilled his shoulders. He stretched himself cautiously along under the sheets and lay down beside his wife. One by one they were all becoming shades. Better pass boldly into that other world, in the full glory of some passion, than fade and wither dismally with age. He thought of how she who lay beside him had locked in her heart for so many years that image of her lover's eyes when he had told her that he did not wish to live.

Generous tears filled Gabriel's eyes. He had never felt like that himself towards any woman but he knew that such a feeling must be love. The tears gathered more thickly in his eyes and in the partial darkness he imagined he saw the form of a young man standing under a dripping tree. Other forms were near. His soul had approached that region where dwell the vast hosts of the dead. He was conscious of, but could not apprehend, their wayward and flickering existence. His own identity was fading out into a grey impalpable world: the solid world itself which these dead had one time reared and lived in was dissolving and dwindling.

A few light taps upon the pane made him turn to the window. It had begun to snow again. He watched sleepily the flakes, silver and dark, falling obliquely against the lamplight. The time had come for him to set out on his journey westward. Yes, the newspapers were right: snow was general all over Ireland. It was falling on every part of the dark central plain, on the treeless hills, falling softly upon the Bog of Allen and, farther westward, softly falling into the dark mutinous Shannon waves.[1] It was falling, too, upon every part of the lonely churchyard on the hill where Michael Furey lay buried. It lay thickly drifted on the crooked crosses and headstones, on the spears of the little gate, on the barren thorns. His soul swooned slowly as he heard the snow falling faintly through the universe and faintly falling, like the descent of their last end, upon all the living and the dead.

⊶ ⊨◇⊠ ⊷

T. S. Eliot
1888–1965

T. S. Eliot was one of the dominant forces in English-language poetry of the twentieth century. When the entire body of Eliot's writing and influence is taken into account—not only his relatively modest poetic and dramatic production, but his literary criticism, his religious and cultural criticism, his editorial work at the British publishing house Faber and Faber, his influence on younger poets coming up in his wake, and quite simply his *presence* as a literary and cultural icon—no one looms larger. As one of those younger poets, Karl Shapiro, has written: "Eliot is untouchable; he is Modern Literature incarnate and an institution unto himself." Eliot's obituary in *Life* magazine declared that "Our age beyond any doubt has been, and will continue to be, the Age of Eliot."

Publicity photo from Barry Hyams, *T. S. Eliot*, 1954.

Thomas Stearns Eliot was born in Saint Louis, Missouri. The roots of Eliot's family tree go deep into American, and specifically New England, soil. His ancestor Andrew Eliot was one of the original settlers of the Massachusetts Bay Colony, emigrating from East Coker, in Somerset, England, in the mid-seventeenth century; he later became one of the jurors who tried the Salem "witches." The Eliots became a distinguished New England family; the Eliot family tree includes a president of Harvard University and three U.S. Presidents (John Adams, John Quincy Adams, and Rutherford B. Hayes). In 1834 the Reverend William Greenleaf Eliot, the poet's grandfather, graduated from Harvard and moved to Saint Louis, where he established the city's first Unitarian church; he went on to found Washington University, and became its chancellor in 1872. It was into this family environment—redolent of New England, New England religion (Unitarianism), and New England educational tradition (Harvard)—that Eliot was born in 1888. And yet in a 1960 essay, Eliot wrote "My urban imagery was that of Saint Louis, upon which that of Paris and London had been superimposed." The sights and sounds of Saint Louis impressed

---

1. Where Ireland's longest river, the Shannon, empties into the sea.

themselves deeply on Eliot's young imagination, especially the looming figure of the Mississippi River (which he was to call "a strong brown god" in *The Dry Salvages*).

From age ten Eliot attended Smith Academy in Saint Louis—also founded by his grandfather—and spent his last year of secondary school at the Milton Academy in Milton, Massachusetts, in preparation for his entrance into Harvard in 1906. Eliot went on to take his A.B. (1909) and M.A. (1910) degrees from Harvard and largely completed a Ph.D. in philosophy from Harvard, first spending a relatively unstructured year in Paris, attending lectures at the Sorbonne and hearing Henri Bergson lecture at the Collège de France. He wrote a doctoral dissertation on the neo-idealist philosopher F. H. Bradley in 1916, which was accepted by the philosophy department at Harvard, but he never returned to Cambridge to defend the dissertation and take the degree. Eliot's year in Paris was crucial in many ways; in addition to breathing in the vital Parisian intellectual and artistic scene, he soaked up the writing of late-nineteenth-century French poets like Jules Laforgue, Tristan Corbière, and Charles Baudelaire.

Eliot's poems are deeply indebted both to French and to British poets. The poem with which Eliot broke onto the modern poetry scene was *The Love Song of J. Alfred Prufrock*, composed between 1910 and 1911. In a strikingly new and jarring idiom, the poem builds on the dramatic monologues of Robert Browning, breaking up the unified voice at the center of Browning's experiments with startling juxtapositions and transitions, and adding the violent and disturbing imagery of the French symbolist poets. The resulting poem is a heavily ironic "love song" in which neither lover nor beloved exists with any solidity outside the straitjacket of "a formulated phrase"; Prufrock, like modern European humanity whom he represents, is unable to penetrate the thick husk of habit, custom, and cliché to arrive at something substantial.

Eliot, and the poem, came to the notice of modern literature impresario Ezra Pound; in 1915 Pound saw to it that *Prufrock* was published in Harriet Monroe's influential *Poetry* magazine, as well as in his own *Catholic Anthology*, which brought Eliot to the notice of the (largely hostile) British literary establishment in the person of reviewers like the *Quarterly Review*'s Arthur Waugh. Eliot wrote three other great poems in this early period, *Portrait of a Lady, Preludes*, and *Rhapsody on a Windy Night*. Like *Prufrock*, the poems deal unflinchingly with loneliness, alienation, isolation; while isolation is hardly a new theme for poetry, Eliot suggests in a particularly modernist form in these poems that our isolation from others derives from, and tragically mirrors, our isolation from ourselves. This internalized alienation was also one of the themes of Eliot's early and influential review essay *The Metaphysical Poets* (1921); in that piece, he suggested that English poetry had suffered through a long drought, dating from about the time of Milton, caused by what Eliot termed a "dissociation of sensibility." At the time of the metaphysical poets (in the seventeenth century), a poet, or any sensitive thinker, was a unified whole; "A thought to Donne," Eliot writes, "was an experience; it modified his sensibility. . . . the ordinary man's experience is chaotic, irregular, fragmentary." That chaotic consciousness seemed to Eliot especially pronounced in the early decades of the twentieth century; though not sanguine of easy solutions, he did believe that modern poets, writing a poetry that would synthesize the seemingly unrelated sensations and experiences of modern men and women, might show a way out of "the immense panorama of futility and anarchy which is contemporary history," as he wrote in 1923 in a review of Joyce's *Ulysses*.

A collection of Eliot's early poems was published in 1917 as *Prufrock and Other Observations* by the Egoist Press, through the offices of Pound. For the remainder of the decade, however, Eliot's poetic output was small; feeling himself at a creative cul de sac, he wrote a few poems in French in 1917, including *Dans le Restaurant* which later appeared, trimmed and translated, as a part of *The Waste Land*. On Pound's suggestion, Eliot set himself, as a formal exercise, to write several poems modeled on the quatrains of Théophile Gautier. Arguably the most significant and influential of Eliot's early writings, however, were his many critical essays and book reviews; between 1916 and 1921 he wrote nearly a hundred essays and reviews, many of which were published in 1920 as *The Sacred Wood*. Critics still disagree as to whether Eliot's poetry or critical prose has been the more influential; the most important of Eliot's critical precepts, such as the "impersonality" of poetry and the inherent difficulty of modern writing, have entered wholesale into the way that modern literature is studied and taught. Eliot's critical principles, complemented and extended by academics such as I. A. Richards, make up the foundation of what came to be known as the New Criticism, a major mode of reading that emphasizes close attention to verbal textures and to poetic ironies, paradoxes, and tensions between disparate elements—all prominent features of Eliot's own poetry.

Eliot lived in modest circumstances for several years, working as a schoolteacher and then a bank clerk between 1916 and 1922. He then edited an increasingly influential quarterly, *The Criterion* (1922–1939), and became an editor at Faber and Faber, a post he retained until his death. His reputation as a poet was confirmed in 1922 with *The Waste Land*, the epochal work that remains Eliot's best-known and most influential poem; Pound called it "about enough . . . to make the rest of us shut up shop." More than any other text of the century, *The Waste Land* forcibly changed the idiom that contemporary poetry must adopt if it were to remain contemporary. Perhaps the poem's most impressive formal achievement, created in no small part through Ezra Pound's judicious editorial work, is its careful balance between structure and chaos, unity and fragmentation; this poise is created in the poem in equal parts by the mythical structures Eliot used to undergird the contemporary action and the pedantic footnotes he added to the poem, after its periodical publication in the *Dial*, to call the reader's attention to those structures. *The Waste Land*—like *Ulysses*, *Finnegans Wake*, Pound's *Cantos*, and a number of other important texts—looks unified largely because we readers look for it to be unified. Such a style of reading is one of the great triumphs of modernism, and one Eliot was instrumental in teaching to readers and teachers alike.

The Waste Land is justly celebrated for giving voice to the nearly universal pessimism and alienation of the early decades of the twentieth century Europe—though Eliot maintained to the end that he was not a spokesperson for his generation or for anything else, and that the poem was "only the relief of a personal and wholly insignificant grouse against life; it is just a piece of rhythmical grumbling." Owing to the development of recording technology, to "give voice" in this case is not merely a metaphor, for Eliot's recording of *The Waste Land,* in what Virginia Woolf called Eliot's "sepulchral voice," has been tremendously influential on two generations of poets and students. Eliot's critical principle of "impersonality," however, has sometimes served to obscure how very personal, on one level, the poem is. The poem was completed during Eliot's convalescence at a sanatorium in Margate, England ("On Margate Sands. / I can connect / Nothing with nothing," the speaker despairs in section 3, "The Fire Sermon") and in Lausanne, Switzerland; the speaker, like the poet, is reduced to shoring the fragments of a disappearing civilization against his ruin. The poem also bears painful testimony to the increasingly desperate state of Eliot's wife Vivien Haigh-Wood, whom he had married in 1915; she suffered terribly from what was at the time called "nervousness," and had finally to be institutionalized in 1938. Whole stretches of one-sided "dialogue" from the "A Game of Chess" section would seem to have been taken verbatim from the couple's private conversations: "My nerves are very bad to-night. Yes, bad. Stay with me. / Speak to me. Why do you never speak? Speak." On the draft of the poem, Pound wrote "photography" alongside this passage. *The Waste Land* remains one of the century's most incisive and insightful texts regarding the breakdown of social, communal, cultural, and personal relationships.

In 1930 Eliot's next important poem, the introspective and confessional *Ash Wednesday,* was published; in the time since the publication of *The Waste Land,* however, Eliot's personal belief system had undergone a sea change. In June 1927 he was baptized into the Anglican church; five months later, he was naturalized as a British citizen. In his 1928 monograph *For Lancelot Andrewes,* Eliot declared himself to be "classicist in literature, royalist in politics, and Anglo-Catholic in religion." His poem *Journey of the Magi,* published as a pamphlet a month after his baptism, addresses the journey Eliot himself had made through death to a rebirth—precisely the rebirth which, in the opening lines of *The Waste Land,* seems an impossibility.

The 1930s also saw Eliot's entry into the theater, with three poetic dramas: *The Rock* (1934), *Murder in the Cathedral* (1935), and *The Family Reunion* (1939). In his later years, these highbrow dramas were complemented with a handful of more popular social dramas, *The Cocktail Party* (1950), *The Confidential Clerk* (1954), and *The Elder Statesman* (1959). Though celebrated by critics at the time for their innovative use of verse and their willingness to wrestle with both modern problems and universal themes, the plays have slipped in popularity in recent years. Nevertheless, as fate would have it, Eliot is the posthumous librettist of one of the most successful musicals in the history of British and American theater: his playful children's book *Old Possum's Book of Practical Cats* (1939), light verse written for the enjoyment of his godchildren, was transformed by Andrew Lloyd Webber in 1980 into the smash-hit musical *Cats*.

Eliot's final poetic achievement—and, for many, his greatest—is the set of four poems published together in 1943 as *Four Quartets*. Eliot believed them to be the best of his writing; "The *Four Quartets*: I rest on those," he told an interviewer in 1959. Structurally—though the analogy is a loose one—Eliot modeled the *Quartets* on the late string quartets of Beethoven, especially the last, the A Minor Quartet; as early as 1931 he had written the poet Stephen Spender, "I have the A Minor Quartet on the gramophone, and I find it quite inexhaustible to study. There is a sort of heavenly or at least more than human gaiety about some of his later things which one imagines might come to oneself as the fruit of reconcilliation and relief after immense suffering; I should like to get something of that into verse before I die."

Eliot's last years were brightened by increasing public accolades, including the Nobel Prize for literature in 1948; he became a very popular speaker on the public lecture circuit, attracting an audience of 15,000, for instance, at a lecture at the University of Minnesota in 1956, later published as *The Frontiers of Criticism*. These public appearances largely took the place of creative writing after 1960. In January 1947 Vivien Eliot died in an institution; a decade later, he married Esme Valery Fletcher, and enjoyed a fulfilling companionate marriage until his death in January 1965. Like Hardy and Yeats, Eliot expressed his wish to be buried in his ancestors' parish church, in his case at East Coker, the home of his ancestor Andrew Eliot; thus, in his death and burial, the opening of his poem *East Coker* is literalized: "In my beginning is my end."

The Love Song of J. Alfred Prufrock

> *S'io credessi che mia risposta fosse*
> *a persona che mai tornasse al mondo,*
> *questa fiamma staria senza più scosse.*
> *Ma per ciò che giammai di questo fondo*
> *non tornò vivo alcun, s'i'odo il vero,*
> *senza tema d'infamia ti rispondo.*[1]

Let us go then, you and I,
When the evening is spread out against the sky
Like a patient etherised upon a table;
Let us go, through certain half-deserted streets,
5   The muttering retreats
Of restless nights in one-night cheap hotels
And sawdust restaurants with oyster-shells:
Streets that follow like a tedious argument
Of insidious intent

1. From Dante's *Inferno* (27.61–66). Dante asks one of the damned souls for its name, and it replies: "If I thought my answer were for one who could return to the world, I would not reply, but as none ever did return alive from this depth, without fear of infamy I answer thee."

10   To lead you to an overwhelming question . . .
      Oh, do not ask, "What is it?"
      Let us go and make our visit.

      In the room the women come and go
      Talking of Michelangelo.

15   The yellow fog that rubs its back upon the window-panes,
      The yellow smoke that rubs its muzzle on the window-panes,
      Licked its tongue into the corners of the evening,
      Lingered upon the pools that stand in drains,
      Let fall upon its back the soot that falls from chimneys,
20   Slipped by the terrace, made a sudden leap,
      And seeing that it was a soft October night,
      Curled once about the house, and fell asleep.

      And indeed there will be time
      For the yellow smoke that slides along the street
25   Rubbing its back upon the window-panes;
      There will be time, there will be time
      To prepare a face to meet the faces that you meet;
      There will be time to murder and create,
      And time for all the works and days of hands
30   That lift and drop a question on your plate;
      Time for you and time for me,
      And time yet for a hundred indecisions,
      And for a hundred visions and revisions,
      Before the taking of a toast and tea.

35   In the room the women come and go
      Talking of Michelangelo.

      And indeed there will be time
      To wonder, "Do I dare?" and, "Do I dare?"
      Time to turn back and descend the stair,
40   With a bald spot in the middle of my hair—
      (They will say: "How his hair is growing thin!")
      My morning coat, my collar mounting firmly to the chin,
      My necktie rich and modest, but asserted by a simple pin—
      (They will say: "But how his arms and legs are thin!")
45   Do I dare
      Disturb the universe?
      In a minute there is time
      For decisions and revisions which a minute will reverse.

      For I have known them all already, known them all—
50   Have known the evenings, mornings, afternoons,
      I have measured out my life with coffee spoons;
      I know the voices dying with a dying fall
      Beneath the music from a farther room.
          So how should I presume?

55   And I have known the eyes already, known them all—
     The eyes that fix you in a formulated phrase,
     And when I am formulated, sprawling on a pin,
     When I am pinned and wriggling on the wall,
     Then how should I begin
60   To spit out all the butt-ends of my days and ways?
          And how should I presume?

     And I have known the arms already, known them all—
     Arms that are braceleted and white and bare
     (But in the lamplight, downed with light brown hair!)
65   Is it perfume from a dress
     That makes me so digress?
     Arms that lie along a table, or wrap about a shawl.
          And should I then presume?
          And how should I begin?
                    . . .
70   Shall I say, I have gone at dusk through narrow streets
     And watched the smoke that rises from the pipes
     Of lonely men in shirt-sleeves, leaning out of windows? . . .

     I should have been a pair of ragged claws
     Scuttling across the floors of silent seas.
                    . . .
75   And the afternoon, the evening, sleeps so peacefully!
     Smoothed by long fingers,
     Asleep . . . tired . . . or it malingers,
     Stretched on the floor, here beside you and me.
     Should I, after tea and cakes and ices,
80   Have the strength to force the moment to its crisis?
     But though I have wept and fasted, wept and prayed,
     Though I have seen my head (grown slightly bald) brought
          in upon a platter,[2]
     I am no prophet—and here's no great matter;
     I have seen the moment of my greatness flicker,
85   And I have seen the eternal Footman hold my coat, and snicker,
     And in short, I was afraid.

     And would it have been worth it, after all,
     After the cups, the marmalade, the tea,
     Among the porcelain, among some talk of you and me,
90   Would it have been worth while,
     To have bitten off the matter with a smile,
     To have squeezed the universe into a ball
     To roll it towards some overwhelming question,
     To say: "I am Lazarus, come from the dead,

---

2. Cf. Matthew 14. John the Baptist was beheaded by Herod and his head was brought to his wife, Herodias, on a platter.

95   Come back to tell you all, I shall tell you all"[3]—
        If one, settling a pillow by her head,
             Should say: "That is not what I meant at all.
             That is not it, at all."

        And would it have been worth it, after all,
100   Would it have been worth while,
        After the sunsets and the dooryards and the sprinkled streets,
        After the novels, after the teacups, after the skirts that trail
             along the floor—
        And this, and so much more?—
        It is impossible to say just what I mean!
105   But as if a magic lantern[4] threw the nerves in patterns on a
             screen:
        Would it have been worth while
        If one, settling a pillow or throwing off a shawl,
        And turning toward the window, should say:
             "That is not it at all,
110   That is not what I meant, at all."
                                . . .
        No! I am not Prince Hamlet, nor was meant to be;
        Am an attendant lord, one that will do
        To swell a progress, start a scene or two,
        Advise the prince; no doubt, an easy tool,
115   Deferential, glad to be of use,
        Politic, cautious, and meticulous;
        Full of high sentence, but a bit obtuse;
        At times, indeed, almost ridiculous—
        Almost, at times, the Fool.
120   I grow old . . . I grow old . . .
        I shall wear the bottoms of my trousers rolled.

        Shall I part my hair behind? Do I dare to eat a peach?
        I shall wear white flannel trousers, and walk upon the beach.
        I have heard the mermaids singing, each to each.

125   I do not think that they will sing to me.

        I have seen them riding seaward on the waves
        Combing the white hair of the waves blown back
        When the wind blows the water white and black.

        We have lingered in the chambers of the sea
130   By sea-girls wreathed with seaweed red and brown
        Till human voices wake us, and we drown.

---

3. Cf. John 11. Jesus raised Lazurus from the grave after he had been dead four days.

4. A device that employs a candle to project images, rather like a slide projector.

Gerontion[1]

Thou hast nor youth nor age
But as it were an after dinner sleep
Dreaming of both.[2]

Here I am, an old man in a dry month,
Being read to by a boy, waiting for rain.
I was neither at the hot gates
Nor fought in the warm rain
5   Nor knee deep in the salt marsh, heaving a cutlass,
Bitten by flies, fought.
My house is a decayed house,
And the Jew squats on the window sill, the owner,
Spawned in some estaminet° of Antwerp,   *café*
10   Blistered in Brussels, patched and peeled in London.
The goat coughs at night in the field overhead;
Rocks, moss, stonecrop, iron, merds.°   *droppings, shit*
The woman keeps the kitchen, makes tea,
Sneezes at evening, poking the peevish gutter.
15   I an old man,
A dull head among windy spaces.

Signs are taken for wonders. "We would see a sign!"[3]
The word within a word, unable to speak a word,
Swaddled with darkness. In the juvescence° of the year   *youth*
20   Came Christ the tiger

In depraved May, dogwood and chestnut, flowering judas,[4]
To be eaten, to be divided, to be drunk
Among whispers; by Mr. Silvero
With caressing hands, at Limoges[5]
25   Who walked all night in the next room;
By Hakagawa, bowing among the Titians;[6]
By Madame de Tornquist, in the dark room
Shifting the candles; Fräulein von Kulp
Who turned in the hall, one hand on the door.
30   Vacant shuttles
Weave the wind. I have no ghosts,

1. From the Greek word meaning "old man." While still working on what was to become *The Waste Land*, Eliot had considered printing *Gerontion* as a kind of prelude; Pound disapproved of the idea, and it was dropped.
2. Loosely quoted from Shakespeare's *Measure for Measure* (3.1.32–34).
3. Eliot here echoes the sermon by Anglican theologican Lancelot Andrewes (1555–1626) on Matthew: "An evil and adulterous generation seeketh after a sign; and there shall no sign be given to it, but the sign of the prophet Jonas." (Matthew 12.39).
4. A flowering shrub-tree, named after Judas Iscariot; according to legend, Judas hanged himself on this type of tree after betraying Jesus.
5. City in France; home of fine china of the same name.
6. Painter of the Italian Renaissance (1477–1576) known for his female nudes.

An old man in a draughty house
Under a windy knob.

After such knowledge, what forgiveness? Think now
35   History has many cunning passages, contrived corridors
And issues, deceives with whispering ambitions,
Guides us by vanities. Think now
She gives when our attention is distracted
And what she gives, gives with such supple confusions
40   That the giving famishes the craving. Gives too late
What's not believed in, or is still believed,
In memory only, reconsidered passion. Gives too soon
Into weak hands, what's thought can be dispensed with
Till the refusal propagates a fear. Think
45   Neither fear nor courage saves us. Unnatural vices
Are fathered by our heroism. Virtues
Are forced upon us by our impudent crimes.
These tears are shaken from the wrath-bearing tree.

The tiger springs in the new year. Us he devours. Think at last
50   We have not reached conclusion, when I
Stiffen in a rented house. Think at last
I have not made this show purposelessly
And it is not by any concitation°   *stirring up*
Of the backward devils.
55   I would meet you upon this honestly.
I that was near your heart was removed therefrom
To lose beauty in terror, terror in inquisition.
I have lost my passion: why should I need to keep it
Since what is kept must be adulterated?
60   I have lost my sight, smell, hearing, taste and touch:
How should I use them for your closer contact?

These with a thousand small deliberations
Protract the profit of their chilled delirium,
Excite the membrane, when the sense has cooled,
65   With pungent sauces, multiply variety
In a wilderness of mirrors. What will the spider do,
Suspend its operations, will the weevil
Delay? De Bailhache, Fresca, Mrs. Cammel, whirled
Beyond the circuit of the shuddering Bear[7]
70   In fractured atoms. Gull against the wind, in the windy straits

7. The constellation Ursa Major, also called the Great Bear or Big Dipper.

Of Belle Isle,[8] or running on the Horn.[9]
White feathers in the snow, the Gulf claims,
And an old man driven by the Trades[1]
To a sleepy corner.

75   Tenants of the house,
Thoughts of a dry brain in a dry season.

THE WASTE LAND   Like Conrad's *Heart of Darkness*—from which Eliot had originally planned to take his epigraph, "The horror! the horror!"—*The Waste Land* has become part of the symbolic landscape of twentieth-century Western culture; the text, like Conrad's, has been appropriated by commentators high and low, left and right, as an especially apt description of the psychosocial and interpersonal malaise of modern Europeans. Late in 1921 Eliot, who was suffering under a number of pressures both personal and artistic, took three months' leave from his job at Lloyd's Bank and went for a "rest cure" at a clinic in Lausanne, Switzerland. On his way he passed through Paris and showed the manuscript of the poem—really manuscripts of a number of fragments, whose interrelationship Eliot was trying to work out—to Ezra Pound; Pound and Eliot went through the poem again as Eliot returned to London in January 1922. Pound's editorial work was considerable, as the facsimile edition of the draft reveals; Pound said that he performed the poem's "caesarian operation," and Eliot dedicated *The Waste Land* to Pound—*il miglior fabbro* ("the better craftsman," a phrase from Dante).

The most obvious feature of *The Waste Land* is its difficulty. Eliot was perhaps the first poet and literary critic to argue that such "difficulty" was not just a necessary evil but in fact a constitutive element of poetry that would come to terms with the modern world. In his review of a volume of metaphysical poetry, Eliot implicitly links the complex poetry of Donne and Marvell with the task of the modern poet: "We can only say that it appears likely that poets in our civilization, as it exists at present, must be *difficult*. Our civilization comprehends great variety and complexity, and this variety and complexity, playing upon a refined sensibility, must produce various and complex results." In the case of *The Waste Land*, the difficulty lies primarily in the poem's dense tissue of quotations from and allusions to other texts; as Eliot's own footnotes to the poem demonstrate, the poem draws its strength, and achieves a kind of universality, by making implicit and explicit reference to texts as widely different as Ovid's *Metamorphoses* and a World War I Australian marching song.

Beyond the density of the poem's quotations and allusions, Eliot hoped to suggest the possibilty of an order beneath the chaos. In his review of Joyce's *Ulysses* (published in November 1923) Eliot was to describe the "mythical method," deploying allusions to classical mythology to suggest an implicit (and recurring) order beneath contemporary history; and while his use of myth was not so methodical as Joyce's, his use of vegetation myth and romance structures points outside the world of the poem to "another world," where the brokenness of the waste land might be healed. At the time of writing the poem, however, Eliot could not see clearly where that healing might come from.

---

8. The passage between Newfoundland and southern Labrador.

9. Cape Horn, the southernmost point of South America.
1. The trade winds, nearly conotant tropical winds.

The Waste Land[1]

"Nam Sibyllam quidem Cumis ego ipse oculis meis vidi in
ampulla pendere, et cum illi pueri dicerent: Σίβυλλα τί
θέλεις; respondebat illa: ἀποθανεῖν θέλω."[2]

FOR EZRA POUND
il miglior fabbro.

I. THE BURIAL OF THE DEAD

April is the cruellest month, breeding
Lilacs out of the dead land, mixing
Memory and desire, stirring
Dull roots with spring rain.
5 Winter kept us warm, covering
Earth in forgetful snow, feeding
A little life with dried tubers.
Summer surprised us, coming over the Starnbergersee[3]
With a shower of rain; we stopped in the colonnade,
10 And went on in sunlight, into the Hofgarten,[4]
And drank coffee, and talked for an hour.
Bin gar keine Russin, stamm' aus Litauen, echt deutsch.[5]
And when we were children, staying at the arch-duke's,
My cousin's, he took me out on a sled,
15 And I was frightened. He said, Marie,
Marie, hold on tight. And down we went.
In the mountains, there you feel free.
I read, much of the night, and go south in the winter.

What are the roots that clutch, what branches grow
20 Out of this stony rubbish? Son of man,[6]
You cannot say, or guess, for you know only
A heap of broken images, where the sun beats,
And the dead tree gives no shelter, the cricket no relief,[7]
And the dry stone no sound of water. Only

---

1. Not only the title, but the plan and a good deal of the incidental symbolism of the poem were suggested by Miss Jessie L. Weston's book on the Grail legend: *From Ritual to Romance* (Cambridge). Indeed, so deeply am I indebted, Miss Weston's book will elucidate the difficulties of the poem much better than my notes can do; and I recommend it (apart from the great interest of the book itself) to any who think such elucidation of the poem worth the trouble. To another work of anthropology I am indebted in general, one which has influenced our generation profoundly; I mean *The Golden Bough*; I have used especially the two volumes *Adonis, Attis, Osiris.* Anyone who is acquainted with these works will immediately recognize in the poem certain references to vegetation ceremonies [Eliot's note]. Sir James Frazer (1854–1941) brought out the 12 volumes of *The Golden Bough*, a vast work of anthropology and comparative mythology and religion, between 1890 and 1915, with a supplement published in 1936.

2. From the *Satyricon* of Petronius (first century A.D.). "For once I myself saw with my own eyes the Sybil at Cumae hanging in a cage, and when the boys said to her, 'Sybil, what do you want?' she replied, 'I want to die.'" The Sybil was granted anything she wished by Apollo, if only she would be his; she made the mistake of asking for everlasting life, without asking for eternal youth.
3. A lake near Munich.
4. A public park in Munich, with a zoo and cafés.
5. I'm not a Russian at all; I come from Lithuania, a true German (German).
6. Cf. Ezekiel 2.1 [Eliot's note]. Line 20. Ezekiel 2.1 reads: "But thou, son of man, hear what I say unto thee; Be not thou rebellious like that rebellious house: open thy mouth, and eat that I give thee."
7. Cf. Ecclesiastes 12.5 [Eliot's note]. "They shall be afraid of that which is high, and fears shall be in the way, and the almond tree shall flourish, and the grasshopper shall be a burden, and desire shall fail."

25 There is shadow under this red rock,
(Come in under the shadow of this red rock),
And I will show you something different from either
Your shadow at morning striding behind you
Or your shadow at evening rising to meet you;
30 I will show you fear in a handful of dust.

> *Frisch weht der Wind*
> *Der Heimat zu*
> *Mein Irisch Kind,*
> *Wo weilest du?*[8]

35 "You gave me hyacinths first a year ago;
They called me the hyacinth girl."
—Yet when we came back, late, from the hyacinth garden,
Your arms full, and your hair wet, I could not
Speak, and my eyes failed, I was neither
40 Living nor dead, and I knew nothing,
Looking into the heart of light, the silence.
Oed' und leer das Meer.[9]

Madame Sosostris, famous clairvoyante,
Had a bad cold, nevertheless
45 Is known to be the wisest woman in Europe,
With a wicked pack of cards.[1] Here, said she,
Is your card, the drowned Phoenician Sailor,
(Those are pearls that were his eyes.[2] Look!)
Here is Belladonna, the Lady of the Rocks,
50 The lady of situations.
Here is the man with three staves, and here the Wheel,
And here is the one-eyed merchant, and this card,
Which is blank, is something he carries on his back,
Which I am forbidden to see. I do not find
55 The Hanged Man.[3] Fear death by water.
I see crowds of people, walking round in a ring.
Thank you. If you see dear Mrs. Equitone,
Tell her I bring the horoscope myself:
One must be so careful these days.

---

8. V. *Tristan and Isolde,* i, verses 5–8 [Eliot's note]. In Wagner's opera, Tristan sings this about Isolde, the woman he is leaving behind as he sails for home: "Fresh blows the wind to the homeland; my Irish child, where are you waiting?"

9. Id. iii, verse 24 [Eliot's note]. Tristan is dying and waiting for Isolde to come to him, but a shepherd, whom Tristan has hired to keep watch for her ship, reports only "Desolate and empty the sea."

1. I am not familiar with the exact constitution of the Tarot pack of cards, from which I have obviously departed to suit my own convenience. The Hanged Man, a member of the traditional pack, fits my purpose in two ways: because he is associated in my mind with the Hanged God of Frazer, and because I associated him with the hooded figure in the passage of the disciples to Emmaus in Part V. The Phoenician Sailor and the Merchant appear later; also the "crowds of people," and Death by Water is executed in Part IV. The Man with Three Staves (an authentic member of the Tarot pack) I associate, quite arbitrarily, with the Fisher King Himself [Eliot's note].

2. From Ariel's song, in Shakespeare's *The Tempest:* "Full fathom five thy father lies; / Of his bones are coral made; / Those are pearls that were his eyes: / Nothing of him that doth fade, / But doth suffer a sea-change" (1.2.399–403).

3. The tarot card that depicts a man hanging by one foot from a cross.

60 Unreal City,[4]
Under the brown fog of a winter dawn,
A crowd flowed over London Bridge, so many,
I had not thought death had undone so many.[5]
Sighs, short and infrequent, were exhaled,[6]
65 And each man fixed his eyes before his feet.
Flowed up the hill and down King William Street,
To where Saint Mary Woolnoth kept the hours
With a dead sound on the final stroke of nine.[7]
There I saw one I knew, and stopped him, crying: "Stetson!
70 You who were with me in the ships at Mylae![8]
That corpse you planted last year in your garden,
Has it begun to sprout? Will it bloom this year?
Or has the sudden frost disturbed its bed?
O keep the Dog far hence, that's friend to men,[9]
75 Or with his nails he'll dig it up again!
You! hypocrite lecteur!—mon semblable,—mon frère!"[1]

II. A GAME OF CHESS[2]

The Chair she sat in, like a burnished throne,[3]
Glowed on the marble, where the glass
Held up by standards wrought with fruited vines
80 From which a golden Cupidon peeped out
(Another hid his eyes behind his wing)
Doubled the flames of sevenbranched candelabra
Reflecting light upon the table as
The glitter of her jewels rose to meet it,
85 From satin cases poured in rich profusion.
In vials of ivory and coloured glass
Unstoppered, lurked her strange synthetic perfumes,
Unguent, powdered, or liquid—troubled, confused
And drowned the sense in odours; stirred by the air
90 That freshened from the window, these ascended
In fattening the prolonged candle-flames,
Flung their smoke into the laquearia,[4]

---

4. Cf. Baudelaire: "Fourmillante cité, cité pleine de rêves, / Où le spectre en plein jour raccroche le passant" [Eliot's note].
5. Cf. Inferno, iii. 55–7: "si lunga tratta / di gente, ch'io non avrei mai creduto / che morte tanta n'avesse disfatta" [Eliot's note]. "Such an endless train, / Of people, it never would have entered in my head / There were so many men whom death had slain."
6. Cf. Inferno, iv. 25–7: "Ouivi, secondo che per ascoltare, / non avea pianto, ma' che di sospiri, / che l'aura eterna facevan tremare" [Eliot's note]. "We heard no loud complaint, no crying there, / No sound of grief except the sound of sighing / Quivering forever through the eternal air."
7. A phenomenon which I have often noticed [Eliot's note].

8. The Battle of Mylae (260 B.C.) in the First Punic War.
9. Cf. the Dirge in Webster's White Devil [Eliot's note].
1. V. Baudelaire, Preface to Fleurs du Mal [Eliot's note]. "Hypocrite reader—my double—my brother!"
2. Cf. Thomas Middleton's drama A Game at Chess (1625), a political satire.
3. Cf. Antony and Cleopatra, II. ii. 190 [Eliot's note].
4. "Laquearia. V. Aeneid, I.726: "dependent lychni laquearibus aureis / incensi, et noctem flammis funalia vincunt." [Eliot's note]. "Burning lamps hang from the gold-panelled ceiling / And torches dispel the night with their flames"; a laquearia is a panelled ceiling. The passage from Virgil's Aeneid describes the banquet given by Dido for her lover Aeneas.

Stirring the pattern on the coffered ceiling.
Huge sea-wood fed with copper
95   Burned green and orange, framed by the coloured stone,
In which sad light a carvèd dolphin swam.
Above the antique mantel was displayed
As though a window gave upon the sylvan scene[5]
The change of Philomel, by the barbarous king[6]
100   So rudely forced; yet there the nightingale[7]
Filled all the desert with inviolable voice
And still she cried, and still the world pursues,
"Jug Jug" to dirty ears.
And other withered stumps of time
105   Were told upon the walls; staring forms
Leaned out, leaning, hushing the room enclosed.
Footsteps shuffled on the stair.
Under the firelight, under the brush, her hair
Spread out in fiery points
110   Glowed into words, then would be savagely still.

"My nerves are bad to-night. Yes, bad. Stay with me.
Speak to me. Why do you never speak. Speak.
    What are you thinking of? What thinking? What?
I never know what you are thinking. Think."

115   I think we are in rats' alley[8]
Where the dead men lost their bones.

"What is that noise?"
                  The wind under the door.[9]
"What is that noise now? What is the wind doing?"
120   Nothing again nothing.

                                 "Do
"You know nothing? Do you see nothing? Do you remember
Nothing?"
I remember
125   Those are pearls that were his eyes.
"Are you alive, or not? Is there nothing in your head?"[1]
                                  But

    O O O O that Shakespeherian Rag—[2]
It's so elegant
130   So intelligent

---

5. "Sylvan scene. V. Milton, *Paradise Lost*, iv. 140 [Eliot's note]. "And over head up grew / Insuperable height of loftiest shade, / Cedar, and Pine, and Fir, and branching Palm, / A Silvan Scene, and as the ranks ascend / Shade above shade, a woody Theatre / Of stateliest view" The passage describes the Garden of Eden, as seen through Satan's eyes.
6. V. Ovid, *Metamorphoses*, vi, Philomela [Eliot's note]. Philomela was raped by King Tereus, her sister's husband, and was then changed into a nightingale.

7. Cf. Part III, l. 204 [Eliot's note].
8. Cf. Part III, l. 195 [Eliot's note].
9. Cf. Webster: "Is the wind in that door still?" [Eliot's note]. From John Webster's *The Devil's Law Case*, 3.2.162. The doctor asks this question when he discovers that a "murder victim" is still breathing.
1. Cf. Part I, l. 37, 48 [Eliot's note].
2. Quoting an American ragtime song featured in Ziegfield's Follies of 1912.

"What shall I do now? What shall I do?"
"I shall rush out as I am, and walk the street
With my hair down, so. What shall we do tomorrow?
What shall we ever do?"

135   The hot water at ten.
And if it rains, a closed car at four.
And we shall play a game of chess,
Pressing lidless eyes and waiting for a knock upon the door.[3]

When Lil's husband got demobbed,° I said—   *demobilized*
140   I didn't mince my words, I said to her myself,
HURRY UP PLEASE ITS TIME[4]
Now Albert's coming back, make yourself a bit smart.
He'll want to know what you done with that money he gave you
To get yourself some teeth. He did, I was there.
145   You have them all out, Lil, and get a nice set,
He said, I swear, I can't bear to look at you.
And no more can't I, I said, and think of poor Albert,
He's been in the army four years, he wants a good time,
And if you don't give it him, there's others will, I said.
150   Oh is there, she said. Something o' that, I said.
Then I'll know who to thank, she said, and give me a straight look.
HURRY UP PLEASE ITS TIME
If you don't like it you can get on with it, I said.
Others can pick and choose if you can't.
155   But if Albert makes off, it won't be for lack of telling.
You ought to be ashamed, I said, to look so antique.
(And her only thirty-one.)
I can't help it, she said, pulling a long face,
It's them pills I took, to bring it off, she said.
160   (She's had five already, and nearly died of young George.)
The chemist[5] said it would be all right, but I've never been the same.
You *are* a proper fool, I said.
Well, if Albert won't leave you alone, there it is, I said,
What you get married for if you don't want children?
165   HURRY UP PLEASE ITS TIME
Well, that Sunday Albert was home, they had a hot gammon,°   *ham*
And they asked me in to dinner, to get the beauty of it hot—
HURRY UP PLEASE ITS TIME
HURRY UP PLEASE ITS TIME
170   Goonight Bill. Goonight Lou. Goonight May. Goonight.
Ta ta. Goonight. Goonight.
Good night, ladies, good night, sweet ladies, good night, good night.[6]

---

3. Cf. the game of chess in Middleton's *Women beware Women* [Eliot's note].
4. A British pub-keeper's call for a last round before closing.
5. Pharmacist.

6. Ophelia speaks these words in Shakespeare's *Hamlet*, and they are understood by the King as certain evidence of her insanity: "Good night ladies, good night. Sweet ladies, good night, good night" (4.5.72–73).

III. THE FIRE SERMON

The river's tent is broken; the last fingers of leaf
Clutch and sink into the wet bank. The wind
175 Crosses the brown land, unheard. The nymphs are departed.
Sweet Thames, run softly, till I end my song.[7]
The river bears no empty bottles, sandwich papers,
Silk handkerchiefs, cardboard boxes, cigarette ends
Or other testimony of summer nights. The nymphs are departed.
180 And their friends, the loitering heirs of City directors;
Departed, have left no addresses.
By the waters of Leman[8] I sat down and wept . . .
Sweet Thames, run softly till I end my song,
Sweet Thames, run softly, for I speak not loud or long.
185 But at my back in a cold blast I hear
The rattle of the bones, and chuckle spread from ear to ear.

A rat crept softly through the vegetation
Dragging its slimy belly on the bank
While I was fishing in the dull canal
190 On a winter evening round behind the gashouse
Musing upon the king my brother's wreck
And on the king my father's death before him.[9]
White bodies naked on the low damp ground
And bones cast in a little low dry garret,
195 Rattled by the rat's foot only, year to year.
But at my back from time to time I hear[1]
The sound of horns and motors, which shall bring[2]
Sweeney to Mrs. Porter in the spring.
O the moon shone bright on Mrs. Porter[3]
200 And on her daughter
They wash their feet in soda water
Et O ces voix d'enfants, chantant dans la coupole![4]

Twit twit twit
Jug jug jug jug jug jug
205 So rudely forc'd.
Tereu

Unreal City
Under the brown fog of a winter noon

7. V. Spenser, *Prothalamion* [Eliot's note]; Spenser's poem (1596) celebrates the double marriage of Lady Elizabeth and Lady Katherine Somerset.
8. Lake Geneva. The line echoes Psalm 137, in which, exiled in Babylon, the Hebrew poets are too full of grief to sing.
9. Cf. *The Tempest*, I. ii [Eliot's note].
1. Cf. Marvell, *To His Coy Mistress* [Eliot's note]. "But at my back I always hear / Time's wingéd chariot hurrying near."
2. Cf. Day, *Parliament of Bees:* "When of the sudden, listening, you shall hear, / A noise of horns and hunting, which shall bring / Actaeon to Diana in the spring, /

Where all shall see her naked skin . . . " [Eliot's note].
3. I do not know the origin of the ballad from which these are taken: it was reported to me from Sydney, Australia [Eliot's note]. Sung by Australian soldiers in World War I: "O the moon shone bright on Mrs. Porter / And on the daughter / Of Mrs. Porter / They wash their feet in soda water / And so they oughter / To keep them clean."
4. V. Verlaine, *Parsifal* [Eliot's note]. "And O those children's voices singing in the dome." Paul Verlaine's sonnet describes Parsifal, who keeps himself pure in hopes of seeing the holy grail, and has his feet washed before entering the castle.

210   Mr. Eugenides, the Smyrna[5] merchant
     Unshaven, with a pocket full of currants
     C.i.f.[6] London: documents at sight,
     Asked me in demotic° French   *vulgar*
     To luncheon at the Cannon Street Hotel[7]
     Followed by a weekend at the Metropole.[8]

215   At the violet hour, when the eyes and back
     Turn upward from the desk, when the human engine waits
     Like a taxi throbbing waiting,
     I Tiresias,[9] though blind, throbbing between two lives,
     Old man with wrinkled female breasts, can see
220   At the violet hour, the evening hour that strives
     Homeward, and brings the sailor home from sea,[1]
     The typist home at teatime, clears her breakfast, lights
     Her stove, and lays out food in tins.
     Out of the window perilously spread
225   Her drying combinations touched by the sun's last rays,
     On the divan are piled (at night her bed)
     Stockings, slippers, camisoles, and stays.
     I Tiresias, old man with wrinkled dugs
     Perceived the scene, and foretold the rest—
230   I too awaited the expected guest.
     He, the young man carbuncular,° arrives,   *pimply*
     A small house agent's clerk, with one bold stare,
     One of the low on whom assurance sits

---

5. Seaport in western Turkey.

6. The currants were quoted at a price "carriage and insurance free to London"; and the Bill of Lading, etc., were to be handed to the buyer upon payment of the sight draft [Eliot's note].

7. A hotel in London near the train station used for travel to and from continental Europe.

8. An upscale seaside resort hotel in Brighton.

9. Tiresias, although a mere spectator and not indeed a "character," is yet the most important personage in the poem, uniting all the rest. Just as the one-eyed merchant, seller of currants, melts into the Phoenician Sailor, and the latter is not wholly distinct from Ferdinand Prince of Naples, so all the women are one woman, and the two sexes meet in Tiresias. What Tiresias *sees*, in fact, is the substance of the poem. The whole passage from Ovid is of great anthropological interest: ". . . Cum Iunone iocos et 'maior vestra profecto est / Quam, quae contingit maribus,' dixisse, 'voluptas.' / Illa negat; placuit quae sit sententia docti / Quaerere Tiresiae: venus huic erat utraque nota. / Nam duo magnorum viridi coeuntia silva / Corpora serpentum baculi violaverat ictu / Deque viro factus, mirabile, femina septem / Egerat autumnos; octavo rursus eosdem / Vidit et 'est vestrae si tanta potentia plagae,' / Dixit 'ut auctoris sortem in contraria mutet, / Nunc quoque vos feriam!' percussis anguibus isdem / Forma prior rediit genetivaque venit imago. / Arbiter hic igitur sumptus de lite iocosa / Dicta Iovis firmat; gravius Saturnia iusto / Nec pro materia fertur doluisse suique / Iudicis aeterna damnavit lumina nocte, / At pater omnipotens (neque enim licet inrita cuiquam / Facta dei fecisse deo) pro lumine adempto / Scire futura dedit poenamque levavit honore" [Eliot's note]. This passage from Ovid's *Metamorphoses* describes Tiresias's sex change: "[The story goes that once Jove, having drunk a great deal,] jested with Juno. He said, 'Your pleasure in love is really greater than that enjoyed by men.' She denied it; so they decided to seek the opinion of the wise Tiresias, for he knew both aspects of love. For once, with a blow of his staff, he had committed violence on two huge snakes as they copulated in the green forest; and—wonderful to tell—was turned from a man into a woman and thus spent seven years. In the eighth year he saw the same snakes again and said: 'If a blow struck at you is so powerful that it changes the sex of the giver, I will now strike at you again.' With these words he struck the snakes, and his former shape was restored to him and he became as he had been born. So he was appointed arbitrator in the playful quarrel, and supported Jove's statement. It is said that Saturnia [i.e., Juno] was quite disproportionately upset, and condemned the arbitrator to perpetual blindness. But the almighty father (for no god may undo what has been done by another god), in return for the sight that was taken away, gave him the power to know the future and so lightened the penalty paid by the honor."

1. This may not appear as exact as Sappho's lines but I had in mind the "longshore" or "dory" fisherman, who returns at nightfall [Eliot's note]. "Hesperus, thou bringst home all things bright morning scattered: thou bringest the sheep, the goat, the child to the mother."

As a silk hat on a Bradford[2] millionaire.
235   The time is now propitious, as he guesses,
The meal is ended, she is bored and tired,
Endeavours to engage her in caresses
Which still are unreproved, if undesired.
Flushed and decided, he assaults at once;
240   Exploring hands encounter no defence;
His vanity requires no response,
And makes a welcome of indifference.
(And I Tiresias have foresuffered all
Enacted on this same divan or bed;
245   I who have sat by Thebes below the wall
And walked among the lowest of the dead.)
Bestows one final patronising kiss,
And gropes his way, finding the stairs unlit . . .

She turns and looks a moment in the glass,
250   Hardly aware of her departed lover;
Her brain allows one half-formed thought to pass:
"Well now that's done: and I'm glad it's over."
When lovely woman stoops to folly and[3]
Paces about her room again, alone,
255   She smoothes her hair with automatic hand,
And puts a record on the gramophone.

"This music crept by me upon the waters"[4]
And along the Strand, up Queen Victoria Street.
O City city, I can sometimes hear
260   Beside a public bar in Lower Thames Street,
The pleasant whining of a mandoline
And a clatter and a chatter from within
Where fishmen lounge at noon: where the walls
Of Magnus Martyr[5] hold
265   Inexplicable splendour of Ionian white and gold.

The river sweats[6]
Oil and tar
The barges drift
With the turning tide

2. An industrial town in Yorkshire; many of its residents became wealthy during World War I.
3. V. Goldsmith, the song in *The Vicar of Wakefield* [Eliot's note]. Oliver Goldsmith's character Olivia, on returning to the place where she was seduced, sings, "When lovely woman stoops to folly / And finds too late that men betray / What charm can soothe her melancholy, / What art can wash her guilt away? / The only art her guilt to cover, / To hide her shame from every eye, / To give repentance to her lover / And wring his bosom—is to die."

4. V. *The Tempest*, as above [Eliot's note].
5. The interior of St. Magnus Martyr is to my mind one of the finest among Wren's interiors. See *The Proposed Demolition of Nineteen City Churches* (P.S. King & Son, Ltd.) [Eliot's note].
6. The Song of the (three) Thames-daughters begins here. From line 292 to 306 inclusive they speak in turn. V. *Gotterdammerung*, III.I: the Rhine-daughters [Eliot's note]. In Richard Wagner's opera, *Twilight of the Gods*, the Rhine maidens, when their gold is stolen, lament that the beauty of the river is gone.

270   Red sails
       Wide
       To leeward, swing on the heavy spar.
       The barges wash
       Drifting logs
275   Down Greenwich reach
       Past the Isle of Dogs.[7]
              Weialala leia
              Wallala leialala

       Elizabeth and Leicester[8]
280   Beating oars
       The stern was formed
       A gilded shell
       Red and gold
       The brisk swell
285   Rippled both shores
       Southwest wind
       Carried down stream
       The peal of bells
       White towers
290   Weialala leia
              Wallala leialala

       "Trams and dusty trees.
       Highbury bore me. Richmond and Kew[9]
       Undid me. By Richmond I raised my knees
295   Supine on the floor of a narrow canoe."

       "My feet are at Moorgate,[1] and my heart
       Under my feet. After the event
       He wept. He promised 'a new start.'
       I made no comment. What should I resent?"

300   "On Margate Sands.[2]
       I can connect
       Nothing with nothing.
       The broken fingernails of dirty hands.
       My people humble people who expect
305   Nothing."

---

7. Greenwich is a borough on the south bank of the River Thames; the Isle of Dogs is a peninsula in East London formed by a sharp bend in the Thames called Greenwich Reach.
8. V. Froude, *Elizabeth*, vol. 1, Ch. iv, letter of De Quadra to Philip of Spain: "In the afternoon we were in a barge, watching the games on the river. (The Queen) was alone with Lord Robert and myself on the poop, when they began to talk nonsense, and went so far that Lord Robert at last said, as I was on the spot there was no reason why

they should not be married if the queen pleased" [Eliot's note].
9. "Cf. *Purgatorio*, V. 133: "Ricorditi di me, che son la Pia, / Siena mi fe', disfecemi Maremma." [Eliot's note]. "Remember me, that I am called Piety; / Sienna made me and Maremma undid me." Highbury, Richmond, and Kew are suburbs of London near the Thames.
1. A slum in East London.
2. A seaside resort in the Thames estuary.

la la
To Carthage then I came[3]

Burning burning burning burning[4]
O Lord Thou pluckest me out[5]
310   O Lord Thou pluckest

burning

IV. DEATH BY WATER

Phlebas the Phoenician, a fortnight dead,
Forgot the cry of gulls, and the deep sea swell
And the profit and loss.
315   A current under sea
Picked his bones in whispers. As he rose and fell
He passed the stages of his age and youth
Entering the whirlpool.
                         Gentile or Jew
320   O you who turn the wheel and look to windward,
Consider Phlebas, who was once handsome and tall as you.

V. WHAT THE THUNDER SAID[6]

After the torchlight red on sweaty faces
After the frosty silence in the gardens
After the agony in stony places
325   The shouting and the crying
Prison and palace and reverberation
Of thunder of spring over distant mountains
He who was living is now dead
We who were living are now dying
330   With a little patience

Here is no water but only rock
Rock and no water and the sandy road
The road winding above among the mountains
Which are mountains of rock without water
335   If there were water we should stop and drink
Amongst the rock one cannot stop or think
Sweat is dry and feet are in the sand
If there were only water amongst the rock
Dead mountain mouth of carious° teeth that cannot spit   *rotting*
340   Here one can neither stand nor lie nor sit

3. V. St. Augustine's *Confessions*: "to Carthage then I came, where a cauldron of unholy loves sang all about mine ears" [Eliot's note].
4. The complete text of the Buddha's Fire Sermon (which corresponds in importance to the Sermon on the Mount) from which these words are taken, will be found translated in the late Henry Clarke Warren's *Buddhism in Translation* (Harvard Oriental Series). Mr. Warren was one of the great pioneers of Buddhist studies in the Occident [Eliot's note].
5. From St. Augustine's *Confessions* again. The collocation of these two representatives of eastern and western asceticism, as the culmination of this part of the poem, is not an accident [Eliot's note]. Augustine writes: "I entangle my steps with these outward beauties, but thou pluckest me out, O Lord, Thou pluckest me out."
6. In the first part of Part V three themes are employed: the journey to Emmaus, the approach to the Chapel Perilous (see Miss Weston's book), and the present decay of eastern Europe [Eliot's note].

There is not even silence in the mountains
But dry sterile thunder without rain
There is not even solitude in the mountains
But red sullen faces sneer and snarl
345 From doors of mudcracked houses
                                    If there were water
And no rock
If there were rock
And also water
350 And water
A spring
A pool among the rock
If there were the sound of water only
Not the cicada
355 And dry grass singing
But sound of water over a rock
Where the hermit-thrush sings in the pine trees
Drip drop drip drop drop drop drop[7]
But there is no water

360 Who is the third who walks always beside you?
When I count, there are only you and I together[8]
But when I look ahead up the white road
There is always another one walking beside you
Gliding wrapt in a brown mantle, hooded
365 I do not know whether a man or a woman
—But who is that on the other side of you?

What is that sound high in the air[9]
Murmur of maternal lamentation
Who are those hooded hordes swarming
370 Over endless plains, stumbling in cracked earth
Ringed by the flat horizon only
What is the city over the mountains
Cracks and reforms and bursts in the violet air
Falling towers
375 Jerusalem Athens Alexandria
Vienna London
Unreal

---

7. This is *Turdus aonalaschkae pallasii*, the hermit-thrush which I have heard in Quebec County. Chapman says (*Handbook of Birds of Eastern North America*) "it is most at home in secluded woodland and thickety retreats. . . . Its notes are not remarkable for variety or volume, but in purity and sweetness of tone and exquisite modulation they are unequalled." Its "water-dripping song" is justly celebrated [Eliot's note].

8. The following lines were stimulated by the account of one of the Antarctic expeditions (I forget which, but I think one of Shackleton's): it was related that the party of explorers, at the extremity of their strength, had the constant delusion that there was one more member than could actually be counted [Eliot's note]. There seems also to be an echo of the account of Jesus meeting his disciples on the road to Emmaus: "Jesus himself drew near, and went with them. But their eyes were holden that they should not know him" (Luke 24.13–16).

9. Cf. Hermann Hesse, *Blick ins Chaos*: "Schon ist halb Europa, schon ist zumindest der halbe Osten Europas auf dem Wege zum Chaos, fährt betrunken im heiligen Wahn am Abgrund entlang und singt dazu, singt betrunken und hymnisch wie Dmitri Karamasoff sang. Ueber diese Lieder lacht der Bürger beleidigt, der Heilige und Seher hört sie mit Tränen" [Eliot's note]. "Already half of Europe, already at least half of Eastern Europe, on the way to chaos, drives drunk in sacred infatuation along the edge of the precipice, singing drunkenly, as though singing hymns, as Dmitri Karamazov sang, The offended bourgeois laughs at the songs; the saint and the seer hear them with tears."

A woman drew her long black hair out tight
And fiddled whisper music on those strings
380 And bats with baby faces in the violet light
Whistled, and beat their wings
And crawled head downward down a blackened wall
And upside down in air were towers
Tolling reminiscent bells, that kept the hours
385 And voices singing out of empty cisterns and exhausted wells

In this decayed hole among the mountains
In the faint moonlight, the grass is singing
Over the tumbled graves, about the chapel
There is the empty chapel, only the wind's home.
390 It has no windows, and the door swings,
Dry bones can harm no one.
Only a cock stood on the rooftree
Co co rico co co rico
In a flash of lightning. Then a damp gust
395 Bringing rain

Ganga[1] was sunken, and the limp leaves
Waited for rain, while the black clouds
Gathered far distant, over Himavant.[2]
The jungle crouched, humped in silence.
400 Then spoke the thunder
DA
Datta: what have we given?[3]
My friend, blood shaking my heart
The awful daring of a moment's surrender
405 Which an age of prudence can never retract
By this, and this only, we have existed
Which is not to be found in our obituaries
Or in memories draped by the beneficent spider[4]
Or under seals broken by the lean solicitor
410 In our empty rooms
DA
Dayadhvam: I have heard the key[5]
Turn in the door once and turn once only
We think of the key, each in his prison

---

1. The river Ganges.
2. The Himalayas.
3. "Datta, dayadhvam, damyata" (Give, sympathize, control). The fable of the meaning of the Thunder is found in the *Brihadaranyaka—Upanishad,* 5, 1. A translation is found in Deussen's *Sechzig Upanishads des Vada,* p. 489 [Eliot's note]. "That very thing is repented even today by the heavenly voice, in the form of thunder, in the form of thunder as 'Da,' 'Da,' 'Da,'. . . . Therefore one should practice these three things: self-control, alms-giving, and compassion."
4. Cf. Webster, *The White Devil,* v. vi: ". . . they'll remarry / Ere the worm pierce your winding-sheet, ere the spider / make a thin curtain for your epitaphs" [Eliot's note].

5. Cf. *Inferno,* xxxiii. 46: "ed io sentii chiavar l'uscio di sotto / all'orrible torre." Also F. H. *Bradley, Appearance and Reality,* p. 346: "My external sensations are no less private to myself than are my thoughts or my feelings. In either case my experience falls within my own circle, a circle closed on the outside; and, with all its elements alike, every sphere is opaque to the others which surround it. . . . In brief, regarded as an existence which appears in a soul, the whole world for each is peculiar and private to that soul" [Eliot's note]. In the passage from the *Inferno,* Ugolino tells Dante of his imprisonment and starvation until he became so desperate that he ate his children: "And I heard below me the door of the horrible tower being locked."

415   Thinking of the key, each confirms a prison
       Only at nightfall, aethereal rumours
       Revive for a moment a broken Coriolanus[6]
       DA
       Damyata: The boat responded
420   Gaily, to the hand expert with sail and oar
       The sea was calm, your heart would have responded
       Gaily, when invited, beating obedient
       To controlling hands
       I sat upon the shore
425   Fishing, with the arid plain behind me[7]
       Shall I at least set my lands in order?
       London Bridge is falling down falling down falling down
       Poi s'ascose nel foco che gli affina[8]
       Quando fiam uti chelidon—O swallow swallow[9]
430   *Le Prince d'Aquitaine à la tour abolie*[1]
       These fragments I have shored against my ruins
       Why then Ile fit you. Hieronymo's mad againe.[2]
       Datta. Dayadhvam. Damyata.
       Shantih   shantih   shantih[3]

RESPONSES
Fadwa Tuqan: In the Aging City[1]

City streets and pavements receive me
with other people, the human tide rushes
me on. I move in this current, but only on
the surface, remaining by myself.
5   The tide overflows to sweep
these sidewalks and streets.
Faces, faces, faces rolling on,

6. In Shakespeare's play of the same name, Coriolanus is a Roman general who is exiled and later leads the enemy in an attack against the Romans.

7. V. Weston, *From Ritual to Romance*; chapter on the Fisher King [Eliot's note].

8. V. *Purgatorio*, xxvi.148: "Ara vos prec per aquella valor / que vos condus al som de l'escalina, / sovegna vos a temps de ma dolor." / Poi s'ascose nel foco che gli affina" [Eliot's note]. In this passage, the poet Arnaut Daniel speaks to Dante: "Now I pray you, by the goodness that guides you to the top of this staircase, be mindful in time of my suffering."

9. V. *Pervigilium Veneris*. Cf. Philomela in Parts II and III [Eliot's note]. Philomel asks, "When shall I be a swallow?"

1. V. Gerard de Nerval, Sonnet *El Desdichado* [Eliot's note]. "The Prince of Aquitane in the ruined tower."

2. V. Kyd's *Spanish Tragedy* [Eliot's note]. The subtitle of Kyd's play is, "Hieronymo's Mad Againe." His son having been murdered, Hieronymo is asked to compose a court play, to which he responds "Why then Ile fit you"; his son's murder is revenged in the course of the play.

3. Shantih. Repeated as here, a formal ending to an Upanishad. "The Peace which passeth understanding" is a feeble translation of the content of this word [Eliot's note]. The Upanishads are poetic commentaries on the Hindu Scriptures.

1. Translated by Patricia Alanah Byrne and Naomi Shihab Nye. Fadwa Tuqan (1917–2003) was born in Nablus, Palestine, to a privileged family during the period when Ottoman sovereignty was being replaced by British rule. She began publishing, under a pen name, while in her early twenties; following the establishment of the state of Israel in 1948, she began writing directly political poetry, becoming one of the most prominent Arab-language poets of her generation, noted for a provocatively political use of modernist poetic techniques. *In the Aging City* stems from an extended visit she made to London in 1962—her first major trip away from home, at age 45. Fascinated by life in the great city, she was also consumed with thoughts of home. Both in its images and in its staccato dialogue, now set into relief against memories of her homeland, this poem recalls T. S. Eliot's depiction of London.

dry and grim, they move on the surface,
remaining without human touch.

10   Here is nearness without being near.
Here is the no-presence in presence.
Here is nothing but the presence of absence!

Traffic light reddens; the tide holds back.
Bats flash across memory:

15   *a tank passes, as I crossed in the Nablus marketplace,*
I moved out of its way.
How well I've learned not to disturb
The path of traffic! How well I've memorized
traffic laws!

20   *now here I am, in the London slave market*
where they sold my parents and people . . .[2]
Here I stand, a part of the profitable deal,
carrying the brunt of the sin—
Mine was that I am a plant

25   *grown by the mountains of Palestine.*
Ah! Those who died yesterday are at rest now.
(I suspect that their corpses cursed me
as I gave way for a tank to pass,
then moved on in the stream.)

30   *Aisha's letter is on my desk,*
Nablus is quiet, life flowing on
Like river water . . .
The prison seal is an eloquent silence
(A guard tells her the trees have fallen,

35   *the woods are not set ablaze anymore.*
But Aisha insists the forest is thick,
Trees standing like fortresses. She dreams
of the forest she left blazing with fire
five years ago. She heard the thunder

40   *of the wind in her dream, tells the guard:*
"I don't believe you, you're one of them,
and you remain the Prophets of the Lie."[3]
Then she crouches in the darkness of prison, dreaming.
Shaded by her standing trees she is joyous at the sound

45   *of the far forest rattling with swords of flame.*
And Aisha dreams and dreams.)

The traffic light clicks green, the tide drives on.
My memory flits away, bats fall into a deep well.
A shadow changes direction, follows me,

50   sends out a bridge.
       —Are you a stranger like I am?
Two drops separate from the tide,

---

2. A reference to the Balfour Declaration, which paved
the way for the establishment of the state of Israel; it is
seen by the Arabs and the Palestinians as unfairly offering
their country to other people.

3. A reference to the Zionists, who claimed that Palestine
is a land without people for people without land.

sit removed in a corner of the park.
    —Do you like Osborne?[4]
55   —Who doesn't?
    —England's elderly and its officers
      setting with the sun of Suez . . . [5]
    —Who do you think will plant tomorrow's tree
      for this country?
60   —The hippie youth.
    —You are sour, very sour.
The hippic tide passes by,
sweeping the city.
London keeps beat with
65 the toll of Big Ben.
    —Around the-corner
      there's a pub and an elegant hotel
      with central heating—will you come?
    —Impossible!
70 A London lady passes, complaining to her dog
of arthritis and a pinched sciatic nerve.
    —Impossible!
    —Aren't you a modern woman?
    —I've grown beyond the days of rashness;
75   sorrow has made me a hundred years old. Impossible!
I remove his arm from my shoulders.
    —I'm besieged by loneliness.
    —We're all besieged by loneliness;
      we're all alone, play along with life alone,
80   suffer alone, and die by ourselves.
      You will remain alone here, even if a hundred
      women embrace you!
City streets and sidewalks swallow us with others,
a human tide sweeping us away in waves of faces.
85 We remain on the surface, touching nothing.

Martin Rowson: from *The Waste Land*

In his graphic novel treatment of *The Waste Land* (1990), British cartoonist Martin Rowson has created a loving parody of Eliot's poem, underscoring its air of mystery and menace by rendering it in the form of the Raymond Chandler-style film noir of the 1940s. While making light of the gravitas of Eliot's poem, Rowson's frames also manage to retain Eliot's sense of real anguish. The parody extends all the way down to Rowson's footnotes, which poke fun at the ersatz erudition of Eliot's footnotes to *The Waste Land*.

---

4. John Osborne (1929–1994), the British playwright who started the movement known as "the angry young men." 5. A reference to the Suez crisis of 1956, when Britain, France, and Israel invaded Egypt and were forced by both the United States and the Soviet Union to retreat. This was a blow for England's postwar attempts to retain the remains of its empire, on which it used to be said that the sun never set.

Not only the title but the layout and a good deal of the incidental imagery of the book were suggested by Mr. T. S. Eliot's poem *The Waste Land* (Faber & Faber). Indeed, so heavily am I indebted, Mr. Eliot's poem will illuminate the complexities of the book much better than my notes can; and I recommend it (apart from the intrinsic interest of the poem itself) to anyone who thinks such illumination worth the trouble. To two cinematic works I am indebted in general; I mean *The Big Sleep* and *The Maltese Falcon*. Anyone who is familiar with these works will immediately recognize in the book certain references to Californian private investigators.

The references are listed by chapter and frame number.

PROLOGUE

Frame 2: Varus quoted by Servius in his note to Virgil, *Eclogues*, vi, 42 [Rowson's note].

I. THE BURIAL OF THE DEAD
Frame 2: For "dried Tuba," read "dried tuber" throughout. [Rowson's note]

Journey of the Magi[1]

"A cold coming we had of it,
Just the worst time of the year
For a journey, and such a long journey:
The ways deep and the weather sharp,
5   The very dead of winter."
And the camels galled, sore-footed, refractory,
Lying down in the melting snow.
There were times we regretted
The summer palaces on slopes, the terraces,
10   And the silken girls bringing sherbet.
Then the camel men cursing and grumbling
And running away, and wanting their liquor and women,
And the night-fires going out, and the lack of shelters,
And the cities hostile and the towns unfriendly
15   And the villages dirty and charging high prices:
A hard time we had of it.
At the end we preferred to travel all night,
Sleeping in snatches,
With the voices singing in our ears, saying
20   That this was all folly.

Then at dawn we came down to a temperate valley,
Wet, below the snow line, smelling of vegetation,
With a running stream and a water-mill beating the darkness
And three trees on the low sky.
25   And an old white horse galloped away in the meadow.
Then we came to a tavern with vine-leaves over the lintel,
Six hands at an open door dicing for pieces of silver,
And feet kicking the empty wine-skins.
But there was no information, and so we continued
30   And arrived at evening, not a moment too soon
Finding the place; it was (you may say) satisfactory.

All this was a long time ago, I remember,
And I would do it again, but set down
This set down
35   This: were we led all that way for
Birth or Death? There was a Birth, certainly,
We had evidence and no doubt. I had seen birth and death,
But had thought they were different; this Birth was
Hard and bitter agony for us, like Death, our death.
40   We returned to our places, these Kingdoms,
But no longer at ease here, in the old dispensation,
With an alien people clutching their gods.
I should be glad of another death.

1927

---

1. The narrative of the poem is based upon the tradition of the three wise men who journeyed to Bethlehem to worship the infant Christ; cf. Matthew 2.1–12.

from FOUR QUARTETS

Burnt Norton[1]

τοῦ λόγου δ' ἐόντος ξυνοῦ ζώουσιν οἱ πολλοί ὡς ἰδίαν
ἔχοντες φρόνησιν.[2]

I. p. 77. Fr. 2

ὁδὸς ἄνω κάτω μία καὶ ὡυτή.[3]

I. p. 89. Fr. 60

Diels: Die Fragmente der Vorsokratiker (Herakleitos).

1

Time present and time past
Are both perhaps present in time future,
And time future contained in time past.
If all time is eternally present
5   All time is unredeemable.
What might have been is an abstraction
Remaining a perpetual possibility
Only in a world of speculation.
What might have been and what has been
10   Point to one end, which is always present.
Footfalls echo in the memory
Down the passage which we did not take
Towards the door we never opened
Into the rose-garden. My words echo
15   Thus, in your mind.
                          But to what purpose
Disturbing the dust on a bowl of rose-leaves
I do not know.
                          Other echoes
Inhabit the garden. Shall we follow?
Quick, said the bird, find them, find them,
20   Round the corner. Through the first gate,
Into our first world, shall we follow
The deception of the thrush? Into our first world.
There they were, dignified, invisible,
Moving without pressure, over the dead leaves,
25   In the autumn heat, through the vibrant air,
And the bird called, in response to
The unheard music hidden in the shrubbery,
And the unseen eyebeam crossed, for the roses
Had the look of flowers that are looked at.
30   There they were as our guests, accepted and accepting.

---

1. A large country house in Gloucestershire, England, named for an earlier house on the site that had burned down in the 17th century.
2. Although the Word governs all things, most people live as though they had wisdom of their own. (From the Greek philosopher Heraclitus, c. 500 B.C.)
3. The way up and the way down are the same.

So we moved, and they, in a formal pattern,
Along the empty alley, into the box circle,
To look down into the drained pool.
Dry the pool, dry concrete, brown edged,
35 And the pool was filled with water out of sunlight,
And the lotos rose, quietly, quietly,
The surface glittered out of heart of light,
And they were behind us, reflected in the pool.
Then a cloud passed, and the pool was empty.
40 Go, said the bird, for the leaves were full of children,
Hidden excitedly, containing laughter.
Go, go, go, said the bird: human kind
Cannot bear very much reality.
Time past and time future
45 What might have been and what has been
Point to one end, which is always present.

2

Garlic and sapphires in the mud
Clot the bedded axle-tree.
The trilling wire in the blood
50 Sings below inveterate scars
Appeasing long forgotten wars.
The dance along the artery
The circulation of the lymph
Are figured in the drift of stars
55 Ascend to summer in the tree
We move above the moving tree
In light upon the figured leaf
And hear upon the sodden floor
Below, the boarhound and the boar
60 Pursue their pattern as before
But reconciled among the stars.
At the still point of the turning world. Neither flesh nor fleshless;
Neither from nor towards; at the still point, there the dance is,
But neither arrest nor movement. And do not call it fixity,
65 Where past and future are gathered. Neither movement from nor towards,
Neither ascent nor decline. Except for the point, the still point,
There would be no dance, and there is only the dance.
I can only say, *there* we have been: but I cannot say where.
And I cannot say, how long, for that is to place it in time.

70 The inner freedom from the practical desire,
The release from action and suffering, release from the inner
And the outer compulsion, yet surrounded
By a grace of sense, a white light still and moving,
Erhebung[4] without motion, concentration
75 Without elimination, both a new world

---

4. Lifting up; the German philosopher Hegel's term for a new stage in understanding.

And the old made explicit, understood
In the completion of its partial ecstasy,
The resolution of its partial horror.
Yet the enchainment of past and future
80   Woven in the weakness of the changing body,
Protects mankind from heaven and damnation
Which flesh cannot endure.
                          Time past and time future
Allow but a little consciousness.
To be conscious is not to be in time
85   But only in time can the moment in the rose-garden,
The moment in the arbour where the rain beat,
The moment in the draughty church at smokefall
Be remembered; involved with past and future.
Only through time time is conquered.

3

90   Here is a place of disaffection
Time before and time after
In a dim light: neither daylight
Investing form with lucid stillness
Turning shadow into transient beauty
95   With slow rotation suggesting permanence
Nor darkness to purify the soul
Emptying the sensual with deprivation
Cleansing affection from the temporal.
Neither plenitude nor vacancy. Only a flicker
100   Over the strained time-ridden faces
Distracted from distraction by distraction

Filled with fancies and empty of meaning
Tumid apathy with no concentration
Men and bits of paper, whirled by the cold wind
105   That blows before and after time,
Wind in and out of unwholesome lungs
Time before and time after.
Eructation° of unhealthy souls   *belching*
Into the faded air, the torpid
110   Driven on the wind that sweeps the gloomy hills of London,
Hampstead and Clerkenwell, Campden and Putney,
Highgate, Primrose and Ludgate. Not here
Not here the darkness, in this twittering world.

Descend lower, descend only
115   Into the world of perpetual solitude,
World not world, but that which is not world,
Internal darkness, deprivation
And destitution of all property,
Desiccation of the world of sense,
120   Evacuation of the world of fancy,
Inoperancy of the world of spirit;

This is the one way, and the other
Is the same, not in movement
But abstention from movement; while the world moves
125   In appetency,° on its metalled ways   *desire*
Of time past and time future.

4

Time and the bell have buried the day,
The black cloud carries the sun away.
Will the sunflower turn to us, will the clematis
130   Stray down, bend to us; tendril and spray
Clutch and cling?
Chill
Fingers of yew be curled
Down on us? After the kingfisher's wing
135   Has answered light to light, and is silent, the light is still
At the still point of the turning world.

5

Words move, music moves
Only in time; but that which is only living
Can only die. Words, after speech, reach
140   Into the silence. Only by the form, the pattern,
Can words or music reach
The stillness, as a Chinese jar still
Moves perpetually in its stillness.
Not the stillness of the violin, while the note lasts,
145   Not that only, but the co-existence,
Or say that the end precedes the beginning,
And the end and the beginning were always there
Before the beginning and after the end.
And all is always now. Words strain,
150   Crack and sometimes break, under the burden,
Under the tension, slip, slide, perish,
Decay with imprecision, will not stay in place,
Willl not stay still. Shrieking voices
Scolding, mocking, or merely chattering,
155   Always assail them. The Word in the desert
Is most attacked by voices of temptation,
The crying shadow in the funeral dance,
The loud lament of the disconsolate chimera.

The detail of the pattern is movement,
160   As in the figure of the ten stairs.[5]
Desire itself is movement
Not in itself desirable;
Love is itself unmoving,
Only the cause and end of movement,
165   Timeless, and undesiring

---

5. St. John of the Cross used this figure to describe the way to achieve mystical union with God.

       Except in the aspect of time
       Caught in the form of limitation
       Between un-being and being.
       Sudden in a shaft of sunlight
170   Even while the dust moves
       There rises the hidden laughter
       Of children in the foliage
       Quick now, here, now, always—
       Ridiculous the waste sad time
175   Stretching before and after.
1935   1935, 1943

Tradition and the Individual Talent
1

In English writing we seldom speak of tradition, though we occasionally apply its name in deploring its absence. We cannot refer to "the tradition" or to "a tradition"; at most, we employ the adjective in saying that the poetry of So-and-so is "traditional" or even "too traditional." Seldom, perhaps, does the word appear except in a phrase of censure. If otherwise, it is vaguely approbative,[1] with the implication, as to the work approved, of some pleasing archaeological reconstruction. You can hardly make the word agreeable to English ears without this comfortable reference to the reassuring science of archaeology.

Certainly the word is not likely to appear in our appreciations of living or dead writers. Every nation, every race, has not only its own creative, but its own critical turn of mind; and is even more oblivious of the shortcomings and limitations of its critical habits than of those of its creative genius. We know, or think we know, from the enormous mass of critical writing that has appeared in the French language the critical method or habit of the French; we only conclude (we are such unconscious people) that the French are "more critical" than we, and sometimes even plume ourselves a little with the fact, as if the French were the less spontaneous. Perhaps they are; but we might remind ourselves that criticism is as inevitable as breathing, and that we should be none the worse for articulating what passes in our minds when we read a book and feel an emotion about it, for criticizing our own minds in their work of criticism. One of the facts that might come to light in this process is our tendency to insist, when we praise a poet, upon those aspects of his work in which he least resembles any one else. In these aspects or parts of his work we pretend to find what is individual, what is the peculiar essence of the man. We dwell with satisfaction upon the poet's difference from his predecessors, especially his immediate predecessors; we endeavour to find something that can be isolated in order to be enjoyed. Whereas if we approach a poet without this prejudice we shall often find that not only the best, but the most individual parts of his work may be those in which the dead poets, his ancestors, assert their immortality most vigorously. And I do not mean the impressionable period of adolescence, but the period of full maturity.

Yet if the only form of tradition, of handing down, consisted in following the ways of the immediate generation before us in a blind or timid adherence to its successes, "tradition" should positively be discouraged. We have seen many such simple currents soon lost in the sand; and novelty is better than repetition. Tradition is a matter of much wider significance. It cannot be inherited, and if you want it you must obtain it by great labour. It involves, in the first place, the historical sense, which we may call nearly

---

1. Approving.

indispensable to any one who would continue to be a poet beyond his twenty-fifth year; and the historical sense involves a perception, not only of the pastness of the past, but of its presence; the historical sense compels a man to write not merely with his own generation in his bones, but with a feeling that the whole of the literature of Europe from Homer and within it the whole of the literature of his own country has a simultaneous existence and composes a simultaneous order. This historical sense, which is a sense of the timeless as well as of the temporal and of the timeless and of the temporal together, is what makes a writer traditional. And it is at the same time what makes a writer most acutely conscious of his place in time, of his own contemporaneity.

No poet, no artist of any art, has his complete meaning alone. His significance, his appreciation is the appreciation of his relation to the dead poets and artists. You cannot value him alone; you must set him, for contrast and comparison, among the dead. I mean this as a principle of aesthetic, not merely historical, criticism. The necessity that he shall conform, that he shall cohere, is not onesided; what happens when a new work of art is created is something that happens simultaneously to all the works of art which preceded it. The existing monuments form an ideal order among themselves, which is modified by the introduction of the new (the really new) work of art among them. The existing order is complete before the new work arrives; for order to persist after the supervention[2] of novelty, the whole existing order must be, if ever so slightly, altered; and so the relations, proportions, values of each work of art toward the whole are readjusted; and this is conformity between the old and the new. Whoever has approved this idea of order, of the form of European, of English literature will not find it preposterous that the past should be altered by the present as much as the present is directed by the past. And the poet who is aware of this will be aware of great difficulties and responsibilities.

In a peculiar sense he will be aware also that he must inevitably be judged by the standards of the past. I say judged, not amputated, by them; not judged to be as good as, or worse or better than, the dead; and certainly not judged by the canons of dead critics. It is a judgment, a comparison, in which two things are measured by each other. To conform merely would be for the new work not really to conform at all; it would not be new, and would therefore not be a work of art. And we do not quite say that the new is more valuable because it fits in; but its fitting in is a test of its value—a test, it is true, which can only be slowly and cautiously applied, for we are none of us infallible judges of conformity. We say: it appears to conform, and is perhaps individual, or it appears individual, and may conform; but we are hardly likely to find that it is one and not the other.

To proceed to a more intelligible exposition of the relation of the poet to the past: he can neither take the past as a lump, an indiscriminate bolus,[3] nor can he form himself wholly on one or two private admirations, nor can he form himself wholly upon one preferred period. The first course is inadmissible, the second is an important experience of youth, and the third is a pleasant and highly desirable supplement. The poet must be very conscious of the main current, which does not at all flow invariably through the most distinguished reputations. He must be quite aware of the obvious fact that art never improves, but that the material of art is never quite the same. He must be aware that the mind of Europe—the mind of his own country—a mind which he learns in time to be much more important than his own private mind—is a mind which changes, and that this change is a development which abandons nothing en route, which does not superannuate either Shakespeare, or Homer, or the rock drawing of the Magdalenian

---

2. The appearance of something additional.   3. A lump; a mass of chewed food.

draughtsmen.[4] That this development, refinement perhaps, complication certainly, is not, from the point of view of the artist, any improvement. Perhaps not even an improvement from the point of view of the psychologist or not to the extent which we imagine; perhaps only in the end based upon a complication in economics and machinery. But the difference between the present and the past is that the conscious present is an awareness of the past in a way and to an extent which the past's awareness of itself cannot show.

Some one said: "The dead writers are remote from us because we *know* so much more than they did." Precisely, and they are that which we know.

I am alive to a usual objection to what is clearly part of my programme for the *métier* of poetry. The objection is that the doctrine requires a ridiculous amount of erudition (pedantry), a claim which can be rejected by appeal to the lives of poets in any pantheon. It will even be affirmed that much learning deadens or perverts poetic sensibility. While, however, we persist in believing that a poet ought to know as much as will not encroach upon his necessary receptivity and necessary laziness, it is not desirable to confine knowledge to whatever can be put into a useful shape for examinations, drawing-rooms, or the still more pretentious modes of publicity. Some can absorb knowledge, the more tardy must sweat for it. Shakespeare acquired more essential history from Plutarch than most men could from the whole British Museum. What is to be insisted upon is that the poet must develop or procure the consciousness of the past and that he should continue to develop this consciousness throughout his career.

What happens is a continual surrender of himself as he is at the moment to something which is more valuable. The progress of an artist is a continual self-sacrifice, a continual extinction of personality.

There remains to define this process of depersonalization and its relation to the sense of tradition. It is in this depersonalization that art may be said to approach the condition of science. I, therefore, invite you to consider, as a suggestive analogy, the action which takes place when a bit of finely filiated[5] platinum is introduced into a chamber containing oxygen and sulphur dioxide.

2

Honest criticism and sensitive appreciation are directed not upon the poet but upon the poetry. If we attend to the confused cries of the newspaper critics and the *susurrus* [buzzing] of popular repetition that follows, we shall hear the names of poets in great numbers; if we seek not Blue-book[6] knowledge but the enjoyment of poetry, and ask for a poem, we shall seldom find it. I have tried to point out the importance of the relation of the poem to other poems by other authors, and suggested the conception of poetry as a living whole of all the poetry that has ever been written. The other aspect of this Impersonal theory of poetry is the relation of the poem to its author. And I hinted, by an analogy, that the mind of the mature poet differs from that of the immature one not precisely in any valuation of "personality," not being necessarily more interesting, or having "more to say," but rather by being a more finely perfected medium in which special, or very varied, feelings are at liberty to enter into new combinations.

The analogy was that of the catalyst. When the two gases previously mentioned are mixed in the presence of a filament of platinum, they form sulphurous acid. This combination takes place only if the platinum is present; nevertheless the newly formed acid contains no trace of platinum, and the platinum itself is apparently

---

4. Drawings of hunting scenes, rendered in caves in France and Spain, c. 13,000–10,000 B.C.

5. Eliot apparently means "made into filaments."
6. Official government publication.

unaffected; has remained inert, neutral, and unchanged. The mind of the poet is the shred of platinum. It may partly or exclusively operate upon the experience of the man himself; but, the more perfect the artist, the more completely separate in him will be the man who suffers and the mind which creates; the more perfectly will the mind digest and transmute the passions which are its material.

The experience, you will notice, the elements which enter the presence of the transforming catalyst, are of two kinds: emotions and feelings. The effect of a work of art upon the person who enjoys it is an experience different in kind from any experience not of art. It may be formed out of one emotion, or may be a combination of several; and various feelings, inhering for the writer in particular words or phrases or images, may be added to compose the final result. Or great poetry may be made without the direct use of any emotion whatever: composed out of feelings solely. Canto XV of the *Inferno* (Brunetto Latini) is a working up of the emotion evident in the situation; but the effect, though single as that of any work of art, is obtained by considerable complexity of detail. The last quatrain gives an image, a feeling attaching to an image, which "came," which did not develop simply out of what precedes, but which was probably in suspension in the poet's mind until the proper combination arrived for it to add itself to.[7] The poet's mind is in fact a receptacle for seizing and storing up numberless feelings, phrases, images, which remain there until all the particles which can unite to form a new compound are present together.

If you compare several representative passages of the greatest poetry you see how great is the variety of types of combination, and also how completely any semi-ethical criterion of "sublimity" misses the mark. For it is not the "greatness," the intensity, of the emotions, the components, but the intensity of the artistic process, the pressure, so to speak, under which the fusion takes place, that counts. The episode of Paolo and Francesca employs a definite emotion, but the intensity of the poetry is something quite different from whatever intensity in the supposed experience it may give the impression of. It is no more intense, furthermore, than Canto XXVI, the voyage of Ulysses, which has not the direct dependence upon an emotion.[8] Great variety is possible in the process of transmutation of emotion: the murder of Agamemnon,[9] or the agony of Othello, gives an artistic effect apparently closer to a possible original than the scenes from Dante. In the *Agamemnon*, the artistic emotion approximates to the emotion of an actual spectator; in *Othello* to the emotion of the protagonist himself. But the difference between art and the event is always absolute; the combination which is the murder of Agamemnon is probably as complex as that which is the voyage of Ulysses. In either case there has been a fusion of elements. The ode of Keats contains a number of feelings which have nothing particular to do with the nightingale, but which the nightingale, partly, perhaps, because of its attractive name, and partly because of its reputation, served to bring together.

The point of view which I am struggling to attack is perhaps related to the metaphysical theory of the substantial unity of the soul: for my meaning is, that the poet has, not a "personality" to express, but a particular medium, which is only a medium and not a personality, in which impressions and experiences combine in peculiar and unexpected ways. Impressions and experiences which are important for the man may take no place in the poetry, and those which become important in the poetry may play quite a negligible part in the man, the personality.

7. He [Brunetto Latini] turned then, and he seemed, / across that plain, like one of those who run / for the green cloth at Verona; and of those, / more like the one who wins, than those who lose (*Inferno*, 15.119–22).
8. Dante's *Inferno*, Canto 5, tells the story of the lovers Paolo and Francesca; Canto 26 tells of the suffering of Ulysses in hell.
9. In Aeschylus's drama *Agamemnon*, Clytemnestra kills her husband Agamemnon for having sacrificed her daughter, Iphigenia, to the goddess Artemis.

I will quote a passage which is unfamiliar enough to be regarded with fresh attention in the light—or darkness—of these observations:

> And now methinks I could e'en chide myself
> For doating on her beauty, though her death
> Shall be revenged after no common action.
> Does the silkworm expend her yellow labours
> For thee? For thee does she undo herself?
> Are lordships sold to maintain ladyships
> For the poor benefit of a bewildering minute?
> Why does yon fellow falsify highways,
> And put his life between the judge's lips,
> To refine such a thing—keeps horse and men
> To beat their valours for her? . . .[1]

In this passage (as is evident if it is taken in its context) there is a combination of positive and negative emotions: an intensely strong attraction toward beauty and an
equally intense fascination by the ugliness which is contrasted with it and which destroys it. This balance of contrasted emotion is in the dramatic situation to which the
speech is pertinent, but that situation alone is inadequate to it. This is, so to speak, the
structural emotion, provided by the drama. But the whole effect, the dominant tone, is
due to the fact that a number of floating feelings, having an affinity to this emotion by
no means superficially evident, have combined with it to give us a new art emotion.

It is not in his personal emotions, the emotions provoked by particular events in his
life, that the poet is in any way remarkable or interesting. His particular emotions may
be simple, or crude, or flat. The emotion in his poetry will be a very complex thing, but
not with the complexity of the emotions of people who have very complex or unusual
emotions in life. One error, in fact, of eccentricity in poetry is to seek for new human
emotions to express; and in this search for novelty in the wrong place it discovers the
perverse. The business of the poet is not to find new emotions, but to use the ordinary
ones and, in working them up into poetry, to express feelings which are not in actual
emotions at all. And emotions which he has never experienced will serve his turn as
well as those familiar to him. Consequently, we must believe that "emotion recollected
in tranquillity"[2] is an inexact formula. For it is neither emotion, nor recollection, nor,
without distortion of meaning, tranquillity. It is a concentration, and a new thing resulting from the concentration, of a very great number of experiences which to the practical
and active person would not seem to be experiences at all; it is a concentration which
does not happen consciously or of deliberation. These experiences are not "recollected,"
and they finally unite in an atmosphere which is "tranquil" only in that it is a passive attending upon the event. Of course this is not quite the whole story. There is a great deal,
in the writing of poetry, which must be conscious and deliberate. In fact, the bad poet is
usually unconscious where he ought to be conscious, and conscious where he ought to
be unconscious. Both errors tend to make him "personal." Poetry is not a turning loose
of emotion, but an escape from emotion; it is not the expression of personality, but an
escape from personality. But, of course, only those who have personality and emotions
know what it means to want to escape from these things.

---

1. From Cyril Tourneur's *The Revenger's Tragedy* (1607),
3.4; the speaker is addressing the skull of his former
beloved, murdered after she refused to respond to an evil
duke's advances. The revenger will make up the skull to
look alive, putting poison on its lips; the evil Duke then
dies when he kisses this supposed maiden in a dusky garden.
2. This is Wordsworth's famous description of poetry in
the Preface to *Lyrical Ballads*; see page 196.

3

ὁ δὲ νοῦς ἴσως θειότερόν τι καὶ ἀπαθές ἐστιν.[3]

This essay proposes to halt at the frontier of metaphysics or mysticism, and confine itself to such practical conclusions as can be applied by the responsible person interested in poetry. To divert interest from the poet to the poetry is a laudable aim: for it would conduce to a juster estimation of actual poetry, good and bad. There are many people who appreciate the expression of sincere emotion in verse, and there is a smaller number of people who can appreciate technical excellence. But very few know when there is an expression of *significant* emotion, emotion which has its life in the poem and not in the history of the poet. The emotion of art is impersonal. And the poet cannot reach this impersonality without surrendering himself wholly to the work to be done. And he is not likely to know what is to be done unless he lives in what is not merely the present, but the present moment of the past, unless he is conscious, not of what is dead, but of what is already living.

Virginia Woolf

1882–1941

Virginia Woolf is the foremost woman writer of the twentieth century, writing in any language; within British literature, Woolf is in the company of James Joyce, T. S. Eliot, William Butler Yeats, and few others as a major author, of whatever gender. To take account of the transformations in modern English literature—in language, in style, and in substance—requires reckoning with Virginia Woolf, one of the chief architects of literary modernism. By 1962 Edward Albee could sardonically title a play *Who's Afraid of Virginia Woolf?*, knowing that her name would signify the greatness of modern literature. Woolf wrote luminous and intricate novels, two pivotal books on sexual politics, society, and war, several volumes of short stories and collected essays, reviews and pamphlets, and thirty volumes of a remarkable diary. Woolf was a woman of letters in an almost old-fashioned sense, one of the century's subtlest observers of social and psychic life, and a hauntingly beautiful prose writer.

From New York World-Telegram & Sun Collection, *Virginia Woolf, 1928.*

Woolf's writing career began in childhood but was officially launched in 1915 with the publication of her first novel, *The Voyage Out,* when she was thirty-three. *The Voyage Out* was an emblematic beginning for her public career as a novelist, with its title suggesting the need to venture forth, to make a voyage into the world and out of the imprisonments of life and language. This novel paid special homage to *Heart of Darkness,* Joseph Conrad's story of a voyage through Africa that uncovers the heart of Europe's imperial encounter with the African continent and its exploited people. The theme resonated for Woolf throughout her books, because she too concentrated on the costs—both social and personal—of attempting to gain freedom. With the exception of *Orlando* (1928), a playful and flamboyant novel with a few scenes set in Turkey and Russia, Woolf was never again to set a novel outside the geographical confines of England. Voyaging out had become a matter of voyaging within. Woolf does not turn away from the larger world; she sets that larger world and its history squarely in England.

3. The mind is doubtless something more divine and unimpressionable (from Aristotle's *De Anima* [*On the Soul*]).

Woolf's own roots went deep in Victorian literary culture. She was born in 1882 into a privileged and illustrious British professional family with connections to the world of letters on both sides. She was the third child of the marriage of Leslie Stephen and Julia Duckworth, both of whom had been widowed; Leslie Stephen had married a daughter of the novelist William Thackeray, and Julia had been the wife of a publisher, and was connected to a long line of judges, teachers, and magistrates. Woolf's father, eventually to become Sir Leslie, was a prominent editor and a striving philosopher, who was appointed president of the London Library. His fame was to come not from his philosophical work but from his massive *Dictionary of National Biography*, a book that placed, and ranked, the leading figures of British national life for many centuries. Woolf's *Orlando*, with its subtitle: *A Biography*, spoofed the entire enterprise of the biography of great men by having *her* great man, Orlando, unexpectedly turn into a woman halfway through the novel.

Woolf grew up as an intensely literary child, surrounded by her father's project of arbitrating the greatness of the (mostly) men of letters she nonetheless sought to emulate. Her mother Julia was a famed beauty, whose magical grace was captured in the photographs of her equally famous relative, the photographer Julia Margaret Cameron. Woolf was to provide a haunting portrait of both her mother and father in her novel *To the Lighthouse* (1927), where the beautiful and consummately maternal Mrs. Ramsay ministers to her irascible and intellectually tormented philosopher husband, Mr. Ramsay, until her sudden death deprives the family and its circle of friends of their ballast in life. Julia Stephen's premature death in 1895 had cast just such a pall over her own family, especially over thirteen-year-old Virginia, who had a mental breakdown. Breakdowns would recur at intervals throughout her life.

The death-haunted life characteristic of the Victorian family was Virginia Woolf's own experience. Two years after Julia died, Woolf's beloved half-sister and mother substitute, Stella Duckworth, died in childbirth at the age of twenty-seven. Woolf was also to lose her difficult but immensely loved father in 1904 (not so coincidentally, the same year Virginia was to publish her first essay and review), and her brother Thoby died of typhoid contracted on a trip to Greece with her in 1906. The novel *Jacob's Room* (1922) deals with a young man named Jacob and his college room, as perceived by his sister after his death in World War I. The items in Jacob's room are cloaked in memory and live in the consciousness of the sister as far more than precious objects—memory infuses them with shared life. The dead return again and again in Woolf's imagination and in her imaginative work; her development of the "moment of consciousness" in her writing, her novels' concentration on the binding powers of memory, and her invocation of the spreading, intertwining branches of human relations persisting even after death, may be the effect of her painful tutelage in loss.

As upper-class women, Woolf and her sisters were not given a formal education, while Thoby and Adrian both went to fine schools and ultimately to university. The sense of having been deliberately shut out of education by virtue of her sex was to inflect all of Woolf's writing and thinking. Education is a pervasive issue in her novels, and an enormous issue in her essays on social and political life, *A Room of One's Own* (1929) and *Three Guineas* (1938). Woolf became an autodidact, steeping herself in English literature, history, political theory, and art history, but she never lost the keen anguish nor the self-doubt occasioned by the closed doors of the academy to women. Education became for Woolf perhaps the key to transforming the role and the perception of women in society, and writing became her own mode of entry into the public world.

In 1912, Virginia Stephen married Leonard Woolf, like herself a member of the Bloomsbury group, but unlike her in being a Jew and coming from a commercial and far less illustrious family. Leonard Woolf was an "outsider" in anti-Semitic Britain no less than Virginia, who as a great woman writer was equally outside the norm. An accomplished writer in his own right, a political theorist and an activist in socialist issues and in anti-imperialist causes, Leonard Woolf devoted himself to Virginia and to her writing career. They established and ran the Hogarth Press together, an imprint that was to publish all of Virginia's books, as well as many important works of poetry, prose, and criticism from others. Virginia Woolf's erotic and emotional ties to women, and, in particular, her romance with Vita

T. S. Eliot and Virginia Woolf.

Sackville-West, while not necessarily explicitly sexual—no one seems to know for a certainty—were indubitably of the greatest importance to her life. Despite this, she placed Leonard Woolf and their marriage at the center of her being, and their rich and complex partnership weathered Virginia's numerous mental breakdowns. When she felt another episode of depression overtaking her in 1941, it was partly her reluctance to subject Leonard to what she saw as the burden of her madness, which tragically led her to drown herself in the river near their home and their beloved press.

Woolf's themes and techniques as a writer are all distilled in her gem of a story *The Lady in the Looking-Glass: A Reflection* (1929), which is a parable about the dangers and the transcendence of writing. The lady of the title is absent for most of the brief story; an invisible narrator builds a world around her absence by recounting only what can be seen or sensed in the mirror to be glimpsed above the mantel. One of the oldest metaphors for literary art is the mirror, and with it, the notion that literature "holds up the mirror to nature," or reality. Literary art was long considered to be an imitation of reality, its mirrored reflection, its "re-presentation." Woolf's story takes the garden shears of her missing character and tears representation to pieces, so to speak. Language cannot simply mirror something, her prose tells us, because it is too mysterious and subtle and wayward to do so. No imitation can ever capture subjective reality, and even inanimate objects are, for Woolf, filled with subjectivity. Finally, the story takes a "lady," a woman, as its subject because Woolf indicates that representation which tries to be realistic or real is instead a cruel violation, almost a form of rape. Truth in art is neither a representation nor a reflection: truth can only be gotten at sideways, in fragments, and with the fluidity of consciousness, in a subjective moment. "Examine for a moment an ordinary mind on an ordinary day," Woolf wrote in an essay on *Modern Fiction* in 1925:

The mind receives a myriad impressions—trivial, fantastic, evanescent, or engraved with the sharpness of steel. From all sides they come, an incessant shower of innumerable atoms; and, as they fall, as they shape themselves into the life of Monday or Tuesday, the accent falls differently from of old; the moment of importance came not here but there; so that, if a writer were a free man and not a slave, if he could write what he chose, not what he must, if he could base his work upon his own feeling and not upon convention, there would be no plot, no comedy, no tragedy, no love interest or catastrophe in the accepted style, and perhaps not a single button sewn on as the Bond Street tailors would have it.

Woolf's stories are written out of her own painfully won freedom of observation; the passages that follow from *A Room of One's Own* and *Three Guineas* meditate on the ways in which society and even human character would have to change in order for such freedom to spread.

The Lady in the Looking-Glass: A Reflection[1]

People should not leave looking-glasses hanging in their rooms any more than they should leave open cheque books or letters confessing some hideous crime. One could not help looking, that summer afternoon, in the long glass that hung outside in the hall. Chance had so arranged it. From the depths of the sofa in the drawing-room one could see reflected in the Italian glass not only the marble-topped table opposite, but a stretch of the garden beyond. One could see a long grass path leading between banks of tall flowers until, slicing off an angle, the gold rim cut it off.

The house was empty, and one felt, since one was the only person in the drawing-room, like one of those naturalists who, covered with grass and leaves, lie watching the shyest animals—badgers, otters, kingfishers—moving about freely, themselves unseen. The room that afternoon was full of such shy creatures, lights and shadows, curtains blowing, petals falling—things that never happen, so it seems, if someone is looking. The quiet old country room with its rugs and stone chimney pieces, its sunken bookcases and red and gold lacquer cabinets, was full of such nocturnal creatures. They came pirouetting across the floor, stepping delicately with high-lifted feet and spread tails and pecking allusive beaks as if they had been cranes or flocks of elegant flamingoes whose pink was faded, or peacocks whose trains were veined with silver. And there were obscure flushes and darkenings too, as if a cuttlefish had suddenly suffused the air with purple; and the room had its passions and rages and envies and sorrows coming over it and clouding it, like a human being. Nothing stayed the same for two seconds together.

But, outside, the looking-glass reflected the hall table, the sunflowers, the garden path so accurately and so fixedly that they seemed held there in their reality unescapably. It was a strange contrast—all changing here, all stillness there. One could not help looking from one to the other. Meanwhile, since all the doors and windows were open in the heat, there was a perpetual sighing and ceasing sound, the voice of the transient and the perishing, it seemed, coming and going like human breath, while in the looking-glass things had ceased to breathe and lay still in the trance of immortality.

Half an hour ago the mistress of the house, Isabella Tyson, had gone down the grass path in her thin summer dress, carrying a basket, and had vanished, sliced off by the gilt rim of the looking-glass. She had gone presumably into the lower garden to pick flowers; or as it seemed more natural to suppose, to pick something light and fantastic and leafy and trailing, traveller's joy, or one of those elegant sprays of convolvulus that twine round ugly walls and burst here and there into white and violet blossoms. She suggested the fantastic and the tremulous convolvulus rather than the upright aster, the starched zinnia, or her own burning roses alight like lamps on the straight posts of their rose trees. The comparison showed how very little, after all these years, one knew about her; for it is impossible that any woman of flesh and blood of fifty-five or sixty should be really a wreath or a tendril. Such comparisons are worse than idle and superficial—they are cruel even, for they come like the convolvulus itself trembling between one's eyes and the truth. There must be truth; there must be a wall. Yet it was strange that after knowing her all these years one could not say what the truth about Isabella was; one still made up phrases like this about convolvulus and traveller's joy. As for facts, it was a fact that she was a spinster; that she was rich; that she had bought this house and collected with her own hands—often in the most obscure corners of the world and at great risk from poisonous stings and Oriental diseases—the rugs, the chairs, the cabinets which now lived their nocturnal life before one's eyes. Sometimes it seemed as if they knew more about her than we, who sat on them, wrote at them, and trod on them so carefully, were allowed to know. In each of these cabinets were many little drawers, and each almost certainly held letters, tied with bows of ribbon, sprinkled with sticks of lavender or rose leaves. For it was another fact—if facts were what one wanted—that Isabella had known many people, had had many friends; and thus if one had the audacity to open a drawer and read her letters, one would find the traces of many agitations, of appointments to meet, of upbraidings for not having met, long letters of intimacy and affection, violent letters of jealousy and reproach, terrible final words of parting—for all those interviews and assignations had led to nothing—that is, she had never married, and yet, judging from the mask-like indifference of her face, she had gone through twenty times more of passion and experience than those whose loves are trumpeted forth for all the world to hear. Under the stress of thinking about Isabella, her room became more shadowy and symbolic; the corners seemed darker, the legs of chairs and tables more spindly and hieroglyphic.

Suddenly these reflections were ended violently and yet without a sound. A large black form loomed into the looking-glass; blotted out everything, strewed the table with a packet of marble tablets veined with pink and grey, and was gone. But the picture was entirely altered. For the moment it was unrecognisable and irrational and entirely out of focus. One could not relate these tablets to any human purpose. And then by degrees some logical process set to work on them and began ordering and arranging them and bringing them into the fold of common experience. One realised at last that they were merely letters. The man had brought the post.

There they lay on the marble-topped table, all dripping with light and colour at first and crude and unabsorbed. And then it was strange to see how they were drawn in and arranged and composed and made part of the picture and granted that stillness and immortality which the looking-glass conferred. They lay there invested with a new reality and significance and with a greater heaviness, too, as if it would have needed a chisel to dislodge them from the table. And, whether it was fancy or not, they seemed to have become not merely a handful of casual letters but to be tablets graven with eternal truth—if one could read them, one would know everything there was to be known about Isabella, yes, and about life, too. The pages inside those marble-looking envelopes must be cut deep and scored thick with meaning. Isabella would come in, and take them, one by one, very slowly, and open them, and read them carefully word by word, and then with a profound sigh of comprehension, as if she had seen to the bottom of everything, she would tear the envelopes to little bits and tie the letters together and lock the cabinet drawer in her determination to conceal what she did not wish to be known.

The thought served as a challenge. Isabella did not wish to be known—but she should no longer escape. It was absurd, it was monstrous. If she concealed so much and knew so much one must prize her open with the first tool that came to hand—the imagination. One must fix one's mind upon her at that very moment. One must fasten her down there. One must refuse to be put off any longer with sayings and doings such as the moment brought forth—with dinners and visits and polite conversations. One must put oneself in her shoes. If one took the phrase literally, it was easy to see the shoes in which she stood, down in the lower garden, at this moment. They were very narrow and long and fashionable—they were made of the softest and most flexible leather. Like everything she wore, they were exquisite. And she would be standing under the high hedge in the lower part of the garden, raising the scissors that were tied to her waist to cut some dead flower, some overgrown branch. The sun would beat down on her face, into her eyes; but no, at the critical moment a veil of cloud covered the sun, making the expression of her eyes doubtful—was it mocking or tender, brilliant or dull? One could only see the indeterminate outline of her rather faded, fine face looking at the sky. She was thinking, perhaps, that she must order a new net for the strawberries; that she must send flowers to Johnson's widow; that it was time she drove over to see the Hippesleys in their new house. Those were the things she talked about at dinner certainly. But one was tired of the things that she talked about at dinner. It was her profounder state of being that one wanted to catch and turn to words, the state that is to the mind what breathing is to the body, what one calls happiness or unhappiness. At the mention of those words it became obvious, surely, that she must be happy. She was rich; she was distinguished; she had many friends; she travelled—she bought rugs in Turkey and blue pots in Persia. Avenues of pleasure radiated this way and that from where she stood with her scissors raised to cut the trembling branches while the lacy clouds veiled her face.

Here with a quick movement of her scissors she snipped the spray of traveller's joy and it fell to the ground. As it fell, surely some light came in too, surely one could penetrate a little farther into her being. Her mind then was filled with tenderness and regret. . . . To cut an overgrown branch saddened her because it had once lived, and life was dear to her. Yes, and at the same time the fall of the branch would suggest to her how she must die herself and all the futility and evanescence of things. And then again quickly catching this thought up, with her instant good sense, she thought life had treated her well; even if fall she must, it was to lie on the earth and moulder sweetly into the roots of violets. So she stood thinking. Without making any thought precise—for she was one of those reticent people whose minds hold their thoughts enmeshed in clouds of silence—she was filled with thoughts. Her mind was like her room, in which lights advanced and retreated, came pirouetting and stepping delicately, spread their tails, pecked their way; and then her whole being was suffused, like the room again, with a cloud of some profound knowledge, some unspoken regret, and then she was full of locked drawers, stuffed with letters, like her cabinets. To talk of "prizing her open" as if she were an oyster, to use any but the finest and subtlest and most pliable tools upon her was impious and absurd. One must imagine—here was she in the looking-glass. It made one start.

She was so far off at first that one could not see her clearly. She came lingering and pausing, here straightening a rose, there lifting a pink to smell it, but she never stopped; and all the time she became larger and larger in the looking-glass, more and more completely the person into whose mind one had been trying to penetrate. One verified her by degrees—fitted the qualities one had discovered into this visible body. There were her grey-green dress, and her long shoes, her basket, and something sparkling at her throat. She came so gradually that she did not seem to derange the pattern in the glass, but only to bring in some new element which gently moved and altered the other objects as if asking them, courteously, to make room for her. And the letters and the table and the grass walk and the sunflowers which had been waiting in the looking-glass separated and opened out so that she might be received among them. At last there she was, in the hall. She stopped dead. She stood by the table. She stood perfectly still. At once the looking-glass began to pour over her a light that seemed to fix her; that seemed like some acid to bite off the unessential and superficial and to leave only the truth. It was an enthralling spectacle. Everything dropped from her—clouds, dress, basket, diamond—all that one had called the creeper and con-volvulus. Here was the hard wall beneath. Here was the woman herself. She stood naked in that pitiless light. And, there was nothing. Isabella was perfectly empty. She had no thoughts. She had no friends. She cared for nobody. As for her letters, they were all bills. Look, as she stood there, old and angular, veined and lined, with her high nose and her wrinkled neck, she did not even trouble to open them.

People should not leave looking-glasses hanging in their rooms.

A ROOM OF ONE'S OWN   *A Room of One's Own* is difficult to categorize—it is a long essay, a nonfiction novella, a political pamphlet, and a philosophical discourse all in one. Its effects have not been so difficult to categorize—Virginia Woolf's idiosyncratic text has been recognized as a classic from the time of its publication in 1929. The book was a departure from Woolf's output until then; she was a major literary figure, having already published such key novels as *Jacob's Room, Mrs Dalloway, To the Lighthouse,* and *Orlando,* and she was an established essayist with a formidable reputation as an arbiter of the literary tradition. One way of characterizing this book is to see that it represents Woolf's scrutiny of her own position as a woman writer, a self-examination of her public position that inevitably became a political document. The focus is not on Woolf's life or her work per se, but rather on the social and psychological conditions that would make such a life generally possible. The book creates a microcosm of such possibility in the "room" of its title; the book itself is a room within which its author contemplates and analyzes the dimensions of social space for women. Woolf recognizes that seemingly neutral social space, the room of cultural agency just as the room of writing, is in truth a gendered space. She directs her political inquiry toward the making and remaking of such rooms.

A Room of One's Own comes from established traditions of writing as well. It draws on the conversational tone and novelistic insight of the literary essay as perfected in the nineteenth century by such writers as Charles Lamb—whose *Oxford in the Vacation* was certainly in Woolf's mind when she wrote the opening chapter of her essay. At the same time, Woolf's book joins a lineage of feminist political philosophy, whose most eloquent exponent prior to Woolf herself was Mary Wollstonecraft, who joined the rhetorical ranks of Rousseau and John Stuart Mill with the publication of *A Vindication of the Rights of Woman,* her passionately reasoned exhortation for the equal and universal human rights of women. (Selections from Wollstonecraft's *Vindication* can be found on page 146.) The century and a half since Wollstonecraft had produced a rich history of feminist agitation and feminist thought. Virginia Woolf draws on this less-known tradition, invoking nineteenth-century figures from the women's movement like Emily Davies, Josephine Butler, and Octavia Hill. She also places her deliberations in the context of the suffragist movement and its fraught history in Britain. Virginia Woolf was strongly engaged in the debates of the suffrage movement, and its divisions over radical action or more conciliatory political approaches. Much of Woolf's long essay is devoted to demonstrating the subversive quality of occupying the blank page and wielding the printed word.

As politically motivated as *A Room of One's Own* is, it is equally a literary text. Woolf draws on all the intricacies of literary tropes and figures to mount her argument for women's education, women's equality, and women's social presence. Not the least of her strategies is her manipulation of the rhetoric of address—in other words, the audience implied by the language of a text. Woolf creates an ironic space, or room, in which she is a playfully ambiguous speaker addressing an uncertain audience: women at the colleges where she has been invited to speak, but also men and women alike who will read her printed text. By doing so, she keeps an ironic tension in play, holding at bay her anger at being censored or silenced by male readers by creating a sense of privacy and secrecy among women. This underscores Woolf's primary argument, the need for autonomy and self-determination. Her modest proposal, although faintly ironic, is also eminently pragmatic—the room of one's own that is her metaphor for the college classroom or the blank canvas or the book's page is at the same time the actual room, paid for and unintruded upon by domestic worries or social codes, whose possession permits a woman to find out who she may be.

from A Room of One's Own
Chapter 1

But, you may say, we asked you to speak about women and fiction—what has that got to do with a room of one's own?[1] I will try to explain. When you asked me to speak about women and fiction I sat down on the banks of a river and began to wonder what the words meant. They might mean simply a few remarks about Fanny Burney; a few more about Jane Austen; a tribute to the Brontës and a sketch of Haworth Parsonage under snow; some witticisms if possible about Miss Mitford; a respectful allusion to George Eliot; a reference to Mrs Gaskell and one would have done.[2] But at second sight the words seemed not so simple. The title women and fiction might mean, and you may have meant it to mean, women and what they are like; or it might mean women and the fiction that they write; or it might mean women and the fiction that is written about them; or it might mean that somehow all three are inextricably mixed together and you want me to consider them in that light. But when I began to consider the subject in this last way, which seemed the most interesting, I soon saw that it had one fatal drawback. I should never be able to come to a conclusion. I should never be able to fulfil what is, I understand, the first duty of a lecturer—to hand you after an hour's discourse a nugget of pure truth to wrap up between the pages of your notebooks and keep on the mantelpiece for ever. All I could do was to offer you an opinion upon one minor point—a woman must have money and a room of her own if she is to write fiction; and that, as you will see, leaves the great problem of the true nature of woman and the true nature of fiction unsolved. I have shirked the duty of coming to a conclusion upon these two questions—women and fiction remain, so far as I am concerned, unsolved problems. But in order to make some amends I am going to do what I can to show you how I arrived at this opinion about the room and the money. I am going to develop in your presence as fully and freely as I can the train of thought which led me to think this. Perhaps if I lay bare the ideas, the prejudices, that lie behind this

1. Woolf delivered her essay in a shorter version to meetings first at two women's colleges, Newnham and Girton College, Cambridge University, in October 1928. 2. Important 19th-century novelists.

statement you will find that they have some bearing upon women and some upon fiction. At any rate, when a subject is highly controversial—and any question about sex is that—one cannot hope to tell the truth. One can only show how one came to hold whatever opinion one does hold. One can only give one's audience the chance of drawing their own conclusions as they observe the limitations, the prejudices, the idiosyncrasies of the speaker. Fiction here is likely to contain more truth than fact. Therefore I propose, making use of all the liberties and licences of a novelist, to tell you the story of the two days that preceded my coming here—how, bowed down by the weight of the subject which you have laid upon my shoulders, I pondered it, and made it work in and out of my daily life. I need not say that what I am about to describe has no existence; Oxbridge is an invention; so is Fernham;[3] "I" is only a convenient term for somebody who has no real being. Lies will flow from my lips, but there may perhaps be some truth mixed up with them; it is for you to seek out this truth and to decide whether any part of it is worth keeping. If not, you will of course throw the whole of it into the wastepaper basket and forget all about it.

Here then was I (call me Mary Beton, Mary Seton, Mary Carmichael[4] or by any name you please—it is not a matter of any importance) sitting on the banks of a river a week or two ago in fine October weather, lost in thought. That collar I have spoken of, women and fiction, the need of coming to some conclusion on a subject that raises all sorts of prejudices and passions, bowed my head to the ground. To the right and left bushes of some sort, golden and crimson, glowed with the colour, even it seemed burnt with the heat, of fire. On the further bank the willows wept in perpetual lamentation, their hair about their shoulders. The river reflected whatever it chose of sky and bridge and burning tree, and when the undergraduate had oared his boat through the reflections they closed again, completely, as if he had never been. There one might have sat the clock round lost in thought. Thought—to call it by a prouder name than it deserved—had let its line down into the stream. It swayed, minute after minute, hither and thither among the reflections and the weeds, letting the water lift it and sink it, until—you know the little tug—the sudden conglomeration of an idea at the end of one's line: and then the cautious hauling of it in, and the careful laying of it out? Alas, laid on the grass how small, how insignificant this thought of mine looked; the sort of fish that a good fisherman puts back into the water so that it may grow fatter and be one day worth cooking and eating. I will not trouble you with that thought now, though if you look carefully you may find it for yourselves in the course of what I am going to say.

But however small it was, it had, nevertheless, the mysterious property of its kind—put back into the mind, it became at once very exciting, and important; and as it darted and sank, and flashed hither and thither, set up such a wash and tumult of ideas that it was impossible to sit still. It was thus that I found myself walking with extreme rapidity across a grass plot. Instantly a man's figure rose to intercept me. Nor did I at first understand that the gesticulations of a curious-looking object, in a cutaway coat and evening shirt, were aimed at me. His face expressed horror and

3. "Oxbridge" was in fact the common slang term for Oxford and Cambridge universities. "Fernham" suggests Newnham College.
4. Three of the four Marys who by tradition were atten-
dants to Mary Queen of Scots (executed in 1567), and who figure in many Scottish ballads; the fourth was Mary Hamilton.

indignation. Instinct rather than reason came to my help; he was a Beadle; I was a woman. This was the turf; there was the path. Only the Fellows and Scholars are allowed here; the gravel is the place for me.[5] Such thoughts were the work of a moment. As I regained the path the arms of the Beadle sank, his face assumed its usual repose, and though turf is better walking than gravel, no very great harm was done. The only charge I could bring against the Fellows and Scholars of whatever the college might happen to be was that in protection of their turf, which has been rolled for 300 years in succession, they had sent my little fish into hiding.

What idea it had been that had sent me so audaciously trespassing I could not now remember. The spirit of peace descended like a cloud from heaven, for if the spirit of peace dwells anywhere, it is in the courts and quadrangles of Oxbridge on a fine October morning. Strolling through those colleges past those ancient halls the roughness of the present seemed smoothed away; the body seemed contained in a miraculous glass cabinet through which no sound could penetrate, and the mind, freed from any contact with facts (unless one trespassed on the turf again), was at liberty to settle down upon whatever meditation was in harmony with the moment. As chance would have it, some stray memory of some old essay about revisiting Oxbridge in the long vacation brought Charles Lamb to mind—Saint Charles, said Thackeray,[6] putting a letter of Lamb's to his forehead. Indeed, among all the dead (I give you my thoughts as they came to me), Lamb is one of the most congenial; one to whom one would have liked to say, Tell me then how you wrote your essays? For his essays are superior even to Max Beerbohm's, I thought, with all their perfection, because of that wild flash of imagination, that lightning crack of genius in the middle of them which leaves them flawed and imperfect, but starred with poetry. Lamb then came to Oxbridge perhaps a hundred years ago. Certainly he wrote an essay—the name escapes me—about the manuscript of one of Milton's poems which he saw here.[7] It was *Lycidas* perhaps, and Lamb wrote how it shocked him to think it possible that any word in *Lycidas* could have been different from what it is. To think of Milton changing the words in that poem seemed to him a sort of sacrilege. This led me to remember what I could of *Lycidas* and to amuse myself with guessing which word it could have been that Milton had altered, and why. It then occurred to me that the very manuscript itself which Lamb had looked at was only a few hundred yards away, so that one could follow Lamb's footsteps across the quadrangle to that famous library where the treasure is kept. Moreover, I recollected, as I put this plan into execution, it is in this famous library that the manuscript of Thackeray's *Esmond* is also preserved. The critics often say that *Esmond* is Thackeray's most perfect novel. But the affectation of the style, with its imitation of the eighteenth century, hampers one, so far as I remember; unless indeed the eighteenth-century style was natural to Thackeray —a fact that one might prove by looking at the manuscript and seeing whether the alterations were for the benefit of the style or of the sense. But then one would have to decide what is style and what is meaning, a question which—but here I was actually at the door which leads into the library itself. I must have opened it, for instantly there issued, like a guardian angel barring the way with a flutter of black gown

5. A beadle is a disciplinary officer. The fellows of Oxbridge colleges typically tutor the undergraduates, who are divided into scholars and commoners. The commoners form the majority of the student body.
6. William Makepeace Thackeray (1811–1863), novelist and journalist, Woolf's father's first father-in-law.

7. Lamb's *Oxford in the Vacation*—describing the locales Lamb himself was too poor to attend in term time. The manuscript of Milton's elegy *Lycidas* (1638) is in the Wren Library of Trinity College, Cambridge, together with that of Thackeray's novel *The History of Henry Esmond* (1852).

instead of white wings, a deprecating, silvery, kindly gentleman, who regretted in a low voice as he waved me back that ladies are only admitted to the library if accompanied by a Fellow of the College or furnished with a letter of introduction.

That a famous library has been cursed by a woman is a matter of complete indifference to a famous library. Venerable and calm, with all its treasures safe locked within its breast, it sleeps complacently and will, so far as I am concerned, so sleep for ever. Never will I wake those echoes, never will I ask for that hospitality again, I vowed as I descended the steps in anger. Still an hour remained before luncheon, and what was one to do? Stroll on the meadows? sit by the river? Certainly it was a lovely autumn morning; the leaves were fluttering red to the ground; there was no great hardship in doing either. But the sound of music reached my ear. Some service or celebration was going forward. The organ complained magnificently as I passed the chapel door. Even the sorrow of Christianity sounded in that serene air more like the recollection of sorrow than sorrow itself; even the groanings of the ancient organ seemed lapped in peace. I had no wish to enter had I the right, and this time the verger might have stopped me, demanding perhaps my baptismal certificate, or a letter of introduction from the Dean. But the outside of these magnificent buildings is often as beautiful as the inside. Moreover, it was amusing enough to watch the congregation assembling, coming in and going out again, busying themselves at the door of the chapel like bees at the mouth of a hive. Many were in cap and gown; some had tufts of fur on their shoulders; others were wheeled in bath-chairs; others, though not past middle age, seemed creased and crushed into shapes so singular that one was reminded of those giant crabs and crayfish who heave with difficulty across the sand of an aquarium. As I leant against the wall the University indeed seemed a sanctuary in which are preserved rare types which would soon be obsolete if left to fight for existence on the pavement of the Strand.[8] Old stories of old deans and old dons came back to mind, but before I had summoned up courage to whistle—it used to be said that at the sound of a whistle old Professor —— instantly broke into a gallop—the venerable congregation had gone inside. The outside of the chapel remained. As you know, its high domes and pinnacles can be seen, like a sailing-ship always voyaging never arriving, lit up at night and visible for miles, far away across the hills. Once, presumably, this quadrangle with its smooth lawns, its massive buildings, and the chapel itself was marsh too, where the grasses waved and the swine rootled. Teams of horses and oxen, I thought, must have hauled the stone in wagons from far countries, and then with infinite labour the grey blocks in whose shade I was now standing were poised in order one on top of another, and then the painters brought their glass for the windows, and the masons were busy for centuries up on that roof with putty and cement, spade and trowel. Every Saturday somebody must have poured gold and silver out of a leathern purse into their ancient fists, for they had their beer and skittles presumably of an evening. An unending stream of gold and silver, I thought, must have flowed into this court perpetually to keep the stones coming and the masons working; to level, to ditch, to dig and to drain. But it was then the age of faith, and money was poured liberally to set these stones on a deep foundation, and when the stones were raised, still more money was poured in from the coffers of kings and queens and great nobles to ensure that hymns should be sung here and scholars taught. Lands were granted; tithes were paid. And when the age of faith was over and

---

8. A thoroughfare in central London.

the age of reason had come, still the same flow of gold and silver went on; fellowships were founded; lectureships endowed; only the gold and silver flowed now, not from the coffers of the king, but from the chests of merchants and manufacturers, from the purses of men who had made, say, a fortune from industry, and returned, in their wills, a bounteous share of it to endow more chairs, more lectureships, more fellowships in the university where they had learnt their craft. Hence the libraries and laboratories; the observatories; the splendid equipment of costly and delicate instruments which now stands on glass shelves, where centuries ago the grasses waved and the swine rooted. Certainly, as I strolled round the court, the foundation of gold and silver seemed deep enough; the pavement laid solidly over the wild grasses. Men with trays on their heads went busily from staircase to staircase. Gaudy blossoms flowered in window-boxes. The strains of the gramophone blared out from the rooms within. It was impossible not to reflect—the reflection whatever it may have been was cut short. The clock struck. It was time to find one's way to luncheon.

It is a curious fact that novelists have a way of making us believe that luncheon parties are invariably memorable for something very witty that was said, or for something very wise that was done. But they seldom spare a word for what was eaten. It is part of the novelist's convention not to mention soup and salmon and ducklings, as if soup and salmon and ducklings were of no importance whatsoever, as if nobody ever smoked a cigar or drank a glass of wine. Here, however, I shall take the liberty to defy that convention and to tell you that the lunch on this occasion began with soles, sunk in a deep dish, over which the college cook had spread a counterpane of the whitest cream, save that it was branded here and there with brown spots like the spots on the flanks of a doe. After that came the partridges, but if this suggests a couple of bald, brown birds on a plate you are mistaken. The partridges, many and various, came with all their retinue of sauces and salads, the sharp and the sweet, each in its order; their potatoes, thin as coins but not so hard; their sprouts, foliated as rosebuds but more succulent. And no sooner had the roast and its retinue been done with than the silent serving-man, the Beadle himself perhaps in a milder manifestation, set before us, wreathed in napkins, a confection which rose all sugar from the waves. To call it pudding and so relate it to rice and tapioca would be an insult. Meanwhile the wineglasses had flushed yellow and flushed crimson; had been emptied; had been filled. And thus by degrees was lit, halfway down the spine, which is the seat of the soul, not that hard little electric light which we call brilliance, as it pops in and out upon our lips, but the more profound, subtle and subterranean glow, which is the rich yellow flame of rational intercourse. No need to hurry. No need to sparkle. No need to be anybody but oneself. We are all going to heaven and Vandyck[9] is of the company—in other words, how good life seemed, how sweet its rewards, how trivial this grudge or that grievance, how admirable friendship and the society of one's kind, as, lighting a good cigarette, one sunk among the cushions in the window-seat.

If by good luck there had been an ash-tray handy, if one had not knocked the ash out of the window in default, if things had been a little different from what they were, one would not have seen, presumably, a cat without a tail. The sight of that abrupt and truncated animal padding softly across the quadrangle changed by some fluke of the subconscious intelligence the emotional light for me. It was as if some one had let fall a shade. Perhaps the excellent hock was relinquishing its hold. Certainly, as I watched

---

9. Sir Anthony Van Dyck, prominent 17th-century society painter.

the Manx cat pause in the middle of the lawn as if it too questioned the universe, something seemed lacking, something seemed different. But what was lacking, what was different, I asked myself, listening to the talk. And to answer that question I had to think myself out of the room, back into the past, before the war indeed,[1] and to set before my eyes the model of another luncheon party held in rooms not very far distant from these; but different. Everything was different. Meanwhile the talk went on among the guests, who were many and young, some of this sex, some of that; it went on swimmingly, it went on agreeably, freely, amusingly. And as it went on I set it against the background of that other talk, and as I matched the two together I had no doubt that one was the descendant, the legitimate heir of the other. Nothing was changed; nothing was different save only—here I listened with all my ears not entirely to what was being said, but to the murmur or current behind it. Yes, that was it—the change was there. Before the war at a luncheon party like this people would have said precisely the same things but they would have sounded different, because in those days they were accompanied by a sort of humming noise, not articulate, but musical, exciting, which changed the value of the words themselves. Could one set that humming noise to words? Perhaps with the help of the poets one could. A book lay beside me and, opening it, I turned casually enough to Tennyson. And here I found Tennyson was singing:

> There has fallen a splendid tear
>   From the passion-flower at the gate.
> She is coming, my dove, my dear;
>   She is coming, my life, my fate;
> The red rose cries, "She is near, she is near";
>   And the white rose weeps, "She is late";
> The larkspur listens, "I hear, I hear";
>   And the lily whispers, "I wait."[2]

Was that what men hummed at luncheon parties before the war? And the women?

> My heart is like a singing bird
>   Whose nest is in a water'd shoot;
> My heart is like an apple tree
>   Whose boughs are bent with thick-set fruit;
> My heart is like a rainbow shell
>   That paddles in a halcyon sea;
> My heart is gladder than all these
>   Because my love is come to me.[3]

Was that what women hummed at luncheon parties before the war?

There was something so ludicrous in thinking of people humming such things even under their breath at luncheon parties before the war that I burst out laughing, and had to explain my laughter by pointing at the Manx cat, who did look a little absurd, poor beast, without a tail, in the middle of the lawn. Was he really born so, or had he lost his tail in an accident? The tailless cat, though some are said to exist in the Isle of Man, is rarer than one thinks. It is a queer animal, quaint rather than beautiful. It is strange what a difference a tail makes—you know the sort of things one says as a lunch party breaks up and people are finding their coats and hats.

---

1. World War I.
2. From Tennyson's *Maud* (1855), lines 908–915.

3. The first stanza of Christina Rossetti's poem *A Birthday* (1857).

This one, thanks to the hospitality of the host, had lasted far into the afternoon. The beautiful October day was fading and the leaves were falling from the trees in the avenue as I walked through it. Gate after gate seemed to close with gentle finality behind me. Innumerable beadles were fitting innumerable keys into well-oiled locks; the treasure-house was being made secure for another night. After the avenue one comes out upon a road—I forget its name—which leads you, if you take the right turning, along to Fernham.[4] But there was plenty of time. Dinner was not till half-past seven. One could almost do without dinner after such a luncheon. It is strange how a scrap of poetry works in the mind and makes the legs move in time to it along the road. Those words—

> There has fallen a splendid tear
>> From the passion-flower at the gate.
> She is coming, my dove, my dear—

sang in my blood as I stepped quickly along towards Headingley. And then, switching off into the other measure, I sang, where the waters are churned up by the weir:

> My heart is like a singing bird
>> Whose nest is in a water'd shoot;
> My heart is like an apple tree—

What poets, I cried aloud, as one does in the dusk, what poets they were!

In a sort of jealousy, I suppose, for our own age, silly and absurd though these comparisons are, I went on to wonder if honestly one could name two living poets now as great as Tennyson and Christina Rossetti were then. Obviously it is impossible, I thought, looking into those foaming waters, to compare them. The very reason why the poetry excites one to such abandonment, such rapture, is that it celebrates some feeling that one used to have (at luncheon parties before the war perhaps), so that one responds easily, familiarly, without troubling to check the feeling, or to compare it with any that one has now. But the living poets express a feeling that is actually being made and torn out of us at the moment. One does not recognize it in the first place; often for some reason one fears it; one watches it with keenness and compares it jealously and suspiciously with the old feeling that one knew. Hence the difficulty of modern poetry; and it is because of this difficulty that one cannot remember more than two consecutive lines of any good modern poet. For this reason—that my memory failed me—the argument flagged for want of material. But why, I continued, moving on towards Headingley, have we stopped humming under our breath at luncheon parties? Why has Alfred ceased to sing

> She is coming, my dove, my dear?

Why has Christina ceased to respond

> My heart is gladder than all these
> Because my love is come to me?

Shall we lay the blame on the war? When the guns fired in August 1914, did the faces of men and women show so plain in each other's eyes that romance was killed?

---

4. Both Girton and Newnham Colleges, established only in the late 19th century, are outside the old university area of Cambridge.

Certainly it was a shock (to women in particular with their illusions about education, and so on) to see the faces of our rulers in the light of the shell-fire. So ugly they looked—German, English, French—so stupid. But lay the blame where one will, on whom one will, the illusion which inspired Tennyson and Christina Rossetti to sing so passionately about the coming of their loves is far rarer now than then. One has only to read, to look, to listen, to remember. But why say "blame"? Why, if it was an illusion, not praise the catastrophe, whatever it was, that destroyed illusion and put truth in its place? For truth . . . those dots mark the spot where, in search of truth, I missed the turning up to Fernham. Yes indeed, which was truth and which was illusion, I asked myself. What was the truth about these houses, for example, dim and festive now with their red windows in the dusk, but raw and red and squalid, with their sweets and their boot-laces, at nine o'clock in the morning? And the willows and the river and the gardens that run down to the river, vague now with the mist stealing over them, but gold and red in the sunlight—which was the truth, which was the illusion about them? I spare you the twists and turns of my cogitations, for no conclusion was found on the road to Headingley, and I ask you to suppose that I soon found out my mistake about the turning and retraced my steps to Fernham.

As I have said already that it was an October day, I dare not forfeit your respect and imperil the fair name of fiction by changing the season and describing lilacs hanging over garden walls, crocuses, tulips and other flowers of spring. Fiction must stick to facts, and the truer the facts the better the fiction—so we are told. Therefore it was still autumn and the leaves were still yellow and falling, if anything, a little faster than before, because it was now evening (seven twenty-three to be precise) and a breeze (from the south-west to be exact) had risen. But for all that there was something odd at work:

> My heart is like a singing bird
>   Whose nest is in a water'd shoot;
> My heart is like an apple tree
>   Whose boughs are bent with thick-set fruit—

perhaps the words of Christina Rossetti were partly responsible for the folly of the fancy—it was nothing of course but a fancy—that the lilac was shaking its flowers over the garden walls, and the brimstone butterflies were scudding hither and thither, and the dust of the pollen was in the air. A wind blew, from what quarter I know not, but it lifted the half-grown leaves so that there was a flash of silver grey in the air. It was the time between the lights when colours undergo their intensification and purples and golds burn in window-panes like the beat of an excitable heart; when for some reason the beauty of the world revealed and yet soon to perish (here I pushed into the garden, for, unwisely, the door was left open and no beadles seemed about), the beauty of the world which is so soon to perish, has two edges, one of laughter, one of anguish, cutting the heart asunder. The gardens of Fernham lay before me in the spring twilight, wild and open, and in the long grass, sprinkled and carelessly flung, were daffodils and bluebells, not orderly perhaps at the best of times, and now wind-blown and waving as they tugged at their roots. The windows of the building, curved like ships' windows among generous waves of red brick, changed from lemon to silver under the flight of the quick spring clouds. Somebody was in a hammock, somebody, but in this light they were phantoms only, half guessed, half seen, raced across the grass—would no one stop her?—and then on the terrace, as if popping out to breathe the air, to glance at the garden, came a bent figure, formidable yet humble, with her great forehead and her shabby dress—could it be the famous scholar, could it be

J——H—— herself?[5] All was dim, yet intense too, as if the scarf which the dusk had flung over the garden were torn asunder by star or sword—the flash of some terrible reality leaping, as its way is, out of the heart of the spring. For youth——

Here was my soup. Dinner was being served in the great dining-hall. Far from being spring it was in fact an evening in October. Everybody was assembled in the big dining-room. Dinner was ready. Here was the soup. It was a plain gravy soup. There was nothing to stir the fancy in that. One could have seen through the transparent liquid any pattern that there might have been on the plate itself. But there was no pattern. The plate was plain. Next came beef with its attendant greens and potatoes—a homely trinity, suggesting the rumps of cattle in a muddy market, and sprouts curled and yellowed at the edge, and bargaining and cheapening, and women with string bags on Monday morning. There was no reason to complain of human nature's daily food, seeing that the supply was sufficient and coal-miners doubtless were sitting down to less. Prunes and custard followed. And if any one complains that prunes, even when mitigated by custard, are an uncharitable vegetable (fruit they are not), stringy as a miser's heart and exuding a fluid such as might run in misers' veins who have denied themselves wine and warmth for eighty years and yet not given to the poor, he should reflect that there are people whose charity embraces even the prune. Biscuits and cheese came next, and here the water-jug was liberally passed round, for it is the nature of biscuits to be dry, and these were biscuits to the core. That was all. The meal was over. Everybody scraped their chairs back; the swing-doors swung violently to and fro; soon the hall was emptied of every sign of food and made ready no doubt for breakfast next morning. Down corridors and up staircases the youth of England went banging and singing. And was it for a guest, a stranger (for I had no more right here in Fernham than in Trinity or Somerville or Girton or Newnham or Christchurch),[6] to say, "The dinner was not good," or to say (we were now, Mary Seton and I, in her sitting-room), "Could we not have dined up here alone?" for if I had said anything of the kind I should have been prying and searching into the secret economies of a house which to the stranger wears so fine a front of gaiety and courage. No, one could say nothing of the sort. Indeed, conversation for a moment flagged. The human frame being what it is, heart, body and brain all mixed together, and not contained in separate compartments as they will be no doubt in another million years, a good dinner is of great importance to good talk. One cannot think well, love well, sleep well, if one has not dined well. The lamp in the spine does not light on beef and prunes. We are all *probably* going to heaven, and Vandyck is, we *hope*, to meet us round the next corner—that is the dubious and qualifying state of mind that beef and prunes at the end of the day's work breed between them. Happily my friend, who taught science, had a cupboard where there was a squat bottle and little glasses—(but there should have been sole and partridge to begin with)—so that we were able to draw up to the fire and repair some of the damages of the day's living. In a minute or so we were slipping freely in and out among all those objects of curiosity and interest which form in the mind in the absence of a particular person, and are naturally to be discussed on coming together again—how somebody has married, another has not; one thinks this, another that; one has improved out of all knowledge, the other most amazingly gone to the bad—with all those speculations upon human nature and the character of the amazing world we live in which spring naturally from such beginnings. While these

5. Jane Harrison, a famous classical scholar.
6. Trinity, Girton, and Newnham are colleges of Cam-

bridge University; Somerville and Christchurch are at Oxford.

things were being said, however, I became shamefacedly aware of a current setting in of its own accord and carrying everything forward to an end of its own. One might be talking of Spain or Portugal, of book or racehorse, but the real interest of whatever was said was none of those things, but a scene of masons on a high roof some five centuries ago. Kings and nobles brought treasure in huge sacks and poured it under the earth. This scene was for ever coming alive in my mind and placing itself by another of lean cows and a muddy market and withered greens and the stringy hearts of old men— these two pictures, disjointed and disconnected and nonsensical as they were, were for ever coming together and combating each other and had me entirely at their mercy. The best course, unless the whole talk was to be distorted, was to expose what was in my mind to the air, when with good luck it would fade and crumble like the head of the dead king when they opened the coffin at Windsor. Briefly, then, I told Miss Seton about the masons who had been all those years on the roof of the chapel, and about the kings and queens and nobles bearing sacks of gold and silver on their shoulders, which they shovelled into the earth; and then how the great financial magnates of our own time came and laid cheques and bonds, I suppose, where the others had laid ingots and rough lumps of gold. All that lies beneath the colleges down there, I said; but this college, where we are now sitting, what lies beneath its gallant red brick and the wild unkempt grasses of the garden? What force is behind the plain china off which we dined, and (here it popped out of my mouth before I could stop it) the beef, the custard and the prunes?

Well, said Mary Seton, about the year 1860—Oh, but you know the story, she said, bored, I suppose, by the recital. And she told me—rooms were hired. Committees met. Envelopes were addressed. Circulars were drawn up. Meetings were held; letters were read out; so-and-so has promised so much; on the contrary, Mr——won't give a penny. The *Saturday Review* has been very rude. How can we raise a fund to pay for offices? Shall we hold a bazaar? Can't we find a pretty girl to sit in the front row? Let us look up what John Stuart Mill said on the subject.[7] Can any one persuade the editor of the——to print a letter? Can we get Lady——to sign it? Lady——is out of town. That was the way it was done, presumably, sixty years ago, and it was a prodigious effort, and a great deal of time was spent on it. And it was only after a long struggle and with the utmost difficulty that they got thirty thousand pounds together.[8] So obviously we cannot have wine and partridges and servants carrying tin dishes on their heads, she said. We cannot have sofas and separate rooms. "The amenities," she said, quoting from some book or other, "will have to wait."[9]

At the thought of all those women working year after year and finding it hard to get two thousand pounds together, and as much as they could do to get thirty thousand pounds, we burst out in scorn at the reprehensible poverty of our sex. What had our mothers been doing then that they had no wealth to leave us? Powdering their noses? Looking in at shop windows? Flaunting in the sun at Monte Carlo? There were some photographs on the mantel-piece. Mary's mother—if that was her picture— may have been a wastrel in her spare time (she had thirteen children by a minister of

7. In 1869 Mill published his essay *The Subjection of Women*, which argued forcefully for women's suffrage and their right to equality with men.
8. "We are told that we ought to ask for £30,000 at least. . . . It is not a large sum, considering that there is to be but one college of this sort for Great Britain, Ireland and the Colonies, and considering how easy it is to raise immense sums for boys' schools. But considering how few people really wish women to be educated, it is a good deal."—Lady Stephen, *Life of Miss Emily Davies* [Woolf's note].
9. Every penny which could be scraped together was set aside for building, and the amenities had to be postponed.—R. Strachey, *The Cause* [Woolf's note].

the church), but if so her gay and dissipated life had left too few traces of its pleasures on her face. She was a homely body; an old lady in a plaid shawl which was fastened by a large cameo; and she sat in a basket-chair, encouraging a spaniel to look at the camera, with the amused, yet strained expression of one who is sure that the dog will move directly the bulb is pressed. Now if she had gone into business; had become a manufacturer of artificial silk or a magnate on the Stock Exchange; if she had left two or three hundred thousand pounds to Fernham, we could have been sitting at our ease tonight and the subject of our talk might have been archaeology, botany, anthropology, physics, the nature of the atom, mathematics, astronomy, relativity, geography. If only Mrs Seton and her mother and her mother before her had learnt the great art of making money and had left their money, like their fathers and their grandfathers before them, to found fellowships and lectureships and prizes and schol-arships appropriated to the use of their own sex, we might have dined very tolerably up here alone off a bird and a bottle of wine; we might have looked forward without undue confidence to a pleasant and honourable lifetime spent in the shelter of one of the liberally endowed professions. We might have been exploring or writing; moon-ing about the venerable places of the earth; sitting contemplative on the steps of the Parthenon, or going at ten to an office and coming home comfortably at half-past four to write a little poetry. Only, if Mrs Seton and her like had gone into business at the age of fifteen, there would have been—that was the snag in the argument—no Mary. What, I asked, did Mary think of that? There between the curtains was the October night, calm and lovely, with a star or two caught in the yellowing trees. Was she ready to resign her share of it and her memories (for they had been a happy fami-ly, though a large one) of games and quarrels up in Scotland, which she is never tired of praising for the fineness of its air and the quality of its cakes, in order that Fernham might have been endowed with fifty thousand pounds or so by a stroke of the pen? For, to endow a college would necessitate the suppression of families altogether. Mak-ing a fortune and bearing thirteen children—no human being could stand it. Consid-er the facts, we said. First there are nine months before the baby is born. Then the baby is born. Then there are three or four months spent in feeding the baby. After the baby is fed there are certainly five years spent in playing with the baby. You can-not, it seems, let children run about the streets. People who have seen them running wild in Russia say that the sight is not a pleasant one. People say, too, that human nature takes its shape in the years between one and five. If Mrs Seton, I said, had been making money, what sort of memories would you have had of games and quar-rels? What would you have known of Scotland, and its fine air and cakes and all the rest of it? But it is useless to ask these questions, because you would never have come into existence at all. Moreover, it is equally useless to ask what might have happened if Mrs Seton and her mother and her mother before her had amassed great wealth and laid it under the foundations of college and library, because, in the first place, to earn money was impossible for them, and in the second, had it been possible, the law denied them the right to possess what money they earned. It is only for the last forty-eight years that Mrs Seton has had a penny of her own. For all the centuries before that it would have been her husband's property—a thought which, perhaps, may have had its share in keeping Mrs Seton and her mothers off the Stock Exchange.[1]

---

1. The late 19th century saw the passage of legislation designed to improve the legal status of women. In 1870 the Married Women's Property Act allowed women to retain £200 of their own earnings (which previously had automatically become the property of her husband); in 1884 a further act gave married women the same rights over property as unmarried women, and allowed them to carry on trades or businesses using their property.

Every penny I earn, they may have said, will be taken from me and disposed of according to my husband's wisdom—perhaps to found a scholarship or to endow a fellowship in Balliol or Kings,[2] so that to earn money, even if I could earn money, is not a matter that interests me very greatly. I had better leave it to my husband.

At any rate, whether or not the blame rested on the old lady who was looking at the spaniel, there could be no doubt that for some reason or other our mothers had mismanaged their affairs very gravely. Not a penny could be spared for "amenities"; for partridges and wine, beadles and turf, books and cigars, libraries and leisure. To raise bare walls out of the bare earth was the utmost they could do.

So we talked standing at the window and looking, as so many thousands look every night, down on the domes and towers of the famous city beneath us. It was very beautiful, very mysterious in the autumn moonlight. The old stone looked very white and venerable. One thought of all the books that were assembled down there; of the pictures of old prelates and worthies hanging in the panelled rooms; of the painted windows that would be throwing strange globes and crescents on the pavement; of the tablets and memorials and inscriptions; of the fountains and the grass; of the quiet rooms looking across the quiet quadrangles. And (pardon me the thought) I thought, too, of the admirable smoke and drink and the deep armchairs and the pleasant carpets: of the urbanity, the geniality, the dignity which are the offspring of luxury and privacy and space. Certainly our mothers had not provided us with anything comparable to all this—our mothers who found it difficult to scrape together thirty thousand pounds, our mothers who bore thirteen children to ministers of religion at St Andrews.

So I went back to my inn, and as I walked through the dark streets I pondered this and that, as one does at the end of the day's work. I pondered why it was that Mrs Seton had no money to leave us; and what effect poverty has on the mind; and what effect wealth has on the mind; and I thought of the queer old gentlemen I had seen that morning with tufts of fur upon their shoulders; and I remembered how if one whistled one of them ran; and I thought of the organ booming in the chapel and of the shut doors of the library; and I thought how unpleasant it is to be locked out; and I thought how it is worse perhaps to be locked in; and, thinking of the safety and prosperity of the one sex and of the poverty and insecurity of the other and of the effect of tradition and of the lack of tradition upon the mind of a writer, I thought at last that it was time to roll up the crumpled skin of the day, with its arguments and its impressions and its anger and its laughter, and cast it into the hedge. A thousand stars were flashing across the blue wastes of the sky. One seemed alone with an inscrutable society. All human beings were laid asleep—prone, horizontal, dumb. Nobody seemed stirring in the streets of Oxbridge. Even the door of the hotel sprang open at the touch of an invisible hand—not a boots was sitting up to light me to bed, it was so late.

from *Chapter 3*

It would have been impossible, completely and entirely, for any woman to have written the plays of Shakespeare in the age of Shakespeare. Let me imagine, since facts are so hard to come by, what would have happened had Shakespeare had a wonderfully gifted sister, called Judith, let us say. Shakespeare himself went, very probably—his mother was an heiress—to the grammar school, where he may have learnt

---

2. Balliol is a college of Oxford University; King's is at Cambridge.

Latin—Ovid, Virgil, and Horace—and the elements of grammar and logic. He was, it is well known, a wild boy who poached rabbits, perhaps shot a deer, and had, rather sooner than he should have done, to marry a woman in the neighbourhood, who bore him a child rather quicker than was right. That escapade sent him to seek his fortune in London. He had, it seemed, a taste for the theatre; he began by holding horses at the stage door. Very soon he got work in the theatre, became a successful actor, and lived at the hub of the universe, meeting everybody, knowing everybody, practising his art on the boards, exercising his wits in the streets, and even getting access to the palace of the queen. Meanwhile his extraordinarily gifted sister, let us suppose, remained at home. She was as adventurous, as imaginative, as agog to see the world as he was. But she was not sent to school. She had no chance of learning grammar and logic, let alone of reading Horace and Virgil. She picked up a book now and then, one of her brother's perhaps, and read a few pages. But then her parents came in and told her to mend the stockings or mind the stew and not moon about with books and papers. They would have spoken sharply but kindly, for they were substantial people who knew the conditions of life for a woman and loved their daughter—indeed, more likely than not she was the apple of her father's eye. Perhaps she scribbled some pages up in an apple loft on the sly, but was careful to hide them or set fire to them. Soon, however, before she was out of her teens, she was to be betrothed to the son of a neighbouring wool-stapler. She cried out that marriage was hateful to her, and for that she was severely beaten by her father. Then he ceased to scold her. He begged her instead not to hurt him, not to shame him in this matter of her marriage. He would give her a chain of beads or a fine petticoat, he said; and there were tears in his eyes. How could she disobey him? How could she break his heart? The force of her own gift alone drove her to it. She made up a small parcel of her belongings, let herself down by a rope one summer's night and took the road to London. She was not seventeen. The birds that sang in the hedge were not more musical than she was. She had the quickest fancy, a gift like her brother's, for the tune of words. Like him, she had a taste for the theatre. She stood at the stage door; she wanted to act, she said. Men laughed in her face. The manager—a fat, loose-lipped man—guffawed. He bellowed something about poodles dancing and women acting—no woman, he said, could possibly be an actress. He hinted—you can imagine what. She could get no training in her craft. Could she even seek her dinner in a tavern or roam the streets at midnight? Yet her genius was for fiction and lusted to feed abundantly upon the lives of men and women and the study of their ways. At last—for she was very young, oddly like Shakespeare the poet in her face, with the same grey eyes and rounded brows—at last Nick Greene the actor-manager took pity on her; she found herself with child by that gentleman and so—who shall measure the heat and violence of the poet's heart when caught and tangled in a woman's body?—killed herself one winter's night and lies buried at some cross-roads where the omnibuses now stop outside the Elephant and Castle.[3]

That, more or less, is how the story would run, I think, if a woman in Shakespeare's day had had Shakespeare's genius. But for my part, I agree with the deceased bishop, if such he was—it is unthinkable that any woman in Shakespeare's day should have had Shakespeare's genius. For genius like Shakespeare's is not born among labouring, uneducated, servile people. It was not born in England among the Saxons and the Britons. It is not born today among the working classes. How, then,

---

3. A tavern on the outskirts of South London.

could it have been born among women whose work began, according to Professor Trevelyan,[4] almost before they were out of the nursery, who were forced to it by their parents and held to it by all the power of law and custom? Yet genius of a sort must have existed among women as it must have existed among the working classes. Now and again an Emily Brontë or a Robert Burns blazes out and proves its presence. But certainly it never got itself on to paper. When, however, one reads of a witch being ducked, of a woman possessed by devils, of a wise woman selling herbs, or even of a very remarkable man who had a mother, then I think we are on the track of a lost novelist, a suppressed poet, of some mute and inglorious Jane Austen, some Emily Brontë who dashed her brains out on the moor or mopped and mowed about the highways crazed with the torture that her gift had put her to. Indeed, I would venture to guess that Anon, who wrote so many poems without signing them, was often a woman. It was a woman Edward Fitzgerald,[5] I think, suggested who made the ballads and the folk-songs, crooning them to her children, beguiling her spinning with them, or the length of the winter's night.

This may be true or it may be false—who can say?—but what is true in it, so it seemed to me, reviewing the story of Shakespeare's sister as I had made it, is that any woman born with a great gift in the sixteenth century would certainly have gone crazed, shot herself, or ended her days in some lonely cottage outside the village, half witch, half wizard, feared and mocked at. For it needs little skill in psychology to be sure that a highly gifted girl who had tried to use her gift for poetry would have been so thwarted and hindered by other people, so tortured and pulled asunder by her own contrary instincts, that she must have lost her health and sanity to a certainty. No girl could have walked to London and stood at a stage door and forced her way into the presence of actor-managers without doing herself a violence and suffering an anguish which may have been irrational—for chastity may be a fetish invented by certain societies for unknown reasons—but were none the less inevitable. Chastity had then, it has even now, a religious importance in a woman's life, and has so wrapped itself round with nerves and instincts that to cut it free and bring it to the light of day demands courage of the rarest. To have lived a free life in London in the sixteenth century would have meant for a woman who was poet and playwright a nervous stress and dilemma which might well have killed her. Had she survived, whatever she had written would have been twisted and deformed, issuing from a strained and morbid imagination. And undoubtedly, I thought, looking at the shelf where there are no plays by women, her work would have gone unsigned. That refuge she would have sought certainly. It was the relic of the sense of chastity that dictated anonymity to women even so late as the nineteenth century. Currer Bell, George Eliot, George Sand,[6] all the victims of inner strife as their writings prove, sought ineffectively to veil themselves by using the name of a man. Thus they did homage to the convention, which if not implanted by the other sex was liberally encouraged by them (the chief glory of a woman is not to be talked of, said Pericles, himself a much-talked-of man), that publicity in women is detestable.[7] Anonymity runs in their blood. The desire to be veiled still possesses them. They are not even now as concerned about the health of their fame as men are, and, speaking generally, will pass a

4. George Trevelyan (1876–1962), historian.
5. Poet and translator (1809–1883).
6. Currer Bell, pen name of Charlotte Brontë; George Eliot, pen name of Mary Ann Evans; George Sand, pen name of Amandine Aurore Lucille Dupin (1804–1876).

7. The Athenian statesman Pericles was reported by the historian Thucydides to have said, "That woman is most praiseworthy whose name is least bandied about on men's lips, whether for praise or dispraise."

tombstone or a signpost without feeling an irresistible desire to cut their names on it, as Alf, Bert or Chas. must do in obedience to their instinct, which murmurs if it sees a fine woman go by, or even a dog, Ce chien est à moi [that dog is mine]. And, of course, it may not be a dog, I thought, remembering Parliament Square, the Sieges Allee[8] and other avenues; it may be a piece of land or a man with curly black hair. It is one of the great advantages of being a woman that one can pass even a very fine negress without wishing to make an Englishwoman of her.

That woman, then, who was born with a gift of poetry in the sixteenth century, was an unhappy woman, a woman at strife against herself. All the conditions of her life, all her own instincts, were hostile to the state of mind which is needed to set free whatever is in the brain. *** There would always have been that assertion—you cannot do this, you are incapable of doing that—to protest against, to overcome. Probably for a novelist this germ is no longer of much effect; for there have been women novelists of merit. But for painters it must still have some sting in it; and for musicians, I imagine, is even now active and poisonous in the extreme. The woman composer stands where the actress stood in the time of Shakespeare. Nick Greene, I thought, remembering the story I had made about Shakespeare's sister, said that a woman acting put him in mind of a dog dancing. Johnson repeated the phrase two hundred years later of women preaching.[9] And here, I said, opening a book about music, we have the very words used again in this year of grace, 1928, of women who try to write music. "Of Mlle. Germaine Tailleferre one can only repeat Dr. Johnson's dictum concerning a woman preacher, transposed into terms of music. 'Sir, a woman's composing is like a dog's walking on his hind legs. It is not done well, but you are surprised to find it done at all.'"[1] So accurately does history repeat itself.

Thus, I concluded, shutting Mr Oscar Browning's life and pushing away the rest, it is fairly evident that even in the nineteenth century a woman was not encouraged to be an artist. On the contrary, she was snubbed, slapped, lectured and exhorted. Her mind must have been strained and her vitality lowered by the need of opposing this, of disproving that. For here again we come within range of that very interesting and obscure masculine complex which has had so much influence upon the woman's movement; that deep-seated desire, not so much that she shall be inferior as that he shall be superior, which plants him wherever one looks, not only in front of the arts, but barring the way to politics too, even when the risk to himself seems infinitesimal and the suppliant humble and devoted. Even Lady Bessborough, I remembered, with all her passion for politics, must humbly bow herself and write to Lord Granville Leveson-Gower:[2] ". . . notwithstanding all my violence in politics and talking so much on that subject, I perfectly agree with you that no woman has any business to meddle with that or any other serious business, farther than giving her opinion (if she is ask'd)." And so she goes on to spend her enthusiasm where it meets with no obstacle whatsoever upon that immensely important subject, Lord Granville's maiden speech in the House of Commons. The spectacle is certainly a strange one, I thought. The history of men's opposition to women's emancipation is more interesting perhaps than the story of that emancipation itself. An amusing book might be made of it if some young student at Girton or Newnham would collect examples and deduce a

8. Victory Road, a thoroughfare in Berlin.
9. Samuel Johnson (1709–1784), poet and man of letters.
1. A Survey of Contemporary Music, Cecil Gray, page 246

[Woolf's note].
2. Lady Bessborough (1761–1821), correspondent of the British statesman Lord Granville.

theory—but she would need thick gloves on her hands, and bars to protect her of solid gold.

But what is amusing now, I recollected, shutting Lady Bessborough, had to be taken in desperate earnest once. Opinions that one now pastes in a book labelled cock-a-doodle-dum and keeps for reading to select audiences on summer nights once drew tears, I can assure you. Among your grandmothers and great-grandmothers there were many that wept their eyes out. Florence Nightingale shrieked aloud in her agony.[3] Moreover, it is all very well for you, who have got yourselves to college and enjoy sitting-rooms—or is it only bed-sitting-rooms?—of your own to say that genius should disregard such opinions; that genius should be above caring what is said of it. Unfortunately, it is precisely the men or women of genius who mind most what is said of them. Remember Keats. Remember the words he had cut on his tombstone. Think of Tennyson; think—but I need hardly multiply instances of the undeniable, if very unfortunate, fact that it is the nature of the artist to mind excessively what is said about him. Literature is strewn with the wreckage of men who have minded beyond reason the opinions of others.

And this susceptibility of theirs is doubly unfortunate, I thought, returning again to my original enquiry into what state of mind is most propitious for creative work, because the mind of an artist, in order to achieve the prodigious effort of freeing whole and entire the work that is in him, must be incandescent, like Shakespeare's mind, I conjectured, looking at the book which lay open at *Antony and Cleopatra*. There must be no obstacle in it, no foreign matter unconsumed.

For though we say that we know nothing about Shakespeare's state of mind, even as we say that, we are saying something about Shakespeare's state of mind. The reason perhaps why we know so little of Shakespeare—compared with Donne or Ben Jonson or Milton—is that his grudges and spites and antipathies are hidden from us. We are not held up by some "revelation" which reminds us of the writer. All desire to protest, to preach, to proclaim an injury, to pay off a score, to make the world the witness of some hardship or grievance was fired out of him and consumed. Therefore his poetry flows from him free and unimpeded. If ever a human being got his work expressed completely, it was Shakespeare. If ever a mind was incandescent, unimpeded, I thought, turning again to the bookcase, it was Shakespeare's mind.

from *Chapter 4*

The extreme activity of mind which showed itself in the later eighteenth century among women—the talking, and the meeting, the writing of essays on Shakespeare, the translating of the classics—was founded on the solid fact that women could make money by writing. Money dignifies what is frivolous if unpaid for. It might still be well to sneer at "blue stockings with an itch for scribbling," but it could not be denied that they could put money in their purses. Thus, towards the end of the eighteenth century a change came about which, if I were rewriting history, I should describe more fully and think of greater importance than the Crusades or the Wars of the Roses. The middle-class woman began to write. For if *Pride and Prejudice* matters, and *Middlemarch* and *Villette* and *Wuthering Heights* matter,[4] then it matters far more

---

3. See *Cassandra*, by Florence Nightingale, printed in *The Cause*, by R. Strachey [Woolf's note].
4. *Pride and Prejudice* (1813), a novel by Jane Austen;

Middlemarch (1871–1872) by George Eliot; *Villette* (1853) by Charlotte Brontë; *Wuthering Heights* (1847) by Emily Brontë.

than I can prove in an hour's discourse that women generally, and not merely the lonely aristocrat shut up in her country house among her folios and her flatterers, took to writing. Without those forerunners, Jane Austen and the Brontës and George Eliot could no more have written than Shakespeare could have written without Marlowe, or Marlowe without Chaucer, or Chaucer without those forgotten poets who paved the ways and tamed the natural savagery of the tongue. For masterpieces are not single and solitary births; they are the outcome of many years of thinking in common, of thinking by the body of the people, so that the experience of the mass is behind the single voice. Jane Austen should have laid a wreath upon the grave of Fanny Burney, and George Eliot done homage to the robust shade of Eliza Carter—the valiant old woman who tied a bell to her bedstead in order that she might wake early and learn Greek. All women together ought to let flowers fall upon the tomb of Aphra Behn[5] which is, most scandalously but rather appropriately, in Westminster Abbey, for it was she who earned them the right to speak their minds. It is she—shady and amorous as she was—who makes it not quite fantastic for me to say to you tonight: Earn five hundred a year by your wits.

Here, then, one had reached the early nineteenth century. And here, for the first time, I found several shelves given up entirely to the works of women. But why, I could not help asking, as I ran my eyes over them, were they, with very few exceptions, all novels? The original impulse was to poetry. The "supreme head of song" was a poetess. Both in France and in England the women poets precede the women novelists. Moreover, I thought, looking at the four famous names, what had George Eliot in common with Emily Brontë? Did not Charlotte Brontë fail entirely to understand Jane Austen? Save for the possibly relevant fact that not one of them had a child, four more incongruous characters could not have met together in a room—so much so that it is tempting to invent a meeting and a dialogue between them. Yet by some strange force they were all compelled, when they wrote, to write novels. Had it something to do with being born of the middle class, I asked; and with the fact, which Miss Emily Davies a little later was so strikingly to demonstrate,[6] that the middle-class family in the early nineteenth century was possessed only of a single sitting-room between them? If a woman wrote, she would have to write in the common sitting-room. And, as Miss Nightingale was so vehemently to complain,—"women never have an half hour . . . that they can call their own"—she was always interrupted. Still it would be easier to write prose and fiction there than to write poetry or a play. Less concentration is required. Jane Austen wrote like that to the end of her days. "How she was able to effect all this," her nephew writes in his Memoir, "is surprising, for she had no separate study to repair to, and most of the work must have been done in the general sitting-room, subject to all kinds of casual interruptions. She was careful that her occupation should not be suspected by servants or visitors or any persons beyond her own family party."[7] Jane Austen hid her manuscripts or covered them with a piece of blotting-paper. Then, again, all the literary training that a woman had in the early nineteenth century was training in the observation of character, in the analysis of emotion. Her sensibility had been educated for centuries by

5. A dramatist and the first English woman to earn a living by writing (1640–1689). Westminster Abbey, in central London, is the burial place of many of the English kings and queens, as well as of famous poets and statesmen.

6. (Sarah) Emily Davies was prominent in the movement to secure university education for women in the 19th century and was chief founder of Girton College, Cambridge (1873).

7. *Memoir of Jane Austen*, by her nephew, James Edward Austen-Leigh [Woolf's note].

the influences of the common sitting-room. People's feelings were impressed on her; personal relations were always before her eyes. Therefore, when the middle-class woman took to writing, she naturally wrote novels, even though, as seems evident enough, two of the four famous women here named were not by nature novelists. Emily Brontë should have written poetic plays; the overflow of George Eliot's capacious mind should have spread itself when the creative impulse was spent upon history or biography. They wrote novels, however; one may even go further, I said, taking *Pride and Prejudice* from the shelf, and say that they wrote good novels. Without boasting or giving pain to the opposite sex, one may say that *Pride and Prejudice* is a good book. At any rate, one would not have been ashamed to have been caught in the act of writing *Pride and Prejudice*. Yet Jane Austen was glad that a hinge creaked, so that she might hide her manuscript before any one came in. To Jane Austen there was something discreditable in writing *Pride and Prejudice*. And, I wondered, would *Pride and Prejudice* have been a better novel if Jane Austen had not thought it necessary to hide her manuscript from visitors? I read a page or two to see; but I could not find any signs that her circumstances had harmed her work in the slightest. That, perhaps, was the chief miracle about it. Here was a woman about the year 1800 writing without hate, without bitterness, without fear, without protest, without preaching. That was how Shakespeare wrote, I thought, looking at *Antony and Cleopatra*; and when people compare Shakespeare and Jane Austen, they may mean that the minds of both had consumed all impediments; and for that reason we do not know Jane Austen and we do not know Shakespeare, and for that reason Jane Austen pervades every word that she wrote, and so does Shakespeare. If Jane Austen suffered in any way from her circumstances it was in the narrowness of life that was imposed upon her. It was impossible for a woman to go about alone. She never travelled; she never drove through London in an omnibus or had luncheon in a shop by herself. But perhaps it was the nature of Jane Austen not to want what she had not. Her gift and her circumstances matched each other completely. But I doubt whether that was true of Charlotte Brontë, I said, opening *Jane Eyre* and laying it beside *Pride and Prejudice*.[8]

I opened it at chapter twelve and my eye was caught by the phrase, "Anybody may blame me who likes." What were they blaming Charlotte Brontë for, I wondered? And I read how Jane Eyre used to go up on to the roof when Mrs Fairfax was making jellies and looked over the fields at the distant view. And then she longed—and it was for this that they blamed her—that "then I longed for a power of vision which might overpass that limit; which might reach the busy world, towns, regions full of life I had heard of but never seen: that then I desired more of practical experience than I possessed; more of intercourse with my kind, of acquaintance with variety of character than was here within my reach. I valued what was good in Mrs Fairfax, and what was good in Adèle; but I believed in the existence of other and more vivid kinds of goodness, and what I believed in I wished to behold.

"Who blames me? Many, no doubt, and I shall be called discontented. I could not help it: the restlessness was in my nature; it agitated me to pain sometimes. . . .

---

8. Woolf goes on to describe parts of the plot of *Jane Eyre*; Jane Eyre, a penniless orphan, having suffered greatly during her schooling, takes up the post of governess to Adele, the daughter of Mr. Rochester, a man of strange moods. Rochester falls in love with Jane, who agrees to marry him; however this is prevented by Rochester's mad wife—whom Rochester has locked in the attic, concealing her existence from Jane—who tears Jane's wedding veil on the eve of the marriage. Rochester at first tells Jane that Grace Poole, a servant, had been responsible for this and other strange events, including the uncanny laughter occasionally heard in the house.

"It is vain to say human beings ought to be satisfied with tranquillity: they must have action; and they will make it if they cannot find it. Millions are condemned to a stiller doom than mine, and millions are in silent revolt against their lot. Nobody knows how many rebellions ferment in the masses of life which people earth. Women are supposed to be very calm generally: but women feel just as men feel; they need exercise for their faculties and a field for their efforts as much as their brothers do; they suffer from too rigid a restraint, too absolute a stagnation, precisely as men would suffer; and it is narrow-minded in their more privileged fellow-creatures to say that they ought to confine themselves to making puddings and knitting stockings, to playing on the piano and embroidering bags. It is thoughtless to condemn them, or laugh at them, if they seek to do more or learn more than custom has pronounced necessary for their sex.

"When thus alone I not unfrequently heard Grace Poole's laugh . . . ."

That is an awkward break, I thought. It is upsetting to come upon Grace Poole all of a sudden. The continuity is disturbed. One might say, I continued, laying the book down beside *Pride and Prejudice,* that the woman who wrote those pages had more genius in her than Jane Austen; but if one reads them over and marks that jerk in them, that indignation, one sees that she will never get her genius expressed whole and entire. Her books will be deformed and twisted. She will write in a rage where she should write calmly. She will write foolishly where she should write wisely. She will write of herself where she should write of her characters. She is at war with her lot. How could she help but die young, cramped and thwarted?

One could not but play for a moment with the thought of what might have happened if Charlotte Brontë had possessed say three hundred a year—but the foolish woman sold the copyright of her novels outright for fifteen hundred pounds; had somehow possessed more knowledge of the busy world, and towns and regions full of life; more practical experience, and intercourse with her kind and acquaintance with a variety of character. In those words she puts her finger exactly not only upon her own defects as a novelist but upon those of her sex at that time. She knew, no one better, how enormously her genius would have profited if it had not spent itself in solitary visions over distant fields; if experience and intercourse and travel had been granted her. But they were not granted; they were withheld; and we must accept the fact that all those good novels, *Villette, Emma, Wuthering Heights, Middlemarch,* were written by women without more experience of life than could enter the house of a respectable clergyman; written too in the common sitting-room of that respectable house and by women so poor that they could not afford to buy more than a few quires of paper at a time upon which to write *Wuthering Heights* or *Jane Eyre.* One of them, it is true, George Eliot, escaped after much tribulation, but only to a secluded villa in St John's Wood. And there she settled down in the shadow of the world's disapproval.[9] "I wish it to be understood," she wrote, "that I should never invite any one to come and see me who did not ask for the invitation"; for was she not living in sin with a married man and might not the sight of her damage the chastity of Mrs Smith or whoever it might be that chanced to call? One must submit to the social convention, and be "cut off from what is called the world." At the same time, on the other side of Europe, there was a young

9. Following a strictly religious childhood, the novelist George Eliot lost her faith and eloped with G. H. Lewes, a married man, with whom she lived for the rest of his life; her family never forgave her.

man living freely with this gipsy or with that great lady; going to the wars; picking up unhindered and uncensored all that varied experience of human life which served him so splendidly later when he came to write his books. Had Tolstoi lived at the Priory in seclusion with a married lady "cut off from what is called the world," however edifying the moral lesson, he could scarcely, I thought, have written *War and Peace*. * * *

* * * I do not want, and I am sure that you do not want me, to broach that very dismal subject, the future of fiction, so that I will only pause here one moment to draw your attention to the great part which must be played in that future so far as women are concerned by physical conditions. The book has somehow to be adapted to the body, and at a venture one would say that women's books should be shorter, more concentrated, than those of men, and framed so that they do not need long hours of steady and uninterrupted work. For interruptions there will always be. Again, the nerves that feed the brain would seem to differ in men and women, and if you are going to make them work their best and hardest, you must find out what treatment suits them—whether these hours of lectures, for instance, which the monks devised, presumably, hundreds of years ago, suit them—what alternations of work and rest they need, interpreting rest not as doing nothing but as doing something but something that is different; and what should that difference be? All this should be discussed and discovered; all this is part of the question of women and fiction. And yet, I continued, approaching the bookcase again, where shall I find that elaborate study of the psychology of women by a woman? If through their incapacity to play football women are not going to be allowed to practise medicine——

Happily my thoughts were now given another turn.

from *Chapter 6*

Next day the light of the October morning was falling in dusty shafts through the uncurtained windows, and the hum of traffic rose from the street. London then was winding itself up again; the factory was astir; the machines were beginning. It was tempting, after all this reading, to look out of the window and see what London was doing on the morning of the twenty-sixth of October 1928. And what was London doing? Nobody, it seemed, was reading *Antony and Cleopatra*. London was wholly indifferent, it appeared, to Shakespeare's plays. Nobody cared a straw—and I do not blame them—for the future of fiction, the death of poetry or the development by the average woman of a prose style completely expressive of her mind. If opinions upon any of these matters had been chalked on the pavement, nobody would have stooped to read them. The nonchalance of the hurrying feet would have rubbed them out in half an hour. Here came an errand-boy; here a woman with a dog on a lead. The fascination of the London street is that no two people are ever alike; each seems bound on some private affair of his own. There were the business-like, with their little bags; there were the drifters rattling sticks upon area railings; there were affable characters to whom the streets serve for clubroom, hailing men in carts and giving information without being asked for it. Also there were funerals to which men, thus suddenly reminded of the passing of their own bodies, lifted their hats. And then a very distinguished gentleman came slowly down a doorstep and paused to avoid collision with a bustling lady who had, by some means or other, acquired a splendid fur coat and a bunch of Parma violets. They all seemed separate, self-absorbed, on business of their own.

At this moment, as so often happens in London, there was a complete lull and suspension of traffic. Nothing came down the street; nobody passed. A single leaf detached itself from the plane tree at the end of the street, and in that pause and suspension fell. Somehow it was like a signal falling, a signal pointing to a force in things which one had overlooked. It seemed to point to a river, which flowed past, invisibly, round the corner, down the street, and took people and eddied them along, as the stream at Oxbridge had taken the undergraduate in his boat and the dead leaves. Now it was bringing from one side of the street to the other diagonally a girl in patent leather boots, and then a young man in a maroon overcoat; it was also bringing a taxi-cab; and it brought all three together at a point directly beneath my window; where the taxi stopped; and the girl and the young man stopped; and they got into the taxi; and then the cab glided off as if it were swept on by the current elsewhere.

The sight was ordinary enough; what was strange was the rhythmical order with which my imagination had invested it; and the fact that the ordinary sight of two people getting into a cab had the power to communicate something of their own seeming satisfaction. The sight of two people coming down the street and meeting at the corner seems to ease the mind of some strain, I thought, watching the taxi turn and make off. Perhaps to think, as I had been thinking these two days, of one sex as distinct from the other is an effort. It interferes with the unity of the mind. Now that effort had ceased and that unity had been restored by seeing two people come together and get into a taxi-cab. The mind is certainly a very mysterious organ, I reflected, drawing my head in from the window, about which nothing whatever is known, though we depend upon it so completely. Why do I feel that there are severances and oppositions in the mind, as there are strains from obvious causes on the body? What does one mean by "the unity of the mind," I pondered, for clearly the mind has so great a power of concentrating at any point at any moment that it seems to have no single state of being. It can separate itself from the people in the street, for example, and think of itself as apart from them, at an upper window looking down on them. Or it can think with other people spontaneously, as, for instance, in a crowd waiting to hear some piece of news read out. It can think back through its fathers or through its mothers, as I have said that a woman writing thinks back through her mothers. Again if one is a woman one is often surprised by a sudden splitting off of consciousness, say in walking down Whitehall,[1] when from being the natural inheritor of that civilisation, she becomes, on the contrary, outside of it, alien and critical. Clearly the mind is always altering its focus, and bringing the world into different perspectives. But some of these states of mind seem, even if adopted spontaneously, to be less comfortable than others. In order to keep oneself continuing in them one is unconsciously holding something back, and gradually the repression becomes an effort. But there may be some state of mind in which one could continue without effort because nothing is required to be held back. And this perhaps, I thought, coming in from the window, is one of them. For certainly when I saw the couple get into the taxi-cab the mind felt as if, after being divided, it had come together again in a natural fusion. The obvious reason would be that it is natural for the sexes to co-operate. One has a profound, if irrational, instinct in favour of the theory that the union of man and woman makes for the greatest satisfaction, the most complete happiness. But the sight of the two people getting into the taxi and the satisfaction it gave me made me

---

1. A main thoroughfare in central London and site of government offices.

also ask whether there are two sexes in the mind corresponding to the two sexes in the body, and whether they also require to be united in order to get complete satisfaction and happiness. And I went on amateurishly to sketch a plan of the soul so that in each of us two powers preside, one male, one female; and in the man's brain, the man predominates over the woman, and in the woman's brain, the woman predominates over the man. The normal and comfortable state of being is that when the two live in harmony together, spiritually co-operating. If one is a man, still the woman part of the brain must have effect; and a woman also must have intercourse with the man in her. Coleridge perhaps meant this when he said that a great mind is androgynous.[2] It is when this fusion takes place that the mind is fully fertilised and uses all its faculties. Perhaps a mind that is purely masculine cannot create, any more than a mind that is purely feminine, I thought. * * *

* * * One must turn back to Shakespeare then, for Shakespeare was androgynous; and so was Keats and Sterne and Cowper and Lamb and Coleridge. Shelley perhaps was sexless. Milton and Ben Jonson had a dash too much of the male in them. So had Wordsworth and Tolstoi. In our time Proust was wholly androgynous, if not perhaps a little too much of a woman. But that failing is too rare for one to complain of it, since without some mixture of the kind the intellect seems to predominate and the other faculties of the mind harden and become barren. However, I consoled myself with the reflection that this is perhaps a passing phase; much of what I have said in obedience to my promise to give you the course of my thoughts will seem out of date; much of what flames in my eyes will seem dubious to you who have not yet come of age.

Even so, the very first sentence that I would write here, I said, crossing over to the writing-table and taking up the page headed Women and Fiction, is that it is fatal for any one who writes to think of their sex. It is fatal to be a man or woman pure and simple; one must be woman-manly or man-womanly. It is fatal for a woman to lay the least stress on any grievance; to plead even with justice any cause; in any way to speak consciously as a woman. And fatal is no figure of speech; for anything written with that conscious bias is doomed to death. It ceases to be fertilised. Brilliant and effective, powerful and masterly, as it may appear for a day or two, it must wither at nightfall; it cannot grow in the minds of others. Some collaboration has to take place in the mind between the woman and the man before the act of creation can be accomplished. Some marriage of opposites has to be consummated. The whole of the mind must lie wide open if we are to get the sense that the writer is communicating his experience with perfect fullness. There must be freedom and there must be peace. Not a wheel must grate, not a light glimmer. The curtains must be close drawn. The writer, I thought, once his experience is over, must lie back and let his mind celebrate its nuptials in darkness. He must not look or question what is being done. Rather, he must pluck the petals from a rose or watch the swans float calmly down the river. And I saw again the current which took the boat and the undergraduate and the dead leaves; and the taxi took the man and the woman, I thought, seeing them come together across the street, and the current swept them away, I thought, hearing far off the roar of London's traffic, into that tremendous stream.

Here, then, Mary Beton ceases to speak. She has told you how she reached the conclusion—the prosaic conclusion—that it is necessary to have five hundred a year and a room with a lock on the door if you are to write fiction or poetry. She has tried

2. The poet Samuel Taylor Coleridge made the remark in September 1832—"a great mind must be androgynous"—and it was duly recorded in his *Table Talk*.

to lay bare the thoughts and impressions that led her to think this. She has asked you to follow her flying into the arms of a Beadle, lunching here, dining there, drawing pictures in the British Museum, taking books from the shelf, looking out of the window. While she has been doing all these things, you no doubt have been observing her failings and foibles and deciding what effect they have had on her opinions. You have been contradicting her and making whatever additions and deductions seem good to you. That is all as it should be, for in a question like this truth is only to be had by laying together many varieties of error. And I will end now in my own person by anticipating two criticisms, so obvious that you can hardly fail to make them.

No opinion has been expressed, you may say, upon the comparative merits of the sexes even as writers. That was done purposely, because, even if the time had come for such a valuation—and it is far more important at the moment to know how much money women had and how many rooms than to theorise about their capacities—even if the time had come I do not believe that gifts, whether of mind or character, can be weighed like sugar and butter, not even in Cambridge, where they are so adept at putting people into classes and fixing caps on their heads and letters after their names. I do not believe that even the Table of Precedency which you will find in Whitaker's *Almanac*[3] represents a final order of values, or that there is any sound reason to suppose that a Commander of the Bath will ultimately walk in to dinner behind a Master in Lunacy. All this pitting of sex against sex, of quality against quality; all this claiming of superiority and imputing of inferiority, belong to the private-school stage of human existence where there are "sides," and it is necessary for one side to beat another side, and of the utmost importance to walk up to a platform and receive from the hands of the Headmaster himself a highly ornamental pot. As people mature they cease to believe in sides or in Headmasters or in highly ornamental pots. At any rate, where books are concerned, it is notoriously difficult to fix labels of merit in such a way that they do not come off. Are not reviews of current literature a perpetual illustration of the difficulty of judgment? "This great book," "this worthless book," the same book is called by both names. Praise and blame alike mean nothing. No, delightful as the pastime of measuring may be, it is the most futile of all occupations, and to submit to the decrees of the measurers the most servile of attitudes. So long as you write what you wish to write, that is all that matters; and whether it matters for ages or only for hours, nobody can say. But to sacrifice a hair of the head of your vision, a shade of its colour, in deference to some Headmaster with a silver pot in his hand or to some professor with a measuring-rod up his sleeve, is the most abject treachery, and the sacrifice of wealth and chastity which used to be said to be the greatest of human disasters, a mere flea-bite in comparison.

Next I think that you may object that in all this I have made too much of the importance of material things. * * * Intellectual freedom depends upon material things. Poetry depends upon intellectual freedom. And women have always been poor, not for two hundred years merely, but from the beginning of time. Women have had less intellectual freedom than the sons of Athenian slaves. Women, then, have not had a dog's chance of writing poetry. That is why I have laid so much stress on money and a room of one's own. However, thanks to the toils of those obscure women in the past, of whom I wish we knew more, thanks, curiously enough, to two wars, the Crimean which let Florence Nightingale out of her drawing-room, and the

---

3. A compendium of general information first published in 1868.

European War which opened the doors to the average woman some sixty years later, these evils are in the way to be bettered. Otherwise you would not be here tonight, and your chance of earning five hundred pounds a year, precarious as I am afraid that it still is, would be minute in the extreme. * * *

Here I would stop, but the pressure of convention decrees that every speech must end with a peroration. And a peroration addressed to women should have something, you will agree, particularly exalting and ennobling about it. I should implore you to remember your responsibilities, to be higher, more spiritual; I should remind you how much depends upon you, and what an influence you can exert upon the future. But those exhortations can safely, I think, be left to the other sex, who will put them, and indeed have put them, with far greater eloquence than I can compass. When I rummage in my own mind I find no noble sentiments about being companions and equals and influencing the world to higher ends. I find myself saying briefly and prosaically that it is much more important to be oneself than anything else. Do not dream of influencing other people, I would say, if I knew how to make it sound exalted. Think of things in themselves.

And again I am reminded by dipping into newspapers and novels and biographies that when a woman speaks to women she should have something very unpleasant up her sleeve. Women are hard on women. Women dislike women. Women . . . but are you not sick to death of the word? I can assure you that I am. Let us agree, then, that a paper read by a woman to women should end with something particularly disagreeable.

But how does it go? What can I think of? The truth is, I often like women. I like their unconventionality. I like their subtlety. I like their anonymity. I like—but I must not run on in this way. That cupboard there,—you say it holds clean table-napkins only; but what if Sir Archibald Bodkin were concealed among them?[4] Let me then adopt a sterner tone. Have I, in the preceding words, conveyed to you sufficiently the warnings and reprobation of mankind? I have told you the very low opinion in which you were held by Mr Oscar Browning. I have indicated what Napoleon once thought of you and what Mussolini thinks now. Then, in case any of you aspire to fiction, I have copied out for your benefit the advice of the critic about courageously acknowledging the limitations of your sex. I have referred to Professor X and given prominence to his statement that women are intellectually, morally and physically inferior to men. I have handed on all that has come my way without going in search of it, and here is a final warning—from Mr John Langdon Davies.[5] Mr John Langdon Davies warns women "that when children cease to be altogether desirable, women cease to be altogether necessary." I hope you will make a note of it.

How can I further encourage you to go about the business of life? Young women, I would say, and please attend, for the peroration is beginning, you are, in my opinion, disgracefully ignorant. You have never made a discovery of any sort of importance. You have never shaken an empire or led an army into battle. The plays of Shakespeare are not by you, and you have never introduced a barbarous race to the blessings of civilisation. What is your excuse? It is all very well for you to say, pointing to the streets and squares and forests of the globe swarming with black and white and coffee-coloured inhabitants, all busily engaged in traffic and enterprise and love-making, we have had

4. Sir Archibald Bodkin was then Director of Public Prosecutions; his office had been responsible for the 1928 prosecution of Radclyffe Hall's novel *The Well of Loneliness* on a charge of obscenity. It was subsequently banned. Woolf had wanted to give evidence in the book's defense at the trial, but expert witnesses were not allowed by the presiding magistrate.

5. *A Short History of Women*, by John Langford Davies [Woolf's note].

other work on our hands. Without our doing, those seas would be unsailed and those fertile lands a desert. We have borne and bred and washed and taught, perhaps to the age of six or seven years, the one thousand six hundred and twenty-three million human beings who are, according to statistics, at present in existence, and that, allowing that some had help, takes time.

There is truth in what you say—I will not deny it. But at the same time may I remind you that there have been at least two colleges for women in existence in England since the year 1866; that after the year 1880 a married woman was allowed by law to possess her own property; and that in 1919—which is a whole nine years ago—she was given a vote? May I also remind you that the most of the professions have been open to you for close on ten years now? When you reflect upon these immense privileges and the length of time time during which they have been enjoyed, and the fact that there must be at this moment some two thousand women capable of earning over five hundred a year in one way or another, you will agree that the excuse of lack of opportunity, training, encouragement, leisure and money no longer holds good. Moreover, the economists are telling us that Mrs Seton has had too many children. You must, of course, go on bearing children, but, so they say, in twos and threes, not in tens and twelves.

Thus, with some time on your hands and with some book learning in your brains—you have had enough of the other kind, and are sent to college partly, I suspect, to be uneducated—surely you should embark upon another stage of your very long, very laborious and highly obscure career. A thousand pens are ready to suggest what you should do and what effect you will have. My own suggestion is a little fantastic, I admit; I prefer, therefore, to put it in the form of fiction.

I told you in the course of this paper that Shakespeare had a sister; but do not look for her in Sir Sidney Lee's life of the poet. She died young–alas, she never wrote a word. She lies buried where the omnibuses now stop, opposite the Elephant and Castle. Now my belief is that this poet who never wrote a word and was buried at the crossroads still lives. She lives in you and in me, and in many other women who are not here tonight, for they are washing up the dishes and putting the children to bed. But she lives; for great poets do not die; they are continuing presences; they need only the opportunity to walk among us in the flesh. This opportunity, as I think, it is now coming within your power to give her. For my belief is that if we live another century or so—I am talking of the common life which is the real life and not of the little separate lives which we live as individuals—and have five hundred a year each of us and rooms of our own; if we have the habit of freedom and the courage to write exactly what we think; if we escape a little from the common sitting-room and see human beings not always in their relation to each other but in relation to reality; and the sky, too, and the trees or whatever it may be in themselves; if we look past Milton's bogey, for no human being should shut out the view; if we face the fact, for it is a fact, that there is no arm to cling to, but that we go alone and that our relation is to the world of reality and not only to the world of men and women, then the opportunity will come and the dead poet who was Shakespeare's sister will put on the body which she has so often laid down. Drawing her life from the lives of the unknown who were her forerunners, as her brother did before her, she will be born. As for her coming without that preparation, without that effort on our part, without that determination that when she is born again she shall find it possible to live and write her poetry, that we cannot expect, for that would be impossible. But I maintain that she would come if we worked for her, and that so to work, even in poverty and obscurity, is worth while.

Katherine Mansfield

1888–1923

Katherine Mansfield was one of the twentieth century's most gifted writers of short fiction. As Elizabeth Bowen has written, Mansfield realized that "the short story . . . is not intended to be the medium either for exploration or long-term development of character. Character cannot be more than *shown*. . . ." Mansfield thus turned the short story away from contrived plot conventions, and toward the illumination of small events as they reveal the fabric of a life, making of short fiction an almost dramatic form.

Mansfield was born in Wellington, New Zealand. She moved to England more or less permanently before her twentieth birthday, but many of her most successful stories return to her childhood and her homeland for their subject. The path to this mature fiction was complicated, however; when she arrived in London in 1908, Mansfield was pregnant. She quickly married and the same day left her husband, who was not the child's father; she went to a German spa, where she miscarried. This tumultuous background is reflected in the bitter stories of her first volume, *In a German Pension*. In 1911 Mansfield met John Middleton Murray, editor and man of letters, with whom she remained until the end of her life.

Paradoxically, the horrors of World War I (in which her brother Leslie was killed) had an uplifting effect on Mansfield's writing. The result of the war, she wrote, is that "Now we know ourselves for what we are. In a way its a tragic knowledge. Its as though, even while we live again we face death. But *through Life:* thats the point. We see death in life as we see death in a flower that is fresh unfolded. Our hymn is to the flower's beauty—we would make that beauty immortal because we *know*."

One important element of Mansfield's "tragic knowledge" was the awareness that she was dying; she suffered her first tubercular hemorrhage in 1918, and never regained her health. She remained dedicated to her art until the very end, however, producing nineteen major stories during the last nineteen months of her life; Virginia Woolf, who admired and even envied Mansfield's talent, wrote, "No one felt more seriously the importance of writing than she did." The story included here, *The Daughters of the Late Colonel*, diagnoses with both tenderness and horror the spiritual death that Mansfield saw around her. It invokes a theme that has been important in twentieth-century literature from Henry James's *The Beast in the Jungle* to Samuel Beckett's *Waiting for Godot*, and beyond: that, as John Lennon put it, "Life is what happens to you / While you're busy making other plans."

The Daughters of the Late Colonel

1

The week after was one of the busiest weeks of their lives. Even when they went to bed it was only their bodies that lay down and rested; their minds went on, thinking things out, talking things over, wondering, deciding, trying to remember where. . .

Constantia lay like a statue, her hands by her sides, her feet just overlapping each other, the sheet up to her chin. She stared at the ceiling.

"Do you think father would mind if we gave his top-hat to the porter?"

"The porter?" snapped Josephine. "Why ever the porter? What a very extraordinary idea!"

"Because," said Constantia slowly, "he must often have to go to funerals. And I noticed at—at the cemetery that he only had a bowler." She paused. "I thought then how very much he'd appreciate a top-hat. We ought to give him a present, too. He was always very nice to father."

"But," cried Josephine, flouncing on her pillow and staring across the dark at Constantia, "father's head!" And suddenly, for one awful moment, she nearly giggled. Not, of course, that she felt in the least like giggling. It must have been habit. Years ago, when they had stayed awake at night talking, their beds had simply heaved. And now the porter's head, disappearing, popped out, like a candle, under father's hat. . . . The giggle mounted, mounted; she clenched her hands; she fought it down; she frowned fiercely at the dark and said "Remember" terribly sternly.

"We can decide to-morrow," she sighed.

Constantia had noticed nothing; she sighed.

"Do you think we ought to have our dressing-gowns dyed as well?"

"Black?" almost shrieked Josephine.

"Well, what else?" said Constantia. "I was thinking—it doesn't seem quite sincere, in a way, to wear black out of doors and when we're fully dressed, and then when we're at home—"

"But nobody sees us," said Josephine. She gave the bedclothes such a twitch that both her feet became uncovered, and she had to creep up the pillows to get them well under again.

"Kate does," said Constantia. "And the postman very well might."

Josephine thought of her dark-red slippers, which matched her dressing-gown, and of Constantia's favourite indefinite green ones which went with hers. Black! Two black dressing-gowns and two pairs of black woolly slippers, creeping off to the bathroom like black cats.

"I don't think it's absolutely necessary," said she.

Silence. Then Constantia said, "We shall have to post the papers with the notice in them to-morrow to catch the Ceylon mail. . . . How many letters have we had up till now?"

"Twenty-three."

Josephine had replied to them all, and twenty-three times when she came to "We miss our dear father so much" she had broken down and had to use her handkerchief, and on some of them even to soak up a very light-blue tear with an edge of blotting-paper. Strange! She couldn't have put it on—but twenty-three times. Even now, though, when she said over to herself sadly. "We miss our dear father so much" she could have cried if she'd wanted to.

"Have you got enough stamps?" came from Constantia.

"Oh, how can I tell?" said Josephine crossly. "What's the good of asking me that now?"

"I was just wondering," said Constantia mildly.

Silence again. There came a little rustle, a scurry, a hop.

"A mouse," said Constantia.

"It can't be a mouse because there aren't any crumbs," said Josephine.

"But it doesn't know there aren't," said Constantia.

A spasm of pity squeezed her heart. Poor little thing! She wished she'd left a tiny piece of biscuit on the dressing-table. It was awful to think of it not finding anything. What would it do?

"I can't think how they manage to live at all," she said slowly.

"Who?" demanded Josephine.

And Constantia said more loudly than she meant to, "Mice."

But the idea of a little Communion terrified them. What! In the drawing-room by themselves—with no—no altar or anything! The piano would be much too high, thought Constantia, and Mr Farolles could not possibly lean over it with the chalice. And Kate would be sure to come bursting in and interrupt them, thought Josephine. And supposing the bell rang in the middle? It might be somebody important—about their mourning. Would they get up reverently and go out, or would they have to wait . . . in torture?

"Perhaps you will send round a note by your good Kate if you would care for it later," said Mr Farolles.

"Oh yes, thank you very much!" they both said.

Mr Farolles got up and took his black straw hat from the round table.

"And about the funeral," he said softly. "I may arrange that—as your dear father's old friend and yours, Miss Pinner—and Miss Constantia?"

Josephine and Constantia got up too.

"I should like it to be quite simple," said Josephine firmly, "and not too expensive. At the same time, I should like—"

"A good one that will last," thought dreamy Constantia, as if Josephine were buying a nightgown. But of course Josephine didn't say that. "One suitable to our father's position." She was very nervous.

"I'll run round to our good friend Mr Knight," said Mr Farolles soothingly. "I will ask him to come and see you. I am sure you will find him very helpful indeed."

5

Well, at any rate, all that part of it was over, though neither of them could possibly believe that father was never coming back. Josephine had had a moment of absolute terror at the cemetery, while the coffin was lowered, to think that she and Constantia had done this thing without asking his permission. What would father say when he found out? For he was bound to find out sooner or later. He always did. "Buried. You two girls had me *buried!*" She heard his stick thumping. Oh, what would they say? What possible excuse could they make? It sounded such an appalling heartless thing to do. Such a wicked advantage to take of a person because he happened to be helpless at the moment. The other people seemed to treat it all as a matter of course. They were strangers; they couldn't be expected to understand that father was the very last person for such a thing to happen to. No, the entire blame for it all would fall on her and Constantia. And the expense, she thought, stepping into the tight-buttoned cab. When she had to show him the bills. What would he say then?

She heard him absolutely roaring, "And do you expect me to pay for this gimcrack excursion of yours?"

"Oh," groaned poor Josephine aloud, "we shouldn't have done it, Con!"

And Constantia, pale as a lemon in all that blackness, said in a frightened whisper, "Done what, Jug?"

"Let them bu-bury father like that," said Josephine, breaking down and crying into her new, queer-smelling mourning handkerchief.

"But what else could we have done?" asked Constantia wonderingly. "We couldn't have kept him, Jug—we couldn't have kept him unburied. At any rate, not in a flat that size."

Josephine blew her nose; the cab was dreadfully stuffy.

"I don't know," she said forlornly. "It is all so dreadful. I feel we ought to have tried to, just for a time at least. To make perfectly sure. One thing's certain"—and her tears sprang out again—"father will never forgive us for this—never!"

6

Father would never forgive them. That was what they felt more than ever when, two mornings later, they went into his room to go through his things. They had discussed it quite calmly. It was even down on Josephine's list of things to be done. *Go through father's things and settle about them.* But that was a very different matter from saying after breakfast:

"Well, are you ready, Con?"

"Yes, Jug—when you are."

"Then I think we'd better get it over."

It was dark in the hall. It had been a rule for years never to disturb father in the morning, whatever happened. And now they were going to open the door without knocking even. . . . Constantia's eyes were enormous at the idea; Josephine felt weak in the knees.

"You—you go first," she gasped, pushing Constantia.

But Constantia said, as she always had said on those occasions, "No, Jug, that's not fair. You're eldest."

Josephine was just going to say—what at other times she wouldn't have owned to for the world—what she kept for her very last weapon, "But you're tallest," when they noticed that the kitchen door was open, and there stood Kate. . . .

"Very stiff," said Josephine, grasping the door-handle and doing her best to turn it. As if anything ever deceived Kate!

It couldn't be helped. That girl was . . . Then the door was shut behind them, but—but they weren't in father's room at all. They might have suddenly walked through the wall by mistake into a different flat altogether. Was the door just behind them? They were too frightened to look. Josephine knew that if it was it was holding itself tight shut; Constantia felt that, like the doors in dreams, it hadn't any handle at all. It was the coldness which made it so awful. Or the whiteness—which? Everything was covered. The blinds were down, a cloth hung over the mirror, a sheet hid the bed; a huge fan of white paper filled the fireplace. Constantia timidly put out her hand; she almost expected a snowflake to fall. Josephine felt a queer tingling in her nose, as if her nose was freezing. Then a cab klop-klopped over the cobbles below, and the quiet seemed to shake into little pieces.

"I had better pull up a blind," said Josephine bravely.

"Yes, it might be a good idea," whispered Constantia.

They only gave the blind a touch, but it flew up and the cord flew after, rolling round the blindstick, and the little tassel tapped as if trying to get free. That was too much for Constantia.

"Don't you think—don't you think we might put it off for another day?" she whispered.

"Why?" snapped Josephine, feeling, as usual, much better now that she knew for certain that Constantia was terrified. "It's got to be done. But I do wish you wouldn't whisper, Con."

"I didn't know I was whispering," whispered Constantia.

"And why do you keep on staring at the bed?" said Josephine, raising her voice almost defiantly. "There's nothing *on* the bed."

"Oh, Jug, don't say so!" said poor Connie. "At any rate, not so loudly."

Josephine felt herself that she had gone too far. She took a wide swerve over to the chest of drawers, put out her hand, but quickly drew it back again.

"Connie!" she gasped, and she wheeled round and leaned with her back against the chest of drawers.

"Oh, Jug—what?"

Josephine could only glare. She had the most extraordinary feeling that she had just escaped something simply awful. But how could she explain to Constantia that father was in the chest of drawers? He was in the top drawer with his handkerchiefs and neckties, or in the next with his shirts and pyjamas, or in the lowest of all with his suits. He was watching there, hidden away—just behind the door-handle—ready to spring.

She pulled a funny old-fashioned face at Constantia, just as she used to in the old days when she was going to cry.

"I can't open," she nearly wailed.

"No, don't, Jug," whispered Constantia earnestly. "It's much better not to. Don't let's open anything. At any rate, not for a long time."

"But—but it seems so weak," said Josephine, breaking down.

"But why not be weak for once, Jug?" argued Constantia, whispering quite fiercely. "If it is weak." And her pale stare flew from the locked writing-table—so safe—to the huge glittering wardrobe, and she began to breathe in a queer, panting way. "Why shouldn't we be weak for once in our lives, Jug? It's quite excusable. Let's be weak—be weak, Jug. It's much nicer to be weak than to be strong."

And then she did one of those amazingly bold things that she'd done about twice before in their lives; she marched over to the wardrobe, turned the key, and took it out of the lock. Took it out of the lock and held it up to Josephine, showing Josephine by her extraordinary smile that she knew what she'd done, she'd risked deliberately father being in there among his overcoats.

If the huge wardrobe had lurched forward, had crashed down on Constantia, Josephine wouldn't have been surprised. On the contrary, she would have thought it the only suitable thing to happen. But nothing happened. Only the room seemed quieter than ever, and bigger flakes of cold air fell on Josephine's shoulders and knees. She began to shiver.

"Come, Jug," said Constantia, still with that awful callous smile, and Josephine followed just as she had that last time, when Constantia had pushed Benny into the round pond.

7

But the strain told on them when they were back in the dining-room. They sat down, very shaky, and looked at each other.

"I don't feel I can settle to anything," said Josephine, "until I've had something. Do you think we could ask Kate for two cups of hot water?"

"I really don't see why we shouldn't," said Constantia carefully. She was quite normal again. "I won't ring. I'll go to the kitchen door and ask her."

"Yes, do," said Josephine, sinking down into a chair. "Tell her, just two cups, Con, nothing else—on a tray."

"She needn't even put the jug on, need she?" said Constantia, as though Kate might very well complain if the jug had been there.

"Oh no, certainly not! The jug's not at all necessary. She can pour it direct out of the kettle," cried Josephine, feeling that would be a labour-saving indeed.

Their cold lips quivered at the greenish brims. Josephine curved her small red hands round the cup; Constantia sat up and blew on the wavy stream, making it flutter from one side to the other.

"Speaking of Benny," said Josephine.

And though Benny hadn't been mentioned Constantia immediately looked as though he had.

"He'll expect us to send him something of father's, of course. But it's so difficult to know what to send to Ceylon."

"You mean things get unstuck so on the voyage," murmured Constantia.

"No, lost," said Josephine sharply. "You know there's no post. Only runners."

Both paused to watch a black man in white linen drawers running through the pale fields for dear life, with a large brown-paper parcel in his hands. Josephine's black man was tiny; he scurried along glistening like an ant. But there was something blind and tireless about Constantia's tall, thin fellow, which made him, she decided, a very unpleasant person indeed. . . . On the veranda, dressed all in white and wearing a cork helmet, stood Benny. His right hand shook up and down, as father's did when he was impatient. And behind him, not in the least interested, sat Hilda, the unknown sister-in-law. She swung in a cane rocker and flicked over the leaves of the *Tatler*.

"I think his watch would be the most suitable present," said Josephine.

Constantia looked up; she seemed surprised.

"Oh, would you trust a gold watch to a native?"

"But of course I'd disguise it," said Josephine. "No one would know it was a watch." She liked the idea of having to make a parcel such a curious shape that no one could possibly guess what it was. She even thought for a moment of hiding the watch in a narrow cardboard corset-box that she'd kept by her for a long time, waiting for it to come in for something. It was such beautiful firm cardboard. But, no, it wouldn't be appropriate for this occasion. It had lettering on it: *Medium Women's 28. Extra Firm Busks*. It would be almost too much of a surprise for Benny to open that and find father's watch inside.

"And of course it isn't as though it would be going—ticking, I mean," said Constantia, who was still thinking of the native love of jewellery. "At least," she added, "it would be very strange if after all that time it was."

8

Josephine made no reply. She had flown off on one of her tangents. She had suddenly thought of Cyril. Wasn't it more usual for the only grandson to have the watch? And then dear Cyril was so appreciative, and a gold watch meant so much to a young man. Benny, in all probability, had quite got out of the habit of watches; men so seldom wore waistcoats in those hot climates. Whereas Cyril in London wore them from year's end to year's end. And it would be so nice for her and Constantia, when he came to tea, to know it was there. "I see you've got on grandfather's watch, Cyril." It would be somehow so satisfactory.

Dear boy! What a blow his sweet, sympathetic little note had been! Of course they quite understood; but it was most unfortunate.

"It would have been such a point, having him," said Josephine.

"And he would have enjoyed it so," said Constantia, not thinking what she was saying.

However, as soon as he got back he was coming to tea with his aunties. Cyril to tea was one of their rare treats.

"Now, Cyril, you mustn't be frightened of our cakes. Your Auntie Con and I bought them at Buszard's this morning. We know what a man's appetite is. So don't be ashamed of making a good tea."

Josephine cut recklessly into the rich dark cake that stood for her winter gloves or the soling and heeling of Constantia's only respectable shoes. But Cyril was most unmanlike in appetite.

"I say, Aunt Josephine, I simply can't. I've only just had lunch, you know."

"Oh, Cyril, that can't be true! It's after four," cried Josephine. Constantia sat with her knife poised over the chocolate-roll.

"It is, all the same," said Cyril. "I had to meet a man at Victoria, and he kept me hanging about till . . . there was only time to get lunch and to come on here. And he gave me—phew"—Cyril put his hand to his forehead—"a terrific blow-out," he said.

It was disappointing—to-day of all days. But still he couldn't be expected to know.

"But you'll have a meringue, won't you, Cyril?" said Aunt Josephine. "These meringues were bought specially for you. Your dear father was so fond of them. We were sure you are, too."

"I *am*, Aunt Josephine," cried Cyril ardently. "Do you mind if I take half to begin with?"

"Not at all, dear boy; but we mustn't let you off with that."

"Is your dear father still so fond of meringues?" asked Auntie Con gently. She winced faintly as she broke through the shell of hers.

"Well, I don't quite know, Auntie Con," said Cyril breezily. At that they both looked up.

"Don't know?" almost snapped Josephine. "Don't know a thing like that about your own father, Cyril?"

"Surely," said Auntie Con softly.

Cyril tried to laugh it off. "Oh, well," he said, "it's such a long time since—" He faltered. He stopped. Their faces were too much for him.

"Even *so*," said Josephine.

And Auntie Con looked.

Cyril put down his teacup. "Wait a bit," he cried. "Wait a bit, Aunt Josephine. What am I thinking of?"

He looked up. They were beginning to brighten. Cyril slapped his knee.

"Of course," he said, "it was meringues. How could I have forgotten? Yes, Aunt Josephine, you're perfectly right. Father's most frightfully keen on meringues."

They didn't only beam. Aunt Josephine went scarlet with pleasure; Auntie Con gave a deep, deep sigh.

"And now, Cyril, you must come and see father," said Josephine. "He knows you were coming to-day."

"Right," said Cyril, very firmly and heartily. He got up from his chair; suddenly he glanced at the clock.

"I say, Auntie Con, isn't your clock a bit slow? I've got to meet a man at—at Paddington just after five. I'm afraid I shan't be able to stay very long with grandfather."

"Oh, he won't expect you to stay *very* long!" said Aunt Josephine.

Constantia was still gazing at the clock. She couldn't make up her mind if it was fast or slow. It was one or the other, she felt almost certain of that. At any rate, it had been.

Cyril still lingered. "Aren't you coming along, Auntie Con?"

"Of course," said Josephine, "we shall all go. Come on, Con."

9

They knocked at the door, and Cyril followed his aunts into grandfather's hot, sweetish room.

"Come on," said Grandfather Pinner. "Don't hang about. What is it? What've you been up to?"

He was sitting in front of a roaring fire, clasping his stick. He had a thick rug over his knees. On his lap there lay a beautiful pale yellow silk handkerchief.

"It's Cyril, father," said Josephine shyly. And she took Cyril's hand and led him forward.

"Good afternoon, grandfather," said Cyril, trying to take his hand out of Aunt Josephine's. Grandfather Pinner shot his eyes at Cyril in the way he was famous for. Where was Auntie Con? She stood on the other side of Aunt Josephine; her long arms hung down in front of her; her hands were clasped. She never took her eyes off grandfather.

"Well," said Grandfather Pinner, beginning to thump, "what have you got to tell me?"

What had he, what had he got to tell him? Cyril felt himself smiling like a perfect imbecile. The room was stifling, too.

But Aunt Josephine came to his rescue. She cried brightly, "Cyril says his father is still very fond of meringues, father dear."

"Eh?" said Grandfather Pinner, curving his hand like a purple meringue-shell over one ear.

Josephine repeated, "Cyril says his father is still very fond of meringues."

"Can't hear," said old Colonel Pinner. And he waved Josephine away with his stick, then pointed with his stick to Cyril. "Tell me what she's trying to say," he said.

(My God!) "Must I?" said Cyril, blushing and staring at Aunt Josephine.

"Do, dear," she smiled. "It will please him so much."

"Come on, out with it!" cried Colonel Pinner testily, beginning to thump again. And Cyril leaned forward and yelled, "Father's still very fond of meringues."

At that Grandfather Pinner jumped as though he had been shot.

"Don't shout!" he cried. "What's the matter with the boy? *Meringues!* What about 'em?"

"Oh, Aunt Josephine, must we go on?" groaned Cyril desperately.

"It's quite all right, dear boy," said Aunt Josephine, as though he and she were at the dentist's together. "He'll understand in a minute." And she whispered to Cyril, "He's getting a bit deaf, you know." Then she leaned forward and really bawled at Grandfather Pinner, "Cyril only wanted to tell you, father dear, that *his* father is still very fond of meringues."

Colonel Pinner heard that time, heard and brooded, looking Cyril up and down.

"What an esstrordinary thing!" said old Grandfather Pinner. "What an esstrordinary thing to come all this way here to tell me!"

And Cyril felt it *was.*

"Yes, I shall send Cyril the watch," said Josephine.

"That would be very nice," said Constantia. "I seem to remember last time he came there was some little trouble about the time."

10

They were interrupted by Kate bursting through the door in her usual fashion, as though she had discovered some secret panel in the wall.

"Fried or boiled?" asked the bold voice.

Fried or boiled? Josephine and Constantia were quite bewildered for the moment. They could hardly take it in.

"Fried or boiled what, Kate?" asked Josephine, trying to begin to concentrate. Kate gave a loud sniff. "Fish."

"Well, why didn't you say so immediately?" Josephine reproached her gently. "How could you expect us to understand, Kate? There are a great many things in this world, you know, which are fried or boiled." And after such a display of courage she said quite brightly to Constantia, "Which do you prefer, Con?"

"I think it might be nice to have it fried," said Constantia. "On the other hand, of course boiled fish is very nice. I think I prefer both equally well . . . Unless you . . . In that case—"

"I shall fry it," said Kate, and she bounced back, leaving their door open and slamming the door of her kitchen.

Josephine gazed at Constantia; she raised her pale eyebrows until they rippled away into her pale hair. She got up. She said in a very lofty, imposing way, "Do you mind following me into the drawing-room, Constantia? I've something of great importance to discuss with you."

For it was always to the drawing-room they retired when they wanted to talk over Kate.

Josephine closed the door meaningly. "Sit down, Constantia," she said, still very grand. She might have been receiving Constantia for the first time. And Con looked round vaguely for a chair, as though she felt indeed quite a stranger.

"Now the question is," said Josephine, bending forward, "whether we shall keep her or not."

"That is the question," agreed Constantia.

"And this time," said Josephine firmly, "we must come to a definite decision."

Constantia looked for a moment as though she might begin going over all the other times, but she pulled herself together and said, "Yes, Jug."

"You see, Con," explained Josephine, "everything is so changed now." Constantia looked up quickly. "I mean," went on Josephine, "we're not dependent on Kate as we were." And she blushed faintly. "There's not father to cook for."

"That is perfectly true," agreed Constantia. "Father certainly doesn't want any cooking now, whatever else—"

Josephine broke in sharply. "You're not sleepy, are you, Con?"

"Sleepy, Jug?" Constantia was wide-eyed.

"Well, concentrate more," said Josephine sharply, and she returned to the subject. "What it comes to is, if we did"—and this she barely breathed, glancing at the door—"give Kate notice"—she raised her voice again—"we could manage our own food."

"Why not?" cried Constantia. She couldn't help smiling. The idea was so exciting. She clasped her hands. "What should we live on, Jug?"

"Oh, eggs in various forms!" said Jug, lofty again. "And, besides, there are all the cooked foods."

"But I've always heard," said Constantia, "they are considered so very expensive."

"Not if one buys them in moderation," said Josephine. But she tore herself away from this fascinating bypath and dragged Constantia after her.

"What we've got to decide now, however, is whether we really do trust Kate or not."

Constantia leaned back. Her flat little laugh flew from her lips.

"Isn't it curious, Jug," said she, "that just on this one subject I've never been able to quite make up my mind?"

11

She never had. The whole difficulty was to prove anything. How did one prove things, how could one? Suppose Kate had stood in front of her and deliberately made a face. Mightn't she very well have been in pain? Wasn't it impossible, at any rate, to ask Kate if she was making a face at her? If Kate answered "No"—and of course she would say "No"—what a position! How undignified! Then again Constantia suspected, she was almost certain that Kate went to her chest of drawers when she and Josephine were out, not to take things but to spy. Many times she had come back to find her amethyst cross in the most unlikely places, under her lace ties or on top of her evening Bertha. More than once she had laid a trap for Kate. She had arranged things in a special order and then called Josephine to witness.

"You see, Jug?"

"Quite, Con."

"Now we shall be able to tell."

But, oh dear, when she did go to look, she was as far off from a proof as ever! If anything was displaced, it might so very well have happened as she closed the drawer; a jolt might have done it so easily.

"You come, Jug, and decide. I really can't. It's too difficult."

But after a pause and a long glare Josephine would sigh, "Now you've put the doubt into my mind, Con, I'm sure I can't tell myself."

"Well, we can't postpone it again," said Josephine. "If we postpone it this time—"

12

But at that moment in the street below a barrel-organ struck up. Josephine and Constantia sprang to their feet together.

"Run, Con," said Josephine. "Run quickly. There's sixpence on the—"

Then they remembered. It didn't matter. They would never have to stop the organ-grinder again. Never again would she and Constantia be told to make that monkey take his noise somewhere else. Never would sound that loud, strange bellow when father thought they were not hurrying enough. The organ-grinder might play there all day and the stick would not thump.

> *It never will thump again,*
> *It never will thump again,*

played the barrel-organ.

What was Constantia thinking? She had such a strange smile; she looked different. She couldn't be going to cry.

"Jug, Jug," said Constantia softly, pressing her hands together. "Do you know what day it is? It's Saturday. It's a week to-day, a whole week."

> *A week since father died,*
> *A week since father died,*

cried the barrel-organ. And Josephine, too, forgot to be practical and sensible; she smiled faintly, strangely. On the Indian carpet there fell a square of sunlight, pale red; it came and went and came—and stayed, deepened—until it shone almost golden.

"The sun's out," said Josephine, as though it really mattered.

A perfect fountain of bubbling notes shook from the barrel-organ, round, bright notes, carelessly scattered.

Constantia lifted her big, cold hands as if to catch them, and then her hands fell again. She walked over to the mantelpiece to her favourite Buddha. And the stone and gilt image, whose smile always gave her such a queer feeling, almost a pain and yet a pleasant pain, seemed to-day to be more than smiling. He knew something; he had a secret. "I know something that you don't know," said her Buddha. Oh, what was it, what could it be? And yet she had always felt there was . . . something.

The sunlight pressed through the windows, thieved its way in, flashed its light over the furniture and the photographs. Josephine watched it. When it came to mother's photograph, the enlargement over the piano, it lingered as though puzzled to find so little remained of mother, except the earrings shaped like tiny pagodas and a black feather boa. Why did the photographs of dead people always fade so? wondered Josephine. As soon as a person was dead their photograph died too. But, of course, this one of mother was very old. It was thirty-five years old. Josephine remembered standing on a chair and pointing out that feather boa to Constantia and telling her that it was a snake that had killed their mother in Ceylon. . . . Would everything have been different if mother hadn't died? She didn't see why. Aunt Florence had lived with them until they had left school, and they had moved three times and had their yearly holiday and . . . and there'd been changes of servants, of course.

Some little sparrows, young sparrows they sounded, chirped on the window-ledge. *Yeep-eyeep-yeep.* But Josephine felt they were not sparrows, not on the window-ledge. It was inside her, that queer little crying noise. *Yeep-eyeep-yeep.* Ah, what was it crying, so weak and forlorn?

If mother had lived, might they have married? But there had been nobody for them to marry. There had been father's Anglo-Indian friends before he quarreled with them. But after that she and Constantia never met a single man except clergymen. How did one meet men? Or even if they'd met them, how could they have got to know men well enough to be more than strangers? One read of people having adventures, being followed, and so on. But nobody had ever followed Constantia and her. Oh yes, there had been one year at Eastbourne a mysterious man at their boarding-house who had put a note on the jug of hot water outside their bedroom door! But by the time Connie had found it the steam had made the writing too faint to read; they couldn't even make out to which of them it was addressed. And he had left next day. And that was all. The rest had been looking after father, and at the same time keeping out of father's way. But now? But now? The thieving sun touched Josephine gently. She lifted her face. She was drawn over to the window by gentle beams. . . .

Until the barrel-organ stopped playing Constantia stayed before the Buddha, wondering, but not as usual, not vaguely. This time her wonder was like longing. She remembered the times she had come in here, crept out of bed in her nightgown when the moon was full, and lain on the floor with her arms outstretched, as though she was crucified. Why? The big, pale moon had made her do it. The horrible dancing figures on the carved screen had leered at her and she hadn't minded. She remembered too how, whenever they were at the seaside, she had gone off by herself and got as close to the sea as she could, and sung something, something she had made up, while she gazed all over that restless water. There had been this other life, running out, bringing things home in bags, getting things on approval, discussing them with Jug, and taking them back to get more things on approval, and arranging father's trays and trying not to annoy father. But it all seemed to have happened in a kind of tunnel. It wasn't real. It was only when she came out of the tunnel into the moonlight or by the sea or into a thunderstorm that she really felt herself. What did it mean? What was it she was always wanting? What did it all lead to? Now? Now?

She turned away from the Buddha with one of her vague gestures. She went over to where Josephine was standing. She wanted to say something to Josephine, something frightfully important, about—about the future and what . . .

"Don't you think perhaps—" she began.

But Josephine interrupted her. "I was wondering if now—" she murmured. They stopped; they waited for each other.

"Go on, Con," said Josephine.

"No, no, Jug; after you," said Constantia.

"No, say what you were going to say. You began," said Josephine.

"I . . . I'd rather hear what you were going to say first," said Constantia.

"Don't be absurd, Con."

"Really, Jug."

"Connie!"

"Oh, *Jug!*"

A pause. Then Constantia said faintly, "I can't say what I was going to say, Jug, because I've forgotten what it was . . . that I was going to say."

Josephine was silent for a moment. She stared at a big cloud where the sun had been. Then she replied shortly, "I've forgotten too."

D. H. Lawrence
1885–1930

D. H. Lawrence's meteoric literary life ended in Venice, Italy, in 1930, where he died at the age of forty-five, far from his birthplace in Nottinghamshire, the coal-mining heart of England. If Lawrence was something of a comet in British literature, arcing across its skies with vibrant energy and controversy while he lived, he was equally visible after his death in the excitement and danger that persisted like a halo around his texts. A formidable poet, an exceptional essayist and literary critic, and a major novelist, Lawrence created works that were pioneering in their defiant eroticism, their outspoken treatment of class politics, and their insistence on seeing British literature as part of world literature in a time of global crisis. Many of his writings were censored and unavailable in England until long after his death, or published in expurgated versions or in private printings. Their frank concentration on sexuality, and on female as well as male desire, continues to make Lawrence's novels provocative and even controversial today.

David Herbert Lawrence was the son of a coal miner. As a primarily self-educated writer who studied and taught at Nottingham University College, instead of Oxford or Cambridge, he was unlike many of his literary peers in being lower-class and outside the privileged literary and social circles they moved in. He essentially invented himself, drawing on the support and encouragement of his mother, and nurturing a clear-eyed and furious analysis of British class structure that pervades many of his novels. The sexual frankness of his work is accompanied by its economic frankness, its willingness to point out all the ways that culture and taste are fashioned by income as much as by ideas. The sense of being an outsider to the gentlemanly world of letters fed Lawrence's need to live and work outside Britain, and he traveled restlessly to Europe and America, to Australia and Mexico. Lawrence is deeply associated with many of the countries and places he lived in; with Italy, above all, in the power of his writing about Italian culture and landscape; with the United States, in classic analysis of American literature, and in works set in New Mexico and San Francisco; with France, Germany, and Switzerland as backdrops for his literary works and their cultural theorizing; with Australia for his commentary on this distant British colony and its indigenous peoples, in novels like *Kangaroo*; with Mexico and the primitivism and exoticism he explored in *The Plumed Serpent* and *Aaron's Rod*.

As peripatetic and as open to experience as Lawrence was, his great writing begins with novels and stories set in England. Some of his early and most exceptional works are, in fact, modernist versions of a central nineteenth-century literary genre, the *bildungsroman*, or the story of a personal education. Lawrence's *Sons and Lovers* (1912) has the autobiographical overtones that often accompany a coming-of-age narrative. Written after the death of his devoted mother Lydia Lawrence in 1910, the book delineates the experience of a young man who was as socially and economically disadvantaged as Lawrence himself, and the almost incestuous love between mother and son that allows him to break free from the crushing life in the mines that might have been his only option, and to follow his deep need for love, imagination, and poetry into the writing of literature. His later novel *The Rainbow* (published in an expurgated version in 1915) is also a *bildungsroman*, but featuring as its protagonist a female character and specifically feminine issues of education and freedom. In a preface to the novel, Lawrence wrote that he insisted on portraying characters that were not the old-fashioned character portraits of the past, relying on "the old stable ego." For Lawrence, people were internally fragmented, not completely self-aware, and above all governed by sexual currents that exceeded their conscious knowledge and control. In this Lawrence was profoundly influenced by Freud's discovery of the prominence and power of the unconscious. All of Lawrence's writing engages with the invisible and largely silent realm of the unconscious, whose wishes and impulses are a kind of dynamic dance running under the surface of the conscious sense of self.

To this dance of the unconscious rhythms of life Lawrence added an abiding fascination with myth. He joined most modernist writers in his interest in showing the persistence of myth in modern culture: Joyce, Woolf, Eliot, and Faulkner all structured work around mythic parallels or mythic figures. For Lawrence, myth loomed importantly because it allowed for the discussion of hidden patterns and cycles in human action and human relationships, patterns that are much larger than the individual human being. Our personalities are illusions, Lawrence's fiction claims, because they mask deeper mythic forms. In *The Rainbow*, Lawrence draws his mythic structure from the Bible, and the cycles of birth, death, and rebirth in the story of Noah and the flood, with the rainbow of God's promise starting the cycle of rebirth over and over again.

One of Lawrence's greatest novels is *Women in Love*, a story of two sisters confronting modern life as they move out of their country's orbit and take on independence, sexual freedom, and careers in the world. He began writing it in 1916, during World War I. The war was as shattering to Lawrence as it was to every other British writer; for Lawrence, it was the apotheosis and the logical conclusion of the machine culture he hated for having spoiled England even before the war wreaked its devastation. Lawrence sharply criticized industrial capitalism, but not from the vantage point of an aristocratic worldview that regretted the loss of the landed estates. He thought and wrote as the son of a worker whose life was maimed by industrial toil in the mines, and as a school teacher of the impoverished children of miners and laborers who had lost their self-sufficient way of life on the land. Lawrence did not dream of a return to a golden feudal age, but he did dissect the ravages of industry and the connections between world war, capital, and modernization. *Women in Love* embraces these themes and more, as it turns to Europe and its classical culture to try to find a way out of the cultural impasse and sterility Lawrence saw around him. However, in this novel and others Lawrence writes of a death instinct visible for him in European culture, including its philosophy and art. At times, Lawrence's intense hatred of modernity led him to flirt with fascism, which occasionally seemed to him to promise a way out of the dead end of modern society and its hideous conflagrations in war. In order to rescue the life-affirming capacities of human society Lawrence sought out exotic and foreign cultures, and what he termed "primitive" cultures around the world—ostensibly unspoiled agricultural societies still predicated on myth rather than machine. These exotic alternatives, as Lawrence saw, were hardly utopian either, and most such societies were contaminated by colonization and Western influences. Lawrence did seek a less rationalized and less materialistic perspective in the "primitive" or archaic worlds he explored, and found that these cultures were more open to the life-giving force of sexuality. At once intense and engaging, his travel writing gives a sense of immediacy mingled with deep reflection.

Sexuality is the force in human life that most clearly derives from unconscious fantasies and desires, and on that basis it is at the heart of Lawrence's writing. Lawrence's work was thought shocking because it takes for granted the erotic elements hidden in the family—what Freud had called the "family romance." The alliances and the divisions between family members have an erotic component for Lawrence; in addition, relations to friends and to all others one encounters are sexualized in mysterious ways, often involving a powerful homoerotic current. Much of Lawrence's fiction seems to idealize a sexual state beyond words and beyond conscious understanding, and to depict this Lawrence draws on a beautiful incantatory style, filled with a highly musical repetition and rhythm.

Lawrence's own erotic career is as famous as his writing. The passion and frustrations of his marriage to the formidable Frieda Weekely (born Frieda von Richthofen) remained a hidden presence in all his writing after their marriage in 1914. When they met, Frieda was a married woman with an impressive erotic career behind her; she became a close partner in his political and cultural essay writing, and in his restless travels. They lived in Germany, Italy, and in Taos, New Mexico, among other locales. After his death in Italy, she and her then lover transported Lawrence's ashes back to Taos, and the two built a kind of shrine to Lawrence on the grounds of what had been his home with Frieda. It was in this region that they had explored Hispanic and Indian cultures under the sponsorship of a patron of the avant-garde, Mabel Dodge Luhan. Up until the mid-1980s it was possible to pay a dollar to the manager of the Taos Hotel and be admitted into his office, where numerous paintings by D. H. Lawrence were on display. Lawrence was a fascinating, if not a major, painter; the exhibits of his paintings in England were subject to the same censorship and public outrage as his novels. A viewer of the paintings could read them as an allegory for many of the disquieting themes of his literary work: the majority of them depict a couple, usually male and female, locked in an embrace that is as urgent as it is suffocating; around the edges of these couplings Lawrence painted menacing wolves and dogs, often with teeth bared or fangs dripping with blood, emblematic of the intensity and even the destructiveness of erotic relationships.

In his 1923 essay *Surgery for the Novel—or a Bomb*, Lawrence expresses his impatience with the endlessly refined analyses of modernists like Proust and Joyce. "What is the underlying impulse in us," he asks, "that will provide the motive power for a new state of things, when this democratic-industrial-lovey-dovey-darling-take-me-to-mama state of things is bust? *What next?*" His own efforts to forge a new mythic realism can be seen in his novella *The Fox*, also from 1923, which explores the interpenetration of human and animal, nature and social constraint, masculinity and feminity, sexual desire and deep aggression. The story's rural setting becomes a place at once of poverty and of beauty, in which Lawrence can counterpoint pursuits and entrapments on several levels, giving symbolic resonance to sharply observed naturalistic detail.

Lawrence's poetry explores related concerns. Like Thomas Hardy before him, Lawrence was equally gifted in both literary endeavors. Lawrence's poetry emanates from the same image-suffused, musically rhythmic, and tautly modern space as his prose works. Like Lawrence himself, his art desires to move *beyond*—beyond the old stable fictions of the ego in his prose, and beyond the old stable fiction of the lyric voice. In his poetry he accomplishes this by a preternatural immediacy, an intensity of "thereness" that includes what might in the past have seemed to be incoherent elements or fragmentary perspectives. What has been silent, veiled, or unconscious, in personal and in public life, rears up and announces itself in Lawrence's writing, appears on the page and defies silencing.

Piano

Softly, in the dusk, a woman is singing to me;
Taking me back down the vista of years, till I see
A child sitting under the piano, in the boom of the tingling strings
And pressing the small, poised feet of a mother who smiles as she sings.

5 In spite of myself, the insidious mastery of song
Betrays me back, till the heart of me weeps to belong
To the old Sunday evenings at home, with winter outside
And hymns in the cosy parlour, the tinkling piano our guide.

So now it is vain for the singer to burst into clamour
10 With the great black piano appassionato. The glamour
Of childish days is upon me, my manhood is cast
Down in the flood of remembrance, I weep like a child for the past.

1908   1913

Song of a Man Who Has Come Through

Not I, not I, but the wind that blows through me!
A fine wind is blowing the new direction of Time.
If only I let it bear me, carry me, if only it carry me!
If only I am sensitive, subtle, oh, delicate, a winged gift!
5 If only, most lovely of all, I yield myself and am borrowed
By the fine, fine wind that takes its course through the chaos of the world
Like a fine, an exquisite chisel, a wedge-blade inserted;
If only I am keen and hard like the sheer tip of a wedge
Driven by invisible blows,
10 The rock will split, we shall come at the wonder, we shall find the Hesperides.[1]

Oh, for the wonder that bubbles into my soul,
I would be a good fountain, a good well-head,
Would blur no whisper, spoil no expression.

What is the knocking?
15 What is the knocking at the door in the night?
It is somebody wants to do us harm.

No, no, it is the three strange angels.[2]
Admit them, admit them.

                           1917

Tortoise Shout

I thought he was dumb,
I said he was dumb,
Yet I've heard him cry.
First faint scream,

---

1. Three sisters who guard a tree with golden apples at the end of the world; Hercules (Heracles) steals the apples as the eleventh of his twelve labors.

2. Probably the three angels who appeared to Abraham in Genesis 18, prior to the destruction of the cities of Sodom and Gomorrah.

5   Out of life's unfathomable dawn,
Far off, so far, like a madness, under the horizon's dawning rim,
Far, far off, far scream.

Tortoise *in extremis*.

Why were we crucified into sex?
10   Why were we not left rounded off, and finished in ourselves,
As we began,
As he certainly began, so perfectly alone?

A far, was-it-audible scream,
Or did it sound on the plasm direct?

15   Worse than the cry of the new-born,
A scream,
A yell,
A shout,
A paean,
20   A death-agony,
A birth-cry,
A submission,
All tiny, tiny, far away, reptile under the first dawn.
War-cry, triumph, acute-delight, death-scream reptilian,
25   Why was the veil torn?
The silken shriek of the soul's torn membrane?
The male soul's membrane
Torn with a shriek half music, half horror.

Crucifixion.
30   Male tortoise, cleaving behind the hovel-wall of that dense female,
Mounted and tense, spread-eagle, out-reaching out of the shell
In tortoise-nakedness,
Long neck, and long vulnerable limbs extruded, spread-eagle over her
        house-roof,
And the deep, secret, all-penetrating tail curved beneath her walls,
35   Reaching and gripping tense, more reaching anguish in uttermost tension
Till suddenly, in the spasm of coition, tupping like a jerking leap, and oh!
Opening its clenched face from his outstretched neck
And giving that fragile yell, that scream,
Super-audible,
40   From his pink, cleft, old-man's mouth,
Giving up the ghost,
Or screaming in Pentecost,[1] receiving the ghost.

His scream, and his moment's subsidence,
The moment of eternal silence,
45   Yet unreleased, and after the moment, the sudden, startling jerk of coition,
        and at once

---

1. The day the Holy Spirit descended on Christ's disciples, which marked the beginning of the Christian church's mission to the world.

The inexpressible faint yell—
And so on, till the last plasm of my body was melted back
To the primeval rudiments of life, and the secret.

So he tups, and screams
50 Time after time that frail, torn scream
After each jerk, the longish interval,
The tortoise eternity,
Age-long, reptilian persistence,
Heart-throb, slow heart-throb, persistent for the next spasm.

55 I remember, when I was a boy,
I heard the scream of a frog, which was caught with his foot in the mouth
    of an up-starting snake;
I remember when I first heard bull-frogs break into sound in the spring;
I remember hearing a wild goose out of the throat of night
Cry loudly, beyond the lake of waters;
60 I remember the first time, out of a bush in the darkness, a nightingale's
    piercing cries and gurgles startled the depths of my soul;
I remember the scream of a rabbit as I went through a wood at midnight;
I remember the heifer in her heat, blorting and blorting through the hours,
    persistent and irrepressible;
I remember my first terror hearing the howl of weird, amorous cats;
I remember the scream of a terrified, injured horse, the sheet-lightning,
65 And running away from the sound of a woman in labour, something like an
    owl whooing,
And listening inwardly to the first bleat of a lamb,
The first wail of an infant,
And my mother singing to herself,
And the first tenor singing of the passionate throat of a young collier,[2] who
    has long since drunk himself to death,
70 The first elements of foreign speech
On wild dark lips.

And more than all these,
And less than all these,
This last,
75 Strange, faint coition yell
Of the male tortoise at extremity,
Tiny from under the very edge of the farthest far-off horizon of life.

The cross,
The wheel on which our silence first is broken,
80 Sex, which breaks up our integrity, our single inviolability, our deep
    silence,
Tearing a cry from us.

Sex, which breaks us into voice, sets us calling across the deeps, calling,
    calling for the complement,
Singing, and calling, and singing again, being answered, having found.

2. A coal miner.

Torn, to become whole again, after long seeking for what is lost,
85   The same cry from the tortoise as from Christ, the Osiris-cry of
         abandonment,[3]
     That which is whole, torn asunder,
     That which is in part, finding its whole again throughout the universe.

                                                                        1921

Snake[1]

A snake came to my water-trough
On a hot, hot day, and I in pyjamas for the heat,
To drink there.

In the deep, strange-scented shade of the great dark carob tree
5   I came down the steps with my pitcher
And must wait, must stand and wait, for there he was at the trough before me.

He reached down from a fissure in the earth-wall in the gloom
And trailed his yellow-brown slackness soft-bellied down, over the edge of
    the stone trough
And rested his throat upon the stone bottom,
10   And where the water had dripped from the tap, in a small clearness,
He sipped with his straight mouth,
Softly drank through his straight gums, into his slack long body,
Silently.
Someone was before me at my water-trough,
15   And I, like a second comer, waiting.

He lifted his head from his drinking, as cattle do,
And looked at me vaguely, as drinking cattle do,
And flickered his two-forked tongue from his lips, and mused a moment,
And stooped and drank a little more,
20   Being earth-brown, earth-golden from the burning bowels of the earth
On the day of Sicilian July, with Etna smoking.

The voice of my education said to me
He must be killed,
For in Sicily the black, black snakes are innocent, the gold are venomous.

25   And voices in me said, If you were a man
You would take a stick and break him now, and finish him off.

But must I confess how I liked him,
How glad I was he had come like a guest in quiet, to drink at my water-trough
And depart peaceful, pacified, and thankless,
30   Into the burning bowels of this earth?

Was it cowardice, that I dared not kill him?
Was it perversity, that I longed to talk to him?

---

3. Osiris was a major god of ancient Egypt; he was slain
and fragments of his corpse scattered; these were found
and buried, and Osiris became ruler of the underworld.

1. Lawrence had an encounter with a snake drinking
from a water trough while living in Taormina, Sicily, in
July 1912.

Was it humility, to feel so honoured?
I felt so honoured.

35   And yet those voices:
If you were not afraid, you would kill him!

And truly I was afraid, I was most afraid,
But even so, honoured still more
That he should seek my hospitality
40   From out the dark door of the secret earth.

He drank enough
And lifted his head, dreamily, as one who has drunken,
And flickered his tongue like a forked night on the air, so black,
Seeming to lick his lips,
45   And looked around like a god, unseeing, into the air,
And slowly turned his head,
And slowly, very slowly, as if thrice adream,
Proceeded to draw his slow length curving round
And climb again the broken bank of my wall-face.

50   And as he put his head into that dreadful hole,
And as he slowly drew up, snake-easing his shoulders, and entered farther,
A sort of horror, a sort of protest against his withdrawing into that horrid
    black hole,
Deliberately going into the blackness, and slowly drawing himself after,
Overcame me now his back was turned.
55   I looked round, I put down my pitcher,
I picked up a clumsy log
And threw it at the water-trough with a clatter.
I think it did not hit him,
But suddenly that part of him that was left behind convulsed in
    undignified haste,
60   Writhed like lightning, and was gone
Into the black hole, the earth-lipped fissure in the wall front,
At which, in the intense still noon, I stared with fascination.

And immediately I regretted it.
I thought how paltry, how vulgar, what a mean act!
65   I despised myself and the voices of my accursed human education.

And I thought of the albatross,
And I wished he would come back, my snake.

For he seemed to me again like a king,
Like a king in exile, uncrowned in the underworld,
70   Now due to be crowned again.

And so, I missed my chance with one of the lords
Of life.
And I have something to expiate;
A pettiness.

1923

Bavarian Gentians

Not every man has gentians in his house
in soft September, at slow, sad Michaelmas.[1]

Bavarian gentians, big and dark, only dark
darkening the day-time, torch-like with the smoking blueness of Pluto's gloom,
5   ribbed and torch-like, with their blaze of darkness spread blue
down flattening into points, flattened under the sweep of white day
torch-flower of the blue-smoking darkness, Pluto's dark-blue daze,[2]
black lamps from the halls of Dis, burning dark blue,
giving off darkness, blue darkness, as Demeter's pale lamps give off light,
10 lead me then, lead the way.

Reach me a gentian, give me a torch!
let me guide myself with the blue, forked torch of this flower
down the darker and darker stairs, where blue is darkened on blueness
even where Persephone goes, just now, from the frosted September
15 to the sightless realm where darkness is awake upon the dark
and Persephone herself is but a voice
or a darkness invisible enfolded in the deeper dark
of the arms Plutonic, and pierced with the passion of dense gloom,
among the splendour of torches of darkness, shedding darkness on the lost
      bride and her groom.

1923, 1929   1932

Cypresses[1]

Tuscan cypresses,
What is it?

Folded in like a dark thought
For which the language is lost,
5   Tuscan cypresses,
Is there a great secret?
Are our words no good?

The undeliverable secret,
Dead with a dead race and a dead speech, and yet
10 Darkly monumental in you,
Etruscan[2] cypresses.

Ah, how I admire your fidelity,
Dark cypresses!

1. The feast of St. Michael the Archangel, 29 September.
2. Persephone was a daughter of Zeus and Demeter, goddess of agriculture; she was abducted by Hades, king of the Underworld (also known as Pluto or Dis), causing Demeter such sorrow that the land became barren. Zeus commanded Hades to release Persephone, which he did, though she was able to emerge from the Underworld each spring, returning in the fall to her husband. The story offers an explanation of seasonal change.
1. An evergreen tree traditionally associated with mourning.
2. A native or inhabitant of Etruria, an ancient country of Italy in modern Tuscany, conquered by the Romans. The Etruscan language is extinct.

Is it the secret of the long-nosed Etruscans?
15 The long-nosed, sensitive-footed, subtly-smiling Etruscans,
Who made so little noise outside the cypress groves?

Among the sinuous, flame-tall cypresses
That swayed their length of darkness all around
Etruscan-dusky, wavering men of old Etruria:
20 Naked except for fanciful long shoes,
Going with insidious, half-smiling quietness
And some of Africa's imperturbable sang-froid[3]
About a forgotten business.

What business, then?
25 Nay, tongues are dead, and words are hollow as hollow seed-pods,
Having shed their sound and finished all their echoing
Etruscan syllables,
That had the telling.

Yet more I see you darkly concentrate,
30 Tuscan cypresses,
On one old thought:
On one old slim imperishable thought, while you remain
Etruscan cypresses;
Dusky, slim marrow-thought of slender, flickering men of Etruria,
35 Whom Rome called vicious.

Vicious, dark cypresses:
Vicious, you supple, brooding, softly-swaying pillars of dark flame.
Monumental to a dead, dead race
Embowered in you!

40 Were they then vicious, the slender, tender-footed
Long-nosed men of Etruria?
Or was their way only evasive and different, dark, like cypress-trees in a wind?
They are dead, with all their vices,
And all that is left
45 Is the shadowy monomania[4] of some cypresses
And tombs.

The smile, the subtle Etruscan smile still lurking
Within the tombs,
Etruscan cypresses.
50 He laughs longest who laughs last;
Nay, Leonardo only bungled the pure Etruscan smile.

What would I not give
To bring back the rare and orchid-like
Evil-yclept[5] Etruscan?
55 For as to the evil

3. Composure.   5. Named (Middle English).
4. Obsession with one idea.

We have only Roman word for it,
Which I, being a little weary of Roman virtue,
Don't hang much weight on.

For oh, I know, in the dust where we have buried
60   The silenced races and all their abominations,
We have buried so much of the delicate magic of life.

There in the deeps
That churn the frankincense and ooze the myrrh,
Cypress shadowy,
65   Such an aroma of lost human life!

They say the fit survive,
But I invoke the spirits of the lost.
Those that have not survived, the darkly lost,
To bring their meaning back into life again,
70   Which they have taken away
And wrapt inviolable in soft cypress-trees,
Etruscan cypresses.

Evil, what is evil?
There is only one evil, to deny life
75   As Rome denied Etruria
And mechanical America Montezuma still.

Fiesole.
1923

Odour of Chrysanthemums
1

The small locomotive engine Number 4, came clanking, stumbling down from Selston[1] with seven full wagons. It appeared round the corner with loud threats of speed, but the colt that it startled from among the gorse,[2] which still flickered indistinctly in the raw afternoon, out-distanced it at a canter. A woman, walking up the railway line to Underwood,[3] drew back into the hedge, held her basket aside, and watched the footplate of the engine advancing. The trucks thumped heavily past, one by one, with slow inevitable movement, as she stood insignificantly trapped between the jolting black wagons and the hedge; then they curved away towards the coppice where the withered oak leaves dropped noiselessly, while the birds, pulling at the scarlet hips beside the track, made off into the dusk that had already crept into the spinney.[4] In the open, the smoke from the engine sank and cleaved to the rough grass. The fields were dreary and forsaken, and in the marshy strip that led to the whimsey, a reedy pit-pond, the fowls had already abandoned their run among the alders, to roost in the tarred fowl-house. The pit-bank loomed up beyond the pond, flames like red sores licking its ashy sides, in the afternoon's stagnant light. Just beyond rose the tapering chimneys and the clumsy black headstocks of Brinsley Colliery. The two wheels were spinning fast up against the sky, and the winding engine rapped out its little spasms. The miners were being turned up.

---

1. Mining village in Nottinghamshire, central England.   3. Small village in central England.
2. Wild, yellow-flowered shrub.   4. A small thicket.

The engine whistled as it came into the wide bay of railway lines beside the colliery, where rows of trucks stood in harbour.

Miners, single, trailing and in groups, passed like shadows diverging home. At the edge of the ribbed level of sidings squat a low cottage, three steps down from the cinder track. A large bony vine clutched at the house, as if to claw down the tiled roof. Round the bricked yard grew a few wintry primroses. Beyond, the long garden sloped down to a bushcovered brook course. There were some twiggy apple trees, winter-crack trees, and ragged cabbages. Beside the path hung dishevelled pink chrysanthemums, like pink cloths hung on bushes. A woman came stooping out of the felt-covered fowl-house, half-way down the garden. She closed and padlocked the door, then drew herself erect, having brushed some bits from her white apron.

She was a tall woman of imperious mien, handsome, with definite black eyebrows. Her smooth black hair was parted exactly. For a few moments she stood steadily watching the miners as they passed along the railway: then she turned towards the brook course. Her face was calm and set, her mouth was closed with disillusionment. After a moment she called:

"John!" There was no answer. She waited, and then said distinctly:

"Where are you?"

"Here!" replied a child's sulky voice from among the bushes. The woman looked piercingly through the dusk.

"Are you at that brook?" she asked sternly.

For answer the child showed himself before the raspberrycanes that rose like whips. He was a small, sturdy boy of five. He stood quite still, defiantly.

"Oh!" said the mother, conciliated. "I thought you were down at that wet brook—and you remember what I told you——"

The boy did not move or answer.

"Come, come on in," she said more gently, "it's getting dark. There's your grandfather's engine coming down the line!"

The lad advanced slowly, with resentful, taciturn movement. He was dressed in trousers and waistcoat of cloth that was too thick and hard for the size of the garments. They were evidently cut down from a man's clothes.

As they went slowly towards the house he tore at the ragged wisps of chrysanthemums and dropped the petals in handfuls among the path.

"Don't do that—it does look nasty," said his mother. He refrained, and she, suddenly pitiful, broke off a twig with three or four wan flowers and held them against her face. When mother and son reached the yard her hand hesitated, and instead of laying the flower aside, she pushed it in her apron-band. The mother and son stood at the foot of the three steps looking across the bay of lines at the passing home of the miners. The trundle of the small train was imminent. Suddenly the engine loomed past the house and came to a stop opposite the gate.

The engine-driver, a short man with round grey beard, leaned out of the cab high above the woman.

"Have you got a cup of tea?" he said in a cheery, hearty fashion.

It was her father. She went in, saying she would mash.[5] Directly, she returned.

"I didn't come to see you on Sunday," began the little greybearded man.

"I didn't expect you," said his daughter.

The engine-driver winced; then, reassuming his cheery, airy manner, he said:

5. Separate tea from the leaves.

"Oh, have you heard then? Well, and what do you think——?"

"I think it is soon enough," she replied.

At her brief censure the little man made an impatient gesture, and said coaxingly, yet with dangerous coldness:

"Well, what's a man to do? It's no sort of life for a man of my years, to sit at my own hearth like a stranger. And if I'm going to marry again it may as well be soon as late—what does it matter to anybody?"

The woman did not reply, but turned and went into the house. The man in the engine-cab stood assertive, till she returned with a cup of tea and a piece of bread and butter on a plate. She went up the steps and stood near the footplate of the hissing engine.

"You needn't 'a' brought me bread an' butter," said her father. "But a cup of tea"—he sipped appreciatively—"it's very nice." He sipped for a moment or two, then: "I hear as Walter's got another bout on," he said.

"When hasn't he?" said the woman bitterly.

"I heerd tell of him in the 'Lord Nelson' braggin' as he was going to spend that b——afore he went: half a sovereign that was."

"When?" asked the woman.

"A' Sat'day night—I know that's true."

"Very likely," she laughed bitterly. "He gives me twenty-three shillings."

"Aye, it's a nice thing, when a man can do nothing with his money but make a beast of himself!" said the grey-whiskered man. The woman turned her head away. Her father swallowed the last of his tea and handed her the cup.

"Aye," he sighed, wiping his mouth. "It's a settler, it is——"

He put his hand on the lever. The little engine strained and groaned, and the train rumbled towards the crossing. The woman again looked across the metals. Darkness was settling over the spaces of the railway and trucks: the miners, in grey sombre groups, were still passing home. The winding engine pulsed hurriedly, with brief pauses. Elizabeth Bates looked at the dreary flow of men, then she went indoors. Her husband did not come.

The kitchen was small and full of firelight; red coals piled glowing up the chimney mouth. All the life of the room seemed in the white, warm hearth and the steel fender reflecting the red fire. The cloth was laid for tea; cups glinted in the shadows. At the back, where the lowest stairs protruded into the room, the boy sat struggling with a knife and a piece of white wood. He was almost hidden in the shadow. It was half-past four. They had but to await the father's coming to begin tea. As the mother watched her son's sullen little struggle with the wood, she saw herself in his silence and pertinacity; she saw the father in her child's indifference to all but himself. She (seemed to be) occupied by her husband. He had probably gone past his home, slunk past his own door, to drink before he came in, while his dinner spoiled and wasted in waiting. She glanced at the clock, then took the potatoes to strain them in the yard. The garden and fields beyond the brook were closed in uncertain darkness. When she rose with the saucepan, leaving the drain steaming into the night behind her, she saw the yellow lamps were lit along the high road that went up the hill away beyond the space of the railway lines and the field.

Then again she watched the men trooping home, fewer now and fewer.

Indoors the fire was sinking and the room was dark red. The woman put her saucepan on the hob, and set a batter-pudding near the mouth of the oven. Then she stood unmoving. Directly, gratefully, came quick young steps to the door. Someone hung on the latch a moment, then a little girl entered and began pulling off her outdoor things, dragging a mass of curls, just ripening from gold to brown, over her eyes with her hat.

Her mother chid her for coming late from school, and said she would have to keep her at home the dark winter days.

"Why, mother, it's hardly a bit dark yet. The lamp's not lighted, and my father's not home."

"No, he isn't. But it's a quarter to five! Did you see anything of him?"

The child became serious. She looked at her mother with large, wistful blue eyes.

"No, mother, I've never seen him. Why? Has he come up an' gone past, to Old Brinsley? He hasn't, mother, 'cos I never saw him."

"He'd watch that," said the mother bitterly, "he'd take care as you didn't see him. But you may depend upon it, he's seated in the 'Prince o' Wales.' He wouldn't be this late."

The girl looked at her mother piteously.

"Let's have our teas, mother, should we?" said she.

The mother called John to table. She opened the door once more and looked out across the darkness of the lines. All was deserted: she could not hear the winding-engines.

"Perhaps," she said to herself, "he's stopped to get some ripping[6] done."

They sat down to tea. John, at the end of the table near the door, was almost lost in the darkness. Their faces were hidden from each other. The girl crouched against the fender slowly moving a thick piece of bread before the fire. The lad, his face a dusky mark on the shadow, sat watching her who was transfigured in the red glow.

"I do think it's beautiful to look in the fire," said the child.

"Do you?" said her mother. "Why?"

"It's so red, and full of little caves—and it feels so nice, and you can fair smell it."

"It'll want mending directly," replied her mother, "and then if your father comes he'll carry on and say there never is a fire when a man comes home sweating from the pit. A public-house[7] is always warm enough."

There was silence till the boy said complainingly: "Make haste, our Annie."

"Well, I am doing! I can't make the fire do it no faster, can I?"

"She keeps wafflin' it about so's to make 'er slow," grumbled the boy.

"Don't have such an evil imagination, child," replied the mother.

Soon the room was busy in the darkness with the crisp sound of crunching. The mother ate very little. She drank her tea determinedly, and sat thinking. When she rose her anger was evident in the stern unbending of her head. She looked at the pudding in the fender, and broke out:

"It is a scandalous thing as a man can't even come home to his dinner! If it's crozzled up to a cinder I don't see why I should care. Past his very door he goes to get to a public-house, and here I sit with his dinner waiting for him——"

She went out. As she dropped piece after piece of coal on the red fire, the shadows fell on the walls, till the room was almost in total darkness.

"I canna see," grumbled the invisible John. In spite of herself, the mother laughed.

"You know the way to your mouth," she said. She set the dust-pan outside the door. When she came again like a shadow on the hearth, the lad repeated, complaining sulkily:

"I canna see."

"Good gracious!" cried the mother irritably, "you're as bad as your father if it's a bit dusk!"

6. Tearing a vein of coal from the earth.   7. Pub; tavern.

Nevertheless, she took a paper spill from a sheaf on the mantelpiece and proceeded to light the lamp that hung from the ceiling in the middle of the room. As she reached up, her figure displayed itself just rounding with maternity.

"Oh, mother——!" exclaimed the girl.

"What?" said the woman, suspended in the act of putting the lamp-glass over the flame. The copper reflector shone handsomely on her, as she stood with uplifted arm, turning to face her daughter.

"You've got a flower in your apron!" said the child, in a little rapture at this unusual event.

"Goodness me!" exclaimed the woman, relieved. "One would think the house was afire." She replaced the glass and waited a moment before turning up the wick. A pale shadow was seen floating vaguely on the floor.

"Let me smell!" said the child, still rapturously, coming forward and putting her face to her mother's waist.

"Go along, silly!" said the mother, turning up the lamp. The light revealed their suspense so that the woman felt it almost unbearable. Annie was still bending at her waist. Irritably, the mother took the flowers out from her apron-band.

"Oh, mother—don't take them out!" Annie cried, catching her hand and trying to replace the sprig.

"Such nonsense!" said the mother, turning away. The child put the pale chrysanthemums to her lips, murmuring:

"Don't they smell beautiful!"

Her mother gave a short laugh.

"No," she said, "not to me. It was chrysanthemums when I married him, and chrysanthemums when you were born, and the first time they ever brought him home drunk, he'd got brown chrysanthemums in his button-hole."

She looked at the children. Their eyes and their parted lips were wondering. The mother sat rocking in silence for some time. Then she looked at the clock.

"Twenty minutes to six!" In a tone of fine bitter carelessness she continued: "Eh, he'll not come now till they bring him. There he'll stick! But he needn't come rolling in here in his pit-dirt, for I won't wash him. He can lie on the floor——Eh, what a fool I've been, what a fool! And this is what I came here for, to this dirty hole, rats and all, for him to slink past his very door. Twice last week—he's begun now——"

She silenced herself, and rose to clear the table.

While for an hour or more the children played, subduedly intent, fertile of imagination, united in fear of the mother's wrath, and in dread of their father's home-coming, Mrs. Bates sat in her rocking-chair making a 'singlet' of thick cream-coloured flannel, which gave a dull wounded sound as she tore off the grey edge. She worked at her sewing with energy, listening to the children, and her anger wearied itself, lay down to rest, opening its eyes from time to time and steadily watching, its ears raised to listen. Sometimes even her anger quailed and shrank, and the mother suspended her sewing, tracing the footsteps that thudded along the sleepers outside; she would lift her head sharply to bid the children 'hush', but she recovered herself in time, and the footsteps went past the gate, and the children were not flung out of their play-world.

But at last Annie sighed, and gave in. She glanced at her wagon of slippers, and loathed the game. She turned plaintively to her mother.

"Mother!"—but she was inarticulate.

John crept out like a frog from under the sofa. His mother glanced up.

"Yes," she said, "just look at those shirt-sleeves!"

The boy held them out to survey them, saying nothing. Then somebody called in a hoarse voice away down the line, and suspense bristled in the room, till two people had gone by outside, talking.

"It is time for bed," said the mother.

"My father hasn't come," wailed Annie plaintively. But her mother was primed with courage.

"Never mind. They'll bring him when he does come—like a log." She meant there would be no scene. "And he may sleep on the floor till he wakes himself. I know he'll not go to work to-morrow after this!"

The children had their hands and faces wiped with a flannel. They were very quiet. When they had put on their night-dresses, they said their prayers, the boy mumbling. The mother looked down at them, at the brown silken bush of intertwining curls in the nape of the girl's neck, at the little black head of the lad, and her heart burst with anger at their father, who caused all three such distress. The children hid their faces in her skirts for comfort.

When Mrs. Bates came down, the room was strangely empty, with a tension of expectancy. She took up her sewing and stitched for some time without raising her head. Meantime her anger was tinged with fear.

2

The clock struck eight and she rose suddenly, dropping her sewing on her chair. She went to the stair-foot door, opened it, listening. Then she went out, locking the door behind her.

Something scuffled in the yard, and she started, though she knew it was only the rats with which the place was over-run. The night was very dark. In the great bay of railway lines, bulked with trucks, there was no trace of light, only away back she could see a few yellow lamps at the pit-top, and the red smear of the burning pit-bank on the night. She hurried along the edge of the track, then, crossing the converging lines, came to the stile by the white gates, whence she emerged on the road. Then the fear which had led her shrank. People were walking up to New Brinsley; she saw the lights in the houses; twenty yards farther on were the broad windows of the 'Prince of Wales', very warm and bright, and the loud voices of men could be heard distinctly. What a fool she had been to imagine that anything had happened to him! He was merely drinking over there at the 'Prince of Wales'. She faltered. She had never yet been to fetch him, and she never would go. So she continued her walk towards the long straggling line of houses, standing back on the highway. She entered a passage between the dwellings.

"Mr. Rigley?—Yes! Did you want him? No, he's not in at this minute."

The raw-boned woman leaned forward from her dark scullery and peered at the other, upon whom fell a dim light through the blind of the kitchen window.

"Is it Mrs. Bates?" she asked in a tone tinged with respect.

"Yes. I wondered if your Master was at home. Mine hasn't come yet."

"'Asn't 'e! Oh, Jack's been 'ome an' 'ad 'is dinner an' gone out. 'E's just gone for 'alf an hour afore bed-time. Did you call at the 'Prince of Wales'?"

"No——"

"No, you didn't like——! It's not very nice." The other woman was indulgent. There was an awkward pause. "Jack never said nothink about—about your Master," she said.

"No!—I expect he's stuck in there!"

Elizabeth Bates said this bitterly, and with recklessness. She knew that the woman across the yard was standing at her door listening, but she did not care. As she turned:

"Stop a minute! I'll just go an' ask Jack if 'e knows anythink," said Mrs. Rigley.

"Oh no—I wouldn't like to put——!"

"Yes, I will, if you'll just step inside an' see as th' childer doesn't come downstairs and set theirselves afire."

Elizabeth Bates, murmuring a remonstrance,[8] stepped inside. The other woman apologised for the state of the room.

The kitchen needed apology. There were little frocks and trousers and childish undergarments on the squab and on the floor, and a litter of playthings everywhere. On the black American cloth of the table were pieces of bread and cake, crusts, slops, and a teapot with cold tea.

"Eh, ours is just as bad," said Elizabeth Bates, looking at the woman, not at the house. Mrs. Rigley put a shawl over her head and hurried out, saying:

"I shanna be a minute."

The other sat, noting with faint disapproval the general untidiness of the room. Then she fell to counting the shoes of various sizes scattered over the floor. There were twelve. She sighed and said to herself: "No wonder!"—glancing at the litter. There came the scratching of two pairs of feet on the yard, and the Rigleys entered. Elizabeth Bates rose. Rigley was a big man, with very large bones. His head looked particularly bony. Across his temple was a blue scar, caused by a wound got in the pit, a wound in which the coal-dust remained blue like tattooing.

"'Asna 'e come whoam yit?" asked the man, without any form of greeting, but with deference and sympathy. "I couldna say wheer he is—'e's non ower theer!"—he jerked his head to signify the 'Prince of Wales'.

"'E's 'appen[9] gone up to th' 'Yew'," said Mrs. Rigley.

There was another pause. Rigley had evidently something to get off his mind:

"Ah left 'im finishin' a stint,"[1] he began. "Loose-all 'ad bin gone about ten minutes when we com'n away, an' I shouted: 'Are ter comin', Walt?' an' 'e said: 'Go on, Ah shanna be but a'ef a minnit,' so we com'n ter th' bottom, me an' Bowers, thinkin' as 'e wor just behint, an' 'ud come up i' th' next bantle[2]——"

He stood perplexed, as if answering a charge of deserting his mate. Elizabeth Bates, now again certain of disaster, hastened to reassure him:

"I expect 'e's gone up to th' 'Yew Tree', as you say. It's not the first time. I've fretted myself into a fever before now. He'll come home when they carry him."

"Ay, isn't it too bad!" deplored the other woman.

"I'll just step up to Dick's an' see if 'e is theer," offered the man, afraid of appearing alarmed, afraid of taking liberties.

"Oh, I wouldn't think of bothering you that far," said Elizabeth Bates, with emphasis, but he knew she was glad of his offer.

As they stumbled up the entry, Elizabeth Bates heard Rigley's wife run across the yard and open her neighbour's door. At this, suddenly all the blood in her body seemed to switch away from her heart.

"Mind!" warned Rigley. "Ah've said many a time as Ah'd fill up them ruts in this entry, sumb'dy 'll be breakin' their legs yit."

She recovered herself and walked quickly along with the miner.

"I don't like leaving the children in bed, and nobody in the house," she said.

---

8. Protestation or objection.
9. Perhaps, maybe.

1. Amount of work to be done.
2. Carload.

"No, you dunna!" he replied courteously. They were soon at the gate of the cottage.

"Well, I shanna be many minnits, Dunna you be frettin' now, 'e'll be all right," said the butty.[3]

"Thank you very much, Mr. Rigley," she replied.

"You're welcome!" he stammered, moving away. "I shanna be many minnits."

The house was quiet. Elizabeth Bates took off her hat and shawl, and rolled back the rug. When she had finished, she sat down. It was a few minutes past nine. She was startled by the rapid chuff of the winding-engine at the pit, and the sharp whirr of the brakes on the rope as it descended. Again she felt the painful sweep of her blood, and she put her hand to her side, saying aloud: "Good gracious!—it's only the nine o'clock deputy going down," rebuking herself.

She sat still, listening. Half an hour of this, and she was wearied out.

"What am I working myself up like this for?" she said pitiably to herself, "I s'll only be doing myself some damage."

She took out her sewing again.

At a quarter to ten there were footsteps. One person! She watched for the door to open. It was an elderly woman, in a black bonnet and a black woollen shawl—his mother. She was about sixty years old, pale, with blue eyes, and her face all wrinkled and lamentable. She shut the door and turned to her daughter-in-law peevishly.

"Eh, Lizzie, whatever shall we do, whatever shall we do!" she cried.

Elizabeth drew back a little, sharply.

"What is it, mother?" she said.

The elder woman seated herself on the sofa.

"I don't know, child, I can't tell you!"—she shook her head slowly. Elizabeth sat watching her, anxious and vexed.

"I don't know," replied the grandmother, sighing very deeply. "There's no end to my troubles, there isn't. The things I've gone through, I'm sure it's enough——!" She wept without wiping her eyes, the tears running.

"But, mother," interrupted Elizabeth, "what do you mean? What is it?"

The grandmother slowly wiped her eyes. The fountains of her tears were stopped by Elizabeth's directness. She wiped her eyes slowly.

"Poor child! Eh, you poor thing!" she moaned. "I don't know what we're going to do, I don't—and you as you are—it's a thing, it is indeed!"

Elizabeth waited.

"Is he dead?" she asked, and at the words her heart swung violently, though she felt a slight flush of shame at the ultimate extravagance of the question. Her words sufficiently frightened the old lady, almost brought her to herself.

"Don't say so, Elizabeth! We'll hope it's not as bad as that; no, may the Lord spare us that, Elizabeth. Jack Rigley came just as I was sittin' down to a glass afore going to bed, an' 'e said: ''Appen you'll go down th' line, Mrs. Bates. Walt's had an accident. 'Appen you'll go an' sit wi' 'er till we can get him home.' I hadn't time to ask him a word afore he was gone. An' I put my bonnet on an' come straight down, Lizzie. I thought to myself: 'Eh, that poor blessed child, if anybody should come an' tell her of a sudden, there's no knowin' what'll 'appen to 'er.' You mustn't let it upset you, Lizzie—or you know what to expect. How long is it, six months—or is it five, Lizzie? Ay!"—the old woman shook her head—"time slips on, it slips on! Ay!"

Elizabeth's thoughts were busy elsewhere. If he was killed—would she be able to manage on the little pension and what she could earn?—she counted up rapidly. If he was hurt—they wouldn't take him to the hospital—how tiresome he would be to nurse!—but perhaps she'd be able to get him away from the drink and his hateful ways. She would—while he was ill. The tears offered to come to her eyes at the picture. But what sentimental luxury was this she was beginning? She turned to consider the children. At any rate she was absolutely necessary for them. They were her business.

"Ay!" repeated the old woman, "it seems but a week or two since he brought me his first wages. Ay—he was a good lad, Elizabeth, he was, in his way. I don't know why he got to be such a trouble, I don't. He was a happy lad at home, only full of spirits. But there's no mistake he's been a handful of trouble, he has! I hope the Lord'll spare him to mend his ways. I hope so, I hope so. You've had a sight o' trouble with him, Elizabeth, you have indeed. But he was a jolly enough lad wi' me, he was, I can assure you. I don't know how it is. . . ."

The old woman continued to muse aloud, a monotonous irritating sound, while Elizabeth thought concentratedly, startled once, when she heard the winding-engine chuff quickly, and the brakes skirr with a shriek. Then she heard the engine more slowly, and the brakes made no sound. The old woman did not notice. Elizabeth waited in suspense. The mother-in-law talked, with lapses into silence.

"But he wasn't your son, Lizzie, an' it makes a difference. Whatever he was, I remember him when he was little, an' I learned to understand him and to make allowances. You've got to make allowances for them——"

It was half-past ten, and the old woman was saying: "But it's trouble from beginning to end; you're never too old for trouble, never too old for that——" when the gate banged back, and there were heavy feet on the steps.

"I'll go, Lizzie, let me go," cried the old woman, rising. But Elizabeth was at the door. It was a man in pit-clothes.

"They're bringin' 'im, Missis," he said. Elizabeth's heart halted a moment. Then it surged on again, almost suffocating her.

"Is he—is it bad?" she asked.

The man turned away, looking at the darkness:

"The doctor says 'e'd been dead hours. 'E saw 'im i' th' lamp-cabin."

The old woman, who stood just behind Elizabeth, dropped into a chair, and folded her hands, crying: "Oh, my boy, my boy!"

"Hush!" said Elizabeth, with a sharp twitch of a frown. "Be still, mother, don't waken th' children: I wouldn't have them down for anything!"

The old woman moaned softly, rocking herself. The man was drawing away. Elizabeth took a step forward.

"How was it?" she asked.

"Well, I couldn't say for sure," the man replied, very ill at ease. "'E wor finishin' a stint an' th' butties 'ad gone, an' a lot o' stuff come down atop 'n 'im."

"And crushed him?" cried the widow, with a shudder.

"No," said the man, "it fell at th' back of 'im. 'E wor under th' face, an' it niver touched 'im. It shut 'im in. It seems 'e wor smothered."

Elizabeth shrank back. She heard the old woman behind her cry:

"What?—what did 'e say it was?"

The man replied, more loudly: "'E wor smothered!"

Then the old woman wailed aloud, and this relieved Elizabeth.

"Oh, mother," she said, putting her hand on the old woman, "don't waken th' children, don't waken th' children."

She wept a little, unknowing, while the old mother rocked herself and moaned. Elizabeth remembered that they were bringing him home, and she must be ready.

"They'll lay him in the parlour," she said to herself, standing a moment pale and perplexed.

Then she lighted a candle and went into the tiny room. The air was cold and damp, but she could not make a fire, there was no fireplace. She set down the candle and looked round. The candlelight glittered on the lustre-glasses, on the two vases that held some of the pink chrysanthemums, and on the dark mahogany. There was a cold, deathly smell of chrysanthemums in the room. Elizabeth stood looking at the flowers. She turned away, and calculated whether there would be room to lay him on the floor, between the couch and the chiffonier.[4] She pushed the chairs aside. There would be room to lay him down and to step round him. Then she fetched the old red tablecloth, and another old cloth, spreading them down to save her bit of carpet. She shivered on leaving the parlour; so, from the dresser drawer she took a clean shirt and put it at the fire to air. All the time her mother-in-law was rocking herself in the chair and moaning.

"You'll have to move from there, mother," said Elizabeth. "They'll be bringing him in. Come in the rocker."

The old mother rose mechanically, and seated herself by the fire, continuing to lament. Elizabeth went into the pantry for another candle, and there, in the little pent-house under the naked tiles, she heard them coming. She stood still in the pantry doorway, listening. She heard them pass the end of the house, and come awkwardly down the three steps, a jumble of shuffling footsteps and muttering voices. The old woman was silent. The men were in the yard.

Then Elizabeth heard Matthews, the manager of the pit, say: "You go in first, Jim. Mind!"

The door came open, and the two women saw a collier backing into the room, holding one end of a stretcher, on which they could see the nailed pit-boots of the dead man. The two carriers halted, the man at the head stooping to the lintel of the door.

"Wheer will you have him?" asked the manager, a short, white-bearded man.

Elizabeth roused herself and came from the pantry carrying the unlighted candle.

"In the parlour," she said.

"In there, Jim!" pointed the manager, and the carriers backed round into the tiny room. The coat with which they had covered the body fell off as they awkwardly turned through the two doorways, and the women saw their man, naked to the waist, lying stripped for work. The old woman began to moan in a low voice of horror.

"Lay th' stretcher at th' side," snapped the manager, "an' put 'im on th' cloths. Mind now, mind! Look you now——!"

One of the men had knocked off a vase of chrysanthemums. He stared awkwardly, then they set down the stretcher. Elizabeth did not look at her husband. As soon as she could get in the room, she went and picked up the broken vase and the flowers.

"Wait a minute!" she said.

The three men waited in silence while she mopped up the water with a duster.

"Eh, what a job, what a job, to be sure!" the manager was saying, rubbing his brow with trouble and perplexity. "Never knew such a thing in my life, never! He'd no busines to ha' been left. I never knew such a thing in my life! Fell over him clean as a whistle, an' shut him in. Not four foot of space, there wasn't—yet it scarce bruised him."

He looked down at the dead man, lying prone, half naked, all grimed with coal-dust.

" 'Sphyxiated', the doctor said. It is the most terrible job I've ever known. Seems as if it was done o' purpose. Clean over him, an' shut 'im in, like a mouse-trap"—he made a sharp, descending gesture with his hand.

4. Chest of drawers.

The colliers standing by jerked aside their heads in hopeless comment.

The horror of the thing bristled upon them all.

Then they heard the girl's voice upstairs calling shrilly: "Mother, mother—who is it? Mother, who is it?"

Elizabeth hurried to the foot of the stairs and opened the door:

"Go to sleep!" she commanded sharply. "What are you shouting about? Go to sleep at once—there's nothing—"

Then she began to mount the stairs. They could hear her on the boards, and on the plaster floor of the little bedroom. They could hear her distinctly:

"What's the matter now?—what's the matter with you, silly thing?"—her voice was much agitated, with an unreal gentleness.

"I thought it was some men come," said the plaintive voice of the child. "Has he come?"

"Yes, they've brought him. There's nothing to make a fuss about. Go to sleep now, like a good child."

They could hear her voice in the bedroom, they waited whilst she covered the children under the bedclothes.

"Is he drunk?" asked the girl, timidly, faintly.

"No! No—he's not! He—he's asleep."

"Is he asleep downstairs?"

"Yes—and don't make a noise."

There was silence for a moment, then the men heard the frightened child again: "What's that noise?"

"It's nothing, I tell you, what are you bothering for?"

The noise was the grandmother moaning. She was oblivious of everything, sitting on her chair rocking and moaning The manager put his hand on her arm and bade her "Sh—sh!!"

The old woman opened her eyes and looked at him. She was shocked by this interruption, and seemed to wonder.

"What time is it?" the plaintive thin voice of the child, sinking back unhappily into sleep, asked this last question.

"Ten o'clock," answered the mother more softly. Then she must have bent down and kissed the children.

Matthews beckoned to the men to come away. They put on their caps and took up the stretcher. Stepping over the body, they tiptoed out of the house. None of them spoke till they were far from the wakeful children.

When Elizabeth came down she found her mother alone on the parlour floor, leaning over the dead man, the tears dropping on him.

"We must lay him out," the wife said. She put on the kettle, then returning knelt at the feet, and began to unfasten the knotted leather laces. The room was clammy and dim with only one candle, so that she had to bend her face almost to the floor. At last she got off the heavy boots and put them away.

"You must help me now," she whispered to the old woman. Together they stripped the man.

When they arose, saw him lying in the naïve dignity of death, the women stood arrested in fear and respect. For a few moments they remained still, looking down, the old mother whimpering. Elizabeth felt countermanded.[5] She saw him, how utterly inviolable he lay in himself. She had nothing to do with him. She

5. Overruled, contradicted.

could not accept it. Stooping, she laid her hand on him, in claim. He was still warm, for the mine was hot where he had died. His mother had his face between her hands, and was murmuring incoherently. The old tears fell in succession as drops from wet leaves; the mother was not weeping, merely her tears flowed. Elizabeth embraced the body of her husband, with cheek and lips. She seemed to be listening, inquiring, trying to get some connection. But she could not. She was driven away. He was impregnable.

She rose, went into the kitchen, where she poured warm water into a bowl, brought soap and flannel and a soft towel.

"I must wash him," she said.

Then the old mother rose stiffly, and watched Elizabeth as she carefully washed his face, carefully brushing the big blond moustache from his mouth with the flannel. She was afraid with a bottomless fear, so she ministered to him. The old woman, jealous, said:

"Let me wipe him!"—and she kneeled on the other side drying slowly as Elizabeth washed, her big black bonnet sometimes brushing the dark head of her daughter-in-law. They worked thus in silence for a long time. They never forgot it was death, and the touch of the man's dead body gave them strange emotions, different in each of the women; a great dread possessed them both, the mother felt the lie was given to her womb, she was denied; the wife felt the utter isolation of the human soul, the child within her was a weight apart from her.

At last it was finished. He was a man of handsome body, and his face showed no traces of drink. He was blond, full-fleshed, with fine limbs. But he was dead.

"Bless him," whispered his mother, looking always at his face, and speaking out of sheer terror. "Dear lad—bless him!" She spoke in a faint, sibilant ecstasy of fear and mother love.

Elizabeth sank down again to the floor, and put her face against his neck, and trembled and shuddered. But she had to draw away again. He was dead, and her living flesh had no place against his. A great dread and weariness held her: she was so unavailing. Her life was gone like this.

"White as milk he is, clear as a twelve-month baby, bless him, the darling!" the old mother murmured to herself. "Not a mark on him, clear and clean and white, beautiful as ever a child was made," she murmured with pride. Elizabeth kept her face hidden.

"He went peaceful, Lizzie—peaceful as sleep. Isn't he beautiful, the lamb? Ay—he must ha' made his peace, Lizzie. 'Appen he made it all right, Lizzie, shut in there. He'd have time. He wouldn't look like this if he hadn't made his peace. The lamb, the dear lamb. Eh, but he had a hearty laugh. I loved to hear it. He had the heartiest laugh, Lizzie, as a lad——"

Elizabeth looked up. The man's mouth was fallen back, slightly open under the cover of the moustache. The eyes, half shut, did not show glazed in the obscurity. Life with its smoky burning gone from him, had left him apart and utterly alien to her. And she knew what a stranger he was to her. In her womb was ice of fear, because of this separate stranger with whom she had been living as one flesh. Was this what it all meant—utter, intact separateness, obscured by heat of living? In dread she turned her face away. The fact was too deadly. There had been nothing between them, and yet they had come together, exchanging their nakedness repeatedly. Each time he had taken her, they had been two isolated beings, far apart as now. He was no more responsible than she. The child was like ice in her womb. For as she looked at the dead man, her mind, cold and detached, said clearly: "Who am I? What have I been doing? I have been fighting a husband who did not exist. He existed all the time. What wrong have I done? What was that I have been living with? There lies the reality, this man." And her soul died in her for fear: she knew she had never seen him, he had never seen her, they had met in the dark and had fought in the dark, not knowing whom they met nor whom they fought. And now she saw, and turned silent in seeing. For she had been wrong. She had said he was something he was not; she had felt familiar with him. Whereas he was apart all the while, living as she never lived, feeling as she never felt.

In fear and shame she looked at his naked body, that she had known falsely. And he was the father of her children. Her soul was torn from her body and stood apart. She looked at his naked body and was ashamed, as if she had denied it. After all, it was itself. It seemed awful to her. She looked at his face, and she turned her own face to the wall. For his look was other than hers, his way was not her way. She had denied him what he was—she saw it now. She had refused him as himself. And this had been her life, and his life. She was grateful to death, which restored the truth. And she knew she was not dead.

And all the while her heart was bursting with grief and pity for him. What had he suffered? What stretch of horror for this helpless man! She was rigid with agony. She had not been able to help him. He had been cruelly injured, this naked man, this other being, and she could make no reparation. There were the children—but the children belonged to life. This dead man had nothing to do with them. He and she were only channels through which life had flowed to issue in the children. She was a mother—but how awful she knew it now to have been a wife. And he, dead now, how awful he must have felt it to be a husband. She felt that in the next world he would be a stranger to her. If they met there, in the beyond, they would only be ashamed of what had been before. The children had come, for some mysterious reason, out of both of them. But the children did not unite them. Now he was dead, she knew how eternally he was apart from her, how eternally he had nothing more to do with her. She saw this episode of her life closed. They had denied each other in life. Now he had withdrawn. An anguish came over her. It was finished then: it had become hopeless between them long before he died. Yet he had been her husband. But how little!

"Have you got his shirt, 'Lizabeth?"

Elizabeth turned without answering, though she strove to weep and behave as her mother-in-law expected. But she could not, she was silenced. She went into the kitchen and returned with the garment.

"It is aired," she said, grasping the cotton shirt here and there to try. She was almost ashamed to handle him; what right had she or anyone to lay hands on him; but her touch was humble on his body. It was hard work to clothe him. He was so heavy and inert. A terrible dread gripped her all the while: that he could be so heavy and utterly inert, unresponsive, apart. The horror of the distance between them was almost too much for her—it was so infinite a gap she must look across.

At last it was finished. They covered him with a sheet and left him lying, with his face bound. And she fastened the door of the little parlour, lest the children should see what was lying there. Then, with peace sunk heavy on her heart, she went about making tidy the kitchen. She knew she submitted to life, which was her immediate master. But from death, her ultimate master, she winced with fear and shame.

Dylan Thomas
1914–1953

One of the most important facts of Dylan Thomas's biography is his birthplace: Swansea, South Wales. Thomas was Welsh first, English second. Although Wales is entirely contained within the borders of England, it has its own language, unrelated to English. The Welsh language is a living and thriving one, and it is visible in Wales in place names, street signs, church music, and a host of other daily manifestations. Thomas uses the words of the English language in making his poems, plays, and stories, but these words are defamiliarized, are made strange, by virtue of their having been laid on top, as it were, of absent Welsh words and phrasings that echo nonetheless through the English lines. A common criticism made about Dylan Thomas's poetry by English critics who were his contemporaries was that the poetry was overly emotional and excessively musical, and that it lacked "rigor." These charges against the poems sound all too familiarly like the complaints against the Welsh and the Irish peoples—too emotional, too lyrical, too irrational. The innovative and densely lyrical patterns of Thomas's poetry and his prose style come partially out of his "Welshification" of English, a process that has effects on both the style and the subject matter of his work. In another register, he can be seen as the last of the Romantic poets, writing precocious lyrics infused with an intense sense of self.

Dylan Thomas's earliest volume, *18 Poems*, appeared in 1934 when Thomas was twenty years old, a suite of poems based on the cycle of life, birth, childhood, and death in Swansea. It caused a sensation for the magic of its wordplay and the intensely personal focus of the poems. The book was received ecstatically in Britain, but not so in Wales, whose provincial proprieties Thomas always viewed with a half-affectionate sarcasm. Like James Joyce, Thomas felt the necessity of escape; at the age of twenty-one he moved to the metropolitan center, to London, to pursue his hopes of a literary career. There he worked for the BBC as a writer and a performer on radio broadcasts. The short stories of his collection *Portrait of the Artist as a Young Dog* (1940) wittily recount, in obvious homage and parody of Joyce's *Portrait of the Artist as a Young Man*, the travails of the would-be writer who hopes to break through the barriers of class and nation. He spent the years of World War II in London as well, but as a conscientious objector, not a combatant, and, as a Welshman, to a certain degree as an outsider within. The war was traumatizing for him as for so many others, and Thomas's pacifism and despair led to the superb poetry of his volume *Deaths and Entrances*.

Poetry alone could not pay the bills and allow Thomas and his young family to live in London. After the war he turned to screenplays and to short stories. The haunting radio play *Return Journey* gives a medley of voices encountered by the poet returning to a Swansea inhabited by the ghost of his youthful self. It can be compared to some of Hardy's memory-filled poetic landscapes and to stories like *Ivy Day in the Committee Room* in Joyce's *Dubliners*; it also anticipates the spare, ironic dramas that Samuel Beckett would write in the 1960s and 1970s.

In the late 1940s, Thomas returned to his poetry, this time less as a poet than as a performer or public reader of his own work. His vibrant and sonorous Welsh-accented voice (akin to that of the Welsh actor Richard Burton), melded with the incantatory lyricism of his poetic language, proved to be irresistible to the public, both in England and in the United States. His brilliant poetry readings instigated a new popularity for poetry itself on both sides of the Atlantic, and his captivating talents as a reader and indeed an actor created for him the persona of Dylan Thomas, Bohemian poet, which he wore until his early death in New York City, after an overdose of whiskey following a poetry reading. He was on his way to California to stay with Igor Stravinsky, with whom he planned to write an epic opera.

The great American poet John Berryman described certain recurrent words as the "unmistakable signature" of Dylan Thomas's poetry. Berryman chose a list of forty "key words" in Thomas's work, including among them: blood, sea, ghost, grave, death, light, time, sun, night, wind, love, and rain. Berryman noted the symbolic value Thomas made these seemingly simple words carry across the span of many poems. Thomas's themes were agreed by most critics to be simple and elemental ones—related to the cycles of life, to nature and childhood, to life's meaning. Berryman argued fiercely that while these were simple themes on the surface, what a poem means *is* its imagery, the way its words are put into relation to one another: "A poem that works well demonstrates an insight, and the insight may consist, not in the theme, but in the image-relations or the structure-relations." Thomas himself aimed at using wordplay and fractured syntax to create sound as a "verbal music." The musicality of his poems and his prose is stunningly evident, and rarely more so than in his play *Under Milk Wood*, a kind of oratorio for disembodied voices. In the play, published posthumously in 1954, Thomas gives voice to the inhabitants of the Welsh village of Llaregyub, whose voices weave together the actions of nature and humans on one single rural day. There is no "plot," and the actors simply stand on stage and read, taking on many voices as these ebb and flow musically through them.

Oral speech and song are more important than written language in rural countries and cultures, especially when one's written language is officially discouraged or even forbidden. Social memory is passed on in story and song; tales and jokes and sermons and performances loom larger in the society of a country town than do written artifacts. Dylan Thomas was very much a writer, yet his poetry and prose are written to be heard, to exist in the ear of the listener as much as the eye of the reader. The lush richness of Thomas's poetic voice is a verbal music that passes on a tradition of oral culture and its precious gifts. The spoken or sung word is a word accompanied by breath; breath is related in most cultures, but certainly in those of Wales and Ireland, to the spirit. One collection of Dylan Thomas's poetry and sketches he titled *The World I Breathe*. This title could as easily be *The Word I Breathe*.

The Force That Through the Green Fuse Drives the Flower

The force that through the green fuse drives the flower
Drives my green age; that blasts the roots of trees
Is my destroyer.
And I am dumb to tell the crooked rose
5   My youth is bent by the same wintry fever.

The force that drives the water through the rocks
Drives my red blood; that dries the mouthing streams
Turns mine to wax.
And I am dumb to mouth unto my veins
10   How at the mountain spring the same mouth sucks.

The hand that whirls the water in the pool
Stirs the quicksand; that ropes the blowing wind
Hauls my shroud sail.
And I am dumb to tell the hanging man
15   How of my clay is made the hangman's lime.

The lips of time leech to the fountain head;
Love drips and gathers, but the fallen blood
Shall calm her sores.
And I am dumb to tell a weather's wind
20   How time has ticked a heaven round the stars.

And I am dumb to tell the lover's tomb
How at my sheet goes the same crooked worm.

1933

Fern Hill

Now as I was young and easy under the apple boughs
About the lilting house and happy as the grass was green,
    The night above the dingle° starry,   *cart*
      Time let me hail and climb
5   Golden in the heydays of his eyes,
And honoured among wagons I was prince of the apple towns
And once below a time I lordly had the trees and leaves
      Trail with daisies and barley
    Down the rivers of the windfall light.

10 And as I was green and carefree, famous among the barns
About the happy yard and singing as the farm was home,
    In the sun that is young once only,
      Time let me play and be
    Golden in the mercy of his means,
15 And green and golden I was huntsman and herdsman, the calves
Sang to my horn, the foxes on the hills barked clear and cold,
      And the sabbath rang slowly
    In the pebbles of the holy streams.

All the sun long it was running, it was lovely, the hay
20 Fields high as the house, the tunes from the chimneys, it was air
    And playing, lovely and watery
      And fire green as grass.
    And nightly under the simple stars
As I rode to sleep the owls were bearing the farm away,
25 All the moon long I heard, blessed among stables, the nightjars.°   *birds*
      Flying with the ricks,° and the horses   *straw*
    Flashing into the dark.

And then to awake, and the farm, like a wanderer white
With the dew, come back, the cock on his shoulder: it was all
30   Shining, it was Adam and maiden,
      The sky gathered again
    And the sun grew round that very day.
So it must have been after the birth of the simple light
In the first, spinning place, the spellbound horses walking warm
35   Out of the whinnying green stable
      On to the fields of praise.

And honoured among foxes and pheasants by the gay house
Under the new made clouds and happy as the heart was long,
    In the sun born over and over,
40   I ran my heedless ways,
    My wishes raced through the house high hay

And nothing I cared, at my sky blue trades, that time allows
In all his tuneful turning so few and such morning songs
    Before the children green and golden
45   Follow him out of grace,

Nothing I cared, in the lamb white days, that time would take me
Up to the swallow thronged loft by the shadow of my hand,
    In the moon that is always rising,
      Nor that riding to sleep
50   I should hear him fly with the high fields
And wake to the farm forever fled from the childless land.
Oh as I was young and easy in the mercy of his means,
    Time held me green and dying
    Though I sang in my chains like the sea.

Poem in October

    It was my thirtieth year to heaven
Woke to my hearing from harbour and neighbour wood
    And the mussel° pooled and the heron   *shellfish*
      Priested° shore   *presided over*
5   The morning beckon
With water praying and call of seagull and rook
And the knock of sailing boats on the net webbed wall
    Myself to set foot
      That second
10   In the still sleeping town and set forth.

    My birthday began with the water-
Birds and the birds of the winged trees flying my name
    Above the farms and the white horses
      And I rose
15   In the rainy autumn
And walked abroad in a shower of all my days.
High tide and the heron dived when I took the road
    Over the border
    And the gates
20   Of the town closed as the town awoke.

    A springful of larks in a rolling
Cloud and the roadside bushes brimming with whistling
    Blackbirds and the sun of October
      Summery
25   On the hill's shoulder,
Here were fond climates and sweet singers suddenly
Come in the morning where I wandered and listened
    To the rain wringing
      Wind blow cold
30   In the wood faraway under me.

Pale rain over the dwindling harbour
And over the sea wet church the size of a snail
    With its horns through mist and the castle
        Brown as owls
35   But all the gardens
Of spring and summer were blooming in the tall tales
Beyond the border and under the lark full cloud.
    There could I marvel
    My birthday
40 Away but the weather turned around.

    It turned away from the blithe° country   *lighthearted*
And down the other air and the blue altered sky
    Streamed again a wonder of summer
        With apples
45   Pears and red currants
And I saw in the turning so clearly a child's
Forgotten mornings when he walked with his mother
    Through the parables°   *religious fables*
    Of sun light
50   And the legends of the green chapels

    And the twice told fields of infancy
That his tears burned my cheeks and his heart moved in mine.
    These were the woods the river and sea
        Where a boy
55   In the listening
Summertime of the dead whispered the truth of his joy
To the trees and the stones and the fish in the tide.
    And the mystery
    Sang alive
60   Still in the water and singingbirds.

    And there could I marvel my birthday
Away but the weather turned around. And the true
    Joy of the long dead child sang burning
    In the sun.
65   It was my thirtieth
Year to heaven stood there then in the summer noon
Though the town below lay leaved with October blood.
    O may my heart's truth
    Still be sung
70 On this high hill in a year's turning.

Do Not Go Gentle into That Good Night

Do not go gentle into that good night,
Old age should burn and rave at close of day;
Rage, rage against the dying of the light.

Though wise men at their end know dark is right,
5   Because their words had forked no lightning they
Do not go gentle into that good night.

Good men, the last wave by, crying how bright
Their frail deeds might have danced in a green bay,
Rage, rage against the dying of the light.

10   Wild men who caught and sang the sun in flight,
And learn, too late, they grieved it on its way,
Do not go gentle into that good night.

Grave men, near death, who see with blinding sight
Blind eyes could blaze like meteors and be gay,
15   Rage, rage against the dying of the light.

And you, my father, there on the sad height,
Curse, bless, me now with your fierce tears, I pray.
Do not go gentle into that good night.
Rage, rage against the dying of the light.

1951

Samuel Beckett

1906–1989

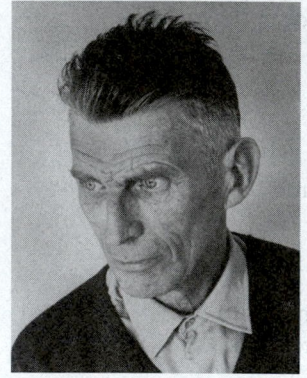

Samuel Beckett, 1971.

On January 5, 1953, *En Attendant Godot* (*Waiting for Godot*) premiered at the Théâtre de Babylone, Paris—and the shape of twentieth-century drama was permanently changed. *Godot* helped to strip the modern stage of everything but its essentials: two characters, seemingly without past or future or worldly possessions, and a spare stage: "A country road. A tree. Evening." Critics would subsequently find in Beckett's bleak stage suggestions of a postnuclear holocaust landscape, as they would in the later *Fin de partie* (*Endgame*, 1957); and for the remainder of his long and productive career, Beckett would continue to explore, with unparalleled honesty and courage, that realm of being that he called in one story *Sans*—"lessness."

April 13, 1906—Good Friday—is the date usually given for Samuel Barclay Beckett's birth, though the birth certificate shows May 13. He was born in the family home of Cooldrinagh in Foxrock, an upper-class Protestant suburb south of Dublin, to William Beckett, surveyor, and Mary (May) Roe, the daughter of a wealthy Kildare family. "You might say I had a happy childhood," Beckett later recalled; "my father did not beat me, nor did my mother run away from home." Beckett attended private academies in Dublin, then in 1920 was enrolled in Portora Royal School in Enniskillen, Northern Ireland, where he excelled more in sports than studies as star bowler on the cricket team, captain of rugby and swimming, and light-heavyweight champion in boxing. In 1923 Beckett entered Trinity College, Dublin, studying modern languages; he also enjoyed the freedom of the city, frequenting the Gate Theatre (for the drama of Pirandello and O'Casey), the music hall, and the movies (especially Charlie Chaplin,

Laurel and Hardy, Buster Keaton, and the Marx Brothers). All would prove formative influences on his later drama and fiction.

In 1927 Beckett received his B.A. degree, first in his class in modern languages, and went off on fellowship to France to teach for two years at the École Normale Supérieure in Paris. While in Paris he became a friend of James Joyce, who influenced him profoundly. Besides aiding Joyce in various ways with his work, Beckett wrote an important essay, *Dante . . . Bruno . . . Vico . . . Joyce*, on *Finnegans Wake*—for a volume of critical writing published before the novel itself was completed. With characteristic understatement, Beckett has said that "Paris in the twenties was a good place for a young man to be"; at the same time, learning the craft of writing in Paris under the shadow of fellow Irish expatriate James Joyce would be enough to provoke the anxiety of influence in even the best of writers. However, Beckett's respect and admiration for Joyce were boundless and never wavered. In 1969 Beckett admitted that Joyce had become "an ethical ideal" for him: "Joyce had a moral effect on me. He made me realize artistic integrity."

The term of his fellowship in Paris having run out, Beckett returned to Dublin to assume teaching at Trinity College. That he was ill-suited to this role was immediately apparent to students, colleagues, and Beckett himself. "I saw that in teaching," Beckett later said, "I was talking of something I knew little about, to people who cared nothing about it. So I behaved very badly." The bad behavior to which Beckett refers was his resignation by mail while on spring holidays in Germany during his second year. Beckett returned briefly to Paris, where it became clear that the unwelcome attentions of Joyce's daughter Lucia were straining Beckett's relationship with the elder writer. He returned to the family home for a time in 1933, where he worked on his first published fiction, the Joycean collection of short stories *More Pricks than Kicks*.

The 1930s found Beckett shuttling back and forth between poverty in London and the frustrating comforts of home in Dublin; Paris seemed to him forbidden, owing to the break with Joyce. In spite of his difficult living circumstances, however, and occasional crippling attacks of clinical depression, Beckett managed to complete his first novel, *Murphy*. The manuscript was rejected by forty-one publishers before being accepted by Routledge in 1937. At the end of 1937, Beckett overcame his reluctance and moved back to Paris. From then on, he wrote largely in French. During the early years of World War II, he attempted to write but found it increasingly difficult to maintain the neutrality required of him by his Irish citizenship in light of the German invasion of France. He abandoned that neutrality in October 1940, when he joined one of the earliest French Resistance groups; he helped in Paris with Resistance activities until his group had been penetrated and betrayed, and just in the nick of time he and his lover Suzanne Deschevaux-Dumesnil (the two had met in 1938, and would eventually marry in 1961) were smuggled into Unoccupied France. At the end of the war Beckett returned to Paris, where he was awarded the *Croix de Guerre* and the *Médaille de la Résistance* by the French government.

While hiding from the Germans from 1942 to 1945 in the village of Roussillon in southeast France, Beckett wrote *Watt*, a complex and aridly witty novel that was never to enjoy the attention devoted to Beckett's other fiction. Meanwhile, Beckett continued his experiments with drama. Though it is drama for which Beckett is best known, he always put more stock in his fiction; "I turned to writing plays," he once said dismissively, "to relieve myself of the awful depression the prose led me into."

At an impasse in the writing of what would prove to be his greatest novels, the trilogy *Molloy*, *Malone Dies*, and *The Unnameable* (1951–1953), Beckett took off three months to write *Waiting for Godot*; it took four years to get the play produced. It is easy enough, in retrospect, to understand the producers' reservations: *Godot* breaks with the conventions of the well-made play at just about every turn, even down to its symmetrical, mirror-image two-act structure. The Irish critic Vivian Mercier wittily described *Godot* as a play in which "nothing happens, twice." *Endgame* (1958) may well be Beckett's bleakest stage production: from its suggestion of Shakespeare's *King Lear*, from which all possibility of heroism and grandeur has been drained away, to its vaguely post-apocalyptic mood and *mise-on-scène*, *Endgame* replicates the despair of *Waiting for Godot* without the earlier play's gallows humor. Beckett's play *Krapp's*

Last Tape (1960) uses a tape recorder (which, at the time of writing, Beckett had never seen) as a stage metaphor for the struggle over memory.

After the success of his plays of the fifties and early sixties, Beckett turned to shorter and shorter forms, both in drama and fiction; he produced a number of very powerful, very short plays (*Not I*, 1973; *Footfalls*, 1976; *Rockabye*, 1981) and short, poetic texts that he called by a variety of self-deprecating names ("fizzles," "residua," "texts for nothing"). He sought an intensified power in the increasing economy of his works. In 1969 Beckett was awarded the Nobel Prize for Literature, for "a body of work," as the citation declares, "that, in new forms of fiction and the theatre, has transmuted the destitution of modern man into exaltation."

Endgame[1]
A Play in One Act

Characters

NAGG   HAMM
NELL   CLOV

Bare interior.

Grey light.

Left and right back, high up, two small windows, curtains drawn. Front right, a door. Hanging near door, its face to wall, a picture. Front left, touching each other, covered with an old sheet, two ashbins. Center, in an armchair on castors, covered with an old sheet, Hamm. Motionless by the door, his eyes fixed on Hamm, Clov. Very red face. Brief tableau.

Clov goes and stands under window left. Stiff, staggering walk. He looks up at window left. He turns and looks at window right. He goes and stands under window right. He looks up at window right. He turns and looks at window left. He goes out, comes back immediately with a small step-ladder, carries it over and sets it down under window left, gets up on it, draws back curtain. He gets down, takes six steps (for example) towards window right, goes back for ladder, carries it over and sets it down under window right, gets up on it, draws back curtain. He gets down, takes three steps towards window left, goes back for ladder, carries it over and sets it down under window left, gets up on it, looks out of window. Brief laugh. He gets down, takes one step towards window right, goes back for ladder, carries it over and sets it down under window right, gets up on it, looks out of window. Brief laugh. He gets down, goes with ladder towards ashbins, halts, turns, carries back ladder and sets it down under window right, goes to ashbins, removes sheet covering them, folds it over his arm. He raises one lid, stoops and looks into bin. Brief laugh. He closes lid. Same with other bin. He goes to Hamm, removes sheet covering him, folds it over his arm. In a dressing-gown, a stiff toque[2] on his head, a large blood-stained handkerchief over his face, a whistle hanging from his neck, a rug over his knees, thick socks on his feet, Hamm seems to be asleep. Clov looks him over. Brief laugh. He goes to door, halts, turns towards auditorium.

CLOV [*fixed gaze, tonelessly*]: Finished, it's finished, nearly finished, it must be
     nearly finished. [*Pause.*] Grain upon grain, one by one, and one day, suddenly,

---

1. Written in French, then translated into English by   director, Roger Blin.
Beckett himself. Beckett dedicated the play to its first   2. A round brimless hat.

there's a heap, a little heap, the impossible heap. [*Pause.*] I can't be punished any more. [*Pause.*] I'll go now to my kitchen, ten feet by ten feet by ten feet, and wait for him to whistle me. [*Pause.*] Nice dimensions, nice proportions, I'll lean on the table, and look at the wall, and wait for him to whistle me.

[*He remains a moment motionless, then goes out. He comes back immediately, goes to window right, takes up the ladder and carries it out. Pause. Hamm stirs. He yawns under the handkerchief. He removes the handkerchief from his face. Very red face. Black glasses.*]

HAMM: Me—[*he yawns*]—to play. [*He holds the handkerchief spread out before him.*]

Old stancher! [*He takes off his glasses, wipes his eyes, his face, the glasses, puts them on again, folds the handkerchief and puts it back neatly in the breast-pocket of his dressing-gown. He clears his throat, joins the tips of his fingers.*]

Can there be misery—[*he yawns*]—loftier than mine? No doubt. Formerly. But now? [*Pause.*] My father? [*Pause.*] My mother? [*Pause.*] My . . . dog? [*Pause.*] Oh I am willing to believe they suffer as much as such creatures can suffer. But does that mean their sufferings equal mine? No doubt. [*Pause.*] No, all is a—[*he yawns*]—bsolute, [*proudly*] the bigger a man is the fuller he is. [*Pause. Gloomily.*] And the emptier. [*He sniffs.*] Clov! [*Pause.*] No, alone. [*Pause.*] What dreams! Those forests! [*Pause.*] Enough, it's time it ended, in the shelter too. [*Pause.*] And yet I hesitate, I hesitate to . . . to end. Yes, there it is, it's time it ended and yet I hesitate to—[*he yawns*]—to end. [*Yawns.*] God, I'm tired, I'd be better off in bed.

[*He whistles. Enter Clov immediately. He halts beside the chair.*]

You pollute the air! [*Pause.*] Get me ready, I'm going to bed.
CLOV: I've just got you up.
HAMM: And what of it?
CLOV: I can't be getting you up and putting you to bed every five minutes, I have things to do. [*Pause.*]
HAMM: Did you ever see my eyes?
CLOV: No.
HAMM: Did you never have the curiosity, while I was sleeping, to take off my glasses and look at my eyes?
CLOV: Pulling back the lids? [*Pause.*] No.
HAMM: One of these days I'll show them to you. [*Pause.*] It seems they've gone all white. [*Pause.*] What time is it?
CLOV: The same as usual.
HAMM [*gesture towards window right*]: Have you looked?
CLOV: Yes.
HAMM: Well?
CLOV: Zero.
HAMM: It'd need to rain.
CLOV: It won't rain. [*Pause.*]
HAMM: Apart from that, how do you feel?
CLOV: I don't complain.
HAMM: You feel normal?
CLOV [*irritably*]: I tell you I don't complain.
HAMM: I feel a little queer. [*Pause.*] Clov!
CLOV: Yes.

HAMM: Have you not had enough?

CLOV: Yes! [*Pause.*] Of what?

HAMM: Of this . . . this . . . thing.

CLOV: I always had. [*Pause.*] Not you?

HAMM [*gloomily*]: Then there's no reason for it to change.

CLOV: It may end. [*Pause.*] All life long the same questions, the same answers.

HAMM: Get me ready.

>   [*Clov does not move.*]

>   Go and get the sheet.

>   [*Clov does not move.*]

>   Clov!

CLOV: Yes.

HAMM: I'll give you nothing more to eat.

CLOV: Then we'll die.

HAMM: I'll give you just enough to keep you from dying. You'll be hungry all the time.

CLOV: Then we won't die. [*Pause.*] I'll go and get the sheet.

>   [*He goes towards the door.*]

HAMM: No!

>   [*Clov halts.*]

>   I'll give you one biscuit per day. [*Pause.*] One and a half. [*Pause.*] Why do you stay with me?

CLOV: Why do you keep me?

HAMM: There's no one else.

CLOV: There's nowhere else. [*Pause.*]

HAMM: You're leaving me all the same.

CLOV: I'm trying.

HAMM: You don't love me.

CLOV: No.

HAMM: You loved me once.

CLOV: Once!

HAMM: I've made you suffer too much. [*Pause.*] Haven't I?

CLOV: It's not that.

HAMM [*shocked*]: I haven't made you suffer too much?

CLOV: Yes!

HAMM [*relieved*]: Ah you gave me a fright! [*Pause. Coldly.*] Forgive me. [*Pause. Louder.*] I said, Forgive me.

CLOV: I heard you. [*Pause.*] Have you bled?

HAMM: Less. [*Pause.*] Is it not time for my pain-killer?

CLOV: No. [*Pause.*]

HAMM: How are your eyes?

CLOV: Bad.

HAMM: How are your legs?

CLOV: Bad.

HAMM: But you can move.

CLOV: Yes.

HAMM [*violently*]: Then move!

[*Clov goes to back wall, leans against it with his forehead and hands.*]

Where are you?

CLOV: Here.

HAMM: Come back!

[*Clov returns to his place beside the chair.*]

Where are you?

CLOV: Here.

HAMM: Why don't you kill me?

CLOV: I don't know the combination of the cupboard. [*Pause.*]

HAMM: Go and get two bicycle-wheels.

CLOV: There are no more bicycle-wheels.

HAMM: What have you done with your bicycle?

CLOV: I never had a bicycle.

HAMM: The thing is impossible.

CLOV: When there were still bicycles I wept to have one. I crawled at your feet. You told me to go to hell. Now there are none.

HAMM: And your rounds? When you inspected my paupers. Always on foot?

CLOV: Sometimes on horse.

[*The lid of one of the bins lifts and the hands of Nagg appear, gripping the rim. Then his head emerges. Nightcap. Very white face. Nagg yawns, then listens.*]

I'll leave you, I have things to do.

HAMM: In your kitchen?

CLOV: Yes.

HAMM: Outside of here it's death. [*Pause.*] All right, be off.

[*Exit Clov. Pause.*]

We're getting on.

NAGG: Me pap!

HAMM: Accursed progenitor!

NAGG: Me pap!

HAMM: The old folks at home! No decency left! Guzzle, guzzle, that's all they think of.

[*He whistles. Enter Clov. He halts beside the chair.*]

Well! I thought you were leaving me.

CLOV: Oh not just yet, not just yet.

NAGG: Me pap!

HAMM: Give him his pap.

CLOV: There's no more pap.

HAMM [*to Nagg*]: Do you hear that? There's no more pap. You'll never get any more pap.

NAGG: I want me pap!

HAMM: Give him a biscuit.

[*Exit Clov.*]

Accursed fornicator! How are your stumps?

NAGG: Never mind me stumps.

[*Enter Clov with biscuit.*]

CLOV: I'm back again, with the biscuit.

[*He gives biscuit to Nagg who fingers it, sniffs it.*]

NAGG [*plaintively*]: What is it?

CLOV: Spratt's medium.

NAGG [*as before*]: It's hard! I can't!

HAMM: Bottle him!

[*Clov pushes Nagg back into the bin, closes the lid.*]

CLOV [*returning to his place beside the chair*]: If age but knew!

HAMM: Sit on him!

CLOV: I can't sit.

HAMM: True. And I can't stand.

CLOV: So it is.

HAMM: Every man his speciality. [*Pause.*] No phone calls? [*Pause.*] Don't we laugh?

CLOV [*after reflection*]: I don't feel like it.

HAMM [*after reflection*]: Nor I. [*Pause.*] Clov!

CLOV: Yes.

HAMM: Nature has forgotten us.

CLOV: There's no more nature.

HAMM: No more nature! You exaggerate.

CLOV: In the vicinity.

HAMM: But we breathe, we change! We lose our hair, our teeth! Our bloom! Our ideals!

CLOV: Then she hasn't forgotten us.

HAMM: But you say there is none.

CLOV [*sadly*]: No one that ever lived ever thought so crooked as we.

HAMM: We do what we can.

CLOV: We shouldn't. [*Pause.*]

HAMM: You're a bit of all right, aren't you?

CLOV: A smithereen. [*Pause.*]

HAMM: This is slow work. [*Pause.*] Is it not time for my pain-killer?

CLOV: No. [*Pause.*] I'll leave you, I have things to do.

HAMM: In your kitchen?

CLOV: Yes.

HAMM: What, I'd like to know.

CLOV: I look at the wall.

HAMM: The wall! And what do you see on your wall? Mene, mene?[3] Naked bodies?

---

3. A phrase that appears written by a supernatural hand on a wall of the Babylonian king Belshazzar's palace in the book of Daniel. The inscription, "mene, mene, tekel, upharsin," is translated by the prophet Daniel as "God has numbered the days of your kingdom and brought it to an end" (Daniel 5.26); Belshazzar is killed the same night.

CLOV: I see my light dying.

HAMM: Your light dying! Listen to that! Well, it can die just as well here, *your* light. Take a look at me and then come back and tell me what you think of *your* light. [*Pause.*]

CLOV: You shouldn't speak to me like that. [*Pause.*]

HAMM [*coldly*]: Forgive me. [*Pause. Louder.*] I said, Forgive me.

CLOV: I heard you.

[*The lid of Nagg's bin lifts. His hands appear, gripping the rim. Then his head emerges. In his mouth the biscuit. He listens.*]

HAMM: Did your seeds come up?

CLOV: No.

HAMM: Did you scratch round them to see if they had sprouted?

CLOV: They haven't sprouted.

HAMM: Perhaps it's still too early.

CLOV: If they were going to sprout they would have sprouted. [*Violently.*] They'll never sprout!

[*Pause. Nagg takes biscuit in his hand.*]

HAMM: This is not much fun. [*Pause.*] But that's always the way at the end of the day, isn't it, Clov?

CLOV: Always.

HAMM: It's the end of the day like any other day, isn't it, Clov?

CLOV: Looks like it. [*Pause.*]

HAMM [*anguished*]: What's happening, what's happening?

CLOV: Something is taking its course. [*Pause.*]

HAMM: All right, be off.

[*He leans back in his chair, remains motionless. Clov does not move, heaves a great groaning sigh. Hamm sits up.*]

I thought I told you to be off.

CLOV: I'm trying.

[*He goes to door, halts.*]

Ever since I was whelped.

[*Exit Clov.*]

HAMM: We're getting on.

[*He leans back in his chair, remains motionless. Nagg knocks on the lid of the other bin. Pause. He knocks harder. The lid lifts and the hands of Nell appear, gripping the rim. Then her head emerges. Lace cap. Very white face.*]

NELL: What is it, my pet? [*Pause.*] Time for love?

NAGG: Were you asleep?

NELL: Oh no!

NAGG: Kiss me.

NELL: We can't.

NAGG: Try.

[*Their heads strain towards each other, fail to meet, fall apart again.*]

NELL: Why this farce, day after day? [*Pause.*]
NAGG: I've lost me tooth.
NELL: When?
NAGG: I had it yesterday.
NELL [*elegiac*]: Ah yesterday!

[*They turn painfully towards each other.*]

NAGG: Can you see me?
NELL: Hardly. And you?
NAGG: What?
NELL: Can you see me?
NAGG: Hardly.
NELL: So much the better, so much the better.
NAGG: Don't say that. [*Pause.*] Our sight has failed.
NELL: Yes.

[*Pause. They turn away from each other.*]

NAGG: Can you hear me?
NELL: Yes. And you?
NAGG: Yes. [*Pause.*] Our hearing hasn't failed.
NELL: Our what?
NAGG: Our hearing.
NELL: No. [*Pause.*] Have you anything else to say to me?
NAGG: Do you remember—
NELL: No.
NAGG: When we crashed on our tandem and lost our shanks.

[*They laugh heartily.*]

NELL: It was in the Ardennes.

[*They laugh less heartily.*]

NAGG: On the road to Sedan.[4]

[*They laugh still less heartily.*]

Are you cold?
NELL: Yes, perished. And you?
NAGG: [*Pause.*] I'm freezing. [*Pause.*] Do you want to go in?
NELL: Yes.
NAGG: Then go in.

[*Nell does not move.*]

Why don't you go in?
NELL: I don't know. [*Pause.*]
NAGG: Has he changed your sawdust?
NELL: It isn't sawdust. [*Pause. Wearily.*] Can you not be a little accurate, Nagg?

---

4. A town in the Ardennes, a wooded region in northern France.

NAGG: Your sand then. It's not important.

NELL: It is important. [*Pause.*]

NAGG: It was sawdust once.

NELL: Once!

NAGG: And now it's sand. [*Pause.*] From the shore. [*Pause. Impatiently.*] Now it's sand he fetches from the shore.

NELL: Now it's sand.

NAGG: Has he changed yours?

NELL: No.

NAGG: Nor mine. [*Pause.*] I won't have it! [*Pause. Holding up the biscuit.*] Do you want a bit?

NELL: No. [*Pause.*] Of what?

NAGG: Biscuit. I've kept you half. [*He looks at the biscuit. Proudly.*] Three quarters. For you. Here. [*He proffers the biscuit.*] No? [*Pause.*] Do you not feel well?

HAMM [*wearily*]: Quiet, quiet, you're keeping me awake. [*Pause.*] Talk softer. [*Pause.*] If I could sleep I might make love. I'd go into the woods. My eyes would see . . . the sky, the earth. I'd run, run, they wouldn't catch me. [*Pause.*] Nature! [*Pause.*] There's something dripping in my head. [*Pause.*] A heart, a heart in my head. [*Pause.*]

NAGG [*soft*]: Do you hear him? A heart in his head! [*He chuckles cautiously.*]

NELL: One mustn't laugh at those things, Nagg. Why must you always laugh at them?

NAGG: Not so loud!

NELL [*without lowering her voice*]: Nothing is funnier than unhappiness, I grant you that. But—

NAGG [*shocked*]: Oh!

NELL: Yes, yes, it's the most comical thing in the world. And we laugh, we laugh, with a will, in the beginning. But it's always the same thing. Yes, it's like the funny story we have heard too often, we still find it funny, but we don't laugh any more. [*Pause.*] Have you anything else to say to me?

NAGG: No.

NELL: Are you quite sure? [*Pause.*] Then I'll leave you.

NAGG: Do you not want your biscuit? [*Pause.*] I'll keep it for you. [*Pause.*] I thought you were going to leave me.

NELL: I am going to leave you.

NAGG: Could you give me a scratch before you go?

NELL: No. [*Pause.*] Where?

NAGG: In the back.

NELL: No. [*Pause.*] Rub yourself against the rim.

NAGG: It's lower down. In the hollow.

NELL: What hollow?

NAGG: The hollow! [*Pause.*] Could you not? [*Pause.*] Yesterday you scratched me there.

NELL [*elegiac*]: Ah yesterday!

NAGG: Could you not? [*Pause.*] Would you like me to scratch you? [*Pause.*] Are you crying again?

NELL: I was trying. [*Pause.*]

HAMM: Perhaps it's a little vein. [*Pause.*]

NAGG: What was that he said?

NELL: Perhaps it's a little vein.

NAGG: What does that mean? [*Pause.*] That means nothing. [*Pause.*] Will I tell you the story of the tailor?

NELL: No. [*Pause.*] What for?

NAGG: To cheer you up.

NELL: It's not funny.

NAGG: It always made you laugh. [*Pause.*] The first time I thought you'd die.

NELL: It was on Lake Como.[5] [*Pause.*] One April afternoon. [*Pause.*] Can you believe it?

NAGG: What?

NELL: That we once went out rowing on Lake Como. [*Pause.*] One April afternoon.

NAGG: We had got engaged the day before.

NELL: Engaged!

NAGG: You were in such fits that we capsized. By rights we should have been drowned.

NELL: It was because I felt happy.

NAGG [*indignant*]: It was not, it was not, it was my story and nothing else. Happy! Don't you laugh at it still? Every time I tell it. Happy!

NELL: It was deep, deep. And you could see down to the bottom. So white. So clean.

NAGG: Let me tell it again. [*Raconteur's[6] voice.*] An Englishman, needing a pair of striped trousers in a hurry for the New Year festivities, goes to his tailor who takes his measurements.

[*Tailor's voice.*]

"That's the lot, come back in four days, I'll have it ready." Good. Four days later.

[*Tailor's voice.*]

"So sorry, come back in a week, I've made a mess of the seat." Good, that's all right, a neat seat can be very ticklish. A week later.

[*Tailor's voice.*]

"Frightfully sorry, come back in ten days, I've made a hash of the crotch." Good, can't be helped, a snug crotch is always a teaser. Ten days later.

[*Tailor's voice.*]

"Dreadfully sorry, come back in a fortnight, I've made a balls of the fly." Good, at a pinch, a smart fly is a stiff proposition. [*Pause. Normal voice.*] I never told it worse. [*Pause. Gloomy.*] I tell this story worse and worse.

[*Pause. Raconteur's voice.*]

Well, to make it short, the bluebells are blowing and he ballockses the buttonholes.

[*Customer's voice.*]

5. A scenic lake in northern Italy.   6. A talented storyteller.

"God damn you to hell, Sir, no, it's indecent, there are limits! In six days, do you hear me, six days, God made the world. Yes Sir, no less Sir, the WORLD! And you are not bloody well capable of making me a pair of trousers in three months!"

[*Tailor's voice, scandalized.*]

"But my dear Sir, my dear Sir, look—[*disdainful gesture, disgustedly*]—at the world—[*pause*] and look—[*loving gesture, proudly*]—at my TROUSERS!"

[*Pause. He looks at Nell who has remained impassive, her eyes unseeing, breaks into a high forced laugh, cuts it short, pokes his head towards Nell, launches his laugh again.*]

HAMM: Silence!

[*Nagg starts, cuts short his laugh.*]

NELL: You could see down to the bottom.

HAMM [*exasperated*]: Have you not finished? Will you never finish? [*With sudden fury.*] Will this never finish?

[*Nagg disappears into his bin, closes the lid behind him. Nell does not move. Frenziedly.*]

My kingdom for a nightman![7]

[*He whistles. Enter Clov.*]

Clear away this muck! Chuck it in the sea!

[*Clov goes to bins, halts.*]

NELL: So white.

HAMM: What? What's she blathering about?

[*Clov stoops, takes Nell's hand, feels her pulse.*]

NELL [*to Clov*]: Desert!

[*Clov lets go her hand, pushes her back in the bin, closes the lid.*]

CLOV [*returning to his place beside the chair*]: She has no pulse.

HAMM: What was she drivelling about?

CLOV: She told me to go away, into the desert.

HAMM: Damn busybody! Is that all?

CLOV: No.

HAMM: What else?

CLOV: I didn't understand.

HAMM: Have you bottled her?

CLOV: Yes.

HAMM: Are they both bottled?

CLOV: Yes.

HAMM: Screw down the lids.

[*Clov goes towards door.*]

---

7. Someone who empties outhouses. Hamm's phrasing alludes to Richard III's call, "My kingdom for a horse!" in Shakespeare's tragedy *Richard III* 5.4.

Time enough.

[*Clov halts.*]

My anger subsides, I'd like to pee.

CLOV [*with alacrity*]: I'll go and get the catheter.

[*He goes towards door.*]

HAMM: Time enough.

[*Clov halts.*]

Give me my pain-killer.

CLOV: It's too soon. [*Pause.*] It's too soon on top of your tonic, it wouldn't act.

HAMM: In the morning they brace you up and in the evening they calm you down.
    Unless it's the other way round. [*Pause.*] That old doctor, he's dead naturally?

CLOV: He wasn't old.

HAMM: But he's dead?

CLOV: Naturally. [*Pause.*] You ask me that? [*Pause.*]

HAMM: Take me for a little turn.

[*Clov goes behind the chair and pushes it forward.*]

Not too fast!

[*Clov pushes chair.*]

Right round the world!

[*Clov pushes chair.*]

Hug the walls, then back to the center again.

[*Clov pushes chair.*]

I was right in the center, wasn't I?

CLOV [*pushing*]: Yes.

HAMM: We'd need a proper wheel-chair. With big wheels. Bicycle wheels! [*Pause.*]
    Are you hugging?

CLOV [*pushing*]: Yes.

HAMM [*groping for wall*]: It's a lie! Why do you lie to me?

CLOV [*bearing closer to wall*]: There! There!

HAMM: Stop!

[*Clov stops chair close to back wall. Hamm lays his hand against wall.*]

Old wall! [*Pause.*] Beyond is the . . . other hell. [*Pause. Violently.*] Closer! Closer!
    Up against!

CLOV: Take away your hand.

[*Hamm withdraws his hand. Clov rams chair against wall.*]

There!

[*Hamm leans towards wall, applies his ear to it.*]

HAMM: Do you hear?

[*He strikes the wall with his knuckles.*]

Do you hear? Hollow bricks!

[*He strikes again.*]

All that's hollow! [*Pause. He straightens up. Violently.*] That's enough. Back!
CLOV: We haven't done the round.
HAMM: Back to my place!

[*Clov pushes chair back to center.*]

Is that my place?
CLOV: Yes, that's your place.
HAMM: Am I right in the center?
CLOV: I'll measure it.
HAMM: More or less! More or less!
CLOV [*moving chair slightly*]: There!
HAMM: I'm more or less in the center?
CLOV: I'd say so.
HAMM: You'd say so! Put me right in the center!
CLOV: I'll go and get the tape.
HAMM: Roughly! Roughly!

[*Clov moves chair slightly.*]

Bang in the center!
CLOV: There! [*Pause.*]
HAMM: I feel a little too far to the left.

[*Clov moves chair slightly.*]

Now I feel a little too far to the right.

[*Clov moves chair slightly.*]

I feel a little too far forward.

[*Clov moves chair slightly.*]

Now I feel a little too far back.

[*Clov moves chair slightly.*]

Don't stay there [*i.e. behind the chair*], you give me the shivers.

[*Clov returns to his place beside the chair.*]

CLOV: If I could kill him I'd die happy. [*Pause.*]
HAMM: What's the weather like?
CLOV: As usual.
HAMM: Look at the earth.
CLOV: I've looked.
HAMM: With the glass?
CLOV: No need of the glass.
HAMM: Look at it with the glass.
CLOV: I'll go and get the glass

[*Exit Clov.*]

HAMM: No need for the glass!

[*Enter Clov with telescope.*]

CLOV: I'm back again, with the glass.

[*He goes to window right, looks up at it.*]

I need the steps.

HAMM: Why? Have you shrunk?

[*Exit Clov with telescope.*]

I don't like that, I don't like that.

[*Enter Clov with ladder, but without telescope.*]

CLOV: I'm back again, with the steps.

[*He sets down ladder under window right, gets up on it, realizes he has not the telescope, gets down.*]

I need the glass.

[*He goes towards door.*]

HAMM [*violently*]: But you have the glass!

CLOV [*halting, violently*]: No, I haven't the glass!

[*Exit Clov.*]

HAMM: This is deadly.

[*Enter Clov with telescope. He goes towards ladder.*]

CLOV: Things are livening up.

[*He gets up on the ladder, raises the telescope, lets it fall.*]

I did it on purpose.

[*He gets down, picks up the telescope, turns it on auditorium.*]

I see . . . a multitude . . . in transports . . . of joy. [*Pause.*] That's what I call a magnifier.

[*He lowers the telescope, turns towards Hamm.*]

Well? Don't we laugh?

HAMM [*after reflection*]: I don't.

CLOV [*after reflection*]: Nor I.

[*He gets up on ladder, turns the telescope on the without.*]

Let's see.

[*He looks, moving the telescope.*]

Zero . . . [*he looks*] . . . zero . . . [*he looks*] . . . and zero.

HAMM: Nothing stirs. All is—

CLOV: Zer—

HAMM [*violently*]: Wait till you're spoken to! [*Normal voice.*] All is . . . all is . . . all is what? [*Violently.*] All is what?

CLOV: What all is? In a word? Is that what you want to know? Just a moment.

[*He turns the telescope on the without, looks, lowers the telescope, turns towards Hamm.*]

Corpsed. [*Pause.*] Well? Content?

HAMM: Look at the sea.

CLOV: It's the same.

HAMM: Look at the ocean!

[*Clov gets down, takes a few steps towards window left, goes back for ladder, carries it over and sets it down under window left, gets up on it, turns the telescope on the without, looks at length. He starts, lowers the telescope, examines it, turns it again on the without.*]

CLOV: Never seen anything like that!

HAMM [*anxious*]: What? A sail? A fin? Smoke?

CLOV [*looking*]: The light is sunk.

HAMM [*relieved*]: Pah! We all knew that.

CLOV [*looking*]: There was a bit left.

HAMM: The base.

CLOV [*looking*]: Yes.

HAMM: And now?

CLOV [*looking*]: All gone.

HAMM: No gulls?

CLOV [*looking*]: Gulls!

HAMM: And the horizon? Nothing on the horizon?

CLOV [*lowering the telescope, turning towards Hamm, exasperated*]: What in God's name could there be on the horizon? [*Pause.*]

HAMM: The waves, how are the waves?

CLOV: The waves?

[*He turns the telescope on the waves.*]

Lead.

HAMM: And the sun?

CLOV [*looking*]: Zero.

HAMM: But it should be sinking. Look again.

CLOV [*looking*]: Damn the sun.

HAMM: Is it night already then?

CLOV [*looking*]: No.

HAMM: Then what is it?

CLOV [*looking*]: Gray.

[*Lowering the telescope, turning towards Hamm, louder.*]

Gray! [*Pause. Still louder.*] GRRAY! [*Pause. He gets down, approaches Hamm from behind, whispers in his ear.*]

HAMM [*starting*]: Gray! Did I hear you say gray?

CLOV: Light black. From pole to pole.

HAMM: You exaggerate. [*Pause.*] Don't stay there, you give me the shivers.

[*Clov returns to his place beside the chair.*]

CLOV: Why this farce, day after day?

HAMM: Routine. One never knows. [*Pause.*] Last night I saw inside my breast. There was a big sore.

CLOV: Pah! You saw your heart.

HAMM: No, it was living. [*Pause. Anguished.*] Clov!

CLOV: Yes.

HAMM: What's happening?

CLOV: Something is taking its course. [*Pause.*]

HAMM: Clov!

CLOV [*impatiently*]: What is it?

HAMM: We're not beginning to . . . to . . . mean something?

CLOV: Mean something! You and I, mean something! [*Brief laugh.*] Ah that's a good one!

HAMM: I wonder. [*Pause.*] Imagine if a rational being came back to earth, wouldn't he be liable to get ideas into his head if he observed us long enough. [*Voice of rational being.*] Ah, good, now I see what it is, yes, now I understand what they're at!

[*Clov starts, drops the telescope and begins to scratch his belly with both hands. Normal voice.*]

And without going so far as that, we ourselves . . . [*with emotion*] . . . we ourselves . . . at certain moments . . . [*Vehemently.*] To think perhaps it won't all have been for nothing!

CLOV [*anguished, scratching himself*]: I have a flea!

HAMM: A flea! Are there still fleas?

CLOV: On me there's one. [*Scratching.*] Unless it's a crablouse.

HAMM [*very perturbed*]: But humanity might start from there all over again! Catch him, for the love of God!

CLOV: I'll go and get the powder.

[*Exit Clov.*]

HAMM: A flea! This is awful! What a day!

[*Enter Clov with a sprinkling-tin.*]

CLOV: I'm back again, with the insecticide.

HAMM: Let him have it!

[*Clov loosens the top of his trousers, pulls it forward and shakes powder into the aperture. He stoops, looks, waits, starts, frenziedly shakes more powder, stoops, looks, waits.*]

CLOV: The bastard!

HAMM: Did you get him?

CLOV: Looks like it.

[*He drops the tin and adjusts his trousers.*]

Unless he's laying doggo.

HAMM: Laying! Lying you mean. Unless he's *lying* doggo.

CLOV: Ah? One says lying? One doesn't say laying?

HAMM: Use your head, can't you. If he was laying we'd be bitched.

CLOV: Ah. [*Pause.*] What about that pee?

HAMM: I'm having it.

CLOV: Ah that's the spirit, that's the spirit! [*Pause.*]

HAMM [*with ardour*]: Let's go from here, the two of us! South! You can make a raft and the currents will carry us away, far away, to other . . . mammals!

CLOV: God forbid!

HAMM: Alone, I'll embark alone! Get working on that raft immediately. Tomorrow I'll be gone for ever.

CLOV [*hastening towards door*]: I'll start straight away.

HAMM: Wait!

[*Clov halts.*]

Will there be sharks, do you think?

CLOV: Sharks? I don't know. If there are there will be.

[*He goes towards door.*]

HAMM: Wait!

[*Clov halts.*]

Is it not yet time for my pain-killer?

CLOV [*violently*]: No!

[*He goes towards door.*]

HAMM: Wait!

[*Clov halts.*]

How are your eyes?

CLOV: Bad.

HAMM: But you can see.

CLOV: All I want.

HAMM: How are your legs?

CLOV: Bad.

HAMM: But you can walk.

CLOV: I come . . . and go.

HAMM: In my house. [*Pause. With prophetic relish.*] One day you'll be blind, like me. You'll be sitting there, a speck in the void, in the dark, for ever, like me. [*Pause.*] One day you'll say to yourself, I'm tired, I'll sit down, and you'll go and sit down. Then you'll say, I'm hungry, I'll get up and get something to eat. But you won't get up. You'll say, I shouldn't have sat down, but since I have I'll sit on a little longer, then I'll get up and get something to eat. But you won't get up and you won't get anything to eat. [*Pause.*] You'll look at the wall a while, then you'll say, I'll close my eyes, perhaps have a little sleep, after that I'll feel better, and you'll close them. And when you open them again there'll be no wall any more. [*Pause.*] Infinite emptiness will be all around you, all the resurrected dead of all the ages wouldn't fill it, and there you'll be like a little bit of grit in the middle of the steppe. [*Pause.*] Yes, one day you'll know what it is, you'll be like me, except that you won't have anyone with you, because you won't have had pity on anyone and because there won't be anyone left to have pity on. [*Pause.*]

CLOV: It's not certain. [*Pause.*] And there's one thing you forget.

HAMM: Ah?

CLOV: I can't sit down.

HAMM [*impatiently*]: Well you'll lie down then, what the hell! Or you'll come to a standstill, simply stop and stand still, the way you are now. One day you'll say, I'm tired, I'll stop. What does the attitude matter? [*Pause.*]

CLOV: So you all want me to leave you.

HAMM: Naturally.

CLOV: Then I'll leave you.

HAMM: You can't leave us.

CLOV: Then I won't leave you. [*Pause.*]

HAMM: Why don't you finish us? [*Pause.*] I'll tell you the combination of the cupboard if you promise to finish me.

CLOV: I couldn't finish you.

HAMM: Then you won't finish me. [*Pause.*]

CLOV: I'll leave you, I have things to do.

HAMM: Do you remember when you came here?

CLOV: No. Too small, you told me.

HAMM: Do you remember your father.

CLOV [*wearily*]: Same answer. [*Pause.*] You've asked me these questions millions of times.

HAMM: I love the old questions. [*With fervour.*] Ah the old questions, the old answers, there's nothing like them! [*Pause.*] It was I was a father to you.

CLOV: Yes. [*He looks at Hamm fixedly.*] You were that to me.

HAMM: My house a home for you.

CLOV: Yes. [*He looks about him.*] This was that for me.

HAMM [*proudly*]: But for me, [*gesture towards himself*] no father. But for Hamm, [*gesture towards surroundings*] no home. [*Pause.*]

CLOV: I'll leave you.

HAMM: Did you ever think of one thing?

CLOV: Never.

HAMM: That here we're down in a hole. [*Pause.*] But beyond the hills? Eh? Perhaps it's still green. Eh? [*Pause.*] Flora! Pomona! [*Ecstatically.*] Ceres![8] [*Pause.*] Perhaps you won't need to go very far.

CLOV: I can't go very far. [*Pause.*] I'll leave you.

HAMM: Is my dog ready?

CLOV: He lacks a leg.

HAMM: Is he silky?

CLOV: He's a kind of Pomeranian.

HAMM: Go and get him.

CLOV: He lacks a leg.

HAMM: Go and get him!

[*Exit Clov.*]

We're getting on.

---

8. Flora, Pomona, and Ceres: the Roman goddesses of flowering plants, fruits, and grains.

[*Enter Clov holding by one of its three legs a black toy dog.*]

CLOV: Your dogs are here.

[*He hands the dog to Hamm who feels it, fondles it.*]

HAMM: He's white, isn't he?

CLOV: Nearly.

HAMM: What do you mean, nearly? Is he white or isn't he?

CLOV: He isn't. [*Pause.*]

HAMM: You've forgotten the sex.

CLOV [*vexed*]: But he isn't finished. The sex goes on at the end. [*Pause.*]

HAMM: You haven't put on his ribbon.

CLOV [*angrily*]: But he isn't finished, I tell you! First you finish your dog and then
   you put on his ribbon! [*Pause.*]

HAMM: Can he stand?

CLOV: I don't know.

HAMM: Try.

[*He hands the dog to Clov who places it on the ground.*]

   Well?

CLOV: Wait!

[*He squats down and tries to get the dog to stand on its three legs, fails, lets it go. The
dog falls on its side.*]

HAMM [*impatiently*]: Well?

CLOV: He's standing.

HAMM [*groping for the dog*]: Where? Where is he?

[*Clov holds up the dog in a standing position.*]

CLOV: There.

[*He takes Hamm's hand and guides it towards the dog's head.*]

HAMM [*his hand on the dog's head*]: Is he gazing at me?

CLOV: Yes.

HAMM [*proudly*]: As if he were asking me to take him for a walk?

CLOV: If you like.

HAMM [*as before*]: Or as if he were begging me for a bone.

[*He withdraws his hand.*]

   Leave him like that, standing there imploring me.

[*Clov straightens up. The dog falls on its side.*]

CLOV: I'll leave you.

HAMM: Have you had your visions?

CLOV: Less.

HAMM: Is Mother Pegg's light on?

CLOV: Light! How could anyone's light be on?

HAMM: Extinguished!

CLOV: Naturally it's extinguished. If it's not on it's extinguished.

HAMM: No, I mean Mother Pegg.

CLOV: But naturally she's extinguished! [*Pause.*] What's the matter with you today?

HAMM: I'm taking my course. [*Pause.*] Is she buried?

CLOV: Buried! Who would have buried her?

HAMM: You.

CLOV: Me! Haven't I enough to do without burying people?

HAMM: But you'll bury me.

CLOV: No I won't bury you. [*Pause.*]

HAMM: She was bonny once, like a flower of the field. [*With reminiscent leer.*] And a great one for the men!

CLOV: We too were bonny—once. It's a rare thing not to have been bonny—once. [*Pause.*]

HAMM: Go and get the gaff.[9]

[*Clov goes to door, halts.*]

CLOV: Do this, do that, and I do it. I never refuse. Why?

HAMM: You're not able to.

CLOV: Soon I won't do it any more.

HAMM: You won't be able to any more.

[*Exit Clov.*]

Ah the creatures, the creatures, everything has to be explained to them.

[*Enter Clov with gaff.*]

CLOV: Here's your gaff. Stick it up.

[*He gives the gaff to Hamm who, wielding it like a puntpole, tries to move his chair.*]

HAMM: Did I move?

CLOV: No.

[*Hamm throws down the gaff.*]

HAMM: Go and get the oilcan.

CLOV: What for?

HAMM: To oil the castors.

CLOV: I oiled them yesterday.

HAMM: Yesterday! What does that mean? Yesterday!

CLOV [*violently*]: That means that bloody awful day, long ago, before this bloody awful day. I use the words you taught me. If they don't mean anything any more, teach me others. Or let me be silent. [*Pause.*]

HAMM: I once knew a madman who thought the end of the world had come. He was a painter—and engraver. I had a great fondness for him. I used to go and see him, in the asylum. I'd take him by the hand and drag him to the window. Look! There! All that rising corn! And there! Look! The sails of the herring fleet! All that loveliness! [*Pause.*] He'd snatch away his hand and go back into his corner. Appalled. All he had seen was ashes. [*Pause.*] He alone had been spared. [*Pause.*] Forgotten. [*Pause.*] It appears the case is . . . was not so . . . so unusual.

9. A fishing pole designed for catching large fish.

CLOV: A madman? When was that?

HAMM: Oh way back, way back, you weren't in the land of the living.

CLOV: God be with the days!

[*Pause. Hamm raises his toque.*]

HAMM: I had a great fondness for him.

[*Pause. He puts on his toque again.*]

He was a painter—and engraver.

CLOV: There are so many terrible things.

HAMM: No, no, there are not so many now. [*Pause.*] Clov!

CLOV: Yes.

HAMM: Do you not think this has gone on long enough?

CLOV: Yes! [*Pause.*] What?

HAMM: This . . . this . . . thing.

CLOV: I've always thought so. [*Pause.*] You not?

HAMM [*gloomily*]: Then it's a day like any other day.

CLOV: As long as it lasts. [*Pause.*] All life long the same inanities.

HAMM: I can't leave you.

CLOV: I know. And you can't follow me. [*Pause.*]

HAMM: If you leave me how shall I know?

CLOV [*briskly*]: Well you simply whistle me and if I don't come running it means I've left you. [*Pause.*]

HAMM: You won't come and kiss me goodbye?

CLOV: Oh I shouldn't think so. [*Pause.*]

HAMM: But you might be merely dead in your kitchen.

CLOV: The result would be the same.

HAMM: Yes, but how would I know, if you were merely dead in your kitchen?

CLOV: Well . . . sooner or later I'd start to stink.

HAMM: You stink already. The whole place stinks of corpses.

CLOV: The whole universe.

HAMM [*angrily*]: To hell with the universe. [*Pause.*] Think of something.

CLOV: What?

HAMM: An idea, have an idea. [*Angrily.*] A bright idea!

CLOV: Ah good.

[*He starts pacing to and fro, his eyes fixed on the ground, his hands behind his back. He halts.*]

The pains in my legs! It's unbelievable! Soon I won't be able to think any more.

HAMM: You won't be able to leave me.

[*Clov resumes his pacing.*]

What are you doing?

CLOV: Having an idea.

[*He paces.*]

Ah!

[*He halts.*]

HAMM: What a brain! [*Pause.*] Well?

CLOV: Wait! [*He meditates. Not very convinced.*] Yes . . . [*Pause. More convinced.*] Yes! [*He raises his head.*] I have it! I set the alarm. [*Pause.*]

HAMM: This is perhaps not one of my bright days, but frankly—

CLOV: You whistle me. I don't come. The alarm rings. I'm gone. It doesn't ring. I'm dead. [*Pause.*]

HAMM: Is it working? [*Pause. Impatiently.*] The alarm, is it working?

CLOV: Why wouldn't it be working?

HAMM: Because it's worked too much.

CLOV: But it's hardly worked at all.

HAMM [*angrily*]: Then because it's worked too little!

CLOV: I'll go and see.

[*Exit Clov. Brief ring of alarm off. Enter Clov with alarm-clock. He holds it against Hamm's ear and releases alarm. They listen to it ringing to the end. Pause.*]

Fit to wake the dead! Did you hear it?

HAMM: Vaguely.

CLOV: The end is terrific!

HAMM: I prefer the middle. [*Pause.*] Is it not time for my pain-killer?

CLOV: No! [*He goes to door, turns.*] I'll leave you.

HAMM: It's time for my story. Do you want to listen to my story?

CLOV: No.

HAMM: Ask my father if he wants to listen to my story.

[*Clov goes to bins, raises the lid of Nagg's, stoops, looks into it. Pause. He straightens up.*]

CLOV: He's asleep.

HAMM: Wake him.

[*Clov stoops, wakes Nagg with the alarm. Unintelligible words. Clov straightens up.*]

CLOV: He doesn't want to listen to your story.

HAMM: I'll give him a bon-bon.

[*Clov stoops. As before.*]

CLOV: He wants a sugar-plum.

HAMM: He'll get a sugar-plum.

[*Clov stoops. As before.*]

CLOV: It's a deal.

[*He goes towards door. Nagg's hands appear, gripping the rim. Then the head emerges. Clov reaches door, turns.*]

Do you believe in the life to come?

HAMM: Mine was always that.

[*Exit Clov.*]

Got him that time!

NAGG: I'm listening.

HAMM: Scoundrel! Why did you engender me?

NAGG: I didn't know.

HAMM: What? What didn't you know?

NAGG: That it'd be you. [*Pause.*] You'll give me a sugar-plum?

HAMM: After the audition.

NAGG: You swear?

HAMM: Yes.

NAGG: On what?

HAMM: My honor. [*Pause. They laugh heartily.*]

NAGG: Two.

HAMM: One.

NAGG: One for me and one for—

HAMM: One! Silence! [*Pause.*] Where was I? [*Pause. Gloomily.*] It's finished, we're finished. [*Pause.*] Nearly finished. [*Pause.*] There'll be no more speech. [*Pause.*] Something dripping in my head, ever since the fontanelles.[1] [*Stifled hilarity of Nagg.*] Splash, splash, always on the same spot. [*Pause.*] Perhaps it's a little vein. [*Pause.*] A little artery. [*Pause. More animated.*] Enough of that, it's story time, where was I? [*Pause. Narrative tone.*] The man came crawling towards me, on his belly. Pale, wonderfully pale and thin, he seemed on the point of—[*Pause. Normal tone.*] No, I've done that bit. [*Pause. Narrative tone.*] I calmly filled my pipe—the meerschaum, lit it with . . . let us say a vesta,[2] drew a few puffs. Aah! [*Pause.*] Well, what is it *you* want? [*Pause.*] It was an extra-ordinarily bitter day, I remember, zero by the thermometer. But considering it was Christmas Eve there was nothing . . . extra-ordinary about that. Seasonable weather, for once in a way. [*Pause.*] Well, what ill wind blows you my way? He raised his face to me, black with mingled dirt and tears. [*Pause. Normal tone.*] That should do it.

[*Narrative tone.*]

No no, don't look at me, don't look at me. He dropped his eyes and mumbled something, apologies I presume. [*Pause.*] I'm a busy man, you know, the final touches, before the festivities, you know what it is. [*Pause. Forcibly.*] Come on now, what is the object of this invasion? [*Pause.*] It was a glorious bright day, I remember, fifty by the heliometer, but already the sun was sinking down into the . . . down among the dead.

[*Normal tone.*]

Nicely put, that.

[*Narrative tone.*]

Come on now, come on, present your petition and let me resume my labors.

[*Pause. Normal tone.*]

There's English for you. Ah well . . .

[*Narrative tone.*]

It was then he took the plunge. It's my little one, he said. Tsstss, a little one, that's bad. My little boy, he said, as if the sex mattered. Where did he come from? He named the hole. A good half-day, on horse. What are you insinuating? That the

---

1. Soft gaps between an infant's skull bones.   2. A match.

place is still inhabited? No no, not a soul, except himself and the child—assuming he existed. Good. I enquired about the situation at Kov, beyond the gulf. Not a sinner. Good. And you expect me to believe you have left your little one back there, all alone, and alive into the bargain? Come now! [*Pause.*] It was a howling wild day, I remember, a hundred by the anenometer.[3] The wind was tearing up the dead pines and sweeping them . . . away.

[*Pause. Normal tone.*]

A bit feeble, that.

[*Narrative tone.*]

Come on, man, speak up, what is it you want from me, I have to put up my holly. [*Pause.*]

Well to make it short it finally transpired that what he wanted from me was . . . bread for his brat? Bread? But I have no bread, it doesn't agree with me. Good. Then perhaps a little corn?

[*Pause. Normal tone.*]

That should do it.

[*Narrative tone.*]

Corn, yes, I have corn, it's true, in my granaries. But use your head. I give you some corn, a pound, a pound and a half, you bring it back to your child and you make him—if he's still alive—a nice pot of porridge, [*Nagg reacts*] a nice pot and a half of porridge, full of nourishment. Good. The colors come back into his little cheeks— perhaps. And then? [*Pause.*] I lost patience. [*Violently.*] Use your head, can't you, use your head, you're on earth, there's no cure for that! [*Pause.*] It was an exceedingly dry day, I remember, zero by the hygrometer. Ideal weather, for my lumbago. [*Pause. Violently.*] But what in God's name do you imagine? That the earth will awake in spring? That the rivers and seas will run with fish again? That there's manna in heaven still for imbeciles like you? [*Pause.*] Gradually I cooled down, sufficiently at least to ask him how long he had taken on the way. Three whole days. Good. In what condition he had left the child. Deep in sleep. [*Forcibly.*] But deep in what sleep, deep in what sleep already? [*Pause.*] Well to make it short I finally offered to take him into my service. He had touched a chord. And then I imagined already that I wasn't much longer for this world. [*He laughs. Pause.*] Well? [*Pause.*] Well? Here if you were careful you might die a nice natural death, in peace and comfort. [*Pause.*] Well? [*Pause.*] In the end he asked me would I consent to take in the child as well—if he were still alive. [*Pause.*] It was the moment I was waiting for. [*Pause.*] Would I consent to take in the child . . . [*Pause.*] I can see him still, down on his knees, his hands flat on the ground, glaring at me with his mad eyes, in defiance of my wishes. [*Pause. Normal tone.*] I'll soon have finished with this story. [*Pause.*] Unless I bring in other characters. [*Pause.*] But where would I find them? [*Pause.*] Where would I look for them? [*Pause. He whistles. Enter Clov.*] Let us pray to God.

NAGG: Me sugar-plum!

CLOV: There's a rat in the kitchen!

---

3. An instrument used to measure wind speed.

HAMM: A rat! Are there still rats?

CLOV: In the kitchen there's one.

HAMM: And you haven't exterminated him?

CLOV: Half. You disturbed us.

HAMM: He can't get away?

CLOV: No.

HAMM: You'll finish him later. Let us pray to God.

CLOV: Again!

NAGG: Me sugar-plum!

HAMM: God first! [*Pause.*] Are you right?

CLOV [*resigned*]: Off we go.

HAMM [*to Nagg*]: And you?

NAGG [*clasping his hands, closing his eyes, in a gabble*]: Our Father which art—

HAMM: Silence! In silence! Where are your manners? [*Pause.*] Off we go. [*Attitudes of prayer. Silence. Abandoning his attitude, discouraged.*] Well?

CLOV [*abandoning his attitude*]: What a hope! And you?

HAMM: Sweet damn all! [*To Nagg.*] And you?

NAGG: Wait! [*Pause. Abandoning his attitude.*] Nothing doing!

HAMM: The bastard! He doesn't exist!

CLOV: Not yet.

NAGG: Me sugar-plum!

HAMM: There are no more sugar-plums! [*Pause.*]

NAGG: It's natural. After all I'm your father. It's true if it hadn't been me it would have been someone else. But that's no excuse. [*Pause.*] Turkish Delight, for example, which no longer exists, we all know that, there is nothing in the world I love more. And one day I'll ask you for some, in return for a kindness, and you'll promise it to me. One must live with the times. [*Pause.*] Whom did you call when you were a tiny boy, and were frightened, in the dark? Your mother? No. Me. We let you cry. Then we moved you out of earshot, so that we might sleep in peace. [*Pause.*] I was asleep, as happy as a king, and you woke me up to have me listen to you. It wasn't indispensable, you didn't really need to have me listen to you. Besides I didn't listen to you. [*Pause.*] I hope the day will come when you'll really need to have me listen to you, and need to hear my voice, any voice. [*Pause.*] Yes, I hope I'll live till then, to hear you calling me like when you were a tiny boy, and were frightened, in the dark, and I was your only hope. [*Pause. Nagg knocks on lid of Nell's bin. Pause. He knocks louder. Pause. Louder.*] Nell! [*Pause. Nagg sinks back into his bin, closes the lid behind him. Pause.*]

HAMM: Our revels now are ended.[4]

[*He gropes for the dog.*]

The dog's gone.

CLOV: He's not a real dog, he can't go.

HAMM [*groping*]: He's not there.

CLOV: He's lain down.

HAMM: Give him up to me.

---

4. Quoting the exiled magician Prospero in Shakespeare's *The Tempest* (4.1): "Our revels are now ended. These our actors / As I foretold you, were all spirits, and / Are melted into air, into thin air."

[*Clov picks up the dog and gives it to Hamm. Hamm holds it in his arms. Pause. Hamm throws away the dog.*]

Dirty brute!

[*Clov begins to pick up the objects lying on the ground.*]

What are you doing?

CLOV: Putting things in order. [*He straightens up. Fervently.*] I'm going to clear everything away! [*He starts picking up again.*]

HAMM: Order!

CLOV [*straightening up*]: I love order. It's my dream. A world where all would be silent and still and each thing in its last place, under the last dust. [*He starts picking up again.*]

HAMM [*exasperated*]: What in God's name do you think you are doing?

CLOV [*straightening up*]: I'm doing my best to create a little order.

HAMM: Drop it!

[*Clov drops the objects he has picked up.*]

CLOV: After all, there or elsewhere. [*He goes towards door.*]

HAMM [*irritably*]: What's wrong with your feet?

CLOV: My feet?

HAMM: Tramp! Tramp!

CLOV: I must have put on my boots.

HAMM: Your slippers were hurting you? [*Pause.*]

CLOV: I'll leave you.

HAMM: No!

CLOV: What is there to keep me here?

HAMM: The dialogue. [*Pause.*] I've got on with my story. [*Pause.*] I've got on with it well. [*Pause. Irritably.*] Ask me where I've got to.

CLOV: Oh, by the way, your story?

HAMM [*surprised*]: What story?

CLOV: The one you've been telling yourself all your days.

HAMM: Ah you mean my chronicle?

CLOV: That's the one. [*Pause.*]

HAMM [*angrily*]: Keep going, can't you, keep going!

CLOV: You've got on with it, I hope.

HAMM [*modestly*]: Oh not very far, not very far. [*He sighs.*] There are days like that, one isn't inspired. [*Pause.*] Nothing you can do about it, just wait for it to come. [*Pause.*] No forcing, no forcing, it's fatal. [*Pause.*] I've got on with it a little all the same. [*Pause.*] Technique, you know. [*Pause. Irritably.*] I say I've got on with it a little all the same.

CLOV [*admiringly*]: Well I never! In spite of everything you were able to get on with it!

HAMM [*modestly*]: Oh not very far, you know, not very far, but nevertheless, better than nothing.

CLOV: Better than nothing! Is it possible?

HAMM: I'll tell you how it goes. He comes crawling on his belly—

CLOV: Who?

HAMM: What?

CLOV: Who do you mean, he?

HAMM: Who do I mean! Yet another.

CLOV: Ah him! I wasn't sure.

HAMM: Crawling on his belly, whining for bread for his brat. He's offered a job as gardener. Before—

[Clov bursts out laughing.]

What is there so funny about that?

CLOV: A job as gardener!

HAMM: Is that what tickles you?

CLOV: It must be that.

HAMM: It wouldn't be the bread?

CLOV: Or the brat. [Pause.]

HAMM: The whole thing is comical, I grant you that. What about having a good guffaw the two of us together?

CLOV [after reflection]: I couldn't guffaw again today.

HAMM [after reflection]: Nor I. [Pause.] I continue then. Before accepting with gratitude he asks if he may have his little boy with him.

CLOV: What age?

HAMM: Oh tiny.

CLOV: He would have climbed the trees.

HAMM: All the little odd jobs.

CLOV: And then he would have grown up.

HAMM: Very likely. [Pause.]

CLOV: Keep going, can't you, keep going!

HAMM: That's all. I stopped there. [Pause.]

CLOV: Do you see how it goes on.

HAMM: More or less.

CLOV: Will it not soon be the end?

HAMM: I'm afraid it will.

CLOV: Pah! You'll make up another.

HAMM: I don't know. [Pause.] I feel rather drained. [Pause.] The prolonged creative effort. [Pause.] If I could drag myself down to the sea! I'd make a pillow of sand for my head and the tide would come.

CLOV: There's no more tide. [Pause.]

HAMM: Go and see is she dead.

[Clov goes to bins, raises the lid of Nell's, stoops, looks into it. Pause.]

CLOV: Looks like it.

[He closes the lid, straightens up. Hamm raises his toque. Pause. He puts it on again.]

HAMM [with his hand to his toque]: And Nagg?

[Clov raises lid of Nagg's bin, stoops, looks into it. Pause.]

CLOV: Doesn't look like it. [He closes the lid, straightens up.]

HAMM [letting go his toque]: What's he doing?

[Clov raises lid of Nagg's bin, stoops, looks into it. Pause.]

CLOV: He's crying. [*He closes lid, straightens up.*]
HAMM: Then he's living. [*Pause.*] Did you ever have an instant of happiness?
CLOV: Not to my knowledge. [*Pause.*]
HAMM: Bring me under the window.

[*Clov goes towards chair.*]

I want to feel the light on my face.

[*Clov pushes chair.*]

Do you remember, in the beginning, when you took me for a turn? You used to hold the chair too high. At every step you nearly tipped me out. [*With senile quaver.*] Ah great fun, we had, the two of us, great fun. [*Gloomily.*] And then we got into the way of it.

[*Clov stops the chair under window right.*]

There already? [*Pause. He tilts back his head.*] Is it light?
CLOV: It isn't dark.
HAMM [*angrily*]: I'm asking you is it light.
CLOV: Yes. [*Pause.*]
HAMM: The curtain isn't closed?
CLOV: No.
HAMM: What window is it?
CLOV: The earth.
HAMM: I knew it! [*Angrily.*] But there's no light there! The other!

[*Clov pushes chair towards window left.*]

The earth!

[*Clov stops the chair under window left. Hamm tilts back his head.*]

That's what I call light! [*Pause.*] Feels like a ray of sunshine. [*Pause.*] No?
CLOV: No.
HAMM: It isn't a ray of sunshine I feel on my face?
CLOV: No. [*Pause.*]
HAMM: Am I very white? [*Pause. Angrily.*] I'm asking you am I very white!
CLOV: Not more so than usual. [*Pause.*]
HAMM: Open the window.
CLOV: What for?
HAMM: I want to hear the sea.
CLOV: You wouldn't hear it.
HAMM: Even if you opened the window?
CLOV: No.
HAMM: Then it's not worth while opening it?
CLOV: No.
HAMM [*violently*]: Then open it!

[*Clov gets up on the ladder, opens the window. Pause.*]

Have you opened it?
CLOV: Yes. [*Pause.*]
HAMM: You swear you've opened it?
CLOV: Yes. [*Pause.*]

HAMM: Well . . . ! [*Pause.*] It must be very calm. [*Pause. Violently.*] I'm asking you is it very calm!

CLOV: Yes.

HAMM: It's because there are no more navigators. [*Pause.*] You haven't much conversation all of a sudden. Do you not feel well?

CLOV: I'm cold.

HAMM: What month are we? [*Pause.*] Close the window, we're going back.

[*Clov closes the window, gets down, pushes the chair back to its place, remains standing behind it, head bowed.*]

Don't stay there, you give me the shivers!

[*Clov returns to his place beside the chair.*]

Father! [*Pause. Louder.*] Father! [*Pause.*] Go and see did he hear me.

[*Clov goes to Nagg's bin, raises the lid, stoops. Unintelligible words. Clov straightens up.*]

CLOV: Yes.

HAMM: Both times?

[*Clov stoops. As before.*]

CLOV: Once only.

HAMM: The first time or the second?

[*Clov stoops. As before.*]

CLOV: He doesn't know.

HAMM: It must have been the second.

CLOV: We'll never know.

[*He closes lid.*]

HAMM: Is he still crying?

CLOV: No.

HAMM: The dead go fast. [*Pause.*] What's he doing?

CLOV: Sucking his biscuit.

HAMM: Life goes on.

[*Clov returns to his place beside the chair.*]

Give me a rug, I'm freezing.

CLOV: There are no more rugs. [*Pause.*]

HAMM: Kiss me. [*Pause.*] Will you not kiss me?

CLOV: No.

HAMM: On the forehead.

CLOV: I won't kiss you anywhere. [*Pause.*]

HAMM [*holding out his hand*]: Give me your hand at least. [*Pause.*] Will you not give me your hand?

CLOV: I won't touch you. [*Pause.*]

HAMM: Give me the dog.

[*Clov looks round for the dog.*]

No!

CLOV: Do you not want your dog?

HAMM: No.
CLOV: Then I'll leave you.
HAMM [*head bowed, absently*]: That's right.

[*Clov goes to door, turns.*]

CLOV: If I don't kill that rat he'll die.
HAMM [*as before*]: That's right.

[*Exit Clov. Pause.*]

Me to play.

[*He takes out his handkerchief, unfolds it, holds it spread out before him.*]

We're getting on. [*Pause.*] You weep, and weep, for nothing, so as not to laugh, and little by little . . . you begin to grieve.

[*He folds the handkerchief, puts it back in his pocket, raises his head.*]

All those I might have helped. [*Pause.*] Helped! [*Pause.*] Saved. [*Pause.*] Saved! [*Pause.*] The place was crawling with them! [*Pause. Violently.*] Use your head, can't you, use your head, you're on earth, there's no cure for that! [*Pause.*] Get out of here and love one another! Lick your neighbor as yourself! [*Pause. Calmer.*] When it wasn't bread they wanted it was crumpets. [*Pause. Violently.*] Out of my sight and back to your petting parties! [*Pause.*] All that, all that! [*Pause.*] Not even a real dog! [*Calmer.*] The end is in the beginning and yet you go on. [*Pause.*] Perhaps I could go on with my story, end it and begin another. [*Pause.*] Perhaps I could throw myself out on the floor.

[*He pushes himself painfully off his seat, falls back again.*]

Dig my nails into the cracks and drag myself forward with my fingers. [*Pause.*] It will be the end and there I'll be, wondering what can have brought it on and wondering what can have . . . [*he hesitates*] . . . why it was so long coming. [*Pause.*] There I'll be, in the old shelter, alone against the silence and . . . [*he hesitates*] . . . the stillness. If I can hold my peace, and sit quiet, it will be all over with sound, and motion, all over and done with. [*Pause.*] I'll have called my father and I'll have called my . . . [*he hesitates*] . . . my son. And even twice, or three times, in case they shouldn't have heard me, the first time, or the second. [*Pause.*] I'll say to myself, He'll come back. [*Pause.*] And then? [*Pause.*] And then? [*Pause.*] He couldn't, he has gone too far. [*Pause.*] And then? [*Pause. Very agitated.*] All kinds of fantasies! That I'm being watched! A rat! Steps! Breath held and then . . . [*He breathes out.*] Then babble, babble, words, like the solitary child who turns himself into children, two, three, so as to be together, and whisper together, in the dark. [*Pause.*] Moment upon moment, pattering down, like the millet grains of . . . [*he hesitates*] . . . that old Greek, and all life long you wait for that to mount up to a life.[5] [*Pause. He opens his mouth to continue, renounces.*] Ah let's get it over!

---

5. Hamm is referring to Zeno of Elea (5th century B.C.), who is known for his philosophical paradoxes. One of them is based on the sound a bushel of millet makes when it falls on the floor: since this sound is caused by the grains, each grain must make a sound when striking the ground. This sound, however, can't be heard, so the apparent sound is really an accumulation of silences.

[*He whistles. Enter Clov with alarm-clock. He halts beside the chair.*]

What? Neither gone nor dead?

CLOV: In spirit only.

HAMM: Which?

CLOV: Both.

HAMM: Gone from me you'd be dead.

CLOV: And vice versa.

HAMM: Outside of here it's death! [*Pause.*] And the rat?

CLOV: He's got away.

HAMM: He can't go far. [*Pause. Anxious.*] Eh?

CLOV: He doesn't need to go far. [*Pause.*]

HAMM: Is it not time for my pain-killer?

CLOV: Yes.

HAMM: Ah! At last! Give it to me! Quick! [*Pause.*]

CLOV: There's no more pain-killer. [*Pause.*]

HAMM [*appalled*]: Good . . . ! [*Pause.*] No more pain-killer!

CLOV: No more pain-killer. You'll never get any more pain-killer. [*Pause.*]

HAMM: But the little round box. It was full!

CLOV: Yes. But now it's empty.

[*Pause. Clov starts to move about the room. He is looking for a place to put down the alarm-clock.*]

HAMM [*soft*]: What'll I do? [*Pause. In a scream.*] What'll I do?

[*Clov sees the picture, takes it down, stands it on the floor with its face to the wall, hangs up the alarm-clock in its place.*]

What are you doing?

CLOV: Winding up.

HAMM: Look at the earth.

CLOV: Again!

HAMM: Since it's calling to you.

CLOV: Is your throat sore? [*Pause.*] Would you like a lozenge? [*Pause.*] No. [*Pause.*] Pity.

[*Clov goes, humming, towards window right, halts before it, looks up at it.*]

HAMM: Don't sing.

CLOV [*turning towards Hamm*]: One hasn't the right to sing any more?

HAMM: No.

CLOV: Then how can it end?

HAMM: You want it to end?

CLOV: I want to sing.

HAMM: I can't prevent you.

[*Pause. Clov turns towards window right.*]

CLOV: What did I do with that steps? [*He looks around for ladder.*] You didn't see that steps? [*He sees it.*] Ah, about time. [*He goes towards window left.*] Sometimes I wonder if I'm in my right mind. Then it passes over and I'm as lucid as before. [*He gets up on ladder, looks out of window.*] Christ, she's under water! [*He looks.*] How can that be? [*He pokes forward his head, his hand above his eyes.*] It hasn't rained. [*He *wipes the pane, looks. Pause.*] Ah what a fool I am! I'm on the wrong side! [*He gets down, takes a few steps towards window right.*] Under water! [*He goes back for ladder.*] What a fool I am! [*He carries ladder towards window right.*] Sometimes I wonder if I'm in my right senses. Then it passes off and I'm as intelligent as ever.

[*He sets down ladder under window right, gets up on it, looks out of window. He turns towards Hamm.*]

Any particular sector you fancy? Or merely the whole thing?

HAMM: Whole thing.

CLOV: The general effect? Just a moment. [*He looks out of window. Pause.*]

HAMM: Clov.

CLOV [*absorbed*]: Mmm.

HAMM: Do you know what it is?

CLOV [*as before*]: Mmm.

HAMM: I was never there. [*Pause.*] Clov!

CLOV [*turning towards Hamm, exasperated*]: What is it?

HAMM: I was never there.

CLOV: Lucky for you. [*He looks out of window.*]

HAMM: Absent, always. It all happened without me. I don't know what's happened. [*Pause.*] Do you know what's happened? [*Pause.*] Clov!

CLOV [*turning towards Hamm, exasperated*]: Do you want me to look at this muck-heap, yes or no?

HAMM: Answer me first.

CLOV: What?

HAMM: Do you know what's happened?

CLOV: When? Where?

HAMM [*violently*]: When! What's happened? Use your head, can't you! What has happened?

CLOV: What for Christ's sake does it matter? [*He looks out of window.*]

HAMM: I don't know. [*Pause. Clov turns towards Hamm.*]

CLOV [*harshly*]: When old Mother Pegg asked you for oil for her lamp and you told her to get out to hell, you knew what was happening then, no? [*Pause.*] You know what she died of, Mother Pegg? Of darkness.

HAMM [*feebly*]: I hadn't any.

CLOV [*as before*]: Yes, you had. [*Pause.*]

HAMM: Have you the glass?

CLOV: No, it's clear enough as it is.

HAMM: Go and get it.

[*Pause. Clov casts up his eyes, brandishes his fists. He loses balance, clutches on to the ladder. He starts to get down, halts.*]

CLOV: There's one thing I'll never understand. [*He gets down.*] Why I always obey you. Can you explain that to me?

HAMM: No . . . . Perhaps it's compassion. [*Pause.*] A kind of great compassion. [*Pause.*] Oh you won't find it easy, you won't find it easy.

[*Pause. Clov begins to move about the room in search of the telescope.*]

CLOV: I'm tired of our goings on, very tired. [*He searches.*] You're not sitting on it?

[*He moves the chair, looks at the place where it stood, resumes his search.*]

HAMM [*anguished*]: Don't leave me there! [*Angrily Clov restores the chair to its place.*] Am I right in the center?

CLOV: You'd need a microscope to find this—[*He sees the telescope.*] Ah, about time.

[*He picks up the telescope, gets up on the ladder, turns the telescope on the without.*]

HAMM: Give me the dog.

CLOV [*looking*]: Quiet!

HAMM [*angrily*]: Give me the dog!

[*Clov drops the telescope, clasps his hands to his head. Pause. He gets down precipitately, looks for the dog, sees it, picks it up, hastens towards Hamm and strikes him violently on the head with the dog.*]

CLOV: There's your dog for you!

[*The dog falls to the ground. Pause.*]

HAMM: He hit me!

CLOV: You drive me mad, I'm mad!

HAMM: If you must hit me, hit me with the axe. [*Pause.*] Or with the gaff, hit me with the gaff. Not with the dog. With the gaff. Or with the axe.

[*Clov picks up the dog and gives it to Hamm who takes it in his arms.*]

CLOV [*imploringly*]: Let's stop playing!

HAMM: Never! [*Pause.*] Put me in my coffin.

CLOV: There are no more coffins.

HAMM: Then let it end!

[*Clov goes towards ladder.*]

With a bang!

[*Clov gets up on ladder, gets down again, looks for telescope, sees it, picks it up, gets up ladder, raises telescope.*]

Of darkness! And me? Did anyone ever have pity on me?

CLOV [*lowering the telescope, turning towards Hamm*]: What? [*Pause.*] Is it me you're referring to?

HAMM [*angrily*]: An aside, ape! Did you never hear an aside before? [*Pause.*] I'm warming up for my last soliloquy.

CLOV: I warn you. I'm going to look at this filth since it's an order. But it's the last time. [*He turns the telescope on the without.*] Let's see. [*He moves the telescope.*] Nothing . . . nothing . . . good . . . good . . . nothing . . . goo—[*He starts, lowers the telescope, examines it, turns it again on the without. Pause.*] Bad luck to it!

HAMM: More complications!

[*Clov gets down.*]

Not an underplot, I trust.

[*Clov moves ladder nearer window, gets up on it, turns telescope on the without.*]

CLOV [*dismayed*]: Looks like a small boy!
HAMM [*sarcastic*]: A small . . . boy!
CLOV: I'll go and see.

[*He gets down, drops the telescope, goes towards door, turns.*]

I'll take the gaff.

[*He looks for the gaff, sees it, picks it up, hastens towards door.*]

HAMM: No!

[*Clov halts.*]

CLOV: No? A potential procreator?
HAMM: If he exists he'll die there or he'll come here. And if he doesn't . . . [*Pause.*]
CLOV: You don't believe me? You think I'm inventing? [*Pause.*]
HAMM: It's the end, Clov, we've come to the end. I don't need you any more. [*Pause.*]
CLOV: Lucky for you. [*He goes towards door.*]
HAMM: Leave me the gaff.

[*Clov gives him the gaff, goes towards door, halts, looks at alarm-clock, takes it down, looks round for a better place to put it, goes to bins, puts it on lid of Nagg's bin. Pause.*]

CLOV: I'll leave you. [*He goes towards door.*]
HAMM: Before you go . . .

[*Clov halts near door.*]

. . . say something.
CLOV: There is nothing to say.
HAMM: A few words . . . to ponder . . . in my heart.
CLOV: Your heart!
HAMM: Yes. [*Pause. Forcibly.*] Yes! [*Pause.*] With the rest, in the end, the shadows, the murmurs, all the trouble, to end up with. [*Pause.*] Clov . . . . He never spoke to me. Then, in the end, before he went, without my having asked him, he spoke to me. He said . . .
CLOV [*despairingly*]: Ah . . . !
HAMM: Something . . . from your heart.
CLOV: My heart!
HAMM: A few words . . . from your heart. [*Pause.*]
CLOV [*fixed gaze, tonelessly, towards auditorium*]: They said to me, That's love, yes, yes, not a doubt, now you see how—
HAMM: Articulate!
CLOV [*as before*]: How easy it is. They said to me, That's friendship, yes, yes, no question, you've found it. They said to me, Here's the place, stop, raise your head and look at all that beauty. That order! They said to me, Come now, you're not a brute

beast, think upon these things and you'll see how all becomes clear. And simple! They said to me, What skilled attention they get, all these dying of their wounds.

HAMM: Enough!

CLOV [*as before*]: I say to myself—sometimes, Clov, you must learn to suffer better than that if you want them to weary of punishing you—one day. I say to myself— sometimes, Clov, you must be there better than that if you want them to let you go—one day. But I feel too old, and too far, to form new habits. Good, it'll never end, I'll never go. [*Pause.*] Then one day, suddenly, it ends, it changes, I don't understand, it dies, or it's me, I don't understand, that either. I ask the words that remain—sleeping, waking, morning, evening. They have nothing to say. [*Pause.*] I open the door of the cell and go. I am so bowed I only see my feet, if I open my eyes, and between my legs a little trail of black dust. I say to myself that the earth is extinguished, though I never saw it lit. [*Pause.*] It's easy going. [*Pause.*] When I fall I'll weep for happiness. [*Pause. He goes towards door.*]

HAMM: Clov!

[*Clov halts, without turning.*]

Nothing.

[*Clov moves on.*]

Clov!

[*Clov halts, without turning.*]

CLOV: This is what we call making an exit.

HAMM: I'm obliged to you, Clov. For your services.

CLOV [*turning, sharply*]: Ah pardon, it's I am obliged to you.

HAMM: It's we are obliged to each other.

[*Pause. Clov goes towards door.*]

One thing more.

[*Clov halts.*]

A last favor.

[*Exit Clov.*]

Cover me with the sheet. [*Long pause.*] No? Good. [*Pause.*] Me to play. [*Pause. Wearily.*] Old endgame lost of old, play and lose and have done with losing. [*Pause. More animated.*] Let me see. [*Pause.*] Ah yes!

[*He tries to move the chair, using the gaff as before. Enter Clov, dressed for the road. Panama hat, tweed coat, raincoat over his arm, umbrella, bag. He halts by the door and stands there, impassive and motionless, his eyes fixed on Hamm, till the end. Hamm gives up.*]

Good. [*Pause.*] Discard. [*He throws away the gaff, makes to throw away the dog, thinks better of it.*] Take it easy. [*Pause.*] And now? [*Pause.*] Raise hat. [*He raises his toque.*] Peace to our . . . arses. [*Pause.*] And put on again. [*He puts on his toque.*] Deuce.

[*Pause. He takes off his glasses.*] Wipe. [*He takes out his handkerchief and, without un-folding it, wipes his glasses.*] And put on again. [*He puts on his glasses, puts back the handkerchief in his pocket.*] We're coming. A few more squirms like that and I'll call. [*Pause.*] A little poetry. [*Pause.*] You prayed—[*Pause. He corrects himself.*] You CRIED for night; it comes—[*Pause. He corrects himself.*] It FALLS: now cry in darkness. [*He repeats, chanting.*] You cried for night; it falls: now cry in darkness. [*Pause.*] Nicely put, that. [*Pause.*] And now? [*Pause.*] Moments for nothing, now as always, time was never and time is over, reckoning closed and story ended. [*Pause. Narrative tone.*] If he could have his child with him. . . . [*Pause.*] It was the moment I was waiting for. [*Pause.*] You don't want to abandon him? You want him to bloom while you are withering? Be there to solace your last million last moments? [*Pause.*] He doesn't realize, all he knows is hunger, and cold, and death to crown it all. But you! You ought to know what the earth is like, nowadays. Oh I put him before his responsibilities! [*Pause. Normal tone.*] Well, there we are, there I am, that's enough. [*He raises the whistle to his lips, hesitates, drops it. Pause.*] Yes, truly! [*He whistles. Pause. Louder. Pause.*] Good. [*Pause.*] Father! [*Pause. Louder.*] Father! [*Pause.*] Good. [*Pause.*] We're coming. [*Pause.*] And to end up with? [*Pause.*] Discard. [*He throws away the dog. He tears the whistle from his neck.*] With my compliments.

[*He throws whistle towards auditorium. Pause. He sniffs. Soft.*]

Clov!

[*Long pause.*]

No? Good.

[*He takes out the handkerchief.*]

Since that's the way we're playing it . . .

[*He unfolds handkerchief.*]

. . . let's play it that way . . .

[*He unfolds.*]

. . . and speak no more about it . . .

[*He finishes unfolding.*]

. . . speak no more.

[*He holds handkerchief spread out before him.*]

Old stancher!

[*Pause.*]

You . . . remain.

[*Pause. He covers his face with handkerchief, lowers his arms to armrests, remains mo-tionless.*]

[*Brief tableau.*]

Curtain

POSTWAR POETS: ENGLISH VOICES

❖

W. H. Auden
1907–1973

Wystan Hugh Auden's fantastically wrinkled face is a familiar icon from photographs taken in his later years. Often depicting Auden posing with his ever-present cigarette against a cityscape or airport, the photographs reveal part of Auden's continuing allure, which is that he was a witness, in his writing and in his person, to the changing scene of life and letters in the middle decades of the twentieth century. Auden came to embody a British literary Golden Age that lived on after the conditions that had brought it into being had changed utterly. His imperturbable face, looking much older than it was, had a sagelike quality of wisdom and the measurement of time passing: a map of modern experience.

Born in York, England, Auden had a pampered childhood, and was too young to see service in World War I. He was of the postwar generation, a group of gifted poets and writers who sought to replace the terrible losses of the war, its literary as well as its human casualties. Auden attended Christ Church College, Oxford, where his precocious literary career began in 1928 with the private publication of his *Poems*, thirty copies of which were put together by his friend and fellow writer Stephen Spender at Oxford. Auden joined a number of his friends and peers in heading to Berlin; his friend Christopher Isherwood's *I Am a Camera* (later the basis for the musical *Cabaret*) documented the phenomenon of these expatriate British writers spending their youthful careers in a decadent and exciting Berlin. Like many of the rest— though some died fighting fascism in Spain—Auden returned to England; he became a teacher in Scotland and England while writing feverishly. The cultural ferment of the thirties led Auden in many directions: chiefly, he wrote poetry, but he also became a noted literary critic, and he collaborated with Isherwood and others on plays and screenplays.

Auden's literary and political wanderlust took him to Iceland in 1936, where he wrote *Letters from Iceland* with Louis MacNeice; to Spain, which resulted in much poetry and occasional writing; to China, Japan, and the United States, culminating in the book *On the Frontier*. In 1939 he took an epochal step: he settled in the United States, where he became a citizen in 1946. In this he was a reverse T. S. Eliot—Eliot was an American who became a British citizen and is usually included as a premier writer of British, not American, literature. Auden was an American citizen who is always included in British anthologies, and rarely, if ever, in American collections. Part of Auden's desire to live in America had to do with his need to escape a stifling set of expectations for him that obtained in England—social, literary, and even personal expectations. In 1935, he had married Thomas Mann's daughter Erika, largely to protect her from political persecution in Germany, since Auden was a homosexual and lived for most of his adult life with the poet Chester Kallman, whom he met in 1939.

It was during Auden's teaching and fellowship years in the United States that he began to produce the large oeuvre of his poetry and his criticism. He taught and lectured at many colleges and universities, and read widely, taking a particular interest in the existentialist theology of Søren Kierkegaard. Increasingly impatient with Marxist materialism, Auden found a renewed commitment to Christianity in his later decades. During these years he published such notable milestones as his *Collected Shorter Poems*, *The Age of Anxiety*, and the critical work *The Enchafèd Flood*. In 1958 his definitive *Selected Poetry* was published, followed in 1962 by his magisterial work of criticism, *The Dyer's Hand*. His peripatetic and sometimes difficult teaching life led him to accept an offer from Oxford in 1956, to spend summers in Italy and in Austria, and to make a final move to Oxford and Christ Church College in 1972. However, he died shortly thereafter in 1973, in Austria, where he shared a summer house with Kallman.

The title of one of Auden's major long poems, *The Age of Anxiety*, summons up a reigning motif of Auden's poetic writing. Auden's poetry is edgy, tense, worried, psychoanalytic and yet despondent of the powers of psychoanalysis to allay anxiety. Anxiety is in some ways Auden's muse. This arises from the seriousness with which Auden had gauged the world political situation. Having witnessed the depression, the rise of Nazism, totalitarianism, World War II, the Holocaust, the atomic bomb, and the Cold War, Auden's political realism is tinged inevitably with disillusionment. Modern history is one primary source for Auden's poetry; in poems like *Spain 1937* and *September 1, 1939*, he makes no retreat to purely aesthetic subject matter, or to the past, or to pure experimentation. Auden's is a poetry of waiting rooms, radio broadcasts, armed battalions, and of snatched pleasures treasured all the more for their fleeting magic.

Paradoxically, Auden's moral and political engagements coexist with an anarchic streak, a wry wit, and a love of leisure and play. Auden developed one of the most seductively varied voices in modern poetry, creating an endlessly inventive style that draws at will on Latin elegy, Anglo-Saxon alliterative verse forms, Norse runes and "kennings," technical scientific discourse, and the meters and language of British music hall songs and of American blues singers. All these elements can be present in a single stanza, to sometimes dizzying effect; in other poems, these radically different materials are blended and modulated into a deceptively plain style of great power.

A topic of special concern for Auden was the survival of literary language. How would poetry make claims for its relevance, given that it was now surrounded by so many other voices, from those of mass culture to the exigent rhetoric of war? Auden often compared himself poetically to William Butler Yeats, as another political poet in a time when poetry was seen as largely irrelevant or even antithetical to politics.

Auden's poetry remains a profoundly lyric poetry: that is, it celebrates the singular human voice that sings its lines. It is not surprising that he wrote opera librettos, notably *The Rake's Progress*, which he wrote with Chester Kallman for Igor Stravinsky. Auden was an intellectual inheritor of Freud and Marx—he knew the ways that the self could remain unknown to itself, and the ways that history could relentlessly rush on oblivious of the human lives swept up in its current. Still, the human voice of poetry goes on, even in the age of anxiety, framing its lyric songs. In the late phase of his poetry, Auden had despaired of systems, and returned even more to the meticulous versification he was so well versed in. His poems become almost defiant vehicles of traditional rhyme and meter, lodged in the modern, everyday world, where "in the deserts of the heart," Auden would "let the healing fountain start."

Musée des Beaux Arts[1]

About suffering they were never wrong,
The Old Masters: how well they understood
Its human position; how it takes place
While someone else is eating or opening a window or just walking dully along;
5   How, when the aged are reverently, passionately waiting
For the miraculous birth, there always must be
Children who did not specially want it to happen, skating
On a pond at the edge of the wood:
They never forgot

---

1. The Musées Royaux des Beaux-Arts in Brussels contain a collection of paintings by the Flemish painter Pieter Brueghel (1525–1569) that includes *The Fall of Icarus*; Brueghel is famous for his acute observation of ordinary life. A figure from Greek mythology, Icarus had wings of wax and feathers but flew too close to the sun, which melted the wax and caused him to fall into the sea.

10   That even the dreadful martyrdom must run its course
       Anyhow in a corner, some untidy spot
       Where the dogs go on with their doggy life and the torturer's horse
       Scratches its innocent behind on a tree.

       In Brueghel's *Icarus*, for instance: how everything turns away
15   Quite leisurely from the disaster; the ploughman may
       Have heard the splash, the forsaken cry,
       But for him it was not an important failure; the sun shone
       As it had to on the white legs disappearing into the green
       Water; and the expensive delicate ship that must have seen
20   Something amazing, a boy falling out of the sky,
       Had somewhere to get to and sailed calmly on.

1938   1940

In Memory of W. B. Yeats
(d. January 1939)

1

       He disappeared in the dead of winter:
       The brooks were frozen, the air-ports almost deserted,
       And snow disfigured the public statues;
       The mercury sank in the mouth of the dying day.
5   O all the instruments agree
       The day of his death was a dark cold day.

       Far from his illness
       The wolves ran on through the evergreen forests,
       The peasant river was untempted by the fashionable quays;
10   By mourning tongues
       The death of the poet was kept from his poems.

       But for him it was his last afternoon as himself,
       An afternoon of nurses and rumours;
       The provinces of his body revolted,
15   The squares of his mind were empty,
       Silence invaded the suburbs,
       The current of his feeling failed: he became his admirers.

       Now he is scattered among a hundred cities
       And wholly given over to unfamiliar affections;
20   To find his happiness in another kind of wood
       And be punished under a foreign code of conscience.
       The words of a dead man
       Are modified in the guts of the living.

       But in the importance and noise of to-morrow
25   When the brokers are roaring like beasts on the floor of the Bourse,[1]
       And the poor have the sufferings to which they are fairly accustomed,
       And each in the cell of himself is almost convinced of his freedom;

1. Stock exchange.

A few thousand will think of this day
As one thinks of a day when one did something slightly unusual.
30   O all the instruments agree
The day of his death was a dark cold day.

2

You were silly like us: your gift survived it all;
The parish of rich women, physical decay,
Yourself; mad Ireland hurt you into poetry.
35   Now Ireland has her madness and her weather still,
For poetry makes nothing happen: it survives
In the valley of its saying where executives
Would never want to tamper; it flows south
From ranches of isolation and the busy griefs,
40   Raw towns that we believe and die in; it survives,
A way of happening, a mouth.

3

Earth, receive an honoured guest;
William Yeats is laid to rest:
Let the Irish vessel lie
45   Emptied of its poetry.

Time that is intolerant
Of the brave and innocent,
And indifferent in a week
To a beautiful physique,

50   Worships language and forgives
Everyone by whom it lives;
Pardons cowardice, conceit,
Lays its honours at their feet.

Time that with this strange excuse
55   Pardoned Kipling and his views,
And will pardon Paul Claudel,[2]
Pardons him for writing well.

In the nightmare of the dark
All the dogs of Europe bark,
60   And the living nations wait,
Each sequestered in its hate;

Intellectual disgrace
Stares from every human face,
And the seas of pity lie
65   Locked and frozen in each eye.

Follow, poet, follow right
To the bottom of the night,

2. Rudyard Kipling (1865–1936), short-story writer, poet, and novelist remembered for his celebration of British imperialism; Paul Claudel (1868–1955), French poet and diplomat noted for his conservative views.

With your unconstraining voice
Still persuade us to rejoice;

70   With the farming of a verse
Make a vineyard of the curse,
Sing of human unsuccess
In a rapture of distress;

In the deserts of the heart
75   Let the healing fountain start,
In the prison of his days
Teach the free man how to praise.

February 1939   1940

Spain 1937[1]

Yesterday all the past. The language of size
Spreading to China along the trade-routes; the diffusion
         Of the counting-frame and the cromlech;[2]
Yesterday the shadow-reckoning in the sunny climates.
5   Yesterday the assessment of insurance by cards,
The divination of water; yesterday the invention
         Of cart-wheels and clocks, the taming of
Horses; yesterday the bustling world of the navigators.
Yesterday the abolition of fairies and giants;
10   The fortress like a motionless eagle eyeing the valley,
         The chapel built in the forest;
Yesterday the carving of angels and of frightening gargoyles.

The trial of heretics among the columns of stone;
Yesterday the theological feuds in the taverns
15   And the miraculous cure at the fountain;
Yesterday the Sabbath of Witches. But today the struggle.

Yesterday the installation of dynamos and turbines;
The construction of railways in the colonial desert;
         Yesterday the classic lecture
20   On the origin of Mankind. But today the struggle.

Yesterday the belief in the absolute value of Greek;
The fall of the curtain upon the death of a hero;
         Yesterday the prayer to the sunset,
And the adoration of madmen. But today the struggle.

25   As the poet whispers, startled among the pines
Or, where the loose waterfall sings, compact, or upright
         On the crag by the leaning tower:
"O my vision. O send me the luck of the sailor."

---

1. Auden visited Spain between January and March 1937, when the civil war between the Spanish government and military-backed Fascist insurgents was at its height. Many foreigners (the so-called "International Brigade") went to Spain at this time to aid the republican forces.
2. Prehistoric stone circle.

And the investigator peers through his instruments
30   At the inhuman provinces, the virile bacillus
                    Or enormous Jupiter finished:
"But the lives of my friends. I inquire, I inquire."
And the poor in their fireless lodgings dropping the sheets
Of the evening paper: "Our day is our loss. O show us
35   History the operator, the
Organiser, Time the refreshing river."

And the nations combine each cry, invoking the life
That shapes the individual belly and orders
                    The private nocturnal terror:
40   "Did you not found once the city state of the sponge,

"Raise the vast military empires of the shark
And the tiger, establish the robin's plucky canton?
                    Intervene. O descend as a dove or
A furious papa or a mild engineer: but descend."

45   And the life, if it answers at all, replies from the heart
And the eyes and the lungs, from the shops and squares of the city:
                    "O no, I am not the Mover,
Not today, not to you. To you I'm the

"Yes-man, the bar-companion, the easily-duped:
50   I am whatever you do; I am your vow to be
                    Good, your humorous story;
I am your business voice; I am your marriage.

"What's your proposal? To build the Just City? I will.
I agree. Or is it the suicide pact, the romantic
55   Death? Very well, I accept, for
I am your choice, your decision: yes, I am Spain."

Many have heard it on remote peninsulas,
On sleepy plains, in the aberrant fishermen's islands,
                    In the corrupt heart of the city;
60   Have heard and migrated like gulls or the seeds of a flower.

They clung like burrs to the long expresses that lurch
Through the unjust lands, through the night, through the alpine tunnel;
                    They floated over the oceans;
They walked the passes: they came to present their lives.

65   On that arid square, that fragment nipped off from hot
Africa, soldered so crudely to inventive Europe,
                    On that tableland scored by rivers,
Our fever's menacing shapes are precise and alive.

Tomorrow, perhaps, the future: the research on fatigue
70   And the movements of packers; the gradual exploring of all the
                    Octaves of radiation;
Tomorrow the enlarging of consciousness by diet and breathing.

Tomorrow the rediscovery of romantic love;
The photographing of ravens; all the fun under
75   Liberty's masterful shadow;
Tomorrow the hour of the pageant-master and the musician.

Tomorrow, for the young, the poets exploding like bombs,
The walks by the lake, the winter of perfect communion;
               Tomorrow the bicycle races
80 Through the suburbs on summer evenings: but today the struggle.

Today the inevitable increase in the chances of death;
The conscious acceptance of guilt in the fact of murder;
               Today the expending of powers
On the flat ephemeral pamphlet and the boring meeting.

85 Today the makeshift consolations; the shared cigarette;
The cards in the candle-lit barn and the scraping concert,
               The masculine jokes; today the
Fumbled and unsatisfactory embrace before hurting.

The stars are dead; the animals will not look:
90 We are left alone with our day, and the time is short and
               History to the defeated
May say Alas but cannot help or pardon.

                                         1937

Lullaby

Lay your sleeping head, my love,
Human on my faithless arm;
Time and fevers burn away
Individual beauty from
5 Thoughtful children, and the grave
Proves the child ephemeral:
But in my arms till break of day
Let the living creature lie,
Mortal, guilty, but to me
10 The entirely beautiful.

Soul and body have no bounds:
To lovers as they lie upon
Her tolerant enchanted slope
In their ordinary swoon,
15 Grave the vision Venus sends
Of supernatural sympathy,
Universal love and hope;
While an abstract insight wakes
Among the glaciers and the rocks
20 The hermit's carnal ecstasy.

Certainty, fidelity
On the stroke of midnight pass

Like vibrations of a bell
And fashionable madmen raise
25   Their pedantic boring cry:
Every farthing of the cost,
All the dreaded cards foretell,
Shall be paid, but from this night
Not a whisper, not a thought,
30   Not a kiss nor look be lost.

Beauty, midnight, vision dies:
Let the winds of dawn that blow
Softly round your dreaming head
Such a day of welcome show
35   Eye and knocking heart may bless,
Find our mortal world enough;
Noons of dryness find you fed
By the involuntary powers,
Nights of insult let you pass
40   Watched by every human love.
1937   1940

September 1, 1939[1]

I sit in one of the dives
On Fifty-Second Street
Uncertain and afraid
As the clever hopes expire
5   Of a low dishonest decade:
Waves of anger and fear
Circulate over the bright
And darkened lands of the earth,
Obsessing our private lives;
10   The unmentionable odour of death
Offends the September night.

Accurate scholarship can
Unearth the whole offence
From Luther[2] until now
15   That has driven a culture mad,
Find what occurred at Linz,[3]
What huge imago made
A psychopathic god:[4]
I and the public know
20   What all schoolchildren learn,

1. Auden arrived in New York City, where he was to spend World War II and much of the rest of his life, in January 1939. German forces marched into Poland on 1 September 1939; Britain and France declared war on 3 September.
2. Martin Luther, German religious reformer (1483–1546), whose criticisms of Roman Catholic doctrine sparked the Protestant Reformation in Europe.
3. Linz, Austria, was Adolf Hitler's birthplace.
4. In the psychological terminology developed by C. G. Jung (1875–1961), an *imago* is an idealized mental image of self or others, especially parental figures.

Those to whom evil is done
Do evil in return.

Exiled Thucydides[5] knew
All that a speech can say
25 About Democracy,
And what dictators do,
The elderly rubbish they talk
To an apathetic grave;
Analysed all in his book,
30 The enlightenment driven away,
The habit-forming pain,
Mismanagement and grief:
We must suffer them all again.

Into this neutral air
35 Where blind skyscrapers use
Their full height to proclaim
The strength of Collective Man,
Each language pours its vain
Competitive excuse:
40 But who can live for long
In an euphoric dream;
Out of the mirror they stare,
Imperialism's face
And the international wrong.

45 Faces along the bar
Cling to their average day:
The lights must never go out,
The music must always play,
All the conventions conspire
50 To make this fort assume
The furniture of home;
Lest we should see where we are,
Lost in a haunted wood,
Children afraid of the night
55 Who have never been happy or good.

The windiest militant trash
Important Persons shout
Is not so crude as our wish:
What mad Nijinsky wrote
60 About Diaghilev

5. Fifth-century Athenian historian and general in the Peloponnesian War between Athens and Sparta (431–404 B.C.). In his famous *History of the Peloponnesian War*, which follows events until 411 B.C., Thucydides records the Athenian statesman Pericles's *Funeral Oration*, given at the end of the first year of the war. In it, Pericles describes the benefits and possible dangers of democratic government as it was then practiced at Athens. Thucydides himself was exiled from Athens in 424 B.C., following a military defeat incurred under his leadership.

Is true of the normal heart;[6]
For the error bred in the bone
Of each woman and each man
Craves what it cannot have,
65   Not universal love
But to be loved alone.

From the conservative dark
Into the ethical life
The dense commuters come,
70   Repeating their morning vow,
"I *will* be true to the wife,
I'll concentrate more on my work,"
And helpless governors wake
To resume their compulsory game:
75   Who can release them now,
Who can reach the deaf,
Who can speak for the dumb?

All I have is a voice
To undo the folded lie,
80   The romantic lie in the brain
Of the sensual man-in-the-street
And the lie of Authority
Whose buildings grope the sky:
There is no such thing as the State
85   And no one exists alone;
Hunger allows no choice
To the citizen or the police;
We must love one another or die.

Defenceless under the night
90   Our world in stupor lies;
Yet, dotted everywhere,
Ironic points of light
Flash out wherever the Just
Exchange their messages:
95   May I, composed like them
Of Eros and of dust,
Beleaguered by the same
Negation and despair,
Show an affirming flame.

1939   1940

---

6. Vaslav Nijinsky (1890–1950), principal male dancer in the Ballets Russes company under the direction of Sergei Pavlovich Diaghilev (1872–1929). The company revolutionized the world of dance, causing a sensation on its visit to Paris in 1909. Auden borrowed the following lines from Nijinsky's (1937) *Diary:* "Diaghilev does not want universal love, but to be loved alone."

In Praise of Limestone[1]

If it form the one landscape that we, the inconstant ones,
    Are consistently homesick for, this is chiefly
Because it dissolves in water. Mark these rounded slopes
    With their surface fragrance of thyme and, beneath,
5   A secret system of caves and conduits; hear the springs
    That spurt out everywhere with a chuckle,
Each filling a private pool for its fish and carving
    Its own little ravine whose cliffs entertain
The butterfly and the lizard; examine this region
10   Of short distances and definite places:
What could be more like Mother or a fitter background
    For her son, the flirtatious male who lounges
Against a rock in the sunlight, never doubting
    That for all his faults he is loved; whose works are but
15   Extensions of his power to charm? From weathered outcrop
    To hill-top temple, from appearing waters to
Conspicuous fountains, from a wild to a formal vineyard,
    Are ingenious but short steps that a child's wish
To receive more attention than his brothers, whether
20   By pleasing or teasing, can easily take.

Watch, then, the band of rivals as they climb up and down
    Their steep stone gennels[2] in twos and threes, at times
Arm in arm, but never, thank God, in step; or engaged
    On the shady side of a square at midday in
25   Voluble discourse, knowing each other too well to think
    There are any important secrets, unable
To conceive a god whose temper-tantrums are moral
    And not to be pacified by a clever line
Or a good lay: for, accustomed to a stone that responds,
30   They have never had to veil their faces in awe
Of a crater whose blazing fury could not be fixed;
    Adjusted to the local needs of valleys
Where everything can be touched or reached by walking,
    Their eyes have never looked into infinite space
35   Through the lattice-work of a nomad's comb; born lucky,
    Their legs have never encountered the fungi
And insects of the jungle, the monstrous forms and lives
    With which we have nothing, we like to hope, in common.
So, when one of them goes to the bad, the way his mind works
40   Remains comprehensible: to become a pimp
Or deal in fake jewellery or ruin a fine tenor voice
    For effects that bring down the house, could happen to all
But the best and worst of us . . .

---

1. This poem is set in the landscape of Yorkshire, where   2. Channels.
Auden was born.

That is why, I suppose,
The best and worst never stayed here long but sought
45   Immoderate soils where the beauty was not so external,
The light less public and the meaning of life
Something more than a mad camp. "Come!" cried the granite wastes,
"How evasive is your humour, how accidental
Your kindest kiss, how permanent is death." (Saints-to-be
50   Slipped away sighing.) "Come!" purred the clays and gravels.
"On our plains there is room for armies to drill; rivers
Wait to be tamed and slaves to construct you a tomb
In the grand manner: soft as the earth is mankind and both
Need to be altered." (Intendant Caesars rose and
55   Left, slamming the door.) But the really reckless were fetched
By an older colder voice, the oceanic whisper:
"I am the solitude that asks and promises nothing;
That is how I shall set you free. There is no love;
There are only the various envies, all of them sad."
60   They were right, my dear, all those voices were right
And still are; this land is not the sweet home that it looks,
Nor its peace the historical calm of a site
Where something was settled once and for all: A backward
And dilapidated province, connected
65   To the big busy world by a tunnel, with a certain
Seedy appeal, is that all it is now? Not quite:
It has a worldly duty which in spite of itself
It does not neglect, but calls into question
All the Great Powers assume; it disturbs our rights. The poet,
70   Admired for his earnest habit of calling
The sun the sun, his mind Puzzle, is made uneasy
By these marble statues which so obviously doubt
His antimythological myth; and these gamins,[3]
Pursuing the scientist down the tiled colonnade
75   With such lively offers, rebuke his concern for Nature's
Remotest aspects: I, too, am reproached, for what
And how much you know. Not to lose time, not to get caught,
Not to be left behind, not, please! to resemble
The beasts who repeat themselves, or a thing like water
80   Or stone whose conduct can be predicted, these
Are our Common Prayer, whose greatest comfort is music
Which can be made anywhere, is invisible,
And does not smell. In so far as we have to look forward
To death as a fact, no doubt we are right: But if
85   Sins can be forgiven, if bodies rise from the dead,
These modifications of matter into
Innocent athletes and gesticulating fountains,
Made solely for pleasure, make a further point:
The blessed will not care what angle they are regarded from,
90   Having nothing to hide. Dear, I know nothing of

3. Street urchins.

Either, but when I try to imagine a faultless love
  Or the life to come, what I hear is the murmur
  Of underground streams, what I see is a limestone landscape.

1948   1948

Philip Larkin
1922–1985

Philip Larkin's lifetime production of poems was quite small, but highly influential; he is best known for his three last volumes, *The Less Deceived* (1955), *The Whitsun Weddings* (1964), and *High Windows* (1974), which together collect fewer than one hundred poems. During his lifetime, however, he fulfilled the role—a role that every society seems to require—of the crotchety traditionalist poet, becoming famous for what the poet and critic Donald Hall has called a "genuine, uncultivated, sincere philistinism."

Born in Coventry, Larkin completed a B.A. and M.A. at Oxford (where he was a friend of the novelist Kingsley Amis), and became a professional librarian, working at the University of Hull from 1955 until his death. After two modestly successful novels (*Jill* and *A Girl in Winter*) and two undistinguished volumes of poetry (*The North Ship* and *XX Poems*), Larkin established himself as a new and important voice in British poetry with his collection *The Less Deceived*. According to most critics, the influence of Thomas Hardy's poetry was decisive; Seamus Heaney writes that the "slips and excesses" of his first two volumes—consisting, primarily, of embarrassing echoes of W. B. Yeats—led Larkin "to seek the antidote of Thomas Hardy."

Larkin was attracted to Hardy's bleak outlook on life, as well as his skilled versification and spare language. Larkin's dark vision remained unremitting as late as *Aubade*, the last poem to be published during his lifetime:

> I work all day, and get half drunk at night.
> Waking at four to soundless dark, I stare.
> In time the curtain-edges will grow light.
> Till then I see what's really always there:
> Unresting death, a whole day nearer now,
> Making all thought impossible but how
> And where and when I shall myself die.

Like the most famous postwar British playwright, Samuel Beckett, the most important postwar British poet was not above having a laugh at his own despair; in an oft-repeated remark, Larkin told an interviewer that "deprivation is for me what daffodils were for Wordsworth."

Larkin is one of the most English of modern British poets; he refused to read "foreign" literature—including most American poetry—or to travel abroad; Hull became the center and circumference of his poetic world. He kept to himself to an extraordinary degree; he never married, nor did he maintain any longstanding intimate relationship. In his obituary for Larkin, Kingsley Amis described him as "a man much driven in upon himself, with increasing deafness from early middle age cruelly emphasizing his seclusion."

Even in his solitude, though, Larkin kept up a running dialogue with the outside world, not only as a poet but as a jazz reviewer for many years. His encyclopedic knowledge of jazz provides the basis for his probing, dyspeptic account of modernity in the opening essay of his collection *All What Jazz*. In this essay as in his verse, Larkin's writing is pointed, skeptical, acerbic—and always self-consciously English.

Church Going

Once I am sure there's nothing going on
I step inside, letting the door thud shut.
Another church: matting, seats, and stone,
And little books; sprawlings of flowers, cut
5 For Sunday, brownish now; some brass and stuff
Up at the holy end; the small neat organ;
And a tense, musty, unignorable silence,
Brewed God knows how long. Hatless, I take off
My cycle-clips in awkward reverence,

10 Move forward, run my hand around the font.
From where I stand, the roof looks almost new—
Cleaned, or restored? Someone would know: I don't.
Mounting the lectern, I peruse a few
Hectoring large-scale verses, and pronounce
15 "Here endeth" much more loudly than I'd meant.
The echoes snigger briefly. Back at the door
I sign the book, donate an Irish sixpence,
Reflect the place was not worth stopping for.

Yet stop I did: in fact I often do,
20 And always end much at a loss like this,
Wondering what to look for; wondering, too,
When churches fall completely out of use
What we shall turn them into, if we shall keep
A few cathedrals chronically on show,
25 Their parchment, plate and pyx[1] in locked cases,
And let the rest rent-free to rain and sheep.
Shall we avoid them as unlucky places?

Or, after dark, will dubious women come
To make their children touch a particular stone;
30 Pick simples° for a cancer; or on some   *medicinal plants*
Advised night see walking a dead one?
Power of some sort or other will go on
In games, in riddles, seemingly at random;
But superstition, like belief, must die,
35 And what remains when disbelief has gone?
Grass, weedy pavement, brambles, buttress, sky,

A shape less recognisable each week,
A purpose more obscure. I wonder who
Will be the last, the very last, to seek
40 This place for what it was; one of the crew
That tap and jot and know what rood-lofts[2] were?
Some ruin-bibber, randy for antique,

---

1. The vessel in which the consecrated bread of the eucharist is kept.

2. Loft at the top of a carved wood or stone screen, separating the nave from the chancel of a church.

Or Christmas-addict, counting on a whiff
Of gown-and-bands and organ-pipes and myrrh?
45 Or will he be my representative,

Bored, uninformed, knowing the ghostly silt
Dispersed, yet tending to this cross of ground
Through suburb scrub because it held unspilt
So long and equably what since is found
50 Only in separation—marriage, and birth,
And death, and thoughts of these—for which was built
This special shell? For, though I've no idea
What this accoutred frowsty° barn is worth,   *stuffy*
It pleases me to stand in silence here;

55 A serious house on serious earth it is,
In whose blent air all our compulsions meet,
Are recognised, and robed as destinies.
And that much never can be obsolete,
Since someone will forever be surprising
60 A hunger in himself to be more serious,
And gravitating with it to this ground,
Which, he once heard, was proper to grow wise in,
If only that so many dead lie round.

1954   1955

High Windows

When I see a couple of kids
And guess he's fucking her and she's
Taking pills or wearing a diaphragm,
I know this is paradise

5 Everyone old has dreamed of all their lives—
Bonds and gestures pushed to one side
Like an outdated combine harvester,
And everyone young going down the long slide

To happiness, endlessly. I wonder if
10 Anyone looked at me, forty years back,
And thought, *That'll be the life;*
No God any more, or sweating in the dark

About hell and that, or having to hide
What you think of the priest. He
15 *And his lot will all go down the long slide*
Like free bloody birds. And immediately

Rather than words comes the thought of high windows:
The sun-comprehending glass,
And beyond it, the deep blue air, that shows
20 Nothing, and is nowhere, and is endless.

1967   1974

Talking in Bed

Talking in bed ought to be easiest,
Lying together there goes back so far,
An emblem of two people being honest.

Yet more and more time passes silently.
Outside, the wind's incomplete unrest
Builds and disperses clouds about the sky,

And dark towns heap up on the horizon.
None of this cares for us. Nothing shows why
At this unique distance from isolation

It becomes still more difficult to find
Words at once true and kind,
Or not untrue and not unkind.

1960   1964

MCMXIV[1]

Those long uneven lines
Standing as patiently
As if they were stretched outside
The Oval or Villa Park,
The crowns of hats, the sun
On moustached archaic faces
Grinning as if it were all
An August Bank Holiday lark;

And the shut shops, the bleached
Established names on the sunblinds,
The farthings and sovereigns,
And dark-clothed children at play
Called after kings and queens,
The tin advertisements
For cocoa and twist, and the pubs
Wide open all day;

And the countryside not caring:
The place-names all hazed over
With flowering grasses, and fields
Shadowing Domesday[2] lines
Under wheat's restless silence;
The differently-dressed servants
With tiny rooms in huge houses,
The dust behind limousines;

1. The year 1914, in the style of a monument to the war dead.   2. The Domesday Book is the medieval record of the extent, value, and ownership of lands in England.

25   Never such innocence,
        Never before or since,
        As changed itself to past
        Without a word—the men
        Leaving the gardens tidy,
30   The thousands of marriages
        Lasting a little while longer:
        Never such innocence again.

1960   1964

→ ⊷≋⊶ ←

Ted Hughes

1930–1998

Ted Hughes can be called a "nature" poet—a somewhat unfortunate label with which he is often tagged—only in a complex and rather dark sense of the word. Critical of Western scientific discourse as leading to nuclear destruction, and finding Christianity depleted of spiritual sustenance, Hughes invokes the "bigger energy" of the natural world—not as a place of tranquil repose or a medium to the sublime, but as a fierce and virile life-force, driven solely by its own relentless will for survival, Tennyson's "nature red in tooth and claw." And yet this force, long neglected by modern humanity, is the source of creativity and regeneration.

Because of their supposed unsevered relationship with nature—their reliance on instinct rather than consciousness—animals, often predatory, provide the subject matter for many of Hughes's poems. Jaguars, crows, foxes, and wolves dominate their respective texts, as Hughes traces through their physicality a deep undercurrent of both human and nonhuman existence. In the much celebrated *Hawk Roosting* (*Lupercal* 1960), the beast provides a voice for nature, in a language as poised and powerful as its speaker: "I kill where I please because it is all mine. / There is no sophistry in my body." In subsequent volumes Hughes's creatures assume complex identities that blur the demarcations of "otherness." *Gog* and *Wodwo*, for instance (*Wodwo* 1967), introduce characters as enigmatic as their names, struggling to understand themselves in relation to their environment. In 1971 Hughes published *Crow*, a poetic-mythology that, among other things, reexamines biblical narratives in light of its grisly protagonist.

Like his modernist predecessors, Hughes was influenced by turn-of-the-century anthropological studies (including Sir James George Frazer's *The Golden Bough*) that infused ancient cultural practices with new meaning and provided disillusioned writers with an alternative symbolic system. Adopting to some extent the model of Robert Graves's *The White Goddess*, Hughes maps out a mythology that places at the center of divinity an earth goddess, the source of true poetry, who has been tragically usurped by patriarchal ideology.

Just as Hughes peers deep into the past for a better understanding of man and nature, his language maintains a toughness and a vitality that harken back to more primitive verse forms. That language was shaped early on by the farms and soggy moors of Mytholmroyd, where he grew up. The torments of war were not eluded there; Hughes's father, after serving four years in Flanders during World War I, brought home the emotional scarring of trench warfare. After working two years as a radio mechanic for the RAF, Hughes went on to study anthropology at Cambridge. There, he met Sylvia Plath, whom he married in 1956, and the tragic relationship that ensued has kindled much interest in both popular and critical circles. *The Birthday Letters,* in which Hughes retrospectively addresses Plath's suicide, met with immediate success after its publication in 1998. Hughes died that same year, after serving fourteen years as Poet Laureate.

Wind

This house has been far out at sea all night,
The woods crashing through darkness, the booming hills,
Winds stampeding the fields under the window
Floundering black astride and blinding wet

5   Till day rose; then under an orange sky
The hills had new places, and wind wielded
Blade-light, luminous black and emerald,
Flexing like the lens of a mad eye.

At noon I scaled along the house-side as far as
10   The coal-house door. Once I looked up—
Through the brunt wind that dented the balls of my eyes
The tent of the hills drummed and strained its guyrope,[1]

The fields quivering, the skyline a grimace,
At any second to bang and vanish with a flap:
15   The wind flung a magpie away and a black-
Back gull bent like an iron bar slowly. The house

Rang like some fine green goblet in the note
That any second would shatter it. Now deep
In chairs, in front of the great fire, we grip
20   Our hearts and cannot entertain book, thought,

Or each other. We watch the fire blazing,
And feel the roots of the house move, but sit on,
Seeing the window tremble to come in,
Hearing the stones cry out under the horizons.

Relic

I found this jawbone at the sea's edge:
There, crabs, dogfish, broken by the breakers or tossed
To flap for half an hour and turn to a crust
Continue the beginning. The deeps are cold:
5   In that darkness camaraderie does not hold;
Nothing touches but, clutching, devours. And the jaws,
Before they are satisfied or their stretched purpose
Slacken, go down jaws; go gnawn bare. Jaws

---

1. Guide or anchoring rope on a ship or, as here, a tent.

Eat and are finished and the jawbone comes to the beach:
10 This is the sea's achievement; with shells,
Vertebrae, claws, carapaces,[1] skulls.

Time in the sea eats its tail, thrives, casts these
Indigestibles, the spars of purposes
That failed far from the surface. None grow rich
15 In the sea. This curved jawbone did not laugh
But gripped, gripped and is now a cenotaph.[2]

Theology

No, the serpent did not
Seduce Eve to the apple.
All that's simply
Corruption of the facts.

5 Adam ate the apple.
Eve ate Adam.
The serpent ate Eve.
This is the dark intestine.

The serpent, meanwhile,
10 Sleeps his meal off in Paradise—
Smiling to hear
God's querulous calling.

Dust As We Are

My post-war father was so silent
He seemed to be listening. I eavesdropped
On the hot line. His lonely sittings
Mangled me, in secret—like TV
5 Watched too long, my nerves lasered.
Then, an after-image of the incessant
Mowing passage of machine-gun effects,
What it filled a trench with. And his laugh
(How had that survived—so nearly intact?)
10 Twitched the curtain never quite deftly enough
Over the hospital wards
Crowded with his (photographed) shock-eyed pals.

I had to use up a lot of spirit
Getting over it. I was helping him.
15 I was his supplementary convalescent.
He took up his pre-war *joie de vivre*.[1]

---

1. A bony shell or shield, such as a turtle's shell.
2. A monument erected in memory of a deceased person whose body is buried elsewhere.
1. Enjoyment of life (French).

But his displays of muscular definition
Were a bleached montage—lit landscapes:
Swampquakes of the slime of puddled soldiers
20   Where bones and bits of equipment
Showered from every shell-burst.

                                    Naked men
Slithered staring where their mothers and sisters
Would never have to meet their eyes, or see
Exactly how they sprawled and were trodden.

25   So he had been salvaged and washed.
His muscles very white—marble white.
He had been heavily killed. But we had revived him.
Now he taught us a silence like prayer.
There he sat, killed but alive—so long
30   As we were very careful. I divined,
With a comb,
Under his wavy, golden hair, as I combed it,
The fragility of skull. And I filled
With his knowledge.

                                    After mother's milk
35   This was the soul's food. A soap-smell spectre
Of the massacre of innocents. So the soul grew.
A strange thing, with rickets[2]—a hyena.
No singing—that kind of laughter.

Leaf Mould

In Hardcastle Crags, that echoey museum,
Where she dug leaf mould[1] for her handfuls of garden
And taught you to walk, others are making poems.

Between finger and thumb roll a pine-needle,
5   *Feel the chamfer,[2] feel how they threaded*
The sewing machines.

                                    And
Billy Holt invented a new shuttle[3]
As like an ant's egg, with its folded worker,
10   *As every other.*
You might see an ant carrying one.

                                    And
The cordite[4] conscripts tramped away. But the cenotaphs[5]
Of all the shells that got their heads blown off
15   *And their insides blown out*

---

2. Disease caused by vitamin D deficiency, resulting in
soft bones.
1. British variant of "mold."
2. A beveled cut, usually in wood.

3. A device that carries thread in a sewing machine.
4. A smokeless explosive powder.
5. A monument erected in memory of a deceased person
whose body is buried elsewhere.

Are these beech-bole[6] stalwarts.

And oak, birch,

Holly, sycamore, pine.

The lightest air-stir

20   Released their love-whispers when she walked
The needles weeping, singing, dedicating
Your spectre-double, still in her womb,
To this temple of her *Missa Solemnis.*[7]

White-faced, brain-washed by her nostalgias,
25   You were her step-up transformer.
She grieved for her girlhood and the fallen.
You mourned for Paradise and its fable.

Giving you the kiss of life
She hung round your neck her whole valley
30   Like David's harp.[8]
Now, whenever you touch it, God listens
Only for her voice.

Leaf mould. Blood-warm. Fibres crumbled alive
Between thumb and finger.
35   *Feel again*
The clogs twanging your footsoles, on the street's steepness,
As you escaped.

Telegraph Wires

Take telegraph wires, a lonely moor,
And fit them together. The thing comes alive in your ear.

Towns whisper to towns over the heather.
But the wires cannot hide from the weather.

5   So oddly, so daintily made
It is picked up and played.

Such unearthly airs
The ear hears, and withers!

In the revolving ballroom of space,
10   Bowed over the moor, a bright face

Draws out of telegraph wires the tones
That empty human bones.

[END OF POSTWAR POETS: ENGLISH VOICES]

---

6. Trunk of a beech tree.
7. The "solemn mass," op. 123 by Ludwig van Beethoven.

8. In the Old Testament book of Psalms, King David plays his harp before the Lord.

Salman Rushdie
b. 1947

Salman Rushdie, c. 1999–2000

Born in Bombay in the heady days leading up to India's independence from Britain, Salman Rushdie was raised in Pakistan after the partition of the subcontinent. He then settled in England, where he soon became one of the most noted writers about the aftermath of empires. His magisterial novel *Midnight's Children* was awarded not only the prestigious Booker McConnell Prize for the best British novel of 1981 but later the "Booker of Bookers," as the best novel in the first twenty-five years of the prize's history. Like Saleem Sinai, the protagonist and narrator of *Midnight's Children*, Rushdie delights in telling its story, in a mixture of history, fantasy, fable, and sheer stylistic exuberance that has come to be known (through the works of Latin American writers like Gabriel Garcia Marquez) as magic realism. At once an Indian and a British writer, Rushdie enjoys a double status as both insider and outsider that allows him to comment both on the history of his native land and on the contemporary politics of Britain with savage and comic incisiveness.

Unfortunately, most who do not know Rushdie's writing well know his name from the publicity surrounding his 1988 novel *The Satanic Verses;* the novel was judged to be an affront to Islam, and on Valentine's Day in 1989 the late Iranian leader Ayatollah Ruhollah Khomeini issued a *fatwa,* or death threat, against both Rushdie and his publisher, carrying a multimillion dollar bounty. As a result, Rushdie was forced to go underground; for nearly ten years he moved from place to place protected by full-time bodyguards, making but unable to receive phone calls, and generally staying out of the public eye and out of harm's way. Under Islamic law, a *fatwa* can be lifted only by the man who imposed it; since Khomeini died with the *fatwa* still in effect, it technically will remain in effect until Rushdie's death, although subsequent Iranian leaders have suggested that the edict would not be enforced. Rushdie has, in recent years, begun a boldly public life in England and the United States.

It is both appalling and intriguing that the written word still has this much power. The book that followed *The Satanic Verses* was *Haroun and the Sea of Stories,* a tale often (mistakenly) labeled "juvenile." It is in fact an allegory of the power of language—its power to liberate, and the desperate attempts of what political philosopher Louis Althusser calls the "ideological state apparatus" to silence this free, anarchic speech. The story did indeed begin as a bath-time entertainment for Rushdie's son Zafar; but as the affair over the *Satanic Verses* grew and festered, the story matured into a parable of the responsibility of the artist to speak from the heart and conscience, regardless of the political consequences. "Chekov and Zulu," playfully but with sinister overtones, adopts the narrative frame of television's *Star Trek* to speak of international terrorism and political violence. "The Courter," one of Rushdie's most tender stories, closes his 1994 volume *East, West,* emphasizing two of his perennial themes: the (sometimes benevolent) influence of transnational popular culture, and the creative magic of everyday language.

The Courter
I

Certainly-Mary was the smallest woman Mixed-Up the hall porter had come across, dwarfs excepted, a tiny sixty-year-old Indian lady with her greying hair tied behind her head in a neat bun, hitching up her red-hemmed white sari[1] in the front and negotiating the apartment block's front steps as if they were Alps. "No," he said aloud, furrowing his brow. What would be the right peaks. Ah, good, that was the name. "Ghats," he said proudly. Word from a schoolboy atlas long ago, when India felt as far away as Paradise. (Nowadays Paradise seemed even further away but India, and Hell, had come a good bit closer.) "Western Ghats, Eastern Ghats, and now Kensington[2] Ghats," he said, giggling. "Mountains."

She stopped in front of him in the oak-panelled lobby. "But ghats in India are also stairs," she said. "Yes yes certainly. For instance in Hindu holy city of Varanasi, where the Brahmins sit taking the filgrims' money is called Dasashwamedh-ghat. Broad-broad staircase down to River Ganga. O, most certainly! Also Manikarnika-ghat. They buy fire from a house with a tiger leaping from the roof—yes certainly, a statue tiger, coloured by Technicolor, what are you thinking?—and they bring it in a box to set fire to their loved ones' bodies. Funeral fires are of sandal. Photographs not allowed; no, certainly not."

He began thinking of her as Certainly-Mary because she never said plain yes or no; always this O-yes-certainly or no-certainly-not. In the confused circumstances that had prevailed ever since his brain, his one sure thing, had let him down, he could hardly be certain of anything any more; so he was stunned by her sureness, first into nostalgia, then envy, then attraction. And attraction was a thing so long forgotten that when the churning started he thought for a long time it must be the Chinese dumplings he had brought home from the High Street carry-out.

English was hard for Certainly-Mary, and this was a part of what drew damaged old Mixed-Up towards her. The letter p was a particular problem, often turning into an f or a c; when she proceeded through the lobby with a wheeled wicker shopping basket, she would say, "Going shocking," and when, on her return, he offered to help lift the basket up the front ghats, she would answer, "Yes, fleas." As the elevator lifted her away, she called through the grille: "Oé, courter! Thank you, courter. O, yes, certainly." (In Hindi and Konkani,[3] however, her p's knew their place.)

So: thanks to her unexpected, somehow stomach-churning magic, he was no longer porter, but courter. "Courter," he repeated to the mirror when she had gone. His breath made a little dwindling picture of the word on the glass. "Courter courter caught." Okay. People called him many things, he did not mind. But this name, this courter, this he would try to be.

2

For years now I've been meaning to write down the story of Certainly-Mary, our ayah,[4] the woman who did as much as my mother to raise my sisters and me, and her great adventure with her "courter" in London, where we all lived for a time in the early Sixties in a block called Waverley House; but what with one thing and another I never got round to it.

Then recently I heard from Certainly-Mary after a longish silence. She wrote to say that she was ninety-one, had had a serious operation, and would I kindly send her

---

1. Traditional Indian woman's wrap dress.
2. Fashionable London neighborhood.
3. Two of India's indigenous languages.
4. Hindi, "nanny."

some money, because she was embarrassed that her niece, with whom she was now living in the Kurla district of Bombay, was so badly out of pocket.

I sent the money, and soon afterwards received a pleasant letter from the niece, Stella, written in the same hand as the letter from "Aya"—as we had always called Mary, palindromically[5] dropping the "h." Aya had been so touched, the niece wrote, that I remembered her after all these years. "I have been hearing the stories about you folks all my life," the letter went on, "and I think of you a little bit as family. Maybe you recall my mother, Mary's sister. She unfortunately passed on. Now it is I who write Mary's letters for her. We all wish you the best."

This message from an intimate stranger reached out to me in my enforced exile from the beloved country of my birth and moved me, stirring things that had been buried very deep. Of course it also made me feel guilty about having done so little for Mary over the years. For whatever reason, it has become more important than ever to set down the story I've been carrying around unwritten for so long, the story of Aya and the gentle man whom she renamed—with unintentional but prophetic overtones of romance—"the courter." I see now that it is not just their story, but ours, mine, as well.

3

His real name was Mecir: you were supposed to say Mishirsh because it had invisible accents on it in some Iron Curtain language in which the accents had to be invisible, my sister Durré said solemnly, in case somebody spied on them or rubbed them out or something. His first name also began with an m but it was so full of what we called Communist consonants, all those z's and c's and w's walled up together without vowels to give them breathing space, that I never even tried to learn it.

At first we thought of nicknaming him after a mischievous little comic-book character, Mr Mxyztplk from the Fifth Dimension, who looked a bit like Elmer Fudd and used to make Superman's life hell until ole Supe could trick him into saying his name backwards, Klptzyxm, whereupon he disappeared back into the Fifth Dimension; but because we weren't too sure how to say Mxyztplk (not to mention Klptzyxm) we dropped that idea. "We'll just call you Mixed-Up," I told him in the end, to simplify life. "Mishter Mikshed-Up Mishirsh." I was fifteen then and bursting with unemployed cock and it meant I could say things like that right into people's faces, even people less accommodating than Mr Mecir with his stroke.

What I remember most vividly are his pink rubber washing-up gloves, which he seemed never to remove, at least not until he came calling for Certainly-Mary . . . At any rate, when I insulted him, with my sisters Durré and Muneeza cackling in the lift,[6] Mecir just grinned an empty good-natured grin, nodded, "You call me what you like, okay," and went back to buffing and polishing the brasswork. There was no point teasing him if he was going to be like that, so I got into the lift and all the way to the fourth floor we sang *I Can't Stop Loving You* at the top of our best Ray Charles voices, which were pretty awful. But we were wearing our dark glasses, so it didn't matter.

4

It was the summer of 1962, and school was out. My baby sister Scheherazade was just one year old. Durré was a beehived fourteen; Muneeza was ten, and already quite a handful. The three of us—or rather Durré and me, with Muneeza trying desperately

---

5. A palindrome is a word that reads the same forwards and backwards.   6. Elevator.

and unsuccessfully to be included in our gang—would stand over Scheherazade's cot and sing to her. "No nursery rhymes," Durré had decreed, and so there were none, for though she was a year my junior she was a natural leader. The infant Scheherazade's lullabies were our cover versions of recent hits by Chubby Checker, Neil Sedaka, Elvis and Pat Boone.

"Why don't you come home, Speedy Gonzales?"[7] we bellowed in sweet disharmony: but most of all, and with actions, we would jump down, turn around and pick a bale of cotton. We would have jumped down, turned around and picked those bales all day except that the Maharaja of B— in the flat below complained, and Aya Mary came in to plead with us to be quiet.

"Look, see, it's Jumble-Aya[8] who's fallen for Mixed-Up," Durré shouted, and Mary blushed a truly immense blush. So naturally we segued right into a quick me-oh-my-oh; son of a gun, we had big fun. But then the baby began to yell, my father came in with his head down bull-fashion and steaming from both ears, and we needed all the good luck charms we could find.

I had been at boarding school in England for a year or so when Abba took the decision to bring the family over. Like all his decisions, it was neither explained to nor discussed with anyone, not even my mother. When they first arrived he rented two adjacent flats in a seedy Bayswater[9] mansion block called Graham Court, which lurked furtively in a nothing street that crawled along the side of the ABC Queensway cinema towards the Porchester Baths. He commandeered one of these flats for himself and put my mother, three sisters and Aya in the other; also, on school holidays, me. England, where liquor was freely available, did little for my father's *bonhomie*,[1] so in a way it was a relief to have a flat to ourselves.

Most nights he emptied a bottle of Johnnie Walker Red Label and a soda-siphon. My mother did not dare to go across to "his place" in the evenings. She said: "He makes faces at me."

Aya Mary took Abba his dinner and answered all his calls (if he wanted anything, he would phone us up and ask for it). I am not sure why Mary was spared his drunken rages. She said it was because she was nine years his senior, so she could tell him to show due respect.

After a few months, however, my father leased a three-bedroom fourth-floor apartment with a fancy address. This was Waverley House in Kensington Court, W8. Among its other residents were not one but two Indian Maharajas, the sporting Prince P— as well as the old B— who has already been mentioned. Now we were jammed in together, my parents and Baby Scare-zade (as her siblings had affectionately begun to call her) in the master bedroom, the three of us in a much smaller room, and Mary, I regret to admit, on a straw mat laid on the fitted carpet in the hall. The third bedroom became my father's office, where he made phone-calls and kept his *Encyclopaedia Britannica*, his *Reader's Digests*, and (under lock and key) the television cabinet. We entered it at our peril. It was the Minotaur's[2] lair.

---

7. "Speedy Gonzales" was a hit in the United States for Pat Boone in 1962.
8. "Jumble-aya" invokes "jambalaya," a cajun stew, but also the title of a Hank Williams song, later recorded by Pat Boone, and a hit for Fats Domino in 1961, and again for John Fogerty (formerly of Creedence Clearwater Revival) in 1973.
9. London neighborhood.
1. Good nature.
2. The Minotaur was the monster of Greek myth, slain by Theseus; his lair lay in the center of the famous labyrinth on Crete.

One morning he was persuaded to drop in at the corner pharmacy and pick up some supplies for the baby. When he returned there was a hurt, schoolboyish look on his face that I had never seen before, and he was pressing his hand against his cheek.

"She hit me," he said plaintively.

"Hai! Allah-tobah! Darling!" cried my mother, fussing. "Who hit you? Are you injured? Show me, let me see."

"I did nothing," he said, standing there in the hall with the pharmacy bag in his other hand and a face as pink as Mecir's rubber gloves. "I just went in with your list. The girl seemed very helpful. I asked for baby compound, Johnson's powder, teething jelly, and she brought them out. Then I asked did she have any nipples, and she slapped my face."

My mother was appalled. "Just for that?" And Certainly-Mary backed her up. "What is this nonsense?" she wanted to know. "I have been in that chemist's[3] shock, and they have flenty nickels, different sizes, all on view."

Durré and Muneeza could not contain themselves. They were rolling round on the floor, laughing and kicking their legs in the air.

"You both shut your face at once," my mother ordered. "A madwoman has hit your father. Where is the comedy?"

"I don't believe it," Durré gasped. "You just went up to that girl and said," and here she fell apart again, stamping her feet and holding her stomach, " '*have you got any nipples?*' "

My father grew thunderous, empurpled. Durré controlled herself. "But Abba," she said, at length, "here they call them teats."

Now my mother's and Mary's hands flew to their mouths, and even my father looked shocked. "But how shameless!" my mother said. "The same word as for what's on your bosoms?" She coloured, and stuck out her tongue for shame.

"These English," sighed Certainly-Mary. "But aren't they the limit? Certainly-yes; they are."

I remember this story with delight, because it was the only time I ever saw my father so discomfited, and the incident became legendary and the girl in the pharmacy was installed as the object of our great veneration. (Durré and I went in there just to take a look at her—she was a plain, short girl of about seventeen, with large, unavoidable breasts—but she caught us whispering and glared so fiercely that we fled.) And also because in the general hilarity I was able to conceal the shaming truth that I, who had been in England for so long, would have made the same mistake as Abba did.

It wasn't just Certainly-Mary and my parents who had trouble with the English language. My schoolfellows tittered when in my Bombay way I said "brought-up" for upbringing (as in "where was your brought-up?") and "thrice" for three times and "quarter-plate" for side-plate and "macaroni" for pasta in general. As for learning the difference between nipples and teats, I really hadn't had any opportunities to increase my word power in that area at all.

5

So I was a little jealous of Certainly-Mary when Mixed-Up came to call. He rang our bell, his body quivering with deference in an old suit grown too loose, the trousers tightly gathered by a belt; he had taken off his rubber gloves and there were roses in

---

3. Pharmacists.

his hand. My father opened the door and gave him a withering look. Being a snob, Abba was not pleased that the flat lacked a separate service entrance, so that even a porter had to be treated as a member of the same universe as himself.

"Mary," Mixed-Up managed, licking his lips and pushing back his floppy white hair. "I, to see Miss Mary, come, am."

"Wait on," Abba said, and shut the door in his face.

Certainly-Mary spent all her afternoons off with old Mixed-Up from then on, even though that first date was not a complete success. He took her "up West" to show her the visitors' London she had never seen, but at the top of an up escalator at Piccadilly Circus, while Mecir was painfully enunciating the words on the posters she couldn't read—*Unzip a banana*, and *Idris when I's dri*—she got her sari stuck in the jaws of the machine, and as the escalator pulled at the garment it began to unwind. She was forced to spin round and round like a top, and screamed at the top of her voice, "O BAAP! BAAPU-RÉ! BAAP-RÉ-BAAP-RÉ-BAAP!" It was Mixed-Up who saved her by pushing the emergency stop button before the sari was completely unwound and she was exposed in her petticoat for all the world to see.

"O, courter!" she wept on his shoulder. "O, no more escaleater, courter, never-more, surely not!"

My own amorous longings were aimed at Durré's best friend, a Polish girl called Rozalia, who had a holiday job at Faiman's shoe shop on Oxford Street. I pursued her pathetically throughout the holidays and, on and off, for the next two years. She would let me have lunch with her sometimes and buy her a Coke and a sandwich, and once she came with me to stand on the terraces at White Hart Lane to watch Jimmy Greaves's first game for the Spurs. "Come on you whoi-oites," we both shouted dutifully. "Come on you *Lily-whoites*." After that she even invited me into the back room at Faiman's, where she kissed me twice and let me touch her breast, but that was as far as I got.

And then there was my sort-of-cousin Chandni, whose mother's sister had married my mother's brother, though they had since split up. Chandni was eighteen months older than me, and so sexy it made you sick. She was training to be an Indian classical dancer, Odissi as well as Natyam, but in the meantime she dressed in tight black jeans and a clinging black polo-neck jumper and took me, now and then, to hang out at Bunjie's, where she knew most of the folk-music crowd that frequented the place, and where she answered to the name of Moonlight, which is what *chandni* means. I chain-smoked with the folkies and then went to the toilet to throw up.

Chandni was the stuff of obsessions. She was a teenage dream, the Moon River come to Earth like the Goddess Ganga, dolled up in slinky black. But for her I was just the young greenhorn cousin to whom she was being nice because he hadn't learned his way around.

She-E-rry, won't you come out tonight? yodelled the Four Seasons. I knew exactly how they felt. Come, *come, come out toni-yi-yight.* And while you're at it, love me do.[4]

6

They went for walks in Kensington Gardens. "Pan," Mixed-Up said, pointing at a statue. "Los' boy. Nev' grew up." They went to Barkers and Pontings and Derry &

4. Hits, respectively, for Frankie Valli and the Four Seasons (1962) and the Beatles (1962).

Toms and picked out furniture and curtains for imaginary homes. They cruised super-markets and chose little delicacies to eat. In Mecir's cramped lounge they sipped what he called "chimpanzee tea" and toasted crumpets in front of an electric bar fire.

Thanks to Mixed-Up, Mary was at last able to watch television. She liked children's programmes best, especially *The Flintstones*. Once, giggling at her daring, Mary confided to Mixed-Up that Fred and Wilma reminded her of her Sahib and Begum Sahiba upstairs; at which the courter, matching her audaciousness, pointed first at Certainly-Mary and then at himself, grinned a wide gappy smile and said, "Rubble."

Later, on the news, a vulpine Englishman with a thin moustache and mad eyes declaimed a warning about immigrants, and Certainly-Mary flapped her hand at the set: "Khali-pili bom marta," she objected, and then, for her host's benefit translated: "For nothing he is shouting shouting. Bad life! Switch it off."

They were often interrupted by the Maharajas of B— and P—, who came downstairs to escape their wives and ring other women from the call-box in the porter's room.

"Oh, baby, forget that guy," said sporty Prince P—, who seemed to spend all his days in tennis whites, and whose plump gold Rolex was almost lost in the thick hair on his arm. "I'll show you a better time than him, baby; step into my world."

The Maharaja of B— was older, uglier, more matter-of-fact. "Yes, bring all appliances. Room is booked in name of Mr Douglas Home. Six forty-five to seven fifteen. You have printed rate card? Please. Also a two-foot ruler, must be wooden. Frilly apron, plus."

This is what has lasted in my memory of Waverley House, this seething mass of bad marriages, booze, philanderers and unfulfilled young lusts; of the Maharaja of P— roaring away towards London's casinoland every night, in a red sports car with fitted blondes, and of the Maharaja of B— skulking off to Kensington High Street wearing dark glasses in the dark, and a coat with the collar turned up even though it was high summer; and at the heart of our little universe were Certainly-Mary and her courter, drinking chimpanzee tea and singing along with the national anthem of Bedrock.

But they were not really like Barney and Betty Rubble at all. They were formal, polite. They were . . . courtly. He courted her, and, like a coy, ringleted ingénue with a fan, she inclined her head, and entertained his suit.

7

I spent one half-term weekend in 1963 at the home in Beccles, Suffolk of Field Marshal Sir Charles Lutwidge-Dodgson,[5] an old India hand and a family friend who was supporting my application for British citizenship. "The Dodo," as he was known, invited me down by myself, saying he wanted to get to know me better.

He was a huge man whose skin had started hanging too loosely on his face, a giant living in a tiny thatched cottage and forever bumping his head. No wonder he was irascible at times; he was in Hell, a Gulliver trapped in that rose-garden Lilliput of croquet hoops, church bells, sepia photographs and old battle-trumpets.

---

5. Charles Lutwidge Dodgson was the birth name of the writer better known as Lewis Carroll, author of *Alice's Adventures in Wonderland* and *Through the Looking Glass*; the latter book uses the game of chess as a structural device. Dodgson was familiarly called "Dodo" by his young companion, Alice Liddell.

The weekend was fitful and awkward until the Dodo asked if I played chess. Slightly awestruck at the prospect of playing a Field Marshal, I nodded; and ninety minutes later, to my amazement, won the game.

I went into the kitchen, strutting somewhat, planning to boast a little to the old soldier's long-time housekeeper, Mrs Liddell. But as soon as I entered she said: "Don't tell me. You never went and won?"

"Yes," I said, affecting nonchalance. "As a matter of fact, yes, I did."

"Gawd," said Mrs Liddell. "Now there'll be hell to pay. You go back in there and ask him for another game, and this time make sure you lose."

I did as I was told, but was never invited to Beccles again.

Still, the defeat of the Dodo gave me new confidence at the chessboard, so when I returned to Waverley House after finishing my O levels, and was at once invited to play a game by Mixed-Up (Mary had told him about my victory in the Battle of Beccles with great pride and some hyperbole), I said: "Sure, I don't mind." How long could it take to thrash the old duffer, after all?

There followed a massacre royal. Mixed-Up did not just beat me; he had me for breakfast, over easy. I couldn't believe it—the canny opening, the fluency of his combination play, the force of his attacks, my own impossibly cramped, strangled positions—and asked for a second game. This time he tucked into me even more heartily. I sat broken in my chair at the end, close to tears. *Big girls don't cry*, I reminded myself, but the song went on playing in my head: *That's just an alibi.*[6]

"Who are you?" I demanded, humiliation weighing down every syllable. "The devil in disguise?"

Mixed-Up gave his big, silly grin. "Grand Master," he said. "Long time. Before head."

"You're a Grand Master," I repeated, still in a daze. Then in a moment of horror I remembered that I had seen the name Mecir in books of classic games. "Nimzo-Indian," I said aloud. He beamed and nodded furiously.

"That Mecir?" I asked wonderingly.

"That," he said. There was saliva dribbling out of a corner of his sloppy old mouth. This ruined old man was in the books. He was in the books. And even with his mind turned to rubble he could still wipe the floor with me.

"Now play lady," he grinned. I didn't get it. "Mary lady," he said. "Yes yes certainly." She was pouring tea, waiting for my answer. "Aya, you can't play," I said, bewildered.

"Learning, baba," she said. "What is it, na? Only a game."

And then she, too, beat me senseless, and with the black pieces, at that. It was not the greatest day of my life.

8

From *100 Most Instructive Chess Games* by Robert Reshevsky, 1961:

> M. Mecir—M. Najdorf
> *Dallas 1950, Nimzo-Indian Defense*

6. "Big Girls Don't Cry" was another falsetto hit for Frankie Valli and the Four Seasons in 1962.

The attack of a tactician can be troublesome to meet—that of a strategist even more so. Whereas the tactician's threats may be unmistakable, the strategist confuses the issue by keeping things in abeyance. He threatens to threaten!

Take this game for instance: Mecir posts a Knight at Q6 to get a grip on the center. Then he establishes a passed Pawn on one wing to occupy his opponent on the Queen side. Finally he stirs up the position on the King-side. What does the poor bewildered opponent do? How can he defend everything at once? Where will the blow fall?

Watch Mecir keep Najdorf on the run, as he shifts the attack from side to side!

Chess had become their private language. Old Mixed-Up, lost as he was for words, retained, on the chess-board, much of the articulacy and subtlety which had vanished from his speech. As Certainly-Mary gained in skill—and she had learned with astonishing speed, I thought bitterly, for someone who couldn't read or write or pronounce the letter p—she was better able to understand, and respond to, the wit of the reduced maestro with whom she had so unexpectedly forged a bond.

He taught her with great patience, showing-not-telling, repeating openings and combinations and endgame techniques over and over until she began to see the meaning in the patterns. When they played, he handicapped himself, he told her her best moves and demonstrated their consequences, drawing her, step by step, into the infinite possibilities of the game.

Such was their courtship. "It is like an adventure, baba," Mary once tried to explain to me. "It is like going with him to his country, you know? What a place, baap-ré! Beautiful and dangerous and funny and full of fuzzles. For me it is a big-big discovery. What to tell you? I go for the game. It is a wonder."

I understood, then, how far things had gone between them. Certainly-Mary had never married, and had made it clear to old Mixed-Up that it was too late to start any of that monkey business at her age. The courter was a widower, and had grown-up children somewhere, lost long ago behind the ever-higher walls of Eastern Europe. But in the game of chess they had found a form of flirtation, and endless renewal that precluded the possibility of boredom, a courtly wonderland of the ageing heart.

What would the Dodo have made of it all? No doubt it would have scandalised him to see chess, chess of all games, the great formalisation of war, transformed into an art of love.

As for me: my defeats by Certainly-Mary and her courter ushered in further humiliations. Durré and Muneeza went down with the mumps, and so, finally, in spite of my mother's efforts to segregate us, did I. I lay terrified in bed while the doctor warned me not to stand up and move around if I could possibly help it. "If you do," he said, "your parents won't need to punish you. You will have punished yourself quite enough."

I spent the following few weeks tormented day and night by visions of grotesquely swollen testicles and a subsequent life of limp impotence—finished before I'd even started, it wasn't fair—which were made much worse by my sisters' quick recovery and incessant gibes. But in the end I was lucky; the illness didn't spread to the deep South. "Think how happy your hundred and one girlfriends will be, bhai," sneered Durré, who knew all about my continued failures in the Rozalia and Chandni departments.

On the radio, people were always singing about the joys of being sixteen years old. I wondered where they were, all those boys and girls of my age having the time of their lives. Were they driving around America in Studebaker convertibles? They certainly weren't in my neighbourhood. London, W8 was Sam Cooke country that summer. *Another Saturday night . . .* [7] There might be a mop-top love-song stuck at number one, but I was down with lonely Sam in the lower depths of the charts, how-I-wishing I had someone, etc., and generally feeling in a pretty goddamn dreadful way.

9

"Baba, come quick."

It was late at night when Aya Mary shook me awake. After many urgent hisses, she managed to drag me out of sleep and pull me, pajama'ed and yawning, down the hall. On the landing outside our flat was Mixed-Up the courter, huddled up against a wall, weeping. He had a black eye and there was dried blood on his mouth.

"What happened?" I asked Mary, shocked.

"Men," wailed Mixed-Up. "Threaten. Beat."

He had been in his lounge earlier that evening when the sporting Maharaja of P— burst in to say, "If anybody comes looking for me, okay, any tough-guy type guys, okay, I am out, okay? Oh you tea. Don't let them go upstairs, okay? Big tip, okay?"

A short time later, the old Maharaja of B— also arrived in Mecir's lounge, looking distressed.

"Suno, listen on," said the Maharaja of B—. "You don't know where I am, samajh liya? Understood? Some low persons may inquire. You don't know. I am abroad, achha? On extended travels abroad. Do your job, porter. Handsome recompense."

Late at night two tough-guy types did indeed turn up. It seemed the hairy Prince P— had gambling debts. "Out," Mixed-Up grinned in his sweetest way. The tough-guy types nodded, slowly. They had long hair and thick lips like Mick Jagger's. "He's a busy gent. We should of made an appointment," said the first type to the second. "Didn't I tell you we should of called?"

"You did," agreed the second type. "Got to do these things right, you said, he's royalty. And you was right, my son, I put my hand up, I was dead wrong. I put my hand up to that."

"Let's leave our card," said the first type. "Then he'll know to expect us."

"Ideal," said the second type, and smashed his fist into old Mixed-Up's mouth. "You tell him," the second type said, and struck the old man in the eye. "When he's in. You mention it."

He had locked the front door after that; but much later, well after midnight, there was a hammering. Mixed-Up called out, "Who?"

"We are close friends of the Maharaja of B—" said a voice. "No, I tell a lie. Acquaintances."

"He calls upon a lady of our acquaintance," said a second voice. "To be precise."

"It is in that connection that we crave audience," said the first voice.

"Gone," said Mecir. "Jet plane. Gone."

There was a silence. Then the second voice said, "Can't be in the jet set if you never jump on a jet, eh? Biarritz, Monte, all of that."

"Be sure and let His Highness know," said the first voice, "that we eagerly await his return."

"With regard to our mutual friend," said the second voice. "Eagerly."

---

7. "Another Saturday Night" was a hit for R&B singer Sam Cooke in 1963.

What does the poor bewildered opponent do? The words from the chess book popped un-bidden into my head. *How can he defend everything at once? Where will the blow fall? Watch Mecir keep Najdorf on the run, as he shifts the attack from side to side!*

Mixed-Up returned to his lounge and on this occasion, even though there had been no use of force, he began to weep. After a time he took the elevator up to the fourth floor and whispered through our letter-box to Certainly-Mary sleeping on her mat.

"I didn't want to wake Sahib," Mary said. "You know his trouble, na? And Be-gum Sahiba is so tired at end of the day. So now you tell, baba, what to do?"

What did she expect me to come up with? I was sixteen years old. "Mixed-Up must call the police," I unoriginally offered.

"No, no, baba," said Certainly-Mary emphatically. "If the courter makes a scan-dal for Maharaja-log, then in the end it is the courter only who will be out on his ear."

I had no other ideas. I stood before them feeling like a fool, while they both turned upon me their frightened, supplicant eyes.

"Go to sleep," I said. "We'll think about it in the morning." *The first pair of thugs were tacticians, I was thinking. They were troublesome to meet. But the second pair were scarier; they were strategists. They threatened to threaten.*

Nothing happened in the morning, and the sky was clear. It was almost impossible to believe in fists, and menacing voices at the door. During the course of the day both Maharajas visited the porter's lounge and stuck five-pound notes in Mixed-Up's waistcoat pocket. "Held the fort, good man," said Prince P—, and the Maharaja of B— echoed those sentiments: "Spot on. All handled now, achha? Problem over."

The three of us—Aya Mary, her courter, and me—held a council of war that af-ternoon and decided that no further action was necessary. The hall porter was the front line in any such situation, I argued, and the front line had held. And now the risks were past. Assurances had been given. End of story.

"End of story," repeated Certainly-Mary doubtfully, but then, seeking to reassure Mecir, she brightened. "Correct," she said. "Most certainly! All-done, finis." She slapped her hands against each other for emphasis. She asked Mixed-Up if he wanted a game of chess; but for once the courter didn't want to play.

10

After that I was distracted, for a time, from the story of Mixed-Up and Certainly-Mary by violence nearer home.

My middle sister Muneeza, now eleven, was entering her delinquent phase a lit-tle early. She was the true inheritor of my father's black rage, and when she lost con-trol it was terrible to behold. That summer she seemed to pick fights with my father on purpose; seemed prepared, at her young age, to test her strength against his. (I in-tervened in her rows with Abba only once, in the kitchen. She grabbed the kitchen scissors and flung them at me. They cut me on the thigh. After that I kept my dis-tance.)

As I witnessed their wars I felt myself coming unstuck from the idea of family it-self. I looked at my screaming sister and thought how brilliantly self-destructive she was, how triumphantly she was ruining her relations with the people she needed most.

And I looked at my choleric, face-pulling father and thought about British citizenship. My existing Indian passport permitted me to travel only to a very few countries, which were carefully listed on the second right-hand page. But I might soon have a British passport and then, by hook or by crook, I would get away from him. I would not have this face-pulling in my life.

At sixteen, you still think you can escape from your father. You aren't listening to his voice speaking through your mouth, you don't see how your gestures already mirror his; you don't see him in the way you hold your body, in the way you sign your name. You don't hear his whisper in your blood.

On the day I have to tell you about, my two-year-old sister Chhoti Scheherazade, Little Scare-zade, started crying as she often did during one of our family rows. Amma and Aya Mary loaded her into her push-chair and made a rapid getaway. They pushed her to Kensington Square and then sat on the grass, turned Scheherazade loose and made philosophical remarks while she tired herself out. Finally, she fell asleep, and they made their way home in the fading light of the evening. Outside Waverley House they were approached by two well-turned-out young men with Beatle haircuts and the buttoned-up, collarless jackets made popular by the band. The first of these young men asked my mother, very politely, if she might be the Maharani of B——.

"No," my mother answered, flattered.

"Oh, but you are, madam," said the second Beatle, equally politely. "For you are heading for Waverley House and that is the Maharaja's place of residence."

"No, no," my mother said, still blushing with pleasure. "We are a different Indian family."

"Quite so," the first Beatle nodded understandingly, and then, to my mother's great surprise, placed a finger alongside his nose, and winked. "Incognito, eh. Mum's the word."

"Now excuse us," my mother said, losing patience. "We are not the ladies you seek."

The second Beatle tapped a foot lightly against a wheel of the push-chair. "Your husband seeks ladies, madam, were you aware of that fact? Yes, he does. Most assiduously, may I add."

"Too assiduously," said the first Beatle, his face darkening.

"I tell you I am not the Maharani Begum," my mother said, growing suddenly alarmed. "Her business is not my business. Kindly let me pass."

The second Beatle stepped closer to her. She could feel his breath, which was minty. "One of the ladies he sought out was our ward, as you might say," he explained. "That would be the term. Under our protection, you follow. Us, therefore, being responsible for her welfare."

"Your husband," said the first Beatle, showing his teeth in a frightening way, and raising his voice one notch, "damaged the goods. Do you hear me, Queenie? He damaged the fucking goods."

"Mistaken identity, fleas," said Certainly-Mary. "Many Indian residents in Waverley House. We are decent ladies; *fleas.*"

The second Beatle had taken out something from an inside pocket. A blade caught the light. "Fucking wogs,"[8] he said. "You fucking come over here, you don't fucking know how to fucking behave. Why don't you fucking fuck off to fucking Wogistan? Fuck your fucking wog arses. Now then," he added in a quiet voice, holding up the knife, "unbutton your blouses."

---

8. Derisive term for a dark-skinned foreigner, especially Indian or Pakistani.

Just then a loud noise emanated from the doorway of Waverley House. The two women and the two men turned to look, and out came Mixed-Up, yelling at the top of his voice and windmilling his arms like a mad old loon.

"Hullo," said the Beatle with the knife, looking amused. "Who's this, then? Oh oh fucking seven?"

Mixed-Up was trying to speak, he was in a mighty agony of effort, but all that was coming out of his mouth was raw, unshaped noise. Scheherazade woke up and joined in. The two Beatles looked displeased. But then something happened inside old Mixed-Up; something popped, and in a great rush he gabbled, "Sirs sirs no sirs these not B—women sirs B—women upstairs on floor three sirs Maharaja of B—also sirs God's truth mother's grave swear."

It was the longest sentence he had spoken since the stroke that had broken his tongue long ago.

And what with his torrent and Scheherazade's squalls there were suddenly heads poking out from doorways, attention was being paid, and the two Beatles nodded gravely. "Honest mistake," the first of them said apologetically to my mother, and actually bowed from the waist. "Could happen to anyone," the knife-man added, ruefully. They turned and began to walk quickly away. As they passed Mecir, however, they paused. "I know you, though," said the knife-man. " '*Jet plane. Gone.*' " He made a short movement of the arm, and then Mixed-Up the courter was lying on the pavement with blood leaking from a wound in his stomach. "All okay now," he gasped, and passed out.

II

He was on the road to recovery by Christmas; my mother's letter to the landlords, in which she called him a "knight in shining armour," ensured that he was well looked after, and his job was kept open for him. He continued to live in his little ground-floor cubby-hole, while the hall porter's duties were carried out by shift-duty staff. "Nothing but the best for our very own hero," the landlords assured my mother in their reply.

The two Maharajas and their retinues had moved out before I came home for the Christmas holidays, so we had no further visits from the Beatles or the Rolling Stones. Certainly-Mary spent as much time as she could with Mecir; but it was the look of my old Aya that worried me more than poor Mixed-Up. She looked older, and powdery, as if she might crumble away at any moment into dust.

"We didn't want to worry you at school," my mother said. "She has been having heart trouble. Palpitations. Not all the time, but."

Mary's health problems had sobered up the whole family. Muneeza's tantrums had stopped, and even my father was making an effort. They had put up a Christmas tree in the sitting-room and decorated it with all sorts of baubles. It was so odd to see a Christmas tree at our place that I realised things must be fairly serious.

On Christmas Eve my mother suggested that Mary might like it if we all sang some carols. Amma had made song-sheets, six copies, by hand. When we did *O come, all ye faithful* I showed off by singing from memory in Latin. Everybody behaved perfectly. When Muneeza suggested that we should try *Swinging on a Star* or *I Wanna Hold Your Hand* instead of this boring stuff, she wasn't really being serious. So this is family life, I thought. This is it.

But we were only play-acting.

A few weeks earlier, at school, I'd come across an American boy, the star of the school's Rugby football team, crying in the Chapel cloisters. I asked him what the matter was and he told me that President Kennedy had been assassinated. "I don't believe you," I said, but I could see that it was true. The football star sobbed and sobbed. I took his hand.

"When the President dies, the nation is orphaned," he eventually said, broken-heartedly parroting a piece of cracker-barrel wisdom he'd probably heard on Voice of America.[9]

"I know how you feel," I lied. "My father just died, too."

Mary's heart trouble turned out to be a mystery; unpredictably, it came and went. She was subjected to all sorts of tests during the next six months, but each time the doctors ended up by shaking their heads: they couldn't find anything wrong with her. Physically, she was right as rain; except that there were these periods when her heart kicked and bucked in her chest like the wild horses in *The Misfits*,[1] the ones whose roping and tying made Marilyn Monroe so mad.

Mecir went back to work in the spring, but his experience had knocked the stuffing out of him. He was slower to smile, duller of eye, more inward. Mary, too, had turned in upon herself. They still met for tea, crumpets and *The Flintstones*, but something was no longer quite right.

At the beginning of the summer Mary made an announcement.

"I know what is wrong with me," she told my parents, out of the blue. "I need to go home."

"But, Aya," my mother argued, "homesickness is not a real disease."

"God knows for what-all we came over to this country," Mary said. "But I can no longer stay. No. Certainly not." Her determination was absolute.

So it was England that was breaking her heart, breaking it by not being India. London was killing her, by not being Bombay. And Mixed-Up? I wondered. Was the courter killing her, too, because he was no longer himself? Or was it that her heart, roped by two different loves, was being pulled both East and West, whinnying and rearing, like those movie horses being yanked this way by Clark Gable and that way by Montgomery Clift, and she knew that to live she would have to choose?

"I must go," said Certainly-Mary. "Yes, certainly. *Bas*. Enough."

That summer, the summer of '64, I turned seventeen. Chandni went back to India. Durré's Polish friend Rozalia informed me over a sandwich in Oxford Street that she was getting engaged to a "real man," so I could forget about seeing her again, because this Zbigniew was the jealous type. Roy Orbison sang *It's Over* in my ears as I walked away to the Tube, but the truth was that nothing had really begun.

Certainly-Mary left us in mid-July. My father bought her a one-way ticket to Bombay, and that last morning was heavy with the pain of ending. When we took her bags down to the car, Mecir the hall porter was nowhere to be seen. Mary did not knock on the door of his lounge, but walked straight out through the freshly polished oak-panelled lobby, whose mirrors and brasses were sparkling brightly; she climbed into the back seat of our Ford Zodiac and sat there stiffly with her carry-on grip on her lap, staring straight ahead. I had known and loved her all my life. *Never mind your damned courter*, I wanted to shout at her, *what about me?*

---

9. Radio service established by the United States government in 1942 for the dissemination of news and information in occupied Europe during WWII.

1. *The Misfits*, a 1961 John Huston western starring Clark Gable, Marilyn Monroe, and Montgomery Clift.

As it happened, she was right about the homesickness. After her return to Bombay, she never had a day's heart trouble again; and, as the letter from her niece Stella confirmed, at ninety-one she was still going strong.

Soon after she left, my father told us he had decided to "shift location" to Pakistan. As usual, there were no discussions, no explanations, just the simple fiat. He gave up the lease on the flat in Waverley House at the end of the summer holidays, and they all went off to Karachi,[2] while I went back to school.

I became a British citizen that year. I was one of the lucky ones, I guess, because in spite of that chess game I had the Dodo on my side. And the passport did, in many ways, set me free. It allowed me to come and go, to make choices that were not the ones my father would have wished. But I, too, have ropes around my neck, I have them to this day, pulling me this way and that, East and West, the nooses tightening, commanding, *choose, choose*.

I buck, I snort, I whinny, I rear, I kick. Ropes, I do not choose between you. Lassoes, lariats, I choose neither of you, and both. Do you hear? I refuse to choose.

A year or so after we moved out I was in the area and dropped in at Waverley House to see how the old courter was doing. Maybe, I thought, we could have a game of chess, and he could beat me to a pulp. The lobby was empty, so I knocked on the door of his little lounge. A stranger answered.

"Where's Mixed-Up?" I cried, taken by surprise. I apologised at once, embarrassed. "Mr Mecir, I meant, the porter."

"I'm the porter, sir," the man said. "I don't know anything about any mix-up."

---

2. Pakistan's largest city and the capital of the province of Sindh.

≈÷ PERSPECTIVES ÷≈

Whose Language?

Though Britain's last major overseas colony, Hong Kong, rejoined China in 1997, at least one important reminder of British rule remains in countries as far-flung as India, South Africa, and New Zealand: the English language itself. Twentieth-century linguists, following on the pioneering work of Benjamin Lee Whorf and Edward Sapir, are nearly unanimous in their belief that languages do not merely serve to describe the world but in fact help to create that world, establishing both a set of possibilities and a set of limits.

The politics of language thus becomes important for writers, especially writers in colonial and postcolonial cultures. In an episode from Joyce's *A Portrait of the Artist as a Young Man*, the Irish protagonist Stephen Dedalus converses with the English-born Dean of Studies at University College, Dublin, where Stephen is a student. In the course of the conversation it becomes clear that Stephen is already a more supple and cunning user of the English language than his teacher, and yet he feels himself at a disadvantage in having to use the language of the invader; he muses: "The language in which we are speaking is his before it is mine. How different are the words *home, Christ, ale, master,* on his lips and on mine! I cannot speak or write these words without unrest of spirit. His language, so familiar and so foreign, will always be for me an acquired speech. I have not made or accepted its words. My voice holds them at bay. My soul frets in the shadow of his language." The Penal Acts of 1695 and 1696 had made the Irish language illegal in Ireland; after 500 years of trying to subdue the "wild Irish," British lawmakers realized that the Irish natives would never be brought under English rule until their tongues were bound. In his poem *Traditions,* Seamus Heaney meditates on the enduring cost of what he has called elsewhere "the government of the tongue":

> Our guttural muse
> was bulled long ago
> by the alliterative tradition,
> her uvula grows
> vestigial, forgotten.

In much colonial and postcolonial writing, however, the confusion of tongues inflicted by British rule has been seen by the writers of Empire as a positive linguistic resource. Nadine Gordimer in South Africa and James Kelman in Scotland both mix local dialect with standard English to take the measure of reality a far cry from London. Salman Rushdie, explaining his decision to use English rather than his native Hindi, writes: "Those of us who do use English do so in spite of our ambiguity towards it, or perhaps because of that, perhaps because we can find in that linguistic struggle a reflection of other struggles taking place in the real world, struggles between the cultures within ourselves and the influences working upon our societies. To conquer English may be to complete the process of making ourselves free." Thus a great deal of contemporary English-language writing—especially in countries where English was once the language of the conqueror (such as Ireland, Scotland, Wales, South Africa, India, and Kenya)—meditates on the blindnesses and insights inherent in using English. Some writers, like the Irish poet Nuala Ní Dhomhnaill, write in defiance of English; if one's native tongue is a minority language like Irish, this decision necessarily narrows a writer's potential audience. More common is the decision made by Rushdie, and by James Joyce before him: to write English as an "outsider," attesting to an alien's perspective on the majority language.

Louise Bennett
b. 1919

Born to working-class parents in Kingston, Jamaica, Louise Bennett left the island in 1945 to pursue her studies in England at the Royal Academy of Dramatic Art. After graduation, she worked with repertory companies throughout England and appeared occasionally on Jamaican television, playing various comedic roles. Her writing has helped bring literary recognition to the Jamaican patois, and her descriptions of life on the island have brought her both critical acclaim and popularity. Her books include *Jamaica Labrish* (1966) and *Anancy and Miss Lou* (1979). She has lectured across the United States and the United Kingdom on Jamaican music and folklore, and served the Jamaican government as a cultural ambassador at large. She has been awarded the Order of Jamaica, the Norman Manley Award for Excellence in the field of arts, and the Institute of Jamaica's Musgrave Silver and Gold Medals for distinguished eminence in the field of arts and culture. In 2001, Bennett was appointed a Member of the Order of Merit for her contribution to the development of Jamaican arts and culture. She has lived for the past decade in Canada.

Back to Africa

Back to Africa, Miss Mattie?
You no know wha you dah seh?
You haf fe come from somewhe fus
Before you go back deh!

5   Me know say dat you great great great
Granma was African,
But Mattie, doan you great great great
Granpa was Englishman?

Den you great granmader fader
10   By you fader side was Jew?
An you granpa by you mader side
Was Frenchie parlez-vous?

But de balance a you family,
You whole generation,
15   Oonoo all barn dung a Bun Grung—[1]
Oonoo all is Jamaican!

Den is weh you gwine, Miss Mattie?
Oh, you view de countenance,
An between you an de Africans
20   Is great resemblance!

Ascorden to dat, all dem blue-yeye
White American
Who-fa great granpa was Englishman
Mus go back a Englan!

---

1. Burned Ground (a place name).

25   What a debil of a bump-an-bore,
      Rig-jig an palam-pam
      Ef de whole worl start fe go back
      Whe dem great granpa come from!

      Ef a hard time you dah run from
30   Tek you chance! But Mattie, do
      Sure a whe you come from so you got
      Somewhe fe come back to!

      Go a foreign, seek you fortune,
      But no tell nobody say
35   You dah go fe seek you homelan,
      For a right deh so you deh!

                                        1966

Colonization in Reverse

      Wat a joyful news, Miss Mattie,
      I feel like me heart gwine burs
      Jamaica people colonizin
      Englan in reverse.

5   By de hundred, by de tousan
      From country and from town,
      By de ship-load, by de plane-load
      Jamaica is Englan boun.

      Dem a pour out a Jamaica,
10   Everybody future plan
      Is fe get a big-time job
      An settle in de mother lan.

      What a islan! What a people!
      Man an woman, old an young
15   Jus a pack dem bag an baggage
      An tun history upside dung!

      Some people doan like travel,
      But fe show dem loyalty
      Dem all a open up cheap-fare-
20   To-Englan agency.

      An week by week dem shippin off
      Dem countryman like fire,
      Fe immigrate an populate
      De seat a de Empire.

25   Oonoo see how life is funny,
      Oonoo see de tunabout?
      Jamaica live fe box bread
      Out a English people mout'.

For wen dem ketch a Englan,
30   An start play dem different role,
Some will settle down to work
An some will settle fe de dole.

Jane say de dole is not too bad
Because dey payin she
35   Two pounds a week fe seek a job
Dat suit her dignity.

Me say Jane will never fine work
At de rate how she dah look,
For all day she stay pon Aunt Fan couch
40   An read love-story book.

Wat a devilment a Englan!
Dem face war an brave de worse,
But me wonderin how dem gwine stan
Colonizin in reverse.

                                                    1966

Independance

Independance wid a vengeance!
Independance raisin Cain!
Jamaica start grow beard, ah hope
We chin can stan de strain!

5   When daag° marga° him head big, an   *dog / thin*
When puss hungry him nose clean,
But every puss an daag no know
What Independance mean.

Mattie seh it mean we facety,°   *proud*
10   Stan up pon we dignity,
An we doan allow nobody
Fe tek liberty wid we.

Independance is we nature
Born an bred in all we do,
15   An she glad fe see dat Government
Tun independant too.

She hope dem caution worl-map
Fe stop draw Jamaica small,
For de lickle speck cyaan show
20   We independantness at all!

Moresomever we must tell map dat
We doan like we position—
Please kindly tek we out a sea
An draw we in de ocean.

25   What a crosses! Independance
Woulda never have a chance

Wid so much hoogooyagga
Dah expose dem ignorance.

Daag wag im tail fe suit im size
30   An match im stamina—
Jamaica people need a
Independance formula!

No easy-come-by freeness tings,
Nuff labour, some privation,
35   Not much of dis an less of dat
An plenty studiration.

Independance wid a vengeance!
Wonder how we gwine to cope?
Jamaica start smoke pipe, ah hope
40   We got nuff jackass rope!¹

1966

Ngũgĩ wa Thiong'o
b. 1938

The great novelist and postcolonial theorist Ngũgĩ wa Thiong'o is a crucial figure to bring into the debate about the ownership of English. Like Nuala Ní Dhomhnaill, the Irish poet who has decided to write in Irish and have her work translated by others into English, even though English is her first language, Ngũgĩ has political reasons for questioning the use of English by African writers who, as he once did, write the literature of modern Africa in European languages. Ngũgĩ achieved prominence in Africa and in Britain and America for his English-language novels of the African struggle for self-determination, especially the revolution in Kenya that led to its independence from Great Britain. After two years of imprisonment by the Kenyan government in 1977 for what it considered a subversive play, Ngũgĩ made the decision to stop writing in English and has since done his creative work in Gĩkũyũ, offering English translations, while continuing to write critical works and political essays in English for worldwide audiences. Despite his love of English and the global impact of his novels, Ngũgĩ wa Thiong'o believes English can never be one of Africa's true languages of liberation and cultural creation.

A Kenyan of the Gĩkũyũ tribe, Ngũgĩ was born James Ngũgĩ, one of twenty-eight children of a peasant farmer who squatted on the land of an African landlord. Kenya was under British colonial rule then, and James's early education was at missionary-run primary schools. Political agitation for independence reached a peak in the 1950s, and when a "State of Emergency" was declared in Kenya in 1952 by the British, English became the official language of instruction. Ngũgĩ won a place at the prestigious Alliance High School and received a thorough training in English literature. The struggle for independence powerfully affected him and his community; upon arriving home on a school vacation, for example, Ngũgĩ found his home destroyed by the colonial soldiers, whose policy of "protecting" villages from insurgency was actually designed to cut off the supply of food the villagers gave to the freedom fighters. This trauma is registered at the heart of Ngũgĩ's writing; his novels almost all contain the motif of a thwarted attempt to return home.

1. Twisted plug tobacco.

Ngũgĩ graduated from Makerere University College in Kampala with an honors degree in English; in the heady postcolonial atmosphere he read not only English classics but was also exposed to the new literature of Africa and the Caribbean by writers like Chinua Achebe and George Lamming. By 1966 James Ngũgĩ had gone to England to study for an M.A. in English at Leeds University, although his main subject was to be Caribbean literature. Ngũgĩ never finished his thesis, which was ironically a boon to world literature, because he was immersed in completing his important novel *A Grain of Wheat* (1966). Two novels had preceded it, the autobiographical *Weep Not, Child* (1964) and *The River Between* (1965). Throughout this time Ngũgĩ continued to write plays; the last work he published as James Ngũgĩ was a collection of short plays *This Time Tomorrow* (1970). While teaching as a visiting professor at several universities, Ngũgĩ wa Thiong'o wrote one of his most impressive novels, *Petals of Blood* (1977). As its title suggests, the novel also treats the bloody trauma of breaking away as a new nation, a nation inevitably haunted by its former colonial existence.

The two years Ngũgĩ spent in prison crystallized his thoughts about decolonization, which he had come to see was not merely a political event but demanded an entire change in the minds of those who had been dominated. The price of becoming free and establishing a viable culture entailed giving up the language of the colonizer. The president of Kenya, Daniel Arap Moi, has permanently banned Ngũgĩ from Kenya as a political threat. From the time of his sentence on, although living in exile and far from his Gĩkũyũ roots in Kenya, Ngũgĩ's fiction, plays, and poetry have been written in the Gĩkũyũ language. His first post-English novel, *Caitaani Muthara-ini* (*Devil on the Cross*, 1980), was written in jail on sheets of the coarse toilet paper provided him in his prison cell and smuggled out by a sympathetic guard. With the strokes of his worn pencil on that rough and precious paper, Ngũgĩ proved his dedication to creating an African literature in its indigenous tongues and ceased to be what he now calls an Afro-European writer. Ngũgĩ has not been back to Kenya since 1982, and his books are banned in his homeland. He has written several novels in the past decade, as well as screenplays for African cinema and many more plays; he founded and edited the first Gĩkũyũ language literary journal *Mutiri*. Ngũgĩ taught all over the world as a visiting professor at such institutions as Beyreuth University, Auckland University, Yale University, and New York University, among others; he is currently a distinguised professor of comparative literature at the University of California, Irvine.

Paradoxically, perhaps, Ngũgĩ wrote his great theoretical analysis of the political and spiritual process of decolonization, *Decolonizing the Mind* (1980), in English, and it has circulated globally as a worldwide touchstone of liberation. An excerpt chosen from this lasting book represents Ngũgĩ's uncompromising answer to the question "whose language?" English can never belong to Africans until the languages of Africa create a literary home where English is not the master, but only an invited guest.

from DECOLONIZING THE MIND

Native African Languages

3

I was born into a large peasant family: father, four wives and about twenty-eight children. I also belonged, as we all did in those days, to a wider extended family and to the community as a whole.

We spoke Gĩkũyũ as we worked in the fields. We spoke Gĩkũyũ in and outside the home. I can vividly recall those evenings of story-telling around the fireside. It was mostly the grown-ups telling the children but everybody was interested and involved. We children would re-tell the stories the following day to other children who worked in the fields picking the pyrethrum flowers, tea-leaves or coffee beans of our European and African landlords.

The stories, with mostly animals as the main characters, were all told in Gĩkũyũ. Hare, being small, weak but full of innovative wit and cunning, was our hero. We identified with him as he struggled against the brutes of prey like Lion, Leopard, Hyena. His victories were our victories and we learnt that the apparently weak can outwit the strong. We followed the animals in their struggle against hostile nature—drought, rain, sun, wind—a confrontation often forcing them to search for forms of co-operation. But we were also interested in their struggles amongst themselves, and particularly between the beasts and the victims of prey. These twin struggles, against nature and other animals, reflected real-life struggles in the human world.

Not that we neglected stories with human beings as the main characters. There were two types of characters in such human-centred narratives: the species of truly human beings with qualities of courage, kindness, mercy, hatred of evil, concern for others; and a man-eat-man two-mouthed species with qualities of greed, selfishness, individualism and hatred of what was good for the larger co-operative community. Co-operation as the ultimate good in a community was a constant theme. It could unite human beings with animals against ogres and beasts of prey, as in the story of how Dove, after being fed with castoroil seeds, was sent to fetch a smith working far away from home and whose pregnant wife was being threatened by these man-eating two-mouthed ogres.

There were good and bad story-tellers. A good one could tell the same story over and over again, and it would always be fresh to us, the listeners. He or she could tell a story told by someone else and make it more alive and dramatic. The differences really were in the use of words and images and the inflexion of voices to effect different tones.

We therefore learnt to value words for their meaning and nuances. Language was not a mere string of words. It had a suggestive power well beyond the immediate and lexical meaning. Our appreciation of the suggestive magical power of language was reinforced by the games we played with words through riddles, proverbs, transpositions of syllables, or through nonsensical but musically arranged words. So we learnt the music of our language on top of the content. The language, through images and symbols, gave us a view of the world, but it had a beauty of its own. The home and the field were then our pre-primary school but what is important, for this discussion, is that the language of our evening teach-ins, and the language of our immediate and wider community, and the language of our work in the fields were one.

And then I went to school, a colonial school, and this harmony was broken. The language of my education was no longer the language of my culture. I first went to Kamaandura, missionary run, and then to another called Maanguũũ run by nationalists grouped around the Gĩkũyũ Independent and Karinga Schools Association. Our language of education was still Gĩkũyũ. The very first time I was ever given an ovation for my writing was over a composition in Gĩkũyũ. So for my first four years there was still harmony between the language of my formal education and that of the Limuru peasant community.

It was after the declaration of a state of emergency over Kenya in 1952 that all the schools run by patriotic nationalists were taken over by the colonial regime and were placed under District Education Boards chaired by Englishmen. English became the language of my formal education. In Kenya, English became more than a language: it was *the* language, and all the others had to bow before it in deference.

Thus one of the most humiliating experiences was to be caught speaking Gĩkũyũ in the vicinity of the school. The culprit was given corporal punishment—three to five strokes of the cane on bare buttocks—or was made to carry a metal plate around the neck with inscriptions such as I AM STUPID or I AM A DONKEY. Sometimes the culprits were fined money they could hardly afford. And how did the teachers catch the culprits?

A button was initially given to one pupil who was supposed to hand it over to whoever was caught speaking his mother tongue. Whoever had the button at the end of the day would sing who had given it to him and the ensuing process would bring out all the culprits of the day. Thus children were turned into witch-hunters and in the process were being taught the lucrative value of being a traitor to one's immediate community.

The attitude to English was the exact opposite: any achievement in spoken or written English was highly rewarded; prizes, prestige, applause; the ticket to higher realms. English became the measure of intelligence and ability in the arts, the sciences, and all the other branches of learning. English became *the* main determinant of a child's progress up the ladder of formal education.

As you may know, the colonial system of education in addition to its apartheid racial demarcation had the structure of a pyramid: a broad primary base, a narrowing secondary middle, and an even narrower university apex. Selections from primary into secondary were through an examination, in my time called Kenya African Preliminary Examination, in which one had to pass six subjects ranging from Maths to Nature Study and Kiswahili. All the papers were written in English. Nobody could pass the exam who failed the English language paper no matter how brilliantly he had done in the other subjects. I remember one boy in my class of 1954 who had distinctions in all subjects except English, which he had failed. He was made to fail the entire exam. He went on to become a turn boy in a bus company. I who had only passes but a credit in English got a place at the Alliance High School, one of the most elitist institutions for Africans in colonial Kenya. The requirements for a place at the University, Makerere University College, were broadly the same: nobody could go on to wear the undergraduate red gown, no matter how brilliantly they had performed in all the other subjects unless they had a credit—not even a simple pass!—in English. Thus the most coveted place in the pyramid and in the system was only available to the holder of an English language credit card. English was the official vehicle and the magic formula to colonial elitedom.

Literary education was now determined by the dominant language while also reinforcing that dominance. Orature (oral literature) in Kenyan languages stopped. In primary school I now read simplified Dickens and Stevenson alongside Rider Haggard. Jim Hawkins, Oliver Twist, Tom Brown—not Hare, Leopard and Lion—were now my daily companions in the world of imagination. In secondary school, Scott and G. B. Shaw vied with more Rider Haggard, John Buchan, Alan Paton, Captain W. E. Johns. At Makerere I read English: from Chaucer to T. S. Eliot with a touch of Graham Greene.

Thus language and literature were taking us further and further from ourselves to other selves, from our world to other worlds.

What was the colonial system doing to us Kenyan children? What were the consequences of, on the one hand, this systematic suppression of our languages and the literature they carried, and on the other the elevation of English and the literature it carried?

9

I started writing in Gĩkũyũ language in 1977 after seventeen years of involvement in Afro-European literature, in my case Afro-English literature. It was then that I collaborated with Ngũgĩ wa Mĩriĩ in the drafting of the playscript, *Ngaahika Ndeenda* (the English translation was *I Will Marry When I Want*). I have since published a novel in Gĩkũyũ, *Caitaani Mũtharabainĩ* (English translation: *Devil on the Cross*) and completed a musical drama, *Maitũ Njugĩra*, (English translation: *Mother Sing for Me*); three books for children, *Njamba Nene na Mbaathi i Mathagu, Bathitoora ya Njamba Nene, Njamba Nene na Cibũ Kĩng'ang'i*, as well as another novel manuscript: *Matigari Ma Njirũũngi*.

Wherever I have gone, particularly in Europe, I have been confronted with the question: why are you now writing in Gĩkũyũ? Why do you now write in an African language? In some academic quarters I have been confronted with the rebuke, "Why have you abandoned us?" It was almost as if, in choosing to write in Gĩkũyũ, I was doing something abnormal. But Gĩkũyũ is my mother tongue! The very fact that what common sense dictates in the literary practice of other cultures is being questioned in an African writer is a measure of how far imperialism has distorted the view of African realities. It has turned reality upside down: the abnormal is viewed as normal and the normal is viewed as abnormal. Africa actually enriches Europe: but Africa is made to believe that it needs Europe to rescue it from poverty. Africa's natural and human resources continue to develop Europe and America: but Africa is made to feel grateful for aid from the same quarters that still sit on the back of the continent. Africa even produces intellectuals who now rationalise this upside-down way of looking at Africa.

I believe that my writing in Gĩkũyũ language, a Kenyan language, an African language, is part and parcel of the anti-imperialist struggles of Kenyan and African peoples. In schools and universities our Kenyan languages—that is the languages of the many nationalities which make up Kenya—were associated with negative qualities of backwardness, underdevelopment, humiliation and punishment. We who went through that school system were meant to graduate with a hatred of the people and the culture and the values of the language of our daily humiliation and punishment. I do not want to see Kenyan children growing up in that imperialist-imposed tradition of contempt for the tools of communication developed by their communities and their history. I want them to transcend colonial alienation.

* * *

Chinua Achebe once decried the tendency of African intellectuals to escape into abstract universalism in the words that apply even more to the issue of the language of African literature:

> Africa has had such a fate in the world that the very adjective *African* can call up hideous fears of rejection. Better then to cut all the links with this homeland, this liability, and become in one giant leap the universal man. Indeed I understand this anxiety. *But running away from oneself seems to me a very inadequate way of dealing with an anxiety* [italics mine]. And if writers should opt for such escapism, who is to meet the challenge?

Who indeed?

We African writers are bound by our calling to do for our languages what Spenser, Milton and Shakespeare did for English; what Pushkin and Tolstoy did for Russian; indeed what all writers in world history have done for their languages by meeting the challenge of creating a literature in them, which process later opens the languages for philosophy, science, technology and all the other areas of human creative endeavours.

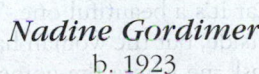

Nadine Gordimer
b. 1923

Nadine Gordimer was born in South Africa to Jewish emigrant parents from London. Thus her childhood, like those of the children of countless middle-class colonial families, was somewhat complex and contradictory. In an interview, Gordimer offers this explanation: "I think when you're born white in South Africa, you're peeling like an orange. You're sloughing off all the conditioning that you've had since you were a child." In Gordimer's case, that "sloughing off" of white, British prejudices and habits of mind has been thorough; the novelist Paul Theroux, for instance, suggests that "Gordimer's vision of Africa is the most complete one we have, and in time to come, when we want to know everything there is to know about a newly independent black African country, it is to this white South African woman . . . that we will turn."

Since Gordimer published her first collection of short stories in 1949 her writing has been praised for its evenhanded and scrupulously honest treatment of the political terrain of South Africa; over the years she has become, in the words of one critic, "the literary voice and conscience of her society." Among her gifts are an ear sensitive to the cadences and idiosyncrasies of spoken English, and a gift for social satire in service of a finally moral purpose. The long-standing subject of Gordimer's writing—her great theme—is, as critic Michiko Kakutani describes it, "the consequences of apartheid on the daily lives of men and women, the distortions it produces in relationships among both blacks and whites." In Gordimer's writing, these distortions are always shown rather than explained; her presentation is essentially dramatic, a trait she shares with modern masters of short fiction like Chekhov and Joyce.

Gordimer has been faulted for the emphasis in politics in her writing. Her response to this charge is eloquent: "The real influence of politics on my writing is the influence of politics on people. Their lives, and I believe their very personalities, are changed by the extreme political circumstances one lives under in South Africa. I am dealing with people; here are people who are shaped and changed by politics. In that way my material is profoundly influenced by politics." To date, Gordimer has published more than ten novels, including the celebrated *A Guest of Honour* (1970) and *The Conservationist* (1974; cowinner of the Booker McConnell Prize), and nine collections of short stories. *Jump and Other Stories*, which includes *What Were You Dreaming?*, was published in 1991, the same year Gordimer was awarded the Nobel Prize for Literature. In this story, the disjunction between black and white South African English is the starting-point for an exploration of blocked communication between races and genders alike. Her thirteenth novel, *Get a Life*, was published in 2005.

What Were You Dreaming?

I'm standing here by the road long time, yesterday, day before, today. Not the same road but it's the same—hot, hot like today. When they turn off where they're going, I must get out again, wait again. Some of them they just pretend there's nobody there, they don't want to see nobody. Even go a bit faster, *ja*. Then they past, and I'm waiting. I combed my hair; I don't want to look like a *skollie* [ruffian]. Don't smile because they think you being too friendly, you think you good as them. They go and they go. Some's got the baby's napkin hanging over the back window to keep out this sun. Some's not going on holiday with their kids but is alone; all alone in a big car. But they'll never stop, the whites, if they alone. Never. Because these *skollies* and that kind've spoilt it all for us, sticking a gun in the driver's neck, stealing his money, beating him up and taking the car. Even killing him. So it's buggered up for us. No white wants some guy sitting behind his head. And the blacks—when they stop for you, they ask for money. They want you must pay, like for a taxi! The blacks!

But then these whites: they stopping; I'm surprised, because it's only two—empty in the back—and the car it's a beautiful one. The windows are that special glass, you can't see in if you outside, but the woman has hers down and she's calling me over with her finger. She ask me where I'm going and I say the next place because they don't like to have you for too far, so she say get in and lean into the back to move along her stuff that's on the back seat to make room. Then she say, lock the door, just push that button down, we don't want you to fall out, and it's like she's joking with someone she know. The man driving smiles over his shoulder and say something—I can't hear it very well, it's the way he talk English. So anyway I say what's all right to say, yes master, thank you master, I'm going to Warmbad. He ask again, but man, I don't get it—*Ekskuus?* Please? And she chips in—she's a lady with grey hair and he's a young chap—My friend's from England, he's asking if you've been waiting a long time for a lift. So I tell them—A long time? Madam! And because they white, I tell them about the blacks, how when they stop they ask you to pay. This time I understand what the young man's saying, he say, And most whites don't stop? And I'm careful what I say, I tell them about the blacks, how too many people spoil it for us, they robbing and killing, you can't blame white people. Then he ask where I'm from. And she laugh and look round where I'm behind her. I see she know I'm from the Cape, although she ask me. I tell her I'm from the Cape Flats[1] and she say she suppose I'm not born there, though, and she's right, I'm born in Wynberg, right there in Cape Town. So she say, And they moved you out?

Then I catch on what kind of white she is; so I tell her, yes, the government kicked us out from our place, and she say to the young man, You see?

He want to know why I'm not in the place in the Cape Flats, why I'm so far away here. I tell them I'm working in Pietersburg.[2] And he keep on, why? Why? What's my job, everything, and if I don't understand the way he speak, she chips in again all the time and ask me for him. So I tell him, panel beater.[3] And I tell him, the pay is very low in the Cape. And then I begin to tell them lots of things, some things is real and some things I just think of, things that are going to make them like me, maybe they'll take me all the way there to Pietersburg.

I tell them I'm six days on the road. I not going to say I'm sick as well, I been home because I was sick—because *she's* not from overseas, I suss that, she know that old story. I tell them I had to take leave because my mother's got trouble with my brothers and sisters, we seven in the family and no father. And s'true's God, it seem like what I'm saying. When do you ever see him except he's drunk. And my brother is trouble, trouble, he hangs around with bad people and my other brother doesn't help my mother. And that's no lie, neither, how can he help when he's doing time; but they don't need to know that, they only get scared I'm the same kind like him, if I tell about him, assault and intent to do bodily harm. The sisters are in school and my mother's only got the pension. *Ja.* I'm working there in Pietersburg and every week, madam, I swear to you, I send my pay for my mother and sisters. So then he say, Why get off here? Don't you want us to take you to Pietersburg? And she say, of course, they going that way.

And I tell them some more. They listening to me so nice, and I'm talking, talking. I talk about the government, because I hear she keep saying to him, telling about this law and that law. I say how it's not fair we had to leave Wynberg and go to the Flats. I tell her we got sicknesses—she say what kind, is it unhealthy there? And I don't have to think what, I just say it's *bad, bad*, and she say to the man, As I told you. I tell about the house we had in Wynberg, but it's not my grannie's old house where we was all living together so long, the house I'm telling them about is more the kind of house they'll know, they wouldn't like to go away from, with a tiled bathroom, electric stove, everything. I tell them we spend three thousand rands fixing up that house—my uncle give us the money, that's how we got it. He give us his savings, three thousand rands. (I don't know why I say three; old Uncle Jimmy never have

1. A small town near Cape Town.
2. A city in northeastern South Africa.

3. A person who does body work on automobiles.

three or two or one in his life. I just say it.) And then we just kicked out. And panel beaters getting low pay there; it's better in Pietersburg.

He say, but I'm far from my home? And I tell her again, because she's white but she's a woman too, with that grey hair she's got grown-up kids—Madam. I send my pay home every week, s'true's God, so's they can eat, there in the Flats. I'm saying, *six days on the road*. While I'm saying it, I'm thinking; then I say, look at me, I got only these clothes, I sold my things on the way, to have something to eat. *Six days on the road*. He's from overseas and she isn't one of those who say you're a liar, doesn't trust you—right away when I got in the car, I notice she doesn't take her stuff over to the front like they usually do in case you pinch something of theirs. Six days on the road, and am I tired, tired! When I get to Pietersburg I must try borrow me a rand to get a taxi there to where I live. He say, Where do you live? Not in town? And she laugh, because he don't know nothing about this place, where whites live and where we must go—but I know they both thinking and I know what they thinking; I know I'm going to get something when I get out, don't need to worry about that. They feeling bad about me, now. Bad. Anyhow it's God's truth that I'm tired, tired, that's true.

They've put up her window and he's pushed a few buttons, now it's like in a supermarket, cool air blowing, and the windows like sunglasses: that sun can't get me here.

The Englishman glances over his shoulder as he drives.

"Taking a nap."

"I'm sure it's needed."

All through the trip he stops for everyone he sees at the roadside. Some are not hitching at all, never expecting to be given a lift anywhere, just walking in the heat outside with an empty plastic can to be filled with water or paraffin or whatever it is they buy in some country store, or standing at some point between departure and destination, small children and bundles linked on either side, baby on back. She hasn't said anything to him. He would only misunderstand if she explained why one doesn't give lifts in this country; and if she pointed out that in spite of this, she doesn't mind him breaking the sensible if unfortunate rule, he might misunderstand that, as well— think she was boasting of her disregard for personal safety weighed in the balance against decent concern for fellow beings.

He persists in making polite conversation with these passengers because he doesn't want to be patronizing; picking them up like so many objects and dropping them off again, silent, smelling of smoke from open cooking fires, sun and sweat, there behind his head. They don't understand his Englishman's English and if he gets an answer at all it's a deaf man's guess at what's called for. Some grin with pleasure and embarrass him by showing it the way they've been taught is acceptable, invoking him as *baas* and *master* when they get out and give thanks. But although he doesn't know it, being too much concerned with those names thrust into his hands like whips whose purpose is repugnant to him, has nothing to do with him, she knows each time that there is a moment of annealment[4] in the air-conditioned hired car belonging to nobody—a moment like that on a no-man's-land bridge in which an accord between warring countries is signed— when there is no calling of names, and all belong in each other's presence. He doesn't feel it because he has no wounds, neither has inflicted, nor will inflict any.

This one standing at the roadside with his transistor radio in a plastic bag was actually thumbing a lift like a townee; his expectation marked him out. And when her

---

4. Tempering by heating.

companion to whom she was showing the country inevitably pulled up, she read the face at the roadside immediately: the lively, cajoling, performer's eyes, the salmon-pinkish cheeks and nostrils, and as he jogged over smiling, the unselfconscious gap of gum between the canines.

A sleeper is always absent; although present, there on the back seat.

"The way he spoke about black people, wasn't it surprising? I mean—he's black himself."

"Oh no he's not. Couldn't you see the difference? He's a Cape Coloured. From the way he speaks English—couldn't you hear he's not like the Africans you've talked to?"

But of course he hasn't seen, hasn't heard: the fellow is dark enough, to those who don't know the signs by which you're classified, and the melodramatic, long-vowelled English is as difficult to follow if more fluent than the terse, halting responses of blacker people.

"Would he have a white grandmother or even a white father, then?"

She gives him another of the little history lessons she has been supplying along the way. The Malay slaves brought by the Dutch East India Company[5] to their supply station, on the route to India, at the Cape in the seventeenth century; the Khoikhoi who were the indigenous inhabitants of that part of Africa; add Dutch, French, English, German settlers whose back-yard progeniture with these and other blacks began a people who are all the people in the country mingled in one bloodstream. But encounters along the road teach him more than her history lessons, or the political analyses in which they share the same ideological approach although he does not share responsibility for the experience to which the ideology is being applied. She has explained Acts, Proclamations, Amendments. The Group Areas Act, Resettlement Act, Orderly Movement and Settlement of Black Persons Act. She has translated these statute-book euphemisms: people as movable goods. People packed onto trucks along with their stoves and beds while front-end loaders scoop away their homes into rubble. People dumped somewhere else. Always somewhere else. People as the figures, decimal points and multiplying zero-zero-zeros into which individual lives—Black Persons Orderly-Moved, -Effluxed, -Grouped—coagulate and compute. Now he has here in the car the intimate weary odour of a young man to whom these things happen.

"Half his family sick . . . it must be pretty unhealthy, where they've been made to go."

She smiles. "Well, I'm not too sure about that. I had the feeling, some of what he said . . . they're theatrical by nature. You must take it with a pinch of salt."

"You mean about the mother and sisters and so on?"

She's still smiling, she doesn't answer.

"But he couldn't have made up about taking a job so far from home—and the business of sending his wages to his mother? That too?"

He glances at her.

Beside him, she's withdrawn as the other one, sleeping behind him. While he turns his attention back to the road, she is looking at him secretly, as if somewhere in his blue eyes registering the approaching road but fixed on the black faces he is trying to read, somewhere in the lie of his inflamed hand and arm that on their travels have been plunged in the sun as if in boiling water, there is the place through which the

---

5. Occupied South Africa from 1652–1795 while it was a Dutch Cape Colony.

worm he needs to be infected with can find a way into him, so that he may host it and become its survivor, himself surviving through being fed on. Become like her. Complicity is the only understanding.

"Oh it's true, it's all true. . . not in the way he's told about it. Truer than the way he told it. All these things happen to them. And other things. Worse. But why burden us? Why try to explain to us? Things so far from what we know, how will they ever explain? How will we react? Stop our ears? Or cover our faces? Open the door and throw him out? They don't know. But sick mothers and brothers gone to the bad—these are the staples of misery, mmh? Think of the function of charity in the class struggles in your own country in the nineteenth century; it's all there in your literature. The lord-of-the-manor's compassionate daughter carrying hot soup to the dying cottager on her father's estate. The "advanced" upper-class woman comforting her cook when the honest drudge's daughter takes to whoring for a living. *Shame,* we say here. Shame. You must've heard it? We think it means, what a pity; we think we are expressing sympathy—for them. *Shame.* I don't know what we're saying about ourselves." She laughs.

"So you think it would at least be true that his family were kicked out of their home, sent away?"

"Why would anyone of them need to make that up? It's an everyday affair."

"What kind of place would they get, where they were moved?"

"Depends. A tent, to begin with. And maybe basic materials to build themselves a shack. Perhaps a one-room prefab. Always a tin toilet set down in the veld,[6] if nothing else. Some industrialist must be making a fortune out of government contracts for those toilets. You build your new life round that toilet. His people are Coloured, so it could be they were sent where there were houses of some sort already built for them; Coloureds usually get something a bit better than blacks are given."

"And the house would be more or less as good as the one they had? People as poor as that—and they'd spent what must seem a fortune to them, fixing it up."

"I don't know what kind of house they had. We're not talking about slum clearance, my dear; we're talking about destroying communities because they're black, and white people want to build houses or factories for whites where blacks live. I told you. We're talking about loading up trucks and carting black people out of sight of whites."

"And even where he's come to work—Pietersburg, whatever-it's-called—he doesn't live in the town."

"Out of sight." She has lost the thought for a moment, watching to make sure the car takes the correct turning. "Out of sight. Like those mothers and grannies and brothers and sisters far away on the Cape Flats."

"I don't think it's possible he actually sends all his pay. I mean how would one eat?"

"Maybe what's left doesn't buy anything he really wants."

Not a sound, not a sigh in sleep behind them. They can go on talking about him as he always has been discussed, there and yet not there.

Her companion is alert to the risk of gullibility. He verifies the facts, smiling, just as he converts, mentally, into pounds and pence any sum spent in foreign coinage. "He didn't sell the radio. When he said he'd sold all his things on the road, he forgot about that."

6. Plains.

"When did he say he'd last eaten?"

"Yesterday. He said."

She repeats what she has just been told: "Yesterday." She is looking through the glass that takes the shine of heat off the landscape passing as yesterday passed, time measured by the ticking second hand of moving trees, rows of crops, country-store stoeps,[7] filling stations, spiny crook'd fingers of giant euphorbia.[8] Only the figures by the roadside waiting, standing still.

Personal remarks can't offend someone dead-beat in the back. "How d'you think such a young man comes to be without front teeth?"

She giggles whisperingly and keeps her voice low, anyway. "Well, you may not believe me if I tell you. . . ."

"Seems odd . . . I suppose he can't afford to have them replaced."

"It's—how shall I say—a sexual preference. Most usually you see it in their young girls, though. They have their front teeth pulled when they're about seventeen."

She feels his uncertainty, his not wanting to let comprehension lead him to a conclusion embarrassing to an older woman. For her part, she is wondering whether he won't find it distasteful if—at her de-sexed age—she should come out with it: for cock-sucking. "No one thinks the gap spoils a girl's looks, apparently. It's simply a sign she knows how to please. Same significance between men, I suppose? A form of beauty. So everyone says. We've always been given to understand that's the reason."

"Maybe it's just another sexual myth. There are so many."

She's in agreement. "Black girls. Chinese girls. Jewish girls."

"And black men?"

"Oh my goodness, you bet. But we white ladies don't talk about that, we only dream, you know! Or have nightmares."

They're laughing. When they are quiet, she flexes her shoulders against the seat-back and settles again. The streets of a town are flickering their text across her eyes. "He might have had a car accident. They might have been knocked out in a fight."

They have to wake him because they don't know where he wants to be set down. He is staring at her lined white face (turned to him, calling him gently), stunned for a moment at this evidence that he cannot be anywhere he ought to be; and now he blinks and smiles his empty smile caught on either side by a canine tooth, and gulps and gives himself a shake like someone coming out of water. "Sorry! Sorry! Sorry madam!"

What about, she says, and the young man glances quickly, his blue eyes coming round over his shoulder: "Had a good snooze?"

"Ooh I was finished, master, finished, God bless you for the rest you give me. And with an empty stummick, you know, you dreaming so real. I was dreaming, dreaming, I didn't know nothing about I'm in the car!"

It comes from the driver's seat with the voice (a real Englishman's from overseas) of one who is hoping to hear something that will explain everything. "What were you dreaming?"

But there is only hissing, spluttery laughter between the two white pointed teeth. The words gambol. "Ag, nothing, master, nothing, all *non-sunce*—"

7. Verandas.   8. An African shrub.

The sense is that if pressed, he will produce for them a dream he didn't dream, a dream put together from bloated images on billboards, discarded calendars picked up, scraps of newspapers blown about—but they interrupt, they're asking where he'd like to get off.

"No, anywhere. Here it's all right. Fine. Just there by the corner. I must go look for someone who'll praps give me a rand for the taxi, because I can't walk so far, I haven't eaten nothing since yesterday . . . just here, the master can please stop just here—"

The traffic light is red, anyway, and the car is in the lane nearest the kerb. Her thin, speckled white arm with a skilled flexible hand, but no muscle with which to carry a load of washing or lift a hoe, feels back to release the lock he is fumbling at. "Up, up, pull it up." She has done it for him. "Can't you take a bus?"

"There's no buses Sunday, madam, this place is ve-ery bad for us for transport, I must tell you, we can't get nowhere Sundays, only work-days." He is out, the plastic bag with the radio under his arm, his feet in their stained, multi-striped jogging sneakers drawn neatly together like those of a child awaiting dismissal. "Thank you madam, thank you master, God bless you for what you done."

The confident dextrous hand is moving quickly down in the straw bag bought from a local market somewhere along the route. She brings up a pale blue note (the Englishman recognizes the two-rand denomination of this currency that he has memorized by colour) and turns to pass it, a surreptitious message, through the open door behind her. *Goodbye master madam.* The note disappears delicately as a tit-bit finger-fed. He closes the door, he's keeping up the patter, *goodbye master, goodbye madam*, and she instructs—"No, bang it. Harder. That's it." *Goodbye master, goodbye madam*—but they don't look back at him now, they don't have to see him thinking he must keep waving, keep smiling, in case they should look back.

She is the guide and mentor; she's the one who knows the country. She's the one—she knows that too—who is accountable. She must be the first to speak again. "At least if he's hungry he'll be able to buy a bun or something. And the bars are closed on Sunday."

1991

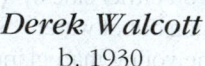

Derek Walcott
b. 1930

Over the last five decades, Derek Walcott has articulated the tensions of living between two worlds—the competing claims and traditions of the West Indies, his home, and Europe. A concern with issues of national identity runs throughout Walcott's large body of poetry and drama; his poetry exploits the resources of a European literary tradition in the service of Caribbean themes and concerns. No poet, as T. S. Eliot insisted, can write important poetry without tapping into some cultural or literary tradition; in the poem *Forest of Europe*, Walcott puts the question this way:

> What's poetry, if it is worth its salt,
> but a phrase men can pass from hand to mouth?
> From hand to mouth, across the centuries,
> the bread that lasts when systems have decayed.

Walcott was born in Castries, Saint Lucia, an isolated, volcanic island in the West Indies. Saint Lucia is a former British colony, and Walcott's education there was thoroughly British. In the introduction to *Dream on Monkey Mountain and Other Plays* (1970), Walcott writes, "The writers of my generation were natural assimilators. We knew the literature of Empires, Greek, Roman, British, through their essential classics; and both the patois of the street and the language of the classroom hid the elation of discovery." Empire and slavery left their impress on the Walcott family; both of his grandmothers were said to be descended from slaves. Walcott attended University College of the West Indies in Jamaica on a British government scholarship; he completed a degree in English in 1953, and from 1954 until 1957 taught in West Indian schools. In 1958 a Rockefeller Fellowship allowed him to spend a year in New York studying theater; the following year he moved to Trinidad and founded the Little Carib Theatre Workshop. It was in his playwriting that Walcott first accomplished the fusion of native and European elements he sought; his 1958 play *Drums and Colours*, for instance, employs calypso music, mime, and carnival masks to "carnivalize" the smooth surface of European drama, creating a literary form which, while written in English, is uniquely Caribbean in character. *O Babylon!* (1976), his most popular play, focuses on the Rastafarians of Jamaica. He is also a talented painter, and his poems are notable for the vivid clarity of their images.

Walcott has written more than fifteen volumes of poetry as well as a dozen plays. His first important poetry collection was *In a Green Night* (1962), which includes his best-known poem, *A Far Cry from Africa*. Africa and Britain serve as the double setting for his trenchant portrait of a foreign aid bureaucrat in *The Fortunate Traveller*. Walcott himself has never settled in one place for long, and for many years he has split his time between his home in Trinidad and a teaching post at Boston University. Walcott's poems create a landscape of historical and personal memory, overlaying empires, centuries, continents, and stages of his own life. He developed his themes most expansively in his verse novel *Omeros* (1991), which rewrites Homer's *Iliad* as a Caribbean story, interspersed with scenes of the poet's own life and travels in Boston, London, and Dublin. Walcott has declared that his 2004 book-length poem, *The Prodigal*, prompted by the death of his twin brother Roderick, will be his last. Walcott was awarded the Nobel Prize for literature in 1992, "for a poetic oeuvre of great luminosity, sustained by a historical vision, the outcome of a multicultural commitment."

A Far Cry from Africa

A wind is ruffling the tawny pelt
Of Africa. Kikuyu,[1] quick as flies,
Batten° upon the bloodstreams of the veldt.°   *fasten/open country*
Corpses are scattered through a paradise.
5   Only the worm, colonel of carrion, cries:
"Waste no compassion on these separate dead!"
Statistics justify and scholars seize
The salients of colonial policy.
What is that to the white child hacked in bed?
10   To savages, expendable as Jews?

---

1. Indigenous people of Kenya.

Threshed out by beaters, the long rushes break
In a white dust of ibises[2] whose cries
Have wheeled since civilization's dawn
From the parched river or beast-teeming plain.
15   The violence of beast on beast is read
As natural law, but upright man
Seeks his divinity by inflicting pain.
Delirious as these worried beasts, his wars
Dance to the tightened carcass of a drum,
20   While he calls courage still that native dread
Of the white peace contracted by the dead.

Again brutish necessity wipes its hands
Upon the napkin of a dirty cause, again
A waste of our compassion, as with Spain,
25   The gorilla wrestles with the superman.
I who am poisoned with the blood of both,
Where shall I turn, divided to the vein?
I who have cursed
The drunken officer of British rule, how choose
30   Between this Africa and the English tongue I love?
Betray them both, or give back what they give?
How can I face such slaughter and be cool?
How can I turn from Africa and live?

1962

Wales
for Ned Thomas

Those white flecks cropping the ridges of Snowdon[1]
will thicken their fleece and come wintering down
through the gap between alliterative hills,
through the caesura[2] that let in the Legions,
5   past the dark disfigured mouths of the chapels,
till a white silence comes to green-throated Wales.
Down rusty gorges, cold rustling gorse,[3]
over rocks hard as consonants, and rain-vowelled shales
sang the shallow-buried axe, helmet, and baldric°   sword belt
10   before the wet asphalt sibilance of tires.
A plump raven, Plantagenet,[4] unfurls its heraldic
caw over walls that held the cult of the horse.
In blackened cottages with their stony hatred
of industrial fires, a language is shared
15   like bread to the mouth, white flocks to dark byres°   sheds

1981

---

2. Wading birds resembling storks.
1. The highest peak in Wales.
2. A break or pause in the middle of a line of verse.

3. Spiny shrub with yellow leaves.
4. English royal house between 1154 and 1485.

The Fortunate Traveller[1]
for Susan Sontag

And I heard a voice in the midst of the four beasts say,
A measure of wheat for a penny,
and three measures of barley for a penny;
and see thou hurt not the oil and the wine.

—*Revelation 6.6*[2]

1

It was in winter. Steeples, spires
congealed like holy candles. Rotting snow
flaked from Europe's ceiling. A compact man,
I crossed the canal in a grey overcoat,
5   on one lapel a crimson buttonhole
for the cold ecstasy of the assassin.
In the square coffin manacled to my wrist:
small countries pleaded through the mesh of graphs,
in treble-spaced, Xeroxed forms to the World Bank
10   on which I had scrawled the one word, MERCY;

I sat on a cold bench
under some skeletal lindens.
Two other gentlemen, black skins gone grey
as their identical, belted overcoats,
15   crossed the white river.
They spoke the stilted French
of their dark river,
whose hooked worm, multiplying its pale sickle,
could thin the harvest of the winter streets.
20   "Then we can depend on you to get us those tractors?"
"I gave my word."
"May my country ask you why you are doing this, sir?"
Silence.
"You know if you betray us, you cannot hide?"
25   A tug. Smoke trailing its dark cry.

At the window in Haiti, I remember
a gecko[3] pressed against the hotel glass,
with white palms, concentrating head.
With a child's hands. Mercy, monsieur. Mercy.
30   Famine sighs like a scythe
across the field of statistics and the desert
is a moving mouth. In the hold of this earth
10,000,000 shoreless souls are drifting.

---

1. Walcott's title invokes Thomas Nashe's tale *The Unfortunate Traveller* (1594). Susan Sontag (b. 1933–2004), American cultural critic and novelist.
2. One of the Four Horsemen of the Apocalypse is decreeing the famine and inflation that accompany wars as the end of the world approaches.
3. A small lizard.

Somalia: 765,000, their skeletons will go under the tidal sand.
35 "We'll meet you in Bristol to conclude the agreement?"
Steeples like tribal lances, through congealing fog
the cries of wounded church bells wrapped in cotton,
grey mist enfolding the conspirator
like a sealed envelope next to its heart.

40 No one will look up now to see the jet
fade like a weevil through a cloud of flour.
One flies first-class, one is so fortunate.
Like a telescope reversed, the traveller's eye
swiftly screws down the individual sorrow
45 to an oval nest of antic numerals,
and the iris, interlocking with this globe,
condenses it to zero, then a cloud.
Beetle-black taxi from Heathrow[4] to my flat.
We are roaches,
50 riddling the state cabinets, entering the dark holes
of power, carapaced in topcoats,
scuttling around columns, signalling for taxis,
with frantic antennae, to other huddles with roaches;
we infect with optimism, and when
55 the cabinets crack, we are the first
to scuttle, radiating separately
back to Geneva, Bonn, Washington, London.

Under the dripping planes of Hampstead Heath,
I read her letter again, watching the drizzle
60 disfigure its pleading like mascara. Margo,
I cannot bear to watch the nations cry.
Then the phone: "We will pay you in Bristol."
Days in fetid bedclothes swallowing cold tea,
the phone stifled by the pillow. The telly
65 a blue storm with soundless snow.
I'd light the gas and see a tiger's tongue.
I was rehearsing the ecstasies of starvation
for what I had to do. *And have not charity*.[5]

I found my pity, desperately researching
70 the origins of history, from reed-built communes
by sacred lakes, turning with the first sprocketed
water-driven wheels. I smelled imagination
among bestial hides by the gleam of fat,
seeking in all races a common ingenuity.
75 I envisaged an Africa flooded with such light
as alchemized the first fields of emmer wheat and barley,
when we savages dyed our pale dead with ochre,

---

4. London's primary airport.
5. "Though I speak with the tongues of men and of angels, and have not charity, I am become as sounding
brass, or a tinkling cymbal" (1 Corinthians 13.1).

and bordered our temples
with the ceremonial vulva of the conch
80 in the grey epoch of the obsidian adze.
I sowed the Sahara with rippling cereals,
my charity fertilized these aridities.

What was my field? Late sixteenth century.
My field was a dank acre. A Sussex don,
85 I taught the Jacobean anxieties: *The White Devil*.[6]
Flamineo's torch startles the brooding yews.
The drawn end comes in strides. I loved my Duchess,
the white flame of her soul blown out between
the smoking cypresses. Then I saw children pounce
90 on green meat with a rat's ferocity.

I called them up and took the train to Bristol,
my blood the Severn's[7] dregs and silver.
On Severn's estuary the pieces flash,
Iscariot's salary,[8] patron saint of spies.
95 I thought, who cares how many million starve?
Their rising souls will lighten the world's weight
and level its gull-glittering waterline;
we left at sunset down the estuary.

England recedes. The forked white gull
100 screeches, circling back.
Even the birds are pulled back by their orbit,
even mercy has its magnetic field.
                              Back in the cabin,
I uncap the whisky, the porthole
105 mists with glaucoma. By the time I'm pissed,[9]
England, England will be
that pale serrated indigo on the sea-line.
"You are so fortunate, you get to see the world—"
Indeed, indeed, sirs, I have seen the world.
110 Spray splashes the portholes and vision blurs.

Leaning on the hot rail, watching the hot sea,
I saw them far off, kneeling on hot sand
in the pious genuflections of the locust,
as Ponce's armoured knees crush Florida
115 to the funereal fragrance of white lilies.

2

Now I have come to where the phantoms live,
I have no fear of phantoms, but of the real.
The Sabbath benedictions of the islands.

---

6. Revenge tragedy (c. 1612) by John Webster.
7. A river running through Wales and England.
8. For betraying Jesus Christ, Judas Iscariot was paid 30

pieces of silver by the Roman authorities.
9. Drunk.

120   Treble clef of the snail on the scored leaf,
the Tantum Ergo[1] of black choristers
soars through the organ pipes of coconuts.
Across the dirty beach surpliced with lace,
they pass a brown lagoon behind the priest,
pale and unshaven in his frayed soutane,[2]
125   into the concrete church at Canaries;
as Albert Schweitzer[3] moves to the harmonium
of morning, and to the pluming chimneys,
the groundswell lifts *Lebensraum, Lebensraum.*[4]

Black faces sprinkled with continual dew—
130   dew on the speckled croton,[5] dew
on the hard leaf of the knotted plum tree,
dew on the elephant ears of the dasheen.[6]
Through Kurtz's teeth, white skull in elephant grass,
the imperial fiction sings. Sunday
135   wrinkles downriver from the Heart of Darkness.
The heart of darkness is not Africa.
The heart of darkness is the core of fire
in the white center of the holocaust.
The heart of darkness is the rubber claw
140   selecting a scalpel in antiseptic light,
the hills of children's shoes outside the chimneys,
the tinkling nickel instruments on the white altar;
Jacob, in his last card, sent me these verses:
"Think of a God who doesn't lose His sleep
145   if trees burst into tears or glaciers weep.
So, aping His indifference, I write now,
not Anno Domini: After Dachau."[7]

3

The night maid brings a lamp and draws the blinds.
I stay out on the verandah with the stars.
150   Breakfast congealed to supper on its plate.

There is no sea as restless as my mind.
The promontories snore. They snore like whales.
Cetus, the whale, was Christ.
The ember dies, the sky smokes like an ash heap.
155   Reeds wash their hands of guilt and the lagoon
is stained. Louder, since it rained,
a gauze of sand flies hisses from the marsh.

---

1. A hymn sung after the Blessed Sacrament has been exposed in the mass.
2. Black robe.
3. German physician, missionary, and musician in Africa; winner of the Nobel Peace Prize in 1952.

4. Space to live in; the term is especially associated with Nazi Germany's territorial expansion.
5. A tropical plant.
6. The taro plant of tropical Asia.
7. Site of the notorious Nazi concentration camp.

Since God is dead,[8] and these are not His stars,
but man-lit, sulphurous, sanctuary lamps,
160   it's in the heart of darkness of this earth
that backward tribes keep vigil of His Body,
in deya, lampion,[9] and this bedside lamp.
Keep the news from their blissful ignorance.
Like lice, like lice, the hungry of this earth
165   swarm to the tree of life. If those who starve
like these rain-flies who shed glazed wings in light
grew from sharp shoulder blades their brittle vans
and soared towards that tree, how it would seethe—
ah, Justice! But fires
170   drench them like vermin, quotas
prevent them, and they remain
compassionate fodder for the travel book,
its paragraphs like windows from a train,
for everywhere that earth shows its rib cage
175   and the moon goggles with the eyes of children,
we turn away to read. Rimbaud[1] learned that.
                           Rimbaud, at dusk,
idling his wrist in water past temples
the plumed dates still protect in Roman file,
180   knew that we cared less for one human face
than for the scrolls in Alexandria's ashes,
that the bright water could not dye his hand
any more than poetry. The dhow's[2] silhouette
moved through the blinding coinage of the river
185   that, endlessly, until we pay one debt,
shrouds, every night, an ordinary secret.

4

The drawn sword comes in strides.
It stretches for the length of the empty beach;
the fishermen's huts shut their eyes tight.
190   A frisson[3] shakes the palm trees.
and sweats on the traveller's tree.
They've found out my sanctuary. Philippe, last night:
"It had two gentlemen in the village yesterday, sir,
asking for you while you was in town.
195   I tell them you was in town. They send to tell you,
there is no hurry. They will be coming back."

In loaves of cloud, *and have not charity,*
the weevil will make a sahara of Kansas,

---

8. So the German philosopher Friedrich Nietzsche declared in his 1882 text *The Gay Science*.
9. A small oil lamp with tinted glass.
1. Arthur Rimbaud (1854–1891), French poet. After abandoning poetry at the age of 20, he traveled in Egypt

and the Sudan, later settling in Ethiopia as a trader and arms dealer.
2. A sailing vessel used by Arabs.
3. Sudden passing excitement.

the ant shall eat Russia.
200   Their soft teeth shall make, *and have not charity,*
the harvest's desolation,
and the brown globe crack like a begging bowl,
and though you fire oceans of surplus grain,
and have not charity,

205   still, through thin stalks,
the smoking stubble, stalks
grasshopper: third horseman,
the leather-helmed locust.[4]

1981

━━━ ⟨⟩ ━━━

Seamus Heaney
b. 1939

More prominently than any poet since Yeats, Seamus Heaney has put Irish poetry back at the center of British literary studies. His first full-length collection, *Death of a Naturalist* (1966), ushered in a period of renewed interest in Irish poetry generally, and Ulster poetry in particular; the subsequent attention to poets like Derek Mahon, Michael Longley, Medbh McGuckian, and Paul Muldoon owes a great deal to the scope of Heaney's popularity.

As a great number of Heaney's early poems bear poignant witness, he spent his childhood in rural County Derry, Northern Ireland; his family was part of the Catholic minority in Ulster, and his experiences growing up were for that reason somewhat atypical. The critic Irvin Ehrenpreis maps the matrix of Heaney's contradictory position as an Irish poet: "Speech is never simple, in Heaney's conception. He grew up as an Irish Catholic boy in a land governed by Protestants whose tradition is British. He grew up on a farm in his country's northern, industrial region. As a person, therefore, he springs from the old divisions of his nation." His experience was split not only along religious lines, then, but also national and linguistic ones; in some of his early poetry Heaney suggests the split through the paired names—"Mossbawn" (the very English name of his family's fifty-acre farm) and "Anahorish" (Irish *anach fhior uisce*, "place of clear water," where he attended primary school). As a result, Heaney's is a liminal poetry—a "door into the dark"—and Heaney stands in the doorway, with one foot in each world. Heaney makes brilliant use of the linguistic resources of both the traditions he inherited, drawing on the heritage of English Romanticism while also relying heavily on Irish-language assonance in lines like "There were dragon-flies, spotted butterflies, / But best of all was the warm thick slobber / of frogspawn that grew like clotted water / In the shade of the banks" (*Death of a Naturalist*).

When he was twelve, Heaney won a scholarship to a Catholic boarding school in Londonderry (now Derry) then went on to Queen's University, Belfast, which was the center of a vital new poetic movement in the 1960s. He was influenced by poets who were able to transform the local into the universal, especially Ted Hughes and Robert Frost. As an "Ulster poet," it has fallen to Heaney to use his voice and his position to comment on Northern Ireland's sectarian violence; ironically enough, however, his most explicitly "political" poems were published before the flare-up of the Troubles that began in 1969, and his most self-conscious response to Ulster's strife, the volume *North* (1975), uses historical and mythological frameworks to address the current political situation obliquely. The Irish critic Seamus Deane has

---

4. The locust, eater of crops, is here identified with the horseman of the Apocalypse quoted in the poem's epigraph.

written, "Heaney is very much in the Irish tradition in that he has learned, more successfully than most, to conceive of his personal experience in terms of his country's history"; for Heaney, as the popular saying has it, the personal is the political, and the political the personal. His most successful poems dealing with Ulster's political and religious situation are probably those treating neolithic bodies found preserved in peat bogs. Heaney was living in Belfast, lecturing at Queen's University, at the inception of the Troubles; as a Catholic, he felt a need to convey the urgency of the situation without falling into the easy Republican—or Unionist, for that matter—rhetoric. It was at this point that Heaney discovered the anthropologist P. V. Glob's *The Bog People* (1969), which documents (with riveting photographs) the discovery of sacrificial victims preserved in bogs for 2,000 years. Heaney intuitively knew that he had found his "objective correlative"—what he has called his "emblems of adversity"—with which to explore the Troubles.

Like Yeats, Heaney has, from the very start, enjoyed both popular and critical acclaim. His poems have a surface simplicity; his early poetry especially relishes the carefully observed detail of rural Irish life.

Punishment[1]

I can feel the tug
of the halter at the nape
of her neck, the wind
on her naked front.

5   It blows her nipples
to amber beads,
it shakes the frail rigging
of her ribs.

I can see her drowned
10   body in the bog,
the weighing stone,
the floating rods and boughs.

Under which at first
she was a barked sapling
15   that is dug up
oak-bone, brain-firkin:[2]

her shaved head
like a stubble of black corn,
her blindfold a soiled bandage,
20   her noose a ring

to store
the memories of love.
Little adulteress,
before they punished you

---

1. A young girl's body, dating from the first century A.D., was recovered from a German bog in 1951. The body exhibited various punishments bestowed upon adulterous women by ancient Germanic peoples.
2. A wooden container.

25   you were flaxen-haired,
      undernourished, and your
      tar-black face was beautiful.
      My poor scapegoat,

      I almost love you
30   but would have cast, I know,
      the stones of silence.
      I am the artful voyeur

      of your brain's exposed
      and darkened combs,
35   your muscles' webbing
      and all your numbered bones:

      I who have stood dumb
      when your betraying sisters,
      cauled³ in tar,
40   wept by the railings,⁴

      who would connive
      in civilized outrage
      yet understand the exact
      and tribal, intimate revenge.

                                                              1975

The Skunk

      Up, black, striped and damasked like the chasuble¹
      At a funeral Mass, the skunk's tail
      Paraded the skunk. Night after night
      I expected her like a visitor.

5   The refrigerator whinnied into silence.
      My desk light softened beyond the verandah.
      Small oranges loomed in the orange tree.
      I began to be tense as a voyeur.

      After eleven years I was composing
10   Love-letters again, broaching the word "wife"
      Like a stored cask, as if its slender vowel
      Had mutated into the night earth and air

      Of California. The beautiful, useless
      Tang of eucalyptus spelt your absence.
15   The aftermath of a mouthful of wine
      Was like inhaling you off a cold pillow.

      And there she was, the intent and glamorous,
      Ordinary, mysterious skunk,

---

3. Capped.
4. In Belfast, women may still be shaven, stripped, tarred
and handcuffed to railings by the Irish Republican Army

for keeping company with British soldiers [Heaney's note].
1. A sleeveless vest worn by priests.

Mythologized, demythologized.
20 Snuffing the boards five feet beyond me.

It all came back to me last night, stirred
By the sootfall of your things at bedtime,
Your head-down, tail-up hunt in a bottom drawer
For the black plunge-line nightdress.

25 Hear it calling out to every creature.
And they drink these waters, although it is dark here
    because it is the night.

I am repining for this living fountain.
Within this bread of life I see it plain
30   although it is the night.

                                1978

The Toome Road

One morning early I met armoured cars
In convoy, warbling along on powerful tyres,
All camouflaged with broken alder branches,
And headphoned soldiers standing up in turrets.
5 How long were they approaching down my roads
As if they owned them? The whole country was sleeping.
I had rights-of-way, fields, cattle in my keeping,
Tractors hitched to buckrakes in open sheds,
Silos, chill gates, wet slates, the greens and reds
10 Of outhouse roofs. Whom should I run to tell
Among all of those with their back doors on the latch
For the bringer of bad news, that small-hours visitant
Who, by being expected, might be kept distant?
Sowers of seed, erectors of headstones. . .
15 O charioteers, above your dormant guns,
It stands here still, stands vibrant as you pass,
The invisible, untoppled omphalos.[1]

                                1979

The Singer's House

When they said Carrickfergus[1] I could hear
the frosty echo of saltminers' picks.
I imagined it, chambered and glinting,
a township built of light.

5 What do we say any more
to conjure the salt of our earth?
So much comes and is gone
that should be crystal and kept,

---

1. The navel, or central point (Greek).

1. Seaport just north of Belfast on the northeast coast of Ireland.

and amicable weathers
10   that bring up the grain of things,
their tang of season and store,
are all the packing we'll get.

So I say to myself *Gweebarra*[2]
and its music hits off the place
15   like water hitting off granite.
I see the glittering sound

framed in your window,
knives and forks set on oilcloth,[3]
and the seals' heads, suddenly outlined,
20   scanning everything.

People here used to believe
that drowned souls lived in the seals.
At spring tides they might change shape.
They loved music and swam in for a singer

25   who might stand at the end of summer
in the mouth of a whitewashed turf-shed,
his shoulder to the jamb, his song
a rowboat far out in evening.

When I came here first you were always singing,
30   a hint of the clip of the pick
in your winnowing climb and attack.
Raise it again, man. We still believe what we hear.

1979

In Memoriam Francis Ledwidge[1]
Killed in France 31 July 1917

The bronze soldier hitches a bronze cape
That crumples stiffly in imagined wind
No matter how the real winds buff and sweep
His sudden hunkering run, forever craned

5   Over Flanders.[2] Helmet and haversack,
The gun's firm slope from butt to bayonet,
The loyal, fallen names on the embossed plaque—
It all meant little to the worried pet

I was in nineteen forty-six or seven,
10   Gripping my Aunt Mary by the hand
Along the Portstewart prom, then round the crescent[3]
To thread the Castle Walk out to the strand.

2. Bay in County Donegal, in the northwest of Ireland.
3. Stiff, waterproof cloth often used as tablecloth.
1. Francis Ledwidge (1891–1917) was friendly with some of the leaders of the 1916 Rising yet, like thousands of Irishmen of the time, felt himself constrained to enlist in the British Army to defend "the rights of small nations" [Heaney's note].
2. Much trench warfare took place here during World War I.
3. Promenade; crescent: curved row of houses.

The pilot from Coleraine sailed to the coal-boat.
Courting couples rose out of the scooped dunes.
15 A farmer stripped to his studs and shiny waistcoat
Rolled the trousers down on his timid shins.

Francis Ledwidge, you courted at the seaside
Beyond Drogheda[4] one Sunday afternoon.
Literary, sweet-talking, countrified,
20 You pedalled out the leafy road from Slane[5]

Where you belonged, among the dolorous
And lovely: the May altar of wild flowers,
Easter water sprinkled in outhouses,
Mass-rocks and hill-top raths and raftered byres.[6]

25 I think of you in your Tommy's uniform,[7]
A haunted Catholic face, pallid and brave,
Ghosting the trenches like a bloom of hawthorn
Or silence cored from a Boyne passage-grave.[8]

It's summer, nineteen-fifteen. I see the girl
30 My aunt was then, herding on the long acre.
Behind a low bush in the Dardanelles
You suck stones to make your dry mouth water.

It's nineteen-seventeen. She still herds cows
But a big strafe[9] puts the candles out in Ypres:
35 "My soul is by the Boyne, cutting new meadows . . .
My country wears her confirmation dress."

"To be called a British soldier while my country
Has no place among nations . . ." You were rent
By shrapnel six weeks later. "I am sorry
40 That party politics should divide our tents."

In you, our dead enigma, all the strains
Criss-cross in useless equilibrium
And as the wind tunes through this vigilant bronze
I hear again the sure confusing drum

45 You followed from Boyne water to the Balkans
But miss the twilit note your flute should sound.
You were not keyed or pitched like these true-blue ones
Though all of you consort now underground.

1979

4. Seaport near the mouth of the Boyne River.
5. The Hill of Slane rises above Slane village, with a commanding view of the Boyne River.
6. Rocks where persecuted Roman Catholics celebrated mass in secret; raths: old circular forts; byres: cow sheds.
7. Uniform of a British soldier in World War I.

8. An underground burial chamber entered through a long tunnel; the Boyne is a river in east Ireland where William III defeated James II.
9. A close-range airplane attack; Ypres: site of three World War I battles.

Postscript

And some time make the time to drive out west
Into County Clare,[1] along the Flaggy Shore,
In September or October, when the wind
And the light are working off each other
5   So that the ocean on one side is wild
With foam and glitter, and inland among stones
The surface of a slate-grey lake is lit
By the earthed lightning of a flock of swans,
Their feathers roughed and ruffling, white on white,
10   Their fully grown headstrong-looking heads
Tucked or cresting or busy underwater.
Useless to think you'll park and capture it
More thoroughly. You are neither here nor there,
A hurry through which known and strange things pass
15   As big soft buffetings come at the car sideways
And catch the heart off guard and blow it open.

1996

A Call

"Hold on," she said, "I'll just run out and get him.
The weather here's so good, he took the chance
To do a bit of weeding."

                         So I saw him
Down on his hands and knees beside the leek rig,
5   Touching, inspecting, separating one
Stalk from the other, gently pulling up
Everything not tapered, frail and leafless,
Pleased to feel each little weed-root break,
But rueful also . . .

                    Then found myself listening to
10   The amplified grave ticking of hall clocks
Where the phone lay unattended in a calm
Of mirror glass and sunstruck pendulums . . .

And found myself then thinking: if it were nowadays,
This is how Death would summon Everyman.

15   Next thing he spoke and I nearly said I loved him.

1996

The Errand

"On you go now! Run, son, like the devil
And tell your mother to try
To find me a bubble for the spirit level
And a new knot for this tie."

1. County in western Ireland.

5   But still he was glad, I know, when I stood my ground,
       Putting it up to him
       With a smile that trumped his smile and his fool's errand,
       Waiting for the next move in the game.

                                                                    1996

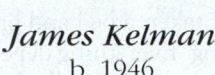

James Kelman
b. 1946

Though his first collection of stories was published (in a very limited edition) back in 1970, it was not until the 1990s that James Kelman emerged as one of the most distinctive voices in British literature. His development as a writer does not fit any of the usual patterns. He was born in Glasgow, Scotland, one of five sons of a frame-maker; he left school at fifteen to apprentice as a compositor. He worked at various manual jobs in Glasgow, London, and Manchester, peppered with regular bouts of unemployment and living "on the giro" (collecting unemployment).

At age twenty-eight, Kelman enrolled at Strathclyde University, where he studied English and philosophy; he left during his third year, however. In the meantime, he continued to write short stories while working at jobs including that of bus driver, which provided material for his grittily realistic first novel, *The Busconductor Hines* (1984). The novel's stark language and lack of dramatic events were ridiculed, however, by London-based critics; and his next novel, *A Chancer* (1985), was largely ignored. His writing, as Kelman well knows, is a slap in the face of the English literary establishment; he describes his work as both "political" and "anti-imperialist." The raw power of his writing could not be overlooked forever, though, and his 1989 novel *A Disaffection* was a finalist for the Booker Prize. Full recognition of Kelman's gifts seems to have come when he won the Booker Prize for his 1994 novel *How Late It Was, How Late*; this award provoked sharp controversy in England over the literary merits of the obscenity-laced musings of Kelman's shiftless, blind protagonist Sammy. The best of Kelman's writing regularly occasions comparisons with the bleak and brutal prose of Samuel Beckett, and has earned him the label "Scotland's Kafka"—a paradoxical term of praise for such a resolutely local writer.

Other writers (notably James Joyce, in his short story collection *Dubliners*) have attempted to chronicle the weary lives of the downtrodden working class on the fringes of the British Empire; unlike Joyce and Beckett, Kelman forswore exile, choosing to remain a member of the local culture he depicts. "I don't earn much money," Kelman has said, "so I'm involved in the culture I write about." His 1987 story *Home for a Couple of Days* shows Kelman's powers of close observation and his keen ear for the vernacular style of Scottish English. The bitten-off cadences of Glasgow dialect at once unite and separate the characters, in a story of estrangement and return.

Home for a Couple of Days

Three raps at the door. His eyes opened and blinked as they met the sun rays streaming in through the slight gap between the curtains. "Mister Brown?" called somebody—a girl's voice.

"Just a minute." He squinted at his wristwatch. 9 o'clock. He walked to the door and opened it, poked his head out from behind it.

"That's your breakfast." She held out the tray as if for approval. A boiled egg and a plate of toast, a wee pot of tea.

"Thanks, that's fine, thanks." He took it and shut the door, poured a cup of tea immediately and carried it into the bathroom. He was hot and sweaty and needed a shower. He stared at himself in the mirror. He was quite looking forward to the day. Hearing the girl's accent made it all even more so. After the shower he started on the grub, ate all the toast but left the egg. He finished the pot of tea then shaved. As he prepared to leave he checked his wallet. He would have to get to a bank at some point.

The Green Park was a small hotel on the west side of Sauchiehall Street. Eddie had moved in late last night and taken a bed and breakfast. Beyond that he was not sure, how long he would be staying. Everything depended.

He was strolling in the direction of Partick, glancing now and then at the back pages of the *Daily Record*, quite enjoying the novelty of Scottish football[1] again. He stopped himself from smiling, lighted a cigarette. It was a sunny morning in early May and maybe it was that alone made him feel so optimistic about the future. The sound of a machine, noisy—but seeming to come from far away. It was just from the bowling greens across the street, a loud lawn-mower or something.

He continued round the winding bend, down past the hospital and up Church Street, cutting in through Chancellor Street and along the lane. The padlock hung ajar on the bolt of the door of the local pub he used to frequent. Farther on the old primary school across the other side of the street. He could not remember any names of teachers or pupils at this moment. A funny feeling. It was as if he had lost his memory for one split second. He had stopped walking. He lighted another cigarette. When he returned the lighter and cigarette packet to the side pockets of his jacket he noticed a movement in the net curtains of the ground floor window nearby where he was standing. It was Mrs McLachlan. Who else. He smiled and waved but the face disappeared.

His mother stayed up the next close.[2] He kept walking. He would see her a bit later on. He would have to get her something too, a present, she was due it.

Along Dumbarton Road he entered the first cafe and he ordered a roll and sausage and asked for a cup of tea right away. The elderly woman behind the counter did not look twice at him. Why should she? She once caught him thieving a bar of Turkish Delight, that's why. He read the *Daily Record* to the front cover, still quite enjoying it all, everything, even the advertisements with the Glasgow addresses, it was good reading them as well.

At midday he was back up the lane and along to the old local. He got a pint of heavy,[3] sat in a corner sipping at it. The place had really changed. It was drastic— new curtains!

There were not many customers about but Eddie recognized one, a middle-aged man of average build who was wearing a pair of glasses. He leaned on the bar with his arms folded, chatting to the bartender. Neilie Johnston. When Eddie finished his beer he walked with the empty glass to the counter. "Heavy," he said and he pointed at Neilie's drink. The bartender nodded and poured him a whisky. Neilie looked at it and then at Eddie.

"Eddie!"

"How's it going Neilie?"

1. Soccer.   3. Stout or porter.
2. Alley.

"Aw no bad son no bad." Neilie chuckled. The two of them shook hands. "Where've you been?"

"London."

"Aw London; aw aye. Well well."

"Just got back last night."

"Good. . ." Neilie glanced at Eddie's suit. "Prospering son eh?"

"Doing alright."

"That's the game."

"What about yourself? still marking the board?"[4]

"Marking the board! Naw. Christ son I've been away from that for a while!" Neilie pursed his lips before lifting the whisky and drinking a fairly large mouthful. He sniffed and nodded. "With Sweeney being out the game and the rest of it."

"Aye."

"You knew about that son?"

"Mm."

"Aye well the licence got lost because of it. And they'll no get it back either neither they will. They're fucking finished—caput! Him and his brother."

Both of them were silent for a time. The bartender had walked farther along and was now looking at a morning paper. Neilie nudged the glasses up his nose a bit and he said, "You and him got on okay as well son, you and Sweeney, eh?"

Eddie shrugged. "Aye, I suppose." He glanced at the other men ranged about the pub interior, brought his cigarettes and lighter out. When they were both smoking he called the bartender: "Two halfs!"

"You on holiday like?" said Neilie.

"Couple of days just, a wee break. . ." he paused to pay for the two whiskies.

Neilie emptied the fresh one into the tumbler he already had. "Ta[5] son," he said, "it's appreciated."

"You skint?"[6]

"Aye, how d'you guess! Giro[7] in two days."

"Nothing doing then?"

"Eh well. . ." Neilie sniffed. "I'm waiting the word on something, a wee bit of business. Nothing startling right enough." He pursed his lips and shrugged, swallowed some whisky.

"I hope you're lucky."

"Aye, ta."

"Cheers." Eddie drank his own whisky in a gulp and chased it down with a mouthful of heavy beer. "Aw Christ," he said, glancing at the empty tumbler.

"You should never rush whisky son!" Neilie chuckled, peering along at the bartender.

"I'm out the habit."

"Wish to fuck I could say the same!"

Eddie took a long drag on the cigarette and he kept the smoke in his lungs for a while. Then he drank more beer. Neilie was watching him, smiling in quite a friendly way. Eddie said, "Any of the old team come in these days?"

"Eh. . ."

"Fisher I mean, or Stevie Price? Any of them? Billy Dempster?"

4. Taking bets.
5. Thanks.
6. Broke.
7. Unemployment check.

"Fisher drinks in T. C.'s."

"Does he? Changed days."

"Och there's a lot changed son, a lot."

"Stevie's married right enough eh!"

"Is that right?"

"He's got two wee lassies."

"Well well."

"He's staying over in the south side."

"Aw."

A couple of minutes later and Eddie was swallowing the last of his beer and returning his cigarettes and lighter to the side pockets. "Okay Neilie, nice seeing you."

Neilie looked as if he was going to say something but changed his mind.

"I'm taking a walk," said Eddie.

"Fair enough son."

"I'll look in later." Eddie patted him on the side of the shoulder, nodded at the bartender. He glanced at the other customers as he walked to the exit but saw nobody he knew.

It was good getting back out into the fresh air. The place was depressing and Neilie hadn't helped matters. A rumour used to go about that he kept his wife on the game.[8] Eddie could believe it.

There was a traffic jam down at Partick Cross. The rear end of a big articulated lorry[9] was sticking out into the main road and its front seemed to be stuck between two parked cars near to The Springwell Tavern. The lines of motors stretched along the different routes at the junction. Eddie stood at the Byres Road corner amongst a fair crowd of spectators. Two policemen arrived and donned the special sleeves they had for such emergencies and started directing operations. Eddie continued across the road.

In T. C.'s two games of dominoes were in progress plus there was music and a much cheerier atmosphere. It was better and fitted in more with the way Eddie remembered things. And there was Fisher at the other end of the bar in company with another guy. Eddie called to him: "Hey Tam!"

"Eddie!" Fisher was delighted. He waved his right fist in the air and when Eddie reached the other end he shook hands with him in a really vigorous way. "Ya bastard," he said, "it's great to see ye!" And then he grinned and murmured, "When did you get out!"[1]

"Out—what d'you mean?"

Fisher laughed.

"I'm being serious," said Eddie.

"Just that I heard you were having a holiday on the Isle of Wight."

"That's garbage."

"If you say so."

"Aye, fuck, I say so." Eddie smiled.

"Well, I mean, when Sweeney copped it . . . Then hearing about you . . .Made me think it was gen."[2]

"Ah well, there you are!"

---

8. Forced his wife to work as a prostitute.

9. Semi truck.

1. Of prison.

2. Genuine.

"That's good," said Fisher and he nodded, then jerked his thumb at the other guy. "This is Mick. . ."

After the introductions Eddie got a round of drinks up and the three of them went to a table at the wall, the only one available. An elderly man was sitting at it already; he had a grumpy wizened face. He moved a few inches to allow the trio more space.

There was a short silence. And Eddie said, "Well Tam, how's Eileen?"

"Dont know. We split."

"Aw. Christ."

"Ah," Fisher said, "she started. . . well, she started seeing this other guy, if you want to know the truth."

"Honest?" Eddie frowned.

Fisher shook his head. "A funny lassie Eileen I mean you never really fucking knew her man I mean." He shook his head again. "You didnt know where you were with her, that was the fucking trouble!"

After a moment Eddie nodded. He lifted his pint and drank from it, waiting for Fisher to continue but instead of continuing Fisher turned and looked towards the bar, exhaled a cloud of smoke. The other guy, Mick, raised his eyebrows at Eddie who shrugged. Then Fisher faced to the front again and said, "I was surprised to hear that about Sweeney but, warehouses, I didnt think it was his scene."

Eddie made no answer.

"Eh. . . ?"

"Mm."

"Best of gear right enough," Fisher added, still gazing at Eddie.

Eddie dragged on his cigarette. Then he said, "You probably heard he screwed the place well he never, he just handled the stuff."

"Aw."

"It was for screwing the place they done him for, but . . ." Eddie sniffed, drank from his pint.

"Aye, good." Fisher grinned. "So how you doing yourself then Eddie?"

"No bad."

"Better than no bad with that!" He gestured at Eddie's clothes. He reached to draw his thumb and forefinger along the lapel of the jacket. "Hand stitched," he said, "you didnt get that from John Collier's. Eh Mick?"

Mick smiled.

Eddie opened the jacket, indicated the inner pocket. "Look, no labels."

"What does that mean?"

"It means it was fucking dear."

"You're a bastard," said Fisher.

Eddie grinned. "Yous for another? A wee yin?"[3]

"Eh. . . Aye." Fisher said, "I'll have a doctor."

"What?"

"A doctor." Fisher winked at Mick. "He doesnt know what a doctor is!"

"What is it?" asked Eddie.

"A doctor, a doctor snoddy, a voddy."

"Aw aye. What about yourself?" Eddie asked Mick.

3. One.

"I'll have one as well Eddie, thanks."

Although it was busy at the bar he was served quite quickly. It was good seeing as many working behind the counter as this. One of things he didnt like about England was the way sometimes you could wait ages to get served in their pubs—especially if they heard your accent.

He checked the time of the clock on the gantry[4] with his wristwatch. He would have to remember about the bank otherwise it could cause problems. Plus he was wanting to get a wee present for his mother, he needed a couple of quid[5] for that as well.

When he returned to the table Fisher said, "I was telling Mick about some of your exploits."

"Exploits." Eddie laughed briefly, putting the drinks on the table top and sitting down.

"It's cause the 2,000 Guineas is coming up. It's reminding me about something!"

"Aw aye." Eddie said to Mick. "The problem with this cunt[6] Fisher is that he's loyal to horses."

"Loyal to fucking horses!" Fisher laughed loudly.

"Ah well if you're thinking about what I think you're thinking about!"

"It was all Sweeney's fault!"

"That's right, blame a guy that cant talk up for himself!"

"So it was but!"

Eddie smiled. "And Dempster, dont forget Dempster!"

"That's right," said Fisher, turning to Mick, "Dempster was into it as well."

Mick shook his head. Fisher was laughing again, quite loudly.

"It wasnt as funny as all that," said Eddie.

"You dont think so! Every other cunt does!"

"Dont believe a word of it," Eddie told Mick.

"And do you still punt?"[7] Mick asked him.

"Now and again."

"Now and again!" Fisher laughed.

Eddie smiled.

"There's four races on the telly this afternoon," said Mick.

"Aye," said Fisher, "we were thinking of getting a couple of cans and that. You interested?"

"Eh, naw, I'm no sure yet, what I'm doing."

Fisher nodded.

"It's just eh. . . "

"Dont worry about it," said Fisher, and he drank a mouthful of the vodka.

"How's Stevie?"

"Alright—as far as I know, I dont see him much; he hardly comes out. Once or twice at the weekends, that's about it."

"Aye."

"What about yourself, you no married yet?"

"Eh. . . " Eddie made a gesture with his right hand. "Kind of yes and no."

Fisher jerked his thumb at Mick. "He's married—got one on the way."

4. Panelling.
5. Pounds sterling.
6. Often used in Scottish slang to refer to men, not sexually but as equivalent to "guy" or "bastard."
7. Bet.

"Have you? Good, that's good." Eddie raised his tumbler of whisky and saluted him. "All the best."

"Thanks."

"I cant imagine having a kid," said Eddie, and to Fisher he said: "Can you?"

"What! I cant even keep myself going never mind a snapper!"

Mick laughed and brought out a 10-pack of cigarettes. Eddie pushed it away when offered. "It's my crash,"[8] he said.

"Naw," said Mick, "you bought the bevy."

"I know but. . . ." He opened his own packet and handed each of them a cigarette and he said to Fisher: "You skint?"

Fisher paused and squinted at him, "What do you think?"

"I think you're skint."

"I'm skint."

"It's a fucking dump of a city this, every cunt's skint."

Fisher jerked his thumb at Mick. "No him, he's no skint, a fucking millionaire, eh!"

Mick chuckled, "That'll be fucking right."

Eddie flicked his lighter and they took a light from him. Fisher said, "Nice . . ."

Eddie nodded, slipping it back into his pocket.

"What you up for by the way?"

"Och, a couple of things."

"No going to tell us?"

"Nothing to tell."

Fisher winked at Mick: "Dont believe a word of it."

"It's gen," said Eddie, "just the maw and that. Plus I was wanting to see a few of the old faces. A wee while since I've been away, three year."

"Aye and no even a postcard!"

"You never sent me one!"

"Aye but I dont know where the fuck you get to man I mean I fucking thought you were inside!"

"Tch!"

"He's supposed to be my best mate as well Mick, what d'you make of it!"

Mick smiled.

Not too long afterwards Eddie had swallowed the last of his whisky and then the heavy beer. "That's me," he said, "better hit the road. Aw right Tam! Mick, nice meeting you." Eddie shook hands with the two of them again.

Fisher said, "No bothering about the racing on the telly then. . . ."

"Nah, better no—I've got a couple of things to do. The maw as well Tam, I've got to see her."

"Aye how's she keeping? I dont see her about much."

"Aw she's fine, keeping fine."

"That's good. Tell her I was asking for her."

"Will do. . . ." Eddie edged his way out. The elderly man shifted on his chair, made a movement towards the drink he had lying by his hand. Eddie nodded at Mick and said to Fisher, "I'll probably look in later on."

A couple of faces at the bar seemed familiar but not sufficiently so and he continued on to the exit, strolling, hands in his trouser pockets, the cigarette in the corner of his mouth. Outside on the pavement he glanced from right to left, then the

8. Treat.

pub door banged behind him. It was Fisher. Eddie looked at him. "Naw eh. . . " Fisher sniffed. "I was just wondering and that, how you're fixed, just a couple of quid."

Eddie sighed, shook his head. "Sorry Tam but I'm being honest, I've got to hit the bank straight away; I'm totally skint."

"Aw. Okay. No problem."

"I mean if I had it. . . I'm no kidding ye, it's just I'm skint."

"Naw dont worry about it Eddie."

"Aye but Christ!" Eddie held his hands raised, palms upwards. "Sorry I mean." He hesitated a moment then said, "Wait a minute. . . " He dug out a big handful of loose change from his trouser pockets and arranged it into a neat sort of column on his left hand, and presented it to Fisher. "Any good?"

Fisher gazed at the money.

"Take it," said Eddie, giving it into his right hand.

"Ta Eddie. Mick's been keeping me going in there."

"When's the giro due?"

"Two more days."

"Garbage eh." He paused, nodded again and patted Fisher on the side of the shoulder. "Right you are then Tam, eh! I'll see ye!"

"Aye."

"I'll take a look in later on."

"Aye do that Eddie. You've actually just caught me at a bad time."

"I know the feeling," said Eddie and he winked and gave a quick wave. He walked on across the street without looking behind. Farther along he stepped sideways onto the path up by the Art Galleries.

There were a lot of children rushing about, plus women pushing prams. And the bowling greens were busy. Not just pensioners playing either, even young boys were out. Eddie still had the *Record* rolled in his pocket and he sat down on a bench for a few minutes, glancing back through the pages again, examining what was on at all the cinemas, theatres, seeing the pub entertainment and restaurants advertised.

No wind. Hardly even a breeze. The sun seemed to be beating right down on his head alone. Or else it was the alcohol; he was beginning to feel the effects. If he stayed on the bench he would end up falling asleep. The hotel. He got up, paused to light a cigarette. Along Sauchiehall Street there was a good curry smell coming for somewhere. He was starving. He turned into the entrance to The Green Park, walking up the wee flight of stairs and in to the lobby, the reception lounge. Somebody was hoovering carpets. He pressed the buzzer button, pressed it again when there came a break in the noise.

The girl who had brought him breakfast. "Mrs Grady's out the now," she told him.

"Aw."

"What was it you were wanting?"

"Eh well it was just I was wondering if there's a bank near?"

"A bank. Yes, if you go along to Charing Cross. They're all around there."

"Oh aye. Right." Eddie smiled. "It's funny how you forget wee details like that."

"Mmhh."

"Things have really changed as well. The people. . . " He grinned, shaking his head.

She frowned. "Do you mean Glasgow people?"

"Aye but really I mean I'm talking about people I know, friends and that, people I knew before."

"Aw, I see."

Eddie yawned. He dragged on his cigarette. "Another thing I was wanting to ask her, if it's okay to go into the room, during the day."

"She prefers you not to, unless you're on full board."

"Okay."

"You can go into the lounge though."

He nodded.

"I dont know whether she knew you were staying tonight. . . "

"I am."

"I'll tell her."

"Eh. . . " Eddie had been about to walk off; he said, "Does she do evening meals as well like?"

"She does." The girl smiled.

"What's up?"

"I dont advise it at the moment," she said quietly, "the real cook's off sick just now and she's doing it all herself."

"Aw aye. Thanks for the warning!" Eddie dragged on the cigarette again. "I smelled a curry there somewhere. . . "

"Yeh, there's places all around."

"Great."

"Dont go to the first one, the one further along's far better—supposed to be one of the best in Glasgow."

"Is that right. That's great. Would you fancy coming at all?"

"Pardon?"

"It would be nice if you came, as well, if you came with me." Eddie shrugged. "It'd be good."

"Thanks, but I'm working."

"Well, I would wait."

"No, I dont think so."

"It's up to you," he shrugged, "I'd like you to but."

"Thanks."

Eddie nodded. He looked towards the glass-panelled door of the lounge, he patted his inside jacket pocket in an absent-minded way. And the girl said, "You know if it was a cheque you could cash it here. Mrs Grady would do it for you."

"That's good." He pointed at the lounge door. "Is that the lounge? Do you think it'd be alright if I maybe had a doze?"

"A doze?"

"I'm really tired. I was travelling a while and hardly got any sleep last night. If I could just stretch out a bit . . . "

He looked about for an ashtray, there was one on the small half-moon table closeby where he was standing; he stubbed the cigarette out, and yawned suddenly.

"Look," said the girl, "I'm sure if you went up the stair and lay down for an hour or so; I dont think she would mind."

"You sure?"

"It'll be okay."

"You sure but I mean . . . "

"Yeh."

"I dont want to cause you any bother."

"It's alright."

"Thanks a lot."

"Your bag's still there in your room as well you know."

"Aye."

"Will I give you a call? about 5?"

"Aye, fine. 6 would be even better!"

"I'm sorry, it'll have to be 5—she'll be back in the kitchen after that."

"I was only kidding."

"If it could be later I'd do it."

"Naw, honest, I was only kidding."

The girl nodded.

After a moment he walked to the foot of the narrow, carpeted staircase.

"You'll be wanting a cheque cashed then?"

"Aye, probably."

"I'll mention it to her."

Up in the room he unzipped his bag but did not take anything out, he sat down on the edge of the bed instead. Then he got up, gave a loud sigh and took off his jacket, draping it over the back of the bedside chair. He closed the curtains, lay stretched out on top of the bedspread. He breathed in and out deeply, gazing at the ceiling. He felt amazingly tired, how tired he was. He had never been much of an afternoon drinker and today was just proving the point. He raised himself up to unknot his shoelaces, lay back again, kicking the shoes off and letting them drop off onto the floor. He shut his eyes. He was not quite sure what he was going to do. Maybe he would just leave tomorrow. He would if he felt like it. Maybe even tonight! if he felt like it. Less than a minute later he was sleeping.

1987

━━━◈━━━

Eavan Boland
b. 1944

The question posed by this final section of the anthology—"whose language?"—asks to whom the English language belongs. The poet Eavan Boland puts a special spin on this question throughout her work. As an Irish writer, she has a complex relationship to the language and the literary tradition shared with England, of course. But the thrust of Boland's questioning is directed more toward Irish literature in English and above all to modern Irish poetry. In that rich poetic tradition, Boland sees an absence, hears a silence: the woman poet in Ireland has been, she argues, shut out of poetry in a distinctive way.

The *Field Day Anthology of Irish Literature* was a monumental undertaking; published to wide acclaim in the early 1990s, and edited by Seamus Heaney and Brian Friel among others, the anthology had an ambitious scope, intending to collect all the major writing in the Irish tradition up to the present day. Eavan Boland made a bold stand in print and in person after its publication, declaring that the absence of more female editors and more works by women was evidence of a long-standing gender problem in Irish literature, even today. Ireland was traditionally represented in poetry and fiction by the figure of a suffering woman, whether she was an old country crone, "the old sow that eats its farrow" in Joyce's *Ulysses*, the beautiful Countess Cathleen Ní Houlihan in Yeats's play, the grieving mother of the famine literature, or the magical ancient Queen Mab. Poetry was written about these metaphorical women, standing in for Ireland and symbolizing the country, but almost never, Boland asserts, in a woman's voice. Women had been sidelined in Irish history altogether, despite having played many active roles, turned by poetic language into beautiful icons or sorrowing mothers in the literature that articulated Irish independence. All of Eavan Boland's complex and distinguished poetry before and since her quarrel with the *Field Day* anthology has been devoted to supplying those absent women's voices. Boland's eloquent poetry is regarded as among the finest women's writing of our time.

Eavan Boland was born in Dublin in 1944; since her father was a diplomat, she spent considerable time outside Ireland growing up, in London when her father was Ambassador to the Court of St. James's from 1950 to 1956, and in New York City from 1956 to 1964 when he served as the Irish ambassador to the United Nations. She returned to Ireland and Dublin for college, receiving a first-class honors degree in English from Trinity College. She spent a year at Trinity as a junior lecturer, but then left the academic life to write full time, raise a family of two children with her novelist husband, and teach sporadically at the School of Irish Studies in Dublin. Her first full-length book of poems, *New Territory*, came out in 1967, followed eight years later by *The War Horse*.

Boland's third collection was a watershed for her: *In Her Own Image* (1980) inaugurated her concentration on bringing the inner lives of women to poetic voice. A fountain of volumes has emerged since then, as well as awards to match them. Among the books are *The Journey and Other Poems* (1983), *Selected Poems 1980–1990* (1990), *In a Time of Violence* (1994), *An Origin Like Water: Collected Poems* (1996), and *The Lost Land* (1998); the awards include a Lannan Foundation Award in Poetry and the American Ireland Fund Literary Award. Eavan Boland is currently almost as well known for her essays and reviews, and for her cultural journalism in the *Irish Times*, as for her prominence as a reader of her own poetry. And she has come full circle since leaving academe; Boland is currently a professor of English at Stanford University.

The poems by Eavan Boland collected for this anthology are diverse and complicated, yet each works to restore missing voices, missing narratives, most of them female. *Anorexic* voices the paradoxical self-destruction of starving for love and power; *The Pomegranate* is a beautiful rewriting of the myth of Persephone, the Greek maiden whose mother, Ceres, the goddess of fertility, was forced to let her daughter spend the winter each year underground with Hades, the god of the underworld, in order to let spring come again. Narrated in the voice of a contemporary mother gazing at her own teenage daughter, separated from her by the girl's need to acquire independence, the poem modernizes the cycle of human seasons and probes the nature of maternal regret. Boland brings the intimacy of such feelings to her meditations on history, violence, and Ireland itself. *Mise Eire* is a dazzling play on words from its title onward; a defiant female voice repudiates Ireland, rejects it for naming her "the woman" in its poetry, not seeing beyond that designation to the real woman who once stood on the deck of the *Mary Belle*, headed to America, a half-dead infant in her arms. "A new language is a scar," the poem tells us. Eavan Boland's poetic task has been to heal those scars by uncovering them, to give voice to the absent throng of women in the Irish past.

Anorexic

Flesh is heretic.
My body is a witch.
I am burning it.

Yes I am torching
5   her curves and paps[1] and wiles.
They scorch in my self-denials.

---

1. Breasts.

How she meshed my head
in the half-truths
of her fevers till I renounced
10   milk and honey
and the taste of lunch.

I vomited
her hungers.
Now the bitch is burning.

15   I am starved and curveless.
I am skin and bone.
She has learned her lesson.

Thin as a rib
I turn in sleep.
20   My dreams probe

a claustrophobia
a sensuous enclosure.
How warm it was and wide

once by a warm drum,
25   once by the song of his breath
and in his sleeping side.[2]

Only a little more,
only a few more days
sinless, foodless.

30   I will slip
back into him again
as if I have never been away.

Caged so
I will grow
35   angular and holy

past pain
keeping his heart
such company

as will make me forget
40   in a small space
the fall

into forked dark,
into python needs
heaving to hips and breasts
45   and lips and heat
and sweat and fat and greed.

                                                        1987

2. These verses recall God's creation of Eve from one of Adam's ribs as he sleeps (Genesis 2.21).

Mise Eire[1]

I won't go back to it—

my nation displaced
into old dactyls,[2]
oaths made
5   by the animal tallows
of the candle—

land of the Gulf Stream,
the small farm,
the scalded memory,
10   the songs
that bandage up the history,
the words
that make a rhythm of the crime

where time is time past.
15   A palsy of regrets.
No. I won't go back.
My roots are brutal:

I am the woman—
a sloven's mix
20   of silk at the wrists,
a sort of dove-strut
in the precincts of the garrison—

who practices
the quick frictions,
25   the rictus[3] of delight
and gets cambric for it,
rice-colored silks.

I am the woman
in the gansy-coat[4]
30   on board the *Mary Belle,*
in the huddling cold,

holding her half-dead baby to her
as the wind shifts East
and North over the dirty
35   water of the wharf

mingling the immigrant
guttural with the vowels
of homesickness who neither
knows nor cares that

1. I am Ireland (Gaelic). Mise Eire also reads as "misery,"
a pun.
2. The English adapted "Eire" to "Ireland," drawing the
word out into dactylic meter.
3. Frozen smile.
4. A cheap cloth coat.

40   a new language
        is a kind of scar
        and heals after a while
        into a passable imitation
        of what went before.

                                                                    1987

The Pomegranate

The only legend I have ever loved is
The story of a daughter lost in hell.
And found and rescued there.
Love and blackmail are the gist of it.
5   Ceres and Persephone the names.
And the best thing about the legend is
I can enter it anywhere. And have.
As a child in exile in
A city of fogs and strange consonants,
10 I read it first and at first I was
An exiled child in the crackling dusk of
The underworld, the stars blighted. Later
I walked out in a summer twilight
Searching for my daughter at bedtime.
15 When she came running I was ready
To make any bargain to keep her.
I carried her back past whitebeams.
And wasps and honey-scented buddleias.
But I was Ceres then and I knew
20 Winter was in store for every leaf
On every tree on that road.
Was inescapable for each one we passed.
And for me.
It is winter
25 And the stars are hidden.
I climb the stairs and stand where I can see
My child asleep beside her teen magazines,
Her can of Coke, her plate of uncut fruit.
The pomegranate! How did I forget it?
30 She could have come home and been safe
And ended the story and all
Our heartbroken searching but she reached
Out a hand and plucked a pomegranate.[1]
She put out her hand and pulled down
35 The French sound for apple and
The noise of stone and the proof

---

1. In the classical myth, Persephone would have emerged from the underworld unharmed except for the fact that she
broke a command to bring nothing back: by plucking a pomegranate, she became liable to death. The next lines recall the
derivation of the term "pomegranate" from Old French *pomme granade*, "seeded apple."

That even in the place of death,
At the heart of legend, in the midst
Of rocks full of unshed tears

40   Ready to be diamonds by the time
The story was told, a child can be
Hungry. I could warn her. There is still a chance.
The rain is cold. The road is flint-coloured.
The suburb has cars and cable television.

45   The veiled stars are above ground.
It is another world. But what else
Can a mother give her daughter but such
Beautiful rifts in time?
If I defer the grief I will diminish the gift.

50   The legend must be hers as well as mine.
She will enter it. As I have.
She will wake up. She will hold
The papery, flushed skin in her hand.
And to her lips. I will say nothing.

                                        1994

A Woman Painted on a Leaf

I found it among curios and silver.
in the pureness of wintry light.

A woman painted on a leaf.

Fine lines drawn on a veined surface

5   in a handmade frame.

This is not my face. Neither did I draw it.

A leaf falls in a garden.
The moon cools its aftermath of sap.
The pith of summer dries out in starlight.

10   A woman is inscribed there.

This is not death. It is the terrible
suspension of life.

I want a poem
I can grow old in. I want a poem I can die in.

15   I want to take
this dried-out face,
as you take a starling from behind iron,
and return it to its element of air, of ending—
so that autumn

20   which was once
the hard look of stars,
the frown on a gardener's face,
a gradual bronzing of the distance,

will be,
25   from now on,
a crisp tinder underfoot. Cheekbones. Eyes. Will be
a mouth crying out. Let me.

Let me die.

1994

⊷ ⊱◈⊰ ⊶

Lorna Goodison
b. 1947

Born in Kingston, Jamaica, to working-class parents, the eighth of nine children, Lorna Goodison studied at the Jamaica School of Art before transferring to the Art Students League of
New York. After completing her studies, she returned to Jamaica to work in advertising. In
1980, Goodison published *Tamarind Seasons: Poems*, a collection that strongly reflects the failure of her marriage in 1972 to a Jamaican radio personality and their divorce in 1978. Her
second book, *I Am Becoming My Mother* (1986), brought Goodison to the attention of the international community and earned her Britain's Commonwealth Poetry Prize. Her sixth collection, *To Us, All Flowers Are Roses* (1995), was given a Gold Star by *Booklist* magazine.
Goodison's poetry portrays the life and character of her fellow Jamaicans, describing folk practices and elegizing her dead mother. She also writes extensively about Jamaica's bloody colonial past as in her poem "About the Tamarind," about the tree that came to the Caribbean
with shipments of African slaves, but her work seeks to lessen the suffering by giving it name,
to ease the pain by spreading it among the entire audience of the world. Goodison has taught
in Canada and the United States, and currently teaches creative writing at the University of
Michigan.

The Mulatta as Penelope[1]

Tonight, I'll pull your limbs through
small soft garments
your head will part my breasts
and you will hear a different heartbeat.
5   Tonight, we said the real goodbye, he and I
But this time I will not sit and spin and spin
the door open to let the madness in.
Till the sailor finally weary of the sea
returns with tin souvenirs and a claim to me.
10   True I returned from the quayside
my eyes full of sand
and his salt-leaving smell
fresh on my hands

---

1. The faithful wife of Odysseus who, in Homer's *Odyssey*, waited twenty years for her husband's return from the Trojan
Wars.

15   but you're my anchor awhile now
        and that holds deep.
        I'll sit in the sun
        and dry my hair
        while you sleep.

                                              1983

On Becoming a Mermaid

        Watching the underlife idle by
        you think drowning must be easy death
        just let go and let the water carry you
        away and under
5   the current pulls your bathing-plaits loose
        your hair floats out straightened by the water
        your legs close together fuse all the length down
        your feet now one broad foot
        the toes spread into
10   a fish-tail, fan-like,
        your sex locked under
        mother-of-pearl scales
        you're a nixie[1] now, a mermaid
        a green-tinged fish/fleshed woman/thing
15   who swims with thrashing movements
        and stands upended on the sea floor
        breasts full and floating buoyed by the salt
        and the space between your arms now always
        filled and your sex sealed forever under
20   mother-of-pearl scale/locks closes finally
        on itself like some close-mouthed oyster.

                                              1986

Annie Pengelly

        I come to represent the case
        of one Annie Pengelly,
        maidservant, late of the San Fleming Estate
        situated in the westerly parish of Hanover.

5   Hanover, where that masif
        mountain range
        assumes the shape of a Dolphin's head
        rearing up in the blue expanse overhead
        restless white clouds round it foaming.

---

1. Nymph or fairy.

10   Those at sea would look up
      and behold, mirrored, a seascape in the sky.

      It is this need to recreate,
      to run 'gainst things, that cause
      all this confusion.

15   The same need that made men
      leave one side of the world
      to journey in long, mawed ships,
      to drogue millions of souls
      to a world
20   that they call the new one
      in competition with the original act
      the creation of the old one.

      So now you are telling me to proceed
      and proceed swiftly.
25   Why have I come here representing Annie?

      Well this is the first thing she asked me to say,
      that Annie is not even her real name.
      A name is the first thing we own in this world.

      We lay claim to a group of sounds
30   which rise up and down and mark out our space
      in the air around us.
      We become owners of a harmony of vowels and consonants
      singing a specific meaning.

      Her real name was given to her
35   at the pastoral ceremony of her outdooring.[1]
      Its outer meaning was, "she who is precious to us."

      It had too a hidden part, a kept secret.
      A meaning known only to those within
      the circle of her family.

40   For sale Bidderman, one small girl,
      one small African girl answering now
      to the name of Annie.

      Oh Missus my dear, when you write Lady Nugent[2]
      to tell her of your splendid birthday
45   of the ivory moire gown you wore
      that you send clear to London for.

      You can tell her too how you had built for you
      a pair of soft, supple leather riding boots
      fashioned from your own last
50   by George O'Brian Wilson

---

1. Christening ceremony in Ghana.   2. Wife of George Nugent, colonial government official
in the early nineteenth century.

late of Aberdeen
now Shoemaker and Sadler of Lucea, Hanover
late occupation,
bruk° Sailor.   *broke*

55   One pair of tortoiseshell combs,
one scrolled silver backed mirror,
one dinner party where they killed
one whole cow
with oaken casks of Madeira wine
60   to wash it down.

And don't forget, one small African girl,
answering now to the name of Annie.

With all that birthday show of affection
Massa never sleep with missus.
65   But I am not here to talk about that,
that is backra° business.   *white people*

I am really here just representing Annie Pengelly.
For Missus began to make Annie
sleep across her feet
70   come December when northers began to blow.

Northers being the chill wheeling tail end
of the winter breezes
dropping off their cold what lef' in Jamaica
to confuse the transplanted Planter.

75   Causing them to remember words like "hoarfrost" and "moors"
from a frozen vocabulary they no longer
had use for.

When this false winter breeze would
careen across canefields
80   Missus would make Annie lie draped,
heaped across her feet
a human blanket
nothing covering her as she gave
her warmth to Missus.

85   So I come to say that History owes Annie
the brightest woolen blanket.
She is owed too, at least twelve years of sleep
stretched out,
free to assume the stage of sleep
90   flat on her back,
or profiled like the characters
in an Egyptian frieze.

Most nights though, Missus don't sleep.
And as Annie was subject to Missus will,

95   Annie was not to sleep as long
        as Missus kept her open-eyed vigil.

        Sometimes Missus sit up
        sipping wine from a cut glass goblet.
        Talking, talking.

100   Sometimes Missus dance and sing
        like she was on a stage,
        sad cantatrice solo
        on a stage performing.

        At the end of her performance
105   she would demand that Annie clap
        clap loud and shout "encore."

        Encouraged by this she would sing
        and dance on,
        her half-crazed torch song of rejection.
110   Sometimes Annie nod off.
        Missus jook° her with a pearl-tipped pin.   *jab*
        Sometimes Annie tumble off the chair
        felled by sleep.
        Missus slap her awake again.
115   Then in order to keep her alert, awake
        she devised the paper torture.

        One pile of newspapers
        a sharp pair of scissors later,
        Annie learned about
120   the cruel make-work task
        that is the *cut-up*
        to *throw-away* of old newspaper.

        For if Missus could not sleep
        Annie gal you don't sleep that night,
125   and poor Missus enslaved by love
        fighting her servitude with spite.

        So I say history owes Annie
        thousands of nights
        of sleep upon a feather bed.
130   Soft feathers from the breast of
        a free, soaring bird,
        one bright blanket,
        and her name returned,
        she who is precious to us.

135   Annie Pengelly O.
        I say, History owe you.

                                                            1995

Agha Shahid Ali
1949–2001

The short but brilliant life and career of Agha Shahid Ali are a monument to the powers of linguistic and cultural cross-pollination. Born in New Delhi, India, Ali was raised a Muslim in Kashmir and was educated at the University of Kashmir, Srinagar, and the University of Delhi. Ali received his doctorate in English from Pennsylvania State University in 1984, and an M.F.A. from the University of Arizona in 1985. His collections of poetry include *Bone Sculpture* (1972), *In Memory of Begum Akhtar and Other Poems* (1979), *The Half-Inch Himalayas* (1987), *A Nostalgist's Map of America* (1991), *The Country Without a Post Office* (1997), *Rooms Are Never Finished* (2001, finalist for the National Book Award), and *Call Me Ishmael Tonight: A Book of Ghazals* (2003). Ali held teaching positions at the University of Delhi, Penn State, SUNY Binghamton, Princeton University, Hamilton College, Baruch College, University of Utah, and Warren Wilson College. He was awarded fellowships from the Guggenheim Foundation, the Pennsylvania Council on the Arts, the Bread Loaf Writers' Conference, the Ingram-Merrill Foundation, and the New York Foundation for the Arts.

Beyond English

No language is old—or young—beyond English.
So what of a common tongue beyond English?

I know some words for war, all of them sharp,
but the sharpest one is *jung*—beyond English!

5   If you wish to know of a king who loved his slave,
you must learn legends, often-sung, beyond English.

Baghdad is sacked and its citizens must watch
prisoners (now in miniatures) hung beyond English.

Go all the way through *jungle* from *aleph* to *zenith*
10   to see English, like monkeys, swung beyond English.

So never send to know for whom the bell tolled,[1]
for across the earth it has rung beyond English.

If you want your drugs legal you must leave the States,
not just for hashish but one—*bhung*—beyond English.

15   Heartbroken, I tottered out "into windless snow,"
snowflakes on my lips, silence stung beyond English.

When the phrase, "The Mother of all Battles," caught on,
the surprise was indeed not sprung beyond English.

Could a soul crawl away at last unshriveled which
20   to its "own fusing senses" had clung beyond English?

---

1. Ali alludes to John Donne's famous Meditation 17, from *Devotions Upon Emergent Occasions* (1624): "Any man's death diminishes me, because I am involved in mankind; and therefore never send to know for whom the bell tolls; it tolls for thee . . ."

If someone asks where Shahid has disappeared,
he's waging a war (no, *jung*) beyond English.

(for LAWRENCE NEEDHAM)

2002

In Arabic
(with revisions of some couplets of "Arabic")

A language of loss? I have some business in Arabic.
Love letters: calligraphy pitiless in Arabic.

At an exhibit of miniatures, what Kashmiri hairs!
Each paisley inked into a golden tress in Arabic.

5   This much fuss about a language I don't know? So one day
perfume from a dress may let you digress in Arabic.

A "Guide for the Perplexed" was written—believe me—
by Cordoba's Jew—Maimonides[1]—in Arabic.

Majnoon,[2] by stopped caravans, rips his collars, cries "Laila!"
10   Pain translated is O! much more—not less—in Arabic.

Writes Shammas:[3] Memory, no longer confused, now is a homeland—
his two languages a Hebrew caress in Arabic.

When Lorca[4] died, they left the balconies open and saw:
On the sea his *qasidas*° stitched seamless in Arabic.   *an Arabic poetic form*

15   In the Veiled One's harem, an adulteress hanged by eunuchs—
So the rank mirrors revealed to Borges[5] in Arabic.

Ah, bisexual Heaven: wide-eyed houris° and immortal youths!   *virginal young*
To your each desire they say *Yes! O Yes!* in Arabic.   *women*

For that excess of sibilance, the last Apocalypse,
20   so pressing those three forms of S in Arabic.

I too, O Amichai,[6] saw everything, just like you did—
In Death. In Hebrew. And (please let me stress) in Arabic.

They ask me to tell them what *Shahid* means: Listen, listen:
It means "The Beloved" in Persian, "witness" in Arabic.

2004

---

1. Moses Maimonides, medieval rabbi and philosopher.
2. The long twelfth-century love poem of Laila and Majnoon is a classic of Persian literature.
3. Anton Shammas (1950–), Hebrew and Arabic writer.
4. Federico Garcia Lorca (1898–1936), Spanish poet and

playwright.
5. Jorge Luis Borges (1899–1986), Argentinian fiction writer and fabulist.
6. Yehuda Amichai (1924–2000), Israel's best-known twentieth-century poet.

Tonight

Pale hands I loved beside the Shalimar

—*Laurence Hope*

Where are you now? Who lies beneath your spell tonight?
Whom else from rapture's road will you expel tonight?

Those "Fabrics of Cashmere—" "to make Me beautiful—"
"Trinket"—to gem—"Me to adorn—How tell"—tonight?

5 I beg for haven: Prisons, let open your gates—
A refugee from Belief seeks a cell tonight.

God's vintage loneliness has turned to vinegar—
All the archangels—their wings frozen—fell tonight.

Lord, cried out the idols, *Don't let us be broken;*
10 Only we can convert the infidel tonight.

Mughal[1] ceilings, let your mirrored convexities
multiply me at once under your spell tonight.

He's freed some fire from ice in pity for Heaven.
He's left open—for God—the doors of Hell tonight.

15 In the heart's veined temple, all statues have been smashed.
No priest in saffron's left to toll its knell tonight.

God, limit these punishments, there's still Judgment Day—
I'm a mere sinner, I'm no infidel tonight.

Executioners near the woman at the window.
20 Damn you, Elijah, I'll bless Jezebel[2] tonight.

The hunt is over, and I hear the Call to Prayer
fade into that of the wounded gazelle tonight.

My rivals for your love—you've invited them all?
This is mere insult, this is no farewell tonight.

25 And I, Shahid, only am escaped to tell thee—
God sobs in my arms. Call me Ishmael tonight.[3]

2004

---

1. Muslim rulers, or emperors, who controlled western India from 1526 to 1858.
2. Jezebel was the wife of Israelite king Ahab; she did not obey the precepts of Jewish law, and the prophet Elijah prophesized that Jezebel would be torn apart by the dogs of Jezreel (1 Kings 21:23), a prophecy which ultimately came to pass.
3. Ali refers here both to the eldest son of the Old Testament patriarch Abraham, who after the birth of his brother Isaac became a wanderer on the earth, and also to the opening of the narrative section of Herman Melville's *Moby-Dick:* "Call me Ishmael."

→ ⁐⧫⧐ →

Paul Muldoon
b. 1951

If reading poetry sometimes appears to be a simple process of translation—a kind of verbal puzzle to be solved—the work of Paul Muldoon should disabuse readers of that notion. Muldoon's poetry celebrates and bears witness to a sense of the mysterious at the heart of everyday existence—the sense, which for Muldoon is a reason to celebrate rather than despair, that life will always elude our attempts to make it all make sense. Indeed, Muldoon's poetry often seems to adopt the motto of one of the bands he writes about in *Sleeve Notes*, the Talking Heads: "Stop making sense."

Like Seamus Heaney, who was later to be his tutor at Queen's University, Belfast, Muldoon was raised Catholic in protestant Northern Ireland. He was born and raised in Portadown, County Armagh; in grammar school his teachers introduced him to poetry, music, and the Irish language. Muldoon's first poems were written in Irish; but when he went to university he switched and began writing in English, fearing that his knowledge of Irish wasn't sufficiently sound. (He has, nevertheless, made English translations of some Irish poetry, including that of Nuala Ní Dhomhnaill.) Queen's University was a crucible of new poetry at the time, with Heaney and Michael Longley the group's established poets, and Medbh McGuckian and Ciaran Carson among his classmates. His first poetry collection, *New Weather*, was published by the prestigious British publisher Faber and Faber while Muldoon was still a student.

Muldoon's now substantial body of poetry—the poems of his first eight collections published with Faber were collected in *Poems 1968–1998* (2001)—covers a very wide geographic and imaginative terrain. His subjects range from ancient Irish legends and sagas, to detective fiction, to popular movies and song; his tastes are, in the lowercase sense of the word, truly catholic.

Since 1990, Muldoon has directed the creative writing program at Princeton University; in 1999 he was elected Professor of Poetry at Oxford. His Clarendon lectures in English literature, delivered at Oxford, were published as *To Ireland, I* in 1998. His most recent poetry collection is *Moy Sand and Gravel* (2002).

Cuba[1]

My eldest sister arrived home that morning
In her white muslin evening dress.
"Who the hell do you think you are,
Running out to dances in next to nothing?
5   As though we hadn't enough bother
With the world at war, if not at an end."
My father was pounding the breakfast-table.

"Those Yankees were touch and go as it was—
If you'd heard Patton[2] in Armagh[3]—
10   But this Kennedy's nearly an Irishman

---

1. The background for the poem is the Cuban Missile Crisis of October 1962, to which the Irish felt some connection through the Irish-American President, John Fitzgerald Kennedy.

2. General George S. Patton (1885–1945), fiery and controversial American military leader in World Wars I and II.
3. An urban district of Northern Ireland.

So he's not much better than ourselves.
And him with only to say the word.
If you've got anything on your mind
Maybe you should make your peace with God."

15 I could hear May from beyond the curtain.
"Bless me, Father, for I have sinned.
I told a lie once, I was disobedient once.
And, Father, a boy touched me once."
"Tell me, child. Was this touch immodest?
20 Did he touch your breast, for example?"
"He brushed against me, Father. Very gently."

1980

Aisling[1]

I was making my way home late one night
this summer, when I staggered
into a snow drift.

Her eyes spoke of a sloe-year,
5 her mouth a year of haws.[2]

Was she Aurora, or the goddess Flora,
Artemidora, or Venus bright,[3]
or Anorexia[4] who left
a lemon stain on my flannel sheet?

10 It's all much of a muchness.

In Belfast's Royal Victoria Hospital
a kidney machine
supports the latest hunger-striker
to have called off his fast, a saline
15 drip into his bag of brine.

A lick and a promise. Cuckoo spittle.
I hand my sample to Doctor Maw.
She gives me back a confident *All Clear*.

1983

Meeting the British

We met the British in the dead of winter.
The sky was lavender

---

1. The *aisling* (pron. "ashling") is a traditional Irish poetic form, in which the poet goes out walking and meets a beautiful lady; he learns that she is the personification of Ireland, and she promises him early deliverance from the yoke of foreign oppressors.
2. Both sloes and haws are shrubs (the blackthorn and hawthorn, respectively); both words have also been used to indicate something of little or no value, as in "not worth a haw."

3. Goddesses of classical mythology, representing, respectively, the morning, vegetation, the hunt, and beauty.
4. Anorexia is no goddess, of course, but the medical condition *anorexia nervosa* in which a young woman (most commonly) denies herself food, sometimes to the point of death. Muldoon here likens the 1981 hunger strikes of the Irish Republican Army "blanket men" in British prisons (like Bobby Sands) to anorexia.

and the snow lavender-blue.
I could hear, far below,

5 the sound of two streams coming together
(both were frozen over)

and, no less strange,
myself calling out in French

across that forest—
10 clearing. Neither General Jeffrey Amherst

nor Colonel Henry Bouquet[1]
could stomach our willow-tobacco.

As for the unusual
scent when the Colonel shook out his hand—

15 kerchief: *C'est la lavande,*
une fleur mauve comme le ciel.[2]

They gave us six fishhooks
and two blankets embroidered with smallpox.

1987

Sleeve Notes

MICK JAGGER: *Rock music was a completely new musical form. It hadn't been around for ten years when we started doing it. Now it's forty years old.*
JANN S. WENNER: *What about your own staying power?*
MICK JAGGER: *I have a lot of energy, so I don't see it as an immediate problem.*
JANN S. WENNER: *How's your hearing?*
MICK JAGGER: *My hearing's all right. Sometimes I use earplugs because it gets too loud on my left ear.*
JANN S. WENNER: *Why your left ear?*
MICK JAGGER: *Because Keith's[1] standing on my left.*

—"JAGGER REMEMBERS," *Rolling Stone,* MARCH 1996

THE JIMI HENDRIX EXPERIENCE: *Are You Experienced?*[2]

"Like being driven over by a truck"
was how Pete Townshend[3] described the effect
of the wah-wah on "I Don't Live Today."

This predated by some months the pedal
5 Clapton used on "Tales of Brave Ulysses"[4]
And I'm taken aback (jolt upon jolt)
to think that Hendrix did it all "by hand."

---

1. General Jeffrey Amherst and Colonel Henry Bouquet: 18th-century British officers who served in the colonial United States.
2. It is lavender, a flower purple like the sky (French).
1. Keith Richards, the Rolling Stones' guitarist.

2. *Are You Experienced?* (1967) was Jimi Hendrix's first album; its best-known tracks are "Purple Haze" and "Fire."
3. Lead guitarist of The Who.
4. Track on the Cream album *Disraeli Gears* (see next page).

To think, moreover, that he used *four*-track
one-inch tape has (jolt upon jolt) evoked
the long, long view from the Senior Study
through the smoke, yes sir, the smoke of battle
on the fields of Laois, yes sir, and Laos.[5]

Then there was the wah-wah on "Voodoo Child
(Slight Return)" from *Electric Ladyland*.[6]

CREAM: *Disraeli Gears*[7]

As I labored over the "Georgiks and Bukolikis"[8]
I soon learned to tell thunder from dynamite.

THE BEATLES: *The Beatles*[9]

Though that was the winter when late each night
I'd put away Cicero or Caesar
and pour new milk into an old saucer
for the hedgehog which, when it showed up right

on cue, would set its nose down like that flight
back from the U.S. . . . back from the, yes sir.
back from the . . . back from the U.S.S.R. . . .
I'd never noticed the play on "*album*" and "white."[1]

THE ROLLING STONES: *Beggar's Banquet*[2]

Thanks to Miss Latimore,
I was "coming along nicely" at piano

while, compared to the whoops and wild halloos
of the local urchins,

my diction
was im-pecc-a-ble.

In next to no time I would be lost
to the milk bars

and luncheonettes
of smoky Belfast,

---

5. Laois is a county and a town (Portlaois) in the mid-lands of Ireland; Laos is a country in Southeast Asia, in which the United States conducted bombing raids during the Vietnam War (about the time that *Are You Experienced?* was released).
6. *Electric Ladyland* (1968) was Hendrix's third album and featured the tracks "All Along the Watchtower" and "Crosstown Traffic."
7. *Disraeli Gears* (1967) was the second album from British "supergroup" Cream, featuring Eric Clapton on lead guitar. The record featured "Sunshine of Your Love" and "Tales of Brave Ulysses."

8. A georgic is a poem on an agricultural theme; a bucolic is a pastoral poem.
9. The Beatles' 1968 double-album release, officially titled *The Beatles* but known colloquially as "The White Album," for its unadorned white cover. Best-known tracks: "While My Guitar Gently Weeps" (on which Eric Clapton plays an uncredited guitar solo), "Blackbird," "Helter Skelter," "Back in the USSR."
1. In the romance languages, the root *alb-* means "white."
2. *Beggar's Banquet* (1968) opens with "Sympathy for the Devil" and also features "Street Fighting Man."

where a troubadour
such as the frontman of Them[3]

had long since traded in the lute
for bass and blues harmonica.

VAN MORRISON: *Astral Weeks*[4]

Not only had I lived on Fitzroy Avenue,
I'd lived there with Madame Georgie Hyde Lees,[5]
to whom I would rather shortly be wed.
Georgie would lose out to The George and El Vino's
5 when I "ran away to the BBC"
as poets did, so Dylan Thomas said.

ERIC CLAPTON: *461 Ocean Boulevard*[6]

It's the house in all its whited sepulchritude[7]
(not the palm tree against which dogs piddle
as they make their way back from wherever
it was they were all night) that's really at a list.

5 Through the open shutters his music, scatty, skewed,
skids and skites from the neck of a bottle[8]
that might turn on him, might turn and sever
an artery, the big one that runs through his wrist.

ELVIS COSTELLO AND THE ATTRACTIONS: *My Aim Is True*[9]

Even the *reductio ad absurdum*[1]
of the *quid pro quo*[2] or "tit for tat"
killing (For "Eilis" read "Alison")

that now took over from the street riot
5 was not without an old-fashioned
sense of decorum, an unseemly seemliness.

WARREN ZEVON: *Excitable Boy*[3]

Somewhere between *Ocean Boulevard* and *Slowhand*[4]
I seemed to have misplaced my wedding band

3. "Them" was the name of Van Morrison's band before
he left to go solo.
4. *Astral Weeks* (1968) is generally considered Morrison's
greatest album, although it did not produce any hits (like
his earlier "Brown-Eyed Girl" and later "Moondance").
5. Georgiana ("Georgie") Hyde-Lees married William
Butler Yeats in 1917.
6. *461 Ocean Boulevard* (1974) produced the hit "I Shot
the Sheriff" (his cover of a Bob Marley song). The cover
shows Clapton standing in front of a whitewashed stucco
house next to a wind-bent palm tree.
7. "Sepulchre" (tomb) and
"pulchritude" (beauty). In *Heart of Darkness*, the narrator
Marlow says that the city from which he embarks, and to
which he returns at the end of his journey, always reminded

him of "a whited sepulchre," a phrase Jesus used to describe
the Pharisees in the New Testament.
8. The smoothed neck of a bottle is often used as a "slide"
in playing slide guitar; Muldoon here also probably alludes to Clapton's severe substance abuse problems of this
period (including heroin addiction), although by the release of *461 Ocean Boulevard* Clapton had kicked heroin.
9. *My Aim Is True* was Costello's first album in 1977, featuring "Alison" and "Less Than Zero."
1. Reduction to absurdity (Latin), a rhetorical strategy.
2. This for that (Latin), or as Muldoon puts it, "tit for tat."
3. *Excitable Boy* (1978) features Zevon's only brush with
pop success, the song "Werewolves of London."
4. Two Clapton albums: *461 Ocean Boulevard* was released in 1974 and *Slowhand* in 1977.

and taken up with waitresses and usherettes
who drank straight gins and smoked crooked cheroots.[5]

5   Since those were still the days when more meant less
Georgie was herself playing fast and loose
with the werewolf who, not so very long before,
had come how-howling round our kitchen door

and introduced me to Warren Zevon, whose hymns
10   to booty, to beasts, to bimbos, boom boom,
are inextricably part of the warp and woof
of the wild and wicked poems in *Quoof*.[6]

DIRE STRAITS: *Dire Straits*[7]

There was that time the archangel ran his thumb along the shelf
and anointed, it seemed, his own brow with soot.

BLONDIE: *Parallel Lines*[8]

It had taken all morning to rehearse
a tracking shot

with an Arriflex[9]
mounted on a gurney.

5   The dream of rain
on the face of a well.

"Ready when you are, Mr. DeMilledoon."[1]
Another small crowd

on the horizon.
10   We should have rented a Steadicam.[2]

BRUCE SPRINGSTEEN: *The River*[3]

So it was I gave up the Oona for the Susquehanna,[4]
the Shannon for the Shenandoah.

LLOYD COLE AND THE COMMOTIONS: *Easy Pieces*[5]

Though not before I'd done my stint on the Cam.
The ceilings taller than the horizon.

The in-crowd
on the outs with the likes of Milton

5. Cigars.
6. Muldoon's 1983 volume of poetry, including the poem *Aisling*.
7. Dire Straits' debut album was released in 1978 and featured their first hit, "Sultans of Swing."
8. *Parallel Lines* (1978) featured Blondie's only venture into "disco," "Heart of Glass," as well as the hit "One Way or Another."
9. A professional movie camera.

1. Muldoon here merges his name with that of legendary Hollywood director Cecil B. DeMille.
2. A consumer-oriented videocamera.
3. *The River* (1980) is seen by many purists as a "sellout," containing the pop-oriented single "Hungry Heart."
4. Muldoon replaces two Irish with two American rivers.
5. *Easy Pieces* (1985) was the title of the American release of Cole's first album (*Rattlesnakes*, 1984, in the UK).

5   and Spenser while Cromwell
     still walked through the pouring rain.

     In graveyards from Urney
     to Ardglass, my countrymen laying down some *Lex*

     talionis:[6] "Only the guy who's shot
10   gets to ride in the back of the hearse."

TALKING HEADS: *True Stories*[7]

You can take the man out of Armagh but, you may ask yourself,
can you take the Armagh out of the man in the big Armani suit?[8]

U2: *The Joshua Tree*[9]

When I went to hear them in Giants Stadium
a year or two ago, the whiff
of kef[1]
brought back the night we drove all night from Palm

5   Springs to Blythe.[2] No Irish lad and his lass
     were so happy as we who roared
     and soared
     through yucca-scented air. Dawn brought a sense of loss,

     faint at first, that would deepen and expand
10   as our own golden chariot
     was showered
     with Zippo[3] spears from the upper tiers of the stands.

PINK FLOYD: *A Momentary Lapse of Reason*[4]

We stopped in at a roadhouse on the way back from Lyonesse
and ordered a Tom Collins and an Old-Fashioned.
As we remounted the chariot

     the poplars' synthesized alamo-alamo-eleison
5   was counterpointed by a redheaded woodpecker's rat-tat-tat
     on a snare, a kettledrum's de dum de dum.

PAUL SIMON: *Negotiations and Love Songs*[5]

Little did I think as I knelt by a pothole

---

6. The principle of "an eye for an eye, a tooth for a tooth."

7. *True Stories* (1986) was the "soundtrack" for the 1986 David Byrne–directed film of the same title; it yielded the hit "Wild Wild Life."

8. In Jonathan Demme's wonderful 1984 documentary about the band, *Stop Making Sense*, David Byrne wears an enormously oversized ecru Georgio Armani suit.

9. The enduringly popular *The Joshua Tree* (1987) yielded the U2 hits, "With or Without You" and "I Still Haven't Found What I'm Looking For."

1. Marijuana.

2. A town in the Mohave Desert in southern California.

3. Disposable lighters.

4. A 1987 album featuring the track, "The Dogs of War."

5. A 1988 greatest-hits compilation of Simon's solo work, including "Mother and Child Reunion," "Still Crazy After All These Years," and many other familiar hits.

to water my elephant with the other elephant drivers,
little did I think as I chewed on some betel[6]

that I might one day be following the river
down the West Side Highway[7] in his smoke-glassed
limo complete with bodyguard-cum-chauffeur

and telling him that his lyrics must surely last:
little did I think as I chewed and chewed
that my own teeth and tongue would be eaten by rust.

5

LEONARD COHEN: *I'm Your Man*[8]

When I turn up the rickety old gramophone
the wow and flutter[9] from a scratched LP
summons up white walls, the table, the single bed
where Lydia Languish will meet her Le Fanu
his songs have meant far more to me
than most of the so-called poems I've read.

5

NIRVANA: *Bleach*[1]

I went there, too, with Mona, or Monica.
Another shot of Absolut.

"The Wild Rover" or some folk anthem
on the jukebox. Some dour

bartender. I, too, have been held fast
by those snares and nets

off the Zinc Coast, the coast of Zanzibar,
                                    lost
                        able
                                    addiction
            "chin-chins"
                                    loos,[2]
"And it's no,
nay, never, no never no more . . . ."

5

10

BOB DYLAN: *Oh Mercy*[3]

All great artists are their own greatest threat,
as when they aim an industrial laser
at themselves and cut themselves back to the root

---

6. An East Indian pepper plant, the leaves of which are chewed.
7. The West Side Highway in Manhattan, running along the Hudson River.
8. A 1988 album featuring the title cut and "First We Take Manhattan."
9. The distortion introduced in playback by a phonograph.

1. *Bleach*, Nirvana's first record, was released on Seattle independent label Sub Pop in 1989 and features the hit single "About a Girl."
2. Toilets.
3. *Oh Mercy* (1989) is thought by many to be Dylan's best album of a rather weak decade for him. It includes the track "Ring Them Bells."

5 so that, with spring, we can never ever be sure
if they shake from head to foot
from an orgasm, you see, sir, or a seizure.

R.E.M.: *Automatic for the People*[4]

Like the grasping for air by an almighty mite
who's suffering from a bad case of the colic.

THE ROLLING STONES: *Voodoo Lounge*[5]

Giants Stadium again . . . Again the scent of drugs
struggling through rain so heavy some young Turks
would feel obliged to butt-hole
surf[6] across those vast puddles

5 on the field. Some might have burned damp faggots[7]
on a night like this, others faked
the ho-ho-hosannas and the hallelujahs
with their "*Tout passe, tout casse, tout lasse.*"[8]

The Stones, of course, have always found the way
10 of setting a burning brand
to a petrol-soaked stack of hay

and making a "Thou Shalt"
of a "Thou Shalt Not." The sky over the Meadowlands[9]
was still aglow as I drove home to my wife and child.

1998

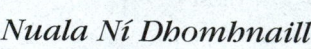

Nuala Ní Dhomhnaill
b. 1952

Nuala Ní Dhomhnaill was born in a coal mining region in England, to Irish parents; she was sent at the age of five, however, to live with relatives in the Gaeltacht (Irish-speaking area) on the Dingle Peninsula in West Kerry—"dropped into it cold-turkey," she says. She thus grew up bilingual, speaking English in the home, Irish out of it. Ní Dhomhnaill quickly learned that translation always picks up and leaves behind meaning; she tells this story: "I recall as a child someone asking my name in Irish. The question roughly translates as 'Who do you belong to?' Still most fluent in English, I replied, 'I don't belong to anybody. I belong to myself.' That became quite a joke in the village." In some ways, Ní Dhomhnaill's poetic career has been the process of discovering who, and whose, she is—and making those discoveries through the medium of the Irish language; her name itself, pronounced *nu-AH-la ne GOE-ne*, sounds different than it looks to English eyes.

---

4. *Automatic for the People* (1992) was R.E.M.'s biggest critical and popular success; it contained the hits "Everybody Hurts," "Drive," and "Man on the Moon," about the late comedian Andy Kaufmann.
5. *Voodoo Lounge* (1994) marked the thirtieth anniversary of the Rolling Stone's career as a rock band.
6. Muldoon plays on the name of the Texas-based band

Butthole Surfers.
7. Cigarettes.
8. Everything passes; everything breaks; everything tires ("all is vanity") (French).
9. The Meadowlands is a popular sports complex and rock venue in New Jersey.

"The individual psyche is a rather puny thing," she has said; "One's interior life dries up without the exchange with tradition." Ní Dhomhnaill's fruitful exchange with the Irish literary tradition has resulted in a poetry rich in the imagery of Irish folklore and mythology, and pregnant with the sense of contradiction and irony that undergirds Irish writing ("We [Celts] are truly comfortable only with ambiguity," she says). Ní Dhomhnaill's poetry in Irish includes the prize-winning volumes *An Dealg Droighin* (1981) and *Féar Suaithinseach* (1984), as well as a selection of poems from her volume *Feis* translated into English by the poet Paul Muldoon. The *Irish Literary Supplement* has called her "the most widely known and acclaimed Gaelic poet of the century"; by continuing to write in Irish, she has helped make it a viable language for modern poetry. Ní Dhomhnaill lives in Dublin and has taught at University College, Cork.

Feeding a Child[1]

From honey-dew of milking
from cloudy heat of beestings
the sun rises up the back
of bare hills,
5   a guinea gold
to put in your hand,
my own.
You drink your fill from my breast
and fall back asleep
10 into a lasting dream
laughter in your face.
What is going through your head
you who are but
a fortnight on earth?

15 Do you know day from night
that the great early ebb
announces spring tide?
That the boats
are on deep ocean,
20 where live the seals and fishes
and the great whales,
and are coming hand over hand
each by seven oars manned?
That your small boats swims
25 óró[2] in the bay
with the flippered peoples
and the small sea-creatures
she slippery-sleek
from stem to bow
30 stirring sea-sand up
sinking sea-foam down.

Of all these things are you
ignorant?
As my breast is explored

---

1. Translated by Michael Hartnett.   2. Soothing nonsense sound in Irish.

35   by your small hand
         you grunt with pleasure
         smiling and senseless.
         I look into your face child
         not knowing if you know
40   your herd of cattle
         graze in the land of giants
         trespassing and thieving
         and that soon you will hear
         the fee-fie-fo-fum
45   sounding in your ear.

         You are my piggy
         who went to market
         who stayed at home
         who got bread and butter
50   who got none.
         There's one good bite in you
         but hardly two—
         I like your flesh
         but not the broth thereof.
55   And who are the original patterns
         of the heroes and giants
         if not you and I?

         1986

Parthenogenesis[1]

         Once, a lady of the Ó Moores
         (married seven years without a child)
         swam in the sea in summertime.
         She swam well, and the day
5   was fine as Ireland ever saw
         not even a puff of wind in the air
         all the bay calm, all the sea smooth—
         a sheet of glass—supple, she struck out
         with strength for the breaking waves
10   and frisked, elated by the world.
         She ducked beneath the surface and there saw
         what seemed a shadow, like a man's.
         And every twist and turn she made
         the shadow did the same
15   and came close enough to touch.
         Heart jumped and sound stopped in her mouth
         her pulses ran and raced, sides near burst.
         The lower currents with their ice
         pierced her to the bone

1. Translated by Michael Hartnett. "Parthenogenesis" is the scientific term for virgin birth.

20   and the noise of the abyss numbed all her limbs
       then scales grew on her skin. . .
       the lure of the quiet dreamy undersea. . .
       desire to escape to sea and shells. . .
       the seaweed tresses where at last
25   her bones changed into coral
       and time made atolls of her arms,
       pearls of her eyes in deep long sleep,
       at rest in a nest of weed,
       secure as feather beds. . .
30   But stop!
       Her heroic heritage was there,
       she rose with speedy, threshing feet
       and made in desperation for the beach:
       with nimble supple strokes she made the sand.
35   Near death until the day,
       some nine months later
       she gave birth to a boy.
       She and her husband so satisfied,
       so full of love for this new son
40   forgot the shadow in the sea
       and did not see what only the midwife saw—
       stalks of sea-tangle in the boy's hair
       small shellfish and sea-ribbons
       and his two big eyes
45   as blue and limpid as lagoons.
       A poor scholar passing by
       who found lodging for the night
       saw the boy's eyes never closed
       in dark or light and when all the world slept
50   he asked the boy beside the fire
       "Who are your people?" Came the prompt reply
       "Sea People."

       This same tale is told in the West
       but the woman's an Ó Flaherty
55   and tis the same in the South
       where the lady's called Ó Shea:
       this tale is told on every coast.
       But whoever she was I want to say
       that the fear she felt
60   when the sea-shadow followed her
       is the same fear that vexed
       the young heart of the Virgin
       when she heard the angels' sweet bell
       and in her womb was made flesh
65   by all accounts
       the Son of the Living God.

                                                    1986

Labasheedy (The Silken Bed)[1]

I'd make a bed for you
in Labasheedy
in the tall grass
under the wrestling trees
5   where your skin
would be silk upon silk
in the darkness
when the moths are coming down.

Skin which glistens
10   shining over your limbs
like milk being poured
from jugs at dinnertime;
your hair is a herd of goats
moving over rolling hills,
15   hills that have high cliffs
and two ravines.

And your damp lips
would be as sweet as sugar
at evening and we walking
20   by the riverside
with honeyed breezes
blowing over the Shannon
and the fuchsias bowing down to you
one by one.

25   The fuchsias bending low
their solemn heads
in obeisance to the beauty
in front of them
I would pick a pair of flowers
30   as pendant earrings
to adorn you
like a bride in shining clothes.

O I'd make a bed for you
in Labasheedy,
35   in the twilight hour
with evening falling slow
and what a pleasure it would be
to have our limbs entwine
wrestling
40   while the moths are coming down.

1986

1. Translated by the author.

As for the Quince[1]

There came this bright young thing
with a Black & Decker
and cut down my quince-tree.
I stood with my mouth hanging open
5   while one by one
she trimmed off the branches.

When my husband got home that evening
and saw what had happened
he lost the rag,
10   as you might imagine.
"Why didn't you stop her?
What would she think
if I took the Black & Decker
round to her place
15   and cut down a quince-tree
belonging to her?
What would she make of that?"

Her ladyship came back next morning
while I was at breakfast.
20   She enquired about his reaction.
I told her straight
that he was wondering how she'd feel
if he took a Black & Decker
round to her house
25   and cut down a quince-tree of hers,
etcetera etcetera.

"O," says she, "that's very interesting."
There was a stress on the "very."
She lingered over the "ing."
30   She was remarkably calm and collected.

These are the times that are in it, so,
all a bit topsy-turvy.
The bottom falling out of my belly
as if I had got a kick up the arse
35   or a punch in the kidneys.
A fainting-fit coming over me
that took the legs from under me
and left me so zonked
I could barely lift a finger
40   till Wednesday.

As for the quince, it was safe and sound
and still somehow holding its ground.

1988

---

1. Translated by Paul Muldoon.

Why I Choose to Write in Irish,
The Corpse That Sits Up and Talks Back[1]

Not so long ago I telephoned my mother about some family matter. "So what are you writing these days?" she asked, more for the sake of conversation than anything else. "Oh, an essay for *The New York Times*," I said, as casually as possible. "What is it about?" she asked. "About what it is like to write in Irish," I replied. There was a good few seconds' pause on the other end of the line; then, "Well, I hope you'll tell them that it is mad." End of conversation. I had got my comeuppance. And from my mother, who was the native speaker of Irish in our family, never having encountered a single word of English until she went to school at the age of 6, and well up in her teens before she realized that the name they had at home for a most useful item was actually two words—"safety pin"—and that they were English. Typical.

But really not so strange. Some time later I was at a reception at the American Embassy in Dublin for two of their writers, Toni Morrison and Richard Wilbur. We stood in line and took our buffet suppers along to the nearest available table. An Irishwoman across from me asked what I did. Before I had time to open my mouth her partner butted in: "Oh, Nuala writes poetry in Irish." And what did I write about? she asked. Again before I had time to reply he did so for me: "She writes poems of love and loss, and I could quote you most of them by heart." This was beginning to get up my nose, and so I attempted simultaneously to deflate him and to go him one better. "Actually," I announced, "I think the only things worth writing about are the biggies: birth, death and the most important thing in between, which is sex." "Oh," his friend said to me archly, "and is there a word for sex in Irish?"

I looked over at the next table, where Toni Morrison was sitting, and I wondered if a black writer in America had to put up with the likes of that, or its equivalent. Here I was in my own country, having to defend the official language of the state from a compatriot who obviously thought it was an accomplishment to be ignorant of it. Typical, and yet maybe not so strange.

Let me explain. Irish (as it is called in the Irish Constitution; to call it Gaelic is not P.C. at the moment, but seen as marginalizing) is the Celtic language spoken by a small minority of native speakers principally found in rural pockets on the western seaboard. These Irish-speaking communities are known as the "Gaeltacht," and are the last remnants of an earlier historical time when the whole island was Irish-speaking, or one huge "Gaeltacht." The number of Irish speakers left in these areas who use the language in most of their daily affairs is a hotly debated point, and varies from 100,000 at the most optimistic estimate to 20,000 at the most conservative. For the sake of a round number let us take it to be 60,000, or about 2 percent of the population of the Republic of Ireland.

Because of the effort of the Irish Revival movement, and of the teaching of Irish in the school system, however, the language is also spoken with varying degrees of frequency and fluency by a considerably larger number of people who have learned it as a second language. So much so that census figures over the last few decades have consistently indicated that up to one million people, or 30 percent of the population of the Republic, claim to be speakers of Irish. To this can be added the 146,000 people

1. Published in the *New York Times Book Review*, January 1995.

in the Six Counties of Northern Ireland who also are competent in Irish. This figure of one million speakers is, of course, grossly misleading and in no way reflects a widespread use of the language in everyday life. Rather it can be seen as a reflection of general good will toward the language, as a kind of wishful thinking. Nevertheless that good will is important.

The fact that the Irish language, and by extension its literature, has a precarious status in Ireland at the moment is a development in marked contrast to its long and august history. I believe writing in Irish is the oldest continuous literary activity in Western Europe, starting in the fifth century and flourishing in a rich and varied manuscript tradition right down through the Middle Ages. During this time the speakers of any invading language, such as Norse, Anglo-Norman and English, were assimilated, becoming "more Irish than the Irish themselves." But the Battle of Kinsale in 1601, in which the British routed the last independent Irish princes, and the ensuing catastrophes of the turbulent 17th century, including forced population transfers, destroyed the social underpinning of the language. Its decline was much accelerated by the great famine of the mid-19th century; most of the one million who died of starvation and the millions who left on coffin ships for America were Irish speakers. The fact that the fate of emigration stared most of the survivors in the eye further speeded up the language change to English—after all, "What use was your Irish to you over in Boston?"

The indigenous high culture became the stuff of the speech of fishermen and small farmers, and this is the language that I learned in West Kerry in the 1950's at the age of 5 in a situation of total immersion, when I was literally and figuratively farmed out to my aunt in the parish of Ventry. Irish is a language of enormous elasticity and emotional sensitivity; of quick and hilarious banter and a welter of references both historical and mythological; it is an instrument of imaginative depth and scope, which has been tempered by the community for generations until it can pick up and sing out every hint of emotional modulation that can occur between people. Many international scholars rhapsodize that this speech of ragged peasants seems always on the point of bursting into poetry. The pedagogical accident that had me learn this language at an early age can only be called a creative one.

The Irish of the Revival, or "book Irish," was something entirely different, and I learned it at school. Although my first literary love affair was with the Munster poets, Aodhagán Ó Rathaille and Eoghan Rua Ó Suilleabháin, and I had learned reams and reams of poetry that wasn't taught at school, when I myself came to write it didn't dawn on me that I could possibly write in Irish. The overriding ethos had got even to me. Writing poetry in Irish somehow didn't seem to be intellectually credible. So my first attempts, elegies on the deaths of Bobby Kennedy and Martin Luther King published in the school magazine, were all in English. They were all right, but even I could see that there was something wrong with them.

Writing Irish poetry in English suddenly seemed a very stupid thing to be doing. So I switched language in mid-poem and wrote the very same poem in Irish, and I could see immediately that it was much better. I sent it in to a competition in *The Irish Times,* where it won a prize, and that was that. I never looked back.

I had chosen my language, or more rightly, perhaps, at some very deep level, the language had chosen me. If there is a level to our being that for want of any other word for it I might call "soul" (and I believe there is), then for some reason that I can never understand, the language that my soul speaks, and the place it comes from, is Irish. At 16 I had made my choice. And that was that. It still is. I have no other.

But if the actual choice to write poetry in Irish was easy, then nothing else about it actually is, especially the hypocritical attitude of the state. On the one hand, Irish is enshrined as a nationalistic token (the ceremonial *cúpla focal*—"few words"—at the beginning and end of speeches by politicians, broadcasters and even airline crews is an example). On the other hand, it would not be an exaggeration to speak of the state's indifference, even downright hostility, to Irish speakers in its failure to provide even the most basic services in Irish for those who wish to go about their everyday business in that language.

"The computer cannot understand Irish" leads the excuses given by the state to refuse to conduct its business in Irish, even in the Gaeltacht areas. Every single service gained by Irish speakers has been fought for bitterly. Thus the "Gaelscoileanna," or Irish schools, have been mostly started by groups of parents, often in the very teeth of fierce opposition from the Department of Education. And the only reason we have a single Irish radio station is that a civil rights group started a pirate station 20 years ago in the West and shamed the Government into establishing this vital service. An Irish television channel is being mooted[2] at present, but I'll believe it when I see it.

You might expect at least the cultural nationalists and our peers writing in English to be on our side. Not so. A recent television documentary film about Thomas Kinsella begins with the writer intoning the fact that history has been recorded in Irish from the fifth century to the 19th. Then there is a pregnant pause. We wait for a mention of the fact that life, experience, sentient consciousness, even history is being recorded in literature in Irish in the present day. We wait in vain. By an antiquarian sleight of hand it is implied that Irish writers in English are now the natural heirs to a millennium and a half of writing in Irish. The subtext of the film is that Irish is dead.

So what does that make me, and the many other writers of the large body of modern literature in Irish? A walking ghost? A linguistic specter?

Mind you, it is invidious of me to single out Thomas Kinsella; this kind of insidious "bad faith" about modern literature in Irish is alive and rampant among many of our fellow writers in English. As my fellow poet in Irish, Biddy Jenkinson, has said, "We have been pushed into an ironic awareness that by our passage we would convenience those who will be uneasy in their Irishness as long as there is a living Gaelic tradition to which they do not belong." Now let them make their peace with the tradition if they wish to, I don't begrudge them a line of it. But I'll be damned if their cultural identity is procured at the expense of my existence, or of that of my language.

I can well see how it suits some people to see Irish-language literature as the last rictus[3] of a dying beast. As far as they are concerned, the sooner the language lies down and dies, the better, so they can cannibalize it with greater equanimity, peddling their "ethnic chic" with nice little translations "from the Irish." Far be it from them to make the real effort it takes to learn the living language. I dare say they must be taken somewhat aback when the corpse that they have long since consigned to choirs of angels, like a certain Tim Finnegan,[4] sits up and talks back to them.

---

2. Debated.
3. Gasp.
4. In the vaudeville song *Tim Finnegan's Wake*, the hero takes a drunken fall and dies. At his wake, however, whiskey is spilled over his body and he comes back to life. James Joyce uses this story as the central structure for *Finnegans Wake*.

The fault is not always one-sided. The Gaels (Irish-language writers) often fell prey to what Terence Browne, a literary historian, has called an "atmosphere of national self-righteousness and cultural exclusiveness," and their talent did not always equal the role imposed on them. Nevertheless, long after the emergence of a high standard of literature in Irish with Seán Ó Riordáin, Máirtin Ó Direáin and Máire Mhac an tSaoi in poetry, and Máirtín Ó Cadhain in prose, writing in Irish was conspicuously absent from anthologies in the 1950's and 60's. Even as late as the 70's one of our "greats," Seán Ó Riordáin, could hear on the radio two of his co-writers in English saying how "poetry in Ireland had been quiescent in the 50's," thus consigning to nothingness the great work that he and his fellow poets in Irish had produced during that very decade. After a lifetime devoted to poetry, is it any wonder that he died in considerable grief and bitterness?

As for the cultural nationalists, Irish was never the language of nationalist mobilization. Unlike other small countries where nationalism rose throughout the 19th century, in Ireland it was religion rather than language that mostly colored nationalism. Daniel O'Connell, the Liberator, a native-Irish-speaking Kerryman, used to address his monster mass meetings from the 1820's to the 40's in English, even though this language was not understood by 70 percent of the people he was addressing. Why? Because it was at the reporters over from *The Times* of London and their readers that his words were being primarily directed. It is particularly painful to recall that while nationalism was a major motivator in developing modern literary languages out of such varied tongues as Norwegian, Hungarian, Finnish and Estonian, during that very same period the high literary culture of Irish was being reduced to the language of peasants. By the time the revival began, the damage had already been done, and the language was already in irreversible decline (spoken by only 14.5 percent in 1880). The blatant myopia of the cultural nationalists is still alive and glaringly obvious in the disgraceful underrepresentation of Irish in the recently published three-volume *Field Day Anthology of Irish Writing*.

It should not be surprising, then, that we poets and fiction writers in Irish who are included in the anthology feel as if we are being reduced to being exotic background, like Irish Muzak. Thus the cultural nationalists, without granting Irish the intellectual credibility of rational discourse or the popular base of the oral tradition, enshrine it instead as the repository of their own utopian fantasies; pristine, changeless, "creative," but otherwise practically useless.

How does all this affect me, as a poet writing in Irish? Well, inasmuch as I am human and frail and prone to vanity and clamoring for attention, of course it disturbs me to be misunderstood, misrepresented and finally all but invisible in my own country. I get depressed, I grumble and complain, I stand around in rooms muttering darkly. Still and all, at some very deep and fundamental level it matters not one whit. All I ever wanted was to be left alone so that I could go on writing poetry in Irish. I still remember a time when I had an audience I could count on the fingers of one hand. I was perfectly prepared for that. I still am.

But it has been gratifying to reach a broader audience through the medium of translations, especially among the one million who profess some knowledge of Irish. Many of them probably had good Irish when they left school but have had no chance of using it since for want of any functional context where it would make sense to use the language. I particularly like it when my poetry in English translation sends them back to the originals in Irish, and when they then go on to pick up the long-lost threads of the language that is so rightly theirs. I also find it pleasant and vivifying to make an occasional trip abroad and to reach a wider audience by means of dual-language readings and publications.

But my primary audience is those who read my work in Irish only. A print run for a book of poems in Irish is between 1,000 and 1,500 copies. That doesn't sound like much until you realize that that number is considered a decent run by many poets in English in Ireland, or for that matter even in Britain or America, where there's a much larger population.

The very ancientness of the Irish literary tradition is also a great source of strength to me as a writer. This works at two levels, one that is mainly linguistic and prosodic and another that is mainly thematic and inspirational. At the linguistic level, Old Irish, though undoubtedly very difficult, is much closer to Modern Irish than, say, Anglo-Saxon is to Modern English. Anyone like me with a basic primary degree in the language and a bit of practice can make a fair job of reading most of the medieval texts in the original.

Thematically too, the older literature is a godsend, though I am only now slowly beginning to assess its unique possibilities to a modern writer. There are known to be well over 4,000 manuscripts in Ireland and elsewhere of material from Old to Modern Irish. Apart from the great medieval codices, only about 50 other manuscripts date from before 1650. Nevertheless, the vast majority of the manuscripts painstakingly copied down after this time are exemplars of much earlier manuscripts that have since been lost. A lot of this is catalogued in ways that are unsatisfactory for our time.

Many items of enormous psychological and sexual interest, for example, are described with the bias of the last century as "indecent and obscene tales, unsuitable for publication." On many such manuscripts human eye has not set sight since they were so described. In addition, most scholarly attention has been paid to pre-Norman-Conquest material as the repository of the unsullied wellsprings of the native soul (those cultural nationalists again!), with the result that the vast area of post-Conquest material has been unfairly neglected. The main advantage of all this material to me is that it is proof of the survival until even a very late historical date of a distinct *Weltanschauung* [worldview] radically different from the Anglo mentality that has since eclipsed it.

Because of a particular set of circumstances, Irish fell out of history just when the modern mentality was about to take off. So major intellectual changes like the Reformation, the Renaissance, the Enlightenment, Romanticism and Victorian prudery have never occurred in it, as they did in the major European languages.

One consequence is that the attitude to the body enshrined in Irish remains extremely open and uncoy. It is almost impossible to be "rude" or "vulgar" in Irish. The body, with its orifices and excretions, is not treated in a prudish manner but is accepted as *an nádúir*, or "nature," and becomes a source of repartee and laughter rather than anything to be ashamed of. Thus little old ladies of quite impeccable and unimpeachable moral character tell risqué stories with gusto and panache. Is there a word for sex in Irish, indeed! Is there an Eskimo word for snow?

By now I must have spent whole years of my life burrowing in the department of folklore at University College, Dublin, and yet there are still days when my hands shake with emotion holding manuscripts. Again, this material works on me on two levels. First is when I revel in the well-turned phrase or nuance or retrieve a word that may have fallen into disuse. To turn the pages of these manuscripts is to hear the voices of my neighbors and my relatives—all the fathers and grandfathers and uncles come to life again. The second interest is more thematic. This material is genuinely ineffable, like nothing else on earth.

Indeed, there is a drawer in the index entitled "Neacha neamhbeo agus nithe nach bhfuil ann" ("Unalive beings and things that don't exist"). Now I am not the greatest empiricist in the world but this one has even me stumped. Either they exist or they don't exist. But if they don't exist why does the card index about them stretch the length of my arm? Yet that is the whole point of this material and its most enduring charm. Do these beings exist? Well, they do and they don't. You see, they are beings from *an saol eile*, the "otherworld," which in Irish is a concept of such impeccable intellectual rigor and credibility that it is virtually impossible to translate into English, where it all too quickly becomes fey and twee and "fairies-at-the-bottom-of-the-garden."

The way so-called depth psychologists go on about the subconscious nowadays you'd swear they had invented it, or at the very least stumbled on a ghostly and ghastly continent where mankind had never previously set foot. Even the dogs in the street in West Kerry know that the "otherworld" exists, and that to be in and out of it constantly is the most natural thing in the world.

This constant tension between reality and fantasy, according to Jeffrey Gantz, the translator of *Early Irish Myths and Sagas*, is characteristic of all Celtic art, but manifests itself particularly in the literature of Ireland. Mr Gantz believes that it is not accidental to the circumstances of the literary transmission but is rather an innate characteristic, a gift of the Celts. It means that the "otherworld" is not simply an anticipated joyful afterlife; it is also—even primarily—an alternative to reality.

This easy interaction with the imaginary means that you don't have to have a raving psychotic breakdown to enter the "otherworld." The deep sense in the language that something exists beyond the ego-envelope is pleasant and reassuring, but it is also a great source of linguistic and imaginative playfulness, even on the most ordinary and banal of occasions.

Let's say I decide some evening to walk up to my aunt's house in West Kerry. She hears me coming. She knows it is me because she recognizes my step on the cement pavement. Still, as I knock lightly on the door she calls out, "An de bheoaibh nó de mhairbh thu?" ("Are you of the living or of the dead?") Because the possibility exists that you could be either, and depending on which category you belong to, an entirely different protocol would be brought into play. This is all a joke, of course, but a joke that is made possible by the imaginative richness of the language itself.

I am not constructing an essentialist argument here, though I do think that because of different circumstances, mostly historical, the strengths and weaknesses of Irish are different from those of English, and the imaginative possibilities of Irish are, from a poet's perspective, one of its greatest strengths. But this is surely as true of, say, Bengali as it is of Irish. It is what struck me most in the Nobel Prize acceptance speech made by the Yiddish writer Isaac Bashevis Singer. When often asked why he wrote in a dead language, Singer said he was wont to reply that he wrote mostly about ghosts, and that is what ghosts speak, a dead language.

Singer's reply touched a deep chord with his Irish audience. It reminded us that the precariousness of Irish is not an Irish problem alone. According to the linguist Michael Krause in *Language* magazine, minority languages in the English language sphere face a 90 percent extinction rate between now and some time in the next century. Therefore, in these days when a major problem is the growth of an originally Anglo-American, but now genuinely global, pop monoculture that reduces everything to the level of the most stupendous boredom, I would think that the preservation of minority languages like Irish, with their unique and unrepeatable way of looking at the world, would be as important for human beings as the preservation of the remaining tropical rain forests is for biological diversity.

Recently, on a short trip to Kerry with my three daughters, I stayed with my brother and his wife in the old house he is renovating on the eastern end of the Dingle peninsula, under the beetling brow of Cathair Chonroi promontory fort. My brother said he had something special to show us, so one day we trooped up the mountain to Derrymore Glen. Although the area is now totally denuded of any form of growth other than lichens and sphagnum moss, the name itself is a dead giveaway: Derrymore from *Doire Mór* in Irish, meaning "Large Oak Grove."

A more desolate spot you cannot imagine, yet halfway up the glen, in the crook of a hanging valley, intricate and gnarled, looking for all the world like a giant bonsai, was a single survivor, one solitary oak tree. Only the top branches were producing leaves, it was definitely on its last legs and must have been at least 200 to 300 years old. How it had survived the massive human and animal depredation of the countryside that occurred during that time I do not know, but somehow it had.

It was very much a *bile*, a sacred tree, dear to the Celts. A fairy tree. A magic tree. We were all very moved by it. Not a single word escaped us, as we stood in the drizzle. At last Ayse, my 10-year-old, broke the silence. "It would just give you an idea," she said, "of what this place was like when it really was a '*Doire Mór*' and covered with oak trees." I found myself humming the air of *Cill Cais,* that lament for both the great woods of Ireland and the largess of the Gaelic order that they had come to symbolize:

> Cad a dhéanfaimid feasta gan adhmad?
> Tá deireadh na gcoillte ar lár.
> Níl trácht ar Chill Cais ná a theaghlach
> is ní chlingfear a chling go brách.

> What will we do now without wood
> Now that the woods are laid low?
> Cill Cais or its household are not mentioned
> and the sound of its bell is no more.

A week later, back in Dublin, that question is still ringing in the air. I am waiting for the children to get out of school and writing my journal in Irish in a modern shopping mall in a Dublin suburb. Not a single word of Irish in sight on sign or advertisement, nor a single sound of it in earshot. All around me are well-dressed and articulate women. I am intrigued by snatches of animated conversation, yet I am conscious of a sense of overwhelming loss. I think back to the lonely hillside, and to Ayse. This is the answer to the question in the song. This is what we will do without wood.

At some level, it doesn't seem too bad. People are warm and not hungry. They are expressing themselves without difficulty in English. They seem happy. I close my notebook with a snap and set off in the grip of that sudden pang of despair that is always lurking in the ever-widening rents of the linguistic fabric of minority languages. Perhaps my mother is right. Writing in Irish is mad. English is a wonderful language, and it also has the added advantage of being very useful for putting bread on the table. Change is inevitable, and maybe it is part of the natural order of things that some languages should die while others prevail.

Nuala Ní Dhomhnaill   1505

And yet, and yet . . . I know this will sound ridiculously romantic and sentimental. Yet not by bread alone. . . . We raise our eyes to the hills. . . . We throw our bread upon the waters.[5] There are mythical precedents. Take for instance Moses' mother, consider her predicament. She had the choice of giving up her son to the Egyptian soldiery, to have him cleft in two before her very eyes, or to send him down the Nile in a basket, a tasty dinner for crocodiles. She took what under the circumstances must have seemed very much like *rogha an dá dhiogha* ("the lesser of two evils") and Exodus and the annals of Jewish history tell the rest of the story, and are the direct results of an action that even as I write is still working out its inexorable destiny. I know it is wrong to compare small things with great, yet my final answer to why I write in Irish is this:

Ceist 'na Teangan

Curirim mo dhóchas ar snámh
i mbáidín' teangan
faoi mar a leagfá naíonán
i gcliabhán
a bheadh fite fuaite
de dhuilleoga feileastraim
is bitiúman agus pic
bheith cuimilte lena thóin

ansan é a leagadh síos
i measc na ngiolcach
is coigeal na mban sí
le taobh na habhann,
féachaint n'fheadaráis
cá dtabharfaidh an sruth é,
féachaint, dála Mhaoise,
an bhfóirfidh iníon Fharoinn?

The Language Issue

I place my hope on the water
in this little boat
of the language, the way a body might put
an infant

in a basket of intertwined
iris leaves,
its underside proofed
with bitumen and pitch,

then set the whole thing down amidst
the sedge
and bulrushes by the edge
of a river

---

5. Echoing three biblical affirmations of the need to look beyond immediate material wants (Matthew 4.4, Psalm 121.1, Ecclesiastes 11.1). In the first passage cited, Jesus is fasting in the wilderness and rejects Satan's tempting suggestion that he turn stones into bread: "he answered, 'It is written, "Man shall not live by bread alone, but by every word that proceeds from the mouth of God." ' "

only to have it borne hither and thither,
not knowing where it might end up;
in the lap, perhaps,
   of some Pharaoh's daughter.[6]

1996

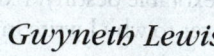

Gwyneth Lewis
b. 1959

Born in Cardiff, Wales, Gwyneth Lewis attended a bilingual school in Pontypridd and went on to Cambridge University, where she studied English. She continued her studies in the United States at Harvard and Columbia, and worked as a freelance journalist in New York before returning to Britain to write for television. Lewis writes in Welsh, her first language, as well as English, and she has published five volumes of poetry in both languages. Her first collection in English, *Parables and Faxes* (1995), won the Aldeburgh Poetry Festival Prize and was short-listed for the Forward Prize for Best First Collection. Her second book, *Zero Gravity* (1998), was short-listed for the Forward Poetry Prize for Best Poetry Collection of the Year, and was inspired in part by the work of astronaut Joe Tanner, Lewis's cousin, in repairing the Hubble telescope in 1997. *Y Llofrudd Iaith* (*The Language Murderer*, 2000) was awarded the Arts Council of Wales Book of the Year Award. In 2002, Lewis published her first nonfiction book, *Sunbathing in the Rain: A Cheerful Book on Depression*, an autobiographical account of her struggle with and triumph over depression. She is a fellow of the Royal Society of Literature. Her latest book of poetry is *Keeping Mum* (2003), and she is currently using a grant from the National Endowment for Science, Technology, and the Arts to conduct research on ports historically linked with Cardiff. In 2004, Lewis was named the first National Poet of Wales.

Therapy

Did you hear the one about the shrink
who let obsessive-compulsives clean his house
      as if their illnesses were his?
They made good caretakers, stayed up all night
      rattling doorknobs, testing locks,
         domesticated poltergeists.

He started an amateur dramatics group
   with the psychotics, who had a ball
   in togas, till they burnt down the hall.
Chronic depressives are always apart,
so he'd check them through his telescope,
   placed them in poses from classical art
and, of course, they'd hardly ever move,
   added a certain style to the grounds.

5

10

6. As happened with Moses when the Israelites were enslaved in Egypt (Exodus 2). Fearing their growing numbers, Pharaoh had ordered all male Hebrew infants to be drowned in the Nile; Moses's mother instead set him adrift in a reed basket, which was found by the Pharaoh's daughter, who adopted him and raised him as an Egyptian. As an adult, Moses led the Israelites out of Egypt to the Promised Land.

15   He recorded Tourette patients' sounds,
     sold them to pop groups as backing tracks.
     Whenever possible, he'd encourage love
     between staff and patients. He had a knack

     with manics, whom he sent out to shop
20   for all his parties, gave tarot cards
     to schizoids so they could read their stars.
     Perhaps he was flip with other people's pain
     but his patients loved him and his hope
     that two or three madnesses might make one sane.

                                                    2002

Mother Tongue

     "I started to translate in seventy-three
     in the schoolyard. For a bit of fun
     to begin with—the occasional 'fuck'
     for the bite of another language's smoke
5   at the back of my throat, its bitter chemicals.
     Soon I was hooked on whole sentences
     behind the shed, and lessons in Welsh
     seemed very boring. I started on printed,
     Jeeves & Wooster, Dick Francis, James Bond,
10   in Welsh covers. That worked for a while
     until Mam discovered Jean Plaidy inside
     a Welsh concordance one Sunday night.
     There were ructions: a language, she screamed,
     should be for a lifetime. Too late for me.
15   I was snorting Simenon
     and Flaubert. Had to read much more
     for any effect. One night I OD'd
     after reading far too much Proust.
     I came to, but it scared me. For a while
20   I went Welsh-only but it was bland
     and my taste was changing. Before too long
     I was back on translating, found that three
     languages weren't enough. The 'ch'
     in German was easy, Rilke a buzz. . .
25   For a language fetishist like me
     sex is part of the problem. Umlauts make me sweat,
     so I need a multilingual man
     but they're rare in West Wales and tend to be
     married already. If only I'd kept
30   myself much purer, with simpler tastes,
     the Welsh might be living. . .
                              Detective, you speak
     Russian, I hear, and Japanese.
     Could you whisper some softly?
35   I'm begging you. Please. . . ."

                                                    2003

Robert Crawford
b. 1959

Born in Bellshill, Scotland, Robert Crawford grew up in and around Glasgow. He studied English at the University of Glasgow and went on to do his postgraduate work at Balliol College, Oxford. He is currently a professor of modern Scottish literature and head of the School of English at the University of St. Andrews. Crawford has published six collections of his poems: *Sharawaggi: Poems in Scots* (with W. N. Herbert, 1990), *A Scottish Assembly* (1990), *Talkies* (1994), *Masculinity* (1996), *Spirit Machines* (1999), and *The Tip of My Tongue* (2003). In addition, he has written a number of critical works, among them *The Savage and the City in the Works of T. S. Eliot* (1987) and *Devolving English Literature* (1992). Much of Crawford's earlier verse is written in Scots, demonstrating his interest in reclaiming Scots as a language suitable for poetry. Through his poetry, he looks at Scotland as it must appear to tourists and adds to the picture of a lovely, wild country the image of a postindustrial Scotland, where connection to the Internet has made the country's small physical size unimportant. In his later work, Crawford considers communication beyond language, as influenced by gender, aging, and awareness of death, and the inescapable physicality of one's body.

The Saltcoats Structuralists
(for Douglas Cairns)

They found the world's new structure was a binary
Gleaming opposition of two rails

That never crossed but ran on parallel
Straight out of Cairo. From small boys

5   On Platform One who listened to the great
Schola cantorum[1] of connecting rods

Dreamed-up by Scots-tongued engineers, they went on
To tame the desert, importing locomotives

From a distant Firth. New wives came out, and one,
10 Shipwrecked off Ailsa Craig, returned to Glasgow,

Caught the next boat; her servants had her wardrobe
Replaced in just four hours from the city shops.

Scotsmen among colonial expats
They learned RP, embarrassing their families

15 In Ayrshire villages where they talked non-stop
About biggah boilahs, crankshawfts. Nicknamed "The Pharaohs,"

They never understood the deconstruction
Visited on Empire when their reign in Egypt

Ran out of steam. They first-classed back to Saltcoats,
20 Post-Nasser,[2] on slow commuter diesels

---

1. Latin, singing school.   2. Gamel Abdel-Nasser, President of Egypt, 1956–1970.

They passed the bare brick shells of loco-sheds
Like great robbed tombs. They eyed the proud slave faces

Of laid-off engineering workers, lost
In the electronics revolution. Along the prom

25   They'd holidayed on in childhood, with exotic walking sticks,
History in Residence, they moved

In Sophoclean raincoats. People laughed
At a world still made from girders, an Iron Age

Of Queen Elizabeths, pea-soupers, footplates,
30   And huge black toilet cisterns named "St Mungo."

Kids zapped the videogames in big arcades
Opposite Arran. Local people found

New energy sources, poems didn't rhyme.
The Pharaohs' grandchildren's accents sounded to them

35   Wee hell-taught ploughmen's. In slow seafront caffs
They felt poststructuralism, tanged with salt.

1990

Alba Einstein

When proof of Einsten's Glaswegian[1] birth
First hit the media everything else was dropped:
Logie Baird,[2] Dundee painters, David Hume[3]—all
Got the big E. Physics documentaries
5   Became peak-viewing; Scots publishers hurled awa
MacDiarmid[4] like an overbaked potato, and swooped
On the memorabilia: *Einstein Used My Fruitshop*,
Einstein in Old Postcards, *Einstein's Bearsden Relatives*.
Hot on their heels came the A. E. Fun Park,
10   Quantum Court, Glen Einstein Highland Malt.
Glasgow was booming. Scotland rose to its feet
At Albert Suppers where The Toast to the General Theory
Was given by footballers, panto-dames, or restaurateurs.
In the US an ageing lab-technician recorded
15   How the Great Man when excited showed a telltale glottal stop.
He'd loved fiddlers' rallies. His favourite sport was curling.[5]
Thanks to this, Scottish business expanded
Endlessly. His head grew toby-jug-shaped,
Ideal for keyrings. He'd always worn brogues.[6]
20   Ate bannocks[7] in exile. As a wee boy he'd read *The Beano*.[8]

---

1. Native of Glasgow, Scotland.
2. Scottish inventor who first publically demonstrated a working television in 1926.
3. Eighteenth-century Scottish philosopher and historian.
4. Hugh MacDiarmid, pen name of Christopher Murray Grieve, Scottish modernist poet.
5. A game played on ice, in which large stones are slid toward a target, developed in Scotland in the sixteenth century.
6. Traditional Scottish shoes.
7. Scottish oatmeal or barley cakes.
8. A popular British comic book series; since 1984 it has been edited by Euan Kerr, a Scotsman.

His name brought new energy: our culture was solidly based
On pride in our hero, The Universal Scot.

1990

⊶ ⇥◊⇤ ⊷

W. N. Herbert
b. 1961

Born in Dundee, Scotland, W. N. Herbert received his doctorate from Brasenose College, Oxford, and has served as Northern Arts Literary Fellow at the Universities of Newcastle and Durham, Writer in Residence on Cumbria Arts in the Education Skylines project, and Writing Fellow for the Wordsworth Trust in Grasmere. He has taught creative writing at Lancaster University, and currently holds a post in creative writing and contemporary Scottish poetry at the University of Newcastle, Tyne. His dissertation on the Scottish poet Hugh MacDiarmid's work was published in 1992 as *To Circumjack MacDiarmid*. His collections include *Dundee Doldrums* (1991), *The Testament of the Reverend Thomas Dick* (1994), *Forked Tongue* (1994), *Cabaret McGonagall* (1996), *The Laurelude* (1998), and *The Bumper Book of Troy* (2002). He has edited various collections and anthologies, including *Strong Words: Modern Poets on Modern Poetry* with Matthew Hollis (2000), and he edits the poetry webzine *Frank's Casket*. Much of his work is in Scots, a language he appreciates for its stanza forms and for its sense of otherness, which helps to hold a reader's attention. He currently lives in a converted lighthouse on the Tyne estuary.

Cabaret McGonagall

Come as ye dottilt,[1] brain-deid lunks,
ye hibernatin cyber-punks,
gadget-gadjies, comics-gecks,
guys wi perfick rat's physiques,
5   fowk wi fuck-aa social skills,
fowk that winnae tak thir pills:
gin ye cannae even pley fuitball
treh thi Cabaret McGonagall.

Thi decor pits a cap oan oorie,[2]
10 ut's puke-n-flock a la Tandoori;
there's a sculpture made frae canine stools,
there's a robot armadillo drools
when shown a phone o thi Pope,
and a salad spinner cerved fae dope:
15 gin ye cannae design a piss oan thi mall
trek thi Cabaret McGonagall.

We got: Clangers, Blimpers, gowks[3] in mohair jimpers,
Bangers, Whimpers, cats wi stupit simpers—
Ciamar a thu,[4] how are you, and hoozit gaun pal,

---

1. Daft, confused [Herbert's gloss].
2. Dirty, tasteless [Herbert's gloss].

3. Fools [Herbert's gloss].
4. "How are you" (Gaelic) [Herbert's gloss].

20 welcome to thi Cabaret Guillaume McGonagall
We got: Dadaists,[5] badass gits, shits wi RADA[6] voices,
Futurists wi sutured wrists and bygets o James Joyce's—
Bienvenue, wha thi fuck are you, let's drink thi nicht away,
come oan yir own, or oan thi phone, or to thi Cabaret.

25 Come as ye bards that cannae scan,
fowk too scared tae get a tan,
come as ye anxious-chicken tykes
wi stabilisers oan yir bikes,
fowk whas mithers waash thir pants,
30 fowk wha drink deodorants:
fowk that think they caused thi Fall
like thi Cabaret McGonagall.

Fur as that's cheesy, static, stale,
this place gaes sae faur aff thi scale
35 o ony Wigwam Bam-meter
mimesis wad brak thi pentameter;
in oarder tae improve thi species' genes,
t'e'll find self-oaperatin guillotines:
bring yir knittin, bring yir shawl
40 tae thi Cabaret McGonagall.

We got: Berkoffs, jerk-offs, noodles wi nac knickers,
Ubuists,[7] tubes wi zits, poodles dressed as vicars—
Gutenaben Aiberdeen, wilkommen Cumbernauld,
thi dregs o Scoatlan gaither at Chez McGonagall.
45 We got: mimes in tights, a MacDiarmidite that'iz ainsel contradicts,
kelpies,[8] selkies,[9] grown men that think they're Picts—[1]
Buonaserra Oban and Ola! tae as Strathsprey,
come in disguise fist tae despise thi haill damn Cabaret.

Panic-attack Mac is oor DJ,
50 thi drugs he tuke werr as Class A,
sae noo he cannae laive thi bog;
thon ambient soond's him layin a log.
Feelin hungry? sook a plook;
thi son o Sawney Bean's oor cook:
55 gin consumin humans diz not appal
treh thi Bistro de McGonagall.

Waatch Paranoia Pete pit speed
intil auld Flaubert's parrot's feed,[2]
and noo ut's squaakin oot in leids

---

5. Avant-garde artistic movement of the early twentieth
century.
6. Royal Academy of Dramatic Arts.
7. After Alfred Jarry's surrealist play *Ubu Roi* (1896).

8. River spirits in the shape of horses [Herbert's gloss].
9. Seals which can take on human form [Herbert's gloss].
1. Ancient inhabitants of Scotland.
2. Languages [Herbert's gloss].

60   naebody kens till uts beak bleeds
        and when ut faas richt aff uts perch,
        Pete gees himsel a boady search:
        thi evidence is there fur all
        at thi Cabaret McGonagall.

65   We got: weirdos, beardos, splutniks, fools,
        Culdees,[3] bauldies, Trekkies, ghouls—
        Airheids fae thi West Coast, steely knives and all,
        welcome to thi Hotel Guillaume McGonagall.
        We got: Imagists, bigamists, fowk dug up wi beakers,
70   lit.mag.eds, shit-thir-beds, and fans o thi New Seekers—[4]
        Doric loons wi Bothy tunes[5] that ploo[6] yir wits tae clay;
        ut's open mike fur ony shite doon at thi Cabaret.

        Alpha males ur no allowed
        amang this outre-foutery[7] crowd
75   tho gin they wear thir alphaboots
        there's nane o us can keep thum oot,
        and damn-aa wimmen care tae visit,
        and nane o thum iver seem tae miss it:
        gin you suspeck yir dick's too small
80   treh thi Cabaret McGonagall.

        There's dum-dum boys wi wuiden heids
        and Myrna Loy[8] is snoggin[9] Steed[1]
        there's wan drunk wearin breeks[2] he's peed—
        naw—thon's thi Venerable Bede;[3]
85   in fack thon auld scribe smells lyk ten o um,
        he's no cheenged'iz habit i thi last millenium:
        gin thi wits ye werr bourn wi hae stertit tae stall
        treh thi Cabaret McGonagall.

        We got: Loplops and robocops and Perry Comatose,
90   Cyclops and ZZ Top and fowk that pick thir nose—
        Fare ye-weel and cheery-bye and bonne nuit tae you all,
        thi booncirs think we ought tae leave thi Club McGonagall.
        But we got: Moptops and bebop bats and Krapp's Last Tapeworm friends,
        Swap-Shop vets and neurocrats, but damn-aa sapiens—
95   Arrevederchi Rothesay, atque vale tae thi Tay,
        Eh wish that Eh hud ne'er set eye upon this Cabaret.

                                                          1996

---

3. Members of the Columban church [Herbert's gloss], named for Scottish St. Columbanus.
4. Ersatz folk-music group formed in 1969.
5. Ballads from the rural North-East [Herbert's gloss].
6. Plough [Herbert's gloss].
7. Excessively fussy [Herbert's gloss].
8. Early American film star (one of whose grandmothers was Scottish).
9. Kissing.
1. Possibly John Steed, secret agent from the television series *The Avengers* which ran through the 1960s.
2. Pants.
3. Seventh/eighth century churchman; author, *Ecclesiastical History of the English People*.

Smirr

The leaves flick past the windows of the train
like feeding swifts: they're scooping up small mouth-
fuls of the midge-like autumn, fleeing south
with the train's hot wake: their feathers are small rain.
5 'Serein' they could say, where I'm passing through,
then just a sound could link rain with the leaves'
symptom, of being sere. But who deceives
themselves such rhyming leaps knit seasons now?
Some alchemist would get the point at once;
10 why I, against the leaves' example, try—
migrating to my cold roots like a dunce.
Thicker than needles sticking to a fir,
Winter is stitching mists of words with chance,
like smears of myrrh, like our small rain, our smirr.

1996

⊬ END OF PERSPECTIVES: WHOSE LANGUAGE? ⊬

CREDITS

Trotter, Alys Fane. "The Hospital Visitor" from *Houses and Dreams*. Oxford: B. Blackwell, 1924. Reprinted by permission of Blackwell Publishing Ltd.

Tuqan, Fadwa. "In the Aging City" trans. by Patricia Alanah Byrne and Naomi Shihab Nye from *Modern Arabic Poetry: An Anthology*, ed. by Salma Khadra Jayyusi. Copyright © 1987 by Columbia University Press. Reprinted with permission of the publisher.

Walcott, Derek. "A Far Cry from Africa;" "The Fortunate Traveller;" Sections L, LII, and LIV from "Midsummer;" and "Wales" from *Collected Poems 1948–1984* by Derek Walcott. Copyright © 1986 by Derek Walcott. Reprinted by permission of Farrar, Straus and Giroux, LLC.

Woolf, Virginia. Excerpts from *A Room of One's Own* by Virginia Woolf. Copyright 1929 by Harcourt, Inc. and renewed 1957 by Leonrad Woolf. Reprinted by permission of the publisher, Harcourt, Inc. "The Lady in the Looking Glass: A Reflection" from *The Complete Shorter Fiction of Virginia Woolf*, edited by Susan Dick. Copyright © 1985 by Quentin Bell and Angelica Garnett, reprinted by permission of Harcourt, Inc. Published by Hogarth Press and reprinted by permission of The Random House Group Ltd.

Wordsworth, Dorothy. From the Grasmere Journals from *Journals of Dorothy Wordsworth*, 2nd edition, edited by Mary Moorman (1988). By permission of Oxford University Press. From *Letters of Dorothy Wordsworth: A Selection*, edited by Alan G. Hill (1985). By permission of Oxford University Press.

Yeats, W.B. "Byzantium" and "Crazy Jane Talks with the Bishop," reprinted with the permission of Scribner, an imprint of Simon & Schuster Adult Publishing Group, from *The Collected Works of W.B. Yeats, Volume I: The Poems, Revised*, edited by Richard J. Finneran. Copyright 1933 by The Macmillan Company; copyright renewed © 1961 by Bertha Georgie Yeats. "Lapiz Lazuli," "The Circus Animal's Desertion," and "Under Ben Bulben," reprinted with the permission of Scribner, an imprint of Simon & Schuster Adult Publishing Group, from *The Collected Works of W.B. Yeats, Volume I: The Poems, Revised*, edited by Richard J. Finneran. Copy- right 1940 by Georgie Yeats; copy- right renewed © 1968 by Bertha Georgie Yeats, Michael Butler Yeats, and Anne Yeats. "Sailing to Byzantium," "Leda and the Swan," "Among School Children," reprinted with the permission of Scribner, an imprint of Simon & Schuster Adult Publishing Group, from *The Collected Works of W.B. Yeats, Volume I: The Poems, Revised*, edited by Richard J. Finneran. Copyright 1928 by The Macmillan Company; copyright renewed © 1956 by Georgie Yeats.

ILLUSTRATION CREDITS

Page 2: Blackburn Museum and Art Galleries; Page 12: Copyright © The British Museum; Page 16; The Royal Collection © 2005 Her Majesty Queen Elizabeth II; Page 42: Courtesy of Princeton University Library; Page 52: The Rosenwald Collection. Reproduced from the Collections of the Library of Congress; Page 55: Reproduced from the Collections of the Library of Congress; Page 58: The Rosenwald Collection. Reproduced from the Collections of the Library of Congress; Page 59: The Rosenwald Collection. Reproduced from the Collections of the Library of Congress; Page 68: Reproduced from the Collections of the Library of Congress; Page 69: Reproduced from the Collections of the Library of Congress; Page 74: Reproduced from the Collections of the Library of Congress; Page 126: Reproduced from the Collections of the Library of Congress; Page 144: Courtesy of Princeton University Library; Page 358: Manchester Art Gallery; Page 515: Courtesy of Susan Wolfson; Page 533: National Portrait Gallery, London; Page 566: Rare Book Division, Department of Rare Books and Special Collections. Princeton University Library; Page 568: The New York Public Library/Art Resource, NY; Page 571; Victoria and Albert Museum, London/Art Resource, NY; Page 576: Columbia University; Page 582: Harvard College Library/Widener Library; Page 585: © Punch Ltd.; Page 592: J. Paul Getty Museum in Los Angeles; Page 620: Bettmann/Corbis; Page 637: Sir Rupert Hart-Davis, Courtesy of Ms. Eva Reichmann; Page 641: Alfred, Lord Tennyson, Poems. London, 1857. William Holman Hunt's illustration of 'The Lady of Shalott. 'Courtesy of Princeton University Library; Page 742: Victoria & Albert Museum, London/Art Resource, NY; Page 807: Public Domain; Page 858L: Mark Samuels Lasner Collection, on loan to the University of Delaware Library, Newark, DE; Page 858R: Mark Samuels Lasner Collection, on loan to the University of Delaware Library, Newark, DE; Page 895: Rare Book Division, Department of Rare Books and Special Collections. Princeton University Library; Page 956: William Andrew Clark Memorial Library, University of California, Los Angeles; 1846–1847; Dover Publications, Inc. Page 1018: Tate Gallery, London/Art Resource, NY; Page 1025: By permission of the Trustees of the Imperial War Museum, London. Crown copyright reproduced by permission of the controller of Her Majesty's Stationery Office; Page 1028: London's Transport Museum © Transport for London; Page 1033: Museum of London/Courtesy of the artist's estate/Bridgeman Art Library; Page 1034: William Vandivert, Life Magazine, © Time Inc./Getty Images; Page 1039: Henry Grossman; Page 1043: Reproduced from the Collections of the Library of Congress; Page 1132: Wadsworth Anthenum Museum of Art, Hartford, CT. The Ella Gallup Sumner and Mary Catlain Sumner Collection Fund.; Page 1182: Reproduced from the Collections of the Library of Congress; Page 1204: Reproduced from the Collections of the Library of Congress; Page 1206: Reproduced with the permission of the Board of the National Library of Ireland; Page 1245: Reproduced from the Collections of the Library of Congress; Page 1287: Princeton University Library, Department of Rare Books.; Page 1358: Time & Life Pictures/Getty Images.

INDEX

INDEX

About suffering they were never wrong, 1396
A bow-shot from her bowereaves, 642
Abstract of the Information laid on the Table of the House of Commons, on the Subject of the Slave Trade, 132
Achebe, Chinua, 1110
"A cold coming we had of it, 1275
Address to the Manchester Chamber of Commerce, 1106
Adonais, 485
Ae fond kiss, 176
Ae fond kiss, and the we server!, 176
A Flower was offered to me:, 71
After Bourlon Wood, 1179
After Death, 892
Ah, did you once see Shelley plain, 756
AH! SUN-FLOWER, 71
Ah Sun-flower! weary of time, 71
Aisling, 1485
A language of loss? I have some business in Arabic., 1482
Alba Einstein, 1509
Ali, Agha Ahahid, 1481
A little black thing among the snow:, 67
A little child, a limber elf, 329
All Religions Are One, 50
All the night is woe, 66
Amazing Grace!, 100
Among School Children, 1195
And has the remnant of my life, 282
Andrea del Sarto, 775
And some time make the time to drive out west, 1460
"And There Was a Great Calm," 1128
And wilt thou have me fashion into speech, 618
An early worshipper at Nature's shrine:, 45
Anecdote for Fathers, 188
Angel, The, 70
Annie Pengelly, 1477
An old, mad, blind, despised, and dying King,—, 477
An omnibus across the bridge, 960
Anorexic, 1471
Anthem for Doomed Youth, 1169
Aphorisms, 1002
Apologia Pro Vita Sua, 725
Apple-Gathering, An, 893
April is the cruelest month, breeding, 1255
Araby, 1207
Arnold, Matthew, 858
As for the Quince, 1497
A simple child, dear brother Jim, 190
As Kingfishers Catch Fire, 927
A snake came to my water-trough, 1336
A Sonnet is a moment's monument,—, 887
A sudden blow: the great wings beating still, 1194
At Francis Allen's on the Christmas-eve,—, 653
At length their long kiss severed, with sweet smart:, 889
A trader I am to the African shore, 106
At the corner of Wood-Street, when day-light appears, 211

Auden, W.H., 1395
Auld Lang Syne, 178
Aurora Leigh, 619
Autumn I love thy latter end to view, 529
Autumn, I love thy parting look to view, 529
'Ave you 'eard o' the Widow at Windsor, 952
A wind is ruffling the tawny pelt, 1447

Back to Africa, 1432
Back to Africa, Miss Mattie?, 1432
Baillie, Joanna, 162
Barbauld, Anna Letitia, 28
Barrington, Pauline, 1178
Bavarian Gentians, 1338
Beachy Head, 45
Beckett, Samuel, 1358
Before one drop of angry blood was shed, 1176
Believe me, if all those endearing young charms, 182
Bellamy, Thomas, 93
Below the thunders of the upper deep:, 638
Benevolent Planters, The, 93
Bennett, Louise, 1432
Bent double, like old beggars under sacks, 1171
Beyond English, 1481
Binsey Poplars, 926
Biographic Literaria or, Biographical Sketches of My Literary Life and Opinions, 338
Bishop Orders His Tomb at Saint Praxed's Church, The, 750
Blake, William, 48
Blast, 1131
Blessed Damozel, The, 884
Blossom, The, 56
Bob Southey! You're a poet, Poet-laureate, 411
Boland, Eavan, 1470
Break, Break, Break, 653
Break of Day in the Trenches, 1172
Bright Star, 561
Bright Star! would I were stead-fast as thou art—, 561
Brontë, Charlotte, 718
Brooke, Rupert, 1163
Browning, Elizabeth Barrett, 613
Browning, Robert, 742
Buried Life, The, 866
Burns, Robert, 172
Burnt Norton, 1276
But bringing up the rear of this bright host, 401
But do not let us quarrel any more, 775
But tell me, tell me! speak again, 309
Bryon, George Gordon (Lord Byron), 134, 347, 401
Bryon's Earlier Heroes, 387
Byzantium, 1197

Cabaret McGonagall, 1510
Call, A, 1460
Can I see anothers woe., 61

Cannan, May Wedderburn, 1176
Canto 1 (Don Juan), 415
Canto 7 (Don Juan), 462
Canto 11 (Don Juan), 463
Canto the Fourth (Childe Harold's Pilgrimage), 405
Canto the Third (Childe Harold's Pilgrimage), 402
Captains of Industry, 597
Carlyle, Thomas, 591
[Carrion Comfort], 927
Casabianca, 518
Channel Firing, 1126
Charge of the Light Brigade, The, 689
Childe Harold's Pilgrimage, 390
"Childe Roland to the Dark Tower Came," 758
Children of the future Age, 75
Child to His Sick Grandfather, A, 165
Chimney Sweeper, The, 57, 67
Christabel, 314
Christmas Carol, 785
Church Going, 1408
Circus Animals' Desertion, The, 1200
City streets and pavements receive me, 1267
Clare, John, 527
Clarkson, Thomas, 119, 129
Clarkson! it was an obstinate Hill to climb;, 129
Clay, 1214
CLOD & the PEBBLE, The, 63
Cloud, The, 498
Cloud-puffball torn turfs, tossed pillows | flaunt forth, then, 929
Clough, Arthur Hugh, 720
Colenso, John William, 722
Coleridge, Samuel Taylor, 291, 392
Colonization in Reverse, 1433
Come. Reason, come! each nerve rebellious bind, 139
Come as ye dottilt, brain-deid lunks, 1510
Come Down, O Maid!, 656
Comin' Thro' the Rye (1), 176
Comin' Thro' the Rye (2), 177
Composed upon Westminster Bridge, Sept. 3, 1802, 231
Congo Diary, 1104
Conrad, Joseph, 1043, 1104
Convergence of the Twain, The, 1125
Corinne at the Capitol, 525
Corsair, The, 387
"Courage!" he said, and pointed toward the land, 645
Courter, The, 1416
Cowper, William, 105
Crawford, Robert, 1508
Crazy Jane Talks with the Bishop, 1198
Crossing the Bar, 701
Cruelty has a Human Heart, 77
Cuba, 1484
Culture and Anarchy, 874
Cypresses, 1338

Darkling Thrush, The, 1124
Darwin, Charles, 702
Daughter of th' Italian heaven!, 525
Daughters of the Late Colonel, The, 1317
Dead, The, 1218
Dead Beggar, The, 44
Dead Man's Dump, 1173

Dear native Brook! wild Streamlet of the West!, 292
Decolonizing the Mind, 1436
Dedication (Don Juan), 411
Defense of Poetry, 505
DEJECTION: An Ode, 334
Democracy, 595
De Profundis, 1004
Detached Thoughts, 134
Dickens, Charles, 712, 782
Did you hear the one about the shrink, 1506
Dipsychus, 721
Dircks, Helen, 1179
Disabled, 1170
DIVINE IMAGE, A, 77
Diving Image, The, 58
Does the road wind up-hill all the way?, 894
Don Juan, 411
Do Not Go Gentle into That Good Night, 1357
Douglas, Alfred (Lord), 958
Dover Beach, 863
Dover Bitch, The, 864
Down a broad river of the western wilds, 519
Doyle, Arthur Conan (Sir), 833
Do you see the OLD BEGGAR who sits at yon gate, 142
Dream, A, 61
Dubliners, 1207
Dulce Et Decorum Est, 1171
Dust As We Are, 1413

Each matin bell, the Baron saith, 322
Early morning over Rouen, hopeful, high, courageous morning, 1177
Earth has not any thing to shew more fair:, 231
Earth rais'd up her head., 63
EARTH'S Answer, 63
Easter 1916, 1189
Ecchoing Green, The, 54
Edinburgh Review, 131
"Education," 1178
Eighteen Hundred and Eleven, 32
Elegiac Sonnets and Other Peoms, 41
Eliot, T.S., 1245
Endgame, 1360
Eolian Harp, The, 293
Epic, The [Morte d' Arthur"], 653
Epilogue from In Memorium A. H. H., 688
Epi-strauss-ium, 720
Epitaph (Hardy), 1130
Equiano, Olaudah, 79
Ere on my bed my limbs I lay, 333
Errand, The, 1460
Eveline, 1211
Evening Prayer, at a Girls' School, 516
Eve of St. Agnes, The, 538
Everybody is in too many pieces, 1119
Everyone Sang, 1168
Everyone suddenly burst out singing;, 1168
Evolution and Ethics, 732
Expostulation and Reply, 192
EXULTING BEAUTY:—phantom of an hour, 136

Far Cry from Africa, A, 1447
Fascination of What's Difficult, The, 1187

Father and Son, 738
Father, father, where are you going, 57
Feeding a Child, 1493
Felix Randal, 926
Felix Randal the farrier, O he is dead then? my duty
    all ended, 926
Fern Hill, 1355
Five years have passed; five summers, with the
    length, 193
Flesh is heretic, 1471
Flower in the Crannied Wall, 701
Flow gently, sweet Afton, 175
Flow gently, sweet Afton, among they green
    braes! 175
FLY, THE, 70
FORCED from home and all its pleasures, 107
*Force That Through the Green Fuse Drives the
    Flower, The, 1354*
Fornicator, The. A New Song, 179
Fortunate Traveller, The, 1449
Four Quartets, 1276
Fra Lippo Lippi, 764
Frankenstein; or The Modern Prometheus, 395
From honey-dew of milking, 1493
Frost at Midnight, 296

Gang of Four, 1119
GARDEN of LOVE, The, 72
Germ of new life, whose powers expanding slow, 31
Gerontion, 1252
Giaour, The, 387
Glenarvon, 393
Glory be to God for dappled things—, 925
Glory of Women, 1166
Goblin Market, 894
God of our fathers, know of old, 953
God's Grandeur, 924
Go, for they call you, shepherd from the hill;, 868
Goodison, Lorna, 1476
Gordimer, Nadine, 1439
Gordon, George. *See* **Bryon, George Gordon
    (Lord Byron)**
Go seek the soul refin'd and strong;, 101
Gospel of Mammonism, 593
Grand-dad, they say you're old and frail, 165
Grasmere—A Fragment, 280
Grasmere Journals, The, 119, 286
Graves of a Household, The, 524
Great Lover, The, 1164
Groping along the tunnel, step by step, 1167
Gosse, Edmund, 737
Gr-r-r—there go, my heart's abhorrence!, 747
Gunga Din, 950

Hail to thee, blithe Spirit!, 480
Half a league, half a league, 689
Hamilton, Cicely, 1176
Hap, 1122
Happy—happier far than thou, 526
Hardy, Thomas, 1120
Harlot's House, The, 959
harp that once through Tara's halls, The, 182
Ha! Whare ye gaun, ye crowlan ferlie!, 174
Heaney, Seamus, 1454

Hear the voice of the Bard!, 62
Heart of Darkness, 1048
Hecht, Anthony, 864
He disappeared in the dead of winter:, 1397
He listened at the porch that day, 616
Hellas, 501
Hemans, Felicia, 397, 514
Herbert, W. N., 1510
Here I am, an old man in a dry month, 1252
Her even lines her steady temper show, 30
He sat in a wheeled chair, waiting for dark, 1170
Higher Pantheism, The, 701
High Windows, 1409
His soul was changed, before his deeds
    had driven, 387
History of Mary Prince, The, a West Indian Slave, 89
*History of the Rise, Porgress, & Accomplishment of
    the Abolition of the African Slave-Trade
    by the British Parliament, The*, 120
"Hold on," she said, "I'll just run out and get
    him.", 1460
HOLY THURSDAY, 59, 64
Home for a Couple of Days, 1461
Homes of England, The, 523
Hooley, Teresa, 1181
Hopkins, Gerard Manley, 923
Hospital Visitor, The, 1180
House of Life, The, 887
How do I love thee? Let me count the ways., 619
How sweet is the Shepherds sweet lot, 54
How the Leopard Got His Spots, 945
Hughes, Ted, 1411
Human Abstract, The, 73
Humanity, 130
Hush! 'tis a holy hour—the quiet room, 516
Huxley, Thomas Henry, 732
Hyde, H. Montgomery, 1011
Hymn to Intellectual Beauty, 474
Hymn to Proserpine, 910

I am poor brother Lippo, by your leave!, 764
I bring fresh showers for the thirsting flowers, 498
I can feel the tug, 1455
I caught this morning morning's minion, king-, 925
I come to represent the case, 1477
I'd make a bed for you, 1496
I Dreamt a Dream! what can it mean?, 70
Idylls of the King, 691
If—, 954
If but some vengeful god would call to me, 1122
"I FEAR thee, ancient Mariner!, 304
If from the public way you turn you steps, 214
If I should die, think only this of me:, 1166
If it form the one landscape that we, the inconstant
    ones, 1405
I found a ball of grass among the hay, 531
I found it among curios and silver., 1475
I found this jawbone at the sea's edge:, 1412
If thou must love me, let it be for nought, 618
If you can keep your head when all about you, 954
I have a boy of five years old, 188
I have been so great a lover: filled my days, 1164
I have heard that hysterical women say, 1198
I have lived long enough, having seen one thing, that
    love hath an end;, 910

I have met them at close of day, 1189
I have no name., 60
I know that I shall meet my fate, 1189
I leant upon a coppice gate, 1124
I Looked Up from My Writing, 1128
I love to rise in a summer morn, 76
Image of Africa, An, 1110
I met a traveller from an antique land, 476
I met the Bishop on the road, 1198
Importance of Being Earnest, The, 962
Impression de Nuit, 958
Impression du Matin, 958
In Arabic, 1482
In a solitude of the sea, 1125
Independence, 1434
Independance wid a vengeance!, 1434
Indian Woman's Death-Song, 519
Indissoluble Matrimony, 1148
I never cared for Life; Life cared for me, 1130
Infant Joy, 60
INFANT SORROW, 73
In futurity, 64
In Hardcastle Crags, that echoey museum, 1414
In Memoriam A. H. H., 659
In Memoriam Francis Ledwidge, 1458
In Memory of W. B. Yeats, 1397
In one of London's most exclusive haunts, 1179
In Praise of Limestone, 1405
"In St. Lucie's distant isle, 109
Inscription for an Ice-House, 30
*Interesting Narrative of the Life of Olaudah
    Equiano*, 80
In the Aging City, 1267
In the stormy east-wind straining, 643
In the sweet shire Cardigan, 186
In this lone, open glade I lie, 865
In Time of "The Breaking of Nations," 1127
Introduction(s)
    Songs of Experience, 62
    Songs of Innocence and Of Experience, 53
In Xanadu, did KUBLA KHAN, 331
I plucked pink blossoms from mine apple tree, 893
Irish Airman Foresees His Death, An, 1189
I said—Then, dearest, since 'tis so, 773
I saw, 1181
I sit in one of the dives, 1402
Isolation. To Marguerite, 861
I sought a theme and sought for it in vain, 1200
"I started to translate in seventy-three, 1507
Is this a holy thing to see, 64
I thought he was dumb, 1333
I thought once how Theocritus had sung, 617
"*It is a beauteous Evening*," 232
It is a beauteous Evening, calm and free;, 232
It is a goodly sight through the clear air, 162
IT is an ancient Mariner, 299
It little profits that an idle king, 649
"*I travell'd among unknown Men*," 267
It seemed that out of battle I escaped, 1169
It seems a day, 212
It was a beautiful and silent day, 259
It was a Christian minister, 115
It was a lovely sight to see, 321
It was in winter. Steeples, spires, 1449
It was my thirtieth year to heaven, 1356
I Wake and Feel the Fell of Dark, Not Day, 928

I walk through the long school-room
    questioning;, 1195
"*I wandered lonely as a Cloud*," 271
I wander thro' each charter'd street, 72
I want a hero: an uncommon want, 415
I was making my way home late one night, 1485
I weep for Adonias—he is dead!, 485
I went to the Garden of Love, 72
I will arise and go now, and go to Innisfree, 1186
I will go back to the great sweet mother, 909
I won't go back to it—, 1473

Jane Eyre, 718
January, 1795, 137
Jeffrey, Francis, 225
Joan of Arc, in Rheims, 520
Journey of the Magi, 1275
Joyce, James, 1204
Just So Stories, 945

Keats, John, 531
Kelman, James, 1461
Kipling, Rudyard, 930
Kraken, The, 638
Kubla Khan: or A Vision in a Dream, 330

Labasheedy (The Silken Bed), 1496
*La belle dame sans merci/LA BELLE DAME SANS
    MERCY*, 548
Labour, 594
Lady in the Looking-Glass, The: A Reflection, 1288
Lady of Shalott, The, 640
Lake Isle of Innisfree, The, 1186
Lamb, Caroline, 393
Lamb, Charles, 228, 229
Lamb, The, 55
Lamplight, 1176
Lapis Lazuli, 1198
Lara, 388
Larkin, Philip, 1407
Last Ride Together, The, 773
Latest Decalogue, The, 721
Lawrence, D. H., 1330
Lay your sleeping hand, my love, 1401
Leaf Mould, 1414
Lectures on Shakespeare, 346
Leda and the Swan, 1194
Leodogran, the King of Cameliard, 691
Letter(s)
    to Charles Brown, 564
    to George and Thomas Keats, 561
    to Mary Ann Rawson, 131
    to Richard Woodhouse, 562
    to Thomas Manning, 229
    to William Wordsworth, 228
Let us go then, you and I, 1248
Lewis, Gwyneth, 1506
Life of Jesus Critically Examined, The, 715
Lift not the painted veil which those who live, 476
Light flows our war of mocking words, and yet, 866
*Lines written a few miles above Tintern
    Abbey*, 193
Lines Written in Kensington Gardens, 865

*Lines Written (Rather Say Begun) on the Morning of
    Sunday April 6ᵗʰ*, 284
Little Black Boy, The, 56
Little Boy found, The, 58
Little Boy Lost, A, 74
Little Boy lost, The, 57
Little Fly, 70
Little Girl Found, The, 66
Little Girl Lost, A, 75
Little Girl Lost, The, 64
Little Lamb who made thee, 55
London (Baillie), 162
LONDON (Blake), 72
London, 1802, 232
Long time hath Man's unhappiness and guilt, 262
Lord Bacon, 711
Lord Randal, 181
Lotos-Eaters, The, 645
Love Among the Ruins, 756
Love seeketh not Itself to please, 63
Love Song of J. Alfred Prufrock, The, 1248
Lucy Gray, 209
Lullaby, 1401
Lyrical Ballads, 186, 196

Macaulay, Thomas Babington, 711
Manfred, 351
Mansfield, Katherine, 1317
Mariana, 638
Matthew and Mark and Luke and holy John, 720
MCMXIV, 1410
Meeting at Night, 753
Meeting the British, 1485
Memorabilia, 756
Merry Merry Sparrow, 56
Michael, 214
Mill, John Stuart, 601
Milton! thou should'st be living at this hour:, 232
Mise Eire, 1473
Modern Painters, 851
Monarch of Gods and Daemons, and all Spirits, 398
Mont Blanc, 470
Moore, Thomas, 181
More, Hannah, 108
Morning and evening, 894
Mother to Her Waking Infant, A, 164
Mother Tongue, 1507
[Mouse's Nest, The], 531
Mouse's Petition to Dr. Priestley, The, 29
Much have I travel'd in the realms of Gold, 535
Mulatta as Penelope, The, 1476
Muldoon, Paul, 1484
Musée des Beaux Arts, 1396
Music, when soft voices die, 482
My aspens dear, whose airy cages quelled, 926
My eldest sister arrived home that morning, 1484
My heart aches, and a drowsy numbness
    pains, 553
"My heart leaps up," 272
My heart leaps up when I behold, 272
My Last Duchess, 749
My mother bore me in the southern wild, 56
My mother groand! my father wept. 73
My pensive Sara! thy soft cheek reclined, 293
My post-war father was so silent, 1413

My Pretty ROSE TREE, 71
My spirit is too weak—Mortality, 536

Native African Languages, 1436
Negro's Complaint, The, 107
Neutral Tones, 1122
Newman, John Henry (Cardinal), 724
Newton, John, 99
Ngũg I wa Thiong'o, 1435
Ní Dhombnaill, Nuala, 1492
No language is old—or young—beyond
    English, 1481
Non-Combatant, 1176
No, no, go not to Lethe, neither twist, 558
No Second Troy, 1186
Not every man has gentians in his house, 1338
No, the serpent did not, 1413
Not, I'll not, carrion comfort, Despair, not feast on
    thee;, 927
Not I, not I, but the wind that blows through
    me!, 1333
Nought loves another as itself, 74
Now as I was young and easy under the apple
    boughs, 1355
Now in thy dazzling half-oped eye, 164
Now, o'er the tesselated pavement strew, 140
No Worst, There Is None, 928
Nuns fret not at their Convent's narrow room;, 230
NURSES Song, 67
Nurses Song, 60
Nutting, 212

*Ode: Intimations of Immortality from Recollections
    of Early Childhood*, 273
Ode to a Grecian Urn, 555
Ode to a Nightingale, 553
Ode to Beauty, 136
Ode to Indolence, 557
Ode to Melancholy, 558
Ode to Psyche, 551
Ode to the West Wind, 477
Odour of Chrysanthemums, 1340
O'er the tall cliff that bounds the billowy main, 141
Oft I had heard of Lucy Gray, 209
Of writing many books there is no end;, 619
O gin a body meet a body, 177
O GODDESS! hear these tuneless numbers,
    wrung, 551
O golden-tongued Romance, with serene lute!, 537
O hear a pensive prisoner's prayer, 29
Oh, Galuppi, Baldassaro, this is very sad to find!, 754
Oh, he is worn with toil! the big drops run, 114
Oh, SLEEP! it is a gentle thing, 306
Oh there is blessing in this gentle breeze, 234
O, Jenny's a' weet, poor body, 176
Old Beggar, The, 142
O, my luve is like a red, red rose, 178
On a Lady's Writing, 30
On Anothers Sorrow, 61
On Becoming a Mermaid, 1477
Once, a lady of the Ó Moores, 1494
Once a dream did weave a shade, 61
Once I am sure there's nothing going on, 1408
Once more the storm is howling, and half hid, 1192

On either side the river lie, 640
One morn before me were three figures seen, 557
One morning early I met armoured cars, 1457
On First Looking into Chapman's Homer, 534
On Liberty, 602
Only a man harrowing clods, 1127
On Seeing the Elgin Marbles, 536
On sitting down to read King Lear once again, 537
On the Departure Platform, 1124
*On the Origin of Species by Means of Natural
    Selection*, 704
On This Day I Complete My Thirty-Sixth Year, 466
"On you go now! Run, son, like the devil, 1460
O Reason! vaunted Sov'reign of the mind!, 140
O Rose thou art sick., 69
Owen, Wilfred, 1168
O what can ail thee Knight at arms, 549
"O where have ye been, Lord Randal, my son?, 181
O wild West Wind, thou breath of Autumn's
    being, 477
Ozymandias, 476

Pains of Sleep, The, 332
Parthenogenesis, 1494
Parting at Morning, 754
Pater, Walter, 915
Pause, A, 892
Pavement slippery, people sneezing, 137
Peaceful our valley, fair and green, 280
*Pentateuch and Book of Joshua Critically
    Examined, The*, 723
Perspectives
    The Abolition of Slavery and the Slave
        Trade, 78
    Religion and Science, 710
Piano, 1333
Pied Beauty, 925
Piping down the valleys wild, 53
Pity would be no more, 73
Poem in October, 1356
Poem on the Inhumanity of the Slave-Trade, A, 101
Poems Concerning the Slave-Trade, 114
Poet of Nature, thou hast wept to know, 469
Pomegranate, The, 1474
Poor Susan, 211
Porphyria's Lover, 745
Postscript, 1460
Prayer for My Daughter, A, 1192
Preface(s)
    The Nigger of the "Narcissus," 1046
    The Picture of Dorian Gray, 960
    Prometheus Unbound, 398
    A Vision of Judgement, 400
Prefatory Sonnet, 230
Prelude, The, or Growth of a Poet's Mind, 234
Prince, Mary, 88
Princess, The, 655
Prometheus, 389
Prometheus Unbound, 398
Promise me no promises, 907
Promises Like Pie-Crust, 907
Punishment, 1455

QUEEN of the silver bow!—by the pale beam, 41

Rear-Guard, The, 1167
Recessional, 953
Records of Woman, 519
Red, Red Rose, A, 178
Relic, 1412
Remember, 891
Remember me when I am gone away, 891
Renaissance, The, 916
Resolution and Independence, 267
Rime of the Ancient Mariner, The (1817), 298
Robinson, Mary, 135
Room of One's Own, A, 1292
Rosenberg, Isaac, 1172
Rossetti, Christina, 889
Rossetti, Dante Gabriel, 882
Rouen, 1177
Round the cape of a sudden came the sea, 754
Rowson, Martin, 1269
Rushdie, Salman, 1416
Ruskin, John, 849

Sailing to Byzantium, 1194
*Sailor Who had Served in the Slave-Trade,
    The*, 115
St. Agnes' Eve—Ah, bitter chill it was!, 538
Saltcoats Structuralists, The, 1508
*Sappho and Phaon, in a Series of Legitimate
    Sonnets*, 138
Sassoon, Siegfried, 1166
Say over again, and yet once over again, 618
Scandal in Bohemia, A, 834
Scholar-Gipsy, The, 868
School-Boy, The, 76
Scorn not the Sonnet, 278
Scorn not the Sonnet; Critic, you have
    frowned, 278
Scott, Walter (Sir), 180
SEASON of mists and mellow fruitfulness, 559
sea view, The, 43
Second Coming, The, 1191
September 1, 1939, 1402
September 1913, 1187
Shelley, Mary Wollstonecraft, 395
Shelley, Percy Bysshe, 398, 467
Shepherd, The, 54
She walks in beauty, 349
She walks in beauty, like the night, 349
Should auld acquaintance be forgot, 178
SICK ROSE, THE, 69
SIGHING I see yon little troop at play;, 43
Simon Lee, 186
Singer's House, The, 1457
Sir Patrick Spence, 171
Skunk, The, 1456
Sleeve Notes, 1486
"slumber did my spirit seal, A," 209
Smirr, 1513
Smith, Charlotte, 40
Smith, Eaglesfield, 108
Snake, 1336
Soldier, The, 1166
Soliloquy of the Spanish Cloister, 747
Song (She sat and sang alway), 891
Song (When I am dead, my dearest), 891
Song of a Man Who Has Come Through, 1333

Songs
    "She dwelt among th' untrodden ways," 209
    Woo'd and Married and A', 168
Songs Eternity, 529
Songs of Experience, 62
Songs of Innocence and Of Experience, 53
Sonnet(s)
    1802–1807 (Wordsworth), 230
    England in 1819, 477
    Lift not the painted veil, 476
    When I have fears, 537
Sonnets from the Portuguese, 617
SONNET TO THE RIVER OTTER, 292
Sorrows of Yamba, The, 109
So there stood Matthew Arnold and this girl, 864
Southey, Robert, 113, 400
So, we'll go no more a-roving, 350
So wildly sweet, its notes might seem, 397
Spain 1937, 1399
Spirit of strength! to whom in wrath 'tis given, 166
Stanley, Henry Morton (Sir), 1106
Stanzas, 466
Statesman's Manual, The, 392
Still the loud death-drum, thundering from afar, 32
Storm-Cloud of the Nineteenth Century, the, 853
"Strange fits of passion have I known," 208
Strange Meeting, 1169
Stranger, approach! within this iron door, 30
Strauss, David Friedrich, 715
Sunday Under Three Heads, 712
Sunset and evening star, 701
Surprized by Joy, 278
Surprized by joy-impatient jas the Wind, 278
Swear by what the Sages spoke, 1201
Sweet and Low, 655
Sweet Meat Has Sour Sauce, 106
Swells then thy feeling heart, and streams thine
    eye, 44
Swinburne, Algernon Charles, 908
Symphony in Yellow, 960

Take telegraph wires, a lonely moor, 1415
Tales, and Historic Scenes, in Verse, 516
Talking in Bed, 1410
Talking in bed ought to be easiest, 1410
Telegraph Wires, 1415
Tennyson, Alfred (Lord), 635
That is no country for old men. The young, 1194
*That Nature Is a Heraclitean Fire and of the Comfort
    of the Resurrection,* 929
That night your great guns, unawares, 1126
That's my last Duchess painted on the wall, 749
The awful shadow of some unseen Power, 474
The Bishop tell us: "When the boys come back, 1167
The blessed damozel leaned out, 884
The boy stood on the burning deck, 518
The bride she is winsome and bonny, 168
The bronze soldier hitches a bronze cape, 1458
The Child is Father of the Man;, 273
The critics say that epics have died out, 632
The curtains were half drawn, the floor was
    swept, 892
The darkness crumbles away—, 1172
The everlasting universe of things, 470
The fascination of what's difficult, 1187
The frost performs its secret ministry, 296
The grey sea and the long black land;, 753
The harp that once through Tara's halls, 182
The king sits in Dumferling toune, 171
The leaves flick past the windows of the train, 1513
The little boy lost in the lonely fen, 58
The Mind, that broods o'er guilty woes, 387
Theology, 1413
The only legend I have ever loved is, 1474
The plunging limbers over the shattered track, 1173
The rain set early in to-night, 745
Therapy, 1506
There are some heights in Wessex, shaped as if by a
    kindly hand, 1123
There came this bright young thing, 1497
There had been years of Passion—scorching,
    cold, 1128
"There is no God," the wicked saith, 721
THERE passed a weary time, Each throat, 302
There sunk the greatest, nor the worst of men, 390
There was a roaring in the wind all night;, 267
The sea is calm to-night., 863
The stately Homes of England, 523
The sun, the moon, the stars, the seas, the hills and
    the plains—, 701
The Sun does arise, 54
THE Sun now rose upon the right:, 301
The Thames nocturne of blue and gold, 958
The time I've lost in wooing, 182
The trees are in their autumn beauty, 1188
The unpurged images of day recede;, 1197
The upland Shepherd, as reclined he lies, 43
The wind flapped loose, the wind was still, 887
The woods decay, the woods decay and fall, 651
—The work of glory still went on, 462
The world is charged with the grandeur of God, 924
The world is too much with us; late and soon, 231
The worship of this sabbath morn, 284
"They," 1167
They found the world's new structure was a
    binary, 1508
They grew in beauty, side by side, 524
They make the chamber sweet with flowers and
    leaves, 892
This Hermit good lives in that wood, 311
THIS LIME-TREE BOWER MY PRISON, 294
This living hand, 560
This living hand, now warm and capable, 560
Thomas, Dylan, 1353
Those long uneven lines, 1410
Those white flecks cropping the ridges of
    Snowdon, 1448
Thou Art Indeed Just, Lord, 929
Though cold as winter, gloomy as the grave, 130
Thoughts on My Sick-bed, 282
Thou hast a charmed cup, O Fame!, 521
Thou large-brained woman and large-hearted
    man, 615
Thou shalt have one God only; who, 721
THOU still unravish'd bride of quietness, 555
Through Groves, so call'd as being void of trees, 463
Thunder, 166
Thus far, O Friend! have we, though leaving
    much, 249
time I've lost in wooing, The, 182

Time present and time past, 1276
Times followed one another. Came a morn, 628
'Tis the middle of night by the castle clock, 315
'Tis time this heart should be unmoved, 466
Titan! to whose immortal eyes, 389
Tithonus, 651
To—, 482
*To a Little Invisible Being Who Is Expected Soon to
        Become Visible*, 31
To a Louse, 174
To a Mouse, 173
To a Sky-Lark, 480
To Autumn, 559
Toccata of Galuppi's, A, 754
To George Sand: A Desire, 615
To George Sand: A Recognition, 616
To Marguerite—Continued, 862
*To melancholy. Written on the banks of the Arun
        October, 1785*, 43
To Mercy Pity Peace and Love, 58
Tonight, 1483
Tonight, I'll pull your limbs through, 1476
Toome Road, The, 1457
"To one who has been long in city pent," 536
Tortoise Shout, 1333
To The Moon, 41
To Toussaint L'Ouverture, 128
Toussaint, the most unhappy man of men!, 128
To Wordsworth, 469
Tradition and the Individual Talent, 1280
Trials of Oscar Wilde, The, 1011
Triumph of Time, The, 909
Trotter, Alys Fane, 1180
True genius, but true woman! dost deny, 616
Tuqan, Fadwa, 1267
Turning and turning in the widening gyre, 1191
TURN to yon vale beneath, whose tangled shade, 139
Tuscan cypresses, 1338
Twas on a Holy Thursday their innocent faces
        clean, 59
Tyger, The, 70
Tyger Tyger, burning bright, 70

Ulysses, 649
Under Ben Bulben, 1201
Up, black, striped and damasked like the
        chasuble, 1456
Up-Hill, 894

Vanity, saith the preacher, vanity!, 750
Vindication of the Rights of Woman, A, 146
Vision of Judgement, The, 401
VORTICIST MANIFESTO, 1133

Walcott, Derek, 1446
Wales, 1448
War Film, A, 1181
Waste Land, The (Pound), 1255
Waste Land, The (Rowson), 1269
Wat a joyful news, Miss Mattie, 1433
Watching the underlife idle by, 1477
We are seven, 190
We caught the tread of dancing feet, 959

Wee, sleekit, cowrin, tim'rous beastie, 173
We kissed at the barrier; and passing through, 1124
Well! If the Bard was weather-wise, who made, 334
Well, they are gone, and here must I remain, 295
We met the British in the dead of winter, 1485
We planned to shake the world together, you
        and I, 1176
Wessex Heights, 1123
West, Rebecca, 1147
We stood by a pond that winter day, 1122
We were apart; yet, day by day, 861
Whate'er he be, 'twas not what he had been:, 388
What from this barren being do we reap!, 405
What is songs eternity, 529
What need you, being come to sense, 1187
What passing-bells for these who die as cattle?, 1169
What smouldering senses in death's sick delay, 888
What Were You Dreaming?, 1440
When a man hath no freedom to fight for at
        home, 466
When do I see the most, beloved one?, 888
When I have fears that I may cease to be, 537
When, in the gloomy mansion of the dead, 141
When I see a couple of kids, 1409
When latest Autumn spreads her evening veil, 43
When my mother died I was very young, 57
When our two souls stand up erect and strong, 619
When proof of Einstein's Glaswegian birth, 1509
When Shall I Tread Your Garden Path?, 284
When the voices of children, are heard on the
        green, 60
When the voices of children are heard on the
        green, 67
When they said Carrickfergus I could hear, 1457
When to my native Land, 129
When yesterday I went to see my friends, 1180
Where are you now? Who lies beneath your spell
        tonight?, 1483
Where the quiet-coloured end of evening
        smiles, 756
Who Goes with Fergus?, 1186
Who will go drive with Fergus now, 1186
Why art thou changed? O Phaon! tell me why? 140
*Why I Choose to Write in Irish, The Corpse That Sits
        Up and Talks Back*, 1498
Why should I blame her that she filled my
        days, 1186
Why, when I gaze on Phaon's beauteous eyes, 139
"Why William, on that old grey stone, 192
Widow at Windsor, The, 952
Wilde, Oscar, 955
Wild Swans at Coole, The, 1188
Wind, 1412
Windhover, The, 925
With blackest moss the flower-plots, 638
Without Benefit of Clergy, 931
Wollstonecraft, Mary, 144
Woman and Fame, 526
Woman Painted on a Leaf, A, 1475
Woodspurge, The, 887
Woolf, Virginia, 1285
Wordsworth, Dorothy, 119, 279
Wordsworth, William, 128, 183
"world is too much with us, The," 231
Written in November, 529
Written in November (manuscript), 529

Yearsley, Ann Cromartie, 100
Year's Spinning, A, 616
Yeats, William Butler, 1182
Ye jovial boys who love the joys, 179
Yes! in the sea of life enisled, 862

Yesterday all the past. The language of size, 1399
You love us when we're heroes, home on
    leave, 1166
You may talk o' gin and beer, 950
YOUNG POETS, 534